August 10-13, 2015
Sydney, NSW, Australia

Association for
Computing Machinery

Advancing Computing as a Science & Profession

KDD '15

Proceedings of the 21st ACM SIGKDD Conference on
Knowledge Discovery and Data Mining

Sponsored by:

ACM SIGKDD and ACM SIGMOD

Supported by:

NSW NOW, Destination NSW, Microsoft, Alibaba Group, Baidu, Facebook, VISA Research, Amazon, Booking.com, Disney Research, Google, Tableau, DataRobot, Twitter, Yahoo Labs, IBM Research, IBM Watson, BOSCH, xuetangx.com, KNIME, Liebert, KDnuggets, NSF, Prof. Ram Kumar Memorial Foundation, and Yandex

Association for
Computing Machinery

Advancing Computing as a Science & Profession

The Association for Computing Machinery
2 Penn Plaza, Suite 701
New York, New York 10121-0701

ISBN: 978-1-4503-3664-2 (Digital)

ISBN: 978-1-4503-4024-3 (Print)

Additional copies may be ordered prepaid from:

ACM Order Department
PO Box 30777
New York, NY 10087-0777, USA

Phone: 1-800-342-6626 (USA and Canada)
+1-212-626-0500 (Global)
Fax: +1-212-944-1318
E-mail: acmhelp@acm.org
Hours of Operation: 8:30 am – 4:30 pm ET

Printed in the USA

Foreword

It is our great pleasure to welcome you to the 21st ACM SIGKDD Conference on Knowledge Discovery and Data Mining (KDD). The annual ACM SIGKDD conference is the premier international forum for data science, data mining, knowledge discovery and big data. It brings together researchers and practitioners from academia, industry, and government to share their ideas, research results and experiences.

KDD-2015 features 4 plenary keynote presentations, 12 invited talks, 228 paper presentations, a discussion panel, a poster session, 14 workshops, 12 tutorials, 27 exhibition booths, the KDD Cup competition, and a banquet at the Dockside Pavilion at the Sydney Darling Harbour. As always, KDD-2015 attracted presenters and delegates from around the world. It is with great pleasure that we bring this international conference for the first time to the southern hemisphere.

This year we again had a strong set of submissions. There were 819 submissions to the Research Track, of which 160 papers were accepted. There were 189 submissions to the Industry & Government Track, of which 68 papers were accepted. All papers submitted to the Research Track and to the Industry & Government Tracks were subjected to a rigorous review process. They were initially screened by the Chairs of the respective tracks, and a small number of papers that did not comply with the formatting requirements or which violated the dual submission policy were summarily rejected. At least three reviewers and a meta-reviewer were assigned to all remaining papers based on the results of a bidding process. The authors were able to read the reviews and provide a response. The meta-reviewers then had an opportunity to consider all reviews and author responses. This then initiated a discussion during which all reviewers of a paper had the opportunity to read each other's reviews and the author responses and to update their reviews as appropriate. In a few cases, the meta-reviewers added another reviewer at this stage to gain expert opinion on specific issues. The meta-reviewers then made recommendations on acceptance or rejection to the track chairs. The track chairs then assessed the meta-reviews, reviews, author responses and discussions to make a final decision. In a few cases, they also solicited further expert reviews and meta-reviews to resolve specific questions. Thus, all papers were assessed by at least four and up to seven discipline experts. All accepted papers were presented both as a 20-minute talk and as a poster.

The Industry & Government Invited Talk Track features 12 talks from world renowned experts who have played a significant role in developing and deploying large-scale data mining applications and systems in their respective fields with clearly measurable and meaningful impact. We trust that this opportunity for the KDD community to hear directly from senior leaders in industry and government will inspire new advances and broader interdisciplinary collaboration between researchers, industry and government counterparts. Featured topics in this year's Industry & Government Invited Talk Track include applications in cloud intelligence, personal finance, insurance, fraud, marketing, advertising, and telecommunications. Additionally, we have focused on key enabling BigData infrastructure for KDD technologies with talks on highly-scalable and open source solutions that are quickly becoming mainstream.

We continued the conference's tradition of strong workshop and tutorial programs. This year there are 9 full-day workshops, 5 half-day workshops, and 12 tutorials.

We would like to thank our generous sponsors who are a very important part of the conference.

The SIGKDD conference series depends on a massive voluntary effort and we thank the members of the Organizing Committee and our other colleagues who have volunteered their time to make this conference a success. Special thanks are due to the Sponsorship Chair, the Treasurer, the Panel Co-Chairs, the Publications Co-Chairs, the KDD Cup Committee, the Awards Chairs and the Awards Committee, and the Publicity Chairs.

We are grateful to the several program committees that provided the advice necessary to put together the program – the Research Track Program Committee, the Research Track Senior Program Committee, the Industry & Government Track Program Committee, the Industry & Government Track Senior Program Committee, the Industry & Government Track Invited Talks Advisory Committee, the Workshop Program Committee, and the Tutorial Program Committee.

This voluntary effort has been supported by the local arrangement team at the Advanced Analytics Institute, the University of Technology Sydney, the Hilton Sydney Hotel, the staff of the CMT online review system, and many other volunteers.

We are further grateful to the Executive Committee which has provided expert advice, guidance and oversight.

We also thank the many contributors to the conference, the authors, keynote and invited speakers, session chairs, tutors, workshop organisers and participants. It is your content that is the core of the conference.

We hope that you will find this program interesting and thought-provoking and that the conference will provide you with a valuable opportunity to share ideas with other researchers and practitioners from around the world.

Longbing Cao and Chengqi Zhang
KDD-2015 General Chairs

Thorsten Joachims and Geoff Webb
KDD-2015 Program Committee Chairs

Dragos Margineantu and Graham Williams
KDD-2015 Industry & Government Track Program Chairs

Rajesh Parekh and Usama Fayyad
KDD-2015 Industry & Government Invited Talks Chairs

Tina Eliassi-Rad and Johannes Fürnkranz
KDD-2015 Workshop Chairs

Jian Pei and Zhi-Hua Zhou
KDD-2015 Tutorial Chairs

Ron Bekkerman and Jie Tang
KDD Cup-2015 Chairs

Premier of New South Wales
Minister for Western Sydney

MESSAGE FROM THE PREMIER

I am delighted to welcome you to Sydney for the 21st ACM SIGKDD Conference on Knowledge Discovery and Data Mining.

The NSW Government is proud to support this major event, which brings together some of the world's brightest minds – facilitating face-to-face interactions, brilliant ideas and new connections.

I would like to acknowledge Prof Longbing Cao and Prof Chengqi Zhang for choosing Sydney as the location for this year's event. With stunning harbours and beaches, world-class entertainment and dining, and a plethora of picturesque locations to explore, the world's best harbour city offers something special for every visiting participant.

I would also like to thank the Advanced Analytics Institute at the University of Technology Sydney for its efforts in ensuring that collaboration and innovation will take centre stage at this year's global conference.

On behalf of the NSW Government, I wish you an enjoyable and inspiring stay in Sydney.

MIKE BAIRD MP
Premier

Table of Contents

Research Paper Presentations (Part 2)

Industry & Government Track Invited Talks

Industry & Government Track Papers

Tutorials

Panel

KDD'15 Chairs and Organizing Committee

Honorary Chair:	Usama Fayyad (ChoozOn Corporation)
General Chairs:	Longbing Cao (University of Technology, Sydney) Chengqi Zhang (University of Technology, Sydney)
Program Chairs:	Thorsten Joachims (Cornell University) Geoff Webb (Monash University)
Industry and Government Track Program Chairs:	Dragos Margineantu (Boeing Research) Graham Williams (Australian Taxation Office)
Industry and Government Track Invited Talks Chairs:	Rajesh Parekh (Groupon) Usama Fayyad (ChoozOn Corporation)
Workshop Chairs:	Johannes Fuernkranz (Technische Universität Darmstadt) Tina Eliassi-Rad (Rutgers University)
Tutorial Chairs:	Jian Pei (Simon Fraser University) Zhihua Zhou (Nanjing University)
KDD Cup Chairs:	Jie Tang (Tsinghua University) Ron Bekkerman (University of Haifa)
Panel Chairs:	Hugh Durrant-Whyte (Nicta) Katharina Morik (Technische Universität Dortmund)
Poster Chairs:	Dacheng Tao (University of Technology, Sydney) Hui Xiong (Rutgers University)
Best Paper Chairs:	Jure Lescovec (Stanford University) Kristian Kersting (Technische Universität Dortmund)
Doctoral Dissertation Award Chair:	Kyuseok Shim (Seoul National University)
Innovation and Service Award Chair:	Ted Senator (Leidos)
Test-of-Time Paper Award Chair:	Martin Ester (Simon Fraser University)
Local Arrangements Chairs:	Jinjiu Li (IDA) Shannon Cunningham (Executivevents) Guandong Xu (University of Technology, Sydney)
Student Travel Award Chairs:	Wei Wang (UCLA) Xingquan Zhu (Florida Atlantic University) Jeffrey Yu (Chinese University of Hong Kong)

Exhibits and Demo Chairs:	Xing Xie (Microsoft Research Asia) Paul Beinat (University of Technology, Sydney) Yanchang Zhao (RDataMining)
Media and Publicity Chairs:	Vincent Tseng (National Cheng Kung University) P.Krishna Reddy (International Institute of Information Technology) Pang-Ning Tan (Michigan State University) Warwick Graco (Australian Taxation Office)
Publications Chairs:	Shou-de Lin (National Taiwan University) Xintao Wu (University of Arkansas)
Social Network Chairs:	Mohak Shah (Robert Bosch LLC) Bernhard Pfahringer (The University of Waikato) Jianping Yin (National University of Defense Technology)
Sponsorship Chair:	Balaji Krishnapuram (IBM)
Registration:	Zhenjiang Lin (University of Technology, Sydney) Brooke Daley (Executivevents, Inc.)
Treasurer:	Zhigang Zheng (University of Technology, Sydney)
Video:	Jiuyong Li (University of South Australia)
Student Volunteer Chair:	Jinyan Li (University of Technology, Sydney)
Webmaster:	Yuming Ou (University of Technology, Sydney) David Hazel (University of Washington)

KDD'15 Research Track Senior Program Committee

Alex Jaimes (Yahoo!)
Andrew Tomkins (Google Research)
Arindam Banerjee (University of Minnesota)
Aristides Gionis (Aalto University)
Arno Siebes,Universiteit Utrecht)
Bart Goethals (University of Antwerp)
Byron Wallace (Brown University)
Charu C. Aggarwal (IBM T. J. Watson Research Center)
Chih-Jen Lin (National Taiwan University)
Chris Ding (University of Texas at Arlington)
Cristian Danescu-Niculescu-Mizil (Cornell University)
Christos Faloutsos (Carnegie Mellon University)
Deepak Agarwal (LinkedIn)
Diane Cook (Washington State University)
Dimitrios Gunopulos (National and Kapodistrian University of Athens)
Eamonn Keogh (UC Riverside)
Edo Liberty (Yahoo! Labs)
Evgeniy Gabrilovich (Google)
Francesco Bonchi (Yahoo Barcelona)
George Karypis (University of Minnesota Twin Cities)
Hong Cheng (Chinese University of Hong Kong)
Hui Xiong (Rutgers)
Ian Davidson (University of California-Davis)
Inderjit Dhillon (UTexas)
James Bailey (University of Melbourne)
Jeffrey Yu (Chinese University of Hong Kong)
Jian Pei (Simon Fraser University)
Jiawei Han (University of Illinois at Urbana-Champaign)
Jie Tang (Tsinghua University)
Jimeng Sun (Georgia Tech)
Johannes Fuernkranz (TU Darmstadt)
Jure Leskovec (Stanford University)
Katharina Morik (TU Dortmund)
Kilian Weinberger (Washington University)
Kristian Kersting (TU Dortmund)
Martin Ester (Simon Fraser University)
Naoki Abe (IBM T J Watson Research Center)
Naren Ramakrishnan (Virginia Tech)
Osmar Zaiane (University of Alberta)
Paul Bradley (MethodCare)
Paul Bennett (Microsoft Research)
Peter Flach (University of Bristol)
Philip S. Yu (UI Chicago)
Prem Melville (Social Alpha)
Qiang Yang (HKUST)
Ravi Kumar (Google)
Rayid Ghani (University of Chicago)
Reza Rawassizadeh (University of California-Riverside)
Saharon Rosset (Tel Aviv University)
Sanjay Chawla (University of Sydney)
Shou-de Lin (National Taiwan University)
Siegfried Nijssen (Universiteit Leiden)
Sofus Macskassy (Facebook)
Srini Parthasarathy (Ohio State)
Stefan Wrobel (Universitaet Bonn)
Suchi Saria (Johns Hopkins University)
Tanya Berger-Wolf (UI Chicago)
Thomas Seidl (RWTH Aachen University, Germany)
Tie-Yan Liu (Microsoft Research)
Tijl de Bie (University of Bristol)
Tina Eliassi-Rad (Rutgers)
Vishwanathan S. V. N. (UCSC)
W. Bruce Croft (UMass)
Wei Wang (UC Los Angeles)
Wray Buntine (Monash University)
Xifeng Yan (UCSB)
Yehuda Koren (Google)
Yisong Yue (Caltech)
Zhi-Hua Zhou (Nanjing University)

KDD'15 Research Track Program Committee

Bruno Abrahao (Cornell University)
Ryan Adams (Harvard)
Amr Ahmed (Google Research)
Bilal Ahmed (Tufts)
Leman Akoglu (SUNY Stony Brook)
Tim Althoff (Stanford)
Gowtham Alturi (University of Minnesota)
Aijun An (York University)
Aris Anagnostopoulos (Sapienza University of Rome)
Annalisa Appice (University of Bari)
Ira Assent (Aarhus University)
Sitaram Asur (HP Labs)
Martin Atzmueller (Uni Kassel)
Ricardo Baeza-Yates (Yahoo Labs Barcelona)
Tony Bagnall (University of East Anglia)
Senjuti Basu Roy (University of Washington Tacoma)
Gustavo Batista (Universidade de Sao Paulo at Sao Carlos)
Christian Bauckhage (Fraunhofer IAIS and University of Bonn)
Luca Becchetti (Sapienza University of Rome)
Ron Bekkerman (Carmel Ventures)
Andrÿs Benczœr (Institute for Computer Science and Control, Hungarian Academy of Sciences)
Fabricio Benevenuto (Federal University of Minas Gerais)
Rubinstein Benjamin (University of Melbourne)
Yuval Benjamini (Stanford University)
Bettina Berendt (K.U. Leuven)
Michele Berlingerio (IBM Research Dublin)
Michael Berthold (KNIME)
Kanishka Bhaduri (Netflix)
Smriti Bhagat (Facebook)
Jinbo Bi (University of Connecticut)
Albert Bifet (University of Waikato)
Mikhail Bilenko (Microsoft Research)
Hendrik Blockeel (KU Leuven)
Christian Boehm (University of Munich)
Petko Bogdanov (University at Albany SUNY)
Klemens Bohm (Karlsruher Institut f r Technologie)
Daniel Boley (University of Minnesota)
Christian Borgelt (European Centre for Soft Computing)
Karsten Borgwardt (ETH Zurich)
Henrik Bostrom (University of Stockholm)
Leon Bottou (Microsoft)
Christos Boutsidis (Yahoo! Labs)
Pavel Brazdil (University of Porto)
Ulf Brefeld (Technische Universität Darmstadt)
David Buttler (Lawrence Livermore National Laboratory)
Rajmonda Caceres (MIT Lincoln Labs)
Deng Cai (Zhejiang University)
RUi Cai (Microsoft Research)
Xiao Cai (abbott laboratories)
Toon Calders (University Libre de Bruxelles)
Berkant Barla Cambazoglu (Yahoo! Research, Barcelona)
John Canny (UC Berkeley)
Jian Cao (Shanghai JiaoTong University)
Longbing Cao (University of Technology Sydney)
Yunbo Cao (Microsoft Research Asia)
Licia Capra (University College London)
Mark Carman (Monash University)
Carlos Castillo (Qatar Computing Research Institute)
James Caverlee (Texas A&M University)
Lawrence Cayton (Context Relevant)
Soumen Chakrabarti (IITB/Google)
Jeffrey Chan (University of Melbourne)
Edward Chang (HTC)
Kai-Wei Chang (Univ of Illionis)
Kevin Chang (University of Illinois at Urbana-Champaign)
Duen Horng Chau (Georgia Tech)
Nitesh Chawla (University of Notre Dame)
Bee-Chung Chen (LinkedIn)
Chine-Yu Chen (National Taiwan University)
Enhong Chen (University of Science and Technology of China)
Haifeng Chen (NEC Research Lab)
Jianhui Chen (Yahoo!)
Lei Chen (Hong Kong UST)
Ming-Syan Chen (Academic Sinica)
Minmin Chen (Criteo Research)
Shuo Chen (Cornell)
Songqing Chen (George Mason University)
Wei Chen (Microsoft Research)
Weizhu Chen (Microsoft)

Wenlin Chen (Washington University in St. Louis)
Yixin Chen (Washington University in St Louis)
James Cheng (Chinese University of Hong Kong)
Justin Cheng (Stanford)
Reynold Cheng (University of Hong Kong)
Junghoo Cho (University of California, Los Angeles)
Peter Christen (Australian National University)
Tat-Seng Chua (National University of Singapore)
Kun-Ta Chuang (National Cheng Kung University)
Liu ChuanRen (Drexel University)
Charles Clarke (University of Waterloo)
Gao Cong (NanyangTechnological University)
Fabio Crestani (University of Lugano)
Bin Cui (Peking University)
Peng Cui (Tsinghua University)
Boris Cule (University of Antwerp)
Alfredo Cuzzocrea (University of Calabria)
Wenyuan Dai (Huawei Noah's Ark Lab)
Abhimanyu Das (MSR)
Barnan Das (Intel Corporation)
Kamalika Das (NASA Ames research Centre)
Mahashweta Das (HP Labs)
Atish Das Sarma (EBay Research Labs)
Anirban Dasgupta (IIT Gandhinagar)
Page David (University of Wisconsin)
Jesse Davis (KU Leuven)
Brian Davison (Lehigh University)
Gianmarco De Francisci Morales (Aalto University)
Gerard de Melo (Tsinghua University)
Dave DeBarr (Microsoft Research)
Dennis DeCoste (Ebay)
Krzysztof Dembczynski (University Poznan)
Alex Deng (Microsoft)
Hongbo Deng (Yahoo!)
Tom Diethe (University of Bristol)
Bistra Dilkina (Georgia Tech)
Nan Ding (Google)
Wei Ding (University of Massachusetts Boston)
Carlos Diuk (Facebook)
Nemanja Djuric (Yahoo!)
Jana Doppa (Washington State University)
Doug Downey (Northwestern University)
Oliver Downs (Globys Inc.)
Gideon Dror (Yahoo! Labs)
Wouter Duivesteijn (TU Dortmund)
Saso Dzeroski (Jozef Stefan Institute)
Khalid El-Arini (Facebook)
Tapio Elomaa (Tampere University of Technology)
Dora Erdos (Boston University)
Stefano Ermon (Stanford)
Alex Fabrikant (Google)
Ad Feelders (Utrecht University)
Elena Ferrari (University of Insubria)
Cesar Ferri (Technical University Valencia)
Dennis Fetterly (Microsoft Research)
Eibe Frank (University of Waikato)
Elisa Fromont (Universite St. Etienne)
Ada Fu (Chinese University of Hong Kong)
Ryohei Fujimaki (NEC Laboratories America)
Benjamin C. M. Fung (McGill University)
Stanislav Funiak (Facebook)
Stephan G nnemann (Carnegie Mellon University)
Thomas Gaertner (University of Bonn)
Esther Galbrun (Boston University)
Joao Gama (University of Porto)
Venkatesh Ganti (Citibank)
Bin Gao (Microsoft Research)
Byron Gao (Texas State University)
Jing Gao (University at Buffalo)
Jake Gardner (Washington University in St. Louis)
Roman Garnett (Washington University in St. Louis)
Matan Gavish (Stanford University)
Yong Ge (University of North Carolina at Charlotte)
Johannes Gehrke (Cornell University)
Pierre Geurts (University of Liege)
Rumi Ghosh (Robert Bosch LLC)
Amol Ghoting (American Express)
Sean Gilpin (Google)
Aris Gkoulalas-Divanis (IBM Research Ireland)
David Gleich (Purdue University)
Ashish Goel (Stanford)
Sreenivas Gollapudi (Microsoft)
Manuel Gomez-Rodriguez (Max Planck Institute)
Amit Goyal (Yahoo!)
Quanquan Gu (University of Virginia)
Ziyu Guan (Northwest Univ. China)
Francesco Gullo (Yahoo Labs)
Sumit Gulwani (Microsoft Research)
Krishna Gummadi (MPI-SWS)
Tias Guns (KU Leuven)
Abhishek Gupta (LinkedIn Corporation)
Manish Gupta (Microsoft-Bing India)

Rahul Gupta (Google)
Reza Haffari (Monash University)
Patrick Haffner (AT&T Research)
Wilhelmiina Hamalainen (Academy of Finland)
Barbara Hammer (Bielefeld University)
Wook-Shin Han (POSTECH)
Yuan Hao (Google)
Ahmed Hassan (Microsoft Research)
Jingrui He (Arizona State University)
Qi He (LinkedIn)
Xiaofeng He (East China Normal University)
Jose Hernandez-Orallo (Technical University Valencia)
Jake Hofman (Microsoft Research)
Katja Hofmann (Microsoft)
Larry Holder (Washington State University)
Geoff Holmes (University of Waikato)
Liangjie Hong (Yahoo!)
Shahriar Hossain (University of Texas El Paso)
Vagelis Hristidis (University of California, Riverside)
Cho-Jui Hsieh (UT Austin)
Hsun-Ping Hsieh (National Taiwan University)
Chun-Nan Hsu (University of California, San Diego)
Bing Hu (Samsung)
Jun Huan (University of Kansas)
Bert Huang (Virginia Tech)
Joshua Huang (Shenzhen University)
Sheng-Jun Huang (Nanjing University of Aeronautics and Astronautics)
Xuanjing Huang (Fudan University)
Eyke Huellermeier (Univ. Paderborn)
Cao Huiping (New Mexico State University)
Seung-won Hwang (Pohang University of Science and Technology)
Tomasz Imielinski (Rutgers University)
Tomoharu Iwata (NTT Communication Science Laboratories)
Arun Iyer (IIT Bombay)
Prateek Jain (Microsoft Research, India)
Mohsen Jamali (Walmart Labs)
Szymon Jaroszewicz (Polish Academy of Sciences)
David Jensen (UMass Amherst)
Shuiwang Ji (Old Dominion University)
Yexi Jiang (Facebook)
Bo Jin (Dalian University of Technology)
Hongxia Jin (IBM Research)
Ruoming Jin (Kent State University)
Wen Jin (Simon Fraser University)
Xiaoming Jin (Tsinghua University)
Ting Kai Ming (Federation University)
Panos Kalnis (King Abdullah University of Science and Technology)
Jaap Kamps (University of Amsterdam.)
Bhargav Kanagal (Google)
U Kang (KAIST)
Ramakrishnan Kannan (Georgia Tech)
Murat Kantarcioglu (University of Texas at Dallas)
Nikos Karampatziakis (Microsoft)
Hisashi Kashima (Kyoto University)
Shiva Kasiviswanathan (Samsung Research America)
Liran Katzir (Final Ltd. Israel)
Sathiya Keerthi (Microsoft)
Arijit Khan (ETH Zurich)
Latifur Khan (University of Texas at Dallas)
Emre Kiciman (Microsoft Research)
Myunghwan Kim (LinkedIn)
Irwin King (Chinese University of Hong Kong)
Dyagilev Kirill (Johns Hopkins University)
Diego Klabjan (Northwestern University)
Ron Kohavi (Microsoft)
Aleksander Kolcz (Twitter)
Tamara Kolda (Sandia Lab)
Deguang Kong (Samsung Research America)
Xiangnan Kong (Worcester Polytechnic Institute)
Christian Konig (Microsoft Research)
Kevin Korb (Monash University)
Michal Kosinski (Stanford)
Nick Koudas (University of Toronto)
Stefan Kramer (University of Mainz)
Andreas Krause (ETH Zurich)
Rui Kuang (University of Minnesota)
Meelis Kull (University of Bristol)
Tsung-Ting Kuo (National Taiwan University)
Matt Kusner (Washington University in St. Louis)
Nicolas Lachiche (University of Strasbourg)
Dmitry Lagun (Emory University)
Laks Lakshmanan (University of British Columbia)
Wai Lam (The Chinese University of Hong Kong)
Sudarshan Lamkhede (Yahoo!)
Theodoros Lappas (Stevens Institute of Technology)
FirstName LastName (Organization)
Silvio Lattanzi (Google)
Victor Lee

Sangkyun Lee (TU Dortmund)
Kristen LeFevre (Google)
Ronny Lempel (Outbrain)
Kristina Lerman (Information Sciences Institute)
Cane Wing-ki Leung (Wisers Research)
Xiaoli Li (A*STAR)
Chengkai Li (University of Texas at Arlington)
Cheng-Te Li (Academia Sinica)
Guoliang Li (USC Information Sciences Institute)
Jiuyong Li (University of South Australia)
Juanzi Li (Tsinghua University)
Lei Li (Samsung Digital Media Solutions Lab)
Lei Li (UC Berkeley)
Ming Li (Nanjing University)
Ping Li (Rugters University)
Wu-Jun Li (Nanjing University)
Xiaolin Li (Nanjing University)
Yuefeng Li (Queensland University of Technology)
Yu-Feng Li (Nanjing University)
Zhenhui Li (Penn State Univ)
Bangyong Liang (Google)
Zhen Liao (Microsoft)
Jefrey Lijffijt (University of Bristol)
Ee-Peng Lim (Singapore Management University)
Hsuan-Tien Lin (National Taiwan Univ)
Jessica Lin (George Mason University)
Yu-Ru Lin (University of Pittsburgh)
Charles Ling (University of Western Ontario)
Nelly Litvak (University of Twente)
Guimei Liu (A*STAR)
Chao Liu (Sogou)
Fei Liu (Carnegie Mellon University)
Huan Liu (Arizona State University)
Nathan Nan Liu (Yahoo! Labs)
Qi Liu (University of Science and Technology of China)
Wei Liu (University of Technology Sydney)
Yan Liu (University of Southern California)
David Lo (Singapore Management University)
Hung-Yi Lo (Shih Chien University, Kaohsiung Campus)
Bo Long (LinkedIn)
Daniel Lowd (University of Oregon)
Eneldo Loza Mencia (TU Darmstadt)
Chang-Tien Lu (Virginia Tech)
Yue Lu (Twitter Inc)
Zhongqi Lu (HKUST)
Dijun Luo (RetailMeNot, Inc.)
Jiebo Luo (Rochester University)
Ping Luo (Chinese Academy of Sciences)
Roger Jie Luo (Yahoo!)
Michael Lyu (Chinese University of Hong Kong)
Emmanuel Müller (Karlsruhe Institute of Technology (KIT))
Hao Ma (Microsoft Research)
Rich Maclin (University of Minnesota-Duluth)
Donato Malerba (University of Bari)
Hiroshi Mamitsuka (Kyoto University)
Nikos Mamoulis (University of Hong Kong)
Julian McAuley (Stanford)
Geoff McLachlan (University of Queensland)
Qiaozhu Mei (University of Michigan)
Wagner Meira Jr (Universidade Federal de Minas Gerais)
Weiyi Meng (Binghamton University)
Pauli Miettinen (MPI Saarbruecken)
Vahab Mirrokni (Google Research)
Prasenjit Mitra (The Pennsylvania State University)
Dunja Mladenic (Institut Jo?ef Stefan)
Martin Mladenov (TU Dortmund)
Marie-Francine Moens (Leuven University)
Claire Monteleoni (George Washington University)
Joshua Moore (Cornell)
Abdullah Mueen (University New Mexico)
Mirco Nanni (KDDLab - ISTI - CNR)
Alexandros Nanopoulos (Catholic University of Eichst?tt-Ingolstadt)
Vivek Narasayya (Microsoft Research)
Franco Maria Nardini (ISTI-CNR)
Olfa Nasraoui (University of Louisville)
Sriraam Natarajan (University of Indiana)
Raymond Ng (University of British Columbia)
See-Kiong Ng
Vincent Ng (University of Texas at Dallas)
Wilfred Ng (Hong Kong University of Science and Technology)
Maximilian Nickel (MIT)
Vlad Niculae (Cornell)
Alexandru Niculescu-Mizil (NEC Laboratories America)
Feiping Nie (University of Texas at Arlington)
Zaiqing Nie (Microsoft Research Asia)
Mathias Niepert (University of Washington)

Xia Ning (Indiana University-Purdue University Indianapolis)
Tim Oates (University of Maryland Baltimore County)
Zoran Obradovic (Temple University)
Brendan O'Connor (UMass Amherst)
Alice Oh (KAIST)
Peder Olsen (IBM Research)
Burkay Orten (Turn Inc.)
Matthew Otey (Google Inc.)
Iadh Ounis (University of Glasgow)
Gerd Paass (Fraunhofer IAIS)
Tapio Pahikkala (University of Turku)
Aditya Pal (IBM Research)
Themis Palpanas (Paris Descartes University)
Rong Pan (Sun Yat-Sen University)
Spiros Papadimitriou (IBM)
Aditya Parameswaran (Stanford University)
Ankur Parikh (CMU)
Laurence Park (Univ. of Western Sydney)
Douglass Parker (UCLA)
Michael Paul (Johns Hopkins University)
Vladimir Pavlovic (Rutgers University)
Wen-Chih Peng (National Chiao Tung University)
Francois Petitjean (Monash)
Bernhard Pfahringer (University of Waikato)
Joel Pfeiffer (Purdue University)
Dinh Phung (Deakin University)
Nico Piatkowski (TU Dortmund University)
Ali Pinar (Sandia National Laboratories)
Claudia Plant (Helmholtz Zentrum M nchen)
B. Aditya Prakash (Virginia Tech)
Kunal Punera (University of Texas at Austin)
Kai Puolam?ki (Finnish Institute of Occupational Health)
Buyue Qian (IBM Watson)
Tao Qin (Microsoft Research)
Novi Quadrianto (University of Sussex)
Kira Radinsky (Sales Predict)
Vladan Radosavljevic (Yahoo!)
Piyush Rai (Duke University)
Ganesh Ramakrishnan (Indian Institute of Technology Bombay)
Karthik Raman (Cornell University)
Huzefa Rangwala (George Mason University)
Sayan Ranu (IIT Madras)
Parisa Rashidi (University of Florida)
S.S. Ravi (SUNY Albany)
Sujith Ravi (Google)
Reza Rawassizadeh (UC Riverside)
Chandan Reddy (Wayne State University)
Xiang Ren (UIUC)
Steffen Rendle (Google)
Chiara Renso (Istituto di Scienza e Tecnologie dell'Informazione)
Matthias Renz (Ludwig Maximilian University of Munich)
Matteo Riondato (Brown University)
Marko Robnik-Sikonja (University of Ljubljana)
Lior Rokach (Ben-Gurion University of the Negev)
Neal Rothleder (CreativeWorx)
Yiye Ruan (Ohio State University)
Salvatore Ruggieri (University of Pisa)
Avishek Saha (Yahoo Labs)
Jorg Sander (University of Alberta)
Scott Sanner (Oregon State University)
Maria Luisa Sapino (University of Turin)
Tamas Sarlos (Google)
Venu Satuluri (Twitter)
Katya Scheinberg (Lehigh University)
Ralf Schenkel (University of Passau, Germany)
Lars Schmidt-Thieme (University of Hildesheim)
Tobias Schnabel (Cornell)
Friedhelm Schwenker (University of Ulm)
Mohak Shah (Bosch Research)
Dafna Shahaf (Microsoft)
James G. Shanahan (Independent Consultant (San Francisco))
Shashi Shekhar (University of Minnesota)
dou Shen (CityGrid Media)
Heng Shen (University of Queensland)
Yi-Dong Shen (Institute of Software, Chinese Academy of Sciences)
Yu-Keng Shih (GraphSQL)
Kyuseok Shim (Seoul National University)
Pannaga Shivaswamy (LinkedIn)
Fabrizio Silvestri (Yahoo Labs)
Gyorgy Simon (University of Minnesota)
Vikas Sindhwani (Google Research, NY)
Yaron Singer (Harvard)
Ambuj Singh (UCSB)
Sameer Singh (University of Washington, Seattle)
Kaushik Sinha (Wichita State University)
Kevin Small (Amazon Research)
Le Song (Georgia Institute of Technology)

Shaoxu Song (Tsinghua)
Yangqiu Song (UIUC)
Sucheta Soundarajan (Rutgers University)
Myra Spiliopoulou (Otto-von-Guericke University Magdeburg)
Eirini Spyropoulou (University of Bristol)
Suvrit Sra (MIT)
Ramakrishnan Srikant (Google)
Michael Steinbach (University of Minnesota)
Nick Street (The University of Iowa)
Gerd Stumme (University of Kassel)
Karthik Subbian (Facebook)
L Subramaniam (IBM Research - India)
Torsten Suel (Polytechnic Institute of New York University)
Masashi Sugiyama (University of Tokyo)
Aixin Sun (Nanyang Technological University)
Jian-Tao Sun (Microsoft Research)
Yizhou Sun (Northeastern Univ)
Einoshin Suzuki (Kyushu University)
Adith Swaminathan (Cornell)
Marcin Sydow (PJIIT and ICS PAS Warsaw)
Andrea Tagarelli (University of Calabria)
Rikiya Takahashi (SmartNews Inc.)
Ichiro Takeuchi (Nagoya Institute of Technology Japan)
Partha Talukdar (CMU)
Ah-Hwee Tan (Nanyang Technological University)
Chenhao Tan (Cornell)
Lu-An Tang (NEC Laboratories)
Dacheng Tao (University of Technology, Sydney)
Yufei Tao (Chinese University of Hong Kong)
Shirish Tatikonda (IBM)
Nikolaj Tatti (Aalto University)
Evimaria Terzi (Boston University)
Alex Thomo (University of Victoria)
YongHong Tian (Peking University)
Hannu Toivonen (University of Helsinki)
Katrin Tomanek (VigLink)
Hanghang Tong (Arizona State University)
Volker Tresp (Ludwig Maximilian University of Munich/Siemens)
Ming-Feng Tsai (National Chengchi University)
Panayiotis Tsaparas (University of Ioannina)
Vincent Tseng (National Cheng Kung University)
Grigorios Tsoumakas (Aristotle University)
Charalampos (Babis) Tsourakakis (Harvard University)
Johan Ugander (Stanford)
Antti Ukkonen (Aalto University)
Jaideep Vaidya (Rutgers Business School)
Laurens van der Maaten (Facebook Research)
Peter van der Putten (Leiden University)
Matthijs van Leeuwen (KU Leuven)
Kush Varshney (IBM Thomas J. Watson Research Center)
Sergei Vassilvitskii (Google)
Suresh Venkatasubramanian (University of Utah)
Nguyen Vinh (University of Melbourne)
Michail Vlachos (IBM Zurich Research Laboratory)
Max Vladymyrov (Yahoo!)
Jilles Vreeken (Max-Planck Institute for Informatics and Saarland University)
Slobodan Vucetic (TempleUniversity)
Bai Wang (Beijing University of Posts and Telecoms)
Chi Wang (Microsoft Research)
Dong Wang (University of Notre Dame)
Fei Wang (University of Connecticut)
Guan Wang (LinkedIn)
Haixun Wang (Google)
Hongning Wang (University of Illinois at Urbana-Champaign)
Jian Wang (LinkedIn)
Jianyong Wang (Tsinghua University)
Ke Wang (Simon Fraser U.)
Lidan Wang (IBM Research)
Shaojun Wang (Wright State University)
Shengrui Wang (Universit? de Sherbrooke)
Xiangjun Wang (Netflix)
Takashi Washio (Osaka University)
Ingmar Weber (Qatar Computing Research Institute)
Xu Wei (New York University)
Gerhard Weikum (Max Planck Institute for Informatics)
Markus Weimer (Microsoft)
Ji-Rong Wen (Renmin University of China)
Tim Weninger (Univ. of Notre Dame)
Robert West (Stanford)
Jenna Wiens (University of Michigan)
Tony Wirth (University of Melbourne)
Ran Wolff (Yahoo!)
Raymond Chi-Wing Wong (Hong Kong University of Science and Technology)

Weng-Keen Wong (Oregon State University)
Junjie Wu (Beihang University)
Xindong Wu (University of Vermont)
Xintao Wu (University of Arkansas)
Yinghui Wu (Washington State University)
Fen Xia (Baidu)
Han Xiao (Technische Universität München)
Keli Xiao (Stony Brook University)
Xiaokui Xiao (Nanyang Technological University)
Yanghua Xiao (Fudan)
Xu Xiaowei (University of Arkansas)
Xing Xie (Microsoft Research)
Jian Xu (Yahoo)
Linli Xu (University of Science and Technology of China)
Xiaobing Xue (UMass)
Takeshi Yamada (NTT Communication Science Laboratories)
Rong Yan (Facebook)
De-Nian Yang (Academic Sinica)
Hongxia Yang (IBM Research)
Jaewon Yang (LinkedIn)
Shuang-Hong Yang (Twitter)
Tao Yang (Ask.com and UCSB)
Jieping Ye (University of Michigan)
Mi-Yen Yeh (Academic Sinica)
En-Hsu Yen (University of Texas at Austin)
Ainur Yessenalina (Amazon)
Dit-Yan Yeung (Hong Kong University of Science and Technology)
Xing Yi (Yahoo!)
Zhen Yi (Georgia Institute of Technology)
Jie Yin (CSIRO)
Jiangang Yu (Microsoft)
Hwanjo Yu (Pohang University of Science and Technology)
Lei Yu (Binghamton University)
Xiao Yu (Google Research)
Yang Yu (Nanjing University)
Zhiguo Yu (University of Texas at Houston)
Nicholas Jing Yuan (Microsoft Research)
Reza Zadeh (Twitter)
Nayyar Zaidi (Monash University)
Carlo Zaniolo (UCLA)
Xiaobo Zhang
Xiaodan Zhang (Drexel University)
Zhenjie Zhang (ADSC)
Dan Zhang (Facebook)
Duo Zhang (Twitter)
Kun Zhang (Max Planck Institute for Intelligent Systems)
Kunpeng Zhang (University of Illinois at Chicago)
Lijun Zhang (Nanjing University)
Min-Ling Zhang (Southeast University)
Nan Zhang (George Washington University)
Peng Zhang (Institute of Information Engineering, Chinese Academy of Science)
Rui Zhang (IBM)
Shichao Zhang (Guangxi Normal University)
xiang Zhang (Case Western Reserve University)
Xiangliang Zhang (KAUST)
Ya Zhang (Shanghai Jiaotong University)
Yu Zhang (Hong Kong Baptist University)
Zhaojun Zhang (UNC)
Zhongfei Zhang (Binghamton University)
Bo Zhao (LinkedIn)
Yuchen Zhao (AppDynamics)
Zheng Zhao (SAS)
Vincent W. Zheng (Advanced Digital Sciences Center)
Yu Zheng (Microsoft Research)
Zijian Zheng (Bing)
Jiayu Zhou (Samsung Research America)
Mianwei Zhou (Yahoo Inc)
Wenjun Zhou (U of Tennessee)
Feida Zhu (Singapore Management Univ.)
Hengshu Zhu (Baidu Inc.)
Jun Zhu (Tsinghua University)
Qiang Zhu (LinkedIn)
xingquan Zhu (Florida Atlantic University)
Fuzhen Zhuang (Institute of Computing Technology)
Arthur Zimek (Ludwig-Maximilians-Universitaet Muenchen)
Albrecht Zimmermann (INSA Lyon)

KDD'15 Industry & Government Track Senior Program Committee

Naoki Abe (IBM T J Watson Research Center)
Greg Cooper (University of Pittsburgh)
Jesse Davis (KU Leuven)
Cesare Furlanello (Fondazione Bruno Kessler)
Rayid Ghani (University of Chicago)
Anne Kao (Boeing Research & Technology)
Prem Melville (Social Alpha Inc.)
Ted Senator (Leidos)
Tomas Singliar (Amazon.com)

KDD'15 Industry & Government Track Program Committee

Kareem Aggour (GE Global Research)
Kamal Ali (Apple Inc.)
Ricardo Baeza-Yates (Yahoo Labs & UPF)
Rohan Baxter (Australian Taxation Office)
Michele Berlingerio (IBM Research Ireland)
Michael Berthold (University of Konstanz)
Christos Boutsidis (IBM)
Tilmann Bruckhaus (Intuit)
Rui Cai (Microsoft Research)
Berkant Barla Cambazoglu (Yahoo Labs)
Longbing Cao (University of Technology Sydney)
Polo Chau (Georgia Tech)
Haifeng Chen (NEC Research Lab)
Jie Chen (University of South Australia)
Michelandgelo D'Agostino (Civis Analytics)
Brian Dalessandro (Dstillery)
Kamalika Das (NASA Ames Research Center)
Denny Denny (University of Indonesia)
Wei Ding (University of Massachusetts Boston)
Seymour Douglas (Google)
Eugene Dubossarsky (Presciient)
Marcus Fontoura (Microsoft)
Ryohei Fujimaki (NEC Knowledge Discovery Laboratories)
Shalini Ghosh (SRI)
Warwick Graco (Australian Taxation Office)
Lifang Gu (Australian Taxation Office)
Melinda Han
Qi He (LinkedIn)
Shawndra Hill (U Penn Wharton)
Jianying Hu (IBM T.J. Watson Research Center)
Zhexue Huang (Industry/China)
Mario Inchiosa (Microsoft)
Sergei Izrailev (Integral Ad Science)
Hongxia Jin (IBM Research)
Warren Jin (CSIRO)
Vanja Josifovski (Pinterest)
Yun Sing Koh (University of Auckland)
Deguang Kong (Samsung Research America)
Christian Konig (Microsoft)
Georgia Koutrika (HP Labs)
Mohit Kumar (Flipkart)
Mounia Lalmas (Yahoo Labs London)
Aleksandar Lazarevic (Aetna)
Kuang-chih Lee (Yahoo)
Bangyong Liang (Google)
Ray Lindsay (Australian Taxation Office)
Chen Ling (Queensland University of Technology)
Lin Liu (University of South Australia)
Xiaomo Liu (Thomson Reuters)
Jiebo Luo (University of Rochester)
Mohammad Mahdian (Google)
Arun Maiya (Institute for Defense Analyses)
Manish Marwah (HP Labs)
Sameep Mehta (IBM Research - India)
Vahab Mirrokni (Google Research)
Vivek Narasayya (Microsoft Research)
Richi Nayak (Queensland University of Technology)
Zaiqing Nie (Microsoft Research Asia)
Kok-Leong Ong (La Trobe University)
Feng Pan (Apple)
Spiros Papadimitriou (IBM)
Jan Pedersen (Microsoft)
Claudia Perlich (Dstillery)
Ned Porter (Census)
Matthew Rattigan (Edgeflip)
Karl Rexer (Rexer Analytics)
Neal Rothleder (Orb Media)
James Schimert (Boeing Research)
Paulo Shakarian (Arizona State University)
Nandita Sharma (Australian Taxation Office)
Amy Shi-Nash (SingTel)
Scott Smith (Boeing Research & Technology)
Glenn Stone (UWS/Australia)
Andrew Stranieri (Federation University)
Jian-Tao Sun (Microsoft)
Shu Tao (IBM Research)
Peter Van der Putten (Pegasystems & Leiden University)
Ranga Vatsavai (North Carolina State University)
Michail Vlachos (IBM Research)
Taifeng Wang (Microsoft Research)
Xing Xie (Microsoft Research)
Debbie Zhang (Australian Taxation Office)
Bo Zhao (LinkedIn)
Yanchang Zhao (Australian Dept. of Immigration)
Zheng Zhao (SAS)
Yu Zheng (Microsoft Research)

KDD'15 Research Track Additional Reviewers

Ashkan Ebadi
Abon Chaudhuri (Intel)
Jiafeng Hu (HKU)
Akhil Arora (XRCI)
Altaf Rahman (Yahoo! Labs)
Akhil Arora
Benjamin Shickel (UF)
Biwei Huang (Max Planck Institute)
Fang-Fei Kuo (Yahoo! Research)
Shiwen Cheng
Daisuke Kimura (University of Tokyo)
Dong Ryeol Lee (Yahoo! Labs)
Defu Lian (UESTC)
Degao Peng (LinkedIn Inc.)
Alexandre V Evfimievski
Yixiang Fang (HKU)
Florian Yger (University of Tokyo)
Freddy Chua
Mingming Gong
Chunqiu Zeng (FIU)
Helena Ahonen-Myka
Shohei Hido (Preferred Networks)
Viet Huynh (Deakin University)
Iyad Batal (General Electric Research)
Jason Zhang (HKUST)
Yi Jia (University of Kansas)
Jonne Pohjankukka (University of Turku)
Jyrki Kivinen (University of Helsinki)
Juho Heimonen (University of Turku)
Yi-Yu Lai (Purdue University)
Le An
Liaoruo Wang (Oracle)
Liang Tang (LinkedIn)
Tang Liang
Mohiuddin Qader
Mianwei Zhou (Yahoo Inc)
Moloud Shahbazi
Luyi Mo (HKU)
Shinichi Nakajima (TU Berlin)
Prithu Banerjee (IBM Research)
Robert Ormandi (Yahoo!)
Hiroaki Sasaki (University of Tokyo)
Shaokun Fan
Mohit Sharma (University of Minnesota)
Silviu Maniu (The University of Hong Kong)
Sina Jafarpour (Turn Inc)
Shan Jiang (UIUC)
Shenshen Liang
(University of California, Santa Cruz)
Song Liu (Tokyo Institute of Technology)
Shouq Sadah
Victor Sheng
Hang Su (Tsinghua University)
Tao Zou
Nhat Le
Teck-Hou Teng (Nanyang Technological University)
Yingzi Wang (Microsoft Research)
Wei (Chang)
Wen Zhong (StonyBrook University)
Weixiang Shao (Univ of Illinois at Chicago)
Xia Zhang (Complete Genomics)
Fei Xie (Hefei University of Technology)
Jia Xu (Guangxi University)
Yuan Fang (Institute for Infocomm Research)
Kui Yu (Simon Fraser University)
Yin Lou (LinkedIn)
Yi Shen
Yu Cheng
Yunlong He (Yahoo! Labs)
Yongxin Tong (HKUST)
Yong Xu (HKU)
Zhiyuan (Chen)
Zhao Chen (HKUST)
Zhen Yue (Yahoo! Labs)
Yuan Zhong (Northeastern University)
Fanwei Zhu (Zhejiang University)
Yudian Zheng (HKU)

KDD 2015 Sponsors & Supporters

Sponsors:

Major Supporters:

Supporters: Platinum

Supporters: Gold

Supporters: Silver

Supporters: Bronze

Supporters: USB Stick and Best Industry & Government Paper Award

Supporter: Best Student Papers, Research Papers & Early Career Paper Awards

Supporter: KDD Cup

Supporter: Lanyard Sponsor

Open for Innovation KNIME

Supporters: Media Sponsor

BIG DATA Mary Ann Liebert, Inc. publishers

KDnuggets™

Supporters: Student Travel Awards

NSF

Prof. Ram Kumar Memorial Foundation

VISA Visa Research

Supporters: Program Ad Sponsor

Yandex

Exhibitors:

sas

cloudera

MathWorks

Contact Singapore contactsingapore.sg

Springer

SALFORD SYSTEMS

Conference Hosts:

UTS:AAi
THE ADVANCED ANALYTICS INSTITUTE

UTS
UNIVERSITY OF TECHNOLOGY, SYDNEY

MORGAN & CLAYPOOL PUBLISHERS

Taylor & Francis
Taylor & Francis Group

Scaling Machine Learning and Statistics for Web Applications

Deepak Agarwal
LinkedIn
Mountain View, CA
dagarwal@linkedin.com

ABSTRACT

Scaling web applications like recommendation systems, search and computational advertising is challenging. Such systems have to make astronomical number of decisions every day on what to serve users when they are visiting the website and/or using the mobile app. Machine learning and statistical modeling approaches that can obtain insights by continuously processing large amounts of data emitted at very high frequency by these applications have emerged as the method of choice. However, there are three challenges to scale such methods: a) scientific b) infrastructure and c) organizational. I will provide an overview of these challenges and the strategies we have adopted at LinkedIn to address those. Throughout, I will illustrate with examples from real-world applications at LinkedIn..

Categories and Subject Descriptors

H.2.8 [**Database Management**]: Database Application — *Data mining*

Keywords

Machine Learning; Statistical Modeling; Web Applications.

Bio

Deepak Agarwal is a big data analyst with 15 years of experience developing and deploying state-of-the-art machine learning and statistical methods for improving the relevance of web applications. He has worked in various positions: chief scientist of large projects, led small and highly technical teams and is also experienced in managing large teams. Deepak currently leads a team that is responsible for all machine learning and optimization efforts at LinkedIn. He is a Fellow of the American Statistical Association, Member Board of Directors for SIGKDD, program chair of KDD in the past, associate editor of two top-tier journals in Statistics, regularly serves on senior program committees of top-tier conferences like KDD, NIPS, CIKM, ICDM, SIGIR, WSDM.

KDD '15, August 10-13, 2015, Sydney, NSW, Australia
ACM 978-1-4503-3664-2/15/08.
http://dx.doi.org/10.1145/2783258.2790452

Hadoop's Impact on the Future of Data Management

Amr Awadallah
Couldera
Palo Alto, CA
aaa@cloudera.com

ABSTRACT

As Hadoop and the surrounding projects & vendors mature, their impact on the data management sector is growing. Amr will talk about his views on how that impact will change over the next five years. How central will Hadoop be to the data center of 2020? What industries will benefit most? Which technologies are at risk of displacement or encroachment?

Categories and Subject Descriptors

H.2.8 [**Database Management**]: Database Application — *Data mining*

Keywords

Hadoop; Data Management; Data Center Technologies.

Bio

Dr. Amr Awadallah, Cofounder/CTO, Cloudera, Inc. Before co-founding Cloudera in 2008, Amr (@awadallah) was an Entrepreneur-in-Residence at Accel Partners. Prior to joining Accel he served as Vice President of Product Intelligence Engineering at Yahoo!, and ran one of the very first organizations to use Hadoop for data analysis and business intelligence. Amr joined Yahoo after they acquired his first startup, VivaSmart, in July of 2000. Amr holds a Bachelor's and Master's degrees in Electrical Engineering from Cairo University, Egypt, and a Doctorate in Electrical Engineering from Stanford University. conferences like KDD, NIPS, CIKM, ICDM, SIGIR, WSDM.

KDD '15, August 10-13, 2015, Sydney, NSW, Australia.
ACM 978-1-4503-3664-2/15/08.
DOI: http://dx.doi.org/10.1145/2783258.2790453

Should You Trust Your Money to a Robot?

Vasant Dhar
New York University
New York City, NY
vdhar@stern.nyu.edu

ABSTRACT

Computers are making more and more decisions for us, and increasingly so in areas that require human judgment. There is a palpable increase in machine intelligence across the touch points of our lives, driven by the proliferation of data feeding into intelligent algorithms capable of learning useful patterns and acting on them. A natural question to ask is how we should be thinking about the role of computers in managing our money. Should we trust our money to a robot? In an era of big data and machines to make sense of it all, do machines have an inherent advantage over humans? There is a surge of interest in Artificial Intelligence for financial prediction. Should we pay attention? Or is this an area where human judgment and input is always essential?

Categories and Subject Descriptors

H.2.8 [**Database Management**]: Database Application — *Data mining*

KDD '15, August 10-13, 2015, Sydney, NSW, Australia
ACM 978-1-4503-3664-2/15/08.
http://dx.doi.org/10.1145/2783258.2790455

Keywords

Computational Finance; Artificial Intelligence; Quantitative Trading

Bio

Vasant Dhar is Professor, Stern School of Business and Center for Data Science at New York University, and Founder of SCT Capital Management. He created the Adaptive Quant Trading (AQT) program, a data-driven learning machine that trades the world's most liquid futures contracts systematically. Dhar has written over 100 research articles and dozens of opinion editorials in media including the Financial Times, Wall Street Journal, Forbes, and Wired Magazine. He is Editor-in-Chief of the Big Data journal.

Data Science at Visa

Waqar Hasan
Visa Inc.
900 Metro Center Blvd
Foster City, CA 94404, USA
wahasan@visa.com

Min Wang
Visa Inc.
900 Metro Center Blvd
Foster City, CA 94404, USA
minwang@visa.com

ABSTRACT

Visa is the payments technology that forms the backbone of the world's financial systems by handling more than 7 trillion dollars of payments annually and our data reflects how the world spends money.

We will describe technical achievements we have made in the area of fraud and cover some open challenges in data science.

Categories & Subject Descriptors: E.0 [General]

Keyword: Data Science

Speakers' Bios

Waqar Hasan

Waqar Hasan joined Visa in 2014 and currently serves as Senior Vice President of Data. He is responsible for Visa's data platform and data-driven products targeted at banks, merchants and consumers in areas like risk and fraud management, loyalty and business intelligence.

Prior to Visa, he was the founder and CEO of InsightsOne, a big data predictive analytics startup, from 2010-2014. At InsightsOne, Hasan formed a company backed by premier venture capital and sold product to Fortune 1000 customers. He led the company through its merger and integration with Apigee. InsightsOne helped make business and consumer interactions both relevant and profitable through cloud-based and on-premise predictive analytics and big data solutions. The combined company (NASDAQ: APIC) had a successful IPO in April 2015.

Prior to Apigee, Hasan was Vice President of Engineering for Data Systems at Yahoo!, where he built and managed Yahoo!'s data platform from 2004 to 2009. He oversaw systems that analyzed data from 500 million consumers, and which remains one of the largest-scale systems in the world, and affect nearly all of Yahoo!'s revenue streams in addition to substantially increasing monetization and consumer engagement.

Before joining Yahoo!, Hasan founded the startup DB Wizards, providing performance accelerators for ERP applications, was an architect at database software provider Informix and a researcher at HP Labs and IBM Almaden.

Waqar received his PhD in Computer Science from Stanford University and a BS in Computer Science from the Indian Institute of Technology, Kanpur. He has published over 20 papers and is a recipient of the ACM SIGMOD Test of Time award.

Min Wang

Dr. Min Wang joined Visa as the Senior Vice President and head of Visa Research in May 2015. Visa Research is a newly created organization as part of the company's continued effort to expand technology research capabilities globally. Visa Research engages with the company's technology and product teams, business partners, academics and governments, to explore and develop technologies that are critical to the payments industry. In her role, Wang leads the research on data analytics, security and the future of payments.

Prior to Visa, Wang was part of Google Research where she was a Senior Staff Research Scientist and research manager focused on knowledge integration and inferencing at Google's headquarters in Mountain View, California. Before Google, Wang was Director of HP Labs China in Beijing, China, where she was also named an HP Distinguished Technologist. Wang also held a senior research role as the manager of the Unified Data Analytics Department at IBM's Thomas J. Watson Research Center in Hawthorne, New York.

Wang has received several distinguished research awards for her work on data management. In 2009, Wang received the ACM SIGMOD Test of Time Award for her 1999 SIGMOD paper, "Approximate Computation of Multidimensional Aggregates of Sparse Data Using Wavelets."

Wang received her PhD in Computer Science from Duke University and BS and MS degrees, both in Computer Science, from Tsinghua University, Beijing, China.

KDD'15, August 10-13, 2015, Sydney, NSW, Australia.
ACM 978-1-4503-3664-2/15/08..
http://dx.doi.org/10.1145/2783258.2790460

How Artificial Intelligence and Big Data Created Rocket Fuel: A Case Study

George John
Rocket Fuel
Redwood Shores, CA
gjohn@rocketfuel.com

ABSTRACT

In 2008, Rocket Fuel's founders saw a gap in the digital advertising market. None of the existing players were building autonomous systems based on big data and artificial intelligence, but instead they were offering fairly simple technology and relying on human campaign managers to drive success. Five years later in 2013, Rocket Fuel had the best technology IPO of the year on NASDAQ, reported $240 million in revenue, and was ranked by accounting firm Deloitte as the #1 fastest-growing technology company in North America. Along the way we learned that it's okay to be bold in our expectations of what is possible with fully autonomous systems, we learned that mainstream customers will buy advanced technology if it's delivered in a familiar way, and we also learned that it's incredibly difficult to debug the complex "robot psychology" when a number of complex autonomous systems interact. We also had excellent luck and timing: as we were building the company, real-time ad impression-level auctions with machine-to-machine buying and selling became commonplace, and marketers became increasingly focused on delivering better results for their company and delivering better personalized and relevant digital experiences for their customers. The case study presentation will present a fast-paced overview of the business and technology context for Rocket Fuel at inception and at present, key learnings and decisions, and the road ahead.

Categories and Subject Descriptors

H.2.8 [**Database Management**]: Database Application — *Data mining*

Keywords

Computational Advertising; Real-time Bidding; Advertising; Artificial Intelligence; Big Data Analytics.

KDD '15, August 10-13, 2015, Sydney, NSW, Australia
ACM 978-1-4503-3664-2/15/08.
http://dx.doi.org/10.1145/2783258.2790458

Bio

George is Chairman and Founder of Rocket Fuel Inc., a smart digital marketing software company that he founded and led as CEO to over 1000 employees and $400 million revenue. Rocket Fuel's software self-optimizes ad campaigns and marketing programs, to drive better results for the business and more relevant digital experiences to customers. The secret sauce is its $100 million investment in artificial intelligence and big data, and Rocket Fuel's moment scoring engine that considers all relevant information just as an ad or message is being delivered. As of Q1 2015, Rocket Fuel powered 96 of the top 100 US advertisers (the "AdAge 100"), plus an increasing number of top global advertisers. Rocket Fuel's DSP (media buying demand-side platform) and DMP (data management platform) have been rated top products in their categories by Forrester and Gartner.

Prior to Rocket Fuel, George led groups at IBM, E.piphany, salesforce.com, and most recently Yahoo!, where he managed behavioral targeting, recommendations, and click fraud. The combined IPO's of E.piphany, salesforce.com, and Rocket Fuel created over $50 billion in peak value for shareholders.

As a kid, George was overly influenced by Star Trek, which led to a short-lived interest in model rocketry (eyebrows grew back after the explosion) and a lifelong interest in Artificial Intelligence. George earned BS, MS, and PhD degrees in Computer Science from Stanford, specializing in AI. During his graduate studies, he won a National Science Foundation fellowship and worked on autonomous spacecraft at NASA, earning his "rocket scientist" credentials.

Optimizing Marketing Impact Through Data-Driven Decisioning

Anil Kamath
Adobe
San Jose, CA
vdhar@stern.nyu.edu

ABSTRACT

Is my marketing working, how much is marketing helping the business and which campaigns and channels are effective? The key challenge for the Chief Marketing Officer is to tie investment in marketing to business results. In an increasingly complex marketing environment – marketing organizations are being called upon to prove and optimize the return on marketing investment across different paid earned and owned marketing channels. In this talk we will show how data science and optimization techniques can be applied to cross channel data to attribute marketing effectiveness, drive media planning and real-time optimization of campaigns. Using terabytes of multi-channel data we answer questions such as what is the impact of different marketing campaigns on our business, how should we allocate our marketing dollars between different channels and when should I spend them and how do we execute our marketing campaigns based on the synergies of the different channels

Categories and Subject Descriptors

H.2.8 [**Database Management**]: Database Application — *Data mining*

Keywords

marketing mix modeling; optimization; data science

Bio

Anil Kamath, Fellow and VP of Technology at Adobe, is a web and technology entrepreneur. At Adobe, he is responsible for data driven algorithms for the Adobe Marketing cloud. He was founder and primary architect of Efficient Frontier, a leading digital ad buying platform, until its acquisition by Adobe. Prior to that Anil, founded an ecommerce company call eBoodle that was acquired by Shopzilla. He has held leadership positions at Shopzilla and DE Shaw and received a PhD in Computer Science from Stanford University and a B.Tech in Computer Science from IIT Bombay.

KDD '15, August 10-13, 2015, Sydney, NSW, Australia
ACM 978-1-4503-3664-2/15/08.
http://dx.doi.org/10.1145/2783258.2790456

Powering Real-time Decision Engines in Finance and Healthcare using Open Source Software

Bassel Ojjeh
LigaDATA
Palo Alto, CA
bassel@ligadata.com

ABSTRACT

Financial services and healthcare companies could be the biggest beneficiaries of big data. Their real-time decision engines can be vastly improved by leveraging the latest advances in big data analytics. However, these companies are challenged in leveraging Open Software Systems (OSS). This presentation covers how, in collaboration with financial services and healthcare institutions, we built an OSS project to deliver a real-time decisioning engine for their respective applications. I will address two key issues. First, I will describe the strategy behind our hiring process to attract millennial big data developers and the results of this endeavor. Second, I will recount the collaboration effort that we had with our large clients and the various milestones we achieved during that process. I will explain the goals regarding big data analysis that our large clients presented to us and how we accomplished those goals. In particular, I will discuss how we leveraged open source to deliver a real-time decisioning software product called Fatafat to these institutions. An advantage of developing applications in Fatafat is that it is already integrated with Hadoop, Kafka for real-time data streaming, HBase and Cassandra for NoSQL data storage. I will talk about how these companies benefited from Fatafat and some of challenges we had in the design of this software. I will provide quantifiable improvements in key metrics driven by Fatafat and interesting, unsolved problems/challenges that need to be addressed for faster and wider adoption of OSS by these companies.

Categories and Subject Descriptors

H.2.8 [**Database Management**]: Database Application — *Data mining*

KDD '15, August 10-13, 2015, Sydney, NSW, Australia
ACM 978-1-4503-3664-2/15/08.
http://dx.doi.org/10.1145/2783258.2790456

Keywords

Financial Services; Healthcare; Real-time Decision Engines; Open Source Software.

Bio

Bassel Ojjeh heads ligaDATA, where he is responsible for the strategic and technological development of an online open-source Big Data learning engine called Fatafat.

Prior to LigaDATA, Ojjeh served as a Senior Vice President of Data Technologies & Products at Yahoo! after the company acquired his Seattle-based data startup, DMX Group. At Yahoo!, his group was responsible for building data products that drive audience engagement and advertising revenues. These products consumed some of the largest data sets in the world, generated by the half a billion users of Yahoo!

Before founding the DMX Group, Ojjeh co-founded digiMine (now Audience Science), where he and his co-founders pioneered behavioral targeting.

Before founding digiMine, Bassel was Group Program Manager in the Internet Business division at Microsoft, where he drove key initiatives in the areas of data warehousing, data mining, personalization and predictive analytics. He started his career as a developer at Fox Software, which was later acquired by Microsoft for $1.5 billion.

Bassel Ojjeh is a Hall of Fame inductee at Bowling Green State University. He also serves on the Board of Directors of the International University of Science and Technology in Syria, which he co-founded.

Clouded Intelligence

Joseph Sirosh
Microsoft
Redmond, WA
jsirosh@microsoft.com

ABSTRACT

Several exciting trends are driving the birth of the intelligent cloud. The vast majority of world's data is now connected data resident in the cloud. The majority of world's new software is now connected software, also resident in or using the cloud. New cloud based Machine Learning as a Service platforms help transform data into intelligence and build cloud-hosted intelligent APIs for connected software applications. Face analysis, computer vision, text analysis, speech recognition, and more traditional analytics such as churn prediction, recommendations, anomaly detection, forecasting, and clustering are all available now as cloud APIs, and far more are being created at a rapid pace. Cloud hosted marketplaces for crowdsourcing intelligent APIs have been launched. In this talk I will review what these trends mean for the future of data science and show examples of revolutionary applications that you can build using cloud platforms.

Categories and Subject Descriptors

H.2.8 [**Database Management**]: Database Application — *Data mining*

Keywords

Cloud Computing; Machine Learning as a Service; Intelligent APIs.

Bio

Joseph Sirosh is the Corporate VP for Machine Learning at Microsoft in the Cloud & Enterprise Group. His team is building the next generation of cloud Machine Learning and Information Management services for transforming data into intelligence. Prior to joining Microsoft in 2013, he was the Vice President of the Global Inventory Platform at Amazon, and also conceived and built the development team for the Amazon Machine Learning service. Prior to joining Amazon in 2004, he was the VP of R&D at FICO. Joseph holds a PhD in Computer Science from the University of Texas at Austin, and a Bachelors in CS from Indian Institute of Technology, Chennai.

KDD '15, August 10-13, 2015, Sydney, NSW, Australia.
ACM 978-1-4503-3664-2/15/08.
DOI: http://dx.doi.org/10.1145/2783258.2790454

Data Science from the Lab to the Field to the Enterprise

Christopher White
Microsoft
Redmond, WA
chwh@microsoft.com

ABSTRACT

DARPA has been investing in data science and building open source tools for applications ranging from counter threat finance, through radar operations and cancer research, to anti-human trafficking. This presentation will cover previous work at DARPA, experience building real-world applications for defense and law enforcement to analyze data, and the future of computer science as an enabler for content discovery, information extraction, relevance determination, and information visualization. The talk will be a mix of background, detailed examples, and software demonstration. It will cover the importance of anchoring in applications, minimization of design-to-testing time, development with users-in-the-loop, error tolerance of machine learning, design for diverse user populations, and the necessity of open source software integration. It will conclude by covering a few next directions for special projects at Microsoft.

Categories and Subject Descriptors

H.2.8 [**Database Management**]: Database Application — *Data mining*

Keywords

Open Source Tools; Data Mining Applications.

Bio

Chris White is a Principal Researcher at Microsoft working on special projects. He was recently a Program Manager at DARPA developing advanced technologies for data science, where he created DARPA's leading programs XDATA, Memex, and the Open Catalog as part of the President's Big Data Initiative. His work has been applied to domains including countering human trafficking and counter terrorism, where it has been featured on 60 minutes, CNN, the Wall Street Journal, TEDx, and Google's Solve for X. He previously served DARPA as the Agency's country lead in Afghanistan. Secretary of Defense Leon Panetta recognized DARPA and his efforts in Afghanistan with a Joint Meritorious Unit Award for support in a combat environment. Prior to DARPA he was a fellow at Harvard's School of Engineering and Applied Sciences and holds a PhD in electrical engineering from the Johns Hopkins University.

KDD '15, August 10-13, 2015, Sydney, NSW, Australia.
ACM 978-1-4503-3664-2/15/08.
http://dx.doi.org/10.1145/2783258.2790461

User Modeling in Telecommunications and Internet Industry

Qiang Yang
Hong Kong University of Science and Technology
Hong Kong
qyang@cse.ust.hk

ABSTRACT

It is extremely important in many application domains to have accurate models of user behavior. Data mining allows user models to be constructed based on vast available data automatically. User modeling has found applications in mobile APP recommendations, social networking, financial product marketing and customer service in telecommunications. Successful user modeling should be aware of several critical issues: who are the target users? How should the solutions be updated when new data come in? How should user feedback be handled? What are the 'pain' points of users? In this talk, I will discuss my own experience on user modeling with big data. I will draw examples from telecommunications and the Internet industry, contrasting and highlighting some lessons learned in these industries.

Categories and Subject Descriptors

H.2.8 [**Database Management**]: Database Application — *Data mining*

Keywords

User Modeling; Recommendations; Internet; Telecommunications.

KDD '15, August 10-13, 2015, Sydney, NSW, Australia
ACM 978-1-4503-3664-2/15/08.
http://dx.doi.org/10.1145/2783258.2788588

Bio

Qiang Yang is the New Bright University Named Professor of Engineering and Chair Professor at Hong Kong University of Science and Technology, where he is the Head of the Department of Computer Science and Engineering. He was the founding head of the Huawei Noah's Ark Lab (2012-2015). He is currently the Technical Advisor to WeChat. His research interests are data mining, machine learning and artificial intelligence. He is a fellow of AAAI, IEEE, IAPR and AAAS, and ACM Distinguished Scientist. He received his PhD degree in Computer Science from University of Maryland, College Park in 1989, and had been a faculty member at University of Waterloo and Simon Fraser University in Canada. He had been the founding Editor in Chief of ACM Transactions on Intelligent Systems and Technology (ACM TIST) between 2009 and 2014, and is the founding Editor in Chief of IEEE Transactions on Big Data. He has been conference and program chair for international conferences such as ACM KDD 2010 and 2012, ACM IUI 2010, IEEE Big Data 2013, ACM RecSys 2013 and International Joint Conference on Artificial Intelligence (IJCAI) in 2015.

The Effectiveness of Marketing Strategies in Social Media: Evidence from Promotional Events

Panagiotis Adamopoulos
padamopo@stern.nyu.edu

Vilma Todri
vtodri@stern.nyu.edu

Department of Information, Operations, and Management Sciences
Leonard N. Stern School of Business, New York University

ABSTRACT

This paper studies a novel social media venture and seeks to understand the effectiveness of marketing strategies in social media platforms by evaluating their impact on participating brands and organizations. We use a real-world data set and employ a promising research approach combining econometric with predictive modeling techniques in a causal estimation framework that allows for more accurate counterfactuals. Based on the results of the presented analysis and focusing on the long-term business value of marketing strategies in social media, we find that promotional events leveraging implicit or explicit advocacy in social media platforms result in significant abnormal returns for the participating brand, in terms of expanding the social media fan base of the firm. The effect is also economically significant as it corresponds to an increase of several thousand additional new followers per day for an average size brand. We also precisely quantify the impact of various promotion characteristics and demonstrate what types of promotions are more effective and for which brands, while suggesting specific tactical strategies. For instance, despite the competition for consumers' attention, brands and marketers should broadcast marketing messages on social networks during the time of peak usage in order to maximize their returns. Overall, we provide actionable insights with major implications for firms and social media platforms and contribute to the related literature as we discover new rich findings enabled by the employed causal estimation framework.

Categories and Subject Descriptors

K.4.4 [**Electronic Commerce**]: Online Shopping; J.4 [**Social and Behavioral Sciences**]: Economics

General Terms

Economics; Experimentation; Measurement

Keywords

Business Analytics; Causal Inference; Event Study; Counterfactual; Social Media; Business Value; Social Commerce

KDD'15, August 10-13, 2015, Sydney, NSW, Australia.
© 2015 ACM. ISBN 978-1-4503-3664-2/15/08 ...$15.00.
DOI: http://dx.doi.org/10.1145/2783258.2788597.

1. INTRODUCTION

Social media are fundamentally changing the way we communicate, collaborate, and consume. They represent one of the most transformative impacts of information technology on business [3] as they drastically change how consumers and firms interact. Harnessing the opportunities that social media generate, marketers nowadays are seeking novel ways to create or further increase the consumers' connection and engagement with their brand. As consumers spend an increasing amount of their time online and the percentage of adults using social media significantly rises, companies invest a growing amount of their marketing budget towards online and social media advertising, invent new ways to establish strong connections with their customers into the online world, and leverage their social connections. Therefore, companies nowadays increasingly compete for consumers' attention and engagement with their brand in the social media space. Content generation, nurture of positive online word-of-mouth (WOM), and utilization of social links among customers are some quintessential effective means of non-paid advertising for companies to spread their message in real time and generate leads associated with key marketing objectives.

Social commerce is a representative example of how e-commerce can leverage the social connections between users to generate leads for a business [31]. The term "social commerce" was first introduced in 2005 by Yahoo! [27] and initially referred to a feature that allowed users to review products on the Yahoo! shopping platform. During the next years, the scope of the term "social commerce" expanded in various directions incorporating peer recommendations, shared shopping lists, product referrals, coupon sharing, team-buying (i.e., a group of customers gathering together in order to bargain with merchants), "deal-of-the-day" websites (i.e., e-commerce websites where a minimum number of purchases should be reached in order an offer to be activated), network-based marketing and integration of online merchandisers with social network platforms, and company-controlled online communities [32]. Towards this direction, American Express Company (Amex) recently pioneered a social commerce venture on the social media platform of Twitter, Inc. based on which a user can purchase a product or claim a promotional offer from a participating brand by sending a short text message, called "tweet", with a designated keyword (i.e., hashtag). The service has already been deployed in large scale offering to users credit of $15 million just in April 2014 [1] and $100 million in total

(Sept 2014).[1] The social commerce initiative of Amex on the social network of Twitter builds on concepts related to the previous social commerce ventures but also exhibits some unique features. For instance, in this setting all the discount claims and transactions are by default visible to the users of the platform, each purchase and offer takes place within the platform itself using only the core feature of the platform (i.e., designated hashtags), the promotions correspond to both online shops and brick-and-mortar businesses, both physical and electronic products are available, and the products and offers are delivered to the user that completed the transaction instead of other users (e.g., Facebook gifts).

The aforementioned unique features of this new venture and the simplicity in completing purchases and claiming offers generate tremendous potentials as they can fundamentally change the way consumers shop online and interact with brands [31]. Wrapping the entire purchase (and discount claim) process into a hashtag, the service makes the transactions fast and easy for the consumers. At the same time, the proposed service capitalizes the unique opportunity for social media to generate direct return on investment. Thus, the *short-term effects* of such an offering seem straightforward for both the consumers, who save money on their purchases, and the marketers, who generate buzz [13] and sales [31] around their brand.

However, this paper assumes the point of view of social brands and organizations and attempts to focus on the *long-term effects* of such social media marketing strategies enabled by the unique salient features of the social medium. Amex essentially turns every single purchase or offer claim into an advertisement as the social neighbors of the customer get exposed to the public advocacy and endorsement of the brand or the product from a fellow friend. The service is an exemplary model of how a highly engaging social media campaign could generate commitment from the consumers and reinforce their loyalty to the brand. Therefore, we attempt to elucidate the role of marketing strategies and promotional events in increasing the user fan base for the participating brand or organization. Any change in the size of the social media fan base of a company is a visible important indicator of firm performance, since a user following a brand on Twitter can be considered as implicit word-of-mouth and recommendation. Besides, companies and organizations are particularly interested into attracting more followers for their social media profiles and capitalize on every opportunity to do so as in the long-run they can more easily generate brand awareness, create engagement, and spur online WOM. Furthermore, a larger fan base might further enhance the company's ability to harness the power and effectiveness of social media in the future as well [31]. According to the hierarchy of effects in marketing, such key marketing objectives are directly linked to increased sales [30] and it has been shown that the corresponding social media-based metrics are significant leading indicators of firm equity value [21].

In this paper, we seek to understand the long-term effectiveness of social media marketing strategies that integrate public advocacy and endorsement features by examining their impact on the image of the participating brands and organizations, specifically their fan base. Focusing on the long-term business value, we employ an event study methodology combining econometric with predictive modeling techniques in a causal estimation framework that allows for more accurate counterfactuals and use a real-world data set consisting of *all* the promotional events by Amex and other participating brands on Twitter, more than 70 million brand-related tweets, and detailed information for more than 3 million users. We find that marketing strategies incorporating implicit or explicit advocacy on social media platforms result in significant abnormal returns for the participating brand, in terms of additional new followers. We also precisely quantify the impact of the various promotion characteristics (e.g., discount, price, flexibility, expected benefit) and demonstrate what types of promotions are more effective towards expanding a brand's social media fan base. Besides, we illustrate for which brands such promotional events are more effective and suggest specific tactical strategies. Overall, we contribute to the related literature discovering new rich findings and provide actionable insights with demonstrable implications for both marketers and social media platforms.

In Section 2 of this paper, we develop the hypotheses pertaining to our research questions and discuss the related work. Then, in Section 3, we describe the particular e-commerce business model as well as the data generating process and, in Section 4, we describe in detail the employed methodology for causal estimation in combination with the deployed data mining techniques. Section 5 presents our empirical results and the real-world value of our discoveries, Section 6 discusses the additional robustness tests we conducted, and Section 7 describes the falsification checks ("placebo" studies) we deployed in order to verify our causal estimates. Finally, Section 8 concludes this paper summarizing our findings as well as the limitations of this work.

2. RELATED WORK AND HYPOTHESES DEVELOPMENT

Employing the hashtag feature of Twitter, American Express effectively transforms the specific social media platform into a social commerce platform, where consumers can directly buy products or claim promotions with the easiness of a tweet and automatically spread the word about the offers. This novel emergent type of e-commerce and user engagement is related to several streams of research from different fields, including Computer Science, Information Systems, Marketing, and Economics. These streams of research include network-based marketing, mobile coupons, real-time marketing, and word-of-mouth (WOM). We review the extant literature to summarize previous work and develop our research hypotheses. Additionally, we discuss the related work regarding the employed causal estimation framework.

Network-based marketing refers to a collection of marketing techniques that take advantage of links between consumers to increase sales and create buzz. Different modes of network-based marketing have been identified in prior literature. For instance, "network targeting" refers to a firm marketing to prior purchasers' social-network neighbors, possibly without any action by the customers, whereas "advocacy" involves particular individuals becoming either vocal advocates (i.e., explicit advocacy) for a product or service recommending it to their friends and acquaintances or implicit advocates through their own actions (e.g., adoption of a specific service or product) [14]. In the particular setting of Twitter and Amex, consumers automatically reveal their

[1]`https://twitter.com/AmericanExpress/status/511591536082296832`

purchases and, thus, contribute to the implicit advocacy. Consumers may additionally choose to personalize the tweet messages they share with their social neighbors and, thus, become explicit advocates. Hence, Amex and its partners using complimentary modes of network-based marketing as an integral part of the purchase process aim at taking full advantage of the social links between customers in order to drive awareness, sales, and engagement. Thus, as the customers spread the word about an offering and advocate the corresponding brand through their product endorsements, more social media users get exposed to the promoting brand and its activities and through a variety of influence processes, including those that raise awareness as well as those that persuade individuals to change their expectations [2], might decide to become social media followers of the particular brand in order to keep up to date with the company's products, services and offerings. On the other hand, promotional events might have a negative impact since such promotions may lead to inferences about the value and quality of the brand and its products. In particular, consumers, especially those that are not familiar with the brand, might interpret these promotions as a signal that the specific product is of low quality or that the firm is in trouble [10, 29]. However, in the online world, thanks to the advancements of modern information systems as well as the valence and volume of online reviews, consumers have easier access to higher quality information, which in combination with the lower search costs improves their ability to compare different brands and products [4], and thus the potential influence of such negative signals is reduced. Besides, because of the increased price competition and the more frequent price adjustments online [6] as well as the increased price sensitivity of consumers [7], such promotions are also less likely to be perceived as negative signals. Hence, promotional events on social media are less likely to have a negative impact. Therefore, we propose that:

*H*1: *A social media marketing strategy incorporating features of implicit and/or explicit advocacy is likely to attract new followers for the participating brand or organization.*

Besides, the current fan base of a brand might affect the potential of social media marketing strategies to attract new followers through online WOM. Research suggests that both volume and valence of WOM have a significant impact [8] while some prior empirical studies indicate that the volume of WOM is more effective than the valence through the awareness effect [20]. Especially in online social media and networks, the large number of users offers the potential for online WOM at much larger scale, causing online social networks to render online WOM more convenient than traditional WOM [9, 35]. Since new customer acquisition is crucial for businesses and given the aforementioned importance of social networks, social media platforms have attracted the attention of many companies who have a perennial interest in leveraging social relationships to extend their customer base [28]. Nonetheless, the current network fan base could either amplify or attenuate the effectiveness of marketing strategies on attracting new followers. For instance, despite the awareness effect of such social media marketing strategies, it might be more difficult for a company with a larger existing fan base to attract new fans due to saturation effects since it is more likely for a user to have already made a conscious decision in the past whether to follow the particular brand or not. On the other hand, a large fan base might positively affect customers' decision to follow a brand through a social influence bias [24] contributing to a "rich-get-richer" effect. Therefore, we hypothesize that:

*H*2*a*: *A social media marketing strategy from a brand with a smaller existing fan base is less likely to attract more followers for the participating brand or organization.*

*H*2*b*: *A social media marketing strategy from a brand with a smaller existing fan base is more likely to attract more followers for the participating brand or organization.*

Moreover, Twitter as a social medium is closely aligned with the trends towards mobile [5] and real-time marketing. Twitter is currently one of the few social platforms that has already captured the "in-the-moment" context and this allows marketers not only to propagate their messages in a timely manner but also to capitalize the context and the mindset in which the consumer is more likely to be receptive and responsive to an advertiser's message [33]. Hence, advertisers who would like to embrace the real-time opportunities of Twitter would be interested into choosing the correct time of promoting such events on the Twitter platform in order to maximize the return on engagement/investment. In particular, someone might argue that the time of peak usage would increase the chances of exposure to a greater audience and thus would attract more followers. However, it could be also the case that at the time of peak usage propagating a promotional message is very competitive and so less effective in attracting consumers' engagement and attention. Therefore, we hypothesize the following:

*H*3*a*: *A promotional message that is broadcasted at the time of peak usage of the social media platform is more likely to attract more followers for the participating brand or organization.*

*H*3*b*: *A promotional message that is broadcasted at the time of peak usage of the social media platform is less likely to attract more followers for the participating brand or organization.*

Furthermore, the ability of a marketer to attract new followers will depend on the perceived benefits of the promotional event as well as the expectations users form about future events. Dickinger and Kleijnen [11] investigate consumers' intentions to redeem mobile coupons since coupon redemption rates are important drivers of sale increases, profits, and market performance [18, 25]. They suggest that the economic benefit is a significant determinant of the coupon usefulness and attractiveness and, consequently, we theorize that, *in a social commerce setting, a promotional event with a larger percentage discount is more likely to attract more followers for the participating brand.* Besides, the ability to claim an offer multiple times allows for additional monetary savings and would be likely to generate more followers who benefit from accumulated savings. Therefore, *a promotional event with an offer that can be claimed multiple times by a single customer is more likely to attract more followers for the participating firm.* While higher savings would be likely to attract more followers, the minimum required amount a customer is required to spend also comes into play. Hence, *a promotional event requiring a larger amount (USD) of minimum spend is less likely to attract more followers for the participating brand.* Additionally, Molitor et al. [23] show that the closer the consumers are to the physical store offering the coupon, the more likely they are to download the mobile coupons. Thus, *in a social commerce setting, a promotional event that is valid only in brick-and-mortar stores and not online is hypothesized to be less likely to attract more followers for the participating brand.* Based on the above discussion, *a promotional event with higher expected benefits for consumers is more likely to attract more followers for the brand* and hence we measure the corresponding effects.

Moreover, our work is closely related to prior research in e-commerce. Studying the consumer behavior in this modern social commerce service, in [31] we elucidate the factors that drive and affect the consumers' decision to adopt this novel service and make a purchase that will be disclosed automatically to the social network. In particular, employing both econometric and predictive models, we study how the characteristics of the user and her social network affect the decision to make a purchase and engage into WOM at the same time, in an attempt to better understand how firms can conduct business through social commerce and spur online conversations. Based on the empirical results, we find that various user characteristics, the brand loyalty and trust of the users, and their familiarity with the platform have significant effects on the likelihood of adoption and social purchases. Additionally, we find that the economic behavior of a user's immediate social network as well as the personalization and the valence of recommendations from the social neighbors of the user have also significant impact on her/his decisions to make such purchases. Besides, observing the WOM episodes, the breadth of their dissemination, and the valence of the recommendations, we are able to study the distinguishing characteristics of the disseminators that are associated with successful post-purchases (i.e., after the transaction of the disseminator has been broadcasted to the network) of their neighbors either due to awareness or influence effects. The derived models provide specific guidelines for marketers to orchestrate WOM in social networks.

As far as the *methodological framework* employed in this paper is considered, event studies represent a relatively underexplored but promising research approach which looks at abnormal returns and reactions to specific events or happenings and measures directly the changes in the quantity of interest. Events studies have been mainly used in economic and finance research where they provide a powerful setting to examine the informativeness and impact of an event, such as investments and acquisitions, on the stock price of a firm. However, at their most general level, event studies do not necessarily include or require stock market information. Instead, there could be a relationship between an event and *any* dependent variable. Thus, the applicability of event studies is not limited to economic and financial research. Event studies have been used, for example, to identify specific factors that influence the outcomes of information technology (IT) investments by publicly traded firms. In recent years, the focus has been extended beyond IT investments to other issues, such as security incidents, IT outsourcing initiatives, e-commerce investments, and standardization projects [26]. Nonetheless, this paper is the first to combine data mining techniques with the econometric methodology of event studies in a causal framework in order to identify the true effect of social media marketing strategies on the user base of brands and organizations. Comparing event studies with other methodologies for estimating average treatment effects (ATE), such as the difference-in-differences (DiD) method or model free approaches, event studies are not limited to only two time periods (i.e., pre-intervention and post-intervention), they do not assume that the event (or treatment) is exactly the same for all treated members, that it has the same effect in every time period, nor that it is static and has no duration, but event studies can include flexible leads and lags. Besides, among other differences, event studies do not necessarily need control groups that consist of the same untreated individual members over time and hence do not suffer from a possible violation of the parallel trend assumption, even though event studies are flexible enough and can include such control groups or "market" observations, if preferable. Similarly, event studies can include synthetic controls (regardless of the scale of the dependent variable across observations and the sign of the correlation between the treated and control units) but they do not need to match individual observations on observed characteristics while assuming that they are also similar on unobserved traits, as in propensity score matching (PSM) techniques. Hence, the proposed methodology can contribute to the formation of synthetic control groups that do not violate the established conditions for causal inference from observation data. In addition, tapping into the advances of predictive modeling and leveraging (big) data of high veracity and variety, the proposed methodology also allows for more accurate counterfactuals, apart from more appropriate control groups. Thus, event studies can be naturally combined with data mining and machine learning approaches for accurate causal inference. In Section 4, we describe in detail the proposed integration of event studies with data mining and machine learning techniques as well as the corresponding assumptions for causal inference.

3. THE BUSINESS MODEL AND DATA GENERATING PROCESS

The data generating process of the specific social commerce case we study differs significantly from traditional online commerce processes. In particular, American Express announces the list of participating brands and organizations and the corresponding promotional sales and offers with their respective terms. The featured promotional products and offers belong to a wide variety of categories, including retail, travel, entertainment, etc.

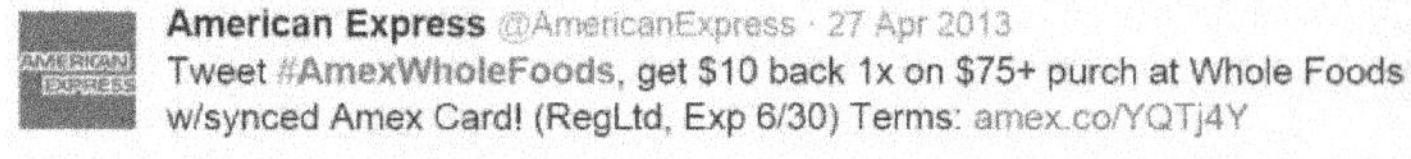

Figure 1: Amex announcing a promotion on Twitter.

A typical announcement for such a promotional offer is the following: *"Tweet #AmexWholeFoods, get $10 back 1x on $75+ purch at Whole Foods w/synced Amex Card! (RegLtd, Exp 6/30) Terms: http://amex.co/YQTj4Y"*, as shown in Figure 1. Respectively, a typical promotional sale announcement is the following: *"Get Xbox 360 4GB for $179.99+tax w/synced Amex Card. Tweet #BuyXbox360Bundle to start purchase! QtyLtd Exp 3/3 Terms http://amex.co/W4X7xa"*.

Then, consumers who are interested into making a purchase or claiming an offer must have a Twitter account and sync their Amex account with Twitter through an easy opt-in process. Once Amex announces the offers, users can purchase the products or claim the offers by posting a tweet (a message of maximum 140 characters) with the designated hashtag or by re-tweeting the specific announcement. Such a tweet is publicly posted on the Twitter profile of the user (private accounts were not eligible to participate in the program) and her/his social network friends will automatically receive the tweet on their own timelines. Amex tracks these tweets that use the designated hashtag in the social network and matches them to the desired product or offer. After the tweet is automatically processed, a reply is sent to the user verifying the terms of the offer or asking to confirm the purchase within fifteen minutes. In the case of a product purchase, once the transaction is confirmed by the user within the designated timeframe, Amex bills the customers or credits the promotional amount in a following eligible purchase, respectively. We should note that a user is not required to follow neither Amex nor the participating brand in order to purchase a product or claim an offer.

Our data set contains *all* the promotional events available by Amex and the participating brands on Twitter. For each promotional event, the available information in our database and the derived variables include, among others, the percentage discount of the promotional event, the minimum amount a user is required to spend in order to be eligible for the promotion, whether the promotion is available only for in-store purchases, whether the promotional event corresponds to a product purchase or a discount offer, whether the promotion can be claimed multiple times from a single user, the number of followers of the participating brand when the announcement of the promotional event was sent, and whether the offer was announced between 12:00pm and 4:00pm, which is the peak of user activity on Twitter platform [34]. The data set spans all the promotional offers and sales that took place since the program was launched, March 2012, until the end of January 2015. Table 1 summarizes the variables of interest and shows the corresponding descriptive statistics computed over all the observations in our data set.

Additionally, using the Twitter API we have access to the daily number of followers, friends, and statuses, since 2011 (or the date the corresponding account was created and verified by Twitter) and for each calendar day, for all the verified accounts on Twitter and all the official brand accounts. Finally, for each brand we have also collected the corresponding economic and market sectors in which it operates as well as their user social network. In summary, we have data on 288 promotional events from 189 brands as well as daily observations for more than 22,000 brands across various industries.

4. EVENT MODEL AND EMPIRICAL ANALYSIS OF MARKETING STRATEGIES

Typical event studies first require identifying the event of interest (e.g., announcement of a merger between two business entities). After the specific event is defined, the period of time over which the corresponding quantity of interest (e.g., stock price of the firm) is adjusted is determined. Then, the quantity of interest is observed and the changes in response to the event, beyond the "normal" or expected level in the absence of the event, are examined to determine the extent to which the event changes the quantity of interest [17]. Nevertheless, event studies are not limited to economic and finance research and do not necessarily include or require stock market information but there could be any relationship between an event and a dependent variable, without the need to presume market efficiency as in stock market studies; however, the motivation and the theories used to generate expectations are likely to differ across disciplines [17]. In such settings, event studies can be a superior framework to various alternative approaches in investigating the response to particular happenings.

In our setting, the main identifying assumption is the absence of confounding events during the estimation and event windows; we describe in detail in the following page how confounding events can be identified employing automated and / or manual processes. Besides, our models for generating expectations (or "normal" returns) are based on data mining techniques and methods following the corresponding machine learning and data mining principles to accurately predict the quantity of interest and avoid problems of over-fitting and data leakage. More formally, the conducted event study assumes that i) a set of features, which is predictive of the outcome variable in the pre-intervention period, would have predicted the outcome also in the absence of the event of interest, and that ii) this set of predictive features has not been affected by the intervention. Even though all causal inference methods require some key model assumptions, the aforementioned assumptions for the identification of the causal impact of the events of interest using the described approach with observational data are less strict and much more realistic compared to the assumptions of the alternatives approaches described in Section 2.

In the following paragraphs we describe in detail the deployed approach following the outline that MacKinlay described in the context of economics and finance [22]. In particular, an event study methodology involves the following steps: (i) identification of the *event of interest*; (ii) definition of the *event window*; (iii) selection of the *sample* set of firms to be included in the analysis; (iv) prediction of the *"normal" return* during the event window in the absence of the event; (v) estimation of the *"abnormal" return* within the event window, where the abnormal return is defined as the difference between the actual and predicted returns without the event occurring; and (vi) testing whether the abnormal return is statistically different from zero.

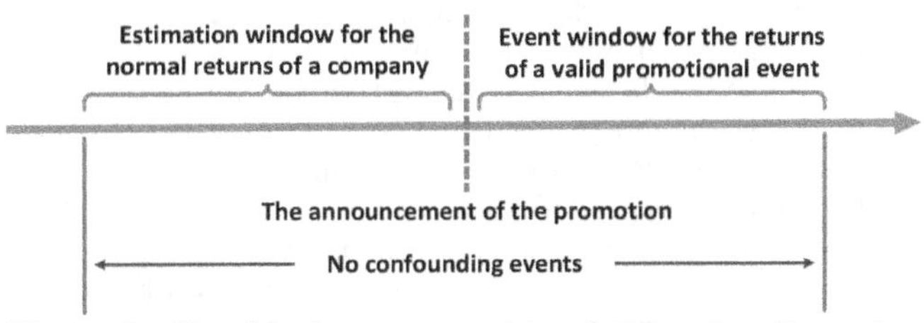

Figure 2: Graphical representation of the estimation window, event, and event window of a promotional event.

In the particular setting of social commerce, participating firms and American Express make announcements on Twitter about specific marketing promotions. Such announcements serve to inform the users about the corresponding terms of each promotion and, for this study, they constitute

Table 1. Variables and Descriptive Statistics

Variable	Description	Mean	Std. Dev	Min	Max
# Followers	The number of followers of the participating brand on Twitter	125,658.60	389,098.70	952	6,864,324
% Discount	The promotional discount	0.2487	0.1700	0.1	1
$ Minimum Price	The minimum amount (USD) a user is required to spend to be eligible for the promotion	126.61	213.10	0	2,500
In-Store Purchase	Whether the promotion is available only for in-store purchases	0.6684	0.4708	0	1
"Pay-By-Tweet"	Whether a user can purchase the promotional product using the 'Pay-By-Tweet' service	0.0320	0.1664	0	1
Unlimited Use	Whether the promotion can be claimed multiple times by a user	0.0285	0.1664	0	1
Social Network Peak Time	Whether the promotion was initially announced between 12:00pm and 4:00pm	0.3656	0.4816	0	1

the *events of interest.* Figure 2 shows the timing of an event relative to the estimation and event windows. If the promotion (i.e., event) is attractive to social media users, a positive response to this promotion is expected from their side. In the short-run, the company benefits from the generation of sale leads and the buzz created around its brand [31]. A central tenet of our approach though is that in the long-run this potential positive response can be translated into an abnormal increase of the user base of the participating brand. On the other hand, if the promotion is unattractive to the users, a negative impact on the user base can occur.

The *"event window"* indicates the number of days before and after the announcement date over which the abnormal returns are accumulated. An event window is typically denoted $(-x, +y)$, where x is the number of days before the announcement day and y is the number of days afterwards, while the announcement day is typically denoted as "day 0". Including days before the announcement captures information leaks, either from the press or internal users [17]. In order to capture such information leaks in this setting, we consider as the starting point of the event window for each promotional event the earliest time of the actual announcement of the promotion or the first message claiming the specific offer, if information leakage occurred; in some cases the first "response" to a promotion is observed a few hours before the actual announcement of the promotion because of information leakage via the employees of Amex or the participating companies. Besides, we narrow the width of the event window to five days refining the effect as precisely as possible and accurately estimating -a lower bound of- the causal impact of the event. This design choice is common in various settings and is motivated by the potential presence of confounding effects over a wide event window. The use of shorter windows reduces the potential for a confounding event to interfere as well as limits the impact of other events on the event of concern. If the event under study affects the dependent variable for a longer period than the selected event window and in the absence of confounding effects after the selected event window and during the influence of the particular event, we underestimate the total causal impact of the event but the results can still be interpreted as the causal impact of the event during the $x + y$ first days or, more generally, as a lower bound of the causal effect. These design choices are also consistent with the suggestions of Konchitchki and O'Leary [17] for effectively designing event studies.

Then, the *sample of firms* is chosen based on the particular event of interest and a combination of both automated and manual techniques. The set of candidate firms consists of all the participants that implemented a social media marketing strategy and had a promotional event on Twitter. The final sample though includes only the firms for which a confounding effect was not observed during the event window and the estimation window for the observations used in estimating normal returns. For instance, one of the candidate firms announced a social media marketing promotion during the time period when it sponsored a major festival and thus we excluded the firm from the final sample, since the change in the dependent variable could not be untangled from the confounding event and attributed to the particular social media marketing promotion. Eliminating such social media marketing promotions that may be tainted by another event or a set of events is an important step towards precisely estimating the causal effect of such promotions. The confounding events during both the event window and the estimation window were independently identified by two appointed graduate students and correspond to a small number of observations. Additionally, the LexisNexis database [19] was also employed in order to identify confounding effects based on full-text articles in newspapers, magazines, and journals from the U.S. and around the world, as in [15].

Besides, the significance of the impact of the event during the event window is usually assessed relative to what is referred to as the *estimation window* (or normal return period) over which a model of the normal returns as well as the variance of abnormal returns are estimated. The observations used to learn the model of normal returns for the counterfactual market response correspond to the specific brand and/or a set of similar companies, the control group, and other predictor variables; the specific set of control time series is described in detail in the following paragraphs. The data mining model learned during the estimation window is used to predict normal returns over the event window (i.e., expected returns at the absence of the event), which are then compared to the abnormal returns. The length of the estimation window is selected to be 120 days, ending immediately prior to the event window.

After estimating both the normal and abnormal (i.e., actual) returns over the event window, we focus on examining

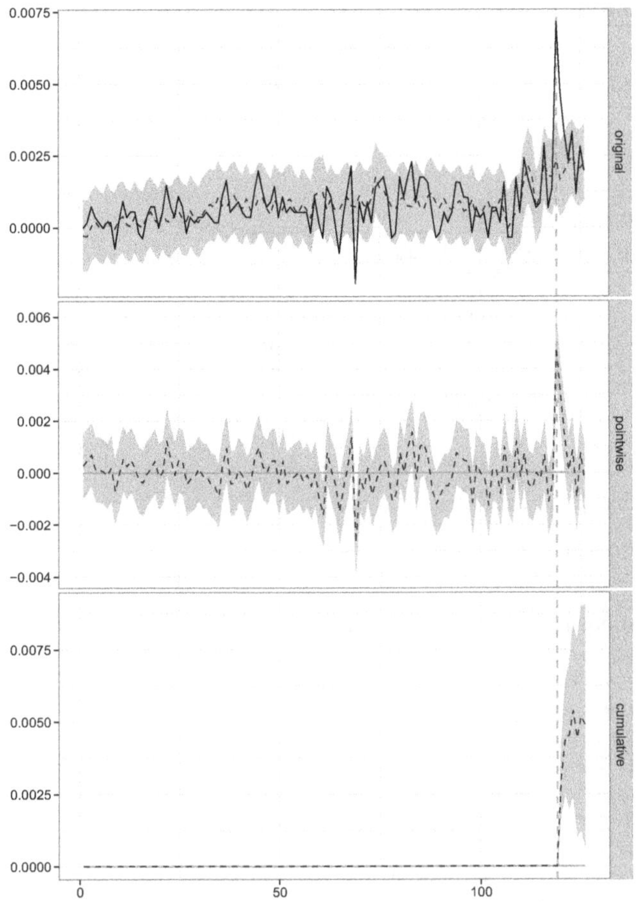

Figure 3: Effect of a promotional event on the number of followers of a participating brand.

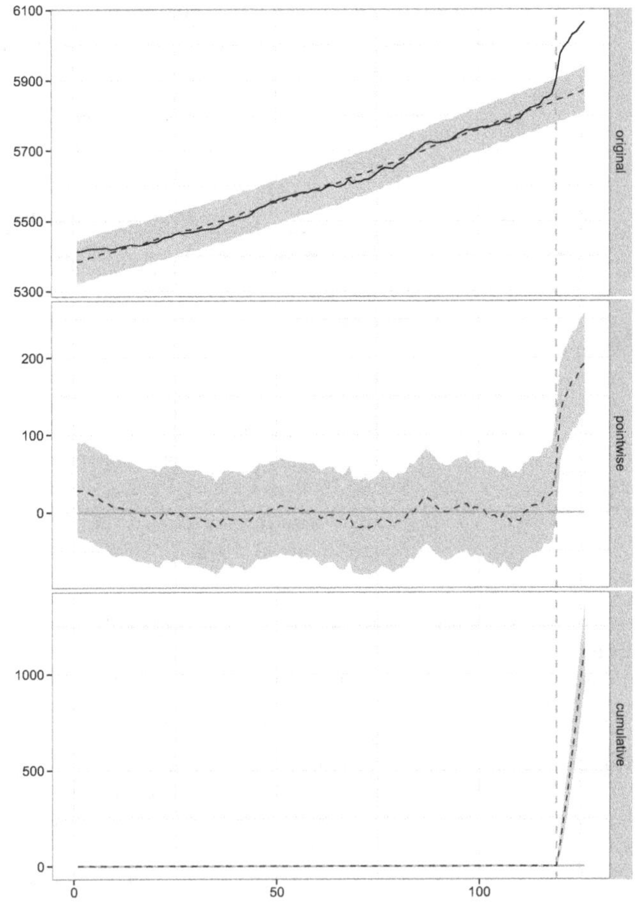

Figure 4: Effect of a promotional event on the number of followers of a participating brand.

the cumulative abnormal return as follows:

$$CAR_i = \sum_{t=-x}^{+y} AR_{it}$$

where $AR_{it} = R_{it} - \mathrm{E}(R_{it})$ is the point-wise difference between the actual observed outcome and the predicted counterfactual at the absence of an intervention, R_{it} the actual return of firm i on day t, $\mathrm{E}(R_{it})$ the corresponding expected return for the same firm and day at the absence of the event (i.e., based on the predictive model learned during the estimation window), and $t \in (-x, y)$. In particular, the predictive model of normal (expected) returns for each firm is

$$R_{it} = y_{it} = \alpha_i + \beta_i \mathbf{x}_{it} + \gamma_i^b \sum_{j \in B} w_{jt}^b + \gamma_i^f \sum_{j \in F} w_{jt}^f + \gamma_i^s \sum_{j \in S} w_{jt}^s + \delta_i s_{it} + \zeta_i z_t + \epsilon_{it}$$

where y_{it} is the natural logarithm of the ratio of number of followers in day t over the number of followers the previous day, $\mathbf{x}_{it}$ is a vector that contains dummy variables about the day of the week and whether there was a bank holiday, w_{jt}^b is the natural logarithm of the ratio of number of followers of brand j in day t over the number of followers at $t-1$ for B firms and organizations that have verified accounts on the social network, w_{jt}^f is correspondingly the logarithm of the ratio of followers for F similar firms (based on common followers), w_{jt}^f is the same metric for S similar firms (based on whether they belong to the same industry and economic sector), s_{it} the number of statuses (i.e., messages) posted on the social network by brand i at time period t, and z_t captures any time trend of the change in performance. These predictive models are then used to predict normal performance during the event window. The aforementioned predictor timeseries and the corresponding control firms of each brand and organization included in the above data mining model were selected based on i) all the officially verified accounts on the social network that correspond to a brand, ii) the relative number of common Twitter followers using the Jaccard coefficient and setting $F = 10$, and iii) all the verified firm-related accounts which belong to the same industry and economic sector.

The use of the specific formulation of the dependent variable allows the comparison of results across brands and better fits the large range of the quantity of interest; alternative formulations are discussed as robustness checks. Figure 3 shows for a specific firm the observed time series and the predicted counterfactual, the abnormal returns per time period, and the cumulative abnormal returns. For illustrative purposes, in Figure 4 we use as dependent variable the num-

Table 2. Cumulative Abnormal Returns Across All Events

Variable	Coefficient		Robust Std. Err.	t-statistic
Cumulative Abnormal Returns	0.0019596	***	0.00058	3.37

Robust standard error are reported
* significant at 10%; ** significant at 5%; *** significant at 1%

Table 3. Model of Abnormal Returns

Variable	Coefficient		Robust Std. Err.	t-statistic
Constant	0.0059222	***	0.0014266	4.15
% Discount	0.0005139	***	0.0000849	6.05
$ Min. Price	-3.70E-06	**	1.25E-06	-2.95
In-store Purchase	-0.0075032	***	0.0016533	-4.54
Unlimited Use	0.0011744		0.0009001	1.30
"Pay-By-Tweet"	-0.0104336	***	0.0023861	-4.37
Initial Brand Followers	0.0000148	**	5.55E-06	2.67
Social Network Peak Time	0.0041712	**	0.0013765	3.03

Robust standard error are reported
* significant at 10%; ** significant at 5%; *** significant at 1%

ber of followers and show the effect for the same brand and promotional event.

The *statistical significance* of the abnormal returns (AR_{it}) as well as the cumulative abnormal returns (CAR_i) can be tested using the corresponding t-statistics and the corresponding sample standard deviation in a time-series approach taking into account also any cross-sectional dependence. Thanks to the narrow event window, the test-statistic is not very sensitive to the benchmark model of abnormal returns or assumptions about cross-sectional or time-series dependence of abnormal returns [17]. Additionally, the significance of the cumulative abnormal returns for all brands as a group can also be estimated.

Finally, we also conduct a complementary explanatory analysis investigating any potential differences in the estimated (cumulative) abnormal returns of the various firms. In particular, we explain the differences in the magnitudes of the returns across brands and organizations in terms of event characteristics using the following econometric model:

$$CAR_i = y_i = \alpha + \beta \mathbf{x}_i + \gamma w_i + \epsilon_i$$

where $\mathbf{x}_i$ a vector of the relevant characteristics of the social media marketing strategy, including the promotional discount, the minimum amount (USD) a user is required to spend to be eligible for the promotion, whether the promotion is available only for in-store purchases, if the promotion can be claimed multiple times from a single user, and whether the marketing promotion was announced between 12:00pm and 4:00pm, which is the peak of user activity on Twitter platform [34], and w_i the initial size of the brand fan base at the time of announcement of the social media marketing promotion.

5. RESULTS

After learning the model of normal returns for each brand using standard data mining techniques and taking into consideration the observations about the brand itself before the "treatment" as well as the behavior of a set of other time series (that were predictive of the target prior to the intervention) and based on their values on the post-treatment period, we compute the daily abnormal returns and the cumulative abnormal returns for each firm. The daily abnormal returns are computed by subtracting the predicted normal return from the actual return for each day in the event window. Then, the cumulative abnormal returns are measured as the sum of the abnormal returns over the event window. As Table 2 shows, the cumulative abnormal returns are positive and statistically significant (0.0020, $p < 0.001$)[2] and thus provide support for the hypothesis that brands which implement social media marketing strategies incorporating explicit and/or implicit advocacy are more likely to attract more followers and expand their fan base ($H1$), illustrating the long-term effects of such marketing strategies on social media platforms.

The identified effect is also economically significant as it corresponds to an increase of about 5,000 additional new followers -*beyond the normal expectations*- for an average size brand. Then, as described in the previous section, we also conduct a complementary analysis investigating the differences in the estimated (cumulative) abnormal returns of the various brands and marketing promotions.

Based on the results presented in Table 3, a social media marketing strategy from a brand with a smaller existing fan base is less likely to attract more followers for the participating brand ($H2a$). Besides, a marketing promotion that is announced at the time of peak usage of the social media platform ($H3a$) is more likely to attract more followers for the participating brand. Consistent with prior literature, a promotional event with a larger percentage discount and a smaller required amount as minimum spend is more effective. Additionally, a promotion that is valid online, corresponds to a discount offer and not a specific product purchase (i.e., "Pay-By-Tweet"), or can be claimed multiple times by a customer (i.e., unlimited use) is more likely to attract more followers. Thus, a promotional event with higher expected benefits for customers is more likely to attract more followers for the brand.[2]

[2]The presented results should be interpreted as the percentage increase in the ratio (slope) of the increase in the number of followers, rather than a simple linear or percentage increase in the number of followers.

Table 4. **Falsification Check (Pseudo Events)**

Variable	Coefficient	Robust Std. Err.	t-statistic
Cumulative Abnormal Returns	-0.0007863	0.00049	-1.59

Robust standard error are reported
* significant at 10%; ** significant at 5%; *** significant at 1%

Table 5. **Falsification Check (Consumer Search Behavior)**

Variable	Coefficient	Robust Std. Err.	t-statistic
Cumulative Abnormal Returns	-0.0159971	0.01247	-1.28

Robust standard error are reported
* significant at 10%; ** significant at 5%; *** significant at 1%

6. ROBUSTNESS CHECKS

Additionally, as robustness checks, we use different dependent variables measuring the performance of social media marketing strategies, such as the percentage change in the number of followers or the number of (new) followers per day, and different numbers (B, F, S) of similar brands as synthetic controls (e.g., $5, \ldots, 50$). Besides, in order to assess the effect of potentially over-fitting our data, apart from using standard approaches such as examining the corresponding learning curves, we also estimate the models using only the performance of brands that belong to the same industry and economic sector or just their average performance, instead of the extended set of control time series that we employed in our main analysis. Similarly, we also evaluate the effect using only similar brands based on the Jaccard coefficient computed using the set of followers of each brand. Furthermore, similar results are observed on average by learning either a pooled regression model of normal performance for all the firms and allowing for firm-specific fixed effects or brand-specific predictive models. Finally, various extra robustness checks are conducted, by varying the length of the event and estimation windows, qualitatively corroborating our empirical findings.

7. FALSIFICATION TESTS

One might think that it is plausible that the previous set of models are simply picking up spurious effects as a result of pure coincidence, a general increase in the corresponding metrics, or other unobserved factors. To assess the possibility that the aforementioned findings are a statistical artifact and the identified positive significant effects were captured by chance or because of other confounding factors, we run a falsification test ("placebo" study) using the same models (in order to maintain consistency) but randomly indicating when each promotional event took place. In particular, we use a standard (pseudo) random number generator in order to create a dummy variable that indicates when each promotional event occurred; when drawing the pseudo event day, we always allow for an estimation window at least 30 days long and a (pseudo) event window that immediately follows this estimation window and does not overlap with the actual event window of the real event. Under this falsification test, since the pseudo event window was not affected by the events of interest, the corresponding variable of interest of abnormal returns should not pick any effect in the falsification models and show that there is no impact. The results of this falsification test are shown in Table 4. We see that, under this check, the corresponding cumulative abnormal returns are negative and *not* statistically significant, indicating that our findings are not a statistical artifact of our specification, but we indeed discovered the actual effects.

In addition, we design and conduct a second set of falsification checks. To assess the possibility that the discovered cumulative abnormal effects are caused by other concurrent events or confounding factors, such as seasonality effects for the specific brand, broader marketing campaigns or offline advertising, we should examine the impact of the specific promotional events under study on other independent marketing objectives that would capture a general increase in consumers' interest for the specific brand. Therefore, we evaluate the potential impact of the promotional events on consumer brand-specific search behavior [16]. In particular, we use as dependent variable the normalized search volume for the brand as captured by Google Trends [12]. Under this falsification test, if the new dependent variable was not affected by the events of interest, the corresponding variable of interest of abnormal returns should not pick any effect in the falsification models and show that there is no impact. The results of this falsification test are shown in Table 5. We see that, under this check, the corresponding cumulative abnormal returns are negative and *not* statistically significant, indicating that our findings are not caused by other confounding factors, but the actual effects we discovered can be attributed to the marketing strategies on the social network.

8. CONCLUSION

Studying the pioneering social media venture of American Express on the social network of Twitter, we contribute to the related literature in social media and e-commerce discovering new rich findings and provide actionable insights with implications for network-based targeting and social media marketing. Based on the proposed combination of data mining and econometric techniques in a causal estimation framework that allows for more accurate counterfactuals, we focus on the long-term business value of this novel application of social media and evaluate the effectiveness of social media marketing strategies towards expanding a brand's social media fan base. Based on our empirical results and a combination of robustness checks and "placebo" studies, we find that social media marketing strategies combined with features enabling implicit or explicit advocacy on social media platforms result in statistically significant positive abnormal returns, in terms of additional new followers for the corresponding brands. In essence, we identify an effective method for brands to attract more followers and expand their social media fan base, which they can later leverage in order to increase awareness, engagement, and word-of-mouth [31]. Besides, we illustrate that social media marketing strategies are more effective for brands that already have a large user base, since they can more effectively propagate their messages. Moreover, we show empirically when consumers are more receptive to such marketing messages on social media and thus suggest specific tactical strategies for firms that would like to capitalize on the real time marketing feature of the Twitter social network. Towards this direction, we precisely quantify the impact of the various marketing promotion characteristics (e.g., discount, price, flexibility, expected benefit) and demonstrate what types of promotions are effective for generating desired long-term effects. We discover that the most important factor in increasing significantly the returns of promotional events is the timing of announcing the promotion and broadcasting the corresponding brand message on social networks. Hence, based on the aforementioned results, one of the tactical strategies with significant monetary implications for brands, organizations, and marketers is that, despite the increased competition for consumers' attention, broadcasting marketing messages on social networks during the time of peak usage maximizes their returns as the messages can be more widely disseminated to the network; even if the effectiveness of a message per user is higher during off-peak hours. Our results highlight the need for future studies to investigate the effect of the timing of marketing messages and public announcements across different social media and social networks. For instance, significantly different tactical strategies might be optimal in the social platform of Facebook where the timelines of the users are algorithmically curated.

A limitation of this study is that selecting a narrow event window we might under-estimate the actual causal effect of the particular social media marketing strategies. Moreover, firms that announced the marketing promotions during other confounding events were excluded from the sample, since the effect could not be untangled from the confounding event and attributed to the particular social media marketing strategy. Such firms might experience even higher abnormal returns because of synergies and complementarity effects. As part of the future work, we plan to study how the effect of social media marketing strategies evolves over time and its decay structure as well as the impact of social media promotional events on consumers' perceptions of participating brands.

9. REFERENCES

[1] American Express Company. $15 Million in Savings Available to Amex Card Members in April 2014. `https://twitter.com/AmericanExpress/status/452456770804674560`. Posted: 2014-04-05, Accessed: 2015-02-20.

[2] S. Aral. Commentary-identifying social influence: A comment on opinion leadership and social contagion in new product diffusion. *Marketing Science*, 30(2):217–223, 2011.

[3] S. Aral, C. Dellarocas, and D. Godes. Introduction to the special issue-social media and business transformation: A framework for research. *Information Systems Research*, 24(1):3–13, 2013.

[4] J. Y. Bakos. Reducing buyer search costs: Implications for electronic marketplaces. *Management science*, 43(12):1676–1692, 1997.

[5] S. Balasubramanian, R. A. Peterson, and S. L. Jarvenpaa. Exploring the implications of m-commerce for markets and marketing. *Journal of the academy of Marketing Science*, 30(4):348–361, 2002.

[6] E. Brynjolfsson and M. D. Smith. Frictionless commerce? a comparison of internet and conventional retailers. *Management science*, 46(4):563–585, 2000.

[7] J. Chevalier and A. Goolsbee. Measuring prices and price competition online: Amazon. com and barnesandnoble. com. *Quantitative marketing and Economics*, 1(2):203–222, 2003.

[8] J. A. Chevalier and D. Mayzlin. The effect of word of mouth on sales: Online book reviews. *Journal of marketing research*, 43(3):345–354, 2006.

[9] C. Dellarocas. The digitization of word of mouth: Promise and challenges of online feedback mechanisms. *Management science*, 49(10):1407–1424, 2003.

[10] D. DelVecchio, D. H. Henard, and T. H. Freling. The effect of sales promotion on post-promotion brand preference: A meta-analysis. *Journal of Retailing*, 82(3):203–213, 2006.

[11] A. Dickinger and M. Kleijnen. Coupons going wireless: Determinants of consumer intentions to redeem mobile coupons. *Journal of Interactive Marketing*, 22(3):23–39, 2008.

[12] Google Inc. Google Trends. `www.google.com/trends/`, 2015.

[13] S. Hill and A. D. Benton. Social tv: Linking tv content to buzz and sales. In *Proceedings of the 33th International Conference on Information Systems*, 2012.

[14] S. Hill, F. Provost, and C. Volinsky. Network-based marketing: Identifying likely adopters via consumer networks. *Statistical Science*, pages 256–276, 2006.

[15] A. H. Huang, A. Y. Zang, and R. Zheng. Evidence on the information content of text in analyst reports. *The Accounting Review*, 89(6):2151–2180, 2014.

[16] M. Joo, K. C. Wilbur, B. Cowgill, and Y. Zhu. Television advertising and online search. *Management Science*, 60(1):56–73, 2013.

[17] Y. Konchitchki and D. E. O'Leary. Event study methodologies in information systems research. *International Journal of Accounting Information Systems*, 12(2):99–115, 2011.

[18] R. P. Leone and S. S. Srinivasan. Coupon face value: its impact on coupon redemptions, brand sales, and brand profitability. *Journal of Retailing*, 72(3):273–289, 1996.

[19] LexisNexis Group. LexisNexis U.S. and World News database. `http://www.lexisnexis.com/`, 2015.

[20] Y. Liu. Word of mouth for movies: Its dynamics and impact on box office revenue. *Journal of marketing*, 70(3):74–89, 2006.

[21] X. Luo, J. Zhang, and W. Duan. Social media and firm equity value. *Information Systems Research*, 24(1):146–163, 2013.

[22] A. C. MacKinlay. Event studies in economics and finance. *Journal of economic literature*, pages 13–39, 1997.

[23] D. Molitor, P. Reichhart, and M. Spann. Location-based advertising: what is the value of physical distance on the mobile internet. *Social Science Research Network, Rochester*, 2012.

[24] L. Muchnik, S. Aral, and S. J. Taylor. Social influence bias: A randomized experiment. *Science*, 341(6146):647–651, 2013.

[25] P. Raghubir. Coupons in context: discounting prices or decreasing profits? *Journal of retailing*, 80(1):1–12, 2004.

[26] N. Roztocki and H. R. Weistroffer. Event studies in information systems research: An updated review. In *Proceedings of the 15th Americas Conference on Information Systems*, 2009.

[27] S. Rubel. Trends to watch part ii: Social commerce. *Micro Persuasion vom*, 23:2005, 2006.

[28] N. Shi, Y. Hong, K. Wang, and P. A. Pavlou. Social commerce beyond word of mouth: Role of social distance and social norms in online referral incentive systems. In *Proceedings of the 34th International Conference on Information Systems*, 2012.

[29] I. Simonson, Z. Carmon, and S. O'curry. Experimental evidence on the negative effect of product features and sales promotions on brand choice. *Marketing Science*, 13(1):23–40, 1994.

[30] G. J. Tellis. *Effective advertising: Understanding when, how, and why advertising works*. Sage Publications, 2003.

[31] V. Todri and P. Adamopoulos. Social commerce: An empirical examination of the antecedents and consequences of commerce in social network platforms. In *Proceedings of the 35th International Conference on Information Systems*, 2014.

[32] C. Wang and P. Zhang. The evolution of social commerce: The people, management, technology, and information dimensions. *Communications of the Association for Information Systems*, 31(5):1–23, 2012.

[33] D. Williamson. Advertising on twitter: Unique opportunities outweigh slowing user growth. *March*, 27:2014, 2014.

[34] D. Zarrella. *The social media marketing book.* " O'Reilly Media, Inc.", 2009.

[35] F. Zhu and X. Zhang. Impact of online consumer reviews on sales: The moderating role of product and consumer characteristics. *Journal of marketing*, 74(2):133–148, 2010.

Personalizing LinkedIn Feed

Deepak Agarwal, Bee-Chung Chen, Qi He, Zhenhao Hua, Guy Lebanon, Yiming Ma,
Pannagadatta Shivaswamy, Hsiao-Ping Tseng, Jaewon Yang and Liang Zhang
LinkedIn Corporation
Mountain View, CA, USA
{dagarwal,bchen,qhe,zhhua,glevanon,yma,pshivasw,htseng,jeyang,lizhang}@linkedin.com

ABSTRACT

LinkedIn dynamically delivers update activities from a user's interpersonal network to more than 300 million members in the personalized feed that ranks activities according their "relevance" to the user. This paper discloses the implementation details behind this personalized feed system at LinkedIn which can not be found from related work, and addresses the scalability and data sparsity challenges for deploying the system online. More specifically, we focus on the personalization models by generating three kinds of affinity scores: Viewer-ActivityType Affinity, Viewer-Actor Affinity, and Viewer-Actor-ActivityType Affinity. Extensive experiments based on online bucket tests (A/B experiments) and offline evaluation illustrate the effect of our personalization models in LinkedIn feed.

Categories and Subject Descriptors

H.4 [**Information Systems Applications**]: Miscellaneous

Keywords

Personalization; Feed Relevance; Large Scale Learning

1. INTRODUCTION

More than 300 million people participate on LinkedIn[1]. By introducing the feed function, LinkedIn dynamically delivers update activities from a user's interpersonal network, ensuring a user always has fresh content to digest at login. Popular update activities include "member shares articles", "company posts jobs", "member connects to member", "member likes another activity", leading to a classification of update activities as (actor, verb, object) triplets.

Due to the large volume of activities in feeds and the fact that the users have limited time to interact with their social network, many users experience information overload. To ensure delivering meaningful content to the user, LinkedIn has introduced a personalized feed that ranks activities according their "relevance" to the user.

[1]https://press.linkedin.com/site-resources/news-releases/2015/linkedin-announces-fourth-quarter-and-full-year-2014-results

KDD'15, August 11 - 14, 2015, Sydney, NSW, Australia.
© 2015 ACM. ISBN 978-1-4503-3664-2/15/08 ...$15.00.
DOI: http://dx.doi.org/10.1145/2783258.2788614.

Users can play two roles simultaneously in LinkedIn's feed: *actors* who are users that produce feed activities and *viewers* who are users that consume feed activities. The *actor* label also includes other content producer entities such as companies, groups, schools, publishing channels, etc. Classic research work in personalized feed recommendation represents and synthesizes a viewer's profile from three aspects [13, 5]: the viewer-to-actor relationship strength, the correlation of activity content to viewer interests, and the underlying social network. However, personalizing the LinkedIn feed brings new challenges because of the following reasons.

- *Scalability*: Given the vast amount of users who visit LinkedIn at any given time, scalability becomes one of the major concerns for personalization. For each viewer visit, computing personalized scores between the viewer and tens of thousands of candidate activities in **real-time** using features such as viewer-actor profile similarity or past interactions between the viewer and actor is time consuming and may cause latency problems.
- *Data Sparsity*: Not all LinkedIn members have significant historical interaction data. Even for "heavy" viewers, the total amount of interactions is skewed towards a small fraction of highly active actors and popular activity types. Modeling rare events to compute personalized scores is often unreliable and noisy [3].

This paper describes our experiences in addressing these challenges at LinkedIn and our work on the personalized production feed. Our previous work [4] has already shown that a simple feed ranking model that considers activity freshness, feed diversity, and viewer-actor connection relationships significantly outperforms the time feed (reverse chronological ordering of feed activities) and ranking by social popularity in terms of click-through rate (CTR) – the probability of a viewer clicks on an activity. In this paper, we describe our continued modeling efforts on the LinkedIn feed with a focus on personalized models.

We consider three types of signals for personalization in this paper: a) Viewer-ActivityType Affinity that models how likely a viewer tends to interact with an activity type, e.g. does an individual working in IT industry like to click on job recommendations? b) Viewer-Actor Affinity which models how likely a viewer tends to interact with an actor. Note that although people tend to interact more with their close friends, sometimes they also like to interact with other types of actors, such as influencers (e.g. CEO of a company), big companies, or good publishing channels, etc. c) Viewer-Actor-ActivityType affinity which is the most granular signal that models the three-way interactions among viewer, actor and the activity type.

Given the challenge of data sparsity, often simply using users' past interactions in LinkedIn feed is not good enough. Therefore in this paper, we apply the feature-based approach which contains thousands of cold-start features from peoples' profiles to model the above three affinity signals. Our experimentation in production shows this approach works pretty well in terms of CTR performance, however it raises a scalability challenge as described above: Scoring a sophisticated model with many features for a large scale of candidate activities in real-time with low latency might be technically infeasible.

To address such scalability concern we divide our feature space into two parts: For features that are more dynamic, e.g. time of the day, they still remain in the online scoring system. For the features that are more stable and do not change rapidly over time, e.g. the three affinity scores mentioned above, we pre-generate them in Hadoop offline and then push them to production periodically. The online scoring system only needs to query by the viewer ID and obtain these scores for each (actor, activity-type) pair; no additional scoring needs to be done for generating these scores online, which saves a lot of computational time.

Though ideally the three affinity scores should be jointly trained, it is actually a significant challenge due to the high dimensionality of the parameter space and sparsity of the data. In this paper, we instead adopted a layman's approach by modeling them independently: We train the Viewer-ActivityType affinity first since it has the richest data. Then, the learned Viewer-ActivityType affinity is treated as a single compound feature and is fixed in the downstream actor-level affinity training.

Contributions: In this paper, we make the following contributions:

- We analyze large-scale LinkedIn data and summarize knowledge mined from massive data for personalized models in Section 3.
- We introduce our personalization modeling efforts for Viewer-ActivityType Affinity based on Gamma-Poisson model in Section 4.
- We introduce the Viewer-Actor Affinity modeling and the Viewer-Actor-ActivityType modeling in Section 5.
- We demonstrate how to deploy the pre-computed affinities online for production in Section 6, to tackle the scalability challenge.
- We report on extensive experiments based on online bucket tests (A/B experiments) and offline evaluation in Section 7 to evaluate our personalization models in LinkedIn feed.

2. RELATED WORK

Personalized feeds attracted more user attention compared to the chronologically ordered feed lists [6, 7] or the global relevance ordered feeds [4]. Hence major social networking sites including Facebook and LinkedIn provide users the personalized News feed as the main portal [1].

Early research in personalized feed recommendation is to rank homogeneous tweet feeds in Twitter [12, 2, 11, 13, 16, 26, 22, 10]. This line of work is essentially close to the earlier personalized news article recommendation work [14], except that they used additional social network features like social voting, social tie strength etc. to model the activity relevance. They provided hints on how various features result in various user preferences to the Tweet feeds. For example, [12] reported that content sources, topic interest of users, and social voting on items are three major considerations corresponding to user interests; [11] examined thread length, topic relevance and social tie-strength contribute to the relevance. To implement a personalized recommendation system, [2, 16, 26, 22] enriched user profiles with their activities, text information of tweets and their neighbors through collaborative filtering, and [10] produced different rankers for different sub-communities of a user's social network, where these rankers are described as topics so that the user can rank his/her social feeds by specific topics.

Researchers also studied the personalized recommendation for feeds with heterogeneous activity types [17, 25, 6, 7, 8, 28]. As different activity types support different kinds of actions (e.g., "share", "comment" on activities), some work leveraged user-action interests in the relevance of feed activities [17, 7, 6]. Researchers also investigated the personalized recommendation for heterogeneous enterprise network activity streams [19, 20]. They concluded that the activity stream based user profile is more productive than entity-based user profile for personalizing the stream.

All the above work paved the way for our studies in LinkedIn feed, enlightening our feature exploration and design. Our personalization efforts in computing viewer's affinity scores at activity type level and actor level essentially belong to user-to-content relationships and user-to-user relationships [5]. However, the above work has not been evaluated on top of large-scale production systems. Instead, we always stick to the feasibility of deploying in production when planning personalization models.

Related work on top of LinkedIn feed includes our earlier work [4] and [21]. In [4], we presented an overview of the end-to-end feed recommendation system in LinkedIn, focusing on the infrastructure and generic modeling framework. In [21], various machine learning techniques including linear models on features and latent factor models (matrix factorization and tensor factorization) were experimented in LinkedIn feed data, irregardless of the online deployment.

The novelty of this paper is to present the end-to-end personalization efforts on LinkedIn production feed and online bucket test results. Our product has been deployed in LinkedIn homepage to serve more than 300 million members for more than one year. One effort of this paper is to disclose the implementation details behind this real system, which can not be found from related work.

3. DATA ANALYSIS

In this section we give a brief overview of the LinkedIn feed and show some interesting characteristics of user behaviors on the LinkedIn feed. Beginning by introducing the LinkedIn feed, we show how different users consume LinkedIn content and interact with other users in different ways. The insights that we gain in this section motivate our personalization models that are developed in the following sections.

3.1 The LinkedIn Feed

Every activity in LinkedIn feed is represented as the triple: (actor, verb, object). Accordingly, the *type* of an activity, named as *activity type*, is a triple of (actor type, verb type, object type). Actor types include member, company, school, service, channel. Verb types are comment, connect, join, like, profile change, job change etc. Object types are article, job, member, picture etc. Various combinations of them consist of around 50 activity types on Linked feed. For example, member connects to member, company publishes article, and member updates the profile picture. More details about the taxonomy of LinkedIn feed activities can be found in [4].

Given a viewer, LinkedIn feed displays the activities that happened in the professional network of the viewer, such as activities done by the user's connections, activities done by the companies or the influencers followed by the viewer, and the news articles that the viewer would be interested in. The goal of LinkedIn feed is to provide a personalized activity stream for each viewer, and there can be many metrics to quantify how good the feed is, such as how often the viewer clicks, how fresh the feed is, or how diverse the feed is [4]. In this paper, among various metrics, we focus on click-through rate (CTR) because click is the most immediate user reaction and is straighforward to quantify.

In the rest of this section, we study how viewers tend to click on activities from the log data. We focus on how the CTR is affected by two different relationships between the viewer and the activity. First is the activity type analysis about how viewers have different levels of interest to different types of activities. Second is the viewer-actor analysis about how viewers interact with activities depending on who the actor is.

3.2 Relationships to activity types

Viewers' responses to different activity types vary for two reasons.

- *Global bias.* Some activity types are inherently more popular than others. Figure 1 shows the CTR of different activity types relative to the average CTR of all types when we serve activities in random orders to the viewers. Each curve corresponds to a particular activity type (we cannot label the curves due to confidentiality). The figure shows that some activity types consistently tend to receive more actions than other types.
- *Personal preference.* Individual viewers have different level of interests to different types of activities. For example, some viewers are heavily interested in building connections (connection activities) while others are interested in information activities such as article sharing. Figure 2 shows a scattered plot of viewers' response to two different activity types. We randomly choose 500 LinkedIn viewers from a random bucket where all activities are randomly ordered, and measure their clicks to two different activity types during one month. We discard the users who have clicked less than 10 times on either types. Each point in Figure 2 corresponds to one of 500 viewers. Not only are the clicks on two activity types not positively correlated to each other, but also we observe a clear division between two groups of viewers, indicating that viewers who are interested in one type are not interested in the other type. In our internal analysis, we could classify two groups of viewers with 70% accuracy simply by their number of connections.

This analysis suggests that, to personalize feed, not only should activity type be used as a feature to remove global bias, but also we must consider individaual affinities to different activity types.

3.3 Relationships to actors

Whether or not they have thousands of contacts in LinkedIn, people are only able to keep up close relationships with a handful of people. Here we study how viewers respond to different actors depending on a few notable features of the viewer-actor pairs.

We look at the past interaction features (e.g., number of past clicks, number of past impressions etc.) between viewer and actor. Figures 3a and 3b illustrate the CTR between viewer and actor as a function of their number of past clicks/impressions. The plots are generated based on a set of random users for a few days on both mobile and desktop platforms. For both platforms, more past clicks between viewer and actor generally translate to higher CTR. However, for impressions, we observe different behaviors. On mobile, a viewer appears to be more tolerant to a repeat showing of the same actor, but on desktop, we observe CTR drop if the same actor showing up multiple times.

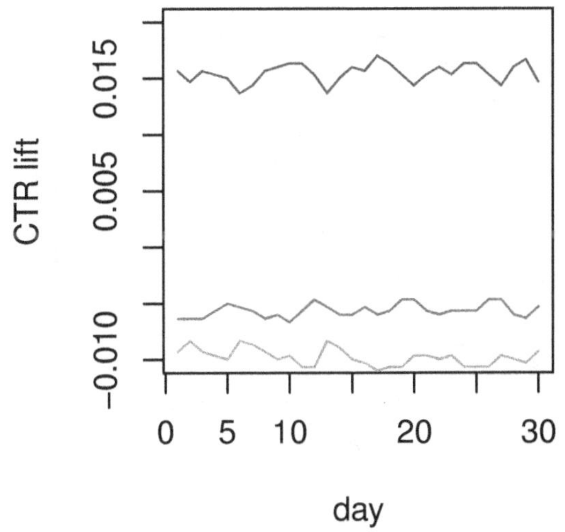

Figure 1: CTR lift of three different acitivity types per day.

Considering the past interaction features are not ubiquitous between viewer and actor, we also look at other features that are always available. Examples of such features include the profile of the viewer and the actor, the interactions in other LinkedIn services outside the feed, and social network features like the number of common connections. In the following we take the number of viewers' connections who have clicked on the actor in the past as the feature for analysis. This feature intuitively makes sense: for example, the more of your connections commented on an article, the more likely you would click on it (Homophily Principle). In fact, researchers have proved that using the connections' responses can improve cold-start recommendation [24]. Figure 4 shows how the CTR between viewer and actor on 4 different activity types positively correlates to the number of the viewer's connections who have clicked on the same actor.

The above two features are just the tip of the iceberg. There are numerous features discoverable in LinkedIn for user-to-user relationships, laying the foundations for the personalization between viewers and actors.

3.4 Discussion

Our data analyses uncover that in LinkedIn feed, not only does the CTR vary on various activity types, but also the CTR should be personalized by actors. In the following sections, we model two kinds of personalized affinities for LinkedIn feed: one is Viewer-ActivityType Affinity that manifests the viewer's topics of interests at the activity type level, and the other is Viewer-Actor Affinity that manifests the viewer's preference to the activity producer. Our personalization strategies are in line with findings of [13] that the source of the activities and the recipient's topics of interest are two major considerations which correspond to user interest.

4. VIEWER-ACTIVITYTYPE AFFINITY

There are about 50 different activity types[2] in LinkedIn feed. In this section, our objective is to compute an affinity score for each

[2]This number varies slightly from time to time as LinkedIn keeps producing new types or retiring old types.

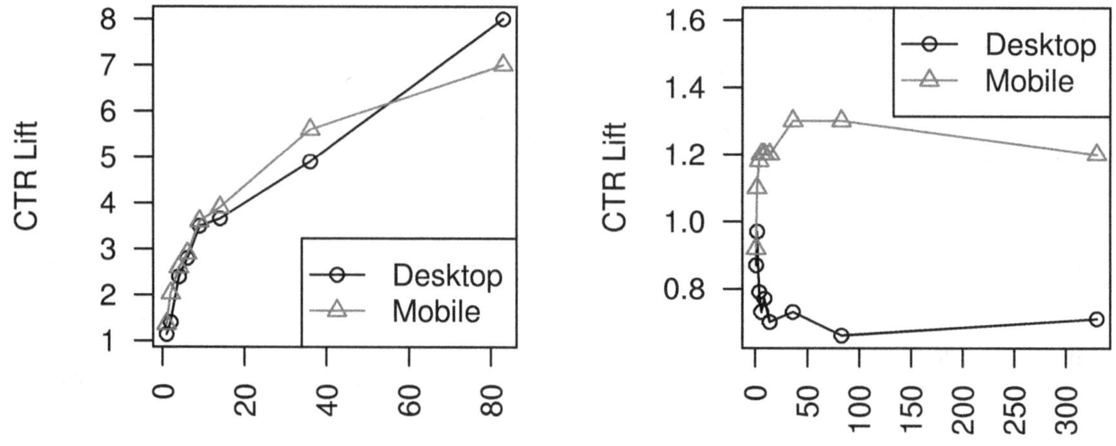

(a) Clicks (b) Impressions

Figure 3: Past interactions versus relative CTR lift.

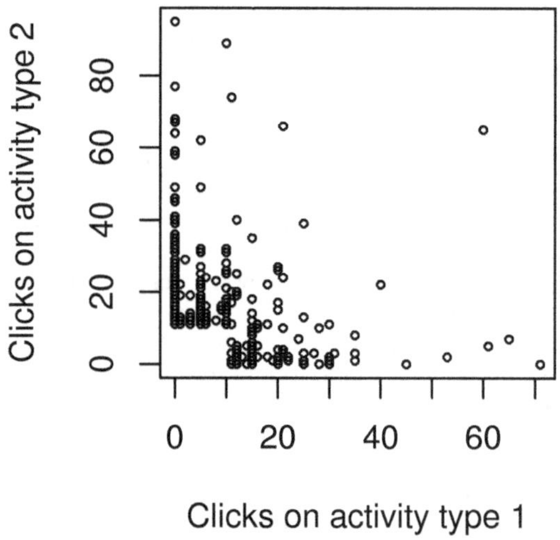

Figure 2: Scatter plot of clicks from 500 random viewers on two different activity types.

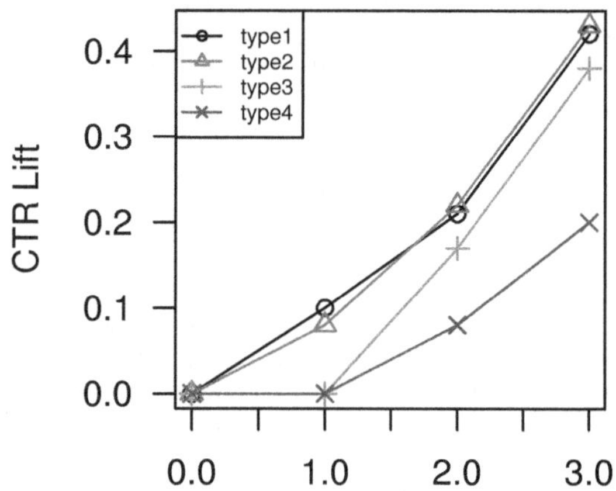

Figure 4: Relations between the relative CTR lift and the number of viewer's connections who have clicked on the same actor.

pair of viewer i and activity type k, which manifests the viewer's topics of interests at the activity type level. In total, we need compute around 300M x 50 affinity scores. We leverage CTR to approximate the affinity, which is defined as:

Definition 1. *Viewer-ActivityType Affinity α_{ik}, the likelihood score of viewer i clicks on the activity type k in LinkedIn feed.*

We describe how we compute the estimator $\hat{\alpha}_{ik}$ for α_{ik}. We are given a set of historical activity impressions $\{e = (y, i, k, m)\}$ where y is viewer i's click to impression m of activity type k. A naive approach to get $\hat{\alpha}_{ik}$ would be to use the CTR of viewer i for type k from a set of historical activity, *i.e.,* we let $\hat{\alpha}_{ik} = S_{ik}/M_{ik}$ where S_{ik} is the number of clicks and M_{ik} is the number of impressions from the viewer i to the activities of type k. However, this CTR is reliable only for large sample sizes, which is not true for computing affinity between viewer and activity type where the majority of viewers are light users with only a few historical impressions. Hence we aim to estimate α_{ik} by applying smoothing via hierarchical probabilistic models.

Denoting by p_e the true CTR for activity impression e with covariates $\mathbf{x}_e$, we assume the following decomposition:

$$p_e = b_e g_{ik}, \tag{1}$$

where b_e is a probability estimate computed from a baseline model which is a function of covariates $\mathbf{x}_e$, and g_{ik} is modeled as the CTR correction factor which is only a function of viewer and activity type pair (i, k) and does not depend on covariates $\mathbf{x}_e$. Logistic regression is a popular choice of the covariate-based baseline models in the literature [27], and is also applied in this paper:

$$\hat{p}_e = \frac{1}{1+e^{-\boldsymbol{\theta}^T \mathbf{x}_e}} \cdot g_{ik}. \tag{2}$$

The covariates $\mathbf{x}_e$ include features that can remove position bias, remove user interface bias, profile viewers, and profile activities etc. Since the baseline model is based on features at the impression level, we have sufficient statistics to estimate b_e using logistic regression.

Now, given the baseline model, we have the expected number of clicks:

$$E_{ik} = \sum_{e \in i,k} b_e. \tag{3}$$

We assume that $S_{ik}|E_{ik}, g_{ik}$ follows Gamma-Poission distribution $S_{ik}|E_{ik}, g_{ik} \sim \text{Poisson}(E_{ik} g_{ik}), g_{ik} \sim \text{Gamma}(1, \gamma)$, since Poisson assumption is reasonable and has been widely used in rare event estimations [15].

As the correction factor, intuitively the value of g_{ik} depends on the O/E (observed-to-expected) ratio S_{ik}/E_{ik}: if $S_{ik}/E_{ik} > 1$, the baseline model under-estimates the CTR, so $g_{ik} > 1$ can force the expected number of clicks equals to the numebr of observed clicks; if $S_{ik}/E_{ik} = 1$, $g_{ik} = 1$ as no need to correct; if $S_{ik}/E_{ik} < 1$, $g_{ik} < 1$ as the baseline model over-estimates the CTR. According to the Gamma-Poisson conjugate property, the posterior of g_{ik} also follows the Gamma distribution with mean $\frac{\gamma+S_{ik}}{\gamma+E_{ik}}$ and variance $\frac{\gamma+S_{ik}}{(\gamma+E_{ik})^2}$. We simply approximate g_{ik} as the posterior mean of Gamma distribution:

$$\begin{aligned} g_{ik} &= \frac{\gamma + S_{ik}}{\gamma + E_{ik}} \\ &= \frac{\gamma + S_{ik}}{\gamma + \sum_{e \in i,k} \frac{1}{1+e^{-\boldsymbol{\theta}^T \mathbf{x}_e}}}. \end{aligned} \tag{4}$$

Can we directly use $\hat{p}_e$ to model the personalized affinity α_{ik}? The answer is no because $\hat{p}_e$ is the estimated CTR binded to activity impression e, yet by definition the Viewer-ActivityType Affinity α_{ik} is impression independent. We extract a subset of the covariates $\mathbf{x}_e$ by only keeping (i, k)-dependent features and rename it as $\mathbf{x}_{i,k}$. Finally, the affinity α_{ik} is modeled as:

$$\hat{\alpha}_{ik} = \frac{g_{ik}}{1+e^{-\boldsymbol{\theta}^T \mathbf{x}_{i,k}}}. \tag{5}$$

There are multiple advantanges of modeling α_{ik} by combining the CTR correction factor with the feature-based CTR. First is that, as we described above, CTR may not be reliable when data is sparse. Smoothing by Gamma-Poisson model mitigates the issues with data sparsity. Second, CTR may contain biases for several reasons: the same activity at different positions attracts different CTRs; the content information of an activity also affects the CTR. We use covariates $\mathbf{x}_e$ to address the effect coming from these factors. Third, it is impractical to discover all possible variates of the CTR function. Computing a baseline model based on covariates $\mathbf{x}_e$ first and then using g_{ik} to model the residue inherited from data is thus easier to implement.

5. VIEWER-ACTOR AFFINITY

5.1 Viewer-Actor Affinity

Many trail-blazing work has studied the strength of social ties in social media for many years [18]. As one kind of social tie strengths, we define

Definition 2. *Viewer-Actor Affinity α_{ij}, the likelihood score of viewer i clicks on any activity produced by actor j in LinkedIn feed.*

The Viewer-Actor Affinity manifests the relationships between the feed recipient (viewer) and activity producer (actor), which have played an important role in scoring feed activity relevance [11]. However, what are the remarkable characteristics of Viewer-Actor Affinity in LinkedIn feed?

Like other commercial social networks, LinkedIn provides a scalable feed for more than 300 millions members to interact with their connections. Given a viewer can see more actors than activity types in feed, the dimension of the Viewer-Actor Affinity is about $40 \sim 50$ times larger than the Viewer-ActivityType affinity on average. Even the number of interactions generated by some viewers may be large, few of them impact a particular actor, making the actor-level interaction data sparse. Due to the absence of activities (zero or a few) between viewer and actor, rate estimates are often unreliable and noisy [3].

Another challenge of Viewer-Actor Affinity is the viewer only interacted with a tiny fraction of actors in the past, comparing to hundreds of millions of LinkedIn entities the viewer can interact. For example, in a one-week testing window, we observed that around half of actors are new to viewers (no past interactions). Hence the Viewer-Actor Affinity heavily suffers from the cold-start problem.

5.2 Viewer-Actor-ActivityType Affinity

We have designed Viewer-ActivityType Affinity and Viewer-Actor Affinity independently. However, an activity is interesting to the viewer often because of both. For example, assuming you like reading articles in general, you may not like reading articles published by sponsors or shared by recruiters. We denote by

Definition 3. *Viewer-Actor-ActivityType affinity α_{ijk}, the likelihood score of viewer i clicks on the activity type k produced by actor j in LinkedIn feed.*

The Viewer-Actor-ActivityType affinity can be seen as a context-aware affinity between viewer and actor, where the context is activity type. It provides a finer-grained affinity between viewer and actor. Undoubtedly, the interaction data of Viewer-Actor-ActivityType are sparser than Viewer-Actor and increase the difficulty of modeling.

5.3 Modeling

Modeling Viewer-Actor Affinities using a counting model like we do for Viewer-ActivityType Affinity is theoretically sound yet heavily suffers from the data sparsity, since the data intensity between viewer and actor is about $40 \sim 50$ times less than the data intensity between viewer and activity type. Modeling zero or few interactions is unreliable and noisy [3]. Hence, we adopt the feature-based regression to model Viewer-Actor Affinities due to simplicity.

Given an activity t from viewer i to actor j on activity type k, to predict the response Y which is 1 if there is a click and 0 otherwise, we use logistic regression where we compute a linear product between a coefficient vector β and a feature vector X_{ijkt}:

$$P(Y = 1) \sim \text{Bernoulli}(\sigma(\beta X_{ijkt})),$$

where σ is the sigmoid function.

We can exclusively classify features in the feature vector X_{ijkt} into three parts: Viewer-Actor features X_{ij}, Viewer-Actor-ActivityType features X_{ijk}, and other activity-dependent features X_t such as the age of the activity and the type of activity which vary on activities and have to be scored online. Though X_{ijk} can be a subset of X_{ij} conceptually, we take it out of X_{ij} for clarity.

We denote the part of β for X_{ij} by β_{ij}, the part of β for X_{ijk} by β_{ijk} and the part of β for X_t by β_t. Accordingly, by linearity of inner product, the score βX_{ijkt} can be decomposed into three parts:

$$\beta X_{ijkt} = \beta_{ij} X_{ij} + \beta_{ijk} X_{ijk} + \beta_t X_t. \quad (6)$$

Since X_{ijk} is about $40 \sim 50$ times sparser than X_{ij}, it may not exist for the activity t. Instead, X_{ij} always exists given the relations between two users are ubiquitous. Our strategy is, by carefully designing indicator features, we can differentiate two scenarios: X_{ijk} exists and X_{ijk} does not exists. If X_{ijk} exists, we name $\hat{\alpha}_{ijk} = \beta_{ij} X_{ij} + \beta_{ijk} X_{ijk}$ as the Viewer-Actor-ActivityType Affinity. No matter X_{ijk} exists or not, we always name $\hat{\alpha}_{ij} = \beta_{ij} X_{ij}$ as the Viewer-Actor Affinity.

5.4 Feature Design and Model Training

When modeling Viewer-Actor Affinities, relation and past interactions between viewer and actor have been shown to be useful [29]. In this subsection, we design a set of past interaction features as "warm-start" features and a set of relation features as "cold-start" features in order to overcome the data sparsity challenge.

Warm-start features: Two nature past interactions from the viewer to the actor are the number of past actions (e..g, clicks, shares, likes, comments, etc.), and the number of past impressions in LinkedIn. Intuitively, more past actions and less past impressions, higher CTR in the future, as shown in Figures 3a and 3b. To enrich the past interaction dynamics, we count the past interactions using multiple time windows. To enrich the past interaction intensity, we extend the time window up to half a year ago. Diverse and long past interactions reduce the data sparsity yet increase the data volume to be processed. This partially leads to our decision of offline computing the affiniy scores later.

The past interaction features can be available for either viewer-actor pairs or viewer-actor-activitytype triples. For example, the number of clicks between viewer and actor in the past 3 months is one feature; and the number of clicks between viewer and actor on "articles shared by the actor" in the past 3 months is another feature.

Cold-start features: The relationships between viewers and actors should be ubiquitous, not limited to viewer-actor pairs with past interactions. Considering the large fraction of new actors who just connected to viewers, we look for cold-start features that enrich relations between viewer and actor.

There are two major sources of cold-start features. One is from the structured member profile where we extract thousands of profile features including education, location, job experiences, and work-related skills etc. We then create millions of binary features by interacting viewer's profile features with actor's profile features. For textual properties like member summaries, we generate binary features by using bag-of-words representations. Top N features are selected by ordering the features using Mutual Information. As shown in Figure 5, we set $N = 2,000$ as the relative CTR lift converges after 2,000 features.

The other source is from the social network underlying the pair of viewer and actor. Graph feature examples considered by us include the number of the viewer's neighbors that took actions on the same actor, the number of common friends between viewer and actor, etc.

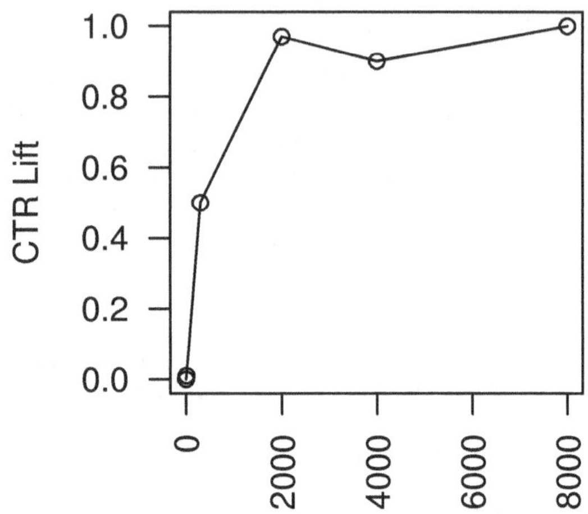

Figure 5: Relative CTR lift over Top N member profile features.

For simplicity, we only consider cold-start features for viewer-actor pairs, not viewer-actor-activitytype triples.

Training large scale logistic regression: From the training data Y and X_{ijkt} that we collect, we aim to learn β using logistic regression. The challenge here is the massive scale of regression, since our training data have billions of activities and we also consider thousands of features for each activity. It is thus not surprising that our regression problem does not fit in a single machine. To overcome this scalability challenge, we solve logistic regression in a distributed fashion, by employing the Alternating Direction Method of Multipliers (ADMM) [9]. ADMM partitions the data and learns a local model from each partition, and then it aggregates all models from partitions and sends back the aggregation results to individual partitions. For more details about how we use ADMM for our regression, refer to [4].

6. AFFINITY DEPLOYMENT FRAMEWORK

In Section 4 and Section 5, we have modeled Viewer-ActivityType Affinity as the CTR estimate and Viewer-Actor Affinities as the partial scores of the CTR estimate respectively. To collectively model all the affinity scores together, we take the following approach: First, we compute Viewer-ActivityType Affinity alone. Then we use Viewer-ActivityType Affinity as one of the baseline features in the joint training of the Viewer-Actor Affinities and the other activity-dependent coefficients. Mathematically, the relevance score used in ranking for viewer i, actor j, activity type k, and activity t, with monotonic logit transformation removed, can be written as

$$\begin{aligned} Y &= \beta_t X_t + \beta_{ik} \alpha_{ik} + \alpha_{ijk}, \text{ if } \alpha_{ijk} \text{ exists}; \\ &= \beta_t X_t + \beta_{ik} \alpha_{ik} + \alpha_{ij}, \text{ else}, \end{aligned} \quad (7)$$

where X_t is the feature vector that corresponds to the more dynamic activity-dependent features, α_{ik} is the Viewer-ActivityType Affinity, α_{ij} is the Viewer-Actor Affinity, α_{ijk} is the Viewer-Actor-ActivityType Affinity, and β_t, β_{ik} are the learned coefficients. Note

Table 1: Offline analysis on the frequency of updating Viewer-Actor Affinities

reward lift at	daily update	hourly update	2-day update
position 1	0.0%	+0.1%	-0.4%

that α_{ijk} or α_{ij} do not have coefficients attached simply because these two are partial results computed from the same model (see Equation (6)). Also, when there is no data to support triple (i, j, k) such that α_{ijk} does not exist, we fall back to α_{ij}.

Ideally the affinities and β should be trained jointly. However, due to the complexity of each affinity scores, high-dimensional feature spaces and data sparsity, we chose this simple yet effective approach for faster model training process. Also, since Viewer-ActivityType affinity has the richest data for warm-start, we choose to model it independently first and treat it as a single compound feature in the model for training Viewer-Actor Affinities.

How to determine the frequency of updating affinities is more an art than a science. We conducted offline analysis in Table 1 for Viewer-Actor Affinities using one week data, and found that increasing the updating frequency from daily to hourly did not change the reward at position 1 [23] significantly (only +0.1% lift). Thus, we choose to update the affinity scores daily in our production pipelines.

Figure 6 depicts the online deployment framework for affinities in LinkedIn feed. The flow starts by the URL request from a viewer i. LinkedIn feed service first fetches all the candidate activities from viewer i's interpersonal social network. Our scoring system then computes the relevance score for each activity and rank activities based on these scores. For each activity t with actor j and activity type k, the online scoring system obtains activity-dependent features X_t, and also fetches affinity scores from Voldemort stores[3] which support distributed key-value storage and queries. The affinity scores are pre-computed offline in Hadoop and updated on the Voldemort store daily. The scoring system finally applies Equation (7) to score and return the top-ranked results to show in people's feed.

Every day we compute tens of billions of Viewer-ActivityType Affinities for all LinkedIn members and all possible activity types (300 millions times 50), and also tens of billions of Viewer-Actor Affinities for both desktop and phone platforms. Note that we only prepare Viewer-Actor Affinities for those pairs with interactions in the past half a year. This strategy largely reduces the dimension of Viewer-Actor Affinities; otherwise, even the offline pre-computation is not feasible. Furthermore, for heavy viewers who interacted with hundreds of thousands of actors, we only store top K Viewer-Actor Affinities in the Voldemort store after offline computation. This strategy avoids the latency timeout when serving heavy viewers online. We set $K = 10,000$ such that it can keep the vast majority of the affinity scores and only lost 0.08% reward at position 1 [23] in the offline analysis for one week data.

7. EXPERIMENTAL RESULTS

7.1 Experimental Setup

Online A/B tests: In LinkedIn, bucket tests (A/B tests) are conducted on a regular basis whenever we believe that we have a better model compared to existing models online (typically based on offline analysis). Once we decide to start testing a model, typically

[3]http://www.project-voldemort.com/voldemort/

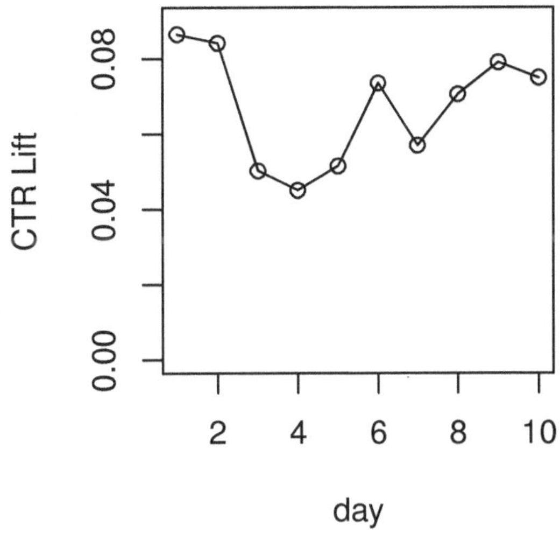

Figure 7: Online CTR lift by Viewer-ActivityType Affinity on desktop.

we launch it on 2% $\sim$ 3% random LinkedIn members. We observe the performance of the model for about two weeks before making a decision to ramp the model to a larger population. Most importantly, we consider engagement, typically measured via CTR (click-through rate), as the evaluation metric. In addition, we also consider other metrics such as freshness of the feed based on the model, diversity of the feed, how many times items are repeated to a user etc. as well in making ramp decisions. However, for the purposes of this paper, we only report CTR metrics. Most of the results reported below are from online A/B tests with offline evaluations when appropriate.

Offline replay analysis: In LinkedIn, after we train a model, we need to evaluate the model offline before deploying it in production. For this, we use a replay methodology for unbiased offline evaluation of online serving schemes [23], where the relative rewards obtained from two different models are typically indicative of which model would perform better in production.

When launching a new model, we also retrain the model with the recent data. This is because, often new activity types are introduced on the feed and sometimes some types are retired. Typically, we retrain both the baseline model and the new model with recent data, and we then evaluate both models offline to decide whether or not the new model is launchable.

We do not always replace the baseline model in production by the baseline model retrained on the recent data, unless we believe retraining itself will create a big performance gap. Therefore, in some of the A/B experiments below, it is possible that the baseline model was not retrained on recent data but the new model was retrained. In such situations, we also provide the offline comparisons.

7.2 Desktop Experiments

In this section, we show results for the models that were launched to improve personalization on desktop.

7.2.1 *Effect of Viewer-ActivityType Affinity*

We tested Viewer-ActivityType Affinity since late 2013. The baseline model consists of activity-dependent features such as age

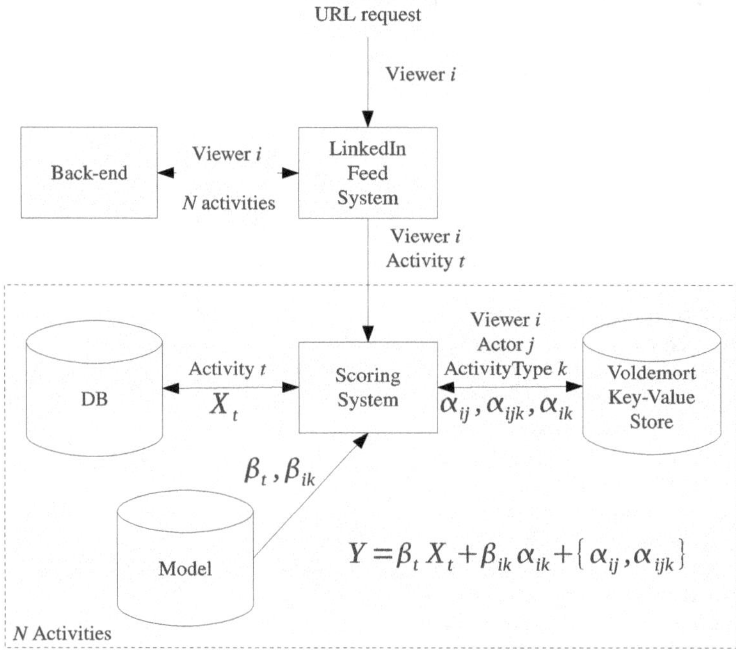

Figure 6: Online deployment framework for affinities.

of an activity, type of an activity etc. and some raw connection strength features between a viewer and an actor. The affinity model applied the Viewer-ActivityType Affinity as a new feature on top of the baseline model. The A/B tests during 10 days between them are shown in Figure 7. The x-axis shows the day index and the y-axis shows the relative CTR lift of the affinity model comparing to the baseline model. Overall, the affinity model achieved a daily CTR lift of about +7.0%. Two models were trained using the same data and tested over the same percentage of LinkedIn members (2%). Hence the comparison is fair except for the bucket bias[4].

7.2.2 *Effect of Viewer-Actor Affinity*

We started testing a model based on Viewer-Actor Affinity since May 2014. Now, the Viewer-ActivityType affinity model in the previous section 7.2.1 becomes the baseline model. The compared affinity model applied the Viewer-Actor Affinity as a new feature on top of the baseline model. The A/B tests between them in Figure 8 showed a CTR lift of about +2.9% on average.

One may wonder why we do not put comparisons in Figure 7 and Figure 8 together in a single plot. They are not numerically comparable simply because two bucket tests were conducted at different time. By the time we started the new bucket tests in May 2014, the baseline model had changed significantly from the Viewer-ActivityType affinity in the previous section 7.2.1. For instance, the new baseline had a few new activity type features, and LinkedIn feed had moved to a paradigm where we always served activities using a relevance model rather than a mixture of relevance feed and real-time feed. However, each bucket test alone is still meaningful because for each bucket test, two compared models have the same test settings and product environment.

Considering the Viewer-Actor Affinity model was trained on newer data, we also have the offline comparison results where both models

[4]Completely removing the bucket bias is impossible because there will always be "noise" inherent to the populations since they're simply not the same people.

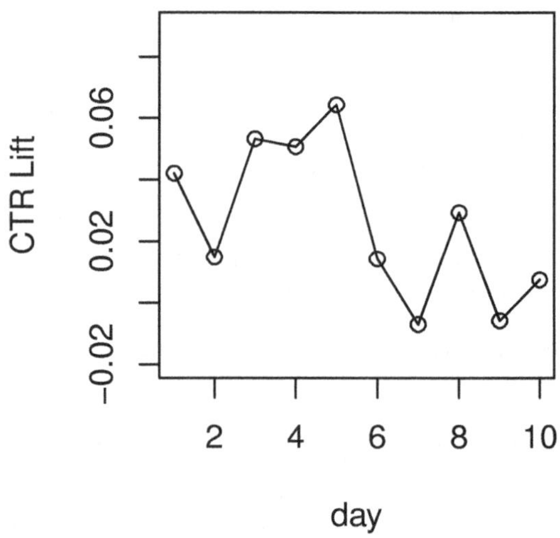

Figure 8: Online CTR lift by Viewer-Actor Affinity on desktop.

were trained and tested on the same data. Comparing to the baseline Viewer-ActivityType Affinity model, the Viewer-Actor Affinity model achieved +3.5% reward lift at position 1 for one week test data, where position 1 has the least position bias in offline replay analysis and is thus the most reliable [23].

7.2.3 *Effect of Viewer-Actor-ActivityType Affinity*

We tested Viewer-Actor-ActivityType Affinity since June 2014. Similarly there were some product design changes since June 2014 in LinkedIn, e.g., showing fresher content on the feed. Thus, we

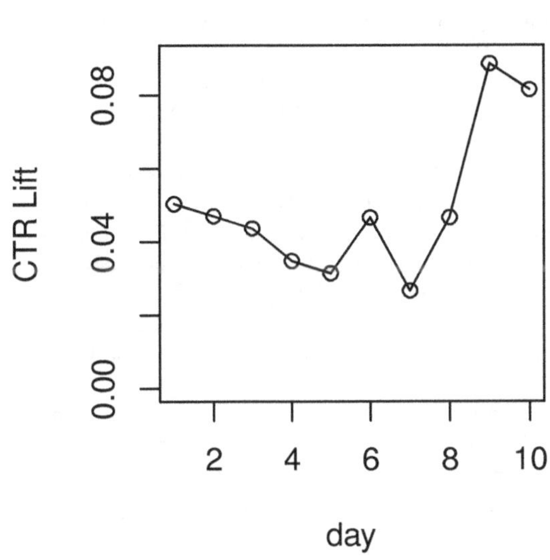

Figure 9: Online CTR lift by Viewer-Actor-ActivityType Affinity on desktop.

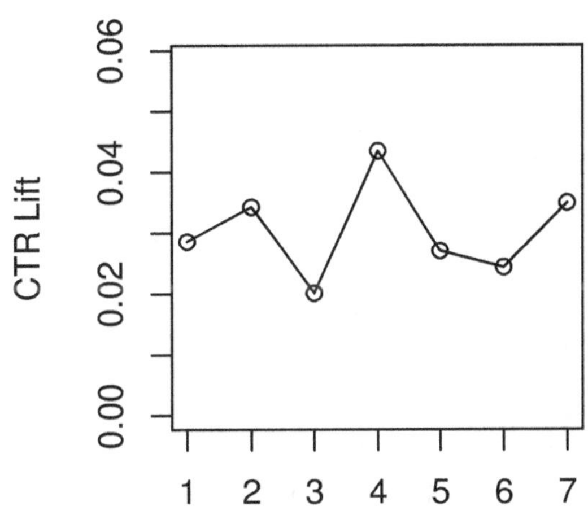

Figure 10: Online CTR lift by Viewer-ActivityType Affinity on mobile.

only look at the comparions in a single bucket test. The baseline model is the Viewer-Actor affinity model in the previous section 7.2.2. The compared affinity model applied the Viewer-Actor-ActivityType Affinity as a new feature on top of the baseline model. The 10-day A/B tests between them in Figure 9 showed an average CTR lift of about +4.3% for each day. During the offline replay analysis where two models were trained and tested on the same data, we found that the Viewer-Actor-ActivityType Affinity model achieved +6.6% reward lift at position 1 for one week test data.

7.2.4 *Discussion*

Experimental results on desktop are promising – we proved that the more granular the affinity, the higher the CTR through both online bucket tests and offline replay analysis. By treating affinities as a compound feature or partial scores of the final response prediction, we only introduced 3 additional arithmatic operations and 1 additional query to the online production, which contributed to less than 10% of online service time.

7.3 Mobile Bucket Test Results

In this section, we show similar results on mobile. Because of the great successfulness of Viewer-Actor-ActivityType Affinity on desktop, we decided to migrate from Viewer-ActivityType Affinity to Viewer-Actor-ActivityType Affinity directly on mobile. So, mobile results of Viewer-Actor Affinity model are skipped.

7.3.1 *Effect of Viewer-ActivityType Affinity*

The comparison has been conducted during one week period in April 2014. The baseline model is the simple model without any affinities described in Section 7.2.1. The compared affinity model applied the Viewer-ActivityType Affinity as a new feature on top of the baseline model. Both models were trained on the same data so no need to additionally provide offline replay analysis. The A/B tests between them in Figure 10 showed a CTR lift of about +3% on average.

7.3.2 *Effect of Viewer-Actor-ActivityType Affinity*

The comparison was conducted during one week period in December 2014. The baseline model is the Viewer-ActivityType Affinity model in the previous section 7.3.1. The compared affinity model applied the Viewer-Actor-ActivityType Affinity as a new feature on top of the baseline model. Both models were trained on the same data so no need to additionally provide offline replay analysis. The A/B tests between them in Figure 11 showed a CTR lift of around +10% on average.

8. CONCLUSION

We studied how to personalize LinkedIn feed in this paper, with a focus on affinity modeling. We generated three kinds of affinity scores offline: Viewer-ActivityType Affinity, Viewer-Actor Affinity, and Viewer-Actor-ActivityType Affinity. All of them are easy to compute, easy to scale, and easy to be deployed in production. We did extensive experiments based on online bucket tests (A/B tests) and offline evaluation to illustrate the effect of these affinities in LinkedIn feed.

Personalizing LinkedIn feed is an open-ended problem given the fact that millions of new members join LinkedIn every month around the world. Our initial study demonstrates that personalization of finer granularity achieves higher CTR, which motivates our future work as below.

- Deepen the personalization to the activity-dependent level, e.g., the affinity between viewer and the content topic of activity.
- Deepen the personalization to the viewer ID level, e.g., each viewer has her own personalization model.

9. REFERENCES

[1] https://www.facebook.com/notes/facebook/new-views-for-your-home-page/162536657130.

[2] F. Abel, Q. Gao, G.-J. Houben, and K. Tao. Analyzing user modeling on twitter for personalized news recommendations. In *UMAP*, pages 1–12, 2011.

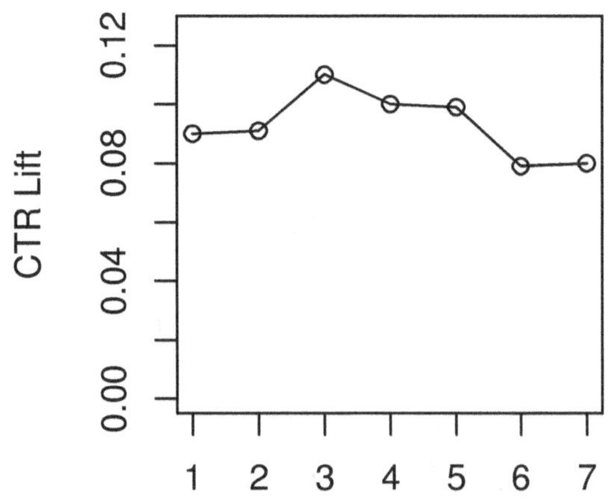

Figure 11: Online CTR lift by Viewer-Actor-ActivityType Affinity on mobile.

[3] D. Agarwal, R. Agrawal, R. Khanna, and N. Kota. Estimating rates of rare events with multiple hierarchies through scalable log-linear models. In *SIGKDD*, pages 213–222, 2010.

[4] D. Agarwal, B.-C. Chen, R. Gupta, J. Hartman, Q. He, A. Iyer, S. Kolar, Y. Ma, P. Shivaswamy, A. Singh, and L. Zhang. Activity ranking in linkedin feed. In *SIGKDD*, pages 1603–1612, 2014.

[5] S. Berkovsky and J. Freyne. Network activity feed: finding needles in a haystack. *LNAI 8940*, pages 21–34, 2015.

[6] S. Berkovsky, J. Freyne, S. Kimani, and G. Smith. Selecting items of relevance in social network feeds. In *UMAP*, pages 329–334, 2011.

[7] S. Berkovsky, J. Freyne, and G. Smith. Personalized network updates: Increasing social interactions and contributions in social networks. In *UMAP*, pages 1–13, 2012.

[8] S. Bourke, M. P. O'Mahony, R. Rafter, and B. Smyth. Ranking in information streams. In *Proceedings of the companion publication of the 2013 international conference on Intelligent user interfaces companion*, pages 99–100, 2013.

[9] S. Boyd, N. Parikh, E. Chu, B. Peleato, and J. Eckstein. Distributed optimization and statistical learning via the alternating direction method of multipliers. Technical report, Stanford University, 2010.

[10] M. Burgess, A. Mazzia, E. Adar, and M. Cafarella. Leveraging noisy lists for social feed ranking. In *AAAI*, 2013.

[11] J. Chen, R. Nairn, and E. H. Chi. Speak little and well: Recommending conversations in online social streams. In *SIGCHI*, pages 217–226, 2011.

[12] J. Chen, R. Nairn, L. Nelson, M. Bernstein, and E. H. Chi. Short and tweet: Experiments on recommending content from information streams. In *SIGCHI*, pages 1185–1194, 2010.

[13] K. Chen, T. Chen, G. Zheng, O. Jin, E. Yao, and Y. Yu. Collaborative personalized tweet recommendation. In *SIGIR*, pages 661–670, 2012.

[14] W. Chu and S.-T. Park. Personalized recommendation on dynamic content using predictive bilinear models. In *WWW*, 2009.

[15] W. DuMouchel and D. Pregibon. Empirical bayes screening for multi-item associations. In *SIGKDD*, pages 67–76, 2001.

[16] G. D. Francisci, A. Gionis, and C. Lucchese. From chatter to headlines: Harnessing the real-time web for personalized news recommendation. In *WSDM*, pages 153–162, 2012.

[17] J. Freyne, S. Berkovsky, E. M. Daly, and W. Geyer. Social networking feeds: Recommending items of interest. In *RecSys*, 2010.

[18] E. Gilbert and K. Karahalios. Predicting tie strength with social media. In *SIGCHI*, pages 211–220, 2009.

[19] I. Guy, I. Ronen, and A. Raviv. Personalized activity streams: Sifting through the "river of news". In *RecSys*, pages 181–188, 2011.

[20] I. Guy, T. Steier, M. Barnea, I. Ronen, and T. Daniel. Swimming against the streamz: search and analytics over the enterprise activity stream. In *CIKM*, pages 1587–1591, 2012.

[21] L. Hong, R. Bekkerman, J. Adler, and B. D. Davison. Learning to rank social update streams. In *SIGIR*, pages 651–660, 2012.

[22] L. Hong, A. S. Doumith, and B. D. Davison. Co-factorization machines: modeling user interests and predicting individual decisions in twitter. In *WSDM*, pages 557–566, 2013.

[23] L. Li, W. Chu, J. Langford, and X. Wang. Unbiased offline evaluation of contextual-bandit-based news article recommendation algorithms. In *WSDM*, pages 297–306. ACM, 2011.

[24] H. Ma, D. Zhou, C. Liu, M. R. Lyu, and I. King. Recommender systems with social regularization. In *WSDM*, pages 287–296, 2011.

[25] T. Paek, M. Gamon, S. Counts, D. M. Chickering, and A. Dhesi. Predicting the importance of newsfeed posts and social network friends. In *AAAI*, 2010.

[26] Y. Pan, F. Cong, K. Chen, and Y. Yu. Diffusion-aware personalized social update diffusion-aware personalized social update recommendation. In *RecSys*, pages 69–76, 2013.

[27] M. Richardson, E. Dominowska, and R. Ragno. Predicting clicks: estimating the click-through rate for new ads. In *WWW*, pages 521–530, 2007.

[28] P.-H. Soh, Y.-C. Lin, and M.-S. Chen. Recommendation for online social feeds by exploiting user response behavior. In *WWW*, 2013.

[29] I. Uysal and W. B. Croft. User oriented tweet ranking: a filtering approach to microblogs. In *CIKM*, pages 2261–2264, 2011.

Whither Social Networks for Web Search?

Rakesh Agrawal
Data Insights Laboratories
ragrawal@acm.org

Behzad Golshan
Boston University
behzad@bu.edu

Evangelos Papalexakis
Carnegie Mellon University
epapalex@cs.cmu.edu

ABSTRACT

Access to diverse perspectives nurtures an informed citizenry. Google and Bing have emerged as the duopoly that largely arbitrates which English language documents are seen by web searchers. A recent study shows that there is now a large overlap in the top organic search results produced by them. Thus, citizens may no longer be able to gain different perspectives by using different search engines.

We present the results of our empirical study that indicates that by mining Twitter data one can obtain search results that are quite distinct from those produced by Google and Bing. Additionally, our user study found that these results were quite informative. The gauntlet is now on search engines to test whether our findings hold in their infrastructure for different social networks and whether enabling diversity has sufficient business imperative for them.

Categories and Subject Descriptors

H.2.8 [**Database Applications**]: Data mining; H.3.3 [**Information Search and Retrieval**]: Search process

Keywords

Web search; social media search; search engine; search result comparison; Google; Bing; Twitter

1. INTRODUCTION

The fairness doctrine contends that citizens should have access to diverse perspectives as exposure to different views is beneficial for the advancement of humanity [19]. The World Wide Web is now widely recognized as the universal information source. Content representing diverse perspectives exist on the Web, on almost on any topic. However, this does not automatically ensure that citizens encounter them [46].

Search engines have become the primary tool used to access the web content [38]. In particular, it is the duopoly of Google and Bing that largely arbitrates what documents people see, especially from the English language web (Yahoo's web search is currently powered by Bing).

KDD'15, August 10-13, 2015, Sydney, NSW, Australia.
© 2015 ACM. ISBN 978-1-4503-3664-2/15/08 ...$15.00.
DOI: http://dx.doi.org/10.1145/2783258.2788571.

A recent study [2] indicates that there is now a large overlap in the top-10 organic search results produced by Google and Bing. These are the results that get most of the clicks as users rarely look at results at lower positions [18, 24]. This overlap was found to be even more pronounced in the top-5 results and the results of queries in which citizens exhibited large interest. The implication is that citizens may no longer be able to gain different perspectives by obtaining results for the same query from different search engines.

This paper investigates whether data mining of social networks can help web search engines imbue their search results with useful diversity [33]. Specifically, we present the results obtained by mining the real-life Twitter data that demonstrate:

1. We are able to obtain search results, even by simply analyzing the retweet graph, which are quite distinct from the web results for the same query.

2. Users have judged those results to be quite informative.

We used Twitter in our study because it is still possible to selectively crawl Twitter.

The structure of the rest of the paper is as follows. We begin by discussing related work in Section 2. In Section 3, we describe the data mining tools we employed for conducting our study. Section 4 gives the experimental setup and Section 5 presents the results of our analysis using data from Google, Bing, and Twitter. Section 6 presents the user study for assessing the usefulness of our findings. We conclude with a summary and future directions in Section 7.

2. RELATED WORK

Three lines of research are most relevant to our work: i) overlap between the results of the search engines, ii) social search technologies, and iii) integration of social search results into web search. We review all three in this section. Note that we use the term "social search" to mean searches conducted over databases of socially generated content, although this term often refers broadly to the process of finding information online with the assistance of any number of social resources such as asking others for answers or two people searching together [49].

2.1 Overlap Studies

Since their advent in early 90's, there has been considerable interest in understanding how distinct are the results produced by the prevalent web search engines. Ding and Marchionini measured and observed in 1996 a low level of result overlap between InfoSeek, Lycos, and OpenText [14]. Around the same time, Selberg and Etzioni found that each of Galaxy, Infoseek, Lycos, OpenText, Webcrawler and Yahoo returned mostly unique results [43]. Also in 1996, Gauch, Wang and Gomez found that a metasearch engine that fused the results of Alta Vista, Excite, InfoSeek, Lycos, Open Text, and WebCrawler provided the highest number of relevant results [21]. Bharat and Broder estimated the overlap between the websites indexed by HotBot, Alta Vista, Excite and InfoSeek in November 1997 to be only 1.4% [8]. Lawrence and Giles, in their study of AltaVista, Excite, HotBot, Infoseek, Lycos, and Northern Light published in 1998, found that the individual engines covered from 3 to 34% of the indexable Web [30]. Spink et al. studied the overlap between the results of four search engines, namely MSN (predecessor of Bing), Google, Yahoo and Ask Jeeves, using data from July 2005. They found that the percent of total first page results unique to only one of the engines was 84.9%, shared by two of the three was 11.4%, shared by three was 2.6%, and shared by all four was 1.1% [44].

One way the users dealt with low overlap was by manually executing the same query on multiple search engines. Analyzing six months of interaction logs from 2008-2009, White and Dumais [52] found that 72.6% of all users used more than one engine during this period, 50% switched engines within a search session at least once, and 67.6% used different engines for different sessions. Their survey revealed three classes of reasons for this behavior: dissatisfaction with the quality of results in the original engine (dissatisfaction, frustration, expected better results, totaling 57%), the desire to verify or find additional information (coverage/verification, totaling 26%, curiosity), and user preferences (destination preferred, destination typically better, totaling 12%). Another way the problem of low overlap was addressed was by developing metasearch engines (e.g. InFind, MetaCrawler, MetaFerret, ProFusion, SavvySearch). A metasearch engine automatically queries a number of search engines, merges the returned lists of results, and presents the resulting ranked list to the user as the search of the query [36]. Note that with either manual or automated approach, the user ends up seeing multiple perspectives.

A recent study, using data from June-July 2014, however, found large overlap between the top-10 search results produced by Google and Bing [2]. This overlap was found to be even more pronounced in the top-5 results and the results of head queries. Some plausible reasons for greater convergence in the search results include deployment of greater amount of resources by search engines to cover a larger fraction of indexable Web, much more universal understanding of search engine technologies, and the use of similar features in ranking the search results. A consequence of this convergence is that the access to diverse perspectives becomes harder.

Contrary to the rich literature on overlap between the web search engines results, the only prior work we could find on overlap between web and social search results appears in Section 5 of [49] (TRM Study). They extracted snippets of all search results from Bing search logs for 42 most popular queries for one week in November 2009. They also obtained all the tweets containing those queries during the same period. They then computed per query average cosine similarity of each web snippet with the centroid of the other web snippets and with the centroid of the tweets. Similarly, they computed the per-query average cosine similarity of each Twitter result with the centroid of the other tweets and with the centroid of the web snippets. All averaging and comparisons are done in the reduced topic space obtained using Latent Dirichlet Allocation (LDA) [9]. They found that the average similarity of Twitter posts to the Twitter centroid was higher than the web results' similarity to the web centroid. The issue of usefulness of Twitter results is not addressed in their paper.

We shall see that our study considers head as well as trunk queries and encompasses both Google and Bing. We also employ different data mining tools in our study. Specifically, our TensorCompare uses tensor analysis to obtain low-dimensional representation of search results since the method of moments for LDA reduces to canonical decomposition of a tensor, for which scalable distributed algorithms exist [4, 25]. Our CrossLearnCompare, uses a novel cross-engine learning to quantify the similarity of snippets and tweets. Additionally, we provide a user study demonstrating the usefulness of the Twitter results. We will have more to say quantitatively about the TRM study when we present our experimental results in Section 5.

2.2 Social Search

In addition to being considered a social media and a social network [28], Twitter may also be viewed as a information retrieval system that people can utilize to produce and consume information. Twitter today receives more than 500 million tweets per day at the rate of more than 33,000 tweets per second. More than 300 billion tweets have been sent since the founding of Twitter in 2006 and it receives more than 2 billion search queries every day. Twitter serves these queries using an inverted index tuned for real-time search, called EarlyBird [11]. While this search service excels at surfacing breaking news and events in real time and it does indeed incorporate relevance ranking, it is a feature that the system designers themselves consider that they have "only begun to explore".[1]

The prevailing perception is that much of the content found on Twitter is of low quality [3] and the keyword search as provided by Twitter is not effective [48]. In response, there has been considerable research aimed at designing mechanisms for finding good content from Twitter. In many of the proposed approaches, retweet count alone or in conjunction with textual data, author's metadata, and propagation information play a prominent role [12, 16, 48, 51]. The intuition is that if a tweet is retweeted multiple times, then several people have taken the time to read it, decide it is worth sharing, and then actually retweeted it, and hence it must be of good quality [50]. But, of course, one needs to remove socware and other spam before using retweet count [35, 39, 42] Other approaches include using the presence of a URL as an indicator [3], link analysis on the follows and retweet graphs [40, 53], clustering taking into account the size and popularity of a tweet, its audience size, and recency [29], and the semantic approaches including topic modeling [54]. See overviews in [51, 54] for additional references.

In this work, we are not striving to create the best possible social search engine, but rather investigate whether the results obtained using signals from a social network could be substantially different from a web search engine and yet useful. Thus, in order to avoid confounding between multiple factors, we shall use a simple social search engine that ranks tweets based on retweet analysis.

2.3 Integration of Web and Social search

Bing has been including a few tweets related to the current query on its search result page, at least since November 2013. However, it is not obvious for what queries this feature is triggered and what tweets are included. For example, on February 12, 2015 at 10:42AM, our query "Greece ECB" brought only one tweet on Bing's result page, which was a retweet from Mark Rauffalo from two days ago. Bing also offered a link titled "See more on Twitter" below this tweet. Clicking this link took us to a Twitter page,

[1]One of the problems with Twitter search has been that, while it is easy to discover current tweets and trending topics, it is much more difficult to search over older tweets and determine, say, what the fans were saying about the Seahawks during the 2014 Super Bowl. Beginning November 18, 2014, however, it has become possible to search over the entire corpus of public tweets. Still, our own experiments indicate that the ranking continues to be heavily biased towards recency.

where the top tweet was from 14 minutes ago with the text "ECB raises pressure on Greece as Tsipras meets EU peers"! Since June 2014, one can also search Bing by hashtag, look up specific Twitter handles, or search for tweets related to a specific celebrity. Google is also said have struck a deal with Twitter that will allow tweets to be shown in Google search results sometime during this year.

There is also research on how web search can be improved using signals from Twitter. For example, Rowlands et al. [41] propose that the text around a URL that appears in a tweet may serve to add supplementary terms or add weight to existing terms in the corresponding web page and that the reputation or authority of the tweeterer may serve to weight both annotations and query-independent popularity. Similarly, Dong et al. [15] advocate using Twitter stream for detecting fresh URLs as well as for computing features to rank them. We propose to build our future work upon some of these ideas.

3. DATA MINING TOOLS

We next review the data mining tools for analyzing and comparing search engine results, introduced in [2]. One, called TensorCompare, uses tensor analysis to derive low-dimensional representation of search results. The other, called CrossLearnCompare, uses cross-engine learning to quantify their similarity.

3.1 TensorCompare

Postulate that we have the search results of executing a fixed set of queries at certain fixed time intervals on the same set of search engines. These results can be represented in a four mode tensor $\underline{\mathbf{X}}$, where (query, result, time, search engine) are the four modes [27]. A result might be in the form of a set of URLs or a set of keywords representing the corresponding pages. The tensor might be binary valued or real valued (indicating, for instance, frequencies).

This tensor can be analyzed using the PARAFAC decomposition [23] into a sum of rank-one tensors: $\underline{\mathbf{X}} \approx \sum_{r=1}^{R} \lambda_r \, \mathbf{a}_r \circ \mathbf{b}_r \circ \mathbf{c}_r \circ \mathbf{d}_r$. where $\mathbf{a}_r, \mathbf{b}_r, \mathbf{c}_r, \mathbf{d}_r$ have been normalized with their scaling absorbed in λ_r. For compactness, the decomposition is represented as matrices $\mathbf{A}, \mathbf{B}, \mathbf{C}, \mathbf{D}$. The decomposition of $\underline{\mathbf{X}}$ to $\mathbf{A}, \mathbf{B}, \mathbf{C}, \mathbf{D}$ gives a low rank embedding of queries, results, timings, and search engines respectively. The factor matrix $\mathbf{D}$ projects each one of the search engines to the R-dimensional space. Alternatively, one can view this embedding as soft clustering of the search engines, with matrix $\mathbf{D}$ being the cluster indicator matrix: the (i, j) entry of $\mathbf{D}$ shows the participation of search engine i in cluster j.

This leads to a powerful visualization tool that captures similarities and differences between the search engines in an intuitive way. Say we take search engines A and B and the corresponding rows of matrix $\mathbf{D}$. If we plot these two row vectors against each other, the resulting plot will contain as many points as clusters (R in our particular notation). The positions of these points are the key to understanding the similarity between search engines.

Figure 1 serves as a guide. The (x, y) coordinate of a point on the plot corresponds to the degree of participation of search engines A and B respectively in that cluster. If all points lie on the 45 degree line, this means that both A and B participate equally in all clusters. In other words, they tend to cluster in the exact same way for semantically similar results and for specific periods of time. Therefore, Fig. 1(a) paints the picture of two search engines that are very (if not perfectly) similar with respect to their responses. In the case where we have only two search engines, perfect alignment of their results in a cluster would be the point $(0.5, 0.5)$. If we are comparing more than two search engines, then we may have points on the lower parts of the diagonal. In the figure, multiple points are shown along the diagonal for the sake of generality.

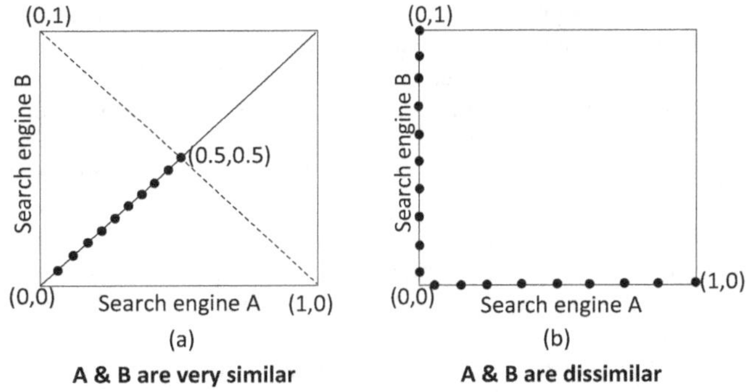

Figure 1: Visualization guide for TENSORCOMPARE.

Figure 1(b), on the other hand, shows the opposite behavior. Whenever a point lies on either axis, this means that only one of the search engines participate in that cluster. If we see a plot similar to this figure, we can infer that A and B are very dissimilar with respect to their responses. In the case of two search engines, the only valid points on either axis are $(0, 1)$ and $(1, 0)$, indicating an exclusive set of results. For generality, multiple points are shown on each axis.

Of course, the cases shown in Fig. 1 are the two extremes, and one expects to observe behaviors bounded by those extremes. For instance, in the case of two search engines, all points should lie on the line $\mathbf{D}(1, j)x + \mathbf{D}(2, j)y = 1$, where $\mathbf{D}(1, j)$ is the membership of engine A in cluster j, and $\mathbf{D}(2, j)$ is the membership of engine B in cluster j. This line is the dashed line of Fig. 1(a).

3.2 CrossLearnCompare

An intuitive measure of the similarity of the results of two search engines is the predictability of the results of a search engine given the results of the other. Say we view each query as a class label. We can then go ahead and learn a classifier that maps the search result of search engine A to its class label, i.e. the query that produced the result. Imagine now that we have results that were produced by search engine B. If A and B return completely different results, then we would expect that classifying correctly a result of B using the classifier learned using A's results would be difficult, and our classifier would probably err. On the other hand, if A and B returned almost identical results, classifying correctly the search results of B would be easy. In cases in between, where A and B bear some level of similarity, we would expect the classifier to perform in a way that it is correlated with the degree of similarity between A and B.

One can get different accuracy when predicting search engine A using a model trained on B, and vice versa. This, for instance, can be the case when the results of A are a superset of the results of B.

4. EXPERIMENTAL SETUP

We next describe the experimental setup of the empirical study we performed, applying the tools just described.

4.1 Social Pulse

For concreteness, we first specify a simple social search engine, which we shall henceforth refer to as Social Pulse. We are not striving to create the best possible search engine, but rather investigate whether the results obtained using signals from a social network could be substantially different from a Web search engine and yet useful. Thus, instead of employing a large set of features (see Section 2.2), we purposefully base the Social Pulse's ranker on one single feature in order to be able to make sharp conclusions and to avoid confounding between multiple factors.

Social Pulse uses Twitter as the social medium. For a given query, Social Pulse first retrieves all tweets that pertain to that query. Multiple techniques are available in the literature for this purpose (e.g. [7, 37, 45, 47]). We choose to employ the simple technique of checking for the presence of the query string in the tweet. Subsequently, Social Pulse ranks the retrieved tweets with respect to the number of re-tweets (more precisely, the number of occurrences of the exact same tweet without having necessarily been formally re-tweeted).

Arguably, one can restrict the attention to only those tweets that contain at least one URL [3]. However, we have empirically observed that highly re-tweeted tweets, in spite of containing no URL, usually provide high quality result. Hence, Social Pulse uses these tweets as well.

4.2 Data Set

We conducted the study for two sets of queries. The TRENDS set (Table 1) contains the most popular search terms from different categories from Google Trends during April 2014. We will refer to them as *head queries*. The MANUAL set (Table 2) consists of hand-picked queries by the authors that we will refer to as *trunk queries*. These queries consist of topics that the authors were familiar with and were following at the time. Familiarity with the queries is helpful in understanding whether two sets of results are different and useful. Queries in both the sets primarily have the informational intent [10]. Many of them are named entities, which constitute a significant portion of what people search. The total number of queries was limited by the budget available for the study.

Albert Einstein	American Idol	Antibiotics	Ariana Grande
Avicii	Barack Obama	Beyonce	Cristiano Ronaldo
Derek Jeter	Donald Sterling	Floyd Mayweather	Ford Mustang
Frozen	Game of Thrones	Harvard University	Honda
Jay-Z	LeBron James	Lego	Los Angeles Clippers
Martini	Maya Angelou	Miami Heat	Miami Heat
Miley Cyrus	New York City	New York Yankees	Oprah Winfrey
San Antonio Spurs	Skrillex	SpongeBob SquarePants	Tottenham Hotspur F.C.
US Senate			

Table 1: TRENDS queries

Afghanistan	Alternative energy	Athens	Beatles	Beer
Coup	Debt	Disaster	E-cigarettes	Education
Gay marriage	Globalization	Gun control	IMF	iPhone
Iran	Lumia	Malaria	Merkel	Modi
Paris	Polio	Poverty	Rome	Russia
San Francisco	Self-driving car	Syria	Tesla	Ukraine
Veteran affairs	World bank	World cup	Xi Jinping	Yosemite

Table 2: MANUAL queries

We probed the search engines during June-July 2014 with the same set of queries at the same time of the day for 21 (17) days for the TRENDS (MANUAL) set. For Google, we used their *custom search API* (code.google.com/apis/console), and for Bing their *search API* (datamarket.azure.com/dataset/bing/ search). Twitter data consists of 1% sample of tweets obtained using Twitter API.

In all cases, we recorded the top-k results. The value of k is set to 10 by default, except in the experiments studying the sensitivity of results to the value of k. Every time, we ran the same code from the same machine having the same IP address to minimize noise in the results. Because we were getting the results programmatically through the API, no cookies were used and there was no browser information used by Google or Bing in producing the results [22].

4.3 Representation of Search Results

While our methodology is independent of the specific representation of search results, we employ the snippets of the search results provided by the search engines for this purpose. The snippet of a search result embodies the search engine's semantic understanding of the corresponding document with respect to the given query. The users also heavily weigh the snippet in deciding whether to click on a search result [34]. The alternative of using URL representation must first address the well-known problems arising from short URLs [5], un-nomalized URLs [31, 32], and different URLs with similar text [6]. Unfortunately, there is no agreed upon way to address them and the specific algorithms deployed can have large impact on the conclusions. Furthermore, the users rarely decide whether to look at a document based on the URL they see on the search result page [34]. In the case of Social Pulse, the entire text of a tweet (including hashtags and URLs, if any) is treated as snippet for this purpose. Snippets and tweet texts respectively have also been used in the study of overlap between the results of web search and social search in [49].

More in detail, for a given result of a particular query, on a given date, we take the bag-of-words representation of the snippet, after eliminating stopwords. Subsequently, a set of results from a particular search engine, for a given query, is simply the union of the respective bag-of-words representations. For TENSORCOMPARE, we keep all words and their frequencies; binary features did not change the trends. For CROSSLEARNCOMPARE, we keep the top-n words and have binary features. Finally, we note that the distribution of the snippet lengths for Google, Bing, and Social Pulse was almost identical for all the queries we tested. This ensures a fair comparison between them.

To assess whether snippets are appropriate for comparing the search results, we conducted the following experiment. We inspect the top result given by Google and Bing for a single day, for each of the queries in both TRENDS and MANUAL datasets. If for a query, the top result points to the same content, we assign the URL similarity score of 1 to this query, and the score of 0 otherwise. We then compute the cosine similarity between the bag-of-word representations of the snippets produced by the two search engines for the same query. Figure 2 shows the outcome of this experiment. Each point in this figure corresponds to one query and

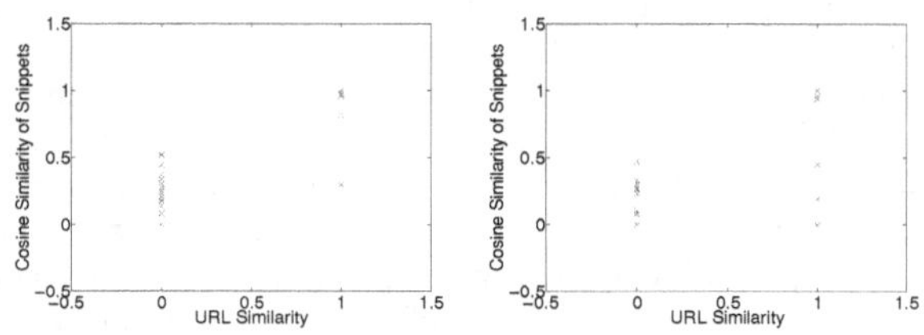

(a) TRENDS query set (b) MANUAL query set

Figure 2: Comparing URL similarity with snippet similarity

We see that for most of the queries for which the snippet similarity is low, the results point to different documents. On the other hand, when this similarity is high, the documents are identical. In both TRENDS and MANUAL, there exist some outliers with pointers to identical documents yet dissimilar snippets. Yet, overall, Fig. 2 indicates that snippets are good vehicles for content comparison.

Note that we do not consider their ordering in our representation of the search results. Instead, we study the sensitivity of our conclusions to the number of top results, including top-1, top-3, and top-5 (in addition to top-10).

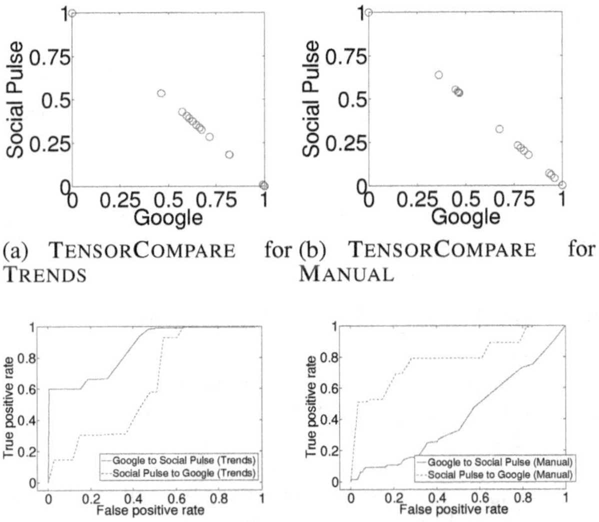

(a) TENSORCOMPARE for TRENDS (b) TENSORCOMPARE for MANUAL

(c) CROSSLEARNCOMPARE for TRENDS (d) CROSSLEARNCOMPARE for MANUAL

Figure 3: Social Pulse vs. Google for top-10 results

	TRENDS →	TRENDS ←	MANUAL →	MANUAL ←
Google- Social Pulse	0.86	0.64	0.42	0.78

Table 3: AUC for CROSSLEARNCOMPARE comparing Google and Social Pulse for top-10 results.

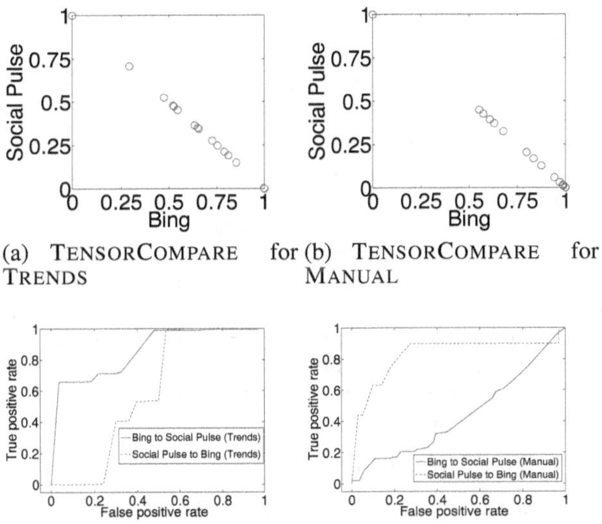

(a) TENSORCOMPARE for TRENDS (b) TENSORCOMPARE for MANUAL

(c) CROSSLEARNCOMPARE for TRENDS (d) CROSSLEARNCOMPARE for MANUAL

Figure 4: Social Pulse vs. Bing for top-10 results

	TRENDS →	TRENDS ←	MANUAL →	MANUAL ←
Bing- Social Pulse	0.86	0.60	0.44	0.83

Table 4: AUC for CROSSLEARNCOMPARE comparing Bing and Social Pulse for top-10 results.

5. FINDINGS

We next present the results of comparing search results of Social Pulse first to that of Google and then Bing.

5.1 Social Pulse Versus Google

Figure 3 and Table 3 show the results. We see in Figs. 3(a), 3(b):

1. There exist a number of results exclusive to either search engine as indicated by multiple points around $(0, 1)$ and $(1, 0)$.
2. For the non-exclusive results, the points are not concentrated on $(0.5, 0.5)$ (which would have indicated similar results), but are rather spread out.

This suggests that Social Pulse and Google provide distinctive results to a great extent.

For the TRENDS dataset in Fig. 3(a), there is a cloud of clusters around $(0.7, 0.3)$, which indicates that Google has greater participation in these results than Social Pulse. Figure 3(c) and AUC in Table 3 also show that using Google to predict Social Pulse works relatively better than the converse for this dataset. This asymmetry suggests that the Twitter users might not retweet much the readily-available, main-stream content on popular topics.

In contrast, for the MANUAL dataset in Fig. 3(b), the non-exclusive points are relatively more dispersed along the line that connects $(0, 1)$ and $(1, 0)$ and there are clusters in which Social Pulse is more prominent. We also find that now predicting Google using Social Pulse works better than the converse (Figs. 3(c) and 3(d)). Collectively, they quantitatively validate the intuition that social networks might have content very different from that indexed by web search engines for non-head queries.

5.2 Social Pulse Versus Bing

We repeated the preceding analysis, but by using Bing search results rather than Google this time. Figure 4 and Table 4 show the results. These results are qualitatively similar to those obtained using Google search results, which is not surprising given the earlier finding that Google and Bing have significant overlap in their search results. However, this sensitivity analysis employing another commercial search engine further reinforces the conclusion that social search can yield results quite different from the ones produced by the conventional Web search.

5.3 Query Level Analysis

In order to gain further insight into mutual predictability of web and social search, we looked at three queries that have the highest and lowest predictability for each search engine and query set, when using CROSSLEARNCOMPARE analysis. Tables 5 and 6 show the results with respect to Google; the insights gained were similar for Bing.

	Google → Social Pulse	Social Pulse → Google
TRENDS	SpongeBob SquarePants	Oprah Winfrey
	Albert Einstein	Maya Angelou
	Tottenham Hotspur F.C.	Albert Einstein
MANUAL	self-driving car	World cup
	gay marriage	gay marriage
	San Francisco	World bank

Table 5: Queries exhibiting highest predictability.

	Google → Social Pulse	Social Pulse → Google
TRENDS	Honda	Game of Thrones
	Antibiotics	Skrillex
	Frozen	Martini
MANUAL	coup	coup
	education	iPhone
	globalization	poverty

Table 6: Queries exhibiting lowest predictability.

We see that the timely queries, like *World cup* or *gay marriage*, have high mutual predictability. Indeed, timeliness creates relevance; the same information gets retweeted and clicked a lot. Queries like *Maya Angelou* and *Albert Einstein* are also highly mutually predictable, in part because people tend to tweet quotes by them, which tend to surface to Web search results as well.

On the other hand, queries such as *globalization* and *poverty* have low predictability. These queries are informational queries with large scope. However, it seems that the content people retweet a lot for these queries is not the same as what is considered authoritative by the web search ranking algorithms. We shall see that the majority of users in our user study found the results by Social Pulse for these queries to be very informative. This suggests a potentially interesting use case of Social Pulse, where the user does not have a crystalized a-priori expectation of the results and the search engine returns a set of results that have been filtered socially.

5.4 Sensitivity Analysis

We repeated our analysis for top-5, top-3 and top-1 search results. The results for Bing exhibited the same trend as Google, so we focus on presenting the results for Google. Figures 5 and Table 7 show the results. Overall we observe that our results are consistent, in terms of showing small overlap between Google and Social Pulse.

We also carried out another experiment in which we took the bottom five results from the top-6 results produced by Social Pulse and treated them as if they were the top-5 results of Social Pulse. We then compared these results to Google's top-5 results. Through this experiment, we wanted to get a handle on the robustness of our conclusions to the variations in Social Pulse's ranking function and the errors in tweet selection. We again found that the trends were preserved. We omit showing actual data.

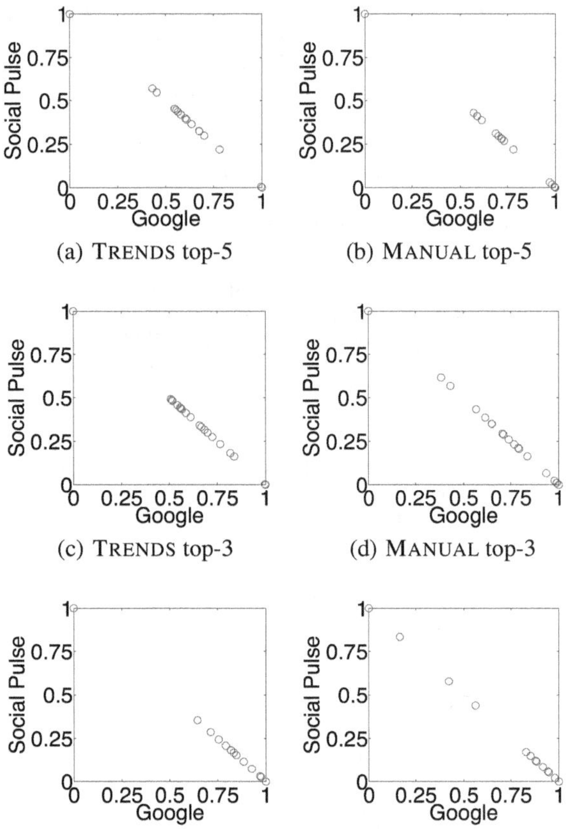

(a) TRENDS top-5 (b) MANUAL top-5

(c) TRENDS top-3 (d) MANUAL top-3

(e) TRENDS top-1 (f) MANUAL top-1

Figure 5: TENSORCOMPARE sensitivity

Google- Social Pulse	TRENDS →	TRENDS ←	MANUAL →	MANUAL ←
top-10	0.86	0.64	0.42	0.78
top-5	0.87	0.70	0.39	0.66
top-3	0.86	0.50	0.35	0.69
top-1	0.79	0.98	0.50	0.53

Table 7: AUC for CROSSLEARNCOMPARE comparing Google and Social Pulse for different number of top results.

5.5 Consistency With TRM Method

Recall our overview of the TRM method [49], given in Section 2. In order to study the consistency between our results with what one would obtain using the TRM method, we conducted another sensitivity experiment. We first apply tensor analysis to the Google and Social Pulse results to obtain their condensed representations. We then compute the centroids for the Google and the Social Pulse results topics, and for every result from Google and Social Pulse (for all queries and days), we compute its cosine similarity to each centroid. While calculating the centroids, we ignore topics that are shared between Google and Social Pulse and keep those that lie on the $(0, 1)$ and $(1, 0)$ points of the TENSORCOMPARE plots. We present the results of this experiments in Table 8.

		To Google centroid	To Social Pulse centroid
TRENDS	From Google result	0.20	0.10
	From Social Pulse result	0.05	0.10
		To Google centroid	To Social Pulse centroid
MANUAL	From Google result	0.22	0.10
	From Social Pulse result	0.05	0.11

Table 8: Similarity from centroids

We again see that Google results in both query sets are more similar to the Google centroid, and Social Pulse results to the Social Pulse centroid. This analysis, this time employing a different method, further reinforces the conclusion that the social search results can be quite different from the conventional Web search results.

6. USER STUDY

So far, we have discovered that the results of Social Pulse are different from Google and Bing. However, one might wonder whether these different results are actually useful, particularly given the apprehension that the content found on Twitter is of low quality [3]. To that end, we conducted a user study on the Amazon Mechanical Turk platform, following the best practices recommended in [1]

6.1 HIT Design

Taking cue from the relevance judgment literature [13], the HIT (Human Intelligence Task) presented to the users consist of a query and a text representing a search result. The users are asked to select whether 1) the text is not informative, 2) the text is informative, or 3) it is hard to tell. They are then asked to explain their answer; any HIT that did not provide this explanation was rejected. Figure 6 shows a sample HIT.

We used the phrase "informative" rather than "relevant" in the instructions, after some initial testing. The choice "not informative" was placed above the positive one to avoid biasing the user's response towards the positive answer. Requiring users to explain their answer turned out to be important: users were forced to have a well justified reason why they selected a particular answer, minimizing random responses and other forms of noise.

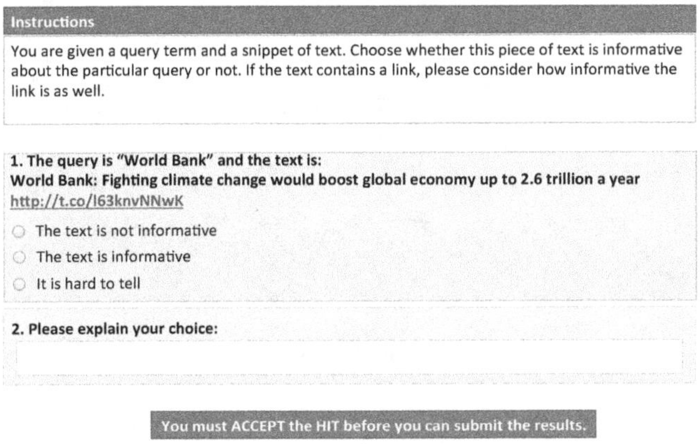
Instructions

You are given a query term and a snippet of text. Choose whether this piece of text is informative about the particular query or not. If the text contains a link, please consider how informative the link is as well.

1. The query is "World Bank" and the text is:
World Bank: Fighting climate change would boost global economy up to 2.6 trillion a year
http://t.co/l63knvNNwK

The text is not informative
The text is informative
It is hard to tell

2. Please explain your choice:

You must ACCEPT the HIT before you can submit the results.

Figure 6: A sample HIT

Considering budget for the study, a subset of the queries were used. Both TRENDS and MANUAL queries were included; the reader can see the complete list in Fig. 10. A HIT was created for every query and each of the top-10 search results for the query. We asked every HIT to be judged by ten users.

6.2 Inter-User Agreement

To ensure there is consistency in the judgments provided by the users, we measured the inter-user agreement using the *Fleiss' kappa* test [20]. In a nutshell, Fleiss' kappa (κ) is a number that indicates the degree of agreement between judges that is statistically significant and not attainable by chance. Its maximum value (for perfect agreement) is 1, and where there is no agreement, it can also take negative values. In exploratory tasks such as ours, a value in the range of 0.2-0.4 shows reasonable agreement and confidence on the results.

Although we had sought 10 judgments for every HIT, the actual deployment yielded the number of good judgments ranging from 4-10. Table 9 shows the κ values for our user study. A column of this table shows the number of search results that were judged exactly by the corresponding number of users as well the κ value. Thus, the column 1 of this table indicates that for twelve of the search results each was judged by exactly four users. We observe that κ is reasonably good in all cases, signifying good inter-user agreement.

# Judges	4	5	6	7	8	9	10
# Results	12	70	92	91	51	25	5
κ	0.19	0.29	0.27	0.26	0.32	0.43	0.22

Table 9: Inter-user agreement. A column of this table provides the number of search results that were judged exactly by the corresponding number of users as well as the κ value.

6.3 Sanity Checks

To further increase our confidence in the conclusions we arrive at, we did two sanity checks: i) visual inspection of the tweets in the result sets, and ii) their quantitative evaluation. We give below the results of both.

6.3.1 *Visual Inspection*

We examined top tweets for which there was high agreement amongst the judges as well as those tweets that had split judgments.

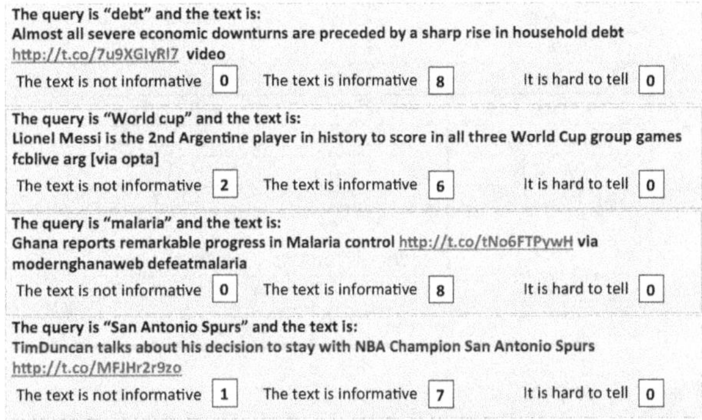
The query is "debt" and the text is:
Almost all severe economic downturns are preceded by a sharp rise in household debt http://t.co/7u9XGlyRl7 video
The text is not informative 0 The text is informative 8 It is hard to tell 0

The query is "World cup" and the text is:
Lionel Messi is the 2nd Argentine player in history to score in all three World Cup group games fcblive arg [via opta]
The text is not informative 2 The text is informative 6 It is hard to tell 0

The query is "malaria" and the text is:
Ghana reports remarkable progress in Malaria control http://t.co/tNo6FTPywH via modernghanaweb defeatmalaria
The text is not informative 0 The text is informative 8 It is hard to tell 0

The query is "San Antonio Spurs" and the text is:
TimDuncan talks about his decision to stay with NBA Champion San Antonio Spurs http://t.co/MFJHr2r9zo
The text is not informative 1 The text is informative 7 It is hard to tell 0

Figure 7: Informative results with high judge agreement

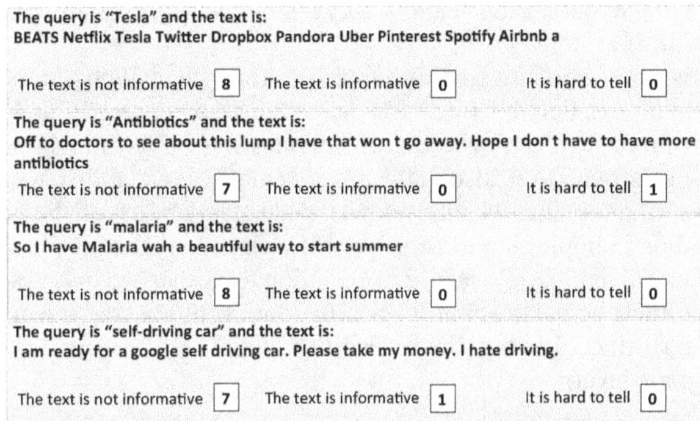
The query is "Tesla" and the text is:
BEATS Netflix Tesla Twitter Dropbox Pandora Uber Pinterest Spotify Airbnb a
The text is not informative 8 The text is informative 0 It is hard to tell 0

The query is "Antibiotics" and the text is:
Off to doctors to see about this lump I have that won t go away. Hope I don t have to have more antibiotics
The text is not informative 7 The text is informative 0 It is hard to tell 1

The query is "malaria" and the text is:
So I have Malaria wah a beautiful way to start summer
The text is not informative 8 The text is informative 0 It is hard to tell 0

The query is "self-driving car" and the text is:
I am ready for a google self driving car. Please take my money. I hate driving.
The text is not informative 7 The text is informative 1 It is hard to tell 0

Figure 8: Not informative results with high judge agreement

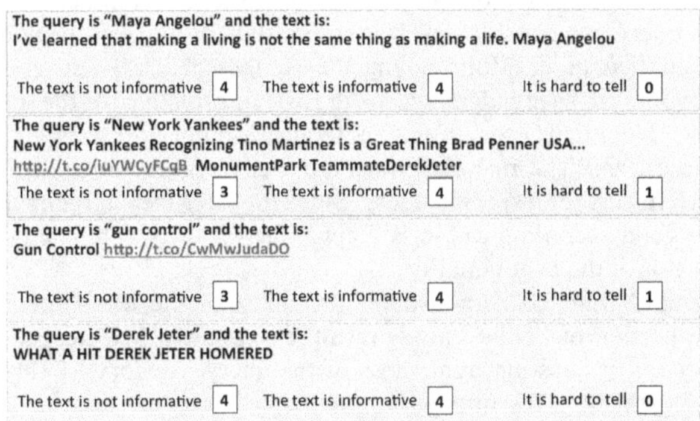
The query is "Maya Angelou" and the text is:
I've learned that making a living is not the same thing as making a life. Maya Angelou
The text is not informative 4 The text is informative 4 It is hard to tell 0

The query is "New York Yankees" and the text is:
New York Yankees Recognizing Tino Martinez is a Great Thing Brad Penner USA... http://t.co/iuYWCyFCqB MonumentPark TeammateDerekJeter
The text is not informative 3 The text is informative 4 It is hard to tell 1

The query is "gun control" and the text is:
Gun Control http://t.co/CwMwJudaDO
The text is not informative 3 The text is informative 4 It is hard to tell 1

The query is "Derek Jeter" and the text is:
WHAT A HIT DEREK JETER HOMERED
The text is not informative 4 The text is informative 4 It is hard to tell 0

Figure 9: Results with poor judge agreement

Figures 7–9 show the top tweets from the two categories for which we had eight judgments each.

It is readily apparent from these figures that the users were quite diligent in arriving at their decisions.

6.3.2 *Readability of the Result Tweets*

It is a common belief that tweets are usually of bad quality, containing a lot of misspellings and illegible terms. But does this belief hold water when we focus on highly retweeted tweets? To quantitatively answer this question, we put the tweets in our result sets through the unix `style` tool. Given a piece of text, this tool computes seven metrics that have been extensively discussed in the literature and applied in practice [17].

Metric	Google	Social Pulse
Kincaid	11.3	7.1
ARI	13.5	9.5
Coleman-Liau	12.9	11.4
Flesch Index	52.9/100	71.2/100
Fog Index	14.2	10.0
SMOG-Grading	12.5	9.6
Lix	49.3 (school year 9)	42.2 (school year 7)

Table 10: Readability of results.

We conducted this study for Google and Social Pulse, for the same set of results that we use for the user study. Due to the nature of the `style` tool, we strip the snippets off any non alpha-numeric character, and we concatenate the snippets of each search engine into a longer passage, and apply `style` to it. The results are shown in Table 10.

It is not surprising that tweets score lower than Web snippets. The latter are derived from Web pages that are generally written much more formally whereas communication on Twitter is relatively informal. Note also that a lower value of a readability metric does not automatically imply lower understandability of the content. For example, the most popular novels are written at the 7th-grade level and people read for recreation texts that are two grades below their actual reading level [26]. Interestingly, we see from Table 10 that Lix pegs the readability of the result tweets at the 7th-grade level.

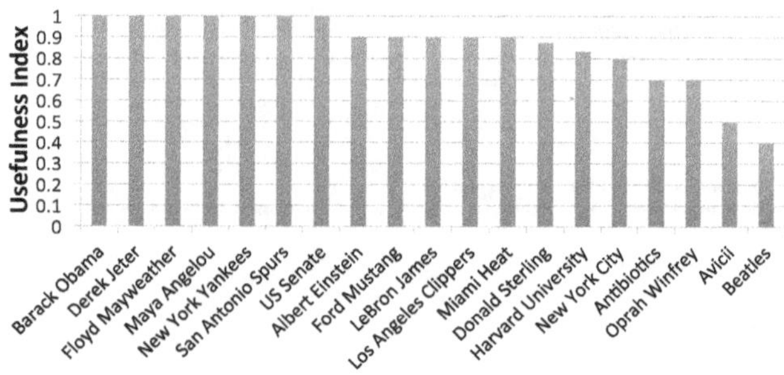

(a) TRENDS

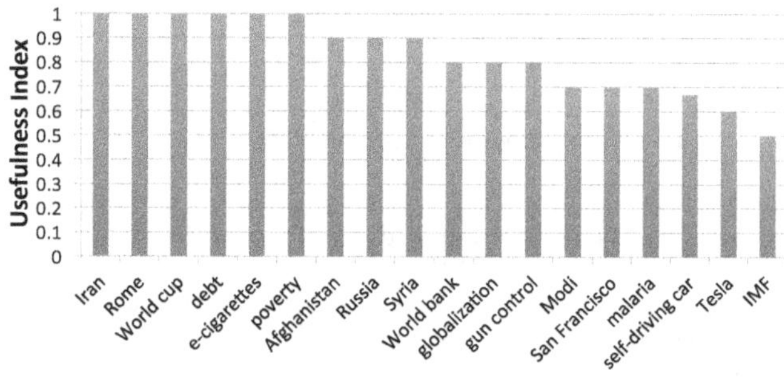

(b) MANUAL

Figure 10: Usefulness index of search results produced by Social Pulse for various queries

6.4 Results of the User Study

We can now finally present the results of our user study. Figure 10 summarizes them. We have plotted the usefulness index separately for each of the queries. For computing the usefulness index for a query, we consider every search result for a query for which we could get at least four judgments. We then check if a strict majority of users have judged the result to be informative for the given query. Note that "hard to tell" is treated as "not informative" for this purpose. The majority votes are then averaged over distinct search results for a specific query. Since the inter-user agreement is quite good according to Fleiss' kappa, the majority vote is a good indicator of the result quality.

Overall, Fig. 10 demonstrates that most of the users found a large portion of Social Pulse's results informative with respect to the query in question, regardless of the query category (TRENDS or MANUAL). This finding is remarkable given the fact that the sole signal we use in order to discover and rank these results is the number of retweets.

7. SUMMARY AND FUTURE WORK

Our major contributions in this work are as follows:

1. Through a rigorous analysis of real data from Google, Bing, and Twitter, we showed that a search engine built using even simple social signals like retweet count can surface tweets whose content is quite different from those provided by the current search engines to the web users. Our extensive user study demonstrated that not only is this content different, but can also be very informative.

   These findings have direct, practical ramifications. Given the central role the commercial search engines play in arbitrating what information is seen by the citizens and the importance of ready access to diverse view points for inculcating an informed citizenry, it behooves the commercial search engines to conduct studies similar to ours in their own infrastructure. They certainly have the financial and computing resources as well as ready availability of data for conducting such explorations and provide the choice of access to diversity to citizens.

2. By successfully reusing the methodology and tools, introduced in [2], for carrying out the present investigation of distinctiveness of social network content from the web content, we reinforced the power of data mining to be able to abstract meaningful insights from massive amount of data.

3. We generated data sets that other researchers might be able to use for making their own discoveries.

Looking ahead, web search engines can start providing search results from social networks in two phases (assuming they see sufficient business imperative for it):

1. Add a social tab to their search result page. Research can contribute by refining algorithms for global and personalized ranking of social results as well as addressing the related infrastructure and environmental issues such as trust and privacy. Other topics for fruitful research include drill down into the differentiating attributes of social results and characterizing the phenomena that underlie the differences [51].

2. Intermix the social results with the web results. Research can contribute by building comprehensive diversity models as well as evaluating and extending algorithms for diversifying search results [13, 33].

Acknowledgements This work was partially done at the erstwhile Microsoft Research in Silicon Valley. E. Papalexakis was partially supported by National Science Foundation Grant IIS-1247489.

8. REFERENCES

[1] *Amazon Mechanical Turk, Requester Best Practices Guide.* Amazon Web Services, June 2011.

[2] R. Agrawal, B. Golshan, and E. Papalexakis. A study of distinctiveness in web results of two search engines. In *24th international conference on World Wide Web, Web Science Track.* ACM, 2015.

[3] O. Alonso, C. Carson, D. Gerster, X. Ji, and S. U. Nabar. Detecting uninteresting content in text streams. In *SIGIR Crowdsourcing for Search Evaluation Workshop*, 2010.

[4] A. Anandkumar, R. Ge, D. Hsu, S. M. Kakade, and M. Telgarsky. Tensor decompositions for learning latent variable models. *Journal of Machine Learning Research*, 15(1):2773–2832, 2014.

[5] D. Antoniades, I. Polakis, G. Kontaxis, E. Athanasopoulos, S. Ioannidis, E. P. Markatos, and T. Karagiannis. we.b: The web of short URLs. In *20th international conference on World Wide Web*, pages 715–724. ACM, 2011.

[6] Z. Bar-Yossef, I. Keidar, and U. Schonfeld. Do not crawl in the DUST: different urls with similar text. *ACM Transactions on the Web*, 3(1):3, 2009.

[7] R. Batool, A. M. Khattak, J. Maqbool, and S. Lee. Precise tweet classification and sentiment analysis. In *IEEE/ACIS 12th international conference on Computer and Information Science*, pages 461–466. IEEE, 2013.

[8] K. Bharat and A. Broder. A technique for measuring the relative size and overlap of public web search engines. *Computer Networks and ISDN Systems*, 30(1):379–388, 1998.

[9] D. M. Blei, A. Y. Ng, and M. I. Jordan. Latent dirichlet allocation. *Journal of Machine Learning Research*, 3:993–1022, 2003.

[10] A. Broder. A taxonomy of web search. *ACM Sigir forum*, 36(2):3–10, 2002.

[11] M. Busch, K. Gade, B. Larson, P. Lok, S. Luckenbill, and J. Lin. Earlybird: Real-time search at Twitter. In *IEEE 28th international conference on Data Engineering*, pages 1360–1369. IEEE, 2012.

[12] C. Castillo, M. Mendoza, and B. Poblete. Information credibility on twitter. In *20th international conference on World Wide Web*, pages 675–684. ACM, 2011.

[13] C. L. A. Clarke, N. Craswell, I. Soboroff, and E. M. Voorhees. Overview of the TREC 2011 web track. Technical report, NIST, 2011.

[14] W. Ding and G. Marchionini. A comparative study of web search service performance. In *ASIS Annual Meeting*, volume 33, pages 136–42. ERIC, 1996.

[15] A. Dong, R. Zhang, P. Kolari, J. Bai, F. Diaz, Y. Chang, Z. Zheng, and H. Zha. Time is of the essence: improving recency ranking using twitter data. In *19th international conference on World Wide Web*, pages 331–340. ACM, 2010.

[16] Y. Duan, L. Jiang, T. Qin, M. Zhou, and H.-Y. Shum. An empirical study on learning to rank of tweets. In *23rd international conference on Computational Linguistics*, pages 295–303. Association for Computational Linguistics, 2010.

[17] W. DuBay. *The principles of readability*. Impact Information, 2004.

[18] E. Enge, S. Spencer, J. Stricchiola, and R. Fishkin. *The art of SEO*. O'Reilly, 2012.

[19] Federal Communications Commission. Editorializing by broadcast licensees. Washington, DC: GPO, 1949.

[20] J. L. Fleiss. Measuring nominal scale agreement among many raters. *Psychological bulletin*, 76(5):378, 1971.

[21] S. Gauch and G. Wang. Information fusion with profusion. In *1st World Conference of the Web Society*, 1996.

[22] A. Hannak, P. Sapiezynski, A. Molavi Kakhki, B. Krishnamurthy, D. Lazer, A. Mislove, and C. Wilson. Measuring personalization of web search. In *22nd international conference on World Wide Web*, pages 527–538. ACM, 2013.

[23] R. A. Harshman. Foundations of the parafac procedure: models and conditions for an" explanatory" multimodal factor analysis. Technical report, UCLA, 1970.

[24] T. Joachims. Optimizing search engines using clickthrough data. In *ACM SIGKDD international conference on Knowledge Discovery and Data mining*, pages 133–142. ACM, 2002.

[25] U. Kang, E. Papalexakis, A. Harpale, and C. Faloutsos. Gigatensor: scaling tensor analysis up by 100 times - algorithms and discoveries. In *18th ACM SIGKDD international conference on Knowledge Discovery and Data mining*, pages 316–324. ACM, 2012.

[26] G. R. Klare and B. Buck. *Know Your Reader: The scientific approach to readability*. Heritage House, 1954.

[27] T. G. Kolda and B. W. Bader. Tensor decompositions and applications. *SIAM review*, 51(3):455–500, 2009.

[28] H. Kwak, C. Lee, H. Park, and S. Moon. What is twitter, a social network or a news media? In *19th international conference on World Wide Web*, pages 591–600. ACM, 2010.

[29] H. W. Lauw, A. Ntoulas, and K. Kenthapadi. Estimating the quality of postings in the real-time web. In *Proc. of SSM conference*, 2010.

[30] S. Lawrence and C. L. Giles. Searching the world wide web. *Science*, 280(5360):98–100, 1998.

[31] S. H. Lee, S. J. Kim, and S. H. Hong. On URL normalization. In *Computational Science and Its Applications–ICCSA 2005*, pages 1076–1085. Springer, 2005.

[32] T. Lei, R. Cai, J.-M. Yang, Y. Ke, X. Fan, and L. Zhang. A pattern tree-based approach to learning URL normalization rules. In *19th international conference on World Wide Web*, pages 611–620. ACM, 2010.

[33] V. Maltese, F. Giunchiglia, K. Denecke, P. Lewis, C. Wallner, A. Baldry, and D. Madalli. *On the interdisciplinary foundations of diversity*. University of Trento, 2009.

[34] M.-C. Marcos and C. González-Caro. Comportamiento de los usuarios en la página de resultados de los buscadores. un estudio basado en eye tracking. *El profesional de la informaciôn*, 19(4):348–358, 2010.

[35] J. Martinez-Romo and L. Araujo. Detecting malicious tweets in trending topics using a statistical analysis of language. *Expert Systems with Applications*, 40(8):2992–3000, 2013.

[36] W. Meng, C. Yu, and K.-L. Liu. Building efficient and effective metasearch engines. *ACM Computing Surveys*, 34(1):48–89, 2002.

[37] K. Nishida, T. Hoshide, and K. Fujimura. Improving tweet stream classification by detecting changes in word probability. In *35th international ACM SIGIR conference on Research and development in information retrieval)*, pages 971–980. ACM, 2012.

[38] K. Purcell, J. Brenner, and L. Rainie. *Search engine use 2012*. Pew Internet & American Life Project, 2012.

[39] M. S. Rahman, T.-K. Huang, H. V. Madhyastha, and M. Faloutsos. Efficient and scalable socware detection in online social networks. In *USENIX Security Symposium*, pages 663–678, 2012.

[40] D. M. Romero, W. Galuba, S. Asur, and B. A. Huberman. Influence and passivity in social media. In *Machine learning and knowledge discovery in databases*, pages 18–33. Springer, 2011.

[41] T. Rowlands, D. Hawking, and R. Sankaranarayana. New-web search with microblog annotations. In *19th international conference on World Wide Web*, pages 1293–1296. ACM, 2010.

[42] I. Santos, I. Miñambres-Marcos, C. Laorden, P. Galán-García, A. Santamaría-Ibirika, and P. G. Bringas. Twitter content-based spam filtering. In *International Joint Conference SOCO'13-CISIS'13-ICEUTE'13*, pages 449–458. Springer, 2014.

[43] E. Selberg and O. Etzioni. Multi-service search and comparison using the metacrawler. In *4th international conference on World Wide Web*, 1995.

[44] A. Spink, B. J. Jansen, C. Blakely, and S. Koshman. A study of results overlap and uniqueness among major web search engines. *Information Processing & Management*, 42(5):1379–1391, 2006.

[45] B. Sriram, D. Fuhry, E. Demir, H. Ferhatosmanoglu, and M. Demirbas. Short text classification in twitter to improve information filtering. In *33rd international ACM SIGIR conference on Research and development in information retrieval*, pages 841–842. ACM, 2010.

[46] N. J. Stroud and A. Muddiman. Exposure to news and diverse views in the internet age. *ISJLP*, 8:605, 2012.

[47] H. Takemura and K. Tajima. Tweet classification based on their lifetime duration. In *21st ACM international conference on Information and knowledge management*, pages 2367–2370. ACM, 2012.

[48] K. Tao, F. Abel, C. Hauff, and G.-J. Houben. Twinder: a search engine for twitter streams. In *Web Engineering*, pages 153–168. Springer, 2012.

[49] J. Teevan, D. Ramage, and M. R. Morris. # twittersearch: a comparison of microblog search and web search. In *4th ACM international conference on Web Search and Data Mining*, pages 35–44. ACM, 2011.

[50] I. Uysal and W. B. Croft. User oriented tweet ranking: a filtering approach to microblogs. In *20th ACM international conference on Information and knowledge management*, pages 2261–2264. ACM, 2011.

[51] W. M. Webberley. *Inferring Interestingness in Online Social Networks*. PhD thesis, Cardiff University, 2014.

[52] R. W. White and S. T. Dumais. Characterizing and predicting search engine switching behavior. In *18th ACM conference on Information and knowledge management*, pages 87–96. ACM, 2009.

[53] M.-C. Yang, J.-T. Lee, S.-W. Lee, and H.-C. Rim. Finding interesting posts in twitter based on retweet graph analysis. In *35th international ACM SIGIR conference on Research and development in information retrieval*, pages 1073–1074. ACM, 2012.

[54] M.-C. Yang and H.-C. Rim. Identifying interesting twitter contents using topical analysis. *Expert Systems with Applications*, 41(9):4330–4336, 2014.

Exploiting Data Mining for Authenticity Assessment and Protection of High-Quality Italian Wines from Piedmont*

Marco Arlorio
Department of Pharmaceutical Sciences
University of Piemonte Orientale
Novara, Italy
marco.arlorio@uniupo.it

Jean Daniel Coisson
Department of Pharmaceutical Sciences
University of Piemonte Orientale
Novara, Italy
jeandaniel.coisson@uniupo.it

Giorgio Leonardi
Computer Science Institute, DiSIT
University of Piemonte Orientale
Alessandria, Italy
giorgio.leonardi@uniupo.it

Monica Locatelli
Department of Pharmaceutical Sciences
University of Piemonte Orientale
Novara, Italy
monica.locatelli@uniupo.it

Luigi Portinale†
Computer Science Institute, DiSIT
University of Piemonte Orientale
Alessandria, Italy
luigi.portinale@uniupo.it

ABSTRACT

This paper discusses the data mining approach followed in a project called TRAQUASWINE, aimed at the definition of methods for data analytical assessment of the authenticity and protection, against fake versions, of some of the highest value *Nebbiolo-based* wines from Piedmont region in Italy. This is a big issue in the wine market, where commercial frauds related to such a kind of products are estimated to be worth millions of Euros. The objective is twofold: to show that the problem can be addressed without expensive and hyper-specialized wine analyses, and to demonstrate the actual usefulness of classification algorithms for data mining on the resulting chemical profiles. Following Wagstaff's proposal for practical exploitation of machine learning (and data mining) approaches, we describe how data have been collected and prepared for the production of different datasets, how suitable classification models have been identified and how the interpretation of the results suggests the emergence of an active role of classification techniques, based on standard chemical profiling, for the assesment of the authenticity of the wines target of the study.

*Authors are listed in alphabetical order.
†Corresponding Author.

KDD '15, August 10-13, 2015, Sydney, NSW, Australia.
 ISBN 978-1-4503-3664-2/15/08...$15.00.
DOI: http://dx.doi.org/10.1145/2783258.2788596.

Categories and Subject Descriptors

I.5.4 [**Computing Methodologies**]: Pattern Recognition—*Applications*; I.5.2 [**Computing Methodologies**]: Pattern Recognition—*Design Methodology*

Keywords

Compliance and Fraud, Multi-label and Multi-class learning

1. INTRODUCTION

The quality and safety profiles of quality wines represent a peculiar case of the notion of *food integrity*, because of the very high value of a single bottle, and because of the complex chemical profile, requiring therefore specific and robust methods for their univocal profiling/authentication. *Vitis vinifera* is the unique grape allowed for the winemaking, but many different genetic varieties (e.g. *Pinot, Nebbiolo, Merlot, Sangiovese, Sirah* and many others) lead to wines with different character and chemical profiles. The industrial processing largely build the wine specificity.

Moreover, the "terroir" (the set of special characteristics that the geography, the geology and the microclimate of a certain region or peculiar location, interacting with grape genetics, express in wine), while bringing to the diversification of the product, complicates significantly the wine chemical profiling under the metabolomics profile and, thus, the process of traceability and identification.

Although specific regulations exist in this matter, and some analytical approaches and protocols are well established for wine tracking and authentication, quality wines are highly subjected to adulteration. Problems with consumption fraud go back a very long time; more or less recently, numerous cases of wine adulteration were worldwide registered, including Austria, France and Italy. Wine fraud is then a big issue worldwide, inducing significant problems for consumers; it also triggers destabilization of the wine market, particularly regarding the quality aspect, with an estimated impact of about 7% of the whole market value.

Although wine can suffer for different type of frauds and different type of counterfeiting, the predominant problem in wine sector is mislabeling, regarding both the used cultivar of grape and the geographical area of origin; it causes an economical impact estimated to be several million of Euros.

The detection of adulterations or declarations which do not correspond to the labeling are actually official tasks of wine quality control and consumer protection. During the last years, analytical methods have been improved in this field. Some of them (stable isotope ratio analysis by nuclear magnetic resonance, and isotope ratio mass spectrometry) have been adopted as official methods by the European Community (EC). In addition, the use of the corresponding analytical devices is expensive and requires a lot of specialization. Moreover, these methods, while playing a key role in detecting adulterations like addition of water and inadmissible sweetening, represent a challenge also regarding the identification of origin, requiring in this case a very large data base.

Non analytical approaches like olograms, trasponder systems or QR codes only partially address the problem of wine authenticity. Finally, regulations, good manufacturing practices and traceability procedures are not always sufficient to guarantee the wine authenticity, considering the falsification of both varietal and geographic origin. For these reasons, a challenge for wine authenticity is to obtain standard analytical procedures to describe a wine proof-of-identity, which could defend consumers from illegal adulteration practices, as well as from unintentional mislabeling due to mistakes during wine production.

There are then two analytical levels: the *chemical* one, concerning the identification of the most relevant standard chemical analyses to perform, and the *data* one, concerning the determination of the relevant data mining and analysis techniques exploiting the features obtained from the chemical level. From the data mining perspective, the main goal of the work is to show that well-established methodologies of classification, from machine learning, can be suitably adopted to fullfill the task of controlling specific wine adulterations, and consequently be capable of generating added value to the quality control process of such high-quality wines.

In the paper we will discuss the experience gained in the TRAQUASWINE project, having as a major goal the assessment of the authenticity and the protection against fake versions of some of the highest quality (and often top priced) *Nebbiolo-based* wines like *Barolo, Barbaresco* and *Gattinara.* Following Wagstaff's scheme [16], we discuss how data have been collected, how they have been prepared, how suitable classification models have been identified and how the interpretation of the results suggests the emergence of an active role of classification techniques, based on standard chemical profiling, for the assesment of the authenticity of the high-quality wines which were target of the study.

The remainder of the paper is organized as follows: section 2 presents the main objectives and the data collection and preparation steps of the study; section 3 discusses the characterization of the data and of the classification algorithms adopted, by presenting results on different datasets with different sets of features; section 4 compares the approach to related works finally, section 5 presents the conclusions, by pointing out to some future evolutions.

2. THE TRAQUASWINE STUDY

2.1 Main Objectives

The TRAQUASWINE project involved both industrial and academic partners in the creation of a network operating in the wine sector, with the aim to trace and authenticate the origin, quality and safety of Piedmont (Italy) wines, with particular interest to high-value and high-quality *Nebbiolo-based* wines. In this context, the principal goals of the project were:

- to define the major characteristics (*chemotype*, with particular interest on bioactive compounds) of Nebbiolo grape and derived wines, identifying molecular markers useful for quality control and wine traceability;
- to establish a comprehensive analytical approach, based on the exploitation of data mining techniques for multivariate analysis to chemotype datasets, useful to the traceability and authentication of high-quality *Nebbiolo-based* wines, produced in different area of Piedmont, by diverse wineries.

The selection of chemical parameters and methods was performed by taking into account two main criteria:

- economical cost of the analyses (particularly regarding the required instrumentation);
- the capacity to work also with common chemical parameters, avoiding the need of pluriannual consolidated databases, as often required by classical isotopic methods.

Important feature has been the use of data of different origin, by considering different producers, different areas of production, different typology of wine (i.e., commercial wines on the market, as well as "model" wines explicitily produced for the study) and different aging of the product. A peculiar approach (use of some *Nebbiolo* wines spiked with different percentages of different wines) was finally exploited in order to check the possibility to highlight the illegal adding of a foreign grape cultivar, so detecting potential frauds.

2.2 Data Collection

Commercial samples of Piedmont *Nebbiolo-based* wines were provided by nine local wineries; producers themselves certified wine's origin and identity. Eight different types of wines at different aging degree (selected on the basis of the mean aging of each type of wine and depending on their commercial availability) were considered. Among them, *Barbaresco* (BRB), *Barolo* (BRL), *Langhe* (LAN), *Nebbiolo d'Alba* (NEB) and *Roero* (ROE) are typical wine productions of the Alba district in Southern Piedmont, while *Gattinara* (GAT), *Ghemme* (GHE) and *Sizzano* (SIZ) are produced in Northern Piedmont (Novara province). The distribution of samples (spanning a period of 10 wine years) resulted in 18 samples of BRB, 18 samples of BRL, 12 samples of LAN, 18 samples of NEB, 6 samples of ROE, 6 samples of GAT, 18 samples of GHE and 6 sample of SIZ. BRL, BRB, GAT, NEB and ROE were certified as produced from 100% Nebbiolo grape, while the other wines contained percentages of different grape varieties (having however Nebbiolo as the primary grape variety).

Beside such commercial wines, a set of experimental wines (model wines) has been specifically prepared, resulting in 56 additional samples. Among them, 12 samples correspond to wines produced without Nebbiolo grape, and in particular with 100% of some grape varieties partially present in some of LAN commercial wines; we labeled them as NON (*NO Nebbiolo*); 26 samples were prepared as more LAN and NEB wines, for a final count (commercial and experimental) of 22 samples of LAN and 34 samples of NEB; 8 samples were prepared as a correct mix for GHE, resulting in a total of 26 samples of GHE. Finally, the remaining experimental wines were produced to model incorrect (i.e., not allowed by the disciplinary of production) blends for GAT wine, resulting in 10 more samples that we labeled as BLE (*Blend*).

As mentioned earlier, the main goal of the study was to develop and assess analytical techniques (both at the chemical and data levels) to effectively support the authenticity of high-value *Nebbiolo-based* wines. To this end, we organized the study as follows: we selected some of the most valued 100%-nebbiolo wines as the high quality class to be protected from fakes, and in particular BRL, BRB and GAT; we also selected LAN and BLE as control wines, the former to simulate not allowed blend for BRL and BRB, and the latter for GAT. We obtained a total of 146 samples with 9 types of wines (i.e., the classes) that we have used to train and test our models. We reserved the 12 samples of NON wines as additional control wines, to test the response of the learned models with respect to simulated fake wines with the absence of Nebbiolo grape, and with the additional complication that no such a kind of wines have been used in the training of the models.

2.3 Data Preparation

Wine samples were mainly characterized for their phenolic composition. The phenolic component of wine is very complex and heterogeneous, and is strongly influenced by several factors related to grape polyphenol composition winemaking procedures, wine aging, and storage conditions. In the present study, we decided to employ common and relatively economic analytical techniques, as well as methods easily reproducible. The adopted analytical (chemical) procedures can be categorized as follows:

- *spectrophotometric methods*, which include not specific and low-cost assays, useful to quantify general class of compounds (total polyphenols, total anthocyans and total tannins) and antioxidant activity;
- *chromatographic methods*, which are more advanced and specific , but are time-consuming and require more expensive instrumentations, which are however generally available in the standardly equipped laboratories for quality control. The chromatographic techniques were employed for the identification and quantification of individual polyphenol compounds in wines.

Considering spectrophotometric methods, the total phenol content is an unspecific parameter; however, due to the complexity of wine's phenolic component, it can be considered an interesting general information. Total anthocyans and total tannins are other peculiar characteristics of wines, related to their organoleptic properties. Antioxidant activity, for which do not exist official methods recommended by international organization for wine analysis , was measured using a rapid chemical model system for the determination of antiradical properties (DPPH assay).

The chromatographic techniques are useful tools to fingerprint wine polyphenols, identifying individual molecules. In this study, different class of compounds were considered: anthocyanins, phenolic acids, hydroxycinnamates and flavonoids. Some of them have been calculated not only as absolute concentrations, but also as relative percentages.

Finally, wine samples were analyzed for the content of resveratrol (both *trans* and *cis* form), important molecule for its beneficial effects on human health, and considered as one of the major compounds responsible for the well-known French Paradox (the fact that French people, having red wines in their dietary habits, have a relatively low incidence of coronary heart disease, while having a diet relatively rich in saturated fats).

3. THE DATA MINING FRAMEWORK

3.1 Data Characterization

From the chemical analyses described in section 2.3, a total of 40 continuous features have been extracted. Besides those described in section 2.3, also wine acidity (the *pH*) and information about the percentage of some grape varieties have been added. Missing values were present in about 1/3 of the dataset, essentially in association with the latter set of attributes (percentage of grape varieties). As reported in section 2.2, we have then obtained a dataset of 146 instances, each one corresponding to a particular class (i.e. the wine type) out of 9 possible classes, and having 40 numerical (continuous) attributes.

We have organized the evaluation of the data mining experimental study as follows. First of all, we have searched for regularities in the profiles of the available wine chemical analyses by means of some *clustering* algorithms. In particular, we tested EM clustering (both with a free number of clusters and with a number of required clusters equal to the number of classes) and a *K-mean* algorithm ($K = 9$). As expected, no definite interpretation of the results have emerged from unsupervised data analysis, suggesting that regularities associated to wines should be better captured through supervised methods.

We then considered classification approaches, by having in mind that the goal of the data mining process was mainly to characterize the misclassification of the target wines, that is high-quality wines (BRL, BRB and GAT) and control wines (LAN and BLE). Thus general classification accuracy has been considered of secondary importance. To test classification approaches, we considered three different data sets: dataset D1 containing all the 146 instances with the whole set of 40 features; dataset D2 containing the 146 instances with a reduced set of 15 features, obtained by automatic feature selection; dataset D3 containing the 146 instances with the set of features of D2 manually reduced to 13 attributes, and in particular by removing all the attributes concerning the percentage of grape varieties which survived automatic feature selection.

We have experimented the learning of the following type of classifiers:

1. A Bayesian Network classifier (BN), with learning performed with standard Cooper/Herskovits algorithm [3], allowing a maximum of 3 parents per node, identifying

	Accuracy	Kappa
BN	87%	0.85
MLP	94%	0.93
SMO	92%	0.91

Table 1: Accuracy and KAPPA statistic for dataset D1.

dependencies among the attributes and thus avoiding the Naive Bayes assumption.

2. A Support Vector Machine (SVM) based on Sequential Minimal Optimization algorithm (SMO) [10] with a Pearson Universal Kernel (PUK) having Lorentzian peak shape [14], and with Platt scaling in such a way to get a probability distribution over the classes [11][1].

3. A Multi-Layer Perceptron (MLP) with one hidden layer of $n = \frac{f+c}{2}$ hidden units (being f the number of features and c the number of classes)

We also experimented with a lazy learner based on 1-NN classification, and with a Decision Tree learner based on the C4.5 algorithm; since this two types of classifier did not perform well for our task, we do not report the corresponding results in the paper.

The BN, SMO and MLP classifier have been learned using the 146 samples and evaluated by means of a 10-fold cross validation. As mentioned before, the main focus was not on general accuracy (even if definitely an important measure), but rather to check the performance of the classifiers with respect to the classes of high-quality wines (BRL, BRB and GAT) and control wines (LAN and BL), by looking at their possible misclassifications.

We have exploited WEKA's algorithms to perform our experimentation[7], and multi-class classification has been perfomed as a *one-agaist-all* approach. In the following subsections we will discuss the results obtained on each of the above datasets.

3.2 Complete Feature Set

In this part we discuss the results obtained by using the whole set of features obtained after the chemical analyses performed on the available wine samples (dataset D1). Table 1 reports the general accuracy and KAPPA statistic of the three classifiers. It can be noticed that the general accuracy (and its significance as measured by KAPPA statistics) is rather high, with the MLP classifier being the most accurate and slightly better than SMO. Figure 1, figure 2 and Figure 3 report the prediction statistics with respect to the classes of interest for BN, MLP and SMO classifier respectively. We also report Matthews Correlation Coefficient (MCC) and F1-measure, with MCC being more significant in our case, since the number of "positive" instances (those of the target class) are much less that the number of "negative" instances (those of all the other classes). Concerning control wines (LAN and BLE), we can notice that classification accuracy is very good, but more importantly, no control wine is misclassified as a high-quality one; on the other hand,

[1]The regularization parameter (a.k.a complexity) has been set to 10, since we are dealing with a multi-class problem with 9 different classes, and it is a good practice to set the parameter close to the number of classes [9].

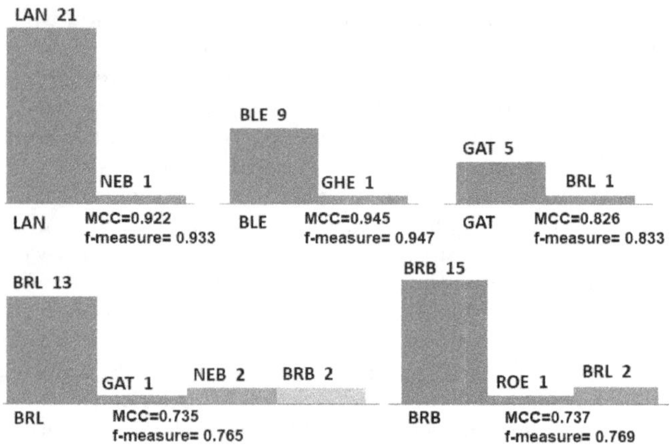

Figure 1: Predictions BN classifier, dataset D1

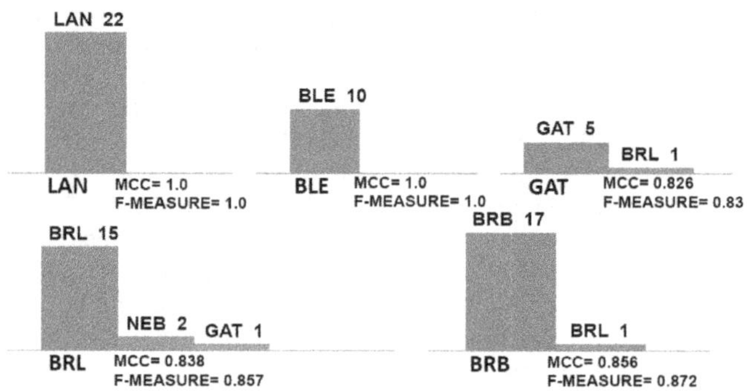

Figure 2: Predictions MLP classifier, dataset D1

high-quality wines (BRL, BRB and GAT) are also recognized very well, with no misclassification predicting control wines. From the diagrams, we can also notice that each misclassification is also not really surprising: for instance in every classifier, BRB is misclassified either as BRL (a very similar wine from the point of view of origin, production and grape composition) or as ROE, which is another 100% Nebbiolo wine. MLP has a perfect performance on control wines (no misclassification). SMO has a misclassification on BLE (but with the other control class LAN) and a perfect classification on BRL (definitely the most valued wine of the set).

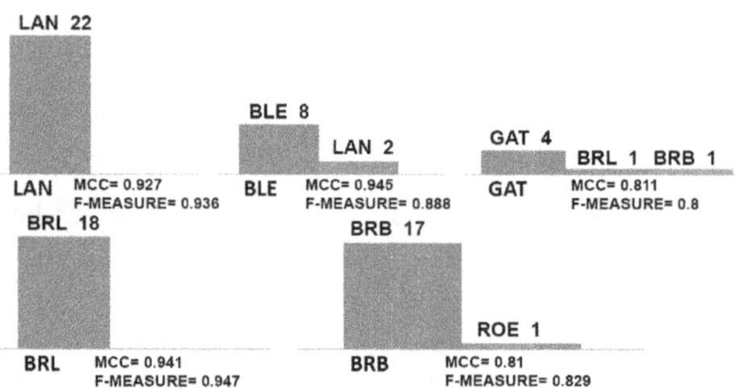

Figure 3: Predictions SMO classifier, dataset D1

	Probability distribution of misclassified predictions								
True Ground	GHE	GAT	SIZ	NEB	BRL	ROE	BRB	LAN	BLE
LAN	0	0	0.02	**0.914**	0	0.056	0.024	0.002	0.002
BLE	**0.893**	0	0	0	0	0	0	0	0.107
GAT	0	0.055	0	0.001	**0.944**	0	0	0	0
BRL	0	**0.827**	0	0.015	0.158	0	0	0	0
	0	0.019	0	**0.918**	0.015	0.048	0	0	0
	0	0.001	0	**0.976**	0.006	0.017	0	0	0
	0	0	0	0.002	0.351	0	**0.647**	0	0
	0	0	0	0	0.299	0	**0.701**	0	0
BRB	0	0	0	0.001	0	**0.898**	0.101	0	0
	0	0	0	0	**0.971**	0	0.029	0	0
	0	0	0	0.192	**0.736**	0	0.072	0	0

Table 2: Probability distribution of misclassifications, dataset D1: BN classifier.

	Probability distribution of misclassified predictions								
True Ground	GHE	GAT	SIZ	NEB	BRL	ROE	BRB	LAN	BLE
GAT	0.003	0.277	0	0.266	**0.449**	0.001	0.003	0	0
BRL	0	0	0	**0.585**	0.408	0.007	0	0	0
	0	0	0	**0.559**	0.437	0.003	0	0	0
	0.089	**0.600**	0	0.008	0.302	0.001	0	0	0
BRB	0	0.003	0	0.001	**0.933**	0.003	0.059	0	0

Table 3: Probability distribution of misclassifications, dataset D1: MLP classifier.

Considering the classes of interest, we also computed, for each classifier, the probability distribution on the predictions that are misclassified. Table 2, table 3 and table 4 show the results for classifiers BN, MLP and SMO respectively. The prediction performed by the classifier corresponds to the entry shown in boldface (the largest probability of prediction). By inspecting such distributions, we confirm the good performance of the classifiers, with MLP and SMO being almost equivalent and sligthly better than BN. All classifiers agree with a very high confidence that a high-quality wine cannot be confused with a control wine (see last two columns of the tables in the rows of high-quality wines). We can also notice that distributions obtained from MLP and SMO are in general less skewed than those of BN, showing more "caution" in the actual prediction, but also very good performance on predicting control wines. For instance SMO, having two misclassification on BLE, predicts BLE as the second most probable class and estimates a probability close to 0 to high-quality wines (exactly 0 for GAT).

As a final investigation on D1, we tested the classifiers using a test set TS composed by the 12 instances of NON wines resulting as discussed in section 2.2. Differently from the wine samples used for training the classifiers, the wine samples in TS do not contain any part of Nebbiolo grape; this implies that acceptable predictions can be those selecting our control wines (LAN and BLE) which are the ones containing parts of the grape varieties contained in the wine samples of TS; in particular, LAN is also a preferred predictions than BLE, because of the way NON wine samples have been prepared. The results are shown in figure 4. SMO shows very reasonable predictions, by identifying very precisely the only class (LAN) containing percentages of the grapes present in the test cases of TS. By considering all the results, we can conclude that, on dataset D1, SMO appears to be the best globally performing classifier.

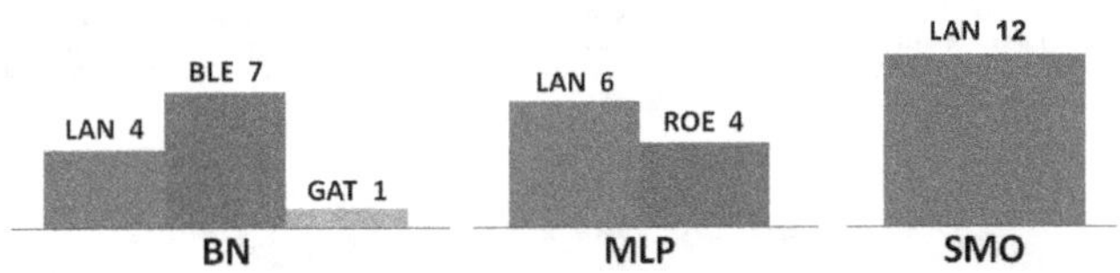

Figure 4: Predictions of NON wines, dataset D1

3.3 Automatic Feature Selection

The second round of experiments we have perfomed takes into account the relevance of the available features of the wine samples, with respect to our target classification task. To this extent, we constructed and evaluated the same set of classifiers considered in section 3.2, but on a dataset with a reduced set of features. In particular, we have perfomed a correlation-based feature selection with sequential forward-backward selection on the original feature space [12, 8], resulting in the selection of 15 analytical attributes out of 40[2]. In particular, all the features representing grape variety percentage, but those of *Nebbiolo* and *Uva Rara* were removed by feasture selection, together with a set of redundant information about polyphenols that were initially provided both as absolute concentrations and relative percentages. As already mentioned, the resulting dataset will be refferred as D2. Table 5 reports the general accuracy and KAPPA statistic of the three classifiers for dataset D2. Results show again a good and significant global accuracy, this time with SMO slightly better than MLP. Figure 5, figure 6 and Figure 7 report the prediction statistics with

[2] An approach based on a PCA transformation of the feature space has also been investigated in the study, with results and considerations similar to those reported in the present papers for the other alternatives.

	Probability distribution of misclassified predictions								
True Ground	GHE	GAT	SIZ	NEB	BRL	ROE	BRB	LAN	BLE
BLE	0.004	0	0	0.117	0.016	0	0.013	**0.599**	0.251
	0.005	0	0	0.154	0.018	0	0.027	**0.620**	0.176
GAT	0.036	0.254	0	0.010	**0.624**	0	0.073	0.002	0.001
	0.014	0.342	0	0.021	0.187	0	**0.433**	0.002	0.001
BRB	0	0	0	0	**0.989**	0	0.011	0	0

Table 4: Probability distribution of misclassifications, dataset D1: SMO classifier.

	Accuracy	Kappa
BN	83%	0.80
MLP	89%	0.87
SMO	90%	0.88

Table 5: Accuracy and KAPPA statistic for dataset D2.

respect to the classes of interest for BN, MLP and SMO classifier respectively. Concerning control wines, we can

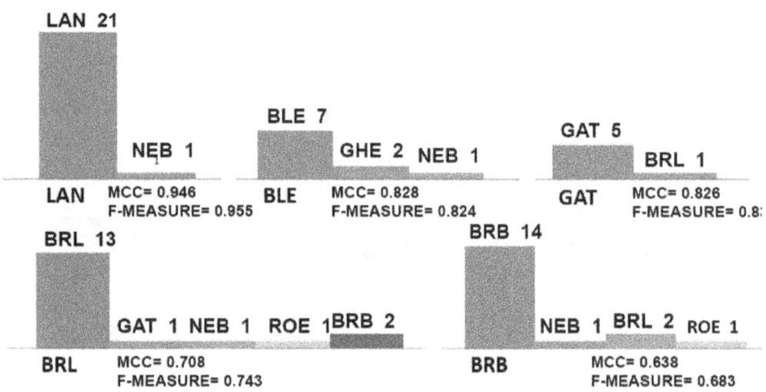

Figure 5: Predictions BN classifier, dataset D2

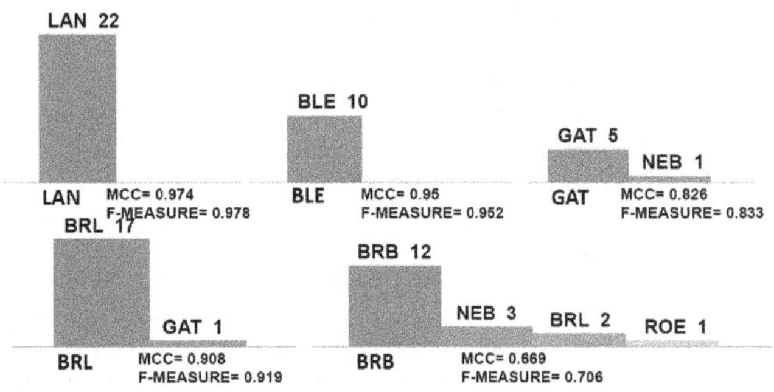

Figure 6: Predictions MLP classifier, dataset D2

notice again a very good classification with high accuracy and no control wine misclassified as a high-quality one; on the other side, high-quality wines are also recognized well (SMO has a perfect prediction on GAT), with no misclassification predicting control wines. As in the previous case, misclassifications can in general be suitably justified: the most interesting result is provided by SMO, where BRL and BRB are each other confused in the corresponding misclassification (which is something definitely acceptable).

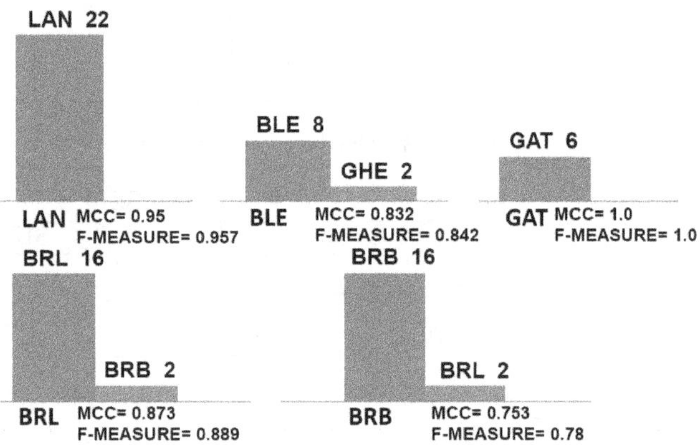

Figure 7: Predictions SMO classifier, dataset D2

As in the case of dataset D1, we also computed, for each classifier, the probability distribution on the predictions that are misclassified, by focusing on the classes of interest. Table 6, table 7 and table 8 show the results for classifiers BN, MLP and SMO respectively. Again, the prediction performed by the classifier corresponds to the entry shown in boldface.

A problem can be noticed in the BN classifier, where the first misclassification of BRB has a a prediction on BLE with a 29% probability, even if the most probable predicted class is NEB. MLP is showing no misclassifications for control wines, even if there are 6 misclassifications of BRB; however, three of them have exactly BRB as the second most probable prediction (with a 48% probability in one case and more than 30% in the others), while the predictions of control wines are either 0 or very close to 0. Concerning SMO, the confusion of BLE with GHE is justified by the fact that samples corresponding to such instances represented mixtures very close to the blend allowed for GHE, while confusion of BRL with BRB and vice versa are justified by the very high similarity of the two wines (as already mentioned).

Finally, we tested the classifiers learned using D2 using the test set TS of NON wines, resulting in the predictions graphically reported in figure 8. BN's prediction appears

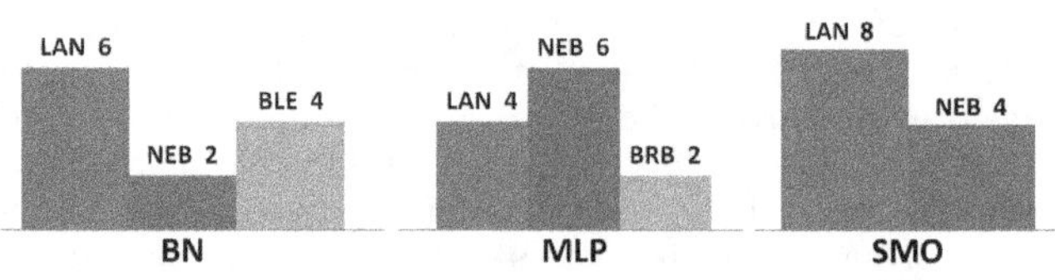

Figure 8: Predictions of NON wines, dataset D2

	Probability distribution of misclassified predictions								
True Ground	GHE	GAT	SIZ	NEB	BRL	ROE	BRB	LAN	BLE
LAN	0	0.002	0.017	**0.917**	0	0.001	0.058	0	0.004
BLE	**0.704**	0	0	0	0	0	0	0	0.295
	0.620	0	0	0	0	0	0	0	0.380
	0.061	0	0	**0.613**	0	0	0	0	0.326
GAT	0	0.017	0	0.101	**0.873**	0.001	0.008	0	0
BRL	0.006	**0.580**	0	0.007	0.406	0	0	0	0
	0	0	0	**0.727**	0.272	0	0	0	0
	0	0.006	0.001	0.066	0.270	**0.467**	0.188	0	0
	0	0	0	0	0.442	0	**0.558**	0	0
	0	0	0	0	0.227	0	**0.772**	0	0
BRB	0	0.007	0	**0.515**	0.056	0	0.128	0.006	0.287
	0.002	0.001	0	0.080	**0.649**	0	0.254	0	0.013
	0	0	0	0	**0.968**	0	0.032	0	0
	0	0	0	0.009	0	**0.991**	0	0	0

Table 6: Probability distribution of misclassifications, dataset D2: BN classifier.

	Probability distribution of misclassified predictions								
True Ground	GHE	GAT	SIZ	NEB	BRL	ROE	BRB	LAN	BLE
GAT	0.002	0.270	0	**0.711**	0.002	0	0.014	0.001	0
BRL	0.068	**0.475**	0	0.008	0.422	0	0.026	0	0
BRB	0	0.012	0	**0.637**	0.001	0	0.349	0	0
	0	0	0	**0.575**	0.003	0.41	0	0	0.011
	0	0.003	0	**0.516**	0	0.001	0.48	0	0
	0.007	0	0	0	**0.691**	0	0.302	0	0
	0	0.015	0	0.001	**0.952**	0.023	0.009	0	0
	0	0	0	0.195	0.007	**0.773**	0	0	0.025

Table 7: Probability distribution of misclassifications, dataset D2: MLP classifier.

	Accuracy	Kappa
BN	79%	0.75
MLP	82%	0.79
SMO	89%	0.87

Table 9: Accuracy and KAPPA statistic for dataset D3.

more reasonable than in the case of D1 (no high-quality wine prediction, even if NEB predictions are not very well justified); MLP's predictions have a problem in the two cases where the sample is recognized as a BRB (in both cases with a rather high probability); SMO's predictions are quite good, even if NEB predictions shows an identification problem on the corresponding samples.

To summarize, also in this situation (i.e., using D2 for training), SMO resulted to be perfoming in general better than the other classifiers.

3.4 Automatic and Manual Feature Selection

A third round of experiments concerned the manual elimination, from the dataset D2, of the information concerning the percentage of grape variety. This resulted in another dataset (D3) with a total of 13 attributes. Table 9 reports the general accuracy and KAPPA statistic of the three classifiers for dataset D3. The accuracy of each classifier slightly reduces again with respect to the previous cases, and SMO results better than MLP, with the lowest accuracy obtained by BN (as in the use of D2). Figure 9, figure 10 and Figure 11 report the prediction statistics with respect to the classes of interest for BN, MLP and SMO classifier respectively. As in the previous cases, no control wine is predicted

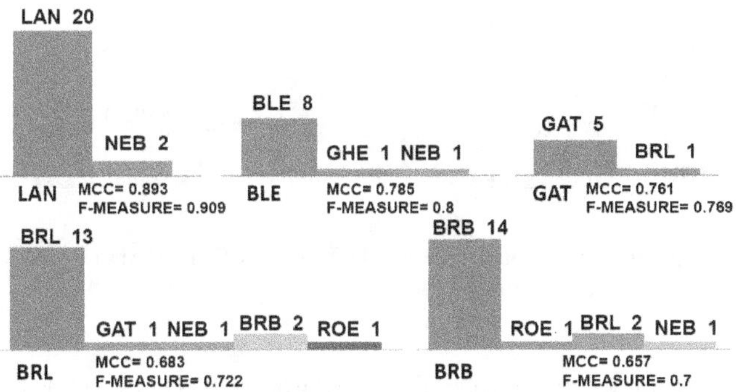

Figure 9: Predictions BN classifier, dataset D3

as a high-quality wine and vice versa. SMO has exactly the same (good) performance as in the case of D2, and also BN produce almost the same results. MLP slightly augment the number of misclassifications, but is still performing better than BN. Thus, the complete elimination of the grape percentages from the dataset does not seem to influence too much the cross validation performance of the classifiers we considered (it is worth noting that in 1/3 of the samples such data were already missing).

	Probability distribution of misclassified predictions								
True Ground	GHE	GAT	SIZ	NEB	BRL	ROE	BRB	LAN	BLE
BLE	**0.990**	0	0	0	0	0	0	0	0.009
	0.962	0	0	0	0	0	0	0	0.037
BRL	0	0	0	0.002	0.199	0	**0.799**	0	0
	0	0	0	0.004	0.358	0	**0.638**	0	0
BRB	0	0	0	0	**0.936**	0	0.063	0	0.013
	0	0	0	0.001	**0.936**	0	0.063	0	0

Table 8: Probability distribution of misclassifications, dataset D2: SMO classifier.

	Probability distribution of misclassified predictions								
True Ground	GHE	GAT	SIZ	NEB	BRL	ROE	BRB	LAN	BLE
LAN	0	0	0	**0.566**	0	0.002	0.002	0.43	0
	0	0	0.005	**0.955**	0	0.001	0.032	0.001	0.005
BLE	**0.611**	0	0	0.002	0	0	0	0	0.387
	0.037	0	0	**0.632**	0.001	0	0	0.015	0.314
GAT	0	0.017	0.001	0.08	**0.893**	0	0.008	0	0
BRL	0.209	**0.419**	0.013	0.004	0.354	0	0	0	0
	0	0	0.001	**0.718**	0.281	0.	0	0	0
	0.011	0	0	0	0.481	0	**0.508**	0	0
	0	0	0	0	0.237	0	**0.763**	0	0
	0	0.037	0.051	0.151	0.313	**0.324**	0.119	0.005	0
BRB	0	0	0	0.009	0	**0.991**	0	0	0
	0.072	0	0	0.035	**0.846**	0	0.044	0	0.004
	0	0	0	0	**0.979**	0	0.021	0	0
	0.01	0.012	0.002	**0.611**	0.086	0	0.186	0.009	0.084

Table 10: Probability distribution of misclassifications, dataset D3: BN classifier.

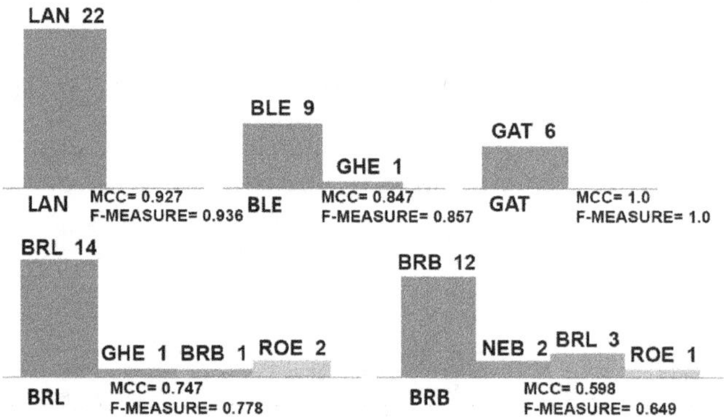

Figure 10: Predictions MLP classifier, dataset D3

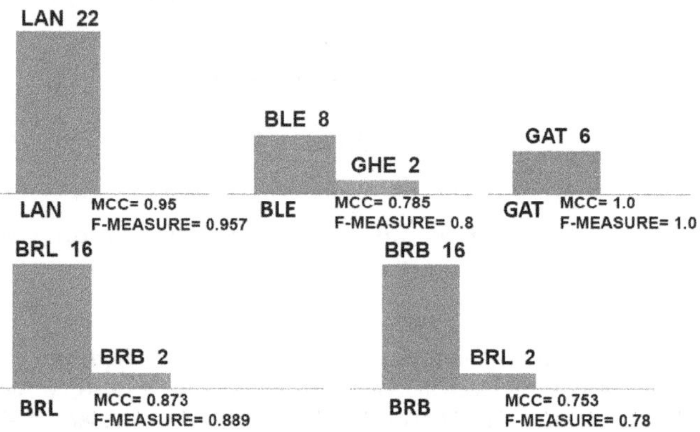

Figure 11: Predictions SMO classifier, dataset D3

Again, as in the case of other datasets, we computed, for each classifier, the probability distribution on the predictions that are misclassified, by focusing on the classes of interest. Table 10, table 11 and table 12 show the results for classifiers BN, MLP and SMO respectively (prediction performed by the classifier corresponding to the boldface entry). It can be noticed the very good performance of SMO, that in case of BRB and BRL (the only high-quality wines having misclassifications) shows a null probability of predicting control wines and in one prediction of BRB (the second misclassification of BRB) has a 31% probability of predicting the correct wine (against a 64% probability of confusing it with the similar BRB). Finally, predictions on BLE (the only misclassified control wine) shows a null or close to null probability of predicting high-quality wines.

Also in this case we finally tested the classifiers learned with D3, using the test set TS of NON wines; results are summurized in figure 12. These results shows that SMO is definitely more robust and stable with respect to the others in presence of control wines on which the classifier was not trained; this proposes, together with the previous results, SMO as the best performing approach on D3 as well.

To conclude, the results of the experiments suggest that standard chemical profiling of Piedmont *Nebbiolo-based* wines, coupled with data mining classification techniques, can be a powerful tool to authenticate high-quality and high-value

	Probability distribution of misclassified predictions								
True Ground	GHE	GAT	SIZ	NEB	BRL	ROE	BRB	LAN	BLE
BLE	**0.471**	0	0.076	0	0.005	0	0	0	0.447
BRL	**0.862**	0.095	0.001	0.001	0.039	0	0	0.002	0
	0.383	0.012	0	0	0.014	0	**0.518**	0	0.072
	0	0	0.21	0	0.064	**0.69**	0.036	0.001	0
	0	0	0.118	0	0.278	**0.59**	0.014	0	0
BRB	0	0	0.025	**0.641**	0.233	0.095	0	0.001	0.004
	0	0	0.014	**0.748**	0	0.233	0	0.001	0.005
	0.004	0.109	0	0.008	**0.543**	0	0.335	0	0
	0	0.041	0.001	0	**0.591**	0.002	0.365	0	0
	0	0.004	0	0.009	**0.878**	0.002	0.107	0	0
	0	0	0.035	0.327	0	**0.626**	0	0.002	0.01

Table 11: Probability distribution of misclassifications, dataset D3: MLP classifier.

	Probability distribution of misclassified predictions								
True Ground	GHE	GAT	SIZ	NEB	BRL	ROE	BRB	LAN	BLE
BLE	**0.99**	0	0	0	0	0	0	0	0.01
	0.747	0	0.059	0.01	0	0	0.002	0	0.182
BRL	0.001	0	0.043	0	0.16	0	**0.795**	0	0
	0.002	0	0.052	0.001	0.309	0	**0.636**	0	0
BRB	0.001	0	0	0	**0.936**	0	0.063	0	0
	0	0	0	0.001	**0.937**	0	0.063	0	0

Table 12: Probability distribution of misclassifications, dataset D3: SMO classifier.

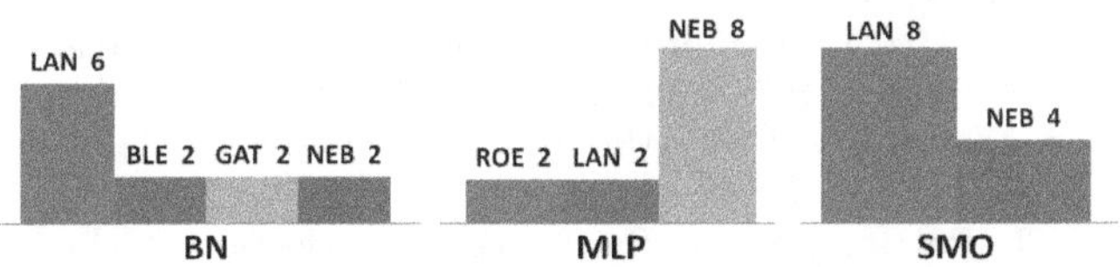

Figure 12: Predictions of NON wines, dataset D3

wines. All the tested classifiers perfomed rather well with respect to the objectives of the work, with BN being the more problematic in some situations, and MLP comparable in performance with SMO, the latter showing a better robustness with respect to possible fake wines.

4. RELATED WORKS

Wine classification and identification through data mining and pattern recognition using chemical descriptors have been approached several times in different settings. Several paper are reported in literature, focused on different analytical targets and techniques, where however the complexity of the data mining task is often proportional to the complexity of the chemical or sensory analyses. Moreover, employed data mining techniques cover essentially all the possible classification or discriminant analysis methods, showing that no "silver bullet" is available in general [2, 15].

Authors in [5] investigate aroma compounds of Galician white wines using a dataset of 42 samples; they show that PCA was not able to accurately separate all the wine varieties, thus different machine learning techniques (SVM, Random Forest, MLP, k-NN and Naive Bayes) were evaluated, obtaining a perfect classification accuracy using the Random Forest algorithm. Differently from our study, the target was maximizing general classification accuracy, and no commercial wine was analyzed.

PCA and Extreme Learning Machine (ELM) were also applied to detect grape varieties: the PCA algorithm was adopted to process chemical components of publicly available wine datasets and classification was performed using the ELM. The experimental results show that the proposed model was useful for general wine classification [17].

Sophisticated analytical methods (even coupled with specific sensory devices such as electronic nose or tongue) have been often used to obtain wine characterization; however, as in our case, [1] shows that simple and nonselective techniques (as UV-visible spectrophotometric methods), in combination with classification approaches, can be demonstrated successful. Here the emphasis is again in improving general classificational accuracy (in this case of several Spanish wines).

Finally, another recent work proposing support vector machine as very promising in this context is presented in [4]; the task here is however completely different, since the goal is to predict (with a suitable score) human wine tasting preferences (that are however closely related to the wine type characteristics).

5. DISCUSSION AND FUTURE WORKS

In this paper we have reported of the results of a study exploiting classification for the assessment of the authenticity of some high-value Italian wines. The problem has been addressed without expensive and hyper-specialized wine chemical analyses, and by learning and suitably evaluating different standard classifiers on the resulting chemical profiles. The proposed approach can be regarded as an instance of the 3-phases Wagstaff's scheme [16]: *Necessary Preparation* has involved the definition of the analyses for data collection and preparation, *Machine Learning Contribution* has regarded the selection of a supervised strategy and of a suitable set of classifiers, while *Impact* has concerned the evaluation of the classification results with respect to the study's objectives. The conclusion is that an SVM classifier like SMO emerges as very promising in this context, both for detecting wrong or illecit blends (not necessarily of low quality, but not compliant with regulations as in the case of LAN and BLE), as well as for avoiding incorrect introductions of unrelated cultivars (as in the case of NON). Moreover, feature selection has pointed out that the number of chemical parameters, needed to get good performances with respect to the authentication objective, can be significantly less than the whole set of parameters initially tought as necessary: performances on datasets D2 and D3 of SMO are in fact comparable, and in some sense even better than those on dataset D1. For instance, in D1, GAT has been misclassified by SMO as BRL and BRB, which are wines similar to GAT, but from different location (Northern vs Southern Piedmont area). Therefore, we can conclude that even a reduced number of chemical analyses (and so a less expensive strategy), together with a suitable classification methodology can be really effective in the considered task.

A weak point of the study could be the not very large number of available samples; however, compared with similar studies, the sample size used in the work is definitely adequate and larger than the usual ones. The practical problem is that obtaining such samples is rather demanding, even if stardard analytical techniques are used. We plan to exploit approaches for generating syntethic data (from the real ones available), in such a way to extend the evaluation of the classifiers to a larger set of data. We have already obtained some interesting preliminary results by learning, using PC algorithm [13], class-specific Linear Gaussian Bayesian Networks [6] as generative models for such synthetic data. The experimental evidence suggests that a data mining classification tool, on wine chemical profiles, can be suitably proposed to address the wine quality control issue.

6. ACKNOWLEDGMENTS

The research was conducted with the financial support of the European Union, Italian Economy and Finance Ministry and the Regione Piemonte (POR-FESR 2007/2013 grants), as a part of TRAQUASWINE project.

7. REFERENCES

[1] F. Acevedo, J. Nez, S. Maldonado, E. Domínguez, and A. Narváez. Classification of wines produced in specific regions by UV-visible spectroscopy combined with support vector machines. *J. Agric. Food Chem.*, 55:6842–6849, 2013.

[2] I. Arvanitoyannis, M. Katsota, E. Psarra, E. Soufleros, and S. Kallithraka. Application of quality control methods for assessing wine authenticity: Use of multivariate analysis (chemometrics). *Trends in Food Science and Technology*, 10:321–336, 1999.

[3] G. Cooper and E. Herskovits. A bayesian method for the induction of probabilistic networks from data. *Machine Learning*, 9(4):309–347, 1992.

[4] P. Corteza, A. Cerdeirab, F. Almeidab, T. Matosb, and J. Reis. Modeling wine preferences by data mining from physicochemical properties. *Decision Support Systems*, 47(4):547–553, 2009.

[5] S. Gòmez-Meire, C. Campos, E. Falqué, F. Dìaz, and F. Fdez-Riverola. Assuring the authenticity of northwest Spain white wine varieties using machine learning techniques. *Food Research International*, 60:230–240, 2014.

[6] M. Grzegorczyk. An introduction to Gaussian Bayesian Networks. In *Systems Biology in Drug Discovery and Development*, volume 662, pages 121–147. Springer, 2010.

[7] M. Hall, E. Frank, G. Holmes, B. Pfahringer, P. Reutemann, and I. Witten. The WEKA data mining software: An update. *SIGKDD Explorations*, 11(1):10–18, 2009.

[8] M. A. Hall. *Correlation-based Feature Subset Selection for Machine Learning.* PhD thesis, University of Waikato, Hamilton, New Zealand, 1998.

[9] D. Mattera and S. Haykin. Support vector machines for dynamic reconstruction of a chaotic system. In B. Schölkopf, C. Burges, and A. Smola, editors, *Advances in Kernel Methods*, pages 211–241. MIT Press, 1999.

[10] J. Platt. Fast training of support vector machines using sequential minimal optimization. In B. Schölkopf, C. Burges, and A. Smola, editors, *Advances in Kernel Methods*, pages 185–208. MIT Press, 1999.

[11] J. Platt. Probability for SV machines. In A. Smola, P. Batlett, B. Schölkopf, and D. Schuurmans, editors, *Advances in Large Margin Classifiers*, pages 61–74. MIT Press, 2000.

[12] L. Portinale and L. Saitta. Feature selection. Technical Report D.14.1, Mining Mart Project, 2002. http://mmart.cs.uni-dortmund.de/content/publications.html.

[13] P. Spirtes, C. Glymour, and R. Scheines. *Causation, Prediction and Search.* Springer Verlag, Berlin, 1993.

[14] B. Üstün, W. Melssen, and L. Buydens. Facilitating the application of support vector regression by using a universal Pearson VII function based kernel. *Chemiometrics and Intelligent Laboratory Systems*, 81:29–40, 2006.

[15] A. Versari, V. Laurie, A. Ricci, L. Laghi, and G. Parpinello. Progress in authentication, typification and traceability of grapes and wines by chemometric approaches. *Food Research International*, 60:2–18, 2014.

[16] K. Wagstaff. Machine learning that matters. In *Proceedings of the 29 th International Conference on Machine Learning (ICML 09)*, Edinburgh, UK, 2012.

[17] Y. Zhao, S. Yu, B. Chu, N. Zhang, and X. Hu. Classification of three wine varieties based on ELM and PCA. In *Lecture Notes in Computer Science*, volume 7751, pages 647–654. 2013.

Predictive Approaches for Low-Cost Preventive Medicine Program in Developing Countries

Yukino Baba[1,2], Hisashi Kashima[3], Yasunobu Nohara[4], Eiko Kai[5], Partha Ghosh[6], Rafiqul Islam[6], Ashir Ahmed[5], Masahiro Kuroda[7], Sozo Inoue[8], Tatsuo Hiramatsu[9], Michio Kimura[10], Shuji Shimizu[4], Kunihisa Kobayashi[11], Koji Tsuda[9], Masashi Sugiyama[9], Mathieu Blondel[12], Naonori Ueda[12], Masaru Kitsuregawa[1,9], Naoki Nakashima[4]
[1]National Institute of Informatics, Tokyo, Japan, [2]JST, ERATO, Kawarabayashi Large Graph Project, Tokyo, Japan
[3]Kyoto University, Kyoto, Japan, [4]Kyushu University Hospital, Fukuoka, Japan
[5]Kyushu University, Fukuoka, Japan, [6]Grameen Communications, Dhaka, Bangladesh
[7]National Institute of Information and Communications Technology, Tokyo, Japan
[8]Kyushu Institute of Technology, Kitakyushu, Japan
[9]The University of Tokyo, Tokyo, Japan, [10]Hamamatsu University School of Medicine, Hamamatsu, Japan
[11]Fukuoka University Chikushi Hospital, Chikushino, Japan
[12]NTT Communication Science Laboratories, Kyoto, Japan

ABSTRACT

Non-communicable diseases (NCDs) are no longer just a problem for high-income countries, but they are also a problem that affects developing countries. Preventive medicine is definitely the key to combat NCDs; however, the cost of preventive programs is a critical issue affecting the popularization of these medicine programs in developing countries. In this study, we investigate predictive modeling for providing a low-cost preventive medicine program. In our two-year-long field study in Bangladesh, we collected the health checkup results of 15,075 subjects, the data of 6,607 prescriptions, and the follow-up examination results of 2,109 subjects. We address three prediction problems, namely *subject risk prediction*, *drug recommendation*, and *future risk prediction*, by using machine learning techniques; our multiple-classifier approach successfully reduced the costs of health checkups, a multi-task learning method provided accurate recommendation for specific types of drugs, and an active learning method achieved an efficient assignment of healthcare workers for the follow-up care of subjects.

Categories and Subject Descriptors

H.2.8 [**Database Management**]: Database Applications—*Data Mining*; J.3 [**Computer Applications**]: Life and Medical Sciences—*Health*

Keywords

Data mining; Healthcare; Preventive medicine

KDD'15, August 10-13, 2015, Sydney, NSW, Australia.
© 2015 ACM. ISBN 978-1-4503-3664-2/15/08 ...$15.00.
DOI: http://dx.doi.org/10.1145/2783258.2788587.

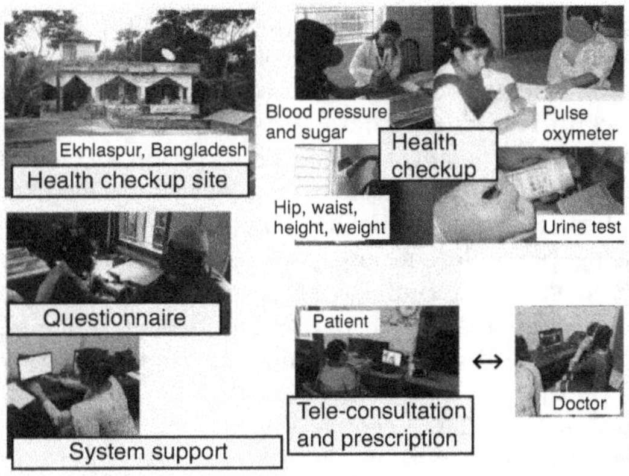

Figure 1: Overview of our two-year-long Portable Health Clinic (PHC) field study in Bangladesh

1. INTRODUCTION

Non-communicable diseases (NCDs), such as heart disease, stroke, cancer, chronic kidney diseases, and diabetes mellitus, have been increasingly prevalent worldwide. The World Health Organization reported that NCDs accounted for 63% (36 million) of the 57 million global deaths in 2008 and approximately 80% of all NCD-related deaths occurred in low- and middle-income countries [1]. In such countries, 29% of NCD-related deaths occurred in the working-age group (in people aged <60 years), which is remarkably higher than that in high-income countries (13%), and contributes to declining labor productivity. The total number of annual NCD-related deaths is estimated to reach 55 million by 2030 [9].

Preventive medicine is undoubtedly the key to combat NCDs. Preventive medicine consists of three levels: primary prevention to maintain healthy conditions, secondary prevention to avoid the development of NCDs, and tertiary prevention to avoid disease progression to serious stages. Over time, the focus of medical services in developed countries has changed from acute and serious diseases to the management of NCDs.

There are two critical issues facing developing countries with respect to the popularization of preventive medicine programs: the cost of preventive medicine and the shortage of healthcare workers. For example, disposables for physical examinations including urine, blood sugar, and hemoglobin tests cost approximately USD 2-3. This price is not affordable in most low-income nations where the average monthly income per household is less than USD 100. In addition, the lack of a healthcare workforce is a severe problem. For instance, there are only 0.36 physicians per thousand population in Bangladesh, one of the developing countries, while the physician density is 2.45 in the United States [8].

We have developed an eHealth system named Portable Health Clinic (PHC); it is an efficient and easy-to-operate preventive medicine service using information and communication technology [6]. PHC is composed of three steps, namely health checkup, tele-consultation and prescription, and follow-up care. These three steps correspond to the three levels of a preventive medicine program. Figures 1 and 2 show an overview of PHC. PHC includes portable packages for health checkups equipped with a tablet computer and consumable goods for physical examination. The tablet computer is connected to a mobile network to send the checkup results to a data server at the medical center. PHC offers tele-consultation and prescription services with a doctor at the medical center to a subject who is suspected to have a health problem. Follow-up checkups are also scheduled using portable checkup packages. Our two-year-long PHC field study in Bangladesh resulted in a collection of health checkup results of 15,075 subjects, 6,607 prescriptions offered by doctors, and follow-up examination results of 2,109 subjects.

Although PHC has been established as a beneficial preventive medicine program, there is still room for improvement to make it a cost-efficient system. In this study, we apply predictive approaches to the collected data and investigate the usage of machine learning methods for providing a low-cost preventive medicine program. We address the following three prediction problems: *subject risk prediction*, *drug recommendation*, and *future risk prediction*. The health checkup procedure in PHC includes low-cost tests, such as measurement of weight or body temperature, that do not require disposables, and high-cost tests, such as urine or blood sugar tests, that use consumable goods for the measurements. The high-cost tests make the preventive medicine program expensive, and if we can reduce the number of administrations of high-cost tests, the preventive medicine program becomes more affordable for developing countries.

The present study first addresses the problem of predicting the subjects' health risks by using the results of low-cost tests and proposes a strategy to select subjects who really need the high-cost tests. We next tackle the drug recommendation problem. If we can predict the drugs that each subject should have, we can reduce the workload of the doctors and allocate the limited human resources more efficiently. In addition, if we provide an accurate recommendation on the basis of the results of low-cost tests, we can reduce the cost of high-cost tests. Finally, we focus on supporting the follow-up process. The aim of this process is to take care of the subjects who still have a health problem. Our goal is to predict the future risk levels by using the previous checkup results to provide priorities on staff assignments to high-risk subjects.

We formalize these problems and investigate the practicability of predictive approaches with respect to a low-cost preventive medicine program. Our key contributions are summarized as follows:

- *Subject risk prediction*: We propose a prediction strategy using multiple classifiers to carefully select the subjects who need to take the high-cost tests. This strategy successfully reduces costs by 50% if it is allowed to have a 1% chance to incorrectly identify a high-risk subject as a low-risk one.
- *Drug recommendation*: Our drug recommendation approach using a multi-task learning method achieves an Area Under the ROC Curve (AUC) of more than 0.8 in 13% of the target drugs. We also find that the same level of accurate recommendations is achieved with only the results of the low-cost tests.
- *Future risk prediction*: Our active learning strategy covers 67% of the high-risk subjects when we are only allowed to use 40% of the total budget, while the original follow-up procedure only covered 46% of such subjects with the same cost constraint.

2. BANGLADESH HEALTH CHECKUP DATASET

We provided eHealth checkups for the population in Bangladesh for two years. We collected the results of questionnaires and health checkups of 15,705 subjects and 6,607 prescriptions for 2,461 subjects. Among all the subjects, 2,109 underwent the checkups in both the first and the second year. In the first year, we conducted the study around Dhaka, the capital of Bangladesh. The sites covered in the second year were Chittagong (south-eastern area), Rajshahi (western area), Thakurgaon (north-western area), and certain areas around Dhaka.

2.1 Data collection procedure

We developed an eHealth system named Portable Health Clinic (PHC). PHC consists of a set of devices in a suitcase, a data transmission system linked to a mobile network, and a data management application. The suitcase is equipped with a tablet and consumable goods for urine, blood sugar, and hemoglobin tests. We also prepared a tele-consultation and tele-prescription service using Skype over a mobile network to gather health data. The checkup and tele-medical procedure is shown in Figure 2. Subjects were first asked to complete a questionnaire, and then, they underwent the health checkup. The checkup results were stored in a tablet and sent to the main server at the medical center in Dhaka. Using the result, we categorized each subject into one of the following four risk groups: *Healthy*, *Caution*, *Affected*, and *Emergency*. For the subjects in the *Affected* or *Emergency* group, we provided a tele-consultation with a doctor at the medical center. If required, the doctors sent tele-prescriptions. Subjects who received a tele-prescription were expected to visit their local pharmacies to purchase the prescribed medicines.

The questionnaire contained 33 questions about basic information, health condition, disease history, and lifestyle.

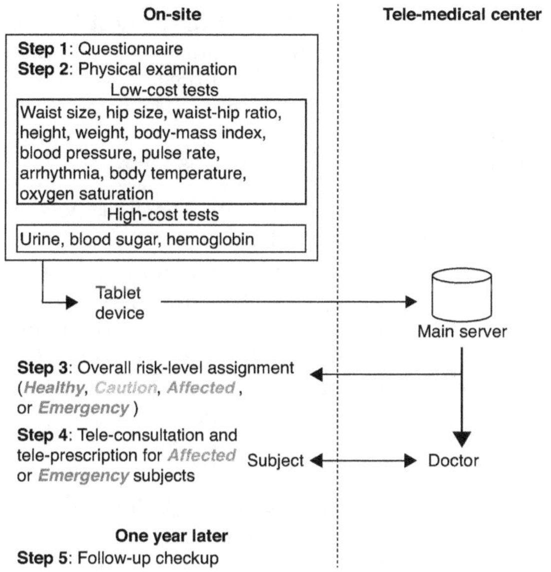

Figure 2: Procedure for our PHC service. When subjects visit the checkup booth, they are asked to fill out a questionnaire (Step 1), and then, they go through a physical examination (Step 2). If a subject is identified as *Affected* or *Emergency* (Step 3), a tele-consultation service with a doctor at the telemedicine center is offered (Step 4). One year later, we provide a follow-up examination for the subjects.

Seven out of the 33 questions were about drug allergies and surgical history, and the subjects who took a teleconsultation were asked to answer these questions mandatorily. All the questions except *age* were given in a multiple-choice format.

We collected the results of checkup items including *hip size*, *height*, *weight*, and those shown in Table 1. Only 2,627 subjects underwent the hemoglobin test. We collected the result of either the blood sugar (fasting) or the blood sugar (postprandial) test of each subject. The costs of urine, blood sugar, and hemoglobin tests were much higher than those of the other tests because these three tests needed a consumable good for each measurement. The consumables cost per measurement is shown in Table 1.

In order to assess a subject's risk level, we established Bangladesh logic [6]. This criterion helped assign one of the four risk levels (*Healthy*, *Caution*, *Affected*, and *Emergency*) to each of the 13 checkup items shown in Table 1.

The overall risk level of a subject was determined by the maximum risk level among all the checkup items. For instance, even if a subject was assigned with Healthy in 12 items and Emergency in one item, the overall risk level of this subject was determined to be *Emergency*. We also categorized the subjects whose overall risk level was *Affected* or *Emergency* as *high risk*, and the others were categorized as *low risk*.

In the tele-consultation, the doctors selected multiple medicines from 49 drugs and prepared a prescription if required. The medicines were categorized by their purposes, such as *drugs for hypertension* or *drugs for cough and cold*.

Table 1: List of consumables cost per measurement

Measurement	Cost (in USD)
Waist	0
Waist/hip ratio	0
Body-mass index	0
Blood pressure (systolic) Blood pressure (diastolic)	0
Blood sugar (fasting) Blood sugar (postprandial)	0.57
Urine-protein Urine-sugar Urine-urobilinogen	0.19
Pulse rate	0
Arrhythmia	0
Body temperature	0
Oxygen saturation	0
Hemoglobin	1.42

2.2 Dataset summary

Our dataset consisted of 8,476 (54.0%) male subjects and 7,229 (46.0%) female subjects. The subjects' ages ranged from 18 to 106 years, and the average age was 35.6 years. There were 3,857 (24.6%) subjects from urban areas, 4,815 (30.7%) subjects from suburban areas, and 7,033 (44.8%) subjects from rural areas. The number of subjects who took the first checkup in the first year was 7,495 (47.7%) and that of subjects who underwent the checkup in the second year was 8,210 (52.3%). We categorized 2,136 (12.5%), 8,483 (53.7%), 4,632 (30.5%), and 454 (3.3%) subjects as *Healthy*, *Caution*, *Affected*, and *Emergency* in terms of the overall risk level, respectively.

The average number of suggested drugs per subject was 2.7 among the subjects who obtained the prescriptions, and the number of suggested drugs ranged from 1 to 10. The average number of prescriptions per drug was 134.8. The minimum number of prescriptions per drug was 1, and the maximum was 1,322.

Among the subjects who took the checkup in both the first and the second year, 326 (15.5%), 1,144 (54.2%), 585 (27.7%), and 54 (2.6%) subjects were categorized as *Healthy*, *Caution*, *Affected*, and *Emergency* in terms of the overall risk level in the first year, respectively. There were 585 (27.7%) subjects whose risk level improved and 632 (30.0%) subjects got worse in the second year.

2.3 Preprocessing

In the following experiments, we processed the results of health checkups and converted them into feature vectors as follows: We encoded the categorical information into feature vectors by using the one-of-K encoding. Categorical information included the results of urine tests and arrhythmia, the risk level of each checkup item, and the response of each question in the questionnaire except age. Continuous values, such as age or the result of physical examination, were scaled to fit the range of 0-1. The transformation was learned on the training data and applied to the rest.

Because not all the subjects underwent the blood sugar (fasting), blood sugar (postprandial), and hemoglobin tests, sometimes, we did not have these values in the training data and hence, failed to scale these parameters by using the minimum and the maximum values. Thus, we predefined the ranges for these values on the basis of the Bangladesh logic. That is, we defined the ranges as $[100, 200]$ for blood sugar (fasting), $[140, 300]$ for blood sugar (postprandial), and $[8, 12]$ for hemoglobin. If the outcome of one of these items was within the defined range, the risk level was *Caution* or *Affected*. After the scaling, the missing values were input as 0.5.

3. SUBJECT RISK PREDICTION FOR CHECKUP COST REDUCTION

We first address the problem of predicting subject risks and discovering low-risk subjects from the outcomes of the questionnaire and low-cost tests. The aim of this prediction is to cut the health checkup costs for the low-risk subjects. Note that all the subjects who are identified as high-risk subjects are required to undergo all the high-cost tests because the doctors need the results to conduct the tele-consultation.

3.1 Problem formulation

Let us assume that there are I subjects who will come for the health checkup. We have J checkup tests where M include a questionnaire and are low-cost tests, and the others are high-cost tests. Each subject will be offered the J tests in a sequence of $(1, 2, \cdots, J)$. Let c_j be the cost of the j-th test. We consider the cost of low-cost test to be considerably smaller than that of any high-cost test; thus, we assume that $c_j = 0$ for all $j \in \{1, 2, \cdots, M\}$, and $c_j > 0$ for all $j \in \{M+1, M+2, \cdots, J\}$. When the i-th subject takes the j-th test, we obtain a d_j dimensional feature vector $\boldsymbol{x}_{ij} \in \mathbb{R}^{d_j}$. Let $m_{ij} \in \{0, 1\}$ indicate whether the i-th subject takes the j-th test ($m_{ij} = 1$) or not ($m_{ij} = 0$).

Let $r_i \in \{0, 1\}$ indicate whether the i-th subject is at a high risk ($r_i = 1$) or not ($r_i = 0$). According to the Bangladesh logic, a subject is at a high risk if at least one of the test result is *high risk*; in such a case, the subject is immediately determined as high risk before he/she takes all the J tests. On the other hand, we cannot completely determine whether a subject is a low-risk one until all the tests are conducted.

Our goal is to predict whether a subject is at a high risk or not, and to output the predictions $\hat{r}_i \in \{0, 1\}$ for all $i \in \{1, 2, \cdots, I\}$. There is a practical constraint that we must offer all the tests to any subject who is predicted as high risk because we use the results in the tele-consultation session. That is, m_{ij} must be set to one for all $j \in \{1, 2, \cdots, J\}$, and for $i \in \{1, 2, \cdots, I\}$ such that $\hat{r}_i = 1$.

3.2 Approaches

An unsophisticated way of obtaining $\{\hat{r}_i\}_{i:I}$ is to have all the subjects take all the tests. Note that we use "$i : I$" to indicate $i \in \{1, 2, \ldots, I\}$ for notational simplicity. This approach correctly determines the risk of all the subjects, i.e., $\hat{r}_i = r_i$ for all $i \in \{1, 2, \cdots, I\}$; however, we need the following amount of money to perform all the tests: $C = I \sum_{j=1}^{J} c_j$. We next discuss predictive approaches to reduce the costs of checkups.

3.2.1 *Strategy with a single classifier*

A simple strategy for applying a predictive approach is to build a single classifier that predicts the subject risks given the results of the low-cost tests. This strategy involves conducting all the tests on a subject if the subject is predicted to be a high-risk one; otherwise, no high-cost test will be offered. Further, the outcomes of a subject who takes all the tests provide the groundtruth label r_i, which can be used to improve the classifier.

The procedure for this strategy is as follows:

Step 1. We offer all the tests to the first N subjects, and obtain their risk outcomes $\{r_i\}_{i:N}$. Then we train a classifier $\hat{f}_M(\cdot)$ by using the results $\{(\{\boldsymbol{x}_{ij}\}_{j:M}, r_i)\}_{i:N}$, where the classifier $\hat{f}_M(\cdot)$ is a function that takes $\{\boldsymbol{x}_{ij}\}_{j:M}$ as the input, and returns whether a subject is considered to be at high-risk or not.

Step 2. For each $i \in \{N+1, N+2, \cdots, I\}$, the i-th subject follows the procedure below:

- *Step 2.1.* We offer the low-cost tests to the subject and obtain $\{\boldsymbol{x}_{ij}\}_{j:M}$.
- *Step 2.2.* If the subject is identified as a high-risk one on the basis of the results of the low-cost tests, or the classifier $\hat{f}_M(\{\boldsymbol{x}_{ij}\}_{j:M})$ predicts that the subject is at high-risk, then the subject will be given all the high-cost tests and we will obtain r_i. We use the sample $(\{\boldsymbol{x}_{ij}\}_{j:M}, r_i)$ to improve the classifier $\hat{f}_M(\cdot)$, and the process for the i-th subject isterminated.
- *Step 2.3.* Otherwise we terminate the process for the i-th subject, and therefore, the subject is not given any high-cost test.

The total execution cost of this strategy is $C = N \sum_{j=1}^{J} c_j + \sum_{i=N+1}^{I} m_{i(M+1)} \sum_{j=1}^{J} c_j$, considering that a subject who takes the $(M+1)$-th test is also offered the other high-cost tests in the procedure above. This procedure enables us to save the costs of high-cost tests for the subjects who are predicted as low-risk subjects; however, it may cause false-negative errors where a high-risk subject is incorrectly predicted as a low-risk one. [1]

3.2.2 *Conservative strategy with multiple classifiers*

One careful strategy to avoid false-negative errors is to separately decide if we should offer each high-cost test to each subject. Suppose a case where a subject is predicted to be a low-risk subject on the basis of the outcomes of the low-cost tests. The strategy using a single classifier will decide that we do not need to offer all the high-cost tests to the subject. If the subject is actually at a high risk, this strategy causes a false-negative error. A careful strategy is designed to perform the first high-cost test (e.g., urine test) even if the classifier considers the subject to be at a low risk. If the urine test indicates an abnormality, the subject will be identified as a high-risk one. If not, we can apply another classifier that uses the result of the urine test as well as that of the low-cost tests to predict the risk. Because this classifier uses additional information, it may provide a more accurate prediction than the first one. When the second classifier also predicts that the subject is at a low risk, this strategy will offer the next high-cost test to the subject.

[1] False-positive errors do not occur in our setting because a subject predicted as a high-risk subject is offered all the tests, and thus, we observe the correct risk outcome.

In a nutshell, this strategy conducts high-cost tests one by one, gradually extracts the subject information, and carefully decides whether we should identify the subject as a low-risk one and skip the high-cost tests. If the subject is considered to be a high-risk one by a classifier, all the rest of the tests will be conducted on the subject. We call this strategy *conservative* and show its detailed operation as follows:

Step 1. We offer all the tests to the first N subjects, and obtain their risk outcomes $\{r_i\}_{i:N}$. For each $j \in \{M, M+1, \cdots, J-1\}$, we train the classifier $\hat{f}_j(\cdot)$ by using the checkup results $\{(\{\boldsymbol{x}_{ik}\}_{k:j}, r_i)\}_{i:N}$, where the classifier $\hat{f}_j(\cdot)$ is a function that takes $\{\boldsymbol{x}_{ik}\}_{k:j}$ as the input, and returns whether a subject is considered to be at a high risk.

Step 2. For each $i \in \{N+1, N+2, \cdots, I\}$, the i-th subject follows the procedure below:

Step 2.1. We offer the low-cost tests to the subject and obtain $\{\boldsymbol{x}_{ij}\}_{j:M}$.

Step 2.2. For each $j \in \{M, M+1, \cdots, J-1\}$, when the j-th test is conducted on the subject and the outcome $\boldsymbol{x}_{ij}$ is obtained,

- If the subject is identified as a high-risk one by the test, or the classifier $\hat{f}_j(\{\boldsymbol{x}_{ik}\}_{k:j})$ predicts that the subject is at a high risk, the subject will be given all the high-cost tests and we will obtain $\{\boldsymbol{x}_{ij}\}_{j:J}$ and r_i. For each $j \in \{M, M+1, \cdots, J-1\}$, we use the sample $(\{\boldsymbol{x}_{ik}\}_{k:j}, r_i)$ to update the classifier $\hat{f}_j(\cdot)$, and terminate the process for the i-th subject.
- Otherwise, when $j \neq J-1$, the $(j+1)$-th test is conducted on the subject. If the subject is predicted to be a low-risk on the basis of the $(J-1)$-th test, we terminate the process for the i-th subject thus the J-th test will not be offered to the subject.

This conservative strategy only cuts the cost of the last high-cost test, and the total checkup cost will be $C = N\sum_{j=1}^{J} c_j + (I-N)\sum_{j=1}^{J-1} c_j + \sum_{i=N+1}^{I} c_J m_{iJ}$. This strategy commits to avoid the false-negative errors rather than substantially reducing the checkup costs.

3.2.3 Aggressive strategy with multiple classifiers

We can consider another strategy that aggressively reduces the costs by omitting the high-cost tests. This *aggressive* strategy does not offer the high-costs tests to subjects if the first classifier predicts that they are at a low risk given the outcomes of the low-cost tests. If the classifier predicts a subject as a high risk, then the first high-cost test will be conducted on the subject and the result is used to make another prediction. In this manner, this strategy excludes all the rest of the high-cost tests and cuts the costs if a classifier predicts the subject as a low-risk one. The procedure for this strategy is given by modifying Step 2.2 in the conservative strategy:

Step 2.2. For each $j \in \{M, M+1, \cdots, J-1\}$, when the j-th test is conducted on the subject and the outcome $\boldsymbol{x}_{ij}$ is obtained,

- If the subject is identified as a high risk by the test, the subject will be given all the high-cost tests. The classifiers are improved by using the results, and the process for the i-th subject is terminated.
- If the classifier $\hat{f}_j(\{\boldsymbol{x}_{ik}\}_{k:j})$ predicts that the subject is at a low riwk, the process for the i-th subject is terminated; thus, the rest of the tests will not be offered to the subject.
- Otherwise, when the $j \neq J-1$, the $(j+1)$-th test will be conducted on the subject. If the subject is predicted to be at a high risk on the $(J-1)$-th test, we will conduct the J-th test on the subject, obtain r_i, and improve the classifiers.

The total execution cost of the aggressive strategy is given by $C = N\sum_{j=1}^{J} c_j + \sum_{i=N+1}^{I}\sum_{j=1}^{J} c_j m_{ij}$.

3.3 Evaluation

We evaluate the approaches using the Bangladesh health checkup dataset and compare their false-negative rates and the total required cost.

3.3.1 Experimental setting

We used the health checkup data of 15,075 subjects. All of the features except for measurements of the hemoglobin level and the responses to the optional questions in the questionnaire were used. In the experiments, we assumed that the subjects would visit the health checkup booth in the original order in our field study.

There were two high-cost tests in the experiments: urine test and blood sugar test. We assumed that all the subjects took the high-costs tests in a fixed order, and we conducted the experiments in both cases where the urine test was offered first and where the blood sugar test was offered first.

We employed an L2-regularized logistic regression implementation (sklearn.linear_model.SGDClassifier) provided by scikit-learn [10]. This implementation incrementally learns the model by using stochastic gradient descent so that we can improve the classifier when we get a new sample. We built classifiers that predict the probability of a subject being at a high risk, returns 1 if the probability is greater than a threshold δ, and returns 0 otherwise. The thresholds were varied in $\{0., 0.01, 0.02, \cdots, 0.09, 0.1, 0.2, \cdots, 1.0\}$. The same threshold was applied to all the classifiers when we evaluated the multiple-classifier strategies. The hyperparameters of the classifiers were determined by using a five-fold cross validation on the training data that was composed of the outcomes of the first N subjects. The size of the training data N was chosen from $N = 785$ (5%), 1570 (10%), and 3141 (20%).

The performances were measured by the false-negative rate and the cost rate. The cost rate indicates the proportion of the cost required by each approach to the cost of offering all the tests to all the subjects.

3.3.2 Results and discussion

The results are shown in Figure 3. It is noticed that across all the sizes of training data, the multiple-classifier strategies with starting with the urine-test substantially reduced the costs of the health checkup while maintaining a small false-negative rate. In particular, in the case where $N = 785$ (5%), our multiple-classifier approach showed a significant cost reduction. The aggressive strategy achieved

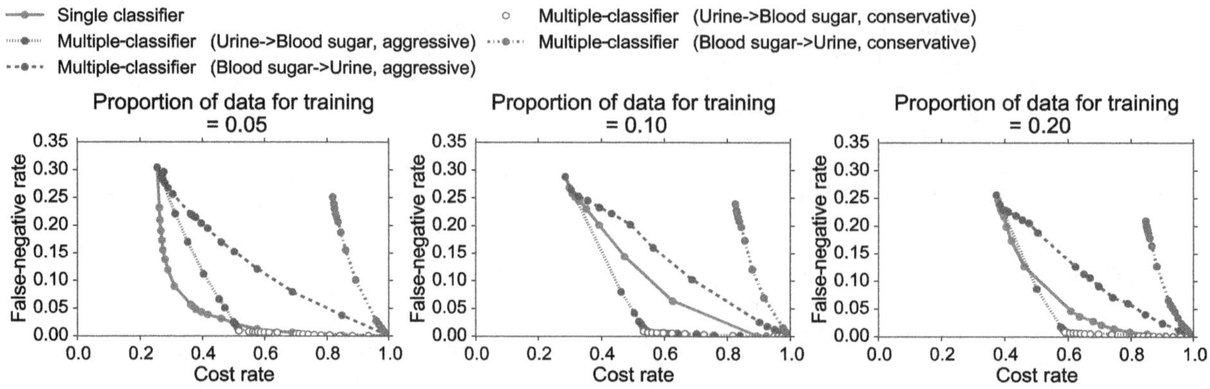

Figure 3: False-negative rate versus the total cost of the health checkup, where a false-negative indicates a case where a subject is identified as a low-risk one when the subject is actually at a high risk. In all the cases, the multiple-classifier strategy starting with the urine test achieves the best trade-off between the cost and the false-negative rate.

false-negative ratio = 1.1% when cost ratio = 51.5%, and the conservative strategy reached false-negative ratio = 0.9% when cost ratio = 51.6%. The two methods successfully reduced the 50% of the costs with the very rare occurrence of a false-negative error. Considering the fact that we need at least 33.7% of the costs to offer the high-cost tests to the subjects who are actually at a high risk, we can conclude that the multiple-classifier approach demonstrated a considerable performance.

We observed that we obtained lower false-negative rates when we first conducted the urine test. The reason behind this is that the classifier using the results of both the low-cost tests and the urine test is more accurate than the one using the results of the low-cost tests and the blood sugar test. Let us compare the AUC of both classifiers that were trained with N = 1,570 (10%) samples. The former classifier achieved an AUC of 0.991, while the latter classifier scored an AUC of 0.844. Incorporating the results of the urine test will be beneficial from two perspectives: the urine test returns three outcomes (urine (protein), urine (sugar), and urine (urobilinogen)), and there is a strong relationship between urine sugar and blood sugar. The latter point is supported by the fact that among the subjects who were classified as *Affected* or *Emergency* on the basis of the blood sugar test, 79.4% were also classified as *Affected* or *Emergency* on the basis of the urine (sugar) test. When the urine test was conducted first, and the results of the test were used to predict whether a subject was at a high risk, we only needed to predict an abnormality of blood sugar so that the information of urine (sugar) contributed to the predictions.

The classifier using the results of the low-cost tests and the blood sugar test needed to predict the overall risk level without observing the outcomes of urine (protein), urine (sugar), and urine (urobilinogen). Although blood sugar and urine sugar are correlated, there was no correlation observed between blood sugar and the other two; thus, the classifier was not as accurate as the one using the results of low-cost tests and the urine test. In addition, the false-negative rate of the multiple-classifier strategy starting with the blood sugar test was higher than that of the single-classifier strategy across almost all the cost rates. Because the classifier using only the results of the low-cost tests achieved an AUC of 0.826, which is comparable to the AUC of the classifier using the results of the low-cost tests and the blood sugar test, it was not helpful to collect the results of the blood sugar test while the test was relatively expensive.

Investigating the trained classification model, we observed several important factors affecting the detection of the subject risk levels. A subject was likely to be at a high risk according to the overall risk level when his/her result of arrhythmia, blood pressure, or body-mass index was categorized as *Affected* or *Emergency*. In contrast, a subject was likely to be at a low risk as per the overall risk level when his/her result of blood pressure, body-mass index, or body temperature was categorized as *Healthy*. We also found that the responses to the questionnaire were helpful for discovering the high-risk subjects. If subjects answered that they periodically took anti-diabetic medicine, they had a high probability of being at a high risk.

For applying our multiple-classifier approach, users need to predefine the strategy, conservative or aggressive, they want to use and the threshold parameter. Because the choice of a suitable setting depends on the requirements of the total cost and the false-negative rate, we recommend that the users first conduct an initial experiment by collecting the results of all the high-cost tests for a small number of subjects, apply the strategies with varying thresholds, and plot the results as shown Figure 3 to determine the appropriate setting to use.

4. DRUG RECOMMENDATION BASED ON HEALTH CHECKUP RESULTS

Next, we address the problem of predicting drugs that should be prescribed for each subject on the basis of the results of the health checkup. The aim of this prediction is to support doctors and to reduce their workloads. We also study the drug recommendation from the outcomes of the low-cost tests. If we provide an accurate recommendation based on them, we can reduce the costs of the high-cost tests.

4.1 Problem definition

Let us assume that there are I subjects and J tests. Using the same method as that described in the Section 3.1, when the i-th subject takes the j-th test, we incur the cost of c_j and obtain the feature vector $\boldsymbol{x}_{ij}$.

We assume that there are L types of drugs. When a doctor conducts a tele-prescription session, the subject will be provided a drug prescription specifying at least one drug. Let $\boldsymbol{p}_i = (p_{i1}, p_{i2}, \cdots, p_{iL})$ denote the prescription for the i-th subject, where $p_{il} = 1$ if the l-th drug is prescribed to the subject, and $p_{il} = 0$ otherwise. Note that the doctors require the outcomes of all the low-cost and high-cost tests of the subject to prepare a prescription for the subject.

Our goal is to predict the prescriptions and to output the predictions $\{\hat{\boldsymbol{p}}_i\}_{i:I}$.

4.2 Approaches

We assume that we have the N prescriptions provided from the doctors, and apply supervised learning methods to train predictors. We study three approaches to build the predictors.

4.2.1 Single-task learning with low-cost and high-cost features

We first present a simple method to train a discrete classifier $\hat{g}_{Jl}(\cdot)$ for each $l \in \{1, 2, \cdots, L\}$. We call this approach *single-task learning*. The classifier $\hat{g}_{Jl}(\cdot)$ takes the feature vectors $\{x_{ij}\}_{j \in 1,2,\cdots,L}$ and returns 1 if the l-th drug should be ordered to the i-th subject; otherwise, it returns 0. When we use the results of all the low-cost and the high-cost tests for the prediction, the total costs of providing recommendations for all the subjects will be $C = I \sum_{j=1}^{J} c_j$.

4.2.2 Multi-task learning with low-cost and high-cost features

One can presume that the order of drugs is associated to one another. Multi-task learning has been proposed for such a case where there are multiple related prediction tasks. A multi-task learning method builds a classifier $\hat{g}_J(\cdot)$ that takes the feature vectors $\{\boldsymbol{x}_{ij}\}_{j:J}$ and returns $\{0,1\}^L$. When we use the results of all the low-cost and the high-cost tests for the prediction, the total costs will be $C = I \sum_{j=1}^{J} c_j$ as well.

4.2.3 Multi-task learning with low-cost features

We also attempt to make predictions only from the results of the low-cost tests. In this case, we build the classifier $\hat{g}_1(\cdot)$ that takes the feature vector $\boldsymbol{x}_{i1}$ as input and returns $\{0,1\}^L$. This approach only needs the cost of training data; thus, the total cost will be $C = N \sum_{j=1}^{J} c_j$, and we can save the cost of offering the high-cost tests to $N - I$ subjects.

4.3 Evaluation

We evaluate the accuracy of the prediction approaches by using the actual prescription data collected through our field study.

4.3.1 Experimental setting

We used the data of 2,461 subjects who took the tele-prescription sessions. When a prediction approach employed the results of all the low-cost and high-cost tests, we used all the checkup items described in Section 2.1.

Table 2: Averages and standard deviations of AUC for all the target drugs

Approach	AUC
Multi-task learning with low- and high-cost features	0.676 ± 0.101
Multi-task learning with low-cost features	0.663 ± 0.095
Single-task learning with low- and high-cost features	0.631 ± 0.125

We employed an implementation of multi-task learning (sklearn.linear_model.MultiTaskLasso) provided by scikit-learn [10], which deploys a multi-task learning method with an L1/L2 mixed-norm regularizer [7]. Further, we applied an implementation of the L1-regularized linear regression method (sklearn.linear_model.Lasso) for comparing the single-task and the multi-task learning methods. Hyperparameters for each method were determined by using a five-fold cross validation on the prescriptions of first $N = 1476$ (60%) subjects. The prescriptions of the rest of the subjects were used for testing. We selected 32 out of 49 drugs that were prescribed to at least five subjects in the test data for a reasonable comparison. We use the AUC values for measuring the accuracy.

4.3.2 Results and discussion

Averages and standard deviations of AUC over all the target drugs are shown in Table 2. It is observed that compared with the single-task method and multi-task methods, the multi-task methods produced more accurate prediction than the single-task method. We also found that the method using only the low-cost features is comparable to the one that uses both the low-cost and high-cost features; the difference between the average AUC of multi-task learning with the low-cost and high-cost features and that of multi-task learning with the low-cost features is only 1.6%.

Prediction performance for each drug is illustrated in Figure 4. Multi-task learning with low-cost and high-cost features achieved an AUC of more than 0.8 in the case of 4 out of 32 drugs. The high scoring drugs are as follows: *oral hypoglycemic drugs*, *drugs for angina and ischaemic heart diseases*, *drugs for hypertension*, and *drugs for iron deficiency anaemias*. The method particularly showed an appreciable recommendation performance with AUC=0.938 for *oral hypoglycemic drugs*. However, the performance for this drug became inferior when we used the multi-task learning with low-cost features; it scored an AUC of 0.761. The results of the blood sugar test, one of the high-cost tests, would be important to make an accurate recommendation of this drug. For the three other drugs, the method without using the results of high-cost tests worked as good as the one using the results of both tests. This is a promising result toward reducing the checkup costs to make recommendations of these three drugs.

We also observed that the standard deviation of the single-task learning method was relatively larger than that of the multi-task learning method. This indicates that the multi-task learning method provides stable drug recommendations.

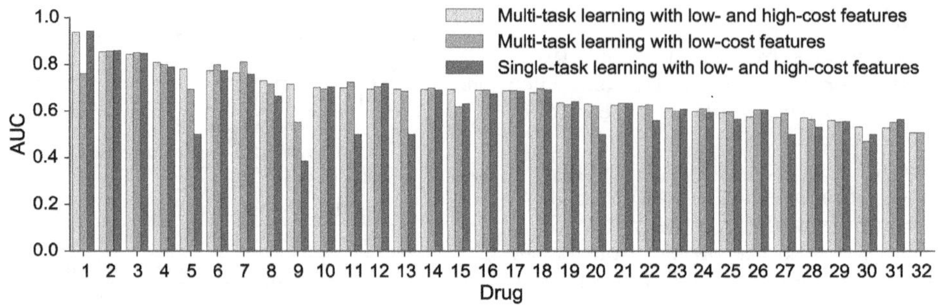

Figure 4: AUC score of drug recommendation. The multi-task learning methods score more than 0.8 in the case of 4 out of 32 drugs, and provide more robust recommendations than the single-task learning method. The multi-task learning method that uses only the low-cost features shows a comparable performance with the one using both the low-cost and high-cost features for most of the drugs.

We examined the model obtained by multi-task learning with the results of the low-cost tests. We found that blood pressure was the main factor for predicting the need for *drugs for angina and ischemic heart diseases* and *drugs for hypertension*. Investigating the classification model built by multi-task learning with the results of the low-cost and high-cost tests, we found that blood sugar was a key factor in determining that subjects required *oral hypoglycemic drugs*. These findings supported our consideration that the results of the blood sugar test were important for providing an accurate recommendation of such a drug.

5. FUTURE RISK PREDICTION FOR EFFICIENT FOLLOW-UP PROCESS

Finally, we target the process of follow-up checkups. The aim of this process is to take care of the subjects who still have a health problem or who become high-risk subjects after a checkup. If we only have a limited budget for the follow-up process, it will be more efficient to set the priority to subjects who are currently classified as high-risk subjects. We discuss the use of prediction approaches to determine the priority.

5.1 Problem definition

Let us assume that there are I subjects who are the targets of the follow-up checkups. We are given the outcomes of the previous checkups $\{\boldsymbol{x}_i\}$ for each $i \in \{1, 2, \cdots, I\}$. Let $q_i \in \{0, 1\}$ indicate the current risk level of the i-th subject. We need to examine whether each subject is currently at a high risk ($q_i = 1$) or not ($q_i = 0$). The cost c is required to investigate the current risk level of each subject; that is, we will be given the current risk of a subject q_i if we spend the cost of c; otherwise, we will not observe it. We also assume that there is a budget constraint C.

Our goal is to determine the priority of subjects on the basis of the results of previous checkups so that we can examine as many of the high-risk subjects as possible under the budget constraint.

5.2 Approaches

We can also apply the prediction approaches to address this problem. First, we offer the follow-ups to N subjects, where N is assumed to be a small number. Using the N sample, we train an initial classifier $\hat{h}(\cdot)$ that takes the outcomes of the previous checkup $\{\boldsymbol{x}_i\}$ as input and predicts the probability of the i−th subject being at high risk, i.e., $\hat{h}(\boldsymbol{x}_i) = \Pr[q_i = 1 \mid \boldsymbol{x}_i]$. We use the output of this classifier to decide the next subject to offer the follow-up checkup. When the i-th subject is investigated, we obtain the new label q_i, which we can use for improving the classifier.

We present two selection strategies that determine the next subject to be taken care of.

5.2.1 Exploitation-only strategy

The first strategy, called *exploitation-only*, always selects the subject who is the most likely to be at high risk. Namely, by using the classifier $\hat{h}(\cdot)$, this strategy selects the i^*-th subject by evaluating

$$i^* = \arg\max_{i \in \mathcal{I}} \hat{h}(\boldsymbol{x}_i), \tag{1}$$

where $\mathcal{I}$ corresponds to a set of subjects who have not had a follow-up yet.

5.2.2 Exploration-and-exploitation strategy with active learning

If we have a well-trained classification and it precisely selects the high-risk subjects, the exploitation-only strategy may work efficiently. However, because of the budget constraint, we have recourse to a classifier trained with a small number of samples and need to incrementally improve the classifier. Choosing the high-risk subjects is not always a good strategy for improving the classifier, because it is likely to collect similar samples. A reasonable solution is to select subjects that are informative in order to improve the classifier as well as the high-risk subjects. Thus, we can achieve a balance between exploration (acquiring new information) and exploitation (taking the most beneficial action based on the knowledge obtained thus far).

A simple strategy called *epsilon-greedy* has been proposed in the area of reinforcement learning to achieve a suitable trade-off between exploration and exploitation [16]. This strategy randomly chooses a sample (i.e., subject) with the probability of ϵ and selects the sample expected to yield the highest return with the probability of $1-\epsilon$. In our problem, the sample selected with the probability of $1-\epsilon$ corresponds to a subject at high risk.

We further modify the epsilon-greedy strategy by incorporating the notion of active learning to make it more appro-

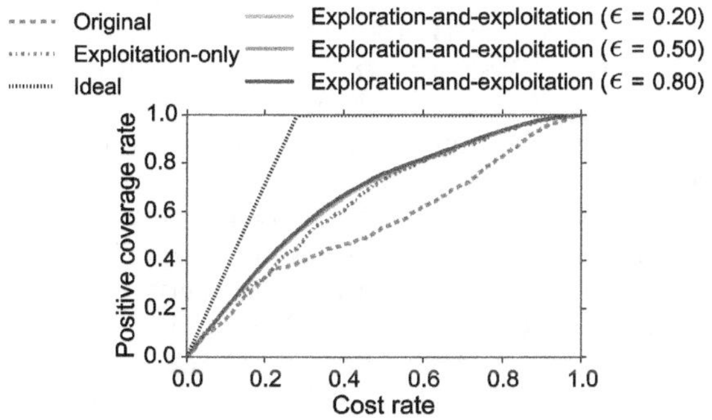

Figure 5: Coverage rate of high-risk subjects versus the cost of follow-up checkup. The exploration-and-exploitation strategy significantly improves the coverage of the original follow-up procedure.

priate for classification problems. Active learning is a framework where an algorithm iteratively selects an informative sample and query whose label. Uncertainty sampling is a common algorithm. In the binary classification case, the algorithm selects the sample with the least certainty of being positive; that is, it chooses the i^*-th subject by evaluating

$$i^* = \arg\min_{i \in \mathcal{I}} \mid \hat{h}(\boldsymbol{x}_i) - 0.5 \mid . \qquad (2)$$

We combine uncertainty sampling and the epsilon-greedy strategy and implement our *exploration-and-exploitation strategy* for determining the priority of the subjects. In each step, our strategy selects the most uncertain subject by using (2) with the probability of ϵ, and selects the subject who is the most likely to be at high risk by using (1) with the probability of $1 - \epsilon$. It is worth noticing that this strategy is applicable in other problems, such as collecting positive samples from an unlabeled multi-relational dataset [2].

5.3 Evaluation

We compare the proposed active learning approach with the original follow-up procedure in terms of the coverage rate under budget constraints.

5.3.1 Experimental setting

We used the data of 2,109 subjects who underwent both the first-year checkup and the second-year checkup. All of the features except for measurements of the hemoglobin level and optional questionnaires were used. We categorized the subjects with *Affected* and *Emergency* risk levels into the high-risk group, and the others are in the low-risk groups; they are used for the class labels. We employed an L2-regularized logistic regression implementation (sklearn.linear_model.SGDClassifier), whose hyperparameters were determined by using a five-fold cross validation on the first $N = 21$ (1%) subjects who underwent the second-year checkups.

The hyperparameter ϵ for the exploration and exploitation strategy was chosen from $\{0.2, 0.5, 0.8\}$; we ran 10 experiments for each of them. We used the coverage rate of high-risk subjects under budget constraints as the performance measure, which is defined as the ratio of the number of high-risk subjects covered by predictions to the total number of high-risk subjects. We investigated the coverage rate by varying the cost rate, and the ratio of the subjects we can offer the follow-up checkups to under the budget constraint. We compared the two strategies, namely, the exploitation-only strategy and the exploration-and-exploitation strategy, with the actual follow-up order and the ideal order.

5.3.2 Results and discussion

Figure 5 shows that both of the proposed active learning strategies reach better high-risk subject coverage for all choices of ϵ, which indicates that they are efficient sampling strategies.

For example, when the budget constraint is at 40%, the actual coverage rate is 46.4%, while the exploitation-only strategy achieved 60.5% and the exploration-and-exploitation strategy with $\epsilon = 0.8$ achieved 66.6% coverage. Among the proposed strategies, not much difference is observed up to 0.15 cost rate. For higher cost rates, higher coverage rates were achieved by the exploration-and-exploitation strategy; this is probably because it selected more informative samples to improve the classifier. The exploration-and-exploitation strategy showed the best and most stable performance at $\epsilon = 0.8$, which puts emphasis the importance of on collecting informative samples.

The trained model indicated that the responses on the questionnaire were helpful for detecting subjects who were still at high risk or who became high-risk subjects after the previous checkup. For example, if subjects answered they did not periodically consult with doctors in the previous checkup , they were likely to be at high risk in the follow-up checkup. Conversely, if subjects answered that they walked faster than the other people of the same sex and similar age, they were expected to be at low risk when the follow-up was conducted.

6. RELATED WORK

There have been many projects aimed at improving healthcare in developing countries. Ramachandran et al. showed that lifestyle modification could prevent type 2 diabetes in Asian Indian subjects [12], Rajput et al. studied an Android-based mHealth system in South Africa [11], and Ramachandran et al. conducted an intervention program in India by using mobile phone messaging for getting advice and support for lifestyle modification [13]. While these authors and we share the ultimate goal, to the best of our knowledge, our work is the first attempt at introducing machine learning approaches for supporting preventive medicine programs in developing countries.

Clinical risk prediction has been studied for specific diseases such as Alzheimer's disease [14, 17, 18], heart failure [17], and leukemia [3]. These studies built prediction models from different types of medical data such as magnetic resonance imaging, positron emission tomography, cerebrospinal fluid, and flow cytometry. Ng et al. developed a general framework for clinical risk prediction using electronic health records (EHR) [5]. Our risk prediction method follows this line; however, we focus on a situation where we do not have much information about subjects and we need to reduce the costs of the checkups. A few drug systems have been proposed for supporting physicians, such as a system that predicts patient abilities to protect themselves from infectious diseases and uses this information for selecting appropriate drugs [15], or a case-based system that retrieves similar patients from previous prescription records [4]. These systems do not consider the costs of collecting information about the patients.

7. CONCLUSION

We have reported on our feasibility study to apply predictive modeling approaches to a low-cost preventive medicine program in Bangladesh. Through the evaluation using real data collected from a field experiment in Bangladesh, we showed that our approach with multiple classifiers successfully reduced the costs of health checkups, a multi-task learning method provided accurate recommendation for specific types of drugs, and an active learning method achieved an efficient assignment of healthcare workers to the follow-up cares of subjects.

One possible future work is to deploy the predictive approaches used in this study to actual preventive medicine programs. Developing more sophisticated methods to assign budgets and human resources in preventive medicine programs is also a promising research direction to popularize preventive medicine.

8. ACKNOWLEDGMENTS

This research has been supported by the Funding Program for World-Leading Innovative R&D on Science and Technology, "Development of the fastest database engine for the era of very large database and experiment and evaluation of strategic social service enabled by the database engine", and a Health Labor Sciences Research Grant, "Study of establishment and diffusion of standards needed for secondary utilization of electronic medical information."

9. REFERENCES

[1] A. Alwan et al. *Global status report on noncommunicable diseases 2010.* World Health Organization, 2011.

[2] H. Kajino, A. Kishimoto, A. Botea, E. Daly, and S. Kotoulas. Active learning for multi-relational data construction. In *Proceedings of the 24th World Wide Web Conference (WWW)*, 2015.

[3] T. Manninen, H. Huttunen, P. Ruusuvuori, and M. Nykter. Leukemia prediction using sparse logistic regression. *PloS one*, 8(8):e72932, 2013.

[4] K. Miyo, Y. S. Nittami, Y. Kitagawa, K. Ohe, et al. Development of case-based medication alerting and recommender system: a new approach to prevention for medication error. In *Proceedings of the 12th World Congress on Health (Medical) Informatics (MEDINFO)*, 2007.

[5] K. Ng, A. Ghoting, S. R. Steinhubl, W. F. Stewart, B. Malin, and J. Sun. PARAMO: A PARAllel predictive MOdeling platform for healthcare analytic research using electronic health records. *Journal of biomedical informatics*, 48:160–170, 2014.

[6] Y. Nohara, E. Kai, P. P. Ghosh, R. Islam, A. Ahmed, M. Kuroda, S. Inoue, T. Hiramatsu, M. Kimura, S. Shimizu, K. Kobayashi, Y. Baba, H. Kashima, K. Tsuda, M. Sugiyama, M. Blondel, N. Ueda, M. Kitsuregawa, and N. Nakashima. Health checkup and telemedical intervention program for preventive medicine in developing countries: Verification study. *Journal of Medical Internet Research (JMIR)*, 17(1):e2, 2015.

[7] G. Obozinski and B. Taskar. Multi-task feature selection. In *Proceedings of the Workshop on Structural Knowledge Transfer for Machine Learning*, 2006.

[8] W. H. Organization. Global health observatory data repository, density of physicians. `http://apps.who.int/gho/data/node.main.A1444`.

[9] W. H. Organization. Non-communicable diseases - a major health challenge of the 21st century. *World Health Statistics 2012*, pages 34–37, 2012.

[10] F. Pedregosa, G. Varoquaux, A. Gramfort, V. Michel, B. Thirion, O. Grisel, M. Blondel, P. Prettenhofer, R. Weiss, V. Dubourg, J. Vanderplas, A. Passos, D. Cournapeau, M. Brucher, M. Perrot, and E. Duchesnay. Scikit-learn: Machine learning in Python. *Journal of Machine Learning Research*, 12:2825–2830, 2011.

[11] Z. A. Rajput, S. Mbugua, D. Amadi, V. Chepng'eno, J. J. Saleem, Y. Anokwa, C. Hartung, G. Borriello, B. W. Mamlin, S. K. Ndege, et al. Evaluation of an Android-based mHealth system for population surveillance in developing countries. *Journal of the American Medical Informatics Association*, 2012.

[12] A. Ramachandran, C. Snehalatha, S. Mary, B. Mukesh, A. Bhaskar, and V. Vijay. The Indian diabetes prevention programme shows that lifestyle modification and metformin prevent type 2 diabetes in Asian Indian subjects with impaired glucose tolerance (IDPP-1). *Diabetologia*, 49(2):289–297, 2006.

[13] A. Ramachandran, C. Snehalatha, J. Ram, S. Selvam, M. Simon, A. Nanditha, A. S. Shetty, I. F. Godsland, N. Chaturvedi, A. Majeed, et al. Effectiveness of mobile phone messaging in prevention of type 2 diabetes by lifestyle modification in men in India: a prospective, parallel-group, randomised controlled trial. *The Lancet Diabetes & Endocrinology*, 1(3):191–198, 2013.

[14] A. Rao, Y. Lee, A. Gass, and A. Monsch. Classification of alzheimer's disease from structural mri using sparse logistic regression with optional spatial regularization. In *Proceedings of the 33rd Annual International Conference of the IEEE Engineering in Medicine and Biology Society (EMBS)*, pages 4499–4502, 2011.

[15] K. Shimada, H. Takada, S. Mitsuyama, H. Ban, H. Matsuo, H. Otake, H. Kunishima, K. Kanemitsu, and M. Kaku. Drug-recommendation system for patients with infectious diseases. In *AMIA Annual Symposium Proceedings*, page 1112, 2005.

[16] R. S. Sutton and A. G. Barto. *Introduction to Reinforcement Learning.* MIT Press, 1st edition, 1998.

[17] F. Wang, P. Zhang, B. Qian, X. Wang, and I. Davidson. Clinical risk prediction with multilinear sparse logistic regression. In *Proceedings of the 20th ACM SIGKDD International Conference on Knowledge Discovery and Data Mining (KDD)*, pages 145–154, 2014.

[18] S. Xiang, L. Yuan, W. Fan, Y. Wang, P. M. Thompson, and J. Ye. Multi-source learning with block-wise missing data for alzheimer's disease prediction. In *Proceedings of the 19th ACM SIGKDD International Conference on Knowledge Discovery and Data Mining (KDD)*, pages 185–193, 2013.

Dynamic Hierarchical Classification for Patient Risk-of-Readmission

Senjuti Basu Roy[†], Ankur Teredesai[†], Kiyana Zolfaghar[†],
Rui Liu[†], David Hazel[†*], Stacey Newman[†], Albert Marinez [◇].
[†] Center for Data Science, UW Tacoma, [◇] MultiCare Health System, [*] Kensci Inc.,
{senjutib,ankurt, kiyana, ruiliu, dhazel, newmsc8}@uw.edu,
albert.marinez@multicare.org, david@kensci.com

ABSTRACT

Congestive Heart Failure (CHF) is a serious chronic condition often leading to 50% mortality within 5 years. Improper treatment and post-discharge care of CHF patients leads to repeat frequent hospitalizations (i.e., readmissions). Accurately predicting patient's *risk-of-readmission* enables care-providers to plan resources, perform factor analysis, and improve patient quality of life. In this paper, we describe a supervised learning framework, *Dynamic Hierarchical Classification (DHC)* for patient's risk-of-readmission prediction. Learning the hierarchy of classifiers is often the most challenging component of such classification schemes. The novelty of our approach is to *algorithmically* generate various layers and combine them to predict overall 30-day risk-of-readmission. While the components of DHC are generic, in this work, we focus on congestive heart failure (CHF), a pressing chronic condition. Since healthcare data is diverse and rich and each source and feature-subset provides different insights into a complex problem, our DHC based prediction approach intelligently leverages each source and feature-subset to optimize different objectives (such as, Recall or AUC) for CHF risk-of-readmission. DHC's algorithmic layering capability is trained and tested over two real world datasets and is currently integrated into the clinical decision support tools at MultiCare Health System (MHS), a major provider of healthcare services in the northwestern US. It is integrated into a QlikView App (with EMR integration planned for Q2) and currently scores patients everyday, helping to mitigate readmissions and improve quality of care, leading to healthier outcomes and cost savings.

1. INTRODUCTION

Hospital readmissions have come to the forefront of healthcare research and discussions in recent years for their recognized universal negative impacts on healthcare systems' budgets and patient loads throughout the world. Within the United States, Centers for Medicare & Medicaid Services (CMS) recently began using readmission rates as a publicly reported quality metric to measure hospital care standards and reimbursements in the fee-for-service model[1]. The severity of the readmissions problem can even be measured in economic terms: the estimated cost of unplanned readmissions is roughly $17.9 billion per year [8]. A significant percentage of these costs are attributable to patients who are often the sickest and most vulnerable: old, critically ill, and suffering from multiple chronic disease conditions. Paradoxically, more than 27% of such readmissions are avoidable [16]. Hence, predicting risk-of-readmission can guide implementation of appropriate interventions to prevent such avoidable readmissions. To that end, this paper investigates the issues faced and challenges addressed in developing and deploying a *framework to predict the risk-of-readmission (RoR)*.

While the deployed framework is extensible by design and includes other chronic conditions, in this paper the chronic condition we focus on is Congestive Heart Failure (CHF) since CHF is one of the leading causes of hospitalization. Studies also indicate that a large percentage of CHF admissions are actually readmissions within a short window of time. The 2005 data for Medicare beneficiaries estimated that 12.5% of Medicare patients admitted due to CHF were followed by readmissions within 15 days, accounting for about $590 million in healthcare costs [12]. In practice, a window of 30-days after discharge for CHF is considered *clinically meaningful* for hospitals and medical communities to take action to reduce readmissions [11] and forms the basis of most readmission risk prediction models.

Current research treats the problem as a binary classification task, where the objective is to identify patients with CHF who are likely to be readmitted within 30 days of discharge as an output of a single binary classifier [21, 19, 18]. A patient readmitted within 30 days = 1 and a patient not readmitted within 30 days = 0. There are several shortcomings to this approach which we address with the DHC framework: the distribution of risk of readmission is highly skewed with a few patients readmitting repeatedly and many patients readmitting once or twice over a period of a year. Traditional classifiers suffer from majority bias and tend to assign patients to the no 30-day-readmission majority class. Moreover, patient characteristics change over time. New diseases and conditions set in; age and vitals continuously change. Thus, including all patients discharged with CHF in the training set to build the classification model introduces noise since patients that were readmitted after a long gap can have characteristics that are very different from pa-

KDD'15, August 10-13, 2015, Sydney, NSW, Australia.
 ISBN 978-1-4503-3664-2/15/08 ...$15.00.
DOI: http://dx.doi.org/10.1145/2783258.2788585.

[1]http://www.cms.gov

tients that were readmitted within a short time (30 days) for the same condition. Hence the team of data scientists and the underlying framework has to handle numerous missing values, discretize attributes, collate comorbidities, extract suitable features and employ the right learning algorithm given the constraints.

This research presents a *Dynamic Hierarchical Classification (DHC)* framework to predict RoR for CHF patients. The primary novelty of the solution is to undertake the prediction problem in *several stages or layers*, leading to the formation of a hierarchy of classification models as the overall solution. Each layer aims at predicting the RoR within *certain days* (cut-points). For example, it may be better to predict whether a CHF patient is likely to (ever) readmit or not before calculating her readmission risk within 30 days of discharge. Each such logical consideration constitutes *a classification layer.* Within a given layer, the problem is of a binary classification design layer by layer[2]. Consider a 70 year old female patient suffering from primary diagnosis of congestive heart failure and various associated conditions such as diabetes and renal failure. If at layer one, DHC predicts her to be likely to be readmitted (ever), then the second layer may predict likely to be readmitted within-60-days of discharge (or not). Subsequently, only when she qualifies to be readmitted with a high confidence at both these layers, would the third layer predict her likelihood to be readmitted within 30 days (or not). This may sound simple conceptually, but the challenge of *how many layers are sufficient and how to design the intermediate layers* remain an open problem. Furthermore, the effectiveness of different features may be different in various layers. Then, the question is, how to select the features? We address this by performing layer specific feature selection. The last challenge is how to perform effective binary classification in each layer. We propose threshold tuning of the classification models for that.

In spite of algorithmic automation as proposed, it is not easy to design these layers and always get it right. Clinical teams may provide initial guidance but there is no clear clinical evidence for how many layers (for decisioning) are appropriate for a given patient population or how to define the time-window for readmission cut-points. Naturally, many of these design decisions are also dataset specific, requiring us to discover these layers for a given patient cohort. In this work, we propose an innovative approach: we design multiple algorithms to discover the actual cut-points assuming that the number of layers is specified as an input. In one of our algorithms, we primarily analyze the characteristics of the underlying patient population and propose greedy algorithms to design the cut-points such that the two consecutive layers generated by our algorithm exhibit the highest difference in the characteristics of the patient population. We also non-trivially adapt one of the frequency based popular discretization algorithms, Chi-Merge [7] (that is primarily used to discretize continuous attributes based on class distribution), to generate these cut-points. After that, to maximize a particular metric (such as AUC, precision, recall, accuracy, etc.), we study how to make use of the training data and the trained classification model in a given layer. We propose novel solutions to the above mentioned problems in this work.

[2]This could be formalized by finding the maximum duration X between two admissions in the dataset; i.e.the task is to predict whether the patient would be readmitted with X days or not.

We present comprehensive experimental results using two real world datasets - we consider 4 years of the State Inpatient Dataset (SID) of Washington State as our large-scale dataset and then we use the real patient dataset provided by MultiCare Health System, a major health system in the northwestern US as the small scale dataset. We empirically evaluate the effectiveness of our proposed solutions with statistical significance analysis using a variety of quality metrics and perform comparative analyses with our hierarchical classifications models against several baseline algorithms. Our results demonstrate that the proposed framework is superior to the baseline algorithms for all quality metrics with statistical significance.

To summarize, we make the following contributions:

1. We initiate the study of designing hierarchical classification models to predict 30-day RoR for CHF patients (Section 2).
2. We propose a *deployed solution for Dynamic Hierarchical Classification (DHC)* framework, empowered with multiple novel solutions to effectively design the prediction hierarchies (Section 3 and and 4).
3. We perform comprehensive experiments using multiple real world patient data sets, demonstrating that the proposed hierarchical model enhances the quality of prediction (Section 5).

2. PRELIMINARIES

It is typical in clinical settings for data to be spread across various relational schemas and flat files; a series of (anonymized) patient record data for various windows of time and modalities of measurements are typically extracted from EMRs and secondary hospital sources to form a data warehouse with appropriate dimensions and measures. Such a schema contains granularities of patient measures related to admission and discharge, other diseases, demographic factors, comorbidities, and post-discharge and follow-up-plans, which are all integrated and preprocessed. Each encounter is uniquely identified by an admission ID. Multiple admissions (i.e., readmissions) of the same patient are identified by the same patient ID and different encounter ID. For a given patient and a given hospital admission, we can calculate the number of days between the current admission and her previous discharge and check if it is less than 30.

Problem definition 1. Given a patient record, the problem of predicting the RoR within γ days of discharge is a hierarchical classification problem. The intuition here is to first predict the readmission window for higher γ values before predicting readmission for $\gamma = 30$ days. Each of these *time intervals* are cut-points, demarcating a classification layer in dynamic hierarchical classification (DHC). Since the 30 day interval is clinically meaningful and tied to reimbursements, that interval is the last layer of risk scoring and outcomes. Each layer can constitute a specific readmission window (for example the very first layer predicts whether a patient would be readmitted at all or not for γ >365 days in a year). Each layer design is to formulate a binary classification model using historical patient data relevant to that interval to predict the RoR within that readmission interval. How many such layers are to be designed, and how to decide the readmission intervals algorithmically, is the key contribution of this work and described in depth in Section 4.

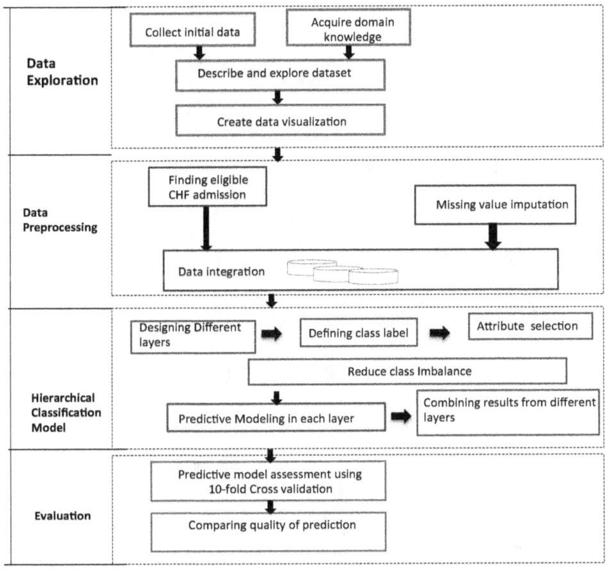

Figure 1: Overall architecture for RoR prediction process includes various stages as seen above including: exploration, preprocessing, modeling, and evaluation.

Data exploration, data pre-processing, hierarchical classification model, and model evaluation are critical for a successful data mining framework, especially at healthcare domain [21, 19, 18]. Figure 1 provides an overview of these major steps. For the DHC framework design we worked closely with cardiologists, nurse practictioners, and other members of the care team to identify critical factors influencing early recurrent readmission. The robustness of these factors and their availability at various points in the care process was an important DHC design consideration.

3. DEPLOYING THE DHC FRAMEWORK

Prior research efforts have focused on the accuracy of modeling to predict the likelihood of patients with chronic conditions to readmit within 30 days[15]. Commercial efforts have been limited and mostly restricted to web based mortality tools or risk calculators where data is manually entered to compute the risk. To the best of our knowledge, ours is the first cloud based scalable EMR integrated effort reported in literature that uses data mining fundamentals to continuously monitor risk of patients and issue risk scores to care providers. We have enabled the platform to deliver the per-patient readmission risk score along with actionable insights, not solely as a business intelligence tool sourced from a data warehouse (see 3.1), but on real-time clinical data, delivered within the clinical workflow, at the point of care.

The DHC framework consists of three main components: a) External Layer, b) Communications Layer, c) Analytics Layer. Within these layers there are multiple subcomponents and processes which are tightly integrated in order to accurately and efficiently score patients for 30 day risk of readmission and deliver these risk profiles to the patients electronic medical record (EMR).

3.1 QlikView Application

The initial deployment scenario envisioned was a single layer binary classifier exposed through a QlikView Readmission App[3]. This would provide system-wide readmission visualization and reporting with facility level, cohort level, and patient level drill down capability. Additionally, the QlikView Readmission App was used to identify and flag patients (within targeted risk categories) for further investigation and focus. It enables exploration of a detailed patient risk profile (30 day risk of readmission score targeting clinical attributes, psychosocial factors, a composite score, and top contributing factors). With the development of the DHC framework, the QlikView risk scores are now computed by the hierarchical classification with algorithmic multi-layer design. A spapshot of the application is presented in Figure 2.

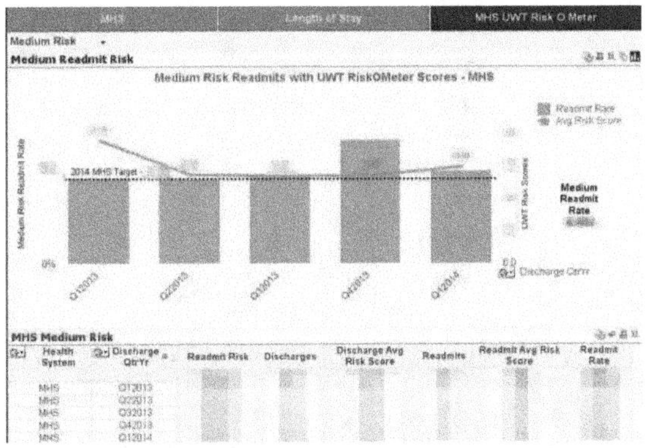

Figure 2: Snapshot of the QlikView Application

Every night it scores discharged patients and creates a ranked list of readmission risk for further review.

3.2 EMR Integration

Business intelligence tools 3.1 are useful for population level reporting and risk management but are not oriented towards the clinical workflow and have limited adoption within that context. To fully leverage our developed framework for CHF readmissions, cardiovascular service line leadership recognized the need to deploy DHC directly into their EMR (Epic).

After extensive user research, the team identified two target Epic integration points: 1) the Heart Failure Dashboard, used by cardiology to see the overview of the patients and help drive interventions during the encounter, 2) Care Management Doc Flowsheet, used to support discharge planning (which begins when the patient is admitted) and bring focus to psychosocial factors and followup care.

The EMR integration roadmap consists of: 1) publishing of a single combined score (clinical + psychosocial) as a "result" [4] in Epic, 2) subcomponents of that result to include discrete clinical and psychosocial scores.

3.3 Patient Data Flows

DHC is available as an on premise deployment or as a series of services hosted on Microsoft Azure. The overall architecture of the system and flow of messages are illustrated in Figure 3.

[3] http://www.qlik.com/us/explore/products/qlikview

[4] In the same way that lab results can be tracked and recorded over time, the insertion of the score as a result, with primary value and multiple sub-components, enables comprehensive trend analysis, reporting capability and intervention exploration.

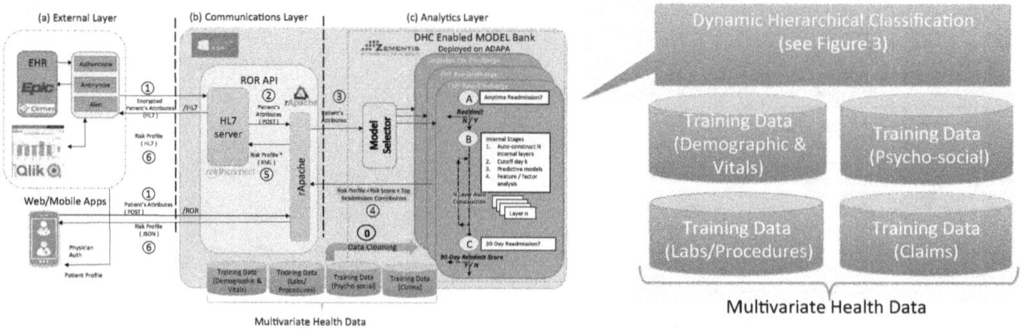

Figure 3: Illustration of the DHC Framework: (a) External Layer, (b) Communications Layer, (c) Analytics Layer. The focus of this paper is the Dynamic Hierarchical Classification in (c) Analytics Layer.

We now return to our example of a 70 year old female patient. She has been admitted to the inpatient setting and within 24 hours her lab results become available. As her medical record within Epic is updated, an HL7 message [5] containing the relevant attributes is generated. This message is then sent from the External Layer (a) to the Communications Layer (b). For cloud deployments, where the data does not stay fully resident within the health system, the tuple of patient data is passed through an anonymization service, which sends only the attributes (+GUID) required for scoring to the API [15].

The HL7 message is then ingested by Mirth Connect service [6] which handles message queuing and translation from HL7 into JSON, used internally by the DHC Enabled Model Bank. For native JSON requests (such as from a mobile device), we would bypass Mirth Connect [15].

After ensuring proper formatting and consumption of the message, it is passed to the Analytics Layer for scoring. We use the Zementis ADAPA Scoring Engine [7] and the DHC Enabled Model Bank. The use of ADAPA brings multiple benefits, among these the ability to scale up to handle a very large volume of messages, as well as the ability to import multiple models (beyond those we have developed for CHF), allowing us to score patients against a number of chronic disease conditions. Additionally, the DHC supports auto selection of cut-points, where the model is trained against MultiVariate Health Data sources outlined in Figure 3 (the significance of this is outlined in Section 4). When a patient tuple is passed to the APIs provided by the ADAPA scoring engine, it is scored against the DHC Model which has been trained for a particular cohort, such as CHF Post-Discharge.

A risk profile, consisting of a risk score as described next in section 4.3 and top correlated factors (identified using Chi-Square test) that contribute to readmission risk, is then generated and returned back to the Communications Layer. In the case of Epic deployment, the JSON response is converted back into HL7 for consumption. This is then returned to the anonymization service, where the risk profile is recoupled with the patient identifier, attached to the patient visit, and published as a result within Epic.

[5]HL7: Messaging format(standards, guidelines and methodologies) by which various health care systems communicate.
[6]http://www.mirthcorp.com/products/mirth-connect
[7]http://zementis.com/products/adapa/

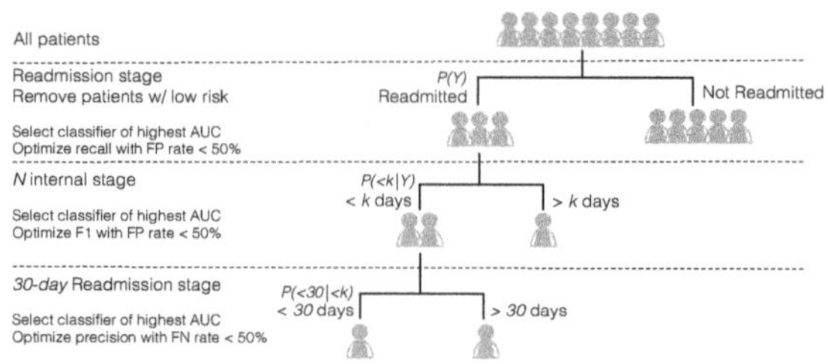

Figure 4: Tree-based hierarchical class structure for predicting 30-day readmission using 1 intermediate layer.

4. DYNAMIC HIERARCHICAL CLASSIFICATION (DHC)

We propose *Dynamic Hierarchical Classification (DHC)* to predict the risk of readmission within 30 days, transforming the problem into a tree-structured class hierarchy. Our approach produces a hierarchical set of classifiers in top-down fashion. The hierarchical setting provides the opportunity to make more specific and accurate predictions and improve knowledge about the problem using factor analysis (Chi-squared test). The framework also allows flexible choices of classifiers at different layers. As the distribution of data changes at each layer, DHC allows us to use the best classifier to optimize different learning objectives for each layer.

For our problem (i.e., predicting 30-day RoR), the hierarchical classification task could be restated as follows: first predict if a patient would ever be readmitted or not. For that task, a binary prediction model is designed using appropriate training data. Then, in the *intermediate layers, a set of classifiers* needs to be designed with each constituting a particular readmission window. Each of these is a subtask towards predicting RoR with a specific time window (cut-point). We design binary classification models for each of these intermediate layers. For simplicity, we assume that the number of intermediate layers is predefined and given [8]. The final layer of the classification is to predict whether a patient would be readmitted within 30 days or not. Similar to all previous layers, this sub-task is also treated as a binary classification problem and the appropriate training dataset is used for that purpose.

[8]However, in our experimental analyses, we empirically decide the number of intermediate layers.

For the purposes of illustration, Figure 4 describes the overall process of predicting 30-day RoR using 1 intermediate layer. The framework involves three stages: *Readmission Stage*, *Internal Stage*, and *30-day Readmission Stage*. Even though the number of layers in the internal stage are given, we still have to identify *the appropriate readmission windows, i.e., cut points* for those layers. Our proposed solutions to design cut-points are described in Section 4.2.

Algorithm 1: DHC Algorithm

Require: Training dataset D, number of internal layers N, cutoff day $k > 30$, Max is the maximum readmission time based on the dataset D

- `[Stage 1]` Design Max-day readmission prediction model using D
- $m = 31$, $n = Max$
- **for** $i = 1$ to $N - 1$ **do**
    - Extract $D' \subset D$, where D' contains only patients who are readmitted within (m, n)-days in D
    - $k \leftarrow$ CutpointFinder(D', m, n)
    - `[Stage 2]` Design (m, k)-day readmission prediction model using D'
    - $D \leftarrow D'$
    - $m = k + 1$
- Design (m, Max)-day readmission prediction model using D', where D' contains only patients who were readmitted within (m, Max) days in D
- Extract $D'' \subset D$, where D'' contains only patients who were readmitted within $(0, 30)$ days in D
- `[Stage 3]` Design $(0, 30)$-day readmission prediction model using D'

Algorithm 1 formalizes the DHC framework. Similar to the multistage screening in medical practice, we impose a maximum error bound while maximizing the recall and precision at different stages. The error bound (i.e. false positive rate) is determined by domain experts. Table 1 provides a tabular view of *Readmission Stage*, *Internal Stage*, and *30-day Readmission Stage*.

4.1 Readmission Stage

The first *Readmission* stage predicts whether a patient will be readmitted at all after being discharged from the hospital. The learning objective is to maximize AUC and recall [7] in order to capture all patients with readmission risk. The maximum false positive rate is set to be 50%. Since this is the root (very top level) of the hierarchical classification model, the goal is to filter out patients who are unlikely to be readmitted.

4.2 Internal Stage

The objective is to maximize AUC and recall while controlling the false positive rate to be lower than 50%. We build N internal layers and, for each layer, derive a cutoff day k. Even when N is a given integer number, we still have to determine N different readmission windows (cut-points). Intuitively, what we intend to do is to choose those cut-points, such that, if one can *create N non-overlapping partitions of the entire patient population based on those cut-points, patients that fall across the stratum are as divergent as possible.* We propose a heuristic algorithm towards that end which iteratively creates N different cut-points.

Algorithm 2 describes the *hill climbing* search heuristic to identify a single cutoff day k that constitutes a layer. Without loss of generality, to find a cut-off day k between a time window (m, n) (note that if $N = 1$, then $m = 31$, $n = Max$, where, for a given dataset D, the highest readmission day is denoted to be Max), we call a pseudo-random number generator between (m, n) to get a k, such that $m < k < n$. We select two candidate cut-points: $k' = k + 5$ and $k'' = k - 5$. After that, we compute two divergences: one based on k' and another based on k''. k then gets updated based on whichever cut-point gives rise to higher divergence. We continue the search until no further improvement is possible. Once a single cut-off point k is found, we run Algorithm 2 twice to find two other cut-off points, one between 31 and k and the other between $k + 1$ and Max. This process is repeated until all N internal layers are identified. Next, we describe two divergence calculation methods used by Algorithm 2.

4.2.1 *Entropy-based Divergence Methods*

Recall Algorithm 2 and note that to select a single cut-point between (m, n) window, the hill climbing algorithm needs to compute the divergence of patient population that constitutes two readmisison windows between (m, k) and $(k + 1, n)$ based on any k, $m < k < n$. In order to use Entropy-based divergence methods, one has to represent each of these patient populations as a probability distribution. To do that, we obtain the *center of the individual patient group*, where the center is the *average* for the numeric attributes and *mode* for categorical attribute, as described in Algorithm 3 (DIVCAL).

In our implementation, we consider two popular divergence methods: Kullback-Leibler Divergence (KL) and Jensen-Shannon Divergence (JSD) [3]. The main difference between the two methods is that unlike KL, JSD is symmetric and always defined. The divergence between two centers p and q of m dimensions, for Kullback-Leibler(KL) and Jensen-Shannon(JSD) methods are calculated as follows [3]:

$$KL(p,q) = \Sigma_{\forall i=1}^{m} ln(\frac{p(i)}{q(i)}) \times p(i)$$

$$JSD(p,q) = \frac{1}{2}\left(\Sigma_{\forall i=1}^{m} ln(\frac{2p(i)}{p(i)+q(i)}) \times p(i) + \Sigma_{\forall i=1}^{m} ln(\frac{2q(i)}{p(i)+q(i)}) \times q(i)\right)$$

Algorithm 2: Subroutine CutpointFinder(D, m, n)

Require: Dataset D, lower boundary of readmission window m, upper boundary of readmission window n

- $k \leftarrow$ RANDOM_NUMBER(m, n)
- **repeat**
    - $k' \leftarrow k + 5$
    - $k'' \leftarrow k - 5$
    - currentDIV $= DIVCAL(k)$
    - **for all** $i \in \{k', k''\}$ **do**
        - **if** $DIVCAL(i) >$ currentDIV **then**
            - $k = i$
            - currentDIV $= DIVCAL(i)$
- **until** $DIVCAL(k) > DIVCAL(k')$ and $DIVCAL(k) > DIVCAL(k'')$
- **return** k

4.2.2 *Chi-Merge Based Solutions*

In addition to Entropy-based methods, we intelligently adapt the popular frequency based Chi-Merge algorithm [10] to design the internal layers.

	`Readmission Stage`	`Internal Stage`	`30-day Stage`
Objective	AUC & Recall	AUC	AUC & Precision
Error Bound	FP Rate < 50%	FP Rate < 50%	NA
# of Layers	1	N	1
Probability	$P(Y)$	$P(< k\|Y)$	$P(< 30\| < k)$

Table 1: Comparison of three stages

Algorithm 3: Subroutine DIVCAL(k)

Require: Dataset D, cutoff day k, center of data V

$D' \leftarrow$ subset of D where readmission day between m, k

$D'' \leftarrow$ subset of D where readmission day between $k+1, n$

$p \leftarrow$ center of D'

$q' \leftarrow$ center of D''

$d \leftarrow KL(p,q) Or JSD(p,q)$

return d

Chi-Merge is traditionally used to discretize continuous attributes based on the class distribution frequency. On the other hand, our objective is to create a set of N intermediate layers (and cut-points thereof) for the variable readmission, where this variable itself is also the class label. This precludes direct adaptation of Chi-Merge in our settings. In fact, to be able to apply Chi-Merge, we need to extend our settings in the following way that we illustrate using a simple example next. Imagine that we have a population of 100 patients in total. Out of these 100 patients, 20 got readmitted within 30 days and 10 never got readmitted. The remaining 70 patients create the positive instances who got readmitted within 30 and Max days. Similarly, Chi-Merge also needs negative instances. If a set of X' patients are readmitted on a day d, then we set the negative instances using the remaining $70 - X'$ patients. After this modification, we apply Chi-Merge to decide the N intermediate layers.

4.3 30-day Readmission Stage

The final stage predicts the readmission $\leq$ 30 days. The sample size has been reduced as we move down toward this final leaf node. We use local information from this subset to train classifiers and assess the likelihood of a given patient being readmitted to the hospital within 30 days – i.e. $P(Readmit \leq 30 | Readmit \leq k)$. The objective of this stage is to maximize the AUC and precision so that the medical resources can be efficiently invested on the right patients.

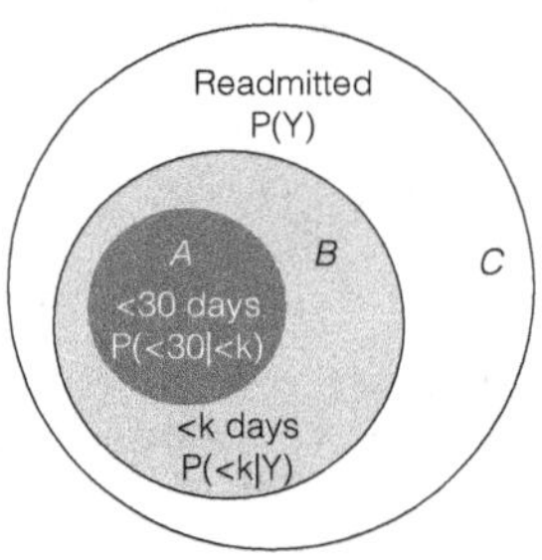

Figure 5: Relationships of predicted probability of three stages considering 1 intermediate layer

Figure 5 shows the relationship of predicted probability of three stages, where circle A is the final stage, circle B is the internal stage (for simplicity we consider 1 internal stage in this example), and circle C is the readmission stage. Intuitively, the predicted probability of 30-day readmission should be the highest in A, lower in B, and the lowest in C. Given the definition of the problem for predicting 30-day readmission, the goal is to estimate $P(\leq 30)$, as below.

$$P(\leq 30 | \leq k) = \frac{P(\leq 30 \wedge \leq k)}{P(\leq k)}$$

Since ≤ 30 is a subset of $\leq k$, we obtain:

$$P(\leq 30 \wedge \leq k) = P(\leq 30)$$

Therefore,

$$P(\leq 30) = P(\leq 30 | \leq k) P(\leq k)$$

Similarity, we can obtain $P(k)$ as follows:

$$P(\leq k | Y) = \frac{P(\leq k \wedge Y)}{P(Y)}$$

Since $\leq k$ is a subset of $Readmission = Y$, we obtain:

$$P(\leq k \wedge Y) = P(\leq k)$$

Thus,

$$P(\leq k) = P(Y) P(\leq k | Y)$$

Therefore,

$$P(\leq 30) = P(\leq 30 | \leq k) P(\leq k) = P(\leq 30 | \leq k) P(\leq k | Y) P(Y)$$

Given the equations above, we can compute $P(\leq 30)$ for all instances in A in Figure 5. We then combine the results using normalization techniques to ensure the correct sequence of instances: $A \prec B \prec C$, if the list is sorted in descending order by the predicted probability. In Figure 5, we identify three mutually exclusive areas – the dark grey area in A, the light grey area in B, and the white area in C. For all instances in A (the dark grey area), we normalize the predicted probability in to the range (0.7,1]. For all instances in the light grey area in B, we normalize the predicted probability to the range (0.3,0.7]. Finally, we fit the predicted probability from the white area in C into [0,0.3]. We compute our evaluation metrics (e.g. AUC, recall etc.) using the combined normalized probability vector.

5. EXPERIMENTS AND EVALUATION

We evaluate performance of proposed DHC framework on Washington State Inpatient Dataset and the Heart Failure cohort data from MultiCare Health Systems (MHS).

5.1 SID Dataset

The State Inpatient Databases (SID) [9] of Washington State (referred as SID-WA) is available for four years 2009-2012. It is discharge abstract data that includes inpatient

[9] http://www.hcup-us.ahrq.gov/sidoverview.jsp

discharge records from community hospitals in the State of Washington with all-payer, encounter-level information.

Each year comprises four files that are associated with hospital encounters: core file (CORE), charges file (CHGS), diagnosis and procedure groups file (DXPRGRPS), and disease severity measures file (SEVERITY). Total 596 attributes for each encounter with an unique identifier KEY, that can be used to link records across files (but NOT across years). We construct a heart failure cohort with patients whose primary or secondary ICD9-CM diagnosis codes are heart failure. Our cardiology partners identified a total of 91 attributes to be related to CHF readmission from a mix of demographic variables such age, gender, and race; as well as comorbidities related to diagnosis information derived from primary and secondary diagnosis codes for that patient. Many features related to utilization services such as thew emergency room, ICU, electrocardiograms services and so on are also included in our prediction models.

The SID-WA attribute DaysToEvent is used to compute the days between two consecutive hospital admissions for each patient. The days since previous hospital discharge is computed using the days between two hospital admissions minus the length of stay of the first admission. We exclude admission records in which the patient passed away while in the hospital, and in which the patient age is less than 1 year (age=0). The dataset then contains a total of $2,051,105$ readmission instances.

5.2 Dataset from MultiCare Health System

The Cardiovascular datamart is our primary source within the MultiCare Health System data. It has about 8,600 patients diagnosed with Heart Failure, serviced over $14,200$ hospital encounters from 2009 to 2013. We consider only patients who are discharged to home, excluding inter-hospital transfers. Encounters where the patient expired are not included. The post cleaning and processing set we used for these experiments includes 6,348 patients diagnosed with CHF and 14,170 hospital encounters. A total of 49 attributes were determined to be related to CHF admission. These are mainly clinical. The key socio-demographic factors related to readmissions are: gender, race, and marital status. Other important factors pertinent to CHF are ejection fraction(EF) [10], blood pressure, primary and secondary diagnosis indicating comorbidities, and APR-DRG codes [11] for severity of illness and risk of mortality. Information about discharges, such as discharge status, discharge destination, length of stay and follow-up plans, are also found to be correlated to CHF readmissions. In addition, we include 34 cardiovascular and comorbidity attributes.

5.3 DHC Evaluation

Our modeling for SID-WA data and corresponding analysis is conducted on Microsoft Azure over virtual machines with 16 cores and 112GB of RAM. For the modeling environment we use R and Python both. Models are then exported in PMML and deployed using the Zementis ADAPA scoring engine. We evaluate quality using measures such as Area Under the Curve(AUC), Precision, Recall, and Accuracy [7].

Depending on the final consumption of RoR predicted score for a patient population, different evaluation measures are appropriate. AUC measure is typically interesting when the dataset is imbalanced and we want to ascertain comparison of performance with other competing tools for risk stratification. Precision is critical if there is a high cost related to incorrectly predicting patients' risk to belong to the *Readmission* class with accompanying reimbursement penalties associated with the decision. Recall is relevant if using the DHC framework to identify patients who belong to *Readmission* class from within an overall population for post-discharge care management. Besides these, we also compute the confusion matrix for all the experiments (each fold) consisting of true positive count (TP), false positive count (FP), true negative count (TN), and false negative count (FN).

In general, we select the classifier that renders the highest AUC for each layer for reporting in this paper. In actual deployment we may vary this choice depending on the end-point where the score is being consumed. We also tune the threshold to optimize the selected evaluation metric for each layer in DHC.

Predictive Models: We use five different predictive models in general. The first one is Logistic Regression (LR) [7], a method that models the outcomes (class labels) as a so-called logit function of the predictive variables. The second one is Naive Bayes (NB) [7], a well-known simple statistical classifier that assumes attribute independence. We also use Random Forests and Adaboost [5], as popular ensemble algorithms (we use 500 decision trees in random forests and 50 CART decision trees in Adaboost). The last implemented model is the Support Vector Machines (SVM) [7] using well-established RBF kernel. For each layer of DHC described in Section 4, we run a 10 fold cross-validation procedure on train set to determine the best classifier.

5.3.1 Comparative study on SID dataset

We follow the holdout method to test the models built on SID-WA data. The data is first partitioned into two independent train and test sets. Three years of data 2009-2011 are allocated to the training set which consists of 1,543,131 admissions and the last year of data (2012), consisting of 507,974 records, is allocated to the test set.

The N internal layers are discovered using either entropy-based divergence calculation methods (Kl-divergence, Jensen Difference), or appropriately adapting frequency based discretization method (Chi-merge), as described in Section 4.

Statistical Significance Test: Wherever applicable, we also perform paired t-test [7] to further understand the statistical significance of the obtained results. To be able to run t-test, we partition the test population into 20 folds, then calculate the quality metric for the competing methods in each fold, and finally run the t-test to investigate whether results are significantly different from each other on each metric. Unless otherewise stated, the significance level is set to p-value < 0.05.

Effect of Number of Internal Layers: We carry out experiments to find the best number of internal layers for each cut-point selection method. We vary the number of layers from 3 to 12. The logic for this range was simply to see if we auto-discover less than 30, 30 to 60, and more than 60 as natural layers. Based on the experiments, the best number of internal layers depends on the cut-point selection methods. However, we observe that the increase in number of layers negatively affects the true positive rate. This

[10]EF is the volumetric fraction of blood pumped out of the ventricle with each heartbeat

[11]All Patient Refined Diagnosis Related Groups Definition

can lead to a significant decrease in recall, while the AUC and the accuracy do not change considerably. The reasoning behind this is as follows: with an increase in the number of layers, more patients are pruned in the initial layers (i.e., predicted readmission is "no") and consequently less patients get promoted to the 30-day readmission layer (which has to be the last layer given the problem formulation). Empirical analyses suggests Chi-Merge to propose 1 (i.e., $N = 1$), and Jensen Divergence optimize at 3 layers overall, while KL-Divergence shows the best performance for 5 internal layers. Table 2 demonstrates the readmission interval for the internal stages as well as the classifier chosen for each stage based on 10 fold cross-validation procedures on training data. Classifiers were chosen based on performance as measured by the appropriate metric from Table 1. It can be seen that Logistic regression (LR) is the dominant classifier for most of the cut-points.

Effect of Cut-Points Selection Algorithms: Recall Section 4 and note that given the number of internal stages as an input, we propose different algorithms to automatically select the N cut-points for the internal stage. The aim of these proposed solutions is to choose cutoff days that discriminates two groups of patients with distinct characteristics as much as possible. As described in previous sections, we vary the value of N experimentally and observe its qualitative effect on different internal hierarchy selection algorithms (Entropy Based Divergence vs Frequencey Based Discretization) and observe that these algorithms lead to different readmission windows (cut-points) for the internal stages. Based on our exhaustive empirical analyses, divergence methods have more stable results in comparison with Chi-Merge, especially when we increase the number of internal stages. Table 3 enlists the best result of each cutoff algorithm based on the best number of layers. The results indicates that, for Recall and AUC, KL Divergence significantly outperforms Jensen Divergence as well as Chi-Merge.

Effect of Threshold Tuning: As discussed in section 4, since the distribution of data changes from layer to layer, we run model selection algorithms at each layer in order to select the classifier that renders the highest AUC. Different data distributions and classifiers at each layer can lead to different probability distribution which may cause some inconsistency in final predictions. DHC allows us to apply scaling, as well as threshold tuning at each stage. This not only solves the problem of varied probability distributions but also enables us to optimize the selected evaluation metric for each stage. The default threshold is set to 0.5. In general, we expect that increasing the threshold throughout the hierarchy will lead to eliminating more patients at upper layers as no-readmission cases. Conversely, decreasing the threshold leaves the classification decision to lower layers. Among evaluation metrics, we focus on recall and AUC, as they provide insight into the performance of classifiers on skewed datasets. We tune the thresholds through the layers such that we improve the overall prediction quality, with the aim of increasing the appropriate objective (see Table 4).

Baseline Algorithms: For comparison, we implement five baseline solutions that employ a single classification model on the full dataset without using a hierarchical structure as proposed in DHC. We consider Logistic Regression, Naive Bayes, SVM, Random Forest, and Adaboost as five classifiers to build our baseline models (prior efforts have demonstrated them to work well for risk of readmission) [21]. Comparing the results in Table 5, the Naive Bayes classifier outperforms other models - it has high AUC, and reasonable recall.

Table 5 compares the result of the baseline models and the best DHC result which was obtained by KL-divergence method with 7 layer (see Table 3 and Table 4). As stated above, we also report the statistical significance of quality results (significance level is set to p-value < 0.05). It can be easily observed that our proposed framework achieves significantly better results for all metrics (AUC, recall, precision and accuracy) compared to the baseline with statistical significance. It is interesting to note that the highest improvement is for the recall and AUC, which are considered as the main metrics when dealing with skewed datasets.

	Random Forests	Adaboost	Naive Baye
Readmit Stage	0.6803	0.6539	0.6000
Internal Stage	0.6014	0.5830	0.5600
30-day Stage	0.6245	0.5900	0.5833

Table 6: MHS data: Classifier Comparison based on AUC for three stages

5.3.2 Comparative study on MultiCare Health System dataset

On MHS internal data, the presented results are representative. We primarily focus on describing the utility of the deployed DHC solution designed using KL-Divergence (as that is the best performing algorithm based on the SID dataset) and compare it with the single stage baseline classification algorithms.

Based on Kl-Divergence, we select one layer in internal stage (i.e., $N = 1$), thereby constituting 3 layers overall (readmit, internal, and the 30-day yes no layer). After getting results from Algorithm 2, the readmission interval for the internal stage was determined to be 65 days. Hence, the problem of predicting 30-day readmission risk is formalized using hierarchical classification as follows: *Readmit Stage*: predicting readmission within 1200 days (based on our dataset, $Max = 1200$), *Internal Stage*: predicting readmission within 65 days, and *30-day Stage*: predicting readmission within 30-days.

DHC Internal Predictive Models for MultiCare Health System: The following three classifiers exhibit the best and somewhat comparable classification performance – Random Forests [2], Adaboost [5], and Naive Bayes [7]– for each layer of DHC described in Section 4. Table 6 shows the AUC of the three classifiers in each layer. As shown in Table 6, Random Forests achieves the highest AUC for all three layers. Therefore, we present the results of Random Forests for all three stages for the rest of our experiments.

Table 7 shows the experimental results for the proposed DHC approach and the prediction quality for each stage. Since, Random Forests achieves the best performance, for brevity, we therefore present our results by comparing DHC with a single-stage baseline Random Forests classifier (500 decision trees). DHC outperforms the baseline on true positive count, recall, and AUC. It is noted that the highest improvement takes place in the *Readmit Stage*, as our predictive model achieves higher AUC at that particular stage. This observation is intuitive as it appears that the quality of prediction can be improved by eliminating negative in-

	layers	Cutpoints
Chi-Merge	3	Readmit(Adaboost),280(LR),30(LR)
KL divergence	7	Readmit(Adaboost),355(svm),240(LR),195(LR),150(LR),110(LR),30(LR)
Jensen Divergence	3	Readmit(Adaboost),280(LR),30(LR)

Table 2: SID Data: Selected cutoffs and classifiers for each cutoff selection methods

	layers	TP	FP	TN	FN	Prec	Recl	Acc	AUC
Chi-Merge	3	34750	103275	329928	40021	0.252*	0.465	0.718*	0.699
KL Divergence	7	38818	118427	314776	35953	0.247	0.519*	0.696	0.701*
Jensen Divergence	3	35762	106907	326296	39009	0.251	0.478	0.713	0.698

Table 3: SID data: Best DHC Results for cutoff selection methods.* denotes whether the result is significantly better than the others among the three variations of cutoff selection methods based on paired-t-test.

stances at an early stage. The overall quality improvement becomes less at the internal stage. This is due to the fact that the data in the internal stage is more homogeneous and no distinct patterns among the patients are identified.

We also have observed that for this dataset the difference in KL-divergence across different k (cut-point) values do not vary greatly (most of them approximately 0.057). After further analysis we realize that such low KL divergence and homogeneity arises due to our use of *mean value* to determine the centroid of each group. In the future we explore alternatives to calculate group centroids, potentially leading to larger values of k for the internal stages. Nevertheless, based on Hill-Climbing we selected $k = 65$.

Factor Analysis: We apply the Chi-Squared test [7] to determine the significant factors. The p-value is set to 0.05 in all cases. We observe that the number of significant factors vary at each stage. There are 32 influential factors for *Readmission Stage* and *Internal Stage* and 16 for *30-day Stage*. Table 8 enlists top-10 most influential factors sorted based on increasing P-values, based on the Chi-Squared test. The importance of a particular factor is different at each stage. For example, *Length of Stay* is an important factor for *Readmission Stage* and *Internal Stage*, but not for *30-day Stage*. It implies that, given that a patient is likely to return to the hospital, care managers can concentrate more on risk factors closely associated to 30-day readmission. Such insights are tremendously useful to the domain experts and the physicians for appropriate prognosis.

Readmission	Internal	30-day
Severity Of Illness	Risk-Of-Mortality	Severity Of Illness
Risk-Of-Mortality	Severity Of Illness	Risk-Of-Mortality
Length-Of-Stay	Length-Of-Stay	Acute coronary syndrome
Renal Failure	Secondary ICD9	Discharge Followup Category
Anemia	Cardio-respiratory Failure	Stroke
Ejection-Fraction	Fluid Disorder	Cardio-respiratory Failure
Pneumonia	Acute coronary syndrome	Fluid Disorder
Fluid Disorder	Discharge Followup Category	Chronic atherosclerosis
Dialysis	Ejection Fraction	Malnutrition

Table 8: MHS data: Factor analysis of three different stages of DHC model

6. RELATED WORK

To the best of our knowledge, no hierarchical classification techniques for risk of readmission risk prediction have been yet reported in literature. Very few cloud based deployed solutions exist today in healthcare and none are for scoring patients for their readmission risk on multiple chronic conditions, in real-time, integrated with EMRs.

Readmission Risk Prediction: An early research result for predicting RoR for CHF patients was termed the Yale Model [11]. Logistic regression was used for 30-day all-cause readmission risk for 65+ year old HF patients. More recently [1], administrative claim data was used to build a regression model on 24,163 patients from 307 hospitals on patients 65 years or older. In collaboration with MultiCare Health Systems, our prior efforts have resulted in accurate solutions [15, 21, 19, 18, 20] to predict 30-day RoR. However, none of these solutions generalizes for any time-interval and automated design, which is one of the primary contributions of the proposed research.

Hierarchical Classification: Hierarchical classification is extensively used in various application areas such as in text mining for web page classification applications [4], Information Retrieval [6], and in signal processing [14]. The use of multistage classification for Bayesian combination of classifiers is explored in literature [13], K-Nearest Neighbor [17], and hierarchical SVMs [9]. Thus we turn to a hierarchical or multi-stage classification process for predicting risk of readmission. The design though is non-trivial to optimize overall prediction quality and ensure good generalization, particularly for high risk patients.

7. CONCLUSION

Predictive models for risk of readmission can significantly improve quality of care. With an increase in the number of patients suffering from chronic conditions, demand for actionable, accurate, and cost-effective solutions to be deployed also increases. In this paper, we describe the algorithm design, deployment challenges, architecture of our

	layers	Thld	TP	FP	TN	FN	Prec	Recl	Acc	AUC
Chi-Merge	3	.55,.55,.45	37921	112700	320503	36850	0.252 †	**0.507***	0.706 †	0.699
KL Divergence	7	.4,.55,.55,.4,.4,.45,.4	40044	121483	311720	34727	0.248	**0.536***†	0.692	0.696
Jensen Divergence	3	.55,.55,.45	39116	118093	315110	35655	0.248	**0.523***	0.697	0.7†

Table 4: SID Data: Threshold tuning for result on table 3.† denotes whether the result is significantly better than the others among the three variations of cutoff selection methods(after threshold tuning).* denotes the result that is significantly higher after threshold tuning compared to result before that. The Thld column describes the selected threshold values from the readmission stage to 30-day stage.

	TP	FP	TN	FN	Prec	Recl	Acc	AUC
logistic regression	52139	264117	169086	22632	0.165	0.697	0.435	0.593
Naive Bayes	37247	120142	313061	37524	0.23666	0.498	0.689	0.678
SVM	3190	2575	430628	71581	0.553	0.043	0.854	0.634
AdaBoost	0	75799	0	432175	NAN	0	0.851	0.696
Random Forests	3150	1434	430741	72649	0.687	0.041	0.854	0.724
DHC (Proposed Technique)	40044	121483	311720	34727	**0.248**†	**0.536**†	**0.692**†	**0.696**†

Table 5: SID-WA data: Single Layer Baseline classifier comparisons. Naive Bayes is the best performing baseline solution.

	Total	Thld	TP	FP	TN	FN	Prec	Recl	Acc	AUC
Baseline (Random Forests)	14,170	0.5	376	139	10,995	2690	0.7301	0.1226	0.8007	0.6492
DHC-combined	14,170	0.5	**1,272**	2,084	9,020	1,794	0.3790	**0.4148**	0.7263	**0.6596**
DHC-Readmit	14,170	0.5	5,119	3,025	3,794	2,232	0.6285	0.6963	0.6290	0.6803
DHC-Internal	8,144	0.46	2,749	4,360	743	292	0.3866	0.9039	0.4287	0.6014
DHC-30Day	6,332	0.7	861	1,230	3,220	1,021	0.4117	0.4574	0.6445	0.6245

Table 7: DHC Results on MHS data: Each stage contains different number of instances (Total column) and uses different threshold (Thld) for classification.

cloud-based deployed framework DHC. MultiCare Health System uses the described DHC framework to predict the 30 day post discharge risk of readmission for their heart failure collaborative. We demonstrate that the proposed framework clearly outperforms baseline solutions for congestive heart failure (CHF). DHC automatically discovers and defines the layers by leveraging the underlying historical patient data. Detailed experimental evaluations on two sizeable real-world datasets statistically validate the utility of DHC and the deployed engineering efforts demonstrate the real-world impact of the framework.

8. ACKNOWLEDGEMENT

We acknowledge MHS and Microsoft Azure for Research for their generous supports in this research.

References

[1] H. BG et al. Incremental value of clinical data beyond claims data in predicting 30-day outcomes after heart failure hospitalization. *Circ Cardiovasc Qual Outcomes*, 2011.

[2] L. Breiman. Random forests. *Machine learning*, 45(1):5–32, 2001.

[3] S.-H. Cha. Comprehensive survey on distance/similarity measures between probability density functions. *City*, 1(2):1, 2007.

[4] S. Dumais et al. Hierarchical classification of web content. In *SIGIR*, 2000.

[5] J. Friedman et al. Additive logistic regression: a statistical view of boosting (with discussion and a rejoinder by the authors). *The annals of statistics*, 2000.

[6] M. Granitzer. Hierarchical text classification using methods from machine learning. 2004.

[7] J. Han and M. Kamber. *Data mining: concepts and techniques.* Morgan Kaufmann, 2006.

[8] S. F. Jencks, M. V. Williams, and E. A. Coleman. Rehospitalizations among patients in the medicare fee-for-service program. *New England Journal of Medicine*, 360(14):1418–1428, 2009.

[9] T. Joachims. Text categorization with support vector machines: Learning with many relevant features, 1998.

[10] R. Kerber. Chimerge: Discretization of numeric attributes. In *Proceedings of the tenth national conference on Artificial intelligence*, pages 123–128. Aaai Press, 1992.

[11] H. M. Krumholz et al. *30-day heart failure readmission measure methodology. Report prepared for the Centers for Medicare & Medicaid Services.*

[12] P. E. Krumholz HM. REadmission after hospitalization for congestive heart failure among medicare beneficiaries. *Archives of Internal Medicine*, 157(1):99–04, Jan. 1997.

[13] M. W. KurzyÅĎski. On the multistage bayes classifier. *Pattern Recognition*, 21(4):355 – 365, 1988.

[14] U. Libal. Multistage pattern recognition of signals represented in wavelet bases with reject option. In *MMAR*, 2012.

[15] V. Rao et al. Readmissions score as a service (raas). 2014.

[16] C. v. Walraven et al. Proportion of hospital readmissions deemed avoidable: a systematic review. *Canadian Medical Association Journal*, 2011.

[17] Y. Yang and X. Liu. A re-examination of text categorization methods. pages 42–49. ACM Press, 1999.

[18] K. Zolfaghar et al. Big data solutions for predicting risk-of-readmission for congestive heart failure patients. In *IEEE Bigdata*, 2013.

[19] K. Zolfaghar et al. Exploring preprocessing techniques for prediction of risk of readmission for congestive heart failure patients. In *DMH Workshop*, 2013.

[20] K. Zolfaghar et al. Predicting risk-of-readmission for congestive heart failure patients: A multi-layer approach. *CoRR*, abs/1306.2094, 2013.

[21] K. Zolfaghar et al. Risk-o-meter: an intelligent clinical risk calculator. In *KDD*, 2013.

ALOJA-ML: A Framework for Automating Characterization and Knowledge Discovery in Hadoop Deployments

Josep Ll. Berral
Barcelona Supercomputing Center (BSC)
Universitat Politècnica de Catalunya (UPC)
Barcelona, Spain

Nicolas Poggi
Barcelona Supercomputing Center (BSC)
Universitat Politècnica de Catalunya (UPC)
Barcelona, Spain

David Carrera
Barcelona Supercomputing Center (BSC)
Universitat Politècnica de Catalunya (UPC)
Barcelona, Spain

Aaron Call
Barcelona Supercomputing Center (BSC)
Barcelona, Spain

Rob Reinauer
Microsoft Corporation
Redmond, USA

Daron Green
Microsoft Corporation
Microsoft Research (MSR)
Redmond, USA

ABSTRACT

This article presents ALOJA-Machine Learning (ALOJA-ML) an extension to the ALOJA project that uses machine learning techniques to interpret Hadoop benchmark performance data and performance tuning; here we detail the approach, efficacy of the model and initial results. The ALOJA-ML project is the latest phase of a long-term collaboration between BSC and Microsoft, to automate the characterization of cost-effectiveness on Big Data deployments, focusing on Hadoop. Hadoop presents a complex execution environment, where costs and performance depends on a large number of software (SW) configurations and on multiple hardware (HW) deployment choices. Recently the ALOJA project presented an open, vendor-neutral repository, featuring over 16.000 Hadoop executions. These results are accompanied by a test bed and tools to deploy and evaluate the cost-effectiveness of the different hardware configurations, parameter tunings, and Cloud services[1].

Despite early success within ALOJA from expert-guided benchmarking [13], it became clear that a genuinely comprehensive study requires automation of modeling procedures to allow a systematic analysis of large and resource-constrained search spaces. ALOJA-ML provides such an automated system allowing knowledge discovery by modeling Hadoop executions from observed benchmarks across a broad set of configuration parameters. The resulting empirically-derived performance models can be used to forecast execution behavior of various workloads; they allow *a-priori* prediction of the execution times for new configurations and HW choices and they offer a route to model-based anomaly detection. In addition, these models can guide the benchmarking exploration efficiently, by automatically prioritizing candidate future benchmark tests. Insights from ALOJA-ML's models can be used to reduce the operational time on clusters, speed-up the data acquisition and knowledge discovery process, and importantly, reduce running costs. In addition to learning from the methodology presented in this work, the community can benefit in general from ALOJA data-sets, framework, and derived insights to improve the design and deployment of Big Data applications.

[1]ALOJA's repository and sources at http://hadoop.bsc.es/

KDD'15, August 11-14, 2015, Sydney, NSW, Australia.

DOI: http://dx.doi.org/10.1145/2783258.2788600.

Categories and Subject Descriptors

C.4 [**Performance of Systems**]: Modeling techniques; D.4.8 [**Operating Systems**]: Performance—*Modeling and Prediction*; I.2.6 [**Artificial Intelligence**]: Learning—*Induction,Knowledge acquisition*

General Terms

Experimentation; Measurement; Performance

Keywords

Data-Center Management; Modeling and Prediction; Machine Learning; Execution Experiences; Hadoop

1. INTRODUCTION

Hadoop has emerged as the *de-facto* framework for Big Data processing deployment [2][19] and its adoption continues at a compound annual growth rate of 58% [12]. Even with this impressive trend, deploying and running a cost-effective Hadoop cluster is hampered by the extreme complexity of its distributed run-time environment and the large number of potential deployment choices. It transpires that many of the software parameters exposed by both Hadoop and the Java run-time have quite a pronounced impact on job performance[9, 8, 10] and therefore a corresponding effect on the cost of execution [13]. Selecting the most appropriate deployment pattern for a given workload, whether for on-premise servers or as part of a cloud service, involves a complex set of decisions. Any *a-priori* information presented as either heuristic or as a specific performance prediction could greatly improve the decision making process resulting in improved execution times and reduced costs.

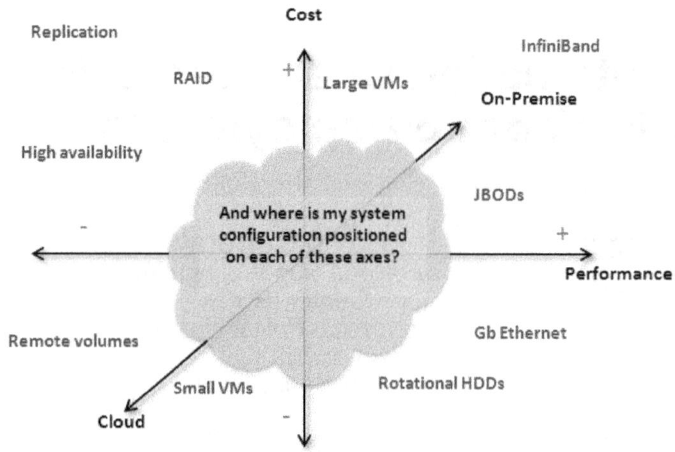

Figure 1: A cloud of points for Cost vs. Performance vs. Cloud or On-premise

Assisting such decision making often requires manual and time-consuming benchmarking followed by operational fine-tuning for which few organizations have either the time or performance profiling expertise. A problem inherent in such complex systems is the difficulty of finding a generalizable *rule of the thumb* for configurations that can be applied to all workloads (Hadoop jobs). To illustrate that complexity, figure 1 presents an example of the search space for evaluating the cost-effectiveness of a particular workload and setup.

ALOJA-ML provides tools to automate both the knowledge discovery process and performance prediction of Hadoop benchmark data. It is the latest phase of the ALOJA initiative which is an on-going collaborative engagement between the Barcelona Supercomputing Center (BSC), Microsoft Product groups and Microsoft Research (MSR). The collaboration explores upcoming hardware architectures and builds automated mechanisms for deploying cost-effective Hadoop clusters. ALOJA-ML's machine-learning derived performance models predict execution times for given a workload and configuration (HW and SW) and provide configuration recommendations for optimal performance of a given task. Given the ability to forecast task performance, the tools can also be used to detect anomalous Hadoop execution behavior. This is achieved using a combination of machine learning modeling and prediction techniques, clustering methods, and model-based outlier detection algorithms.

1.1 Motivation

Dealing with Hadoop optimization necessarily includes running multiple executions and examining large amounts of data, from the information of the environment and configurations, through to the outputs from result logs plus performance readings. In this project we deal with all available data with data mining and machine learning techniques. Selecting which are the relevant features and/or discarding useless information is key to discovering which parameters have the biggest impact on performance, or even the opposite, which features can be freely modified without any detrimental performance impact, allowing the user/operator to adjust configurations not only to me specific performance needs but also to the available resources. Recommending a specific system configuration requires knowledge on how parameter selection will affect various potential goals (e.g., increased performance, reduced execution cost or even energy savings). Modeling and automated learning techniques provide not only the ability to predict the effects of a given configuration, but also they allow exploration of possible configurations *in-vitro*, characterizing how hypothetical scenarios would work. The goal being to demystify the black-art of Hadoop performance tuning by providing Hadoop users and operators with the ability to predict workload performance and empower them with a clear understanding of the effect of configuration selections and/or modifications in both the HW and SW stack.

1.2 Contribution

In ALOJA-ML we aim to provide 1) a useful framework for Hadoop users and researchers characterize and address configuration and performance issues; 2) data-sets of Hadoop experimentation and prediction; and 3) a generalized methodology and examples for automated benchmarking couple to data mining techniques. This is achieved as follows:

1. The ALOJA framework for Big Data benchmarking, including the machine learning enhancements, is available to all the community to be used with own Hadoop data-set executions. Researchers or developers can implement or expand this tool-set through comparing or predicting data from observed task executions and/or by adding new machine learning or new anomaly detection algorithms.

2. All the data-sets collected for ALOJA and ALOJA-ML are public, and can be explored through our framework or used as data-sets in other data analysis platforms.

3. In this work we share our experiences in analyzing Hadoop execution data-sets. We present results on modeling and prediction of execution times for a range of systems and Hadoop configurations. We show the results from our anomalous execution detection mechanisms and model-based methods for ranking configurations depending on relevance. These rankings are used to characterize the minimal set of executions required to model a new infrastructure.

This article is structured as follows: Section 2 presents the preliminaries for this work and current state-of-art. Section 3, presents the datasets, the methodology and results for the Hadoop job execution time predictor model. Section 4 presents two use cases and extension for the predictor model: execution anomaly detection and guided benchmarking, our approach to guide benchmarks executions by predictive value. Finally, sections 5 and 6 the conclusions and future work lines for the project.

2. BACKGROUND

This section presents the background to the project and the current state-of-the art in Hadoop and system performance modeling applying machine learning.

2.1 The ALOJA project

The work presented here is part of the ALOJA Project; an initiative of the Barcelona Supercomputing Center (BSC) that has developed Hadoop-related computing expertise for over 7 years [3]. The efforts are partially supported the

Figure 2: Main components and workflow in the ALOJA framework

Microsoft Corporation, that contributes technically through product teams, financially, and by providing resources as part of its global *Azure4Research* program. ALOJA's initial approach was to create the most comprehensive vendor-neutral open public Hadoop benchmarking repository. It currently features over 16.000 Hadoop benchmark executions, used as the main data-set for this work. The tools on the online platform currently compares not only software configuration parameters, but also *current*, to new available hardware including SSDs, InfiniBand networks, and Cloud services. We also capture the cost of each possible setup along with the run time performance, with a view to offer configuration recommendations for a given workload. As few organizations have the time or performance profiling expertise, we expect our growing repository and analytic tools will benefit Hadoop community to meet their Big Data application needs. The next subsection briefly presets the main platform components, as a more complete description of the scope and goals, the architecture of the underlying framework and the initial findings are presented in [13].

2.1.1 *Benchmarking*

Due to the large number of configuration options that have an effect on Hadoop's performance, it has been necessary previous to this work to characterize Hadoop using extensive benchmarking. Hadoop's distribution includes jobs that can be used to benchmark its performance, usually referred as *micro benchmarks*, however these type of benchmarks usually have limitation on their representativeness and variety. ALOJA currently features the HiBench open-source benchmark from Intel [11], which can be more realistic and comprehensive than the supplied example jobs in Hadoop. For a complete description please refer to [11], and a characterization of the performance details for the benchmarks can be obtained in the *Performance Charts* section of ALOJA's online application [1].

2.1.2 *Current Platform and Tools*

The ALOJA platform[2], is composed of open-source components to achieve an automated benchmarking of Big Data deployments, either on-premise or in the cloud. To achieve this goal, clusters and nodes can be easily defined within the framework, and a set of specialized deployment and cluster orchestration scripts take care of the cluster setup. Then, a set of benchmarks to explore and execute can be selected and queued for execution. As benchmarks execute, results are gathered and imported into the main application —that features a Web interface, feeding the repository. On the Web-based repository of benchmark executions, the user can select to search and filter interesting executions and browse the execution details. Advanced analytic features are also provided to perform normalized and aggregated evaluations of up to thousands of results. The tools include:

- Best configuration recommendation for a given SW/HW combination.
- Speed up comparison of SW/HW combinations.
- Configuration parameter evaluation
- Cost/Performance analysis of single and clustered executions
- Cost-effectiveness of cluster setups

Figure 2 presents the main components of the platform that feed each other in a continuous loop. It is the intent of this work to add data-mining capabilities to the current online tools, to enable automated knowledge discovery and characterization, that is presented in later sections.

The platform also includes a *vagrant* virtual machine with a complete sand-box environment and sample executions that is used for development and early experimentation. In our project's site [1] there is further explanation and documentation of the developer tools.

2.2 Related Work

The emergence and the adoption of Hadoop by the industry has led to various attempts at performance tuning an optimization, schemes for data distribution or partition and/or adjustments in HW configurations to increase scalability or reduce running costs. For most of the deployments, execution performance can be improved at least by 3x from the default configuration [8, 9]. A significant challenge remains: to characterize these deployments and performance, looking for the optimal configuration in each case. There is also evidence that Hadoop performs poorly with newer and scale-up hardware [5]. Scaling out in number of servers can usually improve performance, but at increased cost, power and space usage [5]. These situations and available services make a case to reconsider scale-up hardware and new Cloud services from both a research and an industry perspective.

Previous research focused on the need for tuning Hadoop configurations to match specific workload requirements; for example, the Starfish Project from H. Herodotou [10] proposed to observe Hadoop execution behaviors and use profiles to recommend configurations for similar workload types. This approach is a useful reference for ALOJA-ML when modeling Hadoop behaviors from observed executions, in contrast, we have sought to use machine learning methods to characterize the execution behavior across a large corpus of profiling data.

Some approaches on autonomic computing already tackled the idea of using machine learning for modeling system behavior vs. hardware or software configuration e.g., works on self-configuration like J.Wildstrom [20] used machine learning for hardware reconfiguration on large data-center systems. Similarly, P.Shivam' NIMO framework [16] modeled computational-science applications allowing prediction of their execution time in grid infrastructures. Such efforts are precedents of successful applications of machine learning modeling and prediction in distributed systems workload management. Here we apply such methodologies, not to directly manage the system but rather to allow users, engineers and operators to learn about their workloads in a distributed Hadoop environment.

[2]ALOJA code available at: https://github.com/Aloja/

3. MODELING HADOOP WITH MACHINE LEARNING

The primary contribution of this work is the inclusion of data-mining techniques in the analysis of Hadoop performance data. Modeling Hadoop execution allows prediction of execution output values (e.g., execution time or resource consumption) based on input information such as software and hardware configuration. Modeling the system also enables anomaly detection by comparing actual executions against predicted outputs, flagging as anomalous those tasks whose run-time lies notably outside a machine-learned prediction. Furthermore, compressing system observations using clustering techniques identifies the set of points required for minimal characterization of the system, indicating the most representative tasks needed to model the system or possible sets of tasks needed to learn the behavior of a new system.

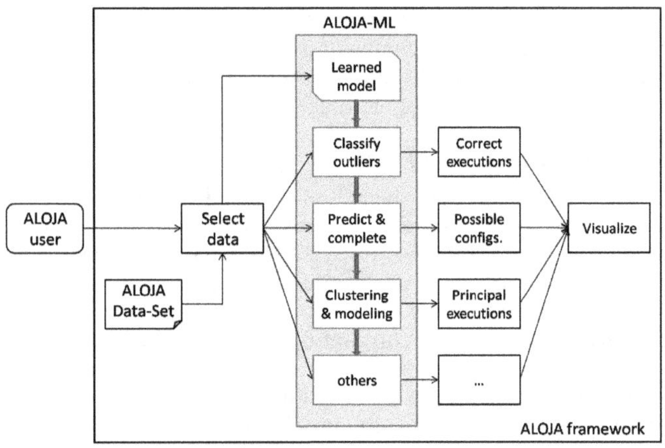

Figure 3: ALOJA-ML inside the ALOJA Framework

The ALOJA framework collates and analyzes data collected from Hadoop task executions and displays it through a range of tools; this helps users understand and interpret the executed tasks. ALOJA-ML complements this framework by adding tools that learn from the data and extract hidden (or not so obvious) information, also adding an intermediate layer of data treatment to complement the other visualization tools. Figure 3 shows the role of ALOJA-ML inside the ALOJA framework.

3.1 Data-sets and Structure

The ALOJA data-set is an open-access collection of Hadoop traces, containing currently over 16.000 Hadoop executions of 8 different benchmarks from the Intel HiBench suite [11]. Each execution is composed of a prepare Hadoop job that generates the data e.g., *teragen*, and a proper benchmark e.g., *terasort*. Although the job of interest is generally the proper benchmark (*terasort*), prepare jobs are also valid jobs that can be also used for training models. This leaves us with over 32.000 executions to learn from. Each benchmark is run with different configurations, including clusters and VMs, networks, storage drives, internal algorithms and other Hadoop parameters. Table 1 shows the data-set relevant features, selected by looking for those providing information into models, and their values.

Figure 4 shows an example execution logged on the ALOJA framework. From here we distinguish the input data, intro-

Benchmarks	
bayes, terasort, sort, wordcount, kmeans, pagerank, dfsioe_read, dfsioe_write	
Hardware Configurations	
Network	Ethernet, Infiniband
Storage	SSD, HDD, Remote Disks {1-3}
Cluster	# Data nodes, VM description
Software Configurations	
Maps	2 to 32
I/O Sort Factor	1 to 100
I/O File Buffer	1KB to 256KB
Replicas	1 to 3
Block Size	32MB to 256MB
Compression Algs.	None, BZIP2, ZLIB, Snappy
Hadoop Info	Version

Table 1: Configuration parameters on data-set

duced by the user executing the benchmark; the result of execution as the total time spent and time-stamps; and other key information that identifies the execution. We focus our interest on the elapsed time for a given execution as this can determine the cost of execution and indicate whether the execution is successful. Other important output data includes resources consumed such as usage statistics for CPU, memory, bandwidth and storage. We center our focus and efforts on learning and predicting the execution time for a given benchmark and configuration as our initial concern is to reduce the number and duration of executions required to characterize (learn) the system behavior.

The collection of traces is part of the ALOJA framework [1] and encourage the academic community and industry to make use of these results and/or to contribute to the corpus of results we have begun to generate.

3.2 Methodology

The learning methodology is a 3-way step model involving training, validation and testing; see Figure 5. Data-sets in ALOJA are split (through random sample) and two subsets used to train and validate the obtained model. A selected algorithm (taken from those detailed in section 3.3) learns and characterizes the system, also identifying and retaining the 'best' parameters (testing them on the validation split) from a list of preselected input parameters. The third subset is used to test the best-from-parameters model. All learning algorithms are compared through the same test subset.

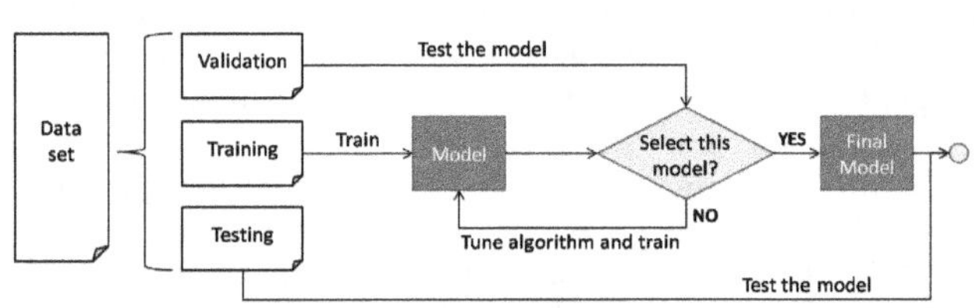

Figure 5: Data-set splitting and learning schema

The tool-set is available as an R library in our on-line *github* repository[3]. In our system the tools are called from the ALOJA web service but access can be initiated from any R-based analysis tool through R's ability to load remote

[3]https://github.com/Aloja/aloja-ml

id_exec	id_cl	bench	exe_time	start_time	end_time	net	disk	bench_type	maps
2	3	terasort	472.000	2014-08-27 13:43:22	2014-08-27 13:51:14	ETH	HDD	HiBench	8

iosf	replicas	iofilebuf	compression	blk_size	# data nodes	VM_cores	VM_ram	validated	version
10	1	65536	None	64	9	10	128	1	1

Figure 4: Example of logged observation on the data-set

functions from the Web. In this way any service or application can call our set of methods for predicting, clustering or treating Hadoop executions. In addition, our machine learning framework can be embedded on Microsoft Azure-ML services, delegating most of the learning process to the Cloud thereby reducing the ALOJA framework code footprint and enabling scaling the cloud. The architecture can be seen in Figure 6. The learning algorithms used here are part of the R *stats* and *nnet* packages, and RWeka [7].

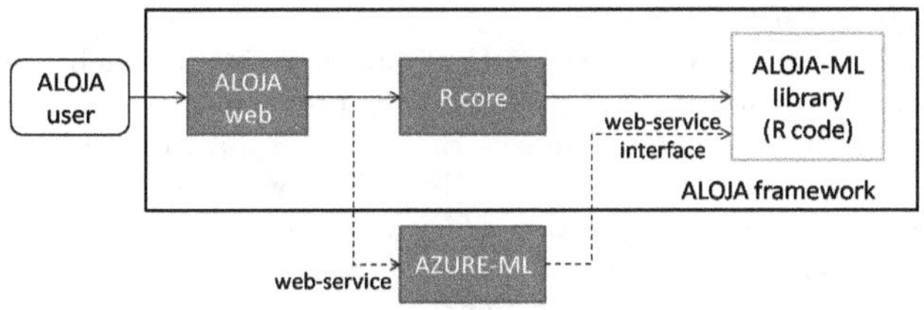

Figure 6: Schema of AZURE-ML on the ALOJA framework

3.3 Algorithms

At this time, the ALOJA-ML user can choose among four learning methods: Regression Trees, Nearest Neighbors, Feed-Forward Artificial Neural Networks, and Polynomial Regression. Each of these has different mechanisms of learning and strengths/weaknesses in terms of handling larges volume of data, being resilient to noise, and dealing with complexity.

Regression tree algorithm: we use the M5P [14, 18] from the RWeka toolkit. The parameter selection (number of instances per branch) is selected automatically after comparing iteratively the prediction error of each model on the validation split.

Nearest neighbor algorithm: we use the IBk [4], also from the RWeka toolkit. The number of neighbors is also chosen the same way as parameters on the regression trees.

Neural networks: we use a 1-hidden-layer FFANN from *nnet* R package [17] with pre-tuned parameters as the complexity of parameter tuning in neural nets require enough error and retrial to not provide a proper usage of the rest of tools of the framework. Improving the usage of neural networks, including the introduction of deep learning techniques, is in the road-map of this project.

Polynomial regression: a baseline method for prediction, from the R core package [15]. Experiences with the current data-sets have shown that linear regression and binomial regression do not produce good results, but trinomial approximates well. Higher degrees have been discarded because of the required computation time, also to prevent over-fitting.

3.4 Execution Time Prediction

Predicting the execution time for a given benchmark and configuration is the first application of the toolkit. Knowing the expected execution time for a set of possible experiments helps decide which new tasks to launch and their priority order (in case of time constraints or the need for immediate insights).

As said previously, the ALOJA data-set is used as training, validation and testing, with separate data splits blindly chosen. Deciding the best sizes for such splits becomes a challenge, as we seek to require as few benchmark executions as possible to train while maintaining good prediction accuracy. Also, at this time, we would like to execute as few jobs as possible to predict the rest of possible executions. Put simply, we look to build an accurate model from the minimum number of observations. As this specific problem is to explore in the next subsection 4.2, here we check the accuracy of predictors given different sizes of training sets. Figure 7 shows the learning and prediction data flow.

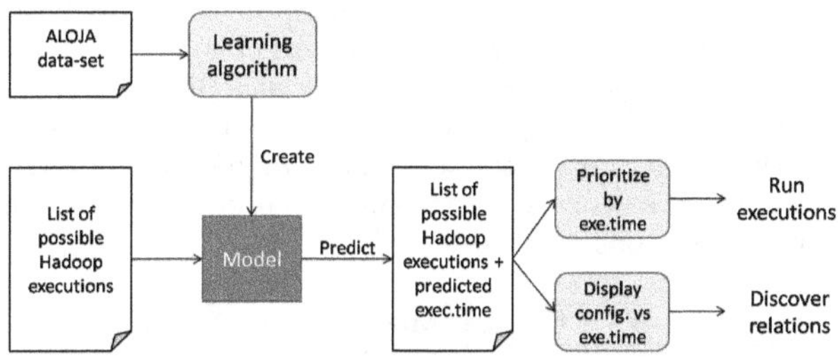

Figure 7: Learning and prediction data-flow schema

Furthermore, in this case we observe how much we can learn from logs and traces obtained from Hadoop executions, how much we can generalize when having different benchmark executions, also how ML improves prediction in front of other *rule of the thumb* techniques applied in the field.

3.4.1 Validation and Comparisons

As explained in subsection 3.3, we have several prediction algorithms from which to create our models, as well as different parameters and choices on the training type. Figure 8 shows the average errors, absolute and relative, for the validation and the testing process for each learning algorithm. In a first exploration, we iterated through some pre-selected parameters and different split sizes for training, validation and testing data-sets. Figure 9 shows how the size of training versus validation affects the model accuracy.

As can been seen in figure 9, using regression trees and nearest neighbor techniques we can model and predict the execution time for our Hadoop traces. We consider that, with a more dedicated tuning, neural networks and deep believe learners could improve results. After testing, linear and polynomial regressions were set aside they achieve poor results when compared with the other algorithms and the time required to generate the model is impractical for the amount of data being analyzed.

Another key concern was whether a learned model could be generalized, using data from all the observed benchmarks,

Algorithm	MAE Valid.	RAE Valid.	MAE Test	RAE Test	Best parameters
Regression Tree	135.19523	0.16615	323.78544	0.18718	M = 5
Nearest Neighbors	169.64048	0.18968	232.01521	0.18478	K = 3
FFA Neural Nets	189.60124	0.24541	333.93250	0.26099	5 neurons (1-hl), 1000 max-it, decay $5 \cdot 10^{-4}$
Polynomial Regression	167.98270	0.2321720	354.93680	0.2541475	degrees = 3

Figure 8: Mean and Relative Absolute Error per method, on best split and parameters found

Algorithm	RAE 50/25/25 Split	RAE 37.5/37.5/25 Split	RAE 20/55/25 Split
Regression Tree	0.18718	0.17903	0.22738
Nearest Neighbors	0.18478	0.21019	0.30529
FFA Neural Nets	0.27431	0.26099	0.27564
Polynomial Regression	0.2541475	0.2602514	0.9005622

Figure 9: RAE per method on test data-set, with different % splits for Training/Validation/Testing

or would each execution/benchmark type require its own specific model. One motivation to create a single general model was to reduce the overall number of executions and to generate powerful understanding of all workloads. Also, there was an expectation that our selected algorithms would be capable of distinguishing the main differences among them (e.g., a regression tree can branch different trees for differently behaving benchmarks). On the other hand, we knew that different benchmarks can behave very differently and generalizing might compromise model accuracy. Figure 10 shows the results for passing each benchmarks test data-set through both a general model and a model created using only its type of observations.

Benchmark	RAE General Model	RAE Specific Model
bayes	0.21257	0.16311
dfsio_read	0.45237	0.18472
dfsio_write	0.26468	0.16861
k-means	0.22700	0.20065
pagerank	0.76518	0.17862
sort	0.42930	0.17535
terasort	0.18190	0.19524
wordcount	0.16282	0.17546

Figure 10: Comparative for each benchmark, predicting them using the general vs. a fitted model with regression trees. The other algorithms show same trends

We are concerned about the importance of not over-fitting models, as we would like to use them for predicting unseen benchmarks similar to the ones already known in the future. Also, the fact that there are some benchmarks with more executions conditions the general model. After seeing the general vs specific results, we are inclined to use benchmark-specific models in the future, but not discarding using a general one when possible.

After the presented set of experiments and derived ones, not presented here for space limitations, we conclude that we can use ML predictors for not only predict execution times of unseen executions, but also for complementing other techniques of our interest, as we present in the following section. Those models provide us more accuracy that techniques used as *rules of thumb* like Least Squares or Linear Regressions (achieving LS with each attribute an average RAE of 2.0256 and Linear Regression a RAE of 0.80451).

3.4.2 *Applicability*

There are several uses on Hadoop scenarios for such prediction capability. One of them is predicting the performance of known benchmarks on a new computing cluster, as far as we are able to describe this new cluster. Having the hardware configuration of such cluster we can predict our benchmark executions with the desired software configuration. In case of a new benchmark entering the system, we can attempt to check if any of the existing models for specific benchmarks fits the new one. And then treat the new benchmark as the known one, or expand or train a new model for this benchmark.

Another important situation is filling values and configurations, or creating new ⟨configuration, execution time⟩ combinations for a benchmark, in order to observe the expected importance of a given parameter or a given range of values on a parameter, with reference to performance.

Further, an important application of such prediction is to know the size in time of a Hadoop workload, aiming to schedule properly the execution inside a cluster. Being able to find the proper combination of parameters for each workload also their allocation in time and placement becomes an interesting problem. Including predictive capabilities into a job scheduling problem can improve consolidation and de-consolidation processes [6], and so reduce resource consumptions by maintaining any quality of service or job deadline preservation.

Finally, the next section presents another specific uses for the predicting model, with high priority in the road-map of the ALOJA project. These are 1) anomaly detection, by detecting faulty executions through comparing their execution times against the predicted ones; and 2) identification of which executions would best model a given Hadoop scenario or benchmark, by clustering the execution observations, and taking the resulting cluster centers as recommended configurations. Next section focuses on these two cases in detail.

4. SELECTED USE CASES

This section exposes two types of experiences on the use of ALOJA with machine learning tools, and some discoveries obtained over the Hadoop data-set.

4.1 Anomaly Detection

Detecting which executions of our data-sets can be considered valid, flagged for revision or directly discarded, is the second application of the prediction models. Detecting automatically executions susceptible of being failures, or even executions not modeled properly, can save time to users who must check each execution, or can require less human intervention on setting up *rules of thumb* to decide which executions to discard.

With Hadoop workload behaviors modeled, model-based anomaly detection methods are applied. Considering the learned model as the 'rule that explains the system', any observation that does not fit into the model (this is, the difference between the observed value and the predicted value is bigger than expected), is flagged as anomalous. Here we flag anomalous data-set entries as *warnings* and *outliers*. A *warning* is an observation whose error respect to the model is n standard deviations from the mean. An *outlier* is a mis-predicted observation where other similar observations are well predicted. I.e an outlier is a warning that, for all its neighbor observations (those ones that differ in less than h attributes, or with Hamming distance $< h$), more than a half are well predicted by the model. Figure 11 shows the anomaly decision making schema.

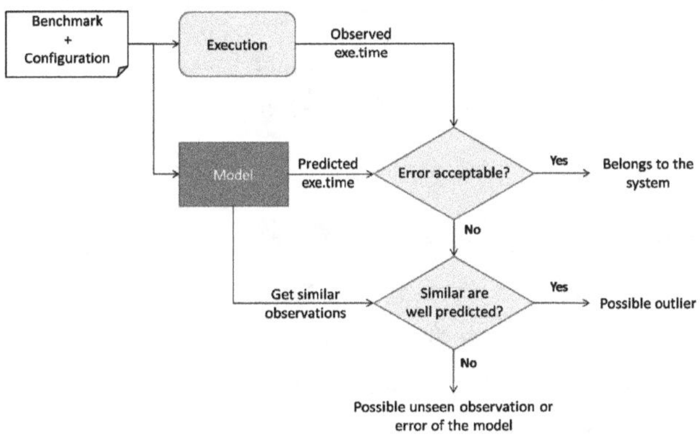

Figure 11: Anomaly detection mechanism schema

In this case we observe how our automatic method can detect outliers or anomalous executions, against a human review and a human-based rules review.

4.1.1 Validation and Comparisons

Once we can model the ALOJA data-set, and knowing that it can contain anomalous executions, we proceed to auto-analyze itself with the anomaly detection method. Here we perform two kind of experiments, one testing the data of a single benchmark with a model learned from all the observations, and one testing it against a model created from its specific kind of observations. We select the observations belonging to the *Terasort* benchmark, with 7844 executions, and the regression trees algorithm from the previous subsection.

After applying our method, using as parameters $h = \{0...3\}$, $n = 3$, and a model learned from all the observed executions, we detect 20 executions of Terasort with a time that does not match with the expected execution time. After reviewing them manually, we detect that those executions are valid executions, meaning that they finished correctly, but something altered their execution, as other repetitions finished correctly and in time. Further, when learning from Terasort observations only (7800), the model is more fitted and is able to detect 4 more executions as anomalous, which in the general model where accepted because of similarities with other benchmark executions with similar times. From here on we recommend to validate outlier executions from models trained exclusively with similar-kind executions.

Testing with different values of Hamming distance shows low variation, as outliers are easily spotted by its error, also confirmed by several neighbors at distance 1. Setting up distance 0, where an observation only is an outlier when there are at least two identical instances with an acceptable time, marks 17:24 observations as warnings, and 7:24 as outliers. Such warnings can be set to revision by a human referee to decide whether are outliers or not. Figure 12 show the comparative of observed versus predicted execution times, marking outliers and warnings.

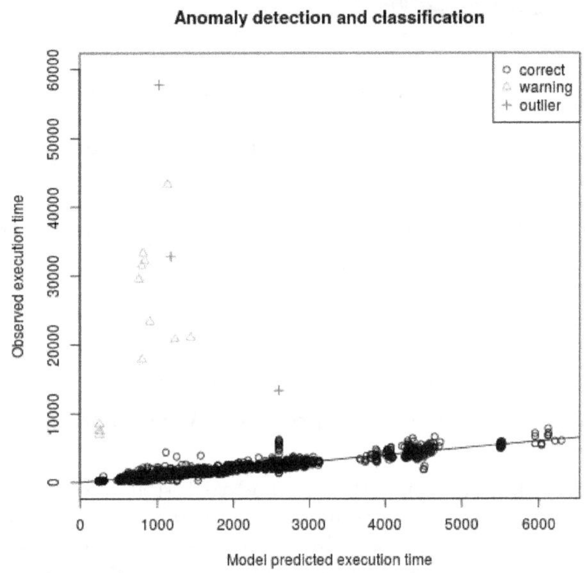

Figure 12: Automatic outlier detection ($h = 0$, $n = 3$)

Notice that the confusion matrix shows anomalies considered legitimate by the automatic method. After human analysis, we discovered that such ones are failed executions with a very low execution time, whose error at prediction is also low, so the method does not detect them. This let us see that for such detection, a manual rule can be set, as if an execution does not exceed a minute, belongs to a failed execution.

Also, we may decide to reduce the number of directly accepted observations by lowering n (standard deviations from the mean) from 3 to 1, putting under examination from a 1% of our data-set up to a 34%. In this situation, we increase slightly the number of detections to 38 (22 warnings and 16 outliers). Figure 13 show the comparative of observed versus predicted execution times, marking outliers and warnings. Also figure 14 shows the confusion matrices for the automatic versus a manual outlier tagging, automatic versus *rule of thumb* (semi-automatic method where ALOJA checks if the benchmark has processed all its data), and automatic warnings versus manual classification as incorrect or "to check" (which is if the operator suspects that the execution has lasted more than 2x the average of its similar executions).

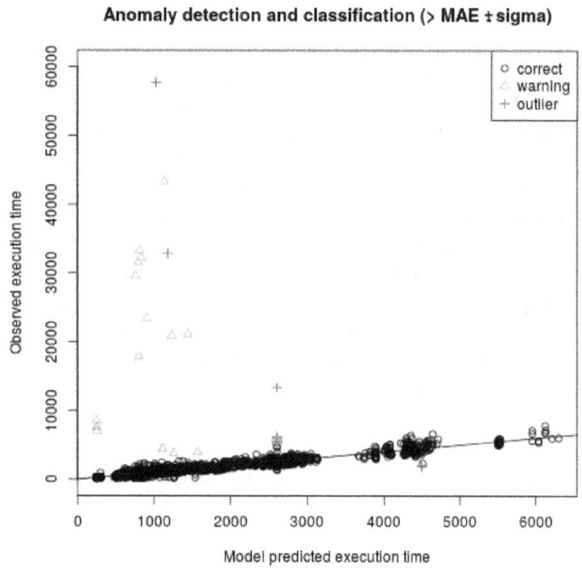

Figure 13: Automatic outlier detection ($h = 0$, $n = 1$)

automatic → manual ↓	Outlier	OK
Anomaly	12	22
Legitimate	4	7786

automatic → *semi-auto.* ↓	Outlier	OK
Anomaly	7	0
Legitimate	9	7786

automatic → manual ↓	Warning	OK
to check	22	0
Legitimate	0	7786

Figure 14: Confusion matrices for different methods

Finally, besides using this method to test new observations, we can re-train our models discarding the observations considered inaccurate. In the first regression tree case, shown in the previous subsection, by subtracting the observations marked as outlier we are able to go from a prediction error of 0.16615 to 0.10873 on validation, and 0.18718 to 0.11912 with the test data-set.

4.1.2 *Use cases*

Spotting failed executions in an automatic way saves time to users, but also let the administrators know when elements of the system are wrong, faulty, or have unexpectedly changed. Further, sets of failed executions with common configuration parameters indicate that it is not a proper configuration for such benchmark; or failing when using specific hardware shows that such hardware should be avoided for those executions.

Furthermore, highlighting anomalous executions is always positive for easing analysis, even more when having more than 16000 executions (and the +300.000 other system performance traces that come with each execution trace). Also it allows to use other learning models less resilient to noise.

4.2 Guided Benchmarking

When modeling a benchmark, a set of configurations, or a new hardware set up, some executions must be performed to observe its new behavior. But executions cost money and time, so we want to run as few sample executions as possible. This is, run the minimum set of executions that define the system with enough accuracy.

We have a full data-set of executions, and we can get a model from it. From it we can attempt to obtain which of those executions are the most suitable to run on a new system or benchmark, and use the results to model it; or we can use the data-set and model to obtain which executions, seen or unseen in our data-set, can be run and used to model. The data-set, as obtained from random or serial executions, can contain similar executions, introduce redundancy or noise. And find which minimal set of executions are the ones that minimize the amount of training data is a combinatorial problem on a big data-set.

Our proposal is to cluster our observed executions (i.e., apply the *k-means* algorithm [15]), obtain for each cluster a representative observation (i.e., its centroid), and use the representatives as the recommended set of executions. Determine the number of clusters (recommendations) required to cover most of the information is the main challenge here. At this time we iterate through a range of k, as figure 15 displays, reconstructing a the model with those recommended observations, and testing it against our data-set or against a reference model. From here on, we decide when the error is low enough or when we exceed the number of desired executions.

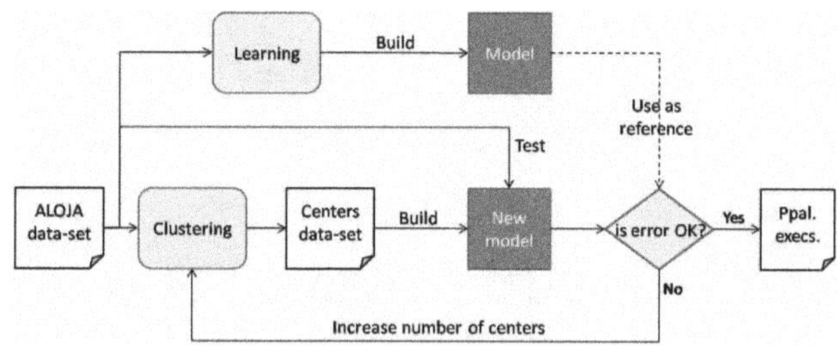

Figure 15: Finding recommended executions schema

4.2.1 *Validation and Comparisons*

For each iteration, looking for k clusters, we compute the error of the resulting model against the reference data-set or model. Also we can estimate the cost of running those executions, as we have the it also we know the average execution cost of 6.85 $\$/hour$ for the clusters we tested. Notice that the estimated execution time is from the seen data-set, and applying those configurations on new clusters or unseen components may increase or decrease the values of such estimations, and it should be treated as a guide more than a strict value. Figure 16 shows the evolution of the error and the execution cost per each k recommendations from our ALOJA data-set. As we expected, more executions implies more accuracy on modeling and predicting, but more cost and execution time.

Further, to test the method against a new cluster addition, we prepared new a setup (on premise, 8 data nodes, 12 core, 64 RAM, 1 disk), and run some of the recommendations obtained from our current ALOJA data-set. We get 6 groups of recommendations with from $k = \{10...60, step = 10\}$, and we executed them in order (first the group of $k = 10$ and so on, removing in this case the repeated just to save experimentation time). We found that with only those 150 recommendations we are able to learn a model with good enough accuracy (tested with all the observed executions of the new cluster), compared to the number of executions needed from the ALOJA data-set to learn with similar accuracy.

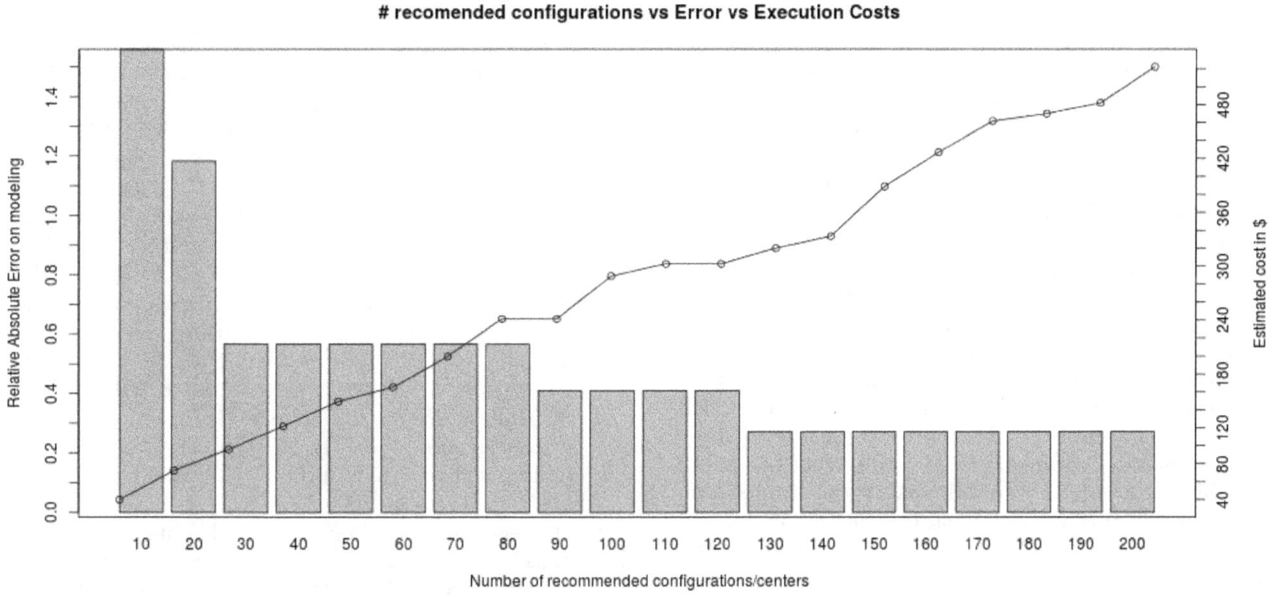

Figure 16: Number of recommended executions vs. error in modeling vs. execution cost

Figure 17 shows the comparative of learning a model with n random observations picked from the ALOJA data-set, seeing how introducing new instances to the selected set improves the model accuracy, against picking the new executed instances (this case in order of recommendation groups), and see how it improves the learning rate of the new cluster data-set. We can achieve low prediction errors very quickly, in front of a random execution selection.

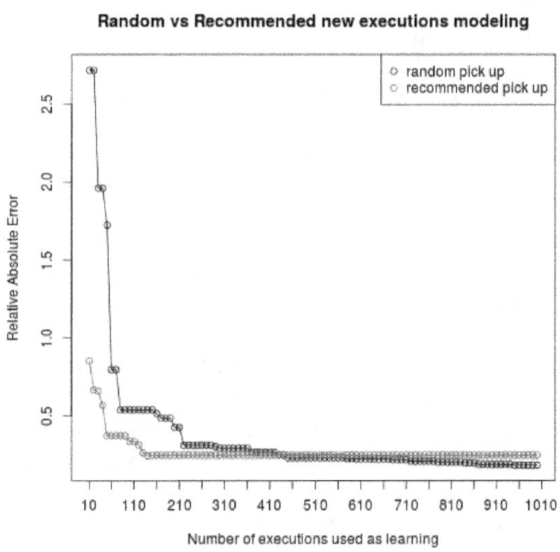

Figure 17: Random vs. recommended executions

4.2.2 Use cases

Often executions on a computing cluster are not for free, or the amount of possible configuration (HW and SW) to test are huge. Finding the minimal set of executions to be able to define the behavior of our Hadoop environment helps to save time and/or money. Also, an administrator or architect would like to prioritize executions, running first those that provide more information about the system, and then run the rest in descending order of relevance. This is useful when testing or comparing our environment after modifications, sanity checks, or validating clone deployments.

Further, it is usual when adding new benchmarks or resources, that the new benchmark is similar in behavior to another previously seen, or that a hardware component is similar in behavior to another. Instead of testing it from random executions, we could use the principal executions for the most similar seen environments to test it, and although results can not fit well with previous models (in fact the new environment can be different), use the new observed results as a starting point to create a new model. The study of how it performs well against other example selection methods for Hadoop platforms and brand new benchmarks is in the ALOJA-ML road-map for near future research.

5. SUMMARY AND CONCLUSIONS

In this article we described ALOJA-ML, a rich tool-set for carrying on automated modeling and prediction tasks over benchmarking data repositories, with particular focus on the BigData domain. The goal of ALOJA-ML is to assist performance engineers, infrastructure designers, data scientists writing BigData applications and cloud providers in minimizing the time required to gain knowledge about deployment variables for BigData workloads. ALOJA-ML takes large performance data repositories available in the ALOJA project and through several Machine Learning techniques identifies key performance properties of the workloads. This information can be later leveraged to predict performance properties for a workload execution on a given set of deployment parameters that have not been explored before in the testing infrastructure. In particular, in this paper we take the case of the Hadoop ecosystem, which is the most widely adopted BigData processing framework currently available, to describe the approach used in ALOJA-ML.

The article describes: a) the methodology followed to process and model the performance date; b) the group of learning algorithms selected for the experiments; c) and the characteristics of the public data set (consisting of more than 16,000 detailed execution logs at the time of the experiments but continuously growing) used for training and validation if the learning algorithms. Through our experiments, we exposed and demonstrated that using our techniques we are able to model and predict Hadoop execution times for given configurations, with a small relative error around 0.20 depending on the executed benchmark. Further we passed out data-set through an automated anomaly detection method, based on our obtained models, with high accuracy respect a manual revision. Also we deployed a new Hadoop cluster, running the recommended executions from our method, and tested the capability of characterizing it with little executions; finding that we can model the new deployment with fewer executions than by randomly selecting executions.

The work presented includes two selected use cases of the ALOJA-ML tool-set in the scope of the ALOJA framework. The fist one is the use of the learning tools for guiding the costly task running experiments for the online performance data-set. In this case, ALOJA-ML assists the framework at the time of selecting the most representative runs of an application that wants to be characterized in a given set of deployment, with the consequent reduction in terms of time and costs to produce relevant executions. The second use case assists in identifying anomalies on large sets of performance testing experiments, which is a common problem of benchmarking frameworks, and that needs to be addressed to get unbiased conclusions on any performance evaluation experiment.

6. FUTURE WORK

The current road-map of ALOJA-ML includes to add new features, tools and techniques, improving the ALOJA framework for Hadoop data analysis and knowledge discovery. Learn how to deal with big amounts of data from Hadoop executions is among our principal interests. This knowledge and capabilities can be used to improve the comprehension and management of such platforms. We are open to new techniques or new kind of applications.

Our next steps are: 1) study techniques to characterize computation clusters and benchmarks, to prepare Hadoop deployments to deal with seen and unseen workloads; 2) introduce new input and output variables, looking new sources of information from the system, and predicting other performance indicators like resource usage; 3) study in detail compatibilities and relations among configuration and hardware attributes, in order to detect impossible setups or executions incompatible with a given deployment; 4) improve the methods to select features, examples and learning parameters. Also introduce new learning algorithms and methodologies like deep-belief networks; 5) and add new executions to the ALOJA data-sets, with new deployments and benchmarks.

7. ACKNOWLEDGMENTS

This project has received funding from the European Research Council (ERC) under the European Union's Horizon 2020 research and innovation programme (grant agreement No 639595). This work is partially supported by the Ministry of Economy of Spain under contracts TIN2012-34557 and 2014SGR1051.

8. REFERENCES

[1] ALOJA Project. `http://hadoop.bsc.es` (Feb 2015).

[2] Apache Hadoop. `http://hadoop.apache.org` (Jan 2015).

[3] BSC-Autonomic. Autonomic systems and big data research group page. `http://www.bsc.es/computer-sciences/performance-tools` (Jan 2015).

[4] D. Aha and D. Kibler. Instance-based learning algorithms. *Machine Learning*, 6:37–66, 1991.

[5] R. Appuswamy, C. Gkantsidis, D. Narayanan, O. Hodson, and A. Rowstron. Scale-up vs scale-out for hadoop: Time to rethink? In *Proceedings of the 4th Annual Symposium on Cloud Computing*, SOCC '13, pages 20:1–20:13, New York, NY, USA, 2013. ACM.

[6] J. L. Berral, R. Gavaldà, and J. Torres. Power-aware multi-data center management using machine learning. In *42nd International Conference on Parallel Processing, ICPP 2013, Lyon, France*, 2013.

[7] M. Hall, E. Frank, G. Holmes, B. Pfahringer, P. Reutemann, and I. H. Witten. The weka data mining software: An update. *SIGKDD Explor. Newsl.*, 11(1):10–18, Nov. 2009.

[8] D. Heger. Hadoop Performance Tuning. `https://hadoop-toolkit.googlecode.com/files/White%20paper-HadoopPerformanceTuning.pdf` (Jan 2015).

[9] D. Heger. Hadoop Performance Tuning - A pragmatic & iterative approach. DH Technologies, 2013.

[10] H. Herodotou, H. Lim, G. Luo, N. Borisov, L. Dong, F. B. Cetin, and S. Babu. Starfish: A self-tuning system for big data analytics. In *CIDR*, 2011.

[11] S. Huang, J. Huang, J. Dai, T. Xie, and B. Huang. The HiBench benchmark suite: Characterization of the MapReduce-based data analysis. *Data Engineering Workshops, 22nd Intl. Conf. on*, 0:41–51, 2010.

[12] L. Person. Global Hadoop Market. Allied market research, March 2014.

[13] N. Poggi, D. Carrera, A. Call, S. Mendoza, Y. Becerra, J. Torres, E. Ayguadé, F. Gagliardi, J. Labarta, R. Reinauer, N. Vujic, D. Green, and J. Blakeley. ALOJA: A systematic study of hadoop deployment variables to enable automated characterization of cost-effectiveness. In *IEEE Intl. Conf. on Big Data 2014, Washington DC, USA*, 2014.

[14] R. J. Quinlan. Learning with continuous classes. In *5th Australian Joint Conference on Artificial Intelligence*, pages 343–348, Singapore, 1992. World Scientific.

[15] R Core Team. *R: A Language and Environment for Statistical Computing.* R Foundation for Statistical Computing, Vienna, Austria, 2014.

[16] P. Shivam, S. Babu, and J. Chase. Active and accelerated learning of cost models for optimizing scientific applications. In *International Conference on Very Large Data Bases*, 2006.

[17] W. N. Venables and B. D. Ripley. *Modern Applied Statistics with S.* Springer, New York, fourth edition, 2002. ISBN 0-387-95457-0.

[18] Y. Wang and I. H. Witten. Induction of model trees for predicting continuous classes. In *9th European Conference on Machine Learning.* Springer, 1997.

[19] T. White. *Hadoop: The Definitive Guide.* O'Reilly Media, Inc., 1st edition, 2009.

[20] J. Wildstrom, P. Stone, E. Witchel, and M. Dahlin. Machine learning for on-line hardware reconfiguration. In *20th Intl. Joint Conference on Artifical Intelligence*, IJCAI'07, 2007.

Multi-View Incident Ticket Clustering for Optimal Ticket Dispatching

Mirela Botezatu
IBM Research
Zurich Switzerland
bot@zurich.ibm.com

Jasmina Bogojeska
IBM Research
Zurich Switzerland
jbo@zurich.ibm.com

Ioana Giurgiu
IBM Research
Zurich Switzerland
igi@zurich.ibm.com

Hagen Voelzer
IBM Research
Zurich Switzerland
hvo@zurich.ibm.com

Dorothea Wiesmann
IBM Research
Zurich Switzerland
dor@zurich.ibm.com

ABSTRACT

We present a novel technique that optimizes the dispatching of incident tickets to the agents in an IT Service Support Environment. Unlike the common skill-based dispatching, our approach also takes empirical evidence on the agent's speed from historical data into account.

Our solution consists of two parts. First, a novel technique clusters historic tickets into incident categories that are discriminative in terms of agent's performance. Second, a dispatching policy selects, for an incoming ticket, the fastest available agent according to the target cluster. We show that, for ticket data collected from several Service Delivery Units, our new dispatching technique can reduce service time between 35% and 44%.

Categories and Subject Descriptors

I.5.3 [**Pattern Recognition**]: Clustering algorithms; I.2.7 [**Natural Language Processing**]: Text analysis; I.2.8 [**Problem Solving, Control Methods, and Search**]: Scheduling

Keywords

Combined affinity matrix; Graph Cut; Spectral Clustering; Fuzzy Clustering, Ticket clustering; Ticket dispatching

1. INTRODUCTION

Enterprises and IT service providers are constantly striving to improve the quality of service and in the same time maintain or reduce the cost of service delivery. One of the major challenges in service delivery is resolving the hundreds of incidents as efficiently as possible. This is an important but labor intensive task, assigned to the service agents that are responsible for solving the customer's incident reports.

In our setting, incidents in the customer environment are submitted to the IT Service Provider in the form of a ticket which is a snippet of text describing a particular IT problem. The reported problems range widely from authentication errors, application crashes, to broken transactions or server unavailabilities.

KDD'15, August 10-13, 2015, Sydney, NSW, Australia.

ACM 978-1-4503-3664-2/15/08 ...$15.00.
DOI: http://dx.doi.org/10.1145/2783258.2788607 .

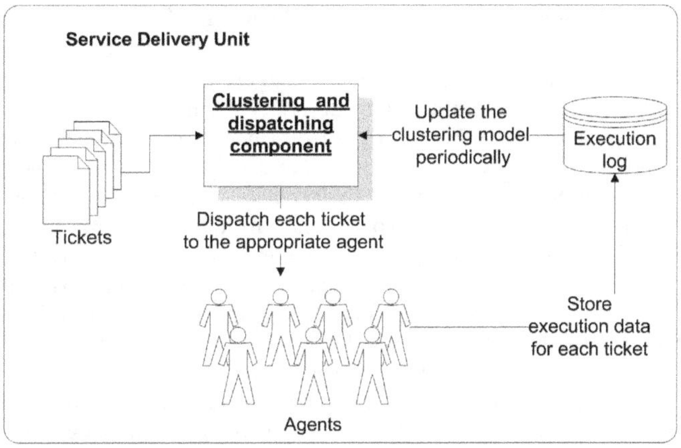

Figure 1: Integration of the clustering and dispatching component.

The dispatching to the service agent is generally done on two levels. First, a human dispatcher reviews the problem description text and decides which delivery unit (a team of service agents) is responsible for addressing that type of ticket. Second, within the delivery unit, a service agent is either chosen by the group leader or on a voluntary basis. The dispatching at this level is based on the qualification of the agents, the availability and the workload of the agents, as well as the complexity of the ticket. At this level we have identified an opportunity for automation and optimization of the dispatching process. Empirical evidence on which agent is most efficient in solving a certain category of tickets is not explicitly taken into consideration. Therefore we derive a method for ticket clustering, which identifies ticket topics (categories) that are discriminative in terms of an agent's performance and dispatches each ticket from every category to the agent that is the most efficient in executing it.

The clustering and dispatching component is designed to be integrated in the IT Service Delivery Environment as shown in Figure 1. In this paper, we show that the existence of such a component that takes informed dispatching decisions, can reduce the resolution time and by extension, the business costs. We demonstrate this by conducting experiments on real data collected from different service delivery units. This data comprises the ticket description and its complexity, the agent who resolved it, the duration recorded for resolving it, etc.

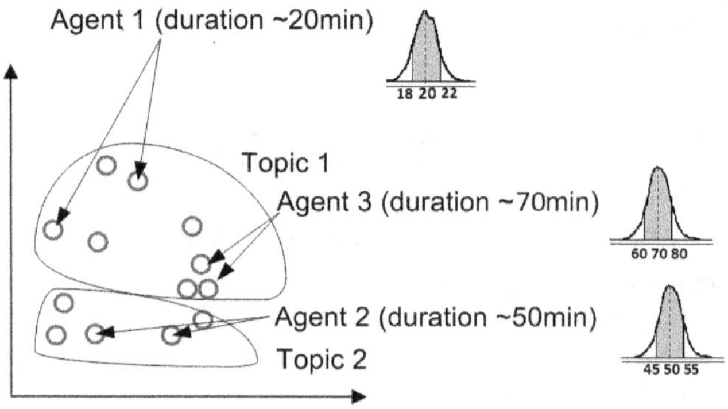

Figure 2: Illustration of a desirable partitioning.

Our approach partitions the tickets into clusters that are relevant with respect to the problem they describe and that are also *homogeneous* in terms of the agent's performance. We achieve this by leveraging multiple views of the ticket data. A cluster is homogeneous in terms of an agent's performance if the variation in the time it takes for an agent to solve tickets from that cluster is small (the distribution is narrow, as illustrated in Figure 2). This way, we can infer the approximate duration needed for an agent to solve the tickets that pertain to a certain cluster from the historical data. Further, we use this information in the dispatching process, by always assigning the ticket of a given cluster, to the agent that is the most efficient in solving tickets of that cluster. The difficulty in finding these clusters is that applying a standard algorithm that groups the tickets based solely on their most prominent topics, leads to clusters that are non-homogenous in terms of the agent's performance. Therefore, we propose a clustering approach that performs a partitioning that can discover meaningful ticket categories with homogeneous agent performance.

Our contributions are manifold:

- A clustering method capable to identify ticket categories that are homogeneous in terms of the agent's performance;
- A data-informed dispatching policy that assigns an incoming ticket to the agent that is the most efficient in resolving it;
- An integrated solution to reduce the service costs.

The outline of this paper is as follows. Section 2 presents the incident ticket clustering method. Section 3 provides an overview of the data-informed dispatching policy. The experimental evaluation on real-world datasets is presented in Section 4, followed by the related work in section 5 and the conclusions in Section 6.

2. INCIDENT TICKET CLUSTERING

We devise a method that partitions the set of tickets into groups of similar tickets both in terms of the incident they report and the time needed for an agent to resolve them. The method utilizes both the matrix of semantic similarities between tickets, and the *divergence matrix* - a matrix which captures information on the difference in the duration of resolution of two tickets assigned to the same agent. More specifically, we first modify the semantic similarity matrix based on the information represented in the divergence matrix, and then, we run a clustering algorithm that operates on the resulting matrix. For each cluster, we derive an estimate for the time each agent needs to resolve tickets pertaining to that cluster. Ultimately, we devise a dispatching policy that assigns each ticket to the agent who is the fastest at resolving it and compute the achieved reduction in terms of service time due to the new assignment.

In the method described above, a small variation in the agent's performance for the clusters is part of the output. We also propose an algorithm that takes a clustering and a target variation for the clusters as an input and then adjusts the clusters structure to achieve the target variation specified in the input.

In Figure 3 we show an example of the desired clustering assuming we had only four tickets. Even though the semantic similarity between tickets T_1 and T_3 and tickets T_2 and T_4 is high, we do not put them in the same cluster due to the large difference in the resolution times. Instead we cut the edge that links them in the similarity graph. Therefore, for this example, instead of reporting the two clusters "servers issues" and "DB issues", we would discover "network issues" (as denoted by bigrams "lost connection" or "ping statistics") and "functional errors" (as denoted by bigrams "server crashed" or "inconsistent state").

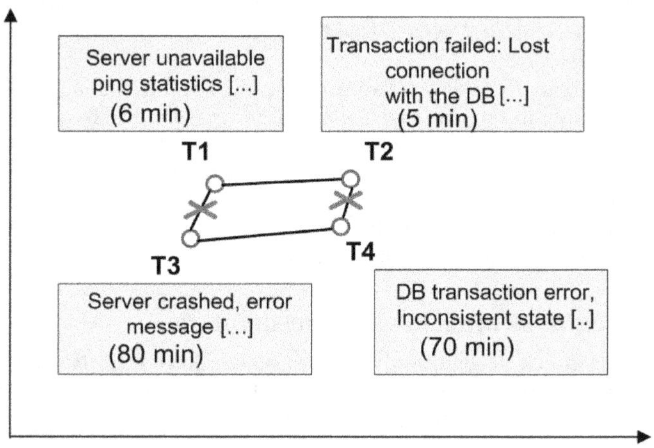

Figure 3: Example of similarity demotion.

2.1 Preliminaries

Let T be a ticket consisting of $|T|$ words $w_1, \cdots, w_{|T|}$ and let $K = \{T_1, T_2, \cdots, T_n\}$ be a set of n tickets. Also, let $A = \{a_1, a_2, \cdots, a_{|A|}\}$ denote the set of agents who resolved the tickets. Each ticket T_i, is associated with several fields: $d^{(i)}$ the duration for resolving it, $a^{(i)}$ the agent who resolved it and $c^{(i)} \in W = \{\text{"A"},\text{"B"},\text{"C"}\}$ the complexity of the ticket (where "A" denotes the highest complexity and "C" the lowest).

For each agent a_i there is a mapping to its skill level $s^{(a_i)} \in W$. An agent with skill level "A" is entitled to resolve tickets of any complexity class, an agent with skill level "B" is entitled to resolve tickets of complexity "B" and "C", and an agent with skill level "C" is entitled to resolve only tickets of complexity "C".

2.2 Multi-view similarity matrix with induced sparsity

The typical approach to measuring the similarity between two blocks of text is to use a lexical matching method, and compute a similarity score based on the number of lexical units (words) that occur in both input texts. Pre-processing the texts via stemming, removal of the stop words, longest subsequence matching and additional normalization and weighting factors have shown to improve the results of such lexical methods [18, 10]. However the lexical similarity measures alone have an important limitation: they fail in identifying the semantic similarity between texts (i.e., the similarity score between "process shutdown" and "application terminated" would be zero).

In this section, we describe the method we used to compute the semantic similarity metric between tickets [19]. It is derived from the semantic-similarity metric between words, described in the next section. We define the semantic similarity between two tickets T_i and T_j, given the semantic similarity between words. Each word w in T_i is assigned a semantic similarity score $maxSim(w, T_j)$, based on the most similar word in T_j. The procedure is applied symmetrically, for each word in T_j. The word similarity scores for each ticket are added and each summation is normalized with the length of its corresponding ticket. The final result is the average of the normalized summation of each ticket:

$$\begin{aligned} Similarity(T_i, T_j) = & \frac{1}{2}\Big(\frac{\sum_{w \in T_i} maxSim(w, T_j)}{|T_i|} + \\ & + \frac{\sum_{w \in T_j} maxSim(w, T_i)}{|T_j|}\Big) \end{aligned} \tag{1}$$

Let $\mathbf{S} \in \mathbb{R}^{n \times n}$ denote the ticket-ticket semantic similarity matrix, where $\mathbf{S}_{ij} = Similarity(T_i, T_j)$.

Another type of proximity relation between tickets is given by the divergence matrix described below. If two tickets T_i and T_j, that are annotated with the same complexity level (i.e., $c^{(i)} = c^{(j)}$) have been resolved by the same agent ($a^{(i)} = a^{(j)}$) and the ratio in their corresponding resolution times is higher than a certain threshold λ then they have different level of difficulty and they should not be clustered in the same group of incidents. We define the divergence matrix $\mathbf{D} \in \mathbb{R}^{n \times n}$:

$$\mathbf{D}_{ij} = \begin{cases} 1 & \text{if } a^{(i)} = a^{(j)} \text{ and } c^{(i)} = c^{(j)} \text{ and} \\ & min(d^{(i)}, d^{(j)}) > \lambda max(d^{(i)}, d^{(j)}); \\ 0 & \text{otherwise} \end{cases} \tag{2}$$

Two tickets which are similar in terms of both their topics and the duration it took an agent to resolve them may reveal stronger connection than two other tickets which are similar only in terms of topic. Motivated by this statement we combine the two proximity relations (views) into one matrix $\mathbf{S}' \in \mathbb{R}^{n \times n}$ as follows:

$$\mathbf{S}' = \mathbf{S} - \mathbf{S} \circ \mathbf{D}. \tag{3}$$

We induced sparsity on $\mathbf{S}$ by setting the similarity scores in $\mathbf{S}$ to 0 when $\mathbf{D}_{ij} = 1$.

2.3 Semantic similarity metric between words

As the same incident may be documented with different words, we are interested in assessing the degree of similarity between words in the specific IT Service Delivery domain.

For extracting the semantic similarity scores between pairs of words, we have explored three corpus-based methods which have been reported to give good results [22, 8]. The methods are: PMI-IR [14], the Google similarity distance (GSD) [6] and LSA [26].

PMI-IR only requires simple statistics about two words: their marginal frequencies and their co-occurrence frequency in a corpus.

$$\text{PMI}_{\text{IR}}(w_1, w_2) = \log \frac{p(w_1, w_2)}{p(w_1) * p(w_2)} \tag{4}$$

where $p(w_i, w_j)$ denotes the probability that words w_1, w_2 co-occur in the same ticket, $p(w)$ is the probability that the word w occurs in a ticket. Please note that we do not need to specify a window size for estimating the co-occurrence frequencies of w_1 and w_2 as the ticket descriptions are usually short ($<$ 20 words).

GSD is based on information distance and Kolmogorov complexity. In the original paper, the authors rely on Google to retrieve pages for co-occurrence statistics. We adapt the extraction of co-occurrence statistics to our setting, as follows:

$$\begin{aligned} \text{GSD}(w_1, w_2) = & \frac{max\{\log(|f(w_1)|, \log(|f(w_2)|\}}{\log(Q) - min\{\log(|f(w_1)|), \log(|f(w_2)|)\}} - \\ & - \frac{\log(|f(w_1, w_2)|)}{\log(Q) - min\{\log(|f(w_1)|), \log(|f(w_2)|)\}} \end{aligned} \tag{5}$$

where $Q = \sum_{w_1 \in T_1, w_2 \in T_2} |f(w_1, w_2)|$ (the sum of the numbers of occurrences of search terms in each ticket, summed over all tickets) and $f(w_1, \cdots, w_k)$ represents the set of all tickets in which the words $w_1, \cdots, w_k$ appear together.

In **LSA**, term co-occurrences in a corpus are captured via dimensionality reduction operated by a singular value decomposition (SVD) on the term-by-document matrix representing the corpus.

While all the methods gave meaningful results regarding the relatedness of words in a broader sense (i.e., flagging associations between pairs of words such as "hung" and "ping" or "disk" and "full" as significant), LSA outperformed the other two methods in identifying synonyms. In order to perform a quantitative evaluation of how well each method performs on our corpus (comprised of a large set of ticket descriptions and ticket resolutions) we did the following:

- We have tagged the words in the corpus into their parts-of-speech and labeled them accordingly (*pos tagging* [25]);
- We selected pairs of words with the same pos tag and with high association score with any of the three methods;
- We asked a domain expert to select out of the pairs given above, pairs of words that are synonyms in the IT Service Delivery domain;
- We evaluated the methods based on their performance in detecting these pairs of synonyms.

The process described above has resulted in a list of 72 pairs of words that are synonyms in the IT Service Delivery domain (e.g., "pingable" and "responsive" or "archive" and "backup"). We consider a method has identified a pair of synonyms (w_1, w_2) if the scaled semantic similarity score between (w_1, w_2) is above the mean of the semantic similarity scores between w_1 and any other word in the corpus (or w_2 and any other word in the corpus).

We count the number of synonyms identified by each method and divide the result by the total number of pairs of synonyms. The results are shown in Table 1.

LSA	GSD	PMI-IR
0.83	0.42	0.3

Table 1: Percentage of synonyms identified.

There are several reasons why LSA outperformed the other two methods. First, the conventional wisdom is that synonym words, with a high degree of relatedness are unlikely to co-occur in a small window size. Second, it is plausible to represent the meaning of a

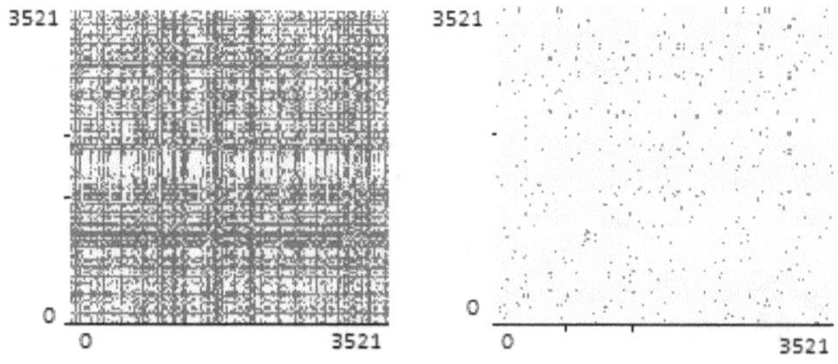

Figure 4: Sparsity: similarity matrix (left), divergence matrix (right).

word by a context vector of co-occuring words and the corresponding co-occurrence counts measured in a text window context. LSA performs this and in addition, it transforms the context vectors to a lower dimensional space by applying singular value decomposition (SVD). The similarity is further reduced to the similarity of the context vectors where the cosine of the angle is employed as a similarity metric.

2.4 Clustering

The tickets are related via two types of similarity measures that originate from different sources: one that comes from the ticket content - the ticket similarity matrix $\mathbf{S}$, and one that comes from the agents who resolved the tickets - the divergence matrix $\mathbf{D}$.

Due to the extreme sparsity shown in Figure 4, the divergence matrix alone does not contain complete information of the structure of the clusters. Since both matrices capture important information, we propose an approach that uses the two matrices in the combined matrix $\mathbf{S}'$ as defined in equation (3) and has the following objectives:

I Cluster similar tickets together (we want to be able to extract topic information from these clusters);

II Minimize the number of pairs of tickets in the same cluster that have similarity equal to zero (we want homogeneous clusters in terms of the agent's performance, which is why we enforced the $\mathbf{S}'_{ij} = 0$ when $\mathbf{D}_{ij} = 1$).

We achieve this using three candidate clustering algorithms namely: hierarchical clustering with complete linkage [7], spectral clustering [20] and our adjusted version of fuzzy k-means [3]: homogeneity optimized fuzzy k-means.

Hierarchical clustering and spectral clustering are *hard clustering* algorithms, i.e., each ticket is a member of exactly one cluster. The input for these algorithms is the matrix $\mathbf{S}'$.

Fuzzy k-means is a *soft clustering* algorithm - and therefore returns a partition of the n tickets $\{T_1, T_2, \cdots, T_n\}$ into k clusters $\{C_1, C_2, \cdots, C_k\}$ specified by a membership matrix $\mathbf{M} \in \mathbb{R}^{n \times k}$, $\mathbf{M}_{ij} \geq 0$ and $\sum_{j=1}^{k} \mathbf{M}_{ij} = 1$, whose components quantify the membership degree of ticket T_i in cluster C_k. The input for fuzzy k-means is the similarity matrix $\mathbf{S}$. We optimize the homogeneity of these clusters by iteratively moving tickets from their most probable clusters to the second, third, up to the least probable clusters, as will be described later on. We selected fuzzy k-means and not LDA [4] because the ticket descriptions are very short, which is too sparse for traditional topic modeling. Therefore we used a soft clustering algorithm that is able to leverage the similarity matrix S.

While hierarchical clustering does not require the specification of the number of clusters, k, spectral clustering and fuzzy k-means take k as input. In order to estimate the optimal number of clusters for the two latter algorithms we use the *silhouette statistic*, a well-balanced coefficient introduced in [11] and which has shown good performance in experiments.

Let $C = \{C_1, C_2, \cdots, C_k\}$ be a clustering of the set of tickets. For each cluster $C_i \in C$, for each complexity class $c \in W$ and for each agent $a_c \in A$ (such that a_c has solved tickets in C_i of complexity c) , one can measure the dispersion in the duration of resolution. The metric we propose for this is the *coefficient of variation* (CV), defined as the ratio of the standard deviation of these durations to their mean:

$$CV = \frac{s_x}{\overline{x}} \tag{6}$$

where s_x is the standard deviation of a set of samples x_i and $\overline{x}$ is their mean.

The motivation for using the coefficient of variation is the following: the standard deviations of two sets are not comparable to each other in a meaningful way to determine which set has greater dispersion because the values in the sets may have different magnitudes. The coefficient of variation does however show the extent of variability in relation to the mean.

2.4.1 *Hierarchical Clustering with Complete Linkage*

The agglomerative hierarchical clustering algorithm with complete linkage, works as follows:(i) the algorithm starts with n clusters, each containing one object; (ii) the most similar pair of clusters C_i, C_j is found using the combined similarity matrix $\mathbf{S}'$ and merged into a single cluster. (iii) the similarity matrix is updated (its order is reduced by one by substituting the individual clusters with the newly merged one). Steps (ii) and (iii) are repeated until a certain stopping criterion is reached.

This method is relevant for our study because of the distance measure that is used between two clusters in the merging step in the algorithm: C_i, C_j: $d_{complete}(C_i, C_j) = max_{l \in C_i, m \in C_j}(1 - \mathbf{S}'_{lm})$. If s_k denotes the similarity of the two clusters merged in step k, this distance measure ensures that no pair of tickets with similarity 0 (distance 1) will be put in the same cluster. The clusters at step k are maximal sets of points that are completely connected with each other by edges of weights (similarity) $s \geq s_k$.

2.4.2 *Spectral Clustering*

Using the combined similarity matrix $\mathbf{S}'$ in a spectral clustering algorithm there will result a partitioning obtained by minimizing the cuts in the input graph and thus implicitly maximally satisfying the objective II above.

Spectral clustering works as follows:

1. Construct the Graph Laplacian $\mathbf{L}$ from the combined similarity matrix $\mathbf{S}'$: $\mathbf{L} = \mathbf{D}^{-\frac{1}{2}}\mathbf{S}'\mathbf{D}^{-\frac{1}{2}}$ where $\mathbf{D}_{ii} = \sum_{j=1}^{n} \mathbf{S}'_{ij}$;

2. Select the first k eigenvalues $\lambda_1, \cdots, \lambda_k$ and determine their corresponding eigenvectors to form a new matix $\mathbf{M} \in \mathbb{R}^{n \times k}$, which needs to be normalized;

3. Perform clustering in the new subspace using K-means.

2.4.3 *Homogeneity Optimized Fuzzy K-means*

We use the similarity matrix $\mathbf{S}$ to perform the soft clustering with fuzzy k-means. The resulting clusters will not be homogeneous in terms of duration because we only pass the semantic similarity matrix to the algorithm. In the following, we propose an approach that utilizes the clusters returned by fuzzy k-means and reduces the variation in duration inside the cluster by iteratively removing tickets.

Let $C = \{C_1, C_2, \cdots, C_k\}$ be the clusters returned by fuzzy k-means and $\Pr(T \mid C_i)$ denote the probability of ticket T belonging to cluster C_i. At each step, the algorithm selects the ticket that minimizes the variation from a sub-cluster $C_i^{(a)(c)} \subseteq C_i$ (subset of tickets in C_i that have been solved by agent a and have complexity c) and removes it from the cluster. The ticket is then tentatively inserted in the the next most probable clusters in an order given by the ranking from fuzzy k-means. A ticket is inserted in another cluster if the variation in duration of the cluster *with* the ticket does not increase. If the ticket can not be inserted in any of the clusters it is dropped. This procedure continues until the variation in duration inside $C_i^{(a)(c)}$ reaches a target value τ. These steps are formalized in Algorithm 1 and Algorithm 2:

Algorithm 1 Optimize homogeneity of the clusters.

function OPTIMIZE(C)
  for all $C_i \subseteq C$ **do**
    for all $C_i^{(a)(c)} \subseteq C_i$ **do**
      while $CV_{C_i^{(a)(c)}} \geq \tau$ **do**
        $T = \text{argmin}_T \, CV_{C_i^{(a)(c)} \setminus \{T\}}$
        $C_i^{(a)(c)} \leftarrow C_i^{(a)(c)} \setminus \{T\}$
        MOVE(T)
      end while
    end for
  end for
end function

Algorithm 2 Move a ticket.

function MOVE(T)
  for $C_i \subseteq C \setminus \{T\}$ sorted in decreasing order of $\Pr(T \mid C_i)$ **do**
    if $CV_{C_i^{(a)(c)} \cup \{T\}} \leq CV_{C_i^{(a)(c)}}$ **then**
      $C_i^{(a)(c)} \leftarrow C_i^{(a)(c)} \cup \{T\}$ **return**
    else
      DROP(T)
    end if
  end for
end function

Homogeneity optimized fuzzy k-means has the following properties: (i) the variation inside the final clusters is not an output of the algorithm but an input parameter of the algorithm and that enables finer control. The variation of the resulting clustering will not exceed the one given as an input. (ii) The algorithm can be used for identifying the outliers in the data set. To achieve this we only move the ticket to the second or the third most probable clusters and drop it if it cannot be placed. The advantage of doing this is that the coherence of the clusters with respect to the topics remains unaltered (unlike the base algorithm where we tradeoff topic relevance for high homogeneity). Additionally one can inspect the set of dropped tickets and observe which type of incidents have inherently higher variation in the resolution time.

3. DISPATCHING

For a given partitioning $C = \{C_1, C_2, \cdots, C_{|C|}\}$, we build a matrix $\mathbf{P} \in \mathbb{R}^{|A| \times |C| \times |W|}$ which stores the median duration for the execution time for each agent in resolving a ticket pertaining to

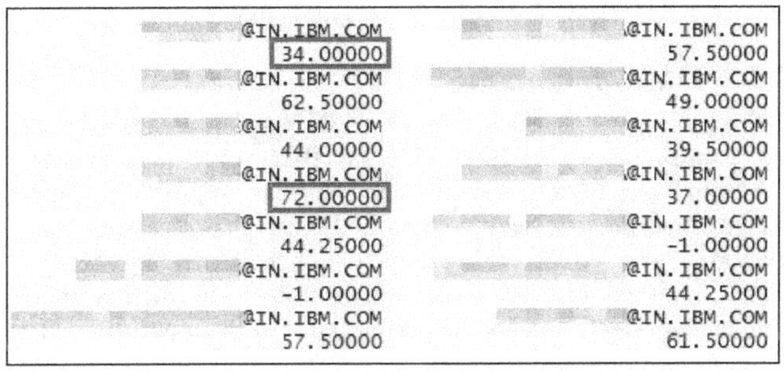

@IN.IBM.COM 34.00000 | @IN.IBM.COM 57.50000
@IN.IBM.COM 62.50000 | @IN.IBM.COM 49.00000
@IN.IBM.COM 44.00000 | @IN.IBM.COM 39.50000
@IN.IBM.COM 72.00000 | @IN.IBM.COM 37.00000
@IN.IBM.COM 44.25000 | @IN.IBM.COM -1.00000
@IN.IBM.COM -1.00000 | @IN.IBM.COM 44.25000
@IN.IBM.COM 57.50000 | @IN.IBM.COM 61.50000

Figure 5: Agent's performance for a given cluster and complexity level.

one of the clusters for a certain complexity class. Some entries in this matrix will be -1. When an entry $\mathbf{P}_{ijk} = -1$ it means that there are no records in the data of agent a_i working on a ticket from cluster C_j of complexity k where k is an id for each complexity class {"A", "B", "C"}.

We implement the data-informed dispatching policy and the non data-informed dispatching policy. Unlike the non data-informed dispatching policy, the data-informed policy, dispatches a ticket $T_j \in C_j$ to the agent that is the most efficient in resolving it from all the agents that are available, i.e., it selects a_i. such that $\mathbf{P}_{ijk}$ is minimal. The implementation of the dispatching aligns to the following setting:

- The maximum working number of hours of an agent is less than 8 hours. When an agent reaches the 8 hours of work in one day, the agent is removed from the pool of available agents to which tickets can be dispatched on that day;
- No tickets are passed from one day to another. This assumption is enforced by the original data, where the ticket resolution is started and completed in the same day in 99.5% of the cases;
- The complexity of the ticket must match the qualification of the resolving agent. Therefore, an agent with skill level "A" is entitled to resolve tickets of any complexity class, an agent with skill level "B" is entitled to resolve tickets of complexity "B" and "C", and an agent with skill level "C" is entitled to resolve only tickets of complexity "C";
- When summing up for the total duration of execution (service time) we did not add any waiting time;
- The arrival order of the tickets based on which we perform the dispatching is the original order, as documented in the dataset.

For the implementation of the dispatching, we split the data in separate chunks for each working day. For every chunk, we store a list with all the agents available that day by mining the log for agents that have tickets associated to their id in that particular day. We also maintain a queue with the tickets that need to be completed that day by extracting the list of tickets from the logs that were recorded as started and completed that day. Ultimately, we run the data-informed dispatching policy and the policy that works under exactly the same assumptions, but without being data-informed (equivalent to the setting when an agent voluntarily selects the next ticket to resolve, provided that the agent has the necessary qualification - skill based dispatching [27]), and compare the recorded service times for each delivery unit.

4. EMPIRICAL EVALUATION

4.1 Data preparation

We use three datasets: DU1, DU2, DU3 from three service delivery units comprising 3696, 2373 and 1916 tickets respectively.

The first step in the analysis is the data cleaning procedure where we take the raw unstructured data and remove unnecessary information such as , email headers, punctuation, html formatting, server names, stop words and we also do stemming. This step is important as it severely impacts the performance of the algorithms. The ticket descriptions are a mixture of machine and human-generated text and contain many domain-specific technical words, some of which are not present in a standard dictionary (e.g., "unpingable", "ssd", "hw"), but are still relevant in identifying the incident category. Some examples of ticket descriptions are given in Table 2.

serverXYXY error : DISK Utilization :Object = /dev/sda3/var : percent full: 95% : MB free: 219 MB
New User Request Form: XYXY backup missed on this server
We are unable to connect to hosts serverXYXY. Please investigate

Table 2: Examples of ticket descriptions.

4.2 Experiments

In the experiments we set the threshold to $\lambda = 0.8$, meaning that for two tickets from the same cluster, solved by the same agent and of the same complexity the variation of duration of executing them is within 20%. Using such small variation is reflected in the connectedness of the similarity graph. In Figure 6 we show how the percentage of deleted edges increases by increasing the value of λ.

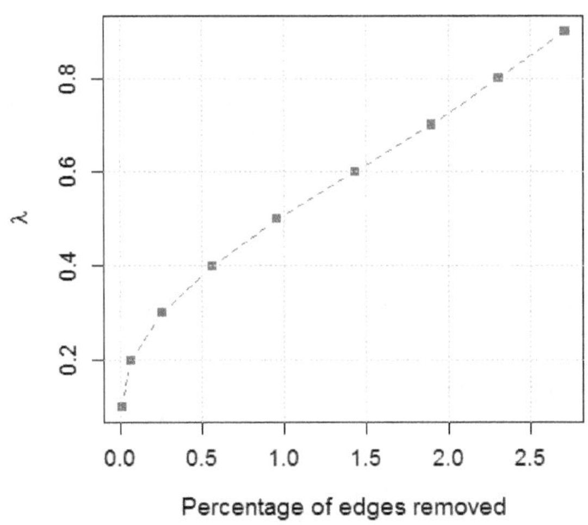

Figure 6: Percentage of edges removed when increasing λ (for DU1).

4.2.1 Clustering

In what follows, we show that spectral clustering and homogeneity optimized fuzzy k-means exhibit the best performance for this task.

We run hierarchical clustering with complete linkage (stopped at dissimilarity threshold 0.8). For DU1 we obtain a large set of clusters (176 clusters) with a low abundance of tickets (on average 19 tickets per cluster), and also the clusters tend to have similar sizes. This is illustrated in Figure 7 where we observe skewed distribution when plotting the cluster abundances. The results remain similar when varying both λ and the dissimilarity threshold for stopping (i.e., for $\lambda = 0.8$, dissimilarity threshold=0.9 we obtain 130 clusters, or for $\lambda = 0.5$, dissimilarity threshold=0.8 we obtain 92 clusters). The resulting clusters are small and with low variation in both topic and resolution time per agent, but they are not unique, i.e., they are fragments of larger clusters.

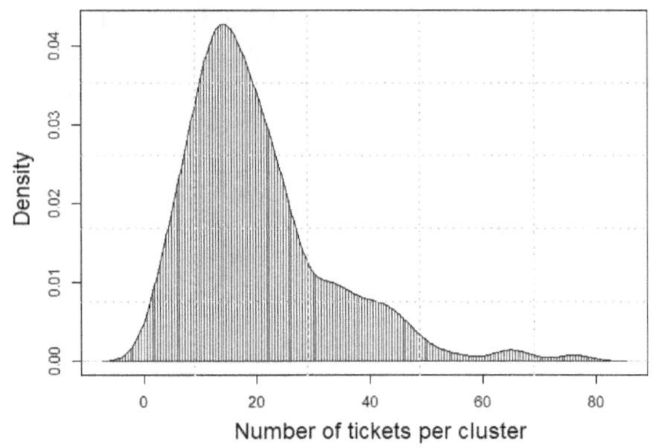

Figure 7: Cluster abundances density plot.

With spectral clustering we obtain 12 clusters with sizes between 193 and 659 tickets for DU1, 7 clusters with sizes between 232 and 601 for DU2 and 5 clusters with sizes between 134 and 385 for DU3. By analyzing the frequent words in the clusters we observe that the algorithm is able to correctly capture relevant incident ticket categories in each cluster. This is shown in the Table 3

Cluster	Frequent words
C_1	*lost, contact, agent*
C_2	*ssd, internal, error*
C_3	*file, system, space, full*
C_4	*prod, issue, faulty, disk*
C_5	*cluster, bottleneck*
C_6	*system, restart, request*
C_7	*backup, error*
C_8	*scsi, retry, failed*
C_9	*server, physical, failure*
C_{10}	*application, problem, not, responding*
C_{11}	*node, down, power, supply*
C_{12}	*limit, exceeded, file*

Table 3: Frequent words in the clusters obtained by spectral clustering using S′ for DU1.

Homogeneity optimized fuzzy k-means exhibits also good performance in identifying incident categories. We obtain 12 clusters with sizes between 195 and 429 tickets for DU1, 7 clusters with sizes between 206 and 387 for DU2 and 5 clusters with sizes between 127 and 368 for DU3.

Delivery Unit	DU1	DU2	DU3
$\tau_{\min}$	0.17	0.23	0.21

Table 4: Values for τ_{min} for each delivery unit

We first run the algorithm such that no tickets are dropped. We choose the minimum value for the target coefficient of variation, τ_{min}, for each delivery unit, such that all the tickets are assigned to a cluster. The values for τ_{min} when no tickets are dropped for each delivery unit are given in Table 4. Note that the values for the coefficient of variation are small, due to the fact that we allow tickets to be assigned to less probable clusters. The frequent words in the clusters discovered are presented in Table 5. We observe that

Cluster	Frequent words
C_1	*monitoring, cluster, disk, replacement*
C_2	*fsd, code, error*
C_3	*command, retry, reboot, server*
C_4	*client, backup, file*
C_5	*ssd, database, memory, corruption*
C_6	*disk, error, scsi*
C_7	*node, down, agent, contact*
C_8	*disk, fan, sensor, faulty*
C_9	*docket, frame, replacement*
C_{10}	*power, supply, fault*
C_{11}	*transport, lost, retry*
C_{12}	*limit, exceeded, file*

Table 5: Frequent words in the clusters obtained homogeneity optimized fuzzy k-means for DU1.

both clustering approaches identify ticket categories documenting "file limit exceeded", problems related to the "power supply", or "backup" related issues. While the clusters obtained with spectral clustering place all the disk related tickets in one single cluster, with the homogeneity optimized fuzzy k-means we obtain two clusters documenting disk errors: one which was documenting disk replacement, and one reporting disk fan sensor issues. Also for homogeneity optimized fuzzy k-means it is not always straightforward to establish the incident category of a certain cluster. One such example is the cluster with top words "ssd, database, memory, corruption". Also, it merged tickets documenting "node down" with tickets documenting "lost, contact, agent". This hints to the fact that for an agent, these two categories of incidents take similar amount of time to be resolved.

When we introduced homogeneity optimized fuzzy k-means we also mentioned the possibility of identifying outliers, tickets that take either too long or too little time to be resolved by an agent relative to the cluster they pertain to. This can be achieved by modifying the algorithm to move tickets only in the first three most likely clusters. This leads to a significant number of tickets dropped and this grows inversely proportional with the value of τ as illustrated in Figure 8. By inspecting the dropped tickets we observe that they mostly document disk errors, and filesystem issues. The recorded duration for the dropped tickets is either very short either very large. This indicates that in the dispatching, for those tickets with larger duration one needs to have some margin with respect to filling the day completely.

In the following we evaluate the quality of the clustering obtained from running spectral clustering with the combined similarity matrix, and homogeneity optimized fuzzy k-means with the minimum values of τ for which no tickets are dropped, τ_{min}. We inspect both the reduction in service time from implementing the data informed dispatching policy and the homogeneity in agent's performance.

4.2.2 Speed-up in service time

Let $C = \{C_1, C_2, \cdots, C_k\}$ be the partitioning of the corpus of tickets C. We measure the service time which is the total number of working hours needed for resolving all the tickets in a given period of time. We use the matrix $\mathbf{P}$ that for each cluster and for each complexity level stores the agent's performance (as depicted in the Figure 5), and we run the data informed dispatching policy, both on the clustering obtained with spectral clustering and with the homogeneity optimized fuzzy k-means. The data informed dispatching policy is evaluated against the dispatching that does not take the insight from the data into account (which agent is fastest in resolving an incoming ticket).

We observe a major reduction in the service time up to 44% (for DU2) when running the data-informed dispatching policy compared to the dispatching policy that does not consider the insight from the data. The reductions are apparent for dispatching based on both the homogeneity optimized fuzzy k-means clustering and the spectral clustering, slightly better in the former one (possibly due to the more uniform cluster sizes). The speedup is shown in Figure 9 where we denote by (DI) the data-informed dispatching policy and by (non-DI) the non data informed dispatching policy.

Figure 11 shows that the discrepancies in agent's performance for a given cluster and complexity are large and exploiting these differences in dispatching leads to a significant reduction in the service time. Also we have identified that agents with skill level "B" are faster than agents with skill level "A" in solving tickets documenting "network errors" of complexity "B", shown in Figure 10. This illustrates that a higher skill (which is established based on experience or training level) does not directly translate into higher speed (which can only be established empirically, by analyzing the historical data). Note that we did not include service level agreements in both dispatching policies In particular we only kept the order of ticket arrival, but assumed that a ticket can be resolved by the optimal agent even if that meant ticket resolution could only start when this agent becomes free. Naturally this might delay ticket resolution potentially conflicting with SLA requirements on resolution times. In contexts with such SLA constraints, a simulation taking arrival patterns into account can yield more precise assessments. Please note however that both dispatching policies considered in our experiments, work under exactly the same assumptions and are therefore comparable.

4.2.3 Homogeneity in terms of agent's performance

As the quality of the clustering is given by the qualities of the individual clusters we define the homongeneity of a clustering as the average of the homogeneity of each cluster:

$$hom(C) = \frac{1}{|C|} \sum_{C_i \subset C} hom(C_i) \tag{7}$$

The homogeneity of the cluster C_i is defined as the average coefficient of variation for the durations recorded for a certain agent and complexity class. Formally, let $C_i^{(a)(c)} = \{d^{(k)} \text{ for } T_k \in C_i | a^{(k)} = a \text{ and } c^{(k)} = c\}$ and $CV_{C_i^{(a)(c)}}$ denote the coefficient of variation of $C_i^{(a)(c)}$. Then, we define the homogeneity of a cluster C_i as:

$$hom(C_i) = \frac{1}{|Z|} \sum_{C_i^{(a)(c)} \in Z} CV_{C_i^{(a)(c)}} \tag{8}$$

where $Z = \{C_i^{(a)(c)} \subseteq C_i \mid C_i^{(a)(c)} \neq \emptyset\}$

For the spectral clustering, the results are shown in Figure 12 where we compared the homogeneity in terms of agent's performance for the algorithm that uses the combined matrix $\mathbf{S}'$ to the algorithm ran on the semantic similarity matrix $\mathbf{S}$.

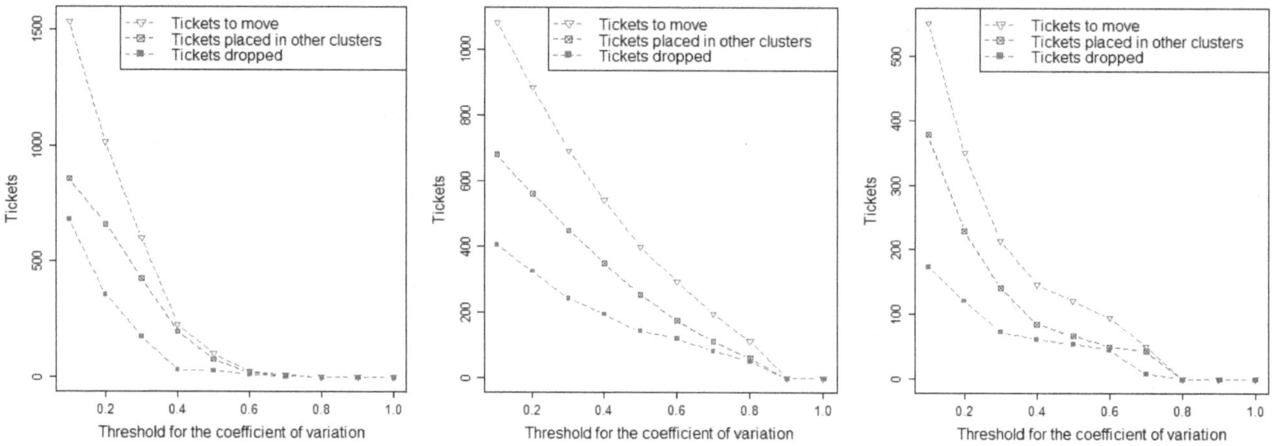

Figure 8: Number of tickets to move, tickets successfully placed in other clusters and tickets dropped for each delivery unit.

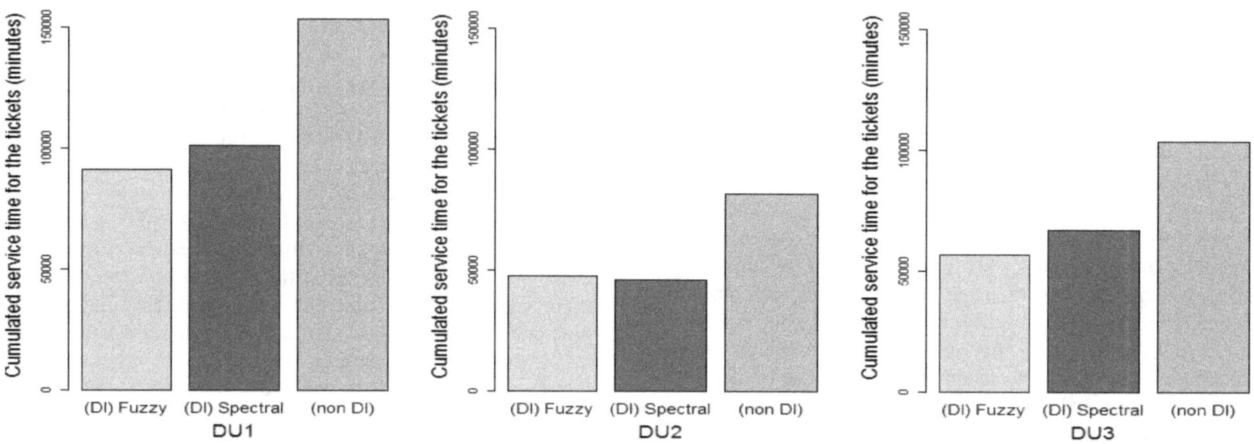

Figure 9: Speed-up in service time for each delivery unit.

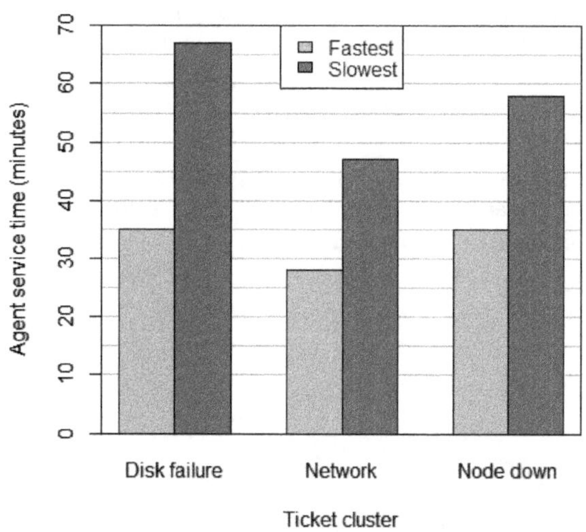

Figure 10: Differences in agent's performance in resolving tickets of the same complexity from different clusters.

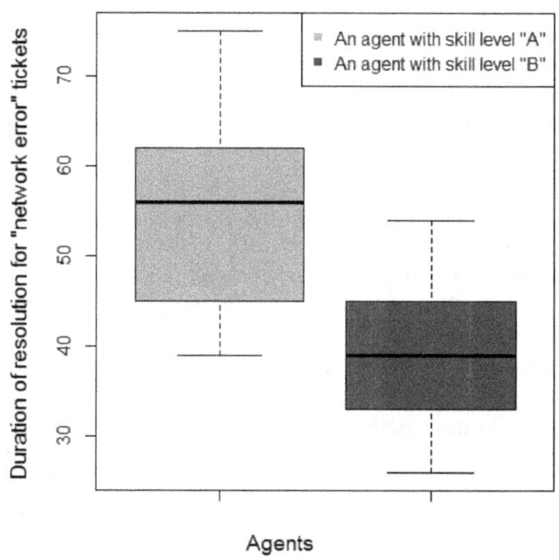

Figure 11: Example of agent with skill level "A" being slower than agent with skill level "B".

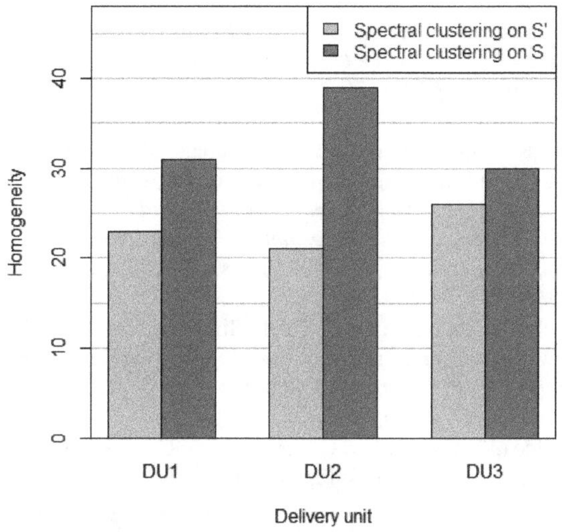

Figure 12: Homogeneity of different clustering methods.

We compare these two version to illustrate the homogeneity gain obtained when using the divergence matrix. This also demonstrates that topics alone are not informative enough for estimating the agent's performance.

For homogeneity optimized fuzzy k-means, the coefficient of variation provided as input will reflect the homogeneity of the final clustering. The minimum values for the coefficient of variation for which no tickets are dropped, for each delivery unit, were given previously in Table 4.

4.2.4 Deployment

As mentioned previously, the clustering and dispatching component is designed to be integrated in the IT Service Delivery Environment and a depiction of the elements the component interfaces with is shown in Figure 1. Our method succeeded in the evaluation phase, demonstrated effectiveness and we work on its deployment.

One important aspect that must be noted in deploying the dispatcher is the handling of a new agent. A new agent is assigned a default duration for solving a ticket of a particular topic, more precisely the median duration across agents for solving tasks of that topic. This way we ensure that enough tickets are sent to the new agent and therefore, the system can rapidly estimate the agent's actual speed.

Another aspect of the dispatching component is that since it favors the best agent for each ticket category, this may potentially lead to uneven workload distribution. To avoid this, one can adjust the greedy dispatching policy to include some regularization.

The performance gaps between agents need to be continuously reduced. Apart from its utility in the automatic dispatching, our system finds execution differences among agents and can show agent training needs and best practices. It can serve in targeted mentoring for ramp-up of skills for new employees which is very useful in a high turn-over environment.

5. RELATED WORK

Several works have previously addressed the possibility of improving the efficiency of ticket routing by mining ticket resolution sequence data or ticket descriptions [23, 1]. The authors in [23] capture the ticket transfer decisions embedded in ticket resolution sequences to develop a model to generate ticket routing recommendations. In [1] supervised learning techniques (SVM) and a discriminative term based heuristic are used to analyze ticket descriptions and predict the most appropriate resolution group. While we also investigate optimal ticket routing based on ticket descriptions, our focus is not matching the correct resolution group for a given ticket but rather on matching the most cost effective agent to resolve the ticket within a resolution group.

Researchers have also previously looked into clustering alerts and incident tickets [16, 17] for both structured and unstructured text using either graph theoretic approaches [16] or a combination of a latent semantic indexing based technique with a hierarchical n-gram based technique [17]. We have observed that standard text similarity measures as Jaccard used by the authors in [16] perform poorly when used in clustering tasks due to data sparseness and the lack of context. We differentiate from these approaches by proposing a similarity metric between tickets that tries to overcome the vocabulary mismatch problem, by using semantic similarity between words inferred from a large corpus.

We are not aware of any previous work on ticket clustering that aims at discovering topics with high homogeneity in the agent's performance. From a theoretical point of view, the problem we are trying to solve is similar to clustering with multiple graphs. Clustering with multiple graphs aims to fully exploit the links between different dimensions of a given network. While there is a rich body of work in the context of single graph clustering [2, 5, 12, 9, 13] the problem of clustering with multiple graphs has gained interest only recently [24, 21, 28]. In [24] the authors propose a factorization method based on linked matrices to solve the multi-graph clustering problem. In this model, each graph is approximated by a graph specific factor with a common factor shared by all the graphs. In [21] the authors propose two multi-graph clustering techniques (one tailored for unweighted graphs and one that performs well also on weighted graphs) with the goal of finding well-defined clusters across all the views of the graph. In [28] the authors propose a generalization of normalized cut for multi-dimensional graphs. Their model leads to a mixture of Markov chains defined on the different graphs.

We want to identify clusters that persist under different measures. Leskovec et al. have shown in [15] that strong communities are still identifiable under various measures. We choose to combine the adjacency matrices in one in a way such that the information in the divergence matrix is manifested in the final matrix as pairwise cannot-link constraints (constraints that express that entity i and entity j should be in different clusters). Having a single matrix, the problem becomes again a single graph clustering problem which we try to solve employing matrix factorization based clustering algorithms or by iteratively adjusting a fuzzy partitioning.

Work by Leskovec et al. has recently demonstrated that, although different quality measures produce differences in terms of specific communities, strong communities persist under a variety of measures

6. CONCLUSION

In this paper, we presented a novel approach that optimizes the service time in IT Service Delivery industry. We demonstrated on real data that considering empirical evidence on which agent is the most efficient on resolving certain incident tickets in the dispatching process significantly reduces service time.

We first build a model able to cluster the tickets into categories that both reflect the problem they document and are homogeneous in the duration time for an agent to solve them. Then we devise a data-informed dispatching policy that assigns an incoming ticket to the agent that is the fastest in resolving it. Experiments conducted on real data from several IBM Service Delivery Units demonstrate the benefits of our approach. More specifically, we compare the data-informed dispatching with the non-data informed dispatching and observe that the former exhibits 35% to 44% reduction in the service time.

7. REFERENCES

[1] S. Agarwal, R. Sindhgatta, and B. Sengupta. Smartdispatch: Enabling efficient ticket dispatch in an it service environment. In *Proceedings of the 18th ACM SIGKDD International Conference on Knowledge Discovery and Data Mining*, KDD '12, pages 1393–1401, New York, NY, USA, 2012. ACM.

[2] C. C. Aggarwal and H. Wang. *Managing and Mining Graph Data.* Springer Publishing Company, Incorporated, 1st edition, 2010.

[3] J. C. Bezdek. *Pattern Recognition with Fuzzy Objective Function Algorithms.* Kluwer Academic Publishers, Norwell, MA, USA, 1981.

[4] D. M. Blei, A. Y. Ng, and M. I. Jordan. Latent dirichlet allocation. *J. Mach. Learn. Res.*, 3:993–1022, Mar. 2003.

[5] Y. Chen, S. Sanghavi, and H. Xu. Clustering sparse graphs. In F. Pereira, C. Burges, L. Bottou, and K. Weinberger, editors, *Advances in Neural Information Processing Systems 25*, pages 2204–2212. Curran Associates, Inc., 2012.

[6] R. Cilibrasi and P. Vitanyi. The google similarity distance. *Knowledge and Data Engineering, IEEE Transactions on*, 19(3):370–383, March 2007.

[7] D. Defays. An efficient algorithm for a complete link method. *Comput. J.*, 20(4):364–366, 1977.

[8] R. El-Yaniv and D. Yanay. Supervised learning of semantic relatedness. In P. Flach, T. De Bie, and N. Cristianini, editors, *Machine Learning and Knowledge Discovery in Databases*, volume 7523 of *Lecture Notes in Computer Science*, pages 744–759. Springer Berlin Heidelberg, 2012.

[9] A. Gionis, H. Mannila, and P. Tsaparas. Clustering aggregation. *ACM Transactions on Knowledge Discovery from Data*, 1(1), Mar. 2007.

[10] T. H. Haveliwala, A. Gionis, D. Klein, and P. Indyk. Evaluating strategies for similarity search on the web. In *Proceedings of the 11th International Conference on World Wide Web*, WWW '02, pages 432–442, New York, NY, USA, 2002. ACM.

[11] L. Kaufman and P. J. Rousseeuw. *Finding Groups in Data: An Introduction to Cluster Analysis*, pages 1–67. John Wiley and Sons, Inc., 2008.

[12] J. Kleinberg. An impossibility theorem for clustering. pages 446–453. MIT Press, 2002.

[13] H.-P. Kriegel, P. Kröger, and A. Zimek. Clustering high-dimensional data: A survey on subspace clustering, pattern-based clustering, and correlation clustering. *ACM Trans. Knowl. Discov. Data*, 3(1):1:1–1:58, Mar. 2009.

[14] T. K. Landauer, P. W. Foltz, and D. Laham. An introduction to latent semantic analysis. *Discourse Processes*, 25:259–284, 1998.

[15] J. Leskovec, K. J. Lang, and M. Mahoney. Empirical comparison of algorithms for network community detection. In *Proceedings of the 19th International Conference on World Wide Web*, WWW '10, pages 631–640, New York, NY, USA, 2010. ACM.

[16] D. Lin, R. Raghu, V. Ramamurthy, J. Yu, R. Radhakrishnan, and J. Fernandez. Unveiling clusters of events for alert and incident management in large-scale enterprise it. In *Proceedings of the 20th ACM SIGKDD International Conference on Knowledge Discovery and Data Mining*, KDD '14, pages 1630–1639, New York, NY, USA, 2014. ACM.

[17] S. Mani, K. Sankaranarayanan, V. S. Sinha, and P. Devanbu. Panning requirement nuggets in stream of software maintenance tickets. In *Proceedings of the 22nd ACM SIGSOFT International Symposium on Foundations of Software Engineering*, FSE 2014, pages 678–688, New York, NY, USA, 2014. ACM.

[18] D. Metzler, S. Dumais, and C. Meek. Similarity measures for short segments of text. In *Proceedings of the 29th European Conference on IR Research*, ECIR'07, pages 16–27, Berlin, Heidelberg, 2007. Springer-Verlag.

[19] R. Mihalcea, C. Corley, and C. Strapparava. Corpus-based and knowledge-based measures of text semantic similarity. In *Proceedings of the 21st National Conference on Artificial Intelligence - Volume 1*, AAAI'06, pages 775–780. AAAI Press, 2006.

[20] A. Y. Ng, M. I. Jordan, and Y. Weiss. On spectral clustering: Analysis and an algorithm. In T. Dietterich, S. Becker, and Z. Ghahramani, editors, *Advances in Neural Information Processing Systems 14*, pages 849–856. MIT Press, 2002.

[21] E. E. Papalexakis, L. Akoglu, and D. Ience. Do more views of a graph help? community detection and clustering in multi-graphs. In *FUSION*, pages 899–905. IEEE, 2013.

[22] G. Recchia and M. Jones. More data trumps smarter algorithms: Comparing pointwise mutual information with latent semantic analysis. *Behavior Research Methods*, 41(3):647–656, 2009.

[23] Q. Shao, Y. Chen, S. Tao, X. Yan, and N. Anerousis. Efficient ticket routing by resolution sequence mining. In *Proceedings of the 14th ACM SIGKDD International Conference on Knowledge Discovery and Data Mining*, KDD '08, pages 605–613, New York, NY, USA, 2008. ACM.

[24] W. Tang, Z. Lu, and I. Dhillon. Clustering with multiple graphs. In *Data Mining, 2009. ICDM '09. Ninth IEEE International Conference on*, pages 1016–1021, Dec 2009.

[25] K. Toutanova, D. Klein, C. D. Manning, and Y. Singer. Feature-rich part-of-speech tagging with a cyclic dependency network. In *Proceedings of the 2003 Conference of the North American Chapter of the Association for Computational Linguistics on Human Language Technology - Volume 1*, NAACL '03, pages 173–180, Stroudsburg, PA, USA, 2003.

[26] P. D. Turney. Mining the web for synonyms: Pmi-ir versus lsa on toefl. In *Proceedings of the 12th European Conference on Machine Learning*, EMCL '01, pages 491–502, London, UK, UK, 2001. Springer-Verlag.

[27] R. B. Wallace and W. Whitt. A staffing algorithm for call centers with skill-based routing. *Manufacturing & Service Operations Management*, 7(4):276–294, Oct. 2005.

[28] D. Zhou and C. J. C. Burges. Spectral clustering and transductive learning with multiple views. In *Proceedings of the 24th International Conference on Machine Learning*, ICML '07, pages 1159–1166, New York, NY, USA, 2007. ACM.

Intelligible Models for HealthCare: Predicting Pneumonia Risk and Hospital 30-day Readmission

Rich Caruana
Microsoft Research
rcaruana@microsoft.com

Yin Lou
LinkedIn Corporation
ylou@linkedin.com

Johannes Gehrke
Microsoft
johannes@microsoft.com

Paul Koch
Microsoft Research
paulkoch@microsoft.com

Marc Sturm
NewYork-Presbyterian Hospital
mas9161@nyp.org

Noémie Elhadad
Columbia University
noemie.elhadad@columbia.edu

ABSTRACT

In machine learning often a tradeoff must be made between accuracy and intelligibility. More accurate models such as boosted trees, random forests, and neural nets usually are not intelligible, but more intelligible models such as logistic regression, naive-Bayes, and single decision trees often have significantly worse accuracy. This tradeoff sometimes limits the accuracy of models that can be applied in mission-critical applications such as healthcare where being able to understand, validate, edit, and trust a learned model is important. We present two case studies where high-performance generalized additive models with pairwise interactions (GA^2Ms) are applied to real healthcare problems yielding intelligible models with state-of-the-art accuracy. In the pneumonia risk prediction case study, the intelligible model uncovers surprising patterns in the data that previously had prevented complex learned models from being fielded in this domain, but because it is intelligible and modular allows these patterns to be recognized and removed. In the 30-day hospital readmission case study, we show that the same methods scale to large datasets containing hundreds of thousands of patients and thousands of attributes while remaining intelligible and providing accuracy comparable to the best (unintelligible) machine learning methods.

Categories and Subject Descriptors

I.2.6 [**Computing Methodologies**]: Learning—*Induction*

Keywords

intelligibility; classification; interaction detection; additive models; logistic regression; healthcare; risk prediction

1. MOTIVATION

In the mid 90's, a large multi-institutional project was funded by Cost-Effective HealthCare (CEHC) to evaluate the application of machine learning to important problems in healthcare such as predicting pneumonia risk. In the study, the goal was to predict the probability of death (POD) for patients with pneumonia so that high-risk patients could be admitted to the hospital while low-risk patients were treated as outpatients. In the study [3, 2], the most accurate models that could be trained were multitask neural nets.[1] On one dataset the neural nets outperformed traditional methods such as logistic regression by wide margin (the neural net had AUC=0.86 compared to 0.77 for logistic regression), and on the other dataset used in this paper outperformed logistic regression by about 0.02 (see Table 2). Although the neural nets were the most accurate models, after careful consideration they were considered too risky for use on real patients and logistic resgression was used instead. Why?

One of the methods being evaluated was rule-based learning [1]. Although models based on rules were not as accurate as the neural net models, they were *intelligible*, i.e., interpretable by humans. On one of the pneumonia datasets, the rule-based system learned the rule "HasAsthama(x) ⇒ LowerRisk(x)", i.e., that patients with pneumonia who have a history of asthma have lower risk of dying from pneumonia than the general population. Needless to say, this rule is counterintuitive. But it reflected a true pattern in the training data: patients with a history of asthma who presented with pneumonia usually were admitted not only to the hospital but directly to the ICU (Intensive Care Unit). The good news is that the aggressive care received by asthmatic pneumonia patients was so effective that it lowered their risk of dying from pneumonia compared to the general population. The bad news is that because the prognosis for these patients is better than average, models trained on the data incorrectly learn that asthma lowers risk, when in fact asthmatics have much higher risk (if not hospitalized).

One of the goals of the study was to perform a clinical trial to determine if machine learning could be used to predict risk prior to hospitalization so that a more informed decision about hospitalization could to be made. The ultimate goal was to reduce healthcare cost by reducing hospital admissions, while maintaining (or even improving) outcomes by more accurately identifying patients that need hospitalization. As the most accurate models, neural nets were a strong candidate for clinical trial. Deploying neural net models that could not be understood, however, was deemed too risky —

[1]SVMs and boosted trees were not in common use yet, and Random Forests had not yet been invented.

KDD'15, August 10-13, 2015, Sydney, NSW, Australia.

ACM 978-1-4503-3664-2/15/08 ...$15.00.
DOI: http://dx.doi.org/10.1145/2783258.2788613 .

if the rule-based system had learned that asthma lowers risk, certainly the neural nets had learned it, too. The rule-based system was intelligible and modular, making it easy to recognize and remove dangerous rules like the asthma rule. While there are methods for *repairing* the neural nets so they do not incorrectly predict that asthmatics are at lower risk and thus less likely to need hospitalization, e.g., re-train without asthmatics in the population, remove the asthma feature, modify the targets for asthmatics to "1" in the data to reflect the care they received (unfortunately confounding care with death), the decision was made to not use the neural nets not because the asthma problem could not be solved, but because the lack of intelligibility made it difficult to know what *other* problems might also need fixing. Because the neural nets were more accurate than the rules, it was possible that the neural nets had learned other patterns that could put some kinds of patients at risk if used in a clinical trial. For example, perhaps pregnant women with pneumonia also receive aggressive treatment that lowers their risk compared to the general population. The neural net might learn that pregnancy lowers risk, and thus recommend not admitting pregnant women, thus putting them at increased risk. In an effort to "do no harm", the decision was made to go forward only with models that were intelligible such as logistic regression, even if they had lower AUC than other unintelligible models. The logistic regression model also learned that having asthma lowered risk, but this could easily be corrected by changing the weight on the asthma feature from negative to positive (or to zero).

Jumping two decades forward to the present, we now have a number of new learning methods that are very accurate, but unfortunately also relatively unintelligible such as boosted trees, random forests, bagged trees, kernelized-SVMs, neural nets, deep neural nets, and ensembles of these methods. Applying any of these methods to mission-critical problems such as healthcare remains problematic, in part because usually it is not ethical to modify (or randomize) the care delivered to patients to collect data sets that will not suffer from the kinds of bias described above. Learning must be done with the data that is available, not the data one would want. But it is critical that models trained on real-world data be validated prior to use lest some patients be put at risk, which makes using the most accurate learning methods challenging.

In this paper we describe the application of a learning method based on high-performance generalized additive models [5, 6] to the pneumonia problem described above, and to a modern, much larger problem predicting 30-day hospital readmission. On both of these problems our GA^{2}M models yield state-of-the-art accuracy while remaining intelligible, modular, and editable. We believe this class of models represents a significant step forward in training models with high accuracy that are also intelligible. The main contributions of this paper are that it: shows that GA^{2}Ms yield competitive accuracy on real problems; demonstrates that the learned models are intelligible; demonstrates that the predictions made by the model for individual cases (patients) also are intelligible, and demonstrates how, because the models are modular, they can be edited by experts.

The remainder of the paper is organized as follows. Section 2 provides a brief introduction to GAM and GA^{2}M. Sections 3 and 4 present our case studies of training intelligible GA^{2}M model on the pneumonia and the 30-day readmission data, respectively. Section 5 discusses a wide range of issues that arise when learning with intelligible models and our general lessons for the research community.

2. INTELLIGIBLE MODELS

Let $\mathcal{D} = \{(\boldsymbol{x}_i, y_i)\}_1^N$ denote a training dataset of size N, where $\boldsymbol{x}_i = (x_{i1}, ..., x_{ip})$ is a feature vector with p features and y_i is the target (response). We use x_j to denote the jth variable in the feature space.

Generalized additive models (GAMs) are the gold standard for intelligibility when low-dimensional terms are considered [4, 5, 6]. Standard GAMs have the form

$$g(E[y]) = \beta_0 + \sum f_j(x_j), \tag{1}$$

where g is the link function and for each term f_j, $E[f_j] = 0$. Generalized linear models (GLMs), such as logistic regression, are a special form of GAMs where each f_j is restricted to be linear. Since the contribution of a single feature to the final prediction can be easily understood by examining f_j, such models are considered intelligible.

To improve accuracy, pairwise interactions can be added to standard GAMs, leading to a model called GA^{2}Ms [6]:

$$g(E[y]) = \beta_0 + \sum_j f_j(x_j) + \sum_{i \neq j} f_{ij}(x_i, x_j). \tag{2}$$

Note that pairwise interactions are intelligible because they can be visualized as a heat map. GA^{2}M builds the best GAM first and then detects and ranks all possible pairs of interactions in the residuals. The top k pairs are then included in the model (k is determined by cross-validation).

There are various methods to train GAMs and GA^{2}Ms. Each component can be represented using splines, leading to an optimization problem which balances the smoothness of splines and empirical error [7]. Other representations include regression trees on a single or a pair of features. Empirical study showed gradient boosting with bagging of shallow regression trees yields as components very good accuracy [5]. Interested readers are referred to [5, 6] for details.[2]

3. CASE STUDY: PNEUMONIA RISK

In this case study we use one of the pneumonia datasets discussed earlier in the motivation [3]. This dataset has 14,199 pneumonia patients. To facilitate comparison with prior work, we use the same train and test set folds from the earlier study: the train set contains 9847 patients and the test set has 4352 patients (a 70:30 train:test split). There are 46 features describing each patient. These range from history features such as age and gender, to simple measurements taken at a routine physical such as heart rate, blood pressure, and respiration rate, to lab tests such as White Blood Cell count (WBC) and Blood Urea Nitrogen (BUN), to features read from a chest x-ray such as lung collapse or pleural effusion. See Table 1 for a complete list.

As discussed earlier, the goal is to predict probability of death (POD) so that patients at high risk can be admitted to the hospital, while patients at low risk are treated as outpatients.[3] 10.86% of the patients in the dataset (1542 patients) died from pneumonia. The GAM/GA^{2}M models are

[2]Code is available at `https://github.com/yinlou/mltk`.

[3]Hospitals are dangerous places, particularly for patients with impaired immune systems. Treating low-risk patients as outpatients not only saves money, but is actually safer.

Patient-history findings			
chronic lung disease	-	age	C
re-admission to hospital	-	gender	-
admitted through ER	-	diabetes mellitus	-
admitted from nursing home	-	asthma	-
congestive heart failure	-	cancer	-
ischemic heart disease	-	number of diseases	C
cerebrovascular disease	-	history of seizures	-
chronic liver disease	-	renal failure	-
history of chest pain	-		
Physical examination findings			
diastolic blood pressure	C	wheezing	-
gastrointestinal bleeding	-	stridor	-
respiration rate	C	heart murmur	-
altered mental status	-	temperature	C
heart rate	C		
Laboratory findings			
liver function tests	-	BUN level	C
glucose level	C	creatinine level	C
potassium level	C	albumin level	C
hematocrit	C	WBC count	C
percentage bands	C	pH	C
pO2	C	pCO2	C
sodium level	C		
Chest X-ray findings			
positive chest x-ray	-	lung infiltrate	-
pleural effusion	-	pneumothorax	-
cavitation/empyema	-	chest mass	-
lobe or lung collapse	-		

Table 1: Pneumonia attributes, grouped by type. Continuous features that will be shaped by GAM/GA^{2}M models are marked with a "C".

trained on this data using 100 rounds of bagging. Bagging is done to reduce overfitting, and to provide pseudo-confidence intervals for the graphs in the intelligible model.

The AUC area for different models trained on this data are shown in Table 2. On this dataset logistic regression achieves AUC = 0.843, Random Forests achieves 0.846, LogitBoost 0.849, GAM 0.854, and GA^{2}M is best with AUC = 0.857.[4] The difference in AUC between the methods is not huge (less than 0.02), but it is reassuring to see the GAM/GA^{2}M methods achieve the best accuracy on this problem. The important question is if the GAM/GA^{2}M models are able to achieve this accuracy while remaining intelligible?

Figure 1 shows 28 of the 56 terms in the GA^{2}M model for pneumonia. Unfortunately, the compact representation necessary for the paper reduces intelligibility. For small models like this with fewer than 100 terms we would prefer to present all terms, possibly sorted by their importance to the model. In the actual deployment, for each term we would also show a histogram of data density for different values of the feature, descriptive statistics about the feature, several different measures of term importance in the model, and links to online resources that provide information about the term, e.g., links to a hospital database, or Wikipedia or WebMD pages that describe features, how they are measured, what the normal ranges are, and what abnormal values indicate. Because of space limitations we have suppressed all of this auxiliary information (including some axis labels!) and just present shape plots for some of the more interesting terms. Presenting the terms in multicolumn format without the auxiliary information further hinders intelligibility — the models are more readable when

[4]The GA^{2}M model uses 10 of the $46 * 45/2 = 1035$ possible pairwise interaction terms (k chosen by cross-validation).

Model	Pneumonia	Readmission
Logistic Regression	0.8432	0.7523
GAM	0.8542	0.7795
GA^{2}M	0.8576	0.7833
Random Forests	0.8460	0.7671
LogitBoost	0.8493	0.7835

Table 2: AUC for different learning methods on the pneumonia and 30-day readmission tasks.

presented in sorted order as a scrollable list of graphs plus auxiliary information.

The 1st term in the model is for age. Age (in years) on the x-axis ranges from 18-106 years old (the pneumonia dataset contains only adults). The vertical axis is the risk score predicted by the model for patients as a function of age. The risk score for this term varies from -0.25 for patients with age less than 50, to a high of about 0.35 for patients age 85 and above. The green errorbars are pseudo-errorbars of the risk score predicted for each age: each errorbar is ± 1 standard deviation of the variation in the risk score measured by 100 rounds of bagging. We use ± 1 standard deviation instead of the standard error of the mean because it is well known that bagging underestimates the variance of predictions from complex models. We believe it is safer to be conservative than to present unrealistically narrow confidence intervals. (See the top of Figure 3(a) for an enlarged version of this graph, and the discussion in Section 5.5 for more detailed analysis of the age feature.)

The 2nd term in the model, asthma, is the one that caused trouble in the CEHC study in the mid-90's and prevented clinical trials with the very accurate neural net model. The GA^{2}M model has found the same pattern discovered back then: that having asthma lowers the risk of dying from pneumonia. As with the logistic regression and rule-based models trained then, but unlike with the neural net models, this term is easy to recognize and fix in the GA^{2}M model. We can "repair" the model by eliminating this term (effectively setting the weight on this graph to zero), or by using human expertise to redraw the graph so that the risk score for asthma=1 is positive, not negative. Because asthma is boolean, it is not necessary to use a graph, and we could present a weight and offset (RiskScore = w*hasAsthma + b) instead. We prefer to use graphs for boolean terms like asthma for three reasons: 1) it is necessary to show graphs for features with multiple or continuous values such as age as well as for interactions between features, and it is awkward for the user to jump from terms presented as graphs to terms presented as equations; 2) we find graphs provide an intuitive display of risk where up implies higher risk, down implies lower risk, and the magnitude of the change in risk is captured by the distance moved; and 3) some users are not as comfortable with numbers as they are with graphs, and it is important that the model is intelligible to real users, whatever their background.

The 3rd term in the model is BUN (Blood Urea Nitrogen) level. Most patients have BUN=0 because, as in many medical datasets, if the variable is not measured or assumed normal it is coded as 0. The model says risk is reduced for patients where BUN was not measured, suggesting that this test typically is not ordered for patients who appear to be healthy. BUN levels below 30 appear to be low risk,

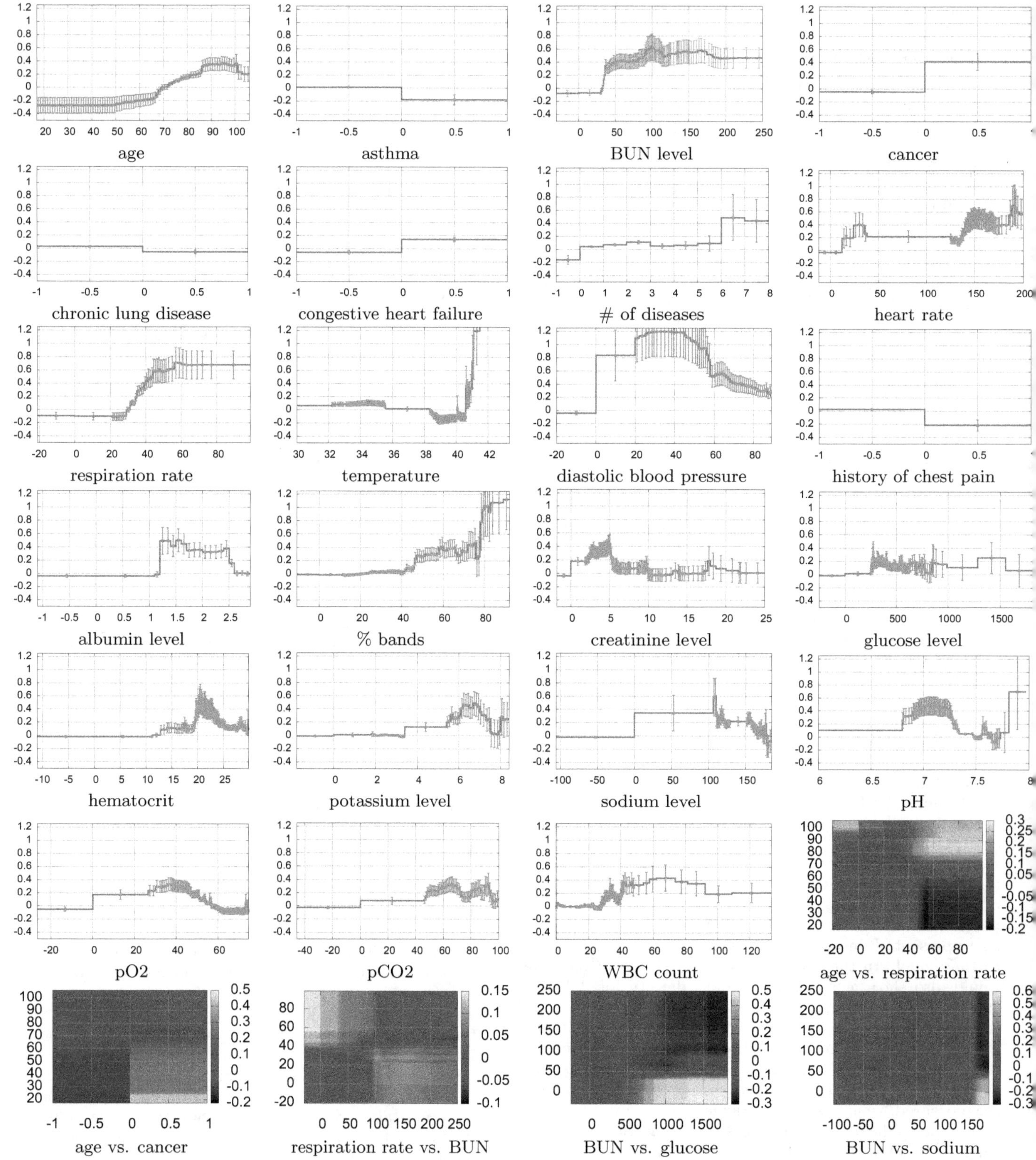

Figure 1: 28 (of 56 total) components for the GA^{2}M model trained on the pneumonia data. The line graphs are terms that contain single features. The heat maps at the bottom are pairwise interaction terms. The vertical scale on all line graphs are the same to facilitate rapid scanning of the relative contribution of each term. The green errorbars are pseudo-errorbars from bagging. Boolean features such as asthma are presented as graphs because this aids interpretation among other features that must be presented as graphs.

while levels from 50-200 indicate higher risk. This is consistent with medical knowledge which suggests that normal, healthy BUN is 10-20, and that elevated levels above 30 may indicate kidney damage, congestive heart failure, or bleeding in the gastrintestinal tract.

The cancer term in the model is clear: having cancer significantly increases the risk of dying from pneumonia, probably because it explains why the patient has pneumonia (either from lung cancer, from immuno suppressive drugs used to treat cancer, or from hospitalization associated with cancer) and/or because it explains the stage of cancer (terminal stages of cancer frequently lead to failing health and being bed-ridden, both of which can lead to pneumonia).

The next term in the model, chronic lung disease, and the history of chest pain term that occurs later, are interesting because the model suggests that chronic lung disease and a history of chest pain both *decrease* POD. We suspect that this may be a similar problem as asthma: patients with lung disease and chest pain may receive care earlier, and may receive more aggressive care. If further investigation suggests this to be the case, both terms would be removed from the model, or edited, similar to the asthma term.

The # of diseases (# of comorbid conditions) is a general measure of illness. The graph suggests that having no diseases other than pneumonia lowers risk, that risk increases slowly as the number of comorbid conditions increases from 1-3, then is flat or decreases until it rises dramatically above 6, but the errorbars are large enough to be consistent with risk being somewhat flat for 3-8 comorbidities.

Heart rate is an unusual looking graph. 91% patients have rate=0, indicating it was not measured or assumed normal. Risk is high for very low heart rates (10-30), and for very high rates (125-200), but the model does not appear to discriminate between patients with heart rates 40-120. On further inspection, there are no patients with heart rate recorded between 40-120! Apparently all patients in this range were considered "normal" and coded as 0. (Normal heart rate in adults is about 60-100, 40-60 for athletes, and somewhat higher than 100 for patients with "White Coat" Syndrome). The unusual shape of the graph for heart rate has lead us to discover a surprising aspect of the data, though it is not clear what risk we would want to model to predict for rates between 40-120 where there is no data?

The respiration rate term is very clear: rate=0 (missing) or 20-28 is low risk, and risk rises rapidly as breathing rate climbs from 28-60. Normal respiration rate for adults is 16-20. In the body temperature term, temps from 36°C-40°C are low risk (normal is 37°C), risk is somewhat elevated at low body temps (32°C-36°C), and greatly elevated for temps above 40.5°C (fever this high often is a sign of serious infection). Having a fever above 41.5°C increases the risk score by a full point or more.[5] Diastolic blood pressure also can dramatically increase risk: low diastolic in the range 20-50 (normal is 60-80) increase risk as much as a full point. % bands is also a strong term (bands in a blood test are a sign of bacterial infection—bacterial pneumonia is more deadly than viral pneumonia): bands above 40% indicate elevated risk, with bands above 80% indicating very elevated risk.

Before leaving pneumonia, let us examine one of the interaction terms. In the age vs. cancer term, we see that risk is highest for the youngest patients (probably cancers acquired in childhood but not cured when the patient reaches age 18), and declines for patients who acquire cancer later in life, but for patients without cancer risk rises as expected with age. This is a classic interaction effect that likely results from the difference between childhood and adult cancers.

Space prevents us from discussing each term individually, or from discussing terms in great detail. See Section 5.5 for a deeper dive on the age term. To summarize this section, the GA^{2}M model discovered the same asthma pattern that created problems in the CEHC study, provides a simple mechanism to correct this problem, and uncovered other similar problems (chronic lung disease and history of chest pain) that were not recognized in the CEHC study but which warrant further investigation and probably repair. As hoped, the GA^{2}M model is accurate, intelligible, and repairable.

4. CASE STUDY: 30-DAY READMISSION

In this section we apply GA^{2}M to a modern and much larger dataset for 30-day hospital readmission. The data comes from a collaboration with a large hospital. There are 195,901 patients in the train set (2011-2012), 100,823 patients in the test set (2013), and 3,956 features for each patient. Features include lab test results, summaries of doctor notes, and details of previous hospitalizations. In this problem, the goal is to predict which patients are likely to be readmitted to the hospital within 30 days after being released from the hospital. All patients in this dataset have already been hospitalized at least once, and the goal is to predict if they will need to return to the hospital unusually quickly (within 30 days). Hospitals with abnormally high 30-day readmission rates are penalized financially because a high rate suggests the hospital did not provide adequate care on the earlier admission, or may have released the patient prematurely, or did not provide adequate instructions to the patient when they were released, or did not perform adequate follow-up after release. In the data 8.91% of patients are readmitted within 30 days. For this problem we use 10 iterations of bagging. Training the 10 models takes 2-3 days on a small cluster of 10 general purpose computers. Table 2 shows the AUC for different models on this data.

In Section 3 we examined the GA^{2}M model for the pneumonia problem. Unfortunately, the readmission dataset contains almost 100 times as many features. Instead of trying to examine the full model, we instead examine the predictions made by the model for three patients. Two of these patients have very high predicted probability of readmission (p=0.9326 and p=0.9264), and one of the patients has a typical readmission probability (p=0.0873). This allows us to demonstrate that the models are intelligible not only taken as a whole, but that the predictions GA^{2}M models make for individual patients also are intelligible.

In Figure 2, each of the three columns is a patient, and each row is a term in the model. Terms are sorted for each patient (in each column) by the risk they contribute to that patient for 30-day readmission. Space limits us to showing the top 6 terms for each patient that contributed most to risk. Patient #1 has a very high probability of readmission within 30 days: p=0.9326. The four terms that contribute most to their high probability of readmission are: their total number of visits to the hospital is 40, they have been an inpatient in the hospital 19 times in the last 12 months, they have been in the hospital 10 times in the last 6 months, and 4 times in the last 3 months. This is not unusual: the most

[5] An increase in risk of 1 point more than doubles the odds of dying. See Section 5.1.

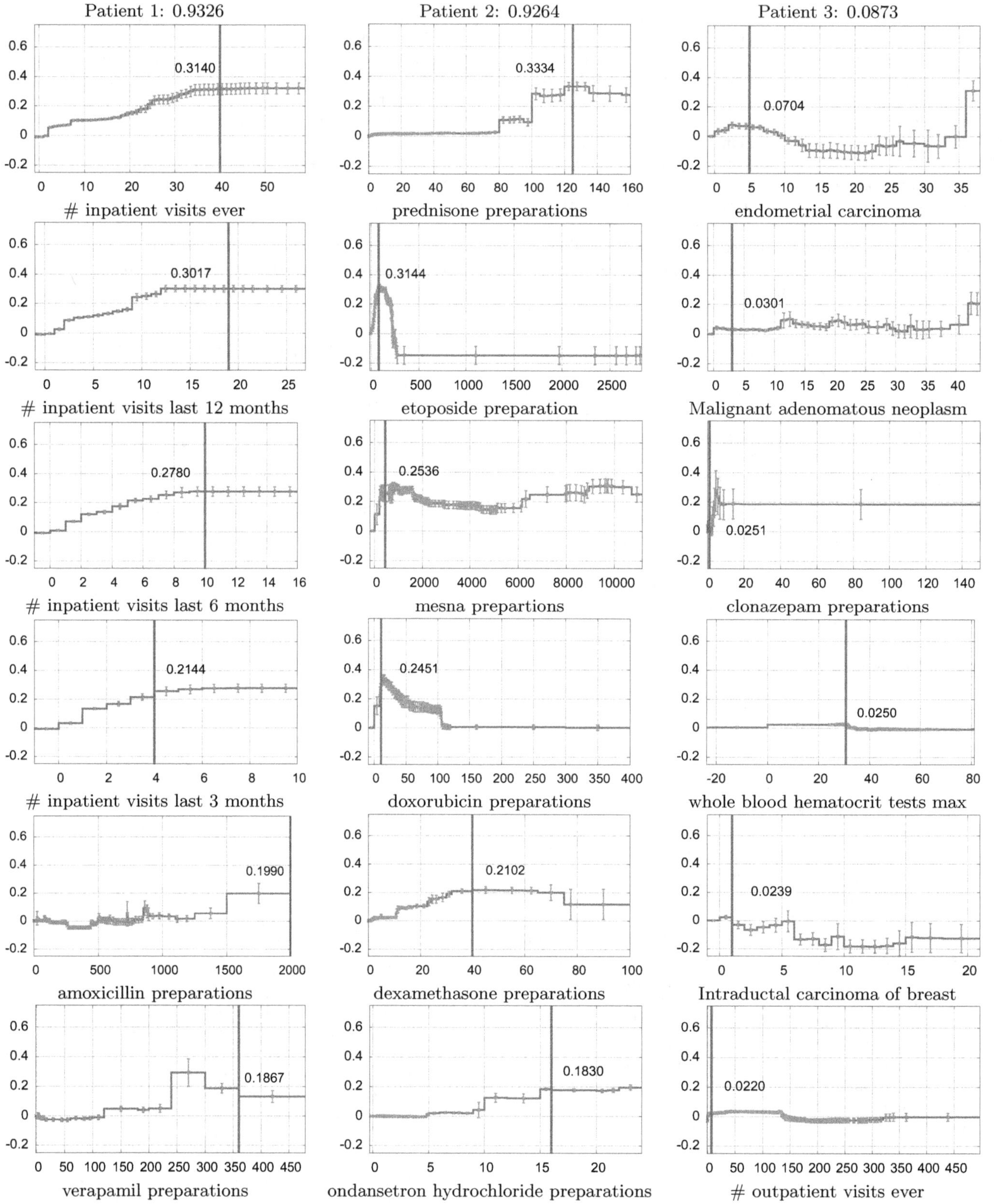

Figure 2: Top 6 terms (of 4456) in the GA^{2}M for three patients. The patients on the left have high risk of readmission. The patient on the right has moderate risk. Terms are sorted by their contribution to risk. Blue lines highlight feature values and corresponding risk scores. Six terms cannot tell the full story for these patients, but even these few terms provide insight into the patients and their risk of readmission.

predictive terms in the 30-day readmission model measure the number of visits patients have made in the last 12 month, 6 months, and 3 months to the ER, as an outpatient, and as an inpatient. As we see with this patient, a large number of recent inpatient visits (admissions) is associated with a high probability of readmission.[6] The next two terms suggest why patient #1 may have been in the hospital often: this patient has received large doses of amoxicillin (an antibiotic used to treat infections like strep and pneumonia) and verapamil (a treatment for hypertension and angina), i.e., they have an ongoing infection that may not be responding to antibiotics, and also probably have heart disease. The main reason this patient is predicted to be likely to return is because they have been in the hospital often in the last year, but the first few terms in the model also give us a hint of the medical conditions that put them at elevated risk.

The terms that are most important for patient #2 (also high risk: p=0.9364) are different from the terms that were important for patient #1. The most important 6 terms are preparations that the patient received during their last visit: prednisone is a corticosteroid used as an imummosuppressant, etoposide in an anticancer drug, mesna is a cancer chemotherapy drug, doxorubicin is a treatment for blood and skin cancers, dexamethosone is another immunosuppressant steroid, and ondansetron is a drug used to treat nausea from chemotherapy. Patient #2 has received doses of each of these preparations that suggest cancer may not be responding well to treatment and that they are receiving aggressive chemotherapy. The contribution to risk from these 6 terms alone is greater than +1.5, i.e., these 6 terms alone triple the odds of their being readmitted within 30-days.

Patient #3 has moderate risk: p=0.0873 (baseline rate is 8.91%). This 6 terms that increase this patient's readmission risk the most are: 1) the patient has endrometrial carcinoma (a cancer common in post-menopausal women that often can be treated effectively by hysterectomy without radiation- or chemo-therapy); 2) a benign abdominal tumor (malignant adenomatous neplasm =3); 3) a relaxant typically prescribed to calm patients or reduce spasms; 4) a fairly typical (i.e. low risk) hematocrit test result; 5) a pre-cancerous non-invasive lesion in the breast; and 6) a small number of outpatient visits suggesting they have been receiving treatment as an outpatient without needing to be hospitalized (the inpatient and ER risk factors for this patient are all low). Patient #3 is a typical patient as far as 30-day readmission is considered. They are post-menopausal, have cancers that respond well to treatment if caught early, the treatments themselves are relatively low-risk, and they have not needed unusual medications or to be hospitalized often in the last year.

The patients above provide a small glimpse of what the GA^2M model learned from a 200,000 patient train set with 4,000 features: we have only been able to examine three patients, and have only looked at the top 6 terms for each of these patients. To a medical expert, the sorted terms

[6]A large number of visits to the ER also is associated with increased chance of readmission, but outpatient visits are more interesting: a small number of recent outpatient visits increases risk of readmission, but a very large number of outpatient visits (100-200 in the last year) indicates lower risk of readmission because the patient is receiving primary care as an outpatient—many of these patients are dialysis patients who visit the hospital 1-2 times per week.

RiskScore	Probability	RiskScore	Probability
-5.0	0.0067	+5.0	0.9933
-4.0	0.0180	+4.0	0.9820
-3.0	0.0474	+3.0	0.9526
-2.0	0.1192	+2.0	0.8808
-1.0	0.2689	+1.0	0.7311
0.0	0.5000		

Table 3: Risk scores (log odds) and the corresponding probabilities.

for each patient present a comprehensive picture of the risk factors that contribute to the probability of readmission predicted for a patient. The model is not causal — it does not say that because the patient has X, they received treatments A, B, and C, and we can see from the amount of A, B, and C they received that they are not responding well. Instead, it learns that high doses of A, B, and C are associated with high risk or readmission, and it is up to the human experts to infer the underlying causal reasons for the feature values and the risk they predict. Nevertheless, compared to an unintelligible model such as an ensemble of 1000 boosted trees or a complex neural net, the model is fairly transparent, and the predictions it makes can be fully "understood", both at the per-patient level, and at the macro-model level.

5. DISCUSSION

5.1 How To Interpret Risk Scores

Each term in the intelligible model returns a risk score (log odds) that is added to the patient's aggregate predicted risk. Terms with risk scores above zero increase risk; terms with scores below zero decrease risk. The term risk scores are added to a baseline risk, and the sum converted to a probability. Both penumonia and 30-day readmission have baseline rates near 0.1, which corresponds to TotalRiskScore = -2.197. So patients with aggregate risk scores above -2.2 have higher than average risk, and patients with total risk scores below -2.2 have lower than average risk scores. A patient with TotalRiskScore = 0 (including the baseline offset) has quite high risk: $p = 1/(1+\exp(-1*TotalRiskSccore) = 1/(1+\exp(0)) = 0.5$. Table 3 shows a sample of total risk scores and the corresponding probabilities.

5.2 Modularity

In the intelligible models discussed in this paper, the average risk score for each graph (i.e., each term: each feature or pair of features) averaged across the training set is set to zero by subtracting the mean score. A single bias term is then added to the model so that the average predicted probability across all patients equals the observed baseline rate. This is done to make models identifiable and modular. Because of this property, each graph can be removed from the model (zeroed out) without introducing bias to the predictions. If all terms were removed from the model, the only remaining term would be the bias term, and the probability predicted for all patients would be the observed baseline rate in the training set. Adding terms (graphs) to the model increases the model's discriminativeness without altering the prior. This is important because it increases modularity and makes it easier to interpret the contribution of each term:

negative scores decrease risk, and positive scores increase risk compared to the baseline risk.

5.3 Sorting Terms by Importance

If a model contains a modest number of terms (e.g., less than 50), it is best to show terms in the model to experts in the order they are most familiar with. Because experts are often used to seeing features in logical groupings, interpretation is aided by preserving these groupings when the model is presented. However, when the number of terms grows large, it becomes infeasible for experts to examine all terms carefully. Term importance often follows a power-law distribution, with a few terms being very important, a modest number of terms being somewhat important, and many terms being of little importance. When this is the case, intelligibility can be improved by sorting terms by a measure of importance such as the drop in AUC when the term is removed, or the skill of the term measured in isolation, or the maximum contribution (positive or negative) that the term can make for any patient. No one measure is correct or best, and we find that a sort that reflects a combination of these metrics seems to work well.

It is much easier to sort terms by importance when making prediction for a single patient: because each term yields a single risk score for each patient at the point where that patient's feature value lies on the term graph, it is possible to sort terms by how much they increase or decrease risk for the patient. This provides a well-defined ordering of the terms for a patient from terms that increase risk most to terms that decrease risk most. Often this ordering quickly identifies the key patient characteristics that best explain the model's prediction, and which help experts quickly understand the patient's condition. This is the method we used to describe the predictions made by the 30-day readmission model — although that model contains more than 4000 terms, the number of terms that are relevant for each patient are, in practice, often quite small (e.g., less than 100).

5.4 Feature Shaping vs. Expert Discretization

Significant effort was made in the CEHC pneumonia study to train accurate models with logistic regression and other methods that could not handle continuous attributes. Medical experts carefully discretized each continuous attribute into clinically meaningful ranges used to define boolean variables. For example, the intervals for age were 18-39, 40-54, 55-63, 64-68, 69-72, 73-75, 76-79, 80-83, 84-88, and 89+. We used these expert-defined intervals for the logistic regression model reported in Table 2. We also trained a GA^2M model with these discretized features, and observed a drop in AUC of about 0.01 on the test set compared to the GA^2M trained with the continuous features, suggesting that the GA^2M model gains some of its accuracy by shaping continuous features more accurately than expert discretization.

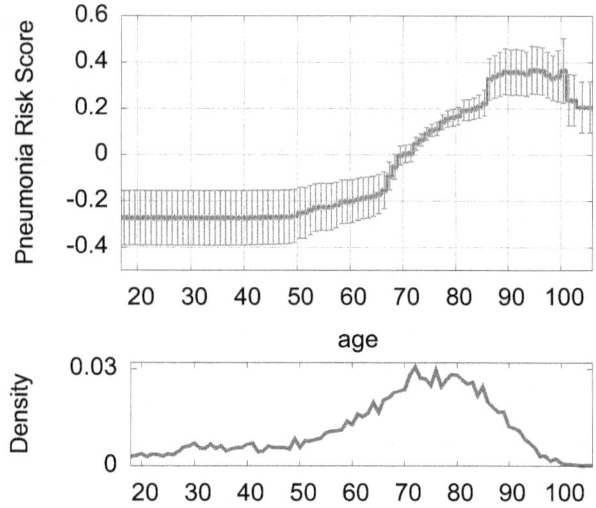

(a) Pneumonia

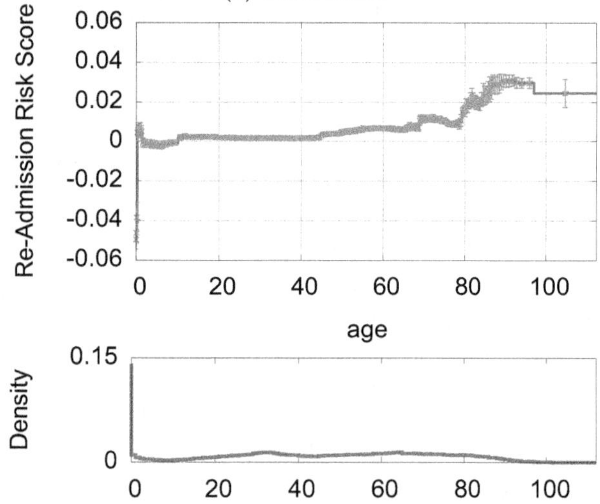

(b) 30-day Readmission

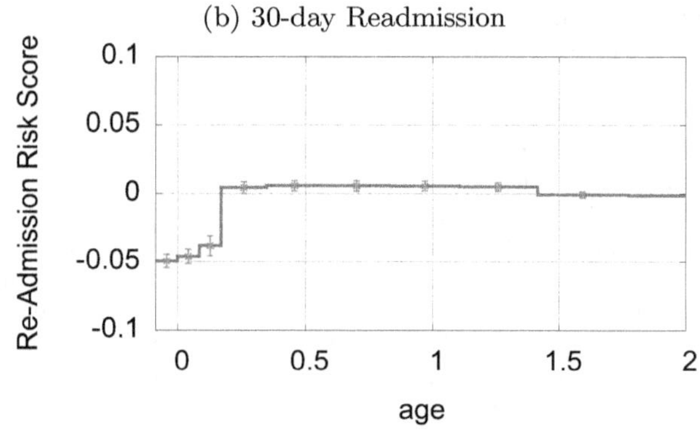

(c) 30-day Readmission (zoomed in)

Figure 3: Risk as a function of Age for the Pneumonia and 30-day Readmission problems.

5.5 Deep Dive: Risk as a Function of Age

In this section we drill down on how the feature "Age" is shaped by the pneumonia and 30-day readmission models. Age is present in both data sets and measured in years. But the relevance of age to the two prediction tasks is very different. In pneumonia, age is a critical factor that can explain why a patient has acquired pneumonia, and what the outcome is likely to be.[7] In 30-day all-cause readmission,

[7]Pneumonia is sometimes called "The Old Man's Best Friend", not because pneumonia is good for elderly patients, but because it often results in rapid death for patients that otherwise could linger for months or years before their primary illness causes death.

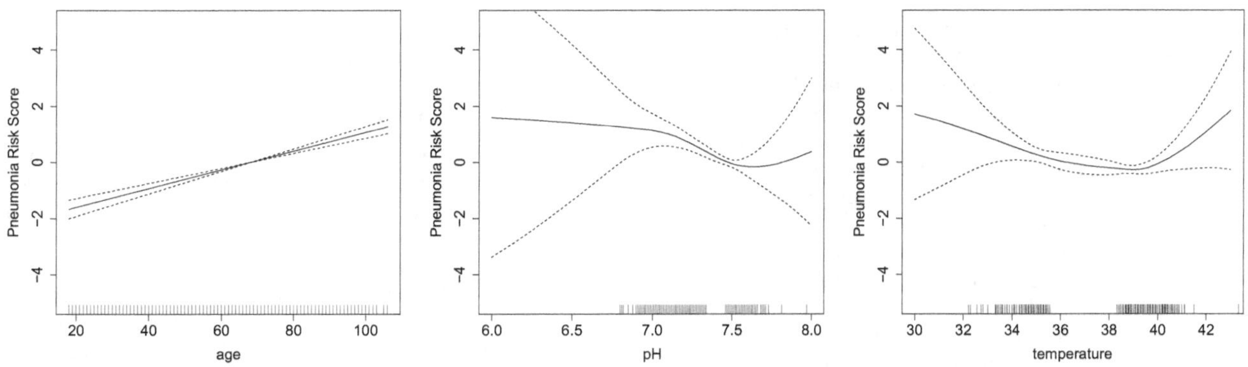

Figure 4: Selected splines in pneumonia dataset.

however, age is just one of thousands of factors that affect a patient's health and course of illness. Moreover, because the prediction task is hospital readmission, not probability of death, age represents a weaker, more generic characterization of patient health and their likeliness to need additional hospitalization within 30 days. If the patient is elderly, but just had a successful hip replacement or kidney stone removed, they are not likely to need to return to the hospital within 30 days for this condition. Similarly, an elderly patient who was admitted to the hospital because of pneumonia, but who is now being released because they responded to treatment, is unlikely to need further care for pneumonia within 30 days if they take proper medications. All-cause readmission is very different from probability of death for a specific condition such as pneumonia.

Figure 3(a) shows the risk profile for age in the pneumonia model, and the distribution of age in the pneumonia data. The majority of pneumonia patients are age 60-90. Qualitatively, the risk of dying from pneumonia is low and constant from age 18-50, rises slowly from age 50-66, then rises quickly from age 66-90, and then levels off at very high risk above age 90. The low-risk region to the left of age 50 is remarkably flat, suggesting that the underlying trees rarely if ever found it useful to split this region into subregions. Note that the risk score for this region is -0.27, suggesting that being young significantly reduces the risk of dying from pneumonia. But risk slowly increases as age increases above 50, though the contribution to risk does not become positive until about 70 years. Beyond 70 years old, the contribution to risk rises rapidly from 0.0 at 70 to +0.20 at age 82 and +0.35 at age 86. According to the model, the increase in risk of going from 70 to 86 is larger than the decrease is risk of going from 70 down to 50 or less.

Beyond the risk vs. age profile described above, there are intriguing details in the graph. 1) There is a small jump in risk at age 67, and again at age 86. The error bars are reasonably tight around age 65-70, suggesting that the jump in risk at 67 may be real. One possible explanation for this is that in a dataset from the 90's, many patients would have retired at around age 65, and that this may yield differences in activity levels, health insurance, and willingness to get access healthcare early enough to improve outcomes — pneumonia responds well to treatment with antibiotics, but can be life threatening if not treated. The 2nd jump in risk around age 86 is harder to explain. It may be that practitioners, either consciously or subconsciously, treat patients older than 85 differently, and that this ultimately increases their POD. Or the jump at 86 may be an artifact of the model — the error bars at age 86 and above are larger. One approach to investigating this issue further would be to train on another sample sample of data (or on different subsamples) to see if the rise at age 86 persists.[8] 2) There is an apparent drop in risk above age 100. We suspect that this drop probably is not real and may be due to mild overfitting — there are very few patients age 95 and older, and the error bars from age 90 to 106 are large and consistent with risk being constant in this region.[9] 3) Surprisingly, there is no evidence that risk, although very high, increases above age 85. Either medical treatments are equally effective for patients older than 85, or other medical conditions are more likely to be responsible for death at this age than pneumonia, or risk does increase above 85 and the model has failed to learn it.

Figure 3(b) shows the age term and density for 30-day readmission. One of the key differences between the pneumonia and 30-day readmission datasets is that pneumonia dataset contains only adult patients age 18 and older, but the readmission dataset contains patients of all age, including newborn infants. The importance of age to 30-day readmission is *very* different. Age has little effect on readmission between age 2 and 50, risk slowly increases from age 50 to 80, and then increases a little more above age 80. The largest increase in score is +0.03 at age 90 and above. There are many reasons why age is less important for readmission than for pneumonia: most patients independent of age would not be released if the hospital thought they were likely to need to be readmitted in less than a month, in this dataset there are thousands of other more specific variables that can better explain variance in the risk of readmission (the model is more illness specific) than age, and some patients who are very elderly will die at home (either unexpectedly or by choice) and thus will not be readmitted.

[8]It is only because the model is so intelligible that we are able to recognize and question such fine detail in the risk vs. age profile. We assume that similar jumps in predicted risk occur in other accurate models such as boosted trees as well, but because those models are less intelligible the jumps are not recognized or investigated.

[9]Or it might be due to *successful agers*, a rare but genetically identifiable class of people with traits that better enable them to survive into old age

An interesting feature of the model for 30-day readmission is highlighted in Figure 3(c) where the x axis has been expanded to show age 0-2. In this dataset newborn infants are born into the hospital, and thus will be treated as readmitted if they need to be hospitalized within 30 days after going home. In part because newborns would not be released if they were at risk, the risk score for newborns age 0-2 months is -0.04—this is a larger negative risk score than the increase in risk for elderly patients. This suggests that most newborns tend to be healthy when they are released from the hospital and are less likely to need to be readmitted within 30 days. But this reduction in risk from being newborn diminishes after 2-3 months, and the model suggests that infants age 3-15 months have slightly higher positive risk of being readmitted to the hospital. Thus infants age 3-15 months have higher risk of readmission than infants that are younger or older, and it is not until age 45 that the risk of readmission rises to this level again.

5.6 Shaping with Splines

Generalized additive models are often fit with splines [7]. Splines allow GAMs to be trained with careful control over regularization and provide more principled error bars. Unfortunately, the spline methods tend to over regularize, yield less accuracy than GA^{2}M models, and yield risk profiles that sometimes miss detail discovered by GA^{2}M models. Figure 4 shows three terms from a spline GAM model trained on the pneumonia data. The 1st term is age, the 2nd is pH, and the 3rd is temperature. Although the splines capture the basic trends (e.g., risk increases with age, pH risk is least around 7.6, and fever risk rises above 40°C), the splines miss detail learned by GA^{2}M. For example, the GA^{2}M model for age is much more nuanced, and the spline model may not properly model temperature in the normal range 36°C-38°C. The spline GAM model has accuracy closer to logistic regression than GA^{2}M, so the extra detail learned by GA^{2}M increases accuracy and probably reflects genuine structure.

5.7 Correlation Does Not Imply Causation

Because the models in this paper are intelligible, it is tempting to interpret them causally. Although the models accurately explain the predictions they make, they are still based on correlation. If features were added to or subtracted and the model retrained, the graphs for some terms that had remained in the model would change because of correlation with the features added or subtracted. Although details of some of the shape plots are suggestive (e.g., does pneumonia risk truly jump as age increases above 65, and again above 85?), it is not (yet) clear if some details like this are due to a) overfitting; b) correlation with other variables; c) interaction with other variables; d) correlation or interaction with unmeasured variables; or e) due to true underlying phenomena such as retirement and change in insurance provider.

Perhaps the strongest statement we can make right now is that the models are intelligible enough to provide a window into the data and prediction problem that is missing with many other learning methods, and that this window allows questions to be raised that will require investigation and further data analysis to answer. In future versions of these models we hope to automate some of these analyses so that it is clearer what features in the intelligible model are "real" or due to random factors such as overfitting and spurious correlation. Adding causal analysis to the models would be tremendously useful, but is, of course, difficult.

6. CONCLUSIONS

We present two case studies on real medical data where GA^{2}Ms achieve state-of-the-art accuracy while remaining intelligible. On the pneumonia case study the GA^{2}M model learns patterns that previously prevented complex machine learning models from being deployed, but because GA^{2}M is intelligible and modular it is possible to edit the model to reduce deployment risk. On the larger, more complex 30-day hospital readmission task the GA^{2}M model achieves excellent accuracy while yielding a manageable, surprisingly intelligible model despite incorporating over 4000 terms. Using this problem we demonstrate how GA^{2}Ms can be used to explain the predictions the model makes for individual patients in a concise way that places focus on the most important/relevant terms for each patient. We believe GA^{2}Ms represent a significant step forward in the tradeoff between model accuracy and intelligibility that should make it easier to deploy high-accuracy learned models in applications such as healthcare where model verification and debuggability are as important as accuracy.

Acknowledgements. We thank Michael Fine, MD, University of Pittsburgh School of Medicine, and Greg Cooper, MD, PhD, University of Pittburgh for help with the Pneumonia data and model. We thank Eric Horvitz, MD, PhD, Microsoft Research Redmond for help with the 30-day hospital readmission data and model. The 30-day hospital readmission experiment was reviewed and approved by the institutional review board at Columbia University Medical Center.

7. REFERENCES

[1] R. Ambrosino, B. Buchanan, G. Cooper, and M. Fine. The use of misclassification costs to learn rule-based decision support models for cost-effective hospital admission strategies. In *Proceedings of the Annual Symp. on Comp. Application in Medical Care*, 1995.

[2] G. Cooper, V. Abraham, C. Aliferis, J. Aronis, B. Buchanan, R. Caruana, M. Fine, J. Janosky, G. Livingston, T. Mitchell, S. Montik, and P. Spirtes. Predicting dire outcomes of patients with community acquired pneumonia. *Journal of Biomedical Informatics*, 38(5):347–366, 2005.

[3] G. Cooper, C. Aliferis, R. Ambrosino, J. Aronis, B. Buchanan, R. Caruana, M. Fine, C. Glymour, G. Gordon, B. Hanusa, J. Janosky, C. Meek, T. Mitchell, T. Richardson, and P. Spirtes. An evaluation of machine-learning methods for predicting pneumonia mortality. *Artificial Intelligence in Medicine*, 9(2):107–138, 1997.

[4] T. Hastie and R. Tibshirani. *Generalized additive models.* Chapman & Hall/CRC, 1990.

[5] Y. Lou, R. Caruana, and J. Gehrke. Intelligible models for classification and regression. In *KDD*, 2012.

[6] Y. Lou, R. Caruana, J. Gehrke, and G. Hooker. Accurate intelligible models with pairwise interactions. In *KDD*, 2013.

[7] S. Wood. *Generalized additive models: an introduction with R.* CRC Press, 2006.

User Conditional Hashtag Prediction for Images

Emily Denton*
New York University
denton@cs.nyu.edu

Jason Weston
Facebook AI Research
jase@fb.com

Manohar Paluri
Facebook AI Research
mano@fb.com

Lubomir Bourdev
Facebook AI Research
lubomir@fb.com

Rob Fergus
Facebook AI Research
robfergus@fb.com

ABSTRACT

Understanding the content of user's image posts is a particularly interesting problem in social networks and web settings. Current machine learning techniques focus mostly on curated training sets of image-label pairs, and perform image classification given the pixels within the image. In this work we instead leverage the wealth of information available from users: firstly, we employ user hashtags to capture the description of image content; and secondly, we make use of valuable contextual information about the user. We show how user metadata (age, gender, etc.) combined with image features derived from a convolutional neural network can be used to perform hashtag prediction. We explore two ways of combining these heterogeneous features into a learning framework: (i) simple concatenation; and (ii) a 3-way multiplicative gating, where the image model is conditioned on the user metadata. We apply these models to a large dataset of de-identified Facebook posts and demonstrate that modeling the user can significantly improve the tag prediction quality over current state-of-the-art methods.

Categories and Subject Descriptors

I.2.6 [**Learning**]: Connectionism and neural nets; I.5.1 [**Models**]: Neural nets; I.5.4 [**Applications**]: Computer vision

Keywords

Social media, user modeling, deep learning, hashtagging, large scale image annotation

1. INTRODUCTION

Hashtags (single words, abbreviations or word concatenations, prefixed by the # symbol) commonly accompany online image content, most notably on social media platforms. Far richer than conventional semantic labels, they provide an incredibly varied and nuanced method of describing images. Some hashtags describe precise labels (`#puppy`, `#craftbeer`). Others contain information about the feelings and intent of the user, e.g. reflecting happiness or sadness (`#awesome`, `#whyme`), or refer to some event in the person's past, present or future (`#happyhour`, `#babyshower`). There are also a wide variety of popular hashtags that convey abstract ideas, and are not necessarily tied to particular image content (`#nofilter`, `#sundayfunday`). Common hashtags that we reference in this paper are defined in Table 7. Hashtags capture the ever-changing distribution of user interests: new hashtags that have never occurred before are constantly being created in response to recent events, products or newly famous people, some of which can become popular very quickly. Finally, a given user, as well as having particular biases of the kind of images they will upload, also have biases of the kind of hashtags they choose to write. Figure 1 shows examples of hashtagged images uploaded to Facebook.

Modern systems for understanding web content make extensive use of machine learning methods for image recognition. In particular, deep learning methods such as convolutional networks have become very popular due to their

#lmao #notevenmad #whatcanyoudo #toqueseason	#camping #vancouverisland	#puppy #archer

#goodluckalgorithm #notmymathin-thebackground	#farm #dog	#toronto #craftbrew #OCW2014

Table 1: Examples of hashtagged images. Images used with owners permission.

*Work done while at Facebook AI Research

KDD'15, August 10-13, 2015, Sydney, NSW, Australia.
 ISBN 978-1-4503-3664-2/15/08 ...$15.00.
DOI: http://dx.doi.org/10.1145/2783258.2788576.

impressive performance [7]. Training such models has typically depended on large sets of manually annotated data (e.g. Imagenet [1]), which is time-consuming and arduous to obtain. Further, such data ignores several aspects of image understanding that are of particular interest to web users: (i) their focus is on precise physical description so aspects such as sentiment are not addressed; (ii) the data distribution differs from online data and it is also unlikely to adapt quickly to changing user interests; and (iii) labels are independent of the users who originally authored the images or image posts (e.g. they are labeled by a Mechanical Turk worker).

In this work, we consider the vast amount of image content on the web where users have provided hashtags as a powerful, alternative training data source. In addition to generating very large amounts of labeled data compared to a manually curated set, we can also directly train on the actual data we wish to capture, rather than one whose distribution differs from user's interests. We thus define our training task as follows: we wish to predict the hashtags for a given *image* uploaded by a given *user*. The learning techniques we employ thus contain feature representations modeling both the image via pixels and the user in the form of metadata. Our hypothesis is that the combination of these sources provides useful information.

We consider several possible architectures based on embedding models. Embeddings are vector representations of images, metadata or text. Embedding models have been successfully used in a variety of contexts such as large scale image annotation [17], zero-shot learning of image categories [2] and hashtag prediction for text posts [18]. An embedding model maps inputs and hashtags into a common embedding space. For a given input, hashtags are ranked according to the dot product between hashtag embedding vectors and the image embedding vector. For the image features, a pre-trained convolutional neural network acts as a feature extractor, converting a raw input image into a concise image descriptor. We present three different methods of embedding inputs. The simplest method learns a linear mapping from image descriptors to embedding space. We then introduce two different methods of incorporating user metadata into the embedding process: (i) simple concatenation; and (ii) a 3-way multiplicative gating, where the image model is conditioned on the user metadata. In our experiments we incorporate the user's gender, age and city into the prediction. Our proposed methods are general, robust and scalable. As such, they can be combined with a variety of machine learning approaches and also deployed in large-scale real-world situations.

Image hashtag prediction has a variety of applications. For example, social media sites could use such a system to recommend hashtags to users as they upload image content. They can also be used for image search or for recommendation and ranking images based on content. Hashtags can also fulfill other roles such as disambiguating synonyms (e.g. jaguar `#car` vs jaguar `#bigcat`), or identifying entities (`#nyc`). In our experiments we apply our models to a large dataset of de-identified Facebook posts and demonstrate that modeling the image and user can significantly improve the tag prediction quality over current state-of-the-art methods.

2. RELATED WORK

As mentioned in Section 1, embedding models have been used in a variety of domains. Of particular relevance to our work is WSABIE, a supervised embedding approach that has been used for large scale image annotation and NLP tasks [17, 3]. Two of the models we present in Section 3 have a linear embedding function based on the WSABIE model and all our models are trained with the ranking loss presented in this work.

The most sophisticated of our proposed embedding models incorporates user information via a three-way tensor product. Multiplicative three-way connections have been used as a feature gating mechanism in restricted Boltzmann machines [15, 20, 9, 14]. More recently, this type of three-way connection has been used to condition neural language models on other modalities [6]. This work is similar to ours in that the tensor product is used to combine inputs from two different domains.

Previous work [18, 5] has addressed the problem of hashtag prediction for text posts. The work of [18] is most similar to our work since we both propose hashtag embedding models trained with a ranking loss. In addition to the obvious difference in domains, our work differs in that we introduce a novel method of incorporating user metadata into hashtag prediction.

Many works have incorporated user modeling into machine learning methods for various applications, for example by considering tensor factorisations for recommendation using music tags [13], web pages [10], using age and gender [4], location [21] and time [19]. However, we are not aware of similar works for our particular application in the image tagging domain.

3. HASHTAG EMBEDDING MODEL

We propose a hashtag embedding model that learns a joint d-dimensional embedding space for hashtags and image posts. Let $y \in \mathcal{Y} = \{1, \ldots, Y\}$ denote an index into a dictionary of possible hashtags. Let $x \in \mathbb{R}^n$ be an image descriptor. The model is of the form:

$$f(x, y) = \Phi_I(x)^\top \Phi_H(y)$$

where $\Phi_I(x) : \mathbb{R}^n \to \mathbb{R}^d$ is an image embedding function and $\Phi_H(y) : \mathcal{Y} \to \mathbb{R}^d$ is a hashtag embedding function.

For a given image, x, possible hashtags, y, are ranked according to $f(x, y)$. We optimize precision at the top of the ranked list using the WARP loss as described in section 3.4.

The hashtag embedding function is given by

$$\Phi_H(y) = V_y$$

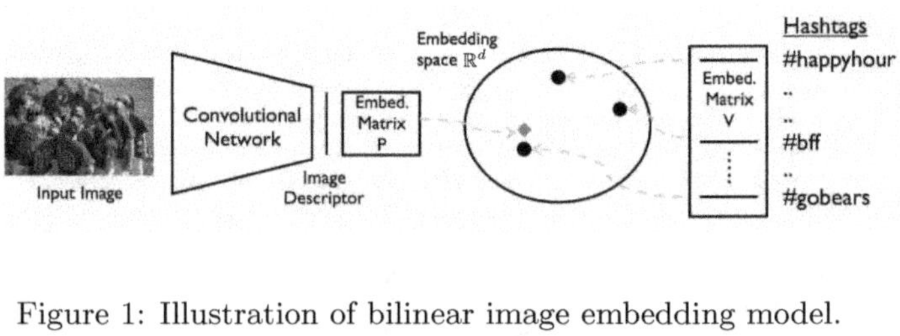

Figure 1: Illustration of bilinear image embedding model.

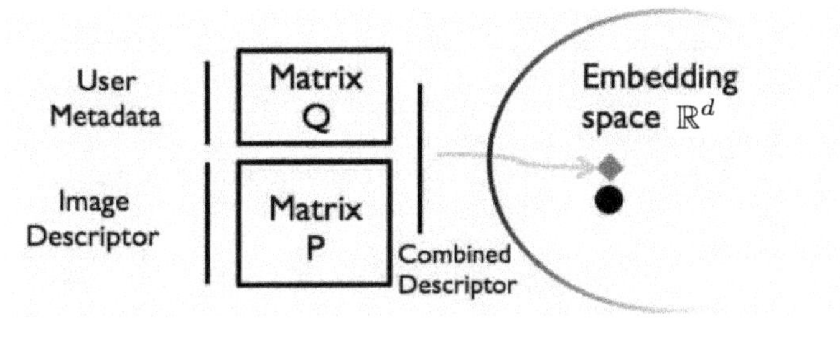

Figure 2: How the user metadata is combined with the image features in the user-biased model

.

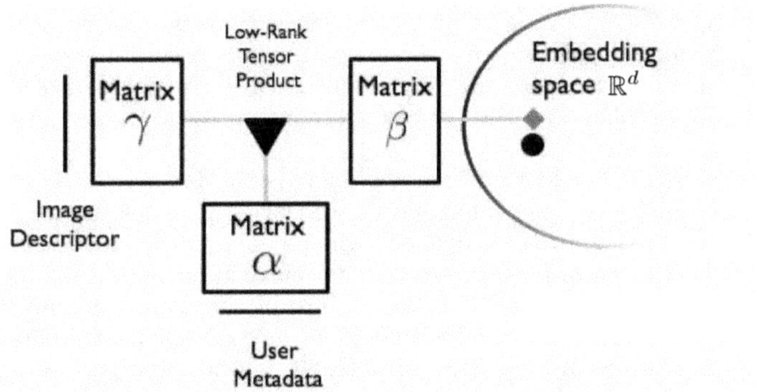

Figure 3: How the user metadata is combined with the image features in the user-multiplicative model.

where $V \in \mathbb{R}^{Y \times d}$ is the hashtag embedding matrix and V_i indexes the ith row of V. Following [17], we constrain the hashtag embedding matrix such that

$$\|V_i\|_2 \leq 1, i = 1, \ldots, Y$$

This regularization technique helps prevent the model from overfitting.

The image embedding function takes an image descriptor as input and produces a d-dimensional embedding vector. We use a pre-trained convolutional neural network [8] as a feature extractor to obtain the image descriptor from the raw image post. The convolutional network was trained separately on ~1 million Facebook images. The network was trained to classify 1000 different concepts which span multiple categories such as Object, Scenes, Actions, Food, Animals, etc. The image descriptors of dimensionality $n = 4096$ are extracted from the final fully connected layer of the network, which has an architecture similar to that of [7].

We propose three different methods of embedding image descriptors. The simplest model does not use any user information and embeds an image descriptor via a linear mapping. We also propose two different methods of incorporating user metadata into the embedding process. The user-biased model introduces a user-dependent additive bias into the image embedding function and the user-multiplicative model has a user descriptor gate, via a multiplication operation, the image embedding function. We now describe each of these models in detail.

3.1 Bilinear Model

The bilinear embedding model [17] does not incorporate any user information into the image embedding function. The image embedding function is a linear map of the form

$$\Phi_I(x) = Px$$

where $P \in \mathbb{R}^{d \times n}$ is the image embedding matrix. As with the hashtag embedding matrix, we constrain the norm of P:

$$\|P_i\|_2 \leq 1, i = 1, \ldots n$$

to help prevent overfitting. The bilinear embedding model is illustrated in Figure 1.

3.2 User-biased Bilinear Model

Assume now that we have information associated with the users responsible for each image post. Let $u \in \mathbb{R}^m$ denote a vector representation of a user. The user-biased model gives a simple method for leveraging user information by adding a user dependent bias term to the image embedding function. In particular, the user-biased image embedding, $\Phi_{I+U}(x, u) : \mathbb{R}^n \times \mathbb{R}^m \rightarrow \mathbb{R}^d$, is defined as

$$\Phi_{I+U}(x, u) = Px + Qu$$

where $Q \in \mathbb{R}^{d \times m}$ is the user embedding matrix. As in the bilinear model, we regularize the model by constraining the norms of P and Q:

$$\|P_i\|_2 \leq 1, i = 1, \ldots, n$$
$$\|Q_i\|_2 \leq 1, i = 1, \ldots, m$$

The user-biased embedding model is illustrated in Figure 2.

3.3 User-multiplicative Tensor Model

The user-multiplicative model provides a more sophisticated method of incorporating user data into the image embedding function by letting the user feature vector, u, gate the image embedding. This allows every user vector to define a different image embedding matrix. The matrix multiplication from the bilinear and user-biased models is replaced with a product between an image descriptor, a user descriptor and an image embedding tensor.

Formally, let $Z \in \mathbb{R}^{m \times d \times n}$ denote the image embedding tensor. Then, for a given user descriptor, u, the user-multiplicative image embedding matrix is

$$P^u = \sum_{i=1}^{m} u_i Z^{(i)}$$

where u_i is the ith component of u and $Z^{(i)} \in \mathbb{R}^{d \times n}$ is a slice of the image embedding tensor specified by the ith index along the first dimension. The user-multiplicative image embedding function is then

$$\Phi_{I \times U}(x, u) = P^u x$$

. The tensor Z has mdn parameters which is impractical to train. We therefore constrain Z to have the following factorized form:

$$Z = \sum_{k=1}^{K} \alpha_k \otimes \beta_k \otimes \gamma_k$$

where $\alpha_k \in \mathbb{R}^m$, $\beta_k \in \mathbb{R}^d$, $\gamma_k \in \mathbb{R}^n$ where $\otimes$ is the tensor outer product operation. K denotes the number of factors and specifies the rank of Z. It is useful to represent the user factors, embedding factors and image factors in matrix form as $\alpha \in \mathbb{R}^{m \times K}$, $\beta \in \mathbb{R}^{d \times K}$ and $\gamma \in \mathbb{R}^{n \times K}$. In this constrained form, Z has $K(m+d+n)$ free parameters. Section A of the appendix explains the 3-way multiplicative model in further detail, including the gradient computations performed during training.

As it is unclear how to choose an appropriate vector representation for user information, we learn one instead. This is done using a neural network which converts the user metadata to an appropriate vector prior to the α matrix in the 3-way connection. The full picture of this model is shown in Figure 3. In our experiments we use a single layer neural network with 24 hidden units (i.e. the user descriptor acted upon by the 3-way connection is 24-dimensional) with Rectified Linear Units [11]. The weights of this network, along with the 3-way factors, are learned jointly. Adding this extra layer makes the model more powerful and also provides a way of extracting concise user vectors from the hidden layer activations, which could potentially be transferred to other tasks, beyond the one considered in this paper.

3.4 Training Algorithm

We train our models by minimizing the weighted approximate-rank pairwise (WARP) loss as described in [17]. The WARP loss approximately optimizes precision at k using a negative sampling technique. This type of loss is ideal for our task since it easily scales to large hashtag vocabularies.

The algorithm proceeds as follows: At every iteration, we sample a positive example, (x, y^+). Up to 1000 negative hashtags, y^-, are then sampled in an attempt to find one such that

$$f(x, y^-) > f(x, y^+) - m$$

where m specifies the margin. We then take a gradient step to minimize

$$|m - f(x, y^+) + f(x, y^-)|_+$$

Following [18], we set $m = 0.1$ in all our experiments.

We minimize the loss with parallel stochastic gradient descent with the hogwild algorithm [12]. Weights were initialized from a zero-mean Gaussian distribution with standard deviation 0.001. The learning rate was initialized to 0.01 and was manually reduced by a factor of 10 when performance stopped improving on a validation set. We used a momentum constant of 0.9. We found training of the 3-way connection was significantly improved by normalizing the image descriptors to have L2 norm of 1 and so this step was performed for all models.

4. EXPERIMENTS

4.1 Dataset

We evaluate our image embedding models on a large Facebook dataset, consisting of 20 million public images uploaded by ~10.4 million de-identified users. The images were collected at random from uploads over a period of several days in October 2014. The images were selected to have at least one hashtag per image, but often had multiple hashtags. In total, the dataset contained ~4.6 million distinct hashtags. The mean number of hashtags per image was 2.7,

Meta data	Possible values
Age	13 − 114
Gender	Male, Female, Unknown
Home City	GPS coordinates
Country	United States, Canada, Great Britain, Australia, New Zealand

Table 2: Summary of user data

with a standard deviation of 3.1. A large fraction of hashtags describe the content of the image, with many synonyms used (e.g. `#cat`, `#catsofinstagram`, `#kitten`). Others describe the sentiment of the user, being only loosely related to the image content (e.g. `#love`, `#happy`, `#blessed`). Another group convey abstract ideas, generally unrelated to the image content (`#nofilter`, `#fundaysunday`, `#latergram`).

Their distribution, shown in Figure 4, is far from uniform: the top 10 hashtags account for 4% of the total; the top 100 for 11%, and 4 million of them appear less than 10 times throughout the whole dataset. Given the difficulties of predicting very infrequent hashtags, we limit our vocabulary to the top 10k most frequent hashtags. In our experiments, we use two different versions of the dataset: *natural* and *balanced*. In the former, we directly use the natural distribution of the 10k most prevalent hashtags (shown in blue in Figure 4). However, the uneven distribution means that the few common hashtags will dominate any error measure, and make it hard to predict infrequent hashtags. Furthermore, many of the most common hashtags (e.g. `#wcw`, `#tbt`, `#mcm`) have little to do with image content, so distract the models from predicting image-relevant hashtags. To remedy this, we create a *balanced* version of the dataset, where the 500 most common hashtags are downsampled to have the same frequency as the 501st. The resulting distribution (shown in red in Figure 4), is much closer to uniform and thus ameliorates both issues. Note that the images and users are the same for both versions of the dataset; only the hashtag distribution changes.

Each de-identified user had 4 pieces of metadata: age, gender, country and city. The metadata is summarized in

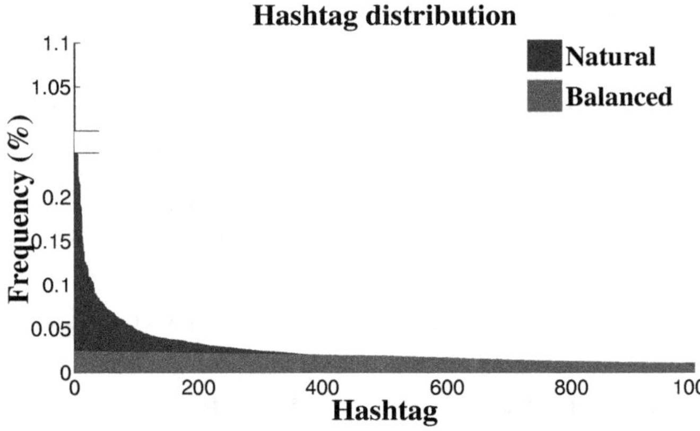

Figure 4: Natural (blue) and balanced (red) hashtag distributions used in our experiments. Note the break in the y-axis.

Method	d	K	P@1	R@10	A@10
Freq. baseline	-	-	3.04%	5.63%	9.45%
Bilinear	64	-	7.37%	11.71%	18.69%
Bilinear	128	-	7.37%	11.69%	18.44%
Bilinear	256	-	6.75%	10.84%	17.25%
Bilinear	512	-	6.50%	10.83%	17.17%
User-biased	64	-	9.02%	13.63%	21.88%
User-biased	128	-	9.00%	13.67%	21.83%
User-biased	256	-	8.48%	13.03%	20.96%
User-biased	512	-	7.98%	12.51%	20.05%
3-way mult.	64	50	8.95%	13.66%	21.82%
3-way mult.	64	100	9.03%	13.81%	22.04%
3-way mult.	64	200	8.96%	13.81%	22.05%
3-way mult.	64	300	9.00%	13.74%	21.96%
3-way mult.	64	400	8.96%	13.65%	21.82%

Table 3: Prediction results for models trained on data with a natural hashtag distribution.

Method	d	K	P@1	R@10	A@10
Freq. baseline	-	-	0.07%	0.36%	0.64%
Bilinear	64	-	3.75%	6.04%	9.81%
Bilinear	128	-	3.73%	5.81%	9.48%
Bilinear	256	-	3.54%	5.57%	9.06%
Bilinear	512	-	3.26%	5.10%	8.38%
User-biased	64	-	3.85%	6.22%	10.34%
User-biased	128	-	3.78%	6.13%	10.06%
User-biased	256	-	3.70%	5.85%	9.50%
User-biased	512	-	3.49%	5.78%	9.64%
3-way mult.	64	50	4.29%	6.94%	11.26%
3-way mult.	64	100	4.25%	6.80%	10.96%
3-way mult.	64	200	4.65%	7.27%	11.77%
3-way mult.	64	300	4.34%	7.02%	11.37%
3-way mult.	64	400	4.25%	7.04%	11.46%

Table 4: Prediction results on the balanced hashtag distribution.

Table 2. We restricted ourselves to images posted by users from five populous English speaking countries to ensure that the hashtags had a common underlying language. Imprecise location information for each de-identified user took the form of the GPS location of their home town/city[1]. The dataset was split into disjoint training and test sets, with each user only appearing in one of them (i.e. no overlap). The test set was 100k images in size, with the remainder used for training.

We construct a 10-dimensional user descriptor based on the 4 pieces of metadata. One dimension represents age as a continuous value, scaled to have value in [0, 1]. Another dimension represents gender, recorded as -1 or 1 for females and males respectively. An unknown gender is represented by 0. The country of origin is encoded as a 1-hot 5d vector for the five different countries. Finally, GPS coordinates are converted to 3-dimensional Cartesian coordinates and scaled to [0,1] range.

4.2 Results

We evaluate the embedding models described in Section 3 on both the natural and balanced versions of our dataset. For all three models, we vary d, the dimensionality of the embedding space to understand its effect on performance. For the 3-way multiplicative model, we also vary the rank K of the tensor factorization, which controls the number of parameters in the embedding function $\Phi_{I\times U}$. We include a simple baseline that ignores the test image and ranks hashtags according to their natural distribution in the training set.

The models are evaluated with three different metrics: precision, recall and accuracy. These are defined as follows: let $\text{Rank}(x, u, k)$ denote the set of top k ranked hashtags by the model for example (x, u) and let $\text{GroundTruth}(x, u)$ denote the set of hashtags actually tagged by the user u for the image x, then:

[1]I.e. the GPS coordinates of the town/city center associated with the user's profile, not the home address of the users, or where the photo was taken.

Precision:

$$\text{P@k} = \frac{1}{N}\sum_{i=1}^{N}\frac{|\text{Rank}(x_i, u_i, k) \cap \text{GroundTruth}(x_i, u_i)|}{|\text{Rank}(x_i, u_i, k)|}$$

Where N is the number of test examples. We show P@1 (i.e. what fraction of the time did the top ranked hashtag match one of the ground truth hashtags for the test image).

Recall:

$$\text{R@k} = \frac{1}{N}\sum_{i=1}^{N}\frac{|\text{Rank}(x_i, u_i, k) \cap \text{GroundTruth}(x_i, u_i)|}{|\text{GroundTruth}(x_i, u_i)|}$$

We show R@10 which gives a measure of the fraction of the relevant hashtags for each test image are ranked in the top 10. Note that if the image has more than 10 ground truth hashtags then this fraction will always be less than 1.

Accuracy:

$$\text{A@k} = \sum_{i=1}^{N}\frac{\text{I}[\text{Rank}(x_i, u_i, k) \cap \text{GroundTruth}(x_i, u_i) \neq \emptyset]}{N}$$

where $\text{I}[\cdot]$ is an indicator function. This metric is useful since it is largely indifferent to the number of ground truth hashtags. We show the accuracy at 10 (A@10) which gives a measure of how often at least one of the ground truth hashtags appears in the top 10 ranked hashtags.

Table 3 shows test results for models on the natural version of the dataset. Given that each image has 10k possible hashtags, the absolute values for all three metrics are low but, as the examples in Table 5 show, the quality of predicted hashtags is nevertheless reasonable. The predicted hashtags convey relevant image content (`#kayaking`, `#glasses`), social cues (`#reunion`, `#party`) and sentiment (`#goodtimes`, `#love`). The results in the table show: (i) all models clearly beating the frequency baseline; (ii) both models that incorporate user information significantly outperform the bilinear model; (iii) the user-multiplicative model performs comparably to the user-biased model; (iv) high values of the embedding dimension d hurt performance, likely due to overfitting and (v) the tensor rank K had little effort on performance.

Table 4 shows results from training on the balanced version of the dataset. The flatter hashtag distribution has higher entropy, relative to the natural version, making the

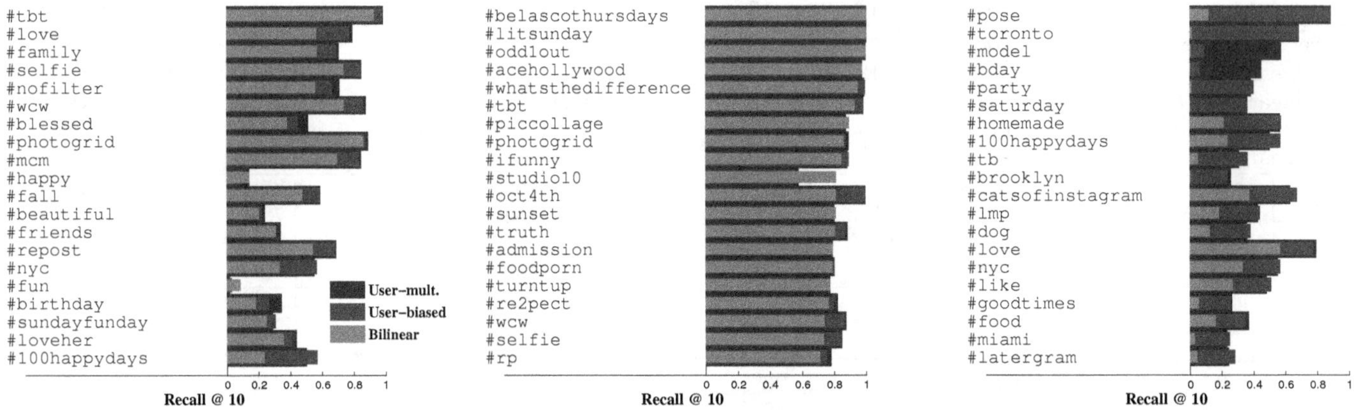

(a) Models trained on natural hashtag distribution.

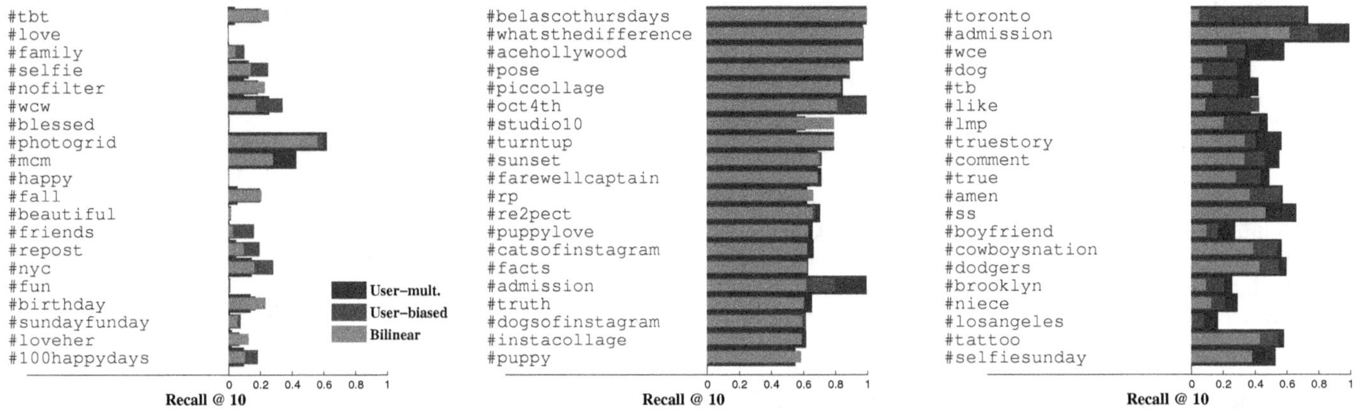

(b) Models trained on balanced hashtag distribution.

Figure 6: Recall at 10 for different subsets of hashtags. Left: The 20 most frequent hashtags are shown. Middle: Top 20 hashtags which have highest recall for the bilinear model. Right: Top 20 hashtags which the difference in performance between the bilinear model and the multiplicative model is greatest.

prediction task harder as evidenced by the significant reduction in frequency baseline performance. In these experiments, the user-biased approach gives slight gains over bilinear. But the user-multiplicative model significantly outperforms both, showing it is able to make effective use of the user metadata. Examples of the predicted hashtags from this model are shown in Figure 5. The predictions can be seen to be far more varied and interesting than those from the same model trained on the natural version of the dataset. For example, very common hashtags such as #tbt, #wcw, #mcm are ranked in the top 10 for almost every photo by the model trained on the natural hashtag distribution. The model trained on the balanced distribution produces less frequent hashtags that are still relevant to the image.

Tables 3 and 4 show precision and recall values for images, averaged over all examples in the test set. Since some hashtags are predicted more accurately than others, we also show precision and recall values for individual hashtags. The average precision and recall at k for a particular hashtag, y, is defined as:

$$\text{R@k}(y) = \frac{\sum_{i=1}^{N} |\text{Rank}(x_i, u_i, k) \cap \{y\}|}{\sum_{i=1}^{N} |\text{GroundTruth}(x_i, u_i) \cap \{y\}|}$$

$$\text{P@k}(y) = \frac{\sum_{i=1}^{N} |\text{Rank}(x_i, u_i, k) \cap \{y\}|}{\sum_{i=1}^{N} |\text{Rank}(x_i, u_i, k)|}$$

Figure 5a plots precision-recall curves for a subset of hashtags for the three models, trained on the natural distribution. Some hashtags are better predicted by the models that leverage user information. For example, cities (#nyc, #london, etc.) see a large boost in performance when user information is incorporated into the model. Other hashtags that are not tied to specific image content but used predominately by certain demographics also see gains from the incorporation of user information. Hashtags such as #100happydays, #wcw and #mcm likely fall into this category. There are also a multitude of hashtags for which the addition of user information makes negligible difference, such as #nature or #sunset. These hashtags likely refer to specific image content, thus the addition of user information adds little signal.

Age	Females	Males
13-17	#mcm	#like
	#bestfriend	#lmp
	#love	#throwback
	#lovehim	#squad
	#mce	#wce
	#latepost	#throwback-
	#bestfriends	#thursday
	#boyfriend	#family
	#loveher	#workflow
	#loveyou	#selfie
		#wcm
43-47	#100happydays	#photoshop-
	#mcm	#express
	#love	#wcw
	#sisters	#goodtimes
	#cousins	#prouddad
	#lovehim	#throwback-
	#latergram	#thursday
	#loveher	#selfie
	#bff	#salute
	#youcampperfect	#blessed
		#zijasummit14
		#familyfirst

Gender	15-17 years old	43-47 years old
Female	#wcw	#100happydays
	#mcm	#blessed
	#bestfriend	#goodtimes
	#tb	#family
	#ss	#love
	#bestfriends	#photogrid
	#throwback	#latergram
	#latepost	#cousins
	#like	#sundayfunday
	#selfiesunday	#friends
Male	#wcw	#goodtimes
	#like	#blessed
	#throwback	#love
	#squad	#family
	#tb	#photoshop-
	#lmp	#express
	#mcm	#photogrid
	#ss	#sundayfunday
	#wce	#friends
	#selfiesunday	#zijasummit14
		#prouddad

Sydney	Toronto
#melbourne	#toronto
#sydney	#tbt
#australia	#canada
#spring	#vancouver
#beach	#fall
#grandfinal	#throwback
#sunshine	#blessed
#sun	#ilovethiscity
#nz	#vancity
#newzealand	#vscocam
#bali	#tb
#happy	#cntower
#nofilter	#goodmorning
#wellington	#hoco
#springbreak	#montreal
#bondi	#wcw
#afl	#tdot
#thailand	#lateupload
#stkilda	#downtown
#city	#beautiful

Table 6: An exploration of our multiplicative model using three different probe images. **Left:** Hashtags most affected by gender, for two different age groups. Left and right columns show hashtags predicted most frequently for female users relative to male users, and vice-versa. **Middle:** Hashtags most affected by age, for female and male users. Left and right columns show hashtags predicted most frequently for younger users relative to older users, and vice-versa. **Right:** Hashtags most affected by location. Left and right columns show hashtags that are predicted most frequently for Sydney users relative to Toronto users, and vice-versa.

Figure 5b plots precision-recall curves of a subset of hashtags for models trained on the balanced distribution. In this case we see the user-multiplicative model performs much better than the bilinear and user-biased models on most hashtags.

Figure 6a and Figure 6b show Recall@10 for several hashtags from the three models trained on the natural and balanced distributions respectively. In the leftmost plot we see the recall values for the 20 most frequent hashtags. For these very frequent hashtags, the models that incorporate user information perform comparably to the bilinear model. By comparing the leftmost plots in Figure 6a and Figure 6b we also see that the most frequent hashtags have much higher recall values for models trained on the natural hashtag distribution than for the models trained on the balanced distribution. The middle plot shows the top 20 hashtags for which the bilinear model has the highest recall, i.e. the hashtags that are predicted well without the aid of additional user information. Many of the hashtags with highest recall (`#belascothursdays`, `#litsunday`, `#acehollywood`) correspond to large event posters. Many different users post the event image and hashtag the image with the event name. Since the images and hashtags are nearly identical, the model is able to achieve nearly perfect recall. The right-hand plot shows the top 20 hashtags for which the difference in performance between the bilinear model and the multiplicative model is greatest. In other words, these figures show the hashtags whose accurate prediction relies most heavily on user information. We see that for these hashtags, the user-biased model and user-multiplicative models perform comparably when trained on the natural distribution. However, when trained on the balanced distribution, the user-multiplicative model tends to outperform both the bilinear and user-biased model.

4.3 Understanding User Information

There are many types of images for which certain hashtags tend to be used more frequently by specific demographics. For example, given a cityscape image, hashtags such as `#toronto` and `#canada` are more likely to be used by individuals living in Toronto. Table 6 explores the user-multiplicative model to see which hashtags are most affected by gender, age and location. Taking gender (left column) as an example, this can be performed by the following procedure: (i) given an initial *probe* image we find a set of close neighbors[2] in the test set using their d-dimensional image descriptors. (ii) from this nearest-neighbor set we pick two different subsets, one for for males and another for females, whose age is constrained to be 13-17 (in the top row; age

[2]We average over a large set of similar images to ensure the results are not specific to an individual image.

Input image	Top 10 ranked hashtags Natural distribution	Balanced distribution
	#tbt	#reunion
	#squad	#goodtimes
	#family	#friends
	#friends	#reunited
	#wcw	#drinks
	#homecoming	#squad
	#goodtimes	#greatnight
	#repost	#party
	#throwback	#drunk
	#party	#fridaynight
	#nofilter	#nature
	#fall	#river
	#autumn	#peaceful
	#beautiful	#lake
	#nature	#sunny
	#vscocam	#sunshine
	#toronto	#trees
	#100happydays	#autumn
	#sunshine	#sun
	#home	#beautifulday
	#selfie	#selfie
	#nofilter	#glasses
	#tbt	#nomakeup
	#love	#haircut
	#wcw	#smiles
	#100happydays	#sundayselfie
	#mcm	#cutie
	#cute	#nofilter
	#beautiful	#selfies
	#happy	#photoshop-express
	#nofilter	#nofilter-needed
	#kingfire	#blueangels
	#sunset	#nofilter
	#fall	#sky
	#tbt	#homesweethome
	#beautiful	#godscountry
	#blessed	#farmlife
	#nofilter-needed	#sunrise
	#vscocam	#countrylife
	#goodmorning	#clouds
	#wcw	#beachday
	#tbt	#beach
	#selfie	#poolside
	#folsom	#beachlife
	#love	#funinthesun
	#beyond-wonderland	#poolparty
	#sundayfunday	#besties
	#family	#beachtime
	#beach	#pooltime
	#mcm	#sandiego
	#tbt	#kayaking
	#kayaking	#pool
	#nofilter	#poolside
	#sundayfunday	#fishing
	#mcm	#funinthesun
	#wcw	#poolparty
	#family	#pooltime
	#familytime	#boating
	#latepost	#boatlife
	#love	#lakelife

Table 5: Top ranked hashtags from user-multiplicative model for sample test images. Left column shows hashtags predicted by model trained on the natural hashtag distribution. Right column shows hashtags from model trained on the balanced hashtag distribution. Photos used with owner permission.

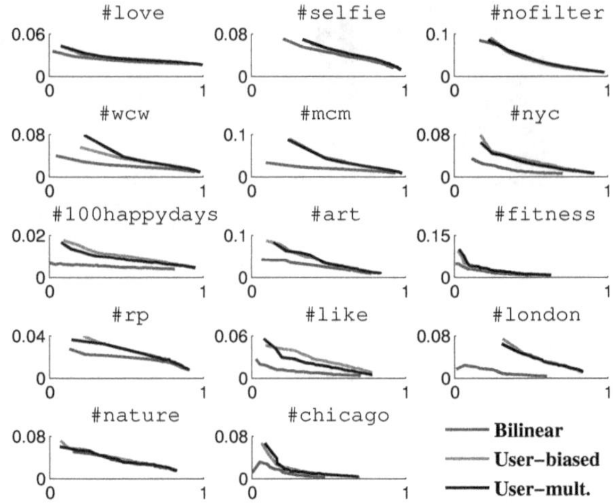

(a) Models trained on the natural hashtag distribution.

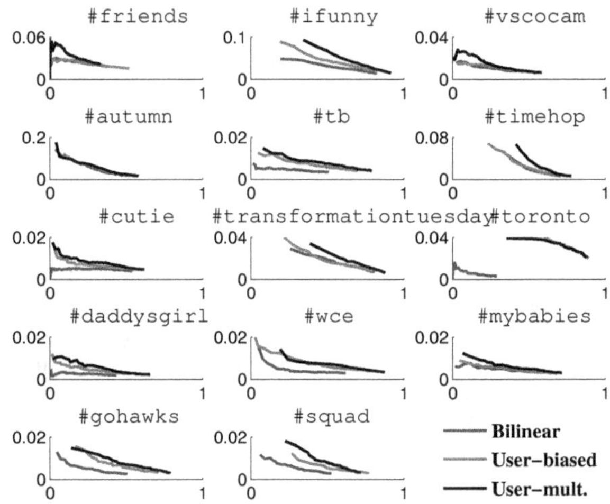

(b) Models trained on the balanced hashtag distribution.

Figure 5: Precision-recall curves of a subset of hashtags. Recall is plotted on the x-axis, precision on the y-axis.

43-47 for the bottom row). (iii) for each image in these two subsets we compute their embedding (using their associated metadata) and find the 10 closest hashtag embeddings. (iv) we compute aggregate counts of hashtags for the male and female subsets and display the hashtags where the *difference* is greatest between the two. The middle and right columns of the table also show how age (holding gender constant) and location affect the hashtag distribution, respectively.

In many cases, the hashtags strongly associated with a particular user attribute make intuitive sense. For example, the hashtags `#mcm`, `#lovehim` and `#boyfriend` are more frequently predicted for young female users than for young male users. The hashtag `#prouddad` is more frequently predicted for older male users than for female users of the same age. We also see that hashtags like `#beach` are predicted more often for Australian users than for those living in Toronto, whereas hashtags like `#cntower` are predicted more for Torontonians.

Figure 7 visualizes the learned user representation in our multiplicative model for 10k users in the test set. The 24-d user descriptors are mapped down to the 2D plane using the

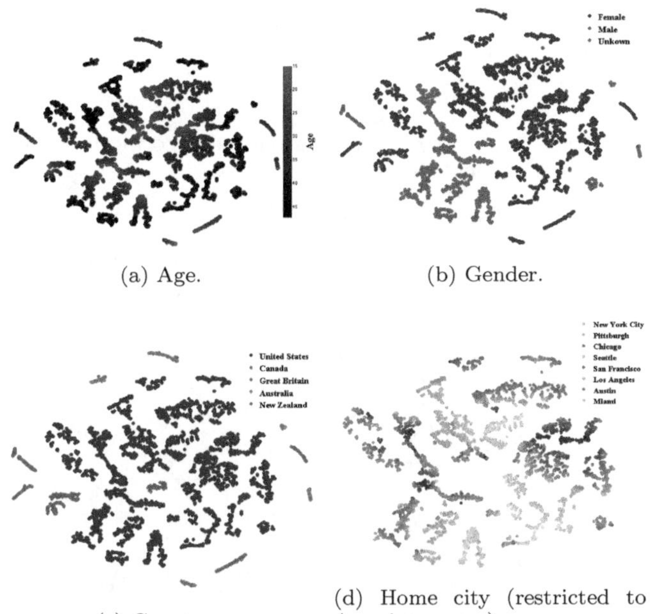

(a) Age. (b) Gender.

(c) Country. (d) Home city (restricted to American users).

Figure 7: t-SNE visualization of user embeddings for 10K different users. Each plot is color coded by a different dimension of the user meta data.

t-SNE algorithm [16]. Four different color codings are used to show different user attributes. Clear structure is apparent in many cases, for example, the radius from the origin seems to correspond to increasing age.

5. CONCLUSIONS

We introduced a set of embedding models that predict highly diverse and relevant hashtags for real-world Facebook images. The simplest of these shows how image features derived from a convolutional neural network can be used to perform image hashtag prediction. We then showed how user metadata could be combined with image features to improve image hashtag prediction. The addition of user information gave a significant performance boost, particularly when incorporated in a multiplicative fashion.

Particular care has to be taken when working on real world datasets rather than curated ones. We addressed the highly skewed hashtag distribution observed in our dataset by downsampling the more frequent hashtags. We show that this technique produces more varied hashtag predictions.

Our models produce hashtags that capture many subtle social and sentiment of the images, and are far richer than the precise semantic descriptions output by many current recognition models. The resulting system is highly scalable and could be used in a number of applications such as automated hashtag suggestion, image search or for recommendation and ranking images based on content.

6. REFERENCES

[1] J. Deng, W. Dong, R. Socher, L.-J. Li, K. Li, and L. Fei-Fei. Imagenet: A large-scale hierarchical image database. In *Conference on Computer Vision and Pattern Recognition*, 2009.

[2] A. Frome, G. S. Corrado, J. Shlens, S. Bengio, J. Dean, M. Ranzato, and T. Mikolov. Devise: A deep visual-semantic embedding model. In *Proc. of Advances in Neural Information Processing Systems*, 2013.

[3] M. Hermann, D. Das, J. Weston, and K. Ganchev. Semantic frame identification with distributed word representations. In *Proc. of ACL*, 2014.

[4] A. Karatzoglou, X. Amatriain, L. Baltrunas, and N. Oliver. Multiverse recommendation: n-dimensional tensor factorization for context-aware collaborative filtering. RecSys '10, pages 79–86, 2010.

[5] E. Khabiri, J. Caverlee, and K. Kamath. Predicting semantic annotations on the real-time web. In *Proc. of 23rd ACM conference on Hypertext and social media*, pages 219–228, 2012.

[6] R. Kiros, R. Salakhutdinov, and R. Zemel. Multimodal neural language models. In *Proc. of The 30th International Conference on Machine Learning*, 2014.

[7] A. Krizhevsky, I. Sutskever, and G. E. Hinton. Imagenet classification with deep convolutional neural networks. In *Proc. of Advances in Neural Information Processing Systems 25*, 2012.

[8] Y. Lecun, L. Bottou, Y. Bengio, and P. Haffner. Gradient-based learning applied to document recognition. *Proceedings of the IEEE*, 86(11):2278–2324, Nov 1998.

[9] R. Memisevic and G. E. Hinton. Learning to represent spatial transformations with factored higher-order boltzmann machines. *Neural Computation*, 22(6):1473–1492, 2010.

[10] A. Menon, K. Chitrapura, S. Garg, D. Agarwal, and N. Kota. Response prediction using collaborative filtering with hierarchies and side-information. In *Proceedings of the 17th ACM SIGKDD international conference on Knowledge discovery and data mining*, pages 141–149. ACM, 2011.

[11] V. Nair and G. Hinton. Rectified linear units improve restricted boltzmann machines. In *Proc. of the 27th International Conference on Machine Learning*, 2010.

[12] F. Niu, B. Recht, C. Re, and S. J. Wright. Hogwild!: A lock-free approach to parallelizing stocastic gradient descent. In *Proc. of Advances in Neural Information Processing Systems 25*, 2011.

[13] S. Rendle and L. Schmidt-Thieme. Pairwise interaction tensor factorization for personalized tag recommendation. In *WSDM*, pages 81–90. ACM, 2010.

[14] K. Sohn, G. Zhou, C. Lee, and H. Lee. Learning and selecting features jointly with point-wise gated Boltzmann machines. In *Proc. of The 30th International Conference on Machine Learning*, pages 217–225, 2013.

[15] G. Taylor and G. E. Hinton. Factored conditional restricted boltzmann machines for modeling motion style. In *Proc. of the 26th International Conference on Machine Learning*, 2009.

[16] L. van der Maaten and G. Hinton. Visualizing data using t-sne. *Journal of Machine Learning Research*, 9(Nov):2579–2605, 2008.

[17] J. Weston, S. Bengio, and N. Usunier. Wsabie: Scaling up to large vocabulary image annotation. In *Proc. of*

the 22nd international joint conference on Artificial Intelligence, 2011.

[18] J. Weston, S. Chopra, and K. Adams. #tagspace: Semantic embeddings from hashtags. In *Conference on Empirical Methods in Natural Language Processing*, pages 1822–1827. Association for Computational Linguistics, 2014.

[19] L. Xiong, X. Chen, T. Huang, J. Schneider, and J. Carbonell. Temporal collaborative filtering with bayesian probabilistic tensor factorization. In *Proceedings of SIAM Data Mining*, volume 2010, 2010.

[20] M. Zeiler, G. Taylor, L. Sigal, I. Matthews, and R. Fergus. Input-output temporal restricted boltzmann machines for facial expression transfer. In *Proc. of Advances in Neural Information Processing Systems 24*, 2011.

[21] V. Zheng, B. Cao, Y. Zheng, X. Xie, and Q. Yang. Collaborative filtering meets mobile recommendation: A user-centered approach. In *Proceedings of the 24rd AAAI Conference on Artificial Intelligence*, 2010.

APPENDIX

A. FACTORED 3-WAY GRADIENT COMPUTATIONS

The user-multiplicative model gates the image embedding matrix by a user descriptor, u. The user conditioned image embedding matrix is

$$P^u = \sum_{i=1}^{m} u_i Z^{(i)}$$

where $Z^{(1)}, \ldots, Z^{(m)}$ are $d \times n$ matrices and u_i indexes the ith component of the user descriptor. Combining each of the $Z^{(i)}$'s into a tensor gives the image embedding tensor $Z \in \mathbb{R}^{m \times d \times n}$. To facilitate learning, Z is constrained to be of the form

$$Z = \sum_{i=1}^{K} \alpha_k \otimes \beta_k \otimes \gamma_k$$

where $\alpha_k \in \mathbb{R}^m$, $\beta_k \in \mathbb{R}^d$, $\gamma_k \in \mathbb{R}^n$ and the user factors, embedding factors and image factors respectively. The parameter K specifies the number of factors.

Letting $\alpha \in \mathbb{R}^{m \times K}$, $\beta \in \mathbb{R}^{d \times K}$ and $\gamma \in \mathbb{R}^{n \times K}$ denote the factors in matrix form, the image embedding matrix can be written as:

$$\begin{aligned} P^u &= \sum_{i=1}^{m} u_i Z^{(i)} \\ &= \sum_{i=1}^{m} u_i \left(\sum_{i=1}^{K} [\alpha_k]_i \beta_k \otimes \gamma_k \right) \\ &= \sum_{k=1}^{K} \left(\alpha_k^\top u \right) \beta_k \otimes \gamma_k \\ &= \beta \mathrm{diag} \left(\alpha^\top u \right) \gamma^\top \end{aligned}$$

The user-multiplicative image embedding function can be re-written as:

$$\phi_{I \times U}(x, u) = P^u x = \beta \mathrm{diag} \left(\alpha^\top u \right) \gamma^\top x$$

Recall from section 3.4 that in every iteration of training a gradient step is taken to minimize

$$L = |m - f(x, u, y^+) + f(x, u, y^-)|$$

where $f(x, u, y) = \phi_{I \times U}(x, u)^\top \phi_H(y)$ is a scoring function. Expanding the loss we get:

$$\begin{aligned} L &= |m - f(x, u, y^+) + f(x, u, y^-)| \\ &= |m - \phi_{I \times U}(x, u)^\top \phi_H(y^+) + \phi_{I \times U}(x, u)^\top \phi_H(y^-)| \\ &= |m - \beta \mathrm{diag} \left(\alpha^\top u \right) \gamma^\top x (V_{y^+} - V_{y^-})| \end{aligned}$$

The gradient of L with respect to the user factors, embedding factors and image factors is:

$$\begin{aligned} \frac{\partial L}{\partial \alpha_k} &= - \left(\sum_{i=1}^{m} u_i \right) \beta \gamma^\top x (V_{y^+} - V_{y^-}) \\ \frac{\partial L}{\partial \beta} &= -\mathrm{diag}(\alpha^\top u) \gamma^\top x (V_{y^+} - V_{y^-}) \\ \frac{\partial L}{\partial \gamma} &= - \left(\beta \mathrm{diag}(\alpha^\top u) \right) \left(x (V_{y^+} - V_{y^-}) \right) \end{aligned}$$

B. DICTIONARY OF COMMON HASHTAGS

Many of the hashtags referenced in this work have non obvious meanings. Table 7 provides definitions of several of the more frequent hashtags.

Hashtag	Meaning
`#tbt`	throw back thursday
`#tb`	throw back
`#mcm`	man crush monday
`#mce`	man crush everyday
`#wcw`	woman crush wednesday
`#wce`	woman crush everyday
`#ss`	selfie sunday
`#rp`	repost
`#lmp`	like my post

Table 7: Definition of common hashtags.

Big Data System for Analyzing Risky Procurement Entities

Amit Dhurandhar
adhuran@us.ibm.com
Mathematical Sciences Dept.
IBM T.J. Watson
1101 Kitchawan Road
Yorktown Heights, NY, USA

Bruce Graves
bruceg@us.ibm.com
Global Procurement Services
IBM GPS
294 ROUTE 100
Somers, NY, USA

Rajesh Ravi
rkravi@us.ibm.com
Mathematical Sciences Dept.
IBM T.J. Watson
1101 Kitchawan Road
Yorktown Heights, NY, USA

Gopikrishnan Maniachari
gopi@us.ibm.com
Mathematical Sciences Dept.
IBM T.J. Watson
1101 Kitchawan Road
Yorktown Heights, NY, USA

Markus Ettl
msettl@us.ibm.com
Mathematical Sciences Dept.
IBM T.J. Watson
1101 Kitchawan Road
Yorktown Heights, NY, USA

ABSTRACT

An accredited biennial 2014 study by the Association of Certified Fraud Examiners claims that on average 5% of a company's revenue is lost because of unchecked fraud every year. The reason for such heavy losses are that it takes around 18 months for a fraud to be caught and audits catch only 3% of the actual fraud. This begs the need for better tools and processes to be able to quickly and cheaply identify potential malefactors. In this paper, we describe a robust tool to identify procurement related fraud/risk, though the general design and the analytical components could be adapted to detecting fraud in other domains. Besides analyzing standard transactional data, our solution analyzes multiple public and private data sources leading to wider coverage of fraud types than what generally exists in the marketplace. Moreover, our approach is more principled in the sense that the learning component, which is based on investigation feedback has formal guarantees. Though such a tool is ever evolving, a deployment of this tool over the past 12 months has found many interesting cases from compliance risk and fraud point of view across more than 150 countries and 65000+ vendors, increasing the number of true positives found by over 80% compared with other state-of-the-art tools that the domain experts were previously using.

Categories and Subject Descriptors

H.2.8 [**Knowledge Management**]: Data Mining

General Terms

Algorithms

KDD'15, August 10-13, 2015, Sydney, NSW, Australia.

DOI: http://dx.doi.org/10.1145/2783258.2788563.

Keywords

Fraud, risk, collusion, social network, online learning, big data, procurement

1. INTRODUCTION

In ideal circumstances, business is carried out between vendors and customers in a manner which is fair and consistent with the law. In practice, however, fair business practices can be subject to fraud, or deliberate deception by one or more individuals or parties for personal gain and/or to cause harm to others persons or parties. A result is an illegal and unfair advantage for a party committing fraud.

Given the subversive nature of fraud, such activities can be well hidden and difficult to identify and trace to the responsible parties. Routing out the cause, including identifying entities indicative of fraud, can be a difficult if not sometimes an insurmountable task. This is mirrored in an accredited 2014 survey conducted across 100+ countries, by the Association of Certified Fraud Examiners (ACFE) [1], who claim that on average 5% of a company's revenue is lost because of unchecked fraud every year. The reason for such heavy losses according to them is that it takes around 18 months for a fraud to be caught and audits catch only 3% of the actual fraud. A large portion of risky activity is caught through whistle blowers. This begs the need for better tools and processes to quickly and cheaply identify potential malefactors.

In the modern era, a phenomenal amount of digital data is involved in nearly every type of business. Modern developments in both software and hardware have allowed for data analysis techniques to be developed and directed to detecting and identifying fraud and its perpetrators. In the art of fraud detection and risk analysis, analytical systems are developed and relied upon to analyze data and make predictions as to the presence of risk/fraud. Despite considerable advances in fraud detection, the ways in which parties can commit fraud have also advanced and become more elusive. There is a persisting need for novel techniques and systems for the detection and identification of fraud and the conspirators responsible, that have a low false positive rate.

We describe one such system in this paper. Though our system architecture and analytics flow would be applicable in a wide variety of domains, we focus our attention on identifying procurement related risk or fraud. In large companies there are procurement groups, which buy goods and services from tens of thousands of vendors/suppliers all across the globe every year amounting to billions of dollars of spend. Given the scale of these operations, it is hard to enforce airtight compliance procedures in the interest of time and money, which makes it a breeding ground for nefarious activity. Here are a couple of real examples of procurement fraud. An employee of a large company bought a few USB drives every month at the company's expense over a couple of years and was selling them in the black market. Since, USB drives are inexpensive they were below the spend clip levels set by the company per purchase order and thus it went undetected for years. Another example was that of a company employee creating a company on his spouse's maiden name and then routing business to that company.

Studying hundreds of such cases of procurement fraud in the last few years, we created a taxonomy ellucidating the broad categories to which these different cases belonged to. This taxonomy is seen in figure 1. The taxonomy, we believe, gives more structure to the problem than just enumerating individual cases. Moreover, it assists us in better understanding the different types of fraud as well as the distribution of the cases across these categories. At a high level there are only two entities namely, company employees and vendors that the company buys from. Hence, fraud occurs through actions of any of the individual entities or through their interactions. In our review of prior fraudulent cases, we found that fraud based on collusion between employee and vendor had the highest occurance. Collusion essentially is secret or illegal cooperation or conspiracy, especially in order to cheat or deceive others. Relative to procurement, collusion involves at least two parties making an arrangement or agreement which provides at least one of the parties an unfair and illegal competitive advantage.

There are a few products that quantify procurement fraud. Based on our study they [3, 9] mostly tackle just the leftmost column in figure 1, that is vendor fraud. Moreover, they are mainly based on business rules with mininmal analytics. Others are based on supervised learning [2] and thus require labelled data, which is often unavalaible in our setting. A few consulting firms also have products mainly relating to text analytics that scan emails and identify employees based on high risk words or phrases. Certain toolboxes in SPSS can identify aliasses [11] of a person or direct relationships [12] such as husband (employee)→ wife (vendor), but not multihop relationships such as husband (employee) → wife → cousin(vendor) in an efficient manner. There are other tools [8], which are mainly used for investigative purposes but not for detection. All of these tools cover small portions of the taxonomy but none of them is even close to being comprehensive.

Our system is the most comprehensive that we know of, since we model collusion detection and all the different types of fraud, not being limited to only certain restricted types. As we will see later, to accomplish this we have the ability to analyze various public and private data sources including social network data to detect collusion. Moreover, our approach is more principled in the sense that our online updating scheme based on investigation feedback has theoretical guarantees, with the goal of reducing false positives and at the same time maintaining interpretability.

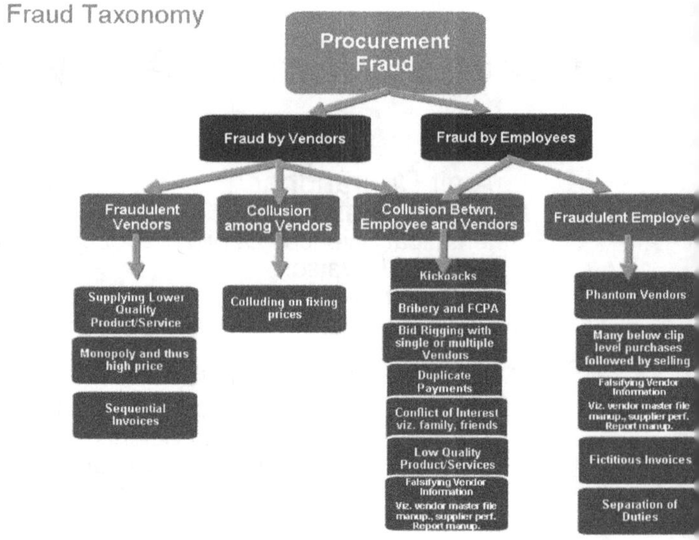

Figure 1: Above we see our taxonomy related to procurement fraud.

The rest of the paper is organized as follows: In Section 2, we describe the different analytical components of our solution and how they interact with each other. We also provide an overview of the system architecture. In Section 3, we discuss findings of the tool in terms of cases that it found and are now under investigation initiated by the domain experts. In Section 4, we discuss issues that could arise in further deployments to other clients and potential remedies.

2. SYSTEM DESIGN

In this section, we provide details of our tool. We first discuss the different analytic components followed by an overview of the overall architecture.

2.1 Analytics Flow

As mentioned before, our system analyzes various public and private data. This data maybe structured or unstructured. It may contain independent instances or the instances maybe linked. To deal with this different types of data and to come up with a credible list of risky individuals (vendors/employees) we intelligently amalgamate various analytical tools such as text analytics, social network analytics, statistical outlier detection techniques, unsupervised learning and online learning with precious domain expertise comprising of business rules and assigning of importance/weights to different anomalous events. An overview of the analytics flow is depicted in figure 2.

2.1.1 Data Sources

There are multiple data sources that feed our tool. Besides the usual transactional data, we access many private and public sources of data, some of which we now mention. This is by no means an exhaustive list but it outlines many important data sources and showcases the diversity of data used. Here are some private data sources other than transactional data.

- *Vendor Master File:* This document contains information of each of the vendors registered with the com-

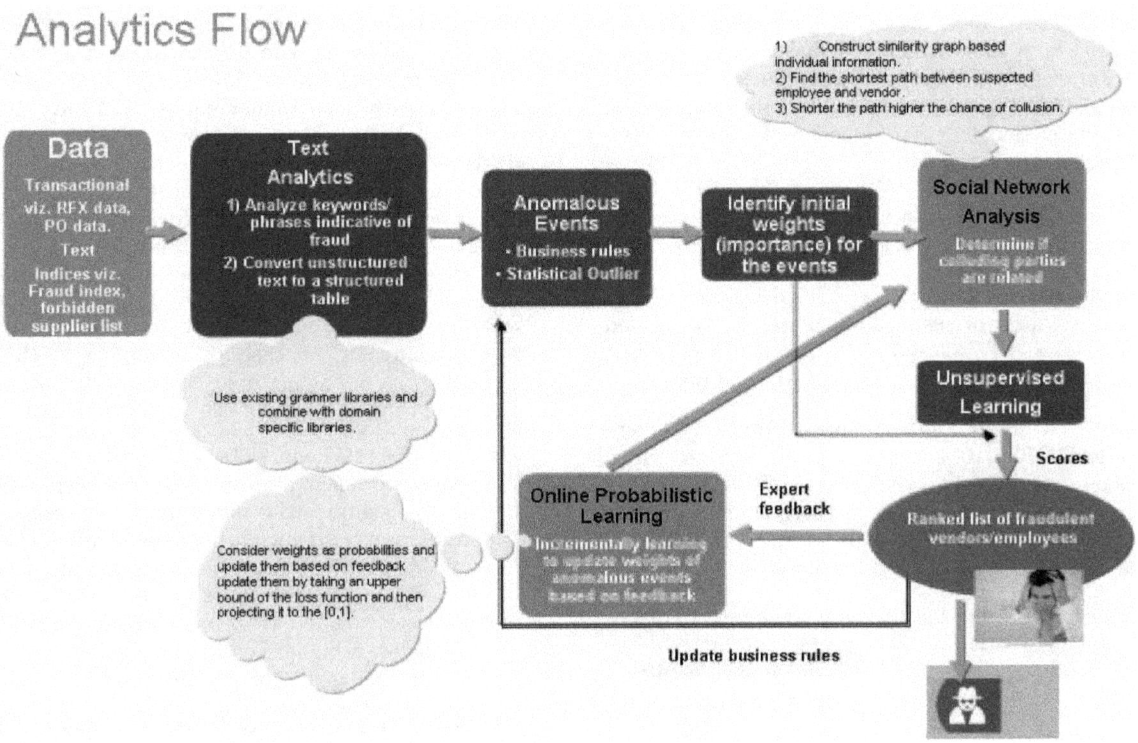

Figure 2: Above we see the different analytical components along with their interactions in our system.

pany. It has their name, addresses, account numbers, the date of registration and other relavant information.

- *RFx data:* This data source contains information about which bids for a particular product or service were sent out by whom in the company and to which vendors. It also has information about who won the bid and what the competitive prices proposed by the different vendors were. In some cases we may also have fair market value for the specific product or service.
- *Risky Vendor Lists:* These are company specific lists, which contain names of fraudulent or high risk suppliers based mostly on undesirable past experiences. It is desired that business not be conducted with these individuals.
- *Vendor Bank Account Numbers:* This is pretty self explanatory. These are accounts that the company pays to for a product or service delivered. They may be actual account numbers or encrypted for privacy.
- *Vendor-Employee Bank Account Matches:* Employee bank accounts are probably more sensitive than vendor bank accounts and hence, acquiring those from human resources could be difficult. However, if we give them the vendor bank accounts they can return the vendors whose account information matched that of any of the employees.
- *Risky Commodity List:* Commodities are high level groupings of products or services. Certain commodities have less stringent checks (viz. higher clip levels) when buying items in that commodity and thus vendors or employees might indicate their item belongs to one of these commodities, when in fact it does not in an attempt to bypass the required checks. Such commodities are thus deemed as risky and it is important for a tool like ours to take into account this information.
- *Global Clip Levels:* Generally speaking clip levels are dollar amount cutoffs for a particular purchase below which the purchase goes through significantly less checks and approvals than a purchase that is above it. These vary from country to country as well as commodity to commodity. It is important for us to know what these clip levels are for catching potential bypasses.
- *Company Risk Reports:* Certain companies privately release risk reports which reflect the global political landscape. Such reports reveal parts of the world where there might be political or even social instabilities. This information could be useful from a risk point of view as vendors located in an unstable place might interrupt supply or might have more incentive to maximize their earnings in a short period of time given the political volatility.
- *Financial Indices:* Many companies maintain statistics based on maturity, stock trends and other financial yardsticks to determine the health of other companies. This information could be useful for us for the vendors that we are interested in monitoring.
- *Social Networking Data:* Company employee emails in terms of content, who they were sent to and how frequently two parties interacted could be useful information. In terms of external sources, certain businesses

sell information about individuals regarding where all and with whom they lived in the last decade. Also information regarding their spouses and other close relatives is available. Some times public profiles on social networking sites could also be accessed to reveal relations between individuals[1].

Besides, the proprietary data sources we access also the following public data:

- *Forbidden Parties Lists:* The US government every year releases lists of suspect businesses. The Denied Persons List (DPL) [6] and the Excluded Parties List (EPL) [13] are two of the more widely used ones.
- *Country Perception Indices:* The corruption perception index (CPI) [10] is another public source, which ranks countries based on the levels of corruption faced by people in their daily lives in these countries. This list is created by different experts around the world such as credible analysts and businessmen.
- *Tax Haven Locations List:* This is again self explanatory. Having vendors located in tax haven locations or their bank accounts being present in such locations could be a red flag especially with other digressions.
- *Advanced Search Engine Searches:* Advanced searches on potentially risky vendors/employees could reveal insightful facts about the individual such as recent lifestyle changes, pending lawsuits and other such facts that might otherwise go unnoticed.
- *DUNS Numbers:* Dun & Bradstreet [5] provides a unique DUNS number and DUNS name for each business registered with them. Having a DUNS id provides a certain level of authenticity to the business.

2.1.2 Text Analytics

There are multiple sources that we use which contain unstructured data. In fact, even the standard transactional data which has invoice and purchase order (PO) information, contains text fields which can serve as a rich source of information. In our system we mine this comments field to check if the work was not authorized by the company by matching certain keywords and phrases. We also try to extract the invoice date and compare it with the PO create date to verify that they occurred in the correct chronological order. Sometimes, no PO is created a priori and it is created as an after thought, which is not acceptable. We can also check if there are indications that the work started prior to PO creation or that the actual commodity code is different from what has been entered into the appropriate structured field indicating category.

Other unstructured sources include risk reports, which can be mined to get a feel for the political situation in a certain country or geography. Employee emails can be mined to see if high risk word or phrases have been used in interaction with vendors indicating possible malicious activity.

2.1.3 Anomalous Events Identification

Anomalous events are a combination of expert provided business rules and analytical techniques such as statistical outlier detection techniques and insights derived from text analytics. Each event can be viewed as an independent feature, which gives us additional insight into the level of risk associated with a particular entity. We have 100s of such events and the list is of course ever growing.

It isn't possible to enumerate and explain all of these events so we provide a sneak peek into some of them to make lucid the kinds of events we are talking about.

- *Vendor Requestor Monopoly:* This rule checks to see if a high percentage (>90%) of invoices from a particular vendor are approved by a single employee in the company. In this case, there is a higher chance of collusion as a single employee has quite some control in accepting or rejecting the vendor invoices.
- *High Spend Vendors:* In this event we want to identify vendors in each country that we are spending (statistically) significantly more than an average vendor in that country. If such a high spend vendor is especially not an expected one we want to flag him. To account for this, we trigger the event for vendors with whom our yearly spend is above a certain confidence level but below a higher confidence level computed for each country using the corresponding vendor yearly spends.
- *Benfords Test:* Benfords law [4] provides an expected distribution of the frequency of the most significant digit in a sequence of numbers given that they were generated from a real-world process. This distribution has been observed in varied domains such as, in surface areas of rivers, molecular weights, death rates, street addresses.

  We can perform statistical testing based on this by comparing the expected distribution with the actual distribution of most significant digit of the invoice numbers for a vendor observed in our data. We can perform the chi-square test, where the null hypothesis states that the invoice numbers were generated from a real source. We trigger the event in this case, if the $p - value \leq 0.05$.
- *PO Create Date after Invoice Date:* A standard procedure is to first create a PO followed by submitting invoices for products sold or services rendered. Sometimes, this procedure may not be followed which is non-compliant behavior. The invoice dates may be indicated in a structured field, however it is sometimes different from the actual invoice date, which can be extracted from a comments field entered by an approver other than the requestor. We can thus check, if both of these invoice dates, which ideally should be the same, are at least after the PO create date, else we trigger the event.
- *Mix of PO and Non-PO Invoices:* Usually a vendor will provide goods or services with a PO corresponding for each such transaction. For some vendors the goods or services are so cheap and frequent that PO is not required to be created. However, having a mix of both is a red flag since, vendors would belong to one of these categories.
- *Invoices with Risky Commodity Code:* As described in the data sources subsection, certain commodity codes

9[1]After acquiring the appropriate approvals.

have higher clip levels after which they go through stringent checks. To bypass these checks an incorrect high clip level commodity may be entered for an invoice, which would trigger this event.

- *Country Corruption:* This event is triggered for countries with CPI below 50. The confidence that is computed for this event is described in the next subsection.
- *Unfair Win:* Once a bid is thrown by a company, if the vendor that wins the bid demands significantly more than the historical/fair market price, then we trigger this event.

2.1.4 Initial Importance Weighting and Confidences of Events

We mentioned before that we do not have labeled data. Hence, we cannot train a supervised model to rank entities based on a fraud score. To limit the number of false positives we come up with an initial weighting signifying the importance of the different events using a combination of domain expertise and the frequency of occurrence of the different events. In particular, we derive a weight in $[0, 1]$, where a higher weight indicates that the event is more important in identifying fraud. These weights are based on evaluation of the events with experts and us devaluing events that occur frequently based on our analysis of real data.

In the design, we insist on weights of individual events being normalized i.e., between $[0, 1]$, so that they are interpretable. The weight of an event can be viewed as the probability that a fraud has occurred given that the particular event was triggered. We believe, such semantics make it easier for the expert not only to be able to interpret the importance of events available in the system, but also in determining the relative importance of new events that may be added in the future. This is not the case if the events have unbounded weights, as is witnessed in some current tools.

Confidences of events are complimentary to their weights. While weights indicate the importance of an event in detecting fraud, confidences signify our belief in the occurrence of the event. For example, if we consider the *vendor requestor monopoly* event, it either occurs or doesn't occur. If the event is triggered our confidence would be 1 else it would be 0. As we can see here, the confidence is different from the weight, which is a fixed number irrespective of if the event occurs or not. We use both of these indicators, that is, confidences and weights to determine the probability of fraud by an entity, which we will visit in detail in subsection 2.1.7.

Confidences for most events are either 1 or 0 depending on if they are triggered or not respectively. However, they are a real number between $[0, 1]$ for some events. A good example is the *country corruption* event. We calculate the confidence for this event as follows: $c_{\mathrm{CPI}} = \frac{100-\mathrm{CPI}}{100}$. CPI lies between $[0, 100]$, where a higher CPI indicates lesser risk. However, in our design we want the confidences to lie in $[0, 1]$, where a higher value indicates a stronger signal for the event.

2.1.5 Social Network Analysis

We have described events on transactional data or RFx data that indicate the possibility of collusion. Analyzing social network data could significantly enhance our confidence in such findings. As mentioned before, there are companies which sell information about individuals regarding where all and with whom they lived in the last decade. In addition, information regarding their spouses and other close relatives is available. Accessing such information could be invaluable in determing collusion. Many times public profiles on social networking sites could also be accessed to reveal relations between individuals.

Algorithm 1 Computing total confidence of collusion based on social networking given collusion confidence based on other (viz. transactional, Rfx) data.

Input: Social network $G_S = (V, E)$, suspect entities (V_1, V_2), confidence of collusion based on other data c_r, social confidence threshold t_s and importance of social network information $\alpha \in [0, 1]$.
Output: c_{tot} {Total confidence of collusion.}
Set $W = \phi$ {Setting list of weights to empty initially.}
for all $E_{ij} \in E$ **do**
  if V_i, V_j are same person **then**
    Set $p = 1$ {p signifies probability that V_i and V_j are colluding based on social network information.}
  else if V_i, V_j are close relatives **then**
    Set $p = 0.95$
  else if V_i, V_j are friends/acquaintences **then**
    Set $p = 0.9$
  end if
  Set $w_{ij} = -log(p)$ {Edge weight for E_{ij}}
  $W = W \cup (w_{ij}, E_{ij})$ {Storing weights with the corresponding edge.}
end for
Set $c_{social} = ETShortestPath(G_S, W, V_1, V_2, t_s)$ {Find the exponentiated shortest path between V_1 and V_2 thresholded by t_s, i.e. if the shortest path length at any intermediate step in Dykstra's algorithm starting at V_1 is $> t_s$ return 0 else return e^{-l_s}, where l_s is the length of the shortest path.}
Return $c_{tot} = min(c_r + \alpha c_{social}, 1)$ {Total collusion confidence is the sum of c_r and discounted social network based collusion.}

In algorithm 1, we observe how information from such data sources could be used to enhance our confidence in the fact that collusion has occurred. c_r can be obtained from transactional or Rfx data. For example, if we consider the event *Unfair Win* being triggered, we could set $c_r = 0.5$ as we are not hundred percent sure that collusion has occurred. Now accessing social network data and using algorithm 1, we can further strengthen our confidence in the finding that the two entities are colluding. t_s is a threshold used in the algorithm to improve efficiency as paths longer than a certain length will lead to very small c_{social} and are not worth calculating. t_s can be easily set by deciding paths lesser than what significance are not worth extending. For example, we could set $t_s = -3log(0.9) = 0.32$ indicating that if V_1 and V_2 have a weaker relationship than being friends of friends of friends, i.e. friends 3 hops away, then they are not socially related. α is just a discount factor for the social part signifying the importance we want to assign to it. Again since we want the confidences to be normalized we let c_{tot} have a maximum value of 1.

Notice that we can further improve efficiency by not weighting the whole graph but rather querying for weights of edges as and when we need them in the shortest path algorithm.

If social data is not available we can use the corporate email network as a weak proxy. Here the weights of the edges would be determined by the frequency of the communication between the various entities and checking the content for high risk words or phrases.

2.1.6 Unsupervised Learning

From experience with dealing with domain experts across different industries, we believe that for them to gain faith in the system it is necessary to have high precision even if it is at the expense of some recall. In other words, many false positives can immediately inhibit interest amongst practitioners and experts for such a tool. Thus, the unsupervised component is of relatively low importance in the initial deployments of this application.

Nevertheless, methods from infrequent pattern mining [7] could be of considerable significance here, in identifying low support but high recall sequences in the data. These methods are of interest in anti-terrorism, where one monitoring suspicious money movements through different bank accounts.

If the patterns found by these methods are interesting they could lead to new rules that need to be checked in the future. This capability should not be ignored as humans are always adapting and hence, it is important to uncover suspicious behaviors not known to be risky by the experts.

2.1.7 Ranking Risky Entities

As we have discussed in previous subsections, each event i is associated with a weight $w_i \in [0,1]$ and given an entity $\mathcal{E}$ we have a corresponding confidence $c_i^{\mathcal{E}} \in [0,1]$ of occurrence. Thus, the probability that an entity is fraudulent/risky is 1 minus the probability that it is not fraudulent. The probability that it isn't fraudulent is the probability that none of events that are triggered for it are fraudulent. Formally, given a total number of n possible events $I = \{1, ..., n\}$ the probability that entity $\mathcal{E}$ is fraudulent is given by,

$$P_f^{\mathcal{E}} = 1 - \prod_{i \in I}(1 - w_i c_i^{\mathcal{E}}) \tag{1}$$

where for any event i, $w_i c_i^{\mathcal{E}}$ is the probability that entity $\mathcal{E}$ is fraudulent given that the event was triggered with confidence $c_i^{\mathcal{E}}$. Notice that for events that are not triggered for entity $\mathcal{E}$, the corresponding confidences $c_i^{\mathcal{E}}$ would be 0, thus not contributing to the overall fraud probability.

We can now rank entities in descending order based on our score namely, the fraud probability $P_f^{\mathcal{E}}$. Entities higher up in the list would be potentially of more interest than those lower down. Information regarding entities of interest can then be passed to other investigative tools. Results of the investigation can be entered into our tool as feedback or can lead to updating of the events as shown in figure 2.

It is clear from the formulation in equation 1 that we can score entities with whatever universe of events we have at a particular stage of the system development. Hence, even without the social networking and unsupervised learning component we can still obtain a ranked list. This is depicted in figure 2 by the thin arrow connecting the weights assignment block to the ranked list block, thus circumventing the blocks described in the previous two subsections.

2.1.8 Online Probabilistic Learning

On presenting the user with a ranked list of possibly fraudulent candidates, the user can further investigate entities

Algorithm 2 A principled method for updating weights based on user feedback for a case/entity that maintains interpretability.

Input: $\{w_1, ..., w_n\}$, $\{c_1^{\mathcal{E}}, ..., c_n^{\mathcal{E}}\}$ and y {Inputs are weights, confidences and the feedback for the case.}
Output: $\{w_1, ..., w_n\}$ {Updated weights.}
Initialise $g_s = 0$ and $\eta = 0$ {η is the learning rate.}
if $y == 0${Feedback is entity is not fraudulent.} **then**
  $\eta = 0.01$
else if $y == 1${Feedback is entity is fraudulent.} **then**
  $\eta = 0.5$
end if
if $\eta \neq 0$ **then**
  for all $i \in I$ **do**
    $g_i = ln(1 - w_i c_i^{\mathcal{E}})$
    $g_s = g_s + g_i$
  end for
  for all $i \in I$ **do**
    if $c_i^{\mathcal{E}} \neq 0${Update weight only if event is triggered.} **then**
      $g_i = g_i - 2\eta(e^{2g_s} + y - 1)$
      $w_i = \frac{(1-e^{g_i})}{c_i^{\mathcal{E}}}$
      $w_i = \mathcal{I}(w_i > 1) + w_i \mathcal{I}(w_i \in [0,1])$ {Projecting to $[0,1]$. $\mathcal{I}(.)$ is an indicator function.}
    end if
  end for
end if
Return $\{w_1, ..., w_n\}$

---

that interest him/her. For each entity he can enter 3 possible outcomes into the system. He can indicate that, i) the entity was fraudulent or ii) the entity was not fraudulent and uninteresting or iii) the entity was not fraudulent but wants to keep monitoring it. Depending on the feedback we want to update the current weights of the events triggerred for that entity. A key aspect of the updating procedure is that we want to *maintain interpretability* of the individual weights. In other words, we want the weights to be in $[0,1]$ after an update. Moreover, we want our efficient online learning procedure to have quality guarantees.

Let y denote the feedback variable, which is 1 for case i), 0 for case ii) and 2 for case iii). For case iii) we maintain the current weights as is seen in algorithm 2, since we neither want to emphasize or deemphasize the relevant events. Hence, we want $P_f^{\mathcal{E}}$ to be as close to 1 when the feedback is i) and to be close to 0 when the feedback is ii). With this we define the following least squares loss function that we want to optimize for our problem,

$$\mathcal{L} = (y - P_f^{\mathcal{E}})^2 \tag{2}$$

where if $\forall i \in \{1, ..., n\}$ $p_i = 1 - w_i c_i^{\mathcal{E}}$, then from equation 1 we have,

$$P_f^{\mathcal{E}} = 1 - \prod_{i \in I} p_i \tag{3}$$

From equations 2 and 3 our loss function can be written as,

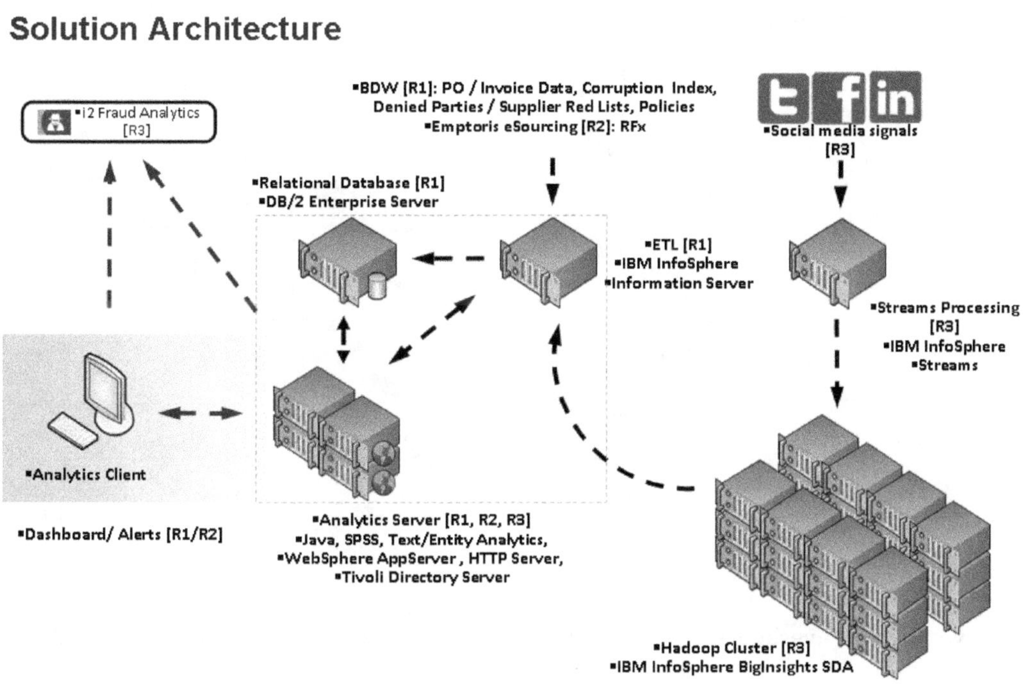

Figure 3: Above we see an overview of the architecture of our system.

$$\mathcal{L} = (y - 1 + \prod_{i \in I} p_i)^2 \tag{4}$$

If we set $g_i = ln(p_i)$ and $b = ln(2(1-y))$ we can rewrite the above equation as,

$$\mathcal{L} = e^{2\sum_{i\in I} g_i} + \frac{1}{4}e^{2b} - e^{\sum_{i\in I} g_i + b} \tag{5}$$

The function in equation 5 is not convex. For convex loss functions however, it has been shown in [14] that online gradient descent with projections onto a convex set, which is [0, 1] in our setting, achieves low regret. For this result to be applicable to us, we need to derive a convex approximation of our loss function. We accomplish this by linearizing the portion in equation 5 after the negative sign, which makes the following new function a convex upper bound of $\mathcal{L}$,

$$\mathcal{L}_u = e^{2\sum_{i\in I} g_i} + \frac{1}{4}e^{2b} - e^b(\sum_{i\in I} g_i + 1) \geq \mathcal{L} \tag{6}$$

Taking partial derivatives of $\mathcal{L}_u$ with respect to (w.r.t.) each of the non-zero g_i's and setting each such derivative to zero, leads to the update procedure described in algorithm 2. The weights are then projected onto [0, 1], where $\mathcal{I}(.)$ is an indicator function, which is 1 when the parametrized condition is true and is 0 otherwise. Thus, our solution achieves low regret w.r.t. $\mathcal{L}_u$, which is a convex upper bound of $\mathcal{L}$.

η in algorithm 2 is the learning rate. We set a significantly higher learning rate for fraudulent cases than for non-fraudulent ones, since in the real world most cases are likely to be non-fraudulent. Given this, we do not want our weights to converge to 0 quickly when feedback on non-fraudulent cases is provided. At the same time we want to quickly emphasize events that lead to entities being fraudulent as they are likely to be far and few but critical. Of course, one can change these settings of η depending on the maturity of a particular company in terms of compliance tools and processes that are in place.

2.2 Architecture

Given that we have a system that runs daily processing and analyzing billions of dollars of spend spread over millions of invoices and tens of thousands of vendors across the world, we need an architecture that is robust and scalable.

The solution architecture primarily comprises of three major components:

- Central data processing system and data warehouse
- Big data processing system
- Risk analytics engine

Firstly, the central data processing system, is implemented using IBM InfoSphere Information Server, which controls and regulates the flow of data in the system. Moreover, it orchestrates the triggering/execution of the different anomalous events and other analytical components. It also uses a number of data adaptors for the various public and private data sources that we have mentioned before, along with an extensible mechanism to add new adapters. One of the major challenges is to integrate the different data sources in a seamless manner so as to perform advanced analytics and report high risk entities. The central data warehouse bares this burden and is implemented using IBM DB2, which uses extensible high dimensional data modeling methods to support scalable data storage and retrieval.

Secondly, the big data processing system, implemented using IBM InfoSphere BigInsights and IBM InfoSphere Streams,

Figure 4: Above we see the average vendor risk score (x100) by country. The darker regions are of higher average risk.

complements the central data processing system for analyzing massive amounts of data. IBM InfoSphere BigInsights is based on an open source Apache Hadoop platform, which includes social media accelerators and text analysis toolkits that can be leveraged to process large structured/unstructured data sources such as social media, email, etc., using low cost commodity hardware. IBM InfoSphere Streams can be used to capture and process data in near real-time.

Finally, the risk analytics engine contains a library of anomalous events and analytic modules based on IBM SPSS, Python and Java that work in a co-ordinated fashion to score and rank risky entities.

3. OPERATIONAL FEEDBACK

Our first client for this system is IBM itself. The reasons for this are at least three-fold: First, if IBM itself is not using the system why would an external client be interested. Second, using IBM as a test bed we can enhance the system by removing kinks and testing it on large amounts of data consisting of billions of dollars of spend with hundreds of thousands of employees and tens of thousands of vendors. Third, a successful deployment within IBM will result in the relevant organizations providing support for the system in front of external clients. Saying this we have already demoed the system to potential external clients with positive feedback.

Our current deployment has been for IBM corporate comprising of experts from *Accounts Payable (AP), and Policies and Practices (P&P)*. The former tries to identify fraudulent entities, while the latter tries to identify entities posing a significant compliance risk. Based on their experience using the tool over the past 12 months, we have received the following feedback:

- They have *significantly better coverage* now. Previously, they could analyze only vendors in 3-4 countries in a month. However, now they can look at vendors across 150 countries daily.
- The tool has increased their efficiency by approximately 80%. What this means in data mining terms is that our top 20 list, which they review every week, has on average *80% more true positives* than the state-of-the-art methods they had been previously using.
- They have found true positives that *weren't in the last 15+ years* because of our text analysis coupled with our scoring scheme.
- They have been able to take *preemptive action* and block invoices of 10s of vendors because of our fuzzy matching with the previously mentioned suspect lists.

Overall, the *main reasons for the improved efficacy are our scoring model, the specific implementations of some of the anomalous events (viz. fuzzy matching, statistical outlier detection, text analysis) and the scalable user friendly architecture of our system.*

Given the closely related but different focus of these two organizations, we provide one example belonging to each of these types of cases that our tool found and were considered high risk by the experts.

Before we describe these cases, we ellucidate the data analyzed. These results are based on analysis of (a rolling window of) one year of real IBM procurement data, which consists of millions of invoices and has over 65000 vendors. In addition to this, we also access the various public and private data sources mentioned before. We have around 200+ DataStage jobs running daily to extract, transform and load data that feeds the analytics engine. *For aesthetic reasons we show the risk/fraud score multiplied by 100 and then rounded* in the screen shots. In figure 4, we have a world view of the risk score computed by our method and then averaged over vendors belonging to a particular country. We see that the average risk score is higher for parts of

Summary:

Vendor	Location	Total Invoice Amount	Average Invoice Amount	No. of Invoices	No. of Events	Profile Risk Score	Transactio Risk Score	Perception Risk Score	Collusion Risk Score	Overall Risk Score
Vendor_3451	US - Illinois	$381,207.05	$8,865.28	43	7	0	82	0	30	87

Events:

Risk Category	Event Name	Risk Score
Collusion	Vendors with high percentage invoices from same requestor	30
Transaction	Consecutive Invoice Numbers	10
Transaction	Vendor with mix of invoices with PO and without PO	29
Transaction	Invoice Amount jumps by 50pct	10
Transaction	Vendor who created PO after Invoice	50
Transaction	Supplier with same material group changes	30
Transaction	Benford Law	10

Figure 5: Above we see the overall risk score (x100) for a potentially fraudulent vendor and the events that were triggered for it.

Summary:

Vendor	Location	Total Invoice Amount	Average Invoice Amount	No. of Invoices	No. of Events	Profile Risk Score	Transactio Risk Score	Perception Risk Score	Collusion Risk Score	Overall Risk Score
Vendor_7549	US - Illinois	$8,524,122.1	$66,594.7C	128	7	0	95	0	0	95

Events:

Risk Category	Event Name	Risk Score
Transaction	Consecutive Invoice Numbers	10
Transaction	Vendor with mix of invoices with PO and without PO	28
Transaction	Vendor who created PO after Invoice	50
Transaction	Vendor who created invoices with risky commodity	30
Transaction	Benford Law	10
Transaction	Invoices were not authorized by IBM (by Text Analysis)	50
Transaction	Work started prior to PO (by Text Analysis)	50

Figure 6: Above we see the overall risk score (x100) for a potentially non-compliant vendor and the events that were triggered for it.

South America, Africa, Asia, Mexico and Eastern Europe. This aggregated view can provide a guideline of regions of the world to focus on.

In figures 5 and 6, we see a more detailed view of two vendors that potentially present high risk and were identified by our tool. In the summary tab in both these figures, we see the (anonymized) vendor name followed by more vendor specific information in the next four columns. The *No. of Events* column, denotes the number of events triggered for this vendor. The last column is the risk score (x100) computed by our method. The preceding four columns are risk scores based on a partition of the universal list of events. Essentially, they act as thumbnails providing a quick sneak peek into where the problem lies for the particular entity. So for example in figure 5, most of the risk for that vendor is associated with its invoice/transactional data. In addition, there is also a collusion risk. Analogously, for the vendor in figure 6 all his risk can be attributed to non-compliant and potentially fraudulent transactions. More details about the particular events that were triggered leading up to these risk scores can be found in the *Events* tab below[2]. The tool also allows the user to perform multiple other tasks such as see the transactional and other accessed data, filter invoices by triggered events, however due to limited space we do not show screen shots for those.

Further delving into the case in figure 5, we see that there is a risk of collusion as a single requestor/employee is approving a bulk of the invoices sent by the vendor. Coupled with this we see that there is more than a 50% jump in spending with this vendor from a six month to the next six month period. Moreover, five other events are triggered making this vendor high on the suspect list.

The case in figure 6, showcases the usefulness of mining unstructured data. The three highest risk events are triggered due to text analysis. Other than these we have the event that checks for risky commodity codes being triggered, which indicates a potential for bypass. These along with triggering of three other lower risk events makes this vendor worth investigating.

4. DISCUSSION

In this paper, we described a daily running system that is currently being used by various organizations within IBM. The plan is to continuously extend and improve the system

9[2]The risk score for each event is its weight multiplied by confidence (x100).

and deploy it with other internal and external clients. The idea is to have a universal list of events with default initial weights that are customizable by the experts in the particular organization. Therefore, every new organization/client will have their own independent instantiation of our system. An effective system such as this will potentially not only identify fraud but will also serve as a deterrent for entities that are currently committing fraud or those that are considering of doing it in the future.

Deploying such a system has many challenges. One of the main challenges is being able to access sensitive private data. For example, some of our events require accessing employee bank account data, which is highly sensitive information. We tackle this problem by letting HR run the specific events in their firewall and returning only the result. Afterall, our system only needs to know if a particular event was triggered for an entity or not. For instance consider the event, where we check to see if a vendor bank account number matches an employee bank account number. This would require knowing the bank account numbers of both these entities. However, we could send HR a list of vendor bank accounts and they could match them against the employee database and return to us the list of vendors that matched. This completely absolves them from sending us the employee bank account numbers. An analogous strategy can be used for other events that require sensitive data, where only the list of entities for whom the event was triggered is returned to us by the responsible party.

Another challenge is the type of data that the client is ready to subscribe to. The client may not want to buy or pay for accessing certain paid data sources that may carry useful signals. In certain cases, a particular geography may have restrictions on the public data that may be used incriminate anyone. For example, in Europe using publicly available social data to accuse an individual is strongly discouraged.

Given these restrictions in regards to accessing different data sources, which could lead us to potentially miss important signals, we can either settle with what we have or try to be more creative. From an analytics perspective a possible way of mitigating the impact of the absence of these data sources is to implement an extrapolated scoring scheme. What we mean by this is that using available data from existing clients (viz. IBM) we can figure out through techniques such as association rule mining the likelihood of certain combination of events to co-occur. Based on these insights we can score entities of a new client with their limited data by seeing the events that have been triggered for each entity and appending those with events that are likely to be triggered if in fact they had the data. In essence, we are extrapolating the score based on our knowledge of other similar clients. This extension could of course be erroneous but its probably our best estimate given the missing data sources.

Another extension to the system would be to come up with joint weights/probabilities for certain groups of events. Of course we cannot consider all possible groups as this list is exponential in the number of events. However, certain groups of events being simultaneously triggered may have more information than multiplying their importances as if they were independent. An alternate way of dealing with this if the groups are disjoint, is to combine the events in each group into a single corresponding composite event with an associated weight, in which case, the machinery described in this paper can be directly applied. Many such improvements are being implemented and tested in the system as we speak. Moreover, we are involved in serious discussions about carrying over the design and adapting the various analytical components to detecting fraud in other related domains.

Acknowledgement

We would like to thank Anthony Mazzati from *Accounts Payable*, Pablo Varela and Kathy Moon from *Policies and Practices*, Brian Hopper from *Global Process Services* and many others from different organizations (FCPA, Auditing) within IBM who continue to help us in improving this tool and are instrumental in its success.

5. REFERENCES

[1] ACFE. Report to the nations. In *Global Fraud Study.* 2014. http://www.acfe.com/uploadedFiles/ACFE_Website/Content/rttn/2014-report-to-nations.pdf.

[2] Alaric. Fraud detection. In *Payment Processing and Fraud Prevention.* 2013. http://www.alaric.com/.

[3] A. Analytixs. Fraud detection. In *yourFirstStrike.* 2013. http://www.apexanalytix.com/firststrike/fraud-detection.aspx.

[4] F. Benford. The law of anomalous numbers. *Proc. of the American Philosophy Soc.*, 78:551–572, 1938.

[5] D. . Bradstreet. Duns numbers. In *US Govt.* 2013. http://fedgov.dnb.com/webform.

[6] I. . S. Bureau. Denied persons list. In *US Dept. of Commerce*, 2013. http://www.bis.doc.gov/index.php/policy-guidance/lists-of-parties-of-concern/denied-persons-list.

[7] D. Haglin and A. Manning. On minimal infrequent itemset mining. In *Proc. of Intl. Conference on Data Mining*, 2007.

[8] i2 IBM. i2 fraud intelligence analysis. In *Planning and Mgmt. Services.* 2013. http://www-03.ibm.com/software/products/en/fraud-intelligence-analysis/.

[9] IBM-RCAT. Rcat. In *ISC.*

[10] T. Intl. Corruption perceptions index. 2013. http://www.transparency.org/research/cpi/overview.

[11] J. Jonas. Entity analytics. In *IBM SPSS.* 2012. ftp://public.dhe.ibm.com/software/analytics/spss/documentation/modeler/15/en/EA_UserGuide.pdf.

[12] J. Jonas. Identity insight. In *IBM SPSS.* 2012. http://www-03.ibm.com/software/products/en/infosphere-identity-insight/.

[13] A. M. System. Excluded parties list. In *US Govt.*, 2013. https://www.sam.gov/portal/public/SAM/.

[14] M. Zinkevich. Online convex programming and generalized infinitesimal gradient ascent. In *Proc. of the 20th Intl. Conference on Machine Learning*, 2003.

Probabilistic Modeling of a Sales Funnel to Prioritize Leads

Brendan Duncan and Charles Elkan
Department of Computer Science and Engineering
University of California, San Diego
La Jolla, CA 90293-0404, USA
{baduncan, elkan}@cs.ucsd.edu

ABSTRACT

This paper shows how to learn probabilistic classifiers that model how sales prospects proceed through stages from first awareness to final success or failure.[1] Specifically, we present two models, called DQM for direct qualification model and FFM for full funnel model, that can be used to rank initial leads based on their probability of conversion to a sales opportunity, probability of successful sale, and/or expected revenue. Training uses the large amount of historical data collected by customer relationship management or marketing automation software. The trained models can replace traditional lead scoring systems, which are hand-tuned and therefore error-prone and not probabilistic. DQM and FFM are designed to overcome the selection bias caused by available data being based on a traditional lead scoring system. Experimental results are shown on real sales data from two companies. Features in the training data include demographic and behavioral information about each lead. For both companies, both methods achieve high AUC scores. For one company, they result in a a 307% increase in number of successful sales, as well as a dramatic increase in total revenue. In addition, we describe the results of the DQM method in actual use. These results show that the method has additional benefits that include decreased time needed to qualify leads, and decreased number of calls placed to schedule a product demo. The proposed methods find high-quality leads earlier in the sales process because they focus on features that measure the fit of potential customers with the product being sold, in addition to their behavior.

1. INTRODUCTION

Customer relationship management systems and marketing automation software have become popular tools for companies with sales and marketing teams. Because these systems store a large amount of historical sales data, they provide great potential for machine learning algorithms to improve the sales process. In theory, companies can use a predictive sales lead scoring or ranking model to prioritize sales and marketing efforts towards leads that are more likely to result in successful sales. This paper shows how to put this theory into practice.

[1]Research performed while Brendan Duncan worked at Fliptop Inc., 594 Howard Street, Suite 400, San Francisco, CA 94105.

KDD'15, August 10-13, 2015, Sydney, NSW, Australia.

ACM 978-1-4503-3664-2/15/08 ...$15.00.
DOI: http://dx.doi.org/10.1145/2783258.2788578 .

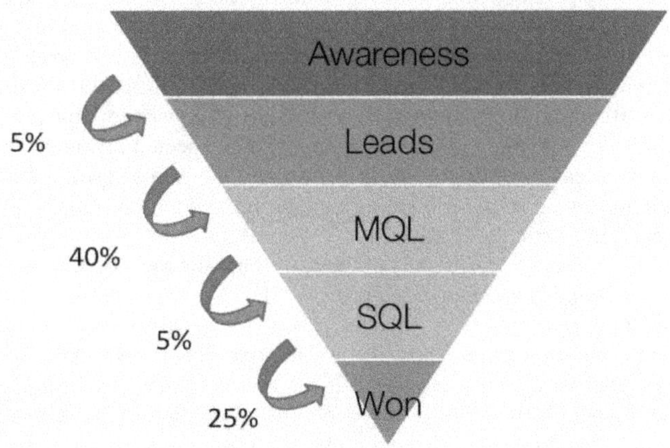

Figure 1: Sales funnel. MQL means marketing-qualified lead, while SQL means sales-qualified lead. Image copyright ©2015 by Fliptop, Inc.

Figure 1 shows a typical sales funnel. The different cross sections of the funnel represent different stages as a lead moves forward in the sales process, from the top of the funnel to the bottom. The decreasing diameter of the funnel represents a smaller and smaller volume of prospects reaching each successive stage.

1.1 Types of prospective customers

In Figure 1, a lead is an initial prospective customer that has not been evaluated in any way. For example, when an individual visits a website, or exchanges contact information with the marketing team, they will begin to be tracked by marketing automation software, as a "cold lead."

As leads are tracked by marketing teams, and by marketing automation software, marketing will qualify leads based on certain criteria, such as the amount of interest they show in the product (behavioral information) and their demographic fit for purchasing the product; see Section 1.3. Leads that are qualified by marketing will be passed along to the sales team and called "marketing-qualified leads."

Once the sales team receives leads from marketing, there is an additional qualification step. So-called teleprospectors or sales development representatives reach out to the individuals and determine if they meet the minimum criteria for becoming a sales opportunity. For example, the person must be in the market for the product or service offered by the seller, and must have the authority and budget to make a purchase within the sales timeline requirements. If an individual meets these criteria, he or she is qualified, called a "sales-qualified lead" (SQL), and becomes a genuine sales opportunity that is assigned to an account executive. This process is called "lead conversion." The majority of SQLs will be pursued by sales representatives, and will result in either a successful sale (closed-won) or a failure (closed-lost).

1.2 Prioritization of leads

According to the company named SiriusDecisions, it is typical for only 6% of MQLs to convert to closed-won status. A major expense for sales teams is the time wasted on dealing with a large volume of low quality MQLs that will not become sales-qualified. In many cases, there will be more leads than can be targeted by the current sales team. Instead of hiring more teleprospectors, or arbitrarily choosing a subset of leads to pursue, sales teams should prioritize their efforts towards those leads that are most likely to reach the next stage. A predictive model can be employed for this prioritization. It can predict the probability of conversion, the probability of becoming closed-won, and/or the expected revenue from a given lead. The last of these allows a sales team to estimate the amount of sales and marketing budget that should be allocated to deal with particular leads.

The most expensive parts of the funnel are the sales qualification process and the actual sales process, that is sales representatives pursuing opportunities, since these stages require the most human work either by teleprospectors or sales representatives. Therefore, a predictive model can add the most value for these two steps of the funnel. Although this paper focuses on predicting lead conversion, the methods proposed are also directly applicable to ranking opportunities at earlier stages of the funnel.

Other reports of data mining techniques applied to sales and marketing include [2] and [1], which includes a chapter on identifying prospects using a CRM. Other analyses of using predictive techniques to gain insights into consumer behavior and to improve marketing operations are given in [11] and [3].

1.3 Conventional lead scoring

Lead scoring is not new. Many companies currently use a manual lead scoring system. Such methods are generally used by the marketing team to identify MQLs. Marketing automation software facilitates the creation of such scoring systems. Although the potential benefit of marketing automation has been recognized for at least 25 years [9], according to SiriusDecisions only 40% of sales teams with marketing automation think that their current marketing automation adds value. These systems still result in low quality MQLs being handed off to sales teams, making the sales qualification process expensive and time consuming. In this section we discuss these conventional scoring methods.

With a manual lead scoring system, scores are hand-tuned by experienced members of the marketing or sales team. These systems typically use a "scorecard" in which the presence or absence of certain positive or negative customer attributes or behaviors are assigned fixed positive or negative values. These individual values are then summed to determine a final score for the lead. For example, Table 1 shows some potential values that might be assigned for different behaviors and attributes.

One issue with conventional lead scores is that they fail to capture nonlinear effects. For example, if a user visits many webinars, they will receive a high lead score, since they accumulate 5 points for each webinar. However, there may be diminishing returns for each webinar visit. The highest quality leads may visit, say, between two and four webinars; attending additional webinars past this may not indicate a significant probability of making a purchase. It may even be the case that visiting many webinars is a negative signal. For example, it could indicate the behavior of a student, or even a competitor, who is researching the marketing functions of the company. In addition, complex interactions of features cannot be represented by scorecard models.

Table 1: An example of a conventional lead scorecard. Values are traditionally hand-selected.

Behavior	Value
Filled out a contact form	+ 10
Attended webinar	+5
Visited webpage or blog	+1
Visited careers page	-10

Attribute	Value
Job title is "VP of sales"	+20
Company is located in Northeast USA	+5
Lead has a consumer email address (Gmail etc.)	-5
Job title is "student"	-10

Another issue with conventional lead scoring is that the hand-selection of values is error-prone. In particular, hand-selection is vulnerable to bias from potentially mistaken business logic. This bias is also a problem for predictive methods, and is discussed further in Section 1.4.

A third disadvantage is that traditional lead scores are unbounded positive or negative values. They do not intuitively map to the probability of lead conversion or opportunity close. Many machine learning methods are probabilistic and therefore can give valid probability scores [13].

A fourth issue is that scorecard systems are often heavily reliant on behavioral data. While such data can be a good indicator of lead interest in the product, it prevents discovering the high quality leads early; they will only be found after enough time has passed for the lead to have taken specific actions. To avoid reliance on behavioral data, one could try to gather additional static features about the customer, but each additional feature adds complexity for hand-selecting an appropriate value.

1.4 Goals for automated lead scoring

The criteria for lead qualification vary greatly by seller. Determining that a lead is an MQL is usually based on simple behavioral and demographic rules. The demographic rules depend on the product or service being sold, and the behavioral rules depend on lead interaction with marketing materials specific to the company. As discussed above, identifying MQLs is an error-prone process, and the volume of MQLs is often greater than can be handled by the sales team. Even if there is not a great volume of leads, teleprospecting low-quality MQLs results in wasted time, and causes tension between the sales and marketing teams. This tension is the subject of research such as [8].

Most companies identify MQLs based on fixed criteria, usually not more sophisticated than a hand-tuned scorecard. Training a machine learning model could simply learn to reproduce these simple linear criteria, and therefore maintain the bias that is present in the existing, hand-tuned model. For example, if a company has focused its sales efforts on Florida, a machine learning model may learn that a prospect being located outside Florida is a negative signal, which may in fact not be the case. We describe below how our design reduces the effect of selection bias [12].

On the other hand, typically all SQLs are pursued by sales representatives. Therefore, there is little selection bias in the later stages of the funnel. This is a major reason why predictive models should be trained with information from later stages of the funnel. Another reason is that the ultimate goal of the sales funnel is to close a successful sale, even if the problem at hand is simply to find leads that are more likely to be qualified by sales.

In the design of the methods described below, we address several major goals:

1. A model should be probabilistic and have a meaningful interpretation, such as expected revenue or probability of successful close.
2. A model should not simply relearn an existing conventional lead classification model.
3. A model should be consistent with a separate opportunity won/lost classification model. That is, it should assign higher scores to leads corresponding to closed-won opportunities than to leads which convert but are not successfully closed.
4. The model should be able to find quality leads quickly, without relying too heavily on activity data.

The design of the models accomplishes goals 1, 2 and 3, while goal 4 is achieved by having good static (non-behavioral) features.

2. DATA FOR EXPERIMENTS

The data in our experiments is provided by Fliptop. It consists of sales and marketing data extracted from Salesforce and Marketo systems, to which Fliptop has appended additional proprietary features. As with conventional lead scoring, the type of features present are of broadly two kinds: static (or demographic) features and behavioral (also called activity) features.

The static features are information about either the individual contact or the company for which the individual works. Fliptop obtains some of these features directly from fields in Salesforce, and uses individual, company, and domain names from Salesforce to append additional features. These features include company level information such as industry codes, number of employees, market value, income, and company location. They also include company hiring features, such as the number of job openings in marketing, sales, business, and other departments. Fliptop appends binary features indicating which technologies are employed by the company. Such features include whether a company uses Java, marketing automation software, HTML5, etc. Finally, the contact's job title is appended as a categorical feature. These static features represent the fit of the individual and the product being sold. The majority of static features are binary or categorical values, and the remainder are numerical features.

Behavioral features represent actions taken by an individual, and capture interest in the seller by the potential customer during a specific period of time. These features are all numerical counts representing the number of times a user has performed a specific action that is tracked by marketing automation software. Examples of actions include visiting a product website, opening a marketing email, attending a webinar or trade-show event, and filling out a particular form, such as a product demo request form or an unsubscribe form.

The remainder of this section describes the data available for two sellers called Company A and Company B. This data consists of lead data pulled from CRM and marketing automation software, to which Fliptop then appended additional features. For additional information on data preprocessing, see Section 3.2.

Company A is a SaaS (software as a service) business with around 200 employees and annual revenue around \$20 million. The training set for Company A consists of 5925 unconverted leads, 1320 leads that became closed-lost opportunities, and 1469 leads that became closed-won opportunities. For this company, we have 243 static features about leads and their employers, along with 350 behavioral features. The median closed price of a sale for Company A is \$99, while the mean closed price is \$9930 The mean is 100 times the median because the pricing varies greatly based on the product type and the number of software licenses sold. The variability in revenue makes identifying the best prospects for Company A especially challenging.

Company B is a software business with over 500 employees and annual revenue around \$100 million. Its training set consists of 25904 unconverted leads, 956 leads that became closed-lost opportunities, and 1097 leads that became closed-won opportunities. For this company, we have 242 static features about prospects, along with 20 behavioral features. The median closed price of a sale is \$29618, and the mean closed price is \$46118.

3. DIRECT QUALIFICATION MODEL

The DQM (direct qualification model) models a sales funnel using a single multiclass classifier. Leads receive different class labels depending on how far along in the sales funnel they progress. We first describe the motivation for this model, then give details on how to construct and label a training set for it, and then describe the predictive algorithm.

3.1 Motivation

Predicting whether a lead will convert is a binary classification problem, and would seem to require only training a binary classifier. There are several reasons why this can be undesirable for lead qualification. The first reason is that it runs the risk of merely learning to reproduce the conventional lead scoring model that the company uses. Since traditional lead scoring models are typically scorecards with linear weights, machine learning models can predict lead conversion with high accuracy. However, this does not provide additional benefit to a sales team.

Another disadvantage of a two-class solution is that a lead that makes it further through the sales funnel is of higher quality than one that does not. Therefore, we would like scores to incorporate information about the chance of a lead to end up as a successful sale. If a lead conversion score incorporates closed-won probability information, it is more likely that the score will be consistent with a separate predictive model that ranks sales opportunities. That is, if lead A has a higher score than lead B, and both leads convert to opportunities A and B, we would like opportunity A to also have a higher score than opportunity B, according to an opportunity scoring model.

We address these potential disadvantages by classifying leads into three classes:

- `NoCON`: Leads that never convert.
- `LOST`: Leads that convert to opportunities that are ultimately lost.
- `WON`: Leads that convert to opportunities that successfully close (closed-won).

3.2 Training set

For the classes `LOST` and `WON`, we include leads that have closed within the last year, so that the model is up-to-date. The numbers given in Section 2 are after performing all the filtering described

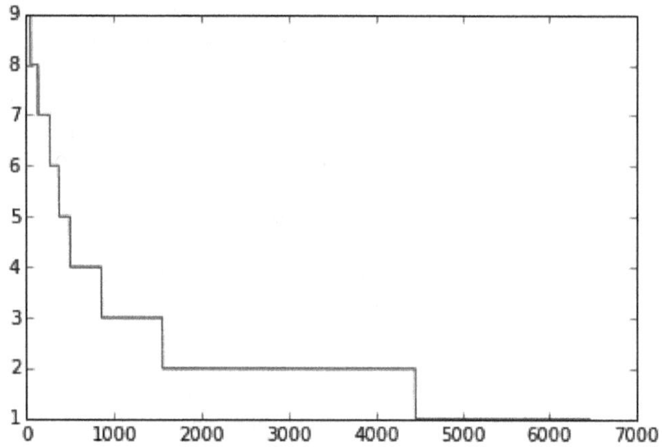

Figure 2: Leads are sorted by number of activities. The horizontal axis value is position in the sort, while the vertical axis value is the corresponding number of activities for that lead.

here. For the class NoCON, we use all leads that have not yet converted. While this class may contain a small number of leads that will eventually convert, that does not greatly affect the performance of our method. Another option would be to treat the unconverted leads as unlabeled, and use a positive-only learning method [4].

For behavioral features, we ensure that the only the most recent year of values is included; for most leads there is much less data than this. To avoid leakers [7], we only include activities that occur before conversion, and we remove activities that indicate actions taken by the marketing team, including administrative or data management actions, rather than by the actual prospective customer.

For company A, the great majority of unconverted leads have fewer than two activities, and similar features in general, meaning that a model could achieve high accuracy by simply identifying this great majority of unconverted leads. In order to investigate how our methods work well for companies with more variety in the class NoCON, we include all the leads with more than one activity, and a number L_1 of leads with fewer than two activities, such that L_1 is roughly equal to the number of leads with exactly two activities. Although this changes the distribution of leads, and therefore also changes the calibration of probabilities, this filtering of the training set is not unlike the process of clearing unpromising leads out of a leads database. Some companies will be more aggressive with deleting leads, so our method must work with different procedures.

For both Company A and Company B, we use 75% of the data for training and 25% of the data for testing. The training and test split was determined based on the time each lead was added to the lead management system. Leads in the test set were added after those in the training set, to approximate the real-world scenario where training the model occurs before lead scoring.

3.3 Training and prediction

We use a three-class gradient boosted tree classifier [5, 6]. The experiments in this paper use the implementation from scikit-learn [10] with the default parameters, and with so-called deviance loss in order for predictions to be probabilities.

After training the classifier on the training set, we use it to perform prediction on a separate test set. For each lead x to be scored in the testing set, the classifier gives three probabilities that sum to one: $p_1(x) = P(l = \texttt{NoCON}|x)$, $p_2(x) = P(l = \texttt{LOST}|x)$, and $p_3(x) = P(l = \texttt{WON}|x)$, where l is a label value conditional on x.

Table 2: AUC values for the DQM method.

Company	Features	AUC_1	AUC_2
A	All	0.992	0.960
A	Static only	0.988	0.940
A	Behavioral only	0.927	0.867
B	All	0.956	0.969
B	Static only	0.928	0.964
B	Behavioral only	0.906	0.922

Table 3: AUC values for the FFM method.

Company	Stage	AUC
A	Lead conversion	0.991
A	Closed-won	0.788
B	Lead conversion	0.952
B	Closed-won	0.912

There are several ways to map the three probabilities into a lead score $s(x)$. We consider linear combinations of p_2 and p_3:

$$s(x) = \alpha p_2(x) + \beta p_3(x).$$

After a linear combination is chosen, leads are sorted based on their score. As linear combinations we consider $(\alpha, \beta) = (0, 1)$, and $(\alpha, \beta) = (1, 1)$. These correspond respectively to maximizing closed-won probability and to maximizing lead conversion probability.

Although we only consider these two weightings, other weightings are possible. Alternative weightings may be desirable as a tradeoff between maximizing conversion of existing leads, which the marketing team is motivated to do, and maximizing closing of opportunities, which the sales team is motivated to do. The weighting can be tuned to demonstrate a sufficient benefit to both teams, which is important because companies who purchase predictive lead scoring solutions often split the cost between the marketing and sales budgets.

4. FULL FUNNEL MODELING

FFM stands for "full funnel modeling." As a prospect advances in a sales funnel, he or she moves through several stages; see Figure 1. The FFM method uses a separate probabilistic classifier for each stage of the funnel, in whatever way the funnel is defined.

For companies A and B, the transitions we are most interested in are from lead to SQL (conversion beyond MQL) and from SQL to won (successful sale). We represent these transitions using two models:

$$P(\text{SQL}|x, \text{lead})$$
$$P(\text{won}|x, \text{SQL}).$$

Note that $P(\text{won}|x, \text{SQL}) = P(\text{won}|x, \text{lead}, \text{SQL})$ because SQL being true logically implies "lead" being true. Additionally, we include a third model for the final stage of the funnel, namely the size of the closed deal:

$$E(\text{revenue}|x, \text{won}).$$

In these expressions, x denotes the feature values describing a given potential customer.

The probability that a lead with characteristics x will become a successful sale is

$$P(\text{won}|x, \text{lead}) = P(\text{SQL}|x, \text{lead}) \cdot P(\text{won}|x, \text{SQL}).$$

The expected revenue from the lead is

$$E(\text{revenue}|x, \text{lead}) = P(\text{won}|x, \text{lead}) \cdot E(\text{revenue}|x, \text{won}).$$

Knowing the expected revenue from a prospect x at the stage when x is only a lead allows a sales organization to estimate better how much budget should be invested in pursuing this individual prospect.

A full funnel model can also make predictions involving prospects currently at the SQL stage. For example, the expected revenue from customer x given that x has reached this stage is

$$E(\text{revenue}|x, \text{SQL}) = P(\text{won}|x, \text{SQL}) \cdot E(\text{revenue}|x, \text{won}).$$

Separating the conversion classifier and the closed-won classifier results in another advantage of FFM. It is often the case that data about leads data and data about sales opportunities are stored in separate databases. In some cases, missing fields make it difficult to link up a lead with its corresponding opportunity, and vice versa. In such a case, an FFM can be learnt, while a DQM cannot, as we do not know whether to label converted leads as class `WON` or class `LOST`.

Filtering and preprocessing the features that describe prospects are done in the same way as described above in Section 3.2, but the training sets and labels differ. In general, FFM requires the construction of a separate training set for each transition that is modeled. Here, we have a training set of leads for modeling the probability $P(\text{SQL}|x, \text{lead})$ and a training set of opportunities for modeling $P(\text{won}|x, \text{SQL})$ and a training set of closed-won customers for modeling $E(\text{revenue}|x, \text{won})$.

We use the same classifier learning algorithm and parameters as in the DQM model, but for binary instead of three-class classification. For regression, we also use gradient boosted trees.

For FFM, we can compute the score $s(x)$ of a lead as either $s(x) = P(\text{won}|x, \text{lead})$ or $s(x) = E(\text{revenue}|x, \text{lead})$. The former definition is analogous to setting $(\alpha, \beta) = (0, 1)$ for DQM. Our experiments only consider scoring based on expected revenue of leads.

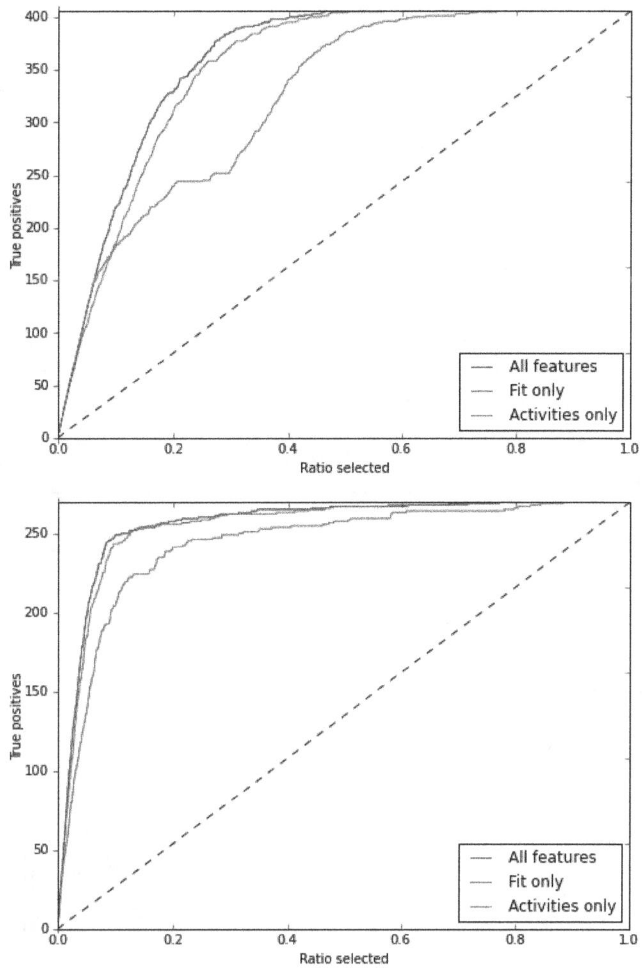

Figure 3: Closed-won lift curves for DQM with $(\alpha, \beta) = (0, 1)$. Top: Company A. Bottom: Company B.

5. RESULTS ON REAL DATA

This section describes empirical results obtained from retrospective analysis of historical data. The next section describes results from actual use in practice of the DQM.

The historical data used for this section is described above. Experiments for DQM report two scalar evaluation metrics: AUC_1, the area under the ROC curve (AUC) for classification of non-converted versus converted leads, that is, class `NoCON` versus class [`WON` or `LOST`], and AUC_2, the AUC for the classification of leads that become closed-won opportunities versus those that do not, that is, class [`NoCON` or `LOST`] versus class `WON`. These correspond to ranking the leads with $(\alpha, \beta) = (1, 1)$ and $(\alpha, \beta) = (0, 1)$, respectively. For FFM we report AUC for the two separate classifiers which predict conversion and closed-won. Note that predicting conversion is the same binary classification task with the DQN and FFM approaches, so AUC_1 and AUC for FFM conversion are in principle the same. Observed differences are due to randomness.

As another evaluation of score quality, we plot lift curves for each of the experiments that show the ratio of converted or closed-won leads as we increase the proportion of selected leads. We also include lift curves that show the expected revenue as we increase the proportion of selected leads.

5.1 AUC measures

Applying the DQM to Company A data results in the AUC metrics given in Table 2. In order to see how the different types of features contribute to the model, we give AUC metrics for a model built with all the features, one built with only behavioral features, and one built with only demographic ("static") features.

AUC scores for the FFM method are given in Table 3. We show the AUC measures for the two classifiers: for predicting lead to SQL conversion, and predicting SQL to closed-won. To keep the paper shorter and more readable, we do not repeat the comparison of static versus behavioral features for FFM, and all FFM experiments use all behavioral and static features.

The AUC_1 scores are high. This is likely because the model can easily learn the existing business rules, that is the linear scorecard for qualifying leads. The way the DQM can add value over existing methods is by using further criteria to prioritize leads, as examined in lift curves for revenue and win rate shown below. A general reason why we are able to achieve high AUCs is that the training data includes all leads tracked in the CRM. Many of these are early stage leads, which are often obviously unlikely to convert.

5.2 Lift curves

To visualize the performance of DQM and FFM, we use lift curves. To understand these, note that the criterion for ordering leads on the horizontal axis is in general different from the quantity measured on the vertical axis. In particular, the DQM orders leads based on scores $s(x)$ corresponding to predicted probability

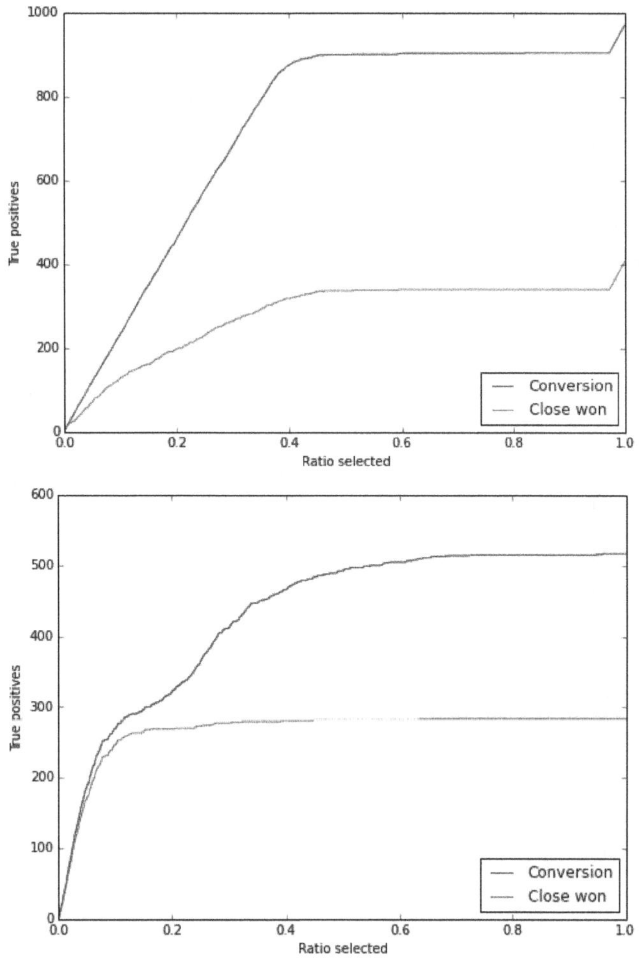

Figure 4: Conversion and closed-won lift curves for FFM. Top: Company A. Bottom: Company B.

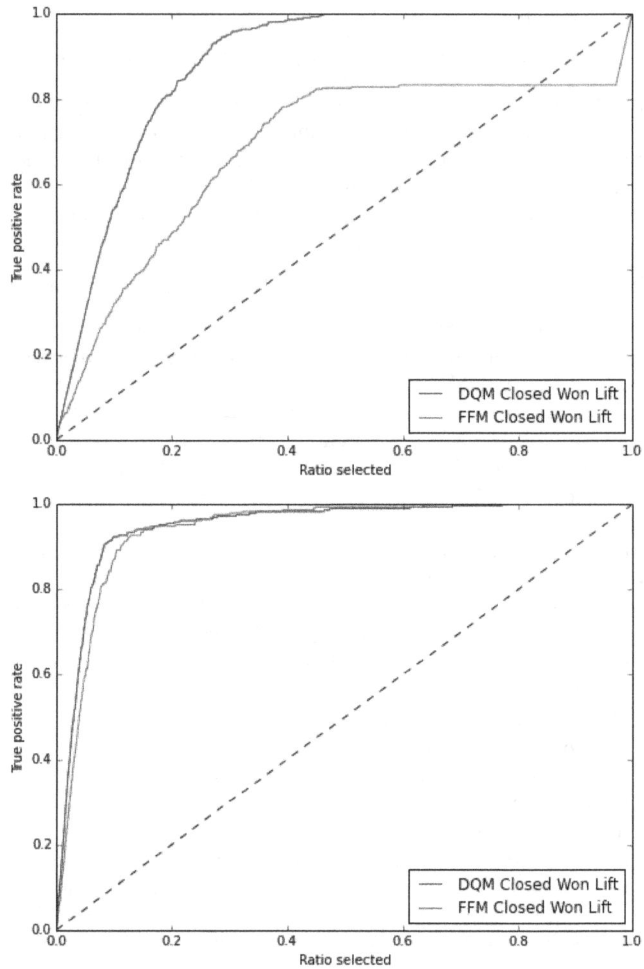

Figure 5: Closed-won lift curves, FFM versus DQM. Top: Company A. Bottom: Company B.

of closed-won, using $(\alpha, \beta) = (0, 1)$. With this same ordering, we compute separate curves that track the number of successful sales and the sales revenue. Similarly, experiments with FFM rank leads based on expected revenue, but with this same ordering we again plot lift curves corresponding to number of conversions, successful sales, and the sales revenue. We use only one ordering for lift curves because this most closely matches the teleprospecting scenario, in which teleprospectors use a single ranking when contacting leads.

5.3 DQM and FFM comparison

Figure 3 shows closed-won lift curves for leads prioritized using $(\alpha, \beta) = (0, 1)$. It compares models obtained using all features, using just behavioral features, and using just static features. For both company A and B, we see that using all features performs best, while using behavioral features alone performs worst.

Figure 4 shows conversion and closed-won lift curves when we prioritize leads according to their expected revenue. For company A, the lift is significantly less in the 50% selected to 95% selected range, than it is in the 95% to 100% selected range. Figure 6 shows that the sales in this later range generate low revenue. It is often the case that bigger contracts have a lower chance of successful closing, but still a higher expected revenue overall.

Figure 5 contrasts the closed-won lift curves for FFM and for DQM with $(\alpha, \beta) = (0, 1)$, both trained using all behavioral and static features. The ranking of leads for DQM is based on expected closed-won probability, while the ranking for FFM is based on expected revenue, so the closed-won curves are better for DQM. This is because the win probability for higher revenue deals tends to be lower, but the expected revenue is still higher for these deals.

Figure 6 compares revenue for the same models. For company A, DQM performs poorly at achieving lift in revenue. This is because the model focuses on closing the less risky, smaller magnitude sales. In general, the DQM method is less appropriate if there is high variance in the sales price. Alternatively, separate DQM models could be built for separate products or price ranges.

In Figure 5, the region to the very right of the FFM curve for company A (the straight line region) indicates that this method gives lowest priority to leads that with high confidence result in a low-revenue win. The DQM method achieves high initial closed-won lift for company A. However, the corresponding revenue curve in Figure 6 shows low initial lift, because DQM prioritizes low-revenue deals for company A. These observations suggests that it is easier to predict confidently low-revenue closes for company A.

As a final comparison, suppose that the sales teams of company A and B only have enough resources to contact 20% of all leads.

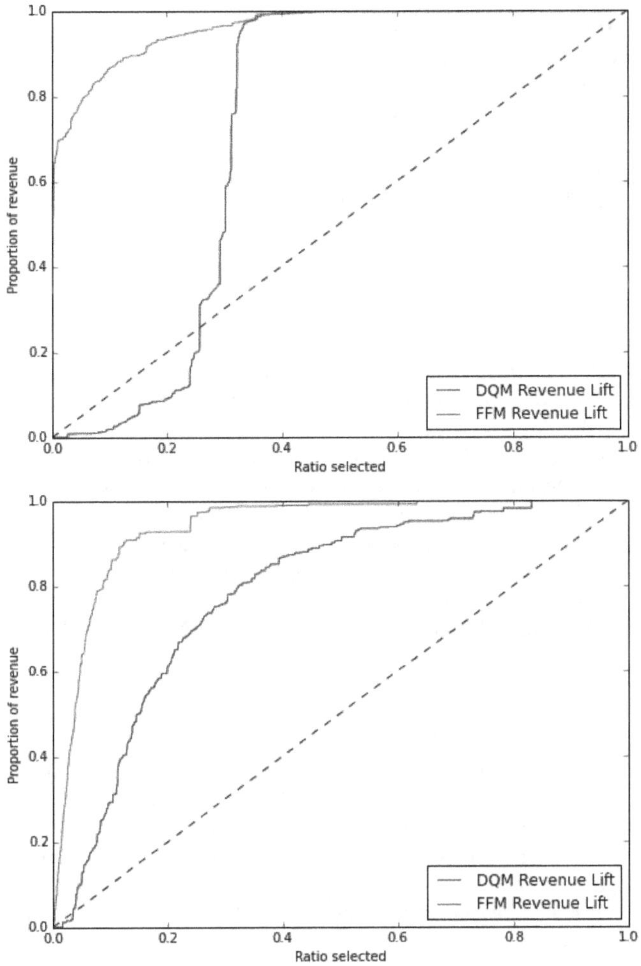

Figure 6: Revenue lift curves, FFM versus DQM. Top: Company A. Bottom: Company B.

Table 4 shows the conversion rates, closed-won rates, and revenue if the companies prioritize leads randomly, using DQM, or using FFM.

6. RESULTS IN PRODUCTION

Fliptop has deployed DQMs for several companies, and the initial results have shown definite benefits for both marketing and sales. Here we describe results for two sellers, called company C and company D.

6.1 Company C

The experiments with historical data show that we can best increase revenue using a full funnel model. However, the main goal of company C was to improve its marketing team's conversion rate, so a DQM was a good solution for it. Instead of giving explicit ranks, the DQM assigned four grades (A, B, C, D) by splitting the leads into deciles based on their ranking. These scores were then made visible in the sales team's CRM system.

The teleprospectors focused on qualifying A and B leads, and during three months (October 2014 to December 2014), Fliptop collected statistics on how the DQM improved the lead conversion rate and time needed to qualify leads. The conversion rate increased from 8% to 17% during these three months. In addition, the company found another unexpected benefit: the average time needed to qualify a lead went from 20 days to 7 days. This last statistic suggests that a three class model that takes into account the class `WON` produces benefits by accelerating the qualification process as well as by closing more sales.

6.2 Company D

This company provides a software tool to a variety of different types of customers. Fliptop built multiple DQM models for company D, with each model corresponding to a different customer type, or "vertical." The company and Fliptop worked together to collect statistics on the performance of DQM for the Dental and Lifestyle verticals. For two months (November and December 2014), they split the sales team into two groups: a control group that did not see Fliptop grades, and a test group that did see A, B, C, and D grades. The company and Fliptop took care that the two separate teams had similar historical conversion rates and rates at which they succeeded in scheduling demos for leads.

The team that used Fliptop for the dental vertical had a 31% higher conversion rate, and the lifestyle vertical had a 37% higher conversion rate. Additionally, the average number of times the sales team called a lead before conversion was 35% worse in the control group (35 calls versus 26 telephone calls) and the average number of demos scheduled per call placed was 28% better in the test group (3.6% versus 2.8%). These metrics indicate that the high quality leads uncovered by DQM are superior even in metrics that we are not optimizing over. The reduction in calls placed and in days to qualify a lead represent a significant decrease in workload for a sales team. Therefore the DQM has an even greater benefit impact, and potentially a positive impact in revenue, than the metrics in Section 5 might indicate.

7. CONCLUSION

This paper introduces two methods for modeling prospective customers moving through a sales funnel, called DQM and FFM. We examine how these two models can be used to perform predictive lead scoring. In order to provide benefit to a sales team, we design these models in such a way that they do not simply learn to duplicate a company's existing lead qualification rules, which can be error-prone and often do not take into account enough features. Instead we focus on predicting events further along in the sales process, in particular the likelihood of a successful close and expected revenue. Experiments show that applying these models to actual company data achieves high accuracy, both for classifying lead conversion and for predicting an ultimately successful future sale.

We also demonstrate that the model is predictive whether or not a lead has activity data, which means that high quality leads can be identified even before they take actions that can be tracked by the marketing team. We compare the two methods directly and conclude that FFM is more advantageous if there is more variance in the average sales price, because it can prioritize based on expected sales price, or if lead and opportunity databases cannot be reliably linked.

Production results show that DQM is successful in deployment, and that it has additional benefits for a sales team, separate from the metrics we are directly optimizing over. These include decreased time needed to qualify leads, and decreased number of phone calls placed by sales representatives in order to qualify leads and move them forward through the sales funnel.

Table 4: Expected results if companies A and B can only contact 20% of leads.

Company	Method	Conversion rate	Close rate	Total revenue ($)
A	Random	39.6%	16.6%	1,545
A	DQM	92.2%	67.6%	346,793
A	FFM	93.7%	40.3%	3,556,043
B	Random	8.4%	4.6%	2,619,493
B	DQM	27.7%	22.1%	8,009,377
B	FFM	26.1%	21.9%	12,149,051

8. REFERENCES

[1] M. J. Berry and G. S. Linoff. *Data mining techniques for marketing, sales, and customer relationship management.* John Wiley & Sons, 2004.

[2] I. Bose and R. K. Mahapatra. Business data mining—a machine learning perspective. *Information & Management*, 39(3):211–225, 2001.

[3] G. Cui, M. L. Wong, and H.-K. Lui. Machine learning for direct marketing response models: Bayesian networks with evolutionary programming. *Management Science*, 52(4):597–612, 2006.

[4] C. Elkan and K. Noto. Learning classifiers from only positive and unlabeled data. In *Proceedings of the 14th ACM SIGKDD international conference on Knowledge discovery and data mining*, pages 213–220. ACM, 2008.

[5] J. H. Friedman. Greedy function approximation: A gradient boosting machine. *Annals of Statistics*, pages 1189–1232, 2001.

[6] J. H. Friedman. Stochastic gradient boosting. *Computational Statistics & Data Analysis*, 38(4):367–378, 2002.

[7] S. Kaufman, S. Rosset, C. Perlich, and O. Stitelman. Leakage in data mining: Formulation, detection, and avoidance. *ACM Transactions on Knowledge Discovery from Data (TKDD)*, 6(4):15, 2012.

[8] P. Kotler, N. Rackham, and S. Krishnaswamy. Ending the war between sales and marketing. *Harvard Business Review*, 84(7/8):68, 2006.

[9] R. T. Moriarty and G. S. Swartz. *Automation to boost sales and marketing*. Harvard Business Review, Reprint Service, 1989.

[10] F. Pedregosa, G. Varoquaux, A. Gramfort, V. Michel, B. Thirion, O. Grisel, M. Blondel, P. Prettenhofer, R. Weiss, V. Dubourg, J. Vanderplas, A. Passos, D. Cournapeau, M. Brucher, M. Perrot, and E. Duchesnay. Scikit-learn: Machine learning in Python. *Journal of Machine Learning Research*, 12:2825–2830, 2011.

[11] M. J. Shaw, C. Subramaniam, G. W. Tan, and M. E. Welge. Knowledge management and data mining for marketing. *Decision support systems*, 31(1):127–137, 2001.

[12] A. Smith and C. Elkan. Making generative classifiers robust to selection bias. In *Proceedings of the SIGKDD International Conference on Knowledge Discovery and Data Mining (KDD)*, pages 657–666. ACM Press, 2007.

[13] B. Zadrozny and C. Elkan. Obtaining calibrated probability estimates from decision trees and naive Bayesian classifiers. In *Proceedings of the 18th International Conference on Machine Learning*, pages 609–616. Morgan Kaufmann, June 2001.

Online Topic-based Social Influence Analysis for the Wimbledon Championships

Varun R Embar
IBM Research, India
varembar@in.ibm.com

Indrajit Bhattacharya
IBM Research, India
indrajbh@in.ibm.com

Vinayaka Pandit
IBM Research, India
pvinayak@in.ibm.com

Roman Vaculin
IBM Research, NY, USA
vaculin@us.ibm.com

ABSTRACT

Various industries are turning to social media to identify key influencers on topics of interest. Following this trend, the All England Lawn Tennis and Croquet Club (AELTC) is keen to analyze the 'social pulse' around the famous Wimbledon Championships. IBM developed and deployed social influence analysis capability for AELTC during the 2014 edition of the Championship. The design and implementation of influence analysis technology in the real world involves several challenges. In this paper, we define various functional and usability criteria that social influence scores should satisfy, and propose a multi-dimensional definition of influence that satisfies these criteria. We highlight the need to identify both all-time influencers and recent influencers, and track user influences over multiple time-scales for this purpose. We also stress the importance of aspect-specific influence analysis, and investigate an approach that uses an aspect hierarchy that annotates tweets with topics or aspects before analyzing them for influence. We also describe interesting insights discovered by our tool and the lessons that we learnt from this engagement.

Categories and Subject Descriptors

H.2.8 [**Database Management**]: Database Application—*Data mining*

Keywords

Social Influence Analysis; Wimbledon; IBM; multi-dimensional; aspect-specific; multiple time-scales; online updates

1. INTRODUCTION

The last few years have seen unprecedented adoption of social media forums all over the world. Analyzing social media data has emerged as one of the best ways to gain insight into social trends, individual preferences, and community behavior. Initially, analysis of social media data largely meant analysis of sentiment, brand value, network structure, etc. Of late, a new aspect of social media forums has been gaining attention. Social media platforms provide various modes of interaction between users, and these interactions carry signals of authority or influence of any user over others in the network. This aspect of analyzing influence signals in social media data is called social influence analysis. Its applications are in marketing, law enforcement, social sciences, etc. Recently, social influence analysis has received concerted attention of the research community as well as the industry. In this paper, we present our experience of deploying a social influence analysis platform for the 2014 Wimbledon Tennis Championship.

The Wimbledon Championship is one the four Grand Slam tennis tournaments, and ranks among the most popular sporting events in the world. In the social and mobile era, the tournament generates large volumes of social conversations throughout the tournament. The All England Lawn Tennis and Croquet Club (AELTC), which organizes the event, has recognized its social footprint and has been particularly keen on analyzing the social buzz and on providing the social media users an immersive experience during the tournament. IBM has been the official technology partner for the tournament since 1990. In 2014, IBM helped AELTC deploy the Social Media Command Center (SMCC) on site at Wimbledon. The SMCC was open for visiting executives, journalists and industry practitioners to get a 'social perspective' of the Wimbledon.

Deploying a robust and useful social influence analysis tool in the real world involves many technical challenges. The first and foremost is coming up with a robust, interpretable and useful definition of social influence. It is important to recognize that social media has many unique features of interaction, and simply borrowing notions of influence from other domains is not sufficient. In order to be useful, influence has to be tied to topics. A user who is an influencer for technology may not be an influencer for the arts. The dynamism of social media interactions makes static notions of influence irrelevant. Influence scores need to evolve all the time taking into account new data that becomes available. Moreover, measuring influence at a single time-scale does not reveal all influencers. To take an analogy from literature, we need to be able to detect the likes of Shakespeare who is an 'all-time' influencer, and also the likes of Stephen King, who is indeed an influencer but at a significantly smaller time-scale. Finally, the tool needs to be able to handle data at very large volumes and update influence

KDD'15, August 10-13, 2015, Sydney, NSW, Australia.
© 2015 ACM. ISBN 978-1-4503-3664-2/15/08 ...$15.00.
DOI: http://dx.doi.org/10.1145/2783258.2788593.

scores at (near) real-time. To give an example, about 200 thousand relevant tweets were generated per hour during the final day at Wimbledon 2014.

Before we proceed, we briefly comment about the various existing social influence analysis tools, techniques and services. We survey these approaches in greater detail in Sec. 2. There are many research papers that are relevant for influence analysis. Some of them focus completely on Twitter data [30], while others consider the more general problem of network inference [16]. The main drawbacks of these approaches are that they are offline in nature yielding static influence scores, and typically require non-trivial adaptation for real-life settings. There are several commercial services offering influence analysis, such as Klout, Kred, etc. These typically provide a single influence score that is hard to interpret and act upon. Most such services have also not been deployed for large scale event analysis.

Given this context, one of our main tasks was understanding what constitutes a good definition of social influence of a user. We came up with two sets of requirements, which we called the functional and usability requirements.

The *functional requirements* state that the definition of influence should cover all the unique features of social media (specifically Twitter) data. Specifically, the influence measure should account for the following:

- the importance of the user in the structure of social network
- the user's engagement with her followers and other users
- the reach and the speed of the user's messages in the network

In comparison, the *usability requirements* state that the influence score should be easy to use and act upon. We elaborate upon its different aspects below.

- The measure should be natural and intuitive. Users who are commonly acknowledged as influencers on any topic should in general score high according to the influence measure. For example, the official Wimbledon Twitter handle and popular tennis star Roger Federer, who tweets frequently and has many active followers, should be natural choices for the top tennis influencers.
- Since the scores will be exposed to the world, they should be easily interpretable. For example, in the case of analyzing node influence in static networks, the pagerank of a webpage has a natural interpretation — it is the probability that a random surfer will be on the webpage at any time. Similarly, the definition of social influence should also have a natural interpretation that is accessible to a typical social user.
- The social influence score should lead to actionable insights. Any user should be able to analyze her influence score and have an understanding of what actions can help in increasing her score. Alternatively, the influence score should help an analyst designing a viral marketing campaign decide which influencers can help propagate the marketing message far and which influencers can spread it quickly.
- The score should be refreshable quickly based on new data. This implies that the score should not be complex. Instead, it should be possible to compute and also update the scores using efficient algorithms.

Given these seemingly conflicting requirements that we set for ourselves, we take a multi-dimensional approach for defining social influence. We develop a suite of scores each of which is individually natural, interpretable, actionable and easily computable. Each score covers a subset of the functional requirements, while the suite as a whole covers the entire set. The individual scores are also topic or aspect specific. The final influence score is obtained by aggregating the individual scores in an appropriate fashion. This multi-dimensional nature ensures robustness of the score, and also helps in speeding up computation since the individual scores can be computed in parallel. We use a two-stage approach for aspect-specific influence analysis, where the posts are first annotated and grouped according to a hierarchy of aspects, and then posts in each of the aspects are independently analyzed for influence. Finally, all the scores are online or time-sensitive. Since our data accumulates over time, we analyze influence for every user at every time step at multiple time-scales. Using short term and long term horizons, we identify both *all-time influencers* and *recent influencers.*

The rest of this paper is organized as follows. We first discuss existing approaches for influence analysis in Sec. 2. We describe our data, and define the social influence analysis problem and the multi-dimensional influence measure in Sec. 3. Next, the algorithms for computing the influence scores in batch and online fashion and for aggregating the individual scores are described in Sec. 4. A description of the overall system architecture is presented in Sec. 5 before discussing actual data and insights from the Wimbledon engagement in Sec. 6. We end by discussing the impact of the engagement and the lessons that we learnt from it in Sec. 7.

2. RELATED WORK

Analysis of social media data has grown into a vast body of research spanning multiple disciplines and has myriad applications. Among the different social platforms, Twitter has emerged as an important source for social media analysis driven by the Twitter APIs and the rich structure of the tweets. The literature on social network analysis of Twitter data is very broad and an exhaustive survey is beyond our scope. It covers whole range of applications such as information filtering [26], sentiment and opinion analysis [21, 25], detecting emerging topics [22], event detection [27], usage during emergency events [19], analysis of political events [10], and marketing [20]. We will focus on influence analysis in the rest of this section.

Influence Analysis on Twitter Graph: A comprehensive study of influence analysis on Twitter data was carried out by Cha et. al [13]. They considered in-degree, number of retweets, and number of mentions as parameters of influence of a user. They studied the influence of about 6 million users on a population of 54 million users and arrived at three key findings: (i) the in-degree of a node is not necessarily an indicator of top influence, (ii) a top influencer is often an influencer on multiple topics, and (iii) influence profile is not built overnight, but through concerted efforts. An similar analysis was carried out by Ye and Wu [30]. Bakshy et.

al [11] conducted influence analysis on Twitter data by looking at the cascade of tiny URLs. They looked at 74 million cascades of tiny URLs among a population of 1.6 million users. Their influence score was a variant of retweet count which roughly looks at 'tiny URL count' . They concluded that the longer cascades were mostly started by influential users. Other papers have adapted the notion of PageRank and its topic-sensitive variant to the Twitter world. The most notably of these is 'Twitterrank' [28]. This approach produces results that are very different from, and sometimes qualitatively better than, those based on counting in-degree, retweets, and mentions.

Relation to Network Inference: The problem of inferring a diffusion network cascade of information through the network was introduced by Gomez-Rodriguez et. al [16] and has evolved into a rich body of research[16, 24, 17, 23, 15]. The idea is to model the cascade as a result of a diffusion process over the network defined by the influence relationships between the nodes. However, such an approach has not so far been used for analysis of real world events, or in an online setting.

Commercial Services: There are several companies that offer influence analysis as a commercial service, such as Klout [2], Kred [3], PeerIndex [5], and Twitalyzer [7] to name a few. Klout provides a "klout score" that ranges from 1 to 100. But the algorithm for the computation of the score is not revealed and hence the score is not interpretable. Kred computes two scores (Influence and Outreach) for each user, and have made their algorithms public. Their influence score reflects the trust reposed on a user by others and Outreach reflects the user's generosity in spreading other user's messages. Klout and Kred have reported influence analysis of some events, but only in offline settings [1, 4]. Services offered by PeerIndex are similar to those of Klout and Kred. Twitalyzer's approach is based on the observation that Klout-like scores change slowly over time. Twitalyzer combines a user's Klout score with analysis of their most recent activities to provide a dynamic view of the user's influence.

Our main innovation in the context of these myriad tools, techniques and services is that we address the problem of online influence analysis considering topics and multiple timescales. We also focus on developing a score that is multidimensional and interpretable. Among the individual scores in our suite, we introduce a new measure based on the network inference literature that captures the rate at which the user's tweets diffuse over her network of followers. Such a score has not previously been explored for influence analysis on Twitter. We also adapt this score to consider topics and to work in an online setting. This multi-dimensional approach proved extremely effective in terms of robustness and the richness of insights that it provided.

3. PROBLEM DEFINITION AND SOCIAL INFLUENCE SCORES

In this section, we formally define the online social influence analysis problem based on the Wimbledon requirement. We begin by discussing Twitter data from the perspective of influence analysis, then formally define the representation of the data that we used for our analysis, and formalize the problem of identifying influential users based on this representation. Finally, we address the definition of user-specific influence scores. While it is possible to generalize our approach to deal with data from other social media applications, we will not dwell further on this topic here.

3.1 Influence Cues in Twitter

The two different aspects of Twitter data relevant for influence analysis are (a) the follower graph and diffusion of tweets over it and (b) the content of the tweets.

Follower graph and Tweet diffusion: Each user in Twitter is identified by her unique id or *handle*. The Twitter network consists of all users and the 'follow' relation between them. We will call the directed graph induced on the Twitter users by the follow relations the *follower graph*. A typical user broadcasts a message of her interest by posting (or *tweeting*) the message on the Twitter network. This tweet then becomes visible to all her followers. The followers can *retweet* the message in turn if they wish, which will then be visible to their followers. The follower graph grows when users choose to become followers of other users. A users acquires followers because of various reasons, but mostly because she is either a celebrity or an expert, whose tweets are of interest to others.

Clearly, the number of followers of any user is an indication of her influence in the network. Higher order notions of 'centrality' of the user in the follower network provide deeper insight into this influence. Additionally, the rate at which tweets of the user spread over the network via retweets is also indicative of her influence.

Content of Tweets: The other unique feature of Twitter data is the content of the tweets. The tweets are short — 140 characters including spaces. As a result of this brevity, tweets are almost always directed towards a very small set of topics, usually just one. A user also has the option of adding interpretable structure in the content of her tweet. She may refer to other users using their handles. These are called *mentions*. She may also include labels in her Tweet, called *hashtags*, which then become available for reuse by her followers and other users.

Using such interpretable structure, it is relatively easy to annotate tweets with additional inferred structure, such as higher level topics. First, these annotations can be used for focused or topic-specific influence analysis, for example counting references to specific topics or to specific users. Secondly, these provide an additional indication of any user's influence through the mentions. Often (but not always), a retweet of a message can be regarded as an endorsement or expression of interest towards the original tweet. Therefore, such annotations carry signals of social influence in the network.

These features highlight the uniqueness of Twitter data from the perspective of influence analysis. In network data such as tele-communication call detail records (CDRs) and emails in the Enron archive for example, the communications are directed. Telephone calls occur between two users, and emails between a sender and small set of recipients. In contrast, Twitter messages are broadcast. Also, unlike in Twitter, there is no specific notion of responding to a phone call, while email responses go back to the sender. As regards content, annotation of phone calls and emails, even assuming that they are acceptable from the privacy view-point, is significantly harder to perform at any acceptable combination of accuracy and computational complexity. Thus, any existing approach of user influence analysis in such networks is not suitable for Twitter. It calls for approaches tailored specifically to handle its unique features, which we address in this paper.

3.2 Influence Analysis: Problem Definition

Having informally identified the various sources of user influence in Twitter data, we now formally define the influence analysis problem. We do this in three parts. We define the representation of annotated Twitter data, the hierarchy of aspects which are used for annotating the data, and then the task of analyzing this annotated data for user influence.

Annotated Twitter Data: Let us denote the Twitter follower graph as $G_f = (U_f, E_f)$ over users U_f and containing directed follow edges $(u, v) \in E_f$ denoting that user u follows user v. Twitter data is made available for analysis through third party providers such as GNIP[1]. Such data does not include the follower graph G_f or the set of all users U_f. Instead, it only contains a collection of tweets.

The data for our problem consists of tweets collected and annotated over a sequence of time intervals or epochs. We represent this data as $D = \{D_t\}_{t=1}^{T}$, where D_t is the data from the tth epoch and there are T epochs in all. In practice, each epoch may correspond to an hour or a day, and the duration T may span several days, weeks or months. The data $D_t = \{D_{t,a}\}_{a=1}^{A}$ for each epoch is grouped according to topics or *aspects* belonging to a given set of aspects A. We will separately discuss the design of the aspect set. The data $D_{t,a}$ for each epoch-aspect combination consists of a collection of tweets $\{d_{t,a,i}\}_{i=1}^{n_{t,a}}$.

Since we do not compare tweets across epochs or aspects in our analysis, we will not use the subscript t, a for individual tweets, unless specifically required. Each tweet d_i contains multiple attributes and is represented as $(u_i, t_i, r_i, m_i, f_i)$. Here u_i is the user posting the tweet and t_i is the time at which the tweet was posted. Note that the set of all users mentioned in $D_{t,a}$ is a subset of all users: $U_{t,a} \subset U_f$. The retweet attribute r_i is a list of attributes of the original tweet for tweets that are retweets, and is empty otherwise. The attribute r_i has complete information about the original tweet, but we only consider $r_i.u$ and $r_i.t$, which denote the user and the posting time of the original tweet. The mention attribute m_i is the set of users mentioned in the textual content of the tweet, and is empty for tweets with no mentions. Finally, the follower attribute f_i denotes the number of followers of the user u_i at time t_i. This attribute is redundant when the follower graph G_f is available at any time. However, since G_f is unknown in our case, f_i is an informative attribute.

Organization of Aspects: The tweets relevant for a popular event such as Wimbledon span a diverse set of topics. So it is important to understand the influence of users at the level of topics, and not analyze all tweets under a single general category. We denote the set of all topics or *aspects* by A. In the case of Wimbledon, the aspects are arranged in the form of a hierarchy. This helps to capture the relationships between aspects and share data across aspects for analysis. Intuitively, each node of this hierarchy is an aspect, and its child nodes are its sub-aspects, capturing more granular topics. The leaves of the hierarchy represent the most fine-grained aspects. Each aspect at level l, which is denoted by A_l, is the child of one of the aspects at level $l - 1$. The number of levels is denoted by L. The root aspect a_0 is also called the *General aspect.* Some example of aspects at the next level ($l = 1$) for Wimbledon were *Grounds, Players, Sponsors,* etc.

Each subset $D_{t,a}$ in the data D_t for an epoch t corresponds to one of the aspects (leaf or internal) of the hierarchy A, and the total number of subsets is $|A|$. Each tweet is labeled with at least one path through the hierarchy starting with the General or root aspect a_0. The set of tweets for aspects at the same level may be overlapping. In other words, the same tweet may belong to multiple paths through the hierarchy.

Such annotation is typically done by rule-based algorithms that consider a set of keywords and hashtags associated with each aspect $a_{l,j}$ and the textual content of a tweet d_i, and use regular expressions for matching the two. While designing such algorithms have their own challenges, we will not discuss such algorithms further in this paper and consider the annotations as input.

Top Influencers: Assume that we are given an appropriate definition $I(u, D)$ of the influence of an user u based on a set of tweets D in our representation. Let $U(D)$ denote all relevant users for tweets D, i.e. the unique users who appear as the user u_i or in the retweet r_i or mention m_i attributes of any tweet $d_i \in D$. Let $D^*_{t,a} = \cup_{t'=1}^{t} D_{t',a}$ denote the accumulated data for aspect a from the first epoch as the start epoch ($t_s = 1$) up to epoch t as the end epoch ($t_e = t$). Given such aspect-annotated tweets and the definition of $I(u, D)$, our task for every epoch t is two-fold. First, we need to identify the *all-time top influencers* over all epochs starting from $t = 1$, e.g. since the beginning of the Wimbledon tournament. For this, we need to compute the influence of each individual user $u \in U(D)$ for tweets $D \in \{D^*_{t,a}\}$ and then find the top-k influencers for each aspect $a \in A$ for each epoch t.

This definition cannot find users who are very influential for some time segment of the tournament, but are not influential over the entire tournament. Therefore, we also need to find the *recent top influencers.* This implies addressing the same problem as above with a start epoch $t_s \neq 1$. For Wimbledon, we needed to find influencers for the last 24 hours.

3.3 Defining Social Influence

We now come to the important task of defining social influence $I(u, D)$ of a user u based on a collection of tweets D. The definition must capture the different features of social media data. We call these *functional requirements.* These require the social influence definition to capture **(a)** the importance of the user in the follower graph, e.g in terms of number of followers and centrality, **(b)** her engagement with her followers and other users, in terms of mentions, retweets, etc., and **(c)** the reach of the users message in the network, in terms of the volume of her tweets and how readily the followers respond to her tweets.

Additionally, there are various requirements elaborated in Section 1 related to the consumption or usage of the influence score by broad spectrum of analysts and users. We refer to these as *usability requirements.* These require the score to be natural and intuitive, interpretable, actionable and refreshable at (near) real-time.

It is difficult to come up with a single social influence score that satisfies all the above requirements. Instead, we focus on developing different influence scoring functions, each of which is individually natural, intuitive, interpretable. Each

[1]https://gnip.com/

score individually covers a subset of the functional requirements, while ensuring that together the scores cover all the functional requirements. One advantage of such a multi-dimensional definition is that these score are simple and independent of each other, so that they can be computed efficiently and in parallel.

Formally, we define K influence scores $\{I_1(u, D), I_2(u, D), \ldots, I_K(u, D)\}$ for each user, which are finally aggregated. We discuss aggregation techniques at the end of this section. We later demonstrate in the paper that this multi-dimensional nature also makes the definition robust. It is essential for a user to score well across multiple dimensions to emerge as influential. In other words, while it is possible for a user who is truly not influential to 'fool' an individual dimension, fooling many dimensions simultaneously is unlikely.

Specifically, we consider 5 different dimensions of social influence:

Follower strength: This is a network-centric measure and refers to the number of followers of a user. We denote this as $I_f(u, D)$. Recall that the number of followers of a user u is available as an attribute in tweets posted by u. Therefore $I_f(u, D) = f_i$, where d_i is the latest post by user u in D.

According to this definition, for each aspect, all users who posted on that aspect are assigned some follower strength. However, this definition is not specific to any aspect or even Wimbledon. Imagine a Hollywood celebrity, with a huge number of followers tweeting about Wimbledon. Her follower score will suggest that she is an influencer, even if none of her followers are interested about Wimbledon. Additionally, the followers may not all be active. We investigate this further in Sec. 6.

Activity: This captures the number of tweets posted by a user. We denote this as $I_a(u, D)$ and define $I_a(u, D) = \sum_{d_i \in D} \delta(u_i = u)$, where $\delta(a = b)$ is the indicator function which evaluates to 1 if the argument is true and to 0 otherwise. This indicates the volume of the user's activity in the network.

Engagement: This is the number of retweets and mentions of a user. This is denoted as $I_e(u, D)$ and we define $I_e(u, D) = \sum_{d_i \in D}(\delta(r_i.u = u) + \sum_{m \in m_i} \delta(m = u))$. This is indicative of the popularity of the user in tweets by other users.

Authority or Network centrality: This captures the centrality of a specific user in an user graph. To capture centrality of a user in a graph, we use the popular PageRank score used for ranking web-pages on the internet [12]. We denote this as $I_c(u, D)$, and define $I_c(u, D) = p(u, \hat{G}(D)$, where $\hat{G}(D)$ is a graph over users reconstructed from tweet set D, and $p(u, G)$ denotes the PageRank score of a vertex u in a graph G. The graph over users may be the follower graph, retweet graph or mention graph. In our work, we used the engagement graph considering retweets and mentions. Note that the follower graph is not directly observed in our data. We discuss reconstruction of the follower graph and other graph construction in Section 4). Also note that when the tweets D correspond to different aspects, we get aspect-specific measures of PageRank.

Response rate or Timeliness: None of the scores above consider the temporal nature of tweet diffusion over the network. While the engagement score captures the volume of response to a user, it is also informative from the perspective of influence analysis to measure how quickly a user's tweets reach her followers. A user who can regularly, consistently and quickly draw a response from a large number of other users is clearly very influential in the network. To capture this, we define response rate as the rate at which other users respond to the user's tweets in the form of retweets. We denote this as $I_r(u, D)$. Assuming that the delays $(t_v - t_u)$ between a tweet by user u and its retweet by user v follow an exponential distribution $f(t_v|t_u; \alpha_{uv}) = \alpha_{uv} \exp(-\alpha_{uv}(t_v - t_u))$ with *transmission rate* parameter α_{uv}, we define $I_r(u, D; t)$ to be the expected number of retweets for a single tweet by user u by all other users within a delay t. Under the assumption of the exponential distribution, this leads to the following definition:

$$I_r(u, D; t) = \sum_{v \in U}(1 - \exp(-\hat{\alpha}_{uv}(D)t)) \qquad (1)$$

where $\hat{\alpha}_{uv}(D)$ is the estimate of parameter α_{uv} from tweets in D. This problem has been studied in the context of network inference [16] but not for influence analysis in Twitter. (We discuss estimation of α_{uv} parameters in Section 4.2). A very significant aspect of this score is its predictive nature — it captures future reach of a user's tweets over the network.

We next investigate how well the scores satisfy the requirements that we had stated upfront. Individually, the metrics are natural and intuitive in that any true influencer is expected to score well according to these metrics. They are easily interpretable by a lay-person. In terms of computational complexity, some are easier to compute than others, and we will show analytically in the next section that all of them admit efficient algorithms that generate good approximations if not the exact scores. Thus, the scores satisfy all our usability requirements.

The scores also satisfy the functional requirements. The follower graph is covered by follower strength, network centrality and response rate scores, user activity and engagement are covered by the activity, engagement and timeliness scores, and readiness of followers is covered by the response rate score.

It is worth mentioning that the *Klout score* of each user is also available in our data as an attribute of each tweet. However, like the follower attribute, this does not have any relevance for any specific subset of tweets, e.g. those relevant for Wimbledon. We will show in our experiments that this score on its own is not very useful for us.

Aggregating Influence Scores: Earlier in the section, we have highlighted the advantages of multi-dimensional influence analysis. However, this approach comes with a challenging overhead. These multiple influence scores need to be aggregated to produce a single influence score for each user. We believe that this in itself is a challenging research problem, that can build upon existing work in rank aggregation [14]. Formally, for each user $u \in U$ we have 5 influence scores $I_a(u)$, $I_f(u)$, $I_e(u)$, $I_c(u)$ and $I_r(u)$. The task is to compute an aggregate score $I^*(u)$ for user u. We discuss algorithms for this in Sec. 4.4

4. ALGORITHMS

In this section, we present the algorithms for computing the influence scores defined in Section 3.3. Recall that one of the key usability requirements is to have efficient algorithms for computation of the scores. Given the scale of tweets for an event like Wimbledon, the computation of the influence scores at the end of epoch t should be 'incremental' in the sense that it should not mean discarding the computations done on data D^*_{t-1} and redoing the computation on D^*_t. In this section, we will consider such online algorithms for influence scores. We have seen in the previous section that we are required to compute influence scores over different subsets of tweets. For example, for each aspect, we need to compute scores on the all-time data and on the recent data. In this section, we define the algorithms to compute each of the scores $I(u, D)$ over a generic set of tweets D. The same algorithm is then run on different tweet collections as required.

User Graph Construction: For many of the influence scores, the algorithms require a graph over users as one of the inputs. As mentioned in Section 3.1, even the follower graph is not directly observed in the data available to us. As a result, such graphs need to be reconstructed from the data. Before moving on to algorithms for computing influence scores, we first address this problem.

Let us first consider the follower graph G_f. Formally, given a collection of tweets D, the task is to estimate from D the follower edges (u, v) indicating that user u follows user v. The only evidence in the tweets about follower edges are the retweets. This is because a user u retweets user v only if u follows v, or in other words, (u, v) is an edge in the follower graph. For any tweet d_i with non-empty r_i, we add an edge $(u_i, r_i.u)$ in the retweet graph G_r. Based on this, the retweet edges from a set of tweets D is $E_r(D) = \cup_{d_i \in D}\{(u_i, r_i.u)\}$. We consider the resultant *retweet graph* $G_r(D) = \{U, E_r(D)\}$ also as the *reconstructed follower graph* $\hat{G}_f(D)$ from tweets D.

Alternatively, some scores may require the *mention graph* $G_m = \{U, E_m\}$, where (u, v) is a mention edge between users u and v if u mentions v in some tweet. Based on this, we construct the mention edges from a set of tweets D as $E_m(D) = \cup_{d_i \in D} \cup_{m \in m_i} \{(u_i, m)\}$. We also consider the *engagement graph* $G_e = \{U, E_e\}$, where (u, v) is an engagement edge if u has either retweeted or mentioned v. This can be obtained simply taking the union of the follower and mention edges.

4.1 Updating Follower strength, Activity and Engagement

The definitions of Follower strength, Activity and Engagement scores, as seen in Sec. 3.3, are quite straight-forward and the scores can be computed very efficiently. Specifically, for Follower strength $I_f(u, D)$, the algorithm initializes all scores to 0 and makes one pass over all the tweets $d_i \in D$. For each tweet d_i, it updates the follower strength $I_f(u_i, D)$ of u_i as f_i. At the end of the pass, the follower strengths of all users appearing in D are available.

The algorithms for Activity score $I_a(u, D)$ and Engagement score $I_e(u, D)$ are similar. On scanning each tweet $d_i \in D$, the algorithm for Activity increments $I_a(u_i, D)$ by 1 and the algorithm for Engagement increments $I_e(r_i.u, D)$ by 1 and $I_e(u_j, D)$ by 1 for all $u_j \in m_i$.

Let us now consider the online settings for these scores, where we have a current score $I(u, D^*_t)$ for each user at the end of epoch t, and it needs to be updated based on a new set of tweets D_{t+1} at epoch $t+1$. A naive approach is to recompute the score $I(u, D^*_{t+1})$ from scratch over the aggregated tweets D^*_{t+1}. However, this completely disregards the existing score $I(u, D^*_t)$, which we would like to reuse and restrict our computation to only the new data D_{t+1}. This online or incremental approach turns out to be straight-forward for all three scores. The algorithm proceeds exactly as in the batch setting, with the scores for each user initialized to their current scores $I(u, D^*_t)$ instead of 0 and then scans over the tweets D_{t+1}.

4.2 Updating Response Rate Scores

We now come to the Response rate score, which is significantly more sophisticated than the three earlier scores. Recall that for computing this score, we need to find the estimate $\hat{\alpha}_{uv}(D)$ of the 'transmission rate' parameter α_{uv} parameter between users u and v from a collection of tweets D. We consider the maximum likelihood (ML) estimate. Since the transmission rate is modeled as an exponential distribution, the ML estimate is given by $\hat{\alpha}_{uv}(D) = \frac{\rho_{uv}(D)}{\Delta_{uv}(D)}$, where $\rho_{uv}(D)$ and $\Delta_{uv}(D)$ are defined as follows [16, 15]:

$$\rho_{uv}(D) = \sum_{d_i \in D} \delta(r_i.u = v)\delta(u_i = u)$$

$$\Delta_{uv}(D) = \sum_{d_i \in D} \delta(r_i.u = v)\delta(u_i = u)(t_i - r_i.t)$$

Intuitively, $\rho_{uv}(D)$ indicates the total number of times u has retweeted v in D, and $\Delta_{uv}(D)$ is the cumulative delay between tweets by v and their retweets by v in D.

Based on this definition of the ML estimate, the batch algorithm for computing the Response rate scores computes $\rho_{uv}(D)$ and $\Delta_{uv}(D)$ from the tweets in D, then the estimate $\hat{\alpha}_{uv}(D)$ for each edge in the retweet graph G_r, and finally the expectations for each user u over all followers v as in Eqn 1. The second and third operations take $O(E_r(D))$ time. Let us now consider the algorithm for computing ρ and Δ. This algorithm is very similar in spirit to those for the first three scores. It initializes all ρ and Δ counts to 0, and makes a single pass over the tweets in D and updates the scores. For tweet $d_i \in D$, if it is a retweet, it increments $\rho_{u_i, r_i.u}(D)$ by 1 and $\Delta_{u_i, r_i.u}$ by $t_i - r_i.t$. The correct $\rho_{uv}(D)$ and $\Delta_{uv}(D)$ values for all follower edges are available at the end of the pass. Thus this algorithm takes $O(|D|)$ time and the end-to-time time to compute Response rate scores is $O(|D|) + O(|E_r(D)|)$.

Now we come to the online algorithm, where we have existing values $\rho_{uv}(D^*_t)$ and $\Delta_{uv}(D^*t)$ at the end of epoch t and we need to update the scores based on data D_{t+1} from the next epoch $t+1$. The approach for this is again straight-forward. Since $\rho_{uv}(D^*_{t+1}) = \rho_{uv}(D^*_t) + \sum_{d_i \in D_{t+1}} \delta(r_i.u = v)\delta(u_i = u)$, we can use exactly the same algorithm as in the batch setting with the initial scores changed from 0 to $\rho_{uv}(D^*_t)$. Online computation of $\Delta_{uv}(D^*_{t+1})$ follows a very similar approach. Once we have the updated ρ and Δ values for all retweet edges, the Response rates for all users can again be updated in $O(|E_r(D_{t+1})|)$ time.

4.3 Computing Network Centrality

We finally come to the most computationally demanding influence score in our suite, which is the Network centrality score. Recall that for the network centrality score $I_n(u, D)$ for a user u based on data D, we need to compute the PageRank $p(u, G_e(D))$ of user u in the engagement graph $G_e(D)$ constructed using tweets in D. The PageRank $p(u, G)$ of a vertex in a graph G is defined recursively in terms of the Pagerank of its neighbors $N(u)$ in the graph. In the simplest version, $p(u, G) = \sum_{v \in N(u)} p(v, G)/d(v, G)$, where $d(v, G)$ is the degree of the vertex v in graph G. A typical PageRank algorithm starts with some initial values for the PageRanks of all vertices, and then iteratively updates the values for each vertex based on the current PageRanks of its neighbors. The algorithm terminates when there is no significant change in the PageRank values.

There are many scalable open-source implementations of PageRank. We experimented with many of these implementations to determine the right framework for the expected number of users for the Wimbledon data. An Apache Giraph implementation of this algorithm exchanges messages between individual vertices and runs on top of MapReduce [2]. The Jung library [3] has an in-memory implementation that uses a Markov Chain representation for the edges between vertices and uses the power method for computing the stationary distribution. For the expected size of the user graph for our use-case, we found a centralized in-memory framework to be more suitable.

Unlike our other scores, incremental computation of PageRank scores is a very challenging problem that has attracted recent research [18]. However, we were able to compute the Pagerank scores from scratch on the accumulated data D_t^* for each epoch in time before the data D_{t+1} for the next epoch arrived. Therefore, we decided to use the batch algorithm for Wimbledon.

4.4 Aggregating Influence Scores

Given 5 influence scores $I_a(u)$, $I_f(u)$, $I_e(u)$, $I_c(u)$ and $I_r(u)$, we now address the problem of computing an aggregate score $I^*(u)$ for user u. A simple aggregation technique is to directly aggregate the scores for each user, for example, using a linear combination: $I^*(u) = \sum_k I_k(u) \times w_k$. However, this has several issues. Individual scores are not normalized, and the best normalization is not obvious. There are many outlier scores, for example in the case of followers, which would drown all other scores in a linear combination. A better option is to bypass the actual scores and consider just the ranking of users for each score, where $R_i(u)$ now indicates the rank of user u for the ith influence score. Then, instead of aggregating scores, we aggregate the ranks of individual users.

Optimal rank aggregation is known to be a hard problem, and the individual ranked lists that we need to aggregate are extremely long since they are over all users. A computationally easier approach is Borda's method [14]. In its simple form, this approach computes the average rank of each user, and then creates the final list by sorting the average rank. This is computationally straight-forward but suffers from some drawbacks. For example, consider a user who is top-ranked in all the lists except one, where she has a low rank. This user's overall rank would be very low in this approach. We considered three different rank scoring functions for each user: (a) *Average rank*, which is essentially the approach above, (b) *Top rank*, which considers the best rank for a user, and (c) *Average Top-k rank* which takes the average of $k(< 5)$ best ranks for a user. The third approach worked best for us, as we demonstrate in Sec. 6.

[2]http://giraph.apache.org/pagerank.html
[3]http://jung.sourceforge.net/doc/api/edu/uci/ics/jung/algorithms/scoring/PageRank.html

5. SYSTEM DESIGN

In this section, we briefly describe the architecture of the Social Influence Analysis tool deployed at Wimbledon.

The Influence Analysis (IA) tool was one component of the larger Social Media Analysis framework that IBM deployed at Wimbledon. This larger framework obtained tweets in JSON format from the GNIP Twitter feed every hour, filtered these to extract tweets relevant for Wimbledon, annotated the Wimbledon-related tweets using the Aspect hierarchy, and deposited the hourly batch files in the IA server. The responsibility of the IA tool was to compute the all-time and daily influence scores for every aspect and expose the scores of the top 100 users through Rest APIs at the end of the hour.

Extraction of tweets relevant for Wimbledon was done using a multi-stage algorithm. First, this includes all tweets that contained words and hashtags from a Wimbledon and tennis-specific dictionary, followed by all tweets posted by users from a pre-specified list including all players participating in the Wimbledon tournament, etc. This was followed by a spam-filtering step, where all tweets matching certain regular expressions were filtered out. These steps were extremely crucial for the success of the engagement, but we do not go into further details in this paper.

On the Influence Analysis server, a cron job monitored the arrival of new data batches. When a data batch arrived, this job invoked the modules that compute the individual influence scores in parallel. These modules, on completion, wrote two sets of influence scores, one for the all-time scores and another for the daily scores, in two JSON files, each containing the scores for every user for every aspect. Once all individual scores were available, the scores for each user were aggregated and the top 100 users and their scores were written into database tables. On invocation through the Rest APIs the scores were retrieved from the database. The entire system was deployed on a cloud platform.

The IA tool also included two user interfaces. The external user interface embedded within the Social Media Analysis tool displayed the top 9 all-time influencers and their individual influence scores. Aside from this, there was an internal user interface containing all details about the influence sores, and included the ability to slice and dice according to days and aspects, sort users according to aggregate and individual scores, and view the original tweets of users. This was primarily meant for verifying the accuracy of the ongoing analysis, and diagnosing any surprises that may appear during the course of the tournament. In Sec. 6, we demonstrate the strength of the internal UI with an example insight that we were able to discover through it.

6. EXPERIMENTAL RESULTS

In this section, we discuss quantitative details of the Wimbledon engagement, including the data and the influence scores, and the some insights that we derived from the scores.

Summary of the data: We first discuss properties of the annotated data for Wimbledon that we were required to analyze for social influence. The 2014 Wimbledon tournament started on Monday, June 23rd, and continued until Sunday, July 6, when the Men's Singles Final was played.

The aspect hierarchy was hand-crafted ahead of time, and had 3 levels and 23 nodes in total. The highest level contained the *General Aspect*, while the aspects in the second level were *Broadcasters, Celebrities, Commentators, Grounds, Players, Sponsors, Tennis, Travel* and *Weather.* There were 14 aspects in the third level, all of them under *Celebrities.*

Table 1: Statistics of the hourly data

	Min	Max	Avg	Std. Dev.
Tweets	0	215,839	8,315	14,458
ReTweets	0	65,224	3,461	5,045
Users	0	130,490	5,979	9,343

We received fresh batches of tweets every hour. In other words, one epoch corresponded to 1 hour. In totality, the data had about 4.8 million tweets, 1.6 million users, 1.5 million retweets and 6.2 million engagements (retweets and mentions). The volume of data per hour varied greatly over the tournament, peaking every day during the matches, and peaking over days before reaching the largest volume on the last day during the Men's Singles Final. In Tab. 1, we record this the summary of this temporal pattern for the total number of tweets, the number of users and the number of retweets for the *General Aspect.* Observe the large range and standard deviation for all 3 characteristics.

Table 2: Kendall Tau (upper triangle) and Jaccard (lower triangle) among top influencers across aspects: Broadcasters, Celebrities, Commentators, Grounds, Players, Sponsors, Tennis and Travel

	Br	Ce	Co	Gr	Pl	Sp	Te	Tr	We
Br		-0.37	-0.33	-0.32	-0.36	-0.46	-0.36	-0.48	-0.40
Ce	0.05		-0.34	-0.28	-0.32	-0.45	-0.29	-0.45	-0.34
Co	0.09	0.09		-0.31	-0.31	-0.43	-0.28	-0.46	-0.37
Gr	0.11	0.13	0.11		-0.31	-0.44	-0.17	-0.45	-0.23
Pl	0.06	0.11	0.09	0.11		-0.45	-0.22	-0.45	-0.35
Sp	0.03	0.02	0.04	0.03	0.02		-0.43	-0.47	-0.41
Te	0.08	0.13	0.12	0.21	0.18	0.04		-0.45	-0.26
Tr	0.00	0.02	0.01	0.02	0.02	0.01	0.02		-0.45
We	0.05	0.07	0.06	0.08	0.08	0.06	0.13	0.02	

Aggregate analysis of influence scores: We now come to the user influence scores computed on top of this data. As mentioned earlier, we maintained two different running influence scores for each user for each aspect. One was the *all-time influence score*, which indicates the influence score for the user since the beginning of the tournament to the current hour (or epoch), and the other was the *recent* or *daily* influence score, which indicates the influence of the user over the previous 24 hour window. Because of space constraints, here we only present details and analysis for the *all time influence score* computed at the end of the tournament.

We first provide some aggregate insight on the influence scores in Tab. 2 and Tab. 3 before analyzing user-specific scores. In Tab. 2, we show the correlation among the top-100 influencers (according to the aggregated influence score) for pairs of second-level aspects. Specifically, for each pair of aspects, we report two scores for their top-100 influencers. The Jaccard score is the ratio of the intersection and the union of the two sets. This score lies in the range $[0, 1]$ and higher scores indicate better agreement. Since this score disregards rank differences, we also calculate the Kendal-Tau rank correlation coefficient. This is defined as (no. concordant pairs - no. of discordant pairs) / total no. of pairs, where concordant pairs are those whose relative orders are preserved in the two rankings, and discordant pairs are those whose orders are flipped. We adjust this definition for top-k rankings, which need not have the same elements, by splitting the pairs missing in one of the lists equally between concordant and discordant. This lies in $[-1, +1]$ where higher scores indicate better agreement. We can see that the largest Jaccard score is 0.21. Even when there is overlap, there is very little agreement in terms of ranking. This shows that influencers vary greatly across aspects, and therefore categorizing influencers according to aspects is important. The scores indicate some shared influencers for (Tennis, Grounds) and (Tennis, Players), which is intuitive, and also for (Celebrities, Grounds), which is not as intuitive.

Table 3: Kendall Tau (upper triangle) and Jaccard (lower triangle) for top influencers across Influence scores

	Activity	Engagement	Followers	Centrality	Resp Rate
Activity		-0.45	-0.50	-0.47	-0.45
Engagement	0.04		-0.39	0.07	0.24
Followers	0.00	0.05		-0.40	-0.38
Centrality	0.02	0.36	0.05		-0.08
Resp Rate	0.03	0.47	0.06	0.28	

Next, in Tab. 3 we similarly analyze correlations between the individual influence scores for the General aspect. The largest correlation is 0.47 with Jaccard (0.24 with Kendall-Tau) between Engagement and Response Rate. Centrality has a Jaccard score of 0.36 with Engagement, being computed on top of the Engagement graph, and of 0.28 with Response Rate. Follower strength and activity are not correlated with the others or with each other. These scores clearly demonstrate the need for the multi-dimensional approach, and that none of the influence scores are redundant.

Analysis of user-specific influence scores: We next present an analysis of influence scores at the level of users. Naturally, no gold-standard rankings were available for evaluation. But we anecdotally verified the rankings and scores through the duration of the tournament for the different influence scores and for different aspects to the extent possible. In Tab. 4, we show the top-5 users in terms of the individual influence scores for the General Aspect. Observe that Activity and Follower strength on their own did not yield meaningful influencers for Wimbledon. Expectedly, the top users for Activity post in huge volumes without much engagement, and those for Follower strength have millions of followers but are not very relevant for Wimbledon. We also show the top users according to the Klout scores, which we did not use though available in our data. We can see that ranking according to raw Klout scores is not very relevant for Wimbledon. The Engagement, Centrality and Response Rate scores are the most interesting. While there is some overlap in these 3 lists, there are differences as well. Many of the top influencers here, such as the official Wimbledon handle, and popular tennis players Federer, Bouchard, Murray, Djokovic, are natural candidates for appearing at the top of the list. However, there are some surprising names as well. For example, popular boy band One Direction members Liam Payne and Niall Horan are not intimately related to tennis or Wimbledon, but appear at the top in these lists. On investigation using our internal UI, we found that both of them posted single tweets about Wimbledon that went viral very quickly, explaining their high Response Rate scores. Notably, both also have millions of followers.

The influence scores over the the duration of the tournament presented many interesting insights. We briefly mention some of them here. Basketball player Shaquille O'Neal was among the top celebrity influencers at the end of the first day (24th hour), by virtue of mentions after he was observed

Table 4: Top 5 General influencers according to different influence scores

Rank	Activity	Engagement	Followers	Centrality	Response Rate	Klout
1	YSMLive	Wimbledon	instagram	Wimbledon	Wimbledon	Forbes
2	yoursportmanuk	rogerfederer	twitter	rogerfederer	NiallOfficial	guardian
3	yoursportmanng	NiallOfficial	NiallOfficial	andy_murray	Real_Liam_Payne	nytimes
4	yoursportman	BritishTennis	cnnbrk	geniebouchard	BBCSport	CNN
5	thatsportman	geniebouchard	Real_Liam_Payne	DjokerNole	ESPNTennis	AP

in the stands, even though he did not tweet about Wimbledon at all. He never appeared among top influencers after that. Similarly, celebrity cricketer Sachin Tendulkar was among the top recent influencers for a few hours on the 10th day (July 2nd). This demonstrates the need for recording the recent influencers, which picks up such notable but temporary trends that are too insignificant in the long term to be picked up by the all-time influencer score. Another interesting insight was that Roger Federer's soccer related tweets (about the World Cup which was also going on at the same time) contributed more to his influence score than his tweets about Wimbledon. This did not show up automatically in our analysis, which did not have a soccer aspect, pointing to the short-coming of having fixed and pre-determined aspects. We were able to pick this up by diagnosing Federer's influence using the internal user-interface, which proved to be very useful during the course of the engagement.

Table 5: Top overall influencers according to different aggregation methods

	Top 1	Top 3	Avg(Top 5)	Wtd. Avg.
1	Wimbledon	Wimbledon	Wimbledon	Wimbledon
2	instagram	NiallOfficial	BBCSport	rogerfederer
3	YSMLive	rogerfederer	livetennis	geniebouchard
4	NiallOfficial	Real_Liam_Payne	MeridianoTV	NiallOfficial
5	rogerfederer	geniebouchard	bbc5live	Real_Liam_Payne

Analysis of influence-aggregation methods: Finally, we do an analysis of different influence aggregation methods. In Tab. 5, we show the top 5 influencers according to different aggregation methods that we discussed in Sec. 4.4. Considering the top-rank for a user does not work very well, as is it not very robust. The average of all ranks is not a good alternative either, since it is unlikely for genuine candidates to rank high across all influence dimensions. Average of top-3 ranks and ranking by weighted average of all scores are much better options. Interestingly, the top 5 users are identical (though reordered) for these two lists.

In summary, our experiments demonstrate that for social influence analysis in a real-world setting an aspect-oriented, multi-dimensional and online approach with multiple temporal resolutions is necessary and useful.

7. IMPACT AND LESSONS LEARNT

In this section, we summarize the real-world impact achieved by the Social Influence Analysis engagement at Wimbledon 2014. We also look at the lessons learnt from this engagement and highlight some research challenges that need to be addressed for greater impact in the future.

Impact: The Social Influence Analysis Engine was deployed as part of the Social Command Center (SMCC) developed by IBM to provide insights about the tournament. The deployment proved to be extremely successful according to multiple metrics.

The deployment got prominent coverage in press. At least four prominent broadcasters (CNBC, Bloomberg, Sky News and BBC), 25 independent articles in national and prestigious media outlets (Wall Street Journal, NewsWeek, Guardian, Reuters, Forbes, Techweek, London Evening Standard, Computer Weekly, eWeek and others) and many Business and Trade forums reported the innovation[6, 9]. AELTC publicly praised the role of the Social Command Center in the success of Wimbledon 2014. Special tours of the Social Command Center at Wimbledon were conducted for at least 300 executives from industry and press. IBM Leaders appeared in TV programs and wrote popular blogs on the capability[8]. Buoyed by the success of the Wimbledon engagement, the Social Influence Analysis capability became part of an announced solution and has since generated interest from clients. The technology has been used successfully in Proofs of Concepts with clients from different industries. As a follow up after Wimbledon 2014, the same capability was also successfully deployed recently at the Australian Open Tennis Championships 2015 with a minimum of effort, demonstrating the reproducibility of the framework and the generalizability of the algorithms within.

Lessons Learnt: In parallel with the overall success, the Social Influence Analysis engagement with Wimbledon also made us aware of some deficiencies in our analysis, which need to be addressed in the future versions of this framework. We highlight some of the main challenges here.

We used a multi-dimensional approach to influence analysis, which was largely successful. However, the individual influence scores have room for improvement. We found that number of followers was not very useful for aspect-specific analysis. The followers also need to be interested and active in that aspect. Also, some scores will be more useful than others, and we expect this usefulness to be engagement specific. Thus, as the size of the influence suite grows, more work will need to be done around score aggregation.

A novel aspect of our analysis was the use of multiple temporal windows for online influence analysis. We scored each user for a specific epoch, for all epochs, and also for the most recent epoch. This proved to be extremely useful and necessary for separating out 'influence blips' from long-term influence. However, we did not have tools for analyzing influence patterns over time, and had to fall back on manual analysis, which yielded many interesting insights. Integrating time-series analysis techniques to detect patterns and anomalies in influence change over time would be an important area of future work.

The aspect hierarchy used for annotating the tweets was fixed and defined ahead of time using domain knowledge about tennis and Wimbledon and the expected consumers of the insights. While simplicity of deployment and interpretability of the aspects are the main motivations of this approach, it can also be a serious shortcoming. Many of the leaf-level aspects did not accumulate enough tweets, indicating that they were either not significant or incompletely defined. Additionally, this leaves no room for surprising topics that were not expected ahead of time and yet generated a lot of conversation, such as soccer-related conversation in our case. Specifically, this calls for online topic detection techniques that can identify new topics on the fly and also allow enhancements and modifications for existing topics. While this area has seen some research recently[29], this needs to be tied seamlessly with influence analysis. On a related note, the filtering algorithm determines a fine balance between precision of the analysis and its coverage. Our filtering algorithm was biased towards high precision, resulting in a smaller volume of very related tweets. This also meant that we could not detect many relevant and possibly important tweets. For example, all tweets of yesteryears star John McEnroe were missed because of his unusual language though they were very relevant for Wimbledon.

The network centrality or PageRank score proved to be a key score in our suite. The volume of data for this engagement could be handled by batch algorithms for PageRank. However, this is unlikely to hold true in all scenarios. Therefore, it is important to have online algorithms for PageRank, in spite of their implementation challenges.

In summary, we have presented our online, multi-dimensional approach for topic-specific social influence analysis which was successfully deployed for the Wimbledon 2014 Tennis Championships. The engagement helped us appreciate both the usefulness and the challenges of social influence analysis in a real-world setting. We believe that our experience will benefit us in improving our tool and also the broader social media analysis community in their understanding of an important problem and its real-world demands.

8. REFERENCES

[1] 75 days of the occupy movement. `http://blog.klout.com/2011/12/75-days-of-the-occupy-movement/`. Accessed: 2015-02-17.

[2] Klout. `https://klout.com/home`. Accessed: 2015-02-17.

[3] Kred. `http://kred.com`. Accessed: 2015-02-17.

[4] Kred analysis. `http://blog.kred.com/category/kred-analysis/`. Accessed: 2015-02-17.

[5] PereIindex. `http://www.peerindex.com/`. Accessed: 2015-02-17.

[6] Roger federer is wimbledon's twitter champion. `http://www.standard.co.uk/news/london/roger-federer-is-wimbledons-twitter-champion-9567728.html`. Accessed: 2015-02-20.

[7] Twitalyzer. `http://www.twitalyzer.com`. Accessed: 2015-02-17.

[8] Wimbledon - Social Media Command Center. `http://jonmell.co.uk/wimbledon-social-media-command-centre/`. Accessed: 2015-02-20.

[9] Wimbledon and IBM get closer to digital tennis fans. `http://www.bbc.com/news/business-27861327`. Accessed: 2015-02-20.

[10] A.Tumasjan, T. Sprenger, P. Sandner, and I. Welpe. Predicting elections with twitter: What 140 characters reveal about political sentiment. In *ICWSM*, 2010.

[11] E. Bakshy, J. Hofman, W. Mason, and D. Watts. Everyone's an influencer: quantifying influence on twitter. In *WSDM*, 2011.

[12] S. Brin and L. Page. The anatomy of a large-scale hypertextual web search engine. *Computer Networks*, 30(1-7), 1998.

[13] M. Cha, H. Haddadi, F. Benevenuto, and P. Gummadi. Measuring user influence in twitter: The million follower fallacy. In *ICWSM*, 2010.

[14] C. Dwork, R. Kumar, M. Naor, and D. Sivakumar. Rank aggregation methods for the web. In *WWW*, 2001.

[15] V. Embar, R. Pasumarthi, and I. Bhattacharya. A bayesian framework for estimating properties of network diffusions. In *SIGKDD*, 2014.

[16] M. Gomez-Rodriguez, J. Leskovec, and A. Krause. Inferring networks of diffusion and influence. *ACM TKDD*, 5(4), 2012.

[17] M. Gomez-Rodriguez and B. Schölkopf. Influence maximization in continuous time diffusion networks. In *Proceedings of the International Conference on Machine Learning (ICML)*, 2012.

[18] D. Hong. Optimized on-line computation of pagerank algorithm. *Arxiv*, 2012.

[19] A. Hughes and L. Palen. Twitter adoption and use in mass convergence and emergency events. *International Journal of Emergency Management*, 6(3), 2009.

[20] B. Jansen, M. Zhang, K. Sobel, and A. Chowdury. Twitter power: Tweets as electronic word of mouth. *Journal of the American Society for Information Science and Technology*, 60(11):2169–2188, 2009.

[21] E. Kouloumpis, T. Wilson, and J. Moore. Twitter sentiment analysis: The good the bad and the omg! In *ICWSM*, 2011.

[22] M. Mathioudakis and N. Koudas. Twittermonitor: trend detection over the twitter stream. In *SIGMOD*, 2010.

[23] S. Myers and J. Leskovec. On the convexity of latent social network inference. In *NIPS*, 2010.

[24] P. Netrapalli and S. Sanghavi. Learning the graph of epidemic cascades. In *ACM SIGMETRICS*, 2012.

[25] A. Pak and P. Paroubek. Twitter as a corpus for sentiment analysis and opinion mining. In *Proceedings of the International Conference on Language Resources and Evaluation, LREC*, 2010.

[26] B. Sriram, D. Fuhry, E. Demir, H. Ferhatosmanoglu, and M. Demirbas. Short text classification in twitter to improve information filtering. 2010.

[27] J. Weng and B. Lee. Event detection in twitter. In *ICWSM*, 2011.

[28] J. Weng, E. Lim, J. Jiang, and Q. He. Twitterrank: finding topic-sensitive influential twitterers. In *WSDM*, 2010.

[29] W. Xie, F. Zhu, J. Jiang, E. Lim, and K. Wang. Topicsketch: Real-time bursty topic detection from twitter. In *ICDM*, 2013.

[30] S. Ye and F. Wu. Measuring message propagation and social influence on twitter.com. *Int. Jour. of Communication Networks and Distributed Systems*, 11(1), 2013.

Collective Spammer Detection in Evolving Multi-Relational Social Networks

Shobeir Fakhraei*
University of Maryland
College Park, MD, USA
shobeir@cs.umd.edu

James Foulds
University of California
Santa Cruz, CA, USA
jfoulds@ucsc.edu

Madhusudana Shashanka†
if(we) Inc.
San Francisco, CA, USA
shashanka@alum.bu.edu

Lise Getoor
University of California
Santa Cruz, CA, USA
getoor@soe.ucsc.edu

ABSTRACT

Detecting unsolicited content and the spammers who create it is a long-standing challenge that affects all of us on a daily basis. The recent growth of richly-structured social networks has provided new challenges and opportunities in the spam detection landscape. Motivated by the *Tagged.com*[1] social network, we develop methods to identify spammers in evolving multi-relational social networks. We model a social network as a time-stamped multi-relational graph where vertices represent users, and edges represent different activities between them. To identify spammer accounts, our approach makes use of structural features, sequence modelling, and collective reasoning. We leverage relational sequence information using k-gram features and probabilistic modelling with a mixture of Markov models. Furthermore, in order to perform collective reasoning and improve the predictive power of a noisy abuse reporting system, we develop a statistical relational model using hinge-loss Markov random fields (HL-MRFs), a class of probabilistic graphical models which are highly scalable. We use *Graphlab Create*™ and *Probabilistic Soft Logic (PSL)*[2] to prototype and experimentally evaluate our solutions on internet-scale data from *Tagged.com*. Our experiments demonstrate the effectiveness of our approach, and show that models which incorporate the multi-relational nature of the social network significantly gain predictive performance over those that do not.

*Contribution partly performed while under internship at if(we) Inc., formerly Tagged Inc.

†Currently with Niara, Inc., Sunnyvale, CA.

[1] *Tagged.com* was founded in 2004, has over 300 million registered members, and is aimed towards fostering new connections between people.

[2] `http://psl.umiacs.umd.edu`

KDD'15 August 11-14, 2015, Sydney, NSW, Australia

ACM 978-1-4503-3664-2/15/08 ...$15.00
DOI: http://dx.doi.org/10.1145/2783258.2788606.

Keywords

Social Networks, Spam, Social Spam, Collective Classification, Graph Mining, Multi-relational Networks, Heterogeneous Networks, Sequence Mining, Tree-Augmented Naive Bayes, k-grams, Hinge-loss Markov Random Fields (HL-MRFs), Probabilistic Soft Logic (PSL), Graphlab.

1. INTRODUCTION

Unsolicited or inappropriate messages sent to a large number of recipients, known as "spam", can be used for various malicious purposes, including phishing and virus attacks, marketing of objectionable materials and services, and compromising the reputation of a system. From printed advertisements to unsolicited phone calls, spam has been a perennial problem in modern human communication. With the emergence of the Internet, spammers have found a cost-effective medium to reach a broader audience than was previously possible. Email spam is almost as old as the Internet itself. The first email spam was sent in 1978 to all several hundred users of ARPANET [1].

More recently, social media has given spammers a new and effective medium to spread their content. Using social media platforms, spammers can disguise themselves as legitimate users and engage in realistic looking interactions. They can use these platforms to send messages to users, leave spam comments on popular pages, and reply to legitimate comments using spam content. Such diversity of choice has often increased spammers' ability to conceal their intentions from traditional spam filters. According to a study by Nexgate [2], social spam grew by more than 355% between January to July of 2013, one in 200 social messages contain spam, and 5% of all social apps are spammy.

While content-based approaches have been shown to be effective in stopping spam in email and the web, they can be manipulated by sophisticated spammers via incorporating content randomness. Unlike in email and the web, social media enables spammers to split their content across multiple messages in order to bypass spam filters. Link-based approaches that leverage the connectivity of the entities, have been combined with content-based methods to build more effective methods. While it is easier to pass traditional content-based filters, behavioral patterns and graph properties of the users' interactions are harder to manipu-

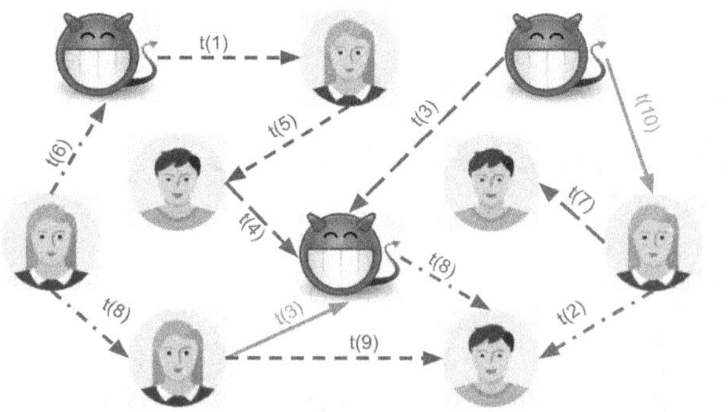

Figure 1: A time-stamped multi-relation social network with legitimate users and spammers. Each link $\langle v_1, v_2 \rangle$ in the network represents an action (e.g. profile view, message, or poke) performed by v_1 towards v_2 at specific time t.

late. Furthermore, many social networks can not monitor all the generated contents due to privacy and resources concerns. Content-independent frameworks, such as the one proposed in this paper, can be applied to systems that provide maximum user privacy with end-to-end encryption.

Perhaps the most important difference between social networks and email or web graphs is that social networks have a multi-relational nature, where users have relationships of different types with other users and entities in the networks. For example, they can send messages to each other, add each other as friends, "like" each other's posts, and send non-verbal signals such as "winks" or "pokes." Figure 1 shows a representation of a social network as a time-stamped multi-relation graph. The multi-relational nature provides more choices for spammers, but it also empowers detection systems to monitor patterns across activity types, and time. In this paper, we propose a content-independent framework which is based on the multi-relational graph structure of different activities between users, and their sequences.

Our proposed framework is motivated by *Tagged.com*, a social network for meeting new people which was founded in 2004 and has over 300 million registered members. More generally, the framework is applicable to any multi-relational social network. Our goal is to identify sophisticated spammers that require manual or semi-automated intervention by the administrative security team. These spammers have already passed initial classifiers and know how to manipulate their accounts and contents to avoid being caught by automatic filters. We show that our framework significantly reduces the need for manual administration to control spam.

Our framework consists of three components. First, we extract graph structure features for each of the relations and show that considering the multi-relational nature of the graphs improves the performance. Second, we consider the activity sequence of each user across these relations and extract k-gram features and employ mixtures of Markov models to label spammers. Third, we propose a statistical relational model based on hinge-loss Markov random fields to perform collective reasoning using signals from an abuse reporting system in the social network.

The following sections formally define the problem and our solution framework along with an experimental validation of our approach on internet-scale data from *Tagged.com*.

2. PROBLEM STATEMENT

We represent a social network as a directed time-stamped dynamic multi-relational graph $\mathcal{G} = \langle \mathcal{V}, \mathcal{E} \rangle$, where $\mathcal{V}$ is the set of vertices of the form $v = \langle f_1, \ldots, f_n \rangle$ representing users and their demographic features f_i, and $\mathcal{E}$ is the set of directed edges of the form $e = \langle v_{src}, v_{dst}, r_i, t_i \rangle$ representing their interactions, relation type r_i, and a discrete time-stamp t_i. The social spam detection problem is to predict whether v_i with an unobserved label is a spammer or not, based on the given network $\mathcal{G}$ and a set of observed labels for already identified spammers. Since the deployed security system could employ different measures based on the classification confidence, we are interested in (un-normalized) probabilities or ranking scores of the likelihood that each user is a spammer. In other words, the problem is assignment of a score (e.g., a probability) to user accounts to rank them from the most to the least probable spammer in the system: $c : v_i \rightarrow [0, 1]$.

3. OUR METHOD

In our framework, we focus on three different mechanisms to identify spammers and malicious activities. We first create networks from the user interactions and compute network structure features from them. As these are evolving networks, each user generates a sequence of actions with the passage of time. Mining these sequences can provide valuable insights into the intentions of the user. We use two methods to study these sequences and extract features from them. We use the output of these methods as features to classify spammers. We then employ a collective model to identify spammer accounts only based on the signals from the abuse reporting system ($\mathcal{G}_{\text{report}}$) as a secondary source to reassure predictions. The following sections discuss our framework and extracted features in more details.

3.1 Graph Structure Features ($\mathbf{x}_{\mathcal{G}}$)

We create a directed graph $\mathcal{G}_r = \langle \mathcal{V}, \mathcal{E}_r \rangle$ for each relation r in the social network, where vertices $\mathcal{V}$ consist of users, and edges $\mathcal{E}_r$ represent interactions of type r between users, e.g. if user$_1$ sends a message to user$_2$ then $\mathcal{G}_{\text{message}}$ will contain v_1 and v_2 representing the two users, and $e_{1,2}$ representing the relation between them. We have ten different graphs each containing the same users as vertices but different actions as edges.

We use *Graphlab Create*™[3] to generate features based on each of these graphs for each user. We use six graph analytics methods m_i to compute the features. Using each m_i we create a set of features for each relation graph $\mathcal{G}_r$ as following:

$$\mathbf{X}_{\mathcal{G}_\mathbf{r}}^{m_i} = \left[\, \mathbf{X}_{\mathcal{G}_{r_1}}^{m_i} \, \ldots \, \mathbf{X}_{\mathcal{G}_{r_n}}^{m_i} \, \right]$$

where m_i is one of the graph analytics methods described below, and r_i is one of the relationships considered in the study.

We then use these features together to get a complete multi-relational graph feature-set, as the following:

$$\mathbf{X}_{\mathcal{G}_\mathbf{r}}^{\mathbf{m}} = \left[\, \mathbf{X}_{\mathcal{G}_\mathbf{r}}^{m_1} \, \ldots \, \mathbf{X}_{\mathcal{G}_\mathbf{r}}^{m_k} \, \right]$$

The graph analytics methods m_i we use to extract the features from each relation network are described in the fol-

[3]http://dato.com/products/create

lowing section. Each of these algorithms provieds different perspectives on the local connectivity of the graph and neighborhood characteristics of each user. Our goal is to capture the structural differences between spammers' and legitimate users' multi-relational neighborhood graph.

PageRank:

PageRank [3], is a well known ranking algorithm proposed for ranking websites, and computes a score for each node by considering the number and quality of links to a node. The algorithm is based on the underlying assumption that important nodes receive more links from other nodes.

Degree:

We compute the total degree, in-degree, and out-degree of each node for each relation, which correspond to the total number of activities a user has been involved in, the number of communications (or actions) a user received, and the number of actions the user performed.

k-core:

k-core [4] is a centrality measure that is based on the graph decomposition via a recursive pruning of the least connected vertices. The value each vertex receives depends on the step in which the vertex is eliminated from the graph. e.g, vertices removed on the third iteration receive the value three.

Graph Coloring:

Graph coloring [5] is an assignment of colors to elements (here vertices) of a graph, such that no two adjacent vertices share the same color. Using a greedy implementation, we obtain the color identifier of each vertex as a feature.

Connected Components:

A connected component [6] is a group of vertices with a path between each vertex and all other vertices in the component. A weakly connected component is a maximal set of vertices such that there is an undirected path between any two vertices in the set. We compute the weakly connected component on each graph and extract the component identifier and size of the component that the vertex participates in as features.

Triangle Count:

The triangle count [7] of a vertex is the number of triangles (a complete subgraph of three vertices) in the graph the vertex participates in. Such number is an indication of the connectivity of the graph around that vertex.

3.2 Sequence-Based Features ($\mathbf{x}_S$)

Sequence classification is used in many domains, including biology and health-informatics, anomaly detection, and information retrieval [8]. In dynamically evolving multi-relational social networks, each user v_i generates a sequence of edges via their actions as the following:

$$\mathcal{S}^{v_i} = \langle r_p, \ldots, r_q \rangle$$

Spammers typically pursue specific purposes in the network and it is likely that their sequence of actions diverge from the norm. In this section we study these sequences and provide two different solutions for classifying users based on their activity sequences. It is important to note that such an approach would not be possible if the network were not multi-relational.

Sequential k-gram Features

The simplest way to represent a sequence with features is to treat each element in the sequence as a feature independently. However, the order of the sequence cannot be captured with this approach. Furthermore, in our scenario the values of these features will be the same as the out-degree for each vertex, which we previously computed in the graph-based features. To address this, a short sequence segment of k consecutive actions, called a k-gram, can be used to capture the order of events [8]. The sequence can be represented as a vector of the frequencies of the k-grams. To keep the feature space computationally manageable we chose bigram sequence features where $k = 2$. For example, the number of times a user v_i sent a *message* after performing a *profile view*, would be the value for the feature $x^{v_i}_{\text{profileview-message}}$. The bigram feature set for the sequence $\mathcal{S}$ will be the following:

$$\mathbf{X}_{\mathcal{S}_B} = \left[\ \mathbf{X}_{r_1 r_1} \ \ldots \ \mathbf{X}_{r_p r_q} \ \ldots \ \mathbf{X}_{r_n r_n}\ \right]$$

where r_i is one of the relationships considered in the study, $\mathbf{X}_{r_p r_q} = \left[x^{v_1}_{r_p r_q} \ldots x^{v_n}_{r_p r_q}\right]^\intercal$, and $x^{v_i}_{r_p r_q}$ is the total number of times user v_i performed an action of type r_q consecutively after performing r_p.

Mixture of Markov Models

While k-gram features capture some aspects of the order of elements in the sequence, they may miss patterns in longer sequences. Increasing k will rapidly increase the feature space, introducing computational barriers and estimation challenges due to feature sparsity. Instead, to capture the salient information from longer sequence chains, and to study the predictive power of this information, we construct a simple generative model for sequence data. The model is equivalent to the chain-augmented naive Bayes model of [9], a special case of the tree-augmented naive Bayes model [10] which has been shown to be effective in language modelling. The model posits that each user's actions are generated via a mixture of Markov models. In more detail, each class (spammer or not spammer) is associated with a mixture component y. Conditional on the class (mixture component) y for a user, that user's sequence of actions are assumed to be generated from a Markov chain specific to that class. The joint probability for a user's class y and action sequence $x_i, \ldots, x_n$ is given by

$$P(y, x) = P(y)P(x_1|y)\prod_{i=2}^{n} P(x_i|x_{i-1}, y) \ ,$$

which we summarize with a directed graphical model diagram in Figure 2. We place symmetric Dirichlet priors on the parameters of the discrete distributions $P(y)$, $P(x_1|y)$, and $P(x_i|x_{i-1}, y)$, and compute maximum a posteriori (MAP) estimates of them, which are readily obtained as the proportion of each outcome in the training data, with the counts first adjusted by adding the Dirichlet smoothing parameter $\alpha = 1$. Finally, at test time we compute the posterior probability of the user's class label given the observed action sequence x via Bayes rule, $P(y|x) \propto P(x|y)P(y) = P(y, x)$.

There are multiple methods to incorporate the predictions from this model into our framework. We simply use the

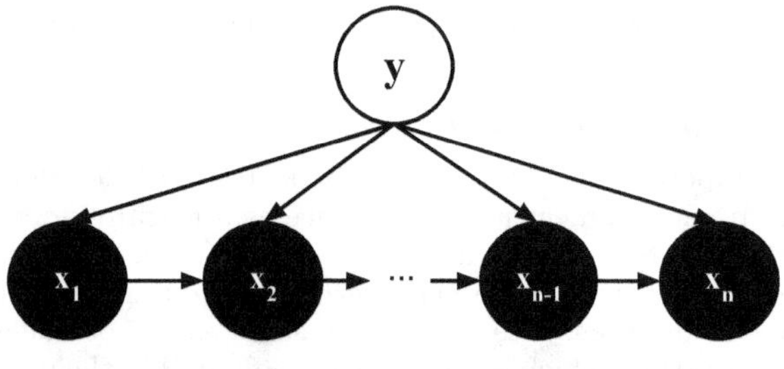

Figure 2: The directed graphical model for the mixture of Markov models / chain-augmented naive Bayes model, for one user. In the diagram, y indicates the label (spammer or not) and x_i represents the ith action performed by the user.

ratio of posterior probabilities and their logarithmic forms as a small feature-set ($\mathbf{X}_{\mathcal{S}_M}$) for our classifier.

3.3 Collective Classification with Reports

Most websites that enable users to publish content also provide an *abuse reporting* mechanism for other users to bring malicious behavior to the system's attention. However, these systems do not necessary offer clean signals. Spammers themselves often randomly report other users (spammers and legitimate users) to increase the noise, legitimate users often have different standards for malicious behaviors, and users may report others for personal gains such as censorship or blocking an opponent in a (social) game from accessing the system. A model that can extract sufficient information from the relational *report* feature, can enhance the administrative team's performance by focusing their attention, and can also provide an additional feature or parallel mechanism for spam classification.

We propose a model based on hinge-loss Markov random fields [11] to collectively classify spammers within the reported users, and assign credibility scores to the users offering feedback via the reporting system. Using this model a better ranking of the reported users based on their probability of being spammers can be provided to the security administration team. The hinge-loss formulation has the advantage of admitting highly scalable inference, regardless of the structure of the network.

Hinge-loss Markov Random Fields

Hinge-loss Markov random fields (HL-MRFs) are a general class of conditional, continuous probabilistic models [11, 12]. HL-MRFs are log-linear models whose features are hinge-loss functions of the variable states. Through constructions based on *soft logic*, hinge-loss potentials can be used to model generalizations of logical conjunction and implication. A hinge-loss Markov random field P over random variables $\mathbf{Y}$ and conditioned on random variables $\mathbf{X}$ defines a conditional probability density function as the following:

$$P(\mathbf{Y}|\mathbf{X}) = \frac{1}{Z(\lambda)} \exp\left[-\sum_{j=1}^{m} \lambda_j \phi_j(\mathbf{Y},\mathbf{X})\right] ,$$

where Z is the normalization constant of the form

$$Z = \int_{\mathbf{Y}} \exp\left[-\sum_{j=1}^{m} \lambda_j \phi_j(\mathbf{Y},\mathbf{X})\right] .$$

In the above, ϕ is a set of m continuous potential of the form

$$\phi_j(\mathbf{Y},\mathbf{X}) = \left[\max\{\ell_j(\mathbf{Y},\mathbf{X}), 0\}\right]^{p_j} ,$$

where ℓ is a linear function of $\mathbf{Y}$, and $\mathbf{X}$ and $p_j \in \{1,2\}$.

Probabilistic Soft Logic (PSL) [12] uses a first-order logical syntax as a templating language for HL-MRFs. HL-MRFs have achieved state-of-the-art performance in many domains including knowledge graph identification [13], understanding engagements in MOOCs [14], biomedicine and multi-relational link prediction [15, 16], and modelling social trust [17]. A typical example of a PSL rule is

$$\lambda : P(a,b) \wedge Q(a) \rightarrow R(b),$$

where P, Q, and R are *predicates*, a and b are *variables*, and λ is the weight associated with the rule, indicating its importance. For instance, $P(a,b)$ can represent a relational edge in the graph such as $\textsc{Reported}(a,b)$, and $Q(a)$ could represent a value for a vertex such as $\textsc{Credible}(b)$. Each grounding forms a ground atom, or logical fact, that has a soft-truth value in the range $[0,1]$. The rules can encode domain knowledge about dependencies between these predicates. PSL uses the *Lukasiewicz* norms to provide relaxations of the binary connectives to soft-truth values. A ground instance of a rule r ($r_{\text{body}} \longrightarrow r_{\text{head}}$) is satisfied when the value of r_{body} is not greater than the value of r_{head}. ℓ is defined to capture the distance to satisfaction for rules:

$$\ell = val(r_{\text{body}}) - val(r_{\text{head}}) .$$

HL-MRFs Collective Model for Reports

The goal of this model is to use reports to predict spammers. We study three HL-MRFs models to incorporate the reporting users' credibility into the reporting system and improve the predictability of the reports. We show that collective reasoning over credibility of the reporting user and the probability of the reported user being an spammer, increases the classification performance of the system.

Our collective HL-MRFs model uses the *report* relation graph ($\mathcal{G}_{\text{report}}$), and is based on the intuition that the credibility of a user's abuse reporting should increase when they report users that are more likely to be spammers. Hence, if a user reports other users whom there are other evidence supporting them being spammers, the credibility of that person should increase. On the other hand, if the user reports another user that is unlikely to be a spammer, the credibility of the reporting user should decrease.

$$\begin{aligned}
\textsc{Credible}(v_1) \wedge \textsc{Reported}(v_1,v_2) &\rightarrow \textsc{Spammer}(v_2)\\
\textsc{Spammer}(v_2) \wedge \textsc{Reported}(v_1,v_2) &\rightarrow \textsc{Credible}(v_1)\\
\neg\textsc{Spammer}(v_2) \wedge \textsc{Reported}(v_1,v_2) &\rightarrow \neg\textsc{Credible}(v_1)\\
\textsc{Prior-Credible}(v) &\rightarrow \textsc{Credible}(v)\\
\neg\textsc{Prior-Credible}(v) &\rightarrow \neg\textsc{Credible}(v)\\
&\neg\textsc{Spammer}(v)
\end{aligned}$$

Figure 3: Collective HL-MRFs model to predict spammers based on the reports from other users.

We propose the model shown in Figure 3 to capture the collective intuition. We incorporate prior credibility of the reporting users based on the past reporting behavior into the model. The negative prior on *SPAMMER* is included in the model to complement the first rule that increases the score of users being spammers. To study the effect of each part of the model, we experimentally compare the proposed collective model with two simpler HL-MRFs models that do not contain the collective reasoning and credibility priors in section 5.4.

4. DATA

The dataset[4] was collected from the *Tagged.com* social network website, which is a network for meeting new people, and has multiple methods for users to make new connections. *Tagged* has various methods to deal with spam. It uses several registration and activation filters to identify and block spam accounts based on traditional methods such as content and registration information and patterns. *Tagged* also employs a reporting mechanism that users can report spammers to the system. An administrative security team also monitors the network for malicious behaviors and manually blocks spammers. Our goal in this study is to identify sophisticated spammers that require manual intervention by the security team. These spammers have already passed initial classifiers and know how to manipulate their content to avoid being caught by automatic filters.

The purpose of the social network affects its susceptibility to spam. A social network which is designed for connecting the users who already know each other, can control spam by limiting the communications between users who are not already connected in the network. However, a social network that promotes finding new connections may like to impose minimum limitations on how users interact. *Tagged*, which is a social network for meeting new people, has multiple venues for users to communicate without much restriction.

Another challenge with identifying spammers in multi-purpose social networks such as *Tagged* is that users join the network for different reasons. For example, users may come to *Tagged* to play social games such as *Pets* and *MeetMe*, to find romantic relationships, or simply to spend time with virtual connections. Not only they will generate different behavioral patterns, they will use security measures such as *abuse reporting* mechanism differently and introduce noise to it.

In our experiments, all the users who had at least one activity in the sampling time frame were included in the sample dataset. More formally our initial sample included the following elements:

$$\mathcal{V} = \{ v \mid \exists\, e = \langle v, v_*, r_*, t_k \rangle \in \mathcal{E}_{\text{all}} \ \wedge \ t_{\text{b}} \leq t_k \leq t_{\text{e}} \}$$
$$\mathcal{E} = \{ e = \langle v_i, v_j, r_*, t_k \rangle \mid \exists\, v_i, v_j \in \mathcal{V} \ \wedge \ t_{\text{s}} \leq t_k \leq t_{\text{e}} \}$$

where v_* indicates any user in the network, r_* indicates any type of action in the study, $\mathcal{E}_{\text{all}}$ indicates all the edges in the *Tagged* network, and t_{b} and t_{e} indicate the time of the beginning and the end of the sampling period.

To perform a retrospective study, we chose t_{b} and t_{e} such that enough time had passed since the sampling period by the time we accessed the data (t_{access}), so that most of the spam accounts were identified and labeled. We then removed the users who had deactivated their accounts themselves by t_{access}, because we could not determine their labels. The remaining users were labeled as spam if their accounts has been manually canceled by a security team by t_{access}. Although the security team cancels accounts for multiple reasons, not just spam, most of the canceled accounts are due to malicious activities. For simplicity, we labeled all the canceled accounts as spammers. Ten different activities on the website were selected during the sampling time frame. The activities included in the study are: viewing another user's profile, sending friend requests, sending messages, sending *luv*, sending *winks*, buying or wishing others in the *Pets* game, clicking yes or no in the *MeetMe* game, and reporting other users for abuse.

There are more effective ways to sample the network in order to conserve its characteristics [18, 19, 20]. However, for practical reasons and ease of deployment, we have chosen the simple time-based sampling method. Further performance improvements may be achieved via better sampling employments. The spammer accounts that were selected for this study could initially bypass *Tagged* deployed preventative measures and successfully perform at least one action in the network. Although they could be identified within a short period of time after their activity, their identification required a manual or semi-automated procedure by the members of the security team. Not only are these spammers harder to identify, they are also very rare in the dataset, causing a huge class imbalance.

Table 1 shows some statistics from the sample we used. These numbers do not represent the statistics of the *Tagged* social network, as they have been altered by limiting the number of action types in the study as well as eliminating users with deactivated accounts at t_{access} (which is later than the sample period). Furthermore, only the users who performed an action in the sampling period were included in the dataset.

Table 1: Data Sample Statistics.

Entity	**Count**
$\lvert\mathcal{V}\rvert$ (total users)	5,607,454
$\lvert\mathcal{E}\rvert$ (total actions)	912,280,409
$\max(\lvert\mathcal{E}_r\rvert)$ (number of actions that are most frequent action type)	350,724,903
$\min(\lvert\mathcal{E}_r\rvert)$ (number of actions that are least frequent action type)	137,550
total users labeled as spammers	(%3.9) 221,305

All of our experiments are based on the relational data in the following form:

$$\langle t_i, v_{\text{src}}, v_{\text{dst}}, r_j \rangle$$

where t_i is the time stamp, v_{src} is the user who initiated the action, v_{dst} is the user the action was towards, and r_i categorizes the type of action.

5. EXPERIMENTAL VALIDATION

We performed four sets of experiments to evaluate the proposed methods. First we study the graph structure properties and compare the multi-relational approach with only considering a single relation. We also study using one graph analytics algorithm as a feature, comparing to having features from multiple methods. We then study the effectiveness of sequence mining features and combine them with graph-based methods to measure the overall performance

[4]An anonymized sample of the multi-relational part of the dataset along with our code for the experiments can be found here: `http://github.com/shobeir/fakhraei_kdd2015`.

enhancements. We then include only three demographics features for each user to measure their influence on the performance. Finally we perform collective reasoning over *abuse reports* and measure the improvement of the predictions with this method.

For our experiments we used *Graphlab Create*^{TM} and the Java-based open-source *Probabilistic Soft Logic (PSL)*,[5] on a single Ubuntu machine with 32GB RAM and 3.2GHz CPU (4 cores). For classification, we used *Gradient-Boosted Decision Trees* which is a collection of decision trees combined through a technique called gradient boosting [21].

The deployment options of the framework and what actions are planned to be taken on the identified spammer accounts determine which performance metrics are more appropriate for this task. High precision lets the spam accounts be blocked without manual intervention, and without concerns of the system harming legitimate users. High recall allows the system to identify the legitimate users with more confidence and clear the environment via deploying measures such as CAPTCHA and additional account verifications for the users with suspicious status. Hence, the appropriate metric to measure the performance of this system is the *Precision-Recall* curve. The *ROC* curve could also be useful, however, due to the high class-imbalance, it would not provide much insight, and unless properly adjusted, it would result in over-optimistic estimates. We report the area under *Precision-Recall* curve (AUPR) and the area under the *ROC* curve (AUROC) for the experiments. We used 10-fold cross-validation to estimate the performance of each method and feature-set. Unless stated otherwise, the reported numbers represent *mean* and *standard deviation* over 10-fold cross-validation.

5.1 Graph Structure Features

Table 2 shows the average results of classification via graph-based features. The first row indicated the best results from using a single relation with features from all the graph-based algorithms. The second row shows the best graph-based feature with all the relations. Comparing the results from the two rows suggests that combining different relations is more effective than combining features from different algorithms on a single relation. Using all algorithms to compute features on all relation graphs results in the best performance for graph-based methods.

Table 2: Classification with graph-based features.

Experiment	AUPR	AUROC
$\left[\mathbf{X}^{\mathbf{m}}_{\mathcal{G}_{r_i}}\right]$ 1 Relation, k Methods	0.187±0.004	0.803±0.001
$\left[\mathbf{X}^{m_i}_{\mathcal{G}_\mathbf{r}}\right]$ n Relations, 1 Method	0.285±0.002	0.809±0.001
$\left[\mathbf{X}^{\mathbf{m}}_{\mathcal{G}_\mathbf{r}}\right]$ n Relations, k Methods	0.328±0.003	0.817±0.001

5.2 Sequence-based Features

Next, we experimentally evaluated the sequence-based features. First, we study their effectiveness independently, and then we measure their performance in combination with the graph-based features. To compute the bigram features, we first sorted all of the activities in our dataset based on user IDs and timestamps via the standard external sort function in Linux. We did a single pass on the sorted file to compute the bigram features.

[5]`http://psl.umiacs.umd.edu`

Table 3: Classification with k-gram features.

Experiment	AUPR	AUROC
$\left[\mathbf{X}_{\mathcal{S}_B}\right]$ k-gram features	0.471±0.004	0.859±0.001
$\left[\mathbf{X}_{\mathcal{S}_B}\ \mathbf{X}^{\mathbf{m}}_{\mathcal{G}_\mathbf{r}}\right]$ k-gram & graph features	0.543±0.005	0.914±0.001

Table 3 shows the results of classification using the bigram features. The second row suggests that a model that uses both graph-based and k-gram features outperforms the ones that use them independently. *Precision-Recall* and *ROC* curves from graph-based and k-gram features are shown in Figure 4.

We further study the sequence-based classification with the Mixture of Markov Models (MMM) approach. We did a single pass on the sorted file we already generated for the bigram features to compute the probabilities for this model. We then used the probabilities generated from this model in logarithmic and ratio forms as features for classification.

Table 4: Classification with mixture of Markov models.

Experiment	AUPR	AUROC
$\left[\mathbf{X}_{\mathcal{S}_M}\right]$ MMM	0.246±0.009	0.821±0.003
$\left[\mathbf{X}_{\mathcal{S}_M}\ \mathbf{X}_{\mathcal{S}_B}\right]$ MMM & k-gram	0.468±0.012	0.860±0.002
$\left[\mathbf{X}_{\mathcal{S}_M}\ \mathbf{X}_{\mathcal{S}_B}\ \mathbf{X}^{\mathbf{m}}_{\mathcal{G}_\mathbf{r}}\right]$ MMM & k-gram & graph	0.550±0.005	0.914±0.002

The results from Table 4 shows the classification performance with these features, which suggests minimal improvement employing longer sequence models. This may suggest that the bigram features can incorporate enough signal to capture spam activity in a multi-relational network. However, computing the Mixture of Markov Models does not impose much overhead when extracting bigram features, and can be done within the same process.

5.3 Demographic Information

Many people use *Tagged* to find new relationships. We anticipate that in such environment users behave differently based on their demographics. To capture this point, we added three features ($\mathbf{X}_{\mathcal{D}}$) to our model: age, gender, and time since registration. Age and gender highly improved the classification results as they tend to be most discriminative of behavioral patterns. Another feature that we included in our model is the time past since registration. As mentioned earlier we labeled all the cancelled accounts for malicious activities as spammers. However, these users have different behavioral patterns, where spammers who mainly mass advertise, may use much newer accounts, in contrast to users who have been blocked due to misbehaviors, and have been active in the system much longer.

Table 5 shows the significant improvements of the results when including these features in different models. Figure 4

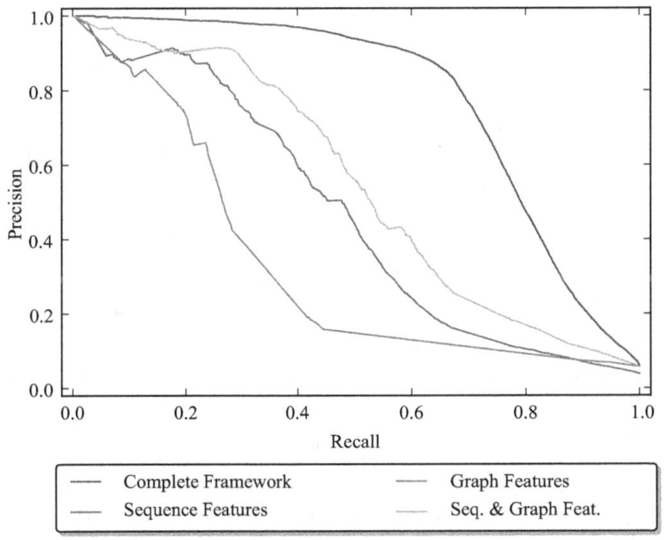

(a) Precision-Recall Curve

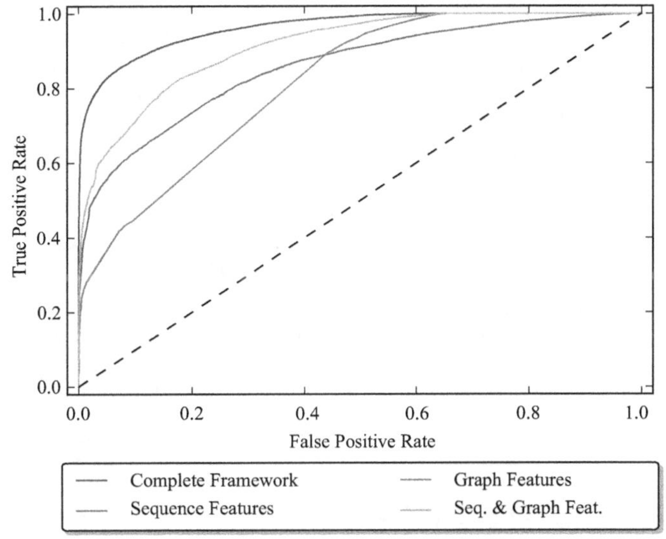

(b) ROC Curve

Figure 4: *Precision-Recall* and *ROC* curves for models with k-gram and graph-based features. Using both features with user demographics significantly improve the results.

shows the *Precision-Recall* and *ROC* curves of the complete framework.

Table 5: Classification when including user demographics information.

Experiment	AUPR	AUROC
$\left[\mathbf{X}_{\mathcal{D}}\ \mathbf{X}_{\mathcal{S}_B}\right]$ Demo. & k-gram	0.689±0.006	0.935±0.001
$\left[\mathbf{X}_{\mathcal{D}}\ \mathbf{X}^{\mathbf{m}}_{\mathcal{G}_\mathbf{r}}\right]$ Demo. & graph	0.701±0.002	0.950±0.001
$\left[\mathbf{X}_{\mathcal{D}}\ \mathbf{X}_{\mathcal{S}_B}\ \mathbf{X}^{\mathbf{m}}_{\mathcal{G}_\mathbf{r}}\right]$ Demo. & k-gram & graph	0.778±0.001	0.963±0.001
$\left[\mathbf{X}_{\mathcal{D}}\ \mathbf{X}_{\mathcal{S}_M}\ \mathbf{X}_{\mathcal{S}_B}\ \mathbf{X}^{\mathbf{m}}_{\mathcal{G}_\mathbf{r}}\right]$ Demo. & MMM & k-gram & graph	0.779±0.002	0.963±0.001

5.4 Collective Classification with Reports

The reporting system can have useful information to detect spammers. We studied the effectiveness of our proposed collective model (in Figure 3) to extract useful signals from this relation. We first designed a baseline model shown in Figure 5a to only use the reports to detect spammers. This model gives similar results to assigning total count of the reports for each user as their score of being a spammer. We then designed the model shown in Figure 5b to use the reports and prior credibility of the reporting user to detect spammers. This model gives similar results to assigning total *weighted* count of the reports for each user as their score of being a spammer, where reports are weighted by the credibility of the reporting users.

To perform the experiments we have only used $\mathcal{G}_{report}$, which is a sparse graph. Our collective model is aimed to propagate information between the reported users' likelihood of being spammer, through the credibility of the reporting users. In order for information to propagate in the model, each reporting user should at least have reported two other users. Hence, we removed the vertices with out-degree less than two. We then performed 10-fold cross validation to compare the three models and study the effectiveness of the collective model. We used the ratio of the correctly reported spammers from the training data as a simple prior on credibility for each user. Potentially more effective priors could incorporate the the count and the frequency of the reports as well.

$$\begin{aligned} \textsc{Reported}(v_1, v_2) \rightarrow\ & \textsc{Spammer}(v_2) \\ & \neg\textsc{Spammer}(v) \end{aligned}$$

(a) HL-MRFs model that only uses the reports to detect spammers. This model would give similar results to assigning total count of the reports for each user as their score of being a spammer.

$$\begin{aligned} \textsc{Credible}(v_1) \wedge \textsc{Reported}(v_1, v_2) \rightarrow\ & \textsc{Spammer}(v_2) \\ \textsc{Prior-Credible}(v) \rightarrow\ & \textsc{Credible}(v) \\ \neg\textsc{Prior-Credible}(v) \rightarrow\ & \neg\textsc{Credible}(v) \\ & \neg\textsc{Spammer}(v) \end{aligned}$$

(b) HL-MRFs model that uses the reports and prior credibility of the reporting user to detect spammers. This model would give similar results to assigning total *weighted* counts of the reports for each user as their score of being a spammer.

Figure 5: Simple HL-MRFs models to compare with the collective model shown in Figure 3.

Table 6 shows the results from our three experiments. Using the collective model significantly increases the performance of the reports in detecting spammers. These predictions can be added to the overall classification framework as a feature. However, since the report graph was sparse relative to the other relation graphs in our dataset, many users could not be classified with this model. Hence, we did not include these predictions as a feature in our framework. This model can be deployed independently to improve the signal from the reports.

Table 6: Classification with collective HL-MRFs model.

Experiment	AUPR	AUROC
Reports (Figure 5a)	0.674±0.008	0.611±0.007
Reports & Credibility (Figure 5b)	0.869±0.006	0.862±0.004
Reports & Credibility & Collective Reasoning (Figure 3)	0.884±0.005	0.873±0.004

6. RELATED WORK

Spam detection in email [22] and the web [23] have been extensively studied, and various methods and features have been proposed for them. Network-based approaches are more closely related to our proposed framework. These methods can be generally categorized based on feature construction and label propagation. Shrivastava et al. [24] generalized the network-based spam detection to random link attacks and showed that the problem is NP-complete. Tseng and Chen [25] used network features to identify email spammers, and incrementally updated the SVM classifier to capture the changes in spam patterns. Oscar and Roychowdbury [26] used a network representation of the emails where nodes were email addresses and links between them indicated a sender-receiver relationship. They used clustering properties of the network to build white and black lists of email addresses and identify spammers. Becchetti et al. [27] proposed a link-based classification for web spam detection, and later combined it with content-based features and used graph topology to improve performance [28]. Since spammers tend to form clusters on the web (unlike in social networks), the authors leveraged clustering and label propagation, to further improve their predictions.

A group of methods are based on label propagation and influenced by PageRank. TrustRank [29] for example, used reputable sites as seeds and propagated reputations through the network. There are multiple variations which propagate dis-trust. Similar to this work, Chirita et al. [30] proposed MailRank which ranked the trustworthiness of a sender based on the network representation of the mail environment. Abernethy et al. [31] proposed a method based on graph regularization and used regularizers that is based on the intuition that linked pages are somewhat similar.

The research focus on spam detection in social networks is relatively more recent. Heymann et al. [32] surveyed different countermeasures to address the spam issue in social networks, and categorized them into methods based on detection, demotion, and prevention. Hu et al. [33] combined information from email, text messages (SMS), and web with Twitter content to detect spammers, and showed improvements in results. Tan et al. [34] proposed an unsupervised spam detection method that focused on identifying a white list of non-spammers from the social network. They argued that legitimate users show more stable patterns in social blogs.

Stein et al. [35] described the spam filtering system in Facebook. They highlighted that attacks on social media use multiple channels, and an effective systems must share feedback and feature data across channels. Gao et al. [36] studied messages between users in Facebook, and used clustering to detect spam campaigns. They identify multiple clusters associated with several campaigns.

Markines et al. [37] studied multiple features and classifiers to detect spam in social tagging systems. Benevenuto et al. [38] used content such as presence or absence of a URL in the post, and user social behaviors such as number of posts to detect spam on Twitter. Lee et al. [39] used honeypots in Twitter and MySpace to harvest deceptive spam profiles. They then used content, posting rate, number of friends, and user demographics such as age and gender as features in their classifier.

Zhu et al. [40] reported that unlike email and web, in social networks, spammers do not form clusters with other spammers, and their neighbors are mostly non-spammers. They use matrix factorization on user activity matrix of data extracted from Renren[6] and use the latent factors as features for classification.

Evolving social networks are of high interest to researchers and have been studied for different purposes [41]. Jin et al. [42] modeled a social network as a *time-stamped heterogeneous network* and used a clustering method to identify spammers. They also used active learning to refine their model. Zhang et al. [43] identified spam campaigns on Twitter by linking accounts with similar malicious URLs in their posts.

Laorden et al. [44] used collective classification to filter spam messages based on their text, to reduce the number of necessary labeled messages. They used implementations in WEKA for collective classification in their evaluation. Geng et al. [45] used a semi-supervised learning algorithm to reduce the labeled training data requirement for web spam detection. Torkamani and Lowd [46] proposed a method to robustly perform collective classification against malicious adversaries that change their behavior in the system.

7. DISCUSSION AND DEPLOYMENT

We have studied the characteristics of time-stamped multi-relational social networks that can be leveraged to detect spammers. We showed that by considering action or relation types and incorporating graph-based features from different relations, one can improve the spammer classification performance. We then showed two sequence mining techniques and their effectiveness to model sequences extracted from time-stamped multi-relational network for spam detection. We also proposed a collective model to refine and improve the signals from the abuse report graph.

Depending on the precision of the results from the model, the security system could either automatically flag a user as spammer and deactivate the account or block its activities in the system, or ask for more verification. Our experimental results show that our model can detect over 65% of the manually detected spammers with higher than 85% precision. These sophisticated spammers had passed the already deployed security measures and performed some activity in the network. Inspecting some of the false positives with the highest spammer probability, we found unlabeled and abandoned spammer accounts, which suggests the real precision

[6] A social network in China: `http://renren.com`

of the proposed framework might actually be higher than reported. These results can significantly reduce the manual overhead of the administrative security team. Furthermore, our results show that the precision at 80% recall, is above 50%, suggesting this portion of users can be asked for additional verification (e.g., CAPTCHA) without affecting many legitimate users.

This model can be deployed as an iterative batch module to complement real-time filters. Except for some parameters such as the user *credibility prior* for the report system that should be set and adjusted globally for the user, the model has to be re-trained from a fresh sample of the network to adjust to the adversarial changes in patterns. Computing the parameters of the models on a relatively low-powered single machine for our experiments suggests that the framework could be run on very short intervals depending on the training size and computational power. The features can also be computed in parallel. Using *Graphlab Create*^{TM}, computing the features is highly efficient. To provide an example, for a graph with 5.6 million vertices and 350 million edges computing PageRank on our experiment machine took approximately 6.25 minutes, triangle counting 17.98 minutes, k-core 14.3 minutes, and graph coloring 143 minutes.

To optimize the model for production, it is possible to perform feature selection and reduce the necessary features. Feature selection [47] may also improve the performance of the model. Our method for collectively refining the signals from the report graph can be used independently or as a feature in the framework. Improved precision of the predictions via reports enables the system to take actions with more confidence, and reduces the manual overhead.

Our method should be retrained with every new sample. An online learning method that can incorporate the changes in the dynamic network can effectively improve the usability of our framework. Another approach that could improve the prediction results significantly could be incorporating this framework with content-based models. Furthermore, spam accounts often do not act independently and are part of spam campaigns. Their targets may often not be at random as well. They may use a white list of legitimate users to target. Our initial observations show that spammers make relations with legitimate users disproportionally to the overall population ratios. A multi-relational model that can classify spammer accounts based on their target accounts, and identify campaigns based on their relational information could potentially improve the results.

Acknowledgements

Part of this work was performed during the first author's internship at *if(we)* formerly *Tagged Inc.* We are highly grateful to Johann Schleier-Smith and Karl Dawson for their extensive help and support. We also thank Dai Li, Stuart Robinson, Vinit Garg, and Simon Hill for constructive discussions, and Jay Pujara and Arti Ramesh for their helpful suggestions and feedback. We also like to thank the *Dato (Graphlab)* team for their insightful guidance and help with using *Graphlab Create*^{TM}for this project, especially Danny Bickson, Brian Kent, Srikrishna Sridhar, Rajat Arya, Shawn Scully, and Alice Zheng. This work is partially supported by the National Science Foundation (NSF) under contract number IIS0746930. Any opinions, findings, and conclusions or recommendations expressed in this material are those of the author(s) and do not necessarily reflect the views of the supporting institutions.

References

[1] Wikipedia. History of email spam — Wikipedia, the free encyclopedia, 2014. URL http://en.wikipedia.org/wiki/History_of_email_spam.

[2] Harold Nguyen. 2013 state of social media spam. Technical report, Nexgate. URL http://go.nexgate.com/nexgate-social-media-spam-research-report.

[3] Lawrence Page, Sergey Brin, Rajeev Motwani, and Terry Winograd. The pagerank citation ranking: Bringing order to the web. Technical report, 1999.

[4] J Ignacio Alvarez-Hamelin, Luca Dall'Asta, Alain Barrat, and Alessandro Vespignani. Large scale networks fingerprinting and visualization using the k-core decomposition. In *Advances in neural information processing systems (NIPS)*, 2005.

[5] Tommy R Jensen and Bjarne Toft. *Graph coloring problems.* John Wiley & Sons, 2011.

[6] S Pemmaraju and S Skiena. Implementing discrete mathematics: Combinatorics and graph theory with mathematica, 2003.

[7] Thomas Schank. Algorithmic aspects of triangle-based network analysis. *Phd in computer science, University Karlsruhe*, 2007.

[8] Zhengzheng Xing, Jian Pei, and Eamonn Keogh. A brief survey on sequence classification. *ACM SIGKDD Explorations Newsletter*, 2010.

[9] Fuchun Peng, Dale Schuurmans, and Shaojun Wang. Augmenting naive Bayes classifiers with statistical language models. *Information Retrieval*, 2004.

[10] Fei Zheng and Geoffrey I Webb. Tree augmented naive Bayes. In *Encyclopedia of Machine Learning*, pages 990–991. Springer, 2010.

[11] Stephen H. Bach, Bert Huang, Ben London, and Lise Getoor. Hinge-loss Markov random fields: Convex inference for structured prediction. In *Uncertainty in Artificial Intelligence (UAI)*, 2013.

[12] S. H. Bach, M. Broecheler, B. Huang, and L. Getoor. Hinge-loss Markov random fields and probabilistic soft logic. arXiv:1505.04406 [cs.LG], 2015.

[13] Jay Pujara, Hui Miao, Lise Getoor, and William Cohen. Knowledge graph identification. In *International Semantic Web Conference (ISWC)*, 2013.

[14] Arti Ramesh, Dan Goldwasser, Bert Huang, Hal Daume III, and Lise Getoor. Learning latent engagement patterns of students in online courses. In *Proceedings of the Twenty-Eighth AAAI Conference on Artificial Intelligence*. AAAI Press, 2014.

[15] Shobeir Fakhraei, Bert Huang, Louiqa Raschid, and Lise Getoor. Network-based drug-target interaction prediction with probabilistic soft logic. *IEEE/ACM Transactions on Computational Biology and Bioinformatics*, 2014.

[16] Shobeir Fakhraei, Louiqa Raschid, and Lise Getoor. Drug-target interaction prediction for drug repurposing with probabilistic similarity logic. In *ACM SIGKDD 12th International Workshop on Data Mining in Bioinformatics (BIOKDD)*. ACM, 2013.

[17] Bert Huang, Angelika Kimmig, Lise Getoor, and Jennifer Golbeck. A flexible framework for probabilistic models of social trust. In *International Conference on Social Computing, Behavioral-Cultural Modeling, & Prediction (SBP)*, 2013.

[18] Nesreen K. Ahmed, Jennifer Neville, and Ramana Kompella. Network sampling: From static to streaming graphs. *ACM Trans. Knowl. Discov. Data*, 2013.

[19] Jure Leskovec and Christos Faloutsos. Sampling from large graphs. In *Proceedings of the 12th ACM SIGKDD international conference on Knowledge discovery and data mining*. ACM, 2006.

[20] Mohammad Al Hasan and Mohammed J. Zaki. Output space sampling for graph patterns. *PVLDB*, 2009.

[21] Jerome H Friedman. Greedy function approximation: a gradient boosting machine. *Annals of statistics*, pages 1189–1232, 2001.

[22] Enrico Blanzieri and Anton Bryl. A survey of learning-based techniques of email spam filtering. *Artificial Intelligence Review*, 2008.

[23] Nikita Spirin and Jiawei Han. Survey on web spam detection: principles and algorithms. *ACM SIGKDD Explorations Newsletter*, 13(2):50–64, 2012.

[24] Nisheeth Shrivastava, Anirban Majumder, and Rajeev Rastogi. Mining (social) network graphs to detect random link attacks. In *Data Engineering, 2008. ICDE 2008. IEEE 24th International conference on*, pages 486–495. IEEE, 2008.

[25] Chi-Yao Tseng and Ming-Syan Chen. Incremental SVM model for spam detection on dynamic email social networks. In *Computational Science and Engineering, 2009. CSE'09. International conference on*, volume 4, pages 128–135. IEEE, 2009.

[26] P Oscar and VP Roychowdbury. Leveraging social networks to fight spam. *IEEE Computer*, 38(4):61–68, 2005.

[27] Luca Becchetti, Carlos Castillo, Debora Donato, Ricardo Baeza-Yates, and Stefano Leonardi. Link analysis for web spam detection. *ACM Transactions on the Web (TWEB)*, 2008.

[28] Carlos Castillo, Debora Donato, Aristides Gionis, Vanessa Murdock, and Fabrizio Silvestri. Know your neighbors: Web spam detection using the web topology. In *Proceedings of the 30th annual international ACM SIGIR conference on Research and development in information retrieval*. ACM, 2007.

[29] Zoltán Gyöngyi, Hector Garcia-Molina, and Jan Pedersen. Combating web spam with trustrank. In *Proceedings of the thirtieth international conference on very large data bases*, pages 576–587. VLDB Endowment, 2004.

[30] Paul-Alexandru Chirita, Jörg Diederich, and Wolfgang Nejdl. Mailrank: using ranking for spam detection. In *Proceedings of the 14th ACM international conference on Information and knowledge management*, pages 373–380. ACM, 2005.

[31] Jacob Abernethy, Olivier Chapelle, and Carlos Castillo. Graph regularization methods for web spam detection. *Machine Learning*, 81(2):207–225, 2010.

[32] Paul Heymann, Georgia Koutrika, and Hector Garcia-Molina. Fighting spam on social web sites: A survey of approaches and future challenges. *Internet Computing, IEEE*, 11(6):36–45, 2007.

[33] Xia Hu, Jiliang Tang, and Huan Liu. Leveraging knowledge across media for spammer detection in microblogging. In *Proceedings of the 37th international ACM SIGIR conference on Research & development in information retrieval*. ACM, 2014.

[34] Enhua Tan, Lei Guo, Songqing Chen, Xiaodong Zhang, and Yihong Zhao. Unik: unsupervised social network spam detection. In *Proceedings of the 22nd ACM international conference on information & knowledge management*. ACM, 2013.

[35] Tao Stein, Erdong Chen, and Karan Mangla. Facebook immune system. In *Proceedings of the 4th Workshop on Social Network Systems*. ACM, 2011.

[36] Hongyu Gao, Jun Hu, Christo Wilson, Zhichun Li, Yan Chen, and Ben Y Zhao. Detecting and characterizing social spam campaigns. In *Proceedings of the 10th ACM SIGCOMM conference on Internet measurement*, pages 35–47. ACM, 2010.

[37] Benjamin Markines, Ciro Cattuto, and Filippo Menczer. Social spam detection. In *Proceedings of the 5th International Workshop on Adversarial Information Retrieval on the Web*, pages 41–48. ACM, 2009.

[38] Fabricio Benevenuto, Gabriel Magno, Tiago Rodrigues, and Virgilio Almeida. Detecting spammers on twitter. In *Collaboration, electronic messaging, anti-abuse and spam conference (CEAS)*, volume 6, page 12, 2010.

[39] Kyumin Lee, James Caverlee, and Steve Webb. Uncovering social spammers: social honeypots+ machine learning. In *Proceedings of the 33rd international ACM SIGIR conference on Research and development in information retrieval*, pages 435–442. ACM, 2010.

[40] Yin Zhu, Xiao Wang, Erheng Zhong, Nathan N Liu, He Li, and Qiang Yang. Discovering spammers in social networks. In *Twenty-Sixth AAAI Conference on Artificial Intelligence*, 2012.

[41] Gueorgi Kossinets and Duncan J Watts. Empirical analysis of an evolving social network. *Science*, 2006.

[42] Xin Jin, Cindy Xide Lin, Jiebo Luo, and Jiawei Han. Socialspamguard: A data mining-based spam detection system for social media networks. *PVLDB*, 2011.

[43] Xianchao Zhang, Shaoping Zhu, and Wenxin Liang. Detecting spam and promoting campaigns in the twitter social network. In *ICDM*, pages 1194–1199, 2012.

[44] Carlos Laorden, Borja Sanz, Igor Santos, Patxi Galán-García, and Pablo G Bringas. Collective classification for spam filtering. *Logic Journal of IGPL*, 2012.

[45] Guang-Gang Geng, Qiudan Li, and Xinchang Zhang. Link based small sample learning for web spam detection. In *Proceedings of the 18th international conference on World wide web*, pages 1185–1186. ACM, 2009.

[46] Mohamadali Torkamani and Daniel Lowd. Convex adversarial collective classification. In *Proceedings of the 30th International Conference on Machine Learning (ICML-13)*, pages 642–650, 2013.

[47] Shobeir Fakhraei, Hamid Soltanian-Zadeh, and Farshad Fotouhi. Bias and stability of single variable classifiers for feature ranking and selection. *Expert Systems with Applications*, 41(15):6945 – 6958, 2014.

Utilizing Text Mining on Online Medical Forums to Predict Label Change due to Adverse Drug Reactions

Ronen Feldman*
School of Business Administration, Hebrew University of Jerusalem
ronen.feldman@huji.ac.il

Oded Netzer
Graduate School of Business, Columbia University
on2110@columbia.edu

Aviv Peretz*
School of Computer Science and Engineering, Hebrew University of Jerusalem
aviv.peretz@mail.huji.ac.il

Binyamin Rosenfeld
grurgrur@gmail.com

ABSTRACT

We present an end-to-end text mining methodology for relation extraction of adverse drug reactions (ADRs) from medical forums on the Web. Our methodology is novel in that it combines three major characteristics: (i) an underlying concept of using a head-driven phrase structure grammar (HPSG) based parser; (ii) domain-specific relation patterns, the acquisition of which is done primarily using unsupervised methods applied to a large, unlabeled text corpus; and (iii) automated post-processing algorithms for enhancing the set of extracted relations.

We empirically demonstrate the ability of our proposed approach to predict ADRs prior to their reporting by the Food and Drug Administration (FDA). Put differently, we put our approach to a predictive test by demonstrating that our methodology can credibly point to ADRs that were not uncovered in clinical trials for evaluating new drugs that come to market but were only reported later on by the FDA as a label change.

Categories and Subject Descriptors

I.2 [**Artificial Intelligence**]: Natural Language Processing—*Text analysis*

General Terms

Algorithms; Experimentation

Keywords

Adverse Drug Reactions; Pharmaceutical Drugs; Hpsg; Medical Forums; Text Mining

*Research supported by Intel ICRI-CI, Israel Science Foundation (ISF) and Israel Ministry of Defense.
*corresponding author

KDD'15, August 10-13, 2015, Sydney, NSW, Australia.
 ISBN 978-1-4503-3664-2/15/08 ...$15.00.
DOI: http://dx.doi.org/10.1145/2783258.2788608.

1. INTRODUCTION

The field of text mining deals with algorithms and techniques by which valuable information can be derived from textual data. Specifically, text mining has been found to be useful when the amount of text is extensive. One such corpus that is characterized by a large body of textual data is Internet forums. In this research we are particularly interested in mining *medical* online forums in an attempt to draw insights and make predictions with respect to pharmaceutical ADRs - medical damages caused by taking a given medication at a normal dose. Several papers have investigated whether mining social media can help detecting ADRs (e.g., [13] and [20]). However, these papers relate the set of reported ADRs to ADRs found in the forum. They do not attempt to predict unreported ADRs that are likely to be found at a later time. Clinical trials are often limited in terms of the number of participants and scope. Accordingly, these trials sometimes fail to indicate ADRs associated with a particular drug. ADRs that were not found in the clinical trials are often reported later on, sometimes even years after a drug has come to market as an FDA label change [20]. Because adverse drug events comprise the fourth leading cause of death in the US [3], the FDA has developed several monitoring channels for physicians, pharmacists, patients and drug companies to report ADR post-marketing of the drugs.

Now, suppose a new drug is introduced to the market. A natural task in terms of text mining would therefore be finding a way to efficiently and accurately utilize the wisdom of crowds, manifested in health related online forums, in order to identify potential ADRs that were not found in clinical trials. Netzer, Feldman, Goldenberg and Fresko [13] portray the curse underlying the abundant supply of user generated content. Practically, one needs to track and quantify an overwhelming amount of information. Furthermore, the data available in user-generated forums, while rich, is highly unstructured. Text in such forums often includes informal jargon, abbreviations, and lack of formal linguistic structure, making the task of parsing a sentence and identifying the role of each part of speech, burdensome.

The goal of this paper is to present a text mining methodology that will allow a rather unlaborious, yet reliable, detection of unreported ADRs that are likely to be identified in the future. Since we cannot prove our predictions on to-be-announced ADRs - not until the future becomes the present - we take a set of ADRs that have been reported by the FDA in a label change post the marketing of the drug, and examine whether signals of these ADRs appear in user-generated health forum prior to the first announcement by the FDA about these ADRs. We find that our approach is able to detect such label changes sometime years prior to the FDA announcement.

2. RELATED WORK

There is a large body of literature on the information and insights that can be elicited from text mining consumer forums [8, 7, 5, 6, 11, 9]. Moreover, the specific task of mining ADRs from health-related social media, has also drawn the attention of researchers. Several papers have taken various approaches to tackle this problem. These papers vary with respect to the way Drug-ADR relations were perceived and, as a result, in the techniques that were used for extracting those Drug-ADR relations. We describe this literature next.

2.1 Co-occurrence Based Approach

Several papers have addressed the problem of relation extraction based on the notion of sheer co-occurrence analysis. These papers explicitly or implicitly assume that a Drug-ADR pair co-occurring within the same sentence, or within a window of n tokens, or even within an entire document, conceals a relation. Recently Segura-Bedmar, PePeña and Martìnez [17] presented a system aimed at detecting ADRs from Spanish medical forums based on co-occurrence of Drug-ADR pairs while considering different window sizes stretching from 10 up to 250 tokens. Similarly, Benton et al. [2] developed a system to extract Drug-ADR pairs from medical message boards using co-occurrence statistics, in which any two terms co-occurring within a window of 20 tokens apart were considered an association rule. In an early paper by Leaman at al. [10] co-occurrence analysis was implicit, as the mined information had been scraped from a website, in which users indicated a specific treatment when posting comments, thus treatments which were not drug-based, were filtered out. In order to mine the ADRs themselves, the terms mentioned in user comments in a bag-of words sliding window were matched against terms in a lexicon. Yang, Yang, Jiang and Tang [21] (followed by [22]), proposed that co-occurrences of a drug and an ADR in online healthcare communities were to be regarded as an association rule, that is, a drug $\Rightarrow$ ADR association. An association rule mining algorithm was employed, in which ADRs were identified by comparing a sliding window of tokens against each term in an ADR lexicon.

The main limitation of using co-occurrence as a measure for Drug-ADR relation is that in many cases co-occurrence of two entities is loosely related to these two entities comprising a relation. Co-occurrence ignores the syntactic and semantic structures of the relation. Moreover, association rules that are derived from co-occurrence don't necessarily have causal direction, rather they simply imply a correlation between a drug and an ADR. The problem exacerbates as the allowed window size for co-occurrence increases. These problems lead to low precision in relation extraction.

2.2 Supervised Learning Based Approach

A few recent papers have tried to harness the power of supervised machine learning to extract Drug-ADR relations. Nikfarjam and Gonzalez [14] applied association rule to mine a set of annotated comments for generating underlying language patterns frequently used for ADR mentions in social media websites. Ensemble classification technique was used by Chee, Berlin and Shatz [3] to classify drugs into those that had undergone label changes or regulatory by the FDA, and those which had not. For their experiments they built hundreds of classifiers. Naïve Bayes and Support Vector Machine (SVM) with a RBF kernel were the two base classification algorithms used. They were able to successfully identify drugs that have been withdrawn from the market based on messages that had been posted before those withdrawals. Patki et al. [15] explored a supervised text classification approach for mining health-related forum. Applying a two-step approach, they first classified whether or not a user comment included a mention of an ADR, and then inferred whether the combined comments for the drug indicated an inordinate incidence of adverse reactions. Two supervised machine learning algorithms were utilized: Multinomial Naïve Bayes (MNB) and SVM. They demonstrate mixed results with respect to the ability of their method distinguishing true ADRs from noise.

While text classification approaches gained popularity in analyzing unstructured, informal texts commonly found in online forums, due to their ability to filter out noise from noisy data, it is worth emphasizing that the supervised nature of the these approaches is quite laborious. Numerous user comments had to be annotated to create the training data, often annotation was performed by domain experts or under the guidance of a pharmacology expert. This effort might not be feasible when researching a large number of drugs and ADRs. Moreover, results are highly dependent on the richness and the representativeness of the training data.

2.3 Semi-Supervised and Unsupervised Learning Based Approach

In light of the above-mentioned limitations of the supervised-based approach, recent papers have tried to evade its chains by suggesting unsupervised or semi-supervised learning methodologies, thus eliminating the need for plentiful human annotations. Wang, Li, Ferguson and Zhai [19] proposed a completely unsupervised, probabilistic topic model to mine, for each drug, the related ADRs mentioned by online health forum users. The model was able to distinguish ADRs from just disease symptoms by explicitly modeling the two components separately, therefore, enabled the mining of meaningful ADRs, some of which have never been reported in the FDA database. Liu and Chen [12] developed a framework for Drug-ADR relation extraction from patient forums, which was based on statistical learning.

Lastly, in a study closest in its methodology to ours, Netzer et al. [13] have utilized consumer-generated data posted on consumer forums to allow commercial marketing analysis. One of the cases investigated Drug-ADR relationships extracted from diabetes online forums. They show firm consistency between ADRs mentioned in diabetes online forums and ADRs reported in formal medical venues. Our methodology, to be described hereinbelow, also resides in the unsupervised learning yard, and will exhibit the following qualities: (1) An end-to-end text mining solution for Drug-ADR detection from online forums, which is unsupervised or semi-supervised with high degree of precision; (2) A text mining technology that is based on a HPSG-based parser; (3) A post-processing algorithm that enhances the set of Drug-

ADR extracted relations in order increase recall and allow statistical testing of the results.

3. METHODOLOGY

At the core of our mechanism for mining the Drug-Symptom relations lies an Unsupervised Relation Extraction (URE) framework. The framework, as thoroughly illustrated by Rozenfeld and Feldman [16], is a domain independent set of tools and methods for building Information Extraction (IE) and Relation Extraction (RE) systems focusing on natural language sentences. The framework includes both supervised and unsupervised methods, as well as allowing arbitrary blends between them. Purely unsupervised methods can be utilized in Open IE task setting (Banko and Etzioni [1]), in which the RE system trains itself to extract all possible target relations without any human input. Among other tools, the URE framework includes a grammar description language, which is able to define arbitrary weighted typed-feature-structure context-free grammars (WTFSCFG-s), a parser for such grammars, and a specific grammar and lexicon for parsing general English sentences. This grammar is a generic, HPSG-based English grammar with an underspecified lexicon. In the lexicon, only the most frequent and functional words have full definitions, while the open classes of words are defined with underspecified lexical entries and tightly-integrated separate PoS and NER components. For general English sentences, URE produces parses of only mediocre quality. However, when its lexicon is augmented with focused domain-specific entries, the quality of parses for precisely the relevant (i.e. containing interesting relations) domain-specific sentences is dramatically improved. The domain-specific lexical entries can be added manually or learned in an unsupervised manner from an unlabeled text corpus.

We utilize the URE framework and augment its lexicon with respect to the medical domain, in an attempt to mine Drug-ADR relations. The URE framework serves as our main processing flow: relation pattern acquisition followed by relation extraction. The downside of using this method, as shown later in our empirical application, is that while being highly accurate, it can suffer from low recall. Only patterns that are both semantically and linguistically meaningful can be directly converted into lexical definitions, which severely restricts the possible pattern forms. To mitigate this problem and increase recall we employ an additional post-processing step.

Next, we outline the steps involved in our text mining methodology.

3.1 Pre-processing

Following are the steps that are taken as part of a pre-processing flow.

1. *Download and Parse*: Download relevant Web pages from various popular medical forums in HTML format. Then, parse each HTML-formatted page and extract vital information from it: thread link, thread ID, thread title. Additionally, for each message in a thread, i.e. the original message and its replies, extract its user name, date and its textual content. These operations are performed using Scrapy[1].

2. *Remove Duplicates*: Filter out identical messages by using the Python Standard Library's *md5* module, which implements RSA's MD5 message-digest algorithm for generating a 128-bit hash value that serves as a fingerprint for each message. The hash value is produced on the string resulting in concatenating a lowered-case message's text, its date and user name.

3. *Break Into Sentences*: Split each message into sentences. This is done using Natural Language Toolkit (NLTK)[2]. More specifically, using a NLTK's *tokenize* module, that uses an unsupervised learning approach to build a model for finding sentence boundaries.

3.2 Relation Pattern Acquisition

After obtaining the pertinent medical forums texts, and after breaking all unique message into sentences, and preparing them for the mining process, we continue to the learning phase, in which relevant Drug-Symptom relation patterns are generated by applying an acquisition process on those unlabeled texts. We follow the Drug and Symptoms entity identification procedure, described in detail in the Web Appendix in [13]. That is, the Drug entity is a dictionary-based entity type, while the Symptom entity is a combination of dictionary-based and pattern-based entity type. The acquisition process amounts to the following steps.

1. Run the Automatic Lexicon Acquisition mode of URE on a sample of the data in order to learn Drug-Symptom relation patterns between the following entity types: Person, Drug, Symptom and, when relevant, Disease.

2. Manually remove irrelevant relations that have been generated. In addition, cluster relation patterns if necessary and promote relevant relation patterns that were discovered but did not cross a predefined threshold for them to be considered sufficiently supported to comprise relation patterns.

3.3 Extraction

After learning the relevant patterns, the URE lexicon acquisition component converts them into HPSG lexical entries and adds them to the lexicon, which is then used to parse the entire input corpus. The output of this process includes all extracted relevant entities (Drug, Symptom, etc.), and relations (Drug-Symptom, Person-Drug, Person-Symptom, etc.) in the form of HPSG semantic structures, which then can be converted into a standard "relation frame" form. The extracted entities are further used during the post-processing stage.

3.4 Post-processing

When taking only straightforwardly extracted Drug-Symptom relations, URE often misses many valuable relations that are mentioned in indirect ways. For example, a relation slot may be missing due to unresolved co-references or because of the main relation verb being in a gerund form or in an actor-less passive form. There are also more elusive syntactic relation forms which cannot be easily learned, and also relations which are semantically implied but not stated directly. Therefore, a post-processing stage has been designed

[1]An open-source web crawling/web scraping framework, which is written in Python. Available at *scrapy.org*.

[2]A suite of libraries for Natural Language Processing (NLP), which is written in Python. Available at *www.nltk.org*.

to try and catch those missing relations, thus boosting the recall while keeping the precision at a high level.

In the following description of the post-processing algorithms, we will refer to Drug-Symptom relations as *full relation* (FE), and to relations that are not themselves Drug-Symptom relations, but contain either a Drug slot or a Symptom slot, as *partial relation*. For example, each of Rel_PERSON_take_DRUG and Rel_PERSON_experience_SYMPTOM are partial relations.

3.4.1 Types of Post-processed Relation Extractions

Apart from the full relation extractions that are straightforwardly extracted by URE, we employ the following three post-processing methods to extract additional relations:

3.4.2 Merging Partial Relations (MPR)

Detect two partial relations that complete each other, either in the same sentence or in adjacent sentences. In our case, it means one that is missing a Drug entity in the relation and the other that is missing a Symptom entity in the relation. For example, from the sentence in Figure 1 two relations are extracted: Rel_PERSON_take_DRUG and Rel_PERSON_suffer_SYMPTOM. Thus, it is very natural and intuitive to deduce a Drug-Symptom relation in this sentence between Lipitor and memory loss.

I took Lipitor **and {I} suffered muscle weakness and memory loss.**

Figure 1: An example of a MPR candidate. (Curly brackets denote an implicit word in the sentence.)

3.4.3 Merging a Partial Relation with an Entity (MPRE)

Detect a partial relation along with an entity of the type that the partial relation lacks, either in the same sentence or in adjacent sentences. For example, in the sentences in Figure 2, the relation Rel_PERSON_take_DRUG is extracted from the first sentence and several Symptom entities, including memory loss, are extracted from the second sentence, allowing us to infer the statins-memory loss relation.

My husband took statins **for 9 years, the last one was Lipitor. Side effects included** severe neck **and** shoulder pain, muscle atrophe, loss of muscle strength **and both short term and long term** memory loss.

Figure 2: An example of a MPRE candidate.

3.4.4 Merging Same Sentence Entities (MSSE)

Detect two complementary entities in the same sentence. This heuristics is a special case of the co-occurrence approach. However, unlike the naïve co-occurrence approach, we severely restrict the extractions by distance between entities, and by requiring the absence of other entities of the same types in the sentence. Naturally, this heuristic is applied after all the other methods, and only if they cannot be applied. These restrictions limits false-positive cases, while serving as a safety net for catching unextracted relations.

This post-processing method also has a development-related aspect, as it can assist us in manually expanding the list of relation patterns by manually reviewing such MSSE extractions in the development set.

3.5 Post-Processing Algorithms

The two algorithms presented hereinafter together implement the post-processing flow. The first algorithm, a relation generation algorithm, is responsible for generating candidates for relations that have been missed by URE. The second algorithm filters possibly superfluous relations generated by the first algorithm. The reason for separating the two algorithms stems from the fact that the relation generation algorithm makes only local decisions, on whether or not to add the current extraction as a relation candidate. On the other hand, the filtering algorithm has a global scope, and checks all relations generated from the message when making its decisions.

Algorithm 1 Post-processing: Relation Generation

```
In: A list of extractions E, EntTyp1, EntTyp2
Out: A list of post-processed extractions PPE
ME ← Group E by message
for all me in ME do
  SenInd2PartExt ← Map me's partial ext. by sentence index
  EntExt1 ← Map me's EntTyp1 ent. by sentence index
  EntExt2 ← Map me's EntTyp2 ent. by sentence index
  for all e in me do
    if |e.drugs| ≥ 1 and |e.symptoms| ≥ 1 then
      e.type ← FE
      PPE ← PPE||addRel(c)
    end if
    twoPartExtSentInd ← sentence indices with
    at least two partial extractions in SenInd2PartExt
    for all si in twoPartExtSentInd do
      twoPartExt ← SenInd2PartExt[si]
      for all (peA, peB) in twoPartExt do
        if |peA.EntTyp1| = 0 and |peA.EntTyp2| ≥ 1
        and |peB.EntTyp1| ≥ 1 and |peB.EntTyp2| = 0
        then
          e ← Merge peA and peB into
          relation e with e.type = MPR
          PPE ← PPE||addRel(e)
        end if
      end for
    end for
    Repeat adding MPR's logic with 1 sentence-distance.
    for all (si, pe) in SenInd2PartExt do
      sentDist ← 0
      missEntTyp ← pe.missEntTyp
      adjSent ← Using relevant EntExti, 0 sentDist sentences
      in relation to si having missEntTyp (excluding anaphora)
      for all s in adjSent do
        e ← Merge pe and entity of type missEntTyp from s tc
        relation e with e.type = MPRE
        PPE ← PPE||addRel(e)
      end for
    end for
    twoEntSentInd ← sentence indices with (at least) two
    entities of different types, based on EntExt1 and EntExt2
    for all si in twoEntSentInd do
      e ← Merge each possible combination of entities into
      relation e with e.type = MSSE
      PPE ← PPE||addRel(e)
    end for
    Repeat adding MPRE's logic with 1 sentDist.
    Repeat adding MPRE's logic with 2 sentDist.
  end for
end for

addRel(e): Break extraction having more than one drug
  and/or symptoms into multiple extractions.
```

Algorithm 2 Post-processing: Relation Filtering

```
In: A list of post-processed extractions PPE, EntTyp1, EntTyp2, A predefined list of weak anaphoras WA
Out: A list of filtered post-processed extractions FPPE
ME ← Group PPE by message
for all me in ME do
  SME ← Sort by sentence distance then by extraction type
  PriorE ← []
  for all e in SME do
    localSkipCond1 ← e.ent1 and e.ent2 are anaphoras
    localSkipCond2 ← e.ent1 in WA or e.ent2 in WA
    if localSkipCond1 or localSkipCond2 then
      continue
    end if
    skipExtraction ← false
    for all pe in PriorE do
      skipCond1 ← e.senDist >0 and e.supSenInd = pe.senInd
      skipCond2 ← e.senDist >0 and e.supSenInd = pe.supSenInd
        and e.senInd <>pe.senInd
      skipCond3 ← e.senDist = 0 and e.senInd = pe.senInd
        and pe.type = FE or pe.type = MPR
      skipCond4 ← e.senDist = 0 and e.senInd = pe.senInd
        and e.ent1 is anaphora or e.ent2 is anaphora
      if any skipCond_i holds then
        skipExtraction = true
        break
      end if
      if not skipExtraction then
        PriorE ← PriorE||e
        FPPE ← FPPE||e
      end if
    end for
  end for
end for
```

3.6 Analysis

We compute a lift measure to evaluate the likelihood of a particular Drug-ADR relationship to occur over and beyond chance. We then use a chi-square statistic to evaluate the statistical significance of the lift measure.

One important indication that sheds light on a Drug-ADR association is the *lift* metrics. The concept of lift, also known as *association ratio* and *point-wise mutual information* ([4, 18]), serves as a method for measuring the strength of the semantic association between words, by calculating the degree of statistical dependence between them. Our methodology aims at obtaining data regarding Drug-Symptom relations rather than mere co-occurrence of Drug and Symptom entities. Thus, given a drug D and a symptom S, we define:

$$\text{lift}(D, S) = \frac{\Pr(D, S)}{\Pr(D) \times \Pr(S)}$$

In this extended definition $\Pr(D, S)$ relates to the probability of a relation extraction, while $\Pr(D)$ and $\Pr(S)$ relates to the probability of an entity extraction.

In calculating lifts in our case the researcher has a decision to make with respect to what is the population of messages to be included in the denominator of the lift probabilities. On the one hand, one can include the entire population of messages whether or not the messages includes a Drug-Symptom relation. This is likely to lead a set of lift measures that are greater than 1, as many of messages include neither drug nor a symptom. An alternative is to include in the denominator only messages that include at least one Drug-Symptom relation. In our empirical application we include both measures of lift.

- *classic-induced lift*:

$$\frac{\Pr(\text{message has } D - S \text{ relation})}{\Pr(\text{message has D entity}) \times \Pr(\text{message has S entity})}$$

  In this formula the population refers to *all* of the messages that were downloaded from the medical forums.

- *relation-driven lift*:

$$\frac{\Pr(D_0 - S_0 \text{ relation})}{\sum_i \Pr(D_i - S_0 \text{ relations}) \times \sum_i \Pr(D_0 - S_i \text{ relations})}$$

  In this calculation the population is the sum of Drug-Symptom relation extractions. Note that this means a message is bound to have a Drug-Symptom relation extraction in order to be taken into account, specifically it is not enough for it to include just Drug and Symptom entity extractions, which don't relate one another. Put in other words, this lift calculation factors only relation extractions and ignores plain entity extractions.

We report these two lift metrics in our empirical applications. In addition to lift measures we use a chi-square test to measure the statistical significance of the difference between the calculated lift measure and a lift value of 1, which represents the lift expected by chance.

4. EMPIRICAL APPLICATIONS

One could use our proposed approach to extract Drug-ADR relations for each drug and compare them to ADRs that are "formally" reported on the drug label and pharmaceutical drug website. Several studies have taken that approach ([13], [21], [22]). However, that approach is descriptive rather than predictive. Specifically, it is not clear whether the mention of the Drug-ADR relation in social media is a reflection of the medical relation between the two or simply recitation of information posted by the FDA and/or pharmaceutical firm about the relation. In this study we wish to put our proposed approach under a tougher test of *predicting* Drug-ADR relations from their mention in social media prior to their reporting by the FDA. We present our above-described methodology applied to two case studies from different sub-domains. In addition to the extracted Drug-ADR mentions in online forums, we collected safety communications, reported by the FDA regarding one or more ADRs that were associated with one or more drugs post-marketing of the drug. Our goal is to test for substantial, statistically significant evidence for Drug-ADR relations mentions in forum messages, that were posted prior to the FDA communications. Such analysis could provide a retrospective proof that those Drug-ADR relations could have been detected beforehand. Before focusing on each case study, here are a few implementation details:

Data: We mined 4 online medical forums and monitored texts spreading over 15 years, from 1999 to 2013.

Extracted Drugs: Apart from a chemical name, each drug has a brand name (trade name). Moreover, often a drug is marketed by more than just one brand name. For example, *Bupropion* is the chemical name for the antidepressant medication *Wellbutrin*, however it is also marketed by other brand names, such as *Aplenzin* and *Zyban*. Furthermore, drugs are occasionally mentioned in online forums by an acronym or with common typos. In keeping with the last example, in several messages *Wellbutrin* was referred to as *WB* or as *Wellbutrine*. Thus, when mining for Drug-ADR relations we searched for all of those variations for the drug name, based on the Drugs.com[3] website, a popular online source of drug information. In the few cases when we stumbled upon a drug name that was missing in our comprehensive Drug dictionary, consisting of nearly 10K entries (see the Web Appendix in [13] for details about forming this dictionary), it was manually added to it. Lastly, for the sake of our analysis we aggregated the results for each drug variation by referencing them all to one *head drug*.

Extracted Symptoms: When reviewing the set of extracted symptoms in our extracted Drug-ADR relations, we aggregated them into a set of disjoint clusters. Each subset in the partition was referenced by a *head symptom*. For instance, *cognitive impairment* is the head symptom of symptoms such as *amnesia*, *blackouts*, *brain fog*, *cognitive problems*, *confusion*, *feeling confused*, *forgetfulness*, etc. Those mappings were done manually, however note that it is a one-time chore for each symptom. Because symptoms are often common across therapeutic areas, as we progressed from one case study to another, less such mappings were left to be done. In the few cases when we came across a variation of a symptom that was missing in our comprehensive Symptom dictionary, consisting of nearly 15K entries (see the Web Appendix in [13] for details about forming this dictionary), it was manually added to it. In general, when deciding on a subset, as well as on its head symptom, we tried to be consistent with symptoms as presented on the WebMD[4] website, so that we will able to later on examine the correlation between our findings and the documented symptoms appearing on this website.

Evaluation: The collection of messages for each case study, was split into development set (25%) and test set (75%). This split was performed for each medical forum that contributed to the collection of messages, as well as for each year out of the 15 years that were surveyed in our case studies, resulting in equivalent sample sets.

Learning: We ran the Automatic Lexicon Acquisition mode of URE while setting the learning thresholds needed for promoting a pattern as follows: A frequency of 2 for a relation (binary or trinary) or modifier and a frequency of 10 for an unary relation. During this process, 194 patterns were learned. Additional 46 patterns were manually added by reviewing the results of the development set, most of them were detected in post-processed results of the above-described *merged same sentence entities* type. All in all, the set was comprised of 246 patterns.

Acquisition: The unsupervised acquisition step was performed on a training set, which was comprised of 150K sentences (from each of the sub-domains). Note that this means training was performed based on a sample that, though equally representing all medical forums and all drugs and symptoms (not just the ones we will focus on in our experiments), comprised only a minority of the entire data.

Analysis: We computed the two measures of lift, the classic-induced and the relation-driven. Each lift with value greater than 1 was considered a potential indicator for a Drug-ADR association. The chi-square test, statistically examined the difference between the lift value and 1.

[3] www.drugs.com

[4] www.webmd.com

#	Class Name	Head Drugs
1	Bile Acid Sequestrants	Welchol, Questran, Colestid
2	Cholesterol Absorption Inhibitors	Zetia
3	Fibric Acid Derivatives (Fibrates)	Tricor, Lopid, Trilipix, Atromid-S
4	Misc. Antihyperlipidemic Agents	Niacin, Vascepa, Choloxin, Jutapid, Kynamro
5	Antihyperlipidemic Combinations	Vytorin, Advicor, Simcor, Caduet, Pravigard Pac, Juvisync, Liptruz
6	Statins	Altoprev, Crestor, Lescol, Lipitor, Mevacor, Pravachol, Zocor, Livalo, Baycol

Table 1: Class names and their belonging head drugs.

Forum	No. of unique messages	No. of sentences	No. of unique usernames
medhelp.org	1,887	14,276	647
exchanges.webmd.com	5,492	32,693	854
healthboards.com	32,665	207,765	3,250
ehealthforum.com	1,042	7,150	562

Table 2: The data collected for the analysis of the Cholesterol Lowering sub-domain.

4.1 The Cholesterol Lowering Sub-Domain

In this experiment, we aimed to follow monitored ADRs, which are related to statins, a class of cholesterol lowering drugs. The cholesterol lowering sub-domain includes several *classes* of drugs. Statin drugs, for example, are often referred to, by patients and doctors as well as in the medical literature, by the use of the collective name: *statins*. This aggregation might affect the output of a text mining task: On the one hand, it naturally thickens the number of extractions for each class of drugs in question. On the other hand it might result in noisy output as not all drugs of a class share the same ADRs. Because our FDA label change was at the level of a class of drugs (statins) we mine Drug-ADR relations at the drug-class level.

We therefore aggregated the cholesterol lowering drugs under their drug classes. We followed the Drugs.com website, a popular online source of drug information, and categorized those drugs into 6 main classes alongside monitoring the class names themselves as drugs when seeking Drug-ADR relations. Table 1 presents the classes and the head drug that belongs to each class. All in all, 119 variations of drugs were monitored for this sub-domain. The collected data for this case study included $41K$ messages from 4 medical forums as detailed in table 2.

4.1.1 Statins and Cognitive Impairment

In February 2012 the FDA approved important safety label changes for statins[5]. Among others, those changes included the addition of label information with regard to

[5] www.fda.gov/Drugs/DrugSafety/ucm293101.htm

Top Extracted ADRs	Class 1	Class 2	Class 3	Class 4	Class 5	Class 6	Total
pain	12	4	12	20	11	453	512
muscle pain	9	0	14	37	9	374	443
flushing	2	0	0	2	180	16	200
heart attack	1	0	4	4	13	172	194
muscle damage	1	2	6	24	7	141	181
feeling weak	1	0	7	20	4	147	179
allergic reaction	3	2	2	8	21	101	137
liver failure	4	0	10	0	42	63	119
diabetes	6	2	2	5	17	78	110
cognitive impairment	1	0	4	2	2	95	104
leg pain	5	0	5	7	7	77	101
muscle problems	2	1	2	8	2	57	72
infection	1	0	2	1	9	59	72
leg cramps	3	2	2	4	2	56	69
muscle weakness	0	2	6	3	0	56	67
cancer	2	0	0	4	4	54	64
head pain	5	2	4	4	10	30	55
heart problems	0	0	1	0	2	51	54
stroke	2	0	2	3	1	42	50
burning sensation	1	0	0	0	4	38	43
Total	61	17	85	156	347	2,160	2,826

Figure 3: Leading extracted relations for the Cholesterol Lowering sub-domain, 1999-2011 (Class 6 is Statins).

Relation-Driven Lift	1	2	3	4	5	6	1	2	3	4	5	6
pain	1.1	1.3	0.8	0.7	0.2	1.2	0.1	0.3	0.0	0.0	0.0	50.3
muscle pain	0.9	0.0	1.1	1.5	0.2	1.1	0.0	0.0	0.0	8.1	0.0	18.6
flushing	0.5	0.0	0.0	0.2	7.3	0.1	0.0	0.0	0.0	0.0	1207.0	0.0
heart attack	0.2	0.0	0.7	0.4	0.5	1.2	0.0	0.0	0.0	0.0	0.0	17.3
muscle damage	0.3	1.8	1.1	2.4	0.3	1.0	0.0	0.8	0.1	22.2	0.0	0.2
feeling weak	0.3	0.0	1.3	2.0	0.2	1.1	0.0	0.0	0.5	11.7	0.0	3.4
allergic reaction	1.0	2.4	0.5	1.1	1.2	1.0	0.0	1.8	0.0	0.0	1.2	0.0
liver failure	1.6	0.0	2.8	0.0	2.9	0.7	0.9	0.0	12.4	0.0	61.1	0.0
diabetes	2.5	3.0	0.6	0.8	1.3	0.9	5.9	2.8	0.0	0.0	1.1	0.0
cognitive impairment	0.4	0.0	1.3	0.3	0.2	1.2	0.0	0.0	0.3	0.0	0.0	13.3
leg pain	2.3	0.0	1.6	1.3	0.6	1.0	3.9	0.0	1.4	0.4	0.0	0.0
muscle problems	1.3	2.3	0.9	2.0	0.2	1.0	0.1	0.8	0.0	4.4	0.0	0.3
infection	0.6	0.0	0.9	0.3	1.0	1.1	0.0	0.0	0.0	0.0	0.0	1.2
leg cramps	2.0	4.8	1.0	1.1	0.2	1.1	1.6	6.2	0.0	0.0	0.0	0.9
muscle weakness	0.0	5.0	3.0	0.8	0.0	1.1	0.0	6.5	8.3	0.0	0.0	1.9

Classic-Induced Lift	1	2	3	4	5	6	1	2	3	4	5	6
pain	0.8	0.8	0.6	1.0	0.1	1.7	0.0	0.0	0.0	0.0	0.0	144.1
muscle pain	1.0	0.0	1.0	2.3	0.2	2.2	0.0	0.0	0.0	23.4	0.0	298.0
flushing	0.5	0.0	0.0	0.3	7.6	0.2	0.0	0.0	0.0	0.0	1017.8	0.0
heart attack	0.1	0.0	0.3	0.3	0.2	0.9	0.0	0.0	0.0	0.0	0.0	0.0
muscle damage	0.3	1.6	1.2	3.4	0.4	2.0	0.0	0.5	0.3	29.8	0.0	76.5
feeling weak	0.2	0.0	0.8	2.4	0.1	1.5	0.0	0.0	0.0	15.8	0.0	29.8
allergic reaction	0.8	1.3	0.3	1.3	1.0	1.4	0.0	0.2	0.0	0.5	0.0	12.6
liver failure	1.6	0.0	2.2	0.0	2.9	1.3	0.9	0.0	6.4	0.0	56.3	4.9
diabetes	0.8	0.8	0.2	0.5	0.5	0.7	0.0	0.0	0.0	0.0	0.0	0.0
cognitive impairment	0.5	0.0	1.3	0.6	0.2	2.0	0.0	0.0	0.2	0.0	0.0	49.3
leg pain	2.2	0.0	1.7	2.0	0.6	2.0	2.5	0.0	1.5	3.1	0.0	49.9
muscle problems	1.6	2.0	1.0	3.8	0.3	2.3	0.4	0.5	0.0	17.3	0.0	58.5
infection	0.2	0.0	0.2	0.1	0.3	0.6	0.0	0.0	0.0	0.0	0.0	0.0
leg cramps	1.7	2.9	0.7	1.4	0.2	1.7	1.0	2.6	0.0	0.5	0.0	18.5
muscle weakness	0.0	3.5	2.6	1.3	0.0	1.9	0.0	3.5	5.9	0.2	0.0	30.6

Figure 4: Lifts and respective chi-square values for leading extracted relations for the Cholesterol Lowering sub-domain, 1999-2011. Each lift cell with value that is greater than 1 is filled with color green, and its chi-square value is calculated. Each such equivalent chi-square value corresponding p-value ≤ 0.05 and p-value ≤ 0.01 is filled with pale blue and blue, respectively.

the potential for non-serious and reversible cognitive side effects, such as memory loss or confusion. This announcement stemmed from post-marketing reports and data that the FDA had reviewed. For instance, the prescribing information for Lipitor, a member of the statins class, was revised to include the following note under post-marketing information clause: *There have been rare post-marketing reports of cognitive impairment (e.g., memory loss, forgetfulness, amnesia, memory impairment, confusion) associated with statin use.*[6]

We implemented our above-described apparatus to mine for Drug-Symptom relations between statins, as well as the other drug classes, and cognitive impairment, as well as other symptoms. Figure 3 presents the number of Drug-Symptom relationships between each drug class and main side effects mined from the test set data from 1999 to 2011 (the year that preceded the FDA's relevant communication). The relationship between statins and cognitive impairment was identified 95 times by our algorithm between 1999 and 2011. It was the 7th most common symptom to be mentioned with statins. Furthermore, the tables in Figure 4, demonstrate that the lift associated with the relationship between statins and cognitive impairment is above 1 and is statistically significant at the 0.01 level. One caveat of that analysis is that it is possible that most of mentions of statins and cognitive impairment appeared in the later years close to the label change announcement when the information about this relation became public. Table 3 presents analysis of the lift between statins and cognitive impairment by year from 2003 and 2011. A strong and significant relationship between statin and cognitive impairment is identified as early as 9 years prior to the FDA label change. Note also that we do not find similar relationship between cognitive impairment and other classes of cholesterol lowering drugs. Indeed, no such association has been reported.

Year	Relation-driven lift	Chi-square value	Classic-induced lift	Chi-square value
2011	1.20	**13.33**	1.99	**49.28**
2010	1.21	**13.24**	1.94	**42.21**
2009	1.22	**13.35**	1.97	**40.03**
2008	1.21	**10.70**	1.89	**31.42**
2007	1.20	**9.95**	2.00	**36.46**
2006	1.21	**10.30**	1.89	**28.20**
2005	1.20	**6.63**	2.04	**25.12**
2004	1.25	3.46	2.18	**12.93**
2003	1.27	1.55	2.16	**5.79**

Table 3: Lifts and respective chi-square values by year for the 9 years that preceded the relevant FDA label change for statin and cognitive impairment. All values in bold are chi-square values ≥ 3.85 or ≥ 6.64, corresponding p-value ≤ 0.05 or ≤ 0.01.

4.2 The Anti-Depression Sub-Domain

This sub-domain presented us with an additional text mining challenge. The ADR in question, agitation, was referred to by user of the medical forums not only as a symptom of drug but as a symptom of depression, or even as a

[6]`www.fda.gov/safety/medwatch/safetyinformation/safety-relateddruglabelingchanges/ucm133531.htm`

Forum	No. of unique messages	No. of sentences	No. of unique usernames
medhelp.org	86,715	729,888	25,049
exchanges.webmd.com	17,403	138,936	1,310
healthboards.com	149,238	1,129,341	16,381
ehealthforum.com	20,634	196,765	9,688

Table 4: The data collected for the analysis of the Anti-Depression sub-domain.

disease of its own. To address this issue we added a new entity type to the framework: DISEASE along with a very basic lexicon of common diseases. After doing so we repeated the acquisition process, this time enabling a richer set of patterns, in which 4 entity types participate: Person, Drug, Symptom and Disease. During this process, we enriched the set of patterns from 246 to 256 patterns.

For this case study we monitored a list of 6 popular anti-depression drugs, whose head drug are the following: *Celexa*, *Effexor*, *Pristiq*, *Wellbutrin*, *Xanax*, and *Zoloft*. All in all, 32 variations of drugs were monitored for this sub-domain. The collected data included $274K$ messages from 4 medical forums as detailed in Table 4.

4.2.1 *Wellbutrin and Agitation*

In an FDA alert from July 2009[7] the manufacturers of Wellbutrin were required to add new box warnings highlighting the risk of serious neuropsychiatric symptoms in patients using the drug. Among those symptoms were agitation and hostility. Healthcare professionals were also instructed to monitor patients taking Wellbutrin for those symptoms. In addition, FDA also required those manufacturers to describe those risks in the Medication Guides for these products.

The table in Figure 5 presents the accumulated Drug-Symptom relations mined from the test set data from 1999 to 2008, the year preceding the FDA's alert discussed above. Wellbutrin was mentioned 77 times in our forums with agitation. Agitation is the 6th most frequently mentioned symptom with Wellbutrin. Looking at the tables in Figure 6, we see that the relationship between Wellbutrin and agitation is statistically significant. Moreover Wellbutrin is the only anti-depression drug that demonstrates that relationship. As can be seen in Table 5, as early as 7 year prior to the FDA communication we find strong and significant relationship between Wellbutrin and agitation.

5. DISCUSSION

We have presented two out of several case studies that we carried out on different medical sub-domains, involving various drugs and ADRs. We used lift measures and corresponding statistical chi-square test primarily to evaluate the quality of our overall approach to predict the eventual outcome of a medical drug-ADR relation. All of those cases demonstrated strong and significant relationship between the drug and the ADR reported by the FDA *prior* to the FDA communication and sometimes years prior to the communication. However, the results are only as good as

[7]http://www.fda.gov/Drugs/DrugSafety/PostmarketDrugSafetyInformationforPatientsandProviders/DrugSafetyInformationforHeathcareProfessionals/ucm169986.htm

Top Extracted ADRs	celexa	effexor	pristiq	wellbutrin	xanax	zoloft	Total
anxiety	217	359	3	343	423	492	1,837
weight gain	71	144	1	130	11	169	526
head pain	56	127	1	100	21	102	407
panic state	44	70	0	19	133	96	362
sleep disorder	43	78	1	86	49	104	361
allergic reaction	46	69	0	67	23	98	303
feeling weak	40	74	3	48	15	60	240
pain	21	74	0	38	30	60	223
tremors	29	59	0	30	43	57	218
agitation	24	46	0	77	11	54	212
nausea	22	89	2	33	7	51	204
sweating	22	103	1	21	5	42	194
seizure	5	16	0	113	40	16	190
dizziness	18	66	1	25	9	50	169
suicidality	15	67	0	18	9	36	145
sexual dysfunction	21	37	0	46	2	28	134
cognitive impairment	10	41	1	17	23	21	113
weight loss	5	23	0	61	2	18	109
mood swings	18	36	0	21	3	27	105
sleepiness	26	32	0	17	5	17	97
Total	753	1,610	14	1,310	864	1,598	6,149

Figure 5: Leading extracted relations for the Anti-Depression sub-domain, 1999-2008.

Relation-Driven Lift	C	E	P	W	X	Z	C	E	P	W	X	Z
anxiety	1.0	0.7	0.7	0.9	1.6	1.0	0.0	0.0	0.0	0.0	174.7	0.9
weight gain	1.1	1.0	0.8	1.2	0.1	1.2	0.8	0.4	0.0	4.0	0.0	11.3
head pain	1.1	1.2	1.1	1.2	0.4	1.0	0.9	5.7	0.0	2.8	0.0	0.0
panic state	1.0	0.7	0.0	0.2	2.6	1.0	0.0	0.0	0.0	0.0	164.0	0.1
sleep disorder	1.0	0.8	1.2	1.1	1.0	1.1	0.0	0.0	0.0	1.5	0.0	1.6
allergic reaction	1.2	0.9	0.0	1.0	0.5	1.2	2.6	0.0	0.0	0.1	0.0	6.7
feeling weak	1.4	1.2	5.5	0.9	0.4	1.0	4.5	2.8	11.5	0.0	0.0	0.0
pain	0.8	1.3	0.0	0.8	1.0	1.0	0.0	5.9	0.0	0.0	0.0	0.1
tremors	1.1	1.0	0.0	0.6	1.4	1.0	0.2	0.1	0.0	0.0	6.0	0.0
agitation	0.9	0.8	0.0	1.7	0.4	1.0	0.0	0.0	0.0	29.5	0.0	0.0
nausea	0.9	1.7	4.3	0.8	0.2	1.0	0.0	33.2	5.3	0.0	0.0	0.0
sweating	0.9	2.0	2.3	0.5	0.2	0.8	0.0	75.1	0.7	0.0	0.0	0.0
seizure	0.2	0.3	0.0	2.8	1.5	0.3	0.0	0.0	0.0	170.4	8.0	0.0
dizziness	0.9	1.5	2.6	0.7	0.4	1.1	0.0	14.9	1.0	0.0	0.0	1.2
suicidality	0.8	1.8	0.0	0.6	0.4	1.0	0.0	30.8	0.0	0.0	0.0	0.0

Classic-Induced Lift	C	E	P	W	X	Z	C	E	P	W	X	Z
anxiety	0.8	0.6	0.3	0.7	2.0	0.9	0.0	0.0	0.0	0.0	211.9	0.0
weight gain	1.4	1.4	0.6	1.6	0.3	1.7	8.8	19.2	0.0	25.9	0.0	51.8
head pain	0.9	1.0	0.5	1.0	0.5	0.9	0.0	0.1	0.0	0.0	0.0	0.0
panic state	1.0	0.8	0.0	0.3	4.2	1.2	0.0	0.0	0.0	0.0	335.2	2.9
sleep disorder	0.9	0.8	0.7	1.1	1.4	1.2	0.0	0.0	0.0	0.6	6.8	2.3
allergic reaction	1.1	0.8	0.0	0.9	0.8	1.2	0.7	0.0	0.0	0.0	0.0	3.8
feeling weak	0.8	0.7	2.0	0.6	0.4	0.7	0.0	0.0	1.6	0.0	0.0	0.0
pain	0.2	0.3	0.0	0.2	0.4	0.3	0.0	0.0	0.0	0.0	0.0	0.0
tremors	1.2	1.1	0.0	0.7	2.2	1.1	0.7	0.5	0.0	0.0	27.2	0.4
agitation	0.9	0.9	0.0	1.8	0.6	1.1	0.0	0.0	0.0	28.8	0.0	0.5
nausea	0.8	1.7	2.4	0.7	0.4	1.0	0.0	24.1	1.6	0.0	0.0	0.0
sweating	1.1	2.4	1.7	0.7	0.4	1.1	0.1	74.2	0.3	0.0	0.0	0.2
seizure	0.3	0.4	0.0	3.5	3.0	0.5	0.0	0.0	0.0	187.4	50.3	0.0
dizziness	0.8	1.4	1.4	0.7	0.6	1.2	0.0	6.6	0.1	0.0	0.0	1.5
suicidality	0.3	0.7	0.0	0.3	0.3	0.5	0.0	0.0	0.0	0.0	0.0	0.0

Figure 6: Lifts and respective chi-square values for leading extracted relations for the Anti-Depression sub-domain, 1999-2008.

our ability to mine the Drug-ADR relations. Therefore, we now discuss the quality of our text mining approach. Given the manageable number of extracted relations we annotated each and every extracted relation of focus for its correct-

Annotated Extracted ADRs / Development Set	Sub-domain	Precision	True Positive Extractions	False Positive Extractions	Total Extractions	Distribution by Impression		Distribution by Extraction			
						Subjective Impressions	Objective Impressions	FE Type	MPR Type	MPRE Type	MSSE Type
cognitive impairment	Cholesterol Lowering	100.0%	38	0	38	76%	24%	32%	8%	29%	31%
agitation	Anti-Depression	89.2%	58	7	65	84%	16%	6%	8%	57%	29%
Total		**93.2%**	**96**	**7**	**103**	**81%**	**19%**	**16%**	**8%**	**47%**	**30%**

Annotated Extracted ADRs / Test Set	Sub-domain	Precision	True Positive Extractions	False Positive Extractions	Total Extractions	Distribution by Impression		Distribution by Extraction			
						Subjective Impressions	Objective Impressions	FE Type	MPR Type	MPRE Type	MSSE Type
cognitive impairment	Cholesterol Lowering	96.9%	125	4	129	55%	45%	32%	5%	39%	24%
agitation	Anti-Depression	83.4%	231	46	277	84%	16%	9%	7%	51%	33%
Total		**87.7%**	**356**	**50**	**406**	**75%**	**25%**	**17%**	**6%**	**47%**	**30%**

Recall	True Positive Extractions	False Negative Extractions	Total Extractions
71.7%	104	41	145
69.1%	105	47	152
70.4%	**209**	**88**	**297**

Figure 7: Annotated Drug-ADR extractions for both the development and test sets.

Year	Relation-driven lift	Chi-square value	Classic-induced lift	Chi-square value
2008	1.70	**29.53**	1.81	**28.79**
2007	1.75	**28.70**	1.83	**26.97**
2006	1.72	**21.13**	1.61	**12.91**
2005	1.69	**16.54**	1.78	**15.90**
2004	1.46	**5.13**	1.51	**5.13**
2003	1.64	**8.03**	2.05	**13.99**
2002	1.78	**6.41**	2.36	**12.25**

Table 5: Lifts and respective chi-square values by year, for the 7 years that preceded the relevant FDA communication for Wellbutrin and agitation. All values in bold are chi-square values ≥ 3.85 or ≥ 6.64, corresponding p-value ≤ 0.05 or ≤ 0.01.

ness. The aggregated results of our annotations are detailed in Figure 7.

One can see that precision rates are indeed high: 88% overall precision for the test set. Precision for the development set is only moderately higher at 93%, suggesting that the manually added rules, which were affected by the development set, were not over-fitted much by the data. By adding the Disease entity type into the set of extracted entities and relations, our results for the test set have been moderately improved from a 80.7% precision to 83.4% precision (the results for the development set have been upgraded from 80.3% to 89.2%). Although the core of our research is in the design of a text mining methodology capable of predicting Drug-ADR relations, we also wanted to have a recall estimation of our relation extractions. Based on the test set messages between 1999-2011 (2012 being the pivotal year), we measured a 71.7% recall for relations involving the cognitive impairment Symptom entity. As for Drug-ADR relations with respect to the agitation Symptom entity, we measured a 69.1% recall on test set messages between 1999-2008 (2009 being the pivotal year). When combining those scores for recall and precision we get 82.4% and 75.6% F1-Scores, respectively.

Next, the distribution by extraction type indicates that without the post-processing step, our analysis would have reached a substantially lower recall. Thus, post-processing comprises a crucial step for establishing our findings.

When annotating the extractions, we also annotated them for their impressions (this concept is elaborated on Table 6). Note that the majority of the relation extractions are characterized as expressing subjective impressions. Patients, as

Impression Type	Definition
Subjective	Extractions, in which a patient was confessing about a personal experience or an experience of a close family member or a friend, e.g., *I had **memory problems** with **Simvastatin** also to the point that I forgot where I was while driving.*
Objective	Extractions, in which the writer either quotes facts from scientific articles or information gained from the media, or states a general saying (e.g. hearsay) about a Drug-ADR connection, e.g., *There are more people out here having **memory loss problems** from **statin** drug that anyone can count.*

Table 6: Different types of annotated impressions.

it seems, do tend to share their user experience with respect to drugs. Notwithstanding, the table also suggests that the dominance of the subjective impression dramatically varies from one ADR to another. It is considerably stronger for the agitation ADR compared to the cognitive impairment ADR. One might suggest it could stem from the characteristics of the ADR, mainly its manifestation in our lives. In this respect, this result coincides with a previous finding by Yang, Yang, Jiang and Tang [21], who show that their proposed technique was promising for detecting ADRs such as heart condition and diarrhea, however not effective for ADRs such as cancer.

6. CONCLUSION AND FUTURE WORK

In this paper we have presented an end-to-end, step-by-step text mining methodology for the process of extracting Drug-ADR relations from online message boards. Our methodology combined several advantages that have made it effective as a tool kit for practical use. Despite being unlaborious, our approach has shown to be precise and more importantly, able to predict Drug-ADR relations that have not been announced at the time of their mention in the medical forums. Using several case studies, we demonstrated that one could find significant traces in medical forums for ADRs related to different drugs years before these ADRs are reported by the FDA.

One can suggest a few research directions, which may enhance our current methodology and its outcomes, including:

Augmenting the pre-processing step by amending irregularities such as corrupt grammar, informal syntax, typos and extensive use of acronyms, aiming at reducing the amount of sentences for which the parse failed; Extending the corpus by mining more online message boards or other social media sources (e.g., Twitter feed), as obtaining more raw data may be crucial when mining less popular sub-domains, when looking into less common drugs, or when addressing less discussed ADRs; Lastly, perfecting our text mining algorithm, among others: Exploring improved approaches to distinguish Drug-Disease relations from Drug-ADR relations as well as bringing to a minimum cases of Drug-ADR false alarms.

7. REFERENCES

[1] M. Banko, O. Etzioni, and T. Center. The tradeoffs between open and traditional relation extraction. In *ACL*, volume 8, pages 28–36. Citeseer, 2008.

[2] A. Benton, L. Ungar, S. Hill, S. Hennessy, J. Mao, A. Chung, C. E. Leonard, and J. H. Holmes. Identifying potential adverse effects using the web: A new approach to medical hypothesis generation. *Journal of Biomedical Informatics*, 44(6):989–996, 2011.

[3] B. W. Chee, R. Berlin, and B. Schatz. Predicting adverse drug events from personal health messages. 2011:217–226, 2011.

[4] K. W. Church and P. Hanks. Word association norms, mutual information, and lexicography. *Computational Linguistics*, 16(1):22–29, 1990.

[5] R. Feldman, M. Fresko, J. Goldenberg, O. Netzer, and L. H. Ungar. Extracting product comparisons from discussion boards. In *International Conference on Data Mining (ICDM)*, pages 469–474, 2007.

[6] R. Feldman, M. Fresko, J. Goldenberg, O. Netzer, and L. H. Ungar. Using text mining to analyze user forums. In *International Conference on Service Systems and Service Management (ICSSSM)*, pages 1–5, 2008.

[7] N. Glance, M. Hurst, K. Nigam, M. Siegler, R. Stockton, and T. Tomokiyo. Analyzing online discussion for marketing intelligence. In *Special Interest Tracks and Posters of the 14th International Conference on World Wide Web*, pages 1172–1173, 2005.

[8] N. Glance, M. Hurst, K. Nigam, M. Siegler, R. Stockton, and T. Tomokiyo. Deriving marketing intelligence from online discussion. In *Proceedings of the Eleventh ACM SIGKDD International Conference on Knowledge Discovery in Data Mining*, pages 419–428, 2005.

[9] S. Hariharan and T. Ramkumar. Mining product reviews in web forums. In *Information Retrieval Methods for Multidisciplinary Applications*, pages 78–94. IGI Global, 2013.

[10] R. Leaman, L. Wojtulewicz, R. Sullivan, A. Skariah, J. Yang, and G. Gonzalez. Towards internet-age pharmacovigilance: Extracting adverse drug reactions from user posts to health-related social networks. In *Proceedings of the 2010 Workshop on Biomedical Natural Language Processing*, pages 117–125, 2010.

[11] T. Y. Lee and E. T. Bradlow. Automated marketing research using online customer reviews. *Journal of Marketing Research*, 48(5):881–894, 2011.

[12] X. Liu and H. Chen. Azdrugminer: An information extraction system for mining patient-reported adverse drug events in online patient forums. In *Smart Health*, pages 134–150. Springer, 2013.

[13] O. Netzer, R. Feldman, J. Goldenberg, and M. Fresko. Mine your own business: Market-structure surveillance through text mining. *Marketing Science*, 31(3):521–543, 2012.

[14] A. Nikfarjam and G. H. Gonzalez. Pattern mining for extraction of mentions of adverse drug reactions from user comments. In *American Medical Informatics Association (AMIA) Annual Symposium Proceedings 2011*, pages 1019–1026. American Medical Informatics Association, 2011.

[15] A. Patki, A. Sarker, P. Pimpalkhute, A. Nikfarjam, R. Ginn, K. O'Connor, K. Smith, and G. Gonzalez. Mining adverse drug reaction signals from social media: Going beyond extraction. In *Proceedings of the 22nd Annual International Conference on Intelligent Systems for Molecular Biology (ISBM)*, pages 9–16, 2014.

[16] B. Rozenfeld and R. Feldman. Unsupervised lexicon acquisition for hpsg-based relation extraction. In *International Joint Conference on Artificial Intelligence (IJCAI)*, pages 1890–1895, 2011.

[17] I. Segura-Bedmar, S. de la Pena, and P. Martınez. Extracting drug indications and adverse drug reactions from spanish health social media. In *Proceedings of the 2014 Workshop on Biomedical Natural Language Processing*, pages 98–106, 2014.

[18] P. D. Turney and M. L. Littman. Measuring praise and criticism: Inference of semantic orientation from association. *ACM Transactions on Information Systems (TOIS)*, 21(4):315–346, 2003.

[19] S. Wang, H. Lin, D. Ferguson, and C. Zhai. Sideeffectptm: An unsupervised topic model to mine adverse drug reactions from health forums. 2014.

[20] R. W. White, N. P. Tatonetti, N. H. Shah, R. B. Altman, and E. Horvitz. Web-scale pharmacovigilance: Listening to signals from the crowd. *Journal of the American Medical Informatics Association (JAMIA)*, 20(3):404–408, 2013.

[21] C. C. Yang, L. Jiang, H. Yang, and X. Tang. Detecting signals of adverse drug reactions from health consumer contributed content in social media. In *Proceedings of ACM SIGKDD Workshop on Health Informatics*, 2012.

[22] C. C. Yang, H. Yang, L. Jiang, and M. Zhang. Social media mining for drug safety signal detection. In *Proceedings of the 2012 International Workshop on Smart Health and Wellbeing (SHB)*, pages 33–40, 2012.

One-Pass Ranking Models for Low-Latency Product Recommendations

Antonino Freno*
Zalando
Berlin, Germany
antonino.freno@zalando.de

Martin Saveski*
MIT Media Lab
Cambridge, USA
msaveski@mit.edu

Rodolphe Jenatton
Amazon
Berlin, Germany
jenatton@amazon.com

Cédric Archambeau
Amazon
Berlin, Germany
cedrica@amazon.com

ABSTRACT

Purchase logs collected in e-commerce platforms provide rich information about customer preferences. These logs can be leveraged to improve the quality of product recommendations by feeding them to machine-learned ranking models. However, a variety of deployment constraints limit the naïve applicability of machine learning to this problem. First, the amount and the dimensionality of the data make in-memory learning simply not possible. Second, the drift of customers' preference over time require to retrain the ranking model regularly with freshly collected data. This limits the time that is available for training to prohibitively short intervals. Third, ranking in real-time is necessary whenever the query complexity prevents us from caching the predictions. This constraint requires to minimize prediction time (or equivalently maximize the data throughput), which in turn may prevent us from achieving the accuracy necessary in web-scale industrial applications. In this paper, we investigate how the practical challenges faced in this setting can be tackled via an online learning to rank approach. Sparse models will be the key to reduce prediction latency, whereas one-pass stochastic optimization will minimize the training time and restrict the memory footprint. Interestingly, and perhaps surprisingly, extensive experiments show that one-pass learning preserves most of the predictive performance. Additionally, we study a variety of online learning algorithms that enforce sparsity and provide insights to help the practitioner make an informed decision about which approach to pick. We report results on a massive purchase log dataset from the Amazon retail website, as well as on several benchmarks from the LETOR corpus.

*Antonino Freno and Martin Saveski contributed to this work while they were at Amazon Development Center Germany.

KDD'15, August 10-13, 2015, Sydney, NSW, Australia.

ACM 978-1-4503-3664-2/15/08 ...$15.00.
DOI: http://dx.doi.org/10.1145/2783258.2788579.

1. INTRODUCTION

Ranking algorithms for document retrieval and (content-based) product recommendation typically work with high-dimensional feature vector representations of the products to be ranked. The available features range from query-independent information (e.g., product category or document topic) to information measuring the match between the user or query and the retrieved product or document (e.g., similarity scores or other relational quantities). The dimensionality of the feature vectors and the complexity of the statistical relationships involved are such that accurate results cannot be achieved by designing the relevant ranking functions manually. Therefore, learning to rank from examples has become the dominant approach when designing and optimizing ranking systems [16, 21].

Learning to rank in web-scale, real-time applications pose at least three major challenges to algorithmic design. First, the learning algorithms must be able to process several gigabytes (when not terabytes) of training data in a limited amount of time. Here, the data set size stems both from the huge number of training examples (in the order of millions to hundreds of millions) and the large number of attributes describing the examples. When a ranking system is deployed to production, a common requirement is to train a new model at regular intervals (e.g., daily) on fresh query logs, which are collected over the past few days. This limits the amount of time available for training to at most a few hours, taking into account the overhead imposed by collateral deployment issues. Second, when the amount of training data is too large, we cannot store anything but a minimal fraction of the available data in memory. This restricts the range of viable learning options to methods characterized by extremely frugal memory requirements. In particular, any learning method whose memory footprint grows with the size of the training data set is a nonstarter in this setting. Third, the learned ranking function must meet strict requirements in terms of latency/throughput. For instance, when the customer of an e-commerce website is browsing the catalogue, we must be able to compute recommendations tied to that particular, dynamically generated context in quasi real time, i.e., at the same time as he or she is loading and scrolling the content of the web page. In practice, this means that, for lists containing hundreds of candidate recommendations, all the products in each list need to be scored/ranked in just a few milliseconds.

The general framework we adopt in order to address these challenges is listwise ranking loss minimization with sparsity-inducing penalties, where optimization is based on single pass of stochastic gradient descent (SGD) updates or variants thereof. In particular, we focus on a set of techniques within the LambdaRank family [3]. The main reasons for this choice are the following. First, LambdaRank provides a straightforward way to customize the loss function in order to accommodate for different ranking evaluation metrics. This allows us to abstract our analysis from a specific application domain, such as product recommendation or document retrieval. Second, SGD requires the smallest memory footprint we might achieve, i.e., one training example for each model update or (small) mini-batches. Third, doing one pass through the training examples minimizes the time needed to stream data from disk or through a network connection, which can be extremely expensive. Finally, we learn sparse models (i.e., models where most of the data attributes play no role at prediction time) to significantly reduce the amount of computation required to score/rank candidates (not only in terms of strict scoring time, but especially in terms of fetching/extracting the required features), which brings us closer to our low-latency requirements.

The impact of sparsity-inducing schemes on ranking quality is a relatively recent topic in the learning-to-rank community. The ℓ_1-based methods that we consider in the next sections are related to the truncated gradient approach [19], which has been applied to text document retrieval in [31]. The authors of [18] also consider a sparsity-inducing approach, but it is based on a different primal-dual optimization scheme. Emphasis on non-convexity issues in sparsity-enforcing ranking loss formulations has been discussed instead in [20]. While we share the same interest in sparsity as the aforementioned studies, at least one point has not been addressed by them (or, to the best of our knowledge, by any related work). Specifically, previous work does not explore the impact (in terms of learning and ranking quality) of working under such constraints as *minimal training time* (i.e., only one pass allowed over the training data) and *minimal prediction latency* (i.e., extremely aggressive sparsity requirements). Furthermore, they evaluate (sparse) ranking models on benchmarks of relatively modest size, both in terms of sample size and in terms of dimensionality. As a concrete illustration, the used benchmarks contained at most 64 features and 148,657 samples (see the summary in [18]). Such a setting is simply not commensurable with the scale of current challenges from the WWW. Therefore, we believe that we are filling a gap in the learning-to-rank research by benchmarking sparsity-inducing schemes in a more realistic scenario.

This paper aims to provide *empirically solid* answers to the following two questions:

1. Can we achieve state-of-the-art ranking quality by one-pass SGD (or variants thereof) over the training data?

2. Can we boost the efficiency of our ranking function to the extent necessary to cope with low-latency (real-time) WWW applications?

Our investigation is rooted in web-scale machine learning practice (as enforced, in particular, in the online retail industry), which we deem to be crucial to back theoretical results with their empirical counterpart.

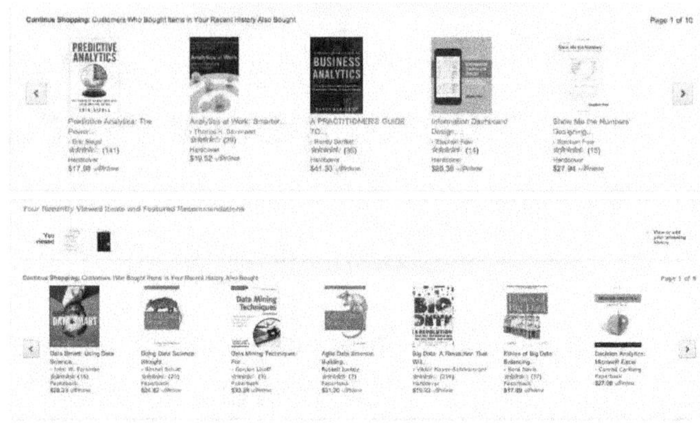

Figure 1: Two examples of Amazon's Recent History Footer (RHF) widget showing 5 (top) and 7 (bottom) products to the customer. The number of products shown depends on the browser's viewing settings.

The paper is organized as follows. We provide an overview of the use case in Section 2 and discuss related ranking evaluation metrics in Section 3. In Section 4, we discuss related work. The listwise ranking model and the on-line learning algorithms are introduced in Section 5. Section 6 describes the Bayesian optimization technique that we use in order to make hyperparameter tuning, both, accurate and efficient. In Section 7, we assess the predictive performance of our approach by looking at three benchmark datasets from the LETOR collection, which is a universally accessible reference for research on learning to rank. After demonstrating the quality of the adopted method on these benchmarks, we investigate the behavior of the proposed approach on a more challenging, web-scale application based on Amazon retail data and discuss the latency/predictive power trade-off (Section 8). The lessons learned from our study are summarized in Section 9.

2. USE CASE: RECOMMENDATIONS BY AMAZON WIDGETS

Consider the two examples shown in Figure 1. Each one is a list of impressions from the recent history footer (RHF) widget. RHF appears at the bottom of many pages on the retail website. The widget displays a number of products which are deemed to be relevant w.r.t. the most recent browsing history of a website visitor (rather than the whole browsing/purchase history, or an aggregate, non-personalized relevance model). When the RHF widget is displayed to a customer, a smaller or larger number of recommendations are actually shown depending on viewport constraints, typically screen resolution, browser font size, etc.

As depicted in Figure 1 the product impressions are shown horizontally. The relative ordering of the products within a widget of size k is not crucial to capture the customer's attention; any product appearing within the top k will be considered relevant. However, once the size k of the widget is determined, it is important to move the products that are most likely to be considered by the customer within the top k positions. If a product which is appealing for the customers is ranked below position k, they do not have the possibility to go directly to the detail page.

Other widgets, with a similar structure, are displayed on the product detail pages from the Amazon retail portal. One such widget is the "Customers Who Bought This Item Also Bought" carousel. Instead of considering relevance to the customer's recent browsing history, this widget focuses on relevance to the currently visited product detail page, based on the criterion of a purchase-to-purchase similarity. Yet, another widget is based on view-to-purchase similarity ("What Other Items Do Customers Buy After Viewing This Item?"). Each widget provides a different type of recommendations by ranking different sets of products.

3. RANKING METRICS

The goal in product recommendation is to recommend products that maximize the click-through rate (CTR) or the purchase rate (PR), which are computed based on the impression logs of these products. CTR and PR express an ordering of the products in the catalog (or any subset of it), which we will call the target ranking. Several ranking evaluation metrics have been proposed in information retrieval [7] to assess the quality of rankings produced, for example, by machine-learned ranking models. These data-driven models try to minimize the discrepancy between the ranking they produce and the target ranking.

Consider a list of n products that is (partially) displayed to one customer. We denote by $\boldsymbol{l} = (l_1, \ldots, l_n)$ the relevance labels associated to the products in this list. Label l_i is the feedback provided by the customer regarding product i. It could be an integer in $\{1, \ldots, n\}$, but it need not be. For example, the feedback could be in some cases continuous, like the purchase price of the product, or ordinal, like a rating by the customer. We will consider the case where every display of a list of products will result in at most one non-zero feedback.

Let $\boldsymbol{r} = (r_1, \ldots, r_n)$ be a ranking of the products in the list. The rank r_i of product i is an integer in $\{1, \ldots, n\}$, where 1 is the first position and n the last one. A popular metric to evaluate the quality of $\boldsymbol{r}$ in light of the relevance labels $\boldsymbol{l}$ is the discounted cumulative gain (DCG):

$$DCG(\boldsymbol{r}, \boldsymbol{l}) = \sum_{i=1}^{n} \frac{2^{l_i} - 1}{\log_2(r_i) + 1}. \quad (1)$$

DCG is non-negative and larger values correspond to better rankings; the contribution of products with low relevance labels that are poorly ranked are downweighted as desired. A closely related evaluation metric is NDCG, which is obtained by normalizing the righthand side of (1) such that the perfect ranking corresponds to a value of NDCG equal to 1 and does not depend on the length of the list. NDCG, can be further parameterized by a threshold $k \in \{1, \ldots, n\}$, such that the summation only runs over the top k products of the proposed ranking $\boldsymbol{r}$. We will call this measure NDCG@K. This variant is appealing in practice as one is usually only interested in an accurate estimation of the rank of the most relevant products.

When the relevance labels are restricted to be binary (i.e. $l_i \in \{0, 1\}$), for example, because we only care about relevant products being ranked at position k or above, we can use recall at k (R@K):

$$R@K(\boldsymbol{r}, \boldsymbol{l}) = \frac{\sum_{i=1}^{n} \mathbb{I}(r_i \leqslant k) l_i}{\sum_{i=1}^{n} l_i}, \quad (2)$$

where $\mathbb{I}(\cdot)$ is the indicator function. R@K is non-negative and larger values correspond to better rankings. This evaluation metric is more suitable than NDCG@K when the relative sorting of the top products does not matter.

Other popular metrics include precision at k, mean average precision, mean reciprocal rank, Kendall's tau and the area under the ROC curve. We refer the interested reader to [5, 22] for in-depth discussions of these metrics, but we will not further discuss them as the most appropriate metric depends on the target application. In Section 7, we report results in terms of NDCG@K as this is the evaluation metric typically used to compare ranking models on the benchmark data sets we consider. In Section 8, we adopt R@K as it matches our use case more closely.

4. BACKGROUND AND RELATED WORK

Learning-to-rank models can be classified into three broad families: pointwise, pairwise, and listwise methods [21]. *Pointwise* approaches postulate a scoring function and attempt to estimate the relevance score of every item. The relevance score is typically the rank of the item in the list or a transformed version of it. At prediction time, the items returned for a query are sorted according to their estimated scores. Linear or logistic regression are examples of scoring functions used in pointwise approaches. *Pairwise* methods score ordered pairs of items instead of individual items. The goal is now to learn the order of such pairs correctly. In other words, the task is to score the more relevant items higher than less relevant ones. In general, this approach is preferable to the pointwise approach, because it does not require to learn absolute relevance scores. RankSVM [12, 16] is one of the most popular pairwise approaches. It formalizes ranking as a binary classification problem of item pairs and uses support vector machines as the underlying binary classifier. Alternatively, one could use Rank Logistic Regression (RankLR), which was shown to work slightly better [29]. RankBoost [11] is another pairwise ranking model, where boosting is used to learn the ranking. The idea is to construct a sequence of 'weak rankers' over iteratively reweighted training data, and then to make rank predictions using a linear combination of the weak learners. While the predictive power of RankBoost is greater in theory, it only marginally improves the quality of the ranking in practice (see Section 7). Finally, *listwise* approaches assume that the training examples are lists of ranked items. They attempt to minimize a loss function defined over the whole list instead of ordered pairs extracted from the list. ListNet [6] is a listwise ranking algorithm, which performs gradient descent over a loss function defined in terms of the cross-entropy. AdaRank [34] is another listwise approach, based instead on boosting. While more costly to learn, in practice these methods perform similarly to pairwise approaches (see Section 7). Recently, gradient-boosted trees (GBTs) have become pretty popular in learning to rank [4, 25]. Although GBTs have been shown to outperform simpler approaches (e.g., plain linear models), training them in the large-scale setting can be very expensive. Moreover, scoring latency is a serious issue for GBTs whenever we are not able to precompute and cache predictions for the task at hand, for the following reasons. In typical real-world applications, several hundreds of base learners (i.e. regression trees) are necessary to reach the desired accuracy, where each tree has about 4 to 8 leaves. This means going through a few thousands of decision rules for each candidate to be scored, which is problematic in our setting. In particular, parallelizing decisions would not be a solution in this case, because single-host multithreading has further latency overhead in terms of spawning the threads, whereas distributing to multiple hosts is even less effective because of inter-host communication. On top of these considerations about scoring latency, one more difficulty is that, without enforcing global feature selection strategies, most or all of the involved features will be used throughout our set of regression trees. This means having to go through the whole feature extraction process, which is often the most expensive side of online candidate scoring. On the other hand, sparse modelling would not suffer from such an overhead by simply dropping features from the scoring function. An alternative model, which has been shown to be very effective for the large-scale setting, is referred to as the WSABIE algorithm [32]. While WSABIE also uses SGD learning, it has not been targeted at the one-pass setting. Moreover, low-dimensional embeddings and data sub-sampling are the main learning tools used by that model, whereas our focus is on sparsity-inducing regularization schemes.

A recent trend in learning to rank is to attempt optimizing the ranking evaluation metric *directly*. This class of approaches typically falls into the listwise approaches, as the ranking metrics are functions of ranked lists (rather than of individual pairs or individual items). In principle, such listwise approaches should be able to outperform pairwise or pointwise methods w.r.t. the ranking metric, as the learning process is more firmly tied to the ranking objective. However, direct optimization of the ranking metric is problematic in practice. Evaluation metrics such NDCG@K and R@K are defined in terms of the resulting ranking, not the scoring functions that induce these rankings. Hence, the ranking metrics are discontinuous (and thus non-differentiable) w.r.t. the parameters of the scoring functions, which in turn means that we cannot apply continuous optimization techniques such as gradient-based methods. One solution to this problem is to construct a continuous approximation of the ranking metric [28], whose optimization will indirectly improve the actual objective. Another solution is to appeal to the idea of an *implicit* ranking metric, called *LambdaRank* [3]. The strategy consists in estimating the parameters of a (differentiable) scoring function while implicitely accounting for the ranking metric. This is achieved by weighting parameter updates proportionally to changes in the ranking metric. We pursue the approach of LambdaRank in the present paper, as discussed at greater length in the next section.

5. RANKING LOSS MINIMIZATION

In this section, we present our regularized formulation of the problem and discuss the different optimization strategies we use. We divide our discussions in two parts, first exposing a convex approach suitable for stochastic optimization strategies and then describing non-convex alternatives. The regularizer we choose leads to sparse solutions to ensure low-latency scoring functions with minimal computation time and memory footprint.

For a given ranking evaluation metric $\mathscr{M}(\boldsymbol{r},\boldsymbol{l})$, we introduce the delta function $\Delta_{\mathscr{M}(\mathrm{r,l})}$, which is given by:

$$\Delta_{\mathscr{M}(\mathrm{r,l})}(i,j) = \mathscr{M}(\boldsymbol{r},\boldsymbol{l}) - \mathscr{M}(\boldsymbol{r}_{i/j},\boldsymbol{l}), \quad (3)$$

where $\boldsymbol{r}_{i/j}$ is the ranking we would obtain by swapping the positions of product i and j in $\boldsymbol{r}$. Intuitively, the delta function $\Delta_{\mathscr{M}(\mathrm{r,l})}$ can be thought of as measuring the importance of sorting i and j correctly in order for $\boldsymbol{r}$ to maximize the value of $\mathscr{M}(\boldsymbol{r},\boldsymbol{l})$.

Further, let $\mathscr{X} = \{\boldsymbol{x}_1,\dots,\boldsymbol{x}_n\}$ be the features associated to the products in the (unsorted) list and suppose that product i is scored by some parametric function $\varphi(\boldsymbol{x}_i)$. We define the ranking loss as follows:

$$\ell_{\mathscr{M}(\boldsymbol{r},\boldsymbol{l})}(\mathscr{X};\varphi) = \sum_{r_i \leqslant r_j} \Delta_{\mathscr{M}(\mathrm{r,l})}(i,j)\cdot \mathscr{P}(\varphi(\boldsymbol{x}_i),\varphi(\boldsymbol{x}_j)), \quad (4)$$

where $\mathscr{P}(x,y)$ is a pairwise loss term. Possible choices for the pairwise loss include the hinge loss, $\mathscr{P}(x,y) = \max\{0, y - x + \epsilon\}$ (for some slack parameter $\epsilon \geqslant 0$), or the logistic loss, $\mathscr{P}(x,y) = \log(1+\exp(x-y))$.

The loss defined in (4) can be understood as follows. If the score of i is higher (or marginally lower) than the score of j, then little loss (or no loss) is incurred. However, if the score of j is higher than the score of i, then the pairwise loss is weighted by $\Delta_{\mathscr{M}(\mathrm{r,l})}(i,j)$, which is the cost of not ranking i and j correctly.

Given a training sample, that is, a list of products to be ranked together with relevance labels, we can learn the parameters in φ by minimizing the ranking loss $\ell_{\mathscr{M}}$ over that sample. This task can be accomplished via standard (sub) gradient descent methods. Any choice for the parametric form of φ, ranging from a simple linear regression to a multilayer perceptron, will be compatible with the ranking metric we are adopting as long as we are able to compute the corresponding (sub)gradients. To satisfy the requirements of our web-scale application, we will restrict ourselves to linear scoring functions. The score of a feature vector $\boldsymbol{x}_i$ is thus given by $\varphi(\boldsymbol{x}_i) = \boldsymbol{w}^\intercal \boldsymbol{x}_i$. This choice preserves the convexity of the ranking loss defined in (4), which is a convenient property for the optimization stage we discuss next.

5.1 Convex approach

In order to induce sparsity in the learned scoring functions, i.e., to zero out some components in the weight vector $\boldsymbol{w}$, we add a ℓ_1-regularization term to the loss defined in (4). This regularized objective is convex (since ℓ_1 is a norm) with, both, theoretical guarantees and efficient algorithmic schemes (e.g., see [26] and references therein). As advocated in large-scale settings (e.g., [24] in the context of online advertising), we additionally consider a squared ℓ_2-term, thus leading to the following regularized ranking loss:

$$\ell^*_{\mathscr{M}(\boldsymbol{r},\boldsymbol{l})}(\mathscr{X};\varphi_{\boldsymbol{w}}) = \ell_{\mathscr{M}(\boldsymbol{r},\boldsymbol{l})}(\mathscr{X};\varphi_{\boldsymbol{w}}) + \lambda_1\|\boldsymbol{w}\|_1 + \frac{1}{2}\lambda_2\|\boldsymbol{w}\|_2^2, \quad (5)$$

where λ_1 and λ_2 are the nonnegative hyperparameters determining, respectively, the weight of the ℓ_1 and ℓ_2 penalties within the overall loss. Note that the resulting regularization is usually referred to as elastic-net [35]. In the remainder of the paper, we will refer to our listwise ranking model as *ElasticRank*.

Our training set is composed of several lists of products $\{\boldsymbol{l}^{(j)},\boldsymbol{r}^{(j)},\mathscr{X}^{(j)}\}$, where $j = 1\dots m$, so that instead of minimising (5), we seek to optimise the *averaged* regularized problem, which is given by:

$$\min_{\boldsymbol{w}} \left\{ \frac{1}{m} \sum_{j=1}^{m} \ell_{\mathcal{M}(\boldsymbol{r}^{(j)},\boldsymbol{l}^{(j)})}(\mathcal{X}^{(j)}; \varphi_{\boldsymbol{w}}) + \lambda_1 \|\boldsymbol{w}\|_1 + \frac{1}{2}\lambda_2 \|\boldsymbol{w}\|_2^2 \right\}. \tag{6}$$

In our web-scale application, m is typically in the order of 10^6. We therefore resort to stochastic optimization tools [2] to solve (6), where the update rule to get the next iterate is based solely on a *single* randomly drawn ranked list. The literature dedicated to the stochastic optimization of functions of the form of (6) is vast (e.g., [9,10,14,23,33]), and we shall focus next on two representative options. Note that we have not considered the recently proposed incremental-gradient schemes (e.g., see [8] and references therein) well-suited to the optimization of (6) because of the their prohibitive memory footprint.

Here, we consider two algorithms that can be implemented efficiently: the update for a single instance is *linear in the number of non-zero features* and independent of the total number of features. In many settings the data are described by a large number of features, but in each individual example only a small subset of these are non-zero. For instance, in text-based applications the number of features corresponds to size of the vocabulary (i.e., the number of unique tokens in the corpus), while each document contains only a small fraction of all the words in the vocabulary. Similarly, one-hot representation of categorical variables that can take many values results in a large number of binary features (as described in Section 8), but typically in each example only one feature is active. Thus, to handle large high-dimensional data sets it is crucial to exploit the sparsity of the examples and perform only the minimum number of operations in each iteration.

Forward-Backward Splitting (FOBOS) [10], on the one hand, solves the regularized optimization problem by alternating between two phases: taking a simple gradient step followed by a proximal step that involves the elastic-net regularization. More specifically, we first perform an unconstrained gradient step:

$$\widetilde{\boldsymbol{w}}_t = \boldsymbol{w}_t - \eta_t \nabla_{\boldsymbol{w}} \ell_{\mathcal{M}(\boldsymbol{r},\boldsymbol{l})}(\mathcal{X}; \varphi_{\boldsymbol{w}}), \tag{7}$$

where η_t is the learning rate at iteration t. Subsequently, we take a proximal step based on the elastic-net regularization (e.g., see Section 3.3 of [1]):

$$w_{t+1,i} = \begin{cases} 0 & \text{if } |\widetilde{w}_{t,i}| \leq \eta_t \lambda_1, \\ \frac{1}{1+\eta_t \lambda_2}(\widetilde{w}_{t,i} - \operatorname{sgn}(\widetilde{w}_{t,i})\eta_t \lambda_1) & \text{otherwise.} \end{cases}$$

Note that the regularization hyperparameter λ_1 is scaled by the learning rate η_t, thus inducing more regularization at earlier iterations.

Regularized Dual Averaging (RDA) [33], on the other hand, adjusts the learning variables by solving a proximal step that involves the running average of *all past gradients* of the loss functions instead of taking a gradient step at each iteration. More formally, the exponentially weighted average is first updated as:

$$\bar{\mathbf{g}}_t = \frac{t-1}{t} \bar{\mathbf{g}}_{t-1} + \frac{1}{t} \nabla_{\boldsymbol{w}} \ell_{\mathcal{M}(\boldsymbol{r},\boldsymbol{l})}(\mathcal{X}; \varphi_{\boldsymbol{w}}).$$

Next, the weights are adjusted as follows:

$$w_{t+1,i} = \begin{cases} 0, & \text{if } |\bar{g}_{t,i}| \leq \lambda_1, \\ -\frac{1}{\lambda_2+\eta_t}(\bar{g}_{t,i} - \operatorname{sgn}(\bar{g}_{t,i})\lambda_1) & \text{otherwise.} \end{cases}$$

Parameter t is the iteration number and parameter η_t the learning rate. We refer the interested readers to [23] for a in-depth discussion about the connections between FOBOS and RDA.

5.2 Non-convex approach

There exists a variety of approaches similar to (6) where, either a non-convex penalty, or some heuristics are used in lieu of the convex ℓ_1 term to promote sparsity. We discuss below two possible options.

As proposed in [19], we can simply enforce sparsity by adding a pruning operation to the l_2-regularized stochastic gradient descent (SGD) update rule. The pruning, scheduled every k gradient steps, simply consists of setting to 0 all the weights w_i such that, for a chosen threshold θ, $|w_i| < \theta$. We refer to this (somehow naïve) strategy as *pruned SGD* (PSGD). Clearly, the higher the value we choose for θ, the sparser the model will get as a result. Despite its simplicity, our experiments show that PSGD applied to (6) with $\lambda_1 = 0$ compares remarkably well to the more sophisticated convex approaches discussed previously.

A more elaborate variation built upon this idea is provided by Truncated Gradient Descent (TGD) [19], which truncates the solutions obtained by standard SGD after every k iterations based on the ℓ_1 norm. It is worth noting that if we restrict FOBOS to only use the ℓ_1 penalty, we end up with an algorithm that is a special case of TGD (as detailed in [19]). In particular, the technique used in [31] is exactly this special variant of TGD, and hence, is equivalent to FOBOS without the ℓ_2 regularization.

6. BAYESIAN OPTIMIZATION OF THE HYPERPARAMETERS

The family of ranking models we are focusing on is parameterised by several hyperparameters. Our formulation depends on the careful choice of the weighting scheme $\Delta_{\mathcal{M}(\mathrm{r},\mathrm{l})}$, the pairwise loss function $\mathcal{P}$, the regularization parameters for both the ℓ_1 and ℓ_2 penalties, and the choice of the online optimization algorithm itself.

While some of these hyperparameters could be tuned *separately* based on tailored heuristics (e.g., the ℓ_1-regularization parameter via homotopy techniques [27]), it becomes much more challenging to optimize them all jointly in a scalable fashion. To this end, we resort to recent progress made in the field of Bayesian optimization applied to the automatic tuning of machine-learning hyperparameters [15,30]. Bayesian optimization is well-suited to carry out the optimization of unknown black-box functions whose evaluation is expensive, which, in our context, corresponds to the entire ranking loss minimization pipeline.

In a nutshell, this class of methods works as follows: while collecting (possibly noisy) observations over the course of the optimization, a probabilistic model of the unknown black-box function is being constructed and maintained. The next point to evaluate is determined based on the posterior distribution of the probabilistic model combined with some surrogate acquisition function, such as the expected improvement [17]. This process is then continued until some predefined budget gets consumed, e.g., expressed as a maximum number of black-box function evaluations. In our settings, we typically run the optimization for 30 evaluations. Note that this hyperparameter-tuning step is made possible thanks to the sufficiently low training- and evaluation-time requirements of our ranking model.

As advocated in [30], for our probabilistic engine we consider a Gaussian process with a 5/2-Matérn covariance function and automatic relevance determination. Moreover, regarding the choice of the acquisition function to drive the optimization, we found that Thompson sampling worked best at trading off exploration and exploitation (e.g., as also recently reported in [13]). Given that our space of hyper-parameters is relatively small (two numerical and three categorical hyper-parameters), we observed that a simple empirical Bayes approach performed well to handle the covariance parameters of the Gaussian process.

It is lastly worth mentioning that in our industrial environment, the different development and deployment phases of our ranking package imply that customer teams with various skills, in particular, without machine-learning expertise, should have access to a simple turn-key interface. Moreover, this interface should at the same time be easy to extend to additional instantiations of the loss family (4). We have found that Bayesian optmization is a good choice in these respects.

7. DOCUMENT RETRIEVAL BENCHMARK

In this section, we conduct experiments on benchmark data sets for text document retrieval. In the next section, we will return to our use case and report results on large-scale experiments with Amazon data.

The goal of the first set of experiments is to assess how the proposed approach compares to a selection of state-of-the-art learning-to-rank models in terms of predictive performance. We focus on the LETOR 3.0 benchmark collection, which provides easy access to a number of authoritative baselines in terms of different evaluation metrics.[1] In particular, we provide results for TD2003, TD2004, and OHSUMED data sets. TD2003 contains 49,058 query-document pairs. Each pair is described by a 64-dimensional, pre-extracted feature vector. The total number of unique queries is 50, and for each query, the corresponding list of results is labeled by a binary relevance judgment for the document. TD2004 has the same number of features and labeling structure as TD2003, except that there are 75 queries overall, i.e., a total of 74,146 query-document pairs. Finally, OHSUMED contains 16,140 query-document examples, described by 45 attributes, for a total number of 106 queries. The relevance judgments are organized on a 3-graded integer scale.

For ease of exposition, our approach is referred to as *ElasticRank*. We compare ElasticRank based on RDA to a selection of alternative methods in the pointwise, pairwise and listwise families, including both linear and non-linear estimators (see Section 4): RankSVM [12, 16], RankBoost [11], ListNet [6], AdaRank-NDCG [34], and simple linear regression. The results are reported in Figure 2. They were obtained based on 5 random splits into train and test.

Overall, ElasticRank is competitive w.r.t. state-of-the-art learning-to-rank models, while only performing a single pass on the data. The other models are allowed to run as many iterations as needed in order to converge to optimal performance. On OHSUMED (Figure 2c), ElasticRank is achieving the highest performance (for $NDCG@1–5$) and on TD2003

[1]Documentation available at `http://research.microsoft.com/en-us/um/beijing/projects/letor/default.aspx`.

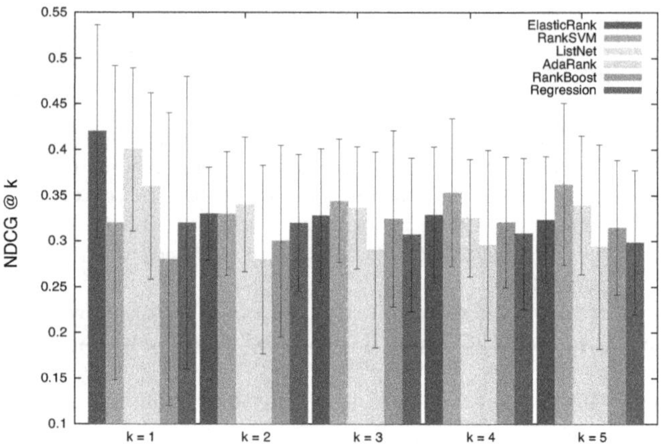

(a) TD2003

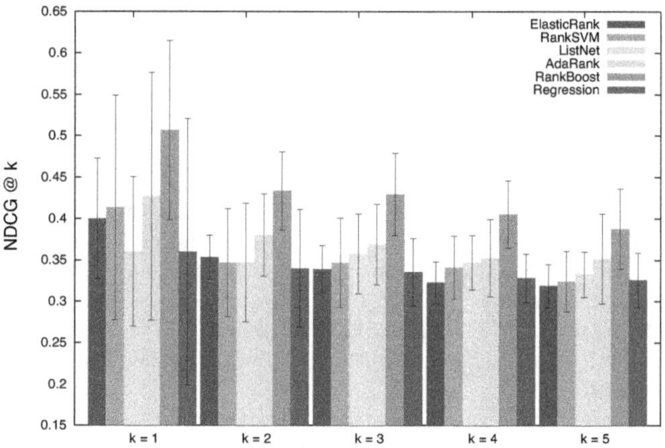

(b) TD2004

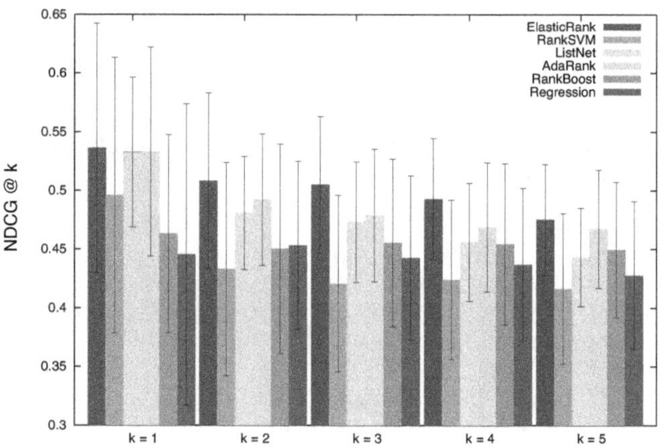

(c) OHSUMED

Figure 2: Predictive performance in terms of NDCG@K measured on three different data sets from the LETOR 3.0 collection: (a) TD2003, (b) TD2004 and (c) OHSUMED. Results are averaged based on 5-fold cross-validation. ElasticRank is competitive w.r.t. the other models, while only performing a single pass on the training data.

Metric	R@1	R@2	R@3	R@4	R@5	NDCG
LR	92.30%	57.27%	35.68%	23.17%	12.83%	18.67%
RankSVM	124.54%	75.36%	47.71%	32.04%	19.80%	25.99%
PSGD	128.73%	**77.21%**	**48.62%**	**32.74%**	**20.00%**	**26.64%**
FOBOS	128.27%	75.73%	48.39%	32.04%	19.16%	26.16%
RDA	**129.03%**	76.26%	48.37%	32.08%	19.13%	26.33%

Table 1: Highest R@K achieved by each one of the considered algorithms (over the test set) after one training pass. R@K is reported in terms of relative improvement (in percentage) over the values achieved by ranking the recommendations uniformly at random. ElasticRank (listwise) is more accurate than RankSVM (pairwise), which in turn outperforms LR (pointwise).

(Figure 2a) it performs best in $NDCG@1$. The performance obtained on TD2004 is less satisfying (Figure 2b), although for $NDCG@1$–2 ElasticRank is still outperforming ListNet and RankSVM. The best results for TD2004 are achieved by RankBoost, which suggests that non-linearities are important here. Unfortunately, nonlinear methods usually do not scale and, in practice, only linear methods are feasible. More data also leads to larger feature sets, which in turn, provide a way to compensate for the absence of nonlinearities.

8. PRODUCT RECOMMENDATION ON AMAZON.COM

In this section, we evaluate ElasticRank on a data set collected on the Amazon retail website. The task is to learn ranking models based on purchase logs. The results we report are based on data collected for a widget similar to the one described in Section 2. We cannot name the actual widget for confidentiality reasons.

We focus on the following questions, which are crucial to provide practical guidance when considering massive, low-latency ranking problems:

i. Which regularization technique leads to the highest predictive performance?

ii. In the one-pass setting, which sparsity-inducing technique is best at trading-off performance for sparsity?

iii. How large is the impact of the number of training passes w.r.t. the quality of the learned models?

In order to run our experiments, we sampled a set of impression log data from a contiguous time interval, and used $\frac{9}{11}$ of the data for training and $\frac{1}{11}$ for validation and testing respectively, leaving the temporal order intact. The sample contains millions of impressions, where an impression is simply one of the items displayed within the widget as a recommendation tied to a particular context. Note that this size is larger than the average size of the LETOR benchmarks by several orders of magnitude. Each item is described by a high-dimensional feature vector, including boolean, numerical, and categorical features. In order to protect sensitive information, we cannot disclose the exact number of features available from our logs, their actual semantics or the way they are engineered. For the purpose of the present experiment we consider up to a few thousand features. We convert categorical features into numerical ones using a sparse, one-hot representation, which may generate hundreds of thousands or even millions of dimensions. We scale the feature values in a listwise fashion, so that the minimum and maximum values of each feature are, respectively, 0 and 1 for each of the processed impression lists. Relevance labels are derived from purchase decisions made by the customers.

Table 1 collects the highest values obtained by ElasticRank in the one-pass setting, both for R@K and NDCG@K. The algorithms described in Section 5, namely RDA, FOBOS and PSGD, are compared to one another. We further compare to a number of alternative ranking models, respectively logistic regression (LR), which falls into the pointwise family, and RankSVM, which falls into the pairwise family.

From the results listed in the table, we can draw at least two conclusions. First, ElasticRank (abstracting from the choice of the specific regularization technique) is more accurate than both LR and RankSVM. The fact that RankSVM performs slightly worse should not be a surprise as it can be seen as optimizing a special case of the objective stated in (4). Indeed, RankSVM simply sets the delta function to 1 and considers a hinge loss. Second, the three variants of ElasticRank are all pretty close to one another in terms of achieved performance. This answers question (*i*) above.

Figure 3 shows the predictive performance of the models learned by different sparsity-inducing formulations, measured by $R@1$ and $R@4$, as a function of the number of non-zero parameters. The plots are obtained by varying the regularization parameter (λ_1 or θ depending on the algorithm). We report results for $K=1$ and $K=4$ to show that the observed trends are not an artifact of the specific values of K. We only report result for R@K because this evaluation metric matches our use case better and it is therefore preferred over NDCG@K. Note, however, that we observed similar trends with the NDCG@K-based delta function, but the results were slightly worse than for R@K-based one (which was not the case in the LETOR experiments).

Next, let us focus on question (*ii*). RDA allows us to smoothly increase the sparsity induced in the model while keeping the model performance under control. In fact, when regularization becomes too aggressive, the ranking quality decreases with a trend which is seemingly monotonic in the growth of λ_1. This relatively smooth decay in ranking quality is what ensures the model sparsity can be safely adapted to the latency requirements of the application without the risk of missing the optimal sparsity/performance trade-off. Interestingly, such smoothness is also observed for PSGD, which is a simple way of reducing the model latency. On the contrary, the curves for FOBOS are pretty bumpy, which means we could get stuck in suboptimal solutions whenever we cannot afford to explore a wide range of λ_1 values.

As a sanity check whether elastic net helps, we also tested the version of TGD adopted in [31], which corresponds to

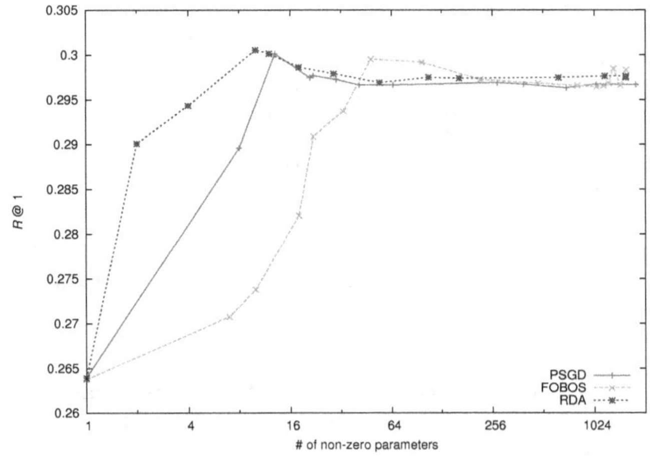

(a) Recall@1, one pass

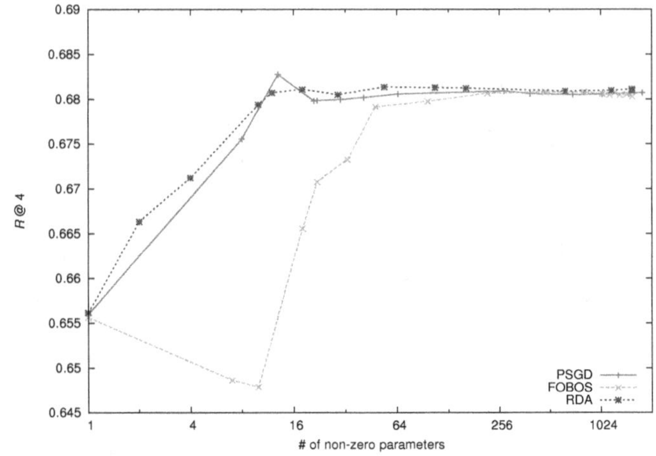

(b) Recall@4, one pass

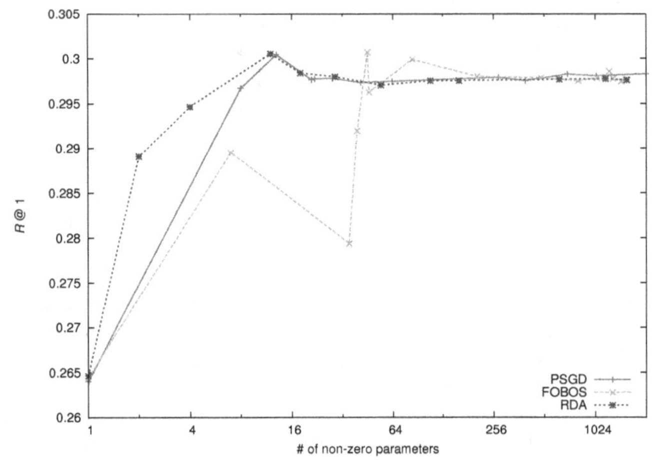

(c) Recall@1, two passes

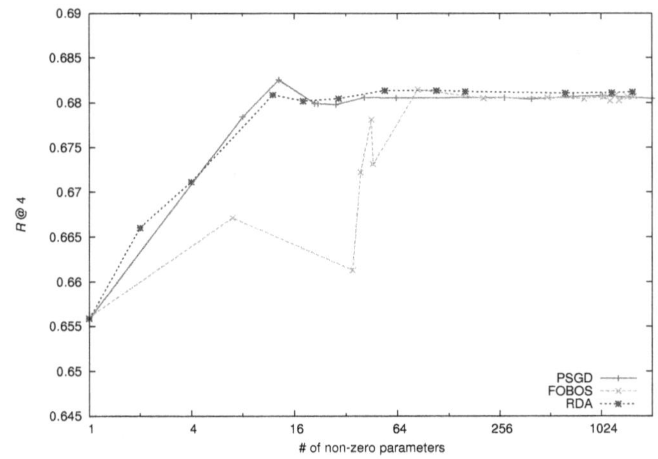

(d) Recall@4, two passes

Figure 3: Predictive performance of the three algorithms: PSGD, FOBOS, and RDA in terms of Recall@1 (left) and Recall@4 (right), over one (top) and two (bottom) passes. RDA and PSGD are more reliable than FOBOS at trading-off model sparsity for predictive performance.

FOBOS without the ℓ_2 penalty. The resulting curves were less stable and less accurate than those reported for FOBOS.

Independently of these stability considerations, ElasticRank based on RDA or PSGD converges faster to the high values regime as a function of model size (i.e., the number of non-zero parameters). In other words, RDA and PSGD enable us to pick more informative features than the ones selected by FOBOS. This is important, because when latency is a mission-critical requirement, we might have to restrict the maximal number of features a priori.

Next, we turn our attention to question (*iii*). Letting the algorithm run for more than one pass over the training data is mostly useful for the algorithm that is slowest in converging to its highest value (i.e., FOBOS). We only show results for up to 2 training passes as additional passes over the data did not improve the quality of the learned models.

We end this section by analyzing the prediction latency, i.e., the time it takes for our model to compute the score of candidate recommendations as a function of the model sparsity. We benchmarked the scoring functions learned over the runs plotted in Figure 3 by averaging the time to score approximately 5 million examples. The results are reported in Table 2.

# of weights	Latency	TPS
4	0.0062 ms	≈ 161,290
29	0.0087 ms	≈ 114,942
1804	0.0109 ms	≈ 91,743

Table 2: Average latency per recommendation and total throughput per second (TPS, i.e., number of scored impressions) for models of decreasing sparsity.

The latency/throughput requirements in web-scale applications can be extremely strict. It is crucial to enforce the desired level of sparsity when learning a ranking model as too many non-zeros can rapidly lead to exceeding these requirements due to the amount of traffic. For example, to meet the requirements of a latency smaller than 0.009 ms, one would not be able to afford more than 29 parameters.

The latency due to the computation of the scoring function might seem very small and it can be noted that it does not grow linearly with the size of the model. However, features are rarely readily available in real-time applications. Even if the features are pre-computed, they might have to be read from disk or transmitted over the network. The time required to access the features is much longer than the time required to process them with the scoring function. Hence, and even though this claim is not fully illustrated here in the time needed to compute the scores alone, model sparsity may be even more impactful when it comes to web-scale deployment of the ranking system.

9. CONCLUSIONS

The core question motivating this work was whether learning-to-rank methods are able to cope with the scale of a global e-commerce platform. In particular, we asked whether the ranking quality, which is typically demonstrated on public learning-to-rank benchmarks, is still achievable when the challenges in terms of training time and memory requirements, as well as prediction latency and throughput, are pushed to their limits. Our results suggest that web-scale efficiency requirements can be met without sacrificing predictive performance. Surprisingly enough, such goal is exemplarily achieved by just sticking to the simplest options available. First, we obtain state-of-the-art results by using a *linear* scoring function as the basic modeling tool. Second, making only *one-pass* over the training data is sufficient for SGD-type algorithms to converge to fairly accurate solutions. Third, *naively pruning* the estimated model weights at regular training intervals leads to models which are nearly as sparse and accurate as those delivered by the best-behaved ℓ_1-based regularization techniques, such as elastic net.

10. ACKNOWLEDGMENTS

We are grateful to Mitchell Goodman, Vijai Mohan, and JJ Tavernier for helping us geting a grip on the log data and model deployment infrastructure at Amazon. We are also indebted to Ralf Herbrich for providing input and feedback on model design.

11. REFERENCES

[1] F. Bach, R. Jenatton, J. Mairal, and G. Obozinski. Optimization with sparsity-inducing penalties. *Foundations and Trends in Machine Learning*, 4(1):1–106, 2011.

[2] L. Bottou and Y. LeCun. Large scale online learning. In *Advances in Neural Information Processing Systems*, volume 16, pages 217–224, 2004.

[3] C. J. C. Burges, R. Ragno, and Q. V. Le. Learning to rank with nonsmooth cost functions. In *Advances in Neural Information Processing Systems (NIPS)*, pages 193–200, 2006.

[4] C. J. C. Burges, K. M. Svore, P. N. Bennett, A. Pastusiak, and Q. Wu. Learning to Rank Using an Ensemble of Lambda-Gradient Models. In *Proceedings of the Yahoo! Learning to Rank Challenge, held at ICML 2010, Haifa, Israel, June 25, 2010*, pages 25–35, 2011.

[5] S. Büttcher, C. L. Clarke, and G. V. Cormack. *Information Retrieval: Implementing and Evaluating Search Engines*. MIT Press, 2010.

[6] Z. Cao, T. Qin, T.-Y. Liu, M.-F. Tsai, and H. Li. Learning to rank: from pairwise approach to listwise approach. In *Proceedings of the 24th International Conference on Machine learning (ICML 2007)*, pages 129–136, New York, NY, USA, 2007. ACM.

[7] B. Croft, D. Metzler, and T. Strohman. *Search Engines: Information Retrieval in Practice.* Addison-Wesley, Boston (MA), 2009.

[8] A. Defazio, F. Bach, and S. Lacoste-Julien. Saga: A fast incremental gradient method with support for non-strongly convex composite objectives. Technical report, preprint arXiv:1407.0202, 2014.

[9] J. Duchi, E. Hazan, and Y. Singer. Adaptive subgradient methods for online learning and stochastic optimization. *The Journal of Machine Learning Research*, 12:2121–2159, 2011.

[10] J. C. Duchi and Y. Singer. Efficient online and batch learning using forward backward splitting. *Journal of Machine Learning Research*, 10:2899–2934, 2009.

[11] Y. Freund, R. Iyer, R. E. Schapire, and Y. Singer. An Efficient Boosting Algorithm for Combining Preferences. *Journal of Maching Learning Research*, 4:933–969, 2003.

[12] R. Herbrich, T. Graepel, and K. Obermayer. Large Margin Rank Boundaries for Ordinal Regression. In Smola, Bartlett, Schölkopf, and Schuurmans, editors, *Advances in Large Margin Classifiers*, chapter 7, pages 115–132. MIT Press, 2000.

[13] M. Hoffman, B. Shahriari, and N. de Freitas. On correlation and budget constraints in model-based bandit optimization with application to automatic machine learning. In *Proceedings of the International Conference on Artificial Intelligence and Statistics (AISTATS)*, pages 365–374, 2014.

[14] C. Hu, J. T. Kwok, and W. Pan. Accelerated gradient methods for stochastic optimization and online learning. In *Advances in Neural Information Processing Systems*, 2009.

[15] F. Hutter, H. H. Hoos, and K. Leyton-Brown. Sequential model-based optimization for general algorithm configuration. In *Proceedings of LION-5*, page 507-523, 2011.

[16] T. Joachims. Optimizing search engines using clickthrough data. In *Proceedings of the Eighth ACM SIGKDD International Conference on Knowledge Discovery and Data Mining*, pages 133–142, New York, NY, USA, 2002. ACM.

[17] D. R. Jones, M. Schonlau, and W. J. Welch. Efficient global optimization of expensive black-box functions. *Journal of Global optimization*, 13(4):455–492, 1998.

[18] H. Lai, Y. Pan, C. Liu, L. Lin, and J. Wu. Sparse Learning-to-Rank via an Efficient Primal-Dual Algorithm. *IEEE Transactions on Computers*, 62:1221–1233, 2013.

[19] J. Langford, L. Li, and T. Zhang. Sparse Online Learning via Truncated Gradient. *Journal of Machine Learning Research*, 10:777–801, 2009.

[20] L. Laporte, R. Flamary, S. Canu, S. Déjean, and J. Mothe. Nonconvex Regularizations for Feature

Selection in Ranking With Sparse SVM. *IEEE Trans. Neural Netw. Learning Syst.*, 25(6):1118–1130, 2014.

[21] T.-Y. Liu. Learning to rank for information retrieval. *Foundations and Trends in Information Retrieval*, 3(3):225–331, 2009.

[22] C. D. Manning, P. Raghavan, and H. Schutze. *Introduction to Information Retrieval.* Cambridge University Press, 2008.

[23] B. H. McMahan. Follow-the-Regularized-Leader and Mirror Descent: Equivalence Theorems and L1 Regularization. In *Proceedings of the Fourteenth International Conference on Artificial Intelligence and Statistics, AISTATS 2011, Fort Lauderdale, USA, April 11-13, 2011*, pages 525–533, 2011.

[24] H. B. McMahan, G. Holt, D. Sculley, M. Young, D. Ebner, J. Grady, L. Nie, T. Phillips, E. Davydov, D. Golovin, et al. Ad click prediction: a view from the trenches. In *Proceedings of the 19th ACM SIGKDD international conference on Knowledge discovery and data mining*, pages 1222–1230. ACM, 2013.

[25] A. Mohan, Z. Chen, and K. Q. Weinberger. Web-Search Ranking with Initialized Gradient Boosted Regression Trees. In *Yahoo! Learning to Rank Challenge*, pages 77–89, 2011.

[26] S. Negahban, P. Ravikumar, M. J. Wainwright, and B. Yu. A unified framework for high-dimensional analysis of M-estimators with decomposable regularizers. In *Advances in Neural Information Processing Systems*, 2009.

[27] M. Y. Park and T. Hastie. L1-regularization path algorithm for generalized linear models. *Journal of the Royal Statistical Society. Series B*, 69(4):659–677, 2007.

[28] T. Qin, T.-Y. Liu, and H. Li. A general approximation framework for direct optimization of information retrieval measures. *Information Retrieval*, 13(4):375–397, 2010.

[29] D. Sculley. Large scale learning to rank. In *NIPS Workshop on Advances in Ranking.* 2009.

[30] J. Snoek, H. Larochelle, and R. P. Adams. Practical bayesian optimization of machine learning algorithms. In *Advances in Neural Information Processing Systems*, pages 2960–2968, 2012.

[31] Z. Sun, T. Qin, Q. Tao, and J. Wang. Robust sparse rank learning for non-smooth ranking measures. In *Proceedings of the 32nd Annual International ACM SIGIR Conference on Research and Development in Information Retrieval, SIGIR 2009, Boston, MA, USA, July 19-23, 2009*, pages 259–266. ACM, 2009.

[32] J. Weston, S. Bengio, and N. Usunier. WSABIE: Scaling Up to Large Vocabulary Image Annotation. In *IJCAI 2011, Proceedings of the 22nd International Joint Conference on Artificial Intelligence, Barcelona, Catalonia, Spain, July 16-22, 2011*, pages 2764–2770, 2011.

[33] L. Xiao. Dual Averaging Methods for Regularized Stochastic Learning and Online Optimization. *Journal of Machine Learning Research*, 11:2543–2596, 2010.

[34] J. Xu and H. Li. Adarank: A boosting algorithm for information retrieval. In *SIGIR '07: Proceedings of the 30th Annual International ACM SIGIR Conference on Research and Development in Information Retrieval*, pages 391–398, New York, NY, USA, 2007. ACM.

[35] H. Zou and T. Hastie. Regularization and variable selection via the elastic net. *Journal of the Royal Statistical Society. Series B*, 67(2):301–320, 2005.

On the Reliability of Profile Matching Across Large Online Social Networks

Oana Goga
MPI-SWS

Patrick Loiseau
EURECOM

Robin Sommer
ICSI/LBNL

Renata Teixeira
Inria

Krishna P. Gummadi
MPI-SWS

ABSTRACT

Matching the profiles of a user across multiple online social networks brings opportunities for new services and applications as well as new insights on user online behavior, yet it raises serious privacy concerns. Prior literature has showed that it is possible to accurately match profiles, but their evaluation focused only on sampled datasets. In this paper, we study the extent to which we can *reliably* match profiles *in practice*, across real-world social networks, by exploiting *public attributes*, i.e., information users publicly provide about themselves. Today's social networks have hundreds of millions of users, which brings completely new challenges as a reliable matching scheme must identify the correct matching profile out of the millions of possible profiles. We first define a set of properties for profile attributes–Availability, Consistency, non-Impersonability, and Discriminability (ACID)–that are both necessary and sufficient to determine the reliability of a matching scheme. Using these properties, we propose a method to evaluate the accuracy of matching schemes in real practical cases. Our results show that the accuracy in practice is significantly lower than the one reported in prior literature. When considering entire social networks, there is a non-negligible number of profiles that belong to different users but have similar attributes, which leads to many false matches. Our paper sheds light on the limits of matching profiles in the real world and illustrates the correct methodology to evaluate matching schemes in realistic scenarios.

1. INTRODUCTION

Internet users are increasingly revealing information about different aspects of their personal life on different social networking sites. Consequently, there is a growing interest in the potential for aggregating user information across multiple sites, by matching user accounts across the sites, to develop a more complete profile of individual users than the profile provided by any single site. For instance, companies like PeekYou [28] and Spokeo [2] offer *"people search"* services that can be used to retrieve publicly visible information about specific users that is aggregated from across a multitude of websites. Some companies are mining data posted by job applicants on different social networking sites as part of background checks [34], while others allow call centers to pull up social profiles when their customers call [32]. The many applications of matching profiles across social networking sites also raise many legitimate and serious concerns about the privacy of users. A debate on the relative merits of leveraging profile matching techniques for specific applications is out of the scope of this paper.

In this paper, our goal is to investigate the *reliability* of techniques for matching profiles across *large real-world* online social networks, such as Facebook and Twitter, using only *publicly* available profile attributes, such as names, usernames, location, photos, and friends. Reliability refers to the extent to which different profiles belonging to the same user can be matched across social networks, while avoiding mistakenly matching profiles belonging to different users. Matching schemes need to be highly reliable because incorrectly matched profiles communicate an inaccurate portrait of a user and could have seriously negative consequences for the user in many application scenarios. For example, Spokeo has been recently sued over providing inaccurate information about a person which caused "actual harm" to the person employment prospects [3]. We focus on publicly available profile attributes because data aggregators today can crawl and leverage such information for matching profiles.

Recently, a number of schemes have been proposed for matching profiles across different social networks [24, 30, 37, 11, 23, 14] (we review them in §9). The potential of these schemes to reliably match profiles in practice, however, has not been *systematically* studied. Specifically, it is not clear how or what properties of profile attributes affect the reliability of the matching schemes. Furthermore, the training and testing datasets for evaluating the matching schemes are often opportunistically generated and they constitute only a small subset of all user profiles in social networks. It is unclear whether the reliability results obtained over such datasets would hold over all user profiles in real-world social networks, where there are orders of magnitude more non-matching profiles than matching profiles (i.e., there is a huge class imbalance).

Our first contribution lies in defining a set of properties for profile attributes–Availability, Consistency, non-Impersonability, and Discriminability (ACID)–that are both necessary and sufficient to determine the reliability of a matching scheme (§3). Analyzing the ACID properties of profile attributes reveals the significant challenges associated with matching profiles reliably in practice (§4). First, data in real-world social networks is often *noisy* – users do not consistently provide the same information across different sites. Second, with hundreds of millions of profiles, there is a non-trivial chance that there exist multiple profiles with very similar attributes (e.g., same name, same location) leading to false matches. Finally, attackers create profiles attempting to impersonate other users, fundamentally limiting the reliability of any profile matching scheme.

KDD'15, August 10-13, 2015, Sydney, NSW, Australia.
 ISBN 978-1-4503-3664-2/15/08 ...$15.00.
DOI: http://dx.doi.org/10.1145/2783258.2788601.

Another key contribution lies in our method for carefully selecting the training and testing datasets for matching profiles (§5). When we evaluate the main types of matching schemes in the literature (based on binary classifiers) using a small random sample of Twitter and Facebook profiles (similar to how these schemes were evaluated originally), the schemes achieve over 90% recall and 95% precision (§6.1). Unfortunately, when we evaluate these schemes over datasets sampled carefully to preserve the reliability that the schemes would have achieved over the larger datasets (full Facebook database), their performance drops significantly (§6.2). We could obtain only a 19% recall for a 95% precision.

We then investigate if we could improve the reliability of matching schemes in scenarios where we know that there is *at most one matching profile* (§7). In such scenarios, we propose a new matching scheme and show that it is indeed possible to improve the recall to 29% at 95% precision. This is still considerably lower than the high recall (90%) reported in the literature.

Thus, we discover a fundamental limitation in matching profiles across existing social networks using public attributes. To further confirm the inherent limits of reliably matching profiles in practice, we compare the reliability of automated matching schemes with that of human Amazon Mechanical Turk (AMT) workers. Under similar conditions, AMT workers are able to match only 40% of the profiles with a 95% precision. Our analysis is the first to highlight that achieving high reliability in matching profiles across large real-world social networks comes at a significant cost (in terms of reduced recall).

2. PROBLEM DEFINITION

In this section, we define the problem of matching profiles, we present the constraints we have to consider and discuss how we approach the problem.

The profile matching problem: We consider that two profiles in two social networks match if they belong to/are managed by the same user. The profile matching problem is: given a profile a^1 in one large social network SN_1, find all its *matching profiles* in another large social network SN_2, if at least one exists. We will denote by a^2 generic profiles in SN_2 and by $\hat{a}^2$ matching profiles of a^1. For conciseness, we will also write a^2-match-a^1 if a^2 is a matching profile of a^1 and a^2-non-match-a^1 otherwise.

Note that we address here the problem of matching *individual* profiles, which is different from the problem of matching two entire social networks or databases. The difference is that we do not assume that we have access to all the data in SN_1 but only to one profile. For example, we cannot match profiles by exploiting patterns in the graph structure of SN_1 and SN_2, and we cannot optimize the matching of a profile in SN_1 based on the matchings of other profiles in SN_1. Thus, we cannot take advantage of some methods proposed for de-anonymizing social graphs [25, 15] and entity matching [8].

Our problem formulation is motivated by practical scenarios. There are many people search engines such as Spokeo that allow users to search for data about a particular person. These services gather data about a person by matching the profiles a person has on multiple social networks.

We are particularly interested in two instantiations of the problem that are motivated by practical scenarios: (1) the *generic case* – a profile can have multiple matching profiles in SN_2; and (2) the *special case* – a profile can have *at most one* matching profile. This case is suited for matching social networks such as Facebook or LinkedIn that enforce users to have only one profile.

Features: In this paper, we investigate the extent to which we can match profiles by exploiting the *attributes* users publicly provide in their profiles such as their *real names, screen names* (aka. username – name that appears in the URL of the profile), *location, profile photos,* and *friends*. Using this information we can ideally match any person that maintains the same persona on different social networks. Also, we choose these attributes because they are essential to find people online and they are present and usually remain public across different social networks even if users make all their other content, such as their posts and photos, private. For profile a^1 (resp. a^2), we denote by v^1 (resp. v^2) the value of a considered attribute. From attribute values, we define a *feature* as the similarity between the values of profiles in SN_1 and SN_2: $s(v^1, v^2)$.

Matching scheme as a binary classifier: Most previous works solved the matching problem by building binary classifiers that, given two profiles a^1 and a^2, determine whether a^1 and a^2 are matching or not [23, 31, 36, 29, 37, 24, 27, 22]. The binary classifier takes as input a feature vector $f(a^1, a^2)$ that captures the similarity between each attribute of a pair of profiles (a^1, a^2); and then outputs the probability p of a^1 and a^2 to match. By selecting a cutoff threshold for p the classifier returns 1 (i.e., matching profiles) if p is larger than the threshold; and 0 otherwise. We say that a matching scheme outputs a *true match* when the matched profiles belong to the same user and outputs a *false match* when the matched profiles belong to different users. The threshold's choice constitutes the standard tradeoff between increasing the number of true match and decreasing the number of false matches.

This solution works well for the generic case of our matching problem. Given a profile a^1, we can use the binary classifier to check, for every pair of profiles (a^1, a^2) such that $a^2 \in SN_2$, whether it is matching or not. We can then output any profile a^2 that the binary classifier declares as matching. In this paper, we test such approach when we represent (a^1, a^2) with five features, each corresponding to the similarity score between a^1 and a^2 for each of the five profile attributes: real name, screen name, location, photo, and friends.

For the special case of our matching problem, the previous approach is vulnerable to output many false matches. For this case, instead of independently judging whether *each* pair (a^1, a^2) is a match or not, we can compare (for a given a^1) the probabilities p for *all* pairs (a^1, a^2) to judge which profile is most likely the matching profile of a^1. We discuss this case in more detail in §7.

Reliability of a profile matching scheme: In this paper our focus is on the reliability of matching schemes. A *reliable matching scheme* should ensure that the profile it finds indeed matches with high probability, i.e., the matching scheme does not have many false matches. If there is no clear matching profile in SN_2 for a^1, then the scheme should return nothing.

Many previous studies used the true and the false positive rate to evaluate their matching schemes. The true positive rate is the percentage of matching profiles that are identified, while the false positive rate is the percentage of non-matching profiles that are false matches. The goal is to have a high true positive rate and a low false positive rate. These metrics are, however, a misleading indicator of the reliability of a matching scheme because they are not suited for scenarios with high class imbalance, i.e., the number of matching profiles is much lower than the number of non-matching profiles. For example, a matching scheme with a 90% true positive rate for a 1% false positive rate might seem reliable, however, if we use it in a scenario where we have 1,000 matching and 999,000 non-matching profiles, the matching scheme would output 900 true matches and 9,990 false matches, which is clearly unreliable. In real-world social networks, the class imbalance is even higher (e.g., for each matching profile we have over 1 billion non-matching profiles in Facebook) thus the scheme would output even more false matches.

This paper argues that better metrics to evaluate the reliability of a matching scheme are the precision and recall. The recall is the percentage of matching profiles that are identified, while the precision is the percentage of all pairs returned by the matching scheme which are true matches. The goal is to have a high recall and a high precision. In the previous example, we would have 90% recall for a 8% precision, which shows the low reliability of the scheme (out of all matched profiles only 8% are true matches). Thus, the best way to show the reliability of a matching scheme is to evaluate its precision and recall with realistic class imbalance. In the rest of the paper, by *reliable* we mean a precision higher than 95%.

3. THE ACID FRAMEWORK

The natural question that arises when investigating the reliability of matching schemes is: what does the reliability depends on? Undoubtedly, the reliability depends on the attributes we consider for matching and on their properties. Thus, given an attribute, what properties should the attribute have in order to enable a reliable profile matching? We propose a set of four properties to help capture the quality of different attributes to match profiles: *Availability, Consistency, non-Impersonability, and Discriminability (ACID).*

Availability: At first, to enable finding the matching profile, an attribute should have its value available in both social networks. If only 5% of users provided information about their "age" across two sites, then "age" has limited utility in matching profiles. To formalize this notion, we model the attribute values of a^1 and each $a^2 \in SN_2$ as random variables and we define the availability of an attribute as:

$$A = Pr\left(v^1 \text{ and } v^2 \text{ available} \middle| a^2\text{-match-}a^1\right).$$

Consistency: It is crucial that the selected attribute is consistent across matching profiles, i.e., users provide the same or similar attribute values across the different profiles they manage. Formally, we define the consistency of an attribute as:

$$C = Pr\left(s(v^1, v^2) > th \middle| a^2\text{-match-}a^1, v^1 \text{ and } v^2 \text{ available}\right),$$

where th is a threshold parameter.

non-Impersonability: If an attribute can be easily impersonated, i.e., faked, then attackers can compromise the reliability of the matching by creating fake profiles that appear to be matching with the victim's profiles on other sites. Some public attributes like "name" and "profile photo" are easier to copy than others such as "friends". To formalize this notion, we introduce the notation a^2-impersonate-a^1 to denote that profile a^2 has been created by an attacker impersonating profile a^1. We denote the probability that there exists at least one profile a^2 impersonating a^1 by $p_I = Pr(a^1 \text{ is impersonated})$ and the probability that there is no profile impersonating a^1 by $p_{nI} = 1 - p_I$. The difficulty to manipulate an attribute is characterized by its non-Impersonability defined as:

$$nI = Pr\Big(\max_{a^2 : a^2\text{-impersonate-}a^1} s(v^1, v^2) < th\Big).$$

Discriminability: Even without impersonations, in order to enable finding the matching profile, an attribute needs to uniquely identify a profile in SN_2. A highly discriminating attribute would have a unique and different value for each profile, while a less discriminating attribute would have similar values for many profiles. For example, "name" is likely to be more discriminating than "gender".

Formally, we define the discriminability of an attribute as:

$$D = Pr\Big(\max_{a^2 : a^2\text{-non-match-}a^1} s(v^1, v^2) < th \big| a^1 \text{ not impersonated}\Big).$$

In practice, it is impossible to estimate D (and nI) unless we are able to identify impersonating profiles. Instead, we estimate:

$$\tilde{D} = Pr\Big(\max_{a^2 : a^2\text{-non-match-}a^1} s(v^1, v^2) < th\Big).$$

$\tilde{D}$ represents the "effective discriminability" taking into account possible impersonations. Since impersonators create non-matching profiles as similar as possible to the original profile, it is reasonable to assume that $\tilde{D} \leq D$. Moreover, by application of Bayes formula, we can show that $D \leq \tilde{D}/p_{nI}$ so that, if p_I is not too large, $\tilde{D}$ gives a good estimate of D. If we assume that the impersonating profiles are independent from the other non-matching profiles, we can also prove that $\tilde{D} = D \cdot (p_{nI} + nI \cdot p_I)$. This clearly shows that $\tilde{D}$ is close to D if either the attribute is hard to impersonate (nI close to one) or the proportion of impersonator is small (p_I small).

The ACID properties are clear and intuitive properties that help understand the potential of an attribute to perform reliable matching, as the following theorem formalizes.[1]

THEOREM 1. *Consider a classifier based on a given attribute that classifies as matching profiles if $s(v^1, v^2) > th$. The performance of the classifier is characterized by the following results.*

(i) We have

$$recall = C \cdot A.$$

(ii) Assume that, for each profile $a^1 \in SN_1$, there is at most one matching profile in SN_2. Then,

$$precision \leq \frac{recall}{recall + 1 - \tilde{D}}.$$

(iii) Assume that $p_I > 0$. Then, $precision = recall = 1$ iif $A = C = nI = D = 1$.

In Theorem 1, the threshold parameter th must be the same as the one in the definitions of C, nI and D. Theorem 1-*(i)* shows that the classifier's recall is simply the product of consistency and availability. Theorem 1-*(ii)* gives a simple upper bound of the precision as a function of the effective discriminability (which itself is a function of the discriminability and of the impersonability, see above). This upper bound gives a good order of magnitude for the precision; moreover, for high precision (which is what we aim), given the small number of false positives, the true precision should be close to the bound. Finally, Theorem 1-*(iii)* confirms that a high value of all four ACID properties is *necessary* and *sufficient* to obtain high precision *and* recall.

Properties A, C and nI are independent of the network scale, however, the discriminability very largely depends on the network scale since having more non-matching pairs decreases the probability that none of them has a high similarity score. This implies that we must estimate the precision and the recall of a matching scheme using datasets that accurately capture the ACID properties of profile attributes of the entire social network. Otherwise, the precision and the recall will be incorrect.

In practice different attributes satisfy the properties to different extent and the challenge is to combine different attributes with imperfect properties to achieve a reliable matching. The next section analyzes the ground truth for several large social networks to understand the limits of matching profiles across different sites.

[1] The proof can be found in the extended version of the paper [12].

Table 1: Number of ground truth matching profiles obtained with Friend Finder (DATASET FF) and Google+ (DATASET G+) for different combinations of social networks.

	DATASET FF	DATASET G+
TWITTER - FACEBOOK	4,182	76,332
LINKEDIN - FACEBOOK	2,561	20,145
TWITTER - FLICKR	18,953	35,208
LINKEDIN - TWITTER	2,515	20,439

4. LIMITS OF MATCHING PROFILES

To understand the limits of matching profiles, we analyze the ACID properties of profile attributes (screen name, real name, location, profile photo, and friends) across six popular social networks (Facebook, Twitter, Google+, LinkedIn, Flickr, and MySpace). First we present our method to gather ground truth of matching profiles and we then analyze each property separately.

4.1 Ground truth of matching profiles

Gathering ground truth of matching profiles spanning multiple social networks is challenging and many previous works manually labeled profiles [18, 36, 29]. Below we describe two automatic methods that we used to obtain our ground truth.

We first obtained ground truth data by exploiting "Friend Finder" mechanisms on many social networks that allow a user to find her friends by their emails. We used a list of email addresses collected by colleagues for an earlier study analyzing spam email [16].[2] These email addresses were collected on a machine instructed to send spam by a large bot network. Since spammers target the public at large we believe that this list of emails catch a representative set of users. To combat abuse, some social networks limit the number of queries one can make with their "Friend Finder" mechanism and employ techniques to make an automated matching of an email to a profile ID impossible. Hence, we were only able to collect the email-to-profile ID matching for Twitter, Facebook, LinkedIn and Flickr. Table 1 summarizes the number of matching profiles we obtained using the Friend Finder mechanism (DATASET FF).[3]

Some previous works obtained ground truth from users that willingly provide links to their profiles in different social networks. Such users might not represent users in general because they want their profiles to be linked and probably expend the effort to keep their profiles synced. To be able to compare our results against previous works we collected DATASET G+ (see Table 1) by exploiting the fact that Google+ allows users to explicitly list their profiles in *other* social networks on their profile pages. Due to space constraints, for the rest of the paper, we show by default the results for profiles in DATASET FF and occasionally, for comparison, we show the results are for DATASET G+.

4.2 Attribute availability

The availability of attributes depends on the social network, for example Twitter does not ask users about their age while Facebook does. The availability also depends on whether users choose to input the information and make it public. Users might choose to let their location public on Twitter while make it private on Facebook.

Table 2 shows the breakdown of attribute availability per social network and pairs of social networks. The availability per social network characterizes the behavior of users, while the availability for pairs of social networks corresponds to the definition of A in §3.

[2]The local IRB approved the collection.

[3]To test the representativeness of DATASET FF, we compare the distribution of properties such as account creation date, number of followers, and number of tweets of Twitter profiles in our dataset with the same properties of random Twitter profiles. We found that the pairs of distributions for each property matched fairly closely.

Table 2: Availability of attributes for DATASET FF.
Legend: Tw = Twitter, Fb = Facebook, Fl = Flickr, Lnk = LinkedIn.

	Screen Name	Real Name	Profile Photo	Location	Friends
TW	100%	100%	69%	54%	86%
FB	100%	100%	98%	52%	60%
FL	100%	30%	29%	11%	40%
LNK	100%	100%	57%	99%	0%
FB - TW	100%	100%	69%	30%	43%
FB - LNK	100%	100%	56%	54%	0%
TW - FL	100%	30%	24%	8%	32%
LNK- TW	100%	100%	44%	54%	0%

First, we find that the availability of the attributes varies considerably across the different social networks. For example, users are more likely to provide their location information on LinkedIn than they are on Facebook or Twitter. The differences in availability are presumably due to the different ways in which users use these sites. For our purposes, it highlights the additional information one could learn about a user by linking her profiles on different sites.

Second, we find that screen name and real name are considerably more available than location or friends. However, the availability of the less available attributes is not negligible – for example, location and friends are available for more than 30% of matching profiles in Twitter and Facebook.

Third, when we compare the availability using DATASET FF and DATASET G+ (not shown), we observe that the availability of attributes for profiles in the DATASET FF is much lower than the availability for profiles in the DATASET G+ (e.g., profile photo is available for only 69% of Twitter users in DATASET FF while it is available for 96% of users DATASET G+). For more results on DATASET G+, we refer the reader to [10]. Thus, users in DATASET G+ are more likely to complete their profiles and consequently there is a higher bound on the recall to match them.

4.3 Attribute consistency

We now study the extent to which users provide consistent attribute values for their profiles on different social networks. Some users deliberately provide different attribute values either out of concerns for privacy or out of a desire to assume online personas different from their offline persona. It would be very hard to match profiles of such users by exploiting their public attributes.

Other users may input slightly different values for an attribute across sites. For example, a user might specify her work place as International Business Machines on one site and International Business Machines Corporation on another site.

Similarity metrics for profile attributes: We borrow a set of standard metrics from prior work in security, information retrieval, and vision communities to compute similarity between the values of attributes: the Jaro distance [9] to measure the similarity between names and screen names; the geodesic distance to measure the similarity between locations; the phash [1] and SIFT [20] algorithms to detect whether two photos are the same; and the number of common friends between two profiles. Please check our extended version of the paper for a full description of these metrics [12].

Similarity thresholds for attribute consistency: Clearly the more similar two values of an attribute, the greater the chance that the values are consistent, i.e., they refer to the same entity, be it a name or photo or location. Here, we want to show consistency results for a "reasonable" threshold beyond which we can declare with high confidence that the attribute values are consistent (irrespective of the tradeoff between consistency and discriminability in §3). The best to judge whether two attribute values are consistent are humans. Thus, we gathered ground truth data by asking Amazon Mechanical Turk (AMT) users to evaluate whether pairs of attribute values are consistent or not. We randomly select 100 pairs each

Table 3: Consistency of attributes for users in DATASET FF; † in parenthesis, the consistency only when information is available in both social networks.

	Screen Name	Real Name	Location	Profile Photo	Friends
Fb - Tw	38%	77%	23% (77%†)	8% (12%)	34% (79%)
Fb - Lnk	71%	97%	44% (83%)	11% (23%)	0%
Tw - Fl	40%	25% (84%)	5% (67%)	5% (22%)	13% (42%)
Tw - Lnk	36%	83%	39% (71%)	13% (31%)	0%

of matching and non-matching Twitter and Facebook profiles from DATASET FF and asked AMT users to annotate which attribute values are consistent and which are not. We followed the guidelines to ensure good quality results from AMT workers [6].

For each attribute, we leverage the AMT experiment to select the similarity thresholds to declare two values as consistent. Specifically, we select similarity thresholds, such that more than 90% of the consistent values, as identified by AMT workers, and less than 10% of the inconsistent values have high similarities. Note that, we only use these thresholds to evaluate whether attribute values in matching profiles are consistent and we do not use them to actually match profiles. Thus, while it is important that the majority of consistent values pass the threshold, it is not critical if some inconsistent values also pass the threshold. Incidentally, this experiment also shows that the similarity metrics we choose are consistent with what humans think is similar. Note that, it is unpractical to use AMT workers to estimate the threshold for friends, thus we manually choose it to be at least two friends in common to avoid noise.

Attribute consistency in matching profiles: Table 3 shows the proportion of users who provide consistent values for an attribute in a pair of social networks out of all users.This proportion corresponds to the recall we can achieve using the attribute given the threshold used, as shown in the previous section. In parenthesis, we also provide the equivalent proportion of users with consistent values only when the attribute value is available in both social networks (corresponding to the definition of C). This proportion better illustrates how likely users are to provide consistent values, i.e., shows the users's attempt to maintain synched profiles.

First, we find that a large fraction of users provides similar *real names* across different social networks. Put differently, most users are not attempting to maintain distinct personas on different sites. This trend bodes well for our ability to match the profiles of a user.

Second, we computed the percentage of matching profiles in Twitter and Facebook for which all public attributes in Table 3 are inconsistent. We find that there are 7% of such users. These users are likely assuming different personas on different sites and it is very hard, if not impossible, to match their profiles using only the public attributes that we consider in this paper. Thus, we can at most hope to match profiles for 93% of users. This percentage represents an upper bound on the recall for matching profiles based on public attributes.

Third, the consistency differs between different social networks. Twitter and Facebook have one of the lowest consistency for each attribute while Facebook and LinkedIn have the highest consistency. Thus, users are more likely to maintain synched profiles across Facebook and LinkedIn than other pairs of social networks.

4.4 Attribute discriminability

The previous section showed that a large fraction of users have consistent attribute values between their profiles. However, the number of profiles that we can match reliably is smaller because attribute values might not uniquely identify a single person.

To evaluate the discriminability of attributes, for each Twitter profile we compare the similarity of the matching Facebook profile with the similarity of the most similar non-matching Facebook profile. Figure 1 shows the CDF of similarity scores in DATASET FF (sample). Zero means no similarity and one means perfect similarity; except for location, where zero means perfect similarity because it corresponds to the distance between locations. The vertical lines represent the similarity thresholds for consistent attribute values used in the previous subsection. Given a threshold, we have perfect discriminability if there are no non-matching profiles with higher similarities. Concretely, for a given similarity threshold (x value), the y value for the distribution for the most similar non-matching profile represents an estimate of the (effective) discriminability $\tilde{D}$, whereas the y value for the distribution of matching profiles represents the complementary of the recall $1 - C \cdot A$.

For the *real name* and *screen name* we see a clear distinction between distributions of matching and non-matching profiles in Figure 1. The highest similarity of non-matching profiles is around 0.75 while a number matching profiles have similarities around 1. This suggests that these attributes have a high discriminability. For *photo*, the two distributions are generally similar. The photo does not appear to have a very good overall discriminability because there are not many Facebook matching profiles that use the same profile photo with the Twitter profile. However, for similarities large than 0.10, when the profile photos are consistent, there are not many non-matching profiles. As expected, the *location* does not have a good discriminability; even in a small dataset there are Facebook non-matching profiles with the same location as the Twitter profile. Finally, *friends* have a good discriminability between matching and non-matching profiles, i.e., it is uncommon to have non-matching profiles with many common friends.

We do not have access to the whole Facebook dataset to evaluate the discriminability of all attributes over an entire social network, however, we exploit the Facebook Graph Search to estimate the discriminability of real names and screen names. For each Twitter profile we use Facebook Graph Search to retrieve all the profiles with the same or similar names and screen names. This procedure samples the non-matching profiles with the highest similarity; therefore it preserves the discriminability of the entire social network. Figure 1a and 1b also presents the discriminability of real names and screen names over the entire Facebook (entire). As expected, the CDF of similarity score for non-matching profiles is much lower than it was at small scale. Furthermore, for 60% of the Twitter profiles, there is a non-matching Facebook profile that has *exactly* the same real name and for 25% exactly the same screen name. Even worse, the CDFs of Figure 1a for non-matching profiles are even below the CDFs for matching profiles which means that in many cases there are non-matching profiles that have even more similar names with the Twitter profile than the matching profile. These results show that names and screen names are actually not so discriminating in practice and consequently shows the difficulty of reliably finding the matching profile in real-world social network. This also shows the risk of evaluating matching scheme over a sampled dataset because attributes have a much higher discriminability than over entire social networks.

4.5 Attribute impersonability

In most social networks a user is not required to prove that her online identity matches her offline person. Since there is a lot of personal data publicly available, it is very easy for attackers to create fake profiles that impersonate honest users. Because such attacks could be a very big source of unreliability for matching schemes, we show evidence that such attacks indeed exist and they are more frequent than previously assumed.

To search for potential cases of impersonation we start with an initial set of 1.4 million random profiles in Twitter. We find that,

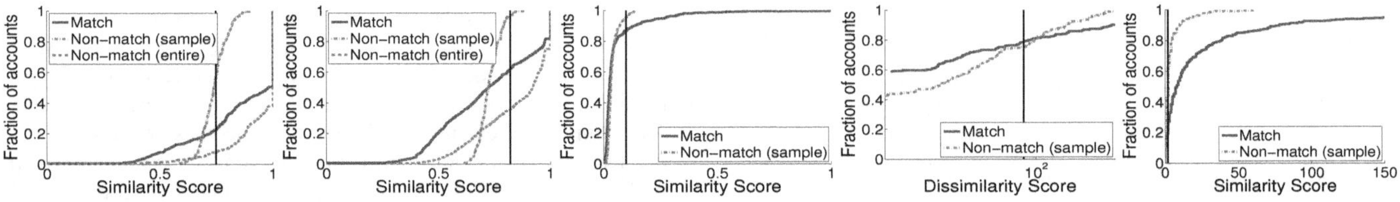

Figure 1: CDF of similarity scores for the matching Facebook profiles and for the most similar non-matching Facebook profile in DATASET FF (sample) and the entire Facebook (entire).

strikingly, a large fraction of profiles could be *potential* victims of impersonation attacks: 18,662 Twitter profiles have at least another Twitter profile with consistent profile attributes. This gives a rough estimate of p_I of 1%. It is beyond the scope of this paper to thoroughly investigate such attacks but in §7 we propose a way to make matching schemes less vulnerable to impersonation attacks.

5. TRAINING & TESTING MATCHING SCHEMES

In this section, we focus our attention on the datasets used to train and evaluate (test) matching schemes. To estimate well the precision and recall in practice, we should test for each profile a^1 the accuracy of finding the matching profiles $\hat{a}^2$ out of all the profiles $a^2 \in SN_2$. If we consider large social networks like Facebook, Twitter, or Google+, SN_2 has hundreds of millions of profiles. Obtaining such complete datasets is impractical, thus, we have to sample a number of profiles in the network.

Most previous studies sampled datasets by picking matching and non-matching profiles at random. Such random sampling fails to capture the precision and recall of matching schemes in practice because it severely over-estimates the discriminability of attributes found in the original social network (as seen in §4.4) and therefore it severely over-estimates precision. To estimate well the reliability of a matching scheme in practice, the sampled dataset needs to preserve the precision and recall of the original social network at least for high values of precision. The key to ensure this is to sample *all potential* false matches, i.e., all profiles that could be mistakenly matched by the matching scheme. Thus, we build two datasets: (1) a *reliability non-preserving sampled dataset* for comparison with previous techniques (as this is the standard evaluation method); and (2) a *reliability preserving sampled dataset* that strives to capture all possible false matches in a social network to better estimate the reliability of matching schemes in practice.

We generate a reliability preserving sampled dataset for matching Twitter and Facebook. Although building such dataset for other social networks is possible, the process is strenuous. Instead, we take two of the most popular social networks to show the limitations for matching profiles across real-world social networks.

Reliability-non-preserving sampling: We randomly sample 850 matching Twitter-Facebook profiles from DATASET FF and we use them to build 722,500 pairwise combinations of Twitter-Facebook profiles (850 positive and 721,650 negative examples). We call the resulting dataset the RANDOM-SAMPLED. The RANDOM-SAMPLED dataset preserves the availability and consistency of attributes in the original social network, but it does not preserve the discriminability and non-impersonability. Thus, the dataset does not preserve the precision of the original social network. Note that, datasets such as DATASET G+, which have been used in previous work, do not even preserve the availability and consistency of attributes because they are biased towards a particular kind of users (as seen in §4.2); hence they do not preserve recall.

Reliability-preserving sampling: To preserve the reliability over the original social network, our sampling strategy is to sample non-matching profiles that have a reasonably high similarity to a^1 and ignore non-matching profiles that have a very small chance of matching. We note the set of most similar profiles to a^1 in SN_2 as $C(a^1) \subset SN_2$. A comprehensive $C(a^1)$ includes all the Facebook profiles which could be potential false matches.

Given that our analysis in §4.3 shows that most Twitter-Facebook matching profiles have consistent real names or screen names, we hope to build a comprehensive $C(a^1)$ by exploiting the Facebook search API, which allows searching for people by name. For each Twitter profile, a^1 (we sample the same Twitter profiles as in RANDOM-SAMPLED), we generate $C(a^1)$ using the Facebook search API to find profiles with the same or similar real name or screen name as a^1. The resulting dataset, which we call EMULATED-LARGE, contains over 270,000 combinations of profiles (a^1, a^2) where $a^2 \in C(a^1)$. Thus, for each Twitter profile the dataset contains in average 320 Facebook profiles with similar names.

Our analysis shows that the matching profile of a^1 is in $C(a^1)$ (i.e., $\hat{a}^2 \in C(a^1)$) for 70% of Twitter profiles. This implies that for 70% of cases we selected at least all non-matching profiles with higher name similarity than the matching profile. Additionally, the median similarity of the least similar real name in $C(a^1)$ is 0.5, while the median similarity of matching profiles is 0.97. This means that we also catch many Facebook profiles with lower name similarity than the matching profiles. Thus, the only possible false matches that we miss are the ones that have very different names.

Note that the reliability preserving sampling does not sample the matching profile when there is little chance for it to match (in 30% of the cases). We actually tried to train and test matching schemes with or without including the unsampled matching profiles in the EMULATED-LARGE and the reliability did not differ significantly.

Our sampling strategy ensures that the discriminability and impersonability of real names and screen names found in the real-world datasets are preserved. It might over-estimate, however, the discriminability of location, friends, and profile photos since we do not sample in $C(a^1)$ profiles with similar location, friends or photos if they do not also have similar names or screen names. Evaluating matching schemes over $C(a^1)$ rather than all SN_2 could lead to an under-estimation of the false matches. Thus, the precision we obtain over this dataset is an upper bound on the precision in practice. This implies that the limits of reliably matching schemes in practice can only be worse than what we show in this paper. We believe, however, that our sampling strategy gives a very good idea of the precision and recall in the real-world datasets because there will be very few false matches (if any) with very dissimilar names even if they have similar location, photo or friends.

Another limitation of the dataset is that it does not contain cases where a profile a^1 has multiple matching profiles in SN_2. This is a consequence of our method to gather ground truth (§4.1) that only gives a single matching profile in SN_2 for each a^1. The implications of this limitation on our evaluation is that there might be some matching profiles that we consider as false matches whereas they are not. Since Facebook enforces the policy that users should only have one profile, we believe there are not many such cases and the reliability we measure is likely close to the real-world reliability.

In practice, there are Twitter users that do not have a matching Facebook profile, but our datasets do not contain such cases. To evaluate how matching schemes perform in such scenarios, we test in §7 the reliability of matching schemes when we remove the matching profile from EMULATED-LARGE.

6. GENERIC MATCHING PROBLEM

This section evaluates the reliability of matching schemes based on classifiers aimed at solving the generic case of the matching problem (see §2). We build classifiers that are conceptually similar to what previous works have done. The primary difference between different previous matching schemes is the features and the datasets they used to train and test classifiers, however, they all use traditional classifier such as SVM and Naive Bayes. The goal of this section is not to build a matching scheme that is better than previous ones but to investigate the limits of such schemes in practice.

We first emulate the methodology employed by previous works: we train and test matching schemes with RANDOM-SAMPLED, using all attributes. Since some profile attributes have a high discriminability in the dataset, it is straightforward to build a matching scheme with high reliability. On top of this, there is little difference between the reliability of naive classification techniques and more sophisticated ones.

We then investigating the reliability of matching schemes in practice by testing them over EMULATED-LARGE. As expected, the precision of the previously built matching schemes drastically decreases to a point that makes them unusable. Thereafter, we investigate the reasons behind such poor reliability and we evaluate different strategies to increase the precision and recall in practice. The resulting schemes are able to achieve a good precision, but the recall is still low. These results show the inherent difficulty of matching profiles reliably in today's large social networks.

6.1 Evaluation over RANDOM-SAMPLED

We use the RANDOM-SAMPLED dataset to train and test four classification techniques to match profiles: Naive Bayes, Decision Trees, Logistic Regression, and SVM. We split RANDOM-SAMPLED in two: 70% for training and 30% for testing.

There are two important aspects to handle when training classifiers to match profiles: (1) *classes are very imbalanced* – there are much more non-matching profiles than matching profiles. Previous works handled this problem by balancing the training instances by under-sampling the majority class [13]. We also adopt this technique and we randomly sample 850 non-matching profiles from the RANDOM-SAMPLED; (2) *features have missing values* – some attribute values may be unavailable hence the similarity value is missing (e.g., users may choose to omit their location or photo). Thus, we must either work with classification techniques that are robust to missing values (e.g., Naive Bayes) or identify methods to impute the missing values.

We use 10-fold cross validation on the training data to evaluate the four classifiers with different combinations of parameters and different methods for imputing the missing feature values. We call the four resulting classifiers with the best optimized parameters the LINKER-NB, LINKER-SVM, LINKER-LR and LINKER-DT.

We investigate the tradeoff between precision and recall for the different classifiers in Figure 2a. Our results show that LINKER-NB out of the box, without imputing the missing values and LINKER-SVM and LINKER-DT when we replace missing values with -1

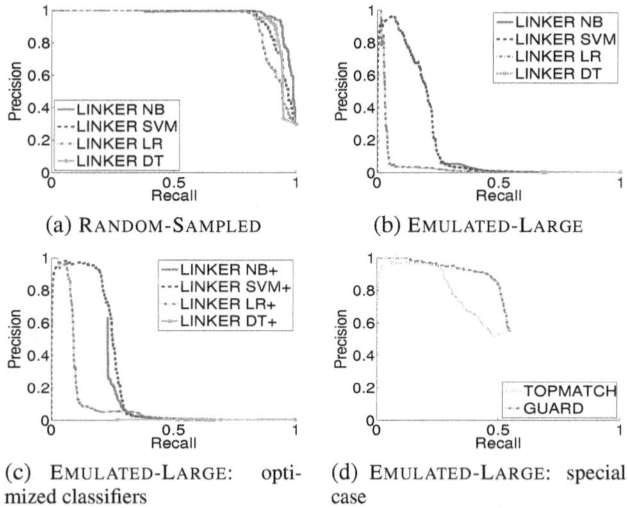

(a) RANDOM-SAMPLED (b) EMULATED-LARGE (c) EMULATED-LARGE: optimized classifiers (d) EMULATED-LARGE: special case

Figure 2: Precision and recall tradeoff for matching Twitter to Facebook profiles using different classifiers when evaluated over RANDOM-SAMPLED and EMULATED-LARGE.

Table 4: Fraction of true, missed and false matches that have available and consistent attributes in RANDOM-SAMPLED.

Feature	Fraction of available and consistent attributes			
	All Matches	True Matches	Missed Matches	False Matches
Real Name	0.77	0.91	0.20	0.62
Screen Name	0.38	0.46	0.07	0.09
Location	0.23	0.25	0.14	0.00
Profile Photo	0.08	0.10	0.01	0.00
Friends	0.34	0.34	0.22	0.38

achieve the highest reliability with a recall over 90% for a 95% precision. LINKER-LR achieves a lower recall, only 85% for the same precision. Thus, as expected, even out of the box classification techniques such as Naive Bayes are able to achieve a high precision and recall over RANDOM-SAMPLED.

Analysis of matched pairs: To understand what pairs of profiles the classifiers are matching, we analyze in Table 4 the availability and consistency of attributes for the *true matches*, the *false matches*, and the *missed matches* (the pairs of matching profiles that are *not* detected by the classifier). We use LINKER-SVM with a threshold on the probability p (outputted by the classifier) corresponding to a 95% precision (and 90% recall) to select the true, missed and false matches. The table shows that the only matching profiles the LINKER-SVM is not able to identify are the ones that do not have available and consistent attributes: only 20% of the missed matches have consistent names and 53% of missed matches do not have *any* consistent and available attribute (not shown in the table). The table also shows that the LINKER-SVM easily mistakes non-matching profiles form matching profiles if they have either consistent names or friends. While in this dataset this is not problematic, in practice this will lead to many false matches.

6.2 Evaluation over EMULATED-LARGE

Figure 2b presents the tradeoff between precision and recall when we evaluate using EMULATED-LARGE the four LINKER classifiers trained on RANDOM-SAMPLED. The figure shows that when matching profiles in practice the reliability of all four classifiers drops significantly compared to RANDOM-SAMPLED (presented in Figure 2a). The best classifier on the RANDOM-SAMPLED, LINKER-NB, achieve only a 4.5% precision for a 23% recall when tested on EMULATED-LARGE. The only classifier that achieves a satisfying 95% precision is LINKER-SVM, however, the recall is only 15%.

These results confirm our intuition that the reliability of a matching scheme over RANDOM-SAMPLED fails to capture the reliability of the matching scheme in practice. Worse, the matching scheme that has the best reliability when testing with RANDOM-SAMPLED (i.e., the LINKER-NB) can be amongst the worst in practice.

Optimizing the binary classifiers

LINKER-NB: We investigate the reasons for the low precision of LINKER-NB in EMULATED-LARGE. The results in Figure 1 show that matching profiles often have consistent names whereas non-matching profiles (from sample) most often do not; there is no such clear distinction for the other attributes. Since Naive Bayes assumes that features are independent, the probability that two profiles match will be mainly determined by their name similarity. In a large social network, however, multiple users can have the same name, which will cause LINKER-NB to output many false matches.

One way to make the classification more accurate is to use two classifiers in cascade instead of one. The first classifier weeds out profiles that are clear non-matches (most of which have different names). Then, the second classifier takes the output of the first and disambiguates the matching profiles out of profiles with similar names. We call this improved classifier LINKER-NB+. For more details about this approach please refer to [10].

Another approach to make the classification more accurate is to use methods based on joint probabilities such as quadratic discriminant analysis. We prefer to move to SVM which also considers features jointly and is not restricted to quadratic boundaries.

LINKER-SVM: LINKER-SVM has a much higher precision in EMULATED-LARGE than LINKER-NB. Intuitively, this is because, as opposed to Naive Bayes, SVM considers the features jointly and hence can distinguish between pairs of profiles with high name similarity that match and pairs of profiles with high name similarity that do not match based on other features. Nevertheless, previous work has shown that SVM performs suboptimally when using under-sampling to deal with imbalanced datasets [5]. By under-sampling the majority class, we are missing informative data points close to the decision boundary.

To improve the reliability of LINKER-SVM, we take advantage of the fact that EMULATED-LARGE contains negative examples close to the decision boundary, to enrich our training set. We build a training set that contains 850 positive examples, 850 negative examples from RANDOM-SAMPLED plus 850 negative examples from EMULATED-LARGE. We call the resulting classifier the LINKER-SVM+. Note that if we only use for training negative examples from EMULATED-LARGE and not from RANDOM-SAMPLED, the resulting classifier will only be able to distinguish the matching profiles out of profiles that look similar and will not be able to distinguish the matching profile out of profiles that are clearly not similar, i.e., it will only work on datasets such as EMULATED-LARGE and not in practice. For LINKER-LR and LINKER-DT we apply the same retraining technique.

Evaluation of optimized classifiers: Figure 2c shows the tradeoff between precision and recall when using LINKER-SVM+, LINKER-NB+, LINKER-LR+, LINKER-DT+ on EMULATED-LARGE. We can see that LINKER-SVM+ is able to achieve a 19% recall (4% improvement over the LINKER-SVM) for a 95% precision. Note that, in DATASET G+, LINKER-SVM+ has 50% recall and 95% precision. Also, LINKER-NB+ achieves a 23% recall for a 88% precision, considerably better than LINKER-NB. Nevertheless, the recall is significantly lower compared with the recall obtained when testing with RANDOM-SAMPLED. Thus, even more sophisticated techniques trained to match profiles in real-word settings fail to match a large fraction of profiles.

Table 5: Fraction of true, missed and false matches that have available and consistent attributes in EMULATED-LARGE.

Feature	Fraction of available and consistent attributes					
	95% precision and 19% recall			0.02% precision and 33% recall		
	True Matches	Missed Matches	False Matches	True Matches	Missed Matches	False Matches
Real Name	0.94	0.73	0.86	0.94	0.69	1.00
Screen Name	0.60	0.33	0.57	0.64	0.26	0.89
Location	0.32	0.21	0.14	0.41	0.15	0.01
Profile Photo	0.14	0.07	0.57	0.16	0.04	0.07
Friends	0.91	0.17	0.57	0.68	0.14	0.00

Analysis of matched pairs: To understand the low recall we obtain in EMULATED-LARGE, we analyze again the availability and consistency of attributes. The precision of LINKER-SVM+ has a sudden drop, to go from a recall of 19% to 33%, the precision goes from 95% to 0.02%. To analyze the drop, we split the pairs of profiles in EMULATED-LARGE in true, missed, and false matches using first a threshold corresponding to a 95% precision (and a 19% recall) and then with a threshold corresponding to a 0.02% precision (and a 33% recall), see Table 5.

Contrarily to our expectation, for most attributes but friends, the availability and consistency of true matches at 0.02% precision is actually slightly higher than the one at 95% precision. Only the availability and consistency of friends decreases from 91% at 95% precision to 68% at 0.02% precision. This means that, to go from 19% to 33% recall we mainly started to match profiles that do not have friends in common. The consequence is that while at 95% precision, the false matches needed to have friends in common, at 0.02% precision, false matches no longer need to have friends in common. This makes the matching scheme have orders of magnitude more false matches at 33% recall than at 19% recall. Thus, even if the features are highly available and consistent, if they are not discriminable enough, they will allow for many false matches which limits the precision and recall we can achieve in practice.

The results suggest that when matching profiles in practice, to maintain a high precision, we need features that are highly discriminable. Indeed, if we exclude friends (one of the most discriminable attributes) from the features we use for the classification, we can only achieve a 11% recall for a 90% precision.

7. SPECIAL MATCHING PROBLEM

The previous section showed that even fine tuned classifiers are vulnerable to output many false matches in practice. Worse, previous matching schemes are not able to protect against impersonation attacks. In this section, we propose ways to mitigate both of these problems in the special case where we know that there exists *at most one matching profile* in SN_2.

The TOPMATCH: The straw man approach is, for each profile a^1, to simply return the profile in $C(a^1)$ with the highest probability p to be the matching profile given by LINKER-SVM+, provided that p is larger than a threshold. We call the most similar profile the TOPMATCH. This approach reduces the number of false matches since the matching scheme outputs at most one false match. Figure 2d displays the tradeoff between precision and recall obtained for different probability thresholds on the p of the TOPMATCH. It shows that TOPMATCH largely improves recall for a given precision: TOPMATCH in EMULATED-LARGE achieves to a 26% recall for a 95% precision.

The GUARD: The strategy of outputting the TOPMATCH considerably increases the recall compared to approaches in §6. However, it is still vulnerable to output false matches in practice when Twitter users who do not have a Facebook profile. Worse, the TOPMATCH is vulnerable to impersonation attacks that also hinder the reliability of the matching scheme. We propose next a simple solution that mitigates both of these problems by comparing the probability to be the matching profile of the most similar profile in $C(a^1)$, p_{1st}, and the probability of the second most similar profile, p_{2nd}. The high level idea is that, to be sure that the most similar profile in $C(a^1)$ is the matching profile, p_{1st} should be much higher than the probability p of any profile in $C(a^1)$, i.e., $p_{1st} \gg p_{2nd}$.

Intuitively, there are two possible scenarios where the TOPMATCH is a false match: The first is if an attacker creates an impersonating profile on SN_2 that is more similar than the true matching profile. It might be possible to detect these cases as both p_{1st} and p_{2nd} will be high and $(p_{1st} - p_{2nd})$ will be very small. The second is when the true matching profile $\hat{a}^2$ is in $C(a^1)$ but a non-matching profile $a^2 \in C(a^1)$ is chosen as output because the classifier assigns it a higher probability p of being the matching profile (due to the lack of attribute availability and/or consistency). Another case is when $\hat{a}^2$ does not exist, forcing the scheme to choose the non-matching profile that is the most similar to a^1 as the output. We might detect these cases as p_{1st} and p_{2nd} will not be very high (none of the profiles in $C(a^1)$ are very similar to a^1) and $(p_{1st} - p_{2nd})$ will be again very small (none of the profiles in $C(a^1)$ is much more similar than the rest).

To incorporate the above logic, we design the GUARD which is a binary classifier that takes as input p_{1st} and p_{2nd} and outputs the probability that the TOPMATCH is the matching profile. Figure 2d shows that the GUARD increases the recall of the matching scheme to 29% for a 95% precision. Although 29% recall is a big improvement over the recall previously obtained, the recall is still low. This shows that in practice, it is hard to achieve a high recall if we want to have a high precision.

The matching schemes in §6 decide independently for each pair (a^1, a^2) where $a^2 \in C(a^1)$ whether it is a match or not. In contrast, the strength of the GUARD is that it exploits the structure of $C(a^1)$ for a given a^1. In particular, since $C(a^1)$ depends on a^1, for a given probability p to be the matching profile of a^1, the TOPMATCH profile a^2 will be declared a match for some a^1 if its attribute values are sufficiently unique, whereas the scheme will return nothing for other a^1 if the attribute values are too common (e.g., Jennifer Clark that lives in New York). This reduces considerably the false matches and, as we have shown, increases a lot the matching recall for a given precision.

Reliability in the absence of a matching profile: To test the reliability of the matching scheme in the absence of a matching profile, we take the EMULATED-LARGE and we remove the matching profiles from the dataset. Then, we evaluate the GUARD over the resulting dataset. Ideally, the GUARD should not return any profile as there is no matching profile in the dataset. Indeed, the GUARD only returns a false match for 1% of the Twitter profiles. We manually investigate the 1% cases: in half the returned profile is a false match; in the other half it is actually a profile that corresponds to the same person (the returned profiles are either impersonators or people that maintain duplicate profiles on Facebook). Thus, the GUARD is reliable when there is no matching profile in SN_2.

8. EVALUATION AGAINST HUMANS

In this section, we confirm the inherent difficulty to obtain a high recall in matching profiles in practice by comparing our results with results obtained by asking human workers to match profiles.

For this we designed an AMT experiment. We randomly select 200 Twitter-Facebook matching profiles from DATASET FF (that are not used for training the matching schemes). In each assignment, we give AMT workers a link to a Twitter profile as well as links to the 10 most similar Facebook profiles (we shuffle their position) and we ask AMT workers to choose the matching profile. We allow workers to choose that they are unable to identify the matching profile. For each assignment we ask the opinion of three different workers. We present the results for majority agreement (two out of three workers decided on the same answer). We design two versions of the experiment: in the first one if the matching profile is not in $C(a^1)$, the matching profile will not be in the list of 10 Facebook profiles; and a second version, where we always put the matching profile the list of 10 Facebook profiles.

In the first version of the experiment, AMT workers were able to match 40% of the Twitter profiles to their matching profiles and 4% are matched to the wrong Facebook profile. This means that AMT workers achieve a 40% recall for a 96% precision, which is better than the GUARD, but far from a 100% recall. In the second version of the experiment, AMT workers were able to match 58% of Twitter profiles. Thus, even humans cannot achieve a recall close to 100% to match profiles in practice.

9. RELATED WORK

We review three primary lines of related research: one proposing schemes to match user profiles across different social networks; one focusing on how anonymized user graphs or databases can be deanonymized to infer user identities; and another about matching entities across databases.

Matching profiles using private user data: Balduzzi et al. [7] match profiles on different social networks using the "Friend Finder" mechanism that social networks provide for users to find their friends using their email addresses. In fact, this is what we use for obtaining our ground truth. Many sites, however, view Friend Finder as leaking users' private data and have since limited the number of queries a user can make which severely limits the number of profiles one can match. In contrast, we are interested in understanding the limits of matching profiles by only using public attributes that anyone can access without assuming that we have access to more private data such as the emails of users.

Matching profiles using public user data: A number of previous studies proposed matching schemes that leveraged different attributes of public user data to match profiles, but without systematically understanding their limitations in real-world social networks. As a result, previous works overlooked a number of methodological aspects: (1) Most works did not train and test their matching schemes on sampled datasets that preserve the reliability of the original social network. Consequently, the reliability of these schemes drops significantly when evaluated in real-world social networks [30, 24, 31, 36, 29, 18, 39, 38]; (2) Most works used attributes without analyzing their properties and their limits to match profiles in practice, consequently, some of these studies use attributes with low availability and thus can only match a small fraction of profiles across a limited number of social networks [11, 14, 19] or use attributes that are prone to give many false matches in practice [23]. On the contrary, we propose a framework to analyze attributes and evaluate their potential to match profiles in practice. (3) Most studies used biased sets of ground truth users that willingly publish links to their profiles on different social networks. Our analysis reveals that such datasets have attributes that are more available and consistent, consequently, the reliability results of such schemes are overly optimistic [27, 22, 30, 39, 21]. Other studies assume that all profiles that have the same screen name are matching [17, 14]. In §4.4 we showed that 20% of profiles with the same screen name in Twitter and Facebook are actually not matching. We further split these studies according to the type of attributes used.

The closest to our work are a number of schemes that leverage information in the *profiles of users* similar to the attributes we use in this paper [24, 30, 22, 27, 4, 37, 36, 31, 26, 29, 18, 39, 38, 37, 17, 33]. Most schemes work by training classifiers to distinguish between matching and non-matching profiles. We simulated these approaches in §6 and we saw that, because they did not consider the problems that come with matching in practice, the matching schemes are very unreliable when evaluated in real-world social networks. A few studies attempted to perform profile matching in practice [22, 27, 4]. These studies, however, just pointed out that profile matching in practice yields a large number of false matches. In contrast, we conduct a systematic analysis of the causes of such false matches and possible ways to eliminate them.

Other schemes use attributes extracted from *user activities* (i.e., the content users generate instead of attributes of the profile) [11, 23, 14]. These schemes reveal how even innocuous activities can help identify a user across social networks. However, they explore attributes with either low availability or low discriminability, which makes them hard to use in practice without sacrificing reliability.

De-anonymizing user identities: De-anonymizing user identities and matching user profiles share common methods. In fact, our work here is inspired by one of the seminal papers of Sweeney [35], which explored the uniqueness of attributes such as date of birth, postal code, and gender to de-anonymize medical records of US citizens. Other studies [25, 15] showed the feasibility to de-anonymize the friendship graph of a social network at large-scale using the *friendship graph* of another social network as auxiliary information. The structure of the social graph is certainly a powerful feature. Nevertheless, in this work, we explicitly assume that we cannot have access to the entire graph structure of the social networks since we only use public APIs to collect data. We leave as future work how to exploit partial graphs that can be obtained trough APIs to improve matching schemes based on binary classifiers.

Entity matching: There is a large body of research in the database and information retrieval communities on matching entities across different data sources [8]. Conceptually there are many similarities between matching profiles across social networks and matching entities (e.g. the way we compute the similarities between attributes or the adoption of a supervised way to detect matches). However, matching profiles has some specific constraints (e.g., not being able to access all records in SN_1) that the entity matching community, to our knowledge, overlooked.

10. CONCLUSION

In this paper, we conducted a systematic and detailed investigation of the reliably of matching user profiles across real-world online social networks like Twitter and Facebook. Our analysis yielded a number of methodological and measurement contributions.

To understand how profile attributes used by matching schemes affect the overall matching reliability, we proposed a framework that consist of four properties – *Availability, Consistency, Impersonability, and Discriminability (*ACID*)*. Our analysis showed that most people maintain the same persona across different social networks – thus it is possible to match the profiles of many users, however, in practice there can be a non negligible number of profiles that belong to different users but have similar attribute values, which leads to false matches.

We showed that the reliability of matching schemes that are trained and tested on reliability non-preserving sampled datasets is not indicative of their reliability in practice. In fact, traditional matching schemes based on binary classifiers can only achieve a 19% recall for a 95% precision to match Twitter to Facebook profiles in practice. To avoid these pitfalls we illustrated the right assumptions we can make about the matching problem and the correct methodology to evaluate matching schemes in realistic scenarios.

Finally, we proposed a matching scheme that is able to mitigate impersonation attacks and reduce the number of false matches to achieve a 29% recall for a 95% precision. Our matching scheme exploits a special case of the matching problem, namely that there exists at most one matching profile. Although we cannot claim that 29% is a high recall, humans cannot do much better (they only detect 40% of matching profiles).

References

[1] Phash. http://www.phash.org.
[2] Spokeo. http://www.spokeo.com/.
[3] Spokeo lawsuit. http://www.ftc.gov/sites/default/files/documents/cases/2012/06/120612spokeocmpt.pdf.
[4] A. Acquisti, R. Gross, and F. Stutzman. Faces of facebook: Privacy in the age of augmented reality. In *BlackHat*, 2011.
[5] R. Akbani, S. Kwek, and N. Japkowicz. Applying support vector machines to imbalanced datasets. In *ECML*, 2004.
[6] Get better results with less effort with Mechanical Turk Masters – The Mechanical Turk blog. http://bit.ly/112GmQI.
[7] M. Balduzzi, C. Platzer, T. Holz, E. Kirda, D. Balzarotti, and C. Kruegel. Abusing social networks for automated user profiling. In *RAID*, 2010.
[8] P. Christen. *Data Matching - Concepts and Techniques for Record Linkage, Entity Resolution, and Duplicate Detection.* Data-centric systems and applications. Springer, 2012.
[9] W. W. Cohen, P. Ravikumar, and S. E. Fienberg. A comparison of string distance metrics for name-matching tasks. In *IIWeb*, 2003.
[10] O. Goga. *Matching User Accounts Across Online Social Networks: Methods and Applications.* PhD thesis, UPMC, 2014.
[11] O. Goga, H. Lei, S. Parthasarathi, G. Friedland, R. Sommer, and R. Teixeira. Exploiting innocuous activity for correlating users across sites. In *WWW*, 2013.
[12] O. Goga, P. Loiseau, R. Sommer, R. Teixeira, and K. P. Gummadi. On the reliability of profile matching across large online social networks, 2015. Technical report, available as arXiv:1506.02289.
[13] H. He and E. A. Garcia. Learning from imbalanced data. *IEEE TKDE*, 2009.
[14] T. Iofciu, P. Fankhauser, F. Abel, and K. Bischoff. Identifying users across social tagging systems. In *ICWSM*, 2011.
[15] N. Korula and S. Lattanzi. An efficient reconciliation algorithm for social networks. *PVLDB*, 2014.
[16] C. Kreibich, C. Kanich, K. Levchenko, B. Enright, G. M. Voelker, V. Paxson, and S. Savage. Spamcraft: An inside look at spam campaign orchestration. In *LEET*, 2009.
[17] S. Labitzke, I. Taranu, and H. Hartenstein. What your friends tell others about you: Low cost linkability of social network profiles. In *SNA-KDD*, 2011.
[18] J. Liu, F. Zhang, X. Song, Y.-I. Song, C.-Y. Lin, and H.-W. Hon. What's in a name?: An unsupervised approach to link users across communities. In *WSDM*, 2013.
[19] S. Liu, S. Wang, F. Zhu, J. Zhang, and R. Krishnan. Hydra: Large-scale social identity linkage via heterogeneous behavior modeling. In *SIGMOD*, 2014.
[20] D. G. Lowe. Distinctive image features from scale-invariant keypoints. *IJCV*, 2004.
[21] C.-T. Lu, H.-H. Shuai, and P. S. Yu. Identifying your customers in social networks. In *CIKM*, 2014.
[22] A. Malhotra, L. Totti, W. Meira, P. Kumaraguru, and V. Almeida. Studying user footprints in different online social networks. In *CSOSN*, 2012.
[23] M. A. Mishari and G. Tsudik. Exploring linkability of user reviews. In *ESORICS*, 2012.
[24] M. Motoyama and G. Varghese. I seek you: searching and matching individuals in social networks. In *WIDM*, 2009.
[25] A. Narayanan and V. Shmatikov. De-anonymizing social networks. In *IEEE S&P*, 2009.
[26] C. T. Northern and M. L. Nelson. An unsupervised approach to discovering and disambiguating social media profiles. In *MDSW*, 2011.
[27] P. K. Paridhi Jain and A. Joshi. @i seek 'fb.me': Identifying users across multiple online social networks. In *WoLE*, 2013.
[28] Peekyou. http://www.peekyou.com/.
[29] O. Peled, M. Fire, L. Rokach, and Y. Elovici. Entity matching in online social networks. In *SocialCom*, 2013.
[30] D. Perito, C. Castelluccia, M. Ali Kâafar, and P. Manils. How unique and traceable are usernames? In *PETS*, 2011.
[31] E. Raad, R. Chbeir, and A. Dipanda. User profile matching in social networks. In *NBiS*, 2010.
[32] R. Schmid. Salesforce service cloud – featuring activision, 2012. http://www.youtube.com/watch?v=eT6iHEdnKQ4&feature=relmfu.
[33] Y. Shen and H. Jin. Controllable information sharing for user accounts linkage across multiple online social networks. In *CIKM*, 2014.
[34] Social Intelligence Corp. http://www.socialintel.com/.
[35] L. Sweeney. Weaving technology and policy together to maintain confidentiality. *Journal of Law, Medicine, and Ethics*, 1997.
[36] J. Vosecky, D. Hong, and V. Shen. User identification across multiple social networks. In *NDT*, 2009.
[37] G.-w. You, S.-w. Hwang, Z. Nie, and J.-R. Wen. Socialsearch: enhancing entity search with social network matching. In *EDBT/ICDT*, 2011.
[38] R. Zafarani and H. Liu. Connecting corresponding identities across communities. In *ICWSM*, 2009.
[39] R. Zafarani and H. Liu. Connecting users across social media sites: A behavioral-modeling approach. In *KDD*, 2013.

E-commerce in Your Inbox: Product Recommendations at Scale

Mihajlo Grbovic, Vladan Radosavljevic, Nemanja Djuric, Narayan Bhamidipati
Yahoo Labs
701 First Avenue, Sunnyvale, USA
{mihajlo, vladan, nemanja, narayanb}@yahoo-inc.com

Jaikit Savla, Varun Bhagwan, Doug Sharp
Yahoo, Inc.
701 First Avenue, Sunnyvale, USA
{jaikit, vbhagwan, dsharp}@yahoo-inc.com

ABSTRACT

In recent years online advertising has become increasingly ubiquitous and effective. Advertisements shown to visitors fund sites and apps that publish digital content, manage social networks, and operate e-mail services. Given such large variety of internet resources, determining an appropriate type of advertising for a given platform has become critical to financial success. Native advertisements, namely ads that are similar in look and feel to content, have had great success in news and social feeds. However, to date there has not been a winning formula for ads in e-mail clients. In this paper we describe a system that leverages user purchase history determined from e-mail receipts to deliver highly personalized product ads to Yahoo Mail users. We propose to use a novel neural language-based algorithm specifically tailored for delivering effective product recommendations, which was evaluated against baselines that included showing popular products and products predicted based on co-occurrence. We conducted rigorous offline testing using a large-scale product purchase data set, covering purchases of more than 29 million users from 172 e-commerce websites. Ads in the form of product recommendations were successfully tested on online traffic, where we observed a steady 9% lift in click-through rates over other ad formats in mail, as well as comparable lift in conversion rates. Following successful tests, the system was launched into production during the holiday season of 2014.

Categories and Subject Descriptors

H.2.8 [**Database applications**]: Data Mining

Keywords

Data mining; computational advertising; audience modeling

KDD '15, August 10-13, 2015, Sydney, NSW, Australia
 ISBN 978-1-4503-3664-2/15/08...$15.00
DOI: http://dx.doi.org/10.1145/2783258.2788627.

1. INTRODUCTION

Hundreds of millions of people around the world visit their e-mail inboxes daily, mostly to communicate with their contacts, although a significant fraction of time is spent checking utility bills, reading newsletters, and tracking purchases. To monetize this overwhelming amount of traffic, e-mail clients typically show display ads in a form of images alongside native e-mail content. Convincing users to exit the "e-mail mode", characterized by a relentless focus on the task of dealing with their mail, in order to enter a mode where they are willing to click on ads is a challenging task. Effective personalization and targeting [11], where the goal is to find the best matching ads to be displayed for each individual user, is essential to tackling this problem, as ads need to be highly relevant to overcome user's inclination to focus narrowly on the e-mail task. In addition to financial gains for online businesses [26], proactively tailoring advertisements to the tastes of each individual consumer also leads to an improved user experience, and can help with increasing user loyalty and retention [2].

Inbound e-mails are still insufficiently explored and exploited for the purposes of ad targeting, while arguably representing a treasure trove of monetizable data. A recent study [13] showed that only 10% of inbound volume represents human-generated e-mails. Furthermore, out of the remaining 90% of traffic more than 22% represents e-mails related to online shopping. Given that a significant percentage of overall traffic has commercial intent, a popular form of targeted advertising is mail retargeting (MRT), where advertisers target users who previously received e-mails from certain commercial web domains. These e-mails present a strong signal useful for targeting campaigns, as they give a broad picture about each customer's interests and relationship with commercial domains. A recent paper [14] proposed to make use of this vast potential and presented a clustering method to generate MRT rules, showing that such rules are more accurate than the ones generated by human experts.

However, in order to go beyond MRT rules that utilize only the fact that users and e-commerce sites communicated, advertisers require more detailed data such as purchased product name and price that are often part of e-mail body. E-mail clients have been working with e-commerce and travel domains to standardize how e-mails are formatted, resulting in schemas maintained by the *schema.org* com-

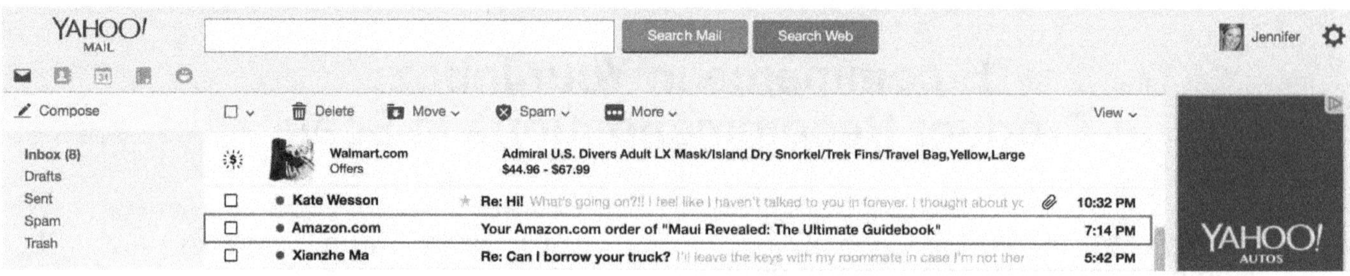

Figure 1: Product recommendations in Yahoo Mail

munity[1]. With more and more e-commerce sites using standard schemas, e-mail clients can provide more personalized user notifications, such as package tracking[2] and flight details[3]. In addition, e-mail receipt extraction brings monetization opportunity through product advertising to users based on their individual purchase history. Availability of purchase data from multiple commercial e-mail domains puts the e-mail provider in the unique position to be able to build better recommendation systems than those based on any one commercial e-mail domain alone. In particular, unlike e-commerce websites that make recommendations of type: "Customers who bought X also bought Y", e-mail providers can make recommendations of type: "Customers who bought X from vendor V_1 also bought Y from vendor V_2", allowing much more powerful and effective targeting solutions.

In this paper we tell the story of an end-to-end development of product ads for Yahoo Mail. The effort included developing a product-level purchase prediction algorithm, capable of scaling to millions of users and products. To this end, we propose an approach that embeds products into real-valued, low-dimensional vector space using a neural language model applied to a time series of user purchases. As a result, products with similar contexts (i.e., their surrounding purchases) are mapped to vectors that are nearby in the embedding space. To be able to make meaningful and diverse suggestions about the next product to be purchased, we further cluster the product vectors and model transition probabilities between clusters. The closest products in the embedding space from the most probable clusters are used to form final recommendations for a product.

The product prediction model was trained using a large-scale purchase data set, comprising more than 280 million purchases made by 29 million users, involving 2.1 million unique products. The model was evaluated on a held-out month, where we tested the effectiveness of recommendations in terms of yield rate. In addition, we evaluated several baseline approaches, including showing popular products to all users, showing popular products in various user groups (called *cohorts*, specified by user's gender, age, and location), as well as showing products that are historically frequently purchased after the product a user most recently bought. To mitigate the cold start problem, popular products in user's cohort were used as back-fill recommendations for users without earlier purchases.

[1]http://schema.org/email, accessed June 2015
[2]yahoomail.tumblr.com/post/107247385566/track-your-packages-now-in-the-yahoo-mail-app, accessed June 2015
[3]venturebeat.com/2014/10/22/yahoo-mail-now-tells-you-about-upcoming-flights-and-events, accessed June 2015

Empirical results show that the proposed product-level model is able to more accurately predict purchases than baseline approaches. In the experimental section we also share results of bucket tests on live traffic, where we compared the performance of the baselines in the same ad slot. Our method substantially improves key business metrics, measured in terms of clicks and conversions. Moreover, our product-prediction technique was successfully implemented at large scale, tested in live buckets, and finally launched in production. The system is able to make near-real-time product recommendations with latency of less than $200ms$. In Figure 1 we show an example of our product recommender, where an offer from *walmart.com* is suggested after related purchase was made on *amazon.com* (marked with red).

2. RELATED WORK

In this section we describe related work in mail-based advertising, as well as neural language models that motivated our product recommendation approach.

2.1 Leveraging e-mail data in advertising

Web environment provides content publishers with a means to track user behavior in much greater detail than in an offline settings, including capturing user's registered information and activity logs of user's clicks, page views, searches, website visits, social activities, and interactions with ads. This allows for targeting of users based on their behavior, which is typically referred to as ad targeting [1]. With the rise of big data applications and platforms, machine learning approaches are heavily leveraged to automate the ad targeting process. Within the past several years, there has been a plethora of research papers that explored different aspects of online advertising, each with the goal of maximizing the benefits for advertisers, content publishers, and users.

For any machine learning technique, features used to train a model typically have a critical influence on the performance of the deployed algorithm. Features derived from user events collected by publishers are often used in predicting the user's propensity to click or purchase [9]. However, these features represent only a weak proxy to what publishers and advertisers are actually interested in, namely, user's purchase intent. On the other hand, commercial e-mails in the form of promotions and purchase receipts convey a strong, very direct purchase intent signal that can enable advertisers to reach a high-quality audience. According to the Direct Marketing Association's "National Client E-mail Report"[4], an e-mail user has been identified as having over 10% more value than the average online customer. Despite these

[4]www.powerprodirect.com/statistics, accessed June 2015

encouraging facts, limited work has been done to analyze the potential of features derived from commercial e-mails. A recent work [14] was among the first attempts to investigate the value of commercial e-mail data. The authors applied Sparse Principal Component Analysis (SPCA) on the counts of received e-mails in order to cluster commercial domains, demonstrating significant promise of e-mail data source.

Outside of the e-mail domain, information about user's purchase history is extensively used by e-commerce websites to recommend relevant products to their users [22]. Recommendation systems predict which products a user will most likely be interested in either by exploiting purchase behavior of users with similar interests (referred to as collaborative filtering [22]) or by using user's historical interaction with other products (i.e., context-based recommendation [29]). Unlike these studies, we are not limited to the data from a single website, as purchases extracted from e-mails enable us to gather information from hundreds of different e-commerce websites that can be exploited to learn better product predictions. To the best of our knowledge, this work represents the first study that offers a comprehensive empirical analysis and evaluation of product predictors using e-mail data of such scale and nature.

2.2 Neural language models

In a number of Natural Language Processing (NLP) applications, including information retrieval, part-of-speech tagging, chunking, and many others, specific objectives can all be generalized to the task of assigning a probability value to a sequence of words. To this end, language models have been developed, defining a mathematical model to capture statistical properties of words and the dependencies among them [3, 20]. Traditionally, language model approaches represent each word as a feature vector using a one-hot representation, where a word vector has the same length as the size of a vocabulary, and the position that corresponds to the observed word is equal to 1, and 0 otherwise. However, this approach often exhibits significant limitations in practical tasks, suffering from high dimensionality of the problem and severe data sparsity, resulting in suboptimal performance.

Neural language models have been proposed to address these issues, inducing low-dimensional, distributed embeddings of words by means of neural networks [5, 8, 28]. Such approaches take advantage of the word order in text documents, explicitly modeling the assumption that closer words in the word sequence are statistically more dependent. Historically, inefficient training of the neural network-based models has been an obstacle to their wider applicability, given that the vocabulary size may grow to several millions in practical tasks. However, this issue has been successfully addressed by recent advances in the field, particularly with the development of highly scalable continuous bag-of-words (CBOW) and skip-gram (SG) language models [23, 24] for learning word representations. These powerful, efficient models have shown very promising results in capturing both syntactic and semantic relationships between words in large-scale text corpora, obtaining state-of-the-art results on a plethora of NLP tasks. More recently, the concept of distributed representations has been extended beyond word representations to sentences and paragraphs [10, 21], relational entities [6, 27], general text-based attributes [19], descriptive text of images [18], nodes in graph structure [25], and other applications.

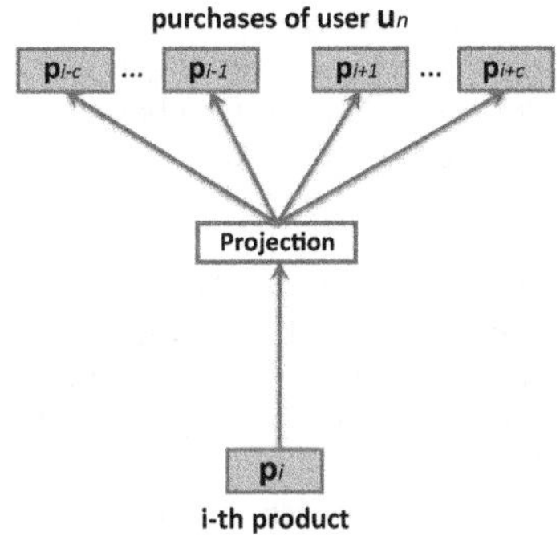

Figure 2: prod2vec skip-gram model

3. PROPOSED APPROACH

In this section we describe the proposed methodology for the task of product recommendations, which leverages information about prior purchases determined from e-mail receipts. To address this task we propose to learn representation of products in low-dimensional space from historical logs using neural language models. Product recommendation can then be performed in the learned embedding space through simple nearest neighbor search.

More specifically, given a set $\mathcal{S}$ of e-mail receipt logs obtained from N users, where user's log $s = (e_1, \dots, e_M) \in \mathcal{S}$ is defined as an uninterupted sequence of M receipts, and each e-mail receipt $e_m = (p_{m1}, p_{m2}, \dots p_{mT_m})$ consists of T_m purchased products, our objective is to find D-dimensional real-valued representation $\mathbf{v}_p \in \mathcal{R}^D$ of each product p such that similar products lie nearby in the vector space.

We propose several approaches for learning product representations that address specifics of the recommendations from e-mail receipts. We first propose *prod2vec* method that considers all purchased products independently. We then propose novel *bagged-prod2vec* method that takes into account that some products are listed as purchased together in e-mail receipts, which results in better, more useful product representations. Finally, we present product-to-product and user-to-product recommendation models that make use of the learned representations.

3.1 Low-dimensional product embeddings

prod2vec. The prod2vec model involves learning vector representations of products from e-mail receipt logs by using a notion of a purchase sequence as a "sentence" and products within the sequence as "words", borrowing the terminology from the NLP domain (see Figure 2 for graphical representation of the model). More specifically, prod2vec learns product representations using the skip-gram model [24] by maximizing the objective function over the entire set $\mathcal{S}$ of e-mail receipt logs, defined as follows

$$\mathcal{L} = \sum_{s \in \mathcal{S}} \sum_{p_i \in s} \sum_{-c \le j \le c, j \ne 0} \log \mathbb{P}(p_{i+j} | p_i), \tag{3.1}$$

where products from the same e-mail receipt are ordered arbitrarily. Probability $\mathbb{P}(p_{i+j}|p_i)$ of observing a neighboring product p_{i+j} given the current product p_i is defined using the soft-max function,

$$\mathbb{P}(p_{i+j}|p_i) = \frac{\exp(\mathbf{v}_{p_i}^\top \mathbf{v}'_{p_{i+j}})}{\sum_{p=1}^{P} \exp(\mathbf{v}_{p_i}^\top \mathbf{v}'_p)}, \tag{3.2}$$

where $\mathbf{v}_p$ and $\mathbf{v}'_p$ are the input and output vector representations of product p, c is the length of the context for product sequences, and P is the number of unique products in the vocabulary. From equations (3.1) and (3.2) we see that prod2vec models context of product sequence, where products with similar contexts (i.e., with similar neighboring purchases) will have similar vector representations. However, prod2vec does not explicitly take into account that e-mail receipt may contain multiple products purchased at the same time, which we address by introducing a *bagged* version of prod2vec described below.

bagged-prod2vec. In order to account for the fact that multiple products may be purchased at the same time, we propose a modified skip-gram model that introduces a notion of a shopping bag. As depicted in Figure 3, the model operates at the level of e-mail receipts instead at the level of products. Product vector representations are learned by maximizing a modified objective function over e-mail sequences s, defined as follows

$$\mathcal{L} = \sum_{s \in \mathcal{S}} \sum_{e_m \in s} \sum_{-n \le j \le n, j \ne 0} \sum_{k=1,\ldots,T_m} \log \mathbb{P}(e_{m+j}|p_{mk}). \quad (3.3)$$

Probability $\mathbb{P}(e_{m+j}|p_{mk})$ of observing products from neighboring e-mail receipt e_{m+j}, $e_{m+j} = (p_{m+j,1} \ldots p_{m+j,T_m})$, given the k-th product from m-th e-mail receipt reduces to a product of probabilities $\mathbb{P}(e_{m+j}|p_{mk}) = \mathbb{P}(p_{m+j,1}|p_{mk}) \times \ldots \times \mathbb{P}(p_{m+j,T_m}|p_{mk})$, each defined using soft-max (3.2). Note that the third sum in (3.3) goes over receipts, so the items from the same e-mail receipt do not predict each other during training. In addition, in order to capture temporal aspects of product purchases we propose to use the directed language model, where as context we only use future products [12]. The modification allows us to learn product embeddings capable of predicting future purchases.

Learning. The models were optimized using stochastic gradient ascent, suitable for large-scale problems. However, computation of gradients $\nabla\mathcal{L}$ in (3.1) and (3.3) are proportional to the vocabulary size P, which is computationally expensive in practical tasks as P could easily reach millions of products. As an alternative, we used negative sampling approach proposed in [24], which significantly reduces the computational complexity.

3.2 Product-to-product predictive models

Having learned low-dimensional product representations, we considered several possibilities for predicting the next product to be purchased.

prod2vec-topK. Given a purchased product, the method calculates cosine similarities to all other products in the vocabulary and recommends the top K most similar products.

prod2vec-cluster. To be able to make more diverse recommendations, we considered grouping similar products into clusters and recommending products from a cluster that is related to the cluster of previously purchased product. We applied K-means clustering algorithm implemented on the top of Hadoop distributed system where we grouped products based on cosine similarity between their low-dimensional representations. We assume that purchasing a product from any of the C clusters after a purchase from cluster c_i follows a multinomial distribution $Mu(\theta_{i1}, \theta_{i2}, \ldots \theta_{iC})$, where θ_{ij} is the probability that a purchase from cluster c_i is followed by a purchase from cluster c_j. In order to estimate parameters θ_{ij}, for each i and j, we adopted a maximum likelihood

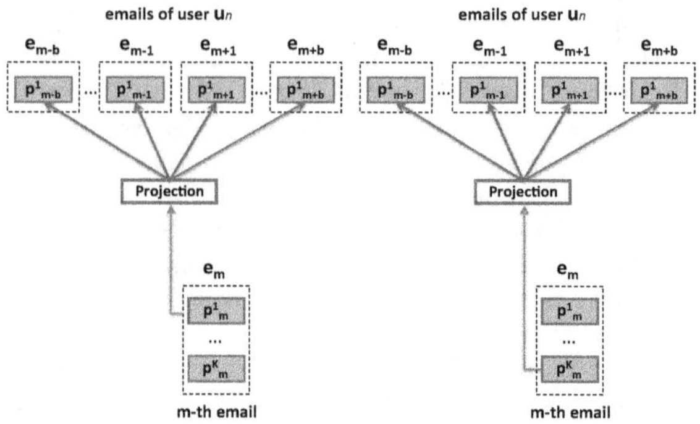

Figure 3: bagged-prod2vec model updates

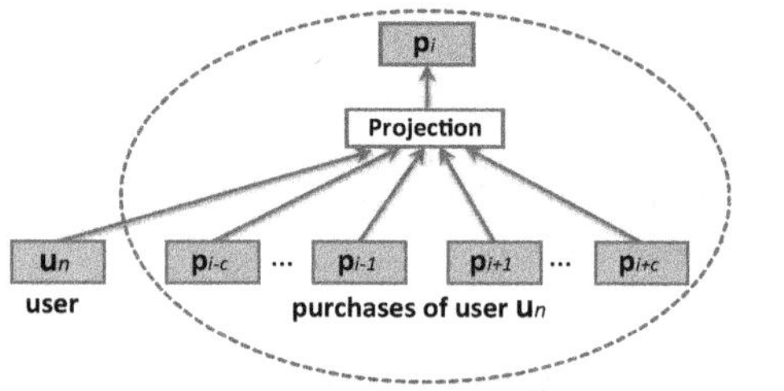

Figure 4: User embeddings for user to product predictions

approach,

$$\hat{\theta}_{ij} = \frac{\#\text{ of times } c_i \text{ purchase was followed by } c_j}{\text{count of } c_i \text{ purchases}}. \quad (3.4)$$

In order to recommend a new product given a purchased product p, we first identify which cluster p belongs to (e.g., $p \in c_i$). Next, we rank all clusters c_j, $j = 1, \ldots, C$, by the value of θ_{ij} and consider the top ones as top-related clusters to cluster c_i. Finally, products from the top clusters are sorted by their cosine similarity to p, and we use the top K products as recommendations.

3.3 User-to-product predictive models

In addition to product-to-product predictions [16, 17], most recommendation engines allow user-to-product predictions as well [15, 30]. Recommendation for a user are typically made considering historical purchases and/or interests inferred using other data sources such as user's online behavior [15], social contacts [30], and others. In this section we propose a novel approach to simultaneously learn vector representations of products and users such that, given a user, recommendations can be performed by finding K nearest products in the joint embedding space.

user2vec. The user2vec model simultaneously learns vector representations of products and users by considering the user as a "global context", motivated by paragraph2vec algorithm [21]. The architecture of such model is illustrated in Figure 4. The training data set was derived from user purchase sequences $\mathcal{S}$, which comprised users u_n and their purchased products ordered by the time of purchase, $u_n = (p_{n1}, p_{n2}, \ldots p_{nU_n})$, where U_n denotes number of items purchased by user u_n. During training, user vectors are updated to predict the products from their e-mail receipts, while product vectors are learned to predict other products in their context. For simplicity of presentation and w.l.o.g.

in the following we present non-bagged version of the language model, however we note that it is straightforward to extend the presented methodology to use the bagged version.

More specifically, objective of user2vec is to maximize the log-likelihood over the set $\mathcal{S}$ of all purchase sequences,

$$\mathcal{L} = \sum_{s\in\mathcal{S}} \Big(\sum_{u_n \in s} \log \mathbb{P}(u_n | p_{n1} : p_{nU_n}) + \sum_{p_{ni}\in u_n} \log \mathbb{P}(p_{ni} | p_{n,i-c} : p_{n,i+c}, u_n) \Big) \tag{3.5}$$

where c is the length of the context for products in purchase sequence of the n-th user. The probability $\mathbb{P}(p_{ni}|p_{n,i-c} : p_{n,i+c}, u_n)$ is defined using a soft-max function,

$$\mathbb{P}(p_{ni}|p_{n,i-c} : p_{n,i+c}, u_n) = \frac{\exp(\bar{\mathbf{v}}^\top \mathbf{v}'_{p_{ni}})}{\sum_{p=1}^{V} \exp(\bar{\mathbf{v}}^\top \mathbf{v}'_p)}, \tag{3.6}$$

where $\mathbf{v}'_{p_{ni}}$ is the output vector representation of p_{ni}, and $\bar{\mathbf{v}}$ is averaged vector representation of the product context including corresponding u_n, defined as

$$\bar{\mathbf{v}} = \frac{1}{2c+1}(\mathbf{v}_{u_n} + \sum_{-c\leq j\leq c, j\neq 0} \mathbf{v}_{p_{n,i+j}}), \tag{3.7}$$

where $\mathbf{v}_p$ is the input vector representation of p. Similarly, the probability $\mathbb{P}(u_n|p_{n1} : p_{nU_n})$ is defined as

$$\mathbb{P}(u_n|p_{n1} : p_{nU_n}) = \frac{\exp(\bar{\mathbf{v}}_n^\top \mathbf{v}'_{u_n})}{\sum_{p=1}^{V} \exp(\bar{\mathbf{v}}_n^\top \mathbf{v}'_p)}, \tag{3.8}$$

where $\mathbf{v}'_{u_n}$ is the output vector representation of u_n, and $\bar{\mathbf{v}}_n$ is averaged input vector representation of all the products purchased by user u_n,

$$\bar{\mathbf{v}}_n = \frac{1}{U_n}\sum_{i=1}^{U_n} \mathbf{v}_{p_{ni}}. \tag{3.9}$$

One of the main advantages of the *user2vec* model is that the product recommendations are specifically tailored for that user based on his purchase history. However, disadvantage is that the model would need to be updated very frequently. Unlike product-to-product recommendations, which may be relevant for longer time periods, user-to-product recommendations need to change often to account for the most recent user purchases.

4. EXPERIMENTS

The experimental section is organized as follows. We first describe data set used in development of our product-to-product and user-to-product predictors. Next we present valuable insights regarding purchase behavior of different age and gender groups in different US states. This information can be leveraged to improve demo- and geo-targeting of user groups. This is followed by a section on effectiveness of recommendation of popular products in different user cohorts, including age, gender, and US state. Finally, we show comparative results of various baseline recommendation algorithms. We conclude with the description of the system implementation at a large scale and bucket results that preceded our product launch.

4.1 Data set

Our data sets included e-mail receipts sent to users who voluntarily opted-in for such studies, where we anonymized user IDs. Message bodies were analyzed by automated systems. Product names and prices were extracted from e-mail messages using an in-house extraction tool.

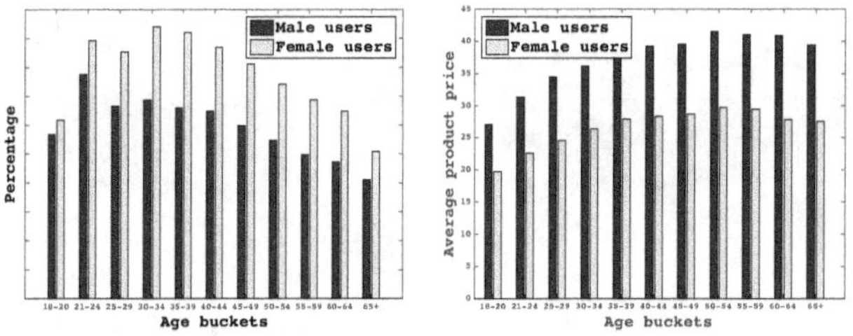

(a) Percentage of purchasing users among all online users (b) Average product price

Figure 5: Purchasing habits for different demographics

Training data set collected for purposes of developing product prediction models comprised of more than 280.7 million purchases made by $N = 29$ million users from 172 commercial websites. The product vocabulary included $P = 2.1$ million most frequently purchased products priced over \$5.

More formally, data set $\mathcal{D}_p = \{(u_n, s_n), n = 1, ..., N\}$ was derived by forming e-mail receipt sequences s_n for each user u_n, along with their timestamps. Specifically, $s_n = \{(e_{n1}, t_{n1}), \ldots, (e_{nM_n}, t_{nM_n})\}$, where e_{nm} is a receipt comprising one or more purchased products, and t_{nm} is receipt timestamp. Predictions were evaluated on a held-out month of user purchases D_p^{ts}, formed in the same manner as D_p. We measured the effectiveness of recommendations using prediction accuracy. In particular, we measured the number of product purchases that were correctly predicted, divided by the total number of purchases. For all models, the accuracy was measured separately on each day, based on the recommendations calculated using prior days. We set a daily budget of distinct recommendations each algorithm is allowed to make for a user to $K = 20$, based on an estimate of optimal number of ads users can effectively perceive daily [7].

4.2 Insights from purchase data

To get deeper insights into behavior of online users based on their demographic background and geographic location, we segregated users into cohorts based on their age, gender, and location, and looked at their purchasing habits. Such information can be very valuable to marketers when considering how and where to spend their campaign budget. We only considered users from the US, and computed statistics per each state separately. First, we were interested in differences between male and female shopping behavior for different age ranges. In addition, we were interested in the following aspects of purchasing behavior: 1) percentage of online users who shop online; 2) average number of products bought; 4) average spent per user; and 4) average price of a bought item. Figures 5 and 6 illustrate the results.

In Figure 5 for each gender and age group we show the percentage of online users who shop online, as well as the average prices of bought items. Expectedly, we see that male and female demographics exhibit different shopping patterns. Throughout the different age buckets percentage of female shoppers is consistently higher than for males, peaking in the 30-34 age range. On the other hand, percentage of male shoppers reaches its maximum in the 21-24

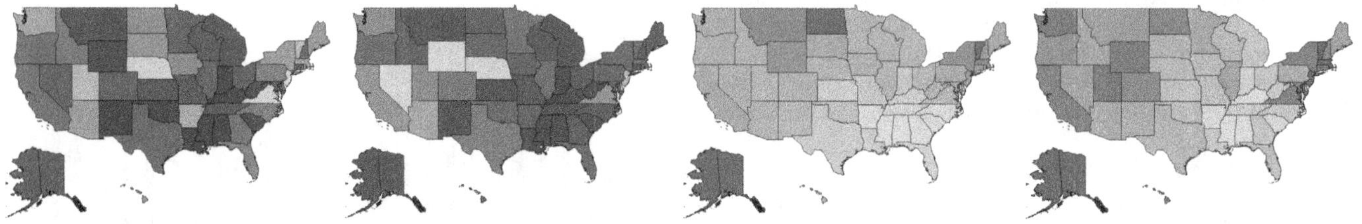

(a) ages 18-20 (b) ages 40-44 (c) ages 18-20 (d) ages 40-44

(e) ages 18-20 (f) ages 40-44 (g) ages 18-20 (h) ages 40-44

Figure 6: Purchasing behavior for different cohorts, dark color encodes higher values: (a, b) Percentage of shoppers among online users; (c, d) Average number of purchases per user; (e, f) Average amount spent per user; (g, h) Average product price

bucket, and from there drops steadily. In addition, we observe that male users buy more expensive items on average.

Furthermore, in Figure 6 we show per-state results, where darker color indicates higher values. Note that we only show results for different locations and age ranges, as we did not see significant differences between male and female purchasing behavior across states. First, in Figures 6(a) and 6(b) we show the percent of online shoppers in each state, for younger (18-20) and medium-age (40-44) populations, where we can see there exist significant differences between the states. In Figures 6(c) and 6(d) we show the average number of purchased products per state. Here, for both age buckets we see that the southern states purchase the least number of items. However, there is a significant difference between younger and older populations, as in northern states younger populations purchase more products, while in the northeast and the western states this holds true for the older populations. If we take a look at Figures 6(e) and 6(f) where we compare the average amount of money spent per capita, we can observe similar patterns, where in states like Alaska and North Dakota younger populations spend more money than peers from other states, and for older populations states with highest spending per user are California, Washington, and again Alaska. Interestingly, users from Alaska are the biggest spenders, irrespective of the age or metric used. Similar holds when we consider average price of a purchased item, shown in Figures 6(g) and 6(h).

4.3 Recommending popular products

In this section we evaluate predictive properties of popular products. Recommending popular products to global population is a common baseline due to its strong performance, especially during holidays (e.g., Christmas, Thanksgiving). Such recommendations are intuitive, easy to calculate and implement, and may serve in a cold start scenarios for newly registered users when we have limited information.

We considered how far back we need to look when calculating popularity and how long popular products stay relevant.

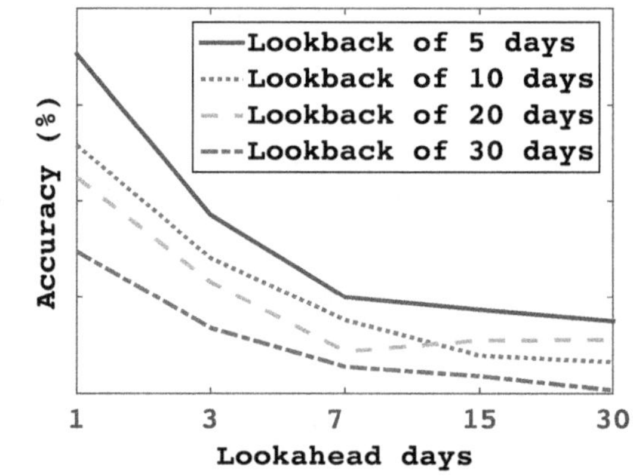

Figure 7: Prediction accuracy and longevity of popular products with different lookbacks

In Figure 7 we give results for popular products calculated in the previous 5, 10, 20, and 30 days of training data D_p, evaluated on the first 1, 3, 7, 15, and 30 days of test data D_p^{ts}. To account for ever-changing user purchase tastes, the results indicate that popular products need to be recalculated at least every 3 days with lookback of at most 5 days.

Next, we evaluated the prediction accuracy of popular products computed for different user cohorts, and compared to the accuracy of globally popular products. In Figure 8 we compare accuracies of popular products in different user cohorts, with the lookback fixed at 5 days. We can observe that popular products in gender cohorts give bigger lift in prediction accuracy than popular products in age or state cohorts. Further, jointly considering age and gender when calculating popular products outperforms the popular gender products. Finally, including geographic dimension contributes to further accuracy lift. Overall, the results indicate that in the cold start scenario the best choice of which popular products to recommend are the ones from the user's (age,

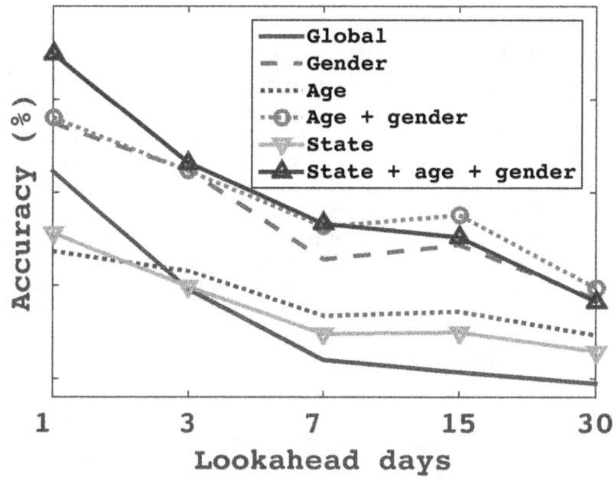

Figure 8: Prediction accuracy of popular products for different user cohorts

gender, location) cohort. The results also suggest that popular products should be recalculated often to avoid decrease in accuracy with every passing day.

4.4 Recommending predicted products

In this section we experiment with recommending products to users based on neural language models described in Section 3. Specifically, we compare the following algorithms:

1) prod2vec-topK was trained using data set D_p, where product vectors were learned by maximizing log-likelihood of observing other products from sequences s, as proposed in (3.1). Recommendations for a given product p_i were given by selecting the top K most similar products based on the cosine similarity in the resulting vector space.

2) bagged-prod2vec-topK was trained using D_p, where product vectors were learned by maximizing log-likelihood of observing other products from e-mail sequences s as proposed in (3.3). Recommendations for a given product p_i were given by selecting the top K most similar products based on the cosine similarity in the resulting vector space.

3) bagged-prod2vec-cluster was trained similarly to the bagged-prod2vec model, followed by clustering the product vectors into C clusters and calculating transition probabilities between them. After identifying which cluster p_i belongs to (e.g., $p_i \in c_i$), we rank all clusters by their transition probabilities with respect to c_i. Then, the products from top clusters are sorted by cosine similarity to p_i, where top K_c from each cluster are used as recommendations ($\sum K_c = K$). Example predictions of bagged-prod2vec-cluster compared to predictions of bagged-prod2vec are shown in Table 2. It can be observed that predictions based on the clustering approach are more diverse.

4) user2vec was trained using data set D_p where product vectors and user vectors were learned by maximizing log-likelihood proposed in (3.5) (see Figure 4). Recommendations for a given user u_n were given by calculating cosine similarity between the user vector u_n and all product vectors, and retrieving the top K nearest products.

5) co-purchase. For each product pair (p_i, p_j) we calculated frequency $F_{(p_i,p_j)}, i = 1, \ldots, P, j = 1, \ldots, P$, with which product p_j was purchased immediately after product p_i. Then, recommendations for a product p_i were given by sorting the frequencies $F_{(p_i,p_j)}, j = 1, \ldots, P$, and retrieving the top K products.

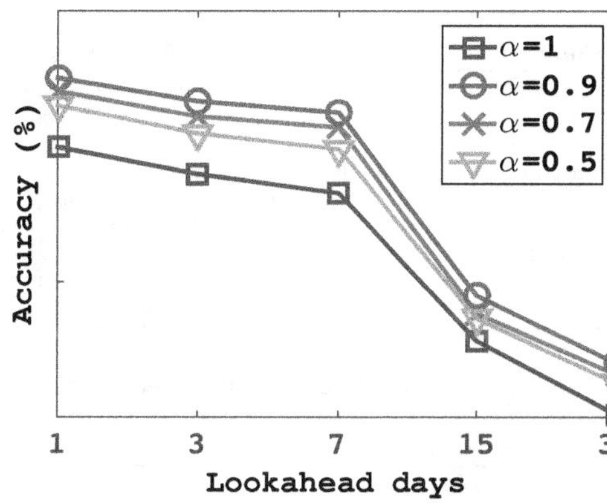

Figure 9: prod2vec accuracy with different decay values

Since user u_n may have multiple products purchased prior to day t_d, separate predictions need to reach a consensus in order to choose the best K products to be shown on that day. To achieve this we propose time-decayed scoring of recommendations, followed by choice of top K products with the highest score. More specifically, given user's products purchased prior to t_d along with their timestamps, $\{(p_1, t_1), \ldots (p_{U_n}, t_{U_n})\}$, for each product we retrieve top K recommendations along with their similarity scores, resulting in the set $\{(p_j, sim_j), j = 1, \ldots, KU_n\}$, where sim denotes cosine similarity. Next, we calculate a decayed score for every recommended product,

$$d_j = sim_j \cdot \alpha^{(t_d - t_i)}, \tag{4.1}$$

where $(t_d - t_i)$ is a difference in days between current day t_d and the purchase time of product that led to recommendation of p_j, and α is a decay factor. Finally, the decayed scores are sorted in descending order and the top K products are chosen as recommendations for day t_d.

Training details. Neural language models were trained using a machine with 96GB of RAM memory and 24 cores. Dimensionality of the embedding space was set to $d = 300$, context neighborhood size for all models was set to 5. Finally, we used 10 negative samples in each vector update. Similarly to the approach in [24], most frequent products and users were subsampled during training. To illustrate the performance of the language models, in Table 1 we give examples of product-to-product recommendations computed using bagged-prod2vec, where we see that the neighboring products are highly relevant to the query product (e.g., for "despicable me" the model retrieved similar cartoons).

Evaluation details. Similarly to how popular product accuracy was measured, we assumed a daily budget of $K = 20$ distinct product recommendations per user. Predictions for day t_d are based on prior purchases from previous days, and we did not consider updating predictions for day t_d using purchases that happened during that day.

Results. In the first set of experiments we evaluated performance of prod2vec for different values of decay factors. In Figure 9 we show prediction accuracy on test data D_p^{ts} when looking 1, 3, 7, 15, and 30 days ahead. Initial prod2vec predictions were based on the last user purchase in the training data set D_p. The results show that discounting of old predictions leads to improved recommendation accuracy, with decay factor of $\alpha = 0.9$ being an optimal choice.

Table 1: Examples of product recommendations made by the bagged-prod2vec model

despicable me	**first aid for the usmle step 1**	**disney frozen lunch napkins**
monsters university	usmle step 1 secrets 3e	disneys frozen party 9 square lunchdinner plates
the croods	first aid basic sciences 2e	disneys frozen party 9oz hotcold cups
turbo	usmle step 1 qbook	disneys frozen party 7x7 square cakedessert plates
cloudy with a chance of meatballs	brs physiology	disneys frozen party printed plastic tablecover
hotel transylvania	rapid review pathology with student consult	disneys frozen party 7 square cakedessert plates
brave	lippincotts microcards microbiology flash cards	disney frozen beverage napkins birthday party supplies
the smurfs	first aid cases for the usmle step 2	disney frozen 9 oz paper cups
wreckit ralph	highyield neuroanatomy	frozen invitation and thank you card
planes	lange pharmacology flash cards third edition	disneys frozen party treat bags

Table 2: Product recommendations for product *cressi supernova dry snorkel*

bagged-prod2vec-topK	**bagged-prod2vec-cluster**	**cluster ID**
jaws quick spit antifog 1 ounce	cressi neoprene mask strap	
cressi neoprene mask strap	cressi frameless mask	cluster 1
cressi frameless mask	cressi scuba diving snorkeling freediving mask snorkel set	
akona 2 mm neoprene low cut socks	akona 2 mm neoprene low cut socks	
tilos neoprene fin socks	tilos neoprene fin socks	cluster 2
cressi scuba diving snorkeling freediving mask snorkel set	mares equator 2mm dive boots	
mares cruise mesh duffle bag	jaws quick spit antifog 1 ounce	
us divers island dry snorkel	aqua sphere kayenne goggle with clear lens clear black regular	cluster 3
us divers trek travel fin	aqua sphere kayenne goggle with clear lens black regular	
us divers proflex ii diving fins	nikon coolpix aw120 161 mp wi-fi and waterproof digital camera	
mares cruise backpack mesh bag	olympus stylus tg ihs digital camera with 5x optical zoom	cluster 4
water gear fin socks	nikon coolpix aw110 wi fi and waterproof digital camera with gps	

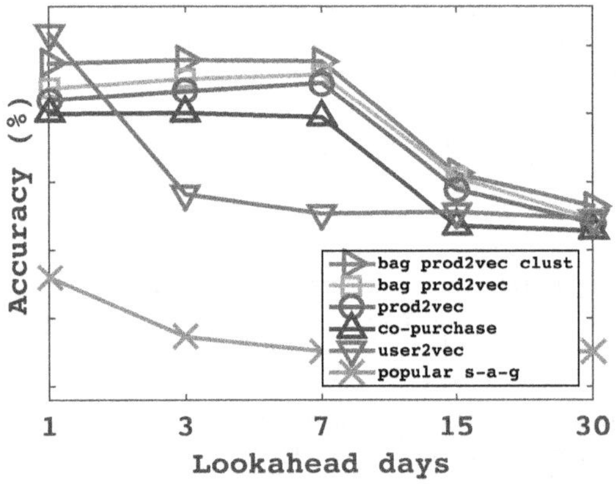

Figure 10: Prediction accuracy of different algorithms

Next, we evaluate different product-to-product and user-to-product methods and compared them to the popular products approach found in Figure 8 to perform the best, namely recommending popular products computed separately for each (state, age, gender) cohort. Results are summarized in Figure 10. We can observe that all neural-based prediction algorithms outperformed method that recommends popular products. Further, even though user2vec model had the best overall accuracy on day 1, its prediction power quickly drops after 3 days. On the other hand, variants of the prod2vec model did not exhibit such behavior, and their performance remained steady across the first 7 days. Of all prod2vec models, the bagged-prod2vec-cluster model achieved the best performance, indicating that diversity in predictions leads to better results. Finally, predictions based on co-purchases did not perform as well as neural language models, supporting the "don't count, predict" claim from [4] where the authors suggest that simple co-occurence approaches are suboptimal.

Table 3: Results from live A/B testing of product recommendations on Yahoo Mail

Metric	**Control (5% traffic)**	**Popular (5% traffic)**	**Predicted (5% traffic)**
CTR	-	+8.33%	+9.81 %
YR		-	+7.63 %

4.5 Bucket results

Following offline evaluation of different product prediction methods, we conducted additional A/B testing experiments on live Yahoo Mail traffic. We ran two buckets with two different recommendation techniques, both on 5% of Yahoo Mail users. In the first bucket, for users with prior purchases the recommendations were based on the bagged-prod2vec-cluster model, while for users without prior purchases they were based on globally popular products. In the second bucket all users were recommended globally popular products. For purposes of a fair bucket test, both models were retrained and refreshed with the same frequency of 7 days.

Both test buckets were evaluated against a control bucket in which products ads were replaced with standard ads from Yahoo Ad serving platform. All three buckets had significant amount of users with prior purchases. Evaluation was done based on the click-through rate (CTR) computed as $\text{CTR} = \frac{\#\text{clicks}}{\#\text{impressions}}$. In particular, we measured the number of clicks on product ads that occurred after the targeted recommendation, divided by the total number of shown (or impressed) product ads. In the control bucket, we computed the same metric for standard ads. For the two product ad buckets we additionally measured the yield rate, calculated as $\text{YR} = \frac{\#\text{conversions}}{\#\text{impressions}}$, where conversion refers to an actual purchase of the recommended product. Conversions were attributed to impression for up to 48 hours since the time users clicked or observed a product ad.

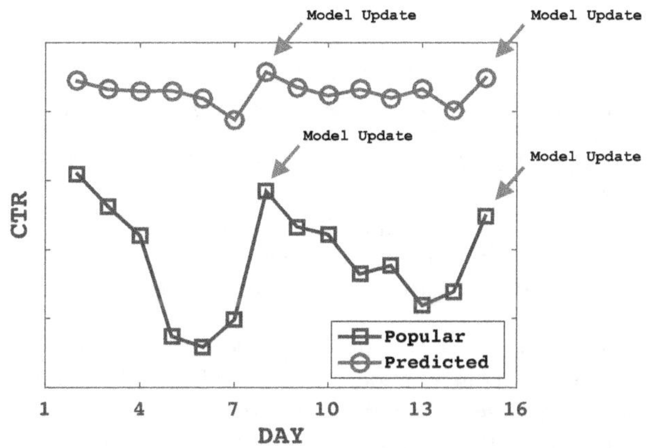

Figure 11: CTR of predicted versus popular recommendations in live bucket test over time

The results are presented in Table 3. We can make several observations. First, both popular and predicted bucket showed better CTR numbers than the control bucket, indicating that the users prefer product ads over standard ads. Second, the prediction bucket achieved slightly better CTR rates than the popular bucket. Finally, the prediction bucket achieved significantly better YR than the popular bucket. This indicates that many times users click on popular products out of curiosity and do not end up buying the product, whereas clicks on targeted products lead to more purchases as they better capture user interests. Overall, the presented results strongly suggest benefits of the proposed approach for the task of product recommendations.

In addition, in Figure 11 we show how CTR rates change over time. Similarly to our offline experiments, it can be observed that popular recommendations become stale much faster than predicted recommendations, as indicated by the steeper CTR drop. They are also more susceptible to novelty bias following model updates, as seen by larger increase in CTR. Another useful finding was that 7 day updates are not sufficient, confirming findings from Figure 7.

5. SYSTEM DEPLOYMENT

In this section we cover the details on our system implementation that led to final product deployment.

5.1 Implementation details

Due to product requirements for near-real-time predictions, we chose to use product-to-product recommendations, with the bagged-prod2vec-cluster model. The model is updated every 5 days with the most recent purchase data. The product vectors are stored on Hadoop Distributed File System (HDFS), and updated via training procedure implemented on Hadoop[5], where we heavily leverage parallel processing with MapReduce. We form purchase sequences using the newest purchased products extracted from e-mail receipts, and incrementally update the product vectors instead of training them from scratch.

Popular products were used as back-fill for users who do not have prior purchase history. Following the experimental results, we recalculated popular products every 3 days, with a lookback of 5 days. More specifically, we extracted 100 most frequently purchased products for every state-age-gender cohort, and showed them in randomized order to users without purchase history.

We implemented a multi-tier architecture in order to productionize product recommendation capability on Yahoo Mail. For data storage we used a custom, high-performance distributed key-value store (similar to Cassandra[6]), which persists user profiles and product-to-product prediction model. The user profile store utilizes user identifier as a key and stores multiple columns representing user prior purchases as values. User profiles are updated hourly with new products, extracted from e-mail receipts. Each purchase record persists in memory with time-to-live (TTL) set to 60 days, after which period it is discarded.

Product-to-product prediction model is stored in a similar key-value store, where purchased product is used as a key and values are multiple columns each representing predicted products ordered by score. Both user and product-to-product stores are updated in batch without impacting real traffic. Separate process performs all processing of querying user purchases and asynchronously retrieves relevant predictions and offers. It then returns selected product ad back to presentation process implemented in JavaScript and HTML which renders it in the browser. The retrieval process is configured such that it can fetch offers from multiple e-commerce websites (affiliate partners). The system runs with a service-level agreement of 500ms and can be improved further by caching interactions with affiliate partners.

Given predictions for a certain user, once the user logs into the e-mail client we show a new recommendation after every user action, including clicking on folders, composing e-mail, and searching the inbox. Recommendation are circled in the order of decayed prediction score, as described in Section 4.4. The product ads are implemented in the so-called "pencil" ad position, just above the first e-mail in the inbox (Figure 1).

6. CONCLUSIONS AND FUTURE WORK

We presented the details of a large-scale product recommendation framework that was launched on Yahoo Mail in the form of product ads. We discussed the recommendation methodology, as well as the high-level implementation details behind our system. To perform recommendations, we described how we employed neural language models capable of learning product embeddings for product-to-product predictions, as well as user embeddings for user-to-products predictions. Several variants of the prediction models were tested offline and the best candidate was chosen for an online bucket test. Following the encouraging bucket test results, we launched the system in production. In our ongoing work, we plan to utilize implicit feedback available through ad views, ad clicks, and conversions to further improve the performance of our product recommendation system.

7. REFERENCES

[1] A. Ahmed, Y. Low, M. Aly, V. Josifovski, and A. J. Smola. Scalable distributed inference of dynamic user interests for behavioral targeting. In *KDD*, pages 114–122, 2011.

[2] J. Alba, J. Lynch, B. Weitz, C. Janiszewski, R. Lutz, A. Sawyer, and S. Wood. Interactive home shopping:

[5]https://hadoop.apache.org, accessed June 2015

[6]http://cassandra.apache.org/, accessed June 2015

consumer, retailer, and manufacturer incentives to participate in electronic marketplaces. *The Journal of Marketing*, pages 38–53, 1997.

[3] R. Baeza-Yates, B. Ribeiro-Neto, et al. *Modern information retrieval*, volume 463. ACM press New York, 1999.

[4] M. Baroni, G. Dinu, and G. Kruszewski. DonÕt count, predict! a systematic comparison of context-counting vs. context-predicting semantic vectors. In *Proceedings of the 52nd Annual Meeting of the Association for Computational Linguistics*, volume 1, pages 238–247, 2014.

[5] Y. Bengio, H. Schwenk, J.-S. Senécal, F. Morin, and J.-L. Gauvain. Neural probabilistic language models. In *Innovations in Machine Learning*, pages 137–186. Springer, 2006.

[6] A. Bordes, N. Usunier, A. Garcia-Duran, J. Weston, and O. Yakhnenko. Translating embeddings for modeling multi-relational data. In *Advances in Neural Information Processing Systems*, pages 2787–2795, 2013.

[7] C.-H. Cho and H. J. Cheon. Why do people avoid advertising on the internet? *Journal of advertising*, 33(4):89–97, 2004.

[8] R. Collobert, J. Weston, L. Bottou, M. Karlen, K. Kavukcuoglu, and P. Kuksa. Natural language processing (almost) from scratch. *The Journal of Machine Learning Research*, 12:2493–2537, 2011.

[9] N. Djuric, V. Radosavljevic, M. Grbovic, and N. Bhamidipati. Hidden conditional random fields with distributed user embeddings for ad targeting. In *IEEE International Conference on Data Mining*, Dec 2014.

[10] N. Djuric, H. Wu, V. Radosavljevic, M. Grbovic, and N. Bhamidipati. Hierarchical neural language models for joint representation of streaming documents and their content. In *International World Wide Web Conference (WWW)*, 2015.

[11] D. Essex. Matchmaker, matchmaker. *Communications of the ACM*, 52(5):16–17, 2009.

[12] M. Grbovic, N. Djuric, V. Radosavljevic, and N. Bhamidipati. Search retargeting using directed query embeddings. In *International World Wide Web Conference (WWW)*, 2015.

[13] M. Grbovic, G. Halawi, Z. Karnin, and Y. Maarek. How many folders do you really need?: Classifying email into a handful of categories. In *Proceedings of the 23rd ACM International Conference on Conference on Information and Knowledge Management*, pages 869–878. ACM, 2014.

[14] M. Grbovic and S. Vucetic. Generating ad targeting rules using sparse principal component analysis with constraints. In *international conference on World Wide Web*, pages 283–284, 2014.

[15] D. J. Hu, R. Hall, and J. Attenberg. Style in the long tail: discovering unique interests with latent variable models in large scale social e-commerce. In *Proceedings of the 20th ACM SIGKDD international conference on Knowledge discovery and data mining*, pages 1640–1649. ACM, 2014.

[16] J. Katukuri, T. Konik, R. Mukherjee, and S. Kolay. Recommending similar items in large-scale online marketplaces. In *Big Data (Big Data), 2014 IEEE International Conference on*, pages 868–876. IEEE, 2014.

[17] J. Katukuri, R. Mukherjee, and T. Konik. Large-scale recommendations in a dynamic marketplace. In *Workshop on Large Scale Recommendation Systems at RecSys*, volume 13, 2013.

[18] R. Kiros, R. Zemel, and R. Salakhutdinov. Multimodal neural language models. In *Proceedings of the 31th International Conference on Machine Learning*, 2014.

[19] R. Kiros, R. S. Zemel, and R. Salakhutdinov. A multiplicative model for learning distributed text-based attribute representations. *arXiv preprint arXiv:1406.2710*, 2014.

[20] V. Lavrenko and W. B. Croft. Relevance based language models. In *SIGIR*, pages 120–127. ACM, 2001.

[21] Q. V. Le and T. Mikolov. Distributed representations of sentences and documents. *arXiv preprint arXiv:1405.4053*, 2014.

[22] G. Linden, B. Smith, and J. York. Amazon.com recommendations: Item-to-item collaborative filtering. *IEEE Internet Computing*, 7(1):76–80, Jan. 2003.

[23] T. Mikolov, K. Chen, G. Corrado, and J. Dean. Efficient estimation of word representations in vector space. *arXiv preprint arXiv:1301.3781*, 2013.

[24] T. Mikolov, I. Sutskever, K. Chen, G. S. Corrado, and J. Dean. Distributed representations of words and phrases and their compositionality. In *NIPS*, pages 3111–3119, 2013.

[25] B. Perozzi, R. Al-Rfou, and S. Skiena. Deepwalk: Online learning of social representations. *arXiv preprint arXiv:1403.6652*, 2014.

[26] D. Riecken. Personalized views of personalization. *Communications of the ACM*, 43(8):27–28, 2000.

[27] R. Socher, D. Chen, C. D. Manning, and A. Ng. Reasoning with neural tensor networks for knowledge base completion. In *Advances in Neural Information Processing Systems*, pages 926–934, 2013.

[28] J. Turian, L. Ratinov, and Y. Bengio. Word representations: a simple and general method for semi-supervised learning. In *Proceedings of the 48th Annual Meeting of the Association for Computational Linguistics*, pages 384–394. Association for Computational Linguistics, 2010.

[29] Y. Zhang and M. Pennacchiotti. Predicting purchase behaviors from social media. In *WWW*, pages 1521–1532, 2013.

[30] X. W. Zhao, Y. Guo, Y. He, H. Jiang, Y. Wu, and X. Li. We know what you want to buy: a demographic-based system for product recommendation on microblogs. In *Proceedings of the 20th ACM SIGKDD international conference on Knowledge discovery and data mining*, pages 1935–1944. ACM, 2014.

Gender and Interest Targeting for Sponsored Post Advertising at Tumblr

Mihajlo Grbovic†, Vladan Radosavljevic†, Nemanja Djuric†,
Narayan Bhamidipati†, Ananth Nagarajan‡
†Yahoo Labs ‡Yahoo, Inc.
701 First Ave, Sunnyvale, CA, USA
{mihajlo, vladan, nemanja, narayanb, ananth}@yahoo-inc.com

ABSTRACT

As one of the leading platforms for creative content, Tumblr offers advertisers a unique way of creating brand identity. Advertisers can tell their story through images, animation, text, music, video, and more, and can promote that content by sponsoring it to appear as an advertisement in the users' live feeds. In this paper, we present a framework that enabled two of the key targeted advertising components for Tumblr, gender and interest targeting. We describe the main challenges encountered during the development of the framework, which include the creation of a ground truth for training gender prediction models, as well as mapping Tumblr content to a predefined interest taxonomy. For purposes of inferring user interests, we propose a novel semi-supervised neural language model for categorization of Tumblr content (i.e., post tags and post keywords). The model was trained on a large-scale data set consisting of 6.8 billion user posts, with a very limited amount of categorized keywords, and was shown to have superior performance over the baseline approaches. We successfully deployed gender and interest targeting capability in Yahoo production systems, delivering inference for users that covers more than 90% of daily activities on Tumblr. Online performance results indicate advantages of the proposed approach, where we observed 20% increase in user engagement with sponsored posts in comparison to untargeted campaigns.

Categories and Subject Descriptors

H.2.8 [**Database applications**]: Data Mining

General Terms

Information Systems, Algorithms, Experimentation

Keywords

Data mining; computational advertising; audience modeling

KDD '15, August 10-13, 2015, Sydney, NSW, Australia
© 2015 ACM. ISBN 978-1-4503-3664-2/15/08 ...$15.00.
DOI: http://dx.doi.org/10.1145/2783258.2788616.

1. INTRODUCTION

In recent years, online social networks have evolved to become an important part of life for online users of all demographic and socio-economic backgrounds. They allow users to easily stay in touch with their friends and family, discuss everyday events, or share their interests with other users with the click of a button. Tumblr is one such social network, representing one of the most popular and fastest growing networks on the web. Hundreds of millions of people around the world come every month to Tumblr to find, follow, and share what they love. Consequently, the Tumblr network represents a gold mine of content, comprising around 200 million blogs on different topics such as travel, sports, or music, with 85 million user posts being published on a daily basis. This wealth of user-generated data opens a great opportunity for advertisers, allowing them to promote their products through high-quality targeting campaigns to both blog visitors and blog owners [19].

The prevalent form of advertising on Tumblr is through *sponsored posts* that appear alongside regular posts in the user's *dashboard*, the central page for a Tumblr user, displaying the most recent posts of followed blogs in the form of a stream. This form of advertising, where advertisements resemble native content in the stream, is often referred to as *native advertising.* Native advertisements are usually aesthetically beautiful and highly engaging, which typically makes them more enjoyable than regular display ads [4]. Tumblr launched its native advertising product in May of 2012. Since then, the number of advertisers (or brands) on the platform has grown steadily and reached a milestone of 100 advertisers in April of 2013. Moreover, 8 of the 10 most valuable brands are advertising on Tumblr[1], while sponsored posts have generated more than 3 billion paid ad impressions since the launch of the Tumblr advertising product[2]. However, a huge marketing potential of Tumblr [19] has not been fully exploited, due to the fact that targeting against specific interest and demographic audiences, a targeting component that Tumblr was missing, has become an industry standard and many advertisers are in need of such a solution.

Building interest targeting products on social and microblogging platforms is an important research topic, discussed previously by several researchers [14]. However, due to its distinct characteristics, Tumblr poses novel challenges, which we explain in detail in this paper. In particular, the

[1] `marketr.tumblr.com`, accessed June 2015
[2] `www.comscore.com`, accessed June 2015

Figure 1: Examples of blog titles (larger, bolded font) and blog descriptions (smaller font)

content and language used on Tumblr have distinct characteristics that needed to be accounted for during the modeling. For instance, users often use tags to summarize the text in their posts. However, the language styles used in the tags and post text are different (e.g., the tag "hp" and the word "hp" found in posts have different meanings, "Harry Potter" and "Hewlett-Packard", respectively). Moreover, unlike the popular social platform Facebook, which contains a large amount of social interactions but a limited amount of content, or the microblogging platform Twitter, which contains an intermediate amount of social interaction and content, Tumblr represents a unique combination of a rich and diverse content platform and a dynamic social network. To make use of this vast advertising potential, in this paper we propose to classify user-generated Tumblr content into a standard multi-level *general-interest taxonomy*[3] that advertisers commonly use for defining their targeting campaigns, opening doors to high-quality audience segmentation and modeling for purposes of ad targeting. However, inferring categories of user posts is a challenging task, given huge quantities of unlabeled data being posted every day and very limited amount of labeled data, typically obtained by editorial efforts. To this end, we propose a novel semi-supervised neural language model, capable of jointly learning embeddings of post keywords, post tags, and category representations in a common feature space. The neural model was trained on a large-scale data set comprising 6.8 billion posts, with only a fraction of manually categorized content.

Targeting pipelines described in this paper are being used to show ads to millions of users daily, and have substantially improved Tumblr's business metrics following the launch. We detail our path to developing targeting capabilities for Tumblr, where one of the key steps was creating user profiles, based on users' activities that include publishing blog posts, following other blogs, or liking posts. Then, we describe how both demographic and interest predictive models were built based on the created profiles.

Lastly, we emphasize that the privacy of users is of critical importance to Yahoo. Therefore, we were constrained in regards to what data we can use. Specifically, user profiles were created solely from data which users share publicly with others, including contents of blog posts, blog titles and descriptions, as well as follow, like, and reblog actions. This data is publicly available through Tumblr Firehose data source[4]. Other user activities, such as user searches on Tumblr, which blogs they visited or where they clicked, are all considered to be sensitive data and were not used in any way for the development of the presented ad targeting models.

2. RELATED WORK

Personalization is defined as "the ability to proactively tailor products and product purchasing experiences to tastes of individual consumers based upon their personal and preference information" [7], and it has become an important and very lucrative topic in the recent years. Personalization of online content may lead to improved user experience and directly translate into financial gains for online businesses [17]. In addition, personalization fosters a stronger bond between customers and companies, and can help in increasing user loyalty and retention [2]. For these reasons it has been recognized as a strategic goal and is the focus of significant research efforts of major internet companies [8, 15].

We consider personalization through the prism of ad targeting [11], where the task is to find the best matching ads to be displayed for each individual user. This improves the user's online experience (as only relevant and interesting ads are shown) and can lead to increased revenue for the advertisers (as users are more likely to click on the ad and make a purchase). Due to its large impact and many open research questions, targeted advertising has garnered significant interest from the community, as witnessed by a large number of recent workshops[5] and publications [5, 9, 14].

One of the basic approaches in ad targeting is to target users with ads based on their demographics, such as age or gender. Historically, this method has proven to work better than targeting random users. However, while for some products this type of targeting may be sufficient (e.g., women's makeup, women's clothing, man's razors, man's clothing), for others it is not effective enough and more involved profiling of users is required. A popular targeting approach that addresses this issue is known as interest targeting, in which users are assigned interest categories based on their historical behavior, such as "sports" or "travel" [1]. Typically, a taxonomy is used to decide on the targeting categories, and a model is learned to categorize user activities and estimate their interest in each category. Interest targeting is known to

[3] `http://www.iab.net/QAGInitiative/overview/taxonomy`, accessed June 2015

[4] `gnip.com/sources/tumblr`, accessed June 2015

[5] `www.targetad-workshop.net`, accessed June 2015

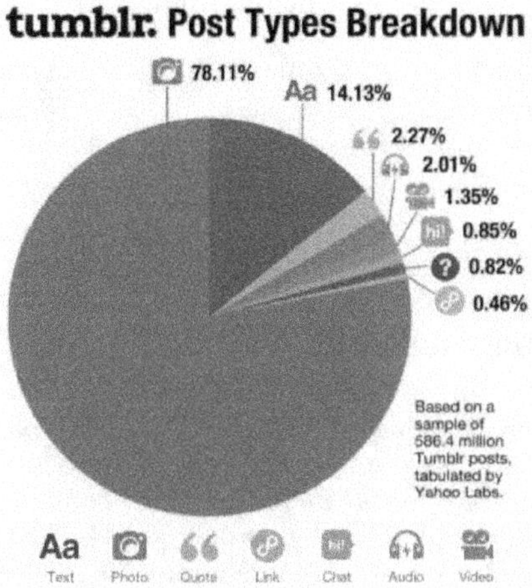

Figure 2: Distribution of Tumblr post types

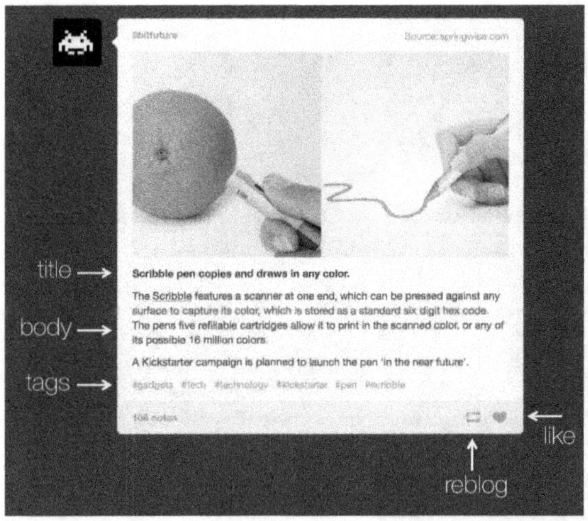

Figure 3: Example of Tumblr blog post

build good brand awareness with relevant audience, which has already shown interest in the corresponding category. In this paper we follow this targeting approach. Alternatively, advertisers may be interested to go a step further and optimize for current intent as opposed to long-term interest of users, typically done by assigning categories to actual ads, and training a machine learning model to estimate the probability of an ad click in that category [10, 20]. For each ad category a separate predictive model can be trained and evaluated on the entire user population, with N users with the highest score selected for ad exposure.

To the best of our knowledge, the Tumblr social network has been considered by only a handful of scientific studies. In [3, 18] the problem of blog recommendation is discussed, while in [6] the authors explore social norms on the social network. However, our work is the first that addresses an important problem of ad targeting on Tumblr.

3. WHAT IS TUMBLR?

Tumblr[6] is one of the most popular social blogging platforms on the web today, where users can create and share posts with the followers of their blogs. According to the data from January 2015[7], there is a total of 221.6 million blogs on Tumblr, which jointly produced over 102.7 billion blog posts. With a large number of new users signing up every day, it is currently the fastest growing social platform[8].

3.1 User activities on Tumblr

To register a Tumblr account, a valid e-mail address is required, along with a primary username (which becomes a part of the blog URL) and a confirmation of age. Once created, a Tumblr blog contains a profile picture, blog title, and blog description appearing at the top (see Figure 1), followed by a stream of blog posts bellow. The first blog created by a registered user is considered their primary blog. In addition, very small portion of users maintains one or more secondary blogs. A Tumblr user is uniquely identified by a blog ID of their primary blog, and throughout the paper we will use terms "blog" and "user" interchangeably.

Common user activities of Tumblr users include the following actions: 1) creating a post on one's blog; 2) sharing a post created by another blog, called *reblogging* (a reblogged post will appear on the user's blog); 3) liking a post by another blog; and 4) following another blog. Similarly to Twitter, follow connections on Tumblr are unidirectional. However, unlike Twitter, users can create longer and richer content in a form of several post types, such as text, photo, quote, link, chat, audio, and video. The posts are shown in user's dashboard, ordered such that more recent posts appear closer to the top. The most popular types of blog posts are photo and text posts, which, based on the analysis published in [21], together cover more than 92% of all content on Tumblr (see Figure 2 for detailed distribution of post types). In addition, any post type can be annotated with words starting with the "#" sign (called *tags*) that concisely describe a post and allow for easier browsing and searching. Additional metadata that describes a post includes photo captions in photo posts, post titles in text posts, and artists names in audio posts. An example photo post is shown in Figure 3. Tags are displayed bellow the photo caption (e.g., *#gadgets* and *#tech*), while buttons for reblog and like actions are located in the bottom right corner.

3.2 Advertising on Tumblr

Advertising on Tumblr is implemented through the mechanism of sponsored (or promoted) posts shown in user's dashboard. This is similar to how advertising works on Twitter and Facebook. A sponsored post can be a video, an image, or simply a textual post containing an advertising message. In Figure 4, we show an example of a sponsored post and how it appears on desktop and mobile dashboards. Similarly to organic (or non-promoted) posts, sponsored posts can propagate from user to user in the network by means of reblogs, and users can also "like" the promoted post. Both likes and reblogs can be seen as an implicit form of acceptance or endorsement of the advertising message. Moreover, just like other posts, sponsored posts are supplemented with notes on who liked and reblogged them.

[6] `www.tumblr.com`, accessed June 2015
[7] `www.tumblr.com/about`, accessed June 2015
[8] `http://t.co/3txHFRJreJ`, accessed June 2015

Figure 4: Example of Tumblr sponsored post

Interestingly, while user-generated, organic posts are reblogged 14 times on average, sponsored posts are reblogged 10,000 times on average[9]. We have observed that 40% of engagements with sponsored posts are reblogs, likes, and follows. Moreover, every four reblogs of a sponsored post result in 6 downstream reblogs from followers, leading to content longevity, while one third of reblogs of sponsored posts are present for 30 days or more after the initial post.

4. TUMBLR DATA

In this section we describe data sets comprising user activities and post contents, which were utilized to create user profiles. In particular, user activities include actions such as posts, likes, follows, and reblogs, while post contents include tags, title and body for text posts, artist names from audio posts, as well as tags and captions for photo posts.

4.1 Used data sets

Once signed into Tumblr, a user can follow other users' blogs. The follow action is one-directional as it does not require the followed user to follow back. For the purpose of this study, we extracted a sub-graph which contained 96.9 million unique nodes (i.e., users) and 5.1 billion edges (i.e., follows), out of which 36.4 million are bidirectional (18.2 million pairs of users that follow each other). The data set included more than 26.1 billion activities on Tumblr. As mentioned earlier, an entire activity log is publicly available through a data feed called Firehose.

To create user profiles for targeting, textual contents of all posts were collected, including photo captions, tags, titles, and bodies. In addition, every time a user performs a post or reblog activity, Firehose lists the user's blog title and blog description, which were also employed to represent a user. As we can see in Figure 1, a blog title and description often provide useful information with respect to targeting, such as the user's first name, age, and even declared interests (e.g., statements such as "fashion addict" or "I love football").

[9] `http://yhoo.it/1vFfIAc`, accessed June 2015

Table 1: User data extracted from Tumblr Firehose

Declared	Content	Actions
blog title	post tags	reblog
blog description	photo captions	like
	text post title	follow
	text post body	
	audio post artists	

4.2 Data processing

In order to obtain useful representations of user profiles, we propose to extract keywords from available blog information, which requires data preparation and processing. Given the extracted blog data, including title, content, and tags, we first removed all HTML tags, followed by the extraction of bigrams and the removal of common English stopwords.

In particular, it is common for certain words to appear together more often than some others (e.g., words "credit" and "card"), and we aim to capture those bigrams and use them in keyword-based user profiles. To detect bigrams, we use a procedure that counts the unigram and bigram appearances, and for each combination of words w_i and w_j calculates the following score,

$$\text{score}(w_i, w_j) = \frac{\text{count}(w_i \text{ and } w_j \text{ together})}{\text{count}(w_i)\ \text{count}(w_j)}. \tag{4.1}$$

Finally, bigrams with a score above a certain threshold were extracted from the blog contents, along with the remaining unigrams. On the other hand, post tags are originally formed as n-grams by the users (e.g., *#chess rules*), and were extracted in their original form.

4.3 User profiles

Available data sources were used to create user profiles. In particular, we extracted three distinct groups of user-related data: 1) declared; 2) content of posts; and 3) actions. The specific components included in each of the data groups are listed in Table 1. From each group we extracted features to represent the users as described below.

Declared data consists of information provided during sign-up, including keywords from the blog title and blog description extracted using the method described in Section 4.2. We counted the keyword frequency in a user's blog title and description, and stored the counts along with a timestamp of the latest log-in as a part of user's profile.

Content features were formed from the textual contents of posts which a user either created or reblogged. The main content feature types include: 1) post tags; 2) keywords from the post title and body; 3) keywords from the captions of photo post; and 4) artist names from audio posts. In this way we collected several millions of distinct keywords that were used to obtain rich representation of user profiles. To illustrate content keyword extraction from the Firehose, consider that user u_i at timestamp t used tag *#hp* five times and tag *#nba* eight times, keyword *football* two times in post titles, and posted ten times an audio post with a song from artist *Shakira*. Then, the resulting user profile would be $u_i = \{tag : \{\#hp, t : 5; \#nba, t : 8\}, title : \{football, t : 2\}, artist : \{shakira, t : 10\}\}$.

Action features include follows, likes, and reblogs. If user u_i follows user u_j at timestamp t, we create an indicator feature $follows : \{j, t : 1\}$ and add it to the u_i user's profile. Similarly, if user u_i likes user's post, we create a feature that

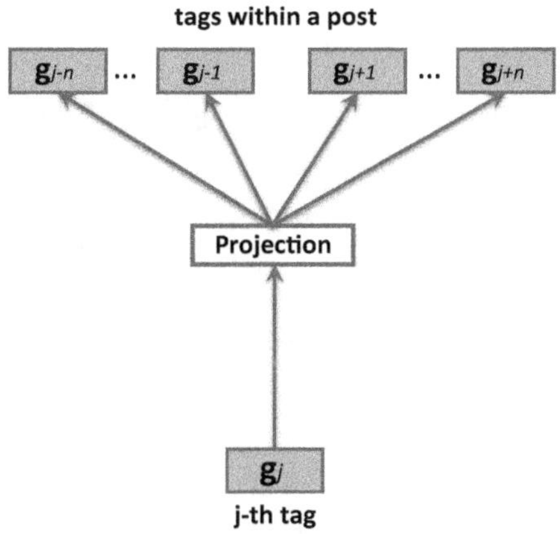

Figure 5: Unsupervised skip-gram model

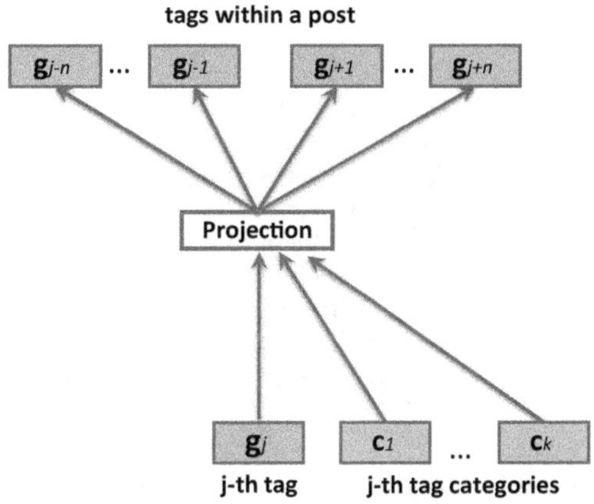

Figure 6: Semi-supervised skip-gram model

keeps record of the number of likes m, as $likes : \{j, t : m\}$, and update the user's profile accordingly.

The timestamps used in feature engineering represent the day on which the activity happened. For the experiments presented in this paper we subsampled Tumblr users to obtain 80 million user profiles. The total number of unique features was 1.4 million, and on average a user had 380 non-zero features.

5. INTEREST PREDICTION

The goal of our work is to identify user groups with interests in certain topics, such as music, travel, cooking, or books, in order to allow advertisers to target segmented Tumblr audiences, as well as to infer user demographics (discussed in Section 6). As the topic interests may be defined at various levels of granularity, to avoid sparsity problems while still providing useful and actionable interest categories, user interests are often classified into a pre-determined hierarchical interest taxonomy that the advertisers commonly use. However, to be able to create effective user interest classifiers, a modeler requires a sufficient amount of labeled data. Yet, for the problem of the scale of Tumblr interest prediction, this can be a daunting task for human editors. For that reason we propose to use a novel semi-supervised classification approach [12] based on the recently proposed word2vec model [16], which efficiently and seamlessly makes use of large amounts of unlabeled and a limited amount of labeled data for learning effective content classifiers.

5.1 User interest taxonomy

We decided to classify keywords into the General Interest Taxonomy (GIT), used by the Yahoo Gemini advertising platform for native advertising[10]. The GIT is carefully derived based on Interactive Advertising Bureau (IAB) taxonomy recommendations, in order to meet advertiser needs and protect Yahoo's interests. The GIT has a two-level hierarchical structure, such that advertisers can adjust the audience reach by utilizing broader or narrower interest categories. The top level of the taxonomy contains 23 nodes (e.g., "Automotive", "Pets", "Travel"), while the second level contains 130 nodes which represent more focused interests (e.g., "Automotive/SUV", "Automotive/Luxury", "Pets/Dogs").

[10]http://gemini.yahoo.com, accessed June 2015

5.2 Semi-supervised classification

In this section, we describe a recently proposed classification approach [12] based on the skip-gram model [16], which is used to categorize keywords into the GIT taxonomy. For conciseness, we describe the proposed model on the assumption that it is applied to tag categorization. However, it is straightforward to use the same methodology for categorization of keywords originating from blog titles and descriptions, as well as from text, audio, and image posts. Thus, we consider the task of tag classification, where the goal is to classify tags into one or more interest categories. In order to address this problem, we learn tag representation in a low-dimensional vector space using neural language models that are applied to historical Tumblr posts.

More specifically, let us assume that we are given N posts. In the post logs found in Firehose, each post p is recorded along with the tags g_j, $j = 1...M$, where M represents the number of tags in the post. Given the data set $\mathcal{D}$ of all posts, the objective is to find a vector representation of tags in which semantically similar tags are nearby in the vector space. For this purpose, we extend ideas originating from recently proposed language models, as described in the remainder of this section.

The skip-gram (SG) model involves learning representations of tags in a low-dimensional space from post logs in an unsupervised fashion, by using the notion of a blog post as a "sentence" and the tags within the post as "words", borrowing the terminology from the Natural Language Processing (NLP) domain (see Figure 5). Tag representations using the skip-gram model [16] are learned by maximizing the objective function over the entire $\mathcal{D}$ set of blog posts defined as follows,

$$\mathcal{L} = \sum_{p \in \mathcal{D}} \sum_{g_j \in p} \sum_{-n \leq m \leq n, m \neq 0} \log \mathbb{P}(g_{j+m} | g_j). \tag{5.1}$$

Probability $\mathbb{P}(g_{j+m}|g_j)$ of observing a neighboring tag g_{j+m} given the current tag g_j is defined using the soft-max,

$$\mathbb{P}(g_{j+m}|g_j) = \frac{\exp(\mathbf{v}_{g_j}^\top \mathbf{v}'_{g_{j+m}})}{\sum_{k=1}^{G} \exp(\mathbf{v}_{g_j}^\top \mathbf{v}'_k)}, \tag{5.2}$$

where $\mathbf{v}_g$ and $\mathbf{v}'_g$ are the input and output vector representations of tag g of user-specified dimensionality d, n defines the length of the context for tag sequences, and G is the

Table 2: Examples of categorized tags

Tag	Category
music	Arts & Entertainment/Music
fashion	Style & Fashion
song	Arts & Entertainment/Music
art	Arts & Entertainment
disney	Arts & Entertainment/Movies
style	Style & Fashion
photography	Hobbies/Photography
teen wolf	Arts & Entertainment/TV
food	Food & Drink

number of unique tags in the vocabulary. Following training of the skip-gram model, tags that co-occur often and tags with similar contexts (i.e., with similar neighboring tags) will have similar vector representations.

The semi-supervised skip-gram (SS-SG) model assumes that some tags are labeled with categories from the GIT taxonomy. Then, we introduce a dummy category vector for each node of the taxonomy, and leverage the tag contexts in blog posts to jointly learn tag vectors and category vectors in the same feature space [12]. Given such setup, after learning the representations every tag from the vocabulary can be categorized by simply looking up the closest category vector in the joint embedding space.

Given a set of categorized tags, we extend $\mathcal{D}$ to obtain data set $\mathcal{D}_{ss}$ where available categories are imputed into post "sentences" p. In particular, labeled tags are accompanied by assigned categories, and every time a vector of a labeled central tag t_j is updated to predict the surrounding tags, vectors of categories assigned to g_j are updated as well. More formally, assuming the central tag g_j is labeled with C_j of C categories in total, $\zeta_j = \{c_1, \ldots, c_{C_j}\}$, the semi-supervised skip-gram learns tag and category representations by maximizing the following objective function,

$$\sum_{p \in \mathcal{D}_{ss}} \sum_{g_j \in p} \sum_{-n \leq m \leq n, m \neq 0} \Big(\log \mathbb{P}(g_{j+m}|g_j) + \sum_{c \in \zeta_j} \log \mathbb{P}(g_{j+m}|c) \Big). \tag{5.3}$$

Probability $\mathbb{P}(g_{j+m}|c)$ of observing tag g_{j+m}, given label c of the current tag g_j, is defined using the soft-max,

$$\mathbb{P}(g_{j+m}|c) = \frac{\exp(\mathbf{v}_c^\top \mathbf{v}'_{g_{j+m}})}{\sum_{k=1}^{G} \exp(\mathbf{v}_c^\top \mathbf{v}'_k)}. \tag{5.4}$$

This procedure allows us to seamlessly incorporate labeled and unlabeled data, and learn tag and category vectors in the common embedding space. Then, classification of tags amounts to a simple nearest-neighbor search among the category vectors. In Figure 6 we show graphical representation of the semi-supervised skip-gram model.

5.2.1 Training

The models are optimized using stochastic gradient ascent, suitable for large-scale problems. However, computation of gradients $\nabla\mathcal{L}$ in (5.1) and (5.3) is proportional to the vocabulary size G, which may be expensive in practice as G could easily reach several million tags. As an alternative, we used a negative sampling approach [16], which significantly reduces the computational complexity.

The data set used during the model training comprised 6.8 billion posts that contained tags. To collect category labels for some of the tags, we sorted the tags in a decreasing order of popularity and through editorial efforts labeled the top ones with one or more categories. This resulted in a total of 8,400 categorized tags used during semi-supervised training. We show examples of categorized tags in Table 2.

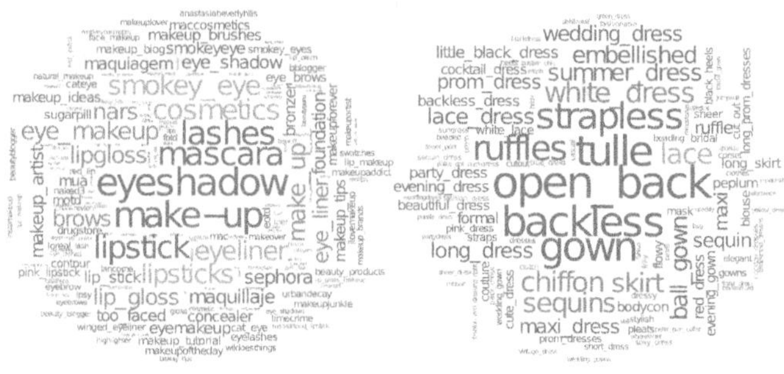

Figure 7: Nearest neighbors of tags: a) *#makeup*; b) *#dress*

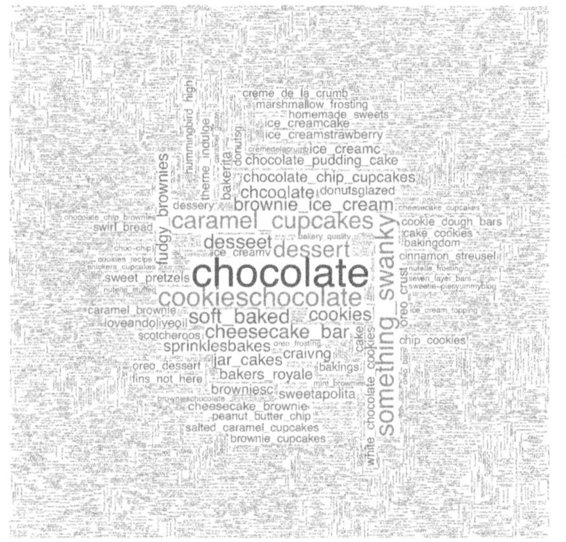

Figure 8: Nearest tags to "Food & Drink/Desserts"

The representations were trained using a machine with 96GB of RAM memory and 24 cores. Dimensionality of the embedding space was set to $d = 300$, and the neighborhood size was set to $n = 5$. Finally, we used 10 negative samples in each vector update. Similarly to [16], most frequent tags were subsampled during training.

5.2.2 Inference

When the vector representations of all tags are learned, we can find similar tags for a given tag by straightforward k-nearest neighbor (k-NN) searches in the representation space. We use cosine distance [16] as a measure of similarity. To illustrate the usefulness of our approach, word clouds of neighboring tags to the tags *#makeup* and *#dress* are shown in Figure 7, where we see that semantically similar tags are grouped in same parts of the embedding space.

Similarly, we can find the most likely category for any tag by finding the nearest category in the vector space. To produce a high-confidence set of categorized tags, we retrieved only tags with a cosine distance of 0.7 or higher to the corresponding category vectors. This threshold was obtained

Figure 9: Nearest tags to "Health & Fitness/Weight Loss"

Table 3: Precision and recall of the competing methods

Method	Precision	Recall
LR-SG	0.71	0.65
k-NN-SG	0.82	0.62
SS-SG	**0.85**	**0.63**

through editorial evaluation of the results. In total, more than 380,000 tags were categorized into one or more categories with high confidence. To illustrate the quality of obtained classifiers, in Figures 8 and 9 we give word clouds of categorized tags for "Food & Drink/Desserts" and "Health & Fitness/Weight Loss" categories, respectively. A demonstration video of our tag categorization tool is available online[11].

5.2.3 *Evaluation*

In order to quantify the benefits of our approach, we trained method by excluding random 2,000 tags from the editorially labeled set, and evaluating on the held-out set by predicting the top-level GIT categories. We compared the SS-SG classification to the state-of-the-art logistic regression (LR) and k-NN methods, trained on the vectors learned by the original SG model. For LR classification (we refer to the method as LR-SG) we trained one classifier per interest category, while for k-NN (we refer to the method as k-NN-SG) for each held-out tag we found $K = 50$ nearest categorized neighbors and predicted its category by a majority vote. We report the results following a 5-fold cross-validation in Table 3. The results indicate that classification based on the proposed approach achieves higher precision than the competing methods, while at the same time maintaining competitive recall measure.

5.2.4 *Blog- and post-specific models*

To be able to map more of Tumblr content to the GIT taxonomy, we trained two additional SS-SG models: 1) for keywords from post titles and bodies; and 2) for keywords

[11] http://youtu.be/ygn5oUBydfM, accessed June 2015

Table 4: Language differences in post tags and post text

Neighbors of tag "hp"	Neighbors of word "hp"
harry potter	hewlett packard
hp movies	hp.com
hp books	hp computers
hp book quotes	hp company
harry potter facts	dell computers
hogwarts	hp printers

from blog titles and descriptions. To train the models, we followed a similar procedure as before. Editors provided 4,700 categorized keywords, which were used to form training data sets for SS-SG model learning. Post keyword vectors were trained using a data set comprising $N = 6.8$ billion posts, while blog title and description keyword vectors were trained using $N = 37.1$ million blogs. Then, to find high-confidence keywords for each category, we calculated cosine distances between learned vectors of categories and of keywords from the vocabulary. We retrieved 184,000 text blog keywords with a cosine distance of 0.7 or higher. We repeated the same procedure for keywords from blog titles and descriptions, resulting in 173,000 categorized keywords.

Note that the three models were trained separately due to language differences between these domains (i.e., between post tags, post text, and blog title and description text). To justify our claim, in Table 4 we show the nearest neighbors of the tag "hp" from the SS-SG model trained on tags and the word "hp" from the SS-SG model trained on post text. As we can see in the table, "hp" has different meanings in post tags and post text domains, referring to "Harry Potter" and "Hewlett-Packard", respectively.

5.3 Forming interest segments

The goal of interest prediction is to identify groups of users with interest in certain topics. In this section we describe method for predicting user interests used in this study.

After we obtained categorized tags and keywords as described in the previous sections, the interest score for user u_i at time t in the k-th interest category was calculated as

$$u^t_{i,cat=k} = \sum_{feat \in \mathcal{A}_i} \alpha^{(t-t_{feat})}\, w_{feat}\, I(feat \text{ is of class } k), \tag{5.5}$$

where $\mathcal{A}_i$ is the set of extracted actions or keywords of user u_i contained in user's profile as described in Section 4.2, w_{feat} is a value of action or keyword feature (with 0/1 values for actions and counts for keywords), while the indicator function $I(\cdot)$ returns 1 if an action or a keyword extracted from a user activity is categorized into class k, and 0 otherwise (note that we postpone description of action categorization to Section 5.3.1). In addition, we used timestamp t_{feat}, representing day on which the activity happened, to exponentially decay less recent activities to account for passing interest (we used $\alpha = 0.99$ in our experiments).

Thus, the value of $u^t_{i,cat=k}$ represents an exponentially time-decayed count of all the activities in the k-th interest category. In order to effectively store user profiles for interest targeting and avoid storing all possible activities with their timestamps, we maintain a decayed sum for each category and update $u^t_{i,cat=k}$ daily. Using this approach we are able to qualify top K users in each category by sorting their interest scores $u^t_{i,cat=k}$, where the choice of K varies from campaign to campaign depending on advertiser's goals. Sev-

Table 5: Examples of interest inference based on categorized user features

User	Inferred interest	User profile
user 1	Arts & Entertainment/Movies	tag:{spoilers:30, shrek:18, hercules:12, cinderella:3, hobbit:123, hulk:21, pokemon:7, thor:58, ... disney:500, tarzan:8, marvel:385, wolverine:21, twilight:2, pixar:87, godzilla:1, x-men:53, ... pocahontas:4, avengers:134} txt:{aladdin:28, batman:10, bambi:12, movies:100} desc:{oscar:1, animation:12, comedy:1, movie:1, dvd:1}
user 2	Style & Fashion	tag:{ womensfashion:110, curls:6, fashiondiaries:133, redhair:2, menswear:125, chanel:4 ... springfashion:50, style:132, streetstyle:132, hairstylist:134, dapper:3, mensfashion:124} txt:{fashion:108}
user 3	Food & Drink	tag:{food:11, dessert:4 , soup:1, brunch:1, fruit:2, chicken:3, smoothie:1, cake:2, breakfast:2, ... ginger:2, salad:5, avocado:1} txt:{food:16, meals:6} follows:{user4542:1, user84852:1, user9332:1, user4524424:1 }
user 4	Home & Garden	tag:{daisies:2, kitchen:20, chair:3, art:81, outdoor:20, chandelier:12, lamp:8, window:2, bath:1 ... floral:17, home:3, wildflowers:1, flowers:102, interior:201, tree:1, flower:49, table:1, stairs:2, ... bedroom:56, wood:2, bathroom:26} txt:{garden:32, interior:17, home:41}
user 5	Automotive/Motorcycles	tag:{cars:24, ride:9, vehicle:22, riding:8, road:18} txt:{bike:8, motorcycle:10, riding:5, ride:9, road:10, vehicle:18, bikes:6, bicycle:2, scooter:1}

Table 6: A/B test results on 10% of user population

Campaign	Control	Targeted
Home & Garden	–	+9.71%
Style & Fashion	–	+42.53%
Sports/Outdoor Sports	–	+19.86%
Arts & Enter./Television	–	+24.37%
Arts & Enter./Video Games	–	+19.02%
Pets/Dogs	–	+27.21%
Arts & Enter. (campaign no. 1)	–	+9.08%
Arts & Enter. (campaign no. 2)	–	+6.54%

eral examples of qualified user profiles are given in Table 5. Note that a user may be qualified into more than one interest category. When the system was deployed in the production, each user was assigned to 13 categories on average.

5.3.1 *Leveraging the follower graph*

In order to target Tumblr users who do not create much content, but actively follow and engage with other blogs, we leverage the follower graph to create additional categorized features. In particular, using equation (5.5) we identify users with high value of $u^t_{i,cat=k}$ (which we term *influencers*). Then, following and liking posts created by influencers in the k-th category can serve as additional evidence of one's interest in that category.

To implement this idea, we labeled 5% of users with the highest interest score in a certain category as influencers, and categorized "follow", and "like" actions directed towards such users into that category. Then, we recompute equation (5.5) with an extended set of categorized activities that includes the categorized actions. This effectively expands the interest segments with users that are not content producers, but mostly act as consumers of content.

5.4 Results

In order to evaluate the generated user interest segments, we performed online A/B testing and worked with several advertisers who ran concurrent interest-targeted and untargeted campaigns. We tracked user engagement with their ads in terms of sponsored post likes, reblogs, and follows, and present the results for 8 targeting campaigns in Table 6. We observed an average increase of 20% in user engagement with sponsored posts in comparison to untargeted campaigns (aggregated over 3 metrics), representing a significant improvement over the baseline approach.

6. GENDER PREDICTION

In this section, we explain the details of our gender prediction model, based on the user profiles described in the previous sections. We first describe the generation process of a golden set of labeled users, which is used to train a predictive model that generalizes well on the remaining unlabeled users. This is followed by a description of the classification model and a discussion of the empirical results.

6.1 Collecting ground-truth labels

In order to train machine learning method for gender prediction, in addition to user profiles we also require labels that present the ground truth (i.e., "male" or "female"). However, Tumblr does not collect gender information during sign-up, leaving open the question of how to obtain such data.

To address this problem, we propose to leverage highly informative blog description data in order to infer user gender. In particular, users often declare their names in their blog descriptions, as illustrated in Figure 1. To extract the declared names, we used several regular expression rules that we found to result in high precision. The obtained results from a large set of name-matching regular expressions were editorially tested for quality. It was found that regular expressions reported in Table 7 yielded the most reliable extracted names (valid names were extracted in more than 95% of the cases).

Next, in order to generate the ground truth, we used US census data of popular baby names[12] from year 1880 to 2013 to create "name → gender" mapping. More specifically, we used male/female empirical ratios as soft labels, with 1 indicating 100% confidence in male and 0 indicating 100% confidence in female name. This approach resulted in 564 thousand female and 395 thousand male users found.

6.2 Proposed approach

Let $\mathcal{D}_g = \{(\mathbf{x}_i, y_i), i = 1, ..., N\}$ denote our gender data set, where N is the total number of labeled users, $\mathbf{x}_i$ is a K-dimensional user feature vector, and $y_i \in [0, 1]$ is a soft gender label. The feature vectors were generated from the

[12]`www.ssa.gov/oact/babynames/limits.html`, 06/15

Table 7: Matching names in blog description

Pattern	Count
my name is *	783,564
my name's *	291,811
me llamo *	47,663
the name's *	38,065
mi nombre es *	9,751
mi chiamo *	9,181
mein name ist *	1,025
meu nome e *	512
mon nom est *	215
mio nome e *	185

Table 8: Accuracy of gender model on hold-out set

Gender	Precision	Recall
female	0.806	0.838
male	0.794	0.689

user profiles as described in Section 5.3 by setting $\alpha = 1$, which turns off the time-decay of feature counts (due to the fact that, unlike interest, gender does not fluctuate). To handle large feature counts, we normalized the values by applying log transformation: assuming that the count is x, we replaced feature value with $\log(1 + x)$.

Our goal is to learn a gender predictor, $f : \mathbf{x} \rightarrow y$. As a classification model, we used logistic regression, parameterized by weight vector $\mathbf{w}$. We assume that the posterior gender probabilities can be estimated as a linear function of input $\mathbf{x}$, passed through a sigmoidal function,

$$\mathbb{P}(y = 1|\mathbf{x}) = f(\mathbf{x}, \mathbf{w}) = \frac{1}{1 + \exp(-\mathbf{x}^{\mathrm{T}}\mathbf{w})}, \tag{6.1}$$

and $\mathbb{P}(y = 0|\mathbf{x}) = 1 - \mathbb{P}(y = 1|\mathbf{x})$. To estimate the parameters $\mathbf{w}$, we minimize the following loss function,

$$\min_{\mathbf{w}\in\mathbb{R}^K} \frac{1}{N} \sum_{i=1}^{N} \left(y_i - f(\mathbf{x}_i, \mathbf{w})\right)^2 + \lambda\|\mathbf{w}\|_1, \tag{6.2}$$

where hyper-parameter λ controls the ℓ_1-regularization, introduced to induce sparsity in the parameter vector and reduce the feature space to a subset of features that are most predictive. In addition, we experimentally observed that the model generalizes better when we trained an initial model with ℓ_1-regularization to find which features have non-zero weight, and then do another round of training without ℓ_1-regularization, by only using features with non-zero weights from the first round to learn a better classifier.

Given a trained LR model, the posterior class probabilities are estimated as $f(\mathbf{x}_i, \mathbf{w}) \in [0, 1]$. Then, the predictions are made by thresholding, as $\hat{y}_i = \mathrm{sign}(f(\mathbf{x}_i, \mathbf{w}) - \theta)$, where threshold $\theta \in (0, 1)$ is set to ensure desired precision and recall according to advertiser's specific requirements.

6.3 Results

To evaluate accuracy of our gender prediction framework, we trained a logistic regression model on 70% of the golden set and tested on the remaining 30%. We used Vowpal Wabbit [13] implementation on Hadoop to train the model. To illustrate the performance of our gender classifier, the performance results in terms of precision and recall measures are presented in Table 8. The threshold value θ was set to a value which ensured precision of 0.8.

Table 9: Editorial evaluation of random user predictions

Prediction	# correct	# wrong	# not sure
female	429	4	298
male	144	5	127

In addition to evaluation on the hold-out set, we editorially evaluated gender predictions on the unlabeled data set of user profiles. We randomly picked 1,007 gender predictions from the population of 64.1 million users and asked editors to visit their profiles and verify their gender. They were instructed to mark our predictions as "correct", "incorrect", or "not sure". The "not sure" grade is to be used when the visual inspection of a profile is inconclusive, as we found was often the case. The editorial judgment came back with 573 "correct" (429 females and 144 males), 9 "incorrect", and 425 "not sure" grades (see Table 9). The fact that there are so many "not sure" grades indicates that in many cases it is hard to infer the gender even after manual efforts, further indicating the benefits of the proposed approach and its superior performance in comparison to humans. Finally, we retrained the model with 100% of the golden set and deployed it in Yahoo production systems. A demonstration video of gender predictive tags is available online[13].

7. DEPLOYED SYSTEM

To keep up with large number of daily activities, we implemented daily scoring of users on Yahoo production servers. We store the activity raw counts as well as decayed counts in Hive tables[14] for efficient retrieval. The decayed counts used in interest prediction are updated on a daily basis by multiplying the old feature values by the decay factor α and adding new activities. In order to infer the gender of new users we implemented daily scoring by leveraging MapReduce on Hadoop[15]. Both interest and gender models are retrained on a regular basis.

After thorough editorial evaluation of the inferred gender and interest targeting, both targeting frameworks were enabled through Gemini self-serve tool. Advertisers can choose to use gender and/or interest targeting with custom segment sizes, allowing for effective targeting campaigns.

8. CONCLUSION

We presented the steps in the development of a large-scale Tumblr gender and interest targeting framework, where we used historical Tumblr activities to create rich user profiles. We described the methodology, including a recently proposed semi-supervised neural language model, as well as the high-level implementation details behind the deployed system. Currently, our gender and interest predictions cover users that generate more than 90% of overall daily activities on Tumblr, and are heavily leveraged by advertisers. In our ongoing work, we are concentrating on creating custom keyword-targeted advertising segments specifically tailored for a particular advertiser, which includes work on addressing the problems of keyword discovery and expansion.

[13] `https://youtu.be/jXGJ0TpOlhg`, accessed June 2015

[14] `https://hive.apache.org`, accessed June 2015

[15] `https://hadoop.apache.org`, accessed June 2015

9. REFERENCES

[1] A. Ahmed, Y. Low, M. Aly, V. Josifovski, and A. J. Smola. Scalable distributed inference of dynamic user interests for behavioral targeting. In *Proceedings of the 17th ACM SIGKDD International Conference on Knowledge Discovery and Data Mining (KDD)*, pages 114–122, 2011.

[2] J. Alba, J. Lynch, B. Weitz, C. Janiszewski, R. Lutz, A. Sawyer, and S. Wood. Interactive home shopping: consumer, retailer, and manufacturer incentives to participate in electronic marketplaces. *The Journal of Marketing*, pages 38–53, 1997.

[3] N. Barbieri, F. Bonchi, and G. Manco. Who to follow and why: Link prediction with explanations. In *Proceedings of the 20th ACM SIGKDD International Conference on Knowledge Discovery and Data Mining (KDD)*, pages 1266–1275. ACM, 2014.

[4] F. Bonchi, R. Perego, F. Silvestri, H. Vahabi, and R. Venturini. Efficient query recommendations in the long tail via center-piece subgraphs. In *Proceedings of the 35th International ACM Conference on Research and Development in Information Retrieval (SIGIR)*, pages 345–354. ACM, 2012.

[5] A. Z. Broder. Computational advertising and recommender systems. In *Proceedings of the ACM conference on Recommender systems*, pages 1–2. ACM, 2008.

[6] Y. Chang, L. Tang, Y. Inagaki, and Y. Liu. What is tumblr: A statistical overview and comparison. *ACM SIGKDD Explorations Newsletter*, 16(1):21–29, 2014.

[7] R. K. Chellappa and R. G. Sin. Personalization versus privacy: An empirical examination of the online consumer's dilemma. *Information Technology and Management*, 6(2-3):181–202, 2005.

[8] A. S. Das, M. Datar, A. Garg, and S. Rajaram. Google news personalization: Scalable online collaborative filtering. In *WWW*, pages 271–280. ACM, 2007.

[9] N. Djuric, M. Grbovic, V. Radosavljevic, N. Bhamidipati, and S. Vucetic. Non-linear label ranking for large-scale prediction of long-term user interests. In *AAAI Conference on Artificial Intelligence (AAAI)*, 2014.

[10] N. Djuric, V. Radosavljevic, M. Grbovic, and N. Bhamidipati. Hidden conditional random fields with distributed user embeddings for ad targeting. In *IEEE International Conference on Data Mining*, 2014.

[11] D. Essex. Matchmaker, matchmaker. *Communications of the ACM*, 52(5):16–17, 2009.

[12] M. Grbovic, N. Djuric, V. Radosavljevic, N. Bhamidipati, J. Hawker, and C. Johnson. querycategorizr: A large-scale semi-supervised system for categorization of web search queries. In *International World Wide Web Conference (WWW)*, 2015.

[13] J. Langford, L. Li, and T. Zhang. Sparse online learning via truncated gradient. *The Journal of Machine Learning Research*, 10:777–801, 2009.

[14] A. Majumder and N. Shrivastava. Know your personalization: Learning topic level personalization in online services. In *Proceedings of the 22nd International Conference on World Wide Web*, pages 873–884, 2013.

[15] U. Manber, A. Patel, and J. Robison. Experience with personalization on Yahoo! *Communications of the ACM*, 43(8):35, 2000.

[16] T. Mikolov, I. Sutskever, K. Chen, G. S. Corrado, and J. Dean. Distributed representations of words and phrases and their compositionality. In *NIPS*, pages 3111–3119, 2013.

[17] D. Riecken. Personalized views of personalization. *Communications of the ACM*, 43(8):27–28, 2000.

[18] D. Shin, S. Cetintas, and K.-C. Lee. Recommending tumblr blogs to follow with inductive matrix completion. In *RecSys 14 Poster Proceedings*, 2014.

[19] T. Singh, L. Veron-Jackson, and J. Cullinane. Blogging: A new play in your marketing game plan. *Business Horizons*, 51(4):281–292, 2008.

[20] S. K. Tyler, S. Pandey, E. Gabrilovich, and V. Josifovski. Retrieval models for audience selection in display advertising. In *Proceedings of the 20th ACM International Conference on Information and Knowledge Management*, pages 593–598. ACM, 2011.

[21] C. Yi, T. Lei, I. Yoshiyuki, and L. Yan. What is tumblr: A statistical overview and comparison. arXiv:1403.5206v2, 2014.

Mining Administrative Data to Spur Urban Revitalization*

Ben Green
Harvard University
Cambridge, MA
bgreen@g.harvard.edu

Alejandra Caro
Carnegie Mellon University
Pittsburgh, PA
alejandra.caro@moodys.com

Matthew Conway†
University of Chicago
Chicago, IL
matt@indicatrix.org

Robert Manduca
Harvard University
Cambridge, MA
rmanduca@g.harvard.edu

Tom Plagge
University of Chicago
Chicago, IL
tplagge@gmail.com

Abby Miller
Innovation Delivery Team
Memphis, TN
abby.miller@memphistn.gov

ABSTRACT

After decades of urban investment dominated by sprawl and outward growth, municipal governments in the United States are responsible for the upkeep of urban neighborhoods that have not received sufficient resources or maintenance in many years. One of city governments' biggest challenges is to revitalize decaying neighborhoods given only limited resources. In this paper, we apply data science techniques to administrative data to help the City of Memphis, Tennessee improve distressed neighborhoods. We develop new methods to efficiently identify homes in need of rehabilitation and to predict the impacts of potential investments on neighborhoods. Our analyses allow Memphis to design neighborhood-improvement strategies that generate greater impacts on communities. Since our work uses data that most US cities already collect, our models and methods are highly portable and inexpensive to implement. We also discuss the challenges we encountered while analyzing government data and deploying our tools, and highlight important steps to improve future data-driven efforts in urban policy.

Categories and Subject Descriptors

G.3 [**Probability and Statistics**]: Statistical computing; H.2.8 [**Database Management**]: Database Applications—*Data mining, Spatial databases and GIS*; J.1 [**Administrative Data Processing**]: Government

Keywords

Neighborhood distress; Social good; Urban revitalization

*This work was completed as part of the 2014 Eric and Wendy Schmidt Data Science for Social Good Summer Fellowship at the University of Chicago, in partnership with the City of Memphis, Tennessee.

†Previous affiliation.

KDD'15, August 10-13, 2015, Sydney, NSW, Australia.

ACM 978-1-4503-3664-2/15/08 ...$15.00.
DOI: http://dx.doi.org/10.1145/2783258.2788568.

1. INTRODUCTION

US cities face a legacy of rapid outward growth and suburbanization. Since the middle of the twentieth century, municipalities across the country implemented policies designed to increase their land area, population, and tax base. As cities invested in growth, however, they neglected to properly maintain their older, central neighborhoods. Populations declined and the housing stock deteriorated, leaving struggling urban cores throughout the United States.

Recent efforts by governments and communities to reinvest in central city neighborhoods have been uneven, especially since the financial meltdown of 2008. While some neighborhoods have rapidly revitalized, many others continue to struggle with foreclosures, crime, and joblessness. These neighborhoods often require more money to deliver services than they generate back in fees and tax revenues, draining city resources. Revitalizing distressed neighborhoods is therefore a primary goal in many American cities.

We define distress as properties in need of structural or cosmetic repairs in order to be brought up to the community's standards. Although distress is perhaps more commonly referred to as blight, we avoid that term here given the negative connotations associated with it. We use distress to refer simply to the physical condition of homes, not as a political label assigned to neighborhoods.

Distress is a symptom of economic malaise, but potentially a cause as well. Distressed properties themselves produce little or no tax revenue and send negative signals to communities and investors. They can depress the value of nearby homes and diminish their neighborhood's quality-of-life [16, 20]. Distressed and abandoned properties also limit social interactions among neighbors, a result linked to higher crime rates, decreased public health, and other negative indicators of community well-being [18].

However, redeveloping traditional core neighborhoods is a challenging goal. The lots and homes tend to be relatively small, many areas face long-standing issues with poverty and crime, and some properties come with tax liens that raise the effective cost to purchase the property. As a result, it often takes encouragement from public or nonprofit investors to kickstart private development in these neighborhoods.[1]

[1]While policymakers must be mindful to avoid causing gentrification or displacement, the more pressing concern in most severely-distressed neighborhoods is improving conditions up to a livable standard.

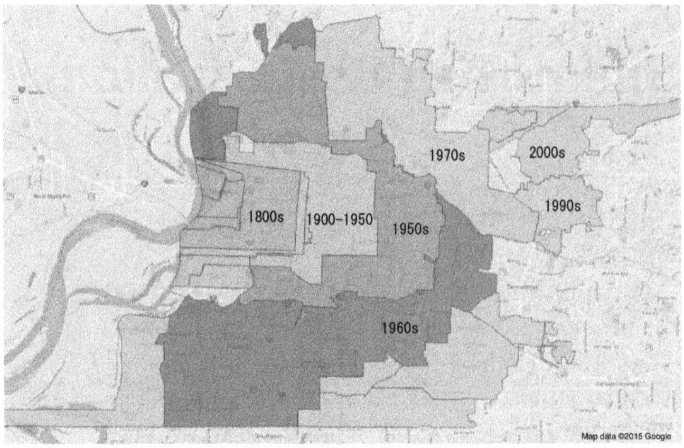

Figure 1: The land area of Memphis has grown more than 350% since 1950 due to annexations.

The City of Memphis, TN is a case study for many of these issues. Over the past several decades, Memphis has pursued a growth strategy of annexing land for suburban-style greenfield development. From 1950–2010, the City's geographic area increased 350% (Figure 1). Yet, in that same timespan, the City's population grew only 161% [3]. Furthermore, Memphis contains more of its regional population than many other American cities (approximately 50%, compared with 20% in Boston), meaning that it is responsible for maintaining a larger portion of its sprawl [1]. This has left the city with a hollowing core and sprawling population. The City's resources are, quite literally, stretched too thin across its geography: a recent report declared "Memphis literally does not have the financial resources to continue with this pattern of growth" [13].

To combat this trend, a coalition of groups including Memphis government agencies and local Community Development Corporations (CDCs) have begun investing in portions of the city's traditional urban core. From the City's perspective, rehabilitation and construction in core neighborhoods are highly productive: they make use of existing infrastructure, increase property tax revenues, and generate additional income from sales taxes and fees. For this and other reasons, the city would like to see such renewal continue.

Yet given the limited resources that governments and CDCs have at their disposal, they must be selective about where to invest money. They want to find the properties and determine the actions that will most impact property values and social well-being.

The work described in this paper was completed in order to aid these efforts in Memphis. We worked with the Innovation Delivery Team, a group in the Mayor's Office funded by Bloomberg Philanthropies that brings innovative approaches to pressing and complex urban challenges.[2] We gathered data from various government departments and neighborhood organizations, which we then analyzed to develop data-driven tools the City can use to improve its neighborhood revitalization strategies.

Of course, urban development cannot simply be optimized using data and algorithms. Politics, funding, community engagement, and individual initiative all impact what actions are possible and expedient. Yet data-driven strategies can help communities better understand which decisions will yield the most beneficial impacts. Proposing policies that are backed by good data and analysis offers useful insights that can inform stakeholders throughout the planning process and increase the likelihood of implementation.

We focus here on three aspects of the problem: identifying distressed properties, characterizing their effects on neighborhoods, and assessing the costs and benefits of remediation strategies. We first describe previous related work and the data used for our analyses (Sections 2 & 3). Section 4 describes the tools we developed that mine neighborhood surveys and administrative data to identify distressed homes. In Section 5, we discuss our efforts to evaluate the impacts of distressed homes and different investment strategies on neighborhood property values. After highlighting our primary impacts in Memphis in Section 6, we discuss in Section 7 important lessons learned while conducting data science analyses for municipal governments. Finally, we discuss future work in Section 8 and conclude in Section 9.

All of our code and some data used in our analyses are available at `https://github.com/dssg/memphis-public`.

2. RELATED WORK

Many studies have attempted to quantify the effects of distressed and abandoned homes on neighborhood property values. A 2001 study conducted in Philadelphia found that "all else being equal, houses on blocks with abandonment sold for $6,715 less than houses on blocks with no abandonment" [16]. The same study also warns against demolishing homes, finding that rehabilitating properties was more effective at stabilizing neighborhoods.

Analyses of vacant homes find that these properties have far-reaching detrimental effects on cities: they are threats to public safety, drive down neighborhood property values, and decrease the community's quality-of-life [20]. Among the challenges identified for cities dealing with this issue is a lack of data about abandoned properties and their costs.

One technique used to target investments within cities is Market Value Analysis. Looking at a variety of neighborhood indicators, cities can use clustering algorithms to segment all of its neighborhoods into a small number of categories (these might include "strong and growing" and "weak and declining"). Cities can then develop common strategies to implement in multiple neighborhoods of the same category. Previous efforts using this approach have been successful in Philadelphia, Baltimore, and other cities [9]. Another study of neighborhood improvement strategies found that revitalization efforts are most successful when investments are clustered in a few neighborhoods rather than distributed evenly across the city [7].

Within Memphis, many partners are working to revitalize core neighborhoods and combat distress. Organizations such as Livable Memphis, Community LIFT, and The Economic Development Growth Engine (EDGE) have spent the past several years implementing programs that emphasize growth, sustainable communities, and economic development.

Starting in October 2012, the Innovation Delivery Team began developing a series of initiatives that revitalize neighborhoods through a simple formula: "clean it, activate it, sustain it." These efforts work in three stages:

Clean Eliminate physical barriers to investment.

[2]`http://innovatememphis.com`

Activate Deploy small-scale and temporary changes to inject energy and demonstrate what is possible.

Sustain Make successful changes permanent through public policy.

To test various approaches to neighborhood vitality, the Innovation Delivery Team has so far focused their efforts on three neighborhoods: South Memphis, Binghampton, and Crosstown. Thus far, the Innovation Delivery Team's work shows the City of Memphis how moderate investments applied in focused ways can generate significant returns for neighborhoods.

3. DATA DESCRIPTION

3.1 Administrative Data

Most of the data we use in this paper was collected by local administrative bodies that regularly gather information about property conditions and neighborhood well-being. One important factor to keep in mind is that this data was not originally collected for assessing and targeting urban revitalization, making the incremental data collection cost for this type of work negligible. While collecting additional data would improve the models we describe later, it would be quite burdensome. By using data that already exists in almost every US city, we highlight methods that are possible across the country without requiring extensive data-collection efforts.

The majority of our data came from the City's internal database of every parcel (plot of land) in Memphis. Our primary source of information was property assessments, which contains information such as appraised value, parcel size, number of rooms, and building condition. This allowed us to consider many specific aspects of each property that may help us understand its health.

Another valuable dataset from the City of Memphis details which properties have had their utilities disconnected, been subject to code violations, or fallen into tax delinquency. These all indicate some level of poor maintenance and so are all valuable for identifying properties in need of reinvestment.

We also obtained data on every foreclosure that occurred in Memphis since 2000. Foreclosures are a clear indicator of distressed properties and financially-struggling homeowners. Because this data came from a separate source than our other property data, we were unable to reliably match foreclosures with specific properties. Instead, we were only able to aggregate foreclosures based on distance to properties and Census block groups.

Our final administrative data sources were the US Census and American Community Survey. Neighborhood-level statistics are valuable for understanding the context of how a given property fits into the fabric of the city.

3.2 Neighborhood Surveys

Critical to our work were several neighborhood windshield surveys conducted by community groups in Memphis. Most useful was the Neighborhood-by-Neighbor survey, which was conducted by The Center for Community Building and Neighborhood Action (CBANA) at the University of Memphis between February 2008 and January 2010 [5]. Volunteers familiar with each neighborhood surveyed the entirety of Memphis, identifying all residential properties not in compliance with the City's anti-blight housing code. Similar surveys were conducted by the Binghampton and Frayser Neighborhood CDCs in 2011 and 2013, respectively.

Although in-person inspections are the most reliable method for labeling property conditions, there are nonetheless a few caveats when using data of this kind. Surveys are completed by volunteers rather than trained professionals, and each person only surveys a small portion of the city. While the organizations running neighborhood surveys typically train volunteers and provide common definitions, there remains potential for inconsistent classifications. This is especially true when comparing results across different surveys.

4. IDENTIFYING DISTRESSED PROPERTIES

A major challenge for cities dealing with distressed neighborhoods is determining which properties need repair. While the identities of a city's most struggling neighborhoods are often widely-known, there is no simple way to determine the condition of specific properties without in-person inspections. Revitalizing communities typically requires a small number of targeted investments, however. If city officials had better data about property conditions, they would be able to invest more effectively.

The most common approach to gather property condition data is a windshield survey, in which a government department or community group organizes volunteers to visually inspect the outside of each home.[3] Windshield surveys are time-consuming and expensive, however, and often require countless volunteer hours and private funding from donors. It is therefore impractical for cities to rely on such surveys to diagnose local housing conditions.

In order to alleviate the need for regular surveys, we designed a system that uses administrative data to estimate the risk that each residential property in Memphis is distressed. We assembled pre-existing data, collected by the City of Memphis for other purposes such as property assessments and utility payments, and built a model by comparing these data to survey results.

While such a model is not as accurate as in-person inspections, relying exclusively on administrative data has an important benefit: it takes little time or money to derive new estimates. All of the data used as features in our model are already collected regularly by the City for other purposes. Estimates of property conditions can therefore be updated annually with little overhead, allowing the City and other stakeholders to efficiently track trends.

This tool obviates the necessity to conduct resource-intensive full-city surveys on a regular basis. Use of the model will highlight hotspots and outliers to help the City set priorities for thorough in-person surveys without requiring expensive preliminary work.

4.1 Data and Features

We built our model using thirty input features contained in the data described in Section 3. These include:

- Total appraised value of the home
- Age of the home

[3]This has traditionally been done from within a car, hence the term windshield.

- Whether the home has had its utilities disconnected in the past
- Percent change in the assessed value of the home over the past four years
- Percent of properties in the Census block of the home that were foreclosed on in the past year

We trained our model using the Neighborhood-by-Neighbor windshield survey conducted in Memphis [5]. This data served as our ground truth and allowed us to identify if a property was distressed or not in 2008.

4.2 Model

We trained a random forest classifier to predict, for multiple years, whether each residential property in Memphis was distressed. The model was built using the `randomForest` [11] package in `R` [15]. We also experimented with other classifiers, specifically decision trees and logistic regression, but we don't report the results here since random forests produced the best results.

Because the labeled data we have for the entire city came from the Neighborhood-by-Neighbor survey in 2008, we used that year's data as our training set. While the survey categorized distressed properties into seven different categories, we reduced the labels to a binary classification of "distressed" and "not distressed." Due to the relatively small sample size for each distressed class and the potential for volunteer surveyors to label similar properties inconsistently, we did not feel confident we could train the model to accurately distinguish between multiple forms of distress. Future work can involve selectively building more detailed models if necessary to classify properties into more groups.

Nonetheless, our estimates of a property's condition were more nuanced than binary classification because we considered the predicted class probabilities rather than just the predicted class. In a random forest classifier, each property in the test set is compared with those most similar in the training set. Roughly speaking, the predicted class probabilities reflect the proportion of similar properties from the training set labeled with each class. If a property is labeled as distressed with a probability of 0.75, for example, 75% of the most similar properties in the training set were labeled as distressed while the other 25% were labeled as not distressed. We define a property's class probability for being distressed as its risk score.

4.3 Validating the Classifier

In addition to testing the classifier using cross-validation (described below), we first wanted to get a more qualitative sense of what our predictions reveal about actual homes. We shared the results of the model with our collaborators in Memphis to get their feedback on some of the properties we had classified.

We then "walked" a few neighborhoods on Google Street View to compare the images for a random sample of properties with the risk scores calculated by our model. The images viewed were taken in August 2013. On one block in the Midtown neighborhood, for example, risk scores range from 0.269 to 0.807. Figure 2 shows two example homes with high and low risk scores. Clear differences are visible between these two properties, such as the differently maintained lawns.

Figure 2: There is a visible difference between homes with a low risk score (0.368, left) and a high risk score (0.807, right).

	Trial 1	Trial 2	Trial 3	Trial 4	Trial 5
AUC	0.829	0.832	0.829	0.832	0.832

Table 1: The results of cross-validation were consistently accurate.

While this test clearly does not validate our model, observing many homes in this manner encourages us to be confident in the model's predictive ability. In general, we find that our risk scores provide accurate insights into the relative conditions of properties.

4.3.1 Cross-Validation

We validated our model using five-fold cross-validation. We randomly selected the data into five groups, and then trained a model on four-fifths of the data and tested on the last fifth. The accuracy of our model was evaluated using a precision-recall curve [6]. Our results were encouraging, with an area-under-curve (AUC) between 0.829 and 0.832 for the five trials (Table 1). The accuracy and consistency of our model shows that it can successfully identify distressed properties.

For further insights into the accuracy of our model, we also measured the accuracy of the risk scores our classifier assigned to properties. We grouped all properties from the test set into bins based on the risk score assigned to them by the classifier, and then measured the proportion of properties in each bin identified as distressed in the Neighborhood-by-Neighbor survey. Figure 3 shows the results of this analysis for one of our cross-validated models (the results for each trial of cross-validation were almost identical). The size of each circle represents the number of properties in that bin. As shown in the figure, the predicted and actual probabilities of distress in the survey are almost identical. This indicates that the risk score assigned to each property by the classifier accurately identifies the probability that the property is distressed.

4.3.2 Test on a Recent Neighborhood Survey

To further test our model on more recent data, we obtained the results from a neighborhood windshield survey conducted by the Frayser Neighborhood CDC on 12,000 properties in 2013. This survey provides Memphis' only labeled property data for years after 2011, and is therefore the only data available from recent years for large-scale evaluation of our model.

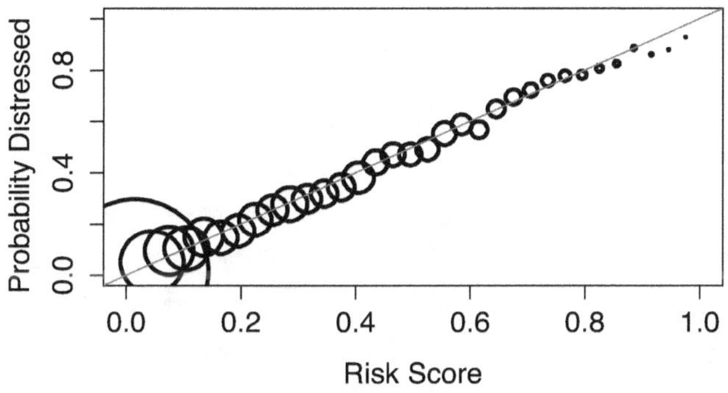

Figure 3: The risk scores assigned to properties accurately estimate the probability that the property is distressed. Circle sizes correspond to the number of properties identified with that risk score. The red line plots the one-to-one correspondence $y = x$.

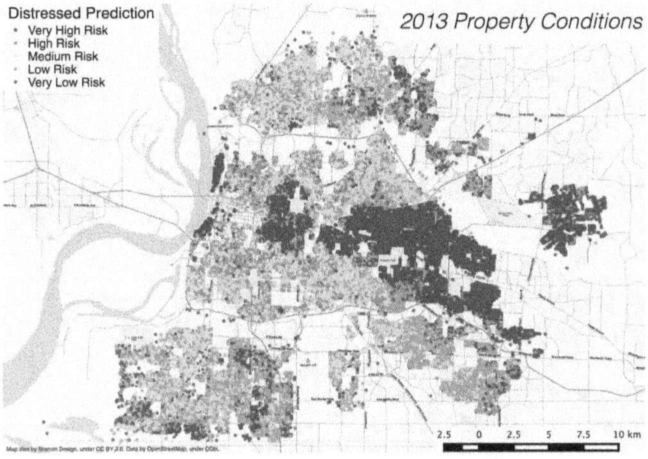

Figure 4: Our model predicts that the most severely distressed properties (marked in red) form a "C" shape around the center of Memphis.

We tested our full model on the 12,000 properties surveyed by the Frayser CDC neighborhood survey in 2013. With an AUC of 0.621, our results suggest that we are able to estimate distressed properties in 2013 with mediocre accuracy. However, we must account for a few sources of error that are likely to diminish the quality of our predictions.

Because the Neighborhood-by-Neighbor and Frayser surveys were completed by separate organizations without coordination, they label properties differently. In particular, while the Neighborhood-by-Neighbor survey identifies properties needing "cosmetic repairs only" as a distinct category (one that we considered as distressed), the Frayser survey groups properties with "possible minor cosmetic issues" and "no structural issues" in the same category (which we considered as not distressed). In other words, the Frayser survey sets a higher threshold for marking a property as distressed.

This may explain why our model significantly overestimates distress for properties it assigns a risk score between 0.4 and 0.7, but accurately predicts distress for properties with higher risk scores. Homes with "minor cosmetic issues" are likely to be classified by our model as moderate risk properties, but appear in the Frayser survey as in good condition. Our model performs better on homes to which it assigns a risk score above 0.7. These homes are likely to appear relatively consistently in both surveys. They are also, for the purposes described here, the most important properties to identify accurately. This sample of properties thus provides a better test for our model — and yields encouraging results about its accuracy.

4.4 Implementation

We used our model to estimate the condition of every residential property in Memphis in 2011, 2012, and 2013. Future years can be added to the model as new data becomes available. Figure 4 shows the estimates from our model for 2013. Note the C-shaped distribution, with distressed properties forming a strip along the north, west, and south of central Memphis. This is known colloquially in Memphis as the "C of poverty."

We have presented these estimates to policymakers and community leaders in Memphis through a web application made using the **shinyapps** package in **R** [4].[4] The site (Figure 5) provides an interactive map where users can zoom in to any neighborhood in Memphis to see each residential property's risk score. The map can display predictions for 2011, 2012, and 2013, allowing users to assess property and neighborhood conditions over time.[5]

Using this site, community groups and city officials can efficiently evaluate neighborhoods to inform investments and policy proposals. Rather than surveying the entire city to obtain estimates of which properties are distressed, they can use this website to estimate neighborhood-level priorities. Once a neighborhood has been identified for attention, the City can invest resources in preparing a much more precise and in-depth analysis of its condition.

5. EVALUATION OF REVITALIZATION STRATEGIES

Identifying distressed properties is only the first step toward revitalizing neighborhoods. The next task for cities is to determine what action to take. When dealing with distressed properties, Memphis typically either demolishes the structure, leaving a vacant lot, or boards the home, leaving an abandoned property. These actions are largely dictated by a lack of available resources. CDCs and private investors occasionally rehabilitate and sell distressed properties, inserting them back into the pool of habitable homes. While studies in other cities have linked rehabilitations with improved neighborhood outcomes [16], officials and developers in Memphis struggle to understand precisely how any individual property contributes to its neighborhood's condition.

In this section, we analyze the impact of distressed homes on neighborhoods in Memphis. Finding that rehabilitated homes are correlated with increased property values throughout their neighborhood, we then develop a tool to predict

[4]Due to restrictions on our data sharing agreement with the City of Memphis, this website is not public but the source code for all this work is available at `https://github.com/dssg/memphis-public`.

[5]We did not feel it would be useful to the City to calculate risk scores for years preceding 2011.

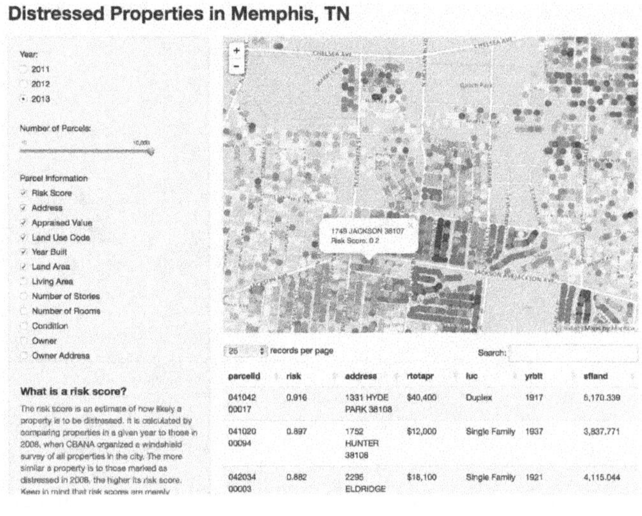

Figure 5: A screenshot of our distressed properties web application. The site contains options to control displayed data (left panel), an interactive map to look at the risk score of every property (top panel), and a data portal with information about each displayed home (bottom panel).

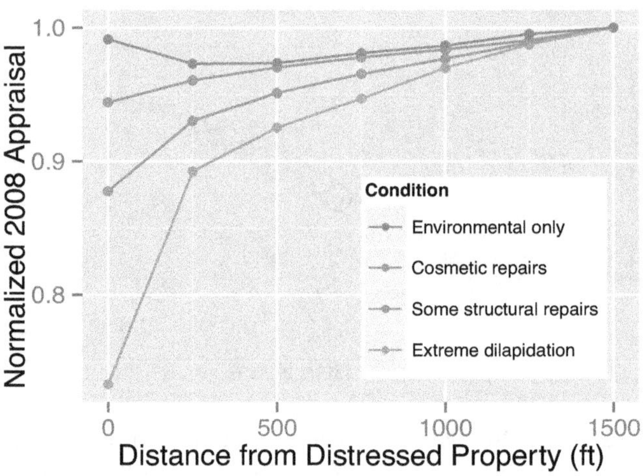

Figure 6: Homes near more severely distressed properties have lower appraised values than those further away.

which homes, if rehabilitated, will generate the greatest impacts. Together, these analyses will help Memphis design cost-effective strategies to invest in neighborhoods.

5.1 The Real Estate Market and Distress

We first studied the relationship between the property values of distressed homes and other homes in their vicinity. We selected each single-family home identified as distressed in the Neighborhood-by-Neighbor survey [5] and averaged the appraised values of the surrounding non-distressed homes as a function of distance from the distressed property. We grouped distressed properties and their neighbors based on the form of distress, as noted in the survey. We then normalized these profiles by the value of homes in the most distant bin (1250 to 1500 feet) and plotted the mean profile in Figure 6. The leftmost point is the average normalized value of the distressed properties themselves, followed by the average of properties between 0 and 250 feet away, and so on.

The results are intuitive: more severely-distressed properties and their immediate neighbors are valued below undistressed homes further away in their neighborhoods. Home values increase as the distance from a distressed property grows. Additionally, homes marked as "extremely dilapidated" show the biggest price decrease relative to their neighbors, indicating that worse forms of distress correlate with more severe reductions in home value.

It is tempting to interpret these results as an estimate of the effect of distress on neighboring home values. However, it could equally easily be interpreted as demonstrating the increased likelihood of distress in areas with unusually low property values — values whose ultimate cause may be something else entirely (crime, little accessibility to jobs, less access to credit, poor health, etc.). Moreover, distressed properties are clustered: a home near one distressed property is likely to be near others as well, which magnifies the observed price decrement. These results should therefore be taken as a characterization of the typical property values surrounding distress, rather than as a measurement of its impacts.

Another confounding factor in this analysis is our use of appraised property value as our metric of a home's worth. Assessors consider the quality of nearby properties when estimating the value of each home, and so it is difficult to untangle whether a distressed home truly impacts the value of its neighbors or simply causes assessors to provide a lower appraisal based on their formulae.

We also studied the appraised values surrounding distressed homes where some remediation was attempted. We identify rehabilitated homes as those that were labeled as distressed in the Neighborhood-by-Neighbor survey and received non-demolition building permits valued over $10,000 between 2008 and 2013. In Figure 7, we compare the neighborhoods of distressed single family homes that were demolished, rehabilitated, or received no treatment.

Unfortunately, building permits are not a perfect indicator for investment in a property. Some improvements may be done without a permit or do not require one (for example, new flowerbeds, trash pickup, or lawn maintenance). Additionally, not all permits are followed through, and some permit activity may not visibly change the house (such as interior repairs). Nonetheless, building permits are the best available proxy to infer when a property has received rehabilitation.

Using appraised values from 2013, we see that rehabilitated properties and their neighbors have a higher relative value for their neighborhood than the neighbors of untouched properties. Meanwhile, demolitions are associated with price decreases. It is not surprising that demolished properties are worth significantly less than their neighbors, since there is no structure on the lot and they were likely in the worst condition initially. The more interesting result is that the neighbors of demolished homes are appraised at lower values than the neighbors of rehabilitated homes, a result that holds at all distances considered. This suggests that rehabilitations may improve neighborhoods while demolitions drive down the value of neighboring properties.

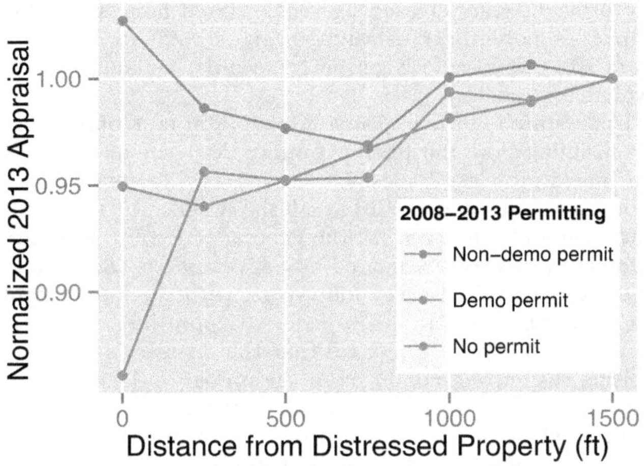

Figure 7: The appraised values of rehabilitated homes and their neighbors are higher than those of demolished homes.

These results are merely descriptive and cannot definitively evaluate the effectiveness of rehabilitation and demolition. They are designed instead to summarize how the City deals with distress and to generate hypotheses for further testing. As above, we note the complex relationships not captured in our analysis. For example, developers are more likely to invest in neighborhoods where property values are increasing, while cities are most likely to demolish properties in the worst neighborhoods. It is not yet clear what impact, if any, rehabilitating or demolishing homes has on neighborhood dynamics.

5.2 Evaluating the Impacts of Rehabilitation

While the previous analysis has shown that rehabilitations are correlated with higher property values, to guide the actions of city governments we would like to understand the causal relationships at play: do any of these interventions change the property value of homes in the neighborhood?

Understanding the indirect impacts of rehabilitations will help cities determine when interventions can be justified economically. Considering properties individually, the answer is usually no: it typically costs more to rehabilitate a property than can be recouped by its sale and increased property tax revenues. However, if the rehabilitation also increases the value of neighboring homes, then the economic calculus changes: the cumulative gains from the rehabilitated property *and* its neighbors may be greater than the cost of investment, thereby financially justifying the intervention.

Questions of causality are best answered using econometrics, controlling outside influences on the outcome of interest to isolate the effects of the variable under study. This is often done using matching, a technique in which each observation in the treatment set is matched to an observation from the control set that has similar characteristics. This method attempts to make the only difference between the treatment and control groups be the treatment itself.

In our case, we wanted to evaluate the impact of interventions on the value of neighboring homes. We looked at recently-sold single and multi-family homes that did not see building permit activity, defining those within 500 feet of rehabilitated homes as the treatment group and those more than 500 feet from rehabilitated homes as the control group. We identified rehabilitations as properties that were marked as distressed in the 2008 Neighborhood-by-Neighbor survey and had since then had been subject to building permits of $10,000 or greater.

Arguably the most common matching method is propensity score matching, in which a model (for instance, a logit) is fit to predict the probability of treatment based on the covariates. The propensity function from that model (in the case of the linear regression, the output of the linear regression before the logit transformation) is then used to match observations between treatment and control. Observations that are similar on the covariates that predict selection are matched. Thus a control group is created of samples that had a similar probability to receive treatment as those that did receive treatment.

The related technique that we used is known as proximity matching [14]. With this technique, a random forest is used to predict treatment, and the proximity matrix from that random forest is used to match observations. Thus, observations that frequently end up in the same leaves of the random forest are more likely to be matched. This shares the quality of propensity score matching wherein observations are matched primarily based on the covariates that are likely to influence selection, but also has the property that observations are matched on the covariates themselves, rather than on a linear combination. Thus one is less likely to see a result where very different observations are matched because they have unrelated traits that happen to yield similar propensity functions. We found that proximity score matching produced better covariate balance, and so we used it for the analysis that follows. We used a random forest with a minimum terminal node size of 20, 3 variables at each split, and 25,000 trees.

Recognizing that our data does not elucidate all salient attributes about each property, we attempted to match unobservable features as best we could. We controlled for location in our matching, requiring each of the control properties to be within two miles of the matched property from the treatment group. Additionally, we used neighborhood-level covariates to ensure that matched properties were in similar neighborhoods. We assume that properties are most similar to those near them, and thus that we can best control for unobserved features by selecting homes from the same region of the city.[6] Two miles is large enough to include potential matching properties, but not so large that a property could be matched with one from a vastly different neighborhood. Unfortunately there is no metric to know how well this parameter we have chosen performs, since the attributes we are controlling for are unobserved.

Performing the matching as described, using spatial restrictions and proximity matching, we found a positive effect of rehabilitations on surrounding property sales: our model estimates a 3.25% increase in property values around rehabilitated homes.[7] This number is not statistically significant

[6]This is Tobler's First Law of Geography: "Everything is related to everything else, but near things are more related than distant things" [21].

[7]The minimum p-value for differences in observed variables between treatment and control was 0.23. The minimum p-value for first-order interactions between observed variables was 0.17. These are Kolmogorov-Smirnov p-values with 1000

($p = 0.312$), however, meaning that we cannot confidently determine whether rehabilitation has an effect. Thus, the results are inconclusive.

The conclusion from this analysis should not be that rehabilitation of distressed properties does not affect neighborhood property values, but rather that we were unable to detect a statistically significant effect of rehabilitation on property values. We believe this is largely because of the small sample size of sales ($n = 200$). Houses, especially in distressed neighborhoods, don't sell very often. Additionally, the hypothesized positive effect of interventions on home values is likely small to begin with, and thus difficult to differentiate from zero effect — no one would expect to see a 50% bump in sale price due to a nearby rehabilitation.

Such insignificant results do not necessarily imply that rehabilitation has no effect on housing price. The direction of the effect is positive, as one might expect; it is simply not measurable at 95% confidence with the data we have. It is possible that collecting more data would allow us to find a stronger effect; as additional homes are renovated in Memphis neighborhoods, and more homes around them are sold, this analysis could be revisited.

One way forward would be to increase the sample size by repeating this research in a larger city, or by extending the period of sales. Another option would be to take a qualitative approach, interviewing new buyers of houses near a rehabilitation and asking questions about how the neighborhood influenced their choice, documenting the effect of the interventions directly.

Model misspecification is another possible problem. One concern is that this model assumes that rehabilitating a distressed property has the same effect on surrounding property values in every part of the city. Perhaps rehabilitation affects property values only in certain neighborhoods. Relaxing this assumption is difficult, though, as the data is sparse: there are relatively few sales around rehabilitated homes, and they do not represent every neighborhood.

5.3 Simulating Tax Appraisals

Memphis has an active set of Community Development Corporations (CDCs) that rehabilitate dilapidated properties and sell them to local residents. However, CDCs cannot rehabilitate many properties because the costs typically exceed the amount that can be recouped from the sale of the property. The Frayser neighborhood CDC, for example, typically spends about $20,000 more rehabilitating a house than it can make back in that home's sale [12].

Based on the previous analyses, however, the benefits of rehabilitating a home appear to extend beyond the sale price of that specific house. This impact can be manifested in many forms. In parts of the city with large amounts of abandoned housing, an extra resident may help stabilize a block, preventing further abandonment. Even in areas that are doing well, an extra resident may contribute to community cohesiveness. Just having a house that is physically well-maintained will reduce the perceived disorder of a neighborhood, and may increase the value of neighboring properties.

Additionally, because recent comparable sales are used to determine the assessed value of properties for tax purposes, a rehabilitation can impact the tax revenues generated by the renovated property as well as its neighbors. Unlike some of the other benefits created by rehabilitated houses, the tax impact is potentially measurable: it is computed entirely from the tax assessor's property records, a dataset made available to us.

Understanding the impacts of rehabilitation required first determining how the Shelby County Assessor of Property calculates property values. Due to external factors we were unable to correspond directly with the Assessor on this issue, but their website describes the general procedure to determine the property taxes owed by a given parcel [2]. Properties are reappraised every four years, with the most recent appraisal occurring in 2013. Prior to appraisal, an inspector visits the house to ensure that the Assessor's database reflects the current condition of the property. The Assessor also records the price and type of all property sales in the county. Once the dataset has been updated, the Assessor uses a Computer-Assisted Mass Appraisal (CAMA) system to estimate each property's value based on its condition and recent sales in the area. This is then multiplied by the assessment rate (25% for residential properties) and the result is multiplied by the tax rate (generally around 3%) to get the final tax paid each year.

We matched each of the 12,486 single family residential properties in Frayser with the five closest sales whose properties were of comparable age, size, and condition. The appraised value was computed as the average of the five prices. The correlation between our estimated appraised values for 2013 and the Assessor's appraised values was 0.74. While by no means perfect, this is high enough to suggest that it captures many of the assessor's formula's underlying mechanisms.

The ability to estimate appraised values from property and sales data allowed us to estimate what would happen to neighborhood tax appraisals following the hypothetical sale of a rehabilitated property. We simulated appraisals where the sale of a rehabilitated home is included as a comparable and one where it is not. Subtracting the second set of values from the first provides an estimate of the impact of the rehabilitation on the tax appraisal of each property. Summing across properties gives the total impact of the new appraisal in the neighborhood.

This will help investors evaluate potential rehabilitations based on their expected impact on property values. To facilitate these estimates, we created a web application that allows users to select a property in Frayser and input a hypothetical selling price (Figure 8). The website then calculates the expected impact that selling the home at that price would have on the total property tax assessed throughout Frayser.

With this tool, the Memphis government and Frayser CDC can better predict their returns for rehabilitating and selling different homes. If they use it to target investments such that they can recoup more money, their model would become more financially stable. If investors and developers did not lose money on most of their rehabilitations, they would have the funds to rehabilitate more homes, thus turning revitalization into a self-sustaining venture.

6. IMPACTS IN MEMPHIS

Our analyses have contributed to Memphis' understanding of neighborhood vitality. By providing a macro view of distress across the city, officials can now see citywide patterns and trends. We have also provided new analyses re-

bootstraps. Indicator variables used a paired sample t-test. Balance was evaluated using the `Matching` package in `R` [19].

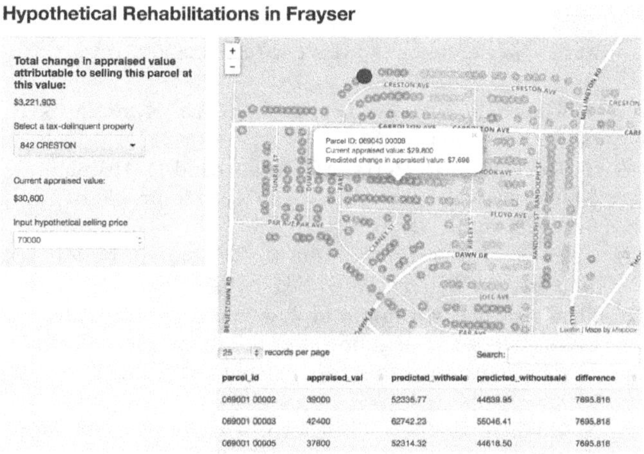

Figure 8: We built a website that predicts the impact of hypothetical rehabilitations on property values for one neighborhood in Memphis.

garding the cost of distress on neighborhoods. As such, the City is better prepared to calibrate neighborhood improvement strategies with a better sense of how it will affect a neighborhood rather than a single parcel.

As Memphis undertakes future revitalization efforts, it can do so with greater ease and to greater effect than was possible before. Its first task is to identify neighborhoods in need of aid. In previous years this would have required expensive and time-consuming neighborhood surveys just to determine which neighborhoods should be evaluated further. This can now be done online using our website described in Section 4.

Once it has decided where to invest in revitalization efforts, the City must determine what actions to take. While it has traditionally boarded or demolished distressed homes, our analyses in Section 5 challenge the suitability of these strategies. Although our results were not entirely conclusive, we found correlations between demolitions and decreased property values in the neighborhood. Rehabilitations, on the other hand, were correlated with increased property values for both the rehabilitated home and its neighbors.

To aid the rehabilitation efforts of City Hall and local CDCs, we developed an application that predicts the impact of proposed rehabilitations on neighborhood property values. They can use this tool to invest in homes that will generate the greatest increase in property values across the entire neighborhood. This will drive down the effective cost of each rehabilitation, freeing up resources to be used for additional rehabilitations or other revitalization efforts.

Our project has also started conversations locally about the need to invest money and human resources into the City's use of data. In order to aid future work by the City of Memphis, we created and handed over a data portal that contains all of the data we gathered from various sources. This affirmed the potential in Memphis for a unified data center that would allow stakeholders to be on one platform and ask questions using common data. The City is currently designing a more sophisticated data warehouse. In addition, officials around Memphis are now exploring new projects that use data to address their needs.

7. DATA SCIENCE CHALLENGES IN GOVERNMENT

Cities across the country are increasing their use of data and technology to guide policy and better interact with citizens [8, 22]. Throughout our work, we encountered many challenges that we believe are typical of efforts to apply data science techniques to aid government policy. We review several here and discuss important steps to improve future data-driven efforts in public policy.

First and foremost, we encourage cities to invest in data collection efforts: data mining algorithms produce results only as good as the data they are given. Cities and citizens should develop common goals for data-driven initiatives. This will involve first identifying problems that data can solve, then determining what data is needed, and finally developing tools to acquire and maintain data.

Our work also highlights the need for municipal bodies to share data while solving complex urban problems. One of our primary challenges was discovering what data exists, identifying who in Memphis controls it, and determining how to access it. We believe that creating a common data warehouse across City Hall will empower government employees to develop more comprehensive data-driven policies.

Another challenge we encountered was determining the proper metrics to evaluate the success of revitalization initiatives. Cities must juggle numerous, often competing, goals: balancing the budget, improving social connectivity, and ensuring the welfare of their most disadvantaged citizens, among others. Because cities are responsible for the well-being of their citizens, they cannot think like a corporation and focus only on earning back the money spent. If a revitalization project increases property values but displaces many citizens through gentrification, we do not believe that should be considered a success. Yet it was difficult to develop metrics for social vitality based on the data in city ledgers. We believe it is important for governments, data scientists, and social scientists to think creatively about novel ways to measure social well-being with existing data as well as new data that should be collected toward this end.

Finally, we encourage data scientists working with public officials to emphasize that their models provide *estimates*, and should be used as one of multiple inputs into the decision making process. There are many caveats that need to be specified (noisy data, sample bias, model assumptions, etc.), and it is important to be open about the limits of our techniques. Therefore, our results came with the attached notice: "Apply local knowledge before drawing conclusions." It is a remark equally about the limits of modeling as it is a reminder to be mindful of the context of one's work.

8. FUTURE WORK

There are multiple approaches we could take to improve our model of distressed properties. Initial attempts should focus on feature selection, in particular generating more complex features from the data. One example would be to consider the number of unique homebuyers, rather than total transaction volume, thus separating the effects of speculation from other types of investment.

Another potential approach is to take advantage of large online resources with images of city streets, such as Google Street View. This technique has recently gained attention as an effective way to study urban conditions [10, 17]. Computer vision algorithms could identify features of the homes labeled as "distressed" and "not distressed" using historical images available on the site. Incorporating images into our model would add a rich layer of information about each home not captured in the City's internal databases.

Finally, it will be valuable to attempt similar applications using more targeted machine learning approaches. In the absence of up-to-date labels of property conditions, we could design a semi-supervised system where only some of the properties require training data.[8] This would ease the burden on officials or volunteers who otherwise would need to assess every property. It would also be worthwhile to attempt multi-class learning methods that can classify homes into more nuanced categories than just "distressed" and "not distressed."

9. CONCLUSIONS

In this paper, we developed tools to aid Memphis, TN's efforts to revitalize neighborhoods. Our methods were successful at identifying distressed properties based on the City's administrative data, allowing stakeholders in Memphis to easily, quickly, and inexpensively evaluate citywide trends and neighborhoods in particular need of aid. We then studied the impacts that distressed properties have on their local neighborhoods. Finding that rehabilitations appear more effective than demolitions at revitalizing neighborhoods, we built a tool to help CDCs and other local investors identify which homes will most affect their neighborhood if rehabilitated.

By using data that municipalities across the United States already collect regularly for administrative purposes, we highlighted approaches that are possible in many cities without requiring extensive upfront data collection. We hope that these analyses will show municipalities how utilizing their existing data and increasing future data-collection efforts can help them better serve citizens and use their resources to the greatest effect. Our work has, in part, spurred Memphis to invest more heavily in data collection and analysis, as well as policymaking based on data processing. This will allow both data scientists and city employees to conduct more rigorous and impactful analyses in the future.

10. ACKNOWLEDGMENTS

This work was completed during the 2014 Eric and Wendy Schmidt Data Science for Social Good Summer Fellowship at the University of Chicago. We are grateful to the entire team of mentors and fellows who contributed their guidance, suggestions, expertise, and camaraderie.

We received invaluable data and assistance from many people and organizations in Memphis. These include George Lord and Tommy Pacello from the Innovation Delivery Team, Nathan Ron-Ferguson and Tk Buchanan from the University of Memphis, the Frayser and Binghampton CDCs, Shelby County ReGIS, and the Shelby County Register of Deeds.

11. REFERENCES

[1] City-data. `http://www.city-data.com`. Accessed: 2015-02-15.

[2] Shelby county assessor of property. `http://www.assessor.shelby.tn.us`. Accessed: 2014-07-21.

[3] Urban areas in the United States: 1950 to 2010. `http://www.demographia.com/db-uza2000.htm`. Accessed: 2015-02-15.

[4] J. Allaire. *shinyapps: Interface to ShinyApps*, 2013. R package version 0.3.63.

[5] T. Buchanan, P. Betts, J. Gilman, and R. Brimhall. Neighborhood-by-neighbor: A citywide problem property audit, 2010.

[6] T. Fawcett. An introduction to ROC analysis. *Pattern Recognition Letters*, 27(8):861–874, 2006.

[7] G. Galster, P. Tatian, and J. Accordino. Targeting investments for neighborhood revitalization. *Journal of the American Planning Association*, 72(4):457–474, 2006.

[8] S. Goldsmith and S. Crawford. *The Responsive City: Engaging Communities Through Data-smart Governance*. John Wiley & Sons, 2014.

[9] I. Goldstein and C. S. Closkey. Market value analysis: Understanding where and how to invest limited resources. *St. Louis, MO: Federal Reserve Bank of St. Louis*, 2006.

[10] J. Hwang and R. J. Sampson. Divergent pathways of gentrification racial inequality and the social order of renewal in Chicago neighborhoods. *American Sociological Review*, 79(4):726–751, 2014.

[11] A. Liaw and M. Wiener. Classification and regression by randomForest. *R News*, 2(3):18–22, 2002.

[12] S. Lockwood. Personal Communication, Aug 2014.

[13] C. Marohn. Strong towns report for the City of Memphis, 2013.

[14] D. I. Miller, H. Tan, and J. Savage. The next generation of matching methods for causal inference. In Preparation.

[15] R Core Team. *R: A Language and Environment for Statistical Computing*. R Foundation for Statistical Computing, Vienna, Austria, 2013.

[16] Research for Democracy. *Blight Free Philadelphia: A Public-Private Strategy to Create and Enhance Neighborhood Value*. Eastern Pennsylvania Organizing Project, 2001.

[17] P. Salesses, K. Schechtner, and C. A. Hidalgo. The collaborative image of the city: Mapping the inequality of urban perception. *PLoS ONE*, 8(7), 2013.

[18] R. J. Sampson. *Great American City: Chicago and the Enduring Neighborhood Effect*. University of Chicago Press, 2012.

[19] J. S. Sekhon. Multivariate and propensity score matching software with automated balance optimization: The Matching package for R. *Journal of Statistical Software*, 42(7):1–52, 2011.

[20] The National Vacant Properties Campaign. Vacant properties: The true costs to communities, 2005.

[21] W. R. Tobler. A computer movie simulating urban growth in the Detroit region. *Economic Geography*, pages 234–240, 1970.

[22] A. M. Townsend. *Smart Cities: Big Data, Civic Hackers, and the Quest for a New Utopia*. WW Norton & Company, 2013.

[8]We thank an anonymous reviewer for this suggestion.

Measuring Causal Impact of Online Actions Via Natural Experiments: Application to Display Advertising

Daniel N. Hill
Amazon.com, Inc.
Palo Alto, CA
daniehil@amazon.com

Robert Moakler
Integral Ad Science
& NYU Stern
New York, NY
rmoakler@stern.nyu.edu

Alan E. Hubbard
Division of Biostatistics
University of California
Berkeley, CA
hubbard@berkeley.edu

Vadim Tsemekhman
OpenDSP
Seattle, WA
vadimt@opendsp.com

Foster Provost
Integral Ad Science
& NYU Stern
New York, NY
fprovost@stern.nyu.edu

Kiril Tsemekhman*
Integral Ad Science
New York, NY
kiril@integralads.com

ABSTRACT

Predictive models are often employed to decide actions in interactive online systems. For example, ads are selectively served to users who are modeled as being inclined to purchase the product being advertised. News feed items are populated based on a model of the user's interests. A common consequence of these predictive models is the creation of a spurious correlation, or confounding, between the action and its desired outcome. In the above examples, the targeted users are likely to buy the product or find the news item regardless of the intervention. This presents a challenge for measuring the true impact of these systems.

Here we present a novel framework for estimating causal effects that relies on neither randomized experiments nor adjusting for the potentially explosive number of variables used in predictive models. We propose the identification and instrumentation of events that mediate the effect of the action. When the effect of an action depends on a mediating event that is not subject to the same confounders, the problem of causal estimation is greatly simplified. We demonstrate this approach in display advertising using ad viewability as a natural experiment that mediates the impact of served ads. Approximately 45% of display ad impressions never make it into a viewable portion of the user's browser. We show that an analysis based on ad viewability can massively reduce the amount of bias in estimating campaign lift. We integrate the use of negative controls as well as the identification and adjustment for residual confounding to further reduce the bias in estimated lift to less than 10%. A system using these techniques is deployed to monitor the daily causal impact of many large-scale advertising campaigns.

*Corresponding author.

KDD '15 August 11-14, 2015, Sydney, NSW, Australia
ACM 978-1-4503-3664-2/15/08.
DOI: http://dx.doi.org/10.1145/2783258.2788622.

Categories and Subject Descriptors

H.2.8 [**Database Management**]: Database Applications—*data mining*; J.4 [**Computer Applications**]: Social and Behavioral Sciences

General Terms

Design, Experimentation, Measurement

Keywords

display advertising, causal analysis, natural experiments, performance measurement, negative controls

1. INTRODUCTION

In today's complex interactive online systems, economically important actions increasingly are taken based on inferences drawn from predictive models. Examples run from classic applications such as automatic credit decisions to contemporary applications such as what content to show a user in a news feed. In this paper we use online display ad targeting as our running example and our domain of application. As has been described comprehensively elsewhere, online display ads are targeted based on various predictive modeling-based strategies, *e.g.*, [13].

When actions are important economically, firms generally would like to assess the impact of the actions. For example, advertisers would like to assess whether their advertisements actually lead to an increase in certain outcomes, such as purchases or other brand actions. Unfortunately, *the use of predictive models substantially increases the difficulty of assessing the true impact of the actions.* In this paper we explain this phenomenon carefully, present a framework for collecting and using data to address this difficulty directly, and provide a demonstration implemented across a variety of real, large-scale ad campaigns.

To understand why predictive modeling makes assessments of impact more difficult, we need to focus on the key difficulty of causal reasoning: confounding. Consider figure 1, which shows a causal directed acyclic graph (DAG) [12] representing a collection of random variables that describe an individual and the causal relationships among them. These

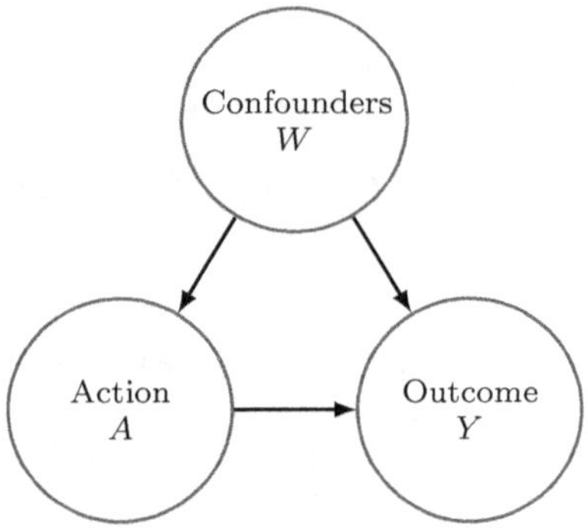

Figure 1: Causal DAG with confounders.

include an action (A), such as whether or not the individual was served an advertisement for a particular product, an outcome of interest (Y), such as whether or not the individual purchased the product, and a set of confounding variables (W). A variable or a set of variables is confounding if it is causally related to both the action and the outcome of interest. In the language of causal reasoning, one must control for confounding if one is to draw valid causal inferences.

We can now state precisely why using predictive modeling creates a problem. Predictive models very often are built to choose actions based on the user's prior inclination towards a particular outcome. For example, an online store may recommend products that the user is modeled as likely to purchase. News feeds may be populated with items that are predicted to be of interest to the user. The very features that predict the outcome for the individual are used to decide actions to further promote that outcome, thus confounding the link between action and outcome. So in our advertising example, predictive models are built based on, say, the web pages that users have visited and those users' purchase behavior. The model identifies the statistical link[1] from web page visits W to purchase behavior Y. Then these predictive models are applied such that users with certain W values are selected for ad targeting. This creates the causal link between W and A, and completes the confounding. The practical upshot is well understood by academics and knowledgeable data scientists, but poorly dealt with in the industry: the models select people who are more likely to purchase even without being shown an ad, a concept known as selection bias. Due to the confounding one cannot judge the effectiveness of the ad campaign easily—estimates that do not control for the confounding will be highly inaccurate [9, 8].

One possible way to address this confounding is by conducting randomized experiments, called A/B tests in the advertising industry. A/B testing can have serious technical challenges, which have been described in detail [6]. Possibly more importantly, A/B testing is expensive. In the case of online display advertising, typically 5-15% of targeted consumers are randomly assigned to a control group and shown campaign-irrelevant public service announcements (PSAs), while the remaining users are assigned to the test group and are shown normal campaign ads. Thus, advertisers or their targeting agents must spend 5-15% of marketing budgets on ads that have no direct effect on outcome, and not surprisingly advertisers are reluctant to spend such sums. Even in cases where they do, usually the A/B tests are conducted over a limited time period that restricts the scope of the assessment. Finally, in certain cases ethics precludes randomized trials. This concern is well known in ethically fraught applications such as medical treatment [1]; it is only beginning to come to attention in online experiments (*e.g.* [7]).

The other major alternative is to use causal analysis to directly adjust for confounders present in observational data. Several factors prevent this from being done efficiently or at all. First, for many modern applications, W can contain tens of millions or more variables, such as all the possible web pages that an ad targeter considers in modeling a user. Correctly controlling for such a huge number of non-independent confounding variables is difficult. Second, for automated actions there is a strong possibility of a violation of the positivity assumption necessary for causal inference [14]. If the action A is taken for every individual with a particular W, then there is no control group for W in which the action was not taken.

Most importantly, the organization interested in the assessment of impact often does not have precise knowledge of the data W on which the actions are taken. For example, it is the brand who cares about the impact of advertisements. A large brand typically will engage a dozen or more targeting firms. For most of those firms, the brand does not know exactly how they are targeting, or even exactly what data they are using. And the brand generally does not have access to those data, which may have been gathered by the targeter, purchased from third parties, or created internally based on inferences from other models. So while targeters themselves can conduct observational causal studies based on their own data [3, 15], the brand generally cannot do so either for individual targeters, or across targeters, *e.g.*, to judge which targeters are generating the best return on ad spend.

Here we offer an alternative, that can complement A/B tests or causal analysis, and that can also be applied in some situations where these techniques break down *or lack statistical significance*. Our framework, as outlined in section 2, is based on the identification and exploitation of an event M that mediates the impact of the action A on the outcome Y (figure 2). When such an event exists and is independent of the predictors W used to decide the action, it can be treated as a natural experiment. This removes or dramatically reduces the need to perform complicated adjustments for W in assessing causal effects. A major contribution of our framework is the proposal to instrument computer systems to observe such mediating events. The framework also integrates the use of negative controls to assess any residual confounding, and the use of methods from causal inference to adjust for residual confounding.

The second main contribution of this paper is the specific application of our framework to assessing the impact of online display advertisements. The key novelty is the instrumentation of the display advertising ecosystem to reveal a mediator M: viewability of ads [11]. More specifically,

[1]Technically, there are some hidden behavioral drivers that cause the individual to have both an increased propensity to visit the web pages and an increased propensity to purchase. We will ignore that distinction for now; it makes the causal graph slightly more complex, but does not affect the confounding by W.

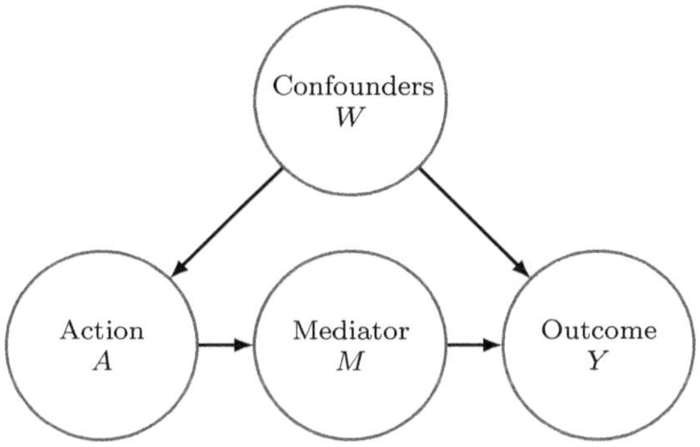

Figure 2: Causal DAG with mediating variable.

it turns out that for various reasons described below, after an ad targeting action A has been taken, online consumers are able to *view* only about 55% of display ads. The reasons for not seeing the ad are largely independent from the predictive modeling and from W, and thus confounding is dramatically reduced. Our results show that indeed the apparent impact of online display ads is dramatically reduced when utilizing viewability as a natural experiment. This concurs with prior results from randomized experiments [2] and from causal modeling with access to W [3, 15]. We then show, by employing negative controls, that the residual confounding is relatively small—though still present. We identify particular confounders that affect the viewability of ads, and further reduce the bias of our estimates through an adjustment. An implementation of our framework that estimates causal performance of display ad campaigns using viewability has been deployed as a product at the corresponding author's company. The system monitors lift for dozens of advertising campaigns on a daily basis. The selection of the right confounders to adjust the performance estimate is a work in progress and will be incorporated into future product releases.

2. MEASUREMENT FRAMEWORK

We now outline our framework for using mediating events to measure the causal impact of an action, as illustrated in figure 3. The workflow is briefly sketched here and then described in more detail in later sections as we work through our application in online advertising.

The process begins with the identification of potential mediators that correspond to the causal model in figure 2. A good candidate must meet several criteria. First is that the event must happen after the action is taken but before the outcome occurs. Second, the mediating event must be necessary for the action to have an effect on the outcome. Third, the event should not be directly influenced by the same predictors W that confound the system in the first place. Finally, the mediating event must fail to occur sometimes for all values of W in order to avoid positivity violations. The mediating event for our application is the viewability of display ads, but another example exists in online advertising that uses real-time bidding (RTB) systems. The effect of targeting a user for ads is mediated by winning an auction. If the auction is lost, the user cannot be influenced by targeting. There are candidates in other domains as well. The effect of adding a recommended song to a playlist is mediated by whether the user remains online long enough for the song to play. The effect of placing an item in a news feed is mediated by whether the user scrolls through all the preceding items.[2] In our framework, once a candidate event is proposed, the next step is to instrument the mediator to collect measurements of M.

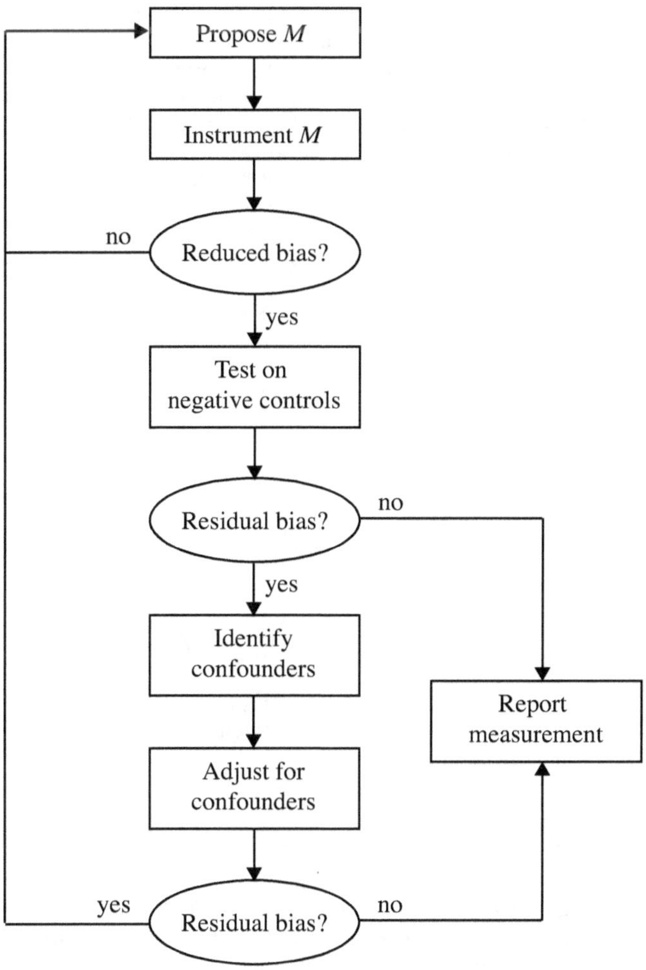

Figure 3: Framework for exploiting mediators.

An ideal or perfect natural experiment results when the treatment status for each user is assigned due to a truly random and naturally occurring event. If the event M results in an ideal natural experiment, then the estimation of a causal effect is straight-forward. For all users who experienced the action A, the probability of outcome Y can be compared directly between users who experienced the mediating event and users who did not, as if a randomized experiment had

[2]Jensen et al. [5] discuss an automated method of discovering natural experiments (what they term "quasi-experimental designs") in observational data. They show that natural experiments can be discovered using a relational database schema, additional information about the temporal durations of specific events, and limited prior knowledge about potential causes.

been conducted.[3] This analysis would be subject to none of the bias associated with a naïve analysis where users who experienced the confounded action A are compared to those who did not experience A. It may be quite helpful for a comparison of both types of analysis to be carried out as a first-pass evaluation of the usefulness of the measurement M as a natural experiment.

It may be the case that M is not a perfect natural experiment, meaning that there exist residual confounders W' between the mediator M and the outcome Y (figure 4). The confounders W' may or may not overlap with W depending on the domain. How can we identify whether there is residual confounding of the mediator? In principle, this could be identified by comparing results from the analysis to that of a randomized experiment. However, it may be that reliable experiments are not available if this framework is being used. If available, a low-cost alternative is to employ *negative controls* as a way to identify confounding of M.

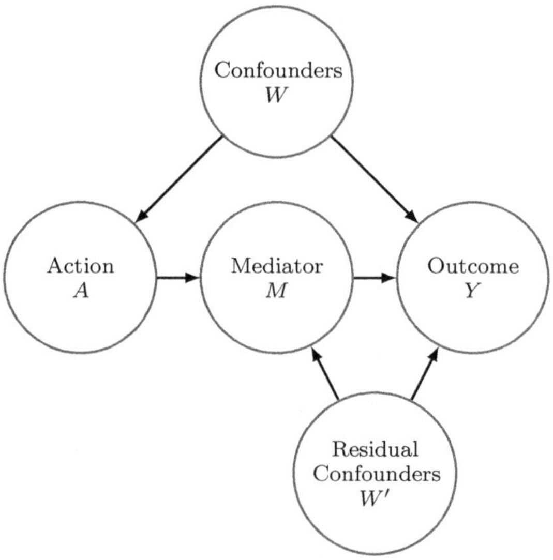

Figure 4: Causal DAG with confounded viewability.

A negative control is an irrelevant but observable outcome Y^- where the action A is known to have no impact (figure 5). Negative controls can help identify bias in causal studies as they provide a test where the analysis should produce an estimate of zero effect [10]. Online entities typically track a large number of actions that a user may take, so negative controls are often readily available. A commonly used negative control in online advertising is a conversion event from an unrelated campaign [3, 15]. In the case of recommender systems, the selection by the user of an unrelated item could serve as a negative control for the recommended item.

A negative control is most useful when it is subject to all of the same confounders W as the original outcome Y. If the negative control conversion has fewer confounders, then it is possible to correctly predict no effect on the negative control while still admitting residual bias on the actual outcome. For this reason, we propose to use a spectrum of negative controls to increase the likelihood that each confounder is covered by at least one control. An additional advantage of using multiple negative controls is the possibility to infer the magnitude of estimation bias. If the negative controls are subject to the same bias as the outcome of interest, they can provide an empirical distribution of this bias.

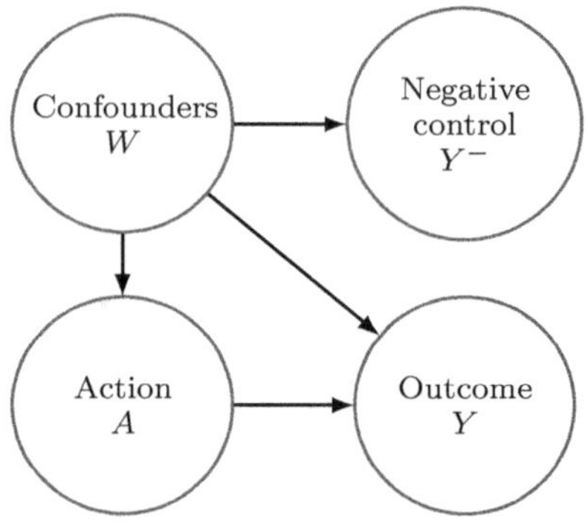

Figure 5: Causal DAG with negative control.

If an analysis based on a mediating event produces significant non-zero effects when analyzed against a spectrum of negative controls, this likely indicates there are residual confounders W'. Below we describe an approach to identifying W' and adjusting for it to revise a causal estimate in the context of online advertising. When successful, adjusting for residual confounders can lead to low-bias estimates of causal effects at the mere cost of instrumenting M. In general, we expect that controlling for confounding of the mediator M to be easier than controlling for the deep confounding of the action A. That being said, if the adjustment for confounders of M estimates large effects on negative controls, then the proposed M should be discarded for a new candidate.

3. AD VIEWABILITY

We apply our framework to online advertising where we identified *ad viewability* as a mediating event. A large fraction of ad impressions that are served to users are never seen because these ads are not loaded to a viewable portion of the user's browser. Unviewable ads cannot have an effect on the user's actions, and so viewability mediates the effect of serving ads. To understand this phenomenon, it is important to know the factors that determine whether an ad becomes viewable.

The most common reason for a display ad to be unviewable is it being served "below the fold." This means the user must scroll down the page for the ad to move into the window of the web browser. If the user leaves the web page before scrolling to the ad's location, the impression will not be seen. Whether an ad is served below the fold is determined by a combination of factors including the web page's layout, the size and location of the ad, the window size of the user's browser, and the monitor's display settings. Each of these factors is subject to a wide degree of variability. For example, ads can be displayed as wide, short banners at the top of a web page, as narrow, tall "skyscrapers" on the border of a page's content, or as rectangular patches distributed at various locations within the page.

Another reason why ads become unviewable is their being "out of focus." Sometimes content is loaded to a browser that is minimized or to a tab that is not currently active. This is commonly a result of auto-refreshing where content is reloaded at regular intervals without the user's intervention.

[3]Please note the similarity between this approach and the front-door criterion described by Pearl [12].

The content is not seen unless the user actively navigates to the hidden or minimized window.

The targeter has very limited information about any of these factors at the time of placing an ad. Typically the targeter bids for placements based on the URL, the ad size, and aspects of the visitor, so detailed information about the likelihood of the ad to be viewable cannot be factored into the decision to serve the ad. This suggests that viewability is a good candidate for our analysis framework since it is not subject to normal targeting bias.

The corresponding author's company has instrumented viewability via JavaScript code that is served along with ads. This code is run in the user's browser, where it queries geometric data and other information from the browser that it uses to determine whether the ad is currently in view. The definition we use for *in view* for this paper is that at least 50% of the ad's pixels are visible on the user's screen. The end result is a measurement of the duration over which the ad was determined to be in view.

Figure 6 shows the distribution of the duration of time in view for a random sample of ads collected from advertising campaigns from a variety of industries. We find that approximately 45% of ads are in view for less than one second. Hereafter, we will refer to such ads as *unviewable*. Impressions that were in view for at least one second will be called *viewable*.

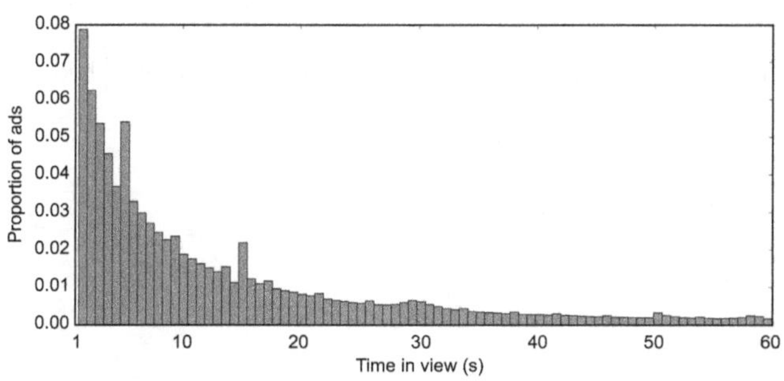

Figure 6: Distribution of time in view for viewable impressions (*i.e.* impressions that have at least 50% of the ad's pixels in a visible portion of the user's screen for at least one second).

Figure 7 summarizes the influence of vertical location of the impression on ad viewability. The median browser window size is depicted as the red box in figure 7a and the frequency of a pixel containing an ad is shown by the green heatmap. We see in figure 7b that less than half of all ads are served above the fold. Furthermore, the probability of the impression being viewable drops quickly around the median location of the bottom of the browser window (figure 7c). In addition, hidden tabs and minimized browser windows account for about 6% of ads being unviewable.

4. REDUCTION IN BIAS

In this section, we use measurements of ad viewability to reduce bias in estimating campaign performance. We compare a viewability analysis to a naïve one where the presence of selection bias is ignored. For both analyses, we use the individual impression as the unit of analysis (see figure 8). The observed data structure is $O = (A, M, Y) \sim P$ where A indicates whether the impression is from the campaign of interest, M indicates whether the impression was viewable, Y indicates whether the user converted in a window after the impression, and P is the underlying probability distribution. We use a conversion window of 7 days from the exact time of the impression. Note that in both analyses it is assumed that the effect of an ad is not modified by preceding or following ads. If a user receives multiple ads, they are considered in isolation of each other. While this assumption is likely to break down in certain scenarios, we use it to simplify our analysis while still addressing the problem of selection bias.

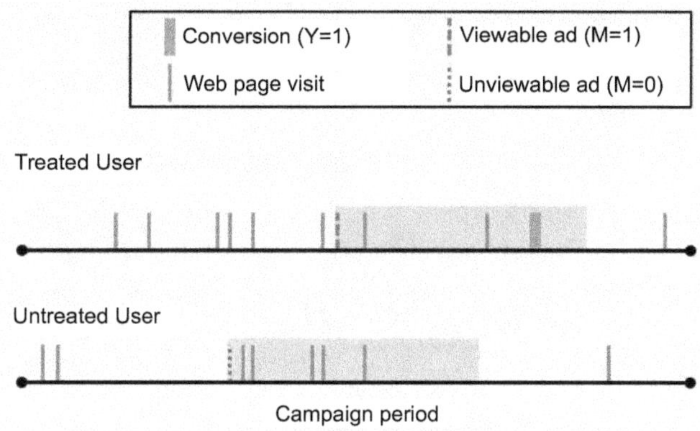

Figure 8: Diagram depicting variable definitions for viewability analysis. Gray boxes indicate the window in which conversions are monitored.

In our naïve analysis, we compare cases where the impression is from the campaign associated with the conversion ($A = 1$) versus cases where the impression is from an unrelated campaign ($A = 0$).[4] We expect this analysis to be biased by strong confounding from ad targeting. The target parameter for this analysis is the campaign lift defined by

$$\begin{aligned}\Phi_{\text{naïve}}(P) &= \frac{E\{Y \mid A=1\}}{E\{Y \mid A=0\}} - 1 \\ &= \frac{p(Y=1 \mid A=1)}{p(Y=1 \mid A=0)} - 1.\end{aligned} \tag{1}$$

For the viewability analysis we focus only on impressions from the campaign ($A = 1$). We compare conversion rates for users who received viewable ads ($M = 1$) with those who had unviewable ones ($M = 0$). The lift in this case is defined by

$$\begin{aligned}\Phi_{\text{viewability}}(P) &= \frac{E\{Y \mid M=1, A=1\}}{E\{Y \mid M=0, A=1\}} - 1 \\ &= \frac{p(Y=1 \mid M=1, A=1)}{p(Y=1 \mid M=0, A=1)} - 1.\end{aligned} \tag{2}$$

Both equations could be interpreted causally in the absence of confounders. However, as we expect strong selection bias in ad targeting, our hypothesis is that utilizing ad viewability will dramatically reduce such bias.

Our data come from seven display advertising campaigns run during the 4th quarter of 2014. The products advertised represented diverse industries including auto insurance,

[4]All the users in data under consideration received at least one impression from some campaign.

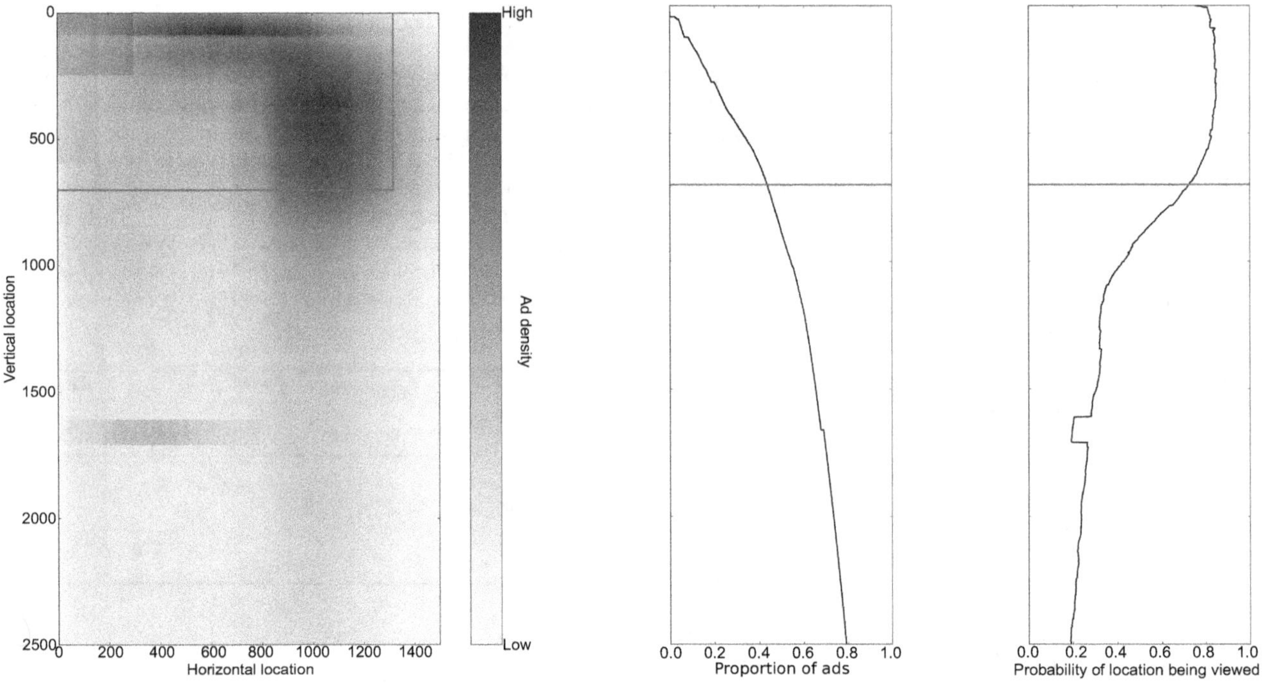

(a) Frequency of ads served at different locations on a page.

(b) Proportion of ads served at or above a particular page height.

(c) Probability of a pixel being brought into a viewable portion of the user's web browser.

Figure 7: Summary of the effect of the page fold on viewability. The red box and line depict the median size of a browser window. Location units are in pixels.

beauty products, finance, and online marketing. Conversions also represented diverse actions such as visiting the advertiser's web page, purchasing a product, or filling out a quote form. The volume of the campaigns ranged from 3 million to 29 million impressions. We define our users via browser cookies. The number of users who converted after receiving an impression ranged between 2,000 and 2 million depending on the campaign. For each campaign, we calculated $\Phi_{\text{naïve}}$ and $\Phi_{\text{viewability}}$ from the empirical probabilities that impressions of each type were followed by conversions. Confidence intervals were derived from the binomial distribution.

We found that across all campaigns values dropped dramatically between $\Phi_{\text{naïve}}$ and $\Phi_{\text{viewability}}$ (figure 9). For example, campaign C saw a drop in lift from 33,000% (95% CI, 28,000%–40,000%) in the naive analysis to 26% (95% CI, 21%–32%) in the viewability analysis. This campaign utilized retargeting practices where users were served ads if they had specifically interacted with the advertising brand in the past. This practice suggests selection bias should be particularly severe. Campaign F saw the smallest difference between the naive and viewability analyses displaying lifts of 65% (95% CI, 62%–69%) and 12% (95% CI, 7%–16%), respectively. The campaign in question was run by a major US consumer banking company which may use rather broad targeting criteria, limiting the amount of selection bias.

While the above data provide compelling evidence that bias can be reduced by using measurements of ad viewability, it is unclear how much residual bias remains. To probe the remaining bias, we turn to negative controls.

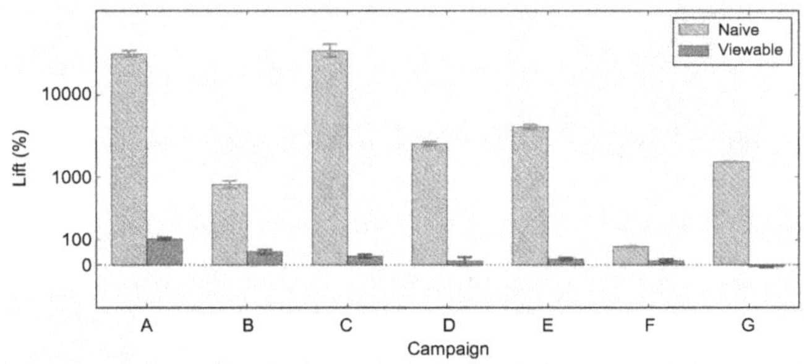

Figure 9: Lifts estimated for the naive analysis and for the analysis using viewable ads to define the treatment group. Note: a log scale is used to depict the difference between lifts.

5. NEGATIVE CONTROLS

As discussed above, negative controls help to identify bias in causal studies as they provide a test where an unbiased estimator should predict zero effect. For each of our seven campaigns, we identified 7–10 conversion events from other campaigns to serve as negative controls. The negative controls were chosen from a different industry from the true conversion in order to minimize any possible interaction. In figure 10 we show the result of campaign B's impressions analyzed against its true conversion event as well as 10 negative controls using the viewability methodology. The lift on the true conversion, 41% (95% CI, 34%–50%), is larger than that of any of the negative controls. However, all but one negative control showed a significant lift despite being irrelevant to the campaign ads ($p < 0.05$).

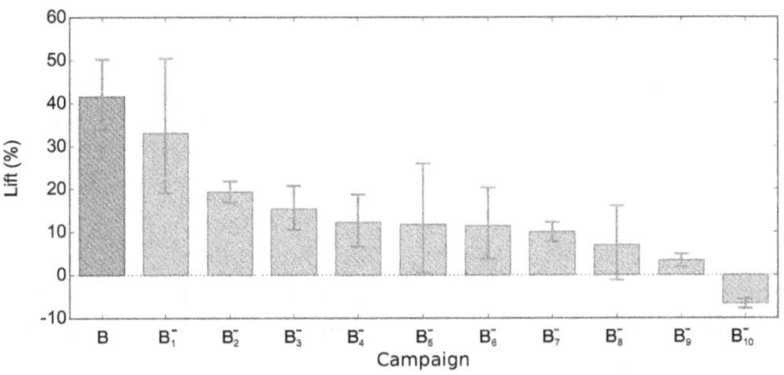

Figure 10: Lift estimated for campaign B's true conversion and several negative controls B_i^- using ad viewability to define treatment.

In total, we had seven campaigns with a combined 60 negative controls. The average absolute effect estimated on the negative controls was 11% ± 8% indicating a modest bias in the viewability analysis. Out of 60 negative controls, 44 showed a significant effect ($p < 0.05$). The most likely explanation for this bias is that ad viewability is not a perfect natural experiment and that there are confounders for the impact of ad viewability on conversion (W' in figure 4). In the next section we proceed to identify and adjust for these confounders.

6. ADJUSTMENT FOR CONFOUNDERS

Confounders are variables that influence both the outcome and the action as described above. A common way to identify such factors is to test for a statistical dependence on a candidate confounder of both the action and outcome. In our case, we are searching for factors X with the properties $M \not\perp X$ and $Y \not\perp X \mid M$. We caution that statistical tests are generally insufficient for identifying a true confounder and that the identification must also rest on true domain knowledge of the system under study [12].

To determine which variables constitute a set of confounders in our new framework, we first identified a set of candidates by drawing on domain knowledge from the online advertising ecosystem. These features are organized into three general categories that encompass user level and campaign level characteristics. A summary of potential confounders is given in table 1. We identified the confounders W' on a campaign-by-campaign basis as those factors that were significantly correlated with both M and Y. This was determined by performing a logistic regression with each factor alone and testing its coefficient for statistical significance ($p < 0.05$).

We adjusted our analysis for these confounders through an extension of our viewability analysis. We continued to use individual impressions as the unit of analysis. The augmented data structure was $O' = (W', A, M, Y) \sim P'$ where the confounders W' have been added while all other variables are as before. The estimation of lift was altered to provide for an adjustment over W'. The equation for the

Category	Description	Examples
Technical	The user's computer setup.	Operating system, browser, screen resolution, aspect ratio
Behavioral	Determined by the user's actions.	Browsing frequency, average viewability for user, previous brand interaction, time of day
Targeting	Parameters of campaign as set by advertiser.	Prospecting or retargeting strategy, average viewability for publisher, targeted web page

Table 1: Summary of potential confounders.

adjusted lift is

$$\begin{aligned}\Phi_{\text{adjusted}}(P') &= \frac{E\{Y \mid M=1, A=1\}}{E\{Y_0 \mid M=1, A=1\}} - 1 \\ &= \frac{p(Y=1 \mid M=1, A=1)}{p(Y_0=1 \mid M=1, A=1)} - 1\end{aligned} \tag{3}$$

where Y_0 indicates whether the outcome would occur if the ad had been unviewable. In the language of causal inference this is a *counterfactual* outcome which can only be identified by performing an adjustment for the confounders W' [12]. This adjustment is given by

$$\begin{aligned}&p(Y_0 = 1 \mid M=1, A=1) \\ &\quad= \sum_{w'} p(Y=1 \mid W'=w', M=0, A=1) \\ &\qquad\quad \times p(W'=w' \mid M=1, A=1) \\ &\quad\approx \frac{1}{N}\sum_{i}^{N} p(Y=1 \mid W'=w'_i, M=0, A=1).\end{aligned} \tag{4}$$

The first equality performs an adjustment over all possible values of the confounder $W' = w'$. The second equality makes an empirical approximation for the distribution of W' among viewable impressions. The final summation is over the N viewable impressions in O' where w'_i represents the confounders of viewability for the ith viewable impression.

To estimate Φ_{adjusted}, we need estimates for the probabilities in the numerator and denominator of equation 3. We estimated the numerator as the empirical probability of conversion among viewable impressions. To estimate the denominator we fit the probability $p(Y = 1|W', M = 0, A = 1)$ with a logistic regression trained on data from unviewable impressions. This model was then substituted into equation 4 and applied to the value of W' for all viewable impressions. Confidence intervals were obtained through 1000 bootstrap samples.

Following our framework, we tested our model on each of the seven campaigns and their corresponding set of negative controls. Both the unadjusted and adjusted viewability model results for campaigns B and G are shown in figure 11. In campaign B, we find the lift on the true conversion, 34% (95% CI, 28%–41%), is larger than that of any of its negative controls. Whereas the unadjusted estimate shows a significant effect ($p < 0.05$) in 9 out of 10 negative controls, this number drops to 4 out of 10 when adjusting for W'. In contrast, the adjusted effect of impressions from campaign G on its true conversion is not significant ($p > 0.05$).

Overall, the average lift across negative controls is -2% suggesting an absence of systematic bias. The average absolute value of the lift estimated for negative controls was $9\% \pm 9\%$ which constitutes only a small decrease when compared to the unadjusted estimate. Out of 60 negative controls, 29 still showed a significant non-zero effect ($p < 0.05$). These results indicate that while adjustment for W' were successful in reducing bias, there is still likely some uncontrolled source of confounding.

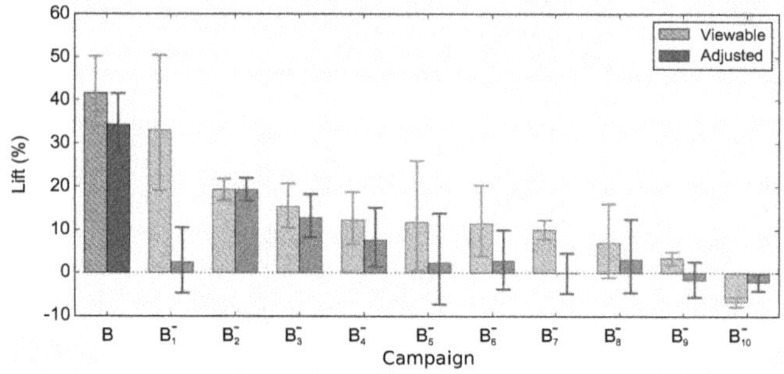

(a) Campaign B

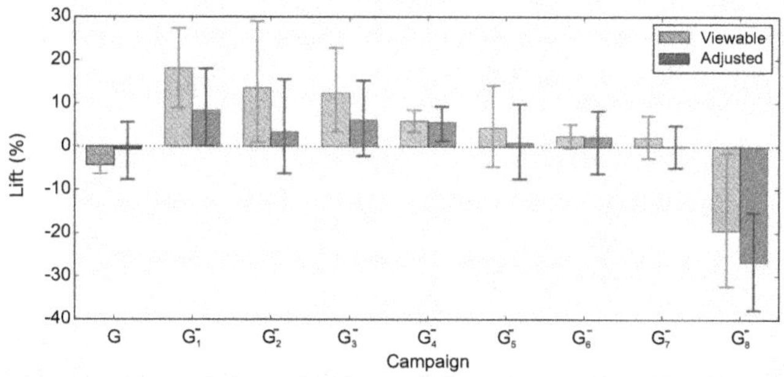

(b) Campaign G

Figure 11: Unadjusted and adjusted lift for campaigns B and G and their corresponding negative controls.

The effect of each campaign on its true conversion is shown in figure 12. Across campaigns we found that the estimate of campaign lift dropped on average from 30% to 10% when adjusting for W'. The adjustment for confounding therefore created substantial revisions in the estimate of lift. The variation in the effect of adjustment on the estimated lift can likely be attributed to large differences in the degree of confounding present in each campaign.

7. DISCUSSION AND CONCLUSION

The results presented above demonstrate that even with intractable confounding, causal estimation is still possible when the effect of an action is mediated through another event. We applied our framework to display advertising where the effect of serving ads is mediated by whether the ad appears in a viewable portion of the user's screen. Despite huge bias in comparing users who receive ads with those who do not, we found a relatively small bias on the order of 10% when comparing the effect of viewable ads to unviewable ones under proper controls. Approximately 50% of display ads are unviewable, so ad viewability represents a perpetual, balanced, and free natural experiment for measuring the impact of ad impressions. An implementation of our analysis has been released in production to monitor the lift of dozens of advertising campaigns on a daily basis. Extensions of this technique are being used to understand the performance of campaigns on a more granular scale, such as different audience segments or targeting strategies.

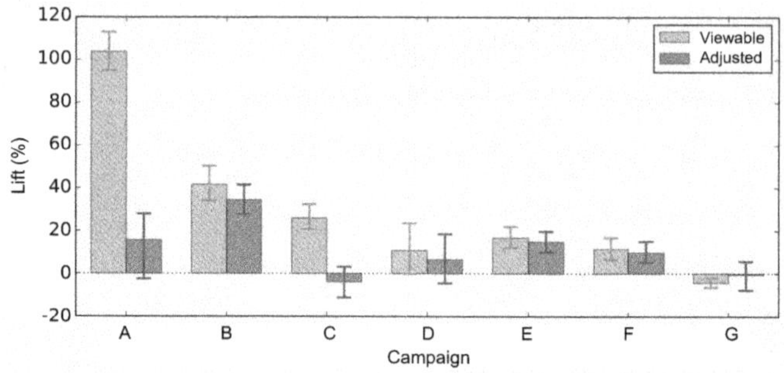

Figure 12: The lift estimates for the campaign's true conversion event when using viewability with and without adjusting for confounding.

We discuss two limitations of our current approach. The first is the assumption that ad impressions can be considered independently from one another. Violations of this assumption may account for some of the residual bias in our analysis. It may be that when a user receives multiple ads from the same campaign that the impressions interact in a non-additive way. Our current research focuses on a *longitudinal* implementation of our viewability analysis [4] in which we consider the evolution of the user's ad experience over the course of the campaign. Second, while we actively collect information related to measuring ad viewability, we do not collect all possible metrics. For example, we do not collect information related to page structure or creative format (*e.g.* static image or animated graphics). With further data mining efforts, other potential confounders can be introduced into our pipeline. The exploration and discovery of these features is the subject of ongoing work.

Our framework has applications beyond advertising as confounding is an almost unavoidable consequence of today's predictive modeling systems. The use of mediating events thus provides an attractive alternative for estimating causal effects when randomized experiments are prohibitive. Companies commonly collect and store an enormous amount of data on their customers. These data could be leveraged to identify causal mediators with minimal additional cost to the company. The instrumentation of mediators has the potential to become a critical step in measuring the performance of automated systems.

8. ACKNOWLEDGMENTS

An earlier version of this work was presented at the Winter Conference on Business Intelligence [11]. We thank Ori Stitelman, Mark van der Laan, Steve Tadelis, Tom Blake, Dominic Coey, Katia Eliseeva, and Gijs Joost Brouwer for useful discussion and suggestions. This work was done while Daniel Hill, Vadim Tsemekhman, and Foster Provost were at Integral Ad Science. Foster Provost thanks Andre Meyer for a Faculty Fellowship.

9. REFERENCES

[1] N. Black. Why we need observational studies to evaluate the effectiveness of health care. *BMJ*, 312(7040):1215–1218, 1996.

[2] T. Blake, C. Nosko, and S. Tadelis. Consumer heterogeneity and paid search effectiveness: A large scale field experiment. Technical report, National Bureau of Economic Research, 2014.

[3] D. Chan, R. Ge, O. Gershony, T. Hesterberg, and D. Lambert. Evaluating online ad campaigns in a pipeline: causal models at scale. In *Proceedings of the 16th ACM SIGKDD international conference on Knowledge discovery and data mining*, pages 7–16. ACM, 2010.

[4] D. Hill, G. J. Brouwer, A. E. Hubbard, and Tsemekhman. It's about time: A longitudinal model for the causal impact of display ads. *Winter Conference on Business Intelligence*, 2014.

[5] D. D. Jensen, A. S. Fast, B. J. Taylor, and M. E. Maier Automatic identification of quasi-experimental designs for discovering causal knowledge. In *Proceedings of the 14th ACM SIGKDD international conference on Knowledge discovery and data mining*, pages 372–380. ACM, 2008.

[6] R. Kohavi, and R. Longbotham. Unexpected results in online controlled experiments. *ACM SIGKDD Explorations Newsletter*, 12(2):31–35, 2011.

[7] A. D. Kramer, J. E. Guillory, and J. T. Hancock. Experimental evidence of massive-scale emotional contagion through social networks. *Proceedings of the National Academy of Sciences*, 111(24):8788–8790, 2014.

[8] R. Lewis and J. M. Rao. The unfavorable economics of measuring the returns to advertising. *Available at SSRN*, 2014.

[9] R. A. Lewis, J. M. Rao, and D. H. Reiley. Here, there, and everywhere: correlated online behaviors can lead to overestimates of the effects of advertising. In *Proceedings of the 20th International Conference on World Wide Web*, pages 157–166. ACM, 2011.

[10] M. Lipsitch, E. T. Tchetgen, and T. Cohen. Negative controls: a tool for detecting confounding and bias in observational studies. *Epidemiology*, 21(3):383–388, 2010.

[11] R. Moakler, V. Tsemekhman, A. Ahuja, D. N. Hill, G. J. Brouwer, F. Provost, and K. Tsemekhman. Causal impact of online advertisements using viewability as a method of treatment. *Winter Conference on Business Intelligence*, 2014.

[12] J. Pearl. *Causality: models, reasoning and inference.* Cambridge University Press, New York, 2000.

[13] C. Perlich, B. Dalessandro, T. Raeder, O. Stitelman, and F. Provost. Machine learning for targeted display advertising: Transfer learning in action. *Machine Learning*, 95(1):103–127, 2014.

[14] M. L. Petersen, K. E. Porter, S. Gruber, Y. Wang, and M. J. van der Laan. Diagnosing and responding to violations in the positivity assumption. *Statistical Methods in Medical Research*, 21(1):31–54, 2012.

[15] O. Stitelman, B. Dalessandro, C. Perlich, and F. Provost. Estimating the effect of online display advertising on browser conversion. *The Fifth International Workshop on Data Mining and Audience Intelligence for Online Advertising at SIGKDD*, 2011.

[16] O. M. Stitelman and M. J. van der Laan. Collaborative targeted maximum likelihood for time to event data. *Int J Biostat*, 6(1):Article 21 2010.

Focusing on the Long-term: It's Good for Users and Business

Henning Hohnhold*
Google, Inc.
Mountain View, CA, USA
henningh@google.com

Deirdre O'Brien*
Google, Inc.
Mountain View, CA, USA
deirdre@google.com

Diane Tang*
Google, Inc.
Mountain View, CA, USA
diane@google.com

ABSTRACT

Over the past 10+ years, online companies large and small have adopted widespread A/B testing as a robust data-based method for evaluating potential product improvements. In online experimentation, it is straightforward to measure the short-term effect, i.e., the impact observed during the experiment. However, the short-term effect is not always predictive of the long-term effect, i.e., the final impact once the product has fully launched and users have changed their behavior in response. Thus, the challenge is how to determine the long-term user impact while still being able to make decisions in a timely manner.

We tackle that challenge in this paper by first developing experiment methodology for quantifying long-term user learning. We then apply this methodology to ads shown on Google search, more specifically, to determine and quantify the drivers of ads blindness and sightedness, the phenomenon of users changing their inherent propensity to click on or interact with ads.

We use these results to create a model that uses metrics measurable in the short-term to predict the long-term. We learn that user satisfaction is paramount: ads blindness and sightedness are driven by the quality of previously viewed or clicked ads, as measured by both ad relevance and landing page quality. Focusing on user satisfaction both ensures happier users but also makes business sense, as our results illustrate. We describe two major applications of our findings: a conceptual change to our search ads auction that further increased the importance of ads quality, and a 50% reduction of the ad load on Google's mobile search interface.

The results presented in this paper are generalizable in two major ways. First, the methodology may be used to quantify user learning effects and to evaluate online experiments in contexts other than ads. Second, the ads blindness / sightedness results indicate that a focus on user satisfaction could help to reduce the ad load on the internet at large with long-term neutral, or even positive, business impact.

*Authors listed alphabetically and contributed equally.

KDD'15, August 10-13, 2015, Sydney, NSW, Australia.
ACM 978-1-4503-3664-2/15/08.
DOI: http://dx.doi.org/10.1145/2783258.2788583.

Categories and Subject Descriptors

G.3 [**Probability and Statistics/Experimental Design**]: controlled experiments; randomized experiments

General Terms

Experimentation; Measurement; Prediction; Management

Keywords

Controlled experiments; A/B testing; predictive modeling; overall evaluation criterion

1. INTRODUCTION

Over the past few years, online experimentation has become a hot topic, with numerous publications and workshops focused on the area and contributions from major internet companies, including Microsoft [12], Amazon [11], eBay [17], Google [18]. There has been a corresponding explosion in online experiments: Microsoft cites running 200+ concurrent experiments [15], Google is running 1000+ concurrent experiments on any day, and start-ups like Optimizely and Sitespect focus on helping smaller companies run and analyze online experiments.

A major discussion in several of those papers has been about developing an OEC (overall evaluation criterion) [12] for online experiments. It has been suggested that OECs should include metrics that reflect an improvement in the long-term (years) rather than metrics that merely optimize for the short-term (days or weeks). In [14], Kohavi et al. show that optimizing for short-term gains may actually be detrimental in the long-term.

We encountered this problem at Google when experimenting with changes to the systems and algorithms that determine which ads show when users search. Optimizing which ads show based on short-term revenue is the obvious and easy thing to do, but may be detrimental in the long-term if user experience is negatively impacted. Since we did not have methods to measure the long-term user impact, we used short-term user satisfaction metrics as a proxy for the long-term impact. When using those user satisfaction metrics, we did not know what trade-off to use between revenue and user satisfaction, so we tended to be conservative, opting for launch variants with strong user experience. The qualitative nature of this approach was unsatisfying: we did not know if we were being too conservative or not conservative enough.

What we needed were metrics to measure the long-term impact of a potential change. However:

- Many of the obvious metrics, such as changes in how often users search, take too long to measure.

- When there are many launches over a short period of time, it can be difficult to attribute long-term metric changes to a particular experiment or launch.
- Attaining sufficient power is a challenge. For both our short- and long-term metrics, we generally care about small changes: even a 0.1% change can be substantive.

It may be due to these and other issues that despite the need for long-term metrics for online experimentation, there has been little published work around how to find or evaluate such long-term metrics.

In this paper, we present an experiment methodology to quantify long-term user learning effects. We show the efficacy of our methods by quantifying both *ads blindness* and *ads sightedness*, i.e., how users' inherent propensity to click on ads changes based on the quality of the ads and the user experience. In addition, we introduce models that predict the long-term effect of an experiment using short-term user satisfaction metrics. This allows us to create a principled OEC that combines revenue and user satisfaction metrics.

We have applied our learnings to numerous launches for search ads on Google. We discuss two examples where, by prioritizing user satisfaction as measured by ads blindness or sightedness, we have changed the auction ranking function [10] and drastically reduced the ad load on the mobile interface. Reducing the mobile ad load strongly improved the user experience but was a substantially short-term revenue negative change; with our work, the long-term revenue impact was shown to be neutral. Thus, with the user satisfaction improvement, this change was a net positive for both business and users.

2. BACKGROUND & RELATED WORK

At Google, and in Google Search Ads in particular, most changes are evaluated via online experiments prior to launch. We have long recognized that optimizing for short-term revenue may be detrimental in the long-term if users learn to ignore the ads, or, even worse, stop using Google. Thus, we have always prioritized **ads quality**, including measurements of both ad relevance and the landing page experience. Our auction ranking algorithm has always been a combination of the advertiser's willingness to pay for a click (bid) and *algorithmically-determined* quality signals, and our measures of ads quality also help determine if an ad is qualified to appear at all [6]. In fact, we do not show ads on most queries, despite having ads targeted to them, because their measures of quality are too low [7].

In the context of serving ads, there are two main situations where trade-offs between ads quality and short-term revenue are made. The first situation occurs when deciding, for a particular query, both whether to show ads at all and what set of ads to show. Broder et al. propose training a classifier that predicts editorial judgments or thresholded click-through-rates and can be used to determine whether to show ads [3]. The second situation occurs when a macro-level decision must be made about whether to launch a change, ranging from how ads are matched to queries to changes in algorithmically-determined quality signals to UI changes. This paper focuses primarily on how to make better decisions in this second situation.

We will not cover the basics (definitions and terminology) of online controlled experimentation, a.k.a. A/B testing, nor the systems to run such experiments. These are adequately covered with ample references elsewhere [12][13][18]. However, we will now define the most relevant terminology and concepts that we use throughout this paper.

Experimental unit is the entity that is randomly assigned to the experiment or the control and presumed to be independent. In this paper, we use a **cookie**, an anonymous id specific to a user's particular browser and computer combination, as our experimental unit. A cookie is an imperfect proxy for a user identifier, and issues that arise from using cookies are discussed in Section 3.3.

We call the set of randomized cookies that we follow over a period of time a **cohort**, which we denote with capital letters, such as E for experiment and C for control. The treatment that a cohort receives is denoted in lower case letters, such as e for the experimental treatment and c for the control treatment; a cohort could be exposed to different treatments at different times, e.g. E might be in treatment e from time 0 to T and then in treatment c.

We use **relative changes** throughout when comparing a metric M in the experiment and control cohorts and define

$$\Delta\mathrm{M} \;=\; \Delta\mathrm{M}(E,C) \;=\; \frac{\mathrm{M}(E)-\mathrm{M}(C)}{\mathrm{M}(C)} \qquad (1)$$

If a measurement is taken at a specific time t we will sometimes make this explicit by writing $\Delta\mathrm{M}(E,C,t)$. Note that all measurements made in this paper are aggregate measurements over a cohort and not on an individual user or cookie. Even when we measure user learning or user satisfaction, those measurements are done over the entire cohort.

An **A/A test**, or uniformity trial, is an experiment where instead of comparing an experimental treatment to a control, two cohorts are exposed to the exact same treatment in order to compare them or their behavior.

User learning was first proposed as Thorndike's Law of Effect [19] and roughly states that positive outcomes reinforce the behavior that caused them and negative outcomes diminish the behavior that caused them. Modeling user learning with statistical models dates back to the 1950's [4][5]. Studies of online behavior associated with user learning have primarily focused on novelty or primacy effects (users being presented with something new and either wanting to explore or needing time to adjust) or change aversion (users simply not liking change).

User learning is rarely studied at scale on large populations, with the exception of [14] that cautions against optimism in online experimentation when seeing novelty / primacy effects by claiming that they rarely, if ever, result in the outcome changing directionality.[1] Kohavi et al. also note that experiments can result in carryover effects, where the treatment from an experiment on a cohort can impact the results from a follow-on experiment on the same cohort. We have independently observed such carryover effects in our systems and our methodology (Section 3) leverages them to study user learning at scale.

In this paper, we focus on a specific user learning effect: **ads blindness and sightedness**, which is when users change how likely they are to click on or interact with ads based on their prior experience with ads. Ads blindness and sightedness have been discussed since banner ads appeared on the web in the late 1990s. In [2], it was shown that users ignore text embedded in rectangular web banners, with location as a primary trigger. Subsequently, increased use of

[1]This is at odds with results we describe in Section 5.

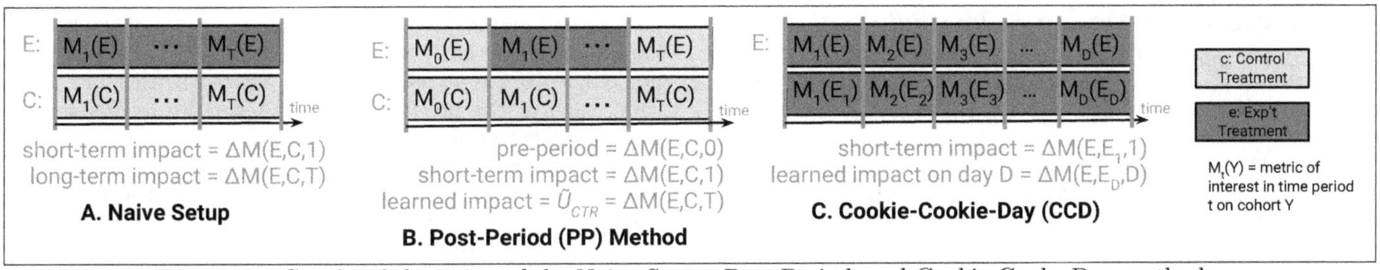

Figure 1: Graphical depiction of the Naive Setup, Post-Period, and Cookie-Cooke-Day methods.

animation was meant to draw user's attention to ads and increase user's rate of ad recognition [1]. A more recent study showed that text ads blindness also occurs, with users skipping sections that were clearly text ads (although sometimes returning later)[16].

All references describe small qualitative studies. Our work, to our knowledge, is the first to quantify, at scale, over millions of users and months of elapsed time, the effect of both ads blindness and sightedness, and apply those results to a large running system, namely Google search, which receives billions of searches per day from hundreds of millions of cookies in 200+ countries across multiple platforms (mobile, tablet, desktop, etc.).

Short-term impact is the measured difference between an experiment and control during the experiment period, typically days or weeks. The **long-term impact** is what would happen if the experiment launched and users received the experiment treatment in perpetuity – in other words, it is the impact in the limit $t \to \infty$. In the context of ads, differences between short- and long-term impact can mainly be attributed to user learning and advertiser response. Here, we focus on measuring and estimating the impact from user learning (the **learned impact**), specifically ads blindness and sightedness. We then approximate the long-term impact as the combination of the short-term and the learned impact.

Long-term revenue is a sensible OEC with an obvious focus on the long-term health of a business. Note that we can decompose revenue into component metrics as follows:

$$\text{Revenue} = \text{Users} \cdot \frac{\text{Tasks}}{\text{User}} \cdot \frac{\text{Queries}}{\text{Task}} \cdot \frac{\text{Ads}}{\text{Query}} \cdot \frac{\text{Clicks}}{\text{Ad}} \cdot \frac{\text{Cost}}{\text{Click}} \quad (2)$$

This decomposition is useful, since it shows us that revenue, measured in the long-term, reflects user satisfaction since users could be:

- So unhappy that users abandon the product altogether (decreased number of users, term 1)
- Unhappy enough to decrease their usage of the product (fewer tasks per user, term 2)
- Sufficiently unhappy that they decrease how often they click on the ads (term 5), as well as which ads they click on (term 6)

The short-term interpretation of (2) suggests that increasing the ad load, i.e., the number of ads per query (term 4), would also increase revenue. One of our main results is that such gains may not persist in the long-term! To see this, first note that in an ad system that aims to show the highest quality ads to users, an increase in ad load usually leads to a decrease in the **click-through rate** (CTR = Clicks/Ad, term 5), even in the short-term. User learning may cause additional decreases in terms 1, 2, and 5 that may more than offset the increase in ad load, leading to reduced revenue in the long-term. In other words, increasing the ad load may increase short-term revenue but decrease long-term revenue since decreased user satisfaction causes ads blindness.

For Google search ads experiments, we have not measured a statistically significant learned effect on terms 1 and 2.[2] Thus, we focus primarily on CTR, i.e., Clicks/Ad.

This discussion motivates the following definition. Consider any system change ('treatment') we may want to launch. *We call the relative change in CTR due to user learning caused by launching the treatment* **Learned CTR**, and we denote it by U_{CTR}. Some remarks:

- This definition does not give U_{CTR} in a computable form. Rather, we imagine the change compared to a counterfactual setting, where no user learning occurs. We explain some of the reasons why U_{CTR} cannot be measured directly in Section 3.3.
- We develop experimental methodology that enables us to measure approximations $\tilde{U}_{CTR}$ of U_{CTR}, e.g., as a percentage change in CTR in an experiment-control setting. We work with relative rather than absolute differences in order to control for the impact of seasonality as well as any system changes that launch during our experiment period.
- It may take months after a launch for the full effect U_{CTR} to develop. We estimate the time it takes for user learning to occur in Section 3.2.1.
- U_{CTR} tells us how users' inherent propensity to click on ads (measured at a population-level) changes due to the treatment. Guided by Thorndike's Law of Effect, we therefore consider U_{CTR} a *user-centric quality metric* (users' response to the treatment reflects their experience). Positive U_{CTR} corresponds to ads sightedness, and negative U_{CTR} to ads blindness.

In addition to describing how to estimate U_{CTR} robustly, we create models that predict U_{CTR} from short-term metrics so that we can predict long-term revenue as our OEC.

3. MEASURING USER LEARNING

Our first goal was to directly measure ads blindness and sightedness. This required new experiment designs and several months to run the experiments. The methodology described in this section is generally applicable for measuring user learning effects, but here we focus on measuring ads blindness and sightedness. We first describe the experimental designs and then lay out our basic ads blindness results. Finally, we discuss why our methodology understates the user learning effects in actual launches.

[2] We suspect the lack of effect is due to our focus on quality and user experience. Experiments on other sites indicate that there can indeed be user learning affecting overall site usage.

3.1 Experiment Design & Methodology

For the experiment methodology, we start with a naive setup before describing two methods, the Post-Period (PP) and the Cookie-Cookie-Day (CCD), that we developed.

3.1.1 Naive Setup

The obvious experiment design is to consider two cookie cohorts, E and C, where E receives some experimental treatment e and C receives a control treatment c, and track their metrics over time. The difference in metrics between E and C at the beginning of the experiment, $t = 1$, is the short-term impact of e, and the difference in metrics between E and C at the end of the experiment, $t = T$, is the long-term impact, including user learning (see Figure 1A). The experiment period will need to last for however long it takes for users to learn, which can be weeks, months, or more.

Unfortunately, even though time is taken to allow for users to learn, this naive setup does not yield reliable user learning measurements. The measured long-term effect at the end of the experiment period may change for many reasons unrelated to user learning: system effects, seasonality, interactions with subsequent launches, etc. Disentangling these effects to measure long-term learning within cohort E over time is, in our experience, very difficult if not impossible.

3.1.2 Post-Period Learning Measurements (PP)

The key insight, in part stemming from observing carry-over effects from prior experiments, is that to measure user learning, we need to compare the two cohorts, E and C, while they receive the same treatment.

To achieve this, we sandwich the treatment period between two A/A test periods: a *pre-period*, where we ensure that there are no statistically significant differences between the cohorts when the study starts[3], and a *post-period* (PP), where any behavioral differences due to user learning are measured. For the purposes of quantifying user learning, the behavior of E while receiving treatment e is not of interest – only the post-period measurement matters (see Figure 1B). Since E and C receive the same treatment in the post-period, differences between the metrics of the two cohorts in the PP can be ascribed to user behavior changes, i.e., to learning that occurred during the treatment period.

In this way, we obtain PP user learning measurements $\tilde{U}^{PP}_{CTR} = \Delta\text{CTR}(E, C, T)$. We give examples in Section 3.2.1. Post-periods have proven to give reliable and reproducible user learning measurements at Google. Nevertheless, there are some caveats and limitations we want to point out.

Ensuring valid measurements. In practice, it may happen that despite receiving the same treatment, E and C do not experience identical serving in the PP due to personalization or other long-term features.[4] In order to ensure a valid learning measurement, one needs to confirm that metrics that should be unaffected by user behavior changes, such as ads per query or the average predicted ad CTR, are consistent across E and C.

Also note that the measurement environment c of the post-period may affect the magnitude or nature of the learning effects observed. As a basic example, if e adds a great new UI feature that users learn to interact with more over time, we will not be able to observe this in a post-period serving c where the feature is absent.

Unlearning. Since both E and C receive the same treatment in the PP, their behavior will become more similar over time, that is, *unlearning* will occur. Thus, our measurement would ideally be taken in a brief period right at the beginning of the PP. However, for a given experiment size, we can increase statistical power by taking the measurement over a longer period of time. The price to pay is measurement bias introduced by unlearning. This bias can be corrected based on (un)learning rates, see Section 3.2.1.

Cookie churn. Cookie churn occurs when users reset or clear their cookies, leading to random movement between experiments. Including new cookies in the experiment and control dilutes the user learning effect measured. This issue can be addressed by restricting the measurement to cookies that were created before the start of the experiment. Note that restricting to old cookies may introduce bias.

Experiment sizing. To ensure that our studies are adequately powered, we use the best practices enshrined in the experiment sizing tool described in [18]. As noted there, using cookies as the experimental unit requires larger sizes than experiments that divert on individual query events, since one has to account for the non-independence of queries coming from the same cookies over time.

Unlearning and cookie churn also affect the statistical power of the experiments. We studied the cookie age distribution to allow us to estimate the number of cookies that would be lost from the post-period comparison because of cookie churn and to scale up the size of E and C as needed.

Intermediate measurements and lagged-starts. One serious disadvantage of the PP method is that the learning measurement is taken *after* the treatment period, i.e., the measurement requires ending the treatment period. No preliminary measurements of learning are obtained along the way. This can be problematic since the required length of the treatment period can depend on the treatment studied and may not be known in advance.[5]

One way of obtaining a preliminary measurement is by adding an extra **lagged-start** cohort E_1. We keep E_1 in the control treatment c while E already receives the experimental treatment e until we want to take a learning measurement, say at time T_1. At T_1 we switch E_1 from c to e. We can now obtain a user learning measurement $\tilde{U}^{LS}_{CTR} = \Delta\text{CTR}(E, E_1, T_1)$ by comparing E, which was exposed to e, to E_1, which was previously exposed to c.

The important point here is that, as in the PP method, the learning measurement is taken when the two cohorts receive the same treatment (here the experiment treatment e). Note that taking this lagged-start measurement does *not* require ending the treatment period of E. We can take several lagged-start measurements during the treatment period, but each additional measurement will require its own lagged-start cohort E_1, E_2, etc.

3.1.3 The Cookie–Cookie-Day Method (CCD)

This method is derived from the idea of continuously tak-

[3]Running a pre-period is good practice for all experiments and not just for measuring user learning.

[4]The problem is typically that the treatments c and e change the distribution of cookie-level long-term features in C and E. These differences may cause C and E to receive systematically different serving even under the same treatment c. Examples of such long-term features are remarketing lists or mute-this-ad data. Care should be taken to minimize such feedback if the goal is to measure user learning.

[5]In Section 3.2.1, we will describe an approach to determine appropriate treatment period durations, but such prior information is not always available.

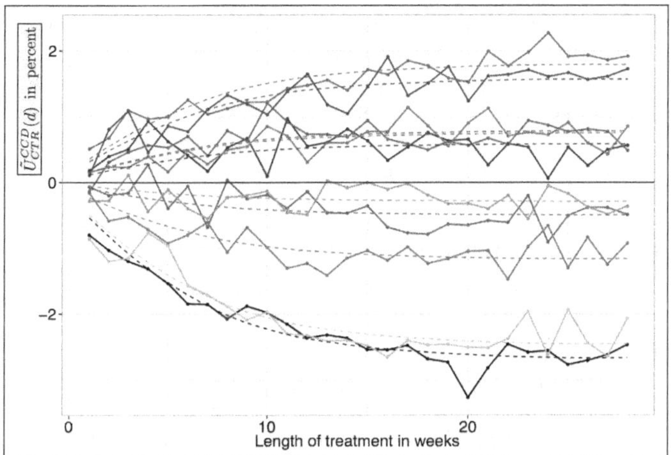

Figure 2: $\tilde{U}^{CCD}_{CTR}(d)$ for a grid of 10 different system parameter changes for mobile devices. The dashed lines give a simple exponential learning model, see Equation (4).

ing lagged-start measurements in order to track user learning while it happens. In fact, we construct *daily measurements* by essentially using a different lagged-start cohort for every treatment day.

Cookie-day experiments. We obtain such cohorts by using an experimental unit that is a combination of the cookie and the date, so that cookies are re-randomized into experiments daily. Experiments based on such experimental units are called *cookie-day experiments.*

In practice, we start with a large pool of cookies, and on each day we randomly assign a fraction of these cookies to the experiment. If the cookie pool is sufficiently large, each cookie will only be assigned to the experiment on very few days so that, in essence, we treat a different cookie cohort on any given day. In particular, each cookie will not receive consistent enough exposure to the experiment treatment to accumulate any learned effect.

The Cookie–Cookie-Day comparison. In the Cookie–Cookie-Day (CCD) method, we compare cookie and cookie-day experiments receiving the same treatment e.[6] In the cookie experiment, cohort E receives the treatment e every day and experiences user learning. In parallel, we run a cookie-day experiment where a different cohort E_d is exposed to e on any given day d. On all other days, E_d receives the control treatment c.[7] As in the lagged-start setting, user learning can be measured on day d by comparing the metrics of E to E_d: this is the CCD comparison (see Figure 1C).

The main advantage of CCD is that learning can be tracked continuously while it is happening: the daily measurements $\tilde{U}^{CCD}_{CTR}(d) = \Delta\text{CTR}(E, E_d, d)$ fit together to yield a time series describing learning over time. This can help inform the length of the study: if learning is still going strong, one might want to extend the experiments, whereas if no effect

[6]Within a single layer, for those familiar with the Overlapping Experiments framework [18].

[7]In our actual implementation, in order to manage experiment traffic more efficiently, the cookie-day cohorts E_d may not receive c on every day $d' \neq d$. Rather, they see a mix of treatments that, on average, is very similar to c and so the learning effects are approximately the same. We usually also run a cookie-day version of the control (on day d cohort C_d will get the the control treatment); by comparing C_d to a control cookie cohort C we can check that cookies in the cookie-day space do not accumulate a learned effect.

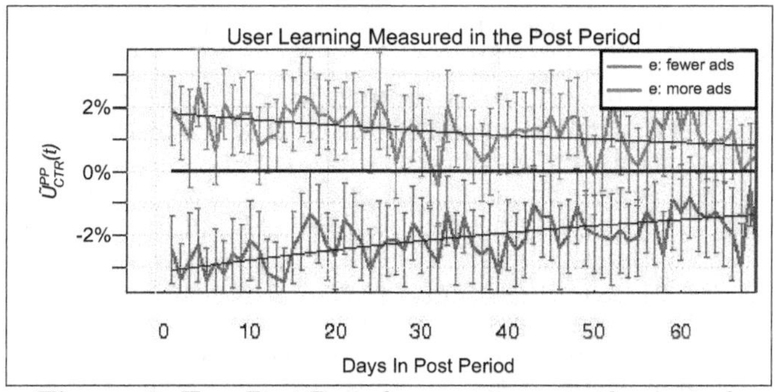

Figure 3: Two Post-Period comparisons to the control.

is visible after two months, chances may be slim to observe anything even when running longer. The time series of learning measurement can also be useful in estimating learning rates and detecting issues in the experiment set-up.

Another upside of CCD is that learning can be measured over a longer period of time than in the PP method since unlearning is not a concern. Such extended measurement periods can significantly reduce noise. The main disadvantages of CCD are the increased infrastructure complexity and the need for a large cookie pool that provides traffic for the cookie-day experiment.

To illustrate the efficacy of the CCD method, Figure 2 shows a time series of learned changes in CTR, i.e. $\tilde{U}^{CCD}_{CTR}(d)$, for a grid of ten settings of a system parameter over six months, along with exponential trends fit to the data.

As a *best practice*, we recommend combining both methods: run a CCD setup and also take a PP measurement on the cookie cohort E after the treatment period is over. We have generally found the measurements $\tilde{U}^{PP}_{CTR}$, $\tilde{U}^{LS}_{CTR}$, and $\tilde{U}^{CCD}_{CTR}$ to produce consistent results.

3.2 Ads Blindness Studies

Since 2007, we have run hundreds of experiments to quantify ads blindness and sightedness. The main output from this work is an OEC that depends only on short-term metrics but predicts the long-term impact (see Section 4). Using this OEC to make launch decisions has improved the ads we show to users. Here we summarize some of the major steps in collecting the data necessary to build these models.

3.2.1 Initial Experiments

The goal of our initial user learning experiments was to explore the magnitude of treatments needed to induce measurable learning effects and to see how long learning takes. These experiments were run before we developed the CCD method, so we used a combination of the PP and lagged-start methods to obtain user learning measurements.

We used two different experimental treatments. One treatment increased the ad load, and the other reduced it. Since we are always trying to show the best ads to our users, any additional ads will have slightly lower quality so that the average quality of ads decreases as the ad load increases. In particular, these treatments conflate ads quality and ad load, something we tried to disentangle in later experiments.

Ads blindness can be measured. This basic result can be seen in Figure 3, which shows the relative change in CTR of the cohorts exposed to the two treatments relative to the control cohort in the post-period. Showing fewer but higher quality ads resulted in ads sightedness (positive

$\tilde{U}^{PP}_{CTR}$); showing more but lower quality ads resulted in ads blindness (negative $\tilde{U}^{PP}_{CTR}$).

User learning takes a long time. A more subtle goal of the initial experiments was to quantify the time period needed for user learning to occur, i.e., determining when the user learning impact on CTR (the change in users' click propensity) would plateau. We used repeated lagged-start measurements to verify that the learned effects still increased, even after many weeks of treatment. In other words, *user learning takes a long time to converge.*

A simple learning model. As mentioned in the discussion in Section 3.1.2, PP measurements are, in practice, taken over an extended period of time. This yields a time series $\tilde{U}^{PP}_{CTR}(t) = \Delta\text{CTR}(E, C, t)$ for $t \geq T$ as in Figure 3.

In order to obtain a quantitative result on the pace of user learning, we fit a simple exponential curve to model $\tilde{U}^{PP}_{CTR}(t)$ (effectively modeling unlearning rather than learning)[8]:

$$\tilde{U}^{PP}_{CTR}(t) = \alpha \cdot e^{-\beta \cdot (t-T)} \quad \text{for } t \geq T \tag{3}$$

Here α estimates the magnitude of learning at the beginning of the post-period T, and β is the (un)learning rate. We assumed a constant learning rate β across different treatments but α was assumed to be treatment dependent (and is the focus of the modeling discussed in Section 4).

The half-life of learning $ln(2)/\beta$ was approximately 60 days (see Figure 3), or $\beta \approx 0.012$ per day. This learning rate was later validated in a CCD study, where we modeled

$$\tilde{U}^{CCD}_{CTR}(t) = \alpha' \cdot (1 - e^{-\beta \cdot t}) \quad \text{for } t \geq 0 \tag{4}$$

with α' estimating the magnitude of learning we would measure in a very long study ($t \to \infty$).[9]

In this section, we have considered learning rates as a function of time. We explored alternatives, such as considering them as a function of the number of user interactions (e.g., searches issued or ads viewed). However, we use time for convenience as it allows us to aggregate all users' activities across a day and do all analysis in this aggregated space.

Standard ads blindness studies. Based on the learning rate estimate $\beta \approx 0.012$, we now typically run long-term desktop experiments for 90 days, which gives a reasonable trade-off between study run-times and captured learning effects. According to (4), the learning observed after 90 days is approximately $1 - e^{-0.012 \cdot 90} = 65\%$ of the learning effect we would see in a very long experiment.[10]

In the following sections, we denote by $\tilde{U}_{CTR}$ ads blindness or sightedness measurements taken in 'standard studies' lasting about 3 months. These may be PP, lagged-start, or CCD measurements.

Note that we can also apply the model (3) to understand the bias in PP measurements due to unlearning. Assume we take the measurement in the first two weeks of the post-period and that each day contains the same amount of data. Then unlearning reduces the effect observed over the 14 days of the measurement to $\frac{1}{14}\sum_{j=1}^{14} \exp(-0.012 \cdot j) = 92\%$.

Hence $\tilde{U}_{CTR}$ measured in the first 14 days of a post-period in a standard learning study is $65\% \cdot 92\% \approx 60\%$ of the effect observed in a very long running study (on desktop).

[8]We also used learning data from lagged-start measurements to fit these models, but do not discuss this here for simplicity.

[9]The exponential trends for the mobile study in Figure 2 were obtained in the same way.

[10]The learning rate may depend on the treatment, e.g., the triggering rate of a feature, but we have found these results to hold for a reasonable variety of system changes.

3.2.2 *The Dropping Study*

While the initial study verified the existence and quantified the rate of user learning for ads blindness and sightedness, we were dissatisfied with the conflation of ads quality and ad load. To address this issue, we devised our next set of experiments, in 2010, to explicitly control the quality of the shown ads. Specifically, we divided the ads into tiers by their ads quality scores. We then ran PP method experiments with the following treatments:

- e: Increase the ad load, with the same conflation of ads quality and ad load as above.
- $e_1, ..., e_n$: We want these treatments to have the same ad load as c but different ads quality. We achieve this through a series of system manipulations. We first increase the ad load and then reduce it back to the level of c by dropping ads from a specific quality tier $i = 1, ..., n$. The ads quality of e_i decreases as i increases.
- e': Same as for e_i, in that we increase the ad load to the same level as e, but we then drop ads uniformly across all quality tiers to achieve the same ad load as c but with an average ads quality comparable to e.

Bringing the corresponding cookie cohorts E, E_1, ... , E_n, E' to post-period, we could determine if quantity was the driver (in which case $\tilde{U}_{CTR}(E, C)$ would be more negative than $\tilde{U}_{CTR}(E', C)$), or if quality was the driver (the effect of E_1, where we dropped the highest quality ads, would be more negative than that of E_2, which would be more than E_3, etc., and E' would be somewhere in the middle).

Our results showed that cohorts that experienced higher ad quality than the control during the treatment had positive $\tilde{U}^{PP}_{CTR}$ (ads sightedness) and that cohorts exposed to lower quality had negative $\tilde{U}^{PP}_{CTR}$ (ads blindness). We did not measure a significant learning effect in the post-period comparison of E and E', $\tilde{U}_{CTR}(E', E)$. Therefore we concluded that ads quality is the main driver of user learning.

Note, however, that in practice ad load *does* matter since it is correlated with ads quality in systems that strive to show the best possible ads to users.

3.2.3 *Subsequent Experiments*

The initial experiments and the dropping study provided our first models for understanding ads blindness and sightedness: the rate of learning, the magnitude of the long-term effects relative to the short-term impact, and the main drivers behind the effect. Over the last eight years, we have run hundreds of long-term experiments to increase our understanding, especially regarding the drivers of user learning. We designed learning studies to address specific questions, such as: Does the type of task matter? How does ad relevance differ from landing page quality in driving the magnitude of the effect? How do UI changes impact user learning?

These studies allowed us to improve the algorithms that select the best ads to show to users. In Section 4, we use data from these experiments to predict the magnitude of ads blindness or sightedness from short-term metrics.

3.3 Underestimation of Results

In this section, we discuss why the PP and CCD methods both yield systematic underestimates of true long-term user learning effect U_{CTR}. By this, we mean that if we launched a treatment to all users, the user learning effect would be larger than the effect $\tilde{U}_{CTR}$ we measure in our experiments.

How severely our measurements underestimate user learning is difficult to estimate since learning is not just a function of time, but also a function of the number, frequency, and consistency of exposure to the treatment.

Number and frequency of exposure. Intensity of exposure to the treatment affects the learning rate. For example, the β derived in Section 3.2.1 depends on how often users search on Google and on how often ads show on their queries. Measuring learning for features that show on more queries than ads can be done using shorter treatment periods (for changes that impact every search results page, we estimate that half the learning has happened after 14-21 days). Conversely, learning on features that show less often than ads may take a lot longer, to the point of being impossible to measure.

Even for ad-centric studies, the learning rates may vary. For example, learning induced by an ad format with low triggering rate or a subtle UI change might take a long time to materialize. Due to this uncertainty, using the CCD methodology to measure learning in real-time is helpful.

Treatment inconsistency. The bigger issue is that cookies are a poor proxy for users. A cookie is simply an anonymous id attached to a browser and a device. Users can clear their cookies whenever they want, and they frequently use multiple devices and multiple browsers. Thus, any learning measured from a cookie-based experiment is diluted since a user is likely seeing non-experiment treatments on other browsers: there is less *consistency* in an experiment than there is when the change is launched. Using a signed-in id may seem to mitigate this issue, but users can have multiple sign-ins and many searches are conducted while signed-out.

Accounting for underestimation. In the discussion of OECs in Section 4.4 below, we want to be explicit about the distinction between user learning when a treatment is launched (U_{CTR}) and the potentially weaker learning effect $\tilde{U}_{CTR}$ we observe in standard PP or CCD measurements. To this end, we introduce a 'fudge factor' Q defined by

$$U_{CTR} \ = \ Q \cdot \tilde{U}_{CTR}. \tag{5}$$

Since the user learning measurement methods we presented here underestimate learning, we have $Q \geq 1$. Both number and frequency of exposures and consistency issues contribute to Q. As a result, Q depends on our decision to run long term experiments for 90 days and, since treatment consistency differs by platform, it also differs by device type.

How large is Q? Generally, this is a difficult question to answer. The exponential learning model from Section 3.2.1 implies that in a 90-day study we would only measure about 65% of the long-term effect simply due to the limited study duration, not even accounting for lack of treatment consistency. Hence we have $Q \geq 1/0.65 = 1.54$ for a standard learning measurement in a desktop study. In practice, we often use values of Q between 2 and 3 for desktop and laptop devices in order to also compensate for treatment inconsistency. This range, though only a rough estimate, has been supported by a study considering learning effects of cohorts of cookies with very high treatment exposure.

Our exponential models for mobile (not discussed here, but observable in Figure 2) suggest that learning is faster on smartphones, and we also believe the consistency issue to be less severe. As a result, we think Q is closer to 1 for mobile and have, in fact, often assumed the minimal possible value $Q = 1$ in this case.

Other sources of user behavior changes. In this section, we have been concerned with underestimates of learning arising from low treatment dose and an imperfect relationship between cookies and users. However, there are factors affecting long-term user behavior on Google search that cannot be captured in experiments at all. For example, perception of poor ads quality may be amplified by word-of-mouth or negative press reports.

4. PREDICTING ADS BLINDNESS

Thus far, we have discussed how to measure user learning in long-term experiments. Now we tackle the issue of predicting the ads blindness or sightedness effect rather than waiting for months to measure it. The simple exponential models we fit in Section 3.2.1 gave us the time that we would have to wait, but not the magnitude of the effects. In order to apply ads blindness to day-to-day decisions, we need to be able to take the short-term measurements and use them to predict the magnitude of the long-term effect.

We now present models doing precisely this. We call them *macro-models* since they make predictions at the population level. To create these models, we use the results from more than 100 long-term ads blindness experiments, collected over several years, that test a range of changes, from new prediction algorithms to optimizing system parameters to changing the keyword matching algorithms and more.

Since all data considered here is from PP or CCD studies, we use $\tilde{U}_{CTR}$ as the user learning metric our models predict (response). The model covariates (predictors) are short-term treatment metrics, i.e. the instantaneous metric changes observed when the treatment is applied in a short-term experiment. In the notation of Figure 1, covariates are defined by $\Delta\mathrm{M} = \Delta\mathrm{M}(E, C, 1)$, for suitable metrics M.

Thus, all metrics on the right-hand side of the models below are short-term quantities that are easy to measure in a standard A/B experiment setup, whereas the left-hand side is the long-term user behavior change we are predicting. All equations below are dimensionless as all metrics are relative changes between experiment and control.

4.1 Ad-Load-based Models

The change in ad load is a good linear predictor for the resulting change in user clickiness when the treatment is just a simple ad load change, as in the initial experiments described in Section 3.2.1 or similar follow-up studies. This is expressed succinctly by the macro model

$$\tilde{U}_{CTR} \ \approx \ -k \cdot \Delta\mathrm{AdLoad} \tag{6}$$

with $k > 0$. This model states that showing more ads results in ads blindness, i.e., a decrease in users' propensity to click on ads. We have observed the relationship (6) for ad load changes of moderate magnitude in various settings (different sites or device types) but with varying values of k.

However, (6) *only* applies to simple ad load changes where ad load and ads quality are directly (negatively) correlated, as in our original experiments. While the applicability of (6) is thus restricted to a small set of treatments, it has nevertheless proven useful (e.g., the mobile example in Section 5).

4.2 Quality-based Models

As discovered in the experiments described in Section 3.2.2, the main driver of ads blindness is the ads quality rather than the ad load. Given those findings, our subsequent and

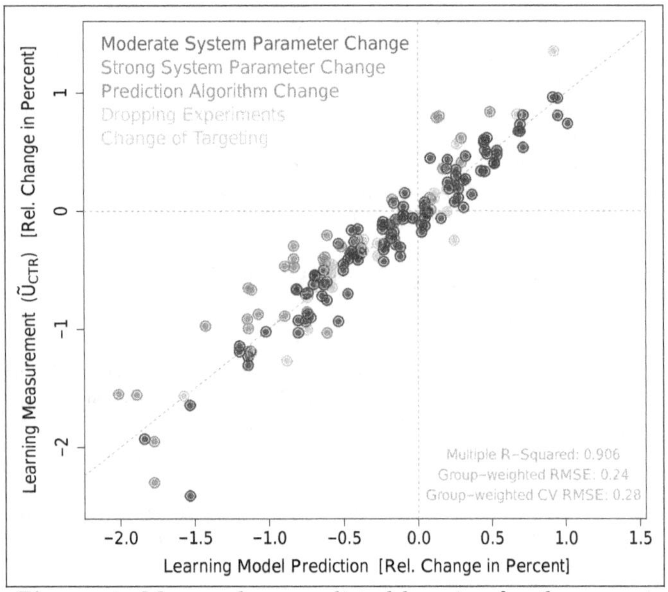

Figure 4: Measured vs. predicted learning for the current desktop macro-model.

more generally applicable macro-models used ads quality-based metrics rather than ad load-based metrics.

Many of these models are of the form

$$\tilde{U}_{CTR} \approx k_1 \cdot \Delta\text{AdRelevance} + k_2 \cdot \Delta\text{LandingPageQuality} \quad (7)$$

with k_1, $k_2 > 0$. The interpretation of (7) is intuitive: better AdRelevance and/or LandingPageQuality increase user engagement with ads. While the form of (7) has been consistent over the last few years, our definitions of the AdRelevance and LandingPageQuality metrics used in the model have evolved over time. The simplest example of an AdRelevance metric is CTR. LandingPageQuality metrics are generally more complex and consider the actual content and experience of the landing site [8].

In our experience, good macro-models require both an ad relevance and landing page quality term: we have not found satisfactory single variable blindness models. In particular, we have found that AdRelevance alone is insufficient to characterize ads quality and that user satisfaction after a click is also very important. This makes sense: if an ad looked good but the user had a horrible experience after the click, the user will remember the bad experience on the landing page and the propensity of future ad clicks decreases.

We have found that ads-quality-based models such as (7) capture ads blindness and sightedness reasonably well for a wide variety of non-UI manipulations such as ad load, ranking function, and prediction algorithm changes. This can be seen in Figure 4, which plots predictions from our current desktop macro-model against the actual measurements $\tilde{U}_{CTR}$ for the 170 observations used to fit the model. We have a similar model for the mobile interface of Google search.

4.3 Remarks on Methodology

The macro-models given above are simple linear models, with weights according to measurement precision. The main reason to stick to such simple models is interpretability. We considered using larger predictor sets and regularization, but the gains in prediction accuracy were rather modest and not worth giving up models with well-understood semantics. Naturally, such simple linear models can only cover a limited range of serving configurations, but we have found their validity to be pretty broad in practice.

Our models were evaluated using cross-validation, with cross-validation folds being manually chosen groups of similar experiments. This was done to avoid overfitting, which is a huge concern given the small sample size.

Another requirement imposed on more general models was that prediction accuracy on simple experiments should not be worse than that of very plain models, such as (6), known to work well in certain cases. The most important criterion for our models is, of course, their prediction accuracy on new data, and we continually validate our models by comparing predictions against measurements in new studies.

The models given here are specific to Google search. Nevertheless, we expect the fundamental principle to apply in other contexts: quality drives user interaction, and suitable user experience signals can be used to predict changes in user engagement (e.g., click-through or page visit rates).

4.4 Long-term Impact and OECs

4.4.1 *Approximations of Learned RPM*

The change of user engagement with ads, as captured by the quality metric U_{CTR}, alters the revenue impact of a system change in the weeks and months after its launch. Analogous to the definition of U_{CTR}, we define U_{RPM} to be the relative change in RPM (revenue per 1000 queries) due to user learning caused by the launched treatment.[11]

If a change in users' propensity to click on ads is the only user learning effect we observe, which is often the case on Google search, then

$$U_{RPM} \approx U_{CTR} . \quad (8)$$

This can be seen from the revenue decomposition (2). For example, if CTR decreases by 1%, then so does revenue. The right-hand side of (8) can be expressed as $Q \cdot \tilde{U}_{CTR}$ via (5), and computed using the models from Sections 4.1/4.2.

When revenue is generated from several segments of ads, one needs to use

$$U_{RPM} \approx Q \cdot \sum_i w_i \cdot \tilde{U}_{CTR,\,i} \quad (9)$$

where we measure $\tilde{U}_{CTR,\,i}$ separately for different segments i, and w_i gives the revenue fraction in the segment. The different segments reflect differences in Learned CTR or major differences in click costs. Cases where this segmentation is particularly important include ad location on the page and geography, where the bids can differ, either due to standards of living, currency exchange, or the number of advertisers.

These approximations of U_{RPM} are needed since measuring $\tilde{U}_{RPM}$ directly in a long-term study is often impossible due to statistical noise.

4.4.2 *Longterm RPM*

We often combine the instantaneous revenue change of a treatment, $\Delta\text{RPM} = \Delta\text{RPM}(E, C, 1)$, and the RPM change due to user learning U_{RPM} into a single long-term metric

$$LT_{RPM} = \Delta\text{RPM} + U_{RPM} . \quad (10)$$

[11] We can use RPM instead of revenue since we have not measured changes in the first three terms of (2).

LT_{RPM} aims to approximate the long-term revenue impact of a launch.[12] The interpretation of (10) is straightforward: the expected long-term RPM effect is given by the observed instantaneous revenue change plus a correction term that expresses how user behavior changes will alter RPM post-launch. Note that (10) defines an OEC that focuses on long-term business health, given that, for Google search, we did not see changes in the first 3 terms of (2) in Section 2.

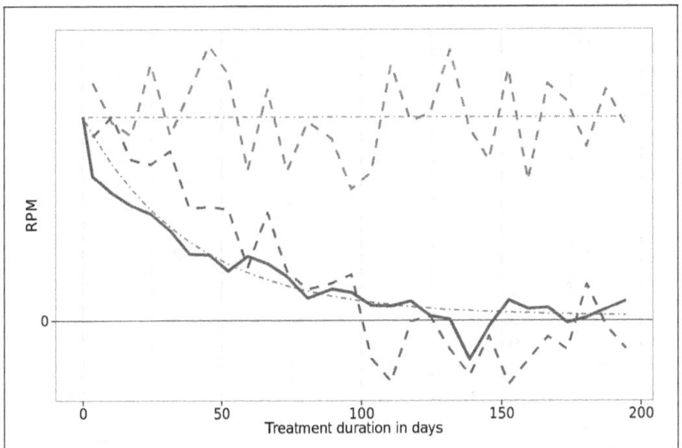

Figure 5: Short-term (pink) and long-term (blue) ΔRPM metrics for simple ad load changes on mobile Google search, restricted to old cookies, 6/26/2013 – 1/9/2014.

Using the approximation (8), we obtain:

$$LT_{RPM} \;=\; \Delta\text{RPM} \;+\; Q \cdot \tilde{U}_{CTR} \qquad (11)$$

Recall that our macro-models allow us to express $\tilde{U}_{CTR}$ in terms of short-term metrics. Thus (11), together with our macro-models, solves the problem of defining an OEC with emphasis on the long-term that can be readily computed from short-term metric measurements, which was our original goal.[13] The two summands in the OEC (11) express that long-term business health depends both on creating revenue *and* providing a good user experience. An obvious aspect missing in (11) is *advertiser value*, which we currently verify through separate metrics. Building an OEC that reflects the launch impact on Google, users, *and* advertisers is an active area of research at Google.

5. APPLICATIONS OF ADS BLINDNESS

Ultimately, the success of our work is measured by whether we improved user satisfaction and affected decision-making for search ads on Google. The answer is unequivocally yes! Understanding ads blindness (Section 3) has changed the nature of the discussions around evaluating changes. We have used the models discussed in Section 4 to predict the long-term impact of experimental treatments to support or reject potential changes. Here are two specific examples.

Ranking function change. In October 2011, our ads blindness work drove a change in the quality score used in the auction ranking function that emphasizes the landing page experience more [10]. We ran numerous studies to understand the long-term impact of the proposed (and ultimately launched) change as well as to validate our prior learnings. While we had taken the identified metrics from Section 4 into account for our OEC prior to this launch, this launch was when we really moved to using what we learned about ads blindness to impact per-query decisions.

[12] The 'long-term revenue impact of a launch' is the relative difference in revenue (a sufficiently long time period after the launch), compared to the counterfactual scenario where the launch did not happen.

[13] For treatments where our macro-models do not work, we often fall back to measuring $\tilde{U}_{CTR}$ directly in a blindness study. This is cumbersome but sometimes necessary.

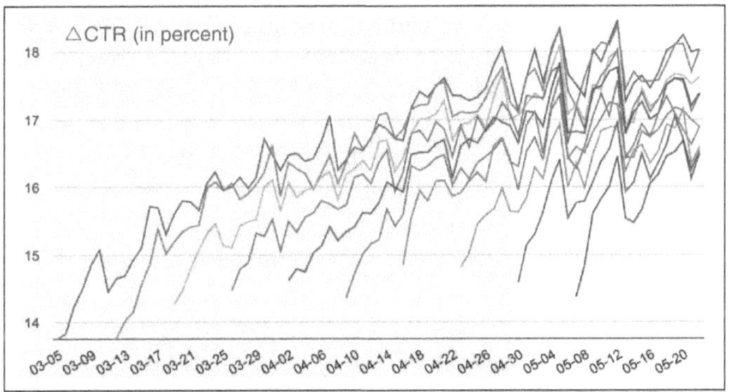

Figure 6: ΔCTR time series for different user cohorts in the launch. (The launch was staggered by weekly cohort.)

Mobile ad load. In another example, our experiments were used to determine the appropriate ad load for searches on Google from mobile devices.

In 2013 we ran experiments that changed the ad load on mobile devices, similar to the experiments described in Section 3. Figure 5 shows results for an experiment that increased the ad load. The dashed lines give weekly RPM measurements for the cookie-day (pink, includes no user learning) and the cookie (blue, reflects learning) experiments of the study. The thinner horizontal pink line gives the cookie-day average: this is the short-term RPM change ΔRPM. The solid blue line gives $\Delta\text{RPM} + \tilde{U}_{CTR}(d)$, which approximates LT_{RPM} (with $Q = 1$) as d gets large. It hugs a smooth curve based on a simple exponential learning model as described in Section 3.2.1. Since the blue curves settle near 0 as the study runs longer, the long-term revenue estimate LT_{RPM} for this treatment is essentially zero – in stark contrast to the significant short-term RPM gains – even under the idealized assumption of complete treatment consistency ($Q = 1$). In reality, the increased ads load is likely long-term negative at the state of the system during the study.

This and similar ads blindness studies led to a sequence of launches that **decreased** the search ad load on Google's mobile traffic by 50%, resulting in dramatic gains in user experience metrics. We estimated that the positive user response would be so great that the long-term revenue change would be a net positive. One of these launches was rolled out over ten weeks to 10% cohorts of traffic per week. Figure 6 shows the relative change in CTR for different cohorts relative to a holdback. Each curve starts at one point, representing the instantaneous quality gains, and climbs higher post-launch due to user sightedness. Differences between the cohorts represent positive user learning, i.e., ads sightedness.

6. CONCLUSIONS & FUTURE WORK

In this paper, we have presented experimental methodology for quantifying long-term user learning and modeling methodology that uses the experimental results to identify which short-term metrics best predict the long-term user-learning impact.

We have applied these methodologies to a concrete use

case, ads blindness and sightedness, and shown that users do in fact change their interaction rate with ads based on the quality of the ads they see and click on. These studies have been highly impactful:

- We created a frequently used OEC that accounts for both short-term and long-term impact.
- They were fundamental to a major conceptual change to our search ads auction that emphasizes landing page experience more.
- Launches that reduced the ad load on the Google search mobile interface by 50% were driven by our results.

Work beyond the scope of this paper includes the application of this methodology to sites other than Google search pages – both search pages on other sites as well as non-search-based interfaces (e.g., YouTube, display ads). One challenge is how to handle the increased heterogeneity of the sites in the modeling. That said, some initial results on other search sites with substantially higher ad load and lower quality are quite promising, with results even stronger than those discussed in Section 5, including impact to query volume and other terms in (2). We have communicated the results of these experiments to several partners, who have reduced their ad load and increased the quality, leading to positive long-term results for users and their business.

We have also applied this methodology to user learning beyond ads, specifically for experiments on bolding and labeling changes on the search results page, as well as other features such as Google Shopping.

We continue to work on better estimates for the correction factor Q. Also, our current models are based solely on (and applicable to) non-UI changes. The key challenge with integrating UI changes is that we have not identified metrics that appropriately capture the impact of UI changes on user experience and could serve as predictors in our model.

Finally, the models we describe in Section 4 predict a population-level learned ads blindness response that can be used at a macro-level, e.g., for launch decisions or validating quality metrics. We are working on "nano-models" that aim to predict the blindness cost of individual ad impressions, i.e., the future revenue loss (or gain) caused by showing an ad to the user. However, these models are substantially more difficult than the macro-models we have presented due to the sparse data available at the impression level and because this problem requires inference from observational data, lacking the clean randomization of an experiment-control setup.

Acknowledgments. Jean Steiner contributed greatly to the experiments and analysis described in Section 3.2.2. Ryan Giordano was a major contributor to ads blindness modeling and in particular the considerations described in Section 3.3. Marc Berndl and Ted Baltz designed and implemented many blindness experiments and drove the auction change launch described in Section 5 (Ted was also critical for the mobile changes), and with Rehan Khan and Bill Heavlin were instrumental in some of the initial framing of ads blindness. Chris Roat and Bartholomew Furrow contributed to the experiment and analysis implementation. Mark Russell worked on the study extending these methodologies to other search sites. An incomplete list of technical contributors includes Amir Najmi, Nick Chamandy, Xiaoyue Zhao, Omkar Muralidharan, Dan Liu, Jeff Klingner, Kathy Zhong, and Alex Blocker. This work was supported through the years (both by adopting the results in decision-making and by allowing us to run very expensive experiments) by Sridhar Ramaswamy, Nick Fox, Jonathan Alferness, Adam Juda, Mike Hochberg, and Vinod Marur. Adam Juda, Ben Smith and Tamara Munzner helped make this paper understandable to a wider audience. (Tamara was also critical in the original Overlapping Experiments publication.) Roberto Bayardo, Sugato Basu, Mukund Sundararajan, Jeff Dean, Greg Corrado, and Maya Gupta gave valuable feedback on preliminary versions of this paper.

7. REFERENCES

[1] M. Bayles. Just how "Blind" Are We to Advertising Banners on the Web? In *Usability News*, 22 2000.

[2] J.P. Benway, D.M. Lane. Banner Blindness: Web Searchers Often Miss "Obvious" Links. `www.ruf.rice.edu`.

[3] A. Broder, M. Ciaramita, M. Fontoura, E. Gabrilovich, V. Josifovski, D. Metzler, V. Murdock, V. Plachouras. To Swing or not to Swing: Learning when (not) to Advertise. In CIKM 2008.

[4] R.R. Bush, F. Mosteller. A Mathematical Model for Simple Learning. In *Psychological Review*, 58 1951.

[5] W.K. Estes. Toward a Statistical Theory of Learning. In *Pyschological Review*, 57 1950.

[6] Google. AdWords Help: Check and understand Quality Score. `support.google.com`.

[7] Google. AdWords Help: Things you should know about Ads Quality. `support.google.com`.

[8] Google. AdWords Help: Understanding Landing Page Experience. `support.google.com`.

[9] G. Hotchkiss. More Ads = Better Ads = Better User Experience: Microsoft's Success Formula? `searchengineland.com`.

[10] A. Juda. Ads quality improvements rolling out globally. `adwords.blogspot.com`.

[11] R. Kohavi, M. Round. Front Line Internet Analytics at Amazon.com. `ai.stanford.edu`.

[12] R. Kohavi, R. Henne, D. Sommerfield. Practical Guide to Controlled Experiments on the Web: Listen to Your Customers not to the HiPPO. In KDD 2007.

[13] R. Kohavi, T. Crook, R. Longbotham. Online Experimentation at Microsoft. In *Third Workshop on Data Mining Case Studies* 2009.

[14] R. Kohavi, A. Deng, B. Frasca, R. Longbotham, T. Walker, Y. Xu. Trustworthy Online Controlled Experiments: Five Puzzling Outcomes Explained. In KDD 2012.

[15] R. Kohavi, A. Deng, B. Frasca, T. Walker, Y. Xu, N. Pohlmann. Online Controlled Experiments at Large Scale. In KDD 2013.

[16] J.W. Owens, B.S. Chaparro, E.M. Palmer. Text Advertising Blindness: The New Banner Blindness? In *Joural of Usability Studies*, May 2011.

[17] G. Sadler. Why Not Treat Marketing Like Sales? `www.dnb.com`.

[18] D. Tang, A. Agarwal, D. O'Brien, M. Meyer. Overlapping Experiment Infrastructure: More, Better, Faster Experimentation. In KDD 2010.

[19] E.L. Thorndike. Animal Intelligence: An experimental study of the associative processes in animals. In *Psychological Monographs: General and Applied*, 2(4) 1898.

Traffic Measurement and Route Recommendation System for Mass Rapid Transit (MRT)

Thomas Holleczek, Dang The Anh, Shanyang Yin, Yunye Jin, Spiros Antonatos,
Han Leong Goh, Samantha Low and Amy Shi-Nash
DataSpark Pte Ltd, Singtel
31B Exeter Road
Singapore 239733
{thomasas, anhkeen}@singtel, yang@swarm.is, {jinyunye, antonatos, hanleong, samlow, amyshinash}@singtel.com

ABSTRACT

Understanding how people use public transport is important for the operation and future planning of the underlying transport networks. We have therefore developed and deployed a traffic measurement system for a key player in the transportation industry to gain insights into crowd behavior for planning purposes. The system has been in operation for several months and reports, at hourly intervals, (1) the crowdedness of subway stations, (2) the flows of people inside interchange stations, and (3) the expected travel time for each possible route in the subway network of Singapore. The core of our system is an efficient algorithm which detects individual subway trips from anonymized real-time data generated by the location based system of Singtel, the country's largest telecommunications company. To assess the accuracy of our system, we engaged an independent market research company to conduct a field study—a manual count of the number of passengers boarding and disembarking at a selected station on three separate days. A strong correlation between the calculations of our algorithm and the manual counts was found. One of our key findings is that travelers do not always choose the route with the shortest travel time in the subway network of Singapore. We have therefore also been developing a mobile app which allows users to plan their trips based on the average travel time between stations.

Categories and Subject Descriptors

H.4.m [**Information Systems Applications**]: Miscellaneous

Keywords

Monitoring system; public transport; cellular networks; call detail records (CDRs)

KDD'15, August 10-13, 2015, Sydney, NSW, Australia.
© 2015 ACM. ISBN 978-1-4503-3664-2/15/08 ...$15.00.
DOI: http://dx.doi.org/10.1145/2783258.2788590.

1. INTRODUCTION

Singapore's public transport system is among the world's most efficient ones in terms of the density of the network, crowdedness and travel times [19, 20]. Its core component is the Mass Rapid Transit (MRT), a railway system spanning the entire city-state, which has been in operation since 1987. Efficiency metrics such as the crowdedness of stations and travel times between stations are instrumental to decision making for operators in ensuring quality of service. Currently, available technical solutions to estimate the crowdedness of stations include:

- Estimations from video footage of camera surveillance systems [16]. However, the performance of these systems depends on various external factors such as the lighting conditions inside stations. Video footage cannot be used to measure travel times between stations.
- Estimations from WiFi captures [18] since Singapore's subway stations are currently equipped with free WiFi [5]. However, this measure does not differentiate between passengers on platforms and passengers on trains. Similarly, travel times cannot be estimated by WiFi captures.
- Smart card system records from when passengers enter of exit the platforms of subway stations [3], which can be used to determine the number of boarding and disembarking at a particular station [14]. Such records include the time of departure and arrival of each passenger. However, these data do not capture activity such as travel routes and transfer activity between lines—factors of importance when considering the crowdedness of platforms, especially in Singapore, where the density of stations and lines is high and route alternatives available to each passenger are numerous.

Cell phone location data are capable of addressing the information gaps in the approaches above. In fact, cell phone location data have been used to various degrees to detect individual trips and categorize them into classes such as walking, cycling, public transport and driving a car. Early studies were based on cell phone fluctuations in GSM signal strength [21, 8] or location feeds picked up by in-build GPS receivers [15, 22]. However, these methods are limited by their sample size and face difficulty scaling up. Approaches that do scale up make use of cell phone call detail records

(CDRs), which are recorded by telcos for billing purposes and include the location of calls and SMS, to spot trips of all cell phone subscribers in a mobile network [17, 9, 10, 13, 14, 23, 11].

In this article, we present a traffic measurement system we have developed and deployed a for a key player in the transportation industry to gain insights into crowd behavior for planning purposes. The system reports, at hourly intervals,

1. the number of people on the platforms of subway stations,
2. the flows of people transferring between lines inside interchange stations, as well as
3. the expected travel time for each possible route in the subway network of Singapore.

The core of our traffic measurement system is an efficient algorithm which detects individual subway trips from anonymized real-time data generated by the location based system of Singtel, Singapore's largest telecommunications company (telco) with a market share of 47 % [4].

2. DATASET

Singtel recognizes that privacy is important to its customers and has implemented security measures to protect their personal data in compliance with the Singapore's Personal Data Protection Act (PDPA) [7]. All processing of mobile customer data for our analysis is conducted in compliance with the PDPA and within the scope of consent obtained from Singtel mobile customers, as set out in the Singtel Data Protection Policy [6]. All references to location data in this article refers to location data in the anonymized state as illustrated below.

For our analysis, we use the anonymized location data of 3.98 million prepaid and postpaid mobile customers of Singtel [4]. Singtel's Location Based Services System (LBS) records the cell tower a cell phone is connected to in case of

- **active network events** such as incoming or outgoing calls or SMS, as well as switching on the cell phone, and
- **passive network events**, for example when the cell phone moves between network zones, switches between 2G, 3G and 4G networks, or after one hour of inactivity.

Unlike location datasets based on call detail records (CDRs), Singtel's LBS also captures passive network events, which account for about 80 % of all recorded locations. The location data is updated in real-time as network events occur and on average, the LBS system records 60 network events per user and day. The location data being analyzed consists of an anonymized ID, latitude, longitude, timestamp and service type. The original unique ID allocated to each mobile customer is anonymized via a two-step non-reversible AES Encryption and Hashing process which makes it impossible to trace back to the original unique ID or the mobile customer. The location data does not contain any personally identifiable information of the mobile customer or any content of calls or SMSes.

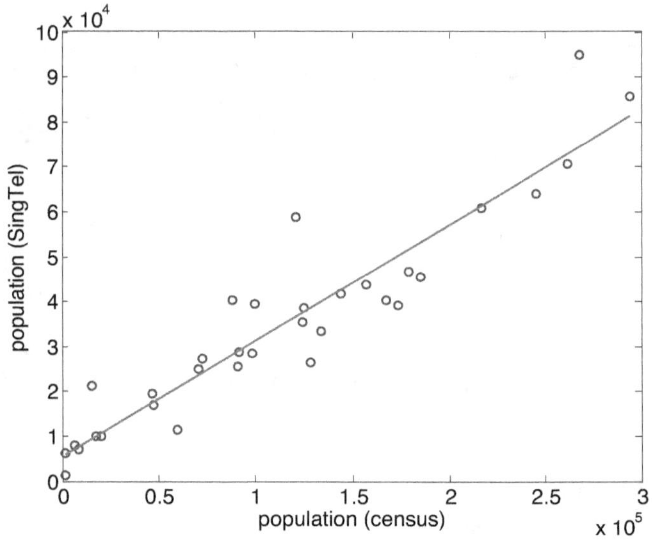

Figure 1: Population in Singapore's 33 residential districts according to the 2010 census versus the population of Singtel customers. With a correlation coefficient of 0.94, the two distributions are highly linearly correlated.

To demonstrate that Singtel's location data is representative of the population in Singapore, we compared the distribution of residences of Singtel's customers with official census data [12]. Singapore is divided into 55 administrative districts, 33 of which are residential [2]. We determined the population of Singtel customers in the 33 residential districts and compared our results with 2010 census data [1]. With a correlation coefficient of 0.94, the two distributions are highly linearly correlated (see Figure 1) [14].

3. METHODOLOGY

The core of our traffic measurement system is an algorithm which detects indoor MRT trips from cell phone data recorded by the location based system of Singtel. In 2015, the MRT system consists of 92 stations, which are connected by five train lines. The stations situated in densely populated, central locations (58 of the 92 stations) are indoors. The platforms and tunnels of these indoor stations are served exclusively by indoor cell towers—cell phones outside the MRT network cannot connect to these dedicated cell towers (see Figure 2). Our algorithm recovers individual MRT trips from cell phone location data by making use of this clear distinction between cell towers which exclusively serve indoor stations and all other cell towers in the Singtel network.

We define an MRT trip as the sequence of indoor stations $\mathbf{s} = [s_1, \dots s_n]$ a passenger α passes during their ride and the corresponding timestamps $\mathbf{t} = [t_1, \dots t_n]$ when each of these stations is reached. s_1 is the boarding station, s_n the station of disembarkation and $s_2, \dots s_{n-1}$ stations α passes during their ride.

Our MRT trip detection algorithm is based on a function that is called for every new LBS location x_i of any cell phone subscriber α. Apart from active network events, a cell phone moving on a train will produce LBS location updates every

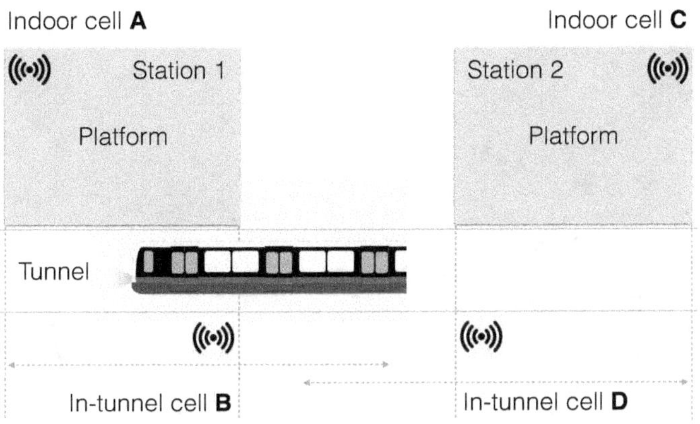

Figure 2: Dedicated indoor cell towers serve the platforms (A and C) and tunnels (B and D) of indoor MRT stations exclusively.

three stations on average. Moreover, there will be a periodic location update every hour for every cell phone. Let x_{i-1} denote the LBS location of α preceding x_i. Then, the following four cases can occur:

- If α is currently outside the MRT network (that is, the last recorded location x_{i-1} was not inside any of the MRT stations) and x_i is inside an MRT station, then α must have boarded the subway some time between x_{i-1} and x_i. Based on x_{i-1} and x_i, we identify the boarding station s_1 of α as follows. Let y denote the MRT station that is closest to x_{i-1} and is on the same train line as the station of x_i. If x_{i-1} is reasonably close to y, i.e. $||x_{i-1} - y|| < \Delta d$ and was not recorded too long ago, i.e. $t(x_i) - t(x_{i-1}) < \Delta t_{\text{timeout}}$, we set the boarding station s_1 as y. Otherwise, we assume α boarded at the station of x_i. Two temporary lists are created for α:

  1. **u**, which stores the stations at which the location of α is recorded during their MRT ride, and
  2. **v**, which stores the corresponding timestamps.

- If α is currently inside the MRT network (that is, the last recorded location x_{i-1} was inside an MRT station) and x_i is not inside the MRT network, then α must have disembarked the subway some time between x_{i-1} and x_i. Based on x_{i-1} and x_i, we identify the disembarking station s_n of α as follows. Let z denote the MRT station that is closest to x_i and is on the same train line as station of x_{i-1}. If x_i is reasonably close to z, i.e. $||x_i - z|| < \Delta d$ and was not recorded too long ago, i.e. $t(x_i) - t(x_{i-1}) < \Delta t_{\text{timeout}}$, we set the disembarking station s_n as z. Otherwise, we assume α disembarked at the station of x_{i-1}.

  Next, the observed sequence of stations is mapped to the MRT network. Let S denote the set of all possible routes from the boarding station s_1 to the disembarking station s_n in the MRT network. We assume that α took that route $\mathbf{s} \in S$ where the size of the intersection with the sequence of observed stations **u** is maximal. In case of multiple such options, we assume α took the shortest of these. Now that the sequence of stations **s** that α passed during their trip has been determined, the complete list of timestamps **t** needs to be recovered from the recorded timestamps **v**. We do this by

  1. linearly extrapolating the times between the boarding station s_1 and the first observed station u_1 as well as between last observed station u_m and disembarking station s_n usingΔ t_{hop}, and
  2. linearly interpolating the times for passed stations without LBS records.

  Now, the complete trip of α has been detected and the function returns.

- If both x_{i-1} and x_i are inside the MRT network, α is assumed to continue his MRT ride. If the station of x_i is not yet part of **u**, we append it to **u**, as well as the corresponding timestamp $t(x_i)$ to **v**. Finally, the function returns.

- If both x_{i-1} and x_i are outside the MRT network, α remains outside the MRT network and the function returns.

Figure 3 illustrates the trip detection algorithm. The algorithm parameters as well as values we choose are summarized in Table 1.

Parameter	Description	Value
Δd	Maximum distance allowed between last location outside and first location inside MRT or last location inside and first location outside MRT	2000 m
$\Delta t_{\text{timeout}}$	Maximum time allowed from last record outside and first record inside MRT or last record inside and first record outside MRT	2700 s
Δt_{hop}	Average travel time between two neighbored stations used for extrapolation (estimated from train schedule)	120 s

Table 1: Parameters of the MRT trip detection algorithm.

4. EVALUATION

To assess the accuracy of our system, we engaged an independent market research company to conduct a field study at Orchard MRT station, a popular shopping destination in Singapore. The number of passengers boarding and disembarking was counted manually at the entry gates of the station on three days (Monday, Friday and Saturday) and aggregated in hourly intervals. We determined the number of Singtel subscribers departing and arriving at Orchard

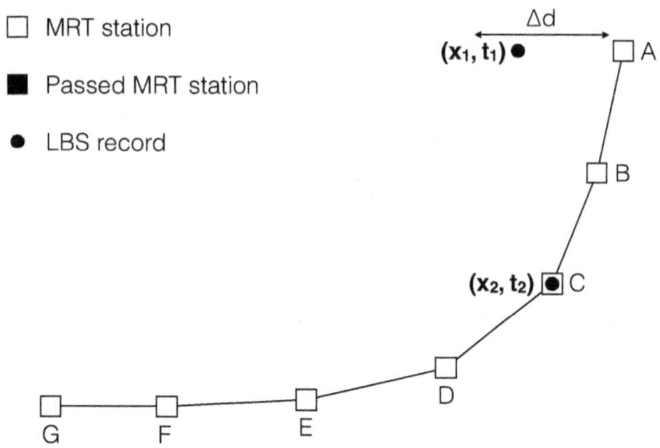

(a) The first location x_1 is recorded outside the MRT network at time t_1, and the second one x_2 is inside the MRT station C at time t_2. Now, the boarding station is identified. The station closest to x_1 is A. Let us suppose that the time difference between t_2 and t_1 is acceptable, i.e. $t_2 - t_1 < \Delta t_{\text{timeout}}$. As the distance between x_1 and A is less than the threshold valueΔ d, we assume that the boarding station is A.

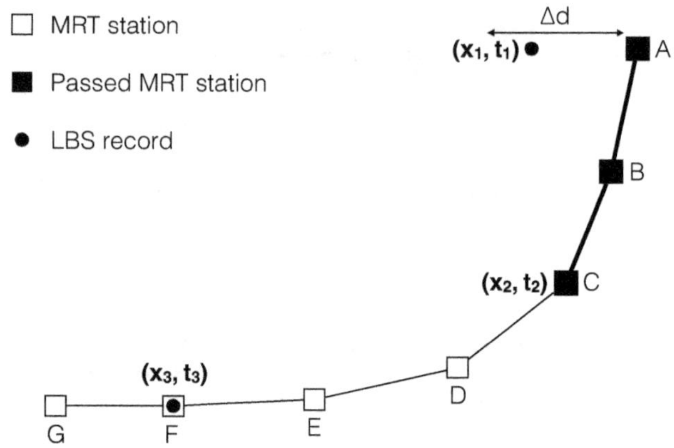

(b) The third location x_3 is still inside the MRT network at station F. The trip is assumed to continue.

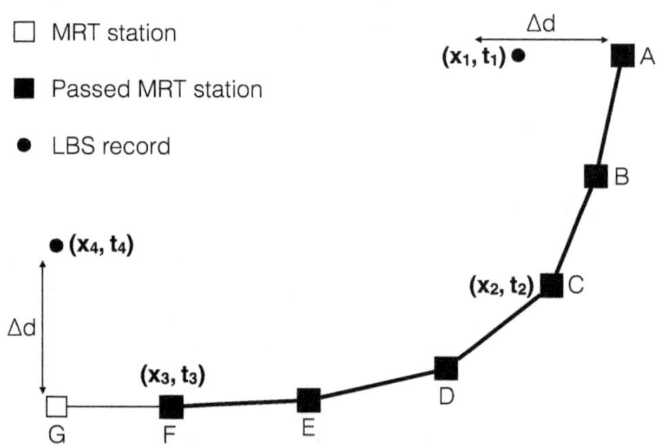

(c) The fourth location x_4 is recorded outside the MRT network, which means that the trip has ended some time between t_3 and t_4. The distance between x_4 to the closest station G exceeds the threshold valueΔ d, which is why we assume that the disembarking station is the last observed station F.

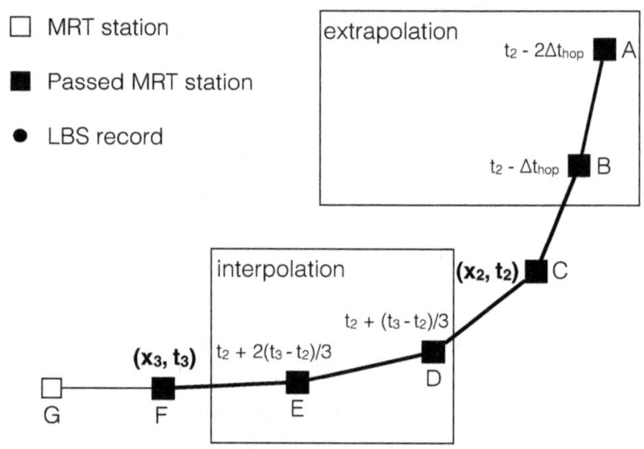

(d) Once the trip has ended and the disembarking station is identified, the timestamps corresponding to the stations without records have to be recovered. We use linear extrapolation from the boarding station A to the first observed station C, as well as linear interpolation for the stations without observation between C and F.

Figure 3: Illustration of the MRT trip detection algorithm.

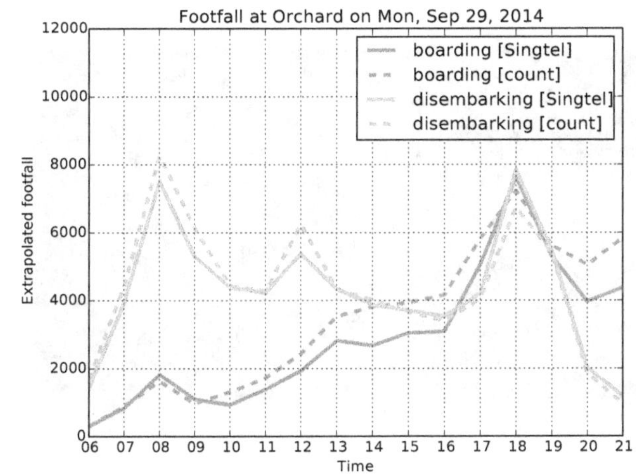

Figure 4: Validation of footfall at Orchard MRT. The solid lines represent the extrapolated number of boarding and disembarking passengers determined from Singtel location data, whereas the dashed lines show manual counts. There is a very good correspondence, with an average hourly discrepancy of 9.5 %.

MRT station during the same three days on an hourly basis using our MRT trip detection algorithm and market extrapolated these numbers with the scaling factor A, which takes into account both Singtel's market share in Singapore as well as the mobile device penetration rate in Singapore:

$$A = \frac{1}{\text{market share} \times \text{device penetration}}. \quad (1)$$

With an average hourly discrepancy of 9.5 %, there is a very good correspondence between the manual counts and the detected number of Singtel subscribers departing and arriving at Orchard MRT station. Figure 4 shows a comparison of data from the manual count against data from Singtel's LBS.

5. DEPLOYMENT

The traffic measurement system was deployed to a key player in the transportation industry in exploration of new applications that can improve the MRT operation efficiency and enhance the traveling experience of commuters. Examples include better planning of free bus bridging services in the event of MRT train disruptions, simulations for infrastructure planning such as the building of new MRT stations and the shaping of new policies which incentivize off-peak traveling. We have implemented the system in the Python programming language and have been detecting MRT trips from Singtel location data over the course of several months. The trip extraction module starts its execution daily at 2am after all passengers have disembarked and the MRT system has closed. The recovered trips are then stored in a database, which can be queried for the following (market extrapolated) efficiency metrics of the MRT system:

1. the crowdedness of subway stations,

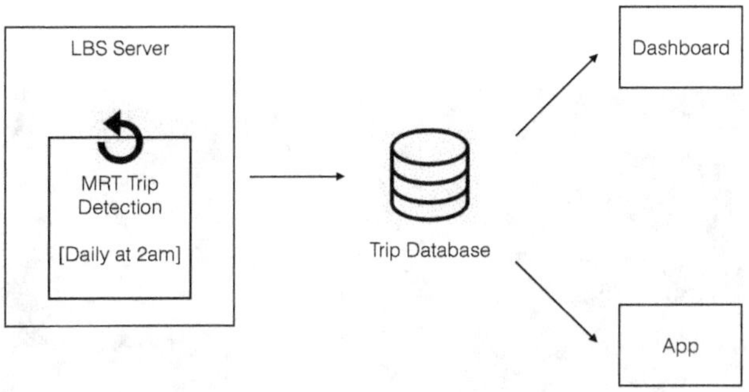

Figure 7: Architecture of the traffic measurement system. The trip extraction module starts its execution daily at 2am. The recovered trips are stored in a database, which can be queried for MRT efficiency metrics from a dashboard as well as a mobile app.

2. the flows of people transferring between lines inside interchange stations, as well as

3. the expected travel time for each possible route in the subway network.

These metrics are reported by a dashboard, which is connected to the trip database (see Figure 5). Users can select the time window as well as the MRT stations they want to inspect. One of our key findings is that travelers do not always choose the route with the shortest travel time in the subway network of Singapore. We have therefore also been developing a mobile app that allows users to plan their trips based on the average travel time between stations as well as the crowdedness of stations (see Figure 6). The app has not yet been released and has not influenced route choices of travelers in our analysis. The overall architecture of the traffic measurement system is illustrated in Figure 7.

5.1 Crowdedness of Stations

The crowdedness of a station, which we also refer to as platform footfall, is the number of of passengers boarding, disembarking or transferring at that station in a given time window—determined from our database by grouping trips according to stations and times Figure 8 shows and interprets the hourly footfall of three selected MRT stations (one located in the Central Business District, one in a residential area, as well as the largest interchange station) on a typical Monday. The station in the CBD is a major destination of trips in the morning and origin of trips in the evening, whereas the opposite is true for the station in the residential area. More than 50 % of the people at the interchange station change between lines.

5.2 Flows of People

The trip database allows us to zoom into any interchange station and analyze the flows of people transferring between the different lines. This is particularly helpful for the operation of escalators (e.g. in which direction should escalators run at which time), or for setting up barriers to help reduce congestion inside the station. Figure 9 shows the flows of people transferring between three lines at Dhoby Ghaut

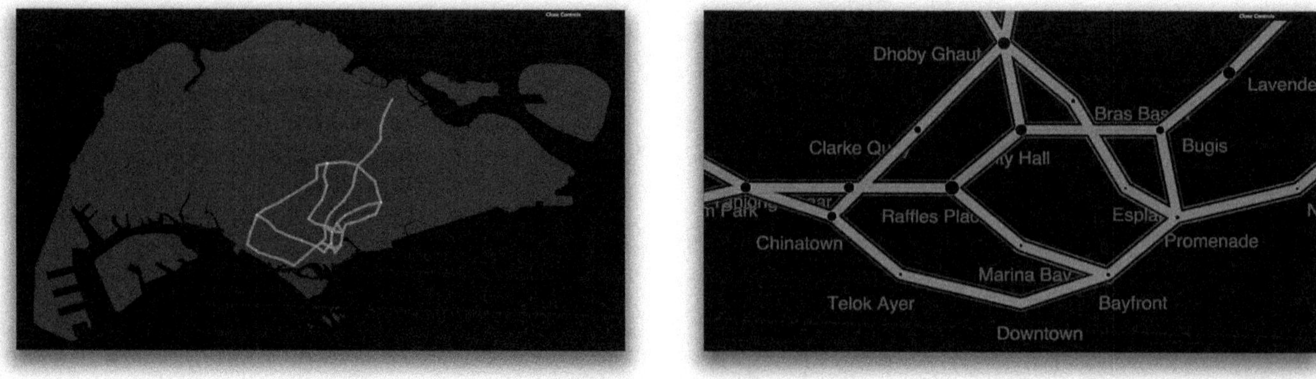

(a) (b)

Figure 5: Dashboard showing the hourly footfall in MRT stations (black circles) as well as the number of people on trains between stations (colored lines).

(a) Users can select the origin and destination of their trip.

(b) The app presents all routes from the selected origin to the destination, along with the average travel time and crowdedness.

(c) Trip details can be viewed on a map as well.

Figure 6: Screenshots of our mobile app, which allows users to plan their trips based on the average travel time between stations as well as the crowdedness of stations. The app has not yet been released and has not influenced route choices of travelers in our analysis.

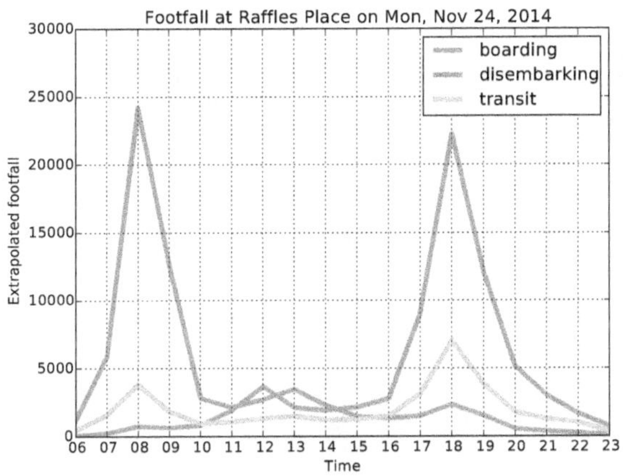

(a) Raffles Place is located in the Central Business District. It is a major destination of trips in the morning and origin of trips in the evening.

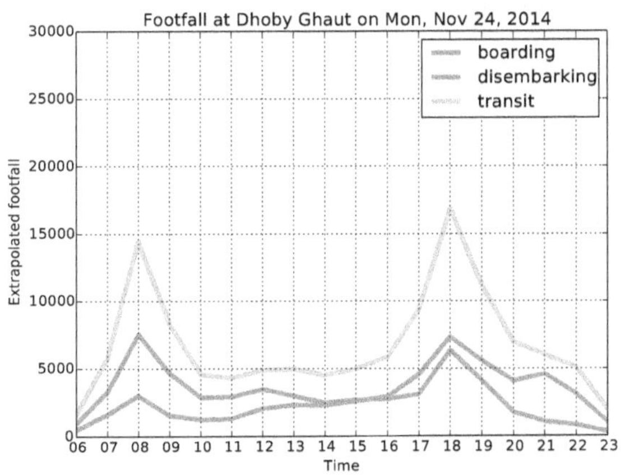

(b) Connecting three train lines, Dhoby Ghaut is the largest interchange station in Singapore. More than 50 % of the platform footfall are passengers transferring between lines.

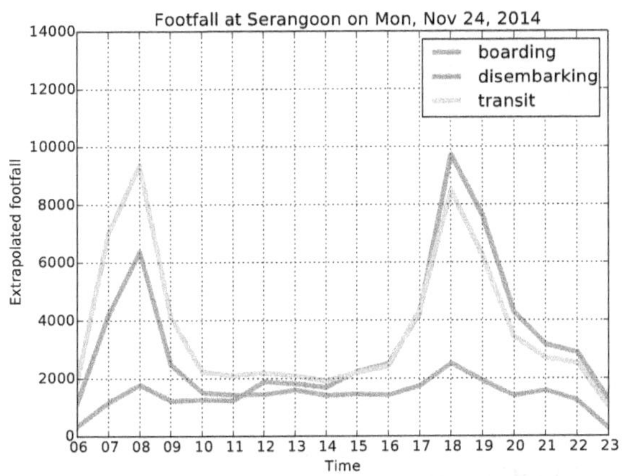

(c) Serangoon is a transit station situated in a residential area, which is also a popular destination for shopping and eating.

Figure 8: Extrapolated hourly platform footfall (broken down into boarding, disembarking and transit) on a typical Monday.

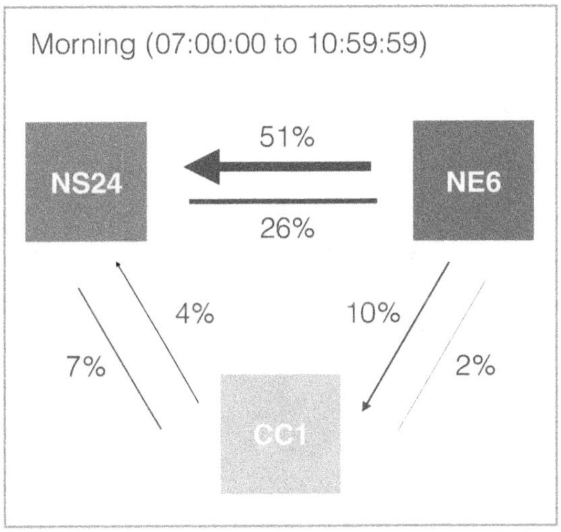

Figure 9: Flows of people transferring at Dhoby Ghaut, the largest interchange station in Singapore, in the morning of a typical working day. NS24 represents the platform of the North-South Line, CC1 the platform of the Circle Line and NE6 the platform of the North-East Line. During the morning peak hours, the majority of people transfer from the North-East to the North-South Line.

MRT, the largest interchange station in Singapore, in the morning of a typical working day.

5.3 Travel Times

Due to the high density of stations and lines in Singapore's core, there can be plenty of route alternatives which passengers can choose from. Sometimes, the shortest distance may also not be the quickest route due to congestion. As such, the most time efficient route between two MRT stations may be difficult to determine for commuters. With the implementation of the trip database, we are able to determine the popularity of routes between stations (i.e. the number of people taking any route between two given stations), as well as the average travel time per route. Figure 10 visualizes the five route options between Kovan, a residential area, and Bugis, an area for dining and going out. Only 23 % of all passengers traveling from Kovan to Bugis take the shortest route via Dhoby Ghaut and City Hall, which has an average travel time of 29 minutes. With 48 %, the majority transfers at Chinatown, a route that takes 36 minutes. The route suggested by Google Maps is via Outram Park and is the third most popular alternative among passengers (20 %), with an average travel time of 36 minutes.

6. CONCLUSION AND OUTLOOK

Understanding how people use public transport is important for the operation and future planning of the underlying transport networks. We have therefore developed and deployed a traffic measurement system for a key player in the transportation industry to gain insights into crowd behavior for planning purposes. The system has been in operation for several months and reports, at hourly intervals,

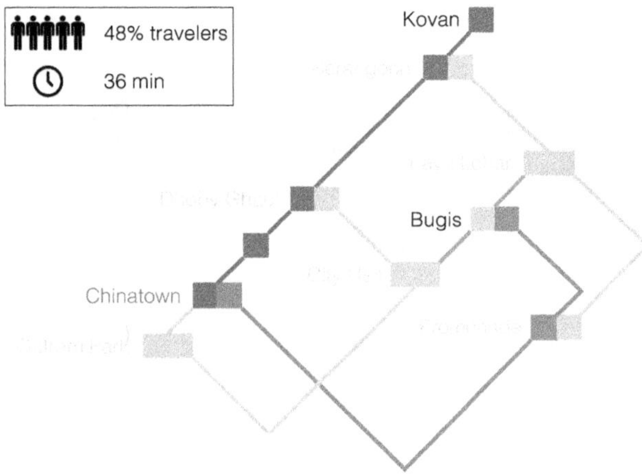

(a) Route via Chinatown.

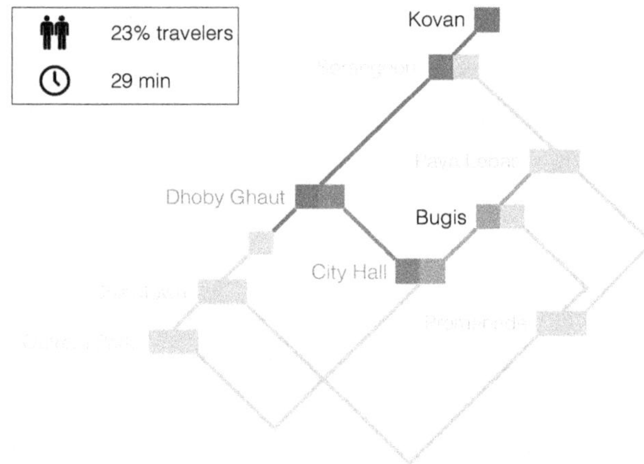

(b) Route via Dhoby Ghaut and City Hall.

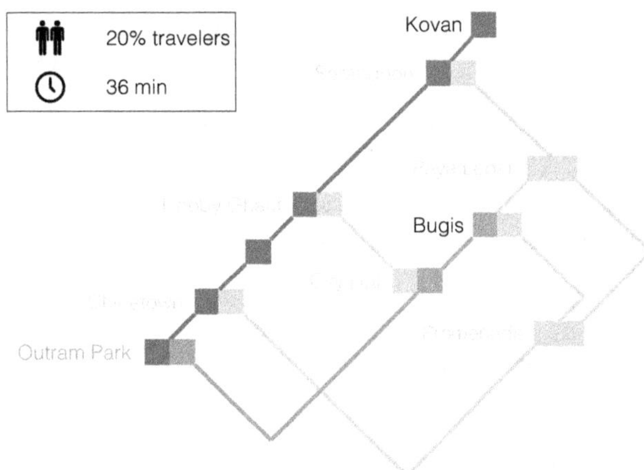

(c) Route via Outram Park.

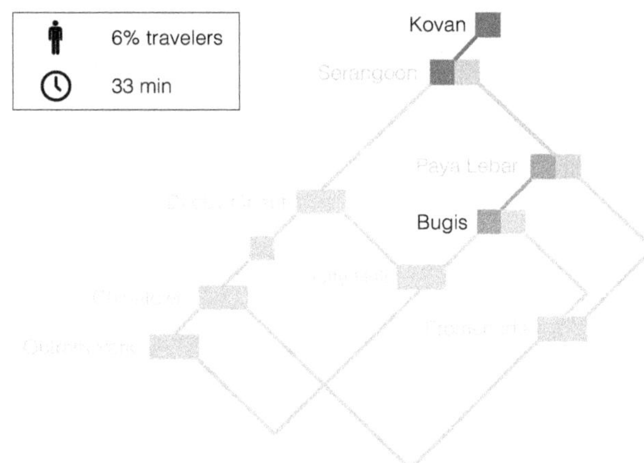

(d) Route via Serangoon and Paya Lebar.

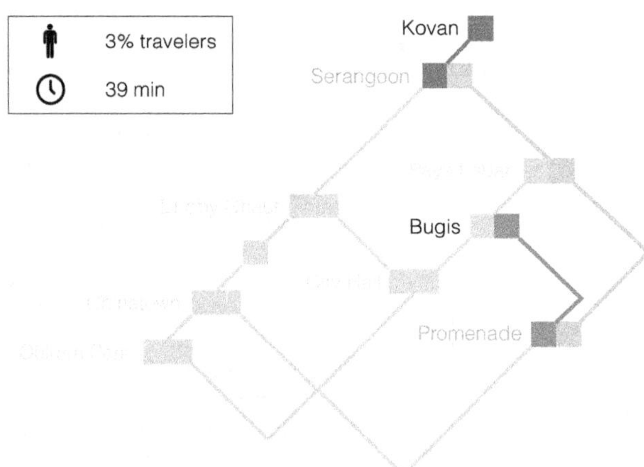

(e) Route via Serangoon and Promenade.

Figure 10: There are five route alternatives between Kovan, a residential area, and Bugis, an area for dining and going out. Apparently, only 23 % of all passengers traveling from Kovan to Bugis take the shortest route via Dhoby Ghaut and City Hall, which has an average travel time of 29 minutes. With 48 %, the majority transfers at Chinatown, a route that takes 36 minutes. The route suggested by Google Maps is via Outram Park and is the third most popular alternative among passengers (20 %), with an average travel time of 36 minutes.

1. the number of people on the platforms of subway stations,
2. the flows of people transferring between lines inside interchange stations, as well as
3. the expected travel time for each possible route in the subway network of Singapore.

The core of our system is an efficient algorithm which detects individual subway trips from anonymized real-time data generated by the location based system of Singtel, the country's largest telecommunications company. To assess the accuracy of our system, we engaged an independent market research company to conduct a field study—a manual count of the number of passengers boarding and disembarking at a selected station on three separate days. A strong correlation between the calculations of our algorithm and the manual counts was found. One of our key findings is that travelers do not always choose the route with the shortest travel time in the subway network of Singapore. We have therefore also been developing a mobile app which allows users to plan their trips based on the average travel time between stations. The traffic measurement system is currently limited to the detection of indoor MRT trips and we are extending our algorithm to detect outdoor trips as well.

7. REFERENCES

[1] Singapore census of population 2010. Technical report, Singapore Department of Statistics, 2010.

[2] Administrative divisions of Singapore. `http://en.wikipedia.org/wiki/Administrative_divisions_of_Singapore`, retrieved on 2012-12-03.

[3] EZ-Link Card. `http://www.ezlink.com.sg/index.php`, retrieved on 2014-12-29.

[4] SingTel Business Review. `http://info.singtel.com/annualreport/2014/business_review/group_consumer/singapore.html`, retrieved on 2014-12-29.

[5] Roll-out of free WiFi at 32 MRT stations to be completed by end-2015. `http://www.todayonline.com/singapore/roll-out-free-wifi-32-mrt-stations-be-completed-end-2015`, retrieved on 2015-02-05.

[6] Singtel's data protection policy. `http://info.singtel.com/personal/dataprotection`, retrieved on 2015-02-05.

[7] Personal Data Protection Act. `https://www.pdpc.gov.sg/legislation-and-guidelines/overview`, retrieved on 2015-02-18.

[8] I. Anderson and H. Muller. Exploring GSM data in pervasive environments. *International Journal of Pervasive Computing and Communications*, 4(1):8–25, 2008.

[9] N. Caceres, J. Wideberg, and F. Benitez. Deriving origin destination data from a mobile phone network. *Intelligent Transport Systems*, 1(1):15–26, 2007.

[10] F. Calabrese, G. Di Lorenzo, L. Liu, and C. Ratti. Estimating origin-destination flows using opportunistically collected mobile phone location data. *Pervasive Computing*, 10(4):36–44, 2011.

[11] M. Dash, K. Koo, J. Decraene, G. Yap, S. Krishnaswamy, W. Wu, J. Gomes, A. Shi-Nash, and X. Li. CDR-To-MoVis: Developing a mobility visualization system from CDR data. In *Proceedings of the IEEE International Conference on Data Engineering (ICDE 2015)*, Seoul, Korea, 2015.

[12] M. Dash, H. L. Nguyen, C. Hong, G. E. Yap, M. N. Nguyen, X. Li, S. Krishnaswamy, J. Decraene, S. Antonatos, Y. Wang, D. T. Anh, and A. Shi-Nash. Home and work place prediction for urban planning using mobile network data. In *Proceedings of the 15th IEEE International Conference on Mobile Data Management (MDM 2014)*, pages 37–42, Brisbane, Australia, 2014.

[13] V. Frias-Martinez, C. Soguero, and E. Frias-Martinez. Estimation of urban commuting patterns using cellphone network data. In *Proceedings of the ACM SIGKDD International Workshop on Urban Computing (UrbComp 2012)*, pages 9–16. ACM, 2012.

[14] T. Holleczek, L. Yu, J. Lee, O. Senn, C. Ratti, and P. Jaillet. Detecting weak public transport connections from cellphone and public transport data. In *Proceedings of the Third ASE International Conference on Big Data Science and Computing (BigDataScience 2014)*, Beijing, China, 2014. ACM.

[15] L. Liao, D. Patterson, D. Fox, and H. Kautz. Learning and inferring transportation routines. *Artificial Intelligence*, 171(5-6):311–331, 2007.

[16] B. Ozer and M. Wolf. A train station surveillance system: Challenges and solutions. *Proceedings of the 2014 IEEE Conference on Computer Vision and Pattern Recognition*, pages 652–657, 2014.

[17] C. Pan, J. Lu, S. Di, and B. Ran. Cellular-based data-extracting method for trip distribution. In *Transportation Research Record: Journal of the Transportation Research Board*, volume 1945, pages 33–39, 2006.

[18] L. Schauer, M. Werner, and P. Marcus. Estimating crowd densities and pedestrian flows using Wi-Fi and Bluetooth. In *Proceedings of the 11th International Conference on Mobile and Ubiquitous Systems: Computing, Networking and Services (MOBIQUITOUS 2014)*, pages 171–177, Brussels, Belgium, 2014. ACM.

[19] V. Shah and M. Manibo. Cities with efficient public transport highly attractive and competitive: study. `http://www.eco-business.com/news/cities-efficient-public-transport-highly-attractive-and-competitive-study/`, retrieved on 2015-02-02.

[20] R. Sim. Study: Singapore's public transport system one of world's most efficient. `http://www.straitstimes.com/news/singapore/transport/story/study-singapores-public-transport-system-one-worlds-most-efficient-20`, retrieved on 2015-02-02.

[21] T. Sohn, A. Varshavsky, A. LaMarca, M. Chen, T. Choudhury, I. Smith, S. Consolvo, J. Hightower, W. Griswold, and E. De Lara. Mobility detection using everyday GSM traces. In *Proceedings of the 8th International Conference on Ubiquitous Computing (Ubicomp 2006)*, pages 212–224, Orange County, CA, USA, 2006. Springer.

[22] L. Stenneth, O. Wolfson, P. Yu, and B. Xu. Transportation mode detection using mobile phones and GIS information. In *Proceedings of the 19th ACM SIGSPATIAL International Conference on Advances in Geographic Information Systems (GIS 2011)*, pages 54–63. ACM, 2011.

[23] W. Wu, Y. Wang, J. Gomes, D. T. Anh, S. Antonatos, M. Xue, P. Yang, G. E. Yap, X. Li, S. Krishnaswamy, J. Decraene, and A. Shi-Nash. Oscillation resolution for mobile phone cellular tower data to enable mobility modelling. In *Proceedings of the 15th IEEE International Conference on Mobile Data Management (MDM 2014)*, pages 321–328, Brisbane, Australia, 2014. IEEE.

Real-Time Bid Prediction using Thompson Sampling-Based Expert Selection

Elena Ikonomovska
Turn Inc.
835 Main St.
Redwood City, California
eikonomovska@turn.com

Sina Jafarpour
Turn Inc.
835 Main St.
Redwood City, California
sjafarpour@turn.com

Ali Dasdan
Turn Inc.
835 Main St.
Redwood City, California
adasdan@turn.com

ABSTRACT

We study online meta-learners for real-time bid prediction that predict by selecting a single best predictor among several subordinate prediction algorithms, here called "experts". These predictors belong to the family of context-dependent past performance estimators that make a prediction only when the instance to be predicted falls within their areas of expertise. Within the advertising ecosystem, it is very common for the contextual information to be incomplete, hence, it is natural for some of the experts to abstain from making predictions on some of the instances. Experts' areas of expertise can overlap, which makes their predictions less suitable for merging; as such, they lend themselves better to the problem of best expert selection. In addition, their performance varies over time, which gives the expert selection problem a non-stochastic, adversarial flavor. In this paper we propose to use probability sampling (via Thompson Sampling) as a meta-learning algorithm that samples from the pool of experts for the purpose of bid prediction. We show performance results from the comparison of our approach to multiple state-of-the-art algorithms using exploration scavenging on a log file of over 300 million ad impressions, as well as comparison to a baseline rule-based model using production traffic from a leading DSP platform.

Categories and Subject Descriptors

I.I [**Symbolic and Algebraic Manipulation**]: Applications; I.2 [**Artificial Intelligence**]: Learning—*Concept learning*; I.6 [**Simulation and Modeling**]: Applications—*Miscellaneous*

General Terms

Performance, Design, Experimentation

Keywords

Randomized probability matching, Bayesian online learning, Online algorithms, Online advertising, Multi-armed bandits

KDD'15, August 10-13, 2015, Sydney, NSW, Australia.
© 2015 ACM. ISBN 978-1-4503-3664-2/15/08 ...$15.00.
DOI: http://dx.doi.org/10.1145/2783258.2788586.

1. INTRODUCTION

With the increasing adoption of real time bidding (RTB), internet advertising models are undergoing a revolution. RTB enables marketers to participate in real time auctions for ad placement that occur seconds before a website loads. This functionality has helped to make advertising much more precise and personalized and enables advertisers to reach their target audiences. Programmatic trading, the technology behind the RTB, offers an immense potential for cost effective advertising. However, in order to realize this potential, advertisers need to intelligently adjust their bids as the market conditions fluctuate and real time feedback is received regarding the efficacy of a campaign. Demand-Side Platforms (DSPs) offer real time bid prediction [25, 18] to help advertisers find the optimal bid value in milliseconds. The goal of real time bid prediction is to maximize campaign performance goals under a budget constraint. Typical performance goals are minimizing cost-per-click (CPC) or cost-per-action (CPA), as well as maximizing click-through-rate (CTR) or action-rate (AR).

Predicting the performance of an ad is a challenging problem for many reasons. First of all, each decision to buy an impression and at what price needs to be made in just few milliseconds. Top DPSs typically receive a few million bid requests per second coming from users that are exploring the web all around the globe. Most of the time, the necessary information to make the optimal bidding decision is missing or delayed. For example, user data is based on cookies rather than real users. In addition, a significant number of visitors are likely to be entirely new with no historical consumption record whatsoever. In many web-based scenarios, the content universe undergoes frequent changes, with content popularity changing over time as well. The situation is similar with respect to advertisers' content (ads and campaigns); this is known as the cold-start problem.

The above problem is known as a feature-based exploration-exploitation problem [21] and to solve this problem we propose learning a pool of simple online prediction algorithms (predictors) with a partial view of the full contextual information. Specifically, for each triple of (user, advertiser, publisher) features we create a prediction strategy (an "expert") that examines only those features and makes predictions based on their values. In our framework the experts may choose to abstain from giving a prediction on a given instance. As in [6, 11], we shall call these experts *specialists*, because they are allowed to abstain when the instance doesn't fall into their areas of expertise, or specialities.

In this paper we shall deal with a pool-based real-time bid prediction. The learner is presented with a fixed pool of *specialists* that learn according to a modified online learning protocol with batch updates. Learning proceeds in a sequence of trials. On each trial the learner receives one instance from a fixed domain and feeds this instance to the *specialists* in the pool. The learner then selects one *specialist* from the pool and uses its estimate towards the bid computation. If the bid wins in the external auction then the learner pays a cost. After some time, the adversary provides the learner with the true labels and then the learner induces an updated set of *specialists* based on the newly received information.

We frame the problem of best specialist selection in the multi-armed bandit framework and propose to use randomized probability matching. An important component of the online learning framework is a loss function that associates a non-negative loss to each pair of prediction and outcome. In the multi-armed bandit framework, however, there is no obvious loss function defined on an instance basis.

Contributions. Our contributions are threefold. First, we describe how randomized probability matching can be naturally applied to settings like real-time bid prediction for online advertising. In particular, we describe a new version of a Thompson Sampling algorithm customized to suit such conditions [1]. It can be viewed as a meta-learning algorithm that selects from a pool of *experts*. Our work is one of the first in trying to use bandit type ideas for sampling from an ensembles of *experts* in real-time bid prediction with budget constraints, and we strongly believe that one can build extremely practical, yet very simple and scalable algorithms by understanding the interplay between multi-armed bandits and learning from a pool of experts. Second, we show that this approach is useful in practice, scales well, and is easily deployed at large-scale in real world industrial systems for real time ad allocation. Finally, we provide empirical support and comparison with several state-of-the-art algorithms using real world campaign data provided by Turn, a leading Demand-Side Platform (DSP).

2. BRIEF SYSTEM OVERVIEW

A simplified illustration of the advertising ecosystem and a typical ad call flow is given in Fig. 1. The figure illustrates a user with a web browser, an ad server, an ad exchange, a Data Management Platform (DMP) and a Demand Side Platform (DSP).

The ad call flow starts from the user's browser. The call is initiated when a user with **uid** opens a webpage at URL **url**. The user's browser then contacts the ad exchange the publisher is integrated with. The ad exchange appends **uid** and **url** to a request submitted to several DSP partners. Using the *uid* and *url*, DSPs return to their decision enginers the information about the given user and the web page that they can find in their stores. Each DSP runs an auction among the eligible ads (normally those that satisfy certain targeting constraints) from its list of existing campaigns. Then, one or more ads, depending on the space and layout characteristics, are chosen for display and ranked based on some function of expected performance and advertiser's bid.

[1]e.g. minimizing effective CPC (eCPC) and maximizing advertiser ROI.

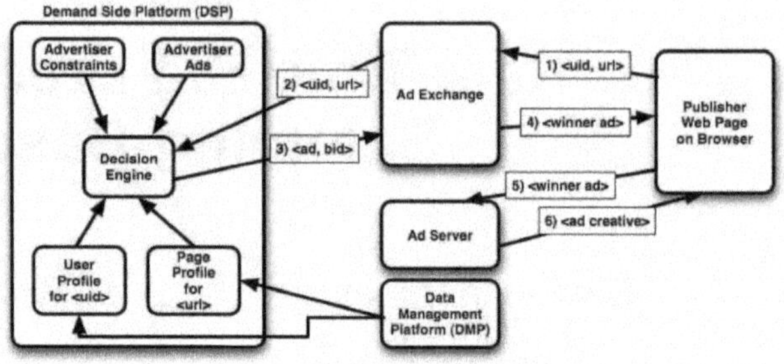

Figure 1: Ad call flow between a web browser and a demand side platform.

The bidding DSPs return back their proposed ad and bid pair back to the ad exchange. Once the ad exchange collects all the bids, it runs an auction (usually a second price auction) and determines the winning bid and the corresponding ad. It then passes the winning ad and the location of its creative back to the browser. The browser then collects the creative and finally returns the page to the user [19].

This entire flow needs to happen within a small portion of a second so that the user can see the page with ads as soon as the page appears on her web browser. This latency and throughput constraints put extreme time constraints on each bidding DSP and their decision engines. Our proposed approach is at the heart of the decision engine and works under such time constraints with a satisfactory performance.

3. PROBLEM FORMULATION

For the sake of clarity, we will only talk about click events, and focus on maximizing the CTR or minimizing the cost-per-click (CPC). Our methodology is equally applicable to other types of events such as conversion events, engagement events, etc. Moreover, without loss of generality, we will focus on the display channel. We provide a bottom-up formulation of the problem that provides the skeleton of our solution constructed on ideas such as: feature hierarchies, randomized probability matching, and sleeping experts.

3.1 Feature space and predictors

In the online advertising context, the feature space is usually constructed along three main dimensions: *user*, *publisher* represented as webpages, *advertisers* represented as ads. Time and other dimensions are extra. Let $\mathcal{U} = \{u_1, u_2, ..., u_l$ $\mathcal{P} = \{p_1, p_2, ..., p_m\}$, and $\mathcal{A} = \{a_1, a_2, ..., a_n\}$ represent all the users, webpages and ads (with creatives) in a DSP, respectively. The goal in bid prediction is then to find among all eligible ads the ad that has the highest probability of a click for a given user on a given webpage. One way to model this is to represent users, webpages, and ads using a set of explicit features and build a classification model. However, due to the sparsity of user-level data, an alternative and better idea is to compute the number of times an ad was displayed to "similar" users on a given website and observe how many of these impressions result in a click. Then, the CTR for this user can simply be estimated as the total number of clicks among all similar users divided by the total number of impressions. This kind of user grouping can either be achieved by explicit clustering based on some similarity metric or it can be implicitly done by using data hierarchies [19].

For example, every ad in the DSP can be considered as belonging to an advertising campaign which in turn belongs to an advertiser (e.g., Advertiser: 'Acme Cars' → Campaign: '2011 Year End Sales' → Ad: 'Incredible Year End Sales Event!'). Similarly, a website on which an ad will be displayed is under a top level domain (TLD) which is owned by a publisher and the publisher itself might belong to some category based on its main content (e.g., Publisher Type: 'News' → Publisher: 'Acme City Times' → Page: 'Auto News'). If we assume that user, publisher, and advertiser data have l_u, l_p, l_a levels in their respective data hierarchies, there are $l_u \times l_p \times l_a$ possible ways of combining count data for a given ($user \times publisher \times advertiser$) triple.

Using these various levels of count data aggregated along the time dimension we can create simple context-dependent predictors that are able to produce a maximum likelihood estimate of the CTR. Experts that use higher-level data will be susceptible to high bias in their estimates. On the other hand, experts that use lower-level data will be susceptible to high variance, due to a limited number of data points from which the estimates are drawn. Naturally, by observing more data points in the lower levels of the data hierarchies the corresponding experts will become more accurate over time. In the next section, we discuss how we can combine these estimators to obtain a final prediction.

3.2 Meta-learning

Let let $\hat{x}^1_{ijk}$, $\hat{x}^2_{ijk}$, ..., $\hat{x}^K_{ijk}$, denote the full set of maximum likelihood estimates of the CTR for user u_i, webpage p_j and ad a_k, at K different level combinations. For clarity, we will drop the indexes and use $\hat{x}^1$, $\hat{x}^2$, ..., $\hat{x}^K$ instead. Recall that each of these levels corresponds to a distinct combination of the user, publisher and advertiser hierarchies and, as such, it is not always clear which one will yield the best estimate of the true CTR p_{ijk}.

Most of the time user-publisher-advertiser data will be missing, and the estimators using these information sources simply will not be computed. For example, a user IDs might not be found in the user profile servers, or the publisher's webpage will not match any of the known categories in the publisher taxonomy, or the advertiser has no past-performance data in the system. Moreover, there may not be sufficient number of click events in one of the hierarchical levels to calculate a reliable estimator output using the past performance observations. As a result, the number of available estimates will change over time, and in some cases might be zero.

One way to aggregate these estimates is to use a learning method that combines the available estimates into a single prediction. For example, Lee et al. [19] have used logistic regression to combine experts estimates for action rate prediction. Further, there exist a number of online learning algorithms designed for the scenario of missing experts from a pool of learners, such as the online SBayes [11]. However, due to the dynamic nature of the problem and the time-varying performance of the experts, these approaches are not most suitable. Rather than trying to combine multiple predictions, in this work we try to pick the best estimator among the K experts. The reasoning behind this decision is two-fold: First, through an online evaluation we have observed that under specific contextual decisions, the experts are able to provide very good estimates of the CTR without merging; second, their performance varies significantly over time. Hence, our problem can be formulated as an online expert selection problem, where the set of available experts changes over time.

3.3 Performance-based bid prediction

At an abstract level, advertisers place their bids in the form of CPC or CPA goals. In pure second-price auctions the dominant bidding strategy for the advertisers is to submit their private true value [10]. Therefore, the value of the impression is typically calculated with the probability of a click (predicted by DSPs) multiplied by the value of the click (given by advertisers). The resulting bid for a given impression at time t would be calculated as:

$$Bid(t) = \theta(t) \times goal$$

where the goal is a fixed number w.r.t. the given campaign that amounts to the monetary value the advertiser assignes to a click, and $\theta(t)$ is the click probability. In practice, however, this is never the case. Besides the additional bid adjustments which are done post-CTR computation, the advertisers can further influence the bid price through multiple scaling factors.

Therefore, when minimizing the eCPC, one needs to take into account the expected cost for the expected number of clicks. In other words, minimizing the eCPC is not equivalent to the CTR maximization strategy. To illustrate this, let's assume that we need to minimize the eCPC, and the total budget is \$1000. Assume further that we have two different prediction strategies whose average estimates for the CTR are: 12×10^{-3} and 20×10^{-3} correspondingly. Due to the difference in the expected values of these estimates and the inherent sampling biases, the bid price would be different though not linearly dependent, so let's assume that the average cost per impression is \$0.05 and \$0.12 correspondingly. That means one could buy on average around 20,000 impressions in the first case and around 8,334 impressions in the second case. This leads us to about 200 clicks with the first strategy and 175 with the second, and correspondingly \$5 and \$5.7 effective cost per click (eCPC). In this case, using the first strategy whose CTR estimate is lower can lead us to a better eCPC.

4. MULTI-ARMED BANDITS

Choosing the best expert for bid prediction can be naturally viewed from the perspective of exploration-exploitation trade-off. The concept of exploration-exploitation is central to problems in decision making under uncertainty, and is best illustrated by the multi-armed bandit (MAB) problem.

In its simplest formulation (generally referred to as stochastic), a bandit problem consists of a set of K probability distributions $< D_1, ..., D_K >$ with associated expected values $< \mu_1, ..., \mu_K >$. Initially, the distributions are unknown to the player. In fact, these distributions are generally interpreted as corresponding to arms on a slot machine; the learning algorithm is viewed as a gambler whose goal is to collect as much money as possible by pulling these arms over many turns. At each turn, $t = 1, 2, ...$, the player selects an arm, with index a_t, and receives a reward $y_t \sim D_j(t)$. The goal of the algorithm is to find out which distribution has the highest expected value, and also to gain as much reward as possible during the course of the game.

The added complexity of using bandit algorithms in bid prediction problems is two-fold: First, we assume that the bandit algorithm has access to a set of experts $S_t \in 1, K$ whose performance can change over time; second, for each turn t the bandit has to pay an unknown variable cost c_t associated with winning the auction. Hence, each trial of the bid prediction problem is a trial between the algorithm and an adversary in a game that consists of the following steps:

1. The adversary choses a set $S_t \subseteq \{1, ..., K\}$ of experts that are available at iteration t.
2. Each available expert $i \in S_t$ provides an estimate $\hat{x}^i$.
3. The algorithm chooses one expert s_j from S_t and uses its estimate to compute a bid.
4. The adversary chooses a cost c_t for buying that impression and a binary outcome $y_t \in \{0, 1\}$ (no click / click).
5. The algorithm pays a cost c_t.

Various strategies have been proposed that maximize the expected reward, but very few consider the inherent cost for playing an arm. As we showed, an algorithm that strives to maximize the expected reward (CTR) can be sub-optimal in minimizing the effective cost-per-click (eCPC). We propose a solution based on *randomized probability matching*, better known as Thompson Sampling [27] (TS). In the next section we provide the details of our solution.

4.1 Randomized probability matching

Randomized probability matching plays each action *randomly* in proportion to its probability of being *optimal*. This approach is known as *Thompson Sampling* and has been shown to be especially successful in systems whose limitations allow only periodic (batch) updates. It is broadly applicable, easy to implement and can be extended to work with a broad class of reward distributions.

We consider a general probabilistic, or Bayesian, formulation in which uncertain quantities are modeled as random variables. Let $\mathbf{y}_t = (y_1, ..., y_t)$ denote the sequence of rewards observed up to time t, such that $y_i \in \{0, 1\}, \forall i = 1, ..., t$. We focus on binary rewards because clicks are binary events. Let a_t denote the played arm at time t. The success of each arm is modeled as an IID random variable, Y_1, Y_2, ..., Y_K living in a space $\mathcal{Y} = \{0, 1\}^K$. Since each random variable has a binary outcome, each arm is modeled with a Bernoulli distribution with success probability θ_a. It follows that each y_t was generated independently from the reward distribution $f_{a_t}(y|\theta)$ of the played arm, where θ is an unknown parameter vector that governs the success probabilities of the Bernoulli distributions of the arms.

Let $\mathbf{c}_t = (c_1, ..., c_t)$ denote the sequence of costs that the algorithm has payed for each observed reward up to time t, such that $c_i \in \mathbb{R}, \forall i = 1, ..., t$. The cost of each arm is modeled as an independent and identically distributed random variable, C_1, C_2, ..., C_K defined in a space $\mathcal{C} = \mathbb{R}^K$. Now, the cost distribution of each arm is modeled with a Gaussian distribution with parameters m_a and σ_a. It follows that each c_t was generated independently from the cost distribution $f_{a_t}(c|m, \sigma)$ of the played arm, where m and σ are unknown parameter vectors.

Let $\mu_a(\theta) = E(y_t|\theta, a_t = a)$ denote the expected reward coming from the reward distribution $f_{a_t}(y|\theta)$. Let $\nu_a(m, \sigma) = E(c_t|m, \sigma, a_t = a)$ denote the expected cost coming from the cost distribution $f_{a_t}(c|m, \sigma)$. If our goal was to maximize the number of clicks without considering the price we are paying for each impression, then the optimal long run strategy would be to always choose the arm with the largest $\mu_a(\theta)$. However, our goal is to minimize the ratio of the total cost and the total number of clicks, i.e., the cost per click. Therefore, we will denote with $\mu_a(\theta, m, \sigma)$ the expected cost per click coming from the reward distribution $f_{a_t}(y|\theta)$ and the cost distribution $f_{a_t}(c|m, \sigma)$.

Let $p(\theta)$ denote a prior probability on θ, and $p(m, \sigma)$ denote a prior probability on m and σ. Assuming that we have a method to compute $\mu_a = \mu_a(\theta, m, \sigma)$, according to the principles of randomized probability matching one can compute the initial allocation probabilities:

$$w_{a,0} = P(\mu_a = \min\{\mu_1, \mu_2, ..., \mu_K\}). \quad (1)$$

Eq. 1 can be expressed as an integral of an indicator function. Let $I_a(\theta, m, \sigma) = 1$ if $\mu_a(\theta, m, \sigma) = \min\{\mu_1(\theta, m, \sigma), ..., \mu_K(\theta, m, \sigma)\}$, and $I_a(\theta, m, \sigma) = 0$ otherwise. Then

$$w_{a,0} = E(I_a(\theta, m, \sigma)) = \int I_a(\theta, m, \sigma) p(\theta) p(m, \sigma) d\theta dm d\sigma. \quad (2)$$

Here we assume that the success variables and the cost variables are independent from each other. The prior distributions represent our beliefs or a-priori knowledge about the success probability of each arm as well as the cost parameters per arm. As rewards and costs from the bandit process are observed, the parameters of the reward and cost distributions are updated through the process of Bayesian updating. After observing the sequence of rewards $\mathbf{y}_t$ and costs $\mathbf{c}_t$ at time t the posterior distribution of θ is

$$p(\theta|\mathbf{y}_t) \propto p(\theta) \prod_{\tau=1}^{t} f_{a_t}(y_\tau|\theta) \quad (3)$$

while the posterior distribution of m and σ is

$$p(m, \sigma|\mathbf{c}_t) \propto p(m, \sigma) \prod_{\tau=1}^{t} f_{a_t}(c_\tau|m, \sigma). \quad (4)$$

Hence, to compute the allocation probabilities in the next iteration all we need is a component that will be able to estimate the expected reward μ_a and up-to-date beliefs represented with the posterior distributions $p(\theta|\mathbf{y}_t)$ and $p(m, \sigma|\mathbf{c}_t)$:

$$\begin{aligned} w_{a,t} &= P(\mu_a = max\{\mu_1, \mu_2, ..., \mu_K\}|\mathbf{y}_t, \mathbf{c}_t) \quad (5) \\ &= E(I_a(\theta, m, \sigma)|\mathbf{y}_t, \mathbf{c}_t). \end{aligned}$$

Eq. 1 and Eq. 5 can be computed using the law of large numbers by simulation. Let $\theta^{(1)}$, ..., $\theta^{(G)}$ be a sample of independent draws from $p(\theta|\mathbf{y}_t)$, and $(m^{(1)}, \sigma)$, ..., $(m^{(G)}, \sigma)$ be a sample of independent draws from $p(m, \sigma|\mathbf{c}_t)$. By the law of large numbers,

$$w_{a,t} = \lim_{G \to \infty} \frac{1}{G} \sum_{g=1}^{G} I_a(\theta^{(g)}, m^{(g)}, \sigma). \quad (6)$$

Eq. 6 estimates the allocation probabilities $w_{a,t}$ by the empirical proportion of Monte Carlo samples in which $\mu_a(\theta^{(g)}, m^{(g)},$ is maximal. Choosing adequate conjugate prior distributions $p(\theta)$ and $p(m, \sigma)$ makes sampling independent draws of θ and m possible. In our case we will be working with a Beta distribution as a prior for the Bernoulli distribution used to model the reward likelihood, and a Gaussian prior for the Gaussian distribution used to model the cost likelihood.

Estimating $\mu_a(\theta, m, \sigma)$ is a separate problem which will not be discussed here in full detail. The method simply estimates the expected cost per click by the method of simulation, using the posterior distributions $p(\theta|\mathbf{y}_t)$ and $p(m, \sigma|\mathbf{c}_t)$. Since posterior draws are all that is needed to compute the allocation probabilities one can apply randomized probability matching with almost any family of reward distributions.

4.2 Thompson Sampling with double priors

The pseudo-code of our proposed Thompson Sampling algorithm is given in Algorithm 1. The algorithm starts from its prior beliefs on the expected success rate and the expected cost, implemented with a Beta and a Gaussian prior distribution, respectively. In each trial, the algorithm first observes the set of available experts S_t and their estimates $\hat{\mathbf{x}}_t^j$ (line 3), and performs a Monte Carlo simulation to calculate the allocation probabilities using Eq. 6 (line 4). The simulation consists of drawing independent samples from the posterior distributions of θ and m. Then the algorithm chooses to play an expert according to the allocation probabilities $\mathbf{w}_t$ (line 5), and uses its estimate of the CTR to calculate the bid. If the bid wins the external auction, the algorithm observes the outcome y_t and the cost c_t (line 8), and updates the posterior distributions by updating their parameters (lines 10-14).

Algorithm 1 Thompson Sampling with double priors

1: Initialize S(1) = 0, F(1) = 0, , T(1)=0, $\hat{m}(1) = 0$
2: **for** $t = 1, 2, ..., T$ **do**
3: Observe S_t and $\hat{\mathbf{x}}_t^j$
4: For $i \in S_t$ calculate the allocation probabilities $w_{i,t}$ using $Beta(S_a(t)+1, F_a(t)+1)$ and $\mathcal{N}(m(t), \sigma(t)^2)$
5: Choose one expert a at random according to $\mathbf{w}_t$
6: Use estimate $\hat{x}_t^a$ to submit a bid b_t
7: **if** b_t won the auction **then**
8: Observe the outcome y_t and the cost c_t
9: Update the posterior distributions of expert a:
10: $S_a(t+1) = S_a(t) + y_t$
11: $F_a(t+1) = F_a(t) + 1 - y_t$
12: $m(t+1) = \frac{\sigma_0^2}{\frac{\sigma^2}{t}+\sigma_0^2} c + \frac{\sigma^2}{\frac{\sigma^2}{t}+\sigma_0^2} m_0$
13: $\sigma(t+1)^2 = \left(\frac{1}{\sigma_0^2} + \frac{t}{\sigma^2}\right)^{-1}$
14: $T_a(t+1) = T_a(t) + 1$
15: **end if**
16: **end for**

Using Beta(α, β) priors is useful for Bernoulli rewards because the Beta distribution is a conjugate prior distribution for Bernoulli. This enables simple Bayesian updates through updating the parameters α and β. At time t having observed $S_a(t)$ successes and $F_a(t)$ failures in $T_a(t)$ plays of arm a, the posterior distribution is Beta($S_a(t)$+ y_t, $F_a(t)$ + 1 - y_t).

Similarly, the conjugate prior distribution for a Gaussian likelihood distribution is Gaussian, which again enables simple updates through the parameters of the distribution. We choose to model the likelihood of the cost $f_a(c|m, \sigma)$ with a Gaussian distribution $\mathcal{N}(m, \sigma^2) \sim \frac{1}{\sigma^t} \exp\left(-\frac{1}{2\sigma^2}\sum_i (c_i - m)^2\right)$.

By choosing a conjugate prior distribution $\mathcal{N}(m_0, \sigma_0^2)$s:

$$p(m_0, \sigma_0) \propto \frac{1}{\sigma_0} \exp\left(-\frac{1}{2\sigma_0^2}(m - m_0)^2\right)$$

where the prior mean m_0 is typically chosen to be 0, and the prior variance σ_0 is some large value, the resulting posterior distribution $p(m|\mathbf{c}_t)$ is obtained by simply multiplying the likelihood $f_a(c|m, \sigma)$ and the prior $p(m_0, \sigma_0)$:

$$\mathcal{N}\left(\frac{\sigma_0^2}{\frac{\sigma^2}{t} + \sigma_0^2} c + \frac{\sigma^2}{\frac{\sigma^2}{t} + \sigma_0^2} m_0, \left(\frac{1}{\sigma_0^2} + \frac{t}{\sigma^2}\right)^{-1}\right) \quad (7)$$

Both of the distributions can be updated using batch updates of their parameters.

5. NON-STATIONARY SYSTEMS

In a variety of practical applications as well as in our system the time evolution of the system, and in particular of the reward distributions, is gradual. Actually, if the relationship between the input features and the target variable is stationary then we can confidently predict that the reward distributions for each cold-started arm will be evolving in a similar way. As the estimates of the experts improve over time we should expect that there will a gradual increase in the running CTRs and a shift towards convergence. All of the experts will be characterized with an initial period of high instability and uncertainty. An example of how one should expect the evolution of the CTR would look like is given in Fig. 2.

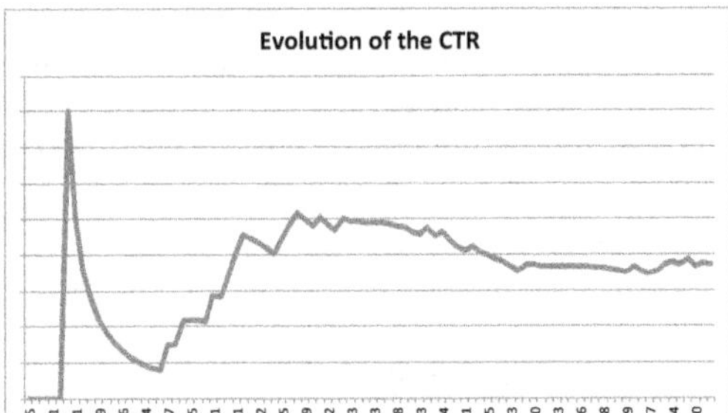

Figure 2: Evolution of the click-through-rate (CTR) for one specialists w.r.t. a given campaign.

Hence, for dynamic multi-armed bandit problems one should prefer policies that take into account the fact that the reward distributions change in a gradual manner, starting from a point of high instability and uncertainty and moving slowly towards a more stable phase. While Thompson Sampling naturally handles this evolution, it can be easily adapted to track potential changes.

5.1 Time-varying reward distributions

As discussed previously the problem we are solving falls in the family of multi-armed bandit problems with non-stationary reward distributions, where the optimal arm changes over time. We have discovered two sources of change in the reward distributions of the experts (arms):

1. Due to the slow increase in the accuracy and prediction power of a cold-started expert i, we expect an

initial period of instability where rewards arrive in an adversarial manner, followed by a gradual increase in the probability of successes S_i obtained in T_i number of Bernoulli trials and a saturation phase.

2. Due to the dynamic nature of the bidding process and the possibility of a change in the bidding landscape or the setup of the campaign, experts that performed well in the past might start to underperform compared to others w.r.t. a given campaign.

To be able to track changes in the probability of success of each expert, we adopt an approach based on exponential smoothing proposed by Gupta et al. [14]. This is a filtering technique that can be easily and efficiently implemented in a large-scale system like ours. The gist of exponential smoothing is exponential weighting of the outcomes in each trial, such that older outcomes get smaller weights and hence contribute less to the current estimate of the success probability θ_i. This is a typical forgetting mechanism used in many online learning algorithms designed for dynamic environments, and has been used for computing prequential (predictive-sequential) error estimates as well, where the sum of losses $L_A(t)$ at time t is computed as:

$$L_A(t) = \alpha L_A(t-1) + L_A(\hat{y}_t, y_t)$$

where $\alpha \in [0, 1]$ is a fading factor that determines the speed with which past errors will be diminished.

As discussed previously the posterior of the reward distribution at time t of expert a is modeled with a Beta($S_a(t)+y_t$, $F_a(t) + 1 - y_t$) distribution, where $S_i(t)$ and $F_i(t)$ denote the successes and the failures up to time t. Exponential smoothing is simply implemented through a new set of update rules on the parameters of the Beta distributions S_i and F_i, $\forall i = 1, ..., K$ and a threshold parameter C which determines the upper bound on the variance of the Beta distribution:

1. If $S_a(t-1) + F_a(t-1) < C$

$$\begin{aligned} S_a(t) &= S_a(t-1) + y_t \\ F_a(t) &= F_a(t-1) + 1 - y_t \end{aligned} \tag{8}$$

2. If $S_a(t-1) + F_a(t-1) \geq C$

$$\begin{aligned} S_a(t) &= (S_a(t-1) + y_t)\tfrac{C}{C+1} \\ F_a(t) &= (F_a(t-1) + 1 - y_t)\tfrac{C}{C+1} \end{aligned} \tag{9}$$

The effect of these update rules are that: 1) they ensure that the sum of $S_a(t)$ and $F_a(t)$ never grows above C; 2):

$$\mu_a(t) = \frac{S_a(t)}{S_a(t) + F_a(t)} = \alpha \mu_a(t-1) + (1-\alpha) y_t \tag{10}$$

where $\alpha = \frac{C}{C+1}$; and 3):

$$0 \leq \sigma_a^2(t) \leq \frac{1}{4(C+1)} \tag{11}$$

The direct effect of bounding the variance of the Beta distribution through the parameter C is to enabling indefinite exploration and through that, detection of relative changes in the expected values of the reward distributions of the experts. Due to the scale of our system and the large number of campaigns with different pacing parameters, the value of the parameter in practice needs to be set individually.

Exponential smoothing, however, is not sufficient to capture the dynamics of the reward distributions that are specific to cold-started experts. For that purpose, our online learning samplers operate on sliding windows. Using a sliding window enables us to discard the counts of successes and failures from the early stages of the specialized learners and maintain estimates using the most recent data.

5.2 Extensions: Factoring in Context

In the traditional, non-contextual multi-armed bandit problem, the learner has no access to arm features and simply competes with pulling the best of K arms in hindsight. As opposed to the traditional K-armed bandit problems, features of the arms may be useful to infer the conditional average payoff of an arm and improve the total average payoff over time. Our idea is to use real-time performance features of each expert, and time decaying functions that model the uncertainty in their performance in the early stages of their learning process as contextual information.

We use a predefined set of performance features and the time span w.r.t. the number of times the specialist was given a chance to learn: 1) the empirical estimate of the success probability $f_1(t) = S_a(t)/T_a(t)$, the running average of the specialist's predictions $f_2(t) = \frac{1}{T_a(t)} \sum_{\tau=1,a_\tau=a}^{t} \hat{y}_{a,\tau}$, the running variance of the specialist's predictions $f_3(t) = \frac{1}{T_a(t)} \sum_{\tau=1,a_\tau=a}^{t} (\hat{y}_{a,\tau} - \bar{\hat{y}}_{a,\tau})^2$, the submitted bid $f_4(t) = b_t$, and the time-decaying function $f_5(t) = \frac{1}{\sqrt{T_a(t)+1}}$.

The most notable example of bandits with side information are contextual bandits with linear payoff functions, which is a well studied problem in statistics and machine learning. Agrawal and Goyal have designed the first extension of Thompson Sampling for the case of the stochastic contextual multi-armed bandit problem, using Gaussian priors and Gaussian likelihood model [3]. We have adopted the same design of a contextual Thompson Sampling algorithm without any changes and used it for CTR estimation.

6. PRACTICAL ISSUES

The practical deployment of the Thompson Sampling algorithm involves the design and implementation of an offline and an online component. The offline component is designed to collect performance data which is being stored and accessed periodically, using Apache Hadoop and Pig. The online component, on the other hand, is executed by the ad servers in real time, and involves the process of sampling from the posterior distribution and calculating the allocation probabilities.

To ingest the data from the outside world, our data processing pipeline defines a process of transformation, join, and compression stages. Raw web logs need to be first synced to a designated location on the Hadoop file system, where they would be picked up by the modules for click attribution. This stage is followed by click de-duplication and fraud detection, and at last the aggregated data becomes accessible for querying. Because of this complicated pipeline, updates to the learners are periodical and can only happen in batches. It becomes clear that algorithms that cannot operate with batch updates cannot be implemented in our platform.

Further, having different campaigns with different budgets, bidding pace, bidding tactics, goals and targeting criteria, the expert selection problem needs to be carried out

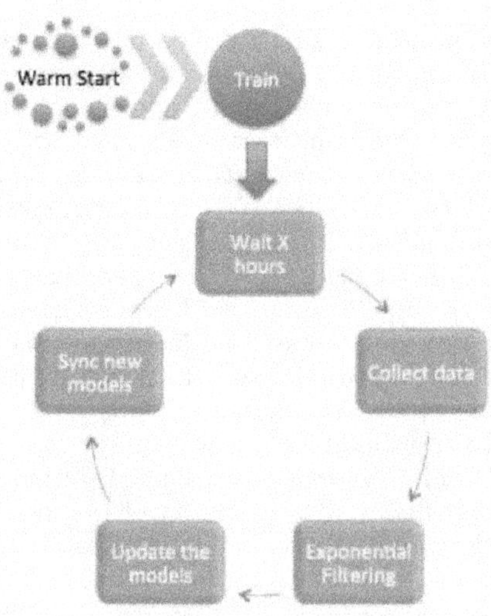

Figure 3: Illustration of the learning flow on HDFS.

at a more granular level. Therefore the data collection and model generation is done on a campaign level. For each campaign and for each expert that has been played, the data collection flow consists of a cyclic repetition of the following stages: collection and aggregation, exponential smoothing, generation of new hyper-parameters, as shown in Figure 3. The resulting model is in essence a key-value map, where the key is a combination of a campaign id and expert id, and value is a list of multiple summary statistics and distribution parameters.

After the new model is generated, it is synced to the 1000s of ad servers on the distributed platform, and its execution proceeds without real-time updates. It is worth mentioning that sampling from a Beta and a Gaussian distribution can be time consuming especially when the whole bid prediction process has to be done within few milliseconds. In order to speed up the sampling, we have used a fast implementation of the Mersenne-Twister algorithm [23] as a replacement of the random sampling function available in Java, as well as an implementation of the Ziggurat algorithm for generating random numbers from a Gaussian distribution [22]. Although using these improved samplers within the algorithms for sampling from a Beta and Gaussian distribution improved the sampling time significantly, due to the extremely sensitive time restrictions for some cases we also used precomputed samples and estimates.

7. RELATED WORK

The exploration / exploitation dilemma is an old problem and has received a significant amount of attention from the statistics and machine learning communities. The Multi-armed bandit problem has close connections to the Boosting method in classification [29], and to sparse recovery and compressed sensing [28]. Various strategies have been proposed throughout the decades, probability matching, greedy, hybrid strategies, methods based on indices such as the upper confidence bounds (UCB) and Gittins indices [12]. Among the oldest heuristics are the *randomized probability matching* or *posterior sampling* strategies. The first version of this Bayesian heuristic is around 80 years old, dating back to Thompson [27].

Thompson Sampling (TS) has only recently been established as a top performer for MABs with Bernoulli distributed rewards, and the reason for this delay has been the lack of theoretical understanding. Several studies [13, 26, 8, 24, 15] have empirically demonstrated the efficacy of TS. Weak guarantees have been provided by [13, 24] with a bound of $o(T)$ on the expected regret in time T. Some significant progress has recently been made by [1, 15, 2], who provided optimal regret bounds on the expected regret; Agrawal and Goyal provided high probability, near-optimal regret bounds for stochastic contextual bandits with linear payoffs [3].

It is useful to mention that one could imagine trying to solve the best specialist selection problem using EXP3- or EXP4-type approaches [5]. In EXP4-type approaches the player's goal is to combine the advice of the experts in such a way that its return is close to that of the best expert. EXP4 stands for "Exponential-weight algorithm for Exploration and Exploitation using Expert advice", hence, it is an algorithm that learns how to mix the probability distributions coming from N experts in order to generate a final mixture distribution over the set of arms of size K. It can be used in a simplified scenario, where each expert corresponds to a deterministic policy that maps a context to only one arm with probability 1.0, and with probability 0.0 to the rest of the arms. EXP3 is in essence a special case of EXP4 for this simplified scenario.

While in the expert-learning framework, each expert corresponds to a contextual policy for arm selection, in our setup experts are not a mapping from a context to an arm, but they are specialized arms whose outputs are the conditional probabilities $f_i(y_t|\theta)$. EXP3- and EXP4-type approaches cannot be easily modified towards more complex reward distributions or optimization goals. Therefore, none of these approaches provide any advantage over Thompson Sampling. Posterior sampling can be applied to a much broader class of problems, and one of its greatest strengths is its ability to incorporate prior knowledge in a flexible and coherent way.

Recently Li [20], motivated by the connection between Thompson Sampling and exponentiated updates, has designed a new family of algorithms called Generalized Thompson Sampling in the expert-learning framework [7]. Generalized Thompson Sampling (GTS) is very similar in structure to EXP4, with the difference of a more general update rule that uses a loss function to adjust the expert's weights. Each expert represents a greedy policy with respect to the probability of success (reward prediction) that maps a context to an arm. As in all existing analysis for Thompson Sampling, the assumption is that one of the experts correctly predicts the expected reward (probability of success). The generalization involves two loss functions: Logarithmic loss and square loss, for which regret bounds are derived. The author shows that Thompson Sampling is a special case of GTS when the logarithmic loss is used [2].

Due to the complexity of the performance-based bid prediction problem, very few algorithms are designed to maximize the expected reward (CTR) having into account budget limitations or costs for playing the arms. To the best of our

[2]The loss function is used to measure how well the expert predicts the average reward, given the context and the selected arm. In general, the loss function and the reward may be completely unrelated.

knowledge, there is only one work that treats the bandit problem with budget constraint and variable costs [9]. The authors propose UCBBV2 an UCB-type algorithm whose expected regret depends on the budget which constrains the total number of pulls. While this algorithm does take into account the variable costs per arms, it is not designed to work with batch updates and as such it is not appropriate for our platform.

8. EVALUATION METHODOLOGY

Our proposed framework of bid prediction has been implemented, tested, and deployed at Turn, a leading DSP. In this section, we present experimental results from our testing environment where we compared different strategies for expert selection. In addition, we also show results from real campaigns that serve large amounts of daily impressions in order to demonstrate the overall performance improvement in terms of CTR, eCPC, and ROI performance metrics. Advertiser's return of investment (ROI) is the total value ($\#click \times value$) divided by the total cost incurred ($\sum_i c_i$).

8.1 Experiments

The first part of our experimental evaluation consists of an offline policy evaluation of the proposed Thompson Sampling algorithm and its extension, the Contextual Thompson Sampling algorithm with a number of state-of-the-art multi-armed bandit strategies. The offline evaluation is performed on a large collection of over 300 million ad impressions, collected by Turn's processing pipeline in a period of 30 days. The impressions belong to 7 top spending advertisers that are running several campaigns on the platform. The second part of our experimental evaluation is an online comparison of Thompson Sampling on production data to our existing baseline algorithm through fair A/B testing. The baseline algorithm is a static, rule-based model that chooses the best expert in a deterministic manner.

First, we would like to emphasize the volatility of the CTR in few top performing estimators through the daily evolution of the CTR shown on Fig. 4. This CTR is computed by ordering our historic impressions based on the time stamp the impression was shown to a user and aggregated by day. We can see that the daily CTR varies significantly, which has strongly discouraged us from running experiments on simulated data.

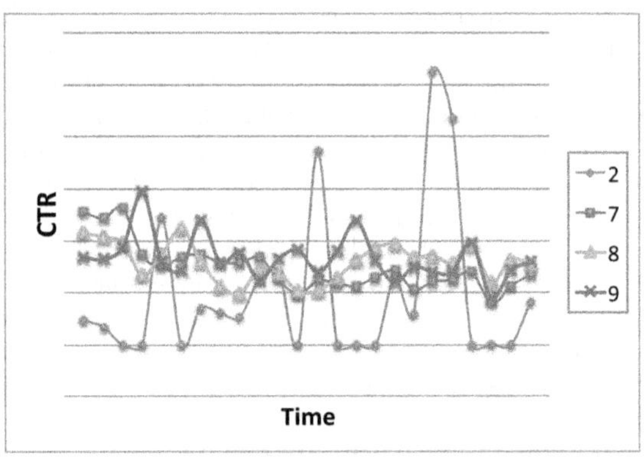

Figure 4: Illustration of the evolution of the CTR per day for the top performing experts.

In the comparison we have used the following state-of-the-art MAB algorithms: Chernoff UCB is an index based UCB-style algorithm with a tight upper confidence bound derived from the Chernoff bound ([16], page 278), EXP3 and EXP3.S [5] are bandit algorithms with experts advice, UCB1 and Tuned UCB1 [4], UCBBV2 [9]. For a fair comparison we ran all of the algorithms without using any explicit change detection or blind concept drift management. All of the algorithms were further tuned for best performance.

As a DSP, we do not have the luxury of executing arbitrary policies on real traffic, and the only viable alternative is to do offline policy evaluation. Offline policy evaluation is the process of evaluating a new strategy for behavior, or policy, using only observations collected during the execution of another policy. The difficulty of this problem stems from the lack of control over available data. In our case we are bounded to use the existing logged impressions and the corresponding choices of the baseline algorithm, which is our exploration policy.

Exploration Scavenging (also known as *offline replay* [17]) is a popular method for offline evaluation of new MAB policies π_i, by using the logged decisions of an existing baseline policy s. This method suggests to calculate an expected reward of a new policy s using the following equation:

$$\hat{R}(\pi) = \frac{1}{T}\sum_{t=1}^{T} r_{s(x_t)}\mathbf{1}[s(x_t) = \pi(x_t)] \sum_{a\in\mathcal{A}} \mathbf{1}[s(x_t) = a] w_{x_t,a}, \quad (12)$$

where T denotes the total number of historic logs used in the replay, A is the set of all possible actions (arms), x_t is the context for impression at time t, $\mathbf{1}$ is the indicator function, and $w_{x,a}$ is a normalization weight calculated from the whole set of impressions with contextual information x as

$$w_{x,a} = \frac{\sum_{t'=1}^{T} \mathbf{1}[x_{t'} = x] \times \mathbf{1}[\pi(x_{t'}) = a]}{\sum_{t'=1}^{T} \mathbf{1}[x_{t'} = x] \times \mathbf{1}[\pi(x_{t'}) = a] \times \mathbf{1}[\pi(x_{t'}) = s(x_{t'})]}.$$

Exploration scavenging first estimates the average reward of each action from the set of impression on which both the evaluation π and the exploration s policies agree on choosing the same action a, then applies the estimate to all the impressions for which the evaluation policy π suggests the action a. Fig. 5 shows the total scavenged CTR for each algorithm computed at the end of the run.

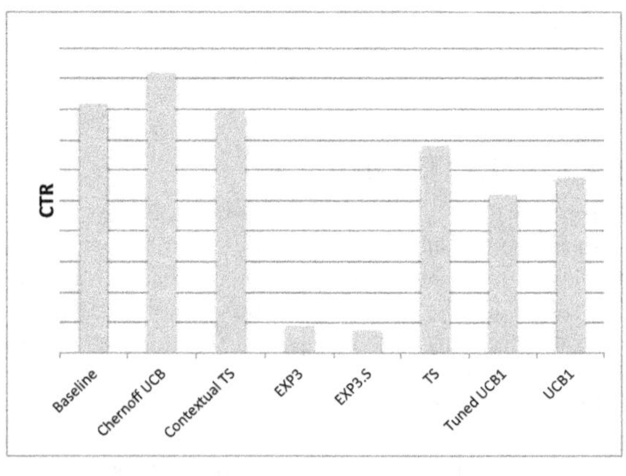

Figure 5: Total scavenged CTR per algorithm.

Beside exploration scavenging we also show results computed using only the impressions on which the evaluation policy agreed with the exploration policy, without applying precomputed estimates of the average reward. We will refer to this approach as the matched CTR. Unlike the exploration scavenging estimates this approach will provide rather optimistic estimates of the CTR. These estimates are highly dependent on the number of matched impressions between the evaluation and the exploration policy. From all algorithms, TS and Contextual TS had the largest overlap with the baseline policy, with Contextual TS having twice as much more matched decisions than TS. Fig. 6 shows a comparison of the total matched CTR for all algorithms at the end of the run.

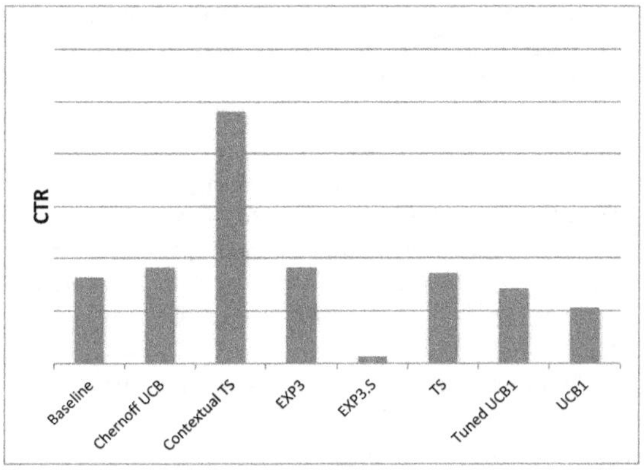

Figure 6: Total matched CTR per algorithm.

At last, Fig. 7 shows relative results in terms of the total ROI at the end of the run, which is our main metric of interest. The top leading algorithms are evidently TS and Contextual TS, with UCBBV2 and the baseline being third. As discussed previously, to work properly, UCB-type of algorithms require updates of the arm's upper confidence bounds instantaneously due to the deterministic indexes. In practice, this is rarely doable. On the other hand, Thompson sampling relies purely on random distribution sampling, and can maintain a reasonable balance between exploration and exploitation in each round while using a batch-updates.

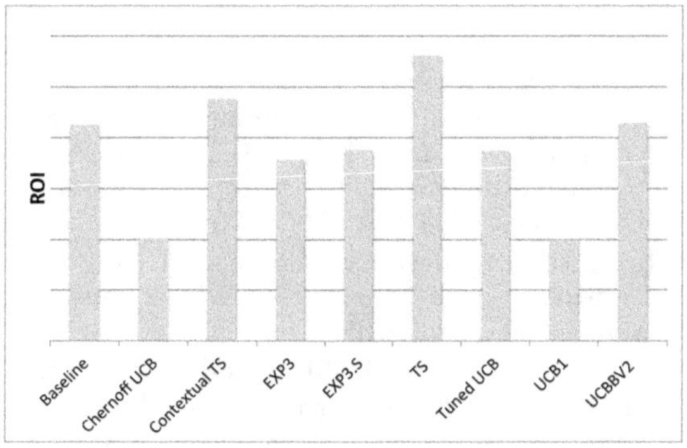

Figure 7: Total ROI per algorithm.

Due to the dynamic behavior of the expert's performance it is important to understand how the performance of each of the top algorithms evolves over time. Due to space limitations we will only show the evolutions of the CTR and the ROI for the Thompson Sampling algorithm and our baseline model evaluated on production traffic over the timeline of one day. Figure 8 and Figure 9 show summaries of the cumulative CTR and ROI on a global level as time proceeds. We can see that Thompson Sampling performs better than the baseline model both in terms of CTR and in terms of global ROI. Similarly, Figure 10 compares the cumulative eCPC of the two models as a function of time. As the plot indicates, TS is able to provide a lower overall eCPC compared to the baseline model.

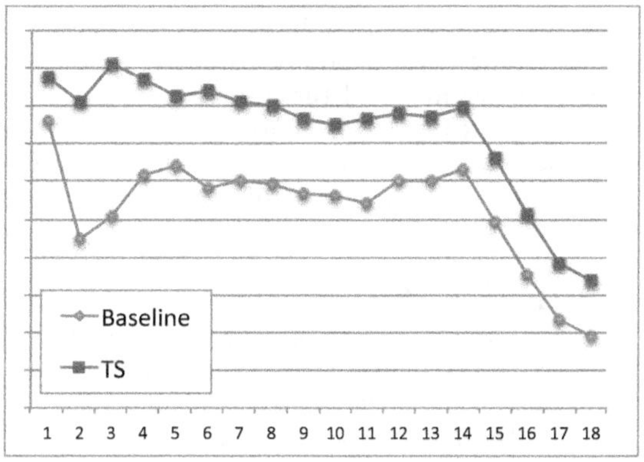

Figure 8: Evolution of CTR on production traffic.

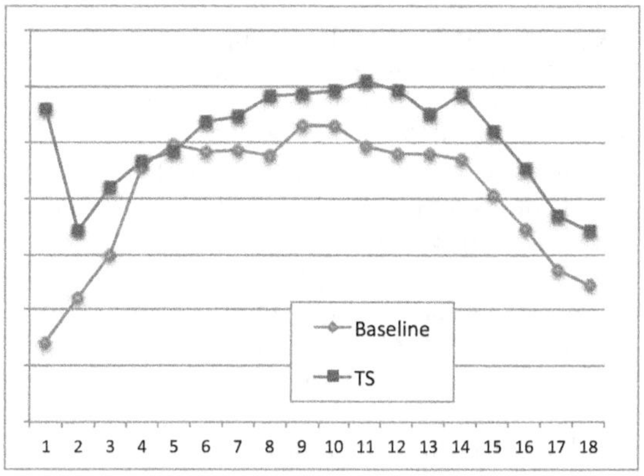

Figure 9: Evolution of ROI on production traffic.

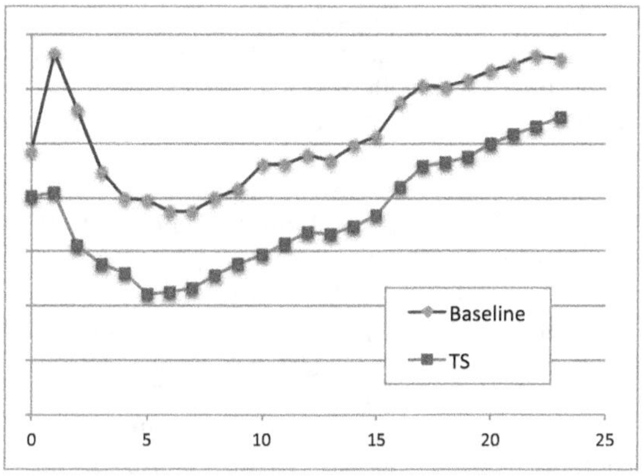

Figure 10: Evolution of eCPC on production traffic.

9. CONCLUSIONS

Multi-armed bandits have an important role to play in modern production systems that emphasize "continuous improvement", where products remain in a perpetual state of feature testing even after they have been launched. In this paper we advocate using randomized probability matching as a superior algorithm, and the industry standard, due to its performance both in terms of accuracy, as well as speed, broad applicability and ease-of-use. Thompson Sampling offers superior real-time bid prediction compared to the baseline algorithm in just a few milliseconds.

10. REFERENCES

[1] S. Agrawal and N. Goyal. Analysis of thompson sampling for the multi-armed bandit problem. In *Proceedings of the 25th Annual Conference on Learning Theory (COLT)*, June 2012.

[2] S. Agrawal and N. Goyal. Further optimal regret bounds for thompson sampling. *CoRR*, abs/1209.3353, 2012.

[3] S. Agrawal and N. Goyal. Thompson sampling for contextual bandits with linear payoffs. *30th International Conference on Machine Learning (ICML)*, June 2013.

[4] P. Auer, N. Cesa-Bianchi, and P. Fischer. Finite-time analysis of the multiarmed bandit problem. *Mach. Learn.*, 47(2-3):235–256, 2002.

[5] P. Auer, N. Cesa-Bianchi, Y. Freund, and R. E. Schapire. The nonstochastic multiarmed bandit problem. *SIAM J. Comput.*, 32(1):48–77, Jan. 2003.

[6] A. Blum. Empirical support for winnow and weighted-majority based algorithms: Results on a calendar scheduling domain. In A. Prieditis and S. J. Russell, editors, *ICML*, pages 64–72. Morgan Kaufmann, 1995.

[7] N. Cesa-Bianchi and G. Lugosi. *Prediction, Learning, and Games.* Cambridge University Press, New York, NY, USA, 2006.

[8] O. Chapelle and L. Li. An empirical evaluation of thompson sampling. In *NIPS*, pages 2249–2257, 2011.

[9] W. Ding, T. Qin, X.-D. Zhang, and T.-Y. Liu. Multi-armed bandit with budget constraint and variable costs. In M. desJardins and M. L. Littman, editors, *AAAI*. AAAI Press, 2013.

[10] B. Edelman, M. Ostrovsky, and M. Schwarz. Internet advertising and the generalized second price auction: Selling billions of dollars worth of keywords. Working Paper 11765, National Bureau of Economic Research, November 2005.

[11] Y. Freund, R. E. Schapire, Y. Singer, and M. K. Warmuth. Using and combining predictors that specialize. In F. T. Leighton and P. W. Shor, editors, *STOC*, pages 334–343. ACM, 1997.

[12] J. C. Gittins. Bandit processes and dynamic allocation indices. *Journal of the Royal Statistical Society. Series B (Methodological)*, 41(2):148–177, 1979.

[13] O. Granmo. Solving two-armed bernoulli bandit problems using a bayesian learning automaton. *International Journal of Intelligent Computing and Cybernetics*, 3(2):207–234, 2010.

[14] N. Gupta, O.-C. Granmo, and A. Agrawala. Thompson sampling for dynamic multi-armed bandits. In *Proceedings of the 2011 10th International Conference on Machine Learning and Applications and Workshops - Volume 01*, pages 484–489. IEEE Computer Society, 2011.

[15] E. Kaufmann, N. Korda, and R. Munos. Thompson sampling: An asymptotically optimal finite-time analysis. In *Proceedings of the 23rd International Conference on Algorithmic Learning Theory*, ALT'12, pages 199–213. Springer-Verlag, 2012.

[16] J. Langford. Tutorial on practical prediction theory for classification. *J. Mach. Learn. Res.*, 6:273–306, 2005.

[17] J. Langford, A. Strehl, and J. Wortman. Exploration scavenging. In *Proceedings of the 25th International Conference on Machine Learning*, pages 528–535, New York, NY, USA, 2008. ACM.

[18] K.-C. Lee, A. Jalali, and A. Dasdan. Real time bid optimization with smooth budget delivery in online advertising. In *Proceedings of the Seventh International Workshop on Data Mining for Online Advertising*, pages 1:1–1:9, New York, NY, USA, 2013. ACM.

[19] K.-c. Lee, B. Orten, A. Dasdan, and W. Li. Estimating conversion rate in display advertising from past erformance data. In *Proceedings of the 18th ACM SIGKDD International Conference on Knowledge Discovery and Data Mining*, KDD '12, pages 768–776, 2012.

[20] L. Li. Generalized thompson sampling for contextual bandits. *CoRR*, 2013.

[21] L. Li, W. Chu, J. Langford, and R. E. Schapire. A contextual-bandit approach to personalized news article recommendation. In M. Rappa, P. Jones, J. Freire, and S. Chakrabarti, editors, *WWW*, pages 661–670. ACM, 2010.

[22] G. Marsaglia and W. W. Tsang. A simple method for generating gamma variables. *ACM Trans. Math. Softw.*, 26(3):363–372, Sept. 2000.

[23] M. Matsumoto and T. Nishimura. Mersenne twister: A 623-dimensionally equidistributed uniform pseudo-random number generator. *ACM Trans. Model. Comput. Simul.*, 8(1):3–30, Jan. 1998.

[24] B. C. May, N. Korda, A. Lee, and D. S. Leslie. Optimistic bayesian sampling in contextual-bandit problems. *J. Mach. Learn. Res.*, 13(1):2069–2106, June 2012.

[25] C. Perlich, B. Dalessandro, R. Hook, O. Stitelman, T. Raeder, and F. Provost. Bid optimizing and inventory scoring in targeted online advertising. In *Proceedings of the 18th ACM SIGKDD International Conference on Knowledge Discovery and Data Mining*, KDD '12, pages 804–812. ACM, 2012.

[26] S. L. Scott. A modern bayesian look at the multi-armed bandit. *Appl. Stoch. Model. Bus. Ind.*, 26(6):639–658, Nov. 2010.

[27] W. R. Thompson. On the likelihood that one unknown probability exceeds another in view of the evidence of two samples. *Biometrika*, 25:285–294, 1933.

[28] S. Jafarpour, V. Cevher, and R. E. Schapire. A game theoretic approach to expander-based compressive sensing. *Proceedings, IEEE International Symposium on Information Theory*, 2011.

[29] R. E. Schapire, and Y. Freund. Boosting: Foundations and Algorithms *MIT Press*, 2012.

Life-stage Prediction for Product Recommendation in E-commerce

Peng Jiang† Yadong Zhu† Yi Zhang‡ Quan Yuan†
† Alibaba Inc, Beijing, China
‡ University of California, Santa Cruz, USA
{jiangpeng.jp, edgewind.zyd, yuanquan.yq}@alibaba-inc.com
{yiz}@soe.ucsc.edu

ABSTRACT

Although marketing researchers and sociologists have recognized the large impact of life stage on consumer's purchasing behaviors, existing recommender systems have not taken this impact into consideration. In this paper, we found obvious correlation between life stage and purchasing behavior in many E-commerce categories. For example, a mum may look for different suitable products when her baby is at different ages. Motivated by this, we introduce the conception of life stage into recommender systems and propose to predict a user's current life-stage and recommend products correspondingly. We propose a new Maximum Entropy Semi Markov Model to segment and label consumer life stage based on the observed purchasing data over time. In the mom-baby product category where the life stage transition is deterministic, we develop an efficient approximate solution using large scale logistic regression and a Viterbi-like algorithm. We also propose a Gaussian mixture model to efficiently handle multi-kids life stage prediction problem. We integrate the life stage information predicted into the recommender system behind the largest online shopping website taobao.com. Both offline and online experiments demonstrate the effectiveness of the proposed life-stage based recommendation approach.

Categories and Subject Descriptors

H.2.8 [**Database Management**]: Database applications–Data mining

Keywords

E-commerce, Recommender System, Life Stage

1. INTRODUCTION

Recommender systems have achieved much commercial success and is one of the most important data mining applications. For example, online stores such as Taobao, Amazon, and Walmart.com provide customized recommendations for additional products or services based on a user's historical purchasing records. It's well known that these recommendations are extremely important and have great impact on consumers' online shopping experience. Thus scholars and industry researchers in the data mining community have spent much effort on further improving recommendation performance, exploring all possible approaches. Most of the existing recommendation approaches can be mainly divided into two categories: content-based approaches [1, 2, 3] and collaborative filtering approaches [4, 5]. The content-based filtering recommend items similar to what a user likes before by representing the user's preferences using item content features, whereas the collaborative filtering approaches assume users with similar preferences on some items may also have similar preferences on other items.

On the other hand, marketing researchers and sociologists have recognized the importance of life stages on consumer's purchasing behaviors for many years[6, 7, 8]. For example, consumers go through various life stages, such as bachelor stage (i.e. young and single), newly married couples (young, no children), full nest (married couple with dependent children), empty nest (i.e. elder married couples with no children living together). Full nest stage can be further divided into a few substage, largely depending on the age of the dependent children; while empty nest stage can be further divided into sub stages such as head in labor force, retired, solitary survivors (i.e. old and single) etc. It's well recognized that both durable products and consumable products are sensitive to changes in life cycle stage.

In our E-commerce system, we also found strong correlation between life cycle stages and consumer purchasing behavior. For example, a woman will buy maternal vitamin during the pregnancy stage, then buy a baby car when her baby is born. A mum will have different purchasing needs during different life stages, which can be illustrated as figure 1. The figure shows that a user's needs and interests are dynamic and determined by her current life stage. Therefore, explicitly modeling and predicting life stages might be very useful for predicting the purchasing timed of products. We expect making recommendations based on this additional information could further improve the recommendation effectiveness. Unfortunately, most of the existing methods do not consider the concept of life stages, which exists in many verticals in E-commerce.

In this paper, we introduce the concept of life-stage into E-commerce recommendation systems. The system first predicts the current life stage of a user, then recommends products to the user based on the prediction and our proposed

KDD'15, August 10-13, 2015, Sydney, NSW, Australia.

DOI: http://dx.doi.org/10.1145/2783258.2788562.

probabilistic recommendation model, which can explicitly incorporate the life-stage information into an E-commerce recommender system.

To predict the life stage of a user, we proposed a new Maximum Entropy Semi Markov model for stochastic life stage segmentation and prediction over the user's past purchasing sequence. Besides, we developed a practical efficient large scale industry solution for life stage segmentation and labeling in mum-baby domain, where the life stage transition is deterministic. More specifically, we utilize the logistic regression classifier to predict the label and associated probability of each behavior sequence, and segment the whole sequence by Viterbi-like approach efficiently. We also handle the multi-kids problem via Gaussian mixture model.

To evaluate the effectiveness of the proposed life-stage based approach, we conduct extensive experiments with both offline data and online user studies for the mum-baby domain. The offline experimental results on a large dataset demonstrate that the proposed approach can significantly improve the performance in terms of prediction accuracy. Online experimental results also demonstrate the effectiveness of introducing life stage concept into a recommendation system. This work is integrated into the largest online shopping web site Taobao.com. Figure 2 is a snapshot of mum-baby product recommender system[1]. On Figure 2, the left side vertical navigation menu contains several life stages: pregnant, new born to 6 months, 6-12 months, 1-3 years, 3-6 years and 6-14 years, which describes the natural growth process of children. The system automatically locates a customer into a predicted (i.e. system selected) life stage. The right side recommends various products corresponding to the selected life stage.

The main contributions of this paper are:

1. We introduced the conception of life stages into E-commerce recommendation systems;

2. We proposed a new Maximum Entropy Semi Markov model for stochastic life stage segmentation and prediction;

3. We developed a practical efficient large scale industry solution for life stage segmentation and labeling in mum-baby domain, where the life stage transition is deterministic;

4. We proposed a probability model which can explicitly incorporate the life-stage information into an E-commerce recommender system.

5. We proposed a solution for modeling multi-kids scenario via Gaussian mixture models.

6. We verified of the effectiveness of the life-stage based approach in both offline and online scenarios.

The rest of the paper is organized as follows. The paper first provides some example based analysis in Section 2. Secondly, the life-stage based recommendation approach proposed is described in Section 3, followed by the analysis and modeling of multi-kids scenario in Section 4. Section 5 presents the experimental results, Section 6 describes the related work, and Section 7 concludes.

[1] http://www.taobao.com/market/baobao/2014/

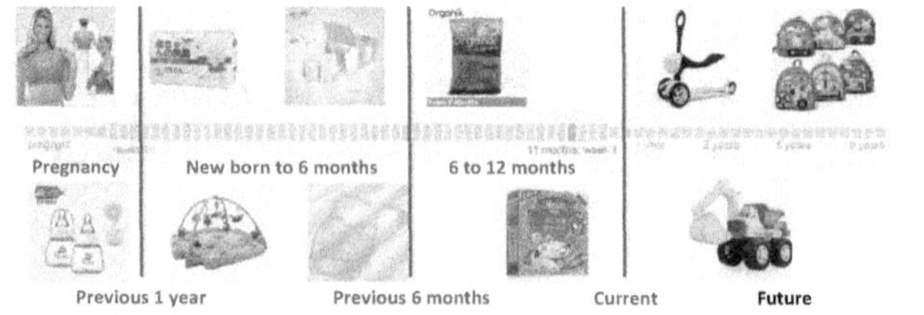

Figure 1: An illustration of the changing needs during different life stages of a baby.

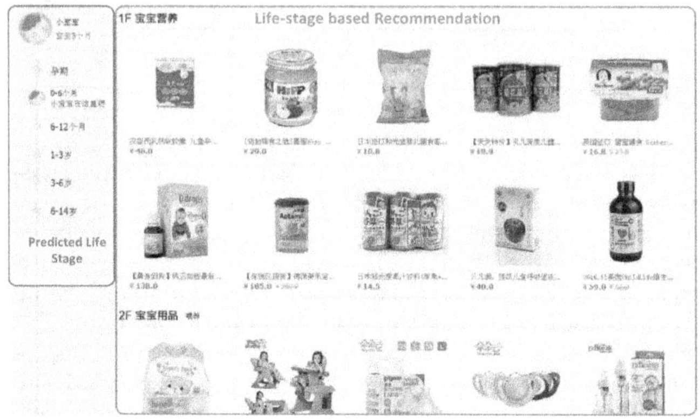

Figure 2: A screenshot of life-stage based recommender system deployed in Taobao.com.

2. LIFE STAGE AND CONSUMER BEHAVIORS

In this paper, we define life stage broadly and assume life stages are linked to certain tasks, which are the hidden reasons behind various purchasing choices. In addition, new purchasing tasks may emerge as a consumer transits from one life stage to the next one. Based on our broad definition, the conception of life stage exists in many vertical domains (i.e. categories) in E-commerce, such as home remodeling, car purchasing and wedding planning.

2.1 Data Analysis in Multiple Verticals

We carried out detailed data analysis in several verticals at taobao.com. We find that the conception of life-stage can be recovered from the purchasing behavior of users. The results on house remodeling vertical are shown in Figure 3. It shows that when a person enters into the house remodeling process, he or she may first buy some tiles for floor and emulsion paints for wall at the early stage. Next, the person may buy ceiling lights and shower faucets, followed by furniture such as dining table and beds. When all the above remodeling are completed, the person may buy formaldehyde clear spray for cleaning and bedding for the final stage decoration. We also find similar temporal purchasing patterns for other complex events that involve multiple stages, such as wedding planning and car purchasing.

2.2 Mum-Baby Domain

Although the proposed idea and major models can be applied to various events, the experiments and large scale solution described in this paper are focusing on the vertical recommendation of mum-baby products. In the mum-baby

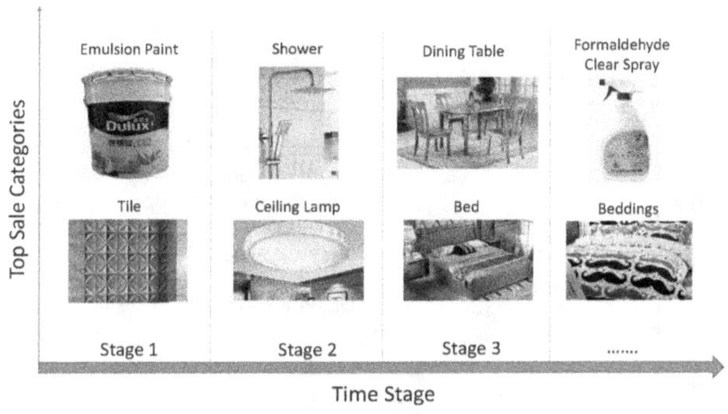

Figure 3: A data analysis of home remodeling in Taobao.com

vertical domain, the effect of life-stage on consumer behavior is the most obvious and very important. At different life stages of a baby, a woman needs to buy different matching products. For example, a woman is likely to buy maternity clothes at the prenatal stage, then she may look for milk powder after the baby is born. For a vertical recommender system, how to predict a user's life stage precisely and recommend appropriate products for the current life stage is a very important and challenging problem.

3. LIFE-STAGE BASED RECOMMENDATION

Life-stage of a user is a predefined set of phases in life, and each life stage spans a period of time. Changes in life stages may lead to changes in a person's purchasing needs. Examples of life-stage in maternal and child domain include pregnancy, new-born-baby, 1 - 3 months old, etc.

In our system, there are two major sub tasks. First, we label each user's behavior sequences so that we can tell a user's current life stage. Second, we generate recommendations based on the predicted life-stage. Thus the key components of life-stage based recommendations include how to model and predict life stages and how to give appropriate product recommendation correspondingly. The details of each component is described in this sections. Our experiments focus on the mum-baby domain, which is a special domain we will describe in more details.

3.1 Notations

The notations to be used in the rest of this paper are:

- X: the behavior sequence of a user. Behavior sequence X of a user is a sequence of user actions ordered by time. User actions in our system include clicking/collecting/buying an item, issuing a query, clicking navigating tips, etc.
- T: the length of X.
- X_t: the observed behavior sequence at time t.
- d_t: the duration of a life stage at time t.
- y_t: the life stage label at time t.
- l_{min},l_{max}: the minimum and maximum lengths of life stage respectively which are defined by domain experts.

3.2 MESMM for Life-stage Prediction and Segmentation

We considered several structured models (e.g. Hidden Semi-Markov Model[9], Maximum Entropy Markov Model[10], Conditional Random Fields[11], etc.) that may be used to model the joint distribution of life stages and user actions. Based on the characteristics of our problem, we propose a Maximum Entropy Semi Markov Model (MESMM) to segment and label consumer life stage based on the observed purchasing data over time. This model is motivated by Maximum Entropy Markov Models and Hidden Semi Markov Models. It is similar to Maximum Entropy Markov model except that the probability of changing the hidden state depends on the amount of time that has elapsed since entry into the current state. This model is general enough to model various scenarios.

In this model(see Figure 4), the probability of life stage y_t at time t depends on the previous life stage y_{t-1} at time $t-1$, how long the user has been in the previous life stage (i.e. d_{t-1}), and the observed user behavior sequence. The variable d changes deterministically. When life stage changes, d is reset to 0. Otherwise d decreases as time goes on. Therefore, d can capture the duration of user being in a life stage.

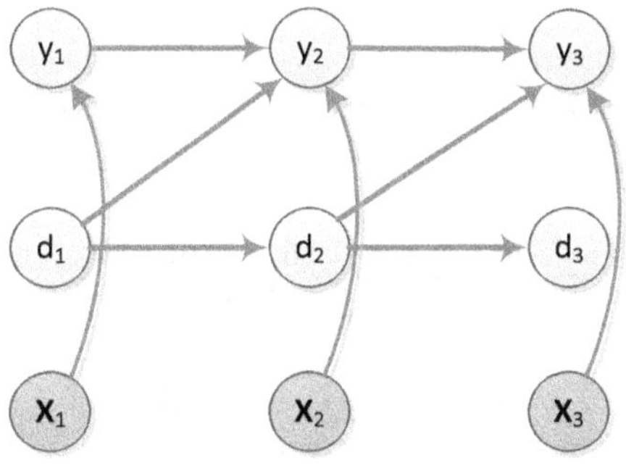

Figure 4: The Maximum Entropy Semi Markov Model for segmenting and labeling consumer life stages based on the observed purchasing data over time

Given an observed behavior sequence X, our goal is to find the best underlying life-stage sequence $y_1, ..., y_k$ and the corresponding duration $d_i, ..., d_k$:

$$\begin{aligned} &\{y_1, ..., y_k, d_i, ..., d_k\} \qquad (1) \\ &= \underset{k,d_t,y_t}{\text{argmax}} \prod_{t=1}^{k} P(y_t|y_{t-1}, d_{t-1}, X_t)P(d_t|d_{t-1}) \\ &\text{s.t. } l_{min} \le d_t \le l_{max} \end{aligned}$$

where X_t denotes the observed behavior sequence at time t. T denotes the length of X. l_{min} and l_{max} are the minimum and maximum lengths of a stage, which are defined by domain experts. $p(y_t|y_{t-1}, d_{t-1}, X_t)$ is the probability of being in y_t at time t given the previous stage y_{t-1}, the previous stage duration d_{t-1} and the observed behavior sequence X_t. The optimal segmentations and labels can be found using dynamic programming.

3.3 Mum-Baby Domain: An Efficient Solution

In our experiments, we mainly focus on the life-stage based recommendation in the mum-baby domain. The candidate life-stage labels/states are shown on Table 1. They are provided by marketing experts based on baby product standards and their domain knowledge.

Although MESMM is very general, learning and inference are computationally expensive for large data set and complex features. Fortunately, in the mom-baby product category, the transition and duration of life stages for a child are deterministic. We only need to find the birthday date, then the whole sequence can be labeled by a baby life stage template with a fixed sequence of life stages and fixed length in each stage.

Since most of our mum-baby consumers only have one child per family (due to the one child policy in our country), we first assume all our training data are from one child families. Multi-kids family scenarios are referred to the next Section.

In this scenario, we only need to focus on the problem of estimating the probability $P(y_t|y_{t-1}, d_{t-1}, X_t)$ in E.q 1. In our system, we train a large scale multinomial logistic regression (LR) model with $l1$ regularization. y_{t-1}, d_{t-1} and X_t are all input features for the LR model. To get training data for the multinomial logistic regression model, we first label users' behavior sequences in our training dataset based on the birth dates provided by users. The prediction and segmentation of life-stage for all users are implemented offline on parallel machines.

Table 1: Life-stage labels for Mom-baby domain

Label	Baby Age Category
0	Pregnant
1	New born - 6 months
2	6 - months
3	1 - 3 years
4	3 - 6 years

3.4 Features for the Classifier

To train $P(y|y', d', X_*)$, we convert each behavior subsequence X_* into a feature vector for training the multinomial logistic regression model. In general, the features fall in the following groups:

Category features: Many user actions are related to some items. Given a behavior sequence, we obtain a set of product IDs and could use a bag of IDs as features. However, this will lead to poor performance because of the sparsity issue. Besides, the set of items available in our system are changing frequently over time. To alleviate this problem, we represent each item using its category.

All items in Taobao are mapped to a category hierarchy. We expect consumer purchasing behavior patterns at different stages are more obvious on the categorical level. For example, a pregnant women is more likely to browse or buy products in 'Maternity Cloths' and 'Pregnant Bras' categories. A new parent is likely to browse 'Baby stroller' category. Figure 5 shows how purchasing ratio of top level categories relates to baby age.

We utilize all parent categories and first level categories an item belongs to as features. In order to reduce the influence of popular categories, the feature weight is set based on the TFIDF equation commonly used in the Information Retrieval community. To do so, each user is treated as a document and each category is treated as a term.

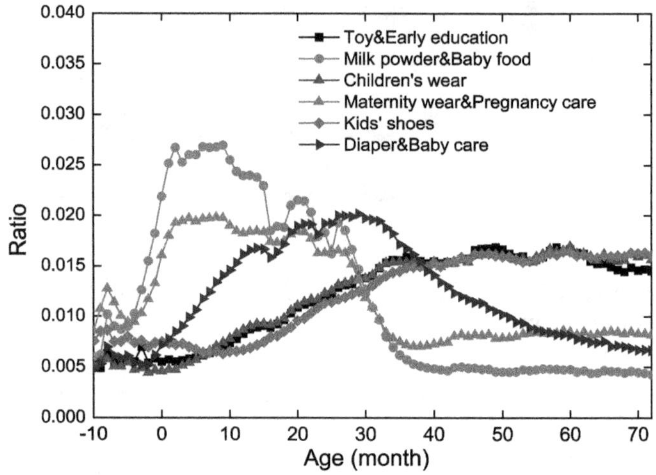

Figure 5: The purchasing ratio of 6 top level categories changes with a baby's age (unit: month). We normalize the value of a category at each time stage using a category specific normalization factor (i.e. the total number of products in the category bought over all those years)

Queries: A user behavior sequence may contain user product search activities. User search queries can directly reflect users' requirements, which can indirectly reflect a baby's age. For example, a user may search "large-size diaper" or "3 years old children's garments". This information is very important for age prediction. Therefore, search queries in E-commerce are also utilized as features. In our system, search queries are pre-processed using Chinese word segmentation and stop words removing techniques, and represented as word vectors.

Product property features: Taobao is a distributed market space where sellers sell products. Many sellers provide meta data about the products. For example, a seller will label 'Size' as "M" or "L" on children clothes, or label 'Age' as "newborn" or "1-3 years" etc. Each product facet-value pair (i.e. a product property) is associated with an unique feature.

Product title features: Product titles are created by sellers who are not affiliated with Taobao. Sellers are very creative about product titles. As a result, many product titles can be very informative about the life stage of the consumer. For example, *'Diaper for new born'* on a product title suggests the product is targeting for consumers with new babies. We preprocess these product titles via Chinese segmentation and phrase extraction techniques. Most of the extracted words are used as features, except stop words and words with very high inverse-document frequency.

Temporal Effect of Features: Whether a user has purchased a diaper 1 month ago or 2 years ago has deferent meanings in terms of predicting the current life stage. To capture the temporal patterns, we divide each consumer behavior time sequence X_* into multiple subsequences with fixed size time windows. A feature vector for each time window is generated. Then we concatenate all the feature

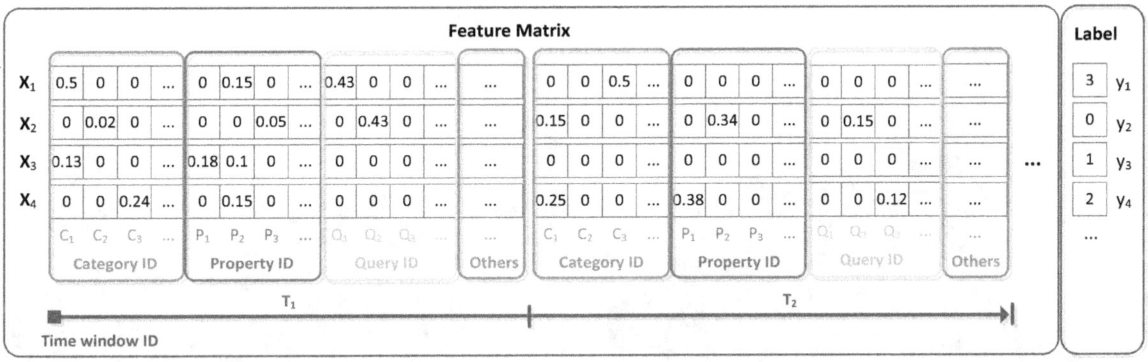

Figure 6: An example of feature matrix in our approach.

vectors into a big feature vector to represent X_*. Figure 6 illustrates an example of feature matrix, where each row corresponds to a training data point.

3.5 Recommendation Based on Life-stage

To make product recommendations, we propose a model to estimate the probability of a user purchasing a product at a specific age a. That is the joint probability $P(p\_product_j, a)$, where a is the baby's age. Let $P(p\_product_j)$ be the probability of the user purchasing the product j, and we calculate it for each user-product pair based on the existed recommendation algorithms. Let $P(a|p\_product_j)$ be the conditional probability of making the purchase at age a given that the user will purchase product j. Based on the chain rule, we have:

$$\begin{aligned}&P(p\_product_j, a)\\&= P(a|p\_product_j)P(p\_product_j)\end{aligned} \tag{2}$$

Given a baby's age a, we can use the above value to rank all candidate products. For a user u without the age information, we first estimate his/her age distribution $p_u(a)$ based on the Gaussian mixture model, which will be introduced in Section 4. Then we rank the products based on:

$$P(p\_product_j)\int p(a|p\_product_j)p_u(a)da \tag{3}$$

where $p(a|p\_product_j)$ is the probability of the age of a random user purchasing product j (i.e. purchasing age), which we assume follows a Gaussian distribution $\mathcal{N}(\mu_j, \sigma_j^2)$. This distribution can be estimated from the age information of all users who have purchased this product. For a user without age information, we estimate the baby's birth date using the life stage prediction and segmentation method described previously, then infer the age of the user when purchasing each product in the past. Figure 7(a) shows an example of fitting a Gaussian distribution ($\mu = 43$) based on the histogram of purchasing age of users who purchased a product. It suggests that the product is most suitable for children at around 43-month old, where μ_j is the expected baby age for product j.

To estimate $P(p\_product_j)$ in E.q 3, we use a large scale logistic regression model:

$$P(p\_product_j) = \frac{1}{1+e^{-\mathbf{w}^T\mathbf{x}}} \tag{4}$$

where x is a feature vector that represents a purchasing action, which includes scores generated by basic recommendation algorithms such as item-item based collaborative filtering, as well as other features that might be useful. $\mathbf{w}$ is learnt by maximizing the likelihood of the training data.

4. MIXTURE MODEL FOR MULTI-KIDS

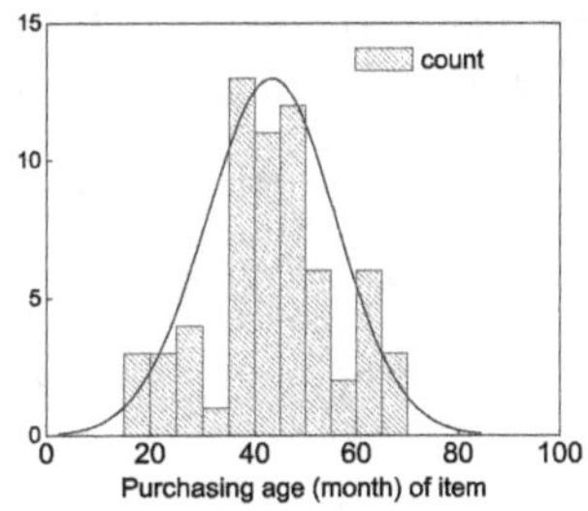

(a)

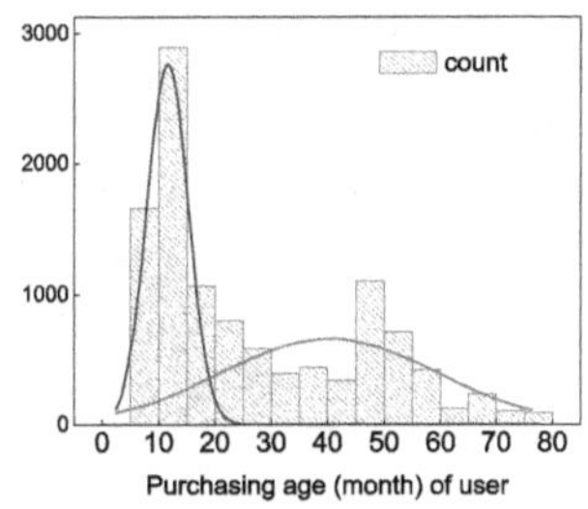

(b)

Figure 7: The distributions of item and user purchasing age (month). (a) Gaussian distribution of item purchasing age. This item is suitable for 41-month old children. (b) Gaussian mixture model with two components for user purchasing age. One component represents 11-month old, and the other one represents 40-month old.

Our previous analysis is based on the assumption that each user account corresponds to a family with only one child, which is very common in our market due to the one-child policy in China. However, we also find about 10% of our users bought maternity dress and baby products together with products for older kids at the same time. Many of those cases do not look like buying gifts for others. Recently, the one child policy is adjusted in China, which leads to an increasing number of families having two or more children. This motivates us to work on multi-kids life stage modeling and prediction.

One of the major challenges is that most of our users who registered their babies' age seldom register for multiple babies, thus we do not have much labeled training data for multi-kids modeling. Therefore we approach this problem based on unsupervised learning techniques.

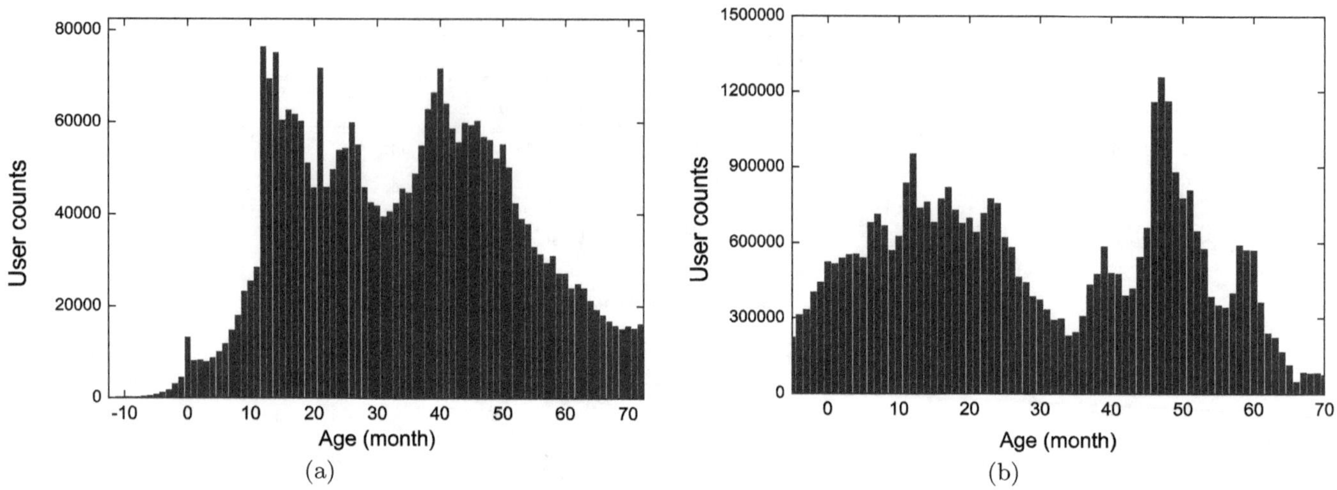

Figure 8: The distribution of user children's age (unit: month): (a) training dataset and (b) predicted dataset.

For a given user account, we observe a sequence of product purchasing behaviors. For each product j purchased by the user at time t_j, we estimate the expected purchasing age of the consumer $a_j = E(a|P(age|p\_product_j))$ at time t_j based on the age information of all consumers who have purchased the product, as described in the previous section. Then we can map the expected purchasing age to the projected age of the user at time t by adding the time difference between t and t_j: $a_{j,t} = a_j + (t - t_j)$.

We model the distribution of $a_{j,t}$ with a Gaussian Mixture Model (GMM):

$$p(a_{j,t}) = \sum_{c=1}^{K} w_c \mathcal{N}(a_{j,t} : \mu_c, \sigma_c^2) \quad (5)$$

where $c \in [1, K]$ is the index for each child, K is the total number of children, μ_c and σ_c are the mean and variance of c-th Gaussian component respectively, and w_c is the mixture weight for the component. Given a fixed K and the set of projected age of the user, the model parameters w_c, μ_c, σ_c can be found by the maximum likelihood estimation. To find the optimal K, we use the Akaike information criterion (AIC) and Bayesian information criterion (BIC) [12]. Based on this model, the age of the cth child at time t follows a Gaussian distribute centered on μ_c with variance σ_c as illustrated by the example in Figure 7(b).

5. EXPERIMENTS

In this section, we will evaluate the effectiveness of our approach empirically. We first introduce the experimental setup, then analyze the classification accuracy on offline dataset. We also give a data analysis of temporal effect. Additionally, we make an analysis of multi-kids situation. Finally, a real online evaluation is launched on Taobao.com.

5.1 Experimental Setup

We collected a dataset[2] with more than 8 millions children birth date information provided by consumers who share the information in order to receive better recommendations or search results. The age distribution till Feb 2015 is shown in Figure 8(a). The distribution is not uniform, because users usually do not disclose the age information when they are in the pregnancy stage. For each user with known birth date, we divided his/her activity sequence over time into different life stages, such as *'pregnant'*, *'new born-6 month'*, *'6-12 months'*, etc, using the fixed baby life stage template. This gives us labeled sequences for further analysis.

[2]The dataset sample can be downloaded from http://tianchi.aliyun.com/datalab/dataSet.htm?id=3

Table 2: Effects of features for maternal and child life-stage prediction.

Features&Approach	Accuracy
Basic	73.86%
Basic+Prop	76.14%
Basic+Prop+Query	76.31%
Basic+Prop+Query+Title	76.83%
Basic+Prop+Query+Title+Temp	81.99%
Basic+Prop+Query+Title+Temp+Seg	83.14%

5.2 Life-stage Prediction and Segmentation

For offline analysis, classification accuracy is used to measure the performance of mum-baby life-stage prediction and template based segmentation. We firstly study the effect of different feature sets and segmentation. For the multinomial logistic regression model, 5-fold cross validation is used. Table 2 shows the performance as more features are added. The logistic regression model with only product category features serves as the basic approach. It shows that the product meta data properties (Prop), title features (Title) and query features (Query) are effective. The biggest contribution is capturing the temporal effect of features (temp) with feature vectors at different time windows.

"+Seg" means the fixed baby life stage template is introduced to segment each user activity sequence, and the best starting point of the template is found to maximize the joint likelihood of the label sequence given the classifiers at each segment. The results show that introducing the template to force consistency improves the performance, as it achieves the goal of smoothing segments with less activities (i.e. poor features) by soft constraints from other segments.

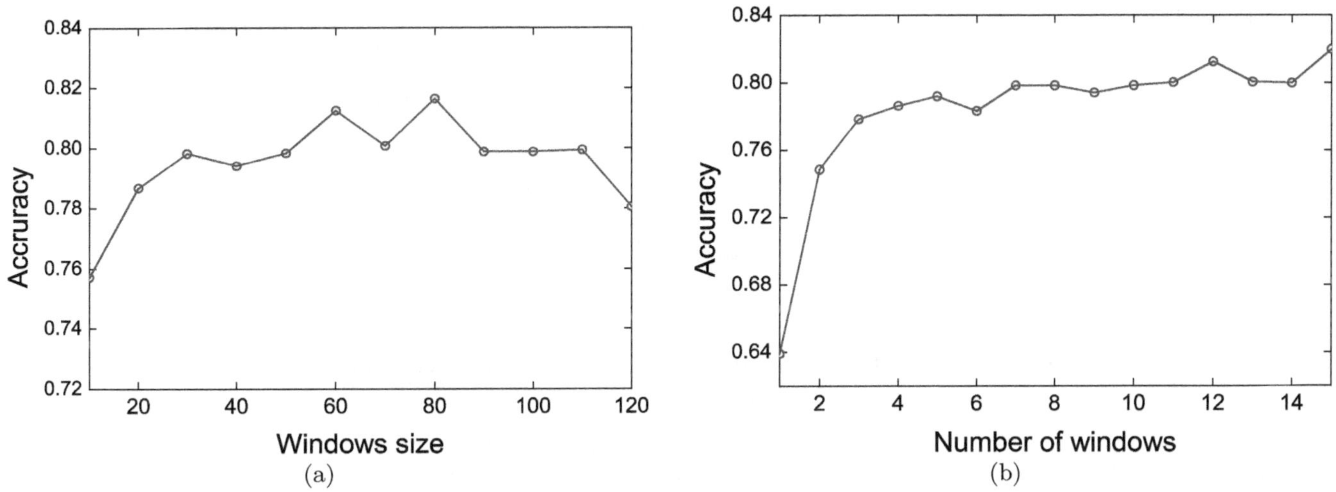

Figure 9: The analysis of window size and number.

The prediction and segmentation module is deployed to taobao.com. The predicted age distribution of all users till Feb. 2015 is shown in Figure 8(b). The KL-divergence is 0.2086 between predicted distribution and the distribution of the training dataset in Figure 8(a). There are relatively more users at the pregnancy stage than that of the training dataset.

5.3 Analysis of Temporal Effect

Temporal patterns play very important roles in baby age stage prediction. We divide each consumer behavior time sequence X_* into multiple time windows. The detailed analysis results are shown as figure 9. As we increase the window size, the prediction accuracy first increases, then does not change much, finally decreases. The best accuracy is achieved when the window size is around 40 to 90 as shown in Figure 9(a). On one hand, when the windows size is too small, the activities in a window are too sparse and limited. On the other hand, the discriminative power of temporal features is too weak when the window size is set too big. In the rest of this paper, the window size for each time span is set to 60, which is within the optimal range.

Given a fixed window size 60, we also change the number of windows from 1 to 15 to see how it affects the performance. As the window number increases, the performance starts to increase significantly before hitting a plateau (Figure 9(b)). This suggests a longer consumer behavior history gives more accurate prediction of the user's current life-stage.

5.4 Analysis of Multi-kids

As discussed before, an increasing number of families in China are having more than one child over the last several years, thus we propose the Gaussian Mixture Modeling approach (GMM) to predict the baby age(s) for each account. Although very few users provide multiple children's birth date, the learned GMMs suggest around 16.03% $(1,133,678)$ users in our training dataset have more than one child.

Figure 10 shows an example of choosing the number of children for an account using AIC and BIC as model selection criteria. And the lower values of y-axis means a better choice for the number of children.

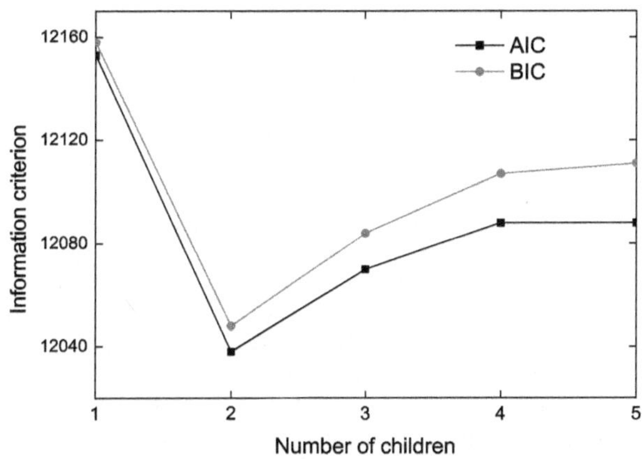

Figure 10: A case of AIC and BIC analysis to determine the number of children.

5.5 Online Experiments

Online experiments with real world E-commerce users are carried out to study the effect of life-stage based product recommendation. We conduct A/B testing based on a recommendation scenario in Taobao.com($100M$+clicks/day). We randomly sample some users with predicted mum-baby life stages and divide them into 2 buckets.

Our system has an independent module to generate candidate mum-baby products, which are the same for both buckets. Then for users in the A bucket (i.e., the baseline group), the system ranks the candidate products based on our existing recommendation solution that predicts $P(p\_product_j = yes)$ based on various factors, such as CF predictions, consumer brand preferences, consumer shop preferences, quantity of sale, consumer purchasing power, etc. For users in the B bucket (i.e., the experimental group), the system integrates life stage prediction and ranks candidate products based on Equation 3, where $P(p\_product_j = yes)$ is estimated in the same way as the A bucket. Therefore, even if a product has high $P(p\_product_j = yes)$ (E.g,. it is more relevant to user past behaviors or is popular), it may not be recommended if it does not match the life stage of the user.

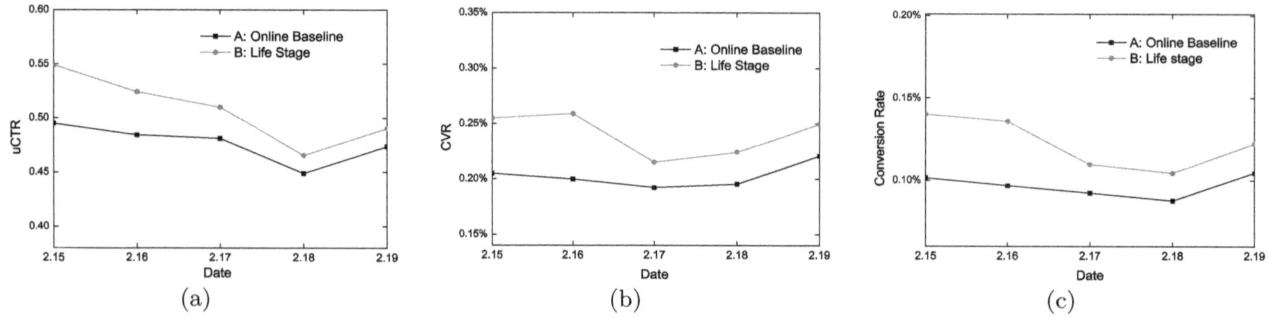

Figure 11: uCTR, CVR and Conversion Rate for two buckets.

We compared the two buckets using user Click Through Rate (uCTR), Click Conversion Rate (CVR) and Conversion Rate:

$$uCTR = \frac{\#user\_click}{\#user\_pv}$$

$$CVR = \frac{\#user\_trade}{\#user\_click}$$

$$Conversion\_Rate = uCTR \times CVR$$

where #user_click is the number of user clicking, #user_pv is the number of user browsing, #user_trade is the number of user trading in the scenario.

The results are shown in Figure 11[3]. We found that the performance on the experimental group (bucket B) is significantly better ($p<0.05$) than that on the baseline group (bucket B) in all three measures. More specifically, the improvement of uCTR means that users are more likely to slide and click. The improvement of CVR implies that after a user's clicks the proposed approach has higher probability to convert the clicking action into a purchasing action. Conversion rate combines both uCTR and CVR, and reflects the probability of a browsing action leading to a purchasing action. The improvement on it is very important for an E-commerce recommendation system and has significant business value.

6. RELATED WORK

Recommender systems are the most important and popular data mining tools that have been utilized by many E-commerce web sites to help consumers find products. There are two major recommendation approaches: content-based filtering and collaborative filtering.

The content-based approach is based on the assumption that explicit features of an item (category, words in title, price, style, size, etc.) a user liked before tell much about a user's preference. Thus the system recommends items that are similar to what the user like before. Various approaches [1, 2, 3] have been proposed, such as vector space models, language models, Bayesian classifiers, clustering models, etc. Although content based filtering has gained popularity in news recommender systems, it is success in E-commerce products recommendation is limited, because content features such as product title words, product style and brands, can hardly describe all the implicit characters of products and the fine-grained preference of users. The content-based approach is useful to increase recommendation coverage. Therefore, it is usually used as a part of solution in a hybrid recommender system [13].

The collaborative filtering approach[4, 5] assumes that users with similar tastes on some items may also have similar preferences on other items. Thus the system recommends items to a user based on other users who share similar behaves similarity preferences on other items. This approach usually operates on a user-item matrix, in which each row is a user vector and each column is an item vector. User-based methods [14, 15] find similar users to the current user. Item-based methods [16, 17] directly find items that are similar to the item that a user has clicked or purchased. Various similarity measures, such as cosine similarity, jaccard similarity, Pearson correlation coefficient, conditional probability-based similarity have been proposed to find the top-n similar items. Compared to user-based method, item-based method is more commonly used in large scale E-commerce systems because of the effectiveness and efficiency. Recently, factorization models, such as such as Singular Value Decomposition (SVD) [18], Probabilistic Matrix Factorization (PMF) [19], have gained much attention from both the research community and industry due to the their good performjance on benchmark datasets. The main benefit of this approach is introducing latent factors of user and item, which better solves the data sparsity issue.

Recently, the effect of time in recommender system has received some research attention [20, 5, 21]. One aspect studied is the drift of user preferences over time [22, 23]. Koren et al.[20] improved movie rating prediction accuracy on Netflix dataset by modeling the temporal dynamics via factorization model. Xiang et al.[22] used graph to explicitly model users' long-term and short-term preferences for top-N recommendation. Rendel et al.[23] proposed a tensor factorization modeling approach that combines Markov chain and matrix factorization for personalized next-basket recommendation. Wang et al.[24] adapted the proportional hazards modeling approach in survival analysis and explicitly incorporate time information to recommend right product at right time. However, we are not aware of any work that tries to explicitly model and predict life stages for product recommendation, especially in the context of a large scale E-commerce system.

[3]Normalized related value instead of the original absolute value of the online measures are shown for business reason. The relative improvement is consistent with real experimental results. The fluctuating performance over time is due to the effect of Chinese New Year.

7. CONCLUSION

We introduce the concept of life stage into recommendation systems research. In particular, we propose a new Maximum Entropy Semi Markov Model to segment and label consumer life stages based on observed purchasing data over time. In the mum-baby product category where the life stage transition is deterministic, we develop an efficient approximate solution using large scale logistic regression and a template based approach. We also propose a Gaussian mixture model to efficiently handle multi-kids cases. We integrate our solution into the largest online shopping website taobao.com. Both the offline and online experiments demonstrate the effectiveness of the proposed approach.

This is the first step towards life-stage based recommendations. In the future, we will study scalable solutions for the more general Maximum Entropy Semi Markov Model and apply it to other categories such as wedding and home remodeling. Besides, we plan to apply life stage labeling to other E-commerce applications such as personalized search and advertising.

8. REFERENCES

[1] Raymond J. Mooney and Loriene Roy. Content-based book recommending using learning for text categorization. In *Proceedings of the Fifth ACM Conference on Digital Libraries*, DL '00, pages 195–204, New York, NY, USA, 2000. ACM.

[2] Michael Pazzani and Daniel Billsus. Learning and revising user profiles: The identification of interesting web sites. *Machine Learning*, 27(3):313–331, 1997.

[3] Pasquale Lops, Marco de Gemmis, and Giovanni Semeraro. Content-based recommender systems: State of the art and trends. In Francesco Ricci, Lior Rokach, Bracha Shapira, and Paul B. Kantor, editors, *Recommender Systems Handbook*, pages 73–105. Springer US, 2011.

[4] G. Linden, B. Smith, and J. York. Amazon.com recommendations: item-to-item collaborative filtering. *Internet Computing, IEEE*, 7(1):76–80, Jan 2003.

[5] Jian Wang, Badrul Sarwar, and Neel Sundaresan. Utilizing related products for post-purchase recommendation in e-commerce. In *Proceedings of the Fifth ACM Conference on Recommender Systems*, RecSys '11, pages 329–332, New York, NY, USA, 2011. ACM.

[6] WILLIAM D. WELLS and GEORGE GUBA. Life cycle concept in marketing research. *Journal of Marketing Research*, 1966.

[7] S. G. Barton. The life cycle and buying patterns. *Consumer Behavior*, 1955.

[8] David C. Bojanic. The impact of age and family life experiences on mexican visitor shopping expenditures. *Tourism Management*, 32(2):406 – 414, 2011.

[9] Shun-Zheng Yu. Hidden semi-markov models. *Artificial Intelligence*, 174(2):215 – 243, 2010. Special Review Issue.

[10] Andrew McCallum, Dayne Freitag, and Fernando C. N. Pereira. Maximum entropy markov models for information extraction and segmentation. In *Proceedings of the Seventeenth International Conference on Machine Learning*, ICML '00, pages 591–598, San Francisco, CA, USA, 2000. Morgan Kaufmann Publishers Inc.

[11] Charles Sutton, Andrew McCallum, and Khashayar Rohanimanesh. Dynamic conditional random fields: Factorized probabilistic models for labeling and segmenting sequence data. *J. Mach. Learn. Res.*, 8:693–723, May 2007.

[12] H. Akaike. A new look at the statistical model identification. *Automatic Control, IEEE Transactions on*, 19(6):716–723, Dec 1974.

[13] Robin Burke. Hybrid recommender systems: Survey and experiments. *User Modeling and User-Adapted Interaction*, 12(4):331–370, 2002.

[14] Badrul Sarwar, George Karypis, Joseph Konstan, and John Riedl. Analysis of recommendation algorithms for e-commerce. In *Proceedings of the 2Nd ACM Conference on Electronic Commerce*, EC '00, pages 158–167, New York, NY, USA, 2000. ACM.

[15] John S. Breese, David Heckerman, and Carl Kadie. Empirical analysis of predictive algorithms for collaborative filtering. In *Proceedings of the Fourteenth Conference on Uncertainty in Artificial Intelligence*, UAI'98, pages 43–52, San Francisco, CA, USA, 1998. Morgan Kaufmann Publishers Inc.

[16] Badrul Sarwar, George Karypis, Joseph Konstan, and John Riedl. Item-based collaborative filtering recommendation algorithms. In *Proceedings of the 10th International Conference on World Wide Web*, WWW '01, pages 285–295, New York, NY, USA, 2001. ACM.

[17] Mukund Deshpande and George Karypis. Item-based top-n recommendation algorithms. *ACM Trans. Inf. Syst.*, 22(1):143–177, January 2004.

[18] Y. Koren, R. Bell, and C. Volinsky. Matrix factorization techniques for recommender systems. *Computer*, 42(8):30–37, Aug 2009.

[19] Ruslan Salakhutdinov and Andriy Mnih. Bayesian probabilistic matrix factorization using markov chain monte carlo. In *Proceedings of the 25th International Conference on Machine Learning*, ICML '08, pages 880–887, New York, NY, USA, 2008. ACM.

[20] Yehuda Koren. Collaborative filtering with temporal dynamics. *Commun. ACM*, 53(4):89–97, April 2010.

[21] Gang Zhao, Mong Li Lee, Wynne Hsu, and Wei Chen. Increasing temporal diversity with purchase intervals. In *Proceedings of the 35th International ACM SIGIR Conference on Research and Development in Information Retrieval*, SIGIR '12, pages 165–174, New York, NY, USA, 2012. ACM.

[22] Liang Xiang, Quan Yuan, Shiwan Zhao, Li Chen, Xiatian Zhang, Qing Yang, and Jimeng Sun. Temporal recommendation on graphs via long- and short-term preference fusion. In *Proceedings of the 16th ACM SIGKDD International Conference on Knowledge Discovery and Data Mining*, KDD '10, pages 723–732, New York, NY, USA, 2010. ACM.

[23] Steffen Rendle, Christoph Freudenthaler, and Lars Schmidt-Thieme. Factorizing personalized markov chains for next-basket recommendation. In *Proceedings of the 19th International Conference on World Wide Web*, WWW '10, pages 811–820, New York, NY, USA, 2010. ACM.

[24] Jian Wang and Yi Zhang. Opportunity model for e-commerce recommendation: Right product; right time. In *Proceedings of the 36th International ACM SIGIR Conference on Research and Development in Information Retrieval*, SIGIR '13, pages 303–312, New York, NY, USA, 2013. ACM.

[25] Steffen Rendle, Christoph Freudenthaler, Zeno Gantner, and Lars Schmidt-Thieme. Bpr: Bayesian personalized ranking from implicit feedback. In *Proceedings of the Twenty-Fifth Conference on Uncertainty in Artificial Intelligence*, UAI '09, pages 452–461, Arlington, Virginia, United States, 2009. AUAI Press.

[26] Steffen Rendle, Zeno Gantner, Christoph Freudenthaler, and Lars Schmidt-Thieme. Fast context-aware recommendations with factorization machines. In *Proceedings of the 34th International ACM SIGIR Conference on Research and Development in Information Retrieval*, SIGIR '11, pages 635–644, New York, NY, USA, 2011. ACM.

Visual Search at Pinterest

Yushi Jing[1], David Liu[1], Dmitry Kislyuk[1], Andrew Zhai[1], Jiajing Xu[1], Jeff Donahue[1,2], Sarah Tavel[1]
[1]Visual Discovery, Pinterest
[2]University of California, Berkeley
{jing, dliu, dkislyuk, andrew, jiajing, jdonahue, sarah}@pinterest.com

ABSTRACT

We demonstrate that, with the availability of distributed computation platforms such as Amazon Web Services and open-source tools, it is possible for a small engineering team to build, launch and maintain a cost-effective, large-scale visual search system. We also demonstrate, through a comprehensive set of live experiments at Pinterest, that content recommendation powered by visual search improves user engagement. By sharing our implementation details and learnings from launching a commercial visual search engine from scratch, we hope visual search becomes more widely incorporated into today's commercial applications.

Categories and Subject Descriptors

H.3.3 [**Information Systems Applications**]: Search Process; I.4.9 [**Image Processing and Computer Vision**]: Application

General Terms

information retrieval, computer vision, deep learning, distributed systems

Keywords

visual search, visual shopping, open source

1. INTRODUCTION

Visual search, or content-based image retrieval [5], is an active research area driven in part by the explosive growth of online photos and the popularity of search engines. Google Goggles, Google Similar Images and Amazon Flow are several examples of commercial visual search systems. Although significant progress has been made in building Web-scale visual search systems, there are few publications describing end-to-end architectures deployed on commercial applications. This is in part due to the complexity of real-world visual search systems, and in part due to business considerations to keep core search technology proprietary.

KDD'15, August 10-13, 2015, Sydney, NSW, Australia.

ACM 978-1-4503-3664-2/15/08 ...$15.00.
DOI: http://dx.doi.org/10.1145/2783258.2788621 .

Figure 1: Similar Looks: We apply object detection to localize products such as bags and shoes. In this prototype, users click on automatically tagged objects to view similar-looking products.

We faced two main challenges in deploying a commercial visual search system at Pinterest. First, as a startup we needed to control the development cost in the form of both human and computational resources. For example, feature computation can become expensive with a large and continuously growing image collection, and with engineers constantly experimenting with new features to deploy, it was vital for our system to be both scalable and cost effective. Second, the success of a commercial application is measured by the benefit it brings to the users (e.g. improved user engagement) relative to the cost of development and maintenance. As a result, our development progress needed to be frequently validated through A/B experiments with live user traffic.

In this paper, we describe our approach to deploy a commercial visual search system with those two challenges in mind. We make two main contributions.

Our first contribution is to present our scalable and cost effective visual search implementation using widely available tools, feasible for a small engineering team to implement. Section 2.1 describes our simple and pragmatic approach to speeding up and improving the accuracy of object detection and localization that exploits the rich metadata available at Pinterest. By decoupling the difficult (and computation-

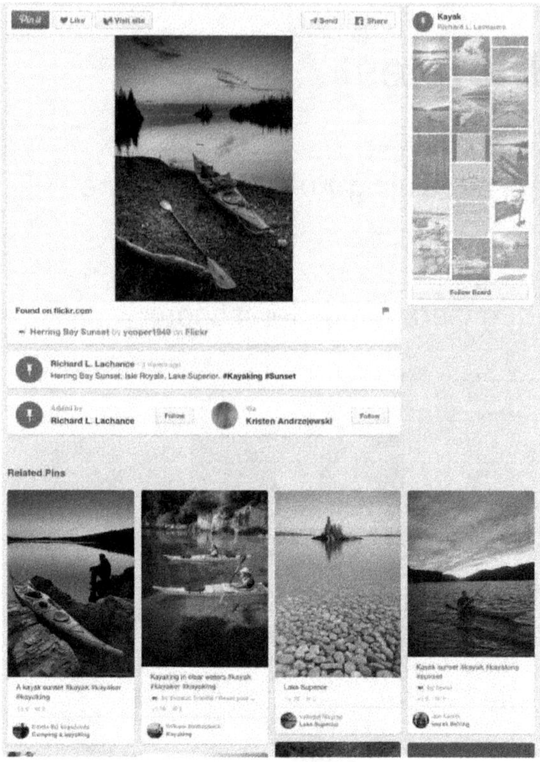

Figure 2: Related Pins is a product feature that shows recommendations based on the Pinterest curation graph.

ally expensive) task of multi-class object detection into category classification followed by per-category object detection, we only need to run (expensive) object detectors on images with a high probability of containing the object. Section 2.2 presents our distributed pipeline to incrementally add or update image features using Amazon Web Services, which avoids wasteful re-computation of unchanged image features. Section 2.3 presents our distributed indexing and search infrastructure built on top of widely available tools.

Our second contribution is to share results of deploying our visual search infrastructure in two product applications: *Related Pins* (Section 3) and *Similar Looks* (Section 4). For each application, we use application-specific data sets to evaluate the effectiveness of each visual search component (object detection, feature representations for similarity) in isolation. After deploying the end-to-end system, we use A/B tests to measure user engagement on live traffic.

Related Pins (Figure 2) is a feature that recommends Pins based on the Pin the user is currently viewing. These recommendations are primarily generated from the "curation graph" of users, boards, and Pins. However, there is a long tail of less popular Pins without recommendations. Using visual search, we generate recommendations for almost all Pins on Pinterest. Our second application, *Similar Looks* (Figure 1) is a discovery experience we tested specifically for fashion Pins. It allows users to select a visual query from regions of interest (e.g. a bag or a pair of shoes) and identifies visually similar Pins for users to explore or purchase. Instead of using the whole image, visual similarity is computed between the localized objects in the query and database images. To our knowledge, this is the first published work on object detection/localization in a commercially deployed visual search system.

Our experiments demonstrate that 1) one can achieve very low false positive rate (less than 1%) with a decent detection rate by combining the object detection/localization methods with metadata, 2) using feature representations from the VGG [22] [3] model significantly improves visual search accuracy on our Pinterest benchmark datasets, and 3) we observe significant gains in user engagement when visual search is used to power Related Pins and Similar Looks applications.

2. VISUAL SEARCH ARCHITECTURE AT PINTEREST

Pinterest is a visual bookmarking tool that helps users discover and save creative ideas. Users *pin* images to *boards*, which are curated collections around particular themes or topics. This human-curated user-board-image graph contains rich information about the images and their semantic relationships. For example, when an image is pinned to a board, it implies a "curatorial link" between the new board and all other boards the image appears in. Metadata, such as image annotations, can then be propagated through these links to describe the image, the image board and the users.

Since the image is the focus of each pin, visual features play a large role in finding interesting, inspiring and relevant content for users. In this section we describe the end-to-end implementation of a visual search system that indexes billions of images on Pinterest. We address the challenges of developing a real-world visual search system that balances cost constraints with the need for fast prototyping. We describe 1) the features that we extract from images, 2) our infrastructure for distributed and incremental feature extraction, and 3) our real-time visual search service.

2.1 Image Representation and Features

We extract a variety of features from images, including local features and "deep features" extracted from the activation of intermediate layers of deep convolutional neural networks (CNNs) [6]. We studied architectures based on AlexNet [15] and VGG [22], extracting feature representations from *fc6* and *fc8* layers. These features are binarized for representation efficiency and compared using Hamming distance. We use the open-source Caffe [12] framework to perform training and inference of our CNNs on multi-GPU machines.

The system also extracts *salient color signatures* from images. Salient colors are computed by first detecting salient regions [25, 4] of the images and then applying k-means clustering to the Lab pixel values of the salient pixels. Cluster centroids and weights are stored as the color signature of the image.

Two-step Object Detection and Localization

One feature that is particularly relevant to Pinterest is the presence of certain object classes, such as bags, shoes, watches, dresses, and sunglasses. We adopted a two-step detection approach that leverages the abundance of weak text labels on Pinterest images. Since images are pinned many times onto many boards, aggregated pin descriptions and board titles provide a great deal of information about the image.

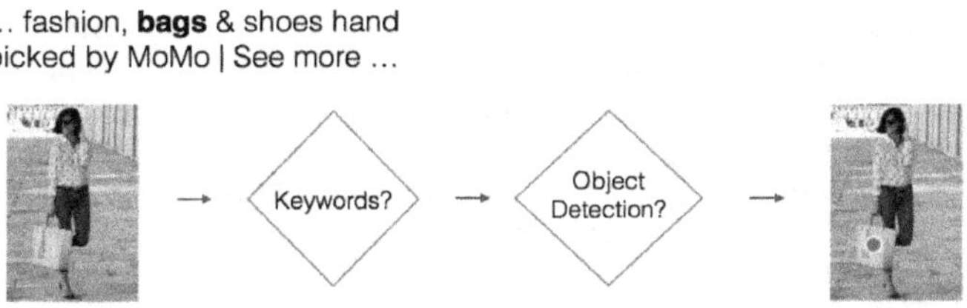

Figure 3: Instead of running all object detectors on all images, we first predict the image categories using textual metadata, and then apply object detection modules specific to the predicted category.

A text processing pipeline within Pinterest extracts relevant annotations for images from the raw text, producing short phrases associated with each image.

We use these annotations to determine which object detectors to run. In Figure 1, we first determined that the image was likely to contain bags and shoes, and then we proceeded to apply visual object detectors for those object classes. By first performing category classification, we only need to run the object detectors on images with a high prior likelihood of matching. This filtering step reduces computational cost as well as false positives.

Our initial approach for object detection was a heavily optimized implementation of cascading deformable part-based models [8]. This detector outputs a bounding box for each detected object, from which we extract visual descriptors for the object. Our recent efforts have focused on investigating the feasibility and performance of deep learning based object detectors [9, 10, 7].

Our experiment results in Section 4 show that our system achieved a very low false positive rate (less than 1%), which was vital for our application. This two-step approach also enables us to incorporate other signals into the category classification. The use of both text and visual signals for object detection and localization is widely used [2] [1] [13] for Web image retrieval and categorization.

Click Prediction

When users browse on Pinterest, they can interact with a pin by clicking to view it full screen ("close-up") and subsequently clicking through to the off-site source of the content (a click-through). For each image, we predict close-up rate (CUR) and click-through rate (CTR) based on its visual features. We trained a CNN to learn a mapping from images to the probability of a user bringing up the close-up view or clicking through to the content. Both CUR and CTR are helpful for applications like search ranking, recommendation systems and ads targeting since we often need to know which images are more likely to get attention from users.

CNNs have recently become the dominant approach to many semantic prediction tasks involving visual inputs, including classification [16, 15, 23, 3, 21, 14], detection [9, 10, 7], and segmentation [18]. Training a full CNN to learn a good representation can be time-consuming and requires a very large corpus of data. We apply transfer learning to our model by retaining the low-level visual representations from models trained for other computer vision tasks. The top layers of the network are fine-tuned for our specific task. This saves substantial training time and leverages the visual features learned from a much larger corpus than that of the target task. We use Caffe to perform this transfer learning.

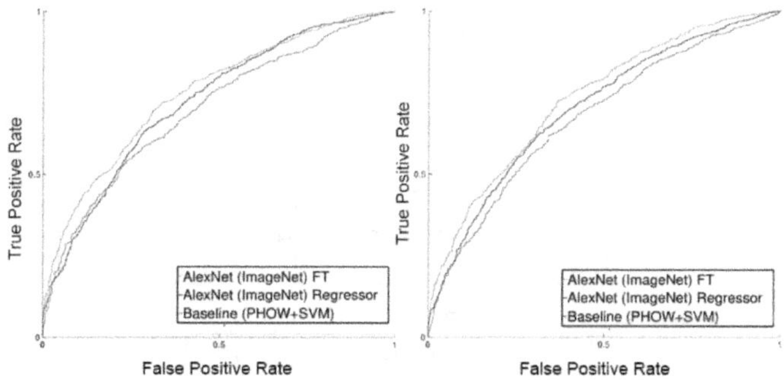

Figure 4: ROC curves for CUR prediction (left) and CTR prediction (right).

Figure 4 depicts receiver operating characteristic (ROC) curves for our CNN-based method, compared with a baseline based on a "traditional" computer vision pipeline: a SVM trained with binary labels on a pyramid histogram of words (PHOW), which performs well on object recognition datasets such as Caltech-101. Our CNN-based approach outperforms the PHOW-SVM baseline, and fine-tuning the CNN from end-to-end yields a significant performance boost as well. A similar approach was also applied to the task of detecting pornographic images uploaded to Pinterest with good results [1].

2.2 Incremental Fingerprinting Service

Most of our vision applications depend on having a complete collection of image features, stored in a format amenable to bulk processing. Keeping this data up-to-date is challenging; because our collection comprises over a billion unique images, it is critical to update the feature set incrementally and avoid unnecessary re-computation whenever possible.

We built a system called the *Incremental Fingerprinting Service*, which computes image features for all Pinterest images using a cluster of workers on Amazon EC2. It incrementally updates the collection of features under two main change scenarios: new images uploaded to Pinterest, and feature evolution (features added/modified by engineers).

Our approach is to split the image collection into *epochs* grouped by upload date, and to maintain a separate feature store for each version of each feature type (global, local, deep features). Features are stored in bulk on Amazon S3, organized by feature type, version, and date. When the data is fully up-to-date, each feature store contains all the epochs. On each run, the system detects missing epochs for each feature and enqueues jobs into a distributed queue to populate those epochs.

This storage scheme enables incremental updates as follows. Every day, a new epoch is added to our collection with that day's unique uploads, and we generate the missing features for that date. Since old images do not change, their features are not recomputed. If the algorithm or parameters

[1]By fine-tuning a network for three-class classification of *ignore*, *softcore*, and *porn* images, we are able to achieve a validation accuracy of 83.2%. When formulated as a binary classification between *ignore* and *softcore/porn* categories, the classifier achieved a ROC AUC score of 93.6%.

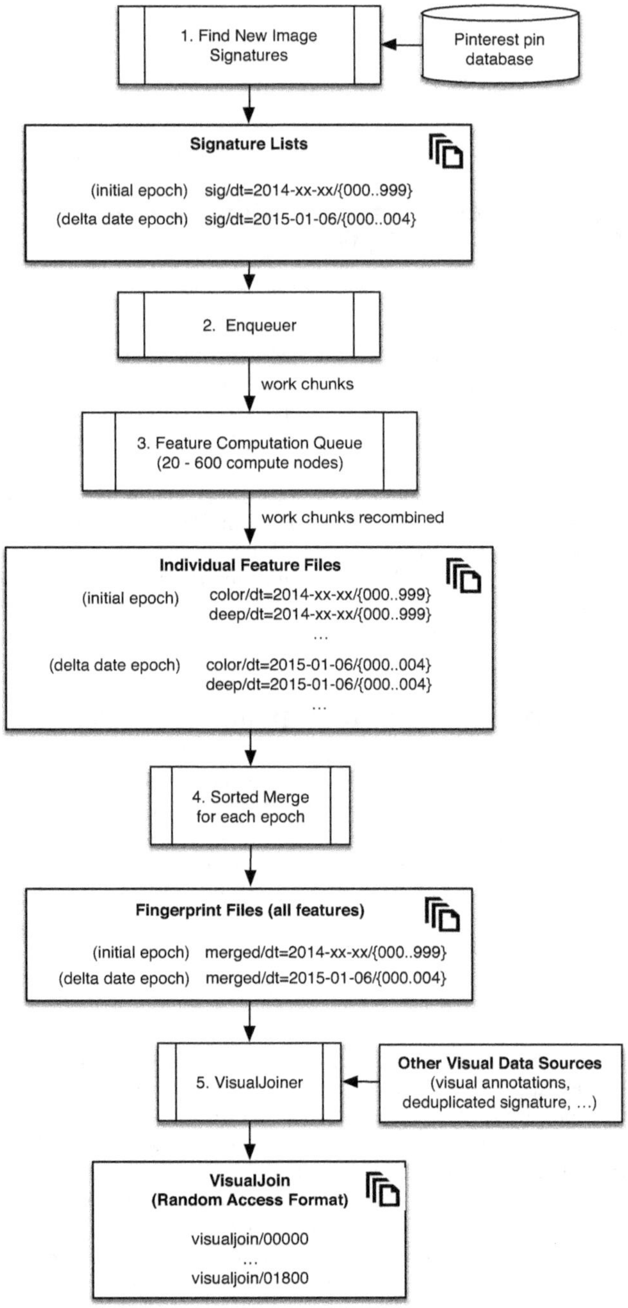

Figure 5: Examples of outputs generated by incremental fingerprint update pipeline. The initial run is shown as 2014-xx-xx which includes all the images created before that run.

for generating a feature are modified, or if a new feature is added, a new feature store is started and all of the epochs are computed for that feature. Unchanged features are not affected.

We copy these features into various forms for more convenient access by other jobs: features are merged to form a *fingerprint* containing all available features of an image, and fingerprints are copied into sharded, sorted files for random access by image signature (MD5 hash). These joined fingerprint files are regularly re-materialized, but the expensive feature computation needs only be done once per image.

A flow chart of the incremental fingerprint update process is shown in Figure 5. It consists of five main jobs: job (1) compiles a list of newly uploaded image signatures and groups them by date into epochs. We randomly divide each epoch into sorted shards of approximately 200,000 images to limit the size of the final fingerprint files. Job (2) identifies missing epochs in each feature store and enqueues jobs into PinLater (a distributed queue service similar to Amazon SQS). The jobs subdivide the shards into "work chunks", tuned such that each chunk takes approximate 30 minutes to compute. Job (3) runs on an automatically-launched cluster of EC2 instances, scaled depending on the size of the update. Spot instances can be used; if an instance is terminated, its job is rescheduled on another worker. The output of each work chunk is saved onto S3, and eventually recombined into feature files corresponding to the original shards.

Job (4) merges the individual feature shards into a unified fingerprint containing all of the available features for each image. Job (5) merges fingerprints from all epochs (along with other metadata) into a sorted, sharded HFile format allowing for random access *(VisualJoins)*.

The initial computation of all available features on all images, takes a little over a day using a cluster of several hundred 32-core machines, and produces roughly 5 TB of feature data. The steady-state requirement to process new images incrementally is only about 5 machines.

2.3 Search Infrastructure

At Pinterest, there are several use cases for a distributed visual search system. One use case is to explore similar looking products (Pinterest Similar Looks), and others include near-duplicate detection and content recommendation. In all these applications, visually similar results are computed from distributed indices built on top of the VisualJoins generated in the previous section. Since each use case has a different set of performance and cost requirements, our infrastructure is designed to be flexible and re-configurable. A flow chart of the search infrastructure is shown in Figure 6.

As the first step we create distributed image indices from VisualJoins using Hadoop. Each machine contains indexes (and features) associated with a randomly sharded subset of the entire image collection. Two types of indexes are used: the first is a disk-based (and partially memory cached) *token index* associating each vector-quantized feature (i.e. visual vocabulary token) with a posting list of image document IDs. This is analogous to a text-based image retrieval system, except text is replaced by visual tokens. The second index is an in-memory store of visual features and metadata such as image annotations and "topic vectors" computed from the user-board-image graph. The first part is used for fast (but imprecise) lookup, and the second part is used for more accurate (but slower) ranking refinement.

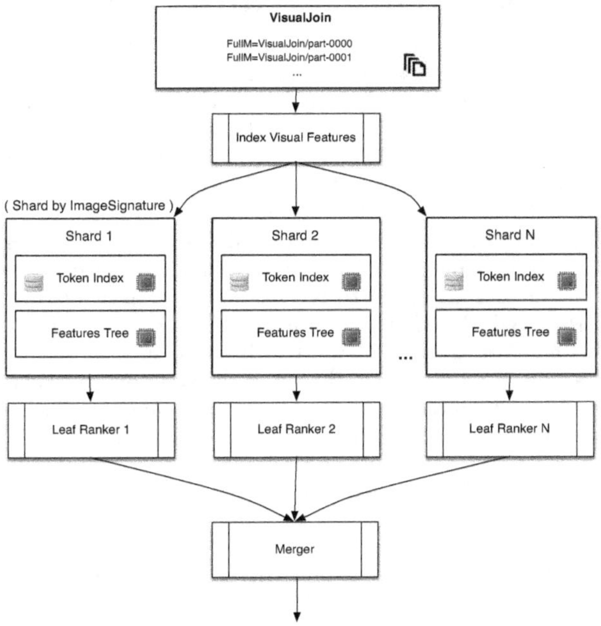

Figure 6: A flow chart of the distributed visual search pipeline.

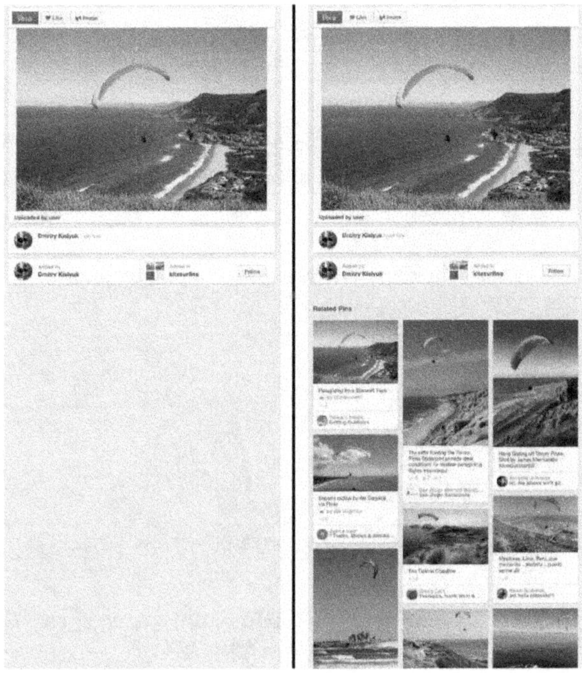

Figure 7: Before and after incorporating Visual Related Pins

Each machine runs a leaf ranker, which computes the k nearest neighbors from the indices using visual features, and then re-ranks the top candidates using additional metadata. In some cases, the leaf ranker skips the token index and directly retrieves the k nearest neighbor images from the feature tree index using approximate KNN methods such as [19]. A root ranker hosted on another machine will retrieve the top results from each of the leaf rankers, merge the results, and return them to the users. To handle new fingerprints generated with our real-time feature extractor, we have an online version of the visual search pipeline where a very similar process occurs. With the online version however, the given fingerprint is queried on pre-generated indices.

3. APPLICATION 1: RELATED PINS

One of the first applications of Pinterest's visual search pipeline was within a recommendations product called Related Pins, which recommends other images a user may be interested in when viewing a Pin. Traditionally, we have used a combination of user-curated image-to-board relationships and content-based signals to generate these recommendations. However, this system is unable to provide recommendations for less popular Pins (which do not have many connections) and newly created Pins (which may not have been indexed yet). As a result, 6% of images at Pinterest have very few or no recommendations. For these images, we used our visual search pipeline to generate *Visual* Related Pins in real time, as shown in Figure 7.

The first step of the Visual Related Pins product is to use the local token index built from all existing Pinterest images to detect if we have near duplicates to the query image. Specifically, given a query image, the system returns a set of images that are variations of the same image but altered through transformation such as resizing, cropping, rotation, translation, adding, deleting and altering minor parts of the visual content. Since the resulting images look visually identical to the query image, their recommendations are most likely relevant to the query image. In most cases, however, we found that there are either no near duplicates detected or the near duplicates do not have enough recommendations. Thus, we focused most of our attention on retrieving visual search results generated from an index based on CNN features.

Static Evaluation of Search Relevance

Our initial Visual Related Pins experiment utilized features from the original and fine-tuned versions of the AlexNet model in its search infrastructure. However, recent successes with deeper CNN architectures for classification led us to investigate the performance of feature sets from a variety of CNN models.

To conduct evaluation for visual search, we used the image annotations associated with the images as proxy for relevancy. This approach is commonly used for offline evaluation of visual search systems [20] in addition to human evaluation. In this work, we used top text queries associated with each image as labels. We retrieved 3,000 images per query for 1,000 queries using Pinterest Search, which yielded a dataset with about 1.6 million unique images. We labeled each image with the query that produced it. A visual search result is assumed to be relevant to a query image if the two images share a label.

With this dataset, we computed *precision@k* for recommendations based on several features: the *fc6* layer activations from the generic AlexNet model (pre-trained for ILSVRC) [15], the *fc6* activations of an AlexNet model fine-tuned to recognize over 3,000 Pinterest product categories, the *loss3/classifier* activations of a generic GoogLeNet [23],

Table 1: **Relevance of visual search.**

Model	p@5	p@10	latency
Generic AlexNet	0.051	0.040	193ms
Pinterest AlexNet	0.234	0.210	234ms
Generic GoogLeNet	0.223	0.202	1207ms
Generic VGG-16	0.302	0.269	642ms

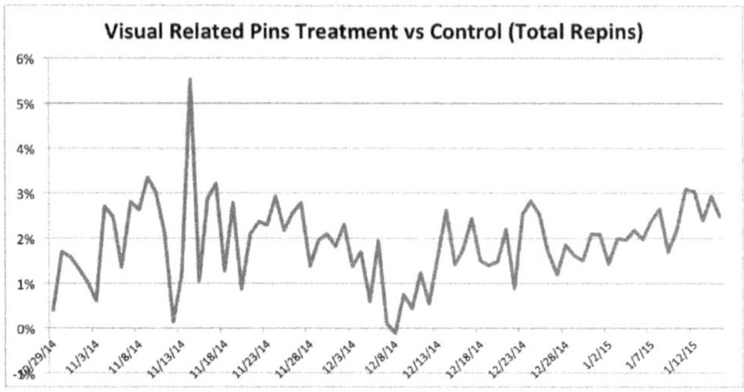

Figure 8: Visual Related Pins increases total Related Pins repins on Pinterest by 2%.

and the *fc6* activations of a generic VGG 16-layer model [3]. Table 1 shows p@5 and p@10 performance of these models, along with the average CPU-based latency of our visual search service, which includes feature extraction for the query image as well as retrieval. Using GPU-based inference dramatically reduces these latencies. We observed a substantial gain in precision against our evaluation dataset when using the FC6 features of the VGG 16-layer model, with an acceptable latency for our applications.

Live Experiments

We set up a system to detect new Pins with few recommendations, query our visual search system, and store their results in HBase to serve during Pin close-up.

For this application, we show visual search results when a majority share a common category (*category conformity thresholding*). We chose to trade off coverage for greater precision in this manner to avoid using visual search when we have relatively low confidence in its results.

We initially launched the experiment to 10% of eligible live traffic; users were eligible when they viewed a Pin close-up that did not have enough recommendations. Eligible users were triggered into either a treatment group (in which we replaced the Related Pins section with visual search results), or a control group (in which we did not alter the experience). We measured the change in total repin activity[2] within the Related Pins section.

By displaying visually similar pins for just the 6% of queries that would otherwise have empty recommendations, we observed a **2% increase** in *total* re-pin actions on Related Pins (Figure 8). Furthermore, we performed another experiment in which we reranked all recommendations using deep CNN feature similarity, achieving a **10% increase** in re-pin and click-through engagement.

[2]Repinning is the action of adding an existing Pinterest Pin to a board. Repins are one of our standard top-line metrics for measuring engagement.

4. APPLICATION 2: SIMILAR LOOKS

One of the most popular categories on Pinterest is women's fashion. However, a large percentage of pins in this category do not direct users to a shopping experience, and therefore are not actionable. There are two challenges towards making these Pins actionable: 1) Many pins feature editorial shots such as "street style" outfits, which often link to a website with little additional information on the items featured in the image; 2) Pin images often contain multiple objects (e.g. a woman walking down the street, with a leopard-print bag, black boots, sunglasses, torn jeans, etc.) A user looking at the Pin might be interested in learning more about the bag, while another user might want to buy the sunglasses.

User research revealed this to be a common frustration, and our data indicated that users are much less likely to click through to the external Website on women's fashion Pins, relative to other categories.

To address this problem, we built a product called "Similar Looks", which localizes and classifies fashion objects (Figure 9). We use object recognition to detect products such as bags, shoes, pants, and watches in Pin images. From these objects, we extract visual and semantic features to generate product recommendations ("Similar Looks"). A user would discover the recommendations via a red dot displayed on the object in the Pin (see Figure 1). Clicking on the red dot loads a feed of Pins featuring visually similar objects (e.g. other visually similar blue dresses).

Related Work

Applying visual search to "soft goods" has been explored both within academia and industry. Like.com, Google Shopping, and Zappos (owned by Amazon) are a few well-known applications of computer vision to fashion recommendations. Baidu and Alibaba also recently launched visual search systems targeting similar problems. There is also a growing amount of research on vision-based fashion recommendations [24, 17, 11]. Our approach demonstrates the feasibility of an object-based visual search system for tens of millions of Pinterest users and exposes an interactive search experience around these detected objects.

Static Evaluation of Object Localization

The first step of evaluating our Similar Looks product was to investigate our object localization and detection capabilities. We chose to focus on fashion objects because of the aforementioned business need and because "soft goods" tend to have distinctive visual shapes (e.g. shorts, bags, glasses).

We collected our evaluation dataset by randomly sampling a set of images from Pinterest's women's fashion category, and manually labeling 2,399 fashion objects in 9 categories (shoes, dress, glasses, bag, watch, pants, shorts, bikini, earnings) on the images by drawing a rectangular crop over the objects. We observed that shoes, bags, dresses and pants were the four largest categories in our evaluation dataset. Shown in Table 2 is the distribution of fashion objects as well as the detection accuracies from the text-based filter, image-based detection, and the combined approach (where text filters are applied prior to object detection).

As previously described, the text-based approach applies manually crafted rules, such as regular expressions, to the Pinterest metadata associated with images (which we treat as weak labels). For example, an image annotated with "spring fashion, *tote* with flowers" will be classified as "bag,"

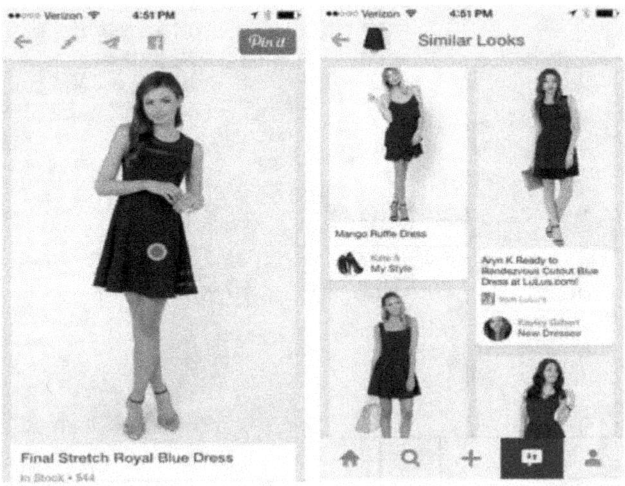

Figure 9: Once a user clicks on the red dot, the system shows products that have a similar appearance to the query object.

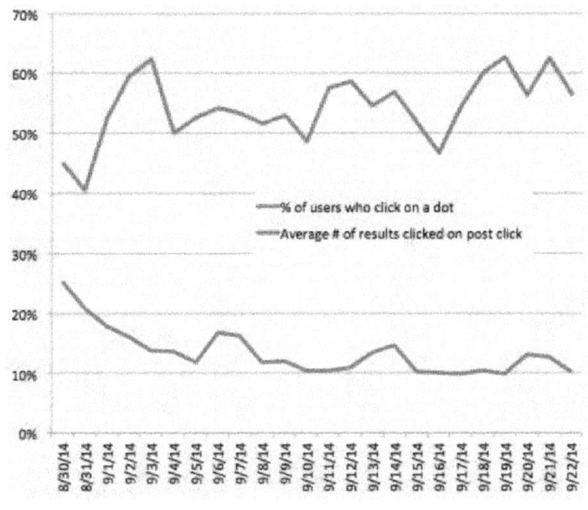

Figure 10: Engagement rates for Similar Looks experiment

Table 2: Object detection/classification accuracy (%)

		Text		Img		Both	
Objects	#	TP	FP	TP	FP	TP	FP
shoe	873	79.8	6.0	41.8	3.1	34.4	1.0
dress	383	75.5	6.2	58.8	12.3	47.0	2.0
glasses	238	75.2	18.8	63.0	0.4	50.0	0.2
bag	468	66.2	5.3	59.8	2.9	43.6	0.5
watch	36	55.6	6.0	66.7	0.5	41.7	0.0
pants	253	75.9	2.0	60.9	2.2	48.2	0.1
shorts	89	73.0	10.1	44.9	1.2	31.5	0.2
bikini	32	71.9	1.0	31.3	0.2	28.1	0.0
earrings	27	81.5	4.7	18.5	0.0	18.5	0.0
Average		72.7	6.7	49.5	2.5	38.1	0.5

and is considered as a positive sample if the image contains a "bag" object box label. For image-based evaluation, we compute the intersection between the predicted object bounding box and the labeled object bounding box of the same type, and count an intersection over union ratio of 0.3 or greater as a positive match.

Table 2 demonstrates that neither text annotation filters nor object localization alone were sufficient for our detection task due to their relatively high false positive rates at 6.7% and 2.5% respectively. Not surprisingly, combining two approaches significantly decreased our false positive rate to less than 1%.

Specifically, we saw that for classes like *glasses*, text annotations were insufficient and image-based classification excelled (likely due to the distinctive shape of glasses). For other classes, such as *dress*, this situation was reversed (the false positive rate for our dress detector was high, 12.3%, due to occlusion and high variance in style for that class, and adding a text filter dramatically improved results). Aside from reducing the number of images we needed to process with our object classifiers, for several object classes (*shoe*, *bag*, *pants*), we observed that text filtering was crucial to achieve an acceptable false positive rate (under 1%).

Live Experiments

Our system identified over 80 million "clickable" objects from a subset of Pinterest images. A clickable red dot is placed upon the detected object. Once the user clicks on the dot, our visual search system retrieves a collection of Pins with other instances of the object class, ranked by visually similarity to the query object. We launched the system to a small percentage of Pinterest live traffic and collected user engagement metrics for one month. Specifically, we looked at the clickthrough rate (CTR) of the dot, the CTR on our visual search results, and we compared engagement on Similar Look results with the engagement on existing Related Pins recommendations.

As shown in Figure 10, on average, 12% of users who viewed a pin with a dot clicked on a dot in a given day. Those users went on to click an average of 0.55 Similar Looks results. Although this data was encouraging, when we compared engagement with all related content on the pin close-up (summing both engagement with Related Pins and Similar Look results for the treatment group, and just Related Pins engagement for the control), Similar Looks actually hurt overall engagement on the pin close-up by 4%. After the novelty effort wore off, we saw a gradual decrease in CTR on the red dots, which stabilized at around 10%.

To test the relevance of our Similar Looks results independently of the newly introduced UI (the clickable object dots), we ran an experiment in which we blended Similar Looks results directly into the existing Related Pins. This gave us a way to directly measure whether users found our visually similar recommendations more relevant than our existing non-visual recommendations. On pins where we detected an object, this experiment increased overall engagement (repins and close-ups) in Related Pins by 5%. Although we set an initial static blending ratio for this experiment (one visually similar result for every three non-visual results), we later adjusted this ratio dynamically using user click data.

5. CONCLUSION AND FUTURE WORK

We demonstrate that, with the availability of distributed computational platforms such as Amazon Web Services and

Figure 12: Samples of object detection and localization results for bags. [Green: ground truth, blue: detected objects.]

Figure 13: Samples of object detection and localization results for shoes.

Figure 14: Samples of object detection and localization results for dresses

open-source tools, it is possible for a handful of engineers or an academic lab to build a large-scale visual search system using a combination of non-proprietary tools. This paper presented our end-to-end visual search pipeline, including incremental feature updating and two-step object detection and localization method that improves search accuracy and reduces development and deployment costs. Our live product experiments demonstrate that visual search features can increase user engagement.

We plan to further improve our system in the following areas. First, we are interested in investigating the performance and efficiency of CNN based object detection methods in the context of live visual search systems. Second, we are interested in leveraging Pinterest "curation graph" to enhance visual search relevance. Lastly, we want to experiment with alternative interactive interfaces for visual search.

6. REFERENCES

[1] S. Bengio, J. Dean, D. Erhan, E. Ie, Q. V. Le, A. Rabinovich, J. Shlens, and Y. Singer. Using web co-occurrence statistics for improving image categorization. *CoRR*, abs/1312.5697, 2013.

[2] T. L. Berg, A. C. Berg, J. Edwards, M. Maire, R. White, Y.-W. Teh, E. Learned-Miller, and D. A. Forsyth. Names and faces in the news. In *Proceedings of the Conference on Computer Vision and Pattern Recognition (CVPR)*, pages 848–854, 2004.

[3] K. Chatfield, K. Simonyan, A. Vedaldi, and A. Zisserman. Return of the devil in the details: Delving deep into convolutional nets. In *British Machine Vision Conference*, 2014.

[4] M. Cheng, N. Mitra, X. Huang, P. H. S. Torr, and S. Hu. Global contrast based salient region detection. *Transactions on Pattern Analysis and Machine Intelligence (T-PAMI)*, 2014.

[5] R. Datta, D. Joshi, J. Li, and J. Wang. Image retrieval: Ideas, influences, and trends of the new age. *ACM Computing Survey*, 40(2):5:1–5:60, May 2008.

[6] J. Donahue, Y. Jia, O. Vinyals, J. Hoffman, N. Zhang, E. Tzeng, and T. Darrell. Decaf: A deep convolutional activation feature for generic visual recognition. *CoRR*, abs/1310.1531, 2013.

[7] D. Erhan, C. Szegedy, A. Toshev, and D. Anguelov. Scalable object detection using deep neural networks. In *2014 IEEE Conference on Computer Vision and Pattern Recognition, CVPR 2014, Columbus, OH, USA, June 23-28, 2014*, pages 2155–2162, 2014.

[8] P. F. Felzenszwalb, R. B. Girshick, and D. A. McAllester. Cascade object detection with deformable part models. In *The IEEE Conference on Computer Vision and Pattern Recognition (CVPR)*, pages 2241–2248, 2010.

[9] R. Girshick, J. Donahue, T. Darrell, and J. Malik. Rich feature hierarchies for accurate object detection and semantic segmentation. *arXiv preprint arXiv:1311.2524*, 2013.

[10] K. He, X. Zhang, S. Ren, and J. Sun. Spatial pyramid pooling in deep convolutional networks for visual recognition. In *Transactions on Pattern Analysis and Machine Intelligence (T-PAMI)*, pages 346–361. Springer, 2014.

[11] V. Jagadeesh, R. Piramuthu, A. Bhardwaj, W. Di, and N. Sundaresan. Large scale visual recommendations from street fashion images. In *Proceedings of the International Conference on Knowledge Discovery and Data Mining (SIGKDD)*, 14, pages 1925–1934, 2014.

Figure 11: Examples of object search results for shoes. Boundaries of detected objects are automatically highlighted. The top image is the query image.

[12] Y. Jia, E. Shelhamer, J. Donahue, S. Karayev, J. Long, R. Girshick, S. Guadarrama, and T. Darrell. Caffe: Convolutional architecture for fast feature embedding. *arXiv preprint arXiv:1408.5093*, 2014.

[13] Y. Jing and S. Baluja. Visualrank: Applying pagerank to large-scale image search. *IEEE Transactions on Pattern Analysis and Machine Intelligence (T-PAMI)*, 30(11):1877–1890, 2008.

[14] A. Karpathy, G. Toderici, S. Shetty, T. Leung, R. Sukthankar, and L. Fei-Fei. Large-scale video classification with convolutional neural networks. In *2014 IEEE Conference on Computer Vision and Pattern Recognition (CVPR)*, pages 1725–1732, 2014.

[15] A. Krizhevsky, S. Ilya, and G. E. Hinton. Imagenet classification with deep convolutional neural networks. In *Advances in Neural Information Processing Systems (NIPS)*, pages 1097–1105. 2012.

[16] Y. LeCun, B. Boser, J. S. Denker, D. Henderson, R. E. Howard, W. Hubbard, and L. D. Jackel. Backpropagation applied to handwritten zip code recognition. *Neural Comput.*, 1(4):541–551, Dec. 1989.

[17] S. Liu, Z. Song, M. Wang, C. Xu, H. Lu, and S. Yan. Street-to-shop: Cross-scenario clothing retrieval via parts alignment and auxiliary set. In *Proceedings of the IEEE Conference on Computer Vision and Pattern Recognition (CVPR)*, 2012.

[18] J. Long, E. Shelhamer, and T. Darrell. Fully convolutional networks for semantic segmentation. *arXiv preprint arXiv:1411.4038*, 2014.

[19] M. Muja and D. G. Lowe. Fast matching of binary features. In *Proceedings of the Conference on Computer and Robot Vision (CRV)*, 12, pages 404–410, Washington, DC, USA, 2012. IEEE Computer Society.

[20] H. Müller, W. Müller, D. M. Squire, S. Marchand-Maillet, and T. Pun. Performance evaluation in content-based image retrieval: Overview and proposals. *Pattern Recognition Letter*, 22(5):593–601, 2001.

[21] O. Russakovsky, J. Deng, H. Su, J. Krause, S. Satheesh, S. Ma, Z. Huang, A. Karpathy, A. Khosla, M. Bernstein, et al. ImageNet large scale visual recognition challenge. *arXiv preprint arXiv:1409.0575*, 2014.

[22] K. Simonyan and A. Zisserman. Very deep convolutional networks for large-scale image recognition. *CoRR*, abs/1409.1556, 2014.

[23] C. Szegedy, W. Liu, Y. Jia, P. Sermanet, S. Reed, D. Anguelov, D. Erhan, V. Vanhoucke, and A. Rabinovich. Going deeper with convolutions. *arXiv preprint arXiv:1409.4842*, 2014.

[24] K. Yamaguchi, M. H. Kiapour, L. Ortiz, and T. Berg. Retrieving similar styles to parse clothing. *Transactions on Pattern Analysis and Machine Intelligence (T-PAMI)*, 2014.

[25] Q. Yan, L. Xu, J. Shi, and J. Jia. Hierarchical saliency detection. In *Proceedings of the IEEE Computer Society Conference on Computer Vision and Pattern Recognition (CVPR)*, 13, pages 1155–1162, Washington, DC, USA, 2013.

Discovering Collective Narratives of Theme Parks from Large Collections of Visitors' Photo Streams

Gunhee Kim*
Seoul National University
Seoul, South Korea, 151-744
gunhee@snu.ac.kr

Leonid Sigal
Disney Research
Pittsburgh PA 15213
lsigal@disneyresearch.com

ABSTRACT

We present an approach for generating pictorial storylines from large collections of online photo streams shared by visitors to theme parks (*e.g.* Disneyland), along with publicly available information such as visitor's maps. The story graph visualizes various events and activities recurring across visitors' photo sets, in the form of hierarchically branching narrative structure associated with attractions and districts in theme parks. We first estimate *story elements* of each photo stream, including the detection of faces and supporting objects, and attraction-based localization. We then create spatio-temporal story graphs via an inference of sparse time-varying directed graphs. Through quantitative evaluation and crowdsourcing-based user studies via Amazon Mechanical Turk, we show that the story graphs serve as a more convenient mid-level data structure to perform photo-based recommendation tasks than other alternatives. We also present storybook-like demo examples regarding exploration, recommendation, and temporal analysis, which may be most beneficial uses of the story graphs to visitors.

Categories and Subject Descriptors

I.4.9 [**Image processing and computer vision**]: Applications

Keywords

Photo storylines; summarization and exploration of multimedia data; user modeling

1. INTRODUCTION

Current technical advances, including widespread availability of mobile photo taking devices and ubiquitous network connectivity, are changing the way we tell our stories. Personal storytelling is becoming more *data-driven* and *vision-oriented*; people can simply capture their memorable moments by a stream of images, and then spontaneously reuse them to deliver their own stories. In addition, with the emergence of social networking, the sharing of such visual stories is becoming effortless. For example, even in a single day, tens of thousands of people visit *Disneyland*, and much of them take and are willing to share large streams of photos that record their experiences with families or friends. Each photo stream tells a slightly different story from its own point of view, but by aggregating them, it is likely that common storylines of *Disneyland* experience emerge. The storylines can summarize a variety of visitors' activity patterns such as popular paths in the theme parks and temporal changes of the flow in and out of the attractions.

In this paper, the term *story* refers to *personal* or *collective narrative*, instead of a *fictional story* as is the case in novels, games, or films. The *personal narrative* describes accounts of specific events that have been personally experienced [9], whereas the *collective narrative* is regarded as a collection of *personal narratives* from different people that share the similar experiences. We consider a photo stream of each visitor as a visual instantiation of his or her personal narrative, and the aggregation of photo streams as that of collective narrative, assuming that photographers take pictures when they encounter scenes or events that they want to remember or tell a story about. We define a photo stream as a set of images that are taken in sequence by a single photographer within a fixed period of time (*e.g.* one day).

Fig.1 summarizes the problem statement. Our goal is to develop an approach for creating and exploring spatio-temporal storylines from large collections of photo streams contributed by visitors to *Disneyland*, along with its public information like visitor's map. We also use meta-data of images such as timestamps and GPS information if available, although they are often noisy and missing (*e.g.* only 19% of photo streams in our dataset has GPS information). Taking advantage of computer vision techniques, we represent the visual contents of images in the form of *story elements* (*e.g.* human faces, supporting objects, and locations), and automatically extract shared key moments and put them together to create a *story graph*, which is a structural summary of branching narratives that visualize various events and/or activities recurring across the input photo sets. To show the usefulness of story graphs, we leverage them to perform photo-based exploration, recommendation, and temporal analysis tasks. For example, once we have story graphs summarizing people's experiences on their *Disneyland* trips, we can recommend pieces of those experiences to new visi-

*This work has been completed when Gunhee Kim was a post-doctoral researcher at Disney Research.

KDD'15, August 10-13, 2015, Sydney, NSW, Australia.
© 2015 ACM. ISBN 978-1-4503-3664-2/15/08 ...$15.00.
DOI: http://dx.doi.org/10.1145/2783258.2788569.

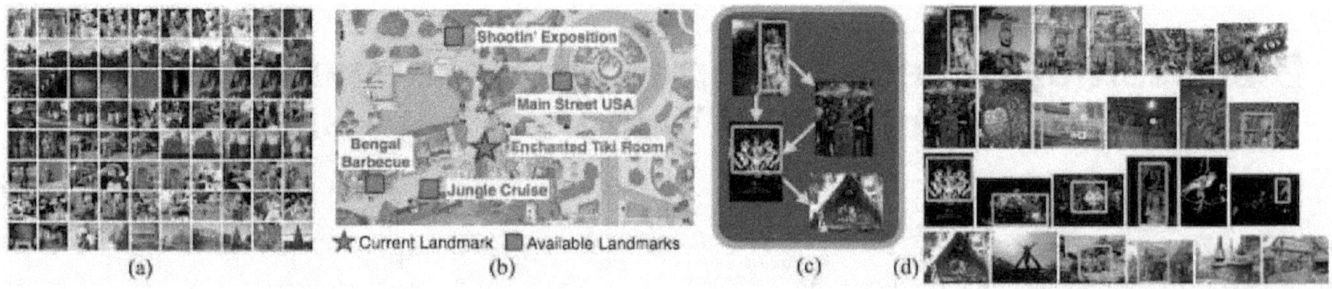

Figure 1: (a) Given large sets of online photo streams shared by visitors to a theme park (*e.g.* Disneyland), and its public information (*e.g.* visitor's map), we create story graphs as a structural summary visualizing various events or activities recurring across the visitors' photo sets. The story graphs are hierarchically created to enable users to explore the stories between attractions in (b), and sub-stories inside the individual attractions in (c)–(d). In (c), we show the connectivity between story subgraphs at the *Enchanted Tiki Room*, and their details are given in (d). The photos in (c) are the first images of story subgraphs in (d).

tors, suggesting attractions, touring plans, or best ways to experience a given attraction at a particular time of the day.

As a problem domain, we focus on *theme parks*, more specifically *Disneyland*, for the following reasons. First, we can easily obtain abundant visual data, because visiting a theme park is a special leisure activity where much of visitors are willing to take and share the pictures of their experiences[1]. Second, stories play an important role in theme parks for the purpose of user modeling, personalization, and recommendation. Theme parks provide different sets of attractions and entertainment, only parts of which are experienced by individual visitors. Thus a large diversity of possible stories exist according to who visits when. Families with children may prefer to play with the characters their kids like. Such storylines may differ from those of young adults who may enjoy more adventurous rides (*e.g.* roller coasters). Finally, our story extraction and exploration in theme parks can be easily extended to other leisure and entertainment domains, such as city tours [15] and museum tours [30], as long as they have sufficient sets of photo streams. Similar to theme parks, cities also consist of multiple attractions that are more sparsely distributed and events, attendance of which differs by preference, time and visitor types.

Our story graphs can be used as mid-level data structure for a variety of applications, including virtual exploration, path planning, travel recommendations, and temporal mining tasks, among many others. Usually theme park operators, including Disney, do not disclose any statistics on the use of attractions. Thus, our story graphs can indirectly hint the visitors' behavior patterns. Compared to guided routes and lists of events by travel agencies, our visual exploration using story graphs directly builds upon consumer-generated pictures, and thus reflects candid and spontaneous peer costumers' experiences in the original visual forms. It could be more synergetic to integrate our results with the official Apps of theme parks (*e.g.* *My Disney Experience* mobile app of *Disneyland*). Not only for visitors, our story graphs can benefit theme park operators by providing an automatic tool for monitoring the popularities of attractions. We also focus on revealing in-depth branching stories at each attraction, which are not easily mined from other sensor modalities. For example, although a GPS tracker can more accurately localize the visitors' paths, it cannot correctly discover the visitors' activities that occur inside individual attractions.

To conclude, we summarize the contributions of this paper as follows. First, to the best of our knowledge, our work is the first approach for creating spatio-temporal story graphs from large sets of online photo streams, especially in the domain of theme parks where the discovery of underlying stories is of a particular importance for user modeling, personalization and recommendation. Through quantitative evaluation and crowdsourcing-based user studies with Amazon Mechanical Turk, we show that the story graphs serve as a convenient and mid-level data structure to which many applications are supported by simple algorithms applied, including photo-based exploration, recommendation, and temporal analysis. Second, we develop a scalable algorithm for creating semantic story graphs, consisting of two components: story element estimation and graph inference. The story element estimation includes the detection of faces and supporting objects, and attraction-based localization. The graph inference algorithm builds a time-varying sparse story graph directly from estimated story elements of photo streams, while addressing several key challenges of large-scale nature of our problems, including global optimality, easy parallelization, and linear computation time.

2. RELATED WORK

We discuss some representative previous studies from four lines of research that are closely related to our work.

Story extraction from Web data. In recent web mining research, much work has been done to build and visualize storylines from online text corpora such as news articles and scientific papers [1, 5, 22, 26]. The work of [5, 22] addresses the problem of extracting diverse story threads from large document collections. In [1], a probabilistic model is presented to group incoming news articles into temporary but tightly-focused storylines, to identify prevalent topics/keywords and evolving structure of stories. In [26], the NIFTY is developed for real-time tracking of *memes* (*e.g.* short textual phrases that travel and mutate on the Web) from blog posts and news articles. From this line of research, our work differs that we leverage image collections instead of text data, to discover and explore the storylines of user data.

Story extraction from visual data. The story has been used as an important concept to build interactive video

[1]For example, *Disneyland* is reported as the most geo-tagged location in the world on Instagram in 2014, as shown in http://time.com/3618002/most-instagram-places-2014/.

summarization or editing [7, 29], in which the objective is to summarize input video clips in a concise form (*e.g.* static images, shorter videos, or language sentences) while preserving key moments of the videos and allowing users to intuitively explore or edit them. In this category of work, input videos usually contain a small number of specified actors in fixed scenes. In contrast, our main technical challenge is the extraction of shared moments from photo streams that are independently taken by multiple visitors at different time.

The story extraction has been also investigated in the image domain as well. In [19], storyline-based summarization is discussed for a small private photo album. However, it is tested with only a small set of about 200 images from a single user's photo collection. This work is also related to our previous work [12] that leverages a large set of Flickr images to create photo storylines. However, [12] exploits only temporal information between images, whereas we additionally consider spatial information that synergetically interplays with time. Thus, our approach also involves an image localization task. Second, the algorithm of [12] defines the nodes of graphs using low-level image features only, whereas we here leverage high-level semantic story elements, including the detection output of faces and supporting objects.

Data mining for tourism. As massive amounts of travel data are available and the location-based systems proliferate, the data mining techniques begin offering significant benefits on tourism analytics in various ways. Some notable examples include customized tour recommendations in urban areas [6], discovery of international human mobility [25], recommendation of travel packages with consideration of both tourists' interests and travel costs [4], to name a few. Geo-referenced Flickr pictures are also leveraged for this purpose. In [14], representative and diverse travel routes are discovered from the histories of tourists' geotagged photos for landmarks. In [31], a diversity ranking method for such trajectory patterns is proposed. Our main novelty is that we take advantage of computer vision techniques to understand image contents, and thus we can possibly use all the images no matter whether GPS information is available or not. In addition, our idea of story-based summarization and exploration is unique in this line of work.

Exploration of large collections of tourists' images. With recent popularity of online image sharing, there has been a significant amount of effort for intuitively exploring large collections of unstructured tourists' photos. The work of [10] organizes the Flickr images of landmarks by analyzing the associated location information, tags, and contents. One of early pioneering work is *Photo Tourism* [24], which calibrates geo-tagged photos of tourist landmarks in a 3-D space, and enables users to interactively browse them. This work has been extended later in many different directions. In [23], tourists' paths around the landmarks are discovered for better navigation of the 3-D scene. In [21], a semantic navigation is established between regions of 3D landmark models and their corresponding reference texts of Wikipedia. In [15], online geo-tagged images are leveraged to create tours of the world's tourist sites on Google Maps. Compared to this line of research, our work differs in that we aim to build storylines, which illustrate a series of spatio-temporal events or episodes without requiring availability of accurate geometric information as input. Therefore, our system can bypass the time-consuming step of reconstructing 3-D models.

	CA	FL	PA	TK	HK	HI	N/A
# PS	6,402	11,437	1,707	1,849	856	120	5,409
# IM	568.8	1,037.2	197.8	196.3	80.1	19.7	413.6

Table 1: The number of photo streams and images ($\times 10^3$) of the Disneyland dataset according to the park locations. Total numbers of images and photo streams are (2,513,367, 27,780), respectively. (CA: California, FL: Florida, PA: Paris, TK: Tokyo, HK: Hong Kong, HI: Hawaii, N/A: unknown or noisy).

	Districts	Attractions	Dining	Entertainment
(DCA)	8	37	29 (1)	4
(DP)	8	63	22 (1)	8

Table 2: The attraction statistics of *Disney California Adventure* (DCA) and *Disneyland Park* (DP). The numbers in parentheses are about *character dining*.

3. PROBLEM FORMULATION

3.1 The Input Data

The input of our approach is two-fold: a set of visitors' photo streams and side information of the parks.

Photo streams. We download 3,602,727 unique images from Flickr by querying multiple *Disneyland* related keywords. Then, using the timestamp and user information associated with each image, we obtain 27,780 photo streams that contain more than 30 images. The input set of photo streams is denoted by $\mathcal{P} = \{P^1, \cdots, P^N\}$, where N is the number of photo streams. We sort the pictures of each photo stream by timestamps. Next we classify the photo streams according to the park locations where they are recorded: {*California, Orlando, Tokyo, Paris, Hong Kong, Hawaii, N/A*}. The *N/A* label is tagged for the photo streams that are not taken in any Disney parks or whose locations are unknown. We use GPS information when available; in our sets, 5,257 (19%) of photo streams include GPS information. Next we exploit the location keywords (*e.g. California, Florida*) in the text data (*e.g.* tags and titles) associated with images. Table 1 summarizes the statistics of our Disneyland dataset.

We apply our algorithm to the set of each park separately. To make our discussion easier and more coherent, we henceforth focus on the two parks at *California*: *Disney California Adventure Park* and *Disneyland Park*.

Side information about attractions. Disneyland parks consist of multiple districts, each of which includes a sets of attractions, dining, and other entertainment (*e.g.* parades and stage shows). Table 2 summarizes the statistics obtained from Disney's official maps. For simplicity, we hereafter use the term *attractions* to indicate attractions, dining, and entertainment events without distinction. We denote the set of attractions by $\mathcal{L}$. For dining, we consider a *character dining* as a separate attraction, and all the others as a single *restaurant* attraction. The *character dining* (*e.g. Ariel's Grotto*) is a restaurant where visitors can take pictures with characters (*e.g. Ariel the little mermaid*). For each attraction, we download at maximum 1,000 top-ranked images from Google and Flickr by querying the attraction name. We use the attraction images as training data for various tasks of story element estimation, such as image localization and supporting object detection, which will be presented in Section 4. We also obtain the GPS

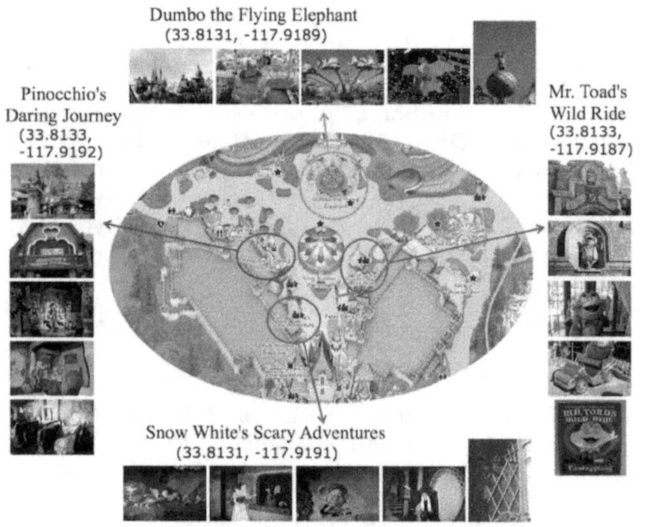

Figure 2: Examples of images and GPS coordinates for four attractions in the *Fantasyland* district of *Disneyland park.* The attractions are identified by Disney's official map, and images are retrieved by Google and Flickr image search. The GPS coordinates are obtained from Google Maps.

coordinates of attractions from Google Maps, except for entertainment events that do not happen in a specific location (*e.g. Mickey's Soundsational Parade*). Fig.2 shows sampled training images and GPS coordinates of four attractions in the *Fantasyland* district. Indeed, each attraction builds on a unique theme, whose visual contents are clearly discriminative with other attractions. Thus, Google and Flickr images found by attraction names yield an excellent repository that captures various canonical views of the attractions.

3.2 The Storylines

The output of our algorithm is two-fold. First, we extract *story elements* from all images of the photo streams using computer vision techniques. Along with two low-level image features denoted by $\mathbf{v}$ (section 4.1), we define four types of *story elements* as story-related, high-level descriptors of images in the context of theme parks: {faces, time, location, supporting objects}, which are represented by four vectors: $\{\mathbf{f}, \mathbf{t}, \mathbf{c}, \mathbf{o}\}$. We will explain each of them in section 4.2–4.4.

Based on the estimated story elements over photo streams, the second output is the story graph $\mathcal{G} = (\mathcal{O}, \mathcal{E})$. The vertices $\mathcal{O}$ correspond to dominant image clusters of the photo streams, and the edge set $\mathcal{E}$ links the vertices that sequentially recur in many photo streams. More rigorous definition will be shown in Section 5.

4. STORY ELEMENT ESTIMATION

We discuss our low-level image description and story element estimation for the input photo streams $\mathcal{P}$.

4.1 Image Features

For low-level image description, we use dense feature extraction with vector quantization, which is one of standard methods in recent computer vision research. We densely extract HSV color SIFT [17] and histogram of oriented edge (HOG) features [3] on a regular grid of each image at steps of 4 and 8 pixels, respectively. We form 300 visual words for each feature type by applying K-means to randomly selected descriptors. Finally, the nearest word is assigned to every node of the grid. As image or region descriptors, we build L_1 normalized spatial pyramid histograms to count the frequency of each visual word at three levels [16]. We define the image descriptor $\mathbf{v}$ by concatenating the two spatial pyramid histograms of color SIFT and HOG features.

4.2 Face and Time Descriptors

Since much of visitors' images contain faces as foregrounds, we define a high-level image descriptor that encodes presence/absence of faces and their spatial layout in the image. For example, we may cluster the images that have similar face sizes and positions (*e.g.* clustering family photos), or bypass the localization step for the images that are fully occupied by faces. For face detection, we use the Fraunhofer engine [20], which returns bounding boxes containing faces with confidence scores. Based on the detection, we compute the following three types of face features. (i) Histogram of face areas: we first make 10 bins in the range of $[0, \sqrt{h \times w}]$, where h and w are image height and width respectively, and count the frequencies of squared areas of detected faces for each bin. (ii) Histogram of face locations: we split the image into 9 evenly split tiles (*i.e.* 3 per dimension), and count the detected face centers in each spatial bin. (iii) Histogram of pairwise face distances: We compute pairwise distances between centroids of all detected faces and make a histogram of 10 bins in the range of [0, diagonal length]. As a final face descriptor vector $\mathbf{f} \in \mathcal{R}^{29}$, we concatenate all the three histogram after L_1 normalization.

The timestamps of images can be trivially obtained from meta-data provided by Flickr. We use month and hour information to define time features because the events in theme parks are seasonally and daily periodic. We define the month feature $\mathbf{t}_m(i) \in \mathcal{R}^{12}$ of image I in which each bin i has a value of Gaussian weighting $\mathbf{t}_m(i) = g(i - m) \propto \exp(-(i-m)^2/\sigma_m)$, where m is the month of image I and $\sigma_m = 1.5$. Its basic idea is that if an image is taken in May, the feature values for nearby months like April and June (*i.e.* $\mathbf{t}_m(4)$ or $\mathbf{t}_m(6)$) are non-zeros as well. The same Gaussian weighting is used for the hour feature with $\sigma_h = 2$. Finally, the two features are L_1-normalized and concatenated into the time descriptor $\mathbf{t}$.

4.3 Localization of Photo Streams

It is important to find out which attraction each image is likely to be taken, because visitors' activities and stories can be modularized according to attractions. Thus, we perform the attraction-based localization, whose objective is to determine the likelihood of each image over attractions. Mathematically, we assign a probability vector $\mathbf{c}_i \in \mathbb{R}^L$ to each image of photo stream $P^n = \{I_1, \ldots, I_{N^n}\}$, where N^n is the number of images in P^n and L is the number of attractions (*i.e.* $L = |\mathcal{L}|$). For notational simplicity, we let $\mathbf{c} = [\mathbf{c}_1, \ldots, \mathbf{c}_{N^n}] \in \mathbb{R}^{L \times N^n}$.

We run localization of each photo stream separately because all photo streams are taken by different users independently of one another. We use a Conditional Random Field (CRF) model to infer the conditional distribution over the attraction labels of each photo stream P^n. The strength of CRF is the flexibility to easily incorporate various pieces of evidence related to localization as energy terms in a single

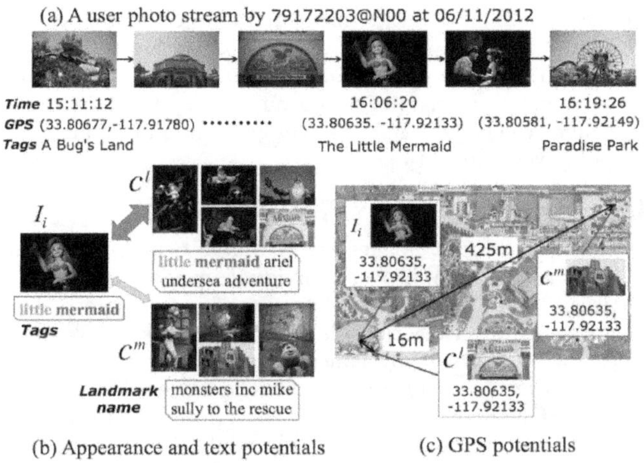

Figure 3: An example of attraction-based localization. (a) An input photo stream with meta-data of timestamps, GPS coordinates, and text tags. (b) The appearance potential of each image is computed by visual similarity with attraction images. The text potential is defined by the tf-idf measure between tags of the image and attraction names. (c) GPS potential is obtained from a normal distribution on the distances between the image and attractions.

unified model. Since each photo stream is a time-ordered sequence of images, it can be modeled by a linear-chain CRF. The conditional probability of the attraction labels $\mathbf{c}$ given a photo stream P^n is defined by

$$\log P(\mathbf{c}|P^n) = \sum_{i=1} \Big(\psi(\mathbf{c}_i, I_i) + \pi(\mathbf{c}_i, I_i) + \lambda(\mathbf{c}_i, I_i)\Big) \quad (1)$$
$$+ \phi(\mathbf{c}_0) \sum_i \phi(\mathbf{c}_i, \mathbf{c}_{i+1}, \Delta_i) - \log Z(P^n)$$

where $Z(P^n)$ is the partition function. In the following, we discuss each term of Eq.(1) in detail.

Appearance potential. The $\psi(c_i^l, I_i)$ represents the likelihood that image I_i is *visually* associated with attraction l. (See Fig.3(b)). Intuitively, $\psi(c_i^l, I_i)$ has a high value if I_i is visually similar to the images of attraction l. Since the training images of attractions are available, the estimation of $\psi(c_i^l, I_i)$ can be accomplished by any image classifier or their combination. In this paper, the potential is computed by summing the normalized scores of two classifiers, a KNN classifier and a linear SVM [28]. For SVM classifiers, we learn multiple classifiers per attraction because the training images of each attraction may contain multiple views; we first split the attraction image set into k different groups using K-means clustering with $k = \min(2.5\sqrt{n}, 200)$, and learn a separate classifier per cluster.

GPS potential. For the 19% of photo streams where GPS information is available, we define the GPS potentials as a normal distribution: $\pi(c_i^l, I_i) = N(x_c^l; x_i, \sigma)$ where x_c^l and x_i are the GPS coordinates of attraction l and image I_i, respectively. (See Fig.3(c)). We set the standard deviation $\sigma = 0.07$ km. That is, if a attraction l is $3\sigma (= 0.21$ km) distant away from I_i, l is very unlikely to be assigned to I_i. This GPS term is ignored for the photo streams without GPS information.

Text potential. We also take advantage of text information when available, as shown in Fig.3(b). We use the tf-idf measure (Term Frequency Inverse Document Frequency).

Figure 4: Examples of detected regions of interest encoding supporting objects of different meanings.

Let us denote the text associated with image I_i by D_i, which is a list of words of the title and tags. For each term $q \in D_i$, we compute the tf measure $tf_{q,i}$, which is the number of occurrences of q in D_i, and the idf measure $idf_q = \log(N/df_q)$ where df_q is the number of images containing q, and N is the total number of images. Then, for each attraction l, we generate a word list using its name, denoted by $\mathbf{q}^l$. The potential $\lambda(c_i^l, I_i)$ of image I_i to attraction l is computed by

$$\lambda(c_i^l, I_i) = \sum_{q \in \mathbf{q}^l} tf_{q,i} \times idf_q. \quad (2)$$

Edge potential. The $\phi(c_i^l, c_i^m, \Delta_i)$ is defined by the likelihood that a pair of consecutive images I_i and I_{i+1} are associated with attraction l and m respectively, given Δ_i that denotes the elapsed time between I_i and I_{i+1}. The edge potential depends on both spatial connectivity between attractions and visitors' walking speed in the park. We define the edge potential as follows. We first build a connectivity graph between attractions $\mathcal{G}_c = (\mathcal{L}, \mathcal{E}_c)$ based on the official park map and the GPS coordinates. Each attraction in $\mathcal{L}$ is linked to its k closest attractions, and the edge weight is given by the walking time between a attraction pair, which is computed by dividing the distance by the human walking speed s_w. we set $s_w = 1$km/h. Inspired by a human mobility study [8], we assume that a visitor stays in the same location with a probability α or moves to one of neighbor attractions with $1-\alpha$. α is sampled from a truncated exponential distribution: $\alpha \propto \exp(-\lambda\Delta_i)$. With probability $1-\alpha$ of moving to another attraction, we use the Gaussian model for a transition likelihood from attraction l to m:

$$\phi(c_i^l, c_i^m, \Delta_i) = \frac{1}{\sigma\sqrt{2\pi}} \exp(-\Delta_i^2/2\sigma^2) \text{ where } \sigma = s_w\Delta_i. \quad (3)$$

where σ is proportional to Δ_i; with a longer Δ_i, farther attractions can be reached.

Inference. Since our model for the localization is a linear-chain CRF, exact inference is possible. We use the Viterbi algorithm to obtain the most probable attraction assignment of the photo stream $\mathbf{c}^* = [c_1^*, \ldots, c_{n^l}^*]$. We also compute the posterior marginals of location labels $\mathbf{c}$ using the forwards-backwards algorithm.

4.4 Detection of Supporting Objects

We detect the regions of interest (ROI) that may include important supporting objects of images for the following two reasons. First, it can be used as another high-level image descriptor, as shown in Fig.4, because supporting objects illustrate the main theme of the images, such as rides, meals, or interaction with characters. Second, it can be exploited

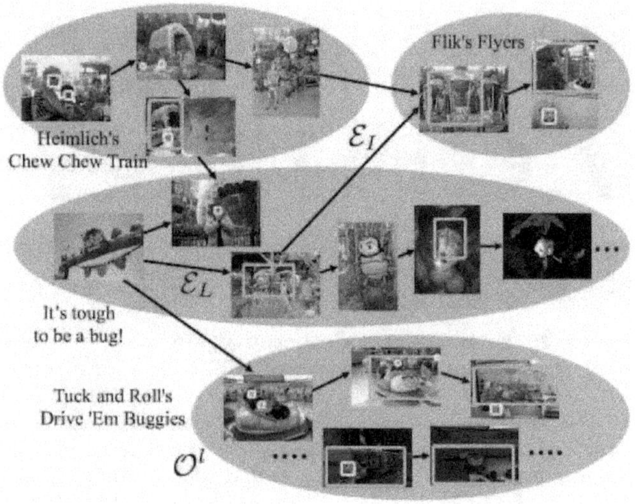

Figure 5: A small piece of story graph between and inside four attractions of *Bug's Land* district of *Disney California Adventure* Park. Each image represents the central image of each vertex.

for user interaction; we allow users to choose ROIs to retrieve the images that share the similar supporting objects, as another control for story exploration. We will introduce examples in Section 7.

For ROI detection, we first learn a set of ROI classifiers of each attraction as follows. We first sample 10 rectangular windows per training image of each attraction using the objectness metric [2], and build a similarity graph between the windows of all training images, using histogram intersection on the color SIFT and HOG features $\mathbf{v}$ of the windows. By applying the diversity ranking and clustering algorithm of [13] to the similarity graph, we discover k representative and discriminative exemplar windows, and cluster windows by associating each window with its closest exemplar. We set $k = \min(2.5\sqrt{n}, 200)$, where n is the size of graph. For each exemplar, we learn KNN and linear SVM classifiers as done for the appearance potential of localization in section 4.3. For a positive training set, we use the exemplar and its 10 nearest neighbors. For a negative training set, we randomly sample 200 windows from the other attractions. As a result, we have k number of classifiers per attraction. We repat this ROI classifier learning for all attractions.

Next we leverage the learned classifiers to detect the ROIs for the images of photo streams. As a pre-processing step, we first sample 100 windows per image using the objectness metric. Our assumption here is that at least some of candidate windows correspond to good potential supporting objects. We then remove the windows if they largely overlap with face detection (*i.e.* if more than 50% of the window area overlaps with any face region), due to redundancy with face detection. Then, if the image is localized as attraction l, we apply a set of learned classifiers for attraction l, and choose one single best window per image as the ROI.

5. STORY GRAPH RECONSTRUCTION

In this section, we discuss how to create a story graph $\mathcal{G} = (\mathcal{O}, \mathcal{E})$ from the results of story element estimation. We build story graphs hierarchically. As shown in Fig.5, the upper-level story graph is defined between attractions, each of which subsumes small story subgraphs that represent sequences of activities inside attraction. That is, in the storyline graph $\mathcal{G} = (\mathcal{O}, \mathcal{E})$, the vertex set can be decomposed into the ones per attraction (*i.e.* $\mathcal{O} = \bigcup_{l \in \mathcal{L}} \mathcal{O}^l$), and the edge set $\mathcal{E}$ consists of two groups: $\mathcal{E} = \mathcal{E}_L \cup \mathcal{E}_I$ where $\mathcal{E}_L$ defines the edges inside each attraction, and $\mathcal{E}_I$ includes edges between attractions.

5.1 Vertices of Story Graphs

Since many input images are redundant, it is inefficient to build a story graph over individual images. Hence, the vertices $\mathcal{O}$ are preferentially defined as *image clusters.* The vertex set $\mathcal{O}^l$ for attraction l is obtained as follows. We first represent each image by concatenating the set of vectors $\{\mathbf{v}, \mathbf{f}, \mathbf{o}, \mathbf{t}\}$, each of which represents the low-level image feature, the face descriptor, the ROI descriptor, and the time descriptor, respectively. We include the ROI descriptor $\mathbf{o}$ to encourage clustering the images that share similar supporting objects. In order to define the vertex set $\mathcal{O}^l$ for each attraction, we first build a similarity matrix between the images localized at attraction l, by applying the histogram intersection to the above descriptors. We then discover k exemplars and clusters using the same diversity ranking and clustering algorithm of [13] with $k = \min(2\sqrt{n}, 200)$. Then, the k clusters constitues the vertex set $\mathcal{O}^l$ for attraction k. We repeat this process for each attraction $l \in \mathcal{L}$. We denote the number of vertices by M (*i.e.* $M = |\mathcal{O}| = \sum_{l \in \mathcal{L}} |\mathcal{O}^l|$).

As a result of clustering for the vertex definition, each image is now associated with a vertex membership vector $\mathbf{x} \in \mathbb{R}^M$, which has only a single nonzero element $x_v = 1$ if the image is a member of vertex $v \in \mathcal{O}$. Therefore, each photo stream $P^n = \{I_1, \ldots, I_{N^n}\}$ can be represented by the membership vectors $P^n = \{\mathbf{x}_1, \ldots, \mathbf{x}_{N^n}\}$.

5.2 Edges of Story Graphs

The edge set $\mathcal{E} \subseteq \mathcal{V} \times \mathcal{V}$, whose adjacency matrix is denoted by $\mathbf{A} \in \mathbb{R}^{M \times M}$, includes directed edges between the vertices that sequentially co-occur across many photo streams. In order for the story graphs to be practical, we enforce the edge set $\mathcal{E}$ to satisfy the following two properties. (i) $\mathcal{E}$ should be *sparse.* If there are too many edges in the graph, the narrative structure is unnecessarily complex. Thus, we retain only a small number of strong story branches per node. (*i.e.* $\mathbf{A}$ has only a few nonzero elements). (ii) $\mathcal{E}$ should be *time-varying*; $\mathcal{E}$ smoothly changes over time in a day $t \in [0, T]$. It means that the preferred transitions between attractions can change over time in the theme parks. For example, in many visitors' photo streams, the images of attraction *Mad Tea Party* are likely to be followed by *dining* images around lunch time, by *fireworks* images at night, or by nearby attraction images like *Pixie Hollow* in other time. Hence, we infer individual $\mathbf{A}^t$ every 30 minutes while changing t from 8AM to 12AM to densely capture such time-varying popular story transitions.

In our previous work [12], we formulate a maximum likelihood estimation for inferring $\{\mathbf{A}^t\}$ given input photo streams $\mathcal{P} = \{P^1, \cdots, P^N\}$, and develop an optimization algorithm that has several appealing properties for large-scale problems, including global optimality, easy parallelization, and linear computation time. We here skip the details of optimization, which can be found in [12]. Instead we denote edge reconstruction procedure by $\{\mathbf{A}^t\}_{t=1}^T = \mathsf{GraphInf}(\mathcal{P}, T)$.

Although we use the similar algorithm for creating edges of graphs with our previous work [12], the story graphs of

Method	Top-1 Attr.	Top-5 Attr.	Top-1 Dist.
(A+T+E+G)	**8.34%**	**20.56%**	**28.03%**
(A+T+E)	5.18%	16.16%	22.87%
(A+T)	4.88%	14.52%	20.12%
(A)	5.02%	15.88%	21.31%
(T)	3.12%	9.17%	17.83%
(VKNN)	5.16%	16.85%	22.12%
(VSVM)	4.63%	15.80%	20.63%
(Rand)	0.93%	4.63%	5.56%

Table 3: Results of image localization. We report top-1/5 attraction accuracies, and top-1 district accuracies. We test our CRF-based approach with different combinations of terms: (T), (A), (G), and (E) indicate appearance, GPS, text, and edge potential.

this work are different from those of [12] in two respects. First, the graphs of [12] are built based on only temporal information between images, whereas here we consider both time and spatial information. Second, the vertices of the graphs of [12] are based on low-level image features only (*e.g.* SIFT and HOG features), whereas we define vertices over *story elements* of high-level semantic image description, including face and object detection. In section 6.2, we empirically compare these two story graphs for the image recommendation tasks.

6. EXPERIMENTS

We evaluate the accuracy of our story element estimation for image localization (Section 6.1). Then, we quantitatively compare the performance of image recommendataion using our story graphs with other candidate methods (Section 6.2).

6.1 Results of Image Localization

We evaluate the performance of our approach for estimating the *locations* of images, which may be considered as the most important story elements. The task here is to find out the attraction that a given image is likely to be taken. We select 108 attractions and restaurants as the classes for localization. We obtain groundtruth by letting human experts to annotate 3,000 images of photo streams. We randomly sample 2,000 images out of them and perform a localization experiment, which is repeated ten times.

For baselines, we implement two vision-based methods, which are solely based on the visual contents of images. We use the training images of each landmark to learn linear-SVM and KNN classifiers, which are denoted by (VSVM) and (VKNN), respectively. In addition, in order to quantize the contribution of terms of our CRF-based localization framework in Eq.(1), we also measure the variation of localization accuracies by changing the combination of the four terms; we use (T), (A), (G), and (E) to indicate appearance, GPS, text, and edge potential, respectively.

Table 3 summarizes the results of our experiments. We also report chance performance (Rand) to show the difficulty of the localization task. Our CRF-based approach outperforms the vision-based methods; the accuracy of our full model (A+T+E+G) is higher than the best vision-based method (VKNN) by 61.6% and 26.7% in terms of the top-1 attraction and those district metric, respectively. We also make three observations from the results. First, the visual content of images is a strong clue for localization. Second, text associated with Flickr images is noisy, and hence provides little to enhance localization accuracy. Third, the edge potential improves the localization accuracy by enforcing temporal constraints between consecutive images.

We note that the task is very difficult, with chance performance of under 1%. In many cases, even human experts feel difficulty in localizing images as content may match multiple locations (*e.g.* Mickey can be observed virtually at any location). We believe overall accuracy can be improved significantly by pre-filtering the images, however, in this experiment, our focus is on assessing the contributions of individual terms toward our CRF localization objective, not absolute performance. Hence, the tendency is important instead of absolute numbers in this experiment.

6.2 Results on Image Prediction

We evaluate the ability of our story graphs to perform photo recommendation, which is one of key practical applications of story graphs. We carry out the following two image sequence prediction tasks: (I) predicting next likely images given a short image sequence, and (II) filling in a missing part of a novel photo stream. The first task simulates the scenario where a visitor takes a small number of pictures during his trip, and the task suggests up the most likely next pictures of attractions by analyzing the photo sets of other users who had similar experience. The second task can show the pictures of alternative paths taken by other visitors. It helps the visitor compare similarity and differences of her trip with others. Fig.6 shows examples of the two prediction tasks.

We use the similar experimental protocol of [12]. We first randomly select 80% of photo streams as a training set and the others as a test set. We reduce each test photo stream into uniformly sampled 100 images, since consecutive images can be often very similar. For task (I), we randomly divide a test photo stream into two disjoint parts. Then, the goal is, given the last 10 images of the first part and next 10 query time points $\mathbf{t}_q = \{t_{q1}, \ldots, t_{q10}\}$, to retrieve the 10 images that are likely to appear at $\mathbf{t}_q$ from the training set. The actual images at $\mathbf{t}_q$ are used as groundtruth. For task (II), we randomly crop out 10 images in the middle of each test photo stream. Then, the goal is to predict the likely images for the missing part given the time points $\mathbf{t}_q$ and five images before and after the missing slots. Since training and test sets are disjoint, each algorithm can only retrieve similar (but not identical) images from training data at best.

As a result of inference of story graphs, we obtain a set of $\{\mathbf{A}^t\}$, which can be regarded as a state transition matrix between vertices of the graph at different time t. We adopt the *state space model* (SSM) to perform all prediction tasks [18]. For example, we can predict next k likely story vertices using the forward algorithm, and infer the best k paths between any two vertices using the top-k Viterbi algorithm.

We compare our approach with the method of [12] and the four baselines used in [12]. The first baseline (Page) is a Page-Rank based image retrieval, which is one of most successful methods to retrieve a small number of canonical images. The second baseline (HMM) is based on the HMM, which has been popularly used for modeling tourists' sequential photo sets. The third (Clust) is a clustering-based summarization on the timeline [11], in which images on the timeline are grouped into 10 clusters using K-means at every 30 minutes. The forth baseline is the method of [12], denoted by (Temp), whose key differences from our approach are (i) use of low-level features only (vs. story elements in our

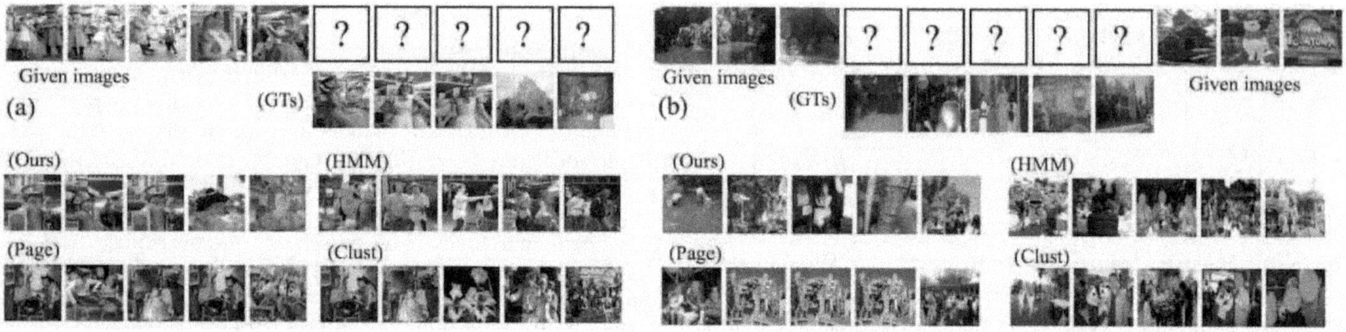

Figure 6: Examples of the two prediction tasks: task (I) (*i.e. predicting likely next images*) in (a), and task (II) (*i.e. filling in missing parts*) in (b). The first row shows a question (*i.e. given* images and five slots to be predicted). In each set, we show hidden groundtruth and predicted images by different algorithms. In AMT preference tests, we show the first row and a pair of predictions by our algorithm and one baseline in a random order. A turker is asked to select the more likely one to occur in the empty slots.

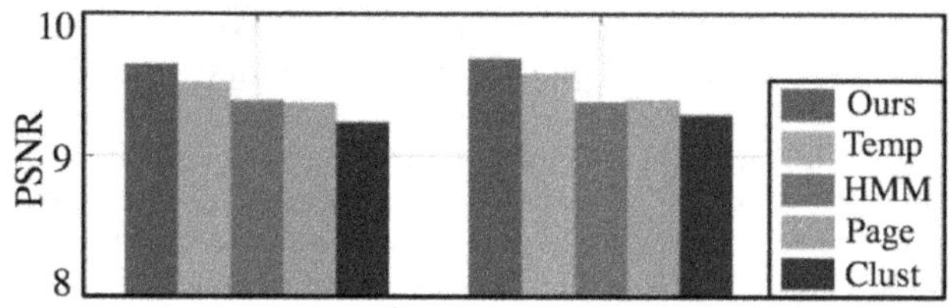

Figure 7: Results of our method and four baselines for the two prediction tasks. The PNSR values are as follows: [(`Ours`) , (`Temp`), (`HMM`), (`Page`), (`Clust`)] = [9.65, 9.51, 9.39, 9.37, 9.24] for task (I), and [9.69, 9.58, 9.38, 9.39, 9.29] for task (II).

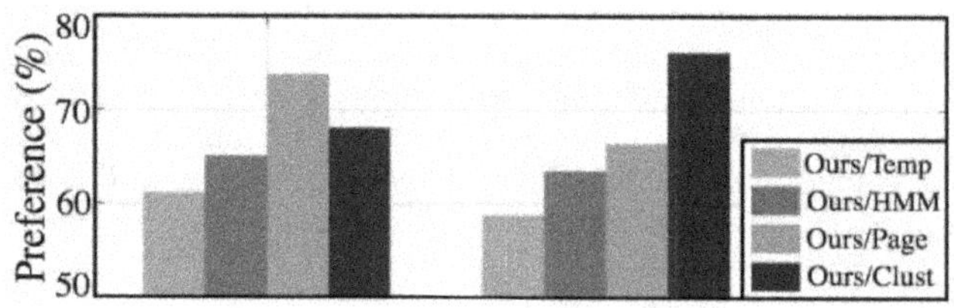

Figure 8: Results of pairwise preference tests via AMT between our method and baselines. The number should be higher than 50% to validate the superiority of our method. The average preferences of our method over (`Temp`), (`HMM`), (`Page`), and (`Clust`) are [61.2, 65.1, 73.9, 68.1] for task (I), and [58.8, 63.5, 66.4, 76.2] for task (II).

approach) for the node definition, and (ii) temporal information only (vs. spatio-temporal information) for the edge definition. We measure the performance in two different ways: quantitative similarity measures and crowdsourcing-based user studies via Amazon Mechanical Turk (AMT).

Quantitative results. We evaluate the prediction accuracy by measuring the similarity between predicted images and groundtruth images of test photo streams. For a similarity metric, we resize the images into 32×32 tiny images [27] to focus on holistic views instead of minor details, and compute peak signal-to-noise ratio (PSNR) between them. A higher value indicates that the two images are more similar.

Fig.7 shows comparison results between our method and four baselines for task (I) and (II). Our algorithm significantly outperforms all the competitors. That is, predicted images by our method are more similar to groundtruths than those by other baselines. For example, our PSNR performance gains (in dB) over the best baseline (`Temp`) are 0.131 and 0.106 for the two prediction tasks, respectively. All the numbers can be found in the caption of Fig.7.

User studies via AMT. Actual users' satisfaction is the most important measure of recommendation. Thus, we here evaluate the performance of image recommendation using user studies via Amazon Mechanical Turk (AMT). We use the same experimental setup with the previous tests, except that the number of images to be estimated is reduced to five for easy evaluation by human subjects. We show *given* images and five empty slots as a question (*e.g.* the first row of Fig.6), and then show a pair of image sequences predicted by our algorithm and one of baselines in a random order, while algorithm names are hidden. A turker is asked to choose one of them that is more likely to come at the empty slots. We obtain such pairwise comparison for each test set from at least five different turkers. In the second row of Fig.6, we show the groundtruth (*i.e.* hidden actual images), and predicted images by our algorithm and three baselines.

Fig.8 shows the quantitative results of pairwise AMT preference tests between our method and four baselines. The number indicates the mean percentage of responses that choose our prediction as a more likely one than that of each baseline. Hence, numbers should be higher than 50% to validate the superiority of our algorithm. Our algorithm significantly outperforms all the baselines; for example, our algorithm (`Ours`) gains 65.1% and 63.5% of votes over the baseline (`HMM`) in the two tasks.

7. APPLICATIONS

Once we build a story graph as a data-driven summary of visitors' activities in the parks, we can leverage it toward several interesting applications. We present preliminary storybook-like demos regarding exploration, recommendation, and temporal analysis, all of which may be beneficial uses of the story graphs to visitors.

Exploration. The first intuitive application is spatio-temporal exploration of the parks. As shown in Fig.9, we can hierarchically explore the stories between or inside attractions, with a single click of controls. In Fig.9.(a), the map on the left shows the current attraction and next available ones that are popularly visited after the current attraction. A user can proceed to a nearby attraction by clicking

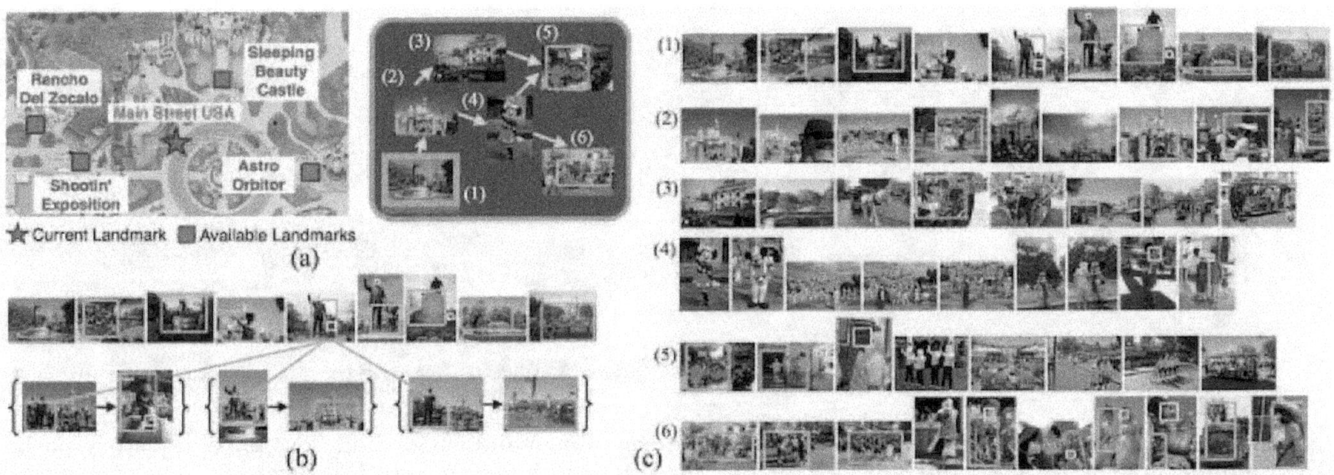

Figure 9: An example of story exploration. (a) The map on the left shows the current attraction and nearby available attractions that are popularly visited from the current location. The right panel illustrates the first images of story subgraphs for the current attraction. The detailed view of each story subgraph is presented in (c). (b) We allows a user to click a region of interest to retrieve its closest neighbors using a simple KNN search. We also show the next most popular transitions from the retrieved images.

one of the blue controls. On the right panel, we show a part of story subgraphs at the current attraction (*i.e.* the *Main Street USA*). Here each photo shows the first image of each story subgraph, whose detailed view is presented in Fig.9.(c). Every story subgraph illustrates a popular coherent story thread, for example, from top to bottom, Fig.9.(c) shows *Walt Disney Statue*, *Sleeping Beauty Castle*, transportation at the main street, character experiences, and parades. Fig.9.(b) shows an example of image retrieval using regions of interest (ROI). By clicking an ROI, we retrieve the closest neighbors using a simple KNN search. For retrieved images, we also show next most popular transitions.

Recommendation. Fig.10 shows an example of predicting the location of a novel image and suggesting next engaging paths. Since we organize images according to attractions in our story graph, we can easily localize the new images using a simple KNN search, as shown in Fig.10.(a). Based on the retrieved images, we suggest several attractions from which the exploration begins. The query image includes *Mickey's Fun Wheel*, which is viewable from most attractions in the *Paradise Pier* district. As done in the exploration example of Fig.9, a visitor is allowed to choose one of nearest attractions for further exploration, or have our system suggest a popular one for them. If a user chooses *California Screamin'*, as shown in Fig.10.(b), we suggest two popular next available attractions, which are *Ariel's Grotto* and *King Triton's Carousel*. On the bottom, we preview the initial segments of story subgraphs of the two attractions.

Temporal analysis. Fig.11 shows an example of temporal analysis that benefits from our story graphs. Every two hours on the timeline, we present exemplar images of two central vertices of the story graph at the *Mickey's Fun wheel*. The ranking scores of vertices at time t can be easily obtained by column-wise summing $\mathbf{A}^t$. As shown in Fig.11, even at a single location, a variety of events happen at different time throughout the day, for example, *Goofy Instant Concert*, *Pixar Play Parade*, *Electrical Parade*, and *World of Color* from 2PM to 10PM. Our story graph can help visitors plan their itinerary beforehand by providing an intuitive way to promptly preview the popular events.

8. CONCLUSION AND DISCUSSION

We presented an approach for creating story graphs from large collections of online photo streams shared by visitors to theme parks. We formulate the story reconstruction as a two-step procedure of story element estimation and inference of sparse time-varying directed graphs. To demonstrate the usefulness of the story graphs, we leverage them to perform photo-based exploration, recommendation, and temporal analysis tasks. Through quantitative evaluation and user studies via AMT, we show that our algorithm outperforms other alternatives for two image prediction tasks.

There are several promising future directions that go beyond the current paper. First, to be more practical for general users, we can leverage guidebooks to infuse semantic meaning for exploration and recommendation. Second, personalization of story graphs is another interesting direction, in order to deliver relevant guidelines to visitors based on the group sizes, people's age and gender, and visiting seasons. Finally, it would be also interesting to implement our technique as a function of Disneyland official mobile apps (*e.g. Disneyland Explorer* and *My Disney Experience*).

9. REFERENCES

[1] A. Ahmed, Q. Ho, J. Eisenstein, E. P. Xing, A. J. Smola, and C. H. Teo. Unified Analysis of Streaming News. In *WWW*, 2011.

[2] B. Alexe, T. Deselaers, and V. Ferrari. What is an Object? In *CVPR*, 2010.

[3] N. Dalal and B. Triggs. Histograms of Oriented Gradients for Human Detection. In *CVPR*, 2005.

[4] Y. Ge, Q. Liu, H. Xiong, A. Tuzhilin, and J. Chen. Cost-aware Travel Tour Recommendation. In *KDD*, 2011.

[5] J. Gillenwater, A. Kulesza, and B. Taskar. Discovering Diverse and Salient Threads in Document Collections. In *EMNLP*, 2012.

[6] A. Gionis, T. Lappas, K. Pelechrinis, and E. Terzi. Customized Tour Recommendations in Urban Areas. In *WSDM*, 2014.

[7] D. B. Goldman, B. Curless, D. Salesin, and S. M. Seitz. Schematic Storyboarding for Video Visualization and Editing. In *SIGGRAPH*, 2006.

Figure 10: An example of predicting the location of a query image and suggesting next engaging story paths. (a) For a query image, we show top 3 most likely attractions. (b) A user selects *California Screamin'* as a next destination from which the story exploration begins. On the bottom, we preview the initial story subgraphs of the two attractions, *Ariel's Grotto* and *King Triton's Carousel*.

Figure 11: Variation of high-ranked vertices in the story graph at *Mickey's Fun Wheel* sampled every two hours. Each image represents the central image of each vertex.

[8] M. C. Gonzalez, C. A. Hidalgo, and A.-L. Barabasi. Understanding Individual Human Mobility Patterns. *Nature*, 453:779–782, 2006.

[9] J. A. Hudson and L. R. Shapiro. From Knowing to Telling: The Development of Children's Scripts, Stories, and Personal Narratives. In A. McCabe and C. Peterson, editors, *Developing Narrative Structure*. LEA, 1991.

[10] L. Kennedy, M. Naaman, S. Ahern, R. Nair, and T. Rattenbury. How Flickr Helps us Make Sense of the World: Context and Content in Community-Contributed Media Collections. In *ACM MM*, 2007.

[11] G. Kim and E. P. Xing. Jointly Aligning and Segmenting Multiple Web Photo Streams for the Inference of Collective Photo Storylines. In *CVPR*, 2013.

[12] G. Kim and E. P. Xing. Reconstructing Storyline Graphs for Image Recommendation from Web Community Photos. In *CVPR*, 2014.

[13] G. Kim, E. P. Xing, L. Fei-Fei, and T. Kanade. Distributed Cosegmentation via Submodular Optimization on Anisotropic Diffusion. In *ICCV*, 2011.

[14] T. Kurashima, T. Iwata, G. Irie, and K. Fujimura. Travel Route Recommendation Using Geotags in Photo Sharing Sites. In *CIKM*, 2010.

[15] A. Kushal, B. Self, Y. Furukawa, D. Gallup, C. Hernandez, B. Curless, and S. M. Seitz. Photo Tours. In *3DIMPVT*, 2012.

[16] S. Lazebnik, C. Schmid, and J. Ponce. Beyond Bags of Features: Spatial Pyramid Matching for Recognizing Natural Scene Categories. In *CVPR*, 2006.

[17] D. G. Lowe. Distinctive Image Features from Scale-Invariant Keypoints. *IJCV*, pages 91–110, 2004.

[18] K. P. Murphy. *Dynamic Bayesian Networks: Representation, Inference and Learning.* PhD thesis, University of California, Berkeley, 2002.

[19] P. Obrador, R. de Oliveira, and N. Oliver. Supporting Personal Photo Storytelling for Social Albums. In *ACM MM*, 2010.

[20] T. Ruf, A. Ernst, and C. Küblbeck. Face Detection with the Sophisticated High-speed Object Recognition Engine (SHORE). *Microelectronic Systems*, pages 237–246, 2011.

[21] B. C. Russell, R. Martin-Brualla, D. J. Butler, S. M. Seitz, and L. Zettlemoyer. 3D Wikipedia: Using Online Text to Automatically Label and Navigate Reconstructed Geometry. In *SIGGRAPH Asia*, 2013.

[22] D. Shahaf, C. Guestrin, and E. Horvitz. Metro Maps of Science. In *KDD*, 2012.

[23] N. Snavely, R. G. S. M. Seitz, and R. Szeliski. Finding Paths through the World's Photos. In *SIGGRAPH*, 2008.

[24] N. Snavely, S. M. Seitz, and R. Szeliski. Photo Tourism: Exploring Photo Collections in 3D. In *SIGGRAPH*, 2006.

[25] B. State, I. Weber, and E. Zagheni. Studying Inter-National Mobility through IP Geolocation. In *WSDM*, 2013.

[26] C. Suen, S. Huang, C. Eksombatchai, R. Sosic, and J. Leskovec. NIFTY: A System for Large Scale Information Flow Tracking and Clustering. In *WWW*, 2013.

[27] A. Torralba, R. Fergus, and W. T. Freeman. 80 Million Tiny Images: A Large Data Set for Nonparametric Object and Scene Recognition. *IEEE PAMI*, 30:1958–1970, 2008.

[28] A. Vedaldi, V. Gulshan, M. Varma, and A. Zisserman. Multiple Kernels for Object Detection. In *CVPR*, 2009.

[29] M. Wang, R. Hong, X.-T. Yuan, S. Yan, and T.-S. Chua. Movie2Comics: Towards a Lively Video Content Presentation. *IEEE T. Multimedia*, 14(3):858–870, 2012.

[30] J. Xiao and Y. Furukawa. Reconstructing the World's Museums. In *ECCV*, 2012.

[31] Z. Yin, L. Cao, J. Han, J. Luo, and T. Huang. Diversified Trajectory Pattern Ranking in Geo-Tagged Social Media. In *SDM*, 2011.

A Machine Learning Framework to Identify Students at Risk of Adverse Academic Outcomes*

Himabindu Lakkaraju
Stanford University
himalv@cs.stanford.edu

Everaldo Aguiar
University of Notre Dame
eaguiar@nd.edu

Carl Shan
University of Chicago
carlshan@uchicago.edu

David Miller
Northwestern University
dmiller@u.northwestern.edu

Nasir Bhanpuri
University of Chicago
nbhanpuri@uchicago.edu

Rayid Ghani
University of Chicago
rayid@uchicago.edu

Kecia L. Addison
Montgomery County Public Schools
Kecia_L_Addison@mcpsmd.org

ABSTRACT

Many school districts have developed successful intervention programs to help students graduate high school on time. However, identifying and prioritizing students who need those interventions the most remains challenging. This paper describes a machine learning framework to identify such students, discusses features that are useful for this task, applies several classification algorithms, and evaluates them using metrics important to school administrators. To help test this framework and make it practically useful, we partnered with two U.S. school districts with a combined enrollment of approximately 200,000 students. We together designed several evaluation metrics to assess the goodness of machine learning algorithms from an educator's perspective. This paper focuses on students at risk of not finishing high school on time, but our framework lays a strong foundation for future work on other adverse academic outcomes.

Categories and Subject Descriptors

I.2.1 [**Artificial Intelligence**]: Applications and Expert Systems

Keywords

evaluation metrics; applications; education; risk prediction;

*Work done as part of the Eric & Wendy Schmidt Data Science for Social Good Summer Fellowship at the University of Chicago [27].

KDD'15, August 10-13, 2015, Sydney, NSW, Australia.
© 2015 ACM. ISBN 978-1-4503-3664-2/15/08 ...$15.00.
DOI: http://dx.doi.org/10.1145/2783258.2788620.

1. INTRODUCTION

One of the perennial challenges faced by school districts is to improve student graduation rates. Though the magnitude of this problem has reduced due to a steady rise in high school graduation rates over the past few years, nearly 730,000 students in the United States do not finish high school on time every year [28]. A myriad of reasons ranging from economic problems, lack of motivation, and unexpected life changes can delay students' graduation or cause them to drop out [7, 13, 24]. Studies have shown that not graduating high school on time impacts a student's future career prospects immensely [1, 18]. In addition, students who do not graduate on time can strain school districts' resources. To address this issue, school districts have been heavily investing in the construction and deployment of intervention programs to better support at-risk students and their individual needs.

The success of these individualized intervention programs depends on schools' ability to accurately identify and prioritize students who need help. Traditionally, schools relied on feedback from instructors and used heuristic rules based on metrics such as GPAs, absence rates, and tardiness to identify at-risk students [8]. Though human judgment and heuristics can often be accurate, they serve as rules of thumb, are static, expensive to maintain, and often error prone [25]. Further, the set of heuristics which might help in identifying at-risk students for a particular cohort of students within one school district might not generalize or transfer to other cohorts and schools.

As alternatives to manually created rule-based systems, recent research has indicated the potential value of machine learning approaches such as Logistic Regression, Decision Trees, and Random Forests [8, 26, 3]. Trained using traditional academic data, these machine learning approaches can often identify at-risk students earlier and more accurately than prior rule-based approaches [3].

Nevertheless, the application of such methods to this particular context is still in its early stages, even for schools with state-of-the-art technology and analytics teams. To build more robust and comprehensive early warning systems, we partnered with two large U.S. school districts with a combined enrollment of approximately of 200,000 students. Following a number of discussions with the district officials who oversee the implementation of early warning systems, we developed an outline of their expectations:

- ***Using historical data:*** Schools have historical data that describe current and past student performances, and would like to use that to identify students at risk in future cohorts.
- ***Ranking students using risk estimates:*** School districts have limited resources for intervention programs, and their exact allocation can fluctuate over time, directly affecting the number of students that can be enrolled to such programs. For that reason, school officials need the ability to pick the top k% students who are at risk at any given point (where k is a variable). This requirement calls for the use of algorithms which can rank students according to some risk metric.
- ***Interpretability:*** It is important to understand the student-level features and how they are being used by each algorithm. In fact, school officials consistently ranked interpretability as a very important factor for any approach. Frequently, simple rule based systems are preferred to *intelligent* algorithms mainly because they can be easily understood and acted upon.
- ***Early predictions:*** Students who are at risk of not graduating should be identified as early as possible so that appropriate help can reach them in a timely manner. This requirement favors algorithms which can identify at-risk students early on.
- ***Identifying risk before off-track:*** It is ideal to identify students who are at risk even before they start failing or repeating grades. School officials acknowledge that it is considerably more difficult to help a student who is already *off-track*.
- ***Visualizing risk scores for each student:*** All of the above information needs to presented in a way that is clear and understandable to professional educators who are not familiar with machine learning. We are currently developing web-based software that can display model predictions for each student, and help teachers and administrators gauge how much support each student needs.

Our interactions with educators revealed that there were several deeper and interesting challenges in this setting, and helped us quickly understand that evaluating algorithms simply using AUC and precision/recall metrics would not be sufficient. In this work, our goal is to investigate how to evaluate the suitability of any given algorithm for the problem at hand so as to ensure that it meets the expectations of educators and school officials. To this end, we apply several off-the-shelf machine learning algorithms to identify at-risk students and analyze their behavior according to several evaluation techniques. To summarize, our major contributions are:

- We present a novel framework for evaluating algorithms which identify students at risk of not graduating high school on time. The evaluation process is designed to cater to the needs of educators, instead of only being focused on commonly used machine learning metrics.
- We present a rigorous qualitative and quantitative comparison of several well known machine learning algorithms using the proposed evaluation process.
- We carry out all our experimentation using data from multiple student cohorts in collaboration with two major school districts in the United States. Unlike recent work where evaluation is carried out via cross validation on a single cohort, we use disjoint cohorts for training and testing. This setting ensures validation of the system's performance in a more realistic manner and makes it possible to directly deploy these systems in all school districts in the US.

2. RELATED WORK

Our interdisciplinary work benefited from prior research at the intersection of educational research and data mining. Educational research provided a basis for selecting and understanding features indicative of adverse academic outcomes, and data mining research helped us use these features in conjunction with statistical techniques to develop robust early warning systems.

Educational research has found that some specific features such as students' grades and attendance are particularly relevant to predicting on-time high school graduation [24, 8]. Bowers et al. [8] systematically reviewed this vast literature, finding that these commonly recorded student features can predict future student outcomes with high accuracy. Most of these studies predominantly advocated usage of rule based models. These studies widely varied in how they combined individual student features when developing such rule based models. For instance, one of the studies suggested that a student should be flagged as at-risk if he/she has both low grades AND low attendance rates, while another study suggested that a student should be flagged if he/she has either low grades OR low attendance rates. Moreover, many studies focused on developing high precision rules, but at the cost of low recall. A major drawback of such rule-based models is that they are not generalizable in the sense that they might work well for a specific district and cohort, but result in poor performance when applied elsewhere.

Recent research in data mining addresses the limitations of such rule based models by advocating the usage of automated learning methods. Several well-known machine learning algorithms such as Random Forests, Logistic Regression, Decision Trees etc. were used to predict student outcomes [26, 12, 3, 2, 11, 22, 31, 12]. These models consistently outperformed rule based models on traditional metrics such as precision, recall, and AUC. In addition, models such as Bayesian networks were employed to identify students who were likely to fail in mathematics courses [29]. Further, machine learning models were also employed to predict trajectories of future learning performance using past history [15].

Though machine learning models are very useful in practice, they are essentially black boxes from an educator's perspective. Furthermore, traditional model evaluation metrics such as AUC are both difficult to interpret for educators and are not well suited to address all the issues at hand [30]. We therefore worked closely with two school districts to identify how to best interpret and evaluate machine learning methods so that they address the districts' educational goals.

3. DATASET DESCRIPTION

The work we describe in this paper is being done in collaboration with two school districts in the United States. One of the districts is among the largest districts in the mid-Atlantic region with over 150,000 students enrolled across 40 schools (District A). The other is a medium-sized district on the east coast with an enrollment of approximately 30,000 students across 39 schools (District B). Both of these districts are instituting several measures to help students and had already recognized the importance of early warning indicator systems for identifying at-risk students. District A had a rule-based early warning system in place which employed several important indicators such as academic performance, behavior, mobility and few demographic attributes. Our partnership with these school districts has been critical in developing a machine learning system that is not only based on real data but also designed for the needs and priorities of educators.

We obtained data from each of these school districts. The dataset provided by District A comprises of two cohorts of 10884 and 10829 students, expected to graduate in 2012 and 2013 respectively. Most of the students in these cohorts were tracked from 6th - 12th grade, while some arrived throughout the study. Students belonging to the latter group have missing data fields for all the years prior to their enrollment in the school district since the school only starts collecting data when students enroll. The data contains several attributes for each of these students such as their GPAs, absence rates, tardiness, gender etc. About 90% of the students in each of these cohorts graduated high school within 4 years of enrollment.

The dataset obtained from District B comprises of two cohorts of 1499 and 1575 students, with expected graduation dates in 2012 and 2013 respectively. In this dataset, most of the students were tracked from 8th - 12th grade and several academic and behavioral attributes of these students were recorded. However, some arrived throughout the study and subsequently have missing data fields for years prior to their enrollment. About 95% of the students in each of these cohorts completed high school on time.

While there could be a variety of reasons for academic difficulties ranging from lack of motivation to economic concerns, recent research has demonstrated that these diverse causes often manifest themselves through a common set of indicators such as academic performance, behavior, and attendance [4, 6]. The data used for this analysis captured most of these indicators. Table 1 provides an exhaustive list of all attributes that we used in the analysis. The availability of each of these attributes in a given dataset is indicated by the two rightmost columns of the table. It can be seen that there are minor variations in the ways data is recorded for the two districts. For instance, GPA is recorded on a quarterly basis for District A and on an yearly basis for District B. Our analysis is not sensitive to such representational variations. In fact, the framework proposed in this paper is generic enough to be applicable to any given set of features.

Student Attributes	District A	District B
Gender	✓	✓
Age	✓	X
Ethnicity	X	✓
City	X	✓
Street	X	✓
School Code	✓	✓
Absence Rates	✓	✓
Tardiness Rates	✓	✓
# of Suspensions	✓	X
# of Unexpected Entries/Withdrawals	✓	✓
Quarterly GPA	✓	X
Cumulative GPA	X	✓
Cumulative Math GPA	X	✓
Cumulative Science GPA	X	✓
Cumulative Social Science GPA	X	✓
Cumulative English GPA	X	✓
MAP-R National Percentile Ranks	✓	X
Math Proficiency Scores (MPS)	✓	X
PSAT Critical Reading	✓	X
PSAT Math	✓	X
Limited English Proficiency	X	✓
Economically Disadvantaged (EDS)	X	✓
Is student new to the school district?	✓	✓
Is student disabled?	X	✓
Was student ever retained?	✓	✓
Did student graduate on time?	✓	✓

Table 1: List of student attributes and their availability in Districts A and B.

4. FRAMEWORK OVERVIEW

In this section, we present an overview of the models that we will be using through out this study. In addition, we also describe in detail the experimental setup that we use for all the prediction tasks. Our experimental setting is designed to match the real world setting as closely as possible.

Problem Setting: In order to provide assistance to students who are at risk of not graduating on time, we first need to accurately identify such students. This can be achieved by using algorithms that can learn from the outcomes of students in the earlier cohorts. Schools have records on which of the students from prior cohorts failed to graduate high school within 4 years. From Table 1, it can be seen that the flag *Did the student graduate high school on time?* captures this aspect and hence can serve as the outcome variable. We compute the complement of this flag which takes the value 1 if the student failed to graduate on time and 0 otherwise. We use the term `no_grad` to refer to this complement variable and use it as the response variable for all our prediction tasks. The problem of identifying students who are at risk of not graduating on time can thus be formulated as a binary classification task with `no_grad` as the outcome variable. All the other variables in Table 1 can be used as predictors.

Models: To predict if a student is at risk of not graduating on time, we experiment with Random Forests (RF), Adaboost (AB), Logistic Regression (LR), Support Vector Machines (SVM), and Decision Trees (DT). We use *scikit-learn* implementations of all these models.

Experimental Setup: Our datasets comprise of cohorts of students graduating in 2012 and 2013. Recent research that deals with the problem of predicting student performance evaluated the models via cross validation on a single cohort [26, 3]. Though this is an acceptable way of estimating any algorithm's performance in general, it is not ideal for the current setting. To illustrate, school districts often have access to outcomes and other features from previous cohorts. The goal here is to predict the future outcomes accurately by training on data from previous cohorts. Thus, an apt way of evaluating an algorithm in this setting is to train a model using data from previous cohorts and use a later cohort as the test set. We carry out all the evaluations in this manner, using the cohort of students graduating in 2012 as the training set and the later cohort of students graduating in 2013 as the test set.

Some of the models that we employ such as Random Forests involve sampling random subsets of data. This creates a certain degree of non-determinism in the estimated outcomes. In order to account for this, we carry out 100 runs with each of these models and average the predictions (and/or probabilities) to compute the final estimates. During our analysis, we also experimented with the leave-k-out strategy. As a part of this approach, we executed 100 iterations for each classification model. During each iteration, every model is trained on $N-k$ randomly chosen data points, where N is the size of the entire dataset and $k = 0.01 * N$.

With this framework in place, we now proceed to present how we evaluate each of the models while taking into account educators' requirements.

5. ANALYSIS OF PREDICTIVE MODELS

School districts are interested in identifying those students who are at risk of not graduating high school on time before they reach the end of middle school. This helps them plan their resource allocation ahead of time. In this section, we focus on this setting by predicting if a student is at risk of not graduating high school on time using the data available prior to the end of middle school. More specifically, we use GPAs, absence rates, tardiness, other scores and flags (listed in Table 1) up until grade 8 along with other demographic attributes and predict the outcome variable `no_grad`. In this section, we address the following questions:

- How well do each of the models perform when evaluated using traditional metrics such as precision, recall, and AUC?
- How can we ensure that the probabilities or confidence score estimates produced by various algorithms are good enough for schools to reliably deploy interventions based on them?
- How can we compare various algorithms based on the goodness of such estimates?

5.1 Evaluation using traditional metrics

Our goal here is to evaluate the performance of various models on the task of predicting if a student is likely to graduate high school on time. Since we are dealing with the prediction of a binary outcome, several standard metrics such as accuracy, precision, recall, and AUC can be readily used. We evaluate the performance of all the models using these standard metrics. Figure 1 shows the ROC curves corresponding to various classification models for districts A and B. It can be seen that the Random Forest model outperforms all the other models for both school districts, with AdaBoost and Logistic Regression being the next best performing solutions for both the datasets. SVMs and Decision Trees exhibit varying performance across the two datasets. While SVM performs on par with Logistic Regression and AdaBoost models on District A, it performs much more poorly when applied to District B.

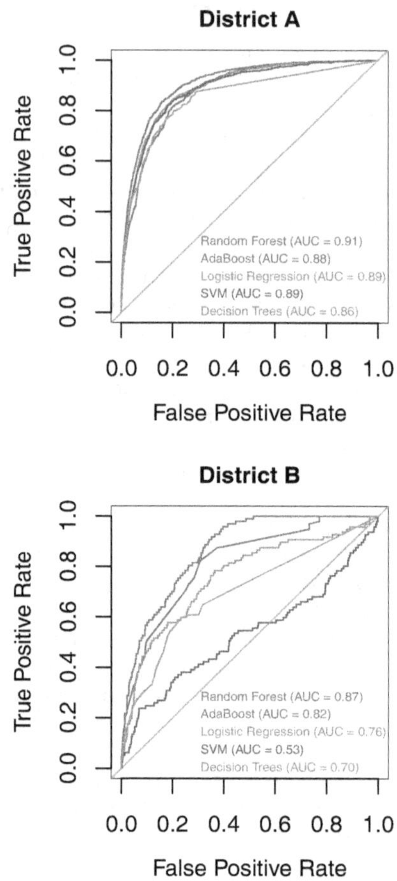

Figure 1: ROC Curves.

Usage of metrics such as AUC for a binary classification task is relatively common in machine learning. Educators on the other hand think about the performance of an algorithm in this context slightly differently. The educators perspective stems from the fact that school districts often have limited resources for assisting students. Furthermore, the availability of these resources varies with time. Due to factors such as the number of students enrolled and budget allocated, the availability of these resources widely varies across districts. For example, District A might have the resources to support 100 students in 2012, however they might be able to target only 75 students in 2013. Further, District B might be able to assist 300 students in 2012 and 500 students in 2013. Building algorithms that can cater to these settings is extremely crucial to address the problem at hand.

After various discussions with our school district partners, we understood that an algorithm that can cater to their needs must provide them with a list of students ranked according to some measure of *risk* such that students at the top of the list are verifiably at higher risk. Once educators have such a ranked list available, they can then simply choose the top K students from it and provide assistance to them. For instance, if District A can only support 75 students in 2013, educators in that district can just choose the top 75 students from this rank ordered list and assist them. Furthermore, as more resources become available, they can

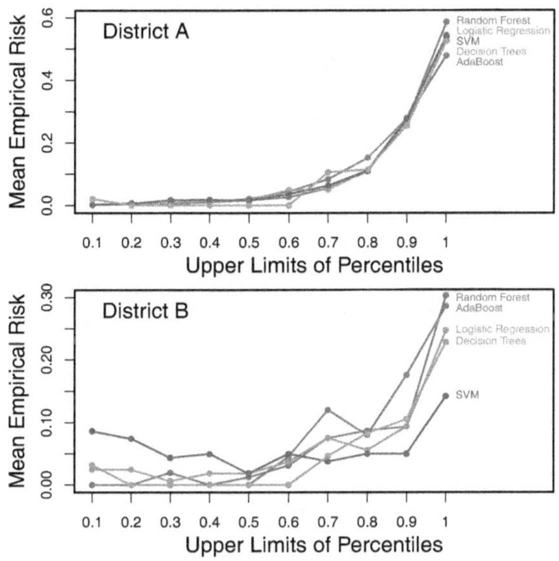

Figure 2: Empirical Risk Curves. The ranking quality of an algorithm is good if this curve is monotonically non-decreasing.

choose more students from this list according to the rank ordering and provide support to those students too.

The challenge associated with ranking students is that the data available to school districts only has binary ground truth labels (i.e., graduated/not-graduated). This effectively means that we are restricted to using binary classification models because other powerful learning to ranking techniques [20] require ground truth that captures the notion of ranking. Fortunately, most of the classification models assign confidence/probability estimates to each of the data points and we can use these estimates to rank students. However, before we begin using these estimates to rank students, we need to ensure that these estimates are indeed correct.

5.2 Ensuring the quality of risk estimates

We begin this section by understanding how to use the confidence scores or probability estimates output by algorithms to rank order students. Then, we discuss how to evaluate the goodness of such estimates produced by various algorithms.

From models to risk estimates: Binary classification approaches output a 0/1 value for each data point. However, most of the classification algorithms involve computation of some form of confidence scores for each data point before the algorithm even assigns a label to it. In this work, we use the probability of not graduating on time as a proxy for estimating risk. While Logistic Regression estimates these probabilities as a part of its functional form, all the other algorithms output proxies to these probabilities. We obtain these proxy scores and convert them into probabilities.

Decision tree assigns each data point to one of its leaf nodes and the probability of not graduating on time for any given data point is equivalent to the fraction of those students assigned to the corresponding leaf node who do not graduate on time [10]. Random Forests involve training a forest of trees on data points and the probability of not graduating on time for a particular data point is computed as the mean of the predicted class probabilities of the trees in the forest [9]. The class probability assigned by any single tree is computed in the same manner as that of a decision tree. Similarly, in the case of AdaBoost which involves multiple learners, the probability assigned to a particular student is computed as the weighted mean of the predicted class probabilities of the classifiers in the ensemble [21]. Support Vector Machines estimate the signed distance of a data point from the nearest hyperplane and Platt scaling can be used to convert these distances into probability estimates [19].

Next, we describe the process of evaluating the goodness of these probabilistic estimates of risk. We use the term *risk scores* to refer to these probabilities from here on.

Measuring the goodness of risk scores: In order to understand the accuracy of the risk scores estimated by various algorithms for ranking students, we propose a simple solution. We first rank students in descending order of their estimated risk scores. We then group students into bins based on the percentiles they fall into when categorized using risk scores. For example, if we choose to create 10 bins, the bottom 10% of students who have the least risk are grouped into a single bin. Students who rank between $10^{th}$and 20th percentile are grouped into the next bin and so on. For each such bin, we compute the *mean empirical risk*, which is the fraction of the students from that bin who actually (as per ground truth) failed to graduate on time. We then plot a curve where values on the X-axis denote the upper percentile limit of a bin and values on the Y-axis correspond to the mean empirical risk of the corresponding bins. We call this curve an ***empirical risk curve***.

An algorithm is considered to be producing good risk scores and consequently ranking students correctly if and only if the *empirical risk curve* is monotonically non-decreasing. If the empirical risk curve is non-monotonic for some algorithm, it implies that the ranking using the algorithm's risk scores may result in scenarios where students with lower risk scores are more likely to not graduate on time compared to students with higher risk scores. Figure 2 shows these curves with 10 student bins for districts A and B respectively. It can be seen that most algorithms exhibit monotonically non-decreasing empirical curves in the case of District A. However, decision tree exhibits some degree of non-monotonicity. On the other hand, for District B, all the models except for Random Forest exhibit non-monotonicity consistently. Therefore, students should be ranked using the scores provided by Random Forest model for District B.

5.3 Comparative evaluation of risk estimates

In the previous section, we discussed how to evaluate the goodness of rankings produced by various models. Here, we continue the discussion and present two metrics which are far more informative to educators than traditional precision recall curves. We already emphasized on the fact that school districts have limited resources and can assist only a certain number of students every year (let us denote this number as K). Consequently, there is a strong need for algorithms which can produce good risk scores to rank students. Given this setting, it would be much more informative to provide precision and recall values of various algorithms at different values of K. We call these curves ***precision_at_top_K curve*** and ***recall_at_top_K curve*** respectively. These curves help educators in readily inferring

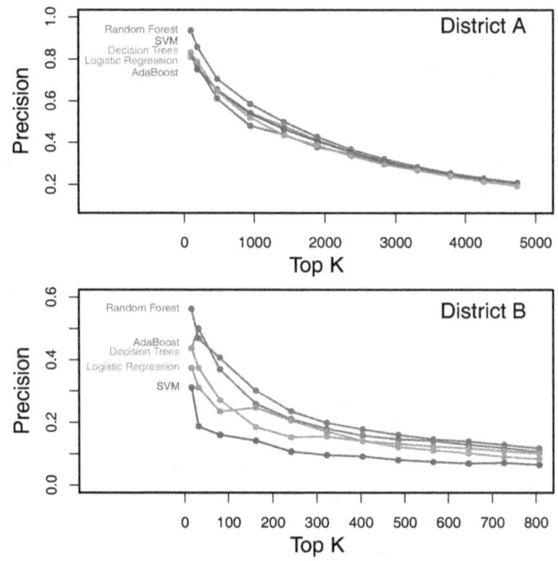

Figure 3: Precision at top K.

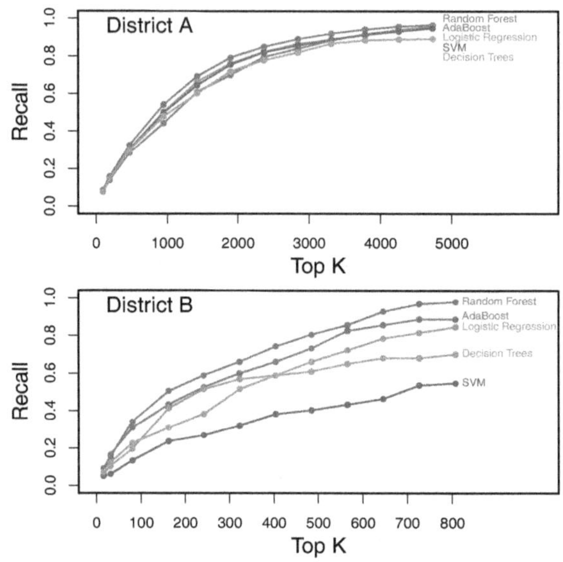

Figure 4: Recall at top K.

the precision and recall of various algorithms at a threshold K of their choice.

Figure 3 shows the precision_at_top_K curves for districts A and B respectively. It can be seen that there are huge differences in the precision of algorithms at smaller values of K, particularly for District B. Note that resource constraints often force educators to set K to small values. Random Forests consistently outperform their counterparts across all K for both districts A and B. The precision of other algorithms, however, varies with K. For instance, we can observe that Logistic Regression has lower precision compared to the decision tree when $K \leq 150$ on District B. Beyond this threshold, Logistic Regression has a higher precision than the decision tree.

Figure 4 shows the recall_at_top_K curves for both districts. Again, Random Forests outperform all other models at all values of K. It can be seen that there is a higher variation in the recall values of algorithms for District B. Further, Support Vector Machines exhibit consistently low recall on District B. The performance of other algorithms depends on the threshold K.

6. INTERPRETING CLASSIFIER OUTPUT

While the construction of models that can precisely identify students at risk is an important step to the design of early warning systems, it is equally important to analyze the output produced by these algorithms to make sure it aligns with the prior knowledge and/or findings of educators. In this section, we study in detail:

- How do we identify features which are heavily used by algorithms?
- How do we characterize patterns of mistakes made by algorithms?
- How can we compare and contrast the sets of students identified as at-risk by various algorithms?

Each of these aspects allows us to obtain a better understanding of the model behavior.

6.1 Feature Importances

In order to ensure that the output of the prediction models can be converted into actionable insights, it is essential to understand which factors contribute most heavily to the predictions. To answer this question, we make use of a variety of feature selection techniques that can be used to rank features according to their level of importance.

The setup we use to evaluate feature importances is similar to that previously described in section 5. We specifically chose to threshold our datasets at the end of 8th grade, as that time stamp marks the students' transition into high school, and has been shown to be an especially opportune moment for targeted interventions [5].

The approaches that we use to compute feature importances are strictly dependent on the algorithms being used. We compute feature importances using both Gini Index (GI) and Information Gain (IG) for Decision Trees [23]. In the case of Random Forest, we consider feature importance to be the ratio of the number of instances routed to any decision tree in the ensemble that contains that feature over the total number of instances in the training set. For AdaBoost, we simply average the feature importances provided by the base-level classifier – CART decision tree with maximum depth of 1 – across all iterations. In the case of Logistic Regression and SVM models, feature importances were simply considered to be the absolute values of feature coefficients.

As discussed earlier, we ran each classification model 100 times and subsequently averaged the importance scores assigned to each feature across all the iterations. We then ranked all the features in descending order of their importance scores derived from the appropriate classifiers. Figure 5 illustrates how features are ranked by various algorithms. Due to space constraints, we only present a subset of 5 features in Figure 5. Table 2 lists the top 5 features as ranked by each of the algorithms.

It can be inferred from Table 2 and Figure 5 that GPA at 8th grade is highly ranked according to most of the algorithms, indicating that academic performance at that particular time stamp is predictive of on-time high school grad-

	Rank	RF	AB	LR	SVM	GI	IG
District A	1	Q4GPA_08	Q4GPA_08	Gender_07=Male	Gender_07=Male	Q4GPA_08	Q4GPA_08
	2	Q3GPA_08	MPS_08	Gender_07=Female	Gender_07=T	MAPR_08	Abs_Rate_08
	3	Q1GPA_08	MAPR_08	Gender_06=Female	Gender_06=Female	Abs_Rate_08	MAPR_08
	4	MAPR_08	Abs_Rate_08	Abs_Rate_08	Abs_Rate_08	Q1GPA_08	Abs_Rate_07
	5	MPS_08	Q4GPA_06	Q2GPA_06	Gender_06=Male	MPS_08	MAPR_06
District B	1	GPA_08	GPA_08	GPA_Science_08	School_Code=317	GPA_08	GPA_08
	2	GPA_ENG_08	Days_Abs_08	Math_Credits_08	GPA_SocSci_08	GPA_Science_08	GPA_SocSci_08
	3	GPA_SocSci_08	Num_Marks_08	GPA_SocSci_08	GPA_Math_08	Exc_Abs_08	Exc_Abs_08
	4	GPA_Math_08	GPA_Science_08	School_Code=317	GPA_Science_08	Num_Marks_08	GPA_ENG_08
	5	GPA_Science_08	Has_Disability_08=N	Has_Disability_08=Y	School_Code_08=315	EDS_08=T	School_Code_08=320

Table 2: List of top 5 features in districts A and B (GI stands for Gini Index and IG is Information Gain).

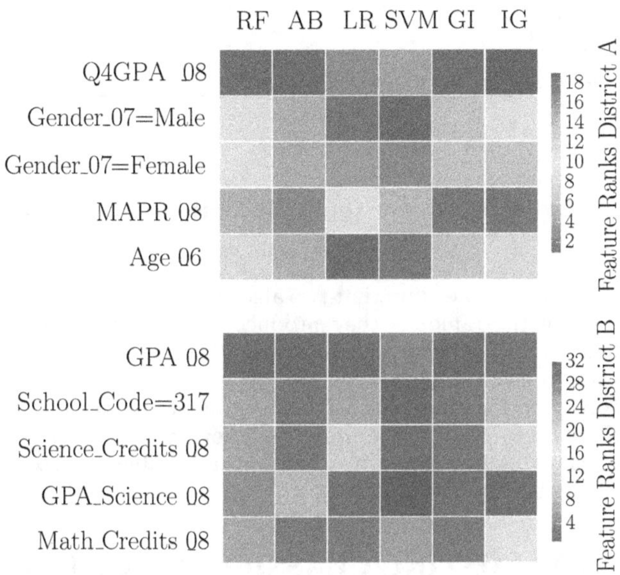

Figure 5: Feature ranking by various algorithms. GPA_08 is ranked consistently high in both the districts by most of the models.

uation. Interestingly, gender was highly ranked by Logistic Regression and SVM methods for one of the cohorts. In addition to GPA, absence rates at 8th grade also show up as prominent features for both districts A and B. Further, some of the algorithms rank features such as economically disadvantaged (EDS) and disability flags highly.

6.2 Characterizing prediction mistakes

School district administrators and educators are often interested in understanding the patterns of mistakes made by algorithms, which in turn helps them decide whether to use that model. For instance, if an algorithm is misclassifying certain kinds of students and educators consider such patterns of misclassifications unacceptable, then they can choose not to use it in spite of the fact that the algorithm might be achieving a high precision and recall.

In order to identify such patterns for any given classification model, we use a simple technique involving frequent itemset extraction. Below is a description of the technique:

1. Identify all frequent patterns in the data using the FP-growth technique [14]. A frequent pattern is a combination of *(attribute, relation, value)* tuples which occur very frequently in the entire dataset. For example, if the pattern *GPA_08 > 2.0 and Abs_Rate_08 <= 0.1* holds true for about 80% of the students, then it can be considered a frequent pattern.

2. Rank students based on risk score estimates from the classification model. The predicted value of `no_grad` is 1 for the top K students from this list and 0 for others. K is a threshold set by the school districts depending on the availability of resources at their end.

3. Create a new field called *mistake*. Set the value of this field to 1 for those data points where the prediction of the classification model does not match ground truth, otherwise set it to 0.

4. For each frequent pattern detected in Step 1, compute the probability of mistake. This can be done by iterating over all the datapoints for which the pattern holds true and computing the fraction of these datapoints where *mistake* field is set to 1.

5. Sort the patterns based on their probability of mistake (high to low) and pick the top R patterns as mistake patterns.

The above procedure helped us identify several interesting mistake patterns for various algorithms. Due to space constraints, we present the patterns for just two of the algorithms (refer Table 3). It can be seen that the models are making mistakes when a student has a high GPA and a high absence rate/tardiness or when a student has a low GPA and low absence rate/tardiness. It is also interesting to note that the Adaboost model is less accurate with respect to students who are economically disadvantaged but do well in Math and Science. This indicates that classification models are prone to making mistakes particularly on those data points where certain aspects of students are positive and others are negative. We found similar patterns with most other algorithms.

6.3 Comparing classifier predictions

Our discussions with school districts revealed that educators placed a lot of importance on exploratory aspects of models. When we present educators with a suite of algorithms, they are keen on understanding the differences in rank orderings produced by each of these algorithms. Here, we address the question: *How similar or dissimilar are the rank orderings produced by any two given models ?* This question can be answered by computing rank correlation metrics such as Spearman rank correlation coefficient,

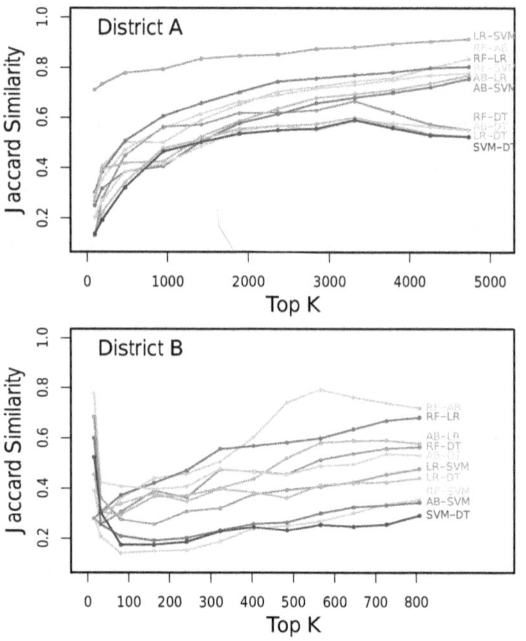

Figure 6: Jaccard Similarity of students at-risk as identified by various algorithms.

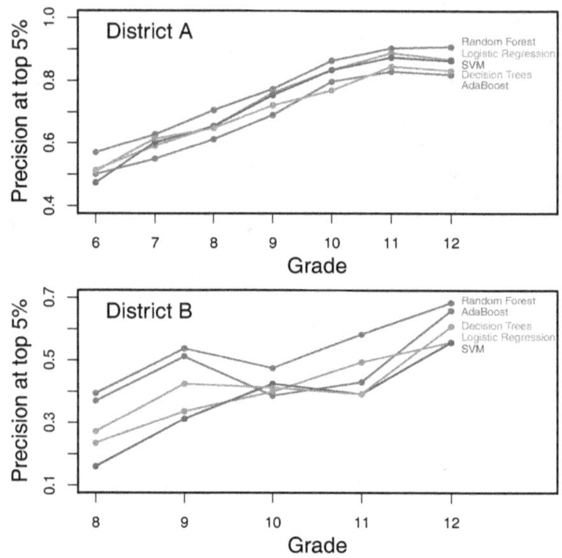

Figure 7: Precision at top 5% across various grades.

Kendall's Tau, and Goodman and Kruskal's gamma [17] for every pair of algorithms. While this is a perfectly reasonable strategy, recall that educators are typically interested in understanding all the metrics as a function of K (the number of students that can be targeted using the available resources).

In order to measure the similarity of rank orderings for various values of K, we use Jaccard similarity metric. Given two sets A and B, Jaccard similarity is the ratio of the number of elements in the intersection of A and B to the number of elements in the union of A and B. The higher the value of Jaccard similarity, the more similar the sets. For a given K, all the algorithms return a set of K students who are likely to not graduate on time based on the risk scores they produce. Similarity between rank orderings of algorithms can now be estimated by computing the Jaccard similarity metric between the set of K students returned by various algorithms.

Figure 6 shows the Jaccard similarity values that we computed for every pair of algorithms at various values of K for Districts A and B respectively. It can be seen that Logistic Regression and SVM produce highly similar outputs for all values of K in District A. Furthermore, the ranking produced by most models is not similar to Decision Trees (RF-DT, AB-DT, LR-DT, SVM-DT curves). In the case of District B, there are interesting variations in the similarity between algorithms as K changes. For small values of K, AdaBoost and Decision Trees flag an identical set of students as at-risk. However, as K increases, Random Forest and AdaBoost produce similar outputs. The rank orderings output by Random Forest and Logistic Regression models are also quite similar. Lastly, we see that results from SVM are least similar to that of any other algorithm in the case of District B (RF-SVM, AB-SVM, LR-SVM, SVM-DT curves).

This analysis helps school districts in understanding which algorithms to retain in their suite and which ones to discard. For instance, if they find that two algorithms are consistently similar in the rankings they produce, they may choose to retain just one of these algorithms based on parameters such as ease-of-use, computational efficiency etc.

Next, we focus on the importance of predicting risk at early stages. We describe in detail an evaluation procedure that helps us determine if an algorithm is able to predict student risk at early stages.

7. EVALUATING CLASSIFIERS FOR EARLY PREDICTIONS

Beyond being able to accurately identify students who are at risk of not graduating on time, it is important to make these predictions early so that educators and administrators have enough time to intervene and guide students back on track. In addition, our interactions with school districts revealed that once a student is retained in a grade, it becomes much harder to ensure timely graduation. Therefore, it is important to identify a student who is at risk before he/she starts failing grades and/or drops out. In this section, we discuss evaluation procedures which help us determine if an algorithm is making timely predictions.

Predicting risk early: Here, we address the questions: *How precise is any given model at the earliest grade for which we have data? How does this performance change over time?* These questions can be answered by examining the performance of the models across all grades. The metrics that we use to evaluate the performance of our models are: *precision_at_top_K* and *recall_at_top_K*. Working with our school district partners revealed that a majority of school districts can afford resources to assist at least 5% of their student population. Therefore, we set K to 5% of the student population for each of the districts.

We evaluate the performance of the models across all grades. Figure 7 depicts the precision at top 5% for each of the algorithms on districts A and B respectively. Random Forest consistently outperforms all other models in both the districts. In the case of District A, the performance im-

Model	Mistake Patterns
Random Forests (District A)	If Q4GPA_08 > 3.0 and Abs_Rate_08 > 0.3 and Tardy_08 > 0.4, then Mistake If Q4GPA_07 > 3.0 and Abs_Rate_07 > 0.4 and Tardy_07 > 0.3, then Mistake
Logistic Regression (District A)	If Q4GPA_08 ≤ 2.0 and Q1GPA_08 ≤ 2.0 and Abs_Rate_08 ≤ -0.2 and Abs_Rate_07 ≤ -0.1, then Mistake If Gender_07 = Female and Q4GPA_08 ≤ 2.0 and Abs_Rate_08 ≤ -0.1, then Mistake
Decision Tree (District B)	If GPA_08 ≤ 2.0 and Tardy_08 ≤ -0.1 and Days_Abs_08 ≤ -0.2, then Mistake If EDS_08 = True and GPA_Math_08 > 3.0 and GPA_Science_08 > 2.0, then Mistake
Adaboost (District B)	If Days_Abs_08 > 0.5 and GPA_Science_08 > 3.0, then Mistake If Has_Disability_08 = True and GPA_Science_08 > 3.0 and Days_Abs_08 > 0.2, then Mistake

Table 3: Classifier Mistake Patterns. The variables corresponding to GPA assume values in the range [0.0,4.0]. All the continuous variables except GPAs are standardized to unit normal distribution. A positive value for such variables indicates above average and a negative value indicates below average.

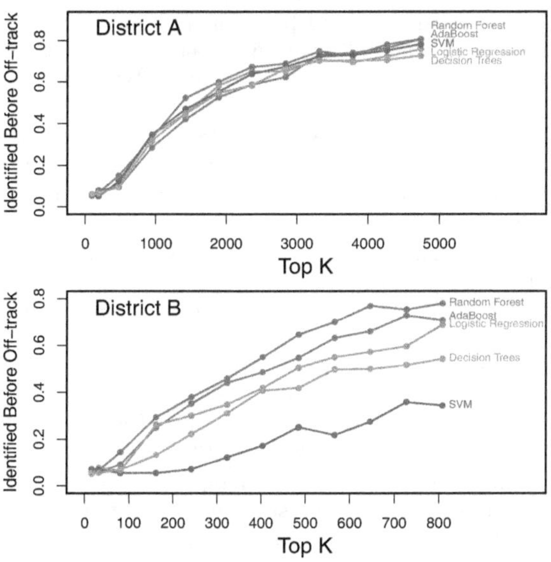

Figure 8: Identification before Off-track.

proves steadily from 6th to 11th grade and then plateaus. AdaBoost and Decision Tree algorithms exhibit poor performance compared to other models across all grade levels for district A. The performance of SVM is consistently poor through out all grades for District B. The corresponding recall curves (omitted due to space constraints) exhibit similar patterns.

Identifying risk before off-track: Recall that an important requirement in this setting is for a model to be able to identify students who are at risk of not graduating on time even before the student begins to fail grades and/or drops out. It is ideal to provide interventions to students before either of these undesired outcomes materialize, as opposed to taking a more reactive approach. A student can be categorized as *off-track* if he or she is retained or drops out at the end of a given grade. An ideal algorithm should be able to predict risk even before students go *off-track*.

Here, we investigate if our models succeed in identifying students before they go *off-track*. In order to do determine this, we use a metric called ***identification before off-track***. This metric is a ratio of the number of students who were identified to be at risk before off-track to the total number of students who failed to graduate on time. For instance, if there are 100 students in the entire dataset who failed to graduate on time, and if the algorithm identifies 70 of these students as at-risk before they fail a grade or drop out, then the value of *identification before off-track* is 0.7. The higher the value of this metric, the better the algorithm is at diagnosing risk before any undesirable outcome occurs. Note that we exclude all those students who graduate in a timely manner from this calculation.

Figure 8 presents the values for *identification before off-track* metric across varying K for districts A and B. The findings here match our earlier results in that Random Forest model outperforms all the other models for both districts. While Decision Tree exhibits poor performance on District A, SVM turns out to be the weaker model for District B.

8. CONCLUSION

In this paper, we outlined an extensive framework that uses machine learning approaches to identify students who are at risk of not graduating high school on time. The work described in this paper was done in collaboration with two school districts in the US (with combined enrollment of around 200,000 students) and is aimed at giving them (as well as other schools) proactive tools that are designed for their needs, and to help them identify and prioritize students who are at risk of adverse academic outcomes. Although the work in this paper is limited to predicting students who are likely to not finish high school on time, we believe that the framework (problem formulation, feature extraction process, classifiers, and evaluation criteria) applies and generalizes to other adverse academic outcomes as well, such as not applying to college, or undermatching [16]. Our hope is that as school districts see examples of work such as this coming from their peer institutions, they become more knowledgeable, motivated and trained to use data-driven approaches and are able to use their resources more effectively to improve educational outcomes for their students.

9. ACKNOWLEDGEMENTS

This work was supported in part by the Eric & Wendy Schmidt Data Science for Social Good Summer Fellowship, and a Robert Bosch Stanford Graduate Fellowship. The authors would like to thank Amy Hawn Nelson for her help in coordinating with one of the school districts, Ben Yuhas for insightful discussions, and Shihching Liu and Marilyn Powell for assisting us with data logistics.

10. REFERENCES

[1] Building a Grad Nation. http://www.americaspromise.org/sites/default/files/legacy/bodyfiles/BuildingAGradNation2012.pdf.

[2] E. Aguiar, G. A. Ambrose, N. V. Chawla, V. Goodrich, and J. Brockman. Engagement vs performance: Using electronic portfolios to predict first semester engineering student persistence. *Journal of Learning Analytics*, 1(3), 2014.

[3] E. Aguiar, H. Lakkaraju, N. Bhanpuri, D. Miller, B. Yuhas, and K. Addison. Who, When, and Why: A machine learning approach to prioritizing students at risk of not graduating high school on time. In *Proceedings of the Learning Analytics and Knowledge Conference(LAK)*, 2015.

[4] E. M. Allensworth and J. Q. Easton. What matters for staying on track and graduating in chicago public high schools. *Chicago, IL: Consortium on Chicago school research. Retrieved December*, 17, 2007.

[5] E. M. Allensworth, J. A. Gwynne, P. Moore, and M. D. L. Torre. Looking forward to high school and college: Middle grade indicators of readiness in chicago public schools. 2014.

[6] R. Balfanz, L. Herzog, and D. J. Mac Iver. Preventing student disengagement and keeping students on the graduation path in urban middle-grades schools: Early identification and effective interventions. *Educational Psychologist*, 42(4), 2007.

[7] A. J. Bowers and R. Sprott. Why tenth graders fail to finish high school: Dropout typology latent class analysis. *Journal of Education for Students Placed at Risk*, 17(3), 2012.

[8] A. J. Bowers, R. Sprott, and S. A. Taff. Do we know who will drop out?: A review of the predictors of dropping out of high school: Precision, sensitivity, and specificity. *The High School Journal*, 96(2), 2013.

[9] L. Breiman. Random forests. *Machine learning*, 45(1), 2001.

[10] N. V. Chawla and D. A. Cieslak. Evaluating probability estimates from decision trees. In *Proceedings of the AAAI Conference on Artificial Intelligence Workshops*, 2006.

[11] G. W. Dekker, M. Pechenizkiy, and J. M. Vleeshouwers. Predicting students drop out: A case study. *International Working Group on Educational Data Mining*, 2009.

[12] E. Er. Identifying at-risk students using machine learning techniques: A case study with is 100. *International Journal of Machine Learning and Computing(IJMLC)*, 2(4), 2012.

[13] D. C. French and J. Conrad. School dropout as predicted by peer rejection and antisocial behavior. *Journal of Research on Adolescence*, 11(3), 2001.

[14] J. Han, J. Pei, and Y. Yin. Mining frequent patterns without candidate generation. In *ACM SIGMOD Record*, volume 29. ACM, 2000.

[15] A. Hershkovitz, R. Baker, S. M. Gowda, and A. T. Corbett. Predicting future learning better using quantitative analysis of moment-by-moment learning. In *Educational Data Mining*, 2013.

[16] C. Hoxby, S. Turner, et al. Expanding college opportunities for high-achieving, low income students. *Stanford Institute for Economic Policy Research Discussion Paper*, (12-014), 2013.

[17] M. Kendall. *Rank correlation methods.* Griffin, London, 1948.

[18] H. M. Levin and C. Belfield. *The price we pay: Economic and social consequences of inadequate education.* Brookings Institution Press, 2007.

[19] H.-T. Lin, C.-J. Lin, and R. C. Weng. A note on platt's probabilistic outputs for support vector machines. *Machine learning*, 68(3), 2007.

[20] T.-Y. Liu. Learning to rank for information retrieval. *Found. Trends Inf. Retr.*, 3(3), 2009.

[21] A. Niculescu-mizil and R. Caruana. Obtaining calibrated probabilities from boosting. In *Proceedings of the Conference on Uncertainty in Artificial Intelligence*, 2005.

[22] K. Pittman. *Comparison of data mining techniques used to predict student retention.* ProQuest, 2008.

[23] J. Quinlan. Induction of decision trees. *Machine Learning*, 1(1), 1986.

[24] R. W. Rumberger and S. A. Lim. Why students drop out of school: A review of 25 years of research. *California Dropout Research Project, Policy Brief 15*, 2008.

[25] J. Soland. Predicting high school graduation and college enrollment: Comparing early warning indicator data and teacher intuition. *Journal of Education for Students Placed at Risk*, 18, 2013.

[26] A. Tamhane, S. Ikbal, B. Sengupta, M. Duggirala, and J. Appleton. Predicting student risks through longitudinal analysis. In *Proceedings of the ACM SIGKDD International Conference on Knowledge Discovery and Data Mining(KDD)*, 2014.

[27] University of Chicago. The Eric & Wendy Schmidt Data Science for Social Good Summer Fellowship. http://dssg.uchicago.edu/. Accessed: 2014-10-01.

[28] U.S. Department of Education, National Center for Education Statistics. The condition of education. 2014.

[29] A. Vihavainen, M. Luukkainen, and J. Kurhila. Using students' programming behavior to predict success in an introductory mathematics course. In *Proceedings of the International Conference on Educational Data Mining*, 2011.

[30] K. L. Wagstaff. Machine learning that matters. In *Proceedings of the International Conference on Machine Learning(ICML)*, 2012.

[31] S. K. Yadav, B. Bharadwaj, and S. Pal. Data mining applications: A comparative study for predicting student's performance. *arXiv preprint arXiv:1202.4815*, 2012.

Probabilistic Graphical Models of Dyslexia

Yair Lakretz
Sagol School of Neuroscience
Tel-Aviv University
69978, Israel
yairlakretz@post.tau.ac.il

Gal Chechik
The Gonda Brain Research Center
Bar-Ilan University
52900, Israel
gal.chechik@biu.ac.il

Naama Friedmann
Sagol School of Neuroscience and School of Education
Tel-Aviv University
69978, Israel
naamafr@post.tau.ac.il

Michal Rosen-Zvi
IBM Research Laboratory
Haifa, Israel
rosen@il.ibm.com

ABSTRACT

Reading is a complex cognitive process, errors in which may assume diverse forms. In this study, introducing a novel approach, we use two families of probabilistic graphical models to analyze patterns of reading errors made by dyslexic people: an LDA-based model and two Naïve Bayes models which differ by their assumptions about the generation process of reading errors. The models are trained on a large corpus of reading errors. Results show that a Naïve Bayes model achieves highest accuracy compared to labels given by clinicians ($AUC = 0.801 \pm 0.05$), thus providing the first automated and objective diagnosis tool for dyslexia which is solely based on reading errors data. Results also show that the LDA-based model best captures patterns of reading errors and could therefore contribute to the understanding of dyslexia and to future improvement of the diagnostic procedure. Finally, we draw on our results to shed light on a theoretical debate about the definition and heterogeneity of dyslexia. Our results support a model assuming multiple dyslexia subtypes, that of a heterogeneous view of dyslexia.

Categories and Subject Descriptors

J.4 [**Computer Applications**]: Social and behavioral sciences

General Terms

Psychology

Keywords

Probabilistic Graphical Models; Dyslexia; Diagnosis; Latent Dirichlet Allocation; Naïve Bayes

1. INTRODUCTION

KDD'15, August 10-13, 2015, Sydney, NSW, Australia.
© 2015 ACM. ISBN 978-1-4503-3664-2/15/08 ...$15.00.
DOI: http://dx.doi.org/10.1145/2783258.2788604.

Reading is an intricate task involving multiple processes located in different areas in the brain [25]. Errors in reading can result from dyslexia, a disorder involving a variety of such errors. Dyslexia is a highly common disorder with estimates of prevalence ranging from 5% to 17.5% [34], pointing to the need for accurate and accessible diagnosis. However, current diagnostic procedures require experts, and are mostly lengthy and expensive. In this study, we aim to provide an accessible, reliable and cheap diagnosis tool for dyslexia. We do this by showing that rich probabilistic graphical models can diagnose dyslexia closely to how experts do, rendering them accurate, reliable and automated tool for diagnosis. Moreover, by providing probability distributions of errors given target words in screening tests, models can be used for future improvement of the diagnosis procedure and understanding of dyslexia. Finally, our results provide a novel and quantitative perspective on an ongoing debate regarding the nature of dyslexia (e.g., [9]).

A dyslexic person may read the word *three* as *there*, as *tree* or as *four*. Despite this heterogeneity, many studies in the field of reading disorders focus on measures of speed and accuracy to characterize dyslexia, thus possibly ignoring the rich structure of types of reading errors. These studies often assume a common phonological [26], [28], [36], [37] or sensorimotor [37] cause to all types of reading errors. However, an alternative approach views dyslexia as an umbrella term for various deficiencies, or dyslexia subtypes, each characterized by specific error types (e.g., [6], [11], [20]). According to this approach, each of the errors above could result from a different subtype of dyslexia. This approach suggests that fundamental aspects of reading disorders lay in the complex structure of reading errors.

We explore the structure of reading errors and the heterogeneity of dyslexia using probabilistic tools. Probabilistic graphical models have several advantages as a framework for modelling reading errors. Probabilistic models allow explicitly capturing a dependency structure among variables in the problem, making learning more efficient. Probabilistic graphical models provide both diagnoses and explicit error distributions per each type of dyslexia and target word, as learned from the corpus data, and can naturally follow an error-generation process.

We use two families of graphical models. First, we construct Naïve Bayes models which are well-known for having a good performance as classifiers with relatively low model complexity (see, e.g., [18]). These models are thus suitable for the classification of reading errors. Next, we construct a Latent Dirichlet Allocation based (LDA-based) model, which has been proven to well capture generation processes in the context of writing and text [1], [31]. In such a model, the generation of reading errors made by a dyslexic person is a more complex process than that in a Naïve Bayes model, as it assumes that errors are generated according to a mixture of subtypes of dyslexia. An LDA model is therefore a natural candidate for dyslexia analysis.

We compare the models on two different tasks. First, we identify the probabilistic model that best performs on the task of diagnosing dyslexia. We achieve this by comparing the diagnoses of the models to those of experts. Secondly, we explore which model best captures the complex structure of the patterns of reading errors. We achieve this by comparing the models on the task of predicting unseen errors. Finally, the performance of the models is used to explore the question of whether reading errors do result from different subtypes of dyslexia, or rather from one general malfunction.

The rest of the paper is organized as follows: section 2 describes the related literature of probabilistic graphical models and of dyslexia. It also provides a summary of the major views of dyslexia in the current literature of reading disorders. Section 3 describes the structure and size of the data that was used in this study. Section 4 provides a detailed description of the probabilistic graphical models. Finally, section 5 describes the results of this study: the performance of the models on the task of diagnosing dyslexia (section 5.1), and the performance of the models in predicting reading errors (section 5.2).

2. RELATED WORK

2.1 Probabilistic graphical models

The LDA model was introduced a decade ago to discover topics in documents, and has been most influential since. Three main algorithms for approximate inference in the model were proposed: Variational Expectation-Maximization [1], the Expectation-Propagation [21], and Collapsed Gibbs Sampling [15]. In this paper we use the latter method. The generative process described by the LDA model commences in Dirichlet priors which are often chosen to be uniform. However, following the demonstration of the importance of using non-uniform priors for this model [39], we use these and not uniform priors in this study.

2.2 Dyslexia and reading errors

Literature on reading disorders presents various accounts of the causes of developmental dyslexia. One central approach describes developmental dyslexia as a disorder that can be reduced into a single cause, and will be referred to hereby as the *single-type* approach. The most influential example of this approach is the *phonological deficit hypothesis.* According to this theory, developmental dyslexia originates from a deficit affecting either the representations and processing of speech sounds [34], [35], [36], or as other authors have argued, from the access to these representations [27]. This hypothesis had influence on much research in neuroscience and brain imaging studies, e.g., [2], [8], [10], [14], [26], [28].

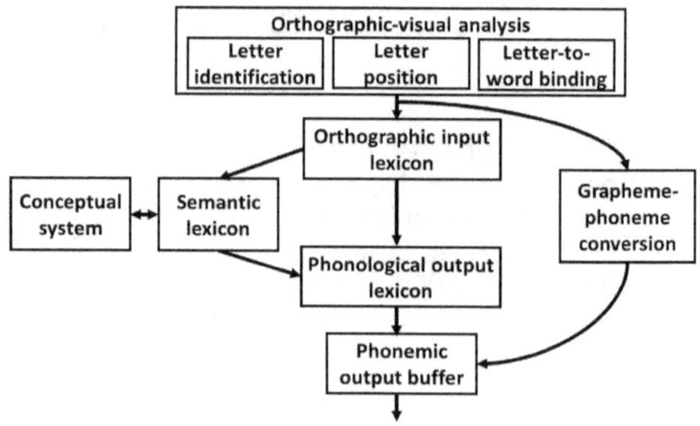

Figure 1: The dual-route model (see, e.g., [11]).

Another central approach describes dyslexia as a heterogeneous disorder, having several different causes, and will be referred to hereby as the *subtypes* approach. The most influential example of this approach derives from the *Dual-Route Reading Model* [5], [6], [20], describing the process of reading by several processing stages and routes (figure 1). According to this approach, there are subtypes of dyslexia, each resulting from a deficit or malfunction in a different stage in the process of reading. For example, reading *signs* as *sings* may result from a specific malfunction in letter position processing during the early visual-orthographic stage, and is in this case ascribed to Letter Position Dyslexia [12]. However, reading *signs* while pronouncing the 'g', may be caused by Surface Dyslexia, characterized by reading irregular words according to the regular grapheme-to-phoneme conversion rules [7]. The deficit leading to Surface Dyslexia occurs in one of two long-term memory lexicons, the orthographic or phonological lexicon, or in the information processing between them. Brain imaging studies following this approach aim to identify the neural correlates of different subtypes of dyslexia, e.g., [16], [19].

The single-type approach and the subtypes approach use different procedures to diagnose dyslexia. The diagnostic procedure based on the single-type approach mainly uses phonological tasks, for example, asking the subject to swap between the first phonemes in the two words *fresh bread* (expecting to get *bresh fread*). When otherwise using reading tasks, the degree of dyslexia is assessed by measuring accuracy and speed in such tasks, while disregarding the types of errors which were made. However, the diagnostic procedure based on the subtypes approach mainly uses reading tasks, asking the subject to read aloud a list of words which are prone to erroneous reading. These tests assess the subtype of dyslexia by counting the errors made of each type.

Another group of studies aim to characterize dyslexia subtypes (e.g., [23]), however the diagnostic procedure in these studies is not based on data of error types in reading tests, but on measures of speed and accuracy in various tasks. Several such studies have proposed probabilistic models to analyze the data (e.g., [24]). See also [30] for analysis of reading aloud data, however in contrast to our study, they were not concerned with error types in reading tests but focused on reading of nonwords by normal subjects.

3. THE DATA

We test our models on reading tests collected from 313 Hebrew-speaking individuals with developmental dyslexia, aged 7 to 62 years, all diagnosed in the Language and Brain laboratory in Tel-Aviv University. Out of the 313 subjects, 97 were diagnosed with an Attention Deficit Disorder (ADD) in addition to dyslexia. This is, to our knowledge, the largest reading-errors corpus used so far (see [22], [29]). The battery of tests has two parts: (1) screening-tests: reading tests given for initial assessment of dyslexia (TILTAN battery, [13]), and (2) varying post-tests which are determined according to the results of the screening-tests. These are used to further specify the diagnosis. Since different subjects take different post-tests, only the corpus of the screening tests was used in this study.

The screening test is composed of 196 target words in Hebrew, which are prone to erroneous readings. The audio responses of subjects are recorded, and then encoded before used in the model. Responses were encoded by experts in dyslexia diagnosis and research, into one of 19 different error types (appendix B, table 2). Each of the 313 subjects therefore read 196 words in the screening-test, resulting in a corpus consisting of a total of 61,348 pairs of target-word and response.

Based on the screening tests and on additional post-tests, had these been conducted, each subject is diagnosed by an expert by marking the subtypes of dyslexia that he or she has. We represent each diagnosis as a multi-label binary vector of length 7, corresponding to seven dyslexia subtypes: 'Letter position dyslexia', 'Attentional dyslexia', 'Neglexia', 'Surface dyslexia', 'Visual dyslexia', 'Vowel letter dyslexia' and 'Normal state'.

The collected data corpus is in Hebrew, therefore it is important to discuss the applicability of this work to other languages, specifically English. The underspecification of vowels in Hebrew makes the Hebrew orthography neighborhood denser than that of languages such as English. An example of this is that in Hebrew, letter transpositions inside a word are more likely to result in another existing word, than in English. This property makes some dyslexias more easily detectable in Hebrew than in English. However, once the relevant stimuli are selected for an English reading task, the same dyslexias with the same properties are detectable in both languages. And indeed, the dyslexias we describe have all been identified in English (For a comprehensive survey of this literature of dyslexia types in English, see for example [6]; for the specific dyslexias that we describe here see Letter position dyslexia: [6]; Attentional dyslexia: [32], [33]; Neglexia: [38]; vowel dyslexia: [17]; Surface dyslexia: [3], [4], [5], [7]). This work can therefore be expanded to English and other languages.

4. THE MODELS

Bayesian models are expressive statistical models. Typically, these are used for mathematically modeling assumptions regarding the manner in which data (in this case, reading errors), is generated. We construct three different probabilistic graphical models for this purpose: a Latent Dirichlet Allocation (LDA) model, and two Naïve Bayes models.

4.1 Naïve Bayes models

We begin to explore the generation process of reading errors with the class of Naïve Bayes models. Naïve Bayes models have shown much success in classification tasks, and could therefore fit the task of classifying reading error into dyslexia subtypes.

The types of the errors made by the subjects are denoted in the models by $e_i (i = 1, \ldots, N)$. This variable takes one of E possible values $e_i \in 1, \ldots, E$, where E stands for the number of possible error-types including a correct response. Another observed variable of the model represents the target-words. We denote it by $w_i (i = 1, \ldots, N)$, where N represents the number of target-words in the screening-test. This variable can have one of W possible values $w_i \in 1, \ldots, W$. Since in our case each target-word is present only once in the screening-test, we have $W = N$.

In all three models, a *dyslexia state* defines a hidden variable that stands for a state associated with a specific subtype of dyslexia, and is characterized by particular reading errors. For example, being in a state of low orthographic attention could be associated with Letter Position Dyslexia (LPD), typically leading to letter migration errors. We denote a dyslexia state by d_i, where d_i can have one of D $d_i \in 1, \ldots, D$ dyslexia states. We have 7 such states as described above.

In all models, S stands for the total number of subjects, N stands for the number of target-words in the screening test, W is the size of the vocabulary of the target-words, and D stands for the total number of dyslexia states. e represents an error type, w a target-word and d a dyslexia state.

4.1.1 Word independent Naïve Bayes Model

Typically, clinicians use the screening test to diagnose dyslexic subjects based on the total counts of different errors types they make. This approach disregards the specific target-words on which the errors were made, for instance, whether it is a word that many subjects misread, or specific subjects only. This diagnosis procedure can be modeled with a Naïve-Bayes model in which the probability of an error-type depends on the dyslexia subtype only. In what follows, we refer to this model as the Naïve Bayes 1 (NB1) model.

Model description.

For test results of a single subject, the joint distribution of the NB1 model factorizes as:

$$p(\bar{e}, \bar{w}, d) = p(d) \prod_{i=1}^{N} p(e_i \mid d) p(w_i)$$

where the subscript i runs over all word-error pairs in the screening-test. Note that each error is independent of the specific target-word on which it was made. Figure 2a describes the plate diagram of the model.

4.1.2 Word dependent Naïve Bayes Model

A more complex model is a Naïve Bayes model in which the probability of an error is dependent on the dyslexia subtype and also on the target-word. We examine this model as well and will refer to it in what follows as the Naïve Bayes 2 (NB2) model.

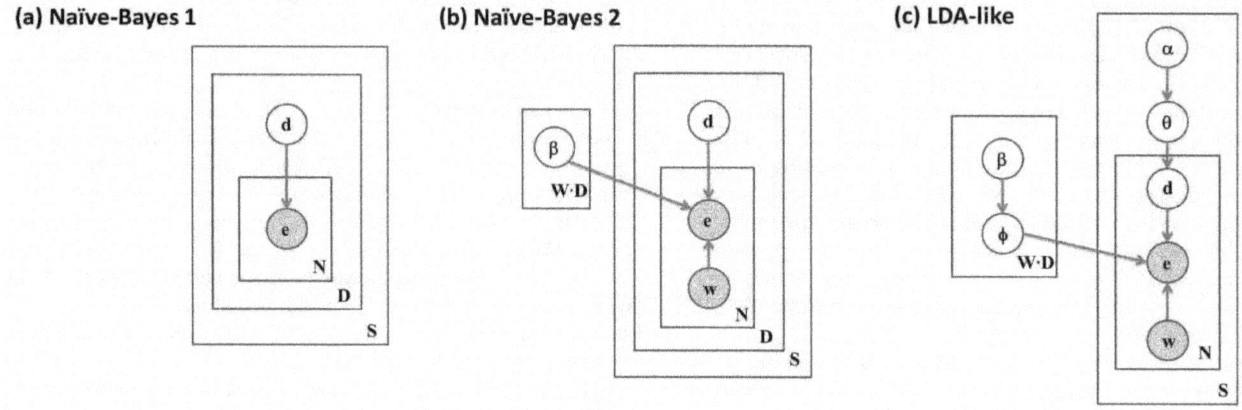

Figure 2: Plate diagrams for all three models. (a) Naïve-Bayes 1 (b) Naïve-Bayes 2 (c) LDA-like model. S represents the total number of subjects, N the number of target-words in the screening test, W the size of the vocabulary of the target-words, and D represents the total number of dyslexia states. e represents an error type, w a target-word and d a dyslexia state. In the LDA model, θ represents a diagnosis, ϕ represents a word-error-dyslexia distribution. α and β are the Dirichlet priors for these distributions respectively.

Model description.

In this model the response of the subject e_i is dependent on the ith target-word w_i and on the dyslexia state d_i. Similarly to the NB1 model, the joint distribution for the NB2 factorizes as:

$$p(\bar{e}, \bar{w}, d; \beta) = p(d) \prod_{i=1}^{N} p(e_i \mid d, w_i; \beta) p(w_i)$$

where the subscript i runs over all word-error pairs in the screening-test as before. Figure 2b describes the plate diagram of the model.

4.2 The LDA model

We continue our inquiry with a particular family of Bayesian models that has attracted much attention in the past decade, the Latent Dirichlet Allocation (LDA) Model [1]. The LDA model enables inferring unobserved variables given observed data, and has shown much success in capturing generative processes of text documents [1], [31].

4.2.1 *Model description*

The LDA model captures the more complex assumption that a person can suffer from a mixture of different dyslexia subtypes. According to this model, each person has a unique distribution over dyslexia subtypes. Additionally, each dyslexia subtype has a unique distribution of expected errors for a given target-word. When a person is reading a target-word, a particular dyslexia subtype is directing the way by which the word is read. The response is then dependent on this dyslexia subtype and the target-word. We therefore define two additional hidden variables. A *diagnosis* θ_s, which is a distribution over dyslexia states d_i for a subject. This distribution is learned from the data. A *word-error-dyslexia distribution* $\phi_{wed} = p(e_i = e \mid w_i = w, d_i = d)$ is a distribution for all subjects in which, given a dyslexia state d and a target-word w, each error has a certain probability of occurring. For example, given an LPD state, and the target-word *three*, the erroneous response *there* would be of high probability, but *tree* would be of a lower one. Similarly, given a normal state, and the target-word *three*, all error responses would have low probabilities except for the (correct) response *three*.

The input to the model is the word-error pairs of all subjects. The hidden variables discovered by the model are: (1) N dyslexia states for each subject; (2) the diagnosis of each subject - θ_s, and (3) a single word-error-dyslexia distribution ϕ_{wed} for all subjects. Figure 2c describes the plate diagram of the dyslexia-state model.

4.2.2 *Dirichlet priors*

The generative process we use to model reading errors uses two Dirichlet priors from which the two distributions θ_s, ϕ_{wed} are sampled. Dirichlet priors are often chosen to be uniform. However, adding priors that adequately describe the generative process could enhance model performance. As the subtype approach to dyslexia has developed ways to detect typical reading errors for each dyslexia subtype, this prior knowledge can be incorporated into the LDA model. We tested the model both with this prior knowledge coded into it and without it.

The expert knowledge is used for sampling the word-error-dyslexia distribution and we denote it by β_{wed}. This knowledge tells us about the error expected for each target-word given a dyslexia state (figure 2c). For example, given an LPD dyslexia-state, the word *three* is more likely to be read as *there* than *tree* or *four*. We incorporate this into the model by assigning a higher prior value β_{high} to the more probable responses of an LPD dyslexia-state, in this example *there*. We also assign a lower prior value β_{low} to the less probable responses, in this case *tree* and *four*. This is repeated for all dyslexia-states, including the normal state.

4.2.3 Parameter estimation

Gibbs sampling is a form of a Markov Chain Monte Carlo (MCMC) method which is widely used for parameter estimation in topic models ([15], [31]). We use Gibbs sampling to construct a Markov chain between dyslexia-states, where the order of the Markov chain is based on the order of target-words in the reading-test. In each step, a dyslexia-state is sampled from its posterior distribution conditioned on all other variables in the model (see *appendix A*):

$$p(d_i = d \mid w_i = w, e_i = e, d_{-i}, w_{-i}, e_{-i}, \alpha, \beta) \propto \frac{C_{wed,-i} + \beta_{wed}}{\sum_{e'} [C_{we'd,-i} + \beta_{we'd}]} \frac{C_{ds,-i} + \alpha_{ds}}{\sum_{d'} [C_{d's,-i} + \alpha_{d's}]} \quad (1)$$

where, $d_i = d$ represents the assignment of the ith word-error pair to dyslexia-state d. $w_i = w$ represents the observation that the ith target-word is w, and $e_i = e$ represents the observation that the ith error type is e. d_{-i} represents all dyslexia-state assignments excluding the current i^{th} instant. w_{-i} represents all target-words observations excluding the current i^{th} instant. Similarly, e_{-i} represents all target-words observations excluding the current i^{th} instant. $C_{wed,-i}$ represents the number of times the word-error pair (w, e) was assigned to the dyslexia-state d, excluding the current instance. $C_{ds,-i}$ represents the number of times the dyslexia-state d was assigned to the dyslexic person s. α_{ds}, β_{wed} are the Dirichlet prior weights (see 4.1.2). At each step of the Markov chain, we update the diagnoses of the subjects $\{\theta_s\}_{s=1}^{S}$ and the word-error-dyslexia distribution ϕ_{wed} according to the dyslexia-state assignments $\bar{d}_s$. These are then used to assess the accuracy and predictive power of the model.

5. EXPERIMENTS

We conduct two experiments with the data. In the first, described in section 5.1, we compare three graphical models to find which model most accurately predicts dyslexia diagnosis. In principle, this model can be used to automate dyslexia diagnosis. In the second experiment, described in section 5.2, we compare the quality by which these three graphical models predict specific reading errors. The best model to predict errors could contribute to the better characterization of dyslexia.

Experimental set-up.

We use two different types of cross validation, first leaving out a set of subjects and then leaving out a set of word readings of the test subjects. Specifically, we randomly split the data into a training-set with 219 subjects (70%) and a test-set with 94 subjects (30%), controlled to have the same proportion of subjects which are also diagnosed with Attention Deficit Disorder. See illustration in figure 3. The test-set is further divided into two equal-sized sets: a ***diagnosis-set*** with 98 pairs of target-words and subject responses, used to infer the diagnosis of test subjects, and a ***prediction-set*** also with 98 word-response pairs, used for assessing the predictions of the models.

5.1 Probabilistic modeling as a dyslexia diagnosis tool

Automation of the diagnosis process could facilitate the accessibility of the process to many people and increase

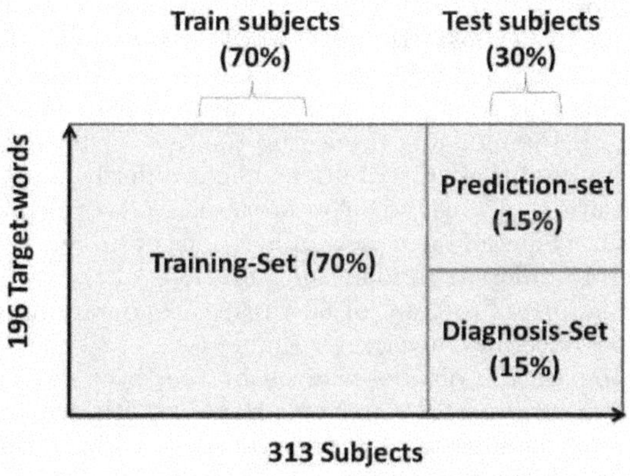

Figure 3: Data is partitioned into 3 sets. The dataset is first divided into a *training-set* which contains reading-tests of 70% of the subjects, and a test-set which contains the remaining 30% of the data. The test-set is further divided into two subsets, a *diagnosis-set* containing the first halves of the reading-tests, and a *prediction-set* containing the remaining reading-tests of the test subjects.

awareness to treatment of specific reading deficits. We compare the automatic diagnosis of the three models – NB1, NB2 and LDA – to those given by experts, to test if the automated tool can indicate the diagnosed dyslexia type with high accordance to diagnoses given by experts. We evaluate the diagnosis quality as follows. The automatic diagnosis is based on the diagnosis-set. This set is used to infer the diagnosis distribution θ_s for each subject. The accuracy of the models is then assessed using the diagnoses given by experts. The prediction-set together with the diagnosis distribution θ_s are later used for the evaluation of the predictive power of the models. The prediction-set is therefore not used in the diagnosis process. Diagnosis quality of the two Naïve Bayes models, is estimated by computing

$$p(d \mid \bar{e}) \propto p(d) \prod_{i=1}^{N} [p(e_i \mid d)]^{C_{e_i}} \quad (2)$$

$$p(d \mid \bar{e}, \bar{w}) \propto p(d) \prod_{i=1}^{N} p(e_i \mid d, w_i) \quad (3)$$

where the dyslexia prior $p(d)$, the probability of error given a dyslexia subtype $p(e_i|d)$, and the probability of an error given a dyslexia-type and a target-word $p(e_i \mid d, w_i)$ are evaluated from the training group.

For the LDA model, we train the model on the training-set together with the diagnosis-set. The model is initialized with random dyslexia state assignments $\{\bar{d}_s\}_{s=1}^{P}$ which are then iteratively sampled according to the sampling rule in (1). At each step of this process, we update the dyslexia distribution per each subject θ_s and the word-error-dyslexia distribution ϕ_{wed} according to the new sampled dyslexia-state.

The reason we train the model on the training-set and the diagnosis-set together is to avoid a discrepancy between the hidden dyslexia-states of the word-error-dyslexia distribution ϕ_{wed}, learned from the training-set, and those of the dyslexia distributions $\{\theta_s\}_{s \in test-set}$, learned from the diagnosis set. If the model is trained on the sets separately, the hidden states of these distributions might differ by a permutation relation. All results below are averages over 5 splits of subjects to train- and test- sets (allocations of subjects), and also over 10 different random initializations of the dyslexia state assignments (a total of 50 runs). 500 iterations were found to suffice for convergence (figure 5A).

We compare the diagnoses given by the three models to those given by experts. The Naïve-Bayes models are known to be strong classifiers and were designed by similar assumptions and guidelines to the ones held by diagnosticians, and therefore their diagnoses are expected to strongly correlate with those given by experts. The LDA model is designed to capture the generative process of the patterns of reading errors, (see section 5.2) but may therefore be a worse predictor of dyslexia subtypes. Note also that the diagnoses of the clinicians are given according to the results of the entire screening-tests and the post-tests results, whereas the diagnoses of the models are based on only halves of the screening-tests. This is expected to lower the maximum accuracy for all models.

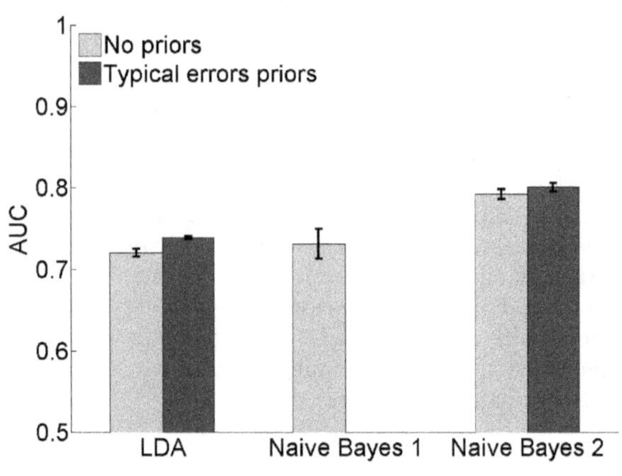

Figure 4: Accuracy results for the three graphical models – LDA, NB1 and NB2, with (dark bars) and without (light bars) typical errors priors to NB2 and LDA.

Figure 4 shows the comparison between the accuracy of the models, table 1 summarizes the resulting AUC values. The highest accuracy is achieved with the NB2 model when it is provided with typical-errors priors β_{wed}. Next are the LDA when it is provided with typical-errors priors and the NB1 Models. Results reflect that the NB2 model is best at replicating diagnoses of experts, and therefore can be used as an automated data-driven tool for dyslexia diagnosis.

Table 1: Accuracy of the models.

	NB1	NB2	LDA
Without priors	0.731 (0.018)	0.792 (0.006)	0.720 (0.005)
With Priors	—	0.801 (0.005)	0.739 (0.002)

AUC values for the three models, standard deviation values in parentheses

As expected, the LDA model reasonably correlates with expert diagnosis. Yet, it predicts the same diagnosis as experts in fewer cases than NB2. In the following section we examine whether this is ought to the LDA model being an inaccurate model of dyslexia, or rather the opposite - it may contribute to expert knowledge in capturing dyslexic phenomena.

5.2 The predictive power of the models

Which model of the proposed models (NB1, NB2, LDA) best captures the hidden error patterns in the data, thereby best characterizing dyslexic errors? We answer this by comparing the predictive power of the three models. We evaluate the predictive power of the models using the prediction-set (figure 3). The perplexity score is commonly used in assessing the predictive power of a language model (e.g., [1]). Here, it reflects the degree of "surprise" of the models to the errors made by the dyslexic person. Formally it is:

$$Perplexity = \exp\left\{ -\frac{\sum_{s=1}^{N_{test}} log(p(\bar{w_s}, \bar{e_s}))}{\sum_{s=1}^{N_{test}} |\bar{w_s}|} \right\} \quad (4)$$

and it is evaluated on the prediction-set, where $\bar{w_s}$ are the observed target-words and $\bar{e_s}$ are the error types in the prediction-set of person p. $|\bar{w_s}|$ represents the number of words in the prediction-set ($|\bar{w_s}| = 98$), and N_{test} is the total number of test subjects ($N_{test} = 219$).

We also compare the predictive power of NB2 to LDA when provided with priors about the typical errors for each dyslexia subtype. Figure 5 shows that the perplexity of these models is lower when provided with priors (figure 5: dark curve in panel A and dark bars in panel B). Incorporating expert knowledge into the model therefore increases its predictive power.

The prior value of the diagnosis distribution was set to be uniform with arbitrary value $\alpha_{dp} = 0.05$. The lower prior for the word-error-dyslexia distribution was set to $\beta_{low} = 0.05$, whereas for the higher prior β_{high}, different values were explored. β_{high} is then chosen to be the value that achieves lowest perplexity $\beta_{high} = 0.7$ (figure 5). The perplexity values for all three models are summarized in figure 5b.

These results show that the best prediction of reading errors is achieved by the LDA model when it is provided with typical-errors priors (figure 5B). This result is consistent for different typical-error priors when compared to the

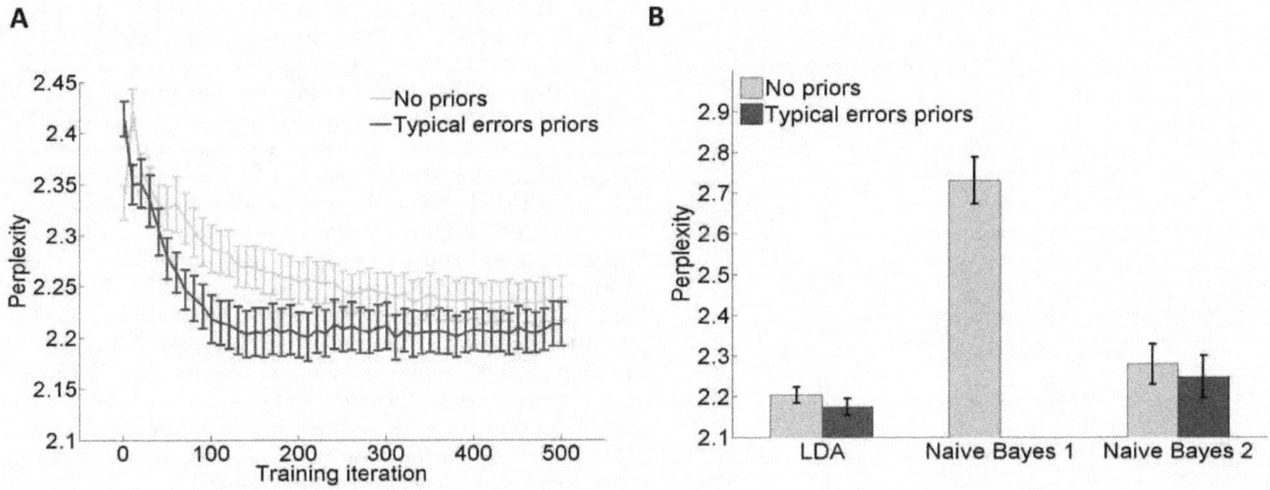

Figure 5: (A) Perplexity values for the prediction set during training of the LDA model, with (dark curve) and without (light curve) typical-error priors. (B) A comparison between perplexity values calculated for the three models, with (dark bars) and without (light bars) typical-error priors to the NB2 and LDA models.

NB2 model (figure 6). These results indicate that the LDA model best captures the hidden structure of reading errors, among all three models.

5.3 The Dyslexia-Attention model of reading

In addition to dyslexia, other factors may contribute to reading errors. For instance, people make reading mistakes due to momentarily lowered attention, which may be caused by an attention deficit or simply because they become tired as the diagnostic procedure progresses. These causes may interact with dyslexia. We hypothesized that we could "clean out" incorrect assignments of reading errors to dyslexia, rather than to an unattended state, by disentangling errors caused by dyslexia from errors caused by low attention. We further hypothesized that by disentangling the two, we could classify between participants which are diagnosed with attention deficit disorder in addition to dyslexia. We therefore designed a model that takes into account the two possible causes of reading errors, specific dyslexia types and a generic low attention state, incorporating the manner in which these change during the diagnostic procedure. Specifically, we added to the LDA-based graphical model a binary random hidden variable marking the attentional state of the subject, attended or unattended, while reading each word. We set these attentional states as a hidden Markov chain, incorporating the dynamics of reading errors in time. We trained the model in a similar way to the LDA-based model, but this time also inferring the hidden attention states and learning the transition probabilities between these states.

When evaluating this model, as in the above experiments, we did not find the Dyslexia-Attention model to improve over the dyslexia-state LDA model. We hypothesize that two reasons may explain the lack of improvement. First, adding the attention hidden variables requires a significantly larger number of parameters, which might be hard to well optimize with the current dataset. It is possible that training the model with an even larger corpus of data would improve the predictions. A second possible reason is that the attentional processes follow a different time scale than the one captured by the current experiments. The time spent in a state in an hidden Markov model follows an exponential distribution, and this may not be an adequate model for switching between attention states. We encourage and intend to further examine this line of research with more accumulating data.

6. DISCUSSION

This study is a first demonstration of using probabilistic graphical models as a method for analyzing reading errors made by dyslexic people. The work has two main novel contributions: (a) it provides an automatic diagnosis tool of dyslexia, based on data of types of reading errors; (b) it provides probabilistic tools which enable exploring dyslexic phenomena based on reading errors data. By using these tools, the hidden structure of reading errors data, such as the probability of an error-type given a dyslexia and a target-word, may be extracted.

We tested three graphical models, a Latent Dirichlet Allocation (LDA) model and two Naïve-Bayes models, all differing by their complexity. The models were trained on a uniquely large data set of reading tests taken by dyslexic people.

Two experiments were conducted with the data to determine: (a) which model best captures the fine structure of the patterns of reading errors, and (b) which model best agrees with expert diagnoses.

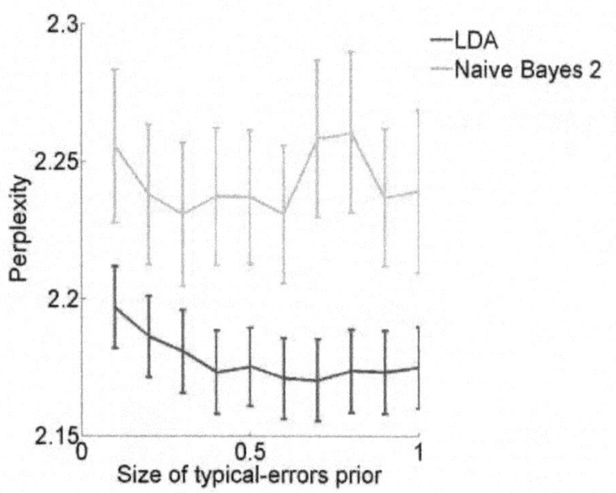

Figure 6: Perplexity values calculated for the NB2 and LDA models for varying size of typical-error prior value β_{high}.

To answer the above questions, multiple models where trained on a large corpus including 313 subjects and 196 target words in each test. Note that the majority of responses on the reading tests are correct responses of the subject, therefore most of the information about the structure of the errors resides in a small proportion of the data ($< 20\%$). We expect accuracy of algorithms to improve as more data is accumulated.

The results show that the LDA model achieves best performance in terms of predicting reading errors, and it is therefore best in capturing the fine structure of the data. This result has both theoretical and practical implications. It may contribute to the understanding of dyslexic phenomena, and it may be used to improve designs of screening tests.

Another result of this study may serve as an application for diagnosis of dyslexia. NB2 was best in replicating diagnoses of experts ($AUC = 0.801$). This is yet another demonstration of Naïve-Bayes models being efficient classifiers. Note that in this study all models were trained on the screening-tests only, whereas diagnoses of clinicians are usually based on the results of the post-tests as well. The data-driven models, and particularly NB2, performed well in detecting the dyslexia subtype without leveraging the post-test information and thus are very effective.

Finally, the predictive power of the Naïve-Bayes and LDA models is improved when the models are provided with priors which are set according to knowledge of experts from the subtype approach. If the subtype approach were wrong, adding these priors would damage the predictive power of the model rather than improving it. The accuracy of these models is also improved when providing the models with such priors. Our work therefore provides support to the subtype approach to dyslexia, and exemplifies the ability of probabilistic graphical models to shed light on theoretical issues from different research fields, such as reading disorders in the case here.

Our vision is to deploy the algorithm of the NB2 model as a mobile application, providing an accessible, cheap and fast screening test, which allows people to obtain initial screening results, helping them decide whether further diagnosis is needed. This can be achieved by a mobile application which presents a series of words, asks the user to read them aloud, recognizes the spoken words, and uses the diagnosis algorithms described here to provide an initial diagnosis. The main challenge in achieving this is having the speech recognition component recognize utterances that are nonwords. Responses of dyslexic people may differ from existing words, whereas automatic speech recognizers (ASRs) are often trained to provide the most likely word elicited. For example, a subject may read an existing word such as *cloud*, as another existing word *could*, but also as a nonword such as *clud*. This kind of distinction is crucial for the diagnosis. This challenge can be addressed by training and assessing ASR tools on data sets of labeled nonwords.

To conclude, this study is a demonstration of the use of probabilistic graphical models as a method of analyzing reading errors data. The progress presented in this paper can also be deployed as a novel, efficient diagnostic tool for dyslexia, based on reading errors only. The Naive-Bayes model tested in this research was compared to labels given by experts in diagnosis of dyslexia, and was found to be an accurate and reliable candidate for an automated tool for initial screening of dyslexia, by its subtypes.

APPENDIX

A. DERIVATION OF THE UPDATE RULE

In this section, we expand on the derivation of the update rule of the Gibbs sampler (section 4.2). The derivation we use follows similar lines as the ones described in [15], with the modification required for our dyslexia-model (figure 2C):

The joint distribution of the model is given by:

$$p(\bar{e}, \bar{w}, \bar{d}, \Theta, \Phi; \alpha, \beta) =$$

$$p(\Phi \mid \beta)p(\beta) \prod_{s=1}^{S} p(\bar{e}_s \mid \bar{d}_s, \bar{w}_s)p(\bar{w}_s)p(\bar{d}_s \mid \Theta_s)$$

$$p(\Theta_s \mid \alpha_s)p(\alpha_s) =$$

$$p(\Phi \mid \beta)p(\beta) \prod_{s=1}^{S} \prod_{i=1}^{N} p(e_{i,s} \mid w_{i,s}, d_{i,s})p(d_{i,s} \mid \Theta_s)p(\Theta_s \mid \alpha_s)$$

$$p(w_{i,s})p(\alpha_s)$$

Given that $p(\Theta_s \mid \alpha_s)$ and $p(\Phi \mid \beta)$ are Dirichlet priors, and that $p(w_{i,s})$ are constant, rewriting the expression for the joint distribution, we get:

$$p(\bar{e}, \bar{w}, \bar{d}, \Theta, \Phi; \alpha, \beta) \propto$$

$$\prod_{s=1}^{S} \prod_{w=1}^{W} \prod_{e=1}^{E} \prod_{d=1}^{D} \phi_{wed}^{C_{wed}+\beta_{wed}-1} \theta_{ds}^{C_{ds}+\alpha_{ds}-1}$$

Table 2: List of error types and possible responsible dyslexia types. NS - Normal State; LPD - Letter Position Dyslexia; VD - Visual Dyslexia; VLD - Vowel Letter Dyslexia; AD - Attentional Dyslexia; ND - Neglect Dyslexia; Other - Other types of dyslexia, such as phonological output buffer dyslexia or deep dyslexia, which are diagnosed based on additional post-tests.

	Error type	Dyslexia type
1	Correct response	NS
2	Consonant migration	LPD, VD
3	Consonant omission	VD
4	Consonant addition	VD
5	Consonant substitution	VD
6	Vowel migration	VLD, LPD, VD
7	Vowel omission	VLD, VD
8	Vowel addition	VLD, VD
9	Vowel substitution	VLD, VD
10	Semantic error	Other
11	Morphological error	Other
12	Surface error	SD
13	Visual error (left side)	ND, VD
14	Function word error	Other
15	Letter doubling, or double omission	LPD, VD
16	Attentional omission	AD
17	Attentional vowel letter error	AD, VLD
18	Attentional migration between words	AD
19	Migration of end letters	VD

Integrating out θ and ϕ, we get:

$$p(\bar{e},\bar{w},\bar{d};\alpha,\beta) \propto$$

$$\iint \prod_{s=1}^{S}\prod_{w=1}^{W}\prod_{e=1}^{E}\prod_{d=1}^{D} \phi_{wed}^{C_{wed}+\beta_{wed}-1}\theta_{ds}^{C_{ds}+\alpha_{ds}-1} d\theta d\phi =$$

$$\int \prod_{s=1} \theta_{ds}^{C_{ds}+\alpha_{ds}-1} d\theta \prod_{w=1}^{W}\prod_{d=1}^{D} \int \prod_{e=1}^{E} \phi_{wed}^{C_{wed}+\beta_{wed}-1} d\phi =$$

$$\frac{\prod_{d=1}^{D}\Gamma(C_{ds}+\alpha_{ds})}{\Gamma(\sum_{d'=1}^{D}(C_{d's}+\alpha_{d's}))} \prod_{w=1}^{W}\prod_{d=1}^{D} \frac{\prod_{e=1}^{E}\Gamma(C_{wed}+\beta_{wed})}{\Gamma(\sum_{e'=1}^{E}(C_{we'd}+\beta_{we'd}))}$$

The posterior distribution for the ith dyslexic state can now be expressed using the expression for the joint distribution:

$$p(d_i = d \mid w_i = w, e_i = e, d_{-i}, w_{-i}, e_{-i}; \alpha, \beta) \propto \frac{p(\bar{e},\bar{w},\bar{d};\alpha,\beta)}{p(\bar{e}_{-i},\bar{w}_{-i},\bar{d}_{-i};\alpha,\beta)}$$

The numerator and denominator of the above fraction, differ only by the counts having the ith pair of word-error in them, whereas all other terms cancel out. The posterior distribution thus results in the following update rule (section 4.2.3):

$$p(d_i = d \mid w_i = w, e_i = e, d_{-i}, w_{-i}, e_{-i}, \alpha, \beta) \propto \frac{C_{wed,-i}+\beta_{wed}}{\sum_{e'}[C_{we'd,-i}+\beta_{we'd}]} \frac{C_{ds,-i}+\alpha_{ds}}{\sum_{d'}[C_{d's,-i}+\alpha_{d's}]}$$

B. LIST OF ERROR-TYPES

The list of all error-types used to encode the data is shown in table 2. Possible dyslexia-types which may be responsible for each error are listed in the second column.

References

[1] D. M. Blei, A. Y. Ng, and M. I. Jordan. "Latent dirichlet allocation". In: *the Journal of machine Learning research* 3 (2003), pp. 993–1022.

[2] B. Boets et al. "Intact but less accessible phonetic representations in adults with dyslexia". In: *Science* 342.6163 (2013), pp. 1251–1254.

[3] Y. M. Broom and Doctor A. E. "Developmental phonological dyslexia: A case study of the efficacy of a remediation program". In: *Cognitive Neuropsychology* 12.7 (1995), pp. 725–766.

[4] A. Castles, T. Bates, and M. Coltheart. "John Marshall and the developmental dyslexias". In: *Aphasiology* 20.9 (2006), pp. 871–892.

[5] A. Castles and M. Coltheart. "Varieties of developmental dyslexia". In: *Cognition* 47.2 (1993), pp. 149–180.

[6] M. Coltheart and S. Kohnen. "Acquired and developmental disorders of reading and spelling". In: *The handbook of the neuropsychology of language*. Ed. by M. Faust. 2012, pp. 892–920.

[7] M. Coltheart et al. "Surface dyslexia". In: *Quarterly Journal of Experimental Psychology* 35.3 (1983), pp. 469–495.

[8] S. Dehaene. *Reading in the brain: The new science of how we read.* Penguin, 2009.

[9] J. G. Elliott and E. L. Grigorenko. *The dyslexia debate.* Cambridge University Press, 2014.

[10] M. van Ermingen-Marbach et al. "Distinct neural signatures of cognitive subtypes of dyslexia with and without phonological deficits". In: *NeuroImage: Clinical* 2 (2013), pp. 477–490.

[11] N. Friedmann and M. Coltheart. "Types of developmental dyslexia". In: *Handbook of communication disorders: Theoretical, empirical, and applied linguistics perspectives.* Ed. by A. Bar-On and D. Ravid. Berlin, Boston: De Gruyter Mouton, in press.

[12] N. Friedmann and A. Gvion. "Letter position dyslexia". In: *Cognitive Neuropsychology* 18 (2001), p. 673.

[13] N. Friedmann and A. Gvion. *TILTAN: Battery for the diagnosis of dyslexias in Hebrew.* Tel Aviv: Tel Aviv University, 2003.

[14] P. Georgiewa et al. "Phonological processing in dyslexic children: a study combining functional imaging and event related potentials". In: *Neuroscience letters* 318.1 (2002), pp. 5–8.

[15] T. L. Griffiths and M. Steyvers. "Finding scientific topics". In: *Proceedings of the National Academy of Sciences.* 5228-5235: 101 (suppl. 1), 2004.

[16] G. Jobard, F. Crivello, and N. Tzourio-Mazoyer. "Evaluation of the dual route theory of reading: a metanalysis of 35 neuroimaging studies". In: *Neuroimage* 20.2 (2003), pp. 693–712.

[17] L. Khentov-Kraus and N. Friedmann. "Dyslexia in vowel letters (DIVL)". In: *Language and Brain* 10 (2011), pp. 65–106.

[18] P. Langley, W. Iba, and K. Thompson. "An analysis of Bayesian classifiers.*AAAI*". In: 90 (1992), pp. 223–228.

[19] J. Levy et al. "Testing for the dual-route cascade reading model in the brain: an fMRI effective connectivity account of an efficient reading style". In: *PLoS One* 4.8 (2009), p. 6675.

[20] J. C. Marshall and F. Newcombe. "Patterns of paralexia: A psycholinguistic approach". In: *Journal of psycholinguistic research* 2.3 (1973), pp. 175–199.

[21] T. Minka and J. Lafferty. "Expectation-propagation for the generative aspect model". In: *In Proceedings of the Eighteenth conference on Uncertainty in artificial intelligence.* 2002, pp. 352–359.

[22] J. Pedler. "Computer correction of real-word spelling errors in dyslexic text". PhD thesis. Birkbeck, University of London, 2007.

[23] B. F. Pennington. "From single to multiple deficit models of developmental disorders". In: *Cognition* 101.2 (2006), pp. 385–413.

[24] B. F. Pennington et al. "Individual prediction of dyslexia by single versus multiple deficit models". In: *Journal of abnormal psychology* 121.1 (2012), p. 212.

[25] C. J. Price. "A review and synthesis of the first 20years of PET and fMRI studies of heard speech, spoken language and reading". In: *Neuroimage* 62.2 (2012), pp. 816–847.

[26] F. Ramus. "Neuroimaging sheds new light on the phonological deficit in dyslexia". In: *Trends in cognitive sciences* 18.6 (2014), pp. 274–275.

[27] F. Ramus and G. Szenkovits. "What phonological deficit?" In: *The Quarterly Journal of Experimental Psychology* 61.1 (2008), pp. 129–141.

[28] F. Ramus et al. "Theories of developmental dyslexia: insights from a multiple case sudty of dyslexic adults". In: *Brain* 126.4 (2003), pp. 841–865.

[29] L. Rello, R. Baeza-Yates, and J. Llisterri DysList. "An Annotated Resource of Dyslexic Errors". In: *In Proceedings LREC* (2014), pp. 26–31.

[30] S. Robidoux and S. Pritchard. "Hierarchical Clustering Analysis of Reading Aloud Data: A New Technique for Evaluating the Performance of Computational Models". In: *Frontiers in Psychology* 5.267 (2014).

[31] M. Rosen-Zvi et al. "The author-topic model for authors and documents". In: *In Proceedings of the 20th conference on Uncertainty in artificial intelligence.* 2004, pp. 487–494.

[32] E. M. Saffran and H. B. Coslett. "Implicit vs. letter-by-letter reading in pure alexia: A tale of two systems". In: *Cognitive Neuropsychology* 15.1-2 (1998), pp. 141–165.

[33] T. Shallice and E. K. Warrington. "The possible role of selective attention in acquired dyslexia". In: *Neuropsychologia* 15 (1977), pp. 31–41.

[34] S. E. Shaywitz and B. A. Shaywitz. "Dyslexia (specific reading disability)". In: *Biological psychiatry* 57.11 (2005), pp. 1301–1309.

[35] M. J. Snowling. *Dyslexia.* Blackwell Publishing, 2000.

[36] M. J. Snowling. "Dyslexia as a Phonological Deficit: Evidence and Implication". In: *Child and Adolescent Mental Health* 3 (1998), pp. 4–11.

[37] J. Stein. "The magnocellular theory of developmental dyslexia". In: *Dyslexia* 7 (2001), pp. 12–36.

[38] G. Vallar, C. Burani, and L. S. Arduino. "Neglect dyslexia: a review of the neuropsychological literature". In: *Experimental Brain Research* 206.2 (2010), pp. 219–235.

[39] H. M. Wallach, D. Minmo, and A. McCallum. "Rethinking LDA: Why priors matter". In: *Neural Information Processing Systems* (2009), pp. 1973–1981.

Promoting Positive Post-Click Experience for In-Stream Yahoo Gemini Users

Mounia Lalmas
Yahoo Labs
London, UK
mounia@acm.org

Janette Lehmann*
Freie Universität Berlin
Berlin, Germany
lehmann.j@fu-berlin.de

Guy Shaked
Yahoo
Tel Aviv, Israel
gshaked@yahoo-inc.com

Fabrizio Silvestri
Yahoo Labs
London, UK
silvestr@yahoo-inc.com

Gabriele Tolomei
Yahoo Labs
London, UK
gtolomei@yahoo-inc.com

ABSTRACT

Click-through rate (CTR) is the most common metric used to assess the performance of an online advert; another performance of an online advert is the user *post-click experience*. In this paper, we describe the method we have implemented in Yahoo *Gemini*[1] to measure the post-click experience on Yahoo mobile news streams via an automatic analysis of advert landing pages. We measure the post-click experience by means of two well-known metrics, *dwell time* and *bounce rate*. We show that these metrics can be used as *proxy* of an advert post-click experience, and that a negative post-click experience has a negative effect on user engagement and future ad clicks. We then put forward an approach that analyses advert landing pages, and show how these can affect dwell time and bounce rate. Finally, we develop a prediction model for advert quality based on dwell time, which was deployed on Yahoo mobile news stream app running on iOS. The results show that, using dwell time as a proxy of post-click experience, we can prioritise higher quality ads. We demonstrate the impact of this on users via A/B testing.

Categories and Subject Descriptors

H.4.0 [**Information Systems Applications**]: General

Keywords

Mobile advertising; Native advertising; Advertising quality; Post-click experience; Dwell time prediction

1. INTRODUCTION

One of the main requirements driving the development of Yahoo Gemini, the Yahoo advertising platform, has been that of caring not only about the sheer number of clicks on ads but also about the user experience. In our case, user experience means to show advertisements[2] that will not discourage users to continue using the platform or, even more challenging, to engage them to click more on ads.

Following from this, we put forward an approach that analyses ad landing pages, and show how these can affect *dwell time* and *bounce rate*. Then we develop a model based on dwell time for predicting the quality of *native* Yahoo Gemini ads, which is currently deployed on Yahoo Gemini. We chose to deploy the version predicting dwell time as we wanted to serve ads on which users spend time, meaning not only they promote a positive post-click user experience but also have the potential of leading to a "conversion" (e.g., making a purchase). Analyzing one month data through A/B testing, we see that returning high quality ads, as measured in terms of the ad post-click experience, not only increases click-through rates by 18%, it has a positive effect on users, as we observe an increase in dwell time (+30%) and a decrease in bounce rate (-6.7%).

As we stated above, we focus in this paper on showing how our approach works on *native* ads. Let us now describe what a native ad is.

Feed-based layouts, or *streams*, are becoming an increasingly common layout in many applications, and a predominant interface in mobile applications. *In-stream* advertising has been increasingly emerging as a popular online advertising because it offers a user experience that fits nicely with that of the stream [9]. It is often referred to as *native advertising*.[3] In-stream (or native) ads have an appearance similar to that of the items in the stream, but are clearly marked with a "Sponsored" label or a currency symbol e.g. "$" to indicate that they are in fact adverts. Major news sites such as the New York Times, Yahoo News, and the Guardian integrate ads into their streams. Yahoo launched *Gemini* in 2013, an unified ad marketplace for mobile search and native advertising. Many of the ads served by Yahoo Gemini are in-streams ads. In this work, we focus on such ads served by Gemini on one of Yahoo mobile news streams.

*This work has been carried out while the author was an intern at Yahoo Labs.

[1] `https://advertising.yahoo.com/Blog/gemini-announcement.html`

[2] For simplicity, "advertisement" and "advert" are referred to as "ad".

[3] Sponsored search is also an instance of native advertising, as sponsored results have a similar look and feel to the organic results, while being clearly indicated as being ads.

KDD'15, August 10-13, 2015, Sydney, NSW, Australia.
© 2015 ACM. ISBN 978-1-4503-3664-2/15/08 ...$15.00.
DOI: http://dx.doi.org/10.1145/2783258.2788581.

We refer to the ad impression shown within the stream as the *creative* of the ad. A user decides if he or she is interested in the ad content by looking at its creative, depending on how attractive it is to users. After a user clicks on the creative he or she is redirected to the ad *landing page*, which is either a web page specifically created for that ad, or the advertiser homepage [2]. It is well known that the way user experiences a landing page, the *ad post-click experience*, is an important factor that, if properly measured, can help differentiating between a high quality and a low quality ad. Indeed, when the post-click experience is negative users may tend to click less on ads in the future, if not stop accessing the service at all with disruptive consequences in the overall number of visitors and therefore in total revenue.

Looking at the post-click experience is particularly important in the context of Gemini in-stream ads because (1) the creatives have mostly the same look and feel, as opposed to display ads, and what differs mostly is their landing pages, and (2) accounting for the post-click experience has led to increased performance in many areas, including sponsored search. In this paper, we develop and deploy a method to identify high quality ads, by analysing their landing pages and relate these to the ad post-click experience. Our focus is on mobile in-stream advertising as offered by Yahoo Gemini.

We measure the post-click experience through well-known engagement metrics, *dwell time* and *bounce rate*. Dwell time is the time between users clicking on an ad creative until returning to the stream; bounce rate is the percentage of "short clicks" (clicks with dwell time less than a given threshold). We demonstrate that they can be used as proxy of ad post-click experience. We also show that a negative post-click experience has a negative effect on user engagement and, in particular, future ad clicks.

2. RELATED WORK

Online advertising. Online advertising has been extensively studied in the context of display advertising [1, 22] and sponsored search [3, 23] for desktop users. Studies have been mostly focussed on predicting how an ad will perform according to various effectiveness measures [1, 12, 24].

Many efforts have been devoted to improve the matching between the textual content of web queries (in sponsored search) or web pages (in display advertising) and the ad textual content (creative and/or bid phrases and title). Most works aim at categorizing the ad textual content within some taxonomy and then matched it against the query category [2, 3] or a web page [5, 14, 18] where the ad could be shown. In particular, [2, 3] studied the effect of landing page categorization on user experience by defining a small taxonomy of landing pages. A year later, [6] studied the effect of landing page features in improving ad relevance in textual advertising. They show that augmenting the ad textual features with features from the content of the page increases relevance metrics. Finally, [11] focused on automatically categorizing display ad images into a taxonomy of relevant interest categories. They demonstrate the effectiveness of using image and textual features extracted from the ad landing page in predicting the category of the display ad. We also exploit landing page features to predict the quality of ads with respect to the post-click experience.

Users spend an increasing amount of their time online through their mobile devices. This presents unique opportunities for advertisers interested in promoting their products beyond the desktop. Previous studies have investigated the degree in which mobile advertising is accepted by users [4] and how users perceive display advertisements on mobile [8]. Findings suggest that personal relevance of the ad is not as important as matching the ad topics to the content of the page, and that utility, context and trust are crucial for acceptance of mobile advertising. Efforts have been put in building models to predict when to show an ad [19, 20]. Finally, as highlighted in [9, 21], the dominance of the feed-based structure on mobile makes pop-ups and banners impractical, whereas in-stream ads provide an optimal format as they are seamlessly incorporated to the main feed, thereby promoting relatively similar experience across all ads. This is not the same for the ad landing pages, as advertisers have total freedom in how they design these, which can vary greatly in terms of quality. In this paper, we study how an ad post-click experience, as measured with dwell time and bounce rate, can inform about the quality of its landing page.

Ad quality measures. Several measures have been proposed to evaluate the "performance" of an ad in terms of the user experience. The most common measure is the ad click-through rate (CTR), which is the number of times the ad was clicked out of the number of times it has been shown (number of ad impressions) [1]. The higher the CTR the better the ad is considered to perform; it attracts the users to click on it. However, CTR does not account for how users experience the ad when they land on the ad site, namely their *post-click experience*, for which other measures are better suited. A positive experience with an ad landing page increases the probability of users "converting" (e.g., purchasing an item, registering to a mailing list, or simply spending time on the site building an affinity with the brand) [3, 22]. Even if no conversion occurs, publishers are keen to serve high quality ads, as doing otherwise may affect user long-term engagement: loosing users would mean less clicks on ads, and lower engagement with the site, which in turn negatively impact revenue. In this paper, we indeed show that when users experienced high quality ads post-click, they were more likely to clicks on an ad in the future.

A positive post-click experience does not necessarily mean a conversion. Therefore, although the former can be measured by the latter (e.g., a high conversion rate), this way of assessing the quality of the post-click experience is restrictive. There may be many reasons why conversion does not happen, independent of the quality of the ad served to users. In addition, conversion rate information is not always available. A good proxy of the post-click experience is the time a user spends on the ad site before returning back to the publisher site: "the longer the time, the more likely the experience was positive". The two most common measures used to quantify time spent on a site are *dwell time* [27] and *bounce rate* [23]. These measures have been used as proxies of post-click experience in online advertising and organic search, e.g., to improve the performance of ranking algorithms [12], as well as in recommender systems, e.g., to estimate the relevance of an item to a user [26]. In this work, we show that these are also good proxies of post-click experience in both the mobile and desktop contexts.

Finally, [3] showed that conversion rates differ significantly depending on the type of landing page. Also, [6] showed that landing pages could be leveraged to better select which ads to return to users in sponsored search. In the context of mobile advertising, whether the landing page of an ad is mobile-optimised or not was shown to affect post-click experience [16]. Our research adds to this body of work by analysing other features of landing pages for mobile advertising, and how these help predict user post-click experience.

3. MEASURING POST-CLICK EXPERIENCE

We show that dwell time and bounce rate are good proxy measures of ad post-click experience.

Datasets and metric definitions. We randomly sampled 4,000 ads from a large set of ads served on Yahoo homepage stream in March 2014 both on desktop and mobile. Although our focus is on mobile devices, we look at both mobile and desktop to demonstrate that dwell time and bounce rate are good measures to act as proxy of ad post-click experience. We defined dwell time and bounce rate as follows:

- The average *dwell time* is the average time between users clicking on the ad and returning to the stream.
- The *bounce rate* is the percentage of ad clicks whose dwell time, unless otherwise specified, is lower than or equal to a fixed threshold.

The threshold used to determine the bounce rate on mobile was set to 5 seconds; this was empirically selected based on the dwell time distribution, which showed a "plateau" just around that value. The threshold on desktop instead was set to 12 seconds; this was chosen so to align with the threshold on mobile, by picking the value which corresponds to the same cumulative frequency of "bouncy" clicks on both dwell time distributions. Both these thresholds fall into the range between 5 and 60 seconds proposed in [15].[4]

In addition, we removed all clicks with a dwell time higher than 10 minutes, as these clicks may correspond to cases when users left the mobile or desktop device and came back later. By doing so we removed 1.74% of the total ad clicks. Finally, we only considered ads with at least 10 clicks.

Dwell Time as a Proxy of Ad Post-Click Experience. The fact that a user takes time to return to the news stream after clicking on an ad seems a good indicator that the experience is positive: the user browsed the site, maybe converted (e.g., purchased a product, registered to the site, shared the page, etc.), and finally went back to the stream. We study the extent to which higher dwell time indeed reflects a positive experience.

We used a random sample of 200K ad clicks on the mobile stream for which we have records of a click on the ad site. For desktop, we matched the page views associated with the ad clicks to those contained in the Yahoo toolbar's browsing data,[5] which results in page views from 30K ad clicks.

For both datasets, the Spearman's rank correlation coefficient between the number of clicks on the ad site and the ad dwell time is, respectively, 0.65 for mobile and 0.54 for desktop; the higher the dwell time, the higher the number of clicks on the ad site. Assuming that clicking on the ad site suggests a positive "ad experience", high dwell time is indicative of a positive post-click experience. The probability of a second click as the percentage of users who clicked

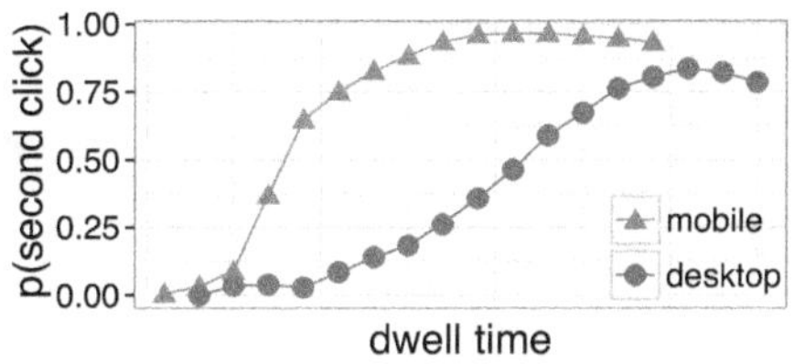

Figure 1: Post-click experience. The probability of a second click given dwell time. The x-axis values (log-scale) are removed for confidential reasons.

on a link on the ad landing page, for given dwell time values, is plotted in Figure 1. This probability increases with the time spent *until* the users return to the news stream for both mobile and desktop, further indicating that dwell time is a good proxy of post-click experience. It is also worth noticing that to get the same probability of a second click on mobile and on desktop, the dwell time has to be far larger in the latter than in the former. This suggests that dwell time is generally greater on desktop than on mobile.

Dwell time is *not* the time spent on the ad site, but the time between the click on the ad until the user returns to the stream. It can happen that users visit other sites during their session before returning. With the Yahoo toolbar dataset, we are able to look into this. We saw that the higher the dwell time, the higher the probability that users visited other websites. However, for all ad clicks with a dwell time up to 3 minutes, this happens for only 7.4% of the clicks. For dwell time higher than 3 minutes, this percentage increases to 23.3%. Therefore, in general dwell time is a good proxy of users spending time on the ad site, with longer dwell time reflecting a positive experience with the ad site. Next, we relate this to the long-term effect on user engagement.

Long-term User Engagement. We now focus on mobile. We investigate the effect of the ad post-click experience, as measured by dwell time and bounce rate, on long-term user engagement. In other words, we examine how users are affected when they experience ads on which they spend little time (reflecting a negative ad experience) compared to the opposite (reflecting a positive ad experience)

We divided our dataset into three time-periods, covering a four-week period of user interaction with the mobile stream:[6]

- user *pre-engagement* in a given two-week period;
- user *post-engagement* in the following two-week period;
- user *ad-click-activity* in the last three days of the pre-engagement period and the first three days of the post-engagement period.

Our objective is to compare the pre- and post-engagement periods depending on the ad-click-activity between the two.

We used the *ad-click-activity* dataset to distinguish between a positive ad post-click experience and a negative one. For each ad a, we calculate its mean dwell time $dt_m(a)$ and its standard deviation $dt_{sd}(a)$. Any click c on ad a with $dt_c(a) \leq dt_m(a) - 0.25 \cdot dt_{sd}(a)$ is referred to as a *short click*, and any click c on ad a with $dt_c(a) \geq dt_m(a) + 0.25 \cdot dt_{sd}(a)$ is referred to as a *long click*. Here, $dt_c(a)$ is the dwell time on ad a for click c. These definitions account for the fact

[4]We also experimented with other thresholds in this range. Similar results were obtained.

[5]A sample of users gave their consent to provide browsing data via the Yahoo toolbar, which is a browser extension providing additional functionalities and direct access to selected websites.

[6]The study was carried out with other datasets and led to the same conclusions.

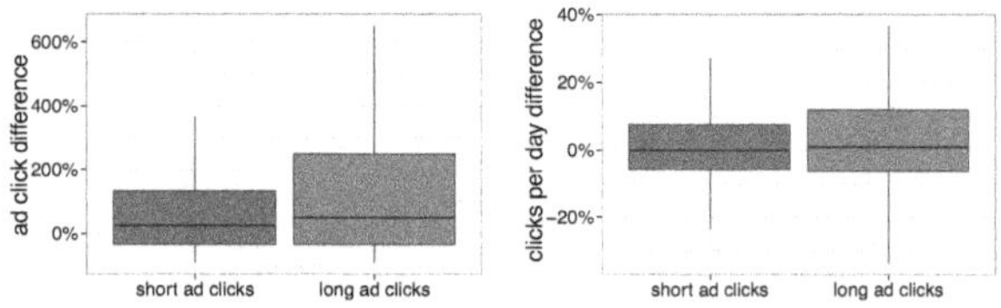

(a) Changes in adClicks. (b) Changes in clicksPerDay.

Figure 2: Changes in engagement depending on whether the users experienced short or long clicks.

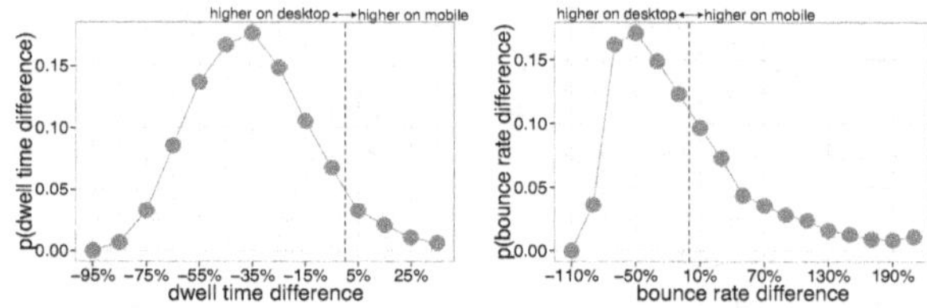

(a) Difference in dwell time. (b) Difference in bounce rate.

Figure 3: Distributions of the differences in post-click experience between mobile and desktop.

Table 1: Changes in engagement for short and long ad clickers. We report the average and median (*avg*|*median*) of the ad clicks and clicks per day difference, and the *p*-values.

	Short ad cl.	Long ad cl.	*p*-value
AdClicks diff.	90.3%|25.0%	122.6%|50.0%	0.002
ClicksPerDay diff.	2.4%|0.0%	5.5%|0.9%	0.000

that ads differ in terms of their average dwell time. For example, we saw that ads related to beauty products have on average a higher dwell time than those related to finance, simply because the ad experience is different (reading about a product versus registering an interest).

For all users that clicked on at least 3 ads, users with only short clicks were said to have had a negative experience (*shortAdClicker*), whereas those with only long clicks were said to have a positive experience (*longAdClicker*). Having a minimum of 3 clicks allow us to select users that have experienced enough ads to be affected by them. These resulted in two sets of similar size, around 800 users each.

We use two metrics to measure pre- and post-engagement:[7]

- *adClicks* is the number of ad clicks of a user over the period considered. This metric shows the effect of the ad post-click experience on that user future ad clicks.
- *clicksPerDay* is the average number of pages a user is viewing within each day over the period considered. This metric shows the effect of the ad post-click experience on the user future interaction with the stream.

We define the change in the engagement between the pre- and post-engagement time periods as follows:

$$\text{eng}_d = (\text{eng}_{\text{post}} - \text{eng}_{\text{pre}})/\text{eng}_{\text{pre}}$$

where eng is either *adClicks* or *clicksPerDay*. A value above (below) 0 indicates that post-engagement increased (decreased) compared to pre-engagement, and the extent of the increase (decrease). Figure 2 shows the distribution of the two metrics for the two user groups (*shortAdClicker* and *longAdClicker*). We also report the average and the mean of the two metrics in Table 1. We use a two-sample Kolmogorov-Smirnov test to check whether the distributions are different. The *p*-values are reported in Table 1.

For both user groups, the ad click activity is increasing. This is likely to reflect that users in both groups are becoming more engaged with the stream and as a result are more likely to click on ads. However, the median $adClicks_d$ for the short ad clicker group is 25.0%; this value is 50.0% for the long ad clicker group. That is, the increase in ad clicks (both in terms of median and average, and distribution) for the long ad clicker group is higher, indicating that a positive ad post-click experience is leading to more ad clicks. The difference is statistically significant (p-value < 0.01).

The metric $clicksPerDay_d$ has a median close to 0.0% for both user groups. This suggests a similar trend in engagement with the stream, some users becoming more engaged, while others becoming less engaged. Looking at our dataset in more depth, we could identify users getting more engaged with the stream as time passed, and users that were very engaged with the stream. As such their future engagement could not increase further (reaching a certain plateau). However, when looking at the average values and the distributions of $clicksPerDay_d$, we see a larger increase for the long click group, compared to the short click group (5.6% and 2.4%, respectively), suggesting a larger increase in engagement with the stream for users in the positive post-click experience group. The difference, although small compared to $adClicks_d$, is significant (p-value < 0.01).

To conclude, using dwell time to measure the ad post-click experience, we showed that a positive experience had a strong effect on users clicking on ads again, and a small effect on user engagement with the stream. The effect is statistically significant for both. Thus, not only can dwell time be used to measure an ad post-click experience, ensuring that high quality ads are served to users is important for long-term engagement. We investigate further the two post-click measures, in particular what they can tell about the mobile post-click experience compared to the desktop one.

Mobile vs. Desktop. We examine the difference in the ad post-click experience, measured by dwell time and bounce rate, between mobile and desktop. First, we compare whether dwell time and bounce rate of an ad differs between the two.

Users experience ads differently depending on the device they are using. In fact, using Spearman's rank correlation coefficient ρ, for dwell time we obtain $\rho = 0.50$; this value is even smaller for bounce rate with $\rho = 0.23$.[8]

Next, we calculate for each ad the difference in percentage of their dwell time and bounce rate, when shown on desktop compared to mobile (*val* refers to dwell time or bounce rate):

$$d_{val} = (val_{mobile} - val_{desktop})/val_{desktop}$$

The distributions of the percentage differences are plotted in Figure 3, (a) for dwell time and (b) for bounce rate. For 92.9% of the ads the dwell time is higher on desktop than

[7]Similar results were observed with other metrics.

[8]Similar correlations were observed when restricting to ads with at least 50 clicks. The correlations are 0.63 and 0.29, respectively.

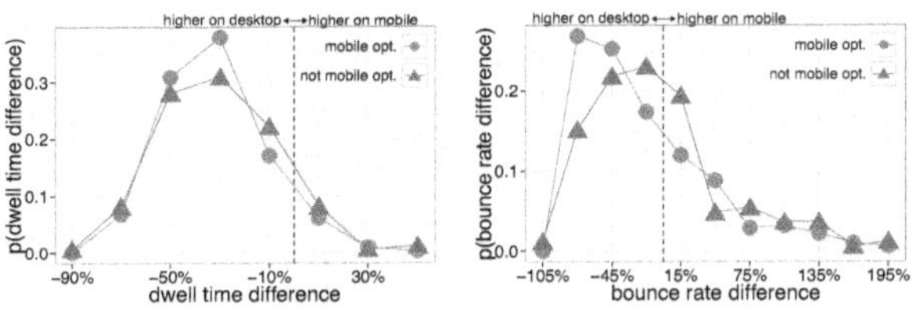

(a) Difference in dwell time. (b) Difference in bounce rate.

Figure 4: Differences in ad post-click experience between mobile and desktop depending on whether the landing page is mobile-optimised or not.

on mobile (Figure 3(a)). This is not surprising, as browsing time on mobile has been shown to be shorter generally outside advertising [25]. The highest decrease in dwell time from desktop to mobile is by 35.0%. From Figure 3(b), we observe that 64.1% of the ads have a higher bounce rate on mobile than on desktop, which is a lower percentage than for dwell time. The highest decrease of bounce rate from desktop to mobile is by 50.0%, which is slightly higher when compared to dwell time. The distribution is skewed to the left however, indicating that many ads have a large increase in bounce rate when shown on mobile. For instance, 18.9% of the ads have a bounce rate increase higher than 50.0%.

Whereas the dwell time differences between desktop and mobile may reflect the browsing behaviour on these two devices (shorter sessions on mobile), the bounce rate differences clearly suggest that the ad post-click experience between mobile and desktop differs. The device has an impact on how users experience the ad.

Mobile-Optimised Ad Landing Pages.

We showed that the ad experience on mobile is different to that on desktop. This can partly be explained by the different ways users interact with their desktop and their mobile. However, a preliminary analysis done on the landing pages of the ads in our dataset showed that, when served on a mobile device, some of the landing pages were *not* mobile-optimised, which is likely to have a negative effect on users [16]. In optimised version, landing pages have typically larger buttons, no long text paragraphs, and a single large image of the product advertised in the middle of the page. To see the effect of this on the ad post-click experience, and the extent to which this reflects the quality of the ad, we designed a mechanism to automatically detect when a landing page is mobile-optimised or not.

We first downloaded the landing pages, rendered them and extracted seven features. We used features such as the size in bytes of the HTML landing page, and whether the page contains an apple touch icon. Next, we manually labelled a sample of 259 ads as mobile-optimised (Opt) or non-optimised (Npt). Our training set consisted of 108 Opt and 151 Npt ads. We fed the feature representation of the landing pages in our annotated dataset to a Gradient Boosted Decision Tree classifier, and we estimated its quality using leave-one-out cross validation (LOOCV). The classifier reached a F_1 score of 0.995, demonstrating its high accuracy.

We then tested if dwell time and bounce rate of a landing page correlates with it being Opt. Using a sample dataset of 500 ads, with approximately 65.0% of them being mobile-optimised and 35.0% non-mobile-optimised, we conducted a similar experiment to the previous section, but with Opt ads and Npt as our classes. The results are shown in Figure 4. We employ a Two-sample Kolmogorov-Smirnov test to look at whether the differences are significant.

The distribution of the dwell time difference is very similar for both groups, Opt and Npt (Figure 4(a)). The average dwell time decreases by 31.8% (*median* = 31.8%) for Opt landing pages, and by 28.9% (*median* = 33.6%) for Npt landing pages. The difference is not significant (p-value = 0.20). *Whether a landing page is optimised does not influence how long users spend on the mobile ad site.*

When considering bounce rate, however, we observe differences (Figure 4(b)). The average bounce rate decreases by 6.9% (median decreases by 30.4%) for Opt landing pages but increases by 13.4% (median decreases by 11.5%) for Npt landing pages. These differences are statically significant (p-value = 0.003). Therefore, *mobile-optimised landing pages have a positive influence on users, as they are less likely to lead to bounce, compared to when shown on the desktop.* Studies looking at ad post-click experience in the mobile context should account for this property of the landing page, which by itself is not surprising. However, since we observe no difference in dwell time other features of the landing pages influence user post-click experience. This is the motivation for the landing page analysis discussed next.

4. PREDICTING HIGH QUALITY ADS

When a landing page has a high dwell time it is likely to be interesting, and *potentially* more likely to lead to a conversion. On the other hand, if a landing page has a high bounce rate it means that most of the users are annoyed by it. The previous section demonstrated dwell time to be a good proxy of user post-click experience and bounce rate provided additional insights on user post-click experience. In this section, we use these metrics to identify *high quality* ads on the basis of their landing pages, as experienced by mobile users on Yahoo mobile news stream.

4.1 High Quality Ads Ranking

Given a request for an ad to be served on Yahoo mobile news stream, we describe how ads are ranked to fulfill that request. Let $P^i_{\text{click}} \in [0,1]$ be the predicted probability of an ad i being clicked, and let $\text{bid}^i \in \mathbb{R}$ be the amount of money the advertiser is willing to pay for its ad to be shown. Ranking the ads is done by computing the *expected cost per click* $\text{eCPC}^i = P^i_{\text{click}} \cdot \text{bid}^i$ for each ad, and later sorting them in descending order of this value. Our aim is to predict P^i_{SAT}, that is the *conditional probability* of a user being satisfied *given* that he or she clicked on an ad i. The goal is thus to estimate the overall *joint probability* of clicking on an ad *and* being satisfied by its landing page. More formally, we want to compute $P^i_{\text{HQ}} = P^i_{\text{click}} \cdot P^i_{SAT}$.[9] Finally, the ranking of ads will be computed as $\text{eCPC}^i_{\text{HQ}} = P^i_{\text{HQ}} \cdot \text{bid}^i$. The ad with the highest $\text{eCPC}^i_{\text{HQ}}$ will then be served.

We thus want to predict a class label $Y_i \in \{-1, 1\}$ for a given landing page X_i represented by a feature vector $\phi(X_i)$. The class label Y_i is 1 if X_i is a high quality page, -1 otherwise. Concretely, we aim at estimating the following probability density function:

$$P(Y_i = -1|\phi(X_i)) = 1 - P(Y_i = 1|\phi(X_i))$$

which, in practice, corresponds to the joint probability P^i_{HQ}.

[9]Note that P^i_{SAT} is conditioned on P^i_{click}.

4.2 Two Definitions of High Quality Ads

In this work, we focus on the quality of an ad as experienced by users on the ad landing page. Within this context, there are many definitions of a *high quality ad* we could use. We consider two definitions, one based on dwell time and the other on bounce rate, which we have shown to be good proxies of the ad post-click experience.

Formally, with a web page X_i accessed by a set of n_{X_i} users we associate two real numbers $\delta_{X_i} > 0$ its mean dwell time computed over the set of n_{X_i} users, and $\beta_{X_i} \in [0, 1]$ its bounce rate computed as the fraction of the n_{X_i} leaving X_i before a given time threshold.

1. *High Dwell Time.* $Y_i = 1$ when $\delta_{X_i} > t_\delta$ where t_δ is a threshold defined on dwell time. Under this assumption $P^i_{\text{HDT}} = P(Y_i = 1|\phi(X_i)) = P(\delta_{X_i} > t_\delta)$.
2. *Low Bounce Rate.* $Y_i = 1$ when $\beta_{X_i} < \tau_\beta$ where $0 < \tau_\beta < 1$ is a bounce rate threshold value. Under this assumption $P^i_{\text{LBR}} = P(Y_i = 1|\phi(X_i)) = P(\beta_{X_i} < \tau_\beta)$.

We experiment with these two definitions, to identify whether they can be predicted based on the ad landing page features. Next we define these features.

4.3 Ad Landing Page Features

Inspired by previous work [2, 3, 6, 11] exploiting features extracted from the landing pages to categorise ads, our understanding of the problem at hand and our own expertise and common sense, we define three sets of features.

CONT (C) Features. This group captures the content including the functionality of the landing page:

- *media*: boolean value stating if the site is responsive.[10]
- *clickToCall*: number of clickables linking to a phone call.
- *imageHeight*: height of the landing page.
- *imageWidth*: width of the landing page.
- *numClickable*: number of clickables.
- *numDropdown*: number of dropdown lists.
- *numImages*: number of images.
- *numInputCheckbox*: number of checkboxes.
- *numInputRadio*: number of radio buttons.
- *numInputString*: number of input strings (usually to elicit users details).
- *tokenCount*: number of tokens (words).
- *viewPort*: a boolean feature represents if the site can be tuned to different screen sizes.
- *windowSize*: total width of all `div` tags on the page, which allows detecting carousels.
- *nounsSumOfScores*: number of nouns.
- *numConceptAnnotation*: number of all Wikipedia *entities* (a concept with a Wikipedia entry).
- *summarizabilityScore*: predicts if the page is a good candidate for extracting a summary, where higher value means the landing page is more "newsy".
- *isMobileOptimised*: the result of the classifier as discussed in Section 3.

SIM (S) Features. This group of features captures the similarity of the landing page with the creative text displayed within the stream. Usually, a user sees the creative and decides to click on the basis of the text written there. If the semantics of the creative text is very different from the semantics of the landing page then the user who clicked may be annoyed and leave immediately the page.

- *similarityNoun*: cosine similarity between creative text and landing page based on nouns.
- *similarityWikiIds*: cosine similarity between creative text and landing page based on Wikipedia entities.

HIST (H) Features. These features captures historical information about the ad past performance.

- *impressions*: number of times the ad was shown.
- *clicks*: number of times the ad was clicked.
- *bouncerate*: bounce rate of the ad.
- *avgdwelltime*: average dwell time of the ad.
- *avgdwelltimenonshort*: average dwell time when short clicks were removed.
- *ctr*: click-through rate of the ad.
- *cpx*: cost per click of the ad.

4.4 Prediction Quality

Using the features listed above we train several models to predict P^i_{HQ} using three well-known learning methods: Logistic Regression (LogReg) [28], Support Vector Machines (SVM) [7], and Gradient Boosted Decision Trees (GBDT) [10]. We use the implementations of these methods available in the Python scikit-learn package.[11] The probability values are extracted using the implementation available with this framework. We adopt standard parameters for each method. For the LogReg classifier we set C, the inverse of regularization strength, to 100, and $L1$ as penalty norm, and 0.01 as the tolerance value for stopping the optimization. For the SVM classifier we adopt a *RBF* kernel with a penalty parameter C of the error term equal to 1.0, 0.0 as the gamma kernel coefficient, and 10^{-3} as the tolerance used in the stopping criterium. Finally, for the GBDT classifier we generate a forest of 100 trees with a max depth of each tree of 4, and a learning rate of 0.01.

4.5 Offline Model Evaluation

To assess the validity of our prediction models, we run a traditional offline evaluation based on historical data.

Experimental Setup. For each definition of high quality ads, we report the performance of predictors using three standard metrics, Area Under the ROC Curve (AUC), F_1, and the Matthews Correlation Coefficient (MCC) [17]. The latter is a correlation measure between predictions and labels taking into account the popularity of each class.

The dataset used to run the experiments is a uniformly generated sample of our ad set. As a training set we extract a sample of 1,500 ads shown in March 2014 to users of the system. The test set contains a sample of 550 ads shown in April 2014. In all the tests we conduct we experiment with several thresholds for dwell time (t_δ) and bounce rate (τ_β). Finally, we test several combinations of features: content-based or C features; similarity-based or S features; and history-based or H features.

Tables 2 and 3 report the results for predicting the probability of high dwell time and low bounce rate. Only for high dwell time, we report the results for the three classification methods (LogReg, SVM, and GBDT). For bounce rate, we report the results using LogReg.

First, the various classification methods perform similarly (with a slight advantage of SVM over the others for high dwell time). Similarity-based features perform bad as they

[10] `http://en.wikipedia.org/wiki/Responsive_web_design`

[11] `http://scikit-learn.org`

never increase (and in some case are detrimental to) both metrics. Finally, history-based features are very important as they boost, for instance, AUC above 0.8 when combined with content. Content-based features alone are already achieving high values with both metrics.

We should note that history-based features are very sparse for ads and, in particular, are non-existing for newly inserted ones. Content-only classifiers can always be used as they provide the perfect solution to the "item cold-start problem" that will be often experienced with many ads.

Features	Method	t_δ	AUC	F_1	MCC
C	LogReg	35	0.71	0.65	0.44
C-S	LogReg	35	0.70	0.64	0.42
C-H	LogReg	35	0.82	0.81	0.64
C-S-H	**LogReg**	**35**	**0.84**	**0.83**	**0.67**
C	SVM	35	0.82	0.81	0.65
C-S	SVM	35	0.82	0.81	0.64
C-H	SVM	35	0.83	0.82	0.66
C-S-H	SVM	35	0.83	0.82	0.66
C	GBDT	35	0.77	0.73	0.55
C-S	GBDT	35	0.77	0.74	0.56
C-H	GBDT	35	0.83	0.82	0.66
C-S-H	GBDT	35	0.83	0.82	0.66
C	LogReg	40	0.70	0.60	0.47
C-S	LogReg	40	0.72	0.63	0.49
C-H	LogReg	40	0.83	0.79	0.66
C-S-H	LogReg	40	0.83	0.79	0.66
C	SVM	40	0.83	0.79	0.67
C-S	SVM	40	0.83	0.79	0.67
C-H	**SVM**	**40**	**0.83**	**0.80**	**0.68**
C-S-H	**SVM**	**40**	**0.83**	**0.80**	**0.68**
C	GBDT	40	0.82	0.77	0.70
C-S	GBDT	40	0.81	0.77	0.68
C-H	GBDT	40	0.83	0.80	0.68
C-S-H	GBDT	40	0.83	0.80	0.68
C	LogReg	45	0.69	0.57	0.48
C-S	LogReg	45	0.70	0.57	0.50
C-H	LogReg	45	0.79	0.72	0.60
C-S-H	LogReg	45	0.79	0.72	0.60
C	SVM	45	0.82	0.76	0.67
C-S	SVM	45	0.82	0.76	0.67
C-H	SVM	45	0.80	0.73	0.61
C-S-H	SVM	45	0.80	0.73	0.61
C	GBDT	45	0.72	0.62	0.56
C-S	GBDT	45	0.71	0.60	0.54
C-H	GBDT	45	0.80	0.73	0.61
C-S-H	GBDT	45	0.80	0.73	0.61

Table 2: Dwell Time prediction performance on models built on ads data from March 2014 and tested on April 2014. We vary t_δ to evaluate the impact of the threshold chosen on the prediction ability of the model (best results in bold).

4.6 Feature Ranking

We show the importance of each set of features, namely C, C-S and C-S-H. We limit our analysis to the GBDT classifier and use the technique implemented in the scikit-learn toolkit. This technique can naturally be used to induce a ranking of the "importance" of features in a regression or classification problem. Table 4 shows the top-15 features ranked according to their importance scores as output by GBDT when trained for predicting ad quality on the basis of dwell time being above a fixed threshold[12]. Each column refers to the ranking of a specific set of features: C, C-S and C-S-H. The i-th row

[12]As explained later in this section, we select 40 seconds as our dwell time threshold.

Features	Method	τ_β	AUC	F_1	MCC
C	LogReg	0.2	0.51	0.78	0.06
C-S	LogReg	0.2	0.59	0.8	0.24
C-H	LogReg	0.2	0.79	0.85	0.58
C-S-H	LogReg	0.2	0.78	0.85	0.57
C	LogReg	0.22	0.61	0.74	0.27
C-S	LogReg	0.22	0.61	0.72	0.23
C-H	LogReg	0.22	0.86	0.86	0.71
C-S-H	**LogReg**	**0.22**	**0.85**	**0.86**	**0.70**
C	LogReg	0.25	0.57	0.63	0.15
C-S	LogReg	0.25	0.63	0.63	0.26
C-H	LogReg	0.25	0.83	0.82	0.67
C-S-H	LogReg	0.25	0.83	0.81	0.66

Table 3: Bounce rate prediction performance on models built on ads data from March 2014 and tested on April 2014. We vary τ_β to evaluate the impact of the threshold chosen on the prediction ability of the model (best result in bold).

contains the i-th ranked feature, along with its category (C, S or H) and importance score, for each set.

When the classifier is trained using only content features (C) or both content and similarity features (C-S), *clickToCall* is the most important signal. The first similarity feature (*similarityNoun*) is ranked 11-th when using the C-S set. This means that similarity features do not provide significant insights to discriminate between high and low quality ads. This is even more evident when using the C-S-H set, where no similarity features appear in the top-15 list. We also observe that features related to the functionality of the landing page (*numDropdown, numInputRadio*) impact more than those related to the content itself (*tokenCount, nounsSumOfScores*) and aesthetic (*isMobileOptimised, media*). Only when considering the similarity features (C-S) as well, two content–related features become more important (*summarisabilityScore* and *numConceptAnnotation*). Finally, for the set C-S-H, the top-3 most important signals come all from historical features; *avgdwelltime* and *avgdwelltimenonshort* play a crucial role. This is not surprising as our classifier uses dwell time as the proxy for ad quality.

Using LogReg, we saw that the functionality features have negative coefficients, suggesting that they affect negatively the post-click experience. These features relate to the existence of a form on the landing page, and as such are a strong deterrent to users. The forms when displayed on a mobile device may not be user-friendly, or users are simply not willing to share private information.

In Section 3, we showed that dwell time was a good proxy of an ad post-click experience. The LogReg solution showed very good performance in predicting high dwell time, i.e. dwell time being above a given threshold. Although SVM performed slightly better, LogReg supports quick update operations, which is important when deployed in production. We therefore decide to deploy such a model using only content-based features to allow full coverage of the ads in the database, and not just those for which we have historical data. We use 40 seconds as our threshold, as in our dataset it corresponds to the *median* of the overall dwell times distribution. We also choose to deploy the version predicting high dwell time as we wanted to serve ads on which users spend time. This means that not only they are of high quality but also have the potential of leading to a "conversion".

Rank	C	C-S	C-S-H
1.	[C] *clickToCall* (0.331)	[C] *clickToCall* (0.313)	[H] *avgdwelltime* (0.480)
2.	[C] *windowSize* (0.125)	[C] *summarizabilityScore* (0.109)	[H] *avgdwelltimenonshort* (0.314)
3.	[C] *numClickable* (0.113)	[C] *numConceptAnnotation* (0.086)	[H] *bouncerate* (0.059)
4.	[C] *numInputRadio* (0.089)	[C] *numInputRadio* (0.086)	[C] *clickToCall* (0.047)
5.	[C] *numDropdown* (0.084)	[C] *numDropdown* (0.077)	[C] *numClickable* (0.019)
6.	[C] *numImages* (0.064)	[C] *numClickable* (0.075)	[C] *numImages* (0.012)
7.	[C] *numInputCheckbox* (0.031)	[C] *numImages* (0.048)	[C] *summarizabilityScore* (0.011)
8.	[C] *imageHeight* (0.029)	[C] *windowSize* (0.036)	[C] *numInputRadio* (0.008)
9.	[C] *nounsSumOfScores* (0.026)	[C] *imageHeight* (0.029)	[C] *numDropdown* (0.008)
10.	[C] *numConceptAnnotation* (0.024)	[C] *nounsSumOfScores* (0.028)	[H] *ctr* (0.007)
11.	[C] *viewPort* (0.021)	[S] *similarityNoun* (0.023)	[C] *numConceptAnnotation* (0.006)
12.	[C] *media* (0.021)	[C] *numInputCheckbox* (0.023)	[H] *clicks* (0.006)
13.	[C] *tokenCount* (0.014)	[C] *viewPort* (0.016)	[H] *cpx* (0.004)
14.	[C] *numInputString* (0.011)	[C] *spaceball_score* (0.014)	[H] *impressions* (0.003)
15.	[C] *imageWidth* (0.010)	[C] *media* (0.012)	[C] *numInputCheckbox* (0.003)

Table 4: Top-15 ranked features using GBDT with three sets of features: C, C-S, and C-S-H.

5. ONLINE BUCKETING EVALUATION

To measure the impact that our ad quality prediction model has on users we conduct an *online* evaluation through A/B testing. We implement an ad ranking scorer on Yahoo *Gemini* based on the Logistic Regression (LogReg) prediction model, and assess its performance on the mobile news stream app running on iOS.

We split the incoming traffic into two *buckets*, i.e. *baseline* and *ad quality*. In the first bucket, ads are served using the existing ranking scheme, i.e. the expected cost per click, whereas in the second bucket ads are served according to the newly proposed ranking scorer that accounts for the ad post-click experience (i.e. the probability that users do not return to the stream within the next 40 seconds).

We measure the user post-click experience with dwell time and bounce rate. Specifically, we compute the *median* of the former to deal with the high variance of dwell times. For the bounce rate we report, instead, the *average* of the values. Bounce rate is already a normalised score in the $[0, 1]$ range and also exhibits small variance.

Experimental Setup. We consider two distinct datasets of ad clicks, randomly sampled from May to June 2014. The first dataset is drawn from the baseline bucket and contains only clicks on ads ranked by the baseline scorer. The second dataset is drawn from the ad quality bucket and contains all the clicks of ads served by the ad quality ranking scorer.

We conduct three analyses, at the *(ad-)click-level*, at the *ad-level*, and at the *user-level*. For all three, we evaluate the two buckets performance. First, we compare the performance accounting for all ads (users) as they appear in the two datasets; we refer to this experimental setting as All. Then, we measure the performance limited to only those ads (users) common to the two datasets; we call this Shared. Finally, we focus only on those ads (users) that appear in only one of the two datasets; we refer to this as Unique.

Click-level Analysis. We discuss how the daily click-through rate behaves on the two buckets. When assessing the effect of any change, e.g., in a ranking algorithm, it is important to do so over a long period of time, as an increased performance shortly after the change may not translate in the long run to better user experience [13].

We collect around 14,500 ads from the dataset relating to the baseline bucket, and about 12,500 ads from the ad quality bucket (All). More than 11,000 ads are shared between the two buckets (Shared), and therefore are very likely high quality ads. Looking at these two settings (All and Shared) we observe that the overall click-through rate (the whole month) increases by about 18% and 13% on the ad quality bucket. Figure 5 shows that for both settings, the click-through rate is always higher for the ad quality bucket. This means that the probability of a user clicking on an ad increases in the ad quality bucket. Interestingly, the two time series are perfectly correlated (Pearson's $r = 1.0$). The *paired t-test* applied to each pair of time series samples shows that the differences between the two samples, though correlated, are statistically significant (p-value $= 0.01$).

If we consider only the (high quality) ads shared between the two buckets the chance of clicking on an ad seems to depend on which bucket the ad is served. Intuitively, if a high quality ad is served together with other, lower quality ads (i.e. baseline bucket) then users may not perceive it as valuable as it is, and thus the probability of clicking on it decreases. However, if the *same* high quality ad is served with other high quality ads (i.e. ad quality bucket) the users may be more likely to click on it because they have been exposed to ads leading to positive experience. Therefore we conjecture that the perception of the ad quality is influenced by the ads to which a user has been "exposed" and by how those have been experienced (either positive or not), which is what Figure 5(b) suggests. This further confirms our results relating ad post-click experience and future ad clicks discussed in Section 3.

Ad-level Analysis. The second analysis shows how dwell time and bounce rate behave on the two buckets, from an "ad perspective". We first remove all the ad clicks with dwell time greater than 10 minutes (following from Section 3). Afterwards, we consider only those ads that received at least 10 clicks. This is done to avoid the effect of outliers and ensure that we have enough clicks to calculate bounce rates. Finally, a click is considered a bounce if its dwell time is less than or equal to 5 seconds. This resulted in around 1,000 ads in the baseline bucket and 700 in the ad quality bucket (All), with around 600 ads common to both buckets (Shared). We should note the ads used in this analysis form a subset of those used in the first click-level analysis.

The results for the All, Shared, and Unique datasets are reported in Table 5. Unique is the dataset comprised of ads that are only in one of the two buckets. Each cell of the table refers to the relative difference (in percentage) between

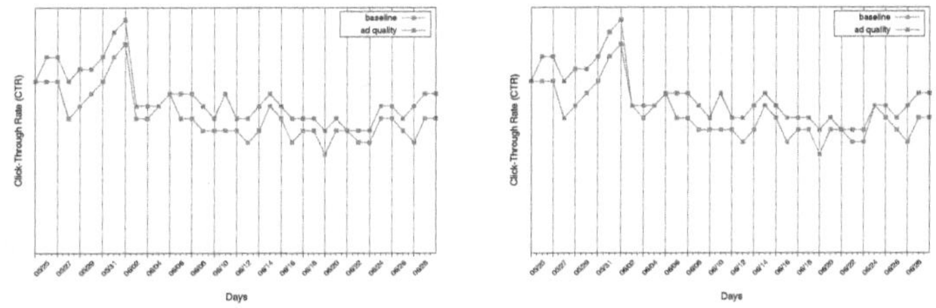

(a) All (b) Shared

Figure 5: Daily Click-Through Rate (CTR): *baseline* vs. *ad quality*.

	All	Shared	Unique
Dwell Time (*median*)	+30.0	+20.0	+35.7
Bounce Rate (*avg*)	-6.7	0.0	-25.0

Table 5: Differences (%) in Dwell Time and Bounce Rate between *ad quality* and *baseline* ads.

	All	Shared	Unique
Dwell Time (*median*)	+25.0	+20.0	+30.0
Bounce Rate (*avg*)	-12.0	-12.5	-12.0

Table 6: Differences (%) in Dwell Time and Bounce Rate between *ad quality* and *baseline* users.

the statistics as computed from the ad quality and baseline buckets, respectively. Note also that while a positive difference is desirable in the case of dwell time (i.e. showing the ad quality bucket exhibits more time spent on the ad landing page), for the bounce rate we aim at reducing the number of short clicks, and so we prefer a negative difference.

In all the experimental settings, the ad quality bucket outperforms the baseline bucket. This is particularly visible when considering Unique ads. Interestingly, when looking at the Shared ads, the median dwell time is still higher when the ads are served as part of the ad quality bucket, compared to the baseline bucket. In Figure 5(b), we can see that the click-through rate for the Shared ads is higher in the ad quality bucket. Therefore, not only serving high quality ads together (i.e. the ad quality bucket) attract more clicks, the post-click experience, as measured with dwell time, is also positively affected: *users engage more with the ads.*

Similarly, the average bounce rate is lower with the ad quality bucket, which implies a lower probability of bouncing back once users click on ads that have been deemed to be of high quality. Interestingly, for Shared ads, there is no difference in bounce rate. Bounce rate is more a reflection of an ad being annoying. This suggests that the property of "being annoying" is a characteristic of the ad itself (i.e. its landing page as experienced on average by users), and does not depend on which other ads are served during the session.

We compare the distribution of dwell time and bounce rate, as observed in the two buckets. We run a Kolmogorov-Smirnov test for two samples on each pair of observations to test if both samples might have been drawn from the same underlying probability distribution. For all cases except one, this is not the case with p-value lower than 0.01. The exception is with the bounce rate on the Shared setting. This however complies with the results in Table 5, where no difference exists between the two buckets for the average bounce rate for Shared, further confirming that "being an annoying" ad or being a *bad ad* comes from the ad "itself".

User-level Analysis. The aim of the last analysis is close to that of the previous one yet from a "user perspective". We remove all the ad clicks having dwell time larger than 10 minutes and a click is considered a bounce as long as its dwell time is at most 5 seconds. Furthermore, we take into account only those users who clicked on at least 2 unique ads. This results into around 16,000 users in the baseline bucket and 11,000 in the ad quality bucket, with about 2,700 individuals shared between the two buckets. Table 6 shows the relative differences (in percentage) of dwell time and bounce rate as computed from the two buckets.

The median dwell time is higher for the ad quality bucket, which means that when users are served ads deemed of high quality, they spend time on the ad landing page before returning to the stream. In particular, looking at the Shared setting (i.e. users appearing in both buckets), serving high quality ads indeed promotes a positive post-click experience. This is further accentuated when users experience only high quality ads (as seen with Unique).

Concerning the average bounce rate, this is computed as the average fraction of bounce clicks for each user. This is different from the actual definition of bounce rate, which instead is formulated at the ad-level. Still, we observe a decrease of the average bounce rate in the ad quality bucket. This relates to the fact that more high quality ads are served in the ad quality bucket, which leads to fewer users bouncing back after clicking on them. Finally, the difference between dwell time and bounce rate distributions is statistically significant (p-value $\ll 0.01$) using Kolmogorov-Smirnov test.

This section shows that returning high quality ads, as measured in terms of the ad post-click experience, is important. Not only this increases CTR, and as a likely consequence revenue in the long-term, it has a positive effect on users, as seen by the increase in dwell time and decrease in bounce rate. Interestingly, when users are served ads deemed of high quality together, their engagement with the ads, in terms of time spent on the ad site, is positively affected. In addition, so called *bad ads* are so because of themselves, and this independently of whether they are served or not with ads deemed of high quality.

6. CONCLUSIONS

We proposed a method to identify high quality ads served on one of Yahoo mobile stream platforms. In this paper, quality refers to the ad post-click experience. We therefore related the ad landing page to the ad post-click experience, which we measured through well known engagement metrics, dwell time and bounce rate. We first showed that these measures were appropriate proxies of ad quality in our context. We also showed that users clicking on ads that promote a positive post-click experience are more likely to click on ads in the future, and their long-term engagement is positively affected. We also compared these measures in the context of mobile versus desktop devices, and found that a positive ad post-click experience is not just about serving ads with mobile-optimised landing pages; other aspects of an landing page affect the post-click experience.

We then put forward an approach that analyses ad landing pages, and shows how these can affect dwell time and bounce rate. We experimented with three types of features, related to the actual content and organization of the ad landing page, the similarity between the creative and the landing page, and ad past performance. We saw that the later type of features were best at predicting dwell time and bounce rate; we also show that content and organization features perform well, and have the advantages to be applicable for all ads, not only for those that have been served. Overall, our offline evaluation showed that, using dwell time as a proxy of post-click experience, we could predict the quality of an ad with good accuracy.

Finally, we deployed our prediction model for ad quality based on dwell time on Yahoo *Gemini*, and validated its performance on the mobile news stream app running on iOS. This was conducted through A/B testing to measure the impact of our approach in a real-world scenario. Finally, dwell time and bounce rate exhibited statistically significant differences, when the ads served took into account their predicted dwell time, using the landing pages features, compared to when they did not. Dwell time increased by 30% whereas bounce rate decreased by 6.7%.

As future work, we plan to train our model on new features, such as readability, PageRank, sentimentality level of the landing pages. We are currently carrying out user studies to understand how users perceive the quality of the landing pages, and how this can be translated into additional features. Finally, we will be studying alternative metrics, for example combining dwell time and bounce rate, but also others, to fully capture the ad post-click experience.

7. ACKNOWLEDGEMENTS

We would like to thank John Agapiou and Andy Haines for their help in obtaining and polishing the data we used in our experiments and the feedbacks on our results.

8. REFERENCES

[1] J. Azimi, R. Zhang, Y. Zhou, V. Navalpakkam, J. Mao, and X. Fern. Visual appearance of display ads and its effect on click through rate. In *CIKM*, 2012.

[2] H. Becker, A. Broder, E. Gabrilovich, V. Josifovski, and B. Pang. Context transfer in search advertising. In *SIGIR*, 2009.

[3] H. Becker, A. Broder, E. Gabrilovich, V. Josifovski, and B. Pang. What happens after an ad click?: Quantifying the impact of landing pages in web advertising. In *CIKM*, 2009.

[4] K. E. Boudreau. Mobile advertising and its acceptance by american consumers. Bachelor thesis, 2013.

[5] A. Z. Broder, M. Fontoura, V. Josifovski, and L. Riedel. A semantic approach to contextual advertising. In *SIGIR*, 2007.

[6] Y. Choi, M. Fontoura, E. Gabrilovich, V. Josifovski, M. Mediano, and B. Pang. Using landing pages for sponsored search ad selection. In *WWW*, 2010.

[7] C. Cortes and V. Vapnik. Support-vector networks. *Machine Learning*, 1995.

[8] M. de Sa, V. Navalpakkam, and E. F. Churchill. Mobile advertising: evaluating the effects of animation, user and content relevance. In *CHI*, 2013.

[9] T. Foran. Native advertising strategies for mobile devices. `http://www.forbes.com/sites/ciocentral/2013/03/14/native-advertising-strategies-for-mobile-devices/`, 2013.

[10] J. H. Friedman. Stochastic gradient boosting. *Computational Statistics and Data Analysis*, 2002.

[11] A. Kae, K. Kan, V. K. Narayanan, and D. Yankov. Categorization of display ads using image and landing page features. In *LDMTA*, 2011.

[12] Y. Kim, A. Hassan, R. W. White, and I. Zitouni. Modeling dwell time to predict click-level satisfaction. In *WSDM*, 2014.

[13] R. Kohavi, A. Deng, B. Frasca, R. Longbotham, T. Walker, and Y. Xu. Trustworthy online controlled experiments: Five puzzling outcomes explained. In *Proceedings of the 18th ACM SIGKDD international conference on Knowledge discovery and data mining*, pages 786–794. ACM, 2012.

[14] J.-H. Lee, J. Ha, J.-Y. Jung, and S. Lee. Semantic contextual advertising based on the open directory project. *ACM TWEB*, 2013.

[15] M. Levene. *An Introduction to Search Engines and Web Navigation.* Addison Wesley Publishing Company, 2005.

[16] H. Liu, W.-C. Kim, and D. Lee. Characterizing landing pages in sponsored search. In *LA-WEB*, 2012.

[17] B. W. Matthews. Comparison of the predicted and observed secondary structure of t4 phage lysozyme. *Biochimica et Biophysical Acta*, 1975.

[18] V. Murdock, M. Ciaramita, and V. Plachouras. A noisy-channel approach to contextual advertising. In *ADKDD*, 2007.

[19] R. J. Oentaryo, E.-P. Lim, J.-W. Low, D. Lo, and M. Finegold. Predicting response in mobile advertising with hierarchical importance-aware factorization machine. In *WSDM*, 2014.

[20] A. Penev and R. K. Wong. Framework for timely and accurate ads on mobile devices. In *CIKM*, 2009.

[21] L. Ritzel, C. V. der Schaar, and S. Goodman. *Native Advertising Mobil.* GRIN Verlag GmbH, 2013.

[22] R. Rosales, H. Cheng, and E. Manavoglu. Post-click conversion modeling and analysis for non-guaranteed delivery display advertising. In *WSDM*, 2012.

[23] D. Sculley, R. G. Malkin, S. Basu, and R. J. Bayardo. Predicting bounce rates in sponsored search advertisements. In *KDD*, 2009.

[24] E. Sodomka, S. Lahaie, and D. Hillard. A predictive model for advertiser value-per-click in sponsored search. In *WWW*, 2013.

[25] Y. Song, H. Ma, H. Wang, and K. Wang. Exploring and exploiting user search behavior on mobile and tablet devices to improve search relevance. In *WWW*, 2013.

[26] X. Yi, L. Hong, E. Zhong, N. Liu, and S. Rajan. Beyond clicks: Dwell time for personalization. In *RecSys*, 2014.

[27] P. Yin, P. Luo, W.-C. Lee, and M. Wang. Silence is also evidence: interpreting dwell time for recommendation from psychological perspective. In *KDD*, 2013.

[28] H.-F. Yu, F.-L. Huang, and C.-J. Lin. Dual coordinate descent methods for logistic regression and maximum entropy models. *Machine Learning*, 2011.

Generic and Scalable Framework for Automated Time-series Anomaly Detection

Nikolay Laptev
Yahoo Labs
Sunnyvale, CA, USA
nlaptev@yahoo-inc.com

Saeed Amizadeh
Yahoo Labs
Sunnyvale, CA, USA
amizadeh@yahoo-inc.com

Ian Flint
Yahoo
Sunnyvale, CA, USA
ianflint@yahoo-inc.com

ABSTRACT

This paper introduces a generic and scalable framework for automated anomaly detection on large scale time-series data. Early detection of anomalies plays a key role in maintaining consistency of person's data and protects corporations against malicious attackers. Current state of the art anomaly detection approaches suffer from scalability, use-case restrictions, difficulty of use and a large number of false positives. Our system at Yahoo, EGADS, uses a collection of anomaly detection and forecasting models with an anomaly filtering layer for accurate and scalable anomaly detection on time-series. We compare our approach against other anomaly detection systems on real and synthetic data with varying time-series characteristics. We found that our framework allows for 50-60% improvement in precision and recall for a variety of use-cases. Both the data and the framework are being open-sourced. The open-sourcing of the data, in particular, represents the first of its kind effort to establish the standard benchmark for anomaly detection.

1. INTRODUCTION

While rapid advances in computing hardware and software have led to powerful applications, still hundreds of software bugs and hardware failures continue to happen in a large cluster compromising user experience and subsequently revenue. Non-stop systems have a strict uptime requirement and continuous monitoring of these systems is critical. From the data analysis point of view, this means non-stop monitoring of large volume of time-series data in order to detect potential faults or anomalies. Due to the large scale of the problem, human monitoring of this data is practically infeasible which leads us to automated anomaly detection using Machine Learning and Data Mining techniques.

An anomaly, or an outlier, is a data point which is significantly different from the rest of the data. Generally, the data in most applications is created by one or more generating processes that reflect the functionality of a system. When the underlying generating process behaves in an unusual way, it creates outliers. Fast and efficient identification of these outliers is useful for many applications including: intrusion detection, credit card fraud, sensor events, medical diagnoses, law enforcement and others [1].

KDD'15, August 10-13, 2015, Sydney, NSW, Australia.
© 2015 ACM. ISBN 978-1-4503-3664-2/15/08 ...$15.00.
DOI: http://dx.doi.org/10.1145/2783258.2788611.

Current approaches in automated anomaly detection suffer from a large number of false positives which prohibit the usefulness of these systems in practice. Use-case, or category specific, anomaly detection models [4] may enjoy a low false positive rate for a specific application, but when the characteristics of the time-series change, these techniques perform poorly without proper retraining. Section 6.3 demonstrates the shortcoming of 'one size fits all' principle in practice.

Our system at Yahoo is called EGADS (Extensible Generic Anomaly Detection System) and it enables the accurate and scalable detection of time-series anomalies. EGADS separates forecasting, anomaly detection and alerting into three separate components which allows the person to add her own models into any of the components. Note that this paper focuses on the latter two components.

EGADS uses a set of default models that are tuned to reduce the number of false positives, which by itself suffices for the average user. More advanced use-cases, however, will require the system to capture some types of anomalies while ignoring others. The anomalies of interest may vary in magnitude, severity or other parameters which are unknown apriori and depend on the use-case. For this reason the alerting component of EGADS uses machine learning to select the most relevant anomalies for the consumer.

To the best of our knowledge EGADS is the first comprehensive system for anomaly detection that is flexible, accurate, scalable and extensible. EGADS is being open-sourced [19] along with the anomaly detection benchmarking data [18]. The open-sourcing of the data and the system will provide the first of its kind benchmarking data and the framework to help the academics and the industry collaborate and develop novel anomaly detection models. At Yahoo, EGADS is used on millions of time-series by many teams daily.

In Section 2 we describe the EGADS architecture. The algorithms and the alerting module are described in Sections 3 and 4 respectively. Previous work is described in Section 5. Experiments are discussed in Section 6 followed by the real-world use-cases and conclusion in Sections 7 and 8 respectively.

2. ARCHITECTURE

The EGADS framework consists of three main components: the time-series modeling module (TMM), the anomaly detection module (ADM) and the alerting module (AM).

Given a time-series the TMM component models the time-series producing an expected value later consumed by the ADM and AM components that, respectively, compute the error and filter uninteresting anomalies. These components are described in detail in Sections 3 and 4.

EGADS was built as a framework to be easily integrated into an existing monitoring infrastructure. At Yahoo, our internal Yahoo Monitoring Service (YMS) processes millions of data-points every second. Therefore, having a scalable, accurate and automated anomaly detection for YMS is critical. We describe the integration details into YMS next.

2.1 System Integration

EGADS operates as a stand-alone platform that can be used as a library in larger systems. Therefore, designing an interface between EGADS and an internal Yahoo monitoring service (YMS) is critical. A key constraint of YMS is scale; the platform needs to evaluate millions of data points per second. As a result, many of the integration architecture decisions are focused on optimizing real-time processing. The integration with YMS is shown in Figure 1.

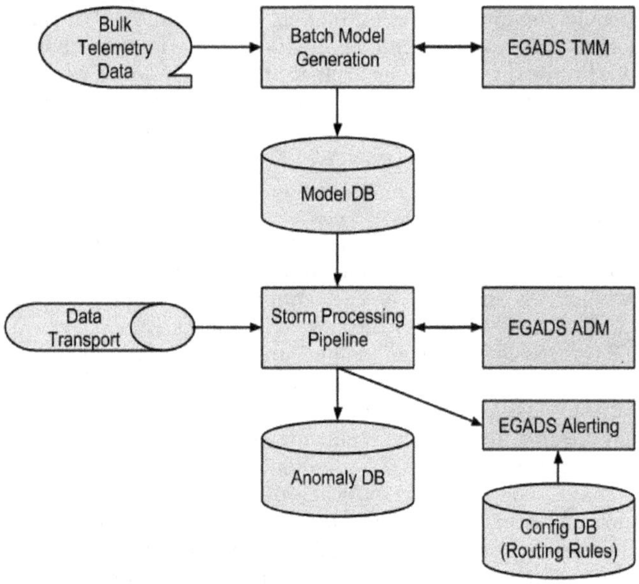

Figure 1: EGADS-YMS Architecture

Several support components are required to drive action based on detected anomalies. First of all, all anomaly detection models are generated in batch and applied in real time. The batch flow is comprised of three steps:

1. Telemetry (i.e. the monitored time-series) data are stored in bulk on a Hadoop cluster.
2. A batch model generator runs against these data and builds models for targeted time-series.
3. The models are stored in a model database.

The online flow then utilizes the stored models.

1. Data flows into a Storm [25] stream-processing topology.
2. One of the bolts (modules) in the topology calls the EGADS ADM to evaluate incoming data points based on models stored in the model database.
3. If an anomaly is present, this is fed to a secondary rule flow, consisting of combinatorial rules and other use-case specific logic (see Section 4).
4. Based on the rules, if the anomaly is an alert event, the event is generated, stored in a status database, and forwarded to an alert routing system.
5. The alert routing system applies routing configuration rules to send the alert to the appropriate support staff.

2.2 Scalability

The monitoring use case for EGADS requires the evaluation of millions of data-points per second, across over one hundred million time-series. This has scalability implications in terms of CPU load, I/O, and memory footprint. The evaluation of a datapoint needs to be as efficient as possible. This means that as much of the model as possible should be precomputed. It is not practical to read a model from disk each time a datapoint arrives because of the rate of inbound traffic. This suggests that the models should be stored in memory. In order to contain costs, the models should be as small as possible.

One optimization is to share models across multiple similar time-series. This is practical in the context of a large web serving environment, since applications are broken into horizontal tiers of similar servers. This optimization will reduce the memory footprint, the batch workload, and I/O against the model database.

Another possible optimization is to investigate self-tuning models; models that update themselves based on a stream of inbound data via online learning rather than requiring periodic batch generation. Models of this type may need to be initialized in batch, but overall they will reduce the batch workload. Depending on implementation, however, they may increase writes against the model database since they are being constantly refined.

Yet another optimization involves a trade-off between model size, training speed and accuracy. Depending on the characteristics of the time-series a light and fast forecasting model can provide similar accuracy as a more sophisticated one. We evaluate some of these optimization approaches in Section 6.2.2.

3. ANOMALY DETECTION ALGORITHMS

In this section, we give a big picture overview of the anomaly detection algorithms supported by EGADS. Currently, EGADS is capable of detecting three classes of anomalies:

(a) **Outliers:** given an input time-series x, an outlier is a timestamp-value pair $\langle t, x_t \rangle$ where the observed value x_t is *significantly* different from the expected value of the time-series at that time, i.e. $\mathbb{E}(x_t)$.

(b) **Change points:** given an input time-series x, a change point is a timestamp t such that the behavior of the time-series is *significantly* different before and after t.

(c) **Anomalous time-series:** given a set of time-series $X = \{x^{(i)}\}$, an anomalous time-series $x^{(j)} \in X$ is a time-series whose behavior is *significantly* different from the majority of the time-series in X.

In the following sections, we give the general sketch of the methods that are currently used in EGADS for detecting the aforementioned anomaly types.

3.1 Outlier Detection

Detecting outliers is the most important functionality in many monitoring applications. For this reason the main focus of this paper is on outlier detection and unless it is explicitly specified, by anomalies, we refer to outliers by default.

EGADS offers two classes of algorithms for detecting outliers, which are described in this section.

3.1.1 Plug-in methods

The first class of methods for time-series outlier detection in EGADS are called *plug-in* methods. These methods *explicitly* model the normal behavior of the time-series such that a significant deviation from this model is considered an outlier. To model the normal behavior of the input time-series we can plug-in a wide range of time-series modeling and forecasting models (e.g. ARIMA [30], Exponential Smoothing [11], Kalman Filter [9], State Space Models [6], etc.) depending on the application and the nature of time-series. That is why we refer to this general strategy as the plug-in methods. It should be noted that all these models are used in EGADS for time-series forecasting which is another feature of our framework; however, since the focus of this paper is on anomaly detection, we do not give more details on modeling and forecasting features of EGADS.

Our proposed Plug-in framework consists of two main components: the time-series modeling module (TMM) and the anomaly detection module (ADM). Given a time-series $X = \{x_t \in \mathbb{R} : \forall t \geq 0\}$, the TMM provides the predicted value of x_t at time t, denoted by u_t. We also refer to this quantity as the expected value of x_t (not to be confused with the mathematical notion of expectation). The TMM can be a machine learned model which makes predictions based on some training data or a rule-based system which encodes expert's knowledge about how x_t behaves at time t. In this paper, we *do not* make any assumption regarding the TMM; that is, the TMM is just a black box module in our proposed method that generates predictions u_t. In this sense, our proposed framework is *generic* and does not depend on any specific time-series modeling framework.

Given the predicted value u_t and the actual observed value x_t, the ADM computes some notion of deviation which we refer to as the deviation metric (DM). The simplest measure of deviation is the prediction error, $PE_t = x_t - u_t$. If the error falls outside some fixed thresholds, an alert is issued. This simple method may work in some cases, but it will not be a good strategy for most because it does not capture the relative error. The *relative error*, RE_t is defined as a factor of u_t:

$$RE_t = \frac{x_t - u_t}{u_t} = \frac{x_t}{u_t} - 1 \qquad (1)$$

By thresholding the relative error, one can detect anomalies while normalizing out the dependence on the magnitude of the expected value. The values of these thresholds, indeed, determine how sensitive the anomaly detection module is. Various thresholding techniques are described in Section 4. Despite its common usage and effectiveness, however, there is no reason to believe the relative error is always the optimal metric for anomaly detection on a given time-series. In fact, the choice of the optimal metric for a given time-series highly depends on the nature of the time-series as well as the TMM performance. For instance, if we are dealing with a very regular time-series for which we have an accurate model, using the prediction error for anomaly detection might be sufficient as it is expected to be Normally distributed. In other cases, the optimal metric might be something between the prediction error and the relative error. For this reason, EGADS tracks a set of deviation metrics by default and the person using the system can create her own error metrics. These error metrics, together with other features, such as the time series characteristics, are used in the alerting module (AM), described in Section 4, to learn consumer's preferences and filter unimportant anomalies.

3.1.2 Decomposition-based methods

The second class of outlier detection methods in EGADS is based on the idea of time-series decomposition. In particular, in the time-series analysis literature, it is a common practice to decompose a time-series into three components: *trend*, *seasonality* and *noise*. By monitoring the noise component, one can capture the outliers. More precisely, if the absolute value of the noise component of point x_t is greater than a certain threshold, one can announce x_t as an outlier.

The decomposition of time-series can be done both in the time-domain via smoothing or in the frequency-domain via spectral decomposition. STL (Seasonal-Trend Decomposition based on Loess) [5] is a famous technique that uses Loess smoothing for decomposition. The frequency-domain methods can be further divided into parameteric and non-parametric methods. For the parametric methods, the basis used for spectral decomposition has a known parametric form (such as Fourier transform [2] or wavelet transform [22]) whereas, for non-parametric methods, the basis is data-driven [21].

3.2 Change Point Detection

Change points are those points in time where the behavior of the time-series starts to deviate from what is expected. The big difference between change points and outliers is that change points correspond to more sustained, long-term changes compared to volatile outliers. A common strategy for detecting change points in the literature is to move two side-by-side windows on the time-series and compute the difference between the behavior of the time-series in the two windows as a measure of the deviation metric [12, 31, 20, 23]. The behavior of the time-series in each window is typically modeled by the distribution of the values, motifs, frequencies, etc. that are present in the time-series. We refer to these techniques as the *absolute* techniques because they do not make explicit assumptions regarding the expected behavior of the time-series.

In EGADS, currently we have taken a different approach which we refer to as the *relative* or *model-based* methods. In these methods, the expected behavior of the time-series is explicitly modeled through one of the modeling techniques mentioned in Section 3.1.1. In particular, we incorporate the plug-in approach described in Section 3.1.1 to compute the sequence of *residuals* (or deviations from the model expectation) for an input time-series. Then we apply the absolute change point detection methods on the series of residuals to detect a change in the distribution of the residuals. We have used Kernel Density Estimation [7] to non-parametrically estimate the distribution of the residuals and the Kullback-Leibler divergence [16] to measure the change in the distribution.

We believe the model-based change point detection methods are more useful than the absolute methods in the practical applications. This is because the change points are meaningful as much as our models cannot explain the behavior of the time-series after a certain time point. However, if the model can explain the time-series behavior even after an absolute change point, from the practical point of view, there is no reason for us to consider that time point as a change point. In other words, the change points are relative to the underlying model used to explain the behavior of the time-series, which in turn gives rise to the relative change-point detection techniques.

3.3 Detecting Anomalous Time-series

Another class of anomaly detection techniques supported by EGADS involves detecting anomalous time-series. An anomalous time-series T is defined as a time-series whose average deviation from the other time-series is significant. Assuming all time-series are homogeneous and come from the same source (i.e. are part of the same cluster) one can simply compute the average deviation for time-series (i) relative to other time-series. In EGADS our current approach involves clustering the time-series into a set of clusters C based on various time-series features including trend & seasonality, spectral entropy, autocorrelation, average Euclidean distance etc. After clustering we perform intra or inter-cluster time-series anomaly detection by measuring the deviation within or among the cluster centroids and the time-series (i). A common use-case for this EGADS anomaly detection type involves triaging. For example if a network engineer wants to find an anomalous server amongst millions of time-series, it can be impractical with the previous approaches because the modeling is done on the *per* time-series basis without taking into account the behavior of other metrics. Another application of this anomaly detection type is in finding similar anomalies, which is the inverse of the previous use-case.

4. ALERTING

The end-goal of anomaly detection is to produce accurate and timely alerts. EGADS achieves this via a two stage process by first generating a set of candidate anomalies by *threshold selection* and then *filtering* the irrelevant anomalies for a given use-case.

4.1 Threshold Selection

The job of threshold selection is to select appropriate thresholds on the deviation metrics produced by the anomaly detection module (ADM). Currently EGADS implements two algorithms for threshold selection based on (a) $K\sigma$ deviation and (b) density distribution.

The first approach is parametric and assumes that the data is normally distributed with a well-defined mean and standard deviation. Relying on the Gaussian distribution we can apply a well known statistical tool called the 'three-sigma rule' which states that 99.73% of all samples lie within three standard deviations of the mean. Therefore, depending on the value of K in $K\sigma$, one can be confident as to the probability of observing a sample at time t. Depending on the desired level of sensitivity, one can measure if a given sample lies within the 95.45% or 68.27% of all the samples for $K = 2$ or 1 respectively. Note that the assumption here was that our deviation metrics are normally distributed.

Time-series feature	Description
Periodicity (frequency)	Periodicity is very important for determining the seasonality.
Trend	Exists if there is a long-term change in the mean level
Seasonality	Exists when a time series is influenced by seasonal factors, such as month of the year or day of the week
Auto-correlation	Represents long-range dependence.
Non-linearity	A non-linear time-series contains complex dynamics that are usually not represented by linear models.
Skewness	Measures symmetry, or more precisely, the lack of symmetry.
Kurtosis	Measures if the data are peaked or flat, relative to a normal distribution.
Hurst	A measure of long-term memory of time series.
Lyapunov Exponent	A measure of the rate of divergence of nearby trajectories.

Table 1: Time-series features used by EGADS

The second approach is non-parametric and is useful for the cases when the deviation metric is not normally distributed. The basic idea is to to find low density regions of the deviation metric distribution. One approach is to use an algorithm such as Local Outlier Factor (LOF) [3] which is based on a concept of a local density, where locality is given by nearest neighbors, whose distance is used to estimate the density. By comparing the local density of an object to the local densities of its neighbors, one can identify regions of similar density, and points that have a substantially lower density than their neighbors. These are considered to be outliers.

4.2 Filtering

Filtering performs the last stage post-processing on the anomalies which are then delivered to the consumer. While the candidate anomalies, which are the input to the filtering stage, are statistically significant, not all of them will be relevant for a particular use-case. For example some consumers are interested in spikes in the time-series, while others are interested in dips, yet others are interested in change points. EGADS provides a simple and intuitive interface which allows users to mark the regions of the time-series that are anomalous. This feedback is then used by EGADS together with time-series and model features to train a classifier that predicts if an anomaly a_i is relevant to user u_j. The time-series features tracked by EGADS are shown in Table 1 and are described in more detail in [29]. Section 6.4 explores the performance of a filtering module for a specific use-case. Like other components of EGADS, the filtering component is extensible in terms of models and features.

Figure 2 shows the feature profile of a sample time-series. Note that the metrics beginning with *dc* are obtained on the adjusted time-series (i.e. after removing trend and seasonality). In Section 6.2 we look at how these time-series characteristics impact the model performance.

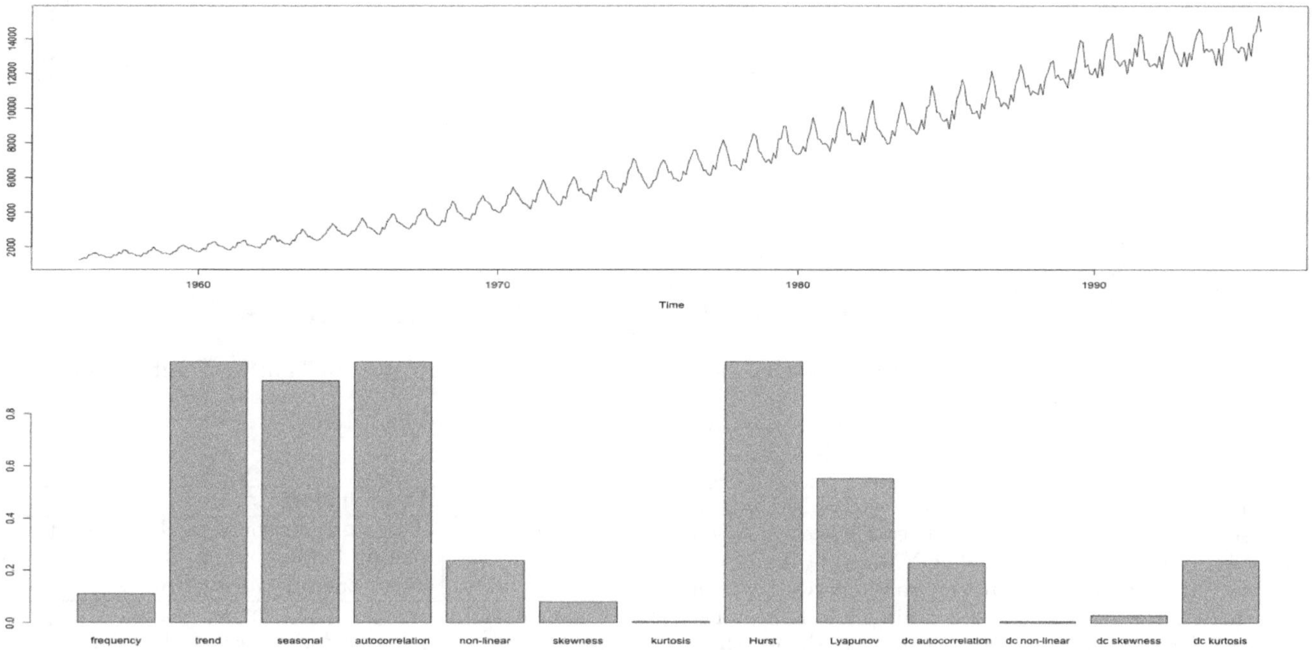

Figure 2: An example of the time-series and its characteristics extracted by EGADS. These characteristics are used by EGADS for filtering and model selection.

5. RELATED WORK

There are a number of anomaly detection techniques in the literature. The techniques range from point anomaly detection algorithms to change-point detection algorithms. In [24] authors propose an outlier detection technique based on hypothesis testing, which is very accurate at detecting extreme outliers. In fact Twitter, [26], uses [24] in conjunction with piecewise approximation of the underlying long-term trends to remove many of the false positives. Twitter's approach is fast and enjoys an impressive precision and recall, however it is specific to the use-case of Twitter. There are also a number of open-source point anomaly detection techniques available including [27, 15].

Authors in [13] provide an anomaly detection technique that finds 'Change Points' or 'Level Shifts'. Change Points (CP) are different form point anomalies or point outliers in that CP reflect a change in underlying statistic of the time-series (e.g., Mean shift). CP typically occurs in a time-series with a launch of a new product feature or a new platform. There are a number of open-source change point detection algorithms available including [14].

In our experience, a particular anomaly detection algorithm is usually applicable to only a specific use-case. As authors in [1] mention the anomalies will have typically a high anomaly score, but the high score alone is not a distinguishing factor for an anomaly. Rather, it is the analyst, who regulates the distinction between noise and anomaly. Similarly, authors in [4] provide a concise overview of the anomaly detection technique per category, citing the fact that only a set of anomaly models are most appropriate for a given anomaly category of interest. Therefore, based on the observation that 'One Size Fits All' is a myth in the anomaly detection world, EGADS uses a strategy where a collection of well trained anomaly detection models with a post-processing use-case-specific anomaly filtering stage is used. Nevertheless, EGADS is not the only generic anomaly detection framework out there. Venkataraman et. al [28] proposed a 'Black Box Anomaly Detection' framework that can be applied to a variety of data sources. Although the proposed framework is generic, it is not fully automated because it still needs a significant degree of user involvement in setting the appropriate models and metrics for a given application. Besides, this framework assumes the input training data to the system is anomaly-free, which is an unrealistic assumption in many real-world use-cases. On the other hand, Lan et. al. [17] proposed a framework for anomaly detection in large-scale systems which is automated but not generic enough to be applied to a general time-series anomaly detection problem. EGADS, however, provides flexible and effective mechanisms which make it both generic, automated and scalable. Furthermore, from the industrial point of view, EGADS has been incorporated in large-scale monitoring systems across Yahoo.

6. EXPERIMENTAL STUDY

We present the experiments for the modeling, anomaly detection and alerting components of EGADS next.

6.1 Data

The dataset used for the experiments is comprised of a mixture (50/50) of synthetic and real data. We have created a synthetic time-series generation tool that is being open-sourced along with the framework [19] and the benchmarking data [18]. Using the tool, each synthetic time-series is generated by specifying the length, magnitude, number of anomalies, anomaly type, anomaly magnitude, noise level,

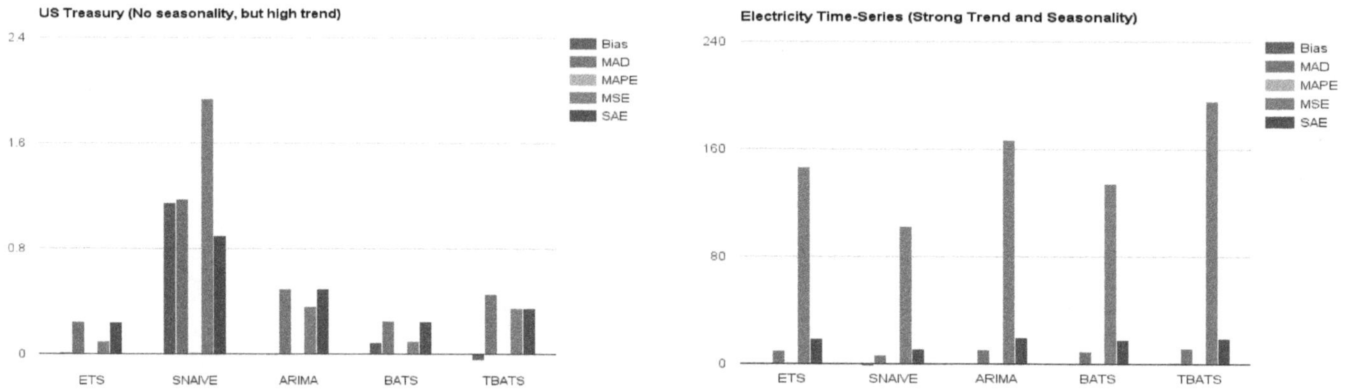

(a) Model performance on TimeSeries with trend.

(b) Model performance on TimeSeries with seasonality.

Figure 3: Model performance on time-series with varying characteristics.

trend and seasonality. These parameters are picked from a fixed distribution. The real dataset is comprised of Yahoo Membership Login (YML) data. The YML data tracks the aggregate status of user logins to the Yahoo network. Both the synthetic and real time-series contain 1400 data-points each, which for the YML data represent 3 months worth of data-points. Unless otherwise stated, all experiments were run on 1000 randomly picked time-series and the results were averaged. Also note that both the synthetic and real-time data have anomaly labels, that are either synthetically or editorially generated, allowing us to measure precision and recall.

6.2 Modeling Experiments

Time-series modeling (captured by the TMM component in EGADS) is a fundamental part of anomaly detection. It is often the case that the anomaly detection is as good as the underlying time-series model. Due to a large number of candidate models, model-selection becomes critical and depends upon time-series characteristics and available resources. In the experiments that follow, we demonstrate the impact of time-series features on the model performance and show the trade-off between accuracy, memory usage and training time. The models and the error metrics used in the experiments are described in Tables 2 and 3 respectively. More details about the models and the metrics can be found in [10] and [29].

6.2.1 *Time-series Characteristics and Model Performance*

To demonstrate the impact of time-series features on model performance we compare the error metrics of different models when fitting time-series with different features (see Section 4.2). Figure 3 shows that time-series characteristics play an important role in model behavior. For example the *Seasonal Naive Model*, performs poorly on a dataset with no seasonality and a strong trend. EGADS keeps track of the historic time-series characteristics and model performance. Using this historical information, EGADS selects the best model (given the time-series features) judged by the error metrics described in Table 3. In practice, performing model selection based on the data features is much faster than performing cross-validation for every model.

Model	Description
Olympic Model (Seasonal Naive)	The naive seasonal model where the prediction for next point is a smoothed average over previous n periods.
Exponential Smoothing Model	A popular model used to produce smoothed time-series. Double and Triple exponential smoothing variants add trend and seasonality into the model. The ETS model used for the experiments automatically picks the best 'fit' exponential smoothing model.
Moving Average Model	In this mode, the forecast is based on an artificially constructed time series in which the value for a given time period is replaced by the mean of that value and the values for some number of preceding and succeeding time periods. The Weighted Moving Average and Naive Forecasting Model are special cases of the moving average model.
Regression Models	Models the relationship between x & y using one or more variable.
ARIMA	Autoregressive integrated moving average.
(T)BATS Family	(Trigonometric) Exponential smoothing state space model with Box-Cox transformation.
Spectral Kalman Filter	An in-house algorithm that implements a fast multi-variate spectral learning method for learning Kalman Filter parameters.

Table 2: Models Used for Modeling Experiments

6.2.2 *Time-series Model Scalability*

As discussed in Section 2 it is often prohibitive to build models for every time-series and optimization techniques are required to support real-time performance over massive (e.g., millions of points every second) data-streams. A fundamental optimization performs a trade-off between model size, training time and accuracy. Such a trade-off is shown in Figures 4(a) and 4(b). From the figure, for example, it is clear that the Seasonal Naive model is quick to train but has a relatively large memory requirement and a high average error. At Yahoo, a target in terms of resources and training

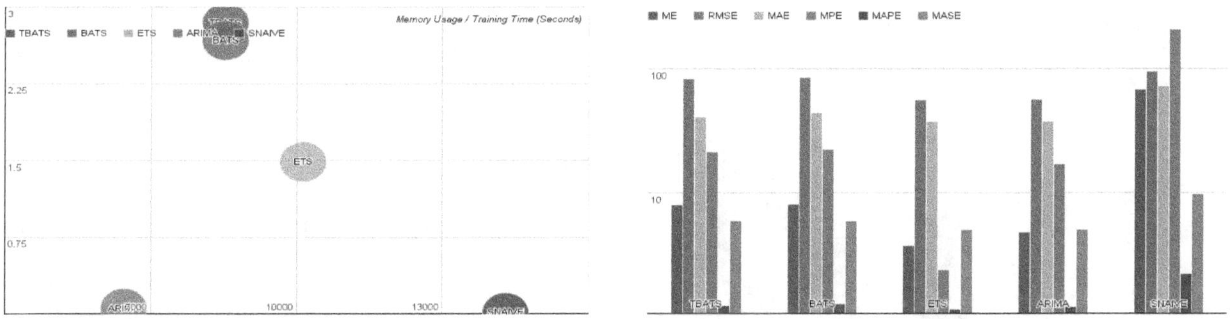

(a) Model Tradeoff: Model Size vs Training Time

(b) Model Accuracy

Figure 4: Model trade-offs

Model	Description
Bias	The arithmetic mean of the errors.
MAD	The mean absolute deviation. Also known as MAE.
MAPE	The mean absolute percentage error.
MSE	The mean square of the errors.
SAE	The Sum of Absolute Errors.
ME	Mean Error.
MASE	Mean absolute scaled error.
MPE	Mean percentage error.

Table 3: Metrics Used for Modeling Experiments

Model	Description
EGADS ExtremeLow-DensityModel Outlier	EGADS density-based anomaly detection.
EGADS CP	EGADS kernel-based change-point detection.
EGADS KSig-maModel Outlier	EGADS re-implementation of the classic k-sigma model.
Twitter Outlier	The Open-Source Twitter-R anomaly detection library based on the Generalized ESD method.
ExtremeI & II R Outlier	Open source univariate outlier detection that threshold the absolute value and the residual to detect anomalies.
BreakOut Twitter CP	A package from Twitter that uses an ESD statistics test to detect change points.
ChangePt1 R CP	An R library that implements various mainstream and specialized change-point methods for finding single and multiple change-points within data. Method I uses a change in variance.
ChangePt2 & 3 R CP	Detects a change in the mean and the variance.

Table 4: Open Source systems used for evaluation

time is first set and then the models are picked accordingly. In other words, the objective is to minimize the errors in Table 3 subject to the resource and model building time constrains. Other optimization techniques including time-series sampling and model sharing are being investigated.

6.3 Anomaly Detection Experiments

In this section we compare open source system against EGADS. The open source systems considered are shown in Table 4. The results on the data described in Section 6.1 are shown in Figure 5. The results are compared in terms of the standard $F_1\text{-}Score = 2 \times \frac{precision \times recall}{precision + recall}$. The results indicate that there is no best anomaly detection model for all use-cases. In particular different algorithms are best at detection different types of anomalies. For example Twitter [13] performs best on the time-series labeled *TS-2* while ExtremeLowDensity model is best on *TS-3*. These datasets contain a mixture of anomaly types (e.g., outliers, change-points), and one might argue that comparing an algorithm that is only meant for change-point detection is not fair. Recall, however, that the motivation for EGADS was that the user should be agnostic to the type of time-series and the type of anomalies that are in the data. The system must be able to gracefully and robustly deal with a wide variety of anomalies present in the data. For this reason, EGADS is built as a library that combines a set of anomaly detection models into a single framework. The anomalies from these models are forwarded to the filtering component for accurate anomaly detection.

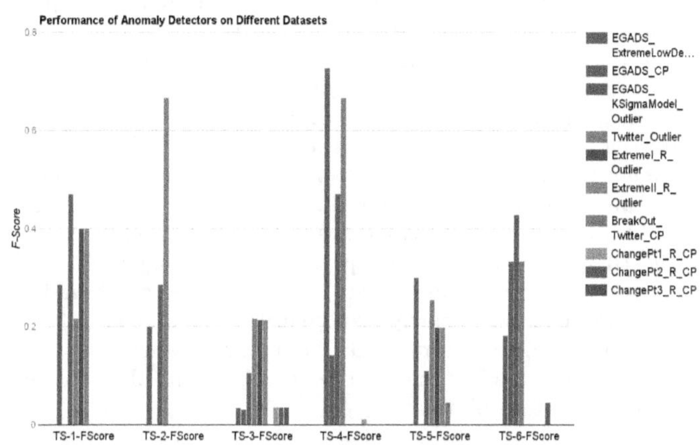

Figure 5: Anomaly model performance on different datasets. Observe that there is no single model that is best on all datasets.

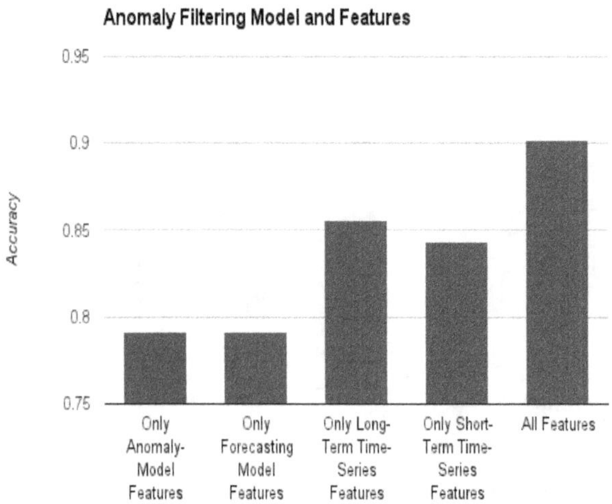

Figure 6: Accuracy of the filtering stage using different types of features.

6.4 Anomaly Filtering Experiments

The importance of an anomaly often depends on the use-case. Specifically, some users may be interested in the time-series behavior that exhibits a malicious attack, while others may be interested in revenue drops. Yahoo Membership (YM) use-case refers to the former set of users. Specifically for the YM use-case, editors supplied feedback to EGADS of instances that exhibited abnormal spikes and level shifts. *Abnormal* in the case of YM meant *seasonal* followed by *non-seasonal* behavior which characterizes most of the attacks. Also the YM editors did not care about *traffic-shift* behavior, where a large drop in traffic was observed in a time-series due to router table being updated.

To address this requirement the filtering stage scanned all anomalies a_i from all models and using a model classified if a_i was a true positive. The model used in the filtering stage for the YM use-case is a boosted tree model based on AdaBoost [8]. The features used in the model are described in Table 1. The core principle of AdaBoost is to fit a sequence of weak learners (e.g., small decision trees) on repeatedly modified version of the data. The final result is then produced via a combined weighted majority vote. On each iteration, the examples that are difficult to predict receive a higher importance in the next iteration and therefore each subsequent weak learner focuses on the examples that are missed by the previous learners in the sequence. Besides the time-series features described in Table 1 we use the model features described in Section 6.2. The experiments in Figure 6 indicate an impressive precision/recall even with just the time-series features compared to just using the model alone without the filtering stage. This experiment underlines an important principle and a critical component of any anomaly detection framework: an anomaly is use-case specific and must be learned automatically for a fully scalable and automated solution.

7. PRACTICAL USE-CASES AT YAHOO

A major use case for anomaly detection at Yahoo is the monitoring of system and business metrics in order to detect infrastructure and product issues. Yahoo currently tracks over one hundred million distinct timeseries emitted by its production systems. In monitoring these timeseries, three broad use categories emerge; system metrics, business KPIs, and groups of like metrics.

7.1 System Metrics

System metrics are broadly defined as measurements of the health of a hardware component in a serving system. Examples include CPU utilization, free disk space, network interface traffic stats, and memory utilization. Some of these metrics, such as CPU utilization, track the overall traffic to a component, and some, like free disk space, are independent of the current traffic levels. What sets system metrics apart from other types of metrics is that due to the redundant nature of Yahoo's serving system, a threshold violation is typically a leading indicator of serving problems. Because of this, alerting against these types of metrics is often not treated as an outage, but instead used to trigger longer term remediations such as adding capacity or clearing disk space.

7.2 Business KPIs

Business KPIs are metrics that directly reflect customers' experiences with Yahoo sites. Examples include things such as page views, serving latency, serving errors, click-through rate, and revenue received. Business KPIs are almost always trailing indicators of site issues, and by definition reflect impact to Yahoo's ability to serve. As a result, anomalies in business KPIs are normally treated with a high degree of urgency. The nature of business KPIs at large scale is that they tend to be highly predictable, so they lend themselves well to automated anomaly detection. Yahoo has had tremendous success in instrumenting business KPIs to discover serving and revenue issues using automated anomaly detection.

7.3 Groups of similar metrics

Most of Yahoo's infrastructure follows a horizontal scaling model, with dozens to hundreds of individual servers making up each serving tier. When triaging and isolating the cause of a suspected incident, it can be difficult to survey an infrastructure of thousands of machines to find the fault. Automated anomaly detection can be used to rank the relative anomalousness, or "interestingness", of each component of the infrastructure, and these characteristics can be ranked in descending order to enable operators to quickly see patterns and isolate issues.

8. CONCLUSION

Anomaly detection is a critical component at the heart of many real-time monitoring systems with applications in fault detection, fraud detection, network intrusion detection and many others. Despite its crucial importance, implementing a fully-automatic anomaly detection system in practice is a challenging task due to the large problem scale and the diverse use-cases residing in the real-world setting. These challenges typically result in solutions that are either not scalable or highly specialized, which would in turn result in a high rate of false positives when applied to other use-cases.

In this paper, we introduced EGADS, the generic anomaly detection system implemented at Yahoo to automatically monitor and alert on millions of time-series on different Yahoo properties for different use-cases ranging from fault detection to intrusion detection. As we described in the paper, the parallel architecture of EGADS on Hadoop as well as its stream processing mechanism through Storm enable it to perform real-time anomaly detection on millions of time-series at Yahoo. Furthermore, EGADS employs different time-series modeling, and anomaly detection algorithms to handle different monitoring use-cases. By incorporating this array of algorithms combined with a machine-learned mechanism in the alerting module, EGADS automatically adapts itself to the anomaly detection use-case that is important to the user. All of these features effectively create a powerful anomaly detection framework which is both generic and scalable. Our showcase experiments on real and synthetic datasets have shown the superior applicability of our framework compared to its rival solutions.

Last but not least, EGADS by its very nature is extendable, providing an easy mechanism to plugin new models and algorithms into the system. This feature specifically creates an oppurtunity for the community to contribute to EGADS. Finally, to further engage with the anomaly detection and monitoring community, our framework together with all its datasets are contributed to the open source repository.

9. REFERENCES

[1] C. Aggarwal. *Outlier Analysis.* Springer New York, 2013.

[2] P. Bloomfield. *Fourier analysis of time series: an introduction.* John Wiley & Sons, 2004.

[3] M. M. Breunig, H.-P. Kriegel, R. T. Ng, and J. Sander. Lof: Identifying density-based local outliers. *SIGMOD Rec.*, 29(2):93–104, May 2000.

[4] V. Chandola, A. Banerjee, and V. Kumar. Anomaly detection: A survey. *ACM Comput. Surv.*, 41(3):15:1–15:58, July 2009.

[5] R. B. Cleveland, W. S. Cleveland, J. E. McRae, and I. Terpenning. Stl: A seasonal-trend decomposition procedure based on loess. *Journal of Official Statistics*, 6(1):3–73, 1990.

[6] J. Durbin and S. J. Koopman. *Time series analysis by state space methods.* Number 38. Oxford University Press, 2012.

[7] V. A. Epanechnikov. Non-parametric estimation of a multivariate probability density. *Theory of Probability & Its Applications*, 14(1):153–158, 1969.

[8] Y. Freund and R. E. Schapire. A decision-theoretic generalization of on-line learning and an application to boosting, 1996.

[9] S. S. Haykin, S. S. Haykin, and S. S. Haykin. *Kalman filtering and neural networks.* Wiley Online Library, 2001.

[10] R. J. Hyndman and A. B. Koehler. Another look at measures of forecast accuracy. *International Journal of Forecasting*, pages 679–688, 2006.

[11] R. H. Jones. Exponential smoothing for multivariate time series. *Journal of the Royal Statistical Society. Series B (Methodological)*, pages 241–251, 1966.

[12] Y. Kawahara, T. Yairi, and K. Machida. Change-point detection in time-series data based on subspace identification. In *ICDM*, pages 559–564. IEEE, 2007.

[13] A. Kejariwal and P. Kumar. Mitigating user experience from 'breaking bad': The twitter approach. In *Velocity*, New York, NY, Sept. 2014.

[14] R. Killick. *changepoint, an R package that implements various mainstream and specialised changepoint methods.*, 2014.

[15] L. Komsta. *outliers, an R package of some tests commonly used outlier detection techniques.*, 2011.

[16] S. Kullback. *Information theory and statistics.* Courier Corporation, 1997.

[17] Z. Lan, Z. Zheng, and Y. Li. Toward automated anomaly identification in large-scale systems. *Parallel and Distributed Systems, IEEE Transactions on*, 21(2):174–187, 2010.

[18] N. Laptev and S. Amizadeh. Online dataset for anomaly detection. http://webscope.sandbox.yahoo.com/catalog.php?datatype=s&did=70, April 2015.

[19] N. Laptev and S. Amizadeh. Egads source code. https://github.com/yahoo/egads, June 2015.

[20] S. Liu, M. Yamada, N. Collier, and M. Sugiyama. Change-point detection in time-series data by relative density-ratio estimation. *Neural Networks*, 43:72–83, 2013.

[21] V. Moskvina and A. Zhigljavsky. An algorithm based on singular spectrum analysis for change-point detection. *Communications in Statistics-Simulation and Computation*, 32(2):319–352, 2003.

[22] D. B. Percival and A. T. Walden. *Wavelet methods for time series analysis*, volume 4. Cambridge University Press, 2006.

[23] B. K. Ray and R. S. Tsay. Bayesian methods for change-point detection in long-range dependent processes. *Journal of Time Series Analysis*, 23(6):687–705, 2002.

[24] B. Rosner. Percentage points for a generalized esd many-outlier procedure. *Technometrics*, 25(2):165–172, 1983.

[25] A. Toshniwal, S. Taneja, A. Shukla, K. Ramasamy, J. M. Patel, S. Kulkarni, J. Jackson, K. Gade, M. Fu, J. Donham, N. Bhagat, S. Mittal, and D. Ryaboy. Storm@twitter. In *SIGMOD*, pages 147–156, New York, NY, USA, 2014. ACM.

[26] O. Vallis, J. Hochenbaum, and A. Kejariwal. A novel technique for long-term anomaly detection in the cloud. In *USENIX*, Philadelphia, PA, June 2014. USENIX Association.

[27] M. van der Loo. *extremevalues, an R package for outlier detection in univariate data*, 2010. R package version 2.0.

[28] S. Venkataraman, J. Caballero, D. Song, A. Blum, and J. Yates. Black box anomaly detection: is it utopian? 2006.

[29] X. Wang, K. Smith-Miles, and R. Hyndman. Rule induction for forecasting method selection: Meta-learning the characteristics of univariate time series. *Neurocomput.*, 72(10-12):2581–2594, June 2009.

[30] W. W.-S. Wei. *Time series analysis.* Addison-Wesley publ, 1994.

[31] Y. Xie, J. Huang, and R. Willett. Change-point detection for high-dimensional time series with missing data. *Selected Topics in Signal Processing, IEEE Journal of*, 7(1):12–27, 2013.

Leveraging Knowledge Bases for Contextual Entity Exploration

Joonseok Lee*
Google Inc.
Mountain View, CA, USA
joonseok@google.com

Ariel Fuxman†
Google Inc.
Mountain View, CA, USA
afuxman@google.com

Bo Zhao†
LinkedIn
Mountain View, CA, USA
bo.zhao.uiuc@gmail.com

Yuanhua Lv
Microsoft Research
Redmond, WA, USA
yuanhual@microsoft.com

ABSTRACT

Users today are constantly switching back and forth from applications where they consume or create content (such as e-books and productivity suites like Microsoft Office and Google Docs) to search engines where they satisfy their information needs. Unfortunately, though, this leads to a suboptimal user experience as the search engine lacks any knowledge about the content that the user is authoring or consuming in the application. As a result, productivity suites are starting to incorporate features that let the user "explore while they work".

Existing work in the literature that can be applied to this problem takes a standard bag-of-words information retrieval approach, which consists of automatically creating a query that includes not only the target phrase or entity chosen by the user but also relevant terms from the context. While these approaches have been successful, they are inherently limited to returning results (documents) that have a syntactic match with the keywords in the query.

We argue that the limitations of these approaches can be overcome by leveraging semantic signals from a knowledge graph built from knowledge bases such as Wikipedia. We present a system called Lewis for retrieving contextually relevant entity results leveraging a knowledge graph, and perform a large scale crowdsourcing experiment in the context of an e-reader scenario, which shows that Lewis can outperform the state-of-the-art contextual entity recommendation systems by more than 20% in terms of the MAP score.

Categories and Subject Descriptors

H.4 [**Information systems applications**]: Data mining

*This work was done during an internship at Microsoft.
†This work was done while working at Microsoft.

KDD'15, August 10-13, 2015, Sydney, NSW, Australia.
© 2015 ACM. ISBN 978-1-4503-3664-2/15/08 ...$15.00.
DOI: http://dx.doi.org/10.1145/2783258.2788564.

Keywords

Entity recommendation, Context, Semantic, Knowledge base, Context-Selection Betweenness

1. INTRODUCTION

Users today are constantly switching back and forth from applications where they consume or create content (such as e-books and productivity suites like Google Docs and Microsoft Office) to search engines where they satisfy their information needs (such as Bing or Google). Unfortunately, though, this leads to a suboptimal user experience as the search engine lacks any knowledge about the content that the user is authoring or consuming in the application [11, 19, 13].

How can we empower users to satisfy their information needs directly within the applications where they consume content? A significant step in this direction is enabling users to interact with anything on the document that they are working on, directly within the productivity application, and recommending results that are contextually relevant to the elements they are interacting with. Productivity suites are starting to incorporate features that realize this scenario, such as the "Insights for Office" feature in Microsoft Word Online.

As an example, consider a user reading on an e-reader the document shown in Figure 1, which describes the Capture of Fort Ticonderoga, an important event in American history. At some point, she finds a mention to a historical figure called "Silas Deane" and decides that she would like to learn more about him. Just sending the query "silas deane" to any of the major commercial search engines returns results such as "Silas Dean High School" which are unrelated to the historical context of the document. A much more compelling user experience is the one shown in Figure 1, where the user has tapped on the phrase "Silas Deane" and is shown contextually relevant articles such as "Revolutionary War", where she can learn about Silas Deane's overall involvement in the American Revolutionary War, and "Benjamin Franklin", where she can learn that Deane and Franklin were the first diplomats in American history, and they were sent together to France as commissioners from the Continental Congress.

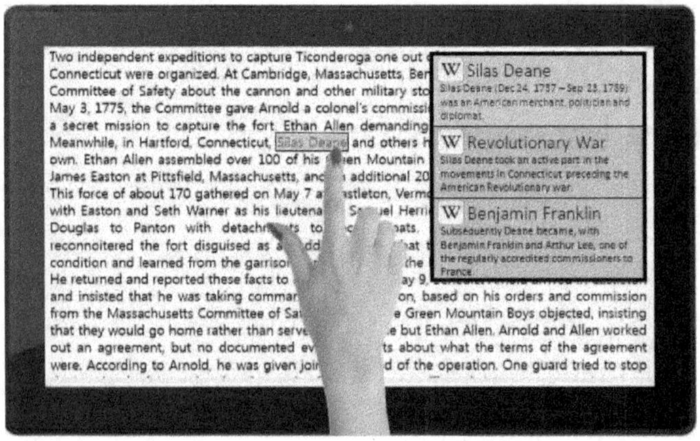

Figure 1: An example of contextual exploration.

Previous efforts in the literature have made significant progress towards realizing this scenario, including systems for *contextual search* [11, 19] and *contextual insights* [13]. These systems take a standard bag-of-word information retrieval approach to the problem, which consists of automatically creating a query that includes not only the target phrase or entity chosen by the user but also relevant terms from the context. More broadly, these approaches are related to relevance feedback in information retrieval [35], where a context (in the case of relevance feedback, the results of a query; in our scenario, the document context) is used to refine an initial query (in our case, the phrase chosen by the user).

While these approaches have been successful, they are inherently limited to returning results (documents) that have a syntactic match with the keywords in the query. For example, the Wikipedia articles for "Revolutionary War" and "Benjamin Franklin" have just a single passing mention to Silas Deane and are thus unlikely to be retrieved by a query that contains the terms "silas deane". To tackle this problem, in this paper we argue that such results can be obtained by more directly modeling the semantic connections between the target concept and the entities in the context where it appears.

To illustrate our approach, consider the graph shown in Figure 2 (henceforth called *knowledge graph*). The black node corresponds to the entity chosen by the user (Silas Deane), the gray nodes correspond to entities mentioned in the context (Green Mountain Boys, Fort Ticonderoga, Connecticut). The edges correspond to hyperlinks in the Wikipedia articles. As we can see, the node for "Revolutionary War" acts as a bridge between Silas Deane and the context concepts Green Mountain Boys (the militia that captured Fort Ticonderoga) and Fort Ticonderoga. Our approach leverages precisely this type of semantic connections to retrieve contextually relevant results.

The contributions of this paper include:

- A framework for leveraging semantic signals from a knowledge graph for the problem of retrieving contextually relevant entity results.
- A system called *Lewis* for retrieving contextually relevant entities leveraging a knowledge graph built from Wikipedia hyperlinks.

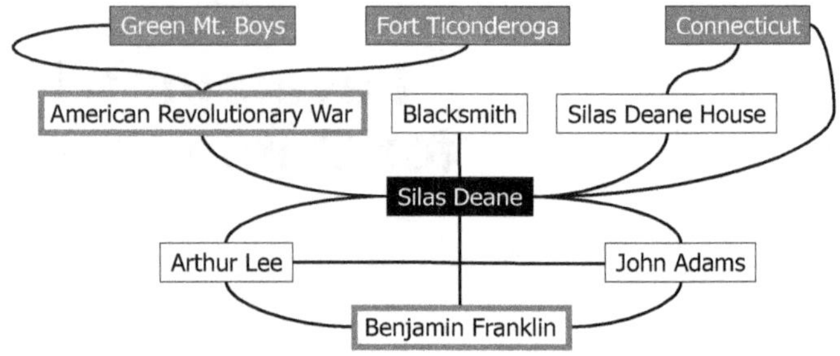

Figure 2: A portion of the focused subgraph for our running example. (Black for the user selection node, gray for context nodes, and white for all other nodes.)

- An algorithm for retrieving contextually relevant entities.
- A large-scale evaluation of the approach in the context of a real-word e-reader application. The results show an improvement of up to 20.8% in terms of the MAP scores with respect to the state-of-the-art methods for contextual insights and pseudo-relevance feedback. We also present a detailed ablation study that shows the importance of the different components of the *Lewis* system.

The rest of this paper is organized as follows. We formally define the contextual entity exploration problem in the next section, followed by a detailed description of our proposed method in Section 3. We evaluate our method in Section 4. Lastly, we review related problems and previous work in Section 5, and provide concluding remarks in Section 6.

2. CONTEXTUAL ENTITY EXPLORATION PROBLEM

The input to the contextual entity exploration problem consists of a *user selection*: the span of text that the user highlights with the mouse or taps with the finger, which implicitly determines the entity she would like to gain insights about (e.g., "Silas Deane"); a *context*, consisting of the content that the user is consuming or authoring; a *knowledge base*, that consists of entities that are candidates to be recommended; and a *knowledge graph*, whose nodes are entities from the knowledge base; and an *text-to-entity* mapping that given some text from the user selection or context produces an entity from the knowledge base.

The *contextual entity exploration problem* is then formally defined as follows:

DEFINITION 1. *Given a quintuple* (s, C, B, G, γ)*, where* s *is a user selection,* C *is some text context,* B *is a knowledge base,* G *is a undirected graph whose nodes are entities in* B*, and* γ *is a text-to-entity mapping; the objective of the* contextual entity exploration problem *is to produce a set of entities* O *such that* $O \subseteq B$ *and every entity in* O *is relevant to* s *in the context of* C*.*

In this work, we will use Wikipedia as our knowledge base B and the hyperlink structure of Wikipedia as the edges of the knowledge graph. In particular, G will be an undirected graph $G = (B, E)$ where there is an edge (x, y) in E if there

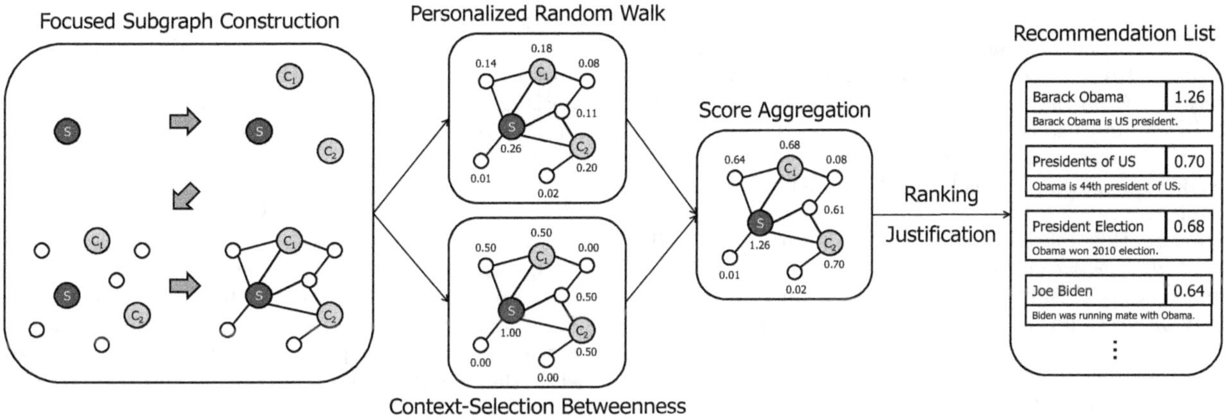

Figure 3: Overall flow of the proposed approach.

is a link to entity y on the Wikipedia page for entity x or vice versa. Notice, however, that the techniques presented in this paper are independent of the actual method used to construct the knowledge graph.

3. OUR APPROACH

In this section, we explain our approach to contextual entity exploration using a knowledge graph. Figure 3 provides an overview of the proposed system. We start by building a focused subgraph from the given knowledge graph for each problem instance, followed by scoring participating nodes in two ways, namely context-selection betweenness and personalized random walk. Ranking the aggregated scores generates a recommendation list, with a human readable justification.

3.1 Focused Subgraph

The first step of the algorithm consists of mapping the user selection s and the context C to nodes in the knowledge graph using the text-to-entity mapping γ. Notice that this mapping is given as input to the contextual entity exploration problem; it can be any off-the-shelf entity linking system (e.g., [9])[1].

Continuing our running example of Figure 1, a mapping γ would map the user selection "Silas Deane" to the entity for Silas Deane in Wikipedia[2]; and extract from the document entities related to the surface forms that appear therein, e.g., "Green Mountain Boys"[3] and "Fort Ticonderoga"[4].

The next step consists of creating a subgraph of the knowledge graph that contains candidate entities to be recommended as contextually relevant results, which we call *focused subgraph.* Its nodes consist of the union of two sets V' and V''. V' is the set of entities obtained by applying the mapping γ in the previous step (i.e., the entities associated to the user selection and context); and V'' is the set of entities reachable from nodes of V' in the knowledge graph G through a path of length one. The edges of the focused subgraph can be obtained by adding the edges induced by $V' \cup V''$ in G, or by any other suitable heuristic.[5] Figure 2 demonstrates an example of the focused subgraph for our running example.

[1]For our experiments, we use an in-house entity linking system. We also conduct experiments where the mapping γ is actually an oracle: i.e., a human manually provides a perfect mapping.

[2]`http://en.wikipedia.org/wiki/Silas_Deane`

[3]`http://en.wikipedia.org/wiki/Green_Mountain_Boys`

[4]`http://en.wikipedia.org/wiki/Fort_Ticonderoga`

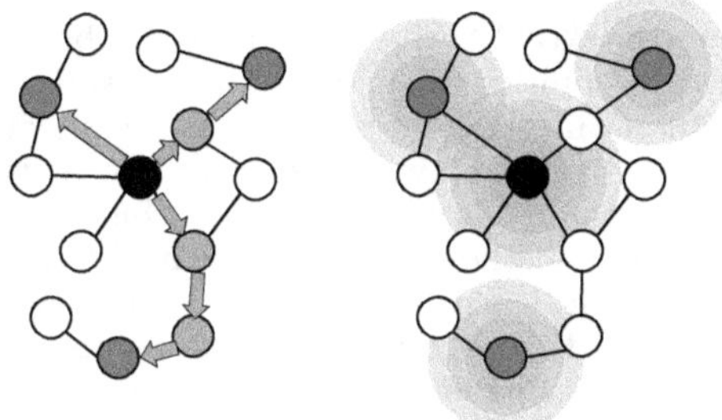

Figure 4: Illustration of retrievable nodes with context-selection betweenness (*left*) and personalized random walk (*right*). (The black node in the center represents the user selection node, and three gray nodes are context pages.)

Once the focused subgraph is constructed, we proceed to scoring each candidate entity in the focused subgraph by capturing the semantic connection among the candidates, the user selection, and the context nodes. We explain the scoring methods in detail next.

3.2 Scoring Methods

We now present the two scoring methods that we use, and how we combine them to produce a final contextual relevance score.

3.2.1 Context-Selection Betweenness

This method captures to what extent a given candidate node serves as a bridge between the user selection node and the context nodes. For example, in Figure 2, "Revolutionary War" gets a higher score than "Blacksmith" because remov-

[5]The heuristic that we employ in the Lewis system consists of adding all the edges that involve at least one context or user selection node; and the edges (x, y) such that either x has inlinks from the user selection node s and y in G (s and y are common parent of x), or x has outlinks to the user selection node s and y in G (s and y are common children of x).

ing the former disconnects "Silas Deane" from two context nodes, whereas removing the latter does not disconnect the selection node from any context node. This makes intuitive sense because while the Revolutionary War is very relevant to Silas Deane and the context of the document, the entity "Blacksmith" is irrelevant to the context (it is just mentioned on the Wikipedia page for Silas Deane because his father was a blacksmith).

We capture this intuition with a measure that we call *context-selection betweenness* (CSB). The measure is inspired by the notion of betweenness centrality [12], which measures how many shortest paths go through a given node v. It is defined as follows:

$$BC(v) = \sum_{v \neq i \neq j} \frac{\sigma_{i,j}(v)}{\sigma_{i,j}}, \quad (1)$$

where $\sigma_{i,j}$ is the total number of shortest paths from node i to j, and $\sigma_{i,j}(v)$ is the number of such paths that pass through node v.

For the contextual entity exploration problem, however, the original definition of betweenness centrality does not suffice. First, in the contextual entity exploration problem, relevance is defined with respect to the context. Thus, the measure should consider only paths connecting the user selection node and the context nodes, not every path connecting two nodes. This can be done by a straight-forward modification of the original definition, by simply by summing over all (s, c) pairs for all $c \in C$, instead of all possible pairs of nodes in the focused graph.

Another reason that we need to modify betweenness centrality is that not all context terms are equally relevant to the user selection. Thus, we need a weighted version of betweenness centrality. To compute this weight, we use Normalized Wikipedia Distance (NWD) [28], a measure of semantic distance of two nodes on graph that is widely used in the entity linking literature. The NWD between two nodes u and v is defined as

$$NWD(u, v) = \frac{\log(\max(|I_u|, |I_v|)) - \log |I_u \cap I_v|}{\log |V| - \log(\min(|I_u|, |I_v|))}, \quad (2)$$

where I_x is the set of incoming edges to the node x, and V is the set of all nodes in Wikipedia. In our modified measure, each path from user selection node s to a context node c is weighted by $\max(1/(\theta - NWD(s, c)), 0)$ with some threshold θ. (In our case, $\theta = 0.5$.) In this way, a context term more relevant to the target mention is more emphasized.

Putting it all together, we define *context-selection betweenness* of a node v as follows:

DEFINITION 2. *Context-Selection Betweenness of a node v is*

$$CSB(v) = \frac{1}{Z} \sum_{c: v \in sp(s,c)} \frac{w(s, c)}{k \cdot l(s, c)}, \quad (3)$$

where $w(s, c) = \max(\theta - NWD(s, c), 0)$, $l(p, c)$ is the length of shortest path between user selection node s and context node c, $sp(s, c)$ is a set of all shortest paths between s and c, $Z = \sum_{c \in C} \frac{w(s,c)}{l(s,c)}$, and k is the number of different shortest paths between s and c.

Intuitively speaking, a higher CSB score means the node is playing a more important role connecting the user selection node s and other context nodes c, which are more relevant to p through shorter and more unique paths.

Figure 4 (left) illustrates how CSB works. We have three context (gray) nodes in this graph. For each user selection - context ($s - c$) path, marked with pink arrows, we assign scores by (3) to all participating nodes on it. As a result, we found three pink nodes including A with nonzero score. All other white nodes are 0, as they are not on any $s - c$ path.

3.2.2 Personalized Random Walk

We also consider a measure of the relevance of a node to the user selection. This measure does not factor in the contributions of context nodes directly, but it does so indirectly since the focused graph is built from context nodes in the knowledge graph. In Section 4, we will show that while this measure does not suffice by itself to obtain an appropriate relevance score, it is quite effective when used in conjunction with the context-selection betweenness measure described above.

We compute this measure by computing a personalized random walk [18]. Intuitively, the random walk is simulating the behavior of a user reading articles in Wikipedia as follows. We assume that a user starts reading the page most directly relevant to the user selection (the page for "Silas Deane" in our example) and then follow an interesting link from that page. She continues surfing articles in this way, until at some point she comes back to the article of the user selection.

Random walk [30] computes the stationary probability that a user would stay in the page. Personalized random walk [18] is a generalization of random walk in that it introduces a set of default pages which the user can jump from anywhere on the web with certain probability. It is proven to always have a unique solution with stationary probability for each page. [18] There are numerous previous works using personalized random walk for graph-based data mining. The most related to ours is WikiWalk [41], which used a general jump probability vector (possibly with different probability to different pages) for measuring similarity of two texts (without a notion of "user selection"). Note that we call this random walk "personalized" only because it is the name known in literature, not because we personalize to the interests of an individual user.

To compute the random walk, we use a vector for all nodes, containing random jump probability to each node. We assign $0 < x_s < 1$ for the user selection node s and $x_c/|C|$ where $0 \leq x_c \leq x_s$ for each context node $c \in C$. All the other nodes are assigned zero probability of random jump. Thus, users can come back to the user selection node during surfing with some probability x_s, as well as to some context page with smaller probability $x_c/|C|$, and restart navigation from there.

Figure 4 (right) illustrates an example of probability distribution from personalized random walk with $x_s > x_c > 0$. The user tends to stay on the user selection node with highest probability, followed by context nodes. Also, nodes close from the user selection and context nodes have slightly higher probability than nodes far from them. In other words, personalized random walk retrieves semantically relevant pages from the query and context terms by assigning higher probability (score) to closely and densely connected nodes from the user selection and context nodes.

3.2.3 Score Aggregation

At this point, we have two scores for each node v: a context-selection betweenness score $CSB(v)$, and a random walk score $RW(v)$. We now explain how to combine them to obtain the final relevance score.

The random walk scores of a node are probability scores and thus sum up to 1. Thus, the expected value of $RW(v)$ gets smaller when we have more nodes in the graph. To counter the effect of graph size, we consider $|V|RW(v)$ instead of $RW(v)$ itself, where V is the set of nodes in the focused graph. As the expected value of $|V|RW(v)$ is always 1 because it sums to $|V|$, we can interpret this score as how many times the node is preferred to visit compared to expectation. If $|V|RW(v) = 3$, for example, we interpret the page v is 3 times more recommendable than others.

Context-selection betwenness, on the other hand, is normalized by the sum over all context nodes. Thus, the $CSB(v)$ score for each node tends to be inversely proportional to the number of context nodes. To counter this effect, we again consider $|C|CSB(v)$ instead of $CSB(v)$, where C is the set of context nodes. As the highest score of $|C|CSB(v)$ is $|C|$, each $s-c$ path distributes 1 to all participating nodes. Thus, we can interpret $|C|CSB(v)$ score as the expected number of shortest paths from user selection s to any context node visiting v in the meanwhile.

We aggregate these scores reflecting their relative importance. First, it is natural to trust context-selection betweenness score more when we have more context terms at hand. On the other hand, we trust context-selection betweenness less when we have a relatively large number of nodes in our focused graph compared to the number of context nodes $|C|$, as this may imply that either nodes in outside the context may not overlap so much (that is, the context is not topically coherent) or user selection and context nodes have large number of connected nodes (so they are general terms, e.g, *Water* or *Human*). In either case, therefore, the importance of $|C|CSB(v)$ should be proportional to the ratio of $|C|$ to $|V|$. With a scaling factor α, we finally propose the following aggregation equation to compute final score for node v:

DEFINITION 3. *Relevance score of a node v is given by*

$$Relevance(v) = |V|RW(v) + \alpha\frac{|C|}{|V|}|C|CSB(v). \tag{4}$$

We sort this score for each entity in decreasing order, and recommend the top-k entities. We recommend nodes v satisfying $|V|RW(v) > 1$ only. That is, we do not recommend pages with lower random walk score even than its expectation. This is to remove some general (so not recommendable) context terms having very high $|C|CSB(v)$ due to a cluster of context pages on the focused subgraph.

4. EVALUATION

In this section, we evaluate our approach and compare it with several baselines using crowd-sourced data in the context of a real-world e-reader application.

4.1 Experimental Setting

Dataset

We employed snapshot of English Wikipedia from January 2nd, 2014 as our knowledge base, considering all pages from namespaces *main* and *category*. We further performed some preprocessing: removing stop words, consolidating redirections[6], and removing disambiguation pages[7] since they connect ambiguous entities which are not quite related with each other. (This is different from category or list pages, which contain semantically relevant pages.)

We performed experiments in the context of an e-reader application, as illustrated in Figure 1. To create suitable test data, we employed a corpus consisting of all English textbooks from the Wikibooks site[8]. The corpus consists of 2,600 textbooks that cover a broad spectrum of topics, such as engineering, humanities, health sciences, and social sciences. We sampled 900 paragraphs from this corpus, and for each paragraph we asked 100 crowd workers to select phrases for which they would like to learn more. Then, we performed weighted random sampling from the user-selected phrases to get 500 test cases (pairs of user selections and contexts). For each test case, we pooled the top 8 results from our system as well as several baselines. For each result in the pool, we showed the original user selection and context to 10 crowd workers and ask them if they thought the recommended page is good in the context. We applied some simple heuristics to remove spam labels, and used majority voting to get the final label.

Model Parameters and Metrics

We considered 100 words before and after the user selection as context for all compared methods. For the personalized random walk, we used $x_s = 0.05$ (random jump probability to the perfect node), $x_c = 0$ (random jump probability to any context node)[9], and iterated up to 50 times. For context-selection betweenness, we used $\theta = 0.5$. We compared Lewis to baselines using Mean Average Precision (MAP) to take both precision and recall into account with a single metric.

User Interface and Justification

Figure 5 shows our user interface for crowd workers to evaluate our recommendation. On the left side, workers can see the original context. The user selection is marked as light green box. On the right side, it shows an entity recommended for the user selection. In order to let the user understand whether the entity is appropriate, we show the Wikipedia page of the entity. The workers are asked to answer how relevant the entity is to the user selection and the given context on the left-bottom of the page. We gave three options: 1) This article is what I'd expect to see if I highlighted the text on the left, 2) This article is not what I'd expected, but I see a connection between the highlighted text and the article, and 3) This article is not what I'd expected, and I don't see a connection between the highlighted text and the article. We regarded 1) and 2) as relevant, and 3) as not relevant.

During this evaluation, we faced the following challenge. As our corpora consist of various topics including literature, history, science, or engineering, it is rather difficult to find a worker sufficiently knowledgeable in all of these areas. Fur-

[6]E.g, "MIT" and "Massachusetts Institute of Technology" refer to the same page. Users might link to this page using either of them.

[7]E.g, "Apple (disambiguation)" page contains links to both the fruit apple and the IT company Apple Inc.

[8]`http://en.wikibooks.org`

[9]We tried some $x_c > 0$, but observed no significant difference.

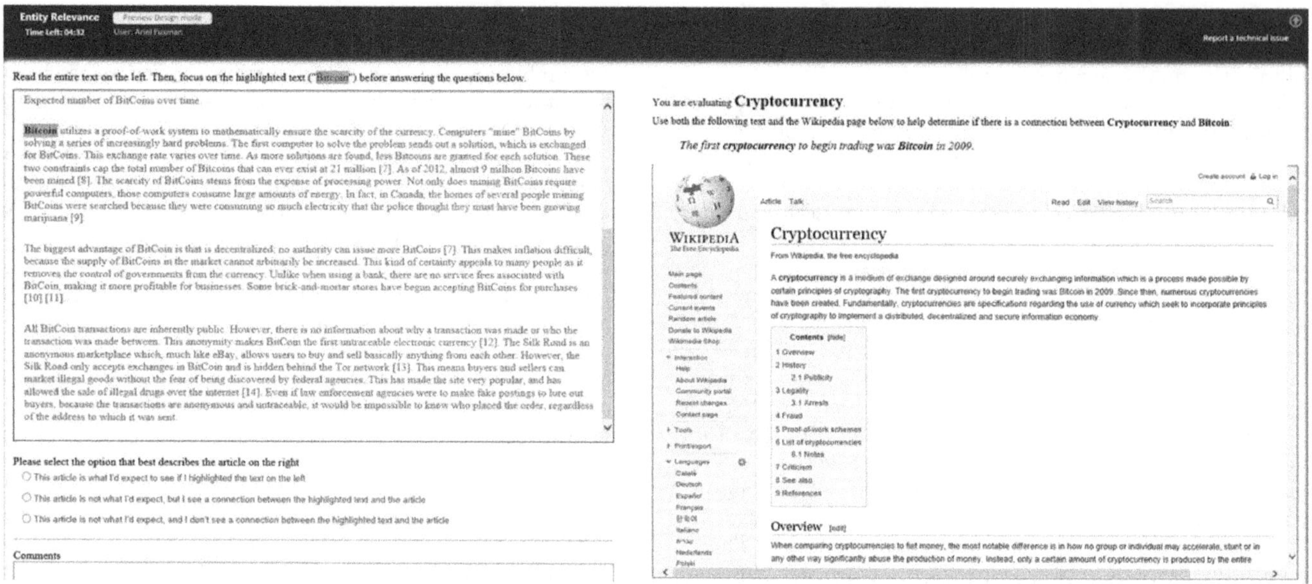

Figure 5: The web page we used for crowd-sourced evaluation.

User selection	Recommend page	Explanation
Wang Mang	Xin Dynasty	**Wang Mang** was a Han Dynasty official who seized the throne from the Liu family and founded the **Xin Dynasty**, ruling AD 9-23.
Malacca	Malaysia	**Malacca** (Melaka, dubbed "The Historic State") is the third smallest **Malaysian** state after Perlis and Penang.
Diolkos	Corinth Canal	Sections of the **Diolkos** have been destroyed by the 19th-century **Corinth Canal**.
Kanji	Chinese characters	**Kanji** are the adopted logographic **Chinese characters** that are used in the modern Japanese writing system along with hiragana and katakana.
Throttle	Automobile	In a motor vehicle the control used by the driver to regulate power is sometimes called the **throttle** pedal or accelerator.

Table 1: Examples of recommendation justification.

thermore, crowd workers tend to answer without close inspection but just relying on their background knowledge.

To resolve this issue, we added a justification sentence in the user interface (on the top-right of the page). There is recent work in the area of justification of recommendations [16, 37, 43, 39, 8], and in our case we used a simple, yet effective, heuristic. From either the perfect page or the recommended page, we chose one sentence which satisfies one of the following conditions: 1) a sentence containing both (the perfect and the recommended) pages' titles with hyperlink, 2) a sentence containing both (the perfect and the recommended) pages' titles without hyperlink, 3) a sentence containing the other page's title with hyperlink, 4) a sentence containing the other page's title without hyperlink. In this way, we prefer a sentence which can explain relationship between the user selection and the recommended page. If we find more than one sentence in the same category, we chose the first occurence, because general explanation tends to come first in Wikipedia articles. If we can find no sentence satisfying any of those four conditions, we choose the first sentence of the recommended page. Table 1 illustrates several examples of our justifications.

We provided the same justifications for all baselines as well as our method to be fair.

4.2 Results and Discussion

Comparison against Baselines

We considered four baselines. The first baseline consists of simply sending the user selection to a commercial search engine, without using any context. The second baseline consists of the widely used semantic relatedness measure Normalized Wikipedia Distance (NWD) [28]. In this baseline, we take the user selection node in the graph and compute NWD with respect to all other nodes in the focused subgraph, and then return the entities with the top-k score. Finally, we consider two approaches that are representative of contextual entity exploration using bag-of-words IR techniques: the Leibniz system [13], and an algorithm based on positional relevance model (PRM) [25, 14], which is a state-of-the-art pseudo-relevance feedback algorithm. Notice that both NWD and Lewis need to perform entity linking to get the user selection entity. In our experiments, we placed the entity proposed by an in-house entity linking system at the top position for NWD and Lewis, which is for the benefit of fair comparison with the search engine and Leibniz, since their top results are generally entity linking results.

Table 2 compares performance of Lewis against the baselines in terms of MAP@8. We can see that Lewis outperforms all the baselines, with a MAP@8 score of 0.291. In particular, it outperforms the state-of-the-art contextual entity recommendation systems: the PRM pseudo-relevance feedback system, which achieves a MAP@8 score of 0.278; and Leibniz, which achieves a MAP@8 score of 0.262. The lowest MAP score of 0.244 corresponds to using NWD as a measure for entity recommendation.

The scores above correspond to the case in which we output up to eight entities. We also analyzed the case when we set a threshold in the maximum number of results. That is, we computed MAP@k, for varying values of k. The results

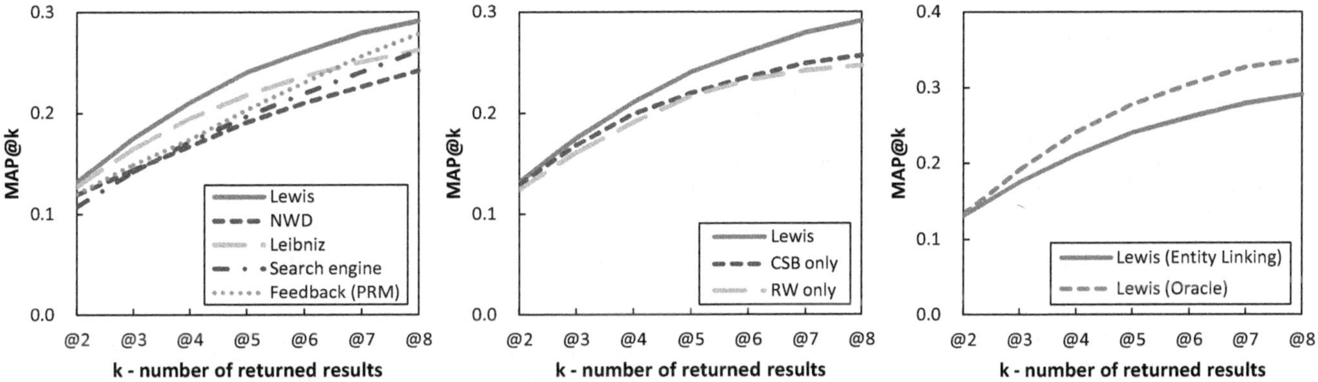

Figure 6: MAP@k for Lewis with baselines (left), for ablation study (middle), and with the user selection entity chosen by entity linking and by human (right).

Method	MAP@8
NWD	0.244
Search Engine	0.261
PRM Relevance Feedback	0.278
Leibniz	0.262
Lewis	**0.291**

Table 2: Comparison of Lewis against baselines.

Method	MAP@8
Random Walk only	0.246
Context-selection betweeness only	0.256
Lewis	**0.291**

Table 3: Ablation study results.

are seen in Figure 6 (left). As we can see, Lewis consistently outperforms all baselines at every value of k.

Ablation Study

We also performed an ablation study where we consider each of the two scoring methods of Lewis in isolation. The results for MAP@8 are shown in Table 3. We can see that the full Lewis system outperforms its ablations. The results for MAP@k for varying values of k are shown in Figure 6 (middle). We can also see that Lewis consistently outperforms the ablations at every value of k. In addition, we see that context-selection betweenness outperforms the random walk method. This means that user selection and context should be considered as first class citizens, as we advocate in this paper.

Effect of Entity Linking

Recall that in the construction of the focused graph, we use a mapping γ to map the user selection to an entity node. All the results given so far are based on the use of an in-house entity linker. But this raises the following question: what is the dependency of Lewis on the actual entity linking method? To address this question, we consider an experiment where the mapping γ is given by an oracle. That is, a human manually produced the correct entity linking result for the user selection. The Lewis system with an entity linking oracle gets a MAP@8 score of 0.336. In contrast, Lewis achieves a MAP@8 score 0.291 when we use our in-house entity linker. This means that if we used a different entity

Rank	Title of Retrieved Page	CSB	RW	Total
1	Silas Deane	402.26	6442.53	6844.78
2	American Revolutionary War	49.58	82.42	131.99
3	Benjamin Franklin	2.46	128.17	130.63
4	Arthur Lee (diplomat)	0.00	107.99	107.99
5	Thomas Jefferson	2.46	98.82	101.28
6	Continental Congress	19.58	74.02	93.60
7	Continental Army	30.25	61.45	89.14
8	Capture of Fort Ticonderoga	49.58	39.56	89.14

Table 4: Score decomposition with *Silas Deane* example.

linker system, the MAP@8 score could be improved by at most 17%. Potential MAP improvement with different k is shown in Figure 6 (right).

Overlap of Results

We also investigated how many entities Lewis and Leibniz return in common. Interestingly, only a small portion of the recommended entities overlap. Specifically, Lewis recommended 3,790 entities for 500 test examples (up to 8 entities for each) and Leibniz did so for 3,032 entities. Among these, only 580 entities (9.3%) were in both sets. Furthermore, if we exclude the user selection entity obtained via the entity linker, the number of overlapping entities drops to 320 (5.6%). This observation leads to a conclusion that IR-based and knowledge-graph based systems tend to retrieve qualitatively different types of entities, and thus the combination of such system is a promising direction of future work.

Graph Construction and Running Time

The focused subgraph we created for each problem instance contained 16,041 nodes and 118,380 edges in average. For each instance, in average, it took 0.3 seconds for constructing focused subgraph. It took 3.3 seconds in average for computing context-selection betweenness score, and 3.2 seconds in average for random walk score. (This excludes all preprocessing steps which were done offline, taking about 30 minutes.) The largest focused subgraph had 155,711 nodes and 1,617,403 edges, taking 0.6 seconds for constructing subgraph, and 32 seconds for each scoring method.

Anecdotal Examples

We present a couple of anecdotal examples. We start with running example of Figure 1, where the user selection is *Silas*

CSB only	RW only	NWD baseline	Leibniz
Silas Deane	**Silas Deane**	**Silas Deane**	**Silas Deane**
Ethan Allen	**Benjamin Franklin**	**Arthur Lee (diplomat)**	Silas Deane House
Noah Phelps	**Arthur Lee (diplomat)**	Hugh Campbell Wallace	Connecticut Route 99
Benedict Arnold	**John Adams**	Somerville Pinkney Tuck	Silas Dean House
Fort Ticonderoga	Thomas Jefferson	Evan G. Galbraith	
American Revolutionary War	**James Monroe**	Howard H. Leach	
Capture of Fort Ticonderoga	William Short	**Jesse I. Straus**	
Green Mountain Boys	Gouverneur Morris	Arthur K. Watson	

Table 5: Retrieved results with Lewis and baselines. Bold faces mean relevant results.

Deane. The original text is as follows, with the user selection *Silas Deane* marked with a surrounding box.

> Two independent expeditions to capture Ticonderoga – one out of Massachusetts and the other from Connecticut – were organized. At Cambridge, Massachusetts, Benedict Arnold told the Massachusetts Committee of Safety about the cannon and other military stores at the lightly defended fort. On May 3, 1775, the Committee gave Arnold a colonel's commission and authorized him to command a secret mission to capture the fort. Ethan Allen demanding the surrender of Fort Ticonderoga Meanwhile, in Hartford, Connecticut, [Silas Deane] and others had organized an expedition of their own. Ethan Allen assembled over 100 of his Green Mountain Boys, about 50 men were raised by James Easton at Pittsfield, Massachusetts, and an additional 20 men from Connecticut volunteered. This force of about 170 gathered on May 7 at Castleton, Vermont.
>
> - Silas Deane
> - American Revolutionary War
> - Benjamin Franklin
> - Arthur Lee (diplomat)
> - Thomas Jefferson
> - Continental Congress
> - Continental Army
> - Capture of Fort Ticonderoga

Lewis retrieved contextually relevant results such as *American Revolutionary War* and *Capture of Fort Ticonderoga*. We see that part of these results were retrieved by the random walk component, while for some others context-selection betweenness contributed more. Table 4 shows decomposed scores for CSB and RW contributions. For example, context-selection betweenness plays an important role to retrieve *American Revolutionary War* and *Capture of Fort Ticonderoga*, because they are semantically connecting user selection *Silas Deane* and context phrase *Fort Ticonderoga*. It also retrieves results for *Benjamin Franklin*, *Arthur Lee*, and *Thomas Jefferson*, who happened to be the other three people who, together with Silas Deane, can be considered to be the first diplomats of the United States. We see that the random walk component indeed plays more important role for retrieving these pages from Table 4. They are recommended due to their close relation with *Silas Deane*, despite they are not directly related to the context above.

Table 5 compares the output of the *Silas Deane* example from baselines. As we have seen above, CSB only retrieves contextually relevant pages. RW only and NWD baseline mostly retrieve pages for close figures of Silas Deane. Many of them are marked as unrelevant, because they are not related to the context in spite of their relatedness to Silas Deane. Interestingly, Leibniz retrieved only 4 results for this example, where none of them except for *Silas Deane* is relevant to the given context. On the other hand, the entire Lewis system retrieves more relevant results to the context and the user selection by combining CSB and RW component.

The other example is an article about pronunciation and location of stress on the Greek word *Ulysses*. The user selection is *Oxford English Dictionary*:

> In 1895, when Joyce was in his third year at Belvedere College, he chose Ulysses as his subject for an essay entitled "My Favourite Hero". In English Ulysses is sometimes stressed on the second syllable, and this is the pronunciation required in most verse translations of the Homeric epics. Joyce, however, always referred to his novel as YOOL-i-seez, with the stress on the first syllable. This pronunciation is sanctioned by the [Oxford English Dictionary] and is used almost universally in Ireland when one is referring to the book. In his design for the cover of the 1949 Random House edition of Ulysses, the American artist Edward McKnight Kauffer emphasized the initial UL, "giving graphic form to the phonetic structure of the title with its accent on the first syllable."
>
> - Oxford English Dictionary
> - Received Pronunciation
> - English language
> - Greek language
> - Old English
> - Standard English
> - New Oxford American Dictionary
> - Concise Oxford English Dictionary

We see in this example that Lewis is returning results relevant to both the user selection and the context again. *Received Pronunciation*, which is regarded as the standard accent of Standard English in the United Kingdom, is directly relevant to the topic as well as the user selection. *Greek language* is also relevant to the context, as the passage is talking about pronunciation of a greek word *Ulysses*. Another interesting result is *Old English*, as this article is talking about historical pronunciation (from 1895) of the word in English.

5. RELATED WORK

Contextual exploration [13, 23] is closely related to several information retrieval problems: entity linking and search, relevance feedback, and content recommendation.

5.1 Entity Linking, Search, and Ranking

The goal of entity linking is disambiguating the mention of an entity in unstructured text to the entity's record in knowledge base, usually by using machine learning techniques and disambiguated training data. There is a rich literature, including [9, 17, 20, 27, 42]. Recently entity linking was applied to text streaming data [40] and broadcasting. [29] Contextual exploration in contrast is not limited to disambiguating an entity mention, but it also explores and recommends articles relevant to the mention as well as the context.

Entity search [31, 5] and related entity search [3] are also related to our work. Entity search aims to answer a query with direct entity answers extracted from documents or entity records in a knowledge base; related entity search/finding takes as input a query entity, the type of the target entity, and the nature of their relation, and outputs a ranked list of related entities. However, the task at hand is principally different, which is to recommend related entities that are related to the user selection, which can be any continuous text (including but not limited to entity mentions), in the context of the document being consumed.

Entity ranking and recommendation is another recent area of research related to our work. Lee et al. [22] utilized random walk based approach for entity ranking, and Agarwal et al. [2] approached the ranking problem for networked entities with Markov walks. Vercoustre et al. [38] proposed a method for ranking Wikipedia entities.

5.2 Relevance Feedback

Relevance feedback has been shown to be effective to expand a query to relax the syntactic mis-matching problem in information retrieval [35, 34, 6]. Specifically, when a user submits a query, an IR system would first return an initial set of result documents, then ask the user to judge whether some documents are relevant or not; after that, the system would expand the query by adding a set of related terms extracted from the user's judgments, and return a set of new results. When there are no real relevance judgments available, alternatively, pseudo-relevance feedback [7, 21, 25, 14] may be performed, which simply assumes that a small number of top-ranked documents in the initial results are relevant. Our work may also be regarded as a pseudo-relevance feedback approach which assumes not only the top-ranked documents but the context around the user selection as pseudo-relevant resources. In contrast to the works above, however, we do not use syntactic query expansion. Instead, we explore a novel way of leveraging Wikipedia semantics to rank the results directly.

In the Experiments section, we showed that our approach outperforms a method based on pseudo-relevance feedback. Furthermore, since the approaches are complementary, a promising direction of future work involves the combination of IR and semantic approaches.

5.3 Content Recommendation

Content recommendation has been studied extensively in the past. Traditional content-based recommendation [33, 1] is usually to recommend documents which reflect users' long-term interests (e.g., a user might generally like sports). However, our work is recommending content related to users' ad hoc interests implied by the user selection when reading a document.

Related content recommendation [24], cumulative citation recommendation [4, 44], and contextual advertising [32] are also in the direction of ad hoc content-based recommendation. They recommend related content, such as news articles, Wikipedia articles, Web documents, or ads, to a target document. However, these works are based on a problem formulation that is insufficient for contextual exploration, as it does not allow for a user selection as part of its input.

5.4 Exploiting Knowledge Graphs

There are also several approaches that exploit the Wikipedia link-structure (or other knowledge base as a graph structure) to compute semantic similarity between text and knowledge base entities. One of the most popular areas exploiting knowledge graph structure is estimating semantic document or word similarity. WikiWalk [41] applied personalized page rank on a graph derived from Wikipedia to estimate semantic relatedness between documents. Gouws et al. [15] proposes a method for computing semantic relatedness by spreading activation energy over the hyperlink structure of Wikipedia. Mihalcea et al. [26] also presents a method for measuring the semantic similarity of short texts, using corpus-based and knowledge-based measures of similarity. Wikipedia link-structure is also exploited for computing concept relatedness [36] and query expansion [10] as well.

We emphasize that contextual entity exploration problem is a fundamentally different task from the vast bodies of work above, in that contextual entity exploration takes as input both an entity and its context. The work on exploiting semantic similarity between documents takes a document as input (our "context") and finds similar documents. However, it does not take a "pivot" entity as input (In our running example, the input entity used as pivot is "Silas Deane"). WikiWalk [41], for example, is very related to part of our approach in the sense that it performs a random walk on the Wikipedia graph. In contrast to our work, however, WikiWalk does not make a difference between the input entity and the context. Most importantly, we show in Section 4 that a baseline that consists exclusively of a random walk (like in WikiWalk) is clearly outperformed by our techniques which combine random walks with methods such as context-selection betweenness that treat the concepts of input entity and context entities as first class citizens. No problems listed above takes both an entity (user selection) and its context as input to recommend relevant entities from knowledge base.

6. CONCLUSIONS

In this paper, we presented Lewis, a system that provides a solution for the contextual entity exploration problem leveraging knowledge bases. A large scale evaluation of the approach shows significant performance improvement with respect to state-of-the art methods for contextual entity exploration. Furthermore, the results indicate that combining IR-based and knowledge-graph based methods for this problem is a promising direction of future work.

7. ACKNOWLEDGEMENTS

We thank Ashok Chandra and Panayiotis Tsaparas for their insightful feedback.

8. REFERENCES

[1] G. Adomavicius and A. Tuzhilin. Toward the next generation of recommender systems: A survey of the state-of-the-art and possible extensions. *IEEE Transactions on Knowledge and Data Engineering*, 17(6):734–749, 2005.

[2] A. Agarwal, S. Chakrabarti, and S. Aggarwal. Learning to rank networked entities. In *Proc. of the ACM SIGKDD International Conference on Knowledge Discovery and Data Mining*, 2006.

[3] K. Balog, A. P. de Vries, P. Serdyukov, P. Thomas, and T. Westerveld. Overview of the trec 2009 entity track. In *Proc. of the Text Retrieval Conference Working Notes*, 2009.

[4] K. Balog and H. Ramampiaro. Cumulative citation recommendation: Classification vs. ranking. In *Proc. of the International ACM SIGIR Conference*, 2013.

[5] I. Bordino, Y. Mejova, and M. Lalmas. Penguins in sweaters, or serendipitous entity search on user-generated content. In *Proc. of the ACM International Conference on Information Knowledge Management*, 2013.

[6] C. Buckley and S. E. Robertson. Relevance feedback track overview: Trec 2008. In *Proc. of the Text Retrieval Conference*, 2008.

[7] C. Buckley, G. Salton, J. Allan, and A. Singhal. Automatic query expansion using smart: Trec 3. In *Proc. of the Text Retrieval Conference*, 1994.

[8] W. Chen, W. Hsu, and M. L. Lee. Tagcloud-based explanation with feedback for recommender systems. In *Proc. of the International ACM SIGIR Conference*, 2013.

[9] S. Cucerzan. Large-scale named entity disambiguation based on wikipedia data. In *EMNLP-CoNLL*, 2007.

[10] J. Dalton, L. Dietz, and J. Allan. Entity query feature expansion using knowledge base links. In *Proc. of the International ACM SIGIR conference on Research and Development in Information Retrieval*, 2014.

[11] L. Finkelstein, E. Gabrilovich, Y. Matias, E. Rivlin, Z. Solan, G. Wolfman, and E. Ruppin. Placing search in context: The concept revisited. In *Proc. of the International World Wide Web Conference*, 2001.

[12] L. C. Freeman. A set of measures of centrality based on betweenness. *Sociometry*, pages 35–41, 1977.

[13] A. Fuxman, P. Pantel, Y. Lv, A. Chandra, P. Chilakamarri, M. Gamon, D. Hamilton, B. Kohlmeier, D. Narayanan, E. Papalexakis, and B. Zhao. Contextual insights. In *Proc. of the Companion Publication of the International Conference on World Wide Web Companion*, 2014.

[14] S. Gottipati and J. Jiang. Linking entities to a knowledge base with query expansion. In *Proc. of the Conference on Empirical Methods in Natural Language Processing*, 2011.

[15] S. Gouws, G. Van Rooyen, and H. A. Engelbrecht. Measuring conceptual similarity by spreading activation over wikipedia's hyperlink structure. In *Proc. of Workshop on The People's Web Meets NLP: Collaboratively Constructed Semantic Resources*, 2010.

[16] J. L. Herlocker, J. A. Konstan, and J. Riedl. Explaining collaborative filtering recommendations. In *Proc. of the ACM Conference on Computer Supported Cooperative Work*, 2000.

[17] J. Hoffart, S. Seufert, D. B. Nguyen, M. Theobald, and G. Weikum. Kore: Keyphrase overlap relatedness for entity disambiguation. In *Proc. of the ACM International Conference on Information and Knowledge Management*, 2012.

[18] G. Jeh and J. Widom. Scaling personalized web search. In *Proc. of the International Conference on World Wide Web*, 2003.

[19] R. Kraft, C. C. Chang, F. Maghoul, and R. Kumar. Searching with context. In *Proc. of the International World Wide Web Conference*, 2006.

[20] S. Kulkarni, A. Singh, G. Ramakrishnan, and S. Chakrabarti. Collective annotation of wikipedia entities in web text. In *Proc. of the ACM SIGKDD International Conference on Knowledge Discovery and Data Mining*, 2009.

[21] V. Lavrenko and W. B. Croft. Relevance-based language models. In *Proc. of the International ACM SIGIR Conference*, 2001.

[22] S. Lee, S.-i. Song, M. Kahng, D. Lee, and S.-g. Lee. Random walk based entity ranking on graph for multidimensional recommendation. In *Proc. of the ACM Conference on Recommender Systems*, 2011.

[23] Y. Lv and A. Fuxman. In situ insights. In *Proc. of the International ACM SIGIR Conference*, 2015.

[24] Y. Lv, T. Moon, P. Kolari, Z. Zheng, X. Wang, and Y. Chang. Learning to model relatedness for news recommendation. In *Proc. of the International World Wide Web Conference*, 2011.

[25] Y. Lv and C. Zhai. Positional relevance model for pseudo-relevance feedback. In *Proc. of the International ACM SIGIR Conference*, 2010.

[26] R. Mihalcea, C. Corley, and C. Strapparava. Corpus-based and knowledge-based measures of text semantic similarity. In *Proc. of the National Conference on Artificial Intelligence*, 2006.

[27] R. Mihalcea and A. Csomai. Wikify!: linking documents to encyclopedic knowledge. In *Proc. of the ACM Conference on Information and Knowledge Management*, 2007.

[28] D. Milne and I. Witten. An effective, low-cost measure of semantic relatedness obtained from wikipedia links. In *Proc. of AAAI Workshop on Wikipedia and Artificial Intelligence*, 2008.

[29] D. Odijk, E. Meij, and M. de Rijke. Feeding the second screen: Semantic linking based on subtitles. In *Proc. of the Conference on Open Research Areas in Information Retrieval*, 2013.

[30] L. Page, S. Brin, R. Motwani, and T. Winograd. The pagerank citation ranking: Bringing order to the web. 1999.

[31] D. Petkova and W. B. Croft. Proximity-based document representation for named entity retrieval. In *Proc. of the ACM Conference on Information and Knowledge Management*, 2007.

[32] B. Ribeiro-Neto, M. Cristo, P. B. Golgher, and E. Silva de Moura. Impedance coupling in content-targeted advertising. In *Proc. of the International ACM SIGIR Conference*, 2005.

[33] S. Robertson and I. Soboroff. The trec 2002 filtering track report. In *Proc. of the Text Retrieval Conference*, 2002.

[34] S. E. Robertson and K. S. Jones. Relevance weighting of search terms. *Journal of the American Society of Information Science*, 27(3):129–146, 1976.

[35] J. J. Rocchio. Relevance feedback in information retrieval. In *In The SMART Retrieval System: Experiments in Automatic Document Processing*. Prentice-Hall Inc., 1971.

[36] M. Strube and S. P. Ponzetto. Wikirelate! computing semantic relatedness using wikipedia. In *Proc. of the AAAI Conference on Artificial Intelligence*.

[37] P. Symeonidis, A. Nanopoulos, and Y. Manolopoulos. Providing justifications in recommender systems. *IEEE Transactions on Systems, Man and Cybernetics, Part A*, 38(6):1262–1272, 2008.

[38] A.-M. Vercoustre, J. A. Thom, and J. Pehcevski. Entity ranking in wikipedia. In *Proc. of the ACM Symposium on Applied Computing*, 2008.

[39] J. Vig, S. Sen, and J. Riedl. Tagsplanations: explaining recommendations using tags. In *Proc. of the International Conference on Intelligent User Interfaces*, 2009.

[40] N. Voskarides, D. Odijk, M. Tsagkias, W. Weerkamp, and M. de Rijke. Query-dependent contextualization of streaming data. In *Proc. of the European Conference on Information Retrieval*, 2014.

[41] E. Yeh, D. Ramage, C. D. Manning, E. Agirre, and A. Soroa. Wikiwalk: Random walks on wikipedia for semantic relatedness. In *Proc. of the Workshop on Graph-based Methods for Natural Language Processing*, 2009.

[42] M. A. Yosef, J. Hoffart, I. Bordino, M. Spaniol, and G. Weikum. Aida: An online tool for accurate disambiguation of named entities in text and tables. *Proc. of the VLDB Endowment*, 4(12):1450–1453, 2011.

[43] C. Yu, L. V. Lakshmanan, and S. Amer-Yahia. Recommendation diversification using explanations. In *Proc. of the IEEE International Conference on Data Engineering*, 2009.

[44] M. Zhou and K. C.-C. Chang. Entity-centric document filtering: boosting feature mapping through meta-features. In *Proc. of the ACM International Conference on Information and Knowledge Management*, 2013.

Click-through Prediction for Advertising in Twitter Timeline

Cheng Li [1]*, Yue Lu [2], Qiaozhu Mei [1], Dong Wang [2], Sandeep Pandey [2]
[1] School of Information, University of Michigan, Ann Arbor, MI, USA
[2] Twitter Inc, 1355 Market St Suite 900, San Francisco, CA, USA
lichengz@umich.edu, yuelu@twitter.com, qmei@umich.edu, dongw@twitter.com, spandey@twitter.com

ABSTRACT

We present the problem of click-through prediction for advertising in Twitter timeline, which displays a stream of Tweets from accounts a user choose to follow. Traditional computational advertising usually appears in two forms: *sponsored search* that places ads onto the search result page when a query is issued to a search engine, and *contextual advertising* that places ads onto a regular, usually static Web page. Compared with these two paradigms, placing ads into a Tweet stream is particularly challenging given the nature of the data stream: the context into which an ad can be placed updates dynamically and never replicates. Every ad is therefore placed into a unique context. This makes the information available for training a machine learning model extremely sparse. In this study, we propose a learning-to-rank method which not only addresses the sparsity of training signals but also can be trained and updated online. The proposed method is evaluated using both offline experiments and online A/B tests, which involve very large collections of Twitter data and real Twitter users. Results of the experiments prove the effectiveness and efficiency of our solution, and its superiority over the current production model adopted by Twitter.

Categories and Subject Descriptors

H.4 [**Information Systems Applications**]: Miscellaneous

General Terms

Algorithms, Experimentation, Measurements

Keywords

Online Advertising; Social Media Stream; Click-through Prediction

1. INTRODUCTION

Users at Twitter could subscribe to other accounts, commonly referred to as followees. These followees continuously produce messages ("Tweets"), corresponding in general to the follower's long term interest. Once posted, Tweets are pushed into the follower's **timeline**, a continuous stream of Tweets from one's followees. To facilitate the consumption of the large amount of real time information, each user's timeline is displayed in a way that new arrivals are presented on the top of the screen, replacing the older ones. When a user refreshes her timeline, only limited number of Tweets are pushed to the user's device. This leads to the concept of **session**, which consists of all the Tweets sent to one user at the same time.

In this paper, we present the problem of click-through prediction for advertising in Twitter timeline, an essential problem in determining ads to be presented and appropriate payments [11]. Stating the problem more specifically, given a user's timeline, the session pushed to this user at a particular time, and a set of ads, we predict the probability that a particular ad will be clicked on if it is displayed at a particular position of this user's timeline. Traditional online advertising usually appears in two forms: *sponsored search* and *contextual advertising*. Sponsored search is designed for web search engines. It is concerned with placing ads onto a search result page of a particular query. In contrast, contextual advertising studies how to display ads on a regular, usually static Web page. Compared with these two traditional paradigms, placing ads into a Twitter user's timeline is particularly challenging given its streamed nature. First, the stream of Tweets are emitted from accounts the user follows, which usually correspond to her long term interest but do not reflect her current status. However, whether the user clicks on an ad or not depends more on her current information need (a.k.a., intent) when the ad is viewed [30]. For example, a user following *@Microsoft* on Twitter is not necessarily looking for a Microsoft product right now. A user who is inquiring about the most recent version of iPhone may not necessarily subscribe to Apple's feeds. Second, every user receives a unique stream of Tweets which update continuously. Compared with sponsored search where an ad can be placed whenever the same query is issued, and to contextual advertising where an ad can be placed whenever a user visits the same Web page, in a Tweet stream few ads are placed in the same session. Moreover, every user has a different timeline which is updated dynamically. This means that we have a unique "page" (i.e., session) for every user at any given time point. As a result, ads inserted at different time points are actually displayed in completely different "pages" (sessions). These factors make it difficult to gather enough user behavioral signals for training a machine learning model and non-trivial to utilize historical clicks on an ad for predicting how likely it will be clicked on in the future. These unique challenges call for a reevaluation of the techniques employed in traditional online advertising scenarios, and for new approaches that could specifically address the unique properties of Tweet streams.

In this paper, We investigate how learning-to-rank and online learning techniques can be utilized and customized to address these

*The work is done while the author was an intern at Twitter Inc.

KDD'15, August 10-13, 2015, Sydney, NSW, Australia.
ACM 978-1-4503-3664-2/15/08.
DOI: http://dx.doi.org/10.1145/2783258.2788582 .

challenges. We examine our solutions by conducting both offline experiments and online experiments (a.k.a., A/B tests), which involve very large collections of Twitter data and real Twitter users. The results prove the efficiency and effectiveness of the proposed method, and its improvement over Twitter's current production model.

The rest of the paper is organized as follows. We discuss related work in Section 2. Section 3 gives an overview of the procedure for advertising in stream. Section 4 describes methods to tackle the challenges, followed by description of infrastructure implementation to conduct online experiments in Section 5. Section 6 describes setup of offline experiments and results, while the report of online experiments is present in Section 7. Finally, we conclude the paper in Section 8.

2. RELATED WORK

The task of click-through prediction for online advertising at Twitter is related to the practice in social media industry, including online advertising in Facebook, LinkedIn, etc. The most relevant work in literature is a recent study of predicting clicks on Facebook ads by He et al. [16]. Their study did not fully address the unique properties of data streams and the challenges of advertising in streams. As a result, they treated the prediction for every ad as a classification problem, a formulation commonly used in conventional online advertising scenarios. We show in this paper that a significant improvement can be obtained by considering the unique properties of data streams and utilizing learning-to-rank techniques. Researchers at Google [1] developed a system that processes training data in a streamed fashion, which was applied to sponsored search. The problem we present is quite different from and arguably much more challenging than theirs, in which an ad is not triggered by a query but by a unique, fast evolving context in the social media stream.

Aside from studies on advertising in streams, we consider three lines of researches that are related to our work: learning to rank, online advertising, and ranking streaming data. Due to the large body of work on learning to rank [21] and online advertising [12], we constrain our focus to predicting click-through rate (CTR) for online advertising through a machine learning approach. That is, we aim at training CTR prediction models using either historical click logs or human annotated examples.

Traditionally, online advertising falls into two categories: sponsored search [18] and contextual advertising [27]. Sponsored search advertising displays advertisements onto the result page of a particular query submitted to a search engine. Google is the first to incorporate click feedback into the model [3]. In order to estimate CTR for new ads, Richardson et al. [28] explored different types of features (ads, terms, and advertisers) to train a logistic regression model. Considering the rapid growth of data volume, Ciaramita et al. [9] employed online learning using the perceptron algorithm. Graepel et al. [15] addressed the same problem by using a scalable Bayesian algorithm.

Contextual advertising refers to ads placement within the content of regular web pages. A large body of work is devoted to learning the relevance of the displayed ads to the page content. Features identifying both semantic and syntactic relationship of words between the Web page and ads are included in [6]. Semantic relationships of words between Web pages and ads are modeled by hidden classes in [26]. Murdock et al. [23] developed a system that uses features derived from statistical machine translation models, aiming to learn a "translation" of vocabularies between ads and target pages. Chakrabarti et al. [8] applied logistic regression to learn the match between ads and Web pages. Bai et al. [2] proposed a supervised version of latent semantic indexing to map the query-document pair to a ranking score. In order to learn the ranking function, genetic programming is adopted by Lacerda et al. [20]. Karimzadehgan et al. [19] proposed a stochastic algorithm to learn a ranking function that directly optimizes IR evaluation metrics, which are usually not differentiable.

Ranking streaming data, such as Tweets, has been widely studied in literature. Duan et al. [10] presented an empirical study on learning to rank of Tweets by considering features like content relevance, account authority and Tweet-specific features such as presence of a URL. Zhang et al. [31] exploited transductive learning, of which the idea is similar to pseudo relevance feedback, to alleviate the problem of few training data in learning to rank. To find out the semantics of Tweet content, Nguyen et al. [24] incorporated topic modeling features into the learning-to-rank procedure. Hong et al. [17] studied ranking LinkedIn social updates by utilizing learning to rank, collaborative filtering, and click-through modeling. Our work is different from these studies as our target is not ranking organic feeds in the stream, but the ads to be inserted into the stream. The organic feeds in the stream instead defines the context of ads. Our study also goes beyond finding the relative order of candidate ads and targets an accurate estimation of click probability.

3. ADVERTISING IN TWITTER TIMELINE

3.1 System overview

We first give an overview of the advertising system designed for Twitter. This system overview could help the readers better understand how advertising in a message stream functions.

The nature of Twitter encourages various forms of advertisements. For instance, advertisers could invite users to follow their Twitter accounts, enhance the popularity of a particular hashtag, and distribute product information via Tweets.[1] Among them, a large proportion of user targeting takes the form of Tweets, which we call *promoted Tweets*. When inserted in user's timeline, promoted Tweets are like regular Tweets: they scroll through the timeline, appear in the timeline just once, and users can engage with the Tweets by a variety of forms. For example, users can click on URLs, retweet, reply to, or favorite the promoted Tweet, just as they do to any other regular Tweets. The only difference is that a user could perform a negative engagement with a promoted Tweet by hitting a "dismiss" button associated with the promoted Tweets.

Figure 1 summarizes the interactions between the client side and the ad server. When a Twitter user refreshes her home timeline, the client side issues an ad display request to the ad server. We refer to this time stamp as *request time*. An initial set of ad candidates are formed according to the information of the user. To decide the winner from these candidates, an auction is run based on two major factors. The first is the bid price, the amount of money advertisers are willing to pay if users engage with their ads. The second factor is the predicted click probability – the target of our prediction task. We call this task the *click-through rate* (**CTR**) prediction, following the literature of online advertising. By clicks, we mean any type of engagements with the Tweets. In this paper, we focus on predicting the probability of any positive engagements, e.g., retweet, reply, and click a URL. Described methods could be easily generalized to prediction of a specific user action, e.g., dismissing a promoted Tweet. Positive engagements are shortened as *engagements* in the rest of the paper if no ambiguity arises. At the end of the auction, there could be zero to K winning ads. No ad will be placed if the system cannot find a good match to the context. Showing ads anyway in this case would hurt user experience in the long run.

[1] https://business.twitter.com/ad-products

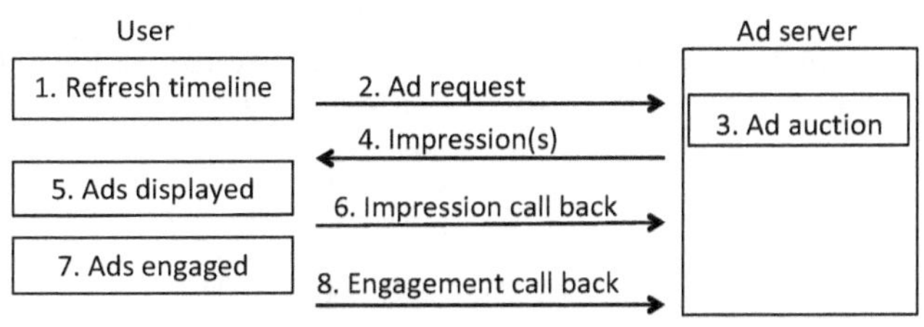

Figure 1: The process of displaying an ad in Twitter timeline. Numbers indicate the order of events.

Due to the same reason, the maximum number of selected ads K is usually set to a very small number.

One thing worth noting is that there are essentially two aspects in the CTR prediction task. On the one hand, we should give a correct estimation of click probability, especially for the winners in the auction. An underestimation could result in no winners while an overestimation incurs user frustration. In addition, inaccurate prediction leads to complications in charging, due to Twitter's adoption of second-price auction [11]. On the other hand, a ranking of the ads are more critical than the actual values of CTR when choosing the best ads to show to every user. This is especially important as there is a very limited number of spots to display ads. A model achieving reasonable CTR estimation does not necessarily output good ranking, and vice versa.

Having chosen the ads to display, the server expects an impression callback from the client, indicating the successful appearance of ads in user's device screen. This time stamp is recorded as *impression callback time*. This callback is necessary given the streamed nature of user's timeline: promoted Tweets might have already been scrolled over before users ever see it. Admittedly, impression callbacks only indicate that promoted Tweets have been displayed in user's screen. It is very possible that the user fails to notice them. However, this is the best signal we can collect that indicates the impression. If, by any chance, the user engages with the promoted Tweet, an engagement callback will be triggered. This point of time is called *engagement callback time*.

4. METHODS

Challenges of CTR prediction at Twitter call for special treatments to the machine learning techniques used in conventional scenarios that could at least address some aspects of these challenges. To this end, our approach in general is to employ learning-to-rank techniques in an online fashion, with careful design of features that addresses the unique properties of data streams. We first introduce a straightforward classification framework, employed as current production model at Twitter, and then investigate possible improvement based on it.

4.1 Pointwise approach

Following the typical machine learning approach to CTR prediction problem, we use a pointwise learning-to-rank approach as our baseline, a method applied as the production model of Twitter. In our particular application, we try to train a probabilistic classifier that assigns a posterior click-through probability to an ad, if it is displayed in user's current session of her timeline. The training data are made up of all historical impressions shown across all users. These data are treated as i.i.d. and the learning algorithm optimizes for the global loss. An instance is represented as $(y, \mathbf{x})$, where $y \in \{\pm 1\}$ is the ground-truth binary label, with value 1 being the presence of clicks. Feature vector $\mathbf{x}$ is extracted from the ad, user, timeline, current session, and possible interactions between any two of the entities. These features should be general enough because no session repeats. Let $D = \{(y, \mathbf{x})\}$ be the set of all instances. The loss function for the pointwise learning can be formulated as [4]

$$L(\mathbf{w}, D) = \sum_{(y,\mathbf{x}) \in D} \ell(y, f(\mathbf{w}, \mathbf{x}))$$

where f is a hypothesis function, $\mathbf{w}$ is function parameters, and ℓ is a loss function for a single instance. In order to quickly capture user's change of information need, and enable large-scale online learning on the huge amount of click data, we use logistic regression to instantiate this learning framework with stochastic gradient descent (SGD) [4] as the optimization algorithm, a strategy also employed by Facebook [16]. Specifically, we have

$$\ell(y, f(\mathbf{w}, \mathbf{x})) = \log(1 + \exp(-y f(\mathbf{w}, \mathbf{x})))$$

where $f(\mathbf{w}, \mathbf{x}) = \mathbf{w}^T \mathbf{x}$, and $y \in \{\pm 1\}$.

4.2 Pairwise approach

In pointwise approaches, the learner takes as input a single instance one at a time, with presence of engagement as target value. Despite its advantage of directly minimizing prediction error, pointwise learning does not take into account the relative order of ads in terms of a particular user's preference, externalized by this user's click probability on each ad. However, as we know, ranking is critical in the auction of determining the winning ads – only top few candidates can be finally displayed, as we discussed as the second aspect of CTR prediction in Section 3.1.

Another significant advantage of directly learning user's relative ads preference is that we can address the training data sparsity challenge if we choose preference data wisely. It is natural that user's interest on ads can change over time. If a user clicked an ad a_A one year ago, and ignored an ad a_B today, it is doubtful to draw the conclusion that this user prefers a_A to a_B, due to a possible shift of interest of this user over a year. However, it is reasonable to assume that user preference is steady during a short time period. For example, two ads are more comparable if they are presented to the same user in one session. Two ads in the same session have almost the exact context, thus directly optimizing the perference order between them can address the sparsity challenge that ads are shown in different unique contexts.

In order to optimize for the relative user preference, we employ a pairwise learning approach [14], which attempts to incur less ranking loss. In particular, we train a pairwise model on ad pairs that are shown to one user in the same session. Let $P = \{((y_A, \mathbf{x}_A), (y_B, \mathbf{x}_B)) \,|\, y_A \neq y_B\}$ be the set of all pairs. The loss function is defined as

$$L(\mathbf{w}, P) = \sum_{((y_A,\mathbf{x}_A),(y_B,\mathbf{x}_B)) \in P} \ell(g(y_A - y_B), f(\mathbf{w}, \mathbf{x}_A) - f(\mathbf{w}, \mathbf{x}_B))$$

where $g(y_A - y_B)$ transforms the difference of two individual instance labels into the label for pairwise learning. We use $g(y) = y/2$ to ensure that $g(y_A - y_B) \in \{\pm 1\}$. For logistic regression, $f(\mathbf{w}, \mathbf{x}_A) - f(\mathbf{w}, \mathbf{x}_B) = \mathbf{w}^T \mathbf{x}_A - \mathbf{w}^T \mathbf{x}_B = \mathbf{w}^T (\mathbf{x}_A - \mathbf{x}_B) = f(\mathbf{w}, \mathbf{x}_A - \mathbf{x}_B)$. Therefore, the logistic loss listed in classification section can still be used with no change [7], bringing the advantage that pairwise learning can be conducted in an online and scalable manner, just as pointwise learning.

4.2.1 *Calibration*

As stated above, pairwise approaches try to minimize ranking loss. Accordingly, the output of pairwise model is interpreted as preference score, rather than predicted click probability. However, estimation of click probability is indispensable for ad auctions, as described in Section 3.1. This means calibration is needed to transform score to click probability. A common practice is to use a sigmoid function [25], where the coefficients are learned through maximizing likelihood on the training set. An advantage of this transformation is that the relative order of instances ranked by score of the original model is preserved.

4.3 Combining pointwise and pairwise learning

Pointwise approaches try to obtain good estimate of click probability, while pairwise approaches aim to learn the ranking of impressions ordered by click probability. This brings their respective downside: pointwise methods are performing poorly on ranking, whereas pairwise methods tend to have the problem of inaccurate CTR estimation. Another practical problem could possibly arise if we resort to pairwise learning: not all sessions have more than one ad. This is especially true for Twitter, where the majority of auctions output no more than one winning ad. Consequently, a large proportion of instances would be wasted at training stage. The above analysis suggests that a combination of two approaches might be a good solution to simultaneously achieve good click probability estimation and ranking. Therefore, we propose an online algorithm, based on a combined optimization framework developed by Sculley [29]:

$$\min_{\mathbf{w}} \alpha L(\mathbf{w}, D) + (1-\alpha) L(\mathbf{w}, P) \quad (1)$$

with α being a trade-off parameter between optimizing towards classification and ranking. In [29], this trade-off is implemented by sampling an instance from D with probability α and a pair from P with probability $1-\alpha$. The sampling practice is perfect for offline static learning. For real online learning, the model receives training data in the form of ad stream, and ads of one session could return at different time points. Therefore, an algorithm adapted to the online setting has to be developed for the combined learning. We defer the description of the new algorithm to Section 5, where we introduce the infrastructure to support this learning approach.

One thing worth noting is that no calibration is necessary for combined learning, attributed to the classification component in the objective function.

4.3.1 *Acquisition of more pairs*

In practice, multiple ads shown in the same user session is still the minority case, because of the need to protect user experience by controlling the ads load. This is especially true for promoted Tweets, which are inserted into the main stream that users consume information from, unlike search ads or contextual ads displayed on the sidebar. As a result, only a small percentage of training instances fed to the model are from a pair of ads. Consequently, the learned model would be biased towards minimizing classification loss, failing to obtain enough pairs to induce a good ranker and mitigate the sparsity issue. To combat this problem, one strategy is to form more pairs artificially by grouping impressions from distinct requests. There are two grouping choices: across different users and within one user. Comparing impressions across users is to compare clicks collected from disparate preferences. It is possible to pair impressions from users sharing similar interests, borrowing the idea of collaborative filtering. For simplicity, in this work we only consider within-user grouping. Though a user's interest shifts over the course of time, it is reasonable to assume that each user's preference is stable within a short period of time. This makes it plausible to form *"pseudo-pairs"* by grouping impressions shown in different sessions but to the same user. To emphasize the time information, we attach importance weight to formed pairs based on time difference. Mathematically, let $S = \{((y_A, \mathbf{x}_A, t_A), (y_B, \mathbf{x}_B, t_B)) | y_A \neq y_B, t_A \neq t_B\}$ be the set of all pseudo-pairs, where t_A, t_B are the request time of impression A and B respectively. The loss function is defined as

$$L(\mathbf{w}, S) = \sum_{((y_A, \mathbf{x}_A, t_A),(y_B, \mathbf{x}_B, t_B)) \in S} \max\left(\min(\log \frac{N}{|t_A - t_B|}, 1), 0\right) \cdot \ell(g(y_A - y_B), f(\mathbf{w}, \mathbf{x}_A) - f(\mathbf{w}, \mathbf{x}_B))$$

where N is acting as the size of a sliding window – the weight of a paired instance is 0 if $|t_A - t_B| \geq N$. The optimization framework incorporating pseudo-pairs can be formulated as:

$$\min_{\mathbf{w}} \alpha_1 L(\mathbf{w}, D) + \alpha_2 L(\mathbf{w}, P) + (1 - \alpha_1 - \alpha_2) L(\mathbf{w}, S) \quad (2)$$

4.4 Summary of methods

We give a summary of methods for future references.

1. **Pointwise learning**, which considers each ad as an individual training instance. This is the production model currently deployed at Twitter.
2. **Pairwise learning**. This method essentially refers to pairwise learning with calibration. Since the performance of pairwise approach before calibration is extremely poor in our empirical studies, we only report results on the calibrated version, which preserves the original ranking performance.
3. **Combined learning**, which takes into account classification and ranking under one framework.
4. **Pseudo**. Based on combined learning, we artificially create more pairwise training instances called pseudo-pairs.

5. ONLINE LEARNING INFRASTRUCTURE

In this section, we introduce the infrastructure at Twitter, an implementation used to conduct live experiments on the learning techniques described in Section 4. Considering the massive behavior data collected from each user's timeline, models that could be updated online are strongly necessary. In this section, we introduce how pointwise and combined learning could be conducted in an online manner, so that large-scale online A/B tests can be performed. Due to its poor estimation of CTR in offline study, we exclude pairwise learning in online experiments. Launching the method pseudo requires a significant change to Twitter's production system, which is unrealistic for this study. Therefore, pseudo is excluded as well. More detailed behavior analysis across all methods are performed via offline experiments.

5.1 Pointwise learning

Online learning requires we obtain new clicks and non-clicks in real-time so that new training instances could be formed to update the model. However, some difficulties surface due to the nature of stream.

The first issue has already been stated in Section 3.1, which is related to deciding whether users have seen the promoted Tweets. Since it is possible that users do not click ads simply because they fail to see it, only ads with impression callbacks will be considered as training examples.

There is yet another problem: the length of time varies for different users to finally see and engage with the promoted Tweets. This leads to a time difference for servers to receive engagement callbacks. The worst case is that users simply ignore these Tweets and servers can never obtain engagement callbacks. Hence comes

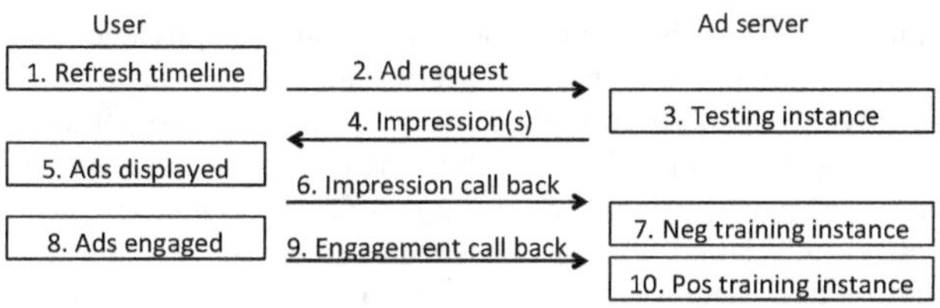

Figure 2: Online pointwise learning process

the problem of deciding the length of time the server should wait for user clicks. Because a training instance is not complete until its label is decided, this waiting time directly determines the lag of online learning. One solution to this problem is to cache impressions, and judge them as negative if no engagement callbacks are returned in a predefined amount of time, as did by Facebook [16]. That is to say, our judgment of labels could be wrong – engagement callbacks could return after the predefined time. The longer we cache ads, the more likely we obtain the ground-truth labels. However, trade-off exists – longer cache time leads to larger cache size and bigger delay of training. Our choice is not to cache at all – impressions are always set as negative and are added to the training set immediately when **impression** callback is received. If ever **engagement** callback returns, this impression is reset as positive to update the model again. This solution saves the large amount of cache space we have to offer and ensures no delay of training. Additionally, considering the rarity of clicking events, only a small percentage of examples need correction. Furthermore, preliminary work showed marginal improvement through caching. A summary of the online learning process is shown in Figure 2.

5.2 Combined learning

Combined learning requires training instances formed from both a single ad and a pair of ads. The procedure of obtaining single ads is identical to the one for pointwise learning. However two problems remain to be solved. First, we need to find a way to collect a pair of ads with click information. For simplicity, in the setting of online tests we only consider ads belonging to one session (request). Second, we have to decide how to trade-off between classification and ranking. That is, how to combine pointwise learning and pairwise learning.

The label for a pair can be decided only if we have click labels for both impressions in the pair. However, engagement callbacks return separately and the time of which varies a lot. To wait for the labels for both impressions, we have no choice this time but to cache them. The cache is accessed by using request id as the key. The cache value is a set of impressions with labels initialized to null. Each cache entry is guaranteed to be alive for 15 minutes. When an impression call back arrives, the label of the correspondent impression is set to negative. Whereas when an engagement call back returns, the label for the associated impression is turned to positive. Update of the model is only necessary when one impression's label changes from negative to positive, namely the moment when an engagement call back occurs. The positive instance is then paired with all negative instances belonging to one session. Chances are that some of the negative instances are clicked later, leading to input of false information to the model. In practice, we ignore such situations as we do not observe much performance loss, possibly due to the rarity of these circumstances.

With regard to the second problem, we assume a simple strategy – always apply pointwise learning for each individual impression, and do both pointwise and pairwise learning when there are more than one impression with differing labels. In this case, the trade-off parameter α in Equation 1 depends on the percentage of requests with a single ad and the number of clicked ads in requests with more than one ad.

Algorithm 1 Update $\mathbf{w}$ using combined learning

Input: *cache*, request ID *req_id*, call back impression ID *imp_id*, call back type *type*, current model parameter $\mathbf{w}$, weight w_p for paired instance
Output: Updated model parameter $\mathbf{w}$

$imp\_map \leftarrow cache.get(req\_id)$
$(y, \mathbf{x}) \leftarrow imp\_map.get(imp\_id)$ // get impression
if $type = impression\_call\_back$ **then**
  $imp\_map.set(imp\_id, (-1, \mathbf{x}))$ // set label to negative
  update $\mathbf{w}$ using $(-1, \mathbf{x})$ by SGD // pointwise learning
else // handle engagement call back
  $imp\_map.set(imp\_id, (+1, \mathbf{x}))$ // set label to positive
  update $\mathbf{w}$ using $(+1, \mathbf{x})$ by SGD // pointwise learning
  $P \leftarrow extract\_pairs(imp\_map, (+1, \mathbf{x}))$
  if $P.length > 0$ **then** // pairwise learning
    for Each pair $((y_A, \mathbf{x}_A), (y_B, \mathbf{x}_B))$ in P **do**
      $\mathbf{x} \leftarrow (\mathbf{x}_A - \mathbf{x}_B)$
      $y \leftarrow g(y_A - y_B)$
      update $\mathbf{w}$ using $(y, \mathbf{x})$ and weight w_p by SGD
    end for
  end if
end if

Therefore we would like to adjust α by changing the percentage of requests with more than one ad. Unfortunately decision of this percentage is complicated, and we have no direct control over it. However, we can still approximately change α by varying the weight w_p of instances formed by a pair of ads.

Note that paired instances are only used at training stage, and are excluded for prediction. In fact, for all approaches, prediction stage stays the same – we predict the click probability of each individual ad candidate at ad request time while running auctions.

Algorithm 1 gives a detailed description of the training procedure for combined learning. Algorithm 2 shows how pairs are extracted from a request. Line 3 to 8 guarantee that we generate positive and negative instances with equal probability.

Algorithm 2 *extract_pairs* (Extract pairs for a particular request)

Input: Impression map *imp_map*, call back impression $(y, \mathbf{x})$
Output: An array of paired instances $P = \{((y_A, \mathbf{x}_A), (y_B, \mathbf{x}_B)) | y_A \neq y_B\}$

1: $P \leftarrow \{\}$
2: **for** Each negative instance $(y^-, \mathbf{x}^-)$ in *imp_map* **do**
3:   Draw z uniformly at random from $[0, 1)$
4:   **if** $z < 0.5$ **then**
5:     Form a pair $p \leftarrow ((y, \mathbf{x}), (y^-, \mathbf{x}^-))$
6:   **else**
7:     Form a pair $p \leftarrow ((y^-, \mathbf{x}^-), (y, \mathbf{x}))$
8:   **end if**
9:   $P \leftarrow P \cup \{p\}$
10: **end for**

6. OFFLINE EXPERIMENT

We evaluate the methods using both offline and online experiments. Online experiments are used to verify the true effectiveness of methods in real setting, while more detailed analysis is done through offline simulation. We introduce the offline experiments in this section, and describe the online tests in Section 7.

6.1 Metrics

6.1.1 NRIG

In order to quantify the accuracy of predicted click probability, we use normalized relative information gain (NRIG), based on relative information gain (RIG) [15]. Given test set T, the empirical CTR of the data is defined as $\bar{p} = \sum_{t=1}^{T} y_t/|T|$, where $y_t \in \{0, 1\}$ is the ground-truth label. The entropy is referred as $H(\bar{p}) = -(\bar{p}\log\bar{p} + (1-\bar{p})\log(1-\bar{p}))$. The empirical cross entropy for a model is $CE = -\frac{1}{|T|}\sum_{t=1}^{T}(y_t \log p_t + (1-y_t)\log(1-p_t))$, where p_t is the model predicted click probability for t-th impression. Then relative information gain could be computed as $RIG = (H(\bar{p}) - CE)/H(\bar{p})$. To normalize RIG, we compute normalized prediction $\hat{p}_t = p_t \times \frac{\bar{p}}{\sum_{t=1}^{T} p_t/|T|}$ This ensures that the average of the normalized prediction equals to $\bar{p}$, the empirical CTR. The subsequent computation of NRIG is almost identical to RIG, with the exception that p_t is replaced by $\hat{p}_t$ when computing CE.

6.1.2 AUC

To measure ranking quality, we compute the area under receiver operator curve (AUC) [13] for the subset of requests containing more than one ad. For each of such requests, we calculate AUC using (1) predicted ranking, formed by the estimated click probability output by the model, and (2) ground-truth, which is the presence or absence of engagements for each ad in the request. We report final AUC as an average over requests with more than one ad.

6.2 Procedure

Instead of k-fold cross-validation, we use an evaluation procedure based on progressive validation [5]. This procedure works in a streamed fashion, simulating the online setting described in Section 5: both test and training data come in a stream, and instances are first used for testing at request time, and are later used for training.

With regard to pseudo, a method not covered in Section 5, we do offline simulation using the following process. Cache time is set to N, the sliding window size. Impressions displayed to the same user that coincide in the same window can form pairs. Similar to combined learning, a positive ad is paired with each of all negative ones.

6.3 Dataset

To conduct offline experiments, we collected data from a random week of year 2014. Given that progressive validation is employed, there is no need to partition the data into training and testing. To give readers a sense of the scale of the dataset, in the third quarter of 2014, there are 181 billion timeline views on Twitter,[2] approximating the number of ad requests.

6.4 Parameters

All parameters, including learning rate of stochastic gradient, parameter controlling regularization, coefficients of calibration model, and the weight w_p of instances formed by a pair of ads, are tuned using the first day's data. This period is excluded in the reports of experiment results. In addition to parameter tuning, the first day training allows the models to warm up.

In combined learning, we have a parameter α to control the importance of classification error against ranking error. As stated in Section 5, we adjust it by varying the weight w_p of instances formed by a pair of ads. In pseudo, we have parameter N, the size of sliding window to form pseudo pairs. Both w_p and N are tuned to optimum using the data of first day, equaling to 20 and 8 hours respectively. Actually in pseudo, we have another two parameters α_1 and α_2 in Equation 2, controlling the importance of single ads, paired ads, and pseudo-pairs. Like α, the importance of pseudo-pairs could be approximated by the maximum possible weight of pseudo-pairs. Due to its similarity to α, we omit the study of it by simply setting the maximum possible weight to 1. A sensitivity study of parameter α and w_p will be performed later in the experiment result section.

[2]https://investor.twitterinc.com/releasedetail.cfm?releaseid=878170

6.5 Features

In order to better catch user's information need, deal with training sparsity problem and capture the unique properties of ads in streams, we design features from four perspectives: ad, user, ad-user interaction, and context of the stream. Unfortunately, we can only give a brief description of features in each category, without disclosing the specific features to be used.

- Ad. Features related to an ad can be further divided into three subcategories. 1) Advertiser profile, such as a set of topics pertinent to an advertiser. 2) Meta information, including ID of an advertiser, type of ad, etc. 3) Click history, an example is past clicks of an ad on the population level.

- User. Analogous to ad, user related features also fall into three subcategories. 1) User profile, such as user related topics. 2) Meta information, including gender and device information. 3) Click history, such as advertisers engaged by a user in the past.

- Ad-user interaction. The interactions can be characterized by ad-user similarity and user click history of ads belonging to the same advertiser. Multiple similarity measures are included, e.g., similarity between user and advertiser's profile, and whether the user is related to certain keywords specified by the advertiser.

- Context of the stream. The context refers to features available within a session, which enables us to find out interactions between ads and organic messages. Because no sessions repeat, these contextual features have to be general enough. Specifically, we include positions of the promoted Tweets, used to correct position bias at training time, and similarity between the promoted Tweets and organic Tweets in one session. To compute the similarity, we consider two forms of text representations: bag of words and word vectors calculated by word2vec [22].

Continuous features are transformed to categorical ones using boosted decision trees, a similar discretization technique reported by Facebook [16].

6.6 Experiment results

6.6.1 Overall performance

Table 1 summarizes performance of different approaches, averaged over one week but excluding the first day. The result is reported based on percentage of improvement using pointwise learning, our production model, as the reference. Though we are not aware of any statistic tests designed for NRIG, empirical studies show that the improvement listed in Table 1 is strongly significant.

Consistent with our expectation, pairwise learning scores relatively high in terms of AUC, but does poorly on NRIG, even with calibration. Therefore, pairwise learning indeed gives a good ranking of ads, but fail at estimating the click probability. This is due to its objective of incurring less ranking loss by attempting to give a correct order of ads, however without taking into any account of the accurate estimation of click probability.

Method	Pairwise	Combined	Pseudo
Relative NRIG (%)	-75.90	$+9.44$	$+10.25$
Relative AUC (%)	$+1.76^{***}$	$+1.91^{***}$	$+2.11^{***}$

Table 1: Summary of performance relative to pointwise learning method. * indicates the improvement over Pointwise method is statistically significant according to Wilcoxon signed rank test at the significance level of 0.001**

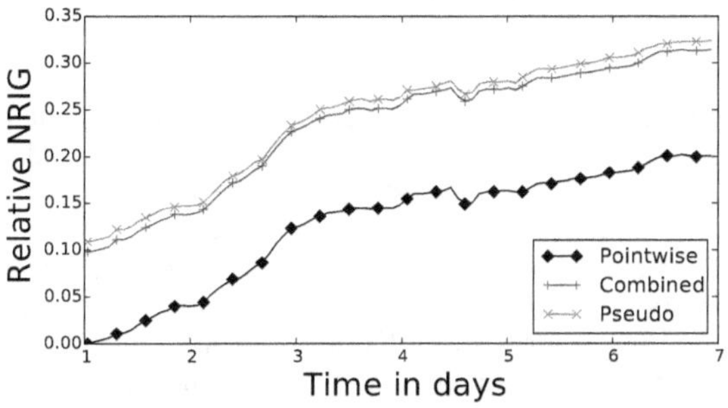

Figure 3: Relative NRIG of one week excluding the first day. The pairwise method is excluded due to its extremely low score.

In contrast, the pointwise model achieves reasonable result on NRIG, but is inferior to all the other methods on ranking. This behavior can be explained by its optimization purely towards minimizing errors of CTR prediction, while ignoring relative ranking of ads.

Combining pointwise and pairwise methods brings a huge performance gain on both CTR estimation and ranking. We suspect the reason behind it is that learning two tasks simultaneously requires the model to put more weight on features that could achieve good CTR prediction as well as good ranking. The enhancement of both NRIG and AUC indicate that combining pointwise and pairwise learning-to-rank techniques indeed helps us better capture user's current interest, and alleviates the training sparsity problem by incorporating relative preference information.

The last column of Table 1 shows the results after adding pseudo-pairs to the combined model. We could find a further improvement over the original combined model. This indicates that these pseudo-pairs could contribute positively, which is good news if we are concerned that showing too many ads in one request could hurt user experience. Pseudo-pairs alleviate this problem and corroborate the assumption that user preference are stable in a short period of time, and can be utilized to capture user's short-term interest.

6.6.2 *Learning behavior*

In addition to the average performance, we are also interested in how different methods behave over the course of time. Figures 3 and 4 show such behavior changes in terms of relative NRIG and AUC. The relative value is computed as the improvement over the performance of pointwise learning at the end of the first day. The pairwise method is excluded in Figure 3, due to its extremely low score and resemblance to other methods in terms of the learning curve.

For both metrics, all the methods exhibit similar patterns: an evident rise of performance in the first day, followed by small, gradual but continual improvement. Though not completely stabilized at last, the increase shows a tendency to level off. This common pattern depicts the learning behaviors of the online models: the effectiveness of the model keeps improving as more and more training

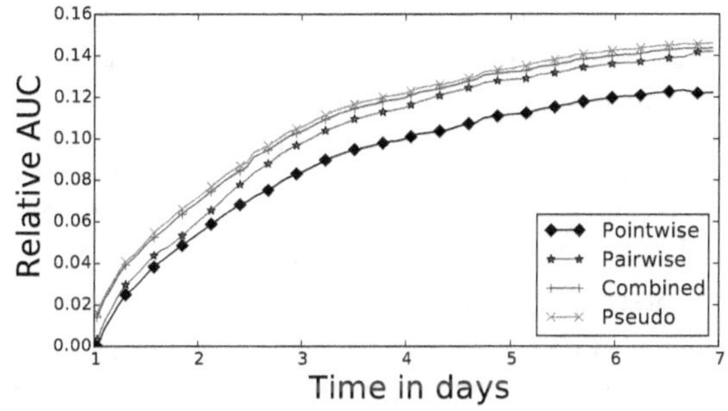

Figure 4: Relative AUC of one week excluding the first day.

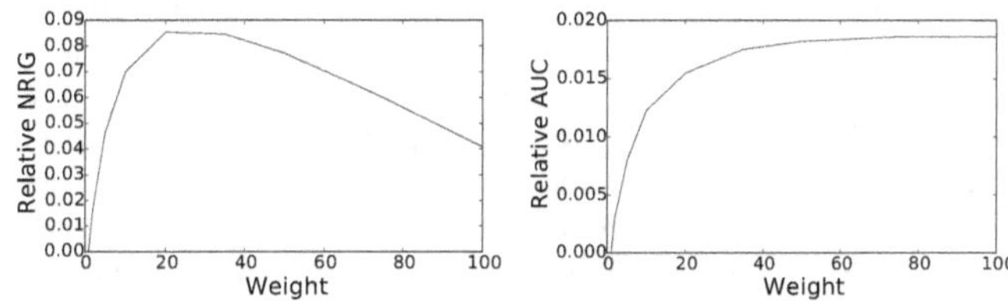

(a) NRIG (b) AUC

Figure 5: Change of performance against weight.

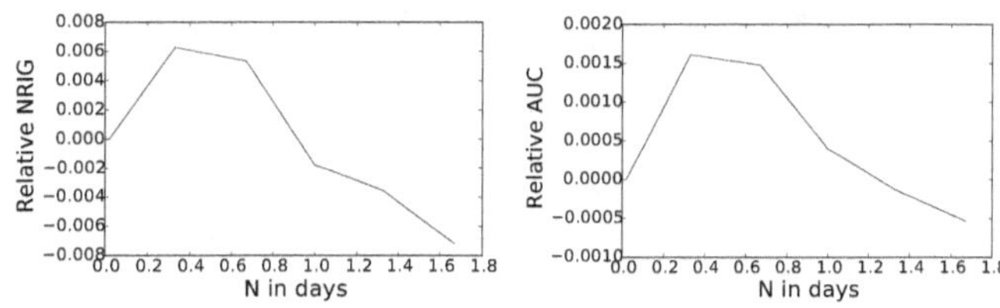

(a) NRIG (b) AUC

Figure 6: Change of performance against N.

examples are revealed. The improvement starts to diminish as the model saturates.

Consistent with our findings from the average performance, pseudo is the winner on both CTR prediction and ranking – it persistently performs better than all other methods across the entire learning process. Pairwise learning achieves reasonable results on AUC, but is way behind other methods on NRIG.

6.6.3 *Parameter sensitivity*

We study two parameters offline: the weight w_p of instances formed by a pair of ads and sliding window size N to form pseudo pairs. The performance changes are plotted in Figures 5 and 6.

Intuitively, the higher the value of w_p, the more likely the model would be optimized towards ranking. This intuition is supported by the experiment result: we observe improved AUC as paired instance weight w_p increases. This improvement flattens out finally. In contrast, The change of NRIG resembles a right-skewed bell shape – an initial increase to a certain point, followed by a decline when weight w_p gets too large. The increase at the beginning might be due to that information brought in by ranking is beneficial to estimation of CTR as well. However, as the model keeps shifting its focus on optimizing towards ranking, the classification quality is finally undermined.

When we vary the size of sliding window N, the performance of classification and ranking exhibit similar patterns. At the beginning, there is an increase of performance resulting from the inclusion of more pairs. However, as the size of sliding window becomes even larger, the model degenerates, likely caused by the formation of training instances from two ads with a bigger time difference. User preference might have changed as time passes by, making two ads incomparable. It might be surprising that the best N is around 8 hours. Actually a user's intent could change rapidly in daily tasks (e.g., choosing restaurants). The context of timeline ads also changes fast and affects the user's perception of ads.

6.7 Feature analysis

As mentioned before, we put features into four categories: advertiser, user, ad-user interaction, and context of the session. To study the importance of different feature categories, we rerun the offline experiments of combined learning by removing one feature category at one time, while keeping all other features present. Figures 7 and 9 show the negated percentage of performance reduction relative to the method using the entire feature set. We negate the values in order to make the figures more graphically intuitive. Each category is colored distinctively, and features belonging to the same major category carry the same color. The left figure plots the result after removing all features belonging to a major category, whereas the right figure is only removing a subcategory. Apart from removing features, we also consider using a single category alone, with all other features excluded. The results are shown in Figure 8 and 10.

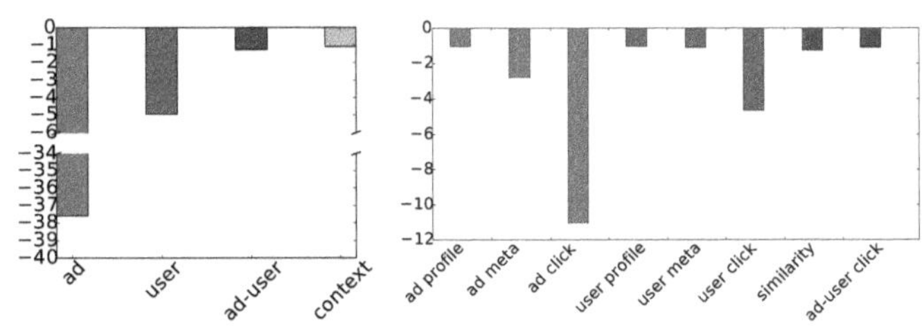

(a) Major categories (b) Subcategories

Figure 7: Negated percentage of NRIG diminished when removing features of a particular category.

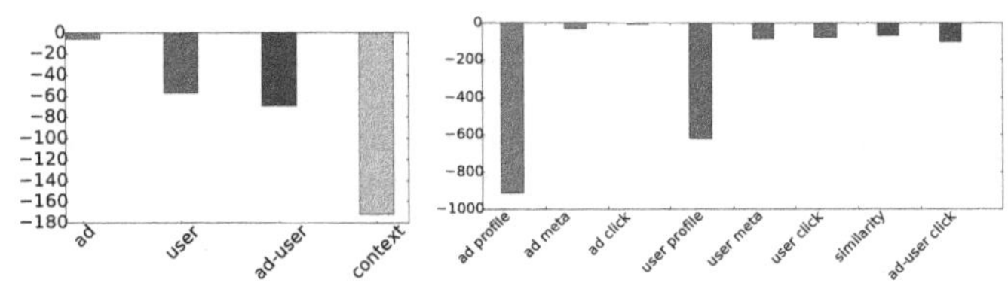

(a) Major categories (b) Subcategories

Figure 8: Negated percentage of NRIG diminished when keeping features of a particular category.

We could analyze feature importance by reading the two types of figures side by side. There are in total four possible outcomes, which are summarized in Table 2.

6.7.1 NRIG

Looking at the major categories depicted in Figure 7 (a) and 8 (a), we can see that in order to achieve a good CTR prediction performance, the ad features play an importance role. Removing user features leads to a significant decrease of model quality as well, but is much less severe than that of ad features. Excluding ad-user features causes a counterintuitively marginal impact. By looking at Figure 8 (a), where ad-user features achieve comparable performance as user features, we could conjecture that features from ad-user category correlate with ad and user features – if a user clicks

Remove	Keep	Interpretation
L	S	Important features
L	L	Does not happen
S	L	Weak features
S	S	Important but possibly covered by other features

Table 2: Possible outcomes for each feature category. "L" under "Remove" column means there is a large drop of performance after removing a feature category. Likewise, "S" means small.

frequently and an ad is popular, there is usually a good interaction between the user and the ad. Context information extracted from a session is not so useful, suggesting that textual information in the context is hard to capture user's current interest.

Investigating the subcategories by reading Figure 7 (b) and 8 (b), click history of both advertisers and users are most important, confirming the result reported by Facebook [16]. Somehow surprisingly, ad meta information imposes a non-negligible effect on CTR estimation. This is due to the existence of advertiser IDs, which act as an indirect way of counting the popularity of advertisers.

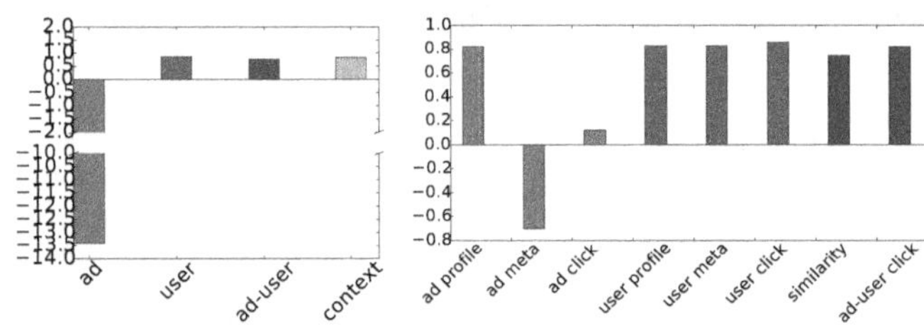

(a) Major categories (b) Subcategories

Figure 9: Negated percentage of AUC diminished when removing features of a particular category.

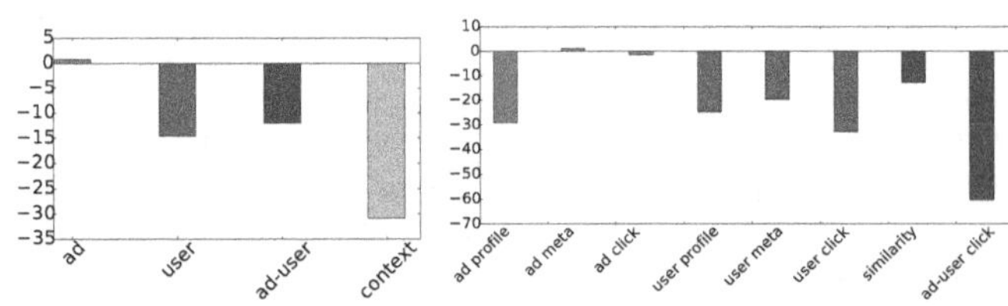

(a) Major categories (b) Subcategories

Figure 10: Negated percentage of AUC diminished when keeping features of a particular category.

6.7.2 AUC

When we study feature importance on ranking, one unexpected observation in Figure 9 and 10 is the existence of positive values, which means AUC is actually improved after removing a feature category or when applying a single category alone. We make two comments on this observation. First, the majority of instances fed to the learning model are formed from single ads, rather than a pair of ads. In other words, the model would optimize towards CTR estimation more than ranking. Consequently, learned features might contribute positively to CTR prediction, even if ranking performance is sacrificed. Second, the sacrifice of AUC is not significantly large – all positive values are no more than 1%.

Having discussed about the abnormality, we move our focus to the feature importance with respect to ranking. We can see from

Method	Pointwise	Combined
Relative CTR (%)	+14.59	+26.10(+10.05)
Relative RPMq (%)	+57.20	+57.89(+0.44)

Table 3: Summary of performance relative to random-pointwise. Numbers in the parentheses indicate performance of combined learning relative to pointwise learning.

Figure 9 (a) and 10 (a) that the ad features are paramount in deciding rankings. However, except for the ad category, removing any other single category causes almost no effect on ranking. Judged from Figure 10 (a), user information and ad-user interaction can to some extent be helpful in ranking. But removing either of them is not hurting the performance, due to the power of ad features. It is reasonable that context features are not strong indicators, as ads in the same session almost face the same context.

According to Figure 9 (b) and 10 (b), excluding a single subcategory does no harm to ranking, as either ad meta or ad click information is strong enough to maintain a good performance. Aside from ad features, similarity between an advertiser and a user could give a relatively good ranking while clicks of a user towards a particular advertiser cannot. The reason is that we have much richer information to calculate similarity, including user's following accounts, and user's Tweets. However, click information is much sparser – typically users seldom click ads, not to mention ads from a particular advertiser.

7. ONLINE EXPERIMENT

7.1 Metrics

For online experiment, we compare the click-through rate (CTR) and revenue per thousand requests (RPMq) of different approaches. We report both metrics because there is a trade-off between CTR and RPMq. A model can play conservatively by only placing ads for requests that are most likely to result in a click, while ignoring most ad requests. In this case, this model could achieve a rather high CTR, but at the cost of RPMq. Conversely, if a model acts aggressively by sending out ads to every request, it could possibly increase RPMq by sacrificing CTR, which hurts user experience and causes negative effects for the company in the long run.

Consequently, a model can be safely claimed to be successful if it can improve one of the metrics, while keeping the other one at least as good as competing methods.

7.2 Procedure

A random week of year 2014 is selected to evaluate pointwise learning and combined learning via online A/B tests. Additionally, a weaker baseline **random-pointwise** is introduced, which adds some randomness in the ad selection process to the pointwise learning model. Users are randomized into different bins by hashing user IDs, with one bin corresponds to 0.5% of all Twitter users. Each method is then evaluated on users belonging to one of the bins.

7.3 Experiment results

To further evaluate the effectiveness of combined learning in real setting, we launched the online experiments, comparing it with the baseline pointwise learning and a weaker baseline random-pointwise. The result averaged over one week can be referred in Table 3.

The performance on each individual day are plotted in Figures 11 and 12, using the result of random-pointwise on the first day as reference. A few observations could be made from the figures. First, both pointwise and combined learning are acting better than random-pointwise, suggesting the benefits of taking learning ap-

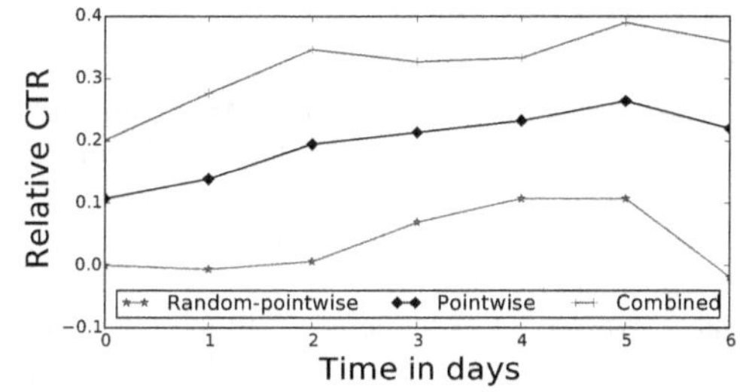

Figure 11: Relative CTR as a function of time.

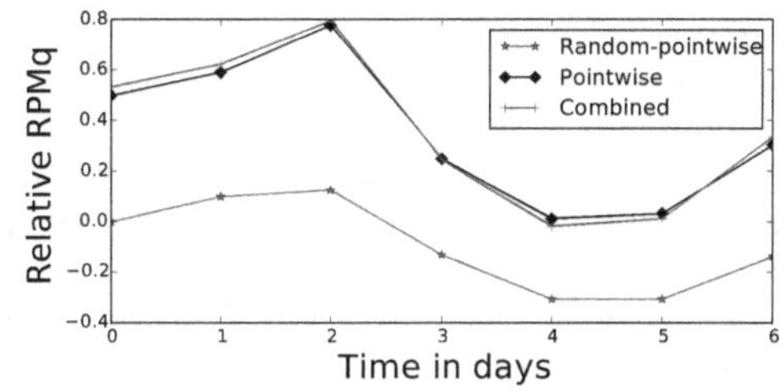

Figure 12: Relative RPMq as a function of time.

proaches towards advertising in stream. Second, combined learning strictly dominates and significantly outperforms pointwise learning on CTR. In terms of RPMq, it performs on par with, and on average slightly better than pointwise learning. As described in Section 7.1, trade-off exists between CTR and RPMq. Improving CTR while maintaining RPMq has proved the superiority of combined learning over pointwise learning. More specifically, the results mean that combined model is showing fewer ads to users. But these ads lead to higher click-throughs, compensating for the revenue loss caused by placing fewer number of ads. Though short-term revenue brought by the two methods stays close, user experience is improved when using combined learning, bringing in more long-term benefits to the company. Moreover, some threshold parameters could be adjusted in the auction system, so that the combined model could distribute more ads. In this way, combined learning can achieve similar CTR score as the pointwise baseline, but with much higher revenue, measured by RPMq.

8. CONCLUSION

In this paper, we presented the problem of click-through prediction for advertising in Twitter Timeline. Compared with traditional computational advertising *sponsored search* and *contextual advertising*, placing ads in a Tweet stream is particularly challenging given the nature of a data stream: the context in which an ad can be placed changes dynamically and few ads could be placed in the same session. This makes the information available for training extremely sparse.

We proposed a learning-to-rank method which not only addresses the sparsity of training signals but also can be trained in real-time with great scalability. The proposed method was evaluated using both offline experiments and online A/B tests, involving very large collections of Twitter data and real Twitter users. We demonstrated that the proposed method not only improved prediction performance in offline simulations but also significantly enhanced actual CTR when deployed to the real Twitter ads-serving system, using the production model as the baseline.

9. REFERENCES

[1] R. Ananthanarayanan, V. Basker, S. Das, A. Gupta, H. Jiang, T. Qiu, A. Reznichenko, D. Ryabkov, M. Singh, and S. Venkataraman. Photon: Fault-tolerant and scalable joining of continuous data streams. In *Proceedings of the 2013 international conference on Management of data*, pages 577–588. ACM, 2013.

[2] B. Bai, J. Weston, D. Grangier, R. Collobert, K. Sadamasa, Y. Qi, O. Chapelle, and K. Weinberger. Learning to rank with (a lot of) word features. *Information retrieval*, 13(3):291–314, 2010.

[3] J. Battelle. *The Search: How Google and Its Rivals Rewrote the Rules of Business and Transformed Our Culture*. Penguin, 2005.

[4] C. M. Bishop et al. *Pattern recognition and machine learning*, volume 1. springer New York, 2006.

[5] A. Blum, A. Kalai, and J. Langford. Beating the hold-out: Bounds for k-fold and progressive cross-validation. In *Proceedings of the twelfth annual conference on Computational learning theory*, pages 203–208. ACM, 1999.

[6] A. Broder, M. Fontoura, V. Josifovski, and L. Riedel. A semantic approach to contextual advertising. In *Proceedings of the 30th annual international ACM SIGIR conference on Research and development in information retrieval*, pages 559–566. ACM, 2007.

[7] C. Burges, T. Shaked, E. Renshaw, A. Lazier, M. Deeds, N. Hamilton, and G. Hullender. Learning to rank using gradient descent. In *Proceedings of the 22nd international conference on Machine learning*, pages 89–96. ACM, 2005.

[8] D. Chakrabarti, D. Agarwal, and V. Josifovski. Contextual advertising by combining relevance with click feedback. In *Proceedings of the 17th international conference on World Wide Web*, pages 417–426. ACM, 2008.

[9] M. Ciaramita, V. Murdock, and V. Plachouras. Online learning from click data for sponsored search. In *Proceedings of the 17th international conference on World Wide Web*, pages 227–236. ACM, 2008.

[10] Y. Duan, L. Jiang, T. Qin, M. Zhou, and H.-Y. Shum. An empirical study on learning to rank of tweets. In *Proceedings of the 23rd International Conference on Computational Linguistics*, pages 295–303. Association for Computational Linguistics, 2010.

[11] B. Edelman, M. Ostrovsky, and M. Schwarz. Internet advertising and the generalized second price auction: Selling billions of dollars worth of keywords. Technical report, National Bureau of Economic Research, 2005.

[12] D. S. Evans. The online advertising industry: Economics, evolution, and privacy. *The journal of economic perspectives*, pages 37–60, 2009.

[13] T. Fawcett. An introduction to roc analysis. *Pattern recognition letters*, 27(8):861–874, 2006.

[14] Y. Freund, R. Iyer, R. E. Schapire, and Y. Singer. An efficient boosting algorithm for combining preferences. *The Journal of machine learning research*, 4:933–969, 2003.

[15] T. Graepel, J. Q. Candela, T. Borchert, and R. Herbrich. Web-scale bayesian click-through rate prediction for sponsored search advertising in microsoft's bing search engine. In *Proceedings of the 27th International Conference on Machine Learning (ICML-10)*, pages 13–20, 2010.

[16] X. He, J. Pan, O. Jin, T. Xu, B. Liu, T. Xu, Y. Shi, A. Atallah, R. Herbrich, S. Bowers, et al. Practical lessons from predicting clicks on ads at facebook. In *Proceedings of 20th ACM SIGKDD Conference on Knowledge Discovery and Data Mining*, pages 1–9. ACM, 2014.

[17] L. Hong, R. Bekkerman, J. Adler, and B. D. Davison. Learning to rank social update streams. In *Proceedings of the 35th international ACM SIGIR conference on Research and development in information retrieval*, pages 651–660. ACM, 2012.

[18] B. J. Jansen and T. Mullen. Sponsored search: an overview of the concept, history, and technology. *International Journal of Electronic Business*, 6(2):114–131, 2008.

[19] M. Karimzadehgan, W. Li, R. Zhang, and J. Mao. A stochastic learning-to-rank algorithm and its application to contextual advertising. In *Proceedings of the 20th international conference on World wide web*, pages 377–386. ACM, 2011.

[20] A. Lacerda, M. Cristo, M. A. Gonçalves, W. Fan, N. Ziviani, and B. Ribeiro-Neto. Learning to advertise. In *Proceedings of the 29th annual international ACM SIGIR conference on Research and development in information retrieval*, pages 549–556. ACM, 2006.

[21] T.-Y. Liu. Learning to rank for information retrieval. *Foundations and Trends in Information Retrieval*, 3(3):225–331, 2009.

[22] T. Mikolov, K. Chen, G. Corrado, and J. Dean. Efficient estimation of word representations in vector space. *arXiv preprint arXiv:1301.3781*, 2013.

[23] V. Murdock, M. Ciaramita, and V. Plachouras. A noisy-channel approach to contextual advertising. In *Proceedings of the 1st international workshop on Data mining and audience intelligence for advertising*, pages 21–27. ACM, 2007.

[24] T.-T. Nguyen, T.-T. Nguyen, and Q.-T. Ha. Applying hidden topics in ranking social update streams on twitter. In *Computing and Communication Technologies, Research, Innovation, and Vision for the Future (RIVF), 2013 IEEE RIVF International Conference on*, pages 180–185. IEEE, 2013.

[25] J. C. Platt. Probabilistic outputs for support vector machines and comparisons to regularized likelihood methods. In *Advances in large margin classifiers*. Citeseer, 1999.

[26] A. Ratnaparkhi. A hidden class page-ad probability model for contextual advertising. In *WWW Workshop*, 2008.

[27] B. Ribeiro-Neto, M. Cristo, P. B. Golgher, and E. Silva de Moura. Impedance coupling in content-targeted advertising. In *Proceedings of the 28th annual international ACM SIGIR conference on Research and development in information retrieval*, pages 496–503. ACM, 2005.

[28] M. Richardson, E. Dominowska, and R. Ragno. Predicting clicks: estimating the click-through rate for new ads. In *Proceedings of the 16th international conference on World Wide Web*, pages 521–530. ACM, 2007.

[29] D. Sculley. Combined regression and ranking. In *Proceedings of the 16th ACM SIGKDD international conference on Knowledge discovery and data mining*, pages 979–988. ACM, 2010.

[30] J. G. Shanahan and G. Kurra. Digital advertising: An information scientist's perspective. In *Advanced Topics in Information Retrieval*, pages 209–237. Springer, 2011.

[31] X. Zhang, B. He, and T. Luo. Transductive learning for real-time twitter search. In *ICWSM*, 2012.

Predicting Voice Elicited Emotions

Ying Li
Jobaline Inc.
620 Kirkland Way, Suite 208
Kirkland, Washington 98033, USA
ying.li@jobaline.com

Jose D. Contreras
Jobaline Inc.
620 Kirkland Way, Suite 208
Kirkland, Washington 98033, USA
jose@jobaline.com

Luis J. Salazar
Jobaline Inc.
620 Kirkland Way, Suite 208
Kirkland, Washington 98033, USA
luis@jobaline.com

ABSTRACT

We present the research, and product development and deployment, of Voice Analyzer™ by Jobaline Inc. This is a patent pending technology that analyzes voice data and predicts human emotions elicited by the paralinguistic elements of a voice. Human voice characteristics, such as tone, complement the verbal communication. In several contexts of communication, "how" things are said is just as important as "what" is being said. This paper provides an overview of our deployed system, the raw data, the data processing steps, and the prediction algorithms we experimented with. A case study is included where, given a voice clip, our model predicts the degree in which a listener will find the voice "engaging". Our prediction results were verified through independent market research with 75% in agreement on how an average listener would feel. One application of Jobaline Voice Analyzer technology is for assisting companies to hire workers in the service industry where customers' emotional response to workers' voice may affect the service outcome. Jobaline Voice Analyzer is deployed in production as a product offer to our clients to help them identify workers who will better engage with their customers. We will also share some discoveries and lessons learned.

Categories and Subject Descriptors
H.2.8 [**Database Management**]: Database Applications - *data mining*; H.5.2 [**Information Interfaces and Presentation**]: User Interfaces *-voice I/O*; I.5.2 [**Pattern Recognition**]: Design Methodology - *pattern analysis*.

General Terms
Algorithms, Design, Experimentation, Human Factors.

Keywords
Voice Analysis, Predictive Modeling, Speech Signal Processing, Deployed System

KDD '15, August 11-14, 2015, Sydney, NSW, Australia.
ACM 978-1-4503-3664-2/15/08.
http://dx.doi.org/10.1145/2783258.2788619

1. INTRODUCTION

This paper presents Jobaline Voice Analyzer, a deployed system that analyzes human voice data and predicts listener emotions elicited by the paralinguistic elements of the voice [9].

The motivation for developing this technology at Jobaline is to automate the screening process of hiring workers for service industries. Jobaline is the leading mobile and bilingual hourly job matching marketplace and training network. Hourly job workers represent approximately two-thirds of the U.S. labor force and more than 50 million people are hired every year in this job category. The hiring of these hourly job workers is typically done through a manual process conducted by human resource personnel to match workers with jobs. Many hourly jobs can not be filled in time even though employers spend nearly one billion hours pre-screening job applicants. To overcome this extreme low efficiency, Jobaline automates the pre-screening and matching of applicants to jobs. The automation includes automated phone interviews whereby applicants record their answers to a set of interview prompts.

At this writing, Jobaline has processed over 700,000 job applications in either English or Spanish with millions of voice clips recorded by job candidates of different cultures, education levels, genders and ages. We resort to the power of data science and predictive modeling to analyze these voice clips to further facilitate the automation of recruiting processes. If we can identify applicants whose voices can elicit positive emotions in a listener, thanks to certain characteristics possessed by the voice, in real-time during the automated interview, our system can rank them higher in the job matching process. This in turn optimizes for best matching between workers and jobs.

We have thus researched and developed a voice data analysis system and built data mining models that can predict human emotions elicited by paralinguistic elements of the voice interview records. Our system utilizes only the paralinguistic elements (how things are said) of a voice and does not involve the lexical contents (what is being said). This has multiple benefits, including privacy preserving and fair hiring across cultural backgrounds.

Our main contributions are: 1) the framing of the problem of predicting listener emotion response to voice by paralinguistic elements; 2) a set of system modules that process and extract features representing voice cues; and 3) a set of data mining models and analyses that derive insights and make predictions about listener emotions in response to voice clips. The prediction results were verified by independent market research, and the system modules and prediction models are deployed into production. In particular, our prediction models quantify, for any given voice clip, the likelihood that a listener may associate certain emotions such as "engaging". The utilization of only paralinguistic (i.e., non-lexical) elements enables us to predict listener response to "how things are said" regardless of what is being said.

One exemplary application of this technology is in the services industry, where hiring workers who can connect with their customers and keep their customers engaged is critically important. Some examples of these jobs include telemarketers, retail store clerks, frontline employees at a quick serve restaurant, or front desk associates at a hotel. By analyzing job applicants' voices with Jobaline Voice Analyzer, companies can predict which job candidates will likely perform better in sales and marketing or customer-facing positions at restaurants, hotels, or call centers. This provides an objective input into recruiters' hiring decision process.

This paper is organized as follows: Section 2 provides some basic definitions and background knowledge about voice data, and a high level overview of the state of the art of speech affect analysis. Section 3 presents our voice analyzer system: from the raw data, to feature extraction, to modeling, and deployment. Section 4 presents a case study where we built models which, given a voice clip, predict the likelihood of an emotion of "being engaged" generated in the listener. We also present validation of our prediction results through third-party market research. In Section 5, we share some discoveries from analyzing job applicants' voices and lessons learned. And lastly, in Section 6, we conclude with business benefits and outline next steps in our research and development.

2. BACKGROUND

For our goal of predicting emotion responses to voices, we envision a framework for research and development to encompass the below elements:

- an "emotion taxonomy" that includes all the emotion responses we want to predict such as "feeling engaged", "feeling soothed", or "trustworthiness"
- a general understanding of voice data that could provide insights for mapping voice characteristics to a feature space of finite quantified dimensions that can be computationally constructed
- a machine learning and data science experimentation framework that will enable us to build the best performing models

Among the many emotion categories and definitions researched and employed by the research fields, we found the framework articulated by "FEELTRACE" [2], screenshot in Figure 1, is most compelling for our purpose in the sense that it is more inclusive of all emotions we want to predict and it describes various emotions by finite quantifiable dimensions (see Figure 1). Whereas other research papers cover only a small set of "strong emotions", such as "fear", "happy", or "angry". The finite dimensions such as negative vs. positive, active vs. passive, could assist us in mapping emotion characteristics to and measure them by known voice paralinguistic features.

Combining emotion research with data science and engineering is a relatively new research and development area [10]. Our focus of predicting listener emotion response to voices would need to employ domain knowledge related to the processing and analysis of human voice data, as well as machine learning and data mining methodologies and techniques. The remainder of this section presents a brief introduction of affects associated with the human voice (Section 2.1), a high level survey of the state of the art in classifying emotions associated with voices (Section 2.2), and an overview of paralinguistic features and their use in existing works (Section 2.3).

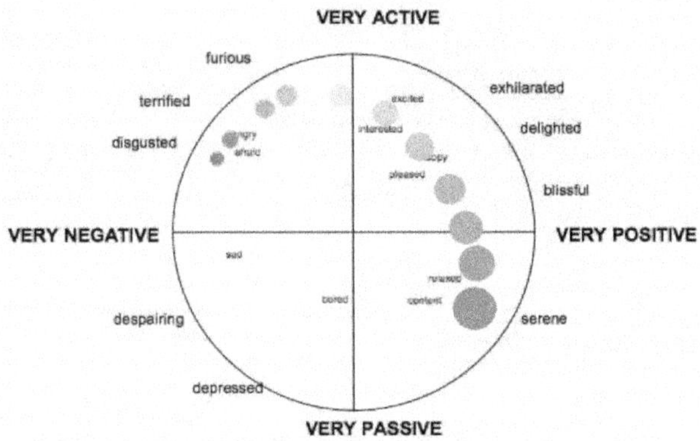

Figure 1. Representation of emotional states [2].

2.1 Affects Related to Human Voice

Attention to the affects of human voice probably existed as long as human existed. Systematic study of affects of human voice dated back centuries ago; Kreiman et al [6] provides a comprehensive survey on the studies of perception of voice quality. Research and studies on the affects in and from human voice can be found in subject areas such as theories of emotions for Information Retrieval [8], Affective Computing (e.g., MIT Media Lab Affective Computing Group), and Speech Communication (e.g., International Speech Communication Association) [14, 16, 17]. Table 1 lists some attributes associated with human voice that have been the subjects of research.

Table 1. Example Attributes Associated with Human Voice

Categories of Attributes	Definition	Examples
speaker trait	characteristics that are permanently associated with speaker	age, gender, personality, likeability
speaker state	attributes of speaker that change over time	affection, deception, interest, intoxication, stress
speaker acoustic behavior	non-linguistic vocal outbursts during speech	sighs, yawns, laughs, cries, hesitations
acoustic affect	non-linguistic attributes carried in the voice	sounds pleasant, cheerful, trustworthy, deceitful
elicited listener emotion	listener reactions immediate upon hearing a speech clip	feels energized, happy, joyful, annoyed, agitated

2.2 Classification of Affects Associated with Voice

There is a rich repertoire of scientific research in speech signal processing and analysis that make classifications of affects based on human voice data. The majority of these research works can be regarded as addressing two sets of goals. One is to recognize the presence of and/or to classify the type of personality traits intrinsically possessed by the speaker. These personality traits can be independent of, or in relation to, when the speech was made. The other set of goals focuses on recognizing the presence of and classifying the types of emotions carried within a speech clip or the context out of which the speech clips arise.

Table 2 lists some previous research works that aimed at classifying speaker traits or presence of emotions in speech.

Table 2. Classification of Speaker Traits or Speaker Emotions.

Speaker Type	Speaker Prompt	Classification Objective
Parkinson's disease patient	portray emotion	presence of emotion in speech speaker trait [18]
Actor	portray emotion	presence of emotion in speech [12]
Actor	portray personality	speaker personality (e.g., Big Five) [11]
Consumer phone recording	customer seeking service and support from commercial service providers	presence of emotion in speech clips acoustic correlates observable with emotions [5]
Medical call center dialog	real life situation without artificial prompt	recognition of speaker emotion (anger, fear, relief, sadness) [3]

Jobaline Voice Analyzer is particularly focused on predicting the elicited emotions based on paralinguistic features of voice clips. We have not come across research works aimed at predicting/classifying listener emotions elicited by voices.

2.3 Paralinguistic Features of Voices

The modeling of the anatomy and physiology of human voice production have been studied in the domain of speech signal processing with established paradigm and methodologies [13]. We list some definitions related to analyzing paralinguistic features in Table 3.

Converting audio signals into data features typically involves:

- Sampling in time domain and frequency domain
- Extracting FFT and energy in frequency domain and information from the time domain signal
- Extracting feature vectors in the time and frequency domain

Generally, frequency and energy variation over time are the major cues used to analyze emotions in audio samples. A number of methods, from mathematical transformations to slicing audio samples into shorter snippets, turn direct acoustic signals into pitch contours, from which statistics can be extracted and analyzed for correlations with emotions.

Table 3. Definitions of some voice features.

Concept	Definition	Data Representation
amplitude	measurement of the variations over time of the acoustic signal	quantified values of a sound wave's oscillation
energy	acoustic signal energy representation in decibels	20*log10(abs(FFT))
formants	the resonance frequencies of the vocal tract	maxima detected using Linear Prediction on audio windows with high tonal content
perceived pitch	perceived fundamental frequency and harmonics	formants
fundamental frequency	the reciprocal of time duration of one glottal cycle - a strict definition of "pitch"	first formant

Existing research on detecting speaker emotions from voice clips has demonstrated that speaker emotions, and the intensity of those emotions, can be recognized from acoustic data with varying accuracy depending on the types of emotions. Pitch has been used as one major cue for emotion recognition. Intensity and speech rate have also been used. Typical transformations include turning a voice clip into pitch contours and measuring various statistics such as max, min, standard deviation, and time-window averages, on the whole clip or on snippets of the clip.

Some features that have proven effective for recognizing speaker emotions include:

- Fundamental frequency and its statistics such as min, max, mean and standard deviation over time
- Pitch contour
- Speech signal amplitude
- Frequency spectrum energy distribution
- Durations: proportion of pauses, duration of syllables, syllable rate, and total duration

In addition, some research also demonstrated associations between voice features and emotions expressed in voices. For example, researchers found that the presence of anger in voice clips was associated with a rise in fundamental frequency and amplitude, whereas despondency was associated with a decreased syllable rate [5]. Researchers have experimented with novel acoustic features and have found that they outrank "classic" features for affect recognition tasks [4]. The use of paralinguistic features has also been demonstrated effective in assisting other features to further disambiguate affects.

The list of features presented at INTERSPEECH competitions, which focused on recognizing speaker emotion and likability through paralinguistic features [15, 16] provided a starting point for our feature space construction for our voice analyzer.

3. JOBALINE VOICE ANALYZER

Intuitively, our common day experience tells us that predicting emotions that might be elicited when we hear a voice clip is a feasible task. For instance, when we hear a voice, we can tell whether the voice makes us feel "being engaged", "at ease", or "soothed". Figure 2 shows the spectrograms of two sample voice clips from job applicants responding to the interview prompt,

"*Greet me as if I am a customer*". One can clearly notice the energy level difference between the two voice clips. The spectrogram on the top (Figure 2(a)) is from a voice clip that would make listeners feel much less engaging than the clips depicted on the bottom (Figure 2(b)).

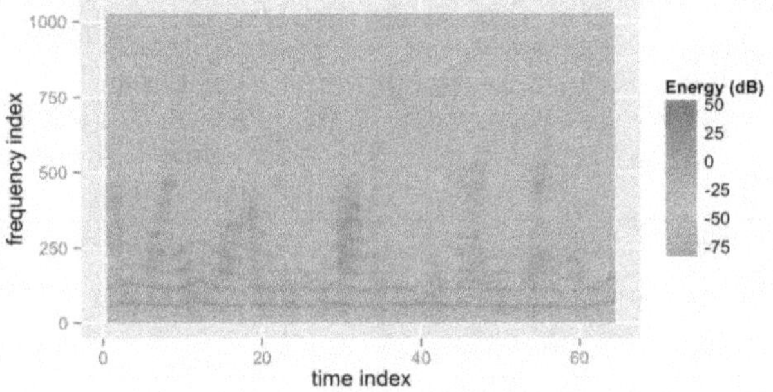

(a) A non-energetic voice.

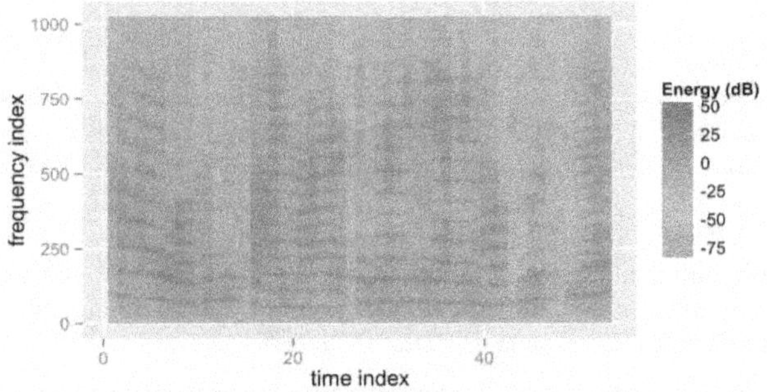

(b) An energetic voice.

Figure 2. Spectrogram of sample voice clips.

At Jobaline, we focused our study on the types and instances of paralinguistic features and their effectiveness in classifying voice recordings. We will describe our system in steps and provide descriptions about the components of our system.

3.1 Overview

Our task is to analyze and model speech affect based on paralinguistic correlates in acoustic data. The desired outcome is a system capable of predicting listeners' emotion response to voice clips elicited by the paralinguistic aspects of the voice clips. The building blocks of our system are drawn in Figure 3. The resulting Jobaline Voice Analyzer accomplishes the tasks through the following steps:

1. Record and sample raw voice clips
2. Extract audio features that represent voice cues
3. Construct data feature space suitable for applying data mining and machine learning algorithms
4. Build models using various algorithms for unsupervised learning, and supervised and semi-supervised learning
5. Engineer scalable data processing pipelines that process voice clips and generate prediction scores by applying the prediction models

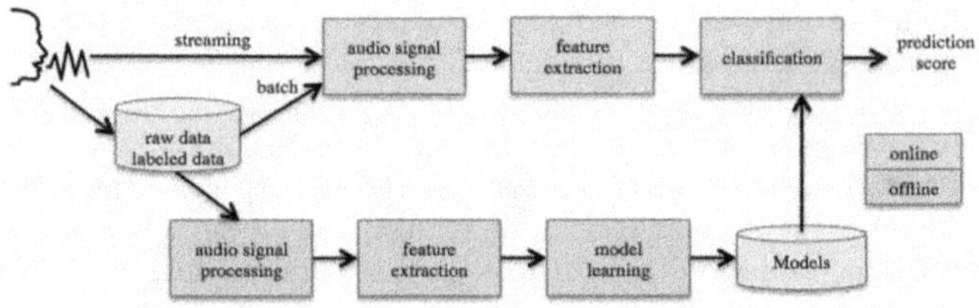

Figure 3. Jobaline Voice Analyzer building blocks.

3.2 Raw Data and Metadata

Our raw data are voice clips from job applicants recorded as audio signals in wave format. Jobaline has served more than one-half million job applicants, where each job applicant may record voice clips as responses to various interview prompts. Typical interview prompts are:

- *Greet me as if I am your customer.*
- *How would you describe excellent customer service?*
- *Tell me about a time you handled an angry customer.*
- *Tell me about a time when you were able to diffuse an escalated customer situation without transferring to a supervisor or other department.*
- *Briefly explain your experience on this type of job.*

The metadata associated with voice clips include job categories for which the applicants were applying and the interview prompts for which the applicants were asked to respond to by the employers. The metadata were used to filter voice clips for building models according to groups of interview prompts. The content of metadata is not used for modeling because we wanted our models to be purely based on voice data.

3.3 Preprocessing of Audio Signals

Our preprocessing tasks involves:

1. Converting audio signal into data in time domain and frequency domain
2. Filtering out voice clips that are unfit for modeling and analysis

Our audio signal processing component transforms voice clips in wave format to the following data elements:

- Short-term Fast Fourier Transform per frame
- Energy measures in frequency domain per frame
- Linear Prediction Coefficient in frequency domain per frame

The result of preprocessing is stored in a json file for each wave file. Our feature space for modeling is subsequently built based on these data elements (more in Section 3.4).

Voice clips that are not suited for modeling or scoring are those that:

- Are too short for any data elements to be meaningful
- Contain too much background noise, leading/trailing noise, or other types of noises

Since our voice clips are free-form speech recorded from job applicants, they do not have a uniform length when they arrive at our system. Figure 4 shows the distribution of voice clip length. We discard voice clips shorter than two seconds because they do not provide enough evidence of qualifications for employers to screen for further information.

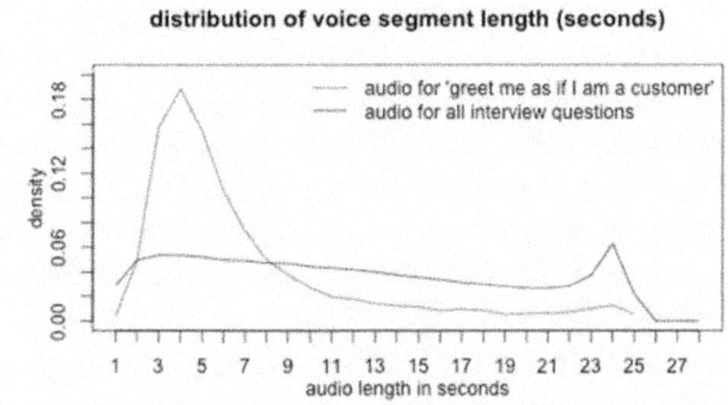

Figure 4. Distribution of voice clip lengths in seconds.

3.4 Feature Space Construction

We experimented with feature construction based on the following dimensions and combinations:

- Signal measurements such as energy and amplitude
- Statistics such as min, max, mean, and standard deviation on signal measurements
- Measurement window in time domain: different time size and entire time window
- Measurement window in frequency domain: all frequencies, optimal audible frequencies, and selected frequency ranges
- Distance metrics: dynamic time warping and Euclidean
- Algorithms: hierarchical clustering, k-means and complete

Combining our explorative analysis with learnings from existing researchers in speech signal processing and speaker emotion classification, we focused on voice energy features and constructed feature space using various statistical measures of energy attributes. We analyzed feature selection against clustering algorithms to determine the effectiveness of the features and to guide us in the final selection of features.

3.5 Model Building

Our modeling goal is to be able to construct prediction models that, given a voice clip, predict listeners' emotion response to it.

In modeling listener emotional response to voice clips, we cannot expect the availability of the absolute ground truth as we have yet to have a mathematical formulation of mappings from voice to emotion. We can jump start with the conventional approach of collecting training data through human labeling (labeled data), however we also note that the labelers' sense of emotion may vary and thus could potentially introduce hidden bias in the labeled data.

When given a set of voice clips without prior knowledge of quantified ground truth or definitive verified examples that represent ground truth, we first utilize unsupervised learning techniques to help us find patterns in unlabeled data. We then constructed training data sets based on evaluation of clustering results combined with independent manual labeling of individual voice clips. The labeled data are then fed to supervised learning routines to build the prediction models.

3.5.1 Unsupervised Learning

We ran clustering analysis on the paralinguistic features of the voice clips (as listed in Section 3.4). We experimented with:

- Various clustering algorithms such as hierarchical clustering and k-means
- Various distance metrics employed within the clustering algorithms, such as dynamic time warping and Euclidean

The clustering results were evaluated based on:

- Cluster quality measurements such as compactness, good separation, connectedness, stabilities, etc.
- Manual validation, including visual inspection of the clusters and/or aural inspection of the voice clips in each cluster, to determine whether the clustering is meaningful

We ran cluster quality measurements on multiple clustering algorithms and multiple choices for the number of clusters to determine which clustering algorithms yield the best results and the number of clusters that are most appropriate for the data. Figure 5 gives an example of those results, which indicates that hierarchical clustering with five clusters gives the best clusters in this particular example.

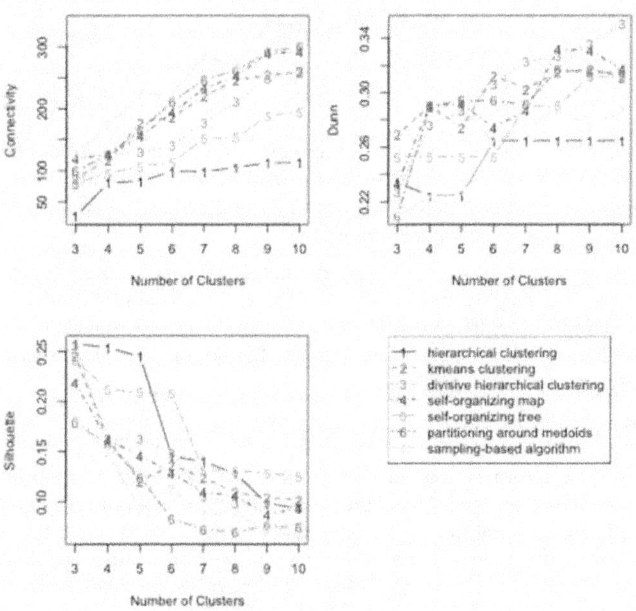

Figure 5. Cluster quality measurement by number of clusters.

We visualized the clustering results by displaying the centroids of clusters by average energy in frequency domain across voice clips in each cluster. Figure 6 shows the results of one such clustering run.

We listened to the voice clips that were clustered together to evaluate whether the voice clips from the same cluster did indeed generate similar listener effect. Based on our listening test, we detected reasonable similarities within clusters and dissimilarities between clusters, and they also mapped to a scaled positive vs. negative response.

For the example shown in Figure 6, we noted that two distinct clusters emerged: one for highly energetic voice clips and one for very low energy voice clips. This indicates that the voice clips and the corresponding extracted feature data have reasonable differentiating power to map the voice clips into clusters that might correlate with listener responses. We combine clustering results with human labeling to produce labeled data for training prediction models.

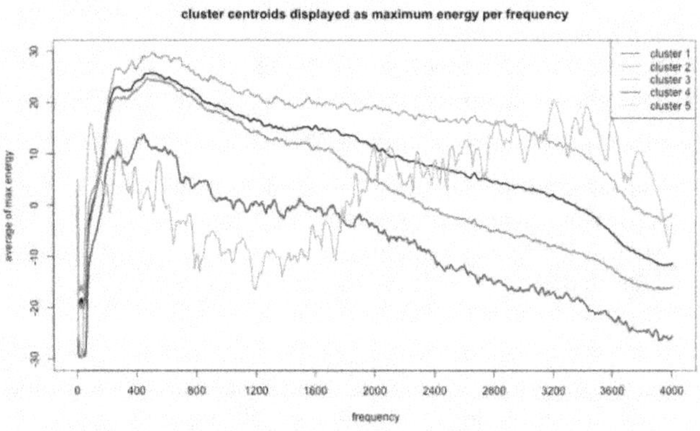

Figure 6. Clustering based on energy features.

3.5.2 Supervised and Semi-Supervised Learning

In building our prediction models, we experimented with various supervised learning algorithms, including:

- Logistic regression
- Support Vector Machine
- Random Forest

where the training data is a combination of clustering results and human labeling. We also experimented with models to predict binary outcome (positive vs. negative) and numerical scores for further classifying listener emotions.

Our experiments show that the predictive models built on top of clustering insights and iterative feedback from listeners produces meaningful results. We will provide detailed accuracy analysis in Section 4 when we present our prediction model for emotion response of "feeling engaged".

In addition to prediction models using the convention methods like SVM and Random Forest, we also conducted experiments with an unsupervised and semi-supervised learning algorithm, called Kodama, which performs feature extraction from noisy and high-dimensional data [1]. The output of Kodama includes a dissimilarity matrix from which we can perform clustering and classification. In Figure 7, we project voice clips onto two-dimensional space from the multidimensional scaling of the Kodama dissimilarity matrix. The voice clips' emotion response label is overlaid with color ("turquoise" for positive response, and "red" for negative response). We can see a fairly good separation of the two types of responses in training data. We use experiments like this to validate the direction of research investigations, and to lead to the final selection of training data and corresponding features to be used in model training.

3.6 Deployed System

The Jobaline Voice Analyzer system is a production system deployed in a cloud infrastructure. The functional components as described in Figure 3 are all deployed to production: voice data arrive at our system after a job applicant records their answers to interview questions; a prediction score is produced by the system; and the result is stored in a database for downstream consumption, such as ranking of applicants. The main architecture consists of: Hadoop clusters; audio signal preprocessing components developed in MATLAB and then converted to Java running on the clusters; various model training and prediction routines written in R.

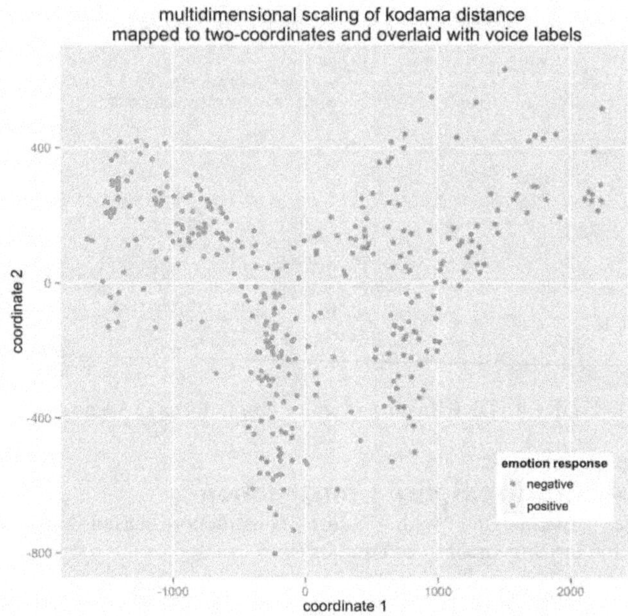

Figure 7. Overlay emotion label on Kodama dissimilarity.

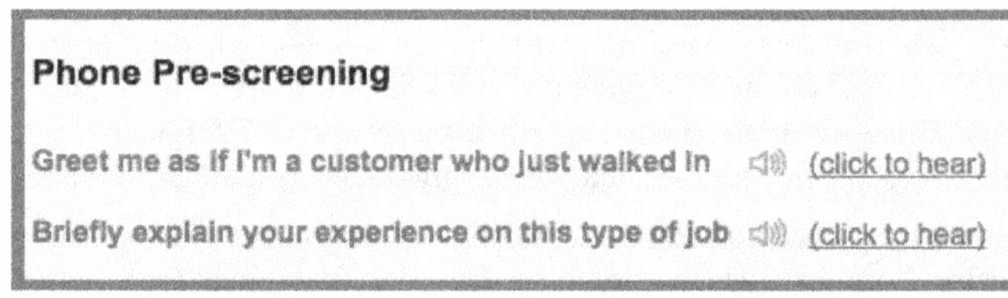

(a) Interview questions and links to voice clips.

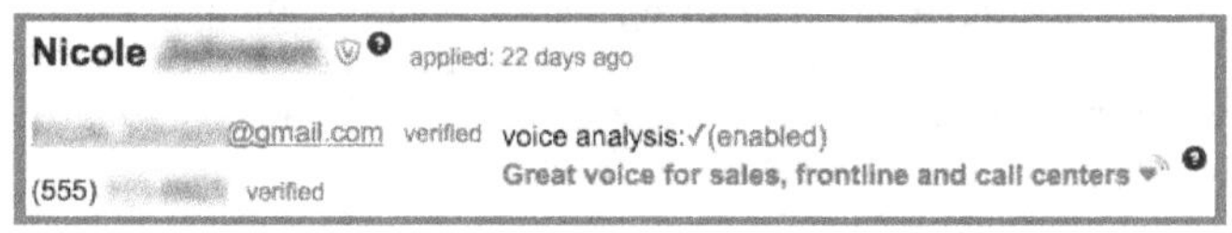

(b) Voice analysis conclusion at lower right.

Figure 8. UI screen shots of how voice analysis is surfaced.

Figure 8 provides two screen shots of Voice Analyzer results that are surfaced to the recruiter UI as in the deployed system. Figure 8(a) shows the UI where a recruiter as a Jobaline user can access the voice recordings left by the job applicants as answers to their interview questions. Once a voice clip went through our system, a notice and flag will show on the UI, as shown in lower right of Figure 8(b), to indicate whether the voice would score high as to elicit a positive response from customers for the types of jobs the candidate is applying for. The blur in Figure 8(b) is added for the purpose of this paper to mask out the candidate's personal data.

At the time of this submission (February 2015), Jobaline had more than 700,000 job applicants on file, processed more than two million voice clips, and Jobaline Voice Analyzer was already available as product offering to clients.

Our work has been focused on the paralinguistic aspects of the voice data. We do not analyze the lexical contents of the voice clips. The result of Voice Analyzer is one additional data point to the recruiting process, not a hiring decision. The use of lexical content of the candidate's answers to the interview questions in the recruiting process is left to the human recruiter.

4. PREDICTING LISTENER EMOTION OF FEELING ENGAGED

We present a case study for predicting listener emotion responses to voices for the purpose of assisting employers in screening job applicants. The business goal is to enable better matching of workers to jobs that require interaction with customers and keeping them engaged. Examples of such jobs are telemarketer, retail store clerk, frontline employee at a quick serve restaurant, or a front desk associate at a hotel.

We incorporate the thinking from the emotion presentation framework by Cowei et al [2] (Figure 1). Instead of taking any specific categorization and definition of one particular emotion (such as "happy") and building a model for it, we chose to start by predicting a positive response vs. negative response. A positive response could be one or multiple perceptions of a "pleasant voice", "makes me feel good", "cares about me", "makes me feel comfortable", or "makes me feel engaged".

While being novel in predicting listener emotion responses, we take the learnings from classifying speaker traits and speaker states by previous research works as guidance. In particular, the effectiveness of certain speech paralinguistic features in identifying the presence of and further classifying speaker emotions helps us decide what features to use to construct our feature spaces.

4.1 Prediction Model for Engaging Effect

We used the methodologies and system components described in Section 3 to obtain the prediction model and deployed the model to production. The production system was built and upgraded in two versions by the time of this writing. We experimented with SVM for version 1 and Random Forest for version 2.

The collection of voice clips that answer the interview prompt of "*Greet me as if I am a customer*" are used for building the models for engaging effect. The training data was obtained by the combination of unsupervised learning and human manual labeling and inspection.

We have achieved accuracy in the range of 76% to 90% as measured by cross-validation for binary classification (positive vs. negative on "feeling engaged", "energetic", etc.). Here we report one model built with random forest algorithm, it has an AUC value of 0.918, the ROC for binary classification performance as shown in Figure 9, and some other performance measures as listed below:

```
##              Accuracy : 0.8605
##                95% CI : (0.7689, 0.9258)
##     P-Value [Acc > NIR] : 5.762e-07
##           Sensitivity : 0.8182
##           Specificity : 0.8868
##        Pos Pred Value : 0.8182
##        Neg Pred Value : 0.8868
```

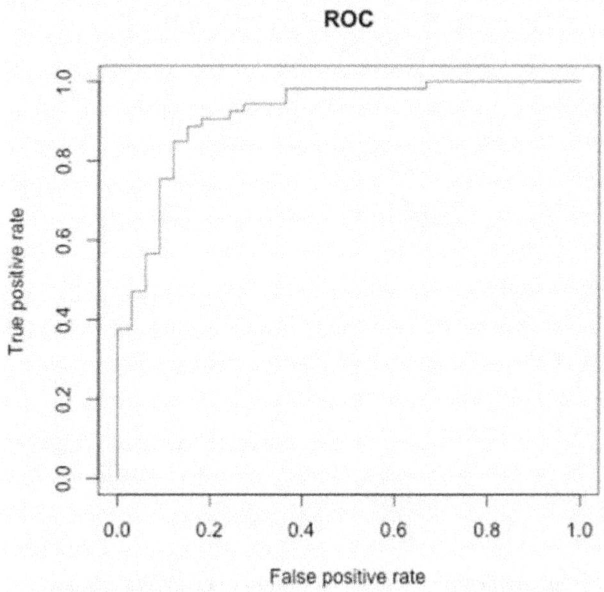

Figure 9. Cross validation ROC for deployed model.

4.2 Prediction Scores for Downstream Applications

The downstream applications of the prediction scores need to be based on a set of well thought out principles. As we iteratively build out our prediction engines for voice elicited emotions, our system is comprised of models built with different training datasets, different predictive modeling algorithms, and different tuning parameters. The prediction scores will have different meaning and implications. Figure 10 shows the spread of the predicted scores on 1000 randomly selected, unseen voice clips, by a support vector regression model (Figure 10(a)), and a random forest classification model (Figure 10(b)). The two sets of scores are directionally parallel, but have to be treated differently, as the model in Figure 10(a) predicts the engaging score and the model in Figure 10(b) produces the probability of positive response to a voice clip.

Each voice clip is very rich in what it expresses; listener response to voices is complex depending on the listener's context such as cultural and demographical factors. Thus, even within the same model, say the random forest model (Figure 10(b)), when applying the scores in downstream applications such as ranking, a more reasonable way to use the prediction scores is to bucketize voice clips directionally, accordingly. As we will continue to improve on all aspects of our efforts, such as feature extraction, feature transformation, combination of training datasets, modeling algorithms, and their parameters, the absolute scored values will undergo changes until a global scaled normalization is found satisfactory.

We can also observe important differences in model behavior from Figure 10. The SVM model in Figure 10(a) tends to be more biased towards predicting positive response than the random forest model. One reason for this behavior is that the training dataset was imbalanced due to our limited labeled training data at the earlier stage of our engine development. We moved our production system to the version 2 model that is random forest based with more balanced training dataset.

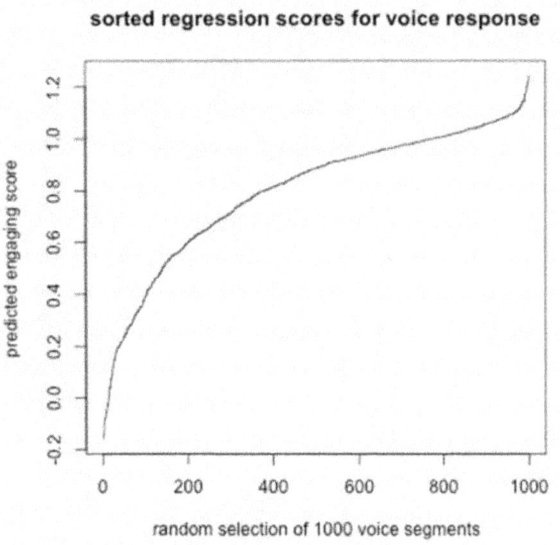

(a) Scores from v1 model of support vector regression.

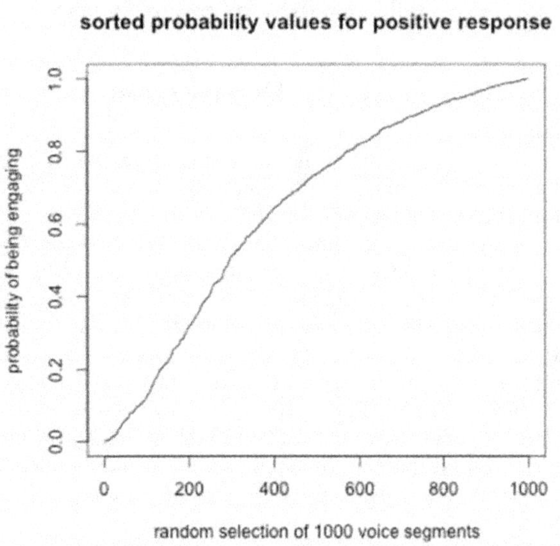

(b) Scores from v2 model of random forest classification.

Figure 10. Sorted prediction scores by two models for 1000 randomly selected voice clips.

4.3 Market Research for Evaluation and Model Refinement

To get third party opinion on our production models, we used market research with a representative U.S. demographic sample (by geographic region, income, ethnicity, gender and age) to manually validate the results.

Jobaline commissioned two independent research firms to validate the output of our prediction models. This validation was done by surveying a representative sample of U.S. residents balanced by geographic region, income, ethnicity, gender and age, comparing their subjective evaluation of voice clips with our prediction results. The survey takers matched the U.S. census in geography, age, ethnicity, income, and gender, at a 95% confidence interval and with a 5% margin of error. Survey responses have to be triple verified in order to be included in calculating agreement between the survey taker and our prediction results. Figure 11 describes the verification process in detail.

The market research concludes that, when asked how the sound of the recorded voice clips made them feel, 75% agreed with the Jobaline Voice Analyzer prediction of an interesting or engaging voice.

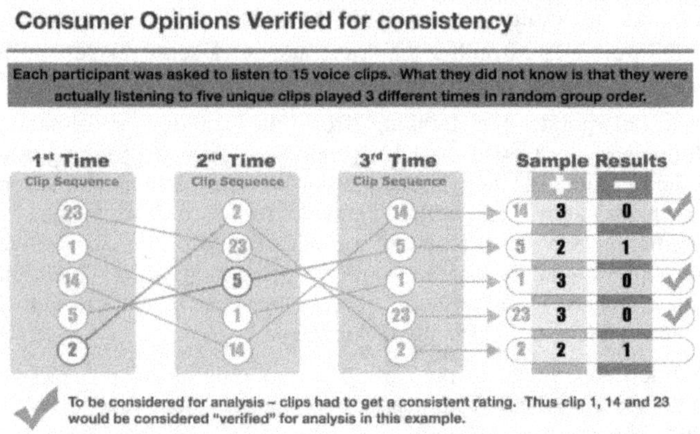

Figure 11. Only those survey responses that were triple-verified are used in validation.

Our market research data could also provide insights to feedback on our feature construction and modeling work. Some key takeaways are:

1. The demographic characteristics of the listener matter. For example, younger listeners (18-29 years old) or people in lower income brackets of less than $29K/year have more strict criteria of how they sense pleasant or engaging. The practical implication is that algorithms can be fine-tuned to the age range of the target audience the workers will speak to. Thus, a retailer that caters to a younger demographic might need individuals with voice characteristics different than a retailer that caters to an older demographic.

2. There is a significant drop in emotional response to voices of similar characteristics when the listener is exposed to voice clips longer than five seconds. More research has to be done to correlate this to various demographics, but this could affect things like defining the optimal length of customer greeting for a telemarketing or customer service firm, or a retailer based on the demographic they serve.

3. No positive or negative correlation was found between the emotion elicited and the age, ethnicity (accent), or education level of the speaker.

4. A slight bias of the respondents toward female voices was noticed. Voices with similar characteristics, but from a female speaker ranked on average 11% better than voices from male speakers. This provides additional input for fine-tuning the algorithms; not based on gender, but on the unique attributes of the voice.

5. DISCOVERIES AND LESSONS LEARNED

Since the launch of Jobaline Voice Analyzer, we have received inquiries from media and interests in collaboration from academia. Here we want to share some of the discoveries we've made while working with our voice data and lessons learned.

5.1 Differences in Voice Characteristics

It is an established knowledge that men and women have different fundamental frequencies in their voices. On average, the fundamental frequency for men is about 115 Hz and 220 Hz for women [8]. We selected one male voice and one female voice from our voice data set and show, in Figure 12, their average fundamental frequencies. The fundamental frequencies of the male voice (top graph) show differences between two interview questions (red vs. blue), whereas the fundamental frequencies of the female voice (bottom graph) are well mixed within the same range for different interview questions.

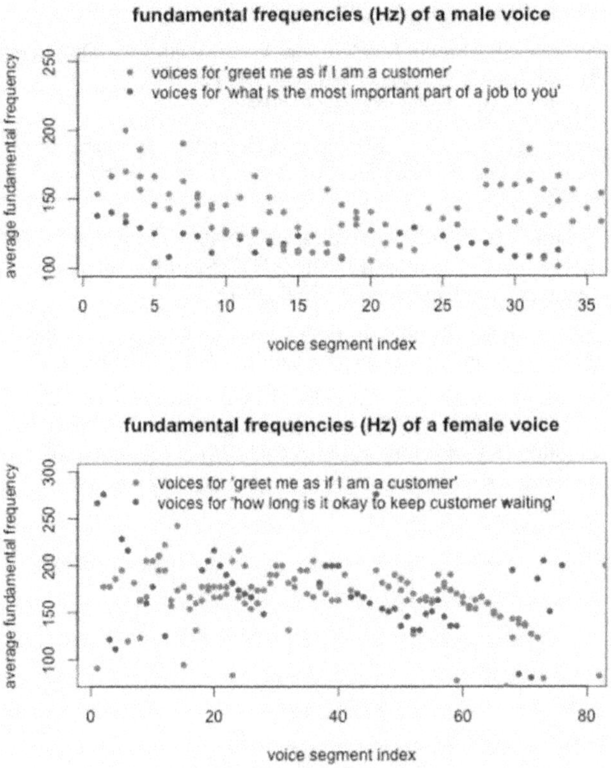

Figure 12. Fundamental frequencies for one male voice (top graph) and one female voice (bottom graph).

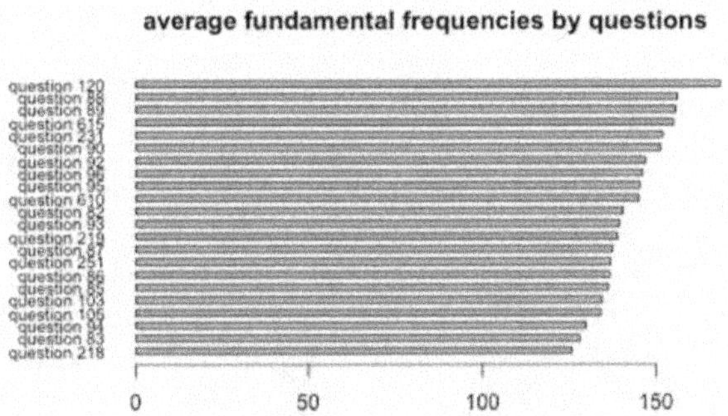

Figure 13. Differences in fundamental frequencies for different interview questions.

Taking all job applicants on all interview questions, we have observed differences in voice characteristics when job applicants answer different interview questions. Shown in Figure 13, the fundamental frequencies from voice clips on the question, "greet me as if I am a customer" (question 120 in Figure 13) are much higher than the fundamental frequencies on question, "tell me about the last time you performed a similar job" (question 218).

5.2 Layering Classification Models by Voice Characteristics Helps Improve Accuracy

Taking into consideration the differences in voice characteristics, we experimented with layering a decision tree by features related to fundamental frequency on top of the random forest classification model. We are able to improve the classification accuracy by nearly 10%. The layered model will need to go through further market research validation as described in Section 4.3 before we put it into production.

5.3 Anomalous Voice Characteristics

A voice paralinguistic feature can sometimes be critical for one classification task and be noise for another. For instance, "silence intervals" can be a useful feature for predicting soothing response when the voice is intentional for keeping a steady rhythm, but it can also be noise for predicting engaging effect when they are indications of low energy in the voice.

Dealing with voice signal often involves trade-offs between time domain and frequency domain. We have learned lessons to be mindful about using statistical features taken over one domain. For instance, when we use the maximum energy in the frequency domain over time as the main feature, it generally works well for voice clips that are of similar time length, but it has potential to overrate a voice clip that is very long in time. Therefore we need to take into account such limitations in the models/features when we use the scores from the model in a production environment where the voice clips were generated in free form. When we removed "silence intervals" in our voice feature construction, it helped remove noise, but it also generated a boundary case where a mostly silent clip actually gets high engaging score.

6. BUSINESS BENEFITS AND FUTURE RESEARCH

With Jobaline Voice Analyzer, employers will be able to identify service workers whose voices will better engage with their customers. Workers and employers will benefit from a shorter hiring cycle, thanks to the automated nature of the process. The deployed Jobaline Voice Analyzer system is starting to provide more quality input into our data science research and will enable more robust product features from Jobaline in the future.

We have a number of exciting future projects that will explore the many rich features of the Jobaline voice database and tap into vast repositories of data science methodologies and techniques. We have started work on building models for predicting emotion response of feeling "calmed" when exposed to voices that the listener feel is soothing. Our current findings indicate that we need to incorporate more paralinguistic features, such as cadence and emotion changes over time.

Over the longer term as we deploy data science on more types of emotion responses, as depicted in Figure 1, we hope to synthesize and establish a set of research methodologies on paralinguistic voice features for modeling listener response for broader application areas such as human-machine interaction, opening the doors for creating artificial voices for machines and allowing for better communication by enabling an emotional machine-listener connection.

7. REFERENCES

[1] Cacciatore, S., Luchinat, C., Tenori, L. 2014. Knowledge discovery by accuracy maximization. In *Proc. Natl. Acad. Sci., USA, vol. 111 no. 14, 5117-5122.*

[2] Cowie, R., Douglas-Cowie, E., Savvidou, S., McMahon, E., Sawey, M., Schröder, M. 2000. FEELTRACE: an instrument for recording perceived emotion in real time. In *ISCA workshop on speech and emotion*, Northern Ireland, pp 19–24.

[3] Devillers, L., and Vidrascu, L. 2006. Real-life emotions detection with lexical and paralinguistic cues on human call center dialogs. *INTERSPEECH.*

[4] Fernandez, R. 2004. A Computational Model for the Automatic Recognition of Affect in Speech. PhD Thesis, Massachusetts Institute of Technology, Cambridge, MA.

[5] Forsell, M. 2007. Acoustic Correlates of Perceived Emotions in Speech. Master Thesis in Speech Communication, Royal Institute of Technology. KTH.

[6] Kreiman, J., Van Lancker-Sidtis, D., and Gerratt, B.R., 2005. Perception of Voice Quality, in The Handbook of Speech Perception, Ed. Pisoni, D.B. and Remez, R.E., Blackwell Publishing, 338-362.

[7] Kreiman, J., Sidtis, D., 2011. Foundations of Voice Studies. Wiley-Blackwell.

[8] Lopatovska, I. and Arapakis, I. 2011. Theories, methods and current research on emotions in library and information science, information retrieval and human-computer interactions. *Information Processing & Management*. 47(4), 575-592.

[9] Mullor, M., Salazar, L., Li, Y., and Contreras, J. (Jobaline, Inc., USA) 2015. Matching and Lead Prequalification Based on Voice Analysis. US Patent Application #14532600.

[10] Picard, R.W. 2010. Emotion research by the people, for the people. *Emotion Review,* Volume 2, Issue 3 (July 2010)

[11] Polzehl, T., Moller, S., and Metze, F. 2010. Automatically assessing personality from speech. *2010 IEEE Fourth International Conference on Semantic Computing (ICSC).*

[12] Polzin, T. S., and Waibel, A. 1998. Detecting emotions in speech. *Proceedings of the CMC.*

[13] Quatier, T. F. 2002. Discrete-Time Speech Signal Processing: Principles and Practice.

[14] Schuller, B., Steidl, S., Batliner, A., Burkhardt, F., Devillers, L., Müller, C. A., et al. 2010. The INTERSPEECH 2010 paralinguistic challenge. *INTERSPEECH.*

[15] Schuller, B. 2011. Voice and speech analysis in search of states and traits. *Computer Analysis of Human Behavior,* 227-253.

[16] Schuller, B., Steidl, S., Batliner, A., Nöth, E., Vinciarelli, A., Burkhardt, F., et. al. 2012. The INTERSPEECH 2012 Speaker Trait Challenge. *INTERSPEECH.*

[17] Weiss, B. and Burkhardt, F. 2012. Is 'not bad' good enough? Aspects of unknown voices' likability. *INTERSPEECH.*

[18] Zhao, S., Rudzicz, F., Carvalho, L. G., Márquez-Chin, C., and Livingstone, S. 2014. Automatic detection of expressed emotion in Parkinson's disease. *2014 IEEE International Conference on Acoustics, Speech and Signal Processing (ICASSP).*

Discovery of Glaucoma Progressive Patterns Using Hierarchical MDL-Based Clustering

Shigeru Maya *
Graduate School of Information Science & Technology,
The University of Tokyo,
Tokyo 113-8656, Japan,
shigeru_maya@mist.i.u-tokyo.ac.jp

Kai Morino
Graduate School of Information Science & Technology,
The University of Tokyo,
Tokyo 113-8656, Japan,
morino@mist.i.u-tokyo.ac.jp

Hiroshi Murata
Department of Ophthalmology,
The University of Tokyo,
Tokyo 113-8655, Japan,
hmurata-tky@umin.net

Ryo Asaoka
Department of Ophthalmology,
The University of Tokyo,
Tokyo 113-8655, Japan,
rasaoka-tky@umin.ac.jp

Kenji Yamanishi
Graduate School of Information Science & Technology,
The University of Tokyo,
Tokyo 113-8656, Japan,
yamanishi@mist.i.u-tokyo.ac.jp

ABSTRACT

In this paper, we propose a method to cluster the spacial patterns of the visual field in glaucoma patients to analyze the progression patterns of glaucoma. The degree of progression in the visual field of glaucoma patients can be divided into several regions by straight line boundaries, we call this specific structure *Direct Product Structure* in this paper. Since we can observe the direct product structure in the visual fields, we propose a bottom-up hierarchical clustering method to embed this structure into the clustering structure. In our method, according to the minimum description length (MDL) principle, we select the best cluster division so that the total code length required for encoding the data as well as the clustering structure is minimum. We can thereby select the clusters that are robust to the noise in the position of the direct product structure for clustering. We demonstrate the effectiveness of our method using an artificial dataset and a real glaucoma dataset. Our proposed method performed better than existing methods for both datasets. For the real glaucoma dataset in particular, our method discovered the characteristic progressive patterns of glaucoma as specific features of clusters. These patterns agree with clinical knowledge. Furthermore, we show that our clusters can be applied to improve the accuracy of predicting glaucoma progression. Thus, our clusters contain rich information of glaucoma, and hence can contribute to further development in glaucoma research.

*The current address is Corporate Research & Development Center, TOSHIBA Corporation.
E-mail: shigeru1.maya@toshiba.co.jp.

KDD'15, August 10-13, 2015, Sydney, NSW, Australia.

ISBN 978-1-4503-3664-2/15/08 ...$15.00.
DOI: http://dx.doi.org/10.1145/2783258.2788574.

Categories and Subject Descriptors

H.2.8 [**Information Systems**]: Database Applications—*Data mining*; J.3 [**Life and Medical Sciences**]: Medical information systems

General Terms

Experimentation, Performance, Algorithm

Keywords

Glaucoma, hierarchical clustering, normalized maximum likelihood distribution, the minimum description length

1. INTRODUCTION

1.1 Background of this Study

Glaucoma is a chronic disease of eyes, which affects the field of vision (*visual field*). The mechanism of the progression of glaucoma is based on an increase in fluid pressure on the eye. As this pressure increases, the optical nerve is damaged which leads to visual field loss. Glaucoma is one of the main causes of blindness worldwide. Patients are surgically treated, according to the progression speed and also the pattern of the disease, hence it is clinically useful to optimize the treatment using mined-knowledge regarding glaucoma.

A major field requiring mined knowledge regarding glaucoma is the prediction of glaucoma progression [10, 12, 13]. In the relevant studies, predicting models embedded with

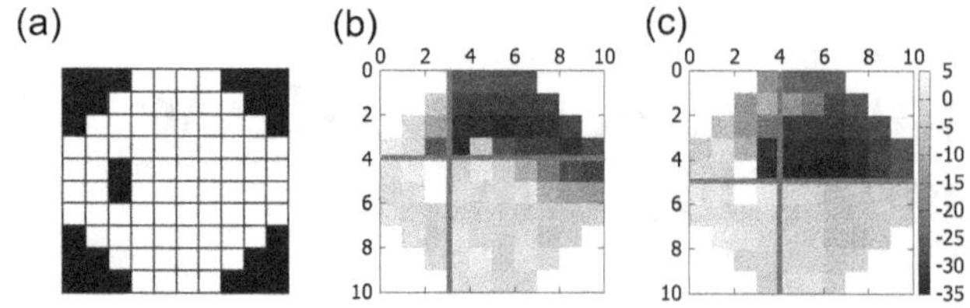

Figure 1: Visual fields of glaucoma. (a) 74 diagnosis points are shown as the white box. (b, c) Direct product structure of real visual field data. Regions are divided by red straight lines.

the characteristic features of glaucoma were constructed. Although these models performed well, many issues remain to be analyzed in order to improve the clinical setting.

Detecting characteristic progressive patterns on the visual fields of glaucoma patients is one of most challenging problems in research on predicting glaucoma progression. Clinical knowledge shows that the progression of glaucoma is deeply correlated with the pattern of optical nerves [6], such as progression from the side of the ear and that from the side of the nose. If we can classify these progressive patterns, we may obtain useful knowledge from clinical data. Such knowledge might help clinicians in numerous ways, such as the visualization of implicit clinical knowledge, the detection of novel progressive patterns, the addition of new information to improve the accuracy of prediction, and the discovery of correlations between the progressive patterns and risk factors of glaucoma and so on. Therefore, we focus on clustering glaucoma visual field data.

In this paper, we propose a clustering method to analyze the progression patterns of glaucoma by using a real glaucoma patient dataset which is given as Figure 1(a). We can observe a characteristic special feature on the visual field of glaucoma eyes as shown in Figure 1(b), (c). The red straight boundaries divide progression areas in both figures. We call this characteristic structure *Direct Product Structure* in this paper. To effectively mine knowledge from the dataset, we embed this direct product structure into our model. Past studies on pattern clustering of glaucoma primarily used a Gaussian mixture model [21] and independent component analysis [3]. These methods could not embed spacial information into the analyses, and the number of clusters had to be given in advance. Therefore, we propose a novel clustering method that embeds specific features of glaucoma into the model, and can automatically choose the best number of clusters. To the best of our knowledge, this is the first approach of its kind in glaucoma analyses.

We focus on spatial information in glaucoma progression. We show two sets of visual field data in Figure 1(b), (c). We can see that the red straight boundaries divide progression areas in both figures. However, these boundaries are similar but in slightly different positions. Therefore, a clustering technique is needed that classifies data with similar direct product structures together by tolerating slight differences in their spatial positions. We implemented this architecture by coding such features into our proposed technique. Under the *minimum description length* (MDL) principle [18], our proposed hierarchical clustering method obtains optimal clustering division where the total code length required for encoding the data as well as the clustering structure is minimum. We specifically employ the *normalized maximum likelihood coding* (NML) [18] for the encoding of data.

Our method worked better than comparative methods in clustering an artificial dataset. We further found progressive patterns in the real glaucoma dataset. Our method sensitively detects the difference of progression stages in glaucoma. Moreover, we applied our clustering method to the prediction of glaucoma progression. Liang et al. [10] recently proposed a framework for predicting glaucoma progression on the basis of spatio-temporal pattern clustering. By using our clusters in the clustering part of Liang et al.'s framework, we were able to significantly improve the prediction accuracy with a few data points in previous works.

1.2 Novelty of this Study

The novelty of our research can be summarized in the following: (1) A novel clustering method of visual field data on glaucoma; (2) Mining deep knowledge in ophthalmology.

We first propose a novel clustering method considering specific features of glaucoma. Many past studies did not use the spatial information of the visual field for clustering visual fields. The relevant spatial information constitutes important knowledge because the progression of glaucoma is deeply correlated with the spatial patterns of the optical nerves. Our proposed method embeds characteristic direct product features into our models and tolerates slight differences in boundary positions of divided ares in glaucoma (see Figure 1(b), (c)). Moreover, we employ bottom-up hierarchical clustering based on the MDL principle, which can automatically determine the number of clusters.

We obtained the following knowledge of glaucoma using this method. Firstly, we can divide visual field data into clusters which correspond to damaged areas of visual field. This was not achieved in previous works. Secondly, we find that obtained clusters can reflect the time evolution of visual field in glaucoma progression. This result agrees with the clinical knowledge. Finally, we find that obtained clusters can contribute to the improvement of the prediction accuracy by applying them into the previous prediction method.

1.3 Related Works

Because numerous studies have been conducted in the field of glaucoma progression prediction, we summarize here a few recent studies involving the embedding of glaucoma-specific features into models. Liang et al. [10] proposed a prediction method based on spatio-temporal clustering. This method collects data regarding patients with similar progressive patterns to form a prediction target patient. Maya et al. [12] proposed a prediction method based on a multi-task learning algorithm. Their method does not apply clustering to patient data for prediction, but instead uses a multi-task learning algorithm. Murata et al. [13] proposed a prediction method based on variational Bayesian learning. Their method involved embedding spatio-temporal patterns of glaucoma patients into their models. Hirasawa et al. [9] investigated the relationship between the inspection points and progression rates. Asaoka [2] clustered the inspection points to understand the feature of regions.

In past research involving the clustering of the progressive patterns of glaucoma, a Gaussian mixture model was used to show the correspondence of the clustering results and the existence of glaucoma [21]. Independent component analysis was employed to show the feature detection of the clusters

[3]. However, these methods embed neither specific feature of glaucoma nor the relevant spatial information into their models. The relationship between the local points of the visual field and optical nerves has also been studied [6].

The visual field data of glaucoma can be treated as image data. The *scale-invariant feature transform* (SIFT) algorithm [11] and the *histogram of oriented gradients* (HOG) feature descriptors [4] have been used in image processing. Although rotated patterns of glaucoma are different features because spatial positions are important, SIFT is consistent for rotating and scaling pictures, i.e., SIFT does not suit our setting. Thus, to apply these features quantities to cluster glaucoma progression patterns, HOG is better than SIFT.

With regard to past studies on clustering methods related to our work here, a method combining the Gaussian mixture model and Laplacian regularization was proposed [7]. Hirai and Yamanishi [8] proposed an automatic decision of the number of clusters using a normalized maximum likelihood distribution. Papadimitriou et al. [14] proposed a top-down hierarchical clustering method based on the MDL principle.

1.4 Organization of this Paper

This paper is organized as follows: In Section 2, we introduce the glaucoma dataset. In Section 3, we show the framework of our proposed method based on the MDL principle. The code length of our model is introduced in Sections 4 and 5. In Section 6, we provide the details of our proposed algorithm. We show the experimental results for the artificial dataset in Section 7 and those for real glaucoma dataset in Section 8. We conclude our paper in Section 9.

2. GLAUCOMA DIAGNOSTIC DATA

The local points over the visual field are shown in Figure 1(a). The black parts are local points where diagnoses are not made. The number of local points is 74, and an integer called *total deviation* (TD), representing the loss of visual strength, is measured at each local point. The range of TD is approximately [-40, 0]. A small value of TD implies advanced damage of glaucoma at the relevant local point.

Glaucoma data are characterized by visual field data that often have direct product structures. The positions of the boundaries to specify the direct structures on visual field are not necessarily congruent (see Figure 1(b), (c)).

As shown in Figure 1(a), the visual field data has a grid-like structure and many points do not correspond to values. We complement these values with neighboring values of TDs for analyses. See Figure 2 for this compliment procedure. Values of the six points on each corner are determined as the mean of the TD of the neighboring four points. Values of the two points (blind spots) located at the center-left are determined as the mean of the TD of neighboring three diagnosis points. Finally, we round these determined values because a value of the TD is an integer. As written above, many missing values in the original data shown as boxes with red line in Figure 2(a) are completed in Figure 2(b).

3. HIERARCHICAL CLUSTERING

Our proposed clustering method divides a set of visual fields of glaucoma patients into several clusters. We employ a *code length* as a criterion to determine the optimal clustering division. Let us express the dataset with a series of codes $\{0, 1\}$, e.g. 010, according to a coding rule. Then,

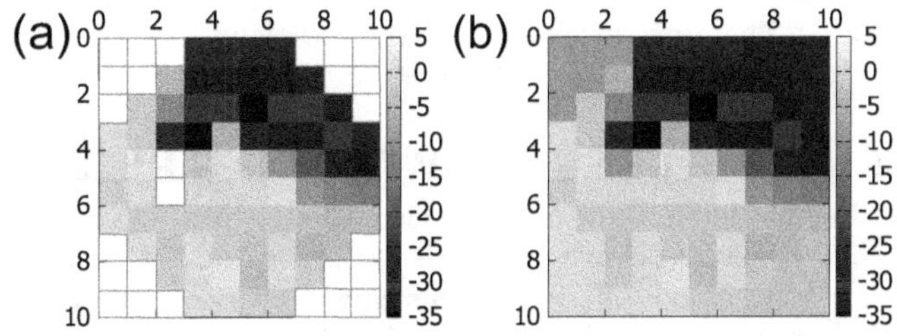

Figure 2: Complementing missing values (red boxes). (a) Original data. (b) Complemented data.

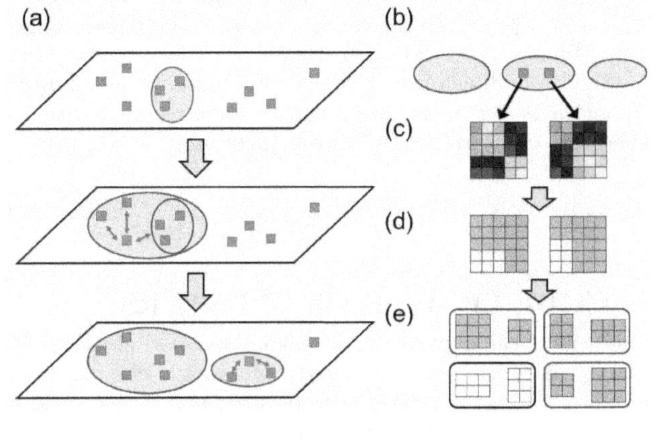

Figure 3: A schematic figure of our proposed method. (a) A sketch of our proposed hierarchical clustering. Each Square is visual field data. Several clusters are merged at each step. (b)-(e) Procedure to obtain the code length. (b) Obtain the code length of the rule of dividing clusters (RCcode). (c) Visual field data belonging to one cluster. (d) Obtain the code length to represent the direct structure (SCB). (e) Obtain the code length to produce elements in each region (SCR).

the dataset can be converted into a series of codes. The code length is the length of this series of codes. Under the *minimum description length* (*MDL*) principle [18], the optimal selection is chosen when it achieves the minimum code length. The code length of our clustering model is composed of two parts: the code length of the rule of clustering divisions (*RCcode*) and the code length of each of the divided clusters (*DCcode*). Under the MDL principle, optimal clustering division is obtained by minimizing the code length of our clustering model. However, it is difficult to obtain optimal clustering division because of its large time complexity due to the large number of possible clustering divisions.

In this paper, we propose a *bottom-up hierarchical clustering method* (BHCM) which clears up this large time complexity by merging several clusters for each step. Furthermore, we embed characteristic spatial structures of the visual fields of glaucoma patients, the direct product structure (see Figure 1), into our model. This idea is effective in clustering glaucoma datasets. Its procedure is schematically shown in Figure 3. Our method obtains clustering divisions by minimizing code length, the sum of RCcode and DCcode. Before introducing the detailed architecture of BHCM, we provide details of RCcode in Section 4 and DCcode in Section 5. The procedure to obtain the code length is schematically illustrated in Figure 3 (b)-(e).

4. CODE LENGTH OF DIVIDING RULE

Let us divide data from N visual fields into M clusters where the size of each cluster is k_m $(m = 1, \dots, M)$. Note that $\sum_{m=1}^{M} k_m = N$. Under this rule of clustering division, the number of possible assignments of the visual filed data is $M_2 := N!/(k_1!k_2! \cdots k_M!)$.

We code the rule of clustering division by considering the information necessary to describe the implementation of the division. In this case, we need $M+2$ natural numbers M, $\{k_m\}$, and M_2. Note that we can record the realized assignments of visual field data using M_2 if we set a counting rule, e.g., the ascending order. The code length of any natural number m is $\log^* m := \log(2.865) + \log m + \log\log m$ [16]. Hence, the code length RCcode is given as

$$\mathrm{RCcode} = \log^* M + \sum_{m=1}^{M} \log^* k_m + \log \frac{N!}{k_1!k_2! \cdots k_M!}. \quad (1)$$

5. CODE LENGTH OF CLUSTERS

DCcode is the sum of the code lengths of all clusters. We focus hereafter on the code length of a single cluster. As in Section 2, the glaucoma visual pattern has direct product structures. We describe embedding this characteristic into our model in Section 5.1. The code length of our model is given as a *stochastic complexity* (*SC*) in Sections 5.2, 5.3, and 5.4. We optimize the code length in Section 5.5.

5.1 Direct Product Structure of Visual Fields

We embed the direct product structure into our model. We assume that a visual field data is an $S \times T$ matrix. We divide this matrix into $G \times H$ *regions* with *boundaries* being normal to the axes. Figure 4(a) is an example. Note that S, T, G, and H are common to all visual field data.

We denote variables as follows: the number of visual field data is n, the ith visual field data is $x_i \in \mathbb{R}^{S \times T}$ $(i = 1, \dots, n)$, the (u, v)th element of x_i is $x_i(u, v)$, the horizontal and vertical boundary positions on the ith visual field data are $\mathbf{y}_{\mathrm{col}}^{(i)} \in \mathbb{Z}^{H+1}$ and $\mathbf{y}_{\mathrm{row}}^{(i)} \in \mathbb{Z}^{G+1}$, respectively. The jth element of $\mathbf{y}_{\mathrm{row}}^{(i)}$ and $\mathbf{y}_{\mathrm{col}}^{(i)}$ are $y_{\mathrm{row}}^{(i)}(j)$ and $y_{\mathrm{col}}^{(i)}(j)$, respectively.

Our proposed method allows different positions of boundaries in visual field data belonging to the same cluster. This is important to eliminate inessential difference in data. Although visual field data showing similar progressive patterns should be combined in the same cluster, slight differences between two sets of patterns might occur, as shown in Figure 4(a). Our proposed method combines these similar data patterns into the same cluster by using code length as a criterion because the code length decreases if the clustered visual field data are similar.

5.2 Stochastic Complexity

Stochastic complexity (SC) is the code length of a dataset given a *normalized maximum likelihood distribution* $P_{\mathrm{NML}}(\cdot)$ [17]. When a data item $\mathbf{x}$ is generated from $P(\mathbf{X}|\theta)$, the *maximum likelihood estimator* $\hat{\theta}$ is obtained. $P_{\mathrm{NML}}(\cdot)$ is then defined as $P_{\mathrm{NML}}(\mathbf{X}) := (P(\mathbf{X}|\hat{\theta}))/(\int P(\mathbf{X}|\hat{\theta})\mathrm{d}\mathbf{X})$. Under this probabilistic distribution, the code length of $\mathbf{x}$ SC is described as $-\log P(\mathbf{x}|\hat{\theta}) + \log \sum_{\mathbf{x}} P(\mathbf{x}|\hat{\theta})$. Although it

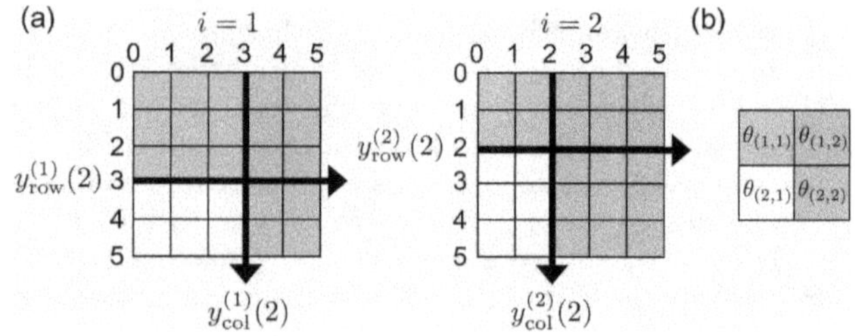

Figure 4: Examples of visual field data. (a) Regions and boundaries are $(n, S, T, G, H) = (2, 5, 5, 2, 2)$ and $\mathbf{y}_{\mathrm{row}}^{(1)} = \{0, 3, 5\}, \mathbf{y}_{\mathrm{col}}^{(1)} = \{0, 3, 5\}, \mathbf{y}_{\mathrm{row}}^{(2)} = \{0, 2, 5\}, \mathbf{y}_{\mathrm{col}}^{(2)} = \{0, 2, 5\}$. (b) Parameters corresponding to regions.

is often difficult to directly obtain SC, Rissanen [15] showed the approximation of SC under certain conditions as follows:

$$\mathrm{SC}(\mathbf{x}) = -\log P(\mathbf{x}|\hat{\theta}) + \frac{k}{2} \log \frac{x}{2\pi} + \log \int \sqrt{|I(\theta)|}\mathrm{d}\theta, \quad (2)$$

where $I(\theta)$ is the *Fisher information matrix*, x is the size of $\mathbf{x}$, and k is the number of parameters. We employed the normal distribution as $P(\cdot)$, i.e., θ represents mean and variance $(k = 2)$. When we restrict the integral intervals of the Fisher information matrix in Eq. (2) to $-2^{\frac{\alpha}{2}} \le \mu \le 2^{\frac{\alpha}{2}}$ and $\sigma^2 \ge 2^{-2\beta}$ [8], $\mathrm{SC}(\mathbf{x})$ is given as $-\log P(\mathbf{x}|\hat{\mu}, \hat{\sigma}^2) + \log(x/(2\pi)) + 1.5 + \beta + \alpha/2$.

5.3 Code Length of Dividing Boundaries

We assume that the boundaries of the data for the ith patient belonging to a cluster are generated by $P(y_{\mathrm{row}}^{(i)}(g)|\psi_{(g-1)}^{\mathrm{row}})$ or $P(y_{\mathrm{col}}^{(i)}(h)|\psi_{(h-1)}^{\mathrm{col}})$, where $\psi_{(g-1)}^{\mathrm{row}}$ and $\psi_{(h-1)}^{\mathrm{col}}$ are parameters. The SC of the gth vertical boundary $\mathrm{SCBR}(g)$ and the hth horizontal boundary $\mathrm{SCBC}(h)$ are then derived as

$$\mathrm{SCBR}(g) = \sum_{i=1}^{n} -\log P(y_{\mathrm{row}}^{(i)}(g)|\hat{\psi}_{(g-1)}^{\mathrm{row}}) + \frac{k}{2} \log \frac{n}{2} + \log \int \sqrt{|I(\psi_{(g-1)}^{\mathrm{row}})|}\mathrm{d}\psi_{(g-1)}^{\mathrm{row}}, \quad (3)$$

$$\mathrm{SCBC}(h) = \sum_{i=1}^{n} -\log P(y_{\mathrm{col}}^{(i)}(h)|\hat{\psi}_{(h-1)}^{\mathrm{col}}) + \frac{k}{2} \log \frac{n}{2} + \log \int \sqrt{|I(\psi_{(h-1)}^{\mathrm{col}})|}\mathrm{d}\psi_{(h-1)}^{\mathrm{col}}. \quad (4)$$

Thus, the code length of the boundaries, defined as SCB, is given as

$$\mathrm{SCB} = \sum_{g=2}^{G} \mathrm{SCBR}(g) + \sum_{h=2}^{H} \mathrm{SCBC}(h). \quad (5)$$

Note that we omit the boundaries $g = 1$ and $h = 1$ because they do not affect the division.

5.4 Code Length of Divided Regions

In this section, we derive the SC of the divided regions. The number of cells $f(g, h)$ within the (g, h)th region is obtained as $f(g, h) = \sum_{i=1}^{n} z_{\mathrm{row}}^{(i)}(g) z_{\mathrm{col}}^{(i)}(h)$, where $z_{\mathrm{row}}^{(i)}(g) := y_{\mathrm{row}}^{(i)}(g+1) - y_{\mathrm{row}}^{(i)}(g)$ and $z_{\mathrm{col}}^{(i)}(h) := y_{\mathrm{col}}^{(i)}(h+1) - y_{\mathrm{col}}^{(i)}(h)$.

Then, the SC of the (g,h)th region $\mathrm{SCRE}(g,h)$ is derived as

$$\mathrm{SCRE}(g,h) = -\log P(x^{(f(g,h))}|\hat{\theta}_{(g,h)}) + \frac{k}{2}\log\frac{f(g,h)}{2\pi} + \log\int\sqrt{|I(\theta_{(g,h)})|}\mathrm{d}\theta_{(g,h)}. \quad (6)$$

We assume that visual field data belonging to the (g,h) region $x^{(f(g,h))}$ are generated from $P(x^{(f(g,h))}|\theta_{(g,h)})$, where $\theta_{(g,h)}$ is the parameter of the (g,h)th region. Thus, the code length of all the regions SCR is given as

$$\mathrm{SCR} = \sum_{g=1}^{G}\sum_{h=1}^{H}\mathrm{SCRE}(g,h). \quad (7)$$

5.5 Optimizing Boundaries

In this section, we describe the optimization of the boundaries $\mathbf{y}^{(i)}_{\mathrm{row}}$ and $\mathbf{y}^{(i)}_{\mathrm{col}}$ by minimizing the total code length of clusters SCC. From Eqs. (5) and (7), SCC is derived as SCC $=$ SCB $+$ SCR. We note that SCB and SCR are functions of the boundaries. In the optimization procedure, procedures A-step and B-step are alternatively repeated five times. In A-step, we update the positions of the boundaries under the condition that the parameters $\theta_{(g,h)}$, $\psi^{\mathrm{row}}_{(g)}$, and $\psi^{\mathrm{col}}_{(h)}$ are fixed. In B-step, we update the parameters $\theta_{(g,h)}$, $\psi^{\mathrm{row}}_{(g)}$, and $\psi^{\mathrm{col}}_{(h)}$ under the condition that the positions of the boundaries are fixed. Following the repetitions, we run an additional B-step to obtain maximum likelihood estimators $\hat{\theta}_{(g,h)}$, $\hat{\psi}^{\mathrm{row}}_{(g)}$, and $\hat{\psi}^{\mathrm{col}}_{(h)}$. Finally, we determine SCC using these estimated parameters. Note that while this architecture provides a local optimal SCC, our experiments indicate that our method is effective. The algorithm is summarized in Alg. 1. The obtained SCC is the criterion for clustering decision described in later Section 6.

5.5.1 A-step

In A-step, we update the positions of the dividing boundaries using *dynamical programming* (*DP*). In particular, we extend *Dynamic Time Warping* [19] to apply to our model. We first modify the code length of a cluster by obtaining the upper bound of SCC, and approximate it as follows:

$$\begin{aligned}
&\sum_{g=1}^{G}\sum_{h=1}^{H} -\log P(x^{(f(g,h))}|\theta_{(g,h)}) \\
&+\frac{k}{2}H\left(\sum_{i=1}^{n}\left(-\frac{1}{2}\frac{G}{G-1}\sum_{g=1}^{G-1}\log\left(\frac{S^2}{S^2-\mathrm{part}^{(i)}_{\mathrm{row}}(g)^2G^2}\right)\right)\right) \\
&+\frac{k}{2}G\left(\sum_{i=1}^{n}\left(-\frac{1}{2}\frac{H}{H-1}\sum_{h=1}^{H-1}\log\left(\frac{T^2}{T^2-\mathrm{part}^{(i)}_{\mathrm{col}}(h)^2H^2}\right)\right)\right) \\
&+\sum_{g=2}^{G}\sum_{i=1}^{n} -\log P(y^{(i)}_{\mathrm{row}}(g)|\psi^{\mathrm{row}}_{(g-1)}) \\
&+\sum_{h=2}^{H}\sum_{i=1}^{n} -\log P(y^{(i)}_{\mathrm{col}}(h)|\psi^{\mathrm{col}}_{(h-1)}). \quad (8)
\end{aligned}$$

Here, we use displacement from equally divided points of row $\{Sg/G\}$ $(g=1,\dots,G-1)$ and column $\{Th/H\}$ $(h=1,\dots,H-1)$. We define the displacement of the boundaries from these points as $\mathrm{part}^{(i)}_{\mathrm{row}}(g) := Sg/G - y^{(i)}_{\mathrm{row}}(g+1)$ and $\mathrm{part}^{(i)}_{\mathrm{col}}(h) := Th/H - y^{(i)}_{\mathrm{col}}(h+1)$. We note that some terms that did not correspond to the position of the dividing boundaries were omitted in Eq. (8). The derivation of Eq. (8) is omitted due to the space limitation.

A crucial modification in Eq. (8) from the original form of the SCC is that we can now separately analyze each patient's visual data. Recall that $f(g,h)$ is the number of cells belonging to the (g,h)th regions of all visual field data within a cluster. Even if a boundary of a visual field data item changes, several values of $f(g,h)$ change. This change affects all visual field data. To overcome this problem, we introduce the displacement of boundaries from equally divided points $\{Sg/G\}$ and $\{Th/H\}$. This idea enables the enhancement of the size of visual field data during DP. Moreover, this allows us to separately calculate the optimizing problem for each patient by modifying the summation of the ith visual field data. Therefore, we can solve an optimization problem for each data item. Hereafter, we use the value obtained from Eq. (8) instead of the original code length.

We now introduce our use of DP. Our goal is to obtain the optimal value of Eq. (8) for the ith visual field $(S\times T)$ with $G\times H$ regions, which is defined as CDP $[S,T,G,H]$. A sub-problem then is to obtain the optimal value of Eq. (8) for the ith visual field $(s\times t)$ with $g\times h$ regions, i.e., CDP $[s,t,g,h]$. Note that $1\le s\le S, 1\le t\le T, 1\le g\le G, 1\le h\le H$.

In DP, a sub-problem for the ith visual field $(s\times t)$ with $g\times h$ regions is generated by adding a new row or column to a smaller sub-problem where the visual fields are $(s-1)\times t$ or $s\times(t-1)$, respectively. This means that the visual field $(s-1)\times t$ enhances to the visual field $s\times t$ by adding a new row and that $s\times(t-1)$ to that $s\times t$ by a new column. Moreover, an option exists whether a new boundary arises or not in the new added row or column. Therefore, a sub-problem originates in four smaller sub-problems, and its CDP$[s,t,g,h]$ is obtained from those of the smaller sub-problems.

Under this procedure, CDP$[s,t,g,h]$ satisfies the following formula as CDP$[s,t,g,h] = \min\{E_1,E_2,E_3,E_4\}$, where

$$\begin{aligned}
E_1 &= \mathrm{CDP}[s-1,t,g,h] + \sum_{v=1}^{t}\left(-\log(P(x_i(s,v)|\theta_{\eta(i,s,v)}))\right), \\
E_2 &= \mathrm{CDP}[s-1,t,g-1,h] - \log(P(y^{(i)}_{\mathrm{row}}(g+1)|\psi^{\mathrm{row}}_{(g)})) \\
&\quad + \sum_{v=1}^{t}\left(-\log(P(x_i(s,v)|\theta_{\eta(i,s,v)}))\right) \\
&\quad + \frac{k}{2}\left(-\frac{GH}{2(G-1)}\log\frac{S^2}{S^2-(sG-gS)^2}\right), \quad (9) \\
E_3 &= \mathrm{CDP}[s,t-1,g,h] + \sum_{u=1}^{s}\left(-\log(P(x_i(u,t)|\theta_{\eta(i,u,t)}))\right), \\
E_4 &= \mathrm{CDP}[s,t-1,g,h-1] - \log(P(y^{(i)}_{\mathrm{col}}(h+1)|\psi^{\mathrm{col}}_{(h)})) \\
&\quad + \sum_{u=1}^{s}\left(-\log(P(x_i(u,t)|\theta_{\eta(i,u,t)}))\right) \\
&\quad + \frac{k}{2}\left(-\frac{GH}{2(H-1)}\log\frac{T^2}{T^2-(tH-hT)^2}\right), \quad (10)
\end{aligned}$$

where $\eta(i,u,v)$ indicates the divided region (g,h) to which $x_i(u,v)$ belongs. Note that we exclude a pass whereby the denominators of Eqs. (9) and (10) are not positive candidates from CDP $[s,t,g,h]$. The initial condition is set at CDP $[u,v,1,1]$ with $u\in[1:S]$ *and* $v\in[1:T]$, where $[a:b] := \{x\in\mathbb{Z}|a\le x\le b\}$. Note that CDP $[u,v,1,1]$ are

Algorithm 1 The code length of visual field data.

INPUT: Visual field data $x_i \in \mathbb{R}^{S\times T}$ $(i = 1,\ldots,n)$ and structures of divided regions $G \times H$.
OUTPUT: Code length of n visual field data within a cluster (SCC).

```
Initialize the boundary positions of n visual field data.
for l = 1 → # of iterations (here, five times) do
    Run B-step: we update θ_(g,h), ψ^row_(g), and ψ^col_(h) through
    maximum likelihood estimation.
    for i = 1 → n do
        Run A-step: we update the boundaries of the ith
        visual field data.
    end for
end for
Run B-step again.
We obtain SCC using the boundaries of all visual field
data and parameters θ̂_(g,h), ψ̂^row_(g) and ψ̂^col_(h).
```

solely obtained because the visual field is undivided. When we finally obtain CDP $[S, T, G, H]$, we can also obtain the boundaries by checking cases where a new boundary arises. The complexity of this DP is $\mathcal{O}(STGH)$ because we need to obtain a table with $S \times T \times G \times H$ cells in DP. For n visual fields, the complexity is $\mathcal{O}(nSTGH)$.

5.5.2 B-step

In B-step, we update $\theta_{(g,h)}$, $\psi^{\text{row}}_{(g)}$, and $\psi^{\text{col}}_{(h)}$ through maximum likelihood estimation using the data $x^{(f(g,h))}$. In the first B-step, we set the initial conditions of the boundaries to $y^{(i)}_{\text{row}}(j) = \text{round}((j-1)S/G)$ $(2 \le j \le G)$ and $y^{(i)}_{\text{col}}(j) = \text{round}((j-1)T/H)$ $(2 \le j \le H)$, where round(r) gives r rounded to the nearest number. We note that only the first terms in Eqs. (3), (4), and (6) correspond to the parameters.

6. PROPOSED HIERARCHICAL CLUSTERING ALGORITHM

We introduce the detailed algorithm of our proposed *bottom-up hierarchical clustering method* (BHCM). An initial condition of BHCM is that the visual field of each glaucoma eye is considered to be one cluster, i.e., the number of clusters is the same as that of visual fields in the dataset. We merge these clusters based on the MDL principle, i.e., we merge some clusters into others to achieve minimum code length. Note that our BHCM tolerates slight differences in the positions of the boundaries between clusters. We realized this by modeling the boundary positions using probabilistic distributions. If some boundaries are similar and should be merged into the same cluster, the code length of our model will be shorter when these boundaries are generated by the same distribution than when they are generated by different distributions. On the contrary, for different boundaries, the code length of our model is longer when both boundaries have been generated by the same distribution than when they have been generated by different distributions.

First, we choose a cluster C_1 with minimum value of SCC from a set of size-one clusters. Note that clusters previously chosen are never chosen again. Second, we obtain SCC as CS_1. Third, we obtain SCC as CS_2 for the case where C_1 and another cluster, C_2, are merged. If CS_2 is shorter than CS_1, we merge C_2 into C_1 in the fourth step. All clusters except C_1 are checked through this process. Fourth, we merge C_1 and the clusters selected in the third step. We repeat this procedure until no cluster can be selected. We choose the cluster with the minimum code length because such a cluster strongly expresses direct product structures, and thus is a reasonable selection as representative of the final cluster.

A benefit of our proposed method is its small time complexity. This is effected by merging clusters all at once in the fourth step. For ordinal bottom-up hierarchical clustering methods, a cluster is merged to only one other cluster. This is the key to applying bottom-up hierarchical clustering to analyses of glaucoma datasets.

7. EXPERIMENT USING ARTIFICIAL DATA

In this section, we compare the performance of our proposed method with several other methods for using three progressive patterns of artificial data. We generated artificial data with three patterns: direct product pattern, tree pattern, and step pattern (see Figure 5).

7.1 Generating Artificial Data

We show how to generate the artificial data. The data structure is constructed as similar to glaucoma data, i.e., the artificial data has direct product structure and is divided into several regions. Based on this condition, Our manner of generating each artificial progressive pattern data item was as follows. We first initiated the data as $\mathbb{R}^{10\times 10}$, i.e., $S = T = 10$. We then generated boundaries dividing the regions on the spatial data. We finally generated values of elements within each region from the normal distribution of which parameters are given based on corresponding regions.

We divided the spacial data into 3×3 regions with boundaries. The boundary positions were denoted by $\mathbf{y}^{(i)}_{\text{row}}, \mathbf{y}^{(i)}_{\text{col}} \in \mathbb{Z}^4$ of the ith data. They were set to $y^{(i)}_{\text{row}}(1) = 0, y^{(i)}_{\text{row}}(2) = \min\{Z_1, Z_2\}, y^{(i)}_{\text{row}}(3) = \max\{Z_1, Z_2\}$, and $y^{(i)}_{\text{row}}(4) = 10$, where Z_1 and Z_2 were given as $Z_1 = \lfloor(3 + Z)\rfloor$ and $Z_2 = \lfloor(6 + Z)\rfloor$. Note that Z was drawn from the normal distribution, with mean 0 and standard deviation 2, and $\lfloor a \rfloor$ indicates the integer part of a. If $Z_1 = Z_2$, we redraw them. The same procedure was repeated in the case of columns.

Generated data has three types of progressive patterns: direct product pattern, tree pattern, and step pattern. Note that tree and step patterns were generated by merging some regions (see Figure 5(b), (c)). Values of data were given by the normal distribution. Its means were defined for each region as Figure 5 and SDs were all set to 1. We prepared 40 spacial data with the same condition and considered them as a cluster. For each pattern, we generated three clusters, i.e., we had 120 spacial data for each progressive pattern.

7.2 Comparative Methods

We introduce comparative methods in this section. A comparative method is defined as a pair of a clustering method and data inputted to the clustering method.

We prepared three types of inputted data as raw data (RAW), smoothing data (SMO), and HOG[4]. When we input the data without change, we call it RAW. In SMO, each element of spacial data is exchanged for the averaged values of the five points: the point itself and the neighboring four points, i.e. SMO gives local space information. HOG is a feature mainly used in image processing, and is useful for

Table 1: **Code length for the artificial data with (G, H).**

(G, H)	(2,2)	(2,3)	(3,2)	(3,3)	(3,4)	(4,3)	(4,4)
Direct product pattern	4.53×10^4	3.71×10^4	3.93×10^4	$\mathbf{3.24 \times 10^4}$	4.05×10^4	3.88×10^4	4.37×10^4
Tree pattern	3.22×10^4	2.75×10^4	$\mathbf{2.65 \times 10^4}$	3.03×10^5	3.58×10^4	3.48×10^4	4.19×10^4
Step pattern	3.53×10^4	3.42×10^4	$\mathbf{3.30 \times 10^4}$	3.40×10^5	3.36×10^4	3.37×10^4	3.54×10^4

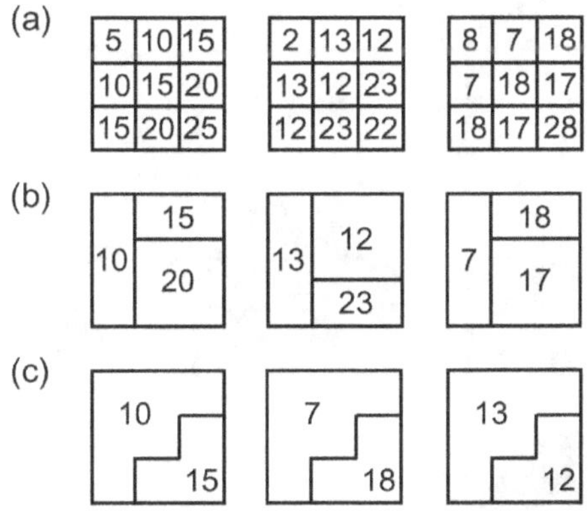

Figure 5: Three spatial patterns. The mean parameters of the normal distribution are shown in each region. (a) Direct product pattern. (b) Tree pattern. (c) Step pattern.

detecting shapes of objects. In HOG, the size of cells and blocks are set at 2 and its dimension was reduced to 100 with principal component analysis due to its high dimension.

For clustering methods, we used Gaussian mixture models with Laplacian regularization (LAP) [7], Gaussian mixture models (GMM), and k-means clustering. We first introduce LAP. Let $x_i \in \mathbb{R}^d$ denotes the ith spacial data, where $d = S \times T = 100$. Then, the similarity matrix $\mathbf{S} \in \mathbb{R}^{N \times N}$ among spacial data is $S(i,j) = \exp\left(-(x_i - x_j)^{\mathrm{T}}\mathbf{D}(x_i - x_j)/d^2\right)$, where $D(u,v) = 1/(\mathrm{dist}(u,v)+1)$. Note that $\mathrm{dist}(u,v)$ is the Euclidean distance between the uth point and vth point. We set the hyperparameter λ to 10^d as in [7]. For these three clustering methods, we set the number of clusters to three which is the true number of clusters. Note that our proposed method automatically determined the number of clusters.

The eight comparative methods are summarized as follows: (RAW + k-means), (RAW + GMM), (RAW + LAP), (SMO + k-means), (SMO + GMM), (SMO + LAP), (HOG + k-means), and (HOG + GMM).

7.3 Evaluation Indices of Clustering

Four evaluation indices of clustering are introduced in this section. We denote a set of spacial data correctly belonging to the ith cluster by L_i, a set of those belonging to the jth cluster by C_j, and N is the number of data items ($N = 120$). We define $\mathrm{Prec}(L_i, C_j) := \frac{|L_i \cap C_j|}{|C_j|}$ and $\mathrm{Rec}(L_i, C_j) = \frac{|L_i \cap C_j|}{|L_i|}$. Then, *Purity* is defined as $\sum_j \frac{|C_j|}{N} \max_i \{\mathrm{Prec}(L_i, C_j)\}$ and *InversePurity* as $\sum_i \frac{|L_i|}{N} \max_j \{\mathrm{Rec}(L_i, C_j)\}$[1]. The *F-measure* is defined as F-measure $= \sum_i \frac{|L_i|}{N} \max_j \{F(L_i, C_j)\}$, where $F(L_i, C_j) = 2\mathrm{Prec}(L_i, C_j)\mathrm{Rec}(L_i, C_j)/(\mathrm{Prec}(L_i, C_j) + \mathrm{Rec}(L_i, C_j))$ [5]. Then, *Normalized mutual information* (NMI) [20] is defined as $\frac{\sum_{i,j} |L_i \cap C_j| \log \frac{N|L_i \cap C_j|}{L_i C_j}}{\sqrt{\sum_i -|L_i| \log \frac{|L_i|}{N}}\sqrt{\sum_j -|C_j| \log \frac{|C_j|}{N}}}$. All four indices were within the range $[0, 1]$, which indicates that the cluster was precise with high values.

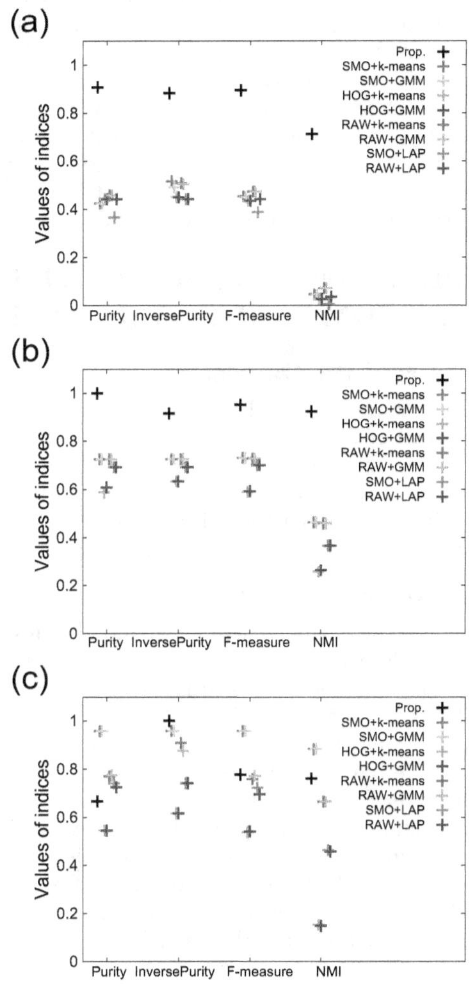

Figure 6: Results using artificial data. (a) Result for direct product pattern. (b) Result for tree pattern. (c) Result for Step pattern.

7.4 Results

In our method, we employed the normal distribution as described in Eqs. (3), (4), and (6). We set (α, β) to $(8, 8)$ in Eqs. (3) and (4), and $(10, 8)$ in Eq. (6). The size of regions $(G \times H)$ was chosen as that giving the shortest code length from $(G, H) = \{(2,2), (2,3), (3,2), (3,3), (3,4), (4,3), (4,4)\}$. As a result, we chose (G, H) as $(3, 3)$ for direct product pat-

Table 2: Code length for the Glaucoma dataset with (G, H).

(G, H)	(2, 2)	(2, 3)	(3, 2)	(3, 3)	(3, 4)	(4, 3)	(4, 4)
code length	$\mathbf{4.77 \times 10^5}$	4.89×10^5	4.82×10^5	4.96×10^5	5.03×10^5	4.99×10^5	5.25×10^5

tern, and $(3, 2)$ for tree and step patterns. The code lengths of (G, H) is shown in Table 1. For each comparative method, we repeated 100 trials by changing initial conditions.

The medians of the evaluation indices of clustering are shown in Figure 6. Our method outperformed all methods in direct product and tree patterns but does not in step pattern. This showed that our method suits the direct product structure like glaucoma special pattern. On the contrary, for the step pattern, they are quite different from the direct product structure, therefore, our method did not work well.

8. EXPERIMENTS INVOLVING VISUAL FIELD DATA FROM REAL GLAUCOMA PATIENTS

8.1 Details of the Dataset

The glaucoma dataset used in this paper was provided by the Department of Ophthalmology, The University of Tokyo. The dataset was composed of diagnoses of 1,086 eyes. Although each eye was diagnosed several times, we selected the visual field data from the initial diagnosis. Therefore, we clustered 1,086 visual field data items.

8.2 Results of Clustering

We employed the normal distribution and determined (G, H) as $(2, 2)$ as in the case of artificial data. We set (α, β) to $(8, 8)$ in Eqs. (3) and (4), and $(12, 8)$ in Eq. (6). The code length with (G, H) is summarized in Table 2.

Our method determined the number of clusters as seven. The progressive patterns of these clusters and sizes of clusters are shown in Figure 7. The progressive patterns are generated by weighted averaging visual field data within each cluster. We omit the details due to the space limitation. Note that we show the values of only 74 local points on the visual field which corresponds to actual diagnosis points (see Fig. 1(a)). We also note that the size of cluster # 7 was only one, therefore, we should consider it as an outlier.

We present the results of the comparative method SMO+GMM. As the comparative method, we employed SMO as input data and GMM for clustering method because this combination performed well on artificial data. We set the number of clusters in GMM to six in keeping with the number of meaningful clusters in our method. The progressive patterns and the sizes of clusters of the comparative method are shown in Figure 8. Each progressive pattern was generated by averaging the visual field data within a cluster.

Here, we show the comparison result of our method and SMO+GMM. Table 3 is a cross-table: The (i, j)th element of this table represents the number of visual field data items belonging to the ith cluster in our proposed method and the jth cluster in SMO+GMM. We can find the significance information in the following four points.

First, our method clearly divides a complex cluster generated by SMO+GMM into two simple clusters. As shown in Table 3, members of the cluster # 5 in SMO+GMM are divided into the clusters # 5 and # 6 in our method. For the clusters # 5 and # 6 in our method, damages of the

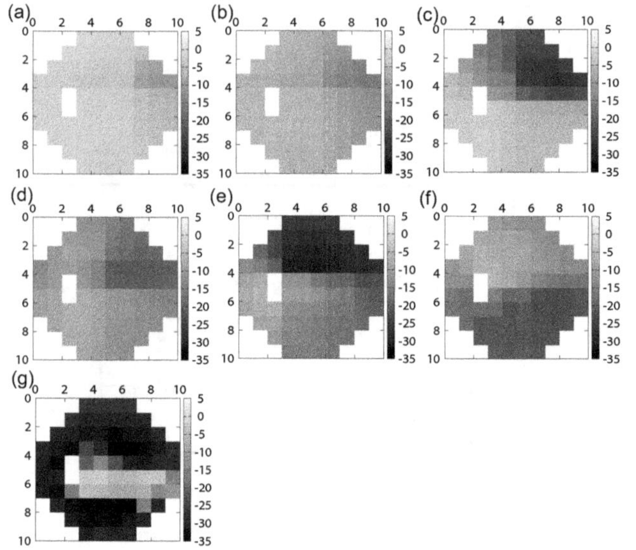

Figure 7: Characteristic features of clusters in our proposed method. (a) The size of the cluster #1 was 569. (b) #2 277. (c) #3 96. (d)#4 49. (e)#5 48. (f) #6 46. (g) #7 1.

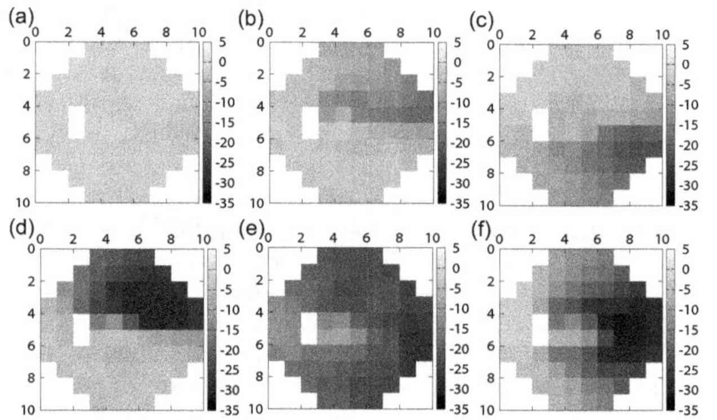

Figure 8: Characteristic features of clusters in SMO+GMM. (a) The size of cluster #1 was 448. (b) #2 221. (c) #3 151. (d)#4 144. (e)#5 63. (f) #6 59.

progressive patterns are on upper and lower area, respectively (Figure 7(e),(f)). On the contrary, for the clusters # 5 in SMO+GMM, damages entirely spread on the visual field. This difference indicates that our proposed method can capture the two different progressive patterns.

Second, our method can sensitively detect the difference of progression stage. As similar to the first point, members of the cluster # 2 in SMO+GMM are divided into the clusters # 1 and # 2 in our method. For the cluster # 2 in SMO+GMM, damages of the progressive pattern are unclear (Figure 8(b)). In our method, however, damages of

Table 3: Cross-table between our proposed and the comparative method.

	Comparative method (SMO+GMM)					
Our method	# 1	# 2	# 3	# 4	# 5	# 6
# 1	359	96	76	25	0	13
# 2	83	85	63	16	0	30
# 3	0	21	0	71	2	2
# 4	5	17	3	12	8	4
# 5	0	0	0	20	22	6
# 6	1	2	9	0	30	4
# 7	0	0	0	0	1	0

the progressive patterns of the cluster # 2 is heavier than that of # 1 (Figure 7(a), (b)). This implies that our method sensitively detects the difference of progression stage.

Third, our method detects the progressive patterns spreading the lower area. For the cluster # 6 in our method (Figure 7(f)), the damages on the visual field clearly shown in the lower area. On the contrary, for the cluster # 3 in SMO+GMM (Figure 8(c)), the damages within the lower area are not so clear. This suggests that our method gathered visual field damaged in the lower area more correctly.

Fourth, our method shows the progressive patterns which agrees with the clinical knowledge. Glaucomatous visual field defect usually starts with nasal step (Figure 7(a)) and/or Bjerrum scotoma. Nasal step and Bjerrum scotoma are the names of areas in the visual field. As the disease progresses these defects expand and can be merged to each other (Figure 7(b), (d), (f)). With the further advancement, hemifield loss in superior or inferior visual field can be observed (Figure 7(c)) sometimes excluding points which are adjacent to a horizontal line (Figure 7(e)). Thus, we see the time evolution of progressive patterns. On the contrary, it is hard to find such time evolution for the clusters of SMO+GMM.

8.3 Predicting Progression of Glaucoma

In this section, we apply our clustering method to the prediction problem of future progression of glaucoma. It is known that damages caused by glaucoma do not recover, therefore, initial treatments to alleviate the progression of glaucoma are seriously important. From this viewpoint, accurate prediction using a few measurements is strongly desired and investigated by many studies [10, 12, 13].

We introduce Liang et al.'s work [10] to use it as an example for the applications of our clustering results into the prediction problem. Recently, Liang et al. [10] proposed a clustering-based prediction method. This method gathers patients who are similar to the target patient using spatio-temporal clustering, and generates a predictor by fitting them to a linear function of time. Thus, by exchanging their clusters for our clusters, we can evaluate the effects of our clustering results on the prediction problem of glaucoma.

Here, we show the settings of our comparison. As the comparative method, we employed the *uv*-em clustering method and the *temporal-shift linear regression* (TSLR) because this combination performed well [10]. The number of clusters of *uv*-em was set to 40 based on [10]. The performance of prediction is measured by the *root mean squared error* (RMSE) defined as $\sqrt{\sum_{i=1}^{74}(\hat{y}_i - y_i)^2/74}$, where $\hat{y}_i$ and y_i are the predicted and actual TD on the ith local point on the visual field at the final data point, respectively. The number of data points used for the learning is denoted by Q. We note that our clusters were generated using only first diagnosis data without use of time information.

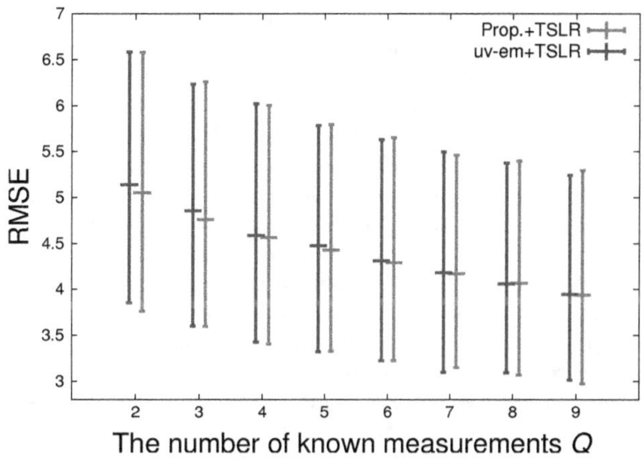

Figure 9: RMSE for the number of known measurements Q. Centers show the median of RMSE and the upper and lower ends show quantiles.

Table 4: The number of wins of proposed and comparative methods.

Q	# of Prop.	# of *uv*-em	# of total	p-value
2	600	486	1086	6.00×10^{-4}
3	585	501	1086	0.0118
4	551	535	1086	0.649
5	555	513	1068	0.210
6	547	507	1054	0.230
7	527	505	1032	0.513
8	472	509	981	0.250
9	429	445	874	0.612

We compared RMSE of both methods varying $Q \in [2:9]$ through 10-fold cross-validation. As shown in Figure 9, our clustering results gave more accurate prediction than the comparative method in the sense of median for $Q = 2$ and 3. Moreover, we counted the number of wins of our method as summarized in Table 4. For $Q = 2$ and 3, our method was significantly better than the comparative method with $p < 0.05$. To check the significance of this result, we conducted a binomial test with a null hypotheses that predictive abilities are equal for both methods. For $Q \geq 4$, the null hypotheses cannot be rejected. This results imply that our clustering contains helpful information for prediction problem.

9. CONCLUSIONS

In this paper, we proposed a bottom-up hierarchical clustering method to embed specific features of the visual field data from glaucoma patients into a model. Our method classifies the visual field data into several clusters based on the code length of the dataset. Under the MDL principle, optimal clusters are selected.

Our proposed method has performed well for an artificial dataset. In the cases involving the artificial dataset with direct product and tree patterns, our method has exhibited the best performance in comparative experiments. However, in case of datasets with step pattern, our method was inferior. This result reflects the architecture of direct product in our proposed method.

Using a real dataset of glaucoma, our method detected the characteristic progressive patterns. This result agrees with clinical knowledge of glaucoma progression. Moreover, we entered our clustering results into a prediction method based on spatio-temporal clustering, and found that prediction performance improved when our clusters were used. This implies that our clusters contain not only characteristic patterns, but also richer information that can extend our method to treat general problems in glaucoma.

In future research, we will investigate the capabilities of our method to provide more information for glaucoma treatment. With a larger patient dataset, we think that our method can provide more detailed features of the progressive patterns of glaucoma. This is supported by the automatic decision regarding the number of clusters in our method. Regardless of the size of the dataset, our method generates suitably sized clusters. Furthermore, our clustering results may be able to contribute to providing classification of glaucoma patients. By combining clustering results in large datasets with other information, such as risk factors, we may obtain deeper knowledge of glaucoma. This will contribute to the treatment of the glaucoma.

10. ACKNOWLEDGEMENTS

The authors thank for Mr. Fujino and Ms. Taketani of the Department of Ophthalmology, The University of Tokyo for providing us useful comments. This work is partially supported by JST-CREST.

11. REFERENCES

[1] J. Artiles, J. Gonzalo, and S. Sekine, "The semeval-2007 weps evaluation: Establishing a benchmark for the web people search task," In *Proceedings of the Fourth International Workshop on Semantic Evaluations*, pp. 64–69, 2007.

[2] R. Asaoka, "Mapping glaucoma patients' 30-2 and 10-2 visual fields reveals clusters of test points damaged in the 10-2 grid that are not sampled in the sparse 30-2 grid," *PloS ONE*, vol. 9(6), e98525, 2014.

[3] R. Choudrey and S. Roberts, "Variational mixture of Bayesian independent component analyzers," *Neural Computation*, vol. 15(1), pp. 213–252, 2003.

[4] N. Dalal and B. Triggs, "Histograms of oriented gradients for human detection," In *Proceedings of 2005 IEEE Computer Society Conference on Computer Vision and Pattern Recognition*, vol. 2, pp. 886–893, 2005.

[5] B. Fung, K. Wang, and M. Este, "Hierarchical document clustering using frequent itemsets," In *Proceedings of SIAM International Conference on Data mining*, Vol. 3, pp. 59–70, 2003.

[6] D. F. Garway-Heath, D. Poinoosawmy, F. W. Fitzke, and R. A. Hitchings, "Mapping the visual field to the optic disc in normal tension glaucoma eyes," *Ophthalmology*, vol. 107(10), pp. 1809–1815, 2000.

[7] X. He, D. Cai, Y. Shao, H. Bao, and J. Han, "Laplacian regularized gaussian mixture model for data clustering," *IEEE Transactions on Knowledge and Data Engineering*, vol. 23(9), pp. 1406–1418, 2011.

[8] S. Hirai and K. Yamanishi, "Efficient computation of normalized maximum likelihood coding for Gaussian mixtures with its applications to optimal clustering," In *Proceedings of the 2011 IEEE International Symposium on Information Theory*, pp. 1031–1035, 2011.

[9] K. Hirasawa, H.Murata, H. Hirasawa, C. Mayama, and R. Asaoka, "Clustering visual field test points based on rates of progression to improve the prediction of future damage," *Investigative ophthalmology & visual science*, IOVS–14, 2014.

[10] Z. Liang, R. Tomioka, H. Murata, R. Asaoka, and K. Yamanishi, "Quantitative prediction of glaucomatous visual field loss from few measurements," In *Proceedings of IEEE the 13th International Conference on Data Mining*, pp. 1121–1126, 2013.

[11] D. G. Lowe, "Object recognition from local scaleinvariant features," In *Proccdings of the Seventh IEEE International Conference on Computer Vision*, pp. 1150–1157, 1999.

[12] S. Maya, K, Morino, and K. Yamanishi, "Predicting Glaucoma Progression using Multi-task Learning with Heterogeneous Features," In *Proceedings of 2014 IEEE International Conference on Big Data*, pp. 261–270, 2014.

[13] H. Murata, M. Araie, and R. Asaoka, "A new approach to measure visual field progression in glaucoma patients using Variational Bayes linear regression," *Investigative ophthalmology & visual science*, vol.55(12), pp. 8386–8392, 2014.

[14] S. Papadimitriou, J. Sun, C. Faloutsos, and P. S. Yu, "Hierarchical, parameter-free community discovery," in *Proceedings of the 19th European Conference on Machine Learning and Principles and Practice of Knowledge Discovery in Databases*, pp. 170–187, 2008.

[15] J. Rissanen, "Fisher information and stochastic complexity," *IEEE Transaction on Information Theory*, vol. 42(1), pp. 40–47, 1996.

[16] J. Rissanen. *Stochastic Complexity in Statistical Inquiry.* World Scientific, 1989.

[17] J. Rissanen, "Stochastic Complexity in Learning," *Journal of Computer and System Sciences* vol. 55(1), pp. 89–95, 1997.

[18] J. Rissanen. *Information and complexity in statistical modeling.* Springer, 2007.

[19] H. Sakoe and S. Chiba, "Dynamic programming algorithm optimization for spoken word recognition," *IEEE Transaction on Acoustics, Speech, and Signal Processing*, vol. 26(1), pp. 43–49, 1978.

[20] A. Strehl and J. Ghosh, "Cluster ensembles—a knowledge reuse framework for combining multiple partitions," *The Journal of Machine Learning Research*, vol. 3, pp. 583–617, 2002

[21] S. Yousefi, M. Goldbaum, M. Balasubramanian, F. Medeiros, L. Zangwill, J. Liebmann, C. Girkin, R. Weinreb, and C. Bowd, "Learning from data: Recognizing glaucomatous defect patterns and detecting progression from visual field measurements," *IEEE Transactions on Biomedical Engineering*, vol. 61(7), pp. 2112–2124, 2014.

Distributed Personalization

Xu Miao
LinkedIn Corporate
605 W Maude Ave
Sunnyvale, USA 94085
xmiao@linkedin.com

Chun-Te Chu
Microsoft Corporate
1 Microsoft Way
Redmond, USA
chch@microsoft.com

Lijun Tang
LinkedIn Corporate
605 W Maude Ave
Sunnyvale, USA 94085
litang@linkedin.com

Yitong Zhou
LinkedIn Corporate
2061 Stierln Court
Mountain View, USA 94043
yizhou@linkedin.com

Joel Young
LinkedIn Corporate
605 W Maude Ave
Sunnyvale, USA 94085
joyoung@linkedin.com

Anmol Bhasin
LinkedIn Corporate
605 W Maude Ave
Sunnyvale, USA 94085
abhasin@linkedin.com

ABSTRACT

Personalization is a long-standing problem in data mining and machine learning. Companies make personalized product recommendations to millions of users every second. In addition to the recommendation problem, with the emerging of personal devices, many conventional problems, e.g., recognition, need to be personalized as well. Moreover, as the number of users grows huge, solving personalization becomes quite challenging. In this paper, we formalize the generic personalization problem as an optimization problem. We propose several ADMM algorithms to solve this problem in a distributed way including a new Asynchronous ADMM that removes all synchronous barriers to maximize the training throughput. We provide a mathematical analysis to show that the proposed Asynchronous ADMM algorithm holds a linear convergence rate which is the best to our knowledge. The distributed personalization allows training to be performed in either a cluster or even on a user's device. This can improve the privacy protection as no personal data is uploaded, while personal models can still be shared with each other. We apply this approach to two industry problems, *Facial Expression Recognition* and *Job Recommendation*. Experiments demonstrate more than 30% relative error reduction on both problems. Asynchronous ADMM allows faster training for problems with millions of users since it eliminates all network I/O waiting time to maximize the cluster CPU throughput. Experiments demonstrate 4 times faster than original synchronous ADMM algorithm.

Categories and Subject Descriptors

H.2.8 [**Database Application**]: Data mining; H.3.4 [**Systems and Software**]: Distributed systems

General Terms

Big Data, Distributed Optimization, Personalization

KDD'15, August 10-13, 2015, Sydney, NSW, Australia.

ACM 978-1-4503-3664-2/15/08 ...$15.00.
DOI: http://dx.doi.org/10.1145/2783258.2788626 .

Keywords

Distributed computing, User modeling, ADMMs

1. INTRODUCTION

Personalization is a key component in many applications such as *advertising* [9, 5, 21], *recommendation* [17, 18], and *personalized medicine* [23], where an impression, a product and a type of drug is predicted according to the user's profile. *Sparse Matrix Factorization* approaches [18, 7, 19] that seek a shared low-dimensional representation for both users and items have inspired significant amount of research. Both theoretical work and empirical work demonstrated that with the *low rank* assumption, i.e., very few dominating factors for individual users, these approaches have achieved state-of-the-arts accuracies on many datasets [7]. However, they are restricted by the matrix formulation, and less flexible to incorporate contextual information, therefore, not general enough to address the personalization aspect in broader machine learning problems. For example, in movie recommendation, extra information about movies like the directors and the budgets are not encoded in the rating matrix. In this paper, we address the personalization differently. Each individual is assigned one model with a regularization term to penalize the difference between individual models and a global consensus model. The regularization term allows individual experiences to be shared among the population, while allowing the models to be different from each other. A parameter in the regularization term controls how much of a difference these models are. This formulation has been proposed under *Multi-task Learning* problem [15, 3] where each individual model is a specific task. These tasks are related to each other, so solving one task provides information to solve others. Our proposed algorithm can be applied to these problem naturally, especially for tasks distributed among a network, e.g., remote sensing and multi-agent planning.

Solving this personalization problem in a distributed environment is quite challenging, especially for data from large companies like LinkedIn and Microsoft. In this paper, we study algorithms based on *alternating direction method of multipliers* (ADMM) [6]. We propose several variants of the original ADMM algorithm including a novel *Asynchronous ADMM* algorithm that frees up the waiting barriers to speed optimization. As the number of worker nodes grows, the processing speed, computation power, network delay usually vary among different worker nodes. Iterating until all nodes finish is expensive as nodes have to wait for the slowest worker node before the next iteration starts. Asynchronous training addresses the problem and achieves better optimization throughput. We provide a mathematical analysis to prove the proposed *Asynchronous ADMM* converges at a comparable rate as the original *Synchronus ADMM*.

We apply our personalization model to solve two industry problems, *facial expression recognition* and *job recommendation*. The experimental results demonstrate a great gain in accuracy, and the proposed Asynchronous ADMM speeds up the training process dramatically.

In summary, our proposed approach enables systematical training of personalized models jointly in a distributed manner. To our knowledge, this is the first solution of large scale personalization problems via asynchronous distributed machine learning. In addition, the proposed asynchronous ADMM is the first algorithm that demonstrates linear convergence both in theory and empirically.

2. DISTRIBUTED OPTIMIZATION

Before detailing the distributed algorithm, we first formulate our personalization framework as an optimization problem. Equation 1 provides a general formalization where $f_i(\mathbf{w}_i)$ is a arbitrary machine learning task for the i-th user, $\mathbf{w}_i$ is the personal model for that user, and $\mathbf{z}$ is the consensus model. Equation 2 shows an example $f_i(\mathbf{w}_i)$ where l is a convex loss function, $\mathbf{x}_{ij}$ is an input feature vector, and y_{ij} is the target to predict. γ is a regularizatino term inversely coupling the individual and consensus models. With only a handful of samples per model, we need a relatively large γ to prevent overfitting.

$$\min_{\mathbf{z},\{\mathbf{w}_1\ldots\mathbf{w}_M\}}\left(\frac{1}{2}\|\mathbf{z}\|^2+\sum_{i=1}^{M}\left(f_i(\mathbf{w}_i)+\frac{\gamma}{2}\|\mathbf{w}_i-\mathbf{z}\|_2^2\right)\right) \quad (1)$$

$$f_i(\mathbf{w}_i)=\sum_{j=1}^{N_i} l(\mathbf{x}_{ij},y_{ij};\mathbf{w}_i) \quad (2)$$

We focus on distributed personalization of classification tasks and as such assume that the number of users is proportional to the total number of samples, and finally, that each user's data is drawn *i.i.d.* from the distribution D_i. These are captured in Assumption 1 where N_i is the number of training samples for user i, N is the total number of training samples, and M is the total number of users.

ASSUMPTION 1. *We make the following assumptions:*

1. *Let* $N=\sum_i^M N_i$ *where* $M=\mathcal{O}(N)$.
2. *For each user* $i\in[1\ldots M]$, $\{\mathbf{x}_{ij},y_{ij}\}\sim\mathsf{D}_i$.
3. *Network latency is i.i.d. with mean* τ.

Applying *distributed stochastic optimization* approaches [1, 10, 2, 12] to this distributed personalization problem is non-trivial. Although the consensus model can be obtained, there aren't enough samples to reliably estimate individual user models. In addition, tracking the learning rate for each user is difficult.

We experiment with a synchronous ADMM algorithm [6, 25] from the literature, a novel versioned adaptation, and propose a faster asynchronous algorithm. A key observation is that alternately optimizing $\mathbf{w}_i$ and $\mathbf{z}$ converges slowly — a low sample count per user drives a large γ large coupling the personal and consensus models which, in turn, leads to histeresis.

2.1 Synchronous ADMM

We first derive a synchronous ADMM to solve Equation 1. By introducing local consensus variables $\mathbf{q}_i$, we rewrite the problem as in Equation 3. Turning it into the augmented Lagrangian, we have Equation 4.

$$\begin{aligned}\min_{\mathbf{z},\mathbf{q},\{\mathbf{w}_i\}} \quad & \sum_{i=1}^{M} f_i(\mathbf{w}_i)+\frac{\gamma}{2}\|\mathbf{w}_i-\mathbf{q}_i\|^2+\frac{1}{2}\|\mathbf{z}\|^2 \\ \text{subject to} \quad & \mathbf{q}_i=\mathbf{z},\forall i\in[1\ldots M]\end{aligned} \quad (3)$$

$$\begin{aligned}\mathcal{L}(\mathbf{z},\{\mathbf{q}_i,\mathbf{w}_i,\boldsymbol{\lambda}_i\}) &= \sum_{i=1}^{M} f_i(\mathbf{w}_i)+\frac{\gamma}{2}\|\mathbf{w}_i-\mathbf{q}_i\|^2+ \\ & \frac{\rho}{2}\|\mathbf{q}_i-\mathbf{z}\|^2+\boldsymbol{\lambda}_i^T(\mathbf{q}_i-\mathbf{z})+\frac{1}{2}\|\mathbf{z}\|^2\end{aligned} \quad (4)$$

An synchronous ADMM solution can be obtained by Equations [5,6,7].

$$\begin{aligned}\mathbf{w}_i^{t+1},\mathbf{q}_i^{t+1} &= \arg\min_{\mathbf{q}_i,\mathbf{w}_i} f_i(\mathbf{w}_i)+\frac{\gamma}{2}\|\mathbf{w}_i-\mathbf{q}_i\|^2+ \\ & \frac{\rho}{2}\|\mathbf{q}_i-\mathbf{z}^t\|^2+\boldsymbol{\lambda}_i^t(\mathbf{q}_i-\mathbf{z}^t) \quad (5)\\ \mathbf{z}^{t+1} &= \arg\min_{\mathbf{z}}\frac{\rho}{2}\|\mathbf{q}_i^{t+1}-\mathbf{z}\|^2+ \\ & \boldsymbol{\lambda}_i^t(\mathbf{q}_i^{t+1}-\mathbf{z})+\frac{1}{2}\|\mathbf{z}\|^2 \quad (6)\\ \boldsymbol{\lambda}_i^{t+1} &= \boldsymbol{\lambda}_i^t+\rho(\mathbf{q}_i^{t+1}-\mathbf{z}^{t+1}) \quad (7)\end{aligned}$$

In Equation 5, $\mathbf{q}_i$ has analytical relation to $\mathbf{w}_i$, we obtain the updating rules in Equation [9,10,11,8], where $\boldsymbol{\mu}=\boldsymbol{\lambda}/\rho$.

$$\begin{aligned}\forall i,\boldsymbol{\mu}_i^{t+1} &= \boldsymbol{\mu}_i^t+\mathbf{q}_i^t-\mathbf{z}^t \quad (8)\\ \forall i,\mathbf{w}_i^{t+1} &= \arg\min_{\mathbf{w}} f_i(\mathbf{w})+\frac{\rho\gamma}{2(\rho+\gamma)}\|\mathbf{w}-\mathbf{z}^t+\boldsymbol{\mu}_i^{t+1}\|^2 \quad (9)\\ \forall i,\mathbf{q}_i^{t+1} &= \frac{\rho}{\rho+\gamma}\mathbf{z}^t+\frac{\gamma}{\rho+\gamma}\mathbf{w}_i^{t+1}-\frac{\rho}{\rho+\gamma}\boldsymbol{\mu}_i^{t+1} \quad (10)\\ \mathbf{z}^{t+1} &= \frac{\sum_{i=1}^{M}\left(\mathbf{q}_i^{t+1}+\boldsymbol{\mu}_i^{t+1}\right)}{M+\frac{1}{\rho}} \quad (11)\end{aligned}$$

From Equation 9, even when γ is huge, the regularization is upper bounded by $\frac{\rho}{2}$ that avoids obtaining a $\mathbf{w}$ over-influenced by $\mathbf{z}$, and leads to faster convergence. Note that we update $\boldsymbol{\mu}_i$ first, and update $\mathbf{z}$ at the end of the iteration for a simpler derivation.

In synchronous ADMM, Equations [8,9,10] are performed in each worker node, while Equation 11 is performed in the master node. The master node waits for all sub-problems to be solved and their local models submitted, before merging and broadcasting a new consensus model, see Figure 1. Waiting for all nodes to finish slows down the distributed computation process, and each user benefits from the latest consensus less frequently. The asynchronous ADMM essentially unblocks the master and allows the consensus model to be updated freely. Therefore, the aggregated knowledge can be shared between individuals more frequently.

2.2 Versioned Synchronous ADMM

Different users have different numbers of samples to optimize, and different workers have different hardware latency. The submitted local models $\mathbf{q}_i$, and dual variables $\boldsymbol{\mu}_i$ come to the master out of order. It is easy to see that $\mathbf{z}$ can be updated whenever the master is ready as long as it is broadcast at the end of the iteration. On the other hand, we can broadcast $\mathbf{z}$ to the workers at any time, and force the remaining workers to restart the sub-problem based on the new consensus $\mathbf{z}$, i.e., at any moment, there is only one version of consensus. Theorem 2 proves that this *Single-Versioned ADMM* converges at the same rate as the original Synchronous ADMM. The convergence analysis for Synchronous ADMM can be found in literature [[16],[22]].

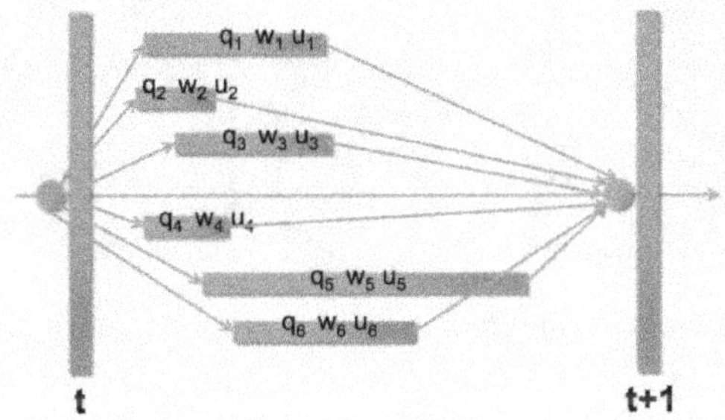

Figure 1: Synchronous ADMM updating schedule. Although all personal models proceed in parallel, the master has to wait for all updates come to merge. This induces a great overhead.

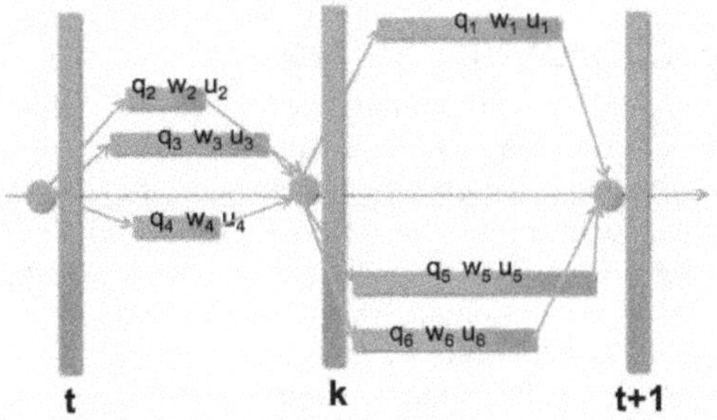

Figure 2: A Single-Versioned ADMM updating schedule. The master updates the consensus periodically to allow faster sharing, but it adds additional barriers that potentially stalls the process more.

THEOREM 2. *Let* $\Theta_i = (\mathbf{w}_i, \mathbf{q}_i, \boldsymbol{\mu}_i)$*, Lagrangian in Equation 4 can be rewritten as* $\mathcal{L}(\{\Theta_i\}, \mathbf{z})$*. Assuming* $\forall i$*,* f_i *is a convex function, at any point, update* $\mathbf{z}_k^{t+1} = \arg\min_{\mathbf{z}} \mathcal{L}(\{\Theta_i^{t+1}\} \cup \{\Theta_i^t\}, \mathbf{z})$*, then any optimization sequence, i.e.,* $\Theta_1 ... \Theta_i^{t+1}, \mathbf{z}_k^{t+1}, \Theta_{i+1}^{t+1} ... \Theta_M^T$*, converges at rate* $o(\frac{1}{T})$ *on expectation.*

PROOF. For any iteration t, Lagrangian $\mathcal{L}^t(\{\Theta_i^t\}, \mathbf{z}_k^t)$ after k intermediate consensus updates, we can verify that

$$\mathsf{E}\left[\mathcal{L}(..., \mathbf{w}_i^t, \mathbf{q}_i^t, \mathbf{z}_k^t, \boldsymbol{\mu}_i^{t+1})\right] \leq \mathsf{E}\left[\mathcal{L}(..., \mathbf{w}_i^t, \mathbf{q}_i^t, \boldsymbol{\mu}_i^{t+1})\right].$$

On the other hand, on expectation, an optimization step $\mathbf{w}_i^t, \mathbf{q}_i^t, \mathbf{z}_k^t, \boldsymbol{\mu}_i^{t+1}$ is equivalent to $\boldsymbol{\mu}_i^t, \mathbf{w}_i^t, \mathbf{q}_i^t$, i.e.,

$$\mathsf{E}\left[\mathcal{L}(..., \boldsymbol{\mu}_i^t, \mathbf{w}_i^t, \mathbf{q}_i^t)\right] \leq \mathsf{E}\left[\mathcal{L}(..., \mathbf{w}_i^t, \mathbf{q}_i^t, \mathbf{z}_k^t, \boldsymbol{\mu}_i^{t+1})\right].$$

Combining these two, the optimization sequence for the *Single-Versioned ADMM* is dominated by the sequence of the original *Synchronous ADMM*. If f_i is convex, both sequences arrive at a saddle point. □

If the master and individual workers optimize independently, it is possibly that users' personal models branch out on different versions of the consensus, and request to merge at different pace. These **delayed** updates do not necessarily dominate the synchronous ADMM optimization. However, we can show that they dominate an optimization sequence for a *multiple block ADMM* formulation [13]. The technique is to create the auxiliary variables for these different versions of consensus models. Assuming for the k-th merge, we have a set of users $B_k \subset [1...M]$ submitted local

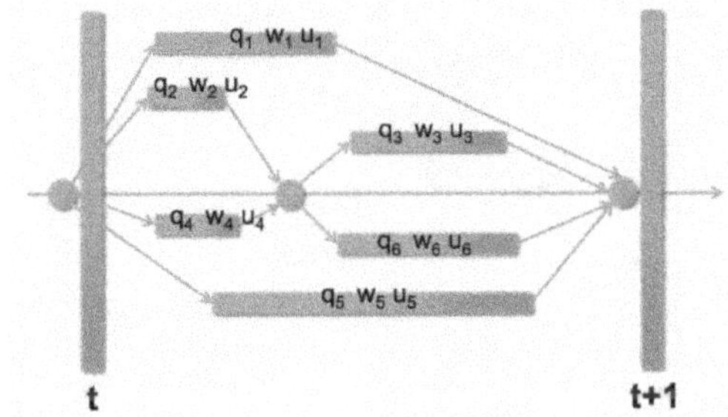

Figure 3: A Multi-Versioned ADMM updating schedule. Similar to Single-Versioned ADMM, this allows the consensus periodically updated, but no additional barriers are added.

updates. For each one of them $j \in B_k$, the sub-problem is solved by using the consensus model $\tilde{\mathbf{z}}_{h(j)}$, where $h(j) \in [1...k-1]$ is the mapping from the user to the consensus model version. We first update $\tilde{\mathbf{z}}_{h(j)}$ for all $j \in B_k$, then update $\mathbf{z}_k$, and broadcast it. The consensus updating rules for this *multi-versioned ADMM* are defined in Equations 12 and 13.

$$\tilde{\mathbf{z}}_{h(j)}^{t+1} = \tilde{\mathbf{z}}_{h(j)}^t + \frac{1}{M + \frac{1}{\rho}}(\mathbf{q}_j^t + \boldsymbol{\mu}_j^t - \mathbf{q}_j^{t-1} - \boldsymbol{\mu}_j^{t-1}) \quad (12)$$

$$\tilde{\mathbf{z}}_k^{t+1} = \frac{1}{|B_k|} \sum_{j \in B_k} \tilde{\mathbf{z}}_{h(j)}^{t+1} \quad (13)$$

REMARK 3. *When* $\forall j, k, h(j) = k-1$, multi-versioned ADMM *reduces to* single-verioned ADMM.

To prove that *multi-versioned ADMM* converges, we first show that a Multi-Block ADMM problem updates using rules in Equations 12 and 13. Consider the optimization problem in Equation 14, where K is the total number of consensus updates. In this problem, we have multiple blocks, $\{\mathbf{q}_i, \mathbf{w}_i\}$, $\tilde{\mathbf{z}}_k$ and $\mathbf{z}$. According to [8], extending the ADMM algorithm directly by alternating optimizations over these blocks achieves the same linear convergence when the equality constraints satisfy the condition in Theorem 4.

$$\begin{aligned} \min_{\mathbf{z}, \{\mathbf{q}_i, \mathbf{w}_i\}, \{\tilde{\mathbf{z}}_k\}} \quad & \sum_{i=1}^{M} f_i(\mathbf{w}_i) + \frac{\gamma}{2}\|\mathbf{w}_i - \mathbf{q}_i\|^2 + \frac{1}{2}\|\mathbf{z}\|^2 \quad (14) \\ \text{subject to} \quad & \mathbf{q}_i = \tilde{\mathbf{z}}_k, \forall i \in B_k \\ & \tilde{\mathbf{z}}_{h(i)} = \tilde{\mathbf{z}}_k, \forall i \in B_k \\ & \tilde{\mathbf{z}}_K = \mathbf{z} \end{aligned}$$

THEOREM 4. *[8] Assuming a constraint optimization has constraint* $A_1 x_1 + A_2 x_2 + A_3 x_3 = 0$*, if* $A_1^T A_2 = 0$ *or* $A_2^T A_3 = 0$*, a direct extension of ADMM converges in* $\mathcal{O}(\frac{1}{T})$*.*

In our case, it is easy to see that A_k for $\tilde{\mathbf{z}}_k$ is canceling each other, and therefore $A_k = 0$. The dual variables for constraints $\tilde{\mathbf{z}}_k = \mathbf{z}$ cancel out, so Equation [12,13] are equivalent to the ADMM updating rules for $\tilde{\mathbf{z}}_k$ and $\mathbf{z}$. Therefore, for any such consensus updating schedules, we can construct a Multi-Block ADMM program that updates correspondingly. The only difference is that Multi-Versioned ADMM also updates $\mathbf{z}$ immediately after $\tilde{z}$ is updated. Similar to Theorem 2, optimizing $\mathbf{z}$ multiple times within the same iteration dominates the original optimization sequence, so we conclude convergence as stated in Theorem 5.

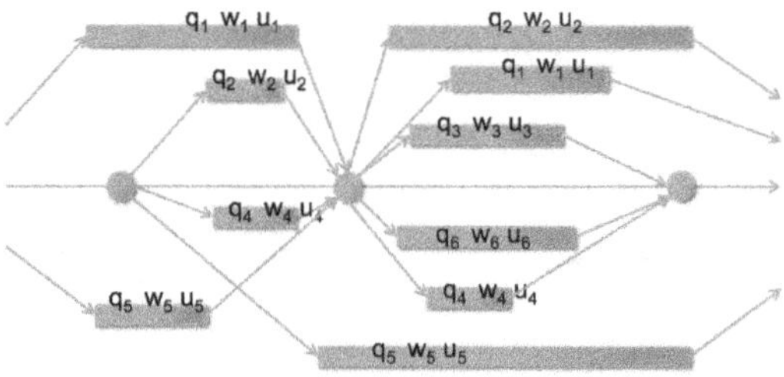

Figure 4: Asynchronous ADMM updating schedule. This algorithm removes the iteration barriers and free up the consensus updates completely.

THEOREM 5. *For any optimization sequence that follows Equation [12,13],* $\Theta_1^1, ...\Theta_i^{t+1}, \tilde{\mathbf{z}}_{h(j)}^{t+1}, \mathbf{z}_k^{t+1}, \mu_{h(j)}^{t+1}, \Theta_{i+1}^{t+1}...\Theta_M^T$, *it converges at rate* $\mathcal{O}(\frac{1}{T})$.

2.3 Asynchronous ADMM

For the algorithms described in previous section, the last synchronous property holds that no one proceeds until the end of the current iteration. The master keeps track of the versions of the consensus models, which are the only dependencies to update the new version of the consensus. We can simply remove this iteration lock, and let the whole process runs. This results in the proposed Asynchronous ADMM algorithm as shown in Algorithm 1.

K *is the latest version number*;
input : $\{\Delta_j, h(j) | j \in B\}$
for $j \in B$ **do**
    $\mathbf{z}_{h(j)} = \mathbf{z}_{h(j)} + \frac{\Delta_j}{M + \frac{1}{\rho}}$;
end
$K = K + 1$;
$\mathbf{z}_K = \frac{1}{B} \sum_{j \in B} \mathbf{z}_{h(j)}$;
`Broadcast` $(\mathbf{z}_K, K)$;

Algorithm 1: Master for ASYNC-ADMM

$\mathbf{z}_k$ *is the current consensus*;
input : $\mathbf{x}, \mathbf{y}, i$
Add $\mathbf{x}, \mathbf{y}$ to samples for user i;
Update $\boldsymbol{\mu}_i, \mathbf{q}_i, \mathbf{w}_i$ according to Equations [8,10,9];
Let $\boldsymbol{\mu}_i^o$ and $\mathbf{q}_i^o$ be the original values;
$\Delta_i = \boldsymbol{\mu}_i + \mathbf{q}_i - \boldsymbol{\mu}_i^o - \mathbf{q}_i^o$;
`Reduce` (Δ_i, k)

Algorithm 2: Worker for ASYNC-ADMM

By assuming that networking latency has an identical distribution with mean τ. We can show that this AsynchADMM converges at a similar rate as synchronous ADMM. Note that the concept of iterations does not exist any more. Here, T refers to the number of operations from the master, and is about M times the number of iterations in Synchronous setting. Therefore, the convergence rate is comparable for both of them.

THEOREM 6. *With assumptions 1, Asynchronous ADMM Algorithms [1,2] converge at* $\mathcal{O}(\frac{M\gamma\tau}{T})$

One interesting fact about the Theorem 6 is that the personalization strength γ influences the convergence too. Intuitively, if the personalized models are independent from the consensus model, i.e., $\gamma = 0$, the local model $\mathbf{q}_i$ can be simply assigned to the consensus $\mathbf{z}$, and the iteration stops. On the other hand, if different persons have very different personal preference, enforcing them to reach the consensus is very difficult. Allowing the models to be diverged effectively improves convergence speed.

Figure 6: Facial expression of happy emotion on different people's faces.

3. FACIAL EXPRESSION

Human emotion study is a critical topic in several fields, including human-computer interaction, psychology research, medical diagnosis and treatment, entertainment, education, etc. Facial expression is one of the most useful non-verbal information for detecting human emotion. For decades, people have already investigated in automatic facial expression analysis through image, video, or audio [20]. As the camera becomes prevalent in modern devices, like mobile phone, laptop, desktop, and even wearable device, automatically recognizing the facial expression from image or video has gained much attention. Great amount of research [4] and industry products [1] [2] are proposed to solve this problem. The state of the art techniques [4] includes three major steps as shown in figure 5. First of all, human face is detected from the video frame, and the landmark points are located, such as eyes, nose, and mouth. After that, features are extracted from the face image. Popular features are optical flow, Gabor filter, gradient feature, local binary patterns, motion signature, geometry displacement, etc. These features can effectively represent the characteristics of different expressions. Given the feature set extracted from the collected data, classifiers have been trained with various machine learning models such as *linear classifier*, *neural networks*, *hidden Markov model*, *random forests*. However, due to different personalities, cultures, ages, and appearances, the facial expressions of the same emotion vary greatly. For instance, in figure 6, three people performs happy face but with different visual appearance. Hence, using a single model is not sufficient enough to represent all the users. Therefore, personalization will be the key to enhance the accuracy and improve the user experience.

To support this, we consider the data set collected for the facial expression recognition app developed by Microsoft in Xbox One Kinect [3]. The following experiments are conducted based on a subset of this data set. The subset includes 151,413 samples collected from 250 users. Conventionally, one model is trained for a classifier of a facial expression. In this way, the individual accuracy is sacrificed for obtaining fair average accuracy. With our Asynchronous ADMM framework, we can train a personalized model for each user which can better represent his/her feature distribution. We follow the state-of-the-art techniques in face and landmarks detection

[1] FaceReader:http://www.noldus.com/human-behavior-research/products/facereader

[2] Kaggle Challenge:https://www.kaggle.com/c/challenges-in-representation-learning-facial-expression-recognition-challenge

[3] http://www.shacknews.com/article/79301/xbox-one-kinect-reading-emotions-and-heart-rate

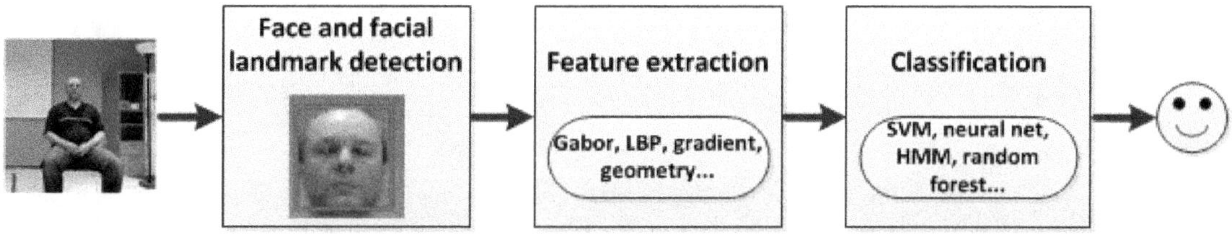

Figure 5: Flow chart of facial expression recognition.

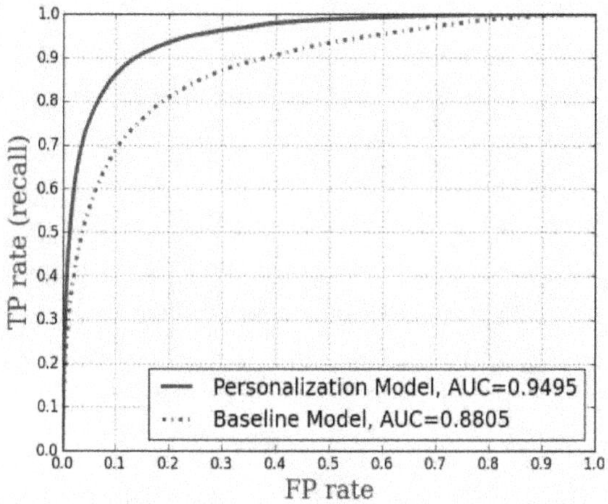

Figure 7: ROC curves of personalized model and baseline (consensus) model in Facial expression data set. γ id set as 50 in this case.

and feature extraction. The features we extract are popular features used in computer vision domain, including, spatial filter responses, temporal filter responses, statistical values, and geometry values.

In addition to the accuracy improvement, our framework reduces the privacy concern of the users. People are usually unwilling to share their privacy data to others, especially this kind of visual data from which the subject's identity can be easily revealed. In the existing framework, in order to train a facial expression classifier, the personal data must be uploaded to somewhere hence loses the privacy. In our distributed framework, training can be performed locally, such as in a smart device or private cluster. The personal data does not need to be uploaded to other places. Although the personal model is still exposed to others, the privacy of the data itself is preserved which largely mitigates the concerns of the privacy.

3.1 Influence of the Personalization

First, we compare the difference between the results with personalization and without personalization in accuracy. For each user, we use 5 positive samples and 5 negative samples for training. Figure 7 shows the ROC curve of the overall accuracy among all the users. When the personalization is considered, the accuracy is better than the one without personalization(baseline model). The baseline model is obtained based on conventional ADMM where all the users train a single consensus model. This result is not surprising since one model does not fit all the users. This result also tells during the real world application, the personalized models would provide better satisfaction to the users than the consensus model.

As we discussed in the previous section, the strength of personalization plays the key role for the generalization ability. To demonstrate such a behavior, we study the accuracies in different γ settings. The larger the γ is, the more the personal model is towards the consensus model. We show the distribution of the ROC curves across different users. We compute the ROC curves for each individual user, and sample the data points along the curve to compute the mean and the variance. Figure 8 represents a mean ROC curve and the standard deviation interval along the curve to show how consistent the model performs across the population. From the figures, we demonstrate that $\gamma = 50$ (chosen by a validation set) produces the best prediction at the testing set (with better mean ROC curve and narrower variance range), while $\gamma = 10^{-6}$ and $\gamma = 10^{6}$ produce inferior results. At one extreme side, $\gamma = 10^{-6}$ corresponds to a model trained completely by using personal data. The overfitted model introduces high variance. On the other extreme side, $\gamma \rightarrow \infty$, everyone is using nearly the same model which is too generalized to represent different users' distribution. By tuning the γ, we find the balance between generalization and personalization. In the future, our vision is γ value can be an user-controlled setting. Users can freely select how personalized their own models should be. Our general recommendation is: when the user has only few data, it is always intuitive to have the consensus model to be the *cold start* model. After the user accumulates the personal data, the model can be relaxed a little bit to support divergence. When the user has enough personal data, the model can be personalized completely, and the consensus model has less and less influence.

3.2 Learning Curves

One of the benefits of the distributed personalization is to leverage community knowledge to improve individual user's learning curve. In this experiment, we vary the number of training samples to show the progress of the accuracy improvement. Figure 9 and 10 show the testing ROC curves using personalized models trained on different amounts of training samples. The training samples are set as 1 sample per user, 3 samples per user, 5 samples per user, and 10% of an user's data for each curve, respectively. The corresponding area under curve (AUC) is shown in Table 1. From 1 sample to 3 samples, the learning speed is really fast that increases the accuracy a lot which demonstrates that our framework enables the users to share the knowledge with each other efficiently. On the contrary, if we use consensus model, the improvement of the accuracy is slow compare to the increase of training samples. It is true that the consensus model performs better than the personalized model when using only 1 training sample per user. It means 1 sample of the personal data is not sufficient enough to represent the intra-user variance for each user. With more training data, it covers the variation within each user, i.e., it adapts individual user well, the accuracy of personalized models starts to outperform the consensus model.

This experiment demonstrates that the learning speed of personalized model is fast as the size of training set increases, i.e., users only need few samples to improve their personal models. This is relatively important when we consider the applications in

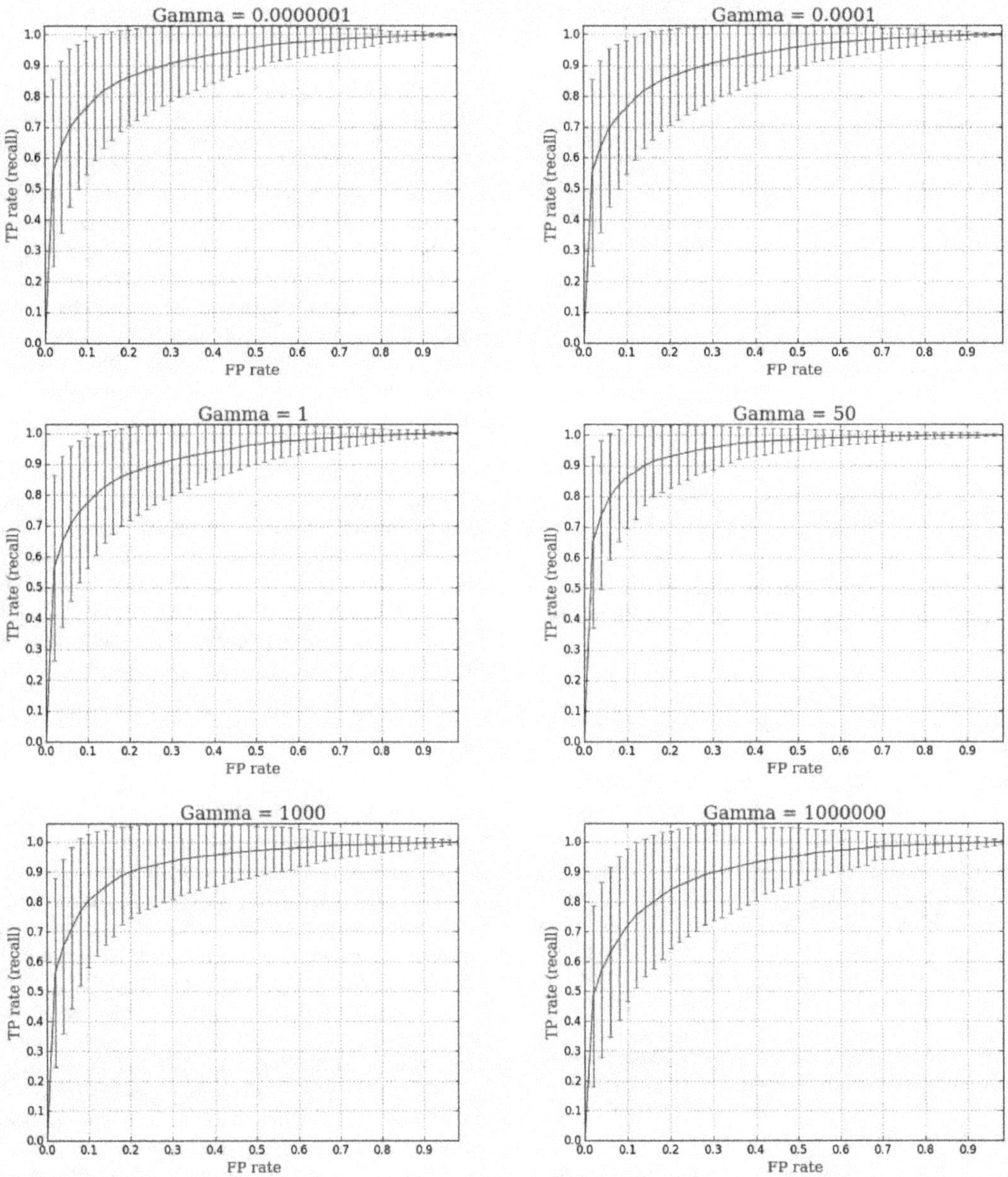

Figure 8: The distributions of the ROC curves of using personalized models for all the users. For each user, we use 5 positive samples and 5 negative samples for training. Each subfigure corresponds to different personalization strengths ($\gamma = 10^{-6}, 10^{-3}, 1, 50, 10^3, 10^6$). The accuracy is the highest when $\gamma = 50$ and drops when γ is too large or small.

commercial products. In most of the existing personalization products/services, e.g., ads, recommendation system, users are usually asked to provide some personal information, answer questions, or do data collection and tagging. However, users sometimes do not have patience to provide so much information. With our framework, even though users only provide little amount of data, the system can make the models adapt quickly. It encourages the users to provide more data since they can feel the improvement of the accuracy. With more data, the models fit individuals better, and the whole community is also benefited from the ability of knowledge sharing in our framework.

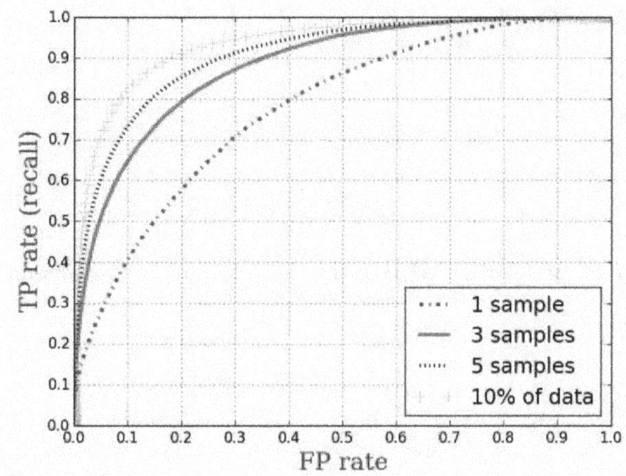

Figure 9: ROC curves of the personalized models trained on different number of samples. $\gamma = 1$ in this experiment.

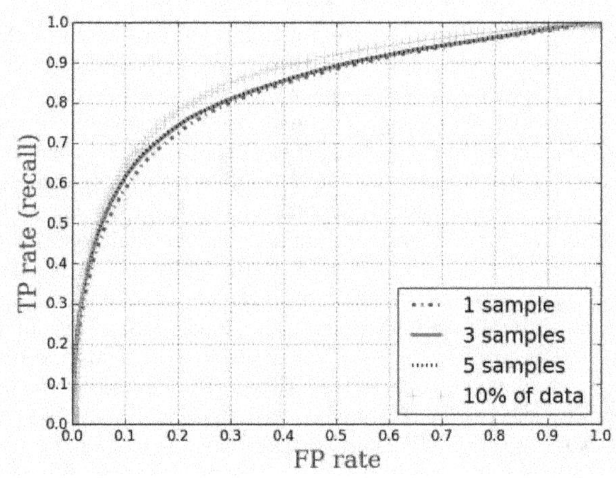

Figure 10: ROC curves of the baseline (Consensus) models trained on different number of samples. $\gamma = 1$ in this experiment.

4. JOBS YOU MIGHT BE INTERESTED IN (JYMBII)

One of the premium member value propositions of LinkedIn is the jobs recommendation product, Jobs You May Be Interested In (JYMBII), where LinkedIn members can impress active job postings relevant to their professional profiles. It is one of most valuable

Table 1: Area under curve in figures[9,10]

Model	1 sample	3 samples	5 samples	10% of data
Personalized	0.7771	0.8812	0.9084	0.936
Baseline	0.8277	0.8373	0.8383	0.8623

product contributing to member engagement on LinkedIn. Members can consume JYMBII recommendations in different channels, such as LinkedIn homepage feeds, Email, and LinkedIn Jobs Home (i.e. the 'jobs' tab on LinkedIn home page).

As many members maintain an up-to-date professional profile on LinkedIn, it is very important that JYMBII can recommend highly relevant and personalized jobs for members, whether they are active job seekers or passive ones who just want gain some awareness of the job market. Without personalization, there are circumstances that a bad job recommendation can significantly impair user's satisfaction, for example, an executive in a large-size company may feel offended by seeing entry-level job recommendation, an experienced professional may feel uncomfortable receiving intern-level job recommendations. Even though current recommendation engine has already taken into consideration of members' personal career characteristics, such as their professional skills, current job position, and their next job preference (either explicit or implicit), the model coefficients for these features are global as we train a single model for all of our members, which inevitably return less satisfactory recommendations for certain members. The Asynchronous ADMM model we propose, on the other hand, will train a personalized model for each member with sufficient job seeking history, and still maintain a global consensus model for those without enough historical record. In doing so, it can provide additional personalization in a way such that it greatly improve user satisfaction for member's personal job seeking experience.

In order to compare personalization ADMM model against current baseline consensus model trained with synchronized ADMM setting, we have trained our personalization ADMM model with different gammas, which controls the strength of personalization, with larger gamma indicating more personalization. Each example is a (member, job, label) tuple, with label being either 1 or 0 indicating whether or not the member has applied the job. The feature set is the same for baseline and treatment, it mainly includes field based content matching features and member preference features. Each content matching feature is a cosine similarity score between the two fields' tf.idf vectors, with one field from member profile and the other field from job posting, for example, member's experience field matching against job's description field, member's profile summary field matching against job's desired skills field, etc. 11 illustrates the field layout of a (member,job) pair on LinkedIn. The member preference features include job location preference, industry preference, and company size preference. They can be members' explicit preference they set on the web UI, or their latent preference mined by a model [24]. The final model includes one hundred of such features for each example, and the dataset includes about a million samples. Figure 12 illustrates the ROC curves and their AUCs for model comparison.

The personalized model has the best AUC of 0.91 with gamma = 100, comparing to AUC of 0.79 for the most personalization model (with gamma = 1), and AUC of 0.86 for the least personalization model (with gamma = 10000). It suggests that neither personalization nor extreme personalization performs the best, but the optimal strength for personalization is somewhere falls in between.

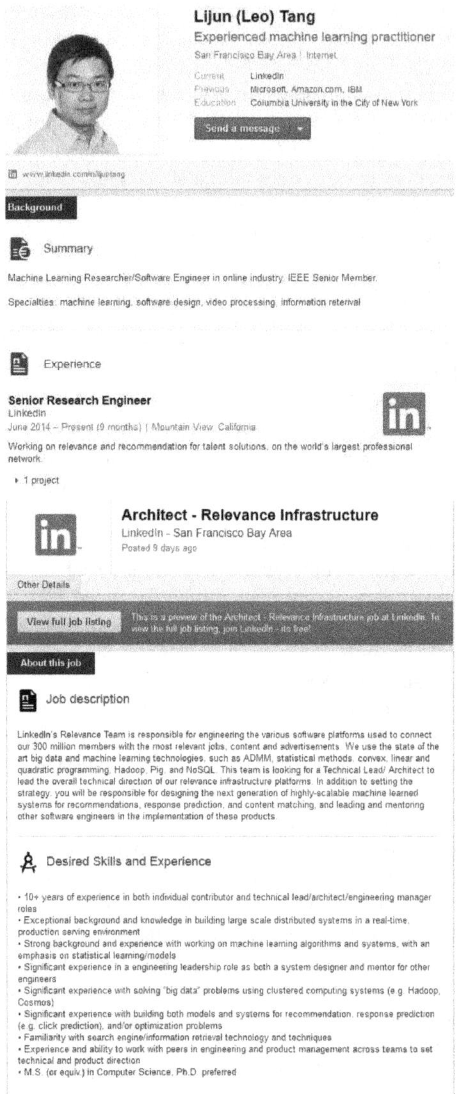

Figure 11: A Member Profile (upper) and A Job Posting (lower)

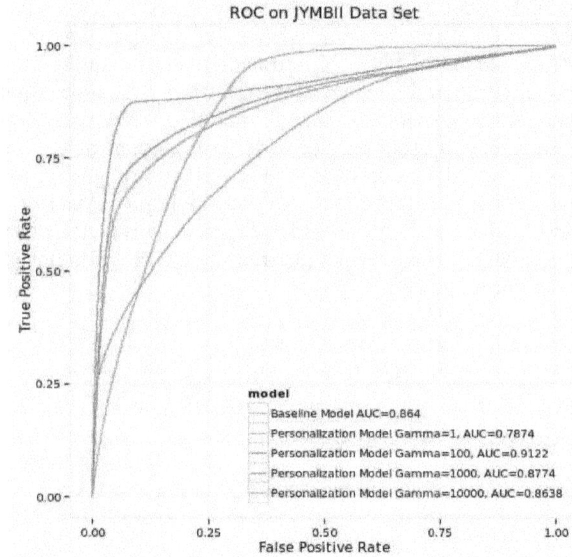

Figure 12: ROC of JYMBII baseline model and personalization models

Comparing to the baseline without personalization (AUC=0.86), it is interesting to see all of the personalization models performs much better in the operation area with low false positive rates (e.g. false positive rate less than 0.1), this area is critical as it aligns better with the online system which observes much more negative examples than positive examples, thus it is a necessity to operate with a low false positive rate all the time.

5. CONVERGENCE EXPERIMENT

Due to the asynchronous nature of Algorithm 1&2, it is difficult to implement such algorithms in a typical Map/Reduce architecture [11], which requires a synchronization step between each map/reduce stage. We develop an asynchronous computation framework based on the Publish/Subscribe message paradigm [14] to facilitate the parallel computation interfaces. The framework consists of a master node and multiple worker nodes. Each worker holds a subset of users and their data, initializes a personal model and subscribes a message channel for each user. The training events are triggered through user interactions. The corresponding worker fetches the current best-known consensus model after receiving a training event, performs a local optimization and sends the updated personal model back to the master. The consensus model then gets updated at the reception of each updating event. In synchronous ADMM (SYNC-ADMM), all personal models start training at the same time using the same consensus model, the next round is triggered after all personal models are merged into the consensus. For multi-versioned ADMM (MV-ADMM), all personal models start training at approximately the same time using their current known consensus model. The consensus model does not block any training event in any single round and merges continuously, but it waits for the completion of all user models before triggering another round. In asynchronous ADMM (ASYNC-ADMM), each user training event only depends on the completion of the user's previous round. The consensus model merges any reported personal model immediately. During the entire experiment process, the total number of training events triggered is more than 10 million. In Figure 13, for each ADMM model, we divide the

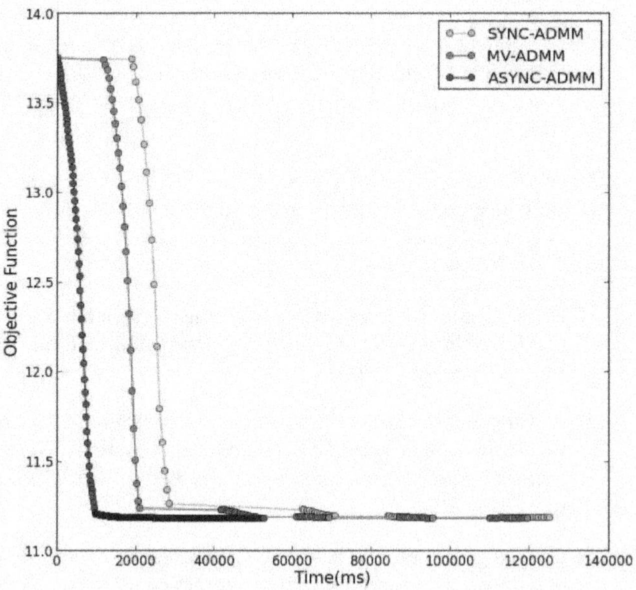

Figure 13: Convergence rate of different ADMM models. Note that the objective function is in log scale.

time window into 300 buckets and only report the average objective function value observed within each time bucket. We choose the starting time when all user models are trained at least once. The flat blank periods within SYNC-ADMM and MV-ADMM models are the blocking periods when they wait for all personal models being merged into the consensus. As demonstrated in Figure 13, ASYNC-ADMM converges at a close-to-identical rate compared to other models, but performs 2∼4 times faster by eliminating all blocking period.

6. CONCLUSION AND DISCUSSION

In this paper, we propose a distributed personalization framework and present its successful application to two industry problems. Our approach enables distributed personalization not only for traditional recommendation problems, but also for recognition. Provided each individual task can be formulated as a convex optimization, our framework can scale, for both training and personalization, to millions of simultaneous users. One of the major contribution that enables this distributed learning system is a novel *Asynchronous ADMM* algorithm that removes all network I/O wait barriers to maximize the CPU throughput. One of the interesting features of our publish/subscribe based distributed computation approach allows worker nodes to execute on personal devices. Unlike other popular distributed learning algorithms, we do not rely on a decaying step size to control convergence. Instead, Asynchronous ADMM keeps track of versions of the consensus model, thereby avoiding complicated learning rate adjustments. In the future, we plan to extend our approach to the real online setting. Problems like warm-start, online model adaptation, and in-session personalization will be studied in-depth. Furthermore, we currently employ only one master to update the consensus. This wastes some network bandwidth. Much research has suggested that a *Minimum Spanning Tree* topology can provide optimal network communication to efficiently leverage computational resources — a natural extension to the proposed algorithm.

References

[1] A. Agarwal, O. Chapelle, M. Dudík, and J. Langford. A reliable effective terascale linear learning system. *J. Mach. Learn. Res.*, 15(1):1111–1133, Jan. 2014.

[2] A. Agarwal and J. C. Duchi. Distributed delayed stochastic optimization. In *Proceedings of the 51th IEEE Conference on Decision and Control, CDC 2012, December 10-13, 2012, Maui, HI, USA*, pages 5451–5452, 2012.

[3] S. Ben-David, J. Gehrke, and R. Schuller. A theoretical framework for learning from a pool of disparate data sources. In *Proceedings of the Eighth ACM SIGKDD International Conference on Knowledge Discovery and Data Mining*, KDD '02, pages 443–449, New York, NY, USA, 2002. ACM.

[4] V. Bettadapura. Face expression recognition and analysis: the state of the art. *arXiv preprint arXiv:1203.6722*, 2012.

[5] M. Bilenko and M. Richardson. Predictive client-side profiles for personalized advertising. In *Proceedings of the 17th ACM SIGKDD International Conference on Knowledge Discovery and Data Mining*, KDD '11, pages 413–421, New York, NY, USA, 2011. ACM.

[6] S. Boyd, N. Parikh, E. Chu, B. Peleato, and J. Eckstein. Distributed optimization and statistical learning via the alternating direction method of multipliers. *Found. Trends Mach. Learn.*, 3(1):1–122, Jan. 2011.

[7] E. CandÃÍs and B. Recht. Exact matrix completion via convex optimization. *Foundations of Computational Mathematics*, 9(6):717–772, 2009.

[8] C. Chen, B. He, Y. Ye, and X. Yuan. The direct extension of admm for multi-block convex minimization problems is not necessarily convergent. *Mathematical Programming*, pages 1–23, 2014.

[9] Y. Chen, D. Pavlov, and J. F. Canny. Large-scale behavioral targeting. In *Proceedings of the 15th ACM SIGKDD International Conference on Knowledge Discovery and Data Mining*, KDD '09, pages 209–218, New York, NY, USA, 2009. ACM.

[10] A. Cotter, O. Shamir, N. Srebro, and K. Sridharan. Better mini-batch algorithms via accelerated gradient methods. In J. Shawe-Taylor, R. Zemel, P. Bartlett, F. Pereira, and K. Weinberger, editors, *Advances in Neural Information Processing Systems 24*, pages 1647–1655. Curran Associates, Inc., 2011.

[11] J. Dean and S. Ghemawat. Mapreduce: Simplified data processing on large clusters. *Commun. ACM*, 51(1):107–113, Jan. 2008.

[12] O. Dekel, R. Gilad-Bachrach, O. Shamir, and L. Xiao. Optimal distributed online prediction using mini-batches. *J. Mach. Learn. Res.*, 13:165–202, Jan. 2012.

[13] W. Deng, M.-J. Lai, Z. Peng, and W. Yin. Parallel Multi-Block ADMM with o(1/k) Convergence. *ArXiv e-prints*, Dec. 2013.

[14] G. Eisenhauer, K. Schwan, and F. E. Bustamante. Publish-subscribe for high-performance computing. *Internet Computing, IEEE*, 10(1):40–47, 2006.

[15] T. Evgeniou and M. Pontil. Regularized multi–task learning. In *Proceedings of the Tenth ACM SIGKDD International Conference on Knowledge Discovery and Data Mining*, KDD '04, pages 109–117, New York, NY, USA, 2004. ACM.

[16] M. Hong and Z.-Q. Luo. On the Linear Convergence of the Alternating Direction Method of Multipliers. *ArXiv e-prints*, Aug. 2012.

[17] Y. Koren. Factorization meets the neighborhood: A multifaceted collaborative filtering model. In *Proceedings of the 14th ACM SIGKDD International Conference on Knowledge Discovery and Data Mining*, KDD '08, pages 426–434, New York, NY, USA, 2008. ACM.

[18] Y. Koren, R. Bell, and C. Volinsky. Matrix factorization techniques for recommender systems. *Computer*, 42(8):30–37, Aug. 2009.

[19] D. D. Lee and H. S. Seung. Algorithms for non-negative matrix factorization. In *In NIPS*, pages 556–562. MIT Press, 2000.

[20] M. Pantic and L. J. M. Rothkrantz. Automatic analysis of facial expressions: The state of the art. *Pattern Analysis and Machine Intelligence, IEEE Transactions on*, 22(12):1424–1445, 2000.

[21] C. Perlich, B. Dalessandro, T. Raeder, O. Stitelman, and F. Provost. Machine learning for targeted display advertising: Transfer learning in action. *Mach. Learn.*, 95(1):103–127, Apr. 2014.

[22] W. Shi, Q. Ling, K. Yuan, G. Wu, and W. Yin. On the linear convergence of the admm in decentralized consensus optimization. *Signal Processing, IEEE Transactions on*, 62:1750–1761, February 2014.

[23] L. Veer and R. Bernards. Enabling personalized cancer medicine through analysis of gene-expression patterns. *Nature*, 452:564–570, 2008.

[24] J. Wang and D. Hardtke. User latent preference model for better downside management in recommender systems. In *International World Wide Web Conference*, WWW '15, Florence, Italy, May 2015.

[25] C. Zhang, H. Lee, and K. G. Shin. Efficient distributed linear classification algorithms via the alternating direction method of multipliers. In *Proceedings of the Fifteenth International Conference on Artificial Intelligence and Statistics, AISTATS 2012, La Palma, Canary Islands, April 21-23, 2012*, pages 1398–1406, 2012.

Voltage Correlations in Smart Meter Data

Rajendu Mitra, Ramachandra Kota, Sambaran Bandyopadhyay, Vijay Arya
IBM Research
{rajendum, rama.chandra, sambandy, vijay.arya}@in.ibm.com

Brian Sullivan, Richard Mueller, Heather Storey, Gerard Labut
DTE Energy, USA
{sullivanbj, muellerrj, storeyh, labutg}@dteenergy.com

ABSTRACT

The connectivity model of a power distribution network can easily become outdated due to system changes occurring in the field. Maintaining and sustaining an accurate connectivity model is a key challenge for distribution utilities worldwide. This work shows that voltage time series measurements collected from customer smart meters exhibit correlations that are consistent with the hierarchical structure of the distribution network. These correlations may be leveraged to cluster customers based on common ancestry and help verify and correct an existing connectivity model. Additionally, customers may be clustered in combination with voltage data from circuit metering points, spatial data from the geographical information system, and any existing but partially accurate connectivity model to infer customer to transformer and phase connectivity relationships with high accuracy. We report analysis and validation results based on data collected from multiple feeders of a large electric distribution network in North America. To the best of our knowledge, this is the first large scale measurement study of customer voltage data and its use in inferring network connectivity information.

Categories and Subject Descriptors

I.5.3 [**Pattern Recognition**]: Clustering—*Algorithms*; J.m [**Computer Applications**]: Miscellaneous

General Terms

Algorithms, Design, Measurement, Experimentation

Keywords

Power Distribution Grids; Voltage Time Series; Topology Inference; Data Mining; Clustering

1. INTRODUCTION

The connectivity model (CM) of the physical distribution network specifies how the devices, assets, and customers are interconnected downstream of a distribution substation. For example, which customer is powered by which distribution transformer, which customer is powered by which phase of the feeder, and so on. CM essentially provides a coarse-grained view of the network topology. A common problem faced by distribution utilities worldwide is an inaccurate or unknown CM of their network when compared to the actual connectivity that exists on the field. The CM may not always be updated or tracked based on changes made by field crews and its accuracy deteriorates over time due to maintenance, repairs, and restoration activities following faults or outages. Moreover during large scale outages, there is often a trade-off between expediting restoration versus tracking changes to the distribution network.

While CM is foundational to planning, operations, and maintenance of distribution networks, the key factors driving utilities to improve its accuracy are effectively faster restoration and the ability to accurately communicate with impacted customers during outages. The annual cost of power interruptions in US is estimated to be \$79B with 106 ± 54 outage minutes per customer. Interruptions in electric service occur from time to time due to a number of reasons including storms, aging assets, excess loading from heat waves, and other system disturbances. Any analysis following a fault in the distribution system uses the CM to identify the root causes and determine the appropriate course of action. An accurate CM minimizes the diagnostic time and the time spent by crew in the field, leading to reduced outage minutes and improved system availability.

During outages, utilities seek to inform customers about the status of restoration and the expected downtimes. The CM is required to localise customers downstream of a faulted device and to map each fault with the right set of outaged customers for communication. An inaccurate CM increases the risk of erroneous communication and limits a utility's ability to provide customized and timely information to their customers, which may negatively impact customer relations. Additionally, an accurate CM is required to localise losses, estimate loading at unmetered points such as distribution transformers, and ensure a balanced infusion of energy back into the distribution grid when customers have behind-the-meter resources such as distributed generation and storage/electric vehicles [4, 6, 9, 10].

Existing techniques to maintain an accurate CM include the use of manual field inspections and power line communications (PLC). Manual inspections are expensive and unsustainable as field configurations change over time and therefore these need to be repeated periodically. The PLC

KDD'15, August 10-13, 2015, Sydney, NSW, Australia.

ACM 978-1-4503-3664-2/15/08 ...\$15.00.
DOI: http://dx.doi.org/10.1145/2783258.2788594 .

approach requires both customer and grid meters to be able to read and write signals onto the power-line and is capital intensive. Additionally, challenges arise as signals may not propagate over long distances or across assets.

Leading utilities are undertaking initiatives to modernize their information management and data analytics capabilities in order to realize the benefits of smart grid deployments. This work focuses on the use of data already available from a distribution network to infer its connectivity model. Our approach to infer connectivity relies on clustering customers using their voltage data. The computed customer clusters may be used to identify inconsistencies in the existing CM or correct an existing CM that may be partially accurate. We observe that voltage time series measurements from customer smart meters exhibit hierarchical correlations which may be exploited to partition customers based on common phase[1], distribution transformer, and feeder. Customers may also be clustered in combination with voltage data from circuit metering points (SCADA) and spatial data from the GIS to verify and correct errors in customer to transformer and phase mapping, which are generally prone to inaccuracies. We report validation results based on the analysis of data collected from multiple feeders of a large distribution network in North America. The data includes average RMS values of voltage recorded once every 5 minutes from more than 10K customers across 5 feeders and 2 substations for about 2 months. The performance of techniques is estimated by comparing the computed connectivity relationships with the ground truth available from existing database and results from field verification. We view the main contributions of this work as follows:

1. Using smart meter measurements, we show that customer voltage data exhibits hierarchical correlations which tend to be consistent with the hierarchical connectivity relationships between customers, distribution transformers, phases, feeders, and substation transformers of a distribution network. Towards this, we transform the voltage measurements into binary fluctuations and conduct different clustering experiments by considering customers within and across different feeders and substations. We show that customers can be partitioned based on common phases and feeders with high accuracy. We point out settings where phase correlations are stronger when compared to feeder correlations.

2. We compare different approaches to infer customer to transformer mapping by clustering customers under a feeder, its individual branches, and within spatial subclusters formed from GIS data. The clustering solutions are compared with the currently available mapping in the database which is known to be accurate. Our results indicate that clustering customers under each branch of the feeder introduces constraints that help improve the accuracy of clustering.

3. To infer customer to phase mapping, customer voltage measurements are clustered in combination with the per-phase feeder measurements obtained from SCADA data which act as centroids of an initial solution. We compare the computed solutions with the mapping that was available both before and after manual field inspections. Our results indicate that the proposed approach is able to correct most of the errors identified during field inspections and may be used as a low cost alternative to help maintain an accurate phase connectivity model.

[1]The concept of *phase* and the structure of the distribution network are explained in Section 2

The rest of the paper is organized as follows. Section 2 explains the topology of the distribution network and the connectivity model. Section 3 summarizes the voltage and spatial data used in this work and our observations on various correlations, while Section 4 describes our clustering methodology. Section 5 presents our analysis of the hierarchical correlations. Sections 6 and 7 describe our techniques and results for inferring customer to transformer and phase connectivity using clustering. Section 8 presents related work and Section 9 concludes.

2. DISTRIBUTION NETWORK, CONNECTIVITY MODEL, AND ERRORS

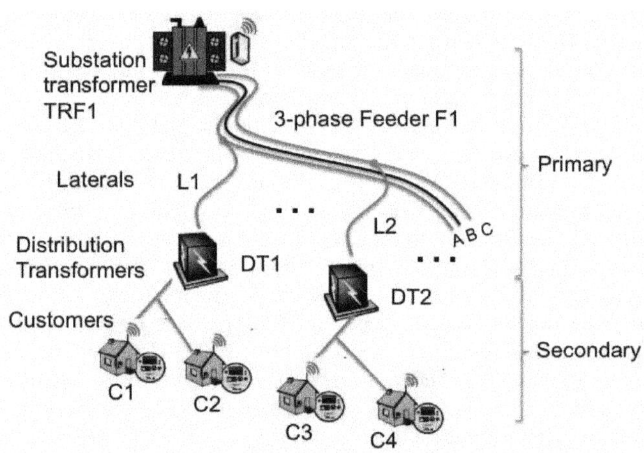

Substation Transformer	Feeder	Distribution Transformer	Cust.	Phase
TRF1	F1	DT1	C1	A
TRF1	F1	DT1	C2	A
TRF1	F1	DT2	C3	C
TRF1	F1	DT2	C4	C

Figure 1: Simplified view of a distribution network and the mapping between customers and assets

Distribution System. The power delivery infrastructure consists of generation, transmission, and distribution systems. Electric power is generated in large power plants as 3-phase AC voltage and reaches distribution via a transmission system. The distribution system starts from the distribution substation and consists of primary and secondary networks. The primary network consists of 3-phase *feeders* which carry power at medium voltage from the *substation transformers* (TRFs) to the *distribution transformers* (DTs). Each TRF may power multiple feeders. Depending on the type and density of customers, a feeder may carry power at different voltages such as 33kV, 13.2kV, and 4.8kV and serve a few hundred distribution transformers. The branches or line segments of a feeder are also known as *laterals*. The secondary network carries power from the distribution transformers to the customers at low voltage (e.g. 120V).

Table 1: Information about the feeder circuits analyzed from the distribution network

Substation, Substation transformer	Feeder circuit	Voltage fed	Length (Miles)	Residential	Non-residential	1-phase transformers	1-phase customers	Missing data
SUB-I, TRF-I	α	13.2kV	34	80%	20%	221	1773	12%
SUB-II, TRF-I	β_1	13.2kV	38	97%	3%	342	2178	1%
SUB-II, TRF-I	β_2	13.2kV	39	91%	9%	306	2363	1%
SUB-II, TRF-II	γ_1	13.2kV	38	92%	8%	363	2497	1%
SUB-II, TRF-II	γ_2	13.2kV	30	94%	6%	281	1561	1%

A 3-phase feeder consists of three transmission lines, usually labelled as A, B and C, which carry AC power with their voltage waveforms shifted by 120°. A DT receives power by tapping onto one of the 3 phases of a feeder and is generally single-phase (1-phase). On average a DT might serve about 8 single-phase residential customers. A few DTs that serve larger loads such as super-markets or office buildings may be 2 or 3-phase. Similarly a feeder branch or lateral may be single, two, or three-phase. [10].

Connectivity Model. The CM of a distribution network specifies the mapping between various assets and customers downstream of a substation. In particular, which customer is powered by which DT, which DT is powered by which feeder and phase, which feeder is powered by which TRF, and so on. For example, the CM of the distribution system in Fig. 1 records that customers C1, C2 are powered by distribution transformer DT1, while C3, C4 are powered by DT2. DT1 is powered by phase A of feeder F1, while DT2 is powered by phase C of F1. Feeder F1 in turn is powered by TRF1. In the above example, since the distribution transformers are single-phase, customer phase is same as transformer phase. The CM may also record other hierarchical relationships such as the mapping between a lateral and the set of transformers that it powers.

Errors. The most common errors in the CM are related to the mapping between customers, DTs, and phases of the feeder. For example, the phase of a customer or its distribution transformer may be recorded incorrectly or missing. Similarly the DT that powers a customer may have been inaccurately recorded. Other types of errors include the mapping of customers to feeders wherein some of the customers under a feeder are recorded as being powered by another feeder. We study these mappings in subsequent sections.

3. DATA CHARACTERISTICS

Power measurements in a distribution network are generally available from customer smart meters and on-grid sensors. The primary network is monitored using a SCADA (supervisory control and data acquisition) system that records feeder level measurements (per-phase voltage, current, active and reactive power, etc.) close to the substation. customer smart meters generally record periodic measurements of load (kWh) and voltage (RMS value) over small time intervals of 5-30 min as setup by the utility.

In this work we use measurements from five anonymized feeder circuits belonging to two substations of a North American distribution network. The mapping between substations, TRFs and feeders is showing in Table 1. Each circuit is fed at 13.2kV and serves more than 2K residential, commercial and industrial customers.

Low-voltage data from smart meters. We analyze two months of voltage measurements from customers which are powered by single-phase distribution transformers. The measurements have average RMS values of voltage in the 120V range. These are recorded once every 5 minutes up to a precision of one decimal place. The measurements also have missing values.

Medium-voltage data from the SCADA system. The feeder circuits are instrumented with SCADA field devices which monitor the feeders close to the substation transformer and periodically report per-phase measurements of voltage, current, and power. We consider two months of voltage measurements from these devices. The measurements are averaged over 5 minute intervals and normalized to 120V range to compare them against the low-voltage data dfrom the customers.

Spatial Data from GIS. Anonymized geospatial locations of customers and DTs are available and used to sub-cluster customers and transformers under a feeder based on geographical proximity. This is utilized in the inference of customer to DT mapping.

Customer to DT mapping (Ground Truth). The existing CM holds the mapping between customers and the DTs. While this mapping is known to have good accuracy for the 5 chosen circuits, it may not be 100% accurate. We use this mapping to estimate the performance of clustering algorithms.

Customer to phase mapping (Ground Truth). The transformer phase is available for all 1-phase distribution transformers (customer phase is same as transformer phase for 1-phase transformers). The phase of overhead (pole top) transformers is available before and after manual field inspections. In case of overhead distribution, field inspections are conducted by linemen using a combination of visual inspections and specialized devices. The devices are reserved to check the phase at certain operating points in the feeder while walking down the line segments and visually inspecting the phase down to individual transformers or customers. The voltage data analyzed in this work was collected before commencing field inspections. The phasing information available during data collection and after field inspections is used to validate algorithms and also identify errors in existing phasing information.

DT to lateral mapping. Accurate mapping from distribution transformers to laterals, i.e. the set of customers powered by each branch of the feeder, is available in the existing CM for each of the circuits. This mapping is used to introduce spatial constraints in the inference of customer to DT mapping.

3.1 Observations on Voltage Data

Fig. 2 shows benchmark plots that give an overview of the voltage measurements obtained from customer smart meters and the SCADA system. Fig. 2 (left) plots the voltage measurements of 3 random customers on different phases

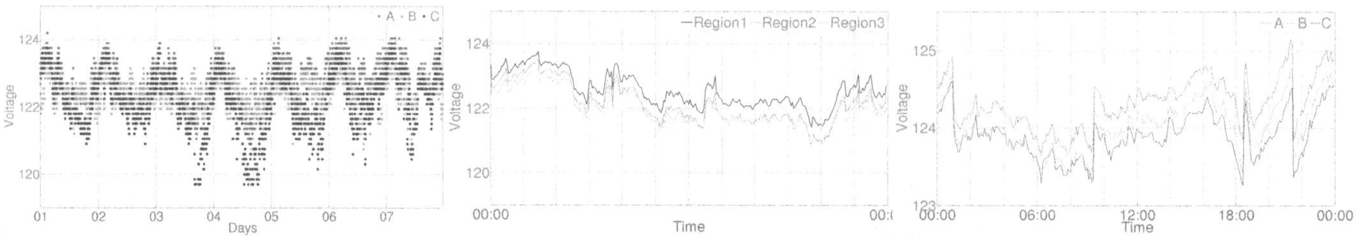

Figure 2: Voltage data from one of the feeders and its customers. (left):Voltage of 3 customers on phases A, B, and C over 7 days, (center): Average voltage of customers in 3 different sections of a feeder circuit over a day, (right): Per-phase feeder measurements taken close to substation over a day.

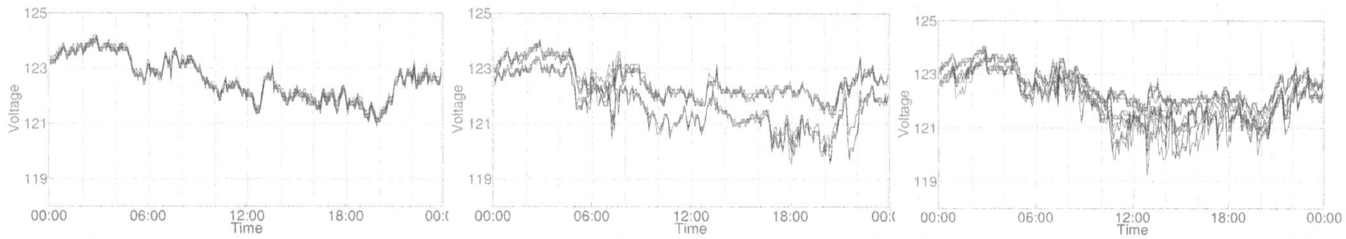

Figure 3: Different types of voltage measurements. Measurements of all customers under each DT.

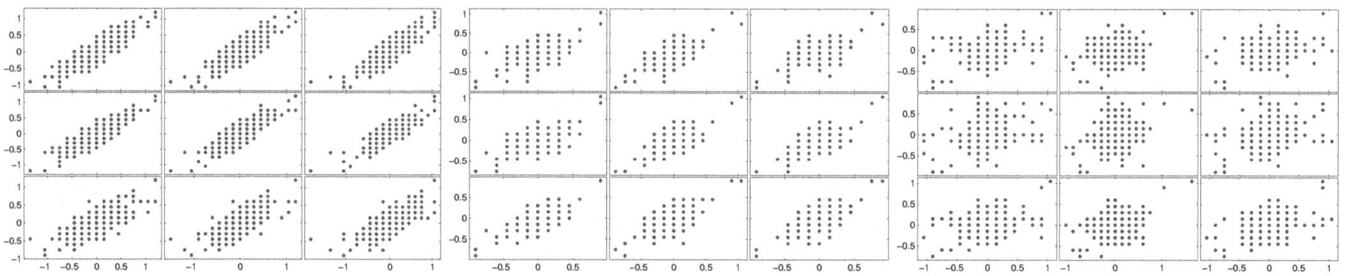

Figure 4: Correlations of customer voltage fluctuations using scatter plot– (left): Two different sets of customers under same transformer (hence same phase) (center): Two sets of customers under different transformers but same phase. (right): Two sets of customers under different phases (hence different transformers).

and under different distribution transformers over a 7 day period. We observe the diurnal cycles of voltage based on energy consumed each day and differences in voltage across customers based on phase. In order to study the voltage observed in different regions of a feeder circuit, we divided the circuit into three sections based on deployed reclosers (circuit breakers). Fig. 2(center) plots the average voltage of customers in each of these regions. Region 1 corresponds to customers which are closer to the distribution substation. These customers observe a slightly higher voltage irrespective of phase. Customers in regions 2 and 3 observe a small voltage drop as they are located further away from the substation. The plot demonstrates that customer voltage also depends on a number of factors other than phases or distribution transformers. Fig. 2(right) plots the per-phase voltage measurements observed at the feeder normalized to 120V range for a day. We see that the voltages on the 3 phases vary together on larger time scales based on aggregate load while each phase shows distinct variations at smaller time scales. Although voltages on the 3 phases differ, the feeder voltage measurements showed low imbalances on average across all days.

Fig. 3 shows voltage plots of customers under different distribution transformers. Fig. 3 (left) shows an example where voltages of all customers under a transformer are very similar and vary together. Fig. 3 (center) shows another transformer where the customer voltages vary within two groups. This may occur due to variable loading or distances of customers from their transformers. Fig. 3 (right) shows a transformer where the voltages of customers show high variation. The plots show that deciphering customer voltage may be challenging as it depends on several factors in the electric network.

Fig. 4 shows the benchmark correlations between voltage fluctuations of customers under one feeder using a matrix of scatter plots. Fig. 4 (left) shows correlations between two different sets of customers which are powered by the same single-phase transformer (hence same phase as well). Each scatterplot shows correlations between a pair of customers. We observe that voltage fluctuations of customers under the same transformer show high correlation and points lie closer to the X = Y line. Fig. 4 (center) shows correlations between two sets of customers powered by different transformers under the same phase of the feeder. We observe that correlations still exist but become weaker in comparison to the same transformer case. Lastly, Fig. 4(right) shows correlations between two sets of customers powered by different phases of the feeder (hence different transformers as well). We see that these customers are even less correlated and points are spread over the X = Y plane. In section 5, we also consider correlations of customers across different feeders.

4. DISTANCE METRICS & CLUSTERING

Our approach to infer connectivity leverages the fact that the voltage variations observed by customers powered by the same DT, phase, or feeder tend to be more "similar". However, there are different measures of similarity and different approaches to compare voltage measurements. In particular, we have studied 3 distance metrics and 3 data transformations which are described below.

4.1 Voltage data transformations

Let $v_{i,t}$ denote the raw RMS voltage measurements from customer i in the tth time step, $t \in \{1, \ldots, m\}$. We compute the continuous voltage fluctuations as $\delta_{i,t} = v_{i,t} - v_{i,t-1}$. We also discretize these to obtain binary fluctuations, which we denote by $b_{i,t}$. Let $\mathbf{V}_i = [v_{i,t}]_{m \times 1}$ denote the m-dimensional *observation vector* that holds the time series of voltage measurements obtained from customer i. Similarly, let Δ_i and $\mathbf{B}_i$ denote the delta and binary observation vectors respectively. We assume that voltage measurements are approximately synchronised across customers, which is the case for our datasets as well.

Thus for each customer i, we have three datasets: (i) *Raw*: original data V_i, (ii) *Delta*: continuous fluctuations Δ_i, and (iii) *Binary*: discretized fluctuations $\mathbf{B}_i$. In order to identify which among the three forms of data is best suited for clustering, we consider the most common problem of partitioning customers of a feeder into 3 groups corresponding to the three phases A, B and C. We apply the K-MEANS algorithm [11] for each dataset with three measures of similarity: (i) L_2 (Euclidean) (ii) Cosine, and (iii) Correlation. To compare the resultant clusters with the true customer to phase mapping, we utilize the labelling procedure described next.

4.2 Cluster Labelling and Accuracy

To determine clustering accuracy, we assign labels to the computed clusters using an existing customer to phase mapping as follows. The computed clusters are intersected with the clusters corresponding to the existing customer to phase mapping and a one to one correspondence is established based on maximum match. Each cluster in the computed solution is assigned the phase of its matching cluster in the existing solution (Fig. 5). The accuracy of the clustering solution is then calculated as the proportion of the customers that were assigned the correct labels. Note that the same procedure may be used to calculate the clustering accuracy for experiments which determine customer to DT or feeder mapping (where the labels correspond feeders or DTs rather than phase). Additionally, the same procedure can also be used to correct an existing customer to phase or DT mapping that may be partially accurate, under the assumption that the accuracy of the existing mapping is not too low.

Fig. 6 shows the accuracy of phase clustering for the three datasets and three similarity measures for a sample feeder. We see that irrespective of the similarity measure, *Binary* performs best. Moreover, the performance of the three similarity measures with *Binary* are comparable to each other. Similar results are observed for other mapping experiments as well (customer–DT & customer–feeder). Fig. 7 shows the cluster scatter plots for two phases A and B, which compare the computed clusters with the ground truth. In each case, correlation is used as a measure of similarity. Again

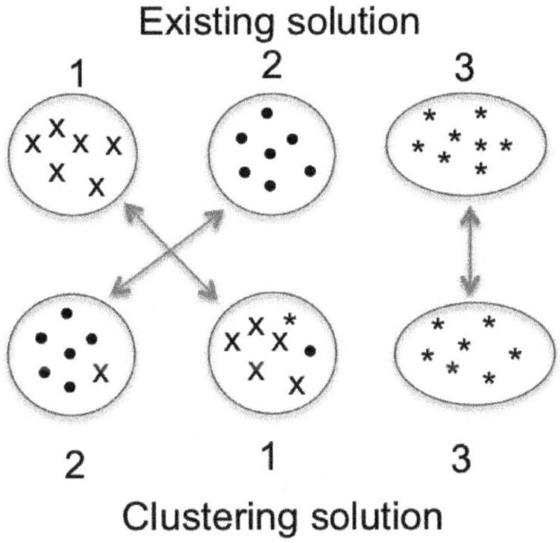

Figure 5: Labelling clusters in the computed solution using labels of an existing solution

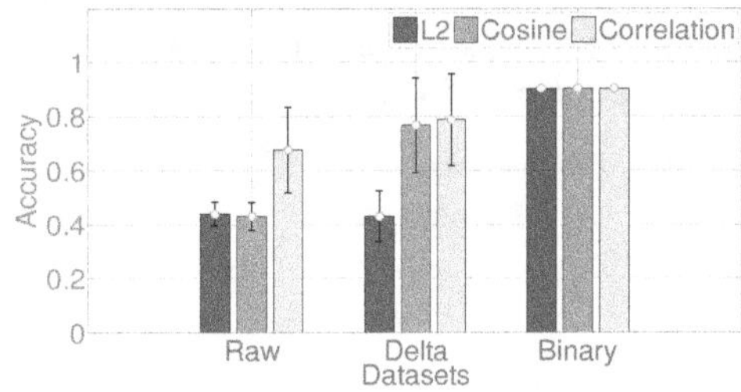

Figure 6: Clustering accuracy for the combination of datasets and similarity measures.

the plots show higher accuracy for *Binary* when compared to *Raw* or *Delta*.

In what follows in the rest of the paper, we apply K-MEANS algorithm for clustering over the binary observation vectors using correlation as a measure of similarity. Apart from K-MEANS being one of the standard techniques, it is especially suitable for our settings because, in all cases, we know the value of k beforehand. This is because we seek clustering to derive the connectivity of customers to feeder, phases or DTs and these remain unchanged despite any changes in the connectivity. For labelling the resultant clusters and calculating the clustering accuracy, we follow the same procedure as detailed above. For the experiments, we break up the datasets into batches of size 4 days and conduct clustering over the different batches, presenting the average accuracy in the results. Experiments over other batch-sizes of $1-7$ days also gave similar results.

5. CUSTOMER TO FEEDER MAPPING

This section describes our analysis towards partitioning customers belonging to different feeders. We consider three possible settings: (i) **Inter-substation:** Feeders powered by different substations, (ii) **Inter-TRF:** Feeders powered by different TRFs of same substation, and (iii) **Intra-TRF:** Feeders powered by same TRF.

For each of these settings, we combine customers belonging to the two feeders (based on the actual ground truth) and then apply voltage-data clustering (using K-MEANS) to separate them into their respective feeders. Furthermore in each case, we selectively combine all customers belonging to the same single phase (A, B or C), same two phases (AB, BC or AC) and all three phases (ABC) across the two feed-

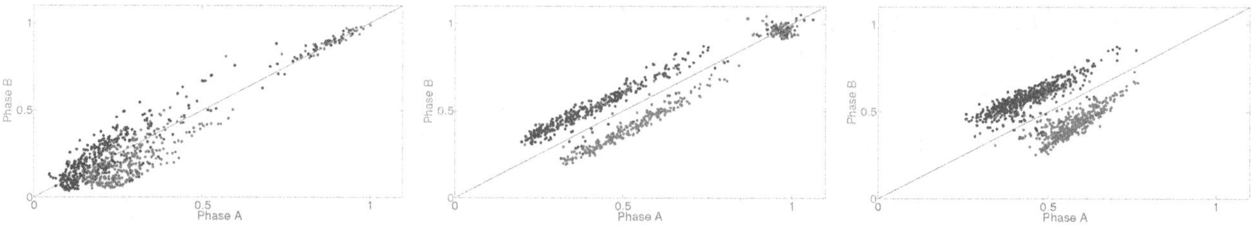

Figure 7: Cluster scatter plots. (left): *Raw* dataset, (center): *Delta* dataset and (right): *Binary* dataset

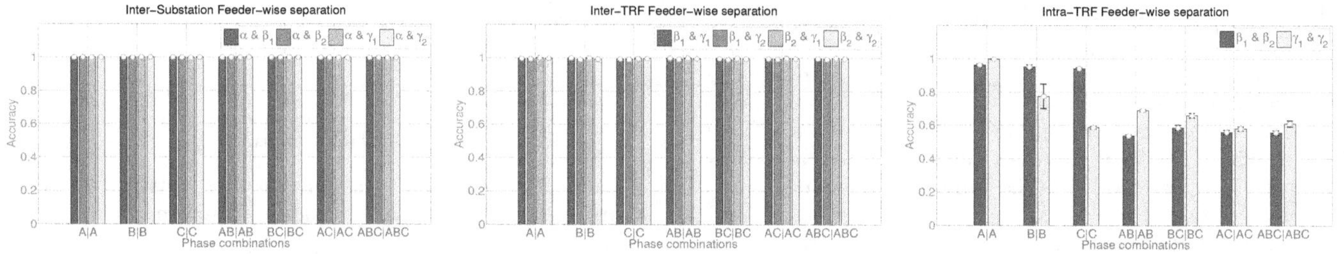

Figure 8: Feeder-wise separation of customers powered by different feeders. (left): feeders of different substations, (center): feeders of different TRFs under the same substation, and (right): feeders of the same TRF

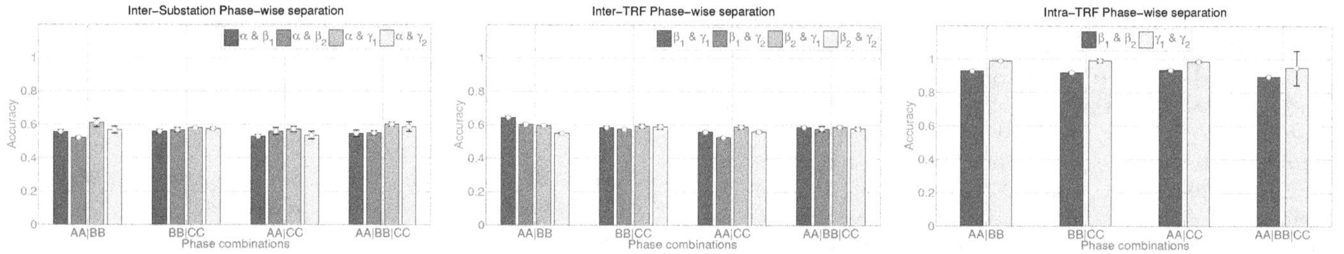

Figure 9: Phase-wise separation of customers powered by different feeders. (left): feeders of different substations, (center): feeders of different TRFs under same substation, and (right): feeders of the same TRF

ers. These experiments allow us to determine settings under which feeder correlations are stronger versus phase correlations. For example, if customers of phases A and B of two feeders (denoted by a_1, b_1, a_2, b_2) are combined and partitioned into 2 clusters, then these may separate as $\{a_1 b_1, a_2 b_2\}$ or $\{a_1 a_2, b_1 b_2\}$ (or other combinations) depending on whether customers are strongly correlated based on phase or feeders.

Feeder-wise separation. Fig. 8 shows the accuracy of feeder separation for INTER-SUBSTATION, INTER-TRF, and INTRA-TRF. The plots show average accuracy and standard deviation over multiple batches of voltage data. We see that for both the INTER-SUBSTATION and INTER-TRF setting, the accuracy of separation is almost 1, for all the phase combinations. This implies that for both these settings, voltage correlations between customers belonging to the same feeder are not only strong, but also much higher than any phase correlations. However, we see that for INTRA-TRF, where we consider feeders powered by the same TRF, the accuracy is much lower. In particular, for cases where two or all three phases are considered together, accuracy drops to 0.6. This occurs because the phase-wise correlations are quite strong among customers belonging to the same TRF, even if they belong to different feeders. Thus, the two obtained clusters do not particularly correspond to the two feeders.

The above results show that as long as customers are not powered by the same TRF, they can easily be separated out into multiple feeders using their voltage data. For instance, given customers powered by s different substations, we can partition these into s groups, one corresponding to each substation, simply by using their voltage measurements.

Phase-wise separation. For this, we conducted the same set of experiments as above, for the three settings, with the aim of obtaining clusters of customers belonging to the same phase. Fig. 9 shows the accuracy of customers being partitioned based on same phase. We observe that the accuracy is low for both INTER-SUBSTATION and INTER-TRF settings. This is expected because, as seen earlier, feeder-wise correlations are much stronger in these cases. However, for INTRA-TRF setting, the accuracy achieved is closer to 1. This goes to show that customers powered by the same TRF are related to each other much more on the basis of their phase rather than their feeder.

In summary, using voltage-data to separate customers belonging to different feeders is accurate when the feeders are powered by different TRFs. When customers belong to the same TRF, they can be accurately separated based on different phases. These results match the underlying structure of the distribution network as feeders under the same TRF are essentially powered by the same 3 phases of the TRF.

6. CUSTOMER DT MAPPING

During maintenance and repair operations, the field crew may switch customers between nearby DTs in order to restore power to the customers. Over time, such changes result in an inaccurate customer to DT mapping. In this section, we present techniques to infer customer to DT mapping solely on the basis of the data available with the utilities: GIS

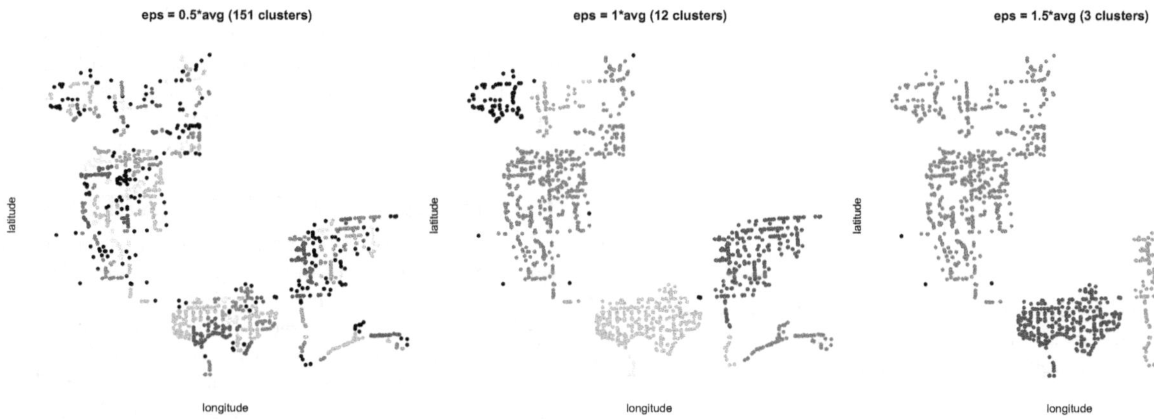

Figure 10: Anonymized spatial clusters of customers and DTs for circuit β_2

data, voltage time-series data, and any existing but partially accurate customer to DT mapping. We present results for 3 feeders: α, β_1 and β_2. Similar results are obtained for other feeders as well.

6.1 Spatial clustering for neighbourhoods

Utilities often possess GIS data of their network which includes the geospatial locations of customers and DTs. Our approach to infer customer to DT mapping leverages the GIS data to divide customers and DTs under a feeder into smaller groups within which voltage-data clustering is applied.

Now, to cluster spatial data, we require a method that is capable of discovering clusters of arbitrary shapes (corresponding to streets or blocks) without much prior information. DBSCAN [8] is a well established clustering method for such purposes. DBSCAN requires two parameters – *MinPts* and *Eps*, which determine the sizes and number of clusters respectively. A typical value of MinPts is 4 (our results do not vary with change in MinPts). On the other hand, Eps, denoting the *neighbourhood distance* of a point, plays a significant role in clustering. As our end goal is to obtain customer–DT connectivity, we used that as the factor for varying Eps. Specifically, avg denotes the average customer–DT distance in a feeder (as per the database); and Eps is varied from $0.5 * avg$ to $2 * avg$ for DBSCAN runs.

Fig. 10 shows the resulting spatial clusters (colour-coded) for one of the circuits, β_2 for three values of Eps. We see that for low value of Eps ($0.5 * avg$), a large number of clusters are obtained, most so small so as to correspond to a single street (or even less), while for higher values of Eps, we obtain well demarcated large neighbourhoods. As the purpose of clustering is to help determine customer–DT mapping, we define the accuracy of clustering as the fraction of customers that were clustered into the same cluster as their DTs. Fig. 11 (left) shows the accuracy values for the three feeders over increasing Eps values. As expected, with increasing Eps, as the cluster sizes increase, the accuracy also increases because larger clusters are more likely to contain the customers and their DTs together (tending to 1 for the full feeder scenario). Nevertheless, it is interesting to note that high accuracy (above 0.9) is achieved for Eps=avg case with only marginal improvement further on.

However, the accuracy measure by itself is not a complete indicator of the effectiveness of clustering. For the purpose of identifying customer–DT connectivity, it is preferable to

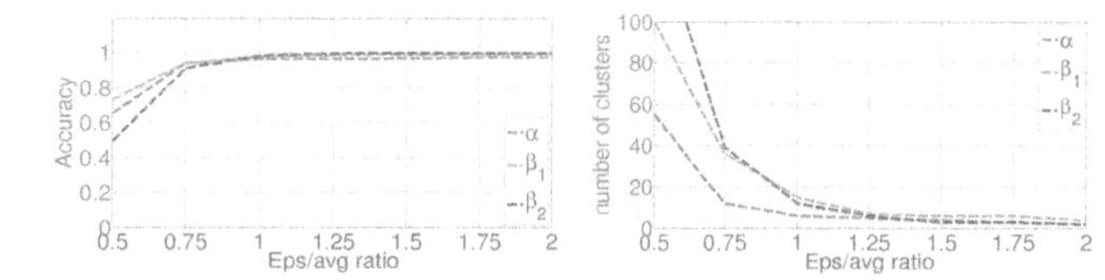

Figure 11: Spatial clustering– (left): clustering accuracy, and (right): number of clusters

have smaller spatial clusters (as long as they are accurate) so that there are fewer candidate DTs for each customer. Fig. 11(right) depicts the number of clusters generated for the three feeders for increasing Eps value. We see that while the number of clusters range from 50 to 150 (for β_2) for Eps=$0.5 * avg$, they fall rapidly to range between 10–20 for the Eps=avg case. Since the accuracy achieved by Eps=avg case is also high, it appears to be a good parameter for generating the right set of clusters.

6.2 Clustering based on Voltage-data

In order to infer the customer–DT connectivity, we apply K-MEANS clustering over the voltage data of the customers, as described in Section. 4, with number of clusters k = number of DTs. The aim is to obtain distinct clusters, each corresponding to one DT and containing only the set of those customers connected to that DT.

Given the set of customers belonging to a feeder, one may apply voltage-data clustering over them directly. However, spatial clustering of customers and DTs provides smaller clusters within each feeder. With the assumption that a customer is likely to be connected to a DT in its vicinity than to one faraway, it may be beneficial to conduct voltage-based clustering of customers within each spatial cluster separately. The final case is to consider the lateral to DT mapping. Although the lateral connectivity may not always be available, it provides good groupings of customers and DTs within each branch of the feeder. Group of customers and number of DTs belonging to a lateral are relatively small in size, however, all the customers in that group are only connected to DTs belonging to that group. Thus, lateral information provides small yet accurate spatial groups over which voltage-based clustering can be performed to obtain customer–DT connectivity.

In summary, we conducted voltage data-based clustering for all the above cases – (i) within spatial clusters (formed

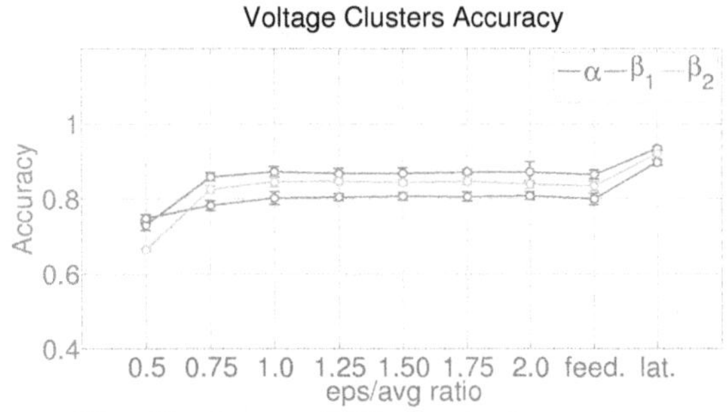

Figure 12: Customer-DT clustering: Accuracy of voltage clustering over spatial clusters formed with different Eps/avg ratios, full feeder and lateral cases.

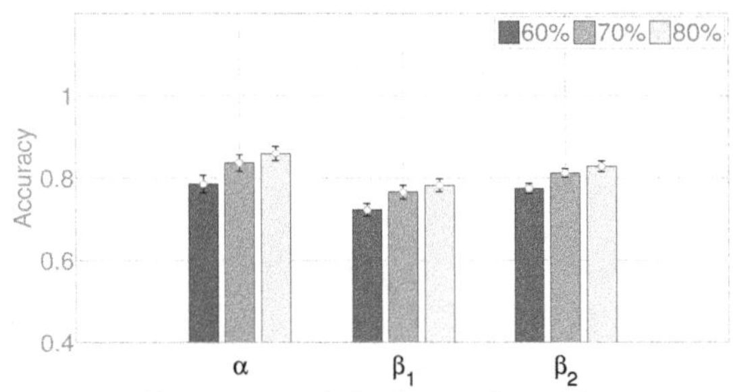

Figure 13: Customer-DT clustering: Accuracy over existing connectivity with different inaccuracies

with Eps ranging from $0.5 * avg$ to $2 * avg$), (ii) within the full feeder and, (iii) within each lateral. For each case, while using K-MEANS, k was set to the number of DTs in that group. Therefore, in the 'feeder' and 'lateral' case, it was equal to the number of DTs belonging to the feeder or the lateral respectively. However, for clustering within each spatial cluster, k value was set to the number of DTs present in that cluster. After the clusters are obtained, DTs are assigned to the clusters based on majority rule using ground truth to determine the accuracy of clustering, as explained in Section. 4.2.

As expected, when using spatial clusters generated with Eps=$0.5 * avg$ and Eps=$0.75 * avg$, the accuracy values are low, since the accuracy of the spatial clusters themselves are low (ref Fig. 11). For Eps=avg and higher, good accuracy is achieved, ranging from 0.78 for β_1 feeder to 0.87 for α feeder. For the feeder case, similar accuracy is achieved, though on average, slightly lower than when compared to the cases of Eps=avg to $1.5 * avg$. Finally, the accuracy when clustering within each lateral is even higher at around 0.9. This is expected as the lateral case represents the best-case scenario. However, lateral information may not always be available.

The previous plots show the accuracy of clustering when compared to ground truth. In practice, our goal is to correct an existing customer-DT mapping that may be partially accurate. To simulate this case, we repeat the above experiments by randomly introducing errors (20-40%) in the existing customer to DT mapping (thus leading to 80%-60% accurate ground truth scenarios). Fig. 13 plots the accuracy for full feeder case, when an existing but partially accurate mapping is used in the labeling of computed voltage-data clusters, as described in section 4.2. We observe that as long as the errors are not too high, the accuracy of the existing mapping can be improved.

In summary, the results show that by performing clustering over the voltage data and then assigning DTs to the clusters, 0.8-0.9 accuracy can be achieved depending on the setting. Moreover, we can see that when lateral-level information is not available, spatial clustering prior to voltage-clustering can lead to slightly better results on average.

7. CUSTOMER TO PHASE MAPPING

This section considers the problem of inferring customer to phase mapping, which is generally prone to more inaccuracies when compared to other mappings. As before we use voltage-data clustering to infer the phase of customers. In order to partition customers based on phases, we cluster them into three groups, *i.e.* no. of clusters $k = 3$ in K-MEANS, one corresponding to each phase A, B, and C. In this case, we compare our results with both the existing mapping available in the database as well as the true mapping that was obtained after conducting manual field inspections for the 3 feeder circuits: α, β_1 and β_2.

In order to assign a phase to each cluster, we utilize the per-phase feeder measurements obtained from the SCADA system. Let $f_{A,t}$ denote the RMS voltage measurement from phase A of the feeder during time step $t \in \{1, \ldots, m\}$ and let $\mathbf{F}_A = [f_{A,t}]_{m \times 1}$. Similarly let $\mathbf{F}_B$ and $\mathbf{F}_C$ correspond to phases B and C respectively. We pass feeder measurements $\{\mathbf{F}_A, \mathbf{F}_B, \mathbf{F}_C\}$ as centroids of the initial solution to the K-MEANS algorithm. Thus each centroid effectively has a phase. The algorithm iteratively updates the centroids and yields the final set of customer clusters. Each cluster is assigned the phase of its centroid. Note that even when data from SCADA system is not available, clustering can still be used to verify if two customers belong to the same phase. Therefore it can identify inconsistencies in the existing customer–phase mapping solely from customer voltage measurements.

As described earlier, we divide the voltage dataset, which covers 2 months, into multiple batches of 4 days each. Thus we may compute a customer to phase mapping for each batch and combine these clustering solutions to obtain the final clusters corresponding to the full dataset. We present results using two different techniques of combining these clustering solutions. (i) Majority Approach, and (ii) Cluster Ensemble.

Majority-rule approach: Each customer may be assigned a different phase based on each batch of voltage data. This simple approach assigns a final phase to a customer based on the majority of all assignments it receives over different batches.

Cluster Ensemble: There exist several cluster ensemble techniques to combine multiple partitionings of data without accessing the original feature values. Specifically, we use *Cluster-based Similarity Partitioning Algorithm* (CSPA) [13] along with k-medoid clustering algorithm to ensemble individual partitionings into a single clustering. We first generate a similarity matrix based on the individual partitionings corresponding to each batch and then apply the k-medoid algorithm to produce the final clustering. CSPA is an intuitive and efficient cluster ensemble algorithm and suits our purpose effectively.

We compare both these above methods with the accuracy averaged multiple batches in Fig. 14. We see that for all the feeders, the performance of *Cluster Ensemble* and *Majority Rule* are comparable to each other and yield close to

Table 2: Effectiveness of Phase Clustering

Feeder	Verified DTs	Positive	Negative	False Positive	False Negative	Flagged as inaccurate but incorrectly assigned	Accuracy of Clustering	Accuracy of database
α	119	100	6	5	7	1	89%	90%
β_1	200	110	78	3	8	1	94%	59%
β_2	233	161	48	13	5	6	90%	71%

Category	database solution = ground truth	database solution = computed solution	computed solution = ground truth
Positives	Yes	Yes	Yes
Negatives	No	No	Yes
False positives	No	Yes	No
False Negatives	Yes	No	No
Flagged Inaccurate but incorrectly assigned	No	No	No

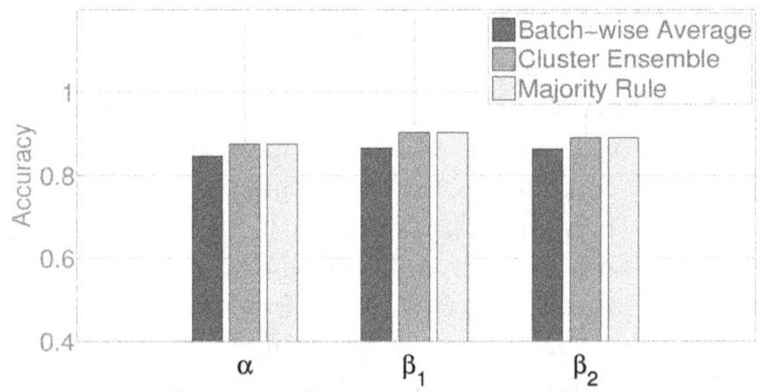

Figure 14: Customer–Phase mapping: Accuracy after applying cluster integration techniques

90% accuracy. Moreover both these methods perform significantly better than the batch-average. We obtain similar results when we use different batch sizes of $1-7$ days. Thus combining clustering solutions obtained from the different batches of voltage-data generates a final set of clusters with improved accuracy.

7.1 Comparison with Field Verified Mapping

Particularly for customer–phase mapping, we possess two mapping solutions. We possess a *Database solution* which refers to the mapping stored in the utility's database and not verified in the field. In addition, we possess the actual *Ground truth*, which was obtained after the phase of DTs was inspected in the field for the 3 feeders. Since the DTs considered are all single-phase, the customers connected to a DT have the same phase as their DTs.

We now compare our clustering-based mapping solution with manual field inspections to determine its effectiveness in identifying and correcting errors in the existing database solution. For this, we use the computed customer–phase mapping and assign a phase to each DT based on the phases of all customers under it. We then compare transformer phases across the computed solution, database solution, and the ground truth. Table 2 presents the results. The second column lists the total number of single-phase DTs which were verified in the field and the last column shows the accuracy of the existing database solution (as compared with ground truth from field inspections). The *positive* and *negative* columns count DTs wherein the computed phase is same as ground truth. The *positive* column counts DTs whose phase remains unchanged after field inspections. The *negative* column counts DTs whose phase was erroneous in the database, but was identified and corrected in the computed solution. The *false positive* counts the DTs which had an erroneous phase in the database solution but were not corrected in the computed solution. The *false negatives* counts DTs which had a correct phase in the database solution, but were identified as incorrect by the computed solution. In summary, the results show that our method of identifying customer–phase based on voltage-data clustering helped improve the accuracy of the database solution significantly in case of β_1 and β_2. For feeder α, there is a negligible drop in the accuracy. As explained above, phase is assigned to DT based on the computed phases of its customers. However, this customer–DTmapping was not verified on the field and can contain errors. These errors possibly lead to the slight drop in accuracy of the α feeder. While field inspections can be used to obtain 100% accuracy, they are expensive and time-consuming. These results show that our analytics approach is a low-cost alternative, which may be used to improve the accuracy of the database solution.

8. RELATED WORK

We know of no prior work that infers customer to feeder or transformer mapping using data already available in the distribution network. This section summarizes prior work on inferring customer phase. Caird [5] discloses a system and method for phase identification with suitably enhanced meters that can detect phases based upon a unique signal injected into the phase line. The disadvantage of signal injection methods or in general those that rely on power-line communication (PLC) is that they require enhanced hardware to transmit and receive signals at different points of the grid, increasing capital and maintenance costs. Moreover in North America, feeders from substations can run for several miles before reaching a customer. Therefore PLC-based solutions become impractical and expensive since the signal may not propagate over long distances or across DTs without repeaters. Our approach on the other hand simply relies on voltage measurements from customers and feeders and therefore does not require any additional hardware other than conventional meters.

Our prior work [1] describes an optimization approach to infer the connectivity model using a time series of customer and grid side load (kWh) measurements. The measurements are used to set up a system of linear equations based upon the principle of conservation of energy. The equations are analyzed to fit a customer to phase mapping that is consistent with the observed time series (i.e. it minimizes the error of fit). Dilek's [7] work on phase prediction in power circuits also uses interval consumption measurements, however the author employs a heuristic Tabu search to determine the phase of attached loads. Voltage-based techniques have two advantages over load-based techniques. Firstly, voltage-based clustering techniques may be used to verify and correct an existing customer to phase mapping solely from customer meter measurements. The load-based optimization approaches require both customer and feeder measurements. Secondly, since load-based optimization techniques are based on the principle of conservation, their accuracy may reduce in the presence of any non-AMI or unmetered loads. The voltage-based approaches however are insensitive to unmetered loads in the system.

In [12], authors analyse measurements from a low voltage network consisting of a 3-phase distribution transformer and its customers. Voltage measurements of individual customers are matched with the per-phase measurements taken at the transformer to determine customer phase. Our prior work [2, 3] studies voltage measurements from a microgrid and a feeder circuit respectively to infer phase relationship. We demonstrate that individually comparing the low voltage measurements from customers with the feeder measurements yields a lower accuracy when compared to clustering, which simultaneously compares customer measurements with each other as well as with the per-phase feeder measurements. This current work, on the other hand, studies voltage data from multiple feeder circuits of a distribution network and reports accuracy results based on manual field inspections. We demonstrate the effectiveness of the clustering in comparison to field inspections for identifying and correcting phase errors. Furthermore we show that voltage measurements exhibit hierarchical correlations which can be exploited to infer customer to feeder and transformer mapping in addition to customer phase.

9. CONCLUSIONS

An accurate connectivity model is required in the planning, operations, and maintenance of distribution networks. It enables faster restoration, accurate and timely communication with customers during outages, and is also needed to efficiently integrate distributed generation sources. Automated inference of customer to distribution transformer and phase mapping using data that is already available from smart meters, feeder sensors, and GIS data allows utilities to periodically validate their connectivity and maintain a more accurate connectivity model of their distribution network without the use of expensive manual inspections.

In this work, we show that customer voltage measurements exhibit hierarchical correlations which are consistent with the hierarchical connectivity relationships that exist between customers, distribution transformers, phases, and feeders of a distribution network. We show that voltage-data clustering may be used to partition customers under different feeders as long as they are powered by different substation transformers. We present a novel analytics approach that can infer both customer-to-transformer and phase mapping with the help of customer voltage measurements in combination with feeder measurements, GIS data and any existing but partially accurate customer to transformer mapping. We showed accuracy results based on analysis of low and medium voltage measurements collected from multiple feeder circuits with more than 10K single-phase customers. Our results indicate that voltage measurements spanning several days could be utilized to infer both customer to transformer and phase mapping with high accuracy.

Future work will evaluate other clustering algorithms such as hierarchical clustering and study their performance using different cluster validity measures. We will study the use of spatio-temporal techniques which may be used to effectively combine voltage and GIS data. We will study the impact of distributed generation on customer voltage measurements and also develop approaches that combine both load (kWh) and voltage measurements to infer customer phase.

10. REFERENCES

[1] V. Arya, T. S. Jayram, S. Pal, and S. Kalyanaraman. Inferring connectivity model from meter measurements in distribution networks. In *e-Energy*, pages 173–182, 2013.

[2] V. Arya and R. Mitra. Voltage-based clustering to identify connectivity relationships in distribution networks. In *SmartGridComm*, pages 7–12, 2013.

[3] V. Arya, R. Mitra, R. Mueller, H. Storey, G. Labut, J. Esser, and B. Sullivan. Voltage analytics to infer customer phase. In *IEEE PES Innovative Smart Grid Technologies(ISGT) Europe*, 2014.

[4] J. Bouford and C. Warren. Many states of distribution. *Power and Energy Magazine, IEEE*, 5(4):24–32, 2007.

[5] K. Caird. Meter Phase Identification. US Patent Application 20100164473, January 2010. Patent No. 12/345702.

[6] G. Clark. A changing map: Four decades of service restoration at alabama power. *Power and Energy Magazine, IEEE*, 12(1):64–69, Jan 2014.

[7] M. Dilek. *Integrated Design of Electrical Distribution Systems: Phase Balancing and Phase Prediction Case Studies.* PhD thesis, Virginia Polytechnic Institute and State University, 2001.

[8] M. Ester, H. Kriegel, J. Sander, and X. Xu. A density-based algorithm for discovering clusters in large spatial databases with noise. In *Proceedings of the Second International Conference on Knowledge Discovery and Data Mining (KDD-96), Portland, Oregon, USA*, pages 226–231, 1996.

[9] J. Fan and S. Borlase. The evolution of distribution. *Power and Energy Magazine, IEEE*, 7(2):63–68, 2009.

[10] J. D. D. Glover and M. S. Sarma. *Power System Analysis and Design.* Brooks/Cole Publishing Co., Pacific Grove, CA, USA, 3rd edition, 2001.

[11] J. A. Hartigan and M. A. Wong. A K-means clustering algorithm. *Applied Statistics*, 28:100–108, 1979.

[12] H. Pezeshki and P. Wolfs. Correlation based method for phase identification in a three phase lv distribution network. In *Universities Power Engineering Conference (AUPEC), 22nd Australasian*, pages 1–7, 2012.

[13] A. Strehl and J. Ghosh. Cluster ensembles—a knowledge reuse framework for combining multiple partitions. *The Journal of Machine Learning Research*, 3:583–617, 2003.

Analyzing Invariants in Cyber-Physical Systems using Latent Factor Regression

Marjan Momtazpour[1], Jinghe Zhang[2], Saifur Rahman[2], Ratnesh Sharma[3], Naren Ramakrishnan[1]
[1]Discovery Analytics Center, Department of Computer Science, Virginia Tech
[2]Advanced Research Institute, Virginia Tech
[3]NEC Laboratories America, Inc.
[1]{marjan,naren}@cs.vt.edu,[2]{jing2014,srahman}@vt.edu,[3]ratnesh@nec-labs.com

ABSTRACT

The analysis of large scale data logged from complex cyber-physical systems, such as microgrids, often entails the discovery of invariants capturing functional as well as operational relationships underlying such large systems. We describe a latent factor approach to infer invariants underlying system variables and how we can leverage these relationships to monitor a cyber-physical system. In particular we illustrate how this approach helps rapidly identify outliers during system operation.

Categories and Subject Descriptors

H.2.8 [**Database Applications**]: Data mining

Keywords

Regression, Latent Factors, System Invariants, Outlier Detection.

1. INTRODUCTION

In recent years, with the rapid growth in data logged from modern devices in a distributed system, the need for having stronger knowledge discovery methods has attracted significant attention [28]. Concomitantly, the size and complexity of these systems have become a burden for administrators in detecting failures and repairing them [13, 25]. These challenges inspired us to characterize and track anomalies in cyber-physical systems by correlating all monitored data across the system.

According to [15], "*detecting anomalies that occur only within individual variables is often trivial, while detecting correlation anomalies is much harder and is practically important in fault analysis of complicated dynamic systems*". In a complex cyber-physical system, such as a smart grid (Fig.1), while some of the relationships between time series can be directly observed, other mutual dependencies are significantly complex to extract computationally. A typical cyber-physical system may include tens of time series with hundreds of mutual dependencies, where a large number of them are not directly observable. In the past, researchers have tried to infer existing linear relations using regression models [17] or by harnessing the structure of causal networks [4]. However, due to the complexity of modern systems, we must go beyond direct linear correlations in understanding them.

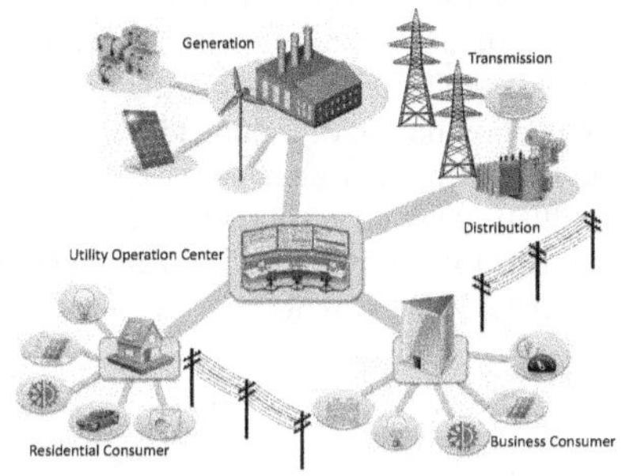

Figure 1: A typical example of a smart grid.

In this paper, we aim to use a more realistic approach to discover hidden patterns and indirect relationships among devices by employing latent variables in regression models. Specifically, we harness hidden factors derived by factor analysis and use them in regression models. We perform various experiments on synthetic and real datasets including wireless sensor networks and microgrid datasets. Furthermore, we use graph representations for better visualization of relationships which aids in discovering system-wide anomalies. Results show that the use of invariants derived with latent factors helps us to monitor large scale complex systems and discover outliers more precisely. We also propose a ranking method to score system-wide anomalies.

Our key contributions are thus:

- Proposing latent factor analysis regression to reveal hidden correlations among time series in a cyber-physical system.
- Summarizing the discovered invariants into an invariant graph of the system.
- Detecting system outliers based on the change in the graph of invariants and ranking time series for fault localization.

2. BACKGROUND

The high complexity of modern distributed cyber-physical systems urges us to enhance the self-management capabilities of these systems. Cyber-physical systems such as microgrid systems have a high degree of heterogeneity (in terms of shape, trend, and periodicity) that requires us to have a general tool to profile a variety of behaviors. Moreover, due to the nature of these systems, we may observe abrupt regime changes, seasonal patterns, and pairwise relationships among time series [11]. Ding et al. proposed an

KDD'15, August 11-14, 2015, Sydney, NSW, Australia.
© 2015 ACM. ISBN 978-1-4503-3664-2/15/08 ...$15.00.
DOI: http://dx.doi.org/10.1145/2783258.2788605.

ensemble of different approaches to tackle these problems in [11]. As stated in [28], traditional computational techniques cannot be used to model complex cyber-physical systems for data analytic purposes in a straightforward manner. There have been multiple research efforts to model complex dynamic systems such as inferring/visualizing the input-output relationships or predicting state switches/changes [28].

Guofei et al. [16] proposed a concept named *flow intensity* and used the ARX (autoregressive exogenous) model to quantify the relationship between each pair of flow intensities. If such a relationship holds all the time, they are considered as invariants of the underlying system. This model has been successful in characterizing complex systems and in supporting different system management tasks such as fault detection and localization. However, one of the main disadvantages of this method, as cited in [13], is that the complexity of algorithm in order to find all invariants is high. In this model, they look at two flow intensities (timeseries) where one of them is considered as input and the other one as output signal. Note that the differentiation of input and output time series are unknown and such labeling can occur only after examining both directions and evaluating which assignments lead to higher scores. The ARX model posits the following relationship between two flow intensities of y (output) and x (input):

$$\begin{aligned} y(t) + a_1 y(t-1) + ... + a_u y(t-u) \\ = b_0 x(t-l) + ... + b_v x(t-l-v) \end{aligned} \quad (1)$$

where u, v, and l are the order of the model and determine the number of previous steps that are affecting the current output. a_i's and b_j's are coefficient parameters that reflect how strongly a previous step is affecting the current output. Equation 1 can be solved using a least squares method (LSM) and the fitness score will indicate whether the model fits the observed data appropriately [16].

3. PROBLEM FORMULATION

Let us assume that we have observed a set of n time series, $\mathcal{D} = \{x_1(t), \dots, x_n(t)\}$, measured at various points in one or more cyber-physical systems. For a time series $x_i(t)$, we represent the vector of samples at time steps $t_k, \dots, t_{k+w}$ as follows:

$$\mathcal{X}_i^{k:k+w} = [x_i(t_k), x_i(t_{k+1}) \dots, x_i(t_{k+w})]^T. \quad (2)$$

Furthermore, we use X_i to represent the time series $x_i(t)$ as a random variable. In other words, $x_i(t)$ is a time series whose samples are drawn from a random distribution represented by random variable X_i.

In any type of cyber-physical system, there are various correlations and inter-dependencies among time series. In large cyber-physical systems, having sufficient level of knowledge about these inter-dependencies is crucial to preform accurate system management tasks. In the following definition, we formally define what we mean by dependency between two time series.

DEFINITION 1. ***(Approximate Dependency):*** *At time step t_m, time series $x_j(t) \in \mathcal{D}$ approximately depends on $x_i(t) \in \mathcal{D}$, if and only if, there exists a function $f : \mathbb{R} \to \mathbb{R}$ that for appropriately small $\epsilon > 0$:*

$$\hat{x}_j(t_m) = f(\mathcal{X}_j^{1:m-1}, \mathcal{X}_i^{1:m}) \quad (3)$$

and

$$|x_j(t_m) - \hat{x}_j(t_m)| < \epsilon. \quad (4)$$

We depict this dependency by $x_j(t) \underset{\epsilon}{\to} x_i(t)\Big|_{t_m}$.

When the dependency between two time series does not change over time, we say that these two time series are system-invariants.

DEFINITION 2. ***(System Invariants):*** *Two time series, $x_j(t) \in \mathcal{D}$ and $x_i(t) \in \mathcal{D}$, are system-invariant up to time T within range of ϵ if and only if at least one of the following rules satisfied:*

$$\exists f : \mathbb{R} \to \mathbb{R} \quad and \quad \forall 0 \le t \le T \quad : \quad x_j(t) \underset{\epsilon}{\to} x_i(t)\Big|_{0 \le t \le T}$$

or

$$\exists f : \mathbb{R} \to \mathbb{R} \quad and \quad \forall 0 \le t \le T \quad : \quad x_i(t) \underset{\epsilon}{\to} x_j(t)\Big|_{0 \le t \le T}.$$

We show invariant time series by $x_i(t) \overset{\epsilon}{\leftrightharpoons} x_j(t)$.

Based on the nature of the system, dependencies between time series can be linear or nonlinear and this is modeled by the function f. In complex cyber-physical systems, when we have a large number of time series, it is appropriate to represent the invariants in the form of a graph.

DEFINITION 3. ***(Invariant Graph):*** *Graph $G = (V, E)$, with the set of vertices $V = \{v_1, \dots, v_n\}$ and the set of edges $E = \{e_1, \dots, e_m\}$, is called an invariant graph of a system with observed time series $\mathcal{D} = \{x_1(t), \dots, x_n(t)\}$, where $e = (v_i, v_j) \in E$ if and only if $x_i(t) \overset{\epsilon}{\leftrightharpoons} x_j(t)$.*

From Definition 3 it is obvious that the vertex v_i is equivalent to the time series $x_i(t)$. It should be noted that system invariants and invariant graph represent features of a system under its normal condition. However, in the presence of anomalies, when the behavior of system deviates from its normal condition, these dependencies may disappear. In other words, while two times series, $x_i(t)$ and $x_j(t)$, may be invariant under normal conditions, the invariant feature may not hold when an anomaly condition appears in the system.

DEFINITION 4. ***(Broken Invariants):*** *We say that system invariant $x_i(t) \overset{\epsilon}{\leftrightharpoons} x_j(t)$ is broken at time $T = t_m$, if and only if, time series $x_i(t)$ and $x_j(t)$ satisfy the following conditions:*

$$\exists f : \mathbb{R} \to \mathbb{R} \quad and \quad \forall 0 \le t < T = t_m :$$

$$\left(x_j(t) \underset{\epsilon}{\to} x_i(t)\Big|_{t<T} \quad \wedge \quad |x_j(t_m) - f(\mathcal{X}_j^{1:m-1}, \mathcal{X}_i^{1:m})| \ge \epsilon \right)$$

or

$$\left(x_i(t) \underset{\epsilon}{\to} x_j(t)\Big|_{t<T} \quad \wedge \quad |x_i(t_m) - f(\mathcal{X}_i^{1:m-1}, \mathcal{X}_j^{1:m})| \ge \epsilon \right).$$

In some cases, the existence of unseen factors has an impact on the observed values of the system which cause them to have a specific behavior. However, uncovering those hidden factors behind all the underlying electro-mechanical devices is a challenging task. Characterizing these factors can help us to reveal the hidden relationships between potential time series whether they have indirect or complex relationships. Figure 2 (a) shows an example of relationships among a set of time series, $(x_1, x_2, \cdots, x_n)$. In reality, the relationships can be direct (solid lines) or indirect (dashed lines). Previous works tried to reveal the direct relationships among time series (which is shown in Figure 2 (b)). However, despite the simplicity of these linear methods, sometimes they result in a sparse graph of invariants where tracking all time series is impossible. Moreover, these methods are not able to capture the underlying hidden relationships and results in poor detection of system outliers. In this paper, we aim to uncover those hidden relationships

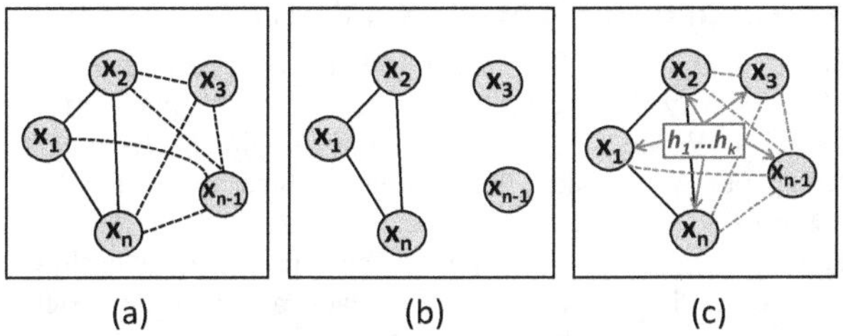

Figure 2: Different models of relationships: (a) Relationships in reality, (b) Relationships in the ARX model and (c) Relationships in ARX with a latent model.

with the help of hidden factors as latent variables. Hidden factors, $(f_1, f_2, \cdots, f_n)$, are considered as a higher level in hierarchy of the system and have an impact on the whole observed variables. An example of relationships in a system with hidden factors is illustrated in Figure 2 (c).

DEFINITION 5. ***(Latent Variable):*** *In a cyber-physical system with the set of observed time series $\mathcal{D} = \{x_1(t), \ldots, x_n(t)\}$, an unobserved time series $h(t)$ is a latent variable when two or more observed time series are functions of $h(t)$. In other words,*

$$\begin{aligned} \exists \mathcal{D}' \subset \mathcal{D} \quad where \quad \forall x(t) \in \mathcal{D}', \quad \exists g_x : \mathbb{R} \to \mathbb{R} \quad : \\ \forall t_m \geq 0, \quad x(t_m) = g_x(\mathcal{H}^{1:m}) \end{aligned} \tag{5}$$

where similar to Eq. 2, $\mathcal{H}^{1:m}$ is defined as follows:

$$\mathcal{H}^{1:m} = [h(t_1), h(t_2) \ldots, h(t_m)]^T.$$

It should be noted that each cyber-physical system may have more than one latent variable. Also, existence of a latent variable does not mean that all the observed time series should be directly related to that variable.

4. INVARIANT DISCOVERY

In this section, we describe a framework for invariant graph discovery and anomaly detection. For this purpose, we first extract latent variables using factor analysis and incorporate hidden factors into the regression model. Then we construct the invariant graph using a search algorithm. Finally, we use the constructed graph as a normal invariant graph and deploy it for the purpose of anomaly detection in the system. By discovering the broken invariants and ranking them, one may be able to find fault(s) and localize them.

4.1 Factor Analysis

Let us assume that we have a set of n random variables (input variables), denoted by X_1, ..., X_n. Also, assume that there are k hidden (latent) factors in the system, denotes by H_1, ..., H_k. Furthermore, assume that the observed variables are modeled as linear combinations of latent variables. Then we derive latent variables using the *factor analysis* method. Factor analysis is a well-studied field and is used to determine the main latent sources behind the observed data variation [9]. Although factor analysis is similar to principal component analysis (PCA), it is used more in predictive models due to its generalizability (e.g., factor loadings can remain consistent for different subsets of variables) [29]. Some might think of the factor model as generative models where the data is produced based on factors.

In factor analysis, for one sample of data extracted from random variable distributions, we have:

$$X_i - \mu_i = \lambda_{i1} H_1 + \ldots + \lambda_{ik} H_k + \zeta_i \tag{6}$$

where μ_i is the expected value of X_i, H_j's are unobserved random variables and λ_{ij}'s are unknown constants ($i \in 1, \cdots, n$ and $j \in 1, \cdots, k$ where $k < n$). Also, ζ_i's are independently distributed error terms with zero mean and finite variance ($Var(\zeta_i) = \psi_i$). In other words, by Eq. 6, each of the X_i's random variables is related to k hidden random variables, known as latent factors.

In matrix notation, we have:

$$\mathbf{X} - \mu = \mathbf{\Lambda H} + \mathbf{Z} \tag{7}$$

where $\mathbf{X} = (X_1, \cdots, X_n)^T$ is a data sample vector, μ is the expected values of data samples, $\mathbf{\Lambda}$ is an $n \times k$ matrix named as loading matrix, $\mathbf{H} = (H_1, \cdots, H_k)^T$ is a vector of latent factors, and $\mathbf{Z} = (\zeta_1, \cdots, \zeta_n)'$ is the vector of error.

It is assumed that $\mathbf{H}$ and $\mathbf{Z}$ are independent, and $E(\mathbf{Z}) = \mathbf{0}$, $E(\mathbf{H}) = \mathbf{0}$, $Cov(\mathbf{Z}) = Diag(\psi_1, ..., \psi_n) = \psi$, and $E(\mathbf{HH^T}) = \mathbf{\Phi}$. Furthermore, it is assumed that the data has a multivariate normal distribution, $\mathbf{X} = \mathcal{N}(\mu, \mathbf{\Sigma})$. Based on these assumptions, we will have:

$$\mathbf{\Sigma} = \mathbf{\Lambda \Phi \Lambda^T} + \psi. \tag{8}$$

Since $\mathbf{X}$ has a multivariate normal distribution, the actual distribution function of elements of sample covariance matrix, $\mathbf{S}$, can be expressed as a Wishart distribution with $m-1$ degrees of freedom, $m\mathbf{S} \sim \mathcal{W}_n(\mathbf{\Sigma}, m-1)$, where m is the number of samples.

The log-likelihood of the Wishart distribution can be expressed as follows:

$$log\, L = -\frac{m-1}{2}(log|\mathbf{\Sigma}| + tr(\mathbf{S\Sigma^{-1}})) \tag{9}$$

where the terms independent of $\mathbf{\Sigma}$ are dropped.

It is obvious that maximization of L is equivalent to minimizing the following function:

$$Q = log\,|\mathbf{\Sigma}| + tr(\mathbf{S\Sigma^{-1}}). \tag{10}$$

One can find the latent variables by taking the partial derivatives of Eq. 10 with respect to the elements of loading matrix and errors constrained by Eq. 8. For simplicity, it is convenient to assume that $\mathbf{\Phi} = \mathbf{I}$ and $\mathbf{\Lambda^T \Psi^{-1} \Lambda}$ is diagonal.

There are different types of criteria to determine the number of factors such as criteria based on eigenvalues, discrepancy of approximation, or overall discrepancy [24]. Here, we use the Kaiser criterion which drops those with eigenvalues of less than 1. Indeed, the number of factors, must be lower than the number of observed variables, $k < n$. More details can be found in [14, 19].

4.2 Latent Factor Auto Regression with Exogenous input (LFRX)

Having n time series, $\mathcal{D} = \{x_1(t), \cdots, x_n(t)\}$, related to a cyber-physical system, similar to the ARX model [16], we can rewrite Eq. 1 as:

$$\hat{x}_j(t) = \sum_{p=1}^{u} a_p x_j(t-p) + \sum_{p=0}^{v} b_p x_i(t-l-p) \tag{11}$$

where $x_i(t), x_j(t) \in \mathcal{D}$.

As acknowledged widely [16, 13, 6, 5, 27], a drawback of ARX is that relationship discovery is done based on the existence of direct linear relationships between two observed time series. In other words, at each time ARX considers a pair of time series without considering the underlying relationships and hidden patterns. To address this issue, we deploy latent factors in the ARX model to recover the complex relationships. If we use latent factors in the

Algorithm 1: Invariant Search Algorithm

Input: x_i, $i \in \{1,..,n\}$: set of time series, Δ: ARX superiority threshold, τ: minimum acceptable score, t_s and t_e: start and end time of training dataset.
Output: G: Invariant Graph.
1 $S_{ARX} = \{\}$;
2 $S_{LFRX} = \{\}$;
3 **for** $i = 1$ *to* n **do**
4   **for** $j = 1$ *to* n **do**
5   **if** $i == j$ **then**
6   Continue;
7   **end**
8   **foreach** $t_s \leq t \leq t_e$ **do**
9   Learn an ARX model, θ_{ji}^{ARX}, using Eq. 11;
10   Calculate $\hat{x}_j^{ARX}(t)$ using θ_{ji}^{ARX};
11   Compute $\mathcal{F}_{ji}^{ARX}(t)$ with Eq. 15;
12   Learn an LFRX model, θ_{ji}^{LFRX}, using Eq. 12;
13   Calculate $\hat{x}_j^{LFRX}(t)$ using θ_{ji}^{LFRX};
14   Compute $\mathcal{F}_{ji}^{LFRX}(t)$ with Eq. 15;
15   **end**
16   **if** $\left(\sum_{t=t_s}^{t_e} \mathcal{F}_{ji}^{ARX}(t) \geq \sum_{t=t_s}^{t_e} \mathcal{F}_{ji}^{LFRX}(t) - \Delta\right)$ *and* $\left(\min_t(\mathcal{F}_{ji}^{ARX}(t)) \geq \tau\right)$ **then**
17       $S_{ARX} = S_{ARX} \cup \{x_i \leftrightharpoons x_j\}$;
18   **end**
19   **if** $\left(\sum_{t=t_s}^{t_e} \mathcal{F}_{ji}^{LFRX}(t) > \sum_{t=t_s}^{t_e} \mathcal{F}_{ji}^{ARX}(t) + \Delta\right)$ *and* $\left(\min_t(\mathcal{F}_{ji}^{LFRX}(t)) \geq \tau\right)$ **then**
20       $S_{LFRX} = S_{LFRX} \cup \{x_i \leftrightharpoons x_j\}$;
21   **end**
22   **end**
23 **end**
24 Construct Graph, $G = (V, E)$, using S_{ARX} and S_{LFRX};
25 **return** G;

above regression model, we will have:

$$\hat{x}_j(t) = \sum_{p=1}^{u} a_p x_j(t-p) + \sum_{p=0}^{v} b_p x_i(t-l-p) + \sum_{p=0}^{w} \sum_{q=1}^{k} c_{pq} h_q(t-p) \tag{12}$$

where $h_p(t)$'s are the latent factor time series that have been built based on the latent factor random variables, as discussed in the previous subsection (Eq. 6). Also, a_p's, b_p's, and c_{pq}'s are the regression weights that are determined in the learning phase. Note that in Eq. 12, in addition to the regression weights, latent factors are also unknown and should be estimated in the learning phase.

It should be noted that here we incorporate the previous values of $x_j(t)$ as well as values of exogenous variable, $x_i(t)$, and hidden variables, $h_q(t)$'s, to estimate new value of $x_j(t)$. In matrix notation, Eq. 12 will change to:

$$\hat{x}_j(t) = \mathbf{A}^T \mathcal{X}_j^{t-u:t-1} + \mathbf{B}^T \mathcal{X}_i^{t-l-v:t-l} + \mathrm{Tr}(\mathbf{C}^T \boldsymbol{\mathcal{H}}) \tag{13}$$

where $\mathbf{A}_{u\times 1}$, $\mathbf{B}_{(v+1)\times 1}$, $\mathbf{C}_{(w+1)\times k}$ are matrices of coefficients. Also, $\boldsymbol{\mathcal{H}}_{(w+1)\times k}$ is a matrix that represents all the latent factors, i.e. $\boldsymbol{\mathcal{H}} = \left[\mathcal{H}_1^{t-w:t} \cdots \mathcal{H}_k^{t-w:t}\right]$. In our experiments, we assume $u = v = w$ and their values are estimated using cross-validation. Also, due to the lack of delay in our datasets, we assume l is zero. In order to solve Eq. 13, first we derive latent factors, $\boldsymbol{\mathcal{H}}$, using factor analysis of Subsection 4.1 and then we incorporate them into the regression model to estimate the weights.

4.3 Invariant Graph Construction

Based on Definition 2, in order to discover system invariants we need to identify time series that have persistent approximate dependencies. While time series may have nonlinear dependencies, in this paper we consider linear relationships and use ARX and LFRX for this purpose.

The search algorithm that extracts system invariants is shown in Algorithm 1. In this algorithm, for each pair of time series, we first assume that they have a direct linear relationship and we fit them using an ARX model (Eq. 11). The ARX model for time series $x_i(t)$ and $x_j(t)$ is illustrated by θ_{ij}^{ARX}. Then, we assume that there might be an indirect relationship through latent variables and hence, we use LFRX model to learn θ_{ij}^{LFRX}. As defined in Definition 1, to determine if $x_j(t)$ depends on $x_i(t)$, we need to compare the estimation error with an acceptable threshold, ϵ. However since in a specific cyber-physical system different time series have different range of values, it is more appropriate to use normalized error measurements. For this purpose, when we estimate $x_j(t)$ based on $x_i(t)$, we can evaluate the relative absolute error (RAE) defined by the following equation:

$$e_{j,i}^{RAE}(t) = \frac{|\hat{x}_j(t) - x_j(t)|}{\sum_{t=t_s}^{t_e} |\bar{x}_j(t) - x_j(t)|} \tag{14}$$

where $x_j(t)$ is the observed value, $\hat{x}_j(t)$ is the estimated value based on $x_i(t)$, and $\bar{x}_j$ is the sample mean of observed values.

According to [17] for each pair of time series, $x_i(t)$ and $x_j(t)$, we calculate a score to measure their dependencies. The following normalized score may be used for the evaluations:

$$\mathcal{F}_{j,i}(t) = 100(1 - e_{j,i}^{RAE}(t)). \tag{15}$$

A higher score indicates stronger dependency between the time series. It should be noted that RAE is a specific example of normalized error measurement and one can easily extend the algorithm to use other error measurement approaches including RMSE, specifically when time series have the same range of variations.

In Algorithm 1, lines 8 to 15 are dedicated to estimate individual values of $x_j(t)$ based on $x_i(t)$ and calculate the scores for ARX and LFRX models. In order to discover invariants and choose between direct or indirect relationships, we consider the following criteria:

- For all the time steps, score should be greater than or equal to a specific threshold. We name this threshold as *minimum acceptable score* and denote it by τ. Then, we should have:

$$\min_t(\mathcal{F}_{ji}(t)) \geq \tau. \tag{16}$$

- Since higher score depict stronger relationships, in choosing between ARX and LFRX, the one with the better overall score is chosen.
- Since linear invariants represent simpler relationships, higher priority is given to ARX-based invariants using a guard bound, Δ, which we name as the *ARX superiority threshold.* In other words, ARX-based invariants are selected when:

$$\sum_{t=t_s}^{t_e} \mathcal{F}_{ji}^{ARX}(t) \geq \sum_{t=t_s}^{t_e} \mathcal{F}_{ji}^{LFRX}(t) - \Delta. \tag{17}$$

When calculated scores satisfy Eq. 16, we will say that $x_i(t)$ and $x_j(t)$ are invariant and based on Eq. 17, the type of invariant is chosen to be direct (ARX) or indirect (LFRX). The resulted invariants are added to the sets of ARX and LFRX invariants denoted by S_{ARX} and S_{LFRX}, respectively. In Algorithm 1, lines 16 to 21 are dedicated to this process.

Algorithm 2: Alerting Algorithm

```
Input: x_i(t), i ∈ {1,..,n}: set of time series,
       G = (V,E): Invariant Graph, t_e: start time of
       monitoring, α: alerting threshold.
foreach t > t_e do
    foreach e_{i,j} ∈ E do
        Use Definition 4 to check if e_{i,j} is broken;
        if e_{i,j} is broken then
            cnt_ij ← cnt_ij + 1;
        else
            cnt_ij ← 0;
        end
        if cnt_ij > α then
            Invoke an alert;
            cnt_ij ← 0;
        end
    end
end
```

After finding system invariants, the final step (line 24 in Algorithm 1) is to construct the invariant graph, $G = (V, E)$. This is a straightforward task which is performed based on Definition 3. The total number of iterations of this algorithm is $O(tn^2)$ where t is the length of time series. At each iteration (lines 9 to 14), models are learned with a time complexity which is a function of t^2 and various constants $(w, v, u, \cdots)$. This results in an overall complexity of $O(Cn^2t^3)$.

4.4 Outlier Detection using Broken Invariants

After constructing the invariant graph (in Subsection 4.3), we can use this graph for detecting abnormalities in the system. For this purpose, using Definition 4, at each time step we check whether each of the graph edges is broken or not. We then rank the time series in order to localize the source of abnormality. In what follows we first describe the alerting algorithm, followed by a metric for alerting threshold estimation and finally the ranking method for fault localization.

Anomaly alerting algorithm: The alerting algorithm is illustrated in Algorithm 2. In this algorithm, in order to prevent generations of multiple alerts consecutively, we use an alert filtering mechanism by imposing a counting strategy with alert threshold of α. When the number of consecutive violations of a specific invariant goes beyond α, the algorithm invokes an alert to the system administrator, who may use this for further investigations. Time complexity of this algorithm is $O(|E|)$ at each time-step.

Anomaly detection threshold: According to model-based FDI methods used in control theory and similar to [27], in order to reduce false alarms the following approach is used for detection of broken invariants. The difference between the predicted value, $\hat{x}_j(t)$, and the actual value, $x_j(t)$, is recorded and whenever this difference deviates more than a predetermined threshold, ϵ_0, an invariant will be broken:

$$|\hat{x}_j(t) - x_j(t)| > \epsilon_0 \tag{18}$$

The threshold ϵ_0 can be estimated based on the observed values in the training period. According to [27], ϵ_0 is assumed to be 10% larger than the tolerance of deviations from the actual values:

$$\epsilon_0 = 1.1 * arg_r \left\{Prob(|\hat{x}_j - x_j| < r) = 0.995\right\} \tag{19}$$

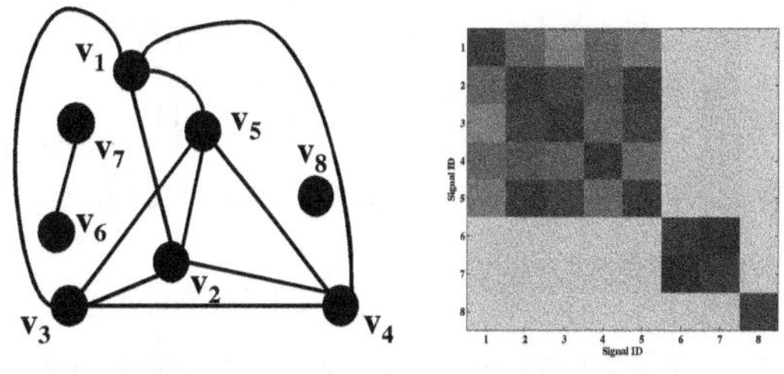

(a) (b)

Figure 3: (a) Invariant graph of synthetic data (b) Correlation matrix of synthetic time series.

where r is greater than 99.5% of the residuals observed in the training data.

Ranking time series for fault localization: In complex cyber-physical systems with a large number of invariants, one single fault in the system may lead to a large number of broken invariants. Hence, for fault localization we need to rank the invariant graph vertices according to the number of their broken edges. Similar techniques have also been used in [12]. For this purpose, we use the following score to rank the vertices after the occurrence of an alarm. Assuming that an alarm is generated at time t, for each vertex, v_j, we calculate the following score:

$$\rho_j = \frac{d_j^{normal} - d_j(t)}{d_j^{normal}} \tag{20}$$

where d_j^{normal} is the degree of v_j in normal condition and $d_j(t)$ is the degree of v_j after alarm generation at time t. It is obvious that higher value of ρ_j indicates v_j has lost more edges which may potentially be due to the occurrence of a fault at $x_j(t)$.

5. EXPERIMENTAL RESULTS

We perform our experiments on several datasets. We aim to show how our method (ARX + LFRX) can discover the invariants, how it can improve the accuracy of system, and how it can find the anomalies happening throughout the network. First, we perform our analysis on a synthetic dataset to recover indirect invariants. Next, we use two datasets from real cyber-physical systems: a wireless sensor network and a microgrid system. In these datasets, there are multiple factors and measurements with various temporal and spatial dependencies.

5.1 Synthetic Data

Dataset Description: At the first step, we perform our experiment on a synthetic dataset to verify our method for the discovery of indirect hidden relationships. For this purpose, we generate eight signals and compare the results of ARX with our method (integration of ARX and LFRX). In this experiment, we add a Gaussian noise with zero mean and standard deviation of 0.1 to one of the time series in order to test the invariant graph under abnormalities. The ground truth graph and its corresponding correlation matrix are shown in Fig. 3 (a) and (b), respectively. As Fig. 3 (a) shows, V_6 and V_7 are correlated to each other. V_8 is isolated and all the remaining nodes are correlated to each other. However, the hidden relationship between signals is not observable in Fig. 3 (a). In fact, V_3, V_4, V_5 are generated using V_1 and V_2. The relationship between signals is given in the following equations:

$$V_1(t) = 0.9V_1(t-1) - 0.02V_1(t-2) - 0.01V_1(t-3) + 0.09 + \eta$$

$$V_2(t) = 2(V_1(t-1) - V1(t-2)) + 0.5(V_2(t-1) + V2(t-2))$$

$V_3(t) = V_1(t-1)+V_2(t)-V_1(t),\ V_4(t) = 3V_1(t-1)+V_2(t-1)$

$$V_5(t) = 3V_1(t-1) - V_2(t-1)$$

$$V_6(t) = 1 + 0.01R(t, 100),\ V_7(t) = 1 - 0.01R(t, 100)$$

$$V_8(t) = 2e^{10^{-4}t} + R(t, 600)e^{-10^{-4}t}$$

where $R(t, T)$ is a rectangular function of t, oscillating between -1 and 1 with period of T and η is a Gaussian noise with zero mean and standard deviation of 0.01.

In order to consider various situations, with and without presence of hidden relationships, we perform multiple experiments with different subset of the above signals.

Results and Discussion: Recovered graph for both methods in normal and abnormal condition are shown in Figure 4. In this figure, each row denotes an experiment involving a subset of synthetic time series, where white nodes represent the one with injected noise. As it is shown, in all cases the ARX + LFRX method has recovered the planted invariants and the recovered graph matches the ground truth. In both methods, in the presence of an anomaly, the invariants attached to the corrupted signal (white node) are broken. However, in some cases such as (a) and (b) where the ARX method cannot recover the existing relationships, at the time of anomaly, it was not able to detect it correctly. In figures (a) to (d), time series V_1 and V_2 are not measured and hence, time series V_3, V_4, and V_5 have indirect relationships. It is obvious from Fig. 4 that the proposed method (ARX + LFRX) is able to discover the corresponding invariants while ARX, with the same parameter settings, has failed to discover them.

5.2 Sensor Motes

Dataset Description: The sensor motes dataset contains measurements from wireless sensors at Intel Berkeley Research lab. There are a total of 54 sensors located at a lab measuring temperature, humidity, light, and voltage between February 28th and April 5th, 2004 [10]. Each sensor was able to record different variables every 31 seconds. Fig. 5 (a) shows the location of each node as well as different part of the lab.

Results and Discussion: Fig. 5 (b) shows the clustering of sensors in the loading matrix (i.e. Λ in Eq. 7) of light measurements. For this purpose, we used a k-means algorithm with $k = 6$. It is interesting to note that the sensors are clustered in a way that reflects their spatial distributions.

We performed invariant graph analysis on each variable (light, temperature, humidity, and voltage), separately. Overall results are illustrated at Table 1. It is obvious from this table that the proposed method results in lower average estimation error on test datasets, compared to the ARX approach. Also, the number of discovered invariants using the proposed method is higher than the one using ARX. This is due to the deployment of latent factors in LFRX method which is beneficial in anomaly detection. In fact, for the purpose of anomaly detection using invariant graphs, anomalies in vertices with a small number of edges cannot be discovered easily. One might think that by increasing the value of ϵ (in Eq. 4) at the time of invariant discovery, we can find larger number of invariants. However, by increasing ϵ, the estimation accuracy decreases dramatically which results in having false invariants. Table 1 shows that the proposed method discovers more invariants with higher accuracy.

Fig. 6 shows an invariant graph of temperature under the normal condition and in the presence of abnormalities. In this figure, direct and indirect invariants are illustrated by blue and red edges, respectively. Fig. 6 (a) shows the invariant graph under the normal condition with 183 edges where 140 of them are derived using LFRX. As we expected, geographic placement of sensors has an effect on the result. Fig. 6 (b) shows the invariant graph at the presence of anomalies. In this figure, the top ten sensors based on the ranking of Eq. 20 are highlighted with red circles. Larger circles represents higher rank of vertices. As this figure shows, variations of environmental temperature in the lab result in distortions in nearby sensors. As an example, sensors 12 to 17 are in the top ten ranking list. Sensors 16 and 37 are both among the highly ranked ones that are susceptible to be the source of anomaly. In Fig. 6(b), we can observe that the LFRX edge between these two vertices is broken. Fig. 7 depicts the corresponding time series of these two sensors. We can easily observe that these two time series have almost similar behavior and are expected to be system invariant. As this figure illustrates, the relationship between these sensors is broken at time $t = 1300$. Abnormal conditions are shown in darker colors.

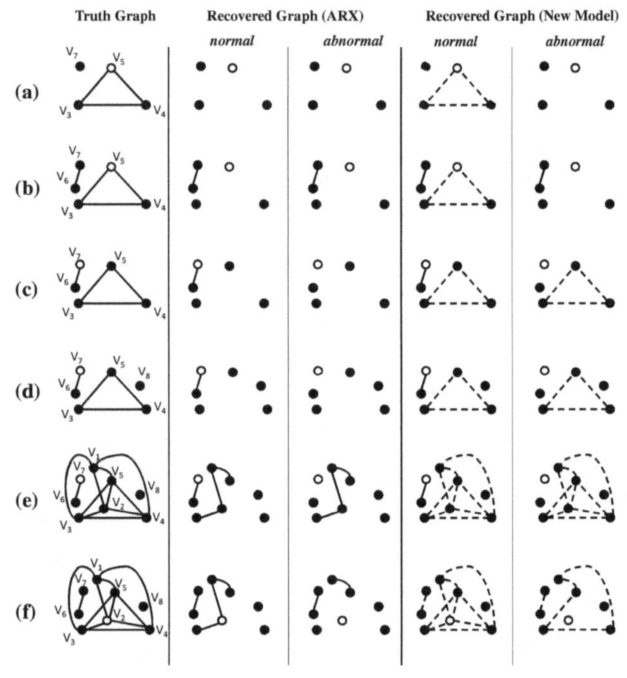

Figure 4: Invariant graphs discovered using ARX and the proposed method (ARX + LFRX) under normal and abnormal conditions. First column shows the ground truth. In the abnormal condition, an anomaly is injected into each graph at one variable (white node). Rows (a) to (f) shows different combinations of time series in Fig. 3. Direct invariants are shown in solid lines and indirect invariants are shown in dashed lines.

Table 1: Performance evaluation result of ARX and (ARX + LFRX) for the Sensor Motes dataset.

Metric	Avg. Error ARX+LFRX	Avg. Error ARX	Edges ARX+LFRX Total	Edges ARX+LFRX Latent	Edges ARX
Voltage	0.0056	0.0070	441	284	170
Temperature	0.3658	0.4971	183	43	145
Humidity	0.6262	0.8632	1142	866	764
Light	81.8377	93.1723	539	269	463

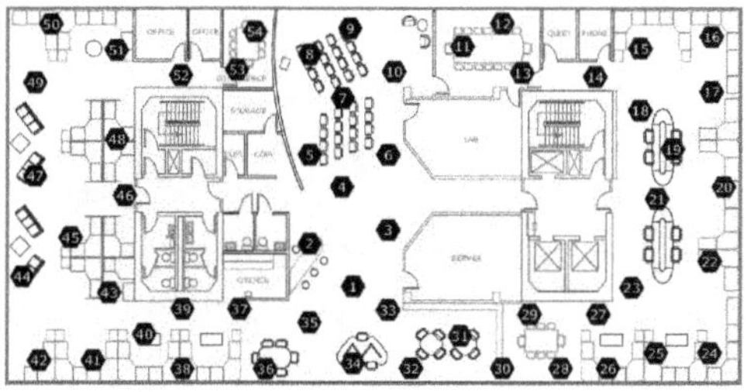

(a)

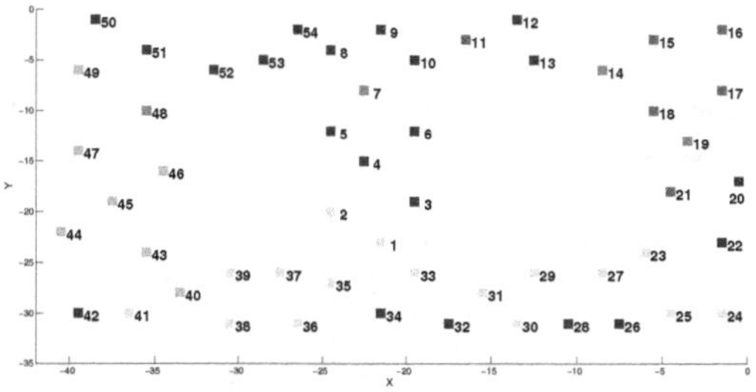

(b)

Figure 5: (a) Geographical location of wireless sensors (taken from [1]). (b) Clustering of sensors based on latent factors of light measurement indicating a high degree of spatial correlation.

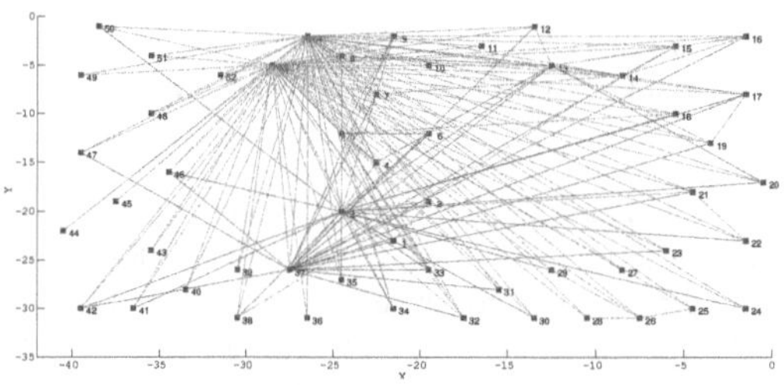

(a)

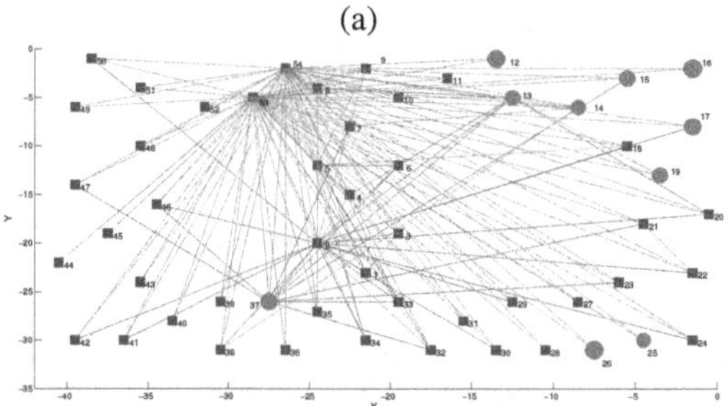

(b)

Figure 6: (a) Invariant graph of sensors based on temperature at normal condition (with 183 edges). ARX-based and LFRX-based invariants are shown with red and blue edges, respectively. (b) Invariant graph with broken edges in the presence of an anomaly (162 edges). Top ten sensors based on the ranking of Eq. 20 are shown with red circles.

5.3 Microgrid

Dataset Description: We performed our experiments on a microgrid system where several devices are operating in a distributed setting (Fig. 8). In this setting, the control unit tries to minimize the amount of energy based on various criteria and hence the microgrid shows a complex behavior in the logged measurements. This dataset which is provided by NEC labs contains logged data from multiple sources such as loads (primary, secondary), battery, PMU

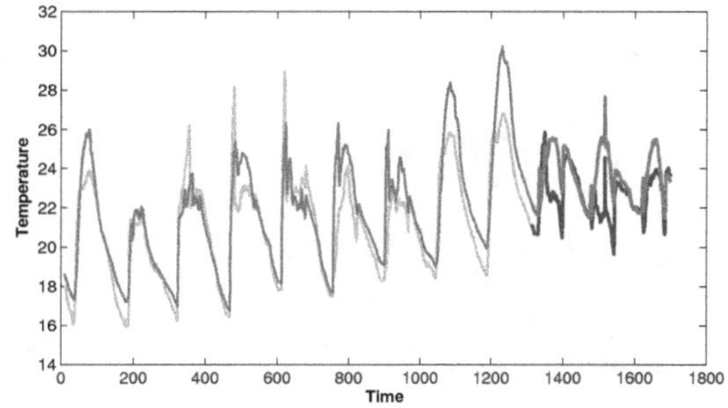

Figure 7: Temperature of sensors 16 (blue) and 37 (red). Outliers are shown in darker color.

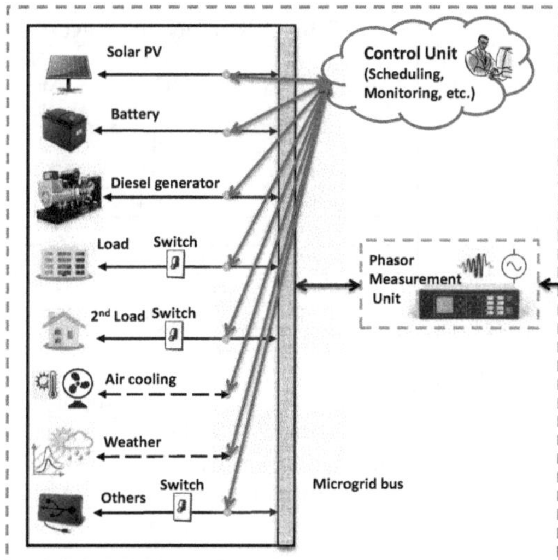

Figure 8: Schematic view of the NEC microgrid setup.

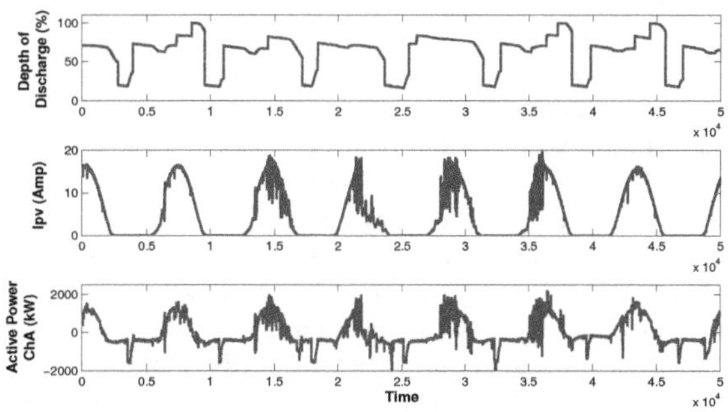

Figure 9: Three different time series of NEC microgrid dataset during one week.

(measurement unit outside of the microgrid), solar system (PV), weather (inside and outside parameters), and air cooling unit. There are total of 84 features measured from July 7th to August 7th, 2014. Due to the different sampling rates of each device, time series are re-sampled with a unique rate to be aligned to a specific window-time. Figure 9 shows a sample plot of three time series from different units during one week.

Results and Discussion: The invariant graph derived by our proposed method is represented in Fig. 10 (a). In this figure, each node represents one of the features and the set of features that belong to

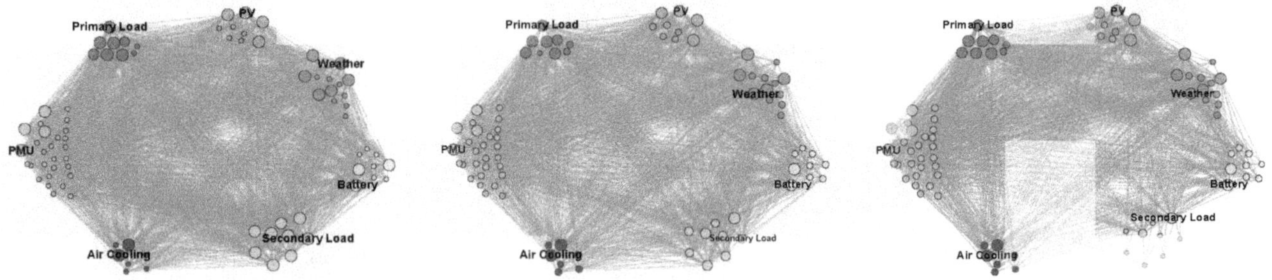

(a) (b) (c)

Figure 10: (a) Invariant graph of microgrid under normal condition (ARX + LFRX) (b) Outlier happens when an additional device is switched off/on in the system. (c) Outlier happens when the secondary load is disconnected.

Table 2: Performance evaluation result of ARX and (ARX + LFRX).

Device (No. of Signals)	Avg. Error (ARX + LFRX)	Avg. Error (ARX)	Intra-Device Edges (ARX + LFRX) Total	Intra-Device Edges (ARX + LFRX) Latent	Intra-Device Edges (ARX)	Inter-Device Edges (ARX + LFRX) Total	Inter-Device Edges (ARX + LFRX) Latent	Inter-Device Edges (ARX)
PMU (28)	0.0028	0.1346	102	73	102	810	265	755
PV (9)	0.0119	0.1146	26	5	26	187	63	175
Battery (9)	3.7×10^{-14}	0.2764	21	12	21	239	81	226
Primary LD (9)	2.2×10^{-4}	0.1460	35	22	29	235	66	236
Secondary LD (9)	2.3×10^{-6}	0.0434	36	0	36	53	19	52
Weather (13)	0	0.1342	57	17	57	260	94	244
Air Cooling (7)	0.2852	0.2903	11	5	11	213	75	203

a specific device are illustrated using the same color. Also, the size of each node is proportional to its degree. Furthermore, invariants derived by ARX and LFRX methods are shown by red and blue edges, respectively. The total number of invariants that ARX + LFRX discovered is 2285 where 797 of them are indirect and 1488 of them are direct invariants.

The average estimation errors of traditional ARX and the proposed method are compared in Table 2. As this table shows, the average error of the proposed method for each device is dramatically lower than the error resulted by ARX approach. This means that invariants are selected with higher accuracy using ARX + LFRX. Also, Table 2 compares the proposed method with ARX in terms of the number of invariants between devices (Inter-Device) and within each device (Intra-Device). Inter-Device edges are visualized in Fig. 11(a) where edge thickness represents the total number of invariants between devices. From this figure, we can observe the high complexity of inter-dependencies between measurements of devices. For example, energy produced by photovoltaics (PV) has effect on battery, PMU, loads, and the temperature of environment.

After occurrence of an abnormal behavior, the topology of the invariant graph changes (i.e., depending on the nature of anomaly, some edges are removed from the graph). By comparing consecutive graphs, one is able to detect outliers in the system. We detect changes in the invariant graph in two different situations: when an additional device is switched off/on and when secondary load is turned off. Results are shown in Fig. 10 (b) and (c), respectively. As we may observe from Fig. 10 (b), two edges connecting the secondary load to PMU and PV are broken. This is due to the change in the energy consumption behavior of the system. On the other hand, as Fig. 10 (c) depicts, a large number of invariants between secondary load and other devices are broken. This is due to the disconnection of the secondary load. It should be noted that measurements of the secondary load were among the top five anomalies returned by our outlier ranking method. Also, the number of remaining invariants between devices are shown in Fig. 11 (b) and (c).

Figure 12 shows some examples of anomalies in the microgrid system. Each figure shows a pair of time series that under normal condition are invariant. Abnormal conditions are shown in darker colors. The gap between occurrence of anomalies and normal time series depicts the time difference between them. As an example, Fig. 12 (a) shows the detection of sudden change in the red curve which is the State of Health (SOH) of the battery. This change is detected using the broken link between SOH and Reactive power in Channel C of the PMU. Detecting such anomalies is crucial for microgrid operators.

It should be noted that since we do not know the labeling of real dataset, we are unable to evaluate our method using precision and recall metrics. Nevertheless, we calculated precision and recall under different scenarios. As an example, when 10 nodes have random injected noise, by looking at the top 10 ranked results, precision and recall were equal. This value is 0.51 for the ARX method, whereas for ARX + LFRX, it is 0.68.

6. RELATED WORK

Smart Grid and Power System Analytics: Power grids comprise a large number of elements and processes that are highly dynamic and complex. Traditionally power system operational studies are primarily based on a quasi-steady-state assumption, with static and explicit models that largely ignores dynamic characteristics of loads and control devices. The classic weighted least square (WLS) estimator, combined with methods such as largest normalized residual test and hypothesis testing identification, is extensively used for system diagnosis and outlier identification [2]. Recent developments in smart grids have revealed to us insight into stochastic operating behaviors and dynamics that we were never able to observe before. In particular, the widespread deployment of smart meters, renewable generation, smart load controls, energy storage, and plug-in hybrid vehicles will require fundamental

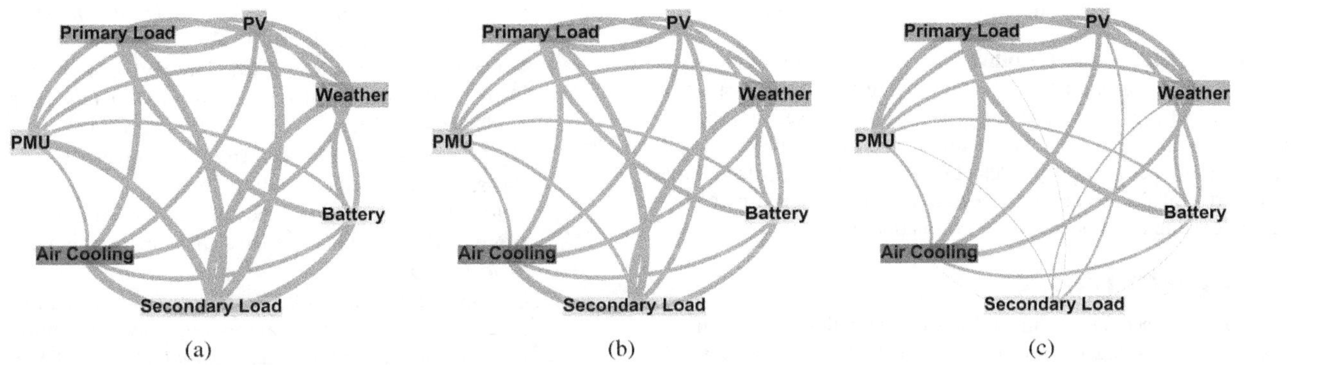

Figure 11: (a) Invariant graph of inter-devices of microgrid (ARX + LFRX) (b) Outlier happens when additional device is switched off/on in the system (c) Outlier happens when secondary load is disconnected.

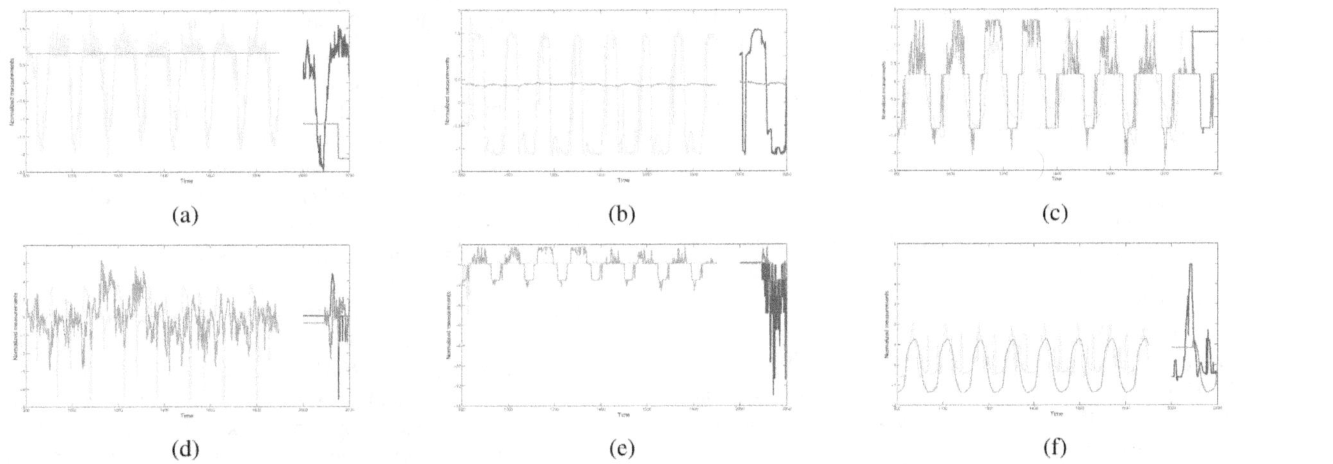

Figure 12: Invariant time series at normal and abnormal conditions: (a) Reactive power Channel C vs. State of Health of Battery (b) Power factor vs. Voltage of channel A in PMU (c) Outside temperature vs. Power Factor of primary load (d) Battery Current vs. Inverter output voltage (e) Peak voltage of secondary load vs. Power factor (f) Current magnitude of Channel A vs. Peak power of primary load.

changes in the operational concepts and principal components of the grid, in order to achieve real-time operation and control.

Fraud detection and particularly detection of energy theft is one of most important concerns in the smart grid [18, 22]. Data analytic methods can play an important role in identifying abnormal consumption trends and possible malicious activities in such systems. Daisuke et al. [22] used ARMA and LOF methods in an adversarial environment to detect attacks in data collected using advanced meter infrastructure (AMI). Rong et al. [18] compared classification-based, state-based, and game theory-based methods in energy-theft detection schemas.

One area that has witnessed significant developments is in the use of phasor measurement units (PMUs). Chen et al. [7] use PCA for online monitoring of PMU data for the purpose of early event detection. Khan et al. [20] proposed a parallel fluctuation approach using MapReduce techniques. At the lower level, Momtazpour et al. [23] proposed an integrated data-driven framework to study the behavior of battery systems in microgrids using clustering, regression, and spectral clustering of time series for the purposes of high level characterization of usage behavior and online parameter estimation.

Invariant Discovery and Structure Learning: Sharma et al. [27] used ARX for invariant discovery in distributed systems and discussed the challenges in fault localization for data centers. Shan et al. [26] have extracted overlay invariants based on pairwise invariant networks for fault detection and capacity planning in distributed systems. Due to the time complexity of invariant discovery of large scale systems, Ge et al. [13] developed an effective pruning techniques based on the identified upper bounds. In some applications, the existence of anomalies in invariant graphs yields many broken links which makes it difficult for a system expert to manually inspect each broken link. Hence, Ge et al. in [12] proposed two different methods of ranking metrics according to the anomaly levels occurring in invariant networks.

In a closely related area, viz. causal modeling of time-series data, Arnold et al. [4] used the concept of Granger causality to infer the structure of the causal network given set of time series. These authors compared performance of the exhaustive Granger method and a Lasso-Granger method with benchmark methods including the VAR and SIN methods. However, in [4], the main goal was to construct causal graphs instead of addressing data with correlated variables. Subsequently, Liu et al. [21] used a hidden Markov random field regression framework to infer temporal causal structures.

Cheng et al. [8] use time order relationships to capture temporal dependence structures underlying multivariate time series.

Anomaly Detection in Graphs: Akoglu et al. [3] provide an extensive survey of anomaly detection methods in graphs spanning different settings: unsupervised, (semi-) supervised approaches, static, dynamic, attributed, and plain graphs. In dependency graphs, for the purpose of anomaly detection, Ide et al. [15] used sparse structure learning to compute correlation anomaly scores of each variable using neighborhood selection approaches.

7. CONCLUSION

Invariant discovery is an exciting research field which aims to discover underlying relationships in cyber-physical systems. We used latent factor regression analysis and combined it with the ARX model (ARX + LFRX) to recover underlying direct and indirect relationships. These invariants are helpful in decision making and monitoring processes such as outlier detection. We tested our models on several datasets and results showed that with the help of latent factors, the accuracy of discovered invariants was higher than traditional methods. Investigating other topologies involving latent variables (such as a mesh network) and heuristic search algorithms to reduce the computational complexity are some of the directions for future research.

8. REFERENCES

[1] Intel Lab Data. `http://select.cs.cmu.edu/data/labapp3/index.html`, 2008. [Online; accessed 03-June-2015].

[2] A. Abur and A. G. Exposito. *Power system state estimation: Theory and implementation*. Marcel Dekker, 2004.

[3] L. Akoglu, H. Tong, and D. Koutra. Graph-based anomaly detection and description: A survey. *Data Min. and Knowl. Disc.*, 28(4), 2014.

[4] A. Arnold, Y. Liu, and N. Abe. Temporal causal modeling with graphical granger methods. In *Proc of KDD'07*, pages 66–75. ACM, 2007.

[5] H. Chen et al. Exploiting local and global invariants for the management of large scale information systems. In *Proc ICDM'08*, pages 113–122, 2008.

[6] H. Chen, G. Jiang, K. Yoshihira, and A. Saxena. Invariants based failure diagnosis in distributed computing systems. In *Proc. IEEE Symp on Reliable Distributed Systems*, pages 160–166, 2010.

[7] Y. Chen, L. Xie, and P. Kumar. Dimensionality reduction and early event detection using online synchrophasor data. In *Power and Energy Society General Meeting (PES), 2013 IEEE*, pages 1–5, July 2013.

[8] D. Cheng, M. T. Bahadori, and Y. Liu. Fblg: A simple and effective approach for temporal dependence discovery from time series data. In *Proc KDD'14*, pages 382–391, 2014.

[9] J. C. F. De Winter and D. Dodou. Common factor analysis versus principal component analysis: a comparison of loadings by means of simulations. *Communications in Statistics - Simulation and Computation*, June 2014.

[10] A. Deshpande, C. Guestrin, S. Madden, J. Hellerstein, and W. Hong. Model-driven data acquisition in sensor networks. In *Proc. Int Conf on VLDB*, 2004.

[11] M. Ding, H. Chen, A. Sharma, K. Yoshihira, and G. Jiang. A data analytic engine towards self-management of cyber-physical systems. In *Proc IEEE ICDCSW'13*, pages 303-308, 2013.

[12] Y. Ge, G. Jiang, M. Ding, and H. Xiong. Ranking metric anomaly in invariant networks. *ACM Trans. Knowl. Discov. Data*, 8(2):8:1–8:30, June 2014.

[13] Y. Ge, G. Jiang, and Y. Ge. Efficient invariant search for distributed information systems. In *Proc. ICDM'13*, pages 1049–1054, 2013.

[14] H. Harman. *Modern Factor Analysis*. University of Chicago Press, Chicago, 3rd ed. edition, 1976.

[15] T. Ide, A. C. Lozano, N. Abe, and Y. Liu. Proximity-based anomaly detection using sparse structure learning. In *Proc SDM'09*, 2009.

[16] G. Jiang, H. Chen, and K. Yoshihira. Discovering likely invariants of distributed transaction systems for autonomic system management. *Cluster Computing*, 9(4):385–399, Oct. 2006.

[17] G. Jiang, H. Chen, and K. Yoshihira. Efficient and scalable algorithms for inferring likely invariants in distributed systems. *IEEE Trans. on Knowl. and Data Eng.*, 19(11):1508–1523, Nov. 2007.

[18] R. Jiang, R. Lu, Y. Wang, J. Luo, C. Shen, and X. S. Shen. Energy-theft detection issues for advanced metering infrastructure in smart grid. *Tsinghua Science and Technology*, 19(2):105–120, April 2014.

[19] K. Joreskog. Some contributions to maximum likelihood factor analysis. *Psychometrika*, 38(2):183–202, 1967.

[20] M. Khan, M. Li, P. Ashton, G. Taylor, and J. Liu. Big data analytics on pmu measurements. In *Proc Int Conf on FSKD'14*, pages 715–719, Aug 2014.

[21] Y. Liu, A. Niculescu-mizil, A. C. Lozano, and Y. Lu. Learning temporal causal graphs for relational time-series analysis. In *Proc ICML'10*, pages 687–694, 2010.

[22] D. Mashima and A. A. Cardenas. Evaluating electricity theft detectors in smart grid networks. In *Research in Attacks, Intrusions, and Defenses*, volume 7462 of *Lecture Notes in Computer Science*, pages 210–229. 2012.

[23] M. Momtazpour, R. Sharma, and N. Ramakrishnan. An integrated data mining framework for analysis and prediction of battery characteristics. In *Proc IEEE ISGT Asia'14*, pages 774–779, 2014.

[24] K. J. Preacher, G. Zhang, C. Kim, and G. Mels. Choosing the optimal number of factors in exploratory factor analysis: A model selection perspective. *Multivariate Behavioral Research*, 48:28–56, 2013.

[25] I. Shafer, K. Ren, V. N. Boddeti, Y. Abe, G. R. Ganger, and C. Faloutsos. Rainmon: An integrated approach to mining bursty timeseries monitoring data. In *Proc KDD'12*, pages 1158–1166, 2012.

[26] H. Shan, G. Jiang, and K. Yoshihira. Extracting overlay invariants of distributed systems for autonomic system management. In *Proc IEEE Int Conf on Self-Adaptive and Self-Organizing Systems*, pages 41–50, 2010.

[27] A. Sharma, H. Chen, M. Ding, K. Yoshihira, and G. Jiang. Fault detection and localization in distributed systems using invariant relationships. In *Proc IEEE Int Conf on DSN'13*, pages 1–8, 2013.

[28] A. B. Sharma, F. Ivancic, A. Niculescu-Mizil, H. Chen, and G. Jiang. Modeling and analytics for cyber-physical systems in the age of big data. *SIGMETRICS Perform. Eval. Rev.*, 41(4):74–77, Apr. 2014.

[29] D. Suhr. Principal component analysis vs. exploratory factor analysis. In *Proceedings of SUGI 30*, pages 203–30, 2005.

Predicting Future Scientific Discoveries Based on a Networked Analysis of the Past Literature

Meena Nagarajan[*,1], Angela D. Wilkins[*,3], Benjamin J. Bachman[*,3], Ilya B. Novikov[3], Shenghua Bao[1], Peter J. Haas[1], María E. Terrón-Díaz[3], Sumit Bhatia[1], Anbu K. Adikesavan[3], Jacques J. Labrie[1], Sam Regenbogen[3], Christie M. Buchovecky[3], Curtis R. Pickering[2], Linda Kato[1], Andreas M. Lisewski[3], Ana Lelescu[1], Houyin Zhang[3], Stephen Boyer[1], Griff Weber[1], Ying Chen[1], Lawrence Donehower[3], Scott Spangler[1*], Olivier Lichtarge[3*]

[1]IBM Almaden Research
San Jose, California

[2]The University of Texas MD
Anderson Cancer Center
Houston, Texas

[3]Baylor College of Medicine
Houston, Texas

ABSTRACT

We present KnIT, the Knowledge Integration Toolkit, a system for accelerating scientific discovery and predicting previously unknown protein–protein interactions. Such predictions enrich biological research and are pertinent to drug discovery and the understanding of disease. Unlike a prior study, KnIT is now fully automated and demonstrably scalable. It extracts information from the scientific literature, automatically identifying direct and indirect references to protein interactions, which is knowledge that can be represented in network form. It then reasons over this network with techniques such as matrix factorization and graph diffusion to predict new, previously unknown interactions. The accuracy and scope of KnIT's knowledge extractions are validated using comparisons to structured, manually curated data sources as well as by performing retrospective studies that predict subsequent literature discoveries using literature available prior to a given date. The KnIT methodology is a step towards automated hypothesis generation from text, with potential application to other scientific domains.

Categories and Subject Descriptors

I.2.6 [**Learning**]: Concept Learning and Knowledge Acquisition

General Terms

Algorithms, Experimentation.

Keywords

Text Mining, Scientific Discovery, Hypothesis Generation.

*These authors contributed equally

KDD '15, August 11-14, 2015, Sydney, NSW, Australia
ACM 978-1-4503-3664-2/15/08.
http://dx.doi.org/10.1145/2783258.2788609

1. INTRODUCTION

Broadening the scientific framework for biological hypothesis generation requires collecting, understanding, and integrating diverse facts. Even many specialized topic areas are becoming too dense to be thoroughly studied and understood by the most well-read experts. For instance, the literature on p53, a single protein with a critical role as a master switch to fight cancer, now exceeds 75,000 published papers. Each one of these papers has observations that may support, contradict or contextualize observations from others. The size, complexity, and growth rate of the literature are even greater for multi-component subjects, such as diseases — the breast cancer literature, for example, now encompasses over 300,000 scientific articles in Medline.

Because biological hypotheses necessarily depend on the limited data, from literature or otherwise, that a single person can read and understand, the challenge in a field with as rich a literature as biology is how to harness the full depth and breadth of the knowledge that already exists in publications so as to formulate logically the best hypotheses consistent with the totality of the data. To do so, we aim: to convert unstructured data sources to structured data via natural language parsing; to represent that knowledge as a network of biological entities; and finally to reason over the resulting graph to identify novel, interesting, and testable hypotheses. Although the literature contains errors and machine translation of text will be incomplete and lack the depth of interpretation that scientists develop over a career, a central hypothesis of this work is that by focusing on only the highest confidence predictions it will be possible to reliably make inferences that lead to new discoveries when tested.

Baylor College of Medicine and IBM Research are engaged in a long-term partnership to create the necessary infrastructure, software, and algorithms to improve scientific discovery in this way. We have focused first on protein-protein interactions (PPIs), which have potential applications in drug discovery and understanding of disease. Our initial, proof-of-principle efforts[45] indicated that new p53 kinases could be predicted using a simple bag-of-words feature space representation combined with a graph diffusion reasoning technique based on labels *manually* curated by experts. In the current paper, we present a more complete, scalable, and general instantiation of the Knowledge Integration Toolkit (**KnIT**) for fully automated discovery.

In what follows, we describe how KnIT discovers PPIs in unstructured documents and then reasons over those interactions to generate hypotheses. The discovery phase comprises extraction and normalization of protein entities followed by extraction of PPIs. The latter task is accomplished by combining a catalog of curated relationship types with rule-based and machine-learning approaches to extract meaningful and accurate PPI triples from parsed text. In the reasoning phase, KnIT can deploy various graph algorithms on protein-network representations to predict new interactions.

We also describe several experiments designed to test KnIT's capabilities. In a time-stamped "retrospective" experiment, we validate predictions based on the literature up to a given date against actual subsequent discoveries. We then show that the discovered triples represent a substantial fraction of known protein-protein interactions, documented in the literature and elsewhere. Finally, we revisit our prior study[45] on phosphorylation of the protein p53 and show how the current version of KnIT avoids the need for manual curation of abstracts and thus can scale to large scientific corpora; in particular, we extend our earlier work to study phosphorylation of *any* protein.

Overall, KnIT embodies an integrated computational approach to formulating novel scientific hypotheses that accelerate laboratory discoveries. KnIT is applicable to practically any industry or domain that is faced with overwhelming data and stagnation in innovation. Information extraction and reasoning components of KnIT are built into Watson Discovery Advisor, an IBM product that aims to accelerate breakthroughs by making connections between different pieces of information. In this work we choose biology as our test bed to demonstrate the capabilities of KnIT.

2. THE HUMAN INTERACTOME

Proteins are the fundamental molecular machinery in the cell, and identifying their functions is a central problem in molecular biology. With $\approx$ 20,000 distinct proteins in humans[24], and tens of thousands of possible biological process annotations, disease associations, and molecular interactions, the number of experiments that would be required to verify every possible function for every protein is well beyond the capabilities of molecular biology experiments for the foreseeable future.

For example, an important characteristic of any protein is the set of other proteins with which it interacts; there are almost 200,000,000 protein pairs to investigate. To further complicate the issue, the types of relationships that can occur between any two proteins vary widely. To name a few, two proteins may have: a *binding* interaction, in which the two physically interact with each other to carry out a task within the cell; a *positive regulatory* interaction, in which the activity of one protein in the cell increases the amount or activity of another protein; a *negative regulatory* interaction, in which the activity of one protein in the cell decreases the amount or activity of another protein; a *modification* interaction (e.g. phosphorylation or ubiquitination), in which one protein causes a chemical change to the structure, and therefore function, of another protein; an *expression* relationship, in which the quantities of two proteins are frequently observed to be highly correlated or anti-correlated with one another; or a *co-localization* interaction, in which the two proteins are often found physically near each other, but not necessarily touching, in the cell. This type of information is often represented as a multimodal graph of relationships between proteins[21], for example StringDB[13]. Such graphs form a partial representation of the human *interactome*, i.e., the totality of protein interactions in humans.

Knowledge about some of these interaction types is already accessible in a structured data format. For example, expression relationships often come from published microarray data, which measure the levels of thousands of messenger RNAs (each encoding a distinct protein) in specific cells or tissues. Many examples of this type of data are available from the GEO database[2]. Binding interactions can also be identified by large-scale screens; however, these expensive experiments are known to have significant false negative and false positive rates[12]. They too, are documented in a slew of databases[5; 6; 15; 16; 27; 55; 56]. However, combined, these databases contain around 100,000 likely binding interactions, only 10,000 of which are considered to be high quality[13], whereas the total number of binding interactions occurring in the human interactome has been estimated[47] to be as high as 600,000, leaving as many as half a million to be discovered. Other structured data result from human reading of the biomedical literature and manual input into databases, such as the PhosphoSitePlus[23] database of protein modification interactions; this approach requires intensive labor to keep up with the latest developments in the scientific community. In summary, some protein relationship information is accessible, but the quality, coverage, and cost of acquisition of this information must be improved.

Natural language processing is a useful tool for the extraction of human interactome data from the biomedical literature. Early text

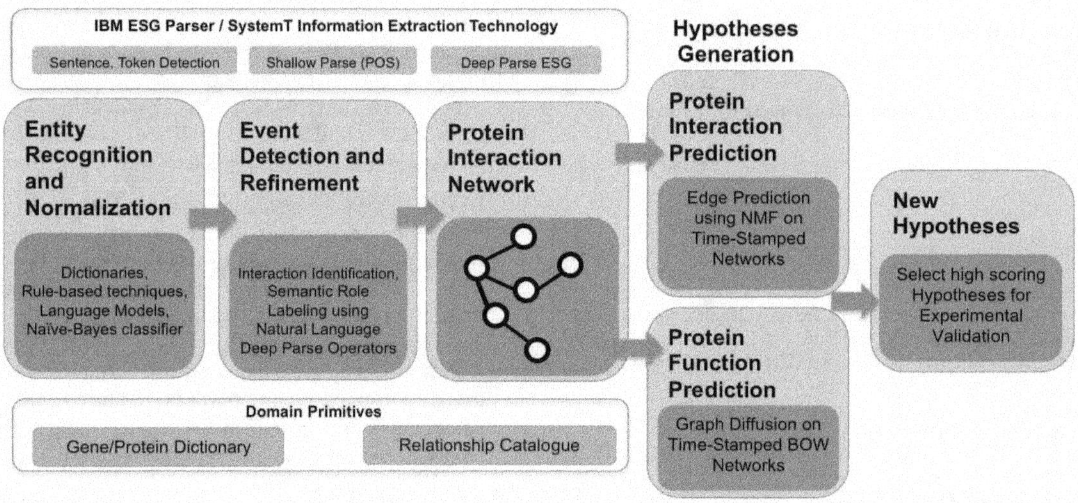

Figure 1 KnIT Extraction and Discovery Pipeline

mining mostly entailed identification of entity co-occurrence within publication text. In recent years, co-occurrence has served as a benchmark for comparison with more sophisticated approaches, but is also still used in many database efforts[13]. Some of the early impactful efforts were iHOP[22] and GeneWays[43]. A recent effort has read the available literature (both abstracts and open access articles) and made their analysis available in the EVEX database[52]. Another effort by Microsoft called Literome[40] allows the user to search genes for possible relationships, and it suggests possible intermediate interactions found in the literature. Although these efforts help inform the scientific community, none have taken the next step in proposing new scientific hypotheses.

As the continuously dropping prices of DNA and RNA sequencing bring personalized genomics closer to reality, we gain vast amounts of raw data on the variations between individuals. However, there remains the challenge of contextualizing these variations in order to understand the source of patient symptoms arising from genetic disease, and to potentially predict mutation effects before they are known to cause a disorder. To help do this, we aim to better understand the human genome by documenting – and generating hypotheses upon – the interactome as described by biomedical scientists across tens of millions of published abstracts.

3. PROTEIN-NETWORK EXTRACTION

Biomedical relationship extraction is a well-studied problem[28; 38]. To identify connections between entities such as proteins, drugs and diseases, rule-based or machine-learning-based approaches[9; 49] typically use a knowledge base that catalogs known interactions, such as MetaMap[1] or GeneOntology,[15; 16] together with a text mining approach. Relationships have been mined using co-occurrence techniques in which two entities in a network are linked simply because they are mentioned within the same sentence[25]. Methods based on clustering similar text have also been used to generate networks between entities[4; 42]. In recent times, syntactic parsing of sentences to identify relationships between entities has also gained popularity[14; 37].

KnIT PPI extraction is guided by a catalog of known biological interaction types and relies on natural language parsing of sentences to establish explicit, directional relationships between known entities. Importantly, KnIT identifies not only direct connections between two proteins, but also *indirect* relationships where there is a secondary interaction or biological process at play. As a result, KnIT protein networks are more expressive and better at predicting heretofore unknown PPIs. KnIT relies on a rule-based approach for learning syntactic relations between known entities and known interactions in a labeled dataset. Learned rules are then applied to a Medline corpus for extraction of PPIs.

The KnIT extraction engine is built using IBM InfoSphere® BigInsights™ SystemT[30] – a powerful information extraction system for extracting structured information from unstructured and semi-structured text. SystemT provides us with basic text analytic capabilities such as sentence splitting, token detection, natural language parse of sentences, and so on. Deep-parsing components of SystemT are derived from an English Slot Grammar (ESG) parser[36] that provides core linguistic analysis.

In this section, we will describe the individual components that are central to KnIT PPI Extraction: (1) entity identification and normalization and (2) event recognition and normalization. (An *event* refers to a particular protein-protein interaction mentioned in the text, such as "Plk1 inhibits RSK1".) Figure 1 presents a detailed pipeline of tasks in KnIT PPI extraction.

3.1 Entity Identification and Normalization

Both rule-based[48] and machine-learning-based[20] approaches have been used for protein extraction and normalization. Recent work has also integrated simple rules with machine learning models. For example, Danger et al., integrate a dictionary look-up and a conditional-random-field classifier for recognizing pertinent entity types in protein-protein interaction contexts[10].

KnIT needs to ignore mentions of generic protein families, such as "Histone", and instead focus on mentions of specific proteins such as "Histone H3". This task can be very challenging. For example, given a mention such as "GRK-1,3 and 5 have strong impact", KnIT needs to extract not only GRK-1, but also GRK-3 and GRK-5. Moreover, KnIT needs to normalize proteins to their canonical forms; a key challenge here is that proteins often share synonyms or abbreviations. Thus KnIT must understand mentions of proteins according to their context and map them to standardized identifiers. To this end, KnIT uses a hybrid model for protein extraction and normalization. The protein annotation process involves three steps: candidate generation, candidate selection, and protein normalization.

3.1.1 Protein Candidate Generation

To ensure high recall for the protein extraction task, KnIT relies upon a comprehensive dictionary of human proteins compiled from NCBI[2; 54], the UniProt KnowledgeBase[51], HUGO[17], and CTD[11]. This dictionary has 340,000 entries, where each entry is mapped to one of over 30,000 protein canonical forms. When generating candidates, KnIT employs a combination of dictionary-matching, pattern-matching, and abbreviation-matching rules to maximize recall while maintaining sufficient precision.

Dictionary-matching rules: Because it is infeasible for a dictionary to capture all possible protein synonyms used in the literature, KnIT supports fuzzy matching of dictionary terms:

- Greek letters matches, e.g., "beta(2)-microglobulin" matches "β(2)-microglobulin";
- Bracket independent matches, e.g., "β(2)-microglobulin" matches "β2-microglobulin";
- Space/Hyphen independent matches, e.g., "β2-microglobulin" matches "β2 microglobulin" and "β2microglobulin".

KnIT also accounts for the different levels of ambiguity in the dictionary terms. During dictionary compilation, each dictionary term is semi-automatically categorized into one of three categories: unambiguous terms like "G protein-coupled receptor kinase 2", ambiguous terms like "ATM", and very risky terms like "C1" and "C2". Terms are categorized according to their length and character complexity; the current dictionary contains roughly 316K, 25K, and 1K terms in each category. Each mention that matches some dictionary term is assigned a confidence score of "high", "medium", or "low", depending on the category of the term. Mentions with a confidence score of medium or low are further verified using the context-based protein classifier described in Section 3.1.2 below.

Pattern-matching rules: Typically, some legitimate proteins do not appear in the dictionary at all, e.g., because researchers may not follow naming conventions or because some exploratory entity names are too new to be added to a dictionary. KnIT therefore enriches protein candidate generation using two types of patterns:

- Entities that contain both upper letters and digits with indicative words like "gene" or "protein" in the context.
- Entities comprising a known protein-family identifier followed by specific IDs, e.g., "BRCA-1, 2, and 3" or "Hemoglobin alpha, beta and gamma".

Abbreviation-matching rules: Abbreviations of proteins are commonly used in the literature. Frequently, the abbreviation itself is either ambiguous or does not appear in the dictionary at all. KnIT therefore detects all definition-abbreviation pairs in an abstract and then maps all mentions of an abbreviation in the abstract to its corresponding definition. For example, if the defining text "Stearoyl-CoA Desaturase (SCD)" appears in an abstract and "Stearoyl-CoA Desaturase" is identified as a protein using the dictionary, then all subsequent appearances of SCD are identified as "Stearoyl-CoA Desaturase" automatically. In this manner, all ad hoc abbreviations whose definitions are in the dictionary are correctly identified and disambiguated.

3.1.2 Protein Candidate Selection

Often, the candidate-generation process identifies entities that are false positives, i.e., they are not proteins. For example, SCD is both an abbreviation for "Stearoyl-CoA Desaturase" and an acronym for "Sickle Cell Disease". Eliminating false-positive candidates is a challenging but important task. Intuitively, the context of a mention that refers to a protein should be very different than the context of the mention when it does not refer to a protein. For example, when proteins are mentioned in literature, the surrounding text often discusses protein-specific biological processes such as regulation or phosphorylation. It may also mention other protein names, or explicitly refer to the entity as a protein. In order to exploit the cues in the surrounding context, we trained a naïve Bayes classifier that uses features derived from the neighboring context of a putative protein mention. KnIT uses the sentence containing the discovered mention as the context span and computes the following features:

- All words present to the left and right of the mention;
- The number of protein mentions in the sentence;
- Whether or not the two immediate words to the left and right of the discovered mention are protein names.

Words appearing in the left context and right context are treated separately. To evaluate the classifier, we used a dataset of 2282 positive examples and 2209 negative examples from BioNLP-ST 2013 tasks for event extraction and pathway curation; we used two-thirds of the data for training and tested on the remaining one-third. Our approach achieved an overall classification accuracy of 77.2%.

3.1.3 Entity Normalization

Researchers commonly refer to proteins by different synonyms or aliases, and KnIT must be able to deal with this phenomenon. Mapping a mention back to the correct canonical protein is a hard problem because different proteins often share the same synonym. For example, synonym "D1" maps back to both the Dopamine Receptor D1 (DRD1) and Leiomoden 1 (LMOD1). Whenever KnIT identifies D1 as a protein mention, it also needs to decide precisely which protein is being referenced. Fortunately, the *context* of a protein mention (i.e., the surrounding words) typically contains sufficient clues to identify the correct canonical protein, allowing disambiguation. For example, a mention of "dopamine" or the family name "GPCR" in the abstract would indicate that the abstract was discussing Dopamine Receptor D1 (DRD1).

KnIT adopts the idea of unigram language models from computational linguistics[35] and builds "context models" for proteins. For a protein g and an abstract d, denote by $S_{g,d}$ the set of sentences in d that reference g. The *context* $C_g(s,d)$ of a protein g in a sentence $s \in S_{g,d}$ is the multiset of terms that occur in s. The *context model* P_g of a protein g is defined as a probability distribution over the terms appearing in the protein's context. In order to estimate this distribution, we query all the abstracts in Medline corpus with the canonical name of the protein and select the set D_g of the 100 most relevant abstracts as ranked by TF-IDF score. We then define the combined context for g as $\tilde{C}_g = \bigcup_{d \in D_g} \bigcup_{s \in S_{g,d}} C_g(s,d)$ and the combined context for the corpus as $\tilde{C} = \bigcup_g \tilde{C}_g$; here we take multiset unions, with the latter union being over all proteins in the corpus. Let $V = \{v_1, v_1, \ldots, v_n\}$ be the vocabulary of all terms in the corpus. Then the probability of observing a term v in the context of protein g is defined as:

$$P_g(v) = \frac{(\text{cardinality of } v \text{ in } \tilde{C}_g) + 1}{(\text{cardinality of } v \text{ in } \tilde{C}) + n}$$

The additive factors in the numerator and denominator are used to smooth the probability distribution so that terms not present in $\tilde{C}_g$ are assigned a non-zero probability. We extend this definition to encompass the likelihood of seeing a given context C (i.e., a given multiset of terms) around g by setting $P_g(C) = \prod_{v \in C} P_g(v)$; i.e., we make a simplifying independence assumption *a la* naïve Bayes. Note that if a term v appears k times in the multiset C, then the foregoing product contains k terms equal to $P_g(v)$.

Whenever KnIT encounters an ambiguous protein mention, it uses the context models to identify the most likely canonical protein in a manner similar to query likelihood models in information retrieval[34]. That is, given an ambiguous mention M, its context C_M, and the set G of possible proteins referred to by M, KnIT determines the canonical protein g^* to maximize the likelihood of the context: $g^* = \text{argmax}_g P_g(C_M)$.

3.2 Event Extraction and Normalization

To extract interaction events, KnIT uses a catalog of PPI types together with natural language parsing of sentences. The catalog is maintained as a list structure similar to that used in the BioNLP 2013 pathway extraction task. The goal of extraction is to obtain triples, each comprising:

1. An *event*: an element appearing in the catalog of interactions described in Section 3.2.1 below.
2. An *agent*: a protein that is causally active in an event.
3. A *theme*: a protein that undergoes the effects of an interaction.

In general, depending on the interaction, extracted triples may or may not possess directionality. Binding relationships, for instance, do not represent directional events, whereas phosphorylation is an example of an interaction that has a clear causal agent and affected theme.

Collect verbs and annotate relationship type

Phosphorylation at Ser-15 may be a critical event in the up-regulation and functional activation of p53 during cellular stress.

up-regulation : Positive Regulation

Overexpression of catalytically inactive **ATR** (ATRki) in human fibroblasts in Ser-15 phosphorylation in response to γ-irradiation and UV light. -damaged

overexpression : Gene Expression

Identify events:

Sentence Labeled for PPI : ATR phosphorylated p53 at Ser-15 and Ser-37 in v suggesting that **p53 is a target for** phosphorylation **by** ATR in DNA-damaged

Event 1 : Agent : ATR Event: Phosphorylated Theme: p53

Event 2 : Agent : ATR Event: Phosphorylation Theme: p53

Figure 2 Curating Process Examples

Catalogue of KnIT Relationship Types

- **Post-translational Modifications**: phosphorylation, dephosphorylation, acetylation, methylation, sumoylation, oxidation, ubiquitylation, etc.
- **Regulation** (no clear sign): regulate, mediate, modulate, control, change, influence, etc.
- **Positive regulation** (implies increase): activate, upregulate, induce, cause, trigger, etc.
- **Negative regulation** (implies decrease): inactivate, inhibit, suppress, downregulate, etc.
- **Gene Expression**: Expression, Translation, Transcription, etc.
- **Localization**: shuttles, transport, accumulate, colocalizes, localize, etc.
- **Binding**: bind, bound, assemble, polymerize, directly interact, etc.
- **Protein dissociation**: depolymerize, dissasemble, etc.
- **Protein degradation**: degradation, degrade, proteolysis, etc.

Figure 3 Relationship Types and Synonyms

KnIT extracts two kinds of triples that capture interactions between proteins – direct and indirect. The first is a simple triple where there is a direct relationship between known entities. The two sentences below express direct relationships between known entities Plk1 and RSK1, and between p53 and Notch1.

In addition, studies on HeLa cells using Plk1 siRNA interference and overexpression showed that phosphorylation of RSK1 increased upon interference and decreased after overexpression, suggesting that Plk1 inhibits RSK1.

These data indicate that p53 negatively regulates Notch1 activation during T cell development.

In addition, KnIT also extracts relationships when the proteins are involved in more complex and indirect interactions. In the examples below we see that KnIT extracts relationships between bcl-2 and p53 that are indirect, since different processes (shown as underlined text) are involved in their interaction.

Silencing of Bcl-2 induced massive p53-dependent apoptosis.

Our data suggests that bcl-2 is able to modulate transmembrane trafficking of p53.

3.2.1 Building the KnIT Relationship Catalog

The KnIT relationship catalog lists many types of protein-protein interaction types (some described in Section 2) that were curated using multiple data sources. Post-translational modification (PTM) interactions were extracted from the Gene Ontology[15; 16], a hierarchy developed to represent functional knowledge for proteins. A second set of relationships (binding, expression, etc.) is adapted from previous studies[41] and community tasks[28; 38]. Finally, we included our curated interactions from the training data described in Section 3.2.2 below.

The curated relationship types and their synonyms were considered valid if confirmed in multiple abstracts in PubMed. We also identified and explicitly added variants of an interaction instead of relying on stems, because we found that several verbs can be ambiguous in their stemmed forms. For example, the stem *sulfat* for the PTM sulfation will also match sulfate or sulfates to indicate the presence of chemical compounds. Finally, the interactions in the list were grouped into nine categories; each category name served as the canonical reference term for its associated set of interactions. Figure 3 shows the categories, along with some sample interactions for each; the current KnIT relationship hierarchy contains 71 interactions in total over all categories.

3.2.2 Training data for Event Detection

In order to learn how PPIs are presented in literature, the subject matter experts (SMEs) on the team labeled abstracts containing PTM interactions. Abstracts were collected using a PTM query "phosphorylate". To ensure that the abstracts also mentioned at least one protein, the query also included p53, a commonly studied protein. To further ensure that there were meaningful and diverse interactions present in the abstracts, an abstract was included in the query result only if the corresponding article was referenced by the manually curated PhosphoSitePlus[23] database. Finally, 400 abstracts were selected at random from the query result to use as training data. Of these abstracts, 60% contained mentions of phosphorylation and 40% contained mentions of other PTMs.

The information labeled in the abstracts included (1) verbs or biological interactions that could potentially apply to proteins (for potential insertion into the KnIT interaction catalog), and (2) the agent, theme and event, if present, in each sentence that contained a PPI. If negation was present, e.g., "ATM did *not* phosphorylate p53", then this feature was recorded as well.

Figure 2 shows examples of interactions collected for cataloguing and a sentence showing two PPIs labeled for Agent, Interaction and Theme instances.

3.2.3 Learning Patterns for Event Extraction

Using the sentences labeled for PPIs (see Section 3.2.2), KnIT learns rules over natural language parse trees for event detection. Each sentence is run through the IBM ESG Parser and the dependency parse structure is examined for syntactic connections between the labeled interaction, agents and themes. Here we show a few examples of rules learned.

(a) The dependency parse structure of a sentence "ATR phosphorylated p53 at Ser-15", reveals that the verb of interest, *phosphorylated,* is connected to a known agent and theme via *nsubj* and *dobj,* (noun-subject and direct-object) relationships. This connection is identified as a rule for semantic role labeling of agents and themes. In more detail, the parse structure is:

```
root(ROOT, phosphorylated)
nsubj(phosphorylated, ATR)
dobj(phosphorylated, p53)
prep_at(phosphorylated, Ser-15)
```

(Here `prep_at` means that the arguments are connected by the preposition "at".) For test sentences that express syntactically similar relationships between known interactions and protein entities, following the *nsubj* and *dobj* connections will result in identification of agents and themes for that interaction. KnIT always relies on the catalog for identifying interactions; the learned rules assign "agent" or "theme" semantic labels to protein entities.

(b) KnIT extracts complex rules where secondary interactions are involved. For example a sentence such as "ATM-mediated phosphorylation of p53 at serine 15." contains an indirect interaction, *mediated*, between the agent and the main interaction, *phosphorylation*, i.e., "ATM-mediated" is an adjective modifying "phosphorylation":

```
amod(phosphorylation, ATM-mediated)
prep_of(phosphorylation, p53)
```

A rule is learned to allow for any secondary interaction (from the KnIT relationship catalog) to act as a connector between an agent and the interaction.

(c) KnIT learns rules where agents and themes are not simply proteins but rather processes or events involving a protein. For example, in the sentence "Our data suggests that bcl-2 is able to modulate transmembrane trafficking of p53." the interaction *modulate* is connected to an entity *p53* via a process that is captured in the phrase *"transmembrane trafficking of p53"*.

Parse structures for every PPI in the labeled training data are examined in the above manner to collect a set of rules that describe how interactions and entities might relate to one another. Rules that have a support of at least three PPIs in the training data are selected for inclusion into KnIT.

Although the rules are learned over interactions that are PTMs, the various sentence structures involved are very similar to those for the other interactions in the KnIT catalog, so that the learned rules are applicable to a wide variety of interactions. Although the set of rules is not exhaustive and will not identify every possible PPI, the high quality of the rules yields precision and recall sufficient to create a network well suited to PPI prediction.

KnIT also learns two kinds of negation patterns. In the first pattern, negation is associated with the verb and is readily available in the dependency parse tree. For example in the sentence, "ATM did not phosphorylate p53" the dependency parse tree shows a connection between the interaction '*phosphorylate*' and negation word '*not*':

```
root(ROOT, phosphorylate)
neg(phosphorylate, not)
nsubj(phosphorylate, ATM)
aux(phosphorylate, did)
dobj(phosphorylate, p53)
```

More complex representations of negation such as an event "was absent", "rarely detected" need special treatment. The SMEs helped curate a list of expressions that are prevalent in PubMed in expressing negative interactions. As with event extraction, negations are predicted by learning rules that connect the known interaction and negation-indicating phrases.

3.2.4 Online Event Extraction

Here we discuss the end-to-end KnIT Extraction pipeline where the learned rules are applied to all 24 million abstracts in Medline, extracting protein entities and their interactions to construct PPI networks. Let us revisit Figure 1 for an overview.

1. KnIT ingests one abstract at a time and performs a sentence split on the title and abstract body. All further extractions in KnIT are at the sentence level.
2. KnIT applies the entity detection and normalization procedure, as described in Section 3.1, to identify all protein mentions and their canonical forms.
3. Every sentence is then checked for the presence of an interaction term from the KnIT relationship catalog (Section 3.2.1). Only sentences that contain an interaction and at least two protein entities proceed to the next step.
4. KnIT performs a natural language parse of the sentence using the IBM parser.
5. The parse tree is then examined using the rules learned between interactions and entities (Section 3.2.3) in order to assign semantic role labels to agent and theme entities.
6. Sentences with interactions, agents and themes are considered as valid triples for the network and are examined for the presence of negation attached to the interaction.

We applied the KnIT extraction engine to a Medline corpus of almost 24 million artifacts. All analysis was restricted to title and abstracts. We were able to extract a total of 171,798 unique triples from 245,833 text occurrences across 167,590 unique abstracts where the agents and themes matched normalized protein entities, i.e. there was no ambiguity in what these entities were.

Examples of interactions between ATM and p53 that can be extracted by KnIT using the learned rules are as follows.

However, IR-activated, ATM-mediated phosphorylation of p53 at serine 15 (human) or 18 (mouse) [Ser15(h)/18(m)], and apoptosis occurred in myoblasts but was impaired in myotubes.

Nuclear accumulation and ATM-dependent phosphorylation of p53 on serine 15 were also observed.

Upon treatment with 5-Aza-CdR, ATM activation was clearly associated with P53 phosphorylation at Ser(15), which was directly responsible for 5-Aza-CdR modified P21(Waf1/Cip1) expression.

Moreover, knockdown of ATM by siRNA significantly reduced p53 phosphorylation and stabilization..

ATM and ATR cannot phosphorylate p53 on Ser-20. **(negation)**

ATM phosphorylates the ***p53 tumor suppressor*** *on a site (Ser15) that regulates transcription activity.*

4. GENERATION OF HYPOTHESES

After extracting (agent, event, theme) triples, KnIT then can use a variety of graph-reasoning techniques to predict heretofore unknown PPIs. There are many possible reasoning techniques[8; 29; 50; 57; 58]. To date, we have primarily investigated two different methods.

Non-negative matrix factorization (NMF): This technique can use the discovered triples directly to simultaneously predict many kinds of PPIs. Originally introduced by Paatero and Tapper in 1994[39], NMF can, given a matrix X, determine (two) smaller matrices that approximate X when multiplied together. If X has dimensions m x n, NMF calculates smaller W and H matrices of dimensions $m \times k$ and $k \times n$, respectively, where the parameter $k \ll \min(m, n)$ determines the granularity of the approximation. In our case, $X_{i,j}$ would have a binary value indicating whether or not KnIT found a connection between proteins i and j, i.e., whether i and j appeared jointly in some triple. There are multiple possible objective functions available for determining "optimal" values W^* and H^* of W and H, but we follow Paatero and Tapper and simply minimize the Frobenius norm of the factorization error: $W^*, H^* = \text{argmin}_{W,H} \|X - WH\|_F$, where $\|A\|_F = \left(\sum_{i,j} a_{ij}^2\right)^{1/2}$.

Matrix factorization is essentially a compression algorithm, where row i of W, corresponding to protein i in the original interaction matrix X, is a small "meta-feature" vector representing the nature of the relationships that row i (protein i) of X has with the columns of X (the other protein), which each have their own meta-feature vector in the H matrix, as shown in Figure 5A. The dot product of the ith row of W with the jth column of H yields a "corrected" value for $X_{i,j}$, which may indicate a new connection if the original value was 0 and the corrected value is not. Berry et al. review many different regularization and parallelization methods[3] that appeared since the first publication, notably Lee and Seung's 1999 paper that rekindled the popularity of NMF [7; 18; 19; 26; 31; 32]. A range of NMF applications already exist in biology, such as for biological image processing[59] and microarray data analysis. The latter produces meta-gene expression levels for each sample, which can then be used for clustering and classification[53]. Applying NMF to PPI networks, we expect it to determine latent variables that indicate the types of interactions each protein takes part in.

BOW-GID: This technique was proposed in Spangler et al.[46] to which we refer the reader for details. Briefly, an event and theme are fixed, and the goal is to find previously undiscovered agents. KnIT constructs a similarity network of proteins based on a bag-of-words (BOW) analysis[44]. Each protein that is a known agent is labeled with a weight of 1 and all other proteins are labeled with a weight of 0. KnIT then uses a graph information diffusion[33] (GID) technique to propagate the weights from known agents to the unknown agents. Candidates with the highest diffused weights are considered to be the most likely to be undiscovered agents.

5. COMPUTATIONAL EXPERIMENTS

In this section, we describe several experiments designed to test the scope and accuracy of the KnIT discovery pipeline. We first describe a retrospective study using the NMF technique, then test KnIT's ability to discover PPIs that are found in sources other than the biomedical literature, and finally show how we can automate, scale up, and generalize the BOW-GID study in Spangler, et al.[46]

5.1 Retrospective Predictions

Our retrospective study was designed to test whether KnIT could predict additional connections that are absent from the network because they are not documented in the literature, could not be parsed, or remain undiscovered. We applied NMF in order to predict, using papers published before a given date, PPIs discovered in papers after that date. The results provide a consistent internal measure of data quality and a realistic assessment of the likelihood KnIT can accurately predict future discoveries. Subgraphs were constructed for each interaction type. The most recent ~20% of edges was removed and used as a test set while the earlier 80% formed the training set for the factorization model. Eight separate datasets, one for each of the most common interaction types, was used, and their results are shown in Figure 5B. The areas under the ROC curves show that each subnetwork was significantly more accurate than chance.

Table 1 – Statistics on the networks created based on each of the 8 most frequently observed relationship types. E/N is the edge to node ratio.

RelationshipType	Edges	Nodes	E/N
RegulationPositive	54278	8296	6.5
RegulationNegative	44091	7812	5.6
Regulation	28717	7063	4.1
Phosphorylation	20991	4280	4.9
Binding	10832	5284	2.1
Expression	5918	2459	2.4
Localization	1335	1526	0.9
Ubiquitination	1155	909	1.3

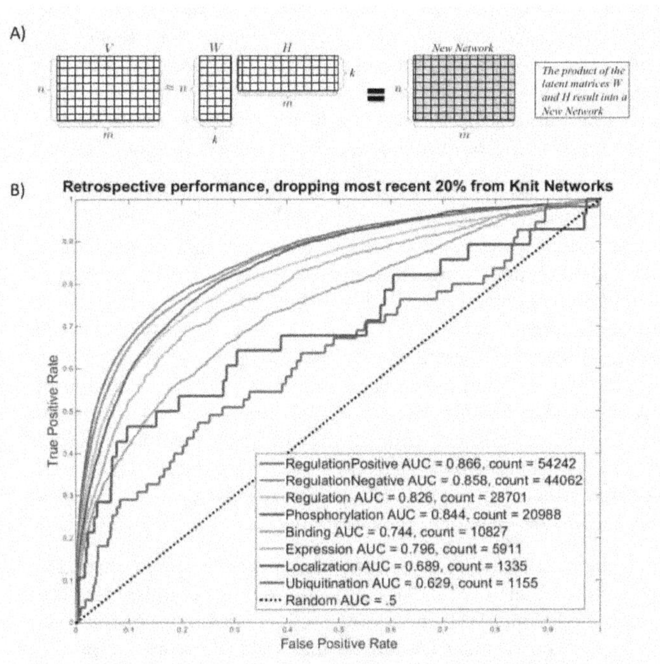

Figure 5. Hypothesis generation on KnIT network. A) Nonnegative matrix factorization was applied for B) retrospective validation in the KnIT network

Notably, the models from networks with more edges did better, suggesting that ultimate performance depends on the richness of the information available in the network to start with. These data demonstrate that the automated KnIT extraction and prediction pipeline can identify new hypotheses that prove correct, i.e., foretell future observations on a large scale in time-stamped experiments designed to mimic realistic conditions.

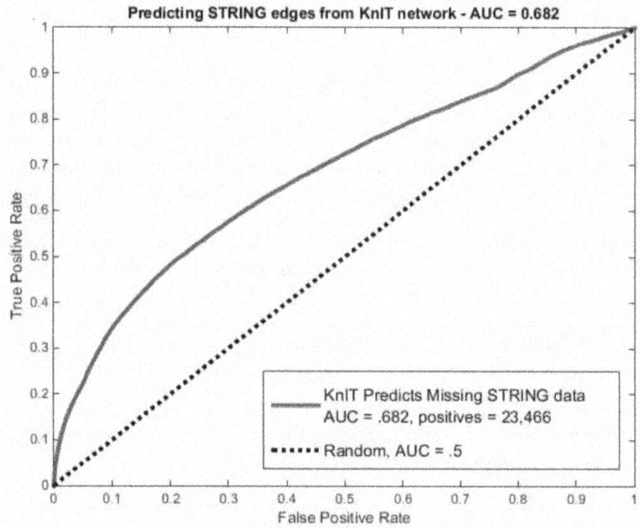

Figure 6. Prospective analysis where the positive set are interactions currently found in StringDB.

5.2 External Validation

In order to examine our ability to mine text for relationships, we compared the state of the KnIT extracted network to StringDB [13]. StringDB is a long-running effort to gather and combine a multitude of information sources on connections between proteins. Particularly useful is its sub database specific to protein-protein interactions with experimental evidence. The data sources, such as BioGRID, BIND, and DIP [13], manually collect information extracted from multiple experimental techniques (yeast two-hybrid experiments, mass spectrometry, genetic interactions, phage display, etc.). Because this information is often taken from large-scale screens, the interactions are unavailable to a literature-mining-only approach. Despite this, we would expect KnIT relationships to have significant correlation with StringDB.

KnIT's extracted network contains 118,864 edges and 11,375 nodes, while StringDB contains 136,734 edges and 13,893 nodes. Although each node represents a protein, not all proteins occur in the underlying data sources, and so only 8,994 nodes are shared between them. Within this shared set of nodes, the KnIT extracted network contains 107,388 edges while StringDB contains 85,954. Had the KnIT extracted network been composed of random edges in this space, only 260 edges would be expected to be shared, but instead, 10,279 edges are in common ($p<0.0001$). This shows that KnIT is significantly aligned with existing structured data, while also finding over 100,000 relationships that were not previously documented by StringDB.

Next, we will show that the information appearing in StringDB that is not detected by KnIT extracted network could potentially be predicted using the factorization method used in section 5.1. To do so, we apply factorization to the KnIT network to predict interactions unique to StringDB. The positive test set was composed of edges that are in StringDB but not detected by our KnIT reading on the literature (75675 interactions), while the negative set is all non-existent edges connecting pairs of proteins that do not have a connection in either network. The NMF analysis of Section 5.1 was repeated, but using the entire KnIT network to train the NMF model. Predicting these edges, the model had a performance, as measured by AU(ROC) (Figure 6) of 0.68. These data show that edge-prediction applied to KnIT relationships can discover true relationships absent from the literature with a significant enrichment over what would be expected by chance.

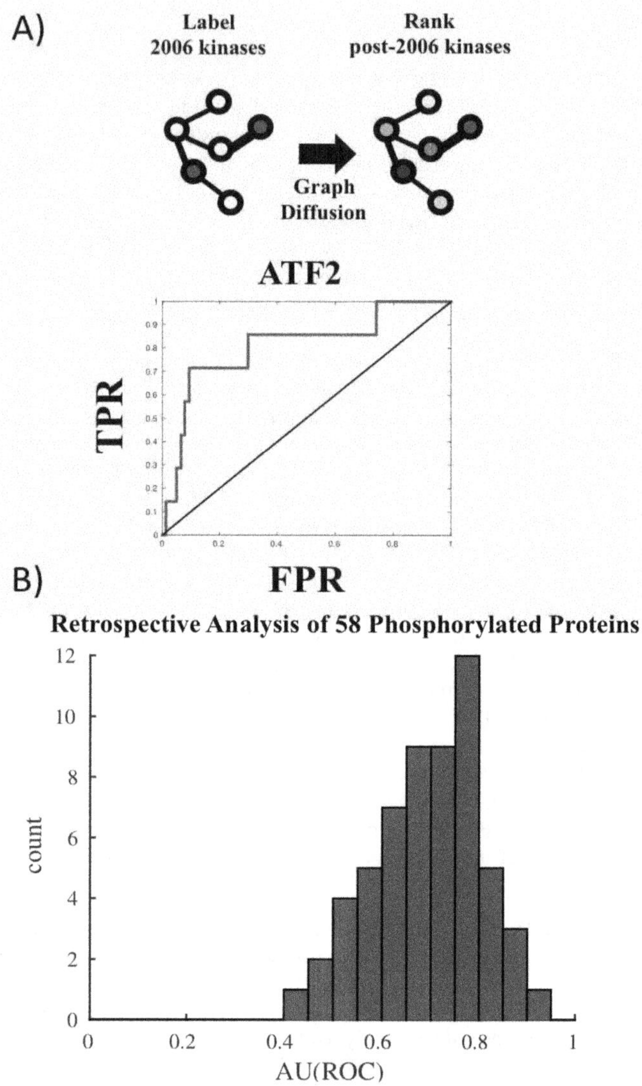

Figure 7 A) Retrospective analysis for kinases phosphorylating B) 58 specific protein targets.

5.3 Automating/Expanding a Prior Analysis

In our final experiment, we tested whether the fully automated KnIT system could eliminate the need for manual, expert-based annotation. Specifically, in a prior study[46], the BOW-GID technique was used to predict p53 kinases, proteins that add phosphate molecules to the tumor-suppressor protein p53. In that retrospective study, abstracts available in 2003 were used to predict subsequent discoveries in the literature. Remarkably, the system identified 7 out of 9 subsequently discovered p53 kinases. This proof-of-principle experiment demonstrated the prediction of novel facts based on the literature, but still required SMEs to manually identify kinases in the abstracts, and in particular to identify kinases that phosphorylated p53 (so that they could receive an initial weight of 1 in the graph diffusion analysis). The goals of our current experiment are (1) to see whether the prior, painstaking manual annotation by experts can be replaced by the new automated triple-extraction technology, thereby allowing KnIT to handle much larger corpora, and (2) to show the potential of such scaling by expanding the prior study to identify kinases that target proteins in general, not just p53.

In more detail, we asked whether the kinases known up to a particular year for a given protein could predict kinases discovered after that year for that same protein, using the (now automated) BOW-GID method. We selected a set of 58 phosphorylated proteins with at least 4 kinases known in 2006 and 4 kinases discovered after 2006. We created a BOW similarity network of 332 kinases based on the literature through 2006, used the triples discovered by KnIT to assign a weight of 1 to known kinases, and then ranked the unknown kinases by their post-diffusion score. Figure 7 shows that 68% of the protein test sets achieved an AU(ROC) > 0.6, and 56% an AU(ROC) > 0.7. The p53-specific result was AU(ROC) = 0.71 compared to AU(ROC) = 0.84 in the prior study, reflecting both the larger search space and the use of an automatically generated initial labeled network rather than one created manually by a human expert. This study shows that, using KnIT in 2006, we automatically modeled the kinase-kinase network and predicted a number of novel kinases found later in publication. Thus, KnIT is effective for predicting novel connections on a large scale without manual intervention.

6. DISCUSSION AND CONCLUSION

This study presents a complete end-to-end discovery pipeline that transforms unstructured data from the biological literature into new scientific hypotheses, significantly enriched for truth. In the process, we show that we can automatically extract relationships from text. These relationship triples are pooled into networks that are reasoned over by diffusing weights or by generating novel edges via matrix completion. Time-stamped studies rigorously assessed the predictive power to foretell discoveries made after a given date, based on what was known prior to that date. We also tested predictions against controls that do not appear in the literature. Finally, we applied KnIT knowledge extraction via triples to obviate the need for manual annotation of abstracts by SMEs when automatically reasoning via BOW-GID. These results point to the quality and predictive power of both the triples and of the network-based reasoning algorithms that we apply to them. KnIT has shown good performance in prospective analysis and, in practice, already suggests thousands of hypotheses that have the potential to efficiently guide biological discoveries.

Baylor College of Medicine and IBM Research are working together to accelerate scientific discoveries, with the long-term goal of taking on the challenge of personalized medicine. In order to understand individual genetic variation, we must be able to contextualize mutations with detailed annotation of genes and proteins. However, to make this practical on a large-scale, data must be structured, and reasoning automated. This study represents the early stages of our effort. In the future, our team will focus on a wider area of biological entities, such as drugs, treatments, and diseases, in order to develop an all-inclusive network of biomedical literature knowledge. The next steps will include a collection of algorithms validated with biological experiments to identify new hypotheses based on the entire network. We will also develop techniques to prioritize the large number of hypotheses generated based on likelihood, value and risk. Such analyses will yield a set of hypotheses that will fill gaps in science, accelerate the pace of discovery and, in turn, improve our understanding of disease to better guide patient care.

7. ACKNOWLEDGMENTS

This work was supported by the Robert and Janice McNair Foundation, DARPA (N66001-14-1-4027), National Science Foundation (NSF DBI-1356569, NSF DBI-0851393), National Institutes of Health (NIH-GM079656, NIH-GM066099), and was supported in part by the IBM Accelerated Discovery Lab.

8. REFERENCES

[1] Aronson, A.R. and Lang, F.M., 2010. An overview of MetaMap: historical perspective and recent advances. *J Am Med Inform Assoc 17*, 3 (May-Jun), 229-236.

[2] Ashburner, M., et al., 2000. Gene ontology: tool for the unification of biology. *Nat Genet 25*, 1 (May), 25-29.

[3] Berry, M.W., et al., 2007. Algorithms and applications for approximate nonnegative matrix factorization. *Comp Statistics & Data Analysis 52*, 1, 155-173.

[4] Brohee, S. and Van Helden, J., 2006. Evaluation of clustering algorithms for protein-protein interaction networks. *BMC Bioinformatics 7*, 1, 488.

[5] Cancer Genome Atlas, N., 2012. Comprehensive molecular characterization of human colon and rectal cancer. *Nature 487*, 7407 (Jul 19), 330-337.

[6] Cancer Genome Atlas Research, N., 2008. Comprehensive genomic characterization defines human glioblastoma genes and core pathways. *Nature 455*, 7216 (Oct 23), 1061-1068.

[7] Catral, M., et al., 2004. On reduced rank nonnegative matrix factorization for symmetric nonnegative matrices. *Linear Algebra and its Applications 393*, 107-126.

[8] Chinnasamy, A., et al., 2006. Probabilistic prediction of protein-protein interactions from the protein sequences. *Comput Biol Med 36*, 10 (Oct), 1143-1154.

[9] Cohen, A.M. and Hersh, W.R., 2005. A survey of current work in biomedical text mining. *Brief Bioinform 6*, 1 (Mar), 57-71.

[10] Danger, R., et al., 2014. Towards a Protein–Protein Interaction information extraction system: Recognizing named entities. *Knowledge-Based Systems 57*, 104-118.

[11] Davis, A.P., et al., 2011. The Comparative Toxicogenomics Database: update 2011. *Nucleic Acids Res 39*, Database issue (Jan), D1067-1072.

[12] Edwards, A.M., et al., 2002. Bridging structural biology and genomics: assessing protein interaction data with known complexes. *Trends Genet 18*, 10 (Oct), 529-536.

[13] Franceschini, A., et al., 2013. STRING v9.1: protein-protein interaction networks, with increased coverage and integration. *Nucleic Acids Res 41*, (Jan), D808-815.

[14] Fundel, K., et al., 2007. RelEx—Relation extraction using dependency parse trees. *Bioinformatics 23*, 3, 365-371.

[15] Gene Ontology, C., 2008. The Gene Ontology project in 2008. *Nucleic Acids Res 36*, Database issue (Jan), D440-444.

[16] Gene Ontology, C., 2010. The Gene Ontology in 2010: extensions and refinements. *Nucleic Acids Res 38*, Database issue (Jan), D331-335.

[17] Gray, K.A., et al., 2013. Genenames.org: the HGNC resources. *Nucleic Acids Res 41*, (Jan), D545-552.

[18] Guillamet, D., et al., 2001. A weighted non-negative matrix factorization for local representations IEEE, I-942-I-947 vol. 941.

[19] Hamza, A.B. and Brady, D.J., 2006. Reconstruction of reflectance spectra using robust nonnegative matrix

factorization. *IEEE Transactions on Signal Processing 54*, 9, 3637-3642.

[20] Hatzivassiloglou, V., et al., 2001. Disambiguating proteins, genes, and RNA in text: a machine learning approach. *Bioinformatics 17 Suppl 1*, suppl 1, S97-106.

[21] Heath, L.S. and Sioson, A.A., 2009. Multimodal networks: structure and operations. *IEEE/ACM Trans Comput Biol Bioinform 6*, 2 (Apr-Jun), 321-332.

[22] Hoffmann, R. and Valencia, A., 2004. A gene network for navigating the literature. *Nat Genet 36*, 7 (Jul), 664.

[23] Hornbeck, P.V., et al., 2015. PhosphoSitePlus, 2014: mutations, PTMs and recalibrations. *Nucleic Acids Res 43*, Database issue (Jan), D512-520.

[24] International Human Genome Sequencing, C., 2004. Finishing the euchromatic sequence of the human genome. *Nature 431*, 7011 (Oct 21), 931-945.

[25] Jenssen, T.K., et al., 2001. A literature network of human genes for high-throughput analysis of gene expression. *Nat Genet 28*, 1 (May), 21-28.

[26] Jia, Y.W.Y. and Turk, C.H.M. ,2004 Fisher non-negative matrix factorization for learning local features. *In Proc. Asian Conf. on Comp. Vision*, 27-30.

[27] Jupe, S., et al., 2012. Reactome - a curated knowledgebase of biological pathways: megakaryocytes and platelets. *Journal of Thrombosis and Haemostasis : JTH,* 10(11), 2399–2402.

[28] Kim, J.D., et al., 2011. Overview of BioNLP shared task 2011 *Association for Computational Linguistics*, 1-6.

[29] Kuchaiev, O., et al., 2009. Geometric de-noising of protein-protein interaction networks. *PLoS Comput Biol 5*, 8 (Aug), e1000454.

[30] Laura, C., et al., 2010. SystemT: an algebraic approach to declarative information extraction. In *Proceedings of the 48th Annual Meeting of the Association for Computational Linguistics*, Uppsala, Sweden, 128-137.

[31] Lee, D.D. and Seung, H.S., 1999. Learning the parts of objects by non-negative matrix factorization. *Nature 401*, 6755 (Oct 21), 788-791.

[32] Lee, D.D. and Seung, H.S., 2000. Algorithms for Non-negative Matrix Factorization. In *NIPS*, 556-562.

[33] Lisewski, A.M. and Lichtarge, O., 2010. Untangling complex networks: risk minimization in financial markets through accessible spin glass ground states. *Physica A 389*, 16 (Aug 15), 3250-3253.

[34] Manning, C.D., et al., 2008. *Introduction to Information Retrieval.* Cambridge University Press Cambridge.

[35] Manning, C.D. and Schütze, H., 1999. *Foundations of statistical natural language processing*. MIT press.

[36] Mccord, M.C. and Bernth, A., 2010. Using slot grammar. *IBM TJ Watson Res. Center, Yorktown Heights, NY, IBM Res. Rep. RC23978.*

[37] Miyao, Y., et al., 2009. Evaluating contributions of natural language parsers to protein-protein interaction extraction. *Bioinformatics 25*, 3 (Feb 1), 394-400.

[38] Nédellec, C., et al., 2013. Overview of BioNLP shared task 2013. *Proceedings of the BioNLP Shared Task 2013 Workshop*, 1–7.

[39] Paatero, P. and Tapper, U., 1994. Positive matrix factorization: A non-negative factor model with optimal utilization of error estimates of data values. *Environmetrics 5*, 2, 111-126.

[40] Poon, H., et al., 2014. Literome: PubMed-scale genomic knowledge base in the cloud. *Bioinformatics 30*, 19 (Oct), 2840-2842.

[41] Pyysalo, S., et al., 2007. BioInfer: a corpus for information extraction in the biomedical domain. *BMC Bioinformatics 8*, 50.

[42] Quan, C., et al., 2014. An unsupervised text mining method for relation extraction from biomedical literature. *PLoS One 9*, 7, e102039.

[43] Rzhetsky, A., et al., 2004. GeneWays: a system for extracting, analyzing, visualizing, and integrating molecular pathway data. *J Biomed Inform 37*, 1 (Feb), 43-53.

[44] Salton, G. and Mcgill, M.J., 1986. *Introduction to Modern Information Retrieval*. McGraw-Hill, Inc.

[45] Scott, S., et al., 2014. Automated hypothesis generation based on mining scientific literature. In *Proceedings of the 20th ACM SIGKDD*, New York, New York, USA, 1877-1886.

[46] Scott, S., et al., 2014. Automated hypothesis generation based on mining scientific literature. In *Proceedings of the 20th ACM SIGKDD*, New York, USA, 1877-1886.

[47] Stumpf, M.P., et al., 2008. Estimating the size of the human interactome. *Proc Natl Acad Sci U S A 105*, 19 (May 13), 6959-6964.

[48] Tanabe, L. and Wilbur, W.J., 2002. Tagging gene and protein names in biomedical text. *Bioinformatics 18*, 8 (Aug), 1124-1132.

[49] Tikk, D., et al., 2010. A comprehensive benchmark of kernel methods to extract protein-protein interactions from literature. *PLoS Comput Biol 6*, 7, e1000837.

[50] Tuncbag, N., et al., 2011. Predicting protein-protein interactions on a proteome scale by matching evolutionary and structural similarities at interfaces using PRISM. *Nat Protoc 6*, 9 (Sep), 1341-1354.

[51] Uniprot, C., 2013. Update on activities at the Universal Protein Resource (UniProt) in 2013. *Nucleic Acids Res 41*, Database issue (Jan), D43-47.

[52] Van Landeghem, S., et al., 2013. Large-scale event extraction from literature with multi-level gene normalization. *PLoS One 8*, 4, e55814.

[53] Wang, H., et al., 2013. Predicting protein-protein interactions from multimodal biological data sources via nonnegative matrix tri-factorization. *J Comput Biol 20*, 4 (Apr), 344-358.

[54] Wheeler, D.L., et al., 2003. Database resources of the National Center for Biotechnology. *Nucleic Acids Res 31*, 1 (Jan 1), 28-33.

[55] Wishart, D.S., et al., 2009. HMDB: a knowledgebase for the human metabolome. *Nucleic Acids Res 37*, Database issue (Jan), D603-610.

[56] Xie, Z., et al., 2010. hPDI: a database of experimental human protein-DNA interactions. *Bioinformatics 26*, 2 (Jan 15), 287-289.

[57] You, Z.H., et al., 2013. Prediction of protein-protein interactions from amino acid sequences with ensemble extreme learning machines and principal component analysis. *BMC bioinformatics 14 Suppl 8*, S10.

[58] Zhang, Q.C., et al., 2012. Structure-based prediction of protein-protein interactions on a genome-wide scale. *Nature 490*, 7421 (Oct 25), 556-560.

[59] Zitnik, M., et al., 2013. Discovering disease-disease associations by fusing systems-level molecular data. *Sci Rep 3*, 3202.

Learning a Hierarchical Monitoring System for Detecting and Diagnosing Service Issues

Vinod Nair, Ameya Raul
Microsoft Research India
{vnair, t-amraul}@microsoft.com

Shwetabh Khanduja
Microsoft Research India
t-shwetk@microsoft.com

Vikas Bahirwani
Microsoft, Redmond, WA
vikasba@microsoft.com

S. Sundararajan
Microsoft Research India
ssrajan@microsoft.com

Sathiya Keerthi
Microsoft, Mountain View, CA
keerthi@microsoft.com

Steve Herbert, Sudheer Dhulipalla
Microsoft, Redmond, WA
{steve.herbert, sudheerd}@microsoft.com

ABSTRACT

We propose a machine learning based framework for building a hierarchical monitoring system to detect and diagnose service issues. We demonstrate its use for building a monitoring system for a distributed data storage and computing service consisting of tens of thousands of machines. Our solution has been deployed in production as an end-to-end system, starting from telemetry data collection from individual machines, to a visualization tool for service operators to examine the detection outputs. Evaluation results are presented on detecting 19 customer impacting issues in the past three months.

1. INTRODUCTION

Consumer and enterprise services increasingly run on large scale distributed storage and computing platforms built on hundreds of thousands of commodity machines. Service quality can be affected by hardware and software failures, unexpected user load changes, and so on, resulting in slow response, unavailability, violation of service level agreements, and ultimately customer dissatisfaction and negative reputation. Therefore monitoring the service to detect and diagnose issues quickly is an important problem. Recently there has been a steady increase in the literature in this area, from designing incident ticket management systems [13, 15], to building large scale textual log and time series analyzers [8, 20], developing specialized machine learning and data mining algorithms for anomaly detection [4, 9, 19], and many others [1, 2, 6, 18, 22].

There are several challenges in building a service monitoring system. *Telemetry data manageability:* A typical service is heavily instrumented by sensors of various kinds (e.g., performance counters, textual logs, event streams), reporting values of thousands of variables in real time. The monitoring system needs to use this data in a scalable manner to accurately detect and diagnose issues, and present to the service operators only the small subset of data that is actually relevant for an issue. *Complexity of service architecture:* Most services consist of sub-systems, components, sub-components and so on. The architecture induces relationships, often unknown, among the variables which need to be taken into account for accurate detection. Furthermore, the complexity can grow over time as more machines and functions get added, giving rise to new issues.

Currently rule-based detection is commonly used in service monitoring. Manually written rules often involve only one or at most a few variables, so the volume of detections becomes large as the number of variables runs into several thousands. They do not take into account the unknown relationships among the large set of variables, and as a result, they tend to produce a large number of false positives. Also, they do not handle changes in the service behavior over time. We consider a machine learning-based approach to building a detection system. Such an approach should process the large volume of telemetry in a scalable manner to detect issues, and present the user only the relevant subset of data to look at in an easily interpretable form. It should automatically discover the unknown relationships among the variables to reduce false positives. It should make use of any domain knowledge available, such as the architecture of the service, and any knowledge about patterns in individual variables that may be partial indicators of issues (e.g., spikes, step changes, trends, etc. in individual variables). It should use minimal supervision for learning because in practice there may not be a large number of past service issues available as labeled examples, and getting labels is expensive. Furthermore, many issues that should have been detected can go undetected, so even apparently "issue-free" data may not be so. Finally, although a fully automated approach would be ideal, here we do not insist on it, as a semi-automated one with semi-supervised learning is more feasible and still highly valuable in practice.

We propose an approach that addresses the above requirements. The main idea is to build a *hierarchical monitoring system* with several levels of detectors, with detectors in each level taking the detector outputs of the previous level as in-

KDD'15, August 11-14, 2015, Sydney, NSW, Australia.
© 2015 ACM. ISBN 978-1-4503-3664-2/15/08 ...$15.00.
DOI: http://dx.doi.org/10.1145/2783258.2788624.

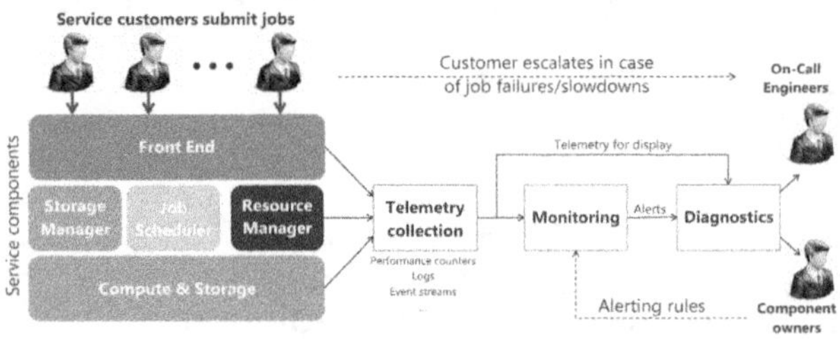

Figure 1: Summary of the service architecture, monitoring infrastructure, and the various types of users involved.

put. The lowest level (i.e., leaf nodes) detectors take raw telemetry data as inputs. The system has the capability to throw alerts at various levels. The hierarchical structure has several advantages. (1) It helps in reducing the data dimensionality progressively in the hierarchy so that at the higher levels the data volume is low. At the lowest level, where the data volume is highest, the computation is embarrassingly parallel over the leaf nodes, which allows the approach to scale to large data volume. (2) A detector's output at a given level can be interpreted by navigating the paths below it to identify the small relevant subset of telemetry data at the leaf nodes. (3) Domain knowledge about service architecture can be used to shape the hierarchy, while knowledge about unusual patterns in individual variables can be used to design the lowest level detectors. (4) It offers a mechanism to reduce false positives as evidence for an issue can be gathered by identifying relationships among variables at each level. Low level detectors can be inaccurate as they are built using individual variables and may only give a partial indication of an issue. By combining these detectors via their relationships, it becomes possible to build a more accurate detector. (5) It requires minimal supervision. Note that although our approach is general and can be applied to different types of telemetry data, in this paper we focus exclusively on time series data from performance counters.

1.1 Contributions

The main contributions of the paper are:

1. We propose a general framework for building a hierarchical monitoring system that addresses the key requirements of a service monitoring application, making it broadly useful. It can be used with different types of telemetry data sources to detect and diagnose service issues.

2. We demonstrate a principled machine learning approach to building a monitoring system using our framework. The system is used to monitor Microsoft's internal distributed data storage and batch computing service that consists of tens of thousands of machines.

3. We have built an end-to-end pipeline for running our monitoring system, starting from telemetry data collection from individual machines, all the way to a visualization tool which service operators use to examine the detection outputs of our system to quickly focus on where the issues are.

4. We have deployed our system in production and present results on detecting 19 customer impacting issues in the past three months.

Outline: The rest of the paper is organized as follows: we begin with a detailed description of our service monitoring application in section 2. Section 3 gives an overview of our solution approach and its deployment in production. Section 4 describes the details of the machine learning techniques we use. Section 5 presents the evaluation of our approach. We then discuss related work (section 7), and conclude with a discussion of possible extensions of our work (section 8).

2. SERVICE MONITORING APPLICATION

The application we consider here is that of monitoring Microsoft's internal distributed data storage and batch computing service. The service is built on several tens of thousands of commodity machines providing fault-tolerant storage and compute. It is used heavily by Microsoft's product groups for running distributed batch jobs on large scale data.

Figure 1 provides a high-level summary of the service and its monitoring infrastructure. The service has a complex architecture with many micro-services, components, subcomponents, and so on. Each of these report their own telemetry. The complexity of the service architecture and the volume of the telemetry necessitates automatic analysis of the data.

Users of monitoring: On-Call Engineers (OCEs) monitor for any issues with the service that need to be immediately addressed to prevent customer impact. They also respond to customer escalations about their jobs failing or executing too slowly (possibly due to service issues), and suggesting work-arounds to customers. Engineering teams who own various components monitor their health and the effect of any updates made to them. Both types of users need to be alerted on any service issues in near-real time so that corrective action can be taken quickly.

Telemetry: *Performance counters* measure quantities such as CPU/memory/disk/network usage, latencies of service operations, number of requests received, etc. at fixed intervals (e.g., once every minute). *Logs* contain various text messages that are generated as the service software executes (e.g., status messages, error messages). *Event streams* are symbolic sequences reporting discrete occurrences in the service, e.g., "Job started". The amount of telemetry is large, e.g., the Storage Manager component by itself reports nearly 26000 counters. (Most of these are accounted by a few hundred unique counters reported by multiple instances of the component.)

Monitoring: As mentioned earlier, a common approach is to use rules, written usually by component owners, to detect issues. Rules are almost always defined on single performance counters, e.g., *If (latency > threshold), then throw alert.* Since one counter provides a limited view of the service behavior, there may not be *any* threshold at which the counter value separates genuine issues from false positives. One is forced to pick a threshold that will detect the issues, but will also result in a large number of false positives. Service operators do not have the time to examine a large number of alerts to pick out the few genuine ones, so the issues are missed anyway. For example, in our application a component team determined that the threshold value for

a single-counter rule that would be required to detect issues of interest to them would generate more than 12000 alerts over a four month period. This is simply too high a volume relative to the manpower available.
Diagnostics: Once an issue is caught, an OCE or a component owner needs to understand it to identify a mitigation for the affected customer or apply a hotfix to the affected component. The subset of performance counters relevant to an issue is typically a small fraction of the full set. Currently OCEs and component owners use domain knowledge and significant manual effort to find the right set of performance counters to visualize. As a result, diagnostics is slow and tedious, and prone to error without domain knowledge. One powerful form of domain knowledge is to know how the various performance counters can be grouped together, both by the service component they belong to, and also by the functionality of that component that they are most closely associated with. Such knowledge helps the user identify the relevant group of performance counters to look at and reduces the manual effort.

3. HIERARCHICAL MONITORING SYSTEM

We give an overview of our solution and then describe its deployment in production.

3.1 Solution overview

We introduce the main ideas behind our learning algorithm. For the purposes of this section, we will define a "detector" abstractly as a function that outputs a scalar score measuring how unusual its inputs are (higher score implies more unusual). Applying the detector across time (e.g., in a sliding window manner) results in a time series of scores.
Issue example: We begin with examples of service issues we are interested in learning detectors for. Figure 2 shows two issue examples ((a) and (b)) which manifest in performance counters. In issue (a), two groups of performance counters shown in blue (counters 1-3) and green (counters 4-6) for the same time interval behave unusually around x-axis value 2.5. (Here the groups were identified using domain knowledge.) For issue (a), the blue group shows a spike *and* the green group simultaneously shows a drop. For issue (b), only the blue group shows a spike. So an issue appears as unusual patterns in individual counter time series, but the unusual pattern in any one counter by itself is not sufficient to detect the issue (the same pattern may occur at non-issue times also), resulting in high false positive rates for single-counter detectors. Therefore it is necessary to discover *groups of unusual patterns* that characterize the issue accurately.

Our algorithm (1) detects unusual patterns in counters, (2) automatically discovers groups of related detectors from a large set, and (3) combines the detectors within each group to detect issues characterized by multiple simultaneous unusual patterns in that group. Detectors with similar score time series are likely detecting the same underlying issues, so grouping them together provides more evidence for detecting them. For example, by grouping together detectors for the blue counters in figure 2 and combining them, a detector for issue (b) can be constructed.

To detect *higher-order* issues, such as issue (a) in figure 2 which involves two groups, one can iteratively apply the same grouping and combining steps to build further levels in the hierarchy:

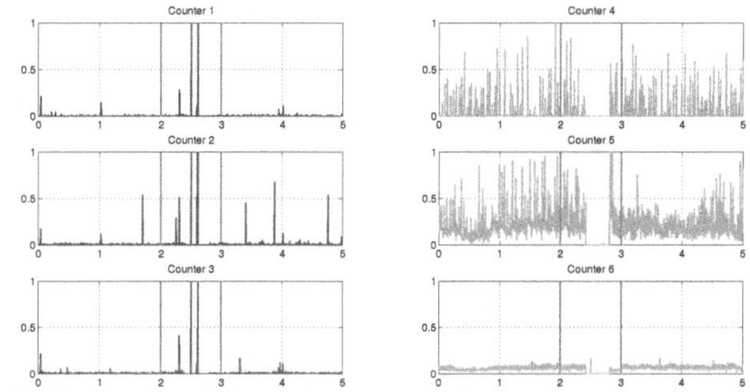

(a) Issue where blue and green counter groups are unusual

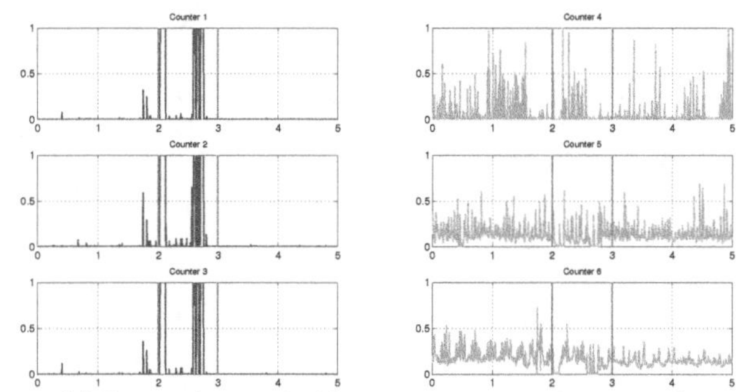

(b) Issue where only blue counter group is unusual

Figure 2: Examples of two different service issues involving (a) two counter groups, denoted by blue and green, and (b) only the blue counter group. The plots show the raw counter time series data with time as x-axis and counter value as y-axis. The issue interval is indicated by two vertical red lines.

- **Grouping:** At level i, find groups of related detectors by the similarity of their score time series.

- **Combining:** For each group found in the previous step, combine their scores to define a detector for level $i+1$.

So, a detector at the $i+1^{st}$ level is a group of ith level detectors which when simultaneously output high scores indicate a higher level issue. For example, by grouping together the detectors for the blue and green groups and combining them, it becomes possible to build a detector that outputs a high score for issue (a).

Note that our algorithm is unsupervised, i.e., it does not use manually marked issue intervals in the counter time series to learn detectors. As a result, the algorithm may learn detectors also for unusual patterns that do not correspond to actual service issues. Such detectors will need to be removed using manual analysis, but since the number of detectors is small, this is not a difficult task.

Figure 3 provides a visual summary of how the algorithm builds the hierarchy. We will refer to the circled numbers in the figure to explain the steps. Consider an example service with two components, A and B, each reporting its own telemetry data consisting of counters, logs, and event streams. (To save space, component B's detectors are shown in less detail than those of A.) *Step 1* is the initialization before the iterations begin. It applies a set of low-level detectors to the raw telemetry data. These detectors will have only a limited view of the service behavior, e.g., an anomaly detector based on a single counter, or a small set of counters within a sub-component. As explained, each detector out-

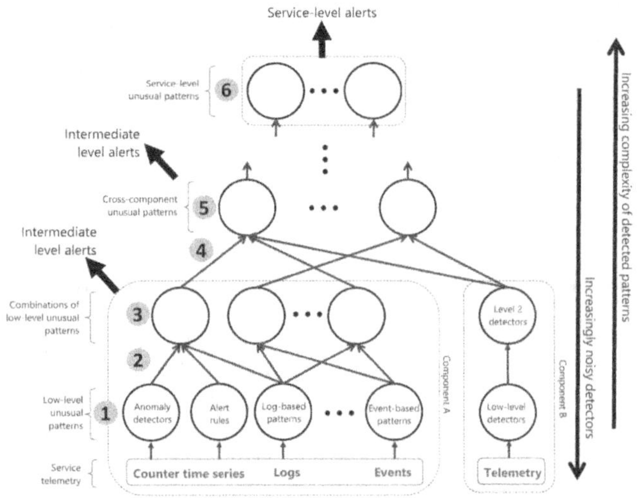

Figure 3: Summary of the main steps of the proposed learning algorithm. Circled numbers refer to the different steps which are explained in section 3.

puts a scalar score time series that measures how unusual its inputs are across time.

As shown in the figure, the low-level detectors can take different forms. Various time series anomaly detection algorithms from the literature can be applied to the counter time series. Alert rules written by service experts can also be plugged in, allowing our approach to leverage the domain knowledge encoded in such rules. Services invest heavily in rule-based alerting before machine learning approaches are adopted. We make direct use of that investment by combining rules with ML, rather than treating them as mutually exclusive. Further detectors based on features extracted from logs and event streams, e.g., frequent itemset mining on event sequences, can also be plugged in, again allowing us to build on the rich literature in this area.

The iterative part starts at *Step 2* with the first grouping operation applied, followed by the combining operation in *Step 3*. Section 4 discusses the algorithmic details of both of these operations. Once *Step 3* is complete, the next-level detectors are defined. At the lower levels of the hierarchy the grouping and combining operations may be restricted to be within a component or a sub-component, as shown by the example in the figure where the second-level detectors are within either component A or B. So the resulting second-level detectors still have a narrow view of the service behavior, but broader than the first-level detectors. Note that alerts need not be generated only at the highest level of the hierarchy. If needed, the lower-level detectors can also be used to throw alerts, e.g., to produce alerts at a component level, as shown in the figure.

Steps 4 and *5* show the next iteration of grouping and combining. As the example shows, at this point detectors across components are combined so that the unusual patterns that require combining information from multiple components can be detected. These two steps can be repeated to learn detectors that have visibility across the entire service, as shown in *Step 6*. As more levels are added, the complexity of the detected unusual patterns increases, and we also expect the detectors to become increasingly sparser in terms of how frequently they output high scores.

3.2 Addressing the requirements

Scalability: By restricting the lowest level detectors to individual counters or small groups of counters, the learning at the lower levels can be made embarassingly parallel. For this reason we avoid joint analysis of a large set of counters at the lowest levels. As further levels are added, the number of detector score time series to consider also drops, and therefore information from across a large set of counters can be efficiently combined at the higher levels. At the higher levels, more expensive joint analysis algorithms can be applied without affecting scalability.

Irrelevant variables: By removing detectors that do not fit into any group well in the grouping operation, irrelevant counters and detectors are automatically removed.

Domain knowledge: Restricting the structure of the hierarchy according to the service architecture and the choice of the level at which to combine detectors across component and sub-component boundaries are powerful ways to incorporate domain knowledge about the service into the detector. Use of rules as low-level detectors provides yet another way.

Lack of labeled data: The algorithm does not require labeled examples to learn the detectors. Evaluating the quality of the detectors still requires labeling. Avoiding or reducing that effort is an open research problem. Supervision is also needed in removing any learned detectors that detect unusual patterns which are not of use for monitoring service health.

Interpretability: Once an alert is thrown at the highest level, the user can trace through the hierarchy to find out which branches contributed the most to the alert. This will directly help identify the components and sub-components involved in the issue.

4. MACHINE LEARNING ASPECTS

This section presents the details of our approach. As explained before, there are two main steps that are repeatedly applied to build each level of the hierarchical detector: 1) discover groups of related detectors from the previous level, and 2) for each such group, combine the scores of its members to compute a score for the group. We present specific choices of algorithms for these two steps. Here we use sparse structure estimation for Gaussian Graphical Model [17] with Affinity Propagation [7] to discover groups of related detectors, and use averaging of scores to compute the group score. We also describe one choice for the low-level detector which is designed to detect a change over time in the probability distribution of a counter.

4.1 Sparse Structure Estimation

Consider a p-dimensional Gaussian random vector $X = (X_1, \dots, X_p) \sim \mathcal{N}(\mu, \Sigma)$ with mean μ, covariance matrix Σ, and precision matrix $K = \Sigma^{-1}$. A *Gaussian Graphical Model* (GGM) is an undirected graph $g = (V, E)$ with a vertex set $V = X_1, ..., X_p$ and an edge set E. The absence of an edge between the vertices X_i and X_j denotes the conditional independence $P(X_i, X_j|X_{-(i,j)}) = P(X_i|X_{-(i,j)})P(X_j|X_{-(i,j)})$ where $X_{-(i,j)}$ denotes the set of all variables in X except X_i and X_j. It can be shown that an edge $(i, j) \in E$ is absent if and only if $K_{ij} = 0$. This is because the conditional distribution $P(X_i, X_j|X_{-(i,j)})$ is also Gaussian with the covariance matrix

$$\bar{\Sigma} = \frac{1}{K_{ii}K_{jj} - K_{ij}K_{ji}} \begin{bmatrix} K_{jj} & -K_{ij} \\ -K_{ji} & K_{ii} \end{bmatrix}. \quad (1)$$

Since K is symmetric, $K_{ij} = K_{ji}$. So if $K_{ij} = 0$, $\bar{\Sigma}$ becomes a diagonal matrix and X_i and X_j become conditionally independent. Therefore the problem of estimating the graph structure of the GGM can be turned into the problem of estimating the non-zero entries of K.

One way to estimate the graph structure from data for the special case of sparsely connected, high-dimensional GGMs is presented by Meinshausen and Buhlmann [17]. This approach uses the fact that the distribution $P(X_i|X_{-(i)})$ is Gaussian with mean $E[X_i|X_{-(i)}] = -\sum_{j\neq i}\frac{K_{ij}}{K_{ii}}X_j$. This is a linear regression model with X_i as the target variable, all remaining variables $X_{-(i)}$ as inputs, and $\beta_{ij} = \frac{K_{ij}}{K_{ii}}$ as the regression coefficient for the input variable X_j. To identify the non-zero entries of K, for each X_i, learn the regression coefficients β_{ij} from data, and $K_{ij} \neq 0$ whenever $\beta_{ij} \neq 0$.

In particular, Meinshausen and Buhlmann propose using squared loss with L_1 regularization to estimate the coefficients (popularly called *Lasso* [23]). Let's denote the training data matrix as $\mathbf{X}$, containing n independent samples of X as the rows and the p variables as the columns. $\mathbf{X}_i$ is the ith column of this matrix, and $\mathbf{X}_{-i}$ is the matrix containing the remaining columns. Let β_i be the vector of regression coefficients when the ith variable is the target. The optimal regression coefficient vector β_i^* is estimated as

$$\beta_i^* = \arg\min_{\beta_i} \frac{1}{n}\|\mathbf{X}_i - \mathbf{X}_{-i}\beta_i\|_2^2 + \lambda\|\beta_i\|_1, \quad (2)$$

where λ is a parameter to control the relative contribution of the L_1 regularizer to the objective function. Meinshausen and Buhlmann show that the resulting algorithm is a consistent estimator of the graph structure for the case of *high dimensional data* (including $p \gg n$) and *sparse graph* (the maximum number of edges for any vertex is $O(n^\kappa)$ with $0 \leq \kappa < 1$). Both of these conditions are relevant for our application – the dimensionality is high due to the large number of performance counters, and the graph is sparse as we expect only a small number of them to be conditionally dependent on each other. So we expect the algorithm to be well-suited for our application. Detailed theoretical results for the algorithm can be found in [17].

In our implementation, for each detector i, we chose λ to be the largest value such that the squared error falls below a fraction above the asymptotic squared error value.

The final output of the algorithm is a pxp graph adjacency matrix A such that $A_{ij} = 1$ if the algorithm has determined that there is an edge between X_i and X_j, and 0 otherwise. A_{ii} is fixed to be 0 for all i.

We apply the algorithm to the output scores of detectors. In practice a detector score may follow a heavier-tailed distribution than a Gaussian, with the score at zero or near zero most of the time and taking high values only during an unusual event. In such a case, the average squared error term in the Lasso objective function (equation 2) is dominated by the prediction error on the high scores. As a result, the algorithm tends to put edges between pairs of detectors that give high scores simultaneously because they can significantly reduce the average squared error.

4.2 Clustering with Affinity Propagation

Once the graph structure is estimated using the Lasso-based algorithm, we want to find groups of detectors that can be combined to form the next-level detectors in the hierarchy. Our approach is to cluster the detectors based on the graph structure such that densely connected subgraphs form the detector groups. One way to achieve this is to use the graph adjacency matrix as a (binary) similarity score matrix between detector pairs in a clustering algorithm. The output is a clustering of the detectors into different groups.

Here we use Affinity Propagation (AP) [7] for clustering. Given a dataset of points and the pairwise similarities between points, AP selects a subset of them as "exemplars", one per cluster, to act as the representative point of each cluster. The remaining points are assigned to one exemplar each, resulting in a partitioning of the dataset. The exemplars and the assignments are selected to maximize the sum of similarities between points and their exemplars. The solution is found using a message passing algorithm.

Unlike k-means clustering, AP does not require pre-specifying the number of clusters. Instead, it uses a "preference" parameter which controls the cost for a datapoint to be selected as an exemplar. The more negative it is, the larger clusters one gets. This parameter can be used to bias the solution towards small/medium/large number of clusters. It also provides a way to incorporate into the clustering domain knowledge about particular data points that should be used as exemplars.

4.3 Combining scores within a detector group

After detector groups are formed using affinity propagation, the scores of the detectors within a group need to be combined to form a single score, which is the output of that group. Here we use averaging, which keeps the group score interpretable. One consequence of this choice is that the detector group score at any level in the detector hierarchy is a linear function of a subset of low-level detector scores.

Other functions can also be used to combine the scores, including nonlinear and/or learned ones. For example, one can use unsupervised learning algorithms such as One Class Support Vector Machine [21] or Local Outlier Factor [3] to learn a nonlinear combiner function. More generally, it can be useful to jointly learn both the detector groups and the combiner function applied to each group by optimizing a single objective function, instead of treating them as two disjoint steps.

4.4 Distribution change detection as a low-level detector

Many issues affecting the service manifest as abrupt changes in the probability distribution of counters (e.g., a jump in the mean value of a counter). One choice for a low-level detector is to find such changes in a single performance counter.

Let $X(t)$ be a univariate counter time series which is generated by independently sampling at each discrete time step from a distribution $P(X;\theta)$ parametrized by θ. Consider a time interval $t \in [t_0, t_1]$ in which a distributional change occurs at time t_c such that $X \sim P(X;\theta = \theta_0)$ for $t \in [t_0, t_c)$ and $X \sim P(X;\theta = \theta_1)$ for $t \in [t_c, t_1]$. t_c can be estimated as the candidate changepoint $t_a \in (t_0, t_1)$ at which the distribution estimated from samples in $[t_0, t_a)$ is maximally different (according to a chosen dissimilarity function) from the distribution estimated from samples in $[t_a, t_1]$. If the maximum dissimilarity is above a threshold, then the detector reports a change in distribution.

We use Poisson distribution for $P(X;\theta)$ for count variables and Squared Hellinger distance to compute the distance between two distributions P and Q. For Poisson-distributed P and Q with parameters λ_P and λ_Q, respectively, Squared Hellinger distance is

$$D^2(P,Q) = 1 - \exp(-\frac{\rho}{2}(\sqrt{\lambda_P} - \sqrt{\lambda_Q})^2), \quad (3)$$

where ρ is a scaling parameter. The advantages of this distance are: 1) it is a function of the change in mean between P and Q, which makes its detection results more visually interpretable, and 2) it produces a score normalized to the interval $[0,1]$, which is needed when combining detectors to form groups. We use an interval size of 12 hours.

To estimate detection quality, we manually evaluated a set of detections. We selected ten counters belonging to five different types of counters (two of each type) and evaluated the ten time intervals over a period of six months which gives the highest change detection score. We found that the precision was 95%.

Setting ρ: The ρ parameter in the Squared Hellinger distance expression above is set such that the detector score saturates at 1 for only a small percentage of time during a six month period, ensuring that the detector stays within its dynamic range most of the time. This percentage is set to 0.1% for all counters. As a result, the appropriate value of ρ for each counter can be estimated automatically from the data.

Alternative approaches: Other choices for the parametric form of the distribution, such as Pareto, Exponential, Log-Normal, etc., can be also be tried. Counters with heavy-tailed distributions are more common in our application, so we expect distributions such as Pareto to be more useful. One can also attempt to automatically identify the best-fitting distribution type for a counter; we leave this as future work. Instead of assuming a parametric form for the counter distribution, one can also use non-parametric two-sample tests such as Kolmogorov-Smirnov test and Maximum Mean Discrepancy [11], or non-parametric change detection using exchangeability Martingales [12].

5. RESULTS

To illustrate the effective working of the various principles underlying our hierarchical monitoring system, we use the data collected from 11 *volumes* (instances of the Storage Manager component of the service), each of which serves the same functionality. Each volume has 75 counter time series. The change detection algorithm described in section 4.4 is applied on each of the counter time series to form 75 low level detector time series. The hierarchical approach was applied on these to form several detectors at the mid level; a second iteration yields one high level detector. The grouping of the low level detectors to form the mid level detectors is done in one of two ways: (a) *Manual* - where an expert identified the grouping at a broad level; and (b) *Auto* - where the Lasso algorithm combined with AP clustering was applied to get the grouping. The manual approach was mainly included to provide a strong baseline for evaluating Auto.

The results are grouped in three parts. (1) First we illustrate the working of the structure discovery process and its effectiveness in bringing about sparsity and removal of irrelevant variables, thus leading to manageability. (2) Then we show how the hierarchical monitoring process leads to a reduction of manual effort via reduction of false positives while retaining alert quality. (3) We quantify this via suitably chosen plots that relate alert quality and manual effort and evaluate the detectors at various levels.

Effectiveness of structure discovery: Figure 4 shows results associated with the formation of the mid level detectors for one volume. The top left gray scale image describes the weights obtained by the Lasso algorithm. Each row (i-th) corresponds to the Lasso weights associated with the prediction model for the i-th variable. Pure black pixels indicate zero weights while gray pixels indicate non-zero weights; as the weight magnitude becomes larger, the pixel becomes more white. It is clear that the solution is very sparse - only a minimal set of important variables are picked up for predicting each variable. The top right plot is the same gray scale image with the variables re-ordered to show the groupings formed by the AP clustering algorithm. The diagonal blocks shown in red or blue describe the groupings.

Note that the AP algorithm is not perfect (it leaves out several good white pixels from the diagonal blocks), which is expected of any soft clustering algorithm. Since the total number of white pixels in the image is small, an alternative to the AP algorithm is to take each white pixel and define a grouping with just the two variables defining the pixel. This means that the groupings can have an intersection, which is quite fine. In general, finding overlapping clusterings may

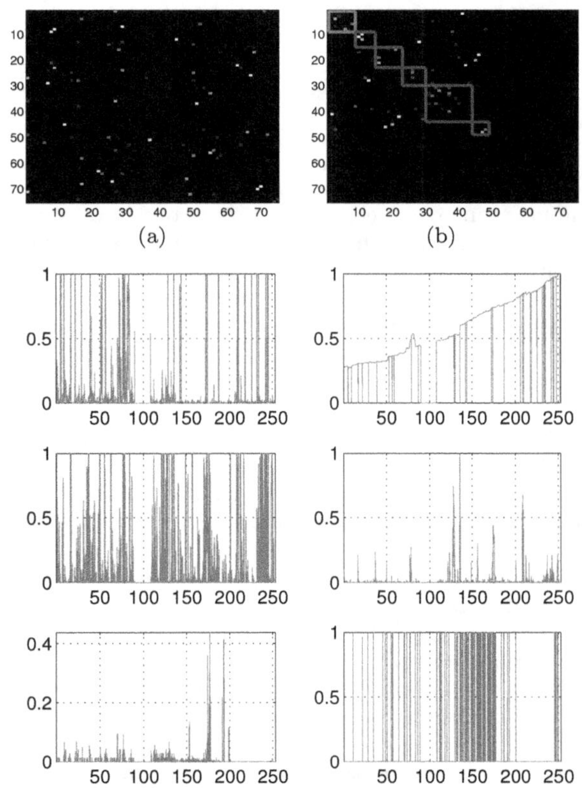

(c)

Figure 4: Illustration of the effectiveness of structure discovery (Lasso and AP clustering). See text for details.

be a good idea for avoiding information loss. We will explore these ideas in future work.

It is useful to note from the top right image of Figure 4 that the last 20 variables do not involve any white pixel. This confirms the ability of our method to separate out variables that do not form any grouping with other variables. While it is usually the case that most of these variables are actually irrelevant, some of them could still be useful; such variables could be identified via supervision - either direct manual specification, or, via supervised learning using data that contains time windows containing issues in the system.

Figure 4(c) shows the low level detector time series (left side plots) and their corresponding raw time series (right side plots) corresponding to a selected subset of three of the eight variables that define the top, red diagonal block of the image in Figure 4(b). In the top two sets of plots in Figure 4(c) one can see that the raw time series of those two variables are quite different, but their detector time series are very close. Thus, as recommended by our method, it is always better to use the detector time series and avoid using the raw time series, at the low level.

The bottom variable in Figure 4(c) has an interesting raw time series with great jumpiness. The distribution detection algorithm is quite effective and leads to a detector with only a small number of high peaks. Thus, this is a case in which the low level detector itself is useful. The other variables of the red block of Figure 4(b) have high peaks that are decently matched with those of the bottom variable - this is the good effect caused by Lasso. It turns out that the mid level detector formed by the red block is even better than the bottom variable in terms of restricting the firings to an even smaller set.

Reduction of manual effort while retaining alert quality: Figure 5 plots the detector time series at the three levels of the hierarchy. The time interval between the two vertical red lines denotes an interval where an issue occurred. For illustration we use a fixed threshold of 0.5 on each detector to define its firing. (Even if the thresholds are changed, the conclusions given below remain nearly the same.) Each firing leads to an alert that adds to the manual effort to investigate and resolve it. Clearly, the number of firings reduces significantly as we move up the hierarchy, and becomes manageably very small - just two - at the high level. These firings also lie in the red interval, thus neatly detecting the issue. It is important to note that this does not mean that firings at the lower levels are unimportant. For example, if we look at the third variable in the mid level, it fires several times around time=150. Other mid level detectors do not fire around the same time, and so the high level detector does not fire here. But it is quite possible that the firings of this variable is indicative of an issue with a mid level component. As pointed out earlier, such firings at lower levels can be determined as important using appropriate supervised learning.

Evaluation of alert quality and manual effort at various levels: Figure 6 plots various quantities accumulated over all 11 volumes of the platform. Here, *#Firings* is the number of times a specified threshold is crossed. Human experts labeled 19 issues in the 11 volumes by locating time intervals where issues occurred in the system. A detector is said to successfully identify an issue if it fires within that issue's time interval. We define *Recall* as the fraction of the set of 19 issues identified by a detector. The figure compares

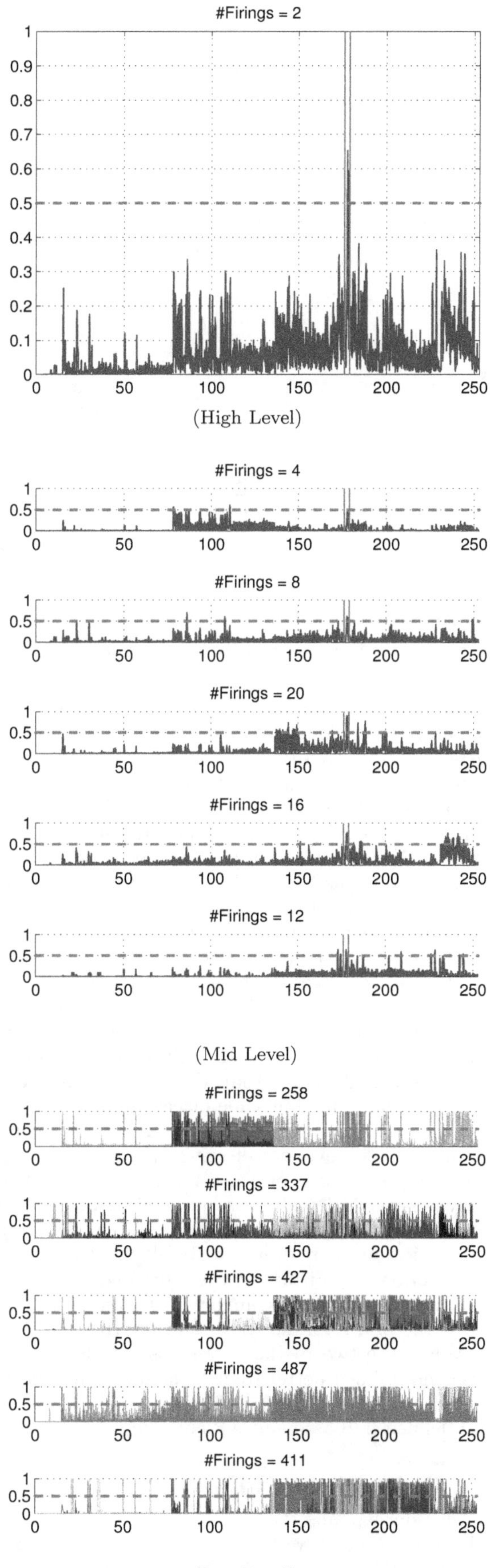

Figure 5: Reduction of the number of firings along levels of the hierarchy. See text for details.

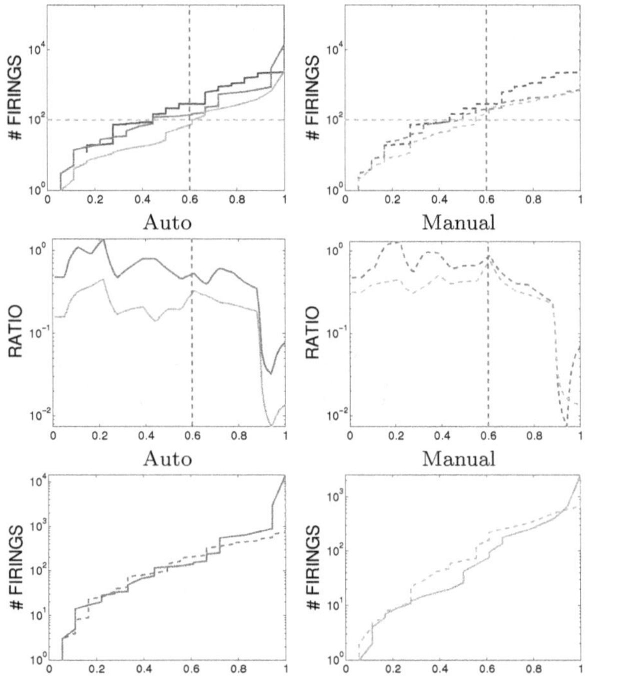

Figure 6: Performance of the hierarchical approach. See text for details.

the performance of detectors at the low (blue), mid (red) and high (green) levels. *Ratio* refers to the ratio of the number of firings of mid or high level to that of the low level; thus, numbers much smaller than 1 indicate much better manageability compared to the low level. The top plots of Figure 6 show the behavior of #Firings against Recall - each curve is drawn by decreasing the threshold of each detector from a large value to a small value. The curves for the Auto and Manual methods are shown respectively as continuous and dotted lines. The plots in the middle row show the variation of Ratio as a function of Recall. Note the use of log scale in the vertical axes of these plots. In all these plots, lower a curve is, the better it is in terms of manageability: a specified recall can be achieved with lesser number of firings.

We can draw the following conclusions. (a) The mid level detectors are overall better than the low level detectors in reducing #Firings, equal in some places and much better in other places. (b) The high level detector is clearly superior to the low and mid level detectors. To get a quantification, (i) horizontal lines are drawn at #Firings=10^2 to get a feel for improvements in Recall for a specified number of firings (fixed amount of inspection time for the system's operators); and (ii) vertical lines are drawn at Recall=0.6 to get an idea of the reduction in #Firings at the same Recall.

The bottom row of plots compares Auto and Manual separately at the Mid level (left plot) and the High level (right plot). While the two methods are close at the mid level, Auto is overall much better than Manual at the High level. This is a clear indication of the effectiveness of the automatic method defined by Lasso and AP clustering.

6. DEPLOYED SYSTEM

This section explains the training pipeline and the real-time detection service we have implemented to deploy our solution in production (fig. 7). Performance counters are

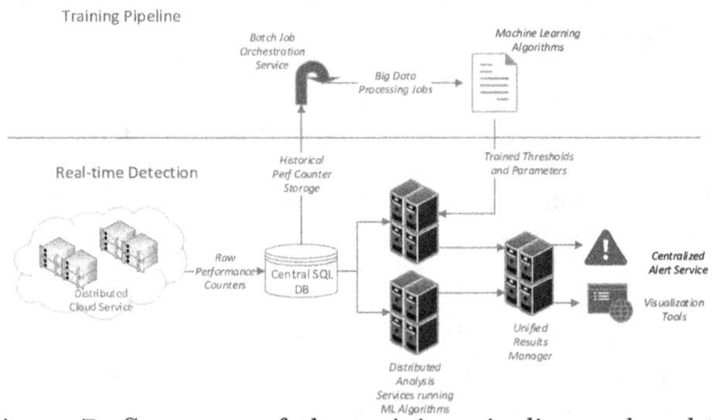

Figure 7: Summary of the training pipeline and real-time detection service for deploying our solution in production.

constantly updated on every machine; however, since there are tens of thousands of machines, these raw counters must be aggregated across time and various machine types for any viable real-time health assessment. Our counter aggregation service generates standard aggregate values such as sum, min, max, and average at specified time intervals (e.g., once per minute). These aggregates are stored in a central database for up to 15 days for real-time querying. Additionally, this data is archived in separate historical counter storage for one year for any offline analysis.

Training Pipeline: The counter data in historical counter storage form the input to the offline learning of the hierarchical detector. A list of past service issues are used for evaluation. The output is a hierarchical detector.

Real-time detection: The goal of our detection service is to detect anomalies as soon as they occur. To achieve this, the service executes the following every 15 minutes:

1. It queries the central database for most recent twelve hours of counter data.
2. The Distributed Analysis module then applies the learned detector (output by the training pipeline) on the counters. The results computed by the detector are used to give health assessments for various components of the service being monitored.
3. Results for each component are sent to the Unified Results Manager, which in turn sends alert decisions to the Centralized Alert Service.
4. Centralized Alert Service sends alerts to relevant stakeholders.

Unified Results Manager: Acting as a bridge between the Distributed Analysis module and the Centralized Alert Service as shown in figure 7, this module groups the detector results, suppresses frequent alert fires, and sends summary reports. Additionally, it sends the detector results to visualization tools used by engineers to debug service issues.

Honoring real-time expectations: To honor real-time expectations, our process must complete in fifteen minutes or less. This necessitates the implementation to be scalable for both data access (querying the central DB) and processing (computing detector results). Our service implements a distributed architecture to achieve scale-out with components communicating with each other using industry standard REST Protocol.

Interactive Monitoring Tool: We have built a tool for visualizing the health of the system, the components and

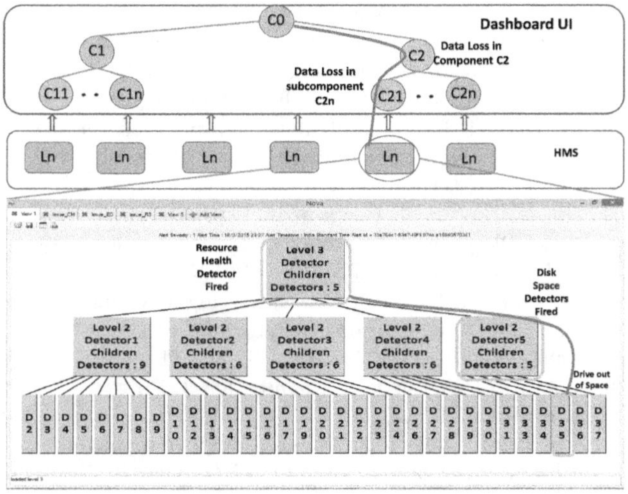

Figure 8: Tool interface for visualizing the hierarchical monitoring system. The red line shows a navigation path for a *data loss* issue starting from component C2 that reports *data loss* and narrowing down to a *drive going out of space* in sub-component C21.

the sub-components in a hierarchical fashion. See Figure 8. The health information is colour coded with colours ranging from green (good health) to red (bad health). The health color information of any node in the hierarchy encodes the aggregated health score computed from the detectors feeding to the node. The health of a higher level component is computed as a weighted combination of the preceding level lower components and, weights are assigned according to the severity of issues that arise in different components. For example, *data loss* could be a more serious issue than *delay in job execution*. Users can monitor the health of any component and navigate down (e.g., to counter level details and views) as they see degrading health or unhealthy signs. As users navigate down, lower level health information (e.g., *response health*, *load health*, *disk access health*) get exposed. For example, *response health* can be computed using alerts signalled through unusual delays in responses (as measured through latency counters). Thus, navigating through a path gives a complete of view of the issues and the components involved in producing the unhealthy state of a higher level component. Furthermore, users can mark patterns or events to detect as they find changing behaviors during their investigation process. Detectors for such patterns get added to the system subsequently. Similarly, users can provide feedback when any harmless unusual patterns get detected, as such patterns falsely score a healthy state as unhealthy. Such labels can be used to adapt the machine learning models.

7. RELATED WORK

The literature in the area of service monitoring and diagnosis can be classified into two categories. Due to space limitation, we briefly discuss a few representative works from each of these categories. The first category covers application oriented works that consider one or more application scenarios (e.g., data centers, internet sites, online services) and develop some heuristics and/or data mining based approaches to solve a selected set of problems. Bodik et al. [2] propose the identification of finger prints that characterize different faulty states of data centers and use such finger prints to classify and identify performance crises quickly. Chen et al. [6] suggest a decision tree based approach to detect failures in large Internet sites such as eBay. Gabel et al. [10] present an unsupervised approach to detect faulty machines by comparing machines that perform the same task. Lin et al. [13] propose a hierarchical approach to cluster alerts and incident tickets using text content in large scale enterprise IT infrastructure scenarios. Chen et al. [5] present a subspace modelling approach that discovers a mapping between workloads and system internal measurements and use this mapping to detect system failures even under varying workload conditions. Fu et al. [8] study the problem of identifying performance issue metrics (e.g., access delay in databases) given a large collection of system metrics for an online services system. Roy et al. [20] describe an automated system for mining service logs to identify anomalies. Lou et al. [15] present a software analytics approach to implement an incident management system that investigates faulty incidents and suggest actions to take. To the best of our knowledge, none of the works develop a principled hierarchical monitoring system that can (a) handle high dimensional time series data, and (b) take system architecture and experts domain knowledge into account.

The second category covers methods that solve more primitive problems such as discovering patterns or detecting anomalies in time series data, text logs and event streams. Fu et al. [9] and Lou et al. [14] develop data mining based approaches to detect anomalies in job execution log files. Liang et al. [22] address the problem of generating system events from logs, with the resulting event streams subsequently used to detect anomalies using techniques such as finite state automaton or frequent item-set mining. Luo et al. [16] suggest to find correlation between time series and event data, and show how such discovered correlations help in the incident diagnosis process. The problem of detecting anomalies in multivariate time series has been studied by several researchers [4, 19]. Qiu et al. [19] propose a Lasso based approach to discover dependency structure among variables and detect anomalies in high dimensional time series data. Chandola et al. [4] suggest a sub-space based approach to convert multivariate time series to univariate time series and use that to detect anomalies. Discovering Motifs or shapelets and detecting rare occurrences of them in time series data have been other related areas of research [1, 18]. All these approaches are relevant to our work from the viewpoint of building low level detectors in our hierarchical monitoring system.

8. DISCUSSION & CONCLUSION

In this paper we have proposed a principled hierarchical approach that scales well to service monitoring applications having large amounts of telemetry data. This approach has been successfully deployed for monitoring a large distributed computing platform.

We briefly cover several important aspects of the system that have possible extensions.

(1) Low level detectors: They broadly belong to three categories: (a) general purpose (e.g., change detection methods, nearest neighbor based local outlier detectors), (b) standard patterns (e.g., frequently occurring spikes, bursts, trends) and (c) user-specified patterns or rules that are specified through a tool. While the first two categories of detectors and using expert rules as detectors are reasonably well-understood, identification and detection of newer patterns can be semi-automated through a motif discovery process [18] and experts suggesting patterns to detect.

(2) Structure discovery models: While our current implementation uses linear models based on the Gaussian assumption, improvements through non-linear and non-Gaussian models are possible. At each level, our method forms non-overlapping groups of variables. Modifying it to allow overlapping groups is easy and can be useful too.

(3) Learning: The learning process can be made more powerful and sophisticated. Our current system is unsupervised. But supervision data usually comes in as specific issues (e.g., machine overload or data loss) get identified by users. Weighted combinations of detectors at various levels can be set up to detect the issues. The supervision data can be used to adjust these weights as well as guide the structure discovery process. In essence, semi-supervised learning can become an important aspect over time. This set up has the potential to pick up important lower level detectors that are useful for detecting issues; see also the discussions in section 5.

(4) Interaction: Human interaction is useful to improve the quality of machine learning solutions. For example, experts can interact with the system to remove some variables from groups during the structure discovery process.

9. REFERENCES

[1] N. Begum and E. J. Keogh. Rare time series motif discovery from unbounded streams. *PVLDB*, 8(2):149–160, 2014.

[2] P. Bodík, M. Goldszmidt, A. Fox, D. B. Woodard, and H. Andersen. Fingerprinting the datacenter: automated classification of performance crises. In *EuroSys 2010*, pages 111–124, 2010.

[3] M. M. Breunig, H.-P. Kriegel, R. T. Ng, and J. Sander. LOF: Identifying density-based local outliers. *SIGMOD Rec.*, 29(2):93–104, May 2000.

[4] V. Chandola, A. Banerjee, and V. Kumar. Anomaly detection for discrete sequences: A survey. *IEEE Trans. Knowl. Data Eng.*, 24(5):823–839, 2012.

[5] H. Chen, G. Jiang, and K. Yoshihira. Failure detection in large-scale internet services by principal subspace mapping. *IEEE Trans. Knowl. Data Eng.*, 19(10):1308–1320, 2007.

[6] M. Y. Chen, A. X. Zheng, J. Lloyd, M. I. Jordan, and E. A. Brewer. Failure diagnosis using decision trees. In *ICAC*, pages 36–43, 2004.

[7] B. J. Frey and D. Dueck. Clustering by passing messages between data points. *Science*, 315:972–976, 2007.

[8] Q. Fu, J. Lou, Q. Lin, R. Ding, D. Zhang, Z. Ye, and T. Xie. Performance issue diagnosis for online service systems. In *SRDS*, pages 273–278, 2012.

[9] Q. Fu, J. Lou, Y. Wang, and J. Li. Execution anomaly detection in distributed systems through unstructured log analysis. In *ICDM*, pages 149–158, 2009.

[10] M. Gabel, R. Glad-Bachrach, N. Bjorner, and A. Schuster. Latent fault detection in cloud services. Technical Report Technical Report, Microsoft Research, 2011.

[11] A. Gretton, K. M. Borgwardt, M. J. Rasch, B. Schölkopf, and A. Smola. A kernel two-sample test. *in JMLR*, 13(1):723–773, Mar. 2012.

[12] S.-S. Ho and H. Wechsler. A martingale framework for detecting changes in data streams by testing exchangeability. *IEEE PAMI*, 32(12):2113–2127, 2010.

[13] D. Lin, R. Raghu, V. Ramamurthy, J. Yu, R. Radhakrishnan, and J. Fernandez. Unveiling clusters of events for alert and incident management in large-scale enterprise it. In *KDD*, pages 1630–1639, 2014.

[14] J. Lou, Q. Fu, S. Yang, Y. Xu, and J. Li. Mining invariants from console logs for system problem detection. In *USENIX*, 2010.

[15] J. Lou, Q. Lin, R. Ding, Q. Fu, D. Zhang, and T. Xie. Software analytics for incident management of online services: An experience report. In *IEEE/ACM ASE*, 2013.

[16] C. Luo, J. Lou, Q. Lin, Q. Fu, R. Ding, D. Zhang, and Z. Wang. Correlating events with time series for incident diagnosis. In *KDD*, pages 1583–1592, 2014.

[17] N. Meinshausen and P. Buhlmann. High-dimensional graphs and variable selection with the lasso. *The Annals of Statistics*, 34(3):1436–1462, June 2006.

[18] A. Mueen. Time series motif discovery: dimensions and applications. *Data Mining and Knowledge Discovery*, 4(2):152–159, 2014.

[19] H. Qiu, Y. Liu, N. A. Subrahmanya, and W. Li. Granger causality for time-series anomaly detection. In *ICDM*, pages 1074–1079, 2012.

[20] S. Roy, A. C. Koíg, I. Dvorkin, and M. Kumar. Perfaugur: Robust diagnostics for performance anomalies in cloud services. In *ICDE, 2015*, 2015.

[21] B. Scholkopf, J. C. Platt, J. C. Shawe-Taylor, A. J. Smola, and R. C. Williamson. Estimating the support of a high-dimensional distribution. *Neural Computation*, 2001.

[22] L. Tang and T. Li. Logtree: A framework for generating system events from raw textual logs. In *ICDM*, pages 491–500, 2010.

[23] R. Tibshirani. Regression shrinkage and selection via the lasso. *Journal of the Royal Statistical Society (Series B)*, 58:267–288, 1996.

Predictive Modeling for Public Health: Preventing Childhood Lead Poisoning

Eric Potash
University of Chicago
epotash@uchicago.edu

Joe Brew
University of Florida
joebrew@ufl.edu

Alexander Loewi
Carnegie Mellon University
aloewi@cmu.edu

Subhabrata Majumdar
University of Minnesota
majum010@umn.edu

Andrew Reece
Harvard University
reece@g.harvard.edu

Joe Walsh
University of Chicago
jtwalsh@uchicago.edu

Eric Rozier
University of Cincinnati
eric.rozier@uc.edu

Emile Jorgensen
Chicago Dept of Public Health
Emile.Jorgensen@cityofchicago.org

Raed Mansour
Chicago Dept of Public Health
Raed.Mansour@cityofchicago.org

Rayid Ghani
University of Chicago
rayid@uchicago.edu

ABSTRACT

Lead poisoning is a major public health problem that affects hundreds of thousands of children in the United States every year. A common approach to identifying lead hazards is to test all children for elevated blood lead levels and then investigate and remediate the homes of children with elevated tests. This can prevent exposure to lead of future residents, but only after a child has been poisoned. This paper describes joint work with the Chicago Department of Public Health (CDPH) in which we build a model that predicts the risk of a child to being poisoned so that an intervention can take place *before* that happens. Using two decades of blood lead level tests, home lead inspections, property value assessments, and census data, our model allows inspectors to prioritize houses on an intractably long list of potential hazards and identify children who are at the highest risk. This work has been described by CDPH as pioneering in the use of machine learning and predictive analytics in public health and has the potential to have a significant impact on both health and economic outcomes for communities across the US.

Categories and Subject Descriptors

J.3 [**Life and Medical Sciences**]: Health; K.4.1 [**Public Policy Issues**]: Human Safety

KDD '15, August 11-14, 2015, Sydney, NSW, Australia

ISBN 978-1-4503-3664-2/15/08 $15.00
DOI: http://dx.doi.org/10.1145/2783258.2788629.

General Terms

Machine Learning, Social Good, Lead Poisoning, Public Health, Public Policy

1. INTRODUCTION

Lead poisoning is a major public health issue, imposing lifelong health and economic costs on hundreds of thousands of children every year in the United States. Although European states banned lead paint as early as 1909 [19], political forces and vested business interests delayed bans on leaded consumer products in the United States until the late 1970s [21]. Throughout most of the 20th century, cars ran on leaded gas, houses were coated with leaded paint, and industry emitted leaded waste products directly into the environment. To this day, lead in paint remains a significant hazard. In Chicago, almost 90% of the housing stock was built before the ban [13].

Exposure to lead has been found to be associated with premature birth and early neurological development issues such as edema, herniation, atrophy, and white-matter degeneration [12, 10]. Lead can cause vomiting; convulsions; paralysis; and, in high concentrations, death [14]. Elevated blood lead levels are associated with lower IQs in children. A retrospective study by Mazumdar *et al* [20] shows that, on average, a 1 μg/dL increase in blood-lead level is associated with a decrease of 1 IQ point among six-month-olds and 2 IQ points among 10 year olds.

Because of the permanent damage it can inflict, lead poisoning imposes significant indirect costs on society. Based on its well-documented effects on IQ and contributions to neuropsychiatric disorders such as ADHD, lead poisoning has been estimated to significantly lower lifetime earnings for individuals and greatly increase the costs of crime prevention and special-education programs for the government. Lead-related child health issues conservatively cost over $40 billion annually [18]. Completely eliminating lead in the United States could indirectly save $200 billion dollars per year [22], ten times more than needed for removal.

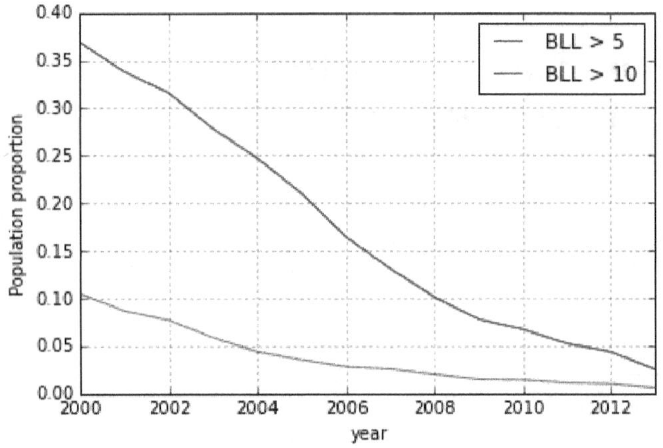

Figure 1: The proportion of blood lead tests conducted each year with a concentration greater than 5 μg/dL (blue) and greater than 10 μg/dL each year (green).

While the Chicago Department of Public Health (CDPH) devotes an enormous and concerted effort to solving the problem of lead exposure, it is like many American departments of public health in its shortage of resources. At current levels of funding and staffing, it would take CDPH 76 years and $98 million to inspect—let alone remediate—the 197,157 older buildings in Chicago. The only hope of making a significant impact with the available budget is to use it efficiently.

In collaboration with CDPH, we focused on identifying children who are at risk of lead poisoning and homes that are likely to contain lead hazards so that the hazards can be remediated *before* the children are poisoned. Our approach uses two decades of blood lead level tests, home lead inspections and remediations, housing records, and census data to build a model that can successfully predict the risk of lead poisoning for individual children.

Based on these results, we are designing experiments to pilot the use of these predictions by CDPH to perform proactive home inspections and targeted education and outreach about lead hazards. In addition, we are working with medical providers in Chicago to deploy our risk score into electronic medical record systems to raise early alerts for blood tests in children with high risk levels. This work has been described by CDPH as pioneering in the use of machine learning and predictive analytics in public health and has the potential to have a significant impact on both health and economic outcomes for communities across the US.

2. CURRENT APPROACHES

The current approaches used to deal with lead poisoning are centered around testing children for lead exposure with blood tests and preventing lead exposure by inspecting homes that contain lead hazards. In this section, we describe those approaches, their shortcomings, and the motivation for our work.

The Center for Disease Control (CDC) recommends all children at risk for exposure get a lead test between one and two years of age. This is known to be the period when children start crawling and exhibiting hand-to-mouth behavior, which puts them most at-risk for lead dust ingestion [17].

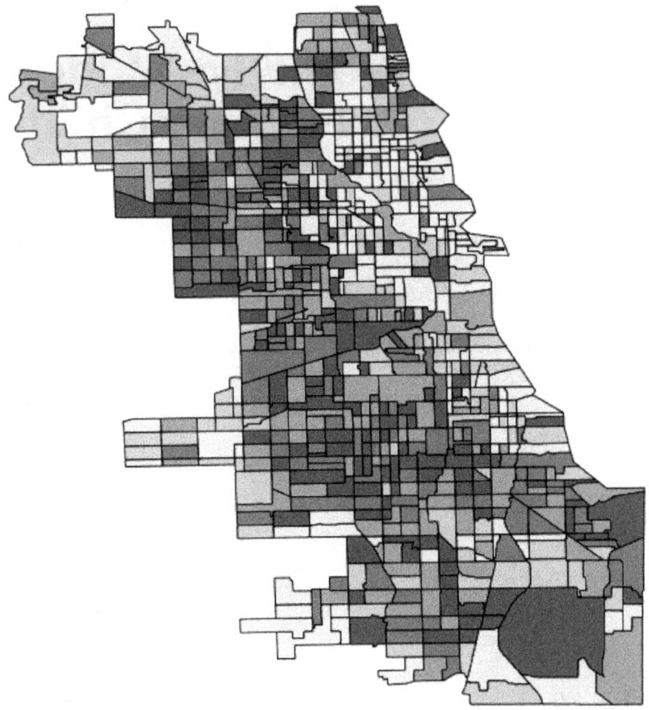

Figure 2: A heatmap of lead poisoning cases in 2012. There are spatial patterns, but space cannot adequately predict lead poisoning alone. There are too many houses in the dark-red (poisoned) areas for the city to inspect.

Our data show that lead levels rise during this period, peaking around age two.

Despite this being well known to public health officials, implementation of these testing recommendations is far from universal. Often, the children least at risk are the most likely to be tested early, and those most at risk do not get tested until well after their period of greatest risk.

In addition to the CDC recommendations, many school districts, including Chicago Public Schools, require children to have had a lead test no more than a year before their matriculation. Again, this requirement may not always be adhered to and misses the most dangerous window—the first two years of the child's life—for lead poisoning. Many of the most vulnerable children are not getting tested early enough.

Screening of blood lead levels in children identifies cases but does not prevent their occurrence. Primary prevention requires that older housing units comply with lead safety standards before they are occupied by children. Though screening and primary prevention work are complementary, the latter is recognized to be more important and far more cost-effective in the effort to eliminate lead poisoning [19].

2.1 Problems with current approaches

Despite these guidelines for testing and prevention, problems remain. First, lead inspections and remediation often come too late, after a child has been poisoned. A positive blood test triggers an inspection, and a positive inspection triggers remediation proceedings. CDPH cannot enforce remediation until a child living in a home tests positive. Second, inspectors may focus too heavily on lead paint. While lead paint is the primary cause of poisoning [15], there are of-

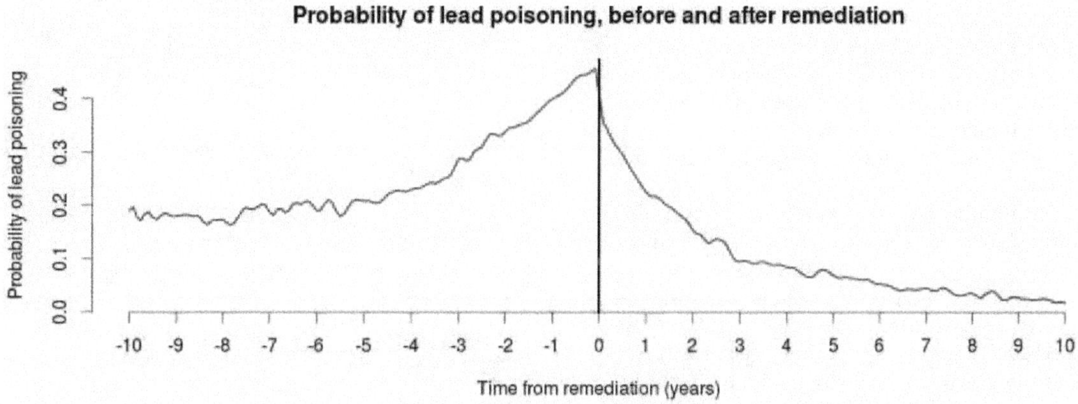

Figure 3: Mean probability of a house having > $5\mu g/dL$ BLL pre- and post-remediation

ten multiple sources of poisoning, especially for higher blood lead levels [11]. In 5% of cases, no source can be identified [8]. Third, lead continues to poison some segments of society more heavily than others. A survey conducted in two of Chicago's riskiest neighborhoods found that 27% of children had elevated blood lead levels and 61% had never been tested previously [13].

Secondary care is a challenge. Lead paint remediation (the removal of leaded paint) and soil abatement, even when conducted by a certified professional, can lead to an increase in BLLs by dispersing lead particulates into the air where they are more accessible to inhalation [9]. In Chicago, most BLLs drop following the intervention (Figure 3), though the extent to which this is environmental as opposed to behavioral is unclear. Worryingly, in 9.3% of the sample, BLLs increased by at least 5 $\mu g/dL$ following remediation. Approximately 46% of children with BLLs over 10 did not receive adequate follow-up testing [16].

2.2 Opportunities for improvement

Since even small quantities of lead are toxic, a transition from secondary (screening) to primary (pre-emptive remediation) care has the potential to dramatically improve health outcomes. However, if not implemented efficiently, prevention could be prohibitively expensive and cannibalize resources for remediating confirmed cases of lead poisoning. This is perhaps the chief impediment to adoption of primary care for lead poisoning.

Fortunately, these challenges of primary care can be mitigated by recent advances in computation. Addressing the scale and complexity of lead-related data is both practical and affordable. Likewise, recent improvements in the quality, scope, and availability of data make the task of predictive lead poisoning prevention feasible. The availability of public infrastructure data, combined with the digitization of medical and inspections and remediation records, offer public-health practitioners the opportunity to model the risk factors associated with lead poisoning, thereby enabling them to target interventions, prevent illness, and use their resources efficiently.

3. OUR SOLUTION

The solution we developed to predict risk for lead poisoning is based on a variety of data sources. We obtained data from the Chicago Department of Public Health that consists of blood lead level (BLL) tests and home-inspection records, combined that with housing records and other public data (described in detail below), and built a classifier to predict the risk of lead poisoning. The city of Chicago has adopted the CDC definition of lead poisoning of a BLL of 5 $\mu g/dL$.

Our system consists of the following components:

1. Data Integration and Cleaning
2. Feature Generation
3. Model Selection and Training
4. Model Validation
5. Deployment and Implementation

The next several sections describe each of the components in more detail.

4. DATA SOURCES

CDPH has two been collecting key data sources that form the basis of our predictions:

1. **Blood Lead Level Tests**: We were given the results of all 2.5 million BLL tests conducted in Chicago from 1993 through 2013. This corresponds to roughly 1 million children (see Section 5 for record linkage), with about 40,000 children born in the city every year and an average of 2.5 tests per child. Clinics submit the BLL test results to the Illinois Department of Public Health (IDPH) and IDPH transfers the results to CDPH daily.

2. **Home Lead Inspection Records**: We were also given 120,000 home-inspection records from the same time period (1993-2013). These reports detail the inspector's findings when they are sent to a home suspected of being hazardous. The most important entries in our model are those corresponding to the date of a house's initial inspection and the date at which it was deemed to be in compliance with lead-safety standards.

We augment these two sources with a variety of publicly available data. The city's building footprint data [1] contains building characteristics such as year of construction, physical condition, number of units, stories (floors), and vacancy status. The city also provides shapefiles of the census tract [2] and ward [3] boundaries. The Cook County Assessor's Office [5] has data on the assessed property value and building classification.

The American Community Five-Year Survey [7] contains census tract variables such as socio-demographics, education, health insurance, and home ownership. We also use the census surname ethnicity data [6], which allows estimates of ethnicity from surname alone. We combine the probability of an ethnicity given a surname with the prior probability of an ethnicity given a census tract to get a local maximum likelihood ethnicity estimate. Ethnicity was anticipated to be a predictive variable because of the history of African Americans being funneled differentially into lower-quality housing, a process known as "redlining."

5. DATA INTEGRATION AND FEATURE GENERATION

Blood test records are recorded manually and individually, so linking multiple records for a single child requires fuzzy matching of error-prone names and birthdates. We perform this using thresholded Levenshtein distances, where date of birth is a 'YYYYMMDD'-formatted string. Because there are millions of records, we use blocking on initials to parallelize and reduce the complexity of the computation. This process finds roughly 12% of records contain errors in these fields.

Home addresses in the blood test records are also prone to typographic error. Roughly 20% match exactly with our address dataset. Another 75% match after cleaning using regular expressions. Another 1% are processed using a fuzzy geocoder, leaving 4% of test addresses unresolved.

After cleaning, we collect and generate three kinds of features:

- Child features: Date of birth, imputed ethnicity (based on census tract and last name using the census surname data), and imputed gender (sometimes missing and sometimes conflicting between linked records). There are a total of 5 child features.
- Spatial features: After geocoding the address, we have a corresponding latitude and longitude. Using the city's shapefiles we can match this to a tract and ward (a neighborhood-scale political boundary in Chicago).

  The city datasets are also aggregated to the tract level, producing features such as the percentage of buildings constructed before 1978 (the year lead paint was banned), the percentage of vacant dwellings, and the average number of units per building. In total there are 44 spatial features plus indicator variables for each of Chicago's fifty wards.
- Spatio-temporal features: These are generated by aggregating the blood test and inspection records in space and time. We do this spatially at the address and tract level. The temporal period depends on the frequency of the event (blood test or inspection) at the given spatial resolution (address or tract). Figure 4 shows the periods chosen using exhaustive search.

scale	event	
	inspections	tests
address	all	3 years; all
tract	all	1 year

Figure 4: The time periods used for aggregating different events at different spatial scales.

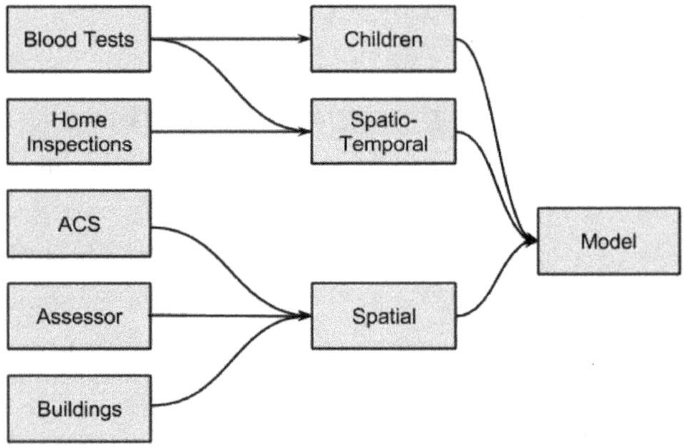

Figure 6: The data pipeline

The aggregate features for inspections and tests are listed and described in Figure 5. At the spatial and temporal scales in Figure 4 there are a total of 63 such features.

For each five year period ending in 2009 to 2013, the 5-year ACS survey gives us tract-level statistics. Features include educational achievement (e.g. percentage of adults who are college graduates), wealth (e.g. percentage of households below the poverty line), and health (e.g. percentage of minors that are uninsured). There are 21 such features.

The data pipeline is visualized in Figure 6. We used PostgreSQL with the geospatial extension PostGIS for data cleaning and aggregation. Deduplication and dataset assembly is done in Python and models are run using the scikit-learn module. The source code is available at the Data Science for Social Good GitHub repository [4].

6. EVALUATION METHODOLOGY

6.1 Cross-validation

To evaluate our models, we use a cross-validation strategy that emulates the way in which our models will be employed by CDPH and provides an accurate performance estimate.

For a given point in time t_0, we train our models only on information available to CDPH before t_0 to avoid training on data from the "future." The length of the training period dt is an additional necessary input to the cross validation, which we measure in years.

Our training set is thus comprised of blood tests occurring in the dt years before the t_0. For recent times t_0, the corresponding training set contains roughly 100,000*dt examples.

Recall that we are interested in predicting childhood lead poisoning and not individual blood samples. Thus the test-

feature	description
count	number of tests
tested	whether there has been a test
poisoned	whether there has been a poisoned test
ebll_count	number of poisoned tests
ebll_prop	proportion of poisoned tests
avg_bll	average blood lead level
median_bll	median blood lead level
max_bll	maximum blood lead level
min_bll	minimum blood lead level
std_bll	standard deviation of blood lead level
kid_count	number of children tested
kid_ebll_here_count	number of children with poisoned tests
kid_ebll_first_prop	proportion of children with poisoned tests
kid_ebll_first_count	number of children with first poisoned test
kid_ebll_first_prop	proportion of children with first poisoned test

(a)

feature	description
count	number of inspections
inspected	whether or not an inspection occurred
hazard_int_count	number of inspections finding interior hazards
hazard_ext_count	number of inspections finding exterior hazards
hazard_int_prop	proportion of inspections finding interior hazards
hazard_ext_prop	proportion of inspections finding exterior hazards
compliance_count	number of inspections in compliances
compliance_prop	proportion of inspections in compliance
avg_init_to_comply_days	average time from inspection to compliance

(b)

Figure 5: Spatio-temporal features for (a) blood tests and (b) home inspections.

ing examples, unlike the training examples, correspond to children, not blood tests. Children are included in the test set if they were born before t_0 and have not been poisoned as of t_0. There are about 50,000 children in the test set for any recent t_0.

Note this evaluation setup dictates that we cannot use the (future) dates of a child's blood test as features in predicting whether those tests will return positive for lead. However, we can use the minimum of the child's age at t_0 and the mean age of blood testing in the training period. Figure 7 shows an example transformation.

Also note that the same child may appear in both the training and test periods if he or she is below the BLL threshold before t_0 but above it after that time. We are modeling *childhood* lead poisoning, so we only consider blood samples up to three years after t_0. Because we train and test our models on data through 2013, we can only test on children born before January 1st, 2011, so that is the maximum t_0 we will consider below.

6.2 Metrics

CDPH would deploy our models to rank children (or buildings) according to their risk for getting (or causing) lead poisoning. Due to limited resources, CDPH can only investigate a subset of cases. Therefore we measure the performance of a model by computing its precision in the examples predicted to be most at risk by that model. In this way we can estimate how many cases of future lead poisoning would be found, and so potentially ameliorated or avoided, if CDPH investigated a given number of cases.

Figure 8 shows the precision at different proportions of intervention for several model types evaluated at two different years. The baseline here and henceforth is given by random classification and so is equal to the incidence of lead poisoning in the test set.

For simplicity the evaluations below will use precision in the top 5% as a representative metric. This choice is based on our observation over hundreds of model runs that this number is representative of precision at the top. That is, if the model A dominates model B at 1% then it unlikely that B dominates A at 10%. Note that 1% to 10% amounts to about 500 to 5,000 children (per year). This range is representative of the numbers that CDPH is considering for various interventions.

After tweaking each model's parameters, we observed similar performance for logistic regression, random forest, and support vector machines. See Figure 9 for a comparison of the best models of each type. Based on this observation, we use logistic regression as a representative model for the following evaluations.

7. MODELS AND RESULTS

Once our dataset is assembled, we train a variety of classification algorithms including logistic regressions, support vector machines, and random forests.

Here we present the results of running a variety of models to find optimal parameters and measure the value of different kinds of features.

By varying the number of years in the training period, we determined that approximately three years of training data

child	birth	inspection	test	BLL
1	2010-1-1	null	2010-9-1	1
1	2010-1-1	null	2012-6-1	7
2	2010-6-1	2011-2-1	2011-3-1	5
3	2011-3-1	2009-1-1	2011-11-1	1

(a)

child	birth	inspection	test	poisoned
1	2010-1-1	null	2010-9-1	True
1	2010-1-1	null	2012-6-1	True
2	2010-6-1	*null*	*null*	False

(b)

Figure 7: Example record transformation with t_0=1/1/2011. Changes to prevent leakage are italicized. The first row is in the training set, the next two are in the test set, and fourth row is discarded.

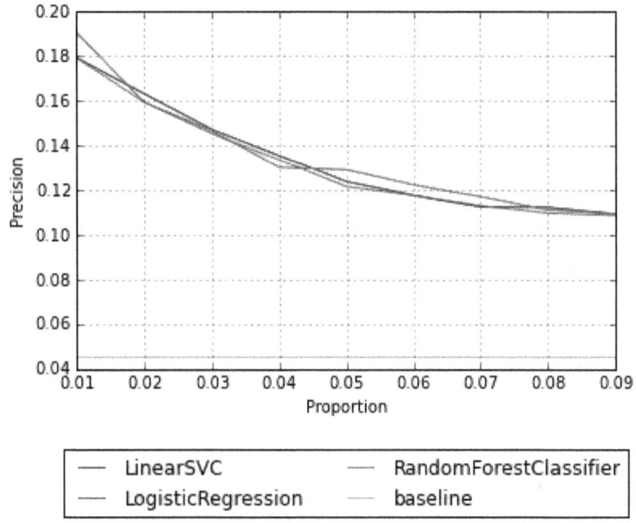

Figure 8: Precision at different proportions of investigation for different model types for the same year.

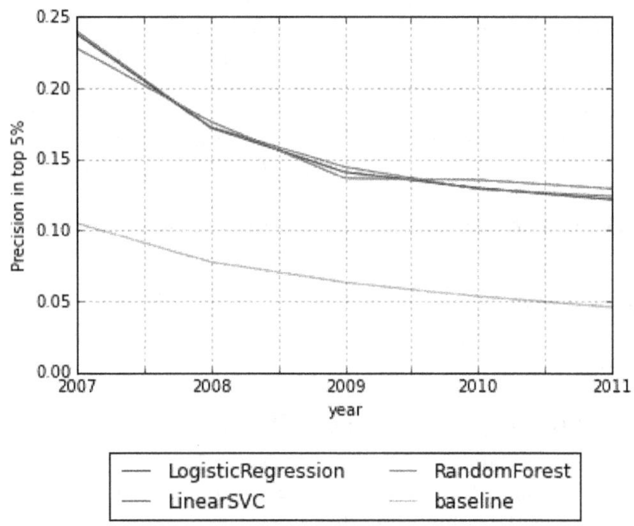

Figure 9: The best models of each class perform comparably across years.

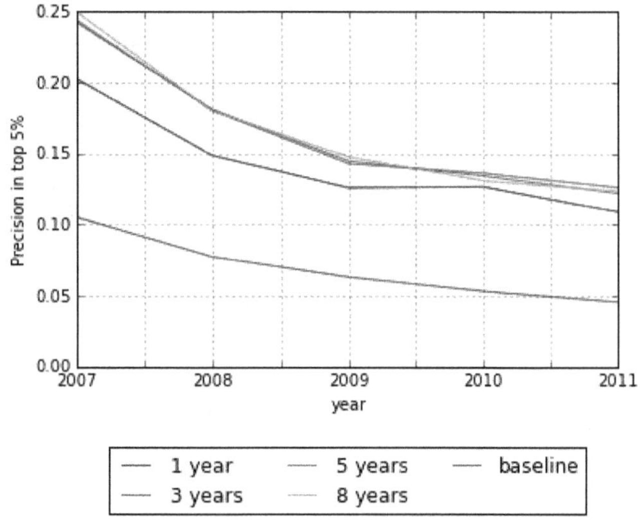

Figure 10: Performance plateaus after about three years of training data.

is optimal. See Figure 10. Note that the training period determines which blood samples are seen by the model but that all training examples include spatio-temporal features that draw on the entire history (blood tests and inspections) of an address or tract.

By fitting the same model on an increasing set of features we can observe the value added by those features. Figure 11 shows that as we refine the spatial scale of our features the model improves dramatically, with address-level features (building age, condition, and history of lead poisoning and inspections) being especially important.

We can also categorize features as they were presented in Section 5. Figure 12 shows that the spatial and spatio-temporal aggregations are very important.

We use the l_1-penalized (inverse regularization coefficient $C = .001$) logistic regression for feature selection. We examine the most important features as measured by the magnitude of their (normalized) coefficients. Figures 14 and 13 show these features having negative and positive coefficients respectively, i.e. corresponding to reduced and increased risk for lead poisoning, respectively. See the captions for a descriptions of the features.

8. IMPLEMENTATION

Based on the encouraging results of our experiments described in the previous section, this section focuses on how CDPH is using our predictive models to prevent lead poisoning. Currently, Chicago requires doctors to determine the

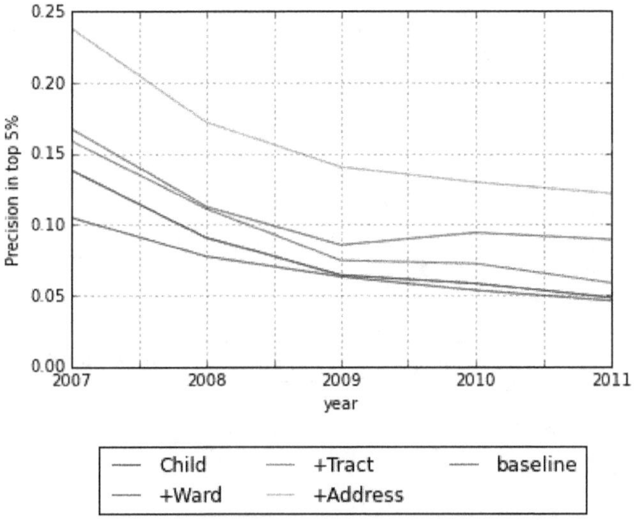

Figure 11: Precision for different feature sets

feature	coefficient
test_kid_age_days	0.224396
address_assessor_age	0.193478
address_tests_3y_kid_ebll_here_prop	0.166018
tract_tests_1y_kid_ebll_here_prop	0.145755
address_tests_3y_kid_ebll_first_prop	0.092541
address_tests_all_ebll_prop	0.052439
address_tests_3y_ebll_count	0.043917
tract_tests_1y_kid_ebll_here_count	0.028020

Figure 13: Features with positive standardized coefficients (increased risk for lead poisoning) in a regularized logistic regression. In order, these are the age of the child at the time of testing, the age of the home according to the assessor, the proportion of children tested at this address in the past three years who were poisoned first at this address, the proportion of children tested at this tract in the last year who were poisoned first at this tract, the proportion of blood tests at this address that were poisoned, the number of blood tests at this address in the past three years that were poisoned, and the number of children poisoned on this tract in the past year.

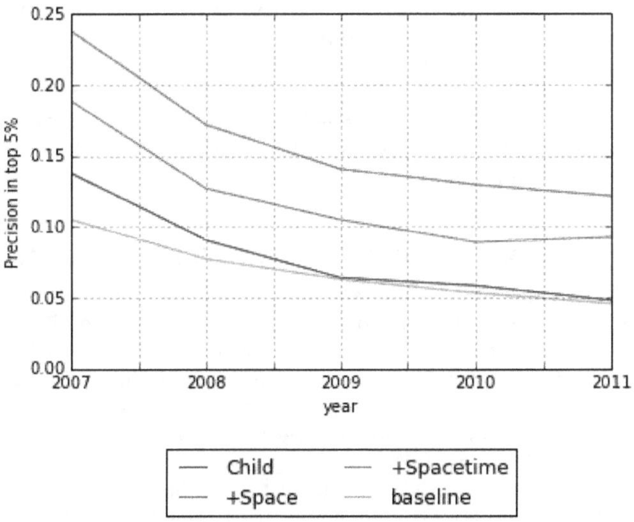

Figure 12: Increasing precision as we supplement the child features with spatial features and spatio-temporal features.

feature	coefficient
acs_5yr_race_pct_white	-0.084256
acs_5yr_health_pct_insured_employer	-0.079481
acs_5yr_edu_pct_ba	-0.020562
tract_inspections_all_compliance_prop	-0.019487
address_building_year	-0.019209
acs_5yr_edu_pct_advanced	-0.012124
address_tests_all_tested	-0.010470
address_lat	-0.007380

Figure 14: Features with negative standardized coefficients (decreased risk for lead poisoning) in a regularized logistic regression. In order, these are the percentage of the census tract that are white, the percentage of the tract that have employer health insurance, the percentage of adults with at least a bachelor's degree, the proportion of all inspections on this tract which have been complied, the year the home was built according to the buildings department, percentage of adults on the tract with an advanced degree, whether or not a child has been previously tested at this address, and the latitude of the address.

BLLs of all young children, regardless of housing age or the absence of other risk factors for lead exposure. This requirement is often ignored. Medicaid also requires two blood tests by age two. In the near future, these requirements will be loosened or will be ignored even more frequently as the risk of elevated lead exposure continues its rapid decline. This will increase the need for and usefulness of a tool that allows stakeholders to better assess risk and take preventative actions as warranted.

There are several ways that CDPH is planning to use the risk model. Each method involves a variation on disseminating the risk score to participants in a young child's life who provide medical care, child rearing, or housing and educating them on how to use this to reduce exposure to lead.

For pregnant women and parents of young children, CDPH is using billboard advertisements to encourage them to request home inspections. The risk score for these homes will be used by CDPH to prioritize inspections. In addition, publishing and publicizing the risk scores of housing allows this target audience to choose low risk housing when they are moving or request an inspection to determine if there are actual lead-based paint hazards. Even when no hazards exist, a high risk score may prompt families to make other behavior changes that minimize exposure from exterior soil (e.g. removing shoes, covering bare soil) and water (e.g. flushing) and more carefully monitor the child's diet to reduce absorption.

For doctors and other health care providers, knowing the risk score for a child can allow them to provide advice to the family regarding inspections and other exposure reducing practices. CDPH is recruiting health and social service providers to facilitate lead-based paint hazard inspections by city inspectors when their patients who are perinatal women live in high-risk housing. In addition, the CDPH is actively trying to pilot an effort where risk scores are incorporated into a child's medical record thus being available to the doctor during well-child visits.

For landlords and housing providers, CDPH is developing a program of outreach and education. For large landlords, CDPH will disseminate risk scores for their properties and encourage them to discuss and negotiate a maintenance plan with the inspectors to reduce the risk of exposure from current hazards and avoid hazardous maintenance and renovation practices. For home owners, CDPH will use the risk score to prioritize free inspections; CDPH has funding to pay for remediation for poorer owners and residents, which reduces the chance that the family will be burdened by unsustainable expenses required after the inspection.

9. THE PROMISE OF LIFETIME TRAJECTORY MODELING

While this paper describes in detail one model that was used, there are many other possible approaches to this problem and several others that are already being explored. One approach attempts to predict later lifetime exposure from infancy, using features on the child at birth, or from early doctors visits. The rationale relies on the idea that trace amounts of lead, perhaps acquired from the air or even from the mother, indicate much higher amounts of environmental lead. The infant is not yet at risk from these sources exclusively because of their inability to crawl. While measured levels at infancy might be below the CDC threshold, not

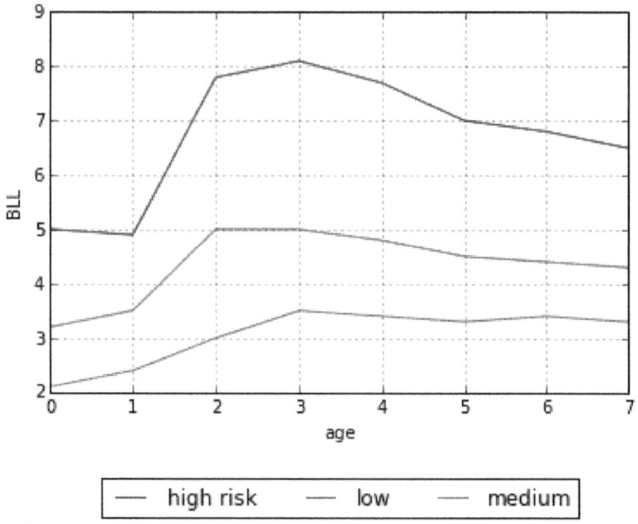

Figure 15: Lifetime trajectories from aggregated data

giving a doctor quantitative cause for concern, they might also be strong indicators that the threshold will be crossed, once crawling begins – allowing a critical window of up to several months for remediation. In addition to being strictly preventative, this approach has the added significant benefit that it could be included as a part of post-natal doctors visits, meaning a schedule of opportunities for an early test is already in place.

While few features and few tests were available for an individual, there was sufficient variation in age at the time of a test to construct rough canonical lifetime trajectories by aggregating tests from many children. In other words, "average BLL at age X" could be calculated easily. One such trajectory was constructed for each census tract in the city, and these trajectories were clustered into low, medium, and high risk. These clusters were cleanly distinguishable even during the period prior to the jump in lead levels that takes place when crawling begins – suggesting that with more features (and aggressive early testing), this approach has significant preventative potential.

10. CONCLUSIONS AND FUTURE WORK

Thousands of Chicago children are poisoned by lead every year, incurring great health and social costs to the city in both the short and long term. We developed this model in conjunction with the Chicago Department of Public Health to help them prioritize their inspection and testing schedule. Using blood tests, home inspections, county land assessments, and census data, the model produces more accurate predictions of lead risk than what CDPH had available.

CDPH is working to implement this model in several ways. CDPH has deployed billboards encouraging families to contact the city for free home lead inspections; CDPH will use the model to prioritize which houses to target first. CDPH also plans to make house-level risk scores available to the public so families can better choose where to live or, if they live there, to minimize their risk. CDPH is working to integrate the model into local electronic medical record systems to encourage health professionals to engage families at risk.

Finally, CDPH plans to use the model to work with large landlords to rid their properties of lead hazards.

11. ACKNOWLEDGMENTS

The work described in this paper was begun as part of the The Eric & Wendy Schmidt Data Science for Social Good Fellowship at the University of Chicago and continued at the Center for Data Science and Public Policy. We thank our collaborators at the Chicago Department of Public Health as well as the mentors and fellows in the fellowship program for their helpful comments and feedback.

12. ADDITIONAL AUTHORS

13. REFERENCES

[1] Chicago building footprints. `https://github.com/Chicago/osd-building-footprints`.

[2] Chicago census tract boundaries. `https://data.cityofchicago.org/Facilities-Geographic-Boundaries/Boundaries-Census-Tracts-2000/pt6c-hxpp`. Accessed: 2014-12-06.

[3] Chicago ward boundaries. `https://data.cityofchicago.org/Facilities-Geographic-Boundaries/Boundaries-Wards/bhcv-wqkf`. Accessed: 2014-12-06.

[4] University of Chicago Data Science for Social Good lead model GitHub repository. `https://github.com/dssg/lead-public`. Accessed: 2015-06-09.

[5] Cook county assessor's office database. `http://www.cookcountyassessor.com/`. Accessed: 2014-12-15.

[6] Demographic aspects of surnames from census 2000. `http://www.census.gov/topics/population/genealogy/data/2000_surnames.html`. Accessed: 2014-11-25.

[7] U.S. census bureau; generated by eric potash; using american factfinder. `<http://factfinder2.census.gov>`. Accessed: 2015-01-05.

[8] Arizona Department of Health Services. *Annual Report 2004*. Phoenix, AZ: Bureau of Epidemiology and Disease Control, Office of Environmental Health, 2005.

[9] A. Aschengrau, A. Beiser, D. Bellinger, D. Copenhafer, and M. Weitzman. Residential lead-based-paint hazard remediation and soil lead abatement: their impact among children with mildly elevated blood lead levels. *Amer. J.Pub. Health*, 87(10):1698–1702, 1997.

[10] D. C. Bellinger. Neurological and behavioral consequences of childhood lead exposure. *PLoS Med.*, 5(5):e115, 2008.

[11] S. M. Bernard and M. A. McGeehin. Prevalence of blood lead levelsâĽě 5 μg/dl among us children 1 to 5 years of age and socioeconomic and demographic factors associated with blood of lead levels 5 to 10 μg/dl, third national health and nutrition examination survey, 1988–1994. *Pediatrics*, 112(6):1308–1313, 2003.

[12] L. M. Cleveland, M. L. Minter, K. A. Cobb, A. A. Scott, and V. F. German. Lead hazards for pregnant women and children: Part 1: Immigrants and the poor shoulder most of the burden of lead exposure in this country. part 1 of a two-part article details how exposure happens, whom it affects, and the harm it can do. *Amer. J. Nursing*, 108(10):40–49, 2008.

[13] T. A. Dignam, A. Evens, E. Eduardo, S. M. Ramirez, K. L. Caldwell, N. Kilpatrick, G. P. Noonan, W. D. Flanders, P. A. Meyer, and M. A. McGeehin. High-intensity targeted screening for elevated blood lead levels among children in 2 inner-city chicago communities. *J. Inform.*, 94(11), 2004.

[14] P. Elliott, R. Arnold, D. Barltrop, I. Thornton, I. M. House, and J. A. Henry. Clinical lead poisoning in england: an analysis of routine sources of data. *Occup.Environ. Med.*, 56(12):820–824, 1999.

[15] C. for Disease Control and Prevention. Screening young children for lead poisoning: guidance for state and local public health officials. In *Screening young children for lead poisoning: guidance for state and local public health officials*. CDC, 1997.

[16] A. R. Kemper, L. M. Cohn, K. E. Fant, K. J. Dombkowski, and S. R. Hudson. Follow-up testing among children with elevated screening blood lead levels. *J. Amer. Med. Assoc.*, 293(18):2232–2237, 2005.

[17] S. Ko, P. D. Schaefer, C. M. Vicario, and H. J. Binns. Relationships of video assessments of touching and mouthing behaviors during outdoor play in urban residential yards to parental perceptions of child behaviors and blood lead levels. *J. Exp. Sci. Environ. Epidemiol.*, 17(1):47–57, 2006.

[18] P. J. Landrigan, C. B. Schechter, J. M. Lipton, M. C. Fahs, and J. Schwartz. Environmental pollutants and disease in american children: estimates of morbidity, mortality, and costs for lead poisoning, asthma, cancer, and developmental disabilities. *Environ. Health Perspect.*, 110(7):721, 2002.

[19] B. P. Lanphear. Childhood lead poisoning prevention: Too little, too late. *J. Amer. Med. Assoc.*, 293(18):2274–2276, 2005.

[20] M. Mazumdar, D. C. Bellinger, M. Gregas, K. Abanilla, J. Bacic, and H. L. Needleman. Low-level environmental lead exposure in childhood and adult intellectual function: a follow-up study. *Environ. Health*, 10(24):1–7, 2011.

[21] H. L. Needleman. Childhood lead poisoning: the promise and abandonment of primary prevention. *Amer. J. Pub. Health*, 88(12):1871–1877, 1998.

[22] S. Zahran, H. W. Mielke, S. Weiler, and C. R. Gonzales. Nonlinear associations between blood lead in children, age of child, and quantity of soil lead in metropolitan new orleans. *Sci. Total Environ.*, 409(7):1211–1218, mar 2011.

Proof Protocol for a Machine Learning Technique Making Longitudinal Predictions in Dynamic Contexts

Kevin B. Pratt
Chief Scientist at ZZAlpha Ltd.[1]
kevin.pratt@zzalpha.com

ABSTRACT:

We demonstrate a protocol for proving strongly that a black-box machine learning technique robustly predicts the future in dynamic, indefinite contexts. We propose necessary components of the proof protocol and demonstrate results visualizations to support evaluation of the proof components. Components include contemporaneously verifiable discrete predictions, deterministic computability of longitudinal predictions, imposition of realistic costs and domain constraints, exposure to diverse contexts, statistically significant excess benefits relative to *a priori* benchmarks and Monte Carlo trials, insignificant decay of excess benefits, pathology detection and an extended real-time trial "in the wild." We apply the protocol to a big data machine learning technique deployed since 2011 that finds persistent, exploitable opportunities in many of 41 segments of US financial markets, the existence of which opportunities substantially contradict the Efficient Market Hypothesis.

Categories and Subject Descriptors

H.3.4 [Information Storage and Retrieval]: Systems and Software - *Performance evaluation (efficiency and effectiveness)* **I.2.6 [Artificial Intelligence]:** - Learning - *Concept learning* **I.6.4 [Simulation and Modeling]:** Model validation and Analysis

Keywords

Experiment design, hypothesis testing, black box, big data, longitudinal study, dynamic context, simulation, pattern analysis, market forecast, prediction.

1. INTRODUCTION

"We think it very interesting to teach machines to understand behaviors that humans cannot describe. But, how do we know they understood?"

How does one prove that a frequently erring method - applied in a constantly evolving environment – is authentic, robust and valuable? Especially where task of proof is aggravated because the method itself is evolving in response to the changing environment and lives hidden inside a "proprietary black box"?

KDD '15, August 10-13, 2015, Sydney, NSW, Australia.

ACM 978-1-4503-3664-2/15/08…$15.00.
http://dx.doi.org/10.1145/2783258.2783273

This question might apply to behaviors of a live anti-viral flu vaccine, to methods of a stock prices prediction engine, to robotic vehicles navigating in a city undergoing wartime destruction or to an ad placement "optimization" system for a multi-national, multi-channel, competitive consumer product. In a broader sense, how does one persuasively answer the skeptic's question of the value of big data analytics in the real and changing world where tomorrow will be different in unknowable ways - and where humans are incapable of doing the data learning and analysis that is being conducted within the "black box"?

In 2010, we set out to prove that a machine learning technique which we were deploying could successfully, repeatedly find exploitable ***future*** stock market inefficiencies at scale. Our goal was to prove that technique's existence and efficacy beyond a reasonable doubt. Part of our task was defining a strong proof protocol. The proof must be strong because the existence and efficacy of such a technique contradicts the Efficient Market Hypothesis[2] for which the Nobel Prize was awarded in 2013.

The learning technique makes early morning recommendations to buy a small, fixed size set of stocks at a price equal to the opening price (whatever it may be) today and to sell those same stocks one week later at the opening price then. It uses input data as of market close the prior day. It thus must work with two great uncertainties (latencies): it does not consider events occurring overnight when making its morning recommendation, and it does not revise recommendations, once made, in view of events in the coming week that affect the market before results of the recommendations (sales) are recorded. Our null hypothesis is that such a technique will produce nothing statistically significant in any market segment.

This article focuses on proof protocol and associated big data behavior visualizations applicable to dynamic contexts, rather than substantive results, which results are presented in another (pending) journal article.

2. PROOF PROTOCOL

Proof protocols and techniques for evaluating data mining validity in stationary contexts have been well developed. N-fold cross validation with holdout test sets, confusion matrices, f-measure weightings and Receiver Operating Curves (ROC) are widely applied and well understood [6]. Statistical dispersion measures for

---

[1] The author is also Senior Analytics Scientist at Teradata Corp. The work described here has no association whatsoever with Teradata Corp. or the author's employment there.

[2] "In the 1960s, Eugene Fama demonstrated that stock price movements are impossible to predict in the short-term…" http://www.nobelprize.org/nobel_prizes/economic-sciences/laureates/2013/fama-facts.html

measurement data, and goodness of fit to parametric descriptions have a long history.

Evaluating big data techniques in dynamic contexts where no situation repeats requires new approaches [3,14]. Data distributions and object interconnectivity change constantly, and assumptions that distributions are "normal" under any parametric description are infrequently valid. Big data analytics feels like navigating mid-ocean on a stormy night with unreliable instruments. Nonetheless, despite the constant changing contexts, we suggest that strict scientific method be applied to avoid squishy evaluation using "pleasing anecdotes."

While longitudinal experimentation is not new [24,26,27] and is applied in a variety of domains [1,2,8,12,19], big data is causing re-examination of the methodologies [5,22,25]. Proving validity of prediction in longitudinal, constantly changing problem spaces suffers from three special challenges. i) Data available today about prior inputs and prior outcomes may have been cleansed (sometimes almost invisibly) by hindsight. An obvious example is survivor bias during "back-testing" in finance [9,13]. A less obvious example we observed is that published data such as stock trading data is silently revised by vendors in later publications when "final numbers" are received. ii) More insidious is the hindsight technique of publishing only favorable results from a panel of "equally well-conceived" trials that had mixed results. This variety of hindsight filtering has been used intentionally in some stock scams, and sometimes naively in drug research where side-effects in some cohorts are dismissed [7,17]. iii) Longitudinal interim results can compound in dynamic feedback systems, whether as part of the contextual environment or as part of the prediction technique. What seems well behaved in early episodes may fluctuate or become brittle - diverging or decaying over time.

A well-defined protocol for proving capability of machine learning in longitudinal, dynamic contexts supports user trust in today's black-box, proprietary technologies [10,18,21,23]. It is also needed for valuation of such technologies for capital investment.

2.1 Components of Proof Protocol

We suggest it is critical to define how success will be measured in advance of an experiment with a learning system, and how to assure the experiment is authentic and sufficient [20,22].

2.1.1 Contemporaneously verifiable discrete predictions

A prediction must be specific. The set of cohorts for which predictions will be made must be defined in advance. The deadline or trigger for each prediction must be established. In order to validate these predictions, all should be consolidated, unalterably archived and time-stamped. In later evaluation of a learning technique, only those predictions meeting this criteria should be included, otherwise one risks "revise as we go" hindsight.

For the ZZAlpha machine learning technique, we defined (in 2010) 41 market segments for which we would produce long and short recommendations before the market opened every day. We also defined 4 size sets for each segment. We aggregated these 320 daily predictions and submitted them to encryption and electronic time-stamping by Digistamp [4] early each morning beginning in late 2011. Digistamp is a trusted third party time stamp authority using an encryption algorithm that does not require deposit of documents with them. Rather a public certificate is provided for unlocking and verifying the date-time of the document. A timestamp costs $0.40 and is commonly used for intellectual property protection.

The learning engine makes predictions for recommendations that are discrete and actionable: buy (or sell) a set of stocks at prescribed prices today.

2.1.2 Deterministic computability of repetitive longitudinal application of predictions

In longitudinal studies with asynchronous triggering events, there is the issue of how to define and calculate the initialization of a fresh context given the resource impact of the sequence of prior decisions. In a stock investment context, that means determining how much cash is now available for purchases after closing prior investments. In an advertising campaign that might mean how to allocate remaining spend after detecting cohort responses to prior channel impressions. In a dynamic real-life context, acting on every prediction causes resource adjustment, and there must be ongoing resource accounting with hard numbers.

For the machine learning evaluation, we created a strict cash flow trading performance evaluator (detailed below) based on a typical tax-free retirement account where margin (borrowing) is prohibited. Thus, a sale must be closed at a defined price with dollar proceeds added to the "pot" before a following purchase can be made.

2.1.3 Imposition of realistic costs and context constraints during evaluation

As part of the resource accounting identified above, there must be imposed realistic transaction costs and context constraints. For example, in a stock trading context, commissions are paid at the time of trade. Short trades cannot be made when brokerages do not have short shares to lend. Institutional investors may be prohibited by self-imposed investment guidelines from trading low priced stocks. These costs and constraints need to be applied during the go-forward accounting of prediction results. Identification of these costs and constraints typically requires consultation with industry subject matter experts and careful modeling. In an advertising campaign this might include lead times, placement premiums, and commission levels.

For the evaluation here, we applied trading commissions, price, liquidity and slippage constraints.

2.1.4 Exposure to diverse contexts

To be deemed robust, a longitudinal technique must survive or thrive when exposed to the unknown - where those unknowns may arise in the future. A general technique, for example a drug therapy, must apply successfully to diverse cohorts and cohort specific stressors, for example cohorts receiving other treatments. Cohorts must be defined in advance of the experiment. If future contextual events will be "excused", those permissible excuses must also be defined in the proof protocol.

For the learning technique experiment here, we identified 41 cohorts spanning diverse market segments, and allowed any trading day as an acceptable context. Impactful events such as the fall of gold prices, Chinese economy slowing, credit card frauds, oil fracking, and very low interest rates were some of the unexpected future unknowns to which the learning technique had to respond, for all cohorts.

2.1.5 Statistically significant excess benefits relative to a priori benchmarks and Monte Carlo trials

In experiment design, the comparison benchmarks must be designated in advance [11]. They need to be appropriate to the cohort, and need to be measurable over the duration of the experiment. Thus, a traditional "status quo" strawman is never available in a dynamic context. There are often hindsight incentives to change to lesser benchmarks so that benefits can be announced from the method being attempted. In the stock domain, Exchange Traded funds indexed to a sector often offer appropriate benchmarks. Stock indexes are less persuasive benchmarks because they are generally capitalization weighted and exclude the compounding benefits of dividends.

Monte Carlo evaluation methods can apply in dynamic contexts, and can be applied to the varying cohorts [23]. Fundamentally each decision of the method being evaluated is replaced with a random selection from the decision set. Evaluation of Monte Carlo results provides both a distributional representation of outcomes, and a sense of whether the chosen dispersion method, such as standard deviation, is appropriate.

Experiment design also requires advance specification of how improvement is to be measured and what value constitutes success. At ZZAlpha we selected an ETF or market index for comparison to each recommendation segment, and built a Monte Carlo trial option into the longitudinal performance evaluator. We chose two measures of success. With respect to a market benchmark, the machine learning method, after expenses, must exceed the annualized returns of the benchmark by 200 basis points. With respect to the Monte Carlo trials, the machine learning method must provide results more than 3 standard deviations (z-score) above the segment mean.

2.1.6 Insignificant decay of excess benefits

In stationary contexts, over-fitting causes brittleness that reduces accuracy when applied to the test sample. In longitudinal dynamic contexts a parallel problem can arise when the method is too strongly tuned to the training episodes [16]. Although one expects a learning method will vary in the success of its predictions as contexts change, the longer term results should not decay. Historic market prices fell 40% or more in 2008 in most stock market segments, but rose again. Some segments have lower returns for several years.

The three years of certified recommendations here do not support evaluation of decay. The 10 year simulated recommendations using the machine learning technique in forward-testing mode are the best available data to respond to decay concerns. We use a requirement of positive regression slope and specifically a more positive slope than that of benchmarks.

2.1.7 Controlled risk and absence of pathologies

Black box techniques in dynamic contexts can exhibit pathological behaviors. In the market price prediction domain we needed to detect and evaluate three: Does the technique repeat or cycle prior predictions? Do individual recommendations within a daily set have high risk (large losses) or are there extended episodes of underperformance? Does the technique only detect opportunities of either price increase (long) or price decrease (short)?

For evaluation of these possible pathologies, we used a quarterly periodicity visualization, a min-max timeline envelope, z-scores of both long and short recommendations, and descriptive statistics of the severity of below regression line risk.

To support the elements of the proof protocol, we prepared over 25 visualizations for each market segment, some of which are included below. These were to confirm the expected and expose the unexpected, to compare to benchmarks, and to support cross-segment interpretation and pathology identification.

2.1.8 Extended duration real-time trial "in the wild"

Simulations can inadvertently omit costs and constraints that occur when participating in dynamic contexts. We suggest it is critical to obtain some portion of ground truth to corroborate lab evaluation techniques, and to uncover experiment misconceptions.

We used daily a few of the machine learning recommendations in the most widely analyzed segment - the stocks in the S&P 500 list - to control actual trading over 15 months with a pot of about $500,000. This parallels a limited clinical trial in the pharmaceutical domain or "back-road" testing of driverless vehicles.

3. MACHINE LEARNING TECHNIQUE

We originated a machine learning technique and tuned that technique in 2009-2010 using portions of 2008 data. We began operating the machine learning technique in 2010 to make daily stock recommendations. The technique continues in autonomous operation today, situated on a large cloud platform. It has no tuning knobs.

To protect proprietary intellectual property, we hide the inner details of the technique. However, in overview, it ingests data, applies transforms, derives features, considers past market dynamics, applies common machine learning technique(s), and predicts stocks likely to rise or fall in price (categorized within 41 market segments Table. 1). [3]

Inputs: The technique consumes 5 types of public data: i) end-of-day daily stock price and volume data, ii) a large set of traditional stock fundamentals updated weekly, iii) Securities and Exchange Commission (SEC) filings on initial public offerings, iv) daily information on merger and acquisition announcements and v) semi-annual data needed to include or exclude stocks in lists of the 41 segments e.g. in the list of S&P 500 stocks or the Health sector or sub-sector of Banks (defined by SIC). All of the data consumed is available on the internet for less than $200 a year in subscription fees. It is also available more quickly from commercial suppliers such as CapitalIQ.

Outputs: The technique outputs daily newsletters on 320 recommendation portfolios, and most importantly a complete, consolidated recommendation list that is encrypted and contemporaneously certified by Digistamp before market open and then archived. The certifications began Nov. 2011.

In 2011 we simulated the machine learning technique to produce 2005-2009 recommendations to confirm its robustness. That simulation involved feeding the machine learner the weekly

[3] This paper does not intend to emphasize the stock recommendation system, but rather to use such a system as an example to focus on the hard, ethically challenging and increasingly important question of "how would one decide" if such a system, and similar systems which must contend with unknown dynamic contexts, would be likely robust and effective.

fundamentals data as originally published at that historic week and providing historic information (including delisted or renamed stocks) of prices and volume (which was split and dividend corrected) as of 2011. The machine learner then issued daily recommendations for the 320 recommendation portfolios day-by-day in a consolidated daily document. This five year simulation took over 9 months of computation.

The goal of the historic simulation (combined with the subsequent go-forward predictions) was to help evaluate possible decay of results over the longer term, and to evaluate the resiliency of the machine learning technique in the extreme contexts of 2007-2008.

Table 1. Segments (cohorts) spanning the US market for predictions. All portfolios are produced for Long and Short positions, and in daily recommendation sizes of 2, 5, 10 and 20 stocks (with a few exceptions).

Listed	**Sectors**
S&P500	S1-Basic Materials
S&PMid400	S2-Capital Goods
S&PSmall600	S4-Cons Cyclical
AllCap (>3$ and >80,000 vol)	S5- Cons Non-Cyclical
Capitalization Rank	S6-Energy
Big100	S7-Financial
Big250	S7-excluding ETFs
Big500	S8-Health
Big750	S9-Services
Big1000	S10-Technology
Big1500	S11-Transportation
Big2000	S12-Utilities
Capitalization ranges	**Sub-sectors**
5Billion +	Banks
1-5 Billion	Insurance
1Billion +	Investmt Services
250m-1B	RealEstate Ops
20m-1B	O&G Ops
2-250m	All Technology
Liquidities	Semiconductors
Very High (>95%)	
High (80-95%)	
Medium (33-66%)	
Low (bottom 33%)	
20m+ (double diamond)	

4. RECOMMENDATION PERFORMANCE EVALUATOR

The evaluator is entirely separate from the machine learning technique. However, it is focused on evaluating the "weekly rolling recommendations" of the type made by the machine learning technique.

The evaluator is cash based [Fig. 1]. It takes a list of k stocks to buy on a day and consumes the available portion of cash for that day to make equal dollar valued (1/k) purchases of the stocks. After n trading days it sells those stocks and contributes the proceeds back to cash. It then repeats. Cash can never be negative. All purchases and sales are made at a price equivalent to the opening price that day. Commissions (either fixed dollar or per share) are applied at each transaction.

We add several constraints to the evaluator: The "pot" of cash is initialized, typically set to $1 million. The pot is initially divided into n portions. On each day, one of the portions is available for purchases. After each day the portions are rebalanced to remain approximately equal. A minimum purchase block size is set to 10. All transactions are "limit order," which prevents price slippage during trades.

Some cash tracking details: If a stock appears in the new "buy" list on the day of "sale", it is treated as held for n additional days and does not contribute to the cash portion on the originally expected day of "sale". If for any reason a stock does not have an opening price on the day of purchase, the stock is not purchased and funds remain in cash. When a stock is not purchased, the cash allocated for that purchase remains unspent in the current portion and becomes again available n days later. The evaluator can also track tax gains and payments.

The evaluator also allows selection of a benchmark, such as the Dow Jones Industrial Index or an S&P500 tracking index fund (for comparison of index fund long term tax treatment "buy and hold").

The evaluator determines results of long positions. It does not evaluate short positions because i) some stocks never or seldom allow shorting and we have not acquired that data, ii) it is impossible to determine whether on a particular day a particular stock has short shares available from a particular brokerage for loan to a particular investor, and iii) regulations sometimes only allow short on uptick. However the evaluator does support a computational concept of "anti-long". Given a list of stocks that are predicted to decline in price (typically used in selecting shorts), it will indicate what results would be if that list had inadvertently been treated as long recommendations.

The recommendation performance evaluator operates in two modes:

Recommendation mode applies the results of the certified ZZAlpha® portfolio recommendations (for a specific portfolio in a market segment and of a specific size). Those results have been historically recorded about 3 days after sale of a position, showing the contemporaneous purchase price and the sale price and relative result (without assuming a quantity of shares purchased). The purchase price is adjusted for dividends and splits to keep it consistent with the sale price. On a few occasions the record is incomplete, typically because of a data provider omission, because the stock price dropped below $3 or trading volume fell below 80,000 shares. Any missing records are treated as "not bought" with no gain or loss. Missing records are logged during the recommendation mode.

Random selection mode operates exactly the same as recommendation mode with two changes. First, instead of a recommendation stock, a stock is selected from the same portfolio market segment at random (using the Java cryptographic random number generator). Second, the purchase and sale prices are obtained from current and archive listings of daily stock prices, adjusted for dividends and splits. On a few occasions the current price record is incomplete, typically because of a data provider omission, because the stock price dropped below $3, because trading volume fell below 80,000 shares or because of delisting. Share price increases due to mergers and acquisitions are typically present in the records. Any missing records are treated as "not bought" with no gain or loss. There are more missing records in random selection mode than in recommendation mode, but seldom more than 10 missing records in a year. Missing records are logged during the random selection mode.

The effect of switching from recommendation mode to random selection mode is to substitute a random choice from the relevant market segment for a machine learning generated recommendation. Thus, operation of the performance evaluator over a period of time (three years in this report) in random selection mode is a Monte Carlo simulation trial, using exactly the same assumptions, constraints, costs and accounting as used in the recommendation mode evaluation. All Monte Carlo trials are repeated 1000 to generate reliable estimates.

5. EVALUATION OF RESULTS PURSUANT TO THE PROOF PROTOCOL

We applied the protocol to the machine learning technique's recommendations. We show visualizations for S1-Basic Industries, one of the market segments, for five recommendations each day.

Contemporaneously verifiable discrete predictions- The daily consolidated recommendations for the 320 set are unalterably time stamped by Digistamp prior to market open. Each recommendation set lists e.g. five stocks to buy at the opening price, which are to be held one week and sold.

Deterministic computability of repetitive longitudinal application of predictions- We use the recommendation Performance Evaluator described in Fig 1 to obtain deterministic results.

Imposition of realistic costs and context constraints during evaluation- In addition to the constraints expressed in the Performance Evaluator, we apply three additional constraints to assure that the recommendations pertain to stocks which institutional investors can purchase under regulatory requirements: $3 recent minimum price, 80,000 daily share volume, and listed on the major US stock exchanges.

Exposure to diverse contexts- The 41 market segments span the US equities market. Each segment suffers somewhat individual stressors, such as falling oil prices or semiconductor innovations. The three years of certified recommendation do not include an episode of price drop of over 10%, and thus lack that diversity. The ten year simulation attempts to overcome that by including the 2007-2008 episode of price drop. Fig. 2 shows the ten years of annual returns.

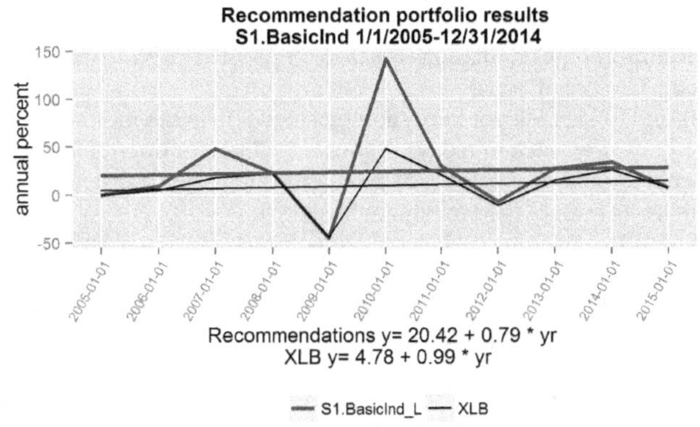

Figure 2. Annual results and benchmark for ten years, showing regression lines used for decay evaluation. Because the recommendation slope of 0.79 is less than the benchmark slope, this suggests the quality of recommendation is declining slightly.

Statistically significant excess benefits relative to a priori benchmarks and Monte Carlo trials- We use z-score to measure significance. Figures 3, 4 and 5 show results for one of the segments - Sector 1-Basic Materials. Both the long and anti-long results have z-scores greater than 3, indicating great significance. In another article we detail that of the 41 recommendation sets of daily size 5, 5 have z-scores greater than 3, 3 have z-scores between 2 and 3, and 9 have z-scores between 1 and 2. Anti-longs show greater significance. Of the 41 portfolios, 23 exceed both their segment means and their benchmarks by 200 basis points (annualized), and another 2 exceed their segment means and their benchmarks by 100 basis points (annualized).

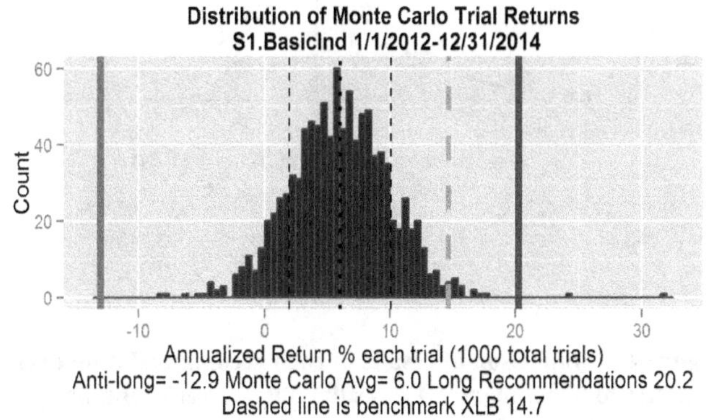

Figure 3. Results compared to benchmarks: 1000 Monte Carlo trials and ETF. Monte Carlo mean and +/- standard deviation shown in black dotted lines. Machine learning recommendation results for long shown in blue line on right, for anti-long in red line on left. Benchmark XLB results indicated by green dashed line.

Select: Portfolio name, Long or anti-long, Recommendation or Monte Carlo mode, Benchmark (optional), Short term and long term tax rates (optional).
Initialize: Pot, Commission (per trade or per share), Portfolio daily size k, Minimum block size, Dates of study period, (and if Monte Carlo mode, number of trials).
Begin: Divide cash pot into n portions (equal to number of hold days = 5).
For each of n days, buy equal value quantities of k recommended (or randomly selected) stocks using that day's portion of the pot at opening price. Determine each purchase commission and apply before each purchase. If stock cannot be purchased, leave cash in that portion. Purchases must exceed minimum block size.
ASSERT: remaining cash is near zero in each of the n portions.
Continue until last date:
For each of the k stocks purchased n days prior, if stock currently held is in current day recommendations, continue to hold. Else, sell stock at opening price and contribute to cash portion after paying commission. If the opening price is not available, treat as sold at original purchase price.
Rebalance the portions by contributing 1/k of sale profits to each.
For each of the recommended stocks, buy equal value quantities of k recommended (or randomly selected) stocks using that day's portion of the pot at opening price (omitting already held stocks). Determine each purchase commission and apply before each purchase. If a stock cannot be purchased (because opening price is not available), leave cash in that portion. Purchases must exceed minimum block size.
If is last day of year, determine tax owing or loss carryforward.
If is Apr 1, reduce total cash by tax owing before making day's purchases.
On last date:
Calculate value of stocks held using purchase prices and add to cash.
Report total value change. Report benchmark change.
If Monte Carlo mode and trials are not complete, reinitialize pot and Begin.

Figure 1. Performance Evaluator pseudo code

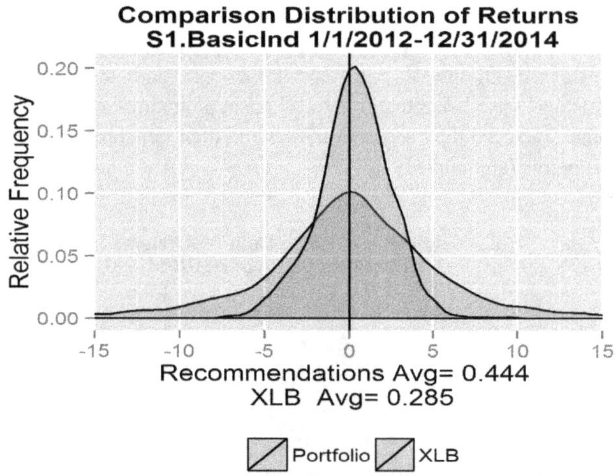

Figure 4. Comparison of results of each recommendation over 3 year test to benchmark ETF results (for all week-long periods). There is a long right tail on the portfolio recommendations in this Cauchy-Lorentz distribution. The figure shows greater dispersion of results for the portfolio, but more positive area under the curve (in the 3 years, 52% of the recommended trades had positive profit).

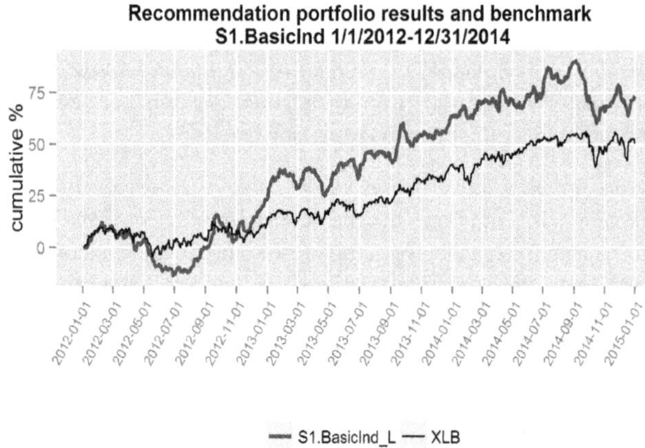

Figure 5. Cumulative results from recommendations in dark blue and benchmark XLB in thin black. This common timeline graph helps quickly identify correlations and anomalies.

Fig. 6 shows persistence of results (both high and low) when comparing average results of individual stocks in the current year with the average results of the same stock in the prior 2 years. The positive correlation and regression slope suggest that a favorable context for a specific stock may repeat. The machine learning technique may be detecting that subtle context within the chaos of the dynamic market. However, this persistence was absent in other segments.

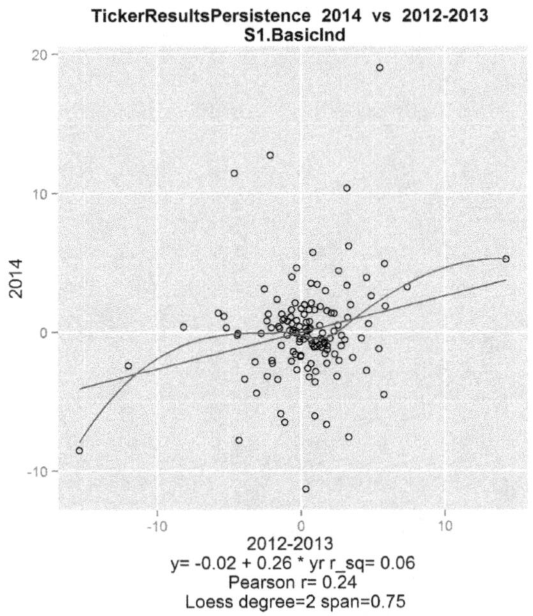

Figure 6. For year 2014 in this segment,, the average returns of a recommended stock in the prior two years are somewhat correlated (Pearson r=0.24) with current year returns. The Loess spline regression emphasizes variations in the regression and indicates discontinuance of positive regression in the middle range, which is not shown by ordinary linear regression line.

Insignificant decay of excess benefits- We identified two varieties of decay. As the number of daily recommendations increase, the recommendation effectiveness decreases: Annualized returns (after commissions) for sizes 2, 5, 10 and 20 declined from 23.8 for size 2 to 20.2, 11.8 and 5.8 in the S1-Basic Materials segment. By changing the commission structure constraint from a fixed $8 per trade to $0.05 per share, the returns for size 20 were increased to 8.6. This is a pattern we saw often across the 41 market segments. Second, looking at annual return rates over 10 years (7 years of simulation and 3 years of certified results), we saw decay in results as shown in Fig. 2.

Controlled risk and absence of pathologies - A machine learning technique in dynamic contexts will likely change its own behaviors. Visualizations from different perspectives are useful. In addition to traditional risk and drawdown statistics, we inspected three suspect behaviors. First, we evaluated the daily range of results to identify spikes or longer duration episodes of extreme results Fig. 7.

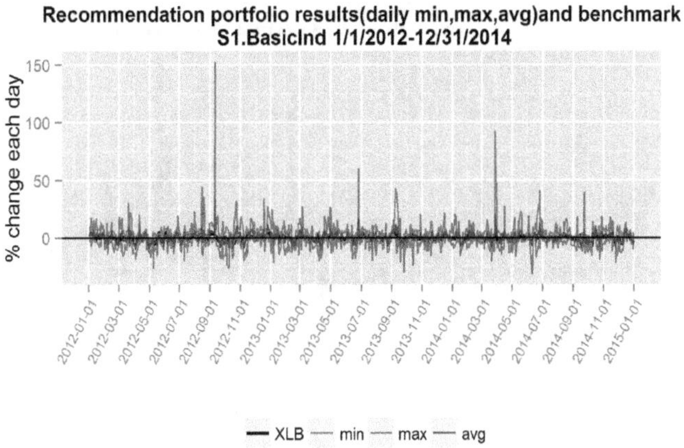

Figure 7. Daily ranges of recommendation results (5 daily recommendations) compared to benchmark. Note that more extreme events were positive, which contributes to rapid compounding of the rolling recommendation results.

We found that although greater mean returns occurred at higher capitalization ranges of the segment, Fig. 8, the greatest total profits derived from the lowest capitalization stocks Fig 9. In Fig. 10, we saw that variation in returns dropped slowly as capitalization increased. Fig 11 indicated a slow change in capitalizations of selected stocks. We inspected recommendations for abnormal periodicity, Fig 12 and found one possible pathology. A few recommendations recurred 4 times on the same day in the 12 quarters of the 3 years, but no significant overall pattern appears in S1-Basic Materials. To further investigate the possible pathology, we looked at the frequencies of individual stock recommendations in the 3 years, which ranged from 90 to one. The existence of several high frequencies suggested some instances of clustered repetitions would not be abnormal. We also maintain extensive operational logs should the need arise to investigate pathologies.

We also investigated how the set of five daily recommendations fit within the rank of all segment members. We expected to see ranked recommendations correlated with ranked results. Use of rank correlation avoids difficulties of comparing absolute results from different contexts, where "good" can mean significantly different absolute results. Fig 13 show almost no rank correlation of the machine learning recommendations to ranked results. However we investigated the extremes in the corners of Fig 13. The histogram in Fig 14 discloses a narrow spike of high result rank correlation to high recommendation rank. This exemplifies the "needle in haystack" that could be lost using ordinary descriptive statistics or down sampling of big data.

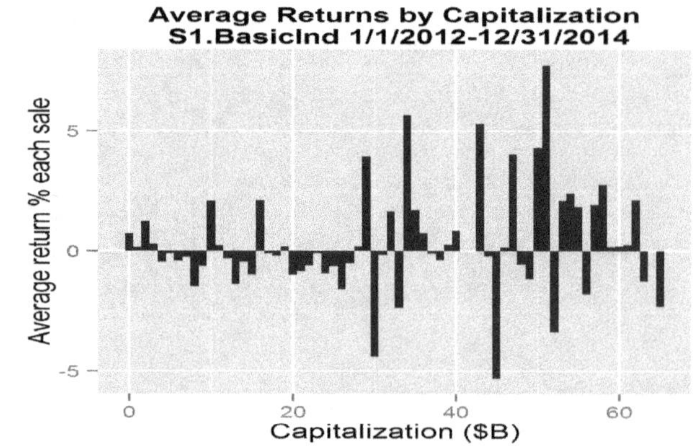

Figure 8. Mean returns by capitalization. Bin size = $1B. This example differs from many of other segments where positive returns were more commonly seen in the smaller cap stocks.

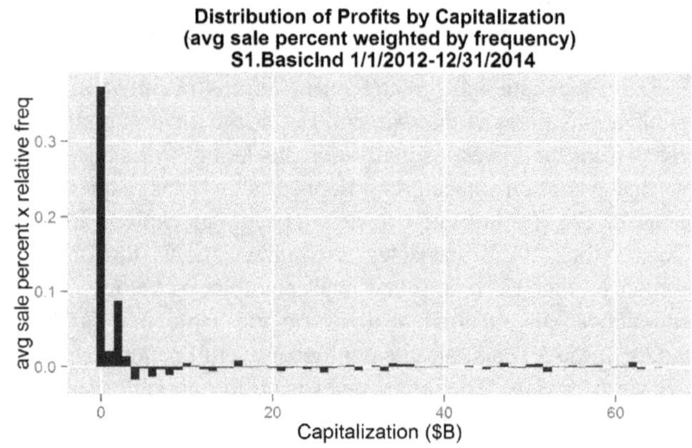

Figure 9. Profit by capitalization. Low capitalization stocks heavily contribute (because they are more often recommended) to recommendation set returns for S1-Basic Materials.

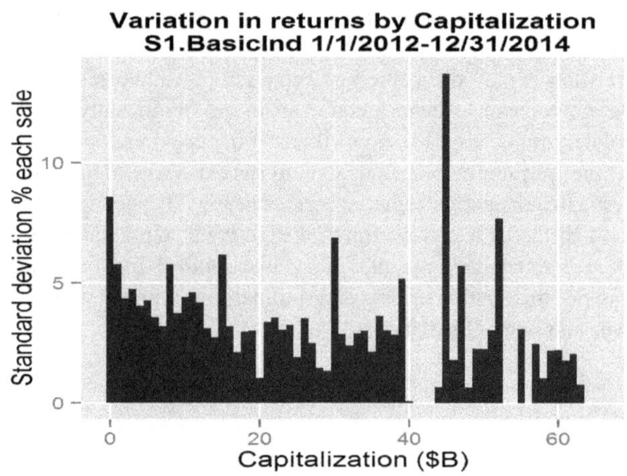

Figure 10. Variation in returns by capitalization. The generally declining variation is as expected. It is one of many "sanity checks" on performance over the 3 years.

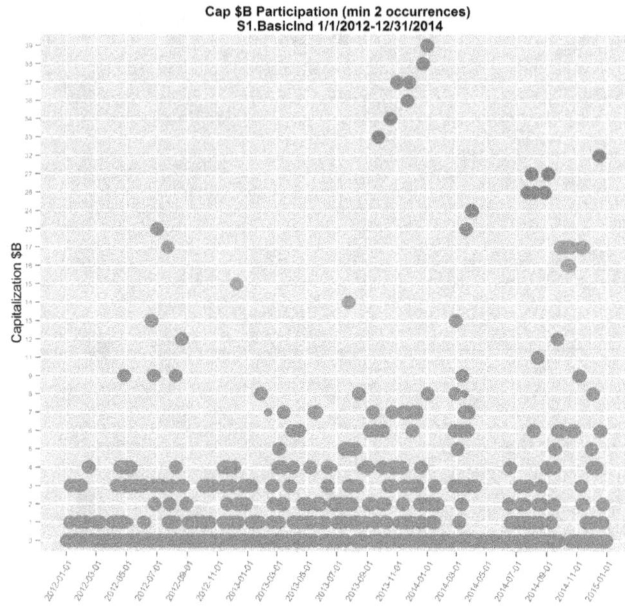

Figure 11. The recommendations included more large cap elements over time. The pink largest cap cluster at the top may indicate a single stock that either issued more shares and/or saw large price increases.

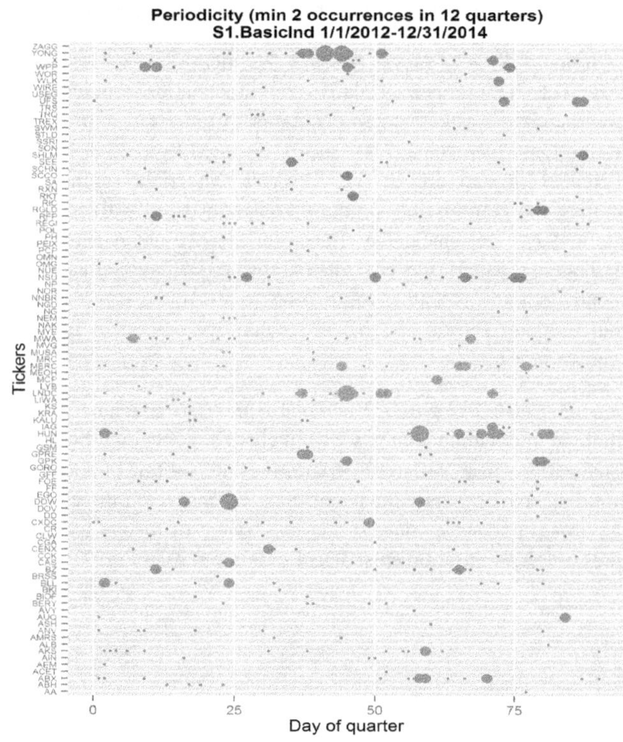

Figure 12. Periodic repetition or recommendations across quarters. Small dots indicate 2x in 12 quarters. Largest dots indicate 4x in 12 quarters. The sequence of large dots at the top middle suggest a possible autocorrelation pathology for examination.

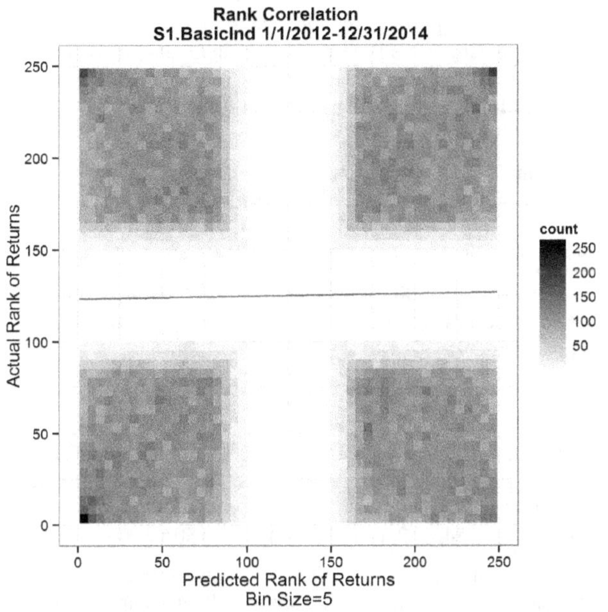

Figure 13. Rank correlation permits comparison across dynamic contexts. For each day, both predictions and results within a segment are ranked. An optimal correlation of result rank to recommendation rank would be a thin scatter running from lower left to upper right. Instead this figure shows almost no correlation, but concentrations in corners. This visualization applies in dynamic contexts where correlation of actual returns would be effectively unusable because a "good" prediction in an up market might be 5% increase compared to a market-wide 2% increase and a "good" prediction in a down market might be a 5% decrease compared to a market-wide 8% decrease. The horizontal and vertical gaps in the center of the figure are artifacts resulting from different sizes of the sample set on different days. To support inspection of the high ranks, both the right and top are aligned for the upper half of the samples. The regression line in the middle of the figure shows the very weak positive slope. The rank correlation patterns seen in the other 40 market segments can vary substantially from this visualization. The recommendation engine is performing differently here than in other segments.

Extended duration real-time trial "in the wild"- We used a pot of about $500,000 for about 15 months (Oct 7, 2013-Dec. 31, 2014) to act upon machine learning recommendations (and no others) for stocks in the SP500 list, using a standard internet discount brokerage account. The actual returns (cumulative), after commissions, exceeded the returns calculated by the Performance Evaluator for that segment and dates (34.1% vs 22.2%). This both provides evidence confirming the ground truth of the Performance Evaluator software, and the reality that the machine learning technique's recommendations were actionable trades in the SP500 segment of the dynamic market. The small trial did not confirm viability at institutional scale.

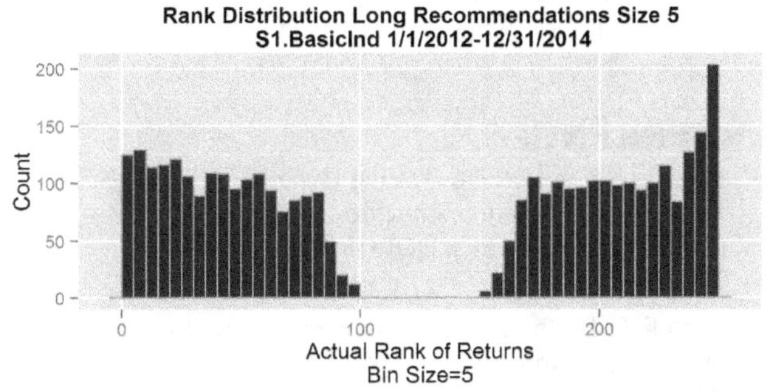

Figure 14. This figure repeats the right-most column of Figure 13 as a histogram. It indicates that for the 5 highest ranked recommendations (the only ones included), there is an unusually high correlation with the highest actual ranks, but most of the actual ranks are spread evenly across lower ranks. An optimal correlation would have higher right-side bars descending to lower left-side bars. This figure discloses an unexpected behavior that may indicate fragility. The center gap is an irrelevant artifact of aligning the right half of the visualization to account for varying sample set sizes.

6. CONCLUSION

We developed and applied this proof protocol to a black box machine learning technique that makes repeated longitudinal recommendations for stocks in the US market. We designed the protocol to support a thorough, trustworthy and persuasive evaluation of the machine learning technique, recognizing that the technique often received erroneous real-time input data, that post recommendation events would materially affect recorded results and that it would need to operate in and be evaluated with respect to unknowable future contexts.

Effective application of a proof protocol requires subject matter expertise to assure appropriate context constraints and relevant benchmarks are applied. Because hindsight filtering is a primary experimental risk in longitudinal experiments, we suggest time-stamp authenticity certification of every evaluated decision is a key minimal requirement. Extensive visualizations of the black box outputs, from many viewpoints help understanding of the performance. Cross-comparison of visualizations among segments add important understanding of broader patterns.

Two proof concerns remain with respect to the machine learning recommendations discussed here: First, the contexts that arose during the three year certified experiment did not include an extended episode of falling prices, or "crash." Second, there is some evidence of learning decay which needs continuing years of study.

It may never be possible to exhaustively evaluate a decisioning/recommending system built for dynamic contexts because of unforeseen factors. Yet, in business, defense, and space exploration final decisions must be made about design, expenditures and testing before deployment non-the-less. Decision makers need the best proof possible.

Finally, we hope insightful, skeptical critiques of the proof protocol will support its extension to other big data longitudinal prediction domains where contexts evolve in unknown ways.

Note: The three year certified recommendations discussed here were deposited for public access with U.Cal.Irvine machine learning repository.

7. REFERENCES

[1] Brooks, J. S. et al. 2006. Testing Hypotheses for the Success of Different Conservation Strategies. *Conservation Biology*, 20, 5 (Oct. 2006), 1528-1538. DOI=10.1111/j.1523-1739.2006.00506.

[2] Canadi, I., Barford, P. and Sommers, J. 2012. Revisiting broadband performance. *In IMC '12 Proceedings of the 2012 ACM conference on Internet measurement conference*. ACM New York, NY (2012), 273-286.

[3] Changa, R. M., Kauffman, R. J. and Kwonc, Y. 2014. Understanding the paradigm shift to computational social science in the presence of big data. *Decision Support Systems*, 63 (Jul. 2014), 67-80. DOI=10.1016/j.dss.2013.08.008.

[4] https://www.digistamp.com/authority/evidence/ (Feb. 2015).

[5] Driscoll, K. and Walker, S. 2014. Big Data, Big Questions Working Within a Black Box: Transparency in the Collection and Production of Big Twitter Data. *Int'l J. of Communication*, 8 (2014).

[6] Han, J. and Kamber, M. 2011. *Data Mining: Concepts and Techniques, 3d Ed.* Morgan Kaufmann (2011).

[7] Heid, I. M. et al. 2009. Meta-Analysis of the INSIG2 Association with Obesity Including 74,345 Individuals: Does Heterogeneity of Estimates Relate to Study Design? (2009) *PLoS Genet.* 5, 10 (Oct. 2009) PMCID: PMC2757909 DOI=10.1371/journal.pgen.1000694.

[8] Hine, D. 2007. Change in a dynamic climate: a single longitudinal case study in a high technology industry. *In Innovative Methodologies in Enterprise Research.* Edward Elgar Pub. (2007).

[9] Hirst, D. E., Koonce, L. and Miller, J. 1999. The Joint Effect of Management's Prior Forecast Accuracy and the Form of Its Financial Forecasts on Investor Judgment. *J. Accounting Research*, 37, Studies on Credible Financial Reporting (1999), 101-124.

[10] Hu, R., and Watt, S. M. 2014. An Agent-Based Financial Market Simulator for Evaluation of Algorithmic Trading Strategies. *In 6th International Conference on Advances in System Simulation*, (2014), 221-227.

[11] Kais, M. et al. 2006. A Multi-Sensor Acquisition Architecture and Real-Time Reference for Sensor and Fusion Methods Benchmarking. *Intelligent Vehicles Symposium, 2006.* IEEE (Tokoyo), 418-423. DOI=10.1109/IVS.2006.1689664.

[12] Knox, S. and Walker, D. 2010. Empirical developments in the measurement of involvement, brand loyalty and their relationship in grocery markets. *J. Strategic Marketing*, (May 2010), 271-286. DOI= 10.1080/0965254032000159072.

[13] Krahnena, J. P. and Weber, M. 2001. Generally accepted rating principles: A primer. *J. Banking Finance* 25, 1 (Jan. 2001), 3-23.

[14] Lebiere, C., Gonzalez, C. and Warwick, W. 2009. A Comparative Approach to Understanding General Intelligence: Predicting Cognitive Performance in an Open-ended Dynamic Task. In Proceedings of the Second Conference on Artificial General Intelligence. Atlantis Press (2009). DOI= 10.2991/agi.2009.2.

[15] Li, Z. and Li, Z. 2015. Optimal robust optimization approximation for chance constrained optimization problem. *Computers & Chemical Engineering*, 74, 4 (Mar. 2015), 89-99.

[16] Lowenstein, R. 2000. *When Genius Failed: the Rise and Fall of Long-Term Capital Management.* Random House Trade Paperbacks, 95–97. ISBN 978-0-375-75825-6.

[17] Magnusson, D. and Bergman, L. R. 1990. *Data Quality in Longitudinal Research.* Cambridge U. Press (1990).

[18] Olden, J. D. and Jackson, D. A. 2002. Illuminating the "black box": a randomization approach for understanding variable contributions in artificial neural networks. *Ecological Modelling*, 154, 1–2, (Aug. 2002), 135–150.

[19] Terry-McElrath, Y.M. et al. 2011. Effects of tobacco-related media campaigns on smoking among 20–30-year-old adults: longitudinal data from the USA. *Tobacco Control* (2011). DOI=10.1136/tobaccocontrol-2011-050208.

[20] Menon, A., et al. 1999. Antecedents and consequences of marketing strategy making: a model and a test. *J. Marketing* (1999).

[21] Pavlou, P. A. and Sawy, O. A. 2011. Understanding the Elusive Black Box of Dynamic Capabilities. *Decision Sciences*, 42, 1 (Feb. 2011), 239-273. DOI= 10.1111/j.1540-5915.2010.00287.x.

[22] Redline, S., Dean, D., and Sanders, M. H. 2013. Entering the Era of "Big Data": Getting Our Metrics Right. *Sleep* 36, 4 (Apr 1, 2013), 465-469. PMCID: PMC3612262 DOI= 10.5665/sleep.2524.

[23] Sen, K., Viswanathan, M. and Agha, G. 2004. Statistical Model Checking of Black-Box Probabilistic Systems. *Computer Aided Verification: Lecture Notes in Computer Science*, 3114 (Springer Link 2004), 202-215.

[24] Sterman, J. D. 1987. Testing Behavioral Simulation Models by Direct Experiment. *Mgmt. Science*, 33, 12 (Dec. 1987), 1572-1592. DOI=10.1287/mnsc.33.12.1572.

[25] Varian, Hal R. 2014. Big Data: New Tricks for Econometrics. *J. Economic Perspectives*, 28, 2 (Spring 2014), 3.

[26] Warbrick-Smith, J. et al. 2009. Three hundred and fifty generations of extreme food specialisation: testing predictions of nutritional ecology. *Entomologia Experimentalis et Applicata*, 132, 1 (Jul. 2009), 65-75. DOI=10.1111/j.1570-7458.2009.00870.

[27] Weiss, R. E. 2005. *Modeling Longitudinal Data: With 72 Figures*. Springer (2005).

An Architecture for Agile Machine Learning in Real-Time Applications

Johann Schleier-Smith
if(we) Inc.
848 Battery St.
San Francisco, CA 94111
johann@ifwe.co

ABSTRACT

Machine learning techniques have proved effective in recommender systems and other applications, yet teams working to deploy them lack many of the advantages that those in more established software disciplines today take for granted. The well-known Agile methodology advances projects in a chain of rapid development cycles, with subsequent steps often informed by production experiments. Support for such workflow in machine learning applications remains primitive.

The platform developed at if(we) embodies a specific machine learning approach and a rigorous data architecture constraint, so allowing teams to work in rapid iterative cycles. We require models to consume data from a time-ordered event history, and we focus on facilitating creative feature engineering. We make it practical for data scientists to use the same model code in development and in production deployment, and make it practical for them to collaborate on complex models.

We deliver real-time recommendations at scale, returning top results from among 10,000,000 candidates with sub-second response times and incorporating new updates in just a few seconds. Using the approach and architecture described here, our team can routinely go from ideas for new models to production-validated results within two weeks.

Categories and Subject Descriptors

H.4.m [**Information Systems Applications**]: Miscellaneous

Keywords

Agile; Recommender Systems; Machine Learning

1. INTRODUCTION

Innovative companies often use short product cycles to gain advantage in fast-moving competitive environments. Among social networks, Facebook is known for especially frequent release cycles [11], and if(we) counts such capabilities as crucial to the early success of the Tagged and hi5 web sites, which today form a social network with more than 300 million registered members. We especially value the quick feedback loop between product ideas and production experiments, with schedules measured in days or weeks rather than months, quarters, or years.

Today, on account of the approach described here, if(we) can develop and deploy new machine learning systems, even real-time recommendations, just as rapidly as we do web or mobile applications. This represents a sharp improvement over our experience with traditional machine learning approaches, and we have been quick to take advantage of these capabilities in releasing a stream of product improvements.

Our system puts emphasis on creative feature engineering, relying on data scientists to design transformations that create high-value signals from raw facts. We work with common and well understood machine learning techniques such as logistic regression and decision trees, interface with popular tools such as R, Matlab, and Python, but invest heavily in the framework for data transformation, production state management, model description, model training, back-testing and validation, production monitoring, and production experimentation,

In what we believe to be a key innovation not previously described, our models only consume data inputs from a time-ordered event history. By replaying this history we can always compute point-in-time feature state for training and back-testing purposes, even with new models. We also have a well-defined path to deploying new models to production: we start out by playing back history, rolling forward in time to the present, then transition seamlessly to real-time streaming. By construction, our model code works just the same with inputs that are months old as with those that are milliseconds old, making it practical to use a single model description in both development and production deployment.

In adopting the architecture and approach described here, we bring to machine learning the sort of rapid iterative cycles that are well established in Agile software development practice [28], and along with this the benefits.

Our approach can be summarized as follows:

- **Event history is primary:** Our models consume data inputs as time-ordered event history, updating model signals represented by *online features*, state variables for which we have efficient incremental update routines with practical storage requirements.

KDD'15, August 10-13, 2015, Sydney, NSW, Australia.
ACM 978-1-4503-3664-2/15/08.
DOI: http://dx.doi.org/10.1145/2783258.2788628.

- **Emphasis on creative feature engineering:** We rely heavily on the insights of data scientists and on their ability to devise data transformations that yield high-value features (or signals) for machine learning algorithms.

- **One model representation:** The same code used by data scientists during model development is deployed to production. Our models are written in Scala, which makes reasonably efficient implementations practical, which offers advanced composability and rich abstractions, and which allows our software engineers to create library code providing a DSL-like environment, one where data scientists can express feature transformations in a natural way.

- **Works with standard machine learning tools:** There exists a tremendous variety of sophisticated tools for training machine learning models. Our approach interfaces cleanly with R, Matlab, Vowpal Wabbit, and other popular software packages.

Key benefits include:

- **Quick iterations:** We routinely need just a few days to go from an idea, a suggestion for a feature that might have increased predictive power, to production implementation and experimental verification. This rapid cycle keeps the cost of trying new ideas low, facilitates iterative progress, and helps data scientists stay engaged and focused.

- **Natural real-time processing:** Although the event history approach can be used in off-line or batch scenarios, using real-time signals carries no additional cost. Even in applications with relaxed update requirements, eliminating batch processing can make a problem easier to reason about. Also, real-time stream processing usually allows for more uniform production workload, which can be easier to manage.

- **Improved collaboration:** In many corporate environments data scientists are inclined to work in silos, and they commonly find it difficult to reproduce one another's work [16]. Our environment offers data scientists the best enablers of modern software development, including version control, continuous integration, automated testing, frequent deployment, and production monitoring. With these tools, plus shared access to a production event history, it becomes much more natural for data scientists to collaborate as they solve problems.

The primary driver of our work has been building the recommendation engine for a dating product, Meet Me, that is offered within Tagged and hi5. Choosing from roughly 10 million active members, and incorporating signals from recent seconds, the system produces an ordered list of profiles to be presented to the user for consideration. We devote Section 2 to a detailed description of this application and the design choices that it spurred. The open source Antelope framework, described in Section 3, generalizes the concepts developed for Meet Me, adds usability improvements, and provides a reference implementation independent from the if(we) codebase and applications.

2. THE MEET ME DATING APPLICATION

2.1 Problem

Among various features offered by the Tagged and hi5 social platform, Meet Me caters most directly to those seeking romantic connections; it serves as the center of the dating offering. The user is presented with one profile at a time, and prompted with a simple question, "are you interested?" In response, the user may select from two options, variously labeled as *yes* or *no*, ✓or ✗. In our terminology, we describe such a response as a *vote*, and in this discussion we standardize on the response terminology *positive* and *negative*. Two users achieve a *match* when both express mutual interest through positive votes for one another, and creating such matches is an important optimization goal for our algorithm. An illustrative screen shot of the Meet Me user interface appears in Figure 1.

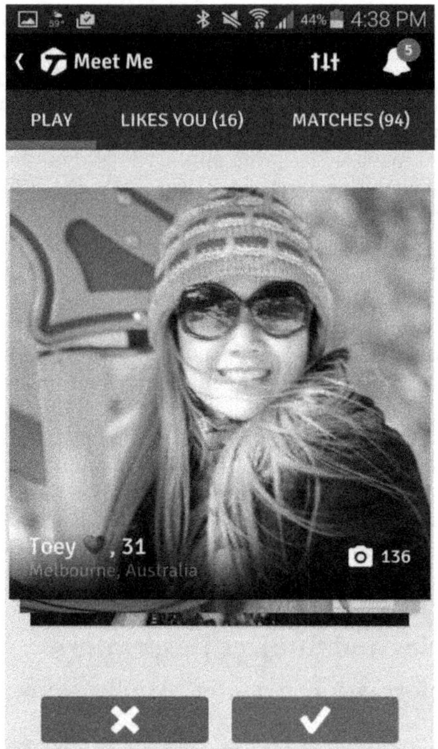

Figure 1: The Meet Me voting interface, shown here in the Tagged Android application. Users can touch the voting buttons at the bottom of the screen, or may swipe the presented profile towards the right to register a positive vote, or towards the left to register a negative vote.

The Meet Me style of matching, adopted by Tagged in 2008 and in 2012 by hi5, following a merger, appears to have been introduced by Hot or Not Inc. in the early 2000s. In recent years it attracted even greater attention as embodied in the Tinder mobile dating app. Notable implementations also include those by online social discovery companies Badoo, a UK company headquartered in London, and MeetMe Inc., a US company headquartered in New Hope, Pennsylvania.

We can view our Meet Me optimization problem from one of several perspectives, but prefer a formulation from the viewpoint of the user, posing the problem as follows: "given the millions of active user profiles matching basic eligibility criteria (principally filter settings), which should we next select to show?" We believe that focusing on the user helps data scientists build empathy for the individual experience, which is an important guide to intuition. It is our conjecture and our hope that separately optimizing for individual users produces a result that is well optimized for all users. Still, in developing a model for the experience of one user, we must account for behavior of other users as well. Most obviously, we recognize that it is not sufficient to derive recommendation from predictions of profiles that a user is likely to be interested in, it is also important that interest is reciprocated and mutual.

We decompose the problem by expressing the match probability in terms of separate conditional probabilities:

$$\begin{aligned} p(match_{a\leftrightarrow b}|vote_{a\rightarrow b}) &= p(vote^{+}_{a\rightarrow b} \wedge vote^{+}_{b\rightarrow a}|vote_{a\rightarrow b}) \\ &= p(vote^{+}_{a\rightarrow b}|vote_{a\rightarrow b}) \times p(vote_{b\rightarrow a}|vote^{+}_{a\rightarrow b}) \\ &\quad \times p(vote^{+}_{b\rightarrow a}|vote_{b\rightarrow a} \wedge vote^{+}_{a\rightarrow b}) \end{aligned} \tag{1}$$

where $match_{a\leftrightarrow b}$ represents a match between user a and user b, $vote_{a\rightarrow b}$ represents a vote, either positive or negative, by user a on user b, and $vote^{+}_{a\rightarrow b}$ represents a positive vote by user a on user b.

In decomposing the match probability into three parts, the first and third represent the likelihood that the voting user issues a positive vote. We represent in $p(vote^{+}_{a\rightarrow b}|vote_{a\rightarrow b})$ the likelihood that the user a will vote positive when we recommend user b. $p(vote_{b\rightarrow a}|vote^{+}_{a\rightarrow b})$ is the likelihood that user b will vote on user a following $vote^{+}_{a\rightarrow b}$, a probability that is itself influenced not only by the behavior of user b, say how active she is and how reliably she returns to Meet Me, but also by the implementation and rules of our algorithm, for example by how we rank user a among other users who have registered positive votes on user b, and by how often our recommendations of user b to others result in positive votes. The third component, $p(vote^{+}_{b\rightarrow a}|vote_{b\rightarrow a} \wedge vote^{+}_{a\rightarrow b})$ can be modeled similarly to the first component, for it represents the likelihood that a vote comes out as positive, yet since our application sometimes highlights match opportunities we do better by distinguishing this situation and training a separate model for it.

Ranking users b according to $p(match_{a\leftrightarrow b}|vote_{a\rightarrow b})$ is a reasonable first approach to the problems of making Meet Me recommendations for a. We will describe improved approaches later but first discuss early attempts at algorithm development.

2.2 Early Attempts

Our first algorithm implementations Meet Me were foundationally heuristic, only later coming to incorporate machine learning. We describe a progression of algorithms before outlining the challenges we encountered. These challenges arose not only from our approach to machine learning, but also from our system architecture, a traditional service-oriented web application, the layout and data flows of which are shown in Figure 2.

2.2.1 *Heuristic Algorithms*

An important early recommendation algorithm employed a patented approach [30] deriving inspiration from PageRank [29]. Ours may be the first commercial application of PageRank to social data, though Twitter also described a similar approach and popularized the notion of personalized PageRank in a social context [12]. Whereas the original PageRank algorithm for web search can be modeled as the likelihood of a page visit by a "random surfer" who starts at a randomly selected page, then traverses the graph along links between pages, at each hop continuing with probability α and stopping with probability $1-\alpha$, the personalized PageRank algorithm starts the graph traversal at the node of interest, in this case at the user who is to receive recommendations.

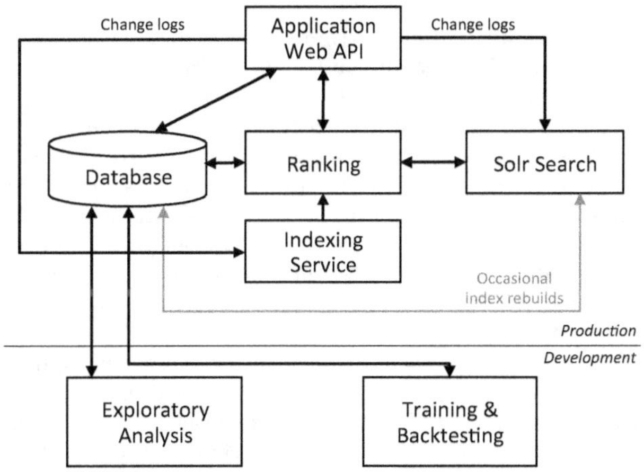

Figure 2: Architecture diagram of an early implementation of the Meet Me recommendation system. The API and database are based on standard web services technologies (PHP and Oracle). Recommendation candidates come from an Apache Solr search instance that first builds an index by querying the database, then stays current by processing change logs from the application. The ranking service (Java) operates similarly in maintaining an in-memory social graph, but also issues on-demand database queries to update user profile data. Data scientists engaged in development activities such as exploratory analysis, training, and backtesting query the database to extract working sets, most often studied using R and Python.

Our early work demonstrated the value of latent information present in social network interactions. For example, even without explicit data on age, gender, or sexual orientation, inspection of top results from a personalized PageRank query on the graph of friend connections or message exchanges gives results that are immediately recognizable as relevant (viewing a grid of photos can be a surprisingly effective way to get a quick and powerful impression of what an algorithm is doing, often proving more useful than statistical measures).

While our approach remained entirely heuristic, involving neither machine learning nor statistics, it provided plenty of parameters for experimentation. We focused on tuning parameters of the personalized PageRank algorithm, as well as parameters involving the level of user activity and the level of inbound positive interest. Lacking a predictive model of user behavior, we proceeded by intuitively guided trial and error, using judgment and quick sequences of A/B tests to maximize the number of users who received matches each day.

2.2.2 Machine Learning

We continue to believe that heuristics are a good way to start building recommendation engines, they test our problem understanding and can lead to good user experiences even with simple implementations. However, limited back-testing ability drives excess need for production experiments, and as the number of parameters rises it becomes increasingly awkward to reason about how to tune them manually. When we saw gains from heuristic improvements plateau we began to incorporate machine learning techniques, pursuing a promise of scaling to greater model complexity.

We chose to implement an SVM-based classifier predicting $p(vote^{+}_{a\rightarrow b}|vote_{a\rightarrow b})$ from a broad range of user details, not only age, gender and location, but also behavioral measures reflecting activity in sending and receiving friend requests and messages. We also included Meet Me activity, profile characteristics such as photos, schools, profile completeness, time since registration, profile viewing behavior, number of profile views received, ethnicity, religion, languages, sexual orientation, relationship status, and expressed reason for meeting people. Our approach might roughly be summed up as using any readily available information as a model feature, a contrast to the deliberate design approach we would later take.

This combination of machine learning with heuristics led to some gains at first, but we again soon found progress faltering. It was particularly troubling that the time between each improvement increased while gains realized in each decreased. In attempting to introduce new features to reflect user behavior better we encountered substantial software engineering challenges, including months spent making changes across multiple services, not only the ranking component but also the web application and database.

Among challenges we identified were the following:

- **Long deployment cycles:** Any algorithm changes required writing a large amount of software: SQL to extract historical data, Java code in models, Java code for processing real-time updates, often PHP code and more SQL to change how data was collected. For live experiments we also needed to consider how new and old implementations would coexist in production.

- **Limited feature transformations:** For the most part our classifier relied on features already available in the application, or those readily queried from the production database. These features represented data useful for display or for business logic, not necessarily for predictions. We lacked a simple and well-defined path for introducing new features, one with less overhead, one requiring effort commensurate to the complexity of the new feature rather than to the complexity of the architecture.

- **Difficulty in generating training data:** The database powering the application might store the current value of a feature, but might not retain a complete change log or history. If we were lucky we had access to a previous snapshot, but such point-in-time images would not accurately reflect the data available for real-time recommendations (see Figure 3). If unlucky, we would need to make new snapshots and wait for training data to accumulate.

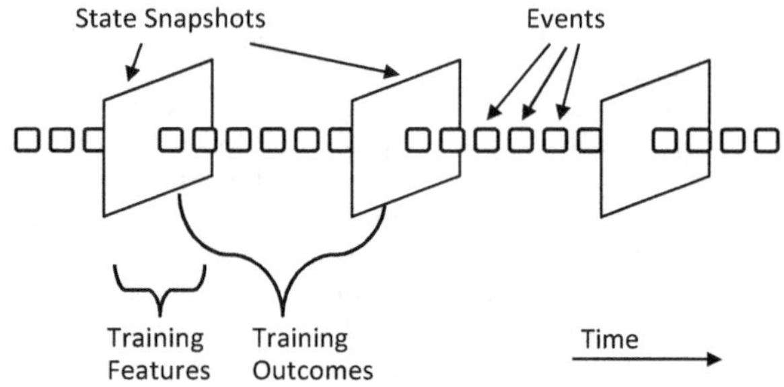

Figure 3: Training data consists of feature snapshots from the application database and outcomes occurring between them. These models are unable to capture feature variation between snapshots, and using real-time data in production introduces an inconsistency between model training and model deployment.

- **Lack of separation between domains:** We relied on computing features mostly in application code, creating a tight coupling between our recommendation system and our general business logic. We also mixed in-application feature computations with in-database computations expressed as SQL, furthering complex couplings.

- **Limited ability to backtest:** While we used training and cross-validation techniques in development of an SVM classifier, our recommendations remained dependent on a number of heuristic rules with tunable parameters. Our only path to tuning such parameters was through production experiments.

- **Limited problem insight:** *Ad hoc* data exploration and focus on statistical measures of performance left data scientists without a strong sense of user experience and, therefore, without the intuition necessary for breakthrough improvements.

- **Limited ability to collaborate:** We lacked a clear path to combine the efforts of multiple data scientists. We had only limited ability to deploy concurrent experiments, and the cost and complexity of implementing new features strained engineering bandwidth.

With so many challenges, we were lucky to have production experiments providing a safety net, protecting us against regressions as we stumbled towards improved recommendation algorithms.

The early approach described here has many shortcomings that leave it far from state-of-the-art. That said, in comparing notes with others we have come to believe that many of the challenges we encountered are common in industry. Our hope is that the solutions we share below will be broadly useful to those who deploy machine learning for high impact, as well as to those who plan to do so.

2.3 The Event History Architecture and Agile Data Science

Our answer to the struggles of previous approaches involves a number of deliberate choices: a departure from our previous software architecture and data architecture, specific ways of constructing machine learning models, and an adherence to certain ways of working with data—and with our team. These choices reinforce one another and allow an agile and iterative approach to delivering real-time recommendations for Meet Me.

2.3.1 Data and Software Architecture

Our architecture is driven by requirements, which can be summarized as follows:

- **Allow rapid experiments:** We should be able to go from ideas to validated results within two weeks.
- **Update in real-time:** Since user sessions are short, ~90s on average, it's important that models update within a few seconds, preferably <1s.
- **Support consumer internet scale and responsiveness:** Millions of active users, thousands of updates per second, subsecond response times for recommendations.
- **Encourage collaborative development practices:** Teams of data scientists and software engineers should make collective progress towards better Meet Me recommendations.

The architecture of our solution drops dependence on the relational database powering the web application, instead relying entirely on an event history log to support our machine learning systems. Importantly, we provide high-speed in-order access to event logs, and allow consumers to access both historical events and real-time streaming events using a single interface (see Listing 1). This architecture, diagrammed in Figure 5, puts the event history repository at the heart of the recommendation application.

It now becomes very natural to generate training and backtesting data for supervised learning algorithms. Whenever we encounter an event that we might want to predict, say $p(vote^{+}_{a \to b} | vote_{a \to b})$, we first write training data comprising the state of the model features just prior to the event occurrence, together with the event outcome. Only then do we update the state to reflect the event occurrence and continue rolling forward in time. Figure 4 illustrates generating training events in this way. The training data can be formatted for use with common statistical software, in our case R and Matlab.

Surprisingly, certain sorts of information that may not appear as event-like can benefit from representation in an event format. Take for instance zip code boundaries, ip-to-geography mappings, ISO country codes, or most any reference information that might naturally be implemented using a static lookup table. In many of these cases information can evolve, if slowly. By structuring such information as *fact update events* we maintain valuable flexibility and uniformity in our abstractions.

Another important benefit of the event history architecture is the symmetry it creates between historical backtesting and real-time streaming. We use the same feature definitions and state management software in development as we do in production. This proves key to quick deployments and rapid iterative data science cycles.

The event history architecture makes it practical to generate detailed training data for newly devised features, makes it straightforward and practical to deploy models based on

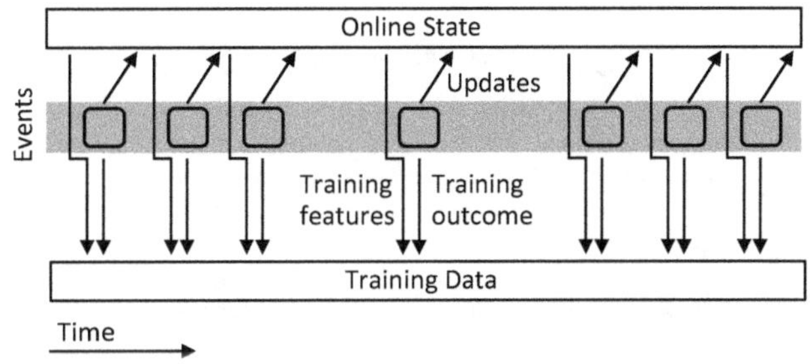

Figure 4: Training data generated from event history has granular alignment of feature state and training outcomes.

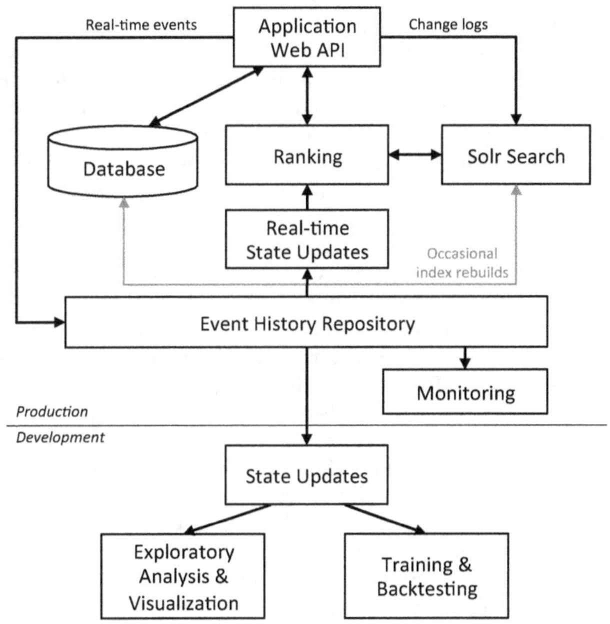

Figure 5: Diagram of the event history architecture. The event history repository serves as a central source of truth for production and development, and supports both historical access and real-time streaming.

such new features in production experiments, and consolidates features in one piece of code that works in both development and production. It provides composable abstractions that allow complex feature definitions, and it provides a single source of truth.

2.3.2 Data Science

A central promise of Agile methodology is a more responsive development cycle, one that generates quick feedback through design, implementation, and validation phases, one that allows continuously incorporating learnings, making corrections, and exploiting opportunities. Another central promise is improving collaboration among team members. All of these are characteristics appealing for data science and for development of machine learning systems, and our approach delivers them in this context.

Figure 6 illustrates our cycle of iterative progress. It starts with data scientists developing problem understanding, and importantly, intuition. From here we propose model im-

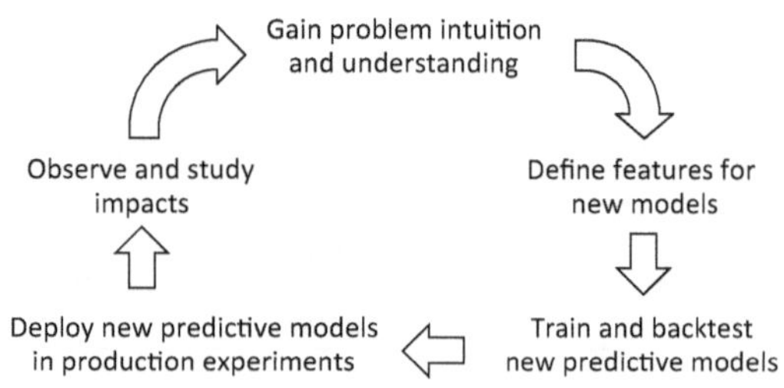

Figure 6: Agile data science cycle.

provements, typically in the form of new features. After training and establishing statistical basis for improvements through backtesting we deploy models to production and study impacts. We often realize gains but always improve our understanding, and enter the next development cycle with even stronger ideas. Additional details follow:

Problem intuition and understanding: Exploratory analysis often proceeds by asking simple questions, generally addressed with descriptive statistics and perhaps simple aggregates. We also encourage visualization, especially of user experience, and often find we can learn more from viewing just 100 faces, sampled from among 100,000, than we can from statistics on the aggregate. Working in this way not only helps us build our intuition but also our user empathy.

Models and feature engineering: We emphasize creative features with otherwise straightforward models. The event history architecture provides us with flexible feature design capabilities, and logistic regression serves us well, integrating signals typically represented by 50–100 features. Rather than learning a model with per-user parameters, we instead construct features that represent individual user characteristics, including how they relate to other users. These features evolve in response to individual user behavior, while the learned parameters of the model, applying to all users, remain fixed.

Training predictive models: Our event history accumulates several thousand events per second, and to compute features we need to process the entire stream. Early sampling is not an option because of the interconnected nature of our social network, and because features often capture interactions between users. On the other hand, since our models contain fewer than 100 parameters we are capable of generating much more training data than we need, at least over much of the domain of the feature space. This suggests that sampling is possible for training, however we are presented with another challenge: we must be careful not to introduce feedback, as occurs when the examples in the training set are biased because they are introduced by a recommendation algorithm. We address this problem by substituting a training recommendation, selected at random, in place of a ranked recommendation in 1% of instances. Doing so proved key to our ability to consistently achieve nonnegative performance changes when retraining models with more recent data, a foundational capability necessary for progress. We can imagine using more sophisticated sampling techniques to generate training examples, but benefiting from an enormous wealth of data we have not yet done so.

Production experiments: Our approach to large scale experiments is similar to that used by other consumer internet companies [18]. We encounter some special needs when testing Meet Me algorithms because performance ultimately depends on interactions between users. To address these, we developed a *split world* approach in which users are assigned at random to one of two partitions, seeing only users with the same "world" assignment in recommendations. Split world experiments are expensive because a reduced candidate pool degrades user experience, and because this drives us to limit ourselves to running one such experiment at a time. While we rely on split world experiments for final model acceptance, we start out evaluating model performance without a split world, assigning an initially small but progressively larger set of randomly selected users to the test group. During experiments we also take care to observe not only the initial effect, but also whether it grows or diminishes as user behavior adapts over time.

Production operations: A number of operating procedures support our Agile data science approach. We continuously monitor model performance, with loss and bias serving as indicators of problems. These measures can be essential for catching bugs that would otherwise go undiscovered amid the complexity of personalized recommendations.

2.4 Productivity and Business Results

Following our implementation of the event history architecture, our replacement of the original heuristic recommendation engine with a fully trained machine learning model implementation, and our adoption of a rapid-cycle Agile data science practice, we readily realized gains against our core optimization objectives. While the progress shown in Figure 7(a) represents contributions from various tuning efforts, including visual layout changes and promotions, results of experiments credit improved machine learning algorithms for over 30% increase in Meet Me usage.

During the course of 12 months our team released 21 changes to the model and adjusted experiment parameters 163 times. During an especially intense 6-month period (May through October 2013) we released 15 changes to our models and adjusted experiments 123 times. We credit our progress to this rapid iteration. Unfortunately, towards the end of this period we suffered from increases in spam abuse (Figure 7(c)), forcing a diversion of attention from improving recommendations to addressing this ever-present threat. We have deployed a number of the techniques developed here in our latest anti-spam measures, but the topic is beyond the scope of this paper.

2.5 The Meet Me Implementation

Here we attempt to provide a flavor for the models we have tested, though the full details of our Meet Me recommendation algorithm remain proprietary.

Optimization objectives: Perhaps the most straightforward approach is to optimize for the total number of matches, yet it quickly becomes clear that additional objectives call for consideration:

- *Total number of matches:* Simple to model by optimizing Equation 1, but gives too much exposure to active users with a high positive vote rate and fails to produce a good experience for many of the users.
- *Total number of individuals experiencing a match each day:* As Equation 1 but only the user's first match of the day counts towards the objective. This requires additional estimation but improves effectiveness.

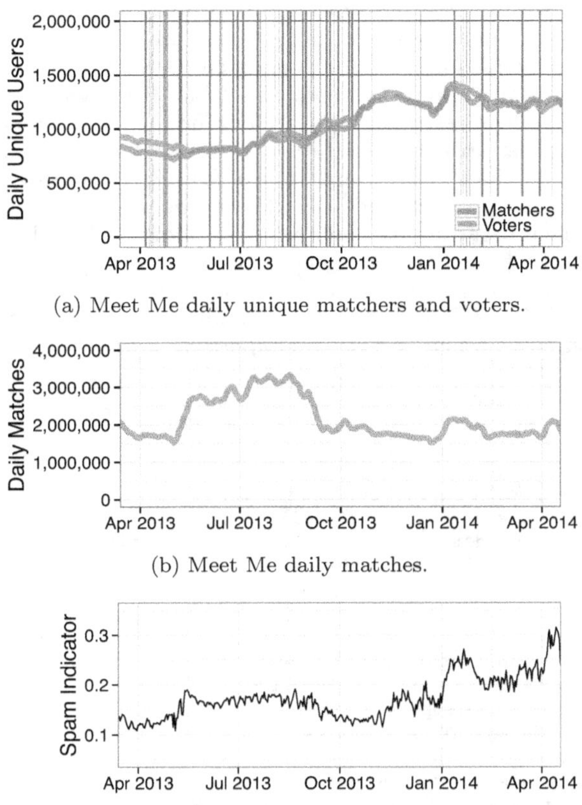

(a) Meet Me daily unique matchers and voters.

(b) Meet Me daily matches.

(c) Meet Me spam index.

Figure 7: Meet Me metrics through a period of focused tuning. (a) shows progress towards increasing activity, with the 7-day average of daily voters and matchers overlaid on production changes. Vertical red lines indicate new algorithm releases, and blue lines indicate adjustments to experiment weights. (b) shows the 7-day average of daily matches, which doesn't correlate with other measures of user activity. Initial models designed to optimize matches led to limited increases in matchers and voters, whereas our later algorithms increased these metrics despite producing fewer total matches. (c) shows an index of spam, here provided by proxy of the female positive vote rate. Spam can contribute to inflated Meet Me metrics, especially matches, but this data indicates stable spam levels through the period of greatest gains. Near the end of the period our efforts shifted to combating increasing spam and away from improving recommendations.

- *Number of conversations following from a match:* We can consider the match successful only after message exchanges, or some other indication of a connection between people of a certain depth. Again, more modeling is required but we can hope for improved effectiveness.
- *Number of users engaged with the Meet Me feature on a daily basis:* Here we model how a recommendation impacts the probability that users involved will come back to the product on a future day. Reasons for re-engaging could include responding to a match opportunity, conversing following a match, or reacting to the present experience, perhaps with encouragement, perhaps with renewed determination to achieve a match.

While we have experimented with all of the approaches listed above, we achieve best results with the last alternative, by optimizing for the number of users predicted to engage with Meet Me on future days.

Models: We separately model the likelihood of a positive vote, either $p(vote^+_{a\to b}|vote_{a\to b})$ or $p(vote^+_{b\to a}|vote_{b\to a} \wedge vote^+_{a\to b})$, and the likelihood of a user returning to vote $p(vote_{b\to a}|vote^+_{a\to b})$. For the positive vote likelihood we use logistic regression, for one because supporting tools are well-developed, but also because it provides a probability as output. This allows us to verify model calibration, and provides a well-defined interface between separate model components. We have also incorporated a decision stump model, but continue to use logistic regression to calibrate it to outcome probabilities.

We estimate time to return using the exponential-response variant of a generalized linear model, with a threshold time to obtain a return vote probability. We note that this approach is a simplified variant of the hazard based approach to user return time prediction developed by Pandora [17].

Features: We use online features only, requiring quick updates for new events and efficient in-memory implementations. Features must also be very quick to access during production ranking, allowing for only a few memory accesses and perhaps some simple arithmetic, e.g., computing a ratio. A good feature is stationary, meaning that with consistent user behavior it asymptotically approaches a fixed value. For example, the number of votes in the past week represents a stationary feature, as does the fraction of all votes that are positive, whereas the total number of votes or the total number of positive votes do not represent stationary features. Some of the features we have implemented include the following, listed along with examples:

- *Binary profile indicator:* Is this user in the US?
- *Factor indicators:* Group all countries into 20 buckets, then provide a binary indicator of user location for each.
- *Combination features:* Product of factor indicators of two users, say (country bucket of user a) $\times$ (country bucket of user b).
- *Arithmetic features:* Age difference, square of age difference, difference of square of age, or any other function of the ages of two users.
- *Regular expression features:* Does the user send messages matching a certain spam indicator?
- *Ratio features:* Fraction of past votes by the user that are positive.
- *Filtered features:* Fraction of past votes by the user that are positive, calculated for each of various recommended user country buckets.
- *Threshold features:* Binary indicator of whether some measure, perhaps a ratio, exceeds a threshold value.
- *Most recent value features:* When was the user most recently active?
- *Transformations relative to current time:* How long ago was the user most recently active?
- *Exponentially smoothed features:* What is the exponentially smoothed voting rate $\sum_i e^{-k(t-t_i)}$ for votes at times t_i, current time t and smoothing constant k?

Our approach stresses the composability of models and features. We routinely rank results according to the combination of several models, and we have experimented with unsupervised models that feed into features of higher-level supervised models. Further details of the features described above are available as part of the Antelope open source software described in Section 3.

2.6 Software Engineering Notes

While if(we) eschews the software development culture of "not invented here", instead making extensive use of both commercial and free software packages, the Meet Me recommendation system consists almost entirely of custom code. Our abstractions and trade-off choices are somewhat different from those used in batch systems such as Hadoop, from those used in relational databases, and from those used by other stream processing software such as Spark Streaming, different enough that we choose to develop our own implementations using Scala and Java.

The event history repository is a service implementing an interface similar to that outlined in Listing 1. This interface highlights the essential character of the event history. It can only do two things: 1. receive and store new events, 2. return events in time-order, possibly applying some filter. By specifying an *endTime* in the future (typically $+\infty$) the client application gains access to real-time streaming, and in a single call to *getEvents* can access both historical and future events.

```
trait EventHistory {
  def publishEvent(e: Event)
  def getEvents(startTime: Date, endTime: Date,
    eventFilter: EventFilter, eventHandler: EventHandler)
}
```

Listing 1: The EventHistory interface (simplified).

We maintain feature state using large arrays of primitives, a packed in-memory representation allowing us to support over 10,000,000 candidate user recommendations on a commodity server. Our framework takes care of mapping feature state to array indexes. Our present implementation supports only a dense feature layout but we can imagine implementing a layout supporting sparse feature vectors. We spent some time considering whether to lay out our features row-major or column-major format, opting for the row-major format so as to keep our implementation simpler.

Our implementation is an efficient one that seeks to limit object allocation and that aims to provide good optimization opportunities to the JVM. While we can rank >50,000 candidate users per second, we see opportunities for order-of-magnitude improvements through optimization.

High availability and scalability are provided by replica ranking servers, while a single feature building server propagates state changes. In the event of feature builder failure we can restart processing from the event history log, accelerating recovery with saved snapshots. Even at our scale, we choose to optimize for performance rather than introduce distributed system complexities. A modern commodity server can handle >10,000 updates per second across 100 or more features, leaving us with ample headroom. We believe that with such implementations even many large businesses have no need for distributed architectures.

3. THE ANTELOPE REAL-TIME EVENTS FRAMEWORK

The event history architecture, our approach to feature engineering, and our approach to Agile data science are general, however the implementation for Meet Me recommendations remains coupled both to the problem and to the if(we) platform. The Antelope open source project[1] aims to make our approach broadly available. It presently represents a demonstration rather than a production tool, yet it fully illustrates the flexibility of the event history architecture, provides concrete examples of feature engineering, and serves as a guide for other implementations.

In our first example application, we address a Kaggle challenge for product search and recommendations [1]. Using the *Feature* interface of Listing 2 in the context of learning to rank [14], we demonstrate use of a simple *Popularity* feature along with a more complex *TfIdfFeature.*

```
trait Feature {
   def score(ctx: ScoringContext): Long => Double
}

class Popularity extends Feature {
  val ct = counter(skuViewed)
  override def score(implicit ctx: ScoringContext) = {
    id => ct(id) div ct()
  }
}

class TfIdfFeature extends Feature {
  val terms = counter(skuUpdated,
    productNameUpdatedTerms)
  val docsWithTerm = set(productNameUpdatedTerms,
    skuUpdated)
  val docs = set(skuUpdated)
  override def score(implicit ctx: ScoringContext) = {
    val queryTerms = ctx.query.normalize.split(" ")
    val n = docs.size()
    id => (queryTerms map { t =>
      val tf = terms(id, t)
      val df = docsWithTerm.size(t)
      sqrt(tf) * sq(1D + log(n / (1D + df)))
    }).sum
  }
}
```

Listing 2: The Feature interface and example implementations (simplified).

In our second example, we simulate user activity in an online dating context, then build recommendations using a model with features similar to those we have deployed for Meet Me (described in Section 2.5).

4. RELATED WORK

We present our review of related work in four parts: Agile data science, design and architecture of machine learning systems, choice of machine learning algorithms, and other approaches to real-time processing. While we find much of this literature to be complementary to the event history architecture described here, we find no direct precedent for our design.

Agile data science: While the Agile methodology [5] is well understood and broadly practiced in many variants by software engineers, the approach is only starting to make impact on data science. Jurney [15] provides a how-to guide for performing analytical tasks using Hadoop, encouraging adoption of Agile values. This work focuses on business understanding and does not address production recommenda-

[1]`https://github.com/ifwe/antelope`

tion engines, as we do. Beyond this, the dearth of literature on Agile data science is remarkable; we imagine this may change in coming years.

Machine learning systems: The work described here has strong philosophical parallels to the Hazy project [22], which states the goal of "making it easier to build and maintain big-data analytics." The emphasis on feature engineering, and the belief that simple machine learning models with more or better features will often outperform more sophisticated algorithms, rings true to our experience. We too emphasize programming abstractions and infrastructure abstractions, but choose rather different implementations. Whereas the Hazy project uses probabilistic logic programming, we use reactive-style Scala code to implement features. Our central infrastructure abstraction is the event history repository, whereas Hazy works against a static data model.

The Hazy team has also described a vision of a data system for feature engineering [4]. In asserting that "feature man-months aren't mythical," they suggest that whereas on traditional software projects adding more people rarely leads to proportionately faster progress [7], in trained systems loose coupling can permit a large team to work toward a common goal with only limited coordination. The proposal, most recently implemented in the DeepDive system [32], facilitates feature engineering as we do, yet does not adopt a time-based data model or provide for real-time updates.

Recent work by the UC Berkeley AMP Lab reveals Velox [10], a low-latency solution to model serving and management. Velox provides important operational capabilities not previously available in open-source machine learning toolkits. In addition to low-latency serving it provides an online update functionality that approximates continuous model retraining, as well as periodic batch retraining. We are not alone in recognizing the gap between the promise of machine learning applications and what is commonplace in industry. In comparison, by using online features only, we achieve continuous production operation without needing batch operations. Furthermore, in addressing feature engineering challenges we contribute additional productivity improvements.

There are a variety of toolkits designed to make machine learning more practical and accessible. MLbase [20] automates many of the technical steps required to build effective machine learning models. The venerable Weka [13] remains a powerful environment for machine learning, offering not only a large number of machine learning algorithms but also a variety of filters for preprocessing data. Our provisions for feature engineering are richer, and we can imagine complementing both of these toolkits.

Machine learning is applied extensively in online advertising, and the production techniques developed at Google are relevant to our work [27, 31]. While there is no mention of a central event history or of using event processing to support iterative development and expressive feature engineering, the importance of real-time processing, of a log-based approach, of keeping machine learning simple, and of thinking carefully about architecture all come through clearly.

Machine learning algorithms: We rank recommendations in Meet Me by ordering candidates according to the optimization objective, matches in early implementations, and predictions for overall engagement in later implementations. Here we review alternatives.

The learning to rank literature is perhaps best developed in the area of information retrieval [25], but its principles can apply to personalized people recommendations as well [14]. Our experience developing examples for Antelope suggests that learning to rank is a natural match with the event history architecture.

People recommendations struggle with the special challenge of a high-dimensionality target space; there are many more candidates than in e-commerce or in entertainment. Collaborative filtering has widely publicized success as part of Amazon's product recommendations [24], and related matrix factorization techniques were used in winning the Netflix prize [19]. While we did not pursue such approaches, it would be interesting to evaluate whether they are practical in our setting.

Contextual-bandit techniques have also been adopted for personalized recommendations [23], in an approach that we believe could be combined with the creative feature engineering described here. In particular, we are encouraged by results showing offline evaluation using previously recorded traffic, which dovetails with an event history approach.

Real-time processing: A number of architectural paradigms exist for processing real-time information.

Complex event processing is well established as an integration pattern that fits naturally with an Agile approach [9]. The MillWheel system described by Google [3] is a platform for reliable stream processing that can execute arbitrary imperative code. A log-centric architecture extolled by Kreps [21] is particularly well aligned with our perspectives on data processing; the immutable log represents the system's single source of truth, just like our event history. Similarly, Event Sourcing and CQRS (Command & Query Responsibility Segregation) [6] patterns for application architecture are particularly well suited to our approach. Streaming query engines are developed in the academic literature [8] and have commercial implementations [2]. All of these platforms and perspectives could serve as a part of an implementation for our architecture.

One approach to real-time recommendations is to build a speed layer on top of a batch system [26]. While this evolutionary approach is sensible, and while some calculations are easier with batch processing, we believe that in most cases such hybrid architecture introduces unnecessary complexity.

5. CONCLUSIONS AND FUTURE WORK

The event history architecture provides a powerful abstraction, allowing teams of data scientists to collaborate actively on machine learning projects. Our production implementation delivers personalized recommendations drawn from millions of candidates, answers queries in under a second and incorporates new information in seconds. We are presently working on Antelope, an open source implementation incorporating the event history paradigm and providing a flexible environment for feature engineering. We have used several machine learning tools alongside the technology developed here, and can envision deeper integrations, including ones with popular data management systems, which only need to implement the interface of Listing 1.

We remain struck by the gulf between sophisticated demonstrations of what is possible in machine learning, and the day-to-day realities of what is practical in most organizations. By bringing Agile capabilities to production data science applications we hope to narrow the gap, to help teams feel the thrill of frequently realized gains, and to help them build and deploy more of what they can imagine.

6. ACKNOWLEDGMENTS

This work reflects the industriousness and ability of the data scientists and engineers of the if(we) Relevance Team. Special thanks go to Karl Dawson and Helena Buhr for leadership and helpful discussions, and to Vinit Garg, Dai Li, Martin Linenweber, and Madhusudana Shashanka for tireless efforts.

7. REFERENCES

[1] Data mining hackathon on (20 mb) Best Buy mobile web site - ACM SF Bay Area Chapter. `http://bit.ly/1O3eDOD`. Accessed: 2015-02-20.

[2] Stream processing explained. `http://www.sqlstream.com/stream-processing/`. Accessed: 2015-02-20.

[3] T. Akidau, A. Balikov, K. Bekiroğlu, S. Chernyak, J. Haberman, R. Lax, S. McVeety, D. Mills, P. Nordstrom, and S. Whittle. Millwheel: Fault-tolerant stream processing at internet scale. *Proc. VLDB Endow.*, 6(11):1033–1044, Aug. 2013.

[4] M. Anderson, D. Antenucci, V. Bittorf, M. Burgess, M. J. Cafarella, A. Kumar, F. Niu, Y. Park, C. Ré, and C. Zhang. Brainwash: A data system for feature engineering. In *CIDR*, 2013.

[5] K. Beck, M. Beedle, A. van Bennekum, A. Cockburn, W. Cunningham, M. Fowler, et al. The Agile manifesto. `http://agilemanifesto.org/`, 2001.

[6] D. Betts, J. Dominguez, G. Melnik, F. Simonazzi, and M. Subramanian. *Exploring CQRS and Event Sourcing: A Journey into High Scalability, Availability, and Maintainability with Windows Azure.* Microsoft patterns & practices, 2013.

[7] F. P. Brooks Jr. *The Mythical Man-Month: Essays on Software Engineering, Anniversary Edition, 2/E.* Addison-Wesley Professional, 1995.

[8] S. Chandrasekaran and M. J. Franklin. Streaming queries over streaming data. In *VLDB*, pages 203–214, 2002.

[9] K. Chandy and W. Schulte. *Event Processing: Designing IT Systems for Agile Companies.* McGraw-Hill, Inc., New York, NY, USA, 2010.

[10] D. Crankshaw, P. Bailis, J. E. Gonzalez, H. Li, Z. Zhang, M. J. Franklin, A. Ghodsi, and M. I. Jordan. The missing piece in complex analytics: Low latency, scalable model management and serving with Velox. *CoRR*, abs/1409.3809, 2014.

[11] D. G. Feitelson, E. Frachtenberg, and K. L. Beck. Development and deployment at Facebook. *IEEE Internet Computing*, 17(4):8–17, July 2013.

[12] P. Gupta, A. Goel, J. Lin, A. Sharma, D. Wang, and R. Zadeh. WTF: The who to follow service at Twitter. In *WWW*, pages 505–514, 2013.

[13] M. Hall, E. Frank, G. Holmes, B. Pfahringer, P. Reutemann, and I. H. Witten. The WEKA data mining software: An update. *SIGKDD Explor. Newsl.*, 11(1):10–18, Nov. 2009.

[14] L. Hong, R. Bekkerman, J. Adler, and B. D. Davison. Learning to rank social update streams. In *SIGIR*, pages 651–660, 2012.

[15] R. Jurney. *Agile Data Science: Building Data Analytics Applications with Hadoop.* O'Reilly Media, 2013.

[16] S. Kandel, A. Paepcke, J. M. Hellerstein, and J. Heer. Enterprise data analysis and visualization: An interview study. *Visualization and Computer Graphics, IEEE Transactions on*, 18(12):2917–2926, 2012.

[17] K. Kapoor, M. Sun, J. Srivastava, and T. Ye. A hazard based approach to user return time prediction. In *KDD*, pages 1719–1728, 2014.

[18] R. Kohavi, A. Deng, B. Frasca, T. Walker, Y. Xu, and N. Pohlmann. Online controlled experiments at large scale. In *KDD*, pages 1168–1176, 2013.

[19] Y. Koren, R. Bell, and C. Volinsky. Matrix factorization techniques for recommender systems. *Computer*, (8):30–37, 2009.

[20] T. Kraska, A. Talwalkar, J. C. Duchi, R. Griffith, M. J. Franklin, and M. I. Jordan. MLbase: A distributed machine-learning system. In *CIDR*, 2013.

[21] J. Kreps. The log: What every software engineer should know about real-time data's unifying abstraction. `http://linkd.in/1fDnlQk`, Dec. 16 2013.

[22] A. Kumar, F. Niu, and C. Ré. Hazy: Making it easier to build and maintain big-data analytics. *Commun. ACM*, 56(3):40–49, Mar. 2013.

[23] L. Li, W. Chu, J. Langford, and R. E. Schapire. A contextual-bandit approach to personalized news article recommendation. In *WWW*, pages 661–670, 2010.

[24] G. Linden, B. Smith, and J. York. Amazon.com recommendations: Item-to-item collaborative filtering. *Internet Computing, IEEE*, 7(1):76–80, 2003.

[25] T.-Y. Liu. Learning to rank for information retrieval. *Found. Trends Inf. Retr.*, 3(3):225–331, Mar. 2009.

[26] N. Marz and J. Warren. *Big Data: Principles and best practices of scalable realtime data systems.* Manning Publications Co., 2015.

[27] H. B. McMahan, G. Holt, D. Sculley, M. Young, D. Ebner, J. Grady, et al. Ad click prediction: A view from the trenches. In *KDD*, pages 1222–1230, 2013.

[28] B. Meyer. *Agile!: The Good, the Hype and the Ugly.* Springer Science & Business Media, 2014.

[29] L. Page, S. Brin, R. Motwani, and T. Winograd. The PageRank citation ranking: Bringing order to the web. 1999.

[30] J. Schleier-Smith. System and method of selecting a relevant user for introduction to a user in an online environment, June 17 2014. US Patent 8,756,163.

[31] D. Sculley, G. Holt, D. Golovin, E. Davydov, T. Phillips, D. Ebner, V. Chaudhary, and M. Young. Machine learning: The high interest credit card of technical debt. In *SE4ML: Software Engineering for Machine Learning (NIPS 2014 Workshop)*, 2014.

[32] C. Zhang, C. Ré, A. A. Sadeghian, Z. Shan, J. Shin, F. Wang, and S. Wu. Feature engineering for knowledge base construction. *CoRR*, abs/1407.6439, 2014.

Scalable Machine Learning Approaches for Neighborhood Classification Using Very High Resolution Remote Sensing Imagery*

Manu Sethi
Department of Computer and Information Science and Engineering
University of Florida
Gainesville, FL 32611
msethi@cise.ufl.edu

Yupeng Yan
Department of Computer and Information Science and Engineering
University of Florida
Gainesville, FL 32611
yupeng@cise.ufl.edu

Anand Rangarajan
Department of Computer and Information Science and Engineering
University of Florida
Gainesville, FL 32611
anand@cise.ufl.edu

Ranga Raju Vatsavai
NC State University and Oak Ridge National Laboratory
890 Oval Drive, Campus Box 8206
Raleigh, NC 27695
rrvatsav@ncsu.edu

Sanjay Ranka
Department of Computer and Information Science and Engineering
University of Florida
Gainesville, FL 32611
ranka@cise.ufl.edu

ABSTRACT

Urban neighborhood classification using very high resolution (VHR) remote sensing imagery is a challenging and *emerging* application. A semi-supervised learning approach for identifying neighborhoods is presented which employs superpixel tessellation representations of VHR imagery. The image representation utilizes homogeneous and irregularly shaped regions termed superpixels and derives novel features based on intensity histograms, geometry, corner and superpixel density and scale of tessellation. The semi-supervised learning approach uses a support vector machine (SVM) to obtain a preliminary classification which is then subsequently refined using graph Laplacian propagation. Several intermediate stages in the pipeline are presented to showcase the important features of this approach. We evaluated this approach on four different geographic settings with varying neighborhood types and compared it with the recent Gaussian Multiple Learning algorithm. This evaluation shows several advantages, including model building, accuracy, and efficiency which makes it a great choice for deployment in large scale applications like global human settlement mapping and population distribution (e.g., LandScan), and change detection.

*This work is partially supported by NSF IIS 1065081

KDD'15, August 11-14, 2015, Sydney, NSW, Australia.
 ISBN 978-1-4503-3664-2/15/08 ...$15.00.
DOI: http://dx.doi.org/10.1145/2783258.2788625.

Categories and Subject Descriptors

H.2.8 [**Database Applications**]: Data Mining; I.5 [**Pattern Recognition**]: Models—*Statistical*

Keywords

Remote Sensing, Segmentation, Neighborhoods

1. INTRODUCTION

The past twenty years have seen an explosion of interest in remote sensing technologies and machine learning algorithms aimed at representing, categorizing and classifying land cover. With applications ranging across agriculture, space exploration and urban planning, remote sensing is a technology with a huge upside with many more applications yet to be envisaged let alone executed. The various improvements in imaging resolution over the past two decades has led to fine-grained classification with several applications; biomass monitoring, urban settlement mapping, climate change projections, etc.

Remote sensing applications have certain characteristics that take them beyond routine application of machine learning algorithms for classification. First, remote sensing data live on a spatio-temporal grid and this fact is fundamentally at odds with the independent and identically distributed (i.i.d.) sample-based approach adopted in present-day machine learning. For this reason, it is vitally important to begin with an image representation which takes the gridded nature of the data into account. We adopt a segmentation-based representation which leverages the spatial remote sensing grid. Second, the range of queries in remote sensing are more complex. Instead of requiring pixel-level classification, newer applications requires us to classify homogeneous regions into single categories while maintaining clear-cut region boundaries between classes (e.g., urban versus forest). This is a far cry from merely labeling individual samples—the usual scenario in standard machine learning. Third, the

Figure 1: An example of the high resolution aerial images obtained from Google Earth that we use in our experiments for terrain classification. The above image contains more than 1 million pixels and represents an area of about 1 sq km on the ground.

underlying volume (terabytes to petabytes) and velocity (gigabytes to terabytes per day) of data produced by these applications is very large and is responsible for carrying us into the bigdata regime. Effective processing requires low complexity and multi-scale algorithms that can exploit modern architectures with deep memory hierarchies. This is an important challenge for existing machine learning techniques. Finally, expert interaction and the demarcation of training and test set regimes are very different in remote sensing. Experts may be called upon to label whole regions, for example, rather than individual pixels. And, since the entire image is available at the time of training, a semi-supervised approach which does not arbitrarily demarcate training and testing regimes is needed. These considerations shape our work presented below. In a nutshell, we leverage a segmentation-driven image representation and perform semi-supervised label propagation within this representation to achieve image classification in our remote sensing application. An example of the images that we are going to use in this paper can be seen in Figure 1:

A fundamental point of departure taken in the present work is the use of superpixel tessellation representations of remote sensing images. When previous work on remote sensing classification is examined in this light, we invariably find that either (i) a pixel-based classification approach is adopted with no consideration given to local region homogeneity, or (ii) rectangular patches of pixels are used, once again with no consideration given to local homogeneity and natural shape of the patch under consideration. In sharp contrast to these previous approaches, we begin with a superpixel tessellation representation of remote sensing images. Coherent local structures are a characteristic, common to remote sensing imagery, and adequately captured by superpixel tessellations. Superpixels are local homogeneous groupings of pixels and superpixel tessellations ensure that the image domain is covered by the superpixels with no overlap. Since region homogeneity is a function of scale, we employ a pyramid of superpixel tessellations with the coarser scales using local groupings of superpixels from finer scales. The result is a scale space of superpixel tessellations—a segmentation driven image representation, fundamental to our approach and rarely used by competing remote sensing classification approaches at the present time.

We now briefly delve into the specifics of the superpixel tessellation approach deployed here. Essentially, we adapt the popular ultrametric contour map (UCM) approach to image segmentation to obtain superpixel tessellations. We briefly summarize UCM and highlight its use as a feature extractor—a novel aspect we have not seen in other recent work. UCM begins by obtaining scale-space image gradient information at each pixel and for different orientations. Next, a graph is constructed by joining any pair of pixels which exhibit good evidence for a line segment connecting them in the actual image. Taking cues from recent developments in graph partitioning and spectral clustering, the top eigenvectors of the graph Laplacian are computed and re-arranged in image space. Then, gradients are computed on the eigenvector images and combined with the original image gradients (from step one) to produce a contour descriptor at each pixel. A oriented watershed algorithm is executed on the gradient image to produce the lowest level superpixel tessellation. These superpixels are combined using grouping heuristics to obtain the final ultrametric contour map (UCM) [2] with superpixel containment across levels. The superpixel tessellation obtained is the image representation used in this work.

Once the hierarchical image representation is in place, we can focus on superpixel classification. As mentioned earlier, we prefer to classify superpixels (at a suitably chosen level) instead of classifying individual pixels of rectangular regions (which lack local homogeneity). A semi-supervised machine learning approach is most suitable in remote sensing and in this context of superpixel tessellation representations. The remote sensing expert is tasked with labeling $O(1)$ superpixels (at a suitably chosen level) with the machine learning algorithm subsequently labeling all the other superpixels. Assume that the expert labels are in place. We now extract features at every superpixel which are consonant with the kind of discrimination required in this application: the separation of remote sensing image data into urban, slum, forest and other labels. To this end, we discovered a novel feature stemming from our chosen UCM-based image representation. The number and type of superpixels (at a suitably chosen level) can function as discriminating features. It turns out that regularly shaped superpixels are better indicative of urban regions and the density of superpixels correlates well with slums. These novel features are combined with more standard color histogram-based features into a superpixel classification algorithm using standard support vector machines (SVMs). Since SVMs do not leverage the underlying spatial grid and indeed have a fundamental limitation as sample-based classifiers, we execute a Laplacian graph-based label propagation algorithm to improve on the result of SVM-based classification.

In this paper, we utilize the above approach for semi-supervised labeling of regions into different land-use land-cover (LULC) classes (urban, slums, forests, sea, sand) in high resolution aerial images. Our approach leverages new features as the traditionally available features such as HOG and SIFT may not be effective in discriminating among different LULC classes pictured in aerial images.

1.1 Application Significance

The applications centered around very high resolution (VHR) imagery have gained huge impetus recently, primarily because images with sub-meter resolution are now available easily—an outcome of a surge in the launch of satellites by private companies like Digital globe (e.g., WorldView-2 in late 2009). Evidently, such imagery provides extensively new avenues for the automatic classification of both natural regions (forest, sea, different kinds of terrain) and man-made structures (residential and commerical buildings, for instance) worldwide. We are developing various new approaches to efficiently process this imagery for monitoring natural and man-made infrastructures (including neighborhoods, nuclear and other energy infrastructures). At the Oak Ridge National Laboratory (ORNL), the Computational Science and Engineering division produces the LandScan [21] high-resolution population database that is widely used by both government agencies and commercial entities across the world. One of the critical inputs to this model is a thematic layer consisting of different neighborhoods generated from the VHR imagery that spans the globe. Generating a global scale neighborhood map at a sub-meter resolution is a daunting task. For the past several decades, ORNL is developing accurate and computationally efficient methods to process VHR imagery. Likewise, a few international agencies like European Commission (EU) Joint Research Center (JRC) are involved in global scale settlement mapping [26] using VHR imagery.

Despite great efforts by the research community across the globe, neighborhood mapping is a challenging task. First of all, neighborhoods are not well defined, which is reflected in the quote by Galster [12]—"Urban social scientists have treated 'neighborhood' in much the same way as courts of law have treated pornography: a term that is hard to define precisely, but everyone knows it when they see it." There is no consistent nomenclature across the countries regarding neighborhoods and no consistent ground-truth, making it very difficult to build machine learning models for global scale problems. In addition, most of the neighborhoods are made up of complex objects (consisting of different types of objects, not just buildings and roads) which makes it very difficult to obtain ground-truth data from images.

Despite these problems and limitations, mapping neighborhoods, especially informal settlements is crucial in terms of national security and on humanitarian grounds as well. This is because these informal settlements arise unplanned and unauthorized in the most hazardous regions and lack basic services, and therefore, pose several challanges to the nations. Even though numerous studies sponsored by World Bank and United Nations emphasize the significance of poverty maps in designing better policies and interventions, manually mapping the slums of the world is a daunting task. The framework provided in this paper is an advancement in terms of computational efficiency and accuracy in the current technology available to detect new settlements (across the globe), and as well as characterize different neighborhoods which is a key input to other programs like LandScan [21]. In addition, neighborhood maps have several other applications, including but not limited to health [17], energy [10], and crime [16].

The rest of the paper is organized as follows. In the next section we briefly discuss the related work in classifying remote sensing image datasets using semi-supervised approaches. Section 3 describes our approach in detail. Section 4 provides experimental validation and section 5 presents conclusions.

2. PREVIOUS WORK

The major steps involved in remote sensing image classification can be abstracted into: (i) extraction of features from the image, (ii) collection of ground-truth (training/test) data for a few sample locations, (iii) building a classification model (e.g. naïve Bayes, decision trees, MLPs), and (iv) predicting labels for the entire image. Most existing classification approaches work with spectral features (e.g., blue, green, red, thermal infrared) and derived features (e.g., texture, band ratios like Normalized Difference Vegetation Index (NDVI), Histogram of Oriented Gradients (HOG)), extracted at each pixel (spatial location). These classification approaches are called pixel-based or single instance learning (SIL) algorithms. A review of these techniques can be found in [29, 14]. Most classification schemes model the correlations in feature space while the spatial locations of those features are often ignored. An improvement over per-pixel classification schemes is to incorporate spatial locations such as MRF [23]. This combination of the two where spatial correlations and feature correlations are modeled simultaneously leads to what is known as spatial classification schemes. This results into much smoother class distributions in the final classified image. However, it should be noted that spatial classification methods are also essentially single instance learners. One way to overcome the single instance limitation is to look at additional features beyond spectral features. For example, features that exploit spatial contextual information have proved quite useful in classifying very high-resolution images. Recent studies [29, 27, 14] show the improved performance of SIL methods when the spectral features are combined with a broad set of extended features such as morphological, texture, and edge density. Although these studies showed that the extended features which exploit spatial contextual information resulted in improved SIL accuracy, the underlying image complexity and interpixel relationships are still not fully exploited.

Complex object recognition requires investigation of spatial regions or image patches. Object based classification schemes [20, 4] exploit the spatial and spectral features in order to group the pixels into coherent regions called objects. One can then use these objects to build a meta classifier on the features (shape, geometry, etc.) that describe the whole object and not just a particular pixel. Another approach has also been to simply aggregate all features for all pixels belonging to a particular object into a single feature vector and then apply any single instance learning algorithm. However, all these approaches lose important structural and spatial properties in the aggregation process. In order to overcome some of the limitations of single instance learning schemes, multiple instance learning (MIL) methods have been developed. The seminal work of Dietterich *et al.* [9], Diverse Density [18], and Citation-KNN [30] are some notable approaches for MIL. In general MIL methods are shown to perform better than single instance learning schemes, and therefore, have seen application in remote sensing image classification as well. For example, in [5], the authors have developed an MIL based binary classification scheme for identifying targets (landmines) in Hyperspectral (HS) imagery. The high computational cost of Citation-KNN has led to the development of an efficient Gaussian Multiple Instance (GMIL) [28] learning algorithm. Both of these algorithms are shown to perform better than most well-known SIL approaches, however leveraging them for global scale problems is difficult due to their computational complexity. We believe that our work which utilizes irregular patches or superpixels (which are mainly homogeneous) along with novel and parallelizable machine learning techniques have the potential to address the scale requirements of target applications. In addition our approach eliminates the need for determining an appropriate grid size which impacts the performance—both in terms of computation and accuracy.

Finally, we summarize the evolution—mainly in the past decade—of graph-based semi-supervised learning (SSL) methodologies. Note that there is no general literature of graph-based SSL for gridded data. Early work on SSL focused on optimization [8] and relationships to transductive inference [15, 25] and multi-view learning [19]. Since then, the use of graphs in SSL has become standard [13]. Graph-based SSL methods attempt to assign node labels using a weighted combination of the neighbors. Different methods use different principles to design objective functions for label propagation. For example, a popular approach [31] iterates a function of the graph affinity matrix until convergence and then uses the sign of the function at each node. A different method adapts the Jacobi iteration for linear systems and obtains a somewhat different weighted combination subsequently used for prediction. Other influential methods [3] use regression to determine the weighted combination. First, they compute the graph Laplacian followed by eigenvector computation. Then a regression objective estimates a weighted combination of the principal eigenvectors on the training samples which is utilized for prediction at the unlabeled nodes. Other methods draw upon random walks on graphs to perform label prediction [7].

Our work mostly extends the work of [22] to color images and adds superpixel density at multiple scales of the UCM hierarchy as a new feature. This is an important augmentation to the feature descriptor needed for terrain classification as we will describe in the following sections.

3. APPROACH

In this paper, we describe an efficient image representation and machine learning approach for analyzing large scale remote sensing imagery to support a wide range of earth science applications. The application involves the labeling of remote sensing imagery given expert labels on a small fraction of data. Typically, the classes are (i) forestry, (ii) slums, (iii) urban and (iv) other (not above). The approach has the following steps:

1. Tessellation of the data into superpixels: This step converts the data into irregular (but coherent) patches called superpixels. Superpixels correspond to coherent patches or areas in 2D. These coherent superpixels reduce the data complexity since processing is moved to the superpixel level from the pixel level. Superpixels also have a huge advantage over partitioning the image into regular patches because regular patches ignore the local variability of the underlying data w.r.t. the grid.

2. Generating multi-pixel features for each superpixel: At this step we generate features which are effective in discriminating between terrains present in the spatiotemporal image data. We exploit intensity, geometry and scale of tessellation to arrive at these features.

3. Building a superpixel graph: This step constructs a superpixel graph with edges corresponding to the spatiotemporal (grid). The nodes of the graph are the superpixels with the edges being the connections between them.

4. Label initialization of superpixels: Labels are only available for a small number of pixels. This information is used to derive the labels for a subset of superpixels. A classifier is then built using these features to provide an initial label for all the nodes of the superpixel graph.

5. Label refinement: The rudimentary labels obtained from the previous step are further smoothed using semi-supervised learning techniques.

These steps are described in detail in the next subsections. We will use the image in Figure 1 as a running example. The size of this image is roughly 1 million pixels.

3.1 Superpixel formation

Since the advent of normalized cuts [24] and graph-cuts [11, 6], there has been considerable interest in segmenting an image into sets of superpixels. There are several techniques available in the image processing literature. The ultrametric contour map (UCM) [2] is a popular method which uses local and global cues to produce a hierarchy of tessellations at different scales ranging from fine to coarse. These tessellations respect the containment property, that is every finer scale tessellation is contained within the next higher (or coarser) scale tessellation. We use UCM in two different ways – (i) The first usage is more traditional and direct in the sense that a finer scale tessellation is obtained which is used for classifying (or labeling) each superpixel (as against each individual pixel). (ii) This second usage is more subtle because we obtain the tessellation at a coarser scale and use it as a feature for classifying the superpixels at the finer scale selected in (i). For example, for the target application, the tessellation at a coarser scale mostly picks up prominent boundaries thus increasing the probability of detecting urban regions. Furthermore, the density of superpixels is greater in slum regions than in urban, forested regions making it a suitable feature for slum detection. In Figure 2, we show the superpixels obtained for the image in Figure 1 corresponding to fine and coarse scales.

The steps in superpixel estimation using UCM are as follows: (i) feature extraction using oriented scale-space gradients, (ii) graph construction, (iii) eigenvector computation, (iv) scale-space gradient computation on the eigenvector image, (v) combination of local and global information and (vi) oriented watershed transform to produce non-uniform tessellations. While this sequence is somewhat of a simplification, the major steps have been highlighted. Note that the UCM approach obtains local and global contour information by combining information from the original image and weighted graph eigenvector "images." This perceptual grouping property is mainly responsible for obtaining good superpixel tessellations. We now detail the individual steps in the overall sequence:

Step 1: Scale space feature extraction from brightness, texture and wavelength channels: Oriented Gaussian derivative filters are executed at multiple scales to obtain

$$I_{\mathrm{local}}(\mathbf{x},\theta)=\sum_{\lambda}\sum_{s(\lambda)}\sum_{i(\lambda)}w_{i(\lambda),s(\lambda)}G(\mathbf{x},\theta;\sigma(i(\lambda),s(\lambda))) \quad (1)$$

where $\{w_{i(\lambda),s(\lambda)}\}$ is a set of weights that depend on the channels and scales. The dependence between the Gaussian filters and the scales can range from the simple to the complex. Here, we have just executed the filters at multiple

(a) Superpixels obtained at the finer scale. (b) Superpixels obtained at a coarser scale.

Figure 2: Superpixels obtained at different scales for Figure 1. Different scales capture different properties. Coarser scales mostly picks up strong boundaries while the finer scale can be leveraged to obtain the varying density of superpixels contained in coarser superpixels. Coarser superpixels contain higher density of finer superpixels near slum regions but lower density in urban and forest regions—a feature which is exploited to get binary urban and slum features as shown in Figure 3.

scales and orientations. This results in a set of *local* features at different orientations which integrates information from the different color channels.

Step 2: Weighted graph construction: A weighted graph (for the purposes of eigenvector computation) is constructed using the local filter responses above. Following the UCM strategy, pixels within a certain distance of each other are linked by a weighted edge using the relation

$$W(\mathbf{x},\mathbf{y}) = \exp\left\{-\alpha \max_{\mathbf{z}(\mathbf{x},\mathbf{y})} \max_{\theta} I_{\text{local}}(\mathbf{z}(\mathbf{x},\mathbf{y}),\theta)\right\} \quad (2)$$

where α is a constant and $\mathbf{z}(\mathbf{x},\mathbf{y})$ is any point lying on the line segment connecting $\mathbf{x}$ and $\mathbf{y}$.

Step 3: Eigenvector computation from the weighted graph $W(\mathbf{x},\mathbf{y})$: Following the standard strategy of spectral clustering, the top eigenvectors of the weighted graph are computed. Since these eigenvectors are in location space, the result is a set $\{e_k(\mathbf{x})\}$ (usually rescaled using the eigenvalues of the weighted graph).

Step 4: Spectral information obtained from the top K eigenvectors: Since gradient information computed from the scaled eigenvectors can be expected to contain complementary spectral information [2], a set of gradient operations in different orientations are computed to obtain

$$I_{\text{spectral}}(\mathbf{x},\theta) = \sum_k \nabla_\theta(e_k(\mathbf{x})). \quad (3)$$

Step 5: Combination of local and spectral information: We linearly combine the information in (1) and in (3) to obtain the final, global contour probability measure. A free parameter is used for the combination and this needs more careful validation (which we reserve for future work).

Step 6: Oriented watershed transform applied to the global contour measure: Since the global contour probability map may not always be closed and therefore may not divide the image into regions, we require another operation to extract closed contours. We have used the Oriented Watershed Transform (OWT) [2] to construct closed contours. Here, the orientation that maximizes the response of the contour detection approach is used to construct a set of regions and further build a hierarchical region tree from the input contours. Real valued weights are associated with each possible segmentation based on their likelihood to be a true boundary. For a specific threshold, the set of the resulting closed contours can be seen either as a segmentation or as the output of the super-pixellization. Further it can be seen that the uncertainty of a segmentation can be represented—at low thresholds, the image can be oversegmented respecting even very least probable boundaries and as you make the threshold higher only very strong boundaries survive (Fig. 3). This has the benefit of introducing a trade off between the extreme ends of the segmentation.

The resulting tessellation for the image in Figure 1 is given in Figure 2. It shows that areas of significant variation require smaller patch sizes while areas with less variations are captured by large patch sizes. We believe that this variability is one of the major strengths of the proposed approach.

3.2 Superpixel descriptor

Each superpixel at a finer level is described using three kinds of features—intensity histograms, corner density and a binary feature derived from the coarser levels. For the intensity histograms, we quantize the grayscale intensities into 52 bins and obtain a 52 dimensional feature vector for each superpixel.

We use the Harris corner detector to obtain a density measure—the number of corners per unit area for each superpixel. Corners are an important feature for discriminating between regions with buildings (for example, slums and urban area) and regions without (for example, forest and sea). To further distinguish between urban and slum dwellings, we compute the density of superpixels at a suitable level. This feature is based on the (visual) observation that slums have a higher superpixel density relative to forest and urban settlements at the same level of the superpixel pyramid. Another key feature for distinguishing between different kinds of human settlements (slums versus urban) is the presence of stronger boundaries around the superpixels representing the urban regions. Traditional features like dense SIFT, HOG etc. can be used to detect these regions but these suffer from the problem of determining the appropriate scale and orientation. Further these features are also not able to pick up the prominent boundaries as detected by UCM tessellations at coarser scales. As UCM inherently involves a combination of dense features like textons and color histograms and only shows stronger boundaries at coarser

(a) Regions overlayed with the binary urban descriptor. Regions overlayed as white correspond to 1 in our binary urban descriptor signifying a high probability of finding urban regions

(b) Regions overlayed with the binary slum descriptor. Regions overlayed as white correspond to 1 in our binary slum descriptor signifying a high probability of finding slums.

Figure 3: Binary urban and slum descriptors.

scales, it greatly simplifies the task of discriminating the urban regions from the slums. The coarser scale UCM provides a binary feature for each finer superpixel as follows. The coarser scale UCM only keeps prominent boundaries and therefore outputs much larger superpixels. Among them, the superpixels which are smaller than a certain size threshold predominantly belong to urban regions. This is because urban regions are usually found with stronger boundaries and hence are more discriminating. The superpixels which are much larger than the size threshold are more likely to be a merger of several different types of smaller superpixels and are often not very discriminating. For example, these superpixels can be a merger of slums and forests or other similar looking regions which do not have as clearly demarcating boundaries as the urban regions. We label the superpixels below the chosen size threshold with ones and the superpixels above this threshold with zeroes in order to get binary features. These binary features are then percolated down the UCM hierarchy to the finer scale superpixels. All the finer superpixels contained in the larger superpixels get the same label as that of their larger parent superpixel.

Additionally, we also compute the density of finer level superpixels contained within each superpixel at the coarser level. This density is high in the regions corresponding to slums and low in the regions corresponding to urban and forest regions. This can be noticed in Figure 2. We choose a density threshold above which we mark all superpixels at the finer level as ones while the remaining as zeros. This approach further simplifies the task of discriminating slums from the rest of the image. Henceforth, we call these two discriminating features for urban and slum regions as binary urban descriptor and binary slum descriptor respectively. The significance of these two features is visually depicted in Figure 3 by overlaying them on top their corresponding regions of the image in Figure 1.

Further, we use average RGB values corresponding to each superpixel as another 3D feature. All these five different kind of features are then concatenated to form a 58 dimensional feature vector which describes each superpixel of the finer tessellation. Other features like HOG and dense SIFT can also be added to the above framework if needed.

3.3 Initializing the graph labels

Given the large size of the underlying datasets it is impractical to expect that the ground truth is available except at a small number of grid points since data sets scale but experts do not. Thus, practical approaches have to be semi-supervised (as opposed to supervised or unsupervised) with the focus restricted on methods with proven scalability. In this work, we achieve semi-supervised learning through a two stage process of (i) classification using either SVM or kNN followed by (ii) graph Laplacian smoothing. Our classification pipeline is similar to [1]. As mentioned above, the ground truth data is available only for a small number of superpixels as labeled by experts. We use this ground truth to train our classifier. A standard linear SVM was used for training. The model obtained from training is then used to determine preliminary labels for all other superpixels.

3.4 Label refinement

Because of the semi-supervised nature of the problem, the classification obtained from above is rudimentary because it is based on a classifier (SVM in our case) derived from limited ground truth data. This classification can lead to artifacts such that neighboring regions which belong to the same class may get labeled incorrectly. To correct this problem and after being inspired by [1], we apply the Laplacian propagation method as detailed here.

Let f_i denote the feature vector corresponding to the ith superpixel and let X_i be the label that is required to be found from the Laplacian propagation. Let Y_i be the initial label as obtained from the first stage of either SVM or kNN. To perform Laplacian propagation, we construct a graph connecting adjacent superpixels in the spatial domain (and not in the feature domain). The edge weight is given as $W_{ij} = \exp\left(-\frac{\|f_i - f_j\|^2}{2\tau^2}\right)$. Our goal is to minimize the following objective function [1] :

$$C(X) = \sum_{i,j=1}^{N} W_{ij} \left| \frac{X_i}{\sqrt{D_{ii}}} - \frac{X_j}{\sqrt{D_{jj}}} \right|^2 + \sum_{i=1}^{N} \lambda \left| X_i - Y_i \right|^2 \tag{4}$$

where $D_{ii} = \sum_{j=1}^{N} W_{ij}$. The objective in (4) is optimized separately for each category in a one versus rest fashion.

$Y_i = 1$ if the superpixel belongs to the category and 0 otherwise. X_i can take a real value and after minimizing the objective in (4) for each category, we assign each superpixel to the category which corresponds to the maximum value of X_i. The objective function in (4) can be directly minimized by solving a linear system of equations [1]:

$$\left(I - (1 - \frac{\lambda}{1+\lambda})S\right) X = \alpha Y \tag{5}$$

where $S = D^{-\frac{1}{2}} W D^{-\frac{1}{2}}$, and $\alpha = \frac{\lambda}{1+\lambda}$.

The image in Figure 4a below shows the preliminary labels obtained after SVM classification and its further refinement by using the graph Laplacian to obtain the final labels in Figure 4b.

4. EXPERIMENTAL RESULTS

To evaluate the accuracy and the efficiency of our approach, we used VHR imagery data from three different geographic settings. The first five images are collected from the Google Earth from Rio, Brazil which is approximately around a million pixels corresponding to 1 square km of area. The Rio images represent two major types of neighborhoods—formal (high-rise apartments and commercial complexes), and informal (favelas). The other two images are from Madison and Milwaukee suburbs from Wisconsin, USA and the last image is from Sterlings Heights city, a suburb of Detroit, Michigan, USA. These images correspond to about 4 square km with the same resolution of 1m as the rio images. The Madison image represents two distinct neighborhoods of commercial complexes and suburban residential communities, while the Milwaukee image consists of downtown and residential neighborhoods. Sterling Heights is the second largest suburb of Metro Detroit and fourth largest city in the state of Michigan. The subregion chosen from Sterling Heights consists of commercial and residential neighborhoods. Apart from the major categories of neighborhoods, these images also contain forests (and isolated trees mixed with houses), grass fields and lawns, undeveloped areas (barren lands and rock outcrops), water bodies, and sandy areas along the shore. As can be seen from these three study regions, they represent diverse set of neighborhoods. The first five Rio images and their classification results are shown in Figure 4 and Figure 5. The Madison, Milwaukee, and Detroit images are shown in Figure 6.

Prior to obtaining superpixels using the method given in [2], we converted the color images to grayscale and performed Gaussian smoothing on the grayscale version of our color images. The support of the Gaussian filter was chosen to be 10 pixels wide and the standard deviation was set to 15. It is important to note that this heavy smoothing of image data as mentioned above was only done for computing UCM [2]. The high resolution detail provided by the images can lead to the generation of an enormous number of superpixels which are not needed for classification purposes. Hence, blurring the images to reduce the number of superpixels is a crucial step. Once UCM was obtained, the original images were used at every other stage of our pipeline, for example in computing features or for classification.

Grayscale intensity histograms, RGB values averaged over each superpixel at multiple levels of the UCM hierarchy, corner density, textons, and descriptors derived from the UCM hierarchy were extracted for each superpixel. As explained

Image	labeled data (%)	misclassification error (%)
Rio-1	1.21	8.49
Rio-2	1.49	7.81
Rio-3	1.14	6.58
Rio-4	1.38	11.46
Rio-5	1.30	7.40
Madison	1.01	9.82
Milwaukee	0.52	12.93
Detroit	0.26	16.71

Table 1: Quantitative results for the image in Figure 1 and the 4 different images shown in Figure 5.

Image	% error grids (GMIL)	% error superpixels (proposed)
Rio-1	15.6	9.2
Madison	6.8	3.09
Milwaukee	17.2	6.73
Detroit	15.39	8.73

Table 2: Results obtained with GMIL for the first Rio image in Figure 1 and the 3 images belonging to Madison, Milwaukee, and Detroit as shown in Figure 6.

in section 3.2, simple descriptors (multilevel superpixel containment density and superpixel area at a coarser UCM level) were extracted from the UCM hierarchy which can be intuitively seen to distinguish urban (residential, commercial) regions, and slums.

The intensity histograms were obtained by quantizing the intensities into 52 bins. The average RGB values comprised a 3-dimensional vector of average color values for each superpixel. The corner density feature obtained was a scalar which was multiplied by a factor of 100. The coarser scale UCM features and multilevel superpixel containment density features were binary valued. These weighted features were concatenated together to obtain a 58 dimensional feature vector describing each superpixel.

For training the SVM, the ground truth labels were provided to only about 1% (see Table 1) of the superpixels at the finest level. Note that this was even lesser for the Milwaukee (0.52%) and Detroit (0.26%) images. The SVM classifier was used to obtain the preliminary labels for all the other superpixels. This was then given as an initialization to the Laplacian propagation algorithm in order to obtain the final labels. The values of τ and λ were kept fixed to be 2 and 0.125 respectively. For all the images, the misclassification error was around 10% (Table 1). The misclassification error was computed by taking the weighted average of each misclassified superpixel where the weights for each superpixel were the ratio of the area covered by them in the image to the total image area.

The total time required for the overall processing (including UCM) was about 20 minutes on a sequential machine.

Our proposed framework is also compared against the recent Gaussian Multiple Instance Learning (GMIL) [28] algorithm which showed good improvement over standard per-pixel based classification schemes. The accuracy estimates for these three images are summarized in Table 2. Results from our approach are comparable to GMIL, however, it should be noted that GMIL is computationally expensive

(a) Preliminary classification obtained after SVM.

(b) Final result obtained after Laplacian smoothing of the labels obtained by the SVM.

Figure 4: Resulting labels for image in Figure 1. The colors red, gray, green, and orange correspond to slum, urban, forest, and barren regions respectively.

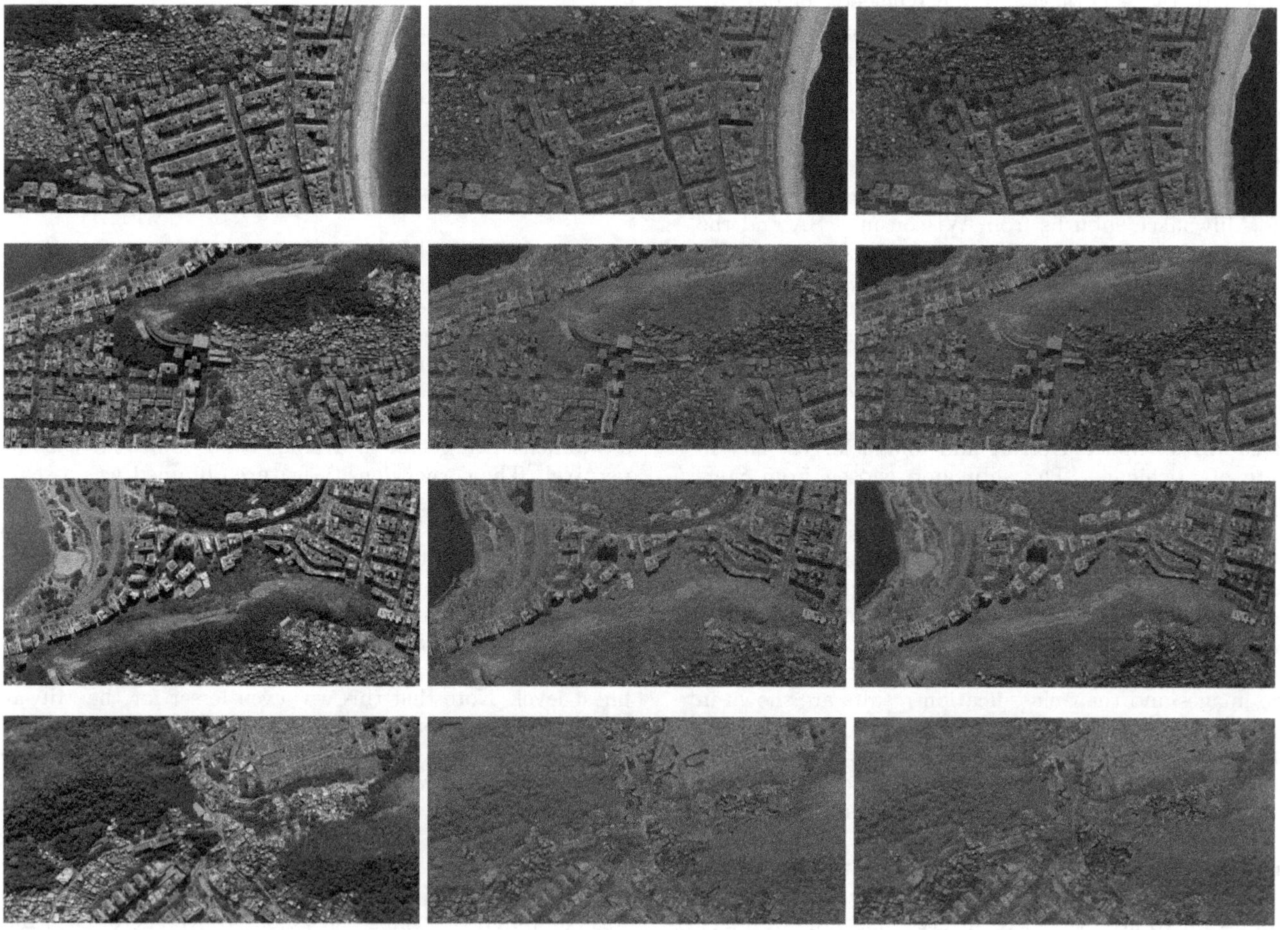

Figure 5: Results for 4 more images from Rio, Brazil. The left column shows the actual images. The middle column shows the preliminary results after SVM classification and the last column corresponds to the final refined results after Laplacian smoothing. The colors red, gray, green, blue, yellow, and orange correspond to slum, urban, forest, sea, sand, and farm regions respectively.

and also requires more ground truth training data compared to our technique.

Analysis

Careful analysis of the workflow and final classification results show following key advantages of the proposed method over GMIL [28].

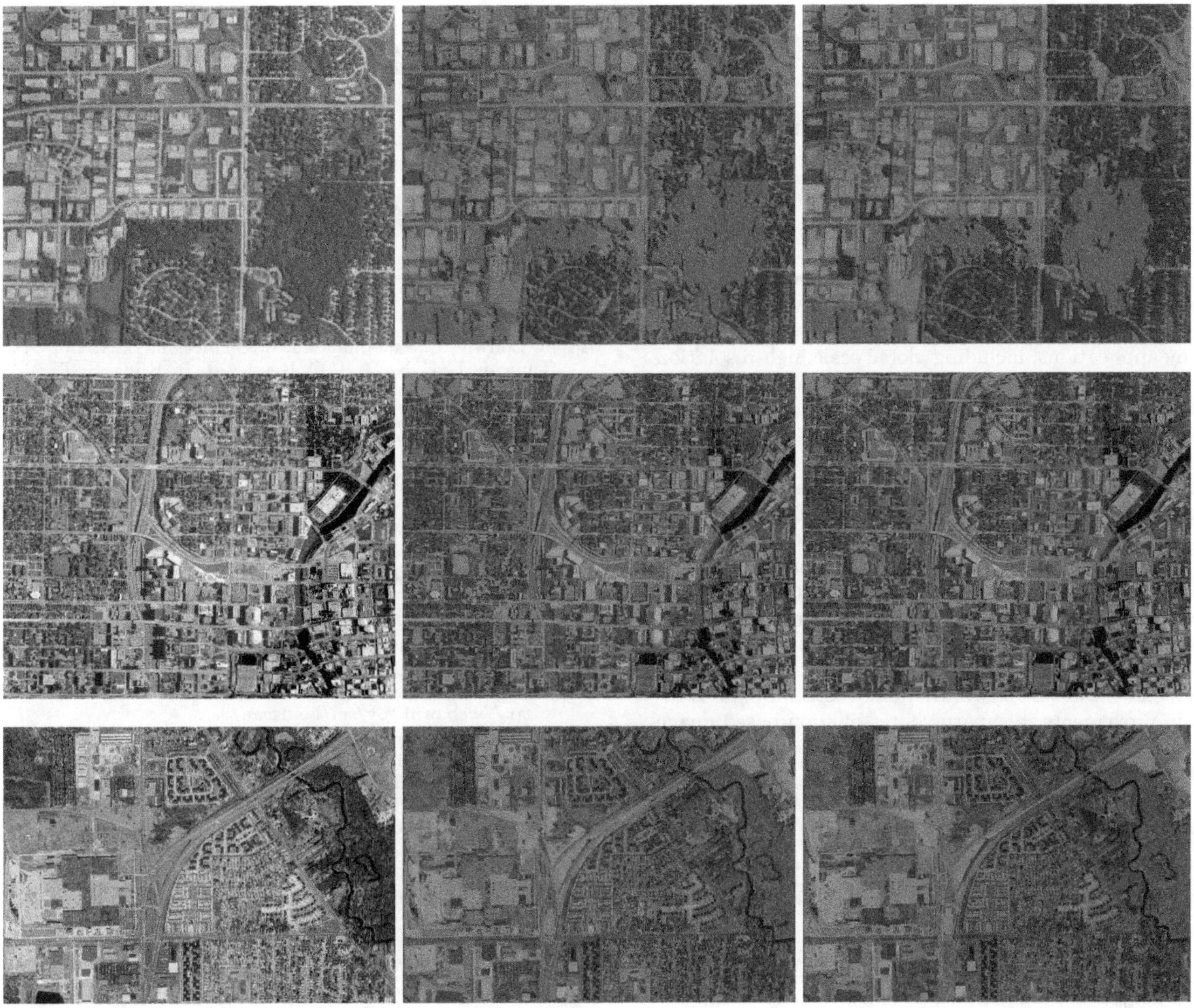

Figure 6: Results for images from Madison (top), Milwaukee (middle), and Detroit (bottom). The left column shows the actual images. The middle column shows the preliminary results after SVM classification and the last column corresponds to the final refined results after Laplacian smoothing. The colors red, gray, dark green, and light green, and blue correspond to residential areas, commercial areas, forests, and grass, and water.

Training One of the most important aspects of supervised learning is obtaining sufficient ground-truth data. GMIL requires a fair amount of ground-truth to capture representative blocks across the image space, as classification is based on patch-matching. On the other hand the proposed approach requires only a fraction of ground-truth points as compared to GMIL, as the ground-truth is for the superpixel. This is an important and notable advantage of the proposed method for global scale applications (e.g., ORNL/LandScan).

Segment vs. Block The basic unit of learning in GMIL is the block. One of the challenges in getting good results from GMIL is determining the appropriate block size. Though trade-offs are known for small and large blocks, determining the appropriate block size requires multiple experiments which is a bottleneck for global scale projects. On the other hand, the proposed method generates superpixel based segmentation, which is far more easier to control than GMIL block size.

Computational Cost GMIL requires each image block (million blocks per sq. km. image at 1m pixel resolution and 10 pixel block size) to be compared against all training blocks (typically on the order of 1000's). This operation is costly as similarity is determined by the Kullback-Leibler (KL) divergence which requires inversion of the covariance matrix. On the other hand, label propagation is computationally much simpler, and furthermore there are far more blocks to classify than the superpixels.

Accuracy Accuracy of both methods are comparable (see Table 2). A visual inspection however shows the proposed method produces a better classification map as the superpixels confirms to natural boundaries of the objects, whereas GMIL produces jagged boundaries (due to arbitrary sized blocks).

Based on these advantages, we are confident that the proposed methods will become operational in global scale applications like LandScan.

5. CONCLUSIONS

We have developed a novel and scalable machine learning framework for classifying neighborhoods in VHR images. Accurate identification of neighborhoods is critical for many applications, including global scale high-resolution population databases (e.g., ORNL/LandScan), national security, human health, and energy. To meet these challenges, we also developed features which can effectively discriminate between different neighborhoods. This approach combines a superpixel image tessellation representation with semi-supervised label propagation (SVM followed by graph Laplacian-based propagation). The superpixel representation naturally coheres with local boundary information and is a major reason for obtaining good classification. Experimental evaluation on three different geographic settings showed good classification performance. The approach taken in this work is extensible to temporal data as well and will be the focus of our future work. In addition, we plan to focus on improvements to superpixel tessellation-based image representations along the lines of improved computational efficiency and contextual level selection.

6. REFERENCES

[1] A. Angelova and S. Zhu. Efficient object detection and segmentation for fine-grained recognition. In *Computer Vision and Pattern Recognition (CVPR), 2013 IEEE Conference on*, pages 811–818. IEEE, 2013.

[2] P. Arbelaez, M. Maire, C. Fowlkes, and J. Malik. Contour detection and hierarchical image segmentation. *IEEE Trans. Pattern Anal. Mach. Intell.*, 33(5):898–916, 2011.

[3] M. Belkin and P. Niyogi. Semi-supervised learning on Riemannian manifolds. *Machine Learning*, 56(1-3):209–239, 2004.

[4] T. Blaschke, S. Lang, and G. Hay. *Object-Based Image Analysis.* Springer, 2008.

[5] J. Bolton and P. Gader. Application of multiple-instance learning for hyperspectral image analysis. *Geoscience and Remote Sensing Letters, IEEE*, 8(5):889 –893, sept. 2011.

[6] Y. Boykov and G. Funka-Lea. Graph cuts and efficient nd image segmentation. *International journal of computer vision*, 70(2):109–131, 2006.

[7] O. Chappelle, B. Schölkopf, and A. Zien, editors. *Semi-supervised learning.* Adaptive Computation and Machine Learning. The MIT Press, 2010.

[8] A. Demiriz and K. Bennett. Optimization approaches to semisupervised learning. In *Complementarity: Applications, Algorithms and Extensions.* Springer, 2001.

[9] T. G. Dietterich, R. H. Lathrop, and T. Lozano-Pérez. Solving the multiple instance problem with axis-parallel rectangles. *Artif. Intell.*, 89(1-2):31–71, 1997.

[10] R. Ewing and F. Rong. The impact of urban form on u.s. residential energy use. *Housing Policy Debate*, 19(1):1–30, 2008.

[11] P. F. Felzenszwalb and D. P. Huttenlocher. Efficient graph-based image segmentation. *International Journal of Computer Vision*, 59(2):167–181, 2004.

[12] G. Galster. On the nature of neighbourhood. *Urban Studies*, 38(12):2111–2124, 2001.

[13] A. B. Goldberg, X. Zhu, and S. J. Wright. Dissimilarity in graph-based semi-supervised classification. In *AISTATS*, pages 155–162, 2007.

[14] J. Graesser, A. Cheriyadat, R. Vatsavai, V. Chandola, J. Long, and E. Bright. Image based characterization of formal and informal neighborhoods in an urban landscape. *Selected Topics in Applied Earth Observations and Remote Sensing, IEEE Journal of*, 5(4):1164 –1176, Aug. 2012.

[15] T. Joachims. Transductive learning via spectral graph partitioning. In *Intl. Conf. Machine Learning*, pages 290–297, 2003.

[16] L. J. Krivo and R. D. Peterson. Extremely disadvantaged neighborhoods and urban crime. *Social Forces*, 75(2):619–648, 1996.

[17] J. Ludwig, L. Sanbonmatsu, L. Gennetian, E. Adam, G. J. Duncan, L. F. Katz, R. C. Kessler, J. R. Kling, S. T. Lindau, R. C. Whitaker, and T. W. McDade. Neighborhoods, obesity, and diabetes: A randomized social experiment. *New England Journal of Medicine*, 365(16):1509–1519, 2011.

[18] O. Maron and T. Lozano-Perez. A framework for multiple-instance learning. In *Advances In Neural Information Processing Systems*, pages 570–576. MIT Press, 1998.

[19] I. Muslea, S. Minton, and C. A. Knoblock. Active + semi-supervised learning = robust multi-view learning. In *Intl. Conf. Machine Learning*, pages 435–442, 2002.

[20] S. Nussbaum and G. Menz. *Object-Based Image Analysis and Treaty Verification.* Springer, 2008.

[21] ORNL. Landscan: High-resolution population database. http://web.ornl.gov/sci/landscan/.

[22] M. Sethi, Y. Yan, A. Rangarajan, R. R. Vatsavai, and S. Ranka. An efficient computational framework for labeling large scale spatiotemporal remote sensing datasets. In *Contemporary Computing (IC3), 2014 Seventh International Conference on*, pages 635–640, Aug 2014.

[23] S. Shekhar, P. Schrater, R. Vatsavai, W. Wu, and S. Chawla. Spatial contextual classification and prediction models for mining geospatial data. *IEEE Transaction on Multimedia*, 4(2):174–188, 2002.

[24] J. Shi and J. Malik. Normalized cuts and image segmentation. *Pattern Analysis and Machine Intelligence, IEEE Transactions on*, 22(8):888–905, 2000.

[25] V. Sindhwani, P. Niyogi, and M. Belkin. Beyond the point cloud: from transductive to semi-supervised learning. In *ICML*, pages 824–831, 2005.

[26] P. M. Thomas Kemper, Nale Mudau and M. Pesaresi. Towards a country-wide mapping & monitoring of formal and informal settlements in south africa. Science and Policy Report JRC92657, Joint Research Centre, European Commission, 2015.

[27] R. R. Vatsavai. High-resolution urban image classification using extended features. In *ICDM Workshops*, pages 869–876, 2011.

[28] R. R. Vatsavai. Gaussian multiple instance learning approach for mapping the slums of the world using very high resolution imagery. In *The 19th ACM SIGKDD International Conference on Knowledge Discovery and Data Mining (KDD)*, pages 1419–1426. ACM, 2013.

[29] R. R. Vatsavai, E. A. Bright, V. Chandola, B. L. Bhaduri, A. Cheriyadat, and J. Graesser. Machine learning approaches for high-resolution urban land cover classification: a comparative study. In *COM.Geo*, page 11, 2011.

[30] J. Wang. Solving the multiple-instance problem: A lazy learning approach. In *In Proc. 17th International Conf. on Machine Learning*, pages 1119–1125. Morgan Kaufmann, 2000.

[31] X. Zhu, Z. Ghahramani, and J. D. Lafferty. Semi-supervised learning using Gaussian fields and harmonic functions. In *ICML*, pages 912–919, 2003.

Early Identification of Violent Criminal Gang Members

Elham Shaabani*, Ashkan Aleali*, and Paulo Shakarian
Arizona State University
Tempe, AZ
{shaabani, aleali, shak}@asu.edu

John Bertetto
Chicago Police Department
Chicago, IL
john.bertetto@chicagopolice.org

ABSTRACT

Gang violence is a major problem in the United States accounting for a large fraction of homicides and other violent crime. In this paper, we study the problem of early identification of violent gang members. Our approach relies on modified centrality measures that take into account additional data of the individuals in the social network of co-arrestees which together with other arrest metadata provide a rich set of features for a classification algorithm. We show our approach obtains high precision and recall (0.89 and 0.78 respectively) in the case where the entire network is known and out-performs current approaches used by law-enforcement to the problem in the case where the network is discovered overtime by virtue of new arrests - mimicking real-world law-enforcement operations. Operational issues are also discussed as we are preparing to leverage this method in an operational environment.

Categories and Subject Descriptors: J.4 [Computer Applications]: Sociology

General Terms: Security; Experimentation

Keywords: Social Network Analysis; Criminology

1. INTRODUCTION

Gang violence is a major problem in the United States [1, 2] - accounting for 20 to 50 percent of homicides in many major cities [10]. Yet, law enforcement actually has existing data on many of these groups. For example the underlying social network structure is often recorded by law-enforcement and has previously been shown useful in enabling "smart policing" tactics [17] and improving law -enforcement's understanding of a gang's organizational structure [19]. In this paper we look to leverage this gang social network information to create features that allows us to classify individuals as potentially violent. While the results of such a classifier are insufficient to lead to arrests, it is able to provide the police leads to individuals who are likely to be involved in violence, allowing for a more focused policing with respect to patrols and intelligence gathering. *Our key aim is to significantly reduce the population of potential violent gang members which will lead to more efficient policing.*

In this paper, we introduce our method for identifying potentially violent gang members that leverages features derived from the co-arestee social network of criminal gangs in a classifier to identify potentially violent individuals. We note that this classification problem is particularly difficult due to not only data imbalances, but also due to the fact that many violent crimes are conducted due to heightened emotions - and hence difficult to identify. Though we augment our network-based features with some additional meta-data from the arrest records, our approach does **not** leverage features concerning the race, ethnicity, or gender of individuals in the social network. We evaluate our method using real-world offender data from the Chicago Police Department. This paper makes the following contributions:

- We discuss how centrality measurements such as degree, closeness, and betweenness when modified to account for metadata about past offenses such as the type of offense and whether the offense was classified as "violent" can serve as robust features for identifying violent offenders.
- We show how the network features, combined with other feature categories provide surprisingly robust performance when the entire offender is known in terms of both precision (0.89) and recall (0.78) using cross-fold validation.
- We then test our methods in the case where the network is exposed over time (by virtue of new arrests) which mimics an operational situation. Though precision and recall are reduced in this case, we show that our method significantly outperforms the baseline approach currently in use by law-enforcement - on average increasing precision and recall by more than two and three times respectively.

In addition to these main results, we also present some side results on the structure and nature of the police dataset we examine. The paper is organized as follows. In Section 2 we motivate this difficult problem within the law-enforcement community. This is followed by a description of our dataset along with technical notation in Section 3. There, we also describe some interesting aspects of the gang arrest dataset and our co-arrestee network. In Section 4 we formally define our problem, describe existing approaches, and then describe the features we use in our approach. Then we present

*These authors contributed equally to this work.

KDD'15, August 10-13, 2015, Sydney, NSW, Australia.
 ISBN 978-1-4503-3664-2/15/08 ...$15.00.
DOI: http://dx.doi.org/10.1145/2783258.2788618.

our results in Section 5 for both cases where we assume the underlying network is known and when we discover the network over time (mimicking an operational scenario). Finally, related work is discussed in Section 6.

2. BACKGROUND

A recent study shows that the network for gunshot victimization is denser than previously believed [16]. According to the authors, within the city of Chicago over 70% of all gunshot victims are contained within only 6% of the total population These findings validate what has been considered common knowledge among police for decades: who you hang out with matters, and if you hang out with those who engage in or are victims of violence you are more likely to become an offender or victim yourself.

Identifying potential offenders of gun violence has also been a staple practice for most law enforcement agencies as an attempt to curtail future victimization. When gang conflicts get "hot," it's common for law enforcement agents to put together a list of known "shooters": those known gang members with an existing criminal history for gun violence and a predilection for engaging in such illegal activity. Law enforcement agents then attempt to make contact with these individuals with the expectation that such direct contact might prevent violence. For most law enforcement agencies, however, this practice is performed in a very ad-hoc manner. Identifying these individuals for intervention has relied primarily on the ability of law enforcement agents to remember and identify at-risk individuals. While feasible for small or discreet networks, the ability to recall multiple individuals in large networks that cross large geographic regions and interact with multiple networks becomes increasing difficult. This difficulty increases significantly as relationships between networks change, known individuals leave the network, and new individuals enter it. In particular, the practice is less than idea because it requires officers to attempt to recall criminal history and network association data that varies between network members. For example, a subject who has been arrested on multiple occasions for carrying a gun or has been arrested for shooting another individual is easy to recall, but recalling and quantifying the risk for a subject with multiple arrests for non-gun violence and a direct association with several offenders and victims of gun violence can be much more difficult. In short, identifying a known "shooter" is relatively straightforward: they are known. The approach in this paper synthesizes network connectivity other attributes of the subject to identify those individuals at risk that law enforcement might not yet know.

Using this information, law enforcement agents may not only more reliably and consistently identify those individuals most likely to engage in acts of violence or become victims of violence due to their personal associations with it, but also to more effectively manage agency resources. Intervention strategies may include service providers outside law enforcement, such as family members, social service providers, current or former educators, and clergy. This diversity in approach not only delivers a more powerful "stop the violence" message but provides a kind of force multiplier for law enforcement, increasing the number of persons involved in the effort to prevent violence. Identifying specific individuals for intervention also allows for a more targeted effort by law enforcement in terms of personnel and geographic areas needing coverage. Blanketing violence reduction strategies that saturate geographic areas with law enforcement agents and rely on direct contact with large numbers of criminal network members are inefficient and resource consuming. Focusing efforts on those individuals most likely to engage in violence allows law enforcement to focus on smaller groups of people and smaller geographic areas (those areas within which those individuals identified are known to frequent). Therefore, our approach can significantly improve such efforts to identify violent individuals. In this paper, we see how our method not only out-performs the current social network heuristic used by police, but also that it provides a much smaller and more precise list of potentially violent offenders than simply listing those with a violent criminal record.

3. GANG CO-OFFENDER NETWORK

In this section, we introduce the necessary basic notation to describe our co-offender network and then provide details of our real-world criminal dataset and study some of its properties.

3.1 Technical Preliminaries

Throughout this paper we shall represent an offender network as an undirected graph $G = (V, E)$ where the nodes correspond with previous offenders and an undirected edge exists between offenders if they were arrested together. We will use $\mathcal{T}$ to denote the set of timepoints (dates). We also have three sets of labels for the nodes: $\mathcal{V}$, $\mathcal{S}$, $gang$ which are the sets of violent crimes, non violent crimes, and gangs. For each time point t and each node v, the binary variable $arr_v^t \in \{\mathsf{true}, \mathsf{false}\}$ denotes if v was arrested at time t and $distr_v^t, beat_v^t, gang_v^t$ to denote the district, beat, and gang affiliation of v at time t (we will assume that time is fine-grain enough to ensure that at each time unit an individual is arrested no more than once). If we drop the t superscript for these three symbols, it will denote the most recent district, beat, and gang associated with v in the knowledgebase. We shall use the sets $\mathcal{V}_v^t$ and $\mathcal{S}_v^t$ to denote the set of violent and non violent offenses committed by v at time t respectively. Note if $arr_v^t = \mathsf{false}$ then $\mathcal{V}_v^t = \emptyset$. We will drop the superscript t for this symbol to denote the union of labels at any time t in the historical knowledgebase. We also note that the edges in the graph also depend on time, but for sake of readability, we shall state with words the duration of time considered for the edges.

For a given violent crime $c \in \mathcal{V} \cup \mathcal{S}$, we will use the notation $V_c^t = \{v \in V \ s.t. \ c \in \mathcal{V}_v^t\}$ (intuitively, the subset of the population who have committed crime c at time t). Again, we will drop the superscript t if v could have committed crime c at any time in the historical knowledgebase. For a set of labels $C \subseteq \mathcal{V} \cup \mathcal{S}$, we will extend this notation: $V_C^t = \{v \in V \ s.t. \ C \cap \mathcal{V}_v^t \neq \emptyset\}$. We will slightly abuse notation here: $V_\emptyset^t = V$. We will use similar notation for denoting a subset of the population that are members of a certain gang. For instance, V_{gang_v} refers to the set of nodes who are in the same gang as node v. Likewise, we shall use the same notation for subgraphs: G_C^t is the subgraph of G containing only nodes in V_C^t and their adjacent edges. We will use the function $d : V \times V \to \mathbb{N}$ to denote the distance between two nodes - which for this paper will be the number of links in the shortest path. For a given node v, the set $N_v^i = \{v' \in V \ s.t. \ d(v, v') = i\}$ – the set of nodes that are

Table 1: Summary of arrest data.

Name	Value
Number of records	64466
Violent offense	4450
Homicide	312
Criminal sexual assault	153
Robbery	1959
Aggravated assault	1441
Aggravated battery	896
Non violent offense	60016

Table 2: Network properties.

Name	Values
Vertices	9373
Edges	17197
Average degree	3.66
Average clustering	0.5
Transitivity	0.62
Connected components	1843
Largest connected component diameter	36
Largest connected component average path length	12.22
Largest connected component average clustering	0.63

whose shortest path is exactly i hops from v. For two nodes v, v', we will use the notation $\sigma(v, v')$ to be the number of shortest paths between v and v'. For nodes u, v, v', $\sigma_u(v, v')$ will be the number of shortest paths between v and v' that pass through u.

For a given subgraph G' of G, we shall use $\mathsf{C}(G')$ to denote the largest connected component of G' and for node $v \in G'$, we will use the notation $\mathsf{C}_v(G')$ to denote the connected component of G' to which v belongs. If we apply a community finding algorithm to subgraph G', we will use the notation $\mathsf{P}_v(G')$ to denote the partition of G' to which v belongs. We will use the notation $|\cdot|$ to denote the size of a set or the number of nodes in a subgraph.

3.2 Overview of Network Data

In this section we describe our police dataset and the associated co-offender network as well as some interesting characteristics that we have noticed.

Police Dataset. Our dataset consists of gang-related arrest incidents gathered from August 2011 - August 2014 in Chicago as well as their immediate associates. This data set includes locations, dates, the links between the joint arrests, and the gang affiliation of the offenders. In Table 1, we summarize some of the important characteristics of the dataset.

Violent Crimes. In our dataset, the set $\mathcal{V}$ consists of the following crimes have been identified by the Chicago Police as violent crimes: homicide (first or second degree murder), criminal sexual assault, robbery, aggravated assault, and aggravated battery. All aforementioned offenses are also FBI "index" crimes as well. A key aspect about the violent crimes is that the dataset is highly imbalanced with much more arrests for non violent crimes vs. arrests for violent crimes (60016 vs. 4450).

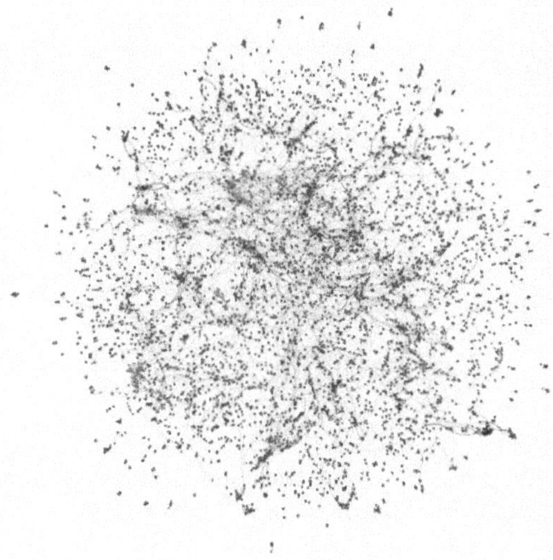

Figure 1: The gang co-offender network. Each color corresponds with a different gang.

Network Properties. From the arrest data, we were able to construct the *co-offender network*. In this network, the isolated vertices are eliminated due to the lack of structural information. A visualization of the network is depicted in Figure 1 and we have included summary statistics in Table 2. In studying this network, we studied its degree distribution (Figure 2). Unlike the degree distribution for other scale free social networks, the degree distribution for the offender network is *exponential* rather than *power law*. However, despite the degree distribution being similar to that of a random (E-R) or small world network topology [27], we noticed other characteristics that indicate differently. The co-offender network has a much higher average clustering coefficient than in a random network and does not follow the properties of the small world topology due to the relative high diameter and average shortest path (computed for the largest connected component.)

Repeat Offenders. There are many instances of repeated offenses from the same offender. Figure 3 shows the distribution of the repeated arrests for each individual in the dataset. This indicates that arrest records have utility in identifying future offenders.

Seasonality of Crime. There is also a higher chance of criminal activities in different months of the year. Figure 4 demonstrates some of these variations. As per police observations, both violent and non-violent crime incidents are lower in the winter months (Dec.-Feb.).

4. IDENTIFYING VIOLENT OFFENDERS

In this section, we describe our problem, some of the existing practical approaches used by law-enforcement, and our approach based on supervised learning with features primarily generated by the network topology.

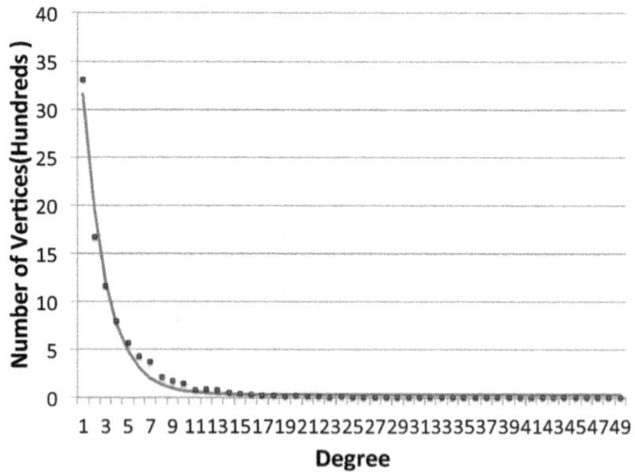

Figure 2: Network degree distribution. The exponential function fits to the distribution ($R^2 = 0.77$).

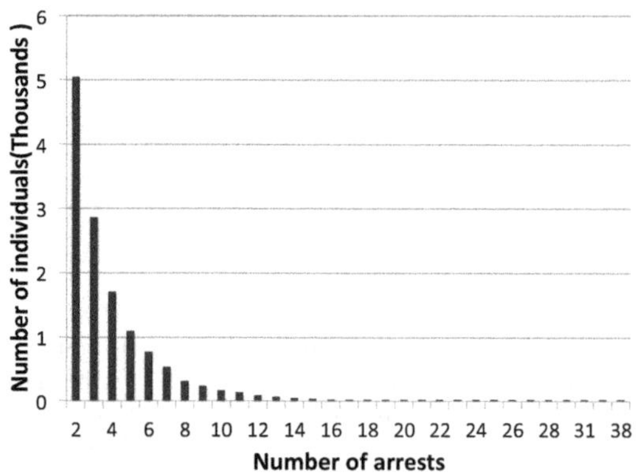

Figure 3: Repeated arrests. 12866 instances of one-time arrests have been removed.

4.1 Problem Statement

Given a co-offender network, $G = (V, E)$ and for each historical timepoint $t \in \tau = \{1, \ldots, t_{\max}\}$ and $v \in V$, we have the values of $arr_v^t, distr_v^t, beat_v^t$ and elements of the sets $\mathcal{V}_v^t, gang_v^t$, we wish to identify set $\{v \in V \ s.t. \ \exists t > t_{\max} \ where \ |\mathcal{V}_v^t| > 0\}$. In other words, we wish to find a set of offenders in our current co-offender network that commit a violent crime in the future.

4.2 Existing Methods

Here we describe two common techniques often used by law-enforcement to predict violent offenders. The first is a simple heuristic based on violent activities in the past. The second is a heuristic that was based on the findings of [17] which was designed to locate future *victims* of violent crime. Both of these approaches are ad-hoc practical approaches that have become "best practices" for predicting violent offenders. However, we are not aware of any data-driven, formal evaluation of these methods in the literature.

Past Violent Activities (PVA). The first ad-hoc approach is quite simple: if an offender has committed a violent crime in the past, we claim that he will commit a violent crime in the future. An obvious variant of this approach is to return the set of violent offenders from the last

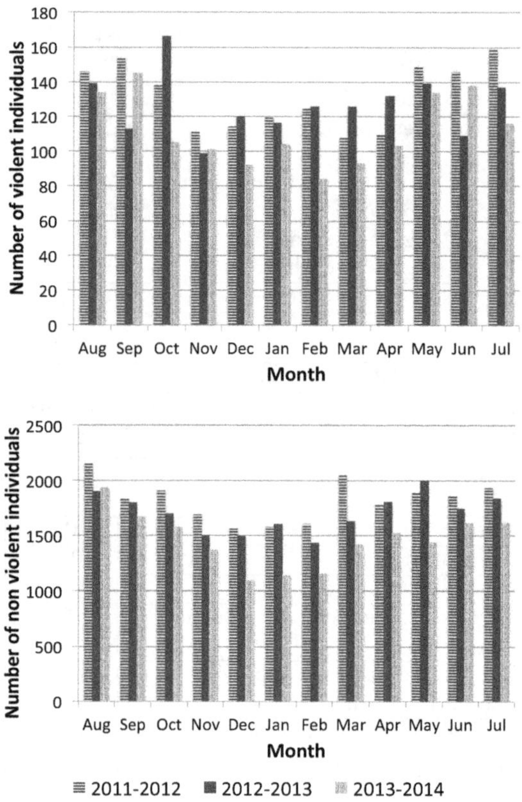

Figure 4: Seasonality of crime.

Δt days. We note in practice, if police also have records of those who are incarcerated, and such individuals would be removed from the list (due to the different jurisdictions of police and corrections in the Chicago area, we did not have access to incarceration data - however discussed re-arrests observed in the data in the previous section).

Two-Hop Heuristic (THH). The two-hop heuristic is based on the result of [17] which investigated a social network of gunshot *victims* in Boston and found an inverse relationship between the probability of being a gunshot victim and the shortest path distance on the network to the nearest previous gunshot victim. Hence, THH returns all neighbors one and two hops away from previous violent criminals (see Algorithm 1 for details on the version we used in our experiments - which was the best-performing variant for our data). The Chicago Police have adopted a variant of this method to identify potential gang victims using a combination of arrest and victim data - the co-arrestee network of criminal gang members includes many individuals who are also victims of violent crime (this is a direct result of gang conflict). We note that victim information did not offer a significant improvement to our approach, except the trivial case that a homicide victim cannot commit any crime in the future.

4.3 Supervised Learning Approach

We evaluated many different supervised learning approaches including Naive Bayes (NB), Linear Regression (LR), Decision Tree (DT), Random Forest (RF), Neural Network (NN),

Algorithm 1 Two-Hop Heuristic

```
procedure TwoHop(G)                          ▷ Offender network G.
    R ← {}                                   ▷ Identified violent offenders.
    VICTIMS ← {u ∈ G | is_homicide_victim(u)}
    for v ∈ VICTIMS do
        N ← N_v^1 ∪ N_v^2                    ▷ Immediate neighbors
        R ← R ∪ {u ∈ N s.t. 𝒱_u = ∅}
    return R
```

and support vector machines (SVM) on the same set of features for the nodes in the network that we shall describe in this section. We also explored combining these approaches with techniques for imbalanced data such as SMOTE [4] and Borderline SMOTE [9], however we do not report the results of Borderline SMOTE as it provided no significant difference from SMOTE. We group our features into four categories: (1.) neighborhood-based (having to do with the immediate neighbors of a given node), (2.) network-based (features that require the consideration of more than a nodes immediate and nearby neighbors), (3.) temporal characteristics, and (4.) geographic characteristics.

4.3.1 Neighborhood-Based Features

Neighborhood-based features are the features computed using each node and its first and/or second level neighbors in G – often with respect to some $C \subseteq \mathcal{V}$. The simplest such measure is the degree of vertex v – corresponding to the number of offenders arrested with v. We can easily extend this for some set of crimes of interest (C) where we look at all the neighbors of v who have committed a crime in C. This generalizes degree (as that is the case where $C = \emptyset$). In our experiments, we found the most useful neighborhood features to be in the case where $C = \mathcal{V}$ though standard degree ($C = \emptyset$) was also used. We also found that using combinations of the following booleans based on the below definition also proved to be useful:

$$maj_v(C, i) \quad = \quad |\{u | u \in (\cup_i N_v^i) \cap V_C\}| \geq 0.5 \times |(\cup_i N_v^i)|$$

Intuitively, $maj_v(C, i)$ is true if at least half of the nodes within a network distance of i from node v have committed a crime in C and false otherwise. Using these intuitions, we explored the space of variants of these neighborhood-based features and list those we found to be best-performing in Table 3.

4.3.2 Network-Based Features

Network-based features fall into two sub-categories that we shall describe in this section: community-based and path-based.

Network-based community features. We use several notions of a node's community when engineering features: the connected component to which a node belongs, the gang to which a node belongs, and what we will refer to as an individual's group. The connected component is simply based on the overall network structure, while the gang is simply the subgraph induced by the individuals in the network who belong to the same gang (the social network of node v's gang is denoted G_{gang_v}. A nodes group is defined as the partition he/she belongs to based on a partition of

Table 3: Neighborhood-Based Features

Description	**Definition**
Degree (w.r.t. C)	$\|\{u \| u \in N_v^1 \cap V_C\}\|$
Fraction of 1-hop neighbors committing a crime in C	$\|\{u \| u \in N_v^1 \cap V_C\}\| / \|N_v^1\|$
Fraction of 2-hop neighbors committing a crime in C	$\|\{u \| u \in N_v^2 \cap V_C\}\| / \|N_v^2\|$
Majority of 1-hop and 2-hop neighbors committing a crime in C	$maj_v(C, 1) \wedge maj_v(C, 2)$
Minority of 1-hop and majority of 2-hop neighbors comitting a crime in C	$\neg maj_v(C, 1) \wedge maj_v(C, 2)$

Table 4: Network-Based Features (Community)

Description	**Definition**
Component size when v is removed	$\|\mathsf{C}(\mathsf{C}_v(G) \setminus \{v\})\|$
Largest component size with a violent node after v is removed	$\max_{v' \in \mathsf{C}(\mathsf{C}_v(G)\{v\} \cap V_{\mathcal{V}}} \|X_{v'}\|$ where $X_{v'} = \mathsf{C}_{v'}(\mathsf{C}_v(G)\{v\})$
Group size	$\|\mathsf{P}_v(G_{gang_v})\|$
Relationships within the group	$\|\{(u, v) \in E \ s.t. \ u, v \in \mathsf{P}_v(G_{gang_v})\}\|$
Number of violent members in the group	$\|\{v' \in \mathsf{P}_v(G_{gang_v}) \ s.t. \ \mathcal{V}_v \neq \emptyset\}\|$
Triangles in group	No. of triangles within subgraph $\mathsf{P}_v(G_{gang_v})$
Transitivity of group	$\frac{\text{No. of triangles in } \mathsf{P}_v(G_{gang_v})}{\text{No. of ``}\vee\text{''s in } \mathsf{P}_v(G_{gang_v})}$
Group-to-group connections	$\|\{u \in \mathsf{P}_v(G_{gang_v}) \ s.t. \ \exists (u, w) \in E \ where \ w \notin \mathsf{P}_v(G_{gang_v})\}\|$
Gang-to-gang connections	$\|\{u \in G_{gang_v} \ s.t. \ \exists (u, w) \in E \ where \ w \notin G_{gang_v}\}\|$

G_{gang_v} found using the Louvain algorithm [5]. We found in our previous work [19] and ensuing experience with the Chicago Police that the groups produced in this method were highly relevant operationally. In this work, we also examined other community finding methods (i.e. *Infomap*, and *Spectral Clustering*) and found we obtained the best re-

Table 5: Network-Based Features (Path)

Description	**Definition**
Betweenness (w.r.t. C)	$\sum_{u,w \in V_C} \frac{\sigma_v(u,w)}{\sigma(u,w)}$
Closeness (w.r.t. C)	$(\lvert V_C \rvert - 1)/\sum_{u \in V_C} d(u,v)$
Shell Number (w.r.t. C)	$shell_C(v)$ (see appendix for further details)
Propagation (w.r.t. C)	1 if $v \in \Gamma_\kappa(V_\mathcal{V})$, 0 otherwise. (see appendix for further details)

sults by using the Louvain algorithm. We provide our best performing network-based community features that we used in Table 4. Of particular interest, we found for individual v that features relating to the size of the largest connected component resulting v' removal of his/her connected component was useful. Another interesting pair of features we noted for both group and gang were the number of edges from members of that group/gang to a different group or gang. We hypothesize that the utility of these features is a result of conflicts between groups/gangs they are connected to as well as the spread of violence amongst different groups (i.e. if two groups are closely connected, one may conduct violent activities on behalf of the other).

Network-based path features. We looked at several features that leveraged the paths in the network by adopting three common node metrics from the literature: betweenness, closeness [6], and shell-number [23] as well as a propagation process based on a deterministic tipping model [8]. The features are listed in Table 5. We examined our modified definitions of closeness, betweenness, and shell number where C was a single element of $\mathcal{V}$, where $C = \mathcal{V}$ and where $C = \emptyset$ (which provides the standard definitions of these measures). Our intuition was that individuals nearer in the network to other violent individuals would also tend to be more violent - and we found several interesting relationships such as that for closeness (where $C = V_\mathcal{V}$) discussed in section 5.1 when we run the classifier on each feature group. Shell number and the propagation process were used to capture the idea of the spread of violence (as shell number was previously shown to correspond with "spreaders" in various network epidemic models [11]). For the propagation process, we set the threshold (κ) equal to two, three, four, five, and six. Further details on shell number and the propogation process can be found in the appendix.

4.3.3 Geographic Features

Geographic features capture the information related to the location of a crime incident. The intuition is that the individuals who commit crimes in violent districts are more likely to become violent than the others. We found that the beat the individual has committed a crime in is an important feature for our problem. This is in accordance with previous well known literature in criminology [3, 21] which studies spatio-temporal modeling of criminal behavior. The complete list is shown in Table 6.

Table 6: Geographic Features

Name	**Definition**
District Frequency	$\lvert\{(t,v') \ s.t. \ arr_{v'}^t = \textsf{true} \wedge \exists t' \ s.t. \ distr_{v'}^t = distr_v^{t'}\}\rvert$
Beat Frequency	$\lvert\{(t,v') \ s.t. \ arr_{v'}^t = \textsf{true} \wedge \exists t' \ s.t. \ beat_{v'}^t = beat_v^{t'}\}\rvert$
Beat Violence	$\lvert\{(t,v') \ s.t. \ arr_{v'}^t = \textsf{true} \wedge \mathcal{V}_{v'}^t \neq \emptyset \wedge \exists t' \ s.t. \ beat_{v'}^t = beat_v^{t'}\}\rvert$
District Violence	$\lvert\{(t,v') \ s.t. \ arr_{v'}^t = \textsf{true} \wedge \mathcal{V}_{v'}^t \neq \emptyset \wedge \exists t' \ s.t. \ distr_{v'}^t = distr_v^{t'}\}\rvert$

4.3.4 Temporal Features

We considered couple of temporal features: average interval month and number of violent groups. Average interval time considers the average time duration of consecutive arrests of the offender. The other feature, which we examine, is number of violent groups appeared over time in the environment. We examined that the number of violent groups has been an important temporal aspect for identifying the violent criminals. The key intuition here is, if at least one member of the offender's groups (formed over time) is violent then we consider the offender as a part of that violent group. For an individual v, we define the partially ordered set $t_C^v = \{t \ s.t. \ arr_v^t = \textsf{true} \wedge V_C^t \neq \emptyset\}$ (intuitively the set of the time points where v has committed at least on of the crimes in C.) We also define $\Delta_i^v(C) = t_i^v - t_{i-1}^v$ for each $t_i^v \in t_C^v$. Considering these definitions, we formally define the temporal features in Table 7.

Table 7: Temporal Features

Name	**Definition**
Average interval time (w.r.t. C)	$\sum_i \Delta_i^v(C)/\lvert t_C^v \rvert$
Number of violent groups	$\lvert\{t \ s.t. \ arr_v^t = \textsf{true} \wedge \exists v' \ s.t. \ arr_{v'}^t = \textsf{true} \wedge \mathcal{V}_v^t \neq \emptyset \wedge v' \in N_v^t\}\rvert$

5. EXPERIMENTAL RESULTS

In this section, we review the results of our experiments. We looked at two types: experiments where the entire co-offender network is known before-hand (Section 5.1) and experiments where the network is discovered over time (Section 5.2). The intuition behind the experiments where the co-offender network is known is that the police often have additional information to augment co-arrestee data. This information can include informant reporting, observed individuals interacting by patrolmen, intelligence reporting, and information discovered on social media and the Internet. In our second type of experiment we discover the network over time in an effort to mimic real-world operations - however, we also show that this makes the problem more difficult as it reduces the power of neighborhood-based and network-based features. Based on our discussions with the Chicago Police, we believe that real-world results will most likely fall somewhere between these two experiments. Operationally, we will not have full arrest data, but the aforementioned augmenting data sources are available (even though we did not have access to them for our experiments).

5.1 Known Co-Offender Network

In this experiment we assume that the entire offender network is known. In other words, to compute the features for each vertex v, we assume that the set $\mathcal{V}_v$ is unknown while the rest of the network is observable. In here we compared our approach with *THH* but not with the *PVA* as we do not utilize time. In each of the experiments described in this section, we conduct 10-fold cross validation. We consider the result of each approach as a set of nodes that the approach considers to be a set of potentially violent individuals. Our primary metrics are precision (fraction of reported violent individual who were actually violent in the dataset), recall (fraction of violent individuals in the dataset reported by the approach), F1 (the harmonic mean of precision and recall) and area under the curve. We conduct two types of experiments: first, we study classification performance using only features within a given category (neighborhood, network, temporal, and geographic), then we study the classification performance when the entire feature set is used but with various different classification algorithms and compare the result to *THH*.

Classification using single feature categories. Here we describe classification results using single feature categories. In this set of experiments, we use a random forest classifier (which we will later show provides the best performance of the classifiers that we examined). Figure 5 shows the performance of RF for the described categories. The network-based features are highly-correlated to violent behavior with average F1 value of 0.72 compared to 0.63 for neighborhood, 0.21 for geographic, and 0.03 for temporal features. In Figure 6, we show the performance of a feature from each category to classify violent vs. non violent crimes; the performance of each example is a good indicator of the performance of its category.

Classification comparison. Table 8 shows the performance of different classification algorithms. According to Table 8, RF provides the best performance (F1=0.83); we also note that using SMOTE for RF, did not improve this result. Figure 8 shows that our algorithm outperforms *THH*. The performance of our features are also illustrated in Figure 7. The area under the curve (AUC) of applying all features is 0.98 – a higher overall accuracy. The AUC for network-based, neighborhood-based, geographic, and temporal categories are 0.92, 0.91, 0.65, and 0.7 respectively. This indicates the importance of network features for this classification task.

5.2 Co-Offender Network Emerges Over Time

In this section, we present a more difficult experiment - where the co-arrestee network is discovered over time (by virtue of arrests). To simulate this phenomenon, we split

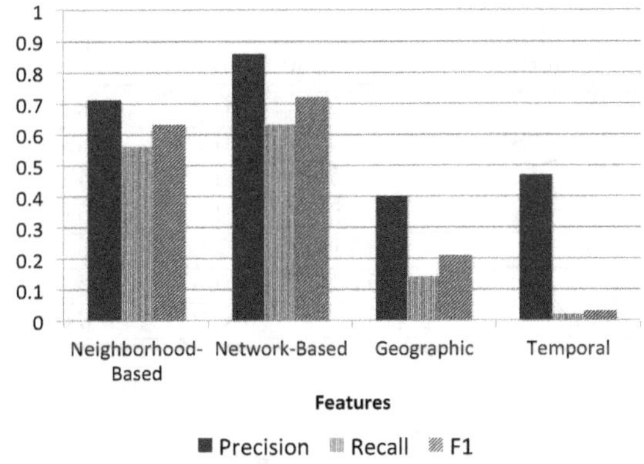

Figure 5: Precision, recall, and F1 comparison between each group of features.

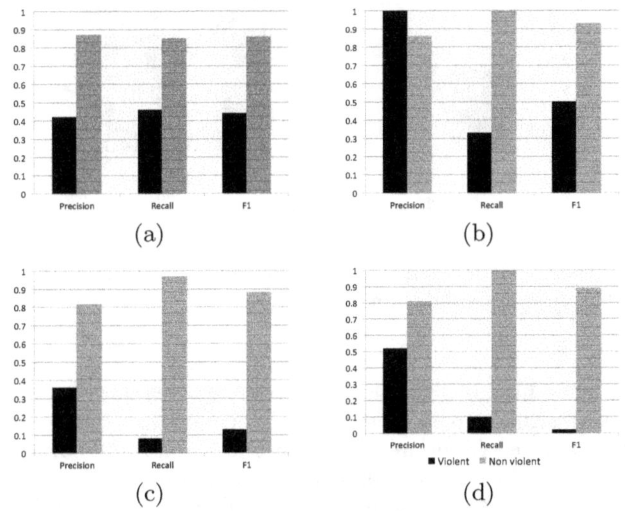

Figure 6: Example features from each category. (a) Neighborhood-based: Minority of 1-hop and majority of 2-hop neighbors committing a crime in C. (b) Network-based: Closeness (w.r.t. $\mathcal{V}$). (c) Geographic: Beat violence. (d) Temporal: Average interval months.

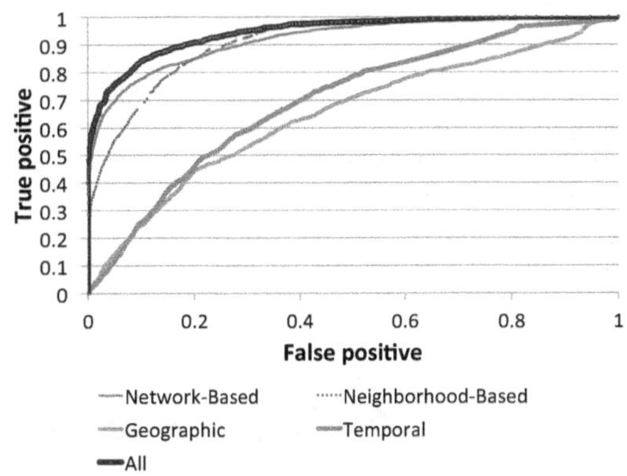

Figure 7: ROC curve for each feature set.

Table 8: K-fold cross validation.

Method	Precision	Recall	F1
RF	0.89	0.78	0.83
RF w. SMOTE	0.86	0.78	0.82
NB	0.45	0.49	0.47
LR	0.68	0.49	0.57
DT	0.71	0.66	0.68
NN	0.64	0.57	0.6
SVM	0.73	0.2	0.31

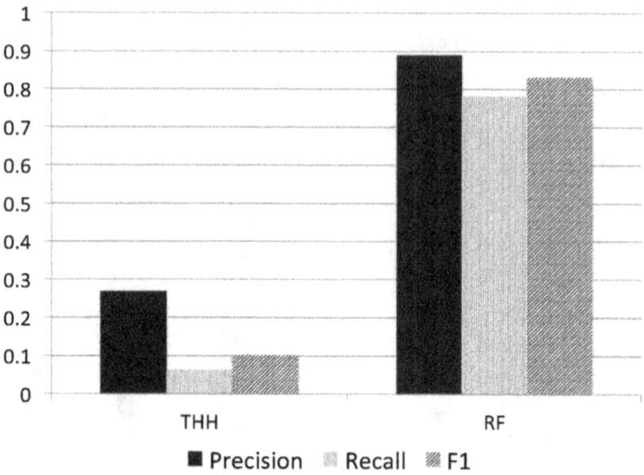

Figure 8: Performance comparison between *THH* and *RF* in K-fold cross validation.

our data into two disjoint sets: the first set for learning and identification, and the second one for measuring the performance. We do monthly split and start from February 2013. To illustrate the difficulty of this test, we show the number of nodes, edges, and violent individuals per month in Figure 9. We note that in the early months, we are missing much of the graphical data (over 40% of nodes and edges in the first two months) - hence making many of our features less effective. However, as the months progress, there are less violent individuals to identify (due to the temporal nature of the dataset) - hence amplifying the data imbalance as time progresses.

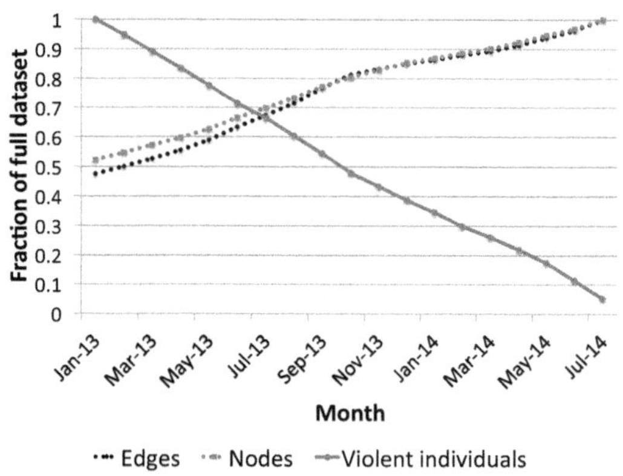

Figure 9: Number of nodes, edges, and violent individuals over time. More training data, less offenders to identify.

In these experiments, we compared our approach using random forests with the full feature set to *THH* and *PVA*. We measure precision, recall, F1, number of true positives, and number of false positives and display the results in Figures 10 and 11. In *FRF* (Filtered Random Forest) we filter the offenders who have not committed any crime in the last 200 days. This simple heuristic increase the precision drastically while preserving the recall. The main advantage of our method, besides the high precision, is its ability to significantly reduce the population of potentially violent offenders when compared to PVA - which for each month had between 1813 and 3571 false positives. Figure 11 compares the number of true and false positives instances for all the approaches for each month except PVA (PVA was omitted due to readability because of the large amount of false positives). While the F1 measure for *PVA* is higher than that of the others, the large number of false positives prevents the law enforcement from using it effectively in practice. Furthermore, as time progresses, PVA likely rises in recall due to the drop in the number of violent criminals to predict.

6. RELATED WORK

Though we believe that the prediction of violent offenders using co-offender social networks is new, there has previously been work on both co-offender networks in general as well as crime forecasting. In this section, we briefly review some of the relevant contributions in both of these areas.

There has been much previous work on co-offender networks. The earlier work that studied these special social networks primarily came from the criminology literature. For instance, [14] utilizes social network analysis techniques to study several case studies where the social network of the criminal organization was known. In [13], the authors study the stability of these networks change over time. More recently, graphical features derived from networks comprised of both offenders and victims has been shown to be related to the the probability of an individual becoming a victim of a violent crime [17, 16]. Previous work has also looked at the relationship between network structure and geography [18] and has leveraged both network and geographic features to predict criminal relationships [25] as well as influence gang members to dis-enroll [24]. There have also been several software tools developed for conducting a wide-range of analysis on co-offender networks including CrimeFighter [20], CrimeLink [22], and ORCA [19]. However, our work departs from this is that we are looking to leverage the network topology and other features to identify violent offenders - which was not studied in any of the previous work.

There has also been a large amount of work on crime forecasting (i.e. [7, 12]) though historically, this work has relied on spatio-temporal modeling of criminal behavior [3, 21] or was designed to identify suspects for specific crimes [26, 15]. None of this previous work was designed to identify future violent offenders nor did it leverage social network structure.

7. CONCLUSION

In this paper we explored the problem of identifying repeat offenders who will commit violent crime. We showed a strong relationship between network-based features and whether a criminal will commit a violent offense providing

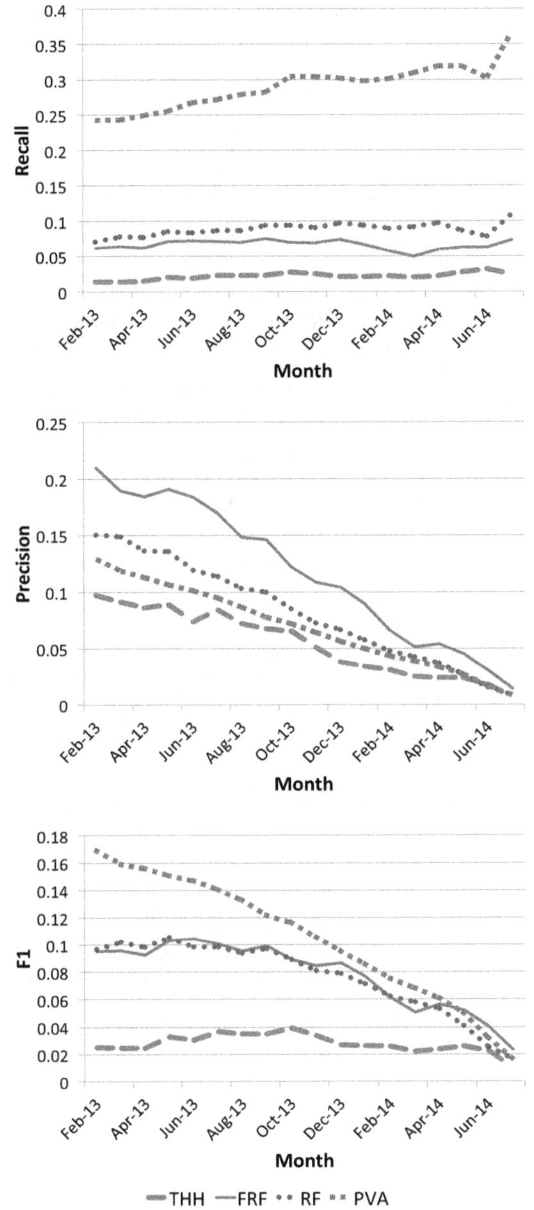

Figure 10: Precision, recall, and F1 over time.

an unbiased F1 score of 0.83 in our cross-validation experiment where we assumed that the underlying network was known. When we moved to the case where the network was discovered over time, our method significantly outperformed baseline approaches significantly increasing precision and recall. We are currently discussing ways to operationalize this technology with the Chicago Police as well as design strategies to best deploy police assets to areas with higher concentrations of potentially violent offenders. We are also working with the police to identify other sources of data to build a more complete social network of the offenders.

Appendix

Shell Number. For a given graph, the k-core is the largest subgraph where each node has at least degree k. The k-shell

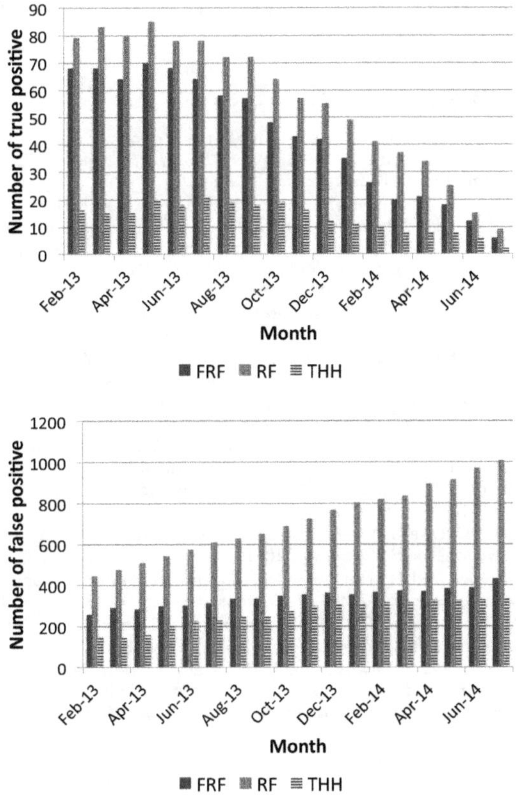

Figure 11: Number of true and false positive instances.

is the set of nodes in core k but not in any higher core. A node's shell number is k value of the shell to which that node belongs. For a given node v and $C \subseteq \mathcal{V}$, we define $shell_C(v)$ as the shell number of node v on the subgraph consisting of v and all nodes v' where $C \cap \mathcal{V}_v \neq \emptyset$. We slightly abuse notation and define $shell_\emptyset(v)$ as the shell number of v on the full network.

Propogation Process. For a given node v and the set of activated nodes V', we define v's active neighbors as follows:

$$act_v(V') = \{u | u \in N_v^1 \cap V'\}$$

We now define an activation function A that, given an initial set of active nodes, returns a set of active nodes after one time step.

$$A_\kappa(V') = V' \cup \{v \in V \ s.t. \ |act_v(V')| \geq \kappa\}$$

We also note that the activation function can be applied iteratively, to model a diffusion process. Hence, we shall use the following notation to signify multiple applications of A (for natural numbers $t > 1$).

$$A_\kappa^t(V') = \begin{cases} A_\kappa(V') & \text{if } t = 1 \\ A_\kappa(A_\kappa^{t-1}(V')) & \text{otherwise} \end{cases}$$

Clearly, when $A_{G,\kappa}^t(V') = A_{G,\kappa}^{t-1}(V')$ the process has converged. Further, this always converges in no more than $|V|$ steps, since the process must activate at least one new node in each step prior to converging. Based on this idea, we define the function Γ which returns the set of all nodes activated upon the convergence of the activation function. We define $\Gamma_\kappa(V') = A_\kappa(V')$ where t is the least value such that $A^t_\kappa(V') = A^{t-1}_\kappa(V')$.

8. REFERENCES

[1] J. Bertetto. Countering criminal street gangs: Lessons from the counterinsurgent battlespace. *Law Enforcement Executive Forum*, 12(3):43, 2012.

[2] A. Braga, D. Hureau, and A. Papachristos. Deterring gang-involved gun violence: Measuring the impact of boston's operation ceasefire on street gang behavior. *Journal of Quantitative Criminology*, pages 1–27, 2013.

[3] P. Brantingham and P. Brantingham. Crime Pattern Theory. In R. Wortley and L. Mazerolle, editors, *Enviromental Criminology and Crime Analysis*, pages 78–93. 2008.

[4] N. V. Chawla, K. W. Bowyer, L. O. Hall, and W. P. Kegelmeyer. Smote: synthetic minority over-sampling technique. *Journal of artificial intelligence research*, 16(1):321–357, 2002.

[5] P. Expert, T. S. Evans, V. D. Blondel, and R. Lambiotte. Uncovering space-independent communities in spatial networks. *Proceedings of the National Academy of Sciences*, 108(19):7663–7668, 2011.

[6] L. C. Freeman. A set of measures of centrality based on betweenness. *Sociometry*, 40(1):pp. 35–41, 1977.

[7] W. Gorr and R. Harries. Introduction to crime forecasting. *International Journal of Forecasting*, 19(4):551 – 555, 2003.

[8] M. Granovetter. Threshold models of collective behavior. *The American Journal of Sociology*, (6):1420–1443.

[9] H. Han, W.-Y. Wang, and B.-H. Mao. Borderline-smote: a new over-sampling method in imbalanced data sets learning. In *Advances in intelligent computing*, pages 878–887. Springer, 2005.

[10] J. C. Howell. *Gangs in America's Communities*. Sage, 2012.

[11] M. Kitsak, L. K. Gallos, S. Havlin, F. Liljeros, L. Muchnik, H. E. Stanley, and H. A. Makse. Identification of influential spreaders in complex networks. *Nat Phys*, 6(11):888–893, Nov. 2010.

[12] H. Liu and D. E. Brown. Criminal incident prediction using a point-pattern-based density model. *International Journal of Forecasting*, 19(4):603–622, Oct. 2003.

[13] J. M. Mcgloin, C. J. Sullivan, A. R. Piquero, and S. Bacon. Investigating the stability of co-offending and co-offenders among a sample of youthful offenders. *Criminology*, 46(1):155–188, 2008.

[14] C. Morselli. *Inside Criminal Networks*. Springer, 2009.

[15] C. Overall and G. Day. The Hammer Gang: an exercise in spatial analyis of an armed robbery series using the probability grid method. In S. Chainey and L. Tompson, editors, *Crime Mapping Case Studies*, pages 55–62. 2008.

[16] A. Papachristos, C. Wildeman, and E. Roberto. Tragic, but not random: The social contagion of nonfatal gunshot injuries. *Social Science and Medicine*, page 139.

[17] B. A. H. D. Papachristos, A. Social networks and the risk of gunshot injury. *J. Urban Health*, 2012.

[18] H. D. B. A. Papachristos, A. The corner and the crew: The influence of geography and social networks on gang violence. *American Sociological Review*, 2013.

[19] D. Paulo, B. Fischl, T. Markow, M. Martin, and P. Shakarian. Social network intelligence analysis to combat street gang violence. In *Proceedings of the 2013 IEEE/ACM International Conference on Advances in Social Networks Analysis and Mining*, ASONAM '13, pages 1042–1049, New York, NY, USA, 2013. ACM.

[20] R. R. Petersen and U. K. Wiil. Crimefighter investigator: A novel tool for criminal network investigation. In *EISIC*, pages 197–202. IEEE, 2011.

[21] D. K. Rossmo and S. Rombouts. Geographic Profiling. In R. Wortley and L. Mazerolle, editors, *Enviromental Criminology and Crime Analysis*, pages 136–149. 2008.

[22] J. Schroeder, J. Xu, and H. Chen. Crimelink explorer: Using domain knowledge to facilitate automated crime association analysis. In H. Chen, R. Miranda, D. Zeng, C. Demchak, J. Schroeder, and T. Madhusudan, editors, *Intelligence and Security Informatics*, volume 2665 of *Lecture Notes in Computer Science*, pages 168–180. Springer Berlin Heidelberg, 2003.

[23] S. B. Seidman. Network structure and minimum degree. *Social Networks*, 5(3):269 – 287, 1983.

[24] P. Shakarian, J. Salmento, W. Pulleyblank, and J. Bertetto. Reducing gang violence through network influence based targeting of social programs. In *Proceedings of the 20th ACM SIGKDD International Conference on Knowledge Discovery and Data Mining*, KDD '14, pages 1829–1836, New York, NY, USA, 2014. ACM.

[25] M. A. Tayebi, M. Ester, U. Glässer, and P. L. Brantingham. Spatially embedded co-offence prediction using supervised learning. In *Proceedings of the 20th ACM SIGKDD International Conference on Knowledge Discovery and Data Mining*, KDD '14, pages 1789–1798, New York, NY, USA, 2014. ACM.

[26] M. A. Tayebi, M. Jamali, M. Ester, U. Glässer, and R. Frank. Crimewalker: A recommendation model for suspect investigation. In *Proceedings of the Fifth ACM Conference on Recommender Systems*, RecSys '11, pages 173–180, New York, NY, USA, 2011. ACM.

[27] D. J. Watts and S. H. Strogatz. Collective dynamics of "small-world" networks. *nature*, 393(6684):440–442, 1998.

Spoken English Grading: Machine Learning with Crowd Intelligence

Vinay Shashidhar, Nishant Pandey and Varun Aggarwal
Aspiring Minds
vinay.shashidhar@aspiringminds.com, nishant.pandey@aspiringminds.com,
varun@aspiringminds.com

ABSTRACT

In this paper, we address the problem of grading spontaneous speech using a combination of machine learning and crowdsourcing. Traditional machine learning techniques solve the stated problem inadequately as automatic speaker-independent speech transcription is inaccurate. The features derived from it are also inaccurate and so is the machine learning model developed for speech evaluation. We propose a framework that combines machine learning with crowdsourcing. This entails identifying *human intelligence* tasks in the feature derivation step and using crowdsourcing to get them completed. We post the task of speech transcription to a large community of online workers (crowd). We also get spoken English grades from the crowd. We achieve 95% transcription accuracy by combining transcriptions from multiple crowd workers. Speech and prosody features are derived by force aligning the speech samples on these highly accurate transcriptions. Additionally, we derive surface and semantic level features directly from the transcription. We demonstrate the efficacy of our approach by predicting expert graded speech sample of 566 adult non-native speakers across two different countries - India and Philippines. Using the regression modeling technique, we are able achieve a Pearson correlation of 0.79 on the Philippines set and 0.74 on the Indian set with expert grades, an accuracy much higher than any previously reported machine learning approach. Our approach has an accuracy that rivals that of expert agreement. We show the value of the system through a case study in a real-world industrial deployment. This work is timely given the huge requirement of spoken English training and assessment.

Categories and Subject Descriptors

I.2.7 [**Artificial Intelligence**]: Natural Language Processing—*Speech Recognition and synthesis*

KDD'15, August 10-13, 2015, Sydney, NSW, Australia.
© 2015 ACM. ISBN 978-1-4503-3664-2/15/08 ...$15.00.
DOI: http://dx.doi.org/10.1145/2783258.2788595 .

Keywords

Spontaneous speech grading; Spoken English evaluation; Crowdsourcing; Speech recognition; Machine Learning

1. INTRODUCTION

The grading of constructed (open) response items, popularly known as subjective evaluation, provides a more holistic and accurate assessment of a candidate's skills as compared to selected response items (multiple-choice questions) [1]. The primary limitation of a selected response item is that it asks the candidate to *choose* the right answer, providing implicit hints and the structure of the solution [2]. However they are traditionally preferred over constructed response as their evaluation can be automated fairly easily. With the recent interest in MOOCs (Massively Online Open Courseware) [3], scalable education/training and automated recruitment assessment [4, 5], the interest in reducing manual effort in the assessment of constructed responses has increased manifolds.

Machine learning has been used to automatically grade these responses. There are many examples of successfully using machine learning for constructed response grading [2, 6]. A framework and general principles for using machine learning to grade constructed responses are presented in [2].

However machine learning techniques fall short of providing accurate assessment for a number of problems [3, 7]. Secondly, these automated approaches have come under criticism since the test-takers can fake high-scoring responses [8]. For instance, automated assessment of spontaneous speech for spoken language evaluation remains largely an unsolved problem [6]. On the other hand, automatic essay grading algorithms can be tricked by inserting the right words in random order or writing long essays [8].

We have identified that one of the key limitations of the current automated techniques is their inability to automatically derive the right set of *features* with high precision for assessing the response. Interestingly, many of these features can be easily derived by (or with help of) *humans*, even if they are non-experts. For instance, word sense disambiguation [9] or gibberish identification for essay grading, text transcription from noisy handwriting [10] and speech transcription [11] for speech grading are easily doable tasks by humans through crowdsourcing [12].

With this insight, we propose an extended machine learning framework with a crowdsourcing layer for constructed response assessment. In this approach, one identifies *human intelligence* tasks in the feature derivation step and posts them to be completed by a non-expert crowd.[1] The responses from the human intelligence tasks are then used to create relevant features for machine learning.

We illustrate our technique for evaluation of spontaneous English speech[2].

Evaluation of spoken English is in high demand for recruitment in the industry and admissions to the universities [17]. Universities teaching in English expect a level of English proficiency in incoming students whereas various job roles require different levels of spoken English capabilities. With the massive increase in the number of applicants applying for both university and companies, there is a great to scale this process by automating it. Having an automated/semi-automated way of evaluation for the purpose of giving feedback to candidates cannot be overstated.

The problem acquires far reaching significance given the evidence that better English leads to better employment outcomes, wages and promotions [18, 19].

Figure 1 shows the application of technique to spoken English grading. In the task of spontaneous speech evaluation, the text of the speech is not known a priori. We post the task of transcription of the sample speech to the crowd who transcribe it fairly accurately [11]. We force-align [18, 20] the speech of the candidate on this text to derive various features which go into a machine learning engine. We also collect non-expert grades of the speech from the crowd, which can be optionally used as additional features. With these accurately identified features with the help of the crowd, machine learning (specifically the modeling step) becomes a powerful technique for constructed response grading.

In summary, our approach is to identify human-intelligence tasks in the feature derivation step and let the crowd complete these in an accurate and reliable way. This enables machine learning to grade spoken English accurately. Our approach is an interesting addition to the extant machine learning only approaches and peer/crowd grading approaches. The approach could help in other grading problems such as that of essay's by outsourcing word sense disambiguation [9], detecting insensible sentences or grammar checks to the crowd. It could also be used to grade handwritten assignments of students [10], where the crowd digitizes the responses. It needs to be seen how one creatively gleans human intelligence tasks for other grading tasks and what is the incremental predictive value added by our technique.

In this paper, we show how we can solve a hitherto unsolved problem [6] of English spontaneous speech evaluation using our approach.

The paper makes the following contributions:

- We introduce a general framework to add a crowdsourcing step for feature derivation in a machine learning based constructed response grading systems. This adds a new alternative to the set of techniques used for automated and semi-automated grading.

- We find that the features derived from crowdsourced transcription do better in predicting expert grades than the machine learning only approach. These features when combined with crowd grades predict spoken English scores with accuracy comparable to expert agreement.

- We provide a scalable and an accurate way to do spoken English grading, a huge requirement in the industry and elsewhere.

The paper is organized as follows– Section 2 describes previous work, compares our technique with current incumbent techniques; Section 3 describes the procedure and aim of the speech assessment task; Section 4 describes the features classes used in the prediction algorithm; Section 5 describes the crowdsourcing framework which is used as input to machine learning methods; Section 6 shows how this framework was used with machine learning techniques to predict a spoken English composite score and a case study of a real world implementations and results; Section 7 discusses the future work and concludes the paper.

2. PREVIOUS WORK

Machine learning and human intelligence have been used in tandem since a long time. The classic application is to use the crowd to label samples and then use supervised learning to predict the labels. Within grading of constructed responses, recently [21] learnt a grade using ML and used its confidence score to determine the number of expert evaluations required for the task. We believe that our work is the first proposal and implementation of using crowdsourcing specifically for the feature derivation step of ML in the context of grading. To our best knowledge, this has not been attempted for other problems either. Some loosely related works include [22, 23, 24].

Our technique, when compared to a ML only approach, has a promise of higher accuracy, but makes some trade-offs. Firstly, there is a cost for every assessment done and the scalability depends on the number of non-expert workers available. These drawbacks are strictly speaking, valid, but they didn't lead to practical challenges in our case. We paid 24 cents for each completely graded sample, a very affordable cost (per assessment) which is significantly lower than that of any expert grading efforts. Recently we have had crowd rate hundreds of samples in a day without any challenge or the need of altering the payment significantly.

Secondly, machine learning based assessments generally provide evaluations in real-time, whereas there is a time lag when using crowdsourcing. This works fine in many scenarios, but doesn't cater well to provide real-time feedback. Real time crowdsourcing has been an active area of research [25, 26] and a focus area for our group as well.

In comparison to peer grading methods [13] or crowdsourcing assessments [14, 15, 16], our technique works differently. In these techniques, the crowd/peers directly evaluates/grades the response on a rubric and a combination of their grades mimics the grades given by experts. We, on the other hand, use the crowd to help complete a human intelligence task, which helps in better feature derivation. One may additionally combine crowd grades too, if needed. This offers a new trade-off point among techniques with interesting possibilities. Crowd grades do not work for evaluating

[1]Our approach is different from peer grading [13] or crowd grading [14, 15, 16] approaches. These approaches directly ask the crowd to grade the response. The primary feature of our technique is using the crowd in the feature extraction step of machine learning. We provide a detailed comparison in Section 2.

[2]Spontaneous speech refers to text–independent speech samples.

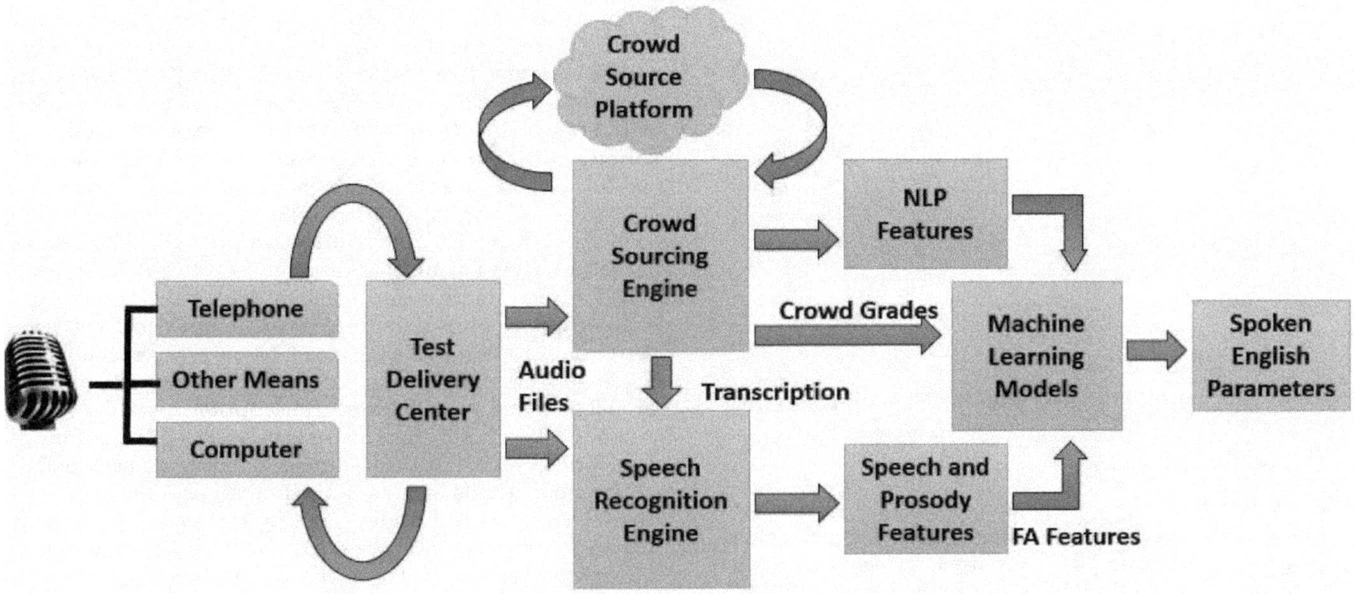

Figure 1: System Design

expert tasks, say a computer program or an advanced electronics question and such evaluations need peers with some exposure to the subject. Our technique has the possibility to make these amenable with cheaper and more scalable crowd, non-expert raters. It may also help improve the accuracy of peer/crowd grading techniques or reduce workers, given that we use a complementary set of information from the crowd. Futuristically, our technique could be more defensible for mid/high stake testing, given it uses the crowd for human intelligence tasks only and not direct evaluation.

In summary, our approach lies somewhere in between the machine learning only approaches and that of drawing grades from the consensus of crowd/experts.

3. GRADING TASK

We want to assess the quality of spoken English of candidates based on their spontaneous speech samples. The speech samples of the candidates were collected using Aspiring Minds' automated speech assessment tool– SVAR [5]. SVAR is conducted over phone as well as on a computer. The test has multiple sections where the candidate is required to: read sentences aloud, listen and repeat sentences, listen to a passage or conversation and answer multiple choice questions and finally spontaneously speak on a given topic. In the spontaneous speech section, the candidates[3] are provided with a topic and given 30 seconds to think, take notes and then speak on the topic for 45 seconds. The topic is repeated to ensure task clarity. The complete test takes 16-20 minutes to complete, depending on the test version.

Currently, SVAR evaluates speech samples from the read and repeat sections with high accuracy [5]. Our goal in this paper is to evaluate the spontaneous speech of the candidate and provide a composite score based on it.

[3]The subjects of our study use English as their second language and hail from various backgrounds, dialects and educational qualifications.

A 5 point rubric for the composite score, similar to CEFR [27], was prepared with the help of experts. This score is a function of the pronunciation, fluency, content organization and grammar quality of the speech sample. Broadly speaking, Pronunciation [28] refers to the correctness in the utterance of the phonemes of a word by the students as per neutral accent. Fluency [29] refers to a desired rate of speech along with the absence of hesitations, false starts and stops etc. Content organization [30] measures the candidate's ability to structure the information disposition and present it coherently. Grammar [31] measures how well the syntax of the language was followed by the candidate.

In the next section we discuss the features which are used in the prediction algorithm.

4. FEATURES

We use three classes of features– Crowd Grades (CG), Force Alignment features (FA) and Natural Language Processing features (NLP). The spoken English samples are posted to the crowd to get the transcription and spoken English grades (Figure 1). Each task was completed by three workers. The crowd grades become one set of features. A second set, i.e., FA features, are derived by aligning [32] the speech sample on the crowdsourced transcriptions. A third set, i.e., NLP features, are also derived from the crowdsourced text. These are explained in the succeeding paragraphs.

- *Crowd Grades:* The crowd transcribes the speech in addition to providing scores on each of the following– pronunciation, fluency, content organization and grammar. These grades are combined to form a composite score per worker per candidate. These are further averaged across workers to give a final score.[4]

[4]Advanced Expectation-Maximization techniques [33] may also be used for an aggregation strategy, once the number of tasks done by every individual worker increases. In our current experiments, this number wasn't very high.

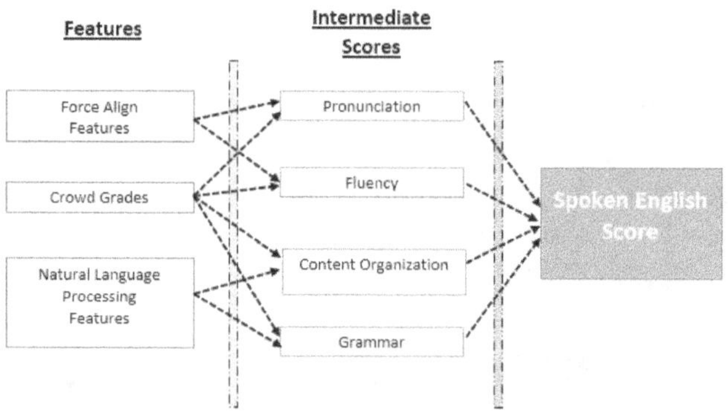

Figure 2: Our intuition of how different features predict the holistic score.

- *FA features:* The speech sample is forced aligned [18, 20] on the crowdsourced transcription using the HTK speech recognizer [34]. We used an acoustic model based on TIMIT [35] for our experiments. TIMIT is a corpus of phonemically and lexically transcribed speech of American English speakers of different sexes and dialects.

  A number of speech quality features are derived, which include– rate of speech, position and length of pauses, log likelihood of recognition, posterior probability, hesitations and repetitions, etc. [36, 6, 37]. These features are predictive of the pronunciation and fluency of the candidate.

- *NLP features:* These features predict the content quality and grammar of the spoken content[5]. They were derived using standard NLP packages [38, 39] on the crowdsourced transcription. The package calculates surface level features such as the number of words complexity or difficulty of words and the number of common words used. It also calculates semantic features like the coherency in text, context of the words spoken, sentiment of the text and grammar correctness. These features are predictive of the grammar and content organization of the sample.

All the features described above were obtained for the spontaneous speech sample. We also derived features similar to FA features for the candidate's read and repeat speech samples collected during his/her SVAR test. The speech and prosody features are calculated by force aligning the speech on the known text. One of the models (RS/LR) in our experiments is based on these features and has been included for comparison. These features do not have any bearing on our final model for spontaneous speech evaluation.

5. CROWDSOURCING

The spoken English sample was given to the crowd to transcribe and provide grades. The task was posted on a popular crowdsourcing platform– Amazon Mechanical Turk (AMT) [40]. AMT is a popular crowdsourcing marketplace. It is inspired by the famous 18th century automated chess playing machine, running on the intelligence of a hidden human operator. It has more than 500,000 online workers from 190 countries [41]. One can post tasks on the platform online and offer fixed remuneration for their completion.

A clean and simple interface was provided to the worker with standard features needed for transcription. Additionally, an advanced audio player was embedded with the ability to play the speech sample in repeat mode, rewind and forward, apart from standard play/pause functionality to help the worker. The different transcriptions were combined using the ROVER algorithm [42]. ROVER is a sophisticated voting algorithm to combine multiple transcriptions with errors, to obtain the best estimate of the correct transcription. It is reported to lead to an error reduction of 20-25%. ROVER proceeds in two stages: first the outputs are aligned and a single word transcription network (WTN) is built. The second stage consists of selecting the best scoring word (with the highest number of votes) at each node.

Several methods have been used in the past for increasing the reliability of the grades given by the crowd by identifying and correcting any biases and removing non-serious/low quality workers [43]. One of the key techniques for this involves inserting gold standard tasks with known answers to get an estimate of the worker's ability [44]. The gold standard tasks are similar to real tasks and the workers have no way to distinguish between the two. Our tasks took workers a reasonable amount of time (8-10 minutes). It wasn't hence feasible to insert a gold standard task, as done typically, with every task to be completed.

To overcome this problem, we propose an innovative approach where a risk is assigned to a worker based on his/her performance on the gold standard tasks. We conceptualized this system as a state machine that determines the risk level of a worker and proposes actions based on it (Refer to Figure 3). All workers started with an initial risk level of 0.2. Gold standard tasks were probabilistically inserted among real tasks based on the worker's risk level. Workers with a higher risk level saw more gold standard tasks. Also, the risk level of the worker was updated based on his/her performance on the gold standard tasks. Workers who consistently performed poorly on gold standard tasks were allocated a higher risk level and a notification was sent to them with a corrective course of action. Beyond a certain level, the worker was barred from attempting future work. We did not do any retrospective correction of the barred worker's completed tasks and simply stopped him/her from attempting newer tasks. This approach allowed us to control for the quality of workers, provide feedback, remove unsuitable workers and also adaptively control the balance between real and gold standard tasks.[6]

We describe the experimental setup and the results in the next section.

6. EXPERIMENTS

We conducted the experiments to answer the following questions:

- Can read/repeat features predict spontaneous speech grades accurately?

[5]We were looking at prompt independent features only, at this point.

[6]Specific details of the implementation are beyond the scope of the paper.

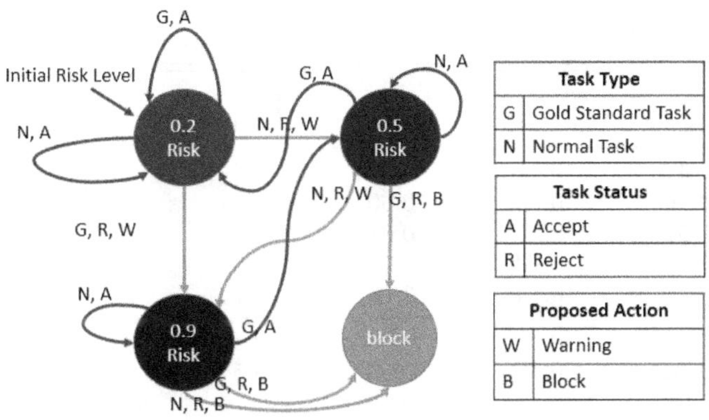

Figure 3: Risk Level State Diagram: In the above figure, each node corresponds to a risk level associated with a worker. The values range between 0 (min) - 1 (max). The worker is either assigned a gold standard task (G) or a normal task (N) on the basis of his/her present risk level. The risk level changes every time a task is Accepted (A) or Rejected (R). Additionally worker may be warned (W) or blocked (B) in case of rejection.

- How accurate is a pure machine learning approach (without crowdsourced transcription) in predicting grades as compared to grades given by human experts?
- How much better is the ML-CS approach in predicting grades as compared to a pure ML approach and to using Crowd Grades only?
- Do Crowd Grades add additional value in predicting grades over and above the features derived from the crowdsourced transcription?

We conducted the experiments on 566 spontaneous speech samples which were graded by expert assessors. Out of these, 319 were of native Indians (IN set), while the remaining 247 were of native Philippines (PH set). To answer the questions stated above, we developed models for the IN and PH sets separately.[7]

In the model building phase, we used different set of features to develop the models and compared their accuracy. The models were built against expert grades using supervised learning techniques. We experimented with three machine learning techniques– Ridge Regression, SVMs and Neural Networks. The data set used in the experiments is discussed in the next section.

6.1 Data Set

Our data set contains a total of 566 spontaneous speech responses comprising of 319 samples from India and 247 samples from Philippines. The speech samples in both sets were from seniors (non–native English speakers in final year of undergraduate education) pursuing bachelor's degree in their respective countries. The candidates were asked to describe one of the following six scenes: *a hospital, flood, a crowded market, an airport, favorite holiday destination* and *a school playground*. The candidates were given 30 seconds to think and take notes and were then asked to speak for the next 45 seconds. The responses were collected on the phone during the SVAR test [5]. Apart from the spontaneous speech response, each candidate was asked to read 12 given sentences and repeat 9 given sentences immediately after listening to each of them. Empty or very noisy responses (not humanly discernible) were not included in the final 566 sample set.

Table 1: Inter-rater correlations

Sample Set	Inter correlation for read/repeat scores	Inter correlation for spontaneous speech score
IN	0.83	0.86
PH	0.80	0.82

The responses in both sets were rated by one common rater with more than thirty years' experience in grading spoken English and one specific rater each who had more than fifteen years' experience. There were two set of scores. The first was a holistic score on the spontaneous speech samples based on its pronunciation, fluency, content characteristics and grammar. The second was a score on the pronunciation and fluency quality of the read/repeat sentences. The correlation between grades given by the two experts is shown below in Table 1. For each of the two scores, the average of the scores by the two expert grades was used for further purposes.

The correlation between the expert scores on spontaneous speech and automated read/repeat speech for IN set was 0.54 and for PH set was 0.56. This shows that there is a considerable unexplained variance (approx. 70%) in the spontaneous speech score, not addressed by the read/repeat scores. This could be due to a difference in the pronunciation quality and fluency of the candidates in reading/repeating text vs. speaking spontaneously and also due to the additional parameters of grammar and content characteristics in the spontaneous speech score. Thus, an automatic score mimicking the read/repeat expert grades, which is a solved problem, is inadequate for our task.

The first score is used for all subsequent discussion and development of models.

6.2 Crowdsourced Tasks

The 566 speech sample assessment task was posted on Amazon Mechanical Turk (AMT). Each task was completed by three workers. In total, 312 unique workers completed the tasks. The majority of workers (90%) belonged to USA and India.

The task took on an average 8–9 minutes to complete and a worker was paid between 6–10 cents per task including a bonus which was paid on completion of every 4 tasks. The average transcription accuracy for a worker was 79.7%[8]. This significantly improved to 94.6% when the transcriptions of the three workers were combined using the ROVER algorithm. In comparison, the accuracy of automatic transcription of a speech recognition engine was 51.6%.

[7]We tried to build a single model over both samples, but it did not get good results. This could be because a good speech in one accent may not be equivalent to the other quantitatively. It may need further techniques for normalization.

[8]PHP similar_text function was used as similarity metric.

Table 2: Regression Results

Technique	Model Code	Feature Type	IN Set Train r	IN Set Validation r	PH Set Train r	PH Set Validation r
Ridge Regression	RR-1	RS/LR	0.42	0.51	0.47	0.44
	RR-2	Pure ML	0.46	0.48	0.60	0.54
	RR-3	Crowd Grades	0.61	0.67	0.61	0.71
	RR-4	ML-CS	0.64	0.70	0.77	0.60
	RR-5	All	0.74	0.74	0.76	0.79
SVM	SVM-1	RS/LR	0.42	0.51	0.49	0.43
	SVM-2	Pure ML	0.44	0.46	0.60	0.54
	SVM-3	Crowd Grades	0.62	0.57	0.60	0.70
	SVM-4	ML-CS	0.60	0.61	0.76	0.61
	SVM-5	All	0.75	0.74	0.75	0.78
Neural Networks	NN-1	RS/LR	0.47	0.51	0.47	0.47
	NN-2	Pure ML	0.60	0.44	0.55	0.49
	NN-3	Crowd Grades	0.61	0.57	0.58	0.63
	NN-4	ML-CS	0.68	0.58	0.62	0.61
	NN-5	All	0.76	0.75	0.76	0.78

6.3 Regression Modeling

Regression Modeling and the steps described herein were performed separately for IN and PH set. Each set was split into two sets: train and validation. The train set had 67% of the sample points whereas the validation set had 33%. The split was done randomly making sure that the grade distribution in both the sets was similar. While learning the model, a 3-fold cross validation was performed on the train sample.

Linear ridge regression, Neural Networks and SVM regression with different kernels were used to build the models. The least cross-validation error was used to select the models. We used some simple techniques for feature selection including forward feature selection and the algorithm which removes all but the k highest correlating features.

In next paragraphs, we explain the steps performed in tuning regression parameters and feature set used to build regression model.

Regression parameters: For linear regression with regularization, optimal ridge coefficient λ, between 1 and 1000, was selected based on the least RMS error in cross-validation. For support vector machines we tested two kernels: linear and radial basis function. In order to select the optimal SVM model, we varied the penalty factor C, parameters γ and ϵ, the SVM kernel and the selected set of values that gave us the lowest RMS error in cross-validation. The Neural Networks model had one hidden layer and 5 to 10 neurons.

Feature sets used: The experiments were carried on five sets of features: first, features generated by automatic speech transcription of spontaneous speech using a speech recognizer (Pure ML approach); second, a set of features generated by force aligning read/repeated by candidates (another ML only approach referred to as RS/LR approach, see Section 4); third, a set of features pertaining to grades given by the crowd; fourth, NLP and FA features generated by force aligning spontaneous speech on crowdsourced transcription (ML-CS approach) and fifth, NLP, FA features from crowdsourced transcription and Crowd Grades.

In the following subsection, the features pertaining to ML-CS approach are referred to as ML-CS, those pertaining to natural language processing on crowdsourced transcription are referred to as NLP features while the one pertaining to crowd grades are referred to as Crowd Grades.

6.4 Observations

The results of the experiments are tabulated in Table 2. We report the Pearson coefficient of correlation (r) for the different models against the expert grades for IN and PH samples. These are the results for the models selected according to least cross-validation error. The best cross-validation error in case of SVMs was obtained for the linear kernel.

All the following observations are based on the validation error. All the three techniques perform similarly with Neural Networks doing slightly worse in some cases. The broad trends across feature–sets remain similar across different modeling techniques. We will be referring to the ridge regression results for further discussion.

Firstly, it is observed that the read/repeat features predict the spontaneous speech score with low accuracy ($r_{\text{PH}} = 0.47$, $r_{\text{IN}} = 0.47$) for both samples. This implies that read/repeat speech and derived features are inadequate to grade a person's spontaneous speech, the ultimate test of a person's spoken language skills. The second observation is that the ML-only approach using spontaneous speech features (Model IN_RR-2, PH_RR-2) is also inadequate to grade spontaneous speech and does worse than approaches that uses features from crowdsourced transcription (Model PH/IN_RR-4). This clearly shows the value of getting accurate transcription from workers towards better features and model.

Further, among the crowdsourcing approaches, we find that the crowd grades (Model RR-3) does equivalently well (and sometimes worse) than the model using features derived from the crowdsourced speech (Model IN/PH_RR-4). However, when we combine all the features from crowdsourcing including the crowd grades, we find much better prediction accuracy ($r_{\text{IN}} = 0.74$ and $r_{\text{PH}} = 0.79$). This shows that the crowd grades feature provides some orthogonal information as compared to the features from the crowdsourced transcription, towards predicting the grade given by experts.

The validation r for Model IN_RR-5 is 0.74 and Model PH_RR-5 is 0.79. We find that the expert agreement on the validation sample is 0.77 and 0.82 respectively for each model. Thus, our predicted score rivals the agreement of experts. This shows great promise for the technique to be used in a high stake test setting.

In summary, we show the following:

- Read/repeat speech features are inadequate to predict spontaneous speech scores.
- ML only approach based on spontaneous speech samples is also inadequate for the purpose.
- Features derived from crowdsourced transcription (or even crowd grades) do better than a ML only approach.
- When considering features from crowdsourced transcription and crowd grades together, we can predict spontaneous speech scores as well as those done by experts.

6.5 Case Study

We studied the deployment of our spontaneous speech scoring algorithm at a hiring event of a potential customer in Philippines. The company was using another automated speech evaluation product. The scoring of this product was based on the read and repeat speech of the candidate and could not do spontaneous evaluation. The customer was not satisfied with the product and experienced high type-1 error. The recruitment event had 500 applicants for the role of a customer support executive, who had to talk to native English speakers. The new scoring algorithm was tested on a subset of 150 students. All these candidates took the complete SVAR test along with the spontaneous speech section. The same set of students also took the existing speech grading product of the other vendor. These candidates were also evaluated by an expert designated by the company. The expert graded each candidate's speech as hirable or not-hireable based on the requirements for the position.

We sweep thresholds across the scores from our spontaneous speech algorithm, read speech scores used by the company and SVAR read speech scores, to enable hirable/ not-hireable decisions. Figure 4 shows the trade-off curve between rejecting good candidates (type-2 error) and selecting bad candidates (type-1 error). The spontaneous speech score ROC curve completely dominates the read speech by both SVAR and the existing product.

Based on one of the trade-off points on the curve, we are correctly able to identify 90% of the hirable candidates while allowing 21% of not-hireable candidates into the final hiring pool. The extant approach however could only identify 69% of the hirable candidates while allowing approximately the same amount of not-hireable candidates. Another trade-off point we consider is with a much lower type-1 error. By selecting an appropriate point, we were able to bring down the percentage of not-hireable candidates in the final set to 15%, while rejecting around 30% of the hirable candidates. On a similar selection percentage of not-hireable candidates, the other scoring algorithms were rejecting around 50% hirable candidates.

The above case study clearly shows the superior candidate selection capabilities of the spontaneous speech scoring algorithm over the score based on the read speech of the candidate. This preliminary case study demonstrates how our approach gives immediate benefit and saves time of the interviewers by massively reducing the number of good candidates being rejected while also reducing the number of bad candidates selected, thus improving the overall hiring quality.

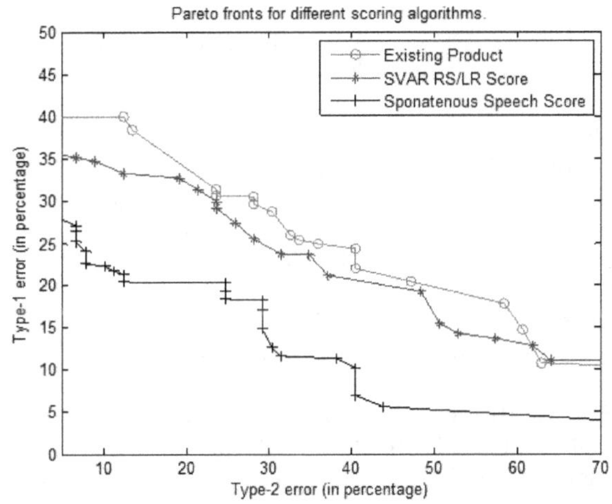

Figure 4: Classification errors of different scoring algorithms

7. CONCLUSIONS

We addressed the problem of evaluating spontaneous speech using a combination of machine learning and crowdsourcing. To achieve this, we post the task of speech transcription to the crowd. Additionally, we also get spoken English grades from the crowd. We are able to derive accurate features by force aligning the speech sample on the crowdsourced text. We experimented our technique on expert–graded speech samples of adult non–native speakers from India and Philippines. Using these features in a regression model, we are able to predict expert grades with much higher accuracy than a machine learning only approach. These features also predict equivalent or better than crowd grades and a combination of these two outperforms all other approaches. Our approach shows an accuracy that rivals that of expert agreement.

Our technique has a promise of higher accuracy but has some trade-offs compared to fully automated approaches. First, there is a cost for every assessment done and the scalability depends on the number of non-expert workers available. Though these drawbacks exist, we were able get tasks done inexpensively. We recently had the crowd rate a hundred samples in a day without any challenge. Second, our approach doesn't provide instant grades. This works fine in many scenarios, but doesn't cater well to providing real-time feedback. Real time crowdsourcing has been an active area of research [25, 26] and is an area for future work for us as well.

8. REFERENCES

[1] Menucha Birenbaum and Kikumi K Tatsuoka. Open-ended versus multiple-choice response formats - it does make a difference for diagnostic purposes. *Applied Psychological Measurement*, 11(4):385–395, 1987.

[2] Varun Aggarwal, Shahank Srikant, and Vinay Shashidhar. Principles for using machine learning in the assessment of open response items: Programming assessment as a case study. *NIPS - Workshop on Data Driven Education*, 2013.

[3] P Mitros, Vikas Paruchuri, John Rogosic, and Diana Huang. An integrated framework for the grading of freeform responses. *MIT Learning International Networks Consortium*, 2013.

[4] Cliff E Beevers and Jane S Paterson. Automatic assessment of problem-solving skills in mathematics. *Active Learning in Higher Education*, 4(2):127–144, 2003.

[5] SVAR. 2014. http://www.aspiringminds.in/talent-evaluation/spoken-english-SVAR.html.

[6] Klaus Zechner, Derrick Higgins, Xiaoming Xi, and David M Williamson. Automatic scoring of non-native spontaneous speech in tests of spoken english. *Speech Communication*, 51(10):883–895, 2009.

[7] Sumit Basu, Chuck Jacobs, and Lucy Vanderwende. Powergrading: a clustering approach to amplify human effort for short answer grading. *TACL*, 1:391–402, 2013.

[8] Donald E Powers, Jill C Burstein, Martin Chodorow, Mary E Fowles, and Karen Kukich. Stumping *e-rater*: challenging the validity of automated essay scoring. *Computers in Human Behavior*, 18(2):103–134, 2002.

[9] Cem Akkaya, Alexander Conrad, Janyce Wiebe, and Rada Mihalcea. Amazon mechanical turk for subjectivity word sense disambiguation. In *Proceedings of the NAACL HLT 2010 Workshop on Creating Speech and Language Data with Amazon's Mechanical Turk*, pages 195–203. Association for Computational Linguistics, 2010.

[10] ASID Lang and Joshua Rio-Ross. Using amazon mechanical turk to transcribe historical handwritten documents. *The Code4Lib Journal*, 2011.

[11] Matthew Marge, Satanjeev Banerjee, and Alexander I Rudnicky. Using the amazon mechanical turk for transcription of spoken language. In *Acoustics Speech and Signal Processing (ICASSP), 2010 IEEE International Conference on*, pages 5270–5273. IEEE, 2010.

[12] Thierry Buecheler, Jan Henrik Sieg, Rudolf M Füchslin, and Rolf Pfeifer. Crowdsourcing, open innovation and collective intelligence in the scientific method-a research agenda and operational framework. In *ALIFE*, pages 679–686, 2010.

[13] Mark Lejk and Michael Wyvill. The effect of the inclusion of selfassessment with peer assessment of contributions to a group project: A quantitative study of secret and agreed assessments. *Assessment & Evaluation in Higher Education*, 26(6):551–561, 2001.

[14] Nathan Van Houdnos. Can the internet grade math? crowdsourcing a complex scoring task and picking the optimal crowd size. *Dietrich College of Humanities and Social Sciences at Research Showcase @ CMU*, 2011.

[15] Joel R Tetreault, Elena Filatova, and Martin Chodorow. Rethinking grammatical error annotation and evaluation with the amazon mechanical turk. In *Proceedings of the NAACL HLT 2010 Fifth Workshop on Innovative Use of NLP for Building Educational Applications*, pages 45–48. Association for Computational Linguistics, 2010.

[16] Nitin Madnani, Joel Tetreault, Martin Chodorow, and Alla Rozovskaya. They can help: using crowdsourcing to improve the evaluation of grammatical error detection systems. In *Proceedings of the 49th Annual Meeting of the Association for Computational Linguistics: Human Language Technologies: short papers-Volume 2*, pages 508–513. Association for Computational Linguistics, 2011.

[17] Sherrie A Kossoudji. English language ability and the labor market opportunities of hispanic and east asian immigrant men. *Journal of Labor Economics*, pages 205–228, 1988.

[18] Elizabeth J Erling and Philip Seargeant. *English and development: Policy, pedagogy and globalization*, volume 17. Multilingual Matters, 2013.

[19] Cahit Guven and Asadul Islam. Age at migration, language proficiency and socio-economic outcomes: Evidence from australia. Technical report, 2013.

[20] Kåre Sjölander. An hmm-based system for automatic segmentation and alignment of speech. In *Proceedings of Fonetik*, volume 2003, pages 93–96. Citeseer, 2003.

[21] Chinmay E Kulkarni, Richard Socher, Michael S Bernstein, and Scott R Klemmer. Scaling short-answer grading by combining peer assessment with algorithmic scoring. In *Proceedings of the first ACM conference on Learning@ scale conference*, pages 99–108. ACM, 2014.

[22] Marina Boia, Claudiu Cristian Musat, and Boi Faltings. Acquiring commonsense knowledge for sentiment analysis using human computation. In *Proceedings of the companion publication of the 23rd international conference on World wide web companion*, pages 225–226. International World Wide Web Conferences Steering Committee, 2014.

[23] Ece Kamar, Severin Hacker, and Eric Horvitz. Combining human and machine intelligence in large-scale crowdsourcing. In *Proceedings of the 11th International Conference on Autonomous Agents and Multiagent Systems-Volume 1*, pages 467–474. International Foundation for Autonomous Agents and Multiagent Systems, 2012.

[24] Sivan Sabato and Adam Kalai. Feature multi-selection among subjective features. *arXiv preprint arXiv:1302.4297*, 2013.

[25] Michael S Bernstein, Joel Brandt, Robert C Miller, and David R Karger. Crowds in two seconds: Enabling realtime crowd-powered interfaces. In *Proceedings of the 24th annual ACM symposium on User interface software and technology*, pages 33–42. ACM, 2011.

[26] Walter S Lasecki, Christopher D Miller, and Jeffrey P Bigham. Warping time for more effective real-time crowdsourcing. In *Proceedings of the SIGCHI Conference on Human Factors in Computing Systems*, pages 2033–2036. ACM, 2013.

[27] Cambridge EOCL Examinations. Using the *CEFR*: Principles of good practice. *at University of Cambridge*, 2011.

[28] Eric John Dobson. *English Pronunciation, 1500-1700: Phonology*, volume 2. Clarendon Press, 1957.

[29] Christopher Brumfit and Christopher J Brumfit. *Communicative methodology in language teaching: The roles of fluency and accuracy*, volume 129. Cambridge University Press Cambridge, 1984.

[30] Robert Stalnaker. The problem of logical omniscience, ii. context and content: Essays on intentionality in speech and thought (pp. 255–273), 1999.

[31] David Brazil. *A grammar of speech.* Oxford University Press, USA, 1995.

[32] Voxforge. 2014. http://www.voxforge.org/home/dev/autoaudioseg.

[33] Mehdi Hosseini, Ingemar J Cox, Nataša Milić-Frayling, Gabriella Kazai, and Vishwa Vinay. On aggregating labels from multiple crowd workers to infer relevance of documents. In *Advances in information retrieval*, pages 182–194. Springer, 2012.

[34] Steve Young, Gunnar Evermann, Mark Gales, Thomas Hain, Dan Kershaw, Xunying Liu, Gareth Moore, Julian Odell, Dave Ollason, Dan Povey, et al. The htk book (for htk version 3.4). *Cambridge university engineering department*, 2(2):2–3, 2006.

[35] John S Garofolo, Lori F Lamel, William M Fisher, Jonathon G Fiscus, and David S Pallett. Darpa timit acoustic-phonetic continous speech corpus cd-rom. nist speech disc 1-1.1. *NASA STI/Recon Technical Report N*, 93:27403, 1993.

[36] Leonardo Neumeyer, Horacio Franco, Mitchel Weintraub, and Patti Price. Automatic text-independent pronunciation scoring of foreign language student speech. In *Spoken Language, 1996. ICSLP 96. Proceedings., Fourth International Conference on*, volume 3, pages 1457–1460. IEEE, 1996.

[37] Catia Cucchiarini, Helmer Strik, and Lou Boves. Quantitative assessment of second language learners' fluency by means of automatic speech recognition technology. *The Journal of the Acoustical Society of America*, 107(2):989–999, 2000.

[38] LightSide. 2013. http://lightsidelabs.com/.

[39] AfterTheDeadline. 2014. http://www.afterthedeadline.com/.

[40] Gabriele Paolacci, Jesse Chandler, and Panagiotis G Ipeirotis. Running experiments on amazon mechanical turk. *Judgment and Decision making*, 5(5):411–419, 2010.

[41] Amazon Mechanical Turk. 2014. https://requester.mturk.com/tour.

[42] Jonathan G Fiscus. A post-processing system to yield reduced word error rates: Recognizer output voting error reduction (rover). In *Automatic Speech Recognition and Understanding, 1997. Proceedings., 1997 IEEE Workshop on*, pages 347–354. IEEE, 1997.

[43] Ahmet Aker, Mahmoud El-Haj, M-Dyaa Albakour, and Udo Kruschwitz. Assessing crowdsourcing quality through objective tasks. In *LREC*, pages 1456–1461. Citeseer, 2012.

[44] Quoc Viet Hung Nguyen, Tam Nguyen Thanh, Tran Lam Ngoc, and Karl Aberer. An evaluation of aggregation techniques in crowdsourcing. In *The 14th International Conference on Web Information System Engineering (WISE), 2013*, number EPFL-CONF-187456, 2013.

Effective Audience Extension in Online Advertising

Jianqiang Shen *
Turn Inc.
901 Marshall Street
Redwood City, CA, USA
jshen@turn.com

Sahin Cem Geyik *
Turn Inc.
901 Marshall Street
Redwood City, CA, USA
sgeyik@turn.com

Ali Dasdan
Turn Inc.
901 Marshall Street
Redwood City, CA, USA
adasdan@turn.com

ABSTRACT

In digital advertising, advertisers want to reach the right audience over media channels such as display, mobile, video, or social at the appropriate cost. The right audience for an advertiser consists of existing customers as well as valuable prospects, those that can potentially be turned into future customers. Identifying valuable prospects is called the *audience extension* problem because advertisers find new customers by extending the desirable criteria for their starting point, which is their existing audience or customers. The complexity of the audience extension problem stems from the difficulty of defining desirable criteria objectively, the number of desirable criteria (such as similarity, diversity, performance) to simultaneously satisfy, and the expected runtime (a few minutes) to find a solution over billions of cookie-based users. In this paper, we formally define the audience extension problem, propose an algorithm that extends a given audience set efficiently under multiple desirable criteria, and experimentally validate its performance. Instead of iterating over individual users, the algorithm takes in Boolean rules that define the seed audience and returns a new set of Boolean rules that corresponds to the extended audience that satisfy the multiple criteria.

Categories and Subject Descriptors

H.3.5 [**Information Storage and Retrieval**]: Online Information Services; I.2.1 [**Artificial Intelligence**]: Applications and Expert Systems

General Terms

Algorithms, Application

Keywords

Online advertising; Targeting; Audience Extension

---

* The authors contributed to this work equally.

KDD'15, August 10-13, 2015, Sydney, NSW, Australia.
 ISBN 978-1-4503-3664-2/15/08 ...$15.00.
DOI: http://dx.doi.org/10.1145/2783258.2788603.

1. INTRODUCTION

Advertising budgets are increasingly moving towards programmatic or digital advertising. In digital advertising, the ecosystem is roughly divided into four main entities: Demand side platforms (DSPs), ad exchanges, supply side platforms (SSPs), and data management platforms (DMPs). Advertisers are on the demand side, i.e. they want to reach the right audience at the right place, cost, and time. Advertisers use DMPs to understand and define their audiences and DSPs to define and execute advertising campaigns to reach those audiences.

Access to an audience occurs through a number of ad formats (such as banner ads, video ads, etc.) on a number of devices (such as desktops, TVs, mobile phones, etc.). The audience is of course on the supply side, paying their attention to publishers through browsing web pages, playing games on mobile phones, shopping on e-commerce sites, etc. SSPs help publishers to monetize what keeps bringing audience to publishers.

Ad exchanges are the bridges between demand and supply sides. Given a user in an online context, ad exchanges perform a match between advertisers (i.e. bids and ads) and publishers (i.e. ad-space) in real-time. It is usually the case that the highest bid wins the match [18].

DMPs have been emerging as a central hub to seamlessly (and rapidly) collect, integrate, manage and activate large volumes of user data [10]. Such user data could be first-party data (i.e., historical user data collected by advertisers in their private customer relationship management systems), or third-party data (i.e., data provided by third-party data partners, typically each specializing in a specific type of data, e.g., demographics, credit scores, buying intentions, etc.). After advertisers utilize DMPs to tie their existing customers to their digital identities (fully anonymous without any personally identifiable information), they could run two kinds of advertising campaigns: retargeting campaigns or prospecting campaigns. The former are run to target existing customers with ads that may help them make more purchases. The latter are run to reach new audiences and convert some portion of them to customers.

In prospecting campaigns, the first and probably the most important question is to define the right audience to reach. By leveraging the data on DMPs, an advertiser can set up a specific segment (groupings of users according to some rules, e.g. "male users in California of ages 25-35") towards which to target their advertisements. For example, to focus on performance, advertisers can target audiences that have previously visited their websites to maximize the likelihood of conversion (e.g. product purchase, subscription, filling out a form, etc.); to promote their brand, advertisers can target audiences that are marked with a given demographic profile by some third-party data provider (e.g. "Parents of Infants" marked by an independent data provider).

Such audience segments are usually manually created for multiple reasons. Most of the time, manual generation of targeted user segments is due to advertiser policy, e.g. a sports company may only target certain age ranges, or a certain income group. Such a choice can be easily justified even if the online performance (clicks or conversions) of such segments is not that good, since the advertiser may want to reach these audiences to improve company recognition (this recognition will help offline purchases etc.). Another reason is to achieve additional filtering on top of automatically generated user audiences to improve performance and obey company policy. The final reason can be listed as simply the intuition of the advertiser, i.e. carrying of advertiser experience/know-how from different domains into the online advertising domain.

In many cases, the manually created segment only covers a small percentage of population and needs to be expanded. Here are two use cases:

- *Predictive targeting*: The advertiser identified a group of clickers. With the assumption that users with similar profiles tend to behave similarly, now they want to find other audiences having similar profiles with those clickers and deliver advertisement impressions to them.
- *Data sparsity*: It is very difficult to collect reliable demographic data on an audience. For example, though there could be plenty of "Parents of Infants" in the audience pool, only a few of them are actually marked as "Parents of Infants". Advertisers want to find other audiences that might also be parents of infants.

In this paper we focus on the topic of what we call *audience extension*. This problem deals with how to best extend the advertiser-provided set of targeted segments so that the new set of users in the extended segment is similar to the original segments' set of users, and performance metrics (such as click-through rate, conversion rate, or return-on-investment which is the ratio of the amount of monetary value received from clicks and conversions to the amount of money spent by the advertiser on showing impressions) are preserved or improved in the extended segments. Furthermore, by extending the initially provided audience, we increase the advertiser's reach of users, as well as the amount of money that can be spent on impressions (spending capacity [13]) by the advertiser. The contributions of this paper are as follows:

- Formal definition of audience extension problem in the online advertising domain,
- Multiple algorithms to extend audiences initially provided by an advertiser,
- Parallel implementation details of our audience extension framework which scales to the terabyte datasets in the online advertising domain,
- Evaluation of different methodologies proposed in terms of their effect on user reach, click/conversion performance etc.

To the best of our knowledge, this is the first paper that focuses on the topic of audience extension, and fills up a significant void in the literature on the methodical examination of this crucial industry problem.

The rest of the paper is organized as follows. We give a more detailed description as well as some explanatory examples of *audience extension* problem in § 2. Previous work in the literature for similar problems is discussed in § 3. Later, we give multiple methodologies for solving audience extension problem in § 4, and the parallel implementation details needed to scale to our domain's large data sizes in § 5. Finally, we conclude the paper with the evaluation of the proposed audience extension methodologies in § 6, followed by the paper's summary as well as our future work suggestions in § 7.

2. PROBLEM DEFINITION

Background and Motivation. In digital advertising, users are usually referred to as the audience (for advertisements). From the business perspective, advertisers wish to learn everything about their audience: their demographics, psychographics, online and offline behavior, and how they respond to different types of advertisements. In Turn's DMP system, each user is essentially a cookie ID with an associated profile data. Examples of data are visits to specific pages or purchases, user demographics (age, gender, income), or user intent (searching for a used car on an auction site). User data can come from an online context (pixels placed on pages) or could be collected offline, through a matching process joined to online users. Data can be owned by the advertiser (first-party) or can be purchased (third-party).

First-party and third-party data usually originate from the data source's own cookie space and identifying the users across all these platforms remains a constant challenge. Inside Turn, we achieve this by syncing cookie IDs, which allows us to incorporate different types of data from a variety of partners and make the data actionable. For example, now advertiser "InfantMilk" might observe that users purchasing their product usually have label "YoungCouple" from a third party. They can then utilize such information so that the impressions are delivered towards this specific population. Advertisers have to pay an impression-based fee for using third-party data, which is called *data cost*; and in reality, it is another reason for audience extension. An advertiser may prefer to utilize the extended audience rules, especially if the third-party data in the extended rules have a lower data cost.

Such a holistic view of the audience data is a key factor to design of highly targeted ad campaigns that would maximize the return-on-investment (ROI). First and third-party data essentially tag users into all kinds of label categories. An advertiser can then decide the audience population for advertisement delivery by designing some rules to check whether a user has some specific labels. In this paper, we focus on how to extend such a manually-selected audience population to improve audience size and preserve the performance metrics. Each user is represented as a bag of data categories $u_i =< c_{i1}, c_{i2}, ..., c_{in} >$, where c_{ij} is category j assigned to user u_i from some data source.

DEFINITION 1. *A* category variable $I_j(u_i)$ *is a boolean indicator which is 1 if user u_i has category label c_j, 0 otherwise. Sometimes we simplify $I_j(u_i)$ as c_j for brevity. An* audience rule *is a propositional logic formula where each variable is a category variable.*

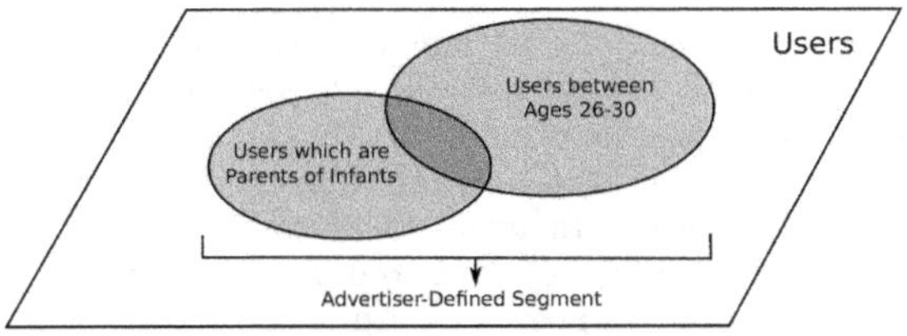

(a) Example of an advertiser-defined segment

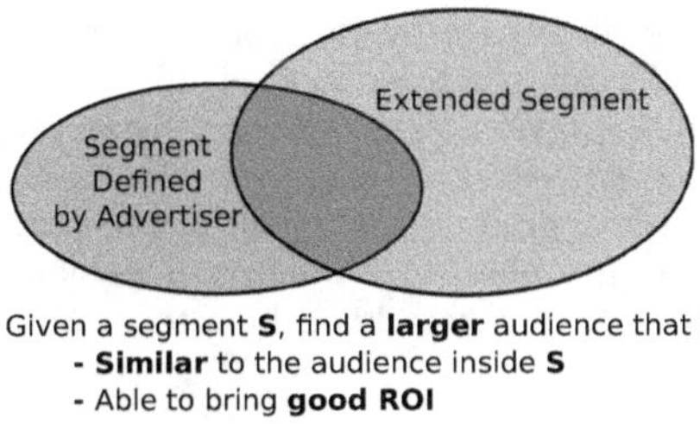

(b) Example for audience extension problem

Figure 1: Explainative examples for advertiser-defined segments and audience extension problem.

DEFINITION 2. *A* segment *is a portion of the online users that qualify for the advertiser-defined audience rule. Such rules are propositional logic formulas operating over user properties that can be first-party or third-party.*

Two examples of advertiser-defined segments are given in Figure 1(a). In the figure, segment "*Age Range 26-30*" is defined as the propositional logic formula

$$(\text{Age26} \vee \text{Age27} \vee \text{Age28} \vee \text{Age29} \vee \text{Age30}),$$

which checks whether a user has one of the given age labels. Segment "*Parents of Infants*" is defined as

$$(\text{ParentOfInfant}),$$

which checks whether a user has label "ParentOfInfant". Both segments are subsets of the total set of users. The intersection of these two segments can further be defined as a new segment which essentially covers young parents of infants. If an advertiser originally targets those young parents of infants and needs to expand its audience pool, *Parents of Infants* or *Age Range 26-30* will be a natural choice.

Research Problem. Given the fact that there are billions of users labeled with all kinds of data categories, advertisers usually conclude that their manually created segment is small and needs to be expanded. This *audience extension* problem can be formally defined as follows:

DEFINITION 3. *Given an advertiser-defined segment rule S,* Audience Extension *recommends a new user population with a segment rule S' such that,*

$$sim(S, S') > \alpha \ ,$$
$$perf(S') - perf(S) > \beta \ , \text{ and}$$
$$|aud(S \vee S')| >> |aud(S)| \ . \qquad (1)$$

Above, *sim* is a similarity score which looks at how similar the two audiences (defined by S and S') are, *perf* is the performance metric (conversion/click rate, ROI etc.) calculated for the two audiences, and finally, $|aud(S)|$ denotes the size (number of users that fall into the rule, or *reach*) of segment S (please note that $|aud(S \vee S')| < |aud(S)| + |aud(S')|$ in most cases due to intersection of users between two segments). Note that there could be multiple definitions to calculate *sim* and *perf*, as we will show later.

An example for the above problem definition is given in Figure 1(b). In the figure, we want the intersection between two segments to be large, and the extended segment to bring additional reach (novel set of users) and have good performance (only ROI has been given in the figure for conciseness). We will be exploring multiple methodologies that we developed for our system in § 4.

There are multiple factors that make audience extension challenging. First, it is usually infeasible to optimize towards each requirement at the same time. Users which are highly similar to the seed audience are usually rare, let alone the set of events (clicks, conversions) that they are involved in, which are necessary to compute their performance. We have to keep a balance among different criteria. Second, computational efficiency is extremely desirable in audience extension. There are tens of thousands of categories in our system and any propositional logic formula of them could be a segment. Given the huge number of possible category combinations, pre-computing the recommendation offline for each possible segment would be expensive. A fast audience extension algorithm is critical for user experience. Finally, advertisers want the extension results to be easily understood, evaluated and modified. This excludes most of black-box machine learning methods for our purpose. In this paper, the search space of S' we focus on is the logical disjunction forms of categories, i.e. $S' = (c_1 \vee c_2 \vee .. \vee c_m)$. Like other overwhelmingly common "*Find Good Items*" tasks in the *recommender systems* literature [15], we would suggest a list of the recommended categories, along with predictions (scores) for how much the advertisers would like them.

3. PREVIOUS WORK

Our problem is significantly different from another audience extension definition used in online advertising [1, 2], which allows publishers to earn extra money by tagging users who visit their websites, so that this information can later be used by themselves or other advertisers to target those users even when they are outside of the publisher's domain. As explained in the introduction section, we focus on methodically increasing the audience population based on an advertiser's manually created rule. Research work in some other domains is related to ours and could potentially be applied.

Understanding User Interests. In order to perform effective advertisement targeting, it is critical to understand user interests. As users interact with content and advertising, their passive behavior can reveal their interests towards advertising [20]. Since there are usually plenty of clicks while other information is not available at a large scale, most existing work in behavioral targeting uses clicks on advertisements as a proxy of interest [8, 22, 27]. Maximizing clicks does not necessarily imply maximizing purchase activities or transactions which directly translate to advertiser's revenue [20]. Recently, advertisers have been willing to share individual responses to advertisements, making it feasible to use machine learning methods to develop models that are specifically optimized for conversions [5, 4]. There have also been some efforts in the literature that approximate user interest with demographics. For example, Joshi et al. [16] aim to generate textual data for each user based on demographic information, by which the authors aim at efficiently matching advertisements to potentially interested users.

User Clustering. User segmentation, which aims at grouping users into user segments with similar behaviors, is crucial to behavioral targeting. If users with similar purchase intentions can be automatically clustered into the same segment, advertisers may gain more profit from advertisement delivery. [24, 3] utilize Latent Dirichlet Allocation (LDA), and [26] utilizes probabilistic latent semantic analysis (pLSA) to group users for advertising, hence generating relevant audience subsets over the available users. In this way, it is possible to evaluate the benefit of each group for each advertiser. While these works are useful in matching appropriate advertisers with appropriate audiences, they do not take into account either advertiser-provided initial segments (our method is basically how to build on top of such prior information), or provide an option for advertisers to choose their audiences. As we will explain later, we provide such an option via weighting of different audience metrics.

Extending Social Networks. Research shows that users connect to both friends they already know offline and new friends they discover on social networking sites [9]. Given the size of social networking sites, finding known contacts and interesting new friends to connect with on the site can both be a challenge. It has been shown that algorithms based on text content or friendship connections are effective in providing people recommendations and can significantly increase the number of friends of a user on the site [6]. An interesting work given in [19] actually may intuitively be utilized as a very feasible way to extend audiences. The authors look at friendship information between users (collected via an online social networking platform) for targeting. It would be intuitive to have the friendship network as a graph (where nodes are online users, and edges represent friendship). Given an initial set of nodes (users) in this graph by the advertiser as the original audiences (i.e. an advertiser-provided subgraph/audience), we can generate an extended audience as the users that have a direct edge (or we can look at n-hop neighborhood depending on advertiser preference or performance metrics etc.) to the original subgraph. [19] does not follow this kind of route, and unfortunately such friendship information is often proprietary (not even available as third-party data).

Recommender Systems. Audience Extension is a special case of making recommendations. There is a wealth of research on recommender systems [15]. One of the most successful technologies for recommender systems, called collaborative filtering, has been developed and improved over the past decade to the point where a wide variety of algorithms exist for generating recommendations. It utilizes similarities of preferences among users to recommend items such as movies for a user to consume. It does not really analyze the actual content of the items, but instead require users to indicate preferences on them, usually in the form of ratings.

Since advertisers typically do not share their created segments, applying many of the existing recommender techniques could potentially be very challenging. To address Audience Extension, we can approach Collaborative Filtering from two perspectives. First, we can treat each segment as an item and find rules used by similar advertisers. This however may raise advertiser privacy concerns. Instead, we could treat each individual audience as an item and find patterns. This is what we adopted in this paper - look into similarity to recommend audiences.

Industry Patents. In terms of patents, there is a single one which is remotely relevant to our work. The authors of [11] describe their approach of Audience Extension, which is quite different from what we propose in this paper. They suggest assigning a score (Audience Extension Score) that reflects the likelihood of each particular user to exhibit a desired behavior, such as desired TV viewing behavior or purchasing behavior. The patent is not specific on how to assign such scores, or how to optimize based on an advertiser's different preferences. Finally, two patents [12, 23] do mention the problem of audience extension, however they do not provide any details on how to recommend extended audiences.

4. METHODOLOGY

Based on the problem formulation, we will present the methodologies we applied to extend advertiser-defined segments. As it will be seen, these are either trying to maximize one single function given in the problem definition, or try to find a balance between them.

4.1 Purely Greedy Approach

As we explained before, the segment(s) provided to us by the advertiser is a propositional rule S, involving n categories $c_1, .., c_n$. This of course does not suggest that the audiences (set of targeted users) belonging to this segment only have these categories. Rather, the users within the segment may have many different properties, but they have been included in this segment due to the fact that they are tagged with the provided set of categories in the segment definition. Therefore, our first method, which we call *purely greedy*, aims to recommend the most frequently occurring set of categories in the segment's audiences, which are **not** in the segment definition. This is a variation of the greedy set cover algorithm, where we want to either completely cover the original segment's audience, or until our newly recommended segment's audience reaches a certain size. Details are given in Algorithm 1.

There are multiple disadvantages of the purely greedy approach. First is the way we generate the extension. Since the algorithm is basically the application of the set cover algorithm, the original segment is a subset of the extended audience. Other than this, the algorithm neither looks at the additional reach of the extended segment (covering the original segment does not mean the extended segment added new users to the original segment, since it can be very close in size to the original audience), nor the performance. Extension is based directly on the set cover algorithm, and at no point of this scheme do we check the return-on-investment (ROI) or any other metric of the newly recommended users. This effect can be seen with a sample we picked from our system which is given in Table 1. The original advertiser-defined segment in this example is a single rule to pick up users in the age range 20-30 (we receive this tag info from the third-party data provider "TP 1"). As it can be seen, the extended audience is not really a gain since it basically either divides the age range to partitions, or presents some obvious facts (the user is a child in the family, i.e. is not the head of household, or makes under 15K dollars a year),

Algorithm 1: Greedy approach to extend an audience

Input: S: original segment, m: desired audience size

$\Omega \leftarrow aud(S)$;

Collect $C \leftarrow c_{n+1 \to n+m}$, all categories from the users in $aud(S)$ that are not in definition of S, such that
$C \cap S = \emptyset$ and,
$\forall c_j \in C, \exists\, u_i \in aud(S)\ s.t.\ u_i \in aud(c_j)$;

$\forall c_j \in C$, count the # of users in Ω that have c_j ;

Order C into C_{sorted} according to the number of users belonging to each category $c_j \in C$, descending ;

$S' \leftarrow \emptyset$ //extended audience is empty at the beginning;

while $|aud(S \vee S')| < m$ *and* $C \neq \emptyset$ **do**

  Get $c_j \in C_{\text{sorted}}$ which is the most frequent ;

  $S' \leftarrow S' \vee c_j$;

  $C \leftarrow C - c_j$;

  $\Omega \leftarrow \Omega - aud(c_j)$;

  $\forall c_j \in C$, recalculate the number of users ;

  Recalculate C_{sorted} from the new C ;

Recommend $S \vee S'$ as the new segment

Table 1: Extended audiences generated in our system for the age range 20-30 according to the purely greedy approach.

Rule Property	Data Source	Rule Parent	Rule Definition
Original Rule	TP 1	Age Range	20-30
Extended Rule	TP 1	Family Position	Child
Extended Rule	TP 1	Age Range	22-25
Extended Rule	TP 1	Age Range	26-35
Extended Rule	TP 1	Income	< 15K $

which comes up with an audience too big, and naturally does not follow the characteristics of the original segment. Second disadvantage with this method is on the running time. Our data have the strict mapping of users to segment rules (not vice versa), hence the set cover logic takes a long processing time, since at every point we need to recalculate the set of users that belong to a segment (this is costly in both sequential and parallel implementation, since we have to go through the audience once for each step, and our user space is in the order of hundreds of millions). Please note that we need the extension to be fast since the advertiser wants to constantly generate new segments and extend them in an interactive application (which we provide in our advertising platform). The rest of the section will be our explanation of a faster algorithm we applied with a much more feasible (better similarity, reach, and performance) recommended audience extension.

4.2 Weighted Criteria-based Algorithm

As we have shown, the greedy approach presented before does not necessarily recommend extended audiences with high reach or performance. In this section, we will present our proposed approach in balancing the necessary metrics as given in the problem definition (Eq. 1). To be exact, we start with an original advertiser-defined segment (set of categories/rules), and come up with an extended audience in a fast manner, while optimizing over the following metrics:

- **Interest:** This metric measures the similarity of the extended and original segments (directly related to *sim*(S, S') in Eq. 1),
- **Novelty:** This metric measures the additional audience size generated by the extended audience segment (directly related to *aud*$(S \vee S')$ in Eq. 1),
- **Quality:** This metric measures the performance (ROI, click-through rate or conversion rate) of the extended audience (directly related to function *perf* in Eq. 1).

Next, we will explain the calculation methods for all three of the above criteria.

4.2.1 *Calculation of* Interest *Criterion*

We have explored two methodologies for the computation of the interest criteria: (*i*) Category correlation, and (*ii*) A simple probabilistic solution (that we decided to apply in the end) which is computationally cheaper, and works well in practice.

Let's first talk about the correlation between categories. This means that if our newly recommended category (to be included in the extended segment) correlates well with the original categories then it has a high interest score. Correlation (*Pearson* correlation coefficient) of the recommended new category with an original category can be calculated as:

$$corr(c_{new}, c_{old}) = \frac{\left[\sum_{u_i \in U} (I_{c_{new}}(u_i) - \mu_{new}) (I_{c_{old}}(u_i) - \mu_{old})\right]}{\sum_{u_i \in U} \sigma_{new}\sigma_{old}} \tag{2}$$

where,

$$\mu_k = \frac{\sum_{u_i \in U} I_{c_k}(u_i)}{|U|},$$

and,

$$\sigma_k = \sqrt{\frac{\sum_{u_i \in U}(I_{c_k}(u_i) - \mu_k)^2}{|U|}}.$$

Above, $I_{c_k}(u_i)$ is the indicator function that returns 1 if c_k is a category that u_i belongs to or 0 otherwise (please also see Definition 1 in § 2). Basically, the above formulation goes over all users and calculates a metric on the overlap of two categories. Please note that in the above formulation, any category can be replaced with a segment (i.e. set of categories) and the formulas can be applied as is.

Correlation is actually a pretty valid similarity criteria, but we have decided not to use it in our proposed method due to the following reasons. The first reason is data sparsity, since most users belong to a few categories, we have observed that the computed correlation values are very close to each other (and very small) for most category pairs. Furthermore, we observed that correlation values are either too small (this is the prominent case), or too high (match perfectly), in which case the extended audience would match perfectly to the original audience, hence would be redundant.

As listed above, the second possibility we explored (and the method of computation we chose) for the interest criteria is based on a simple probabilistic formula. This formulation gives the overlap between the original segment and a newly recommended category, and is as follows:

$$sim(c_{new}, S) = p(c_{new}|S) = \frac{|aud(c_{new}) \cap aud(S)|}{|aud(S)|}.$$

This formula basically answers the following question: "If a user belongs to segment S, what is the probability that

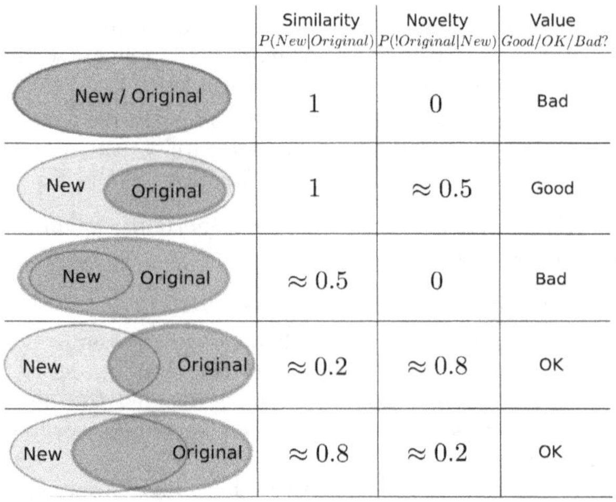

Figure 2: Examples of similarity vs. novelty in original and extended audiences.

the same user also belongs to category c_{new}?". This value measures how well the extended audience covers the original audience. Please note that the purely greedy solution we describe in § 4.1 maximizes this, but as we will show in the rest of the section, we look at *novelty* and *quality* as well.

4.2.2 *Calculation of* Novelty *Criterion*

Novelty is directly related to the size of new audience (novel audience, i.e. that does not belong to the original audience) in the newly recommended extension. Since we may have different sizes of original or extended audiences, we need a normalized value (rather than just the absolute value of the novel audience) for the novelty of a new category, which is given as the following probability:

$$nov(c_{new}, S) = p(!S|c_{new}) = 1 - p(S|c_{new})$$

$$= 1 - \frac{|aud(c_{new}) \cap aud(S)|}{|aud(c_{new})|} \quad .$$

The above formulation can easily be applied to a segment, and answers the following question: "If a user belongs to our newly recommended extended category, what is the probability that it will **not** belong to the original advertiser-provided segment/audience, hence is *novel*?". We show an interpretation of the balance between *similarity* and *novelty* in Figure 2. It can be easily seen that we need both values to be balanced, since the *goodness* of the extended audience does not depend on a single one of the metrics. Furthermore, we give some demonstration of how the metrics of *similarity* (probabilistic formula), *novelty*, and *correlation* (this is what we explored, but ended up not using, for similarity metric) look like for different segments' extensions in Tables 2, 3, and 4. Please note that the tables are created using a set of categories generated by different first/third-party providers and do not necessarily represent ground-truth (since all providers only have access to, and can reliably tag a certain subset of all users).

4.2.3 *Calculation of* Quality *Criterion*

Quality criteria can be calculated in multiple ways, depending on an advertiser's preferences. We can calculate

Table 2: Extended category similarity, novelty, and correlation metrics for the original advertiser-provided segment of "Interest: Gossip" (ordered by similarity).

Category	Sim	Nov	Corr
Interest: Arts & Entertainment	0.746	0.91	0.251
Gender: Female	0.37	0.912	0.173
Interest: News	0.328	0.911	0.163
Interest: TV & Video	0.231	0.966	0.077
Interest: Movies	0.189	0.964	0.073

Table 3: Extended category similarity, novelty, and correlation metrics for the original advertiser-provided segment of "State: California" (ordered by similarity). "*Ethnicity: CA*" represents users who were tagged by a third-party as born in California.

Category	Sim	Nov	Corr
Age: 18-34	0.642	0.721	0.415
Gender: Male	0.554	0.670	0.419
Ethnicity: CA	0.465	0.699	0.365
Politics: Democrat	0.415	0.674	0.36
Politics: Unaffiliated	0.285	0.644	0.312

click-through rate (CTR), conversion rate (CVR), or return-on-investment (ROI) for an extended category c_{new} generated for an advertiser adv as follows:

$$CTR_{c_{new}} = \frac{\sum_{u \in aud(c_{new})} click(u, adv)}{\sum_{u \in aud(c_{new})} imp(u, adv)} \quad , \tag{3}$$

$$CVR_{c_{new}} = \frac{\sum_{u \in aud(c_{new})} conv(u, adv)}{\sum_{u \in aud(c_{new})} imp(u, adv)} \quad , \tag{4}$$

$$ROI_{c_{new}} = \frac{\sum_{u \in aud(c_{new})} value(u, adv)}{\sum_{u \in aud(c_{new})} cost(u, adv)} \quad . \tag{5}$$

Above, we have

- $click(u, adv)$ is the number of clicks that user u (having category c_{new}) performed on impressions provided to it by advertiser adv,
- $imp(u, adv)$ is the number of impressions shown to user u (having category c_{new}) by advertiser adv,
- $conv(u, adv)$ is the number of conversions that user u (having category c_{new}) performed on impressions provided to it by advertiser adv,
- $cost(u, adv)$ is the amount of money spent by advertiser adv to show impressions to user u (having category c_{new}),

Table 4: Extended category similarity, novelty, and correlation metrics for the original advertiser-provided segment of "Financial: Makes Stock Trades" (ordered by similarity).

Category	Sim	Nov	Corr
Activity: Uses Financial Advisor	0.938	0.142	0.897
Trade Style: Online	0.845	0.24	0.8
Activity: Research Financial Prod.	0.779	0.366	0.702
Investment Type: Real Estate	0.774	0.443	0.655
Member: Credit Rewards Program	0.765	0.418	0.665

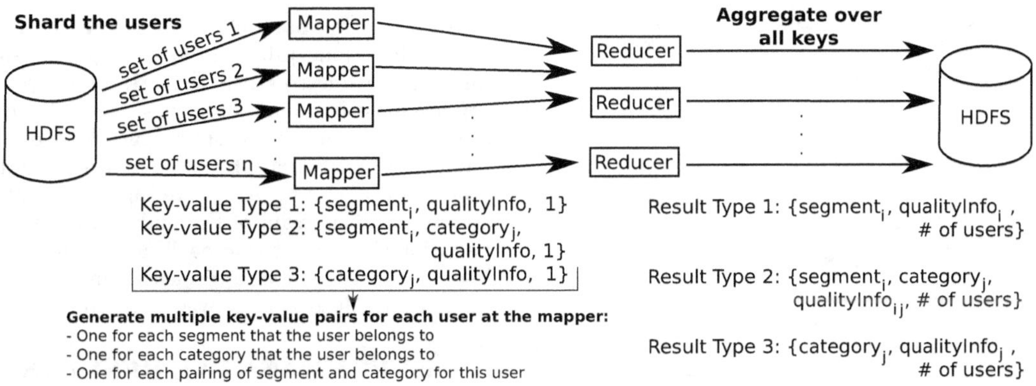

Figure 3: Implementation Details for Weighted Criteria-based Audience Extension

- $value(u, adv)$ is the amount of value (by the clicks and conversions performed) provided by user u (having category c_{new}) to advertiser adv.

Obviously, we want our new segment/audience/category to have a quality value (chosen to be any of above three) as high as possible, while having both good similarity and novelty compared to the original advertiser-provided audience /segment. The need for such balancing implies a weighted audience extension scheme, which is given next.

4.2.4 Weighted Audience Extension

Given the original segment S, our audience extension method combines the previously defined metrics *similarity* (sim), *novelty* (nov), and *quality* (q) and defines the score for a newly recommended category c_{new} as:

$$score \propto sim(c_{new}, S) \times nov(c_{new}|S) \times q(c_{new}) \quad .$$

The intuition for the above formula is to capture the extra return (via $nov(c_{new}|S) \times q(c_{new})$) from the right audience (via $sim(c_{new}, S)$). To avoid numerical instability, we take log of both sides,

$$logScore \propto log(sim(c_{new}, S)) \; + \; log(nov(c_{new}|S)) \; + \; log(q(c_{new})).$$

To make the recommending more flexible and allow advertisers to balance between criteria, we can assign weights to the log metrics, and when we replace the metrics with the formulations from the previous section, we have:

$$logScore(c_{new}|S) = \theta_1 \, log(p(c_{new}|S)) + \theta_2 \, log(1 - p(S|c_{new})) \; + \; \theta_3 \, log(q(c_{new})) \; . \quad (6)$$

The θ values are application specific, but we can furthermore entitle different extension choices to the advertiser (according to different θs), giving them the option to choose as they please. Also, the reason we did not elaborate on the formulation of *quality* metric above is because there might be different choices, and Equations 3, 4, or 5 can all be inserted in place of $q(c_{new})$.

Based on the formulation, we can sort different categories, and recommend the top-k ones to the user. Furthermore, it is always possible to pre-compute a segment-to-category matrix of goodness metrics, and immediately calculate the score online for an advertiser's application-use experience.

5. SYSTEM IMPLEMENTATION

In this section, we give implementation details on how we achieved large-scale audience extension at Turn; in specific, the weighted scheme presented in § 4.2. In the online advertising domain, we typically have to deal with virtual users (cookie spaces) in the orders of hundreds of millions. To be able to check the segment or category information, as well as calculate quality metrics such as ROI or CTR, we need to apply parallel algorithms.

System Architecture. Our audience extension system leverages our in-house data warehouse system, called Cheetah [7] built on top of the Hadoop framework [25]. It is designed specifically for our online advertising application to allow various simplifications and custom optimizations. User facts are stored within nested relational data tables.

We present the first step of the audience extension implementation in Figure 3. This figure gives the basic parallel process on generating the data to calculate segment to category similarity, novelty, and quality values. We distribute the whole segment and category data, as well as quality information (e.g. number of impressions as well as number of clicks for one or multiple advertisers) for each user to different mappers. Within each mapper, we generate three types of key-value pairs:

- **Key → {segmentId}, Value → {qualityInfo,1}:** For each user, we create one of these keys for each segment the user belongs to. Quality info is the numerator and denominator values for one of the Equations 3, 4, or 5 for a single or multiple advertisers.
- **Key → {categoryId}, Value → {qualityInfo,1}:** For each user, we create one of these keys for each category the user belongs to. Quality info is the numerator and denominator values for one of the Equations 3, 4, or 5 for a single or multiple advertisers.
- **Key → {segmentId,categoryId}, Value → {qualityInfo,1}:** For each user, we create one of these keys for each (segment,category) pair the user belongs to. We can further exclude the (segment, category) pairs where the category is part of the segment (since we do not want to recommend an already utilized category in our extension). Quality info is the numerator and denominator values for one of the Equations 3, 4, or 5 for a single or multiple advertisers.

After these keys are generated, in the reducer phase we can count the number of users as well as quality information for

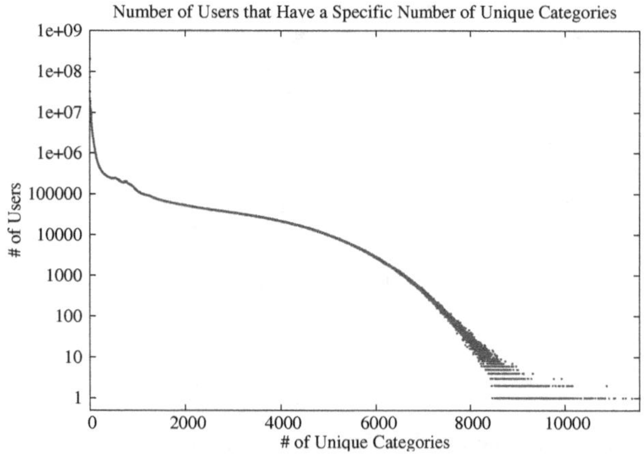

Figure 4: We count how many users have the specified number of unique categories. The plot shows a power-law degree distribution for the number of categories.

each segment, category, or segment-category intersections. These values are then used to calculate similarity, novelty, and quality information as in § 4.2. For this purpose, we need to join segment and category values on the different types of outputs of reducers, again in a parallelized manner. This way we can generate segment-to-category matrices of similarity, novelty, and quality values. At the extension time, it is trivial for each (segment,category) pair to calculate the scores according to given different θ values. We can then sort categories for each segment to be extended and recommend as possible audience extension candidates. The advertiser can then select the extension categories according to their internal metrics or *data cost* to utilize the new categories at run-time for targeting.

Handling Data Skew. Pair-wise computation is expensive in big data systems, since this potentially can involve $O(n^2)$ complexity. Skewed data could create imbalanced load on both mappers and reducers, which makes such an operation much more costly. Varying execution times result in low resource utilization and high overall execution time, since the next MapReduce cycle can only start after all mappers/reducers are done [14, 17]. Our user data is highly skewed. Without any mitigation, counting co-occurrences can lead to significantly longer job execution times and significantly lower cluster throughput.

More specifically, our data skew comes from two dimensions – users and categories. The *user skew* is caused by some long-tail users, which have significantly more category labels than others. They could be bots or spam users. We count the number of each user's unique categories and plot the histogram in Figure 4. Like many other scientific data, a user's count of categories roughly fits the power-law function and a small percentage of users have unusually many categories. Sometimes data providers could introduce *category skew* into the data – advertisers pay a data cost if they use the data provider's data for deciding to deliver an impression. Data providers are motivated to tag more users. In some cases, a category could tag so many users that it loses its discriminative power. For example, the most frequent category, "Traveler" in our data covers more than 55% of our users.

We take two approaches to mitigate data skew. First, we ignore those long-tail users and categories, since they introduce little value to advertisers. In our implementation, the top 5% most frequent categories and 15% most tagged users are removed from the computation. Second, we take the load balance into account when we partition the data: before we do the actual computation, we sample the input records and compute a histogram of the underlying key space. We then partition the data so that each mapper has roughly the same load. With those two approaches implemented, the recommendation speed is improved by more than 450% *.

6. EXPERIMENTAL RESULTS

In this section, we will give some preliminary results on the extended audiences that our proposed algorithms return. As given in Eq. 6, we can assign different weights to *similarity*, *novelty*, and *quality*. This is advertiser/application-specific, i.e. there is no single correct assignment of parameters, but rather we leave it to the advertisers to choose according to their needs.

For our experiments, we have utilized 15 days of user profile data collected at Turn's online advertising platform within 2014. From this data we can calculate how many users fall into any advertiser-defined segment, or how many users will fall into our recommended extended audience. We present our results for mainly four original segments (whose exact names and properties are not shown here due to privacy reasons):

- **Segment 1** picks up users that have bought a certain brand car in a certain state,
- **Segment 2** picks up users that have interest in a certain winter sport,
- **Segment 3** picks up users that have stayed at a specific hotel chain,
- **Segment 4** picks up users that have bought a new certain type of vehicle and are within a certain age range.

We have performed two experiments which optimize fully, either *similarity score*, or *quality score*, and we present the results below. We compare *Weighted* which is our proposed system from § 4.2 to two other methods: *Manual* gives the human-generated extension (which picks up the top k most frequent categories from the advertiser's original segment population), and *P. Greedy* is the purely greedy approach given in § 4.1 (set-cover algorithm).

6.1 Population Recovery

In this experiment, we are examining whether given a subset of an original advertiser-provided segment, we can extend this subset to *recover* the original segment. The exact steps of this experiment is as follows:

1. Pick up the users that belong to an advertiser-provided segment (consisting of k disjoint categories),
2. Sample n (we took this to be 50K for this instance) users from the audience,
3. Pick up the top $k/2$ categories from this user sample, and generate a new segment,

* Exact computation time is not shown here for confidentiality reasons.

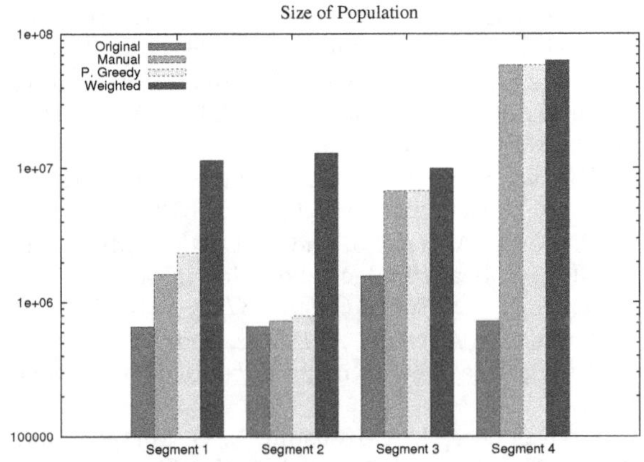

(a) Sizes of audiences for the original segment and different recommended extensions.

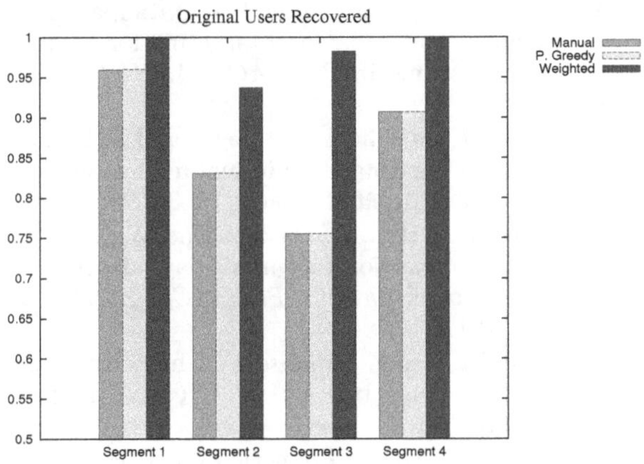

(b) Amount of original audience covered by different recommended extensions.

Figure 5: Results of Population Recovery Experiment

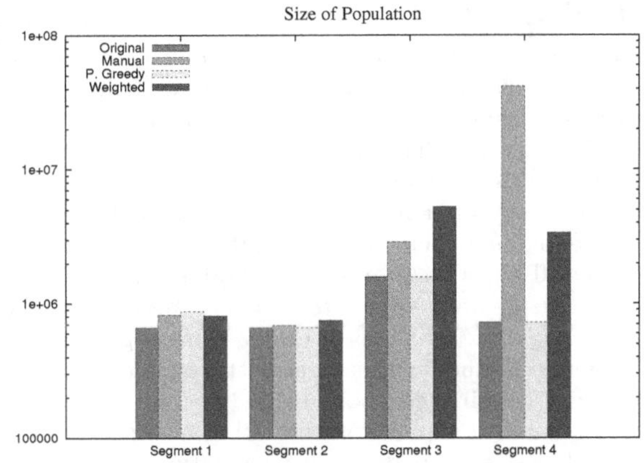

(a) Sizes of audiences for the original segment and different recommended extensions.

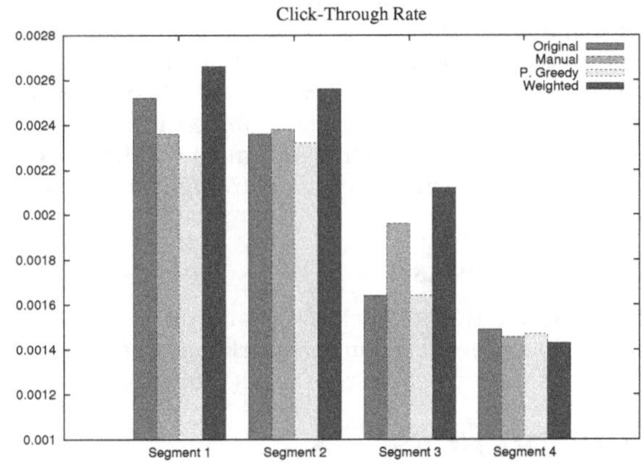

(b) CTR values for the original segment and different recommended extensions.

Figure 6: Results of Performance Optimization Experiment

4. Using different algorithms, generate $k/2$ recommended categories and check how much this new audience population covers the original segment (the one in Step 1, defined by k disjoint categories).

Results of *population recovery* experiment is given in Figure 5. In Figure 5(a), we present the audience sizes for the *original* segments (Segments 1-4 which consist of $k_{1\rightarrow 4}$ categories), and then we present the audience sizes for different extension algorithms (extension is made on top of the subset, and our aim is to recover the original segment). For the weighted case, we have chosen to fully optimize similarity ($(\theta_1, \theta_2, \theta_3)$=(1,0,0) in Eq. 6) since this is the most intuitive, and gave the best result in our experience for population recovery. It can be seen from the figure that although *Manual* and *P. Greedy* each employ a different logic to choose the extension categories, audience size results are pretty close. *Weighted* extension returns the largest audience, which also is significantly larger than the original (further boost to novelty, although we were not optimizing towards it).

Figure 5(b) gives the percentage of users (of the original audience) that were covered by the extension algorithms. Our aim for the experiment was to cover as much of the original segment as possible by extending the subset. It can be seen that our weighted scheme provides significantly higher coverage in all cases ($p < .001$).

6.2 Performance Optimization

In this experiment, we try to recommend an extended population with high quality scores. We chose click-through rates (CTRs, as described in Eq. 3) as our quality metric. For this purpose, we set the parameters $(\theta_1, \theta_2, \theta_3)$=(0,0,1) according to Eq. 6, which fully optimizes according to *quality* score, which we take to be CTR.

The results of the *optimize CTR* experiment is given in Figure 6. We extend the four segments according to different approaches with one recommended category. We can see that our weighted approach comes up with reasonably larger audiences (Figure 6(a)), and the CTR of the extended audience is the largest in most cases (Figure 6(b)). Please note that we have modified the actual CTR values with a constant multiplier for all cases, for privacy purposes. In 3 out of 4 cases, our weighted scheme provides significantly higher CTR values than other methods ($p < .001$). Since the purely greedy approach does not look into the quality of extended audience, it usually produces audiences with a smaller click-through rate compared to the original segments.

7. CONCLUSIONS AND FUTURE WORK

In this paper, we presented the problem of audience extension in online advertising. We provided two solutions, one purely greedy that applies a set-cover algorithm on the original audience, while the other one with different weights on similarity, novelty, and quality of the extended audience. We compared these different approaches on our real-world data set, and explained their implementation in our advertising platform at Turn. Our proposed method is computationally efficient, can flexibly adjust to different needs and shows good performance. To the best of our knowledge, this is the first paper to methodically examine the audience extension problem and possible solutions to it.

There are multiple paths of interesting future work. First, we would like to explore different formulations of the metrics that are optimized for extension, as well as different parameter settings on the weights of similarity, novelty, and quality metrics. Second, our current search space of extension is the logical disjunction forms of categories. It is possible to extend the recommendation to other simple logical formulas, if we can design some heuristics to limit the search space. Lastly, in the future we would like to mine the common rules that advertisers utilize to define a segment and leverage such rules to help recommendations by adapting transfer learning techniques [21].

Acknowledgments

We thank many talented scientists and engineers at Turn for their help and feedback in this work, and the anonymous reviewers for their valuable comments and suggestions.

8. REFERENCES

[1] http://digitalmarketing-glossary.com/what-is-audience-extension-definition, 2011.

[2] http://www.knowonlineadvertising.com/sharing-knowledge/audience-extension/, 2013.

[3] A. Ahmed, Y. Low, M. Aly, V. Josifovski, and A. J. Smola. calable distributed inference of dynamic user interests for behavioral targeting. In *Proc. ACM KDD*, pages 114–122, 2011.

[4] M. Aly, A. Hatch, V. Josifovski, and V. K. Narayanan. Web-scale user modeling for targeting. In *Proc. ACM WWW*, pages 3–12, 2012.

[5] N. Archak, V. S. Mirrokni, and S. Muthukrishnan. Mining advertiser-specific user behavior using adfactors. In *Proc. ACM WWW*, pages 31–40, 2010.

[6] J. Chen, W. Geyer, C. Dugan, M. Muller, and I. Guy. Make new friends, but keep the old: recommending people on social networking sites. In *Proc. CHI*, pages 201–210, 2009.

[7] S. Chen. Cheetah: a high performance, custom data warehouse on top of mapreduce. *Proc. VLDB Endowment*, 3(1-2):1459–1468, 2010.

[8] Y. Chen, D. Pavlov, and J. F. Canny. Large-scale behavioral targeting. In *Proc. ACM KDD*, pages 209–218, 2009.

[9] N. B. Ellison et al. Social network sites: Definition, history, and scholarship. *Journal of Computer-Mediated Communication*, 13(1):210–230, 2007.

[10] H. Elmeleegy, Y. Li, Y. Qi, P. Wilmot, M. Wu, S. Kolay, A. Dasdan, and S. Chen. Overview of turn data management platform for digital advertising. *Proc. VLDB Endowment*, 6(11):1138–1149, 2013.

[11] J. Evans and T. Liebowitz. System and method for targeting advertisements, Nov. 8 2012. WO Patent App. PCT/US2012/032,539.

[12] F. Falcon. Audience measurement system, Aug. 3 2011. EP Patent App. EP20,080,875,725.

[13] S. C. Geyik, A. Saxena, and A. Dasdan. Multi-touch attribution based budget allocation in online advertising. In *Proc. ACM ADKDD*, pages 1–9, 2014.

[14] B. Gufler, N. Augsten, A. Reiser, and A. Kemper. Handling data skew in mapreduce. In *Proc. CLOSER*, 2011.

[15] J. L. Herlocker, J. A. Konstan, L. G. Terveen, and J. T. Riedl. Evaluating collaborative filtering recommender systems. *ACM Trans. Information Systems*, 22(1):5–53, 2004.

[16] A. Joshi, A. Bagherjeiran, and A. Ratnaparkhi. User demographic and behavioral targeting for content match advertising. In *Proc. ACM ADKDD*, pages 53–60, 2011.

[17] Y. Kwon, M. Balazinska, B. Howe, and J. Rolia. Skewtune: mitigating skew in mapreduce applications. In *Proc. ACM SIGMOD*, pages 25–36, 2012.

[18] K.-C. Lee, B. Orten, A. Dasdan, and W. Li. Estimating conversion rate in display advertising from past performance data. In *Proc. ACM KDD*, pages 768–776, 2012.

[19] K. Liu and L. Tang. Large-scale behavioral targeting with a social twist. In *Proc. ACM CIKM*, pages 1815–1824, 2011.

[20] S. Pandey, M. Aly, A. Bagherjeiran, A. Hatch, P. Ciccolo, A. Ratnaparkhi, and M. Zinkevich. Learning to target: what works for behavioral targeting. In *Proc. ACM CIKM*, pages 1805–1814, 2011.

[21] C. Perlich, B. Dalessandro, T. Raeder, O. Stitelman, and F. Provost. Machine learning for targeted display advertising: Transfer learning in action. *Machine Learning*, 95(1):103–127, 2014.

[22] F. Provost, B. Dalessandro, R. Hook, X. Zhang, and A. Murray. Audience selection for on-line brand advertising: privacy-friendly social network targeting. In *Proc. ACM KDD*, pages 707–716, 2009.

[23] C. Sugnet, J. Shoop, P. Sutter, and K. Feldman. Audience segment selection, Aug. 6 2013. US Patent 8,504,905.

[24] S. Tu and C. Lu. Topic-based user segmentation for online advertising with latent dirichlet allocation. In *LNCS 6441*, pages 259–269, 2010.

[25] T. White. *Hadoop: The Definitive Guide.* O'Reilly Media, Sebastopol, CA, 2012.

[26] X. Wu, J. Yan, N. Liu, S. Yan, Y. Chen, and Z. Chen. Probabilistic latent semantic user segmentation for behavioral targeted advertising. In *Proc. ACM ADKDD*, pages 10–17, 2009.

[27] J. Yan, N. Liu, G. Wang, W. Zhang, Y. Jiang, and Z. Chen. How much can behavioral targeting help online advertising? In *Proc. ACM WWW*, pages 261–270, 2009.

Going In-Depth: Finding Longform on the Web

Virginia Smith
UC Berkeley
Berkeley, CA
vsmith@berkeley.edu

Miriam Connor
Google Inc.
Mountain View, CA
mkconnor@google.com

Isabelle Stanton
Google Inc.
Mountain View, CA
stanton@google.com

ABSTRACT

tl;dr: Longform articles are extended, in-depth pieces that often serve as feature stories in newspapers and magazines. In this work, we develop a system to automatically identify longform content across the web. Our novel classifier is highly accurate despite huge variation within longform in terms of topic, voice, and editorial taste. It is also scalable and interpretable, requiring a surprisingly small set of features based only on language and parse structures, length, and document interest. We implement our system at scale and use it to identify a corpus of several million longform documents. Using this corpus, we provide the first web-scale study with quantifiable and measurable information on longform, giving new insight into questions posed by the media on the past and current state of this famed literary medium.

Categories and Subject Descriptors

I.5 [**Computing Methodologies**]: Pattern Recognition; [**Design Methodology**]: Classifier Design and Evaluation

1. INTRODUCTION

The *longform article* is a traditional publishing format encompassing a variety of reporting types, from features to investigative journalism. The format is tied together not by content type or writing guidelines, but by a focus on quality and a deep understanding of the subject matter; longform articles are not produced overnight on a deadline. Classic longform pieces include those by authors considered some of the greatest journalists and writers of our time, e.g. "The Duke in his Domain" by Truman Capote [11], "Frank Sinatra Has a Cold" by Gay Talese [52], and "The String Theory" by David Foster Wallace [54].

In this paper, we seek a method to automatically identify longform content. Given longform's prominence, being able to identify this kind of content enables a variety of applications. These include but are not limited to: building a corpus as the foundation of a web-search system [38]; improving quality or diversity of articles for content recommendation; providing analytical background content in news applications; or even in creating UI hints for article layout. Here, we demonstrate an additional use of our system, creating a corpus of longform documents for scientific discovery.

In particular, we use our novel system to give clarity to the *the longform debate*: Despite longforms' prevalence historically, in a time where 140-character tweets are fast becoming the norm, its future is now unclear. Editorial pieces have abounded recently proclaiming that one of three movements is afoot: (1) a death of longform, (2) a renaissance of longform, or (3) a backlash against the genre. Those from group 1 argue that longforms' relative expense to produce makes it a prime target for cuts, particularly when long-revered publishing institutions are losing classic revenue streams from print advertising [46, 1, 51, 20, 35, 12]. Proponents of the renaissance (group 2) posit that the the web is a transformational platform for this style and that its popularity is on the rise [15, 25, 45, 19, 5]. Finally, members of group 3 have mixed opinions, believing that longform *did* gain interest, but that an over-abundance of poorly-produced longform has caused a backlash against the genre [28, 7, 34, 50].

Leveraging our classifier, we provide concrete, quantifiable answers to these questions as they pertain to web publishing. We first develop a robust classifier to identify longform and then, using a massive web crawl with historical signals, aggregate a comprehensive corpus of longform documents on the web. We query this corpus to provide statistical answers regarding the status of longform online, rather than relying on journalists' opinions. Though prior attempts to quantify the status of longform exist (using hand analysis) [51], a study of this scale has never been performed. This work demonstrates the impact of our classification system, and highlights key techniques needed to carry out similar large-scale studies on the web.

1.1 What is Longform?

Longform is closely aligned with the traditional publishing styles of feature writing and investigative journalism, as well as literary non-fiction and non-fiction storytelling [5]. With the advent of the web, the definition must be broadened to include articles on publications that are web-only, like `qz.com` and `vox.com`, or are self-published on websites like `medium.com` and personal blogs. An initial definition is that longform articles are long, interesting, well-researched, well-written and have a longer 'shelf-life' than standard news articles, i.e., they continue to be relevant for months to more than fifty years [5], also known as *evergreen* [26]. We include a few more requirements – that the work must be *original*; *analytical*, i.e., a narrative or commentary, rather than re-

KDD'15, August 10-13, 2015, Sydney, NSW, Australia.
 ISBN 978-1-4503-3664-2/15/08 ...$15.00.
DOI: http://dx.doi.org/10.1145/2783258.2788599.

porting of an event; and aim to *entertain*, i.e., there is a focus on the writing style, and the goal is not just to inform the reader but also to be interesting or thought-provoking.

Longform is perhaps best defined through a series of illustrative examples. For instance, longform includes feature pieces in print magazines on subjects like The New Yorker's history of elevators [42] or Michael Lewis's profile of President Obama [30]; investigative journalism like Glenn Greenwald and Ewen MacAskill's article on the PRISM revelations [22] or a series of 24 reports on Scientology from the Los Angeles Times [48]; as well as feature pieces from online publications like a piece on the history of the Street Fighter movie in Polygon Magazine [43]. One easy way to familiarize yourself with the genre is to peruse a curated longform website like `thefeature.net` or `longform.org`.

Longform is not limited to US publishers, with other examples including Canada's *McLean Magazine* and *The Walrus*; Great Britain's *The Spectator*, *The Economist* and *Financial Times*; and Australia's *The Monthly*. Nor is it limited to English, with sources like Germany's *Der Speigel* and France's *Le Monde* and *XXI*. However, it is widely considered that US publishers are the "powerhouse" [5], and we thus focus our study on English language longform.

Longform is also not defined solely by length. For example, a long personal blog post would generally not qualify as it is neither broadly interesting, well-researched, nor evergreen. The vast majority of newspaper articles (regardless of the length) would not qualify as they report the events of the day and are neither analytical nor evergreen. We confirm this empirically (Section 4.3), showing that a classifier from length features alone performs poorly. Finally, we note that the definition of longform cannot be made entirely crisp, as new online sources continue to blur the lines. We ultimately resolve this issue by deferring to human opinion, using human raters to label training data (Section 4.2).

1.2 Contributions

In this paper we make several contributions. First, we give a formal definition of longform and provide a crowdsourcing experiment that can be used to obtain labeled data. Using this data (a training set of less than 16,000 labeled samples), we build a highly accurate classifier of English language longform. This is notable given the huge variety in topic and presentation of longform, and that we develop the classifier using a relatively simple set of features relating only to writing style, word usage, length, and human interaction. The features used by this classifier are publicly available, relying only on access to a web crawl and a natural language syntactic parser. Our use of grammatical language features is surprisingly successful given that previous work using these types of features has focused on more distinct categories, such as distinguishing pieces of news from fiction novels or government documents [49]. Given the breadth and ambiguity of the definition in Section 1.1, it was initially unclear that such a classifier could exist.

While this classifier itself is of independent interest and application, we additionally demonstrate its utility by building a corpus of longform articles to aid in scientific discovery. Using the corpus we provide concrete answers to questions raised by the publishing community. No prior work has been able to systematically create a comprehensive corpus of longform from across the web, and doing so is a testament to the accuracy and scalability of our classification system.

The rest of this paper is organized as follows. In Section 2, we discuss related work on web mining and classification systems, as well as background on longform. In Section 3 we present the novel classifier used to build our corpus, and evaluation of this classifier is discussed in Section 4. Insights and observations gained from the generated corpus are highlighted in Section 5 and we offer conclusions in Section 6.

2. RELATED WORK

Building a substantive corpus of longform has required mining large amounts of web data. The mining of web data to measure cultural, societal, or technological changes is not new. Web mining has been used for a number of diverse applications, from predicting public mood and political uprisings from Twitter data, to detecting cultural differences in geo-tagged images, to measuring linguistic change in online communities [10, 53, 29, 13]. Several researchers have looked specifically at mining web-scale datasets related to news [31, 3, 33, 55, 2]. However, most of these developments were aimed solely at improving news recommendation systems, and none have focused specifically on longform content or on characterizing the nature of this content over time.

We note the importance of the classifier used to create our longform corpus. The use of classifiers to predict specific web content is commonplace throughout applications in document ranking, recommendation, and discovery [8, 21]. To develop our corpus from web-crawled data, we implement a logistic regression classifier, the effectiveness of which has been well-studied and demonstrated by numerous web-mining applications. We use a two-step procedure to develop this model, as described in Section 3.

Lastly, an important subset of features in the classifier leverage natural language processing techniques to detect whether an article's writing style makes it a longform candidate. Prior work on automatic style and genre detection has used signals derived from syntactic parses and other linguistic cues to identify a document's style and genre, for example to distinguish between opinion pieces and standard news articles [4, 17, 16] or to identify membership in various online genres (e.g., news, blog posts, and search pages) [47, 49]. Similar techniques have been used to predict whether a piece of writing is well-written and high quality [32, 6].

The Longform Debate.

As discussed in Section 1, there has been much debate recently about the fate of longform, and accordingly, many attempts to investigate the state of the genre. The ubiquity of the web and rise of digital journalism initially caused concern that interest in long content was waning, with notable pieces like Slate's "You Won't Finish This Article," and American Journalism Review's "The Death of Slow Journalism" [35, 12]. Some argued that, even if interest did exist, the return on investment would not be enough to justify its production cost: This trend was recently documented in studies on the state of news media, indicating that costly investigative reporting styles have undergone major cuts across a number of media outlets [1, 51, 20].

Alternatively, many others have recently declared that longform is undergoing a "renaissance" online [15, 25, 45, 19, 5]. Of these, Arnold's monograph [5] has the most research-intensive approach, synthesizing accounts from those involved in journalism at all levels, including publishers, writers, editors, teachers, and readers, the ultimate goal being to determine whether or not longform journalism remains lucrative for media organizations. Her account documents six 'major-players' of longform journalism, including Atavist, Seattle's The Magazine, Longform.org, The Blaze, Byliner, and The Seattle Times. There are additional reports of other "longform startups", such as Jill Abramson's offer of up to $100k advances for longform stories [36]. A history of longform leading to the current purported rise is documented in [37].

Finally, a third camp argues that there is a backlash to the heralded longform renaissance afoot [28, 7, 34, 50]. This side consists mostly of opinion pieces from longform editors and writers, giving nuanced arguments about the hype around longform and importance of quality above quantity. However, some hope to quantify this movement, urging publishers to develop metrics like "dwell time" in order to more accurately measure the popularity of longform [41]. Clearly, it is still undecided as to whether or not longform will maintain its spot as a forerunner in journalistic styles. With a corpus of more than 5.2 million longform documents in hand, this is exactly the question we aim to illuminate.

3. BUILDING A LONGFORM CLASSIFIER

In this section we describe our two-step classifier for identifying longform content. Such a classifier is useful for a variety of applications, including search systems, content recommendation, news applications, or in aiding UI development. Using a classifier is necessary due to the scale of the problem (i.e., identifying a subset of the web), as well as the importance of objectivity and standardization in ratings. We aim to develop a classifier that is simple, transparent, and accurate. These practical design traits ensure that our classification system will be scalable and reliable, as well as easy to maintain. Through extensive testing, model selection, and feature-engineering, we have developed a classifier that exactly meets these needs.

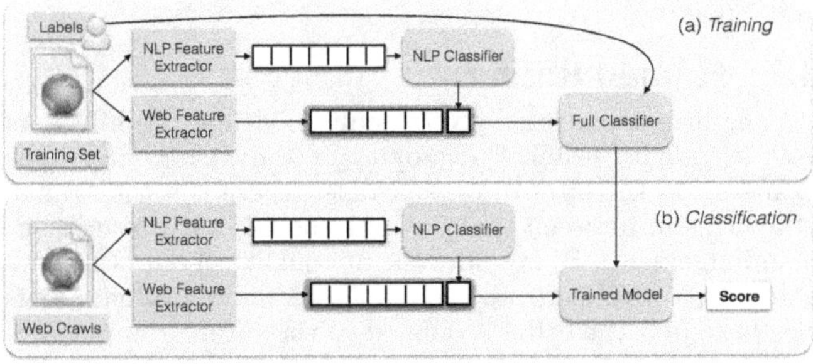

Figure 1: Workflow for developing and using the longform classifier. Classification includes using the NLP classifier as part of the full classifier in a two-step procedure.

Workflow.

Our workflow for developing and using our classifier is shown in Figure 1. We begin by sampling a training set representative of the diverse documents on the web, a task made difficult by the huge number of possibly irrelevant pages (Section 4.1). We then label this set using a crowd-sourced rater system (Section 4.1). Next, we extract a number of features from the documents, which are described in detail in Section 3.1. The features relate broadly to categories of length, document interest, and document quality.

Two-Step Classification.

The extracted features are utilized in a *two-step* procedure. In particular, we construct two classifiers, which we will refer to as the *full classifier* and *NLP classifier* (or natural language processing classifier). The features of the NLP classifier are based on grammatical parse structures from a natural language parser, described in Section 3.1. We use predicted output of the NLP classifier as a feature source in the full classifier. This two-step procedure allows us to separately tune and adjust the features related specifically to natural language, and has the added benefits of reducing the dimensionality of the final model, helping to prevent over-fitting, and mitigating effects of correlation amongst variables. The two classifiers are trained independently on separate datasets, making this distinct from related work on multilevel, nested, or hierarchical models that consider estimation on the full model [56, 44].

Both the full classifier and NLP classifier employ logistic regression, a probabilistic classification model for predicting binary variables $y^{(1)}, \ldots, y^{(n)} \in \{0,1\}^n$ from features $\mathbf{x}^{(1)}, \ldots, \mathbf{x}^{(n)} \in \mathbb{R}^d$, with success probability:

$$p(y^{(i)} = 1|\beta_0, \beta, x^{(i)}) = \frac{1}{1 + \exp(-\beta_0 - \beta^T x^{(i)})}$$

The true values are predicted according to the discriminant function, a linear combination of the input features $\mathbf{x}_j^{(i)}$:

$$\beta_0 + \sum_{j=1}^{d} \beta_j x_j^{(i)}$$

Finally, in order to generate a corpus of longform documents, we utilize the classifier on a massive set of web crawls, passing the features to the fully trained model in order to determine each document's final score (Figure 1b). By thresholding this score, a value between 0 and 1, we restrict our web-scale dataset to a corpus containing only longform documents as identified by our classifier. The observations we generate from this final corpus are given in Section 5.

3.1 Longform Features

We look for three major cues in categorizing longform: document length, interest, and quality. These are measured by calculating repeated structure counts, anchor count and quality, and document language and structure, respectively. We collect the following features:

- **Article length**: We use a state-of-the-art system for parsing HTML structure and identifying the main article content from other parts of the page, like comments or the boilerplate. We find the number of characters in the article and bucket this feature into 4 groups: short (<5,000 characters), medium (5,000–10,000), long (10,000–20,000), and very long (>20,000).

- **Anchors**: The number of *off-domain* anchors, as well as the presence of recently occurring anchors (i.e., those newly observed within the last three months). These measure interest in the document from external sources.

- **NLP Classifier score**: A measure of the quality of the document, classifying longform articles based on language and grammatical structure. This feature is bucketed into three buckets: high score, low score, and score aggregated over all articles from a site.

Including the intercept term, this amounts to a total feature size of 10, using 4 features for article length, 2 for anchors, and 3 for NLP classification. However, the NLP classifier itself (described below) uses many thousands of features.

NLP Classifier.

Beyond the length of a document and the interest level of its readers, the measure of a successful longform article lies in the content of the article itself, and particularly in the writing style. A detailed news report on a breaking topic might be long and frequently cited, but will lack the inventive, entertaining, and analytical language definitive of the longform genre. We therefore need a signal for our full classifier that indicates the quality of the article text itself. To capture this, we train a separate classifier on natural language features and use the output of this classifier as a feature to the longform classifier. Like the full classifier, this classifier is a logistic regression model [9].

To train the NLP classifier, we extract natural language signals from the text of each web page. We obtain syntactic parses of the document text with a shift-reduce transition-based parser [39] using standard features and a linear kernel SVM for classification. The parser is trained on dependency parse trees that are generated by applying the Stanford converter [14] (version 1.6.2) to the OntoNotes treebank data [24]. We describe our natural language features below.

- **Token ngrams**: The most common two-, three-, and four-word sequences of tokens in the page text.
- **Parse tree ngrams**: We run our dependency parser over the page text and extract ngrams by traversing the parse tree. For example, the sentence "the furry dog barked" would generate the ngram: *determiner* → *nominal subject* → *sentence root.*
- **Adjacent parse label ngrams**: The most common sequences of parse labels from adjacent tokens, for ngram lengths three and four. An adjacent parse label of length three in "the furry dog barked" would be *determiner* → *adjectival modifier* → *nominal subject.*
- **Part-of-speech ngrams**: The most common sequences of part-of-speech tags from adjacent tokens, for ngram lengths two and three.
- **Sentence length**: Average length of sentences on page.
- **Pronoun person distribution**: The relative frequency of first-, second-, and third-person pronouns.
- **Punctuation frequency**: The relative frequency of different punctuation mark tokens in the text.
- **Delimiting punctuation frequency**: As above, but only considering sentence-final punctuation marks.

As we use multiple ngram-based features, the feature space for the NLP classifier is quite large. We use feature hashing to reduce the feature space and to add regularization [18].

Intuitively, the NLP classifier on its own should not be sufficient to identify longform articles. It does not, for example, capture the veracity of an article or whether its topic is broadly interesting—the anchor features may be better indicators of this. We confirm this intuition experimentally by evaluating the quality of the NLP classifier independent of the full classifier in Section 4.3.

4. EVALUATION

In this section we evaluate the classifier proposed in Section 3. We validate the performance in a number of ways, including thoughtfully constructing training and testing data (Section 4.1); using feedback from crowd-sourced human raters (Section 4.2); and assessing the classifier with a number of statistical metrics (Section 4.3).

4.1 Challenges in Generating Training Data

When dealing with a corpus the size of the web, finding good representative positive and negative training examples is both incredibly important and quite challenging. In this work, we must identify a subset of the web ordering millions of pages from a corpus of trillions. Techniques like random sampling will both find no positive examples, and find relatively "easy" negative examples unrelated to journalism, leading to poor generalization during learning. Instead, we craft our training examples based on intuition for the problem and then show through evaluation that this approach produces a classifier that generalizes well.

Our labeled training data consists of 16,000 examples. For negative examples, we include a random sample of 6,000 articles consisting of at least 1,500 characters from a large collection of news articles. These documents are all are given a negative label, with knowledge that the vast majority of news articles do not qualify as longform. We include the length requirement to reduce training bias and ensure that that feature alone is not used in identifying longform (we demonstrate in Section 4.3 that a length-only classifier performs very poorly). In addition, we take a sample of documents that ranked highly in Google's In-Depth Article Search system, an independent ranking service that uses a host of signals orthogonal to those in our classifier [38]. Using these candidate articles, we have a set of in-house, well-trained human raters label the examples, a process which is described in detail in Section 4.2. From this second set of experiments, we obtain an additional 8,000 positive examples and 2,000 negative examples.

4.2 Human Ratings

Longform is surprisingly difficult to define. While it is easy to identify stellar examples of the genre, and non-examples in the form of news articles, there is a wide range of articles in-between that can only be labeled through human judgement. To evaluate the full quality of our classifiers across this spectrum, we use human raters to evaluate articles based on the criteria defined in the rater prompt (Section 4.2.1). We use this rater task to both generate training data as well as evaluate the quality of classifier scores with additional human judgements.

The answer to each question translates into ratings between 0 and 4. Ratings from each rater can then be averaged for each article in order to determine a single numeric score. In our evaluation, this average score is scaled to between 0 and 1. While we are only interested in the final question about in-depth, we found that constructing the rating task with the first four questions resulted in higher accuracy from the raters as they were forced to consider each component of longform before generating their final rating. An article with an average unnormalized score less than 1 for in-depth is considered to have a clear negative label, while an article with average score of at least 3 is considered to have a clear positive label.

4.2.1 Rater Prompt

Instructions: In this task, you will be asked to rate an "in-depth article". Please carefully read and consider the description below before completing the task. For the this task, an "in-depth article" has the following properties:

- The content is a text article with the intent to provide information to the user, as opposed to helping the user perform a task or navigate to content.
- The content is interesting to consume while also being informative. Reference materials primarily used to consult or look up facts are not in-depth articles.
- The content has a narrative form. A user would typically read the content from beginning to end, as opposed to skipping to a section of interest.
- The landing page is from a high quality, authoritative source.
- The content is long and detailed enough to be more than just a general summary of a topic. A user who is already familiar with the general subject area would find the content interesting.
- The content has original opinions, research, or synthesis. It is more than a statement of facts that could be found elsewhere.
- The content has broader relevance than a typical news story and would still be interesting to a reader many months from now. For example, a biography or profile of an athlete would meet this criterion but a recap of that athlete's most recent game would not.

Is the content from an authoritative source?
[**Yes** - The author or website is known for its high quality journalism and/or expertise in the main content's subject matter.] [**Mostly**] [**Somewhat** - The author or website is not particularly renowned and/or has expertise in a different subject.] [**A Little**] [**No**] [**Can't Tell**]

Does the content include detailed, original content?
[**Yes** - Substantial effort went into researching or creating the content. It has information that is not readily available on other websites.] [**Mostly**] [**Somewhat** - The content is original but brief, or it is detailed but a summary of facts available elsewhere.] [**A Little**] [**No** - Someone else could easily create a webpage that achieves the same purpose as the content.] [**Can't Tell**]

Look for the date the content was published and consider how the content relates to events at that point in time. About how long would it take for the article to become substantially less relevant, compared to when it was first posted?
[**Never or Almost never** - The content will most likely be permanently relevant.] [**Several Years**] [**Three months to a year** - The content does not directly relate to current events but may become less relevant over time.] [**Up to three months**] [**Days** - The content is "newsy" or about current events.] [**Can't Tell**]

Is the content interesting to a user today? Is the content currently relevant and not stale (regardless of its age)?
[**Yes** - The content is on-topic and currently relevant.] [**Mostly**] [**Somewhat** - The content is somewhat stale, but still provides interesting context on the subject.] [**A Little**] [**No** - The content is outdated.] [**Can't Tell**]

Overall, is the content of the landing page an "in-depth article"?
[**Yes** - The content has all of the characteristics of an "in-depth article".] [**Mostly**] [**Somewhat** - The content has most of the characteristics of an "in-depth article".] [**A Little**] [**No** - The content has few or none of the characteristics of an "in-depth article".] [**Can't Tell** - Could not view content (Page did not load, or content behind a pay wall).]

4.3 Performance of Classifiers

We evaluate the performance of the classifiers on both holdout training data as well as unseen generalization data, using a number of standard statistical metrics.

Performance on Holdout Data.

Figure 2 shows ROC curves with respect to data held out from our training set, for the full longform classifier (red, solid); NLP classifier (green, dotted); and a classifier trained from only length features (blue, dashed). We train the models using a random sample of 80% of the data, with the holdout set containing the remaining 20%. Numerical results are given in Table 1.

Length features alone do not provide enough performance to warrant using as a classifier, receiving low accuracy and poor AUC results. Though the NLP classifier has a high precision value of .8580, the recall for the NLP classifier is quite low. This discrepancy emphasizes the need to combine the natural language signal with our other signals in order to achieve both high-quality and high-coverage identification of longform articles. We see that the low recall of the NLP classifier is mitigated by the full longform classifier, which achieves precision .9138 and recall .8690.

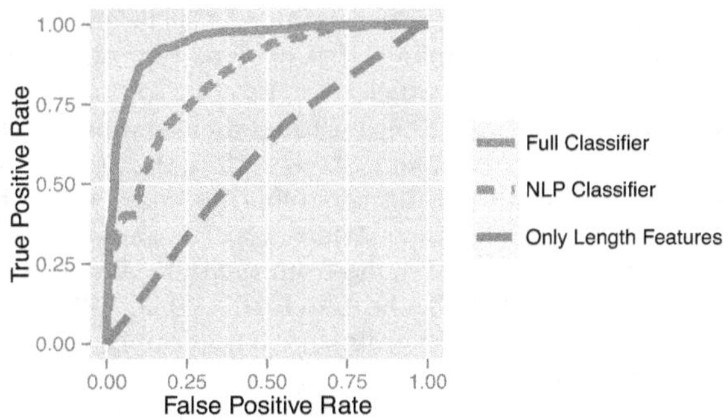

Figure 2: ROC Curves for the full classifier and NLP classifier on the hold-out set from the training data.

Table 1: Performance of Classifiers on Holdout Data.

	Length Features Only	NLP Classifier	Longform Classifier
AUC	.5782	.8319	.9424
Accuracy	.6128	.6202	.8783
Precision	.7317	.8580	.9138
Recall	.6870	.4031	.8690

Performance on Unseen Generalization Data.

Next, we generalize to a set of randomly selected, previously unseen webpages, evaluating how well the scores generated by the classifiers correlate with human ratings. To guarantee an accurate evaluation, regardless of the distribution of the classifier scores on the articles, we use a stratified sampling method with a reservoir sampler to generate an equal number of articles for each classifier score bucket, i.e. between 0 and 0.1, 0.1 and 0.2, etc. These are then rated using the experiment in Section 4.2. We take the average of the rated scores for each data point, and scale this number to match the output of the classifiers between 0 and 1.

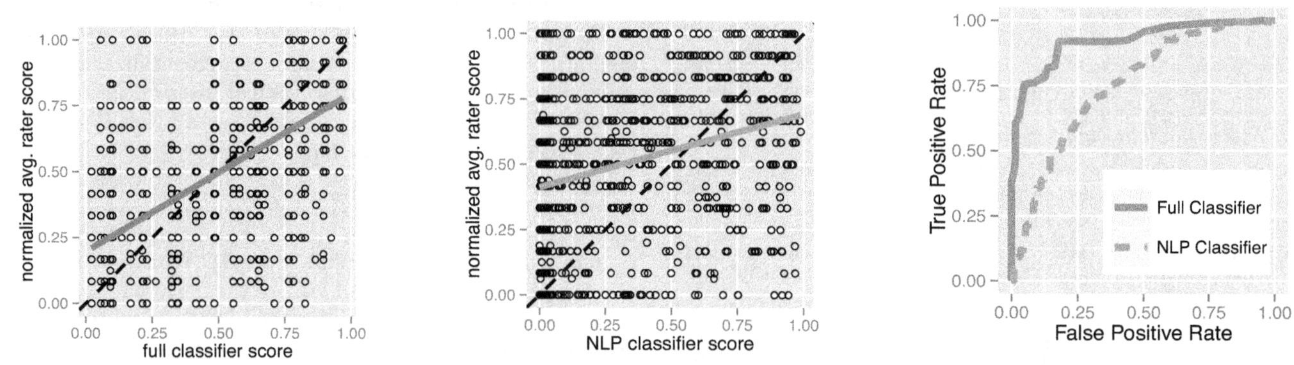

(a) Average rater score vs. full classifier score (red) as compared to optimal (black, dashed).

(b) Average rater score vs. NLP classifier score (green) as compared to optimal (black, dashed).

(c) ROC curves for full classifier (red, solid) and NLP classifier (green, dashed) on highly confident (normalized score < 0.25 or > 0.75) generalization data.

Figure 3: Generalization Results for the Longform and NLP Classifiers.

In Figure 3a, we show the correlation between the average rater score and the score given by the full classifier, for a new sample of 1,000 previously unrated webpages. Figure 3b shows analogous results for the NLP classifier. Even after considering the sampling, it is evident that the scores are somewhat stratified, which is a product of a number of integer-valued features limiting the dimensionality of the space. Comparing these plots, we see that the full classifier is able to more accurately match the scores given by the raters. The optimal correlation (y=x) is shown in the black, dotted line, and the results from the full classifier (the solid line in Figure 3a) closely match this. The full classifier achieves an adjusted R^2 value of 0.34, as opposed to the NLP classifier, which has an R^2 value of 0.06.

It is important to remember when viewing these results that the average rater scores are not an ideal predictor as there are discrepancies amongst the raters themselves: If humans can't perfectly agree, it seems unrealistic to expect the classifier to do so. The variation in rater scores is particularly high when answers to the questions were in the middle range, i.e. were rated 1-3 instead of 0 or 4. For documents that were rated on average between $1-3$, the average deviation from the mean for scores was $\sigma = 1.57$. This is in contrast to scores with average ratings of < 1 or > 3, which had a standard deviation less than .5. Thus, another metric to consider is whether the classifier performs well in areas of high confidence. To investigate this, we additionally consider the performance of the classifier only on data points where the raters are very confident. The classification results of this are shown in an ROC curve, Figure 3c. We see that the full classifier performs quite well in these areas of high confidence, achieving an AUC of 0.91 as compared to 0.75 for the NLP classifier.

Finally, we briefly discuss the relative weights of the features of the trained full classifier, as shown in Table 2. The three specified qualities of longform (length, popularity, and quality) each have a significant impact on the classifier, with feature weights spread roughly uniformly amongst each feature type. In terms of length, articles that are very short are given a negative score, as well as articles that are quite long (e.g., a novella or online book should not be considered an article). The NLP classifier also has a large impact on determining the outcome of longformed-ness, with low NLP scores negatively impacting the outcome, and high scores for the article or site giving positive impact. The popularity of the page also plays an important role in determining this outcome, with both the number of recent anchors and the number of off-domain anchors being positive indicators.

Table 2: Classifier Feature Weights.

Feature Type	Feature	Weight
	intercept	-0.8795
length	short	-1.9357
	medium	-0.2873
	long	-0.0620
	very long	-0.7678
quality	low NLP score	-1.2197
	high NLP score	0.8067
	site-based NLP score	1.2012
popularity	existence of recent anchors	1.2012
	# of off-domain anchors	1.5936

5. A STUDY OF LONGFORM ON THE WEB

In this section, we demonstrate the utility of our classification system by using it to create a corpus of over 5.2 million longform documents on the web. Using this corpus, we provide concrete numbers that address editorials on the current and future state of longform, i.e., is it dying, or facing a new boom? If there is a boom, are people sick of the trend? For reference, the three dominant arguments are as follows: that there is (1) a decline of longform, (2) a renaissance of longform, or (3) a backlash against the genre.

Surprisingly, despite the seeming opposition of these statements, our analysis of the longform corpus provides evidence for all three camps, as we describe below. Longform is not dying; we see a steady increase in the amount of longform published on the web over the years. However, news publishing on the web is increasing at a faster rate, and so the relative amount of longform published *is* dropping. With regards to a "longform renaissance," we see that longform appears to be increasingly popular: Interest in longform relative to news is growing and more sites than ever before are producing longform content. As for the backlash, we do not find evidence to directly support this hypothesis, but we do see a significant spike in the number of new sites producing longform. This provides evidence that longform is a ballooning trend, which forms the basic assumption required for a backlash to develop.

5.1 Building a Longform Corpus

Though we have developed a high quality classifier for distinguishing English language longform articles, additional finesse is required to build a corpus from a web crawl. In order to reduce the space of possible documents, we begin building our corpus by using two additional systems: one for identifying webpages with commercial intent (e.g. Amazon product pages), and one for attributing an author to webpages [27]. We use these systems to filter out clear negative examples to improve the efficiency and quality of our corpus.

The next challenge faced is multi-page articles. In physical print it is necessary that longform articles be paginated, and this tradition is sometimes carried onto the web, making it important to determine whether an article spans just one page or several. We use a clustering system for identifying duplicate content on different URLs, as well as multi-page articles [23] with which we translate the corpus from labeled individual pages on the web to clusters of pages that represent articles. This is vital to avoid skewing volume-related metrics about longform. Finally, we are interested not only in questions about what longform looks like on the web but also how it compares with the general news publishing ecosystem, and thus include a large corpus of news articles as a baseline.

5.2 Extracted Data

To investigate longform along several dimensions, we extract many different signals from the data when developing our corpus. A number of these signals leverage internal systems that have previously generated the signal but for other purposes. For instance, we leverage systems that find the publication or byline date of each article (which, note, may differ dramatically from the first crawled date in instances where an archive has been brought online), as well as systems that determine the root site for a given url (which can be a difficult task given the number of possible domains and sub-domains under which a site could be hosted). A complete list of the signals collected is given in Table 3.

Table 3: Signals extracted for longform study.

Signal	Description
classifier score	score from the longform classifier
byline date	date the article was published
document date	date the article was first crawled
site name	name of the site the article is hosted on
anchor distribution	number of anchors observed and their observation dates

5.3 Results

With the corpus of longform documents in hand, we analyze numerous aspects of this corpus, performing an extensive study of longform on the web. Major aspects we consider are the current distribution of longform on the web (Section 5.3.1); the change to this distribution over time (Section 5.3.2); and characteristics unique to longform (Section 5.3.3). We obtain the following observations:

OBSERVATION 1. *Distribution: The distribution of sites publishing longform is heavy-tailed: longform can be found on many sites with a few high volume publishers. For some publishers, longform forms a significant fraction of published material. (Figure 4)*

OBSERVATION 2. *Volume: The sheer amount of longform content published each year is increasing though increasingly more slowly than the volume of news content published. Despite the decrease as a ratio, we observe an ever increasing amount of interest in longform when compared with news. (Figures 5b, 5b and 5c)*

OBSERVATION 3. *Sites: An increasing number of new sites are publishing longform. The increase in volume of longform publishing is due to many sites, not single large outliers. (Figures 6a and 6b)*

OBSERVATION 4. *Interest: There exists a quantifiable difference between how both publishers and readers interact with longform vs news content – readers interact with the content for longer, and publishers are more likely to bring older longform content online. (Figures 7 and 8)*

5.3.1 Distribution of Longform on the Web

In total, our corpus consists of more than 5.2 million documents currently available on the web and identified as longform, which we compare to a separate corpus of nearly 92 million news documents. To provide some initial insight into this corpus, in Figure 4 we chart the distribution of sites publishing longform. Not unexpectedly for web data, Figure 4a shows that this distribution is heavy-tailed: that is, there are many websites publishing just a few pieces of longform, and relatively few publishing many longform articles. The plot is shown in log-scale – the number of sites publishing beyond $e^7 \approx 1,000$ articles is hardly visible.

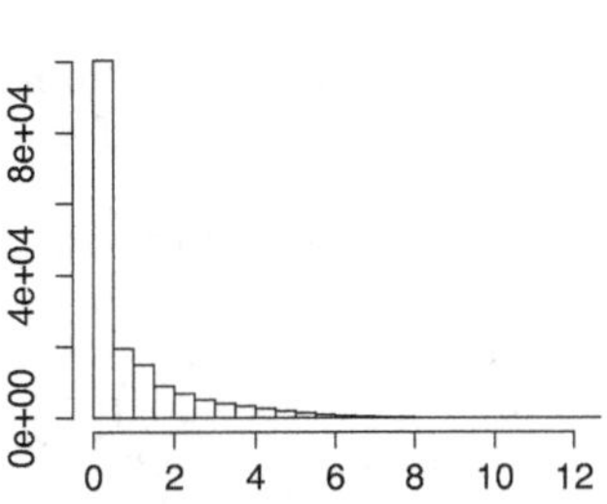

(a) Histogram of sites publishing different volumes of longform (log-scale).

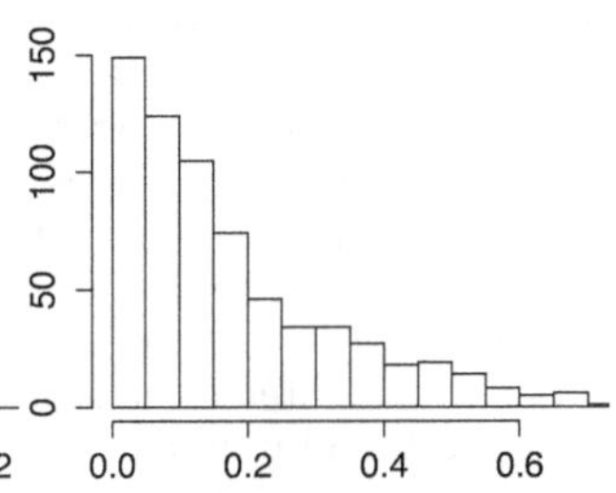

(b) The percentage of longform found on high-volume sites (>1,000 articles).

Figure 4: The distribution of sites that publish longform is quite heavy-tailed (4a). Amongst high-publishing sites, several sites publish longform as a majority of their articles (4b) but many more include longform as a key component.

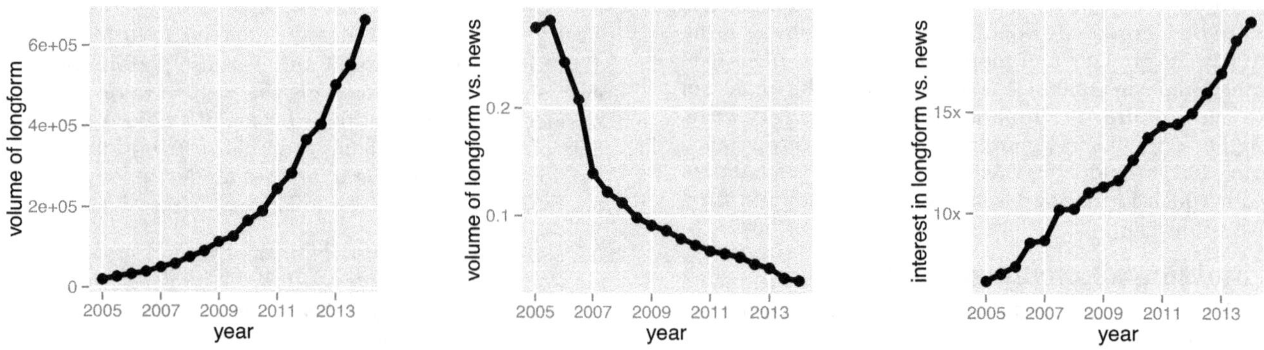

(a) Volume of longform produced every six months, for the past 10 years.

(b) Ratio of the volume of longform produced vs. news for the past 10 years.

(c) Average ratio of anchors in longform to news (a proxy for interest) over time.

Figure 5: Changes in the volume of and interest in longform produced over time. Although the number of longform articles produced yearly is increasing, the volume of longform produced relative to news is decreasing significantly. Despite this decrease, *interest* in longform with respect to news, measured via the ratio of average anchors, is steadily increasing.

A natural question about the few high-publishing sites (>1,000 articles per site) is whether they produce solely longform or if longform is a by-product of sites that publish a large amount of many article types. In Figure 4b, we see that amongst these sites, longform is a non-trivial amount of total production (> 10%) for many of the sites, and in some cases, it is the majority of what is being produced. This indicates that longform plays an important role on these high-producing sites.

5.3.2 Changes in Longform over Time

Next, we investigate how longform has changed over time. We have both the byline date of each article and the first crawled date, a reasonable estimate for when the document was made available on the web. With these, we analyze temporal changes in longform. Our results here are biased by the existence of documents created in the past that have since been taken offline, a confounding factor that is unavoidable.

Some temporal trends are shown in Figure 5. In Figure 5a, we see that the volume of longform produced has increased significantly over the past 10 years, by a factor of more than 30 since 2005. However, as the web itself is growing, we must compare to other, similar sources. Figure 5b shows that the volume of longform published every six months has actually decreased significantly when compared to the volume of news articles produced in the same time period (by a factor of more than 7 since 2005). This decrease in volume relative to news may be evidence of cases where longform has been cut for other sources [51].

Despite the decrease in longform volume relative to news, Figure 5c shows that *interest* in longform compared to news has risen over the past 10 years, from 6 times to nearly 20 times as much. Interest in each of these groups was approximated via the total number of off-domain anchors, a classic measure of popularity used in e.g. PageRank [40]. All articles were grouped by publication date over 6 month periods, and the average number of off-domain anchors accrued (as of creation date) for articles in that period was calculated. Though older articles have had many years to accrue anchors, we find that average anchors for both longform and news are increasing, meaning that new content is popular for both. The fact that interest in longform is growing even more strongly provides evidence for a renaissance [5].

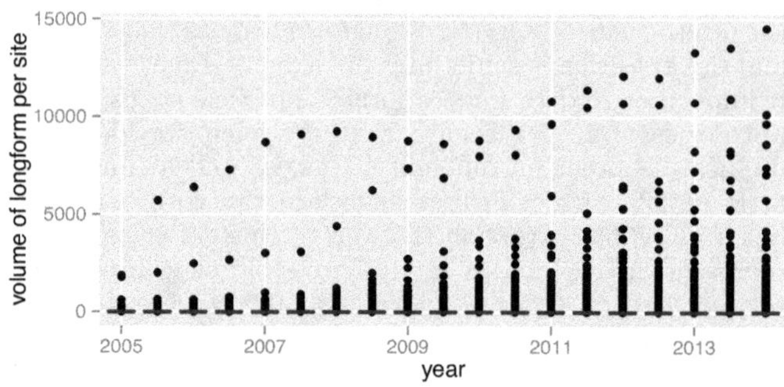

(a) The distribution of top sites over the past 10 years.

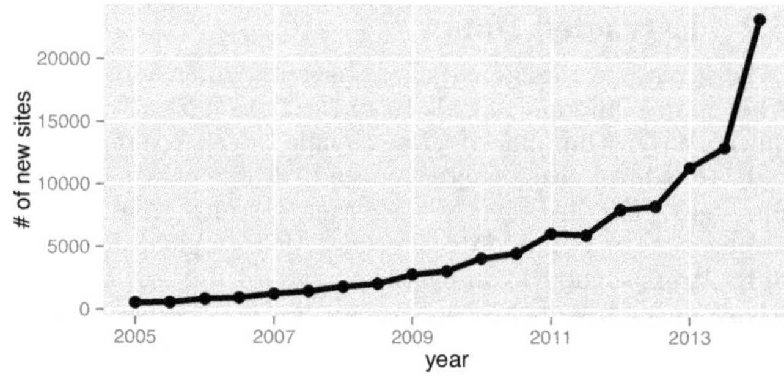

(b) The number of new longform sites added every 6 months.

Figure 6: The increase longform volume includes older sites producing more longform, as well as new sites producing longform for the first time.

Given the increase in longform volume, we aim to answer whether just a few sites are leading the movement, or if increases are apparent everywhere. Some answers to this are illustrated in Figure 6a, where we capture box plots of the volume of longform published at all sites over time. In particular, we aggregate the amount of longform published at each site during a six-month period, and then plot the distribution of these volumes, as in Figure 4a. This data is shown at six month intervals over a 10 year period. Given the heavy-tailed distribution of longform producing sites as described in 5.3.1, the box plots themselves are not visible.

However, it is interesting to see the outliers: there is not just a single site increasing in volume, but the number of total outliers and the degree of these outliers is increasing. This indicates that there are many, rather than just a few, sites that are driving the increase in longform volume.

We further investigate this in Figure 6b. This plot shows the number of new sites publishing longform, as indicated by the first longform byline date found on any article at that site. This indicates that it is not just that older sites are deciding to publish more longform, but rather new sites are either choosing to begin publishing longform (e.g. `buzzfeed.com` hiring a Longform Editor) or coming into existence for the purpose of publishing longform (e.g. `byliner.com` and other longform startups [36]).

5.3.3 Characteristics of Longform Interaction

Though we utilized several defining characteristics of longform while developing our classifier (Section 3), the corpus provides another opportunity to gather new insights about how different parties interact with longform versus news.

One such party is the publishers themselves. We measure their perception of the value of longform by measuring whether they bring older articles online, as this can be a laborious process. The "age" of an article at publication is calculated by taking the difference in the document crawl date and publication date.

Figure 7 plots the distribution of article ages for both longform and news. These numbers are scaled by the total number of longform or news articles, respectively, so that they can be fairly compared. Older longform articles at all ages are nearly twice as likely to be put online than news, including quite old articles, such as those published 15 years prior to coming online. This indicates that there may be more interest in these archived articles, either from the readers or publishers themselves. Given the low relative frequencies for both groups, however, it is also clear that the great majority of both longform and news articles on the web are put online directly after publication.

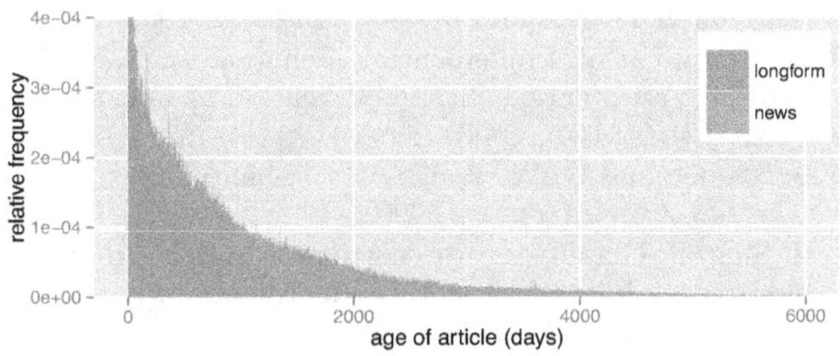

Figure 7: Distribution of the age of articles for longform and news. We see that longform articles are more likely to be put online after their by-line date than news articles.

In Figure 8, we investigate claims that longform is "evergreen", or that it stays relevant longer than other journalistic styles [26]. We measure this by looking at the number of days until 2 months pass without our webcrawler finding any new anchors pointing to the document, which signifies that a systematic loss of interest has occurred. We show boxplots for these numbers over all news and longform articles. Though the results for both are quite heavy-tailed (most articles receive links for just a few days), longform articles tend to maintain external links, a proxy for interest, longer than typical news articles. Some of the larger longform outliers retain anchors for nearly three months, which is significant given that most articles fall out of popular interest within a single day of being published.

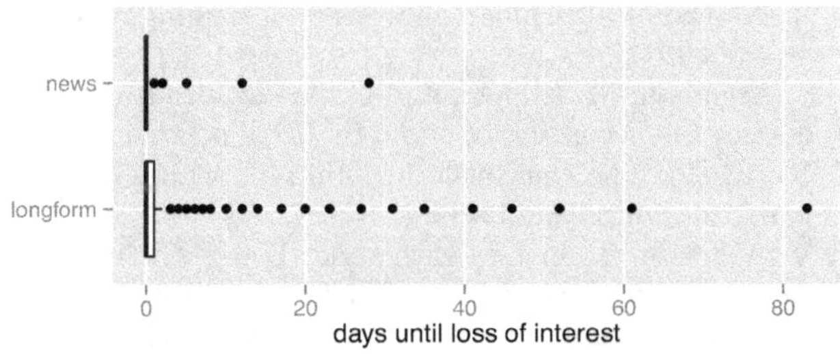

Figure 8: The distribution of the number of days until a loss of interest (i.e. a break of 8 weeks of anchors) occurs in longform vs news. We see that longform tends to stay interesting for a longer period of time than news.

6. CONCLUSIONS

In this paper, we provide a way of selecting features to build a classifier that can successfully differentiate between longform and non-longform articles. Despite the huge variety in writing that is considered acceptable for a longform piece (as opposed to, for example, news reports), we show that using language features like parse structures, in combination with other simple document features, is surprisingly successful. We demonstrate how to generate viable training data and provide an experiment for labeling it with crowdsourced raters. Our workflow in developing and using our classification system serves as an example for others hoping to successfully utilize the web for similar purposes.

Using the developed classifier, we build a corpus of longform and news documents from a web crawl and make several scientific discoveries about the longform ecosystem. Our findings include that the longform ecosystem is growing, both in terms of sheer number of documents published, as well as sites on the web creating this content, but that it is growing more slowly than other forms of publications, like online news reporting. While the average article published online does not receive sustained reader interest, we do find that successful longform articles live up to the 'hype' that they are more relevant and interesting for longer. These findings contribute to our general knowledge of what digital publishing looks like now and how it has changed over the past decade.

As to the future of longform, we believe that defining exactly what longform is will continue to grow more difficult, as it begins to include more immersive and multimedia content as all publishing moves online (see early examples like the New York Times' "Snow Fall: The Avalanche at Tunnel Creek"). As a result of our study, the supply to the ecosystem appears to be quite healthy, though we reserve the right not to prognosticate about how this will change over the next decade. We leave the final word to Naomi Arnold that the future is "cautiously hopeful" [5].

Acknowledgements. The authors are grateful for help and advice from Pavan Desikan, Anand Shukla and Amar Subramanya, and to Dean Weesner for designing the rater experiment.

7. REFERENCES

[1] The state of news media, *Pew Research Center*, 2013.

[2] S. Abbar et al. Real-time recommendation of diverse related articles. In *WWW*, 2013.

[3] A. Ahmed et al. Unified analysis of streaming news. In *WWW*, 2011.

[4] S. Argamon, M. Koppel, and G. Avneri. Routing documents according to style. In *IIS Workshop*, 1998.

[5] N. Arnold. The cautiously hopeful renaissance of longform journalism, 2014.

[6] V. Ashok et al. Success with style: Using writing style to predict the success of novels. *Poetry*, 2013.

[7] J. Bennet. Against 'long-form' journalism, *The Atlantic*, 2013.

[8] P. N. Bennett, K. Svore, and S. T. Dumais. Classification-enhanced ranking. In *WWW*, 2010.

[9] A. Berger, S. Pietra, and V. Pietra. A maximum entropy approach to natural language processing. *Computational Linguistics*, 1996.

[10] J. Bollen, H. Mao, and A. Pepe. Modeling public mood and emotion: Twitter sentiment and socio-economic phenomena. In *ICWSM*, 2011.

[11] T. Capote. The duke in his domain, *New Yorker*, 1957.

[12] C. Cooper. The death of slow journalism, *American Journalism Review*, 2009.

[13] C. Danescu-Niculescu-Mizil et al. No country for old members: User lifecycle and linguistic change in online communities. In *WWW*, 2013.

[14] M.-C. de Marneffe, B. MacCartney, and C. Manning. Generating typed dependency parses from phrase structure parses. In *LREC*, 2006.

[15] L. DVorkin. Inside forbes: How longform journalism is finding its digital audience, *Forbes*, 2012.

[16] A. Finn and N. Kushmerick. Learning to classify documents according to genre. *JASIST*, 2006.

[17] A. Finn, N. Kushmerick, and B. Smyth. Genre classification and domain transfer for information filtering. In *Advances in Information Retrieval*. 2002.

[18] K. Ganchev and M. Dredze. Small statistical models by random feature mixing. In *Workshop on Mobile NLP at ACL*, 2008.

[19] M. Garber. Sit back, relax, and read that long story on your phone, *The Atlantic*, 2014.

[20] M. Gaulon-Brain. Print media and television: Is longform bound for extinction?, *Ina Global*, 2013.

[21] S. Gollapalli et al. Researcher homepage classification using unlabeled data. In *WWW*, 2013.

[22] G. Greenwald and E. MacAskill. Nsa prism program taps in to user data of apple, google and others, *The Guardian*, 2013.

[23] M. Henzinger. Finding near-duplicate web pages: A large-scale evaluation of algorithms. In *SIGIR*, 2006.

[24] E. Hovy, M. Marcus, M. Palmer, L. Ramshaw, and R. Weischedel. Ontonotes: the 90% solution. In *NAACL-HLT*, 2006.

[25] C. Johnston. What buzzfeed's evolution says about the future of longform journalism, *Poynter*, 2012.

[26] Kaggle. Stumbleupon evergreen classification challenge, 2013. `https://www.kaggle.com/c/stumbleupon`.

[27] S. Kamdar. Highlighting content creators in search results. Inside Search, Google Search Blog, 2011.

[28] S. Kandell. What i learned from a year of doing longform at buzzfeed, *The Big Round Table*, 2013.

[29] H. Kwak et al. What is twitter, a social network or a news media? In *WWW*, 2010.

[30] M. Lewis. Obama's way, *Vanity Fair*, 2012.

[31] J. Liu, P. Dolan, and E. Pedersen. Personalized news recommendation based on click behavior. In *IUI*, 2010.

[32] A. Louis and A. Nenkova. What makes writing great? first experiments on article quality prediction in the science journalism domain. *TACL*, 1:341–352, 2013.

[33] Y. Lv et al. Learning to model relatedness for news recommendation. In *WWW*, 2011.

[34] J. Mahler. When 'long-form' is bad form, *The New York Times*, 2014.

[35] F. Manjoo. You won't finish this article, *Slate*, 2013.

[36] K. McBride. Jill abramson startup to advance writers up to $100k for longform work, *Poynter*, 2014.

[37] I. Meuret. A short history of long-form journalism, *Ina Global*, 2013.

[38] P. Nayak. In-depth articles in search results. Inside Search, Google Search Blog, 2013.

[39] J. Nivre et al. The conll 2007 shared task on dependency parsing. In *EMNLP-CoNLL*, 2007.

[40] L. Page, S. Brin, R. Motwani, and T. Winograd. The pagerank citation ranking: Bringing order to the web. Technical report, Stanford InfoLab, 1999.

[41] S. Parker. Buzzfeed's success does not mean we should be slaves to clicks, *The Guardian*, 2014.

[42] N. Paumgarten. Up and then down, *New Yorker*, 2008.

[43] C. Plante. Street fighter: The movie - what went wrong, *Polygon Magazine*, 2014.

[44] S. W. Raudenbush and A. S. Bryk. *Hierarchical linear models: Applications and data analysis methods*. 2002.

[45] R. Rieder. Long-form journalism makes a comeback, *USA Today*, 2013.

[46] Salmon. Jeff bezos and his journalists. *Reuters*, 2013.

[47] M. Santini et al. Implementing a characterization of genre for automatic genre identification of web pages. In *COLING/ACL*, 2006.

[48] J. Sappell and R. W. Welkos. The scientology story. *The Los Angeles Times*, 1990.

[49] S. Sharoff. Classifying web corpora into domain and genre using automatic feature identification. In *Web as Corpus Workshop*, 2007.

[50] B. Smith. What the longform backlash is all about, *Medium.com*, 2014.

[51] D. Starkman. Major papers' longform meltdown, *Columbia Journalism Review*, 2013.

[52] G. Talese. Frank sinatra has a cold, *Esquire*, 1966.

[53] A. Tumasjan et al. Predicting elections with twitter. In *ICWSM*, 2010.

[54] D. F. Wallace. The string theory, *Esquire*, 1996.

[55] H. Wang et al. Joint relevance and freshness learning from clickthroughs for news search. In *WWW*, 2012.

[56] G. Wong and W. Mason. The hierarchical logistic regression model for multilevel analysis. *Journal of the American Statistical Association*, 1985.

Early Prediction of Cardiac Arrest (Code Blue) using Electronic Medical Records

Sriram Somanchi
Carnegie Mellon University
Pittsburgh, USA
somanchi@cmu.edu

Samrachana Adhikari
Carnegie Mellon University
Pittsburgh, USA
asamrach@andrew.cmu.edu

Allen Lin
Harvard University
Cambridge, MA
allenlin@g.harvard.edu

Elena Eneva
Accenture
San Francisco, USA
elena.eneva@accenture.com

Rayid Ghani
University of Chicago
Chicago, USA
rayid@uchicago.edu

ABSTRACT

Code Blue is an emergency code used in hospitals to indicate when a patient goes into cardiac arrest and needs resuscitation. When Code Blue is called, an on-call medical team staffed by physicians and nurses is paged and rushes in to try to save the patient's life. It is an intense, chaotic, and resource-intensive process, and despite the considerable effort, survival rates are still less than 20% [4]. Research indicates that patients actually start showing clinical signs of deterioration some time before going into cardiac arrest[1][2][3], making early prediction, and possibly intervention, feasible. In this paper, we describe our work, in partnership with NorthShore University HealthSystem, that preemptively flags patients who are likely to go into cardiac arrest, using signals extracted from demographic information, hospitalization history, vitals and laboratory measurements in patient-level electronic medical records. We find that early prediction of Code Blue is possible and when compared with state of the art existing method used by hospitals (MEWS - Modified Early Warning Score) [4], our methods perform significantly better. Based on these results, this system is now being considered for deployment in hospital settings.

Categories and Subject Descriptors

I.2.1 [**Artificial Intelligence**]: Applications and Expert Systems—*Medicine and science*

Keywords

Machine Learning; Data Mining; SVM; Code Blue; Cardiac Arrest; Electronic Medical Records; Early Prediction

KDD'15, August 11-14, 2015, Sydney, NSW, Australia.
 ISBN 978-1-4503-3664-2/15/08 ...$15.00.
DOI: http://dx.doi.org/10.1145/2783258.2788588.

1. INTRODUCTION

Code Blue is used to alert a rapid response team (RRT) in a hospital when a patient goes into cardiac arrest and needs resuscitation. The rapid response team intervenes, dropping other tasks they are attending to at the time, and rushes to the Code Blue patient to possibly improve his or her deteriorating condition. More than 200,000 adult in-hospital cardiac arrests occur in the United States each year, and as many as 80% of these incidents result in the death of the patient [4]. Medical professionals believe that if Code Blues can be predicted in advance, applying medical interventions can prevent some of these deaths. In addition to saving lives, early Code Blue prediction can also provide time for a hospital to plan for interventions and allocate resources accordingly, such that other patients do not suffer because of sudden shifts of resources during Code Blues.

There are some existing early warning systems [4] being used to predict which patients are at risk of entering Code Blue. However, these systems have some shortcomings:

1. They require continuous monitoring of patients by clinical staff. This might be possible for patients in the ICU, but around 50% of Code Blues take place in wards outside the ICU, where monitoring is only intermittent, and the interval between visits could very well be as long as 8 hours [5].
2. They use only limited patient characteristics. With increased use of electronic medical records (EMRs), we believe that using all the existing patient characteristics can result in a more effective early warning system.
3. They classify patients into two classes (positive or negative) without ranking them, making it difficult to prioritize within the group of patients classified as likely to go into Code Blue.

The goal of this work is to flag (and rank) patients who are at risk of cardiac arrest, so that doctors can intervene early before a cardiac arrest (Code Blue event) occurs. The questions we consider are: i) how early can we make a prediction? ii) how precise are our predictions? and iii) how many Code Blues do we catch before they happen?

The sooner we can make a prediction, the sooner the intervention can be administered, and the more time a hospital has to plan for this and adjust schedules of response teams and availability of equipment. At the same time, our predictions need to balance the false positive rate to avoid unnecessary interventions (and associated opportunity costs) with making sure that we catch and prevent as many future cardiac arrests as possible. These factors can be considered as tradeoffs in our system since we could possibly increase the precision by waiting until a few seconds before a cardiac arrest to predict such events very accurately, but doing so makes the alert mostly useless since it may be unpreventable with just a few seconds of lead time. We model this problem as a prediction problem and use data collected by monitoring different vitals and lab results of patients leading up to the current time to flag patients who are at risk of entering Code Blue in the next several hours. We treat this as a classification problem and use support vector machines and logistic regression. We compare their performance to the early warning method currently used by hospitals (MEWS) and find that our methods significantly outperform the MEWS method and result in earlier, more precise Code Blue predictions. The methods we develop in this paper are focused on a much broader class of patients (ward patients), unlike the Multiparameter Intelligent Monitoring in Intensive Care II (MIMIC-II) database, which consists of data coming only from ICU patients at a much higher frequency through continuous monitors. This makes our approach especially important for ward patients who are not under constant monitoring but are still at risk of cardiac arrest.

The rest of the paper is organized as follows. We begin by introducing our project partner and data in Section 2. We then explain the model setup and the classification methods used in Section 3. In Section 4 we explain, in detail, our method for feature extraction. We also briefly mention other methods that could potentially improve our method, and are part of future work. In the next two Sections (5 and 6), we explain construction of training and evaluation sets, along with a method for assessing the performance of different models, and for estimating variability in prediction. Finally, we end with our findings in Section 7, and a short discussion about the results and deployment plans in Section 8.

2. DATA AND PROJECT PARTNER

The work described in this paper was done in partnership with NorthShore University HealthSystem. This hospital system contains four individual facilities in the Chicago area. We used patient-level information for about 133,000 in-hospital patients extracted from electronic medical records (EMR) from 2006 to 2011. Code Blue was called for only 0.5% of the 133,000 patients in the hospital. Some of the patients had multiple hospital encounters: the data consists of around 232,000 encounters, and Code Blue alerts were called on only 815 encounters (for patients in the general medical-surgical ward, as well as in the Intensive Care Unit). This extremely skewed class distribution makes the prediction task very difficult.

The data extracted from the EMR system includes information on demographics, past hospitalization history and real-time vitals and laboratory tests for these patients. Demographic features include patient's age, gender, race and ethnicity. We have information on twenty-nine different vitals and lab tests measured at different times since the patient was admitted in the hospital. Some examples of vitals are respiratory rate, systolic and diastolic blood pressures, pulse oximetry and temperature. Lab tests include hemoglobin, platelet count, hematocrit, creatinine and sodium levels. Figure 1 is a summary plot of different vitals and labs in the data.

These measurements are neither taken at equally spaced time points nor at the same frequency for different vitals and lab tests, as demonstrated in Figure 2. We did not perform any sampling and obtained the data exactly as it was recorded in the EMR system. Figure 2 displays the readings of 5 different vitals of a patient who went into Code Blue (at the time indicated by the vertical red line). As we can see in the plot, vitals like heart rate and blood pressure are recorded frequently and periodically. However, vitals like carbon dioxide level are recorded less frequently. Moreover, different patients were admitted in the hospital for different lengths of time. This nature of the data makes the application of typical time series algorithms difficult. We need a good and valid procedure to incorporate temporal property of the data along with information embedded in inconsistencies in data collection. Our method for feature extraction is discussed in Section 4.

We approach this problem as a two stage estimation problem. First stage is to estimate trend and temporal properties of the variables that were recorded at irregular time points in the last 24 hours. Because the length of stay is different for different patients, we use vitals information in the last 24 hours for estimating trends, and use length of stay as a feature. This truncation was necessary to have a uniform comparison across patients. Next, using the estimated trend and temporal properties along with other time constant features, we use standard classification methods like support vector machine and logistic regression, to classify patients who went into code-blue in their hospital stay. We briefly discuss the classification model in the next section.

3. CLASSIFICATION METHODOLOGY

We use classification methods to predict whether Code Blue will occur for a patient in the next h hours, from a given time point, using information leading up to that time. The time point at which prediction is made is denoted as T^P. Time when the event occurs, i.e. h hours after T^P, is called event time and is denoted as T^E. We are interested in predicting the outcome (Y_i) at T^E where:

$$Y_i = \begin{cases} 1 \text{ if patient i goes into Code Blue by } T^E \\ 0 \text{ if patient i does not go into Code Blue by } T^E \end{cases}$$

We create features with medical information up to T^P for both patients who went into Code Blue at T^E (case patients) and those who did not (control patients). Next, given the features at T^P and before, we want to predict how likely a patient is going to go into Code Blue h hours after T^P, such that $T^E - T^P = h$. In our analysis, $h \in \{1, 2, 3, 4\}$, implying that we have four different classification problems. Also note that there is not a well-defined T^E for patients who never go into Code Blue. It ranges from the time a patient was admitted to when the patient was discharged. As the patient never went into Code Blue, the patient can be a negative example in the entire period. We provide an argument on why choice of T^E for control patients matters, and give some intuition on how we went about choosing it for training in Section 5. Figure 3 is a pictorial representation of the problem setup.

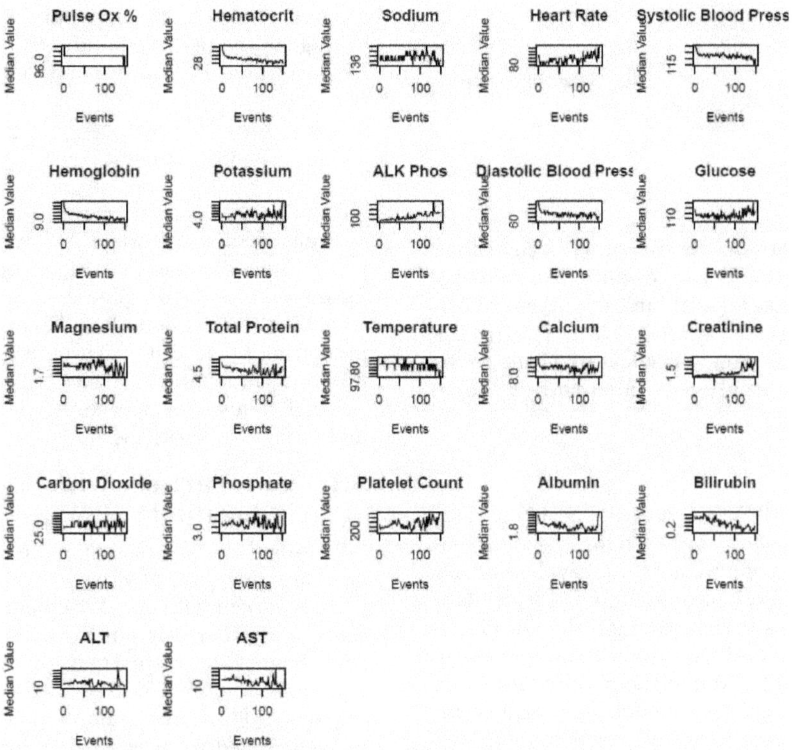

Figure 1: Summary plot of different vitals and labs for patients who go into Code Blue: Along the x-axis are different time points for which data was collected for at least one patient in the last 150 time points. Note that the event times are not regular. Along the y-axis are the median measurements for patients at that time point. This plot shows the variation in population medians of different vitals and lab measurements available for patients right before Code Blue.

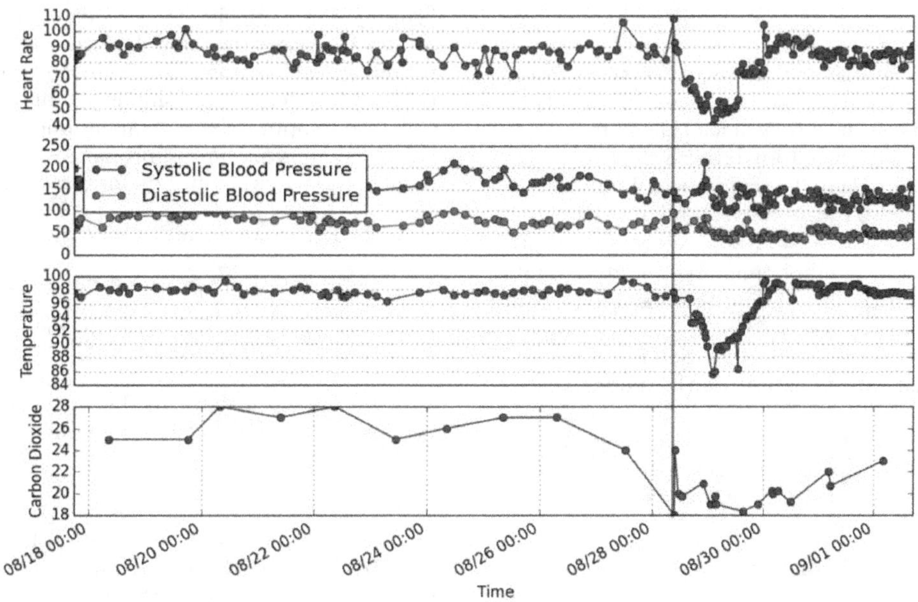

Figure 2: Example of patient-level data for five different vitals. The vertical red line represents the time of Code Blue.

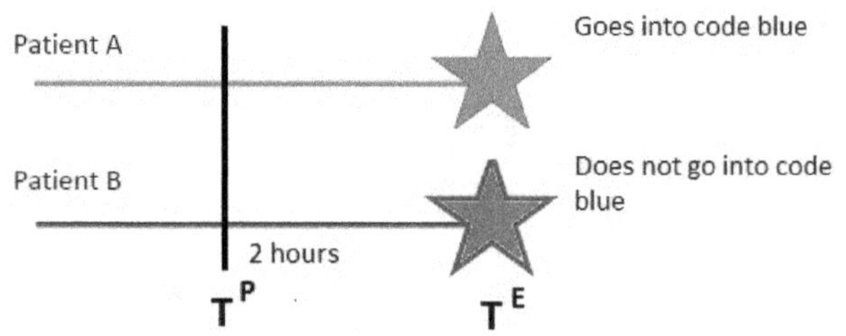

Figure 3: Pictorial representation of the problem setup. We want to classify the events labeled by blue star (=1) and red star (=0), using information before T^P. Time interval between T^P and T^E in this example is 2 hours. We vary prediction time from 1 to 4 hours to see how early we can predict Code Blue.

Support vector machine (SVM) with radial kernel and logistic regression with lasso penalty are used for classification. We train these classifiers on training data, and evaluate their performance by making predictions on held-out (future) test data. SVM with radial basis kernel results in better classification performance but we find that the logistic regression models are more interpretable. While the main goal of this paper is building a good predictive model, it is also of interest to explore how logistic regression perform compared to SVM and what are the important features selected by logistic regression.

Define Y^n as a vector of n outcomes and $X^{(n \times p)}$ as a matrix of p features, for each classification problem. Recall that SVM is formulated as a following optimization problem [11]:

$$\min_{\beta,\beta_0} \frac{1}{2}||\beta||^2 + C\sum_{i=1}^{N}\psi_i \quad \text{subject to } \psi_i \geq 0, y_i(x_i^T\beta + \beta_0) \geq 1 - \psi_i \forall i.$$

Here C is the cost parameter that regulates the number of overlaps in training points, and ψ is the proportion by which the prediction is on the wrong side of the margin, also called slack variables. We want to maximize the separation while minimizing the overlap. For non-linear boundary in original space kernelized SVM is used. Radial basis kernel is given by $K(x,x^{'}) = exp(-\gamma||x - x^{'}||^2)$, where γ is a scale parameter. C and γ are tuning parameters chosen by 5-fold cross-validation in training data to find the best model that fits the selection criteria defined below.

Similarly, in logistic regression classification is done by estimating probability of $(Y_i = 1|X_i)$ using the model, $\text{logit}(P(Y_i = 1|X_i)) = X_i^T\beta$. When the dimension of X is large relative to the number of observation, logistic regression with lasso penalty helps to select sparse predictive models [10]. In this framework the coefficients, $\hat{\beta}$s, are estimated by solving following problem:

$$\min_{\beta} -\text{log likelihood } (\beta) + \lambda|\beta|.$$

λ is a tuning parameter of the model which controls the amount of regularization, and hence the sparsity in the estimated coefficients [11]. λ is selected by 5-fold cross-validation on training data to find the best model that fits the selection criteria.

We use F_1 score as a selection criteria. It is a measure of a test's accuracy. F_1 score can be interpreted as a weighted average of the precision and recall, where an F_1 score reaches its best value at 1 and worst score at 0. F_1 score is given by:

$$F_1 = 2\frac{\text{precision} \times \text{recall}}{\text{precision} + \text{recall}}$$

Recall (true positive rate) is computed as the proportion of true predicted Code Blue events over all the observed Code Blue, whereas FPR (false positive rate) is the ratio of false predicted Code Blue over total number of events that were observed as non-Code Blue. Since we are interested in predicting Code Blue with high recall and precision, we use this criteria for model selection in cross-validation.

Finally, note that the columns of the features are centered and scaled for these methods.

3.1 Comparison with existing methods used in hospitals

Modified Early Warning Score (MEWS) is a composite index commonly used by hospital staff to determine the severity of a patient's illness. We calculate MEWS by individually scoring the aberration of five vital signs (systolic blood pressure, heart rate, respiratory rate, temperature, and level of consciousness) on a scale of 0 to 3 and summing the resulting scores [4] at the time of prediction. A score of five or more is linked to increased likelihood of Code Blue [9]. We will use 5 as a threshold for predicting whether a patient will go into Code Blue. Because MEWS is frequently used in hospitals as a criteria in activating rapid response teams, it serves as an appropriate basis to compare our results to.

4. FEATURE EXTRACTION

A key aspect in the medical domain (and in any application of data mining) is building effective features for classification. We worked with physicians from NorthShore University HealthSystem as well as researched prior work to determine good features. For Code Blue prediction, it was important to incorporate using irregularly spaced and sparsely collected temporal data. As mentioned earlier, vitals and lab information have atypical properties that hinder in applying regular time series methods for classification:

1. They are not recorded at regular time intervals
2. Some vitals are recorded more regularly than others
3. For a given vital, there is more data at some time intervals compared to others
4. Since patients stay in the hospital for different periods of time, lengths of available data are not uniform across patients

We want to incorporate these properties of the data in our feature set. Along with information like trend and range of the variables at different time intervals, we also want to use information on how often the vital was recorded and when it was missing as features. We believe that they are important to identify the features of the data and of the data collection process that lead to the event.

For the analysis presented in this paper, we start with a simple approach to construct features. We divide the timeline of the patient's stay in the hospital into different windows to estimate temporal features and trends from the vitals and lab tests that change over time in an encounter [8] [6]. The timeline for temporal variables before prediction time, T^P, was divided into three windows. The first window contains information up to 3 hours before T^P, the second window contains information between 3 to 9 hours before T^P, and the third one contains information between 9 to 18 hours before T^P. We truncated the data at 18 hours for uniformity across patients, since we did not have information beyond 18 hours for some of the patients. We also use total length of stay of a patient as a feature. For each window and each patient, we compute the first and second moments of the empirical distribution of a variable in that window, along with minimum and maximum values, and the frequency of data collection. We estimate the trend in each window by segmented regression [6]. We fit a regression line in each window and record the slope of the line to include increasing or decreasing trend information in feature set.

This process results in 381 features using our data. These include both time constant features and the features we built for time varying variables. Missing values are replaced by the feature's mean for that time window.

We realize that this is still a rather naive approach to estimating trends, but is better than taking the average over all the periods, or considering each measurement of a vital for a patient at different time points as independent (i.i.d) (which they certainly are not). Currently we are fitting separate (discontinuous) least squares in each window that is of uniform size across patients. Ideally, we would like to use all available measurements of a vital for a patient to fit a piecewise linear function that estimates underlying linear trend and use its summary as features for classification [7].

There are more sophisticated methods in the literature (mostly in economics) related to trend filtering in time series or temporal data analysis, that will be a good guidance to further advance this work. We are especially interested in implementing l_1 trend filtering approach proposed by Kim et. al [7] for continuous temporal data. We are currently exploring ways to incorporate this method in our framework.

5. TRAINING

Since our goal is to build a system that will be deployed in the hospital response system, it is critical that the classifier works in a real-time hospital setting. We train our model on historical data, and use it to predict Code Blue on future holdout data. Our goal is to classify patients who will go into Code Blue as early as possible. We train different models for each early warning time threshold: one model that predicts if a patient goes into Code Blue in the next one hour, another in the next two hours, and so on. We choose the best parameters through 5-fold cross-validation of each model on training data.

One of the important considerations in our classifier is to choose the number of negative examples that should be considered to learn the differences in the two classes (Code Blue and non-Code Blue). Note that this is a highly unbalanced classification problem, where Code Blue is a rare event. We use a nested case-control approach to match control patients to every case patient, so that a classifier can learn the differences in training data easily. We match Code Blue patients to non-Code Blue patients with similar demographic features only, such that there remain differences in their physiological and hospitalization histories. We create a training set that is less skewed by sampling the data, to account for the unbalance of the two class labels. We vary the ratio of cases to controls in our training set as 1:1, 1:4 and 1:10, and we decide on the appropriate ratio based on the prediction results from the training data. It is important to note that we do not change the distribution of the test set. We only vary the number of controls sampled to construct the training set for our classifiers, but we use the natural distribution of the data for the test set. This is done to make sure the models we build are applicable when put in production and the results are still consistent with the initial experiments.

Further, we need to select time of comparable event (T^E) for control patients, so that we can build up the negative examples. For patients who go into Code Blue, time when they go into Code Blue defines the positive event. However, for patients who never go into Code Blue, we have the time from when they were admitted to the time when they were discharged as a choice for the negative event. Most of the patients who get discharged are healthier at the time of discharge than they were during (or at the beginning of) their stay. This makes using time of discharge as a comparable event a bad choice, as the classification problem will become artificially easy. Using time close to admission will not give us enough information to build an accurate model. In this analysis, we vary the time of event for control patients, as the 25th, 50th and 75th percentile of their stay time in the hospital, and select the value that performs best in the training data.

We experiment with using support vector machine (SVM) with radial kernel and sparse logistic regression with lasso penalty as classifiers [11]. γ and C for SVM and λ for logistic regression are selected by cross-validation with maximizing F_1-score as a criteria. Once we select optimal parameters, we refit on the entire training set using these tuning parameters for each method, and use the estimates for prediction on test data.

6. EVALUATION AND ESTIMATION OF STANDARD ERRORS

For every hour in the evaluation set, we take the features of all the patients in the hospital present at that hour. Using these features, we predict which patients would go into Code Blue 1, 2, 3 and 4 hours from that time point. This evaluation is used to compare classifiers and compute the best parameters for those classifiers, using recall and false positive rate (FPR) as metrics. Recall is computed as the proportion of true predicted Code Blue events over all the observed Code Blue, whereas FPR is the ratio of false predicted Code Blue over total number of non-Code Blue events. Also, receiver operation characteristics (ROC) curve for aggregate monthly predictions along with area under the curve (AUC) are compared among classifiers to evaluate their performance.

Our first training set consists of data before January 1, 2011. We use events in the month following the training period as test data. We then sequentially add additional months to the existing training data, and hence create 7 new training data. Estimates from each training set is evaluated on the test data in the following month. Following this procedure we have 8 training and test data. We compute mean recall and FPR, along with the standard error of the mean, over the 8 test data. We also compute MEWS scores for patients in the test data. Patients with MEWS scores greater than or equal to 5 are predicted to go into Code Blue in the next 4 hours. Note that, the first training data is contained in the next training set and so on. This is a time dependent data, where the Code Blues in the past might affect how hospital deals with Code Blues in the future. Hence, we believe that the hospital system learns from the past, so we use the past data to predict the future events. At the same time, multiple training and testing datasets give us a valid way to estimate standard errors of the mean recall and false positive rates for different models. Also, receiver operation characteristics (ROC) curve for aggregate monthly predictions along with area under the curve (AUC) are compared among classifiers to evaluate their performance.

7. RESULTS

Based on mean recall and false positive rate from predictions on multiple test data, we find that using 1:4 case to control (positive to negative class) ratio and 75% percentile time point as a comparative event for the control group in training gives the best results in terms of AUC. The rest of the results presented in this section are based on using these parameters.

We were able to predict Code Blue with around 80% recall and 20% false positive rate at 4 hours ahead of the event. We find that SVM performs better than the current method used by medical practitioners (MEWS) in terms of mean recall and FPR, as shown in Figure 4, and in terms of ROC and AUC, as shown in Figure 5. We also ran sparse logistic regression on the similar framework. Prediction from SVM has significantly lower false positive rate compared to logistic regression. Even though predictions from SVM have higher mean recall, they are not significantly higher for all time points. Both, SVM and logistic regression performed better than MEWS in terms of recall. False positive rate estimated from MEWS has bigger standard errors, and thus we could not be certain about the performance of our method compared to MEWS. As we can observe from the results, the benefit of using our machine learning methods increases as we make our predictions earlier. MEWS gets much worse (especially in terms of recall) compared to SVM as we make our predictions earlier in time. This is critical since our goal is to make these predictions as early as possible to enable the hospital to intervene early, as well as modify the schedules for physicians and nurses to optimize overall quality of care for all patients.

One of the advantages of logistic regression is its popularity among medical practitioners because of its interpretability in terms of understanding important features. From our analysis, we see that the mean, the variability, and the trend (rate of acceleration/deceleration) of features like heart rate, respiratory rate, diastolic blood pressure, and pulse oxygen levels are important features for predictions at all hours. Moreover, the frequency at which lab measurements are taken is also a good predictive feature, and its importance increases as we make earlier predictions. Figure 6 shows the top features selected in the 1 hour ahead prediction. One interesting finding is that as we try to predict further out into the future, more features become relevant. For example, 72 features were selected as important features in the 1 hour ahead as compared to 100 features for the 2 hours ahead prediction. We think that this is because prediction gets more difficult as we try to predict Code Blue earlier, and the model needs (and uses) more features to perform effectively. However, we do not have any measure of uncertainty of these estimates, and while these features are helpful to understand their effect on Code Blue, it is difficult to make any inferences. The important features selected by our model are shown in Figure 6, where we also provide the coefficients of features in the sparse logistic regression. The coefficients represent the log odds ratio of the feature in predicting Code Blues.

8. CONCLUSIONS AND FUTURE WORK

In this paper, we described a system we are building to create an early warning prediction system for in-hospital cardiac arrests that surpasses the existing methods used by hospitals and medical practitioners. This gives hospital staff the ability to intervene before the patient becomes critical, thus averting some potential Code Blue occurrences, and ultimately saving more lives. This also reduces the opportunity cost of the medical personnel having to drop their current hospital activities to rush to attend to Code Blue patients, and facilitates more efficient and effective planning and scheduling. We found that this prediction can be made as early as 4 hours before the Code Blue event with high recall and relatively low false positive rate. Most importantly, we verified the hypothesis that patients show clinical signs of deterioration before going into cardiac arrest, and vital signs and lab measurements can be used to determine these signals.

There are certainly approaches that would improve the performance of these models by adding additional features that we did not have access to, such as using diagnosis information from patient records. Also, the extreme imbalance in class labels in the data had caused some difficulties in creating test and training sets. A good future direction would be to combine data from different hospital systems, so the algorithm can be trained on more positive examples, which should improve predictions further.

While we have significantly higher recall compared to the currently used score (MEWS), we are only slightly better than MEWS in mean FPR. A future step would be to work with medical practitioners and understand this trade-off in deployed systems.

Lastly, as mentioned in Section 4, there is a lot of potential for improving estimation with trends in time-varying features. Exploring more sophisticated and statistically sound time-series methods is a priority for future work.

9. DEPLOYMENT PLANS

The work described here was done in partnership with NorthShore University HealthSystem. We collaborated with the team in the hospital and presented these methods and results to a set of doctors and researchers. Based on our results that outperform the currently used MEWS score, we are now in discussions with NorthShore Hospital as well as with other hospitals and analytical providers to determine the best way to deploy such a system. One approach we are considering is converting the classifier into a set of database queries that runs on top of the EMR system and feeds into an alerting system. This alerting system would raise an alert when a potential Code Blue is about to happen in the next

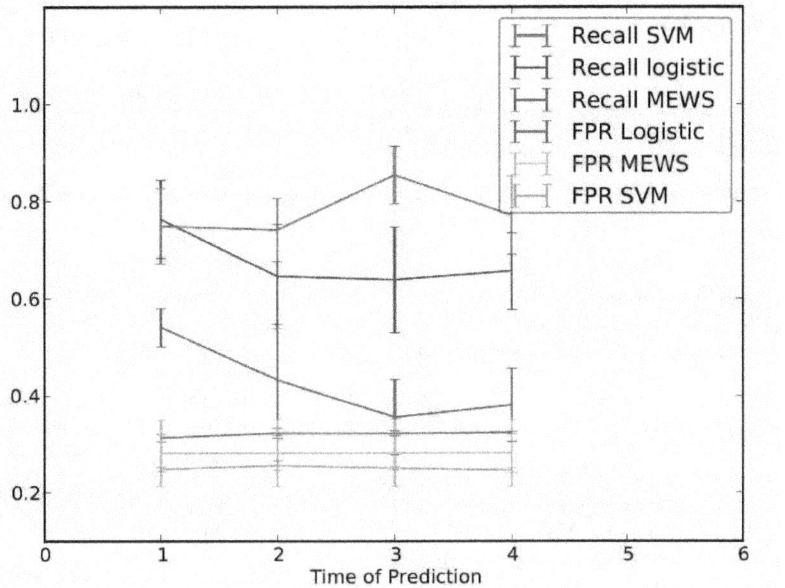

Figure 4: Comparison of the performance of SVM, Logistic Regression and MEWS. Along the x-axis is time of prediction before Code Blue. For example, 4 on the x-axis means the prediction is made 4 hours before the event. Along the y-axis is recall or false positive rate. Different colors are for different classification methods.

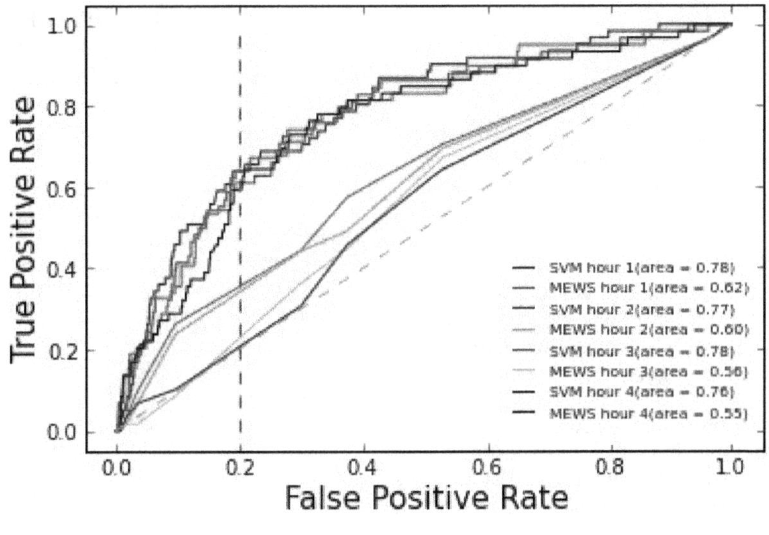

Figure 5: ROC curves for comparing the performance of SVM and MEWS. Area under the curve for each method, along with the number of hours ahead when making the prediction, is mentioned in the legend.

Number of Previous Code Blues	0.23
Number of Previous Discharges to Home	0.16
Emergency Admission	0.15
Number of Previous Encounters	0.13
Minimum Potassium	0.24
Platelet Count Window 0	0.22
GFR Count	0.12
Glucose Count	0.19
Glucose Count Window 2	0.11
Hematocrit Count Window 1	0.16

Average Respiratory Rate	0.20
Average Heart Rate Window 1	0.11
Minimum Heart Rate	0.14
SD Respiratory Rate Window 1	0.29
SD Heart Rate Window 0	0.13
SD Heart Rate Window 2	0.21
SD Diastolic Blood Pressure Window 2	0.16

Figure 6: The top features selected by our sparse logistic regression for the 1 hour ahead prediction.

n hours. In addition, the classifier would also provide input to the hospital scheduling system that will allow administrators to optimize the overall quality of care they provide to patients.

10. ACKNOWLEDGEMENTS

This work was supported by the 'Eric and Wendy Schmidt Data Science for Social Good' Summer Fellowship at the University of Chicago in 2013. We also thank Dr. Jonathan Silverstein, Vice President and Head of the Center for Clinical and Research Informatics at NorthShore University Health Systems, for his valuable inputs, access to data and supporting our efforts to deploy the methods into their hospitals.The data from this study were obtained as part of a collaboration between the University of Chicago and NorthShore University Health Systems, which was funded by an institutional Clinical and Translational Science Award grant (UL1 RR024999; PI: Dr. Julian Solway). We are grateful to Drs. Dana Edelson, Matthew Churpek, Ari Robicek and Christopher Winslow for study conception and/or data acquisition. In addition, Poome Chamnankit, Kelly Bhatia, Audrey Seitman and Justin Lakemen extracted the data.

References

[1] C. A. Alvarez, C. A. Clark, S. Zhang, E. A. Halm, J. J. Shannon, C. E. Girod, L. Cooper, and R. Amarasingham. Predicting out of intensive care unit cardiopulmonary arrest or death using electronic medical record data. *BMC Medical Informatics and Decision Making*, 13:28, 2013.

[2] M. Buist, E. Jarmolowski, P. Burton, S. Bernard, B. Waxman, and J. Anderson. Recognising clinical instability in hospital patients before cardiac arrest or unplanned admission to intensive care. a pilot study in a tertiary-care hospital. *Med Journal*, 171, 1999.

[3] P. Chan, A. Kalid, L. Longmore, R. Berg, M. Kosiborod, and J. Spertus. Hospital-wide code rates and mortality before and after implementation of a rapid response team. *JAMA*, 300, 2008.

[4] M. M. Churpek, T. C. Yuen, M. T. Huber, S. Y. Park, J. B. Hall, and D. P. Edelson. Predicting cardiac arrest on the wards, a nested case-control study. *American College of Chest Physicians*, 11-1301, 2012.

[5] D. A. Jones, M. A. DeVita, and R. Bellomo. Rapid-response teams. *New England Journal of Medicine*, 365(2), 2011.

[6] E. Keogh, S. Chu, D. Hart, and M. Pazzani. Segmenting time series: A survey and novel approach. *Data Mining in Time Series Databases*, 2004.

[7] S.-J. Kim, K. Koh, S. Boyd, and D. Gorinevsky. l1 trend filtering, 2009.

[8] C. Sian and L. David. Effective probability forecasting for time series data using standard machine learning techniques. *Proceeding of the third international conference on advances in pattern recognition*, August 2005.

[9] C. Subbe, M. Kruger, P. Rutherford, and L. Gemmel. Validation of a modified early warning score in medical admissions. *QJM*, 94(10):521–526, 2001.

[10] R. Tibshirani. Regression shrinkage and selection via the lasso. *Journal of the Royal Statistical Society, Series B*, 58:267–288, 1994.

[11] H. Trevor, T. Robert, and F. Jerome. *The Elements of Statistical Learning*. Springer Series in Statistics. Springer New York Inc., New York, NY, USA, 2001.

When-To-Post on Social Networks

Nemanja Spasojevic, Zhisheng Li, Adithya Rao, Prantik Bhattacharyya
Lithium Technologies | Klout
San Francisco, CA
{nemanja, zhisheng.li, adithya, prantik}@klout.com

ABSTRACT

For many users on social networks, one of the goals when broadcasting content is to reach a large audience. The probability of receiving reactions to a message differs for each user and depends on various factors, such as location, daily and weekly behavior patterns and the visibility of the message. While previous work has focused on overall network dynamics and message flow cascades, the problem of recommending personalized posting times has remained an underexplored topic of research.

In this study, we formulate a *when-to-post* problem, where the objective is to find the best times for a user to post on social networks in order to maximize the probability of audience responses. To understand the complexity of the problem, we examine user behavior in terms of post-to-reaction times, and compare cross-network and cross-city weekly reaction behavior for users in different cities, on both Twitter and Facebook. We perform this analysis on over a billion posted messages and observed reactions, and propose multiple approaches for generating personalized posting schedules. We empirically assess these schedules on a sampled user set of 0.5 million active users and more than 25 million messages observed over a 56 day period. We show that users see a reaction gain of up to 17% on Facebook and 4% on Twitter when the recommended posting times are used.

We open the dataset used in this study, which includes timestamps for over 144 million posts and over 1.1 billion reactions. The personalized schedules derived here are used in a fully deployed production system to recommend posting times for millions of users every day.

Categories and Subject Descriptors

J.4 [**Computer Applications**]: Social and Behavioral Sciences; H.1.2 [**Information Systems**]: Models and Principles—*User/Machine Systems*; J.4 [**Computer Applications**]: Information Systems Applications

KDD '15, August 10-13, 2015, Sydney, NSW, Australia.
ACM 978-1-4503-3664-2/15/08..
DOI: http://dx.doi.org/10.1145/2783258.2788584

Keywords

user modeling; personalization; behavior analysis; recommended systems; online social networks; posting times;

1. INTRODUCTION

Social networks have emerged as major platforms for communication in recent years, with hundreds of millions of interactions created by users every day. Though the underlying mechanisms may vary, a large number of active interactions may be classified under (a) users posting messages, or (b) users reacting to messages. Posted messages may sometimes be intended for a few friends and family members, while other times they may be geared towards larger audiences. The latter is especially true for users such as brands, marketers and public figures, who leverage social media as platforms for broadcasting messages.

One of the goals while broadcasting messages is to capture the attention of audience members so that they may react to the posted message. The probability that an audience member reacts to a message may depend on several factors, such as his daily and weekly behavior patterns, his location or timezone, and the volume of other messages competing for his attention. The problem of broadcasting messages at the right time in order to elicit responses from one's audience is therefore a complex one with many dimensions.

A large body of research in this area has focused on the problem of influence maximization and related topics, where the goal is to target a specific subset of users in order to create information cascades in the network. However, the dynamics of broadcasting to entire audiences, rather than picking specific individuals to target, has been an under-explored topic of study. Further, since each user has a unique audience, any recommendations for posting times need to be personalized to be effective, as we show in this study. We hence formulate a *when-to-post* problem here, where the objective is to find the best times for a user to post on social networks in order to increase audience responses.

Apart from introducing the problem, our contributions in this work are three-fold. First, in order to understand the complexity of the *when-to-post* problem and the factors that affect it, we perform in-depth **user reaction behavior analysis**, which includes:

1. *Post-to-reaction behavior:* We analyze the delays between posting and reaction times across different social networks and user in-degrees.

2. *Cross-network analysis:* We examine the similarities and differences of audience behavior on Twitter and Facebook.

3. *Cross-city analysis:* We compare cycles of daily and weekly user activity in different cities, and present analysis on how location affects posting schedules.

Second, we formally define the *when-to-post* problem in a probabilistic setting, and propose multiple approaches for **recommending personalized posting schedules**. Among these are the *First-Degree* and the *Second-Degree* schedules, and their corresponding weighted counterparts. We empirically assess these schedules against two global baselines, on a real-world set of 0.5 million active users observed over a 56 day period. We define a metric called *Reaction Gain* that helps us evaluate the effectiveness of the two approaches, and show that users see an average reaction gain of up to 17% for Facebook and upto 4% for Twitter.

Third, we open a public dataset consisting of anonymized user ids and timestamp data that could help future research in this area. This dataset contains timestamps for **144 million** posts and **1.1 billion** reactions from a 120-day period.

We performed our study and analysis on a full production system deployed on *klout.com.* Klout[1] is a social media platform that aggregates and analyzes data from social networks [14] such as Twitter, Facebook, Google+ and others. Our system recommends personalized posting schedules for millions of users to share content on Twitter and Facebook.

2. RELATED WORK

The subject of user behavior dynamics on social networks has attracted significant research attention [10, 6, 2]. Wu et al. [16] categorized Twitter users into elite and casual users and analyzed the differences in how they generate and consume information. In their study, they showed that regardless of the type of content, all content had very short life spans that usually dropped exponentially after a day. Another study in [1] also showed that only a few topics lasted for a long time on social media platforms, while most topics faded away quickly in the order of 20-40 minutes.

Besides the life span of messages, researchers have also analyzed the effects of timezone and location on user activity patterns. Kwak et al. [9] analyzed the timezone characteristics of user audiences on Twitter and reported that the average timezone difference between a user and her friends varied with the number of friends. In our study, we further analyze the impact of audience location on the volume of responses towards a message.

There have been several studies on modeling the dynamics of social network events [12, 15]. For example, the work in [15] used different convolution functions to analyze the flow of news events and sentiments through Twitter. While the approach of these studies has been to analyze the overall temporal characteristics on social media, here we take the further step of analyzing reaction behavior from the point of view of each individual user, thereby enabling personalized recommendations for posting messages.

Another line of related research is in the area of information flow and diffusion. Studies such as [11, 13, 5] have analyzed how factors such as the topological structure of social networks play a role in information cascades. Yang et al. [17] presented results on analyzing message flow based on Twitter mentions, and found that long-term historical user properties such as the rate of previous mentions were as important as the tweet content. The authors in [18] studied the importance of hashtag adoption in determining the popularity and spread of tweets. The study in [7] proposed a predictive approach to model dynamics of diffusion in social networks based on social, semantic and temporal dimensions. However, the problem of examining the flow of messages in the entire network differs significantly from the one in our study. Here we are instead concerned with the reactions received by a single user in a short time window.

A large body of research has also focused on influence maximization [8, 4, 3], which also differs from the *when-to-post* problem. Influence maximization aims to find a subset of users in a social network, such that targeting them with a message maximizes the propagation or adoption of the message throughout the network. However, the effects of broadcasting messages to entire audiences, rather than targeting specific individuals, has not been as well studied. It is this problem that we propose and analyze here, by examining the temporal aspects of broadcasting to one's audience, in order to get a large volume of responses.

3. PROBLEM SETTING

In this section, we formulate the *when-to-post* problem and provide details about the system and dataset used.

3.1 Problem Statement

The actions taken on any social networking site may be categorized as passive or active in nature. The passive category may include actions such as *views*, while the active category may broadly be classified into two groups – *post* and *reaction*. Typical *post* behavior may include creating and sending messages, sharing photos, or posting news articles on a social network. Typical *reaction* behavior includes resharing, liking, commenting, endorsing or replying to posts created by other users. We restrict the scope of this study to the *post* and *reaction* behavior of users.

Sometimes the *post* behavior is used in the context of one-on-one or personal communication, while other times it may be geared towards a larger audience. Here we focus on the latter case, where one of the motivations behind posting is to reach a large audience and to capture their attention. In particular, we examine the time-related aspects of this behavior and frame a *when-to-post* problem as follows:

Problem Statement: *For a user on a social network, find the* **best time to post** *a message within a specified time period in order to maximize the probability of receiving audience reactions.*

Note that we only consider first-degree reactions such as replies and retweets on Twitter and comments on Facebook, and not those caused by an audience member resharing the original post. In other words, we focus mainly on the reactions a post receives by the user's immediate audience, and not on how the post propagates through the network.

3.2 System Overview

We collect user posts from Facebook through the oauth-token provided by registered users on Klout. We also use the oauth-token-based approach to collect the friend graph of users on Facebook and the follower graph for users on

[1]Klout platform is a part of Lithium Technologies, Inc.

Twitter. Klout partners with GNIP to collect public data generated in the Twitter Mention Stream[2]. For location analysis, we use the city, state and country information provided by registered users on the Klout application.

The collected data is written out to a Hadoop cluster[3] that uses HDFS as the file system, HBase as the serving datastore, and Hive[4] to process, query and manage the large datasets. We implement independent Java utilities with Hive UDF (User Defined Function) wrappers, with functions to process user locations and timezones, and operators such as discrete convolution to process time-series vectors. The combination of Hive Query Language and UDFs allows us to build map-reduce jobs that can scale up to analyze billions of messages posted to social platforms every day. A pipeline run on a 150-node cluster has a cumulative I/O footprint of 224GB of reads, 78GB of writes, and 9.62 days of CPU usage. Fig. 1 shows an overview of the system.

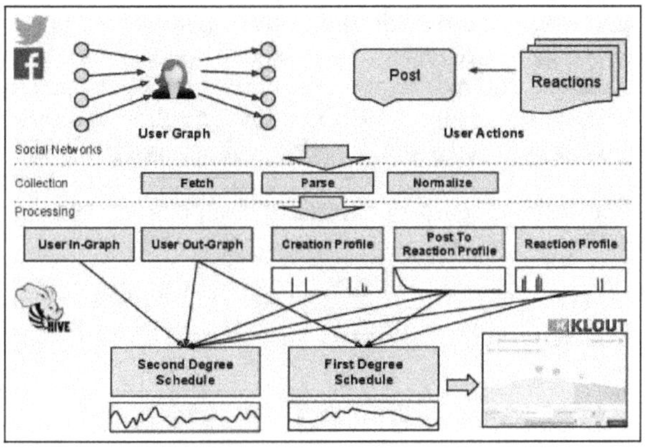

Figure 1: System Overview

3.3 Dataset

The dataset used to run experiments and build models has been opened at `https://github.com/klout/opendata`. The corpus has event timestamps for posts that were created between October 15, 2014 and February 11, 2015 and received at least one reaction. The dataset was generated from more than **1 million** users apiece from Facebook and Twitter, with accounts registered on Klout.com. For Facebook the dataset includes more than **25 million** post timestamps and **104 million** reaction timestamps, while for Twitter these numbers are **119 million** and **1 billion** respectively. In order to preserve privacy, timestamps were slightly perturbed and user and post ids were **anonymized** using custom fingerprint functions.

4. BEHAVIOR ANALYSIS

In this section we perform in-depth user behavior analysis across temporal and local dimensions, such as post-to-reaction delay, user location and the network of activity. This analysis provides some interesting observations and valuable insights into the *when-to-post* problem.

4.1 Post to Reaction Time Analysis

To start with, we note that there is always an inherent delay between when a post was created and when a user reacts to it. This delay is crucial to consider when we study the *when-to-post* problem.

[2]`https://gnip.com/sources/twitter`

[3]`http://wiki.apache.org/hadoop/`

[4]`http://hive.apache.org/`

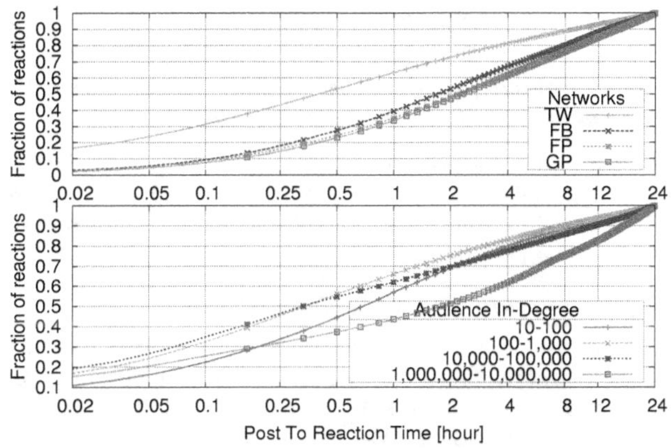

Figure 2: Cumulative Reactions within first 24 hours

	Networks			
$\mathcal{T}_{24h}(p)$	TW	FB	FP	GP
0.25	00:03	00:25	00:31	00:35
0.50	00:24	01:42	02:12	02:19
0.75	02:24	05:65	07:26	07:36
0.90	08:53	13:14	14:57	15:16
	Audience In-Degree (Twitter)			
$\mathcal{T}_{24h}(p)$	10-100	100-1K	10K-100K	1M-10M
0.25	00:08	00:03	00:03	00:06
0.50	00:41	00:20	00:20	01:48
0.75	02:53	01:58	03:11	07:52
0.90	08:49	07:50	11:22	16:26

Table 1: $\mathcal{T}_{24h}(p)$, Post-to-Reaction Times [hh:mm]

Specifically, we are concerned with the post-to-reaction delay within a short time window, and we choose this window to be 24 hours. This is also in accordance with previous studies such as [16] that have shown that messages on social media are short-lived with exponential dropoff after a day. In the limiting case when there is no dropoff and the delay is infinite all posts have the same probability of getting responses. Thus it is because of this dropoff within a finite duration that the *when-to-post* problem becomes important. Further, since most reactions occur in narrow time windows for both networks, the goal should be to recommend posting times in narrow time buckets. To examine the speed of reactions, we define a metric $\mathcal{T}_d(p)$ as follows:

Definition 1. *Let R be the total number of reactions received by all posts within a time period d since posting time. Then $\mathcal{T}_d(p)$ is defined as the amount of time that passes between posting time and the time when the cumulative reaction count is equal to a fraction p of R.* □

Along with the reaction counts, we use this metric $\mathcal{T}_d(p)$ to further analyze post-to-reaction behavior across different dimensions of the problem. Fig. 2 plots the fraction of cumulative reaction counts occurring within 24 hours of posting and Table 1 shows the $\mathcal{T}_{24h}(p)$ values respectively.

Further, we would also like to understand the probability distribution of a reaction occurring within a given time window since the time of post creation. In order to do this, we define a *Post-to-Reaction Filter* function as follows:

Definition 2. **Post To Reaction Filter** *For a time interval d, the post-to-reaction filter function $PTR(d)$ is defined as a discrete probability distribution over the event that a reaction occurs within time d of creating a post.* □

We estimate the post-to-reaction filter function $PTR(d)$ by aggregating reaction times across all observed messages and reactions in a network. This filter function will be used in Sec. 5 when we derive personalized user schedules.

4.1.1 Reaction Times By Network

Posting and reaction behavior varies on social networks because of many factors, such as manner of posting, presentation of posts to users and the set of possible reactions that a user can perform. We compare post-to-reaction times across three major social networks – Twitter (TW), Facebook (FB) and Google+ (GP). We also treat Facebook Fan Pages (FP) as a separate network, since the dynamics of posting and reacting on these pages diverge significantly from personal Facebook pages. The top halves of Fig. 2 and Table 1 show the reaction times for different networks.

We observe that Twitter exhibits a much higher speed of reactions compared to the Facebook. On Twitter, 25% of the reactions take place in the first 3 minutes, 50% within the first half hour, and 90% within the first 9 hours. Other networks exhibit slightly slower speeds compared to Twitter, with 50% of reactions on Facebook, Facebook Pages and Google+ taking place within the first 2 hours of posting. Interestingly, we see that the Facebook Pages network shows more similar reaction times to Google+ rather than Facebook, indicating that similar responses can be elicited from users belonging to completely disjoint user sets, if the underlying dynamics of interactions are similar.

In the rest of this paper, we mainly focus on Twitter and Facebook, which show significant variations in post-to-reaction delays. The distribution of post-to-reaction delay for Twitter is narrower and falls off more quickly compared to Facebook. The $\mathcal{T}_{24h}(p)$ values in Table 1 suggest that a 15 minute bucket can capture the necessary granularity of reactions, which we choose as the length of our time buckets.

These variations also highlight that social networks operate on different timescales, and the post-to-reaction filter function needs to be computed separately for each network during comparison. Next, we consider the dependence of reaction behavior on the in-degree of users posting messages.

4.1.2 Reaction Times By User In-Degrees

Next, we explore the hypothesis that network sizes of users may be a factor that affects reaction times. To do so, we analyze how an audience member's in-degree affects his reaction behavior. Fig. 2 (bottom) plots the fractions of 24 hour reaction counts against the time elapsed, for different sets of in-degrees of audience members on Twitter. Table 1 (bottom) shows the reaction times at various $\mathcal{T}_{24h}(p)$ values.

We find that a large section of audience members with in-degrees between 100 to 100k exhibit similar behavior. More than 60% of the reactions from such users are created in the first 1 hour. Users with low in-degrees between 10-100 have slower response times, perhaps they may not be very active users. The users with in-degrees of greater than 1M have the slowest reaction times among all users. This may be attributed to such users being celebrities and brands who may not react to messages as quickly as other users do, because of the large volume of messages they see.

Thus, a large portion of audience members show similar reaction behavior, though they may have differing in-degrees. We can therefore infer that the *when-to-post* problem does not have a large dependency on the network sizes of audience members, unless these sizes are very small or very large. This permits us to use a common post-to-reaction filter function for all users in a given network.

4.2 Network and Location Analysis

User post and reaction behaviors are multi-dimensional and are highly dependent on the location, network and timezone of the user. In this section, we analyze normalized aggregated user audience reaction behaviors $\mathcal{S}(u)$, for user cohorts within and across various cities as well as across Facebook and Twitter within a given city. For behavior analysis we use correlation and cosine similarity metrics. Correlation and cosine similarity between finite time series $\mathcal{S}(u_1)$ and $\mathcal{S}(u_2)$ are defined in Equations 1 and 2 respectively.

Cosine similarity reveals the overlap between time series, while correlation reveals closeness in time dependent patterns between them. We observe metric distributions for 10 to 50 million user pairs, depending on the cohorts compared, where u_1 is selected from the first cohort and u_2 from the second. In addition to the metrics above, we compare the raw time series to gain further insights into reaction behaviors in Figs. 4 and 5.

$$corr(\mathcal{S}(u_1), \mathcal{S}(u_2)) = \frac{\sum_{i=1}^{N}(s_{u_1,i} - \bar{s}_{u_1})(s_{u_2,i} - \bar{s}_{u_2})}{\sqrt{\sum_{i=1}^{N}(s_{u_1,i} - \bar{s}_{u_1})^2 \sum_{i=1}^{N}(s_{u_2,i} - \bar{s}_{u_2})^2}} \tag{1}$$

$$sim(\mathcal{S}(u_1), \mathcal{S}(u_2)) = \frac{\mathcal{S}(u_1) \cdot \mathcal{S}(u_2)}{||\mathcal{S}(u_1)||\ ||\mathcal{S}(u_2)||} \tag{2}$$

4.2.1 Network Level Analysis

In this section, we analyze the user reaction profiles across Twitter and Facebook for users in New York City (NYC). Fig. 3 top shows expected audience reactions, aggregated across all users in NYC.

We observe that the daily seasonality is more pronounced for Twitter than Facebook, with taller peaks and deeper troughs. Twitter usage seems to peak during working hours and drops quickly thereafter. Both networks also exhibit secondary peaks at around 7-8pm daily. The amplitude of expected reactions on Twitter is around twice that of Facebook's, meaning posting on Twitter at the right times can lead to comparatively larger gains. Also, compared to Twitter, Facebook usage is more consistent throughout the day.

With respect to weekly trends, we find that Twitter activity falls to almost half of its weekday amplitude on Saturday and Sunday, whereas Facebook activity seems to be less affected by weekends. It is interesting to note that Facebook is most consistently used throughout the day on Sundays.

We compare aggregated user audience reaction behaviors $\mathcal{S}_{FB}(u_1)$ and $\mathcal{S}_{TW}(u_1)$ for Facebook and Twitter respectively using Eq. 1 and 2 in Fig. 3 bottom. We observe that correlation is positive, and relatively uniform in the $0.3 - 0.8$ range, which means that daily audience patterns across Twitter and Facebook are only moderately correlated. Both the similarity and correlation curves suggests that although audience reactions exhibit some similarity and cor-

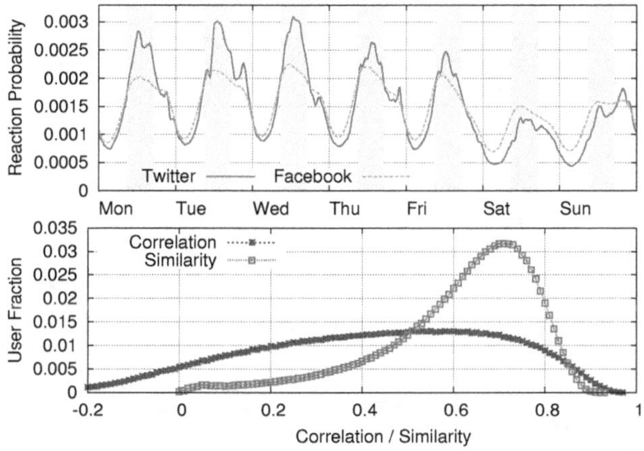

Figure 3: *Top:* Per-Network Globally Aggregated User Audience Reaction Behaviors. *Bottom:* Distribution of Cross-Network Cosine Similarity and Correlation Calculated Per-User. *Both:* All data plotted for users in New York City.

relation across networks for a given user, there are still significant differences. This again reinforces the need for any recommended schedules to be personalized per network.

4.2.2 Cross-City Analysis

In this section we analyze differences in behavior for multiple cities across Facebook and Twitter. Figs 4a and 5a show reaction behaviors, shifted to the local timezone of the city, for Facebook and Twitter respectively.

Observing the Facebook reactions in Fig. 4a, we notice that the US cities of San Francisco and New York exhibit similar shapes, where reactions peak at the beginning of work hours. For Paris, the reactions peak in the second half of working hours, while for London most reactions are expected towards the end of working hours. Finally, the pattern for Tokyo is quite different from the rest with two peaks, both occurring off working hours.

The Twitter reactions in Fig. 5a have similar patterns as Facebook. The notable difference is that Twitter reactions for US cities have more pronounced daily peaks, while for London, Paris and Tokyo the behavior seems more consistent throughout the day. All the curves show significant drops on weekends, and Saturday has noticeably lower activity than Sunday. We also observe that New York schedules lag slightly as compared to San Francisco, which may be explained due to lifestyle differences in the two cities.

In addition to the visual analysis, we also analyze similarity and correlations for reaction behaviors between cities, calculated according to Eq. 1 and 2. The time series compared in this case are the reactions aggregated across users in two cities, denoted by $\mathcal{S}(\mathcal{C}_1)$ and $\mathcal{S}(\mathcal{C}_2)$. Figures 4b-4e, 5b-5e show these distributions for Facebook and Twitter within the same city and across different cities.

Interestingly in US cities (New York and San Francisco) cross-city correlation and similarity for both Facebook and Twitter are not very different from their within city metrics. Globally Twitter reaction behavior compared to Facebook seems to be more correlated and similar. On Facebook, behavior correlation and similarity within city are lowest for London and Tokyo, and have high deviation. This indicates that users within these cities exhibit more diverse behavior patterns compared to US cities. Therefore a city level model built for London may not apply to all users within the city.

5. PERSONALIZED SCHEDULES

The analysis in the previous section highlights the importance of having personalized posting schedules. Here we present multiple approaches to derive such schedules.

5.1 Notation and Definitions

To start with, we simplify the computation by bucketizing time within a period P into discrete time intervals t_i. Based on the analysis in Sec. 4, we use 15 minute time intervals within a period of one week for a total of $4 \times 24 \times 7 = 672$ buckets, though the methods described here are applicable to any time interval and period. Because the number of reactions in one bucket in each period is usually small for most users, we aggregate the actions from multiple periods into the same bucket. For example, all the actions taken by a user between 00:00 to 00:15 on Mondays, in a 90 day time window, will be grouped into the first bucket t_1.

We also define the following sets associated with a user:

Definition 3. *For a user u, the set $U_{out}(u)$ is defined as the set of all users who are connected to u, and can potentially* ***react to*** *the posts created by u.*

Definition 4. *For a user u, the set $U_{in}(u)$ is defined as the set of all users to whom u is connected, and whose posts can be potentially be* ***reacted upon*** *by u.*

Note that though we treat the above sets as separate entities in order to differentiate between the post and reaction behavior, we do not assume that they are disjoint sets. [5]

Let N be the number of time buckets within the time period P under consideration. To represent the actions associated with a user with respect to time, we create time-based action profiles for each user computed from a user's actions in the period P, and aggregated into the buckets t_k. These profiles can thus be represented as vectors of length N.

We define four primary action profiles for each user:

- First, for each user u, we define a **Created Posts** profile $\mathcal{C}(u)$ that represents the posts created by the user in each time bucket.
- Inversely we can also define a **Visible Posts** profile $\mathcal{V}(u)$, which represents the potentially reactionable posts from $U_{in}(u)$ that are visible to the user.
- Based on the posts that a user sees, he may respond to them in some manner. We can represent these responses as a **Self Reaction** profile $\mathcal{R}(u)$ for the user.
- Finally, we define an **Estimated Audience Reaction** profile $\mathcal{Q}(u)$ that estimates the number of reactions received by the user from his audience $U_{out}(u)$ in each time bucket.

As noted in previous works such as [1] and [15], and as analyzed in Sec. 4, there is usually a time difference between when a post is created by a user in $U_{in}(u)$, and when the user u may react to it. Thus a specific post may be visible in the time bucket t_k in $\mathcal{V}(u)$, but may only be reacted upon in a later time bucket $t_{k'}$ in $\mathcal{R}(u)$. The post-to-reaction filter function defined in the previous section represents this lag in terms of a time interval d, discretized into time buckets

[5]For some bi-directional relationships such as Facebook Friends, $U_{out}(u)$ and $U_{in}(u)$ are equivalent.

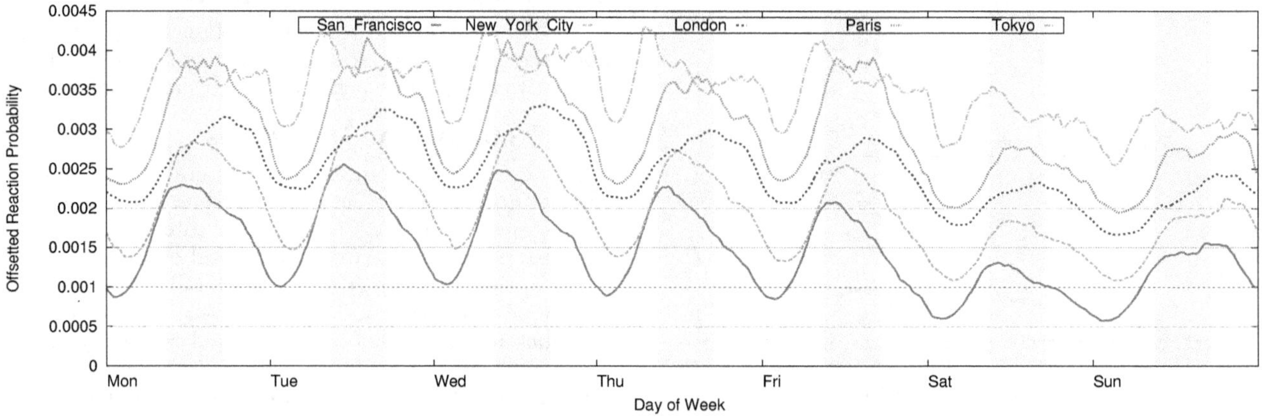

(a) Time Series Capturing City-Level Reaction Behaviors

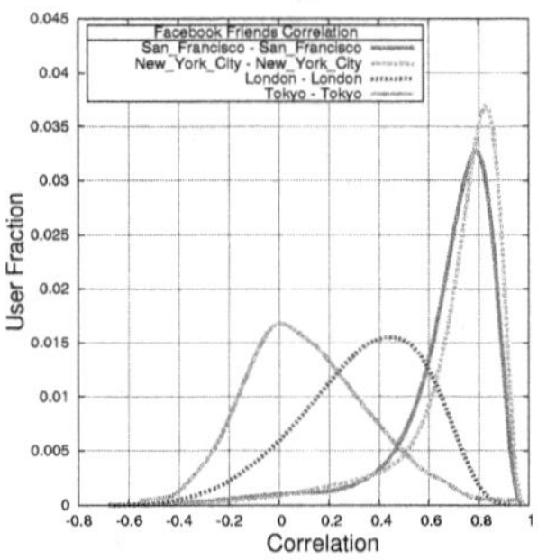

(b) Same-City Correlation

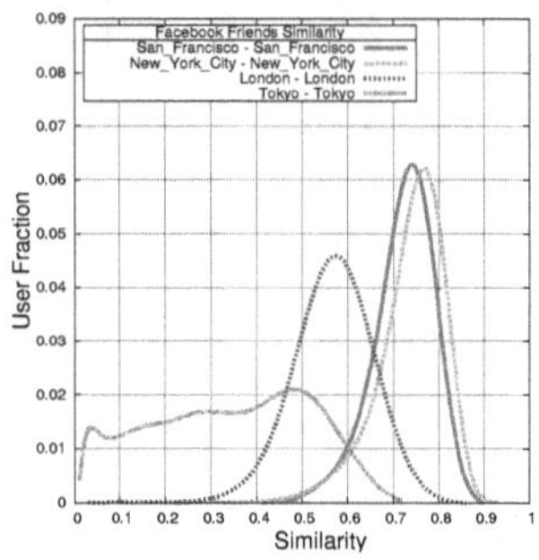

(c) Same-City Similarity

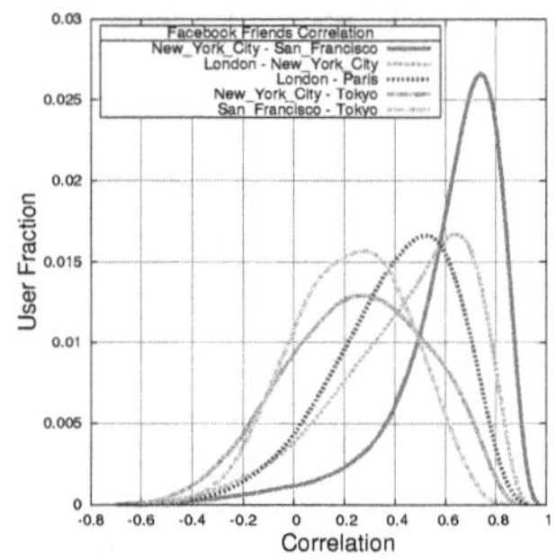

(d) Cross-City Correlation

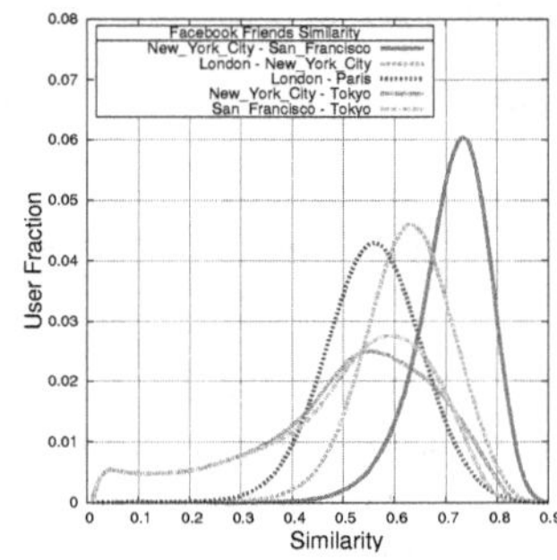

(e) Cross-City Correlation

Figure 4: **Facebook** - City-Level Reaction Behavior

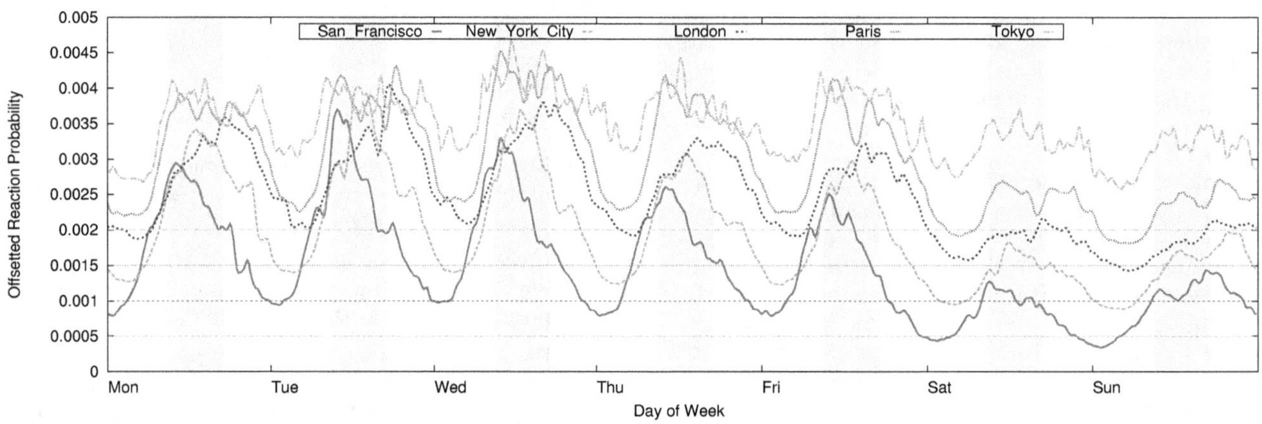

(a) Time Series Capturing City-Level Reaction Behaviors

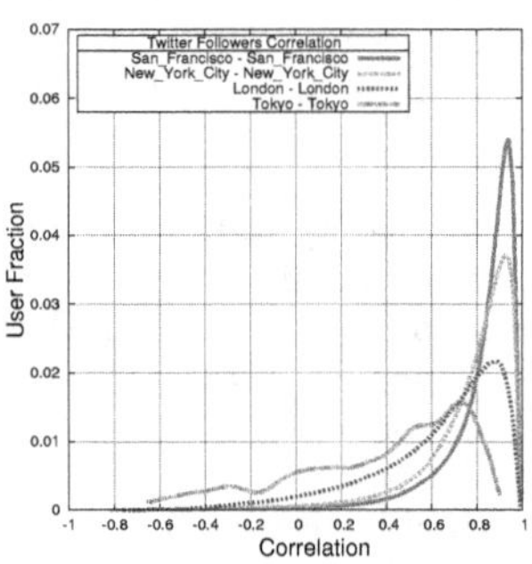

(b) Same-City Correlation

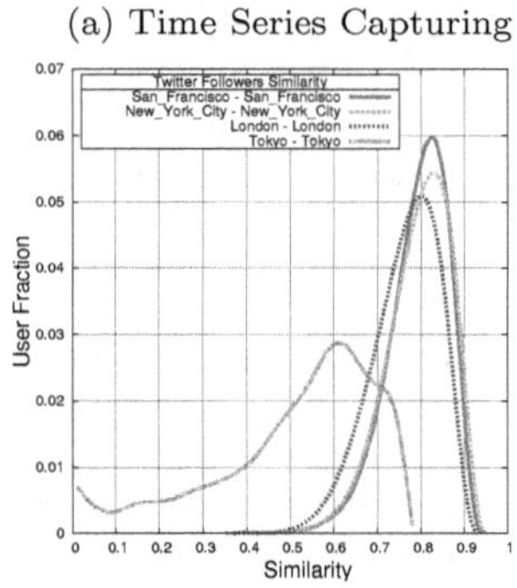

(c) Same-City Similarity

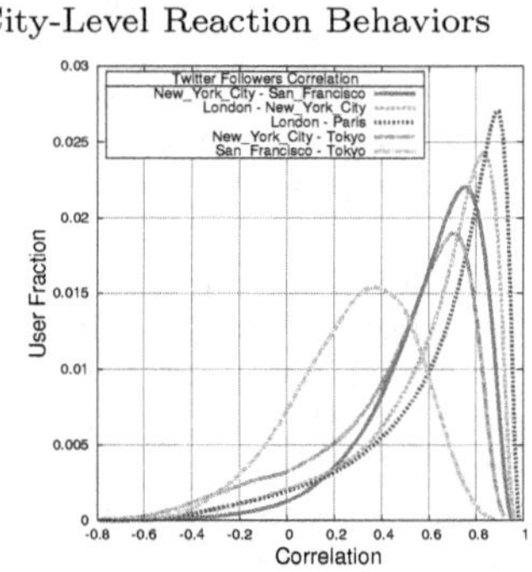

(d) Cross-City Correlation

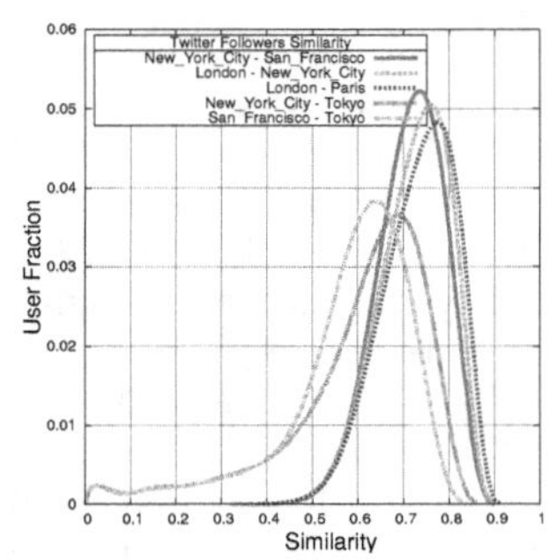

(e) Cross-City Similarity

Figure 5: **Twitter** - City-Level Reaction Behavior

of size t_k. We can therefore compute a **Delayed Reaction Profile** for a user by performing a discrete convolution operation of the original reaction profile with the post-to-reaction filter function.

$$\mathcal{R}_d(u) = \mathcal{R}(u) * PTR(d) \quad (3)$$

where $*$ is the discrete convolution operator.[6]

Each element $r_{d,k}(u)$ in the delayed reaction profile represents the number of reactions that the user u would generate in the time interval d following the bucket t_k. Thus for a post created by a user in the current time bucket, using $\mathcal{R}_d(u)$ for his audience members provides a better estimate of anticipated future reactions.

These estimates for $q_i(u)$ could be computed in multiple ways, as described in the following section. Once $\mathcal{Q}(u)$ is known, we can determine a probability mass function which represents a post schedule for the user. These probabilities $s_i(u)$ can be computed as:

$$s_i(u) = q_i(u) / \sum_{j=1}^{N} q_j(u) \quad (4)$$

Finally, the vector consisting of these probabilities determine the **Post Schedule** for the user. Once we have $\mathcal{S}(u)$, we simply pick the buckets with the highest values of $s_i(u)$, which are the desired best times to post. Next, we describe multiple approaches to compute $\mathcal{S}(u)$ using the above notation and definitions, which are summarized in Table 2.

5.2 Recommended Schedule Derivation

To illustrate the *when-to-post* problem with a concrete example, consider a simplified social network graph, as represented in Fig. 6. For the user a_0, her audience is made up of other users b_i, so we have: $U_{out}(a_0) = \{b_0, b_1, b_2, ..., b_m\}$.

When a_0 creates a post, it may be potentially seen by all the members b_i of her audience. Let us focus on a particular audience member b_0. This audience member b_0 also belongs to the audience sets of other users a_i, and may see posts that are created by each of them. We can represent this relationship between the users as: $U_{in}(b_0) = \{a_0, a_1, a_2, ..., a_n\}$.

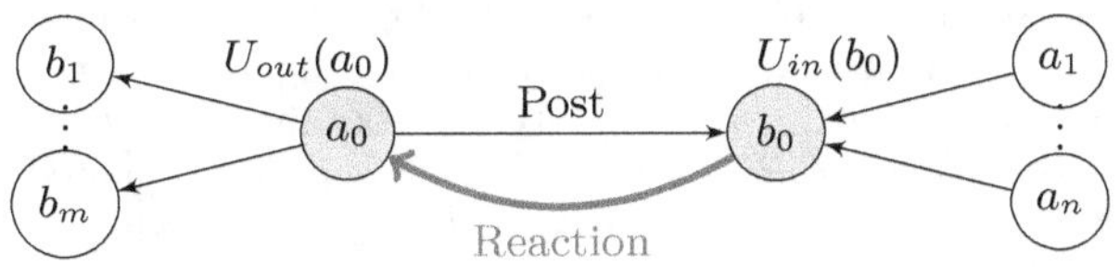

Figure 6: Simplified representation of a user's social graph

We would like to derive the post schedule $\mathcal{S}(a_0)$ for the user a_0. In order to do so, we want to answer the following question: *For the user a_0, what is the expected number of reactions received from $U_{out}(a_0)$ for a post created in the time bucket t_k?* We describe two approaches below to answer this question and compute the recommended schedule.

5.2.1 First-Degree Reaction Schedule

In this approach, we consider the reactions of a_0's audience $U_{out}(a_0)$, ignoring the second-degree effects of the other posting users a_i. With respect to Fig. 6, we consider only the left part of the diagram that represents a_0 and $U_{out}(a_0)$ (including b_0), and ignore all other a_i.

Since we know the reaction profiles $R(b_j)$ for the members of a_0's first-degree graph, we can accumulate these reaction counts per time bucket to get the combined audience reaction profile. However, since this does not take into account the post-to-reaction delay, a better approach is to aggregate the delayed reaction profiles $R_d(b_j)$ for all b_j in $U_{out}(a_0)$.

This sum of delayed reactions per bucket gives us the estimated audience reaction profile $Q(a_0)$ for the user, where the elements of the vector are given by:

$$q_k(a_0) = \sum_{j=0}^{m} r_{d,k}(b_j) \quad (5)$$

Thus in this case, the probability of receiving a reaction in any given time bucket $s_k(a_0)$ can then be computed from $Q(a_0)$ as per Eq. 4. These probabilities determine the *First-Degree Reaction* posting schedule $\mathcal{S}_1(a_0)$.

Note that $\mathcal{S}_1(a_0)$ does not take into account the behavior of an audience member b_j with respect to posts from other users a_i. In other words, this approach only takes into account the first-degree dependency for the user a_0. We therefore describe another approach that takes into account the second-degree dependency as well.

5.2.2 Second-Degree Reaction Schedule

In Fig. 6, the actions of the users a_i represent the second-degree effects for user a_0, since they affect how a_0's first-degree connection b_0 reacts to messages. To consider these second-degree effects, we define a *Second-Degree Reaction* schedule $\mathcal{S}_2(a_0)$, which can be derived by answering the following questions first, before the original one above.

- When do the users a_i create posts?
- When does a specific audience member b_0 react to the posts created by a_i?
- What is the probability that b_0 reacts to a post in a certain time bucket t_k?

The answer to the first question is given by the post creation profiles $\mathcal{C}(a_i)$ for each user a_i, computed by aggregating the past history of post creation events for the user into time buckets. To answer the second question, we first compute the reaction profile $R(b_0)$. Again, this profile is computed by aggregating the past history of reaction events for b_0, which tells us how often he reacts in any given time bucket. The answer to when b_0 reacts with respect to posting times is then given by the delayed reaction profile $R_d(b_0)$, which takes into account the post-to-reaction delay.

For the third question, let $p(b_0, t_k)$ be the probability that user b_0 reacts to a post in time bucket t_k. This event can be modeled as a Bernoulli random variable $X_{b_0,k}$, with the probability of the reaction given by $p(b_0, t_k)$, thus:

$$E(X_{b_0,k}) = p(b_0, t_k) \quad (6)$$

From the point of view of b_0, the probability that he reacts to some post in the time bucket t_k depends on the number of posts that he sees, and his usual reaction behavior in t_k[7].

To estimate the number of posts that are potentially visible to the user b_0 in each time bucket, we aggregate the

[6]For two functions f, g defined on the set of integers $\mathbb{Z}$, the discrete convolution of f, g is given by:
$(f * g)[n] = \sum_{m=-\infty}^{\infty} f[m] \cdot g[n-m]$

[7]Since we are concerned only with the time aspects here, we assume that the posts seen by the user are equally likely to be reacted upon in all other aspects.

Table 2: Notation for Action Profiles

User Action Profile	Vector Notation	Element Notation	Element Description for user u in time bucket t_k
Created Posts	$\mathcal{C}(u)$	$c_k(u)$	aggregated number of posts created by user
Visible Posts	$\mathcal{V}(u)$	$v_k(u)$	aggregated number of posts visible to user
Self Reactions	$\mathcal{R}(u)$	$r_k(u)$	aggregated number of reactions generated by user
Delayed Self Reactions	$\mathcal{R}_d(u)$	$r_{d,k}(u)$	aggregated number of reactions generated by user in the time interval d following t_k
Estimated Audience Reactions	$\mathcal{Q}(u)$	$q_k(u)$	estimated number of reactions received by user
Post Schedule	$\mathcal{S}(u)$	$s_k(u)$	probability of receiving a reaction on a post created by user

post creation profiles for all a_i. The number of posts that are actually visible to the user may be modeled as a linear function of the total created posts. Thus for a given time bucket t_k, the number of posts visible to b_0 is given by:

$$v_k(b_0) = \alpha \cdot \sum_{i=0}^{n} c'_k(a_i) + \beta \tag{7}$$

Where α and β are constants and $c'_k(a_i)$ is a rescaled version of $c_k(a_i)$. These constants may depend on network-specific factors, and we assume that the factor is globally applicable to all users in a given network.

With this information, the *a priori* probability in Eq. 6 can now be computed as:

$$\begin{aligned} p(b_0, t_k) &= \frac{\text{number of delayed reactions by } b_0 \text{ in } t_k}{\text{number of posts visible to } b_0 \text{ in } t_k}. \\ &= \frac{r_{d,k}(b_0)}{v_k(b_0)} \end{aligned} \tag{8}$$

Now we turn our attention back to the original user a_0. Let $Y_{a_0,k}$ to be the random variable representing the number of reactions that a_0 receives for a post created in a specific time bucket t_k. We would like to find the expected number of reactions $E(Y_{a_0,k})$, which can be computed as:

$$\begin{aligned} E(Y_{a_0,k}) &= E(\sum_{j=0}^{m} X_{b_j,k}) = \sum_{j=0}^{m} E(X_{b_j,k}) \\ &= \sum_{j=0}^{m} p(b_j, t_k) = \sum_{j=0}^{m} \frac{r_{d,k}(b_j)}{(\alpha \cdot \sum_{i=0}^{n} c'_k(a_i) + \beta)} \end{aligned} \tag{9}$$

Thus, these expected values computed from the observed $\mathcal{R}_d(u)$ and $\mathcal{C}(u)$ give us the estimates for the number of reactions received by a_0. The elements of the audience reaction profile $\mathcal{Q}(a_0)$ are hence given by:

$$q_k(a_0) = E(Y_{a_0,k}) \tag{10}$$

Finally, we can infer the desired posting schedule $\mathcal{S}_2(a_0)$ for the user a_0 as the probability mass function for the discrete random variable $Y_{a_0,k}$. Again, the elements of $\mathcal{S}_2(a_0)$ are computed from $\mathcal{Q}(a_0)$ as per Eq. 4.

5.2.3 User Weighted Schedules

In the sums computed above for the first- and second-degree schedules, all audience members are treated equally. However, audience members may have differing tendencies to react to the user's posts depending on their affinity to the user. These differences can be accounted for by associating a weight with each audience member who may react to the user, computed based on previous actions as follows:

$$w(a_0, b_i) = \frac{\text{total reactions received by } a_0 \text{ from } b_i}{\text{total overall reactions received by } a_0} \tag{11}$$

Eq. 5 can now be modified with this weight as:

$$q_k(a_0) = \sum_{j=0}^{m} w(b_j, a_0) \cdot r_{d,k}(b_j) \tag{12}$$

Similarly, the expected number of reactions for the second-degree schedule in Eq. 9 can also be modified as:

$$E(Y_{a_0,k}) = \sum_{j=0}^{m} w(b_j, a_0) \cdot E(X_{b_j,k}) \tag{13}$$

We denote these weighted schedules as $\mathcal{S}_{1,w}(u)$ and $\mathcal{S}_{2,w}(u)$ respectively. In Sec. 6 we evaluate the performance of all four schedules described above.

6. SCHEDULE EVALUATION

In this section, we evaluate the user post schedules derived above – $\mathcal{S}_1(u)$, $\mathcal{S}_2(u)$ and their respective weighted counterparts. We evaluate them on empirical observations of real user behavior over a 56-day period for 0.5 million users and more than 25 million messages.

6.1 Baseline Schedules

Because there are no previous baselines on the *when-to-post* problem, we design two schedules to compare our approaches with. We consider all users in a given timezone and aggregate their behavior to create these baseline schedules. Both the baselines are thus uniquely determined for each timezone and are not personalized per user.

One natural baseline can be created by observing the most frequently used time buckets for posting, aggregated across all users in each timezone T. We thus obtain our first baseline, the *Most Frequently Used (MFU) Schedule*, denoted as $\mathcal{BS}^{mfu}(T)$, with bucket values $bs_i^{mfu}(T)$ computed as:

$$bs_i^{mfu}(T) = \sum_{u \in U_T} c_i(u) / \sum_{i=1}^{N} \sum_{u \in U_T} c_i(u) \tag{14}$$

where U_T is the set of users in the timezone T.

As explained in Sec. 5, the *First-Degree Reaction Schedule* for a user is based on his first degree audience behavior. To generate another baseline for global behavior, we simply aggregate the first-degree reaction schedules from all users in the timezone. We call this second baseline schedule *Aggregated First-Degree (AFD) Schedule*, denoted as $\mathcal{BS}^{afd}(T)$, whose bucket values are given by:

$$bs_i^{afd}(T) = \sum_{u \in U_T} q_i(u) / \sum_{i=1}^{N} \sum_{u \in U_T} q_i(u) \tag{15}$$

where U_T is the set of users in the timezone T who have a first-degree reaction schedule $\mathcal{Q}(u)$.

Once we have the baseline schedules, we pick the buckets with the highest values of $bs_i(T)$ as the best recommended times to post for users in timezone T.

6.2 Evaluation metrics

For the purposes of evaluation of schedules, we propose a **ReactionGain** metric, which we compute as below.

Let $\mathcal{U}$ be the user sample set under consideration, observed over M days. Let us first consider a single user u in this sample. For this user u, we can rank the posting time buckets as recommended by a schedule $\mathcal{S}(u)$ over a period of 24 hours, with the first bucket being the best time to post and the last one being the worst.

For the kth ranked bucket as per $\mathcal{S}(u)$ we compute the average *reactions per message*, $RPM(u,k)$:

$$RPM(u,k) = \Big(\sum_{j=1}^{M} r_{k,j}(u)\Big) / \Big(\sum_{j=1}^{M} c_{k,j}(u)\Big) \tag{16}$$

where $r_{k,j}(u)$ and $c_{k,j}(u)$ are respectively the reactions received and the posts created by the user in the time bucket corresponding to the k-th rank, on the j-th day. As before, we compute $r_{k,j}(u)$ as the reactions received in the first 24 hours after the posting time.

We similarly define $RPM(u)$ as the ratio of all the reactions received to all the posts created by the user in the same 56-day period, across all the time buckets. We now compute the *ReactionGain*, $RG(u,k)$, for the k-th bucket for the user as:

$$RG(u,k) = \frac{RPM(u,k)}{RPM(u)} \tag{17}$$

This ratio tells us the increase or decrease in reactions received by the user when she posts in a specific bucket, compared to the average reactions per message she receives.

Finally, we compute the global average reaction gain for each bucket $RG_{avg}(k)$ as the average of $RG(u,k)$ values over all the users in the sampled population $\mathcal{U}$ who created posts in that bucket. We use this average reaction gain metric to evaluate the schedules below.

6.3 Real-world Evaluation

We evaluate real user behavior and measure schedule performance based on how many reactions were received when the recommended times were used.

In our experiments, we sampled 0.25 million active users each from Twitter and Facebook from the dataset described in Sec 3.3. For each sampled user u, we compute $\mathcal{S}_1(u)$, $\mathcal{S}_2(u)$ and their corresponding weighted schedules as described in Sec. 5, for a 63-day time period. We empirically chose the α and β parameters to be both 1.0, and $c_k(a_i)$ rescaled to $c'_k(a_i)$ with the mean. We then evaluate the recommended times on 25 million messages generated by the sampled users in a 56-day time period, with no overlap over the time period used to derive schedules.

To compare the performance of the top posting times recommended by the schedules, we compute the average reaction gain $RG_{avg}(k)$ for the bucket rank k, for each schedule. Fig. 7 plots these values for the top 32 buckets for a weekday[8], for both Facebook and Twitter.

[8]We exclude weekends here since they show diverging behavior compared to weekdays, as shown in Sec. 4, but a similar analysis can also be performed for weekends.

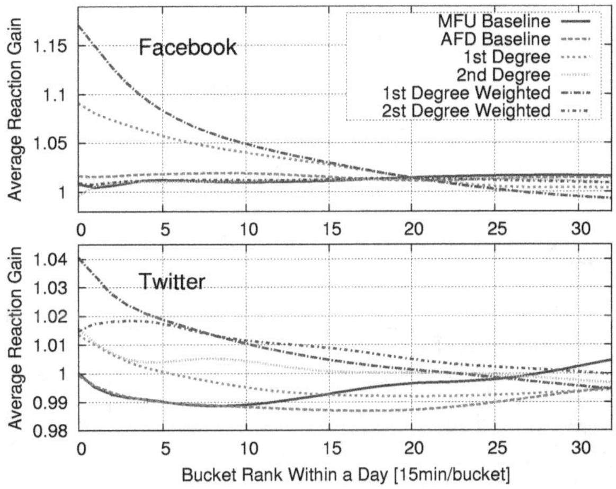

Figure 7: Average Reaction Gain for Ranked Buckets

We observe from Fig. 7 that the *First-Degree Weighted Schedule* outperforms all the others on both Facebook and Twitter. On Facebook, this schedule shows a reaction gain of more than 17% in the highest bucket, and on Twitter the highest gain is 4%. The second best schedule on Facebook is the *First-Degree Schedule*, while that on Twitter is the *Second-Degree Weighted Schedule*. Both the *MFU* and the *AFD* baseline schedules show a reaction gain that is slightly above 1.0 on Facebook, and mostly below 1.0 on Twitter, showing that users who post according to these schedules see little to no increase in reactions received.

Both the second-degree schedules on Facebook show only a small reaction gain, very similar to the baseline schedules. The superior performance of the first-degree schedules on Facebook suggests that second-degree effects on this network are less dominant. This may stem from the inherent nature of the interactions on Facebook, and the manner in which users are shown posts that they could react upon.

On Twitter, we observe that the weighted schedules for the first degree as well as second degree perform better than the baselines and the non-weighted ones. Thus the mutual relationships between a user and his audience members play an important role on Twitter in determining the expected reactions. This observation highlights the importance of treating each edge in a user graph differently.

Note that a good recommended schedule should show a decreasing trend in reaction gains from the higher to the lower ranked buckets, such that posting at the higher recommended times leads to higher reaction gains. The baseline schedules fall short in this regard, and show a decreasing trend only in the first 10 buckets on Twitter, and none at all on Facebook. The global baseline schedules thus prove to be less effective in magnitude of reaction gains, as well as ordering of buckets, validating our hypothesis that personalized recommendations show better performance.

As an example of recommended schedules, Fig. 8 shows the reaction profiles and schedules for a sample user on Twitter. The purple curve in Fig. 8 shows the probability distribution of post-to-reaction delay on Twitter, which is plotted by aggregating reactions observed in a 63-day period. Note that this function falls off steeply in the first few hours from posting time, and almost vanishes after 12 hours. The dashed curve plots the aggregated audience reactions for the user, without the post-to-reaction delay. The red and the blue curves show the *First-Degree Weighted Schedule* and

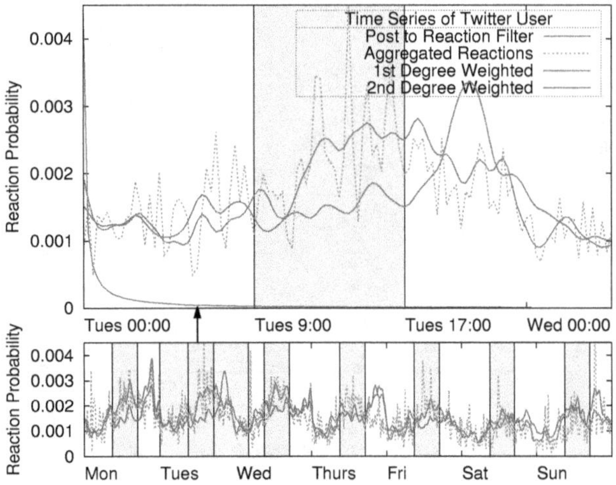

Figure 8: Example Schedules and Filter Function

the *Second-Degree Weighted Schedule* respectively. The recommended best times to post over one day and one week are the peaks in the plot.

7. CONCLUSION AND FUTURE WORK

In this study, we introduce and formulate a *when-to-post* problem to find the best times to post on social networks in order to increase the number of received reactions.

We analyze various factors that affect audience reactions on a dataset containing over a billion reactions on hundreds of millions of messages. We find that a majority of reactions occur within the first 2 hours of posting times on most networks. Audience behavior differs significantly on different networks, with Twitter having larger reaction volumes in shorter time windows as compared to Facebook. We also perform location analysis and find interesting similarities and differences between cities in terms of reaction patterns. Future studies could also study other factors such as content and topical relevance of posted messages.

Further, we present multiple approaches for deriving personalized posting schedules for users, and compare them to two baselines. We evaluate these schedules on empirical data from 0.5 million real-world users and 25 million messages observed over a 56-day period. We find that the *First-Degree Weighted Schedule* performs the best among all, providing a reaction gain of 17% on Facebook and 4% on Twitter. Both first-degree schedules perform better on Facebook and both weighted schedules perform better on Twitter. These schedules are deployed on a full production system that recommends posting times to millions of users daily.

We hope that this study and the accompanying dataset provided enables further research in this area.

8. ACKNOWLEDGEMENTS

We thank Gaurav Ragtah, Sarah Ellinger, Tyler Singletary and Trevor D'Souza for their valuable contributions towards this study. We also thank Sunil Rajasekar and Sateesh Chilukuri for their support throughout this work.

9. REFERENCES

[1] S. Asur, B. A. Huberman, G. Szabo, and C. Wang. Trends in social media: persistence and decay. In *ICWSM*, 2011.

[2] A. Bennamane, H. Hacid, A. Ansiaux, and A. Cagnati. Visual analysis of implicit social networks for suspicious behavior detection. In *DASFAA*, 2011.

[3] S. Bharathi, D. Kempe, and M. Salek. Competitive influence maximization in social networks. In *WINE*, 2007.

[4] W. Chen, Y. Wang, and S. Yang. Efficient influence maximization in social networks. In *Proc. of ACM Conference on Knowledge Discovery and Data Mining (KDD)*, 2009.

[5] J. Cheng, L. Adamic, P. A. Dow, J. M. Kleinberg, and J. Leskovec. Can cascades be predicted? In *Proc. of ACM Conference on World Wide Web (WWW)*, 2014.

[6] R. Crane and D. Sornette. Robust dynamic classes revealed by measuring the response function of a social system. *Proceedings of the National Academy of Sciences*, 105(41), 2008.

[7] A. Guille and H. Hacid. A predictive model for the temporal dynamics of information diffusion in online social networks. In *Proc. of ACM Conference on World Wide Web (WWW)*, 2012.

[8] D. Kempe, J. Kleinberg, and E. Tardos. Maximizing the spread of influence through a social network. In *Proc. of ACM Conference on Knowledge Discovery and Data Mining (KDD)*, 2003.

[9] H. Kwak, C. Lee, H. Park, and S. Moon. What is twitter, a social network or a news media? In *Proc. of ACM Conference on World Wide Web (WWW)*, 2010.

[10] J. Lehmann, B. Gonçalves, J. J. Ramasco, and C. Cattuto. Dynamical classes of collective attention in twitter. In *Proc. of ACM Conference on World Wide Web (WWW)*, 2012.

[11] K. Lerman and R. Ghosh. Information contagion: An empirical study of the spread of news on digg and twitter social networks. *ICWSM*, 2010.

[12] J. Leskovec, L. Backstrom, and J. Kleinberg. Meme-tracking and the dynamics of the news cycle. In *Proc. of ACM Conference on Knowledge Discovery and Data Mining (KDD)*, 2009.

[13] J. Leskovec, M. McGlohon, C. Faloutsos, N. S. Glance, and M. Hurst. Patterns of cascading behavior in large blog graphs. In *SDM*, 2007.

[14] N. Spasojevic, J. Yan, A. Rao, and P. Bhattacharyya. Lasta: Large scale topic assignment on multiple social networks. In *Proc. of ACM Conference on Knowledge Discovery and Data Mining (KDD)*, KDD '14, 2014.

[15] M. Tsytsarau, T. Palpanas, and M. Castellanos. Dynamics of news events and social media reaction. In *Proc. of ACM Conference on Knowledge Discovery and Data Mining (KDD)*, 2014.

[16] S. Wu, J. M. Hofman, W. A. Mason, and D. J. Watts. Who says what to whom on twitter. In *Proc. of ACM Conference on World Wide Web (WWW)*, 2011.

[17] J. Yang and S. Counts. Predicting the speed, scale, and range of information diffusion in twitter. In *ICWSM*, 2010.

[18] J. Yang and J. Leskovec. Patterns of temporal variation in online media. In *WSDM*, 2011.

Mining for Causal Relationships: A Data-Driven Study of the Islamic State

Andrew Stanton, Amanda Thart, Ashish Jain, Priyank Vyas, Arpan Chatterjee, Paulo Shakarian*
Arizona State University
Tempe, AZ 85287
{dstanto2, althart, ashish.jain.1, pvyas1, achatt14, shak} @asu.edu

ABSTRACT

The Islamic State of Iraq and al-Sham (ISIS) is a dominant insurgent group operating in Iraq and Syria that rose to prominence when it took over Mosul in June, 2014. In this paper, we present a data-driven approach to analyzing this group using a dataset consisting of 2200 incidents of military activity surrounding ISIS and the forces that oppose it (including Iraqi, Syrian, and the American-led coalition). We combine ideas from logic programming and causal reasoning to mine for association rules for which we present evidence of causality. We present relationships that link ISIS vehicle-bourne improvised explosive device (VBIED) activity in Syria with military operations in Iraq, coalition air strikes, and ISIS IED activity, as well as rules that may serve as indicators of spikes in indirect fire, suicide attacks, and arrests.

Categories and Subject Descriptors

J.4 [**Social and Behavioral Sciences**]: Sociology

General Terms

Security

Keywords

Rule learning, causality, security informatics

1. INTRODUCTION

Since its rise to prominence in Iraq and Syria in June, 2014, The Islamic State of Iraq and al-Sham (ISIS) – also known as The Islamic State of Iraq and the Levant (ISIL) or simply the Islamic State, has controlled numerous cities in Sunni-dominated parts of Iraq and Syria. ISIS has displayed a high level of sophistication and discipline in its military operations in comparison to similar insurgent groups, which perhaps may be the source of its success. We have meticulously encoded and recorded 2200 incidents of military activity conducted by ISIS and forces that oppose it (including Iraqi, Syrian, and the American-led coalition) in a relational database. Our goal was to achieve a better understanding of how this group operates - which can lead to new strategies for mitigating ISIS's operations. Specifically, we sought to analyze the behavior of ISIS using concepts from logic programming (in particular APT logic [14, 15]) and causal reasoning [10, 18]. By combining ideas from these fields, we have been able to conduct a thorough search for rules whose precondition consists of multiple atomic propositions, and we provide evidence of causality by comparing rules with the same consequence. So, in addition to considering the probability of a rule (p), we also study a measure of its causality denoted ϵ_{avg} (previously introduced in [10]) – which, informally, can be thought of as the average increase in probability a rule's precondition provides when considered with each of the comparable rules. Using this approach, we have found interesting relationships - consider the following:

- Weeks where ISIS conducts infantry operations in Iraq that are accompanied by indirect fire are indicative of vehicle-bourne improvised explosive device (VBIED) operations in Syria in the following week ($p = 1.0$, $\epsilon_{avg} = 0.92$).
- Weeks in which ISIS conducts operations in Tikrit and conducts a significant number of executions are followed by a large spike in improvised explosive device (IED) usage in Iraq and Syria combined ($p = 1.0, \epsilon_{avg} = 0.97$)
- Air strikes by the Syrian government are followed by mass arrests by ISIS in the following week ($\epsilon_{avg} = 0.91, p = 0.67$), and such massive arrests were *always* proceeded by Syrian air strikes in our dataset.
- In the week after coalition air strikes are conducted against Mosul while ISIS is conducting operations in Al-Anbar province, ISIS greatly increases its IED activity in Iraq ($p = 0.67, \epsilon_{avg} = 0.97$). However, if there are also significant ISIS operations occurring in Syria, the increase in IED usage experienced there is ($p = 0.67, \epsilon_{avg} = 0.79$).

Our findings have also led us to several interesting theories about ISIS behavior that we have developed as a result of this data mining effort. These include the following:

*Paulo Shakarian is also affiliated with ASU Center on the Future of War.

KDD '15, August 11 - 14, 2015, Sydney, NSW, Australia.
© 2015 ACM. ISBN 978-1-4503-3664-2/15/08 ...$15.00.
DOI: http://dx.doi.org/10.1145/2783258.2788591.

- ISIS may employ suicide VBIED operations in Baghdad prior to significant infantry operations in other locations to prevent the deployment of Iraqi army/police reinforcements.
- ISIS tends to leverage indirect fire (IDF) as a precursor to infantry operations - more in keeping with a traditional military force as opposed to a primary use of IDF for harassment purposes (as was typically seen by insurgent groups during Operation Iraqi Freedom).
- As we found relationships between coalition air operations and an increase in ISIS usage of IEDs - and not other, larger weapons systems (i.e. VBIEDs), this may indicate that ISIS resorts to more distributed, insurgent-style tactics in the aftermath of such operations.

To our knowledge, this study represents both the first publicly-available, data-driven study of ISIS as well as the first combination of APT logic with the causality ideas of [10]. The rest of the paper is organized as follows. In Section 2, we describe our approach and recall key concepts from APT logic and causal reasoning. This is followed by a description of our corpus of military events surrounding the actions of ISIS from June-December, 2014 in Section 3. In Section 4, we describe our implementation and discuss our results. Finally, related work is reviewed in Section 5.

2. TECHNICAL APPROACH

2.1 APT Logic

We now present a subset of our previously-introduced APT logic [14, 15]. Our focus here is on the syntax of the language utilized with an alternate semantics that is based on the rule-learning approach described in [14]. This is due to the fact that we are only concerned with learning the rules in this paper and determining their level of causality – we leave problems relating to deduction (i.e. the entailment problem studied in [15]) to future work. APT logic considers a two-part semantic structure: threads (sequences of events) and interpretations (probability distributions over such sequences). Initially, we focus on a semantics restricted to threads.

We assume the existence of a set of ground atoms, $\mathcal{A}$ which in this case correspond with events over time and use the symbol n to denote the size of this set. We shall partition the ground atoms into two subsets: action atoms $\mathcal{A}_{act}$ and environmental atoms $\mathcal{A}_{env}$. Action atoms describe actions of certain actors, and environmental atoms describe aspects of the environment. We will use n_{act}, n_{env} to denote the quantity of ground atoms in $\mathcal{A}_{act}, \mathcal{A}_{env}$, respectively. We can connect atoms using $\neg, \wedge, \vee$ to create formulas in the normal way. A *world* is a subset of atoms that are considered to be true. A *thread* is a series of worlds, each corresponding to a discrete time-point, which are represented by simple natural numbers in the range $1, \ldots, t_{\max}$. We shall use $Th[t]$ to refer to the world specified by Th at time t. A thread (Th) at time t *satisfies* a formula f (denoted $Th[t] \models f$) by the following recursive definition:

- For some $a \in \mathcal{A}$, $Th[t] \models a$ iff $a \in Th[t]$
- For $f = \neg f'$, $Th[t] \models f$ iff $Th[t] \models f'$ is false
- For $f = f' \wedge f''$, $Th[t] \models f$ iff $Th[t] \models f'$ and $Th[t] \models f''$
- For $f = f' \vee f''$, $Th[t] \models f$ iff $Th[t] \models f'$ or $Th[t] \models f''$

We also note that based on how often a given formula occurs within a thread, we can obtain a prior probability for that formula. For instance, consider formula g. We can compute its prior probability (w.r.t. thread Th) as the fraction of time points where g is satisfied:

$$\rho = \frac{|\{t | Th[t] \models g\}|}{t_{\max}} \tag{1}$$

Note that we use the notation $|\cdot|$ for the cardinality of a set. Our goal in this section is for some event g to identify previously occurring event c such that the conditional probability of g occurring given c is greater than p_g. In this paper, we shall only look at finding APT rules where c occurs in the time period right before g. The case where multiple time periods elapse between c and g is left to future work. Hence, we introduce an APT rule of the following form: $c \rightsquigarrow_p g$, which intuitively means that "c is followed by g in one time-step with probability p." We shall refer to c as the precondition and g as the consequence. We say thread $Th \models c \rightsquigarrow_p g$ iff:

$$p = \frac{|\{t \ s.t. \ Th[t] \models c \ and \ Th[t+1] \models g\}|}{|\{t \ s.t. \ Th[t] \models c\}|} \tag{2}$$

This alternate definition of semantics is not new: it is a variant of rule satisfaction with the existential frequency function of [14] and also of "trace semantics" used for a PCTL variant in [9]. In this paper, we are focused on learning rules where c is a conjunction of positive atoms and g is a single positive atom. The number of atoms in the conjunction c is referred to as the "dimension" of the rule $c \rightsquigarrow_p g$. We will also be concerned with two other measures of a given rule: the "negative probability" (used to describe the probabilistic rules of [17]) and the notion of support (a standard concept in association rule learning). First, we define "negative probability" – denoted p^* – for a given rule of the aforementioned format.

$$p^* = \frac{|\{t \ s.t. \ Th[t] \models g \ and \ Th[t-1] \not\models c\}|}{|\{t \ s.t. \ Th[t] \models g\}|} \tag{3}$$

Simply put, p^* is the number of times that the consequence of a rule occurs without the head occurring prior. We can think of p as a measure of precision of a given rule while p^* is more akin to a measure of recall. Next, we formally define the notion of support (s) as follows.

$$s = |\{t \ s.t. \ Th[t] \models c\}| \tag{4}$$

For a given rule r, we shall use the notation p_r, p^*_r, s_r, respectively. We will also use the notation ρ_r to denote the prior probability of the consequence. When it is obvious from context which rule we are referring to (as in the experimental results section), we will drop the subscript.

2.2 Determining Causality

Next, we describe how for a given action, g, we identify potential causes based on a set of rules for which g is the consequence. In considering possible causes, we must first identify a set of *prima facie* causes for g [10, 18]. We present the definition in terms of APT logic below.

Definition 2.1 (Prima Facie Cause [10, 18]). *Given APT logic formulas c, g and thread Th, we say c is a **prima facie** cause for g w.r.t. Th if:*

1. *There exists time t such that* $Th[t] \models g$ *(g occurs with a probability greater than zero)*

2. *There exists* t, t' *where* $t < t'$ *such that* $Th[t] \models c$ *and* $Th[t'] \models g$ *(c occurs before g)*

3. *For* $r \equiv c \rightsquigarrow_p g$ *where* $Th \models r$*, we have* $p > \rho_r$ *(the probability of the consequence occurring after the precondition is greater than the prior probability of the consequence)*

As we will assume the existence of a single thread, *Th* (which is our historical corpus of data), we will often use the language "prima facie causal rule" or "PF-rule" to describe a rule $c \rightsquigarrow_p g$ where c is a prima facie cause for g w.r.t. *Th*.

Next, we adopt the method of [10] to determine if an APT rule is causal. First, in determining if a given PF-rule is causal, we must consider other, related PF-rules. Intuitively, a given rule $r \equiv c \rightsquigarrow_p g$ explains why some instances of g occur within a thread. Another rule $r' \equiv c' \rightsquigarrow_{p'} g$ is related if it also explains why some of those same instances occur. Formally, we say r and r' are related if there exists t such that $Th[t] \models c \wedge c'$ and $Th[t+1] \models g$. Hence, we will define related PF-rules (for a given rule $r \equiv c \rightsquigarrow_p g$) as follows.

$$\mathbf{R}(r) = \{r' \ s.t.\ r' \not\equiv r \ and\ r, r' \ are\ related\}$$

Next, we will look at how to compare two related rules. The key purpose from [10] behind doing so is to study how the probability of the rule changes in cases where both preconditions co-occur in comparison to the probability where exactly one of the preconditions occurs. So, given rules r, r' as defined above, we have the following notation: $p_{r,r'}$ and $p_{\neg r,r'}$, which are defined as the point probabilities that will cause the following two rules to be satisfied by *Th*.

$$c \wedge c' \rightsquigarrow_{p_{r,r'}} g$$
$$\neg c \wedge c' \rightsquigarrow_{p_{\neg r,r'}} g$$

So, $p_{r,r'}$ is the probability that g occurs given both preconditions, and $p_{\neg r,r'}$ is the probability that g occurs given just the precondition of the second rule and not of the first. The idea is that if $p_{r,r'} - p_{\neg r,r'} > 0$, then there is something about the precondition of r that causes g to occur that is not present in r'. Following directly from [10], we measure the average of this quantity to determine how causal a given rule is as follows:

$$\epsilon_{avg} = \frac{\sum_{r' \in \mathbf{R}(r)} p_{r,r'} - p_{\neg r,r'}}{|\mathbf{R}(r)|}$$

Intuitively, $\epsilon_{avg}(r)$ measures the degree of causality exhibited by rule r. Additionally, using this same intuition, we find it useful to include a few other related measures when examining causality. First, we define ϵ_{min}, defined below:

$$\epsilon_{min} = \min_{r' \in \mathbf{R}(r)} (p_{r,r'} - p_{\neg r,r'})$$

This tells us the "least causal" comparison of r with all related rules. Another measure we will use is ϵ_{frac}, defined as follows:

$$\epsilon_{frac}(r) = \frac{|\{r' \ s.t.\ (p_{r,r'} - p_{\neg r,r'}) \geq 0\}|}{|\mathbf{R}(r)|}$$

This provides a fraction of the related rules whose probability remains the same or decreases if the precondition of r is not present. Hence, a number closer to 1 likely indicates that r is more causal. By using multiple causality measurements, we can have a better determination of more significant causality relationships.

2.3 Algorithms

Next, given a thread, we provide a variant of the APT-Extract algorithm [14] that we call PF-Rule-Extract. Essentially, this algorithm generates all possible $\mathcal{A}_{env}$ up to a certain size (specified by the argument $MaxDim$) and then searches for correlation. It returns rules whose precondition occurs a specified number of times (a lower bound on support for a rule) - specified with the argument $SuppLB$. We make several modifications specific to our application to support reasoning.

- We reduce the run-time of the algorithm considerably over APT-Extract. As APT-Extract explores all possible combinations of atoms up to size $MaxDim$, it runs in time $O(\binom{n_{env}}{MaxDim})$. However, PF-Rule-Extract only examines combinations of atoms that occur in a given time period – hence, reducing run-time to $O(\binom{\max_t(n_t)}{MaxDim})$ where n_t is the number of atoms in $\mathcal{A}_{env}$ true at time t. We find in practice that $\max_t(n_t) << n_{env}$.
- We further reduce the run-time by not considering elements of $\mathcal{A}_{env}$ that occur less than the lower bound on support - as they would never appear in a rule.
- We guarantee that all rules returned by PF-Rule-Extract are PF-rules.

Algorithm 1 PF-Rule-Extract

Require: Thread *Th*, sets of atoms $\mathcal{A}_{act}, \mathcal{A}_{env}$, positive natural numbers $MaxDim, SuppLB$, real number $minProb$
Ensure: Set of rules $\mathbf{R}$

1: Set $\mathbf{R} = \emptyset$
2: **for** $g \in \{a \in \mathcal{A}_{act}\ s.t.\ \exists t\ where\ Th[t] \models a\}$ **do**
3:   $preCond(g) = \emptyset$
4:   **for** $t \in \{1, \ldots, t_{\max}\ s.t.\ Th[t+1] \models g\}$ **do**
5:     Let X be the set of all combinations of size $MaxDim$ (or less) of elements in $Th[t] \cap \mathcal{A}_{env}$ that occur at least $SuppLB$ times.
6:     $preCond(g) = preCond(g) \cup X$
7:   **end for**
8:   **for** $c \in preCond(g)$ **do**
9:     Compute ρ, p, s, as per Equations 1,2, and 4
10:     **if** $(s \geq SuppLB) \wedge (p > \rho) \wedge (p \geq minProb)$ **then**
11:       $\mathbf{R} = \mathbf{R} \cup \{r\}$
12:     **end if**
13:   **end for**
14: **end for**
15: **return** Set $\mathbf{R}$

Note that APT-Extract allows for multiple time periods between preconditions and consequences – PF-Rule-Extract can also be easily modified to find rules of this sort through a simple modification of line 4. Next, we provide some formal results to show that PF-Rule-Extract finds rules that meet the requirements of Definition 2.1 and show that it explores all possible combinations up to size $MaxDim$ that are supported by the data that meet the requirement for minimum support even with our efficiency improvements.

PROPOSITION 2.1. *Given thread Th as input, PF-Rule-Extract produces a set of rules* $\mathbf{R}$ *such that each* $r \in R$ *is a prima facie causal rule.*

PROOF. The first requirement for a prima facie cause is met by line 2 of PF-Rule-Extract, as the algorithm only considers consequences that have occurred at least once in Th – hence, they have a prior probability greater than zero. The second requirement is met by line 4, as we only consider atoms that occurred immediately before the consequence when constructing the precondition. Finally, the third condition is met by the if statement at line 10 which will only select rules whose probability is greater than the prior probability of the consequence. □

PROPOSITION 2.2. *PF-Rule-Extract finds all PF-rules whose precondition is a conjunction of size* $MaxDim$ *or a size containing fewer atoms and where both the precondition occurs at least* $SuppLB$ *times in* Th *and the probability is greater than* $minProb$.

PROOF. By Proposition 2.1, every consequence that could be used in a PF-rule is considered, so we need only to consider the precondition. Suppose that there is a PF-rule whose precondition occurs at least $SuppLB$ times that has a size of $MaxDim$ or smaller. Hence, the precondition is comprised of $m \leq MaxDim$ atoms: $a_1, \ldots, a_m$. Clearly, as this precondition occurs at least $SuppLB$ times in Th, each of $a_1, \ldots, a_m$ must also occur $SuppLB$ times by line 5 - so that the precondition must be considered at that point. The only condition that would prevent the rule from being returned is line 10, but again, clearly these are met by the statement of the proposition. Hence, we have a contradiction. □

Once we have identified the PF-rules using PF-Rule-Extract, we must then compare related rules with each other. The algorithm PF-Rule-Compare returns the top k rules for each consequence. Again, here we take advantage of our specific application to reduce the run-time of this comparison. In particular, for a given rule, we need not compare it to all the rules returned by PF-Rule-Extract; we only need to compare it to those that share the consequence. By sorting the rules by consequence - a linear time operation (line 3), we are able to reduce the cost of the quadratic operation for the rule comparisons (a brute-force method would take $O(|\mathbf{R}|^2)$ while this method requires $O((\max_g |\mathbf{R}_g|)^2 + |\mathbf{R}|)$ – and we have observed that $\max_g |\mathbf{R}_g| << |\mathbf{R}|$).

Algorithm 2 PF-Rule-Compare

Require: Set of rules $\mathbf{R}$, natural number k
Ensure: Set of rules $\mathbf{R}'$

1: Set $\mathbf{R}' = \emptyset$.
2: **for** $g \in \mathcal{A}_{act}$ **do**
3: Set $\mathbf{R}_g = \{c \leadsto_p g \in \mathbf{R}\}$
4: **for** $r \in \mathbf{R}_g$ **do**
5: Calculate ϵ_{avg} for rule r (Equation 5 by comparing it to all related rules in $\mathbf{R}_g \setminus \{r\}$)
6: **end for**
7: From the set $\mathbf{R}_g$, add the top k rules by ϵ_{avg} to the set $\mathbf{R}'$
8: **end for**
9: **return** Set $\mathbf{R}'$

3. ISIS DATASET

We collected data on 2200 military events that occurred from June 8th through December 31st, 2014 that involved ISIS and forces opposing ISIS. Events were classified into one of 159 event types - and these were used as predicates for APT logic atoms. We list a sampling of the predicates we used in Table 1. Many predicates are unary because they correspond with ISIS actions (i.e. armedAtk) while those dealing with operations by other actors (i.e. airOp) and predicates denoting spikes in activity (i.e. VBIEDSpike) accept more than one argument. Nearly every predicate has one argument that corresponds to the location in which the associated event took place. See Figure 1 for a sampling of locations in the ISIS dataset.

We obtained our data primarily from reports published by the Institute for the Study of War (ISW) [5], and we augmented it with other reputable sources including MapAction [4, 6], Google Maps [3], and Humanitarian Response [2]. We devised a code-book as well as coding standards for events, and one of our team members functioned as a quality-control to reduce errors in human coding.

Figure 1: Map illustrating cities associated with events in the ISIS dataset.

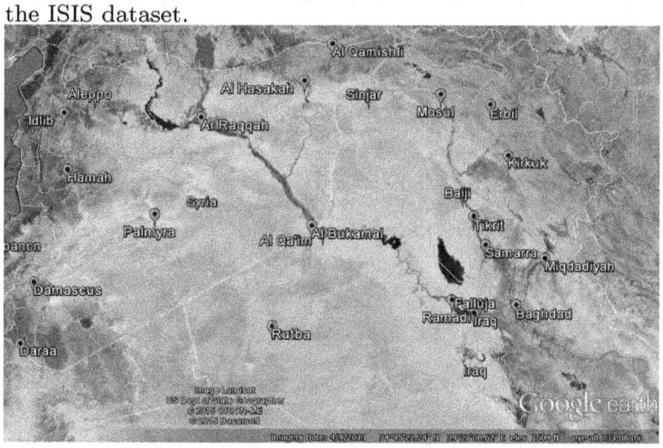

4. RESULTS AND DISCUSSION

4.1 Experimental Setup

We implemented our PF-Rule-Extract and PF-Rule-Compare in Python 2.8x and ran it on a commodity machine equipped with an Intel Core i5 CPU (2.7 GHz) with 16 GB of RAM running Windows 7. The time periods we utilized were weeks - hence, we had 30 time periods in our thread. We had 980 distinct environmental atoms ($\mathcal{A}_{env}$). Our action atoms ($\mathcal{A}_{act}$) corresponded to weeks where the number of incidents for certain activity rose to or past one or two moving standard deviations (denoted $1 \times \sigma, 2 \times \sigma$ respectively, computed based on the previous 4 weeks) above the four-week moving average (computed based on the previous 4 weeks). We refer to these atoms as "spikes" and show some sample atoms denoting such spikes in Table 1. The spikes are designated for three locations: Iraq, Syria, or both theaters combined. We also included these spikes in the set of environmental atoms as well ($\mathcal{A}_{act} \subset \mathcal{A}_{env}$).

We set the parameters of PF-Rule-Extract as follows: $MaxDim = 3$, $SuppLB = 3$, $minProb = 0.5$. For PF-Rule-

Table 1: A sampling of predicate symbols used to describe events in the ISIS Dataset

Predicate	Intuition
airOp(X,Y)	Actor X (typically "Coalition," "Syrian Government," or "U.S.") conducts an air campaign against ISIS in the vicinity of city Y.
armedAtk(X)	ISIS conducts an armed attack (a.k.a. infantry operation) in city X.
IED(X)	ISIS conducts an attack using an improvised explosive device (IED) in city X.
indirectFire(X)	ISIS conducts an indirect fire operation (i.e. mortars) near city X.
VBIED(X)	ISIS conducts an attack using a vehicle-bourne improvised explosive device (VBIED or car-bomb) in city X.
armedAtkSpike(X,Y)	There is a spike in ISIS armed attacks in country X that is Y amount over the 4-month moving average (Y is expressed in terms of moving standard deviations).
VBIEDSpike(X,Y)	There is a spike in ISIS VBIEDs in country X that is Y amount over the 4-month moving average (Y is expressed in terms of moving standard deviations).

Compare, we did not set a particular k value. Instead, we used ϵ_{avg} to rank the rules by causality for a given consequence. In this paper, we report the top causal rules (in terms of ϵ_{avg}) for some of the consequences. We also note that the number of related rules provides insight into that rule's significance - we discuss this quantity in our analysis. We examine some of the top rules in terms of ϵ_{avg} and describe the military insights that they provide. Our team includes a former military officer with over a decade of experience in military operations that includes two combat tours in Operation Iraqi Freedom. In addition to ϵ_{avg}, we also examined the rule's probability (p) - the fraction of times the consequence follows the precondition, the negative probability (p^*) - the fraction of times the consequence is not proceeded by the precondition, the prior probability of the consequence (ρ), and the additional causal measures introduced in this paper - $\epsilon_{min}, \epsilon_{frac}$. The relationship specified in the rule can be considered more significant if $p >> \rho$, p^* is closer to 0, $\epsilon_{min} \geq 0$, and $\epsilon_{avg}, \epsilon_{frac}$ are close to 1. These measures are discussed in more detail in Section 2.

4.2 Algorithm Efficiency

In Section 2, we described some performance improvements that we utilized in PF-Rule-Extract (which is based on APT-Extract [14]) that are specific to this application. The first performance improvement was the reduction in the number of atoms used to generate the preconditions (which were conjunctions of atoms of up to size 3 in our experiments). First, we limited the number of atoms to be used in such combinations based on the weeks in which they occurred. Even though we had 980 environmental atoms, no more than 93 occurred during any given week (this is the value $\max_t(n_t)$ from Section 2). Further, by eliminating atoms that occurred less than the $SuppLB$ from consideration, this lowered it further to 49 atoms per week at the most. This directly leads to fewer combinations of atoms generated for the precondition. A comparison is shown in Table 2. Note that the values for APT-Extract are exact, while the remaining are upper bounds. Again, this substantial, multiple-order-of-magnitude savings in the number of rules explored is a result of the relative sparseness of our dataset and the fact that our preconditions consisted of conjunctions of positive atoms. This efficiency is primarily what enabled us to find and compare rules in a matter of minutes on a commodity system.

Table 2: Improvement in Algorithm Efficiency

Technique	Atoms	Combinations Explored
APT-Extract [14]	980	$182,122,025$
$\max_t(n_t)$	93	$8,853,042$
$\max_t(n_t)$ and consider only atoms that occur more than $SuppLB$ times	49	$1,296,834$

4.3 ISIS Military Tactics

In this section, we investigate rules that provide insight into ISIS's military tactics – in particular, we found interesting and potentially casual relationships that provide insight into their infantry operations, use of terror tactics (i.e. VBIEDs), and decisions to employ roadside bombs and to launch suicide operations.

Table 3: Causal Rules for Spikes in Armed Attacks (Iraq and Syria Combined)

No.	Precondition	ϵ_{avg}	p	p^*
1.	indirectFire($Baiji$)$\wedge$ armedAtk($Balad$)	0.81	0.67	0.50
2.	indirectFire($Baiji$)$\wedge$ armedAtk($Balad$)$\wedge$ VBIED($Baghdad$)	0.81	0.67	0.50

Armed Attacks. The prior probability of large spikes ($2 \times \sigma$) (see figure 2) for ISIS armed attacks for Iraq and Syria was 0.154. However, for our two most causal rules for this spike (Table 3), we derived this probability as 0.67. Such spikes likely indicate major infantry operations by the Islamic State. Rule 1 states that indirect fire at Baiji (attributed to ISIS) along with an armed attack in Balad leads to a spike in armed attacks by the group in the next week while rule 2 mirrors rule 1 but adds VBIED activity in Baghdad as part of the precondition. We note the relatively high p^* (0.5 in this case), which indicates that each spike in armed attacks of this type are not necessarily proceeded by this precondition, despite the relatively high value for ϵ_{avg}, hinting at causality (each of these rules was compared with 265 related rules and had $\epsilon_{frac} = 1$ and $\epsilon_{min} = 0$ – showing little indication of a related rule being more causal). We believe that the strong causality and the high value for p^* indicate that these rules may well be "token causes" – causes for a specific event - in this case, we think it is likely ISIS offensive operations in Baiji. This makes sense, as a common military tactic is to prepare the battlefield with indirect fire (which it seems ISIS did in the prior week). It is unclear if the VBIED incidents in Baghdad are related due to the co-occurrence. That said, it is notable that VBIED operations are often used as "terror" tactics as opposed to part of a sustained operation. If so, this may have been part of a preparatory phase (that included indirect fire in Baiji), and the purpose of the VBIED events in Baghdad was to prevent additional Iraqi Security Force deployment from Baghdad to Baiji. We note in one case supporting this rule (on July 25th, 2014) that ISIS also conducted IED attacks on power-lines that support Baghdad - which may have also been designed to hinder deployment of reinforcements. Here, it is also important to note the ongoing Infantry operations in Balad (specified in the precondition) - which would consume ISIS resources and perhaps make it more difficult to respond to further deployment of government security forces. Though this is likely a token cause, this may be indicative of ISIS tactics when preparing to concentrate force on certain objectives (in this case Baiji) while maintaining ongoing operations (Balad), as a spike in armed attacks likely indicates a surge of light infantry-style soldiers into the area (a manpower-intensive operation).

Figure 2: ISIS Spikes in Armed Attacks in Iraq and Syria per Week

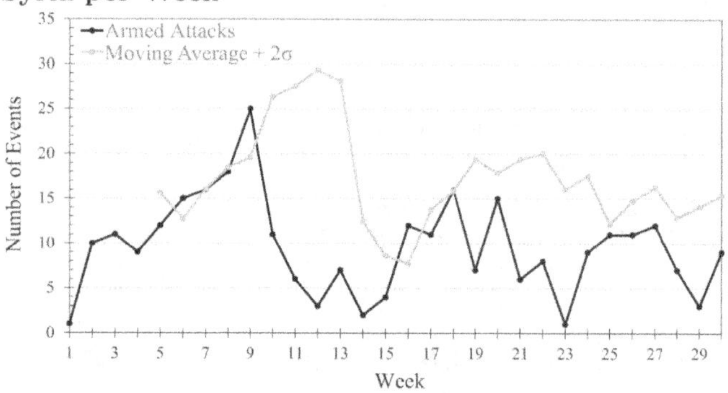

Spikes in VBIED Incidents. VBIED incidents have been a common terror tactic used by religious Sunni extremist insurgent groups in Iraq in the past – including Al Qaeda in Iraq, Ansar al Sunnah, Ansar al Islam, and now ISIS. We found two relationships that are potentially causal for spikes in VBIED activity in Iraq and Syria combined, shown in Table 4.

Rule 3 states that if infantry operations in Balad accompanied by indirect fire operations in Baiji occur, we should expect a major ($2 \times \sigma$) spike in VBIED activity (see figure 3) by ISIS (Iraq and Syria combined). We believe this rule provides further evidence of the use of VBIEDs to pull security forces away from other parts of the operational theater. It is interesting to note that the negative probability

Table 4: Causal Rules for Spikes in VBIED Incidents in Iraq and Syria Combined

No.	Precondition	ϵ_{avg}	p	p^*
3.	armedAtk($Balad$)∧ indirectFire($Baiji$)	0.95	1.00	0.25

is only 0.25 - which means that most of the VBIED spikes we observed were related to operations in Balad and Baiji. This highlights the strategic importance of these two cities to ISIS: Baiji is home to a major oil refinery while Balad is near a major Iraqi air base. We also found solid evidence of causality for this rule - based on 209 related rules, we found $\epsilon_{min} = 0.5$ which means adding a second precondition to this rule increases the probability of the second rule by at least 0.5

Figure 3: Spikes in ISIS VBIED Activity in Iraq and Syria per Week

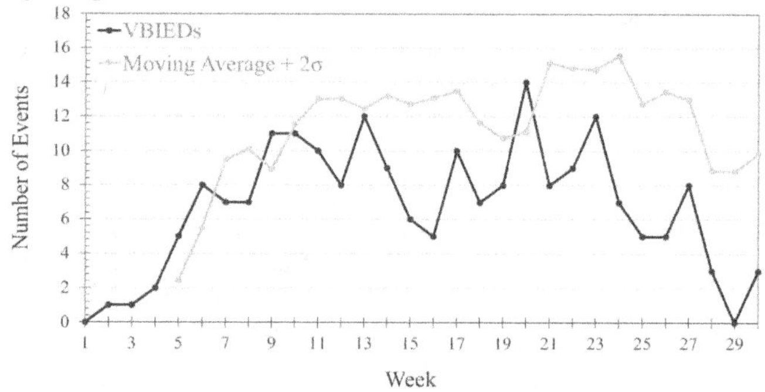

Spikes in IED Incidents. Improvised explosive device (IED) incidents have been a common tactic used by Iraqi insurgents throughout the U.S.-led Operation Iraqi Freedom. Though the IED comprises a smaller weapons system normally employed by local insurgent cells, spikes in such activity could be meaningful. For instance, it may indicate action ordered by a strategic-level command that is being carried out on the city level, or it may indicate improved logistic support to provide local cells the necessary munitions to carry out such operations in larger numbers. Such spikes only occur with a prior probability of 0.19. In Table 5, we show a rather strong precondition for such attacks that consist of infantry operations in Tikrit and a spike in executions. In this Table, rule 4 states that infantry operations in Tikrit, when accompanied by a spike in executions, lead to a spike ($1 \times \sigma$) (see figure 4) in Iraq and Syria combined - with a probability of 1.0 - much higher than the prior of the consequence. With ϵ_{avg} of 0.97 (based on a comparison with 1180 other rules), this relationship appears highly causal ($\epsilon_{frac} = 1.0, \epsilon_{min} = 0.0$) although 40% of $1 \times \sigma$ IED spikes were not accounted for by this precondition.

4.4 Relationships between Iraqi and Syrian Theaters

ISIS has clearly leveraged itself as a force operating in both Iraq and Syria, and the identification of relationships between incidents in relation to the two theaters may indicate some sophisticated operational coordination on their

Figure 4: Spikes in ISIS IEDs in Iraq and Syria per Week

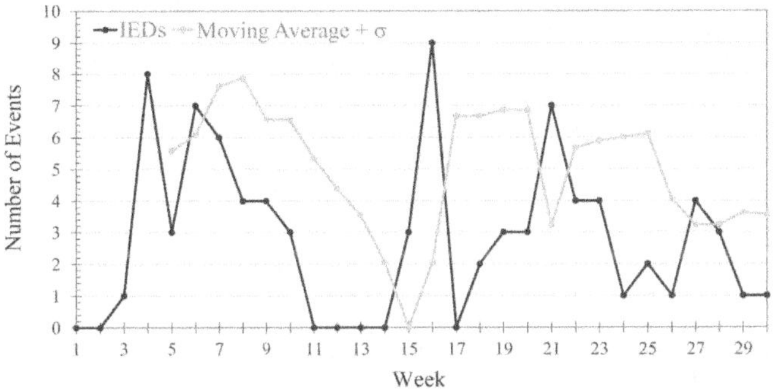

Table 5: Causal Rules for Spikes in IED Incidents in Iraq and Syria Combined

No.	Precondition	ϵ_{avg}	p	p^*
4.	armedAtk($Tikrit$)$\wedge$ executionSpike($Total, 2\sigma$)	0.97	1.00	0.40

part. We have found some evidence of these cross-theater relationships with regard to suicide operations in Iraq (potentially affected by other events in Syria) and VBIED operations in Syria (potentially affected by other operations in Iraq).

VBIED Spikes in Syria. Table 6 shows our most causal rules whose consequence is a $1\times\sigma$ spike (over the four-month moving average) (see figures 5, 6) in ISIS VBIED events in Syria. Rule 5 provides a precondition of a spike in armed attacks in Iraq that includes a major spike in indirect fire activity while rule 6 has the same precondition but includes an additional VBIED event in Baghdad. We believe that the spike in armed attacks indicates major ISIS operations in Iraq and the inclusion of indirect fire events also indicates that ISIS soldiers specializing in weapon systems such as mortars may also be concentrated in Iraqi operations. Taken together, this may indicate a shift in ISIS resources toward Iraq - which may mean that operations have shifted away from Syria. Hence, VBIED attacks, which once prepared, are less manpower-intensive, nevertheless provide a show-of-force in the secondary theater. We also note that the probability of these rules (1.00) is significantly higher than the prior of these spikes (0.19) and that the causality value is also high for each of the 983 related rules, as the probability either remains the same or increases when considering one of these preconditions (in other words, $\epsilon_{frac} = 1$ and $\epsilon_{min} = 0$).

Operations Shifting to Syria. In rules 5 and 6 of Table 6, we saw how increased operations in Iraq led to the use of VBIEDs in Syria – perhaps due to a focus on more manpower-heavy operations in Iraq. Interestingly, rule 7 shown in Table 7 indicates that less manpower-intensive operations in Iraq that have a terror component seem to have a causal relationship (based on $\epsilon_{avg} = 0.97, \epsilon_{frac} = 1.0, \epsilon_{min} = 0.5$ found by comparing to 95 related rules) with

Figure 5: Spikes in ISIS VBIEDs in Syria per Week

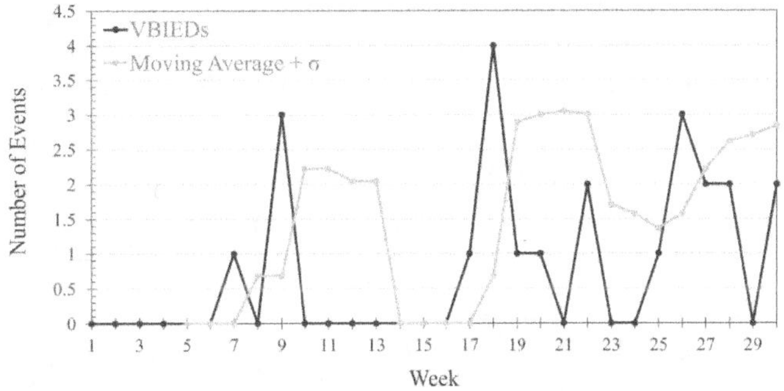

Figure 6: Comparison of ISIS Armed Attacks and VBIEDs in Syria per Week

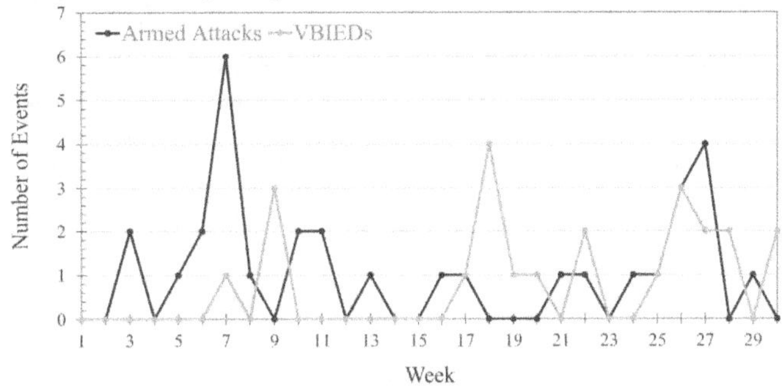

Table 6: Causal Rules for Spikes in VBIED Operations in Syria

No.	Precondition	ϵ_{avg}	p	p^*
5.	armedAtkSpike($Iraq, \sigma$)$\wedge$ indirFireSpike($Iraq, 2\sigma$)	0.92	1.00	0.20
6.	armedAtkSpike($Iraq, \sigma$)$\wedge$ indirFireSpike($Iraq, 2\sigma$)$\wedge$ VBIED($Baghdad$)	0.92	1.00	0.20

significant indirect fire operations in Syria (that occur with a prior probability of 0.08). As discussed earlier, indirect fire is normally used to "prepare the battlefield" for infantry operations, so this rule may be indicative of a shift in manpower toward Syria - and the use of a VBIED tactic in Baghdad (less manpower-intensive but very sensational) seems to always proceed a major ($2\times\sigma$ over the moving average) spike in indirect fire activity in Syria in our data (hence, a negative probability of 0.0).

Table 7: Causal Rules for Spikes in Indirect Fire Operations in Syria

No.	Precondition	ϵ_{avg}	p	p^*
7.	IED($Baghdad$)$\wedge$ VBIED($Ramadi$)	0.97	0.67	0.00

4.5 ISIS Activities Related to Opposition Air Strikes

Table 8: Causal Rules for Spikes in Arrests (Iraq and Syria Combined)

No.	Precondition	ϵ_{avg}	p	p^*
8.	airStrike($SyrianGov, Damascus$)	0.91	0.67	0.00

Reaction to Syrian Government Air Strikes. Rule 8, shown in Table 8, tells us that a $2 \times \sigma$ spike in arrests (see figure 7) was *always* ($p^* = 0.0$) proceeded by an air strike conducted by the Syrian government. The prior probability for such a spike in arrests is 0.08. Further, we found evidence of causality - the actions of the Syrian government raised the probability of each of 33 related rules by at least 0.5. One potential reason to explain why arrests follow Syrian air operations is that unlike western nations, Syria generally lacks advanced technical intelligence-gathering capabilities to determine targets, and Syria likely relies on extensive human intelligence networks - especially within Iraq and Syria. Successful targeting from the air by the Syrian government may then indicate that ISIS's counter-intelligence efforts (activities designed to locate spies within its ranks) may have failed and so the organization perhaps then decides to conduct massive arrests.

Figure 7: Spikes in ISIS Arrests in Iraq and Syria per Week

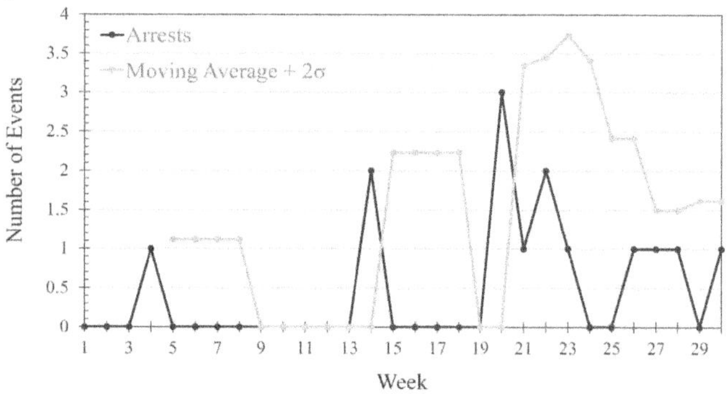

Table 9: Causal Rules for Major Spikes in Suicide Operations in Iraq

No.	Precondition	ϵ_{avg}	p	p^*
9.	airStrike($IraqGovt, Baiji$)$\wedge$ armedAtk($Balad$)$\wedge$ VBIED($Baghdad$)	0.71	0.67	0.60

Reaction to Iraqi Government Air Strikes. In Table 9, rule 9 tells us that a $2 \times \sigma$ spike (see figure 8) in suicide operations in Iraq is related to a precondition involving Iraqi aerial operations in Baiji, ISIS infantry operations in Balad, and a VBIED in Baghdad. The rule shows that these spikes in suicide operations are 3.5 times more likely with this precondition. Though ϵ_{avg} is lower than some of the other rules presented thus far, it has a value for ϵ_{min} of 0.3 - the minimum increase in probability afforded to any of the 82 related rules to which we add the precondition of rule 9. The precondition indicates that ISIS may have recently expended a VBIED (expensive in terms of equipment) while it has ongoing infantry operations in Balad (expensive in terms of personnel) - hence, it may seek a more economical attack (in terms of both manpower and equipment) that still has a significant terror component - and it would appear that a suicide attack provides a viable option to respond to such air strikes.

Figure 8: Spikes in ISIS Suicide Operations in Iraq per Week

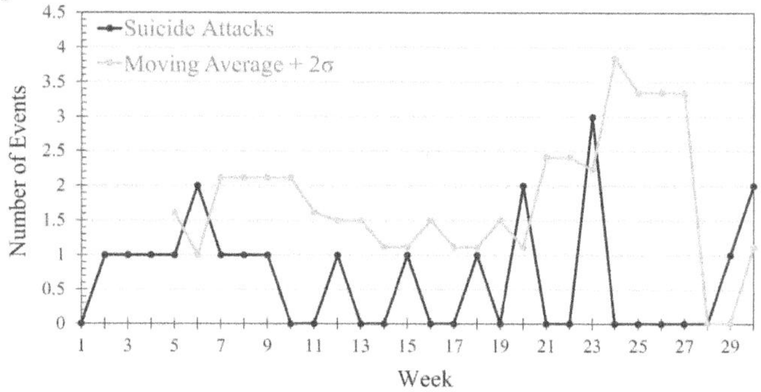

Table 10: Causal Rules for Major Spikes in IED Operations in Iraq

No.	Precondition	ϵ_{avg}	p	p^*
10.	airStrike($Coalition, Mosul$)$\wedge$ armedAtk($Fallujah$)	0.97	0.67	0.33

Table 11: Causal Rules for Major Spikes in IED Operations in Syria

No.	Precondition	ϵ_{avg}	p	p^*
11.	airStrike($Coalition, Mosul$)$\wedge$ armedAtk($Ramadi$)$\wedge$ armedAtkSpike($Syria, \sigma$)	0.79	0.67	0.33

Reaction to Air Strikes by the U.S.-led coalition. Rules 10 ($\epsilon_{frac} = 1.0, \epsilon_{min} = 0.5$, 562 related rules) and 11 ($\epsilon_{frac} = 1.0, \epsilon_{min} = 0.38$, 81 related rules) - shown in Tables 10 and 11 - illustrate two different outcomes from coalition air operations in Mosul. In both cases, ISIS has active operations in the Al-Anbar province – both Ramadi and Fallujah have similar demographics. Hence, the major difference is that the precondition of rule 11 also includes significant infantry operations in Syria. So, even though both rules result in an increase in IED activity ($2 \times \sigma$ above average, a spike that in both cases occurs with a prior probability of 0.12) (see figures 9, 10) - the increase occurs in Iraq for rule 10 and Syria for rule 11. It may be the case that ISIS is increasing IED activity in response to coalition air strikes in the location of their main effort. Further, the relatively low negative probability (0.33) along with relatively high values for ϵ_{min} may indicate that coalition air strikes in Mosul are likely viewed as important factors contributing to ISIS decisions to increase IED activity. We may also note that the use of IED activity in the aftermath of coalition air strikes could also be due to the size of the weapon. An IED can be fairly small, easily disassembled and stored in an innocuous location - hence, it is weapon system that the coalition cannot sense and target from the air.

Figure 9: Spikes in ISIS IEDs in Iraq per Week

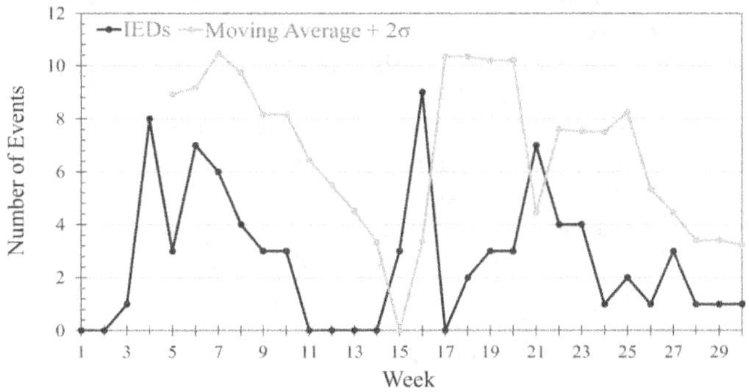

Figure 10: Spikes in ISIS IEDs in Syria per Week

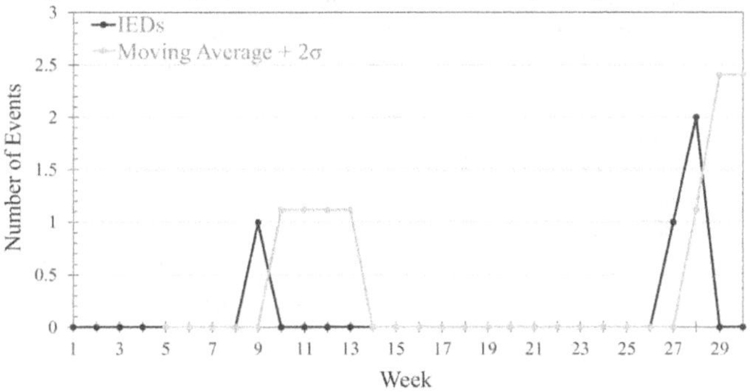

5. RELATED WORK

To the best of our knowledge, this paper represents the first purely data-driven study of ISIS, and it is also the first to combine the causality framework of [10] with APT-Logic. However, there has been a wealth of research conducted where rule-based systems have been applied to terrorist and insurgent groups, as well as other work on modeling insurgent actions. Here, we review this related work and also discuss other approaches to causal reasoning.

Rule-based systems. Previously, there has been a variety of research on modeling the actions of terrorist and insurgent groups. Perhaps most well-known is the Stochastic Opponent Modeling Agents (SOMA) [11, 12], which was developed with the goal of better understanding different cultural groups along with their behaviors. This is also based on a rule-based framework known as action-probabilistic (AP) rules [8], which is a predecessor of APT-logic used in this paper [14, 15]. The SOMA system produces a probabilistic logic representation for understanding group behaviors and reasoning about the types of actions a group may take. In recent years, this system has been used to better understand terror groups like Hamas [12] and Hezbollah [11] through probabilistic rules. However, it can also be used with cultural, religious, and political groups - as it has been demonstrated with other groups in the Minorities at Risk Organizational Behavior (MAROB) dataset [1]. The work on SOMA was followed by an adoption of APT-Logic [14, 15], which extended AP-rules with a temporal component. APT logic was also applied to the groups of the MAROB dataset as well as Shi'ite Iraqi insurgent groups circa 2007 (present during the American-led Operation Iraqi Freedom) [15] [1]. Perhaps most significantly, APT-Logic was applied to another dataset for the study of the terror groups Lashkar-e-Taiba (LeT) and Indian Mujahideen (IM) in two comprehensive volumes that discuss the policy implications of the behavioral rules learned in these cases [17, 16]. The main similarity between the previous work leveraging SOMA, AP-rules, and/or APT-logic and this paper is that both leverage probabilistic rule learning. However, all of the aforementioned rule-learning approaches only discover correlations, while this work is focused on rules that are not only of high probability, but also have a likely casual relationship. We also note that none of this previous work studies ISIS but rather other terrorist and insurgent groups.

Analysis of insurgent military tactics. We also note that the previous rule-learning approaches to understanding terrorist and insurgent behavior have primarily focused on analyzing political events and how they affect the actions of groups such as LeT and IM. However, with the exception of some of the work on APT-Logic which studies Shi'ite Iraqi insurgents [14], the aforementioned work is generally not focused on tactical military operations - unlike this paper. However, there have been other techniques introduced in the literature that have been designed to better account for ground action. Previously, a statistical-based approach leveraged leaked classified data [19] [2] to predict trends of violent activity during the American-led Operation Enduring Freedom in Afghanistan. However, this work was primarily focused on prediction and not identifying causal relationships of interest to analysis as in this work. We also note that this work does not rely on the use of leaked classified data, but rather on open-source information. Another interesting approach is the model-based approach of [7], in which subject matter experts create models of insurgent behavior using a combination of fuzzy cognitive maps and complex networks to run simulations and study "what-if" scenarios. However, unlike this paper, the work of [7] is not as data-driven an approach.

Causal reasoning. The comparison of rules by ϵ_{avg} as a measure of causality was first introduced in [10] and further studied in [9]. It draws on the philosophical ideas of [18]. However, this work has primarily looked at preconditions as single atomic propositions. Further, it did not explore the issue of efficiency. As we look to identify rules whose precondition consists of more than one atomic proposition, we

[1]ISIS is a Sunni group and did not exist in its present form in 2007.

[2]Resulting from WikiLeaks in 2010.

introduce a rule-learning approach. Further, moving beyond previous rule-learning approaches such as that introduced in [8] and [14], we show practical techniques to improve efficiencies of such algorithms. Further, we also improve upon the efficiency of computing ϵ_{avg} - a practical issue not discussed in [10, 9]. We note that neither this previous work on causality nor APT-logic makes independence assumptions. This differs substantially from earlier work on causality such as [13], which relies on graphical models that make relatively strong independence assumptions. Our goal was to avoid such structures in order to provide a more purely data-driven approach. A key aspect of this work as opposed to previous studies on causality is that we leverage the intuitions of APT logic and AP rules, in which the rule-learning algorithm searches for combinations of atomic propositions that are related to a given consequence.

6. CONCLUSION

In this paper, we conducted a data-driven study on the insurgent group ISIS using a combination of APT-logic, rule learning, and causal reasoning to identify cause-and-effect behavior rules concerning the group's actions. We believe our approach is of significant utility for both military decision making and the creation of policy. In the future, we look to extend this work in several ways: first, we look to create non-ground rules that generalize some of the preconditions further. This would allow us to understand the circumstances in which ISIS conducts general operations (as opposed to operations specific to a given city or to a geographic area). We also look to study more complex temporal relationships – possibly using a more fine-grain resolution for time and studying rules where the cause is followed by the effect in more than one unit of time. We also look to leverage additional variables about the environment, including data about weather, information (including social media operations), and the political situation to find more interesting relationships.

7. REFERENCES

[1] V. Asal, C. Johnson, and J. Wilkenfeld. Ethnopolitical violence and terrorism in the middle east. In J. J. Hewitt, J. Wilkenfeld, and T. R. Gurr, editors, *Peace and Conflict 2008*. Paradigm Publishers, 2007.

[2] Districts of iraq. United Nations Office for the Coordination of Humanitarian Affairs, 2014. http://www.humanitarianresponse.info/operations/iraq/search?search=governorate+district.

[3] Google maps. Google Inc., 2014. https://www.google.com/maps/.

[4] Iraq - district reference maps. MapAction, 2014. http://www.mapaction.org/component/search/?searchword=iraq+map&ordering=newest&searchphrase=all&limit=100&areas[0]=maps.

[5] Situation reports. Institute for the Study of War, 2014. http://understandingwar.org/.

[6] Syria: Governorate and district reference maps. MapAction, 2014. http://www.mapaction.org/district-reference-maps-of-syria.html.

[7] P. Giabbanelli. Modelling the spatial and social dynamics of insurgency. *Security Informatics*, 3:2, 2014.

[8] S. Khuller, M. V. Martinez, D. Nau, A. Sliva, G. I. Simari, and V. S. Subrahmanian. Computing most probable worlds of action probabilistic logic programs: scalable estimation for $10^{30,000}$ worlds. *Annals of Mathematics and Artificial Intelligence*, 51(2-4):295–331, 2007.

[9] S. Kleinberg. A logic for causal inference in time series with discrete and continuous variables. In *IJCAI 2011, Proceedings of the 22nd International Joint Conference on Artificial Intelligence, Barcelona, Catalonia, Spain, July 16-22, 2011*, pages 943–950, 2011.

[10] S. Kleinberg and B. Mishra. The temporal logic of causal structures. In *UAI 2009, Proceedings of the Twenty-Fifth Conference on Uncertainty in Artificial Intelligence, Montreal, QC, Canada, June 18-21, 2009*, pages 303–312, 2009.

[11] A. Mannes, M. Michael, A. Pate, A. Sliva, V. S. Subrahmanian, and J. Wilkenfeld. Stochastic opponent modeling agents: A case study with Hezbollah. *First International Workshop on Social Computing, Behavioral Modeling, and Prediction*, April 2008.

[12] A. Mannes, A. Sliva, V. S. Subrahmanian, and J. Wilkenfeld. Stochastic opponent modeling agents: A case study with Hamas. *Proceedings of the Second International Conference on Computational Cultural Dynamics (ICCCD)*, September 2008.

[13] J. Pearl. *Causality: Models, Reasoning, and Inference.* Cambridge University Press, 2000.

[14] P. Shakarian, A. Parker, G. I. Simari, and V. S. Subrahmanian. Annotated probabilistic temporal logic. *ACM Transactions on Computational Logic*, 2011.

[15] P. Shakarian, G. I. Simari, and V. S. Subrahmanian. Annotated probabilistic temporal logic: Approximate fixpoint implementation. *ACM Transactions on Computational Logic*, 2012.

[16] V. S. Subrahmanian, A. Mannes, A. Roul, and R. K. Raghavan. *Indian Mujahideen - Computational Analysis and Public Policy*, volume 1 of *Terrorism, Security, and Computation.* Springer, 2013.

[17] V. S. Subrahmanian, A. Mannes, A. Sliva, J. Shakarian, and J. P. Dickerson. *Computational Analysis of Terrorist Groups: Lashkar-e-Taiba.* Springer, 2013.

[18] P. Suppes. *A probabilistic theory of causality.* North-Holland Pub. Co., 1970.

[19] A. Zammit-Mangion, M. Dewar, V. Kadirkamanathan, and G. Sanguinetti. Point process modelling of the afghan war diary. *Proceedings of the National Academy of Sciences*, 109(31):12414–12419, 2012.

Transfer Learning for Bilingual Content Classification*

Qian Sun[1], Mohammad S. Amin[2], Baoshi Yan[2], Craig Martell[2], Vita Markman[2], Anmol Bhasin[3], and Jieping Ye[4]
[1]Arizona State University, qsun21@asu.edu
[2]LinkedIn Corporation, {mamin, byan, cmartell, vmarkman}@linkedin.com
[3]Groupon, Inc., abhasin@groupon.com
[4]University of Michigan, jpye@umich.edu

ABSTRACT

LinkedIn Groups provide a platform on which professionals with similar background, target and specialities can share content, take part in discussions and establish opinions on industry topics. As in most online social communities, spam content in LinkedIn Groups poses great challenges to the user experience and could eventually lead to substantial loss of active users. Building an intelligent and scalable spam detection system is highly desirable but faces difficulties such as lack of labeled training data, particularly for languages other than English. In this paper, we take the spam (Spanish) job posting detection as the target problem and build a generic machine learning pipeline for multi-lingual spam detection. The main components are feature generation and knowledge migration via transfer learning. Specifically, in the feature generation phase, a relatively large labeled data set is generated via machine translation. Together with a large set of unlabeled human written Spanish data, unigram features are generated based on the frequency. In the second phase, machine translated data are properly reweighted to capture the discrepancy from human written ones and classifiers can be built on top of them. To make effective use of a small portion of labeled data available in human written Spanish, an adaptive transfer learning algorithm is proposed to further improve the performance. We evaluate the proposed method on LinkedIn's production data and the promising results verify the efficacy of our proposed algorithm. The pipeline is ready for production.

Categories and Subject Descriptors

H.2.8 [**Database Management**]: Database applications-Data Mining

General Terms

Algorithm

*Major part of this work was done when Qian Sun interned at LinkedIn.

KDD'15, August 11-14, 2015, Sydney, NSW, Australia.

DOI: http://dx.doi.org/10.1145/2783258.2788575.

Keywords

transfer learning, classification, text mining, NLP

1. INTRODUCTION

Spam content posted in group discussion at LinkedIn will jeopardize other user's return visit on the site. Figure 1 is one of the spam examples in group discussion[1], where A.A puts a job post in reply to S.S's profile update. A.A's response would probably annoy S.S since her reply is not related to S.S's update. Simply blocking A.A's account is not a smart solution for LinkedIn, as she may be a legitimate user and may also put informative posts somewhere else on the site. A better solution is to examine each piece of content and filter those deemed to be spammy. With the development of globalization in social network, LinkedIn is available in more than 20 languages. Therefore such spam content may be written in different languages, such as English, Spanish, Chinese, etc. Efficient tools for spam detection in multiple languages are highly desired at LinkedIn. The multilingual text categorization problem has gained its attention recently [1, 13, 15, 23, 26].

Figure 1: A sample of spam. S.S posted a status update at LinkedIn. A.A replied with a post searching for jobs, which is clearly a spam in this case.

One may solve this multi-lingual spam detection problem by enriching data representation with machine translated features in different languages [2, 21], as illustrated in Figure 2. If we are dealing with multilingual spam detection problem in English, Spanish and French, we can

[1]For the purpose of privacy protection, we anonymize the name and profile pictures in all examples.

translate any content into the other two languages. In this way, we will have bag-of-words features concatenated from three languages, and each piece of content needs to be translated into multiple languages in order to apply the uniform model. However, the machine translation to multiple languages leads to higher latency and consumes more budget. Therefore, the uniform model is not the best choice for an online product.

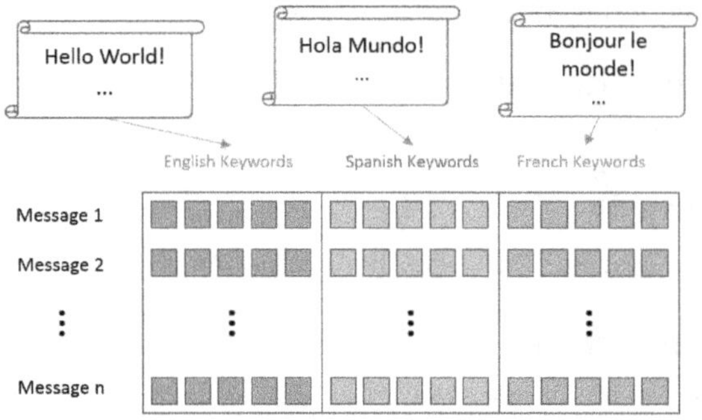

Figure 2: Multi-lingual uniform model. Messages are translated into other languages at first. The keywords for all the languages are then extracted. Frequency based values are assigned to each entry of the data matrix.

Considering the problem from an online product view, we propose to build a generic pipeline for each language. Thus we will keep a model pool in our system which contains models for different languages. The main idea of the pipeline is illustrated in Figure 3. When a piece of content is posted and transferred to the server, we first detect the language in which it is written, then apply the corresponding model to do the spam detection. If it is a spam, the system takes appropriate action. We will start with Spanish spam detection first, as Spanish is the second most widely used language in the US. The pipeline can be petentially well generalized to many other languages, such as French, German, etc.

Problem Setup: In this paper, we aim to develop a framework to deal with the Spanish spam detection problem without training data at LinkedIn. The challenge of Spanish spam detection is that we do not have enough labeled Spanish data in our database, so we cannot train an accurate model from real Spanish data. Instead we have a lot of labeled English content available. Asking human experts to help us label the Spanish data is both time and labor consuming. It is more efficient to translate Spanish content with the emergence of machine translation tools [19, 7].

There are two ways to do the translation: the first one is to translate the features (unigram) in English to Spanish, and the second one is to translate the whole content from English to Spanish and then generate the unigram features based on the machine translated Spanish. To simply translate the features in English to Spanish will lose the intended meaning of the unigrams due to the loss of the context surrounding them. For example, **Python** can be translated into one kind of programming language, and it can also be translated into snake, depending on its surrounding text. Furthermore, for certain languages there is no one-to-one correspondence in translation. For example, one unigram feature in English may be translated into several characters in Chinese. Therefore, we will follow the second way to do the translation.

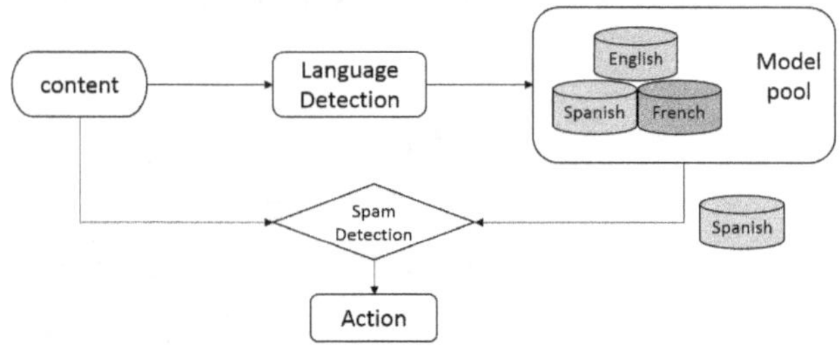

Figure 3: High-level idea for multilingual spam detection. Given a piece of content, we first detect which language it is written in. The corresponding model is then extracted from the model pool to do spam detection. Action will be taken thereafter.

Contributions: In this paper, we propose a generic pipeline to solve the multi-lingual spam detection problem. Job posting is the most common category of spam under group discussion, therefore we target at the job classification here. Starting with Spanish, we utilize the machine translation to obtain the training content in the target language. Google translator is applied in translating the labeled English content into Spanish content. We also collected job posts in Spanish that were originally written by human for model evaluation. It can be shown that the machine translated Spanish and the human written Spanish have different distributions. We therefore propose a two-stage transfer learning algorithm to migrate the knowledge learnt from machine translated Spanish to human written Spanish. In the first stage, we apply the Kernel Mean Matching (KMM) to reweight the instances in the machine translated Spanish to match the human written Spanish. In the second stage, we adaptively update the model if a small amount of label information is available in the human written Spanish domain. Our experiments on LinkedIn's production data show that the proposed two-step transfer learning algorithm achieves much better performance in terms of precision and recall compared with baseline algorithms.

Organization: The rest of the paper is organized as follows. In Section 2, we briefly review the spam detection problem in group discussion module at LinkedIn. In Section 3, we introduce our generic pipeline to solve multi-lingual spam detection problems in detail. Next, we propose our two-step transfer learning algorithm for the bilingual spam detection problem in Section 4, which consists of an instance re-weighting algorithm as step one and an adaptive learning approach as step two. In Section 5, we evaluate our proposed algorithm on LinkedIn's production data. Section 6 discusses some related work and the differences from ours. Finally, we conclude the paper in Section 7.

2. BACKGROUND

LinkedIn is the world's largest professional network with more than 332 million members in over 200 countries and territories. LinkedIn provides a wide variety of products and services that allow members to connect with one another in order to be more productive and successful in their professional lives. LinkedIn Groups in particular is a product which allows professionals in the same industry or with similar interests to gather, share content, find answers to questions, post and view jobs, make business contacts, and establish themselves as industry experts. LinkedIn members are able to freely join public groups, or may be invited to private groups by a group manager. So far, there are more than 2 million groups at LinkedIn, and 154,000 pieces of content are being posted every day. Members who use Groups are 5 times more likely to get profile views from people outside their network. Figure 4 shows a LinkedIn group for professional interior designers, and a snapshot of discussions amongst designers sharing expertise and knowledge about their industry. The best way to participate in LinkedIn groups in general is to focus on intelligent, meaningful posts that add value to a discussion and that will benefit other members.

There are rules for participating in LinkedIn Groups discussions. First, different groups have different norms and expectations around discussions, established by the participants in the group and the group manager(s). For example, different groups have different tolerance for promotional content in group discussions. Some groups encourage members to freely share links to their own websites, blog posts, or other promotional materials, whereas other groups ask their members to confine this sort of content and sharing to a Promotions area within the group. Some groups provide a Jobs area for posting job openings, talking about the current job market, asking job related questions, or starting career discussions. Other groups allow neither promotions nor job postings. In other words, users posting to a group should understand the community norms and expectations for that group, and use good judgement when making a post. Content posted to a group that does not adhere to the group's norms and expectations is considered spam.

The motivation of this work is to develop a computational method to automatically maintain the order of group discussion, i.e., to detect and filter the unwanted posts. For each group, spam detection is conducted based on its specific rules. For example, in the groups which do not allow job posting, any posts related to job annoucement are considered as spam and appropriate actions need to be taken. Users who post spam content under group discussion are not necessarily spamers, instead they may be legitimate users but unfamiliar with the rules of the group. For this reason, we choose to build a content classifier rather than to block the users' accounts.

Users can post their updates in up to 20 different languages (Figure 5). Thus, to maintain the order of group discussion, spam detection is required to work in different languages. From the perspective of production, we build one content classifier for each language and keep a classifier pool in our system.

In summary, the key contributions of this paper are as follows: (1) We design a generic pipeline for spam detection in different languages. (2) Starting with Spanish, we develop a two-step adaptive learning approach to solve the cross-language spam detection problem. (3) We test and validate the proposed algorithm on real data from LinkedIn. The resulting pipeline is production ready.

3. PROPOSED PIPELINE

In this section, we introduce the proposed pipeline to tackle the multi-lingual spam detection problem at LinkedIn. Specifically, we design a generic pipeline to do the spam detection for different languages. Here, we start with the spam detection in Spanish, as Spanish is the second most widely used language in the US. The pipeline can be easily generated to any other language than Spanish by substituting the target language of the machine translator. The pipeline contains four steps, as shown in Figure 6. To make use of labeled English samples in the server, we collect the English labeled data for translation in the first step. During the collection step, we first apply the language detector [12] to make sure that the selected samples are written in English. After collecting a large set of labeled English content, we use machine translation tools to translate the English content into Spanish. We select the Google translate API in the second step as it is one of the most popular machine translators. The second step results in a large set of machine translated Spanish content, which can be considered as the training samples for building a Spanish spam detector. Due to the distribution difference between the machine translated Spanish and the human written Spanish, we propose a two-step transfer learning algorithm to generate a Spanish spam classifier. Finally, we evaluate our model on hunman written Spanish content.

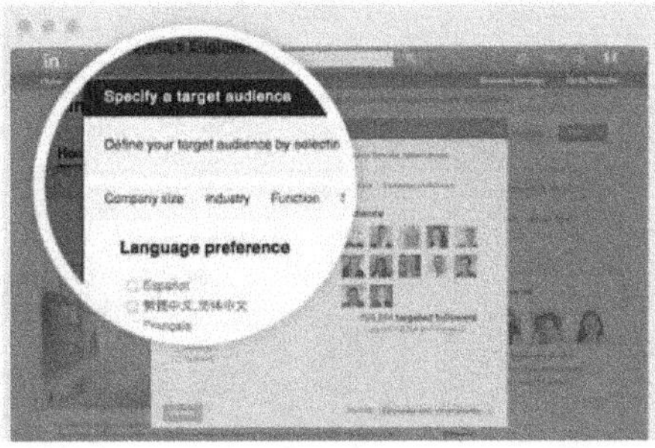

Figure 5: Supported languages at LinkedIn. The site is available in 20 languages, including Chinese, English, French, German, Italian, Portuguese, etc.

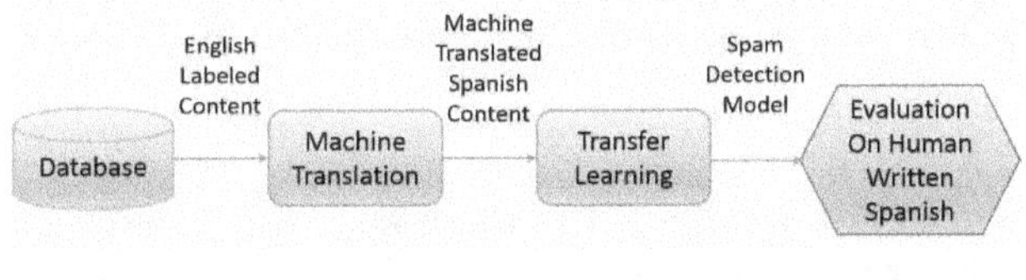

Figure 6: Proposed pipeline for Spanish spam detection. Machine Translator is employed to translate the English labeled content into Spanish. We adopt transfer learning to build a spam detection model. Evaluation is done on human written Spanish.

3.1 Feature Generation

In the aforementioned pipeline, a collection of machine translated Spanish data is available after the machine translation. We generate tf-idf features to represent both machine translated Spanish and human written Spanish data. The features are then used for building transfer learning models.

Term frequency-inverse document frequency (tf-idf) is a numerical statistic that is intended to reflect how important a word is to a document in a collection of corpus. The tf-idf value increases proportionally to the number of times a word

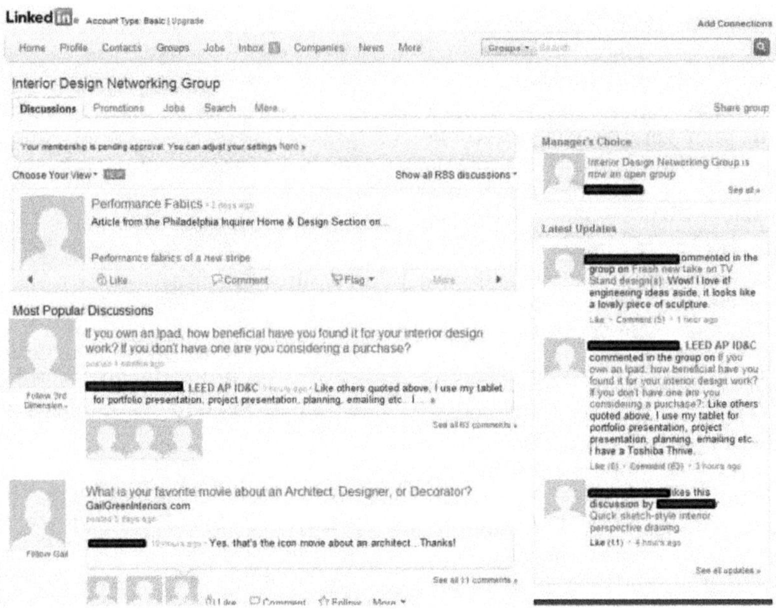

Figure 4: One example of group discussions at LinkedIn. Members in this group interact with each other by posting questions about interior design and answering other members' question.

appears in the document, but is offset by the frequency of the word in the corpus. The offset is necessary since some words are generally more common than others.

Tf-idf is the product of two statistics, including term frequency (tf) and inverse document frequency (idf). Various ways for determining the exact values of both statistics exist. We apply the Scikit-learn (`http://scikit-learn.org/stable/`) [16] package to generate the tf-idf features, where tf, idf and tf-idf are defined as follows:

- $tf(t, d) = 1$ if term t occurs in document d.
- $idf(t, D) = log\frac{N}{|d \in D: t \in d|}$ where N is total number of documents in the corpus, and $|d \in D : t \in d|$ is the number of documents that include term t.
- $tfidf(t, d, D) = tf(t, d) \times idf(t, D)$.

A high weight in tf-idf is reached by a high term frequency (in the given document) and a low document frequency of the term in the whole collection of documents; the weights hence tend to filter out common terms.

3.2 Feature selection

The vocabulary of the corpus is large, and the data matrix for the tf-idf features is sparse. To study the distribution of machine translated Spanish and human written Spanish, we first select the top features using the labels.

Here, we apply Lasso [22] to do the feature selection. Lasso is essentially a linear regression problem with an l_1 norm regularizer. It is often adopted as an efficient tool to perform the feature selection and its extension remains as a hot topic in recent research [27, 25]. Denote the feature matrix as A, the label as y, and the model as x. Lasso can be formulated as the following optimization problem:

$$\min_{x} \frac{1}{2}\|Ax - y\|_2^2 + \lambda\|x\|_1 \tag{1}$$

where λ is a parameter that controls the balance between the loss function and the penalty. The Lasso problem can be solved efficiently by FISTA algorithm [3]. After we get the solution x, the non-zero entries in x correspond to the selected features in A.

We apply Lasso to both machine translated Spanish and human written Spanish to investigate the characteristics of these two domains. The top 20 selected features are listed in Table 1. It can be verified that most of the features relate to jobs. We can see there are some top features shared by machine translated Spanish documents and human written Spanish documents, but about half of the features are different between the two domains. This is not surprising: the machine translated jobs and the manually constructed jobs were taken from non-overlapping data sources. The former was translated job posts from English jobs on LinkedIn, while the latter was obtained by crawling the web and finding job posts written in Spanish. While the top 20 features in both data sets are related to the broad topic of jobs, e.g. business, information, employee, opportunity, development, team, management (Table 1), we cannot expect the features to be 100% identical over both data sets. We only expect stop words to be invariant across different data sets, not nouns, verbs, or adjectives. Furthermore, some of the top 20 features in the manually constructed and the machine translated sets are morphological cognates such as **buscamos** = **we look** and **buscando** = **looking**; **cliente** = **client** and **clientes** = **clients**, which further illustrates that the top 20 features are semantically very close in both data sets.

Despite the above issues, the machine translated content has the same overall intended meaning as the human written content. In addition, as we select more unigram features, we find larger overlaps of selected features between the two domains. Thus, transfer learning is a viable approach to solve the problem. Consider the machine translated Spanish as the source domain, and the human written Spanish as the target domain, transfer learning aims to borrow the

Table 1: unigram features for two domains

Machine Translated Spanish		Human written Spanish	
Selected Spanish Features	English translation	Selected Spanish Features	English translation
años	years	buscamos	look for
buscando	search for	clientes	customers
cliente	customer	comercial	business
clientes	customers	conocimientos	background
desarrollo	development	cv	cv
empresa	company	desarrollo	development
empresas	companies	gestión	management
equipo	team	equipo	team
están	are	españa	Spain
experiencia	experience	experiencia	experience
favor	please	funciones	functions
gestión	management	manejo	management
http	http	millones	million
información	information	más	more
mundo	world	proyectos	projects
más	other	responsable	responsible
oportunidad	opportunity	seguimiento	follow up
posición	position	turismo	travel
servicios	services	ventas	sales
web	web	área	area

knowledge learnt from source domain and apply it to target domain. The details of our two-step transfer learning algorithm are presented in the next section.

4. TRANSFER LEARNING

In this paper, we propose a two-step transfer learning algorithm to learn the content classifier from machine translated Spanish and apply it to human written Spanish. To our best knowledge, this is the first work that transfers the knowledge from machine translation corpus to human written corpus in social network. This paper is different from a related two-stage transfer learning algorithm [20] in the sense that the number of domains are different. The previous work [20] focuses on multiple source domain transfer learning, in which the second stage utilized the smoothness assumption among hypotheses from multiple sources. However, this paper focuses on single source domain transfer learning where the smoothness assumption cannot be established. The proposed algorithm is a general algorithm that can be adopted to any other languages as well as any binary classification problem.

Denote the machine translated Spanish as the source domain T, and the human written Spanish as the target domain H. We have shown in Section 3 that the distributions of the T and H could be different while the support can be the same with the increase of feature dimension. Therefore, we make an assumption that the distribution difference mainly lies in the marginal probability rather than the conditional probability. Based on the assumption, we propose our first step of transfer learning: instance re-weighting. The main idea of instance re-weighting is to calculate the weights for the data in the source domain, and re-weight the source domain for matching the marginal distribution with the target domain.

After the first step, we train a logistic regression model on the re-weighted source data, then apply it to the target domain. In addition, if there are some labels available in the target domain, we propose an adaptive learning algorithm as the second step to update our model learnt in the first step. The adaptive learning algorithm penalizes the misclassification errors in the target domain while minimizes the modifications of the model. The second step will also make up the conditional distribution difference between T and H if our assumption in the first step does not hold.

4.1 Instance Re-weighting

The first step in the proposed transfer learning framework is the Kernel Mean Matching (KMM) algorithm [9], which is a nonparametric method to directly infer weights for source domain without distribution estimation. KMM utilizes the unlabeled data to build a bridge for connecting two domains. In general, the estimation problem with two different distributions $Pr(x, y)$ and $Pr'(x, y)$ is unsolvable, as the two terms could be arbitrarily far apart. In particular, for arbitrary $Pr(y|x)$ and $Pr'(y|x)$, there is no way to infer a good estimator based on the available training samples in the source domain. Hence a simplified version makes assumption that $Pr(x, y)$ and $Pr'(x, y)$ only differ via $Pr(x)$ and $Pr'(x)$, i.e., the conditional probability remains unchanged: $Pr(y|x) = Pr'(y|x)$. This particular case of transfer learning has been termed as covariate shift.

The basic assumption behind KMM approach is that between the two domains, the key difference lies in the marginal distribution $Pr(x)$ rather than the conditional distribution $Pr(y|x)$. The idea of KMM is to find the appropriate weights for T which minimize the discrepancy between the mean values of T and H in the common projected space. Denote x_i as the i-th sample in T and x'_i as the i-th sample in H. The mean differences after projection can be formulated as:

$$\min_{\alpha} \left\| \frac{1}{m} \sum_{i=1}^{m} \alpha_i \Phi(x_i) - \frac{1}{m'} \sum_{i=1}^{m'} \Phi(x'_i) \right\|^2 . \qquad (2)$$

where α_i $(i = 1, \ldots, m)$ is the weight we want to learn, m is the number of samples in T, m' is the number of samples in H, and Φ is a mapping which maps the raw features into a latent space.

The formulation is actually a constrained QP (Quadratic Programming) problem. After weighting, we still want to ensure $\alpha Pr(x)$ is close to a distribution, so there are two constraints that need to be added: $\alpha_i \in [LB, UB]$ and $|\frac{1}{m}\sum_{i=1}^{m} \alpha_i - 1| \leq \epsilon$, where LB and UB is the lower bound and the upper bound of α_i respectively. Denote $K_{ij} = k(x_i, x_j)$ and $\kappa_i = \frac{m}{m'}\sum_{j=1}^{m'} k(x_i, x'_j)$. We can rewrite the formulation (2) as:

$$\begin{aligned} \min_{\alpha} \quad & \frac{1}{m^2}\alpha^T K\alpha - \frac{2}{m^2}\kappa\alpha, \\ \text{s.t.} \quad & \left|\frac{1}{m}\sum_{i=1}^{m}\alpha_i - 1\right| \leq \epsilon, \\ & LB \leq \alpha_i \leq UB. \end{aligned} \tag{3}$$

It can be solved by many optimization algorithms, such as interior point methods or any other successive optimization procedure. We simply apply the **optimize** module in **SciPy** to calculate the solution.

After we obtaining α, we multiply each sample in T with the corresponding α_i, then build a regularized logistic regression model w_0 as follows:

$$\min_{w_0} \sum_{i=1}^{m} log(1 + \exp(-y_i w_0^T \alpha_i x_i)) + \lambda \|w_0\|^2. \tag{4}$$

If there is no labeled data available in target domain, we apply the model learnt in Equation (4) to the target domain for Spam detection. There are many different classification models can be adopted to solve this problem, such as Naive Bayes [11] and SVM [28]. The reason of choosing the logistic regression to build our classification model lies in three folds: (1) Logistic regression has achieved great success in many real-world applications; (2) The processing time for an online product should be as small as possible, and logistic regression is a perfect match; (3) It is easy to be generalized to a distributed version.

4.2 Adaptive Learning

KMM targets at the scenario that there is no labeled data available in the target domain. So far, we have not touched any label information in the target domain. There are scenarios under which a small portion of labeled target data $\{x''_i, y''_i | i = 1, \ldots, m''\}$ is available. For example, the samples may be labeled by crowdsourcing. Next, we show how to improve our model w_0 learnt from KMM by using additional labeled instances in H. We propose an adaptive learning strategy, which aims to learn a perturbation $\Delta f(x) = \Delta w^T \phi(x)$ on the basis of w_0 to further compensate for domain mismatch. Denote the classifier we learnt through KMM as w_0, the target classifier we aim to learn as w, we have the following relation: $w = w_0 + \Delta w$.

Based on the aforementioned assumption that the difference between the distributions of machine translated Spanish and human written Spanish mainly lies in the marginal distribution, the intuition of the proposed adaptive learning is that the difference of w and w_0 should be as small as possible. There are related previous work [6, 8], which were proposed to learn a perturbation of the source hyperplane,

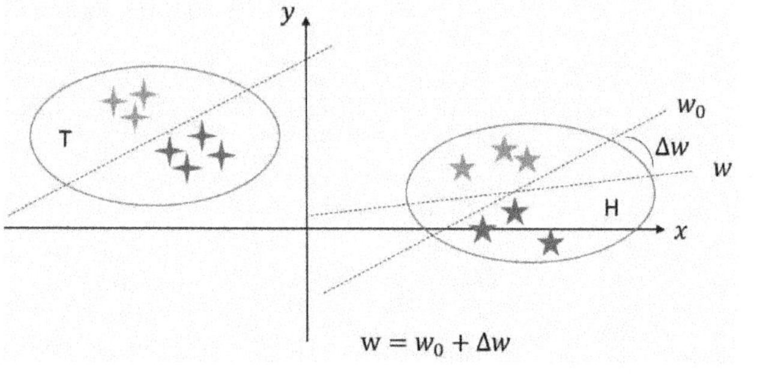

Figure 7: Illustration of adaptive learning. Model w_0 is borrowed from the domain T, and the model w for the domain H should be similar to w_0. Δw is a small perturbation we aim to learn.

by minimizing the classification error on labeled examples in the target domain. The pertubation can also be considered as new feature representations that correct for the domain change. The intuition of our adaptive learning algorithm is consistent with the online learning, thus this step can be put into online learning system.

Our adaptive learning step aims to learn a perturbation Δw such that the difference between prediction $f(x) = w^T x$ and $f_0(x) = w_0^T x$ is small (Figure 7). The following equation holds: $f(x) = f_0(x) + \Delta f(x) = w_0^T \phi(x) + \Delta w^T \phi(x)$, where Δw is the difference to be learnt here. Therefore, we formulate the adaptive learning as the following optimization problem:

$$\begin{aligned} & \min_{\Delta w} \sum_{i=1}^{m''} \log(1 + exp(-y''_i w^T x''_i)) + \lambda \|\Delta w\|_2^2 \\ = & \min_{\Delta w} \sum_{i=1}^{m''} \log(1 + exp(-y''_i (w_0 + \Delta w)^T x''_i)) + \lambda \|\Delta w\|_2^2, \end{aligned} \tag{5}$$

where the logistic loss is utilized with the penalty that encourages the perturbation $\|\Delta w\|$ to be small. Here λ is a tuning parameter to control the balance between the loss function and the penalty. Problem (5) involves a convex smooth function, which can be solved efficiently by gradient-based method. Adaptive learning can make up for the potential issue that there are also conditional differences in the distributions between the machine translated Spanish and human written Spanish. It can also serve as an online update algorithm when more and more labeled target data become available.

Finally, we obtain the model $w = w_0 + \Delta w$ after the proposed two-step transfer learning algorithm. We summarize our two-step transfer learning algorithm in Algorithm 1.

5. EXPERIMENTS

In this section, we demonstrate the effectiveness of our proposed machine learning pipeline using production data at LinkedIn.

Following the pipeline 6, we collect 12000 pieces of English content in group discussions at LinkedIn. The content is collected from the groups where job posts are not allowed, i.e., job related content are considered as spam in these groups. The English content is kept balanced for the two classes: job-related posts and non-job posts. It is used for translation

Algorithm 1 A two-step transfer learning algorithm for bilingual spam detection

Require: a large set of labeled samples in T: $\{x_i, y_i\}$, a large set of unlabeled samples in H: $\{x'_i, y'_i\}$, (optional) a small set of labeled samples in H: $\{x''_i, y''_i\}$, $\Delta w = 0$

Ensure: w

1: Calculate weights α by solving

$$\min_{\alpha} \left\| \frac{1}{m}\sum_{i=1}^{m} \alpha_i \Phi(x_i) - \frac{1}{m'}\sum_{i=1}^{m'} \Phi(x'_i) \right\|^2$$

2: Compute w_0 by solving

$$\min_{w_0} \sum_{i=1}^{m} log(1 + \exp(-y_i w_0^T \alpha_i x_i)) + \lambda \|w_0\|^2$$

3: (Optional) Compute Δw by solving

$$\min_{\Delta w} \sum_{i=1}^{m''} \log(1 + exp(-y''_i (w_0 + \Delta w)^T x''_i)) + \lambda \|\Delta w\|_2^2$$

4: **return** $w = w_0 + \Delta w$

into Spanish to form the source domain. We translated all the collected human labeled content from English to Spanish with Google translate API.

In addition, we also collect 12000 pieces of human written Spanish content (balanced) by crowdsourcing, which serves as the target domain. Inside the target domain, there are 50 pieces of comments considered as labeled samples used in our adaptive learning step and the remaining ones are treated as test data for evaluation. We generate tf-idf features for both machine translated Spanish and human written Spanish, and it turns out that the feature spaces of the two domains differ from each other, as shown in Table 1.

5.1 Experimental Settings

Based on the source domain corpus and the target domain corpus, we first generate the tf-idf features for each domain, and then use the intersection of selected features to build the Spanish spam detector.

Scikit-learn (`http://scikit-learn.org/stable/`) [16] is a powerful machine learning package in python which provides feature generation, feature selection as well as classification functions. We make use of scikit-learn to carry out the experiment: first, we generate the tf-idf features for both domains by use of *feature_extraction.text.TfidfTransformer* class; then we build the classification model via *linear_model-.LogisticRegression* class.

In our experiment, it turns out that stemmer would not help in classification tasks, as it reduced the feature dimension of the problem. There are overlapped unigram features between machine translated Spanish and human written Spanish, but the feature spaces of these two domains are not identical. We simply choose the intersection as our feature space to conduct the transfer learning.

We implement our proposed two-step transfer learning algorithm in Python, and we solve the optimization problem in both KMM and adaptive learning by calling the scipy.optimize module (`http://docs.scipy.org/doc/scipy/reference/optimize.html`). We increase the tf-idf feature dimension to leverage the loss of information introduced by performing intersection. To verify the efficacy of the proposed two-step transfer learning algorithm, we compare it with four other algorithms:

- Baseline: We train a model on T, and directly apply it to the test data in H.
- SLT (Small Labeled dataset for Training): We train a model on a small portion of labeled data in H (50 samples), and apply it to the test data in H.
- KMM: We calculate the weights for data in T via KMM, then train a model on weighted data in T, and apply it to the test data in H.
- Adaptive Learning: We apply the adaptive learning (Equation (5)) to build a model on the basis of model generated from Baseline, and apply it to the test data in H.

We choose the above four algorithms for comparison because they are both straight forward and practically viable algorithms for an online product. To further test the robustness of different approaches, we conduct our experiments by varying the dimension of feature space as follows:

- We generate 600 features for both T and H, and use the intersection (380 features) as the feature space.
- We generate 800 features for both T and H, and use the intersection (504 features) as the feature space.
- We generate 1000 features for both T and H, and use the intersection (629 features) as the feature space.
- We generate 2000 features for both T and H, and use the intersection (1260 features) as the feature space.

From our experience, the more features we generated, the better it will generalize to unseen data.

5.2 Experimental Results

The results of all five algorithms are shown in 8 and Table 2. To encourage the model to achieve the desired performance for production, we set the threshold of logistic regression so as to make the precision fixed at 0.95.

The experimental results exhibit the efficacy of our proposed algorithm in the following aspects:

- SLT works better than Baseline. The reason is that baseline trains a model in the source domain and tests it in a different domain, while SLT trains and tests the data from the same domain. The domain difference makes the baseline perform worse even with a large amount of training data.
- KMM works better than SLT. The reason lies in two folds: KMM trains the model based on the re-weighted source domain data, which leverages the difference between the two domains. In addition, the training data size of KMM is much larger than that of SLT.
- Adaptive learning works better than SLT, but worse than KMM. Since the reference model in adaptive learning here comes from baseline, which ignores the distribution difference between the two domains. However, it utilizes more information from the related source domain, which makes it perform better than SLT.

Table 2: Results for different dimensions of features

tf-idf dimension	intersection dimension	algorithm	precision	recall	f1-score	AUC
600	320	baseline	0.95	0.44	0.60	0.87
		SLT	0.95	0.42	0.63	0.93
		KMM	0.95	0.46	0.64	0.94
		adaptive	0.95	0.57	0.71	0.93
		twoStage	0.95	0.65	0.77	0.95
800	504	baseline	0.95	0.47	0.63	0.87
		SLT	0.95	0.51	0.66	0.93
		KMM	0.95	0.66	0.78	0.94
		adaptive	0.95	0.57	0.71	0.93
		twoStage	0.95	0.65	0.77	0.95
1000	629	baseline	0.95	0.46	0.62	0.88
		SLT	0.95	0.52	0.67	0.93
		KMM	0.95	0.66	0.78	0.94
		adaptive	0.95	0.61	0.74	0.93
		twoStage	0.95	0.79	0.86	0.95
2000	1260	baseline	0.95	0.50	0.65	0.89
		SLT	0.95	0.58	0.72	0.93
		KMM	0.95	0.73	0.82	0.95
		adaptive	0.95	0.70	0.80	0.94
		twoStage	0.95	0.82	0.88	0.96

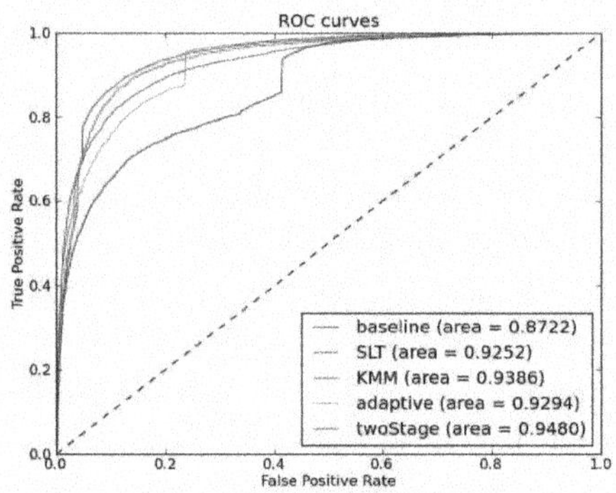

(a) AUC curves for 600 features

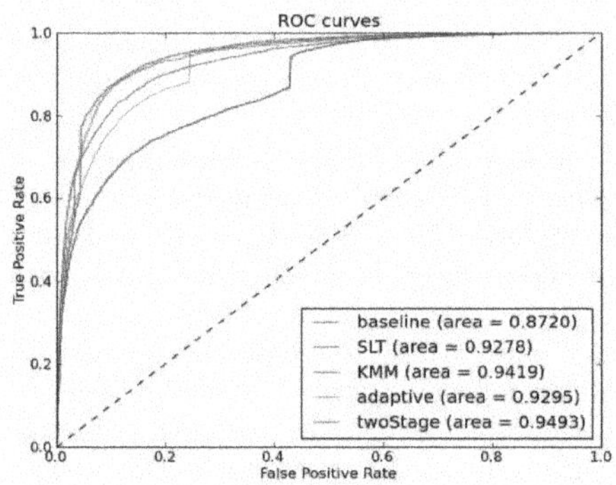

(b) AUC curves for 800 features

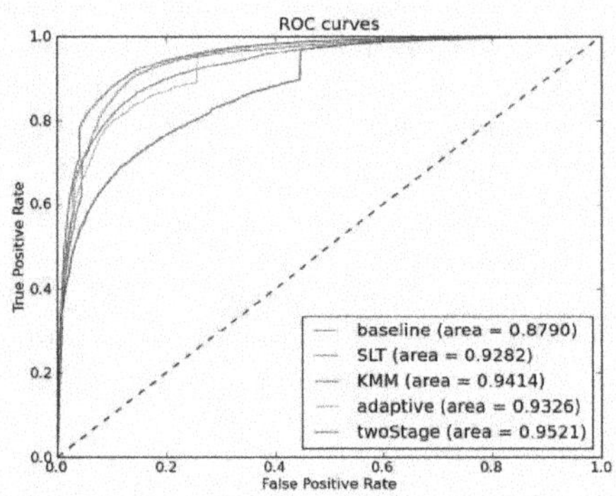

(c) AUC curves for 1000 features

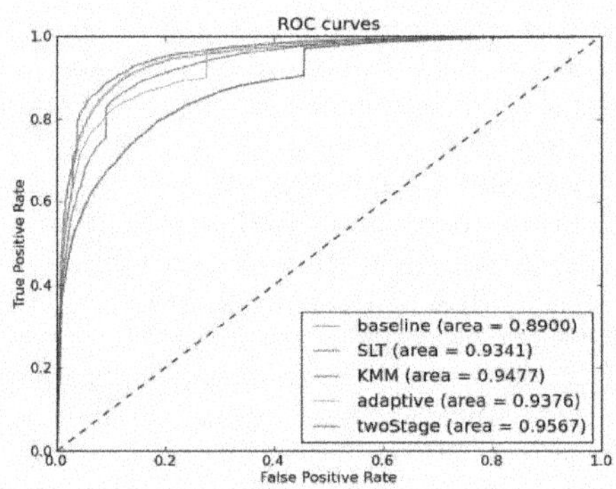

(d) AUC curves for 2000 features

Figure 8: Experiment results for varied dimensions of features: 600, 800, 1000 and 2000. In all these settings, our proposed algorithm achieves the best performance compared with other algorithms.

- Our proposed two-step algorithm produces the best performance, as it combines the advantages of KMM and adaptive learning.

From the results, we conclude that each of the two steps (Instant Weighting and Adaptive Learning) improves the performance compared to the baseline method, while combining the two steps works the best. As the feature dimension increases, the performance also improves. To avoid overfitting and ensure the efficiency as an online product, we stop at 2000 features.

The results also verify our assumption about the distributions of two domains, that is, the main difference lies in the marginal distribution rather than the conditional difference. The proposed two-step transfer learning algorithm achieves the required performance for production.

5.3 Use of less unlabeled samples in H

In real applications, we may not have enough labeled samples in H. In addition, we may not have enough unlabeled samples in H in advance for KMM. As the mean value of projected distribution for the target domain cannot be captured, KMM may fail to match the difference between the source domain and target domain.

To verify whether the KMM algorithm works with a small sample size in the target domain, we further design a series of experiments with varied sizes of samples in the target domain. Specifically, We vary the amounts of unlabeled samples from 20 to 1000 in human written Spanish to test the KMM algorithm, and the results can be seen in Table 3.

Table 3: KMM results for a small number of samples in the target domain

sample size in H	precision	recall	f1-score	AUC
20	0.95	0.28	0.44	0.89
50	0.95	0.56	0.71	0.93
100	0.95	0.62	0.75	0.94
200	0.95	0.68	0.79	0.95
500	0.95	0.82	0.82	0.96
1000	0.95	0.86	0.86	0.97

We want to emphasize that even with a small sample size (100) in H, we can get the desired performance for production. The explanation behind the experiment results lies in the fact that as long as the target samples are balanced, KMM can capture the mean value of the distribution in the projected space even with small sample size. This is critical for an online product: as in the real world, we want to ensure the model to work even with small amounts of human written content. As more and more human written Spanish data become available, we can apply the second step to incrementally update the model, which can also be considered as online learning.

6. RELATED WORK

Cross-lingual content classification is an important topic in natural language processing area, and it gains more attention as the social network becomes global [1, 17, 14, 13, 15, 18, 24, 4]. The transfer learning research on text mining [5, 10] mainly focus on transferring the knowledge from different topics in the same language. The work done by Vinokourov [23] can be considered as the unsupervised cross-lingual learning, where the correlation between two languages are learnt by Canonical Correlation Analysis. In this work, the high correlation between English and French words indicates that they represent the same semantic information. It is different from our work as we deal with supervised learning problems. There is related research that focus on modeling the multi-view representations in which each language is considered as a separate source, and a joint loss is minimized while the consistency between languages is ensured [1]. One related work [15] also represents the data from two languages views and proposes a non-negative matrix tri-factorization (BNMTF) model for the cross-lingual sentiment classification problem. These methods aim to utilize the labeled data in two languages and build a joint model for multi-view learning, which differs from our work as we do not have labeled data in both languages, and for an online product, it is not practical to translate every piece of message into the other language.

The most relevant work was done by Ling et al. [13]. In their work, they translated the Chinese web pages into English, and the common parts of two languages are extracted and used for classification. Specifically, the KL divergence between the feature distribution and the label distribution is minimized to generate the classification model. This work bridges the translated English and label set by common features, and uses a parametric algorithm to build the classifier. In our work, we make use of non-parametric transfer learning algorithm to migrate the information learnt from the machine translated Spanish and apply it to the human written Spanish. To the best of our knowledge, this is the first attempt to take care of the distribution difference between the machine translated corpus and human written corpus in social network. Moreover, we propose an adaptive learning algorithm to update the model online.

7. CONCLUSIONS

In this paper, we develop a machine learning pipeline to tackle the multilingual spam detection problem at LinkeIn. We propose to build a model pool in which one model works for one language, and we start with Spanish as it is widely used in US. Due to the lack of labeled data in Spanish, we first translate the English labeled content into Spanish content via machine translation. Since the distributions of machine translated Spanish and human written Spanish are not identical, we propose a two-step transfer learning algorithm to transfer the knowledge learnt from machine translated Spanish to human written Spanish. In the first step, KMM is applied in order to match the marginal distribution difference between the two domains. If there is a small portion of labeled data available in the human written Spanish, we propose a second step to incrementally update the model obtained from the first step. Results show that our proposed pipeline achieves the requirements in Spanish spam detection for industrial products.

The proposed pipeline is a generic system which can be applied to any other languages by substituting the target lanaguage in machine translation. We plan to extend our proposed algorithms to solve the French and Chinese spam detection problems in the future. In addition, the classification pipeline can deal with different kinds of classification problems as long as there are labeled samples available. We also plan to apply the pipeline to other text classification problems at LinkedIn. Furthermore, the adaptive learning algorithm we propose in the second step can serve as an online learning model. When more labeled data in Spanish become available, the model will be adaptively updated.

8. REFERENCES

[1] M.-R. Amini and C. Goutte. A co-classification approach to learning from multilingual corpora. *Machine learning*, 79(1-2):105–121, 2010.

[2] C. Banea, R. Mihalcea, and J. Wiebe. Multilingual subjectivity: are more languages better? In *Proceedings of the 23rd International Conference on Computational Linguistics*, pages 28–36. Association for Computational Linguistics, 2010.

[3] A. Beck and M. Teboulle. A fast iterative shrinkage-thresholding algorithm for linear inverse problems. *SIAM Journal on Imaging Sciences*, 2(1):183–202, 2009.

[4] W. De Smet, J. Tang, and M.-F. Moens. Knowledge transfer across multilingual corpora via latent topics. In *Advances in Knowledge Discovery and Data Mining*, pages 549–560. Springer, 2011.

[5] C. Do and A. Y. Ng. Transfer learning for text classification. In *NIPS*, 2005.

[6] L. Duan, I. W. Tsang, D. Xu, and S. J. Maybank. Domain transfer svm for video concept detection. In *Computer Vision and Pattern Recognition, 2009. CVPR 2009. IEEE Conference on*, pages 1375–1381. IEEE, 2009.

[7] G. Foster, C. Goutte, and R. Kuhn. Discriminative instance weighting for domain adaptation in statistical machine translation. In *Proceedings of the 2010 Conference on Empirical Methods in Natural Language Processing*, pages 451–459. Association for Computational Linguistics, 2010.

[8] J. Hoffman, E. Rodner, J. Donahue, K. Saenko, and T. Darrell. Efficient learning of domain-invariant image representations. In *International Conference on Learning Representations*, 2013.

[9] J. Huang, A. Gretton, K. M. Borgwardt, B. Schölkopf, and A. J. Smola. Correcting sample selection bias by unlabeled data. In *Advances in neural information processing systems*, pages 601–608, 2006.

[10] J. Jiang. *Domain adaptation in natural language processing*. ProQuest, 2008.

[11] A. M. Kibriya, E. Frank, B. Pfahringer, and G. Holmes. Multinomial naive bayes for text categorization revisited. In *AI 2004: Advances in Artificial Intelligence*, pages 488–499. Springer, 2005.

[12] D. Kurokawa, C. Goutte, and P. Isabelle. Automatic detection of translated text and its impact on machine translation. *Proceedings. MT Summit XII, The Twelfth Machine Translation Summit International Association for Machine Translation Hosted by the Association for Machine Translation in the Americas*, 2009.

[13] X. Ling, G.-R. Xue, W. Dai, Y. Jiang, Q. Yang, and Y. Yu. Can chinese web pages be classified with english data source? In *Proceedings of the 17th international conference on World Wide Web*, pages 969–978. ACM, 2008.

[14] X. Meng, F. Wei, X. Liu, M. Zhou, G. Xu, and H. Wang. Cross-lingual mixture model for sentiment classification. In *Proceedings of the 50th Annual Meeting of the Association for Computational Linguistics: Long Papers-Volume 1*, pages 572–581. Association for Computational Linguistics, 2012.

[15] J. Pan, G.-R. Xue, Y. Yu, and Y. Wang. Cross-lingual sentiment classification via bi-view non-negative matrix tri-factorization. In *Advances in Knowledge Discovery and Data Mining*, pages 289–300. Springer, 2011.

[16] F. Pedregosa, G. Varoquaux, A. Gramfort, V. Michel, B. Thirion, O. Grisel, M. Blondel, P. Prettenhofer, R. Weiss, V. Dubourg, J. Vanderplas, A. Passos, D. Cournapeau, M. Brucher, M. Perrot, and E. Duchesnay. Scikit-learn: Machine learning in Python. *Journal of Machine Learning Research*, 12:2825–2830, 2011.

[17] J. C. Platt, K. Toutanova, and W.-t. Yih. Translingual document representations from discriminative projections. In *Proceedings of the 2010 Conference on Empirical Methods in Natural Language Processing*, pages 251–261. Association for Computational Linguistics, 2010.

[18] P. Prettenhofer and B. Stein. Cross-language text classification using structural correspondence learning. In *Proceedings of the 48th Annual Meeting of the Association for Computational Linguistics*, pages 1118–1127. Association for Computational Linguistics, 2010.

[19] J. Slocum. A survey of machine translation: its history, current status, and future prospects. *Computational Linguistics*, 11(1):1–17, 1985.

[20] Q. Sun, R. Chattopadhyay, S. Panchanathan, and J. Ye. A two-stage weighting framework for multi-source domain adaptation. In *Advances in neural information processing systems*, pages 505–513, 2011.

[21] J. Tang, X. Wang, H. Gao, X. Hu, and H. Liu. Enriching short text representation in microblog for clustering. *Frontiers of Computer Science*, 6(1):88–101, 2012.

[22] R. Tibshirani. Regression shrinkage and selection via the lasso. *Journal of the Royal Statistical Society. Series B (Methodological)*, pages 267–288, 1996.

[23] A. Vinokourov, N. Cristianini, and J. S. Shawe-taylor. Inferring a semantic representation of text via cross-language correlation analysis. In *Advances in neural information processing systems*, pages 1473–1480, 2002.

[24] C. Wan, R. Pan, and J. Li. Bi-weighting domain adaptation for cross-language text classification. In *IJCAI Proceedings-International Joint Conference on Artificial Intelligence*, volume 22, page 1535, 2011.

[25] J. Wang, J. Zhou, P. Wonka, and J. Ye. Lasso screening rules via dual polytope projection. In *Advances in Neural Information Processing Systems*, pages 1070–1078, 2013.

[26] P. Wang and C. Domeniconi. Towards a universal text classifier: Transfer learning using encyclopedic knowledge. In *Data Mining Workshops, 2009. ICDMW'09. IEEE International Conference on*, pages 435–440. IEEE, 2009.

[27] S. Xiang, T. Yang, and J. Ye. Simultaneous feature and feature group selection through hard thresholding. In *Proceedings of the 20th ACM SIGKDD international conference on Knowledge discovery and data mining*, pages 532–541. ACM, 2014.

[28] J. Yang, R. Yan, and A. G. Hauptmann. Cross-domain video concept detection using adaptive svms. In *Proceedings of the 15th international conference on Multimedia*, pages 188–197. ACM, 2007.

FrauDetector: A Graph-Mining-based Framework for Fraudulent Phone Call Detection

Vincent S. Tseng[1*], Josh Jia-Ching Ying[1], Che-Wei Huang[2], Yimin Kao[3], and Kuan-Ta Chen[4]

[1] Department of Computer Science, National Chiao Tung University, Taiwan, ROC

[2] Department of Computer Science and Information Engineering, National Cheng Kung University, Taiwan, ROC

[3] Gogolook Co. Ltd., Taiwan, ROC

[4] Institute of Information Science, Academia Sinica, Taiwan, ROC

*Correspondence: vtseng@cs.nctu.edu.tw,

jashying@gmail.com, weiiboy@idb.csie.ncku.edu.tw, yiminkao@gogolook.com, swc@iis.sinica.edu.tw

ABSTRACT

In recent years, fraud is increasing rapidly with the development of modern technology and global communication. Although many literatures have addressed the fraud detection problem, these existing works focus only on formulating the fraud detection problem as a binary classification problem. Due to limitation of information provided by telecommunication records, such classifier-based approaches for fraudulent phone call detection normally do not work well. In this paper, we develop a graph-mining-based fraudulent phone call detection framework for a mobile application to automatically annotate fraudulent phone numbers with a "fraud" tag, which is a crucial prerequisite for distinguishing fraudulent phone calls from normal phone calls. Our detection approach performs a weighted HITS algorithm to learn the trust value of a remote phone number. Based on telecommunication records, we build two kinds of directed bipartite graph: i) CPG and ii) UPG to represent telecommunication behavior of users. To weight the edges of CPG and UPG, we extract features for each pair of user and remote phone number in two different yet complementary aspects: 1) duration relatedness (DR) between user and phone number; and 2) frequency relatedness (FR) between user and phone number. Upon weighted CPG and UPG, we determine a trust value for each remote phone number. Finally, we conduct a comprehensive experimental study based on a dataset collected through an anti-fraud mobile application, *Whoscall*. The results demonstrate the effectiveness of our weighted HITS-based approach and show the strength of taking both DR and FR into account in feature extraction.

Categories and Subject Descriptors

H.2.8 [Database Management]: Database Applications – *Data Mining*

General Terms: Measurement, Experimentation.

Keywords: Telecommunication Fraud, Trust Value Mining, Fraudulent Phone Call Detection, Weighted HITS Algorithm.

1. INTRODUCTION

In our daily life, fraudulent activities can be seen on different communication channels, such as telecommunication networks, on-line banking, and e-commerce. Fraud is increasing rapidly with the development of modern technology and global communication. As the result, millions of people suffer terribly with these fraudulent activities. To protect people against potential losses caused by fraudulent activities, many anti-fraud mechanisms have been proposed, whereas such mechanisms for telecommunication are still in its infancy stage. Currently, all of the anti-fraud mechanisms for telecommunications more or less rely on the annotations made by the crowd. A person may annotate a phone number as fraud after he receives a fraudulent phone call given an appropriate reporting tool. However, frauders can still approach innocent people via the remote phone number before that particular number is blacklisted as fraudulent. Because not everyone who receives fraudulent calls is willing to annotate a fraudulent phone number, it is possible that the frauders can make fraudulent calls through the phone number for days, weeks, or even months. We denote this phenomenon as the *time lag* in the fraud detection problem. Consequentially, dealing with time lag of fraud detection problem for fraudulent phone calls detection has been a critical issue to be explored.

Figure 1. A screenshot of *Whoscall*, an anti-fraud mobile app.

In recent years, a new breed of smartphone applications for anti-fraud such as *Whoscall*[1], *Pindrop*[2], and *Truecaller*[3], have emerged. This type of smartphone applications identify background information of incoming unknown calls in sub-seconds through tags reported by other users, Internet search results, and yellow/white pages. Obviously, such applications heavily rely on annotations made by the crowd to detect fraudulent remote phone numbers and broadcast the list of detected fraudulent remote phone numbers to each anti-fraud application user. As mentioned earlier, the principle of crowd annotation is the source for the time lag problem in fraud detection; fortunately, mobile applications make the collection of telecommunication records much easier. Figure 1 shows a screenshot of an anti-fraud mobile application, *Whoscall*. We can observe that phone numbers can be recorded when a person makes a

KDD '15, August 11 - 14, 2015, Sydney, NSW, Australia

© 2015 ACM. ISBN 978-1-4503-3664-2/15/08$15.00

DOI: http://dx.doi.org/10.1145/2783258.2788623

[1] http://whoscall.com/

[2] http://www.pindropsecurity.com/

[3] http://www.truecaller.com/

phone call on the smartphone. Furthermore, the timestamps of receiving incoming phone calls, starting conversation, and ending communication can also be recorded. After taking an incoming phone call, users can annotate the remote phone number whether it is fraudulent. Therefore, we can discover the characteristics of fraudulent remote phone numbers through mining these communication and annotation records. Based on the discovered characteristics of fraudulent remote phone numbers, we can develop models that can detect fraudulent phone numbers.

Intuitively, as shown in Formula (1), given a set of remote phone numbers P, the fraudulent remote phone number detection can be formulated as predicting the trust value of a given remote phone number:

$$f(p) \rightarrow \square, \text{where } p \in P \text{ and } \square \in [0, 1] \quad (1)$$

In daily life, a person may receive a large number of normal phone calls relatively compared with fraudulent phone calls. In other words, remote phone numbers tagged with "fraud" would be rarely seen in telecommunication records. Hence, fraudulent remote phone number detection from telecommunication records can be addressed as an *imbalance-label prediction problem* [5] [21]. While imbalance-label prediction techniques have been developed for many fraud detections, such as credit card fraud detection [6], telecommunications fraud detection [7] and insurance fraud detection [19], the problem has not been well explored under the context of communication records, where we operate over telecommunication activities for certain phone calls.

Although the issues of telecommunication fraud detection have been discussed in many literatures, existing studies mostly consider only on the *classifier-based fraud detection* [7] [9] [10] [28] in which the fraud detection problem is formulated as a binary classification problem. Notice that a fundamental issue of classifier-based fraudulent phone call detection is to identify and extract a number of descriptive features for each remote phone number. Selecting the right features is important because the selected features have a direct impact on the effectiveness of the classification task. As a result, the behavior of users who receive a phone call are aggregated into a single value of a feature for the remote phone number. For example, as Figure 2 shows, $user_1$ and $user_2$ directly hang up the call, $user_3$ answers the call and talks for a while, while $user_4$ and $user_5$ miss the call and call back later. Thus, the values of some features that reflect the call duration of users to the known phone should be increased by the behaviors of $user_4$ and $user_5$. Accordingly, the features may not distinguish the fraudulent remote phone numbers from normal remote phone numbers because both categories of remote phone numbers have similar call durations with users. Additionally, frauders tend to make fraud calls to the same group of users because the frauders have those users' profiles.

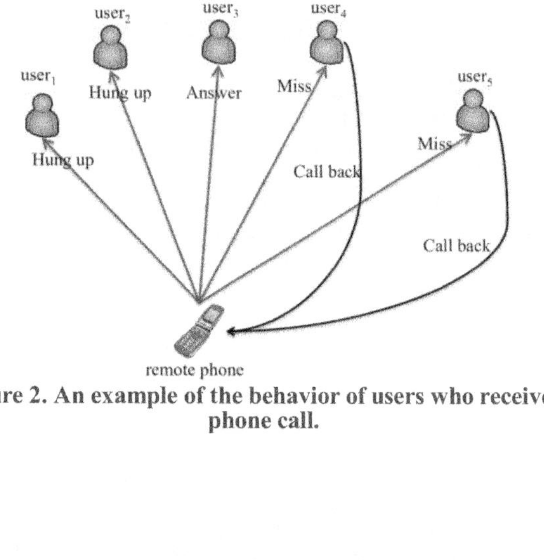

Figure 2. An example of the behavior of users who receive a phone call.

Therefore, the classifier-based fraud detection requires the analysis of users' profiles to produce useful features. However, the analysis of users' profiles costs a lot of effort and may violate the privacy policy.

In this paper, we propose a novel graph-mining-based fraudulent phone call detection framework, *FrauDetector,* to evaluate the trust value of an unknown remote phone number. The framework consists of two major modules: 1) an offline learning module, and 2) an on-line detection module. In the offline learning module, we adopt the notion of *weighted Hyperlink-Induced Topic Search* (*HITS*) *model* to learn users' experience values and trust values of remote phone numbers. The notion of *Hyperlink-Induced Topic Search* (*HITS*) has been proposed by Kleinberg *et al.* [12] [13]. Basically, the HITS algorithm is a link analysis algorithm that rates the importance of web pages. The idea behind Hubs and Authorities was originally based on a particular insight from the networks of web pages. Certain web pages, known as hubs, do not actually provide authoritative information; rather, they provide a number of links which point users to other authoritative pages. Meanwhile, a good hub represents a page that points to many other pages, where a good authority represents a page that is pointed by many hubs. In the context of telecommunication networks, we consider an experienced user as a hub, which has a high capability to propagate "trusts". Therefore, the *hubs* of a telecommunication network can represent experienced users who mostly accept normal phone calls and reject suspicious and fraudulent calls. Take Figure 2 as an example. Suppose the phone calls made by the "remote phone" are fraudulent, $user_1$ and $user_2$ directly hang up the call, $user_3$ answers the call and talks for a while, implying that $user_1$ and $user_2$ are more experienced than $user_3$. Similarly, a good *authority* in the communication network represents a phone number that was answered by many experienced users (i.e., hubs).

Accordingly, we can easily realize that fraudulent phone call detection can inherently be formulated as a learning problem of hubs and authorities. Here, we treat the authority value of a remote phone number as its "trust value" and the hub value of a user as his "experience value". When an unknown remote phone number is seen in the telecommunication record, its trust value will be contributed by the experience values of the user who answered the calls made by the phone number. Although the HITS algorithm has widely been applied in many research areas, such as social network analysis [31], to our best knowledge, this is the first work that explores the HITS-based learning for fraud detection in telecommunications. To support our proposed weighted HITS model, we propose two kinds of directed bipartite graphs, *contact_book-remote_phone_number graph* (*CPG*) and *user-remote_phone_number graph* (*UPG*). Due to Android's privacy design, mobile apps are not allowed to obtain the phone number associated with the device, we do not have an one-to-one mapping between user ID and phone number from the *Whoscall* dataset. Therefore, the two partite sets of the bipartite graphs are users' ID and remote phone numbers, respectively. To weight the edges of CPG and UPG, we extract features for each pair of user ID and remote phone number in two different but complementary aspects: 1) duration relatedness (DR) between a user and a remote phone number; and 2) frequency relatedness (FR) between a user and a remote phone number. In the on-line prediction module, based on the computed experience values of users, we evaluate the trust value of an unknown remote phone number to determine whether it is fraudulent or not. To our best knowledge, this is the first work on detecting fraudulent phone calls by exploiting the weighted HITS model. Through an experimental evaluation, we show that the proposed fraudulent phone calls detection delivers excellent performance.

The contributions of our research are six-fold:

- We propose the *FrauDetector* framework, a novel approach for fraudulent phone call detection. The problems and ideas in *FrauDetector* have not been explored previously in the research community.
- We develop the weighted HITS algorithm to learn experience values for individual users and trust values for remote phone numbers.
- We develop two kinds of structures to support the weighted HITS algorithm. One is contact_book-remote_phone_number graph (CPG) which reflects whether the remote phone number occurs in the user's contact book. The other is user-remote_phone_number graph (UPG) which reflects whether the remote phone number has had telecommunications with the user.
- We propose two kinds of features to weight CPG and UPG. The proposed features can represent each pair of user and remote phone number in two different but complementary aspects: 1) duration relatedness (DR) between a user and a remote phone number; and 2) frequency relatedness (FR) between a user and a remote phone number.
- Based on the learned experience values for individual users and trust values for remote phone numbers, we propose a fraud detection strategy to detect fraudulent phone calls.
- We use a dataset from *Whoscall* in a series of experiments to evaluate the performance of our proposal. The results show superior performance over other classifier-based fraud detection techniques in terms of precision, recall, F-measure and AUC.

The rest of this paper is organized as follows. We briefly review the related work in Section 2 and provide an overview of our graph-mining-based fraudulent phone call detection framework in Section 3. We detail the proposed trust value mining in section 4 and describe our fraudulent phone call detection in Section 5. Finally, we present the evaluation result of our empirical performance study in Section 6 and discuss our conclusions and future work in Section 7.

2. RELATED WORK

In this section, we briefly introduce three popular kinds of fraud detection, Telecommunications Fraud Detection, Insurance Fraud Detection, and Credit Card Detection. As mentioned earlier, most fraud detection techniques formulate the detection problem as a binary classification problem. Such classifier-based approach requires sufficient features to build classification model. Therefore, very limited numbers of literatures have address the telecommunications fraud detection because the phone users usually provide limited profile for applying a phone number such that we can not compute sufficient features only from telecommunication records.

2.1 Fraud Detection in Telecommunications

The histories of fraud detection at AT&T have been described in [1], one of the companies to address the fraud detection and discuss some techniques used to address them. Pal *et al.* [20] describe how data mining techniques help the telecommunication in many applications. Weatherford *et al.* [28] focus on neural networks, which utilize current user profiles that store long-term information to define normal patterns of use. After training the model, the behavior of fraud is probably different than the normal one. To detect frauders' phone numbers, Onderwater [18] adopts outlier detection techniques to identify unusual user profiles. Yusoff [32] proposed an approach using Gaussian mixed model (GMM), a probalistic model which is successful applying on speech recognition problems where the model can apply on it as well. Based on LDA, [17] detects the fraud using a threshold-type classification algorithm. Cahill *et al.* [7] builds upon the adaptive fraud detection framework [10] by using an event-driven approach of assigning fraud scores to detect fraud as it happens, and weighting recent mobile phone calls more heavily than earlier ones. The new framework [7] can also detect types of fraud using rules, in addition to detecting fraud in each individual account, from large databases. This framework has been applied to both wireless and wire line fraud detection systems with over two million customers. The adaptive fraud detection framework presents rule-learning fraud detectors based on account-specific thresholds that are automatically generated for profiling the fraud in an individual account. The system, based on the framework, has been applied by combining the most relevant rules, to uncover fraudulent usage that is added to the legitimate use of a mobile phone account [9] [10].

2.2 Fraud Detection in Other Field

Insurance Fraud Detection. Pocard [22] provide a survey of recent development on economic analysis of insurance fraud. Ngai *et al.* [16] proposed a series of classification schemes used for financial fraud detection, and 49 journals are analysed and 6 classification approaches are utilized. Ormerod *et al.* [19] proposed a Mass Detection Tool (MDT) for early detection of insurance fraud. The MDT uses a dynamic Bayesian Belief Network (BBN) of fraud indicators, whose weights are extracted from the rule generator's outcomes and claims handlers to keep up with the evolving fraudulent behaviors. The approach of fraudulent types evolves when the fraudulent behavior changes while capturing unexpected anomalies detected by claims handlers. Williams *et al.* demonstrated insurance and fraud applications [29], which have been applied, to health care for the Australian Health Insurance Commission. This methodology first performs clustering, *k-means* for cluster detect, and applies *C4.5* algorithm to build the model and evaluate the rules from the domain knowledge, statistical summaries and visualization. Williams [30] proposed an approach to hot spot data mining in which the measure of interestingness and the description of groups evolved according to a user guide the system towards significant discovery. Brockett *et al.* [4] utilized the similar methodology of self-organizing Map to uncover automobile bodily injury claims fraud. [11] used the method of two-class neural network classification for medical practice developed at the Health Insurance Commission. Like the hot spot methodology, this approach can be applied on instances of the Australian Health Insurance Commission health practitioners' profiles. Šubelj *et al.* [26] described an expert system for insurance fraudsters and the experiments shows the better effectiveness.

Credit Card Detection. Credit card fraud detection is of great importance to financial institutions. Raj *et al.* [24] provided a complete survey of techniques for credit card fraud detection and evaluate the effectiveness of each approach. Bhattacharyya *et al.* [2] focus on two advanced approaches: 1) support vector machine 2) random forests 3) regression to achieve better performance on credit fraud detection. Maes *et al.* [14] applied two machine learning techniques: Artificial Neural Network (ANN) and Bayesian Belief Networks (BBN) to the problem and show the results on the real-world financial dataset. Comparative results show that BBNs were more accurate and much faster while BBNs are slower when applied to new instances. Chan *et al.* [6] proposed a method of combining multiple fraud detectors under cost model to evaluate C4.5, CART, Ripper and NB classification models. The result shows that partitioning the large dataset into small subsets to utilizing different classification algorithms used for detecting fraud improves the cost of savings by using stacking to combine multiple models and the method was applied to credit card transactions from two major US banks, Chase Bank and First Union Bank. Weatherford [28] describes the FairIsaac, which produces software for detecting credit card fraud, and utilizing the BP neural network to detect fraudulent activities.

According to above-mentioned three kinds of fraud, we can observe that all existing work formulate the fraud detection as a binary classification problem and try to extract features from users' profile. This strategy is reasonable for detecting insurance and credit card fraud because people should provide details of their profile when they apply insurance or credit card. However, the telecommunication is much different from insurance or credit card. We only can collect very simple profile, which is insufficient to build a precise classifier. As the result, in the next section, we propose a novel fraudulent phone call framework, based only on telecommunication records.

3. OVERVIEW OF OUR PROPOSED *FrauDetector* FRAMEWORK

With the notion of weighted HITS algorithm, we propose a novel fraudulent phone call framework, namely, *FrauDetector,* based only on telecommunication records. The *FrauDetector* framework consists of 1) a trust value mining module, and 2) a HITS-based fraudulent phone call detection module. Figure 3 shows the framework and its flow of data processing. The idea is to explore the telecommunication behaviors of mobile users, captured in telecommunication records, to reveal trust value of a remote phone number. As shown in Figure 3, the trust value mining module is an offline module which includes three steps. The first step, called *UPG and CPG construction,* transforms users' telecommunication as directed graph. The second step, called *weights assignment,* extracts features to weight the edges of CPG and UPG. Meanwhile, two different but complementary aspects, 1) duration relatedness (DR) between user and remote phone number and 2) frequency relatedness (FR) for each pair of user and remote phone number are proposed. The third step, called *trust value discovery,* perform weighted HITS algorithm on the weighted CPG and UPG to learn experience value for individual users and trust value for remote phone numbers. The HITS-based fraudulent phone call detection module is an on-line module in which we propose a scoring function to evaluate the probability for a remote phone number to be fraudulent. We then details the value mining module in next section and the HITS-based fraudulent phone call detection module in the section 5.

4. TRUST VALUE MINING

To learn the trust value for each remote phone number and the experience value for each user without users' profile, we perform a weighted HITS algorithm based on the telecommunication records. To support weighted HITS algorithm, we proposed two kinds of directed graph, CPG and UPG, to represent behavior of users' telecommunications. To weight our proposed CPG and UPG, we propose two different but complementary aspects, 1) duration relatedness (DR) between user and remote phone number and 2) frequency relatedness (FR) for each pair of user and remote phone number.

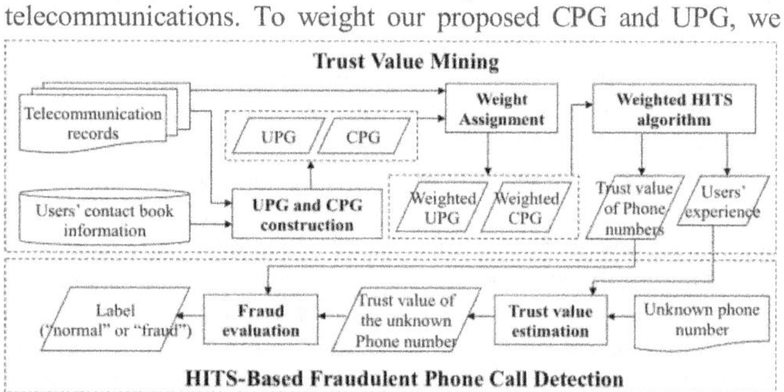

Figure 3. The *FrauDetector* framework for fraudulent phone call detection.

4.1 CPG and UPG Construction

Since original idea of HITS is that a good hub represented a web page that pointed to many other pages, and a good authority represented a web page that was linked by many different hubs. Therefore, constructing a directed graph to represent the relation between users and remote phone numbers is required. Intuitively, it inherently represents the relation between a user and a remote phone number to see if the user has a call from/to the remote phone number. Based on this idea, we propose a directed bipartite graph, *user-remote_phone_number graph* (*UPG*), of which edges represent call directions.

Definition 1. User-remote_phone_number graph (UPG). Given a telecommunication record set T, a user set U and a remote phone number set P, the *User-remote_phone_number graph* is a directed bi-partite graph $UPG = (V, E)$ with the vertex set $V = U \cup P$ the edge set $E = \{(u, p) \mid u \in U, p \in P$, and $\exists$ a call from u to p in $T\} \cup \{(p, u) \mid u \in U, p \in P$, and $\exists$ a call from p to u in $T\}$.

Example 1. Table 1 shows an example of telecommunication record set. The vertex set should be $\{u_1, u_2, u_3, u_4, p_1, p_2, p_3, p_4, p_5\}$, and the edge set should be $\{(p_1, u_1), (p_1, u_2), (p_2, u_2), (u_2, p_1), (u_2, p_2), (u_2, p_5), (u_2, p_3), (u_2, p_4), (p_4, u_3), (u_3, p_5), (u_3, p_4), (p_5, u_3), (p_3, u_4), (p_5, u_4), (u_4, p_5)\}$. The illustration of user-remote_phone_number graph is shown in Figure 4.

Table 1. An example of telecommunication record set.

Users	*Remote Phone Numbers*	*Receiving /Dialing Time*	*Starting Time*	*Ending Time*	*Call Direction*
u_1	p_1	17:01:48	17:02:08	17:06:08	in
u_2	p_1	17:07:48	-	-	in
	p_2	17:02:08	17:02:28	17:04:08	in
	p_1	18:05:21	18:05:30	18:06:01	out
	p_2	18:07:08	18:07:17	18:10:31	out
	P_5	19:00:08	-	-	out
	p_3	19:10:08	-	-	out
	p_4	19:12:32	19:12:38	19:22:01	out
	p_5	19:22:55	19:23:01	19:23:58	in
u_3	p_4	16:22:01	16:22:21	16:25:40	in
	p_5	16:25:41	-	-	out
	p_4	16:25:45	16:26:02	16:30:10	out
	p_5	16:32:01	16:32:13	16:33:50	in
u_4	p_3	17:09:01	17:09:08	17:12:02	in
	p_5	17:12:18	17:12:33	17:30:08	in
	p_5	19:01:05	19:01:16	19:02:28	out
	p_5	20:02:17	20:02:28	20:40:08	in

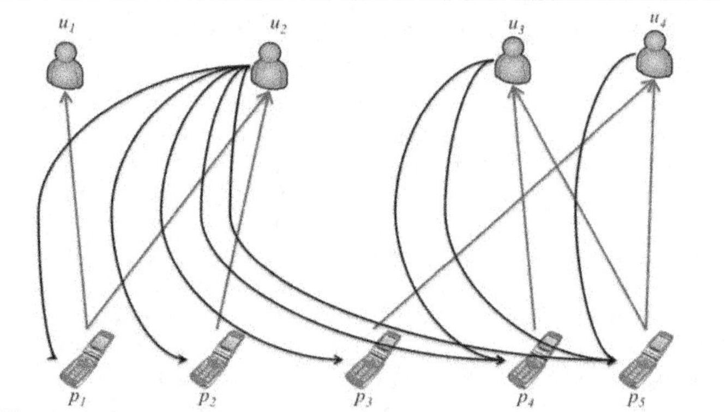

Figure 4. An example of user-remote_phone_number graph (UPG).

Actually, the telecommunication activities can be classified into two categories. One is telecommunication with someone who is well known, and the other is telecommunication with stranger. Accordingly, if the users provide the contact book information for our model building, we could utilize this information to construct the directed graph for HITS algorithm. Based on this idea, we formally define a directed graph, *contact_book-remote_phone_number graph* (*CPG*), as follows:

Definition 2. Contact book phone number (CP). Given a user u, the *Contact book phone number* of u, formally denoted as $CP(u)$, is set list of phone numbers that are recorded in u's contact book.

Example 2. Table 2 shows an example of contact book of each user. The contact book phone number of u_2 should be $\{p_2, p_3, p_4, p_5\}$, i.e., $CP(u_2) = \{p_2, p_3, p_4, p_5\}$

Table 2. An example of contact book of each user.

Users	*Contact Book Phone Numbers*
u_1	p_2, p_4
u_2	p_2, p_3, p_4, p_5
u_3	p_4, p_5
u_4	p_2, p_5

Definition 3. Contact_book-remote phone number graph (CPG). Given a telecommunication record set T, a user set U and a remote phone number set P, the *Contact_book-remote_phone_number graph* is a directed bi-partite graph $CPG = (V, E)$ with the vertex set $V = U \cup P$ the edge set $E = \{(u, p) \mid u \in U, p \in CP(u)$, and $\exists$ a call from u to p in $T\} \cup \{(p, u) \mid u \in U, p \in CP(u)$, and $\exists$ a call from p to u in $T\}$.

Example 3. Table 1 shows an example of telecommunication record set, and Table 2 shows an example of contact book of each user. The vertex set should be $\{u_1, u_2, u_3, u_4, p_1, p_2, p_3, p_4, p_5\}$, and the edge set should be $\{(p_2, u_2), (u_2, p_2), (u_2, p_5), (u_2, p_3), (u_2, p_4), (p_4, u_3), (u_3, p_5), (u_3, p_4), (p_5, u_3), (p_5, u_4), (u_4, p_5)\}$. The illustration of contact_book-remote_phone_number graph is shown as Figure 5.

Here, we can observe that CPG can precisely represent relation between users and remote phone numbers. However, some remote phone numbers would easily be isolated in a CPG, such as p_1 in Figure 5. This phenomenon might lead the HITS algorithm does not work well. As the result, both UPG and CPG are potentially useful for leaning trust values of remote phone numbers.

4.2 Weights Assignment

Based on our observation, users' telecommunication behaviors could be categorized into two types. One is to make phone call to someone familiar, and the other is to make phone call to someone who is a colleague. Usually, people would chatter to someone

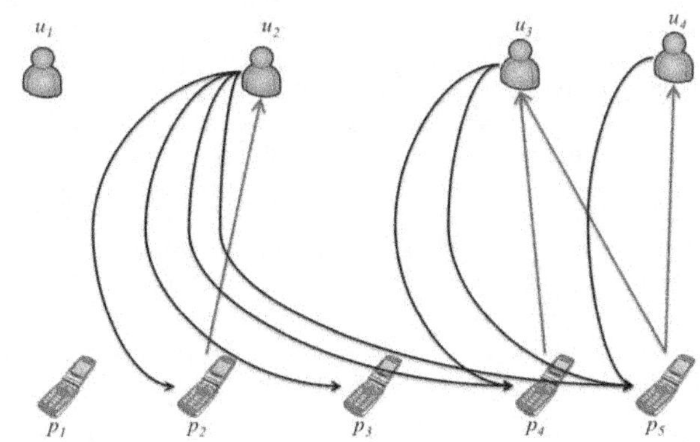

Figure 5. An example of contact_book-remote phone number graph (CPG).

familiar for a while and frequently talk to colleagues. That means user usually has call to/from normal remote phone number either frequently or for a while. Therefore, to weight a specific user-remote_phone_number pair, we explore the telecommunication behaviors in two different but complementary aspects: 1) duration relatedness (DR) between user and remote phone number; and 2) frequency relatedness (FR) between user and remote phone number. Before introducing the duration relatedness features, we first describe the formal definitions for illustrating the duration relatedness features:

Definition 3. Conditional Telecommunication Record Set (CT). Given a telecommunication record set T, a user u, a remote phone number p and call direction d, the *Conditional Telecommunication Record Set*, denoted as $CT(T, u, p, d)$, is a subset of T in which user is u, remote phone number is p, and call direction is d.

Example 3. Consider Table 1 as an example of telecommunication record set T, the conditional telecommunication record set $CT(T, u_4, p_5, in)$ is shown as Table 3.

Table 3. An example of conditional telecommunication record set.

Users	*Remote Phone Numbers*	*Receiving /Dialing Time*	*Starting Time*	*Ending Time*	*Call Direction*
u_4	p_5	17:12:18	17:12:33	17:30:08	in
	p_5	20:02:17	20:02:28	20:40:08	in

4.2.1 Duration Relatedness

Our goal is to extract duration relatedness features for pairs of users and remote phone numbers. Intuitively, users have different telecommunication duration for different people due to the nature of relationship between the users and the remote phone numbers. As a result, different call durations, naturally formed in aggregated behaviors of users to various kinds of remote phone numbers, are embedded in the users' telecommunication activities which are logged in telecommunication records. In a telecommunication record, the most important information is remote phone number and duration, besides the user himself. In the following, we propose to extract two duration features to depict relation between users and remote phone numbers as below.

- **Total Call Duration (TCD).** Intuitively, the user is likely to share some interests with his or her friends or someone familiar. Thus, if a user spends much time for a phone call to/from to a remote phone number, he may contribute his trust to the remote phone number. Accordingly, aggregating user's call duration of a remote phone number can be used to infer the probability that a user trusts that remote phone number. Formally, given a telecommunication record set T, a user u and a remote phone number p, total call duration from u to p and that from p to u are respectively formulated as:

$$\begin{cases} TCD(u \to p \mid T) = \sum_{r \in CT(T,\, u,\, p,\, out)} (r.ending\ time - r.starting\ time) \\ TCD(p \to u \mid T) = \sum_{r \in CT(T,\, u,\, p,\, in)} (r.ending\ time - r.starting\ time) \end{cases} \quad (2)$$

- **Average Call Duration (TCD).** It is trivial that the total call duration includes two aspects, duration of each phone call and phone call frequency. That might weaken the significance of duration relatedness. For example, if a user makes short duration calls to a remote phone number many times, the total call duration might be pretty long. Accordingly, averaging user's call duration of a remote phone number can adjust this bias evaluation. Formally, given a telecommunication record set T, a user u and a remote phone number p, average call duration from u to p and that from p to u are respectively formulated as:

$$\begin{cases} ACD(u \rightarrow p \mid T) = \dfrac{TCD(u \rightarrow p \mid T)}{CT(T,\ u,\ p,\ out)} \\ ACD(p \rightarrow u \mid T) = \dfrac{TCD(p \rightarrow u \mid T)}{CT(T,\ u,\ p,\ in)} \end{cases} \quad (3)$$

Take Table 1 as telecommunication record set T. The total call duration from p_5 to u_4 is (17:30:08 − 17:12:33) + (20:40:08 − 20:02:28) = (00:17:35) + (00:37:40) = 3315 (sec.), and the average call duration from p_5 to u_4 is 3315/2 = 1657.5 (sec.).

4.2.2 Frequency Relatedness

As mentioned earlier, user usually has call to/from normal remote phone number either frequently or for a while. The above-proposed duration relatedness features have completely represented the aspect, having a call for a while. In this subsection, our goal is to extract frequency relatedness feature for pairs of users and remote phone numbers. Intuitively, users have different telecommunication frequencies for different people due to the needs of communication between the users and the remote phone numbers. Thus, we also can realize that different call frequency are embedded in the users' telecommunication activities that can be utilized to distinguish fraudulent remote phone numbers from normal remote phone numbers. In the following, we propose to extract a call frequency feature to depict relation between users and remote phone numbers.

Based on the observation, each person's call frequency is different from other person's call frequency. Some active person might frequently make phone calls to other people. Therefore, we should not directly utilize call frequency as the feature to represent relation between users and remote phone numbers. Accordingly, we propose a Normalized Call Frequency (NCF) to capture relation between users and remote phone numbers. Formally, given a telecommunication record set T, a user u and a remote phone number p, normalized call frequency from u to p and that from p to u are respectively formulated as:

$$\begin{cases} NCF(u \rightarrow p \mid T) = \dfrac{CT(T,\ u,\ p,\ out)}{\max\limits_{p^* \in P} \{CT(T,\ u,\ p^*,\ out)\}} \\ NCF(p \rightarrow u \mid T) = \dfrac{CT(T,\ u,\ p,\ in)}{\max\limits_{p^* \in P} \{CT(T,\ u,\ p^*,\ in)\}} \end{cases} \quad (4)$$

```
Input:  Weighted directed bipartite graph UPG (or CPG)
Output: Trust value vector of remote phone number τ
        Experience value vector of user u
1   X ← transform UPG to user-by-phone matrix
2   Y ← transform UPG to phone-by-user matrix
3   for each user i //initial experience value
4       u[i] ← 0.
5   End for
6   for each remote phone number j //initial trust value
7       if jth remote phone number is fraudulent
8           τ[j] ← -1
9       otherwise
10          τ[j] ← 1
11      End if
12  End for
13  for iteration < N
14      τ ← τ × 1/norm(τ) // normalize by norm
15      u ← u + X^T×τ
16      u ← u × 1/norm(u) // normalize by norm
17      τ ← τ + Y^T×u
18  End for
19  Return τ and u
```

Figure 6. Weighted HITS algorithm.

Take Table 1 as telecommunication record set T. The normalized call frequency from p_5 to u_4 is 2/4.

4.3 Trust Value Learning

Based on the weighted CPG and UPG, we can perform a weighted HITS algorithm to learn trust value for each remote phone number and experience value for each user. Given m users and n remote phone numbers, we build an $m \times n$ weighted adjacency matrix X and an $n \times m$ weighted adjacency matrix Y for the UPG or CPG. Formally, $X = [v_{ij}]$ and $Y = [w_{ji}]$,$0 \leq i < m$; $0 \leq j < n$, where v_{ij} represents the weight of the edge linking the from ith user to the jth remote phone number, and v_{ij} represents the weight of the edge linking from the jth remote phone number to the ith user. Formally, the random walk model applied to the UPG or the CPG can be described as follows:

$$\begin{aligned} u_{user}^{k+1} &= u_{user}^{k} + Y^T \square \frac{1}{norm(u_{phone}^{k})} u_{phone}^{k} \\ u_{phone}^{k+1} &= u_{phone}^{k} + X^T \square \frac{1}{norm(u_{user}^{k+1})} u_{user}^{k+1} \end{aligned} \quad (5)$$

where k indicates the number of iterations; Y indicates the phone-to-user stochastic matrix (computed by UPG or CPG); X indicates the user-to-phone stochastic matrix (computed by UPG or CPG); and norm() indicates the "Euclidean norm [4] of a vector," which represents the length of a trust value vector (respectively experience value vector).

As we described earlier, there are three types of weight, normalized call frequency (denoted as FR), total call duration (denoted as DR_T) and average call duration (denoted as DR_A), and there are two kinds of graph, CPG and UPG. Therefore, there are six kinds of weighted graph (3×2 = 6). Based on one of the six kinds of weighted graph, we perform the weighted HITS algorithm, as shown in Figure 6, to calculate the trust value for each remote phone number and experience value for each user. First, the weighted adjacency matrix X and Y are generated from input UPG or CPG (see lines 1 through 2 of Figure 6). Then, the initial state of each user and each remote phone is obtained (see lines 3 through 12 of Figure 6). For each iteration, we aggregate trust value (τ) into experience value (u) and experience value (u) into trust value (τ) (see lines 13 through 18 of Figure 6). Finally, we can obtain the trust value (τ) and experience value (u) (see lines 9 through 11 of Figure 6). As the result, we can use the learned trust value for each remote phone number and experience value for each user to build the fraudulent phone call.

5. HITS-BASED FRAUDULENT REMOTE PHONE NUMBER DETECTION

After learning trust value and experience value, we must estimate the trust value of unknown remote phone number based on the learned trust value and experience value. Intuitively, we can insert the unknown remote phone number in UPG or CPG and use the learned users' experience values to estimate the trust value of the unknown remote phone number. Since frauders make phone call first before they receive any phone call, there is no in-direct edge point to the vertex, which represents the unknown remote phone number in UPG or CPG. However, the fraudulent phone call detection should detect the fraud as soon as possible. Thus, we assume one of user might call back. Accordingly, we directly use the weighted average experience value to estimate the possible trust value of the unknown remote phone number. Given an unknown

[4] http://en.wikipedia.org/wiki/Euclidean_distance

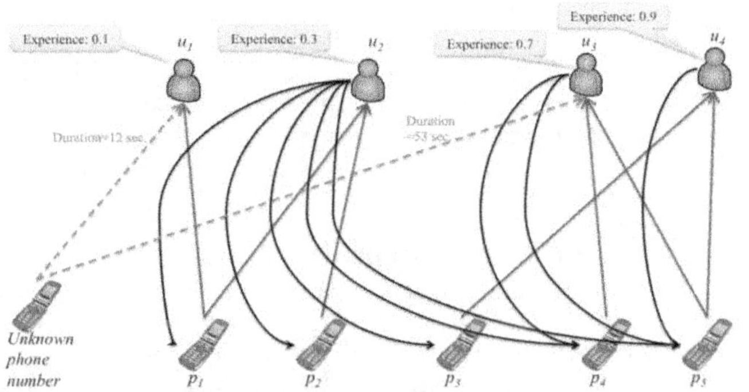

Figure 7. An example of estimation of trust value for an unknown remote phone number.

phone number p^*, a telecommunication record set T and user set U, the estimated trust value of p^* is formally defined as follows:

$$\frac{\sum_{u \in U}\left[\left(w(p^* \to u \mid T) \times u.experience\right)+\left(w(u \to p^* \mid T) \times u.experience\right)\right]}{\sum_{u \in U}\left(w(p^* \to u \mid T)+w(u \to p^* \mid T)\right)}, \quad (6)$$

where $w()$ is the weighting function utilized for UPG or CPG. Take Figure 7 as an example. The unknown phone number has have a phone call to the user u_1 and u_2, and the graph is weight total call duration. The estimated trust value of the unknown phone number should be

$$\frac{12 \square 0.1+53 \square 0.7}{12+53}=0.59 \cdot$$

After estimating possible trust value of the unknown remote phone number, we then determine whether the unknown remote phone number is fraudulent according to the possible trust value. Accordingly, a suitable threshold is required for evaluate whether the possible trust value provide significant evidence to prove the unknown remote phone number is fraudulent. Intuitively, we can use the distribution of learned trust value of phone numbers, utilized for HITS, to compute the threshold. Figure 8 shows the distributions of learned trust values of normal remote phone numbers and that of fraudulent remote phone numbers, learned from *Whoscall* telecommunication record set. Although the distribution of learned trust values of normal remote phone numbers is significantly different from that of fraudulent remote phone numbers, there is a quite portion of fraudulent remote phone numbers get high trust value. To avoid the effect of these outliers, we utilize the k percentile[5] of distribution of learned trust values of fraudulent remote phone numbers as the threshold. Based on the threshold, we classify the unknown remote phone number into the "fraud" category if the possible trust value of it is lower than the threshold.

6. EXPERIMENTAL EVALUATIONS

In this section, we present the results from a series of experiments to evaluate the performance of *FrauDetector* using dataset provided by *Whoscall*. All the experiments are implemented in Java JDK 1.6 on an Intel Xeon CPU W3520 2.67 GHz machine with 48 GB of memory running Microsoft Windows 7. We first describe the preparation of the datasets, and then introduce the evaluation methodology. Finally, we present and discuss our experimental results.

6.1 Dataset Description

We use a dataset provided by *Whoscall*, which is a smartphone application on Android for detecting whether an incoming call

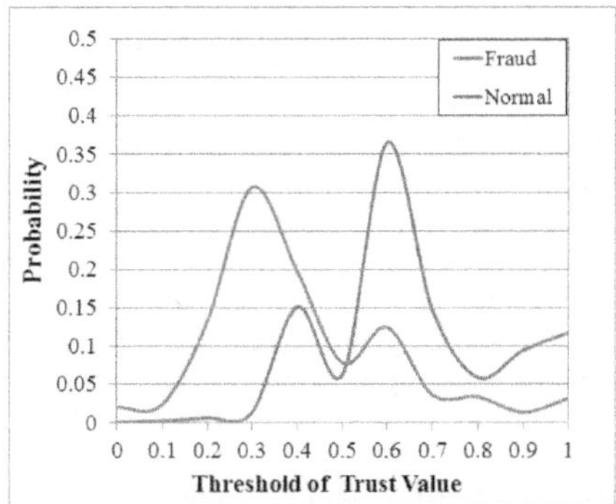

Figure 8. Distributions of learned trust values.

belongs to tele-marketing, harassment, call centers, or frauds, based on known information such as yellow pages and Internet forums. The dataset was collected for a month in August 2014 from a group of voluntary users in Taiwan. The dataset was contributed by 1,324,217 voluntary Whoscall users, who collectively contributed a total of 14,573,937 remote phone numbers and 218,060,640 call records during the period (see Table 4). With those users' consents, each call record comprise the time, user id, remote phone number, duration of calls, ringtone type, whether the incoming call is in contact book, the country code of the incoming call, whether the call is missed, etc. In Table 5, we show the normal remote phone number and fraudulent remote number in the training data and testing data, where the fraudulent remote phone numbers are marked by the *Whoscall* users. According to the call records, we extract the total volumes of each remote phone number, the call duration of each remote phone number, whether the incoming call is in the user's contact books, which we take as the attributes used for classification. Note that, we focus on the fraudulent remote phone numbers, but in our dataset, most of the remote phone numbers are normal. Therefore, the dataset is an imbalance-label dataset, which the proportion of fraudulent remote phone numbers and normal remote phone numbers is about 1:400. Thus, in our experiment, with baseline methods, we solve the imbalance-label problem with our proposed method mentioned before. Otherwise, we came up with the approach to fraudulent detection using the web search engine algorithm Hyperlink Induced Topic Search (HITS), which is compared with in the later section.

Table 4. Basic statistics of the *Whoscall* dataset.

	# of calls in August,2014, Taiwan
# of call records	218,060,640
# of phone numbers	14,573,937
# of voluntary users	1,324,217

Table 5. Distributions of training and testing dataset.

	Training Data	*Testing Data*
# of fraudulent numbers	26,807	10,030
# of normal numbers	10,905,721	3,631,379

6.2 Performance Metrics

To compare with the performance of each approach, we can evaluate the effectiveness by the following standards that we focus on the fraudulent remote phone numbers: (1) Precision: the number of correct positive results divided by the number of all positive results (i.e., of all the classified fraudulent remote phone numbers, the rate of truely classified as fraudulent remote phone numbers). (2) Recall: the number of correct positive results divided by the number of positive results that should have been returned (i.e., of all the real fraudulent remote phone numbers, the rate of truely classified as fraudulent remote phone numbers). (3) F1-Measure: the F1-Measure can be interpreted as a weighted average of the precis4ion

[5] http://en.wikipedia.org/wiki/Percentile

and recall, where an F1 score reaches its best value at 1 and worst score at 0. (4) ROC curve: A graphical plot that illustrates the performance of a binary classifier system as its discrimination threshold is varied. The curve is created by plotting the *True Positive* rate against the *False Positive* rate. When making decision, ROC analysis can not be cost impact, and give the objective and neutral advices. (5) AUC: the area under the ROC curve, representing to the probability that a classifier will rank a randomly chosen positive instance higher than a randomly chosen negative one. In the next section, we will evaluate the performance using the standards.

6.3 Evaluation on Baseline Approaches

Due to the imbalance-label problem, first we use chi-square to select the features that are useful; second, take each remote phone number as a raw data, cluster the remote phone numbers using *k-means* into groups which we prune the normal remote phone numbers that are prone to fraudulent remote phone numbers; third, use sampling approaches [5] (e.g., *over-sampling, down-sampling, SMOTE*) to eliminate the imbalance. After these steps, we use five existing approaches as baseline approaches that are listed below.

- **Naïve Bayes.** Naïve Bayes classifiers are a family of probabilistic classifier based on Bayes' theorem with naïve independence assumptions between the features [17]. In some applications, the effectiveness of classification is better than ANNs and decision trees. Naïve Bayes classifier is sometimes used for large dataset and it sometimes obtains predictive and effective classified results [15] [25].
- **Random Forests.** Random Forests first proposed by Amit and Geman in 1997, after that it was completely integrated by Leo Breiman and Adele Cutler [3]. This algorithm combines the thought of "Bootstrap aggregating" and the method of "random subspace" to construct a multitude of decision trees at training time and output the class with the most popular class.
- **C4.5 decision tree.** An algorithm used to generate a decision tree by Ross Quinlan [23]. C4.5 is an extension of Quinlan's earlier ID3 algorithm, and the decision trees that C4.5 create is not only used for classification, but for statistical classifier.
- **Support Vector Machines (SVM).** SVMs are supervised learning models with associated learning algorithms which analyze data and recognize patterns, and used for classification and regression analysis. SVMs are classification algorithms that can apply in linear data and nonlinear data, and can transform the initial data into higher dimension for more accurate classification [8].
- **Artificial Neural Networks (ANNs).** ANNs are one of statistical algorithms that inspired by biological neural networks [27]. In most cases, ANNs are a self-adaptive system that can change infer-structure based on the input data, and ANNs are a nonlinear statistical tool, which usually building models for complicated relationship between input data and output data. Like other machine learning methodologies, ANNs have been solved a wide variety of tasks including computer vision and speech recognition.

6.4 Internal Experimental Results

As mentioned in the Section 4, we have various weighted directed graphs, which can capture some aspects of users' telecommunication activities. In this section, we compare them and seek the best parameter settings. To conveniently present our experimental results, we give the abbreviations of our proposed HIST-based model under various weighted directed graph as shown in Table 6.

Table 6. Abbreviation of our proposed weighted HITS.

Directed Graph	*Weighting fuction*	*Abbreviation*
UPG	none	*UPG*
	TCD (see section 4.2.1)	*UPG_TCD*
	ACD(see section 4.2.1)	*UPG_ACD*
	NCF(see section 4.2.2)	*UPG_FR*
CPG	none	*CPG*
	TCD (see section 4.2.1)	*CPG_TCD*
	ACD(see section 4.2.1)	*CPG_ACD*
	NCF(see section 4.2.2)	*CPG_FR*

Figure 9 (a) indicates the precision of Graph-mining-based models with different weighting strategies under various threshold setting. Here, the x-axis represents *k* percentile of distribution of learned trust values of the fraudulent remote phone number. In other words, 0.2 means we set threshold as the learned trust value of the fraudulent remote phone number, which is higher than the learned trust values of 20% the fraudulent remote phone numbers. As shown in Figure 9 (a), we can recognize that the precision of most of the lines increase stably and reach the highest peak when threshold is set as 30 percentile. Besides, the precision decrease rapidly down to zero when threshold is set as greater than 0.4. The reason is that a large volumes of normal remote phone numbers are determined as fraud (False Alarm) when threshold is set as greater than 40 percentile so that the false alarm occupy in majority. Furthermore, we can figure out that the UPG_ACD has the highest precision 0.765 when threshold is set as 30 percentile.

Figure 9 (b) shows the recall of Graph-mining-based models with different weighting strategies under various threshold setting. Unlike the precision shown in Figure 9 (a), the recall increases rapidly until threshold is 30 percentile and increases smoothly when threshold is set as greater than 30 percentile. The reason for the

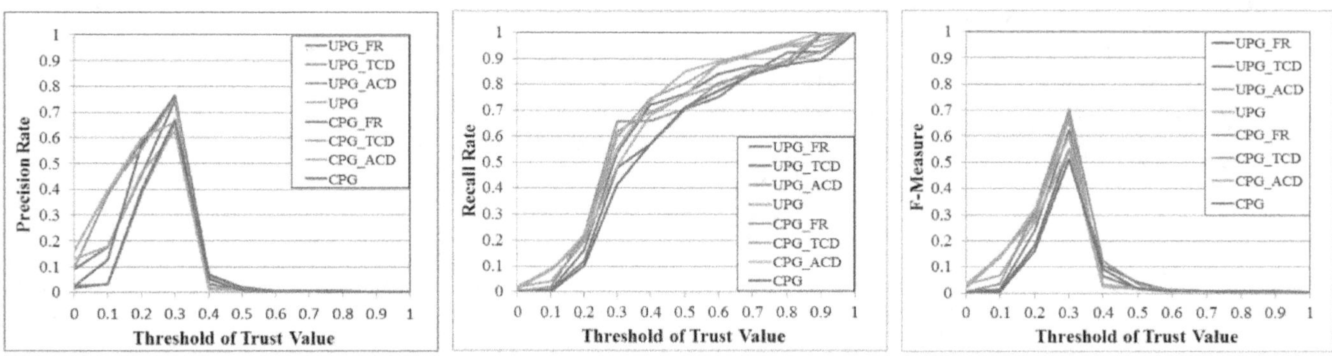

(a) (b) (c)

Figure 9. Precision, Recall and F1-Measure of weighted HITS models.

former phenomenon is a large number of fraudulent remote phone numbers which are determined as fraudulent remote phone numbers (True Positive), and the latter phenomenon is the number of decreasing increased rate. Besides, we can see that the trends of the all models are quite similar, and when threshold is set as greater than 30 percentile, the CPG_ACD performs higher recall than all the other features, and the recall of CPG shows lowest recall.

Figure 9 (c) indicates the F1-Measure of Graph-mining-based models with different weighting strategies under various threshold setting. Taking into account of precision and recall, F1-Measure provides more comprehensive effectiveness evaluation. As shown in Figure 9 (c), the highest peak occurs when threshold is set as about 30 percentile, and the F1-Measure decrease down to zero when threshold is set as greater than 30 percentile. It is reasonable because the precision is very close to zero when threshold is set as greater than 30 percentile. We also can observe that the F1-Measure of all models show the highest peak when threshold is set as 30 percentile. Meanwhile, the F1-Measure of the CPG_FR is up to 0.71 and the F1-Measure of the CPG is 0.51, which means that weighting strategy has played an important role on the weighted HITS model.

Table 7. AUC of weighted HITS models.

HITS model	UPG_ FR	UPG_ TCD	UPG_ ACD	UPG	CPG_ FR	CPG_ TCD	CPG_ ACD	CPG
AUC	0.813	0.808	0.824	0.746	0.829	0.816	0.821	0.791

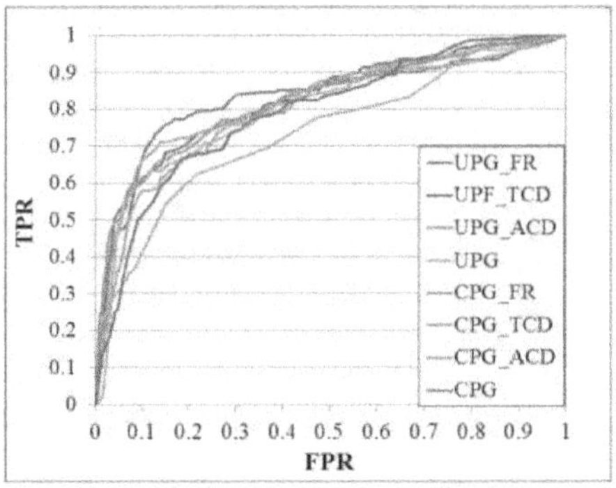

Figure 10. ROC curve of weighted HITS models.

Figure 10 shows the ROC curve of Graph-mining-based models with different weighting strategies. As shown in Figure 10, the true positive rates of all models are increased rapidly while the false positive rates of all models are low. It means that all HITS-based approaches we propose have excellent ability for dealing with imbalance-label problem. We also can observe that the curve of UPG lies below than other models. This phenomenon shows that all weighting functions are useful. Table 7 shows the AUC of Graph-mining-based models with different weighting strategies. We can see that the AUC of all Graph-mining-based models with different weighting strategies are greater than 0.8 except for the CPG, of which is 0.791, and the UPG, of which is 0.746.

In this internal experiment, we can conclude that 1) CPG_FR has the optimal effectiveness and 2) all models have best effectiveness when threshold is set as 30 percentile. As the result, we select the CPG_FR with threshold is set as 30 percentile to represent our proposed method in following experiments.

6.5 Comparison with Classifier-based Fraud Detection

Table 8 shows the AUC and execution time of comparison with classifier-based fraud detection approaches. As t shown in Figure 13, the AUC of our proposed HITS-based approach (CPG_FR) is 0.829, and the highest AUC of the classifier-based fraud detection approach (NaiveBayes) is 0.656. Compared with the best of classifier-based fraud detection approaches, our proposed HITS-based approach achieve 26.4% improvement rate (i.e., (0.829 – 0.656)/ 0.656). Besides, we also can observe that our approach required reasonable training time and detection time compared with the existing Classifier-based Fraud Detection approaches.

Table 8. AUC and execution time of comparison with classifier-based fraud detection approaches.

Approach	CPG_FR	Neural Network	C4.5	SVM	Random Forests	Naïve Bayes
AUC	0.829	0.636	0.613	0.586	0.646	0.656
Detection time (s)	33	35	15	17	32	58
Training time (s)	1427	2894	975	131	2379	246

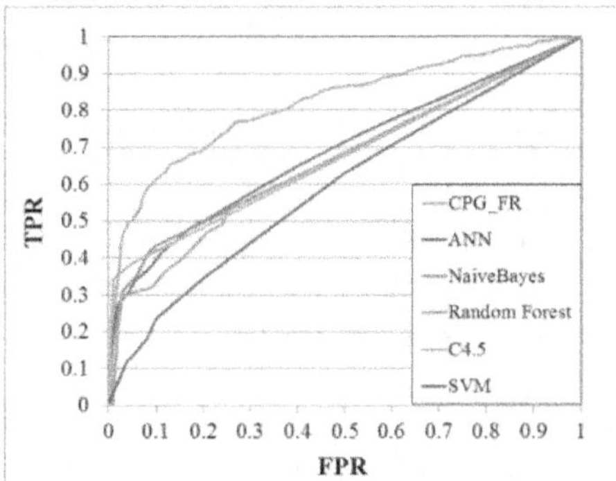

Figure 11. ROC curve of comparison with classifier-based fraud detection approaches.

Figure 11 indicates the ROC curve of comparison of our proposed HITS-based approach with classifier-based fraud detection approaches. As shown in Figure 11, our proposed HITS-based approach outperforms than the classifier-based fraud detection approaches. Besides, we can observe that SVM is significantly worse than other classifier-based fraud detection approaches. The reason is that SVM requires sufficient features to achieve quite high effectiveness, but our proposed HITS-based approach does not.

6.6 Discussions

Some lessons are learned from the above experimental results:

1. The experiments results show that our proposed approaches outperform the classifier-based methods significantly. One observation is that most classifiers require quite sufficient features which might not be provided in this application. Another observation leads to that HITS algorithm is a good solution for this application since the data which could be modeled as a network when the information shown in the data is very limited.

2. CPG_FR shows the best performance in our proposed approaches. It means that contact book and call frequency are the two most important kinds of information for identifying fraudulent phone calls.

3. In *Whoscall* dataset, the 30 percentile of trust values of fraudulent remote phone numbers is a good criteria for identifying fraudulent phone calls. It means there still are many fraudulent remote phone numbers that can get high trust value. Accordingly, although our proposed HITS-based approach is not exactly perfect, the weakness can easily be fixed through a series internal experiments.

7. CONCLUSION AND FUTURE WORK

In this paper, we have proposed a novel framework named HITS-based fraudulent phone call detection (FrauDetector) for detecting fraudulent phone calls by mining users' telecommunication records. We also tackled the problem of mining trust value from telecommunication activity, which is a crucial prerequisite for fraud detection. The core task of fraudulent phone call detection is conveniently transformed to the problem of trust value prediction. We evaluated the trust value of each phone number by training a weighted HITS model. In the proposed FrauDetector, we consider two kinds of telecommunication activities to build the directed graphs, CPG and UPG. Furthermore, we have explored 1) duration relatedness (DR) and 2) frequency relatedness (FR) by exploiting telecommunication to extract descriptive features to weight the CPG and UPG. To the best of our knowledge, this is the first work on fraudulent phone call detection that considers mining trust value of remote phone number by performing weighted HITS algorithm on telecommunication records. Through a series of experiments using a dataset provided by Whoscall, we have validated the proposed FrauDetector and shown that it has excellent performance compared with state-of-the-art classifier-based fraud detection methods under various conditions. In future work, we plan to design more sophisticated methods to enhance the quality of our proposed FrauDetector for various urban computing service applications.

ACKNOWLEDGMENTS

This research was partially supported by Ministry of Science and Technology, Taiwan, R.O.C. under grant no. 101-2221-E-006-255-MY3. This work would not have been possible without the valuable dataset offered by Whoscall and the support by Jeff Kuo from Gogolook, Inc.

REFERENCES

[1] R. A. Becker, C. Volinsky, and A. R. Wilks. Fraud Detection in Telecommunications: History and Lessons Learnd. *Technometrics*, vol. 52, No. 1, pp. 20–33, February 2010.

[2] S. Bhattacharyya, S. Jha, K. Tharakunnel, J. Westland. Data mining for credit card fraud: a comparative study. *Decision Support Systems*, 50 (3), pp. 602–613, 2011

[3] L. Breiman. Random forests. *Machine Learning*, 45(1):5–32, 2001.

[4] P. Brockett, X. Xia and R. Derrig. Using Kohonen's Self Organising Feature Map to Uncover Automobile Bodily Injury Claims Fraud. *Journal of Risk and Insurance*, USA, 1998

[5] J. Burez, D. Van den Poel. Handling class imbalance in customer churn prediction. *Expert Systems with Applications*, 2009

[6] P. Chan, W. Fan, A. Prodromidis and S. Stolfo. Distributed Data Mining in Credit Card Fraud Detection. *IEEE Intelligent Systems,* **14,** pp67-74, 1999.

[7] M. Cahill, D. Lambert, J. Pinheiro and D. Sun. Detecting Fraud In The Real World. *The Handbook of Massive Data Sets*, Kluwer, pp911-930, 2002.

[8] C. Cortes and V. Vapnik. Support-vector network. *Machine Learning*. 20, 273–297, 1995.

[9] T. Fawcett and F. Provost. Combining Data Mining and Machine Learning for Effective User Profiling. In *Proceedings of the 2nd International Conference on Knowledge Discovery and Data Mining*, Oregon, USA, 1996.

[10] T. Fawcett and F. Provost. Adaptive fraud detection. *Data Mining and Knowledge Discovery,* Kluwer, **1**, pp291-316, 1997

[11] H. He, J. Wang, W. Graco and S. Hawkins. Application of Neural Networks to Detection of Medical Fraud. *Expert Systems with Applications*, 13, pp329-336, 1997.

[12] J. Kleinberg. Hubs, Authorities, and Communities. *Cornell University*, December 1999.

[13] J. Kleinberg. Authoritative sources in a hyperlinked environment. *ACM Computing Surveys*, 46 (5): 604–632, 1999.

[14] S. Maes, K. Tuyls, B. Vanschoenwinkel and B. Manderick. Credit Card Fraud Detection Using Bayesian and Neural Networks. In *Proceedings of the 1st International NAISO Congress on Neuro Fuzzy Technologies,* Havana, Cuba, 2002.

[15] K. P. Murphy. Naive Bayes classifiers. *http://www.cs.ubc.ca/murphyk/Teaching/CS340-Fall06/reading/NB.pdf*

[16] E. W. T. Ngai, Y. Hu, Y. H. Wong, Y. Chen, X. Sun. The application of data mining techniques in financial fraud detection: A classification framework and an academic review of literature. *Decision Support Systems*, 50 (3) (2011), pp. 559–569

[17] D. Olszewski. A probabilistic approach to fraud detection in telecommunications. *Knowledge Based Systems,* Volume 26, pp.246-258, 2012

[18] M. Onderwater. Detecting unusual user profiles with outlier detection techniques. VU University Amsterdam, 2010.

[19] T. Ormerod, N. Morley, L. Ball, C. Langley and C. Spenser. Using Ethnography To Design a Mass Detection Tool (MDT) For The Early Discovery of Insurance Fraud. In *Proceedings of ACM CHI Conference,* Florida, USA, 2003.

[20] S. H. Pal, J. N. Patel. Data Mining in Telecommunication: A Review. *International Journal of Innovative Research in Technology*, 2014

[21] C. Phua, D. Alahakoon and V. Lee. Minority Report in Fraud Detection: Classification of Skewed Data. *ACM SIGKDD Explorations Newsletter,* vol. 6, no. 1, pp. 50-59, 2004.

[22] P. Picard. Economic analysis of insurance fraud. G. Dionne (Ed.), Handbook of Insurance, Kluwer Academic Press, Boston (2000), pp. 315–362

[23] J. R. Quinlan. C4.5: Programs for Machine Learning. *Morgan Kaufman*, 1993.

[24] S. B. E. Raj and A. A. Portia. Analysis on Credit Card Fraud Detection Methods. In *Proceedings of International Conference on Computer, Communication and Electrical Technology – ICCCET2011*, 18th & 19th March, 2011

[25] I. Rish. An empirical study of the naive bayes classifier. In *Proceedings of IJCAI-01 workshop on Empirical Methods in AI, International Joint Conference on Artificial Intelligence*, 2001, pages 41– 46.

[26] L. Šubelj, S. Furlan and M. Bajec. An expert system for detecting automobile insurance fraud using social network analysis. Expert Systems with Applications, 38(1), 1039-1052, 2011.

[27] S.C. Wang. Interdisciplinary Computing in Java Programming Language. *Dordrecht the Netherlands, Kluwer Academic Publishers*, 2003.

[28] M. Weatherford. Mining for Fraud. *IEEE Intelligent Systems*, July/August Issue, pp4-6, 2002.

[29] G. Williams and Z. Huang. Mining the Knowledge Mine: The Hot Spots Methodology for Mining Large Real World Databases. In *Proceedings of the 10th Australian Joint Conference on Artificial Intelligence*, Perth, Australia, 1997.

[30] G. Williams. Evolutionary Hot Spots Data Mining: An Architecture for Exploring for Interesting Discoveries. In *Proceedings of the 3rd Pacific-Asia Conference in Knowledge Discovery and Data Mining*, Beijing, China, 1999.

[31] J. J.-C. Ying, E. H.-C. Lu, W.-N. Kuo and V. S. Tseng. Mining User Check-in Behavior with a Random Walk for Urban Point-of-interest Recommendations. *ACM Transactions on Intelligent Systems and Technology (TIST)* Volume 5 Issue 3, September 2014, Article No. 40

[32] M. I. M. Yusoff. Fraud detection in telecommunication industry using Gaussian mixed model. *Mathematical Problems in Engineering*, Volume 2013

Efficient Long-Term Degradation Profiling in Time Series for Complex Physical Systems

Liudmila Ulanova *
UC Riverside
lulan001@ucr.edu

Tan Yan
NEC Laboratories America
yan@nec-labs.com

Haifeng Chen
NEC Laboratories America
haifeng@nec-labs.com

Guofei Jiang
NEC Laboratories America
gfj@nec-labs.com

Eamonn Keogh
UC Riverside
eamonn@cs.ucr.edu

Kai Zhang
NEC Laboratories America
kzhang@nec-labs.com

ABSTRACT

The long term operation of physical systems inevitably leads to their wearing out, and may cause degradations in performance or the unexpected failure of the entire system. To reduce the possibility of such unanticipated failures, the system must be monitored for tell-tale symptoms of degradation that are suggestive of imminent failure. In this work, we introduce a novel time series analysis technique that allows the decomposition of the time series into trend and fluctuation components, providing the monitoring software with actionable information about the changes of the system's behavior over time. We analyze the underlying problem and formulate it to a Quadratic Programming (QP) problem that can be solved with existing QP-solvers. However, when the profiling resolution is high, as generally required by real-world applications, such a decomposition becomes intractable to general QP-solvers. To speed up the problem solving, we further transform the problem and present a novel QP formulation, Non-negative QP, for the problem and demonstrate a tractable solution that bypasses the use of slow general QP-solvers. We demonstrate our ideas on both synthetic and real datasets, showing that our method allows us to accurately extract the degradation phenomenon of time series. We further demonstrate the generality of our ideas by applying them beyond classic machine prognostics to problems in identifying the influence of news events on currency exchange rates and stock prices. We fully implement our profiling system and deploy it into several physical systems, such as chemical plants and nuclear power plants, and it greatly helps detect the degradation phenomenon, and diagnose the corresponding components.

1. INTRODUCTION

The long term operation of physical systems causes degradation of their components. Degradations, such as wearing out or aging [1], lead to condition changes expressed in deviations in mean values, amplitudes or frequencies in the sensed signals of the system, and are an unavoidable property of any system. However, well-timed detection and profiling of an aging phenomenon or trend help avoid consequences and problems it may cause and are crucial tasks in the modern machinery. It is important to note, if one component of a system fails, it may lead to the stoppage of the whole system, and, as already well known, even short interruption in production process may cause huge money waste and serious business related issues [9].

The problem of trend analysis and extraction in time series has attracted significant attention recently, and a plethora of methods have been designed [4, 14]. However, the proposed schemes mainly focus on extracting general trend behavior from time series, and none of them specifically addresses the aging detection and profiling without any prior knowledge of the time series properties (i.e., seasonality, level of noise, etc.).

The *aging phenomenon* profiling is a critical task in detection and analysis of the degradation behavior in time series obtained from sensors on machinery. Such a problem is complicated because a system is usually operated with strong patterns. The aging behavior is usually invisible due to high noise and operational signals, and thus is too small to be detected. Figure 1 shows an example of a one-year-long time series collected from a pipe of a chemical plant. A component inside the pipe started wearing out at the beginning of January 2013, and another started at the beginning of March. This leads to the degradation of the whole pipe. Such aging phenomenon is too tiny to be captured by human eyes but may cause damage to the whole system.

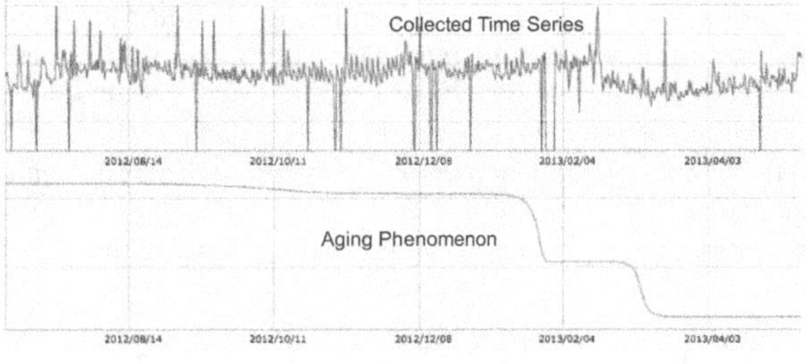

Figure 1: Example of time series showing aging (long-term degradation) phenomenon.

To resolve this issue, in this paper, we aim to provide a time series analysis technique that accurately extracts the aging phenomena of given time series, analyzes the aging behavior, and ranks its severity. We observe that in physical systems, the aging usually is generated in long-term and incremental fashions, such as buildups or component wear out, and thus, naturally, the aging behavior

*Work done during an internship at NEC Laboratories America, Princeton.

[1]We use terms *degradation* and *aging* interchangeably in this paper.

KDD'15 , August 11 - 14, 2015, Sydney, NSW, Australia.

DOI: http://dx.doi.org/10.1145/2783258.2788572.

can be modeled as a monotonic signal. Moreover, for systems under normal operations, the long-term operational signal should be stationary. For example, it does not make sense if a system is normally operated to always increase/decrease temperature, water flow, or pressure for five years, although the instant value can fluctuate at different time points. Under such observations, we want to develop an aging profiling engine that decomposes the given time series into two components - a *monotonic aging trend* that captures all the degradation phenomena in the time series and a *fluctuation term* that represents the normal operational signals and noises. In decomposition, we analyze the aging trend to profile its changes and evolutions including the slope and the shape that indicates the severity and starting point of the degradation.

More particularly, we formulate the aging extraction problem as an optimization problem. Its objective function consists of two parts: (1) Minimizing the reconstruction error to ensure an accurate profiling, and (2) Ensuring flatness of the fluctuation term over time so that the aging trend captures as much degradation signal as it can. Under such objectives, the solution must also satisfy two constraints: (1) the extracted aging trend needs to be monotonic to satisfy the nature of the component wearing out, and (2) all the extracted signals need to be real valued and non-negative. We analyze the formulated objective function and convert this problem statement to a Quadratic Programming (QP) formulation [11] that can be solved with existing well-known solvers. However, when the profiling resolution is high, as generally required by real-world applications, such a problem becomes intractable to general QP-solvers. To further speed up the problem solving, we propose a matrix transformation technique to simplify the constraints and reduce the number of constraints from two to one – only non-negativity constraint. We convert the problem to a Non-negative QP problem and solve it much more efficiently using iterative updates [21]. We show that, using the optimization techniques proposed in this paper, the solution of the problem is tractable, and thus applicable to large-scale time series profiling.

We design two scoring functions to give an aging score and a confidence score to analyze the extracted aging component of the time series. Based on such scores, our aging profiling engine reports the result of decomposition with a ranking of the aging severity and the corresponding confidence level of the extraction, which can assist the domain experts to further diagnose the system.

We demonstrate our ideas on both synthetic and real data, showing that our method allows us to accurately divorce the trend and the shape of rapidly arriving time series. We further demonstrate the generality of our ideas by applying them beyond classic machine prognostics to problems in identifying the influence of news events on currency exchange rates. We fully implement our aging profiling system and deploy it into several physical systems, such as a chemical plant and a nuclear power plant in Japan, which greatly helps detect the aging phenomenon and diagnose the corresponding components.

To summarize, in this paper we make the following three contributions:

- We formulate an objective function for extracting trend and fluctuation terms and build a model to transit the aging profiling requirements into mathematical formulation;
- We demonstrate that the problem is a convex problem, convert it to a QP formulation, and provide a fast optimization technique to solve the problem with Non-negative QP formulation;
- We fully develop the system and deploy it into several real-world complex systems.

The rest of the paper is organized as follows. In Section 2 we provide our detailed scheme and problem formulation. Section 3 gives optimization techniques to efficiently solve our problem. Section 4 presents the conducted experiments. The related work is presented in Section 5. We conclude this paper in Section 6.

2. THE AGING PROFILING ALGORITHM

In this section, we describe our approach for aging profiling in time series data. First, we present the formal definition of the problem. Then, we form the objective function and formulate it to a Quadratic Programming Problem, a subclass of the convex problems whose optimal solution can be obtained with existing solvers. After that, we present the scoring functions to rank the aging severity of the input time series and the confidence level of out system.

2.1 Problem Statement

In physical and other complex systems, the monitored signals (time series) generally are a mixture of aging phenomena, system operational signals, and noises. Our goal is to extract and profile the aging components/phenomena/signals out of the given time series. The aging extraction problem can be defined as follows: given an input time series of length T, $\mathbf{s} \in \mathbf{R}^{T\times 1}$, we want to decompose it into the following terms:

$$\mathbf{s} = \mathbf{x}_a + \mathbf{x}_f \tag{1}$$

where $\mathbf{x}_a$ is the aging term and $\mathbf{x}_f$ is the fluctuation term. Illustration of the desired decomposition is presented in Figure 2.

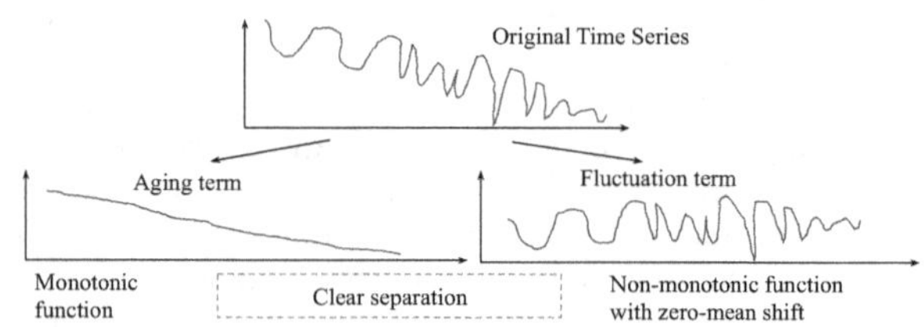

Figure 2: The desired decomposition of a time series to extract the aging trend: the clear separation of the two components – the aging trend and the fluctuation term.

We require the trend component to be monotonic – either non-increasing or non-decreasing [2], and the fluctuation term to be flat, i.e., stationary, to make sure it does not interfere with the aging trend. Having this problem statement, we formulate our problem into an objective function optimization in the following section.

2.2 Quadratic Programming Formulation

To ensure that the trend $\mathbf{x}_a$ is monotonic, we can simply write the constraint of the objective function as

$$\mathbf{x}_a(t) \leq (or \geq) \mathbf{x}_a(t+1). \tag{2}$$

To make the fluctuation term stationary and do not have the mean change over the time, we segment the time series, and ensure the mean value difference of each segment to be as small as possible. More specifically, given a time series, we partition it into K segments, each having mean value m_k, $k = 1, 2, ..., K$. Then, we minimize the difference between mean values of each pair of the segments to ensure flatness of the fluctuation term over time as:

$$\min \sum_{i,j=1}^{K} (m_i - m_j)^2 \mathbf{W}_{ij} \tag{3}$$

[2]For other aging behaviors, such as frequency or variance change, they can always be transformed to value change and modeled as monotonic signals.

Here $\mathbf{W}$ is a weight matrix, each entry $\mathbf{W}_{ij}$ of which specifies the weight we want to assign in order to minimize the mean difference between the segment pair m_i and m_j. If $\mathbf{W}$ is set to be all 1's, then all the segments have equal weight. In practice, to ensure the long-term mean change being minimized, we can increase weights when the distance of the segment pair increases (e.g., linear growth of the weight based on the distance between segments m_i and m_j). In this way, the farther the two segments are apart from each other, the more weight is given to minimize their mean difference.

We formulate the objective function of the optimization problem as minimizing the reconstruction error $\|\mathbf{s}-\mathbf{x}_a-\mathbf{x}_f\|^2$ and ensuring flatness of the fluctuation term over time (Equation (3)), which is subject to the following constraints: (1) monotonicity constraint and (2) non-negativity constraint. The monotonicity constraint can be represented using Equation (2). The non-negativity constraint means that the extracted aging trend and fluctuation term must have only non-negative values. It assumes that the original time series has only non-negative values as well, but if it is not the case it can be easily shifted up by summing up the original values with the absolute value of the minimum (negative) value of the time series. Combining this with Equations (2) and (3), the whole objective function can be written the following way:

$$\begin{aligned} \min \quad & \|\mathbf{s}-\mathbf{x}_a-\mathbf{x}_f\|^2 + \sum_{i,j=1}^{K} (m_i - m_j)^2 \mathbf{W}_{ij} \\ s.t. \quad & \mathbf{x}_a(t) \le (or \ge) \mathbf{x}_a(t+1),\ \forall_{t=1,2,\ldots,T-1} \\ & \mathbf{x}_a \ge 0, \mathbf{x}_f \ge 0 \end{aligned} \tag{4}$$

However, Equation (4) cannot be solved in the form presented above. We now transform it to a Quadratic Programming formulation whose optimal solution can be obtained. We begin with rewriting Equation (3), the flatness objective. For each of the segments m_i, we define an indicator vector $\mathbf{e}_i$ as follows:

$$\mathbf{e}_i = [\underbrace{0,0,\ldots,0}_{1st\ seg},\ \underbrace{0,0,\ldots,0}_{2nd\ seg},\ \ldots, \underbrace{\frac{1}{l},\frac{1}{l},\ldots,\frac{1}{l}}_{ith\ seg}, \underbrace{0,0,\ldots,0}_{Kth\ seg}\ ]^\top, \tag{5}$$

where l is the length of the segment. We let

$$\mathbf{E} = [\mathbf{e}_1,\ \mathbf{e}_2, \ldots, \mathbf{e}_K]^\top,$$

and then such flatness objective (Equation (3)) can be written as

$$\min \mathbf{x}_f^\top \left(\mathbf{E}^\top \mathbf{L} \mathbf{E}\right) \mathbf{x}_f \tag{6}$$

where $\mathbf{L} = \mathbf{D} - \mathbf{W}$ and $\mathbf{D} = diag(\mathbf{W} \cdot \mathbf{1})$.

After that, in Equation (4), we replace the original form of the flatness objective with its new form in Equation (6) and obtain the following formulation:

$$\begin{aligned} \min \quad & \|\mathbf{s}-\mathbf{x}_a-\mathbf{x}_f\|^2 + \lambda \cdot \mathbf{x}_f^\top \left(\mathbf{E}^\top \mathbf{L} \mathbf{E}\right) \mathbf{x}_f \\ s.t. \quad & \mathbf{x}_a(t) \le \mathbf{x}_a(t+1),\ \forall_{t=1,2,\ldots,T-1} \\ & \mathbf{x}_a \ge 0, \mathbf{x}_f \ge 0. \end{aligned} \tag{7}$$

Then, we rewrite Equation (2), the monotonicity constraint. We define $\mathbf{x} = [\mathbf{x}_a^\top, \mathbf{x}_f^\top]^\top$, $\mathbf{E}_2 = [\mathbf{I},\ \mathbf{I}]$, $\mathbf{E}_1 = [\mathbf{0},\ \mathbf{I}]$, where $\mathbf{I}$ is a $T \times T$ identity matrix. We define matrices $\mathbf{B}$ and $\mathbf{C}$ as follows:

$$\mathbf{B} = \begin{bmatrix} 1 & -1 & & & \\ & 1 & -1 & & \\ & & & \ddots & \\ & & & 1 & -1 \end{bmatrix}, \mathbf{C} = [\mathbf{B},\ \mathbf{0}_{T-1 \times T-1}]$$

Under such a definition, the monotonicity constraint can be written as

$$\mathbf{C}\mathbf{x} \ge 0, \tag{8}$$

and the non-negative constraints can be written as

$$\mathbf{x} \ge 0. \tag{9}$$

We further rewrite the objective function in Equation (7) and obtain its form as follows:

$$\begin{aligned} \min \quad & \mathbf{x}^\top \left(\mathbf{E}_2^\top \mathbf{E}_2 + \lambda \mathbf{E}_1^\top \mathbf{E}^\top \mathbf{L} \mathbf{E} \mathbf{E}_1\right) \mathbf{x} - 2(\mathbf{E}_2^\top \mathbf{s})^\top \mathbf{x} \\ s.t. \quad & \mathbf{C}\mathbf{x} \ge 0 \\ & \mathbf{x} \ge 0 \end{aligned} \tag{10}$$

Now, the Equation (10) has a form of a Quadratic Programming optimization problem. Later in Section 3 we propose an efficient optimization method to solve this problem.

2.3 Scores of Aging Severity and Confidence

We decompose a given time series into the aging part (trend) and the fluctuation part. During the decomposition, the reconstruction error is introduced, and thus, the confidence of such decomposition must depend on the value of the error. We use scores to assess the severity of the aging as well as the confidence our tool provides. Essentially, the aging score can be described by the slope of the aging trend, while the confidence score depends on the closeness of the slope of the extracted aging trend to the slope of the original time series. We tune two sigmoid functions to quantify the two scores. For the aging score, we use the slope of the extracted aging trend as the input of the sigmoid function, that gives a value from 0 (no aging expressed) to 1 (severe aging). For confidence score, we use the difference ratio between the slope of the original time series and the slope of the extracted aging trend, i.e., $(ori.\_slope - ext.\_slope)/ori.\_slope$, as the input. The higher the ratio is, the lower the confidence score will be. The two scoring functions can be flexibly tuned according to different application requirements. For example, for five-year monitoring of a physical system, we can pre-tune aging score to give 0 for zero-slope aging trend, while giving 1 when the slope is greater than 0.015, as shown in Figure 3(a). The confidence score function can be tuned so that it scores 1 when the ratio is 0, while it scores 0 when the ratio is close to 1, as shown in Figure 3(b).

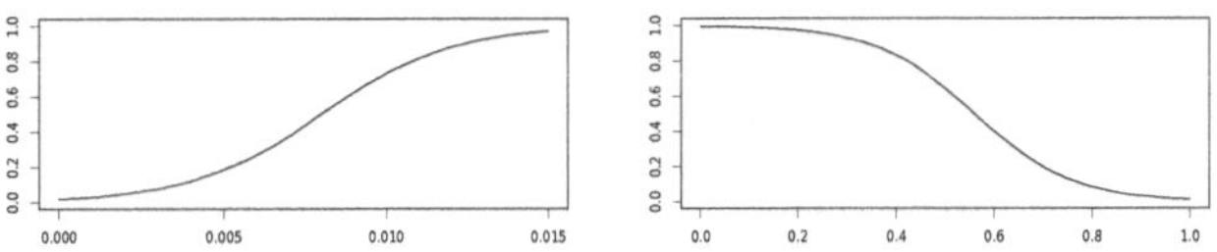

(a) Aging score (b) Confidence score

Figure 3: Aging score and confidence score sigmoid functions

To summarize, the design of the aging profiling system is illustrated in Figure 4.

3. SOLVING PROBLEM (10) EFFICIENTLY

We formulate the underlying aging profiling problem to a QP problem. However, the general QP-solvers are used for a wide range of purposes and are considerably slow, especially for large time series (e.g., more than 1000 data points). Essentially, finding a solution for a time series of 1000 data points is equivalent to

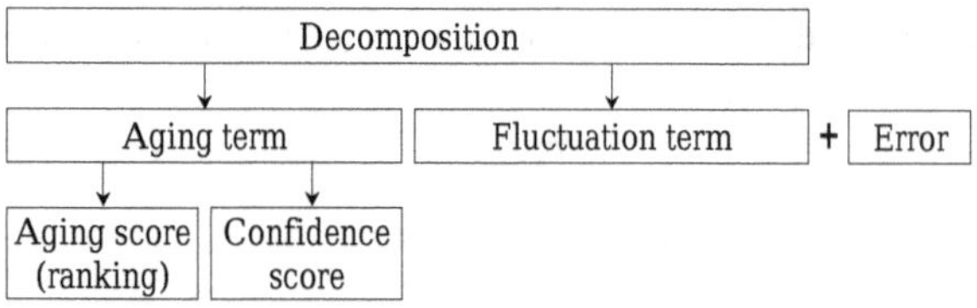

Figure 4: The system overview. A time series is decomposed into the aging and fluctuation terms. Based on the aging term we obtain the aging score (ranking) and the confidence score for it.

solving a system of equations with 1000 variables, which is very computationally costly, and thus, is not tractable.

In this section, we aim to reduce the computational cost and provide a tractable solution for reasonably long time series. Our idea is to further rewrite the QP formulation in Equation (10) to eliminate the monotonicity constraint and only keep the non-negativity constraint to make the problem much easier to solve.

3.1 Non-negative Formulation

We observe that *monotonicity constraint expresses the fact that the difference between two neighboring elements is non-negative* [3]. Based on the observation, we introduce a transition variable $\bar{\mathbf{x}}_a$, and change the problem statement to the following way: instead of using $\mathbf{x}_a$ as a part of the variables, we can use the following surrogate $\bar{\mathbf{x}}_a$ as the variable, which satisfies the equality

$$\begin{aligned} &\mathbf{x}_a(1) = \bar{\mathbf{x}}_a(1) \\ &\mathbf{x}_a(2) = \bar{\mathbf{x}}_a(1) + \bar{\mathbf{x}}_a(2) \\ &\dots \\ &\mathbf{x}_a(k) = \bar{\mathbf{x}}_a(1) + \bar{\mathbf{x}}_a(2) + \dots + \bar{\mathbf{x}}_a(k). \end{aligned}$$

In other words, the first element in $\bar{\mathbf{x}}_a$ is equal to the first element of $\mathbf{x}_a$, and the remaining elements in $\bar{\mathbf{x}}_a$ represent the difference between two neighboring elements of $\mathbf{x}_a$.

The relationship between x_a and $\bar{x}_a$ can be written in the following way:

$$\mathbf{x}_a = \Delta \bar{\mathbf{x}}_a \tag{11}$$

where $\Delta = \Delta^-$ if the trend is nonincreasing, while $\Delta = \Delta^+$ if the trend is nondecreasing

$$\Delta^- = \begin{bmatrix} 1 & & & & \\ 1 & 1 & & & \\ 1 & 1 & 1 & & \\ \dots & & & & \\ 1 & 1 & 1 & \dots & 1 \end{bmatrix} \tag{12}$$

$$\Delta^+ = \begin{bmatrix} 1 & & & & \\ 1 & -1 & & & \\ 1 & -1 & -1 & & \\ \dots & & & & \\ 1 & -1 & -1 & \dots & -1 \end{bmatrix} \tag{13}$$

An example of a trend x_a and its difference values $\bar{x}_a$ is illustrated in Figure 5.

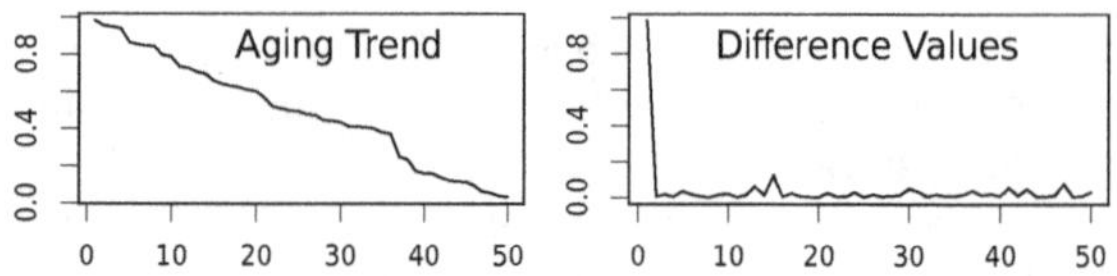

Figure 5: Aging trend x_a and its difference values $\bar{x}_a$

We let $\bar{\mathbf{x}} = [\bar{\mathbf{x}}_a^\top \ \mathbf{x}_f^\top]^\top$. By using this transform, we can merge the monotonicity constraint $\mathbf{C}\mathbf{x} \geq 0$ in Equation (8) and non-negative constraint $\mathbf{x} \geq 0$ in Equation (9) to just one constraint:

$$\bar{\mathbf{x}} \geq 0. \tag{14}$$

We let $\bar{\mathbf{E}}_2 = [\Delta \ \mathbf{I}]$. The original QP problem in Equation (10) can be written in the following form with the only one constraint:

$$\begin{aligned} \min \quad & \bar{\mathbf{x}}^\top \left(\bar{\mathbf{E}}_2^\top \bar{\mathbf{E}}_2 + \lambda \mathbf{E}_1^\top \mathbf{E}^\top \mathbf{L} \mathbf{E} \mathbf{E}_1 \right) \bar{\mathbf{x}} - 2(\bar{\mathbf{E}}_2^\top \mathbf{s})^\top \bar{\mathbf{x}} \\ s.t. \quad & \bar{\mathbf{x}} \geq 0 \end{aligned} \tag{15}$$

We further define

$$\begin{aligned} \mathbf{Q} &= \left(\bar{\mathbf{E}}_2^\top \bar{\mathbf{E}}_2 + \lambda \mathbf{E}_1^\top \mathbf{E}^\top \mathbf{L} \mathbf{E} \mathbf{E}_1 \right) \\ \mathbf{c} &= \bar{\mathbf{E}}_2^\top \mathbf{s}, \end{aligned} \tag{16}$$

then the problem can be written as a simple *non-negative* QP problem:

$$\begin{aligned} \min \quad & \bar{\mathbf{x}}^\top \mathbf{Q} \bar{\mathbf{x}} - 2\mathbf{c}^\top \bar{\mathbf{x}} \\ s.t. \quad & \bar{\mathbf{x}} \geq 0 \end{aligned} \tag{17}$$

After solving Equation (17), the obtained aging trend $\mathbf{x}_a$ can be recovered with $\bar{\mathbf{x}}_a$ as it is shown in E. q. (11). The next section shows that indeed such a non-negative QP problem can be solved much more efficiently than a general QP problem.

3.2 Avoiding General QP-solver

The advantage of using the non-negative QP formulation is that it makes the structure simpler, since non-negativity constraints are much easier to handle than linear inequality constraints. Typically they lead to closed-form iterations that can be computed very efficiently. For example, the multiplicative update studied in [21] can be used to obtain the solution. Let $\mathbf{Q}^+$ and $\mathbf{Q}^-$ be defined as

$$\mathbf{Q}_{ij}^+ = \begin{cases} \mathbf{Q}_{ij}, & \mathbf{Q}_{ij} \geq 0 \\ 0, & otherwise \end{cases} \quad \mathbf{Q}_{ij}^- = \begin{cases} |\mathbf{Q}_{ij}|, & \mathbf{Q}_{ij} < 0 \\ 0, & otherwise \end{cases} \tag{18}$$

Then, the update can be written as

$$\bar{\mathbf{x}}_{i+1} \leftarrow \bar{\mathbf{x}}_i \left[\frac{-\mathbf{c}_i + \sqrt{\mathbf{c}_i^2 + 4(\mathbf{Q}^+\bar{\mathbf{x}})_i(\mathbf{Q}^-\bar{\mathbf{x}})_i}}{(2\mathbf{Q}^+\bar{\mathbf{x}})_i} \right], \tag{19}$$

where $\mathbf{x}_i$ is the vector $\mathbf{x}$ obtained after i iterations.

A good initialization can improve convergence. One can use $|(\mathbf{Q}^{-1}\mathbf{c})|$ suggested in [21] as the starting solution. To compute $\mathbf{Q}^{-1}$, one can use low-rank approximation techniques which is linear complexity.

This avoids using general QP-solvers that are typically designed for general purpose formulations with both linear and nonlinear constraints, and thus, makes the solving process much more efficient. A comprehensive comparison between solving efficiency using general QP-solvers and the proposed method is later shown in Section 4.1.3.

3.3 Formal Algorithm Definition

The formal presentation of our algorithm for time series decomposition can be found in Algorithm 1.

[3] In case of nonincreasing sequence every preceding element is greater or equal to the following, and in case of nondecreasing sequence, vice versa, each following element is greater or equal to the preceding one.

Algorithm 1 The aging profiling algorithm

Notations:

s: intput time series of lenght T
x_a: aging trend (array of length T)
x_f: fluctuation term (array of length T)
$\bar{x}_a$: difference values of aging trend x_a
x: concatenation of aging trend and fluctuation term, $x = x_a + x_f$
$\bar{x}$: concatenation of $\bar{x}_a$ and $\mathbf{x}_f$
Δ: transform matrix from $\bar{x}_a$ to x_a
ϵ: small value used as an algorithm stopping criterion

1: Check the slope of s
2: **if** slope is negative **then**
3: $\quad \Delta = \Delta^-$
4: **else**
5: $\quad \Delta = \Delta^+$
6: **end if**
7: Compute Q, c
8: $\bar{x}_a = |(\mathbf{Q}^{-1}\mathbf{c})|$
9: $f_{old} = 0, difference =$ Infinity
10: **while** $difference > \epsilon$ **do**
11: $\quad$ Compute $\bar{x}$ by (19)
12: $\quad f_{new} = \bar{x}^\top \mathbf{Q}\bar{x} - 2\mathbf{c}^\top \bar{x}$
13: $\quad difference = |(f_{old} - f_{new}|)$
14: $\quad f_{old} = f_{new}$
15: **end while**
16: $\bar{x}_a = \bar{x}[1 : T], x_f = \bar{x}[(T+1) : 2T]$
17: $x_a = \Delta\bar{x}_a$
18: **return** x_a, x_f

In the algorithm, the first step is to check the slope of the input time series and decide if Δ^+ or Δ^- should be used. Then, the next step in line 7 is to compute $\mathbf{Q}$ and $\mathbf{c}$ according to the Equation (16). In line 8, we assign initial value of $\bar{x}_a$ to be $|(\mathbf{Q}^{-1}\mathbf{c})|$. After that, we execute the iterative updates until the difference between objective function values becomes less than ϵ, e.g., 0.001. In line 16, we split the $\bar{x}_a$ into its two components - the aging trend difference values and the fluctuation term, and recover the aging trend by multiplying Δ by $\bar{x}_a$ in line 17. The algorithm returns the extracted aging trend and the fluctuation term.

4. EXPERIMENTS

We have fully developed our aging profiling system and deployed it into several physical systems, such as chemical plants and nuclear power plants in Japan. In this section, we first evaluate the aging profiling accuracy, computational complexity, and the intuition of the parameter tunning of the scheme by applying it to synthetic datasets with different properties. Then, we demonstrate the good profiling and diagnosis performance by applying it to the real-world data collected from one of the systems it is deployed in. Finally, we further demonstrate the generality of our scheme by applying it beyond classic machine prognostics to problems in identifying the influence of news events on currency exchange rates and stock prices.

4.1 Synthetic Data with Different Properties

We generate synthetic data that covers time series with different properties in trend, seasonality, and noise. For trend component, we generate three types of aging trends: no trend, linear trend, and nonlinear trend. Figure 6 summarizes trends that are used in the synthetic data generation. Essentially, to generate a linear trend, we applied the slope in the whole length of time series. For a nonlinear trend, its first half is a flat line (no trend), and the non-linear curve starts in the middle of the time series. We intentionally generate the nonlinear trend this way to test whether our scheme can detect the starting point of the aging. Moreover, all the generated trends are very small (can be seen from their slope values) in order to ensure that the aging trend is not obvious or visible by eyes.

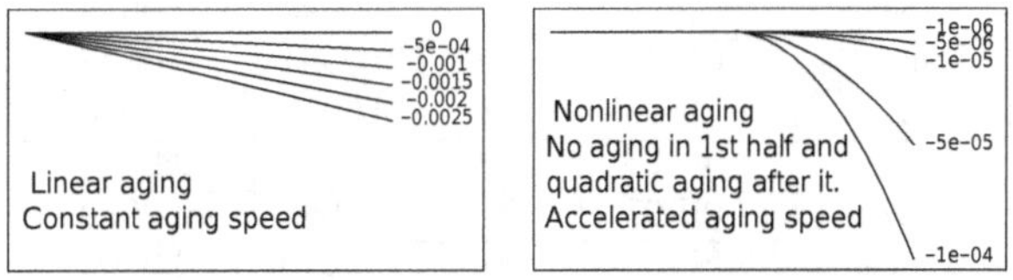

Figure 6: Trends used in synthetic data generation

The fluctuation terms are built according to the following scheme:

- sine wave: $\sin(a\pi t), a = [1/16, 1/8, 1/4, 1/2, 1]$,
- noise: $b * rand(0, 1), b = [1/4, 1/2, 1, 2, 4]$,
- combination of noise and sine wave: $\sin(a\pi t) + b * rand(0, 1)$.

Combinations of possible trends and fluctuations give nine families of time series, presented in Figure 7. In total, we generated 385 synthetic time series, each containing 5000 points. The next section explains parameter setup for the experiments and their justification.

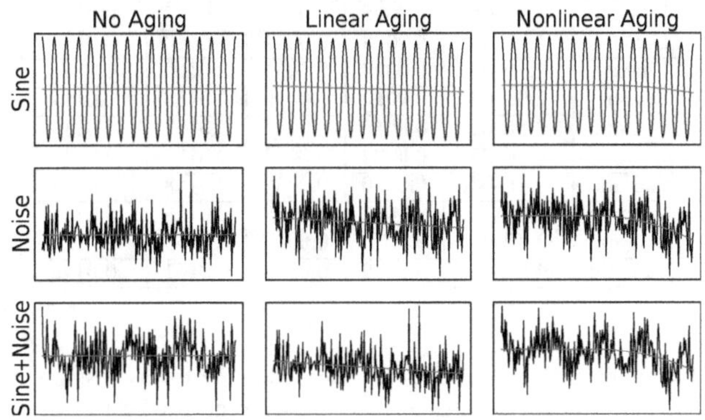

Figure 7: Synthetic Data Examples

4.1.1 *Robustness to Different Parameter Values*

As a careful reader could notice, our model has several parameters, namely λ, K, and $\mathbf{W}$. λ balances the minimization weights between reconstruction error and flatness of the fluctuation term. K control the resolution of the flatness of the fluctuation term. $\mathbf{W}$ adjusts the weights in the fluctuation term and can be set to linearly increase depending on the distance between the pairwised segments (e.g., $1, 2, 3, \ldots$).

To evaluate the effect of different parameter values, we list a range of values for each parameter and try all the combinations to all the synthetic time series. In Table 1, for each time series, we record the best and worst profiling accuracies that are the minimum and the maximum values of the distances between the estimated and actual trends normalized by the time series length. As we can observe, the difference between the reconstruction results is not significant. Thus, our system is not sensitive to the values of the parameters. In practice, based on our extensive experiments, we suggest to set $\lambda = 0.1$ and $K = 5$.

Table 1: Best and Worst Reconstruction Results

Family	Slope (C)	Best	Worst	Difference
Linear	0	0	0.0094	0.0094
Linear	5.0E-04	0.0005	0.0081	0.0077
Linear	1.0E-03	0.0007	0.0076	0.0068
Linear	1.5E-03	0.0009	0.0077	0.0068
Linear	2.0E-03	0.0011	0.0093	0.0082
Linear	2.5E-03	0.0014	0.0116	0.0102
Quadratic	4.8E-05	0.0002	0.0095	0.0092
Quadratic	2.4E-04	0.0009	0.0093	0.0083
Quadratic	4.8E-04	0.0015	0.0090	0.0075
Quadratic	2.4E-03	0.0040	0.0135	0.0095
Quadratic	4.8E-03	0.0048	0.0183	0.0135

4.1.2 *Aging Profiling Accuracy*

To evaluate the decomposition quality, we compute the Euclidean distances between the extracted and actual trends. We compare our method with Singular Spectrum Analysis (SSA), Moving Average (MA), and Wavelet. Table 2 presents the results of the comparison.

Table 2: Euclidean distance between actual and extracted trends

Family	Slope (C)	Ours	SSA	SMA	Wavelets
Linear	0	**0.0004**	0.0036	0.0158	0.0112
Linear	5.0E-04	**0.0005**	0.0034	0.0157	0.0112
Linear	1.0E-03	**0.0008**	0.0034	0.0160	0.0115
Linear	1.5E-03	**0.0010**	0.0034	0.0160	0.0116
Linear	2.0E-03	**0.0012**	0.0036	0.0158	0.0117
Linear	2.5E-03	**0.0015**	0.0035	0.0157	0.0119
Quadratic	4.8E-05	**0.0004**	0.0033	0.0157	0.0111
Quadratic	2.4E-04	**0.0010**	0.0035	0.0158	0.0111
Quadratic	4.8E-04	**0.0017**	0.0037	0.0158	0.0111
Quadratic	2.4E-03	0.0070	**0.0055**	0.0159	0.0124
Quadratic	4.8E-03	0.0099	**0.0068**	0.0161	0.0146

From this table we can see that our method performs best among the majority of the compared schemes with the smallest error between the extracted trend and the ground-truth trend. Especially when the slope is small and the aging phenomenon is tiny, our method performs about 10 times better SSA and 30 betters than SMA and Wavelets. Moreover, although in two cases our method gets higher error than SSA, the aging trend extracted by our scheme is monotonic and satisfies the nature of the aging behavior, while SSA, SMA or Wavelets does not have such advantage as they have no monotonic constraint in extracting the trend. A comparison of extracted slopes with our method and actual trends is shown in Figure 8, which demonstrates how the extracted trends correspond to the actual trends.

In addition, Figure 9 demonstrates an example of outputs from our tool. From this figure, we can see our profiling scheme accurately detects and profiles the aging shape of the input time series.

4.1.3 *Computational Complexity*

Any algorithm that utilizes iterative updates opens a question on how fast it converges upon a solution. This answer depends on the choice of ϵ that satisfies the accuracy of the results and gives a reasonable speed of computation. For all our experiments we fixed ϵ value to be 0.001, and set the initial values for the solution to be $|(\mathbf{Q}^{-1}\mathbf{c})|$. Figure 10 shows the average converge speed for time

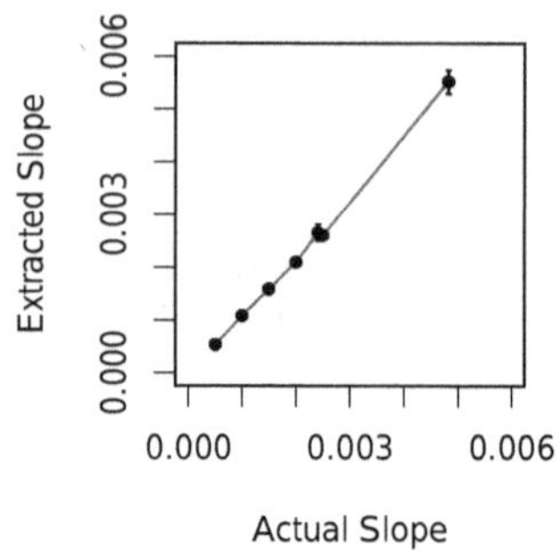

Figure 8: The slopes of the actual and extracted trends

series with 300 data points. From this figure, we can see that the algorithm converges within about 60 iterations.

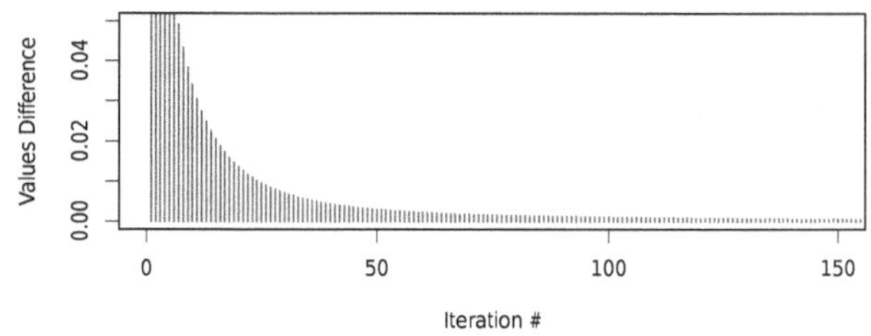

Figure 10: Convergence speed for time series length of 300 data points

To compare the efficiency of the original formulation solved with QP-solvers and the optimized non-negative QP formulation with iterative updates (named *No QP-solver*), we run load tests for different length of time series and plot the execution time for time series with length from 500 to 5000 in Figure 11. The running time is based on a PC with CPU i7-920 3.0GHz with 8 cores [4]. From this figure, it is obvious to see that our approach outperforms general QP-solver based technique, and its speed is about 30 times faster than general QP-solvers. Please note that, since our goal is to capture long-term degradations in physical systems, we do not need a very fine granularity and usually 2000 points is enough for 5-years of monitoring data.

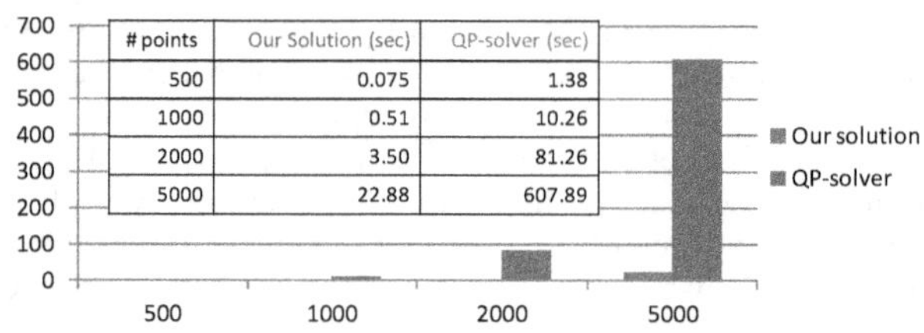

Figure 11: Solution time for QP-solver and without QP-solver

4.1.4 *Aging Trend Ranking and Confidence Score*

We use sigmoid functions to define the aging and confidence scores shown in Figure 3(a) and (b). The aging scores of time series with different slopes of trends are shown in Figure 12. From this figure, we can see that the aging score computed based on the

[4]The algorithm can be easily parallelized along multiple time series, as there is no need of memory sharing between different time series.

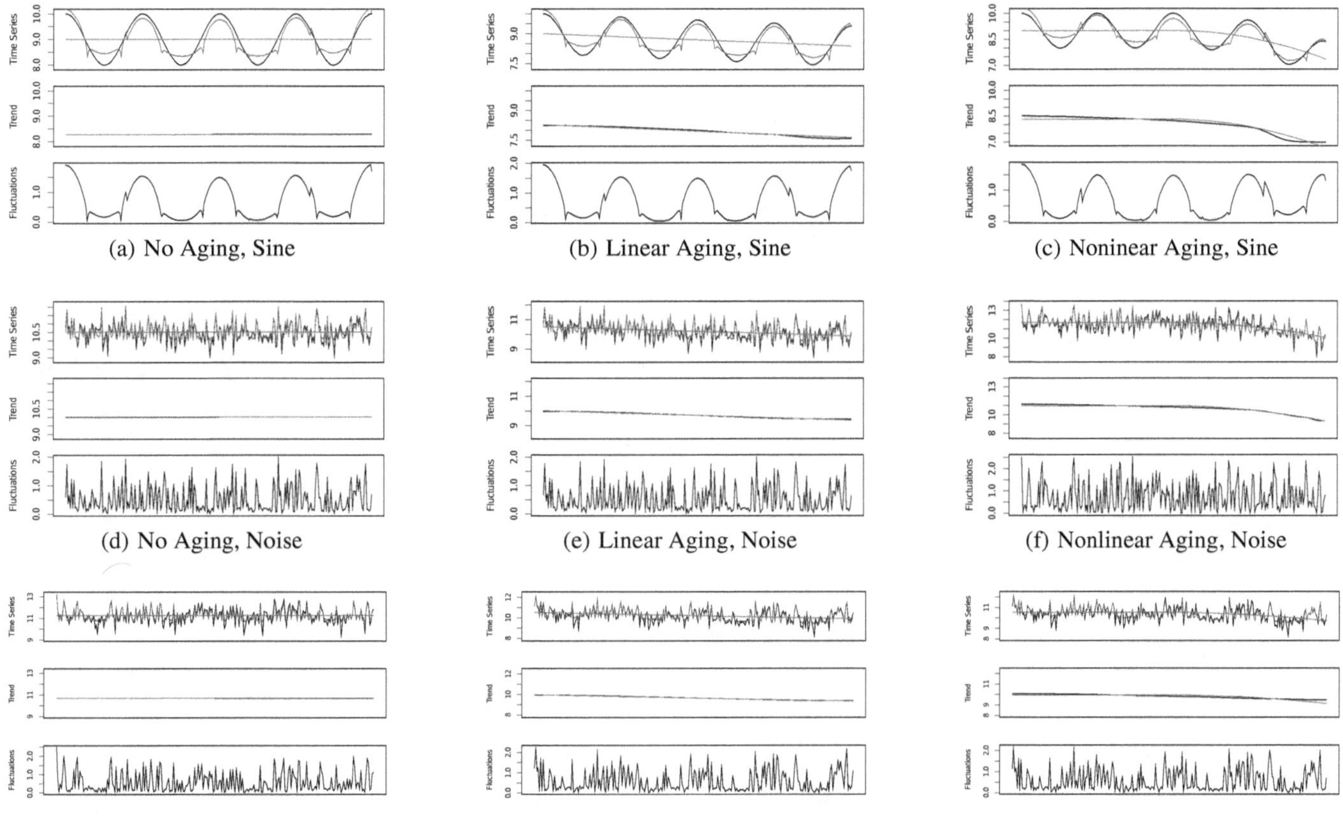

(a) No Aging, Sine (b) Linear Aging, Sine (c) Noninear Aging, Sine

(d) No Aging, Noise (e) Linear Aging, Noise (f) Nonlinear Aging, Noise

(g) No Aging, Sine+Noise (h) Linear Aging, Sine+Noise (i) Nonlinear Aging, Sine+Noise

Figure 9: The examples of graphical output of our tool. The left column is a set of time series without aging; the center column is a set of time series with linear trends; the right column is for the time series with quadratic trends starting from the middle. In each plot, the first row shows the original time series (in black), its reconstructed curve, and its actual trend (in red). The second row shows the actual (in red) and extracted (in black). The bottom row shows the reconstruction error of the whole time series.

extracted aging trend highly correlates with the slope value of the actual aging trend.

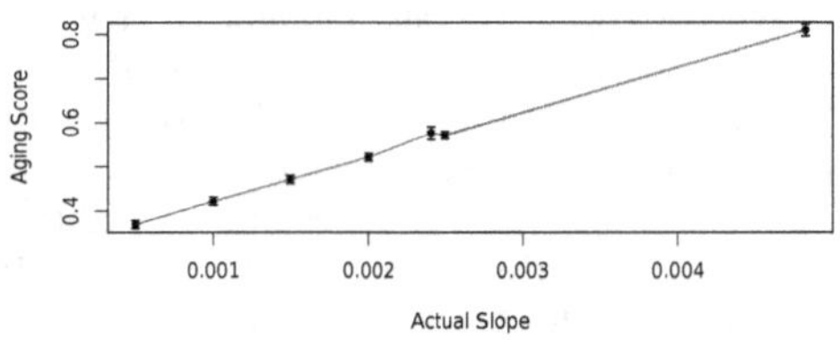

Figure 12: Aging Score Values

Similarly, the confidence scores presented in Figure 13 show the closeness of the slopes of the original time series and the extracted trend. From this figure we can see that when the slope of the actual trend is greater than 0.001, our scheme can have a confidence score higher than 0.99.

4.2 Case Studies with Real-World Data

In this section, we evaluate the profiling performance of our method using real-world datasets collected from different markets: (1) multi-variant time series collected from sensors in a manufacture system of a chemical plant, (2) time series from current exchange rate between Russian Rubles and Ukrainian Hryvnias, and (3) time series from the US stock price of Apple Inc.

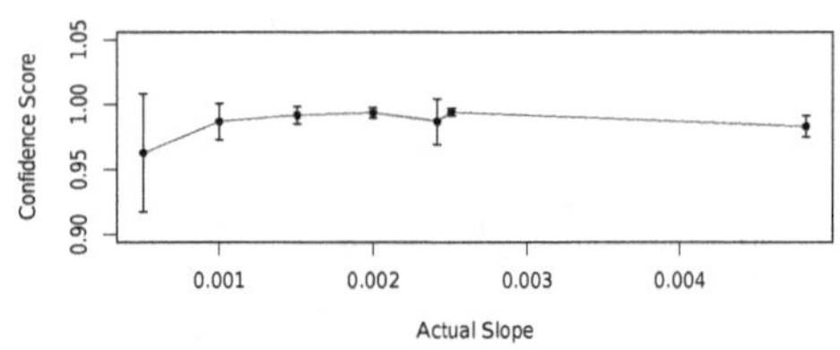

Figure 13: Confidence Score Values

4.2.1 Degradation in Manufacturing Systems

We deploy our profiling system to 8 chemical plants, and collect time series that contain more than 2000 sensors. The sensors are distributed to monitor pressures, temperatures, water flows and sound frequencies of the system. The data has more than 20,000 points, which includes 6 years of monitoring of the system to make sure it captures aging behavior, if any. Since we only focus on long-term behavior, we sample 800 points for each time series and index them using integers from 1 to 800.

After deployment, we run our system on all the collected time series and list the top 9 sensors, showing both strong aging behavior and confidence score, in Table 3. We also plot their original time series and extracted aging curves in Figure 14. From this figure, we can see that the system parts start to have aging behavior at around

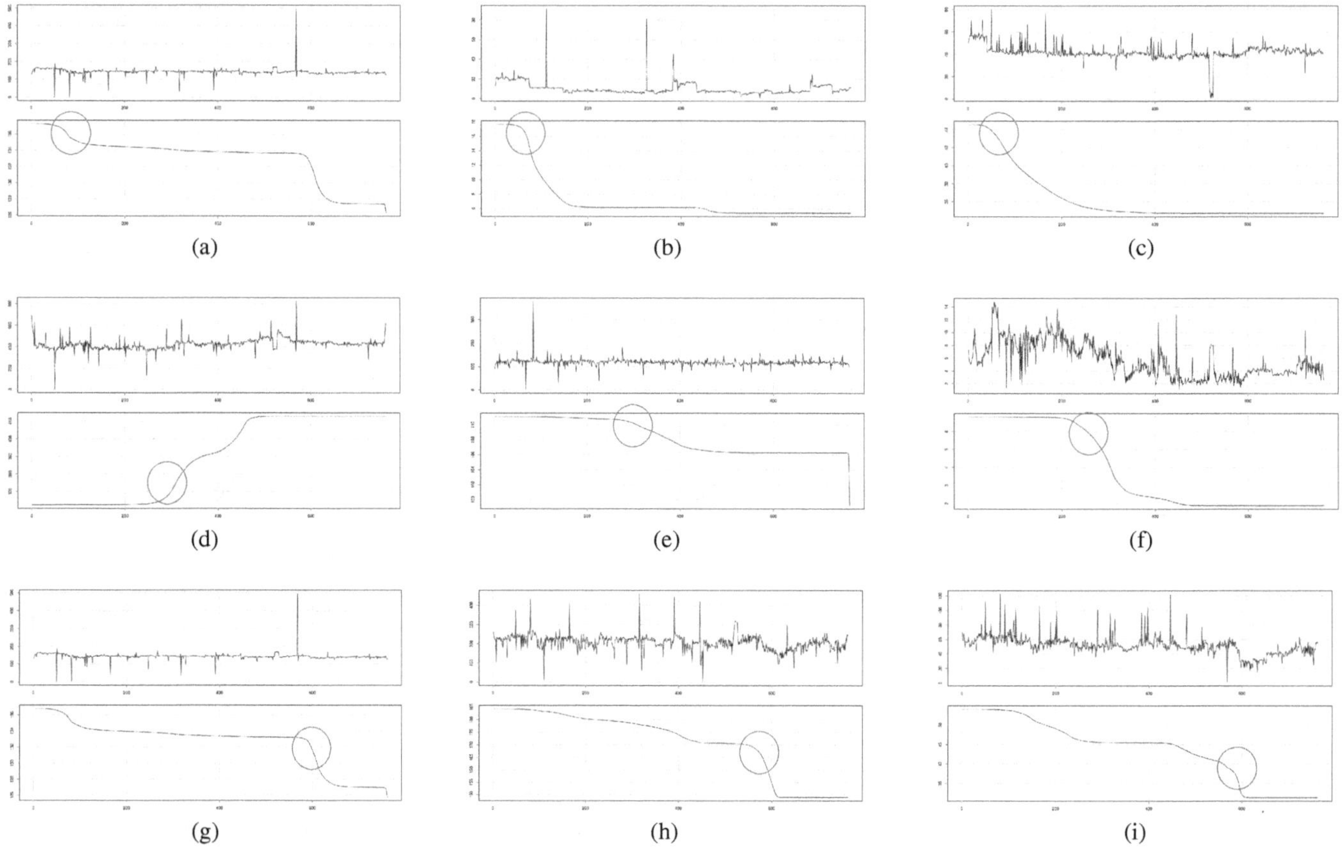

Figure 14: Aging profiling of a chemical plant. (a)-(c), (d)-(f), (g)-(i) show aging behavior start at around 80_{th}, $290th$, 580_{th} points, respectively. Each figure contains the original time series (upper) and the extracted aging curve (lower).

Table 3: Top 9 sensors with highest aging scores

Sensor Name	Aging score	Confidence score
a	0.99	0.99
b	0.99	0.94
c	0.99	0.92
d	1.00	0.96
e	0.99	0.98
f	0.99	0.99
g	0.99	0.99
h	1	0.99
i	0.99	0.99

80_{th}, 290_{th}, 580_{th} points. This is confirmed with domain experts that operate the systems. At around these three points, the pipes of the system that the 9 sensors are monitoring start to have buildups, and the quality of product starts to decrease. This shows our aging profiling engine can accurately profile the aging behavior of the system and observe aging phenomena that cannot be captured by eyes or simple statics.

4.2.2 Currency Exchange Rates

Although this paper mostly considers aging trends expressed in physical systems, our techniques are not limited to this domain and can be applied in many scenarios with long term monotonic changes.

Particularly, we demonstrate how our approach may be used to detect certain events that had influence on the currency exchange rates. Note that we are not claiming applicability of our techniques to the general currency exchange rates monitoring, however, in case of special circumstances our techniques are helpful to detect certain events. Recent events in Ukraine [3] led to a significant decrease of Russian and Ukrainian currencies - Russian Rubles and Ukrainian Hryvnias. Significant changes in the trend appeared in the beginning of 2014 when an unrest started in Ukraine. Figure 15 demonstrates exchange rates between the United States Dollar and aforementioned currencies. Our maximum slope change happens at exactly the same time as that event happens. We obtained currency exchange data from [1] and retrieved the relevant time frame.

4.2.3 Stock Prices

Another application our approach can find is the profiling of long term stock prices. This tracking may be useful to observe changes in a given company success and also to monitor if anything particular happens at some certain time. There are many web resources that provide the information on stock and share prices. For this case study we used data obtained from Yahoo Finance [2] web site and investigated the changes in stock prices of Apple Inc. Figure 16 demonstrates stock prices of Apple Inc. during last 5 years. We can see that the fastest slope change of the trend happened in November 2011 - about the time where iPhone 4S was released, which is detected by our scheme.

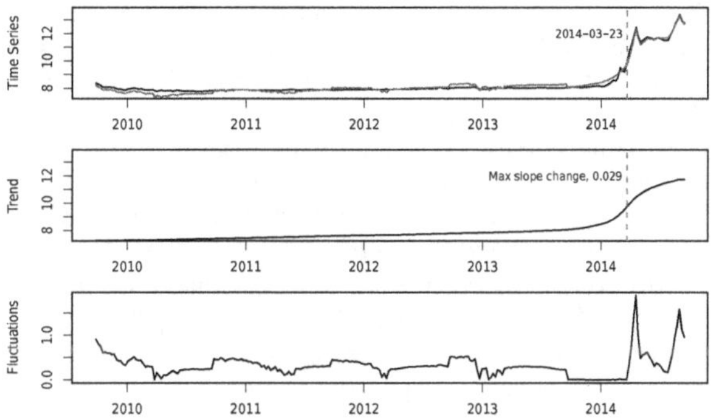

(a) Ukrainian Hryvnia

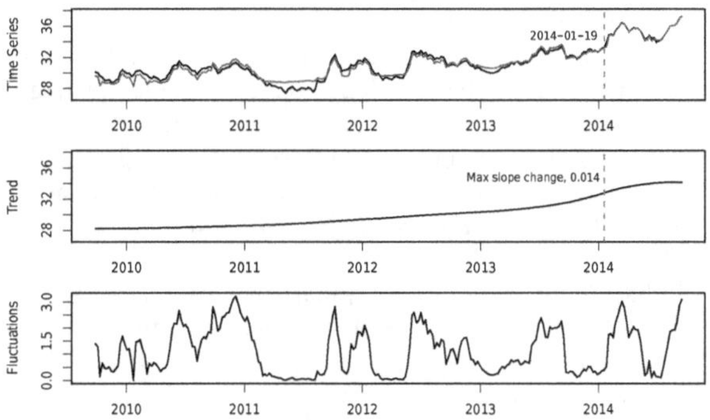

(b) Russian Ruble

Figure 15: Currency Exchange Rates with USD

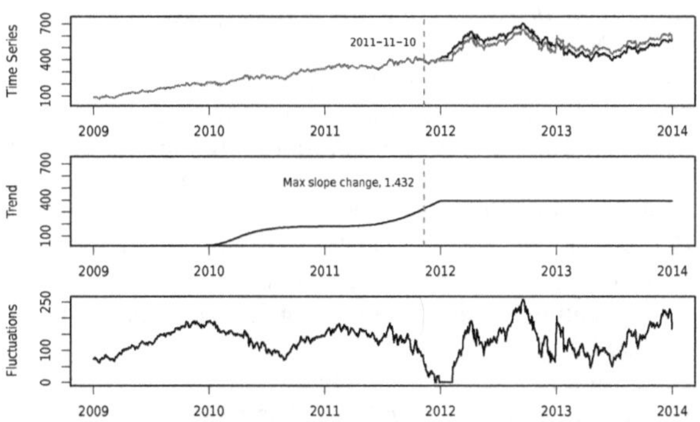

Figure 16: Apple Stock Prices

5. RELATED WORK

In this section, we discuss related work that has been done in two directions: in time series decomposition and in prediction and analysis of technical system failures.

5.1 Time Series Decomposition Techniques

The time series research, especially trend extraction, has attracted significant efforts in recent decades. In this section, we highlight some relevant techniques and refer an interested reader to a recent survey [4] and therein.

One of the simplest approaches to determine if a time series has a trend is a null hypothesis testing for its presence/absence (H_0 = no change/shift between two time segments) [16]. The other approach is smoothing or filtering [14, 20]. It can be done using different techniques, including wavelets [12] and the centered moving average that allows getting mean values of a time series in each certain period of time, thus, detecting any systematic change. Another intuitive possibility for trend extraction is fitting a linear or higher level model to the time series data [6]. The common way of fitting a model is a method of least squares [7].

AutoRegressive Integrated Moving Average (ARIMA) is a model-based technique that allows extracting trend and seasonal components from the time series [5]. This approach can be used for both modeling and forecasting, and it is especially useful when there is a certain seasonal component like a yearly change in temperatures or water levels. The drawback of this model is that, in case of absence of domain information about the time series, the user must provide the parameters that may be very subjective, and thus, leading to inadequate results. Therefore, model-based approaches, as it follows from the name, are model sensitive and can be used when there is available information about the model.

One of the parameter free decomposition techniques for time series is Singular Spectrum Analysis (SSA) [10]. SSA allows extraction of alleged trend, seasonal and noise components from time series. The name comes from singular decomposition of a matrix into its spectrum of eigenvalues. The time series can be reconstructed by regrouping different important components. The SSA method is well-known and is used in a broad spectrum of domains [10]. However, it has some drawback that we are aiming to mitigate. We define the trend for aging behavior as a *monotonic* change, whereas, SSA decomposition can return the trend component of arbitrary shape that is not suitable for the problem at hand. In other words, it cannot give clear interpretation of the obtained components, and the trend and high-frequency components are not ensured to be separated.

Another method of time series decomposition is Independent Component Analysis (ICA) [8]. This method allows decomposing of a time series into several additive subparts assuming they are statistically independent and have non-Gaussian distribution. There are two possibilities of how to define the independence of the extracted components. One of them is minimization of mutual information and the other is maximization of negentropy (a measure of distance to normality). This method has the drawback similar to SSA for our problem application: it does not provide necessary condition of trend monotonicity. Moreover, we assume that the signal may change drastically over time, thus, cannot compose the proper ICA set using pieces of different time segments.

5.2 Aging and Degradation Analysis

The problem of aging and performance degradation has attracted significant attention in the research community because this aspect is very important for virtually all technical systems [17, 19]. Here, we discuss only some recent and relevant works.

Djurdjanovic *et al.* [9] proposed a comprehensive framework for analysis and monitoring of the systems based on the time series analysis. They were concerned more with methodology of the collecting and analysis of the data than with the methods of decomposing time series and extracting necessary features. In contrast, in this work we are solving a problem of aging behavior detection that can be expressed as a monotonic change in some properties (particularly, mean value of the time series over time).

The aging behavior also can be expressed in software systems [13]. It was observed that long running software tends to be more failure prone over time, and thus, generally, it is suggested to restart the software systems. However, the definition of a time point when the software must be restarted requires some investigation and research. Authors of [13] demonstrated that the periodical restart may not work well because the aging mostly depends on the system workload. Thus, it is critical to analyze the aging behavior over time to determine when the system must be restarted.

A similar claim that the scheduled maintenance does not always help avoid the failures and degradation in performance is also presented in [22], in relation to the hardware systems. The work is concerned with log-based predictive analysis in order to monitor the conditions of the operating equipments and provide timely maintenance. The authors built a model in order to classify events and collections of the events as "positive" or "negative" with respect to the failure occurrence. After this, they used this model to predict if the system had come or is coming to a degrading state. The method deals with extracted features and not the shape of the time series.

For data centers failure monitoring, recently a probabilistic method that takes into account network topology and ping data was proposed [15]. This approach is domain specific and initially builds a network model. In our work, as we mentioned above, we are aiming to provide a general approach that could deal with any domain and decompose the time series without usage of a model.

Incident diagnosis from a different prospective was proposed in [18]. Authors presented an approach that allows finding correlation between actual events and time series in order to diagnose incidents. Their approach is able to match events with certain subsequences of time series in order to give a real explanation of the time series shape. However, this work is mostly concerned with finding patterns in time series, whereas our method is dealing with the whole length of time series in order to detect monotonic degradation of an underlying system.

Acknowledgments

We gratefully acknowledge funding from NSF IIS-1161997 II.

6. CONCLUSIONS

In this paper, we profile the long-term degradation in time series by decomposing them into aging and fluctuation components. We formulate the underlying decomposition problem to an optimization problem, and convert it to the Quadratic Programming (QP) formulation whose optimal solution can be obtained. To efficiently solve the formulated problem, we further transform it to a Non-negative QP problem and propose a method to obtain its solution with iterative updates, which is much faster than using general QP-solvers. We implement and deploy our approach to various physical systems, and evaluate our algorithm with both synthetic and real data. We demonstrate that the proposed approach can approximate the true aging trend with fine resolution (with slope coefficient as small as 10^{-6}), which greatly helps diagnose the corresponding system components.

7. REFERENCES

[1] Currency Exchange Rates. `http://www.oanda.com/currency/historical-rates/`.

[2] Yahoo Finance. `http://finance.yahoo.com/`.

[3] 2014 Ukrainian revolution. `http://en.wikipedia.org/wiki/2014_Ukrainian_revolution`, 2014.

[4] Theodore Alexandrov, Silvia Bianconcini, Estela Bee Dagum, Peter Maass, and Tucker S McElroy. A review of some modern approaches to the problem of trend extraction. *Statistics*, page 3, 2008.

[5] George EP Box, Gwilym M Jenkins, and Gregory C Reinsel. Linear nonstationary models. *Time Series Analysis, Fourth Edition*, pages 93–136, 1976.

[6] K Hung Chan, Jack C Hayya, and J Keith Ord. A note on trend removal methods: the case of polynomial regression versus variate differencing. *Econometrica: Journal of the Econometric Society*, pages 737–744, 1977.

[7] Abraham Charnes, EL Frome, and Po-Lung Yu. The equivalence of generalized least squares and maximum likelihood estimates in the exponential family. *Journal of the American Statistical Association*, 71(353):169–171, 1976.

[8] Pierre Comon. Independent component analysis, a new concept? *Signal processing*, 36(3):287–314, 1994.

[9] Dragan Djurdjanovic, Jay Lee, and Jun Ni. Watchdog agent – an infotronics-based prognostics approach for product performance degradation assessment and prediction. *Advanced Engineering Informatics*, 17(3):109–125, 2003.

[10] James B Elsner and Anastasios A Tsonis. Singular spectrum analysis. *NY: Wiley*, 1996.

[11] Donald Goldfarb and Ashok Idnani. A numerically stable dual method for solving strictly convex quadratic programs. *Mathematical programming*, 27(1):1–33, 1983.

[12] Alexander Grossmann and Jean Morlet. Decomposition of hardy functions into square integrable wavelets of constant shape. *SIAM journal on mathematical analysis*, 15(4):723–736, 1984.

[13] Michael Grottke, Lei Li, Kalyanaraman Vaidyanathan, and Kishor S Trivedi. Analysis of software aging in a web server. *Reliability, IEEE Transactions on*, 55(3):411–420, 2006.

[14] Robert Henderson. Note on graduation by adjusted average. *Transactions of the Actuarial Society of America*, 17:43–48, 1916.

[15] Herodotos Herodotou, Bolin Ding, Shobana Balakrishnan, Geoff Outhred, and Percy Fitter. Scalable near real-time failure localization of data center networks. In *Proceedings of the 20th ACM SIGKDD international conference on Knowledge discovery and data mining*, pages 1689–1698. ACM, 2014.

[16] Denis Kwiatkowski, Peter CB Phillips, Peter Schmidt, and Yongcheol Shin. Testing the null hypothesis of stationarity against the alternative of a unit root: How sure are we that economic time series have a unit root? *Journal of econometrics*, 54(1):159–178, 1992.

[17] C Joseph Lu, William Q Meeker, and Luis A Escobar. A comparison of degradation and failure-time analysis methods for estimating a time-to-failure distribution. *Statistica Sinica*, 6(3):531–546, 1996.

[18] Chen Luo, Jian-Guang Lou, Qingwei Lin, Qiang Fu, Rui Ding, Dongmei Zhang, and Zhe Wang. Correlating events with time series for incident diagnosis. In *Proceedings of the 20th ACM SIGKDD international conference on Knowledge discovery and data mining*, pages 1583–1592. ACM, 2014.

[19] Felix Salfner, Maren Lenk, and Miroslaw Malek. A survey of online failure prediction methods. *ACM Computing Surveys (CSUR)*, 42(3):10, 2010.

[20] Abraham Savitzky and Marcel JE Golay. Smoothing and differentiation of data by simplified least squares procedures. *Analytical chemistry*, 36(8):1627–1639, 1964.

[21] Fei Sha, Lawrence K Saul, and Daniel D Lee. Multiplicative updates for nonnegative quadratic programming in support vector machines. In *Advances in neural information processing systems*, pages 1041–1048, 2002.

[22] Ruben Sipos, Dmitriy Fradkin, Fabian Moerchen, and Zhuang Wang. Log-based predictive maintenance. In *Proceedings of the 20th ACM SIGKDD international conference on knowledge discovery and data mining*, pages 1867–1876. ACM, 2014.

Interpreting Advertiser Intent in Sponsored Search

Bhanu C. Vattikonda, Santhosh Kodipaka*, Hongyan Zhou*,
Vacha Dave*, Saikat Guha†, and Alex C. Snoeren
University of California, San Diego
*Microsoft, Redmond, Washington,
†Microsoft Research, Bangalore, India

ABSTRACT

Search engines derive revenue by displaying sponsored results along with organic results in response to user queries. In general, search engines run a per-query, on-line auction amongst interested advertisers to select sponsored results to display. In doing so, they must carefully balance the revenue derived from sponsored results against potential degradation in user experience due to less-relevant results. Hence, major search engines attempt to analyze the relevance of potential sponsored results to the user's query using supervised learning algorithms. Past work has employed a bag-of-words approach using features extracted from both the query and potential sponsored result to train the ranker.

We show that using features that capture the advertiser's intent can significantly improve the performance of relevance ranking. In particular, we consider the ad keyword the advertiser submits as part of the auction process as a direct expression of intent. We leverage the search engine itself to interpret the ad keyword by submitting the ad keyword as an independent query and incorporating the results as features when determining the relevance of the advertiser's sponsored result to the user's original query. We achieve 43.2% improvement in precision-recall AUC over the best previously published baseline and 2.7% improvement in the production system of a large search engine.

Categories and Subject Descriptors

H.3.3 [**Information Search and Retrieval**]: Relevance feedback; I.5.4 [**Applications**]: Text processing

General Terms

Algorithms, Supervised learning, Experimentation

Keywords

Sponsored search; ad relevance; online advertising

KDD '15, August 11–14, 2015, Sydney, NSW, Australia

ACM 978-1-4503-3664-2/15/08$15.00
DOI: http://dx.doi.org/10.1145/2783258.2788566.

1. INTRODUCTION

Search engines deliver two types of results in response to a user query: organic and sponsored search results. Organic results are identified from around the web based on their relevance to the query. Sponsored results—i.e., advertisements—on the other hand, are selected from submissions made by advertisers interested in attracting the user. These additional results are chosen based on a combination of relevance of the ad to the query and the expected revenue the search engine will derive from displaying the ad [22].

When providing advertisements to the search engine, an advertiser specifies for which user queries, e.g., "shirts", "polos", "jersey", etc. it would like to show each ad. These words, referred to as ad keywords, are the basic mechanism through which advertisers can target their ads. Often ads are shown to users when the ad keyword matches the query—resulting in what is known as an exact match. But, it is challenging for an advertiser to enumerate all the queries for which they would like to advertise. Hence, many search engines provide an option of matching the ad keywords with a broader range of relevant user queries, e.g., alternative spellings, synonyms, etc., potentially resulting in what we term a broad match. Typically, when an ad is chosen and displayed to the user, the advertiser only pays the search engine if the user clicks on the ad, incentivizing the search engine to keep even broad matches relevant to the user's query.

Yet sponsored results are generally perceived to degrade user experience on search engines [23]. An aggressive pursuit to maximize revenue from each search impression could therefore hurt the user experience—and, in the long run, the search engine's popularity and profitability. Thus, in some cases, it may be desirable to show few or even no ads if they do not meet some minimum relevance threshold [9]. For example, if the query is "weather", an ad for "cold weather jackets" might occasionally generate revenue, it is not likely if the user is simply seeking the current temperature—and especially if the temperature is currently warm. In this case not showing the ad would be the prudent choice. Another canonical example where sponsored results are frequently ill advised is a so-called navigational query like "Macys", where ads other than those from the retail chain Macy's could elicit a negative user response.

Hence, one of the key challenges for search engines is to quantify the relevance of ads to a user's query. Our partner search engine considers an ad relevant to the query if the following four components are aligned [5]: *i*) query; i.e., what the user is looking for, *ii*) ad creative; what is being promised to the user, *iii*) ad landing page; the web page actually delivered to the user if the ad is clicked, and *iv*) ad keyword; which indicates the type of traffic the advertiser seeks to attract.

Interpreting a user's query is hard mainly because it is very short: 2.5-words long on average [33]. Over time search engines have in-

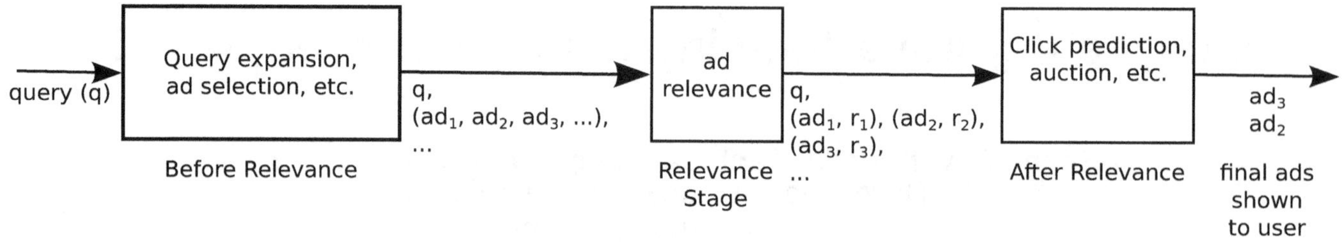

Figure 1: Abstract pipeline for selecting search ads. In this paper we focus on the relevance stage.

corporated large amounts of associated metadata such as the user's search pattern within a session [6] and click-through data [21], as well as employed various other query augmentation techniques [7, 25, 26, 28, 37] in attempts to accurately interpret user queries.

Similarly, various techniques have been used to understand the creative and landing page to improve ad selection [14]. Such approaches are effective because the creative is often a good reflection of what is being advertised and the landing page offers a rich set of features. However, the creative itself offers very little information (a typical creative is a few tens of characters, see Figure 2) and landing pages are known to be noisy [14]. These approaches are even more challenging to apply in the case of broad match since the query and advertisement may not be textually similar. For example, an ad bidding on "sneakers" might be quite relevant for the query "shoes" but there may be little textual similarity between them.

In this work, we complement prior approaches by interpreting the ad keyword as well. Unlike the creative and landing page, both of which are to be displayed to the end user, the ad keyword represents an unconstrained opportunity for the advertiser to be direct about their desires without concern of offending or dissuading the user. Hence, we argue that it represents a very strong signal that should be mined to the fullest extent. We build on the fact that—as discussed above—search engines are good at interpreting a query. In particular, we determine advertiser intent by submitting the ad keyword to the search engine and use organic results that the search engine returns to provide additional context with which to interpret the ad keyword. Specifically, given an advertisement to be scored for relevance against a particular query—we denote this as a (query, ad) pair in the remainder of the paper—-we send the ad keyword associated with the ad to the search engine and use the top organic results returned to get additional information about the ad keyword. We then use features extracted from both these results and the organic results for query itself to measure the similarity between the advertiser's and user's intents.

We consider introducing two complimentary sets of features: 54 features that can be generated using just the query issued by the user and another 21 that require information capturing user intent, which we get by using organic results generated for the user query. We evaluate the benefits of adding each of these feature sets by comparing the performance of the resulting ranker to the best previously published baseline [29] and the production system at a large search engine. We achieve a 43.2% improvement in precision-recall area under the curve (AUC) over the baseline and 2.7% improvement over the highly engineered production system.

2. BACKGROUND

In the sponsored search model advertisers provide an ad comprising of *i*) the creative, a short textual ad that is shown to the user, see Figure 2, *ii*) ad keyword, user queries the advertiser would like to target, *iii*) match type, how the search engine is allowed to match

Figure 2: Creative has a title, description and display URL.

the ad keyword to user queries, *iv*) destination URL, the web page to which the user should be redirected upon clicking the ad, and *v*) bid value, the cost that advertiser is willing to pay for a click.

2.1 Ads pipeline

When the user makes a query, the search engine has to decide which ads (if any) should be displayed along with the organic results. While the production pipeline has many stages, in this paper we abstract it into three stages as shown in Figure 1 with our primary contribution being to the relevance stage. Before the relevance stage, the query (q) is expanded to create expanded queries which are related to the original query depending on the match type indicated by the advertiser [10]. Each expanded query is then used to select candidate ads ($\text{ad}_1, \text{ad}_2, \ldots$) to be further evaluated. The goal at this stage is to identify all ads that are potentially related to the set of expanded queries.

In the relevance stage each ad picked thus far in the pipeline is evaluated for relevance to the original query. While the previous stages choose ads that are related to the expanded queries, this stage performs deeper inspection of the relevance of each ad (ad_1, ad_2, $\ldots$) to query. The output of this stage is a score for each ad (ad_1, $\text{ad}_2, \ldots$) on how relevant it is to query (i.e., generate $r_1, r_2, \ldots$). For example, an ad for "nike shirts" would be scored higher for the query "shirts" than would an ad for "jackets". To do so, the relevance stage trains a learning ranker [35] using a labeled training set of (query, ad) pairs and features computed for each (query, ad) pair. The trained ranker is then deployed to measure the relevance of an ad to the query. In this work we study features that can be used to improve the performance of the ranker.

After the relevance stage, the ads pipeline involves estimating the probability (click-through rate) that an ad would be clicked and conducting the second-price auction. The relevance of ad to query is a factor when estimating the click probability [1]. The probability estimate allows the search engine to calculate the expected revenue to be derived by showing a particular ad. These predictions are made using information about the ad from previous impressions of the ad [31]. For rare or new ads where such information is not available, information from semantically similar ads is used [16]. In both the cases, the relevance of ad to query can be used as one of the features to predict the click-through-rates. So, while click-through-rate estimates do filter out ads, accurate relevance scores complement these efforts. Subsequently, most search engines rank ads by the product of click probability and advertiser bid value in an attempt to maximize expected revenue for the second-price auction [10, 20].

In this paper we evaluate the gains that can be achieved using two different sets of features. The first set of features use just the query that has been submitted by the user and advertiser intent captured using the ad keyword associated with the ad. The second set of features capture the similarity between user and advertiser intent by further considering the organic results the search engine generates in response to the user query, leading to additional improvements in relevance ranking.

2.2 Performance metrics

Search engines use metrics like share of queries with ads, ads per query, clicks per search impression, and clicks per ad [20] to evaluate the performance of the overall ads pipeline. A range of factors including user click probability and bid values play a role in the final decision to show an ad. Because we are focused exclusively on changes to the relevance stage—and, more to the point, do not have access to the various additional inputs used in latter stages of the pipeline—we instead measure the performance of the ranker and its feature set in terms of precision-recall values on a hold out validation set.

3. RELATED WORK

As discussed above, a lot of work has been done to interpret and expand the user query [10, 21]. User click behavior [15, 21, 32] and electronic dictionaries [34] have been used to enhance the query and expand it. The expanded queries are then used to retrieve relevant ads from the corpus of ads. These techniques rely on the fact that relevance of words to a particular query is correlated to the user click behavior or the semantic similarity between words.

Query expansion techniques have also used categorization of the query and topical information to achieve improvements [11, 24, 32] in ranking documents. These approaches use human-judged datasets to classify web pages into hierarchical categories. These categories are then used to find ads that may not be textually similar but belong to same category as the query. Bennett et al. [8] use documents classified under the Open Directory Project (ODP) [2] to train a classifier and show that using such techniques can improve ranking of relevant documents. Broder et al. [10] use search engine results to create an augmented query and then select ads using the augmented query.

Blind relevance feedback techniques have also been used to expand the query and retrieve relevant documents. These techniques [10, 18, 26, 36], like ours, assume that the top results returned by search engine are relevant to the query issued. Such cross-corpus learning techniques have been used to transfer knowledge from one task to another [17, 30].

The most relevant and related work is by Hillard et al. [20], addressing the problem of relevance using human-judged datasets. The authors use translation models to predict click-through rates from click logs. The predicted click-through rates are then used along with baseline features, to train a classifier to predict ad relevance. They also highlight challenges in predicting relevance of an ad to a query given the relatively short nature of queries and creatives.

Other work [20, 35] has explored the use of different supervised learning algorithms to improve the accuracy and performance of the relevance rankers. In this paper, we work with the ranker used by a large search engine and explore the advantages of using new features. As He et al. [19] point out, identifying the right features for the ranker is important. The focus of our work, then, is to illustrate the advantages of using features extracted from the ad keyword associated with an ad.

4. MOTIVATION

The goal of the relevance stage is to compute the relevance of the ad to query in each (query, ad) pair that has been selected by the previous stages. While the stages prior to the relevance stage focus on casting a wide net to rapidly identify as many related ads as possible, the relevance stage uses a broader range of features to measure the relevance of ad to the query.

4.1 Capturing advertiser intent

The learning ranker used to compute a score measuring the relevance of ad to query in a (query, ad) pair is trained using a set of features computed for each pair. For the task of feature computation, the key fields available in the ad are: *i*) creative (Figure 2), *ii*) ad keyword and *iii*) landing page. Features that are currently used by the production system include text similarity features between query and these fields along with other external sources of information — including the click-through rate of the ad from past impressions [5].

We expand the ad keyword and use the resulting features to measure relevance of ad to query. Our key insight here is that the ad keyword captures advertiser intent more accurately than the creative itself. The ad keyword is the only field in the entire ads pipeline through which an advertiser can explicitly express the type of traffic that they would like to attract. Other attributes of the ad, like the creative and landing page, are seen by the user which could prevent the advertiser from freely expressing their intent. Hillard et al. [20] observe that, for example, an ad for "limo rentals" would be quite relevant to a user query for "prom dresses". An advertiser might, thus, list an advertisement for "limo rentals" and bid for the keyword "prom dresses". In the absence of an understanding of the ad keyword, such an ad would be considered completely irrelevant to the user query "prom dresses". If one had a way to identify that that prom dresses and limos are frequently used together, however, better relevance scores could be computed improving the quality of ads delivered.

We choose to solve this problem at the relevance stage because it is expensive to perform a deep evaluation of all possible variations of the query computed by the query expansion algorithms employed in the stages prior to the relevance stage. However, ad keywords associated with the ads provide us with a defined set of keywords on which deeper analysis can be performed.

4.2 Broad match opportunity

The importance of understanding the ad keyword is highlighted in the case of broad match when the query is expanded before being matched against the ad keyword, increasing the likelihood that the user's original intent may not align with the advertiser's. To illustrate this, we compare the performance of a previously published baseline relevance ranker on (query, ad) pairs matched using exact match to those matched using broad match. The performance of the relevance ranker is evaluated using precision/recall values over a hold out validation set. This approach allows for evaluation of the ranker independent of other factors like click probability and bid values which play a significant role in the final decision to show an ad to the user.

Figure 3 plots the precision/recall curve obtained by scoring (query, ad) pairs in the validation set using a relevance ranker trained on baseline features [29] (detailed in Section 5.3). High precision values indicate that a large fraction of the ads being selected are relevant — enhancing the user experience. Whereas, high recall

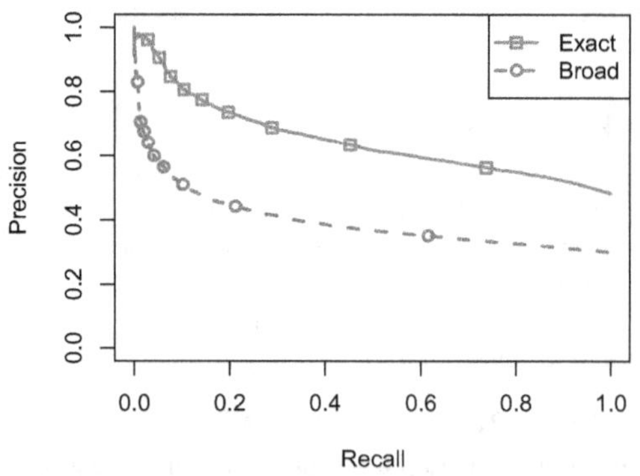

Figure 3: Ads chosen through exact match can be scored more accurately with previously published baseline features than those chosen through broad match.

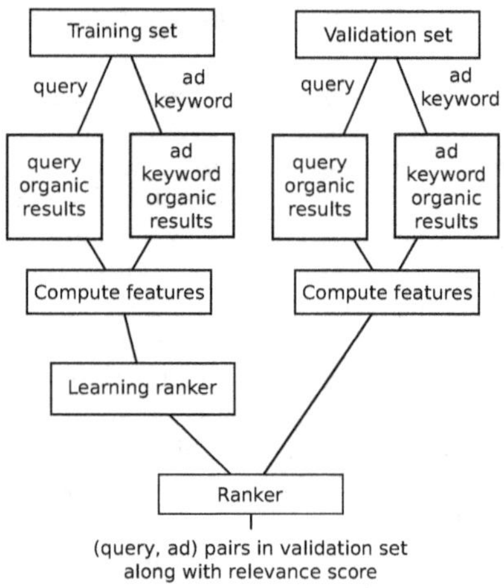

Figure 4: Feature construction and system evaluation overview.

values indicate that a greater number of relevant ads are being selected — improving revenue opportunity for the search engine. Unsurprisingly, the baseline features that measure similarity between only the query and the ad to determine relevance do not work as well in the case of broad match.

5. METHODOLOGY

In this section we present our methodology for using the capabilities of the search engine to create features that represent the advertiser intent. Using the search engine to interpret a query, which is usually short, allows us to leverage years of research. Using the organic web search results corresponding to the ad keyword provides us with detailed information about advertiser intent. We use these features to improve the performance of a learning ranker used to measure the relevance of an ad to a query. For comparison purposes we build upon a baseline ranker using the 19 features described by Hillard et al. [29].

This section starts with a description of the datasets, learning ranker, and baseline features that we use. We then introduce our additional features, starting with features that can be extracted using just the user query along with organic results for the ad keyword. We then explore features of the organic results for the query which act as a proxy for user intent information allowing us to capture the overlap between advertiser and user intent.

5.1 Data overview

The key datasets in our system are the training and validation sets comprising of (query, ad) pairs. Each ad described in Section 2 has an associated ad keyword indicating the type of queries from which the advertiser would like to attract traffic. As shown in Figure 4, in the first phase, we obtain the top 40 organic results associated with the query and the ad keyword in an approach similar to the one taken by Hillard et al. [10].

Each of the 40 organic results returned for a query submitted to the search engine has the following fields associated with it: *i*) title of the web page as shown in the web results, *ii*) snippet, a small piece of text displayed on the results page providing a view into the result page itself, *iii*) description, a small piece of text from the web page which most accurately describes the web page, *iv*) ODP category, the ODP [2] category to which the result belongs, and *v*) URL of the result.

To clean up these fields, we remove stop words [3] and stem the title, snippet, and description of each result using the Porter stemmer [27]. We then concatenate all the titles, snippets, descriptions of results associated with each query to create a bag-of-words representation.

5.2 Ranker

For each (query, ad) pair in the training and validation sets, we compute features as described in the following sections. We train the LambdaMART learning ranker [12] on the features obtained over the training dataset. LambdaMART has been shown to be very effective in solving real-world ranking problems [8, 13]. LambdaMART is known to be robust to features that take a range of values and produces a tree-based model. In our evaluation, the algorithm is trained at a learning rate of 0.12, with 120 leaves and 2,000 trees. The model produced by the ranker can be used to determine a ranked list of the features on which the ranker was trained. We use this attribute of LambdaMART to identify the importance of features we discuss in this paper.

5.3 Baseline features

We use the features described by Hillard et al. [29] as a baseline against which to compare the gains offered by the additional features. Hillard proposes 19 features: query length and 6×3 features obtained by computing the following: *i*) word unigram overlap, *ii*) word bigram overlap, *iii*) character unigram overlap, *iv*) character bigram overlap, *v*) ordered word bigram overlap, and *vi*) cosine similarity between the query and each of the title, description, and display URL of the creative.

Each of the overlap features is the overlap coefficient of the corresponding sets, computed as:

$$\text{overlap}(X, Y) = \frac{|X \cap Y|}{\min(|X|, |Y|)}.$$

For example, the word unigram overlap coefficient between "black shoes" and "shoes at contoso inc" would be 0.5.

5.4 Query features

The first set of features that we introduce rely on using only the information that can be computed based upon the ad and the query in each (query, ad) pair. In the next section we discuss more advanced features that can be computed using organic results for the query which allows us to better measure the similarity between user and advertiser intent.

Feature Type	Details	Count
Creative	ad title ∩ bk. titles	6
	ad text ∩ bk. desc.	6
	ad text ∩ bk. snip.	6
Landing Page	title ∩ bk. titles	6
	snippet ∩ bk. desc.	6
	snippet ∩ bk. snip.	6
Query	query ∩ bk. titles	6
	query ∩ bk. desc.	6
	query ∩ bk. snip.	6
Total		54

Table 1: Query features computed using organic results for the ad keyword.

For each ad, we compute features to determine whether the ad creative and landing page are consistent with the ad keyword the advertiser supplies. Specifically, we compute the same six similarity features as Hillard et al. [29], but between the organic results returned for the ad keyword and aspects of the ad creative and landing page. For the creative, we compare the ad title to the search result titles, and the ad text to both the search result description and snippets. For the landing page, we compare its title to the search result titles, and the snippet to both result descriptions and snippets.

We further compute features that measure the similarity of query to the results of searching for the ad keyword. For this, we compute the same six similarity features, but this time between the query and the titles, snippets and descriptions associated with the ad keyword search results, respectively. These features are easy to implement because organic results for ad keyword can be precomputed, and when the query is received in the online system, feature construction is a matter of computing overlap features. While in each case we use the same overlap and cosine similarity features as in Section 5.3, there is no limitation against using other similarity measures like Jacquard index or edit distance. In total, we add the 54 features shown Table 1. We call these query features.

5.5 Query search features

We also consider features that can be computed if the ads pipeline can interpret user intent in the same way the search engine does to generate organic results for query. We use the organic results generated for query as a proxy to capture user intent in much the same way as we use organic results for the ad keyword to capture advertiser intent. Once we have the organic results for the query, we compute six overlap features for each pair of titles, snippets and descriptions obtained from results of query and ad keyword.

5.5.1 *Category feature*

Each web page in the search index is classified using ODP data [2] into categories by an internal classification engine at indexing time as described by Bennett et al. [8]. Each organic result (which is chosen from the index) is thus classified into one of the 219 categories at the top two levels of the hierarchy. For the query and ad keyword, we obtain the categories to which the corresponding organic results belong. We then compute the cosine similarity between the categories of the two organic results:

$$\text{score} = \frac{\sum_c n_{qc} \times n_{kc}}{\sqrt{\sum_c n_{qc}^2} \times \sqrt{\sum_c n_{kc}^2}},$$

Feature Type	Details	Count
Query Search	query titles ∩ bk. titles	6
	query desc. ∩ bk. desc.	6
	query snip. ∩ bk. snip.	6
Category overlap	query ∩ bk. categories	1
Domain count	domain in query results	1
	domain in bk. results	1
Total		21

Table 2: Query search features constructed using organic results for query and ad keyword.

where, n_{qc} and n_{kc} are the number of times a result belonging to category c is present in organic results for the query and ad keyword respectively.

As has been argued by Broder et al. [10], this feature allows us to identify scenarios when the query and ad keyword might not have a strong overlap but are relevant to each other because they belong to the same category. For example, for the query "shoes", the ad keyword "sneakers" does not result in a text overlap, but is very relevant.

5.5.2 *Domain features*

The last set of features that we introduce captures the presence of the ad domain (e.g., `contoso.com`) in the organic results for query and ad keyword. The ad domain of an ad is determined to be relevant to a query if the ad domain is present in the organic results for the query. Similarly, the the presence of the ad domain in organic results for the ad keyword associated with the ad indicates that the ad domain is relevant to the type of traffic the advertiser wants to attract by bidding on the particular ad keyword. We introduce two features to capture the relevance of ad domain to query and the ad keyword. Specifically, the features are computed as number of times the ad domain is present in organic results for both the query and ad keyword.

In sum, we call these additional $18 + 1 + 2 = 21$ features query search features and summarize them in Table 2. Together with the 54 features computed in Section 5.4 they form a total of 75 features that we consider.

6. EVALUATION

In this section we quantify the improvements in relevance ranking obtained by incorporating advertiser intent. We present the gains in precision and recall over both a published baseline [29] and the production system for a large search engine.

The baseline system [29] is rudimentary and captures only the similarity between query and the ad creative for each (query, ad) pair. However, as far as we are aware this is the best-performing published system in this space. The features that we introduce use much richer information from the organic results to capture advertiser and user intent. As a result, we achieve extraordinary gains over the baseline. Our benefits over the production system—which uses hundreds of features—are less dramatic, but still significant in practice.

6.1 Datasets

The learning ranker that we use is trained using a sample of 1.28 million hand-scored (query, ad) pairs drawn from the ground-truth the production system uses. The scores ranges between one and five with five representing high relevance between the query and the ad. For offline testing of the model, the holdout validation dataset has

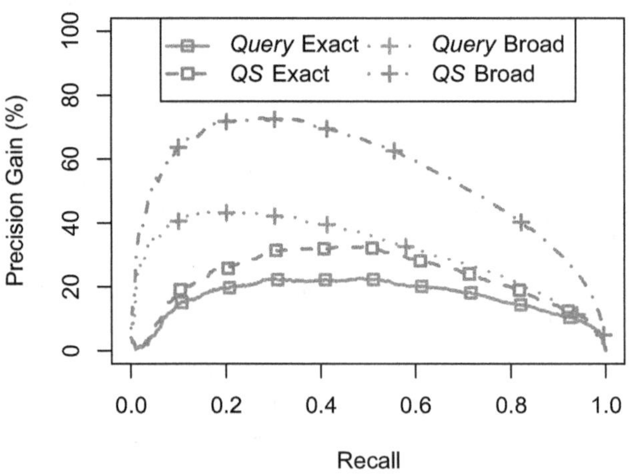

Figure 5: Improvement in precision for different recall values using the new ranker.

		Ground-Truth Scores			
		All	3+	4+	5
Query Features	All	27.5	70.3	60.1	21.6
	Exact	16.6	37.6	35.7	11.5
	Broad	32.2	90.3	82.6	58.8
Query Search Features	All	43.2	103.5	122.7	79.6
	Exact	22.7	50.0	67.9	52.2
	Broad	55.7	165.3	228.6	145.8

Table 3: Relative (%) improvement in precision-recall AUC over baseline for different types of ads.

320,000 similarly sampled (query, ad) pair scores. The training and validation datasets are retrieved from the ad corpus using information retrieval methods used by the selection stage [10]. They contain queries from all search frequency deciles.

We obtain the organic results corresponding to the query and the ad keyword by submitting each of them to the search engine. We also use the ODP [2] categorization of the organic results returned for query and ad keyword.

6.2 Baseline comparison

We start by evaluating the gains that the new features provide over the baseline [29]. For now, we consider an ad to be not relevant to the query if the (query, ad) pair is judged to be a one. We return to consider more stringent cutoffs in Section 6.2.3.

6.2.1 *Query features*

As discussed in Section 5, for each (query, ad) pair in the training and the validation sets, we add 54 new features. Among these, 18 features compute the similarity of query to the title, snippets and descriptions associated with organic results for the ad keyword. Similarity between creative, landing page and ad keyword organic results is captured in another 36 of these features. We compare the performance of a ranker trained with these features to a ranker trained using only the 19 baseline features.

The "Query Exact" and "Query Broad" lines in Figure 5 show the relative improvement in precision at different recall values over the baseline obtained by using the ranker trained on query features over (query, ad) pairs matched through exact and broad match, respectively. The relative change in the area under curve for the precision-recall curves is presented in the All column of Table 3.

The results show that adding information from organic results for the ad keyword provides a large improvement in precision over the baseline. Also, note that the improvement is higher for (query, ad) pairs matched through broad match. Intuitively, the improvement is because information from organic results for the ad keyword increases the possibility of a match between the query and ad when the ad is relevant to the query. In the case of exact match, the baseline features already capture the overlap between the ad and the query because the creative likely contains the ad keyword and hence contains the query.

6.2.2 *Query search features*

In this section, we measure the benefit of adding new features which capture the similarity between user and advertiser intent by using organic results for the query and ad keyword. We introduce a total of 21 features which capture the similarity between user intent and the advertiser intent along with 54 features introduced in the previous section.

As described in Section 5 we use query organic results as a proxy for interpreting the user intent. Note that in an online system generating both organic and sponsored results, the results for query themselves may not be needed, instead techniques used to process the query and identify organic results would be enough to interpret the query.

The organic results of a query give us titles, snippets and the descriptions associated with the query. For each of these fields we compute six features which measure similarity to the corresponding field from organic results for ad keyword. This gives us a total of 6×3 new features. In addition to this, we also add one feature which captures the similarity between the categories of results for the query and ad keyword. Two additional features use organic results to capture how relevant the ad domain itself is to the query and ad keyword.

The "QS Exact" and "QS Broad" lines in Figure 5 show the improvement in precision at different recall values using the model obtained by training the ranker with query search features for exact and broad match types, respectively. These results show that using search results for the ad keyword to interpret advertiser intent provides a large improvement in the accuracy of the relevance ranker over using just the baseline features. Again, the relative change in precision-recall AUC is presented in the All column of Table 3.

6.2.3 *Identifying good ads*

While achieving high overall precision-recall numbers is important to distinguish between relevant and irrelevant ads, a good relevance ranker should be especially adept at identifying high-quality ads accurately. So, techniques which lead to gains in overall precision should not negatively impact the ability of the search engine to identify ads scored three or higher. The ability to identify good ads accurately is a desirable feature for the model used by search engines because it allows search engine to show good ads to the users and not just suppress bad ads. While suppressing bad ads is good for user experience, a ranking model which does not identify good ads would lead to lower revenue.

We measure the ability of the new features to distinguish between ads scored three or higher and ads scored lower than three. We consider ad scored one or two as irrelevant to the corresponding query in the (query, ad) pairs. The relative improvement in precision-recall AUC over the baseline model is shown by the 3+ column in Table 3. We perform a similar analysis for ads scored

		All	3+	4+	5
Query Features	All	0.5	1.0	0.8	0.6
	Exact	0.4	0.6	0.1	0.1
	Broad	0.6	1.8	2.7	1.9
Query Search Features	All	2.7	3.7	5.7	8.9
	Exact	0.7	1.6	2.6	5.4
	Broad	3.9	7.3	12.3	13.2

Table 4: Relative (%) improvement in precision-recall AUC over the production ranker for different types of ads.

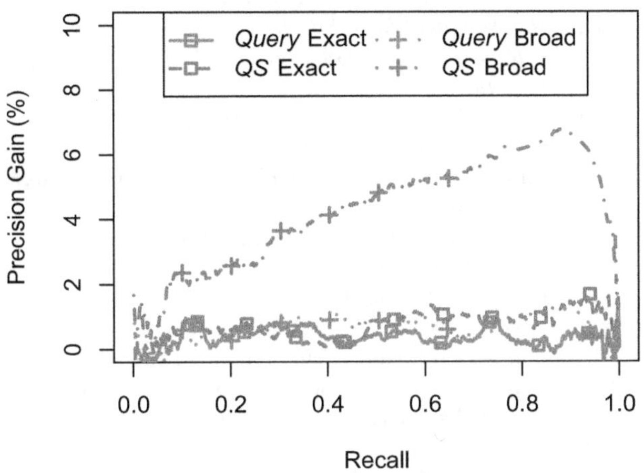

Figure 6: Gains in precision with the introduction of features capturing advertiser intent.

four or higher, and five by considering the remaining ads to be irrelevant respectively.

We see that the understanding of advertiser intent works especially well for identifying high-quality ads. Ads scored four or better and those scored three or better see greater improvement than the overall pool of ads. This behavior is expected because the ad keyword organic results of good ads are more likely to have pattern overlap with the query organic results.

6.3 Production comparison

The results in the previous sections demonstrate that the new features provide significant gains over a published baseline proposed by Hillard et al. [29]. It stands to reason, however, that highly engineered production systems employed by major search engines exhibit better performance and may, in fact, already consider many of the features we suggest. In this section, we consider the gains our new features bring to the production pipeline of a large search engine. We add the above mentioned features to the existing production features and train the production ranker on the combined feature set. The production features capture a variety of attributes about the query and ad, including quality of the ad domain, historical click-through-rates of the ad and landing page attributes [5].

Precision gain over the production system at different recall values with the introduction of query features for exact and broad match are shown using "Query Exact" and "Query Broad" lines in Figure 6. The results show that there is a small improvement in precision-recall curves due to the introduction of query features. The relative change in the precision-recall AUC is presented in the All column of Table 4. The gains are smaller than those over baseline but are nevertheless significant in a production system. As before, the new features perform best for highly-relevant ads in broad searches.

Moreover, we find that the production ranker improves significantly with the addition of query search features. The improvement in precision at different recall values is shown in Figure 6 by the lines labeled "QS Exact" and "QS Broad". The relative improvement in AUC is presented in the All column of Table 4. As before, the new features work even better for high-quality ads.

To capture improvement in the accuracy of the ranker, we measure precision-recall values at max F-score. Table 5 shows the precision and recall values for the production ranker and the ranker trained using query search features at max F-score.

Ranker	Precision	Recall	Max F-Score
Query	-1%	+2.3%	+0.3%
Query Search	+1.7%	+2.9%	+2.2%

Table 5: Gains achieved in precision, recall and max F-Score compared to the production system of a large search engine.

6.4 Feature importance

The value of the features we introduce can also be seen in the importance given to them by the LambdaMART ranker. The tree based model that is produced after training the ranker allows us to determine the ranked list of features. The importance of query search features is very clear in the ranking of the features. We find that the tree created by training the ranker on a combination of existing features and query search features ranks the following as the top three features: *i)* ad domain count in query organic results, *ii)* ordered bigram overlap between snippets of organic results for query and ad keyword and *iii)* ad domain count in ad keyword organic results. These features rank higher than many other highly engineered features.

The benefits of adding query features are smaller than those when compared to the baseline as we in Section 6. But, the value of interpreting the ad keyword is reflected in the ranking of the new features. Two of the 54 features are among the top 30 features in the final tree produced by the ranker. These are: *i)* word unigram overlap between query and snippets in organic results for ad keyword and *ii)* order word bigrams between query and titles of the organic results for ad keyword.

7. DISCUSSION

The gains we see over the production system are naturally lower than the gains over the baseline. However, they are significant in production [4]. Moreover, the features that we propose can be obtained using the datasets and learning experience already at the disposal of the search engine.

Quantifying the impact of these improvements on the revenue of the search engine and user experience is complicated. We see significant improvements in ranking accuracy. However, it may be possible that the ads which have been more accurately scored will not be shown to the user for a host of other reasons including low click probability, low bid values by the advertiser, and so on. In this case, improvements to the relevance ranker would not enhance the user experience. Increase in recall values, however, would lead to the identification of more ads that are truly relevant to the user query, leading to greater competition in the auction—and higher revenue for the search engine.

An immediate extension of our work is to study the benefits of incorporating these features over a slice of live traffic handled by the production system. Such a study would allow us to measure the impact of new features on metrics (e.g., share of queries with ads, ads per query, clicks per search impression and CTR) that have a direct bearing on user experience and search engine revenue.

8. CONCLUSION

The ad keyword is the only field in a sponsored search ad that allows an advertiser to express the type of traffic that they would like to attract. At the same time the ad keyword, like the user query, is very short which makes the task of interpreting advertiser intent hard. In this work, we leverage the ability of modern search engines to interpret the intent behind a user's query to similarly understand the advertiser's intent as conveyed in the ad keyword.

We make three main contributions in this paper. First, we show that using organic engine results to expand the ad keyword provides us with a rich source of information from which we can interpret advertiser intent. Second, we identify the features to be extracted from these organic results which can be used to improve the relevance ranker. Among these, 54 features can be implemented with few changes to the existing system and another 21 features would require user intent information as well. Finally, we evaluate the benefits of these features using training and validation datasets of 1.28M and 320,000 samples sampled from a corpus of ground-truth (query, ad) pair scores respectively. We show that using features which capture user and advertiser intent leads to 43.2% improvement in precision-recall AUC over the baseline and a 2.7% improvement over the production ranker for a large search engine.

Acknowledgments

We thank Greg Buehrer for initial discussions on the idea of using web relevance feedback for improving ad relevance. We also thank the anonymous reviewers for their feedback. This work was funded in part by the National Science Foundation through grant CNS-1237264.

9. REFERENCES

[1] Click Modeling in Search Advertising: Challenges & Solutions. http://advertise.bingads.microsoft.com/en-us/editorial-relevance-quality-guidelines.

[2] DMOZ - the Open Directory Project. http://www.dmoz.org.

[3] English Stop Words (CSV). http://www.textfixer.com/resources/common-english-words.txt.

[4] Personal communications with Bing Ads Relevance Team.

[5] Relevance and quality guidelines - Bing Ads. http://advertise.bingads.microsoft.com/en-us/editorial-relevance-quality-guidelines.

[6] E. Agichtein, E. Brill, and S. Dumais. Improving Web Search Ranking by Incorporating User Behavior Information. In *Proceedings of the 29th Annual International ACM SIGIR Conference on Research and Development in Information Retrieval*, SIGIR '06, pages 19–26, 2006.

[7] L. Ballesteros and W. B. Croft. Phrasal Translation and Query Expansion Techniques for Cross-language Information Retrieval. In *Proceedings of the 20th Annual International ACM SIGIR Conference on Research and Development in Information Retrieval*, SIGIR '97, pages 84–91, 1997.

[8] P. N. Bennett, K. Svore, and S. T. Dumais. Classification-Enhanced Ranking. In *Proceedings of the 19th International Conference on World Wide Web*, WWW '10, pages 111–120, 2010.

[9] A. Broder, M. Ciaramita, M. Fontoura, E. Gabrilovich, V. Josifovski, D. Metzler, V. Murdock, and V. Plachouras. To Swing or Not to Swing: Learning when (Not) to Advertise. In *Proceedings of the 17th ACM Conference on Information and Knowledge Management*, CIKM '08, pages 1003–1012, 2008.

[10] A. Z. Broder, P. Ciccolo, M. Fontoura, E. Gabrilovich, V. Josifovski, and L. Riedel. Search Advertising Using Web Relevance Feedback. In *Proceedings of the 17th ACM Conference on Information and Knowledge Management*, CIKM '08, pages 1013–1022, 2008.

[11] A. Z. Broder, M. Fontoura, E. Gabrilovich, A. Joshi, V. Josifovski, and T. Zhang. Robust Classification of Rare Queries Using Web Knowledge. In *Proceedings of the 30th annual international ACM SIGIR conference on Research and development in information retrieval*, SIGIR '07, pages 231–238, 2007.

[12] C. Burges, R. Ragno, and Q. Le. Learning to Rank with Non-Smooth Cost Functions. In *Advances in Neural Information Processing Systems 19*. MIT Press, Cambridge, MA, January 2007.

[13] C. J. Burges. From RankNet to LambdaRank to LambdaMART: An Overview. Technical Report MSR-TR-2010-82, June 2010.

[14] Y. Choi, M. Fontoura, E. Gabrilovich, V. Josifovski, M. Mediano, and B. Pang. Using Landing Pages for Sponsored Search Ad Selection. In *Proceedings of the 19th International Conference on World Wide Web*, WWW '10, pages 251–260, 2010.

[15] M. Ciaramita, V. Murdock, and V. Plachouras. Online Learning from Click Data for Sponsored Search. In *Proceedings of the 17th International Conference on World Wide Web*, WWW '08, pages 227–236, 2008.

[16] K. S. Dave and V. Varma. Learning the Click-through Rate for Rare/New Ads from Similar Ads. In *Proceedings of the 33rd International ACM SIGIR Conference on Research and Development in Information Retrieval*, SIGIR '10, pages 897–898, 2010.

[17] C. B. Do and A. Y. Ng. Transfer learning for text classification. In Y. Weiss, B. Schölkopf, and J. Platt, editors, *Advances in Neural Information Processing Systems 18*, pages 299–306. MIT Press, 2006.

[18] E. N. Efthimiadis and P. V. Biron. UCLA-Okapi at TREC-2: Query Expansion Experiments. In *In Proceedings of the Second Text Retrieval Conference*, pages 500–215, 1994.

[19] X. He, J. Pan, O. Jin, T. Xu, B. Liu, T. Xu, Y. Shi, A. Atallah, R. Herbrich, S. Bowers, and J. Q. n. Candela. Practical Lessons from Predicting Clicks on Ads at Facebook. In *Proceedings of the Eighth International Workshop on Data Mining for Online Advertising*, ADKDD'14, pages 5:1–5:9, 2014.

[20] D. Hillard, S. Schroedl, E. Manavoglu, H. Raghavan, and C. Leggetter. Improving Ad Relevance in Sponsored Search. In *Proceedings of the Third ACM International Conference on Web Search and Data Mining*, WSDM '10, pages 361–370, 2010.

[21] K. Hui, B. Gao, B. He, and T.-J. Luo. Sponsored Search Ad Selection by Keyword Structure Analysis. In *Proceedings of the European Conference on Information Retrieval*, ECIR '13, pages 230–241, 2013.

[22] B. J. Jansen and T. Mullen. Sponsored search: an overview of the concept, history, and technology. *International Journal of Electronic Business*, 6(2):114–131, 2008.

[23] B. J. Jansen and M. Resnick. An examination of searcher's perceptions of nonsponsored and sponsored links during ecommerce Web searching. *Journal of the American Society for Information Science and Technology*, 57(14):1949–1961, 2006.

[24] P. Kowalczyk, I. Zukerman, and M. Niemann. Analyzing the Effect of Query Class on Document Retrieval Performance. In G. Webb and X. Yu, editors, *AI 2004: Advances in Artificial Intelligence*, volume 3339 of *Lecture Notes in Computer Science*, pages 550–561. Springer Berlin Heidelberg, 2005.

[25] D. Metzler, S. Dumais, and C. Meek. Similarity Measures for Short Segments of Text. In G. Amati, C. Carpineto, and G. Romano, editors, *Advances in Information Retrieval*, volume 4425 of *Lecture Notes in Computer Science*, pages 16–27. Springer Berlin Heidelberg, 2007.

[26] M. Mitra, A. Singhal, and C. Buckley. Improving Automatic Query Expansion. In *Proceedings of the 21st Annual International ACM SIGIR Conference on Research and Development in Information Retrieval*, SIGIR '98, pages 206–214, 1998.

[27] M. F. Porter. An algorithm for suffix stripping. *Program*, 14(3):130–137, 1980.

[28] F. Radlinski, A. Broder, P. Ciccolo, E. Gabrilovich, V. Josifovski, and L. Riedel. Optimizing Relevance and Revenue in Ad Search: A Query Substitution Approach. In *Proceedings of the 31st Annual International ACM SIGIR Conference on Research and Development in Information Retrieval*, SIGIR '08, pages 403–410, 2008.

[29] H. Raghavan and D. Hillard. A Relevance Model Based Filter for Improving Ad Quality. In *Proceedings of the 32nd international ACM SIGIR conference on Research and development in information retrieval*, SIGIR '09, pages 762–763, 2009.

[30] R. Raina, A. Y. Ng, and D. Koller. Constructing Informative Priors Using Transfer Learning. In *Proceedings of the 23rd International Conference on Machine Learning*, ICML '06, pages 713–720, 2006.

[31] M. Richardson, E. Dominowska, and R. Ragno. Predicting Clicks: Estimating the Click-through Rate for New Ads. In *Proceedings of the 16th International Conference on World Wide Web*, WWW '07, pages 521–530, 2007.

[32] D. Sculley, R. G. Malkin, S. Basu, and R. J. Bayardo. Predicting Bounce Rates in Sponsored Search Advertisements. In *Proceedings of the 15th ACM SIGKDD International Conference on Knowledge Discovery and Data Mining*, KDD '09, pages 1325–1334, 2009.

[33] Y. Song, H. Ma, H. Wang, and K. Wang. Exploring and Exploiting User Search Behavior on Mobile and Tablet Devices to Improve Search Relevance. In *Proceedings of the 22nd International Conference on World Wide Web*, WWW '13, May 2013.

[34] E. M. Voorhees. Query Expansion Using Lexical-semantic Relations. In *Proceedings of the 17th Annual International ACM SIGIR Conference on Research and Development in Information Retrieval*, SIGIR '94, pages 61–69, 1994.

[35] Q. Wu, C. Burges, K. Svore, and J. Gao. Adapting boosting for information retrieval measures. *Information Retrieval*, 13(3):254–270, June 2010.

[36] J. Xu and W. B. Croft. Improving the Effectiveness of Information Retrieval with Local Context Analysis. *ACM Trans. Inf. Syst.*, 18(1):79–112, Jan. 2000.

[37] W. V. Zhang, X. He, B. Rey, and R. Jones. Query Rewriting Using Active Learning for Sponsored Search. In *Proceedings of the 30th Annual International ACM SIGIR Conference on Research and Development in Information Retrieval*, SIGIR '07, pages 853–854, 2007.

Client Clustering for Hiring Modeling in Work Marketplaces

Vasilis Verroios*
Stanford University
verroios@stanford.edu

Ramesh Johari*
Stanford University
ramesh.johari@stanford.edu

Panagiotis Papadimitriou
Elance-oDesk
papadimitriou@elance-odesk.com

Hector Garcia-Molina
Stanford University
hector@cs.stanford.edu

ABSTRACT

An important problem that online work marketplaces face is grouping clients into clusters, so that in each cluster clients are similar with respect to their hiring criteria. Such a separation allows the marketplace to "learn" more accurately the hiring criteria in each cluster and recommend the right contractor to each client, for a successful collaboration. We propose a Maximum Likelihood definition of the "optimal" client clustering along with an efficient Expectation-Maximization clustering algorithm that can be applied in large marketplaces. Our results on the job hirings at oDesk over a seven-month period show that our client-clustering approach yields significant gains compared to "learning" the same hiring criteria for all clients. In addition, we analyze the clustering results to find interesting differences between the hiring criteria in the different groups of clients.

1. INTRODUCTION

Online work marketplaces such as oDesk.com, Elance.com and Freelancer.com help "clients" and "contractors" across the globe to connect with each other and work for more than $1 billion in annual contractor earnings just in 2014. Typically, in such marketplaces, contractors apply to a job posted by a client and clients hire the applicant(s) that seems to be the best fit for the job posted. As these platforms grow, a fundamental problem they have to solve is the understanding of successful client hiring practices so that they can help clients make the right hiring decisions. Without such help, clients will have to deal with the friction of screening tens to hundreds of contractors to determine the ideal candidates for their jobs. The screening process is not only time-consuming, but it is also error-prone, since clients often lack the necessary knowledge to assess the qualifications of contractors (e.g., education and work experience from schools and companies that are unknown to a client).

Understanding and modeling the hiring behavior of clients is challenging not only due to the variety of jobs that are posted and the diversity of contractors, but also due to the heterogeneity of client hiring criteria. For example, two different clients that have posted two seemingly similar jobs looking for "php developers" may be looking for totally different people. Say that the first client is a *quality* optimizer that is willing to pay a high hourly rate to get the most qualified contractor while the second client is a *cost* optimizer who is willing to take the risk of working with an inexperienced contractor to reduce his costs. To make recommendations that satisfy both of these clients we would ideally develop a dedicated model for each client. However, in practice, developing a model for each client is not an option, since the marketplace rarely has sufficient data points for a single client to make training possible.

*Work done while authors were at Elance-oDesk

KDD'15, August 10-13, 2015, Sydney, NSW, Australia.
 ISBN 978-1-4503-3664-2/15/08 ...$15.00.
DOI: http://dx.doi.org/10.1145/2783258.2788589.

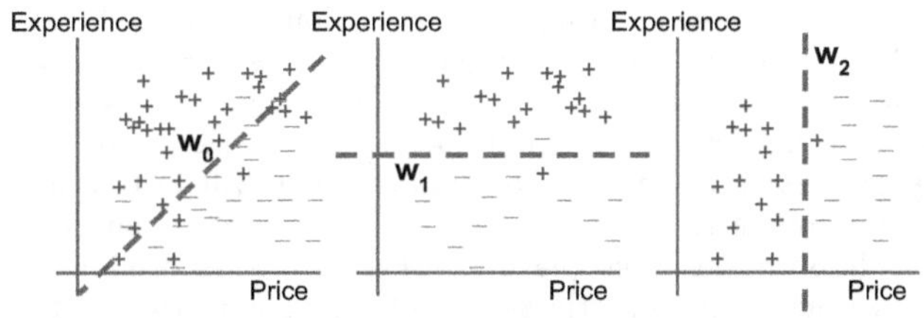

Figure 1: Left: The hiring decisions of all of the marketplace clients in a two-dimensional feature space. Middle: The hiring decisions of quality optimizers. Right: The hiring decisions of cost optimizers.

Although all clients are not the same, there are usually sufficiently large groups of clients with similar hiring criteria that can provide us with data for model training. To illustrate our hypothesis, we show in Figure 1 the hiring decisions in a marketplace that is composed of quality and cost optimizers. In the first plot of the figure we illustrate the hiring decisions of all clients in a two-dimensional feature space. Each "+" point looks at an application that ended up in a hire while a "−" point looks at an application that got rejected. The point positions on the X-axis indicate the bid prices asked by the contractors and the positions on the Y-axis indicate the years of contractor experience. A linear model trained on all of the client decisions would "learn" a linear separator $\mathbf{w_0}$ to distinguish hired from rejected applications. Such a separator would misclassify many rejected applications as hires ("-" points to the left of $\mathbf{w_0}$) and many hires as rejected applications ("+" points to the right of $\mathbf{w_0}$). However, if we could split the clients into quality (middle plot) and cost optimizers (right plot) we could then learn a different model for each client group. The derived separators $\mathbf{w_1}$ and $\mathbf{w_2}$ would then almost perfectly separate the hires in each of the two groups.

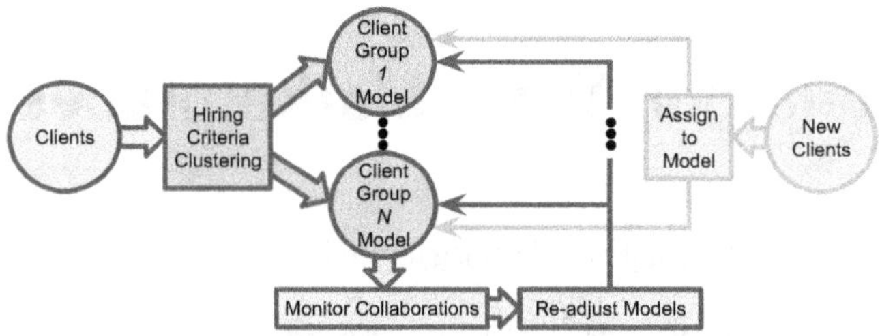

Figure 2: The Hiring Criteria Clustering component in the overall oDesk recommendations workflow.

Clustering clients based on their hiring criteria is a critical component in our oDesk recommendations workflow. Figure 2 depicts the overall workflow and shows how the clustering component fits in the workflow. The clustering component generates groups of clients along with one hiring model per group. Our first objective is to predict more accurately who is the right contractor for a client's task, based on the hiring practices of that client. Nevertheless, predicting accurately the contractor that a client will hire is not our only objective. We observed that very often unsuccessful collaborations take place because of clients relying on the "wrong" hiring practices. Therefore, we have to monitor the collaborations in each group of clients and "intervene" when we detect that a group's hiring practices often lead to unsuccessful collaborations. We "intervene" by adjusting the group's hiring model based on the "problematic" criteria that we detected. For example, we may adjust a hiring model when we detect that clients are biased against working with contractors from specific countries, while we "know" that those countries provide a large pool of experts for the tasks posted by those clients.

The monitoring and re-adjustment components typically require both algorithmic models and manual effort. Hence, it is important to use human-interpretable hiring models in our workflow (see also paper [18]). Furthermore, our workflow also involves a component that assigns new clients without any hiring history to the right group/model. (Note that a positive experience for new clients is particularly important for the marketplace.)

In this paper, we choose to focus on the hiring-criteria clustering component, which forms the basis for the overall workflow and is the most interesting component both from an applied and a research perspective. Below we discuss two classic approaches for client clustering and point out why they are not suitable for our context.

Traditional Clustering Methods: One straightforward approach for client clustering is to apply an algorithm like k-means using client attributes like age or occupation. However, as we observed in the oDesk platform, clients that have the exact same characteristics (age, occupation, etc.), often have very different criteria on hiring contractors. Clearly, a clustering method suitable for our problem must be based on the clients' decisions and not just attributes like age and occupation. Of course, we can also include client attributes related to their past decisions. However, we decided not to rely on a "custom" approach, where we would have to come up with past decisions' attributes and a distance metric to represent the distance between clients. (Instead, we rely on a bayesian approach, as we discuss later in the introduction.)

Collaborative Filtering (CF) Methods: CF techniques, like the ones presented in papers [2, 5, 7, 10, 11, 19, 24, 31], fit well in domains like electronic commerce or streaming media recommendations, but have an inherent limitation for online job marketplaces: each contractor cannot be considered as a "fixed" item as with movies or products. For instance, a contractor may be much more appropriate for a task involving Fortran debugging than Python debugging if she is a Fortran expert but a Python novice. That is, clients do not really "vote" for a contractor when they hire her but "vote" for her application on a specific task.

Since the quality of the client clustering drastically affects the percentage of successful collaborations, we had to develop a new approach tailored to our context. The approach we developed is driven by our findings in papers [4] and [18]. In summary, in those two papers we studied the problem of learning how to rank the applicants on a specific task posted by a client. Our main finding was that a simple sparse logistic regression model, using the accepted applications as positive examples and the rejected ones as negatives examples, proves to be very effective for applicant ranking. Hence, the approach we propose in this paper for the hiring-criteria clustering problem, builds on top of a logistic regression model: we develop a Finite Mixture Logit model and a simple, yet effective and scalable algorithm based on Expectation Maximization with *hard* assignments (hard EM). In simple words, the algorithm starts with a random assignment of clients into clusters and for each cluster it applies sparse logistic regression to learn the hyperplane expressing the client criteria in this cluster. It then re-assigns a client to the hyperplane/cluster that best "explains" her choices. These two steps are repeated until convergence, i.e., until no re-assignments are needed. After the last step, the algorithm has computed a partition of clients into clusters along with the criteria of clients in each cluster; given by sparse logistic regression.

Although our model bears some resemblance to models proposed in the past (e.g., mixture models proposed for clusterwise regression [8, 27], mixtures of Support Vector Machines [3, 9, 32] or models found in the marketing and economics literature [1, 15, 20, 23, 30]), there are some important differences that do not allow previous models to be applied in the context discussed here:

1. Most previous models (e.g., [3, 6, 8, 9, 27, 32]) apply clustering directly on the samples of the dataset. On the contrary, our clustering takes place in a different level: we cluster the clients that produced the samples.
2. As previous models were designed to solve different problems, they do not capture important aspects of the problem discussed in this paper. (For example, in most of the models in the marketing and economics literature, a client's decision refers to the selection of a product or brand from a set of "fixed" alternatives, while in our case a client's decision refers to a "unique" application.) Moreover, most of those models come with unnecessary complexity and in large-scale platforms like oDesk, any unnecessary model or algorithmic complexity incurs a critical cost in terms of computational overhead and software maintenance.

In our experiments, we use the 865,000 accept/reject decisions made by oDesk clients in a seven-month period. As our results show, the predictive hiring models trained on the clusters yielded by our algorithm can improve the performance of a global model (i.e., a single hiring model for all clients) by 43%. Furthermore, our analysis on the clusters produced by our method reveals some very interesting differences on the hiring practices of different client groups. To the best of our knowledge, our study is the first one on the detection and analysis of the differences between hiring practices in online work marketplaces.

In summary, our contributions are the following:

- We provide a Maximum-Likelihood formulation of the hiring-criteria clustering problem, in Section 2.
- We present a hard EM algorithm for this problem, in Section 3.
- We present our model for oDesk job applications, in Section 4.2, and we study the impact of client clustering for different sizes of training sets and sets of features, in Section 4.3.
- We study the hiring criteria in different groups of clients to discover some very interesting differences on how clients choose the contractor they work with, in Section 4.4.

1.1 Running Example

We will use a running example throughout the definition of our model and algorithm in Sections 2 and 3.

For simplicity, let us assume that there are only **three** features, experience, score, bidding, affecting a client's decision and that all information for the contractors' applications are organized in a single table:

Apps(clientID, experience, score, bidding, decision)

The semantics of the 5 columns are the following:

1. clientID: The client that opened the task to which the current application refers.
2. experience: The total number of hours the contractor(applicant) has worked in the platform, i.e., the total number of hours in the contractor's past contracts with clients.
3. score: The aggregated rating of the contractor based on the past reviews from the clients she worked for.
4. bidding: The amount asked by the contractor for performing the task.
5. decision: The decision of the client ("APPROVED"/ "REJECTED") on this application.

In practice, the three features, experience, score, bidding, are normalized so that their value range is $[0.0, 1.0]$. For example, the bidding can be normalized by the maximum amount a contractor may ask for a task; a restriction that could be enforced by the platform's provided functionality.

In our example, the dataset consists of only **four** clients, each having **ten** contractor applications approved and **ten** contractor applications rejected. In addition, we want to form **two** clusters, i.e., we want to split the four clients into two groups such that the clients in each group have "very similar" criteria regarding the experience, score, and bidding of an application. Our model in the next section quantifies the notion of "similar" by defining the *optimal* clustering.

2. MODEL

In this section, we formally define the problem of finding the optimal client partition based on the clients' hiring criteria. Intuitively, our definition requires that the reject/accept applications in each cluster of clients are as "well-separated" as possible. For example, the reject/accept applications ("−"s/"+"s) in the middle and right side of Figure 1 are "well-separated"; a different partition of clients into two clusters could result in having "+"s diffuse over the "−"s area, and the opposite. We use a logit model to quantify how "well-separated" the applications in one cluster are. Based on the cost defined by the logit model, the optimal partition of clients is the one minimizing the cost across all clusters.

We start by describing the dataset notation and the cost for a single cluster and then define the clustering optimization problem (equations (11) to (13)).

2.1 Dataset Notation

All the past applications are stored in a single table:

Apps(clientID, a1, a2, ..., aF, decision)

The features describing each application are denoted by a1, a2, ..., aF and they are normalized so that their value range is $[0.0, 1.0]$. In our running example, we use only three features: a1 $\equiv$ experience, a2 $\equiv$ score, a3 $\equiv$ bidding.

We denote by $\mathbf{x_i}$ the row i in table Apps (Apps[i]), projected over columns a1, a2, ..., aF. Thus, in our running example, each $\mathbf{x_i}$ is a 3-dimensional vector, e.g., if an application involves an experience of 0.2, a score of 0.9, and a bidding of 0.8, then $\mathbf{x_i} = (0.2, 0.9, 0.8)^T$.

In addition to $\mathbf{x_i}$, we use $\mathbf{u_i}$ to express the clientID of row i (Apps[i].clientID), in a 1-of-K scheme. In our running example, where we have $K = 4$ clients, if the second client approved/rejected application i, then $\mathbf{u_i} = (0, 1, 0, 0)^T$.

To simplify notation we split past applications into two subsets $\{\mathcal{P}, \mathcal{N}\}$, such that:

$$\mathcal{P} = \{(\mathbf{x_i}, \mathbf{u_i}) \mid \text{Apps}[i].\text{decision} = \text{APPROVED}\} \quad (1)$$

$$\mathcal{N} = \{(\mathbf{x_i}, \mathbf{u_i}) \mid \text{Apps}[i].\text{decision} = \text{REJECTED}\} \quad (2)$$

In the running example, $|\mathcal{P}| = 40$ since each of the four clients has approved ten contractor applications, and $|\mathcal{N}| = 40$ since each of the four clients has rejected ten applications.

Moreover, we denote with:

- K: the number of clients.
- C: the number of clusters.
- F: the number of features.

2.2 Single-Cluster Cost

The single-cluster cost is based on the logistic regression model. Here, we give a brief overview of logistic regression in the context of our running example. Note that, in this section, we focus only on the applications $\{\mathcal{P}, \mathcal{N}\}$ of the clients that belong to a single cluster.

We denote by $\mathbf{w}$ the vector expressing the criteria of clients for approving/rejecting the applications. Note that all the clients of a cluster share the same $\mathbf{w}$. In the running example, a $\mathbf{w} = (1.0, 0.0, 0.0)^T$ expresses that clients prefer contractors with a lot of experience and do not care about the score and the bidding in an application. (In practice, $\mathbf{w}$ involves an additional coefficient for the general bias. That is, in our running example, an application $\mathbf{x_i} = (0.2, 0.9, 0.8)^T$ would be extended with a constant term on a fourth dimension: $\mathbf{x_i}$ would become $(0.2, 0.9, 0.8, 1.0)^T$, and $\mathbf{w}$ would become a 4-dimensional vector.)

In logistic regression, the probability of an application i being approved is given by the logistic function:

$$g(\mathbf{w^T x_i}) = \frac{1}{1 + e^{-\mathbf{w^T x_i}}} \quad (3)$$

That is,

$$P(\mathbf{x_i}\ approved|\mathbf{w}) = g(\mathbf{w}^\mathbf{T}\mathbf{x_i}) \quad (4)$$

$$P(\mathbf{x_i}\ rejected|\mathbf{w}) = 1 - g(\mathbf{w}^\mathbf{T}\mathbf{x_i}) \quad (5)$$

Therefore, as the value of the dot product $\mathbf{w}^\mathbf{T}\mathbf{x_i}$ approaches $+\infty$, $P(\mathbf{x_i}\ approved|\mathbf{w})$ approaches 1.0, while when $\mathbf{w}^\mathbf{T}\mathbf{x_i}$ approaches $-\infty$, $P(\mathbf{x_i}\ rejected|\mathbf{w})$ approaches 1.0.

The objective in logistic regression is finding the criteria $\mathbf{w}$, maximizing the likelihood:

$$P(\{\mathcal{P},\mathcal{N}\}|\mathbf{w}) = \prod_{\mathcal{P}} g(\mathbf{w}^\mathbf{T}\mathbf{x_i}) \prod_{\mathcal{N}} (1 - g(\mathbf{w}^\mathbf{T}\mathbf{x_i})) \quad (6)$$

Taking into account regularization, the cost of a single cluster is the negative log-likelihood plus a regularization term involving a hyperparameter λ and the 1-norm of the criteria vector $\mathbf{w}$:

$$Cost(\mathbf{w}) : \lambda\|\mathbf{w}\|_1 - \sum_{\mathcal{P}} \ln(g(\mathbf{w}^\mathbf{T}\mathbf{x_i})) - \sum_{\mathcal{N}} \ln(1 - g(\mathbf{w}^\mathbf{T}\mathbf{x_i})) \quad (7)$$

2.3 Optimal Client Partitioning

In this section, we generalize the model to many clusters. Thus, our dataset $\{\mathcal{P},\mathcal{N}\}$ refers to the applications from all clients.

We use the matrix $\mathbf{M} = [\mathbf{m_1}, \ldots, \mathbf{m_C}] \in \{0,1\}^{K \times C}$ to express the clients' membership, i.e., how the K clients are partitioned into C clusters. Column j, $\mathbf{m_j}$, gives the clients that belong to cluster j, while we denote by $\mathbf{m'_k}$ the row k of $\mathbf{M}$, which gives the cluster where client k belongs. In our running example, suppose that the first cluster contains only the third client while the second cluster contains the other three clients. In that case,

$$\mathbf{m_1} = \begin{pmatrix} 0 \\ 0 \\ 1 \\ 0 \end{pmatrix}, \ \mathbf{m_2} = \begin{pmatrix} 1 \\ 1 \\ 0 \\ 1 \end{pmatrix}, \ \mathbf{M} = \begin{pmatrix} 0 & 1 \\ 0 & 1 \\ 1 & 0 \\ 0 & 1 \end{pmatrix}$$

and

$$\mathbf{m'_1} = (0,1),\ \mathbf{m'_2} = (0,1),\ \mathbf{m'_3} = (1,0),\ \mathbf{m'_4} = (0,1)$$

Therefore, the dot product $\mathbf{u_i^T}\mathbf{m}_j$ is 1 if the client that approved/rejected application i belongs to cluster j and 0 otherwise. For instance, if the second client approved/rejected application i and we have the same clustering as in the example above, $\mathbf{u_i^T}\mathbf{m_1} = (0,1,0,0)(0,0,1,0)^T = 0$, while $\mathbf{u_i^T}\mathbf{m_2} = (0,1,0,0)(1,1,0,1)^T = 1$.

The criteria vector for cluster j is given by $\mathbf{w_j}$. We use the matrix $\mathbf{W} = [\mathbf{w_1}, \ldots, \mathbf{w_C}] \in \mathbb{R}^{F \times C}$ to refer to the union of vectors for all clusters.

The likelihood of the evidence $P(\{\mathcal{P},\mathcal{N}\}|\mathbf{W},\mathbf{M})$ becomes:

$$\prod_{j=1}^{C} \left(\prod_{\mathcal{P}} g(\mathbf{w_j^T}\mathbf{x_i})^{\mathbf{u_i^T}\mathbf{m_j}} \prod_{\mathcal{N}} (1 - g(\mathbf{w_j^T}\mathbf{x_i}))^{\mathbf{u_i^T}\mathbf{m_j}} \right) \quad (8)$$

Note that the term for a cluster j involves only the applications of clients that belong to that cluster. (For all of these applications the exponent $\mathbf{u_i^T}\mathbf{m_j}$ is 1, while for all other applications that do not belong to the cluster j the exponent $\mathbf{u_i^T}\mathbf{m_j}$ is 0.)

The log-likelihood, $\ell(\mathbf{W},\mathbf{M})$, becomes:

$$\sum_{j=1}^{C} \left(\sum_{\mathcal{P}} \mathbf{u_i^T}\mathbf{m_j} \ln(g(\mathbf{w_j^T}\mathbf{x_i})) + \sum_{\mathcal{N}} \mathbf{u_i^T}\mathbf{m_j} \ln(1 - g(\mathbf{w_j^T}\mathbf{x_i})) \right) \quad (9)$$

Algorithm 1

Input: C: the number of clusters
$\mathcal{P}$: applications approved
$\mathcal{N}$: applications rejected
Output: $\mathbf{W}$: local-optimum criteria matrix
$\mathbf{M}$: local-optimum membership matrix

```
M:= randomly assign the clients into C clusters
while M ≠ M_pre do
    M_pre := M
    W := solve problem of (11)-(13), with M fixed (M step)
    M := solve problem of (11)-(13), with W fixed (E step)
end while
```

Therefore, the cost of a client partition defined by membership and criteria matrices $\mathbf{M}$ and $\mathbf{W}$, is:

$$Cost(\mathbf{W},\mathbf{M}) : \lambda \sum_{j=1}^{C} \|\mathbf{w_j}\|_1 - \ell(\mathbf{W},\mathbf{M}) \quad (10)$$

Note that the cost involves the sum of the regularization terms for each cluster.

Our objective is to find the membership and criteria matrices that solve the following optimization problem:

$$\min_{\mathbf{W},\mathbf{M}} \quad Cost(\mathbf{W},\mathbf{M}) \quad (11)$$

$$\text{s.t.} \quad \|\mathbf{m'_k}\|_1 = 1,\ \forall k \in \{1,\ldots,K\} \quad (12)$$

$$\mathbf{M} \in \{0,1\}^{K \times C},\ \mathbf{W} \in \mathbb{R}^{F \times C} \quad (13)$$

The constraint (12) expresses that each client must be part of exactly one cluster, i.e., we do not allow overlapping clusters.

3. ALGORITHM

The exhaustive approach for solving the optimization problem in equations (11)-(13) involves a $O(C^K)$ time complexity; for C clusters and K clients. Therefore, we propose a scalable algorithm based on Expectation Maximization with hard assignments. In each iteration two steps are involved:

- *E step:* compute the optimal client memberships, i.e., the optimal $\mathbf{M}$, while keeping $\mathbf{W}$ fixed.
- *M step:* compute the optimal client criteria for each cluster, i.e., the optimal $\mathbf{W}$, while keeping $\mathbf{M}$ fixed.

Our algorithm is given by Algorithm 1. The input is the set of all clients' applications, $\{\mathcal{P},\mathcal{N}\}$, along with the number of clusters C. Note that in practice there are many ways to compute the number of clusters to use as input. The simplest approach is to try several different C values and keep the one maximizing a metric like Mean Average Precision or Discounted Cumulative Gain on a testing set.

In each E step, the value of the objective function in (11) decreases or remains the same; in the worst case there are no changes in the client memberships that would decrease the value of the objective function. Likewise, in each M step the value of the objective function always decreases; or at least remains the same. Hence, the algorithm eventually converges to a minimum; when the client memberships remain the same for two consecutive iterations. Nevertheless, the minimum may be a local minimum and not a global one, since the problem of (11)-(13) is not convex. In practice, we run Algorithm 1 more than once, using different initial assignments of clients to clusters, and keep the solution that gives the lowest value for the objective function. In our technical report [29], we examine how the number of runs affects the convergence of our algorithm to the global minimum using synthetic data; so that the true global optimum is known to us in advance.

One of the main advantages of our algorithm is its scalability. In the E step, a single pass over the clients is needed. (For each client we find the cluster that "explains" better her decisions on her applications, while keeping the criteria for each cluster fixed.) In the M step, we just need to solve C sparse logistic regression problems, i.e., one problem per cluster. (Solving sparse logistic regression problems is a process that has been highly optimized for large datasets, e.g., [14], [17].) In Section 4.1.4, we discuss our scalability experiments and results.

3.1 E step

In the E step, we keep criteria matrix $\mathbf{W}$ fixed and we find for each client the cluster that "explains" better her decisions. That is, if U_a is the set of applications that were approved/rejected by a client a, we compute for each cluster j the log-likelihood $\ell(\mathbf{W}; j, U_a)$:

$$\sum_{\mathcal{P}\cap U_a} \ln(g(\mathbf{w_j^T x_i})) + \sum_{\mathcal{N}\cap U_a} \ln(1 - g(\mathbf{w_j^T x_i})) \quad (14)$$

Then, we assign client a to the cluster that gives the highest $\ell(\mathbf{W}; j, U_a)$ (or, equivalently, the lowest negative log-likelihood). In our running example, if the second cluster gives the highest $\ell(\mathbf{W}; j, U_3)$ for the third client, the third row of $\mathbf{M}$, i.e., $\mathbf{m_3'}$, becomes $(0, 1)$.

At the end of E step, the assignment changes for each client will be reflected on the membership matrix $\mathbf{M}$.

3.2 M step

In the M step, we keep $\mathbf{M}$ fixed and we find for each cluster j the criteria vector $\mathbf{w_j}$ that best "explains" the clients' decisions in that cluster. That is, for a cluster c, if U is the set of applications that were approved/rejected by the clients in c, we solve the following sparse logistic regression problem:

$$\min_{\mathbf{w_c}} \left(\lambda \|\mathbf{w_c}\|_1 - \sum_{\mathcal{P}\cap U} \ln(g(\mathbf{w_c^T x_i})) - \sum_{\mathcal{N}\cap U} \ln(1 - g(\mathbf{w_c^T x_i})) \right) \quad (15)$$

The optimal solutions to the logistic regression problems form the $\mathbf{W}$ for the next E step.

4. EXPERIMENTAL RESULTS

Our experiments are organized in three parts:

- Before applying our algorithm on production data, we wanted to test the algorithm's behavior on synthetic data where we know in advance the ground truth, i.e., the number of client groups and the hiring criteria in each of the groups. The results from the synthetic data experiments allow us to better interpret the results on the production site.
- In Section 4.3 we evaluate the performance of our algorithm on oDesk transactions. The results show that our clustering approach can scale to large datasets and improve the accuracy of base classifiers by more than 40%. We also observe that the improvements of our algorithm are negligible in cases where the training dataset is small relatively to the model complexity, since the formed clusters do not contain sufficient training data for model learning.

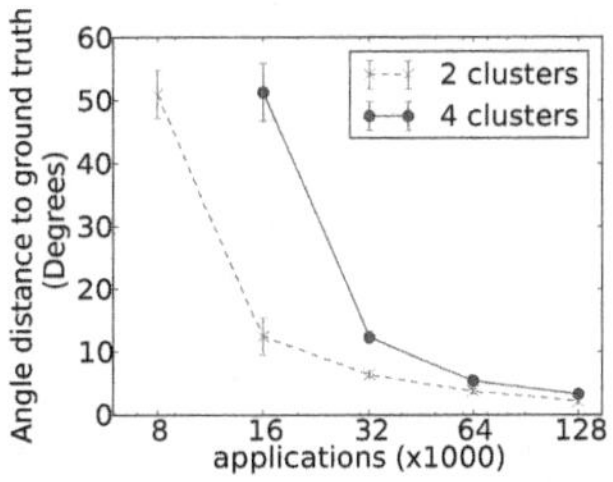

Figure 3: Angle distance to ground truth, as we increase the number of samples(applications) from 8 to 128 applications per client, for 2 and 4 clusters.

- Finally, in Section 4.4 we present a qualitative analysis of the clusters that are formed by our algorithm. The analysis shows that client clustering not only improves the accuracy of hiring predictions, but it also reveals latent characteristics of clients that use the work marketplace in different ways.

4.1 Synthetic Data

In this section, we briefly discuss our experiments with synthetic data. A detailed description of the settings and the synthetic data generation process can be found in our technical report [29].

4.1.1 *Number of samples*

We first try to quantify how our algorithm is affected by the number of samples available. Figure 3 depicts the behavior of our algorithm as we increase the number of applications (X-axis) from 8000 to 128000, for a fixed number of $K = 1000$ clients. The number of dimensions (i.e., the features that affect a client's decision) is fixed to 8. The Y-axis gives the average angle distance between the vectors (hiring criteria) computed by our algorithm and the ground truth vectors. We run experiments for $C = 2$ and 4 clusters and we plot one curve for each C value.

For $C = 2$ we see a huge increase in accuracy (the distance to the ground truth drops from 50 to 12 degrees) when we go from 8 to 16 applications per client. As we keep increasing the number of applications, the accuracy further increases and approaches a zero-degree distance to the ground truth (less than 3 degrees for 128 applications per client).

For $C = 4$ the steep decrease in the distance to the ground truth, happens from 16 to 32 applications per client. In fact, if we look closely at the two curves we observe that for 4 clusters we need, roughly, twice as many applications as we need for 2 clusters, to reach the same distance to the ground truth. This can be explained by the fact that we have twice as many clusters and, hence, each cluster is assigned half the applications.

4.1.2 *Number of dimensions*

In Figure 4(a), we plot the number of applications needed (Y-axis) to reach within a 10-degree distance to the ground truth, as we increase the number of dimensions, from 4 to 24 (X-axis). The number of clusters, C, is 4 and the number of clients, K, is 1000

As we increase the number of dimensions from 4 to 12, the number of applications needed for the 10-degree distance, increases slowly. For more than 12 dimensions, there is a steep increase for the number of applications needed, reaching almost 500 per client for 24 dimensions.

We also tried a second experiment showing the behavior of our approach when the number of dimensions increase,

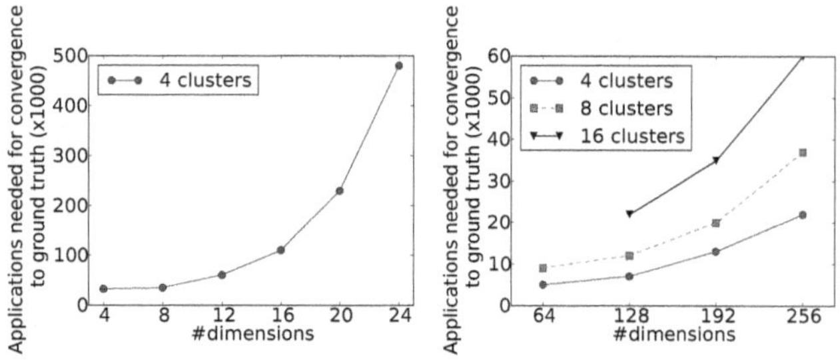

(a) *non-sparse* case (b) *sparse* case

Figure 4: In the *non-sparse* case, we plot the number of applications needed to get a 10-degree angle distance to ground truth, as we increase the number of dimensions from 4 to 24, for 4 clusters. In the *sparse* case, we increase the number of dimensions from 64 to 256, for 4, 8, and 16 clusters.

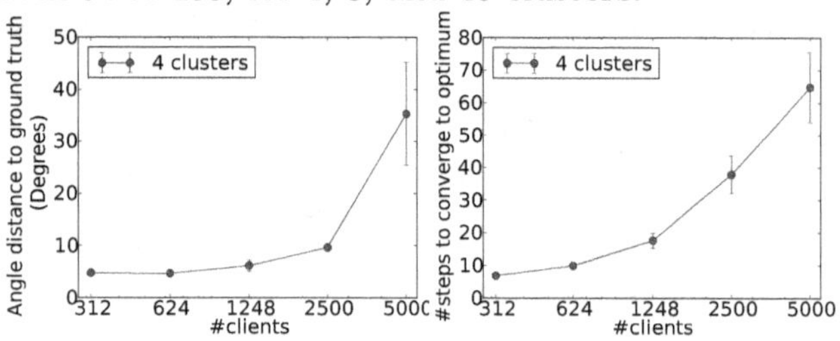

(a) Distance to ground truth (b) #iterations

Figure 5: Distance to ground truth and number of iterations needed for convergence, when we increase the number of clients while we keep the number of total samples(applications) fixed.

however, this time we used *sparse* ground-truth criteria vectors. That is, out of all dimensions/criteria only a few of them play an important role in the clients' decisions (for details see our technical report [29]).

As in Figure 4(a), Figure 4(b) depicts the number of applications needed (Y-axis) to reach a 10-degree distance to the ground truth, as we increase the number of dimensions (X-axis), for the *sparse* case. For 4 clusters, although the number of dimensions is much greater than the number of dimensions in the *non-sparse* case of Figure 4(a), the number of applications needed for the 10 degree distance, is two orders of magnitude lower; requiring around 20 applications per client for 256 dimensions.

For a larger number of clusters, i.e., $C = 8$ and $C = 16$ clusters, we need considerably more applications to reach the 10-degree distance, compared to $C = 4$ clusters. Still, even for $C = 16$ and 256 dimensions, we need less than 60 applications per client, which is an order of magnitude lower than the 500 applications per client for $C = 4$ and 24 dimensions, in the *non-sparse* case of Figure 4(a).

4.1.3 Number of clients

The experiments we discussed until now had a fixed number of 1000 clients. The next direction we explore is to keep the total number of applications fixed, and vary the number of clients, K, that decide upon those applications. We use 64000 applications for 8 dimensions and $C = 4$ clusters.

Figure 5(a) depicts the distance to the ground truth, as K increases from 312 to 5000. For K up to 2500, the distance to the ground truth stays below 10 degrees. However, if we increase K further, to 5000 clients, the distance steeply increases from 10 degrees to 35 degrees. Moreover, there is a significant increase in the variance for $K = 5000$.

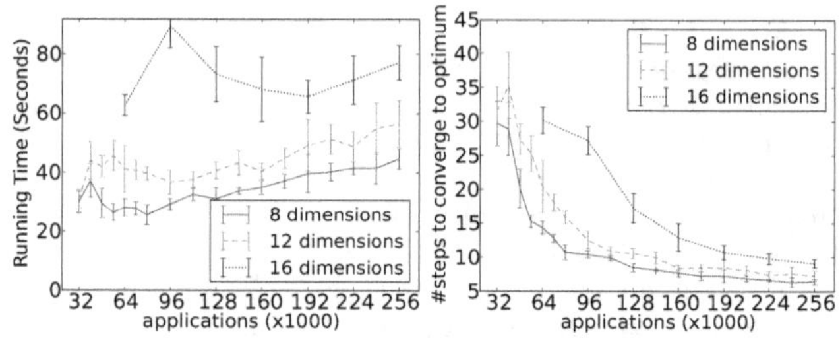

(a) Running Time (b) #iterations

Figure 6: Running time and number of iterations needed for convergence, when we increase the number of samples(applications) and dimensions.

The steep increase from $K = 2500$ to $K = 5000$ can be explained by the decrease in the number of samples per client; 12.8 per client on average for 5000 clients. Note that when having a small number of samples per client, it is "difficult" to accurately predict in which cluster a client should be assigned, in the E step. Therefore, while the total number of samples remains constant, the convergence of the algorithm to the ground truth vectors becomes more "difficult", as we keep decreasing the number of samples per client.

The above fact is confirmed by the number of iterations, until converging to an optimum, for the experiments of Figure 5(a). As we see in Figure 5(b), the number of iterations steadily increases as K increases from 312 to 5000.

4.1.4 Scalability

In this section, we study the scalability of our algorithm as we increase the number of samples and dimensions. In Figure 6(a), we plot the running time of our algorithm (Y-axis) on a 1.8 GHz Intel Core i5 processor with 4 GB of RAM. The algorithm is implemented in Python using scikit-learn, and the local optima are explored in parallel. We use the same *non-sparse* setting with the one used in Figure 4(a).

The computational overhead for solving the sparse logistic regression problems increases as the number of samples increases (X-axis). Surprisingly, though, the overall time of our algorithm is not monotonically increasing: up to a point it is constant or decreasing and then slowly increases. Moreover, that point is different for each number of dimensions.

The outcome of Figure 6(a) is due to the trade-off between the computational overhead for solving the logistic regression problems and the number of iterations needed to converge to an optimum. As the number of samples increases, the computational overhead increases but the number of iterations decreases, as Figure 6(b) shows. This causes the overall running time to decrease or remain constant. In addition, the point where the number of iterations essentially stops decreasing is different for 8, 12, and 16 dimensions: the more the dimensions, the more the samples needed for the number of iterations to stop decreasing. This explains why the overall time starts to slowly increase in different points for each number of dimensions, in Figure 6(a).

4.2 oDesk Job Applications

We start with a brief overview of the datasets, the features, and the metric, and then we discuss our findings.

Training and Testing Datasets: We collected all the applications of contractors to tasks opened by clients in the oDesk platform, from September 1st of 2012 to December 15 of 2012. In addition, we filtered this set of applications in order to keep only the applications rejected/approved by

Feature	Description	Tiers
Contractor's Score	A score summarizing how good the contractor is, based on the feedback received from clients that worked with the contractor.	1, 2, 3, 4
Matched Skills	Jaccard similarity between the set of skills the contractor has in her profile and the set of skills required for the task.	1, 2, 3, 4
Contractor's Total Hours	The aggregated number of hours for the contracts the contractor had in the platform.	1, 2, 3, 4
Bid Amount	The fixed amount of money the contractor asks for completing the task she applies for.	1, 2, 3, 4
Bid Rate	The hourly rate earnings the contractor asks for completing the task she applies for.	1, 2, 3, 4
Independent Contractor	Indicates if the contractor is a company or agency that runs a profile in the platform.	2, 3, 4
Contractor's Assignments	The number of tasks the contractor is assigned to and haven't been completed yet.	2, 3, 4
Contractor's Total Revenue	The aggregated earnings of the contractor in the platform.	2, 3, 4
Contractor's Tests Passed	The number of tests that the contractor has taken and successfully completed in the platform.	2, 3, 4
Contractor's Bill Rate	The hourly rate the contractor charges for the tasks he gets. Contractors usually set their bill rate in their profile to indicate the "quality" of their work.	2, 3, 4
Contractor's Experience	A score summarizing the working experience of the contractor based on her resume.	3, 4
Contractor's Portfolio Items	The number of items the contractor has in her portfolio.	3, 4
Matched Cost	The distance between the asking price and the price the client indicates she is willing to pay for the task.	3, 4
Matched Region	Indicates if the contractor's geographical region matches one of the regions the client prefers.	3, 4
Matched Task Category	Indicates if the task category is one of the categories the contractor has specified in her profile, as her areas of expertise.	3, 4
Contractor's Recent Activity	A score summarizing the contractor's recent activity, e.g., tasks recently completed or the date she completed the last task.	4
Contractor's English Skills	A score summarizing how fluently the contractor speaks english.	4
Contractor's Profile Information	A score summarizing how detailed the contractor's profile information is, e.g., full name appearing or not.	4
Contractor's Active Interviews	The number of pending applications the contractor has made, where the client has responded back to him; and are thus considered as the active interviews.	4
Contractor's Rank Percentile	For each test a contractor passes she receives a score. This feature gives in which percentile the contractor belongs, based on her test scores.	4

Table 1: Features representing each application

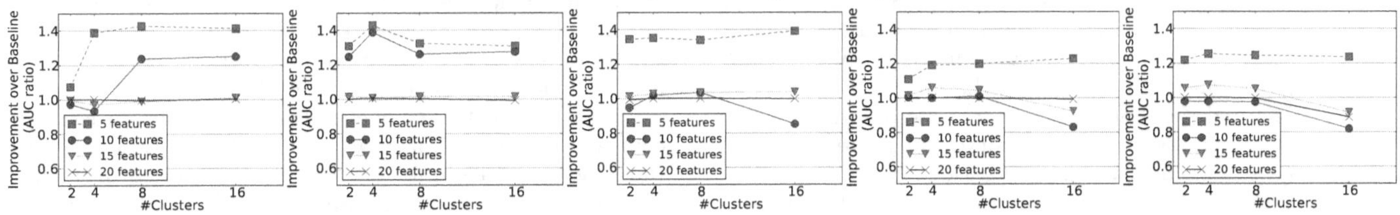

(a) $approved = 10$ (b) $approved = 20$ (c) $approved = 30$ (d) $approved = 40$ (e) $approved = 50$

Figure 7: AUC ratio(Y-axis) for different numbers of clusters(X-axis). Each curve refers to a different feature tier (Table 1) and each plot to a different pair of training and testing sets (Table 2).

approved	*clients*	*training*	*testing*
10 apps	2281	760k apps	105k apps
20 apps	480	260k apps	32k apps
30 apps	172	120k apps	22k apps
40 apps	84	80k apps	13k apps
50 apps	48	50k apps	12k apps

Table 2: Datasets used in experiments

clients who had a "sufficient" number of approved applications within this period. For example, consider a threshold of 10 approved applications, a client A that had 9 approved applications within that period, and a client B with 11 approved applications: all the applications for tasks opened by A are excluded from the training set, while all applications for tasks opened by B are included in the training set.

In particular, we generated 5 training sets using 5 different thresholds: 10, 20, 30, 40, and 50 approved applications. Note that each of these sets is a subset of the previous one. Table 2 summarizes the details for the 5 training sets: column *approved* refers to the threshold of approved applications, column *clients* refers to the number of clients satisfying the respective threshold constraint, and column *training* refers to the number of rejected/approved applications by those clients, i.e., the actual samples in the training set.

Furthermore, we generated the 5 testing sets corresponding to the 5 training sets: for each training set we kept the clients that satisfy the respective threshold constraint, and we collected the rejected/approved applications for their tasks from 01/15/2013 to 03/01/2013 (*testing* in Table 2).

Features: We ran experiments with 4 different tiers of features: tier 1 includes 5 features, tier 2 includes the 5 features of tier 1 plus 5 more features and so on. Table 1 gives the names and descriptions of the features, along with the tiers that include each feature. Note that each application in our training/testing sets is represented by the values for those features the moment the application is made. We normalize all the feature values to $[0.0, 1.0]$, taking into account what is the maximum value the feature may have. For example, for the contractor's score that has a maximum of 5.0 stars, the score in each application is divided by 5.0.

Metric: The metric we use is the area under the ROC curve (AUC). Moreover, when there are more than one clusters, we compute a separate AUC for each cluster. Let us describe how we quantify the improvement over the single-cluster approach through an example. Consider running Algorithm 1 with 2 clusters as input. For each cluster i Algorithm 1 computes, we use the criteria $\mathbf{w_i}$ learned for this cluster, and we compute the AUC: assume an $AUC_1 = 0.8$ for cluster 1 and an $AUC_2 = 0.9$ for cluster 2. Note that in order to compute AUC_i, we use the testing-set applications of the clients that were placed in cluster i. In addition, we run Algorithm 1 using a single cluster as input (i.e., we run the classic logistic regression model) and we compute the criteria $\mathbf{w_s}$ for a single cluster. For each of the 2 clusters Algorithm 1 initially produced, we use $\mathbf{w_s}$ to compute the AUC for the testing-set applications that belong to that cluster: assume an $AUC'_1 = 0.8$ and an $AUC'_2 = 0.5$. Then, we compute the ratio $\frac{AUC}{AUC'}$ for each cluster and the weighted average of all ratios: assume that in the testing set of cluster 1 there are 200 approved applications and in the testing set of cluster 2 there are 800 approved applications. The combined ratio will be: $\frac{200}{1000}\frac{AUC_1}{AUC'_1} + \frac{800}{1000}\frac{AUC_2}{AUC'_2} = 1.64$, indicating an improvement of 64% over the single-cluster approach.

It is important to note that the AUC cannot be greater than 1.0 and will not be less than 0.5; assuming a prediction accuracy not worse than random. Hence, the combined AUC ratio will always be less than 2.0, or in other words, the improvement over the single-cluster approach cannot be more than 100%.

4.3 Improvement over a Global Model

Figure 7 depicts the ratio between the AUC for the multi-cluster approach and the AUC for the single-cluster approach (baseline) on the Y-axis, as we increase the number of clusters (X-axis). Each curve refers to a different feature tier (see Table 1): *a)*5 features in tier 1, *b)*10 features in tier 2, *c)*15 features in tier 3, and *d)*20 features in tier 4. In Figure 7(a), we used the training/testing set for an *approved* threshold of 10, in Figure 7(b), we used the training/testing set for an *approved* threshold of 20, and so on.

There are three main factors that can explain the results in Figure 7. First, as we increase the number of dimensions (features), the improvement over the baseline (same criteria for all clients) drops: note that in most cases the curves for fewer features stay above the curves for more features. This factor is aligned with our observations in Section 4.1.2, i.e., as the number of features increase, our algorithm needs more samples and at some point the number of samples in the respective training set is not sufficient to improve over the prediction accuracy of the baseline approach.

Second, if we increase the number of clusters beyond a certain point, there is no improvement over the baseline (in fact, the baseline gives a higher AUC): in Figure 7(c) for 16 clusters, the curve for 10 features falls below 1.0, in Figure 7(d) for 16 clusters, both curves for 10 and 15 features fall below 1.0, and in Figure 7(e) for 16 clusters, the curves for 10, 15, and 20 features fall below 1.0. This observation is aligned with the discussions for Figures 3 and 4(b).

Third, if we reduce the number of samples (applications) beyond a certain point, the improvement over the baseline diminishes: the curve for 5 features drops from a 30%-40% improvement over the baseline in Figures 7(a)-7(c) to a 20% improvement in Figures 7(d)-7(e), while the curve for 10 features does not show any improvement over the baseline (or even drops below 1.0) in Figures 7(c)-7(e). This observation is aligned with the discussion in Section 4.1.1.

Nevertheless, the three factors discussed above, fail to explain why in some cases where the number of samples decreases, the improvement over the baseline increases. For example, from Figure 7(a) to Figure 7(b), there is a large increase in the curves for 5 and 10 features, for 2 and 4 clusters. (Or, from Figure 7(b) to Figure 7(c), the improvement for 5 features increases from 30% to almost 40%, for 16 clusters.) This behavior is the outcome of an important trade-off: by increasing the *approved* threshold, the number of samples in the training set drops from 760000 to 50000, from Figure 7(a) to Figure 7(e), however, the number of applications per client increases. Hence, we have more samples per client in order to accurately "learn" her criteria and place her in the "right" cluster. (The positive effect of having more samples per client was also discussed in Section 4.1.3.)

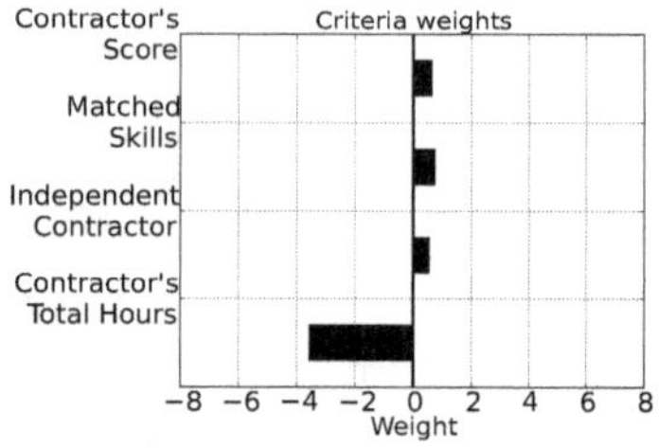

Figure 9: Weights of the criteria vector when a single cluster is used (traditional logistic regression).

4.4 Clients Hiring Criteria

Let us now focus on one of the most interesting outcomes of our algorithm: The 4 clusters produced for 10 features and an *approved* threshold of 20, an outcome achieving a substantial 40% improvement over the baseline, in Figure 7(b). (As we discussed in the description of the metric, the improvement cannot be greater than 100%.)

Figures 8(a) to 8(d) depict the values of the criteria vectors, $\mathbf{w_1}$ to $\mathbf{w_4}$, for the 4 clusters. Specifically, the figures show the 4, out of 10, criteria for which at least one of the vectors had a non-zero value. As these figures indicate, there are important differences in the criteria of clients for: *a)* clusters 1 and 3 (Figures 8(a) and 8(c)), *b)* cluster 2 (Figure 8(b)), and *c)* cluster 4 (Figure 8(d)).

Clients in cluster 2 have a strong tendency in selecting contractors whose skills match well with the task they post (large positive weight for the "Matched Skills" feature), clients in cluster 4 tend to reject contractors that have completed many hours working in the platform (large negative weight for "Contractor's Total Hours"), and clients in clusters 1 and 3 decide based on the contractor's score, skills, and agency independence (see Table 1 for a description of the features).

Before discussing further the differences between client criteria in different clusters, let us compare these criteria with those learnt when using a single cluster, i.e., when learning the same criteria for all clients. Figure 9 depicts the non-zero values of the criteria vector when a single cluster is used, i.e., when we run the traditional logistic regression. There are two main inconsistencies in those values: 1) they do not capture the fact that only a specific group of clients (cluster 4) has a negative bias towards contractors with a lot of hours completed in the platform, and 2) they miss the strong positive bias of a group of clients (cluster 2) towards contractors with the appropriate skills for a task. These two inconsistencies explain why our algorithm gives this substantial 40% improvement (Figure 7(b)) over the baseline approach of learning the same criteria for all clients.

Some of the differences in the clients' criteria can be explained by observing the IT/KPO and FP/HR percentages of the applications in the different clusters. IT stands for Information Technology and refers to applications for all tasks related to software development and administration, e.g., web development, DB administration, or software for scientific experiments. Applications for all other tasks fall under the Knowledge Processing Outsourcing (KPO) category, e.g., translation, marketing, or logo design. A second categorization for tasks is the Fixed Price(FP)/Hourly Rate(HR) categorization that refers to whether a fixed amount will be given to the contractor upon the completion of the task or the client and the contractor will get into a contract with

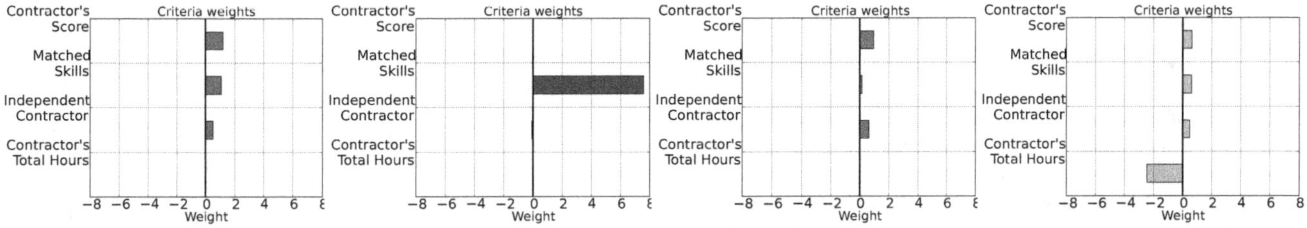

(a) criteria vector $\mathbf{w_1}$ (b) criteria vector $\mathbf{w_2}$ (c) criteria vector $\mathbf{w_3}$ (d) criteria vector $\mathbf{w_4}$

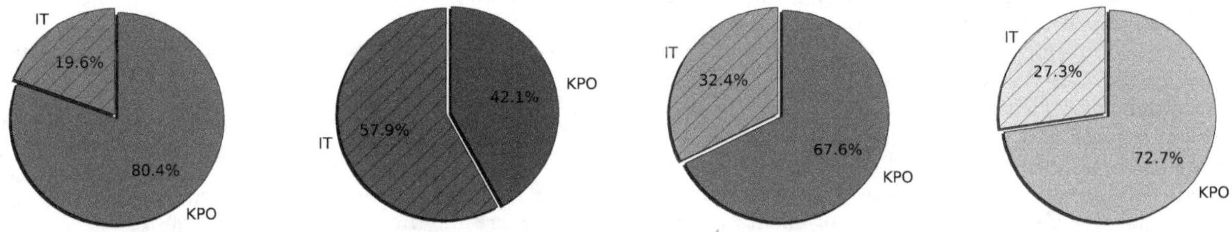

(e) IT vs KPO cluster 1 (f) IT vs KPO cluster 2 (g) IT vs KPO cluster 3 (h) IT vs KPO cluster 4

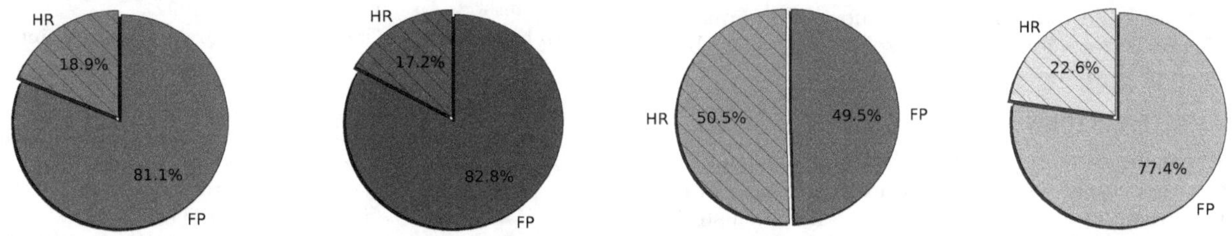

(i) FP vs HR cluster 1 (j) FP vs HR cluster 2 (k) FP vs HR cluster 3 (l) FP vs HR cluster 4

Figure 8: Figures (a) to (d) depict the weights of the criteria vectors in each of the 4 clusters computed for 10 features and an *approved* threshold of 20. Figures (e) to (h) depict the percentage of Information Technology tasks in each cluster, while figures (i) to (l) depict the percentage of Hourly Rate tasks.

predefined hourly-rate earnings. Figures 8(e) to 8(h) depict the IT/KPO percentages, while Figures 8(i) to 8(l) depict FP/HR percentages, in the 4 clusters.

In cluster 2 there is a large percentage of IT tasks (57.9%), as we see in Figure 8(f). This large percentage provides an explanation for the criteria in cluster 2. Most IT contractors receive good reviews by clients; although clients are not always fully satisfied with the contractor's work (e.g., software consistent with the specifications that does not do exactly what the client had in mind). As a result, IT contractors tend to have a very high score and, hence, the contractor's score stops being a powerful signal for a client to base her decision. On the other hand, the technologies where the contractor is an expert, in many cases indicate if a contractor is a good fit for an IT task. Therefore, the clients in cluster 2 have a good reason to base their decisions on the "Matched Skills" (Figure 8(b)).

Although the criteria in clusters 1 and 3 (Figures 8(a) and 8(c)) seem similar, there is an interesting difference: clients in cluster 1 give a large weight to the "Matched Skills" while the value for this feature in cluster 3 is almost zero. As Figures 8(i) and 8(k) point out, there is an important difference in the percentage of the HR tasks in the two clusters: in cluster 1 only 18.9% of the tasks are HR, while in cluster 3 50.5% of the tasks are HR. The "Matched Skills" signal is usually more useful for FP tasks that require expertise in a very specific piece of work that needs to be completed, while HR tasks mostly require a good collaboration between the client and the contractor.

As for the large negative weight on the "Contractor's Total Hours" for cluster 4 (Figure 8(d)), it appears that the IT/KPO and HR/FP percentages cannot provide any plausible explanation. Cluster 4 simply consists of clients that prefer to work with contractors that are "new" to the platform. In fact, there is a good reason for selecting such contractors: in many cases "new" contractors are eager to produce a high-quality outcome in order to build a good reputation in the system.

5. RELATED WORK

A problem similar to the one we study is addressed by collaborative filtering (CF) approaches (see [28] for a recent survey). Traditional memory-based CF approaches estimate the preference of a user U to an item I using the ratings of U for items "similar" to I or the ratings of users "similar" to U for I [11, 26]. Other CF approaches are based on latent factor models such as matrix factorization [24, 31], latent Dirichlet allocation [2], Boltzmann machines [25], Latent Semantic Analysis [12], or user/item co-clustering [7, 10], while others [19] have proposed models that combine the memory and model based approaches.

The hetereogeneity of user preferences is also studied by Lenk et al [21]: user preferences depend on users' spatial region, in that study. User partitioning can also be based on whether a user is an "innovator" or "imitator" [13]: innovators make decisions based on their own preferences, while imitators decide based on a product's stage of maturity.

The main limitation for directly applying CF methods to the problem discussed in this paper, is the fact that contractor applications to a task posted by a client are "unique". That is, while most CF methods assume that users rate, explicitly or implicitly, the same products, in our case, clients do not actually rate the same contractors but their applications to a specific task.

The effect of clients having different preferences when selecting among alternatives, is studied thoroughly in the economics/marketing literature [15, 23, 20, 1]. In particular, most studies focus on how a market is partitioned in segments, with each segment having clients with same preferences when selecting among brands. Most related to our work, are the studies using Finite Mixture Logit models [22, 15, 23]. An important difference of those studies with our work is that we don't focus on "learning" the distribution of market segments. On the contrary, we focus on partitioning the existing clients, with each client belonging to exactly one segment; instead of belonging to any segment with some probability (see [16] for an analysis of the tradeoffs between "hard" and "soft" assignments). Moreover, as noted earlier in the discussion for CF, the preferences of clients refer to "unique" applications in our model, as opposed to a fixed set of alternatives, e.g., brands. Our model is simpler than the Finite Mixture Logit models used in economics and marketing studies, and aims for a scalable solution to a problem met in most of the online work marketplaces.

6. CONCLUSION

Identifying the groups of clients with similar hiring criteria is of great importance in online work marketplaces. In this paper, we presented our model for hiring-criteria clustering and we developed a clustering algorithm that can be applied effectively on large datasets. When applied on oDesk job applications, our approach significantly improves the prediction accuracy for future hirings of clients.

Furthermore, the analysis of the clusters generated by our algorithm reveals some interesting facts about the way different groups of clients choose contractors for their tasks: some clients are positively biased to contractors that are "new" to a marketplace (probably because many new contractors are eager to build a competitive profile), while other clients ignore the contractor's reputation and focus on how well the contractor's skills match to the task requirements. Our approach discovers such differences in client hiring criteria and can drastically improve the matching between clients and contractors in work marketplaces.

7. REFERENCES

[1] G. M. Allenby and P. E. Rossi. Marketing models of consumer heterogeneity. *J. Econometrics*, 89:57–78, 1998.

[2] D. M. Blei, A. Y. Ng, and M. I. Jordan. Latent dirichlet allocation. *J. Machine Learning Research*, 3:993–1022, 2003.

[3] R. Collobert, S. Bengio, and Y. Bengio. A parallel mixture of SVMs for very large scale problems. In *NIPS*, 2002.

[4] M. Daltayanni, L. de Alfaro, and P. Papadimitriou. Workerrank: Using employer implicit judgements to infer worker reputation. In *WSDM*, 2015.

[5] A. S. Das, M. Datar, A. Garg, and S. Rajaram. Google news personalization: Scalable online collaborative filtering. In *WWW*, 2007.

[6] O. Dekel and O. Shamir. There's a hole in my data space: Piecewise predictors for heterogeneous learning problems. In *AISTATS*, 2012.

[7] M. Deodhar and J. Ghosh. Scoal: A framework for simultaneous co-clustering and learning from complex data. *ACM Trans. Knowl. Discov. Data*, 4(3):11:1–11:31, 2010.

[8] W. DeSarbo and W. Cron. A maximum likelihood methodology for clusterwise linear regression. *J. of Classification*, 5(2):249–282, 1988.

[9] Z. Fu, A. Robles-Kelly, and J. Zhou. Mixing Linear SVMs for Nonlinear Classification. *IEEE Trans. Neural Networks*, 21(12):1963–1975, 2010.

[10] T. George and S. Merugu. A scalable collaborative filtering framework based on co-clustering. In *ICDM*, 2005.

[11] J. L. Herlocker, J. A. Konstan, A. Borchers, and J. Riedl. An algorithmic framework for performing collaborative filtering. In *SIGIR*, 1999.

[12] T. Hofmann. Latent semantic models for collaborative filtering. *ACM Trans. Information Systems*, 22:89–115, 2004.

[13] K. Hu, W. Hsu, and M. L. Lee. Utilizing users' tipping points in e-commerce recommender systems. In *ICDE*, 2013.

[14] S. in Lee, H. Lee, P. Abbeel, and A. Y. Ng. Efficient l1 regularized logistic regression. In *AAAI*, 2006.

[15] W. A. Kamakura and G. Russell. A probabilistic choice model for market segmentation and elasticity structure. *J. Marketing Research*, XXVI:379–390, 1989.

[16] M. J. Kearns, Y. Mansour, and A. Y. Ng. An information-theoretic analysis of hard and soft assignment methods for clustering. In *UAI*, 1997.

[17] K. Koh, S.-J. Kim, and S. Boyd. An interior-point method for large-scale l1-regularized logistic regression. *J. Machine Learning Research*, 8:1519–1555, 2007.

[18] M. Kokkodis, P. Papadimitriou, and P. G. Ipeirotis. Hiring behavior models for online labor markets. In *WSDM*, 2015.

[19] Y. Koren. Factorization meets the neighborhood: A multifaceted collaborative filtering model. In *KDD*, 2008.

[20] P. J. Lenk, W. S. DeSarbo, P. E. Green, and M. R. Young. Hierarchical bayes conjoint analysis: Recovery of partworth heterogeneity from reduced experimental designs. *Marketing Science*, 15:173–191, 1996.

[21] J. J. Levandoski, M. Sarwat, A. Eldawy, and M. F. Mokbel. Lars: A location-aware recommender system. In *ICDE*, 2012.

[22] G. Mclachlan and D. Peel. *Finite Mixture Models*. Wiley, 2000.

[23] D. C. J. Pradeep K. Chintagunta and N. J. Vilcassim. Investigating heterogeneity in brand preferences in logit models for panel data. *J. Marketing Research*, 28:417–428, 1991.

[24] R. Salakhutdinov and A. Mnih. Probabilistic matrix factorization. In *NIPS*, 2007.

[25] R. Salakhutdinov, A. Mnih, and G. Hinton. Restricted boltzmann machines for collaborative filtering. In *ICML*, 2007.

[26] B. Sarwar, G. Karypis, J. Konstan, and J. Riedl. Item-based collaborative filtering recommendation algorithms. In *WWW*, 2001.

[27] H. Späth. Algorithm 39 clusterwise linear regression. *Computing*, 22(4), 1979.

[28] X. Su and T. M. Khoshgoftaar. A survey of collaborative filtering techniques. *Advances in Artificial Intelligence*, 2009.

[29] V. Verroios, P. Papadimitriou, R. Johari, and H. Garcia-Molina. Client clustering for hiring modeling in work marketplaces. *Technical report, Stanford University, available at* `http://ilpubs.stanford.edu:8090/1106/`.

[30] M. Wedel and J.-B. E. M. Steenkamp. A clusterwise regression method for simultaneous fuzzy market structuring and benefit segmentation. *J. Marketing Research*, 28(4):385–396, 1991.

[31] J. Yuan, B. Kanagal, V. Josifovski, L. Garcia-Pueyo, A. Ahmed, and S. Pandey. Focused matrix factorization for audience selection in display advertising. In *ICDE*, 2013.

[32] J. Zhu, N. Chen, and E. Xing. Infinite svm: a dirichlet process mixture of large-margin kernel machines. In *ICML*, 2011.

Discerning Tactical Patterns for Professional Soccer Teams: an Enhanced Topic Model with Applications

Qing Wang[1]*, Hengshu Zhu[2], Wei Hu[2], Zhiyong Shen[2], Yuan Yao[1]

[1]School of Mathematical Science, Peking University, [2]Big Data Lab, Baidu Research

{wangqing09,zhuhengshu,huwei05,shenzhiyong}@baidu.com, yuany@math.pku.edu.cn

ABSTRACT

Analyzing team tactics plays an important role in the professional soccer industry. Recently, the progressing ability to track the mobility of ball and players makes it possible to accumulate extensive match logs, which open a venue for better tactical analysis. However, traditional methods for tactical analysis largely rely on the knowledge and manual labor of domain experts. To this end, in this paper we propose an unsupervised approach to automatically discerning the typical tactics, i.e., *tactical patterns*, of soccer teams through mining the historical match logs. To be specific, we first develop a novel model named Team Tactic Topic Model (T^3M) for learning the latent tactical patterns, which can model the locations and passing relations of players simultaneously. Furthermore, we demonstrate several potential applications enabled by the proposed T^3M, such as automatic tactical pattern discovery, pass segment annotation, and spatial analysis of player roles. Finally, we implement an intelligent demo system to empirically evaluate our approach based on the data collected from La Liga 2013-2014. Indeed, by visualizing the results obtained from T^3M, we can successfully observe many meaningful tactical patterns and interesting discoveries, such as *using which tactics a team is more likely to score a goal* and *how a team's playing tactic changes in sequential matches across a season.*

Categories and Subject Descriptors

H.2.8 [**Database Management**]: Database Applications — Data Mining; H.4.m [**Information Systems Applications**]: Miscellaneous

Keywords

Tactical Patterns; Professional Soccer; Topic Model

*The paper was done when the first author was an intern in Baidu Research - Big Data Lab under the supervision of the fourth author.

KDD'15, August 10–13, 2015, Sydney, Australia.

 ISBN 978-1-4503-3664-2/15/08 ...$15.00.

DOI: http://dx.doi.org/10.1145/2783258.2788577.

1. INTRODUCTION

As the most popular sport in the world, soccer stimulates more than 3 billion loyal fans [2] and tens of billions of dollars in revenue each year [7]. A growing interest along this line is to provide professional tactical analysis for the soccer industry, which can facilitate the decision making of soccer coaches and improve the watching experiences of match audiences. Recently, with the rapid development of wearable devices and sensor technology, the mobility information of players/ball and match events can be recorded as extensive match logs. Indeed, these large-scale and fine-grained data open a venue for better professional tactical analysis, and thus attract a lot of research attentions [18, 26, 4, 24, 17]. However, traditional methods for tactical analysis largely rely on the knowledge and manual labor of domain experts, which are very expensive and unscalable for the entire industry. Therefore, it is very appealing to have an effective and automatic approach for learning the typical tactics, i.e., *tactical patterns*, of soccer teams. Specifically, here we define a tactical pattern as a series of frequently used ball-passing combinations that are characterized by the players who make the passing or receiving actions, and their corresponding locations.

In the literature, while there are some related studies on sports data mining, such as [18, 17, 26, 3, 4, 16, 24, 10, 9], the problem of mining tactical patterns for soccer teams is still under-explored. It is because that the tactical patterns are high-level features and only low-level data can be observed, such as the positions of players and the ball over time. To this end, in this paper we propose an unsupervised probabilistic approach to automatically discerning the tactical patterns of soccer teams through mining the historical match logs. To be specific, we first present a novel generative model named Team Tactic Topic Model (T^3M) for learning the latent tactical patterns, which can model the locations and passing relations of players simultaneously. Furthermore, several potential applications enabled by the proposed T^3M are demonstrated, such as automatic tactical pattern discovery, pass segment annotation, and spatial analysis of player roles. Finally, an intelligent demo system is implemented to empirically evaluate our approach based on the data collected from La Liga 2013-2014. Indeed, by visualizing the results obtained from T^3M, many meaningful tactical patterns and interesting discoveries can be observed, such as *using which tactics a team is more likely to score a goal* and *how a team's playing tactic changes in sequential matches across a season.* Particularly, the contributions of this paper can be summarized as follows.

Table 1: A sampled match log of FC Barcelona, where match segments are separated by horizontal lines.

Event ID	Timestamp	Passer ID	Receiver ID	Start position	End position
1574	02:27	[D]J.Alba	[D]J.Mathieu	(44.2,100.0)	(29.8,92.2)
1575	02:30	[D]J.Mathieu	[D]J.Mascherano	(25.5,81.7)	(17.8,42.9)
1576	02:33	[D]J.Mascherano	[D]D.Alves	(20.9,34.8)	(30.6,5.6)
⋮	⋮	⋮	⋮	⋮	⋮
1588	03:06	[M]I.Rakitic	[D]J.Mathieu	(52.4,14.4)	(45.2,56.7)
1589	03:10	[D]J.Mathieu	[M]A.Iniesta	(46.2,58.5)	(56.5,79.3)
1599	03:54	[G]C.Bravo	[M]S.Busquets	(4.8,40.6)	(21.9,49.8)
1600	04:01	[M]S.Busquets	[D]J.Mascherano	(33.6,49.6)	(36.7,20.7)
1601	04:06	[D]J.Mascherano	[M]I.Rakitic	(46.7,17.1)	(52.8,25.9)
1602	04:07	[M]I.Rakitic	[D]J.Mascherano	(52.8,25.9)	(45.1,17.8)
1611	04:43	[M]A.Iniesta	[D]J.Alba	(60.5,97.7)	(70.2,96.9)
1612	04:44	[D]J.Alba	[F]M.E.Haddadi	(70.2,96.9)	(80.4,82.8)
1613	04:45	[F]M.E.Haddadi	[F]L.Messi	(80.4,82.8)	(77.1,62.5)

- To the best of our knowledge, this work is the first attempt to leverage unsupervised modeling approach for automatically discerning the tactical patterns of soccer teams by mining match logs.
- We propose a novel generative model T^{3}M for learning the latent tactical patterns. Comparing to existing models, our model can learn the locations and passing relations of players simultaneously, yielding more meaningful and spatially localized tactical patterns.
- Further, we build an intelligent demo system to evaluate our approach. By visualizing the results obtained from T^{3}M, we show that our model can promote many related applications, including automatic tactical pattern discovery, pass segment annotation, and spatial analysis of player roles.

Overview. The remainder of this paper is organized as follows. Section 2 introduces the details of the proposed generative model T^{3}M. In Section 3, we further discuss the T^{3}M and introduce several potential applications. Then in Section 4, we report the evaluation results based on our intelligent system and a real-world data set. And Section 5 provides a brief review of related works and our innovations. Finally, we conclude the paper in Section 6.

2. MODELING THE TACTICAL PATTERNS FOR SOCCER TEAMS

In this paper, we are interested in the problem of automatically finding a team's tactical patterns in sequential matches across a season. Specifically, a team may have a number of tactical patterns in terms of attacking and defending, such as *how to break through the defense on the sideline*, and *how to keep possession of the ball.* Thus, in this section, we propose an unsupervised approach to modeling the tactical patterns for soccer teams based on the analysis of match logs.

2.1 Data Description

The match log of a specific team contains many event records, such as pass event, foul event, ball-out event and tackle event. In this paper, we define a tactical pattern as a series of frequently used ball-passing combinations that are characterized by the players who make the passing or receiving actions, and their corresponding locations. Therefore, here we mainly focus on the records related to the pass events in the match logs. We further split the pass events into several segments by stoppages and turnovers in matches [17]. A stoppage means the game is paused, usually due to a ball-out or a foul; a turnover means the opponent team takes the possession of the ball, without pausing the game. We label the corresponding events in match logs as stoppages and turnovers. Then the passes before and after a stoppage or a turnover are considered as in two disjoint segments. For example, Table 1 shows a sampled match log of FC Barcelona with three different match segments, where each row in the table represents a successful pass event. Specifically, each event record contains a unique *Event ID*, a *Timestamp*, a *Passer* with corresponding *Start Position* and a *Receiver* with corresponding *End Position* (i.e., each position is scaled to 100×100).

2.2 Team Tactic Topic Model (T^{3}M)

Here we introduce the details of the proposed T^{3}M for modeling tactical patterns. Specifically, let us denote a team as a set of players Q, of which the match log can be split into multiple segments D. For the i-th pass in segment d, $i = 1, \dots, N_d$, we denote the passer as $u_{d,i}$ and the receiver as $v_{d,i}$. Meanwhile, the pass of the ball can be denoted as a directed edge from the passer to the receiver, i.e., $w_{d,i} = (u_{d,i}, v_{d,i})$. And the end position of a pass is denoted as $x_{d,i}$. The end position is used instead of the start position since the end position can better describe the receiver's movement without the ball. To write compactly, a token $f_{d,i}$ in our model is defined by $f_{d,i} = (w_{d,i}, x_{d,i})$.

We assume each team has several tactical patterns $k = 1, \dots, K$, each consists of a passing pattern and a team positioning. Specifically, a passing pattern is a transition frequency matrix between players that is modeled as a multinomial distribution on the Cartesian product between players $(Q \times Q)$ (i.e., parameterized by ϕ_k); A team positioning indicates where the ball is most likely passed to the receiver v. In particular, we assign a Gaussian distribution parameterized by $\psi_{k,v} = (\mu_{k,v}, \Sigma_{k,v})$ to each receiver $v \in Q$ for each pattern k respectively, resulting in $M = K \times |Q|$ Gaussian distributions in total. Furthermore, for each pass $f_{d,i}$ in segment d, we assume there is a latent variable $z_{d,i} \in \{1, \dots, K\}$, indicating which tactical pattern the team is currently playing in this pass. And the latent pattern $z_{d,i}$ in segment d is consid-

Table 2: Mathematical notations.

Symbol	Description
K	The predefined number of tactical patterns.
D	The pass segments of a team. $D = \{d_1, \dots, d_{\|D\|}\}$.
Q	The squads (set of players) for a team.
ϕ_k	Passing pattern for pattern k.
$\psi_{k,v}$	Gaussian parameters of player v's location in pattern k. $\psi_{k,v} = (\mu_{k,v}, \Sigma_{k,v})$
θ_d	Distribution of tactical patterns for segment d.
$w_{d,i}$	The pass from $u_{d,i}$ to $v_{d,i}$. $w_{d,i} = (u_{d,i}, v_{d,i})$.
$x_{d,i}$	The end position of the pass. $x_{d,i} \in \mathbb{R}^2$.
$f_{d,i}$	The players and the end position of a pass. $f_{d,i} = (w_{d,i}, x_{d,i})$.
$z_{d,i}$	Latent tactical pattern of pass $f_{d,i}$.
α	Hyperparameter of the Dirichlet prior on θ_d.
β	Hyperparameter of the Dirichlet prior on ϕ_k.
γ	Hyperparameter of the NIW prior on $(\mu_{k,v}, \Sigma_{k,v})$. $\gamma = (\mu_0, \Sigma_0, \Lambda_0, \nu_0)$

ered as drawn from the multinomial distribution $\text{Mult}(\theta_d)$. As a result, the actual pass $f_{d,i}$ is regarded as drawn according to $z_{d,i}$. To be more specific, given $z_{d,i} = k$, each $w_{d,i}$ conforms a multinomial distribution parameterized by ϕ_k; and the end position $x_{d,i}$ follows a Gaussian distribution with parameters $(\mu_{k,v_{d,i}}, \Sigma_{k,v_{d,i}})$.

In this paper, we leverage the Bayesian approach for the modeling process, where conjugate priors are placed for respective distributions. Specifically, the generative process of our model is demonstrated as follows:

1. Draw K tactical patterns from its prior distribution.
   - (a) Draw ϕ_k from the Dirichlet prior $\text{Dir}(\beta)$ for $k = 1, \dots, K$.
   - (b) Draw $\psi_{k,v}$ from $\text{NIW}(\gamma)$ for $k = 1, \dots, K$ and $v \in Q$.
2. Draw θ_d from the Dirichlet prior $\text{Dir}(\alpha)$ for $d \in D$.
3. For each observation i in segment d:
   - (a) Draw latent assignment $z_{d,i}$ from the segment's specified distribution $\text{Dir}(\theta_d)$.
   - (b) Draw the pass $w_{d,i}$ from $\text{Dir}(\phi_{z_{d,i}})$.
   - (c) Draw the player location $x_{d,i}$ from $N(\mu_{\phi_{z_{d,i}}, v_{d,i}}, \Sigma_{\phi_{z_{d,i}}, v_{d,i}})$.

In summary, we illustrate the important mathematical notations in Table 2, and the graphical representation of T^{3}M in Figure 1. The full model parameterizations are

$$\begin{aligned}
w_{d,i} | z_{d,i} = k, \phi_k &\sim \text{Mult}(\phi_k) \\
x_{d,i} | z_{d,i} = k, v_{d,i} = v, \mu_{k,v}, \Sigma_{k,v} &\sim N(\mu_{k,v}, \Sigma_{k,v}) \\
z_{d,i} | \theta_d &\sim \text{Mult}(\theta_d) \\
\theta_d &\sim \text{Dir}(\alpha) \\
\phi_k &\sim \text{Dir}(\beta) \\
\psi_{k,v} &\sim \text{NIW}(\gamma),
\end{aligned}$$

where the NIW denotes the Normal-Inverse-Wishart distribution [19].

2.3 Model Inference

To estimate the model parameters, here we exploit an iterative approach called collapsed Gibbs sampling (CGS) [11], which is a Monte Carlo Markov Chain (MCMC) algorithm to approximate the posterior distribution of model parameters. Specifically, in CGS procedure we first assign a random tactical pattern to each pass. Then in each iteration of CGS, a new tactical pattern for each pass is drawn from the posterior distribution conditioned on other assignments. Finally, under some regularity conditions, the distribution of assignments for each pass converges to the posterior distribution as the number of iteration increases.

If we denote the latent assignments for the passes in all segments except the i-th pass in segment d as $z_{-(d,i)}$, and the latent assignments for all the passes in segment d except the i-th pass as $z_{d,-i}$ (similar notations hold for x, w, f, etc.), the probability for assigning the tactical pattern k for the i-th pass in segment d conditioned on the other assignments can be computed as

$$\begin{aligned}
& P(z_{d,i} = k | x_{d,i}, w_{d,i}, z_{-(d,i)}, x_{-(d,i)}, w_{-(d,i)}) \quad (1) \\
\propto\ & P(z_{d,i} = k | z_{-(d,i)}) \\
& \cdot P(w_{d,i} | z_{d,i} = k, z_{-(d,i)}, w_{-(d,i)}) \\
& \cdot P(x_{d,i} | z_{d,i} = k, z_{-(d,i)}, x_{-(d,i)}),
\end{aligned}$$

where we have

$$P(z_{d,i} = k | z_{-(d,i)}) = \frac{n^{(k)}_{(d,-i),\cdot} + \alpha}{(N_d - 1) + \alpha K} \quad (2)$$

$$P(w_{d,i} | z_{d,i} = k, z_{-(d,i)}, w_{-(d,i)}) = \frac{n^{(k)}_{-(d,i),w_{d,i}} + \beta}{n^{(k)}_{-(d,i),\cdot} + \beta |Q|^2} \quad (3)$$

$$P(x_{d,i} | z_{d,i} = k, z_{-(d,i)}, x_{-(d,i)}) = P(x_{d,i} | X_{d,i}). \quad (4)$$

The notation $n^{(k)}_{a,b}$ means the frequency of f_a labeled as tactic k while $w_a = b$. And N_d represents the number of passes in segment d. To have a compact representation, we use the notation $X_{d,i} = \{x_{d',i'} : (d', i') \neq (d, i), z_{d',i'} = z_{d,i}, v_{d',i'} = v_{d,i}\}$. The posterior predictive distribution for $P(x_{d,i} | X_{d,i})$ is a multivariate Student-T distribution with parameters [19]:

$$\begin{aligned}
P(x|X) &= t_{\nu_n - 1}\left(\mu_n, \frac{\Lambda_n(\kappa_n + 1)}{\kappa_n(\nu_n - 1)}\right) \quad (5) \\
\mu_n &= \frac{\kappa_0}{\kappa_0 + n}\mu_0 + \frac{n}{\kappa_0 + n}\bar{x} \\
\kappa_n &= \kappa_0 + n \\
\nu_n &= \nu_0 + n \\
\Lambda_n &= \Lambda_0 + \textstyle\sum_{j=1}^{n}(x_j - \bar{x})(x_j - \bar{x})^T \\
&\quad + \frac{\kappa_0 n}{\kappa_0 + n}(\bar{x} - \mu_0)(\bar{x} - \mu_0)^T
\end{aligned}$$

where $n = |X_{d,i}|$ and $\bar{x}$ is the sample mean for $x_j \in X_{d,i}$.

3. APPLICATIONS & DISCUSSION

In this section, we firstly introduce how our T^{3}M can promote various applications in the sports analytic industry, including automatic tactical pattern discovery, pass segment annotation, and spatial analysis of player roles. And then we discuss the improvements of our T^{3}M over basic topic models (e.g., Latent Dirichlet Allocation (LDA) [6]).

3.1 Applications

With T^{3}M, we can study the tactical patterns discovered from a team's passing data, and understand what tactic the team is most likely to use, as well as who is the key player in each tactical pattern. The analysis results of tactical patterns can help soccer coaches to better plan a match.

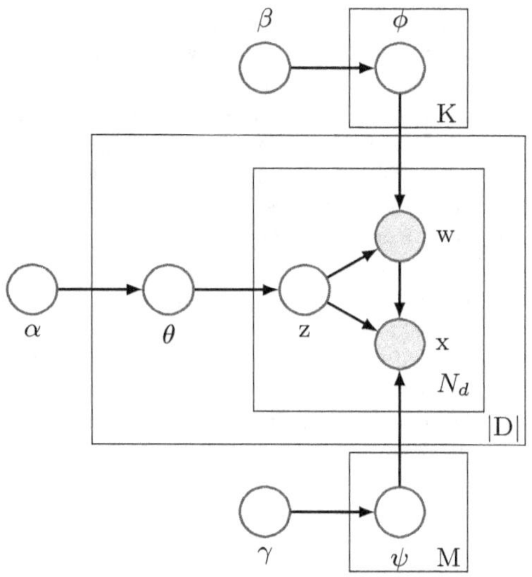

Figure 1: The graphical representation of T³M, where K is the number of tactical patterns, N_d is the number of passes in segment d, $|D|$ is the total number of segments, and $M = K \times |Q|$ is the total number of player position distributions.

3.1.1 *Automatic Team Tactical Pattern Discovery*

Team tactical pattern discovery is an important topic in soccer data analysis. Existing methods include using entropy maps of ball movement patterns to study the spatial variability of tactics (e.g., [17]), and motif finding method to characterize the passing patterns between players (e.g., [10]). In this work, our method can be viewed as a simultaneous analysis on the passing patterns between players and the spatial patterns in the pitch. For a given team, we can find K tactical patterns with our T³M. And for each pattern, we can know its passing patterns ϕ_k on the graph of players, and receiving locations for each player v. By the visualization of these learned tactics, we can study the playing styles of a team in a higher level. Therefore, we can understand the learned tactical patterns in a semantic way, and help coaches and sports analysts to give quantitative and objective analysis of a team's playing styles. With the help of our system, we can also answer the questions like *what is the most successful tactical pattern of a team (resulting in the most goals)* and *who is the central player (strategic center) of a playing style of this team.* Empirical evaluations of this application are demonstrated in Section 4.2.

3.1.2 *Pass Segment Annotation*

In addition to automatic team tactical pattern discovery, we can also study the progress of a match as dynamic changes of tactics. For each segment d in a match, we can find the posterior distribution (parameterized by θ_d) of tactical patterns for the passes in this segment. We can then annotate these disjoint segments in a match with different colors according to the dominating tactical pattern

$$k^* = \text{argmax}_k \theta_d. \tag{6}$$

Following the above approach, we can use our unsupervised method to cluster similar playing styles, and color the pass segments in a series of matches of a team, then analyze the dynamic change of a team's favorite tactical pattern across a season. Meanwhile, we can then study the team's tactical changes, as well as the strategic interaction between the team and different opponent teams. Furthermore, the annotation of pass segments also provides a natural summarization and abstraction of match playing progress. Empirical evaluations of this application can be found in Section 4.3.

3.1.3 *Spatial Analysis of Player Role*

Furthermore, our model is useful for individual analysis as well. Specifically, a joint analysis of team's tactical patterns and the roles a player plays in different tactics can help us define the participation measure of players in different tactics, and players' spatial roles at different regions of the playing field.

Given a player v, we can find in which tactical pattern player v plays a key role. Formally, for a passing pattern $\phi_k \in Q \times Q$ of pattern k, a player v's participation measure is defined as

$$\text{score}(k, v) = \phi_{k,v,\cdot} + \phi_{k,\cdot,v}, \tag{7}$$

which is equal to the sum of the weights for the passes in ϕ_k from or to player v. A visualization of the player scores is given in Figure 6 as an example. Furthermore, denoting the scores for player v as

$$S_v = (\text{score}(1, v), \dots, \text{score}(K, v)), \tag{8}$$

we can then perform clustering algorithms on S_v to study the different player groups with respect to their playing roles.

Finally, we can also study a player's active regions in different tactical patterns. A player may appear in different locations with different roles to play. To visualize the diversity, we can collect the locations where player v receives the ball in different tactics respectively, and plot the heat map for each pattern as

$$P(x_{d,i}|v_{d,i} = v) = \sum_{k=1}^{K} P(x_{d,i}, z_{d,i} = k|v_{d,i} = v). \tag{9}$$

The distribution of $x_{d,i}$ where $v_{d,i} = v$, $z_{d,i} = k$, can be seen as the active region for player v in pattern k. Experiment results of this application are given in Section 4.4.

3.2 Discussion: LDA vs. T³M

Actually, T³M can be seen as an extension of classic topic model LDA. Therefore, here we discuss the differences between T³M and LDA in terms of modeling tactical patterns.

Specifically, for modeling passes between players, we note that both LDA and T³M can capture the prominent passing styles in the our data set. However, without using the location information (e.g., fitting with classical LDA), the learned patterns are not spatially clustered. As in Figure 2, we depict the learned tactical patterns by LDA (i.e., top two rows) and T³M (i.e., bottom two rows) respectively. In this figure, heat maps of receiving positions of the passes that assigned to each learned tactical pattern are drawn to represent the spatial distribution of these patterns. From these figures, we can observe that the location information incorporated in our T³M can help to assess the latent playing styles with more compact spatial patterns in the pitch.

In addition, T³M aims to connect the player locations with latent tactical patterns, so that we can find the different roles or locations of a player in different tactics. For example, player A can play the role of attacking midfielder in both

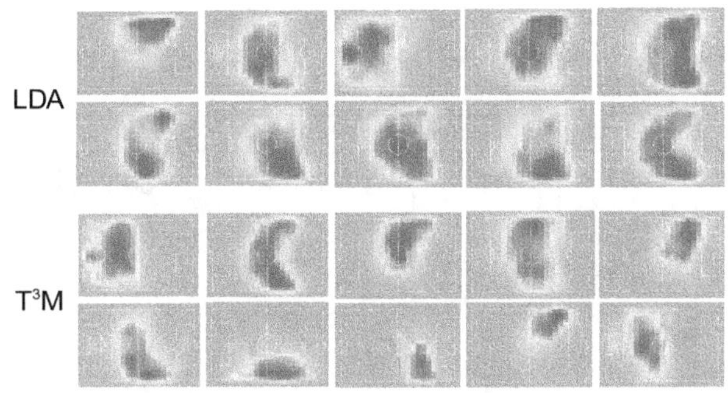

Figure 2: Heat maps for the 10 tactical patterns of Barcelona learned by LDA and T^{3}M.

left side and right side, and player B is a strategic midfielder who usually passes the ball to player A. In classical LDA, the location information of the players is invisible to the model so that the passes from B to A are all categorized as the same tactical pattern. However, with the proposed T^{3}M, the location where player A received the ball is related to the latent tactics he was playing, so it is likely that the passes from B to A will be classified into two distinct patterns, namely one is to attack in the left side and the other in the right side. In this manner, we can give a spatial analysis of each player's roles as described in Section 3.1.3.

4. EXPERIMANTAL RESULTS

In this section, we empirically study several novel applications enabled by our model, including soccer team tactical patterns discovery, team tactics analysis over matches, player role analysis, and a specific case study on Barcelona vs. Real Madrid.

In particular, we have developed a web-based demo system[1] for evaluating different applications. This system can visualize the results obtained from T^{3}M, provide in-depth analysis and objective quantification of team performance, and enhance better watching experience for soccer fans. Figure 3 shows a screenshot of our prototype system for automatic soccer tactic analysis. In the middle of the page, we plot the spatial positions of major players in each tactical pattern, with various statistics below the plot. On the right side, we plot the heatmaps of receiving positions for each tactical pattern.

4.1 Evaluation Setup

For the evaluation of our approach and system, we used match logs from a commercial sports data provider [1], which contains 241 (out of 380) matches in La Liga 2013-2014, resulting in 401,105 events in the match logs. The match logs were preprocessed according to the descriptions in Section 2. To facilitate understanding, we mainly use FC Barcelona, a leading team in La Liga, as an example for evaluating our approach in the following subsections. Specifically, we extracted 24 matches of Barcelona in this season, and split the 13,367 passes into 2,652 playing segments according to the description in Section 2.

In our experiments, the number of CGS iterations was chosen as 10,000 to ensure convergence. The number of tactical patterns was empirically chosen as 10 for evaluation. Note that, although a team may arguably have much more tactics

[1]This demo system will be publicly available soon.

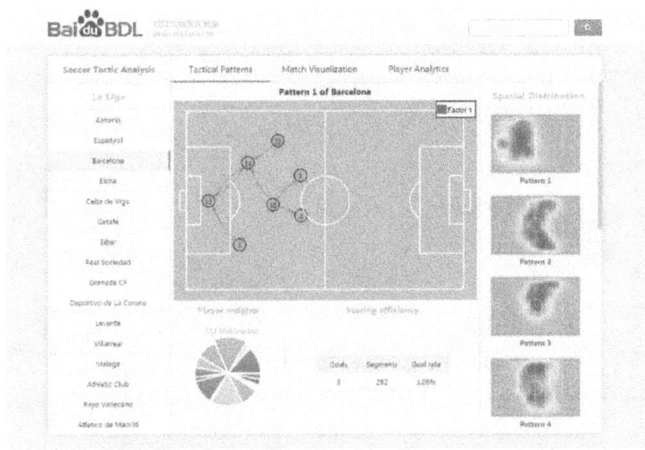

Figure 3: A screenshot of our system for automatic soccer tactic analysis.

than 10, here we only aim to learn the typical tactical patterns. In addition, we set $\alpha = 0.01$ and $\beta = 0.001$ for both LDA and T^{3}M [11]. For NIW prior, we set $\mu_0 = (50, 50)^T$, $\kappa_0 = 2$, $\Lambda_0 = \begin{pmatrix} 100 & 50 \\ 50 & 100 \end{pmatrix}$, $\nu_0 = 2$. Indeed, empirically we find that the results are not sensitive to the choice of NIW prior when we set small values for both κ_0 and ν_0.

4.2 Visualization of Tactics for Barcelona

As one of the most successful soccer clubs in the world, FC Barcelona is well known for its world-class superb players, top-tier records and achievements in various competitions, as well as the famous *Tiki-taka* tactical style. Specifically, Tiki-taka tactical style is characterized by maintaining ball-possession with short passes and movements, which is considered as a diversion from the traditional thinking of formations to a concept derived from zonal play [25]. As an example, here we propose to study the tactical patterns of Barcelona with our approach and system.

First, we fit T^{3}M as described in Section 2 with corresponding match logs. For each pass $f_{d,i}$ in these segments, our model can compute a latent tactical pattern $z_{d,i}$ assigned to the pass. Then, we can collect the passes with the same latent pattern k, and plot the corresponding end positions as a heat map visualized in Figure 2.

Indeed, the learned tactical patterns are meaningful and interpretable. Combining Figure 2 and Figure 4, we can have a simultaneous analysis of passing patterns and spatial patterns. For example, Pattern 1 can be seen as a defensive pattern, with frequent passes between the defenders (Mascherano, Adriano, Pique) and the goalkeeper (Pinto), while Pattern 2 indicates an attacking pattern in the two wings. Specifically, Pattern 5 and Pattern 9 are offensive styles in the left wing, with Iniesta as the playmaker, while Pattern 8 is an offensive style in the right wing, centered on the midfielder Xavi. It should also be noted that, for most patterns there is a central player in the passing network, usually acting as a strategic center or a playmaker.

Further, statistics of the scoring efficiency for the tactical patterns are shown in Table 3. For each goal in the matches, we find the last segment of passes before the goal, and attribute the goal to the most frequent tactical pattern

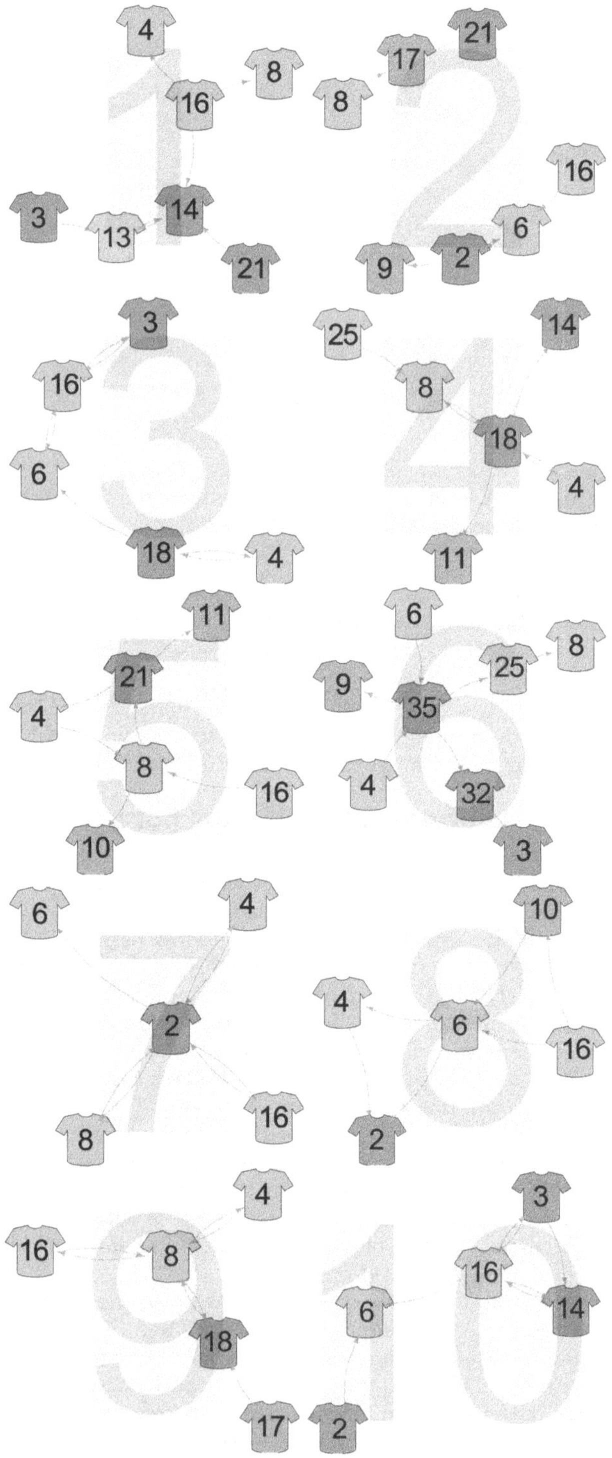

Figure 4: The 10 learned passing patterns for players of Barcelona. Goalkeepers, defenders, midfielders, and forwards are colored in grey, blue, green and red respectively. Players are represented by their jersey numbers (13:[G]Pinto, 35:[D]M.Montoya, 14:[D]J.Mascherano, 21:[D]Adriano, 3:[D]G.Pique, 32:[D]M.Bartra, 18:[D]J.Alba, 2:[D]D.Alves, 4:[M]F.Fabregas, 6:[M]Xavi, 16:[M]S.Busquets, 8:[M]A.Iniesta, 25:[M]A.Song, 11:[F]Neymar, 9:[F]A.Sanchez, 17:[F]P.Rodriguez, 10:[F]L.Messi).

Table 3: Goals statistics for different tactical patterns of Barcelona.

Pattern	# Goals	# Segments	Goal rate
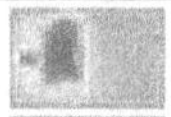	3	282	1.06%
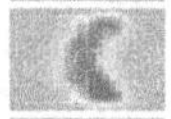	4	327	1.22%
	9	280	3.21%
	1	208	0.48%
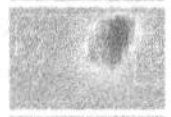	13	325	4.00%
	8	280	2.86%
	3	201	1.49%
	6	280	2.14%
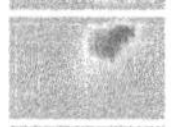	7	189	3.70%
	2	280	0.71%

of the segment. Comparing to existing methods for match statistics, which only attribute shots and goals to teams and players, our model can directly show the scoring statistic for each tactical pattern, which is more meaningful and useful for subsequent analysis.

From the above statistics we can see that some of the tactical patterns are more likely to score a goal. For example, Pattern 5 is an attacking pattern in the left wing, with Adriano and Iniesta as playmakers, passing balls to Neymar, Fabregas, Busquets and Messi. In a total of 325 segments with this pattern as the dominating tactical pattern, there are 13 segments finished with a goal, resulting in a 4.00% scoring rate. The pattern with the second highest scoring efficiency is Pattern 9, which is also an attacking pattern in the left, with Iniesta as the strategic center and ball passes with Fabregas, Busquets, Alba and Pedro. This pattern is also an effective attacking pattern, with 7 of 189 segments ended with goals.

4.3 Visualization of Tactics over Matches

A team's major tactical pattern often changes over time for several reasons, e.g., the coach's experiments with new strategies, or the transfers of core players. Indeed, when deciding which tactic to play before a match, coaches and club managers may also consider the opponent team's major tactics and player conditions of his own team. Therefore, the actual playing tactics usually vary over matches.

Here we also give an analysis of Barcelona's playing patterns for evaluation. Based on the match logs of Barcelona, we plotted the tactical patterns in the first half of each match in Figure 5. The matches are arranged from top to bottom according to the natural order of match dates. Passing segments are colored according to the dominating tactical patterns, as described in Section 3.1.2. It can be seen that at the beginning, Barcelona's favorite tactical patterns are Pattern 6 (vs. Villarreal on 20131215, vs. Elche on 20140105, vs. Sevilla on 20140210, vs. Real Sociedad on 20140223) and Pattern 3 (vs. Levante on 20140120, vs. Malaga on 20140127,

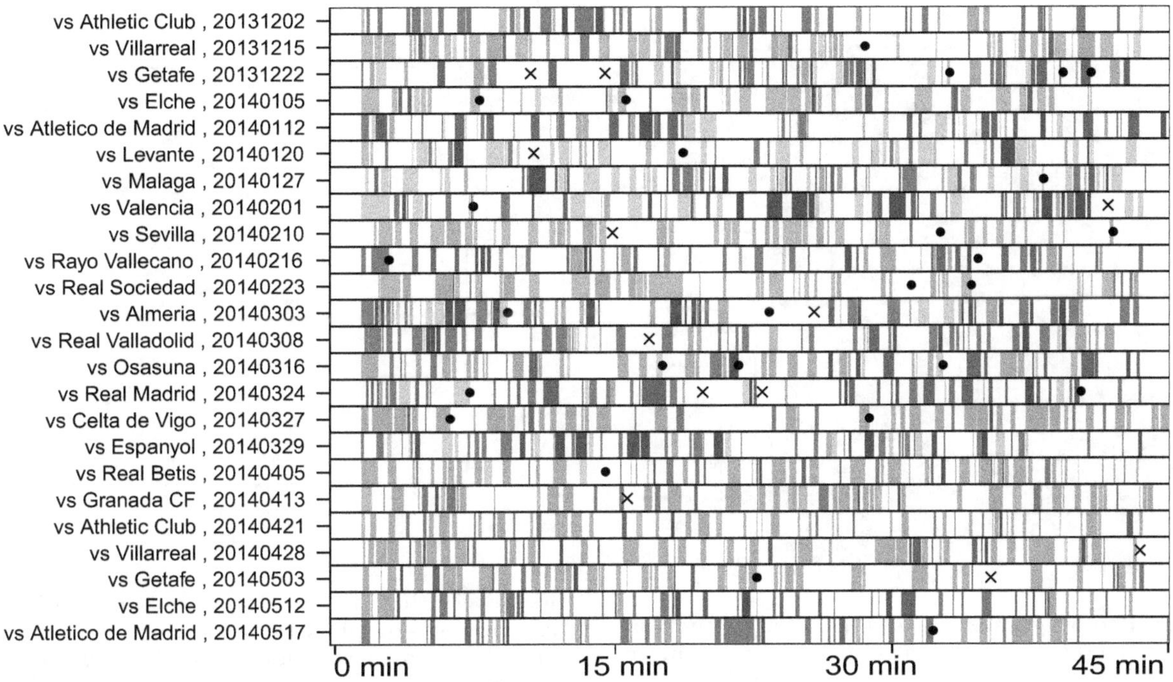

Figure 5: Visualization of tactical patterns over multiple matches, with different colors representing different patterns from 1 to 10 (colored as 1 2 3 4 5 6 7 8 9 10), solid dots representing goals scored, and crossings representing goals conceded.

vs. Valencia on 20140201). And at the end of the season, Barcelona's major patterns are Pattern 2 (vs. Osasuna on 20140316, vs. Real Betis on 20140405, vs. Athletic Club on 20140421, vs. Villarreal on 20140428, vs. Getafe on 20140503) and Pattern 4 (vs. Celta de Vigo on 20140327, vs. Granada CF on 20140413). The dynamic of playing patterns reflects the change of tactical strategies of coach Martino, who experimented with different starting lineups for the team during the first stage of the season. From our analysis, we can also see that although the starting lineup changed from match to match, the actual playing styles shared some similarity between matches.

In addition, it should be noted that, Barcelona tends to have more variation on the tactics when playing against stronger teams. From Figure 5, we can see that when playing against teams like Real Madrid and Atletico de Madrid, Barcelona did not stick to a single tactical pattern and played in different styles, as the match summarization bars are colored with more colors. On the other hand, when playing with other teams like Villarreal and Celta de Vigo, the bars are colored with one color mostly, indicating the match playing was dominated by a single tactical pattern.

We find that this kind of visualization can also improve the watching experience of match audiences. The annotation of pass segments to different tactical patterns provides a natural summarization of the match playing progress (an example is given in Section 4.5).

4.4 Player Role Analysis for Barcelona

We can also give a player role analysis with our T^{3}M. For the 10 tactical patterns learned with the passing data of Barcelona, we compute the scores indicating the importance of each player as described in Section 3.1.3. The results for major players are plotted in Figure 6.

From Figure 6, we can see that midfielders often make more passes in most tactical patterns, while forwards usually have less passes comparing to midfielders and defenders. And players with similar positions and roles in a team tend to have similar distributions of scores, that is, having similar representations on the basis of tactical patterns. In Figure 7, we plot the results of Principle Component Analysis (PCA) on the player scores defined in Section 3.1.3. The positions of the players are determined by the top 2 principle components. We can find that the players are roughly clustered according to their roles. Specifically, we know that both Lionel Messi's and Alexis Sanchez's common positions at Barcelona are right forward, while Neymar shows up as left forward more often. And Pedro Rodriguez can play at both sides as attacking winger in different tactics. We find that they have similar positions in the embedding space of PCA in this figure as well.

Furthermore, we can give a spatial analysis of player roles in different tactical patterns. As an example, Pedro's multifacet characteristic is studied here in details. In Figure 8, we plot the heat map of his receiving points in all the tactical patterns as the collection of the receiving points in each tactical pattern (indeed, this is a visualization of equation 9, see Section 3.1.3 for details). Heat maps for the top 4 tactical patterns are plotted, with the percentage of the passes annotated with each tactical pattern labeled above the corresponding plot. By studying these heat maps, we can find Pedro's active regions in different tactical patterns, which can reflect the different roles he actually plays. In the first 3 patterns (Pattern 2, Pattern 9 and Pattern 3), Pedro's active regions are in the left side of the playing field, while in the fourth pattern (Pattern 8) he mostly appears in the right wing. In fact, Pedro is a player who can play well as both left and right winger. Usually he plays as a left winger in

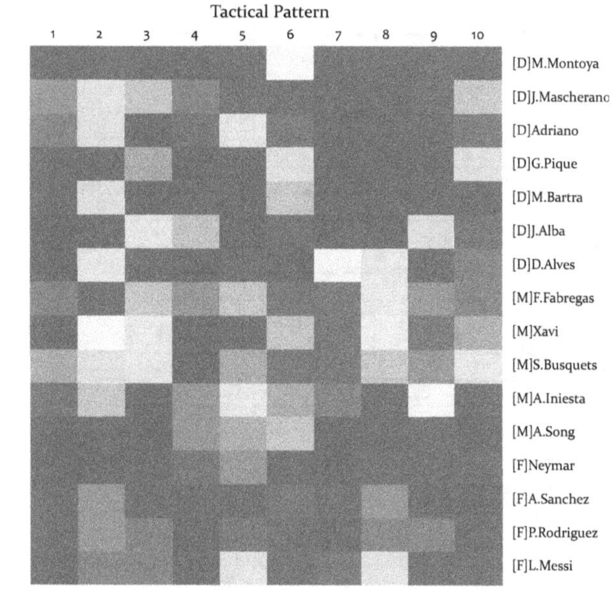

Figure 6: The weights of players in different tactical patterns. Brighter color means the player having a more important role in the tactical pattern (involved in more passes of the pattern).

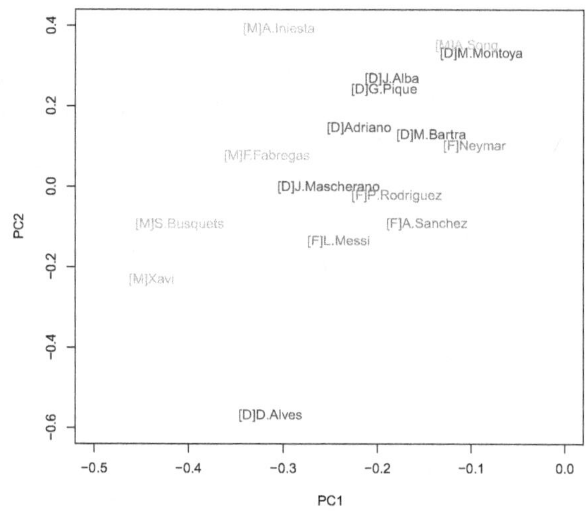

Figure 7: Plot of the players by the top 2 principle components on player scores. Defenders, midfielders and forwards are colored in blue, green and red, respectively.

Barcelona. However he is also considered as a good substitute for Lionel Messi in the right forward field. With T^{3}M, we can automatically recognize Pedro's multi-facet characteristic, which makes him a valuable player in the team.

4.5 Case Study: Barcelona vs. Real Madrid

As an example, here we study how to use T^{3}M to analyze a match between Barcelona and Real Madrid in La Liga 2013-2014. The match finished in 4:3, in favor of Barcelona. A visualization of the first half of the match is given in Figure 9. Both teams scored two goals before the break.

In this match, Iniesta scored first for Barcelona, with Messi's assist from the attacking region outside penalty area. This segment of passes was actually a cooperation between various players in the mid-field (e.g., Fabregas, Alba, Xavi, Busquets), which is recognized by T^{3}M as an offending pattern with these players in the mid-field (see top-left of Figure 9 and Pattern 3 in Figure 2.) In both the 20th and 24th minute, Real Madrid's Benzema finished a Di Maria cross from the left wing of the pitch. Using our model, we successfully recognize the playing pattern of Di Maria setting up chances in the left channel (bottom-left of Figure 9). And just before the break, Messi scored for Barcelona with a shot in the close range. The attack started from the left side by Alba and Iniesta, which is also successfully recognized by our model as an offending tactical pattern in the left wing (Pattern 2 in the bottom-left of Figure 9).

Indeed, the recognized patterns for the segments leading to goals in this match are very effective scoring patterns, with a scoring rate of 3.21% for Pattern 3 and 3.70% for Pattern 9, which are consistent with our analysis in Section 4.2. Furthermore, we can also find that Barcelona possesses the ball more often, noticing that the colored regions are thicker in the top band than the second. In fact, Barcelona is a team good at ball controlling, while Real Madrid is considered to be good at countering back.

5. RELATED WORK

Generally, the related works of this paper can be grouped into two major categories, namely *strategy analysis for soccer matches* and *topic modeling and its applications.*

5.1 Strategy Analysis for Soccer Matches

In almost all team sports, coordination and collaboration between players plays an important role. However, with only low-level observations, it is usually difficult to give a high-level description of a team's playing styles and strategies. We note that there are some related works tackling this problem, which inspired many subsequent works on team playing style analysis and other high-level pattern recognition applications. In a pioneering work [14], Intille *et al.* studied the problem of representing and recognizing complex multi-agent action in American football with probabilistic methods. For soccer playing style analysis, Lucey *et al.* [16, 17] studied the problem of automatic team strategy assessing. In their works, team behaviors were characterized via a study on entropy maps. And in the work of Gyarmati *et al.* [10], the problem of finding playing style in soccer was tackled with motif finding in pass networks, which allowed them to study the playing styles across different teams. For basketball, Fewell *et al.* [9] studied the ball-movement network over player roles. A connected team network was constructed and analyzed to find the probable paths of transition and playing. And in tennis, IBM SlamTracker [12] is a real-time platform providing player statistics and styles of play for a player to win a match.

As the sports data essentially have a spatial-temporal structure, there are also a number of works on analyzing sports activities with locations and/or temporal information. Recently, Yue *et al.* [26] tackled the problem of predictive modeling of dynamic team play in basketball. They used player location information from both teams, and learned semantically meaningful representations of team playing dynamics. For analysis on soccer data, in addition to various

Figure 8: Pedro's active region in the pitch, decomposed by tactical patterns.

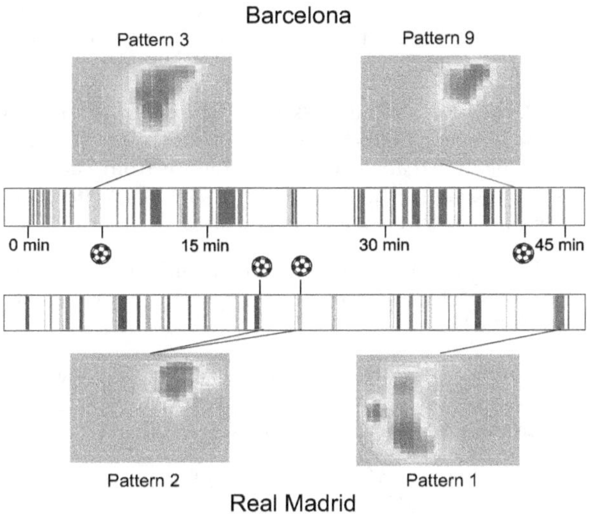

Figure 9: Visualization of the first half of the match between Barcelona and Real Madrid in La Liga on 24th Mar 2014. Segments of play are colored according to the different tactical patterns. We also plot the learned spatial patterns for typical pass segments (e.g., ended with goals).

works discussed above, Bialkowski *et al.* [4, 3] analyzed the player positions over time using an entire season's player and ball tracking data. Using an EM approach, they assigned players to roles and discovered the team's overall role distributions. In another work [24], the authors studied the problem of assigning players to roles at each frame. In addition, they studied the formations used by various teams, and found the most likely formation patterns for a team with spatiotemporal data. There are also some works on players and ball tracking as well as team plays detection with a visual system. We refer interested readers to the corresponding part of Lucey *et al.* [16] for related works.

Our work differs from these previous works as we use an unsupervised probabilistic model on the natural pass segments split by turnovers and stoppages to study the high-level tactical patterns. In addition, we take both the structure of the pass graph between players and the players' locations into our model, so that we can have a simultaneous analysis of *what kind of tactic a team prefers to play,* and *where on the pitch this tactical pattern is usually performed.* With these improvements and innovations, our approach can give realistic results of soccer team tactic analysis, which can promote various applications as described in Section 3 and potential future directions.

5.2 Topic Modeling and Its Applications

Topic models are tools for clustering co-occurrent words into various topics. Many topic models have been proposed, such as probabilistic latent semantic indexing (pLSI) [13], Latent Dirichlet Allocation (LDA) [6], author-topic model [21], correlated topic model (CTM) [15], and dynamic topic model (DTM) [5], etc. By assuming a latent assignment for each word to a topic, these models can perform unsupervised clustering analysis of various kinds of data sets. In addition to the traditional applications of text retrieval and information extraction, topic models have also been widely used for unsupervised analysis in several domains, e.g., activities discovery with sequential data and videos, object categorization in images, and sentiment analysis, etc. For example, Shen *et al.* [22] studied the problem of temporal activities discovery, and showed that with a topic modeling approach, they could obtain improved next activity prediction and sequence clustering results. For action discovery in videos, Wang *et al.* [23] applied unsupervised hierarchical Bayesian models to the problem of activity perception in video scenes, and tackled the problem of high-level semantic analysis and typical activities summarizing with their video based system. Also, in [20], Niebles *et al.* studied the problem of automatic human action categorization from video sequences. For applications in object categorization, Fergus *et al.* [8] applied a topic model (TSI-pLSA) to visual words in images and obtained competitive performance on standard test set with existing method. And for sentiment analysis, Zhu *et al.* [27] proposed several novel models (eToT,meToT,eDTM) based on topic models and demonstrated the effectiveness of these models.

In a similar manner, we use topic models to perform unsupervised clustering of soccer passing data in match logs, which is to our knowledge, the first work on applying topic model to soccer tactic analysis. In addition, enhanced by location information, the proposed model T^3M can learn the players' pass graphs and the spatial patterns of passes simultaneously, with hybrid data of discrete passing events and continuous receiver locations.

6. CONCLUSION AND FUTURE WORK

In this paper we proposed an unsupervised approach to automatically discerning the typical tactics, i.e., tactical patterns, of soccer teams through mining the historical match logs. To be specific, we first developed a novel model named Team Tactic Topic Model (T^3M) for learning the latent tactical patterns. A unique perspective of T^3M is that it can model the locations and passing relations of players simultaneously. Furthermore, we also demonstrated several potential applications enabled by the proposed T^3M, such as automatic tactical pattern discovery, pass segment annotation, and spatial analysis of player roles. Finally, we conducted extensive empirical evaluations for our approach based on the data collected from La Liga 2013-2014. In fact, by visualizing the results obtained from T^3M, many meaningful tactical patterns and interesting discoveries have been obtained, which validated the effectiveness of our approach.

In the future, we plan to develop more novel applications based on T^3M, such as winning rate prediction, and integrate them into our soccer intelligent system.

Acknowledgments

We are especially grateful to the Baidu Big Data Group for their assistance with the collection of our data. We would also like to thank the anonymous reviewers for their helpful feedback and suggestions. This work was supported in part by National Natural Science Foundation of China: 61402019, and in part by China Postdoctoral Science Foundation: 2014M550015.

References

[1] Opta. `http://optasports.com/`.

[2] World's most popular sports by fans, 2015. `http://www.topendsports.com/world/lists/popular-sport/fans.htm` [Online; accessed Feb 11, 2015].

[3] A. Bialkowski, P. Lucey, P. Carr, Y. Yue, S. Sridharan, and I. Matthews. Identifying team style in soccer using formations learned from spatiotemporal tracking data. In *ICDM, Workshop on Spatial and Spatio-temporal Data Mining (SSTDM)*, 2014.

[4] A. Bialkowski, P. Lucey, P. Carr, Y. Yue, S. Sridharan, and I. Matthews. Large-scale analysis of soccer matches using spatiotemporal tracking data. In *ICDM*, 2014.

[5] D. M. Blei and J. D. Lafferty. Dynamic topic models. In *ICML*, 2006.

[6] D. M. Blei, A. Y. Ng, and M. I. Jordan. Latent dirichlet allocation. *Journal of Machine Learning Research*, 2003.

[7] H. Collignon, N. Sultan, and C. Santander. The sports market - major trends and challenges in an industry full of passion, 2015. `http://www.atkearney.com/documents/10192/6f46b880-f8d1-4909-9960-cc605bb1ff34` [Online; accessed Feb 11, 2015].

[8] R. Fergus, L. Fei-Fei, P. Perona, and A. Zisserman. Learning object categories from google's image search. In *Tenth IEEE International Conference on Computer Visio (ICCV)*, 2005.

[9] J. H. Fewell, D. Armbruster, J. Ingraham, A. Petersen, and J. S. Waters. Basketball teams as strategic networks. *PLoS ONE*, 2012.

[10] L. Gyarmati, H. Kwak, and P. Rodriguez. Searching for a unique style in soccer. *arXiv preprint arXiv:1409.0308*, 2014.

[11] G. Heinrich. Parameter estimation for text analysis. Technical report, University of Leipzig, Germany, 2005.

[12] D. Henschen. IBM serves new tennis analytics at wimbledon, Jun 22, 2012. `http://www.informationweek.com/software/information-management/ibm-serves-new-tennis-analytics-at-wimbledon/d/d-id/1104987` [Online; accessed Feb 11, 2015].

[13] T. Hofmann. Probabilistic latent semantic indexing. In *22nd Annual International ACM SIGIR Conference on Research and Development in Information Retrieval*, 1999.

[14] S. S. Intille and A. F. Bobick. A framework for recognizing multi-agent action from visual evidence. In *National Conference on Artificial Intelligence (AAAI)*, 1999.

[15] J. D. Lafferty and D. M. Blei. Correlated topic models. In *NIPS*, 2005.

[16] P. Lucey, A. Bialkowski, P. Carr, E. Foote, and I. Matthews. Characterizing multi-agent team behavior from partial team tracings: Evidence from the english premier league. In *Twenty-Sixth AAAI Conference on Artificial Intelligence (AAAI)*, 2012.

[17] P. Lucey, D. Oliver, P. Carr, J. Roth, and I. Matthews. Assessing team strategy using spatiotemporal data. In *KDD*, 2013.

[18] A. Miller, L. Bornn, R. Adams, and K. Goldsberry. Factorized point process intensities: A spatial analysis of professional basketball. In *ICML*, 2014.

[19] K. P. Murphy. *Machine learning: a probabilistic perspective*. The MIT Press, 2012.

[20] J. C. Niebles, H. Wang, and L. Fei-Fei. Unsupervised learning of human action categories using spatial-temporal words. *International Journal of Computer Vision (IJCV)*, 2008.

[21] M. Rosen-Zvi, T. Griffiths, M. Steyvers, and P. Smyth. The author-topic model for authors and documents. In *20th Conference on Uncertainty in Artificial Intelligence (UAI)*, 2004.

[22] Z. Shen, P. Luo, Y. Xiong, J. Sun, and Y. Shen. Topic modeling for sequences of temporal activities. In *ICDM*, 2009.

[23] X. Wang, X. Ma, and W. E. L. Grimson. Unsupervised activity perception in crowded and complicated scenes using hierarchical bayesian models. *IEEE Transactions on Pattern Analysis and Machine Intelligence (PAMI)*, 2009.

[24] X. Wei, L. Sha, P. Lucey, S. Morgan, and S. Sridharan. Large-scale analysis of formations in soccer. In *International Conference on Digital Image Computing: Techniques and Applications (DICTA)*, 2013.

[25] Wikipedia. Tiki-taka - wikipedia, the free encyclopedia, 2015. `http://en.wikipedia.org/wiki/Tiki-taka` [Online; accessed Feb 11, 2015].

[26] Y. Yue, P. Lucey, P. Carr, A. Bialkowski, and I. Matthews. Learning fine-grained spatial models for dynamic sports play prediction. In *ICDM*, 2014.

[27] C. Zhu, H. Zhu, Y. Ge, E. Chen, and Q. Liu. Tracking the evolution of social emotions: A time-aware topic modeling perspective. In *ICDM*, 2014.

Predicting Serves in Tennis using Style Priors

Xinyu Wei
Queensland University of Technology

Patrick Lucey
Disney Research Pittsburgh

Stuart Morgan
Australian Institute of Sport

Peter Carr
Disney Research Pittsburgh

Machar Reid
Tennis Australia

Sridha Sridharan
Queensland University of Technology

ABSTRACT

In professional sport, an enormous amount of fine-grain performance data can be generated at near millisecond intervals in the form of vision-based tracking data. One of the first sports to embrace this technology has been tennis, where Hawk-Eye technology has been used to both aid umpiring decisions, and to visualize shot trajectories for broadcast purposes. These data have tremendous untapped applications in terms of "opponent planning", where a large amount of recent data is used to learn contextual behavior patterns of individual players, and ultimately predict the likelihood of a particular type of serve. Since the type of serve selected by a player may be contingent on the match context (i.e., is the player down break-point, or is serving for the match etc.), the characteristics of the player (i.e., the player may have a very fast serve, hit heavy with topspin or kick, or slice serves into the body) as well as the characteristics of the opponent (e.g., the opponent may prefer to play from the baseline or "chip-and-charge" into the net). In this paper we present a method which recommends the most likely serves of a player in a given context. We show by utilizing a "style prior", we can improve the prediction/recommendation. Such an approach also allows us to quantify the similarity between players, which is useful in enriching the dataset for future prediction. We conduct our analysis on Hawk-Eye data collected from three recent Australian Open Grand-Slam Tournaments and show how our approach can be used in practice.

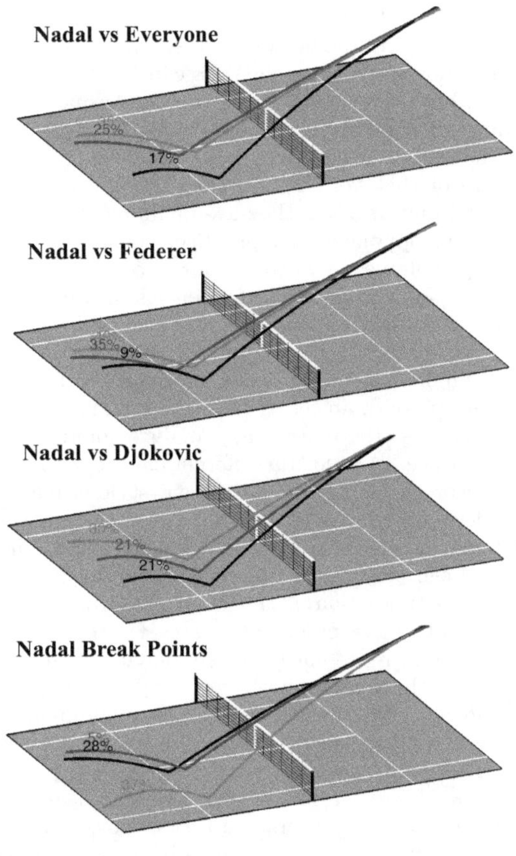

Figure 1: Top 3 likely serves from Nadal against different players for varying match-contexts. Percentage indicates the likelihood of the serve type. Top Row: First serves against different opponents; 2nd Row: First serves against Federer; 3rd Row: First serves against Djokovic; Bottom Row: First serves when down-break point.

1. INTRODUCTION

In recent times, a new innovation which has enhanced the second-screen experience of grand-slam tennis matches has been achieved through IBM Slamtracker [13]. One compelling aspect behind this platform has been the use of predictive analytics which utilizes over 41 million data points to recommend actions a player needs to do against their opponent to succeed in a match. Another innovation that has been utilized in professional tennis over the last decade has been the deployment of the Hawk-Eye tracking system [10], which tracks the trajectory of the ball during a match as well as the player's feet position. This tracking technology has been used to aid both umpiring decisions, and to visualize shot trajectories for broadcast purposes. Although both technologies have revolutionized the way broadcast viewers, players, coaches and commentators have analyzed tennis,

KDD'15, August 10-13, 2015, Sydney, NSW, Australia.

DOI: http://dx.doi.org/10.1145/2783258.2788598.

current tennis analytics have only used generic event-based features, and fine grained analyses and predictions of ball trajectories have been omitted. In this paper, we present a method which accurately predicts the most likely trajectory a player will hit.

Specially, we focus on "serving" where distinct patterns of behavior unique to each player and situation are observable. Serving in tennis is an especially useful insight into the patterned behavior of a player because it is self-paced, and (within the game rules) the type and location of serve is entirely the choice of the server. An example of our approach is shown in Fig. 1 – in the top plot we show the most likely serves Nadal will hit against all opponents regardless of the context of the match. In the second plot, we show how these percentages change when he plays Federer. In the third plot, we show how Nadal's serving behavior changes when he is facing Djokovic and the bottom plot shows what Nadal does when he is down a break-point. As can be seen from these four plots, both the type of serve and the frequency of each serve varies depending on the opponent as well as the context of the match score.

The aim of this work is to create an "assistive tool" for coaches and players when they are planning to play against an upcoming opponent. In practice, coaches and players review large volumes of video in efforts to ascertain the patterned behavior and strategic tendencies of a potential opponent. Due to the time it takes to segment video clips, view and analyze player patterns, it is often the case that there is only enough time to view a single match (often it is the most recent match). In terms of predictive analytics, this is less than ideal as the match they analyze could be: i) on a different surface, ii) against a different calibre of player (e.g., better or worse), iii) against a different style of player (e.g., serve-and-volleyer or baseliner), iv) the opponent could be of a different handedness (e.g., left or right), or v) the game may have been played in a different environment (i.e., temperature and time-of-day). These confounding factors can lead coaches to miss important strategic features in an opponent, or to misrepresent the likely playing strategy of the opponent in other matches.

A significant contribution of this paper is our method of capturing the "style" of a player. We utilize a latent factor model, where we represent the style of a player as a distribution of serve types. Before we can learn the different style types for players, we first discover the types of serves that players use more generally in professional tennis. We compare this learnt dictionary of serves to both an expert's opinion, as well as reconstruction error. We then use a similar method to learn the receiver's behavior which helps boost prediction performance. Such an approach also allows us to quantify the similarity between players. This work was conducted on Hawk-Eye data from the 2012-2014 Men's Australian Open Grand-Slam Tournament.

2. RELATED WORK

With the recent deployment of player and ball tracking systems in professional sports such as basketball, soccer and tennis, new research has been conducted on how to use such data sources. These works can be generally categorized into two areas: 1) knowledge discovery, 2) prediction. We review recent relevant work in these areas which are related to dealing with spatiotemporal tracking data in sports. Additionally, as we are leveraging a high-level description of player behavior which encompasses their unique characteristics or *style*, we also review works in this domain (trajectory clustering is discussed in Section 4).

Knowledge Discovery: Some of the first works using player tracking data have used STATS SportsVU position data from NBA basketball [27]. One of these works was by Goldsberry [9] who used the data to rank the best shooters in the NBA according to their shot location. Maheswaran et al. [21, 22] used the tracking data to analyze the best method to obtain a rebound. Similarly, Wiens et al. [32] looked at optimizing player positions for teams to "crash the boards" (to aggressively approach the basketball ring to regain the ball after a missed shot). Recently, Lucey et al. [19] used tracking data to discover how teams achieved open three-point shots in basketball and found that the distance and number of role-swaps of the defense were the most predictive factors. Bocskocksy et al. [4] re-investigated the hot-hand theory (i.e., a shooter is more likely to make the next shot if he/she made the previous one) using the data and found that the next shot taken by a shooter who just made a shot is often more difficult due to the tighter defense and increased distance from the basket. In soccer, Bialkowski et al. [3] examined the rigidity of a team's formation across a season and showed that home teams tended to player higher up the pitch both in offense and defense. This followed the work in [20], which showed that home teams had significantly more possession in the forward third which strongly correlated with the number of shots and goals. Wei et al. [31] used player tracking data to cluster different methods of how teams score using a role-representation. Knauf and Brefeld [15] proposed a spatio-temporal convolution kernels for clustering trajectories in soccer games. Morgan et al [24] used decision tree induction to learn the movement player patterns that are consistent with eliminating opponents in small-sided hockey games.

Prediction: Cervone et al. [6] used basketball tracking data to predict points and decisions made during a play. They did this via an expected possession value model that assumes the decision the ball-handler makes depends only on the current spatial configuration of the team in possession via a spatial occupancy map. Carr et al. [5] used real-time player detection data to predict the future location of play and point a robotic camera in that location for automatic sport broadcasting purposes. Adams et al., [1], used probabilistic matrix factorization via Gaussian processes to predict the scores of professional basketball games using only team identity, venue and date information of the game. Ganeshapillai and Guttag [8] used SVMs to predict the performance of a pitcher in the next innings in baseball and Sinha et al. [26] recently used Twitter feeds to predict the outcomes in NFL games. In terms of tennis, Wei et al. [30, 29] used Hawk-Eye data to predict the type and location of the next shot during a rally.

Style Analysis: Although latent factor models have been widely used for applications using text data, this is less so for other forms of unstructured data such as images/video as well spatiotemporal tracking data. In vision, the seminal work on separating style from content was by Tenenbaum and Freeman [28] where they used a bilinear model for a host of recognition tasks. By decoupling the raw content from the particular style, they showed how this acted as a useful prior in extrapolating to unseen tasks such as translation of faces to unseen illuminants and of fonts to unseen letters. More recently, Doersch et al. [7] used discriminative clustering to discover the attributes that distinguished images of one city from another ("What makes Paris look like Paris?"). They followed this work by exploring the visual style of objects (e.g., cars and houses) and how they vary over time [17]. Hu et al. [11] used Latent Dirichlet Allocation to discover trending categories for clothes based on a shopper's "aesthetic preferences" which has improved many key business metrics. In sports, detecting a team's style of play was initially conducted by Lucey et al. [18], where they used entropy maps to characterize a soccer team's ball movement patterns using data from Opta [25]. Recently, Miller et al. [23] use non-negative matrix factorization to characterize different types of shooters in basketball by modeling shot attempts as a point-process. Similarly, Yue et al., [33] used a similar approach to incorporate model player behaviors of defense, passing behaviors as well as ball-retention factors to boost prediction performance. No previous work modeling a player's style has been used in tennis analysis.

3. TENNIS DATASET

In this paper, we used Hawk-Eye data from 3 years of the Australian Open Men's draw (2012-2014). In total, the dataset consisted of 4758 first serves and 2292 second serves. As players hit serves with their racquets with either their right or left hand, the side of the court is important in predicting what type of serve will be hit. As such, we refer to the *deuce-court* to the instance when a player hits a serve from their right-hand side to their left-hand side (Fig. 2(bottom) – in blue). The *ad-court* refers to the instance when a player serves from their left-hand side across to their right-hand side see Fig. 2(top) – in red). In the dataset, we had a total of 3658 serves to the deuce-court while 3392 serves were to the ad-court[1]. There were a total of 371 aces and 221 double faults. As Grand-Slam tournaments in tennis are in a *knock-out* format (i.e., if a player loses, they do not play any more matches), we focussed our analysis on the top 10 players who played the most matches in the three years we analyzed. Details of the serve of each player used in the dataset are shown in Table 1. The Hawk-eye system records the (x, y, z) position of the ball as a function of t, as well as the foot position of each player at 20 Hz. For each point, metadata about the point, such as current score, time duration, server, receiver etc., is provided which allows us to drill down to the specifics of player behavior.

4. DISCOVERING SERVE DICTIONARY

In tennis parlance, coarse descriptions are used to describe serves such as "fast, down the T", "kick-serve", "swinging serve", "heavy serve" as well as "body serve". Although these terms are commonly used, they are rather vague and subjective as they have different meanings/interpretations between people. Instead of relying on expert labels which are subjective – our approach was to use an unsupervised method of discovering the types of serves directly from the data. By doing this, we effectively learn a dictionary of serves which we can describe the myriad of serves that exist. The mechanism in which we did this, was via trajectory clustering which also incorporates the semantics of the game. Before any clustering can be conducted however, we first require to

[1]All games in tennis start with serves from the deuce-court side

Player	First	Second	Ace%	Double Err%
Djokovic	598	378	8.86%	15.34%
Nadal	638	215	4.08%	6.05%
Federer	396	187	11.87%	7.49%
Murray	457	239	7.22%	9.21%
Berdych	488	244	8.13%	10.21%
Ferrer	355	166	7.04%	9.47%
Nishikori	267	126	5.77%	6.95%
Tomic	434	246	8.22%	7.45%
Tsonga	469	212	7.69%	7.19%
Wawrinka	656	279	9.49%	8.81%
Total	**4758**	**2292**	**7.81%**	**9.64%**

Table 1: Details of the types of serves the top 10 players utilized in the dataset. Ace% is the number of aces over total number of first serves. Double Err% is the number of double faults over total number of second serves.

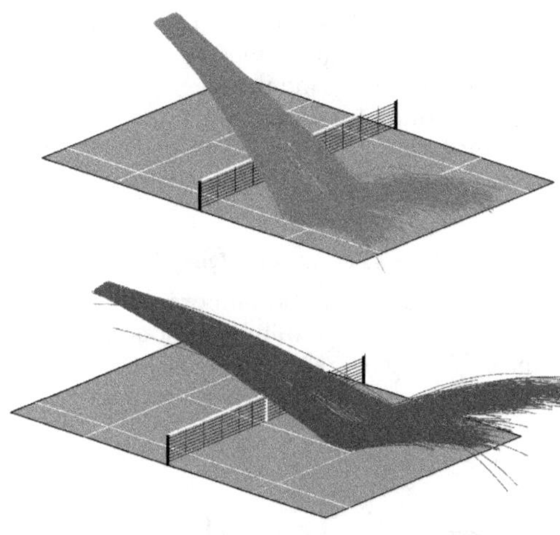

Figure 2: All serves collected in the tournaments. Red trajectories are serves to the ad court while blue are serves to the deuce court.

an accurate parameterization of each serve trajectory to preserve important nuances which can adequately discriminate between different types of serves.

4.1 Trajectory Parameterization

Each serve consists of a set of 3D trajectories – an example is shown in Fig. 3(top). A way of interpreting the serve is by obtaining the absolute location (x, y, z) at t_0, which is the location when the player's racquet impacts the ball for the serve. Due to the rules of tennis, depending on what side of the court comes from, the ball has to travel over the net and bounce in the service box which is diagonally opposite from where the ball is starting from. We refer to the time of flight from the initial impact of the server's racquet on the ball, to the point the ball subsequently bounces on the other side of the net t_1. After the ball bounces in play (if it bounces within the diagonal service box it is legal, if it is outside it is deemed a "fault"), the ball continues on a second trajectory until it is struck by the opponent's racquet or until it has passed the receiver and again hits the court or background (this is referred to as an "ace"). We refer to the time of flight from the bounce to the subsequent impact point on the receiver's racquet t_2. As can be seen in Fig. 3, each serve can be described via two trajectories. Partitioning a serve into sub-trajectories is attractive as we can develop specific metrics for each trajectory segment which can better capture the nuances of the serve, instead of one measure which may fail to capture these slight variations [16]. In this paper, we represented each serve as two sub-trajectories.

In terms of parameterization of each sub-trajectory, there are many representations that can be used. One method which has been used recently is to extract features such as impact speed, angle and bounce mark location [29]. Although intuitive, these hand-crafted features may not capture all the important characteristics of the trajectory (e.g., spin), and only capture the first segment of the trajectory. Another method of parameterization is via the coefficients of a 3rd or 4th order polynomial. Even though such methods are lossless, the coefficients are non-linear meaning the weighted metrics are required for each parameter making it hard to interpret (e.g., what does a 0.1 change of the second coefficient mean?). To allow for interpretability, we sample the trajectory at various time-steps to obtain the absolute position in x, y, z at these moments. Specifically, we uniformly sample n points from segment 1 (between t_0 and t_1) and $n-1$ points from segment 2 (between t_1+1 and t_2). The entire trajectory F can then be represented as:

$$F = \{f_1, ...f_n, ..., f_{2n-1}\}, \quad (1)$$

where the f_i represent the spatiotemporal location of the ball at the ith location. f_i include information of both location and dynamics, $f_i = [x, y, z, \dot{x}, \dot{y}, \dot{z}]$. We set n to 100 in our experiments.

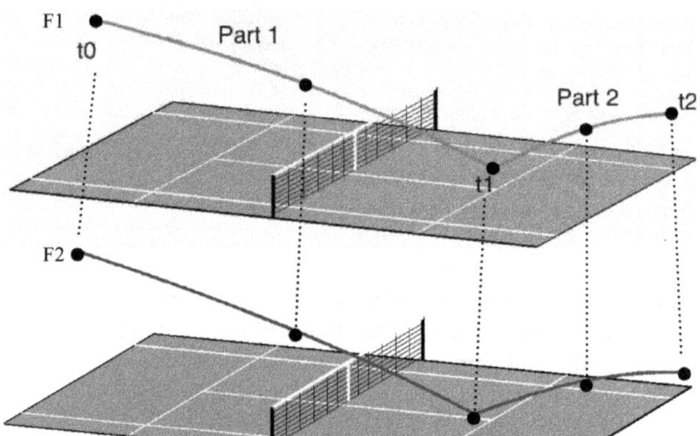

Figure 3: Examples of two serve trajectories F_1 and F_2 from Hawk-eye data when $n = 3$.

4.2 Trajectory Clustering

Once the parameterization of each sub-trajectory has been performed, serve trajectories can be clustered into representative groups. In terms of similarity measures, there is a large number of candidate approaches that can be used. One such method was initially proposed by Hu [12], where the average Euclidean distance between points on two trajectories is used. Instead of working in the trajectory coordinate space, PCA [2] can be used to transform the trajectories into a lower dimensionality subspace. To deal with variable length trajectories, Dynamic Time Warping (DTW) [14] can be applied to compare signals of unequal length by finding a warp that minimizes the total distance between matching points. For our problem, PCA is not ideal as we want the parameterization/thresholds to be interpretable which PCA space is not amenable to. Alternatively DTW is good for aligning for different trajectory lengths, but this loses vital information about the serve (i.e., serve velocity). As such, we use the HU distance as our similarity function. A simplified example illustrated how we compare two trajectories is shown in Fig. 3. Given trajectory F_s and F_k, we define the distance as:

$$Dist(F_s, F_k) = 1/(2n) \sum_{i=1}^{2n} d_E(f_{s,i}, f_{k,i}), \quad (2)$$

where $f_{s,i}$ is the ith point in trajectory f_s. This distance measures the mean of the pairwise Euclidean distance between two corresponding points. There are many different clustering methods that can be used to obtain our serve dictionary (e.g, k-means, spectral methods, agglomerative), but due to the rules of the game of tennis it is most important to: i) incorporate semantics, and ii) allow the clusters to be interpretable. To satisfy the first requirement, we devised a hierarchy of serve types which can be seen in Fig. 4. Based on each of these semantic roots (or serve-contexts), we first assigned all serves to one of these groups. These hard-assignments were based on whether the serve was valid (or in-play), or a fault. We then further assigned these serves on which side the server is serving to (i.e., deuce or ad-court). Once serves were separated by semantic groups, we performed k-means clustering. As we broke the trajectory into segments which should be locally linear, we clustered the first trajectory segments and the second trajectory segments separately. In the first segment, we found 3 groups (down-the-T, body and wide). Each of these groups were then partitioned into further groups which resulted in 7 different serve types for each side of the court. We choose $K = 7$ as the reconstruction error starts to smooth out after this value. A visualization of the clustering results for left and right side is shown in Fig. 5 and Fig. 6 respectively. Given $2k$ cluster. A visualization of the centroids are shown in Fig. 7 and Fig. 8. The reconstruction error as a function of the number of clusters is shown in Fig. 9. A description of these serve types given by a tennis expert is given in Table 2.

5. STYLE

5.1 Representing Serve Style

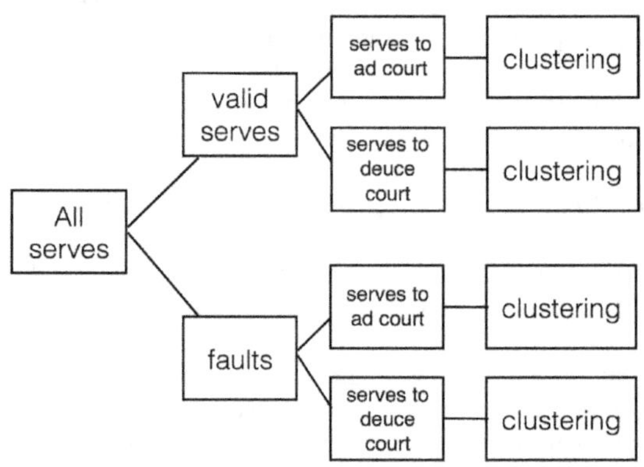

Figure 4: Clustering scheme.

Serve ID	Side	Direction Angle	Speed (KM/HR)
1	ad	wide	172
2	ad	down the T	173
3	ad	down the T	185
4	ad	wide	188
5	ad	body	184
6	ad	down the T	194
7	ad	down the T	161
8	deuce	down the T	193
9	deuce	body	165
10	deuce	down the T	178
11	deuce	wide	184
12	deuce	down the T	196
13	deuce	down the T	183
14	deuce	wide	175

Table 2: Experiment results of serve prediction.

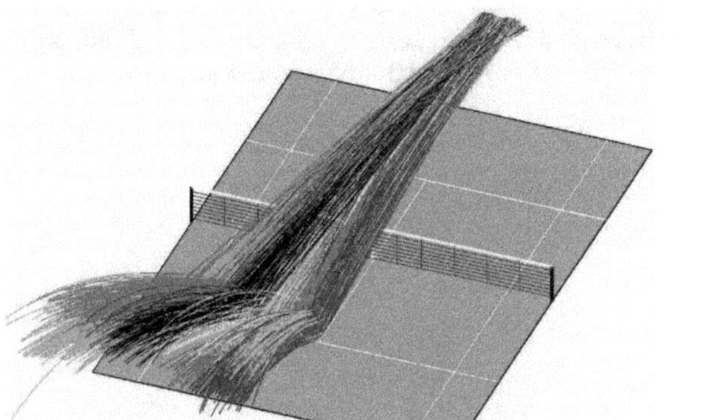

Figure 5: Clusters of serve trajectories to the ad the court.

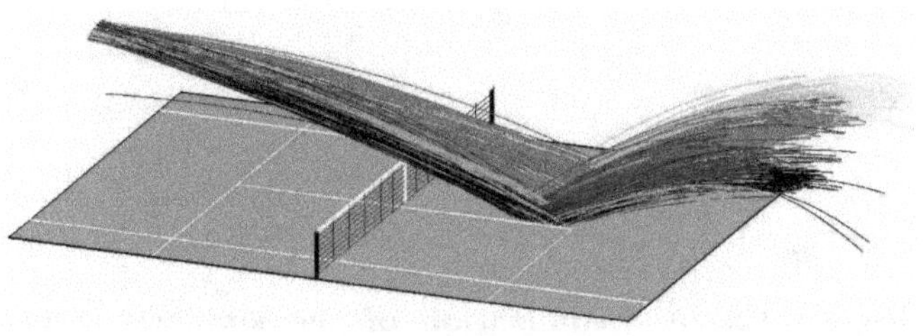

Figure 6: Clusters of serve trajectories to the deuce court.

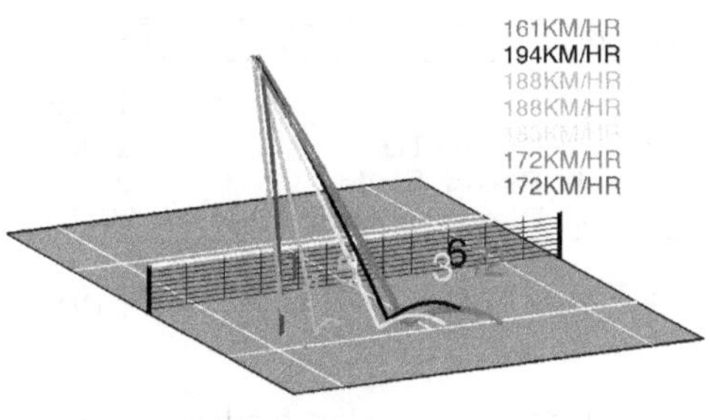

Figure 7: The median trajectory for each cluster to the ad-court.

Describing the playing style of a tennis player can be an extremely subjective task. Depending on the expertise of the observer, it can be very coarse (e.g., "this player hits the ball really hard") or fine-grained (e.g., "the way the player rotates his wrist at the point of contact for his single-handed backhand is beauty personified"). In terms of measuring the similarities, we need a more quantifiable method. As obtaining labels from experts which describe style with high agreeability is a challenging endeavor, another approach is to use a Latent Dirichlet Allocation (LDA) method to capture these high-level semantics. To do this, we can utilize the serve dictionary, $\mathcal{D}$, and represent the serving behavior of each player as a normalized histogram of each serve type. As we have 14 different serve types in our dictionary, this means that we can represent each player's style via a 14-dimensional feature vector, where each feature varies between 0 and 1. The distributions of each of the 10 players we analyzed in this paper are shown in Fig. 10.

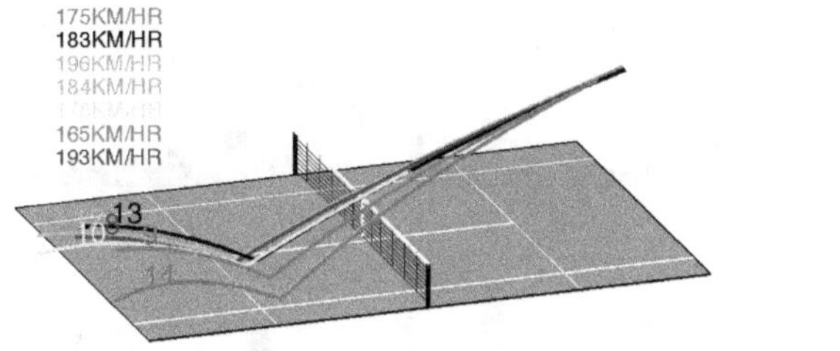

Figure 8: The median trajectory for each cluster to the deuce-court.

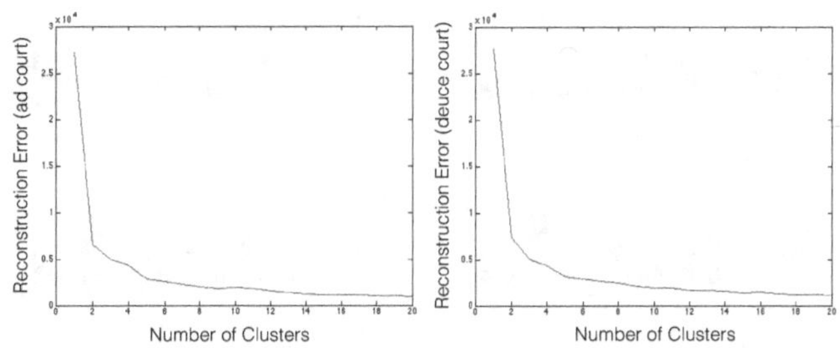

Figure 9: Reconstruction error of serves in terms of Euclidean distance (left=ad-court, right=deuce-court).

Now that we have a style descriptor of each player, we can estimate the similarity between players. A simple method of comparing two style descriptors is to find the sum of differences between them. A visualization of player's pairwise differences is shown in Fig. 11. We also have constructed a graph to visualize player serve similarity (see Fig. 12).

5.2 Serve Prediction using Style Prior

Although quantifying player similarities is an interesting endeavor, it ultimately has little meaning or use in its current form. A method to evaluate whether the style descriptor is useful or not is through a series of prediction experiments. In this paper we ask the following question, *for a given game situation, as well as the identity of the server and receiver, how well can we predict the next serve trajectory?*. To simplify, we interpreted this task as a classification problem where we aim to correctly classify which of the 7 serves to each side of the court the player was most likely to hit. Formally, the problem is: given the current game context feature $\mathbf{x}$ for a particular player, we want to predict the la-

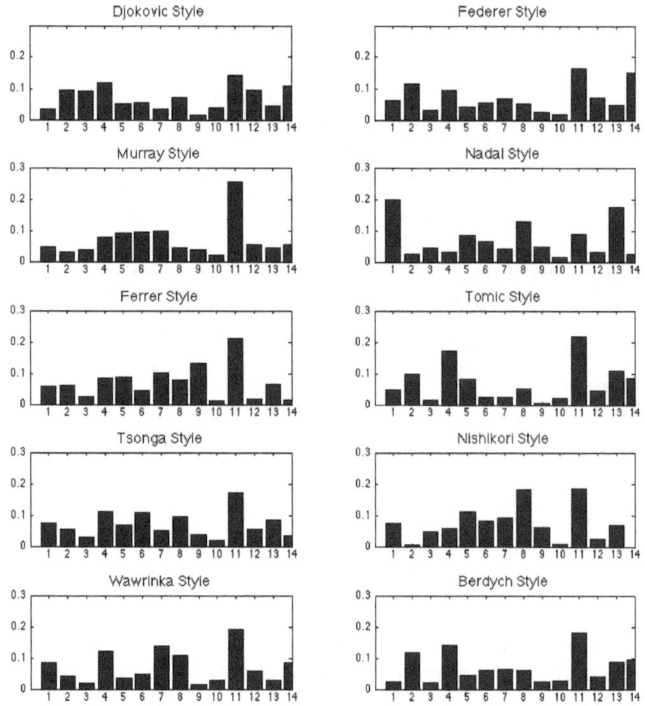

Figure 10: Styles of four top players in the tournaments.

bel of the next serve y, where $y \in \mathcal{Y}$ and $\mathcal{Y} = \{y_1, y_2, ..., y_m\}$, where y_i is a particular serve type in the serve dictionary and m is the total number of serve types in the dictionary (m=7). Our classifier takes the form of a Random Decision Forest, which is robust against the overfitting that might occur via bootstrapping. It also has good local-feature space adaptivity via randomly splitting the feature space at multiple levels of each tree.

To test the style descriptor, we conducted four sets of experiments using different types of prior information: 1) game-context features only, 2) game-context features plus player ID and 3): game-context, player ID plus style features of the player, and 4) game-context features plus style features of both the player and the opponent. As tennis is an adversarial sport, the behavior of the opponent will have an impact on the type of serve a player will use. To incorporate the opponent style, we appended their style descriptor to $\mathbf{x}$.

For all the experiments, we use 60% of the data for training and 40% for testing. We measured the performance of the prediction using the classification rate, which is simply the hit rate of the prediction. Each experiment was conducted 10 times and the average performance is reported in Table 3. As is evident in these results, incorporating the style prior helps boost prediction performance. Perhaps even more interesting, is that by incorporating the style of the serve *return*, we enhance prediction further.

6. APPLICATION: OPPONENT PLANNING

As mentioned earlier, the aim of this work is to create an "assistive tool" for coaches and players when they are planning to play against an upcoming opponent. The idea is that a coach or player would be able to interact with our

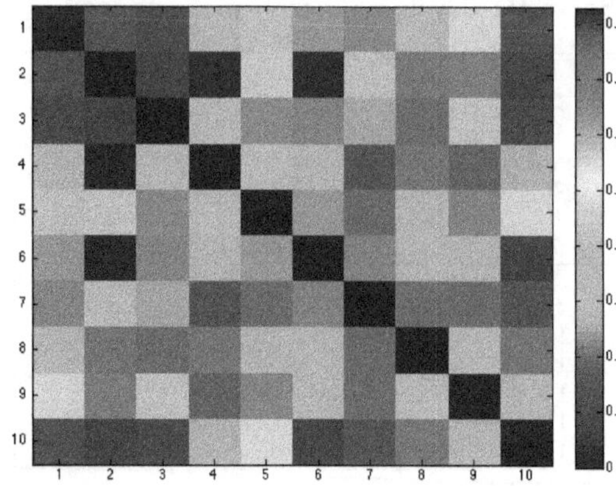

Figure 11: A visualization of the similarities between players. 1- Djokovic; 2 - Nadal; 3 - Federer; 4 - Murray; 5 - Berdych; 6 - Ferrer; 7 - Nishikori; 8 - Tomic; 9 - Tsonga; 10 - Wawrinka.

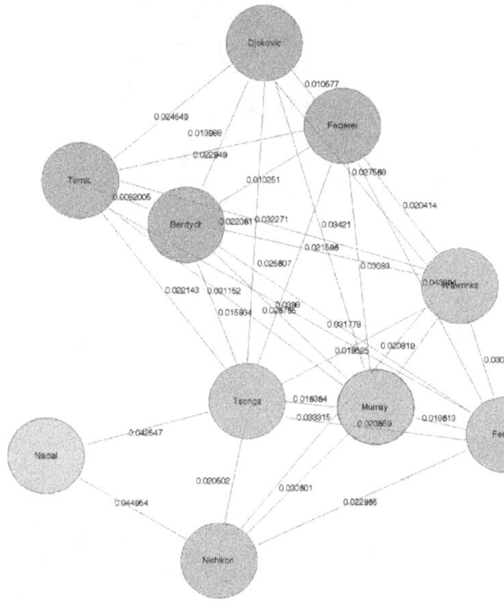

Figure 12: A visualization of the similarities between players. Edges indicate the differences between players. Edges whose distance is greater than the overall mean distance are removed.

Feature	Accuracy
Random	14.3%
Score	17.4%
Score & Player ID	21.6%
Score & Player Style	24.4%
Score & Player & Opp Style	**27.8%**

Table 3: Experiment results of serve prediction.

"serve predictor" tool to see what tendencies opponents have in a very quick and efficient manner (i.e., instead of spending time "cutting tape" just to view a couple of serves, the player would have all previous serves of an opponent stored in database, and would be able to select different match contexts (or opponents) and see how the serves vary. In this instantiation, we display the top 3 likely serves along with

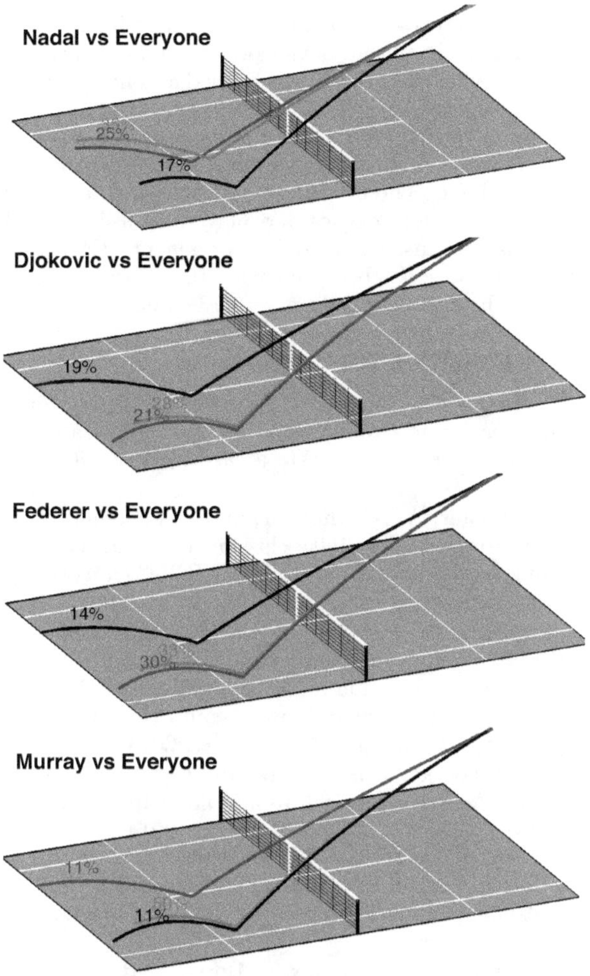

Figure 13: Player serving behavior against all opponents. Percentage indicates the likelihood of the serve type.

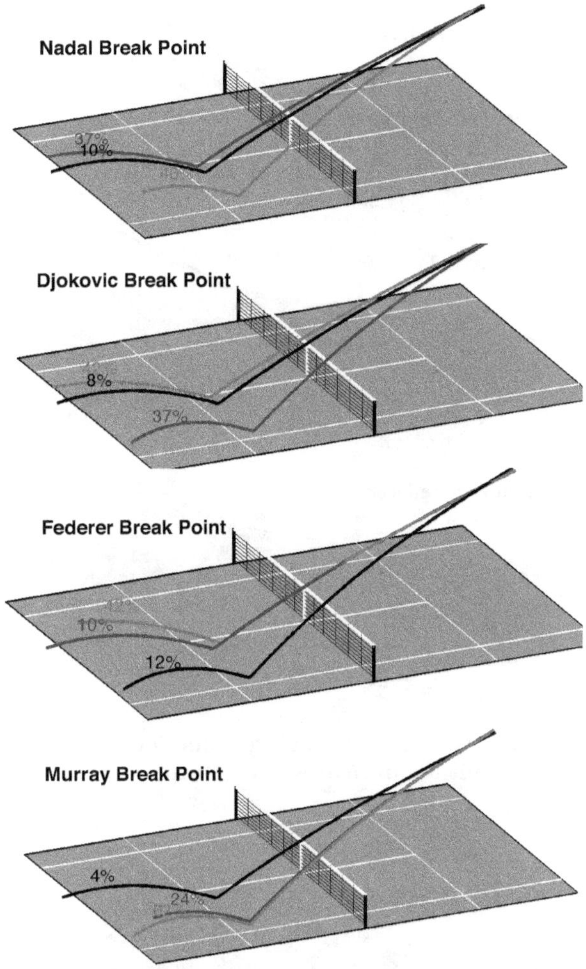

Figure 14: Player serving behavior against all opponents at break-point. Percentage indicates the likelihood of the serve type.

percentages, but this could be altered to the satisfy the requirements of the user. Below we give specific examples of serving behaviors for the "big-four" (i.e., Nadal, Djokovic, Federer and Murray). We first analyze their global behaviors, meaning that on average these are the top 3 serves each player hits to the deuce-court regardless of opponent (see Fig. 13). The second example we show is the player behavior to the deuce-court when they are break-point down (see Fig. 14). The comparison between these two figures is important. For Nadal, in normal situations his main serve tends to be down the line. In break-point situations however, almost half the time (48%) he serves wide of the court which is totally different. Djokovic on the other-hand does the opposite, in normal points he tends to serve wide but in break-points he goes down the middle. The same pattern can be seen for Federer - normally he serves out wide but at break-point he goes down the middle. The change for Murray however, is not as drastic as he tends to subtly change his behavior but not at the same magnitude of the other big three.

In terms of individual serving behavior against specific opponents, our approach can help us pick-up on interesting behavior. In Fig. 15, we can see that Federer's serving scheme does not tend to differ against other opponents generally. In contrast, when we drill down on the serving behaviors against a specific opponent, we can see some interesting patterns. An example of serving behavior against Federer is shown in Fig. 16. We can see that Nadal prefers to hit his serves to Federer's backhand, while the most popular serve for Murray and Tomic is to Federer's forehand side. This is very interesting as Nadal has a tremendous record against Federer with the tactic of hitting shots directly to his backhand. For illustrative purposes we have just chosen these specific examples, but this approach can be used to model the behavior of any player given the tracking data.

7. SUMMARY

In this paper, we presented an approach to predict the most likely serve a player will hit in a given match-context, against a specific opponent using Hawk-Eye data collected from three recent Australian Open Grand-Slam Tournaments. To do this we first learnt a dictionary of "serve prototypes", depending on the side of the court (ad-court, or deuce court), as well as the game-context (i.e., first serve, second serve)

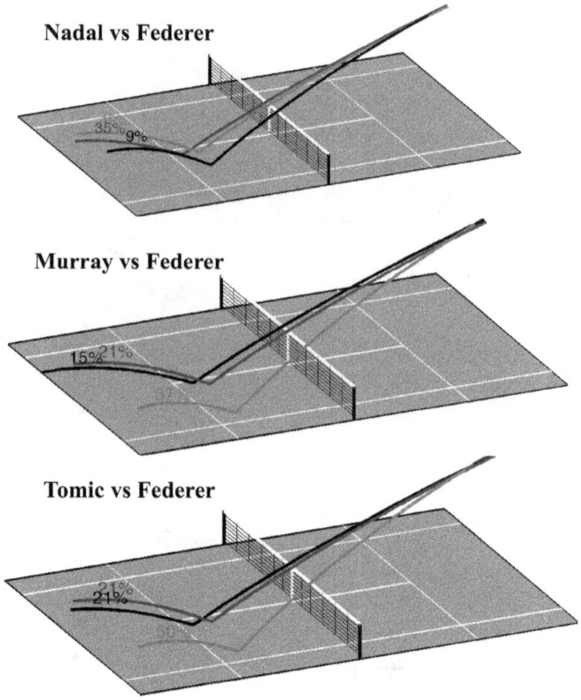

Figure 16: Individual serving behavior against Federer. Percentage indicates the likelihood of the serve type.

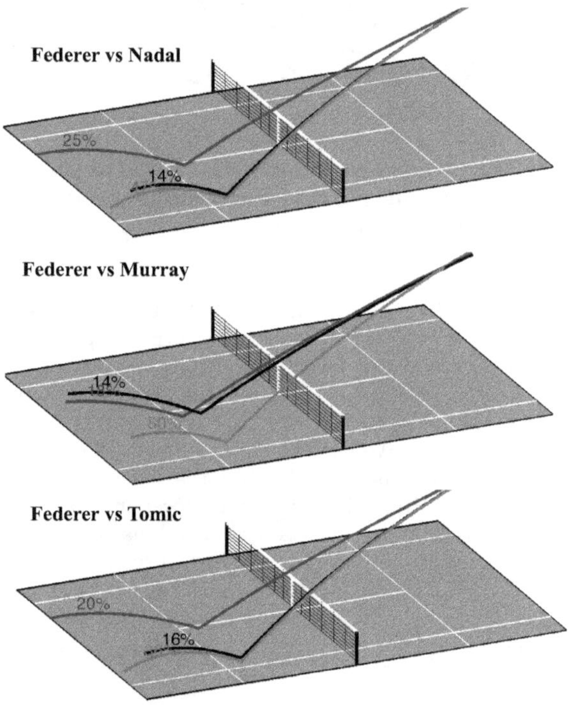

Figure 15: Individual serving behavior of Federer against Nadal, Murray and Federer. Percentage indicates the likelihood of the serve type.

and game-score (i.e., normal point, serving for the game or down break-point). We did this by parameterizing the serve trajectory into two segments, and then clustering in a hierarchical manner. To obtain better prediction performance, we utilized a "style prior" which was formed as a normalized histogram of serve types. We also incorporated the return style of the opponent to further boost performance. Our approach also allowed the similarity of serving styles between players to be quantified. The overall goal of this work is to create an assistive tool for coaches and players to use when planning to play against an upcoming opponent. Even though good performance has been achieved, this work is still in the discovery phase with a system yet to be deployed.

8. REFERENCES

[1] R. Adams, G. Dahl, and I. Murray. Incorporating Side Information in Probabilisitc Matrix Factorization with Gaussian Processes. *arXiv preprint arXiv:1003.4944,*, 2010.

[2] F. I. Bashir, A. A. Khokhar, and D. Schonfeld. Object trajectory-based activity classification and recognition using hidden markov models. In *IEEE Trans. Image Process*, volume 16, pages 1912–1919, 2007.

[3] A. Bialkowski, P. Lucey, P. Carr, Y. Yue, and I. Matthews. "win at home and draw away": Automatic formation analysis highlighting the differences in home and away team behaviors. In *MIT Sloan Sports Analytics Conference*, 2014.

[4] A. Bocskocsky, J. Ezekowitz, and C. Stein. The Hot Hand: A New Approach to an Old "Fallacy". In *MIT Sloan Sports Analytics Conference*, 2014.

[5] P. Carr, M. Mistry, and I. Matthews. Hybrid Robotic/Virtual Pan-Tilt-Zoom Cameras for Autonomous Event Recording. In *ACM Multimedia*, 2013.

[6] D. Cervone, A. D'Amour, L. Bornn, and K. Goldsberry. POINTWISE: Predicting Points and Valuing Decisions in Real Time with NBA Optical Tracking Data. In *MIT Sloan Sports Analytics Conference*, 2014.

[7] C. Doersch, S. Singh, A. Gupta, J. Sivic, and A. Efros. What Makes Paris Look Like Paris? *ACM Transactions on Graphics (SIGGRAPH)*, 31(4), 2012.

[8] G. Ganeshapillai and J. Guttag. A Data-Driven Method for In-Game Decision Making in MLB. In *MIT Sloan Sports Analytics Conference*, 2014.

[9] K. Goldsberry. CourtVision: New Visual and Spatial Analytics for the NBA. In *MIT Sloan Sports Analytics Conference*, 2012.

[10] Hawk-Eye. `www.hawkeyeinnovations.co.uk`.

[11] D. Hu, R. Hall, and J. Attenberg. Style in the Long Tail: Discovering Unique Interests with Latent Variable Models in Large Scale Social E-commerce. In *ACM SIGKDD*, 2014.

[12] W. Hu, D. Xie, Z. Fu, W. Zeng, and S. Maybank. Semantic based surveillance video retrieval. In *IEEE Trans. Image Process*, volume 16, pages 1168–1181, 2007.

[13] IBMSlamtracker. `www.ausopen.com/en_AU/slamtracker/slamtracker.html`.

[14] E. Keogh and M. Pazzani. Scalling up dynamic time warping for datamining applications. In *KDD*, pages 285–289, 2000.

[15] K. Knauf and U. Brefeld. Spatio-temporal convolution kernels for clustering trajectories. In *KDD Workshop on Large Scale Sports Analytics*, 2014.
[16] J.-G. Lee, J. Han, and K.-Y. Whang. Trajectory clustering: a partition-and-group framework. In *ACM SIGMOD*, 2007.
[17] Y. Lee, A. Efros, and M. Hebert. Style-Aware Mid-Level Representation for Discovering Visual Connections in Space and Time. In *ICCV*, 2013.
[18] P. Lucey, A. Bialkowski, P. Carr, E. Foote, and I. Matthews. Characterizing Multi-Agent Team Behavior from Partial Team Tracings: Evidence from the English Premier League. In *AAAI*, 2012.
[19] P. Lucey, A. Bialkowski, P. Carr, Y. Yue, and I. Matthews. How to Get an Open Shot: Analyzing Team Movement in Basketball using Tracking Data. In *MIT Sloan Sports Analytics Conference*, 2014.
[20] P. Lucey, D. Oliver, P. Carr, J. Roth, and I. Matthews. Assessing team strategy using spatiotemporal data. In *ACM SIGKDD*, 2013.
[21] R. Masheswaran, Y. Chang, A. Henehan, and S. Danesis. Destructing the Rebound with Optical Tracking Data. In *MIT Sloan Sports Analytics Conference*, 2012.
[22] R. Masheswaran, Y. Chang, J. Su, S. Kwok, T. Levy, A. Wexler, and N. Hollingsworth. The Three Dimensions of Rebounding. In *MIT Sloan Sports Analytics Conference*, 2014.
[23] A. Miller, L. Bornn, R. Adams, and K. Goldsberry. Factorized Point Process Intensities: A Spatial Analysis of Professional Basketball. In *ICML*, 2014.
[24] S. Morgan, W. DM., and C. Barnes. Applying decision tree induction for identification of important attributes in one-versus-one player interactions: A hockey exemplar. *Journal of Sports Sciences*, 31:1031–1037, 2013.
[25] Opta. `http://www.optasports.com/`.
[26] S. Sinha, C. Dyer, K. Gimpel, and N. Smith. Predicting the NFL Using Twitter. In *ECML Workshop on Machine Learning and Data Mining for Sports Analytics*, 2013.
[27] Stats. `http://www.stats.com/`.
[28] J. Tenenbaum and W. Freeman. Separating Style and Content with Bilinear Models. *Neural Computation*, 12(6):1247–1283, 2000.
[29] X. Wei, P. Lucey, S. Morgan, and S. Sridharan. Predicting Shot Locations in Tennis using Spatiotemporal Data. In *DICTA*, 2013.
[30] X. Wei, P. Lucey, S. Morgan, and S. Sridharan. Sweet-Spot: Using Spatiotemporal Data to Discover and Predict Shots in Tennis. In *MIT Sloan Sports Analytics Conference*, 2013.
[31] X. Wei, L. Sha, P. Lucey, S. Morgan, and S. Sridharan. Large-Scale Analysis of Formations in Soccer. In *DICTA*, 2013.
[32] J. Wiens, G. Balakrishnan, J. Brooks, and J. Guttag. To Crash or Not to Crash: A quantitative look at the relationship between the offensive rebounding and transition defense in the NBA. In *MIT Sloan Sports Analytics Conference*, 2013.
[33] Y. Yue, P. Lucey, P. Carr, A. Bialkowski, and S. Sridharan. Learning Fine-Grained Spatial Models for Dynamic Sports Play Prediction. In *ICDM*, 2014.

Smart Pacing for Effective Online Ad Campaign Optimization

Jian Xu, Kuang-chih Lee, Wentong Li, Hang Qi, and Quan Lu
Yahoo Inc.
701 First Avenue, Sunnyvale, California 94089
{xujian,kclee,wentong,hangqi,qlu}@yahoo-inc.com

ABSTRACT

In targeted online advertising, advertisers look for maximizing campaign performance under delivery constraint within budget schedule. Most of the advertisers typically prefer to impose the delivery constraint to spend budget smoothly over the time in order to reach a wider range of audiences and have a sustainable impact. Since lots of impressions are traded through public auctions for online advertising today, the liquidity makes price elasticity and bid landscape between demand and supply change quite dynamically. Therefore, it is challenging to perform smooth pacing control and maximize campaign performance simultaneously. In this paper, we propose a *smart pacing* approach in which the delivery pace of each campaign is learned from both offline and online data to achieve smooth delivery and optimal performance goals. The implementation of the proposed approach in a real DSP system is also presented. Experimental evaluations on both real online ad campaigns and offline simulations show that our approach can effectively improve campaign performance and achieve delivery goals.

Categories and Subject Descriptors

H.1.0 [**Information Systems**]: Models and Principles—*General*; D.2.8 [**Software Engineering**]: Metrics—*Performance Measures*

Keywords

Campaign Optimization;Demand-Side Platform;Budget Pacing

1. INTRODUCTION

Online advertising is a multi-billion dollar industry and has been enjoying continued double-digit growth in recent years. The market has witnessed the emergence of search advertising, contextual advertising, guaranteed display advertising, and more recently auction-based advertising exchanges. We focus on the auction-based advertising exchanges, which is a marketplace with the highest liquidity, i.e., each ad impression is traded with a different price through a public auction. In this market, Demand-Side Platforms (DSPs) are key players who act as the agents for a number of different advertisers and manage the overall welfare of the ad campaigns through many direct buying ad-networks or real-time bidding (RTB) ad exchanges in order to acquire different ad impressions. The objectives of an advertiser on a DSP can be summarized as follows:

- *Reach the delivery and performance goals:* for *branding* campaigns, the objective is usually to spend out the budget to reach an extensive audience and meanwhile make campaign performance as good as possible; for *performance* campaigns, the objective is usually to meet the performance goal (e.g. eCPC[1] no more than \$2) and meanwhile spend as much budget as possible. Objectives of other campaigns are usually in-between these two extremes.
- *Execute the budget spending plan:* advertisers usually expect their ads to be shown smoothly throughout the purchased period in order to reach a wider range of audience, have a sustainable impact, and increase synergy with campaigns on other medias such as TV and magazines. Therefore, advertisers may have their customized budget spending plans. Figure 1 gives two examples of budget spending plan: even pacing and traffic based pacing.
- *Reduce creative serving cost:* apart from the cost to be charged by DSPs, there is also creative serving cost charged by typically 3rd-party creative server providers. This is even more important nowadays that more and more ad campaigns are in the form of video or rich media. The creative serving cost of such type of impressions can be as much as premium inventory cost, so the advertisers will always be willing to reduce this cost and deliver impressions to the right users effectively and efficiently.

However, it becomes more and more challenging to achieve all the above objectives simultaneously. In the individual campaign level, each campaign may have its own budget, budget spending plan, targeted audiences, performance goal, billing method, creative serving cost, and so on. In the network level, an increasing number of DSPs compete with each other simultaneously to acquire inventory through public auctions in many ad exchanges, and therefore the price elasticity and bid landscape between demand and supply

KDD'15, August 10-13, 2015, Sydney, NSW, Australia.
© 2015 ACM. ISBN 978-1-4503-3664-2/15/08 ...\$15.00.
DOI: http://dx.doi.org/10.1145/2783258.2788615.

[1]Effective cost per click - The cost of a campaign divided by the total number of clicks received. Effective cost per action (eCPA) is defined similarly.

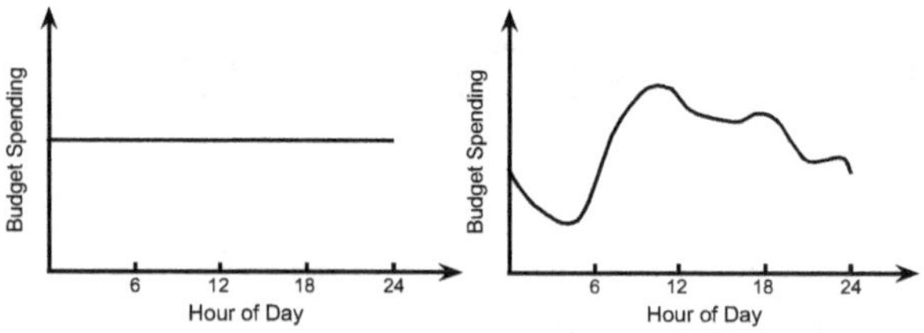

(a) Even pacing (b) Traffic based pacing

Figure 1: Different budget spending plans.

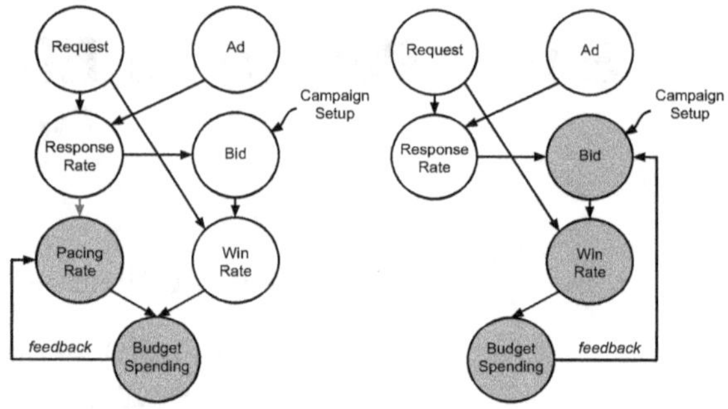

(a) Probabilistic throttling (b) Bid modification

Figure 2: Factor dependency graph in Probabilistic Throttling v.s. Bid Modification. Factors in grey are involved in budget pacing control. Adding dependency between pacing rate and response rate is one of the key ideas of our work.

change dynamically. All those varieties in both campaign and network level make the optimization extremely difficult even for a single campaign.

Fortunately, thanks to the rapid growth of emerging internet industries such as mobile apps and user-generated content platforms, the online advertising industry has observed a sharply increasing availability of advertising inventory. A DSP nowadays typically receives tens of billions of ad requests from dozens of Supply-Side Platforms (SSPs) everyday and hence has more flexibility than before to spend budget on a vast amount of advertising opportunities. In this paper, we consider a problem motivated by these trends in the online advertising industry: *can we smartly decide on which inventories the budget should be spent so that all the objectives of an ad campaign are achieved?* We study this problem with a real DSP and explore models and algorithms to effectively serve ad campaigns it manages. Our contributions can be summarized as follows:

- We formulate the above multi-objective optimization problem with a comprehensive anatomy of real ad campaigns and propose to solve it through *smart* pacing control.
- We develop a control-based method which learns from both online and offline data in order to optimize budget pacing and campaign performance simultaneously.
- We implement the proposed approach in a real DSP and conduct extensive online/offline experimental evaluations. The results show that our approach can effectively improve campaign performance and achieve delivery goals.

The rest of the paper is organized as follows: we review the related work in section 2. In section 3, we present the notations and formal problem statement. We describe our models and algorithms in section 4 and 5. Section 6 and 7 focus on experiments and implementation respectively. We conclude our work and discuss future work in section 8.

2. RELATED WORK

Most existing work related to campaign optimization focuses on estimating the click through rate (CTR)/action rate (AR) or bid landscape, which helps to setup the bid price in the impression level. For a comprehensive survey of all those methods, please refer to [7]. However, those approaches do not take into account of the smooth delivery constraint.

Another research direction deals with the ad allocation problem. Chen et al. [8] and Bhalgat et al. [4] proposed to perform online ad allocation and solve the optimization problem for all campaigns in the marketplace level. Their focus is to find the best allocation plan to optimize revenue on the publisher side while we focus on maximizing the delivery and performance for each campaign. Bhalgat et al. [5] proposed a different approach to perform ad allocation based on the inventory quality, which shares some common thoughts with our work. We both assume that the inventory is much larger than advertiser demand and therefore both of our solutions focus on how to select high quality inventory. However, their approach focuses on the allocation problem and the smooth delivery constraint does not appear in the formulation. Zhang et al. [13] proposed to combine budget allocation and bid optimization in a joint manner. We claim that the budget allocation can be complementary to our work in the campaign level. After the budget allocation is done, our approach of budget pacing can take place to further optimize the campaign goals in the impression level.

Mehta et al. [12], Abrams et al. [1], and Borgs et al. [6] suggested using *bid modification* while Agarwal et al. [3] and Lee et al.[10] used *probabilistic throttling* to achieve pacing control. In this paper, we use probabilistic throttling for several considerations: 1) Probabilistic throttling directly influences budget spending while bid modification changes the win-rate to control spending, which is not preferred in the RTB environment. First, the bid win-rate curve is usually not smooth so modifying bid can cause significant changes in budget spending. Second, our observation on real serving data is that the bid landscape can be changed dramatically over time. Both issues make pacing control extremely difficult through bid modification. 2) SSPs usually set reserve prices so pacing control may fail if the bid need to be modified to be below the reserve price [3]. 3) As shown in Figure 2, throttling with a pacing rate decouples pacing control from bid calculation. This is an appealing feature because the pacing control can be developed independently and combined with any bid optimization implementation. In the rest of this paper, we assume the bid is already given by a preceding bid optimization module.

3. PROBLEM FORMULATION

We focus on two most prevailing campaign types: 1) branding campaigns that aim at spending out the budget to have an extensive reach of audiences, and 2) performance campaigns that have specific performance goals (e.g. eCPC

$\leq$ \$2). Other types of campaigns typically lie in-between these two extremes. A campaign of either type may have its unique budget spending plan. We first formulate the problem to be resolved and then outline our solution.

3.1 Preliminaries

Let Ad be an ad campaign, B be the budget of Ad, and G be the performance goal of Ad if there is. A *spending plan* is a sequence of budgets over a number K of time slots, specifying the desired amount of budget to be spent in each time slot. We denote by $\mathbf{B} = (B^{(1)}, ..., B^{(K)})$ the spending plan of Ad, where $B^{(t)} \geq 0$ and $\sum_{t=1,...,K} B^{(t)} = B$. Let Req_i be the i-th ad request received by a DSP. As we discussed in section 2, we use probabilistic throttling for budget pacing control in our work. Thus we denote by:

$s_i \sim Bern(r_i)$ the variable indicating whether Ad participates the auction for Req_i, where r_i is the *point pacing rate* of Ad on Req_i. $r_i \in [0, 1]$ quantifies the probability that Ad participates the auction for Req_i.

w_i the variable indicating whether Ad wins Req_i if it participates the auction, which depends on the bid bid_i given by the bid optimization module.

c_i the advertiser's cost if Ad is served to ad request Req_i. We note that the cost consists of both the inventory cost and the creative serving cost,

$q_i \sim Bern(p_i)$ the variable indicating whether the user performs some desired response (e.g. click) if Ad is served to Req_i, where $p_i = Pr(respond|Req_i, Ad)$ is the probability of such response.

$C = \sum_i s_i \times w_i \times c_i$ the total cost of ad campaign Ad.

$P = C / \sum_i s_i \times w_i \times q_i$ the performance (e.g. eCPC if the desired response is click) of ad campaign Ad.

$\mathbf{C} = (C^{(1)}, \ldots, C^{(K)})$ the *spending pattern* over the K time slots, where $C^{(t)}$ is the cost in the t-th time slot, $C^{(t)} \geq 0$ and $\sum_{t=1,...,K} C^{(t)} = C$.

Given an ad campaign Ad , we define Ω to be the penalty (error) function that captures how the spending pattern $\mathbf{C}$ is deviated from the spending plan $\mathbf{B}$. A smaller value will indicate a better alignment. As an example, we may define the penalty as follows:

$$\Omega(\mathbf{C}, \mathbf{B}) = \sqrt{\frac{1}{K}\sum_{t=1}^{K}(C^{(t)} - B^{(t)})^2} \tag{1}$$

3.2 The Problem of Smart Pacing for Online Ad Campaign Optimization

Advertisers look for spending budget, executing spending plan, and optimizing campaign performance simultaneously. However, there may be multiple *Pareto* optimal solutions to such an abstract multi-objective optimization problem. In real scenarios, advertisers usually prioritize these objectives for different campaigns. For branding campaigns, advertisers typically put budget spending at the top priority, followed by aligning with spending plan while performance is not a serious concern. At serving time (i.e. the ad request time), since we use probabilistic throttling, the only thing that we can have full control is r_i. Thus the problem of ***smart pacing for ad campaigns without specific performance goals*** is defined as determining the values of r_i so that the following measurement is optimized[2]:

$$\begin{aligned} &\min_{r_i} \ P \\ &s.t. \ C = B, \ \Omega(\mathbf{C}, \mathbf{B}) \leq \epsilon \end{aligned} \tag{2}$$

where ϵ defines the tolerance level on deviating from the spending plan. On the contrary, for performance campaigns that have specific performance goals, achieving the performance goal is the top priority. Sticking to the spending plan is usually the least important consideration. We define the problem of ***smart pacing for ad campaigns with specific performance goals*** as determining the values of r_i so that the following measurement is optimized:

$$\begin{aligned} &\min_{r_i} \ \Omega(\mathbf{C}, \mathbf{B}) \\ &s.t. \ P \leq G, \ B - C \leq \varepsilon \end{aligned} \tag{3}$$

where ε defines the tolerance level for not spending out all the budget. Given the dynamics of the marketplace, even both the single-objective optimization problems are extremely difficult to resolve. Existing methods that are widely used in the industry deal only with capturing either the performance goal or the budget spending goal. One example for achieving performance goal is always bidding the retargeting beacon triggered ad requests. Unfortunately, there is no guarantee to avoid overspending or underspending. Another example for smooth pacing control is introducing a global pacing rate so that all ad requests have the same probability to be bid by a campaign. However, none of these existing approaches can solve the smart pacing problem we formulate here. To tackle this problem, we examine the prevailing campaign setups and make some key observations that motivated our solution:

- *CPM campaigns*: advertisers are charged a fixed amount of money for each impression. For branding advertisers, the campaign optimization is as defined in Equation 2. As long as budget can be spent and spending pattern is aligned as the plan, high responding ad requests should have a higher point pacing rate than low responding ones so that the performance can be optimized. For performance advertisers (i.e. with eCPC, eCPA goal), the campaign optimization is as defined in Equation 3. Apparently, high responding ad requests should have higher point pacing rate to achieve the performance goal.
- *CPC/CPA campaigns*: advertisers are charged based on the sheer number of clicks/actions. There is implicit performance goal to guarantee that DSP does not lose money when bidding on behalf of the advertisers. So it falls in the category of optimization defined in Equation 3. Granting high responding ad requests high point pacing rates will be more effective from both the advertisers' and DSPs' perspectives: advertisers pay less on creative serving cost while DSP can save more ad opportunities to serve other campaigns.
- *Dynamic CPM campaigns*: DSP charges a dynamic amount of money for each impression instead of a fixed amount. These campaigns usually have specific performance goals so the optimization problem falls in Equation 3. Similar with CPC/CPA campaigns, high

[2]Based on our performance definition (i.e. eCPC or eCPA) a smaller value means a better performance.

responding ad requests are more preferred in order to reduce creative serving cost and save ad opportunities.

3.3 Solution Summary

Motivated by these observations, we develop novel heuristics to solve the smart pacing problem. The heuristics try to find a feasible solution that satisfies all constraints as defined in Equation 2 or 3, and then further optimize the objectives through feedback control. We first learn from offline serving logs to build a response prediction model to estimate $p_i = Pr(respond|Req_i, Ad)$, which helps distinguish high responding ad requests from low responding ones. Second, we reduce the solution space by grouping similarly responding ad requests together and the requests in the same group share the same *group pacing rate*. Groups with high responding rates will enjoy high pacing rates (refer to the blue arrow in Figure 2(a)). Third, we develop a novel control-based method to learn from online feedback data and dynamically adjust the group pacing rates to approximate the optimal the solution. Without loss of generality, we assume campaign setup is CPM billing with or without an eCPC goal. Our approach can be applied to other billing methods and performance types as well as other grouping strategies such as grouping based on p_i/c_i (the expected response per cost).

4. RESPONSE PREDICTION

Our solution depends on an accurate response prediction model to estimate p_i. There are plenty of work in the literature addressing this problem as we have reviewed in section 2. Here we briefly describe how we perform this estimation. We use the methodology introduced in [2, 11] and make some improvements on top of that. In this method, we first leverage the hierarchy structures in the data to collect response feedback features at different granularities. For example, at ad side, starting from the root and continuing layer after layer are *advertiser category, advertiser, campaign*, and finally *ad*. Historical response rates at different levels in the hierarchy structures are used as features to derive a machine learning model (e.g. LR, GBDT, etc) to give a raw estimation of p_i, say $\hat{p}_i$. Then we utilize attributes such as user's age, gender to build a shallow tree. Each leaf node of the tree identifies a disjoint set of ad requests which could hardly be further split into subsets with significantly different average response rates. Finally, we calibrate $\hat{p}_i$ within the leaf node Req_i is classified using a piecewise linear regression to estimate the final p_i. This scheme results in a fairly accurate response prediction.

5. A CONTROL-BASED SOLUTION

As we have discussed in section 3, it is extremely difficult to reach the exact optimal solution to the problems defined in equations 2 and 3 in an online environment. We explore heuristics to reduce the solution space of the original problems. More specifically, with the response prediction model described in section 4, similarly responding ad requests are grouped together and they share the same *group pacing rate*. Different groups will have different group pacing rates to reflect our preferences on high responding ad request groups. The original problem of solving the point pacing rate of each r_i is reduced to solving a set of group pacing rates. We employ a control-based method to tune the group pacing rates so that online feedback data can be leveraged immediately for campaign optimization. In other words, the group pacing rates are dynamically adjusted throughout the campaign life time. For simplicity, *pacing rate* and *group pacing rate* are interchangeable in the rest of this paper, and we denote by r_l the group pacing rate of the l-th group.

5.1 A Layered Presentation

For each ad campaign, we maintain a layered data structure in which each layer corresponds to an ad request group. We keep the following information of each ad request group in the layered structure: average *response rate* (usually in the form of CTR, AR, etc) derived from the response prediction model; *priority* of the ad request group; *pacing rate* i.e. the probability to bid an ad request in the ad request group; and the campaign's *spending* on the ad request group in the latest time slot. The principles here are: 1) layers correspond to high responding ad request groups should enjoy high priorities, and 2) the pacing rate of a high priority layer should not be smaller than that of a low priority layer.

For each campaign, when the DSP receives an eligible ad request, it first decides which ad request group the ad request falls in and refers to the corresponding layer to acquire the pacing rate. The DSP then bids the ad request on behalf of the campaign with a probability that equals to the retrieved pacing rate at the price given by a preceding bid optimization module.

5.2 Online Pacing Rate Adjustment

We employ a control-based method to adjust the pacing rate of each layer based on real-time feedbacks. Suppose we have L layers, the response rate estimation by response prediction model for each layer is $\mathbf{p} = (p_1, \ldots, p_L)$, and hence if the desired response is click, the estimated eCPC of each layer is $\mathbf{e} = (e_1, \ldots, e_L)$ where $e_i = \frac{CPM}{1000 \times p_i}$. Let the pacing rate of each layer in the $(t-1)$-th time slot be $\mathbf{r}^{(t-1)} = (r_1^{(t-1)}, \ldots, r_L^{(t-1)})$, and the spending of each layer be $\mathbf{c}^{(t-1)} = (c_1^{(t-1)}, \ldots, c_L^{(t-1)})$, the control-based method will derive $\mathbf{r}^{(t)} = (r_1^{(t)}, \ldots, r_L^{(t)})$ for the coming t-th time slot based on campaign objectives.

5.2.1 Campaigns without Performance Goals

We first describe the adjustment algorithm for ad campaigns without specific performance goals. Recall that for such campaign type, the primary goal is to spend out the budget and align with the budget spending plan. Thus at the end of each time slot, the algorithm needs to decide the amount of budget to be spent in the next time slot and adjust the layered pacing rates to spend exact that amount.

The budget to be spent in the next time slot is determined based on the current budget spending status. Given an ad campaign, suppose its total budget is B, budget spending plan is $\mathbf{B} = (B^{(1)}, ..., B^{(K)})$, and after running for m time slots, the remaining budget becomes B_m. We need to decide the desired spending in each of the remaining time slots, denoted as $\widehat{C}^{(m+1)} \ldots \widehat{C}^{(K)}$ so that the total budget can be spent out and the penalty is minimized.

$$\begin{aligned} &\underset{\widehat{C}^{(m+1)},\ldots,\widehat{C}^{(K)}}{\arg\min} \quad \Omega \\ &s.t. \sum_{t=m+1}^{K} \widehat{C}^{(t)} = B_m \end{aligned} \tag{4}$$

Algorithm 1 AdjustWithoutPerformanceGoal

Input: $\mathbf{c}^{(t-1)}$, $\mathbf{r}^{(t-1)}$, R

Output: $\mathbf{r}^{(t)}$

1: **if** $R == 0$ **then**
2:     return $\mathbf{r}^{(t)} = \mathbf{r}^{(t-1)}$
3: **else if** $R > 0$ **then**
4:     **for** each layer l in $(L, \ldots, l')$ **do**
5:         $r_l^{(t)} = min(1.0, r_l^{(t-1)} \times \frac{c_l^{(t-1)}+R}{c_l^{(t-1)}})$
6:         $R = R - c_l^{(t-1)} \times \frac{r_l^{(t)} - r_l^{(t-1)}}{r_l^{(t-1)}}$
7:     **end for**
8:     $r_{l'-1}^{(t)} = trial\ rate$ **if** $l' \neq 1$ **and** $r_{l'}^{(t)} > trial\ rate$
9: **else**
10:     **for** each layer l in $(l', \ldots, L)$ **do**
11:         $r_l^{(t)} = max(0.0, r_l^{(t-1)} \times \frac{c_l^{(t-1)}+R}{c_l^{(t-1)}})$
12:         $R = R - c_l^{(t-1)} \times \frac{r_l^{(t)} - r_l^{(t-1)}}{r_l^{(t-1)}}$
13:         **if** $R \geq 0$ **then**
14:             $r_{l-1}^{(t)} = trial\ rate$ **if** $l \neq 1$ **and** $r_l^{(t)} > trial\ rate$
15:             **break**
16:         **end if**
17:     **end for**
18: **end if**
19: **return** $\mathbf{r}^{(t)} = (r_1^{(t)}, \ldots, r_L^{(t)})$

in which if we adopt the definition of Ω as in equation 1, we have the following optimal solution:

$$\widehat{C}^{(t)} = B^{(t)} + \frac{B_m - \sum_{t=m+1}^{K} B^{(t)}}{K - m} \tag{5}$$

where $t = m+1, \ldots, K$. We omit the details of how $\widehat{C}^{(t)}$ is derived because of page limit. In an online environment, suppose the actual spending in the latest time slot is $C^{(t-1)}$, we define $R = \widehat{C}^{(t)} - C^{(t-1)}$ to be the *residual* which can help us to make adjustment decisions.

Algorithm 1 gives the details of how the adjustment is done. Suppose index L represents the highest priority, index 1 refers to the lowest priority, and let l' be the last layer with non-zero pacing rate (the principles in section 5.1 guarantee the existence of l'). If R equals 0, no adjustment is needed. If $R > 0$, which means delivery should speed up, pacing rates are adjusted in a top-down fashion. Starting from layer L, the pacing rate of each layer is increased one-by-one until layer l'. Line 5 calculates the desired pacing rate of the current layer in order to offset R. We give layer $l' - 1$ a *trial rate* to prepare for future speedups if layer $l' \neq 1$ and its updated pacing rate $r_{l'}^{(t)} >$ *trial rate*. Figure 3 gives an example of how the speedup adjustment is done. If $R < 0$, which means delivery should slow-down, pacing rate of each layer is decreased in a bottom-up fashion until R is offset. Line 11 derives the desired pacing rate of the current layer to offset R. Suppose l is the last layer adjusted, $l \neq 1$ and its new pacing rate $r_l^{(t)} >$ *trial rate*, we give layer $l-1$ the trial rate to prepare for future speedups. Figure 4 is an example how delivery is slowed down.

We note that this greedy strategy tries to approach the optimal solution to Equation 2 in an online environment. Within each time slot, it strives to invest on inventories with

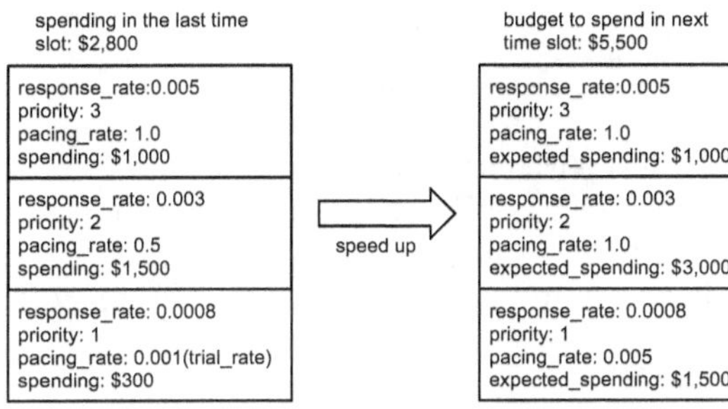

Figure 3: An example to speed up budget spending

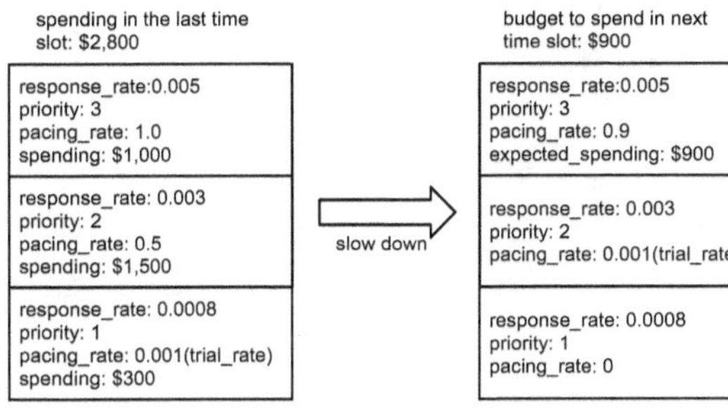

Figure 4: An example to slowdown budget spending

the best performance under the total budget and spending plan constraints.

5.2.2 *Campaigns with Performance Goals*

For campaigns with specific performance goals (e.g. eCPC $\leq$ \$2), pacing rate adjustment is a bit complicated. It is difficult to foresee the ad request traffic in all the future time slots and the response rate distribution can be time-varying. Therefore, given budget spending objectives, exploiting all the ad requests in current time slot that meet performance goal may not be an optimal solution to Equation 3. Algorithm 2 describes how the adjustment is done for such kind of campaigns. We adopt the heuristic that a further adjustment based on performance goal is appended to Algorithm 1. If the expected performance after Algorithm 1 does not meet the performance goal, the pacing rates are reduced one-by-one from the low priority layers until the expected performance meets the goal. Line 7 derives the desired pacing rate of current layer to make the overall expected eCPC meet the goal. Function ExpPerf($\mathbf{c}^{(t-1)}, \mathbf{r}^{(t-1)}, \mathbf{r}^{(t)}, \mathbf{e}, i$) in Line 2 and 4 estimates the expected joint eCPC of layers $i, \ldots, L$ if pacing rates are adjusted from $\mathbf{r}^{(t-1)}$ to $\mathbf{r}^{(t)}$, where e_j is the eCPC of layer j.

$$\text{ExpPerf}(\mathbf{c}^{(t-1)}, \mathbf{r}^{(t-1)}, \mathbf{r}^{(t)}, \mathbf{e}, i) = \frac{\sum_{j=i}^{L} \frac{c_j^{(t-1)} \times r_j^{(t)}}{r_j^{(t-1)}}}{\sum_{j=i}^{L} \frac{c_j^{(t-1)} \times r_j^{(t)}}{r_j^{(t-1)} \times e_j}} \tag{6}$$

5.3 Number of Layers, Initial and Trial Rates

It is important to set proper number of layers, initial and trial pacing rates. For a new ad campaign without any delivery data, we identify the most similar existing ad campaigns in our DSP and estimate a proper global pacing rate r_G at which we expect the new campaign can spend out its budget. Then the number of layers is set as $L = \lceil \frac{1}{r_G} \rceil$. We note

Algorithm 2 AdjustWithPerformanceGoal

Input: $\mathbf{c}^{(t-1)}$, $\mathbf{r}^{(t-1)}$, R, $\mathbf{e}$, $goal$
Output: $\mathbf{r}^{(t)}$

$\mathbf{r}^{(t)}$=AdjustWithoutPerformanceGoal($\mathbf{c}^{(t-1)}$, $\mathbf{r}^{(t-1)}$, R)
if ExpPerf($\mathbf{c}^{(t-1)}, \mathbf{r}^{(t-1)}, \mathbf{r}^{(t)}, \mathbf{e}, 1$) $> goal$ **then**
  for each layer l in $(1, \ldots, L)$ **do**
    if ExpPerf($\mathbf{c}^{(t-1)}, \mathbf{r}^{(t-1)}, \mathbf{r}^{(t)}, \mathbf{e}, l+1$) $> goal$ **then**
      $r_l^{(t)} = 0.0$
    else
      $r_l^{(t)} = r_l^{(t-1)} \times \frac{\sum_{i=l+1,\ldots,L} c_i^{(t-1)} \times (\frac{goal}{e_i} - 1)}{c_l^{(t-1)} \times (1 - \frac{goal}{e_l})}$
      if $l \neq 1$ **then**
        $r_{l-1}^{(t)} = trial\ rate$
      end if
      break
    end if
  end for
end if
return $\mathbf{r}^{(t)} = (r_1^{(t)}, \ldots, r_L^{(t)})$

that a moderate number of layers is more desirable than an excessive one for two reasons: 1) the delivery statistics of each layer is not significant if there are too many layers; 2) from the system perspective, excessive number of layers may use up bandwidth and/or memory.

Once the number of layers is determined, we run the campaign at the global pacing rate r_G in the first time slot. We call this step an *initialization phase* in which the delivery data can be collected. We group equal amount of impressions into the desired number of layers based on their predicted response rate to identify the layer boundaries. In the next time slot, the pacing rate of each layer is reassigned based on planned budget in the next time slot and high responding layers will have rates of 1.0 while low responding ones will have rates of 0.0.

In the adjustment algorithms, the direct successive layer next to the layer with non-zero pacing rate is assigned a trial pacing rate. The purpose is to collect delivery data in this layer and prepare for future speedups. This trial rate is supposed to be quite low. We derive such a rate by reserving a certain portion λ (e.g. $\lambda = 1\%$) of budget to be spent in the next time slot. Let the trial layer be the l-th layer and the budget for next time slot is $\widehat{C}^{(t)}$, recall that we have historical spending and pacing rate of this layer from at least one time slot (the initialization phase), the trial pacing rate is derived as $trial\ rate = r_l^{(*)} \times \frac{\lambda \times \widehat{C}^{(t)}}{c_l^{(*)}}$, where $c_l^{(*)}$ and $r_l^{(*)}$ are the historical spending and pacing rate of the l-th layer.

As a quick summary, we employ a layered presentation of all the ad requests based on their predicted response rate and execute budget pacing control in the layer level to achieve delivery and performance goals. Both the spending in the current time slot and the remaining budget are considered to calculate the layered pacing rates in the next time slot. We also tried the alternative to control a threshold so that only ad requests with predicted response rate above the threshold were bid. The outcome of such alternative, however, was not satisfactory. The main reason is that ad requests are usually not smoothly distributed over response rate, and therefore it is difficult to realize smooth control with a single threshold.

6. EXPERIMENTAL EVALUATIONS

We conduct extensive experiments on both real ad campaigns and offline simulations to evaluate the effectiveness of our approach. Without further specification, the following setting is used throughout the experiments: the baseline approach is our approach with only one layer (i.e. using a global pacing rate), the timespan and time slot interval are 24 hours and 15 minutes respectively, the spending plan is even pacing, and the initial pacing rate and trial budget fraction in our approach are $r_G = 0.01$ and $\lambda = 1\%$ respectively. We look at all the three aspects discussed throughout this paper: 1) performance, 2) budget spending, and 3) spending pattern. Since the value of the penalty Ω as defined in Equation 1 is hard to interpret, we transform it into the following metric: $AvgErr = (\frac{B}{K})^{-1} \times \Omega$, which quantifies the relative deviation of the actual spending from the average planned spending per time slot, where K is the number of time slots and B is the total budget.

6.1 Results from Real Campaigns

We pick up from our DSP system 3 campaigns for online A/B test and another 4 campaigns for online over-time test. All these 7 campaigns are CPM campaigns and two of them have specific eCPC goals.

In the A/B test, we deploy 8 layers of group pacing rates in our approach. Campaign 1, 3 are without performance goals while campaign 2 has an eCPC goal of \$2.5. Figure 5 shows the test result for these campaigns. Our approach is surprisingly effective in boosting the performance. Compared to the baseline, the eCPC reductions are -72%, -67%, and -79% for the three campaigns respectively. We note that for Campaign 2, the baseline solution fails to meet the eCPC goal. On the other hand, the total spendings and spending patterns of our approach are as good as the baseline. The $AvgErr$ comparisons of the baseline and our approach are 6.4% : 6.8%, 9.1% : 9.2%, and 10.2% : 9.8% for the three campaigns respectively. Campaign 3 has experienced spending fluctuations and we found there was another competing campaign went offline at time slot 25 so the win-rate of Campaign 3 surged. Our algorithm can recover very soon from the environment changes and continue to deliver smoothly.

The result of over-time test is summarized in Table 1. In this test, we run 4 campaigns for 2 weeks with baseline solution in the first week and our approach with 3 layers in the second week. Among the 4 campaigns, only Campaign 4 has a specific eCPC goal of \$7. Our approach successfully reduces the eCPC of all the 4 campaigns. The most significant reduction almost comes to -50%. Our approach does not show significant eCPC reduction on Campaign 7 because its average pacing rate $AvgPR$ is already around 0.6 and there is not much room to improve its performance. We note that the baseline fails to achieve the eCPC goal of Campaign 4. In real applications, compromising the performance goal may permanently lose the advertiser, which should always be avoided. From the delivery perspective, both the baseline and our approach manage to spend out the total budget smoothly with less than 13.9% deviation from the spending plan.

6.2 Offline Simulations

We also conduct extensive offline simulations to further assess the effectiveness of our approach. We randomly select from our demand pool an ad campaign to generate the

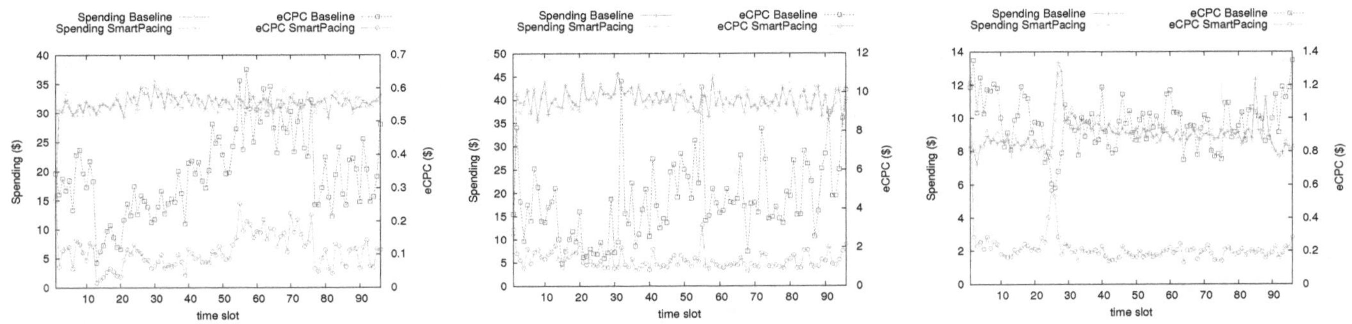

(a) Campaign 1: budget:\$3K, CPM:\$0.5, even pacing. (b) Campaign 2: budget:\$3.8K, CPM:\$2.9, even pacing, search retargeting, eCPC goal:\$2.5. (c) Campaign 3: budget:\$1K, CPM:\$1.5, even pacing, demographic targeting.

Figure 5: Online A/B test result of 3 real campaigns running on our DSP system (# layers: 8).

Campaign Setup				Baseline (1st week)					Smart Pacing (2nd week)					
ID	Budget	CPM	eCPC goal	Spending	Omega	AvgErr	eCPC	AvgPR	Spending	Omega	AvgErr	eCPC	AvgPR	**eCPC reduction**
4	\$35K	\$3.10	\$7.00	\$35.2K	20.43	5.6%	\$10.20	0.0024	\$35.3K	20.72	5.7%	\$5.93	0.0026	**-41.9%**
5	\$20K	\$3.00	No goal	\$20.4K	12.21	5.9%	\$14.78	0.019	\$20.2K	12.32	5.9%	\$7.51	0.017	**-49.19%**
6	\$2K	\$3.35	No goal	\$1.97K	2.89	13.9%	\$10.56	0.017	\$2.01K	2.79	13.4%	\$8.61	0.015	**-18.47%**
7	\$7.5K	\$3.00	No goal	\$7.37K	9.08	11.6%	\$9.90	0.59	\$7.58K	9.19	11.8%	\$9.02	0.65	**-8.89%**

Table 1: Online over-time test result of 4 real campaigns (# layers: 3).

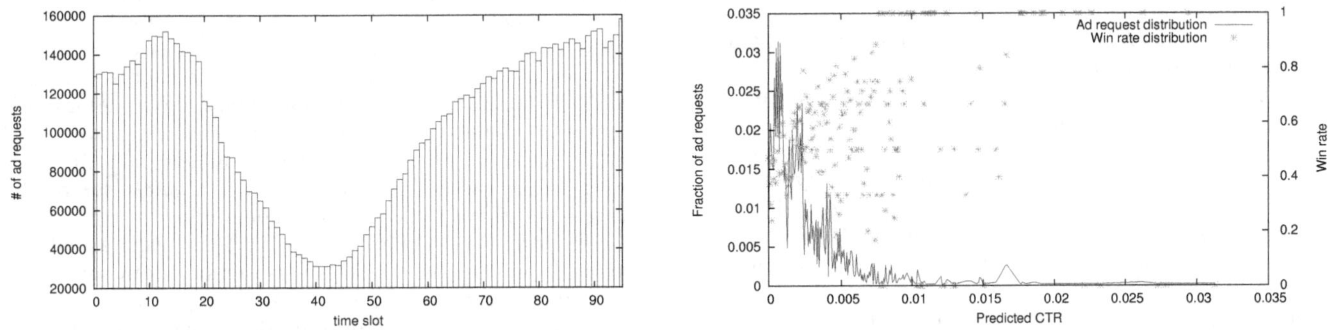

(a) Ad request distribution over time slots (b) Ad request and win-rate distribution over predicted CTR

Figure 6: Offline simulation setup: simulation data is collected from real serving logs of the DSP.

simulation data. First, the eligible ad request distribution over 24 hours is collected (Figure 6(a)). Second, the traffic as well as the win-rate distribution over predicted CTR is collected (Figure 6(b)). We further assume the total number of ad requests is 10,000,000 and billing CPM is \$5. The campaign may or may not have a specific eCPC goal.

We are interested in how our approach performs when compared with the state-of-the-art budget pacing method proposed by Agarwal et al [3]. In their method, a global pacing rate is dynamically adjusted by $\pm 10\%$ every one minute to make the cumulative spending align with the allocated budget. The budget allocation is based on forecasted cumulative traffic. In our experiment, the traffic pattern in Figure 6(a) is further granulized into one minute per time slot, and we use the average traffic of previous seven days as the forecasted traffic to determine budget allocation. Figure 7(a) shows the cumulative traffic and allocated budget curves. Please note that the budget spending plan here is not even pacing. Since their method does not consider performance, no eCPC goal is set. We use 8 layers of pacing rates in our approach. From the result shown in Figure 7(b), both approaches successfully align the cumulative spending curves to the allocation curve. A subtle difference is that their spending curve has fluctuations around the allocation curve. If we look at the *AvgErr* which captures the relative deviation in the per time slot level, their approach gets a surprisingly high error of 96% while our approach generates a much smaller error of 18%, which means our approach can produce smoother pacing result even with very granular time slots. From the control theory perspective, their approach depends on a *conventional feedback controller* while our approach essentially uses an *adaptive controller* whose parameters are adaptive to the spendings in the current time slot and planned budget in the next time slot. In the RTB environment, where the *plant* is complex and time-varying, an adaptive controller usually performs better than a conventional feedback controller [9]. Moreover, since our approach models the quality of the ad requests, it achieves a -70% lower eCPC compared to their approach.

We continue to further study the behaviors of our method. When no eCPC goal is specified, we first fix the campaign budget at \$2,000 and vary the number of layers. As we can

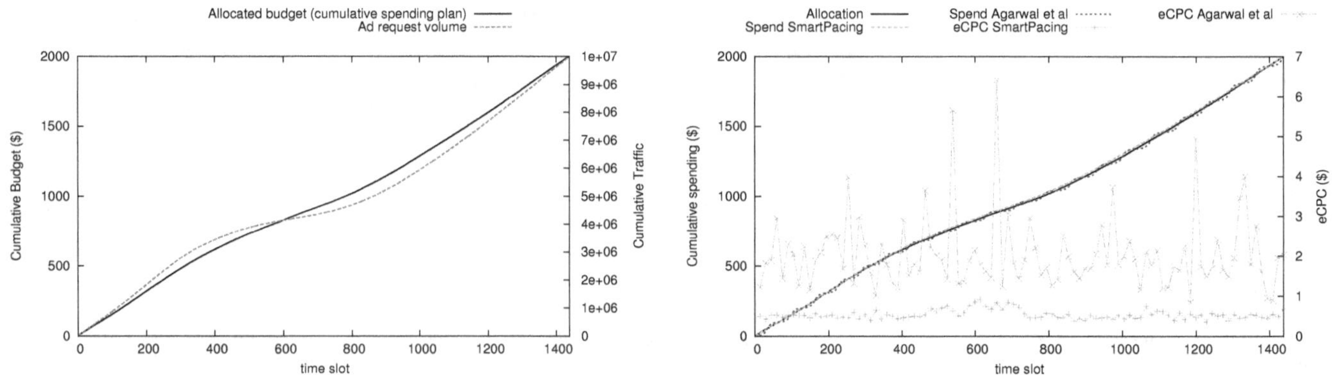

(a) Allocated budget v.s. ad request volume

(b) Actual spendings and eCPCs comparison (eCPC is calculated every 15 minutes to collect sufficient number of clicks)

Figure 7: Comparison with state-of-the-art approach with arbitrary spending plan

observe from Figure 8(a), the top objective to spend out budget as much and as smooth as possible are all achieved except when the number of layers is extremely large (i.e. # layers = 256). The reason is that an excessive number of layers delays the layer-by-layer adjustment to adapt to traffic changes. The difference of eCPCs as shown in Figure 8(c) speaks of the advantage of our approach. When we increase the number of layers, we have more discernability and flexibility to *cherry-pick* high performing ad requests - especially in those time slots when the ad request volume is high. Then we fix the number of layers at 8 and vary the total budget. As Figure 8(b) shows, when the budget keeps going up, there are relatively less available supply so that the budget spending pattern will be more influenced by ad request volume fluctuations. Another interesting observation is that the campaign performance is better when the budget is less (Figure 8(d)). This is because a small budget means our approach can cherry-pick the best performing ad requests without compromising the budget spending objectives.

When a specific eCPC goal is specified, keeping eCPC below this goal is the most important task. Our simulation results in this scenario are shown in Figure 9 when the eCPC goal is set to $0.8. Please note that whenever the pacing rate of every layer is adjusted to zero, which means the performance goal cannot be achieved based on our estimation, we reset the pacing rates of all the layers so that only the top priority layer has a *trial rate*. Again, we first fix budget at $2,000 and vary the number of layers. Different from when no eCPC goal is set, we find that the spendings are extremely low when there are only 1 or 2 layers (Figure 9(a)). Because in such cases, the eCPC goal can never be achieved and the pacing rates are kept being reset. It can be reconfirmed by looking at Figure 9(c), in which only when number of layers is 4, 8, or 256 the average eCPC is below $0.8. When we fix the number of layers at 8 and vary the budget, we also observe different results from when there is no eCPC goal, e.g. Figure 9(b) shows quite different spending pattern from Figure 8(b). The reason is that to achieve eCPC goal, sometimes we need to sacrifice budget spending objectives - especially when the traffic is low. This is even more apparent when the budget increases (Figure 9(d)). We note that it is desired and is exactly one of our contributions.

7. SYSTEM IMPLEMENTATION

In a large scale online ad serving system, there are many infrastructure and implementation issues need to be addressed such as data consistency, service availability, and fault tolerance, that are, however, out of the scope of this paper. In this section, we mainly focus on the following challenges. *rapid feedback of layered statistics:* as described in section 5, the pacing rate adjustment is mainly based on the layered delivery statistics. Therefore, how to collect the online feedback data efficiently and reliably becomes a major implementation challenge. *Overspending prevention:* overspending should always be avoided since it undermines either the advertiser or the DSP's interest. Thus, a *quick stop* mechanism is necessary to prevent overspending.

We address these challenges by implementing a real time feedback pipeline as well as an in-memory data source. As illustrated in Figure 10, impression serving boxes receive impression/click events and produce delivery messages into the message queue. The in-memory data source consumes messages from the message queue and performs aggregations on top of these messages. Finally the controller refers to the in-memory data source to send quick stop notifications or adjusted pacing rates to the bidders.

7.1 Real Time Feedback

Traditional ad serving systems log events such as ad requests, bids, impressions, clicks to an offline data warehouse, and perform offline processing on top of it. However, the delay is too high to fit in our scenario. Therefore, building a separate pipeline to provide real time feedback to online serving system becomes an essential requirement.

We implement both *message queue* and *remote procedure call* (RPC) in our system to transfer messages. Message queue is used to send delivery messages from impression serving boxes to in-memory data source while RPC is used to send pacing rates and quick stop notifications to ad request bidders. Message queue works in asynchronous mode, which means producer and consumer are decoupled and producer has no idea whether consumer has consumed the message or not. The asynchronous nature makes it easy to achieve high throughput and low latency. RPC works in synchronous mode, which means caller will get success or failure responses from callee. Therefore, the motivation to

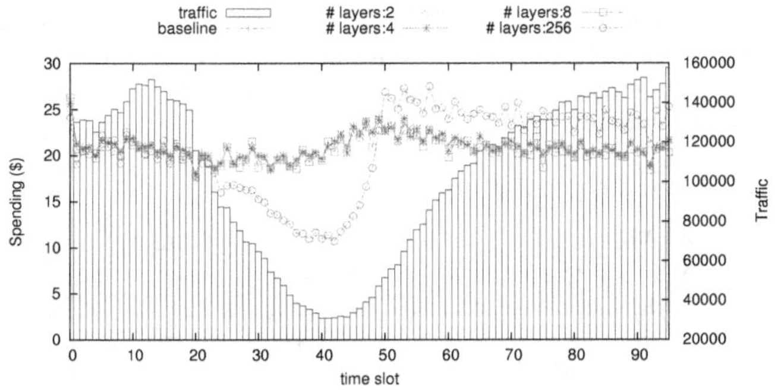

(a) Spendings over time with different # of layers (Budget:$2,000. Budget spending plan is compromised when # of layers is excessive.)

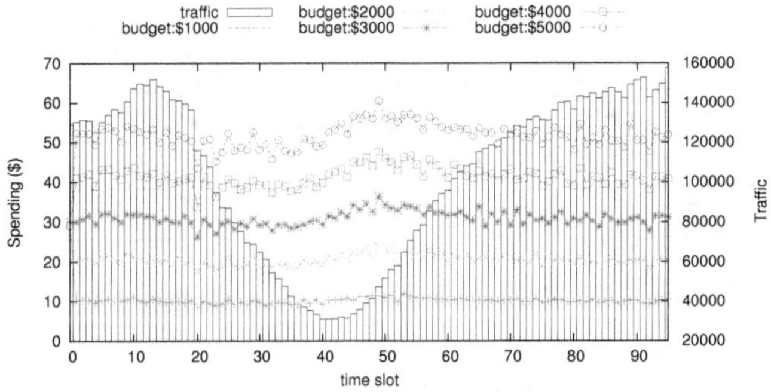

(b) Spendings over time with different budget (# of layers: 8)

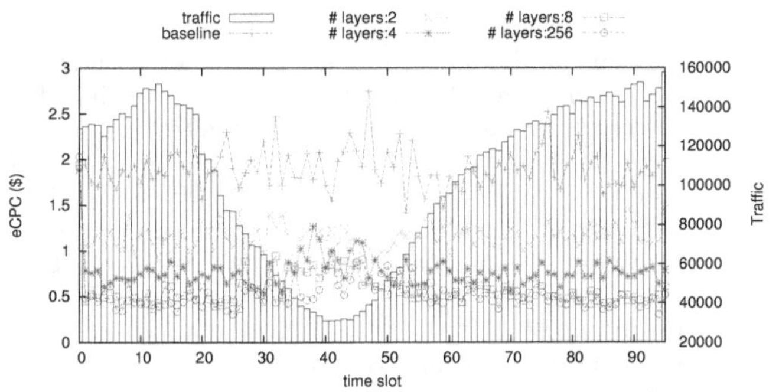

(c) eCPC over time with different # of layers (Budget:$2,000)

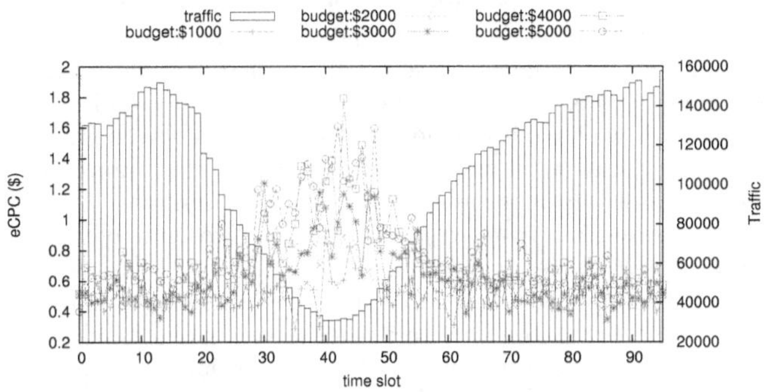

(d) eCPC over time with different budget (# of layers: 8)

Figure 8: Simulation result on campaign without performance goal

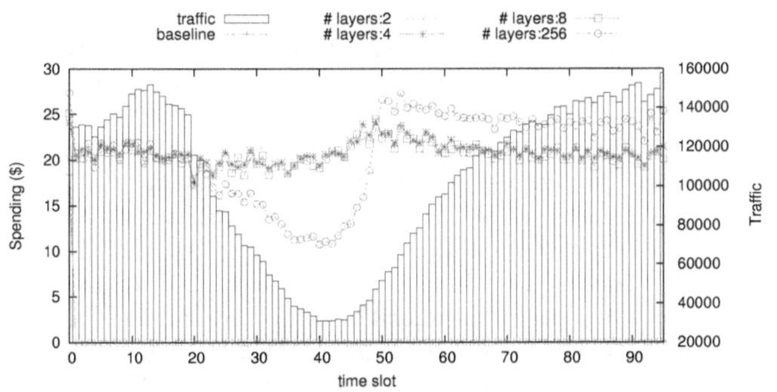

(a) Spendings over time with different # of layers (Budget:$2,000)

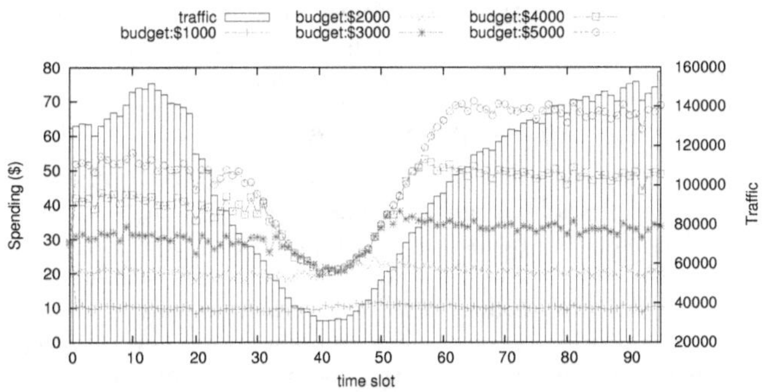

(b) Spendings over time with different budget (# of layers: 8. Budget spending plan is sacrificed to meet the eCPC goal when traffic volume is low.)

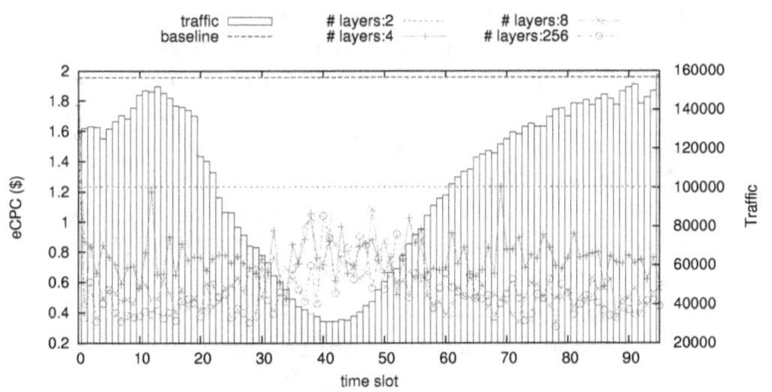

(c) eCPC over time with different # of layers (Budget:$2,000. For baseline and # layers=2, we plot their overall eCPC since only limited number of time slots have clicks)

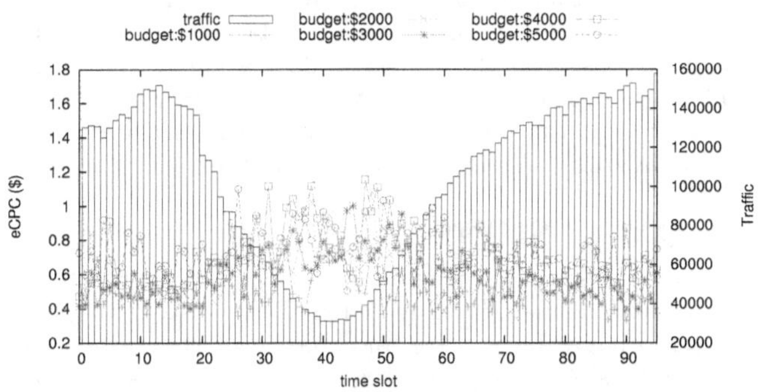

(d) eCPC over time with different budget (# of layers: 8)

Figure 9: Simulation result on campaign with performance goal eCPC $\leq$ \$0.8

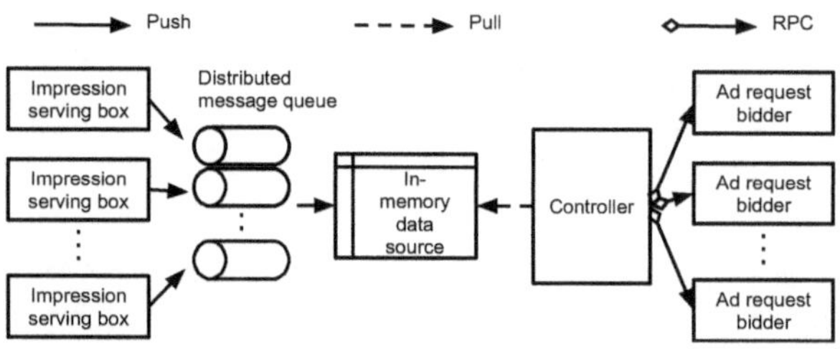

Figure 10: The implementation architecture.

implement both mechanisms is clear: to achieve extremely high throughput (typically billions of impressions per day), impression serving boxes do not need to track whether the messages have been consumed as long as there is no message lost. On the contrary, to make sure the pacing rates and quick stop messages are sent and applied to each bidder, the controller needs to get responses from all the bidders.

Although we have implemented a message queue to transfer delivery messages asynchronously, the huge amount of delivery information requires some further designs. *Batch processing* and *micro-aggregation* are the two endeavors to further drive efficiency. At impression serving boxes side, a batch accumulates hundreds of delivery messages into a single request over the wire to reduce network overhead and amortize transmission delay. This is especially useful for high latency links such as those between data centers. At message queue side, a batch groups multiple small I/O operations into a single one to improve efficiency. Another practice we have is aggregating the delivery messages under certain conditions without information loss, e.g. aggregating impressions of the same campaign with the same predicted response rate within a certain time period.

7.2 In-memory Data Source

The in-memory data source stores the layered delivery information of each campaign. The main challenges of implementing such an in-memory storage are: 1) how to avoid data loss in case of failure, and 2) how to control memory usage. In order to address the potential data loss problem in system failures, we employ a snapshot plus commit log approach. We observe that the message queue itself can be a commit log as long as it honors the order of message sequence. With the help of message queue, we can easily recover the state using the message sequence number and the snapshot data. We address the memory usage issue by aggregation. As described in section 5, the pacing rate adjustment is based on the delivery information of the most recent time slot and therefore only raw messages within configurable recent time need to be stored. Historical data is stored in aggregated form to minimize the memory usage.

8. CONCLUSIONS

We have presented a general and principled approach as well as its implementation in a real DSP system to perform smooth pacing control and maximize the campaign performance simultaneously. Experimental results showed that, compared to state-of-the-art budget pacing method, our proposed approach can significantly boost the campaign performance and achieve smooth pacing goals.

Our future work will mainly focus on trying out different pacing schemes such as pacing based on performance with the help of supply and performance forecasting techniques, combining the proposed approach with other control methods to make it more intelligent and robust, and studying the competitions and interactions among multiple campaigns in pacing control.

9. REFERENCES

[1] Z. Abrams, O. Mendelevitch, and J. Tomlin. Optimal delivery of sponsored search advertisements subject to budget constraints. In *Proceedings of the 8th ACM conference on Electronic commerce*, pages 272–278. ACM, 2007.

[2] D. Agarwal, R. Agrawal, and R. Khanna. Estimating rates of rare events with multiple hierarchies through scalable log-linear models. *ACM SIGKDD Conf. on Knowledge Discovery and Data Mining*, 2010.

[3] D. Agarwal, S. Ghosh, K. Wei, and S. You. Budget pacing for targeted online advertisements at linkedin. In *Proceedings of the 20th ACM SIGKDD international conference on Knowledge discovery and data mining*, pages 1613–1619. ACM, 2014.

[4] A. Bhalgat, J. Feldman, and V. Mirrokni. Online allocation of display ads with smooth delivery. *ACM SIGKDD Conf. on Knowledge Discovery and Data Mining*, 2012.

[5] A. Bhalgat, N. Korula, H. Leontyev, M. Lin, and V. Mirrokni. Partner tiering in display advertising. *The Eighth ACM International Conference on Web Search and Data Mining*, 2014.

[6] C. Borgs, J. Chayes, N. Immorlica, K. Jain, O. Etesami, and M. Mahdian. Dynamics of bid optimization in online advertisement auctions. In *Proceedings of the 16th international conference on World Wide Web*, pages 531–540. ACM, 2007.

[7] O. Chapelle, E. Manavoglu, and R. Rosales. Simple and scalable response prediction for display advertising. *ACM Transactions on Intelligent Systems and Technology*, 2014.

[8] Y. Chen, P. Berkhin, B. Anderson, and N. R. Devanur. Real-time bidding algorithms for performance-based display ad allocation. *ACM SIGKDD Conf. on Knowledge Discovery and Data Mining*, 2011.

[9] I. Landau, R. Lozano, M. M'Saad, and A. Karimi. *Adaptive Control: Algorithms, Analysis and Applications*. Communications and Control Engineering. Springer, 2011.

[10] K.-C. Lee, A. Jalali, and A. Dasdan. Real time bid optimization with smooth budget delivery in online advertising. *The Seventh International Workshop on Data Mining for Online Advertising*, 2013.

[11] K.-C. Lee, B. Orten, A. Dasdan, and W. Li. Estimating conversion rate in display advertising from past performance data. *ACM SIGKDD Conf. on Knowledge Discovery and Data Mining*, 2012.

[12] A. Mehta, A. Saberi, U. Vazirani, and V. Vazirani. Adwords and generalized online matching. *Journal of the ACM (JACM)*, 54(5):22, 2007.

[13] W. Zhang, Y. Zhang, B. Gao, Y. Yu, X. Yuan, and T.-Y. Liu. Joint optimization of bid and budget allocation in sponsored search. *ACM SIGKDD Conf. on Knowledge Discovery and Data Mining*, 2012.

From Infrastructure to Culture: A/B Testing Challenges in Large Scale Social Networks

Ya Xu, Nanyu Chen, Adrian Fernandez, Omar Sinno, Anmol Bhasin
LinkedIn Corp, 2029 Stierlin Court, Mountain View, CA 94043
{yaxu, nchen, afernandez, osinno, abhasin}@linkedin.com

ABSTRACT

A/B testing, also known as bucket testing, split testing, or controlled experiment, is a standard way to evaluate user engagement or satisfaction from a new service, feature, or product. It is widely used among online websites, including social network sites such as Facebook, LinkedIn, and Twitter to make data-driven decisions. At LinkedIn, we have seen tremendous growth of controlled experiments over time, with now over 400 concurrent experiments running per day. General A/B testing frameworks and methodologies, including challenges and pitfalls, have been discussed extensively in several previous KDD work [7, 8, 9, 10]. In this paper, we describe in depth the experimentation platform we have built at LinkedIn and the challenges that arise particularly when running A/B tests at large scale in a social network setting. We start with an introduction of the experimentation platform and how it is built to handle each step of the A/B testing process at LinkedIn, from designing and deploying experiments to analyzing them. It is then followed by discussions on several more sophisticated A/B testing scenarios, such as running offline experiments and addressing the network effect, where one user's action can influence that of another. Lastly, we talk about features and processes that are crucial for building a strong experimentation culture.

Categories and Subject Descriptors

G.3 Probability and Statistics/Experimental Design: controlled experiments, randomized experiments, A/B testing.

General Terms

Measurement, Design, Experimentation

Keywords

Controlled experiments, A/B testing, social network, online experiments, network A/B testing, measurement.

1 INTRODUCTION

A/B testing, also called controlled experiment, has become the gold standard for evaluating new product strategies and approaches in many internet companies, including Amazon, eBay, Etsy, Facebook, Google, Groupon, LinkedIn, Microsoft, Netflix and Yahoo [9, 10]. As experimentation gains popularity, so does the need for properly designing, managing and analyzing experiments.

KDD '15, August 11 - 14, 2015, Sydney, NSW, Australia

 ISBN 978-1-4503-3664-2/15/08…$15.00

DOI: http://dx.doi.org/10.1145/2783258.2788602

The theory of controlled experiment dates back to Sir Ronald A. Fisher's experiments at the Rothamsted Agricultural Experimental Station in England in the 1920s [11]. Since then, many textbooks and papers from different fields have provided theoretical foundations [20, 21, 32, 33] for running controlled experiments. While the theory may be straightforward, the deployment and mining of experiments in practice and at scale can be complex and challenging [13, 14]. In particular, several past KDD papers have discussed at length the experimentation systems used at Microsoft Bing and Google [8, 9], including best practices and pitfalls [7, 10]. Facebook also introduces the PlanOut language which provides a toolkit for parameter-based experiments [12].

At a high level, we follow similar practices and methodology for experimentation at LinkedIn. However, many of the challenges we face arise particularly because LinkedIn is a member-based social network (we call our logged-in users "members"). In this paper, we focus on how we address these challenges as we scale to run more experiments. We share how we built XLNT (pronounced "excellent"), the end-to-end A/B testing platform at LinkedIn, to not only meet the day-to-day A/B testing needs across the company, but to also address more sophisticated use cases that are prevalent in a social network setting.

When we launched XLNT, the platform only supported about 50 experiments per day. Today, that number has increased to more than 400. The number of metrics supported has grown from 60 to more than 1000. Such tremendous growth is not only attributed to our scalable platform but also to our continuous emphasis on embedding experimentation deeply into LinkedIn's decision-making process and culture. We include in the paper several XLNT features we built to enable us to take education and evangelization past the "classroom".

A/B testing is truly the driver behind LinkedIn's product innovation. The areas we experiment on are extremely diverse, ranging from visual changes on our home page, to improvements on our job recommendation algorithm, to personalizing the subject line of our emails. We begin this paper with two example experiments that we recently ran.

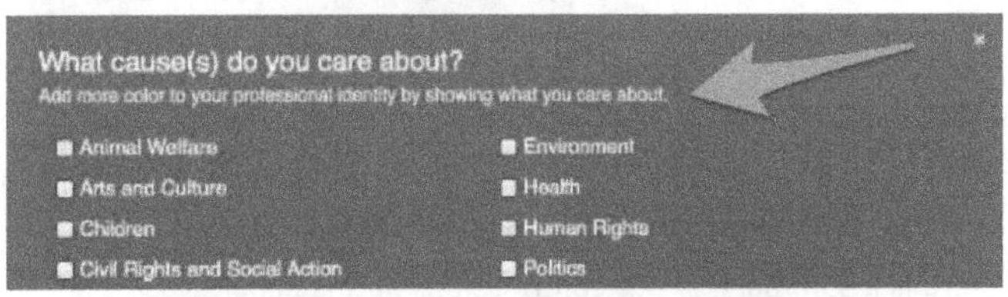

Figure 1: Guided edit experiment on profiles.

The first experiment was on members' profile pages (Figure 1). In order to encourage members to better establish their professional identity, we displayed a small module at the top of their profile. The experiment was to include an additional line of text to call out the benefits and values a complete profile provides. For instance, the example in Figure 1 encourages members to add volunteer experience to their profile. This small change turned out to be extremely successful. Results from the A/B test showed a 14% increase in profile edits on volunteer experience!

Another experiment was an entire redesign of the Premium Subscription's payment flow (Figure 2). Apart from providing a cleaner look and feel, we reduced the number of payment checkout pages and added an FAQ. The experiment showed an increase of millions of dollars in annualized bookings, about 30% reduction in refund orders and over 10% lift in free trial orders.

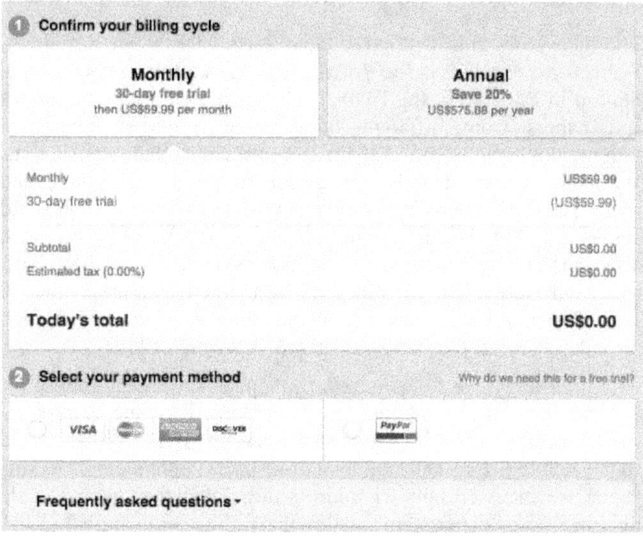

Figure 2: New Premium Subscription payment flow.

In both cases, the XLNT platform made it feasible to quickly measure the impact of both small and large changes at low cost. This enables us to identify features with a high Return-On-Investment (ROI) and moreover, to quantify the impact in a scientific and controlled manner. A screen shot of our analysis dashboard is shown in Figure 3.

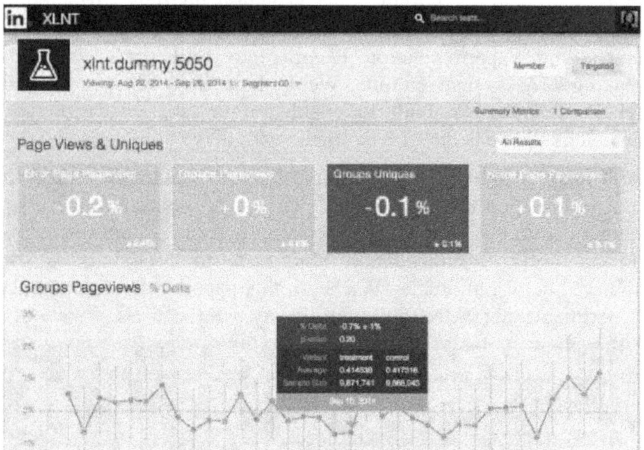

Figure 3: XLNT analysis dashboard.

Here is a summary of our contributions in this paper:

- We share the details of how we built our experimentation platform, including the engineering challenges we faced and how we addressed them.
- We discuss several challenging A/B testing scenarios we face at LinkedIn. Some of these challenges, particularly the ones that are specific to experimentation on social networks, are discussed and shared in a public paper for the first time.
- We discuss several concepts and novel features we introduced at LinkedIn that have significantly shaped our experimentation culture.
- Many real A/B test examples are shared for the first time in public. Even though the examples may be LinkedIn specific, most of the lessons and best practices we share are applicable to experimenting on social networks in general.

The paper is organized as follows. Section 2 introduces XLNT and how it is built to address several fundamental challenges. Section 3 discusses several more sophisticated A/B testing use cases. Section 4 discusses the XLNT features that help create a stronger experimentation culture and Section 5 concludes.

2 THE XLNT PLATFORM

We realized early on that ad-hoc A/B testing was not a scalable approach to sustain the high speed of innovation at LinkedIn. We required an A/B testing platform to allow us to quickly quantify the impact of features. Additionally, this needed to be achieved in a scientific and controlled manner across the company. Thus, we built XLNT.

The XLNT platform is aimed at encompassing every step of the testing process, from designing and deploying experiments to analyzing them. In particular, it was built to address the following concerns and challenges:

1. **Scalability.** We continue to see tremendous growth in both the number of concurrent experiments and the amount of data collected per experiment. The platform needs to scale to handle not only today's data volume but also tomorrow's.
2. **Incorporating Existing Practices**. Over time LinkedIn developed many A/B testing practices. For instance, we have a strong tradition on targeting (Section 2.1.2) as we believe each one of our members is special and unique. It is important to incorporate these practices as part of the platform.
3. **Engineering Integration**. The platform has to be well integrated into LinkedIn's engineering infrastructure. The experimentation platform architecture that works at other companies is unlikely to work for us due to different structure and tooling constraints.
4. **Flexibility**. Although the basic A/B testing requirements are similar across the organization, teams usually have their own special needs, given the diversity of the products they work on. The platform needs to offer enough flexibility to accommodate such customization.
5. **Usability.** A/B testing is not limited only to the R&D organizations. To make it truly a platform for everyone, we needed to provide an intuitive User Interface (together with APIs) for designing, deploying and analyzing experiments.

Taking these challenges into consideration, we share the details of the XLNT platform in this section, with the overall architecture outlined in Figure 4 below.

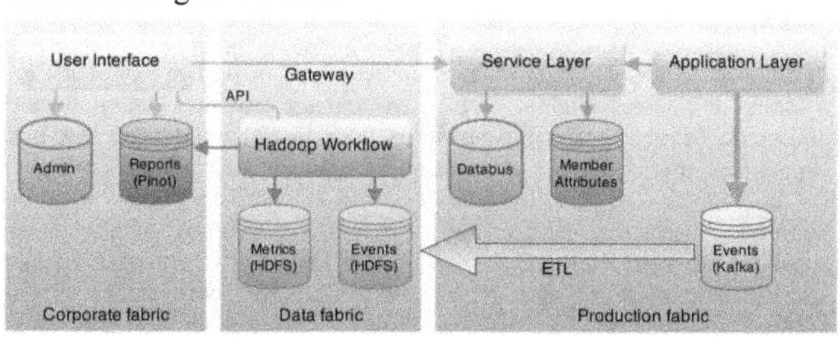

Figure 4: XLNT Platform overall architecture.

2.1 Design

Experimental design is arguably the most important step in the testing workflow to get good and meaningful results. As Sir R. A. Fisher put it [27] "To consult the statistician after an experiment is finished is often merely to ask him to conduct a post mortem examination. He can perhaps say what the experiment died of." To this end, we have built the platform to incorporate the standard practice at LinkedIn while providing capabilities to enable better designs and prevent common pitfalls. In this section, we first start with introducing a few key concepts that are fundamental to our experiment model and then focus on targeting, a critical component used in designing experiments at LinkedIn.

2.1.1 Experiment Definitions

Most experimentation terminologies used at LinkedIn are standard and can be found in any experimental design textbooks [28]. We focus here on only a few definitions that are key to our platform.

To run an experiment, one starts by creating a *testKey*, which is a unique identifier that represents the concept or the feature to be tested. An actual *experiment* is then created as an instantiation of the testKey. Such hierarchical structure makes it easy to manage experiments at various stages of the testing process. For example, we want to investigate the benefits of adding a background image. We begin by diverting only 1% of US users to the treatment, then increasing the allocation to 50% and eventually expanding to users outside of the US market. Even though the feature being tested remains the same throughout the ramping process, it requires different experiment instances as the traffic allocations and targeting changes. In other words, an experiment acts as a realization of the testKey, and only one experiment per testKey can be active at a time.

Every experiment is comprised of one or more *segments*, with each segment identifying a subpopulation to experiment on. A common practice is to set up an experiment with a "whitelist" segment containing only the team members developing the product, an "internal" segment consisting of all LinkedIn employees and additional segments targeting external users. Because each segment defines its own traffic allocation, the treatment can be ramped to 100% in the whitelist segment, while still running at 1% in the external segments. Note that segment ordering matters because members are only considered as part of the first eligible segment. After the experimenters input their design through an intuitive User Interface, all the information is then concisely stored in a DSL (Domain Specific Language). For example, the line below indicates a single segment experiment targeting English-speaking users in the US where 10% of them are in the treatment variant while the rest in control.

```
(ab (= (locale) "en_US")[treatment 10% control 90%])
```

It is important to mention that each experiment is associated with a *hashID*, which serves as an input to an MD5 based algorithm used to randomize users into variants. By default, all experiments of the same testKey share the same hashID, and different testKeys have different hashIDs. This ensures that a user receives consistent experience as we ramp up a treatment. More importantly, as we have hundreds of experiments running in parallel, different hashIDs imply that the randomizations between active experiments are orthogonal. The platform also allows manually overwriting the hashIDs, and the applicable usage cases will be discussed in Section 3.1.

2.1.2 Targeting

We recognize that not only are our products diverse, each one of our users is special and unique. With that in mind, many of the experiments we run at LinkedIn focus on how to provide the most improved user experience possible for specific user groups. This is achieved by creating different segments in an experiment targeting different subpopulations, as we have mentioned in Section 2.1.1. Deciding on the right population to target is the most important part of experiment design. There are three targeting capabilities provided by the platform:

Built-in Member Attributes. The platform provides more than 40 built-in member attributes for experimenters to leverage. They range from static attributes such as a member's country to dynamic attributes such as a member's last login date. These attributes are computed daily as part of our data pipelines and pushed to Voldemort, a distributed key-value data storage system [22], for real-time targeting.

Customized Member Attributes. Frequently experimenters need a targeting criterion beyond the default ones provided by XLNT. The platform provides a seamless onboarding process to include member attributes generated regularly from external data pipelines. It is even more straightforward if this is a static list generated from a one-off job, as one can simply "upload" it to the platform. These customized attributes are pushed to Voldemort on a daily basis and can be used the same way as any of the built-in ones.

Real-time Attributes. These attributes are only available at runtime, such as the browser type or mobile device. XLNT provides an integrated way to target using these attributes, or any parameters passed during a runtime request. For example, to target only requests coming from iPhones, one just needs to inform the platform that an attribute called "osName" is to be evaluated at runtime, and target only those with the value equal to "iPhone". This feature is used extensively for mobile experiments, as new mobile features are usually only rolled out for particular mobile app versions. This is also beneficial when experimenting on guest users where no information is available prior to the request. Section 3.2.1 includes more discussions on this case.

2.2 Deployment

The XLNT A/B testing platform is a key component of LinkedIn's Continuous Deployment framework [23]. It spans across every fabric and stack of LinkedIn's engineering infrastructure, providing A/B testing capabilities universally. Once the design is completed, deploying an experiment involves the following two components:

1. **Application Layer.** This includes any production artifacts, e.g. web applications and offline libraries. Each application requires a thick client dependency in order to run experiments locally, track experiment result events and interface with the service layer. The implementation in the application layer includes two parts: (1) making a simple one-line call to determine the variant, and (2) creating a code path to reflect the new variant behavior accordingly. For example, to decide the right color to show to a user in a "buttonColor" experiment, we just need to include the line below

   ```
   String color = client.getTreatment(memberID,
   "buttonColor").
   ```

   The second step is then simply changing the color of the button depending on the value of "color" returned above. This is the same across all application stacks including frontend, backend, mobile or even email experiments.

2. **Service Layer.** This is a distributed cache and experiment definition provider that implements *Rest.li* endpoints [29]. It is capable of executing experiments remotely and querying the built-in member attributes store described in Section 2.1.2. After the internal testing phase is passed, the experiment owner requests to activate the experiment. An SRE (Site Reliability Engineer) then reviews the specifications and, if no red flags are found, deploys the experiment to production. Experiment deployments are propagated via the Databus [24] relay and listeners. The new experiment definition is then distributed across LinkedIn's service stacks with updates sent to application clients every 5 minutes. This makes A/B testing totally independent of application code releases and can easily be managed through a centralized configuration UI.

At runtime, a simple experiment that does not involve targeting on pre-defined attributes can be executed locally at the application layer, which takes no time delay at all. Experiments that require member attributes for targeting (see Section 2.1.2) are sent to execute at the service layer. The results are then communicated back to the application client with a total delay of 1msec on average. Because these are high throughput services with about 20k to 30k QPS, we need to establish strict SLAs and enforce it with timeouts. These timeout durations can be fully customized according to experiment specific latencies.

2.2.1 Logging

To support monitoring and analysis, an event is logged during the "getTreatment" call at the application layer, with information such as the timestamp, testKey, experiment name, ID (experimental unit), variant, etc. These events are stored in Kafka topics [25] and periodically ETL'd to our HDFS clusters to be used in our data workflows.

It is important to note that these experiment events are fired only when the "getTreatment" code is called, and not for every request to LinkedIn.com. This not only reduces the logs footprint, but also enables us to do *triggered analysis,* where only users who were actually impacted by the experiment are included in the A/B test analysis. For example, LinkedIn.com could have 20 million daily users, but only 2 million of them visited the "jobs" page where the experiment is actually on. Without such trigger information, it is hard to isolate the real impact of the experiment from the noise, especially for experiments with low trigger rates.

Even with triggered logging, the volume of events generated presents a challenge. Currently, an average of 10 billion events are generated daily, and that number is growing quickly as more experiments are run on an increasing user base. We have visited the event schema and generation conditions several times in the past to remove derivable attributes and encode values. Continued effort is necessary for incremental improvement and to identifying new solutions addressing this challenge going forward.

2.3 Offline Analysis

Automated analytics is crucial in popularizing experimentation. It not only saves teams from time-consuming ad hoc analysis, but also ensures that the methodology behind the reports is solid, consistent and scientifically founded.

To paint with a broad brush, the analytics pipeline computes user engagement metrics such as pageviews and clicks, and joins them with the experiment assignment information from online logs described in Section 2.2.1. The data are then aggregated based on the experiment and time range to produce summary statistics that are sufficient to compute not only the difference between any two variants, but also the statistical significance information such as p-values and confidence intervals.

Approximately 4TB of metrics data and 6TB of experiment assignment data are processed every day to produce over 150 million summary records. Much of this computation utilizes the large scale joins-and-aggregations solution provided by the Cubert framework [34, 35]. All these data are stored in Pinot [26], our in-house distributed storage system, to be queried by the UI applications.

2.3.1 Metrics

LinkedIn has many diverse products. Even though there are a handful of company metrics that everyone optimizes towards, every product has several product-specific metrics that are most likely impacted by experiments in their "area". As LinkedIn's products evolve and new products emerge, it is impossible for the experimentation team to create and maintain all metrics for all products (currently more than 1000 of them). Therefore, to maintain the metrics, we follow a hybrid of centralized and decentralized model.

Metrics are categorized into 3 tiers: 1) Company wide 2) Product Specific 3) Feature Specific. A central team maintains tier 1 metrics. Ownership of tier 2 & 3 metrics is decentralized – each team owns the logic for these metrics while the central team is responsible for the daily computation and operations. XLNT computes all tier 1 and tier 2 metrics for all experiments while tier 3 metrics are only computed on an ad-hoc basis.

2.3.2 Multi-Dimensional Deep-Dive

When a metric is impacted, experimenters frequently want to dig deeper and get more actionable insights. For this reason, XLNT provides several slicing and dicing capabilities. Experimenters can leverage both user and non-user based dimensions and even apply multiple dimensions at once. As an example, the metric total pageviews can be narrowed down to homepage pageviews on the iOS app for Spanish speaking members across the US, South America and Spain.

As one can easily imagine, this is computational extremely heavy especially when over 1000 metrics are involved across multiple days for hundreds of experiments. At a high level there are two use cases we need to address within experiment reporting: 1) Enable a *broad* understanding of the impact across LinkedIn 2) Enable a *deep* understanding in the areas most heavily impacted by the experiment.

Knowing that this functionality clearly falls in the second use case, we decided to provide multi-dimensional drill-down only for the subset of metrics likely to be impacted by the experiment. Furthermore, from the dozens of dimensions available, teams decide what dimensions are most relevant for their experiments and at what level of combinations. This saves us from unnecessarily crunching data that is not relevant and no one uses. Even with such savings, our pipeline still generates about 150 million records daily on average, where each record includes summary statistics for the tuple of experiment, variant, date range, metric and dimension combination.

3 BEYOND THE BASICS

We have described the components in XLNT that enable the basic workflow for running experiments at LinkedIn. In this section, we discuss, with real examples, how we address a few challenging scenarios. Even though the examples may be LinkedIn specific, most of the lessons and best practices we share here are applicable to experimenting on social networks in general.

3.1 Interactions between Experiments

As mentioned in Section 2.1, experiments at LinkedIn are fully overlapping *by default*. In other words, a member is simultaneously in all applicable experiments. Unique hashIDs are used for each experiment to ensure the randomizations between experiments are orthogonal. The simple parallel experimentation structure allows us to scale the number of experiments easily in a de-centralized manner. It is sufficient for most of our A/B testing needs as many of our experiments affect entirely different products and are unlikely to interfere or interact with each other. However, there are cases where interactions are expected. For example, one experiment was testing whether or not to include a LinkedIn Pulse module on the homepage, while simultaneously we had another experiment investigating the number of stories to include in the same module. Clearly, when the module does not exist, the second experiment is ineffective. Another example of potential interaction is between two email experiments. When a member receives two emails from LinkedIn, he or she is likely to open only one of them. Hence two email experiments both improving the subject line are in fact competing with each other. Each of them would have enjoyed a larger gain if the experiments were run on two disjoint user spaces.

Google's experimentation system uses layers and domains to divide up the user space to avoid such conflicts or interactions [8]. Microsoft Bing has a similar approach but their system includes detection in addition to prevention [9]. Different from these two systems, the XLNT platform takes a de-centralized approach that is closely integrated with the LinkedIn engineering infrastructure. We describe here how we use XLNT to address the three most common concerns and use cases related to interactions at LinkedIn.

Gating Key. Using the LinkedIn Pulse module example, a testKey is created that acts as a gating key to control whether the module is on or off. A second testKey is then used to split the traffic to test different number of stories. The second testKey would only be evaluated if the gating key indicates that the module is "on". This nested structure ensures that users do not see five stories without the module. The same gating key concept is also used to create disjoint traffic for multiple experiments. For instance, we always have several experiments running simultaneously on the homepage; some are improving the feed relevance while others are modifying UI elements. When one is concerned about potential interaction between N of them, he or she can create a gating key with N variants and each variant acts as a bucket that sends traffic only to one of the N experiments.

Factorial Design. Even though LinkedIn has over 300 million members, there are product areas where the user base is relatively small in comparison to other parts of the site. Some of these products are heavily experimented on, for example, the Subscription acquisition page. Small UI changes on the subscription page can make a big difference monetarily. With multiple UI experiments running in parallel, there is valid concern regarding interference. However, splitting up the traffic makes it even harder to have sufficient power to detect changes. It is also not practical to run experiments sequentially since each experiment runs for at least a month to monitor long-term user impact. On the other hand, if we set up these experiments independently (the default setup) each experiment becomes a factor in a full factorial design. We can then analyze to see if these experiments do interact and if so, what their effects would be without interaction. Of course, if there is no significant interaction, each experiment can be analyzed separately and each gets to enjoy the full amount of traffic available for maximum power.

Dependent Experiments. There are cases where people are interested in only *certain* combinations of different factors, but not all. For instance, we have one experiment testing the maximum number of sponsored updates to include in one's feeds per day, while another experiment varying the gap between two consequent sponsored updates. What is the best combination of these two factors? Some combinations, for example, a maximum of 25 sponsored updates with a gap of 3 organic updates in between, should never be launched due to bad user experience. Testing these combinations not only wastes valuable traffic, but also hurts the member experience. In most cases, creating a single test that combines the two factors is impractical, but we can align them using the same hashID so that members are randomized identically in both experiments. We can then create the variants for the second experiment such that when combined with the first they generate the right combinations. Figure 5 illustrates the idea.

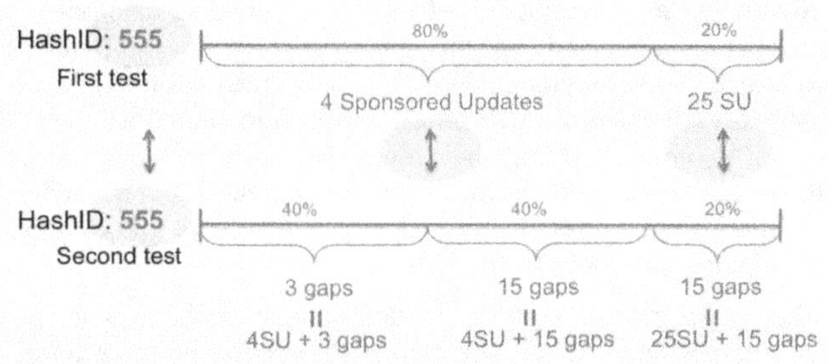

Figure 5: Using the same hashID to align two experiments.

3.2 Experimental Units

The first decision to make when running an experiment is whom to run it on. The experimental unit refers to both the entity randomly assigned to treatment and control (randomization unit) and the unit metrics are calculated and averaged over (analysis unit). We assume these two units are the same in our discussion. The most common case when they do differ (e.g. computing the metric Click-Through-Rate when experimenting on users) is well discussed in the literature [8, 13] and hence omitted in this paper.

In this section, we use guest experimentation as an example to discuss how XLNT supports different experimental units and some of the challenges we encounter. In addition, we introduce an interesting problem that arises particularly in a social network setting where the same user can play two different roles with each needing to be tested separately.

3.2.1 Guest Experiments

Most of our experiments focus on optimizing the member experience. However, we also run experiments on public pages such as the registration page and public profiles. Providing an excellent user experience on these pages is critical because they ultimately drive sign-ups.

The XLNT platform makes it easy to run an experiment on guest users (or any other unit the experimenter requires). A browser ID, instead of a member ID, is usually used to identify guest users and is passed to the "getTreatment" call the same way as a member ID (see Section 2.2). The browser ID is associated with a different URN type called "guest" which is then recorded as part of the experiment logs (Section 2.2.1). Targeting is also possible. Even though there is no rich profile data associated with a browser ID, properties that are available at run time such as the browser type, or the geographic location computed by reversing the IP address can all be used for targeting (Section 2.1.2). Our offline analysis pipeline uses the URN type to differentiate between experimental units and automatically joins metrics with the corresponding experiment assignment information. This enables us to have a single workflow to handle analysis on various experimental units.

One challenge is to handle transitions between member and guest status of the same user during an experiment. There are mainly two cases when this happens: a guest user becoming a member, or a member transitioning between logged-in and logged-out states. The latter is less of a concern since a member's logged out activities on the site is very limited and has little influence over our experiments. The former, however, is of particular concern for experiments optimizing registration and onboarding flow as one unified experience. For example, we have one guest experiment promoting registration using the "Signup with Facebook" option, in which case certain information can then be automatically filled during the onboarding process to provide a better member experience. Even though the experiment is randomized on the browserID, we need to have a measurement based on both browserID and memberID. This is a common use case as information collected on the guest side helps us tailor the experience on the member side. To achieve the continuity, we can make a small customization on the application client (Section 2.2) to emit two pieces of tracking events, one based on the browserID (the default one) and the other on the memberID. The analysis workflow then automatically picks up both events and generates two reports, one for each ID.

Other experimental units have their unique challenges as well. Take experimenting on LinkedIn groups as an example. A member can belong to multiple groups, so we can no longer assume independence between units. This presents a similar challenge as the network A/B testing problem to be discussed in Section 3.4.

3.2.2 Dual Roles of a User

There are different experimental units even when we only consider members on the site. This is the case because every member holds two different roles in a social network as both the one performing an action and the one receiving an action. For example, a member can view others' profiles or receive profile views. Similarly, they can endorse someone or be endorsed.

It is important to know which role we are experimenting on and analyze accordingly. If an experiment is randomizing on endorsers, endorsees are going to be evenly distributed across treatment and control. Therefore, analyzing the number of endorsements received gives no indication on how the experiment performs. Similarly, an experiment that encourages members to send more invitations should not be evaluated based on the number of invitations received. Essentially, even though the total number of actions is the same counting by either role, how the actions are attributed needs to be aligned with the experimental unit. Moreover, some attributions, such as the number of invitations accepted, are time-lagged, in which case we need to create additional metrics to capture the time dimension (e.g. invitation accepted by day X).

We need to be even more careful when we have experiments aiming at assessing impacts on both sides. As an example, we recently considered allowing members to include a custom background image on their profile page. We wanted to evaluate whether members would view more profiles and receive more profile views. Two experiments (testKeys) were created, one allowing a member to upload an image (viewee experiment) and the other allowing a member to see the image if there is one (viewer experiment). However, these two experiments cannot be fully independent because viewer and viewee are simply opposite perspectives of the same member. Members who are able to upload background images should also be able to see them, especially on their own profiles. To address this issue, we applied the same hashID to both experiments to ensure the same treatment assignments. A more subtle but important point is that the experiment effect depends on the percentage of members receiving the treatment. Clearly, if only 1% of profiles have the background image, a viewer's behavior is less likely to be impacted compared to if all profiles had a background image. Therefore, the bias is smallest when the treatment is ramped close to 100%. On the other hand, running the experiments at 50/50 gives the least variance. It is thus a bias and variance trade-off that the team has to keep in mind when evaluating the experiment results.

3.3 Offline Experiments

In an online experiment, users trickle into the A/B test as they visit LinkedIn. The experimenter has no prior information on who will be in the experiment, and users' engagement is measured through their activities on the site, e.g. pageviews and clicks. Many of the experiments we run at LinkedIn are such online experiments. However, because LinkedIn is a member-based social network, there are also many experiments that are "offline", in which case the experiment users do not necessarily have an online activity. We walk through three scenarios below.

Email Experiments. Emails are usually sent to members independent of whether they visit the online site or not. For example, a member would receive a notification email if another member sends them an invitation to connect. Not everyone who gets an email would come to the site. Therefore, if we only consider active members when analyzing an email experiment we are likely to introduce a bias. For instance, if the treatment email has a more attractive subject line that encourages more members to click and visit the online site, we are likely to see a drop in many key metrics (e.g. average pageviews) if only active members are taken into account because the email tends to drive less engaged members to visit LinkedIn. In other words, the experiment population cannot be determined only with online user activity. It needs to take into account all users who received the email. To make it even more complex, we also have experiments that attempt to reduce the email footprint by filtering out emails that are less relevant to members. In these cases, it is not sufficient to only look at users who actually receive the email, but to also include users who would have received the email had there been no relevance filtering.

Email Campaign. We have recently revamped the Who Viewed My Profile page. The product team wants to measure through an A/B test if the new changes are indeed better, and if so, by how much. The marketing team wants to create a buzz around the new page by starting an email campaign. This is a very common scenario, but how can the A/B test and the email campaign coexist? Clearly, we can only send campaign emails to the treatment group as there is nothing new for members in control. However, this would contaminate the online A/B test because the campaign encourages more members from the treatment to visit. To make sure the experiment samples are unbiased, similar to an email experiment discussed earlier, we need to identify the matching population who would have received the email in the control group as well. For instance, if the emails are sent to treatment members selected through process X, the same process needs to be applied to the control group to select those who would have received the email if they were in treatment. It is important to note that even though these two populations are unbiased, the difference between the two populations is no longer just the effect of the newer page, but a compounded effect of both the email campaign and the new page. It may be a subtle point, but this combination is in fact a better representation of the final impact we would like to measure from launching the new page. It is, however, crucial to realize that email campaigns have a strong novelty effect that dies out over time, so we need to keep the experiment running for a longer time period till the effect stabilizes. There are also occasions where one wants to measure the impact of these two factors separately, in which case we would either create a separate treatment bucket that receives no email campaign, or measure the A/B test first before setting off the campaign.

Cohort Experiments. It is common practice at LinkedIn to run A/B tests on a cohort of members who are pre-selected offline. As an example, we tested a new feature where members get a push notification on their LinkedIn profile page if they have not visited the homepage for a while. The first thing the experimenter did was to gather a list of members who have not visited the homepage for more than 7 days and used it to create a customized targeting attribute (Section 2.1.2). These targeted members are then split between treatment and control, and the notification was presented to only members in the treatment cohort. Such cohort experimentation is a great way to leverage the capability of the XLNT platform to test out ideas without having to build a full-fledged product. Another advantage of cohort experiments is to be able to measure long-term member impact without the dilution of members newly added to experiments. However, one common pitfall is that people try to update the cohort selection during the experiment, while the selection criteria is directly related to the experiment outcome. In the push notification example, the treatment encourages more members to visit LinkedIn homepage, though once a member visits the homepage, he or she would disappear from the updated cohort list. Therefore the updated treatment bucket would end up with fewer members which creates a bias. Our suggestion is to use a static cohort or to include the previous cohort in the analysis if an update is necessary.

3.4 Network A/B Testing

In our discussion thus far, we have assumed the Rubin causal model [1], a standard machinery of testing framework, when conducting and analyzing A/B tests. A key assumption made in Rubin causal model is the "Stable Unit Treatment Value Assumption" (SUTVA), which states that the behavior of each sample in the experiment depends only on their own treatment and not on the treatments of others.

This is a plausible assumption in most practical applications. For example, a user who is served better search results is more likely to click, and that behavior is entirely independent of others using the same search engine. However, such assumption does not always hold in experiments run on social networks. In a social network setting, a user's behavior is likely impacted by that of their social neighborhood [2, 3, 4]. In most cases, a user would find a new feature more valuable and hence more likely to adopt it as more of their neighbors adopt it. For example, video chat is a useless feature unless one's friends use it too. In an A/B experiment, this implies that if the treatment has a significant impact on a user, the effect would spill over to his/her social circles, regardless whether his/her neighbors are in treatment or control.

This poses a special challenge for running A/B tests in many online social and professional networks like Facebook, Twitter and LinkedIn. Many features tested there are likely to have network effects. For example, a better recommendation algorithm in treatment for the People You May Know module on LinkedIn encourages a user to send more invitations. However, users who receive such invitations can be in the control variant and when they visit LinkedIn to accept the invitation they may discover more people they know. If the primary metric of interest were the total number of invitations sent, we would see a positive gain in both the treatment and the control groups. The treatment effect estimated ignoring network effect would be biased and would not fully capture the benefit of the new algorithm. Such bias exists in testing almost any features that involve social interactions, which is truly ubiquitous in a social network environment.

To address this challenge, we need to take users' network connections into consideration when sampling them into treatment and control [19]. Essentially, we take the following two-stage procedure:

1. Partition the users into clusters.
2. Treat each cluster as a unit for randomization so all users in one cluster have the same experiment assignment.

The estimation for the treatment effect can then be based on either the sample means, or more sophisticated estimators summarized in [19]. We have noticed strong network effects from the network A/B tests we have run at LinkedIn based on this sampling and estimation framework.

4 FOSTERING AN EXPERIMENTATION CULTURE

Running large scale A/B tests is not just a matter of infrastructure and best practices, establishing a strong experimentation culture is also key to embedding A/B testing as part of the decision making process. Apart from building the basic functionalities any A/B testing platform requires, we have identified four necessary ingredients that have helped us instill experimentation deeply into our culture at LinkedIn. We share them in the rest of the section.

4.1 Integration with Business Reporting

XLNT produces over 1000 metrics for A/B test reports. Similar metrics are often used in business reporting for decision making as well. These two sets of metrics used to be computed separately and much effort was spent on investigating differences when they happened.

We realized the importance of using the same definitions of metrics across reporting and experimentation, and hence have worked with various teams at LinkedIn to evolve our metrics pipeline to be the *unified* metrics pipeline leveraged by the entire company. By making our experiment results and business reports "comparable", we have made it possible for R&D teams to relate changes in business numbers with experiment launches. Moreover, the integration also provides the foundation that enables other organizations such as Finance to bake A/B test results into business forecasting.

4.2 Leveraging Site Wide Impact

In addition to providing product development with a directional signal, A/B testing is often utilized to measure impact and assess ROI (Return-On-Investment). A report based on triggered analysis (Section 2.2.1) is great at providing a directional signal, however, it does not accurately represent the *global* lift that will occur when the winning treatment is ramped to 100% (holding everything else constant). The reason is two-fold: 1) Most experiments only *target* a subset of the entire user population. 2) Most experiments only *trigger* for a subset of their targeted population. In other words, triggered analysis only provides evaluation of the local impact, not the global impact of an experiment.

To address this concern, we compute the Site Wide Impact, defined as the percentage delta between two parallel universes: one with treatment applied to only *targeted* users and control to the rest, the other with control applied to all. With site wide impact provided for all experiments, teams are able to compare results across experiments regardless of their targeting and triggering conditions. Moreover, Site Wide Impact from multiple segments of the same experiment can be added up to give an assessment of the total impact, which is particularly helpful when each segment is running at different percentages and has to be analyzed separately to avoid Simpson's Paradox [31].

However, computing Site Wide Impact explicitly for every metric and report we generate would be more than doubling our current computation effort. It turns out that Site Wide Impact depends only on (1) the summary statistics that are already computed as part of the triggered report, and (2) the global total with a matching analysis date range as the experiment report (see Appendix A). For most of our metrics that are additive across days, we can simply keep a daily counter of the global total and add them up for any arbitrary date range. However, there are metrics, such as the number of unique visitors, which are not additive across days. Instead of computing the global total for all date ranges we generate reports for (an $O(n^2)$ problem), we estimate them based on the daily totals (see Appendix A for more details), saving more than 99% of the computation cost without sacrificing much accuracy.

One interesting phenomenon we observe is that the local impact (percentage delta from triggered analysis) and the Site Wide Impact can sometimes disagree directionally for ratio metrics such as CTR. For example, in a recent experiment testing "connection request" emails targeting English speaking members with fewer than 50 connections, we observed a -9.4% local impact on CTR while a +0.5% Site Wide Impact. Mathematically, this is an instance of Simpon's Paradox as the overall site wide CTR is essentially a linear combination of the within-segment and outside-segment CTR. The real challenge, however, is to decide which number to use for decision making. We believe that even though Site Wide Impact has a stronger business implication, the local impact is a better indication of user satisfaction in this case.

4.3 Simplifying Multiple Testing

Multiple testing is a common problem in the field of A/B testing [30] and LinkedIn is no exception. With over 1000 metrics computed for each experiment, this issue is so prevalent that the most common question we hear from experimenters is "why is this irrelevant metric significant?"

Even though we have tried to educate people on the topic of multiple testing, many are still clueless as what they should do when a metric is unexpectedly significant. What's worse, some people even lost trust in our A/B reports because they couldn't tell whether a metric is moved for real or simply due to multiple testing.

To this end, we have come up with a two-step rule-of-thumb for experimenters to follow:

1. Divide all metrics into three groups: 1) First order metrics are those expected to be impacted by the experiment; 2) Second order metrics are those potentially impacted, e.g. through cannibalization; 3) Third order metrics are those unlikely to be impacted.
2. Apply tiered significance levels to each group. We recommend our experimenters to use 0.05, 0.01 and 0.001 respectively.

Our rule-of-thumb is in fact based on an interesting Bayesian interpretation. It boils down to how much we believe the null hypothesis (H_0) is true before we even run the experiment. Believing that the posterior probability on H_0 should be consistent across all metrics, given different priors on H_0, we essentially vary the probability of observing the data given H_0, which is the definition of p-value in the frequentist interpretation. Since the significance level is the cutoff used for p-values, this leads to adjusting the thresholds accordingly. In particular, the three significance levels 0.05, 0.01 and 0.001 reflect that we believe an experiment having a prior probability of 1/2, 1/6 and 1/51 impacting each of the three metric groups.

This interpretation establishes a simple mathematical equivalence between people's prior belief on whether a metric is impacted and the significance level. Thus for those who are a bit more sophisticated they can easily come up with their own significance level tiers to match their prior beliefs.

4.4 Tracking the Most Impactful Experiments

LinkedIn is a deeply interconnected site. When it comes to experimentation, each team in fact plays two different roles. On the one hand, they run experiments to improve their metrics; on the other hand, they are also responsible for the global health of the same metrics, even when they may be impacted by experiments from other teams. Recognizing the importance of the second responsibility, we launched a feature called "Most Impactful Experiments" (MIE) to allow metric owners to follow experiments that impact the metrics they care about.

MIE is a major milestone for experimentation at LinkedIn. Not only does it drive greater transparency regarding experiment launch decisions, it also encourages more discussions to occur which in turn increases the overall knowledge of experimentation in the company.

To ensure MIE only listed the most relevant experiments, we use the following three-step algorithm:

1. Filter out all the experiments that have potential quality issues based on our alerting system.
2. For each metric, control False Discovery Rate using the Benjamini-Hochberg algorithm [17].
3. Score the experiments from step 2 based on three factors: Site Wide Impact, treatment percentage and experiment duration. These factors are then combined using the Analytical Hierarchy Process [18]. To scale to over 1000 metrics, we use empirical cumulative density functions to automatically control the fraction of experiments selected for each metric. Furthermore, historical experiments are used to ensure the relevance of selected experiments is not affected by the number of high-impact experiments available at any given time.

There are a couple of interesting observations and lessons learnt while developing this capability:

- **Large Initial Impact**. We observed that it is common for newly activated experiments to have overly positive or negative impacts. However, for these experiments the impact tends to shrink over time or become statistically insignificant. While such scenario can be due to novelty effect, most of them are just statistical artifact as explained in [7]. Controlling the false positive rate was helpful in eliminating these, but to further alleviate the problem, we only consider experiments with results over at least three days and penalize short experiments in our ranking algorithm.

- **Personalizing Threshold**. Picking the optimal threshold presents a challenging trade-off between precision and recall. Interestingly, three months after launching MIE, we have noticed that there are two well-separated groups of users. The first group is the functional users, including engineers, product managers and data scientists who themselves own experiments. The second group is the managerial users, including top-level managers and executives. Most users from the first group tend to follow metrics that are mostly impacted by their experiments. A higher recall can allow them to see more experiments beyond the ones they own. On the other hand, we want to keep a higher threshold for the second group of users to maintain a high precision.

5 CONCLUSION

In this paper, we shared the details of building a powerful and flexible experimentation platform that enables teams across LinkedIn to make informed decisions faster and at scale. Furthermore, we discussed several challenging A/B testing scenarios and shared many real examples applicable to social networks. Realizing the importance of a strong experimentation culture, we discussed four ingredients that helps us instill experimentation deeply into every decision making process at LinkedIn, even across roles outside of R&D.

One challenge we have not discussed here is how to provide guided insights to the experiment owners. Traditionally, controlled experiments have been used to answer "what" has been impacted, but not to answer "why". By utilizing the amount of information we have available for each experiment, in terms of both the metrics and dimensions, we hope to automatically generate insights that can better guide product development.

There are also cases where it is not possible to run an A/B test due to practical reasons, so we have to leverage quasi-experimental designs where users in treatment and control groups are matched post hoc using techniques such as propensity score matching.

Lastly, we hope that the topics we covered will lead to further research and development of A/B testing in large scale social networks.

6 ACKNOWLEDGMENTS

The authors wish to thank June Andrews, Drew Moxon, Karan Ahuja, Alexis Baird, Caroline Gaffney, Udi Milo and Xin Fu for insightful discussions on several of the examples. We have been fortunate to be part of the team developing the experimentation platform and we wish to thank *all* members of the XLNT team, including Adam Smyczek who made significant contributions before leaving LinkedIn. Finally, we wish to thank many people for being strong advocates of experimentation at LinkedIn, especially Igor Perisic.

7 REFERENCES

[1] **Rubin, Donald B.** Estimating causal effects of treatments in randomized and nonrandomized studies. *Journal of educational Psychology*, 66(5):688, 1974.

[2] **Ugander, Johan, Karrer, Brian, Backstrom, Lars and Kleinberg, Jon.** Graph cluster randomization: network exposure to multiple universes. *Proceedings of the 19th ACM SIGKDD international conference on Knowledge discovery and data mining*, pages 329–337. ACM, 2013.

[3] **Katzir, Liran, Liberty, Edo and Somekh Oren.** Framework and algorithms for network bucket testing. *Proceedings of the 21st international conference on World Wide Web*, pages 1029–1036. ACM, 2012.

[4] **Toulis, Panos and Kao, Edward.** Estimation of causal peer influence effects. *Proceedings of The 30th International Conference on Machine Learning,* pages 1489–1497, 2013.

[5] **Eckles, Dean, Karrer, Brian and Ugander, Johan.** Design and analysis of experiments in networks: Reducing bias from interference. arXiv preprint arXiv:1404.7530, 2014.

[6] **Aronow, Peter M, and Samii, Cyrus.** Estimating average causal effects under general interference. arXiv preprint arXiv:1305.6156, 2013

[7] **Kohavi, Ron, et al.** Trustworthy online controlled experiments: Five puzzling outcomes explained. *Proceedings of the 18th Conference on Knowledge Discovery and Data Mining.* 2012, www.exp-platform.com/Pages/PuzzingOutcomesExplained.aspx.

[8] **Tang, Diane, et al.** Overlapping Experiment Infrastructure: More, Better, Faster Experimentation. *Proceedings 16th Conference on Knowledge Discovery and Data Mining.* 2010.

[9] **Kohavi, Ron, et al.** Online Controlled Experiments at Large Scale. KDD 2013: *Proceedings of the 19th ACM SIGKDD international conference on Knowledge discovery and data mining. 2013.* http://bit.ly/ExPScale.

[10] **Kohavi, Ron, et al.** Seven Rules of Thumb for Web Site Experimenters. KDD 2014: *Proceedings of the 20th ACM SIGKDD international conference on Knowledge discovery and data mining.* 2014.

[11] **Yates, Frank,** Sir Ronald Fisher and the Design of Experiments. *Biometrics,* 20(2):307–321, 1964.

[12] **Bakshy, Eytan, Echles, Dean and Bernstein, Michael S.** Designing and Deploying Online Field Experiments. *Proceedings of the 23rd international conference on World Wide Web,* pages 283-292, ACM, 2014

[13] **Kohavi, Ron. et al.** Controlled experiments on the web: survey and practical guide. *Data Mining and Knowledge Discovery.* February 2009, Vol. 18, 1, pp. 140-181. http://www.exp-platform.com/Pages/hippo_long.aspx.

[14] **Crook, Thomas, et al.** Seven Pitfalls to Avoid when Running Controlled Experiments on the Web. [ed.] Peter Flach and Mohammed Zaki. KDD '09: *Proceedings of the 15th ACM SIGKDD international conference on knowledge discovery and data mining.* 2009, pp. 1105-1114. http://www.exp-platform.com/Pages/ExPpitfalls.aspx.

[15] **Ioannidis, John PA.** "Why most published research findings are false." *PLoS medicine* 2.8 (2005): e124.

[16] **Wacholder, Sholom, et al.** "Assessing the probability that a positive report is false: an approach for molecular epidemiology studies." *Journal of the National Cancer Institute* 96.6 (2004): 434-442.

[17] **Benjamini, Yoav, and Yosef Hochberg.** "Controlling the false discovery rate: a practical and powerful approach to

multiple testing." *Journal of the Royal Statistical Society. Series B (Methodological)* (1995): 289-300.

[18] **Saaty, Thomas L.** "How to make a decision: the analytic hierarchy process."*European journal of operational research* 48.1 (1990): 9-26.

[19] **Gui, Huan, Xu, Ya, Bhasin, Anmol, Han Jiawei.** Network A/B Testing: From Sampling to Estimation. *Proceedings of the 24rd international conference on World Wide Web,* ACM, 2015

[20] **Box, George EP, J. Stuart Hunter, and William G. Hunter.** "Statistics for experimenters: design, innovation, and discovery." *AMC* 10 (2005): 12.

[21] **Gerber, A. S., and Green, D. P.** Field Experiments: Design, Analysis, and Interpretation. WW Norton, 2012

[22] **Sumbaly, Roshan, et al.** "Serving large-scale batch computed data with project voldemort." *Proceedings of the 10th USENIX conference on File and Storage Technologies.* USENIX Association, 2012.

[23] **Tate, Ryan.** The Software Revolution Behind LinkedIn's Gushing Profits. [Online] http://www.wired.com/2013/04/linkedin-software-revolution

[24] **Auradkar, Aditya, et al.** "Data infrastructure at LinkedIn." *Data Engineering (ICDE), 2012 IEEE 28th International Conference on.* IEEE, 2012.

[25] **Kreps, Jay, Neha Narkhede, and Jun Rao.** "Kafka: A distributed messaging system for log processing." *Proceedings of 6th International Workshop on Networking Meets Databases (NetDB), Athens, Greece.* 2011.

[26] **Naga, Praveen Neppalli,** Real-time Analytics at Massive Scale with Pinot. [Online] September 29, 2014 http://engineering.linkedin.com/analytics/real-time-analytics-massive-scale-pinot

[27] **Fisher, Ronald A.** Presidential Address. *Sankhya: The Indian Journal of Statistics.* 1938, Vol. 4, 1. http://www.jstor.org/stable/40383882.

[28] **Montgomery, Douglas C.** *Design and analysis of experiments.* John Wiley & Sons, 2008.

[29] **Betz, Joe, Tagle, Moira.** Rest.li:RESTful Service Architecture at Scale. [Online] February, 19, 2013 https://engineering.linkedin.com/architecture/restli-restful-service-architecture-scale

[30] **Romano, Joseph P. Azeem M. Shaikh and Michael Wolf.** 2010b Multiple Testing. *New Palgrave Dictionary of Economics.* http://citeseerx.ist.psu.edu/viewdoc/download?doi=10.1.1.418.4975&rep=rep1&type=pdf

[31] **Wikipedia.** Simpson's Paradox. [Online] http://en.wikipedia.org/wiki/Simpson%27s_paradox

[32] **McFarland, Colin.** Experiment!: Website conversion rate optimization with A/B and multivariate testing. s.1. : New Riders, 2012.978-0321834607

[33] **Eisenberg, Bryan.** How to Improve A/B Testing. ClickZ Network. [Online] April 29, 2005. www.clickz.com/clickz/column/1717234/how-improvem-a-b-testing.

[34] **Vemuri, Srinivas, Varshney, Maneesh, Puttaswamy, Krishna and Liu, Rui.** Execution Primitives for Scalable Joins and Aggregations in Map Reduce. *Proceedings of the VLDB Endowment, Vol. 7, No. 13*

[35] **Varshney, Maneesh, Vemuri, Srinivas.** Open Sourcing Cubert: A High Performance Computation Engine for Complex Big Data Analytics [Online] November 11, 2014 https://engineering.linkedin.com/big-data/open-sourcing-cubert-high-performance-computation-engine-complex-big-data-analytics

APPENDIX

A. Site Wide Impact

We use the average number of clicks as an example metric to show how we compute Site Wide Impact. Let Let $X_t, X_c, X_{seg} and\ X_{global}$ denote the total number of clicks in the treatment group, the control group, the whole segment (including the treatment, the control and potentially other variants) and globally across the site, respectively. Similarly, let $n_t, n_c, n_{seg} and\ n_{global}$ denote the sample sizes for each of the four groups mentioned above.

It is easy to see that the total number of clicks in the *treatment (control) universe* can be estimated as

$$X_{tUniverse} = \frac{X_t}{n_t} n_{seg} + (X_{global} - X_{seg})$$

$$X_{cUniverse} = \frac{X_c}{n_c} n_{seg} + (X_{global} - X_{seg})$$

Then the Site Wide Impact is computed as

$$SWI = (\frac{X_{tUniverse}}{n_{tUniverse}} - \frac{X_{cUniverse}}{n_{cUniverse}}) / \frac{X_{cUniverse}}{n_{cUniverse}}$$

$$= (\frac{\frac{X_t}{n_t} - \frac{X_c}{n_c}}{\frac{X_c}{n_c}}) \times (\frac{\frac{X_c}{n_c} n_{seg}}{\frac{X_c}{n_c} n_{seg} + X_{global} - X_{seg}})$$

$$= \Delta \times \alpha$$

which indicates that the Site Wide Impact is essentially the local impact Δ scaled by a factor of α, and X_{global} is the only ingredient that is not already computed as part of summary statistics for the triggered analysis.

For metrics such as average number of clicks, X_{global} for any arbitrary date range can be computed by summing over clicks from corresponding single days. However, for metrics such as average number of unique visitors, de-duplication is necessary across days. To avoid having to compute α for all date ranges we generate reports for, we estimate cross-day α by averaging the single-day α's.

There is one other group of metrics that are ratio of two metrics. One example is Click-Through-Rate, which equals Clicks over Impressions. The derivation of Site Wide Impact for ratio metrics is similar, with the sample size replaced by the denominator metric.

Tornado Forecasting with Multiple Markov Boundaries

Kui Yu[*,1], Dawei Wang[*,2], Wei Ding[†,2]
Jian Pei[1], David L. Small[3], Shafiqul Islam[3], Xindong Wu[4,5]
[1]School of Computing Science, Simon Fraser University, Burnaby, BC, Canada
[2]Department of Computer Science, University of Massachussets Boston, Boston, USA
[3]Department of Civil and Environmental Engineering, Tufts University, Boston, USA
[4]Department of Computer Science, Hefei University of Technology, Hefei, China
[5]Department of Computer Science, University of Vermont, Burlington, USA
{kuiy,jpei}@cs.sfu.ca, {dawei.wang,ding}@umb.edu
{David.Small,Shafiqul.Islam}@tufts.edu, xwu@uvm.edu

ABSTRACT

Reliable tornado forecasting with a long-lead time can greatly support emergency response and is of vital importance for the economy and society. The large number of meteorological variables in spatiotemporal domains and the complex relationships among variables remain the top difficulties for a long-lead tornado forecasting.

Standard data mining approaches to tackle high dimensionality are usually designed to discover a single set of features without alternating options for domain scientists to select more reliable and physical interpretable variables.

In this work, we provide a new solution to use the concept of multiple Markov boundaries in local causal discovery to identify multiple sets of the precursors for tornado forecasting. Specifically, our algorithm first confines the extremely large feature spaces to a small core feature space, then it mines multiple sets of the precursors from the core feature space that may equally contribute to tornado forecasting. With the multiple sets of the precursors, we are able to report to domain scientists the predictive but practical set of precursors.

An extensive empirical study is conducted on eight benchmark data sets and the historical tornado data near Oklahoma City, OK in the United States. Experimental results show that the tornado precursors we identified can help to improve the reliability of long-lead time catastrophic tornado forecasting.

Categories and Subject Descriptors

I.5.4 [**Pattern Recognition**]: Applications-Weather Forecasting

*K. Yu and D. Wang contributed equally to this work
†Corresponding Author

KDD'15, August 10-13, 2015, Sydney, NSW, Australia.
© 2015 ACM. ISBN 978-1-4503-3664-2/15/08 ...$15.00.
DOI: http://dx.doi.org/10.1145/2783258.2788612.

Keywords

Tornado Forecasting, Multiple Markov boundaries, Distributed feature data, Core feature space

1. INTRODUCTION

1.1 Tornado Forecasting

A tornado is one of the most powerful, unpredictable and destructive weather phenomena on Earth. Tornado disasters result in billions of dollars of damages each year and cause more loss of life than most other weather-related hazards. For example, in the year of 2013, 811 confirmed tornadoes cause 55 fatalities and damages up to $3.6 billion in the United States[1]. Reliable tornado forecasts with a long-lead time can greatly support emergency response and are of vital importance for the economy and society. Currently National Weather Service (NWS) issues tornado warnings based on "detection": a tornado threat is broadcasted after being observed, either on-site or through radars [3]. Simulation based warning systems can increase the prediction lead time up to several hours, but most of the predictions are false alarms [15].

Comparing to other domains like electronic advertising, the success of big data-induced process in studying the weather system is limited [7, 19]. Among all the reasons accounting for the slow progress, for data-driven methods trying to model weather dynamics the main difficulty lies in addressing the high dimensionality and the complex relationships among variables. The number of meteorological variables contributing to tornadoes, from the Cartesian product between the spatial and temporal domains, is enormous. Tornadoes are usually developed from thunderstorms and the quasi-geostrophic theory [8] demonstrates that the development of storm events requires a coupling between upper and lower levels of the atmosphere. The atmospheric variables related to this vary both horizontally and vertically and have complex relationships between each other. Even the most efficient Monte Carlo methods will suffer from computational infeasibility for such high dimensional and complex data sets.

Dimension reduction is the standard machine learning approach to deal with high dimensionality [10, 20, 21]. These methods usually report a single subset of features without

[1]http://www.spc.noaa.gov/climo/torn/STATIJ13.txt

alternative options. In our study, the tornado precursors identified are meteorological predictor variables with certain spatial and temporal information, but due to the complex interactions within the variables, the problems of only identifying a single choice precursors are as follows.

(1) Key interpretable precursors may be missed. Due to spatial and temporal adjacency, many precursors contain equivalent information for prediction, because these precursors are not physically independent of one another. For example, when there is a dropping in sea level pressure (anomalously low sea level pressure is an important characteristic of atmospheric regimes, which may lead to extreme precipitations), at the same location there must also be convergence of the winds near the surface and divergence of the winds at the top of the atmosphere. Also, the field of pressure vertical velocity may be strongly negative. In this case, the low level winds, high level winds, and vertical motions in the same location are considered equivalent precursors. A typical feature selection method will only identify one of the three equivalent precursors, the others will not be reported to the domain scientists.

(2) The precursors identified may be considered impractical. It is useful to explore alternative cost-effective but equally effective solutions in the cases where different precursors may have different costs/utilities associated with their acquisition/quality in a forecasting model at the next step. For instance, although the three precursors mentioned in the above example are considered as equivalent precursors, compared to high level and low level winds, vertical motion is a noisy and unreliable precursor. Using vertical motion as a precursor in a prediction model introduces extra uncertainty. Accordingly, if we know all of the three precursors containing equivalent information for forecasting, we can select the low level winds or high level winds for reliable prediction.

1.2 Multiple Markov Boundaries for Tornado Forecasting

It is an important yet new research topic to identify multiple Markov boundaries from data using Bayesian inference in the domain of causal discovery [17]. A Bayesian network is presented by a directed acyclic graph G and a joint probability distribution P over a set of features F [11]. If every conditional independence entailed by G is present in P, G is said to be faithful to P [11]. If a data distribution and an underlying Bayesian network which models that domain are faithful to each other, the Markov boundary of a node is unique and contains its parents, children, and the parents of the children (spouses) [11, 1]. In the past decade, people focused on identification of a single Markov boundary under the faithfulness assumption for causal discovery [1, 18]. However, tornado and other many real-world data distributions often violate the faithfulness condition due to various factors, such as (but not limited to) small sample size, noise in data, and hidden variables. Thus the Bayesian networks built from such data often contains multiple Markov boundaries [12, 17]. Developing methods of discovery of multiple Markov boundaries would improve the discovery of the underlying mechanisms to avoid overlooking key causal variables, and thus this can be useful to explore alternative cost-effective but equally effective solutions in prediction in applications where different variables may have different costs/utilities associated with their acquisition/quality.

1.3 Our Contributions

Our contributions to tornado forecasting are below.

- To cope with high-dimensionality, we define a new concept of a core feature space to represent the feature space of all possible Markov boundaries of a target variable, and then confine mining multiple Markov boundaries to this core feature space instead of the original entire feature space.
- To discover this core feature space from distributed feature data sets, we process distributed feature data sets in a sequential scan without loading the whole tornado data set in memory in advance. Specifically, we process each distributed tornado data set one at a time, and features in each set are processed one-by-one in a sequential scan.
- We design and implement the MB-DEA algorithm, to discover multiple Markov Boundaries from Distributed fEature dAta for tornado forecasting. MB-DEA firstly discovers the core feature space from which multiple Markov boundaries are mined.
- We apply the MB-DEA algorithm to study the historical tornado data near Oklahoma City, OK. Our empirical study includes 810,000 features of 35 years data. We are able to identify physically meaningful and practical tornado precursors which may lead to reliable and long-lead time of catastrophic tornado forecasting.

The remainder of the paper is organized as follows. Section 2 presents related work. Section 3 describes the tornado data set and Section 4 proposes the MB-DEA algorithm, respectively. Section 5 reports our experimental results on tornado forecasting. Finally, Section 6 concludes the paper.

2. RELATED WORK

We will give a brief review of tornado forecasting and multiple Markov boundaries in this section. Tornadoes are usually developed within thunderstorms and most tornado warning systems are based on the prediction of thunderstorms [3]. One official National Weather Service product is the tornado watch, which is based on weather forecasting model outputs and observations, with a lead time up to several hours. Simulations of supercell thunderstorms are performed in [16] with the aim of discovering precursors of tornadoes. Such process usually resulted in a large number of false alarms (false positives) because only very few storms would produce tornadoes. A three-dimensional (in space and time) object identification algorithm is applied in [4] for forecasting tornado path lengths through the predictions of hourly maximum updraft helicity as a measure of storm severity. In [13] the authors implement principal component analysis (PCA) on the outputs from a simulation model (the Weather Research and Forecasting model), and build a tornado prediction model using supported vector machine with the PCA results. They have achieved an accuracy of 0.7 with a one day lead time.

Causal discovery is of fundamental and practical interest in many areas of science and technology [11]. Global causal induction attempts to learn a complete Bayesian network over all features on training data. However, global causal induction is not scalable and cannot even handle thousands of features [5]. Local causal discovery aims to learn a local causal structure closely related to a target feature of interest, i.e., a Markov boundary of a target feature of interest. If a joint probability distribution satisfies the faithful condition, it is guaranteed to have a unique Markov boundary for every node in a Bayesian network [1]. Accordingly, in the past decade, most of the existing algorithms of local causal discovery focused on identification of a single Markov boundary under the faithfulness assumption [1, 12, 18].

However, many real-world data distributions often violate the faithfulness condition due to small sample sizes, noise in data, and hidden variables, and thus contain multiple Markov boundaries [12, 17, 22]. Algorithms of multiple Markov boundaries attempts to discover all Markov boundaries of a target feature containing in data without missing causative variables [17]. Among the most notable advances in the field of discovery of multiple Markov boundaries are the KIAMB algorithm and the TIE* algorithm [17]. Peña et al. [12] proposed a stochastic Markov boundary algorithm, called KIAMB by employing a stochastic search heuristic that repeatedly disrupts the order in which features are selected for inclusion into a Markov boundary with the probability p at each round, thereby introducing a chance of identifying alternative Markov boundaries of a target feature. The limitation is that we do not know how many iterations the KIAMB algorithm needs to run because the exact number of Markov boundaries of a target feature is unknown and varies in different data. To solve this problem, Statnikov et al. [17] recently proposed the TIE* (Target Information Equivalence) algorithm and proved that TIE* can discover all Markov boundaries under the non-faithful condition.

Integrating the drawbacks of the existing work for long-lead tornado forecasting and multiple Markov boundaries, it provides a natural choice to find multiple precursors for long-lead tornado prediction using multiple Markov boundaries. However, both the KIAMB and TIE* algorithms focus on mining multiple Markov boundaries from data on a single feature set. With the real-world tornado data, the KIAMB and TIE* algorithms face the challenges of both very high dimensionality and multiple feature sets. This motivates us to further investigate new algorithms of multiple Markov boundaries for long-lead tornado prediction.

3. THE TORNADO DATA SET

The tornado data set contains eight explanatory variables and tornado information near Oklahoma City, OK, one of the most tornado-prone areas in the United States. All the explanatory variables are sampled at the spatial domain of $90°E$ to $357.5°E$ and $0°N$ to $90°N$ with a horizontal resolution of $2.5° \times 2.5°$ (totally $2,700$ locations) and a daily temporal resolution for the months of March, April and May (MAM, when the highest frequency of violent tornadoes occurs in the studied area) for the years 1979-2013. The tornado study area near Oklahoma City is located in the spatial region of $261.25°E - 263.75°E$ and $33.75°N - 36.25°N$. The eight variables at different levels (Table 1) are selected from the NCEP-NCAR Reanalysis data set [9] by the domain scientists (co-authors of the paper) for the study. In particular, the Relative Humidity data only goes from 1000hPa to 300hPa because the amount of water in the upper troposphere was thought to be negligible when the dataset was designed. Two variables only have one single level (for Sea Level Pressure, the values represent the surface level; for Precipitable Water, the values are column integrated from all the levels). A particular day of the tornado study area is labeled as a positive instance if one or more $EF1$(Enhanced Fujita scale [6]) or above tornadoes are reported, otherwise a negative instance. In total there are 98 tornado days (positive instances) out of the $3,045$ days study period.

We set our "look ahead" days as 5. For example, to forecast tornado situations at tomorrow ($day0$) in the study area, we will look at the explanatory variables from today (day-1) back to previous five days (day-5). The tornado data set presents two characteristics of a difficult task:

- Extremely high dimensionality. With such a setting, the total number of precursors (features) for one instance is $810,000$ in the tornado data set (e.g., the variable of Relative Humidity has 8 levels, 5 days, and 2700 locations. In total there are $8 \times 5 \times 2700$=$108,000$ features). Any existing algorithm of multiple Markov boundaries cannot cope with such large number of features.
- Distributed feature data. The whole tornado data set is large (more than 13GB in total), and thus we have the data distributed in eight data sets according to the eight explanatory variables and one class attribute set. On average each explanatory variable set still has more than $100,000$ features. Mining multiple Markov boundaries from multiple feature data sets is an untouched research topic.

4. MACHINE LEARNING FORMULATION

In this section, we discuss the MB-DEA algorithm for tornado forecasting. The algorithm tackles the discovery of multiple Markov Boundaries from Distributed fEature dAta. The design of the MB-DEA algorithm consists of (1) finding the core feature space from the distributed tornado data, and (2) mining multiple Markov boundaries from the core feature space.

4.1 Notations and Definitions

Given a training data set D containing N training instances and M features, we define a distributed feature data set as that D is vertically divided into W feature blocks without overlapping features between each block, that is, $D = \{B_1, B_2, \cdots, B_W\}$ which is distributed in W files. F_i $(1 \leq i \leq M)$ is an feature within B_j $(1 \leq j \leq W)$ and C is the class attribute. Let P be a joint probability distribution on a set of random variables F via a directed acyclic graph G. We call the triplet $\langle F, G, P \rangle$ a Bayesian network if $\langle F, G, P \rangle$ satisfies the Markov condition: every variable is conditionally independent of any subset of its non-descendant variables given its parents [11].

In the rest of the paper, the terms "variable" and "feature" are used interchangeably. To measure the statistical relationships between features, we adopt the measure of mutual information [14]. Given two variables X and Y, the mutual information between X and Y is defined as follows.

$$I(X;Y) = H(X) - H(X|Y) \tag{1}$$

where $H(Y)$ and $H(Y|Z)$ are computed as follows.

$$H(X) = -\sum_{x_i \in X} (P(x_i) \log_2(P(x_i)) \tag{2}$$

Table 1: Meteorological variables

Name	Level(hPa)
Temperature	200,250,300,400,500,600,700,850,925,1000
Geopotential Height	200,250,300,400,500,600,700,850,925,1000
Meridional Wind	200,250,300,400,500,600,700,850,925,1000
Zonal Wind	200,250,300,400,500,600,700,850,925,1000
Pressure Vertical Velocity	200,250,300,400,500,600,700,850,925,1000
Relative Humidity	300,400,500,600,700,850,925,1000
Sea Level Pressure	–
Precipitable Water	–

$$H(X|Y) = -\sum_{y_j \in Y} P(y_j) \sum_{x_i \in X} (P(x_i|y_j)\log_2(P(x_i|y_j))) \quad (3)$$

From Equations (1) to (3), the conditional mutual information is computed by

$$\begin{aligned} &I(X;Y|Z) \\ &= H(X|Z) - H(X|YZ) \\ &= -\sum_{z_i \in Z} P(z_i) \sum_{x_j \in X} \sum_{y_k \in Y} P(x_j y_k|z_i) \log_2 \frac{P(x_j y_k|z_i)}{P(x_j|z_i)P(y_k|z_i)} \end{aligned} \quad (4)$$

The lower cases x_i, y_i, and z_i in the above equations denote possible values that the variables X, Y and Z take.

Definition 1 (Faithfulness). *[11] Give a Bayesian network $\langle F, G, P\rangle$, G is faithful to P over F if and only if every independence present in P is entailed by G and the Markov condition. P is faithful if and only if there exists a directed acyclic graph G such that G is faithful to P.* ■

Definition 2 (Markov boundary). *[11] If a Bayesian network satisfies the faithfulness, the Markov boundary of any node T in this Bayesian network is unique with the set of parents, children and spouses (the parents of the children of T) of T.* ■

However, if a Bayesian network does not satisfy the faithfulness, the Markov boundary of any node may not be unique [17]. We use Theorem 1 to explicitly construct and verify multiple Markov boundaries when the distribution P violates the faithful condition.

Theorem 1. *[17] If MB_1 is a Markov boundary of T that contains a feature set S_1, and there exists a subset S_2 such that $MB_2 \subseteq (MB_1 - S_1) \cup S_2$, if $I(T; MB_1|MB_2) = 0$, then MB_2 is also a Markov boundary of T.* ■

In Theorem 1, both MB_1 and MB_2 are Markov boundaries of T, since $S_1 \subset MB_1$ and $S_2 \subset MB_2$ contain the equivalent information about T.

4.2 The Core Feature Space

According to the design of the MB-DEA algorithm, the key to the algorithm is how to discover the core feature space from distributed feature data. The core feature space we are looking for is defined as a feature space that contains all possible Markov boundaries of a target feature. By theorem 1, we get Corollary 1 below.

Corollary 1. *Assuming MB_1 is a Markov boundary of T and $MB_2 \subseteq \{MB_1 - \{F_i\} \cup \{F_j\}\}$, if $I(C; F_j|F_i) = 0$, MB_2 is also Markov boundary of T.* ■

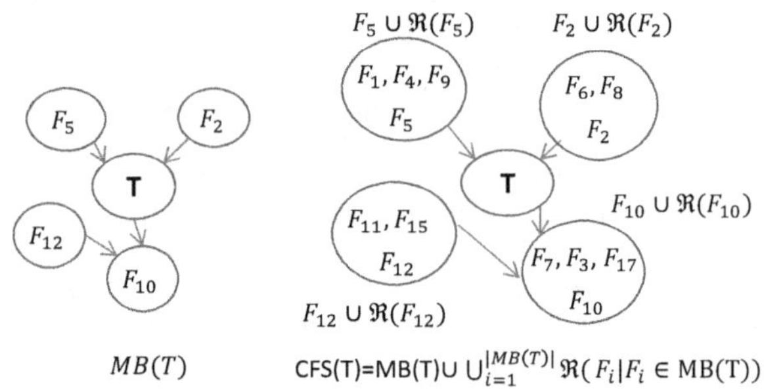

Figure 1: An example of $MB(T)$ and $CFS(T)$

Definition 3. *Assuming $MB(C)$ is a Markov boundary of C and $F_i \in MB(C)$, we define $\Re(F_i)$ as the set of features that satisfies the term $\forall F_j \in \Re(F_i)$ s.t. $I(C; F_j|F_i) = 0$.* ■

By Corollary 1 and Definition 3, we define the core feature space of C as follows.

Definition 4 (Core feature space). *Assuming $MB(C)$ is a Markov boundary of C and $F_i \in MB(C)$, the core feature space (CFS) of C is defined as*

$$CFS(C) = \{MB(C) \cup \bigcup_{F_i \in MB(C)} \Re(F_i)\}.$$

■

With Definition 4, our first problem is how to find $MB(C)$ efficiently. To find $MB(C)$, in general, we can use the existing single Markov boundary algorithms, such as HITION-MB [1] and MMMB [18]. For example, assuming a data set contains 20 features $F = \{F_1, F_2, \cdots, F_{20}\}$ and feature F_{20} is considered as a target feature T, if $MB(T) = \{F_5, F_2, F_{12}, F_{10}\}$, a Markov blanket of T, is found by HITION-MB or MMMB and $\Re(F_5) = \{F_1, F_4, F_9\}$, Figure 1 illustrates the relationships between $MB(T)$ (the left figure) and $CFS(T)$ (the right figure).

To find the core feature space from distributed feature data, we further analyze the relationships between features F_i and F_j in Corollaries 2 and 4 as follows.

Corollary 2. *A feature X is correlated to Y with respect to a feature subset S if $I(X; Y|S) > 0$.*

Proof. By Eq.(4), we can see that the term $I(X; Y|S) = 0$ holds only when X and Y are conditionally independent given S. The corollary is proven accordingly. ■

Corollary 3. *If F_i is correlated to C and $I(C; F_j|F_i) = 0$ holds, then $I(F_i, C) > I(F_j, C)$.*

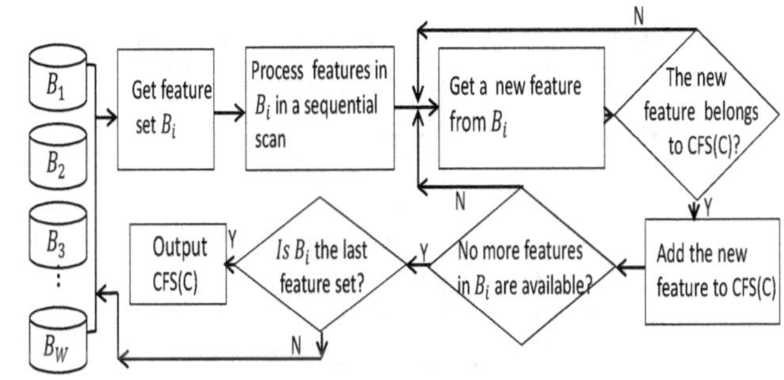

Figure 2: Discovery of the core feature space of C from distributed feature data

Proof. By $I(A;B|C)-I(A;B)=I(A;C|B)-I(A;C)$, we get $I(C;F_j|F_i)-I(C;F_j)=I(C;F_i|F_j)-I(C;F_i)$. Since the term $I(C;F_j|F_i)=0$ hold, then $I(C;F_i)=I(C;F_i|F_j)+I(C;F_j)$. By Corollary 2, the corollary is proven. ∎

Corollary 4. *If both MB_1 and $MB_2 \subseteq (MB_1-\{F_i\})\cup\{F_j\}$ are Markov boundaries of C and $I(F_j;C|F_i)=0$ holds, then $I(F_i;F_j)\geq \max(I(F_i;C),I(F_j;C))$.*

Proof.

$$\begin{aligned} I(F_j;F_i,C) &= I(F_j;F_i)+I(F_j;C|F_i) \\ &= I(F_j;C)+I(F_j;F_i|C) \end{aligned} \tag{5}$$

Since $I(F_j;C|F_i)=0$ holds and F_i and F_j are correlated, we can get $I(F_i;F_j)\geq I(F_j;C)$. And at the same time, the following equation also holds.

$$\begin{aligned} I(F_i;F_j,C) &= I(F_i;F_j)+I(F_i;C|F_j) \\ &= I(F_i;C)+I(F_i;F_j|C) \end{aligned} \tag{6}$$

By Corollary 1, we can also get $I(F_i;C|F_j)=0$. By Eq.(6), we have $I(F_i;F_j)\geq I(F_i;C)$. With the equations (5) and (6), Corollary 4 is proved. ∎

By Corollaries 3 and 4, we can get the following.

Observation 1. *If $I(F_i;C)>I(F_j;C)$ and $I(F_i;F_j)\geq max(I(F_i;C),I(F_j;C))$, then F_i is in a Markov boundary of C ($MB(C)$), and F_j is included by $\Re(F_i)$.* ∎

Algorithm 1: *The MB-DEA Algorithm*

```
Data: D = {B_1, B_2, ..., B_W};
      MB(C) = {} ; CFS(C) = {} ; i = 0;
      δ = max(I(Y;C), I(F_i;C))
1  /*Steps 2-25: Mining the core feature space CFS*/
2  for j=1 to W do
3      Get-new-feature-set(B_j);
4      repeat
5          i = i + 1;
6          Get-new-feature(F_i, B_j);
7          if I(F_i;C) = 0 then
8              Discard F_i; goto step 23;
9          end
10         for each feature Y ∈ MB(C) do
11             if I(Y;C) > I(F_i;C) and I(F_i;Y) ≥ δ then
12                 ℜ(Y) = ℜ(Y) + F_i;
13                 ℜ = ℜ + F_i;
14                 Goto step 23;
15             end
16             if I(F_i;C) > I(Y,C) and I(F_i;Y) ≥ δ then
17                 MB(C) = MB(C) − Y;
18                 ℜ(F_i) = ℜ(F_i) + Y;
19                 ℜ = ℜ − ℜ(Y);
20             end
21         end
22         MB(C) = MB(C) ∪ F_i;
23     until F_i is the last feature of B_j;
24 end
25 CFS(C) = MB(C) ∪ ℜ
26 /*Steps 27-35: Mining Markov boundaries from CFS*/
27 Use HITION_PC to learn a Markov boundary MB_1 of
   C from D over CFS(C) (the original distribution);
28 Output MB_1;
29 repeat
30     Generate a data set D_e from the embedded
       distribution by removing a subset of features within
       the discovered Markov boundaries from CFS(C);
31     Use HITION_PC to learn a Markov boundary
       MB_new of C from D_e;
32     if acc(MB_new) ≥ acc(MB_1) then
33         output MB_new;
34     end
35 until all data sets D_e generated have been considered;
```

4.3 Discovery of Multiple Markov Boundaries from Distributed Feature Data

Figure 2 gives the new framework to efficiently find the core feature space of C from distributed feature data. In Figure 2, each feature block B_i is processed independently at a time, and as a feature block B_i arrives, features in B_i are processed one-by-one in a sequential scan.

As illustrated in Figure 2, we discuss the pseudocode of the MB-DEA algorithm in Algorithm 1. To achieve a relatively low computational complexity to deal with high-dimensional yet distributed tornado data, according to Observation 1, Corollaries 3 and 4, the MB-DEA algorithm uses online pairwise comparisons as the selection criterion for adding features into the core feature space.

In Algorithm 1, $\Re(F_i)$ keeps the set of features correlated to F_i that satisfies Definition 3; $\Re$ dynamically keeps the features in $\bigcup_{i=1}^{|MB(C)|}\Re(F_i)$; $MB(C)$ is defined in Definition 4; and $CFS(C)$ denotes the core feature space of C. Two key stages are given in Algorithm 1. One is to mine $CFS(C)$ from Steps 2 to 25, and the other is to discover Markov boundaries from $CFS(C)$ from Steps 27 to 35.

Steps 2 to 25. As a feature set B_j is achieved, features within B_j are processed one-by-one in a sequential scan. Step 7 is to determine whether a new coming feature F_i is correlated to C; if $I(F_i;C)>0$, then we consider F_i is correlated to C; otherwise, F_i is discarded.

If F_i is correlated to C, Step 11 determines whether to keep F_i given the current set $MB(C)$. If not, F_i is added to $\Re$ and $\Re(Y)$, respectively. If F_i can be added to $MB(C)$ at Step 11, Step 16 further prunes $MB(C)$ due to F_i's inclusion. If Y in $MB(C)$ is removed, the set $\Re(Y)$ is removed from $\Re$ accordingly. Meanwhile, Y is added to $\Re(F_i)$. With the MB-DEA algorithm, we can discover $\Re$ without any additional computation costs.

Table 2: Summary of the benchmark data sets

	Data set	♯ features	♯ training set	♯ testing set
1	arcene	10,000	100	100
2	dexter	20,000	300	300
3	dorothea	100,000	800	300
4	colon	2,000	42	20
5	leukemia	7,129	48	24
6	lung-cancer	12,533	121	60
7	ovarian-cancer	2,190	144	72
8	thrombin	139,351	2,000	543

Table 3: The F-ratio and MB-ratio

Data set	F-ratio	MB-ratio
arcene	0.1157	1
dexter	0.0057	-
dorothea	0.0636	1
colon	0.033	0.5
leukemia	0.0537	1
lung-cancer	0.0.0608	1
thrombin	0.0249	-
ovarian-cancer	0.1685	1

Steps 27 to 35. We integrate the TIE* algorithm into our MB-DEA algorithm to mine Markov boundaries from the discovered core feature space. The main idea of TIE* [17] is to first identify a Markov boundary of a target feature T in the original data distribution and then iteratively run a single Markov boundary induction algorithm from the embedded distributions that are obtained by removing subsets of features from the original Markov boundary in order to identify new Markov boundaries in the original distribution. From Steps 27 to 35, with the core feature space, the TIE* algorithm can search for multiple Markov boundaries in a smaller feature space.

Step 27 uses a single Markov boundary induction algorithm HITION_PC [1] to learn a Markov boundary, called MB_1, from the data set D defined on the feature set $CFS(C)$ (i.e., in the original distribution). Step 30 generates a data set D_e (the embedded distribution) that removes a subset of features from CFS (Regarding how to generate an embedded distribution, please see the IGS algorithm in [17], Page18, Figure 9). The motivation is that D_e may lead to identification of a new Markov boundary of T that was previously "invisible" to a single Markov boundary induction algorithm, because it is shielded by another subset of features within the discovered Markov boundaries. Step 32 uses prediction accuracy as a criterion to verify whether a discovered feature set from the embedded distribution is a new Markov boundary or not. If the prediction accuracy of MB_{new} in Step 32 is not less than that of MB_1, MB_{new} is also considered as a Markov boundary of C. Steps 30-34 are repeated until all data sets D_e generated have been considered.

5. EMPIRICAL STUDY

In this empirical study, since the state-of-the-art multiple Markov boundary discovery algorithm, the TIE* algorithm [17], cannot deal with the high-dimensional yet distributed tornado data set, we will first validate the effectiveness and efficiency of the MB-DEA algorithm against the TIE* algorithm using the benchmark data sets, and then use the MB-DEA algorithm for tornado prediction.

5.1 Experiments on the Benchmark Data Sets

We have chosen eight benchmark data sets as described in Table 2, which cover a wide range of real-world application domains. In Table 2, for the first four NIPS 2003 challenge data sets and the *hiva* data set from the WCCI 2006 performance prediction challenge, we use the originally provided training and validation sets; for the other five data sets we adopt the first 2/3 instances for training and the last 1/3 instances for testing. As for discrete data sets, we

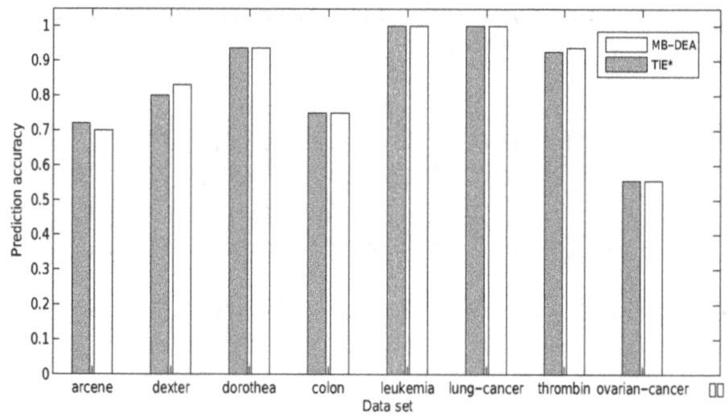

Figure 3: Prediction (classification) accuracies of MB-DEA against TIE*

use mutual information to compute the correlation between features while for the continuous data sets, the Fisher's Z-test is employed [2] in which the significance level for the Fisher's Z-test is set to 0.01. All experiments on the benchmark data sets are conducted on a computer with Intel(R) i7-3770 3.4GHz CPU and 32GB memory.

In our experiments, each training data set in Table 2 is partitioned into ten feature sets evenly to simulate distributed feature data for MB-DEA while TIE* is directly implemented on each training data set. TIE* is parameterized with HITON_PC [1] as the base Markov blanket induction algorithm, and classification accuracy as a criterion is used to verify whether a new feature subset is a Markov boundary or not. The parameter alpha of HITION_PC is set to 0.01.

In the following figures and tables, we report the comparison results of MB-DEA and TIE*. The running time on the *dexter* and *thrombin* data sets exceed 3 days for TIE* and we do not show the experimental results of TIE* on those two data sets.

Table 3 reports the F-ratio and MB-ratio. An F-ratio is the ratio of the number of features of the core feature space discovered by MB-DEA divided by the number of total features on the same data set. An MB-ratio is the ratio of the number of Markov boundaries discovered by MB-DEA in the number of Markov boundaries identified by TIE*. In Table 3, we can see that on each data set, the number of features within the core feature space is a very small fraction of the total number of features. Furthermore, from the MB-ration, except for the *madelon* and *thrombin*, MB-DEA discovers the same number of Markov boundaries as TIE* on the remaining data sets. For the *dexter* and *thrombin* data sets, we do not have their MB-ratios due to long running time of TIE* and denote them as "-".

Table 4: **Efficiency of MB-DEA vs.TIE*(seconds)**

Data set	TIE*	MB-DEA
arcene	19	6
dexter	-	17,091
dorothea	6,465	25
colon	5	1
leukemia	15	6
lung-cancer	79	16
thrombin	-	24,935
ovarian-cancer	6	3

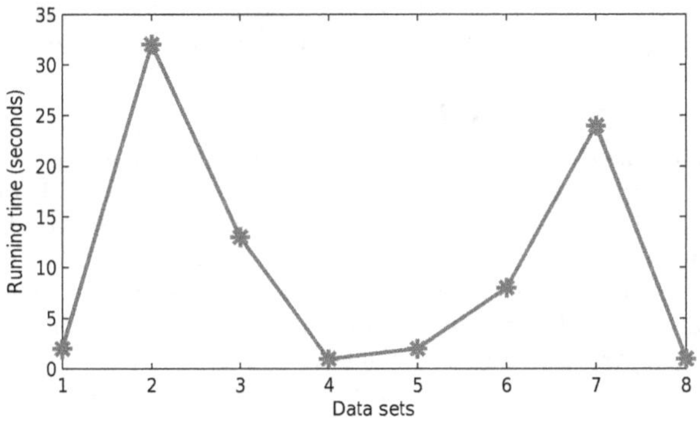

Figure 4: Running time of the discovery of the core feature space. The labels of the x-axis in both figures from 1 to 8 denote the data sets:1.arcene, 2.dexter, 3.dorothea, 4.colon, 5.leukemia, 6.lung-cancer, 7.thrombin, 8.ovarian-cancer.

Meanwhile, Figure 3 gives prediction (classification) accuracies of MB-DEA against TIE* using the K Nearest Neighbor classifier. We select the highest prediction accuracy among all of the Markov boundaries discovered by MB-DEA and TIE*, respectively. From Figure 3, we can see that with the core feature space, MB-DEA gets the same prediction accuracy as TIE*. Although MB-DEA does not find all of Markov boundaries on the *colon* data set, it still gets the Markov boundaries with the highest prediction accuracies.

Figure 4 gives the running time of the discovery of the core feature space from Steps 2 to 25 in Algorithm 1. From Figure 4, we can see that the computational cost of the discovery of the core feature space is very low due to identifying the $\Re$ feature set (see Definition 3) without additional time costs. Table 4 gives the running time of MB-DEA against TIE*. From Table 4, we can see that in term of efficiency, MB-DEA is faster than TIE* on all of ten data sets. From the *dorothea*, *dexter*, and *thrombin* data sets in Table 4, with the core feature space, MB-DEA can efficiently deal with data with very high-dimensionality while TIE* is very expensive, or even impossible due to its exhaustive search over the entire feature space.

In summary, with the above results, we can conclude that the core feature space that the MB-DEA algorithm has discovered is only a small fraction of the entire feature space, but MB-DEA gets a very promising prediction accuracy with a reasonable running time. Therefore, the MB-DEA algorithm is a scalable and accurate method to deal with distributed feature data.

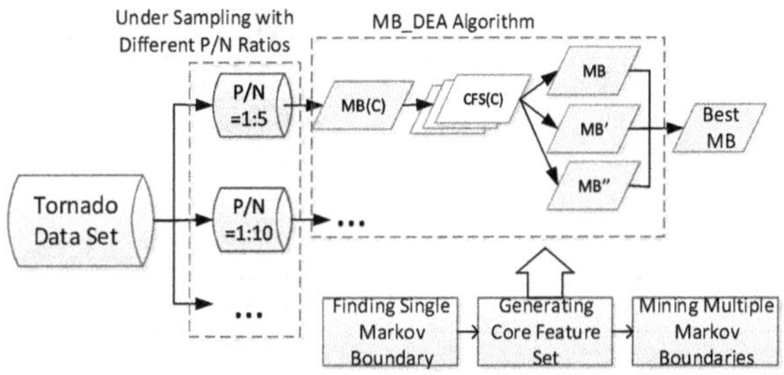

Figure 5: Flow chart of the experimental process. Using an undersampled data set as input, MB-DEA outputs the multiple Markov Boundaries and a best Markov Boundary, or the tornado precursor set, can be found according to the interesting measures.

5.2 Tornado Forecasting

5.2.1 Experiment Setup

Tornadoes are rare events even during the most frequent months. The positive and negative instances ratio in our study is about 1:30. We use both accuracy (Equation 7) and F1 score (Equation 8) as the performance metrics in our empirical study.

$$Accuracy = \frac{TP + FP}{TP + TN + FP + FN} \tag{7}$$

$$F1 = \frac{2TP}{2TP + FP + FN} \tag{8}$$

where TP is the number of true positives, FP is the number of false positives, TN is the number of true negatives, and FN is the number of false negatives.

We divide the data set into two sets, 30 years (1979-2008, 2,610 days with 81 positive instances) as the training set and 5 years (2009-2013, 435 days with 17 positive instances) as the test set. As illustrated in Figure 5, we randomly under sample the negative instances to achieve class ratios of positive: negative (P/N) examples that are equal to 1:5, 1:10, 1:20, and 1:25 respectively. At each ratio level we perform the random process 10 times and run the MB-DEA algorithm with the correspondent training data set to identify tornado precursors from multiple Markov boundaries. We apply the tornado precursors to the K Nearest Neighbor classifier with K=1 on the test set. The average and best prediction results are reported in Table 5, in which the average values are calculated using the best precursors identified from each training data set. We plot the experimental results in Figures 6 to 7.

5.2.2 Results and Discussion

Our goal is to identify key interpretable tornado precursors that can latterly be used in forecasting models. As discussed earlier, we start from a single Markov boundary, then derive a core feature set from it, eventually identify the best tornado precursors. The average F1 values of the best tornado precursor sets are much higher than those of the initial single Markov boundaries at all the sampling levels (Table 5). The best average forecasting result (average accuracy=0.93, average F1=0.31) is achieved at the undersampling level of P/N ratio 1:20 and the best predicting

Table 5: The average and best prediction results

P/N Ratio	Ave. F1 of $MB(C)$	Ave. Size of CFS(C)	Ave. Acc.	Ave. F1	Best Acc.	Best F1
1:5	0.1041	269	0.9097	0.1907	0.9241	0.2667
1:10	0.1333	217	0.9218	0.2440	0.9253	0.2917
1:15	0.1579	233	0.9296	0.2688	0.9448	0.2941
1:20	0.1739	243	0.9255	**0.3129**	0.9310	0.3478
1:25	0.1778	245	0.9264	0.3018	0.9402	**0.3500**
Without Undersampling	0.1429	238	–	–	0.9218	0.2778

result (accuracy=0.94, F1=0.35) is achieved with P/N ratio of 1:25, in which we have successfully predicted 7 tornado events one day ahead out of 17 during the testing period (MAM 2009-2013, 435 days), with 16 false positives. To the best of our knowledge, our result among the most promising tornado forecasting results at daily level compared to the state-of-the-art algorithms [3].

Figure 6 uses our empirical results to explain how MB-DEA works. We plot the single Markov Boundary ($MB(C)$ in Algorithm 1), the core feature set $CFS(C)$, and the tornado precursors (the best Markov boundary according to the criteria of prediction powers) with respect to the experiment having best prediction results (F1=0.35) in Figure 6. Firstly, the single Markov boundary $MB(C)$ is learned from the tornado data set (Figure 6a), then the core feature set $CFS(C)$ is built based on the $MB(C)$ (Figure 6b-6e); finally, the best Markov boundary according to prediction powers, is reported (Figure 6f). Different variables in the core feature set $CFS(C)$ fall into clusters in the spatial domains (blue circles in Figure 6b-6e). The arrows from Figure 6a to Figure 6d show that how a feature from the field of Pressure Vertical Velocity helps to generate a cluster of related features (mostly from the field of Pressure Vertical Velocity and Relative Humidity), and later contributes to the identification of precursor 12 (Figure 6f). The variables from the same field closed to each other in the spatial domains will tend to have similar values due to the spatial autocorrelation effect [23]. These spatial clusters can be considered as real-world examples of the $CFS(C)$ illustrated in Figure 2. Our algorithm picks individual precursors out of each cluster and successfully finds the best combination (Markov Boundary) according to the forecasting task.

As an algorithm of discovering multiple Markov boundaries, MB-DEA is not limited to finding the feature set with the best prediction result. MB-DEA is able to report different precursor sets with similar prediction powers according to other domain interests. For example, compared to other variables in the tornado data set, the Pressure Vertical Velocity is considered as a noisy and unreliable variable. In the feature set with the best prediction result (Figure 6f, b-set for short), we have two features (No.7 and No.12) from the field of Pressure Vertical Velocity. From all the MB-DEA outputs generated from the same input data set, we are able to find a feature set whose features are all from fields other than Pressure Vertical Velocity (Figure 7, we call it the "most reliable" set, or m-set for short.) and have similar prediction power (F1=0.3265). From Figure 6f and Figure 7, we find that more than half of the features in the two sets (No.1,2,3,4,8,10,and 11) are exactly the same, and others (except No.6) are from the same spatial clusters in the core feature set. In the m-set instead of Pressure Vertical Velocity, variables from Relative Humidity are selected (No.5 and No.7 in m-set, compared to No.12 and No.7 in b-set, respectively). MB-DEA provides a new approach of bridging data-driven and knowledge-driven processes for better data interpretation to be used in various forecasting models.

6. CONCLUSION

The development of reliable tornado forecasting techniques able to provide warnings at a long lead-time is crucial to help human beings better prepare and respond to disastrous events. In this paper, we propose the MB-DEA algorithm to identify multiple sets of the precursors for reliable tornado forecasting using multiple Markov boundaries. Our empirical study reveals that the precursors identified by our algorithm are considered more reliable and practical than the ones identified by the single Markov boundary discovery algorithm, and lead to advancements in reliable and long-lead time of catastrophic tornado forecasting.

7. ACKNOWLEDGMENTS

This work is partly supported by a PIMS Post-Doctoral Fellowship Award of the Pacific Institute for the Mathematical Sciences, Canada, the Program for Changjiang Scholars and Innovative Research Team in University (PCSIRT) of the Ministry of Education, China (under grant IRT13059), the National 973 Program of China (under grant 2013CB329604), the National Natural Science Foundation of China (under grants 61229301 and 61305064), an NSERC Discovery grant and a BCIC NRAS Team Project. All opinions, findings, conclusions and recommendations in this paper are those of the authors and do not necessarily reflect the views of the funding agencies.

8. REFERENCES

[1] C. F. Aliferis, A. Statnikov, I. Tsamardinos, S. Mani, and X. D. Koutsoukos. Local causal and markov blanket induction for causal discovery and feature selection for classification part i: Algorithms and empirical evaluation. *Journal of Machine Learning Research*, 11:171–234, 2010.

[2] T. W. Anderson, T. W. Anderson, T. W. Anderson, and T. W. Anderson. *An introduction to multivariate statistical analysis*, volume 2. Wiley New York, 1958.

[3] J. Brotzge and W. Donner. The tornado warning process: A review of current research, challenges, and opportunities. *Bulletin of the American Meteorological Society*, 94(11):1715–1733, 2013.

[4] A. J. Clark, J. S. Kain, P. T. Marsh, J. Correia Jr, M. Xue, and F. Kong. Forecasting tornado pathlengths using a three-dimensional object identification algorithm applied to convection-allowing forecasts. *Weather and Forecasting*, 27(5):1090–1113, 2012.

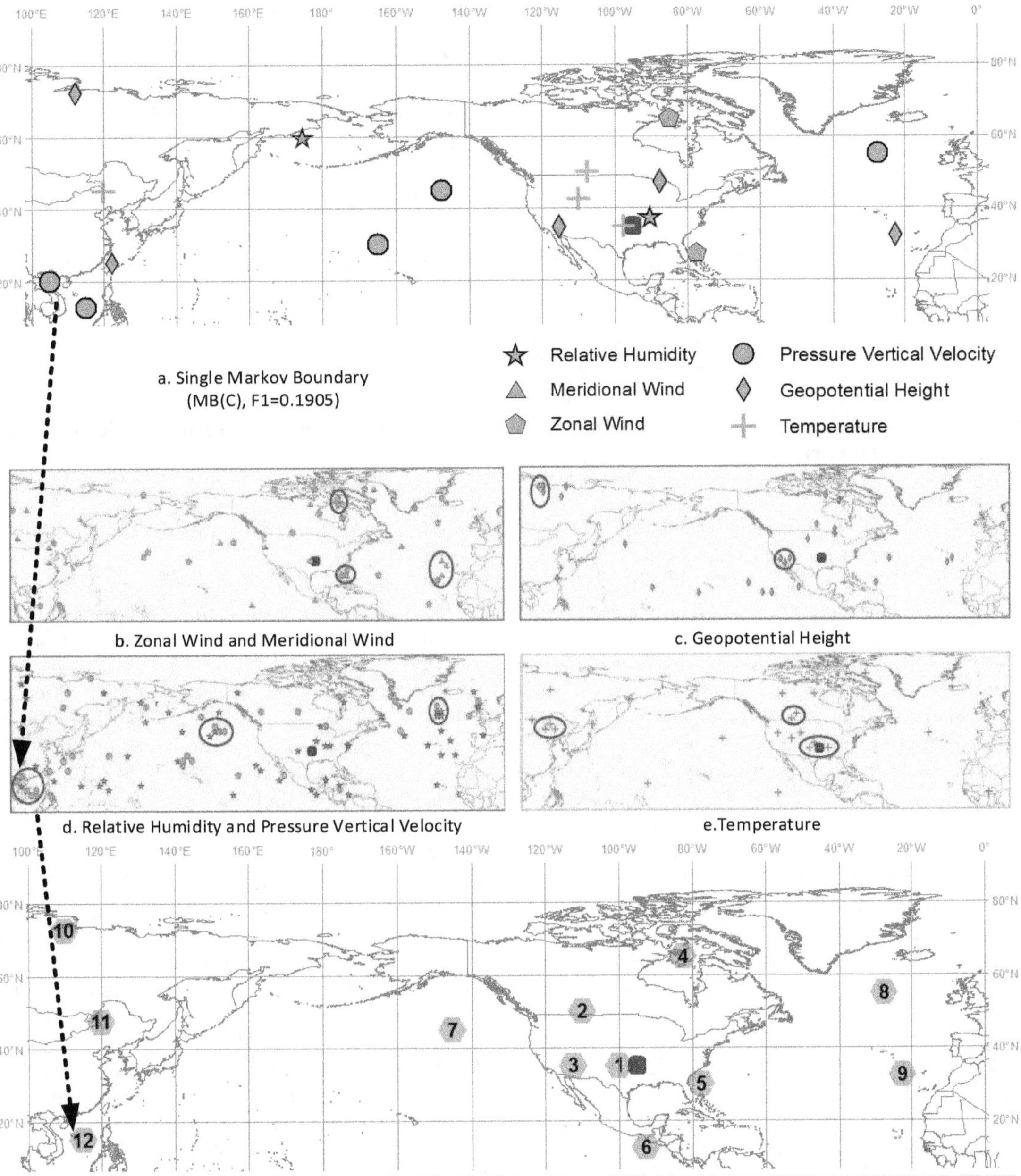

No.	Name	Level	Look Ahead Days	No.	Name	Level	Look Ahead Days
1	Temperature	1000	-1	7	Pressure Vertical Velocity	1000	-4
2	Temperature	1000	-3	8	Relative Humidity	850	-5
3	Geopotential Height	925	-1	9	Meridional Wind	1000	-3
4	Zonal Wind	1000	-5	10	Geopotential Height	700	-4
5	Zonal Wind	600	-4	11	Temperature	1000	-3
6	Relative Humidity	1000	-5	12	Pressure Vertical Velocity	400	-3

Figure 6: A real world example on the processes of how MB-DEA works. MB-DEA firstly discovers a single Markov Boundary (Figure (a): $MB(C)$ from Algorithm 1). The partial CFS (Figures (b) to (e)) shows feature clusters in the spatial domain built based on features from $MB(C)$, and finally the best feature set (b-set (Figure (f)), according to the prediction power) is found from CFS. The red square in each map is the target area for tornado labeling.

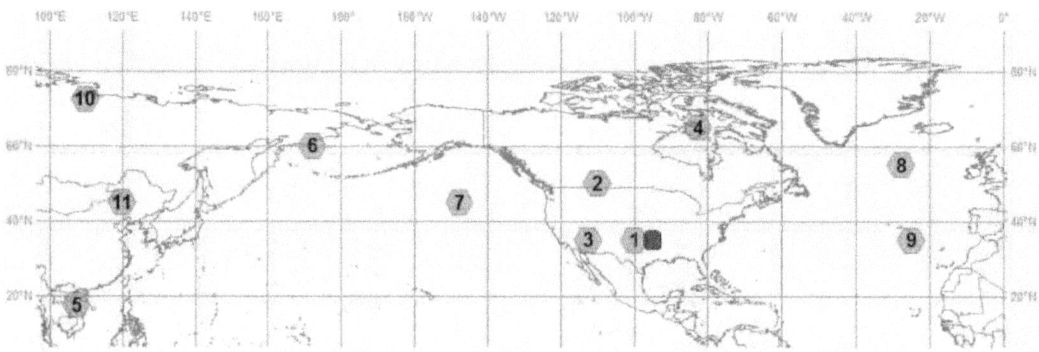

Feature Set with Most Reliable Variables (F1=0.3265)

No.	Name	Level	Look Ahead Days	No.	Name	Level	Look Ahead Days
1	Temperature	1000	-1	7	Relative Humidity	1000	-4
2	Temperature	1000	-3	8	Relative Humidity	850	-5
3	Geopotential Height	925	-1	9	Meridional Wind	1000	-3
4	Zonal Wind	1000	-5	10	Geopotential Height	700	-4
5	Relative Humidity	1000	-3	11	Temperature	1000	-3
6	Relative Humidity	1000	-4				

Figure 7: The most reliable feature set (according to the types of variables in the set). The red square in the map is the target area for tornado labeling.

[5] C. P. De Campos and Q. Ji. Efficient structure learning of bayesian networks using constraints. *Journal of Machine Learning Research*, 12:663–689, 2011.

[6] C. A. Doswell, H. E. Brooks, and N. Dotzek. On the implementation of the enhanced fujita scale in the usa. *Atmospheric Research*, 93(1):554–563, 2009.

[7] J. H. Faghmous and V. Kumar. A big data guide to understanding climate change: The case for theory-guided data science. *Big data*, 2(3):155–163, 2014.

[8] I. M. Held, R. T. Pierrehumbert, S. T. Garner, and K. L. Swanson. Surface quasi-geostrophic dynamics. *Journal of Fluid Mechanics*, 282:1–20, 1995.

[9] E. Kalnay, M. Kanamitsu, R. Kistler, W. Collins, D. Deaven, L. Gandin, M. Iredell, S. Saha, G. White, J. Woollen, et al. The ncep/ncar 40-year reanalysis project. *Bulletin of the American meteorological Society*, 77(3):437–471, 1996.

[10] H. Liu and L. Yu. Toward integrating feature selection algorithms for classification and clustering. *Knowledge and Data Engineering, IEEE Transactions on*, 17(4):491–502, 2005.

[11] J. Pearl. *Probabilistic reasoning in intelligent systems: networks of plausible inference*. Morgan Kaufmann, 1988.

[12] J. M. Peña, R. Nilsson, J. Björkegren, and J. Tegnér. Towards scalable and data efficient learning of markov boundaries. *International Journal of Approximate Reasoning*, 45(2):211–232, 2007.

[13] C. M. Shafer, A. E. Mercer, L. M. Leslie, M. B. Richman, and C. A. Doswell III. Evaluation of wrf model simulations of tornadic and nontornadic outbreaks occurring in the spring and fall. *Monthly Weather Review*, 138(11):4098–4119, 2010.

[14] C. E. Shannon. A mathematical theory of communication. *ACM SIGMOBILE Mobile Computing and Communications Review*, 5(1):3–55, 2001.

[15] K. Simmons and D. Sutter. *Economic and societal impacts of tornadoes*. Springer Science & Business Media, 2013.

[16] N. Snook and M. Xue. Effects of microphysical drop size distribution on tornadogenesis in supercell thunderstorms. *Geophysical Research Letters*, 35(24), 2008.

[17] A. Statnikov, J. Lemeir, and C. F. Aliferis. Algorithms for discovery of multiple markov boundaries. *Journal of Machine Learning Research*, 14(1):499–566, 2013.

[18] I. Tsamardinos, L. E. Brown, and C. F. Aliferis. The max-min hill-climbing bayesian network structure learning algorithm. *Machine learning*, 65(1):31–78, 2006.

[19] D. Wang, W. Ding, K. Yu, X. Wu, P. Chen, D. L. Small, and S. Islam. Towards long-lead forecasting of extreme flood events: a data mining framework for precipitation cluster precursors identification. In *Proceedings of the 19th ACM SIGKDD international conference on Knowledge discovery and data mining*, pages 1285–1293. ACM, 2013.

[20] X. Wu, K. Yu, W. Ding, H. Wang, and X. Zhu. Online feature selection with streaming features. *Pattern Analysis and Machine Intelligence, IEEE Transactions on*, 35(5):1178–1192, 2013.

[21] K. Yu, X. Wu, W. Ding, and J. Pei. Towards scalable and accurate online feature selection for big data. In *Data Mining (ICDM), 2014 IEEE International Conference on*, pages 660–669. IEEE, 2014.

[22] K. Yu, X. Wu, Z. Zhang, Y. Mu, H. Wang, and W. Ding. Markov blanket feature selection with non-faithful data distributions. In *Data Mining (ICDM), 2013 IEEE International Conference on*, pages 857–866. IEEE, 2013.

[23] P. Zhang, Y. Huang, S. Shekhar, and V. Kumar. Exploiting spatial autocorrelation to efficiently process correlation-based similarity queries. In *Advances in Spatial and Temporal Databases*, pages 449–468. 2003.

Gas Concentration Reconstruction for Coal-Fired Boilers Using Gaussian Process

Chao Yuan
Siemens Corporate Research
Princeton, United States
chao.yuan@siemens.com

Matthias Behmann
Siemens Energy
Karlsruhe, Germany
matthias.behmann@siemens.com

Bernhard Meerbeck
Siemens Energy
Offenbach am Main, Germany
bernhard.meerbeck@siemens.com

ABSTRACT

The goal of combustion optimization of a coal-fired boiler is to improve its operating efficiency while reducing emissions at the same time. Being able to take measurements for key combustion ingredients, such as O2, CO, H2O is crucial for the feedback loop needed by this task. One state-of-the-art laser technique, namely, Tunable Diode Laser Absorption Spectroscopy (TDLAS) is able to measure the average value of gas concentration along a laser beam path. A active research direction in TDLAS is how to reconstruct gas concentration images based on these path averages. However, in reality the number of such paths is usually very limited, leading to an extremely under-constrained estimation problem. Another overlooked aspect of the problem is that how can we arrange paths such that the reconstructed image is more accurate? We propose a Bayesian approach based on Gaussian process (GP) to address both image reconstruction and path arrangement problems, simultaneously. Specifically, we use the GP posterior mean as the reconstructed image, and average posterior pixel variance as our objective function to optimize the path arrangement. Our algorithms have been integrated in Siemens SPPA-P3000 control system that provides real-time combustion optimization of boilers around the world.

Categories and Subject Descriptors

J.6 [**Computer Applications**]: COMPUTER-AIDED ENGINEERING; I.4.5 [**Computing Methodologies**]: IMAGE PROCESSING AND COMPUTER VISION—*Reconstruction*

Keywords

Gaussian process; TDLAS; combustion optimization

1. INTRODUCTION

The capability of reconstructing gas (e.g., of O2, CO) concentration images inside the combustion zone is very useful for visualizing, optimizing and monitoring the performance of a coal-fired boiler. The technique of tunable diode laser absorption spectroscopy (TDLAS) has received increasing interests due to its fast responsive speed, high sensitivity and non-invasiveness[7]. A single TDLAS setup consists of a laser transmitter sending laser beams over a path through the combustion region to a laser receiver. Each TDLAS path measures an average value of the gas concentrations along the path. Our goal is to reconstruct the 2D gas concentration image based on multiple path averages (or projections), as illustrated in Fig.1.

There are two challenges for this task. First, given the paths, how can we accurately reconstruct the image? This concept is similar to that of computed tomography (CT) (Chapter 3 in [9]). However, most widely used CT algorithms such as filtered back-projection require a lot of projections (multiple views and dense projections per view) to achieve a good resolution. In contrast, only a very small number of paths are typically set up on a boiler; for example, it is not uncommon that we only have five to 15 paths (projections), which leads to an extremely under-constrained problem. Second, how do we best arrange paths such that the reconstructed image is even more precise? In reality,

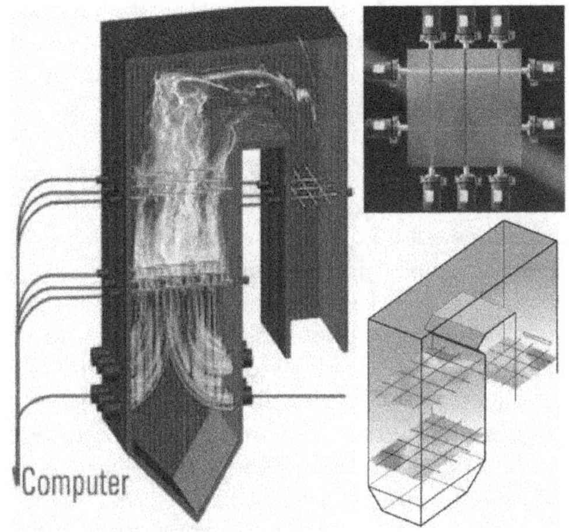

Figure 1: Illustration of gas concentration reconstruction. The left plot shows the geometry of an operating coal-fired boiler. Our goal is to reconstruct 2D cross section gas concentration images (bottom right). To achieve this, TDLAS paths are installed on the wall of a boiler. Each path reads the average gas value along the path (top right).

KDD'15, August 10-13, 2015, Sydney, NSW, Australia.

ISBN 978-1-4503-3664-2/15/08 ...$15.00.
DOI: http://dx.doi.org/10.1145/2783258.2788617.

there are some constraints to consider. For example, a path may not be installed at a location or a direction (view) that we desire because of certain restrictions or mounting difficulties of a boiler. For the first estimation problem, many previous methods have been proposed, however, few of them have tackled the case with only about ten paths that we study here [12, 11, 1, 6, 20]. In addition, to the best of our knowledge, we haven't seen an existing approach addressing the second optimization problem.

In this paper, we present a Bayesian approach based on Gaussian process to tackle both estimation and optimization problems under the same framework. The 2D unknown image is modeled by a Gaussian process, a multivariate Gaussian distribution with pixel coordinates as its inputs. This naturally introduces long-range smoothness constraints such that neighboring pixels have similar values. Given the path projections, the image has a posterior Gaussian distribution with a posterior mean and covariance. We use the mean as the reconstructed image because it is optimal in terms of mean squared error. The posterior covariance indicates the uncertainty of the image. We propose to use the trace of this covariance matrix, or the sum of posterior variances for all pixels, as the objective function of a path arrangement. By minimizing this function, we become more certain about our reconstruction and thus expect to get more accurate results. In addition, our objective function offers a fast and effective way to evaluate and compare existing path arrangements. Our algorithms have been integrated in Siemens SPPA-P3000 control system for real-time combustion optimization applications.

The rest of this paper is organized as follows. In Sect.2, we review previous work. In Sect.3, we define our reconstruction problem. The proposed model is described in Sect.4. We present test results in Sect.5 and conclude this paper in Sect.6.

2. RELATED WORK

Tomographic techniques such as algebraic reconstruction technique (ART) have been proposed to handle the issue of a small number of projections [9, 20, 12]. However, ART updates the estimate only using one path in each iteration, which usually leads to a slow convergence and "salt-and-pepper" noise [6]. Extensions such as simultaneous iterative reconstructive technique (SIRT) [9], simultaneous algebraic reconstruction technique (SART) [9] and multiplicative algebraic reconstruction technique (MART) [6] can update estimation using all paths in each iteration. Although proven to find an image complying to path projections, these ART-based approaches don't offer a way to check if the reconstructed image is realistic or not.

Smoothness constraints among neighboring pixels are introduced as prior information to help addressing this under-constrained problem. Smoothness can be incorporated via smooth basis functions [15, 3]. [15, 3] also apply 1D smooth basis functions to multiple path averages under the same view. [1] correlates two pixels if they are both close to a path. However, such smoothness constraints are local and cannot capture long-range correlation among pixels.

Longer range smoothness can be achieved via the Tikhonov regularization (TR) [6]. This algorithm explicitly enforces a local smoothness constraint: every pixel value should be similar to the average of its neighbors'. Two pixels far apart are implicitly linked via all such local smoothness constraints between them. The TR method can be viewed as a special case of Gaussian random fields [22], which assign weights to every pair of pixels in the image (instead of only neighboring pixels as done in the TR). Gaussian process is widely used in computer vision for applications such as super resolution [18, 17], which motivates our previous work [21]. It has been revealed that both Gaussian random fields and Gaussian process model long range smoothness via the covariance matrix of a Gaussian distribution, but they do this differently. The former models the inverse of the covariance while the latter directly depicts the covariance [22].

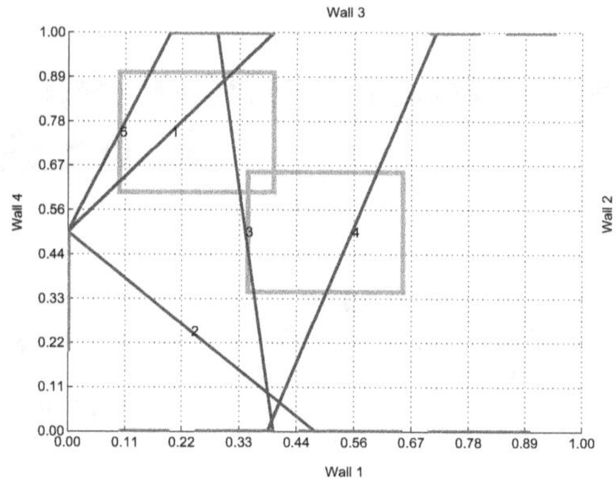

Figure 2: Gas concentration reconstruction problem definition. Paths, available regions and region of interest (ROI) are denoted by blue lines, red lines and green boxes, respectively. The boiler cross section, as shown, has a width of 1 and a height of 1. There are $M = 5$ paths. The image size is $N = 10 \times 10 = 100$.

Finally, all previous gas concentration approaches assume a fixed path arrangement. The most widely used configurations involve multiple views, each with multiple parallel paths [12, 11, 1, 6, 20]. These approaches may not be feasible if there are mounting restrictions about where a path can or cannot be installed. In contrast, we present an optimization approach, taking these restrictions into consideration, to find the best path arrangement that can produce more accurate reconstruction results.

3. PROBLEM DEFINITION

Our goal is to reconstruct an $w \times h$ gas concentration image $\mathbf{v}$ from M path averages (projections), denoted by an M-dimensional vector $\mathbf{b}$. w and h are the width and height of the image, respectively. The projections $\mathbf{b}$ and image $\mathbf{v}$ have the following relation

$$\mathbf{b} = \mathbf{A}\mathbf{v}. \tag{1}$$

$\mathbf{A}$ is an $M \times N$ *projection matrix.* Once the paths are configured, $\mathbf{A}$ becomes a constant matrix. Typically, we represent the image $\mathbf{v}$ as a N-dimensional vector for easy algebraic manipulation, where $N = w \times h$. To visualize the image, we then convert it into the matrix format. In the example shown in Fig.2, we have $w = h = 10$, $M = 5$ paths and we want to estimate the gas concentration at each of the $N = 100$ grid pixels. There are two tasks involved, reconstruction and path arrangement optimization.

3.1 Reconstruction

If the paths are already configured, how can we reconstruct the image? We first introduce some terminology. The sum of the m-th row and the sum of the n-th column of $\mathbf{A}$ are respectively defined by $A_{m,+} = \sum_{n=1}^{N} A_{m,n}$ and $A_{+,n} = \sum_{m=1}^{M} A_{m,n}$. A m-th pixel is termed as *observed* if there is at least one path crossing it or $A_{+,n} > 0$. Otherwise, it is *unobserved*.

We now describe how to determine a projection weight $A_{m,n}$ in the projection matrix $\mathbf{A}$. One way is to treat each pixel as a small rectangle, and then compute the ratio of the length of the m-th path intercepted by the n-th pixel to the total length of the m-th path in the domain of interest [21, 6]. One drawback of this approach is that if a pixel doesn't intersect with a path, it has no impact on the path average even if they are next to each other. We adopt a new strategy by treating each pixel as a point (as in Fig.2). We evenly place 1000 sample points along each path. For each sample point, we locate the closest four pixels (vertices of a small rectangle) and compute the bilinear weights of the four pixels regarding this sample point. Then the contribution of a pixel is the sum of its weights for all sample points. By doing this, we can get a smoother projection matrix because more pixels are involved. Finally, we normalize every row such that $A_{m,+} = 1$, because path projection is a weighted average along the path.

Our reconstruction problem is essentially solving a linear equation (1) with both $\mathbf{A}$ and $\mathbf{b}$ known. If $\mathbf{A}$ is an invertible square matrix, where $M = N$, then we have $\mathbf{v} = \mathbf{A}^{-1}\mathbf{b}$ as done by [11]. If $M > N$ and $\mathbf{A}$ has full rank, based on linear least square we have

$$\mathbf{v} = (\mathbf{A}^T\mathbf{A})^{-1}\mathbf{A}^T\mathbf{b}. \tag{2}$$

However, our problem is very under-constrained because of $M \ll N$. In such a case, we have multiple solutions satisfying the same equation (1).

Simultaneous algebraic reconstruction technique (SART) is one of the most widely used ART algorithms [9]. It has the following iterative procedure

$$v_n^{(q+1)} = v_n^{(q)} + \frac{\lambda}{A_{+,n}} \sum_{m=1}^{M} A_{m,n} \frac{b_m - (\mathbf{A}\mathbf{v}^{(q)})_m}{A_{m,+}}. \tag{3}$$

$v_n^{(q)}$ denotes the current reconstructed image after the q-th iteration. $(\mathbf{A}\mathbf{v}^{(q)})_m$ indicates the estimated m-th projection from the current image. Note that in our problem $A_{m,+} = 1$ and can be omitted from (3), but in general it has a non-zero value. (3) can be understood as follows. The residual between the true projection b_m and the estimated projection $(\mathbf{A}\mathbf{v}^{(q)})_m$ indicates in which direction $v_n^{(q+1)}$ should move from $v_n^{(q)}$ to reduce this residual. The final direction is determined by the weighted average of all M projections, each with a weight of $A_{m,n}$ normalized by $A_{+,n}$. The magnitude of this movement is adjusted by a parameter λ.

The SART algorithm is proven to converge to a solution of (1) if $A_{+,n} \neq 0$ [8]. However, there is no guarantee whether the found solution, out of all possible solutions, is realistic or not. In addition, in our application, the path configuration can be arbitrary. It often happens that $A_{+,n} = 0$ for some columns so the n-th pixel is unobserved. In such cases, division-by-zero problem will happen and (3) will stop working.

Tikhonov regularization (TR) is another technique to regularize linear equations [6]. TR adds another set of equations $\mathbf{L}\mathbf{v} = \mathbf{0}$ to enforce smoothness constraint. $\mathbf{L}$ is a $N \times N$ regularization matrix, where each row requires a pixel's value to be identical to the average of its neighbors. $\mathbf{A}\mathbf{v} = \mathbf{b}$ and $\mathbf{L}\mathbf{v} = \mathbf{0}$ are treated similarly in the objective function of $(\mathbf{A}\mathbf{v} - \mathbf{b})^T(\mathbf{A}\mathbf{v} - \mathbf{b}) + \lambda(\mathbf{L}\mathbf{v})^T(\mathbf{L}\mathbf{v})$ (to be minimized). λ is a parameter. It can be proved that the solution of TR is

$$\mathbf{v} = (\mathbf{A}^T\mathbf{A} + \lambda\mathbf{L}^T\mathbf{L})^{-1}\mathbf{A}^T\mathbf{b}. \tag{4}$$

The only difference between (4) and (2) is due to the regularization term.

3.2 Path arrangement optimization

We previously assume that paths are already configured. How can we arrange paths such that we can get better reconstruction results. The boiler cross section is denoted by a rectangle. It has four walls with ID=$1, 2, 3, 4$ as shown in Fig.2. For some applications, users may only focus on certain *region of interest* (ROI) (green boxes in Fig.2). By default, ROI is the whole cross section.

Ideally, for every path, it can be mounted between any of these wall pairs. However, under certain circumstances, some regions on a particular wall are not available and thus cannot be used to install a path. The red lines in Fig.2 indicates *available regions* that can be used for installation. In other words, every end point of a path must be located within an available region.

In either case, we have a combinatorial optimization problem. Suppose that there are K available regions, leading to about of $(K-1)K/2$ region pairs. Then there are about $((K-1)K/2)^M$ possible arrangements just for assigning region pairs to paths. This complexity has not included the efforts about where the end point of a path should be in a particular available region.

To the best of our knowledge, no prior work has addressed this path arrangement optimization problem. One possible solution is to randomly generate many path arrangements and evaluate each of them against a large number of tests to see which one produce the most accurate reconstruction results. However, due to the aforementioned complexity, it is prohibitive for this approach to find the best path arrangement especially for a relatively large M.

4. MODEL DESCRIPTION

4.1 Reconstruction using Gaussian process

In our previous study [1], we presented a Bayesian algorithm about how to reconstruct $\mathbf{v}$ from $\mathbf{b}$. We model $\mathbf{v}$ as a multivariate Gaussian distribution

$$P(\mathbf{v}) = \mathcal{N}(\mathbf{v}|\mathbf{m}, \mathbf{C}), \tag{5}$$

where $\mathbf{m}$ and $\mathbf{C}$ are the N-dimensional mean vector and $N \times N$ covariance matrix, respectively. Because $\mathbf{v}$ represents a 2D image, its distribution is also referred to as a Gaussian process (GP) [14]. We assume that this GP is homogeneous since we don't have a priori knowledge about the differences between different pixels. Thus, the cross-covariance C_{n_1,n_2} between v_i and v_j in $\mathbf{v}$, where $1 \leq i, j \leq N$, is defined as

$$C_{i,j} = f \exp(-\frac{(x_i - x_j)^2 + (y_i - y_j)^2}{r^2}). \tag{6}$$

(x_i, y_i) and (x_j, y_j) are the coordinates for pixels i and j, respectively. f and r are two parameters. (6) indicates that if neighboring pixels should have high correlation while far apart pixels should have low correlation. This global smoothness constraint aids us to solve our extremely under-constrained reconstruction problem.

We introduce noise to the projection model in (1) to make it probabilistic

$$P(\mathbf{b}|\mathbf{v}) = \mathcal{N}(\mathbf{b}|\mathbf{A}\mathbf{v}, \sigma^2\mathbf{I}). \quad (7)$$

σ^2 is the noise variance and $\mathbf{I}$ is a $M \times M$ identity matrix. The projections $\mathbf{b}$ can thus be modeled as another multi-variate Gaussian distribution given the 2D image $\mathbf{v}$

We can now write the joint probability between image $\mathbf{v}$ and projection $\mathbf{b}$, $P(\mathbf{v}, \mathbf{b}) = P(\mathbf{v})P(\mathbf{b}|\mathbf{v})$

$$P(\mathbf{v}, \mathbf{b}) = \mathcal{N}(\begin{bmatrix}\mathbf{v}\\ \mathbf{b}\end{bmatrix} | \begin{bmatrix}\mathbf{m}\\ \mathbf{Am}\end{bmatrix}, \begin{bmatrix}\mathbf{C} & \mathbf{CA}^T\\ \mathbf{AC} & \mathbf{ACA}^T + \sigma^2\mathbf{I}\end{bmatrix}). \quad (8)$$

From (8), we can write the posterior distribution of $\mathbf{v}$ given $\mathbf{b}$

$$P(\mathbf{v}|\mathbf{b}) = \mathcal{N}(\mathbf{v}|\widetilde{\mathbf{m}}, \widetilde{\mathbf{C}}), \quad (9)$$

where the posterior mean and covariance are

$$\widetilde{\mathbf{m}} = \mathbf{CA}^T(\mathbf{ACA}^T + \sigma^2\mathbf{I})^{-1}(\mathbf{b} - \mathbf{Am}) + \mathbf{m}, \quad (10)$$

$$\widetilde{\mathbf{C}} = \mathbf{C} - \mathbf{CA}^T(\mathbf{ACA}^T + \sigma^2\mathbf{I})^{-1}\mathbf{AC}, \quad (11)$$

respectively.

In our previous work [21], we propose to use the posterior mean $\widetilde{\mathbf{m}}$ as the reconstructed image

$$\widetilde{\mathbf{v}} = \widetilde{\mathbf{m}}. \quad (12)$$

This is our solution to the reconstruction problem and is optimal in the sense of minimizing mean squared error. The complexity of calculating (10) is $\mathcal{O}(MN^2)$ (assuming $M < N$). (10) can also be rewritten as

$$\mathbf{v} = (\mathbf{A}^T\mathbf{A} + \sigma^2\mathbf{C}^{-1})^{-1}(\mathbf{A}^T\mathbf{b} + \sigma^2\mathbf{C}^{-1}\mathbf{m}). \quad (13)$$

If we set $\mathbf{m} = \mathbf{0}$ and let $\mathbf{C}^{-1} = \mathbf{L}^T\mathbf{L}$, (13) has a identical form to (4), the solution of TR. The difference is that we model the covariance $\mathbf{C}$ directly while TR models the inverse of covariance by $\mathbf{L}^T\mathbf{L}$. In practice, we dynamically set each element of $\mathbf{m}$ equally to the average of all M path projections.

We note that one prior approach also models the image as a Gaussian distribution [13]. However instead of using parametric covariance matrix as we do in (6), they propose to estimate the covariance via images simulated by computational fluid dynamics (CFD). This demands a large number of training images, which can be expensive to obtain.

4.2 Reconstruction uncertainty

We have assumed that the path arrangements are already given and thus $\mathbf{A}$ is known. In this section, we describe how to find the best path arrangements or to determine the projection matrix $\mathbf{A}$ that can produce more accurate reconstruction.

4.2.1 Approximating projection matrix

We define the *reconstruction uncertainty* as the average posterior pixel variance

$$F(\mathbf{\Theta}) = \frac{1}{N} trace(\mathbf{C} - \mathbf{CA}^T(\mathbf{ACA}^T + \sigma^2\mathbf{I})^{-1}\mathbf{AC}), \quad (14)$$

which is proportional to the trace of the posterior covariance in (11). Since posterior variance indicates the uncertainty of our prediction, minimizing such variance is expected to reduce uncertainty and thus improve our reconstruction result. Here $\mathbf{\Theta} = \{\boldsymbol{\theta}_1, \boldsymbol{\theta}_2, ..., \boldsymbol{\theta}_M\}$ are path arrangement parameters for all paths and determine projection matrix $\mathbf{A}$. Each $\boldsymbol{\theta}_m = [x_{m,1}\ y_{m,1}\ x_{m,2}\ y_{m,2}]^T$ is a column vector indicating the coordinates of two end points for the m-th path. Note that because an end point is located on a wall so either x or y is a constant. Therefore, each $\boldsymbol{\theta}_m$ only has two tunable parameters. If we have a ROI smaller than the whole cross section, we simply process the pixels within that ROI (instead of applying the trace operator for the whole image).

Using the posterior covariance or variance of GP has been considered in other applications. For example, [5] propagates such uncertainty into multi-step ahead forecasting of time series. [10] performs clustering based the principle that highly populated area should have low uncertainty while less populated area should have high uncertainty.

We now describe how to compute $F(\mathbf{\Theta})$. Because $\mathbf{C}$ is a constant, we just need to compute the projection matrix $\mathbf{A}$. We have been using sample points and bilinear weights to compute the contributions of a pixel to a path and then determine $\mathbf{A}$ as noted in Sect.3.1. However, using the same method is not a good option here, because then we don't have an analytical form to work with. Therefore, we propose the following approximation for computing $\mathbf{A}$ based on the distance between a pixel and the path.

The m-th path is a line and every point (x, y) on this line can be represented by the following equation

$$g_m(x, y) = (y_{m,2} - y_{m,1})x - (x_{m,2} - x_{m,1})y + y_{m,1}(x_{m,2} - x_{m,1}) - x_{m,1}(y_{m,2} - y_{m,1}) = 0 \quad (15)$$

To compute the contribution of the $n-$th pixel (x_n, y_n) (a grid point in Fig.2), where $n = 1, 2, , N$. to this path, we first compute the squared distance between the pixel to the line

$$d_{m,n}^2 = \frac{g_m(x_n, y_n)^2}{(y_{m,2} - y_{m,1})^2 + (x_{m,2} - x_{m,1})^2}. \quad (16)$$

The contribution of this pixel to the path is defined as $\exp(-\gamma d_{m,n}^2)$, where γ is a parameter. The rationale behind this is that the smaller the distance is, the higher impact the pixel has on the path. Finally, we define the m-th row of the projection matrix A_m as

$$\mathbf{A}_m = \frac{1}{\sum_{n=1}^{N}\exp(-\gamma d_{m,n}^2)}[\exp(-\gamma d_{m,1}^2)\ ...\ \exp(-\gamma d_{m,N}^2)]. \quad (17)$$

The normalization term in (17) is to make sure that the sum of this row is equal to one, because the projection is the weighted average of all pixel values on the path. Now the full projection matrix $\mathbf{A}$ is simply $\mathbf{A} = [\mathbf{A}_1^T\ ...\ \mathbf{A}_M^T]^T$.

The largest advantage of using this approximated project matrix is that now our objective function $F(\mathbf{\Theta})$ is differentiable with respective to parameter $\mathbf{\Theta}$. Thus, we can easily compute gradient and employ gradient-based algorithm such as interior point algorithm to solve the problem [2, 19]. This greatly speeds up the optimization process. The error introduced by this approximation is mainly due to pixels located at corners. When we compute the distance between such a pixel and a path, the projection of this pixel on the path can be located outside the cross section. Therefore, ideally, such a pixel should not have any impact on the path average. However, our approximation method is not able to check this. Fortunately, the number of such pixels is very small and we don't expect such error to be a big issue.

Note that our reconstruction uncertainty can be used to compare existing path arrangements and help selecting the best one. This is much faster and more effective than simulating and evaluating against a large number of test images as we show in Sect.5.4.

4.2.2 *Adding region pair constraints*

We have introduced an unconstrained objective function $F(\mathbf{\Theta})$. However, the end points of a path can only be located on a wall or certain regions of a wall and cannot go unbounded. We will add such constraints to our optimization problem.

Suppose that we have K available regions $R_1, R_2, ..., R_K$. Each region is a line segment indicated by $R_k = [wall_k, x_{k,1}, y_{k,1}, x_{k,2}, y_{k,2}]$. $wall_k = 1, 2, 3, 4$ denotes which wall this region is located on (see Fig.2). $(x_{k,1}, y_{k,1})$ and $(x_{k,2}, y_{k,2})$ denote the starting and ending points of the region, respectively. They have a fixed order such that $(x_{k,1} \leq x_{k,2})$ and $(y_{k,1} \leq y_{k,2})$. Note that either $x_{k,1} = x_{k,2}$ or $y_{k,1} = y_{k,2}$ because an available region must be located on one of the four walls.

For example, the available region on Wall 4 in Fig.2 is (4, 0, 0.2, 0, 0.5) indicating $wall_k = 4$, $x_{k,1} = 0$, $y_{k,1} = 0.2$, $x_{k,2} = 0$ and $y_{k,2} = 0.5$. We will use k to exclusively indicate an available region, not to be confused with the path indicator m. So $x_{k,1}$ and $x_{m,1}$ are referring to locations on a region and a path differently even if $k = m$. The red lines on each wall of Fig.2 show such available regions. Every end point of all paths must be located within an available region.

We define *region pair* as a pair of available regions (R_{k_1}, R_{k_2}) All region pairs are denoted by a set $\mathbf{\Omega}=\{(R_{k_1}, R_{k_2})|wall_{k_1} < wall_{k_1}\}$. We require that $wall_{k_1} < wall_{k_1}$ because (R_{k_1}, R_{k_2}) is the same as (R_{k_2}, R_{k_1}) and only needs to be considered once. Conceptually, each path can span two regions to form a total of $K(K-1)/2$ possible region pairs. However, the number is usually smaller because we do not consider two regions on the same wall. We use $|\mathbf{\Omega}|$ to indicate the cardinality of the set $\mathbf{\Omega}$.

The region pair where the m-th path is located is denoted by H_m satisfying $H_m \in \mathbf{\Omega}$. By considering region pairs, we define our final constrained optimization problem as follows

$$\min_{\substack{H_m \in \mathbf{\Omega} \\ \text{for } m=1,2,...,M}} \left[\min_{\substack{LB(H_m) \leq \boldsymbol{\theta}_m \leq UB(H_m) \\ \text{for } m=1,2,...,M}} F(\boldsymbol{\theta}_1, \boldsymbol{\theta}_2, ..., \boldsymbol{\theta}_M) \right]. \tag{18}$$

$LB(.)$ and $UB(.)$ are lower bound and upper bound operators, respectively. They ensure that end points of a path are located within an available region. If we denote $H_m = (R_{k_1}, R_{k_2})$, we have $LB(H_m) = [x_{k_1,1}\ y_{k_1,1}\ x_{k_2,1}\ y_{k_2,1}]^T$ and $UB(H_m) = [x_{k_1,2}\ y_{k_1,2}\ x_{k_2,2}\ y_{k_2,2}]^T$ to bound four parameters in $\boldsymbol{\theta}_m$. Because the end points of both available regions and paths are located on a wall, two parameters in $\boldsymbol{\theta}_m$ are actually constants and don't need to be optimized over. If we let $\mathbf{H} = \{H_1, H_2, ..., H_M\}$, we can write bounds in a more compact form by $\mathbf{LB}(\mathbf{H}) \leq \mathbf{\Theta} \leq \mathbf{UB}(\mathbf{H})$.

4.2.3 *Optimization using simulated annealing*

The constrained optimization problem defined by (18) requires us to search for both M region pairs $H_1, H_2, ..., H_M$ and M path arrangement $\boldsymbol{\theta}_1, \boldsymbol{\theta}_2, ..., \boldsymbol{\theta}_M$. This problem is challenging to solve because it is a combinatorial optimization problem. There are $|\mathbf{\Omega}|^M$ possible cases for region pair assignment $\mathbf{H}$. For each assignment, the gradient-based search takes $\mathcal{O}(MN^2)$. Therefore, the total complexity is $\mathcal{O}(|\mathbf{\Omega}|^M MN^2)$. This is prohibitive for slightly large M and K value.

Therefore, we resort to stochastic optimization scheme [4]. It works as follows. For each iteration, we randomly perturb the current path arrangement by changing the region pair assignment and also initializing the end point positions of affected paths. Then we find the new best objective function in (18) by fixing the pair assignment. Next, we make a decision whether we keep this perturbation or switch back to the previous iteration result. The above process is then repeated until certain criterion is met. Different stochastic optimization methods differ in how we perturb and how we make a decision about the perturbation.

In this paper, we use simulated annealing (SA). For perturbation, we randomly select a path, randomly assign a region pair to it and then randomly initialize its end point positions on this region pair. For the decision, suppose that the newly optimized objective function value is F_{new} and the previous objective function value is F_{old}. We keep the new change if

$$\exp(\frac{F_{old} - F_{new}}{T_0 \epsilon^q}) \geq \delta. \tag{19}$$

Here T_0 and $0 < \epsilon < 1$ are two constants. q is the current iteration number. $0 \leq \delta \leq 1$ is a randomly generated number during each iteration. The idea behind (19) is that if new object function F_{new} is no more than F_{old} (indicating a nice move) the left side is no less than 1. So no matter what the value δ is, (19) is satisfied and we will keep the new perturbation. Otherwise, the left side of (19) will be a value between 0 and 1, so whether we keep the change is determined randomly on how large δ is. The concept of annealing is to reduce the temperature term $T_0 \epsilon^q$ gradually so the left side of (19) is less likely to be larger than δ over time unless F_{new} is surely no more than F_{old}. We exit SA if the number of consecutive iterations without improvement exceeds 100.

By using the simulated annealing, we finally reduce the complexity from $\mathcal{O}(|\mathbf{\Omega}|^M MN^2)$ to $\mathcal{O}(QMN^2)$, where Q is the maximum number of iterations needed and is typically smaller than 1000. This makes our algorithm practical. Alternatively, one can use Genetic algorithm to search for region pair assignments [4]. Algorithm 1 shows the pseudo codes of the complete optimization process.

5. TEST RESULTS

5.1 Test setup

Simulated datasets. In order to evaluate our algorithms, we need to compare the reconstructed image with the ground truth image. However, it is difficult to measure gas concentration inside the combustion region if not impossible. Thus, we resort to simulated tests. In all our tests, the resolution of an image is 200×200, representing a square boiler cross section with a width of 1 and a height of 1. Note that the proposed methodology can be applied to any rectangular cross section.

```
input  : M, Ω
output: F_best, H_best, Θ_best
F_best ← inf, F_old ← inf, i = 0, q = 0;
Randomly select H_new from Ω ;
while i ≤ 100 do
    Apply interior point algorithm to solve
    Θ_new = arg min_{LB(H_new) ≤ Θ ≤ UB(H_new)} F(Θ);
    F_new ← F(Θ_new);
    if F_new < F_best then
        F_best ← F_new, H_best ← H_new,
        Θ_best ← Θ_new;
        i = 0;
    else
        i ← i + 1;
    end
    δ ← random number between 0 and 1;
    if exp((F_old − F_new)/(T_0 ε^q)) ≥ δ then
        F_old ← F_new, H_old ← H_new,
        Θ_old ← Θ_new;
    end
    m ← random number from [1, 2, ..., M] ;
    H*_m ← random item from Ω ;
    Randomly sample θ*_m based on H*_m ;
    H_new ← H_old with H_m replaced by H*_m ;
    Θ_new ← Θ_old with θ_m replaced by θ*_m ;
    q ← q + 1 ;
end
```

Algorithm 1: The proposed path arrangement optimization algorithm. q is the current total number of iterations. i indicates the consecutive number of iterations without improvement; the algorithm exits if $i > 100$.

A ground-truth image is generated by summing L 2D smooth functions (similar to the covariance function in (6)). In particular, the n-th pixel value v_n is produced as follows

$$v_n = \sum_{l=1}^{L} h_l \exp\left(-\frac{(x_n - \mu_{xl})^2 + (y_n - \mu_{yl})^2}{s_l^2}\right). \quad (20)$$

(x_n, y_n) is the corresponding 2D coordinates of v_n. The l-th smooth function is defined by $h_l \exp(-\frac{(x-\mu_{xl})^2+(y-\mu_{yl})^2}{s_l^2})$, where $l = 1, 2, ..., L$. There are four parameters for each function, h_l, s_l, μ_{xl} and μ_{yl}, representing the peak, width and center locations of the function, respectively.

We fix $L = 10$ for all our tests. To produce a 2D image, we randomly create each of the $L = 10$ smooth functions by randomly selecting h_l between 0 and 1, s_l between 0.1 and 0.4, μ_{xl} and μ_{yl} between 0 and 1, respectively. Then all the L functions are summed to form the final ground-truth image $\mathbf{v}$ as in (20). The image created in this way is smooth, and usually multi-peaked and with an irregular shape, which resembles a realistic gas concentration image. We create a total of 100 images using this approach. One example is shown in Fig.6g.

Reconstruction algorithms We compare our GP algorithm with SART and TR. For our algorithm, we fix the GP parameters $f = 1$, $\sigma^2 = 0.001$ and $r = 1.0$. This setting gives us high enough signal-to-noise ratio $f/\sigma^2 = 1000$ and at the same time helps to avoid matrix singularity before the matrix inverse in (10) and (11). Our algorithm is not sensitive to r when it is between 0.5 and 1.5. We set $\gamma = 300$ used in projection matrix approximation such that only pixels right next to a path will have impact on its projection. Parameters in simulated annealing are set as $T_0 = 1$ and $\epsilon = 0.95$. For SART, we set its $\lambda = 1$ in (3) and for TR, we set its $\lambda = 0.1$ in (4). Both values produce the best results for these two algorithms. To further reduce computation, for all three algorithms, we reconstruct images with a lower resolution of $N = 10 \times 10$ and then apply bi-cubic interpolation to render the 200×200 image.

Path arrangement methods Before our study, most previous methods have been using view-based path arrangement scheme. In an *orthogonal* path arrangement, there are two views and a path is parallel to one of the four walls like top right plot in Fig.1. In a *diagonal* path arrangement, there are also two views and a path is parallel to one of the two diagonal directions (via rotating the orthogonal arrangement by 45 degrees). Siemens energy has mostly used these two simple methods to configure paths. We can combine these two schemes and form the *multi-view* path arrangement such that all paths will be arranged under four evenly spaced views. Note that these view-based approaches will not work in the case of mounting restrictions.

We also consider two additional baseline methods. The first one is to replace our objective function in (14) with a much simpler $\max_{n=1}^{N} \min_{m=1}^{M} d_{m,n}^2$. The rationale behind it is that each pixel should have at least one path nearby. We will refer to this method as "max min". The second one is a random path arrangement by randomly selecting a region pair and randomly generating end point positions on the region pair for a path. We will compare our optimized path arrangement with all above five path arrangement schemes.

Evaluation Note that a reconstruction algorithm and a path arrangement method can be arbitrarily combined. For each such combination, we conduct 100 tests. For each test, we use one of the 100 simulated image as our ground truth. Based on the path arrangement, the projections are generated. Then different reconstruction algorithm is applied to produce the reconstructed image. We compare this image $\tilde{\mathbf{v}}$ with the ground truth image $\mathbf{v}$ using root mean squared error $RMSE = \sqrt{\frac{\sum_{n=1}^{N}(\tilde{v}_n - v_n)^2}{N}}$. After all 100 tests, the average RMSE is used to judge the performance of this combination. All tests conducted in this paper are implemented in Matlab.

5.2 Reconstruction test

In this test, we focus on comparing the performances of three reconstruction algorithms based on the same path arrangement method (orthogonal, diagonal, multi-view, random or optimized). Fig.3 shows the average RMSE scores for different algorithms for different number of paths (M from 5 to 100). More details about the optimized path arrangement will be given in the next section.

Our GP algorithm produces the lowest RMSE for all six tests. Note that due to the way we generate synthetic images (Sect.5.1), a ground truth pixel value is usually between 0 and 3. Thus, RMSE=0.028 roughly means a relative error of $0.01 (= 0.028/3)$. To check the statistical significance, we conduct the one-sided paired t-test of GP vs. TR which appears to be the second performer. Table 1 shows the p value for all six tests for different number of paths. With a confidence level at 0.05, our results are significantly better than those of TR except five cases. SART performs worst for all

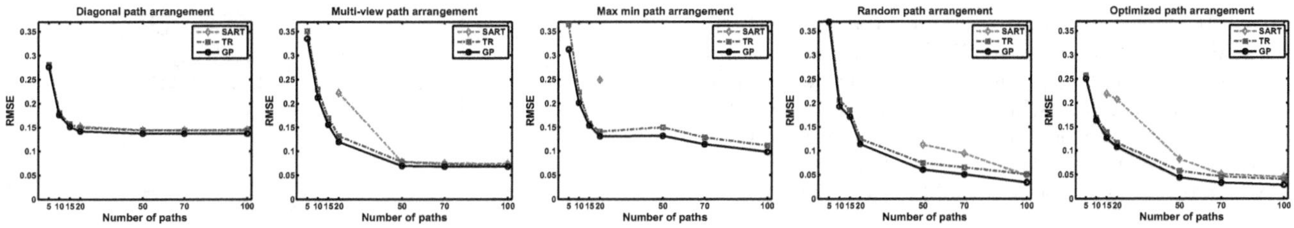

(b) (c) (c) (d) (e)

Figure 3: Comparing reconstruction algorithms using different path arrangement methods.

# paths	5	10	15	20	50	70	100
Orth	0.039	0.013	0.006	0.004	0.032	0.045	**0.057**
Diag	**0.127**	0.025	0.001	0.000	0.001	0.002	0.003
Mult	0.048	0.023	0.001	0.000	0.000	0.000	0.006
MaxMin	**0.056**	0.006	**0.123**	0.001	0.001	0.000	0.001
Rand	**0.269**	0.002	0.003	0.000	0.000	0.000	0.000
Opti	0.005	0.006	0.002	0.003	0.000	0.000	0.000

Table 1: p-value of one-sided paired t-test on RMSE scores comparing our GP algorithm to TR. 0.000 **indicates that p-value is smaller than** 0.001. **A bold entry indicates a failed t-test with a confidence interval of** 0.05.

# paths	5	10	15	20	50	70	100
Mult	0.335	0.212	0.155	0.119	0.069	0.068	0.068
Rand	0.369	0.193	0.172	0.114	0.061	0.050	0.034
Opti	**0.250**	**0.163**	**0.126**	**0.107**	**0.043**	**0.033**	**0.028**

Table 2: RMSE scores for three path arrangement methods using GP reconstruction algorithm. The best score for each column is highlighted in bold.

cases. In addition, due to the previously noted division-by-zero problem SART often fails to produce scores. Therefore, using smoothness regularization like GP and TR helps to overcome this severely under-constrained situation.

If we look across all plots in Fig.3, it appears that the best path arrangement method is our optimization method, followed by random method and then multi-view method. The performance of the diagonal scheme does not improve after 20 paths. The orthogonal method (not shown) follows a similar trend but is worse than the diagonal method. The multi-view method also stops improving after 50 paths. This implies that when the number of paths increases, we should distribute them using more views. Therefore, when the number of paths is more than 50, more than 4 views should help to further improve the multi-view approach. However, this is not the focus of this paper and is not explored here. The "max min" method doesn't perform well, most likely due to the fact that it only focuses on the closest path to a pixel by ignoring the others. Table 2 compares the performance of top three path arrangement methods using the same GP algorithm. Our path optimization method produces the best results for all cases, which also passes the t-test against both multi-view and random methods with a confidence interval of 0.05.

5.3 Path optimization test

We now test the performance of our path arrangement optimization algorithm with different number of paths from 5 to 100. We assume that all walls are available for installing a path and the ROI is the whole cross section.

We initialize the simulated annealing by randomly assigning a region pair to a path and randomly selecting the path's end points within the corresponding available region. Fig.4a shows the total time taken by our optimization algorithm to converge. When the number of paths is very small such as 5, the optimization time is only one and half minute. When the number of paths increases to 100, the time increases to 20 hours. The number of iterations needed ranges between 200 and 600. Fig.4b shows how the current lowest uncertainty (best objective function value) varies with the number of iterations for the case of $M = 10$, which takes a total of 359 iterations. The uncertainty usually improves quick at the beginning, but improvement slows down gradually.

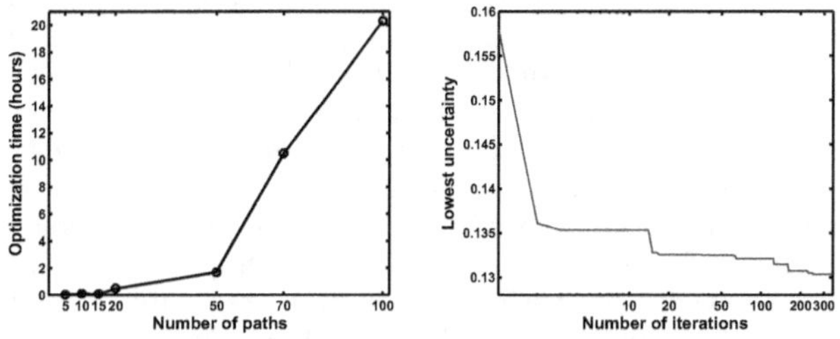

(a) (b)

Figure 4: Path arrangement optimization results. (a) shows the optimization time for different number of paths. (b) shows the evolution of objective function value over number of iterations (in log scale) for the case of $M = 10$ **paths.**

Fig.5 shows the optimized path arrangements for $M = 5$ and $M = 10$ cases. It worthy noting that for both cases, corner areas have more path presence than some center areas. We attribute this to the fact that it is harder to infer corner areas from other areas because they are less correlated with others. Therefore, dedicating some paths to corner areas help to reduce the overall uncertainty.

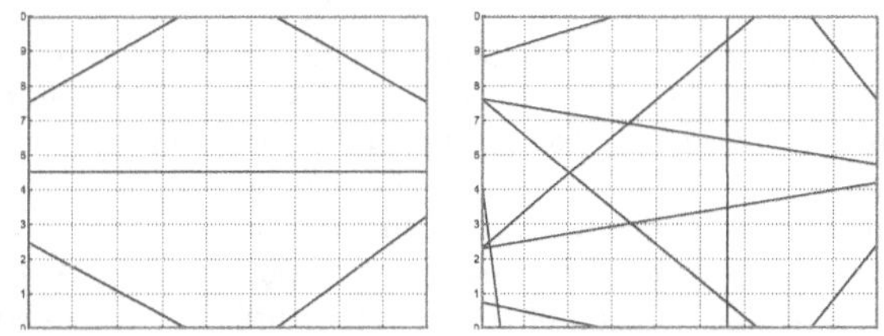

(a) 5 paths (b) 10 paths

Figure 5: Examples of optimized path arrangements.

By using the optimized path arrangements, we can also evaluate reconstruction algorithms as already shown in Fig.3e.

Fig.6 visually shows how reconstruction improves with the increasing number of paths using GP. The ground truth image (Fig.6g) appears to have four peaks. When M is small such as 5 and 10, the algorithm is only able to recover two peaks due to limited projection information. When M increases to 50, three peaks are recovered. The reconstructed image with $M = 100$ closely resembles the ground truth image.

5.4 Path optimization test with restrictions

In this section, we consider a more realistic test case as shown in Fig.2. First, mounting restrictions exist. On the first wall, there are four available regions with a range of [0.1 0.2], [0.25 0.4], [0.45 0.65] and [0.7 0.9], respectively. There is no available region on the second wall. The third wall has three available regions: [0.2 0.4], [0.7 0.8] and [0.85 0.95]. There is only one available region [0.2 0.5] on the fourth wall. In addition, ROI consists of two rectangles. The lower left corner and upper right corner of the first rectangle are located at $(0.1, 0.6)$ and $(0.4, 0.9)$, respectively. The lower left corner and upper right corner of second rectangle are located at $(0.35, 0.35)$ and $(0.65, 0.65)$, respectively. Our objective function will only sum up the posterior variances for pixels within ROI. We only consider $M = 5, 10, 15$ paths, because these small numbers are of more practical use.

So far, we show that our optimized path arrangement is better than multi-view and random path arrangement. This is not so impressive considering that the latter two methods are very simple and straightforward. Even if we don't have other path arrangement algorithms to compare with, we seek the answer to the following question: how does our result compare with ground truth best path arrangement in terms of RMSE measure? Because such ground truth is never known to us, we may attempt to randomly sample paths in the hope that one of the randomly generated path arrangements might be close to the ground truth.

To be able to achieve this, we randomly generate 10000 path arrangements. For each arrangement, we apply a reconstruction algorithm and compute the average RMSE. The random arrangement with the lowest RMSE is treated as the *best random* path arrangement. Fig.7 compares the RMSE of the best random path arrangement with that of our optimization result. Only TR and GP are used as the reconstruction algorithms, which leads to four RMSE curves. The GP based on optimized path arrangement (represented by "Optimized+GP") produces the lowest RMSE. This is significantly better than the second performer "Optimized+TR" with the highest p value at 0.002 for all cases.

Note that for this test, there are 19 region pairs. Even with $M = 5$, we have a total of $19^5 \approx 2.5 \times 10^6$ region pair to path assignments. This hasn't considered the end point locations of a path on an available region (continuous numbers). Therefore, the pool of 10000 random samples is too small to be able to include the ground truth best path arrangement. However, even with this "small" pool size, it takes 16 hours to find the best random path arrangement in the case of $M = 5$. In contrast, our optimization algorithm takes about 1 minute, 2 minutes and 4 minutes to converge for $M = 5$, $M = 10$ and $M = 15$, respectively.

Fig.2 show the final optimized path arrangement in the case of $M = 5$ paths. Comparing Fig.2 with Fig.5a, the optimization result without restrictions, we can see that in Fig.5a, paths tend to cover wider regions. This is because

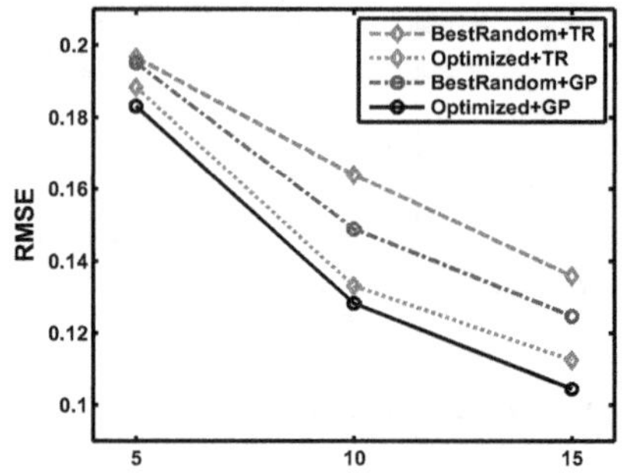

Figure 7: Comparing our optimized path arrangement with best random path arrangement.

the ROI for Fig.5a is the whole cross section while the ROI for Fig.2 is mostly upper left corner and center area. One may expect that in this case with such a small number of paths, all paths should cross the ROI area. Surprisingly, the 2-th path in Fig.2 doesn't follow this intuition. This can be attributed to the fact that a good path arrangement should not only gain information about ROI but also remove ambiguity caused by non-ROI areas. Path 1, 3, 4 and 5 already have a good coverage over ROI, but their projection values are also influenced by pixels around lower left corner. Instead of using path 2 to gain additional information for ROI, our algorithm chooses to use it to gain information about those non-ROI pixels. This turns out to reduce the overall uncertainty even more.

6. SUMMARY

Gas concentration reconstruction for coal-fired boiler is an important task in power industry. There are two aspects of this problem: how do we construct the image and how do we arrange paths. We propose to use Gaussian process to address both aspects under the same framework. We use the posterior mean as the reconstructed image and average posterior pixel variance as the objective function for path arrangement. A variety of tests are conducted to show the advantages of the proposed method.

Our algorithms have been implemented in Java and deployed in Siemens SPPA-P3000 control system as a important component in its combustion optimization module [16]. Combustion optimization is aimed at improving boiler efficiency and reducing emissions. A closed-loop optimization is achieved by manipulating fuel and air levels, with the help of our reconstructed image for key combustion components such as O2, CO, H2O and temperature. Fig.8a shows the work flow diagram of combustion optimization. Our algorithm is located in the block of "distribution calculation based on CAT" (CAT represents computer-aided tomography). Fig.8b shows that O2 distribution becomes better balanced with the closed loop control, which improves the boiler efficiency.

Fig.9 shows a separate user interface for path arrangement optimization, which mainly runs off-line. This software takes a boiler configuration file (with boiler geometry, number of paths, constraints and etc.) as input and exports the optimized path arrangement in an output file. The user can then use the output to design the TDLAS layout plan.

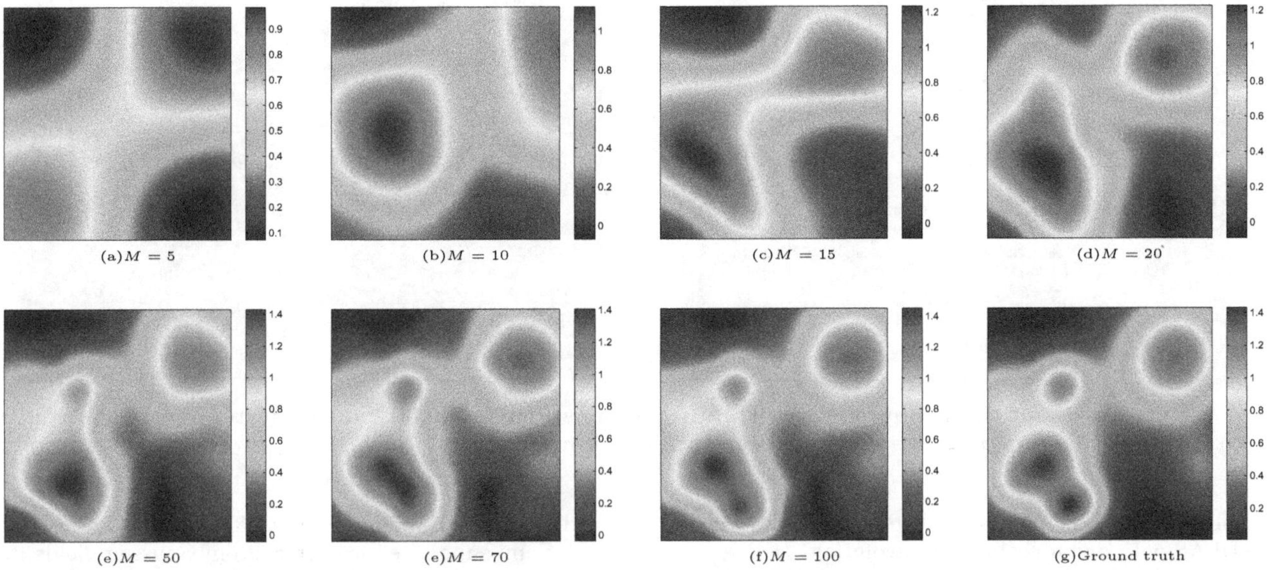

Figure 6: Comparing the reconstructed results with the ground truth with different number of paths.

Note that in our reconstruction algorithm, the reconstructed image is unbounded, which may cause a pixel value to be negative. This is against reality: a gas concentration cannot have negative values. We have improved this by converting the Gaussian process posterior distribution in (9) into a quadratic loss function. After introducing user specified lower and upper bound (e.g, lower bound is zero), we form a quadratic programming problem, which can be easily solved. The details are omitted here.

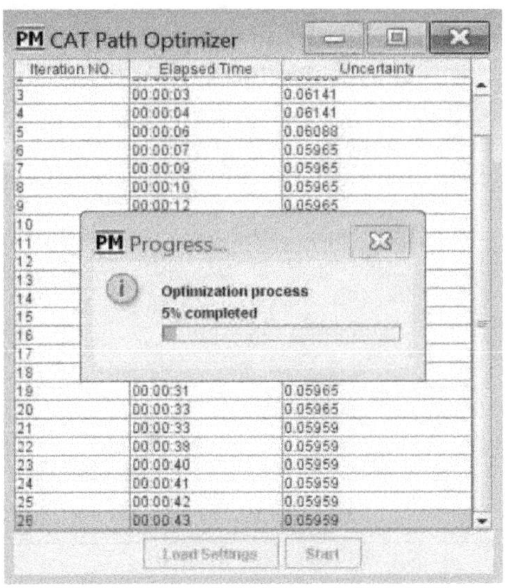

Figure 9: Path arrangement optimization user interface.

7. REFERENCES

[1] S. Angeli and E. Stiliaris. An accelerated algebraic reconstruction technique based on the Newton-Raphson scheme. In *IEEE Nuclear Science Symposium Conference Record*, 2009.

[2] S. Boyd and L. Vandenberghe. *Convex Optimization.* 2004.

[3] K. B. Chung, F. C. Gouldin, and G. J. Wolga. Experimental reconstruction of the spatial density distribution of a nonreacting flow with a small number of absorption measurements. *Applied Optics*, 34:5492–5500, August 1995.

[4] D. Fouskakis and D. Draper. Stochastic optimization: a review. *International Statistical Review*, 2002.

[5] A. Girard, J. Candela, R. Murray-smith, and C. E. Rasmussen. Gaussian process priors with uncertain inputs - application to multiple-step ahead time series forecasting. In *Advances in Neural Information Processing Systems*, 2002.

[6] A. Guha and I. Schoegl. Simulation of 2D tomographic TDLAS using algebraic reconstruction and Tikhonov regularization. In *8th US National Combustion Meeting*, 2013.

[7] R. K. Hanson, P. A. Kuntz, and C. H. Kruger. High-resolution spectroscopy of combustion gases using a tunable IR diode laser. *Applied Optics*, 16:2045–2048, August 1977.

[8] M. Jiang and G. Wang. Convergence of the simultaneous algebraic reconstruction technique (SART). *IEEE Trans. on Image Processing*, 12:957–961, August 2003.

[9] A. C. Kak and M. Slaney, editors. *Principles of Computerized Tomographic Imaging.* SIAM Press, 2001.

[10] H. Kim and J. Lee. Clustering based on Gaussian processes. *Neural Computation*, 19:3088–3107, 2007.

[11] C. Liu, L. Xu, Z. Cao, and H. McCann. Reconstruction of axisymmetric temperature and gas

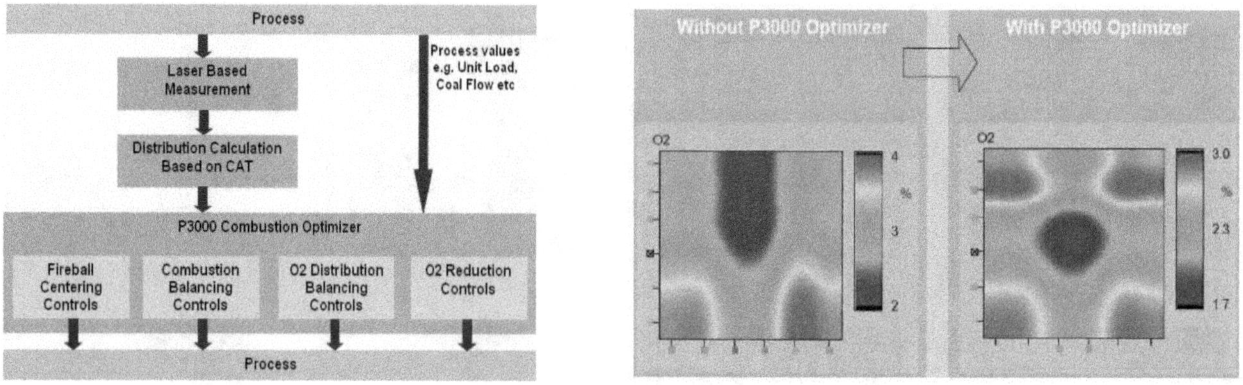

(a) (b)

Figure 8: Integration of the proposed algorithm in Siemens SPPA-P3000 control system (copied from [16]). (a) system work flow diagram. (b) combustion optimization example.

concentration distributions by combining fan-beam TDLAS with onion-peeling deconvolution. *IEEE Transactions on Instrumentation and Measurement*, 63:3067–3074, 2014.

[12] C. Liu, L. Xu, and Z.Cao. Measurement of axisymmetric temperature distributions using single view fan-beam TDLAS tomography. In *IEEE International Instrumentation and Measurement Technology Conference*, 2013.

[13] Z. Nadir, M. S. Brown, M. L. Comer, and C. A. Bouman. Tomographic reconstruction of flowing gases using sparse training. In *IEEE International Conference on Image Processing*, 2014.

[14] C. E. Rasmussen and C. K. I. Williams. *Gaussian Processes for Machine Learning.* MIT Press, 2006.

[15] M. Ravichandran and F. C. Gouldin. Reconstruction of smooth distributions from a limited number of projections. *Applied Optics*, 27:4084–4097, October 1988.

[16] S. Thavamani, M. Behmann, and T. Spaeth. Plant performance improvements by enhanced combustion through laser-based optimization. In *ISA Power Industry Division (POWID) Symposium*, 2012.

[17] J. Tian and K. Ma. A survey on super-resolution imaging. *Signal, Image and Video Processing*, 5:329–342, 2011.

[18] M. E. Tipping and C. M. Bishop. Bayesian image super-resolution. In *Advances in Neural Information Processing Systems*, 2002.

[19] A. Wächter and L. T. Biegler. On the implementation of a primal-dual interior point filter line search algorithm for large-scale nonlinear programming. *Mathematical Programming*, 106:25–57, 2006.

[20] F. Wang, Q. Wu, Q. Huang, H. Zhang, J. Yan, and K. Cen. Simultaneous measurement of 2-dimensional H_2O concentration and temperature distribution in premixed methane/air flame using TDLAS-based tomography technology. *Optics Communications*, 346:53–63, 2015.

[21] C. Yuan. A Bayesian approach for gas concentration reconstruction based on tunable diode laser absorption spectroscopy. In *International Conference on Acoustics, Speech, and Signal Processing*, 2012.

[22] X. Zhu, J. Lafferty, and Z. Ghahramani. Semi-supervised learning: From Gaussian fields to Gaussian processes. *Technical Report CMU-CS-03-175, Carnegie Mellon University*, 2003.

Annotating Needles in the Haystack without Looking: Product Information Extraction from Emails*

Weinan Zhang[1], Amr Ahmed[2], Jie Yang[2], Vanja Josifovski[3], Alex J. Smola[4]
[1]University College London, [2]Google Inc.
[3]Pinterest, [4]Carnegie Mellon University
w.zhang@cs.ucl.ac.uk, {amra,yangjie}@google.com
vanja.josifovski@gmail.com, alex@smola.org

ABSTRACT

Business-to-consumer (B2C) emails are usually generated by filling structured user data (e.g. purchase, event) into templates. Extracting structured data from B2C emails allows users to track important information on various devices.

However, it also poses several challenges, due to the requirement of short response time for massive data volume, the diversity and complexity of templates, and the privacy and legal constraints. Most notably, email data is legally protected content, which means no one except the receiver can review the messages or derived information.

In this paper we first introduce a system which can extract structured information automatically without requiring human review of any personal content. Then we focus on how to annotate product names from the extracted texts, which is one of the most difficult problems in the system. Neither general learning methods, such as binary classifiers, nor more specific structure learning methods, such as Conditional Random Field (CRF), can solve this problem well.

To accomplish this task, we propose a hybrid approach, which basically trains a CRF model using the labels predicted by binary classifiers (weak learners). However, the performance of weak learners can be low, therefore we use Expectation Maximization (EM) algorithm on CRF to remove the noise and improve the accuracy, *without* the need to label and inspect specific emails. In our experiments, the EM-CRF model can significantly improve the product name annotations over the weak learners and plain CRFs.

Keywords

Structured information extraction, Business intelligence

1. INTRODUCTION

Email is arguably one of the most successful applications on the Internet. In the early days email was primarily used for short textual user-to-user communication. Today, this role has been largely overtaken by chat and social network platforms. Now email increasingly serves as a repository of transactional information such as receipts from many business-to-consumer (B2C) interactions. Email messages have several properties that make them appealing for such communication: the communication is asynchronous — it does not require both parties to be present at the same time; it is virtually infallible; email provides persistent storage; finally it is mostly private, requiring authentication for access.

While email is a very suitable communication *medium* for such information exchange, it was originally designed for PC screens with manageable amount of messages. However, nowadays more and more people are checking emails from mobile devices with smaller screens. It will be much more convenient and efficient for users to track important information without having to read every email on mobile devices. Actually it is a key feature of Google Now, just as those displayed in Figure 1.

Most B2C emails are generated by filling a template with values from databases. We call it a templatized email. For example, retailers make receipt emails by populating order details (order number, items and prices, etc.) into a predefined template, and shipment details (tracking number, delivery date, etc.) into another template. Usually users only look for those details, not the templates or static contents. In other words, users only want to see the structured data from databases, which is embedded in the templates. In this paper we will propose a system to extract those data from emails, also known as "wrapper" [12] or "parser" [19] in the literature.

A simple but accurate way is to manually create a parser for each template. However, due to the privacy constraints, it will rely on the vendors to provide the templates, or hire people to craft the extraction rules using donated emails of this template. However, both approaches are not scalable and are vulnerable to changes of the template.

Another more desirable approach is to automatically extract the structured data from those templatized emails: construct the template from similar documents, extract the data, and annotate the semantic types (i.e., price, shipping address, delivery date, etc.) of those data entries. Eventually, the extracted structure data can be rendered in a different UI and served to the users, as what Google Now does. We will introduce such a system in section 3.

1.1 Challenges

Privacy. By law and by policy commercial email providers are held to a very high privacy standard. Users can assume rightfully that their messages are not read by other humans. Most major Internet companies have established protocols to ensure such guarantees automatically. This makes it impossible to generate broad training data of annotated emails, or to visually inspect the results of extractors applied to emails. In other words, unlike traditional information extraction scenarios, we have no access to *both the input and output* of the extractors, except a very small amount of donated emails.

*Work done while all the authors were at Google.

KDD'15, August 11-14, 2015, Sydney, NSW, Australia
ACM 978-1-4503-3664-2/15/08.
http://dx.doi.org/10.1145/2783258.2788580.

Figure 1: Structured information presentation in Google Now (1/2014) from B2C shipping emails on Android 4.4. The product name, shipping date, quantity and retailer are extracted and annotated. The user can check shipment details via the extracted tracking number rather than needing to read the original emails.

Every design and implementation shall respect and protect user privacy. That is why it is hard for us to get more samples to analyze, find heuristics and train good models over the data we cannot see.

Diversity. Different websites have very different templates, the same site can have multiple templates (order confirmation, cancellation, etc.), and even the same template may yield different variants for personalized experience. In general, we are generating millions of templates from billions of emails. Each template has its own contents and characteristics, but we only have some donated emails from a small number of templates to train models, which in turn could yield very biased models with poor performance when apply to new templates. For example, a wrapper or model trained from Google Play receipts may not work well on Newegg.com receipts, but the problem is that we do not have donated training samples from Newegg, nor allow to view any personal emails from Newegg.

Complexity. In early days, many email templates only have one or a few simple tables, but now the HTML codes used in email become much more complex and nested for better visual presentation. In addition, a template consists of various semantic types. For instance, a purchase receipt may contain customer ID, order number, tracking number and URL, delivery date, shipping address, product name, total price, and so on, while an event email can have a totally different set of types.

Scalability. We are dealing with extremely large data, and have to process it in a very short time since people expect emails to arrive instantly. The daily volume of emails are a number of times larger than the web pages indexed per day by well known search engines, and it grows fast. Therefore, efficiency and scalability are the key issues of the system.

In summary, rigid user privacy constraints, diversity, complexity and lack of data are new challenges to wrapper techniques proposed previously for scalable email systems.

1.2 Problem Scope and Contributions

In this paper we address the problem of extracting personal structured information in the presence of reviewing restrictions and variations in emails. We take advantage of the repetitive structure of emails to induce templates. For the content that is not part of the template, i.e., the text regions changing in every email, we need annotate the semantic type so that it can be properly rendered to the user. Some types are easy to annotate, such as date, address, price, etc. We can pre-annotate them using some existing annotators. This paper focuses on non-trivial types without mature annotators, particularly the product name in email receipts, which was one of the most difficult problems in the system. Specifically, after we extract a text without any pre-annotated type, we need to predict if it is a product name or not. We can also apply the same solution to other non-trivial types.

Due to the diversity and lack of training data on all templates, general supervised learning models, such as binary classifiers, have poor performance for this task, although they can be trained with limited data. On the other hand, structure learning methods, such as Conditional Random Field (CRF), are more specific and accurate for inducing structures in templates of sufficient training samples, but it usually requires training labels of every template. Please note, here the elements of the structure learned by CRF are semantic types, not the HTML nodes or text regions. When we apply CRF on a templatized email, it can annotate the types of each node or region[1], such that we can use it to predict the type of any extracted text. If we train a CRF model from some templates and then apply to others templates, its predictions still could be poor, again due to diversity of the data and complexity of the model.

To solve this dilemma, we propose a hybrid method, which takes advantages of both the generality of classifiers and specificity of structure learners. The former can generate sufficient training labels, although it has low quality, and then we rely on the latter to remove the noise and discover high accurate structures, by applying an Expectation Maximization (EM) algorithm. In our experiments, the EM-CRF model can significantly improve the product name annotations over the weak learners and simple CRFs. In sum, our main contributions are:

- We describe the problem of extracting private structured information from email messages under privacy constraints and propose an appropriate training mechanism that does not require labels or human review.
- We propose an EM-style algorithm to compensate for the noise of the weak classifier using a CRF.
- We demonstrate the effectiveness of the framework over a large scale of emails, achieving 30% improvement in F1 measure.

2. RELATED WORK

Information extraction on the Web. Information extraction is a well-studied problem. In particular, since most commercial emails contain HTML, it is reasonable to assume that tools developed for Web pages could conceivably be extended to apply to emails, too. In fact, we will take advantage of this strategy in our model.

[7, 15] present heuristic rules to extract data from Web pages using characteristics of HTML files. [8] uses HTML tag strings to find useful patterns for extraction. In [30, 44], the data records from the Web pages are detected by visual features such as gaps between blocks, and then tagged based on the pre-detected tree structure in the HTML. In [12, 13], different extraction rules are incorporated in an automatic fashion. The above work heavily relies on the induced Web page templates and lack of the advantages of leveraging the other annotated data fields to adaptively improve the extraction/annotation performance, which can be problematic when the templates are mismatched. Therefore, learning based methods are proposed. In [46], the authors infer a hierarchical CRF model to simultaneously detect the data records and label the attributes. [45] exploits additional information about page element alignment by using a 2D-CRFs model. A more integrated model which dynamically learns the hierarchical structure of the Web page and labels the attributes is proposed in [47]. A prerequisite of these works is that the Web pages in the training data should be

[1]Region means the text of a particular node in the DOM tree [18] of the email HTML. It is the unit for labeling here.

fully labeled to train the CRFs models. This is impractical in our scenario where emails are not human accessible.

Email. Email is always among the most sensitive data on the Internet due to users' privacy concerns. Thus data availability is one of the main constraints for any of research or product work on emails [26]. Most work on emails content mining is concerned with anti-spam [4, 9], where the task is to perform binary classification to figure out whether an email is a spam or not [13, 20]. Moreover, classification [26, 24] and clustering [29, 27] techniques are explored for email message categorization into the user's predefined hierarchical folders. This task has some unique challenges [6], such as the varying of users' email filing habits, and the strong imbalance of different email folders. In previous works on email content mining, the email data used is always in the bag-of-words form [26], even if there are some sections (e.g. `from`, `to`, `subject` and `body`). This is quite different from our email data, where the HTML structure and tags can be heavily utilized to improve performance and dynamically include content (such as up-to-date advertisements). For machine generate emails, templating and threading are also studied to help re-organize the email list presenting [1]. Such work is different with our problem because it does not need to recognize the type of each text field (or region). Besides the email content mining, there are some works on email social network analysis and mining [3, 14] to infer email priority [12], to detect spam [41], and to analyze the social hierarchy [38] inherent in the data.

Semi-supervised Learning. To supplement expensive or even unavailable labeled data researchers have started devising semi-supervised learning algorithms which take advantage of additional unlabeled data. See e.g. [48] for an extensive summary and review. Usually semi-supervised algorithms take advantage of a reasonable hypothesis based on which the unlabeled data could be utilized to improve the learning model [49]. In the context of NLP, such a hypothesis can be modeled e.g. via generalized expectation criteria [31] which assumes that conditional class probabilities satisfy moment constraints; regularization via posterior constraints [17]; or by using extrinsic objectives [19]. Optimization proceeds e.g. via Lagrangian relaxation and dual decomposition [39, 40].

In our work we define a hypothesis class using structured extraction via a CRF and employ automatically generated (low-accuracy) annotations as (inconsistent) training data. In other words, we learn constraints between adjacent labels as a mechanism for extracting information about the structure of the documents. Moreover, we cannot assess the quality of the results directly since, due to privacy constraints, we are not allowed to view the extractions. This is what makes it highly challenging to apply moment constraints directly, since this would require knowledge about the commercial content of the emails in question.

Note that our work also links to information extraction with weak supervision, which was originally proposed for biomedical entity recognition [11] and then applied in other scenarios such as entity recognition from multi-lingual corpora [25] and search queries [34], and entity relation extraction [32, 21]. The 'weak' supervision, in previous work, normally comes from direct text matches with some knowledge bases. However, as pointed out in [37, 21], when the target text is very diverse and not aligned with the knowledge bases, supervision helps little. In our scenario with emails as input, the text is quite different and most of the entities such as product names and addresses have multiple variants. Thus it provides little help from the direct match of the entity names. Our approach can be viewed as a form of weak supervision with a novel notion of weak signals (i.e. low-accuracy annotations) coupled with domain adaptation.

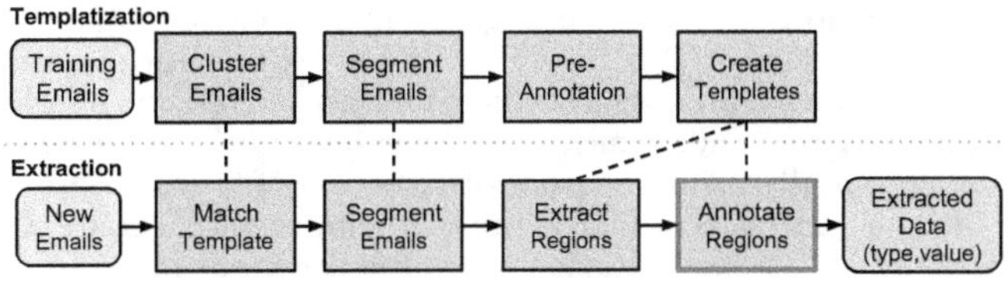

Figure 2: System components overview.

3. SYSTEM OVERVIEW

This section introduces the information extraction system, or wrapper, we developed for large scale email systems.

Some regions in a templatized email are static and do not change for different users or orders, which we call "fixed regions". Other regions vary in every document, such as `Order Number`, `Product` name. We call them "transient regions". Usually only transient regions contain user relevant data, and the template is made from fixed regions. We need to separate transient regions from fixed ones and annotate the semantic type of each transient region.

Figure 2 illustrates the components of our system. Basically, the system has the following major components.

Clustering. The very first step is to split emails by senders, then cluster similar emails which may be generated from a common template. Emails from the same sender are not necessarily from the same template, for instance some retailers may use one email address to send both order confirmation and shipment notification emails. It is also possible that multiple senders share the same template, which can be solved by merging clusters of different senders.

To preserve user privacy and avoid templatizing consumer-to-consumer (C2C) emails, we only induce templates from large clusters which contain many receivers and similar e-mails. Besides, it is easier to distinguish transient regions and fixed regions using lots of similar emails from the same cluster.

Templatization. We induce a template from emails of each cluster. First we segment each email into regions. The major difference between HTML and text emails is how we segment and locate the regions. Each HTML page has a DOM tree [18] and we can regard a text node as a region and use XPath to locate a node in the tree, while for plain text emails we need construct a finite-state machine (FSM) to represent the structure. Moreover, HTML pages may contain tables or hyperlinks, which can be used to get more features. The processes are similar for HTML and text emails. Without loss of generality, we only consider HTML emails below.

We declare regions with high document frequency as fixed. The rest is transient. Eventually a template consists of a dictionary of values in fixed regions (e.g. "Your order of", "Thank you!") and the location (XPath) of transient regions.

We also pre-annotate easy types, such as `Price`, `Address`, `Date` and store the mapping from XPath to its pre-annotated semantic type in the template, because usually the same node among templatized emails has a consistent type. For example, the cell of third row and fourth column of the second table is always `Price`. In case it is inconsistent, we store all the possible types with their probability.

Extraction. The previous steps are done offline, while extraction is performed online. That is, when a non-spam B2C email is received, we find its cluster and template, segment the email to regions, match the regions in the template, decide if it is a fixed region or transient, and finally get its type by the annotation module. The outcome is a list of (type, value) tuples, the structured data we need.

Annotation. If a transient region only has one pre-annotated type, we assign it this type. For regions with multiple candidate types, we either use the most likely type, or let the annotator to decide which one to use based on the text value, potentially using the prior distribution of types, or apply some heuristics according to the surrounding texts (context). Usually only a small portion of transient regions in an email have pre-annotated types. The others are `Unknown`.

For purchase emails, we currently only have one annotator to predict whether the value of an unknown regions is `Product`. However, it is a non-trivial task. Different products may have very similar names, and the same product could have quite different names as well, because the retailers can choose any form to present the products to users. Some product names are very short, such as "9" (a movie) or "hi" (a song). It is very common to include some product specifications in the name, or intentionally add some terms for "search engine optimization". In addition, many emails include recommendations or ads, which also contain production names. As the growing of products available online, it is almost impossible to maintain a database of product names.

The rest of the paper focuses on how to annotate product name in transient regions of unknown type.

4. STATISTICAL MODEL

4.1 Weak Annotations

The low accuracy estimators that we have at our disposal are all binary. That is, for a given position they estimate e.g. the probability of it being a number, or a product name, or a date. In other words, for each position i for document x_j we have the probability

$$\pi_{ij} := p_{\text{weak}}(y_i = y_i^* | i, x_j) \tag{1}$$

indicating the probability of the label y_i, as inferred from a weak, low-accuracy heuristic p_{weak}, being equal to the true label y_i^*. Note that there is no need that these probabilities are properly normalized, i.e. typically we will have $\sum_{y_i} \pi_{ij} \neq 1$, as another form of normalization will be given in (10). We simply require that the probabilities are bounded, i.e. $\pi_{ij} \in [0, 1]$.

To convert this information into an actionable statistical model we follow the lines of [23]. That is, we treat the above problem as one of observing the correct label (denoted as t_i = TRUE) with probability π_{ij} for every position i, as specified by the low-accuracy estimator. In this case, the probability of inferring the correct labels for x_j is given by

$$p(\text{correct}|x_j, \theta) = \sum_{(y_1,\ldots,y_n)} \Big[\prod_{i=1}^{n} \pi_{ij}\Big] p(y_1, \ldots, y_n | x_j, \theta). \tag{2}$$

Here $p(y_1, \ldots y_n | x_j, \theta)$ denotes the CRF modeling a non-trivial joint probability over annotations. Moreover, we assume that the correct label distribution factorizes, hence the $\prod_i \pi_{ij}$ term to capture the joint probability of the inferred labels $(y_1, \ldots, y_n)$ being correct. The model of Figure 3 captures the basic idea.

In the special case of unstructured estimation this reduces to the model of [23]. Moreover, in the case where $\pi_{ij} \in \{0, 1\}$ this reduces to the setting where we simply sum over a subset of possible label combinations. Unfortunately, in all the above settings $p(\text{correct}|x, \theta)$ is not log-concave in $p(y|x, \theta)$. This complicates matters in terms of inference and we will need to resort to DC programming [22], often also referred to loosely as Expectation Maximization in this context, for optimization. Before going into specifics let us briefly describe the statistical model.

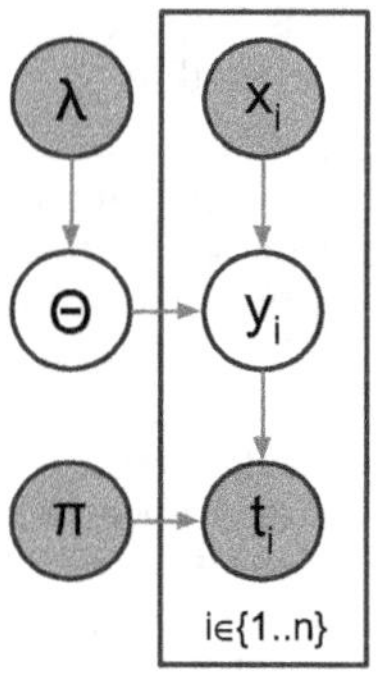

Figure 3: Partial observation model. Data x_i is generated iid from some underlying distribution $p(x_i)$, and labels are drawn from $p(y_i|x_i, \theta)$, as parameterized by θ in the form of a CRF. In turn, θ comes with its prior $p(\theta|\lambda)$ e.g. in the form of a Normal distribution. Finally, t_i, the binary variable showing whether the label y_i is the correct label y_i^*, is generated according to π_{ij}. We dropped dependency of y_i on x_{-i} as in standard CRF and the document index j for figure simplicity (see text for more details).

4.2 Conditional Random Fields

The primary benefit of using a CRF is that we may exploit structural correlation between adjacent labels [28]. This is achieved by expressing the entire chain of labels as a conditional undirected graphical model by multiplying adjacent clique potentials. In other words, we posit that the conditional label distribution is given by an exponential family model

$$p(y|x_j, \theta) = \exp\Big(\langle \phi(x_j, y), \theta \rangle - g(\theta|x_j)\Big), \tag{3}$$

where $\phi(x_j, y)$ is the feature function and the parameter θ acts as the coefficients of the features. Here $g(\theta|x_j)$ is the so-called conditional log-partition function ensuring that $p(y|x_j, \theta)$ is properly normalized as a distribution over y. It is well known that $g(\theta|x_j)$ is a convex function in θ. Computing $g(\theta|x_j)$ and its derivatives can be accomplished by dynamic programming. For this purpose we exploit that

$$g(\theta|x_j) = \log \sum_y \exp\left(\langle \phi(x_j, y), \theta \rangle\right), \tag{4}$$

$$\partial_\theta g(\theta|x_j) = \sum_y \phi(x_j, y) \exp\left(\langle \phi(x_j, y), \theta \rangle - g(\theta|x_j)\right) \tag{5}$$

$$= \mathbf{E}_{y \sim p(y|x_j, \theta)} \left[\phi(x_j, y)\right]. \tag{6}$$

Since the sufficient statistics $\phi(x_j, y)$ decomposes into terms on maximal cliques $(\ldots \phi(y_i, x_j), \phi(y_i, y_{i+1}, x_j), \ldots)$, it is sufficient to have access to $p(y_i|x_j, \theta)$ and $p(y_i, y_{i+1}|x_j, \theta)$ if we deal with the chain CRF [28]. Both terms can be efficiently computed using dynamic programming for $\mathbf{E}_{y_i|x_j,\theta}\left[\phi(y_i, x_{ij})\right]$ and $\mathbf{E}_{(y_i, y_{i+1})|x_j, \theta}\left[\phi(y_i, y_{i+1}, x_j)\right]$ respectively. The forward-backward algorithm suffices since we are dealing with a chain model. For more sophisticated structural evaluation models we would need to resort to a matching strategy satisfying the conditions of the Generalized Distributive Law [2] on the (log,+) semiring.

4.3 Expectation Maximization

Compared with standard CRF models, the key challenge in our scenario is that we do not have access to the correct labels y^* directly but rather only via π_{ij} as obtained by rather much weaker models. Hence, instead of dealing with the log-likelihood $\log p(y|x_j, \theta)$ from (3), we are dealing with $\log \sum_y [\prod_i \pi_{ij}] p(y|x_j, \theta)$ from (2), which is a nonconvex objective function. More specifically, in the case of a CRF the objective decomposes via

$$\log \sum_y \Big[\prod_i \pi_{ij}\Big] p(y|x_j, \theta) \tag{7}$$

$$= \log \sum_y \Big[\prod_i \pi_{ij}\Big] \exp\left(\langle \phi(x_j, y), \theta \rangle\right) - g(\theta|x_j). \tag{8}$$

As can be seen, the first term is convex and the second is concave. Hence, for the purpose of maximizing the log-likelihood

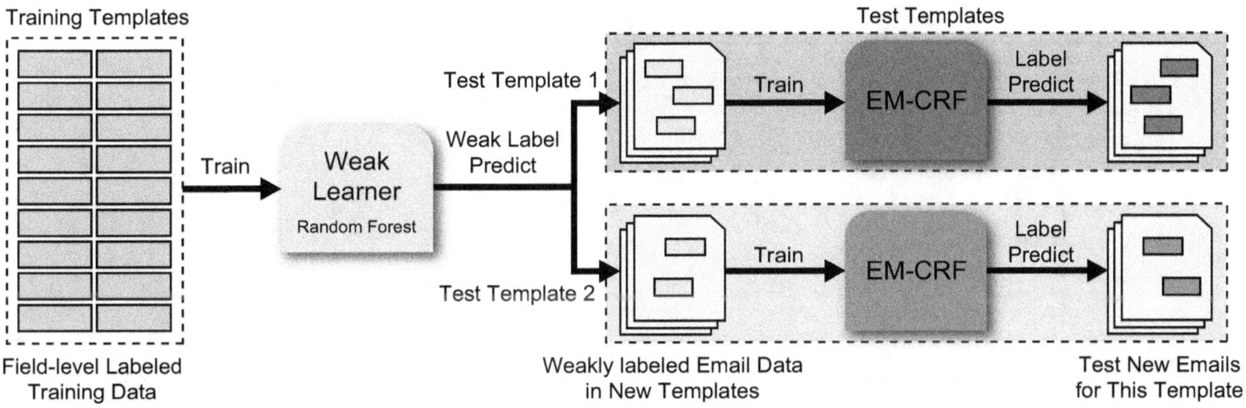

Figure 4: Data flow for training and evaluating the EM-CRF model. Auxiliary annotated regions are used to generate a random forest classifier as low-accuracy annotator of the template-specific emails. This data is then fed into the EM-CRF model to perform prediction on new documents.

Algorithm 1 CRF Inference with Side Labels (EM-CRF)

Require: Document set $\{x_j\}$
Require: Initial distributions $q_j(y)$, e.g. $q_j(y) = \text{const.}$
  Initialize CRFs parameters θ, e.g. $\theta = 0$.
  while not converged **do**
    for each document x_j **do**
      E-step: Update label distribution $q_j(y)$ via (10)
    end for
    M-Step: Train CRFs parameters θ maximizing (7)
  end while
  return θ

we can lower-bound it by linearizing the first term via a Taylor approximation. This yields

$$\begin{aligned}&\log \sum_y \Big[\prod_i \pi_{ij}\Big] p(y|x_j,\theta)\\ \geq& c + \Big\langle \theta, \partial_\theta \log \sum_y \Big[\prod_i \pi_{ij}\Big] \exp\left(\langle \phi(x_j,y),\theta\rangle\right)\Big\rangle - g(\theta|x_j)\\ =& c + \Big\langle \theta, \sum_y q_j(y)\phi(x_j,y)\Big\rangle - g(\theta|x_j),\end{aligned} \tag{9}$$

where the distribution $q_j(y)$ is given by

$$q_j(y) = \frac{[\prod_i \pi_{ij}] \exp\left(\langle \phi(x_j,y),\theta\rangle\right)}{\sum_{y'} [\prod_i \pi_{ij}] \exp\left(\langle \phi(x_j,y'),\theta\rangle\right)} \propto \Big[\prod_i \pi_{ij}\Big] p(y|x_j,\theta). \tag{10}$$

Comparing with (3), the likelihood calculation in (9) takes the weighted average of $\phi(x_j, y)$ across the candidate labels y w.r.t. $q_j(y)$. In other words, we re-weight the conditional label estimates according to the outcomes of the low-accuracy annotators and the CRF model prediction using the current weight θ. Subsequently terms are renormalized.

Optimization proceeds by alternating between maximization of the lower bound of the log posterior over θ using the current estimate of label distribution $q_j(y)$ and by recomputing a new approximation $q_j(y)$ using the current estimate of CRF-weights θ. Note that by construction the lower bound is tight at the point of expansion. This follows directly from the fact that Taylor expansions are exact at the point of expansion. To train the CRF in the M-step, we generate a set of candidate labels for each sequence and weight each of them using $q_j(y)$, and then use a standard convex solver to maximize (7). We add an L_2 penalty on the weights θ of the CRF for regularization as is common in structured estimation. Algorithm 1 summarizes the inference procedure.

5. NEEDLES IN THE HAYSTACK

5.1 Setup

The key challenge in the experimental setup is to demonstrate the efficacy of the algorithm without the need for explicitly labeled training or test data and without the need to inspect the data, e.g. by means of editors. Yet, at the same time we want to have more directly quantifiable quantities than, say, predictive log-likelihoods. This makes assessment of the approach rather difficult.

The assumption is that while the templates might differ, we can at the very least assume that within a given template, the structure is sufficiently similar to apply a given CRF model. That is, we assume that each template comes with its own CRF model. In production, the data flow is as follows:

1. Human labeled region data from text unrelated to user's emails is used to train a random forest as the low-accuracy learner. This data contains only two possible labels — `Product` and `Other`. All the training data are performed over emails and templates that do not occur in test templates.
   Given the low quality estimator, we apply it to unlabeled emails to infer new templates. This allows us to mark up potential regions as `Product`.
2. In addition to the manually labeled auxiliary data we use a set of pre-annotators (independent of the email) to annotate easy types such as `Price`, `Email Address` and `Order Number` based on the textual description of the field. These annotators can be made from some heuristics or regular expressions.
3. For each new template (i.e. the templates from other senders or the new templates from the same senders) use the weak learner's prediction as weighted labels to train an EM-CRF model.
4. For each new email in the template we use the corresponding EM-CRF to predict the labels.

Figure 4 describes the data flow in such an environment. Note that training and test set are entirely disjoint. That is, emails required for testing the EM-CRF model are not used in the training of the EM-CRF.

In the above description, we assumed that the HTML template structure is fully given, that is, the template is entirely static with the only changes being relevant fields in question (e.g. purchase emails from a given sender). Section 6.2 provides results on the performance of the EM-CRF model in this context. Secondly, whenever the HTML structure is variable, with a similar method from [1], we can induce vari-

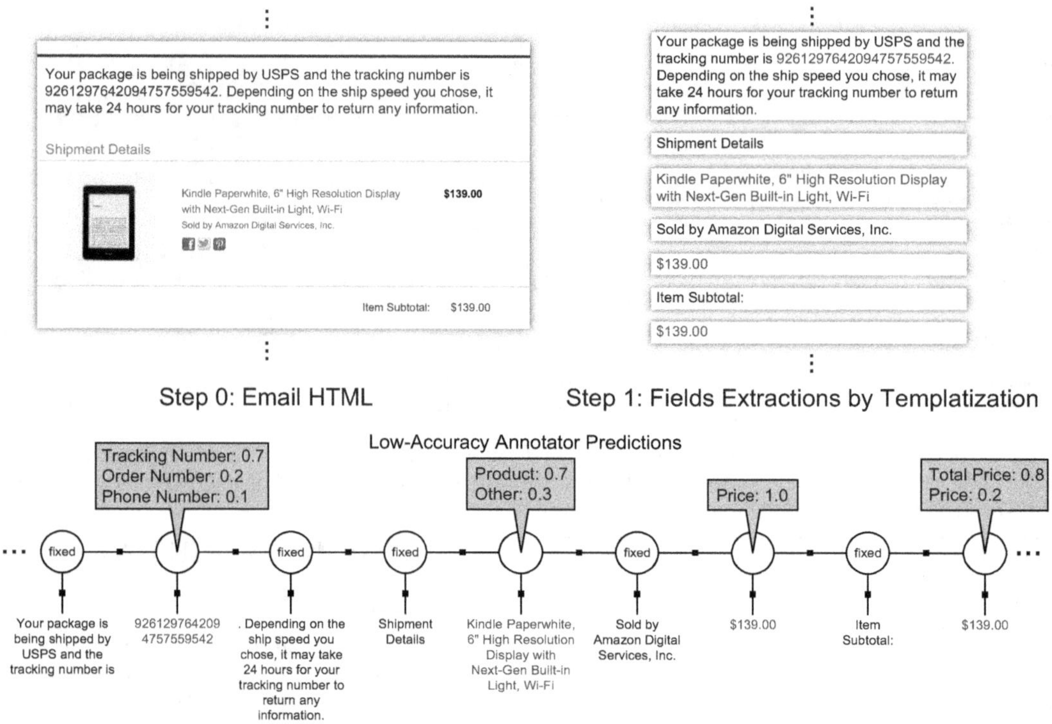

Figure 5: Ingestion of an HTML email. Text is segmented into snippets according to the DOM tree. The labels for the variable regions are unknown. The low-accuracy predicted labels are used to initialize the CRF.

able and static contents using standard automatic methods based on text frequencies across emails in the same template.

5.2 From Email HTML to CRFs Data

Given an email in HTML, we need to transform it into a representation amenable to a CRF. This requires two stages — the actual segmentation and the annotation of content with low-accuracy classifiers, as illustrated in Figure 5.

Step 1. We begin by segment emails to regions using the system we described in section 3. The sequence of the text regions follows their order in the DOM tree of the HTML file. Some text regions are fixed, as part of the template, and some are transient, which may already have semantic types from pre-annotators. Moreover, some text regions may be highly relevant and specific to a receipt although they share the same DOM tree node with surrounding template text. For example, the order number 9261297642094757559542 as shown in step 1 of Figure 5. In such cases, the text regions will be further segmented (see step 2 of Figure 5).

Step 2. We align these text regions to build the linear CRFs data. The label of each fixed region of the template is set as `Fixed`, while the other regions will be given by the low-accuracy annotator (e.g. `Product`, `Other`) and pre-annotated types (e.g. `Price`, `Email Address`, etc.)

Compared with a more traditional word-level CRF annotator, we allow for the segments to contain several words. As such a possible problem is that the text features may not match across documents. In practice this turns out to be less of a problem than anticipated. This is due to two reasons: firstly, the template text regions are almost always repetitive; secondly, even for a new non-template node text, its label can be initially induced by the low-accuracy annotator or the manually crafted rules.

5.3 Training the Low-accuracy Annotator

The low-accuracy annotators are essentially binary classifiers which generate a conditional class probability. There are 32 high-level features of the following categories:

Content Based Number of words, number of digits, having a hyper-link, inside a table, etc.

Context Based Minimum and average distance to regions of price, order number, table header, etc.

Search Based If we send this text as a query to a search engine, how many results are from retailer domains.

Knowledge Based Find the knowledge graph entities in the text, and see how many of them are related to product or brand.

Annotation Based How much this text look like a price, date, address, time, etc.

We tried using N-Gram features, but it did not work well because first it largely increases the dimensionality, and second the feature distribution from one domain can be very different from another domain. Feature selection or reduction does not help either.

In total, we have 66,494 labeled regions generated from 2,310 *user donated* emails. Among these labeled regions, there are 2,740 `Product` regions and 45,637 non-product (`Other`) regions. As noted before, some of these regions are pre-annotated as `Price`, `Date`, `Time`, `Email Address`, `Address`, etc. These are highly accurate for easy fields and we regard them as ground truth throughout the experiments. We only focus on the harder task of detecting product name in the emails. We use this data to train the low-accuracy annotator. In total, we compare 7 different binary classifiers, as illustrated in Table 1.

LogRegL2 Logistic regression with ℓ_2 penalization [20]
LogRegL1 Logistic regression with ℓ_1 penalization [35]
CART Classification and Regression Trees [33]
MARS Multivariate Adaptive Regression Splines [16]
GBM Generalized Boosted Regression Models [36]
RandFor Random Forests [5]
SVM Support Vector Machines [10]

Model selection parameters inherent in the above algorithms are adjusted using cross validation in an automatic fashion.

Table 1: Low-accuracy annotator performance. The estimators are trained on dataset that is not used anywhere else in the rest of the experiments.

model	precision	recall	F1	AUC	runtime
LogRegL2	0.701	0.329	0.448	0.938	9.51
LogRegL1	0.692	0.399	0.507	0.943	11.26
CART	0.701	0.452	0.549	0.834	2.55
MARS	0.727	0.294	0.418	0.949	3.51
GBM	0.780	0.284	0.417	0.950	20.37
RandFor	**0.872**	**0.664**	**0.754**	**0.974**	17.02
SVM	0.846	0.445	0.583	0.935	957.66

`LogRegL2`, `LogRegL1` and `SVM` are linear models, the others are all nonlinear. We observe that `RandFor` provides the best prediction performance while having high computational efficiency. This is not too surprising given that it approximates a nonlinear Pitman estimator in the version space of trees. Consequently we use Random Forests as our low-accuracy region annotator in our work.

5.4 Training the EM-CRF

Based on the low-accuracy annotation we next infer the EM-CRF model as discussed in Section 4. More specifically, the low-accuracy annotator is used to obtain an initial estimate $q_j(y)$ of a region being a product. This allows us to tag the emails for new (or unseen) templates. These are then used to train the EM-CRF model for each template. We proceed by alternating between computing a convex upper bound on the negative log-posterior of the model, i.e. the negative log-likelihood and the Gaussian log-prior, and by invoking an off-the-shelf CRF inference algorithm using the probability estimates $q_j(y)$ for a weighted set of labels.

We perform 4-fold cross validation to test our model. For each test template we sample 75% of its emails and remove their labels to simulate regular unlabeled data. We apply a hand-tuned region annotator to detect specific regions such as `Price`, `Email Address`, and `Order Number`. For the regions labeled as `Product` or `Other`, we apply the weak learner to generate a probability of this region being labeled as `Product`. After that, we train an EM-CRF model for this template using the weighted (and noisy) labeled emails. Finally, for each template we test the EM-CRF model on the remaining 25% labeled emails.

6. EXPERIMENTAL RESULTS

6.1 Baseline

To illustrate the benefit of the EM-CRF approach over a plain CRF model we also trained a CRF model directly using the low-accuracy annotator's predictions. In this case we used the maximum likelihood annotation of the regions rather than the label probabilities. It is to be expected that this approach will still benefit from the regularity properties of the document. For instance, if in a template the `Product` region is always followed by a `Quantity` region and then a `Price` region, one would expect that the potential $\langle\phi(y_i, y_{i+1}), \theta_{yy}\rangle$ capturing adjacent labels would model this correlation. We call this model **CRF-Max** (since it used the maximum likelihood estimation of the low-accuracy annotator).

A second very natural baseline is to use the Weak Learning (**WL**) directly, i.e. to output just the prediction of the low-accuracy estimator. We expect this to perform the worst.

As has been noted previously, we focus the evaluation on the accuracy of tagging `Product` regions, which is the most difficult one. We use precision, recall and the F1 measure to illustrate overall accuracy.

6.2 Templates with Known Structure

We first focus on analyzing the performance of our approach when the template structure is well known. By template structure we mean which regions in the DOM tree are fixed for all emails in the template and which regions are specific to a given email instance from that template (e.g. **`recipient name`**, **`address`** and **`product`**(s) in the purchase). We use this setup to conduct a detailed analysis of our proposed approach. Large scale experiments with variable structure are reported in Section 6.5.

We used 4 frequent templates of user donated emails, and for any given template we manually engineer a template parser to annotate data with almost perfect precision as fixed or variable. This is a costly exercise. It is not scalable since an engineer needs to analyze HTML code to accomplish this task. Moreover, it requires us to continue investing resources whenever the template changes.

template	1	2	3	4
emails	36	105	50	60
products	78	191	59	231

As can be seen, even the frequent templates only consist of a rather small number of labeled emails.

6.3 Model Comparison

Figure 6 provides a comparison of F1, precision, and recall scores for all three algorithms (WL, CRF-Max and EM-CRF). To render the results comparable we tuned all models for maximum F1 score performance.

- EM-CRF outperforms all other algorithms on all test templates. It provides a 30% improvement relative to the WL annotator.
- The CRF-Max model also improves annotations generated by the WL model, albeit only by 26%. This confirms that training CRFs on noisy labels can lead to a *denoising* estimator.
- Compared to the plain CRF-Max model, EM-CRF is approximately 3.5% better. This shows that the EM iterations are helpful in reducing the noise further.

Particularly, for three out of these four templates, WL's achieved precision is lower than recall, which seems to be inconsistent with the `RandFor` figures in Table 1. This is just because the figures in Table 1 are calculated on the data across all the templates while the performance would be different for each individual template.

Besides these three algorithms compared in Figure 6, we also checked the performance of a CRF trained on the data across all other templates. The F1 performance on all four tested templates is almost 0, caused by the structure inconsistency brought from the huge difference across templates. This supports our motivation of training a CRF per template. Another observation is EM-CRF can still boost from WL although WL's precision is lower than 0.5 (F1 is still higher than 0.5). This is because T4 emails contains many (3.85) products on average, which help CRFs learn from abundant repeated structures.

Figure 7 illustrates the distribution of the F1 score across a range of hyperparameter values. Note that the variance of the EM-CRF model is lower than that of its alternatives. Not only is the model more accurate, it also provides a more reliable performance in large scale experiments where we do not have access to a development set for each template.

Figure 6 illustrates precision and recall when the hyperparameters have been tuned for the best F1 score for all models. Again, we may observe improved performance of CRF-Max and EM-CRF over WL. Compared to EM-CRF, the CRF-Max model occasionally exhibits higher precision but lower recall. This is because CRF-Max is trained directly on the labels predicted by the low-accuracy estimator. For

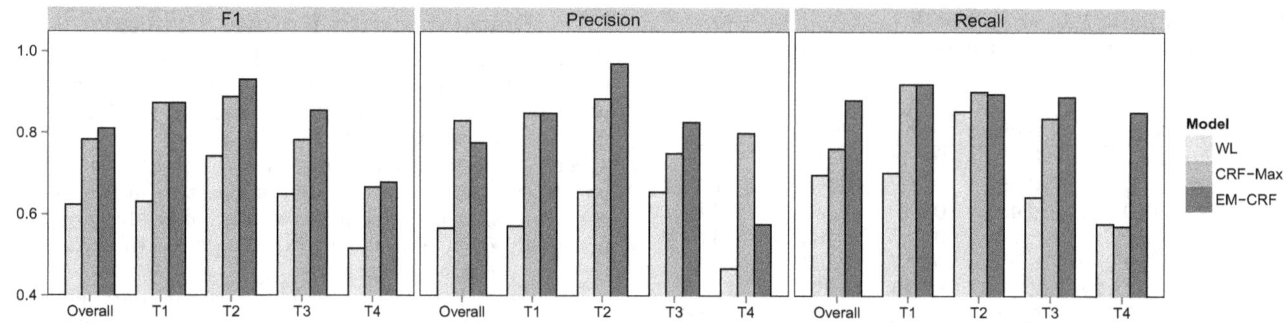

Figure 6: Comparison between the low-accuracy annotator (WL), a conventional conditional random field (CRF-Max), and the proposed algorithm (EM-CRF). We report F1 scores, precision and recall overall and on all four templates (T1 to T4).

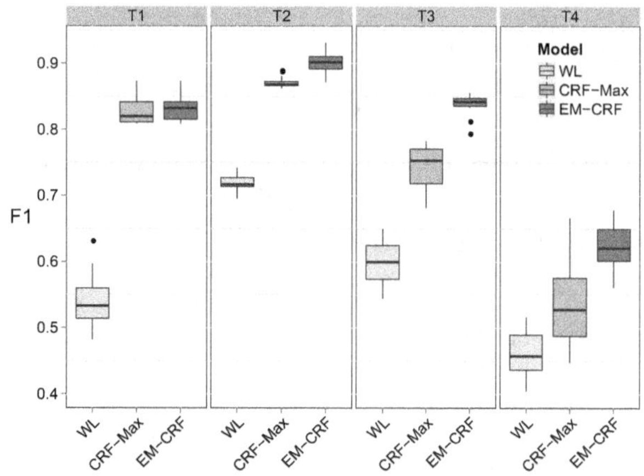

Figure 7: Distribution of F1 performance scores on four templates over a range of hyperparameters.

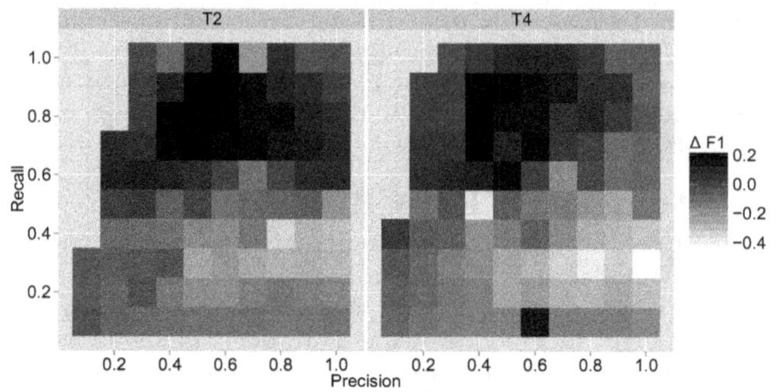

Figure 8: Improvement in F1 score of EM-CRF over WL as a function of precision and recall for templates 2 (left) and 4 (right). Some precision-recall regions are missing since the associated conditions cannot be satisfied.

the `Product` regions, which are correctly labeled by WL, the CRF-Max will train good parameters to predict them. On the other hand, the `Product` regions which are incorrectly labeled as `Other`, CRF-Max will be relatively easily induced to annotate these regions as `Other`. On the contrary, for EM-CRF, when WL provides the wrong prediction on `Product` regions, it just labels it as `Product` with a less-than-half probability. However, this probability will not be ignored during the EM-CRF training. EM-CRF will evaluate the posterior probability of when this region is labeled as `Product`, and usually increases the probability of this region being labeled as `Product` if it finds there is higher structural consistency.

Note that by construction the CRF-Max estimate is what the EM-CRF algorithm obtains in its first iteration with only max-likelihood label sequences. That is, EM-CRF creates a continuum between the decidedly suboptimal annotations of the low-accuracy annotators and the better CRF estimates to a fully self-consistent estimate.

6.4 Ablation Study

Precision and Recall of the low-accuracy estimator. Since EM-CRF is built on data labeled by the low-accuracy WL annotator, it is important to analyze under which conditions the EM-CRF results can improve. To conduct this study we simulated a weak learner with performance that spans the possible range of precision and recall. This can be achieved by oversampling the weight of positive product instances when training the low-accuracy annotators. We then compare the performance difference between EM-CRF and WL to the precision and recall of WL. The results on two large templates (2 and 4) are shown in Figure 8.

As can be seen, the results of both templates are qualitatively similar. That is, improvements are highest for WL whenever the recall is sufficiently high. This is quite possibly due to the fact that we use conditional independence assumptions on the weak learners, i.e. their estimates enter as products of probabilities $\prod_i \pi_{ij}$. Hence, poor recall immediately leads to a strong bias against the presence of a given attribute. A more refined model to capture correlation between the weak learners would probably ameliorate these issues. By and large, for over 50% recall improvements are pervasive.

Number of candidates in the E-Step. In (10) the posterior probability of each possible label combination y for the current document x_j needs be calculated. A potential problem here is that when there are many uncertainties over the labeling of regions in one email, as there could be exponentially large number of possible label combinations (2^N), which much reduces the efficiency of training. In our solution, we pick the top K candidate sequence labels with largest posterior probability in the step of recalculating distribution $q_j(y)$. This reduces the time of the costly M-step (7) significantly.

This raises the question as to how much the hyperparameter K influences the EM-CRF performance? We train models with K ranging from 1 to 500 and evaluate the EM-CRF performance on each template for each K, as shown in Figure 9. As can be seen, the F1 measure overall improves, albeit it does not change dramatically with varying K. This suggests that small values of K are perfectly acceptable. We finally set $K = 100$.

Regularization of CRF weights. We tune the L_2 regularization penalty during the training of the CRF given the current belief on each label combination $q_j(y)$. That is, we add $\lambda \|\theta\|^2$ to the negative log-likelihood in (7). Figure 10

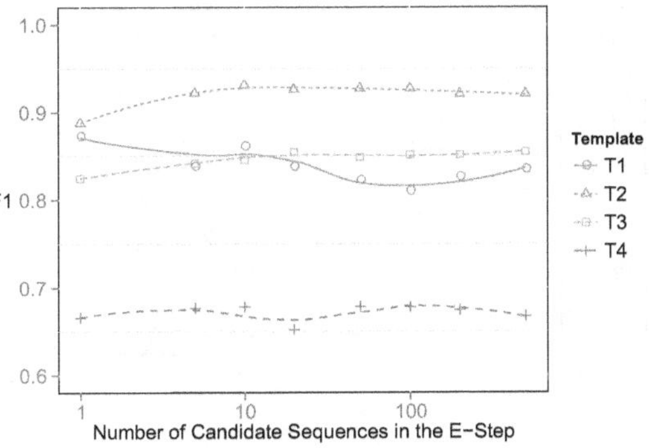

Figure 9: F1 as a function of the number of candidate sequences in the E-step. As can be seen, it is highly robust to sparse approximations.

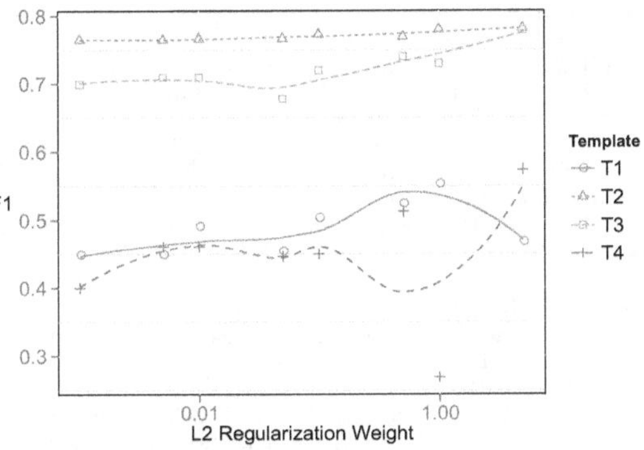

Figure 10: F1 as a function of the L2 regularization parameters. More regularization improves accuracy.

show the accuracy as a function of the regularization parameter for $\lambda \in [10^{-3}, 10]$. As expected, increasing regularization improves generalization up to some point, since it restricts the model class. Beyond that, accuracy decreases again due to underfitting. Empirically, we set L2 regularization as 10^{-2} for the large scale experiments below.

6.5 Templates with Inferred Structure

In this section we demonstrate the behavior of our method by a larger scale evaluation study on 200 templates. The number of emails in each template ranges from 10 to 2500 emails.

We used simple frequency counting with exact textual match as simple template extraction method. Those fixed regions are labeled as `Fixed` during our CRF analysis, however, their textual context is used to as feature for the CRF based models. We use the low-accuracy WL estimator from Section 5.3 which was trained over a separate dataset as our weak learner. The training method proceeds as discussed earlier over each template separately. Once we learn a structural model for each template, we apply this model to predict product regions in new and unseen emails under the same template. We compare the performance of the three methods: WL, CRF-Max and EM-CRF. Those unseen emails are donated with user consent and as such we hand-labeled them strictly for evaluation purposes. During training of the CRF-based models, no labels are needed and as such we do not perform any manual tuning of the hyperparameters and we rather fix them, across all templates, to default values acquired in the previous section. The training of EM-CRF is efficient because in practice we find the performance gets convergence within 10 EM iterations. The average real runtime on a single machine is 1.6s for the large templates studied in this section.

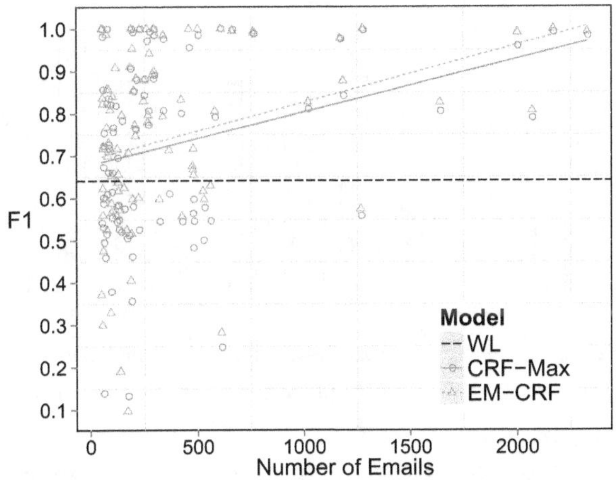

Figure 11: F1 performance as a function of the number of unlabeled emails in a given template.

We first compare the performance of the three methods as a function of the number of emails in each template. As show in Figure 11, both EM-CRF and CRF-Max provide a higher overall performance than WL, which verifies the effectiveness of structural information extraction on large-scale data. Furthermore, as the template email number increases, the improvement over WL becomes more significant. This is reasonable since more emails help CRF models learn the template structure pattern better. Moreover, EM-CRF results in higher improvement for templates with large number of emails (> 1000 emails) while its performance is similar to the CRF-Max model for templates with small number of emails. Thus one can use CRF-Max for cold start situations (new templates) and then switch to using EM-CRF for large templates (with over 1000 emails). We further focus on the performance of the largest 20 templates and give a detailed break-down of the performance in Figure 12. The performance break-down over templates with small number of emails is similar to the one shown in Figure 6 and is omitted due to space constraints.

7. CONCLUSIONS AND FUTURE WORK

In this paper, we addressed the challenging problem of information extraction from commercial emails. While supervised information extraction itself is a relatively well-studied area, information extraction from emails presents distinct privacy challenges that prevent us from even looking at the emails to either annotate fields for training or tune the hyper-parameters of the learning method.

We tackled this problem using a fully automatic approach that requires almost no manual tuning and is unsupervised in nature. The approaches presented in this paper (EM-CRF and CRF-Max) make use of low-accuracy annotators trained using weak features on a separate dataset. Our methods leverage those weak signals to learn, in an unsupervised fashion, structural patterns specific to each template and then use those patterns to extract information from future emails in the same template. We provided a thorough evaluation of our approach over large scale emails and showed that our proposed approaches result in significant performance improvement. Moreover, we analyzed the model and data conditions which could lead large improvement.

In the future we plan to investigate joint approaches for template extraction and structural learning as well as exploring the efficacy of transfer learning approaches of structural patterns across different email templates.

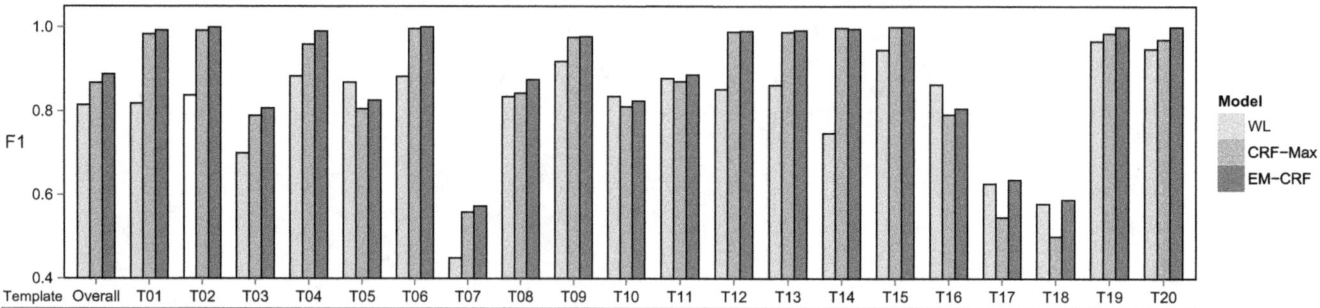

Template	Overall	T01	T02	T03	T04	T05	T06	T07	T08	T09	T10	T11	T12	T13	T14	T15	T16	T17	T18	T19	T20
Emails	22,566	2,328	2,169	2,070	2,001	1,641	1,275	1,267	1,184	1,170	1,021	1,020	762	761	662	608	581	560	526	501	459
Products	39,035	2,336	2,171	2,102	2,027	4,694	1,275	2,574	3,376	1,224	4,777	3,781	765	769	874	608	2,627	565	530	501	459

Figure 12: F1 performance on the 20 large email templates and the email & product numbers of each template.

Acknowledgements.

We sincerely thank Andrei Broder for helpful advices and support for the project. Also, we thank the team and collaborators for the excellent work.

8. REFERENCES

[1] N. Ailon, Z. S. Karnin, E. Liberty, and Y. Maarek. Threading machine generated email. In *WSDM*. ACM, 2013.
[2] S. M. Aji and R. J. McEliece. The generalized distributive law. *IEEE Transactions on Information Theory*, 46(2), 2000.
[3] C. Bird, A. Gourley, P. Devanbu, M. Gertz, and A. Swaminathan. Mining email social networks. In *Workshop on Mining software repositories*, pages 137–143. ACM, 2006.
[4] E. Blanzieri and A. Bryl. A survey of learning-based techniques of email spam filtering. *Artificial Intelligence Review*, 29(1):63–92, 2008.
[5] L. Breiman. Random forests. *Machine learning*, 45(1), 2001.
[6] J. D. Brutlag and C. Meek. Challenges of the email domain for text classification. In *ICML*, pages 103–110, 2000.
[7] D. Buttler, L. Liu, and C. Pu. A fully automated object extraction system for the world wide web. In *ICDCS*, 2001.
[8] C.-H. Chang and S.-C. Lui. Iepad: information extraction based on pattern discovery. In *WWW*, pages 681–688. ACM, 2001.
[9] G. V. Cormack. Email spam filtering: A systematic review. *Foundations and Trends in Information Retrieval*, 1(4), 2007.
[10] C. Cortes and V. Vapnik. Support-vector networks. *Machine learning*, 20(3):273–297, 1995.
[11] M. Craven, J. Kumlien, et al. Constructing biological knowledge bases by extracting information from text sources. In *ISMB*, volume 1999, pages 77–86, 1999.
[12] V. Crescenzi, G. Mecca, P. Merialdo, et al. Roadrunner: Towards automatic data extraction from large web sites. In *VLDB*, volume 1, pages 109–118, 2001.
[13] N. Dalvi, R. Kumar, and M. Soliman. Automatic wrappers for large scale web extraction. *Proceedings of the VLDB Endowment*, 4(4):219–230, 2011.
[14] J. Diesner, T. L. Frantz, and K. M. Carley. Communication networks from the enron email corpus "it's always about the people. enron is no different". *Computational & Mathematical Organization Theory*, 11(3):201–228, 2005.
[15] D. W. Embley, Y. Jiang, and Y.-K. Ng. Record-boundary discovery in web documents. *ACM SIGMOD Record*, 28(2):467–478, 1999.
[16] J. H. Friedman. Multivariate adaptive regression splines. *The annals of statistics*, pages 1–67, 1991.
[17] K. Ganchev, J. Graça, J. Gillenwater, and B. Taskar. Posterior regularization for structured latent variable models. *JMLR*, 99:2001–2049, 2010.
[18] S. Gupta, G. Kaiser, D. Neistadt, and P. Grimm. Dom-based content extraction of html documents. In *WWW*, 2003.
[19] K. Hall, R. McDonald, J. Katz-Brown, and M. Ringgaard. Training dependency parsers by jointly optimizing multiple objectives. In *EMNLP*, pages 1489–1499, 2011.
[20] T. Hastie, R. Tibshirani, and J. J. H. Friedman. *The elements of statistical learning*, volume 1. Springer New York, 2001.
[21] R. Hoffmann, C. Zhang, X. Ling, L. Zettlemoyer, and D. S. Weld. Knowledge-based weak supervision for information extraction of overlapping relations. In *ACL*, 2011.
[22] R. Horst and N. V. Thoai. Dc programming: overview. *Journal of Optimization Theory and Applications*, 103(1):1–43, 1999.
[23] R. Jin and Z. Ghahramani. Learning with multiple labels. In *NIPS*, pages 897–904, 2002.
[24] S. Kiritchenko and S. Matwin. Email classification with co-training. In *CASCON*, pages 301–312. IBM Corp., 2011.
[25] A. Klementiev and D. Roth. Weakly supervised named entity transliteration and discovery from multilingual comparable corpora. In *ACL*, pages 817–824, 2006.
[26] B. Klimt and Y. Yang. The enron corpus: A new dataset for email classification research.
[27] A. Kulkarni and T. Pedersen. Name discrimination and email clustering using unsupervised clustering and labeling of similar contexts. In *IICAI*, pages 703–722, 2005.
[28] J. Lafferty, A. McCallum, and F. C. Pereira. Conditional random fields: Probabilistic models for segmenting and labeling sequence data. In *ICML*, 2001.
[29] H. Li, D. Shen, B. Zhang, Z. Chen, and Q. Yang. Adding semantics to email clustering. In *ICDM*, 2006.
[30] B. Liu, R. Grossman, and Y. Zhai. Mining data records in web pages. In *KDD*, pages 601–606. ACM, 2003.
[31] G. S. Mann and A. McCallum. Generalized expectation criteria for semi-supervised learning with weakly labeled data. *JMLR*, 11:955–984, 2010.
[32] M. Mintz, S. Bills, R. Snow, and D. Jurafsky. Distant supervision for relation extraction without labeled data. In *ACL*, pages 1003–1011, 2009.
[33] L. B. J. F. R. Olshen and C. J. Stone. Classification and regression trees. *Wadsworth International Group*, 1984.
[34] M. Paşca. Weakly-supervised discovery of named entities using web search queries. In *CIKM*, pages 683–690. ACM, 2007.
[35] P. Ravikumar, M. J. Wainwright, and J. D. Lafferty. High-dimensional ising model selection using l1-regularized logistic regression. *The Annals of Statistics*, 38(3), 2010.
[36] G. Ridgeway. Generalized boosted regression models. *Documentation on the R Package 'gbm', version*, 1(5):7, 2006.
[37] S. Riedel, L. Yao, and A. McCallum. Modeling relations and their mentions without labeled text. In *ECML*, 2010.
[38] R. Rowe, G. Creamer, S. Hershkop, and S. J. Stolfo. Automated social hierarchy detection through email network analysis. In *WebKDD and SNA-KDD*, pages 109–117. ACM, 2007.
[39] A. M. Rush. A tutorial on dual decomposition and lagrangian relaxation for inference in natural language processing. 2012.
[40] A. M. Rush, D. Sontag, M. Collins, and T. Jaakkola. On dual decomposition and linear programming relaxations for natural language processing. In *EMNLP*, pages 1–11, 2010.
[41] C.-Y. Tseng, J.-W. Huang, and M.-S. Chen. Promail: using progressive email social network for spam detection. In *Advances in Knowledge Discovery and Data Mining*. 2007.
[42] S. Yoo, Y. Yang, F. Lin, and I.-C. Moon. Mining social networks for personalized email prioritization. In *KDD*, 2009.
[43] S. Youn and D. McLeod. A comparative study for email classification. In *Advances and Innovations in Systems, Computing Sciences and Software Engineering*. 2007.
[44] Y. Zhai and B. Liu. Web data extraction based on partial tree alignment. In *WWW*, pages 76–85. ACM, 2005.
[45] J. Zhu, Z. Nie, J.-R. Wen, B. Zhang, and W.-Y. Ma. 2d conditional random fields for web information extraction. In *ICML*, pages 1044–1051. ACM, 2005.
[46] J. Zhu, Z. Nie, J.-R. Wen, B. Zhang, and W.-Y. Ma. Simultaneous record detection and attribute labeling in web data extraction. In *KDD*, pages 494–503. ACM, 2006.
[47] J. Zhu, Z. Nie, B. Zhang, and J.-R. Wen. Dynamic hierarchical markov random fields for integrated web data extraction. *JMLR*, 9:1583–1614, 2008.
[48] X. Zhu. Semi-supervised learning literature survey. *Computer Science, University of Wisconsin-Madison*, 2:3, 2006.
[49] X. Zhu and A. B. Goldberg. *Introduction to Semi-supervised Learning*. Number 6. Morgan & Claypool Publishers, 2009.

Forecasting Fine-Grained Air Quality Based on Big Data

Yu Zheng[1,2], Xiuwen Yi[2,1], Ming Li[1], Ruiyuan Li[1], Zhangqing Shan[3,1], Eric Chang[1], Tianrui Li[2]
[1]Microsoft Research, Beijing, China
[2]Southwest Jiaotong University, Chengdu, Sichuan, China
[3]Fudan University, Shanghai, China
{yuzheng, v-xiuyi, mingl, v-ruiyli, v-zhasha, echang}@microsoft.com, trli@swjtu.edu.cn

ABSTRACT

In this paper, we forecast the reading of an air quality monitoring station over the next 48 hours, using a data-driven method that considers current meteorological data, weather forecasts, and air quality data of the station and that of other stations within a few hundred kilometers. Our predictive model is comprised of four major components: 1) a linear regression-based temporal predictor to model the local factors of air quality, 2) a neural network-based spatial predictor to model global factors, 3) a dynamic aggregator combining the predictions of the spatial and temporal predictors according to meteorological data, and 4) an inflection predictor to capture sudden changes in air quality. We evaluate our model with data from 43 cities in China, surpassing the results of multiple baseline methods. We have deployed a system with the Chinese Ministry of Environmental Protection, providing 48-hour fine-grained air quality forecasts for four major Chinese cities every hour. The forecast function is also enabled on Microsoft Bing Map and MS cloud platform Azure. Our technology is general and can be applied globally for other cities.

Categories and Subject Descriptors

H.2.8 **[Database Management]**:□Database Applications - *data mining, Spatial databases and GIS*;

Keywords

Urban computing; urban air; air quality forecast; big data.

1. INTRODUCTION

People are increasingly concerned with air pollution, which impacts human health and sustainable development around the world. Many cities have built air quality monitoring stations to inform people about urban air quality, e.g. the concentration of PM2.5 (particulate matter) and PM10, every hour. Besides monitoring, there is a rising demand for the prediction of future air quality, which can inform people's decision making (e.g. whether to go for picnic or jogging in a park) and governments' policy making (such as issuing pollution alerts or performing a pollution control).

Predicting urban air quality, however, is very challenging for the following three reasons: *First*, while urban air quality is affected by multiple complex factors, such as traffic flow, meteorology, and land use [11][14], we do not have sufficient and accurate data to model each factor. For example, it is almost impossible to obtain the accurate pollution emissions data of every vehicle and factory in a real time manner. Likewise, weather forecasts have not been able to tell us exactly when a wind will blow and how long it will last for.

KDD '15, August 11 - 14, 2015, Sydney, NSW, Australia
 ISBN 978-1-4503-3664-2/15/08…$15.00
DOI: http://dx.doi.org/10.1145/2783258.2788573

Second, urban air changes over location and time significantly because of these complex factors. As shown in Figure 1 A), there are 22 air quality monitoring stations in Beijing's urban areas. If we calculate the gap between the maximum and minimum AQIs (Air Quality Indexes) of PM2.5 from these stations at the same hour, as illustrated in Figure 1 B), about 40 percent of time slots have a gap larger than 100, which denotes a two-level difference in pollution (i.e. when the air quality of a location is moderate, another one is unhealthy). Moreover, as depicted in Figure 1 C), the AQIs of three stations change over time very differently. For instance, while the readings of S_1 and S_2 increasing in early part of Oct. 19, 2014, that of S_3 was decreasing. So, we need to predict the air quality of different stations (or even the different time slots of the same station) by using different models. In other words, a general prediction of the overall air quality in a city is not useful enough to inform people's decision making.

Third, there are some inflection points where air quality changes very sharply. This may be caused by unusual weather conditions, such as rain storms or strong winds. As such inflection instances are very rare in observation, a general statistic model will be dominated by normal instances, and therefore cannot predict such inflections or sudden changes very well.

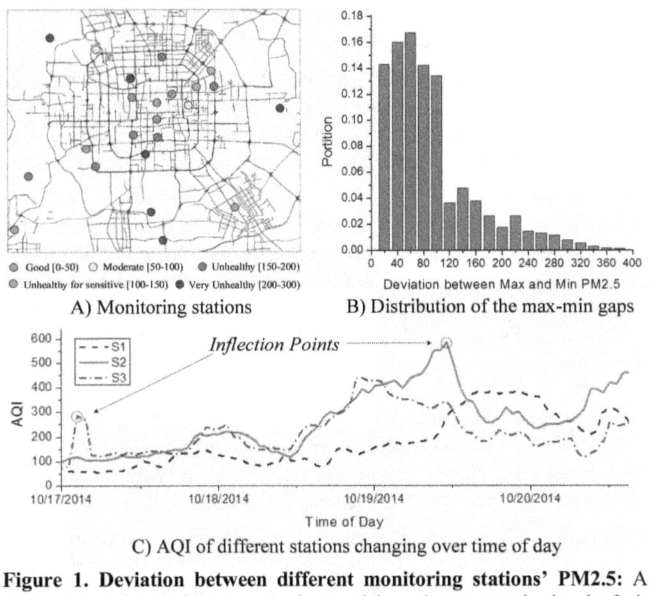

Figure 1. Deviation between different monitoring stations' PM2.5: A circle shown in A) denotes a station, and its color means the level of air pollution, as described in the bottom of the figure. The air quality of these stations were dramatically different at 10am Mar. 13, 2014.

To address the aforementioned issues, we predict the air quality over the next 48 hours for each monitoring station. As shown in Figure 2, in the first 6 hours, we predict a real-valued AQI for each kind of air pollutant, at each hour in each station. For the next 7-12, 12-24, and 24-48 hours, we predict a max-min range of AQIs at the corresponding time interval. That is, a coarser granularity of forecast is provided for a farther future. We continuously predict these values every hour for each station.

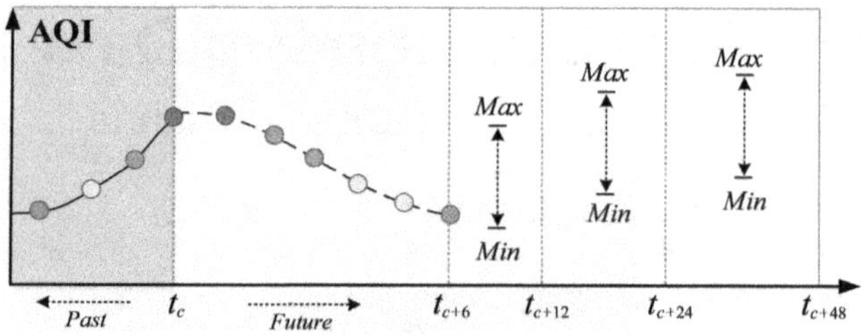

Figure 2: Format of the air quality forecasts

In our method, we train a hybrid predictive model for each kind of pollutant at each station and in different time slots, based on the following three types of data over a period of time: 1) The air quality at the current time and over the past few hours; 2) The meteorological data (such as humidity, temperature, and wind speed) at the current time and over the past few hours; 3) Weather forecasts at the future time we are going to predict. More specifically, for the first two datasets, we need the data of the station we are going to predict and those of other stations within a circle distance (of a few hundred kilometers) to the station. For the first six hours, we train a model for each hour at each station. With respect to the following three ranges, we train a model to predict the maximum and minimum AQIs respectively. Our contribution has four parts:

- We propose a multi-view-based hybrid model that predicts future air quality with inaccurate and insufficient data. The model handles the spatial correlation of air quality among different locations and the temporal dependency of air quality at a location, using non-overlapped features and different machine learning models. It then combines the spatial and temporal predictions dynamically according to weather conditions.
- The inflection predictor in our hybrid model significantly improves the capability of predicting sudden changes of air quality caused by extreme weather conditions.
- We evaluate our model with data from 43 cities in China, achieving a precision greater than 0.75 in the first six hours. Our method significantly outperforms baselines when dealing with general instances, and has a 1.5 times higher accuracy when handling sudden drops.
- The system has been deployed, using a framework that combines the cloud with clients. The cloud is located at Microsoft Azure, continuously collecting real-time data and forecasting air quality. People can access the fine-grained air quality information by using either a mobile app, called Urban Air [2], or through a public website [1]. The technology has also been shipped into Bing Maps China [3]. Additionally, we have deployed the system in Chinese Ministry of Environmental Protection, providing fine-grained air quality for the current time and future hours to inform governments' decision making. The datasets have been released in [17].

The rest of the paper is organized as follows: In Section 2, we present an overview of our system. Section 3 details the predictive model. We evaluate our method in Section 4. Section 5 summarizes related work. We draw conclusions in Section 6.

2. OVERVIEW

2.1 System Architecture

Figure 3 presents the architecture of our system, which consists of three parts: External Data Sources, Cloud and Clients. The Data Sources include a list of public websites and public/private web services providing real-time meteorological data, weather forecasts, and air quality data of different cities. The Cloud is based on Microsoft Azure, hosting five major components of our system. The Data Collector continuously collects real-time data from external data sources, through web service interfaces or by crawling web pages. The collected data is stored in a cloud database. For various reasons, a few air quality monitoring stations occasionally may not have readings; same with the meteorological data. Thus, the Data Supplement component tries to fill the missing values in the collected data based on their spatial or temporal neighbors. The Predictive Model components is comprised of a collection of models, each of which predicts the air quality for a station and at a time interval. The prediction results are then stored in the cloud database for the access of the Web Service component, which provides interfaces to two types of clients: mobile apps and websites. To have a stable and robust system, we set a monitor to continuously check the availability of data sources and the performance of web services as well as the status of other components.

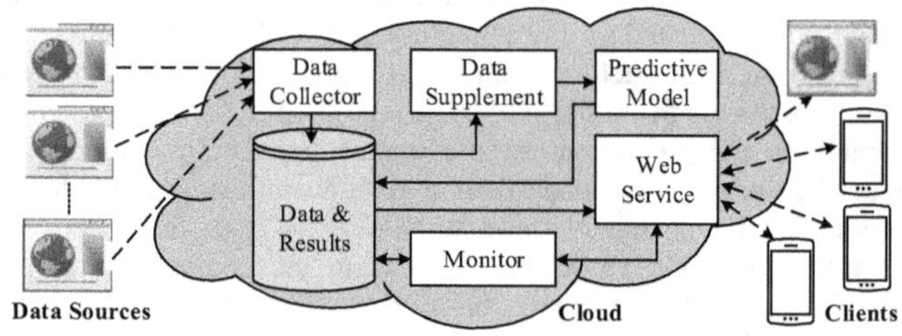

Figure 3. Architecture of our system

2.2 User Interfaces

Figure 4 presents the website of Urban Air [1], where an icon on the map stands for a monitoring station and the number associated with an icon denotes its AQI; the smaller the number is, the better the air quality is. The color of an icon is determined in accordance with its air quality, e.g. "green" means a "good" and "yellow" denotes "moderate" by Chinese AQI standards. After clicking the most right (trend) tab on the floating tool bar, we will see a time line, with which a user can check air quality forecasts of a specific future time interval. Users can also check the future air quality of all stations changing over time by clicking the start button on the left terminal of the time line. By clicking a specific station on the map, users will see a pop-up chart showing a curve of air quality forecast. The number on the top of each time segment is an accuracy of the prediction measured by the data at the station in the past 48 hours. The accuracy of a maxi-min range is measured by its mean value against the mean value of the true range.

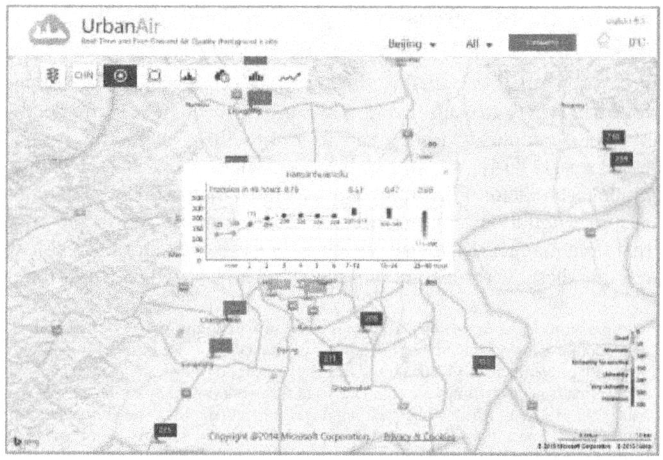

Figure 4. Web user interface of Urban Air

Figure 5 presents the user interface of mobile clients. As depicted in Figure 5 A), a user has selected four locations, such as home and work places, to monitor on their mobile phone. Here, each banner represents one location and the number shown in each banner is the AQI of the location. Each location was selected by pressing and holding the corresponding venue on a map, as shown in Figure 5B), where an icon stands for a venue that a user has selected. Our mobile client will automatically name a selected venue according to the titles of POIs and road networks around the venue. Users can then modify the name to some semantic title, such as home. By clicking a banner in the location list, users can see not only the historical air quality of a location in the past 24 hours but also the forecast of next 48 hours, as illustrated in Figure 5 C).

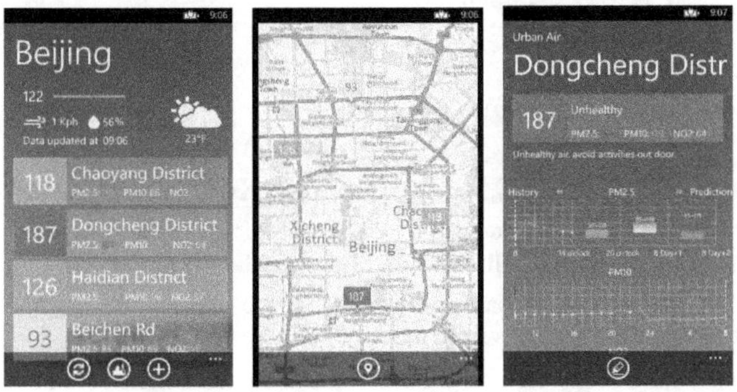

A) List view B) Map view C) Chart view

Figure 5. Mobile interface of Urban Air

2.3 Framework of the Predictive Model

Figure 6 presents the framework for the predictive model, consisting of four components: a (local) temporal predictor, a (global) spatial predictor, an inflection predictor, and a prediction aggregator.

The *Temporal Predictor* predicts the air quality of a station in terms of the data about the station, such as local meteorology, AQIs from the past few hours and the weather forecast for where the station is located. Alternatively, we can say the temporal predictor predicts air quality using *local* data, considering the prediction more from its own historical and future conditions. Specifically, the temporal predictor is based on a linear regression (*LR*), which models the local air quality regression process.

Instead, the *Spatial Predictor* considers spatial neighbor data, such as the AQIs and the wind speed at other stations, to predict a station's future air quality. Intrinsically, the air quality of different locations has a spatial correlation as pollutants are dispersed from one place to another. The *Spatial Predictor* is based on an artificial neural network (*ANN*), modeling the spatial correlation and predicting air quality from other locations' points of view.

The two predictors generate their own predictions independently for a station, which are combined by the *Prediction Aggregator* dynamically according to the current weather conditions of the station. Sometimes, local prediction is more important, while spatial prediction should be given a higher weight on other occasions (e.g. when a wind blows strongly). As the deviation between two consecutive hours' AQIs (ΔAQI) is usually smaller than the AQI itself, the two predictors predict the deviation rather than the original AQI.

There are three reasons we need to devise three separate (spatial, temporal, and aggregator) predictors rather than a single predictor: 1) *From the feature space's perspective*, the features used by the spatial and temporal predictors do not have any overlap, providing different views on a station's air quality. 2) *From the model's perspective*, the spatial and temporal predictors model local factors and global factors respectively, which have significantly different properties. For example, the local is more about a regression problem, while the global is more about a non-linear interpolation. Thus, they should be handled with different techniques. 3) *From the parameter learning's perspective*, feeding all features into a single model results in a big model with many parameters to learn. However, the training data is limited. For instance, we only have one year of AQI data for a city. Decomposing a big model into three organically coupled small models scales down the parameter spaces tremendously, leading to more accurate learning and therefore prediction.

In some cases, e.g. when strong winds or rain storms come, the air quality of a location drops tremendously in a short time period. Such kind of sharp drops are hard to predict, as their presence is very small in the entire observation. To address this issue, we pick out such sudden drop instances to train a separate *Inflection Predictor*. We also learn some conditions that significantly differentiate these drop instances from normal cases, e.g. when the wind speed is higher than a threshold. Once one of these conditions holds, the *Inflection Predictor* will be invoked to generate a ΔAQI, which will be appended to the original AQI with the output of the *Prediction Aggregator* to calculate the final prediction.

As different stations are located in different environments and different air pollutants vary by location and time, we build such a hybrid model for each kind of air pollutant, at each station and for different time intervals. More specifically, we train a model respectively for each hour in the next six hours, and two models for each time interval (from 7 to 48 hours) to predict its maximum and minimum values. All these models are re-trained every a few months in an offline process and generate an online prediction every hour.

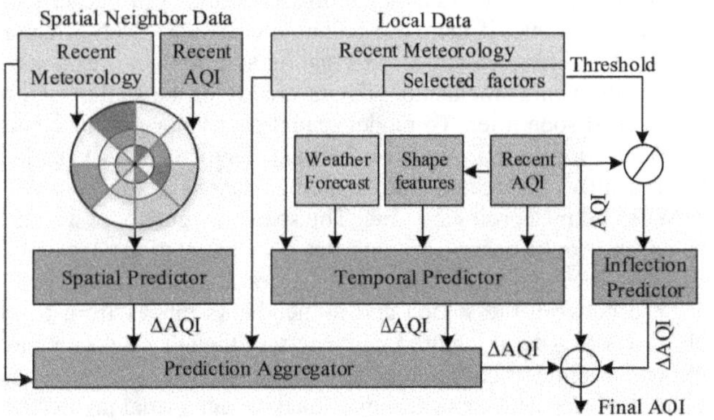

Figure 6. Framework of the predictive model

3. Hybrid Predictive Model

3.1 Temporal Predictor

The temporal predictor models the trend of air quality of a station based on four types of data: 1) the AQIs of the past h hours at the station; 2) the local meteorology (such as sunny/overcast/cloudy/foggy, humidity, wind speed, and direction) at the current time t_c; 3) time of day and day of the week; 4) the weather forecasts (including sunny/overcast/cloudy, wind speed, and wind direction) of the time interval we are going to predict. These features have been proven relevant to air quality in past literature [4][11][14].

Intuitively, the current status has different degrees of impact to different future time intervals. Thus, as illustrated in Figure 7, we pair the inputs (shown in the broken rectangle) with the air quality of different time intervals ($t_{c+1}, t_{c+2}, \dots, t_{c+48}$) to formulate different training sets, which are used to respectively train different models corresponding to different time intervals. Each blue broken arrow shown in Figure 7 denotes a temporal predictor. Over the next six hours, we train a model for each hour. With respect to the next 7 to 48 hours, which are divided into three time intervals (7-12, 13-24, 25-48), we train two models to predict the maximum and minimum AQIs of each time interval respectively. This is the same for spatial predictors which will be detailed later. The first three parts of inputs are the same in different temporal predictors, while the only difference between different predictors' inputs lies in the weather forecast (i.e. the fourth part).

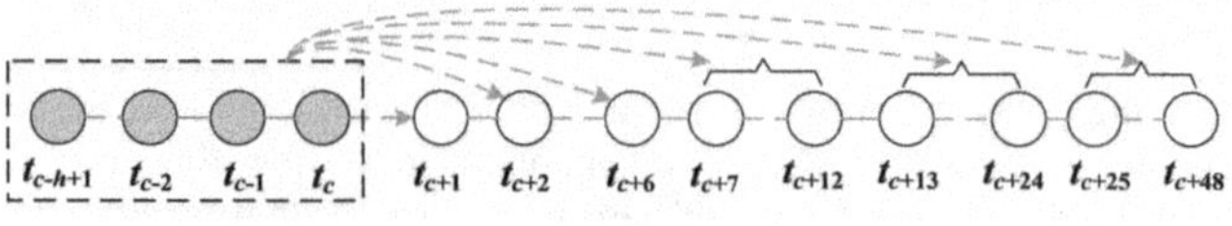

Figure 7. Illustration of the temporal predictor

A linear regression is employed to model the local change of air quality. The categorical features are converted into numeric values, e.g. using (0, 1) to denote (not sunny, sunny) respectively. We do not conduct an iterative moving prediction (e.g. using the prediction of t_{c+1} as an input to predict later hours) for two reasons. First, the new prediction will bring errors to later rounds of prediction. Second, a weather forecast is coarser and less accurate than current meteorological data. Some features (e.g. humidity) are even missing in the weather forecast of many cities. Though one can capture the general trends in air quality at a location using a regression process, the temporal predictor has its weaknesses, e.g. it cannot well handle sudden changes and pollution coming from other places.

3.2 Spatial Predictor

Beside local emissions, the air quality of a location also depends on its neighbors, as air pollutants are dispersed among different locations. For example, if there are pollution emissions from a factory that is 20 kilometers away from a station and the wind happens to blow them towards the station, the air quality of the station will be become bad soon after. To model spatial correlations in air quality at different locations, we devise a spatial predictor which predicts the air quality of a location based on other stations' status consisting of AQIs and meteorological data. The spatial neighbors of a station include not only nearby stations but also the stations located in adjacent cities. To model the impact from different locations, the distance between the station and its neighbors ranges from a few kilometers to several hundred kilometers. Although we do not have first-hand pollution emission data, the stations that have been built can be regarded as sensors sending signals to our spatial predictors.

As shown in Figure 8 A), to build a spatial predictor for a station s, we first partition the spatial space into regions by using three circles with different diameters. The outmost circle has the largest diameter (e.g. 300km), and the innermost one has the least (e.g. 30km). The three circles share a common center (i.e. station s denoted by the black point) and are further segmented by four lines pointing to different angles. We then project other stations onto the regions bound by the line fragments and circles, according to each station's geo-coordinates. To simplify the model, the stations falling outside the biggest circle are not considered in the spatial predictor. As illustrated in Figure 8 B), we aggregate the meteorological data and air quality readings from the stations that are located in the same region. When a region has more than one station, we calculate the average AQI for a given kind of air pollutant; same for temperature and humidity. The wind direction of a region is determined by the mode of the data. As a result, each region will only have one set of aggregated air quality readings and meteorology, which will be fed into the spatial predictor to predict the future air quality for s. We conduct the same process of spatial partition and aggregation for different stations.

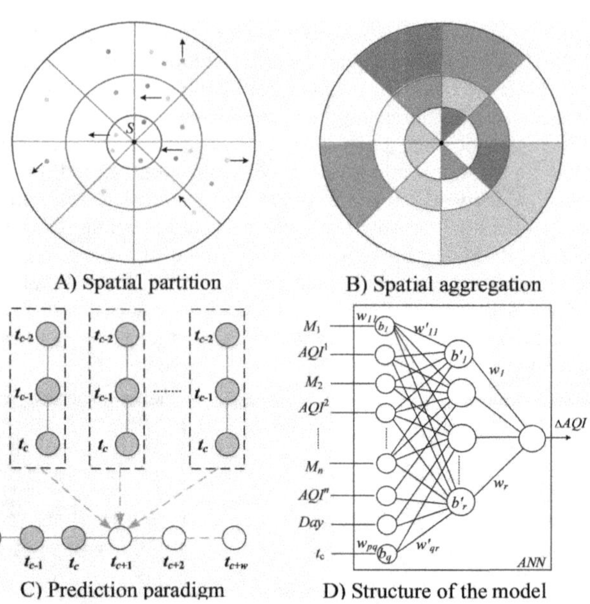

Figure 8. Illustration of the spatial predictor

The reason that we partition a spatial space into regions and then aggregate the readings from other stations are threefold:

1) If we directly feed all the data from a station's neighbors into a machine learning model, the number of parameters increases quickly in proportion to the number of stations. This causes a trouble for model training and therefore prediction. Remember that we do not have sufficient data to train a very big model. The more parameters involved in a model, the more training data we need to find a set of proper parameters. The partition and aggregation significantly reduces the number of inputs, enhancing training quality. It also sets an upper bound for the input (no matter how many new stations will be built in the future), as the number of regions is fixed given the spatial partition process.

2) The information from nearby stations is somehow redundant or even sometimes contradictory. For example, the wind directions of two nearby stations could be opposite, as wind may be affected by urban canyons. Without a proper aggregation, the spatial predictor will be confused by the chaotic input.

3) The partition and aggregation carry a semantic meaning, denoting different regions' impacts (to station s) varying by distance and angle. By setting different diameters for different circles, the partition provides a coarser granularity for a farther region and a finer granularity for closer regions. In other words, we aggregate the data of a larger area for the regions located in a more outward ring.

As demonstrated in Figure 8 C), after the spatial partition and aggregation, we formulate a time series for each region with at least one station. Other regions without stations are called empty regions, which are not considered in a spatial predictor. In the time series (denoted as a broken-bound box), each node stands for the aggregated information of a corresponding hour. For a non-empty region i, we extract the following features from its time series: the AQI of the past three hours ($\boldsymbol{AQI^i}$) and meteorological features (M^i), including the wind speed and direction, at the current time t_c. As depicted in Figure 8 D), $\boldsymbol{AQI^i}$ and M^i of the non-empty regions are fed into an artificial neural network whose output is the AQI of the station at the specific time interval we are going to predict. In the implementation, we predict the deviation between the AQIs of current time t_c and the future time interval t_{c+w}, i.e. $\Delta AQI = AQI_{t_c} - AQI_{t_{c+w}}$, because the distribution space of ΔAQI is much narrower than $AQI_{t_{c+w}}$. For example, Figure 9 A) presents the distribution of AQI in Beijing in 2014, which ranges from 0 to 500. Figure 9 B) shows the distribution of ΔAQI, where w=2. The majority of ΔAQIs fall in a range between -100 and 100, which is much narrower than [0, 500]. The upper bound of ΔAQI's range is [0, 500], no matter how big w is.

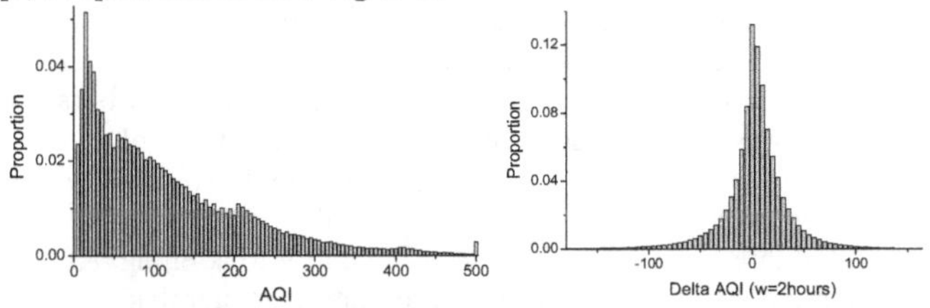

Figure 9. Distributions of AQI and ΔAQI in Beijing

The number of layers in the neural network depends on the scale of inputs, i.e. the number of non-empty regions, and the training data. For example, when there are 150 features and a one-year training dataset, we set a four-layer neural network (i.e. two hidden layers). By pairing the same inputs with the ΔAQIs of different time intervals we are going to predict, we train multiple spatial predictors corresponding to different future time intervals. This occurs in a similar fashion as with temporal predictors.

3.3 Prediction Aggregator

The prediction aggregator dynamically integrates the predictions that the spatial and temporal predictors have made for a location. The spatial and temporal predictors use non-overlapped features to predict the air quality of a location, offering different points of view (local and global) on the prediction. Sometimes, local information is more important than global information, e.g. when the air circulation between different places is weak. On the contrary, global dispersion may be a major factor in determining a place's air quality, e.g. when the wind speed is very high. As a result, we consider the current meteorology of the location, such as the wind speed, wind direction, humidity, and sunny/cloudy/overcast/foggy, to calculate a dynamic weight for the two predictions.

Specifically, we train a Regression Tree (*RT*) [5][9] to model the dynamic combination of these factors and predictions. A Regression Tree can be regarded as an integration of a Decision Tree and a Linear Regression. In general, it hierarchically partitions the data into groups based on some discriminative features and then learns a linear regression for each group of data in a leaf node. While the first step of a RT is similar to a Decision Tree, a RT can handle continuous and discrete features simultaneously. When handling continuous features, it uses the decrease in variance (somehow similar to information gain in a Decision Tree) in the data to determine partition thresholds. The feature that results in the most decreases in variance or information gain will be selected as the first node to partition the data into two parts. The process is performed in each part of the data iteratively, until some criteria have been satisfied, e.g. the depth of a tree or the number of instances in a leaf node.

To train such a regression tree, we deposit the predictions generated by the spatial and temporal predictors with the local meteorological data of the time interval in a feature set. The feature set is then paired with the corresponding ΔAQI (from the ground truth). The spatial and temporal predictors have been trained before we start training the prediction aggregator. Figure 10 presents a RT we train to predict the air quality of a station in Beijing, where an ellipse denotes a feature selected to partition the ΔAQIs; each square leaf node stands for a linear model (LM) that combines different features to calculate ΔAQI; the number associated with each edge is the threshold of a selected feature. All features have been normalized into [0,1]. For instance, when the value of a spatial predictor (*Spatial*) is smaller than 0.003 and the temporal prediction (*Temporal*) is greater than -0.08, we use LM4 to calculate ΔAQI. The weights of a feature in different LMs are different. For example, as presented in the right part of Figure 10, when wind speed is higher than 6.62, we select LM2, which gives temporal prediction a higher weight, to calculate ΔAQI. On the contrary, in LM3, spatial prediction is given a high weight. Each station has its own prediction aggregators that correspond to different time intervals to be predicted. So, the combination of spatial and temporal predictors changes over time and stations dynamically. The features that are not discriminative to determine the combination are ignored by the model automatically.

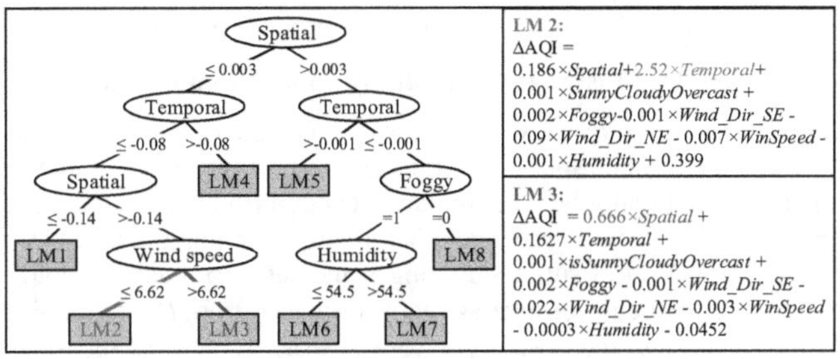

Figure 10. An example of Regression Tree

3.4 Inflection Predictor

In some cases, the air quality of a location changes sharply in a few hours, which may be caused by a strong wind or a rain storm. Being able to predict such sudden changes is vital to informing people's decision making. However, the presence of such cases is very infrequent among entire observations; e.g. within one year of air quality data in Beijing, the presence of sudden drop instances is less than 1.1%. As a result, to predict them becomes almost impossible for the spatial and temporal predictors, which make a prediction based on the majority of observations.

To address this issue, we propose an inflection predictor, which is invoked to handle sudden changes when some criteria are satisfied. The predictor is built by the following four steps:

Step 1. Selecting the sudden drop instances D_i from historical data D: This step can be done by selecting the instances (from all the stations) whose AQI is bigger than 200 and decreases over a threshold in the next few hours, e.g. 50 in the coming one hour, or 100 in the coming two hours, or 150 in the coming three hours. In this study, we only focus on the sudden drop instances, as sudden increases of AQI are very rare in the real world. Even if a factory emission occurs, the air quality of the surrounding places usually becomes worse smoothly (because the volume of sources is much smaller than the capacity of the environment). This is also true when a foggy day is coming. Thus, such increasing cases can be handled by the spatial and temporal predictors. As depicted in Figure 11 A), the selected sudden drop instances are denoted by red points, while the rest are represented by gray points.

Step 2. Finding surpassing ranges and categories: We respectively calculate the distribution of each feature in the sudden drop instance set D_i and the entire dataset D. By comparing the two distributions of a feature, we find the ranges (for continuous features) or the categories (for discrete features) whose proportion in D_i is higher than the rest of the data (i.e. $D - D_i$). We call them surpassing ranges and categories. For example, as shown in Figure 11 B), the two curves denote the distributions of a continuous feature in D_i and $D - D_i$ respectively. We find that a feature's probability in ranges (a_1, a_2) and (a_3, a_4) in D_i is higher than $D - D_i$. Likewise, as illustrated in Figure 11 C), another discrete feature's proportions of category c_3 and c_4 in D_i are higher than that of $D - D_i$. These may suggest that the features in these ranges or categories could be potential factors affecting sudden drop instances. Thus, some of them may be used as thresholds to invoke the inflection predictor. That is, once an instance has a feature's value falling in the surpassing ranges or categories, we send the instance simultaneously to the inflection predictor (besides the spatial and temporal predictors).

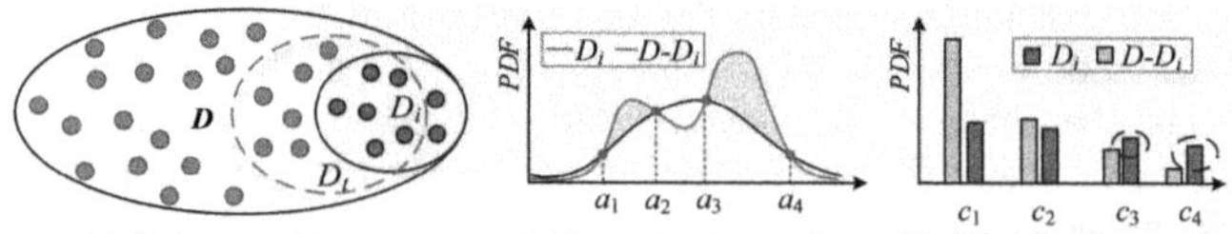

Figure 11. Illustration of building an infection predictor

Step 3: Selecting surpassing ranges and categories as thresholds. While there are multiple surpassing ranges and categories, some of them may not really be discriminative enough (to be a threshold) to invoke the inflection predictor. To improve training quality, we need to find a set of surpassing ranges and categories as thresholds, with which we can retrieve as many instances from D_i as possible while involving the instances from $D - D_i$ as few as possible. Formally, the problem can be defined as finding a set of surpassing ranges (or categories) that maximizes Equation 1:

$$E = Max[(\frac{|x_1|}{|D_i|} - \frac{|x_2|}{|D-D_i|}) \times \frac{\Delta|x_1|}{\Delta|x_2|}; \quad (1)$$

Where $D_t = x_1 \cup x_2$ is a collection of instances retrieved by a set of surpassing ranges and categories; $x_1 \subset D_i$ is a collection of instances in D_t that belong to D_i; $x_2 \subset (D - D_i)$ is a collection of instances in D_t that belong to $D - D_i$; $|x|$ stands for the number of instances in collection x; $\Delta|x_1| = |x_1| - |x'_1|$ denotes the increment of instances (belonging to D_i) after adding a new surpassing range or category; x'_1 is the predecessor of x_1; likewise, $\Delta|x_2| = |x_2| - |x'_2|$ stands for the increment of instances belonging to $D - D_i$ after adding a surpassing range or category. The problem can be solved by using Simulated Annealing when there are many surpassing ranges and categories. Otherwise, we can find the most optimal combination through a brute force search.

Step 4. Training an inflection predictor with D_t: Using the thresholds selected from Step 3, we can retrieve a collection of instances D_t from the entire dataset D. We then train an inflection predictor based on D_t. Note that the selected surpassing ranges and categories are only used as thresholds to control when to invoke the inflection predictor. The features used in the inflection predictor to determine the specific drop values are the same as those of the temporal predictor. In implementation, the inflection predictor is based on a RT, which achieves a slightly better performance than using a linear regression, as some sudden drop instances may not follow a linear relationship with the features used. The output of the inflection predictor is a delta of AQI to be appended to the final result. As D_t contains instances from $D - D_i$, the prediction could be a non-dropping value. Thus, even when a non-sudden drop instance is sent to the inflection point, we can still predict them correctly.

Example: Table 1 shows an example of selecting surpassing ranges and categories based on the data of Beijing (from May 1st, 2014 to April 30th, 2015). Using the method proposed in Step 1, we find 3,184 sudden drop instances (D_i) from 292,167 instances D. By comparing the distributions of each features in D_i and D, we find six surpassing ranges and categories listed in the first column. The second column presents the percentage of instances (retrieved by only using a surpassing range or category) in D_i. The third column shows the percentage in $D - D_i$. These surpassing ranges and categories are sorted in a descending order by the ratio between the two percentages. The fourth column denotes the third part of Equation 1, and the fifth column presents the final score E. After adding the surpassing ranges or categories one by one (starting from the *WindSpeed*), the value of E increases until the fourth surpassing category is added. This is also the global maximum of E in all combinations of items shown in the first column. In the last two columns, the values shown at the i-th row are calculated based on the *first i* surpassing ranges and categories in the first column. For example, E=0.149 is the score when selecting *Wind Speed (13.9-max), Humidity (1-40)*, and *Downpour*. In the deployed system, we select the three surpassing ranges and category for Beijing. As long as a coming instance has a wind speed feature greater than 13.9m/s, and/or humidity lower than 40, and/or downpour, the instance will be sent to the inflection predictor (besides being sent to the spatial and temporal predictors).

Table 1. Example of selecting surpassing ranges/categories

Ranges/categories	$\|x_1\|/\|D_i\|$	$\|x_2\|/\|D\text{-}D_i\|$	$\Delta\|x_1\|/\Delta\|x_2\|$	E
WinSpeed:13.9-	**0.130**	**0.031**	**0.065**	**0.006**
Humidity:1-40	**0.380**	**0.173**	**0.128**	**0.026**
Downpour	**0.382**	**0.174**	**0.714**	**0.149**
Wind Northwest	0.478	0.263	0.078	0.017
Sunny	0.643	0.405	0.084	0.020
Moderate rainy	0.680	0.437	0.087	0.020

After using our method, D_t has a much higher presence of sudden drop instances than D, leading to a quality model predicting sudden drops online. For example, in Beijing the presence has been increased from 1.1% in D to 14.6% in D_t. Note that we would never be able to find some thresholds that can completely exclude instances from $D - D_i$ while embracing all instances from D_i. Thus, we cannot train the inflection predictor using D_i whose distribution differs from coming instances in online predictions.

4. EVALUATIONS

4.1 Settings

4.1.1 Datasets

Air quality data: Our system collects air quality data every hour from 2,296 stations in 302 Chinese cities. Figure 12 A) presents the geographical distribution of these stations, where each icon stands for a station. Each air quality instance consists of the concentration of six air pollutants: NO_2, SO_2, O_3, CO, PM2.5 and PM10. We convert these concentrations into corresponding (individual) AQIs for each air pollutant according to Chinese AQI standards (but without doing a 24-hour moving average over the AQIs). In total, over 12 million air quality instances have been collected from August 2012 to May 2015. As the cities are added into our system at different stages, the specific time spans of the AQI data in particular cities are different.

Meteorological data: The system collects meteorological data from 3,514 cities/districts/stations; Figure 12 B) shows these locations. Most major cities have a district-level (or even finer) granularity for the data, while small cities only have a city-level report. The location of a district (or city)-level meteorological report is represented by the geographical center of a district (or a city). Each meteorological record consists of sunny/cloudy/overcast/foggy/snowy/rainy, temperature, humidity, wind speed, and wind direction. Regarding rain and snow, there are different levels, such as minor rain, moderate rain, heavy rain and rainstorm. The meteorological data updates every hour, generating 16 million instances in total until April 30th, 2015.

Weather forecasts: The system collects weather forecasts for 2,612 cities/districts. The geographical granularity of a weather forecast is very similar but slightly coarser than the meteorological data (a district-level at most) in some cities. We collect the forecast for the next three days for each update, which is usually segmented into multiple 3-hour (or six-hour) time intervals. A weather forecast for each time interval consists of sunny/cloudy/overcast/foggy/snowy /rainy, wind speed, and wind direction. The updating frequency of the forecasts varies by city (some cities are updated every 3 hours; some are 6 hours and 12 hours). In total, 203 million weather forecasts have been recorded until April 30th, 2015.

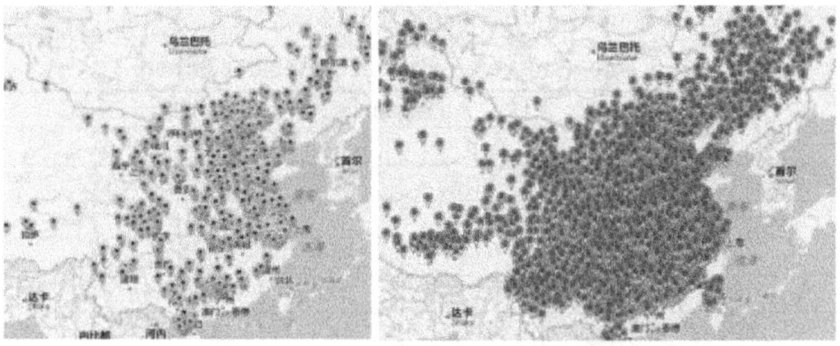

A) Air quality stations B) Meteorological sources

Figure 12 Sources of air quality and meteorological data

In this section, we present the evaluation of 4 major Chinese cities (Beijing, Tianjin, Guangzhou and Shenzhen) whose datasets have been detailed in Table 2. For example, Beijing has 36 air quality monitoring stations, 17 meteorological sources and 17 weather forecasting sources, respectively generating 278,085 air quality instances, 116,867 meteorological instances and 390,702 weather forecasts from May 1st, 2014 to April 30th, 2015. To predict the air quality of the 36 stations in Beijing, 233 air quality monitoring stations from 14 cities that are within 300km to Beijing are retrieved. Figure 13 A) shows the geographical distribution of these stations, which generate 1,272,979 air quality instances in the given time span. In addition, 177 meteorological sources from the 14 nearby cities are used in Beijing's evaluation, generating 1,006,814 meteorological instances. As the weather forecasting source is similar to the meteorological source, we only plot the geographical distribution of the latter in Figure 13 B).

Table 2. Some Details of Datasets

	Datasets	Beijing	Tianjin	Guangzhou	Shenzhen
	Time span	2014/5/1-2015/4/30	2014/5/1-2015/4/30	2014/5/1-2015/4/30	2014/5/1-2015/4/30
	Nearby cities	14	17	19	19
AQI	In-city stations	36	27	42	11
	In-city instances	278,085	191,167	283,735	88,154
	Drop instances	3184	1945	134	8
	Ave. PM2.5	106.4	104.3	59.5	44.9
	Neighbor Sta.	233	267	145	148
	#. of instances	1,272,979	1,436,051	1,002,877	1,068,543
Meteorology	In-city sources	17	20	5	7
	In-city instances	116,867	106,614	30,305	55,632
	Nearby sources	177	195	115	122
	Near instances	1,006,814	1,108,873	626,418	665,463
Forecast	In-city sources	17	20	5	6
	In-city instances	390,702	361,624	106,380	51,870
	Nearby sources	184	182	110	114

In total, the data from another 39 cities has been involved in prediction for the four major cities. Since PM2.5 (Particulate Matter with a diameter smaller than 2.5 micrometers) is the most reported (and also the most difficult-to-predict) air pollutant, we focus the evaluation on PM2.5. Our method can be generally applied to other pollutants and countries. We partition the data into non-overlapped training and test data by a ratio of 2:1. For example, we select the data in March, June, September and December as the test set, and the other months as the train dataset. The data set has been released to the public in [17].

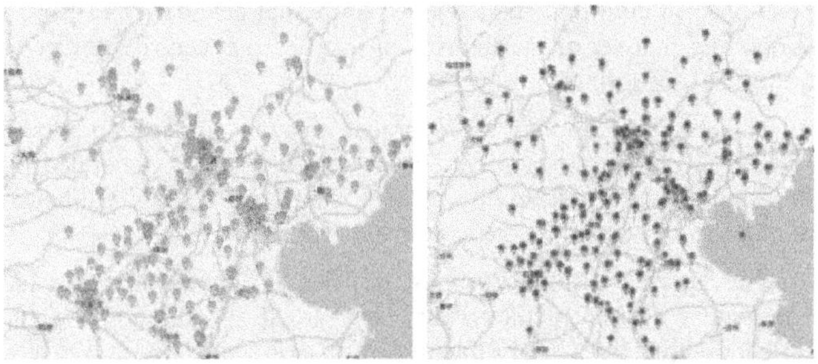

A) Nearby AQI stations for Beijing B) Meteorological sources for Beijing

Figure 13. Geo-distributions of the data sources for Beijing

Figure 14 shows the distributions of PM2.5'AQIs in the four cities, where the six AQI spans are defined by Chinese standards, respectively corresponding to *Good, Moderate, Unhealthy for Sensitive Group, Unhealthy, Very unhealthy and Hazardous*. As Beijing has the biggest population and the most complicated air quality, we focus on Beijing's data when comparing with different baselines, while showing overall results for the other three cities.

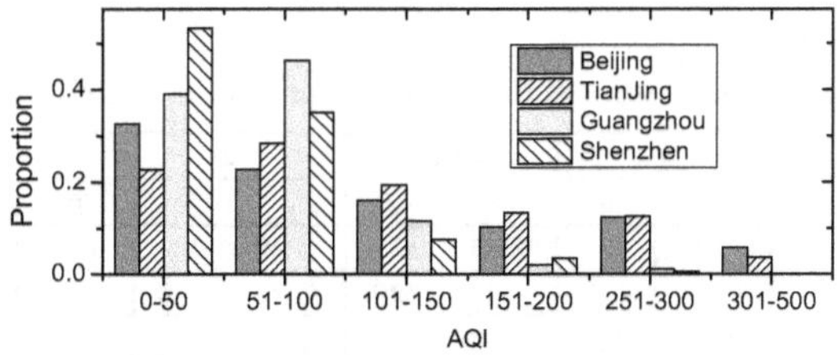

Figure 14. Distributions of AQI in PM2.5

4.1.2 Metrics and Ground Truth

We predict the air quality of a station as we can obtain the ground truth from its later readings. For the next 1-6 hours, we measure the prediction of each hour $\hat{y}_i$ against its ground truth y_i, calculating the accuracy according to Equation 2. With respect to the next 7-12, 13-24, 25-48 hours, we measure the mean of the predicted maximum and minimum values against the mean of the truth AQIs during the interval. As a result, we generate an accuracy for the four time intervals respectively at each station. We also calculate the absolute error of each time interval according to Equation 3, where n is the number of instances measured for a time interval.

$$p = 1 - \frac{\sum_i |\hat{y}_i - y_i|}{\sum_i y_i}; \tag{2}$$

$$e = \frac{\sum_i |\hat{y}_i - y_i|}{n}. \tag{3}$$

We aggregate the accuracy of the same time interval from all the stations in a city into a final result for the city. Finally, a city will have four overall accuracies and four absolute errors in 1-6, 7-12, 13-24, and 25-48 hours.

4.1.3 Baselines

We compare our method, entitled *FFA* (*TP+SP+PA+IP*), with four sets of baselines:

1) *ARMA*: Auto-Regression-Moving-Average (*ARMA*) is a well-known model for predicting time series data. ARMA predicts the air quality of a station solely based on the AQIs of the station. This baseline justifies the advantages of using weather forecasts and meteorological data.

2) This set of baselines feeds all features into a single model, e.g. linear regression (*LR_ALL*), neural network (*ANN_ALL*), and regre-

ssion tree (*RT_ALL*), without treating different features differently. Defining these baselines is to justify the advantages of using a combination of multiple models. As *LR*, *RT* and *ANN* have also been used in environmental science to predict air quality [4][5][6], surpassing this set of baselines also justifies our contribution over traditional approaches.

3) This baseline applies the classical weather forecasting model (*WFM*) to predict air quality. The results of *WFM* is generated by the Beijing Municipal Environmental Monitoring Center, published at http://zx.bjmemc.com.cn/ at 8am and 8pm every day.

4) The fourth set of baselines justifies the necessity of each component of our method. For example, if we do not use the inflection predictor (*IP*), or the prediction aggregator (*PA*).

4.2 Results

4.2.1 Results of Temporal Predictors

We first check if the features we feed into the temporal predictor are really useful. As shown in Table 3, by adding AQIs from the past three hours (*A*), time of day and day of the week (*T*), meteorological features (*M*), and weather forecasts (*F*) step by step, we see a clear improvement on the accuracy p and a decrease on the absolute error e at every future time interval we are going to predict. The results are generated by solely applying the temporal predictor to the test instances.

Table 3. Results of the temporal predictor in Beijing

Time	1-6h		7-12h		13-24h		25-48h	
Features	*p*	*e*	*p*	*e*	*p*	*e*	*p*	*e*
A	0.702	28	0.515	63.9	0.449	70.0	0.448	68.5
A+T	0.706	27.7	0.519	63.3	0.443	70.8	0.433	70.3
A+T+M	0.711	27.2	0.548	59.4	0.470	67.4	0.442	69.2
A+T+M+F	**0.713**	**27.0**	**0.560**	**57.9**	**0.477**	**66.5**	**0.461**	**66.8**

4.2.2 Results of Spatial Predictors

Table 4 presents the results of the spatial predictors respectively using (*ANN_Par*) and without using (*ANN_Raw*) the spatial partition and aggregation. According to the results of 7-12, 13-24, 24-48, the spatial partition and aggregation significantly improves the performance of the spatial predictor. Without this process, there are too many inputs for an *ANN*, leading to too many parameters in the model. Consequently, we cannot learn a set of accurate parameters for the *ANN* based on the limited training data. Additionally, the computational load of *ANN_Raw* is very heavy due to a large number of parameters involved. We also tested a linear regression model in the spatial predictor. In general, *LR* has a similar performance in predicting normal instances but less effective (2% lower) than *ANN* in dealing with sudden drops.

Table 4. The results of the spatial predictor in Beijing

Time	1-6h		7-12h		13-24h		25-48h	
	p	*e*	*p*	*e*	*p*	*e*	*p*	*e*
ANN_Raw	0.693	36.9	0.482	88.1	0.409	98.3	0.318	109.8
ANN_Par	**0.742**	**24.3**	**0.587**	**54.4**	**0.471**	**67.3**	**0.384**	**76.4**

4.2.3 Results of Prediction Aggregator

The results presented in Table 5 justify the advantages of the prediction aggregator (*PA*) which combines the predictions generated by the spatial and temporal predictors (*TP+SP+PA*). This table aggregates the accuracies and absolute errors of four different time intervals. First, *PA* improves the performance of individual spatial and temporal predictors, particularly in predicting sudden drop instances. Second, the combination of (*TP, SP, PA*) outperforms the second set of baselines: *LR_ALL* and *ANN_ALL*, which feed all features into a single model (*LR* or *ANN*).

Table 5. The results of prediction aggregator in Beijing

Methods	All Instances		Sudden Drops	
	p	*e*	*p*	*e*
Temporal Predictor (TP)	0.642	39.2	-0.314	125.2
Spatial Predictor (SP)	0.655	38.2	0.116	85.8
LR_ALL	0.667	36.7	0.015	94.4
ANN_ALL	0.647	39.0	0.150	82.0
TP+SP+PA	**0.670**	**36.4**	**0.173**	**80.5**

4.2.4 Results of Inflection Predictors

We learn the thresholds for the inflection predictor (*IP*) from the D_i of the entire dataset. The surpassing ranges and categories on the first three rows of Table 1 are selected as thresholds for Beijing. We then use these thresholds to find D_t from the training set and the test set respectively. As a result, 4,768 instances are used for training and 2,933 for testing, generating the results shown in Table 6. We find *RT* outperforms *LR* in predicting the sudden drops when used individually and in conjunction with *TP+SP+PA*. The *IP* also brings significant improvement over *TP+SP+PA*. The results of sudden drops in Table 5 are based on D_i while Table 6 is derived from D_t. Some drop instances are not retrieved by the thresholds.

Table 6. Results of the Inflection Predictor in Beijing

Metrics	Individually		*TP+SP+PA+IP*		*TP+SP+PA*
	LR	*RT*	*LR*	*RT*	
p	0.001	0.025	0.253	**0.262**	0.125
e	87.7	86.15	72.1	**72.9**	77.8

4.2.5 Overall results

Table 7 presents the overall results of different methods, where our method *FFA* outperforms all the baselines. *ARMA*-2 means an *ARMA* considering the recent 2 hours for a moving average. First, the meteorological data and weather forecasts bring improvements to air quality prediction. Second, as compared to *LR_ALL* and *ANN_ALL*, our method has a stronger capability of predicting the air quality of farther future and the sudden drops. The results justify the contribution of using a combination of three components rather than feeding all the features into a single model. The results also show that *ANN* is more capable of dealing with sudden changes than *LR*. In many real-world problems, we may not be able to get sufficient data to train a big model. Thus, a deep understanding of the data and the merit of different kinds of models is important.

Table 7. Comparison among different methods: in Beijing

Time	1-6h		7-12h		13-24h		25-48h		Sudden Changes	
Methods	*p*	*e*	*p*	*e*	*p*	*e*	*p*	*e*	*p*	*e*
AMRA-2	0.663	40.4	0.499	84.2	0.371	104.4	0.2	128.8	-0.622	179.1
AMRA-6	0.607	46.9	0.475	88.0	0.365	105.3	0.203	128.0	-0.523	170.6
LR_ALL	0.744	24.1	0.594	53.4	0.496	64.1	0.449	68.3	0.015	94.4
ANN_ALL	0.733	25.2	0.586	54.4	0.457	69.0	0.383	76.4	0.150	82.0
TP+SP+PA	0.75	23.6	0.601	52.4	0.498	63.9	0.444	69	0.173	80.5
FFA (TP+SP+PA+IP)	**0.749**	**23.7**	**0.601**	**52.4**	**0.498**	**63.9**	**0.444**	**69**	**0.262**	**72.1**

Third, the inflection predictor does not comprise the performance of our method, while significantly enhancing our method's capability of predicting sudden changes.

In Table 8, we compare our method *FFA* with *WFM*, which uses a weather forecasting model to predict air quality, during the time span: September 1st 2014 to April 30th 2015. The Beijing Municipal Environmental Monitoring Center (using *WFM*) only provides a district-level forecast for the next 12 hours, updating the forecast twice a day at 8am and 8pm. So, *FFA* has more accuracy predictions with a finer granularity and a farther forecasting period over *WFM*. In addition, *FFA* can update every hour, which indicates less online computational cost than *WFM*.

Table 8. Compare *FFA* with WFM in Beijing

Methods	1-6 hours		7-12 hours		Update	Grained
	p	e	p	e	Hours	Level
FFA	0.839	33.4	0.795	60.0	1	Station
WFM	0.761	49.6	0.777	65.3	12	District

Table 9 details the average absolute error at different time intervals and in different AQI ranges. For example, when predicting the air quality of the next 1 to 6 hours, the average absolute error for the air quality whose AQI falls in the range of [0, 50] is 17.5. Regarding the instances whose AQI falls into 50-100, the average absolute error is 21.2. According to the values shown in the last row, we can achieve an absolute error less than 38 when the real AQI is under 200. As the training instances falling into 300-500 are very small (refer to Figure 15), the error is relatively high in the range of [300-500].

Table 9. Average absolute error in different AQI ranges

Time	0-50	50-100	100-150	150-200	200-300	300-500
1-6	17.5	21.2	23.9	29.5	38.9	61.6
7-12	43.4	45.2	44.2	50.0	62.2	105.2
13-24	68.5	47.8	45.9	56.5	78.1	141.1
25-48	100.3	56.3	40.9	51.8	86.3	181.8
Total	35.2	30.7	30.5	37.3	51.1	88.6

Table 10 presents the results of our method in Beijing, Tianjin, Guangzhou and Shenzhen. Our method has a better performance in the latter two cities, as their air quality falls drastically in the range of [0,150] (see Figure 14) and the number of sudden changes is much smaller than Beijing and Tianjin (refer to Table 2). In short, their air quality is easy to predict. In such kinds of cities, our method does not show clear advantages beyond *TP+SP+PA*. We also compare our method with different baselines based on Tianjin's data, finding a similar trend there.

Figure 15 A) shows the prediction of our method at the next 6th hour against the ground truth in Beijing from Sep. 1, 2014 to Sep. 30, 2014. Figures 15 B), C) and D) present those of Tianjin, Guangzhou and Shenzhen. In general, Beijing and Tianjin have much more complicated air quality (changing over time) than Guangzhou and Shenzhen. Our model is very accurate in tracing the ground truth curves (including sudden changes) in the four cities. Figure 15 E) presents the average of the maxi-min predictions of our method for the next 7-12 hours against the ground truth (i.e. the gray area).

4.2.6 Efficiency and Resources

Table 11 presents the resources we use on the cloud (MS Azure) to enable the forecasting service. It also shows the time consumed by each component of our method to predict the air quality for a station at a time interval. On average, our method can generate a prediction in 3ms, finishing the forecast of the next 48 hours for a station in 36ms (recall that we have 12 models: 6 for the first six hours, 2 for each of the three time intervals). Given such a configuration, our service can answer over 40,000 request per hour. By adding more instances for the Azure Website, we easily upgrade our service to answer more queries.

Table 11. Configuration of Cloud and inference performance

Services	Configurations	Models	Time (ms)
Azure WebSite	S2 Standard (2 cores, 3.5G Memo)	*Feature*	1.778
	3 instances	*TP*	0.010
Cloud Service	A1 (1 core, 1.75 GB Memory)	*SP*	0.108
	1 instance	*PA*	0.247
Database	Standard S0 (10 DTUs)	*IP*	0.508

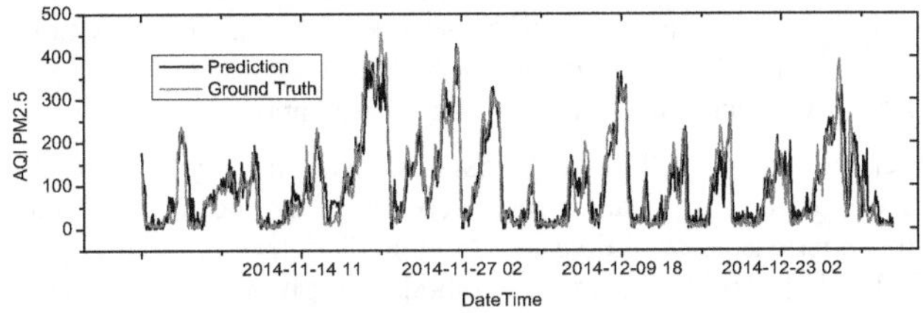

A) 6-hour PM2.5 prediction of HaidianWanliu Station, Beijing

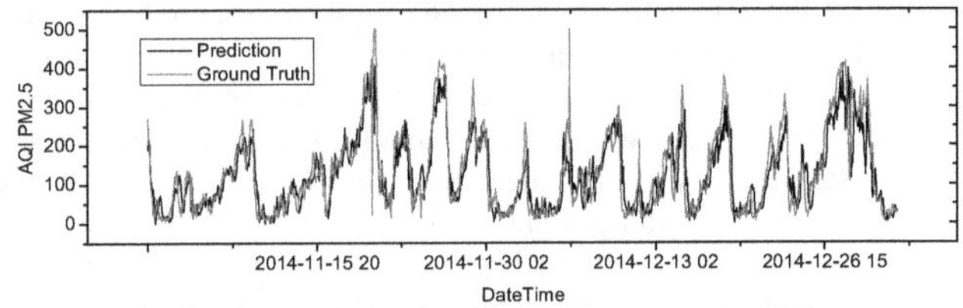

B) 6-hour PM2.5prediction of Dazhigu Station in Tianjin

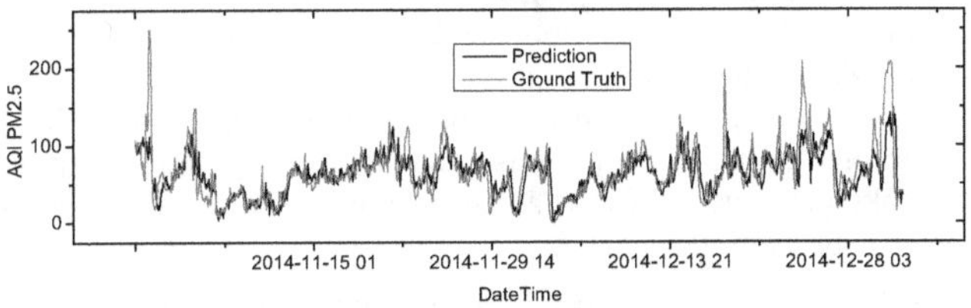

C) 6-hour PM2.5 prediction of Luhu School, Guangzhou

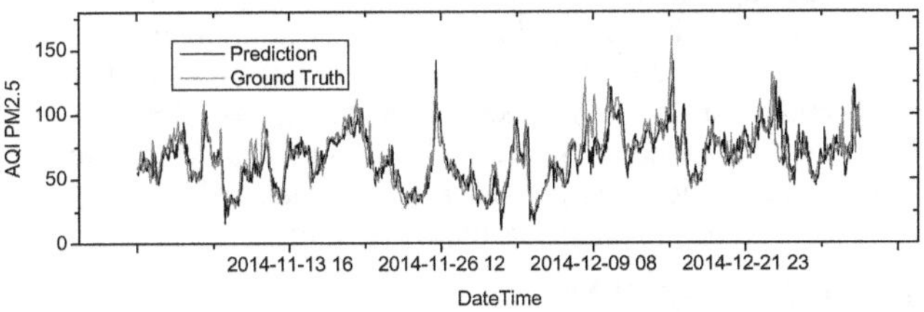

D) 6-hour PM2.5 prediction of Nanyou station in Shenzhen

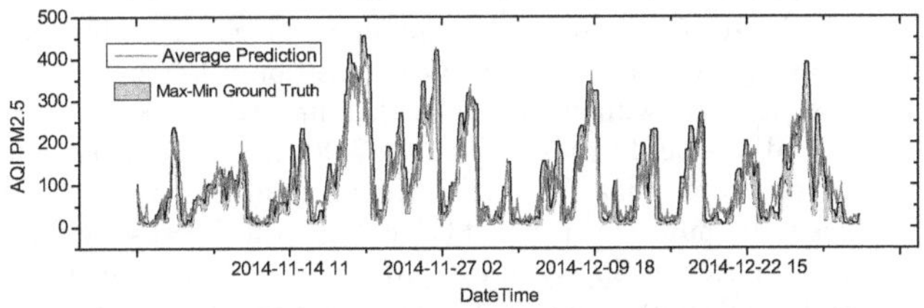

E) 7-12 hours PM2.5 prediction at HaidianWanliu in Beijing

Figure 15. *FFA*'s Predictions against ground truths

5. RELATED WORK

Existing air quality prediction methods in Environmental Science are usually based on classical dispersion models, such as Gaussian Plume models, Operational Street Canyon models, and Computational Fluid Dynamics [11].

Table 10. Overall results of our method in four major cities of China

Time	1-6h		7-12h		13-24h		25-48h		Sudden Changes	
Cities	*p*	*e*	*p*	*e*	*p*	*e*	*p*	*e*	*p*	*e*
Beijing	0.749	23.7	0.601	52.4	0.498	63.9	0.444	69	0.262	72.1
Tianjin	0.754	24.2	0.63	50.1	0.582	54.7	0.578	54.2	0.395	66.5
Guangzhou	0.797	11.3	0.717	22.4	0.676	25.2	0.644	27.5	0.572	45.9
Shenzhen	0.832	7.5	0.753	15.7	0.72	17.7	0.7	18.9	0.791	18.3

These models are in most cases a function of meteorology, street geometry, receptor locations, traffic volumes, and emission factors (e.g. g/km per single vehicle), based on a number of empirical assumptions and parameters that might not be applicable to all urban environments [11]. As these parameters are difficult to obtain precisely, the results generated by such kinds of models may not be very accurate [14]. We instead use a data-driven method to predict air quality rather than empirical model-based approaches.

Over the past decade, some statistic models, like linear regression, regression tree [5][9] and neural networks, have been employed in atmospheric science to do a real-time prediction of air quality [4][6][7][12][13]. However, these methods simply feed a variety of features about a location into a single model to predict the future air quality of the location. Our method is distinguished from these approaches in three ways. First, besides the data of the location we predict, we also incorporate the data from other spatial neighbors (e.g. nearby stations), which send signals to the predictive model thereby significantly improving prediction accuracy. Second, we feed different data sources into different models, capturing the spatial correlation of air quality in different locations and the temporal dependency of air quality in a location simultaneously. These models are then aggregated organically to provide a more accurate prediction than solely feeding all the data into a single model. Third, our method is more capable of forecasting sudden changes in air quality than these other simple approaches. Being able to predict sudden changes is vital to informing people's decision making, but very difficult given such little presence in the entire body of observations.

More recently, there has been a trend of applying big data to solve urban challenges in the form of urban computing [15]. For example, in 2013, we used big data to infer the real-time and fine-grained air quality throughout an entire city [14][16]. Hsieh et al. [8] suggested the locations for air quality monitoring stations based on big data. Shang et al. [10] used GPS trajectories of sample of vehicles to infer the city-wide vehicular emissions. However, none of these technical works is concerned with forecasting air quality.

6. CONCLUSION

In this paper, we report on a real-time air quality forecasting system that uses data-driven models to predict fine-grained air quality over the following 48 hours. The system is based on a framework that connects the cloud with clients, collecting air quality, meteorological data and weather forecasts from over 3,000 sources (e.g. stations /districts/cities) in China. The mobile client, entitled Urban Air, and the website are public available at [1] and [2]. The forecasting function has also been deployed on Bing Map China at [3]. The system has also been deployed with the Chinese Ministry of Environmental Protection. We evaluate our predictive method with data from 43 cities, presenting the results of four major cities: Beijing, Tianjin, Guangzhou and Shenzhen. By combining four major components, consisting of temporal predictor, spatial predictor, prediction aggregator, and inflection predictor, our method outperforms four sets of baselines significantly, including the baseline approach using weather forecasting models to predict air quality. In general, our method can achieve an accuracy of 0.75 for the first 6 hours and 0.6 for the next 7-12 hours in Beijing. It predicts the sudden changes of air quality much better than baseline methods. With a very light resource strain on the cloud, on average, our method can generate predictions for the following 48 hours for a station in 36ms.

7. REFERENCES

[1] Urban Air Website: http://urbanair.msra.cn/

[2] Urban Air Windows Phone Client: http://www.windowsphone.com/en-us/store/app/urban-air/f36d5a33-2ccc-45f5-afd2-0c1afc5fc6dc

[3] Air Quality Forecasting on Bing Map: http://cn.bing.com/ditu/

[4] Air Quality Research Subcommittee of the Committee on Environment and Natural Resources CENR. Air Quality Forecasting: A Review of Federal Programs and Research Needs, June 2001

[5] Burrows, W.R., Benjamin, M., Beauchamp, S., Lord, E.R., McCollor, D., Thomson, B., 1995. CART Decision-Tree Statistical Analysis and Prediction of Summer Season Maximum Surface Ozone for the Vancouver, Montreal, and Atlantic Regions of Canada. J. Appl. Meteor. Climatol. 34.

[6] Donnelly, A., Misstear, B., Broderick, B. Real Time Air Quality Forecasting using Integrated Parametric and Nonparametric Regression techniques. *Atmospheric Environment* 103 (2015), pp. 53–65.

[7] Environmental Protection. Guideline for Developing an Ozone Forecasting Program. EPA-454/R-99-009. July 1999

[8] Hsieh, H. P., Lin, S. D., Zheng, Y. Inferring Air Quality for Station Location Recommendation Based on Big Data. In Proc. of *KDD 2015*, 2015.

[9] Lewis, R. J. An Introduction to Classification and Regression Tree (CART) Analysis. Presented at the 2000 Annual Meeting of the Society for Academic Emergency Medicine.

[10] Shang, J., Zheng, Y., Tong, W., Chang, E. and Yu, Y. "Inferring Gas Consumption and Pollution Emission of Vehicles throughout a City," In Proc. of *KDD'14,* pp. 1027-1036, 2014.

[11] Vardoulakis, S., Fisher, B. E. A., Pericleous, K., Gonzalez-Flesca, N. Modelling Air Quality in Street Canyons: A Review. *Atmospheric Environment* 37 (2003), pp. 155-182.

[12] Zhang, Y., Bocquet, M., Mallet, V., Seigneur, C., Baklanov, A., Real-time Air Quality Forecasting, Part I: History, techniques, and current status, Atmospheric Environment 60 (2012), pp. 632–655.

[13] Zhang, Y., Bocquet, M., Mallet, V., Seigneur, C., Baklanov, A., Real-time Air Quality Forecasting, Part II: State of the science, current research needs, and future prospects, *Atmospheric Environment* 60 (2012), pp. 656–676.

[14] Zheng, Y., Liu, F., Hsieh, H. P. U-Air: When Urban Air Quality Inference Meets Big Data. In Proc. of *KDD 2013*, pp. 1436-1444, 2013.

[15] Zheng, Y., Capra, L., Wolfson, O., Yang, H. "Urban Computing: Concepts, Methodologies, and Applications," *ACM Trans. Intelligent Systems and Technology*, vol. 5, no. 3, pp. 38-55, 2014.

[16] Zheng, Y., Chen, X., Jin, Q., Chen, Y. Qu, X., Liu, L., Chang, E., Ma, W.Y., Rui, Y., Sun, W., A Cloud-Based Knowledge Discovery System for Monitoring Fine-Grained Air Quality. MSR-TR-2014-40

[17] Released Data: http://research.microsoft.com/apps/pubs/?id=246398

Building Discriminative User Profiles for Large-scale Content Recommendation

Erheng Zhong, Nathan Liu, Yue Shi and Suju Rajan
Personalization Sciences, Yahoo Labs, CA, USA
{erheng,nanliu,yueshi,suju}@yahoo-inc.com

ABSTRACT

Content recommendation systems are typically based on one of the following paradigms: user based customization, or recommendations based on either collaborative filtering or low rank matrix factorization methods, or with systems that impute user interest profiles based on content browsing behavior and retrieve items similar to the interest profiles. All of these systems have a distinct disadvantage, namely data sparsity and cold-start on items or users. Furthermore, very few content recommendation solutions explicitly model the wealth of information in implicit negative feedback from the users. In this paper, we propose a hybrid solution that makes use of a latent factor model to infer user interest vectors. The hybrid approach enables us to overcome both the data sparsity and cold-start problems. Our proposed method is learned purely on implicit user feedback, both positive and negative. Exploiting the information in the negative feedback allows the user profiles generated to be discriminative. We also provide a Map/Reduce framework based implementation that enables scaling our solution to real-world recommendation problems. We demonstrate the efficacy of our proposed approach with both offline experiments and A/B tests on live traffic on Yahoo properties.

Categories and Subject Descriptors: H.4 [Information Systems Applications]: Miscellaneous

General Terms: Design, Experimentation

Keywords: Collaborative filtering, content-based recommendation, large scale recommender systems, latent factor models, user profiling.

1. INTRODUCTION

The explosion of online content from news sites, digital magazines, self-publishing platforms and blogs has necessitated an industry around the concept of personalized content recommendation. Products, such as the Yahoo Stream, LinkedIn Feed, Google News and Facebook Feeds, attempt to surface content that is relevant to each user. At any given instance, each of those products attempt to discover and present the most relevant news items from a corpus of around a few million items to the millions of users visiting their sites [8]. While there is a slew of work around recommendation systems, classical methods of recommendation, such as collaborative filtering methods or low rank factorization models [11] assume a long shelf life of items to be recommended, such that each item can garner sufficient user interaction over time. Such assumptions do not hold true in the domain of news content recommendation. Thus, even such a paradigm has been shown to work very well for content items with a long-shelf life, such as movies or consumer products [6], they are generally less effective for news item recommendations as news items tend to expire quickly.

A simple solution to solving the problem of personalized news recommendation is to allow the user to configure personal filters or provide explicit input on news providers, topics or entities that the user would like to be shown content on. Examples of such products are Flipboard, Zite, MyYahoo etc. Needless to say moving the burden of configuration is non-ideal as the user has to continually update his interests to keep pace with the ever-changing nature of news topics or be satisfied with following a limited number of providers.

To overcome these problems, in this paper, we propose another approach by building user interest imputation or user profiling based on the user's feedback on content items. The feedback can be explicit, in the form of ratings or binary preference indicators or implicit, i.e. inferred from the user's interaction with the content item. As with explicit interest declarations, assuming the presence of explicit feedback is infeasible. On the other hand, there is a rich set of implicit feedback that can be obtained from the user's behavior on a content item. As an example, a user can indicate positive preference by clicking on an item or dwelling on it beyond a threshold [29], while a negative feedback can be construed from a lack of click or very low time spend on an item. Given the user feedback on a set of content items, one can then attempt to characterize or build a profile for the user.

Although user profiles can be specialized for every specific product domain, in a general sense, a user profile can be thought of as a numeric representation that indicates the user's interest in a feature space. For example, in the case of Netflix Prize competition [11], the user profile can be seen as a vector of ratings over all the items, i.e., the item space is then the feature space. Such a setting leads itself to collaborative filtering based solutions to the recommendation problem. Alternatively, a user profile can also be built using

KDD'15, August 10-13, 2015, Sydney, NSW, Australia.
© 2015 ACM. ISBN 978-1-4503-3664-2/15/08 ...$15.00.
DOI: http://dx.doi.org/10.1145/2783258.2788610.

the features of the content items that the user has interacted with. Examples of content features for news items are topical categories the content belongs to, the set of named entities in the content item or even the word tokens that appear in item. The feature space of the user profile is then the same as the space of content features and the feature value in the user profile indicates the relevance of the content feature to the user. At the time of serving content items to users, the relevance between a user and an item can be measured based on the similarity between the user's profile and the content features of the item.

The advantage of building such user interest profiles is that this method suffers less from the item cold-start case. That is, even if the user is the very first person to interact with that item, it can be deemed as being relevant to the user as long as there is an overlap in the user interest profile and the item's features. Furthermore, as will be demonstrated later, such profile building methods can be built from a combination of explicit, implicit positive or negative feedback from the user. Thus, building user profiles is a viable solution to the content recommendation systems [15]. However, there are also a few challenges to building an effective user profiling method.

- **Scalability:** Online companies may serve millions of users and items everyday, and thus, personalized recommendation is by default a task at a very large scale. In addition, the content features, based on which the user profiles are built, may probably lie in a very high dimension space, e.g., one text document can be represented by thousands of word tokens or n-grams. As a result, building profiles for individual users requires computation over a massive feature space.
- **Complex implicit feedback:** Explicit feedback from the user, such as ratings, is a sparse signal. A more practical solution is to rely on the implicit feedback provided by the user. For example, a click on an item from a user may indicate that the user is interested in the item, and thus, we can infer that the content features of the item are relevant to the user. However, there can be multiple types of user feedback happening between users and items beyond clicks. In particular, those signals that can be seen as negative feedback of the users are of great value, since they open the possibilities to improve the discriminative ability of user profiles. Then, one of the key challenges is considered as how to effectively exploit the complex implicit feedback data for modeling user profiles.
- **Data sparsity:** While profiling based content recommendation suffers less from the item cold-start case, the problem could still exist. Since user interest profiles are built on a high-dimensional feature space, it is often that a user could have only a small set of observed content features in his profile. Such a case is common for users who interact with a limited number of news items. In an extreme case, the feature set in a user's profile can be so small that it has no intersection with the content features of any items in the corpus. Furthermore, limited interaction data between a user and a content item makes it difficult to confidently estimate the relevance of the corresponding content features to the user. In other words, the number of available instances can be insufficient for an accurate estimation of user profiles.

In this work, we propose a method for performing personalized news recommendation that addresses the drawbacks of the current approaches. Our solution follows the paradigm of imputing user interest vectors or user profiles that can then be used to retrieve relevant content items for the user. The proposed approach tackles the challenges mentioned above by making use of a hybrid approach that combines user interest inference with latent factor models. Unlike conventional approaches that only build user profiles based on positive implicit feedback such as click events [26], we also exploit the rich signal that is present in the negative feedback of users on items. By incorporating both positive and negative user feedback, we train user interest profiles that are not only discriminative but also more effective than the conventional approaches. A straightforward baseline is to build a linear model for each individual user based on the user's positive and negative feedback on items. However, such linear model still suffers from the data sparsity issue, as it requires sufficient training examples for each individual user. Motivated by this observation, we propose to build user profiles by leveraging the latent factor model formulation. We project each user into a latent feature space, i.e., each user is represented by a vector of latent factors. We also project each content **feature** into the same latent space, i.e., each content **feature** is also represented by a vector of latent factors. The underlying principle is then the inner product of the latent factors of a user and a content feature indicates the relevance between the two. Based on the positive and negative user feedback, we learn the latent factor of users and content features through a well-defined optimization framework. The key advantage of this model lies in the fact that the latent factors of the content features are shared across all the users. As a result, even users with limited interaction data could still be represented with a richer content feature interest vector.

Our system is built on the Hadoop-based Map/Reduce framework. This implementation can compute user profiles for millions of users in a few hours, thus making it suitable for real-world content recommendation problems. Besides performing large-scale offline experiments, the proposed method is also A/B being tested in an online test on the Yahoo Recommends (to be detailed in Section 2) property, which is a news recommendation product serving millions of users.

The main contributions of this paper are:

- We propose a user interest profile generation method based on latent factor models that effectively alleviates the data sparseness issue. An added benefit of our model is that it allows us to bootstrap even users with limited content interaction data by learning from the collective set of users.
- We provide a method to leverage the rich signal in the negative implicit feedback provided by the user.
- We provide a Map-reduce framework that can scale to building user interest vectors for millions of users in a few hours.
- We demonstrate the effectiveness of our user profiling model through large-scale offline experiments and A/B testing on real-world applications.

The paper is organized as follows. In Section 2, we introduce the Yahoo Recommends product, as an example of a content recommendation system that can benefit from our proposed approach. We then present the details of latent factor based model used to infer user interest profiles in Section 3. We then introduce the Map-Reduce framework design in Section 4. The offline and real-world experimental results are demonstrated in Section 5, followed by Section 6 that differentiates our work from other related approaches. Section 7 concludes the paper.

2. USE CASES OF USER PROFILE

We introduce two use cases of user profile in Yahoo. The first one is the Yahoo stream, where we recommend items for the content feed or stream on the Yahoo's homepage, shown in Figure 1. In this module, news and ads are ranked based on the relevance of the item to the user and on its popularity. The second one is Yahoo Recommends, which is a recently released product that generates personalized content recommendations and a native advertising experience for users on external publishers. The product makes it easier for users to discover the publisher's content. The Yahoo Recommends product has been deployed on several hundreds of websites including CBS, Vox, and Hearst and is driving several millions of clicks on these partner sites every day. Figure 2 presents an example of the Yahoo Recommends module on an external site. Any external publisher can insert a Yahoo Recommends module on their site by filling out a simple form on the recommends.yahoo.com portal. The module is activated by including a JavaScript snippet for the page, which then triggers content crawling, and event logging and invokes the visible module on the page.

In these products, items are extracted at real time from a content corpus and ranked via a machine learned ranker. The machine learned ranking models makes use of the following classes of features which attempt to characterize three types of relevance:

Universal relevance: Features that capture the popularity and trendiness of a content item by tracking dozens of time series that characterize how users engage with each piece of content within the module, on a publisher site, on social media, and on search engines.

Contextual relevance: Features that capture the context of the page the recommendation module is shown in by leveraging a knowledge graph to measure content relatedness as well as a collaborative filtering style approach to uncover novel patterns about "people who read X who would also read Y.". For example, if a user is currently reading an iPhone 6 review, it may be better to recommend other articles about smartphones or Apple products, and if one user prefers to read sport news in the morning, it is also straightforward to display sport news for this user in the morning time in future.

Personal relevance: Features that cater to the individual preferences of the users. These features are computed using the similarities between user profiles and item features.

The variety and the scale of available user interaction data make the content stream on Yahoo homepage and Yahoo Recommends very relevant applications for testing out the efficacy of the proposed user interest profiling method. We explain the nature of the data collected and the experimental setup for both offline and online A/B tests in Section 5.

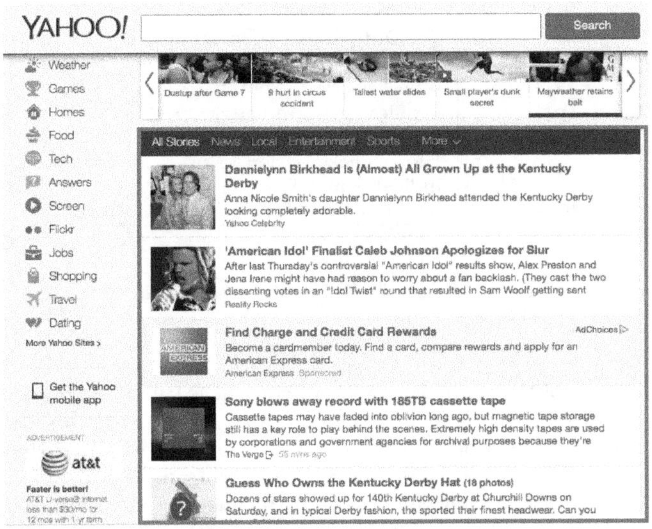

Figure 1: Stream on Yahoo Homepage (Red Box)

Figure 2: Yahoo Recommends

3. USER PROFILE MODELING

The modeling of user interest profiles is a key component of the content recommendation system. In this section, we first formulate the task of user profile modeling and then discuss the three types of models that are tested in our experiments. As baselines we describe two generative statistical models, namely TF-IDF and Chi Square (CS) based models and an independent learning model (ILM). We then describe our proposed solution the latent factor model (LFM).

3.1 Problem Formulation

Generally, user profile modeling in content recommendation system aims to represent user interests in the same space as that of the content features in order to effectively retrieve content items that are relevant to the user. Assume, there are m users, n items and f item features. Also, assume that the user is presented with a ranked list of items on which they provide implicit feedback. As an example of implicit feedback, users can either click or not click (skip) each item in the list. This implicit positive and negative feedback from the users on content items is represented as a sparse matrix C with $m \times n$ dimensions, where $\mathcal{C}_{ij} = +1$ means user $\mathbf{u}_i$ clicked an item $\mathbf{x}_j$ and $\mathcal{C}_{ij} = -1$ means $\mathbf{u}_i$ skipped item $\mathbf{x}_j$. There are still many missing values ? in $\mathcal{C}$ as each user may interact with only a few items. We further represent the items as another matrix $\mathcal{X}$ with $n \times f$ dimensions, where $\mathcal{X}$ is sparse and each entry represents a content

Table 1: Definition of notations

Notation	Description
$\mathcal{X} = \{\mathbf{x}_i\}_{i=1}^n$	Item features, a sparse matrix, $\mathbf{x}_i \in \mathcal{R}^f$
$\mathcal{P} = \{\mathbf{p}_i\}_{i=1}^m$	Profiles, a sparse matrix, $\mathbf{p}_i \in \mathcal{R}^f$
$\mathcal{C} \in [0, 1, ?]^{m\times n}$	User-item interactions, 1 for a click, -1 for a skip, ? for unknown
$\mathcal{I} \in [0, 1]^{m\times n}$	Indicator matrix
$\ell(\cdot)$, $R(\cdot)$	Loss function and regularization term
m	Number of users
n	Number of items
f	Number of features

feature of the item. Examples of content features are named entities, topical categories, noun phrase tokens, n-grams etc. Then, the user profiling problem is to build a model Ω that can construct a sparse matrix $\mathcal{P}\in\mathcal{R}^{m\times f}$ from $\mathcal{X}$ and $\mathcal{C}$, i.e., $\mathcal{P} = \Omega(\mathcal{C}, \mathcal{X})$. Generally, we aim to construct such a model in an optimization framework by minimizing the following objective:

$$\min_{\Omega} \ell(\Omega, C, X) + \lambda R(\Omega) \tag{1}$$

where ℓ is the loss function, λ is the regularization parameter and R is the regularization function to control the model complexity.

3.2 Generative Statistical Model

An intuitive solution to building profiles is to combine all features of items clicked by the user using some statistical models, such term-frequency. The motivation is that if a user interacts a lot with content items containing a specific feature, that feature may be highly relevant to this user and the user may like to read other items that contain the feature as well. A user interest profile can then be represented as a vector over content features.

$$\mathbf{p}_i = \sum_{C_{ij}=1} \mathbf{x}_j \tag{2}$$

However, some content features, such as stop words, may exist in all items and using these features to build the user profile is pointless. Thus, we need to introduce several normalization strategies to adjust the value of each feature. We introduce two methods for normalization. One is a classical document vector model, the term frequency-inverse document frequency (TF-IDF) [24] based model. The main idea of TF-IDF is to use document frequency to penalize those features that are common to all users, and highlight those specific features that can distinguish one user from another. Formally, the score of each feature $p_{ik} \in \mathbf{p}_i$ is defined as follows:

$$p_{ik} = \bar{p}_{ik} \times \log \frac{m}{|\{\bar{\mathbf{p}}_c : \bar{p}_{ck} > 0.0\}|} \tag{3}$$

$$\bar{p}_{ik} = \sum_{C_{ij}=1} \mathbf{x}_{jk} \tag{4}$$

If one feature is common in many users, then the value of the second part in Eq.(3) becomes small and thus lowers the value of the feature.

Another statistical method is derived from the Chi-Square test [19]. Its motivation is to select those features, which have much higher values for the user as compared to the expected value. This means that if one user reads items containing a specific feature at a rate that is statistically significantly above the average rate for that feature, that feature will be included in the user interest profile. Formally, the score of each feature is

$$p_{ik} = \frac{\bar{p}_{ik} + \kappa}{e_{ik} + \kappa} \tag{5}$$

$$e_{ik} = \sum_k \bar{p}_{ik} \times \frac{\sum_c \bar{p}_{ck}}{\sum_k \sum_c \bar{p}_{ck}} \tag{6}$$

where κ is the smoothing term. One advantage of this method over TF-IDF is that it can estimate the confidence of each feature value by using the z-test. The confidence value can be used for further feature selection.

$$z_{ik} = \frac{\log(\bar{p}_{ik} + \kappa)}{\sqrt{e_{ik} + \kappa}} \tag{7}$$

We can observe that generative statistical models are intuitive and easy to compute. However, these methods only use the positive feedback signal. By not taking into account, the rate at which a feature appears in the items with negative feedback such user profiles can misrepresent the relevance of the feature to the user. In other words, these models lack the ability to represent discriminative user interests.

3.3 User Independent Learning Model

In order to build user profiles that contain discriminative user interest features, we propose to leverage supervised learning algorithms that construct models from both positive and negative users' feedbacks on items and use the model coefficients on the content features as user profiles. Specifically, for each user the click or skip feedback on displayed items is used to construct the training data for that user, where each item is a feature vector with labels, click or skip. Due to the reason that we use inner product between user profiles and item features to get the relevance score for the ranking model, we apply a linear model that uses the value of coefficients as the users profiles. Generally, we aim to construct a vector $\mathbf{p}_i$ for each user to minimize the following objective

$$\min_{\mathcal{P}} \sum_{i=1}^{m}\sum_{j=1}^{n} I_{ij}\ell(C_{ij}, \mathbf{p}_i\mathbf{x}_j^T) + \lambda R(\mathbf{p}_i) \tag{8}$$

where I is an indicator matrix. $I_{ij} = 1$ if $\mathcal{C}_{ij}$ is not empty and $I_{ij} = 0$ otherwise. There are multiple approaches to get $\mathbf{p}_i$ by using different loss functions and regularization terms, such as linear support vector machine, logistic regression, linear discriminant analysis and etc. In this paper, we use logistic regression with L2-norm regularization as the learning model. Specifically, we aim to minimize the following objective

$$\min_{\mathcal{P}} \sum_{i=1}^{m}\sum_{j=1}^{n} I_{ij}\gamma(C_{ij}\mathbf{p}_i\mathbf{x}_j^T) + \lambda \parallel \mathbf{p}_i \parallel_2 \tag{9}$$

where $\gamma(x) = \log(1 + \exp(-x))$ is the logistic loss. To guarantee efficiency and minimize effects from noisy data, we use the Stochastic Gradient Descent (SGD) technique to optimize the learning objective. Besides having the property of selecting those features that are preferred by the user, another advantage of this kind of models is that they can also represent the content features that the users do not want to engage with. Despite these properties, there is still a fundamental drawback in this approach. Most users may interact with only a few items and thus the generated labeled data is limited. If we build independent models for each user, we may overfit the rare or noisy observations and fail to produce profiles that generalize well. In addition, as with the statistical models, the system has no natural property that will allow us to explore user interests.

3.4 Latent Factor Model

As stated above, although the independent learning model produces user interest features that are discriminative, the data sparsity problem can still affect the model performance. To solve this aforementioned challenge, we propose to construct each user's profile by using data from all users. The main idea is to construct a latent space for all users, where users' interests can be distinguished while still learning from all available data. Motivated by the success of matrix factorization methods in the domain of multi-task learning [30] and collaborative filtering [11], we introduce a matrix factorization based latent factor model to build profiles. Specifically, we decompose each user's profiles into two components, one is a common mapping from content item features to latent factors, which is shared by all users; and the other contains the latent factors of each user. Each latent factor represents the user's interests in that latent topic. As the membership of each item feature to latent factors is stable for all users, these feature factors can be considered as a bridge to propagate knowledge across users. Thus users who lack interaction data, can benefit from the enriched information provided by interactions from other users. In addition, each user's latent factor membership distribution is specific thereby allowing the model to reflect the users' personalized interests.

We formally describe this model as follows. Firstly, each user is represented as a latent factor vector $\mathbf{u}_i \in \mathcal{R}^{1\times k}$ that indicates users' distribution over latent factors, where k is the number of latent factors. We define $\mathcal{U} = \{\mathbf{u}_i\}_{i=1}^{m}$ as the latent factor matrix for the whole user set. To further build the correlation between item features and latent factors, we introduce another latent matrix $\mathcal{S} \in \mathcal{R}^{k\times f}$ to represent the mapping from item features to latent factors. The user profile matrix can be constructed as $\mathcal{P} = \mathcal{US}$. Then the problem is turned into how to learn $\mathcal{U}$ and $\mathcal{S}$. Following the matrix factorization framework, we propose to use $\mathcal{U}$, $\mathcal{S}$ and $\mathcal{X}$ to approximate users' interaction records $\mathcal{C}$ as $\mathcal{C} \approx USX^T$. By replacing Ω in Eq.(1) as $\mathcal{U}$ and $\mathcal{S}$, we can obtain the following objective function:

$$\min_{\mathcal{U},\mathcal{S}} \ell(\mathcal{US}\mathcal{X}^T, \mathcal{C}) + \lambda_u R_u(\mathcal{U}) + \lambda_s R_s(\mathcal{S}) \tag{10}$$

where λ_u and λ_s are the regularization parameters for $\mathcal{U}$ and $\mathcal{S}$ respectively. In practice, we can choose different loss functions and regularization terms according to different tasks. In this paper, we use L2-norm and three loss functions to handle different types of user feedback. The first one uses square loss for rating feedbacks:

$$\min_{\mathcal{U},\mathcal{S}} \sum_{i=1}^{m}\sum_{j=1}^{n} I_{ij}(\mathcal{C}_{ij} - \mathbf{u}_i\mathcal{S}\mathbf{x}_j^T)^2 + \lambda_u \parallel \mathcal{U} \parallel_2 + \lambda_s \parallel \mathcal{S} \parallel_2 \tag{11}$$

The second one uses logistic loss for binary feedback, such as the click vs. skip feedback in our problem setting:

$$\min_{\mathcal{U},\mathcal{S}} \sum_{i=1}^{m}\sum_{j=1}^{n} I_{ij}\gamma(\mathcal{C}_{ij}\mathbf{u}_i\mathcal{S}\mathbf{x}_j^T) + \lambda_u \parallel \mathcal{U} \parallel_2 + \lambda_s \parallel \mathcal{S} \parallel_2 \tag{12}$$

The last one uses AUC loss for ranking problems [20], when only implicit feedback, such as clicks are available.

$$\min_{\mathcal{U},\mathcal{S}} \sum_{i=1}^{m}\sum_{j\in I_i^+}\sum_{k\in I_i^-} \ln\sigma(\mathbf{u}_i\mathcal{S}\mathbf{x}_j^T - \mathbf{u}_i\mathcal{S}\mathbf{x}_k^T) + \lambda_u \parallel \mathcal{U} \parallel_2 + \lambda_s \parallel \mathcal{S} \parallel_2 \tag{13}$$

where $\sigma(x) = \frac{1}{1+\exp(-x)}$ is the logistic transform and I_i^+ contains the indices of positive feedbacks (e.g., clicks) and I_i^- contains that of negative ones.

Optimization In this paper, we use Stochastic Gradient Descent (SGD) to optimize the proposed LF model. The gradients with respect to $\mathcal{U}$ and $\mathcal{S}$ of one training instance are calculated as

1. Square Loss

$$\nabla\mathbf{u}_i = (\mathbf{u}_i\mathcal{S}\mathbf{x}_j^T - \mathcal{C}_{ij})\mathbf{x}_j\mathcal{S}^T + \lambda_u\mathbf{u}_i \tag{14}$$
$$\nabla\mathcal{S} = (\mathbf{u}_i\mathcal{S}\mathbf{x}_j^T - \mathcal{C}_{ij})\mathbf{u}_i^T\mathbf{x}_j^T + \lambda_s\mathcal{S} \tag{15}$$

2. Logistic Loss

$$\nabla\mathbf{u}_i = \frac{-\mathcal{C}_{ij}\mathbf{x}_j\mathcal{S}^T}{1+\exp(\mathcal{C}_{ij}\mathbf{u}_i\mathcal{S}\mathbf{x}_j^T)} + \lambda_u\mathbf{u}_i \tag{16}$$
$$\nabla\mathcal{S} = \frac{-\mathcal{C}_{ij}\mathbf{u}_i^T\mathbf{x}_j^T}{1+\exp(\mathcal{C}_{ij}\mathbf{u}_i\mathcal{S}\mathbf{x}_j^T)} + \lambda_s\mathcal{S} \tag{17}$$

3. AUC (Area Under Curve) Loss

$$\nabla\mathbf{u}_i = \frac{\exp(-y_{ijk})}{1+\exp(-y_{ijk})}(\mathbf{x}_j - \mathbf{x}_k)\mathcal{S}^T + \lambda_u\mathbf{u}_i \tag{18}$$
$$\nabla\mathcal{S} = \frac{\exp(-y_{ijk})}{1+\exp(-y_{ijk})}\mathbf{u}_i^T(\mathbf{x}_j - \mathbf{x}_k)^T + \lambda_s\mathcal{S} \tag{19}$$
$$y_{ijk} = \mathbf{u}_i\mathcal{S}\mathbf{x}_j^T - \mathbf{u}_i\mathcal{S}\mathbf{x}_k^T \tag{20}$$

To calculate the gradients for AUC loss, we employ a bootstrap strategy that samples a positive-negative feedback pair randomly. Then the updates of U and S are performed alternatively till convergence using the following equations.

$$\mathcal{U} \leftarrow \mathcal{U} - \epsilon\nabla U \tag{21}$$
$$\mathcal{S} \leftarrow \mathcal{S} - \epsilon\nabla\mathcal{S} \tag{22}$$

In practice, we update $\mathcal{S}$ user-wisely. In each round, we randomly shuffle the user set to make the order of input data different. Then, for each interaction of this user, we update the users' latent factors using SGD but keep the feature factor mapping $\mathcal{S}$ the same. After renewing the user's factors with all interactions, we go through the interactions again to update $\mathcal{S}$. The motivation is that one interaction record may be related to only a few item features and will not affect the values too much. So we can update it only once for each user. This approach also provides savings on computation time, which is critical in real-world systems. These two steps are performed alternatively till the optimization convergence.

Discussion We shall emphasize that the key contribution in our latent factor model lies in the feature factor matrix $\mathcal{S}$, which is shared across different users. Through $\mathcal{S}$ those users who have limited data can benefit from the interaction data of other users. This characteristic specifically addresses the issue we mentioned in Section 1, i.e., even if a user is only associated with a narrow range of features via his own interaction with items, we can still extrapolate his profile to a wide range of features by using the feature factor matrix

$\mathcal{S}$. Therefore, the latent factor model can substantially contribute to improving the recall of the user interest profiles. In addition, as we maximize the correlation between user-item similarities ($\mathcal{USX}^T$) and interactions ($\mathcal{C}$) by using both positive and negative feedbacks, the selected features will have higher discriminative ability which further contributes to improving the precision of the system.

4. MAP/REDUCE FRAMEWORK FOR LARGE-SCALE PROFILE BUILDING

In real-world applications, the number of users (m) can be in the order of hundreds of millions, the number of items (n) can be up to tens of millions and the number of user-item interactions can be tens of billions. Thus, making the proposed model scale up is crucial in real-world application. We propose to address this issue through the Map/Reduce [9] implementation: Hadoop. The data is partitioned based on each user and the partitioned data is stored on different machines. The computation of each model is then abstracted into two parts. We need to utilize data from multiple users to obtain global statistics or models. This means that the different machines needs to communicate to exchange data. These operations require both Map and Reduce jobs. Generally, in Map phase, we calculate sub models based on the partial data and combine all pieces of results in the Reduce phase. This applies for both computing the global statistics of generative statistical models and the learning process of the feature-factor mapping in latent factor models. The remaining operations only use the local data, such as the learning of coefficients of each user in the independent learning model and the construction of user factors in the latent factor model. This can be done locally without communications with other machines and thus only the Map job is needed. The general paradigm to generate user profiles using all these three proposed profiling building approaches through Map/Reduce is shown in Figure 3. The details are described as follows.

Generative Model In the first Map operation, we calculate the feature counts of each user and then combine all pieces of results in the Reduce phase to obtain the global statistics, such as the document frequency for TFIDF, and the general expectation of each feature of Chi-Square test. After that, as these statistics are small, they can be loaded into the distributed cache for usage in second step. Distributed cache is a feature of Hadoop and can be understood as a small dataset maintained in the memory by all machines. In the second Map phase, we calculate the term frequency locally for each user and use the global statistics to normalize the values and obtain the profiles for each user.

Independent Learning Model In this model, we consider each user independently, so for each user, we only require the relevant data of this user to build profiles. Thus, we build profiles in the first step by using logistic regression in Map phase using Eq.(9). We can also do some optional operations in the first step to provide a prior for all users, such as training a global logistic regression and using the model coefficients as the initial profiles for each user.

Latent Factor Model Basically, in the first step, we aim to construct the feature factors $\mathcal{S}$ that is shared by all users. So, in the first Map phase, we build a sub model, $\hat{\mathcal{S}}$ and $\hat{\mathcal{U}}$, based on only those users' data in the same machine locally. Then in the Reduce phase, we use an averaging strategy to obtain the final feature factors as $\mathcal{S} = AVG(\hat{\mathcal{S}})$. In the second step, we first load $\mathcal{S}$ into the distributed cache and then learn $\mathbf{u}_i$ for each user using Eq.(21) with fixed $\mathcal{S}$. Finally, we use inner product between users' and features' latent factors to get the profiles. Considering that the correlation between factors and features may be stable in a long term, we can also first construct $\mathcal{S}$ using only the feedbacks from active users and then construct factors for all users. We compare these two strategies in our experiments.

For data communication and storage, we also define a message format for user signals required by profiling models using protocol buffers [27]. One user signal record contains user ID, timestamp, item ID with features, as well as the related action:

```
message UserSignals {
    optional string user_id = 1;
    optional string item_id = 2;
    optional fixed32 timestamp = 3;
    repeated Feature features = 4;
    optional Action action_type = 5;
}
message Feature {
    optional string name = 1;
    optional float value = 2;
}
enum Action {
    SKIP = 0;
    CLICK = 1;
}
```

After grouping all messages by user, we can obtain one input instance for the framework as

```
public class User {
    String userID;
    List<UserSignals> signals;
}
```

The advantage is that, a protocol message can be serialized efficiently and methods to access data are also automatically included, that makes us focus on the model logic without worrying about the data manipulation details. In addition, it also provides a unified data interface for other data and model pipelines in the system.

5. EXPERIMENTS

In this section, we present both the offline and online experiments to evaluate the performance of our proposed user profiling models. The purpose of our experiments is to verify the usefulness of discriminative user profiles and their impact on news recommendation systems.

5.1 Offline Experiments

Our offline experiments are conducted based on the a sample of the event log data from Yahoo Recommends, as described in Section 2, collected over a period of four months. Overall, this dataset contains over 2.4 billion click events from $\sim$ 67 million users and $\sim$ 54 million news items. The number of content features of the news items is $\sim$ 500,000, which defines the feature space of our user profiles.

In order to evaluate the quality of user profiles, we split the dataset into a training set and a test set according to the timestamps of events. We use the data from all weeks but the last one as training data and the data of last week

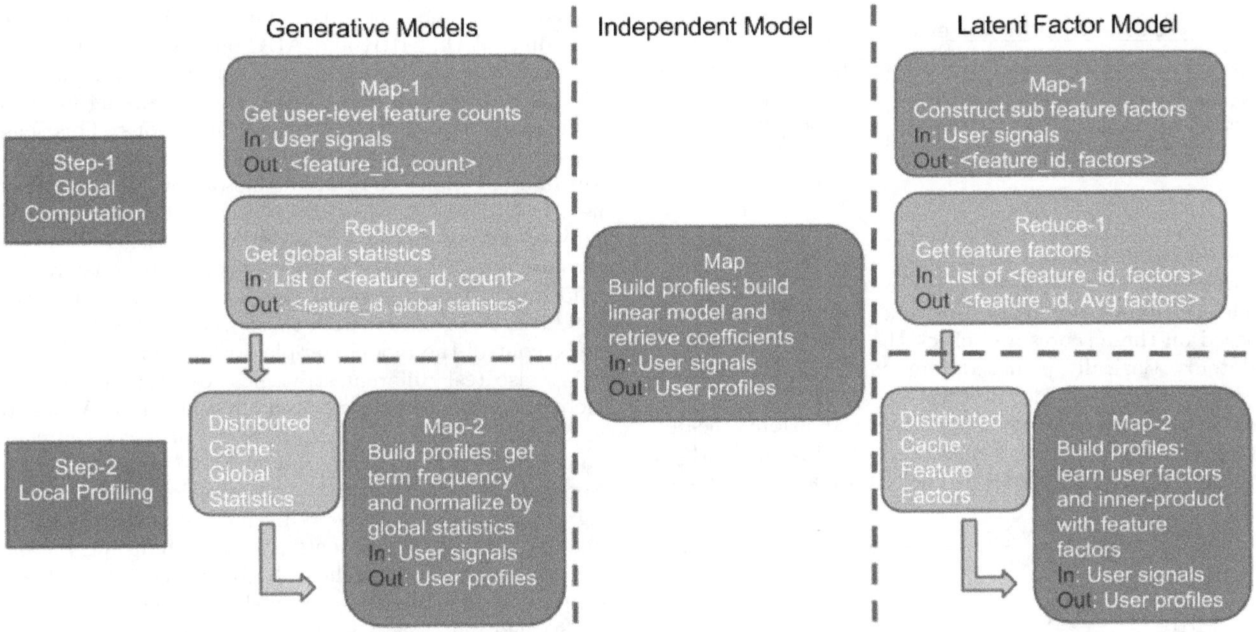

Figure 3: Map/Reduce Framework for User Profile Building

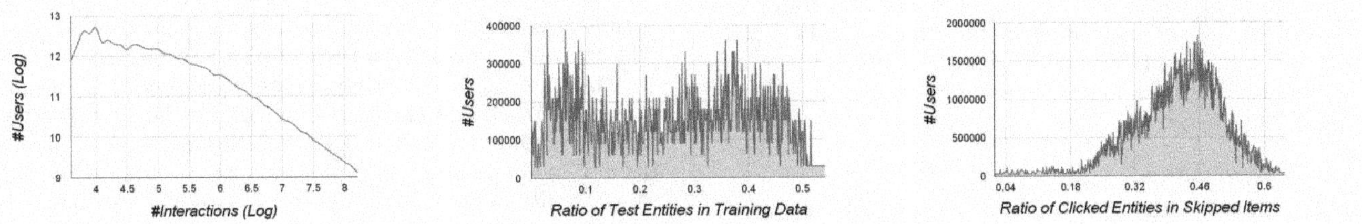

(a) (b) (c)

Figure 4: Data Analysis. (a) User distribution over interactions, which follow the power-log distribution with a long tail. (b) User distribution over ratio of test entities that exist in training data. (c) User distribution over ratio of clicked entities that also appear in skipped items.

as the test set. Specifically, the training set contains about 2.2 billion click events, and the test set contains about 230 million click events. The training set is used to train the user profile models, i.e., each user's profile is built based on the data from the training set. In the test set, we generated for each user a ranked list of news items based on the users' profiles, and measure the performance of ranking against the ground truth labels. As explained earlier, the labels on the data comes from the implicit positive and negative feedback on the content items.

We first highlight some challenges of building user profiles. In Figure 4(a), we show the distribution of users in terms of the number of their interactions with content items. We can observe that the distribution follows a long-tail, indicating that a large number of users only have a limited number of interactions with items. This observation justifies our choice of utilizing the data from multiple users collectively to solve the data sparsity problem.

In addition, we calculated the number of common features in both training set and test set for each user. In other words, we quantify how large is the overlap between the features in the user profile and the features that appear in the test set. As shown in Figure 4(b), we can observe that all users have at least 40% new content feature terms in their profiles , and a large number of users have more than 90% features that do not make it into the user profiles because of its absence in the training data. This again implies that if we only use the clicked events for each individual user, it would result in a situation in which a large number of items will have a zero relevancy score for the user. Finally, we calculate the number of features that exist in both clicked and skipped items for each user. In Figure 4(c), we can see that on average 45% features in clicked entities are shared in both of these items of each user. Thus, if we select profile features only based on clicked items, these features also end up being present in items that are skipped. When such user profiles are used to measure relevancy of a content item to the user, they end up providing misleading information. This observation motivates our model choice to enforce user profile terms to be discriminative.

Table 2: Offline Performance

Metrics	MAP	MRR	AUC
TFIDF	0.61053	0.65085	0.78427
Chi-Square Test	0.62360	0.66807	0.78875
Independent Learning Model	0.64478	0.69366	0.80565
Latent Factor Model (K=50)	0.66278	0.70490	0.82139

In the experiments, we use inner-product value between user profiles and item features to generate the ranking score for each user-item pair. Then we rank the items for each user based on these scores and check the positions of those clicked items. Basically, if clicked items can be ranked higher than skipped items, model performance is better. Three ranking metrics are used in our offline evaluation: mean average precision (MAP), and mean reciprocal rank (MRR) and area under the curve (AUC). The criteria are defined as

$$\text{MAP} = \frac{1}{m}\sum_{i=1}^{m}\frac{\sum_{k=1}^{n_i}P(k)}{n_i} \tag{23}$$

$$\text{MRR} = \frac{1}{m}\sum_{i=1}^{m}\frac{1}{r_i^1} \tag{24}$$

$$\text{AUC} = \frac{1}{m}\sum_{i=1}^{m}\frac{(\sum_j r_i^j) - P_i(P_i+1)/2}{P_i * N_i} \tag{25}$$

where $P(k)$ is precision at k, n_i is the number of items related to user $\mathbf{u}_i$, r_i^1 is the rank of the first clicked item of user $\mathbf{u}_i$, r_i^j is the position of the j-th clicked item of user $\mathbf{u}_i$, P_i is the number of clicked items and N_i is the number of skipped items of user $\mathbf{u}_i$.

5.1.1 Performance

Table 2 summarizes the results of our offline evaluation for all the four approaches investigated in our work. Latent factor model (LFM) consistently outperforms other baselines on all metrics. LFM on average achieves better MAP, compared to TFIDF, Chi-Square (CS) test, and independent learning model (ILM) respectively. LFM also shows significant improvements on MRR and AUC. The better performance of LFM over the independent model can be ascribed to the fact that, LFM considers more knowledge from different users collectively and captures more aspects of users' interests. Due to the data sparseness, not all users' interests can be reflected using only the data from the user. Due to the transferability of the feature factors, relevant but unobserved features can be included into users' profiles confidently. This gives us the added advantage of exploring users' interests. Thus the recall of the model can be improved. On the other hand, although generative statistical models consider data from multiple users and select those features that can distinct the user from others, they do not consider discriminability of those features for each user. Thus, they may introduce unnecessary features from irrelevant items. However, LFM not only captures the cross-user influences but keeps the user-specific distribution over factors and maximizes the dependency of profiles and users' feedbacks, hence solving the above problems.

5.1.2 Latent Factor Model Analysis

In this section, we analyze the performance of latent factor model in depth by studying its convergence and the effectiveness of the number of dimensions, K. We plot the metrics, including MAP, MRR and AUC on training data with different numbers of iterations to check the convergence. From Figure 5(a), we can observe that, all of ranking metrics become stable and close to 1 after 40 iterations. This suggests that the proposed model can fit the data well. In addition, for different numbers of latent factors, we plot its effectiveness in Figure 5(b). As can be seen, the performance improves as the number of factors increases. However, when the number of factors is large enough, the relative performance gain becomes small. For example, the metrics with 100 factors are similar with those with only 50 factors. This helps control the model complexity to avoid overfitting.

We also test different strategies to construct the feature factors $\mathcal{S}$ under the distributed environments. As we stated in Section 4, the learning of $\mathcal{S}$ requires communications among different machines under the Map/Reduce framework. If we implement the optimization fully distributed, e.g., collecting sub gradients from each machine, broadcasting the aggregated gradients and then updating the model, the communication overhead becomes very high. Thus, we propose to use a pseudo parallel approach which averages all learned matrices $\mathcal{S}$ from all machines. As a comparison, we also introduce a baseline that learns $\mathcal{S}$ in a single machine based on those users with sufficient historical data (1 million users in our experiment). The results can be found in Figure 5(c), where $AVG1$ means only one averaging operation is executed and $AVG2$ means we use the averaging result from the first iteration as the initialization value, call the learning process again to get new sub models from each machine and do the second averaging operation. The motivation is to ensure the entity factors can be updated based on the updated user factors to obtain a better representation as averaging may not guarantee to get an optimal value. The results show that, after two averaging operations, the performance of the model using averaging strategy is similar to that trained on a single machine. This suggests the effectiveness of our training strategy. We are still developing a more general solution based on parameter server [13], which can achieve better performance.

5.2 Online A/B Tests

We also tested our proposed models via A/B tests with live traffic on Yahoo Stream. As detailed in Section 2, items from a large corpus are ranked using a machine learned ranking model that uses three broad classes of features. In our experimental setup, a random sample of users were partitioned into a control and a treatment group. The users in the control group had their profiles built via the Chi-Square test model and the users in the treatment group had their profiles built via LFM. Holding all other features constant, the only difference between the control and treatment group was the computation of the relevance score between the corresponding profile and the content item. The performance of the two models was measured by CTR (click-through-rate). The experiment was run till the CTR metric achieved statistical significance. As indicated by the offline experiments, the LFM showed a substantial, statistically significant, lift of $\sim 10\%$ as compared to the control bucket with the Chi-Square based model. In the future, we plan to test out all baselines not only on the news stream but in other content recommendation properties, including Yahoo Recommends.

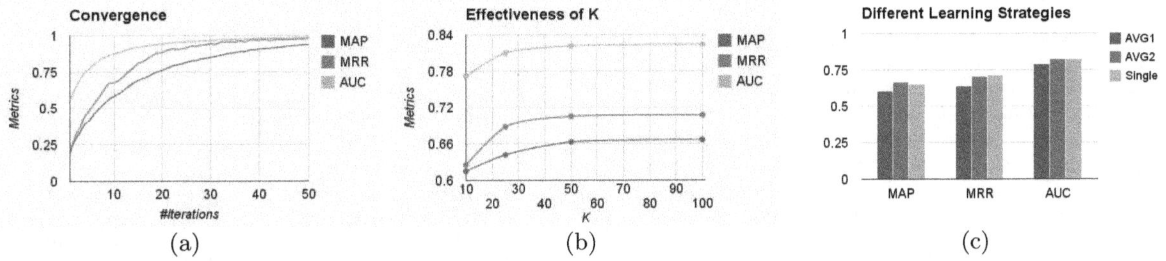

Figure 5: Model Analysis. (a) shows the convergence of LFM with increasing number of iterations. (b) shows the performance of LFM with increasing number of latent factors. (c) shows the performance with different approaches to construct $\mathcal{S}$.

6. RELATED WORK

Our work in this paper is in the intersection of three research areas, user profiling, recommendation systems and latent factor models.

User profiling in principle is to find a representation of the user's interest in the same feature space as that of the items being recommended [7]. One of the most typical tasks involving user profiling is content recommendation [18, 28, 32]. A recent review of the interaction between user profiling and content-based recommendation can be found in [15]. User profiling was also applied on personalized web search to enhance the user experience [26, 22]. However, previous approaches only focus on features that users click or read, that is positive interactions, and ignore the negative feedback. Such profiles may fail to detect the true user interests and lack discriminability in prediction. In addition, the proposed LFM model can leverage relevant features from other users and thus provide an exploration function while prior work does not.

Recommendation systems aim to push relevant content to users based on users' preference. Basically, there are two kinds of recommendations, collaborative filtering and content-based recommendation. Collaborative filtering is the process tof filtering information or patterns using techniques involving collaboration among users, etc. Typical methods include nearest neighborhood models [21] and matrix factorization [11] methods. Content-based recommendation differentiates itself from collaborative filtering mainly in the sense that explicit content features of items (and/or users) are exploited [1]. In addition, content-based recommendation is particularly critical for applications where a significant number of *cold start* items constantly appear, which is a typical case in the domain of news recommendation. A variety of methods have been proposed and shown to be effective for news recommendation, such as spatial-temporal model [3], probabilistic models [14], click shaping [4], hyper graph learning [12] and activity ranking [5]. The method proposed in this paper can be considered as a hybrid method that embeds content-based recommendation in a collaborative filtering framework. Besides this, our work exploits latent factor models that learns user profiles via addressing a multi-task learning problem. Our focus is to improve user profiling and demonstrate its efficacy for content recommendation. The user profiles generated by our models can be easily integrated with previous work to further improve content recommendation. We also noticed that some techniques were proposed to correct click and position bias in real-world applications [5], which can be applied on our framework as well to improve the effectiveness.

Last but not least, our contribution is closely related to latent factor models, a particular set of models well-suited for recommendation systems [2, 11]. Conventionally, latent factor models decompose user-item relation matrix into latent user factors and latent item factors, which can be used for future recommendation. Our proposed model learns latent user factors for each individual user, and in meanwhile, a latent correlation matrix of content features that is shared across all the users. Note that our model is similar to the general framework of collective matrix factorization [23], but our model is specialized for the content recommendation domain, and the joint factorization is designed to learn improved user profiles. Recently, large-scale matrix factorization is also gaining much traction [31, 10, 25]. There are also some open-source products that are developed to handle big data, such as MLlib [17] and GraphLab [16]. However, comparing to these prior works, we integrate our end-to-end user profiling system into real products, demonstrating how such systems work in real-world applications.

7. CONCLUSIONS

In this paper, we proposed a user profiling method based on latent factor models for large-scale content recommendations. We tackled three challenges in real-world applications: data sparsity and cold-start items, complex implicit feedback and large scale applications. The proposed latent factor model (LFM) collectively exploits positive and negative implicit feedback from all users on content items to construct both user and feature factors. We then leverage the LFM to represent each user as an interest vector. Thus, brand new items with no user interaction can still be retrieved for recommendation using the users' interest vectors. In addition, since the feature factors are shared by all users, we can bootstrap profiles even for users who have very limited data. We also proposed a large-scale framework based on Map/Reduce to cope with massive amounts of interaction data. The proposed framework can easily accommodate different loss functions. We conducted empirical studies on real-world datasets from Yahoo Recommends, where LFM significantly outperforms other baselines. A/B test on the Yahoo Stream also indicates that LFM can work well in real-world applications. In future, we plan to develop a fully distributed version of our model by decoupling the learning process using the parameter server implementation [13].

8. REFERENCES

[1] G. Adomavicius and A. Tuzhilin. Toward the next generation of recommender systems: A survey of the state-of-the-art and possible extensions. *IEEE Trans. on Knowl. and Data Eng.*, 17(6):734–749, 2005.

[2] D. Agarwal and B.-C. Chen. Regression-based latent factor models. In *Proceedings of KDD*, pages 19–28. ACM, 2009.

[3] D. Agarwal, B.-C. Chen, and P. Elango. Spatio-temporal models for estimating click-through rate. WWW '09, pages 21–30, 2009.

[4] D. Agarwal, B.-C. Chen, P. Elango, and X. Wang. Personalized click shaping through lagrangian duality for online recommendation. SIGIR '12, pages 485–494, 2012.

[5] D. Agarwal, B.-C. Chen, R. Gupta, J. Hartman, Q. He, A. Iyer, S. Kolar, Y. Ma, P. Shivaswamy, A. Singh, and L. Zhang. Activity ranking in linkedin feed. In *Proceedings of the 20th ACM SIGKDD International Conference on Knowledge Discovery and Data Mining*, KDD '14, pages 1603–1612, New York, NY, USA, 2014. ACM.

[6] J. Bobadilla, F. Ortega, A. Hernando, and A. GutiéRrez. Recommender systems survey. *Know.-Based Syst.*, 46:109–132, July 2013.

[7] L. Chen and P. Pu. Survey of preference elicitation methods. Technical Report EPFL-REPORT-52659, EPFL, 2004.

[8] A. S. Das, M. Datar, A. Garg, and S. Rajaram. Google news personalization: scalable online collaborative filtering. In *Proceedings of the 16th International Conference on World Wide Web*, pages 271–280. ACM, 2007.

[9] J. Dean and S. Ghemawat. Mapreduce: Simplified data processing on large clusters. *Commun. ACM*, 51(1):107–113, Jan. 2008.

[10] R. Gemulla, E. Nijkamp, P. J. Haas, and Y. Sismanis. Large-scale matrix factorization with distributed stochastic gradient descent. In *Proceedings of the 17th ACM SIGKDD International Conference on Knowledge Discovery and Data Mining*, KDD '11, pages 69–77, New York, NY, USA, 2011. ACM.

[11] Y. Koren, R. Bell, and C. Volinsky. Matrix factorization techniques for recommender systems. *Computer*, 42(8):30–37, Aug. 2009.

[12] L. Li and T. Li. News recommendation via hypergraph learning: Encapsulation of user behavior and news content. WSDM '13, pages 305–314, 2013.

[13] M. Li, D. G. Andersen, J. W. Park, A. J. Smola, A. Ahmed, V. Josifovski, J. Long, E. J. Shekita, and B.-Y. Su. Scaling distributed machine learning with the parameter server. In *Proceedings of the 11th USENIX Conference on Operating Systems Design and Implementation*, OSDI'14, pages 583–598, Berkeley, CA, USA, 2014. USENIX Association.

[14] J. Liu, E. Pedersen, and P. Dolan. Personalized news recommendation based on click behavior. IUI '10, 2010.

[15] P. Lops, M. De Gemmis, and G. Semeraro. Content-based recommender systems: State of the art and trends. In *Recommender systems handbook*, pages 73–105. Springer, 2011.

[16] Y. Low, D. Bickson, J. Gonzalez, C. Guestrin, A. Kyrola, and J. M. Hellerstein. Distributed graphlab: A framework for machine learning and data mining in the cloud. *Proc. VLDB Endow.*, 5(8):716–727, Apr. 2012.

[17] X. Meng, J. K. Bradley, B. Yavuz, E. R. Sparks, S. Venkataraman, D. Liu, J. Freeman, D. B. Tsai, M. Amde, S. Owen, D. Xin, R. Xin, M. J. Franklin, R. Zadeh, M. Zaharia, and A. Talwalkar. Mllib: Machine learning in apache spark. *CoRR*, abs/1505.06807, 2015.

[18] S. E. Middleton, N. R. Shadbolt, and D. C. De Roure. Ontological user profiling in recommender systems. *ACM Trans. Inf. Syst.*, 22(1):54–88, 2004.

[19] K. Pearson. On the criterion that a given system of deviations from the probable in the case of a correlated system of variables is such that can be reasonably supposed to have arisen from random sampling. *Philosophical Magazine*, 50:157–175, 1900.

[20] S. Rendle, C. Freudenthaler, Z. Gantner, and L. Schmidt-Thieme. Bpr: Bayesian personalized ranking from implicit feedback. In *Proceedings of the Twenty-Fifth Conference on Uncertainty in Artificial Intelligence*, UAI '09, pages 452–461, Arlington, Virginia, United States, 2009. AUAI Press.

[21] B. Sarwar, G. Karypis, J. Konstan, and J. Riedl. Item-based collaborative filtering recommendation algorithms. In *Proceedings of the 10th International Conference on World Wide Web*, WWW '01, pages 285–295, New York, NY, USA, 2001. ACM.

[22] A. Sieg, B. Mobasher, and R. Burke. Web search personalization with ontological user profiles. In *Proceedings of the Sixteenth ACM Conference on Conference on Information and Knowledge Management*, CIKM '07, pages 525–534, New York, NY, USA, 2007. ACM.

[23] A. P. Singh and G. J. Gordon. Relational learning via collective matrix factorization. In *Proceedings of the 14th ACM SIGKDD international conference on Knowledge discovery and data mining*, pages 650–658, 2008.

[24] K. Sparck Jones. Document retrieval systems. chapter A Statistical Interpretation of Term Specificity and Its Application in Retrieval, pages 132–142. Taylor Graham Publishing, London, UK, UK, 1988.

[25] D. H. Stern, R. Herbrich, and T. Graepel. Matchbox: Large scale online bayesian recommendations. In *Proceedings of the 18th International Conference on World Wide Web*, WWW '09, pages 111–120, New York, NY, USA, 2009. ACM.

[26] K. Sugiyama, K. Hatano, and M. Yoshikawa. Adaptive web search based on user profile constructed without any effort from users. In *Proceedings of the 13th International Conference on World Wide Web*, WWW '04, pages 675–684, New York, NY, USA, 2004. ACM.

[27] K. Varda. Protocol buffers: Google's data interchange format. Technical report, Google, 6 2008.

[28] G. I. Webb, M. J. Pazzani, and D. Billsus. Machine learning for user modeling. *User Modeling and User-Adapted Interaction*, 11:19–29, 2001.

[29] X. Yi, L. Hong, E. Zhong, N. N. Liu, and S. Rajan. Beyond clicks: Dwell time for personalization. In *Proceedings of the 8th ACM Conference on Recommender Systems*, RecSys '14, pages 113–120, New York, NY, USA, 2014. ACM.

[30] J. Zhang, Z. Ghahramani, and Y. Yang. Flexible latent variable models for multi-task learning. *Mach. Learn.*, 73(3):221–242, Dec. 2008.

[31] Y. Zhuang, W.-S. Chin, Y.-C. Juan, and C.-J. Lin. A fast parallel sgd for matrix factorization in shared memory systems. In *Proceedings of the 7th ACM Conference on Recommender Systems*, RecSys '13, pages 249–256, New York, NY, USA, 2013. ACM.

[32] I. Zukerman and D. W. Albrecht. Predictive statistical models for user modeling. *User Modeling and User-Adapted Interaction*, 11:5–18, 2001.

Stock Constrained Recommendation in Tmall

Wenliang Zhong
Alibaba Group
Hangzhou, Zhejiang, China
yice.zwl@alibaba-inc.com

Rong Jin
Alibaba Group
Hangzhou, Zhejiang, China
jinrong.jr@alibaba-inc.com

Cheng Yang
Alibaba Group
Hangzhou, Zhejiang, China
charis.yangc@alibaba-inc.com

Xiaowei Yan
Alibaba Group
Hangzhou, Zhejiang, China
xiaowei.yanxw@alibaba-inc.com

Qi Zhang
Alibaba Group
Hangzhou, Zhejiang, China
john.zhangq@alibaba-inc.com

Qiang Li
Alibaba Group
Hangzhou, Zhejiang, China
zaikuan@tmall.com

ABSTRACT

A large number of recommender systems have been developed to serve users with interesting news, ads, products or other contents. One main limitation with the existing work is that they do not take into account the inventory size of of items to be recommended. As a result, popular items are likely to be out of stock soon as they have been recommended and sold to many users, significantly affecting the impact of recommendation and user experience.

This observation motivates us to develop a novel aware recommender system. It jointly optimizes the recommended items for all users based on both user preference and inventory sizes of different items. It requires solving a non-smooth optimization involved estimating a matrix of $n \times n$, where n is the number of items. With the proliferation of items, this approach can quickly become computationally infeasible. We address this challenge by developing a dual method that reduces the number of variables from n^2 to n, significantly improving the computational efficiency. We also extend this approach to the online setting, which is particularly important for big promotion events. Our empirical studies based on a real benchmark data with 100 millions of user visits from Tmall verify the effectiveness of the proposed approach.

Categories and Subject Descriptors

H.1.0 [**Information Systems Applications**]: Models and Principles General; I.2.6 [**Artificial Intelligence**]: Learning

General Terms

Model,Optimization

Keywords

Recommendation; Tmall; Online Learning

1. INTRODUCTION

KDD'15, August 10-13, 2015, Sydney, NSW, Australia.

ACM 978-1-4503-3664-2/15/08 ...$15.00.
DOI: http://dx.doi.org/10.1145/2783258.2788565 .

Tmall (`www.tmall.com`), a business unit of Alibaba group, is the largest third-party platform for brands and retailers in China. Since 2008, it has served more than 100 millions of costumers and 100 thousands of merchants, including a large number of Chinese and international famous brands. According to the public report [1], the Gross Merchandise Volume (GMV) of Tmall exceeds 45 billion dollars in the last quarter of 2014, and 9 billion dollars for the 11/11 day of 2014.

In order to help customers find products of interests and improve the chance of making online purchase, online recommendation techniques have been studied and deployed extensively on the Tmall platform, resulting in significant increase in revenue. In this paper, we are focused on the recommendation function on detailed pages, named "also view": before a consumer decides to purchase an item (i.e. a product) from Tmall, he/she will first visit the "detail page" of the item that contains information such as title, description and reviews of items. To effectively utilize the traffic to detail pages, "also view" recommends to consumers a subset of items that are closely related to the displayed item on the detailed page. Fig. 1 shows the detail page of a silk blouse as an example, together with recommended items highlighted by a circle. Many computational approached have been developed to support the recommendation function in literature. For example, click-through rate (CTR) models have been developed [9, 30, 15] that aim to recommend items with the largest CTRs. Multiple similarity functions have been explored [10, 27, 28] recommend items with the largest similarities to the displayed one. Markov chain or matrix factorization methods [22, 31, 20] have been developed to recommend items with the highest potential for next-to-buy.

One main limitation of the existing works in e-commerce is that they did not take into account the inventory size of items to be recommended. Given the limited number of items stocked by merchants, a naive recommender system could encounter the situation where all/most the recommended items for certain user visits are out of stock, significantly reducing the impact of recommendation. We found that this issue is particularly severe when coming to the big promotion day, in which popular items are often sold out in the first a few hours and as a result, our recommendation system was unable to make appropriate recommendation for many user visits. This observation motivates to develop a stock aware recommender system that select recommended items based on both the user pref-

[1] `http://www.alibabagroup.com/en/global/home`

Figure 1: An example of detail page and recommendations by "also view".

erence and the inventory size of items. The key contributions of this work are:

- To the first of our knowledge, this is the first recommendation work that takes into account the inventory size of items.
- The computational problem requires solving an optimization problem with matrix of size $n \times n$, where n is the number of items. With the proliferation of item-intensive applications, this approach will quickly become computationally infeasible. We address this limitation by developing a dual method that reduces the number of variables from n^2 to n, significantly improving the computational efficiency. We also extend this approach to the online setting.
- We have successfully deployed the algorithm to the Tmall platform and carry out an experiment with more than 100 millions of user visits.

The rest of this paper is organized as follows. Section 2 gives reviews on recommendation systems and budget constrained advertising methods. Section 3 then describes the proposed model, followed by its online extension. Experimental results are presented in Section 5, and the last section gives some concluding remarks.

Notations: In the sequel, we denote by '$\top$' the transpose of vector/matrix, by '$\circ$' the elementwise matrix (vector) multiplication and by π_Ω the projection onto convex set Ω.

2. RELATED WORK

2.1 Recommender System

In the past decade, recommender system has been examined extensively in literature [3, 23]. Most recommender systems can be classified into four categories, including demographic filtering [12], collaborative filtering [6, 24], content-based filtering [13, 25] and hybrid filtering [21]. None of these methods take into account the stock condition either on training or recommending stage.

2.2 Online Advertising

Our work is also closely related to online advertising systems [1, 11, 16]. Given a query, the search engine will display proper ads to users based on their relevance scores and the auction result, and advertisers will pay for every click they receive. Once the budget constraints are taken into consideration, the problem becomes similar to ours. Without assuming the distribution of queries, budget restricted advertising can be approximately casted into an online learning problem, and multiple error bounds have been established [5, 16]. Multiple settings of budget restricted advertising, e.g. "unreliable estimation" and "random permutation", have been proposed and studied in [14, 7]. Besides revenue, Karande *et al.* [11] develop a system and algorithms for various objectives, such clicks and ad quality. Recently, Agarwal *et al.* [1] propose a budget pacing algorithm such that the advertisers may stay on the platform longer before using up their budgets.

Although budget restricted online advertising share similarity with stock aware recommend, the specific approaches developed for online advertising are unsuitable for our problem due to the following reasons

- Most online advertising approaches model the relationship between queries and ads by a bipartite graph, while we examine a more general graph among items, i.e. item-to-item recommendation;
- Most online advertising approaches employ a generalized second price [26] as a reward, which is absent from our setting;
- A budget constraint is usually related to a large number of queries while each stock constraint corresponds to a unique item. As a result, the computational approaches developed for budget restricted advertising may be too complicated for stock aware recommendation.

3. STOCK AWARE RECOMMENDATION

Let n be the number of items to be purchased online, and each item $i \in \{1, 2, \ldots, n\}$ is associated with an unique detail page. For each item i, we introduce a tuple $\{p_i, s_i, f_i, r_i\}$ to represent its price, its inventory size, its expected traffic flow, and its estimated conversion rate, respectively. In particular,

- $f_i \geq 0$, the expected traffic flow, i.e. the average number of visits to the detail page of item i from different sources (e.g web search and online advertisement and etc.) except for the recommendation from "also view"
- $r_i \in [0, 1]$, the conversion rate, i.e. the probability for any to purchase the corresponding item after visiting the detail page.

We note that both f_i and r_i are estimated from the historical data. Let $C = (\mathbf{c}_1, \mathbf{c}_2, \ldots, \mathbf{c}_n)^\top \in [0, 1]^{n \times n}$ be the CTR matrix, where $C_{i,j}$ denotes the probability of clicking the ad for item j from the detail page of item i, and can be estimated from the log data. Note that C is usually extremely sparse. Throughout this work, we assume that CTR matrix C is pre-computed.

The objective of stock aware recommendation is to revise the CTR matrix C by explicitly taking into the stock information in s_i as well as other information of items (i.e. the price p_i, expected traffic flow f_i, and conversation rate r_i). To this end, we introduce the recommendation matrix $A = (\mathbf{a}_1, \mathbf{a}_2, \ldots, \mathbf{a}_n)^\top \in [0, 1]^{n \times n}$, where $A_{i,j}$ represents the chance of recommending item j when someone is visiting the detailed page of item i. Our goal is to optimize A, based on C and the stock information of items.

3.1 Recommendation with Stock Constraints

Using the introduced notations, the expected sales for item i can be computed as follows:

$$\min\left[s_i, r_i\left(f_i + \left[(C \circ A)^\top \mathbf{f}\right]_i\right)\right], \tag{1}$$

where $C \circ A$ is the element wise product between two matrices, and $\left[(C \circ A)^\top \mathbf{f}\right]_i$ measures the additional number of visits to the detail page of item i via our recommender system. Since $f_i + \left[(C \circ A)^\top \mathbf{f}\right]_i$ computes the expected traffic, including both the direct visits and the traffics through recommendation,

$$r_i\left(f_i + \left[(C \circ A)^\top \mathbf{f}\right]_i\right)$$

calculates the average number of sales for item i. By taking the minimum value between s_i and $r_i\left(f_i + \left[(C \circ A)^\top \mathbf{f}\right]_i\right)$, the expression in (1) yields the sales for item i that takes into account the stock size. By adding up the expected sales from all items, the total sales is computed as

$$R(A) := \sum_{i=1}^{n} p_i \min\left[s_i, r_i\left(f_i + \left[(C \circ A)^\top \mathbf{f}\right]_i\right)\right].$$

Directly optimizing $R(A)$ may not be desirable because CTR matrix C, traffic flow f_i, and conversation rate r_i are estimated from historical data and are therefore noisy when computing A. To alleviate the impact of estimated noise in C, f_i and r_i, we regularize the solution for A by introducing the entropy function as a regularizer, which is defined for probability vector $\mathbf{a}$ as

$$\mathcal{H}(\mathbf{a}) = -\sum_{j=1}^{n} a_j \log a_j.$$

Combining the objective $R(A)$ and the regularizer $\mathcal{H}(\mathbf{a})$, we have the following optimization for stock aware recommendation

$$\max_{A \in \Omega} R(A) + \beta \sum_{j=1}^{n} f_i \mathcal{H}(\mathbf{a}_i), \tag{2}$$

where parameter β balanced the tradeoff between the objective and the regularizer, and domain Ω is defined as

$$\Omega = \begin{bmatrix} A_{i,j} \geq 0, & \forall i,j \in \{1,2,\ldots,n\} \\ \sum_{j=1}^{n} A_{i,j} = 1, & \forall i \in \{1,2,\ldots,n\} \\ A_{i,j} = 0, & \text{if } C_{i,j} = 0 \text{ or } i = j \end{bmatrix}.$$

The first set of constraints $A_{i,j} \geq 0$ ensures that all elements in A are non-negative. The second set of constraints enforces each column vector to be a probability distribution. This follows the fact that the recommendation in one detail page is modeled as a unit resource to be allocated to all other items. The last set of constraints ensures that both A and C share the same sparse pattern, which is very important for reducing computational cost given hundreds of millions of items to be handled in our case.

3.2 Optimization Algorithm

There are two challenges in solving the optimization problem in (2). First, the number of variables to be optimized in (2) is $O(n^2)$, making it computationally challenging. Second, the objective function $R(A)$ is piece wise linear and therefore non-smooth in terms of variable A, leading to relatively slow convergence rate. We address the computational challenges by developing a dual formation for (2) in which the objective function is smooth and the number of variables to be optimized is linear in n.

To develop our dual formation for (2), we need the following proposition to deal with $\min(\cdot,\cdot)$.

PROPOSITION 1. *Given any scalar $\{a, b\}$, following equality holds:*

$$p\min[a,b] \equiv \min_{\kappa \in [0,p]} (p-\kappa)a + \kappa b.$$

Using the above proposition, we introduce dual variables $\boldsymbol{\kappa} = \{\kappa_1, \kappa_2, \ldots, \kappa_n\}$ to $[\min(\cdot)]$s' in (2) and rewrite the optimization problem in (2) as an optimization problem in terms of dual variables $\boldsymbol{\kappa}$, as revealed by the following theorem.

THEOREM 1. *The dual problem of (2) is given by*

$$\min_{\kappa \preceq \mathbf{p}} \quad G(\kappa) =$$

$$-\kappa^\top \mathbf{g} + \beta \sum_{i=1}^{n} f_i \log\left(\sum_{j=1}^{n} I(C_{i,j} > 0) \exp\left(\frac{\kappa_j r_j C_{i,j}}{\beta}\right)\right) \tag{3}$$

and the solution to A is given by

$$A_{i,j}(\boldsymbol{\kappa}) = \frac{I(C_{i,j} > 0)}{Z_i(\boldsymbol{\kappa})} \exp\left(\frac{\kappa_j r_j C_{i,j}}{\beta}\right) \tag{4}$$

where where $I(z)$ is an indicator faction that outputs 1 if z is true and zero otherwise, and

$$Z_i(\boldsymbol{\kappa}) = \sum_{j=1}^{n} I(C_{i,j} > 0) \exp\left(\frac{\kappa_j r_j C_{i,j}}{\beta}\right).$$

PROOF. Using the dual variable $\boldsymbol{\kappa}$, we rewrite (2) into convex-concave optimization problem

$$\max_{A \in \Omega} \min_{\mathbf{0} \preceq \boldsymbol{\kappa} \preceq \mathbf{p}} \sum_{i=1}^{n} \{(p_i - \kappa_i)s_i +$$

$$\kappa_i r_i \left(f_i + \left[(C \circ A)^\top \mathbf{f}\right]_i\right) + \beta f_i \mathcal{H}(\mathbf{a}_i)\}$$

$$\Rightarrow \max_{A \in \Omega} \min_{\mathbf{0} \preceq \boldsymbol{\kappa} \preceq \mathbf{p}} -\boldsymbol{\kappa}^\top \mathbf{g} + \mathbf{f}^\top (C \circ A)(\boldsymbol{\kappa} \circ \mathbf{r}) + \beta \sum_{i=1}^{n} f_i \mathcal{H}(\mathbf{a}_i)$$

$$\Rightarrow \min_{\mathbf{0} \preceq \boldsymbol{\kappa} \preceq \mathbf{p}} \max_{A \in \Omega} -\boldsymbol{\kappa}^\top \mathbf{g} + \mathbf{f}^\top (C \circ A)(\boldsymbol{\kappa} \circ \mathbf{r}) + \beta \sum_{i=1}^{n} f_i \mathcal{H}(\mathbf{a}_i) \tag{5}$$

where $\mathbf{g} = \mathbf{s} - (\mathbf{r} \circ \mathbf{f})$ and the last step follows the Von-Newman lemma. To compute the optimization over A, we use the following lemma.

LEMMA 1. *The optimization problem*

$$\min_{a_i \geq 0, \sum_{i=1}^{n} a_i = 1} \quad \mathbf{a}^\top \mathbf{b} - \beta \mathcal{H}(\mathbf{a})$$

admits a unique optimal solution

$$a_i = \frac{\exp\left(\frac{-b_i}{\beta}\right)}{Z} \text{ and } Z = \sum_{i=1}^{n} \exp\left(\frac{-b_i}{\beta}\right).$$

The above lemma can be found in the standard literature for convex optimization, e.g. [18, 29]. Using Lemma 1, it is straightforward to obtain the expression for A in (4). Z_i is the normalization factor that ensure the sum of each row of A is 1 and is given by

$$Z_i(\boldsymbol{\kappa}) = \sum_{j=1}^{n} I(C_{i,j} > 0) \exp\left(\frac{\kappa_j r_j C_{i,j}}{\beta}\right).$$

Since $A_{i,j}$ can be expressed in terms of dual variables κ, for each row i we obtain

$$\begin{aligned} & \max_{A_{i\cdot}} A_{i,j} f_i \kappa_j r_j C_{i,j} + \beta f_i \mathcal{H}(\mathbf{a}_i) \\ = \; & f_i \sum_{j=1}^{n} (A_{i,j}(\boldsymbol{\kappa}) \kappa_j r_j C_{i,j} - \beta A_{i,j}(\boldsymbol{\kappa}) \log(A_{i,j}(\boldsymbol{\kappa}))) \\ = \; & f_i \beta \sum_{j=1}^{n} A_{i,j}(\boldsymbol{\kappa}) \log(Z_i(\boldsymbol{\kappa})) \\ = \; & f_i \beta \log(Z_i(\boldsymbol{\kappa})) \end{aligned}$$

Plug above equation into (5), we can find the optimal κ by solving the following the optimization problem

$$\min_{\kappa \preceq \mathbf{p}} \quad G(\kappa) =$$

$$-\kappa^\top \mathbf{g} + \beta \sum_{i=1}^{n} f_i \log \left(\sum_{j=1}^{n} I(C_{i,j} > 0) \exp\left(\frac{\kappa_j r_j C_{i,j}}{\beta} \right) \right) \quad (6)$$

□

One nice feature of the dual formulation in (6) is that its objective function is smooth, making it possible to solve the optimization problem significantly more efficiently than the one in (2). This property is revealed by the following theorem.

THEOREM 2. *The optimization problem (6) is convex and smooth w.r.t.* $\boldsymbol{\kappa}$. *Moreover, the Hessian matrix* $H(\boldsymbol{\kappa})$*of the objective function is upper bounded by*

$$H(\boldsymbol{\kappa}) \preceq \frac{1}{\beta} \sum_{i=1}^{n} f_i diag((\mathbf{r} \circ \mathbf{c}_i)^{\cdot 2}), \quad (7)$$

where $diag(\mathbf{v})$ *denotes a diagonal matrix* V *with* $V_{i,i} = v_i$ *and* $\mathbf{v}^{\cdot 2} = (v_1^2, v_2^2, \ldots, v_n^2)$ *is elementwise square for a vector* v.

PROOF. To prove the theorem, we need to introduce two useful lemmas.

LEMMA 2. *[17] The duality of a* β*-strongly convex function* [2] *is convex and* $\frac{1}{\beta}$ *smooth.*

LEMMA 3. *[4] The maximum over a set of linear function is convex, i.e.* $\mathcal{F}(\mathbf{a}) \equiv \max_i \mathcal{F}_i(\mathbf{a})$ *is w.r.t.* $\mathbf{a}$ *when* $\mathcal{F}_i s$*' are linear functions.*

It is well known that $-\mathcal{H}(\mathbf{a})$ is a 1-strongly convex w.r.t. norm $\|\cdot\|_1$ over the simplex [18, 29], then $-\sum_{i=1}^{n} f_i \mathcal{H}(\mathbf{a}_i)$ is also strongly convex as $f_i \geq 0, \forall i$. Moreover,using Lemma 3 we have the function $\max\left[-s_i, -r_i\left(f_i + \left[(C \circ A)^\top \mathbf{f}\right]_i\right)\right]$ convex. As a result, the negative of (2) is ($\beta \min_i f_i$)-strongly convex, thus its dual(i.e. (6)) is convex and ($\frac{1}{\beta \min_i f_i}$)-smooth.

Now we consider the second part. Noting that the Hessian of

$$\log \left(\sum_{j=1}^{n} I(C_{i,j} > 0) \exp\left(\frac{\kappa_j r_j C_{i,j}}{\beta} \right) \right)$$

is H^i with

$$H^i_{j,k}(\boldsymbol{\kappa}) = \begin{cases} \frac{r_j r_k C_{i,j} C_{i,k} A_{i,j}(\boldsymbol{\kappa}) A_{i,k}(\boldsymbol{\kappa})}{\beta^2}, & \text{if } j \neq k, \\ \frac{r_j^2 C_{i,j}^2 A_{i,j}(\boldsymbol{\kappa})(1 - A_{i,j}(\boldsymbol{\kappa}))}{\beta^2}, & otherwise. \end{cases}$$

It is easy to show that $H^i \preceq \frac{1}{\beta^2}\text{diag}((\mathbf{r} \circ \mathbf{c}_i)^{\cdot 2})$, and taking the summation over $i = 1, 2, \ldots, n$, the conclusion follows. □

Finally, since our approach is a first order method In addition, we need to calculate the gradient of $G(\cdot)$, which is given as

$$\nabla G(\boldsymbol{\kappa}) = -\mathbf{g} + \mathbf{r} \circ \left[(A(\boldsymbol{\kappa}) \circ C)^\top \mathbf{f} \right].$$

[2]A function $\mathcal{F}(\mathbf{a})$ is α-strongly convex w.r.t. some norm $\|\|$ over a compact set $\mathcal{S}$ if the following inequality holds for any $\mathbf{a}, \tilde{\mathbf{a}} \in \mathcal{S}$

$$\mathcal{F}(\mathbf{a}) \geq \mathcal{F}(\tilde{\mathbf{a}}) + \nabla \mathcal{F}(\tilde{a})^\top (\mathbf{a} - \tilde{\mathbf{a}}) + \frac{\beta}{2} \|\mathbf{a} - \tilde{\mathbf{a}}\|^2.$$

Algorithm 1 Accelerated Gradient Descent

1: Initialization: $p = q = 1$, $\boldsymbol{\kappa}^0 = \boldsymbol{\kappa}^1 = \frac{\mathbf{p}}{2}$, $\eta_{\max} = 10000$

2: Compute the diagonal Hessian

$$\mathbf{w} = \frac{1}{\beta} \sum_{i=1}^{n} f_i (\mathbf{r} \circ \mathbf{c}_i)^{\cdot 2}$$

3: **for** $t = 1, \ldots, T$ **do**

4: Compute auxiliary solution $\tilde{\boldsymbol{\kappa}}$ as

$$\tilde{\boldsymbol{\kappa}}^t = \boldsymbol{\kappa}^t + q(p^{-1} - 1)(\boldsymbol{\kappa}^t - \boldsymbol{\kappa}^{t-1})$$

5: Set $p = q$

6: Compute matrix $A(\tilde{\boldsymbol{\kappa}}^t)$ as (4)

7: Compute the gradient as

$$\nabla G(\tilde{\boldsymbol{\kappa}}^t) = -\mathbf{g} + \mathbf{r} \circ \left[(A(\tilde{\boldsymbol{\kappa}}^t) \circ C)^\top \mathbf{f} \right]$$

8: Set $\eta = \eta_{\max}$

9: Update the solution of κ by

$$\kappa_i^{t+1} = \pi_{[0,p_i]} \left(\tilde{\kappa}_i^t - \frac{\eta [\nabla G(\tilde{\boldsymbol{\kappa}}^t)]_i}{w_i} \right),$$

10: **if** the inequality (8) fails to hold **then**

11: Set $\eta = \eta/10$ and goto 9

12: **end if**

13: Compute

$$q = \frac{\sqrt{q^4 + 4q^2} - q^2}{2}$$

14: **end for**

Return solution $A(\boldsymbol{\kappa}^T)$

Together with the upper bound of Hessian matrix, we have the solution updated from $\boldsymbol{\kappa}^t$ to $\boldsymbol{\kappa}^{t+1}$ by

$$\kappa_i^{t+1} = \pi_{[0,p_i]} \left(\kappa_i^t - \frac{[\nabla G(\boldsymbol{\kappa}^t)]_i}{w_i} \right)$$

where

$$w_i = \frac{1}{\beta} \sum_{j=1}^{n} f_j (r_i C_{j,i})^2.$$

This update scheme admits a special case of adaptive gradient descent methods [8] and has a strong convergence guarantee.

We can further improve the convergence of the above algorithm by exploring the accelerated gradient methods [2, 19]. In particular, we introduce a parameter η and auxiliary solution $\tilde{\boldsymbol{\kappa}}$ into the algorithm, such that

$$\kappa_i^{t+1} = \pi_{[0,p_i]} \left(\tilde{\kappa}_i^t - \frac{[\nabla G(\tilde{\boldsymbol{\kappa}}^t)]_i}{L w_i} \right),$$

$\tilde{\boldsymbol{\kappa}}$ is a combination of $\boldsymbol{\kappa}^t$ and $\boldsymbol{\kappa}^{t+1}$. It is introduced to take advantage of the smoothness of the objective function to speed up the convergence. One of the key component of the accelerated gradient descent method is to determine the step size. We follow the Nesterov's approach. It starts with a large step size η and gradually reduces it until the following inequality holds

$$G(\boldsymbol{\kappa}^{t+1})$$
$$\leq G(\tilde{\boldsymbol{\kappa}}) + (\boldsymbol{\kappa}^{t+1} - \tilde{\boldsymbol{\kappa}})^\top \nabla G(\tilde{\boldsymbol{\kappa}}) + \frac{1}{2\eta} \sum_{i=1}^{n} w_i (\kappa_i - \tilde{\kappa}_i)^2 . (8)$$

More details are given in Algorithm 1. Note that since $\text{diag}(\mathbf{w})$ is the upper bound of Hessian, L in Algorithm 1 is lower bounded by 1. The convergence rate of accelerated gradient descent method is $O(1/T^2)$ [17, 19, 2]. It is also known that the Nesterov's method achieves the optimal convergence rate for optimizing smooth objective function.

4. EXTENSION TO ONLINE SETTING

One problem with the offline optimization method presented in the last section is that it relies on the estimated quantities for $\mathbf{f}$ and $\mathbf{r}$. It is known that these quantities, despite the best efforts, can not be estimated accurately and reliably. Below, we list two examples that illustrate these quantities can be seriously affected by unpredictable things:

- There is a famous website call "what are worth to buy" in China, which recommends economic but popular items to costumers everyday. For items recommended by this website, their traffic flows are dramatically underestimated;
- Many Tmall sellers run big promotions occasionally (e.g. 50+% discounts and cash coupons) in order to attract a large number of fresh buyers. As a result, the conversion rate of corresponding items will be significantly changed.

The above observations motivate us to develop an online learning framework for stock aware recommendation that can utilize online information to make better estimation for quantities f and $\mathbf{r}$. But, on the other hand, due to the limited computational resources that are available for online updating, we need to develop efficient updating algorithms that allow us to effectively update the dual variables without having to accurately solve the optimization problem in (6).

Let $t = 1, \ldots, T$ be T different time points, and let $\mathbf{s}^t$, $\mathbf{r}^t$, $\mathbf{f}^t$ and C^t be the stock, conversation rate, traffic data, and CTR that are online computed based on the real-time user feedbacks. Using the online data $\mathbf{s}^t$, $\mathbf{r}^t$, $\mathbf{f}^t$, and C^t, the regularized overall sales revenue can be written as

$$\min_{A\in\Omega} \sum_{t=1}^{T}\left\{\sum_{i=1}^{n} p_i \min\left(s_i^t, \mathbf{r}_i^t\left(f_i^t + \left[(C^t\circ A)^\top \mathbf{f}^t\right]_i\right)\right) + \beta\sum_{i=1}^{n}\mathcal{H}(\mathbf{a}_i)\right\}.$$

It is easy to verify that the objective is indeed the same to (2) in the view of optimization.

Now, instead of using the same solution A over all time points, we introduce $A^t = (\mathbf{a}_1^t, \ldots, \mathbf{a}_m^t)$ as the solution at time t, and therefore the objective function becomes

$$\min_{A^t\in\Omega} \sum_{t=1}^{T}\left\{\sum_{i=1}^{n} p_i \min\left(s_i^t, \mathbf{r}_i^t\left(f_i^t + \left[(C^t\circ A^t)^\top \mathbf{f}^t\right]_i\right)\right) + \beta\sum_{i=1}^{n}\mathcal{H}(\mathbf{a}_i^t)\right\}.$$

Similar to that in Section 3.2, we rewrite the objective as $\sum_{t=1}^{T} G^t(\boldsymbol{\kappa}^t)$, where

$$G^t(\boldsymbol{\kappa}^t) = -[\boldsymbol{\kappa}^t]^\top \mathbf{g}^t + \beta\sum_{i=1}^{n} f_i^t \log\left(\sum_{j=1}^{n} I(C_{i,j}^t > 0)\exp\left(\frac{\kappa_j^t r_j^t C_{i,j}^t}{\beta}\right)\right)$$

As a result, we will online update the dual variables, instead of the dual variables, because the number of dual variables is significantly smaller than the number of primal variables.

Our online updating approach is based on the fact that function $G^t(\boldsymbol{\kappa}^t)$ is smooth. In particular, its Hessian H^t is upper bound in a similar way:

$$H^t \preceq \frac{1}{\beta}\sum_{i=1}^{n} f_i^t \text{diag}((\mathbf{r}^t \circ \mathbf{c}_i^t)^{\cdot 2}) \preceq LI,$$

where $L = \max_j \frac{1}{\beta}\sum_{i=1}^{n} f_i^t (r_i^t \circ C_{i,j}^t)^2$ and I is a proper identity matrix.

At the beginning of the $t-$th time slot, we do not know the true traffic flow $\mathbf{f}^t$, $\mathbf{r}^t$ and C^t then have to estimate from the past information. One possible estimation will be

$$\hat{C}^t = C^{t-1},\ \mathbf{r}^t = \mathbf{r}^{t-1},\ \hat{\mathbf{f}}^t = \mathbf{f}^{t-1},\ \widehat{\mathbf{g}}^t = \mathbf{s}^t - (\mathbf{r}^{t-1}\circ \mathbf{f}^{t-1})$$

Since $\mathbf{s}$, the total inventory stock, is known before hand, we can compute $\mathbf{s}^t$ based on the difference between the consumption and $\mathbf{s}^{t-1}$. Thus, we will assume $\mathbf{s}^1, \ldots, \mathbf{s}^T$ are known to the online updating process.

Our algorithm is based on the extra gradient algorithm that was originally developed for smooth objective function. Different from most optimization algorithm, it maintains two sets of solutions, i.e. real solutions $\boldsymbol{\kappa}^1, \boldsymbol{\kappa}^2, \ldots, \kappa^T$ and auxiliary solution $\hat{\boldsymbol{\kappa}}^1, \hat{\boldsymbol{\kappa}}^2, \ldots, \hat{\boldsymbol{\kappa}}^T$. We start with some initial solution $\boldsymbol{\kappa}^1 = \hat{\boldsymbol{\kappa}}^1$. At each time point t, we employ $\{\hat{\mathbf{r}}^t, \hat{\mathbf{f}}^t, \hat{C}^t\}$ to construct a function $\hat{G}^t(\hat{\boldsymbol{\kappa}})$ that aims to approximate the function $G^t(\boldsymbol{\kappa})$. Formally, we define $\hat{G}^t$ as

$$\hat{G}^t(\hat{\boldsymbol{\kappa}}^t) = -[\hat{\boldsymbol{\kappa}}^t]^\top \hat{\mathbf{g}}^t + \beta\sum_{i=1}^{n} \hat{f}_i^t \log\left(\sum_{j=1}^{n} I(\hat{C}_{i,j}^t > 0)\exp\left(\frac{\hat{\kappa}_j^t \hat{r}_j^t \hat{C}_{i,j}^t}{\beta}\right)\right)$$

Using $\hat{G}^t(\cdot)$, we update the solution κ^t by

$$\boldsymbol{\kappa}^t = \pi_{\boldsymbol{\kappa}\in\tilde{\Omega}}\left(\hat{\boldsymbol{\kappa}}^t - \eta\nabla\hat{G}^t(\hat{\boldsymbol{\kappa}}^t)\right)$$

where $\eta > 0$ is the step size and is often set as $1/\sqrt{2}L$ and

$$\tilde{\Omega} = \{\boldsymbol{\kappa} : \mathbf{0} \preceq \boldsymbol{\kappa} \preceq \mathbf{p}\}$$

This computed $\boldsymbol{\kappa}^t$ will then be used to compute $A^t(\boldsymbol{\kappa}^t)$ for recommendation. After time point t, we observe the true quantities $\mathbf{r}^t$, $\mathbf{f}^t$, C^t, and update the auxiliary solution $\hat{\boldsymbol{\kappa}}^t$ by

$$\hat{\boldsymbol{\kappa}}^{t+1} = \pi_{\hat{\boldsymbol{\kappa}}\in\tilde{\Omega}}\left(\hat{\boldsymbol{\kappa}}^t - \eta\nabla G^t(\boldsymbol{\kappa}^t)\right).$$

The auxiliary step can be regarded as a calibration $\hat{G}^t(\cdot)$.

REMARK 1. *As there may be not enough traffic flow at time $t-1$ to estimate an accurate $\{\mathbf{r}^t, \mathbf{f}^t, C^t\}$, one may use a decay update as*

$$\mathbf{r}^t = \lambda\mathbf{r}^{t-1} + (1-\lambda)\tilde{\mathbf{r}}^t,$$

where $\tilde{\mathbf{r}}^t$ the true conversion rate at time t. Moreover, we set $\tilde{r}_i^t = r_i^{t-1}$ if $\tilde{f}_i^t$ is little. So do $\mathbf{f}^t$ and C^t.

5. EXPERIMENTAL RESULTS

5.1 Comparison with CTR-first Approach

We deployed the Algorithm 1 on `www.Tmall.com`, and perform experiments on a large volume of real traffic. Our first baseline is the CTR-first recommender system that always recommends items with highest $C_{i,j}$s.

5.1.1 Data and Setting

- **Training phase:** In this experiment, millions of items sold on our platform are taking into consideration, covering more than 10 fashion categories, such as clothing and shoes, electronic and computers, beauty and healthy, etc. Since the "out of stock" usually occurs among popular items, we filter out those extremely unpopular goods (e.g. the amount of impression is less than 30 in the past month). As introduced in Section 3, the proposed method takes parameter β and $\{\mathbf{p}, \mathbf{s}, \mathbf{f}, \mathbf{r}, C\}$ as input. Price $\mathbf{p}$ and inventory size $\mathbf{s}$ are provided by sellers and stored in our system. The expected traffic flow $\mathbf{f}$ is computed by taking the average of the impressions in the past week while the conversion rate $\mathbf{r}$ is the average number over last month. Estimation of the CTR C could be computationally demanding, as it needs to estimate for n^2 pairs variables, which is larger than $1,000,000,000,000$ in our case. Since the observed data is far beyond enough for a full approximation, only the top 50 CTRs from the same shop are considered for each item. This finally leads to a block diagonal and sparse matrix C, with $\mathcal{O}(10^8)$ non-zero elements. To choose a proper β, an off-line tuning stage is carried out on a relative small data set with millions impressions and thousands items. Training is performed at the begging of everyday, and the resulted model is used for testing.
- **Testing phase:** The online status can be quite complex and fluctuates significantly from day to day. For example, the user behavior on work days may vary a lot compared with that on weekend. And the promotion and advertisement may also affect the result, not to mentioned the modification of price and stock condition during our experimental period. To get a reliable result, around 10 millions of registered users are randomly divided into two groups: one will be severed with the CTR-first algorithm while the proposed method for the other group. Roughly speaking, for every result reported below, it is calculated based on at least 1 million impressions.
- **Measurements:** The proposed method is designed to maximize the sale revenue while the baseline method is in favor of CTR. To have a fair evaluation, we trace both the revenues and the numbers of clicks on the recommended items for one week. Namely, only the impressions induced by the recommender system and its following actions will be counted for comparison. We then scale the numbers such that the CTR-first method always receives a unit of click or revenue at the end of each day. In this way, the improvements made by the proposed method is more obvious to observe.

5.1.2 Results

We first report the result for all item as a whole and then zoom in on four representative categories to see more details.

- **Overall Comparison:** Figure 2 shows the comparison in terms of clicks. The vertical axis represents the (scaled) number of clicks while the horizontal one represents the running time (hours). Since only a small portion of costumers logs in Tmall.com during $00{:}00 - 08{:}00$, the gap between two models is small, while it stably increases after eight O'clock. As expected, the CTR-first method (red curve) outperforms the proposed method by 14% on average under in terms of clicks (see Table 1). On the other hand, opposite results are observed when coming to revenue, i.e. the proposed stock aware recommendation method is leading the CTR-first method by 16%, indicating it results in more deals even with fewer clicks. Moreover, we observe that the improvement in revenue is closely related to the loss in clicks: according to Figure 5(h), 2(f), 3(d) and 3(f), the larger the gap in clicks the bigger the improvement in revenue is also greater (see Figure 3(d) and Figure 3(f)).
- **Comparison across different categories:** Another interesting question is whether the improvement in revenue is consistent across different categories. The answers lie in Figure 4, where each point corresponds to a ratio between two models in revenue. As can be seen, though overall the proposed model enjoys better revenue than the CTR-first method, the improves fluctuate in a wide range. Take the category "electronics and computer" as example. The improvement can be as high as 80% for some day. On the other hand, the result for "clothing and shoes" is fairly stable over different days. As to the "Furniture and Decoration", negative optimization can take place, reminding us training different models for various categories may be necessary.

Table 1: Performance w.r.t. "Scaled #clicks" and "Scaled sales revenue" at the end of each day.

Day	Scaled #clicks		Scaled sales revenue	
	CTR-first	Our-Batch	CTR-first	Our-Batch
Monday	1	0.898201	1	1.121998
Tuesday	1	0.906122	1	1.136914
Wednesday	1	0.908609	1	1.164695
Thursday	1	0.748895	1	1.162689
Friday	1	0.921550	1	1.137332
Saturday	1	0.725727	1	1.230340
Sunday	1	0.887555	1	1.143656
Improvement	-14.33%		15.76%	

5.2 Comparison with CTR*CVR Approach

Since considering the conversion rate (CVR) may help the improvement of sale revenue, our second baseline is the CTR*CVR approach. The experimental setting is identical to that in Section 5.1. Due to the space limitation, we only report results of four days. As can be seen in Figure 5, the proposed stock aware recommendation system outperforms the CTR*CVR method in terms of both the number of clicks and the sales revenue in all cases, where the overall improvements for clicks and revenue are 11.31% and 12.48%, respectively. This result indicates that the proposed approach is more effective than a simple CTR*CVR based method in making the tradeoff between CTR and revenue.

5.3 Evaluation for the Online Setting

Due to engineering issues, we don't have the evaluation result for the proposed online algorithm with live traffic. Instead, we demonstrate the effectiveness of online stock aware recommendation using synthetic data sets with 100 items that are generated as follows: price $\mathbf{p}$, the inventory size $\mathbf{s}$ and conversion rates $\mathbf{r}$ are generated by sampling numbers from a uniform distribution while traffic flows $\mathbf{f}$ and CTR matrix C are created by sampling numbers from Gaussian distributions. The parameter β is manually chosen to maximize the performance.

At the prediction stage, a stream of customers (as the traffic flow f but in random order) arrives and takes actions following param-

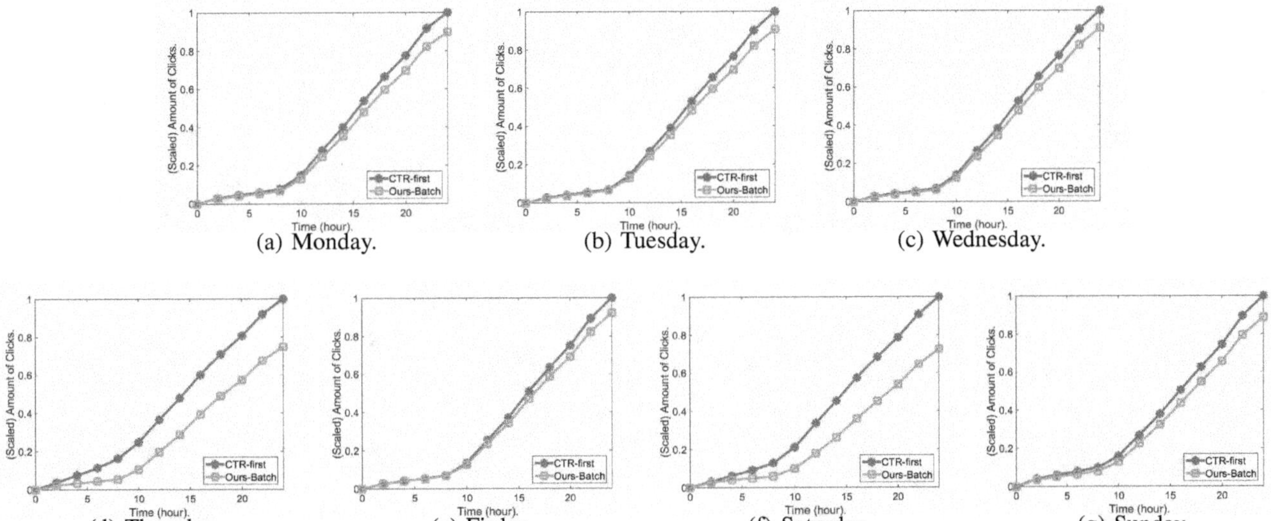

(a) Monday. (b) Tuesday. (c) Wednesday.

(d) Thursday. (e) Firday. (f) Saturday. (g) Sunday.

Figure 2: Scaled amount of clicks versus running time on seven consecutive days.

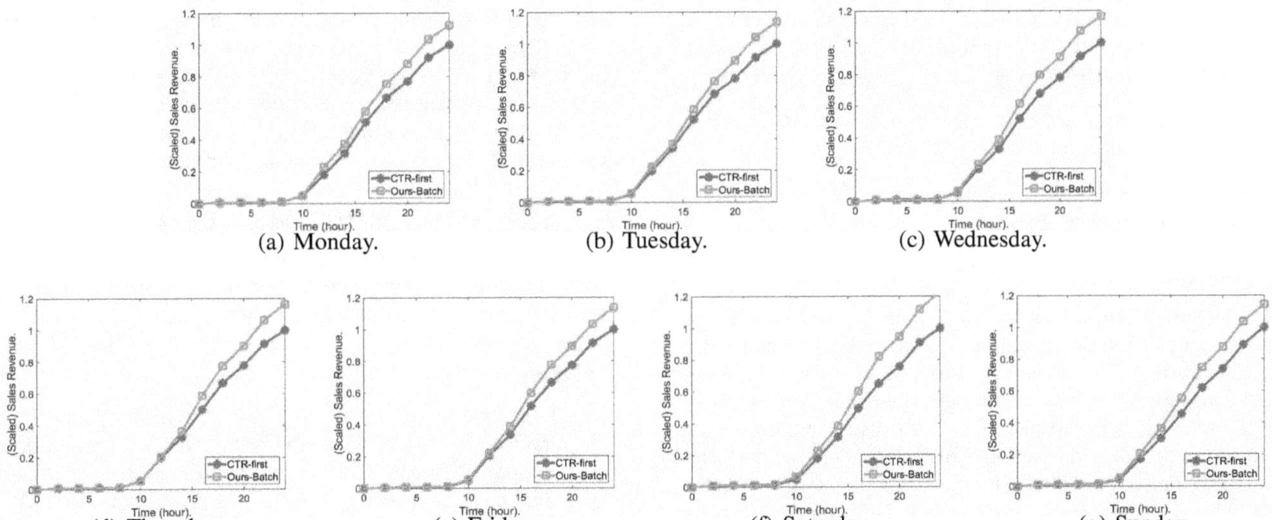

(a) Monday. (b) Tuesday. (c) Wednesday.

(d) Thursday. (e) Friday. (f) Saturday. (g) Sunday.

Figure 3: Scaled sales revenue versus running time on seven consecutive days.

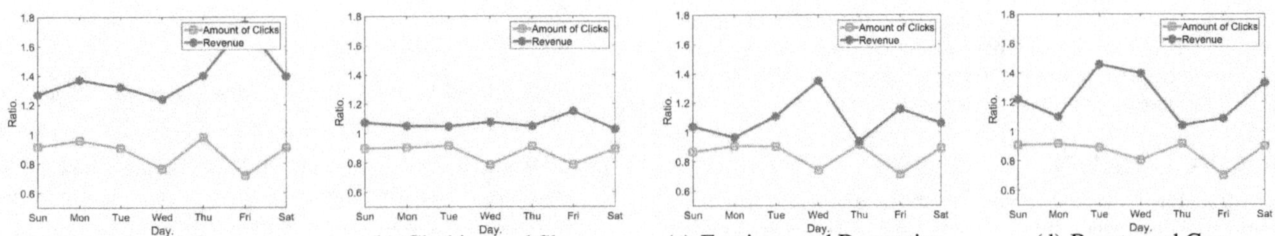

(a) Electronic and Computers. (b) Clothing and Shoes. (c) Furniture and Decoration. (d) Beauty and Care.

Figure 4: Performance versus running time in different categories.

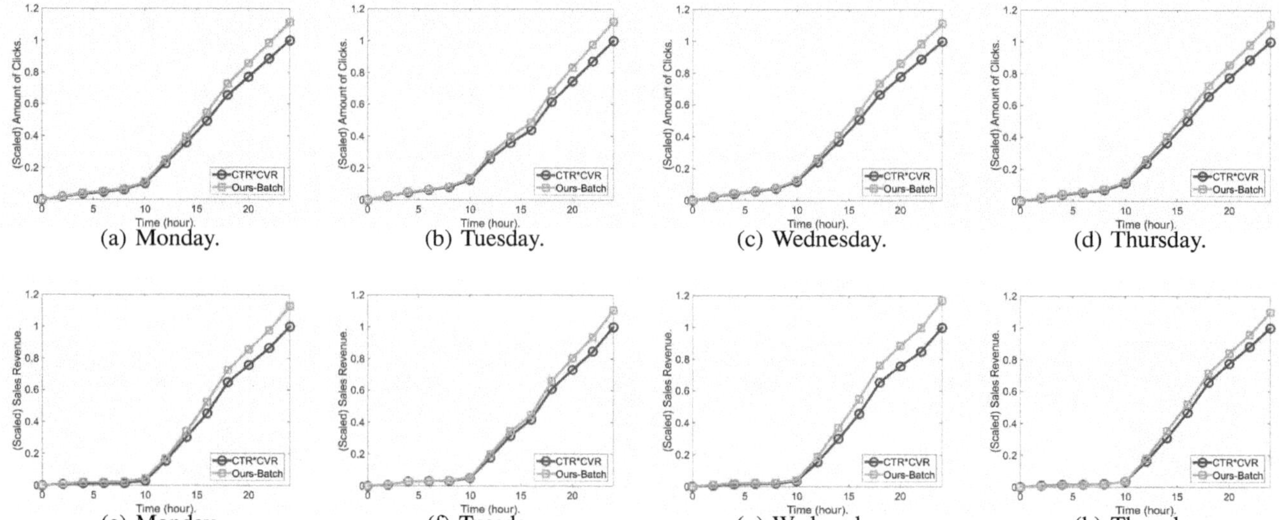

(a) Monday. (b) Tuesday. (c) Wednesday. (d) Thursday.

(e) Monday. (f) Tuesday. (g) Wednesday. (h) Thursday.

Figure 5: Comparison with CTR*CVR approach. Upper:Scaled amount of clicks. Bottom: Scaled sales revenue.

eters $\{\mathbf{p}, \mathbf{s}, \mathbf{r}, C\}$. The sales revenue is then recorded as performance measure. Since the main motivation of online algorithm is to catch the changes in traffic flow and conversion rate [3], we modify $\mathbf{f}$ and $\mathbf{r}$ before testing as following.

- Adding traffic flow with mean Δf to a few items (to simulate looming costumers for suddenly hot items);
- Increase the conversion rate with mean Δr of a few items (to simulate discounts/coupons);
- Modification of both above at the same time.

The online algorithm uses its batch counterpart as an initial solution, and updates the dual solutions based on the procedure described in Section 4. To reduce the impact of variance, all the experiments are repeated for 10 times. Average results are shown in Figure 6. We observe the results that are consistent with the ones reported in the previous subsections: the CTR*CVR method performs slightly better than the CTR-first method in terms of sales revenue, while the proposed batch learning algorithm outperforms both methods, particularly when the number of impression is sufficiently large. It is not surprising to observe that the proposed online learning method yields the best performance since it can catch the change in information and therefore is most sensitive to the case of out of stock. The advantage of the proposed online learning algorithm is further illustrated in Figure 7 where we show the number of out of stock views. We clearly observe that the online learning algorithm yields the smallest number of out of stock views. It is slightly to our surprise that the CTR*CVR performs even worse than CTR-first in terms of out of stock views.

6. CONCLUSION

In this paper, we propose a stock aware recommender system in e-commerce and extend it to online setting. The key idea is to optimize the recommendation selection for individual users based on both user preference and the limit of stock supply. We deploy this system to Tmall.com, the Chinese largest B2C platform, and verify the effectiveness of our approach using the live traffic from Tmall. Experiments with more than 100 million use visits shows that the proposed method can significantly improve the sales revenue of item-to-item recommendation. In the future, we will continue working on the online setting for stock aware recommendation and verify its effectiveness using the real traffic from Tmall.

[3]The CTR of "click ads of item j in the detail page of item i" is relative stable, so we keep it as constant here.

7. ACKNOWLEDGEMENTS

Our research was partially supported by Tianchi Research platform "http://tianchi.aliyun.com/". We thank the reviewers for very detailed and valuable comments.

References

[1] D. Agarwal, S. Ghosh, K. Wei, and S. You. Budget pacing for targeted online advertisements at linkedin. In *Proceedings of the 20th ACM SIGKDD international conference on Knowledge discovery and data mining*, pages 1613–1619. ACM, 2014.

[2] A. Beck and M. Teboulle. A fast iterative shrinkage-thresholding algorithm for linear inverse problems. *SIAM Journal on Imaging Sciences*, 2(1):183–202, 2009.

[3] J. Bobadilla, F. Ortega, A. Hernando, and A. Gutiérrez. Recommender systems survey. *Knowledge-Based Systems*, 46:109–132, 2013.

[4] S. Boyd and L. Vandenberghe. *Convex optimization*. Cambridge Univ Pr, 2004.

[5] N. Buchbinder, K. Jain, and J. S. Naor. Online primal-dual algorithms for maximizing ad-auctions revenue. In *Algorithms–ESA 2007*, pages 253–264. Springer, 2007.

[6] L. Candillier, F. Meyer, and M. Boullé. Comparing state-of-the-art collaborative filtering systems. In *Machine Learning and Data Mining in Pattern Recognition*, pages 548–562. Springer, 2007.

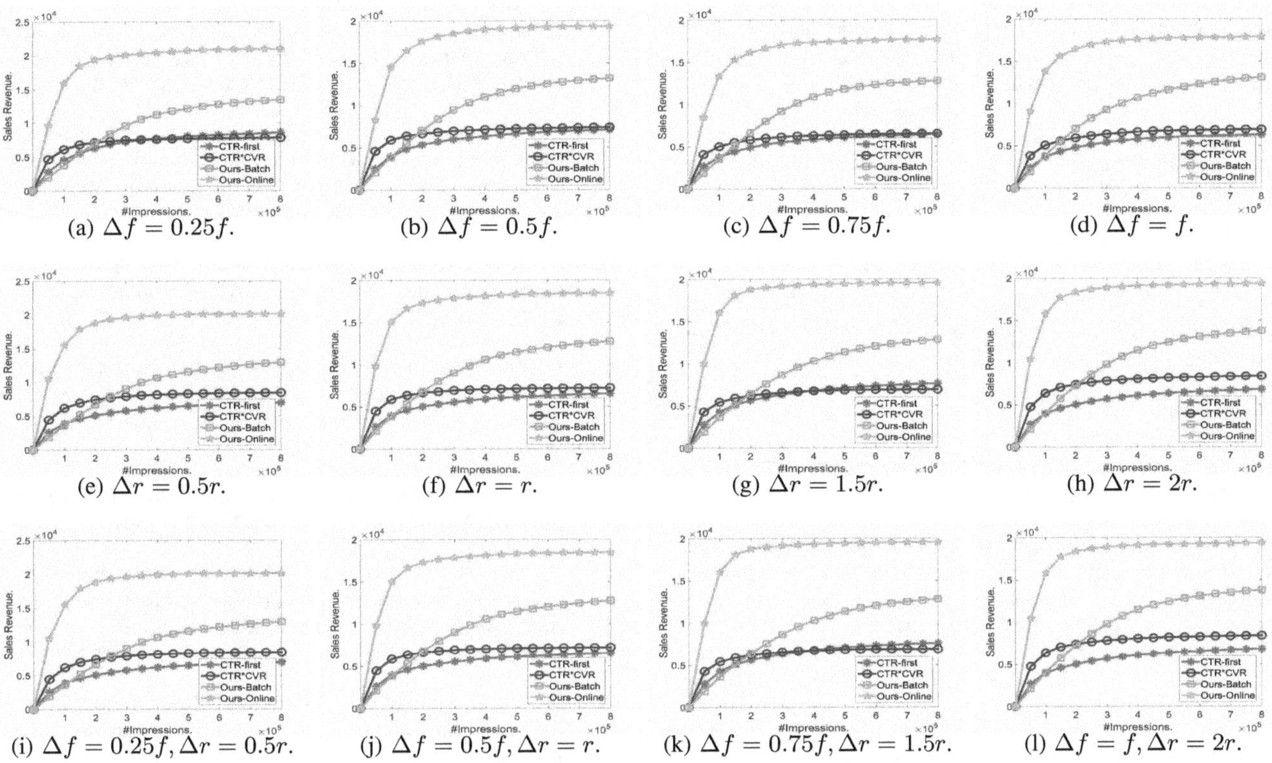

(a) $\Delta f = 0.25f$. (b) $\Delta f = 0.5f$. (c) $\Delta f = 0.75f$. (d) $\Delta f = f$.

(e) $\Delta r = 0.5r$. (f) $\Delta r = r$. (g) $\Delta r = 1.5r$. (h) $\Delta r = 2r$.

(i) $\Delta f = 0.25f, \Delta r = 0.5r$. (j) $\Delta f = 0.5f, \Delta r = r$. (k) $\Delta f = 0.75f, \Delta r = 1.5r$. (l) $\Delta f = f, \Delta r = 2r$.

Figure 6: Revenue versus number of impressions in online setting.

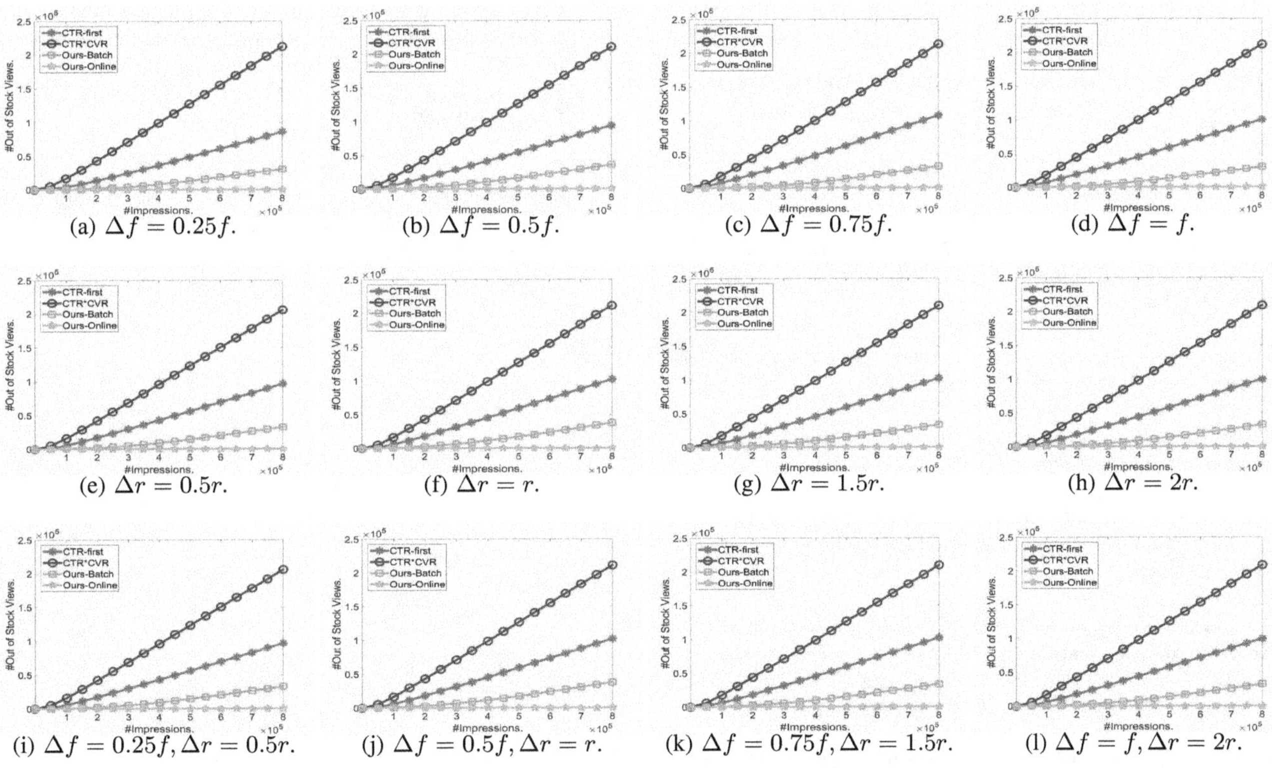

(a) $\Delta f = 0.25f$. (b) $\Delta f = 0.5f$. (c) $\Delta f = 0.75f$. (d) $\Delta f = f$.

(e) $\Delta r = 0.5r$. (f) $\Delta r = r$. (g) $\Delta r = 1.5r$. (h) $\Delta r = 2r$.

(i) $\Delta f = 0.25f, \Delta r = 0.5r$. (j) $\Delta f = 0.5f, \Delta r = r$. (k) $\Delta f = 0.75f, \Delta r = 1.5r$. (l) $\Delta f = f, \Delta r = 2r$.

Figure 7: Number of out of stock views versus number of impressions in online setting.

[7] N. R. Devanur and T. P. Hayes. The adwords problem: online keyword matching with budgeted bidders under random permutations. In *Proceedings of the 10th ACM conference on Electronic commerce*, pages 71–78. ACM, 2009.

[8] J. Duchi, E. Hazan, and Y. Singer. Adaptive subgradient methods for online learning and stochastic optimization. *Manuscript*, 2010.

[9] T. Graepel, J. Q. Candela, T. Borchert, and R. Herbrich. Web-scale bayesian click-through rate prediction for sponsored search advertising in microsoft's bing search engine. In *Proceedings of the 27th International Conference on Machine Learning*, pages 13–20, 2010.

[10] T. Hofmann. Learning the similarity of documents: An information-geometric approach to document retrieval and categorization. In *Advances in Neural Information Processing Systems 13*. Citeseer, 2000.

[11] C. Karande, A. Mehta, and R. Srikant. Optimizing budget constrained spend in search advertising. In *Proceedings of the sixth ACM international conference on Web search and data mining*, pages 697–706. ACM, 2013.

[12] B. Krulwich. Lifestyle finder: Intelligent user profiling using large-scale demographic data. *AI magazine*, 18(2):37, 1997.

[13] N. Landia and S. Anand. Personalised tag recommendation. pages 83–86, 2009.

[14] M. Mahdian, H. Nazerzadeh, and A. Saberi. Allocating online advertisement space with unreliable estimates. In *Proceedings of the 8th ACM conference on Electronic commerce*, pages 288–294. ACM, 2007.

[15] H. B. McMahan, G. Holt, D. Sculley, M. Young, D. Ebner, J. Grady, L. Nie, T. Phillips, E. Davydov, D. Golovin, et al. Ad click prediction: a view from the trenches. In *Proceedings of the 19th ACM SIGKDD international conference on Knowledge discovery and data mining*, 2013.

[16] A. Mehta, A. Saberi, U. Vazirani, and V. Vazirani. Adwords and generalized online matching. *Journal of the ACM*, 54(5):22, 2007.

[17] Y. Nesterov. *Introductory lectures on convex optimization: A basic course*. Springer Netherlands, 2004.

[18] Y. Nesterov. Smooth minimization of non-smooth functions. *Mathematical Programming*, 103(1):127–152, 2005.

[19] Y. Nesterov. Gradient methods for minimizing composite objective function. Technical Report 76, Catholic University of Louvain, 2007.

[20] M. Nickel, V. Tresp, and H.-P. Kriegel. Factorizing yago: Scalable machine learning for linked data. In *Proceedings of the 21st International Conference on World Wide Web*, WWW '12, pages 271–280, New York, NY, USA, 2012. ACM.

[21] C. Porcel, A. Tejeda-Lorente, M. Martínez, and E. Herrera-Viedma. A hybrid recommender system for the selective dissemination of research resources in a technology transfer office. *Information Sciences*, 184(1):1–19, 2012.

[22] S. Rendle, C. Freudenthaler, and L. Schmidt-Thieme. Factorizing personalized markov chains for next-basket recommendation. In *Proceedings of the 19th international conference on World wide web*, pages 811–820. ACM, 2010.

[23] A. Said and A. Bellogín. Comparative recommender system evaluation: benchmarking recommendation frameworks. In *Proceedings of the 8th ACM Conference on Recommender systems*, pages 129–136. ACM, 2014.

[24] X. Su and T. M. Khoshgoftaar. A survey of collaborative filtering techniques. *Advances in artificial intelligence*, 2009:4, 2009.

[25] R. Van Meteren and M. Van Someren. Using content-based filtering for recommendation. In *Proceedings of the Machine Learning in the New Information Age: MLnet/ECML2000 Workshop*, pages 47–56, 2000.

[26] H. R. Varian. Position auctions. *international Journal of industrial Organization*, 25(6):1163–1178, 2007.

[27] W. Wu, H. Li, and J. Xu. Learning query and document similarities from click-through bipartite graph with metadata. In *Proceedings of the sixth ACM international conference on Web search and data mining*, pages 687–696. ACM, 2013.

[28] W. Wu, Z. Lu, and H. Li. Learning bilinear model for matching queries and documents. *The Journal of Machine Learning Research*, 14(1):2519–2548, 2013.

[29] L. Xiao. Dual averaging methods for regularized stochastic learning and online optimization. *Journal of Machine Learning Research*, 11:2543–2596, 2010.

[30] C. Xiong, T. Wang, W. Ding, Y. Shen, and T.-Y. Liu. Relational click prediction for sponsored search. In *Proceedings of the Fifth ACM International Conference on Web Search and Data Mining*, WSDM '12, pages 493–502, New York, NY, USA, 2012. ACM.

[31] G.-E. Yap, X.-L. Li, and S. Y. Philip. Effective next-items recommendation via personalized sequential pattern mining. In *Database Systems for Advanced Applications*, pages 48–64. Springer, 2012.

Predicting Ambulance Demand: a Spatio-Temporal Kernel Approach

Zhengyi Zhou
Center for Applied Mathematics
Cornell University
Ithaca, NY 14853
zz254@cornell.edu

David S. Matteson
Department of Statistical Science
Cornell University
Ithaca, NY 14853
matteson@cornell.edu

ABSTRACT

Predicting ambulance demand accurately at fine time and location scales is critical for ambulance fleet management and dynamic deployment. Large-scale datasets in this setting typically exhibit complex spatio-temporal dynamics and sparsity at high resolutions. We propose a predictive method using spatio-temporal kernel density estimation (stKDE) to address these challenges, and provide spatial density predictions for ambulance demand in Toronto, Canada as it varies over hourly intervals. Specifically, we weight the spatial kernel of each historical observation by its informativeness to the current predictive task. We construct spatio-temporal weight functions to incorporate various temporal and spatial patterns in ambulance demand, including location-specific seasonalities and short-term serial dependence. This allows us to draw out the most helpful historical data, and exploit spatio-temporal patterns in the data for accurate and fast predictions. We further provide efficient estimation and customizable prediction procedures. stKDE is easy to use and interpret by non-specialized personnel from the emergency medical service industry. It also has significantly higher statistical accuracy than the current industry practice, with a comparable amount of computational expense.

Categories and Subject Descriptors

H.2.8 [**Database Management**]: Database Applications—*Data mining*; G.3 [**Probability and Statistics**]: Nonparametric statistics

Keywords

kernel density estimation; non-homogeneous Poisson point process; emergency medical service

1. INTRODUCTION

The emergency medical service (EMS) industry aims to minimize response times to emergencies and keep operational costs low. Accurate spatio-temporal demand predictions are critical to staff / fleet management and dynamic deployment. Predictions are required at high temporal and spatial resolutions for operational decision-making; the industry typically predicts for every hour and every 1 km^2 region. We are motivated to predict spatio-temporal ambulance demand in Toronto, Canada.

KDD'15, August 11-14, 2015, Sydney, NSW, Australia.

ACM 978-1-4503-3664-2/15/08 ...$15.00.
DOI: http://dx.doi.org/10.1145/2783258.2788570.

There are several typical challenges to predicting ambulance demand. First, ambulance demand data is often sparse at the prediction resolution. For instance, Toronto receives only 23 highest priority events per hour on average; 96% of the 1 km^2 spatial regions in Toronto have zero event in any hour. Also, ambulance demand frequently exhibits complex temporal dynamics, some of which are location-specific. For example, ambulance demand in Toronto has weekly and daily seasonality and short-term serial dependence of a few hours [12, 25]. Among these patterns, daily seasonality and short-term dependence are more pronounced downtown and in denser neighborhoods [25]. Lastly, ambulance demand data in large cities is usually large-scale; Toronto dispatches for about 200,000 priority events per year. This may present computational challenges, especially since predictions are needed hourly.

The current industry practice for predicting ambulance demand often uses a simple averaging formula. Demand in a 1 km^2 spatial region over an hour is typically predicted by averaging a small number of historical counts, from the same spatial region and over the corresponding hours from previous weeks or years [8]. In current practice, Toronto EMS averages four historical counts in the same hour of the year over the past four years, while the EMS of Charlotte-Mecklenburg, North Carolina averages twenty historical counts in the same hour of the preceding four weeks for the past five years (the MEDIC method) [20]. Averaging so few historical counts, which are mostly zeros, produces highly noisy and flickering predictions, resulting in haphazard and inefficient deployment. Such methods are also sensitive to how the spatial domains are partitioned [8].

Many studies have accurately predicted aggregate ambulance demand as a temporal process. These studies have considered autoregressive moving average models [4], factor models [12] and spectrum analysis [21]. However, very few studies have modeled spatio-temporal ambulance demand well. One study uses artificial neural networks (ANN) to predict ambulance demand on discretized time and space, but fails to improve predictive accuracy over typical industry practice due to data sparsity [20]. Another more recent study predicts ambulance demand in discrete time and continuous space [25]. It proposes a time-varying Gaussian mixture model (GMM) to incorporate location-specific temporal patterns in the demand, giving higher predictive accuracy than industry approaches. However, its estimation procedure via Bayesian sampling may present computational challenges and require special expertise, making it difficult to use by non-specialized personnel from the EMS industry.

Kernel density estimation (KDE) is a powerful tool for non-parametric density estimation in spatio-temporal data. It has been widely applied to visualize or forecast spatio-temporal crime incidence [3, 14], disease spread [24, 23], product demand [11], and data streams [1, 16]. In most cases, the time dimension is treated differently from the space dimension(s). The most traditional approach is to build a separate spatial KDE for each discrete time period. However, this approach may result in uneven subset size and sparse subsets with too little data for accurate density estimates. Recent studies assume a multiplicative orthogonal relationship between the time and space dimensions. For example, [1] multiplies a spatial kernel with a linear function in time. Studies such as [3, 14, 24] multiply a spatial kernel and a temporal kernel with different bandwidths and kernel functions for the two kernels.

Extending these multiplicative spatio-temporal KDE methods, we propose a fast and accurate method for predicting spatio-temporal ambulance demand that is practical and scalable in industrial settings. We follow [25] in predicting in discrete time and continuous space. We propose a novel specification of spatio-temporal kernel density estimation (stKDE). First, we learn parametrically the temporal and spatial characteristics of the demand. Each historical observation is annotated with a weight based on what we have learned. This spatio-temporal weight function scales how helpful different historical observations are to a given predictive task. Then we construct a spatial kernel density estimator weighted by the informativeness weight function, and use the resulting kernel density estimates as predictions. In this way, we efficiently emphasize the historical data most important to prediction and, as far as possible, exploit the spatial and temporal characteristics in the data. This approach has three main advantages

(a) accessibility: stKDE is fully automated and robust. It is easy to interpret and use by non-specialized personnel, while approaches such as ANN or GMM may need special expertise (e.g., tuning, MCMC diagnostics).

(b) efficiency: stKDE has low computational complexity. It is faster than GMM; inferring latent component label in GMM is costly. It can afford more frequent parameter estimation updates and online predictions.

(c) accuracy: stKDE gives more accurate predictions than current industry practice with similar computational expense. It also outperforms naive KDE methods (and ANN via [20]); it is at least as accurate as GMM.

We implement this method on ambulance demand data from Toronto, Canada from years 2007 and 2008. The data consist of 391, 296 priority emergency events received by Toronto EMS for which an ambulance was dispatched. Each record contains the time and the location to which the ambulance was dispatched. This includes some calls not requiring lights-and-sirens response, but does not include scheduled patient transfers. We include only the first event in our analysis when multiple responses are received for the same event; explanatory analysis did not reveal any spatial or temporal pattern for these cases, and we treat them as a single ambulance dispatch. We have removed all calls with no times or locations. There was no call received for more than two hours on March 10, 2007 due to a recording system malfunction, and we have also removed all calls from that day. These removals totaled less than 2% of the data. For example, Figure 1 shows the locations of all ambulance demand from January to July 2008.

Our proposed method, stKDE, gives significantly more accurate predictions than current industry practice with similar computational expense. It also compares favorably to the state-of-the-art in ambulance demand prediction research.

We propose the stKDE model in §2 and discuss computational methods in §3. We show the empirical results on Toronto ambulance demand in Section §4, and conclude in §5.

2. METHODOLOGY

We model Toronto's ambulance demand on a continuous spatial domain $\mathcal{S} \subseteq \mathbb{R}^2$ and a discretized temporal domain of one-hour intervals $\mathcal{T} = \{1, 2, \ldots\}$. Let $\mathbf{s}_{t,i}$ be the location of the i-th ambulance demand arising from the t-th time period, for $i \in \{1, \ldots, n_t\}$, where n_t is the total number of ambulances demanded in the t-th period. Since a non-homogeneous Poisson process (NHPP) is a natural model for a spatial point process [5, 13], we assume $\{\mathbf{s}_{t,i} : i = 1, \ldots n_t\}$ for each time period t independently follow an NHPP over $\mathcal{S}$, with positive intensity function λ_t. We decompose intensity function as $\lambda_t(\mathbf{s}) = \delta_t f_t(\mathbf{s})$, for $\mathbf{s} \in \mathcal{S}$. Here, $\delta_t = \int_{\mathcal{S}} \lambda_t(\mathbf{s})\, ds$ is the aggregate demand intensity over the spatial domain, and $f_t(\cdot)$ is the continuous spatial *density* of the demand at time t such that $f_t(\mathbf{s}) > 0$ and $\int_{\mathcal{S}} f_t(\mathbf{s}) ds = 1$. Hence, for each t, $n_t|\lambda_t \sim \text{Poisson}(\delta_t)$ and $\mathbf{s}_{t,i}|\lambda_t, n_t \overset{iid}{\sim} f_t(\cdot)$ for $i \in \{1, \ldots, n_t\}$. As mentioned before, numerous studies have proposed sophisticated and accurate methods for estimating $\{\delta_t\}$. We thus focus on predicting the spatio-temporal demand density $\{f_t\}$, which has received far less attention in the literature. With the predicted $\{f_t\}$, we can furthermore predict spatio-temporal demand volume by multiplying our $\{f_t\}$ with $\{\delta_t\}$ from studies such as [12].

2.1 Spatio-Temporal Kernel Density Estimation

Suppose we observe and utilize historical ambulance demand from a set of past time periods $\mathcal{T}_{obs}$, and we would like to forecast demand for a future time period u. We propose to predict f_u using a spatio-temporal weighted kernel density estimator. We place a bivariate spatial kernel K at the location of each past observation in $\mathcal{T}_{obs}$, and weight each kernel by the informativeness of the corresponding observation in predicting for the uth time period. Specifically, we have for $\mathbf{s} \in \mathcal{S}$

$$f_u(\mathbf{s}) = \frac{\sum_{t \in \mathcal{T}_{obs}} w(\mathbf{s}_{t,i}, u)\ K_{\boldsymbol{H}}(\mathbf{s} - \mathbf{s}_{t,i})}{\sum_{t \in \mathcal{T}_{obs}} w(\mathbf{s}_{t,i}, u)}. \tag{1}$$

Here, $w(\mathbf{s}_{t,i}, u)$ is the informativeness weight function multiplied by the spatial kernel of the past observation $\mathbf{s}_{t,i}$. This weight function is defined in detail in §2.2. K is the chosen bivariate spatial kernel with bivariate bandwidth $\boldsymbol{H}$, i.e.,

$$K_{\boldsymbol{H}}(\mathbf{s} - \mathbf{s}_{t,i}) = \frac{1}{|\boldsymbol{H}|} K\left(\boldsymbol{H}^{-1/2}(\mathbf{s} - \mathbf{s}_{t,i})\right).$$

2.2 Weight Function

The weight function w aims to capture the utility of a past observation in predicting demand at a future period. Specifically, we would like to incorporate in w the spatial and temporal dependencies in the demand. Domain knowledge on EMS demand densities focuses our attention on weekly and daily seasonalities and short-term serial dependence of a few hours, which have varying strengths in different neighborhoods.

We can therefore discretize the spatial domain into C large spatial cells, representing a rough division into neighborhoods. We assume that temporal dependencies within each cell remain constant in space. Let w_c denote the weight function local to each discretized cell $c \in \{1, \ldots, C\}$. Within this cell, we further assume that the informativeness of a past observation from time t in predicting for future time u only depends on how far back t is from u. We use the weight function to measure how positively correlated two demand densities $(u-t)$ periods apart are in each cell. We model the weight function as

$$w_c(u-t) = \rho_{1,c}^{u-t} + \rho_{2,c}^{u-t} \rho_{3,c}^{\sin^2\left(\frac{\pi(u-t)}{T_1}\right)} \rho_{4,c}^{\sin^2\left(\frac{\pi(u-t)}{T_2}\right)}, \quad (2)$$

for $c \in \{1, \ldots, C\}$. We combine all w_c to have

$$w(\mathbf{s}_{t,i}, u) = \sum_{c=1}^{C} w_c(u-t) \mathbb{1}_{\{\mathbf{s}_{t,i} \in \text{cell } c\}}. \quad (3)$$

Here, $\{\rho_{1,c}\}, \{\rho_{2,c}\}, \{\rho_{3,c}\}$ and $\{\rho_{4,c}\}$ for $c \in \{1, \ldots, C\}$ are all constrained to take values in $[0, 1]$. We use a separate ρ parameter to capture each typical EMS patterns for easy interpretation and comparisons across locations (e.g., downtown vs suburbs) and times (e.g., winter vs summer). The term $\rho_{1,c}^{u-t}$ describes any potential short-term serial dependence. Its parametric form is the same as a stationary first-order autoregressive model, AR(1), and is also equivalent to the squared exponential function often used in Gaussian processes [17]. The term with $\rho_{3,c}$ describes any potential daily seasonality with $T_1 = 24$, whereas the term with $\rho_{4,c}$ describes any potential weekly seasonality with $T_2 = 24 \times 7 = 168$. The parametric form of these two terms corresponds to the periodic function used in Gaussian processes [17]. These two seasonality terms are multiplied, and further discounted by a squared exponential function, $\rho_{2,c}^{u-t}$. Finally, we sum the short-term dependency effect and the seasonality effects. The different ρ terms are combined in similar to the typical approach to combining covariance functions in Gaussian processes. . There may be other weight functions that work similarly; we draw inspirations from Gaussian processes because these functions are well-studied and have some nice properties (e.g., infinite differentiability). This parametrization of the weight function is easy to interpret and visualize, and flexible to experiment with, even for non-experts.

The weight function is bounded between 0 and 2. We avoid negative weights to avoid negative kernels in the kernel density estimator, which complicates bandwidth selection, results in negative density estimates that need to be floored at zero, and produces discontinuities in the derivatives of the estimates [19]. The magnitudes of the weights are nominal, as long as they are comparable across all C regions, since they are normalized in Equation (1).

Equations (1), (2) and (3) together form the model.

2.3 Computational Methods

We must select or estimate the kernel function K and bivariate bandwidth $\boldsymbol{H}$ in Equation (1), as well as the spatial discretization C and $4C$ number of ρ parameters in the weight function (2). Since the nature of ambulance demand does not change drastically over time, these estimations may be performed infrequently in practice (at most several times a year).

For K, we can use the typical Gaussian kernel, or for additional computational savings, the Epanechnikov kernel with bounded support. We can select the bandwidth $\boldsymbol{H}$ via the plug-in method [22] or smoothed cross-validation [6]. We can also adopt one of many fast computational methods for KDE, including kd-trees [2], ball trees [15], dual trees [10] and statistical regular pavings [18].

For the weight function (2), we can choose the discretization mesh or C *a priori* or via cross validation. A larger value of C allows personalized temporal patterns on a finer grid, but if C is too large, data may become too sparse for accurate estimation of temporal dependencies. In our application, C is best chosen to be close to 20, yielding discrete regions that are roughly 5 km by 5 km each. The $4C$ number of ρ parameters in the weight function could be chosen in a number of standard ways; for instance we could use stochastic gradient ascent to maximize the joint likelihood of training data. For accurate estimation, we would need to use training data with tens of thousands of observations, and incur non-trivial computational cost. Here we introduce a much faster alternative method to estimate these parameters.

In Equation (2), w_c measures how positively correlated two demand densities $(u-t)$ periods apart are at cell c. We can directly estimate this correlation as follows. For each cell c, we can approximate its demand density for any period by the proportion of observations arising from this cell out of all observations from that period. We can then obtain a time series of proportions and compute its (discrete) autocorrelation function $A_c(\ell)$ for lag $\ell \in \{1, \ldots, L\}$, where L is the maximum lag considered. Typically L can be taken to be around several weeks (hundreds of one-hour periods). The non-negative part of this autocorrelation, $A_c^+(\ell)$, or a smoothed version of it, is precisely what w_c aims to capture. For example, Figure 2 (a) shows an example of the autocorrelation function $A_c(\ell)$, and the grey lines in Figure 2 (b) shows the corresponding $A_c^+(\ell)$, for $\ell \in \{1, \ldots, 672\}$ (up to 4 weeks of one-hour periods).

The goal is to find appropriate ρ parameters such that w_c best fits the shape of A_c^+. To do this, we would like to minimize the sum of squared errors between $\rho_{0,c} w_c(\ell)$ and $A_c^+(\ell)$ at all time lags ℓ from 1 to L. We can find the optimal $\rho_{0,c}$ to $\rho_{4,c}$ for this minimization using gradient descent or grid search. The extra parameter $\rho_{0,c}$ is needed to scale w_c to curve-match the magnitude of A_c^+, and is of no real significance. Of greater importance is curvature or shape of A_c^+, which is captured in $\rho_{1,c}$ to $\rho_{4,c}$. To make w_c comparable across all C cells, we need to normalize w_c such that the area under w_c up to L is the same across different cells.

In summary, we estimate the ρ parameters in C minimization problems: for each $c \in \{1, \ldots, C\}$,

$$\min_{\rho_{j,c}, \forall j \in \{0,\ldots,4\}} \sum_{\ell=1}^{L} \left(A_c^+(\ell) - \rho_{0,c} w_c(\ell)\right)^2 \tag{4}$$

$$\text{s.t.} \sum_{\ell=1}^{L} w_c(\ell) = 1.$$

This computation is much more efficient than the joint estimation of $4C$ parameters by maximizing likelihood. Here, we do not need to involve the kernel density estimator, nor loop through tens of thousands of ambulance demand observations. We can easily compute the C minimization problems in parallel. For each cell, we have a low-dimensional (5 parameters) problem with a small number of observations L (around hundreds of hours of time lags). A wide array of standard algorithms for solving optimization problems can be applied. For example, we can Lagrangian relax the constraint into the objective and use the genetic algorithm or particle swarm.

Once the infrequently performed parameter estimation is done, predictions for any future time period can be calculated instantaneously using short sliding windows of length L. We can additionally refine or customize the prediction procedure in the following two ways.

First, to boost predictive accuracy, we can bilinearly interpolate the weight values smoothly over the spatial domain instead of taking only C sets of values on a discretized grid. This is appropriate since we believe that the temporal patterns vary smoothly across the spatial domain. It also mitigates the sensitivity to predictions induced by choices of C.

Secondly, we can impose an omission threshold value, $\mathcal{O}$, for the weights. If the weight of a past observation $\boldsymbol{s}_{t,i}$ is below this threshold, i.e., if $w(\boldsymbol{s}_{t,i}, u) < \mathcal{O}$, we can omit this observation in the calculation of weighted KDE by overriding $w(\boldsymbol{s}_{t,i}, u) = 0$. The threshold can be chosen to balance the tradeoff between computational expense and predictive accuracy.

3. PREDICTING TORONTO AMBULANCE DEMAND

The computation has two stages. In the first stage, we estimate or choose all parameters, including the kernel K, bandwidth $\boldsymbol{H}$, discretization C and $4C$ number of ρ parameters. This estimation only needs to be performed infrequently. For this parameter estimation, we use Toronto ambulance data from January to July 2008. Figure 1 shows the spatial locations of all observations from this 7-month period. In the second stage, we predict future ambulance demand on a sliding window of length $L = 672$ (4 weeks, around 15,000 observations) for each one-hour period from August to December 2008.

In estimation, we choose the Gaussian kernel for K, select the bandwidth $\boldsymbol{H}$ via the plug-in method [22] and discretize Toronto into $C = 21$ equally-sized regions. We estimate the ρ parameters in the weight function using the method detailed in §3. As an example, we outline the cell c covering downtown Toronto in Figure 1. We show in Figure 2 (a) the autocorrelation function A_c for the proportions of observations arising from this downtown cell out of all observations across hourly time periods. This autocorrelation function indicates weekly, daily seasonalities and low-order serial dependence. Figure 2 (b) shows in grey A_c^+ and in black the fitted weight function $\rho_{0,c} w_c$ for downtown, with $\rho_{1,c} = 0.95$ (short-term serial dependence), $\rho_{3,c} = 0.001$ (daily seasonality), $\rho_{4,c} = 0.145$ (weekly seasonality) and $\rho_{2,c} = 0.9995$ (discounting for seasonalities). The fitted weight function provides an interpretable basis for understanding exactly which historical observations are the most important for prediction. For example, from Figure 2 (b), an EMS manager can recognize that at downtown, ambulance demand in the past day or two and corresponding hour of the past few weeks are the most important. Cross-correlations among the 21 weight functions estimated at different regions show that neighboring weight functions have some association, but those far apart are not correlated.

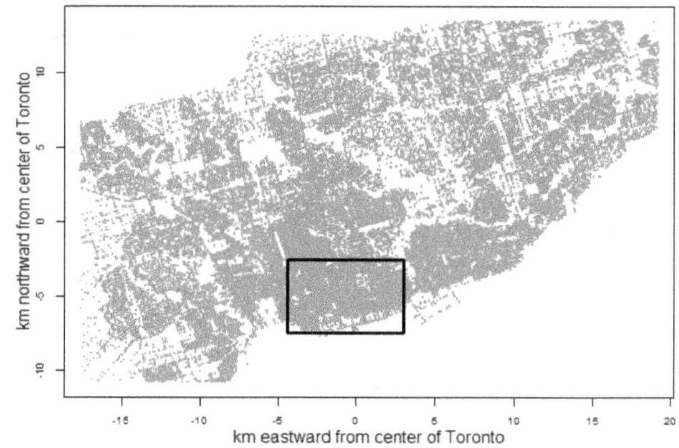

Figure 1: Spatial locations of all Toronto ambulance demand data from January to July 2008. To evaluate location-specific weight functions, we discretize the spatial domain into 21 cells, and here we outline the cell containing downtown Toronto.

Once parameter estimation is done, we predict forward using a sliding window of 4 weeks for each one-hour period from August to December 2008. Figure 3 shows the predictive densities on August 6, 2008 (Wednesday) at two different time periods. The ambulance demand is, not surprisingly, concentrated at the heart of downtown during day time on Wednesday (Figure 3 (b)), and more spread out throughout the city during night time on Wednesday (Figure 3 (a)). This illustrates that stKDE can differentiate temporal patterns at different time periods and locations.

We compare stKDE to the following competing methods

(a) The MEDIC method, which is an industry practice implemented in Charlotte-Mecklenburg, NC (§1). We implement this method as far as we have data. The cell count in a 1-km^2 region and a 1-hour period is predicted by the average of corresponding cell counts in the preceding 4 weeks in the past two years. The log predictive density produced by MEDIC for August 6, 2008 (Wednesday) at 2 - 3 am is shown in Figure 4. Compared to Figure 3 (a), the MEDIC prediction appears much noisier.

(b) Two naive KDEs, (i) using data from the most recent hour to predict the next hour, and (ii) using all data

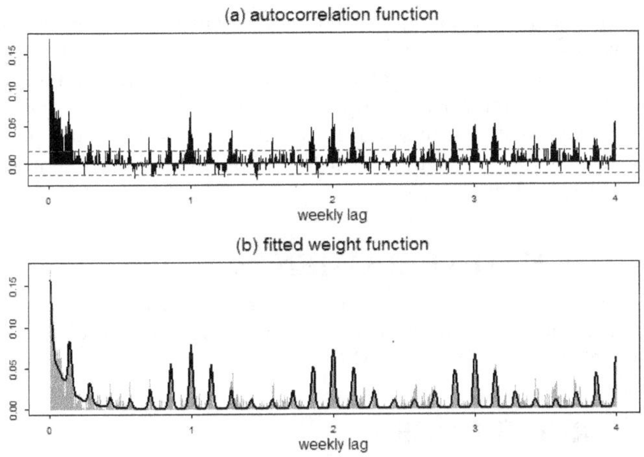

Figure 2: (a) The autocorrelation function of the proportions of observations arising from the rectangle in Figure 1 over all observations across one-hour periods. (b) The fitted weight function (black) against the nonnegative part of the autocorrelation function (gray).

from the past four weeks with equal weights (this produces a spatial only model, with almost no temporal variation).

(c) A time-varying Gaussian mixture model. We quote results from [25] implemented on Toronto data with different training / testing months and various modeling specifications (e.g., number of components). The computational expense is considerable.

To compare the statistical predictive accuracies of our model and the comparison methods, we use the metric of average log score [9]. This performance measure is widely used because it is a strictly proper scoring rule closely related to Bayes factor and Bayes information criterion [7]. It is the average log likelihood of test data, and is defined as

$$\text{Accuracy}(\{\tilde{\mathbf{s}}_{u,i}\}) = \frac{1}{\sum_{u\in\mathcal{T}_{test}} n_t} \sum_{u\in\mathcal{T}_{test}} \sum_{i=1}^{n_t} \log \hat{f}_u(\tilde{\mathbf{s}}_{u,i}),$$

in which $\mathcal{T}_{test}$ are the test time periods, $\{\tilde{\mathbf{s}}_{u,i}\}$ are the test data, and $\hat{f}_u(\cdot)$ is the predictive density for the u-th period obtained either by various methods. Intuitively, it measures the probability that we observe test data given a model. Thus a less negative (higher) average log score indicates that the model is better at capturing the test data.

We show in Table 1 the predictive accuracies produced by stKDE and the comparison methods. We present three variations of stKDE prediction: (i) using the estimated discretized weight functions w_c as they are, (ii) spatially interpolating the estimated weight values, and (iii) imposing an omission threshold on the estimated weight values such that each prediction uses a comparable amount of data as the industry method (about 200 observations).

The stKDE method significantly outperforms the MEDIC method (industry practice). It also outperforms the naive KDE methods, demonstrating the utility of incorporating spatio-temporal patterns via the weight functions. Our performance is comparable to time-varying GMM as it is im-

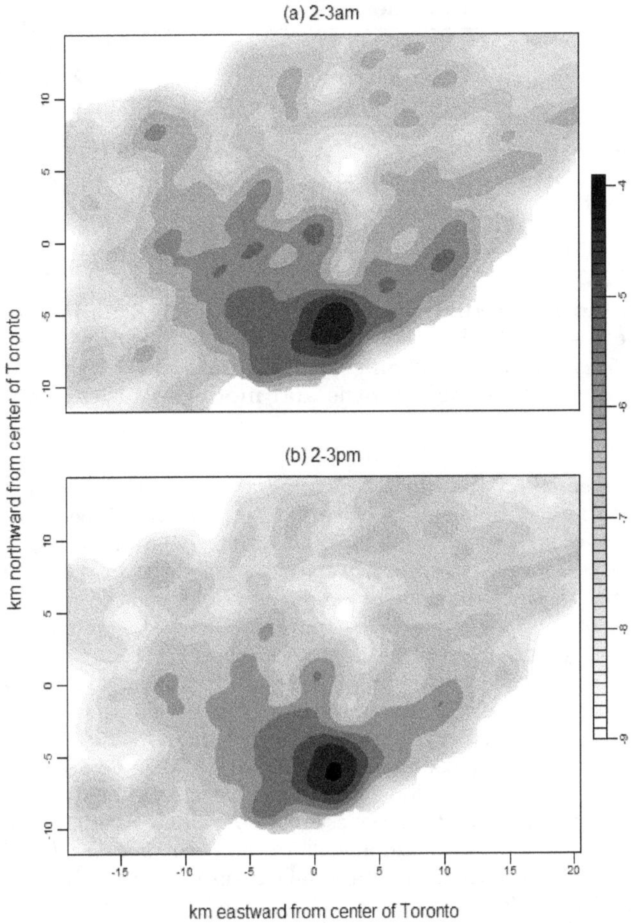

Figure 3: Log predictive density using stKDE for Aug 6, 2008 (Wednesday) at (a) 2 - 3 am (demand more spread out at night) and (b) 2 - 3 pm (demand concentrated at downtown during the day).

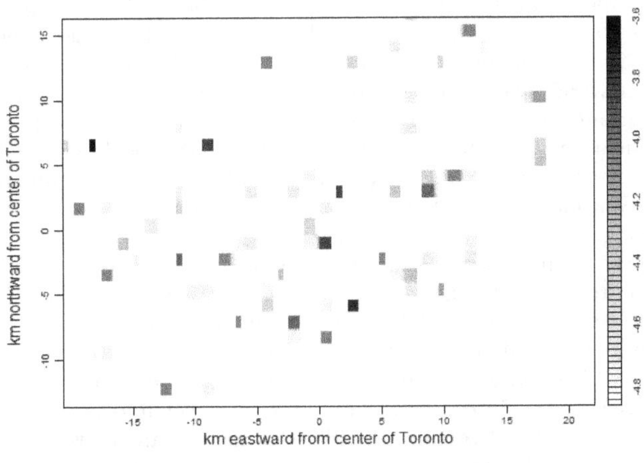

Figure 4: Log predictive density using industry method for Aug 6, 2008 (Wednesday) at 2 - 3 am. Figure 3 (a) shows a less noisy density for the same period predicted by stKDE.

Prediction method		Accuracy
stKDE		−6.106
	+ interpolation	−6.102
	+ threshold (less data)	−6.635
MEDIC		−8.642
naiveKDE	most recent hour	−6.921
	all equal weights	−6.254
GMM		−6.072 to −6.149

Table 1: Predictive accuracies of stKDE and competing methods. Results of GMM are quoted from [25] implemented on Toronto data with various training / testing months and model specifications.

plemented on Toronto data with different training / testing months and modeling specifications. Among the three variations of stKDE, allowing for bilinear interpolation of weight values improves the predictive accuracy slightly. In the third variation, including the omission threshold leads to a small loss of accuracy but reduces computational cost significantly to be comparable to the industry method.

The infrequent estimation of weight functions and bandwidth takes several hours on a personal computer. This offline training is significantly shorter than that of GMM (inferring latent component labels in GMM is costly). It does not take much longer than estimating bandwidths for naive KDE methods. Once estimation is done, making each new prediction is instantaneous (a few seconds). We could further reduce the computational expense of stKDE by parallelizing weight estimation, using a tree-based algorithm for fast KDE computation, using a bounded kernel function, or creating a look-up table of densities (none of these was done).

4. CONCLUSIONS

Fine-resolution spatio-temporal ambulance demand predictions are crucial to optimal ambulance planning. The EMS industry practice and early studies either sacrifice predictive accuracy for fast computation, or incur substantial computational cost in pursuit of high accuracy. We provide a much-needed prediction method that is both accurate and fast. We predict spatio-temporal ambulance demand in Toronto with higher accuracy and comparable computational cost as a typical industry practice.

We propose a spatio-temporal weighted kernel density estimator. The spatial kernel of each historical observation is multiplied with a weight value to indicate the informativeness of this historical observation to the current predictive task. The spatio-temporal weight functions are inferred from dependencies in data, are unique to each neighborhood and can be updated regularly. This is an improvement from the ad hoc heuristic that only accounts for the weekly and yearly seasonality across the entire city. The weight functions are also flexible to represent various spatial and temporal characteristics. They are easy to experiment with, visualize and interpret by non-experts. Moreover, stKDE easily handles missing data by placing zero weight and scaling up weights on other data proportionally. It can also easily predict many hours or days into the future.

The proposed method provides efficient estimation of the weight function, and offers customizable prediction to balance the tradeoffs between accuracy and computational cost. It is straightforward to implement by non-specialized users and scalable to large-scale datasets, and can be easily generalized to a wide range of other applications with spatial-temporal point process data.

5. ACKNOWLEDGMENTS

The authors sincerely thank Toronto EMS for sharing their data, and support from a Xerox Faculty Research Award and NSF grant DMS-1455172.

6. REFERENCES

[1] C. C. Aggarwal. A framework for diagonosing changes in evolving data streams. In *ACM SIGMOD International Conference on Management of Data*, pages 575 – 586, 2003.

[2] J. L. Bentley. Multidimensional binary search trees used for associative searching. *Communications of the ACM*, 1975.

[3] C. Brunsdon, J. Corcoran, and G. Higgs. Visualising space and time in crime patterns: a comparison of methods. *Computers, Environment and Urban Systems*, 31:52 – 75, 2007.

[4] N. Channouf, P. L'Ecuyer, A. Ingolfsson, and A. Avramidis. The application of forecasting techniques to modeling emergency medical system calls in calgary, alberta. *Health Care Management Science*, 10:25–45, 2007.

[5] P. J. Diggle. *Statistical Analysis of Spatial Point Patterns.* Arnold, London, second edition, 2003.

[6] T. Duong and M. L. Hazelton. Cross-validation bandwidth matrices for multivariate kernel density estimation. *Scandinavian Journal of Statistics*, 32:485–506, 2005.

[7] T. Gneiting and A. Raftery. Strictly proper scoring rules, prediction, and estimation. *Journal of the American Statistical Association*, 102:359–378, 2007.

[8] J. B. Goldberg. Operations research methods for the deployment of emergency service vehicles. *EMS Management Journal*, 1:20–39, 2004.

[9] I. J. Good. Rational decisions. *Journal of the Royal Statistical Society: Series B*, 14:107–114, 1952.

[10] A. G. Gray and A. W. Moore. Nonparametric density estimation: toward computational tractability. In *Proceedings of the SIAM International Conference on Data Mining*, 2003.

[11] E. M. Jansenberger and P. Staufer-Steinnocher. Dual kernel density estimation as a method for describing spatio-temporal changes in the upper Austrian food retailing market. In *AGILE Conference on Geographic Information Science*, 2004.

[12] D. S. Matteson, M. W. McLean, D. B. Woodard, and S. G. Henderson. Forecasting emergency medical service call arrival rates. *Annals of Applied Statistics*, 5:1379–1406, 2011.

[13] J. Møller and R. P. Waagepetersen. *Statistical Inference and Simulation for Spatial Point Processes.* Chapman & Hall/CRC, London, 2004.

[14] T. Nakaya and K. Yano. Visualising crime clusters in a space-time cube: an exploratory data analysis approach using space-time kernel density estimation and scan statistics. *Transactions in GIS*, 14:223 – 239, 2010.

[15] S. M. Omohundro. Five balltree construction algorithms. *International Computer Science Institute Technical Report*, 1989.

[16] C. M. Procopiuc and O. Procopiuc. Density estimation for spatial data streams. *Advances in Spatial and Temporal Databases*, 3633:109 – 126, 2005.

[17] C. E. Rasmussen and C. K. I. Williams. *Gaussian Process for Machine Learning*. MIT, Boston, 2006.

[18] R. Sainudiin, G. Teng, J. Harlow, and D. Lee. Posterior expectation of regularly paved random histograms. *ACM Transactions on Modeling and Computer Simulation*, 23, 2013.

[19] D. W. Scott. *Multivariate Density Estimation: Theory, Practice and Visualization*. John Wiley and Sons, New York, 1992.

[20] H. Setzler, C. Saydam, and S. Park. EMS call volume predictions: A comparative study. *Computers & Operations Research*, 36:1843–1851, 2009.

[21] J. L. Vile, J. W. Gillard, P. R. Harper, and V. A. Knight. Predicting ambulance demand using singular spectrum analysis. *Journal of the Operations Research Society*, 63:1556–1565, 2012.

[22] M. P. Wand and M. C. Jones. Multivariate plug-in bandwidth selection. *Computational Statistics*, 9:97–116, 1994.

[23] J. W. Wilesmith, M. A. Stevenson, C. B. King, and R. S. Morris. Spatio-temporal epidemiology of foot-and-mouth disease in two counties of great britain in 2001. *Preventive Veterinary Medicine*, 61:157 – 170, 2003.

[24] Z. Zhang, D. Chen, W. Liu, J. S. Racine, S. H. Ong, Y. Cheng, G. Zhao, and Q. Jiang. Nonparametric evaluation of dynamic disease risk: a spatio-temporal kernel approach. *PLoS ONE*, 6, 2011.

[25] Z. Zhou, D. Matteson, D. Woodard, S. Henderson, and A. Micheas. A spatio-temporal point process model for ambulance demand. *Journal of the American Statistical Association*, 110:6–15, 2015.

Web Personalization and Recommender Systems

Shlomo Berkovsky and Jill Freyne
CSIRO
PO Box 76
Epping NSW Australia
firstname.lastname@csiro.au

ABSTRACT

The quantity of accessible information has been growing rapidly and far exceeded human processing capabilities. The sheer abundance of information often prevents users from discovering the desired information, or aggravates making informed and correct choices. This highlights the pressing need for intelligent personalized applications that simplify information access and discovery by taking into account users' preferences and needs. One type of personalized application that has recently become tremendously popular in research and industry is recommender systems. These provide to users personalized recommendations about information and products they may be interested to examine or purchase. Extensive research into recommender systems has yielded a variety of techniques, which have been published at a variety of conferences and adopted by numerous Web-sites. This tutorial will provide the participants with broad overview and thorough understanding of algorithms and practically deployed Web and mobile applications of personalized technologies.

Categories and Subject Descriptors

H.3.5 [**Information Storage and Retrieval**]: Online Information Services – *Web-based services, commercial services.*

General Terms

Algorithms, Design, Experimentation, Human Factors.

Keywords

Web personalization, recommender systems, user modeling.

1. INTRODUCTION

The sheer quantity of accessible online information has been growing relentlessly and has far exceeded limited processing capabilities of users. Although this abundance of information may be perceived as valuable, it often also prevents users from discovering the desired information, or aggravates making informed and correct choices. This situation manifests in many domains and use cases, and is referred to in the literature as the *information overloading* problem.

The information overloading highlights the pressing need for intelligent *personalized* applications that ease information access discovery by taking into account the preferences and needs of their users. These are exploited in nowadays Web-based and mobile environments for a variety of purposes, such as finding relevant news items, filtering out junk emails, recommending products to purchase, summarizing long textual documents, re-ordering purchase lists, or adaptively visualizing content for the user. The basis for the personalization in these cases is the so-called *user models*, which encapsulate a representation of the user's interests and information needs, as derived from their past behavior and interactions with the system and other users.

One type of personalized application that has recently become popular in the research community as well as in the commercial Web-sites is *recommender systems*. These provide to users personalized recommendations about services and products they may be interested to examine or purchase. In a sense, recommender systems can be considered complementary to established information filtering tools – the former recommend on desired items, whereas the latter filter out the undesired ones. The generation of recommendations typically exploits information collected during the past interactions of users with the system and other users, and other available domain information. Two fundamental groups of methods are used in recommender systems: social methods that leverage the "wisdom of the crowd" and knowledge-based methods that exploit the available domain and expert-engineered knowledge.

Research works around the areas of personalization and recommendation technologies have been tremendously popular at recent. In the last decade, extensive research into personalized technologies has yielded a spectrum of algorithmic techniques and practical systems, which have been published at a wide variety of conferences (WWW, IJCAI, AAAI, KDD, ICDM, CHI, SIGIR, JCDL, WSDM, ICWSM, and more). These techniques turned out to be practically important and have been adopted by many popular commercial Web-sites (Google, Yahoo, eBay, LinkedIn, Facebook, Twitter, Netflix, and more).

The tutorial will overview this exciting area of research and practice, and the participants will gain a thorough understanding of algorithmic techniques exploited by personalized technologies. The tutorial will also include a number of examples and Web-based systems, which will demonstrate the challenges raised by practical deployment of the personalized and recommendation technologies. Topics related to interaction data analysis, decision making, and scalability of recommender systems will give the participants the flavor of challenges and constraints posed by real-life large-scale personalized technologies. The tutorial on personalized technologies and recommender systems is timely and important. It can draw the attention of the KDD community to these topics, and trigger more works looking at the application of core KDD methods to personalized user-facing systems.

KDD '15, August 11-14, 2015, Sydney, NSW, Australia.
ACM 978-1-4503-3664-2/15/08.
http://dx.doi.org/10.1145/2783258.2789995

2. PRESENTERS

Shlomo Berkovsky is a Senior Researcher at the Digital Productivity Flagship, CSIRO. Shlomo received his PhD (summa cum laude) from the University of Haifa, where his research focused on mediation of user models in recommender systems. At CSIRO he was the Research Leader of the Personalized Information Delivery team and worked on a project focusing on personalized eHealth applications. Shlomo's broad research interests include user modeling, Web personalization, and recommender systems. Specifically, he is interested in collaborative and content-based recommenders, personalized persuasion, privacy-enhanced personalization, ubiquitous user modeling, personalization on the Social Web, and context-aware recommender systems. Shlomo is the author of more than 80 refereed papers published in journals, books, and conference proceedings. He published in broad venues (ACM TIST, AI Review, WWW, IJCAI) and in venues focused on personalization and recommender systems (UMUAI, ACM TiiS, RecSys, IUI, UMAP). His paper won the Best Paper Award of the AH conference and 2 iAward prizes. Shlomo presented 3 keynote talks and 8 tutorials on personalization and recommender systems, including at WWW, UMAP, and WISE. He served on the organizing committee of 9 conferences (as general, PC, workshops, tutorials, or DC chair) and chaired 14 workshops.

Jill Freyne is a Senior Research Scientist at the CSIRO Digital Productivity Flagship. Jill received her PhD from University College Dublin, where her research focused on collaborative, community based Web search. Jill continued her research into personalization and recommender technology as a Postdoctoral Fellow at the Clarity Center for Sensor Web technologies and IBM Research in Cambridge, MA where she worked primarily on influence in social networking. Since her commencement at CSIRO, Jill's research has focused on recommender and persuasive technologies to impact attitude and behaviour in the health domain. Jill is the author of over 70 publications published in top quality journals and conferences. She holds a strong international reputation and has been invited to speak at highly regarded institutions including MIT, CMU, and IBM Research. Jill has co-chaired the International Conference on Persuasive Technologies 2013, has organized a national conference, served on the organizing committees of IUI, Hypertext and Recommender Systems conferences, and run several workshops on Recommender System and Social Web. Jill serves as a senior PC member of RecSys and has reviewed for many other journals and international conferences. Jill has taught courses on information retrieval, recommender systems and social media.

3. REFERENCES

[1] Adomavicius, G., Tuzhilin, A.: Toward the next generation of recommender systems: A survey of the state-of-the-art. IEEE Trans. on Knowledge and Data Engineering, 17(6):734–749, 2005.

[2] Amatriain, X.: Mining large streams of user data for personalized recommendations. SIGKDD Explorations. Newsletter, 14(2):37–48, 2013.

[3] Balabanovic, M., Shoham, Y.: Content-based, collaborative recommendation. Communications of ACM, 40(3):66–72, 1997.

[4] Berkovsky, S., Kuflik, T., Ricci, F.: Cross-representation mediation of user models. User Modeling and User-Adapted Interact., 19(1-2):35–63, 2009.

[5] Berkovsky, S., Kuflik, T., Ricci, F.: The impact of data obfuscation on the accuracy of collaborative filtering. Expert Systems with Applications, 39(5):5033-5042, 2012.

[6] Brusilovsky, P.: Methods and techniques of adaptive hypermedia. User Modeling and User-Adapted Interact., 6(2-3):87–129, 1996.

[7] Burke, R.: Hybrid web recommender systems. In: The Adaptive Web, 2007.

[8] Burke, R.: Knowledge-based recommender systems. In: Encyclopedia of Library and Information Systems, 2000.

[9] Fisher, G.: User modeling in human-computer interaction. User Modeling and User-Adapted Interact. 11:65–86, 2001.

[10] Freyne, J., Berkovsky, S., Smith, G.: Recipe recommendation: accuracy and reasoning. In: Conference on User Modeling, Adaptation, and Personalization, 2011.

[11] Golbeck, J.: Generating predictive movie recommendations from trust in social networks. In: Trust Management Conference, 2006.

[12] Herlocker, J.L., Konstan, J.A., Terveen, L.G., Riedl, J.T.: Evaluating collaborative filtering recommender systems. ACM Trans. on Information Systems 22(1):5–53, 2004.

[13] Knijnenburg, B.P., Willemsen, M.C., Gantner, Z., Newell, C.: Explaining the user experience of recommender systems. User Modeling and User-Adapted Interact., 22(4–5):441–504, 2012.

[14] Kobsa, A.: Generic User Modeling Systems. User Model. User-Adapt. Interact., 11(1–2):49–63, 2001.

[15] Konstan, J.A., Riedl, J.: Recommender systems: from algorithms to user experience. User Modeling and User-Adapted Interact., 22(1-2):101–123, 2012.

[16] Koren, Y., Bell, R.M., Volinsky, C.: Matrix factorization techniques for recommender systems. Computer, 42(8):30–37, 2009.

[17] Krulwich, B.: Lifestyle finder: intelligent user profiling using large-scale demographic data. Artificial Intelligence, 18(2):37–45, 1997.

[18] Linden, G., Smith, B., York, J.: Amazon.com recommendations: item-to-item collaborative filtering. IEEE Internet Computing, 7(1):76–80, 2003.

[19] Lops, P., de Gemmis, M., Semeraro, G.: Content-based recommender systems: State of the art and trends. In: Recommender Systems Handbook, 2011.

[20] Maes, P.: Agents that reduce work and information overload. Communications of ACM 37(7):31–40, 1994.

[21] Resnick, P., Iacovou, N., Suchak, M., Bergstrom, P., Riedl, J.: Grouplens: An open architecture for collaborative filtering. In: Conference on Computer-Supported Cooperative Work, 1994.

[22] Tiroshi, A., Berkovsky, S., Vallet, D., Kuflik, T.: Graph-based recommendations: make the most out of social data. In: Conference on User Modeling, Adaptation, and Personalization, 2014.

Graph-Based User Behavior Modeling: From Prediction to Fraud Detection

Alex Beutel
Carnegie Mellon University
Pittsburgh, PA, USA
abeutel@cs.cmu.edu

Leman Akoglu
Stony Brook University
Stony Brook, NY, USA
leman@cs.stonybrook.edu

Christos Faloutsos
Carnegie Mellon University
Pittsburgh, PA, USA
christos@cs.cmu.edu

ABSTRACT

How can we model users' preferences? How do anomalies, fraud, and spam effect our models of normal users? How can we modify our models to catch fraudsters? In this tutorial we will answer these questions - connecting graph analysis tools for user behavior modeling to anomaly and fraud detection. In particular, we will focus on the application of subgraph analysis, label propagation, and latent factor models to static, evolving, and attributed graphs.

For each of these techniques we will give a brief explanation of the algorithms and the intuition behind them. We will then give examples of recent research using the techniques to model, understand and predict normal behavior. With this intuition for how these methods are applied to graphs and user behavior, we will focus on state-of-the-art research showing how the outcomes of these methods are effected by fraud, and how they have been used to catch fraudsters.

Categories and Subject Descriptors

H.2.8 [**Database Applications**]: Data mining;
H.3.5 [**Information Systems**]: Information Storage and Retrieval—*On-line Information Services*

Keywords

User Behavior Modeling; Fraud Detection; Anomalous Behavior; Outlier Detection; Recommendation Systems

1. TUTORIAL PERSPECTIVE

In this tutorial we focus on understanding anomaly and fraud detection through the lens of normal user behavior modeling. The data mining and machine learning communities have developed a plethora of models and methods for understanding user behavior. However, these methods generally assume that the behavior is that of real, honest people. On the other hand, fraud detection systems frequently use similar techniques as those used in modeling "normal" behavior, but are often framed as an independent problem. However, by focusing on the relations and intersections of the two perspectives we can gain a more complete understanding of the methods and hopefully inspire new research joining these two communities.

KDD '15, August 10-13, 2015, Sydney, NSW, Australia.
ACM. ISBN 978-1-4503-3664-2/15/08.
DOI: http://dx.doi.org/10.1145/2783258.2789985.

2. TARGET AUDIENCE

This tutorial is aimed at anyone interested in modeling and understanding user behavior, from data mining and machine learning researchers to practitioners from industry and government. For those new to the field, the tutorial will cover the necessary background material to understand these systems and will offer a concise, intuitive overview of the state-of-the-art. Additionally, the tutorial aims to offer a new perspective that will be valuable and interesting even for researchers with more experience in these domains. For those having worked in classic user behavior modeling, we will demonstrate how fraud can effect commonly-used models that expect normal behavior, with the hope that future models will directly account for fraud. For those having worked in fraud detection systems, we hope to inspire new research directions through connecting with recent developments in modeling "normal" behavior.

3. INSTRUCTORS

Alex Beutel is a fifth year Ph.D. candidate at Carnegie Mellon University in the Computer Science Department. He previously received his B.S. from Duke University. His Ph.D. research focuses on large scale user behavior modeling, covering both recommendation systems and fraud detection systems. He has interned at Facebook on both the Site Integrity and News Feed Ranking teams, at Microsoft in the Cloud and Information Services Laboratory, and at Google Research. His research is supported by a Facebook Fellowship and the National Science Foundation Graduate Research Fellowship Program. More details can be found at `http://alexbeutel.com`.

Leman Akoglu is an Assistant Professor in the Department of Computer Science at Stony Brook University. She received her Ph.D. from the Computer Science Department at Carnegie Mellon University in 2012. She also worked at IBM T. J. Watson Research Labs and Microsoft Research at Redmond during summers. Her research interests span a wide range of data mining and machine learning topics with a focus on algorithmic problems arising in graph mining, pattern discovery, social and information networks, and especially anomaly mining; outlier, fraud, and event detection. Dr.

Akoglu's research has won 4 publication awards; Best Research Paper at SIAM SDM 2015, Best Paper at ADC 2014, Best Paper at PAKDD 2010, and Best Knowledge Discovery Paper at ECML/PKDD 2009. She also holds 3 U.S. patents filed by IBM T. J. Watson Research Labs. Dr. Akoglu is a recipient of the NSF CAREER award (2015) and Army Research Office Young Investigator award (2013). Her research is currently supported by the National Science Foundation, the US Army Research Office, DARPA, and a gift from Northrop Grumman Aerospace Systems. More details can be found at `http://www.cs.stonybrook.edu/~leman`.

Christos Faloutsos is a Professor at Carnegie Mellon University. He has received the Presidential Young Investigator Award by the National Science Foundation (1989), the Research Contributions Award in ICDM 2006, the Innovations award in KDD'10, 20 "best paper" awards, and several teaching awards. He has served as a member of the executive committee of SIGKDD; he has published over 200 refereed articles, 11 book chapters and one monograph. He holds five patents and he has given over 30 tutorials and over 10 invited distinguished lectures. His research interests include data mining for graphs and streams, fractals, database performance, and indexing for multimedia and bio-informatics data. More details can be found at `http://www.cs.cmu.edu/~christos/`.

Acknowledgements

This material is based upon work supported by the National Science Foundation under Grant No. IIS-1247489, IIS-1217559, CNS-1314632, IIS-1408924, IIS-1408287, CAREER 1452425, DGE-1252522, by the Defense Threat Reduction Agency under contract No. HDTRA1-10-1-0120, by the Army Research Laboratory under Cooperative Agreement Number W911NF-09-2-0053, by the U.S. Army Research Office (ARO) and Defense Advanced Research Projects Agency (DARPA) under Contract Number W911NF-11-C-0088, and by the ARO Young Investigator Program under Contract No. W911NF-14-1-0029.

This work is also partially supported by a Google Focused Research Award, a Facebook Fellowship, a Facebook Faculty Gift, an R&D grant from Northrop Grumman Aerospace Systems, and the Stony Brook University Office of Vice President for Research. Any opinions, findings, and conclusions or recommendations expressed in this material are those of the author(s) and do not necessarily reflect the views of the National Science Foundation, or other funding parties. The U.S. Government is authorized to reproduce and distribute reprints for Government purposes notwithstanding any copyright notation here on.

Data-Driven Product Innovation

Xin Fu
LinkedIn
2029 Stierlin Ct
Mountain View, CA 94043
xfu@linkedin.com

Hernán Asorey
Salesforce.com
One Market, Suite 300
San Francisco, CA, 94105
hasorey@salesforce.com

1. ABSTRACT

Data Science is an increasingly popular area of Knowledge Discovery and Data Mining. Leading consumer Web companies such as Amazon, Facebook, eBay, Google and LinkedIn, as well as B2B companies like Salesforce, possess Petabytes of data. Through effective mining of this data, they create products and services that benefit millions of users and generate tremendous amount of business value. It is widely acknowledged that Data Scientists play key roles in the creation of these products, from pattern identification, idea generation and product prototyping to experiment design and launch decisions. Nonetheless, they also face common challenges, such as the gap between creating a prototype and turning it into a scalable product, or the frustration of generating innovative product ideas that do not get adopted.

Organizers of this tutorial have many years of experience leading Data Science teams in some of the most successful consumer Web companies. In this tutorial, we introduce the framework that we created to nurture data-driven product innovations. The core of this framework is the focus on scale and impact - we take the audience through a discussion on how to balance between velocity and scale, between product innovation and product operation, and between theoretical research and practical impact. We also share some guidelines for successful data-driven product innovation with real examples from our experiences.

We end the tutorial by discussing the organizational perspective of data-driven product innovation: how to structure Data Science teams so Data Scientists collaborate effectively with other functions, and how to hire and grow talents into Data Scientist roles.

Categories and Subject Descriptors

K.6.1 [**Management of Computing and Information Systems**]: Project and People Management – *life cycle, staffing, strategic information systems planning, systems analysis and design*

General Terms

Management, Measurement, Experimentation

Keywords

Data Science; Data Product; Innovation

KDD '15, August 11-14, 2015, Sydney, NSW, Australia
ACM 978-1-4503-3664-2/15/08.
http://dx.doi.org/10.1145/2783258.2789994

2. OUTLINE

The total duration of the tutorial is 1.5 hours. The topics to be covered are:

1. Introduction (15 minutes)
   a. Motivating the audience with prominent examples of data-driven products
   b. Overview of approaches to Data Science in consumer Web industry with B2C and B2B mindsets
   c. Understanding of audience background and learning objectives
2. Data-driven product innovation framework (40 minutes)
   a. Product life cycle and the role of data
   b. Key challenges around scale: organizational perspective (how to create cross-functional leverage, how to quantify the impact of a product idea)
   c. Key challenges around scale: technological perspective (how to create the right technology that improve the speed and quality of product decisions)
3. Case Studies (20 minutes)
   a. End-to-end walkthrough of a data-driven product
   b. Discuss 1 or 2 ideas from the audience and apply the framework to turn it into a data product
4. Talents (15 minutes)
   a. Positioning Data Scientists for maximum impact in a product organization
   b. Preparing for Data Scientist roles: skill set versus mind set

3. INTENDED AUDIENCE

We welcome all participants of KDD 2015 to attend this tutorial, but we believe it will be most beneficial for Data Scientists working in product environments (Web or Mobile), Data Mining practitioners who are interested in a career transition to Data Science, and Data Science leaders looking for ways to scale. Students considering industry jobs in Data Science may also find this tutorial valuable. Becoming a Data Scientist is one of the most popular career choices for students with quantitative backgrounds, not only from some of the more "mainstream" Data Mining programs in statistics and computer science, but also increasingly from more diverse backgrounds such as physics, computational biology, economics, and social sciences. Giving them exposure to real life examples of industry practices should help them make informed career choices.

As one of the first tutorials on this topic in a KDD conference, it complements other tutorial topics which often focus on theories of knowledge discovery and data mining, or focus on teaching specific technologies to build data products. We believe that as experienced or aspiring Data Scientists within the KDD community grow interested in more applied roles, they will benefit from tutors with real industry experience and the lessons learned through the process of bringing ideas into reality.

4. PRESENTER INFORMATION

Xin Fu is a Director of Data Science at LinkedIn. He and his team are responsible for driving product innovation through creative use of data, ranging from inferential analysis and online experimentation, to creation of analytics platforms and data products. Xin holds a PhD in Human-Computer Interaction and a MS in Statistics from the University of North Carolina at Chapel Hill. Prior to joining LinkedIn, Xin worked at Google and Microsoft. He has authored over 50 refereed papers and journal articles in the areas of information organization and retrieval, Web search interface, and online user behavioral measurement.

Hernán Asorey is the VP of Product Data Science at Salesforce. In this key leadership position, Hernán and team are responsible for transforming product ideation, development, and customer engagement to an evidence-driven culture where intelligence becomes an intrinsic part of the product to ship. Hernán manages, grows, and inspires a world-class team of data experts across all information spectrum: information engines (digest), analytics engines (visualize), data science (apply), experimentation and optimization (test and learn). Prior to Salesforce, Hernán held different roles in fields related to large-scale data analytics, data warehousing, business intelligence, data mining, social media analytics, and HR analytics at companies such as Sears Holdings, Hewlett Packard, eBay, and Microsoft. Hernán has a degree in Information Systems Engineering with specialization on Applied Math; additionally, he graduated in 2011 from Stanford Executive Program, Graduate School of Business. Hernán also spent 5 years in academia as a lecturer at the Math Department in The School of Engineering in Buenos Aires, Argentina on Discrete Math, Calculus, and Fractal Theory.

Dense Subgraph Discovery

KDD 2015 tutorial

Aristides Gionis
HIIT and Dept. of Computer Science
Aalto University
aristides.gionis@aalto.fi

Charalampos E. Tsourakakis
Center of Research on Computation and Society
Harvard University
babis@seas.harvard.edu

ABSTRACT

Finding dense subgraphs is a fundamental graph-theoretic problem, that lies in the heart of numerous graph-mining applications, ranging from finding communities in social networks [11, 16], to detecting regulatory motifs in DNA [8] and to identifying real-time stories in news [2]. The problem of finding dense subgraphs has been studied extensively in theoretical computer science [1, 5, 6, 7, 10], and recently, due to the relevance of the problem in real-world applications, it has attracted considerable attention in the data-mining community [4, 16, 18, 20, 21].

In this tutorial we aim to provide a comprehensive overview of (*i*) major algorithmic techniques for finding dense subgraphs in large graphs and (*ii*) graph mining applications that rely on dense subgraph extraction. We will present fundamental concepts and algorithms that date back to 80's, as well as the latest advances in the area, from theoretical and from practical point-of-view. We will motivate the problem of finding dense subgraphs by discussing how it can be used in real-world applications. We will discuss different density definitions and the complexity of the corresponding optimization problems. We will also present efficient algorithms for different density measures and under different computational models. Specifically, we will focus on scalable streaming, distributed and MapReduce algorithms. Finally we will discuss problem variants, extensions, and will provide pointers for future research directions.

Outline

The tutorial will cover the following topics:

- Part 1: Introduction and motivating applications
- Part 2: Measures of density
  - Edge density
  - k-core, k-plex, k-club [12]
  - Quasi-cliques [21]
  - Degree density [9]
  - k-clique density [20]
  - (α, d, L)-decompositions [5]
- Part 3: Efficient algorithms for static graphs
  - Goldberg's algorithm [9]
  - Charikar's algorithms [6]
  - Khuller-Saha algorithms [10]
  - Tsourakakis' algorithms [20]
  - MapReduce algorithmics [3]
  - Distributed streams [5]
- Part 4: Efficient algorithms for dynamic graphs
  - Streaming algorithms [3, 5]
  - Space- and time-efficient algorithm for maintaining dense subgraphs
    on one-pass dynamic streams [5]
- Part 5: Problem variants
  - Incorporating vertex weights [14]
  - Incorporating temporal information [15]
  - Finding top-k dense subgraphs [4]
  - Organizing cocktail parties [16, 19]
  - Streaming graph partitionings [13, 17, 22]
- Part 6: Conclusions, open problems and discussion

KDD'15, August 11-14, 2015, Sydney, NSW, Australia.
ACM 978-1-4503-3664-2/15/08.
http://dx.doi.org/10.1145/2783258.2789987.

Biography of the instructors

Aristides Gionis is an associate professor in the department of computer science of Aalto university. He is the director of the Algorithmic Data Analysis (ADA) programme in HIIT and he leads the Data Mining group in Aalto University. Previously he has been a senior research scientist in Yahoo! Research. He received his Ph.D. from the Computer Science department of Stanford University in 2003. He is currently serving as an associate editor in the IEEE Transactions of Knowledge and Data Engineering (TKDE) and the ACM Transactions of Knowledge Discovery from Data (TKDD), and as a managing editor in Internet Mathematics. He has served in the PC of numerous premium conferences, including being the PC chair for WSDM 2013 and ECML PKDD 2010. He has published over 100 papers and his Google scholar h-index is 40.

Charalampos E. Tsourakakis is currently a postdoctoral fellow in the Center of Research on Computation and Society (CRCS) at Harvard University. He received his Ph.D. from the Algorithms, Combinatorics and Optimization (ACO) program at Carnegie Mellon University in 2013. He also holds a Master of Science from the Machine Learning Department at CMU. He did his undergraduate studies in the School of Electrical and Computer Engineering (ECE) at the National Technical University of Athens (NTUA). He is the recipient of a best paper award in IEEE Data Mining and has designed two graph mining libraries for tera-scale graphs. The former is officially used by Windows Azure, and the latter was a research highlight of Microsoft Research. He has served in the PC of premium conferences. He has published over 30 papers in the fields of data mining, discrete mathematics, theoretical computer science and computational biology. He has delivered two tutorials in the ACM SIGKDD Conference on Knowledge Discovery and Data Mining. His Google scholar h-index is 17. His research interests include algorithm design for large-scale datasets, data science and mathematical optimization.

1. REFERENCES

[1] R. Andersen and K. Chellapilla. Finding dense subgraphs with size bounds. In *WAW*, pages 25–37, 2009.

[2] A. Angel, N. Sarkas, N. Koudas, and D. Srivastava. Dense subgraph maintenance under streaming edge weight updates for real-time story identification. *VLDB Endowment*, 5(6):574–585, 2012.

[3] B. Bahmani, R. Kumar, and S. Vassilvitskii. Densest subgraph in streaming and mapreduce. *Proceedings of the VLDB Endowment*, 5(5):454–465, 2012.

[4] O. D. Balalau, F. Bonchi, T. Chan, F. Gullo, and M. Sozio. Finding subgraphs with maximum total density and limited overlap. In *WSDM*, pages 379–388, 2015.

[5] M. Bhattacharya, Sayan Henzinger, D. Nanongkai, and C. Tsourakakis. Space- and time-efficient algorithms for maintaining dense subgraphs on one-pass dynamic streams. In *47th ACM Symposium on Theory of Computing (STOC)*, 2015.

[6] M. Charikar. Greedy approximation algorithms for finding dense components in a graph. In *APPROX*, pages 84–95, 2000.

[7] U. Feige, D. Peleg, and G. Kortsarz. The dense k-subgraph problem. *Algorithmica*, 29(3):410–421, 2001.

[8] E. Fratkin, B. T. Naughton, D. L. Brutlag, and S. Batzoglou. Motifcut: regulatory motifs finding with maximum density subgraphs. *Bioinformatics*, 22(14):e150–e157, 2006.

[9] A. V. Goldberg. Finding a maximum density subgraph. *UCB technical report*, 1984.

[10] S. Khuller and B. Saha. On finding dense subgraphs. In *Automata, Languages and Programming*, pages 597–608, 2009.

[11] R. Kumar, P. Raghavan, S. Rajagopalan, and A. Tomkins. Trawling the Web for emerging cyber-communities. *Computer Networks*, 31(11–16):1481–1493, 1999.

[12] V. E. Lee, N. Ruan, R. Jin, and C. Aggarwal. A survey of algorithms for dense subgraph discovery. In *Managing and Mining Graph Data*, pages 303–336. Springer, 2010.

[13] J. Nishimura and J. Ugander. Restreaming graph partitioning: simple versatile algorithms for advanced balancing. In *Proceedings of the 19th ACM SIGKDD international conference on Knowledge discovery and data mining*, pages 1106–1114. ACM, 2013.

[14] P. Rozenshtein, A. Anagnostopoulos, A. Gionis, and N. Tatti. Event detection in activity networks. In *KDD*, pages 1176–1185, 2014.

[15] P. Rozenshtein, N. Tatti, and A. Gionis. Discovering dynamic communities in interaction networks. In *ECML PKDD*, pages 678–693. Springer, 2014.

[16] M. Sozio and A. Gionis. The community-search problem and how to plan a successful cocktail party. In *KDD*, pages 939–948, 2010.

[17] I. Stanton and G. Kliot. Streaming graph partitioning for large distributed graphs. In *Proceedings of the 18th ACM SIGKDD international conference on Knowledge discovery and data mining*, pages 1222–1230. ACM, 2012.

[18] N. Tatti and A. Gionis. Density-friendly graph decomposition. In *WWW*, 2015.

[19] H. Tong and C. Faloutsos. Center-piece subgraphs: problem definition and fast solutions. In *Proceedings of the 12th ACM SIGKDD international conference on Knowledge discovery and data mining*, pages 404–413. ACM, 2006.

[20] C. Tsourakakis. The k-clique densest subgraph problem. *WWW*, 2015.

[21] C. Tsourakakis, F. Bonchi, A. Gionis, F. Gullo, and M. Tsiarli. Denser than the densest subgraph: Extracting optimal quasi-cliques with quality guarantees. In *KDD*, pages 104–112, 2013.

[22] C. Tsourakakis, C. Gkantsidis, B. Radunovic, and M. Vojnovic. Fennel: Streaming graph partitioning for massive scale graphs. In *WSDM*, pages 333–342. ACM, 2014.

Diffusion in Social and Information Networks: Research Problems, Probabilistic Models & Machine Learning Methods

Manuel Gomez-Rodriguez
MPI for Software Systems
manuelgr@mpi-sws.org

Le Song
Georgia Institute of Technology
lsong@cc.gatech.edu

ABSTRACT

In recent years, there has been an increasing effort on developing realistic models, and learning and inference algorithms to understand, predict, and influence diffusion over networks. This has been in part due to the increasing availability and granularity of large-scale diffusion data, which, in principle, allows for understanding and modeling not only macroscopic diffusion but also microscopic (node-level) diffusion. To this aim, a bottom-up approach has been typically considered, which starts by considering how particular ideas, pieces of information, products, or, more generally, *contagions* spread locally from node to node apparently at random to later produce global, macroscopic patterns at a network level. However, this bottom-up approach also raises significant modeling, algorithmic and computational challenges which require leveraging methods from machine learning, probabilistic modeling, event history analysis and graph theory, as well as the nascent field of network science. In this tutorial, we will present several diffusion models designed for fine-grained large-scale diffusion data, present some canonical research problem in the context of diffusion, and introduce state-of-the-art algorithms to solve some of these problems, in particular, network estimation, influence estimation and influence control.

1. TARGET AUDIENCE, AIMS AND PREREQUISITES

This tutorial is meant for a broad audience at KDD, including students and researchers specifically interested in models and machine learning methods in the context of diffusion over networks. It will provide an introduction to research problems, probabilistic models and machine learning methods in the context of diffusion of information, influence and behaviors over networks. No specific knowledge will be required beyond basic probability and graph theory; the tutorial is self-contained and most of the foundational concepts are introduced during the tutorial.

The participants will learn about the fundamental problems in diffusion networks, including network inference, influence estimation and influence control. We will present a concise overview of the main models and algorithms, the most recent theoretical results, and an overview of empirical results. We will provide pointers to code implementation of most of the algorithms, to allow participants to carry out a hands-on further investigation. Finally, the participants will also learn about open problems in the context of diffusion over networks.

KDD'15, August 10-13, 2015, Sydney, NSW, Australia.
ACM 978-1-4503-3664-2/15/08.
DOI: http://dx.doi.org/10.1145/2783258.2789991.

2. OUTLINE OF THE TUTORIAL

We will divide our tutorial into four parts. In the first section, we will introduce different discrete time and continuous time models of diffusion over networks and introduce several canonical problems in the context of diffusion over networks. The remaining sections will be devoted to three of the above mentioned problems: network inference, influence estimation and influence control. For each problem, we will present and compare different algorithms, highlighting their assumptions and theoretical properties, as well as their performance in practice and limitations. We will focus on principled flexible methods, which can be adapted to different experimental setups and data sources.

2.1 Diffusion Models (45 minutes)

We will provide an introduction to modeling diffusion of information, influence, behaviors, products, or, more generally, *contagions* over networks. We will start with describing several idealized discrete-time models [18], and then continue introducing several continuous-time models, which allow to more realistically fit both non-recurrent [10, 13] and recurrent [17, 22] real diffusion data. We will conclude by introducing several canonical problems in the context of diffusion over networks, where we will highlight the importance of each problem and the progress that has been made so far in each of them. In the remaining parts of the tutorial, we will focus on three of these canonical problems: network inference, influence estimation and influence control.

2.2 Network Estimation (45 minutes)

Given a set of cascades and a diffusion model, the network inference problem consists of inferring the edges (and possibly model parameters) of an unobserved underlying network. The network inference problem has attracted significant attention in recent years, since it is essential to reconstruct and predict the paths over which information can spread, and to maximize sales of a product or stop infections. Here, we will first present several algorithms that allow us to infer the structure (edges) of a network [1, 12, 16], using a natural diminishing property of the problem, submodularity. Then, we will introduce a family of algorithms that allow us to infer not only the structure but also the model parameters [7, 10, 11], using convex programming, and will outline a theoretical analysis of their sampling complexity [4]. We will then show how to extend the latter algorithms to support dynamic networks [14], topic modeling [8], and recurrent events [22, 23].

2.3 Influence Estimation (45 minutes)

Given a diffusion model and an arbitrary set of nodes that initially adopt a piece of information, idea or product, the influence estimation problem which is the basis for subsequent influence control consists of estimating the average number of follow-ups these nodes can trigger. These estimation problems in various diffusion models are often NP-hard [2], and hence call for efficient approximation algorithms with provable guarantees. Furthermore, the problem can be complicated by additional constraints such as estimating influence given a time windows. Here, we will formally define the problem, and briefly overview various algorithms for different diffusion models [2, 3, 5, 6, 15]. We will then focus on two algorithms for continuous-time diffusion models with provable guarantees [6, 15], and show how they provide solutions to influence estimation problem with additional timing constraints, and exploit randomization to scale to networks with million of nodes.

2.4 Influence Control (45 minutes)

Given a diffusion model, the influence control problem aims to manipulate either the information sources or the diffusion networks themselves in order to achieve certain outcome of the diffusion processes. For instance, in influence maximization, one aims to find a set of nodes whose initial adoptions of certain piece of information, idea or product can trigger the largest expected number of follow-ups. In influence blocking, one aims to remove a set of diffusion channels from a diffusion network such that rumor spread can be controlled, or, in influence facilitation, to add a set of diffusion channels such that an important announcement can reach people early. In influence shaping, one aims to drive the overall usage of a service to a certain level per user by incentivizing a small number of users to take more initiatives. Here, we will formally define the influence maximization, influence blocking and influence shaping problems and present several algorithms to solve them under different discrete-time diffusion models [2, 3, 18, 20, 21] and continuous-time diffusion models [6, 9, 15, 19].

3. TUTORS' BIO AND EXPERTISE

Manuel Gomez Rodriguez is an tenure-track independent research group leader at Max Planck for Software Systems. Manuel develops machine learning and large-scale data mining methods for the analysis and modeling of large real-world networks and processes that take place over them. He is particularly interested in problems motivated by the Web and social media and has received several recognitions for his research, including an Outstanding Paper Award at NIPS´13 and a Best Research Paper Honorable Mention at KDD´10. Manuel holds a PhD in Electrical Engineering from Stanford University and a BS in Electrical Engineering from Carlos III University in Madrid (Spain), and has been a Barrie de la Maza Fellow and a Caja Madrid Fellow.

Le Song is an assistant professor in the College of Computing, Georgia Institute of Technology. His principal research interests lie in the development of machine learning methodology, especially in kernel methods, probabilistic graphical models, temporal data and network analysis. Le Song received his Ph.D. in Computer Science from University of Sydney in 2008, and then conducted his post-doctoral research in the School of Computer Science, Carnegie Mellon University, between 2008 and 2011. Before he joined Georgia Institute of Technology, he worked briefly as a research scientist at Google. He is the winner of Outstanding Paper Award at NIPS´13 and Best Paper Award at ICML´10.

References

[1] B. Abrahao, F. Chierichetti, R. Kleinberg, and A. Panconesi. Trace complexity of network inference. In *KDD*, 2013.

[2] W. Chen, C. Wang, and Y. Wang. Scalable Influence Maximization for Prevalent Viral Marketing in Large-Scale Social Networks. In *KDD*, 2010.

[3] W. Chen, Y. Wang, and S. Yang. Efficient Influence Maximization in Social Networks. In *KDD*, 2009.

[4] H. Daneshmand, M. Gomez-Rodriguez, L. Song, and B. Schölkopf. Estimating diffusion network structures: Recovery conditions, sample complexity & soft-thresholding algorithm. In *ICML*, 2014.

[5] N. Du, Y. Liang, M. Balcan, and L. Song. Influence function learning in information diffusion networks. In *ICML*, 2014.

[6] N. Du, L. Song, M. Gomez-Rodriguez, and H. Zha. Scalable Influence Estimation in Continuous-Time Diffusion Networks. In *NIPS*, 2013.

[7] N. Du, L. Song, A. Smola, and M. Yuan. Learning Networks of Heterogeneous Influence. In *NIPS*, 2012.

[8] N. Du, L. Song, H. Woo, and H. Zha. Uncover topic-sensitive information diffusion networks. In *AISTATS*, 2013.

[9] M. Farajtabar, N. Du, M. Gomez-Rodriguez, I. Valera, H. Zha, and L. Song. Shaping social activity by incentivizing users. In *NIPS*, 2014.

[10] M. Gomez-Rodriguez, D. Balduzzi, and B. Schölkopf. Uncovering the Temporal Dynamics of Diffusion Networks. In *ICML*, 2011.

[11] M. Gomez-Rodriguez, J. Leskovec, D. Balduzzi, and B. Schölkopf. Uncovering the Structure and Temporal Dynamics of Information Propagation. *Network Science*, 2014.

[12] M. Gomez-Rodriguez, J. Leskovec, and A. Krause. Inferring Networks of Diffusion and Influence. In *KDD*, 2010.

[13] M. Gomez-Rodriguez, J. Leskovec, and B. Schölkopf. Modeling Information Propagation with Survival Theory. In *ICML*, 2013.

[14] M. Gomez-Rodriguez, J. Leskovec, and B. Schölkopf. Structure and Dynamics of Information Pathways in On-line Media. In *WSDM*, 2013.

[15] M. Gomez-Rodriguez and B. Schölkopf. Influence Maximization in Continuous Time Diffusion Networks. In *ICML*, 2012.

[16] M. Gomez-Rodriguez and B. Schölkopf. Submodular Inference of Diffusion Networks from Multiple Trees. In *ICML*, 2012.

[17] T. Iwata, A. Shah, and Z. Ghahramani. Discovering latent influence in online social activities via shared cascade poisson processes. In *KDD*, 2013.

[18] D. Kempe, J. M. Kleinberg, and E. Tardos. Maximizing the Spread of Influence Through a Social Network. In *KDD*, 2003.

[19] E. B. Khalil, B. Dilkina, and L. Song. Scalable diffusion-aware optimization of network topology. In *KDD*, 2014.

[20] M. Kimura, K. Saito, and H. Motoda. Minimizing the spread of contamination by blocking links in a network. In *AAAI*, 2008.

[21] H. Tong, B. A. Prakash, T. Eliassi-Rad, M. Faloutsos, and C. Faloutsos. Gelling, and melting, large graphs by edge manipulation. In *CIKM*, 2012.

[22] K. Zhou, H. Zha, and L. Song. Learning social infectivity in sparse low-rank networks using multi-dimensional hawkes processes. In *AISTATS*, 2013.

[23] K. Zhou, H. Zha, and L. Song. Learning triggering kernels for multi-dimensional hawkes processes. In *ICML*, 2013.

Social Media Anomaly Detection: Challenges and Solutions

Yan Liu
University of Southern California
941 Bloom Walk
Los Angeles, CA 90292
yanliu.cs@usc.edu

Sanjay Chawla
Qatar Computing Research Institute and
University of Sydney
schawla@qf.org.qa

ABSTRACT

Anomaly detection is of critical importance to prevent malicious activities such as bullying, terrorist attack planning, and fraud information dissemination. With the recent popularity of social media, new types of anomalous behaviors arise, causing concerns from various parties. While a large body of work haven been dedicated to traditional anomaly detection problems, we observe a surge of research interests in the new realm of social media anomaly detection. In this tutorial, we survey existing work on social media anomaly detection, focusing on the new anomalous phenomena in social media and most recent techniques to detect those special types of anomalies. We aim to provide a general overview of the problem domain, common formulations, existing methodologies and future directions.

Categories and Subject Descriptors

H.2.8 [**Database Applications**]: Data Mining; J.4 [**Social and Behavioral Sciences**]: Sociology

General Terms

Algorithms

Keywords

Anomaly detection; Social media analysis

1. INTRODUCTION

Social media systems provide convenient platforms for people to share, communicate, and collaborate. The emergence and detection of anomalous behaviors in social media may shed light into early indication of important events, such as natural disasters and disease outbreak, which provides crucial extra time to take actions. Meanwhile, many malicious behaviors, such as cyber attacks, bullying, terrorist attack planning, and fraudulent information dissemination, also exist on social media. Therefore it is extremely important that we can detect these abnormal activities as accurately and early as possible to prevent disasters and attacks. Needless to say, as more social information becomes available, the most challenging question is what useful patterns could be extracted from this influx of time-series social media data to help with the detection task.

Different from traditional anomaly detection scenarios, social media provides us with additional information between users (e.g. social networks between users). We can summarize the anomalies into two types: one is point anomaly, which refers to the abnormal behaviors of individual users. The other type of anomaly is group anomaly, which involves hidden groups of people (also known as tribe) working collectively to achieve a malicious goal. Another way to summarize the anomalies is by their input type, which usually consists of sequential data, unstructured texts, and graphs.

This tutorial aims to provide the participants a broad and comprehensive coverage on the foundations and recent developments on anomaly detection social media. We will provide both theoretical and practical results as well as illustrative demos. In contrast to previous tutorials on anomaly detection, we will focus on presenting and discussing a broad coverage of the emerging approaches to anomaly detection in the context of scalability and practicability. We will also offer useful and complementary information to the SIGKDD community and suggest directions for future research.

2. OUTLINE OF THE TUTORIAL

The 3-hour tutorial consists of two parts and a break in the middle. In Part 1, we will provide an introduction to anomaly detection for social media data, including an overview of anomaly detection, data types and properties of social media data, anomaly detection in network data [1, 2, 7, 12], and anomaly detection in temporal data [3, 4, 8, 9]. In Part 2, we will discuss recent advances in anomaly detection for social media data, including point anomaly detection in social media [6, 10], group anomaly detection in social media [5, 11], as well as applications and systems.

To summarize, we will

- Present a balanced review of the area of anomaly detection for social media data by presenting topics of both practical and theoretical interest
- Describe the state-of-the-art and emerging analysis technologies on massive social media data in order to identify the recent and future trends
- Provide a good starting point, including tutorial slides, supplementary survey paper, implementation packages

KDD'15, August 10-13, 2015, Sydney, NSW, Australia.
ACM 978-1-4503-3664-2/15/08.
DOI: http://dx.doi.org/10.1145/2783258.2789990.

and data repository with real application datasets, for researchers entering this active research area by looking at both system- and algorithmic-level developments.

3. ACKNOWLEDGMENTS

Yan Liu's research was partly sponsored by the NSF research grants IIS-1134990 and IIS-1254206, and U.S. Defense Advanced Research Projects Agency (DARPA) under Anomaly Detection at Multiple Scales (ADAMS) program and Social Media in Strategic Communication (SMISC) program. Sanjay Chawla's research is partially supported by the Australian Research Council, Capial Markets CRC, CRC for Alertness, Sleep and Productivity. The views and conclusions are those of the authors and should not be interpreted as representing the official policies of the funding agency, or the U.S. Government.

4. REFERENCES

[1] L. Akoglu and M. McGlohon. Anomaly detection in large graphs. *CMU-CS-09-173 Tech- nical, (November)*, 2009.

[2] L. Akoglu, M. McGlohon, and C. Faloutsos. Oddball: Spotting anomalies in weighted graphs. In *Advances in Knowledge Discovery and Data Mining*, pages 410-421. Springer, 2010.

[3] V. Chandola, A. Banerjee, and V. Kumar. Anomaly detection for discrete sequences: A survey. *IEEE Trans. on Knowl. and Data Eng.*, 24(5):823-839, May 2012.

[4] H. Cheng, P.-N. Tan, C. Potter, and S. Klooster. Detection and characterization of anomalies in multivariate time series. In *Proceedings of SDM '09*, pages 413-424, 2009.

[5] L. Friedland and D. Jensen. Finding tribes: identifying close-knit individuals from employment patterns. In *Proceedings of KDD '07*, pages 290-299, New York, NY, USA, 2007. ACM.

[6] Y. Ge, H. Xiong, C. Liu, and Z.H. Zhou, A Taxi Driving Fraud Detection System. In *Proceedings of ICDM '11*, pages 181 - 190, 2011.

[7] J. Sun, H. Qu, D. Chakrabarti, and C. Faloutsos. Neighborhood formation and anomaly detection in bipartite graphs. In *Proceedings of ICDM '05*, pages 418 - 425,Washington, DC, USA, 2005. IEEE Computer Society.

[8] H. Qiu, Y. Liu, N. Subrahmanya, W. Li. Granger Graphical Models for Time-Series Anomaly Detection. In *Proceedings of ICDM' 2012*, Pages 1074-1079, 2012.

[9] P. Sun, S. Chawla, and B. Arunasalam. Mining for outliers in sequential databases. In *Proceedings of SIAM '06*, pages 94-105, 2006.

[10] W.-K. Wong, A. Moore, G. Cooper, and M. Wagner. Bayesian network anomaly pattern detection for disease outbreaks. In *Proceedings of ICML '03*, 2003.

[11] Q. Yu, X. He, and Y. Liu. GLAD: Group anomaly detection in social media analysis. In *Proceedings of KDD '14*, Pages 372-381, 2014.

[12] H. Tong, C.-Y. Lin. Non-Negative Residual Matrix Factorization with Application to Graph Anomaly Detection. In *Proceedings of SDM '2011*, pages 143-153, 2011.

Automatic Entity Recognition and Typing from Massive Text Corpora: A Phrase and Network Mining Approach

Xiang Ren[†], Ahmed El-Kishky[†], Chi Wang[‡], Jiawei Han[†]
[†] University of Illinois at Urbana-Champaign, Urbana, IL, USA
[‡] Microsoft Research, Redmond, WA, USA
[†] {xren7,elkishk2,hanj}@illinois.edu [‡]chiw@microsoft.com

ABSTRACT

In today's computerized and information-based society, we are soaked with vast amounts of text data, ranging from news articles, scientific publications, product reviews, to a wide range of textual information from social media. To unlock the value of these unstructured text data from various domains, it is of great importance to gain an understanding of entities and their relationships.

In this tutorial, we introduce data-driven methods to recognize typed entities of interest in massive, domain-specific text corpora. These methods can automatically identify token spans as entity mentions in documents and label their types (*e.g.*, people, product, food) in a scalable way. We demonstrate on real datasets including news articles and tweets how these typed entities aid in knowledge discovery and management.

Introduction

Motivation: Entity recognition/typing and structured analysis of massive text corpora. The success of database technology is largely attributed to the efficient and effective management of structured data. The construction of a well-structured database is often the premise of consequent applications. Although the majority of existing data generated in our society is unstructured, big data leads to big opportunities to uncover structures of real-world entities, such as people, products and organizations, from massive amount but inter-related unstructured data. By mining token spans of entity mentions in documents, labeling their structured types and inferring their relations, it is possible to construct semantically rich structures and provide conceptual summarization of such data. The uncovered structures will facilitate browsing information and retrieving knowledge that are otherwise locked in the data.

Example: Entity recognition and typing in Yelps reviews. In a business review corpus like Yelp reviews[1], entities such as food, locations and restaurants are mentioned in the documents. For example, from the sentences "*The best BBQ I've tasted in Washington! I had the pulled pork sandwich with coleslaw for lunch.*", it is desirable to identify "*BBQ*", "*pulled pork sandwich*", and "*coleslaw*" as food, and "*Washington*" as location. However, existing work encounters several challenges when handling such a *domain-specific* text corpus.

1. The lack of annotated data for domain-specific corpus presents a major challenge for adapting traditional supervised named-entity recognition techniques. Fortunately, a number of semantically rich knowledge-bases are available, which provides chances for *automatically* recognizing entities by *distant supervision.*

2. Many entity detection tools such as noun phrase chunkers are trained on general-domain corpora (*e.g.*, news articles), but they do not work effectively nor efficiently on domain-specific corpora such as Yelp reviews (*e.g.*, "*pulled pork sandwich*" cannot be detected). A domain-agnostic phrase mining algorithm is required to efficiently generate entity mention candidates with minimal linguistic assumptions.

3. Entity surface names are often ambiguous—multiple entities many share the same surface name (*e.g.*, "*Washington*" may refer to the U.S. government, the capital city or a sport team). Although the contexts surrounding each entity mention provide clues on its types, challenges arise due to the diversity on paraphrasing. With data redundancy in a massive corpus, it is possible to disambiguate entities and resolve synonymous contexts using correlated textual information structured in an information network for holistic analysis.

Target Audience and prerequisites

Researchers and practitioners in the field of data mining, text mining, information extraction, information retrieval, web search, database systems, and information systems. While the audience with a good background in these areas would benefit most from this tutorial, we believe the material to be presented would give general audience and newcomers an introductory pointer to the current work and important research topics in this field, and inspire them to learn more. Only preliminary knowledge about text mining, information extraction, data mining, algorithms, and their applications are needed.

[1]http://www.yelp.com/dataset_challenge

KDD'15, August 10-13, 2015, Sydney, NSW, Australia.
ACM 978-1-4503-3664-2/15/08.
DOI: http://dx.doi.org/10.1145/2783258.2789988.

Tutorial Outline

This tutorial presents a comprehensive overview of the techniques developed for entity recognition in recent years. We will discuss the following key issues.

Recognition and typing of entities from massive, unstructured text corpora
We introduce the background of entity recognition and typing problem. We will provide examples on different documentary data collections where entities are explicitly typed and linked with documents, or need to be extracted or inferred from the text data. We demonstrate the growing needs on recognizing and typing entities for a wide range of applications including information extraction and knowledge base population.

Entity mention detection
We discuss different paradigms and methodologies for detecting entity mention in text data, ranging from supervised learning, unsupervised approaches, to distant supervised methods. We introduce efforts to combine corpus statistics from massive document collection with a variety of document-level features, and to leverage distant supervision from structured knowledge bases. We demonstrate the benefits of various phrase mining-based approaches over traditional supervised entity detection methods.

Entity recognition in a single document
We outline different supervised methods for recognizing typed entities in a single, general-domain document. We discuss the limitations of these methods when they are applied to single, domain-specific document such as business review and tweet. We introduce previous work on designing methods that can specifically handle different domains. We further demonstrate efforts towards recognizing fine-grained entity types and adopting distant supervision from large amount of external knowledge sources.

Entity recognition in a massive, domain-specific text corpus
Often times, it is hard to obtain label data for a large, domain-specific and dynamic text corpus. We demonstrate efforts on data-driven entity recognition and typing methods to more effectively model the data redundancy in the massive text corpus. We focus on the problem of entity recognition and typing with distant supervision and demonstrate the benefits of leveraging rich entity information in structured, semantically-rich knowledge bases. We demonstrate how creating information networks that embody the interaction between different text units in text can assist in high-quality entity typing. We argue that such a network mining approach can holistically model the corpus-level information in a principled way.

Evaluation, Case Studies and Recent Progress
We outline different evaluation metrics and benchmark datasets for named-entity recognition (NER), and introduce several popular NER systems and NER shared tasks. We discuss the findings from applying different NER methods on new article domain and Yelp review domain. We outline the recent progress on combining entity recognition with other related text mining tasks, extracting entities from multiple data sources, integrating NER results from multiple systems, and applying deep learning for NER.

Instructors

Xiang Ren is a Ph.D. candidate of Department of Computer Science at Univ. of Illinois at Urbana-Champaign. His research focuses on knowledge acquisition from text data and mining linked data. He is the recipient of C. L. and Jane W.-S. Liu Award and Yahoo!-DAIS Research Excellence Gold Award in 2015. He received Microsoft Young Fellowship from Microsoft Research Asia in 2012.

Ahmed El-Kishky is a Ph.D. candidate at Univ. of Illinois at Urbana-Champaign. His research interests include mining large unstructured data, text mining, and network mining. He is the recipient of both the National Science Foundation Graduate Research Fellowship as well as National Defense Science and Engineering Fellowship.

Chi Wang is a researcher in Microsoft Research, Redmond, Washington. He has been researching into discovering knowledge from unstructured and linked data, such as topics, concepts, relations, communities and social influence. His book *Mining Latent Entity Structures* is published by Morgan Claypool Pub. in the series of *Synthesis Lectures on Data Mining and Knowledge Discovery.* He is a winner of Microsoft Research Graduate Research Fellowship.

Jiawei Han is an Abel Bliss Professor of Department of Computer Science at Univ. of Illinois at Urbana-Champaign. His research areas encompass data mining, data warehousing, information network analysis, etc., with over 600 conference and journal publications. He is Fellow of ACM, Fellow of IEEE, the Director of IPAN, supported by Network Science Collaborative Technology Alliance program of the U.S. Army Research Lab, and the Director of KnowEnG: a Knowledge Engine for Genomics, one of the NIH supported Big Data to Knowledge (BD2K) Centers.

Acknowledgments

Research was sponsored in part by the U.S. Army Research Lab. under Cooperative Agreement No. W911NF-09-2-0053 (NSCTA), National Science Foundation IIS-1017362, IIS-1320617, and IIS-1354329, HDTRA1-10-1-0120, and grant 1U54GM114838 awarded by NIGMS through funds provided by the trans-NIH Big Data to Knowledge (BD2K) initiative (www.bd2k.nih.gov), and MIAS, a DHS-IDS Center for Multimodal Information Access and Synthesis at UIUC.

VC-Dimension and Rademacher Averages: From Statistical Learning Theory to Sampling Algorithms

Tutorial Outline

Matteo Riondato
Dept. of Computer Science
Brown University
Providence, RI 02912
matteo@cs.brown.edu

Eli Upfal
Dept. of Computer Science
Brown University
Providence, RI 02912
eli@cs.brown.edu

ABSTRACT

Rademacher Averages and the *Vapnik-Chervonenkis dimension* are fundamental concepts from statistical learning theory. They allow to study simultaneous deviation bounds of empirical averages from their expectations for classes of functions, by considering properties of the functions, of their domain (the dataset), and of the sampling process. In this tutorial, we survey the use of Rademacher Averages and the VC-dimension in sampling-based algorithms for graph analysis and pattern mining. We start from their theoretical foundations at the core of machine learning, then show a generic recipe for formulating data mining problems in a way that allows to use these concepts in efficient randomized algorithms for those problems. Finally, we show examples of the application of the recipe to graph problems (connectivity, shortest paths, betweenness centrality) and pattern mining. Our goal is to expose the usefulness of these techniques for the data mining researcher, and to encourage research in the area.

Categories and Subject Descriptors

H.2.8 [**Database Management**]: Database Applications—*Data mining*; G.3 [**Probability and Statistics**]: [Probabilistic algorithms (including Monte Carlo)]

Keywords

Betweenness Centrality; Frequent Itemsets; Graph Mining; Pattern Mining; Randomized Algorithms; Tutorial

1. INTRODUCTION

Random sampling is a natural technique to speed up the execution of algorithms on very large datasets [6]. The results obtained by analyzing only a random sample of the dataset are an approximation of the exact solution. When only a single value must be computed, the trade-off between the size of the sample and the accuracy of the approximation can be studied through probabilistic bounds for the deviation of the quantity of interest in the sample from its exact value in the dataset, e.g., the Chernoff-Hoeffding bounds [7]. In many data mining problems, the number of quantities of interest can be extremely large (e.g., betweenness centrality requires to compute one quantity for each node in a graph [4, 13], and Frequent Pattern Mining requires the computation of a potentially exponential number of quantities). In these cases, *uniform* (i.e., *simultaneous*) bounds to the deviations of all quantities are needed in order to have good approximations of all the values of interest. Classical techniques like the Union bound [11] are insufficient because excessively loose due to their worst-case assumptions that do not hold in many data mining problems, e.g., the assumption that the quantities of interest are independent from each other. *Rademacher Averages* [3] and the *Vapnik-Chervonenkis dimension* [18] have been developed by the statistical learning theory community to study the (rate of) convergence of the empirical risk of a learned function to its expectation. One of the goals of this tutorial is to show that these techniques are very flexible and powerful and their field of use is much broader. In particular, they overcome the weakness of the Union bound: they obtain much stricter uniform deviation bounds by taking into account the nature of the problem (i.e., of the quantities of interest) and properties of the dataset and of the sampling process. They have been used with success in the analysis of sampling algorithms for data and graph analysis problems on very large datasets [1, 5, 9, 13–16].

KDD'15, August 10-13, 2015, Sydney, NSW, Australia.
ACM 978-1-4503-3664-2/15/08.
DOI: http://dx.doi.org/10.1145/2783258.2789984 .

2. OUTLINE

The tutorial is structured as follows.

Introduction. We start with a short introduction about the use of random sampling in data mining, discussing its advantages and the challenges for the algorithm designer. The goal is to lay forward the key questions that will be answered in the rest of the tutorial. In particular, we start with an example involving Frequent Itemset Mining through sampling [14, 15], showing the limitations of the Union bound in solving this problem. By generalizing our settings to general data mining problem, we then introduce the key problem of learning, known as the *Glivenko-Cantelli problem for classes of functions* [18], which clarifies the strong connection with the area of statistical learning theory.

First Part: Theoretical Foundations. The theoretical foundations are presented in the first part, where we introduce the Rademacher Averages [3, 10] and the VC-dimension [19], showing how they allow to answer the questions posed in the introduction, and how they are related to each other. In particular, we show the key theorems that allow to compute an upper bound to the sample size sufficient to obtain a high-quality approximation of the quantities of interest, uniformly. The bounds depend linearly on the Rademacher averages and on the VC-dimension. We then focus on computing, estimating, and bounding the Rademacher averages and the VC-dimension, which is a key step in the process of using them to develop algorithms. We show a number of basic examples of classes of functions with finite and infinite VC-dimension and discuss different techniques for developing analytical bounds and empirical estimations. The examples will range from toy examples (e.g., axis-aligned rectangles, half-spaces, and sinusoidal functions) to much more complex instances that are presented in research papers (e.g., graph neighborhood functions, neural networks [2], and shortest paths [1]).

Second Part: Applications. The second part focuses on showing how to use Rademacher averages and VC-dimension to develop sampling-based algorithms for data and graph mining problems. We start by presenting a generic recipe for developing such algorithms, which eases the application of the techniques and the analysis of the algorithms. We then show a number of examples of application of this technique for different graph and data analysis problems, including network connectivity [9], shortest paths algorithms [1], betweenness centrality computation [13], and frequent pattern mining [14–16], and set covering [5].

Third part: Advanced Material. In the third part, we will focus on more advanced material, to encourage the audience to further explore the field of statistical learning theory, and to stimulate discussion and research on using the results from this field to develop data mining algorithms. Specifically, we will discuss: PAC-Bayesian bounds [3, 17], which show a connection between the typical frequentist approach followed in statistical learning theory to the Bayesian probabilistic approach and may be useful for data mining algorithms on uncertain or probabilistic data, and a selection of the extensions of VC-dimension to real-valued or non-binary functions, including pseudodimension [12], Natarajan dimension, and fat-shattering dimension [8].

3. WEBSITE

We set up a mini-website (`http://bigdata.cs.brown.edu/vctutorial`) with links to the slides that we use for the presentation, and a bibliography of theoretical and application-oriented works about VC-dimension and Rademacher Averages.

4. ACKNOWLEDGMENTS

This work was supported by NSF grant IIS-1247581 and NIH grant R01-CA180776.

5. REFERENCES

[1] I. Abraham, D. Delling, A. Fiat, A. V. Goldberg, and R. F. Werneck. VC-dimension and shortest path algorithms. ICALP'11, 2011.

[2] M. Anthony and P. L. Bartlett. *Neural Network Learning - Theoretical Foundations.* Cambridge University Press, 1999.

[3] S. Boucheron, O. Bousquet, and G. Lugosi. Theory of classification : A survey of some recent advances. *ESAIM: Probability and Statistics*, 9:323–375, 2005.

[4] U. Brandes. A faster algorithm for betweenness centrality. *J. Math. Sociol.*, 25(2):163–177, 2001.

[5] H. Brönnimann and M. Goodrich. Almost optimal set covers in finite vc-dimension. *Discrete & Computational Geometry*, 14(1):463–479, 1995.

[6] G. Cormode and N. Duffield. Sampling for big data: A tutorial. ACM KDD'14, 2014.

[7] W. Hoeffding. Probability inequalities for sums of bounded random variables. *J. American Statistical Assoc.*, 58(301):13–30, 1963.

[8] M. J. Kearns and R. E. Schapire. Efficient distribution-free learning of probabilistic concepts. IEEE FOCS'90, 1990.

[9] J. M. Kleinberg, M. Sandler, and A. Slivkins. Network failure detection and graph connectivity. *SIAM J. Comput.*, 38(4):1330–1346, 2008.

[10] V. Koltchinskii. Rademacher penalties and structural risk minimization. *IEEE Trans. Inf. Theory*, 47(5): 1902–1914, July 2001.

[11] M. Mitzenmacher and E. Upfal. *Probability and Computing: Randomized Algorithms and Probabilistic Analysis.* Cambridge University Press, 2005.

[12] D. Pollard. *Convergence of stochastic processes.* Springer-Verlag, 1984.

[13] M. Riondato and E. M. Kornaropoulos. Fast approximation of betweenness centrality through sampling. ACM WSDM'14, 2014.

[14] M. Riondato and E. Upfal. Efficient discovery of association rules and frequent itemsets through sampling with tight performance guarantees. *ACM Trans. Knowl. Disc. from Data*, 8(4):20, 2014.

[15] M. Riondato and E. Upfal. Mining frequent itemsets through progressive sampling with rademacher averages. ACM KDD'15.

[16] M. Riondato and F. Vandin. Finding the true frequent itemsets. SIAM SDM'14.

[17] S. Shalev-Shwartz and S. Ben-David. *Understanding Machine Learning: From Theory to Algorithms.* Cambridge University Press, 2014.

[18] V. N. Vapnik. *The Nature of Statistical Learning Theory.* Springer-Verlag, 1999.

[19] V. N. Vapnik and A. J. Chervonenkis. On the uniform convergence of relative frequencies of events to their probabilities. *Theory of Probability and its Applications*, 16(2):264–280, 1971.

Large Scale Distributed Data Science using Apache Spark

James G. Shanahan
NativeX and
University of California, Berkeley
875 Howard Street
San Francisco, CA, USA
James.Shanahan@NativeX.com

Liang Dai
NativeX
875 Howard Street
San Francisco, CA, USA
Liang.Dai@NativeX.com

ABSTRACT
Apache Spark is an open-source cluster computing framework for big data processing. It has emerged as the next generation big data processing engine, overtaking Hadoop MapReduce which helped ignite the big data revolution. Spark maintains MapReduce's linear scalability and fault tolerance, but extends it in a few important ways: it is much faster (100 times faster for certain applications), much easier to program in due to its rich APIs in Python, Java, Scala (and shortly R), and its core data abstraction, the distributed data frame, and it goes far beyond batch applications to support a variety of compute-intensive tasks, including interactive queries, streaming, machine learning, and graph processing.
This tutorial will provide an accessible introduction to Spark and its potential to revolutionize academic and commercial data science practices.

Categories and Subject Descriptors
D.3.3 [**Concurrent Programming**]: • Distributed programming.
G.3 [**PROBABILITY AND STATISTICS**] • Statistical computing.

General Terms
Algorithms, Measurement, Performance, Design, Reliability, Experimentation, Security, Languages.

Keywords
Distributed Systems, Hadoop, HDFS, Map Reduce, Spark, Large Scale Machine Learning, Data Science.

1. INTRODUCTION
Big data is a broad term for data sets so large or complex that traditional data processing applications are inadequate. Concretely, imagine an average size laptop (4-8 gig of memory, dual-core, with one terabyte (TB) of disk space) that gets overwhelmed with a machine learning task involving a 3-4 gig dataset; imagine the same laptop taking 3 hours to read one TB of data. Clearly, this type of single node sequential computing is inadequate for processing terabytes/petabytes of data, which are commonplace in modern day society where both machines (internet of Things (IoT)) and humans generate petabytes of data every day (Figure 1).

KDD '15, August 10-13, 2015, Sydney, NSW, Australia.
ACM 978-1-4503-3664-2/15/08..
DOI: http://dx.doi.org/10.1145/2783258.2789993

Until recently "big data" was very much the purvey of database management and summary statistics systems such as Hadoop (HDFS and MapReduce) and was largely underleveraged by machine learning. These systems though useful suffered from their limited utility (challenging to code up; lack of purpose built tools and libraries). This course builds on and goes beyond this collect-and-analyze phase of big data by focusing on how machine learning algorithms can be rewritten and in some cases extended to scale to work on petabytes of data, both structured and unstructured, to generate sophisticated models that can be used for real-time predictions. Predictive modeling at this scale can lead to huge boosts in performance (typically in the order of 10-20%) over small scale models running on standalone computers that require one to significantly down-sample, and necessarily simplify big data.

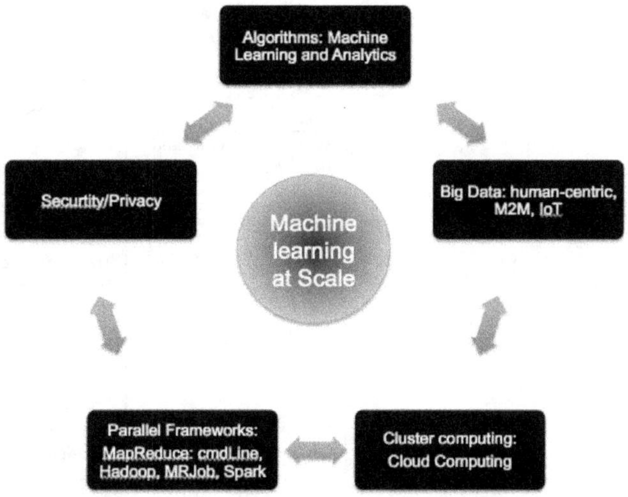

Figure 1. Core concepts of data science at scale

Concretely, this tutorial focuses on how the Map-Reduce design pattern from parallel computing can be extended and more faithfully leveraged to tackle the somewhat "embarrassingly parallel" task of machine learning (a lot of machine learning algorithms fit this mold).

In this tutorial, this is accomplished via the Apache Spark project and it many related sub projects. Spark has emerged as the next generation big data processing engine, overtaking Hadoop MapReduce which helped ignite the big data revolution. Spark maintains MapReduce's linear scalability and fault tolerance, but extends it in a few important ways: it is much faster (100 times faster for certain applications), much easier to program in due to its rich APIs in Python, Java, Scala (and R), and its core data abstraction, the distributed data frame, and it goes far beyond batch applications to support a variety of compute-intensive tasks, including interactive queries, streaming, machine learning, and graph processing

2. Tutorial Outline

This tutorial provides an accessible introduction to Spark and its potential to revolutionize academic and commercial data science practices. It is divided into two parts:

- the first part will cover fundamental Spark concepts, including Spark Core, data frames, the Spark Shell, Spark Streaming, Spark SQL and vertical libraries such as MLlib and GraphX;
- the second part will focus on hands-on algorithmic design and development with Spark (developing algorithms from scratch such as decision tree learning, graph processing algorithms such as pagerank/shortest path, gradient descent algorithms such as support vectors machines and matrix factorization.

Industrial applications and deployments of Spark will also be presented. Example code will be made available in python (pySpark) notebooks. We also review some of the limitations of Spark in its current form. See Table 2 for a list of the subject matter that will be covered in this tutorial.

3. BIBLIOGRAPHY

[1] Karau, H., Konwinski. A., Wendell, and P., Zaharia, M.. 2015. *Learning Spark: Lightning-Fast Big Data Analysis*. O'Reilly Media.

[2] Owen, S., Ryza, S., Laserson, U., and Wills, J.. 2015. *Advanced Analytics with Apache Spark*. O'Reilly Media.

[3] Zaharia, M.. 2011. Spark: In-Memory Cluster Computing for Iterative and Interactive Applications. *Invited Talk. NIPS Big Learning Workshop: Algorithms, Systems, and Tools for Learning at Scale* (Granada, Spain. December 12-17, 2011)

[4] Apache Foundation. 2014. *Cluster Mode Overview - Spark 1.2.0 Documentation - Cluster Manager Types*. Apache Org.

[5] Databricks. 2015. *Databricks Spark Reference Applications*. https://www.gitbook.com/book/databricks/databricks-spark-reference-applications/details

[6] Shanahan, J. G., and Kurra, G., 2010. *Web Advertising: Business Models, Technologies and Issues in Information Retrieval*, Edited by Melucci, M., and Baeza-Yates, R..

[7] Panda, B., Herbach, J. S., Basu, S., and Bayardo, R. J.. 2009. PLANET: massively parallel learning of tree ensembles with MapReduce. *Proc. VLDB Endow.* 2, 2 (August 2009), 1426-1437. DOI=10.14778/1687553.1687569 http://dx.doi.org/10.14778/1687553.1687569

[8] Takács, G. et al. 2008. Matrix factorization and neighbor based algorithms for the Netflix prize problem. In: *Proceedings of the 2008 ACM Conference on Recommender Systems*, Lausanne, Switzerland, October 23 - 25, 267-274.

[9] Ott, P. 2008. *Incremental Matrix Factorization for Collaborative Filtering*. Science, Technology and Design, Anhalt University of Applied Sciences.

Table 2: Tutorial subject matter outline

Section	Topics
Spark Introduction and Hello World	History of Spark Introduction to data analysis with Spark Downloading Spark and getting started on your local machine
Core Spark	Spark intro and basics Functional programming Transformations and actions DataFrames RDDs (no keys) PySpark Pair RDDs Scala, Spark Shell Broadcast variables
Data analysis and handling with Spark	Tools for exploratory data analysis Standardization Reservoir Sampling SparkSQL; Join Statistics in Spark
Algorithms and programming in Spark	Algorithmic design and development with Spark Developing algorithms from scratch • Decision tree learning • Naïve Bayes Graph processing algorithms • PageRank • Shortest path • Friend of friends • TextRank Unsupervised algorithms • Expectation maximization Gradient descent algorithms • Support vector machine • Matrix factorization
Spark at scale	Run Spark on an EC cluster
Spark libraries	SparkSQL, MLlib, GraphX, Spark streaming
Spark deployments and case studies	Mobile advertising Recommendation engines

Medical Mining

KDD 2015 Tutorial

Myra Spiliopoulou
Faculty of Computer Science
Otto-von-Guericke-University
Magdeburg, Germany
myra@iti.cs.uni-magdeburg.de

Pedro Pereira Rodrigues
CINTESIS & LIAAD
Faculty of Medicine
University of Porto, Portugal
pprodrigues@med.up.pt

Ernestina Menasalvas
Biomedical Technology Center
Polytechnic University Madrid
Madrid, Spain
ernestina.menasalvas@upm.es

ABSTRACT

In year 2015, we experience a proliferation of scientific publications, conferences and funding programs on KDD for medicine and healthcare. However, medical scholars and practitioners work differently from KDD researchers: their research is mostly hypothesis-driven, not data-driven. KDD researchers need to understand how medical researchers and practitioners work, what questions they have and what methods they use, and how mining methods can fit into their research frame and their everyday business. Purpose of this tutorial is to contribute to this learning process. We address medicine and healthcare; there the expertise of KDD scholars is needed and familiarity with medical research basics is a prerequisite. We aim to provide basics for (1) mining in epidemiology and (2) mining in the hospital. We also address, to a lesser extent, the subject of (3) preparing and annotating Electronic Health Records for mining.

Target Audience and Prerequisites

This tutorial is intended for conference participants who are interested in medicine (including healthcare and medical research) as application domain for mining. Background on data mining is expected, since we will not explain the learning approaches (e.g. artificial neural networks, density-based clustering etc) but only how each approach has been adjusted to a medical mining task. Experts in some field of medical mining (e.g. knowledge discovery from medical images, machine learning for brain signals) may be familiar with some part of the tutorial but not with all of them.

Benefit for the KDD participants

There is abundance of medical data and of applications that require KDD methods. One serious obstacle in deploying mining in medical research is that this research is hypothesis-driven and follows workflows, which do not agree with the way mining scholars work. Many medical researchers are willing to offer their data for mining, but it is the task of mining scholars to analyze the data in a way that can be understood and exploited by medical researchers. A most disappointing experience for a mining scholar, especially for novice ones, is to hear a medical researcher say "nice results but I will not use them". We discuss this kind of experience in our tutorial and elaborate on reasons that lead to it. Our purpose is to provide underpinnings, guidelines and examples that will help KDD scholars avoid such experiences.

KDD'15, August 10-13, 2015, Sydney, NSW, Australia.
ACM 978-1-4503-3664-2/15/08.
DOI: http://dx.doi.org/10.1145/2783258.2789992 .

Instructors

Myra Spiliopoulou is Professor of Business Information Systems at the Otto-von-Guericke-University Magdeburg, Faculty of Computer Science. Her publications are on mining evolving objects, adapting models to drift and building models that capture drift. In her research she focuses on two application areas: business (mainly opinion stream mining and adaptive recommenders) and medical research (mainly learning from epidemiological studies). She has held tutorials on advanced mining topics at KDD 2009, PAKDD 2013 and in many ECML PKDD conferences.

Pedro Pereira Rodrigues is Professor at the Department of Health Information and Decision Sciences, Faculty of Medicine of the University of Porto, and a researcher at the Biostatistics and Intelligent Data Analysis group of the Center for Health Technologies and Services Research. His publications are on big (stream) data analysis, health data analysis, health informatics and clinical research. He is currently devoted to Bayesian networks applications to clinical research and decision support, and has co-organized tutorials in IBERAMIA 2012 (on streams) and ECMLPKDD 2014 (on medical mining).

Ernestina Menasalvas is Professor at the Department of Computer Systems Languages and Sw Engeneering, Faculty of Computer Science of Universidad Politecnica de Madrid (UPM) and a member of the MIDAS, Data Mining and data simulation group, at the Center of Biotechnology at UPM. Her subject area is Data Mining, and most recently using medical data. She has also participated in a range of projects related to data integration and mining on mobile devices. She has published three international books on web mining (edited by Springer in 2003, 2004 and 2009 respectively) as well as in several key international journals.

Acknowledgments

Part of the work reported by Myra Spiliopoulou was funded by the German Research Foundation project SP 572/11-1 "IMPRINT: Incremental Mining for Perennial Objects".

Big Data Analytics: Optimization and Randomization

Tianbao Yang
Assistant Professor,
Department of Computer Science,
The University of Iowa

Qihang Lin
Assistant Professor,
Management Science Department,
The University of Iowa

Rong Jin
Professor,
Department of Computer Science and Engineering,
Michigan State University

Abstract: As the scale and dimensionality of data continue to grow in many applications of data analytics (e.g., bioinformatics, finance, computer vision, medical informatics), it becomes critical to develop efficient and effective algorithms to solve numerous machine learning and data mining problems. This tutorial will focus on simple yet practically effective techniques and algorithms for big data analytics. In the first part, we plan to present the state-of-the-art large-scale optimization algorithms, including various stochastic gradient descent methods, stochastic coordinate descent methods and distributed optimization algorithms, for solving various machine learning problems. In the second part, we will focus on randomized approximation algorithms for learning from large-scale data. We will discuss i) randomized algorithms for low-rank matrix approximation; ii) approximation techniques for solving kernel learning problems; iii) randomized reduction methods for addressing the high-dimensional challenge. Along with the description of algorithms, we will also present some empirical results to facilitate understanding of different algorithms and comparison between them.

Classification: I.2.6 Computing Methodologies, ARTIFICIAL INTELLIGENCE: Learning

Keywords: machine learning;optimization;randomized approximation;randomized reduction

KDD '15, August 10-13, 2015, Sydney, NSW, Australia.
ACM 978-1-4503-3664-2/15/08.
http://dx.doi.org/10.1145/2783258.2789989

Data Driven Science

SIGKDD Panel

Prof. Dr. Katharina Morik
TU Dortmund University
Dortmund, Germany
katharina.morik@udo.edu

Prof. Dr. Hugh Durrant-Whyte
University of Sydney
Sidney, Australia
hugh.durrantwhyte@sydney.edu.au

Dr. Gary Hill
University of Adelaide
Adelaide, Australia
ghill@amanda.wisc.edu

Prof. Dr. Dietmar Müller
University of Sydney
Sidney, Australia
dietmar.muller@sydney.edu.au

Dr. Tanya Berger-Wolf
University of Illinois, Chicago
Chicago, Illinois, USA
tanyabg@uic.edu

Panel Summary

The panel session, *Data Driven Science* discusses application and use of knowledge discovery, machine learning and data analytics in science disciplines; in natural, physical, medical and social science; from physics to geology, and from neuroscience to population health.

Knowledge discovery methods are finding broad application in all areas of scientific endeavor, to explore experimental data, to discover new models, to propose new scientific theories and ideas. In addition, the availability of ever larger scientific data sets is driving a new data-driven paradigm for modeling of complex phenomena in physical, natural and social sciences.

The purpose of this panel is to bring together users of knowledge discovery, machine learning and data analytics methods across the science disciplines, to understand what tools and methods are proving effective in areas such as data exploration and modeling, to uncover common problems that can be addressed in the KDD community, and to explore the emerging data-driven paradigm in science.

Categories and Subject Descriptors

J.2 [**Computer Applications**]: Physical Sciences and Engineering—*Earth and atmospheric sciences,Physics*; J.3 [**Computer Applications**]: Life and Medical Sciences—*Biology and genetics*; H.2.8 [**Database Management**]: Database Applications—*Data Mining*

Keywords

Knowledge Discovery, Data Mining, Data Driven Science, Data Science

KDD'15, August 10-13, 2015, Sydney, NSW, Australia.
ACM 978-1-4503-3664-2/15/08.
DOI: http://dx.doi.org/10.1145/2783258.2788703.

Outcomes

The aim of this panel session is to explore a number of key questions around the emerging paradigm of data-driven science:

- Do data-driven knowledge discovery methods provide a new way of doing science – or are they just another technique in a scientist's *tool bag*?
- Does access to large amounts of data change the scientific process itself in any fundamental way; in discovery, in hypothesis validation or in which ways?
- Can data-driven knowledge discovery and machine learning methods deliver scientific results, which could not be achieved by classical means? What examples, if any, are there of this?
- Should every scientist be able to do data science or will this remain the task of specialists from KDD?

Panelists

Chair: Prof. Dr. Hugh Durrant-Whyte, *University of Sydney, Australia*
Professor Durrant-Whyte holds a position at the School of Information Technologies at the University of Sydney, Australia. He received his bachelor degree in nuclear engineering at the University of London in 1983 and his MSE and Ph.D at the University of Pennsylvania in 1985 and 1986 respectively. From 2010 to 2014 he was CEO of NICTA, Australia's largest organization dedicated to Information Communications Technology research. His research focuses on probabilistic methods in robotics, including data fusion of noisy sensor data.

Chair: Prof. Dr. Katharina Morik, *TU Dortmund University, Germany*
Professor Morik is the head of the artificial intelligence research group at the Department of Computer Science of TU Dortmund University and the speaker of the collaborative research center SFB 876 consisting of 13 projects, 20 professors and about 50 Ph.D students. Katharina Morik received her Ph.D at the University of Hamburg, Germany, 1981, her habilitation at the TU Berlin 1988 and became full tenured professor at TU Dortmund in 1991. She is interested in theoretically well-based applications of machine learning, which is obvious in her past and current projects that include applications in medicine and genome biology, astrophysics including the Ice-Cube project, ubiquitous systems, and industrial processes.

Dr. Gary Hill, *University of Wisconsin-Madison, USA*
Dr. Hall is a physicist from the University of Adelaide, Australia, and is now working at the Ice-Cube south-pole neutrino observatory project. The Ice-Cube detector encompasses a cubic kilometer of south-polar ice and searches for nearly massless subatomic particles called neutrinos. It measures about 275 million cosmic rays every day, which amounts to about one terabyte of unfiltered data every day. In this vast amount of data, the project aims at finding information to probe the most violent astrophysical sources: events like exploding stars, gamma-ray bursts, and cataclysmic phenomena involving black holes and neutron stars using methods from data mining.

Prof. Dr. Dietmar Müller, *University of Sydney, Australia*
Professor Müller is full professor of Geophysics at the School of Geosciences at the University of Sydney. He received his undergraduate degree from the Christian-Albrechts University of Kiel in Germany, followed by a Ph.D in Earth Science from the Scripps Institution of Oceanography in San Diego, California, in 1993. After joining the University of Sydney as a Lecturer in Geophysics in 1993, he established the University of Sydney Institute of Marine Science and built the EarthByte e-research group. In 2013 he started a project working together with the data-mining experts at NICTA and SIRCA to tackle grand scientific challenges of geosciences and earth dynamics in completely new ways.

Dr. Tanya Berger-Wolf, *University of Illinois, Chicago, USA*
Dr. Berger-Wolf is an Associate Professor at the Department of Computer Science and an Adjunct Associate Professor at the Department for Bioengineering at the University of Illinois, Chicago. She received her undergraduate degrees in computer science and mathematics at the Hebrew University in Jerusalem, Israel, in 1995 and her Ph.D in computer science at the University of Illinois, Urbana-Champaign in 2002. In 2005 she started her position at the University of Illinois, Chicago. Her research focuses on the development and application of qualitative algorithmic methods to problems in population biology of plants, animals, and humans, from genetics to social interactions. She brings together data mining methods from computer science and problems from biology.

Author Index

www.ingramcontent.com/pod-product-compliance
Lightning Source LLC
LaVergne TN
LVHW080107011026
849160LV00013B/1051
* 9 7 8 1 4 5 0 3 4 0 2 4 3 *